A SINHALESE-ENGLISH DICTIONARY

A
SINHALESE-ENGLISH DICTIONARY

BY

THE REV. B. CLOUGH

WESLEYAN MISSIONARY

NEW AND ENLARGED EDITION

Under the Patronage of

The Government of Ceylon

GYAN

Published by

Gyan Publishing House
5, Ansari Road
Daryaganj, New Delhi-110002
Phone: 011-47034999, 9811692060
E-mail: books@gyanbooks.com

Distribution Network
gyanbooks.com
India, USA, Canada, UK, Australia, France

ISBN : 978-81-212-3049-0 (PB)
First Published, 1892

2nd Impression 2020

Printed at: Gyan Press, Delhi.

A

SIṆHALESE-ENGLISH DICTIONARY,

BY

THE REV. B. CLOUGH,

WESLEYAN MISSIONARY.

NEW AND ENLARGED EDITION.

Under the Patronage of

The Government of Ceylon.

COLOMBO:

WESLEYAN MISSION PRESS, KOLLUPITIYA.

1892.

INTRODUCTION

TO THE SECOND EDITION OF

CLOUGH'S SINHALESE ENGLISH DICTIONARY.

THE first edition of this work was published in 1830. It proved to be most valuable to students of the Siṇhalese language. The book has for many years been out of print and copies have been obtained only at very high prices. The issue of a new edition has therefore been long felt to be necessary; but the preparation of it involved a great amount of labour and rendered delay unavoidable. The work was begun by the Rev. George Baugh but the greater part was executed by the Rev. Robert Tebb. After these missionaries left Ceylon the whole has been very carefully revised and no pains have been spared to ensure accuracy. As it has been difficult to find time amid more pressing claims for this work, it is hoped that the delay which has occurred and also any errors and omissions which may be discovered will be regarded leniently. It has not been as a labour of love, but as the discharge of what appeared to be a public duty in the supply of a long felt want, that the execution has been persevered in.

The entire book has had the careful supervision of the eminent Pandit, Bartholomew Guṇasékara Esquire, Mudaliyar, of the Colonial Secretary's Office. At his suggestion a number of Páli and Sanskrit words which appeared in the first edition have been omitted in this, as they did not in any sense belong to the Siṇhalese language. But many other words have been added, and the total number of words in this volume will, it is believed, be much greater than the number included by Mr. Clough. We are much indebted to Mr. Guṇasékara for the care and time he has devoted both to the revision of the copy and the correction of the proof sheets, and we are sure that those who use the book may rely with confidence on the results of his labours.

Botanical terms were a leading feature of the original edition, as might be expected in a dictionary of the language of a people residing in a country enriched with such a profuse and diversified vegetation as that of Ceylon. This edition has the advantage of appearing subsequently to the publication of the "Systematic catalogue of the flowering plants and ferns indigenous to or growing wild in Ceylon, with the Vernacular names and with references to Thwaites's 'Enumeratio,' compiled by Henry Triemen M. B., F. L. S. Director of the Royal Botanical Gardens Ceylon." In the present work all the plants the vernacular names of which are sanctioned by Dr. Triemen's authority are distinguished by the insertion of the natural orders to which they belong. Besides these an immense number of other names appeared in the first edition for which the Botanical names were taken, it is believed, from Moon's catalogue. Many of such names are found only in the medical and other books and are not in common use by the people in general. No pains have been spared to identify these; in many instances the species and genera have been corrected according to Dr. Triemen's catalogue and wherever possible the colloquial names have been added. In some instances a few words of description extracted from Mr. Morris's catalogue of Péradeniya Gardens or from Roxburgh's *Flora Indica* (Carey's edition) are added; and a number of other plants chiefly medicinal are included. It is hoped that Botanical authorities will forgive any inaccuraces they may find in this department.

The scientific names of birds are taken from the printed "list of Ceylon Birds showing the species represented in the Colombo Museum": those of the "reptile fauna" are from the pamphlet of the late Wm. Ferguson Esq. F. L. S. This lamented gentleman took a warm interest in our present undertaking and was ever ready to aid us with advice as well as with information from his abundant stores of scientific knowledge.

Words in other departments of Natural History are represented by the scientific names as far as we have been able to discover them. It is to be regretted that the descriptions appearing in the valuable works on the natural History of Ceylon frequently do not give the vernacular names of the specimens, which thus cannot be easily identified by persons not having special knowledge.

As many words are found only in books and are not used or perhaps understood by the people in general, the colloquial forms have in a large number of such cases been added.

The above remarks will, we trust, make it evident that much has been done for the improvement of Clough's Dictionary by removing blemishes and bringing the information it affords up to the present level of knowledge. It should however be understood that this is not a new Dictionary, but a new edition of an old and approved one. We have not altered anything for altering's sake; and the quaint language and curious definitions of the original are largely left untouched, while at the same time vigilance has been exercised to ensure accuracy throughout.

We believe that to Europeans learning Siŋhalese this book will be indispensable; that Siŋhalese students will find in it assistance which they will constantly and increasingly value; and that all public officials and other persons taking an interest in Ceylon will deem their libraries to be incomplete without it.

There is one feature in this edition to which we would call particular attention: namely that every Siŋhalese word is given in English as well as in native characters. This has been done according to the plan adopted by the Government of Ceylon and now generally followed. It will, we do not doubt, prove a great help to planters, business men and others who, though having transactions with the Siŋhalese, have not acquired a knowledge of the Siŋhalese characters. As the book contains a large number of technical terms as well as all the ordinary colloquial words, such persons will not fail to find it a great help in daily life.

The same fact, viz. that Siŋhalese words are printed in English letters, will we believe make this work of value to those in other countries (especially India and Europe) who take an interest in Indian subjects. The late Professor Childers (to whose Páli Dictionary we are under great obligations in the preparation of this edition) says that the Siŋhalese language is "a rich though as yet almost unexplored philological mine." This dictionary will be found to give compendious but complete descriptions of the doctrines, books and usages of Buddhism (now attracting so much attention,) of Hindu mythology and oriental literature; while it throws a flood of light on the customs, institutions and modes of thought of the natives of Ceylon.

The printing, will go on without intermission, but considering the limited resources of a Mission printing office for an undertaking of this kind and also the time required for the careful reading several times of each proof sheet, we cannot promise that the whole will be completed very speedily. It is in contemplation to add a list (with derivations as of all the important words in the Dictionary) of the more characteristic Siŋhalese names of families and of places; but this will largely depend on the wishes of purchasers.

Wesleyan Mission House,
Kollupitiya, Colombo,
November 1887.

JOHN SCOTT.

THE SIŅHALESE ALPHABET.

N. B:—The equivalents in Roman letters are given according to the Minute of the Government of Ceylon of August 28, 1866 ; with some additions.

VOWELS:

Initial forms ; * අ a, ආ á; ඉ i, ඊ í; උ u, ඌ ú; († ඍ ṛi, ඎ ṛí; ඏ ḷu, ඐ ḷú;) එ e, ඒ é; ඓ ai. ඔ o; ඕ ó; ඖ au [‡ අං aŋ; අඃ aḥ; guttural] ඇ ę, (sounded like *a* as in hat) ඈ ę́, the same sound lengthened.

CONSONANTS.

The following are sounded with *a* as final inherent vowel, and are given separately for the sake of convenience in referring to the Dictionary.

Gutturals: ක ka, ඛ kha; ග ga, ඝ gha; ඞ ńa.
Palatals: ච cha, ඡ chha; ජ ja, ඣ jha; ඤ ña.
Cerebrals: ට § ṭa, ඨ ṭha; ඩ § ḍa, ඪ ḍha; ණ ṇa.
Dentals: ත ta, ථ tha; ද da, ධ dha; න na.
Labials: ප pa, ඵ pha: බ ba, භ bha; ම ma.
Semi-vowels: ය ya, ර ra; ල la, ව va or wa.
Sibilants and aspirate: ශ ṣa, ෂ sha; ස sa, හ ha, ළ ḷa.

When a consonant is final by being deprived of its inherent vowel the sign ් or ් (called *al*) is added to it, as ක්, ච්, unless the consonant is conjoined with another consonant.

* The vowels to be sounded as in the Italian alphabet: අ a, like a in America.
† These characters are taken from the Sanskrit alphabet, the first is seldom the second never used.
‡ These signs (ං and ඃ) are always preceded by vowels.
§ The common English t and d.

The following is a full table of the consonants as combined with final vowels:

ක ka කා ká කි ki කී kí කු ku කූ kú [* කෘ kṛi කෲ kṛí කෟ kḷu කෳ kḷú] කෙ ke කේ ké කෛ kai කො ko කෝ kó කෞ kau කං kaṉ කඃ kaḥ.

ඛ kha ඛා khá ඛි khi ඛී khí ඛු khu ඛූ khú ඛෙ khe ඛෛ khai ඛො kho ඛෞ khau ඛං khaṉ ඛඃ khaḥ.

ග ga ගා gá ගි gi ගී gí ගු gu ගූ gú ගෙ ge ගේ gé ගෛ gai ගො go ගෝ gó ගෞ gau ගං gaṉ ගඃ gaḥ.

ඝ gha ඝා ghá ඝි ghi ඝී ghí ඝු ghu ඝූ ghú ඝෙ ghe ඝෛ ghai ඝො gho ඝෞ ghau ඝං ghaṉ ඝඃ ghaḥ.

ඞ ṅa ඞා ṅá ඞි ṅi ඞී ṅí ඞු ṅu ඞූ ṅú ඞෙ ṅe ඞෛ ṅai ඞො ṅo ඞෞ ṅau ඞං ṅaṉ ඞඃ ṅaḥ.

ච cha චා chá චි chi චී chí චු chu චූ chú චෙ che චේ ché චෛ chai චො cho චෝ chó චෞ chau චං chaṉ චඃ chaḥ.

ඡ chha ඡා chhá ඡි chhi ඡී chhí ඡු chhu ඡූ chhú ඡෙ chhe ඡෛ chhai ඡො chho ඡෞ chhau ඡං chhaṉ ඡඃ chhaḥ.

ජ ja ජා já ජි ji ජී jí ජු ju ජූ jú ජෙ je ජේ jé ජෛ jai ජො jo ජෝ jó ජෞ jau ජං jaṉ ජඃ jaḥ.

ඣ jha ඣා jhá ඣි jhi ඣී jhí ඣු jhu ඣූ jhú ඣෙ jhe ඣෛ jhai ඣො jho ඣෞ jhau ඣං jhaṉ ඣඃ jhaḥ.

ඤ ña ඤා ñá ඤි ñi ඤී ñí ඤු (ඤු) ñu ඤූ (ඤූ) ñú ඤෙ ñe ඤෛ ñai ඤො ño ඤෞ ñau ඤං ñaṉ ඤඃ ñaḥ.

ට ṭa ටා ṭá ටි ṭi ටී ṭí ටු ṭu ටූ ṭú ටෙ ṭe ටේ ṭé ටෛ ṭai ටො ṭo ටෝ ṭó ටෞ ṭau ටං ṭaṉ ටඃ ṭaḥ.

ඨ ṭha ඨා ṭhá ඨි ṭhi ඨී ṭhí ඨු ṭhu ඨූ ṭhú ඨෙ ṭhe ඨෛ ṭhai ඨො ṭho ඨෞ ṭhau ඨං ṭhaṉ ඨඃ ṭhaḥ.

ඩ ḍa ඩා ḍá ඩි ḍi ඩී ḍí ඩු ḍu ඩූ ḍú ඩෙ ḍe ඩේ ḍé ඩෛ ḍai ඩො ḍo ඩෝ ḍó ඩෞ ḍau ඩං ḍaṉ ඩඃ ḍaḥ.

ඪ ḍha ඪා ḍhá ඪි ḍhi ඪී ḍhí ඪු ḍhu ඪූ ḍhú ඪෙ ḍhe ඪෛ ḍhai ඪො ḍho ඪෞ ḍhau ඪං ḍhaṉ ඪඃ ḍhaḥ.

ණ ṇa ණා ṇá ණි ṇi ණී ṇí ණු ṇu ණූ ṇú ණෙ ṇe ණේ ṇé ණෛ ṇai ණො ṇo ණෝ ṇó ණෞ ṇau ණං ṇaṉ ණඃ ṇaḥ.

ත ta තා tá ති ti තී tí තු tu තූ tú තෙ te තේ té තෛ tai තො to තෝ tó තෞ tau තං taṉ තඃ taḥ.

ථ tha ථා thá ථි thi ථී thí ථු thu ථූ thú ථෙ the ථෛ thai ථො tho ථෞ thau ථං thaṉ ථඃ thaḥ.

ද da දා dá දි di දී dí දු du දූ dú දෙ de දේ dé දෛ dai දො do දෝ dó දෞ dau දං daṉ දඃ daḥ.

ධ dha ධා dhá ධි dhi ධී dhí ධු dhu ධූ dhú ධෙ dhe ධෛ dhai ධො dho ධෞ dhau ධං dhaṉ ධඃ dhaḥ.

න na නා ná නි ni නී ní නු nu නූ nú නෙ ne නේ né නෛ nai නො no නෝ nó නෞ nau නං naṉ නඃ naḥ.

ප pa පා pá පි pi පී pí පු pu පූ pú පෙ pe පේ pé පෛ pai පො po පෝ pó පෞ pau පං paṉ පඃ paḥ.

ඵ pha ඵා phá ඵි phi ඵී phí ඵු phu ඵූ phú ඵෙ phe ඵෛ phai ඵො pho ඵෞ phau ඵං phaṉ ඵඃ phaḥ.

බ ba බා bá බි bi බී bí බු bu බූ bú බෙ be බේ bé බෛ bai බො bo බෝ bó බෞ bau බං baṉ බඃ baḥ.

භ bha භා bhá භි bhi භී bhí භු bhu භූ bhú භෙ bhe භෛ bhai භො bho භෞ bhau භං bhaṉ භඃ bhaḥ.

ම ma මා má මි mi මී mí මු mu මූ mú මෙ me මේ mé මෛ mai මො mo මෝ mó මෞ mau මං maṉ මඃ maḥ.

ය ya යා yá යි yi යී yí යු yu යූ yú යෙ ye යේ yé යෛ yai යො yo යෝ yó යෞ yau යං yaṉ යඃ yaḥ.

ර ra රා rá රි ri රී rí රු ru රූ rú රෙ re රේ ré රෛ rai රො ro රෝ ró රෞ rau රං raṉ රඃ raḥ.

ල la ලා lá ලි li ලී lí ලු lu ලූ lú ලෙ le ලේ lé ලෛ lai ලො lo ලෝ ló ලෞ lau ලං laṉ ලඃ laḥ.

ව va වා vá වි vi වී ví වු vu වූ vú වෙ ve වේ vé වෛ vai වො vo වෝ vó වෞ vau වං vaṉ වඃ vaḥ.

ශ ṣa ශා ṣá ශි ṣi ශී ṣí ශු ṣu ශූ ṣú ශෙ ṣe ශේ ṣé ශෛ ṣai ශො ṣo ශෝ ṣó ශෞ ṣau ශං ṣaṉ ශඃ ṣaḥ.

ෂ sha ෂා shá ෂි shi ෂී shí ෂු shu ෂූ shú ෂෙ she ෂෛ shai ෂො sho ෂෞ shau ෂං shaṉ ෂඃ shaḥ.

ස sa සා sá සි si සී sí සු su සූ sú සෙ se සේ sé සෛ sai සො so සෝ só සෞ sau සං saṉ සඃ saḥ.

හ ha හා há හි hi හී hí හු hu හූ hú හෙ he හේ hé හෛ hai හො ho හෝ hó හෞ hau හං haṉ හඃ haḥ.

ළ ḷa ළා ḷá ළි ḷi ළී ḷí ළු ḷu ළූ ḷú ළෙ ḷe ළේ ḷé ළෛ ḷai ළො ḷo ළෝ ḷó ළෞ ḷau ළං ḷaṉ ළඃ ḷaḥ.

Double letters:—ඟ ṉga ච ṉcha ජ ṉja ඬ ṉṭa ඬ ṉḍa ඳ ṉda ඞ ddha ඹ ṉba ව dwa කැ kẹ කෑ kẹ́.

The vowels ඇ ẹ and ඈ ẹ́ are represented by the symbols ැ and ෑ respectively as in කැ *kẹ* and කෑ *kẹ́*. These vowels occur only in pure Siṉhalese words, and are not found in the Pali or Sanskrit.

The above lists of vowels and consonants with the addition of the vowel sounds in කැ *kẹ* and කෑ *kẹ́* repeated for each of the consonants, will contain about 550 characters.

The diacritical mark – under "n" denotes half of the nasal sound in the case of purely Siṉhalese words, such a අඟ *aṉga* horn, ගඟ *gaṉga* river, but when attached to Páli words E. G. පච *paṉcha* five අජලි *aṉjali* clasped hands &c., it stands for the full sound.

* These Sanskrit forms are not repeated for the other consonants.

SINHALESE ENGLISH DICTIONARY.

සිංහල ඉංග්‍රීසි අකාරාදිය.

අ

I. The first letter in the Alphabet, pronounced like *a* in *what*. But in composition it is subject to several modifications: (a) In closed syllables the primary sound is generally retained, thus ගල් *gal*, stones, but in open syllables a change is often met with; thus in ගල්වල *galwala*, of stones, the second syllable has the sound of *a* in *syllable*. (b) In කරණවා *karaṇawá*, do, and its participle කළ *kaḷa*, the sound of *a* in ක is like that of *a* in the word *negative*, while in කල *kala*, time, ක has an open sound like ගල් in ගල්වල.

II. It inherently follows every consonant, unless some other vowel or sign be attached; thus බණ is *baṇa*, but බාන is *bána*, බෙනෙ is *bene*, බිණි is *biṇi*, බොන is *bona*, and බන් is *ban*.

III. In composition it is both a negative and privative particle, being substituted for න *na*, and becoming අන් *an*, before a vowel, thus කටයුතු *kaṭayutu*, proper, අකටයුතු *akaṭayutu*, improper; අන්ත *anta*, end, අනන්ත *ananta*, endless; here අ *a* and අන්ත *anta* form අනන්ත *ananta*, endless.

අං, *an̥*, *s.* horns; (plural of අඟ *an̥ga.*)

අංක, *An̥ka*, *s.* see අඞ්ක *aṅka*.

අංකරය, *An̥karaya*, *s.* anchor.

අංකිත, *An̥kita*, *part.* see අඞ්කිත *aṅkita*.

අංකුට්ටා, *An̥kuṭṭá*, *s.* a small kind of prickly fish; lame person, cripple.

අංකුර, *An̥kura*, *s.* see අඞ්කුර *aṅkura*.

අංකුශ, *An̥kuṣa*, *s.* see අඞ්කුශ *aṅkuṣa*.

අංකෙන්ද, *An̥kenda*, *s.* name of a plant, *Acronychia laurifolia (Rutaceæ)*, used for medicinal purposes.

අංග, *An̥ga*, *s.* see අඞ්ග *aṅga*.

අංගම, *An̥gama*, *s.* the power by which sorcerers or demon priests are said to command demons; spells, incantations, necromancy. pl. අංගං *an̥gan̥*.

අංගණ, *An̥gaṇa*, *s. Timonious Jambosella. (Rubiac.)*

අංගරාග, *An̥garága*, *s.* see අඞ්ගරාග *aṅgarága*.

අංගවිකෘති, *An̥gavikrati*, *s.* see අඞ්ගවිකෘති *aṅga-vikṛiti.*

අංගාර, *An̥gára*, *s.* see අඞ්ගාර *aṅgára*.

අංගුට්ටා, *An̥guṭṭá*, *s.* see අංකුට්ටා *an̥kuṭṭá*.

අංජනං එළිය, *An̥janan̥-eliya*, *s.* the light which a sorcerer or demon priest is said to make, see අඤ්ජනං *añjanan̥*.

අංශ, *An̥ṣa*, *s.* part, share, portion; side, (in this sense used chiefly of the human body).

අංශක, *An̥ṣaka*, part, partner, kinsman or relation, coheir; an astronomical number; dowry; indigent person.

අංශු, *An̥ṣu*, *s.* sun-beam, ray of light, light, splendour, effulgence.

අංශුක, *An̥ṣuka*, *s.* clothes; fine cloth, muslin; a linen garment worn round the upper part of the body.

අංශුධර, *An̥ṣudhara*, *s.* (අංශු light, ධර which holds or bears) the sun.

අංශුමාලා, *An̥ṣumálá*, *s.* (අංශු and මාලා garland) garland of light, halo.

අංශුමාලි, *An̥ṣumáli*, *s.* (අංශුමාලා and ඉන් *in*, aff.) the sun.

අංශුපති, *An̥ṣupati*, *s.* (අංශු and පති chief) the sun.

අංස, *An̥sa*, *s.* shoulder blade, side of the body; sometimes written අංශ *an̥ṣa*, meaning part or portion.

අංසකූට, *An̥sakúṭa*, *s.* (අංස and කූට peak) a bull's hump, the protuberance between the shoulders of an Indian ox against which the yoke presses when drawing.

අංසභාග, *Ansabhága*, *s.* palsy.

අංසමර්දක, *Ansamardaka*, *s.* (අංස and මර්දක which oppresses) one of the eighty morbid airs; it produces sharp pain in the side.

අඃ, *aḥ*, *Interj.* O!, alas, ah.

අක්, *Ak*, *s.* end, termination, summit; the eye; mark; dice used in gambling; name of plant, *terminalia belerica*, (not in common use); sometimes written අග *aga* which see.

අක්කන්ඩි, *Akkandi*, *s.* respectful term for an elder sister.

අක්කපාන, *Akkapána*, *s.* a plant commonly found in the low country, *bryophyllum calycinum*, *(Crassulaceæ)*.

අක්කරය, *Akkaraya*, *s.* acre; a superficial measure containing as much ground as sixteen kurunies, or two bushels, will sow.

අක්කා, *Akká*, *s.* elder sister; pl. අක්කාලා *akkálá*.

අක්කාරන්, *Akkáran*, } *s.* a disease of infants,
අක්කාරම්, *Akkáram*, } scurf or fur on the tongue, thrush.

අක්කි, *Akki*, } *s.* sort of rash or cutaneous
අක්කී, *Akkí*, } eruption.

අක්කිත්ත, *Akkitta*, } *s.* (අක් point, ඉත්ත
අක්කිනිත්ත, *Ak-kinitta*, } stalk) extremity of a cluster of fruit or flowers, end of a twig, extreme point of a branch.

අක්ත, *Akta*, } *s.* a paper signed by some
අක්තය, *Aktaya*, } one and giving authority to
අක්තෙ, *Akte*, } another person; warrant of appointment to an office.

අක්දිවි, *Akdivi*, *s.* (අක් dice, දිවි playing) gambler, dicer; Sanskrit අක්ෂදෙවී *akshadeví*.

අක්දෙරිය, *Akderiya*, *s.* straining cloth for purifying water. [Colloquial: පෙරහන්කඩය *perahankaḍaya*.]

අක්පතුරු, *Akpaturu*, *s.* a tree, *terminalia belerica*, the fruit of which is used in medicine. [Colloq. බුළු *bulu*.]

අක්බඹුරු, *Akbamburu*, *a.* (අග *aga*, end, බඹුරු twisted, curled) curly (used of hair). [Colloq. වකුටු *vakuṭu*.]

අක්මාව, *Akmáwa*, *s.* liver.

අක්මෙල්ල, *Akmella*, *s.* a medicinal plant. *Spilanthes acmella. (Compositæ.)*

අක්මුල්, *Akmul*, *a.* (අක් end, මුල් beginning) root and top, the whole; the beginning and end: compare English phrase "root and branch."

අක්මුල් නැති, *Akmulneti*, *a.* same as above negatively, without beginning or end; wearisome, confused.

අක්‍රපට්ටා, *Akrapaṭṭá*, *s.* a kind of medicinal bark.

අක්‍රාන්ත, *Akránta*, *a.* (අ neg. ක්‍රාන්ත passed) not passed, unsurpassed.

අක්‍රූර, *Akrúra*, *a.* (අ and ක්‍රූර cruel) gentle, not cruel.

අක්‍රෝධ, *Akródha*, *a.* (අ and ක්‍රෝධ anger) not angry, dispassionate, not malicious, calm, even-tempered. *s.* restraint of anger, one of the ten duties of an ascetic.

අක්ෂ. *Aksha*, *s.* a die for gambling; contest, lawsuit, legal proceedings; an organ of sense, the eye; wheel of a carriage; a tree bearing a medicinal fruit, *terminalia belerica;* a kind of seed or small nut, *elæocarpus*, used by Hindus for rosaries, in which sense it chiefly occurs in composition; a weight of sixteen Másha seeds.

අක්ෂධූර්ත, *Akshadhúrta*, *s.* (අක්ෂ die, ධූර්ත rogue) gambler.

අක්ෂණ, *Akshaṇa*, *a.* (අ neg. ක්ෂණ moment) unseasonable.

අක්ෂම, *Akshama*, *a.* impatient, intolerant.

අක්ෂමා, *Akshamá*, *s.* (අ neg. ක්ෂමා patience) envy, impatience of another's success.

අක්ෂමාලා, *Akshamálá*, *s.* (අක්ෂ kind of seed or bead, මාලා necklace) rosary, string of beads, especially the seeds of the Elœocarpus used by the Hindu mendicants; name of Arundhatí wife of Vaṣishṭha from her wearing a rosary.

අක්ෂය, *Akshaya*, *a.* (අ neg. ක්ෂය to waste or decay) durable, permanent, undecaying, imperishable.

අක්ෂර, *Akshara*, *s.* letter of alphabet; a plant, *achyranthes aspera, (Amarantaceæ,)* [Colloquial: කරල්හැබ *karalhęba*]; eternal blessedness or exemption from further transmigration. *a.* imperishable.

අක්ෂරජීවක, *Aksharajívaka*, *s.* (අක්ෂර and ජීවක who lives) one who gets a livelihood by his pen, scribe.

අක්ෂරතූලිකා, *Aksharatúliká*, *s.* (අක්ෂර and තූලිකා a brush) pen.

අක්ෂරලිඛිතය, *Aksharalikhitaya*, *s.* (අක්ෂර and ලිඛිතය writing) writing.

අක්ෂරලෝපය, *Aksharalópaya*, *s.* (අක්ෂර and ලෝප a cutting off) grammatical term for the elision of letters.

අක්ෂරවින්‍යාස, *Aksharavinyása*, *s.* (අක්ෂර and වින්‍යාස an assemblage) metre, division of letters in verses to show their rhythm &c; alphabet, spelling, writing.

අක්ෂරශාස්ත්‍රය. *Aksharaṣástraya*, *s.* (අක්ෂර letter, ශාස්ත්‍ර science) science of letters.

අක්ෂරසංස්ථාන, *Aksharasaṇsthána*, *s.* (අක්ෂර and සංස්ථාන placing, collecting) formation of letters.

අක්ෂරාගම, *Aksharágama*, *s.* (අක්ෂර and ආගම augment) grammatical term for the augmentation or insertion of letters.

අක්ෂරාදිය, *Aksharádiya*, *s.* dictionary, corrupt form of අකාරාදිය *akárádiya*.

අක්ෂරාදේශය, *Aksharádéṣaya*, *s.* (අක්ෂර and ආදේශ substitution) substitution of letters.

අක්ෂාන්ති, *Akshánti*, *s.* (අ neg. ක්ෂාන්ති forbearance) envy, impatience of another's success. [Colloq. නොඉවසීම *no-ivasíma*.]

අක්ෂි, *Akshi*, *s.* the eye. [Colloq. ඇස *ęsa*.]

අක්ෂිකූටක, *Akshikúṭaka*, *s.* (අක්ෂි and කූටක ball) eyeball.

අක්ෂිගත, *Akshigata*, *a.* (අක්ෂි and ගත gone) affecting the eyes, as a disease; hateful.

අක්ෂිගූථ, *Akshigútha*, *s.* (අක්ෂි and ගූථ rheum) rheum in sore eyes, mucus.

අක්ෂිගෝල, *Akshigóla*, *s.* (අක්ෂි and ගෝල a ball) eyeball.

අක්ෂිධාර, *Akshidhára*, *s.* (අක්ෂි and ධාර which flows) tears. [Colloq. කඳුළු *kaṇḍuḷu*.]

අක්ෂිපක්ෂ්ම, *Akshipakshma*, *s.* (අක්ෂි and පක්ෂ්මන් lash) eyelash. [Colloq. ඇසිපිය *ęsipiya*.]

අක්ෂිපටල, *Akshipaṭala*, *s.* (අක්ෂි and පටල coat) cataract in the eye.

අක්ෂිභෛෂජ, *Akshibhéshaja*, *s.* (අක්ෂි and භෛෂජ remedy) a tree, *gomphocarpus volubilia;* any medicament or collyrium for the eye.

අක්ෂිමණ්ඩලය, *Akshimaṇḍalaya*, *s.* (අක්ෂි and මණ්ඩල circumference, disc) eyeball; design shewing alphabet classification at one view.

අක්ෂිරුජ, *Akshiruja*, } *s*, (අක්ෂි and රුජ to ache)
අක්ෂිරුජා, *Akshirujá*, } that one of the eighty morbid airs which causes weak eyes.

අක්ෂිරෝම, *Akshiróma*, *s.* (අක්ෂි and රෝම hair) eyelashes.

අක්ෂීණ, *Akshíṇa*, *s.* (අ neg. ක්ෂීණ decaying) imperishable, unfading.

අක්ෂීර, *Akshíra*, *s.* (අ and ක්ෂීර milk) without milk, milkless.

අක්ෂෞහිණී, *Akshauhiṇí*, *s.* (අක්ෂ *aksha*, a carriage, ඌහිණී *úhiṇí*, an assemblage) a complete army consisting of 109350 foot, 65610 horse, 21870 chariots and 21870 elephants.

අක්සන් *Aksan*, *s.* letters numbering the pages of a book.

අක්සනු, *Aksanu*, *s.* screen, curtain, awning.

අක්සරය, *Aksaraya*, *s.* letter of the alphabet; corrupt form of අක්ෂරය. [Colloq. අකුර *akura.*]

අක්සුන්, *Aksun*, *s*, (අක් end, සුන් cut) any thing having the end cut or pruned; anything rough or fierce.

අක්සුම, *Aksuma*, *s.* wrath, rage.

අක, *Aka*, *s.* sign, mark; little, small quantity; a weight of 16 máshas; pain, affliction; a tree, *asclepias gigantea.*

අකක්, *Akak*, *a.* little. [Colloq. ටිකක් *ṭikak.*]

අකටයුතු, *Akaṭayutu*, *a.* improper to be done.

අකටැබ්බෙ, *Akaṭatębbé*, *a.* improper, irreligious. *s.* mishap, unintended fault.

අකටවිකට, *Akaṭavikaṭa*, *s.* a low word to express raillery, nonsense, clownish antics.

අකණ්ඩ, *Akaṇḍa*, incorrectly for අඛණ්ඩ *akhaṇḍa*, which see.

අකණ්ඩකරණවා, *Akaṇḍakaraṇawá*, see අඛණ්ඩකරණවා *akhaṇḍakaraṇawá*.

අකන, *Akana*, *s.* lightning; want of rest or leisure; Nirváṇa.

අකනිට්ඨා, *Akaniṭṭhá*, *s.* Páli form of the following word; highest, sublime.

අකනිෂ්ඨා, *Akanishthá*, *s.* eldest daughter of a family; the sublime gods who are to inherit Nirváṇa. *a.* elder, superior.

අකප, *Akapa*, *a.* improper, unfit, unlawful; correctly written අකැප *Akępa*.

අකම්ප්‍ය, *Akampya*, } *a.* (අ neg. කම්ප්‍ය shaking)
අකම්ප, *Akampa*, } firm, stable, immovable.

අකම්පාල, *Akampála*, *a.* unshaken, unmoved; in common conversation it is used in a different sense, viz. compassionate, sympathetic, distress or pain of mind.

අකම්පාලවෙනවා, *Akampálawenawá*, *v*, to be sorry, to sympathize.

අකම්පාව, *Akampáwa*, *s.* stability; (in common use) compassion, sympathy.

අකම්පිත, *Akampita*, *part.* (අ neg. කම්පිත shaken) unshaken, unmoved, firm, not agitated.

අකම්පියා, *Akampiyá*, *a.* careless, negligent, inadvertent, forgetful.

අකම්බස්, *Akambas*, *a.* (අ and කම්බස් obedient) disobedient, unruly, ungovernable, unmanageable. [Colloq. අකීකරු *akíkaru.*]

අකමැත්ත, *Akametta*, *s.* unwillingness.

අකමැති, *Akameti*, } අකෑමැති, *Akęmeti*, } *a.* unwilling, indisposed, disinclined.

අකමැතිකම, *Akametikama*, *s.* unwillingness, dislike.

අකමැතිවූ, *Akametiwú*, *a.* not liking, displeased.

අකර්කශ, *Akarkaṣa*, *a.* (අ neg. කර්කශ hard) soft, mild, not harsh, not cruel.

අකර්ණ, *Akarṇa*, *a.* (අ and කර්ණ ear) deaf, heedless, inattentive. *s.* deaf person, one without ears.

අකර්තව්‍ය, *Akartawya*, *a*, (අ and කර්තව්‍ය to be done) not to be done, improper, impracticable. *s.* unlawful or improper act, gross or indecent affair.

අකර්ම, *Akarma*, *s.* (අ and කර්ම an act) actionless, inactive; absence of occupation; crime.

අකර්මක, *Akarmaka*, *a.* without work, inactive, disengaged.

අකර්මණ්‍ය, *Akarmaṇya*, *a.* (අ and කර්මන් *karman*, act, යන් *yan*, aff.) not to be done, improper.

අකර, *Akara*, *s.* letter, Nirváṇa.

අකරණීය, *Akaraṇíya*, *a.* (අ and කරණීය fit to be done) not to be done, improper, impracticable. [Colloq. නොකටයුතු *nokaṭayutu.*]

අකරතැබ්බේ, *Akaratębbé*, *a.* improper, irreligious, *s.* unforeseen occurrence.

අකරුණ, *Akaruṇa*, *a.* (අ and කරුණ cause) causeless, groundless.

අකරුණාව, *Akaruṇáwa*, *s.* (අ and කරුණාව kindness) unkindness, ungraciousness, severity.

අකරුණාවන්ත, *Akaruṇáwanta*, *a.* (අ and කරුණාවන්ත kind) unkind, ungenerous, unmerciful.

අකල්පලිතෙ, *Akalpalite*, *s.* premature greyness of the hair.

අකල්ව, *Akalwa*, *adv.* not in proper time or season.

අකල්‍ය, *Akalya*, *a.* (අ and කල්‍ය well) sick, diseased.

අකල්‍යාණ, *Akalyáṇa*. *a.* (අ and කල්‍යාණ prosperous) unlucky, inauspicious.

අකල, *Akala*, *a.* (අ and කල time) irregular, or unusual as time or season. *s.* premature or unseasonable time,

අකලංක, *Akalanka*, } අකලඞ්ක, *Akalańka*, } *s.* (අ and කලංක blemish) freedom from blemish, immaculate, spotless.

අකැලක, *Akalaka*, *a.* (අ and කලක dirt) clean, pure, free from spots or dirt.

අකලහ, *Akalaha*, *s.* (අ and කලහ tumult) peace, quietness, calmness.

අකළමනා, *Akaḷamaná*, *s.* (අ and කළමනා proper) improper deed, unlawful act, unjustifiable procedure.

අකාම, *Akáma*, *a.* (අ and කාම lust) free from lust or desire.

අකාමකා අරිණවා, *Akámaká ariṇawá*, *v.* to hide a fault, to make excuse; to connive at, to overlook a fault.

අකාර්‍ය, *Akárya*, *a.* (අ and කාර්‍ය to be done) improper to be done. *s.* improper act.

අකාරණ, *Akáraṇa*, *a.* (අ and කාරණ cause) non-existence of a cause, causeless, groundless.

අකාරය, *Akáraya*, *s.* letter අ *a.*

අකාරාදිය, *Akárádiya*, *s.* (අකාර *akára*, the first letter of the alphabet, ආදි *ádi*, and so forth) from the first letter of the alphabet onward, *i. e.* a dictionary.

අකාරුණිකයා, *Akáruṇikayá*, *s.* a merciless, cruel man.

අකල්ව, *Akalwa*, } අකාල, *Akála*, } *a.* (අ priv. කාල time) out of season, unseasonable, premature, inauspicious, unfortunate; also, not black.

අකාලකර්මය, *Akálakarmaya*, *s.* (අකාල unseasonable, කර්ම act or deed) mishap, misfortune, untimely event.

අකාලපලිතය, *Akálapalitaya*, *s.* premature greyness of hair.

අකිඤ්චන, *Akiñchana*, *a.* (අ priv. කිඤ්චන something) having nothing, destitute, penurious, poor.

අකිඤ්චනතා, *Akiñchanatá*, *s.* (the foregoing with the nominal affix තා) state of poverty, voluntary poverty.

අකිත්, *Akit*, *s.* (අ neg. කිත් from කීර්ති *kírti*, fame) infamy, dispraise, public odium; a sort of jasmine, *jasminum sambac* [Colloquial: පිච්ච *pichcha*]; a creeper, *borago zeylanica;* sometimes written in Páli form අකිත්ති *akitti*, infamy.

අකිරිය, *Akiriya*, *a.* (අ and කිරිය act) unpractical, useless, dull; also used in the sense of irreligious or heathenish.

අකිරියවාදියා, *Akiriyavádiyá*, *s.* (අ and කිරිය act, වාදියා who says) one who denies the retribution of acts in a future state, a heathen.

අකීකරු, *Akíkaru*, *a.* (අ and කීකරු obedient) disobedient, selfwilled.

අකිකරුකම්කරණවා, *Akíkarukamkaraṇawá*, *v.* to act disobediently.

අකිකරුකම, *Akíkarukama*, *s.* disobedience.

අකීකරුවා, *Akíkaruwá*, *s.* disobedient person, rebel.

අකිකරුවෙනවා, *Akíkaruwenawá*, *v.* to be disobedient, to be rebellious.

අකිර්තිත, *Akírtita*, *part.* (අ and කිර්තිත said) not said, untold, not celebrated.

අකීර්ති, *Akírti*, *s.* (අ reverse, කීර්ති fame) infamy, disgrace, dispraise, public odium.

අකුඩා, *Akuḍá*, *a.* (අ neg. කුඩා small) not small, large.

අකුණ, *Akuṇa*, *s.* the electric fluid, lightning; thunder bolt, thunder, pl. අකුණු *akuṇu*.

අකුණුගහනවා, *Akuṇugahanawá*, *v.* to explode as the electric fluid, to strike with lightning.

අකුණුවිදුලි, *Akuṇuviduli*, *s.* the stream of fire caused by the explosion of the electric fluid, forked lightning.

අකුණුහඬ, *Akuṇuhaṇḍa*, *s.* the sound caused by the explosion of the electric fluid, thunder.

අකුදුනු. *Akudunu*, *s.* screen, curtain, veil.

අකුධාතු, *Akudhátu*, *s.* (අකු collar, ධාතු relic) the collar bone relic of Buddha.

අකුප්‍ය, *Akupya*, *s.* (අ neg. කුප්‍ය base metal) pure metal, gold, silver. *a.* improper, unfit.

අකුර *Akura*, *s.* letter of the alphabet, flaw, any character written or engraved; bud, young shoots of leaves; little stone. pl. අකුරු *akuru*.

අකුරකින් විදිනවා, *Akurakin vidinawá*, *v.* to throw stones ominously by placing them between the fore-fingers of the left and right hand. This art is described in the native books as that of a certain class of men possessing such a power in their fingers that they could project stones in the way already mentioned, and by throwing them against the leaves and bark of trees could augur future events by the appearance of the impressions made.

අකුරු මඩුව, *Akuru maḍuwa*, *s.* (අකුරු letters, මඩුව shed) place where letters are taught; school.

අකුරු මඬල, *Akuru maṇḍala*, *s.* (අකුරු letters, මඬල plan) scheme exhibiting the alphabet at one view according to the classes of the letters, group of letters.

අකුල, *Akula*, *s.* live hedge, grove, thicket, bush, bushy place; withered branch; pl. අකුල් *akul*.

අකුලනවා, *Akulanawá*, *v.* to fold, roll up, twist, twine, enwrap. Pret. ඇකුළුවා *ękuluwá*.

අකුලීන, *Akulína*, *a.* (අ neg. කුලීන of a good family) mean, low, vile, of low origin or race. [Colloq. නීච *nícha*.]

අකුලීනයා. *Akulínayá*, *s.* one having no caste, of low or base extraction.

අකුව, *Akuwa*, *s.* collar bone.

අකුස්ස, *Akussa*, *s.* hook or goad used for guiding an elephant when travelling, pl. අකුසු *akusu*.

අකුසල, *Akusala*, *s.* (අ neg. කුසල merit) demerit, bad-luck or misfortune, applied to persons labouring under any particular misfortune or deformity, in consequence of misdeeds in a former state of existence and considered as retributive inflictions. pl. අකුසල් *akusal*. *a.* not clever, without merit.

අකොස්, *Akos*, } *s.* abuse, curse.
අකොස, *Akosa*. }

අකෝප්‍ය, *Akópya*, *a.* (අ neg. කෝප්‍ය violate) inviolate, unaltered; not angry, not irritative.

අකෝමල, *Akómala*, *a.* (අ and කෝමල soft) hard, rough, disagreeable, disgusting.

අකැප, *Akępa*, *a.* (අ and කැප proper) improper, unfit, unlawful, used chiefly of religious matters or religious offerings.

අකැමති, *Akęmati*, see අකමැති *akamęti*.

අකැමැත්ත, *Akęmętta*, see අකමැත්ත *akamętta*.

අකෘච්ඡ්‍ර, *Akṛichch'hra*, *a*, (අ neg. කෘච්ඡ්‍ර difficult) without difficulty, easy, unobstructed; also freedom from pain or sorrow.

අකෘත්‍ය, *Akṛitya*, *a.* (අ and කෘත්‍ය to be done) improper to be done. *s.* improper act.

අකෘත, *Akṛita*, *a.* (අ and කෘත done) undone, neglected, incomplete. *s.* any act unperformed.

අකෘතඥ, *Akṛitajña*, *a.* (අ and කෘතඥ grateful) ungrateful. [Colloquial: කෙළෙහි ගුණනැති *keḷehi guṇanęti*.]

අකෘතඥයා, *Akṛitajñayá*, *s.* one insensible of anything done for him, ungrateful man.

අකෞශල්‍ය, *Akauṣalya*, *s.* (අ and කෞශල්‍ය skill) want of skill.

අඛණ්ඩ, *Akhaṇḍa*, *a.* (අ and ඛණ්ඩ broken) all, entire, unbroken, inviolate.

අඛණ්ඩකරණවා, *Akhaṇḍakaraṇawá*, *v.* (අඛණ්ඩ and කරණවා to do) not to violate, not to break; also to violate, to break; this word is chiefly used in the sense of violating.

අඛණ්ඩන, *Akhaṇḍana*, *s.* (අ and ඛණ්ඩන breaking) time; unbroken whole.

අඛාද්‍ය, *Akhádya*, *a.* (අ and ඛාද්‍ය to be eaten) improper to be eaten.

අඛිල, *Akhila*, *a*, (අ and ඛිල separated) all, entire. [Colloq. සියලු *siyalu.*]

අග්, *Ag*, more correctly අග *aga*, which see.

අග්ගල, *Aggala*, *s.* (අග *aga*, higher, ගල *gala*, stone) upper millstone; sometimes improperly written අක්ගල *akgala*.

අග්ගලා, *Aggalá*, *s.* kind of sweetmeat, ball of dough made of flour and jaggery, globe-cake.

අග්ගිස්ස, *aggissa*, *s.* end, extremity, apex, top.

අග්දත්, *Agdat*, *a.* knowing the end, discerning the result of things.

අග්දෙරය, *Agderaya*, *s.* the eaves of a roof.

අග්නි *Agni*, *s.* fire; also a Hindu deity so called in consequence of his being considered the god of fire; he presides over burnt offerings. Agni is also the sovereign of the south east quarter of the world which after him is called අග්නි කෝණ *agni kóṇa* or ගිනි කොණ *gini koṇa*. Name of a plant රත්නිටුල් *ratnitul*, *plumbago zeylanica;* fire of the stomach, bile or the digestive faculty, appetite. In history it is the name of the *tretá* or the second age of the Hindus.

අග්නික්‍රීඩා, *Agnikríḍa*, *s.* (අග්නි fire, ක්‍රීඩා play) illuminations, fireworks.

අග්නිකාර්‍ය්‍ය, *Agnikárya*, *s.* (අග්නි and කාර්‍ය්‍ය an act) maintaining a sacred fire.

අග්නිකාරිකා, *Agnikáriká*, *s*, (අග්නි and කාරිකා making) that which produces fire, firewood; but among the Hindus it is the production of sacrificial fire by means of melted butter; maintaining a sacrificial fire.

අග්නිකාෂ්ඨ, *Agnikáshṭha*, *s.* (අග්නි and කාෂ්ඨ wood) firebrand; agallochum or aloe wood.

අග්නිකෝණ, *Agnikóṇa*, *s.* (අග්නි and කෝණ corner) south east.

අග්නිගර්භ, *Agnigarbha*, *s.* (අග්නි and ගර්භ womb) crystal, sun stone, a fabulous stone supposed to contain and impart solar heat.

අග්නිජ්වාල, *Agnijwála*, *s.* (අග්නි and ජ්වාල flame) flame of fire; plant bearing red blossoms used by dyers, *grislea tomentosa*, [Colloq. මල ඉත්ත *mala-itta*].

අග්නිදිග, *Agnidiga*, *s.* (අග්නි and දිග direction) south east. [Colloq. ගිනිකොණ *ginikoṇa.*]

අග්නිදේව, *Agnidéva*, *s.* (අග්නි and දේව a god) the god of fire; one of the names of the pleiades or 3rd lunar mansion, so called in consequence of අග්නි the god of fire being considered the ruling deity of this constellation.

අග්නිධාතු, *Agnidhátu*, *s.* (අග්නි and ධාතු root, source,) bile.

අග්නිනාශ, *Agninâṣa*, } *s.* (අග්නි and නාශ
අග්නිනාස, *Agninása*, } destroyer) anything that extinguishes fire, fire extinguisher; water.

අග්නිබල, *Agnibala*, *s.* (අග්නි and බල power) sensation caused by hunger.

අග්නිමණි, *Agnimaṇi*, *s.* (අග්නි and මණි a jewel or gem) crystal; sun stone.

අග්නිමන්ද, *Agnimanda*, *s.* (අග්නි and මන්ද deficiency) scarcity of bile, indigestion.

අග්නිමුඛ, *Agnimukha*, *s.* (අග්නි and මුඛ mouth) oblations passed through fire as though it were the mouths of the gods; name of plant, රත් නිටුල් *ratniṭul*, *plumbago zeylanica.*

අග්නිරක්ෂණ, *Agnirakshaṇa*, *s.* (අග්නි and රක්ෂණ preserving) preservation of sacred fire.

අග්නිරාශි, *Agniráṣi*, } *s.* (අග්නි and රාශි a collec-
අග්නිරාසි, *Agnirási.* } tion) a conflagration.

අග්නිවල්ලභ, *Agnivallabha*, *s.* (අග්නි and වල්ලභ friend) resin, so called from its befriending fire. [Colloq. දුම්මල *dummala.*]

අග්නිශිඛ, *Agniṣikha*, *s.* (අග්නි and ශිඛ crest, flame) flame of fire.

අග්නිශිඛා, *Agniṣikhá*, *s.* flame; a plant, නියඟලා *niyangalá*, *gloriosa superba.*

අග්නිස්කන්ධ, *Agniskandha*, *s.* (අග්නි and ස්කන්ධ multitude) flame, flake or pillar of fire, ascending flame.

අග්නිස්තම්භය, *Agnistambhaya*, *s.* (අග්නි and ස්තම්භය pillar) flame arising from a large fire.

අග්නිශාලාව, *Agniṣáláwa*, *s.* (අග්නි and ශාලාව a room) place where water is heated for bathing.

අග්නිහෝත්‍ර, *Agnihótra*, *s.* (අග්නි and හෝත්‍ර burnt offerings) Hindu custom of keeping sacrificial fire constantly burning.

අග්න්‍යාලය, *Agnyálaya*, *s.* (අග්නි *agni*, and ආලය *álaya*, asylum) a place where consecrated fire is kept.

අග්‍ර, *Agra*, *a.* chief, principal, first, prior, excellent, exalted, best, much, most, fore, front. *s.* end, top, summit, point, upper part, a weight equal to one *pala.*

අග්‍රාමාත්‍යයා, *Agrámátyayá*, s. (අග්‍ර *agra*, chief, අමාත්‍යයා *amátyayá*, a minister) prime minister.

අග්‍රකාය, *Agrakáya*, s. (අග්‍ර and කාය body) the upper part of the body, a person having a handsome figure.

අග්‍රජ, *Agraja*, s. (අග්‍ර first, ජ who is born) first born, elder brother or sister; Brahmin.

අග්‍රජාතක, *Agrajátaka*, s. (අග්‍ර and ජාතක who is born) man of high caste, Brahmin.

අග්‍රජාති, *Agrajáti*, see the last.

අග්‍රජිහ්වා, *Agrajihvá*, s. (අග්‍ර end, ජිහ්වා tongue.) tip of the tongue. [Colloq. දිව අග *diva aga.*]

අග්‍රදාක්ෂිණ්‍ය, *Agradákshinya*, s. (අග්‍ර and දාක්ෂිණ්‍ය who is fit to be offered to) venerable person, sage, rahat.

අග්‍රදාන, *Agradána*, } s. (අග්‍ර and දාන alms)
අග්‍රදානය, *Agradánaya*, } excellent alms.

අග්‍රදින, *Agradina*, s. (අග්‍ර and දින day) high day, great day.

අග්‍රදේව, *Agradéva*, s. (අග්‍ර and දේව a god) chief of the gods; Indra.

අග්‍රනඛ, *Agranakha*, s, (අග්‍ර and නඛ nail) end of the nail, very beautiful nail.

අග්‍රනාසිකා, *Agranásiká*, s. (අග්‍ර and නාසිකා the nose) end of the nose, a fine looking nose.

අග්‍රප්‍රාප්ත, *Agraprápta*, a. (අග්‍ර and ප්‍රාප්ත arrived) attained, summit literally or metaphorically.

අග්‍රපුද්ගල, *Agrapudgala*, s. (අග්‍ර and පුද්ගල a man) person of eminence, one of the names of Buddha.

අග්‍රපුරෝහිත, *Agrapuróhita*, s. (අග්‍ර and පුරෝහිත family priest) king's chief Brahmin; prime minister.

අග්‍රමහේෂිකාව, *Agramahéshikáva*, s. (අග්‍ර and මහේෂිකාව queen) empress.

අග්‍රමාර්ග, *Agramárga*, s. (අග්‍ර and මාර්ග path) the path or stage which leads to Nirváṇa; also good path.

අග්‍රයා, *Agrayá*, s. a chief.

අග්‍රරාජ, *Agrarája*, s. (අග්‍ර and රාජ king) emperor.

අග්‍රව්‍රීහි, *Agravríhi*, s. best paddy or rice.

අග්‍රශ්‍රාවකයා, *Agraṣrávakayá*, s. (අග්‍ර and ශ්‍රාවක pupil) the chief pupil priest who attended Buddha during his personal ministry. See අගසව් *agasav*.

අග්‍රසර, *Agrasara*, s. (අග්‍ර and සර who goes) leader. a. going before, preceding.

අග්‍රශස්‍ය, *Agraṣasya*, s. (අග්‍ර and ශස්‍ය corn) best paddy, best thriving paddy; first fruits.

අග්‍රහායණ, *Agraháyaṇa*, s. (අග්‍ර and හායණ year) name of a month, *i, e.* the eighth of the lunar year of the Hindus when the moon is full near the head of Orion, or about November and December.

අග්‍රහාර, *Agrahára*, s. endowment of lands or villages conferred on Brahmins; village inhabited by Brahmins.

අග, *Aga*, s. end, front, extremity, great depth, profundity, sorrow, distress, house, rock, stone, fear, body, fire, medicine, part, portion, sun, snake, *cobra capella*. a. first, noble, principal, chief.

අගණන, *Agaṇana*, s. (අ neg. ගණන price) unfair price, extra charge.

අගණනීය, *Agaṇaníya*, a. (අ and ගණනීය to be numbered) not to be numbered or reckoned.

අගණිත, *Agaṇita*, *part.* (අ and ගණිත counted) not reckoned, not counted.

අගති, *Agati*, s. (අ and ගති manner) wrong course, evil course or state.

අගතිගමන, *Agatigamana*, s. (අගති and ගමන journey or passing off) evil course; inauspicious event, unfavourable occurrence; there are four things that are unfavourable to just and righteous determinations, viz. *lust*, *anger*, *fear*, and *ignorance*, and should these four or any of them be found in a judge, his judicial decrees cannot be according to equity; the determinations of such a judge are called අගතිගමන.

අගතිරහිත, *Agatirahita*, a. (අගති and රහිත not) proper, right, frank, candid, open to conviction, impartial.

අගතිසි, *Agatisi*, s. The ṛishi or sage commonly called Agasti.

අගද, *Agada*, s. (අ and ගද disease) medicament, medicine, drug; a. healthy, free from disease.

අගදෙවි, *Agadevi*, s. the chief god; Indra.

අගන, *Agana*, } a. excellent, worthy, valuable;
අගනා, *Aganá*, } rare, scarce.

අගනිට්ටාබඹලොව, *Aganiṭṭábambalowa*, s. a corrupt form of අකනිටාබඹලොව *akaniṭábambalowa*, (අ priv. කනිටා or කනිෂ්ඨා *kanisṭhá*, small, බඹ Brahma, ලොව world). In Hindu mythology the chief or highest of the material Brahma lókas or worlds.

අගපති, *Agapati*, } s. (අග chief, පති lord)
අගපතියා, *Agapatiyá*, } the first minister of state, man of great power and authority.

අගබමුණු, *Agabamuṇu*, s. (අග and බමුණු Brahmin) chief Brahmin.

අගබ්භසෙය්‍යා, *Agabbhaseyyá*, a. (අ neg. ගබ්භ womb, සෙය්‍යා lying) not liable to be born again in this world, freedom from transmigration. s. state of the Rahats; this state is acquired by a rigid adherence to the prescribed rules of Buddhism.

අගබිසව, *Agabisava*, s. (අග and බිසව queen) chief wife of a king, empress. pl. අගබිසවරු *agabisavaru*.

අගම්, *Agam*, s. religion; grammatical term for the augmentation of letters.

අගම්පඩිසේනාව, *Agampaḍisénáwa*, s. servants or retainers, paid in grain only, who attend to any business in the interior of a palace.

අගම්‍ය, *Agamya*, a. (අ and ගම්‍ය to be gone to) not to be visited or approached, difficult of acquirement, inaccessible.

අගමග, *Agamaga*, s. (අග and මග way) the way to Nirváṇa; the supreme path.

අගමැතියා, *Agameṭiyá*, s. (අග and මැතියා from මන්ත්‍රියා *mantriyá*, councillor) prime minister, chief minister of state.

අගමුල, *Agamula*, s. (අග end, මුල root) root and top of a tree, beginning and end.

අගමුලනැති, *Agamulaneṭi*, a. (අග and මුල beginning, නැති not) without beginning or end, irregular, confused; also used in the sense of infinite, innumerable.

අගමුල නැති වැල්, *Agamula neṭi wel*, s. name of a creeper, *cuscuta reflexa* (*Convolvulaceæ*).

අගමෙහෙසි, *Agamehesi*, s. (අග chief, මෙහෙසි queen) empress. pl. අගමෙහෙසුන් *agamehesun*.

අගය, *Agaya*,
අගේ, *Agé*, } s. price, worth, value, cost.

අගර්භශය්‍යා, *Agarbhasayyá*, a. see අගබ්භසෙය්‍යා *agabbhaseyyá*,

අගර, *Agara*, s. beauty.

අගරජ, *Agaraja*, s. (අග chief, රජ king) emperor. pl. අගරජවරු *agarajawaru*.

අගරා, *Agará*, s. an unguent for anointing the body.

අගරු. *Agaru*, s. agallochum or aloe wood.

අගරු, *Agaru*, a. (අ neg. ගරු honour) dishonourable, disrespectful, degraded, impudent.

අගරුකරණවා, *Agarukaraṇawá*, v. (අගරු and කරණවා to do) to dishonour, to degrade, to despise.

අගල්අඳුර, *Agaládára*, s. tree, *adhatoda vasica*. (*Acanthaceæ*.)

අගල්ලනවා, *Agallanawá*, v. pret, අගල්ලෑවා *agalléwá*; see අගලදමනවා *agaladamanawá*.

අගල, *Agala*, s. ditch, trench.

අගලදමනවා, *Agaladamanawá*, v, to cut a ditch.

අගලමැඩහැස්විම, *Agalameḍaheswima*, s. filling up a ditch or trench.

අගළු, *Agaḷu*, s. nonsense.

අගව්රව, *Agawrawa*, see අගෞරව *agawrawa*.

අගවත්, *Agawat*, a. invaluable or incalculable, good.

අගවිප්, *Agavip*,
අගවිපු, *Agavipu*, } s. (අග and විප් Brahmin) a chief Brahmin.

අගස්, *Agas*, s. (අග *aga*, and සස් *sas* grain, the initial ස *sa* cut off) first fruits, best grain. a. precious, valuable.

අගස්ති, *Agasti*,
අගස්ත්‍ය, *Agastya*, } s. a celebrated saint of Hindu mythology, the son of both Mitra and Varuṇa by Úrvasi; he is represented of short stature, and is said by some to have been born in a water jar; he is said to have once swallowed the ocean when it had given him offence, but restored it again by urinary evacuation. He is spoken of in the Rámáyaṇa, Skandana and other works, and is said to have framed the Tamil language. He is also said to be the regent of the star Canopus. He was a Ṛishi, a sanctified personage. A kind of valuable red stone; a tree, *murunga*.

අගස්තික, *Agastika*, s. a tree, *murunga*.

අගස් දන, *Agas-dana*,
අගස් දානය, *Agas-dánaya*, } s. (අගස් first fruits, දන giving) an offering of the first fruits.

අගසව්, *Agasaw*, s. (අග from, අග්‍ර *agra* chief, සව් from ශ්‍රාවක *śrávaka*, disciple) name given to the two chief disciples of Buddha, who accompanied him in all his travels for the purpose of recording the facts of his history and his public discourses, one called සැරියුත් *Seriyut* was always on his right hand, the other called මුගලන් *Mugalan*, was always on the left. Every Buddha has two chief disciples.

අගසෙන්, *Agasen*, s. (අග chief, සෙන් an army) principal army, leader, general.

අගහන, *Agahana*, a. (අ neg. ගහන crowded) not crowded, not populous, thinly inhabited.

අගහර, *Agahara*, s. village inhabited by Brahmins.

අගහිග, *Agahiga*, *s.* want, need.

අගහිත, *Agahita*, } *a.* (අ and ගහිත legal) counterfeit, illegal, improper.
අගහිත, *Agahíta*,

අගාධ, *Agádha*, *s.* (අ and ගාධ fixed place) hole, chasm, fathomless abyss. *a.* very deep, bottomless.

අගාධ ජලය, *Agádha-jalaya*, *s.* (අගාධ deep, ජලය water) lake, very deep water.

අගානිගා, *Agánigá*, *s.* sorrow, distress, need, necessity, uneasiness, either in body or mind.

අගාරක, *Agáraka*, *s.* (අගාර house, ක aff.) layman, *a.* lay, not clerical.

අගාරය, *Agáraya*, *s.* (අග mountain, ඍ *ṛi* to go, rising like a hill) house, dale, or valley.

අගාරික, *Agárika*, *a.* lay, not clerical, see අගාරක *agáraka*.

අගාරික රත්නය, *Agárika-ratnaya*, *s.* (අගාර *agára* house, ඉක *ika* aff, රත්නය ornament) ornaments of a house, furniture; one of the names of a *Chakravarti*, king of the universe.

අගිනවා, *Aginawá*, *v.* to be worth, value.

අගිල්, *Agil*, *s.* agallochum, the aloe.

අගිය, *Agíya*, *s.* (අ and ගිය verse) prose.

අගුකරුණි, *Agukaruni*, *s.* plant, *geophíla reniformis (Rubiaceæ.)*

අගුකොණ, *Agukoṇa*, *s.* (අගු roof, කොණ angle) the angle of the roof of a house. pl. අගුකොන් *agukon*.

අගුණ, *Aguṇa*, *a.* (අ and ගුණ good qualities) void of good qualities, bad, inefficacious, unwholesome. *s.* defect, fault.

අගුණය, *Aguṇaya*, } *s.* disagreeableness, badness, inefficacy; evil disposition or conduct, indisposition arising from improper diet, impure air &c.
අගුණේ, *Aguṇé*,

අගුප්ත, *Agupta*, *a.* (අ and ගුප්ත hidden) unhidden, unconcealed.

අගුපලඳනාව, *Agupalaṇdanáva*, *s.* (අගු from අඞ්ග armlet, පලඳනාව ornament) arm ornament.

අගුබලන්නා, *Agubalanná*, *s.* (අගු taste, බලන්නා examiner) the king's food taster.

අගුබලනවා, *Agubalanawá*, *v.* to examine the taste of food for kings or noblemen before eating.

අගුරු, *Aguru*, *s.* (අ priv. ගුරු heavy) name of a fragrant wood, aloe wood, also අගිල් *agil*.

අගුල් කණුව, *Agul-kaṇuwa*, *s.* piece of iron which catches the bar.

අගුල් දිව, *Agul-diva*, *s.* bolt.

අගුල් පොල්ල, *Agul-polla*, *s.* bar for fastening a door, door bar.

අගුල, *Agula*, *s.* bolt, bar, pl. අගුල් *agul*.

අගුල දමනවා, *Agula-damanawá*, } *v.* (අගුල bolt, දමනවා or ලනවා to put) to bolt, to bar, to lock up.
අගුල ලනවා, *Agula-lanawá*,

අගුව, *Aguwa*, *s.* eaves of a roof, ground below the eaves of a house.

අගුස, *Agusa*, *s.* sort of fried grain used by the natives, sometimes as food and sometimes as medicine.

අගේ, *Agé*, *s.* value, price, worth.

අගේ ඇති, *Agé eti*, } *a.* valuable, precious.
අගේ ඇතිවූ, *Agé etiwú*,

අගේ කරණවා, *Agé karaṇawá*, *v.* (අගේ value, කරණවා to make) to make valuable, to overvalue; to esteem, to boast.

අගේ වඩන, *Agé waḍana*, *a.* (අගේ worth, වඩන increasing) worth increasing, value augmenting, respectable, valuable.

අගේ වඩනවා, *Agé waḍanawá*, *v.* (අගේ price, වඩනවා to increase) to increase the price, to enhance the value, to overvalue.

අගෞරව, *Agaurawa*, *s*, (අ priv. ගෞරව honour) dishonour, disrespect, irreverence.

අගෞරවකරණවා, *Agaurawa karaṇawá*, *v. a.* to dishonour, to disgrace, to treat with disrespect.

අගෞරවවූ, *Agaurawawú*, *a.* dishonourable, disgraceful.

අඟ, *An̲ga*, *s.* a horn. pl. අං *an̲*.

අඟ, *An̲ga*. *s.* (Sans. අඞ්ග *aṅga*) limb, member, part, mode, manner, body.

අඟං, *An̲gan̲*, *s.* (prop: written අංගං *an̲gan̲*) power by which jugglers are supposed to command demons.

අඟණ, *Angaṇa*, *s.* space in front of a house, court, yard. [Colloq. මිදුල *midula*.]

අඟන, *An̲gana*, *s.* woman. pl. අඟනන් *an̲ganan*.

අඟනා, *An̲ganá*, *s.* woman.

අඟනි, *An̲gani*, *s.* an assembly.

අඟපසඟ, *An̲gapasan̲ga*, *s.* the collective members of the body. The Elu form of the Sanskrit word අඞ්ගප්‍රත්‍යඞ්ග *aṅgapratyaṅga*.

අඟම, *An̲gama*, *s.* sort of magic. pl. අඟං *an̲gan̲*, improperly written for අංගම *angama* which see.

අඟය, *An̲gaya*, *s.* body, limb, manner; corruption of අඞ්ගය *aṅgaya* which see.

අඟරක්ෂක, *An̲garakshaka*, *s.* see අඞ්ගරක්ෂක *aṅgarakshaka*.

අඟරක්‍ෂකයා, *Angarakshakayá*, *s.* see අඞ්ගරක්‍ෂකයා *aṅgarakshakayá*.

අඟරදඟර පානවා, *Angaradangara pánawá*, *v.* to exhibit gestures of body as a dancing girl.

අඟරය, *Angaraya*, *s.* gesture, applied chiefly to women, the particular gesture of the Malabar dancing girls; pretended shyness of women.

අඟරා, *Angará*, *s.* see අඞ්ගරාග *aṅgarága*.

අඟරේණ, *Angaréṇa*, *s.* (අඟ horn, රේණ a cord) cord tied to the horns of wild bullocks and buffaloes.

අඟල, *Angala*, *s.* distance from first to second joint of the forefinger when bent, inch. pl. අඟල් *angal*.

අඟලක්‍ෂණය, *Anga lakskaṇaya*, see අඞ්ගලක්‍ෂණය *aṅgalakshaṇaya*.

අඟවන, *Angawana*. *a.* explanatory, shewing the meaning of.

අඟවනවා, *Angawanawá*, *v.* to intimate by signs, to make known, to inform, pret. ඇඟෙව්වා; see හඟවනවා *hangawaṇawá*.

අඟහරුවා, *Angaharuwá*, *s.* planet Mars.

අඟහරුවාදා, *Angaharuwádá*, *s.* (අඟහරුවා Mars, දා day) Tuesday.

අඟාණි, *Angáṇi*, *s.* stall in market where provisions are sold, especially meat.

අඟාරි, *Angári*, *s.* see අඞ්ගාරි *aṅgári*.

අඟිර, *Angíra*, *s.* see අඞ්ගිර *aṅgíra*.

අඟිරස, *Angírasa*, *s.* see අඞ්ගිරස *aṅgírasa*.

අඟු, *Angu*, *s.* thumb, arm ornament.

අඟුට, *Anguṭa*, *s.* (from අඞ්ගුෂ්ඨ Sans.) thumb.

අඟුටු, *Anguṭu*, *a.* having horns or prickles; short.

අඟුටෙ, *Anguṭe*, *s.* toe.

අඟුණ, *Anguṇa*, *s.* name of a plant, *hoya (Asclepiadeæ)* of which there are several species in Ceylon; Sanskrit අඞ්කෝල *aṅkola*. a woman.

අඟුණ වැල, *Anguṇawela*, *s.* see the foregoing.

අඟුණු, *Anguṇu*, *a.* woman, from අඟනා *anganá*.

අඟුපලඳනාව, *Angupalandanáwa*, *s.* (අඟු from අඞ්ගුෂ්ඨ *aṅgushṭha* the thumb and පලඳනාව an ornament) ring.

අඟුර, *Angura*, *s.* charcoal or carbon. pl. අඟුරු *anguru*.

අඟුරස්, *Anguras*, *s.* a *Ṛishi* so called; one of the seven principal sages; planet Jupiter.

අඟුරුකොක්ක, *Angurukokka*, *s.* (අඟුරු charcoal, කොක්ක a hook) blacksmith's fire hook, iron for branding cattle. pl. අඟුරු කොකු *angurukoku*.

අඟුල් පොල්ල, *Angulpolla*, *s.* (අඟුල double canoe, පොල්ල pole) cross timber of double canoe which joins two canoes together. pl. අඟුල් පොලු *Angulpolu*.

අඟුල, *Angula*, *s.* double canoe, two or more canoes lashed together so as to form one boat having a flat floor at the top; from first to second joint of the forefinger, inch. pl. අඟුල් *angul*.

අඟුලි, *Angulí* *s.* see අඞ්ගුලි *aṅgulí*.

අඟුළුවා, *Anguḷuwá*, *s.* kind of fish with prickles.

අඟුව, *Anguwa*, *s.* ring.

අඟුත්තර, *Anguttara*, *s.* see අඞ්ගුත්තර *aṅguttara*.

අඟොත්තර, *Angottara*, *s.* see අඞ්ගොත්තර *aṅgottara*.

අඞ්ක, *Aṅka*, *s.* mark, spot, stain; sign, badge, vestige; cypher; impression; line, stroke; flank or part of the body above the hip.

අඞ්කිත, *Aṅkita*, *a.* marked, spotted, stained, counted.

අඞ්කුර, *Aṅkura*, *s.* germ, bud of leaves, scion, shoot, sprout, sucker, plant just appearing above ground; name applied to a king and a god.

අඞ්කුශ, *Aṅkuṣa*, } *s.* hook used for driving the
අඞ්කුස, *Aṅkusa*, } elephant. [Colloq. හෙණ්ඩුව *henḍuwa*.]

අඞ්ග, *Aṅga*, *s.* limb, member, part, mode, manner; body; a country so called; among the Hindus it means a certain division of learning comprehending such science as is dependent on the Vedas, hence also it is called Védánga or works on six subjects viz. pronunciation, grammar, prosody, explanation of obscure terms, description of religious rites, and astronomy.

අඞ්ගණ, *Aṅgaṇa*, } *s.* court or yard; [Colloquial:
අඞ්ගන, *Aṅgana*, } මිදුල *midula*].

අඞ්ගනා, *Aṅganá*, }
අඞ්ගනාව, *Aṅganáwa*, } see අඟනා *anganá*.

අඞ්ගනාප්‍රිය. *Aṅganápriya*, *s.* (අඞ්ගනා woman, ප්‍රිය pleasing) plant, *jonesia asoca* (not in common use); a kind of worship being performed by women to this plant. [Colloq. හෝපළු *hópaḷu*.]

අඞ්ගප්‍රත්‍යඞ්ග, *Aṅgapratyaṅga*, *s.* (අඞ්ග body, ප්‍රත්‍යඞ්ග limbs) members of the human body expressed collectively, equivalent to the term *cap a pie*.

අඞ්ගය, *Aṅgaya*, see අඞ්ග *aṅga*.

අඞ්ගරක්‍ෂක, *Aṅgarakshaka*, *s.* (අඞ්ග body, රක්‍ෂක guardian) protector of body; armour.

අඞගරක්‍ෂකයා, *Aṅgarakshakayá*, *s.* one who protects a king's person. (see the foregoing.)

අඞගරාග, *Aṅgarága*, *s.* (අඞග body, රාග anointing) anointing the body after bathing with perfumes made from sandal wood.

අඞගලක්‍ෂණය, *Aṅgalakshaṇaya*, *s.* (අඞග body, ලක්‍ෂණ beauty) beauty of person.

අඞගවික්‍ෂෙප, *Aṅgavikshepa*, *s.* (අඞග and වික්‍ෂෙප moving) gesture, gesticulation.

අඞගවිකෘත, *Aṅgavikṛita*, } අඞගවිකෘති, *Aṅgavikṛiti*, } *s.* (අඞග body, විකෘති change of condition) disfiguration of the body by being born with more limbs than is usual or born without a limb; gesture; syncope.

අඞගවිකෘති, *Aṅgavikrati*, *s.* see අඞගවිකෘති *aṅgavikṛiti*.

අඞගවෛකෘත්‍ය, *Aṅgawaikṛitya*, *s.* (අඞග and වෛකෘත, ඓ *ai* is substituted for ඉ *i* in විකෘත) deformity of the limbs, sign, token, intimation given by a private sign.

අඞගාර, *Aṅgára*, } අඞගාරක, *Aṅgáraka*, } *s.* charcoal, burning or not, but generally the latter; planet Mars, from his resemblance in colour to burning charcoal.

අඞගාරක මණි, *Aṅgáraka maṇi*, *s.* (අඞගාරක and මණි gem) coral.

අඞගාරි, *Aṅgári*, *s.* fiftyseventh year of the Indian cycle.

අඞගිර, *Aṅgíra*, *s.* sixth year of the Indian cycle.

අඞගිරස, *Aṅgírasa*, *s.* (අඞග *aṅga* body, ඊ *í* aug, රස ray) name of Buddha; planet Jupiter.

අඞගුත්තර, *Aṅguttara*, *s.* fourth and fifth divisions of the Sútra Piṭakas, containing 15 books.

අඞගුලි, *Aṅguli*, *s.* finger; tip of an elephant's trunk.

අඞගුලීයක, *Aṅgulíyaka*, *s.* ring, finger.

අඞගුෂ්ඨ, *Aṅgushṭha*, *s.* thumb; great toe. [Colloq. මාපට ඇඟිල්ල *mápaṭa ęngilla*.]

අඞගොත්තර, *Aṅgottara*, see අඞගුත්තර, *aṅguttara*.

අඞග්‍රි, *Aṅghri*, *s.* a foot, [Colloq. පය *paya*]; the ankle bone.

අච්චර, *Achchara*, *a.* (vulg.) so much as that, so many.

අච්චාරු, *Achcháru*, (Portuguese) *s.* pickles.

අච්චුක්කේඩුව, *Achchukkéḍuwa*, *s.* punishment, penalty, degradation, vexation.

අච්චුකරණවා, *Achchukaraṇawá*, *v.* (අච්චු and කරණවා to do) to punish.

අච්චුගසනවා, *Achchugasanawá*, } අච්චුගහනවා, *Achchugahanawá*, } *v.* to print, to stamp.

අච්චුව, *Achchuwa*, *s.* punishment; mould, die, or stamp, *(a modern use.)* pl. අච්චු *achchu*.

අච්ඡිද්‍ර, *Achchhidra*, *a.* (අ neg. ඡිද්‍ර *chhidra*, hole) whole, sound, pure. [Colloq. සිදුරුනැති *siduruneti*.]

අච්ඡෙද්‍යවූ, *Achchhedyawú*, *a.* inseparable, that cannot be cut.

අචණ්ඩ, *Achaṇḍa*, *a.* (අ and චණ්ඩ passionate) not passionate, gentle.

අචපල, *Achapala*, *a.* (අ priv. චපල fickle in temper) calm, thoughtful, steady.

අචර්මච්ඡෙද්‍යය, *Acharmachhedyaya*, *s.* (අ neg. චර්ම skin, ඡෙද්‍ය cutting) uncircumcision.

අචර්මච්ඡෙද්‍යවූ, *Acharmachchhedyawú*, *a.* uncircumcised.

අචල, *Achala*, *a.* (අ priv. චල shaken) unshaken, fixed, immovable.

අචිත්තක, *Achittaka*. *s.* (අ priv. චිත්ත thought) absence of mind, want of thought. careless, forgetful. *a.* having no mind.

අචින්ත්‍ය, *Achintya*, } අචින්ත්‍යවූ, *Achintyawú*, } *a.* (අ neg. චින්ත්‍ය conceivable) incomprehensible, inconceivable, unimaginable.

අචින්තෙය්‍ය, *Achinteyya*, *a.* beyond thought, incomprehensible,

අචිර, *Achira*, *s.* little time, not long.

අචිරවතී, *Achirawati*, *s.* name of one of the five great rivers which proceeded from the lake Anótatta in the Himálaya forest.

අචෙතන, *Achetana*, *a.* (අ neg. චෙතනා consciousness) thoughtless, unconscious, insensible, senseless; inanimate.

අචෙතනික, *Achetanika*, } අචෙතස්ක, *Achetaska*, } අචෙතසික, *Achetasika*, } *a.* see the preceding.

අචෙලක, *Achelaka*, *a.* (අ and චෙලක clothes) unclothed, naked; [Colloq. නිර්වස්ත්‍ර *nirwastra*]. *s.* a sort of religious mendicants who go naked.

අචොර, *Achora*, *a.* (අ and චොර thief) honest, upright.

අජ්ඣාරොහණ තිමිය, *Ajjhárohaṇa timiya*, *s.* (අධි *adhi* very, රුහ *ruha* to ascend, ණ්‍ය *nya* aff.) fabulous fish so called, probably alluding to its size; see තිමිය: *a.* ascending.

අජ, *Aja*, *s.* he goat. [Colloq. එළුවා *eḷuwá*.]

අජන, *Ajana*, *a.* uninhabited, desolated, waste. *s.* forest.

අජනක, *Ajanaka. a.* (අ and ජනක generator) one not a parent or producer, unproductive, ungenerative.

අජනනි, *Ajananí, s.* (අ and ජනනි birth) privation of birth: used in Sanskrit as an imprecation; in Páli it means motherless from අ priv. ජනනි mother.

අජපාල, *Ajapála, s.* (අජ a goat, පාල keeper) goatherd; the banyan tree under which Buddha sat in the seventh week after he attained the Buddhaship.

අජමොජ, *Ajamoja,* } *s.* sort of parsley, *apium*
අජමොජක, *Ajamojaka,* } *involucratum;* name of
අජමොද, *Ajamodá,* } a plant, kind of lovage, *lígusticum ajwaen;* [Colloq. අසමෝදගන් *asamódagan*].

අජර, *Ajara, a.* (අ and ජර decay) imperishable, undecaying, unfading, ever young; [Colloq. නොදිරණ *nodirana*]. *s.* deity.

අජා, *Ajá, s.* she goat. [Colloq. එළුදෙන *eḷudena.*]

අජාතශත්‍රු, *Ajátasatru. s.* (අජාත unborn, ශත්‍රු enemy) one who never made an enemy, one of the names of *Yudhishṭhira.*

අජාදනි, *Ajádaní, s.* (අජ *aja* goat, අදනි *adaní* eating) a small species of prickly night shade.

අජාරෝහිණී, *Ajáróhiṇi, s.* fabulous sea monster; see අජ්ඣාරොහණ *ajjhárohaṇa.*

අජින, *Ajina, s.* sort of antelope; skin of the antelope.

අජින චර්ම, *Ajina-charma, s.* (අජින and චර්ම skin) hide of the antelope or any kind of tiger, skin used as a seat or bed by the Hindu religious mendicants and students; also used by mendicants as a cloak.

අජීර්ණ, *Ajírṇa,* } *s.* (අ and ජීර්ණ digestion)
අජීර්ණය, *Ajírṇnaya,* } indigestion, flatulence.

අජීව, *Ajíwa. s.* (අ and ජීව life) death, non existence. *a.* ugly, cadaverous.

අජීවක, *Ajíwaka, s.* kind of Hindu religious mendicant who goes about naked as a proof that he has destroyed his passions.

අජීවික, *Ajívika, a.* without life.

අජුව, *Ajúwa, a.* disfigured, discoloured. *s.* ugliness. [a low word.]

අජෝඩුව, *Ajóḍuwa, s.* accidental impediment, mishap.

අජෑර, *Ajera, s.* teacher, preceptor.

අජන, *Anjana,* } *s.* antimony; collyrium or ap-
අඤ්ජන, *Añjana,* } plication to the eye lashes to darken and improve them, very generally used among the natives of India as adding to the beauty of the face; the name of a plant; *echites antidysenterica;* elephant of the west.

අජනං, *Anjanaṉ,* } *s.* witchcraft, necromancy,
අඤ්ජනං, *Añjanaṉ,* } sorcery of every kind; medicine rubbed inside the eye when a person is very sick.

අජනංකාරයා, *Anjanaṉkárayá,* } *s.* (අඤ්ජනං
අඤ්ජනංකාරයා, *Añjanaṉkárayá,* } witchcraft,, කාරයා doer) magician, dealer in the black art.

අජනකූටය, *Anjanakúṭaya,* } *s.* (අඤ්ජන an-
අඤ්ජනකූටය, *Añjanakúṭaya,* } timony, කූට rock) native antimony; a rock resembling antimony in colour.

අජනකෙශී, *Anjanakeṣí,* } *s.* a vegetable per-
අඤ්ජනකෙශී, *Añjanakeṣí,* } fume.

අජනදෙවි, *Anjanadeví,* } *s.* (අඤ්ජන witchcraft,
අඤ්ජනදෙවි, *Añjanadeví,* } දෙවි goddess) goddess of magic, mother of Hanuman a noted demon by whose aid the magicians discover lost articles.

අජනාවතී, *Anjanáwatí,* } *s.* female elephant of
අඤ්ජනාවතී, *Añjnnáwatí,* } the north east.

අජලාවා, *Anjaláwá,* } *s.* a fish, the young of the
අඤ්ජලාවා, *Añjaláwá,* } තෝරා *tórá*, or seer fish.

අජලි, *Anjali,* } *s.* cavity formed by putting the
අඤ්ජලි, *Añjali,* } hands together and hollowing the palms as if to receive water in the manner of the *Hindús,* so as to avoid contact with the giver. [Colloq. දෝත *dóta.*]

අජලිපුට, *Anjalípuṭa,* } *s.* the placing the palms
අඤ්ජලිපුට, *Añjalípuṭa,* } of the hands together and raising them towards the forehead, in the attitude of salutation or worship.

අඤ්ඤ, *Añña, a.* other, another.

අඥ, *a. Ajña, a.* stupid, ignorant.

අඥාත, *Ajñáta, a.* (අ neg. ඥාත known) unknown.

අඥාන, *Ajñána, a.* (අ priv. ඥාන knowledge) foolish, stupid, ignorant, unwise.

අඥානයා, *Ajñánayá, s.* fool, idiot, ignorant person.

අට්ටම්වෙනවා, *Aṭṭamwenawá, v.* to get out of the way, to stand aside. [a low word.]

අට්ටම, *Aṭṭama, adv.* (vulg.) aloof, out of the way.

අට්ටාලය, *Aṭṭálaya, s.* hut on poles on which a watchman sleeps, observatory.

අට්ටික්කා, *Aṭṭikká, s.* tree, *Ficus glomerata, (Urticaceæ).*

අට්ටු බඳිනවා, *Aṭṭu bandinawá, v.* to adhere, to stick, to soil, to contract filth, to become dirty or soiled.

අට්ටුව, *Aṭṭuwa*, *s.* any glutinous substance, any thing that soils, dirt, filth.

අට, *Aṭa*, *s.* eight; an age; war.

අටකර, *Aṭakara*, *s.* (අට eight, කර arm) name of Brahma.

අටකොණ, *Aṭakoṇa*, *s.* (අට and කොණ corner) the four points of the compass with their intermediate four half points; an octagon, anything with eight sides.

අටගන්නවා, *Aṭagannawá*, *v.* to grow as trees and all things that have life; to conceive in the womb, to be produced.

අටඟමග, *Aṭanga maga*, *s.* (අට eight, අඟ limb or part, මග way) eightfold way leading to Nirvána, viz: 1. සම්‍යක්දෘෂ්ටිය *Samyakdrishṭiya*, pure religion, 2. සම්‍යක් සංකල්පනාව *Samyaksankalpanáwa*, holy thought, 3. සම්‍යක් වචනය *Samyak vachanaya*, holy words, 4. සම්‍යක් කර්මාන්තය *Samyak karmántaya*, holy works, 5. සම්‍යක් ආජීවය *Samyak ájíwaya*, purity of conduct respecting food, 6. සම්‍යක් ව්‍යායාමය *Samyak vyáyámaya*, holy exertions in religious matters, 7. සම්‍යක් ස්මෘතිය *Samyak smṛitiya*, purity of thought, mental abstraction similar to that practised by Hindús to obtain dominion over the passions, 8. සම්‍යක් සමාධිය *Samyak samádhiya*, holy tranquillity of mind.

අටඟමිණ *Aṭangamiṇa*, *s.* (අට and අඟ part or section, මිණ gem) the octagonal gem, or the precious stone given by Ṣakra to king Kuṣa who had been rejected by his wife on account of his being ugly; he rubbed his face with this stone which rendered him beautiful, and his wife received him again.

අටතුනු, *Aṭatunu*, *s.* (අට and තුනු body) a name of Siva referring to his being evident in the sky, air, water, fire, earth, offering, moon, and sun.

අටතුරා, *Aṭaturá*, *a.* (අට and උතුරු *uturu* subsequent) eight more, more by eight.

අටතුරාසිය, *Aṭaturásiya*, *s.* (අට and උතුරු more, සිය a hundred) magical number of 108.

අටතුරු, *Aṭaturu*, *a.* see අටතුරා *aṭaturá*.

අටදිග්පතින්, *Aṭadigpatin*, } *s.* (අට and දිග
අටදිග්පාලයෝ, *Aṭadigpálayó*, } *diga* place, පාල යෝ keepers) the eight tutelary gods who have charge of the eight parts of the world given in the following word.

අටදිග, *Aṭadiga*, *s.* the four points of the compass with their intermediate four half points.

අටනෙත්, *Aṭanet*, *s.* (අට and නෙත් eyes) eight eyed, one of the names of Brahma.

අටපට්ටම් කරණවා, *Aṭapaṭṭam karaṇawá*, *v.* to make octagonal, to make eight sides.

අටපට්ටම, *Aṭapaṭṭama*, *a.* octagonal, having eight sides. *s.* an octagon. pl. අටපට්ටම් *aṭapaṭṭam*.

අටපිරිකර, *Aṭapirikara*, *s.* (අට and පිරිකර ornaments, utensils) the eight articles that are given to a priest of Buddha on the day of his consecration or ordination, consisting of three robes, one dish out of which to eat his rice, one belt or girdle for the loins, a razor, a needle, and a water strainer.

අටපිරිස, *Aṭapirisa*, *s.* (අට and පිරිස attendants) the eight companies of celestial guards who attended Buddha during his ministry in this world, viz. tautisádéva, brahmayas, kings, máradévatá, grahapati, ṣramaṇa or priests, cháturmahárájika déva, Brahma.

අටමගල, *Aṭamagala*, *s.* magical diagram made by forming an octagonal figure with ashes, and used for propitiatory purposes; also an octagonal ornament worn on the waist. pl. අටමගල් *aṭamagal*.

අටමහනිරය, *Aṭamahanirаya*, *s.* (අට and මහනිරය great hell) the eight chief hells: 1. සංජීව *sanjíwa*, the living hell, or punishments inflicted by others; 2. කාලසූත්‍ර *kálasútra*, black lined hell; 3. සංඝාත *sangháta*, the crushing hell; 4. රෞරව *raurawa*, terrible hell; 5. මහාරෞරව *mahá raurawa*, the very terrible hell; 6. තාප *tápa*, fire hell; 7. ප්‍රතාප *pratápa*, excessive fire-hell; 8. අවීචි *avíchi*, hell of endless torments.

අටමහරෝගය, *Aṭamaharogaya*, *s.* (අට and මහ great රෝගය sickness) the eight chief diseases with which men are afflicted: වාතරෝගය *wátarogaya*, windy complaint; අශ්මරීරෝගය *aṣmarírogaya*, stone; කුෂ්ඨරෝගය *kushṭharogaya*, leprosy; ප්‍රමේහරෝගය *prameharogaya*, urinary complaints, suppression of urine from an excess of venery; උදරරෝගය *udararogaya*, dropsy; භගන්දරරෝගය *bhagandararogaya*, fistula in ano; අර්ශස්රෝගය *arṣasrogaya*, piles; ග්‍රහණීරෝගය *grahaṇirogaya*, dysentery or chronic diarrhœa.

අටරස, *Aṭarasa*, *s.* (අට and රස for දස *dasa*, ten) eighteen; also නාට්‍ය රස අට *náṭya rasa, aṭa*, the eight poetical tastes or sentiments, viz, love, mirth, tenderness, anger, heroism, terror, disgust and surprise. (Námávali. 67.)

අටල්පහුර, *Aṭalpahura*, / **අටල්පහුරු**. *Aṭalpahuru*, } *s.* buffoonery, *a.* (vulg.) clownish, confused, perplexed.

අටල්ල, *Aṭalla*, *s.* high tower or observatory, built of wood, for the purpose of surveying the surrounding country; pl. **අටලු** *aṭalu*.

අටවක් දින, *Aṭawakdina*, / **අටවක් පොහොදින**, *Aṭawak pohodina*, } *s.* the eighth day after the new and full moon on which the Buddhists subscribe to the eight silas.

අටවක, *Aṭawaka*, *s.* (**අට** and **වක** a lunar day twenty-four of our hours or sixty Siṇhalese,) the eighth day after the new and full moon.

අටවකමිණ, *Aṭawakamiṇa*, *s.* see **අටඟමිණ** *aṭaṇgamiṇa*.

අටවනවා, *Aṭawanawá*. *v.* to set a trap; to draw a bow, pret. **ඇටෙව්වා**. *eṭewwá*.

අටවි, *Aṭavi*, *s.* forest. [Colloquial: **වනාන්තරය** *wanántaraya*.]

අටවිසි පිරිත, *Aṭavisi pirita*, *s.* pirit, or recitation consisting of the attributes of twenty-eight Buddhas, with a view to secure protection from demons and for the curing or keeping away of diseases.

අටවී, *Aṭaví*, *s.* see **අටවි** *aṭavi*.

අටවෙනි, *Aṭaweni*, *a.* eighth.

අටවෙනුව, *Aṭawenuwa*, *adv.* eighthly.

අටස්, *Aṭas*, *a.* octagonal.

අටසිල්, *Aṭasil*, *s.* (**අට** and **සිල්** prescribed duties) the eight silas or commands of Buddha. See **අෂ්ටාඞ්ගශීලය**, *ashṭáṅga ṣílaya*.

අටළොස්, *Aṭaḷos*, *a.* eighteen. [Colloq. **දහඅට** *daha aṭa*.]

අටි, *Aṭi*, *s.* pleasure, desire.

අටිවඩනවා, *Aṭiwaḍanawá*, *s.* to excite desire towards a woman; to desire, to covet, to grow fond of.

අටුකොස්, *Aṭukos*, *s.* dried pieces of jack fruit.

අටුමානා, *Aṭumáná*, *s.* species of heron, adjutant bird; used also as a term of ridicule to a long legged man.

අටුමැස්ස, *Aṭumessa*, *s.* elevated wicker frame for keeping paddy, etc.

අටුව, *Aṭuwa*, *s.* barn, granary; see foregoing word. pl. **අටු** *aṭu*.

අටුවා කථාව, *Aṭuwá katháwa*, *s.* discourse upon interpretation, exegesis.

අටුවාව, *Aṭuwáwa*, *s.* glossary, commentary.

අටෝරාසිය, *Aṭórásiya*, *s.* hundred and eight.

අටැස්, *Aṭes*, *a.* octagonal.

අඩ, *Aḍa*, *a.* half.

අඩංගුකරණවා, *Aḍaṇgukaraṇawá*, *v.* to make to consist, to include; to humble, to bring low, to subject, to control.

අඩංගුව, *Aḍaṇguwa*, *s.* the being included; containing.

අඩංගුවෙනවා, *Aḍaṇguwenawá*, *v.* to consist, to be contained, to contain.

අඩක්කම. *Aḍakkama*, *s.* fire work, box filled with all kinds of fireworks and which throws up a jet of fire like a fountain.

අඩකොටස, *Aḍakoṭasa*, *s.* (**අඩ** half **කොටස** part) half part, portion.

අඩගෝත්‍රය, *Aḍagótraya*, *s.* (**අඩ** and **ගෝත්‍රය** tribe) half tribe.

අඩඟුකරණවා, *Aḍaṇgukaraṇawá*, *v.* see **අඩංගුකරණවා** *aḍaṇgukaraṇawá*.

අඩඟුව, *Aḍaṇguwa*, *a.* see **අඩංගුව** *aḍaṇguwa*,

අඩඟුවෙනවා, *Aḍaṇguwenawá*, *v.* see **අඩංගුවෙනවා** *aḍaṇguwenawá*.

අඩතබනවා, *Aḍatabanawá*, / **අඩතියනවා**, *Aḍatiyanawá*, } *s.* to place a support.

අඩදඩ, *Aḍadaḍa*, *s.* hurrying, confusion, puzzle.

අඩදෙනිව, *Aḍadeṇiwa*, *a.* (**අඩ** and **දෙනි** or **දන** *dana* knee **ව** *wa* aff.) kneeling on one knee as a token of reverence.

අඩන්තේට්ටම්කරණවා, *Aḍanteṭṭamkaraṇawá*, *v.* to assault, to commit a rape, to oppress, to arrest, to use personal violence.

අඩපණ, *Aḍapaṇa*, *s.* (**අඩ** and **පණ** life) half dead, nearly extinct.

අඩබැල්ම, *Aḍabelma*, *s.* (**අඩ** and **බැල්ම** sight) side look, leer; pl. **අඩබැලුම්** *aḍabelum*.

අඩමදට, *Aḍamadaṭa*, *s.* (**අඩ** and **මදට** a small red berry) weight used in weighing medicine, half manchádi. [Colloq. **මංචාඩිබාගය** *manchádi bágaya*.]

අඩමස, *Aḍamasa*, *s.* (**අඩ** and **මස** month) half of a lunar month, fortnight.

අඩමානය, *Aḍamánaya*, / **අඩමානේ**, *Aḍamáné*, } *a.* overweighed, overbalanced; *s.* a common word for doubt.

අඩය, *Aḍaya*, *s.* prop, plug, stopper.

අඩයටි, *Aḍayaṭi*, *s.* javelin, missile weapon. [Colloq. **හෙල්ල**, *hella*.]

අඩයටිදර, *Aḍayaṭidara*, *s.* (**අඩයටි** javelin, **දර** bearing) the god of war, one of the names of *kataragama deviyo*.

අඩයාලම, *Aḍayálama*, *s.* brand, mark, type. pl. අඩයාලම් *aḍayálam.*

අඩලය, *Aḍalaya*, } *s.* part, also (common use) අඩලේ, *Aḍalé*, } small portion of the cocoanut left in the shell after the other part has been rasped out for culinary purposes. pl. අඩල *aḍala.*

අඩවල්ලනවා, *Aḍawallanawá*, *s.* to dance with violent bodily action, to throw a somersault.

අඩව්ව, *Aḍawwa*, *s.* dance, somersault.

අඩවල්කරණවා, *Aḍawalkaraṇawá*, *v.* to half shut the door, to put the door or window shutter ajar.

අඩවිය, *Aḍaviya*, *s.* wilderness, large forest, uninhabited or thinly populated district. [Colloq. වනාන්තරය *wanántaraya.*]

අඩස්සිය, *Aḍassiya*, *s.* shortness of breath, oppression in breathing; imprisoning, confinement; obstruction, impediment.

අඩසද, *Aḍasada*, *s.* suppressed sound, arrow.

අඩසඳ, *Aḍasaṉda*, *s.* (අඩ half, සඳ moon) half-moon.

අඩසඳ පනාව, *Aḍasaṉda panáwa*, *s.* see අඩහඳ පනාව *aḍahaṉda panáwa.*

අඩසෙන්, *Aḍasen*, *s.* arrow, detachment in an army,

අඩහඳ පනාව, *Aḍahaṉda panáwa*, *s.* (අඩහඳ half moon, පනාව comb) a comb of the shape of half moon used as an ornament by women.

අඩා, *Aḍá*, *s.* (Tamil,) a low word, used in calling to persons of low caste. [Colloquial: බොල *bola.*]

අඩාල, *Aḍála*, *a.* unfinished, remaining incomplete.

අඩි, *Aḍi*, *s.* plural of අඩිය *aḍiya*, foot, when joined with some verbs it signifies fixing.

අඩිඅල්ලනවා, *Aḍiallanawá*, *s.* to settle, to fix, to remain, to take up an abode; to fix a stand or support.

අඩිකෝඩ කරණවා, *Aḍikóḍa karaṇawá*, *s.* terrifying by ghosts, playing at ghosts.

අඩිකෝල, *Aḍikóla*, *s.* shame, shyness, timidity, fear.

අඩිකෝලම, *Aḍikólama*, *s.* fun, foolery. pl. අඩිකෝලම් *aḍikólam.*

අඩිගහන, *Aḍigahana*. *a.* stamping with the foot.

අඩිගහනවා, *Aḍigahanawá*, *v.* to stamp with the foot.

අඩිගැස්ම, *Aḍigesma*, *s.* the sound made in walking, also a sound caused by ghosts to resemble that of men when walking; mark or track made by the foot of animals, which enables their pursuer to follow them; the sound of birds or animals, by means of which they are discovered by the sportsmen.

අඩිතාලම, *Aḍitálama*, *s.* (අඩි foot, තාල from ස්ථල *sthala* place) foundation.

අඩිපාර, *Aḍipára*, *s.* track made by the feet of animals or of men, foot-path.

අඩිය, *Aḍiya*, *s.* foot, footstep, the bottom of anything; twelve inches.

අඩිහපනවා, *Aḍihapanawá*, *v.* to stamp with the foot as when angry.

අඩී, *Aḍí*, *s.* the vocative of you (feminine) used only to inferiors. (vulg:) [Colloq. තී *tí.*]

අඩු, *Aḍu*, *a.* less, deficient, inferior, low, mean; a grammatical term for abbreviation.

අඩුක්කරණවා, *Aḍukkaraṇawá*, } *v.* to pack අඩුක්කුකරණවා, *Aḍukkukaraṇawá*, } up, to pile up, to heap together.

අඩුක්කුව, *Aḍukkuwa*, *s.* pile, heap of things placed one upon another, assortment of provisions ready dressed. pl. අඩුක්කු *aḍukku.*

අඩුකම, *Aḍukama*, *s.* (අඩු less, කම aff.) state of being less, deficiency, abatement, disgrace.

අඩුකරණවා, *Aḍukaraṇawá*, *v.* to make deficient, to make less, to subtract, to deduct.

අඩු කලය, *Aḍu kalaya*, *s.* (අඩු and කලය pot) pot half filled.

අඩු කලාව, *Aḍu kaláwa*, *s.* small portion of the moon's disc.

අඩුකුලය, *Aḍukulaya*, *s.* low caste, mean birth.

අඩුකුලේ, *Aḍukulé*, *a.* of low caste.

අඩු ගණන, *Aḍu gaṇana*, *s.* (අඩු less, ගණන account) low price, deficient number, unfinished account. pl. අඩුගණන් *aḍuganan.*

අඩු ජාතිය, *Aḍu játiya*, *s.* (අඩු low, ජාතිය birth) low caste, base born.

අඩුත්තු, *Aḍuttu*, *a.* belonging to, part of, appertaining to.

අඩුත්තුවෙනවා, *Aḍuttuwenawá*, *v.* to appertain to.

අඩුතරම, *Aḍutarama*, *a.* base, low, mean, degraded; *s.* inferiority, meanness, degraded state. pl. අඩුතරම් *aḍutaram.*

අඩුපාඩු, *Aḍupáḍu*, *a.* (අඩු less, පාඩු same) deficient, wanting, needful.

අඩුපාඩුව, *Aḍupáḍuwa*, *s.* deficiency, want, need.

අඩුලුහුඬු, *Aḍuluhuṉḍu*, see අඩුපාඩු *aḍupáḍu.*

අඩුලුහුඬුකම, *Aḍuluhuṉḍukama*, see අඩුලුහුඬුව *aḍuluhuṉḍuwa.*

අඩුලුහුඩුකරණවා, *Aḍuluhunḍukaraṇawá*, *v.* to keep in want. to make short of, to lessen.

අඩුලුහුඩුව, *Aḍuluhunḍuwa*, *s.* deficiency, want.

අඩුලුහුඩුවෙනවා, *Aḍuluhunḍuwenawá*, *v.* to want, to be short of.

අඩුව, *Aḍuwa*, *s.* evil, misfortune, curse; part, portion, deficiency.

අඩුවැඩිය, *Aḍuwẹḍiya*, *s.* goods, effects, tools.

අඩුවෙනවා, *Aḍuwenawá*, *v.* to decrease, to become deficient, to be abated.

අඬ, *Anḍa*, *s.* sound, voice.

අඬ, *Anḍa*, properly අණ්ඩ *anḍa*, which see.

අඬගසනවා. *Anḍagasanawá*, } *v.* to call, to invite,
අඬගහනවා, *Anḍagahanawá*, } to sound, to cry out.

අඬජ, *Anḍaja*, see අණ්ඩජ *anḍaja*,

අඬදබරය, *Anḍadabaraya*, *s.* (අඬ noise, දබරය quarrel) noisy squabbling, quarrelling, fighting.

අඬදමනවා, *Anḍadamanawá*, *v.* to make a noise.

අඬනවා, *Anḍanawá*, *v.* to weep, to cry. pret. ඇඬුවා *ẹnḍuwá*. p. p. අඬා *anḍá*.

අඬනහිරිය, *Anḍanahiriya*, *s.* two species of *Crotalaria*; *(Legum.)*

අඬබෙරය, *Anḍaberaya*, *s.* tom tom, or native drum for publishing orders; a corrupt form of අණබෙරය *aṇaberaya*.

අඬබෙරකාරයා, *Anḍaberakárayá*, *s.* drummer, tom tom beater.

අඬබෙරගහනවා, *Anḍaberagahanawá*, *v.* to publish by beat of tom tom, see අණබෙරලනවා *aṇaberalanawá*.

අඬය, *Anḍaya*, *s.* see අණ්ඩය *anḍaya*.

අඬලනවා, *Anḍalanawá*, *v.* to cry or chirp as birds or fowls, to crow.

අඬවාතය, *Anḍawátaya*, } *s.* see අණ්ඩවාතය *anḍa-*
අඬවායුව, *Anḍawáyuwa*, } *wátaya*.

අඬසද්දෙක දුර, *Anḍasddeka dura*. *s.* (අඬ voice, සද්දෙ sound, දුර distance) the distance to which the sound of the voice can be heard when a person is calling or hallooing; this is a common mode of reckoning the distance from one place to another among the natives.

අඬහැරලනවා, *Anḍahẹralanawá*, *v.* to chant or make a noise, as when persons are ploughing or driving cattle.

අඬුව, *Anḍuwa*, *s.* pincers, tongs.

අණ්ඩ, *Anḍa*, *s.* egg, testicle, scrotum.

අණ්ඩජ, *Anḍaja*, *s.* (අණ්ඩ egg, ජ born) one born from an egg, bird; *a.* oviparous, produced from eggs.

අණ්ඩය, *Anḍaya*, *s.* patch.

අණ්ඩරදෙමළ, *Anḍarademaḷa*, } *s.* nonsense, a
අණ්ඩරදෙමළෙ, *Anḍarademaḷe*, } confused unmeaning talk; (a low word).

අණ්ඩවාතය, *s.* (අණ්ඩ scrotum, වාතය wind) hydrocele: see next.

අණ්ඩවායිය, *Anḍawáyiya*, } *s.* (අණ්ඩ scrotum, වායු
අණ්ඩවායු, *Anḍawáyu*, } wind) a disease, hernia of the scrotum.

අත්, *At*, *s.* self, individuality; body from ආත්ම *átma*: hand and arm from හත්ථ *hattha;* within, interior from අන්ත *anta;* wealth, meaning interpretation, from අර්ථ *arttha;* west, see අස්ත *asta;* castor oil plant; end of an age or yuga.

අත්, *At*, *s.* hand, generally used as the plural, the singular being අත *ata*.

අත්අකුර, *At-akura*, *s.* a letter written with the hand, handwriting. pl. අත්අකුරු *at-akuru*.

අත්අතුර, *At-atura*, *s.* breast, part between the arms. [Colloq. ලැපැත්ත *lẹpẹtta*.]

අත්අරිණ, *At-ariṇa*, *a.* leaving, abandoning, forsaking.

අත්අරිණවා, *At-ariṇawá*, *v.* to leave, to abandon, to forsake.

අත්ඇරදමනවා, *At-ẹradamanawá*, *v.* to give up, to forsake, to leave off, to abandon.

අත්ඇරදැමීම, *At-ẹradẹmíma*, *s.* the verbal noun of the last.

අත්ඇරයනවා, *At-ẹrayanawá*, *v.* to leave off, to forsake, to abandon.

අත්ඇරීම, *At-ẹríma*, the verbal noun of අත්අරිණවා *atariṇawá*. leaving, forsaking.

අත් ඉනත්කරණවා, *At-inatkaraṇawá*, *v.* to vaccinate. [Colloq. අත්විදිනවා *atvidinawá*.]

අත්කර, *Atkara*, *s.* the wrist. [Colloq. මැණික් කටුව *mẹnikkaṭuwa*.]

අත්කරගන්නවා, *Atkaragannawá*, *v.* to take possession of.

අත්කුඩය, *Atkuḍaya*, *s.* hand umbrella.

අත්ගල, *Atgala*, *s.* hand stone, upper round stone in a set of curry stones; stone used by potters in smoothing their pots.

අත්ගිර, *Atgira*, } *s.* (අත් west, ගිරි mountain) the
අත්ගිරි, *Atgiri*, } western mountain behind which the sun is supposed to set.

අත්ගුණය, *Atguṇaya*, *s.* (අත් hands, ගුණ virtue) virtue of the hand; power supposed to be possessed by some doctors to give efficacy to the medicines prescribed by them.

අත්ගොබය, *Atgobaya*, } *s.* lower part of the arm
අත්ගොබෙ, *Atgobe*, } from the elbow to the wrist.

අත්ත, *Atta*, *s.* branch. pl. අතු *atu.*

අත්තට්ටුව, *Attaṭṭuwa*. *s.* see අත්තටුව *attaṭuwa.*

අත්තටුගසනවා, *Attaṭugasanawá*, } *v.* to flutter
අත්තටුගහනවා, *Attaṭugahanawá*, } the wings, to flap the wings.

අත්තටුව, *Attaṭuwa*, *s.* wing.

අත්තටුහපනවා, *Attaṭuhapanawá*, *v.* see අත්තටු ගහනවා *attaṭugahanawá*,

අත්තන, *Attana*. *s.* thorn apple, a medicinal plant, *datura fastuosæ, (Solanaceæ).*

අත්තම්, *Attam*, *s.* Elu form of හස්තකර්ම *hasta-karma* (ත *ta* being substituted for ක *ka*,) manufacture, but it is generally used to express chance, fortune etc; also a provincial term for tilling or ploughing a field for another who has ploughed one's own field for him, as අත්තම් කොටනවා *attamkoṭanawá*. [Colloquial: හස්ත කර්මාන්තය *hastakarmántaya.*]

අත්තම, *Attama*, *s.* portion or share of work to be done, pl. අත්තම් *attam.*

අත්තල, *Attala*, *s.* the palm of the hand; cymbals.

අත්තානුදිට්ඨිය, *Attánudiṭṭhiya*, *a.* (අත්ත self, අනු with, දිට්ඨිය sight) close thought, embracing another religion, free thinking.

අත්තානුවාදය, *Attánuwádaya*, *s.* (අත්ත and අනු වාද blame) the upbraidings of conscience in consequence of some secret evil act.

අත්තාලම, *Attálama*, *s.* cymbal. pl. අත්තාලම් *at-tálam.* [Colloq. කයිතාලම *kaytálama.*]

අත්තික්කා, *Attikká*, *s.* a tree, *ficus glomerata, (Urticaceæ)*: see අට්ටික්කා *aṭṭikká.*

අත්තිකාරම, *Attikárama*, *s.* earnest money, deposit money, pl. අත්තිකාරම් *attikáram.*

අත්තිවාරම, *Attiwárama*, *s.* foundation, pl. අත්ති වාරම් *attiwáram.*

අත් තුවක්කුව, *At-tuwakkuwa*, *s.* fowling piece, ordinary small gun, musket.

අත්දකිනවා, *At-dakinawá*, *v.* to experience, to prove, to come at the knowledge or truth of a thing by experiment.

අත් දණ්ඩ. *At-daṇḍa*, *s.* (අත් and දණ්ඩ a stick) walking stick, staff; arm from the elbow to the wrist.

අත්දම, *Atdama*, *s.* handcuff. pl. අත්දම් *atdam.*

අත්දැකීම, *Atdękíma*, *s.* experience.

අත්නූල් බඳිනවා, *Atnúl-bandinawá*, *v.* tying thread on the hands or arms as a charm.

අත්පත්කරගන්නවා, *Atpatkaragannawá*, *v.* to possess, to take possession of, to take possession of by force; to attain.

අත්පස, *Atpasa*, *s.* the space inclosed by the arms placed horizontally the elbows kept by the side; eatables presented to a priest must be placed in that space before he can lawfully accept them; side, part.

අත් පා, *Atpá*, *a.* hands and feet; used in various senses; as අත් පා මෙහෙකරන්නා *at pá mehe-karanná*, a servant of all work.

අත් පා මෙහෙය, *Atpámeheya*, *s.* (අත්පා and මෙහෙය service) rubbing the feet or hands when attacked with pain, any kind of menial service.

අත්පිට, *Atpiṭa*, *adv.* in hand, now, in advance, immediately, readily.

අත්පිඩිගසනවා, *Atpiḍigasanawá*, } *v.* see අත්පොළසන් දෙනවා
අත්පුඩිගසනවා, *Atpuḍigasanawá*, } *atpoḷasandenawá.*

අත්පොර අල්ලනවා, *Atpora-allanawá*, *v.* to seize by the hand as a trial of strength.

අත්පොරය, *Atporaya*. *s.* (අත් hands, පොර war) wrestling, seizing by the hand as a trial of strength.

අත්පොරව, *Atporawa*, *s.* hatchet, pl. අත්පොරෝ *atporó.*

අත්පොවනවා, *Atpowanawá*, *v.* to dip the hands; to touch.

අත්පොළසන්, *Atpoḷasan*, *s.* (අත් hands, පොළ striking, සන් sound) the sound of clapping the hands.

අත්පොළසන්දෙනවා, *Atpoḷasandenawá*, *v.* to clap the hands.

අත්බඹරය, *Atbambaraya*, } *s.* top such as boys
අත්බඹරෙ, *Atbambare*, } play with; that kind of top which is spun by winding a string round the lower part of it.

අත්බර, *Atbara*, *s.* hand bundle, *a.* ill.

අත්බැව, *Atbęwa*, *s.* Elu form of the Páli අත්තභාව *attabháwa*, the body.

අත්මාංචුව, *Atmánchuwa*, *s.* handcuff.

අත්මානංකාරයා, *Atmánankárayá*, *s.* one who throws stones ominously, by placing them between the forefingers of the left and right hand. See අකුරකින් විදිනවා, *akurakin vidina-wá.*

අත්මානන්, *Atmánan*, *s.* name of a game, throwing up several balls at one time.

අත්මාරුගසනවා, *Atmárugasanawá*, *v.* (**අත්** and මාරු changing or crossing, ගසනවා to beat) to beat a drum or tom tom with the hands and elbows at the same time, putting them into various postures.

අත්මිදීම, *Atmidíma*, *s.* release, redemption.

අත්මිදෙනවා, *Atmidenawá*, *v.* to be released.

අත්මුදල, *Atmudala*, *s.* one's own money, *i. e.* money in possession with power to dispose of it; ready cash. pl. **අත්මුදල්** *atmudal.*

අත් මේස්, *At-més*, *s.* gloves.

අත්‍යන්ත, *Atyanta*, *ad.* (අති *ati* beyond, අන්ත *anta* end) very much, exceeding. [Colloquial. ඉතාම *itáma.*]

අත්‍යන්තොපකාර, *Atyantopakára*, *a.* (අත්‍යන්ත *atyanta* and උපකාර *upakára* help) much wanted, very useful.

අත්‍යර්ථ, *Atyartha*, *a.* (අති *ati* and අර්ථ *artha* substance) excessive, much. [Colloq. අධික *adhika.*]

අත්‍යල්ප, *Atyalpa*, *a.* (අති *ati* very, අල්ප *alpa* small) very small, minute.

අත්‍රිලිඞ්ග, *Atrilińga*, *s.* (අ neg. ත්‍රි three, ලිඞ්ග gender) without the three genders; grammatical term used to express verbs and particles that are without gender.

අත්ල, *Atla*, *s.* palm of the hand: sometimes අල්ල *alla*; pl. අතුල් *atul.*

අත්ලස, *Atlasa*, *s.* bribe; pl. අත්ලස් *atlas*; sometimes **අල්ලස්** *allas.*

අත්වසනවා, *Atwasanawá*, *v.* to conceal.

අත්වාච්චිය, *Atwáchchiya*, *s.* knack, peculiar skill or efficacy, especially in administering medicine.

අත්වාරුව, *Atwáruwa*, *s.* support.

අත්විදිනවා, *Atvidinawá*, *v.* to bore the hands, to lance, to spear; to vaccinate, to inoculate for small pox.

අත්විලංගුව, *Atvilanguwa*, *s.* handcuff.

අත්වෙනවා, *Atwenawá*, *v.* to become possessed of, to come into the hands of.

අත්වැට, *Atweṭa*, *s.* hand lamp, candle.

අත්වැඩ, *Atweḍa*, *s.* profit, (in a future state derived by a person from good actions) merit; hand work; self interest.

අත්වැරැද්ද, *Atwereḍda*, *s.* accident, mishap; pl. අත්වැරදි *atweradi.*

අත්වැල, *Atwela*, *s.* rail or string to hold by in passing over a plank thrown acros a river. pl. **අත්වැල්** *atwel.*

අත්වැස්, *Atwes*, *s.* see **අත්වැසියා** *atawesiyá.*

අත්වැස්ම, *Atwesma*, *s.* (**අත්** hands, වැස්ම cover) gloves, cover for the hand; the hilt of a sword.

අත්වැස්සා, *Atwéssá*, } *s.* subject, dependant, ser-
අත්වැසියා, *Atwesiyá*, } vant, pupil.

අත්වෑය, *Atwéya*, *s.* small adze.

අත්සන්කරණවා, *Atsankaraṇawá*, *v.* to sign.

අත්සන, *Atsana*, *s.* signature, pl. අත්සන් *atsan.*

අත්සුනු, *Atsunu*, *s.* a mixture of dried flour mixed with sugar.

අත්හදාබලනවා, *At-hadábalanawá*, *v.* to test, to prove for oneself.

අත්හපාගන්නවා, *At-hapágannawá*, *v.* to strike with the hands (as a sign of pain, anger, joy etc.)

අත්හරි, *At-hari*, *a.* equal, (in force).

අත්හරිණවා, *At-hariṇawá*, *v.* to forsake, to abandon, to dismiss.

අත්හිටවනවා, *At-hiṭawanawá*, *v.* to cause to stop, to hinder, cause to cease, to prevent; to abolish, to adjourn; to stop, to discontinue.

අත්හිටවීම, *At-hiṭavíma*, *s.* suspension, prohibition.

අත්හිටිනවා, *At-hiṭinawá*, *v.* to stop, to discontinue, to cease from action.

අත්හිස, *At-hisa*, *s.* (**අත්** arm, හිස the top) the shoulder blade, scapula.

අත්හුරු, *At-huru*, *s.* ability of the hand, dexterity.

අත්හැන්ද, *At-henda*, *s.* wing. pl. **අත්හැඳි** *athendi.* see also **අත්තටුව** *attaṭuwa.*

අත්හැරදමනවා, *At-heradamanawá*, *v.* to forsake, to turn away, (as a servant,) to cancel a debt, to drop.

අත, *Ata*, *s.* hand, arm, side or quarter, pl. **අත්** *at.*

අතංගුව, *Atanguwa*, *s.* hand net.

අත අරිණවා, *Ata-ariṇawá*, *v.* to forsake, to abandon.

අත උළුක්කරණවා, *Ata-uḷukkaraṇawá*, *v.* to elevate the hand with the intention to strike.

අත කබරයා, *Atakabarayá*, *s.* man with a kind of leprosy in the hands or with spotted hands.

අතකර ආයිත්තම, *Atakara-áyittama*, *s.* ornaments worn by women, comprehending all the articles of jewellery.

අතකුරු, *Atakuru*, *s.* handwriting: see **අත් අකුර** *at-akura.*

අතකුරුගසනවා, *Atakurugasanawá*, *v.* see **අකුර කින් විදිනවා** *akurakin vidinawá.*

අතකොළුව, *Atakoluwa*, *s.* mallet.

අතකෑටියා, *Atakeṭiyá*, *s.* plant, *randia gardneri*, *(Rubiaceæ).*

අතගගා ඉන්නවා, *Atagagá innawá*, *v.* to grope, to feel with the hand; to delay, to neglect.

අතගසනවා, *Atagasanawá*, } *v.* to take by the
අතගහනවා, *Atagahanawá*, } hand, to support by the hand, to strike the hands in pain, to reach with the hand; to strike a bargain.

අතගානවා, *Atagánawá*, *v.* to rub, to stroke, to grope, to feel, to touch.

අතතය, *Atataya*, *s.* shallow drum with only one skin.

අතතුරු, *Ataturu*, *s.* the breast. [Colloq. ලය *laya.*]

අතදමනවා, *Atadamanawá*, *v.* to put the hand in, to meddle.

අතදෙනවා, *Atadenawá*, *v.* to give the hand, to shake the hand.

අතන, *Atana*, *s.* that place, in that place.

අත නගණවා, *Ata-naganawá*, *v.* to raise the hands, to raise the hands as an appeal to God, also give consent or to draw attention.

අතපසුකරණවා, *Atapasukaranawá*, } *v.* to delay,
අතපහුකරණවා, *Atapahukaranawá*, } to fail in performing, to neglect, to put off a thing, to procrastinate.

අතපානවා, *Atapánawá*, *v.* to hold the hands, to stretch the hands.

අතපුරා, *Atapurá*, } *a.* handful.
අතපුරම, *Atapuráma*, }

අතපෙරවනවා, *Ataperawanawá*, *v.* to fold the arms across the breast from cold.

අතපොවනවා, *Atápowanawá*, *v.* to handle, to touch, to dip the hand; to reach with the hand. pret. අතපෙව්වා *atapewwá*.

අතපැන් වත්කරණවා, *Atapen watkaranawá*, *v.* (අත hand, පැන් water, වත්කරණවා to pour) to pour water into the hand, referring to a custom among the Buddhists, when a person makes a vow to offer a gift of importance to the priests or the temple, he ratifies it by pouring water into the hand of the priest; also to pour water into the hands of each other at the marriage ceremony to ratify their promise.

අතබරකම, *Atabarakama*, *s.* magnitude, serious illness, heaviness.

අතබර ලෙඩා, *Atabara ledá*, *s.* excessively diseased person.

අතබාලයා, *Atabálayá*, *s.* younger person.

අතඹුල, *Atambula*, *s.* kind of precious stone which when held in the hand towards any part every object in that direction becomes visible; kind of prism; a nelli fruit, *phyllanthus* or *myrobalana emblica.*

අතමිටනැති, *Atamitaneti*, *a.* (අත hand, මිට fist, නැති not) needy, destitute, helpless, poor.

අතමුගුර, *Atamugura*, *s.* staff, club, mace, carpenter's hammer.

අත යට, *Ata-yata*, *ad.* (අත and යට under) underhand.

අතර, *Atara*, *prep.* between, in, amongst, during the space of; *s.* middle, interval, from අන්තර *antara; adv.* whilst, in the meantime, from අන්තරා *antará.*

අතරණ, *Atarana*, *s.* cloth for covering a chair, table, or couch.

අතරණ මල්, *Ataranamal*, *s.* flowers spread.

අතරතුර, *Ataratura*, *prep.* amongst, in the midst. *s.* intermediate space.

අතරනැති, *Ataraneti*, *a.* coarse, gross, without intermission.

අතරමංකරණවා, *Ataramankaranawá*, *v.* to abandon, to distress, to render helpless, to forsake, to leave unprotected.

අතරමංවෙනවා, *Ataramanwenawá*, *v.* to be astray, wander; to be left unprotected.

අතරමග, *Ataramaga*, *s.* (අතර in, මග road) on the road; or a middle path. pl. අතරමං *ataraman.*

අතරවාරය, *Atarawáraya*, *s.* intermediate tune, an interval.

අතරවාරෙ, *Atarawáre*, *adv.* amidst, in the meantime; seldom.

අතරෙහි, *Atarehi*, } locative of අතර *atara*; mid-
අතරේ, *Ataré*, } dle, amongst, in the midst of.

අතල, *Atala*, *s.* (අ neg. තල bottom) bottomless, that portion of the world immediately below the earth, one of the hells, a particular division in hell; *a.* spread, strewn.

අතලනවා, *Atalanawá*, *v.* (අත and ලනවා to put) to put the hand in, to meddle.

අතලමයා, *Atalamayá*, *s.* infant in arms, a word of fondness like darling in English.

අතල ස්පර්ශ, *Atalasparsa*, *a.* (අ neg. තල bottom, ස්පර්ශ touch) bottomless, very deep, unfathomable. [Colloq. ඉතා ගැඹුර *itá gembura.*]

අතලේ, *Atalé*, *s.* water pot to carry in the hand; [Colloq. අත් කලය *atkalaya*]. mug; pl. අතල *atala.*

අතලොස්ස, *Atalossa*, *s.* kind of measure; *i. e.* as much as can be contained in one hand, handful. pl. අතලොසු *atalosu*, අතලොහු *atalohu.*

අත වනනවා, *Ata-wananawá*, *v.* to beckon with the hand.

අතවිදිනවා, *Ata-vidinawá*, *v.* to let blood, to bleed the arm; to vaccinate.

අතවැස්සා, *Atawęssá*, } *s.* disciple, pupil, dependant, servant.
අතවැසියා, *Atawęsiyá*,

අතහඳ, *Atahanda*, *s.* net. [Colloq. දැල *dęla*.]

අතහන්කරණවා, *Atahankaranawá*, *v.* to sign.

අතහන, *Atahana*, *s.* signature.

අතහරිණවා, *Atahariṇawá*, *v.* see අතඅරිණවා *ata-ariṇawá*.

අති, *Ati*, *ad.* much, very, exceedingly, over, beyond.

අතිඋඩයන්, *Atiudayan*, *s.* see අතිවිඩයන් *atividayan*.

අතික්‍රමණ, *Atikramaṇa*, *s.* (අති beyond, ක්‍රමණ going) transgression, contrariety, opposition; a daring affair.

අතික්‍රාන්ත, *Atikránta*, *a.* (අති exceeding, ක්‍රාන්ත going beyond) in the highest degree, analogous to English words, infinity, beyond all expression; transgressed, surpassed.

අති ගම්භිර, *Ati gambhíra*, *s.* see අතිගැඹුරු *ati-gęmburu*.

අති ගර්විත, *Ati garvita*, *a.* (අති and ගර්ව *garwa* pride, ඉත *ita* aff.) very proud, arrogant. [Colloquial: ඉතා උඩඟු *itá-udangu*.]

අති ගුප්ත, *Ati gupta*, *a.* (අති and ගුප්ත hidden) very secret, closely hidden or concealed,

අති ගැඹුර, *Ati gęmbura*, *s.* great depth, see next.

අති ගැඹුරු, *Ati gęmburu*, *a.* (අති and ගැඹුර deep) very deep, profound, difficult, hard to be understood; used of the abstruse sciences.

අති ජව, *Ati jawa*, *a.* (අති and ජව quick) swift, fleet, marching fast. [Colloq. ඉතා වේගවත් *itá wégawat*.]

අති ජාගර, *Ati jágara*, *a.* (අති and ජාගර wakeful) sleepless, watchful.

අති තණ්හා, *Ati tanhá*, *s.* intense desire, longing.

අති තීක්ෂණ, *Ati tíkshṇa*, *a.* (අති and තීක්ෂණ sharp) very sharp, very pungent.

අතිථි, *Atithi*, *s.* person entitled to the rites of hospitality, guest. [Colloq. ආගන්තුකයා *ágantukayá*.]

අති දක්ෂ, *Ati daksha*, *a.* (අති and දක්ෂ clever) exceedingly clever, generally used mentally.

අති දුර්ලභ, *Ati durlabha*, *a.* (අති and දුර් *dur* difficult, ලභ *labha* receiving) exceedingly scarce, very difficult to obtain.

අති දුෂ්කර, *Ati dushkara*, *a.* extremely difficult.

අති පාන, *Ati pána*, *s.* much drinking, chiefly used of water.

අති භාෂන, *Ati bhásana*, *s.* (අති and භාෂන speaking) loquaciousness; lustre.

අති මනොහර, *Ati manohara*, *a.* (අති and මනොහර beautiful) very beautiful, very lovely, very pleasing.

අති මර්‍යාදා, *Ati maryádá*, *ad.* (අති and මර්‍යාදා limit) much, excessive, unlimited.

අති මාන්නය, *Ati mánnaya*, *s.* (අති and මාන *mána* pride) vainglory, conceit.

අතිය, *Atiya*, *s.* remnant, (Námávali. 287). Colloq. ඉතිරිදෙය *itiri deya*.

අතියුව, *Atiyuwa*, *a.* (අති and යුව young) childish, infantine.

අතිර, *Atira*, *a.* (අ neg. තිර firm) not lasting, unstable, changeable.

අති රක්ත, *Ati rakta*, *a.* (අති and රක්ත red) very red.

අතිරස, *Atirasa*, } *s.* (අති and රස taste) the name of a kind of cake made of sugar and flour; *a.* very fine tasted.
අතිරහ, *Atiraha*,

අතිරික්ත, *Atirikta*, *a.* (අති and රික්ත flowing) overflowing abundant, excessive, exceeding. [Colloq. ඉතිරි *itiri*.]

අති වාද, *Ati wáda*, *s.* (අති overcoming, වාද to speak) abuse, opprobrious speech.

අතිවිඩයන්, *Atividayan*, *s.* medicinal drug; *Lagenandra lancifolia, (Araceæ)*. see also අතිවිෂා *ativishá*.

අති විශාල, *Ati viśála*, *s.* very great, very extensive; see අතිවිසාල *ativisála*.

අතිවිෂා, *Ativishá*, *s.* (අති overcoming, විෂ poison) name of a tree used in medicine, and said to be an antidote to poison, the bark is also employed in dyeing, it is of three kinds; white, red, and black, *Atis* or *Betula*. [Colloq. අතිවිඩයන් *atividayan*.]

අති විස්තර, *Ati vistara*, *a.* very explanatory, very descriptive, very plain.

අතිවිස, *Ativisa*, *s.* medicinal plant; deadly poison.

අතිවිසා, *Ativisá*, see අතිවිෂා *ativishá*.

අති විසාල, *Ati visála*, *a.* (අති very, විසාල large) very large, very extensive, very deep.

අතිශය, *Atiṣaya*, *a.* much, excessive.

අතිශයින්, *Atiṣayin*, *a.* (අතිශය and ඉන් *in* aff,) exceedingly.

අතිශොභන, *Atiṣóbhana*, *a.* (අති and ශොභන beautiful) very pleasing, very agreeable, very beautiful, extremely handsome.

අතිසාර, *Atisára, a.* (අති excessively, සාර that which goes) dysentery; *a.* very fruitful.

අති සියුම්, *Ati siyum, a.* (අති and සියුම් sharp) exceedingly sharp, as a razor; very profound.

අති සුව, *Ati suwa, s.* (අති and සුව health) great happiness, great health; great riches.

අති සූක්‍ෂම, *Ati súkshma, a.* very profound, very deep, very lofty.

අතිහාස, *Atihása, s.* (අති much, හාස laughter) violent laughter, horse laugh. [Colloquial: තද සිනාව *tada sináwa.*]

අතීත, *Atíta, a.* passed, gone, belonging to former times; *s.* the past.

අතීත කථාව, *Atíta katháwa, s.* ancient story.

අතීත කාලය, *Atíta kálaya, s.* past time; in grammar the preterite tense.

අතීන්‍ද්‍රිය, *Atíndriya, a.* (අති *ati* beyond, ඉන්‍ද්‍රිය *indriya* organ of sense) imperceptible, unattainable by the senses.

අතු, *Atu,* plural of අත්ත *atta* a branch; branches.

අතුගාණවා, *Atugáṇawá, v.* to sweep, as with a broom.

අතුගේ, *Atugé, s.* small house or hut made of cocoanut leaves and attached to a dwelling house to bathe in etc. The common word among the natives for a privy or necessary; thatched house or hut.

අතුන, *Atuna, s.* the bowels; [Colloq. බඩවැල *baḍawela*]. pl. අතුනු *atunu.*

අතුනුබහන, *Atunubahana,* } *s.* (අතුනු bowels, බාන string) the caul which encloses the bowels.
අතුනුබාන, *Atunubána,*
අතුනුවැටිය, *Atunuweṭiya,*

අතුපතර, *Atupatara, s.* (අතු branch, පතර leaf) branch with its leaves.

අතුපාර, *Atupára, s.* path branching from the high road, bye path.

අතුබලේ, *Atubalé, s.* prop, support.

අතුර, *Atura, s.* tying cocoanut trees to each other from the top, so as to enable the toddy drawers to walk from one tree to the other without descending when they are extracting toddy; interval. pl. අතුරු *aturu.*

අතුරගහනවා, *Aturagahanawá, v.* to draw lines, to make furrows by the plough for sowing seed, or irrigation. [Colloq. හීහානවා *híhánawá.*]

අතුරණවා, *Aturaṇawá, v.* to spread, to scatter. pret. ඇතුරුවා *ẹturuwá* or අතුළා *atuḷá.*

අතුරු, *Aturu, s.* space, intermission; furrow; heart; also plural of අතුර *atura.*

අතුරු ඇඳනවා, *Aturu ẹndanawá, v.* (අතුරු and ඇඳනවා to yoke together) to tie cocoanut trees together from the top so as to pass from one to the other without descending when extracting toddy.

අතුරු කථාව, *Aturu katháwa, s.* story added by way of explanation to the principal subject.

අතුරු කප, *Aturu kapa, s.* (අතුරු intermediate, කප kalpa) an inferior or intermediate kalpa.

අතුරුදන්, *Aturudan, s.* Elu form of අන්තර්ධාන *antardhána;* disappearing, vanishing.

අතුරුදන්වෙනවා, *Aturudanwenawá, v.* to vanish, to disappear.

අතුරුපස, *Aturupasa, s.* food taken between meal times.

අතුරුමග, *Aturumaga, s.* middle of the way, midway.

අතුරෙහි, *Aturehi, prep.* amongst, between, in the midst.

අතුරේන්දකාරයා, *Aturéndakárayá, s.* one who takes a rent from the principal renter; subrenter; sharer, partner in the purchase of government rents.

අතුරේන්දය, *Aturéndaya, s.* sub rent.

අතුල්, *Atul, a.* (අ neg. තුල් equal) unequal, unlike; [Colloq. අසමාන *asamána,*] *s.* the palm of the hand. [Colloq. අල්ල *alla.*]

අතුල්පහර, *Atulpahara,* } *s.* blow with the palm of the hand.
අතුල්පාර, *Atulpára,*

අතුල්‍ය, *Atulya, a.* (අ neg. තුල්‍ය equal) unequal, unlike. [Colloq. සමනොවන *samanowana.*]

අතුල්ලනවා, *Atullanawá, v.* (අතුල් the palm, ලනවා to apply) to rub off, to knead the limbs; to rub or apply as ointment. pret. ඇතුල්ලුවා *ẹtulluwá.*

අතුළ, *Atuḷa, s.* covering, coverlet, the palm of the hand; *a.* unlike, see අතුල්‍ය *atulya; p. p.* of අතුරණවා *aturaṇawá* to spread.

අතෘප්ති, *Atripti, a.* (අ not, තෘප්ති satisfaction) unsatisfied, greedy.

අථර්වණ, *Atharwaṇa, s.* name of the fourth Véda.

අද්දර, *Addara, s.* edge, border, margin.

අද්දොණේ, *Addóné, s.* vessel for washing the hands.

අද්භුත, *Adbhuta, a.* wonderful, extraordinary.

අද්‍යතන, *Adyatana, s.* period of a current day, from midnight to midnight, but sometimes reckoned from sunset to sunset.

අද්‍රව්‍ය, *Adrawya*, *a.* (අ neg. ද්‍රව්‍ය matter) immaterial.

අද්‍රි, *Adri*, *s.* mountain; tree; sun.

අද්‍රි රජ, *Adri-rája*, *s.* (අද්‍රි and රජ king) the king of mountains; one of the names of the Himálaya mountains.

අද්‍රිෂ්ට, *Adrishṭa*, see අදෘෂ්ට *adrishṭa*.

අද්‍රිස්‍ය, *Adrisya*, see අදෘශ්‍ය *adriṣya*,

අද්වයවාදින්, අද්වයවාදින්, } *Adwayawádin*, *s.* (අ neg. ද්වය two, වාදින් who speaks) one who acknowledges but one principle, he who never contradicts his own word; one of the names of Buddha.

අද්වේෂි, අද්වේෂි, } *Adweshi*, *a.* (අ neg. ද්වේෂ *dwesha* malice) not malicious, harmless.

අද, *Ada*, *ad.* today, this day; another form of හද *hada* (Elu form of හෘදය *hridaya*) the heart.

අදක්ෂ, *Adaksha*, *a.* (අ neg. දක්ෂ clever) not clever, unskilful; *s.* bungler.

අදක්ෂිණාර්හ, *Adakshináiha*, *a.* (අ not, දක්ෂිණ *dakshiṇa* offering, අර්හ *arha* proper) unholy, unfit for offering religiously; *s.* disobedience to the precepts of Buddha.

අදකෙළි, *Adakeḷi*, *s.* cohabitation.

අදත්තාදානය. *Adattádánaya*, *s.* (අ not, දත්ත *datta* given, ආදාන *ádána* taking) taking things that are not given, robbery, theft. [Colloq. සොරකම *sorakama.*]

අදන්මග, *Adanmaga*, *s.* long way.

අදනා, *Adaná*, *v.* the participle of අදිනවා *adinawá*.

අදම්, *Adam*, *a.* Elu form of අධර්ම *adharma;* unrighteous, unjust; *s.* unrighteousness, injustice, false doctrine.

අදම්‍ය, *Adamya*, *a.* (අ not, දම්‍ය tamed) unruly, unmanageable.

අදර්ශනය, *Adarṣanaya*, *s.* (අ neg. දර්ශන sight) invisibility, absence, being out of sight, disappearance.

අදර්ශනීය, *Adarṣaníya*, *a.* (අ and දර්ශනීය agreeable to the sight) ugly, unpleasant to the sight, arising from deformity.

අදර, *Adara*, *s.* the lip; honour, love, affection, esteem arising from affection; name of the locative case in grammar; a receptacle; favour, help.

අදවත, *Adawata*, *s.* see හදවත *hadawata*.

අදසුන්, *Adasun*, *s.* see අදර්ශනය *adarṣanaya*.

අදහනවා, *Adahanawá*, *v.* to believe, to trust, to worship. pret. ඇදහුවා *ẹdahuwá*.

අදහස, *Adahasa*, *s.* motive, design, intention, thought.

අදහාගන්නවා, *Adahágannawá*, *v.* to believe, to confide in.

අද හෙට, *Ada heṭa*, *ad.* today or tomorrow, in these days.

අදායකයා, *Adáyakayá*, *s.* (අ neg. දායකයා who gives) one not disposed to religious offerings; an illiberal man; an uncharitable man; *i. e.* one who does not give to the poor.

අදාරණවා, *Adáraṇawá*, *v.* to read, to say lessons; pret. ඇදෑරුවා *ẹdẹruwá*. see හදාරණවා *hadáraṇawá*. [Colloq. පාඩම් කියනවා *páḍam kiyanawá*.]

අදාළ, *Adáḷa*, *a.* appertaining to, adapted to, fit for; said, repeated, spoken; from අදාරණවා *adáraṇawá*.

අදාළවෙනවා, *Adáḷawenawá*, *v.* to appertain to, to belong to.

අදික, *Adika*, *a.* more, great, excessive; see අධික, *adhika*.

අදිකරණ, *Adikaraṇa*, *s.* cause, suit, trial; court, bar, subject of discourse.

අදිකාරම, *Adikárama*, *s.* a Kandian chief, adigar, minister of state; pl. අදිකාරම්වරු *adikáramwaru*. See අධිකාරම *adhikárama*.

අදින්නාදානය, *Adinnádánaya*, *s.* taking what is not given; theft.

අදිනවා, *Adinawá*, *v.* to pull, to draw, to drag, to haul. pret. ඇද්දා *ẹddá*.

අදිප්පුව, *Adippuwa*, *s.* lattice, frame.

අදිපති, *Adipati*, see අධිපති *adhipati*.

අදිපතිකම් කරණවා, *Adipatikam karaṇawá*. *v.* to exercise chief control, to perform the functions of a chief or prime minister; see අධිපතිකම් කරණවා *adhipatikam karaṇawá*.

අදිපතියා, *Adipatiyá*, *s.* see අධිපතියා *adhipatiyá*.

අදියර, *Adiyara*, *s.* Elu form of අධිකාර *adhikára*, chapter.

අදිස්, *Adis*, see අදිසි *adisi*.

අදිස්සි, *Adissi*, *a.* sudden, unforeseen.

අදිස්සිය, *Adissiya*, *s.* accident, chance, sudden event, haste.

අදිසි, *Adisi*, *a.* (අ neg. දිස *disa* seeing) invisible, out of sight; [Colloq. අදෘශ්‍යමාන *adriṣyamána*].

අදු, *Adu*, *s.* gambling; (Námávali. 231.) [Colloq. දූකෙළිය *dúkeliya*].

අදුප්පුව, *Aduppuwa*, *s.* see අදිප්පුව *adippuwa*.

අදෘශ්‍ය, *Adriṣya*, *a.* (අ neg. දෘශ්‍ය to be seen) invisible, not to be seen; improper to be beheld.

අදෘශ්‍යමාන, *Adriṣyamána*, *a.* invisible, out of sight, obscure.

අදෘශ්‍යය, *Adriṣyaya*, *s.* (අ and දෘශ්‍යය sight) that which is invisible.

අදෘෂ්ට, *Adrishṭa*, *a.* (අ and දෘෂ්ට seen,) unseen, unforeseen, absent; *s.* casual and unseen danger (as from conflagration or inundation), fear.

ආදෙස්, *Ades*, } *s.* mirror; grammatical term for
ආදෙස, *Adesa*, } substitute; see ආදේශ *ádéṣa*. (Námávali. 177.)

ආදේ, *Adé*, *s.* one of the twenty-seven lunar stations, the sixth in the order of reckoning according to native astronomers; Elu form of the Sanskrit ආර්ද්‍රා *árdrá*.

ආදෝනාව, *Adónáwa*, *s.* mourning, lamentation; whine usually made by beggars.

ආදෝ මාර්ගය, *Adó-márgaya*, *s.* corrupt form of අධොමාර්ගය *adhomárgaya* which see.

අඳ, *Anda*, *s.* see අන්ධ *andha*.

අඳනය, *Andanaya*, *s.* under garment of a priest.

අඳනා, *Andaná*, *p. a.* dressing.

අඳනාකඩ, *Andanákaḍa*, *s.* lower robe of a priest, dress.

අඳනේ, *Andané*, *s.* the lower robe of a priest. [Colloq. අඳින සිවුර *andina siwura*.]

අඳය, *Andaya*, *s.* share, portion, part.

අඳිනවා, *Andinawá*, *v.* to dress, to robe, to wear, to put on, to paint, to draw; pret. ඇන්ද *endá*.

අඳුතලා, *Andutalá*, *s.* plant, species of the *Ocymum*, generic name in Hindi and Bengali Toolsi. (Roxburg Flora Indica 465.) See හින්තලා *hintalá* and මදුරුතලා *madurutalá*.

අඳුන්, *Andun*, *s.* Elu form of අඤ්ජන *añjana*, collyrium or application to the eyelashes to darken and improve them; eyesalve; antimony; lamp black.

අඳුන්කුළු, *Andunkuḷu*, *s.* ink, also kind of paint.

අඳුන්ගිර, *Andungira*, *s.* (අඳුන් and ගිර mountain) name of a mountain.

අඳුන්දිවියා, *Andundiviyá*, *s.* spotted tiger.

අඳුන්වනවා, *Andunwanawá*, *v.* (*Causative*) to make acquainted with, to introduce; pret. ඇඳින්නෙවුවා *endinnewuwá*.

අඳුන් වළ, *Andun waḷa*, *s.* the part under the eye which the natives of India make black with antimony.

අඳුන්වැන්න, *Andunwenna*, *s.* a plant; *Wrightiana* (*Ilicineæ*).

අඳුන, *Andana*, *s.* see අඳුන් *andun*.

අඳුනන, *Andunana*, *p. a.* acquainted with, known, familiar.

අඳුනනවා, *Andunanawá*, *v.* to be acquainted with, to know, to recognize; pret. ඇඳින්නා *endinná*.

අඳුර, *Andura*, *s.* darkness, dimness.

අඳුරු, *Anduru*, *a.* dark.

අඳුරු රුපු, *Anduru rupu*, *s.* (අඳුරු and රුපු enemy) the sun.

අධ්‍යක්ෂ, *Adhyaksha*, *s.* superintendent, overseer; *a.* perceptible, present to the senses. [Colloq. ප්‍රධානියා *pradhániyá*.]

අධ්‍යයන, *Adhyayana*, *s.* study, reading, especially of the sacred books; one of the six duties of a Brahmin.

අධ්‍යාපක, *Adhyápaka*, *s.* teacher, instructor in the sacred books of the Hindus.

අධ්‍යාපන, *Adhyápana*, *s.* instruction in the sacred books of the Hindus; one of the six duties of the Brahmins.

අධ්‍යාශය, *Adhyáṣaya*, *s.* wish, intention. [Colloq. අදහස *adahasa*.]

අධ්‍යාහාර, *Adhyáhára*, *s.* adding a word or words to complete a sentence, supplying an ellipsis; reasoning, argument.

අධ්‍රුව, *Adhruwa*, *a.* (අ neg. ධ්‍රුව fixed) unstable, unfixed, uncertain, transient. [Colloq. අස්ථිර *asthira*.]

අධ්ව, *Adhwa*, *s.* road, way. [Colloq. මග *maga*.]

අධ්වග, *Adhwaga*, *s.* (අධ්ව and ග who goes) traveller, camel, the sun. [Colloq. ගමන්කාරයා *gamankárayá*.]

අධම්මික, *Adhammika*, *s.* not doctrinal. Páli form of අධර්මික *adharmika*, which see.

අධම, *Adhama*, *a.* inferior, low, mean, base, vile.

අධමකම, *Adhamakama*, *s.* (අධම and කම aff.) baseness, meanness, vileness.

අධමයා, *Adhamayá*, *s.* person of low caste, mean or base person.

අධර්මය, *Adharmaya*, *s.* (අ priv. ධර්ම virtue &c.) unrighteousness, injustice; all behaviour contrary to religious and legal institutes.

අධර්මික, *Adharmika*, *a.* unjust, unrighteous, irreligious, wicked.

අධර්මිෂ්ඨ, *Adharmishṭha*, *a.* very wicked, unrighteous, improper, irreligious.

අධර්මිෂ්ඨකම, *Adharmishṭhakama*, *s.* wickedness, unrighteousness.

අධර්මිෂ්ඨයා, *Adharmishṭhayá*, *s.* wicked person, unrighteous man.

අධර, *Adhara*, *a.* (අ neg. ධර to hold) low, inferior, below, vile; *s.* under lip.

අධරෞෂ්ඨය, *Adharoshṭhaya*, *s.* corrupt form of the following.

අධරෞෂ්ඨය, *Adharaushṭhaya*, *s.* (අධර *adhara* below, ඔෂ්ඨ *oshṭha* the lip) the under and upper lips.

අධස්, *Adhas*, *ind.* down, downwards, below; [Colloq. පහත *pahata.*] *s.* pudendum muliebre.

අධස්තාත්, *Adhastát*, see last.

අධාර්මික, *Adhármika*, *a.* (අ neg. ධාර්මික virtuous) unjust, wicked.

අධි, *Adhi*, *ind.* over, above, upon, etc. *a.* perposition and prefix to verbs implying superiority in place, quality, quantity.

අධික්‍රම, *Adhikrama*, *s.* (අධි and ක්‍රම to go) ascendancy, superiority; invasion.

අධික, *Adhika*, *a.* more, great, exceeding, excessive, surpassing, superabundant, more than.

අධිකතර, *Adhikatara*, *ad.* exceeding, very much, more, comparatively more.

අධිකරණ, *Adhikaraṇa*, *s.* justice, judgment, suit, trial; matter of dispute. In grammar the locative case.

අධිකරණ නායකයා, *Adhikaraṇa náyakayá*, *s.* a judge.

අධිකවශයෙන්, *Adhikawasayen*, *ad.* more, more so, more than.

අධිකාරම, *Adhikárama*, *s.* prime minister, judge, (principally applied to judges of the superior court), an adigar. pl. අධිකාරම්වරු *adhikáramwaru.*

අධිකාරය, *Adhikáraya*, *s.* (අධි over, කාර what makes) chapter, section; [Colloq. පරිච්ඡේදය *parichchhédaya.*] authority, supremacy; the bearing of royal insignia.

අධිකෘත, *Adhikṛita*, *a.* (අධි over, කෘත made) superintended, guided; *s.* superintendent.

අධිගත, *Adhigata*, *a.* (අධි and ගත gone) approached, attained, acquired, gone through or over; [Colloq. පැමිණුන *pemiṇuna.*] literally or figuratively as read, studied: *s.* ecstasy, trance.

අධිගම, *Adhigama*, } අධිගමන, *Adhigamana*, } *s.* (අධි excellent, ගම going) used to express the way taken to attain Nirváṇa, the attainment of *Arhatship*, *i. e.* an entire freedom from all impure, or improper passions; attainment, reading, study.

අධිගමාන්තර්ධාන, *Adhigamántardhána*, *s.* (අධිගම *adhigama* and අන්තර්ධාන *antardhána*, disappearing) loss of the road to Nirváṇa, age in which perfect purity cannot be obtained (as the present), the age of sin, inability to impart purity, (applied only to the time when there is no Buddha in the world.)

අධිගෘහීත, *Adhigṛihíta*, *a.* (අධි power, ගෘහීත seized for the purpose of dwelling) taking for a dwelling place, applied only to demons whether good or bad, who after having beheld a place suitable for a residence as upon the tops of mountains or trees, seize it as their own: any person intruding on the dwelling of the demon, without his permission would be destroyed, unless possessed of perfect purity. This word is incorrectly written අධිග්‍රහීත *Adhigrahíta.*

අධිත්‍ය සමුත්පත්තිය, *Adhitya samutpattiya*, *s.* (අධිත්‍ය uncaused, සම් *sam* with, උත්පත්තිය *utpattiya* birth) transmigration, one of the four states or divisions of the animate world, signifying the present state of things; state in which men or animals are now in a state of migration. [Colloq. අහෙතුක උත්පත්ති ඇති *ahetuka utpatti ęti.*]

අධිප්‍රාය, *Adhipráya*, } අධිප්‍රාව, *Adhipráwa*, } *s.* see අභිප්‍රාය *abhipráya.*

අධිප, *Adhipa*, *s.* (අධි and ප who preserves from) master, chief, owner, ruler, king.

අධිපති, *Adhipati*, *s.* (අධි and පති master) master, owner, chief ruler, lord.

අධිපතිකම් කරණවා, *Adhipatikam karaṇawá*, *v.* to rule, to hold sway, to exercise influence, to reign.

අධිපතියා, *s.* lord, chief; see අධිපති *adhipati.*

අධිමාත්‍ර, *Adhimátra*, *s.* (අධි more, මාත්‍ර the whole) more than necessary, excessive, superfluous.

අධිමාසය, *Adhimásaya*, *s.* (අධි and මාස month) an intercalary month, formed of the aggregate days omitted in reckoning the lunar year.

අධිරොහිණී, *Adhirohiṇí*, *s.* ladder, pair of steps. [Colloq. ඉණිමග *iṇimaga.*]

අධි වචන, *Adhiwachana*, *s.* (අධි and වචන speech) name, appellation.

අධිවර, *Adhiwara*, *a.* (අධි and වර chief) supreme. [Colloq. ඉතා උත්තම *itá uttama.*]

අධිවාස, *Adhiwása*, *s.* dwelling, abode, residence, house; perfuming the person.

අධිවාසන, *Adhiwásana*, *s.* perfuming or scenting the person; [Colloquial: සුවඳගැල්වීම *suwaṇdagęlvíma.*] consent, assent, acceptance; abiding.

අධිෂ්ඨානය, *Adhishṭhánaya*, *s.* remaining immovable, resolution, determination; applied chiefly to intensity of mind when engaged on subjects that require deep thought and from which nothing can move the mind.

අධිෂ්ඨිත, *Adhishṭhita*, *a.* (අධි and ස්ථිත *sthita* stationed) fixed, determined, established, engaged in meditation, overruled.

අධීන, *Adhína*, *a.* (අධි and ඉන *ina* master) servile, docile, dependant. [Colloq. යටහත් *yaṭahat.*]

අධීශ්වර, *Adhíṣwara*, *s.* (අධි and ඊශ්වර *íṣwara* lord) lord paramount, emperor. [Colloq. අගරජ *agaraja.*]

අධීශ, *Adhíṣa*, *s.* (අධි and ඊශ *íṣa* master) master, lord. [Colloq. ස්වාමියා *swámiyá.*]

අධුනා, *Adhuná*, *ad.* now, at present. [Colloq. දැන් *dẹn.*]

අධො, *Adho*, *ad.* down, under, underneath.

අධොක්ෂරය, *Adhoksharaya*, *s.* correction written under the line.

අධොගත, *Adhogata*, *a.* (අධස් *adhas* down, ගත gone) dishonoured, gone down, base.

අධොගම වාතය, *Adhogama wátaya*, *s.* (අධස් *adhas* below, ගම going, වාත wind) breaking wind, one of the five vital airs.

අධො භාගය, *Adho-bhágaya*, *s.* (අධස් and භාග part) the lower part; from the hips downward; bottom.

අධො භුවන, *Adho-bhuwana*, *s.* (අධස් beneath, භුවන world) infernal regions, hell, the nága world. [Colloq. පාතාලය *pátálaya.*]

අධො මාර්ගය, *Adho-márgaya*, *s.* fundament. [Colloq. මල මග *mala-maga.*]

අධොමුඛ කරණවා, *Adhomukha karaṇawá*. *v.* to look down, to blush, to turn the mouth (as of a vessel) downwards.

අධො මුඛය, *Adho-mukhaya*, *s.* (අධස් downwards, මුඛ mouth) mouth turned down; *adj.* looking downwards; inverted, turned upside down; *adv.* headlong.

අධොලිපිය, *Adholipiya*, *s.* letter or letters below the line to correct errors, foot-note.

අධොලොක, *Adholoka*, *s.* (අධස් and ලොක world) regions below the earth.

අධො ශීර්ෂ, *Adho-ṣirsha*, } *s.* (අධස් and ශීර්ෂ head)
අධශ්ශීර්ෂ, *Adhaṣṣirsha*, } the head downwards, suspension by the heels.

අධඃ, *Adhaḥ*, *adv.* downwards, below, under, low. [Colloq. පහත *pahata.*]

අධඃක්ෂිප්ත, *Adhaḥkshipta*, *a.* (අධස් *adhas* down, ක්ෂිප්ත part past of ක්ෂිප් *kship* to throw) precipitated, thrown down. [Colloq. පහත දැමූ *pahata dẹmú.*]

අධඃ කාය, *Adhaḥ-káya*, *s.* haunches, lower part of the body.

අන්, *An*, *a.* other, foreign; *s.* horns, plural of අඟ *aṅga:* in this sense, more correctly අං *aṅ*; also a negative particle.

අන්ජලාවා, *Anjaláwá*, *s.* kind of sea fish, the young of the sea fish.

අන්ඩෙ, *Aṇḍe*, *s.* patch; testicle.

අන්ත්‍ය, *Antya*, *a.* (අන්ත *anta* end, යත් *yat* aff.) last, ultimate; inferior, low; *s.* man of low caste, last constellation රේවතී *Réwatí*, last sign of the zodiac, last letter of the alphabet. [Colloquial: කෙළවර *kẹlawara.*]

අන්ත්‍රාව, *Antráwa*, *s.* see අන්තරාව *antaráwa.*

අන්ත, *Anta*, *s.* boundary, limit; death; *a.* final, ultimate.

අන්තක, *Antaka*, *s.* (අන්ත death, ක aff. of agency) name of Mára, the king of death, in Hindu mythology called Yama; Wasawarti the enemy of Buddha.

අන්තක රිපු, *Antaka ripu*, *s.* (අන්තක and රිපු enemy) enemy or destroyer of death, enemy of Mára and Yama; one of the names of Buddha.

අන්තග, *Antaga*, } *a.* dead, departed; crossing,
අන්තගත, *Antagata*, } going to the end.

අන්තය, *Antaya*, *s.* limit, end, conclusion: religious penance, religious offerings made to procure a place in Kámalóka.

අන්තයා, *Antayá*, *s.* worst or meanest person.

අන්තර්ගත, *Antargata*, *a.* (අන්තර් *antar* within ගත gone) forgotten, intermediate; included, belonging to, comprehended.

අන්තර්ගෘහ, *Antargriha*, *s.* (අන්තර් and ගෘහ house) an inner apartment. [Colloq. ඇතුල්ගෙය *ẹtul geya.*]

අන්තර්ජඨර, *Antarjaṭhara*, *s.* අන්තර් and ජඨර belly) stomach. [Colloq. ආමාශය *ámáṣaya.*]

අන්තර්දාහ, *Antardáha*, *s.* (අන්තර් and දාහ burning) internal heat or fever.

අන්තර්ධාන, *Antardhána*, *s.* vanishing, disappearing, concealing. [Colloquial: නොපෙණීයාම *nopẹṇí-yáma.*]

අන්තර්ධාන වෙනවා, *Antardhána wenawá*, *v.* to fade away, to disappear, to vanish.

අන්තර්භූත, *Antarbhúta*, *a.* (අන්තර් and භූත been) internal, inner, within.

අනතර්හිත, *Antarhita*, *a.* (අනතර් and ධා *dhá* to hold with ක්ත *kta* aff; හි *hi* substituted for ධා *dhá*) concealed, hidden, vanished, disappearing.

අනතර, *Antara*, *ad.* within, without, between, amongst; except, outside; *s.* end, conclusion, intermediate space, other; *a.* different.

අනතරවාසක, *Antarawásaka*, *s.* Buddhist priest's under clothing, one of the three garments worn by a Buddhist priest.

අනතරා, *Antará*, *prep.* between, without, except, in the middle, on the way, near at hand; see අනතර *antara*.

අනතරා, *Antará*, *s.* danger, obstacle, impediment, hindrance, accident, end.

අනතරාංශ, *Antaráṇsa*, *s.* (අනතර *antara* between, අංශ *aṇsa* part) inner parts. [Colloq. මැද පංගු *męda paṇgu.*]

අනතරාකරණවා, *Antarákaraṇawá*, *v.* to endanger, to imperil, to hurt, to injure; to hinder.

අනතරා මරණය, *Antará maraṇaya*, *s.* sudden death.

අනතරාය, *Antaráya*, see අනතරා *antará*.

අනතරාව, *Antaráwa*, *s.* danger, accident, injury.

අනතික, *Antika*, *a.* (අනත *anta* end, ඉ *i* inserted, ක aff.) near, proximate. [Colloquial: සමීපවූ *samípawú.*]

අනතිම, *Antima*, *a.* final, ultimate, last, very near.

අනතිමය, *Antimaya*, *s.* end, termination, acme.

අනතිමෙ, *Antime*, *s.* at the end; see අනතිමය *antimaya.*

අනෙතවාසික, *Antewásika*, *s.* (අනත and වාසික who dwells) one that lives near another, *i. e.* pupil, scholar; servant.

අනෙතවාසින්, *Antewásin*, *s.* (අනෙත loc. case of අනත near, වාසින් dweller) pupil. [Colloquial: ගෝලයා *gólayá.*]

අනෙතාර, *Antora*, *s.* inner town. (Námávali. 103.) see ඇතොර *ętora.*

අනතඃ, *Antaḥ*, *a.* inner.

අනතඃ කල්පය, *Antaḥ-kalpaya*, *s.* 1,774,080,000 years.

අනතඃ පුරය, *Antaḥ-puraya*, *s.* (අනතර් *antar* inner, පුර house) queen's apartments, inner court; citadel.

අන්ද, *Anda*. *a.* see අන්ධ *andha.*

අන්දකාරය, *Andakáraya*, *s.* darkness.

අන්දන් තබනවා, *Andan tabanawá*, *v.* to clip the beard into shape.

අන්දම, *Andama*, *s.* mode, manner, state, condition; pl. අන්දම් *andam.*

අන්දයා, *Andayá*, *s.* see අන්ධයා *andhayá.*

අන්දර, *Andara*, *s.* a sort of tree, *(acacia)* of which there are about seven or eight species in Ceylon; *Dichrostachys cinerea, (Legum).*

අන්දවනවා, *Andawanawá*, *v.* to dress another, to clothe; pret. ඇන්දෙව්වා *ęndewwá.*

අන්දායම, *Andáyama*, *s.* fortified entrenchment, camp, barricade. pl. අන්දායම් *andáyam.*

අන්ඳිටු, *Andiṭu*, *s.* (අන් other දිටු religion) heathen, pagan.

අන්දෝරුව, *Andóruwa*, *s.* Kandian palanquin.

අන්ධ, *Andha*, *a.* blind; dark.

අන්ධක, *Andhaka*, *s.* name of a country, probably Behar; name of a king, a *muni*, and an Asur. *a.* blind.

අන්ධකම, *Andhakama*, *s.* darkness.

අන්ධකාර, *Andhakára*, *s.* (අන්ධ blind, කාර what makes) darkness.

අන්ධයා, *Andhayá*, *s.* blind man.

අන්ධවෙනවා, *Andhawenawá*, *v.* to become blind.

අන්න, *Anna*, *s.* boiled rice; food.

අන්න, *Anna*, *int.* particle of exclamation, look, behold, there!

අන්නක්කා, *Annakká*, *s.* pine apple; *provincial.* [Colloq. අන්නාසි *annási.*]

අන්නපාන, *Annapána*, *s.* (අන්න food, පාන *pána* drink) meat and drink, food.

අන්නමඩේ, *Annamadé*, අන්නමලය, *Annamalaya*, } *s.* (අන්න striking, මලය weapon) spear or spike used in the chase for spearing animals.

අන්නනවා, *Annanawá*, *v.* to cause to strike or beat; to cause to fight with the horns. pret. ඇන්නෙව්වා *ęnnewwá.*

අන්නවා, *Annawá*, *v.* to strike, to stab, to pierce. pret. ඇන්නා *ęnná.*

අන්‍ය, *Anya*, *a.* other, not this, different, foreign, strange; unlike.

අන්‍ය ගති, *Anya-gati*, *s.* another nature, strange nature.

අන්‍ය ගතික, *Anya-gatika*, *a.* of another kind, of another sample.

අන්‍ය ජාතිය, *Anya-játiya*, *s.* (අන්‍ය and ජාතිය race) another race, another caste.

අන්‍යතර, *Anyatara*, *pron.* other, different, either of the two; applied chiefly to words that refer to two things.

අන්‍ය දෘෂ්ටි, *Anya-drishṭi*, *a.* (අන්‍ය strange, දෘෂ්ටි sight) apostate, heretical, heathen.

අන්‍ය දෘෂ්ටිකයා, *Anya-drishṭikayá*, *s.* apostate, heathen.

අන්‍ය පුෂ්ට, *Anya-pushṭa*, *s.* (අන්‍ය and පුෂ්ට nourished) Indian cuckoo, supposed to be reared by the crow.

අන්‍ය භෘත, *Anya-bṛita*, *s.* (අන්‍ය and භෘත nourished) the *kókila* or Indian cuckoo. This bird is supposed to lay its eggs in the nests of other birds (generally the crow) to be hatched by them. [Colloq. කොහා *kohá*.]

අන්‍ය රසය, *Anya-rasaya*, *s.* (අන්‍ය and රසය taste) another taste.

අන්‍ය ලබ්ධි, *Anya-labdhi*, *a*, (අන්‍ය and ලබ්ධි sect, faith) heretical, false in religion.

අන්‍ය වර්ධිත, *Anya-wardhita*, *a.* (අන්‍ය and වර්ධිත grown) brought up by another, fostered

අන්‍යවාදින්, *Anyawádin*, *s.* (අන්‍ය otherwise, වාදින් who speaks) one who speaks inconsistently, prevaricator.

අන්‍යූන, *Anyúna*, *a.* (අ neg. න්‍යූන defective) complete, entire. [Colloq. සම්පූර්ණ *sampúrṇa*.]

අන්‍යොදක, *Anyodaka*, *s.* (අන්‍ය *anya* and උදක *udaka* water) other water; fever ague taking effect every twenty-four hours.

අන්වනවා, *Anwanawá*, *v.* to cause to pierce or butt, and is used of horned animals to make them fight. pret. ඇන්නෙව්වා *ennewwá*. See අන්නනවා *annanawá*.

අන්වය, *Anwaya*, *s.* generation, lineage, succession; the natural order or connection of words in a sentence or stanza.

අන්වෙෂණ, *Anweshaṇa*, *s.* research, investigation of duty by reasoning. [Colloq. සෙවීම *sewíma*.]

අන්වෙෂිත, *Anweshita*, *a.* (අනු *anu* and ඉෂිත *ishita* desired) sought, searched.

අන්වෙස, *Anwesa*, *s.* another figure or form.

අන්සකය, *Ansakaya*, } *s.* part, portion; see අංසය
අන්සකේ, *Ansaké*, } *aṇsaya*.

අන්සත්, *Ansat*, *s.* spine. [Colloquial: මුදුන් ඇටය *mudun eṭaya*.]

අන්සතු, *Ansatu*, } *a.* belonging to another.
අන්සන්තක, *Ansantaka*, }

අන්සය, *Ansaya*, *s.* see අංශය *aṇsaya*.

අන්සල්, *Ansal*, *s.* lute, rock, stability, firmness.

අන්සින, *Ansína*, *s.* a person deprived of some members of his body.

අන්සු, *Ansu*, see අංසු *aṇsu*.

අන, *Ana*, *s.* command, an order, authority; in Páli books it means sound: more correctly අණ *aṇa*.

අන කරණවා, *Ana-karaṇawá*, *v.* to order, to command: more correctly අණකරණවා *aṇakaraṇawá*.

අන කියනවා, *Ana-kiyanawá*, *v.* prohibit, to threaten: more correctly අණ කියනවා *aṇa-kiyanawá*.

අනගාරික, *Anagárika*, *s.* (අන් *an* not, අගාර *agára* house) houseless, an epithet applied to a certain class of ascetics who live in woods, name for a certain kind of saints, it may be applied to Buddhist priests as they are not householders.

අනගි, *Anagi*, *a.* Elu form of අනර්ඝ *anargha*, which see.

අනඞ්ග *Ananga*, *a.* (අන් *an* neg. අඞ්ග *anga* body) bodiless, an epithet of Káma, the Hindu god of love, which name he bears in consequence of having been reduced to ashes by the eye of Sivá for having disturbed his devotions, and rendered him enamoured of the goddess Párvati; also the sky, heart.

අනඞ්ගපිය, *Anangapiya*, *s.* asóka tree, *(jonesia asoca.)* [Colloq. දියරතඹලා *diyaratambalá*, also හෝපළු ගස *hópaḷu-gasa*.]

අනඞ්ගයා, *Anangayá*, see අනඞ්ග *ananga*.

අනඞ්ගප්‍රිය, *Anańgapriya*, *s.* see අනඞ්ගපිය *ananga piya*.

අනඞ්ගයා, *Anańgayá*, *s.* (අන් *an* neg. අඞ්ග *ańga* body) name of Káma, the Hindu deity of love; see අනඞ්ග *ananga*; also, general name for the gods which they bear in consequence of their beauty.

අනච්ඡ, *Anachchha*, *a.* (අන් *an* and අච්ඡ *achchha* clear) not clear, turbid, muddy as the disturbed waters of a river or pond.

අනඩු, *Anaḍu*, *a.* (අ not, නඩු justice) unjust, contrary to law, iniquitous.

අනඩු පොලිය. *Anaḍu poliya*, *s.* (අනඩු and පොලිය interest) usury.

අනඩුව, *Anaḍuwa*, *s.* injustice; that which is contrary to law.

අනත්, *Anat*, *s.* king of Nágalóka or world of snakes; *a.* endless; see අනන්ත *ananta*.

අනත, *Anata*, *a.* Elu form of the Sanskrit word අනන්ත *ananta*, endless, infinite.

අනතයා, *Anatayá*, *s.* poor man, needy person.

අනතික්‍රාන්ත, *Anatikránta*, *a.* (අන් *an* not, අතික්‍රාන්ත *atikránta* going beyond duty) keeping within bounds, unsurpassed, unexceeded, untransgressed.

අනතුර, *Anatura*, *s.* peril, danger, unforeseen calamity; pl. අනතුරු *anaturu*.

අනතුරු, *Anaturu*, *a.* (අන් *an* and අතුරු *aturu* space) without intermission, constant, continual;

dangerous; next immediately following, next of kin or in succession, next. This word occurs also in the Elu books as a form of the Sanskrit අන්තරාය *antaráya*.

අනද, *Anada*, *a*. (අ priv. නද sound) silent; but it is used as expressive of being joyless; *s*. the name of a famous disciple of Buddha.

අනදර, *Anadara*, *s*. (අන් *an* not, අදර *adara* respect) disrespect: unkindness, injury, injustice.

අනදිවර, *Anadiwara*, *s*. Elu form of අනධිවර *anadhiwara* which see.

අනදෙනවා, *Anadenawá*, *v*. to command: more correctly අණදෙනවා *aṇadenawá*.

අනධිවර, *Anadhiwara*, *s*. (අන් *an* neg. අධිවර *adhiwara* a chief) without a superior, epithet of Buddha.

අනන්ත, *Ananta*, *a*. (අන් *an* not, අන්ත *anta* end) endless, eternal, infinite; *s*. name of the king of the Nágalóka or the world of snakes; the sky, the atmosphere.

අනන්තර, *Anantara*, see අනතුරු *anaturu*.

අනන්ත ශීර්ෂා, *Ananta ṣírshá*, *s*. (අනන්ත many ශීර්ෂ head) the wife of Vásuki, king of serpents.

අනන්‍ය, *Ananya*, *a*. (අන් *an* neg. අන්‍ය *anya* other) without any other, same.

අනන්‍ය වෘත්ති, *Ananya vritti*, *a*. (අන් *an* and අන්‍ය *anya* other, වෘත්ති profession) closely attentive, having the mind fixed on one object.

අනනවා, *Ananawá*, *v*. to knead, to mix as dough, to mingle; pret. ඇනුවා *enuwá*.

අනනුයොන්, *Ananuyon*, *s*. question. [Colloquial: ප්‍රශ්නය *praṣnaya*.]

අනපරාධ, *Anaparádha*, } *s*. (අන් *an* and අපරාධ *aparádha* offence) innocence. *a*. innocent, sinless, guiltless.
අනපරාධි, *Anaparádhi*, }

අන පොල්ල, *Anapolla*, *s*. (අණ order, පොල්ල staff) baton, mace, constable's staff: more correctly අණ පොල්ල *aṇapolla*. pl. අණපොලු *aṇapolu*.

අනබෙරකාරයා, *Anaberakárayá*, *s*. one who publishes orders by beat of drum: more correctly අණබෙරකාරයා *aṇaberakárayá*. pl. අණබෙර කාරයෝ *aṇaberakárayó*.

අනබෙරය, *Anaberaya*, *s*. drum by which orders are published: more correctly අණබෙරය *aṇaberaya*.

අනබෙරලන්නා, *Anaberalanná*, *s*. see අනබෙරකාරයා *anaberakárayá*.

අනබෙරලනවා, *Anaberalanawá*, *v*. to publish orders by beat of drum: more correctly අණබෙර ලනවා *aṇaberalanawá*.

අනභ්‍යාස, *Anabhyása*, *s*. (අන් *an* neg, අභ්‍යාස *abhyása* practice, custom) want of practice, inexperience. [Colloq. නුපුරුද්ද *nupurudda*.]

අනභ්‍ර, *Anabhra*, *a*. (අන් *an* and අභ්‍ර *abhra* cloud) not cloudy; without plumbago.

අනභිඥ, *Anabhijña*, *a*. (අන් *an* and අභිඥ *abhijña* wise) unwise, stupid.

අනභිධ්‍යා, *Anabhiddhyá*, *s*. (අන් *an* and අභිධ්‍යා *abhiddhyá* covetousness) freedom from covetousness.

අනභිනන්ද, *Anabhinanda*, *a*. (අන් *an* and අභිනන්ද *abhinanda* delightful) not pleased. [Colloquial: සතුටු නැති *satuṭuneti*.]

අනභිභව, *Anabhibhawa*, *s*. (අන් *an* and අභිභව *abhibhawa* defeat) freedom from obstruction or defeat.

අනභිභවනීය, *Anabhibhawaníya*, *a*. (අන් *an* and අභිභවනීය *abhibhawaníya* conquerable) unconquerable. *s*. that which cannot be subdued.

අනභිභූත, *Anabhibhúta*, *a*. (අන් *an* and අභිභූත *abhibhúta* subdued) unsubdued, unobstructed; not confused; not happened.

අනභිමත, *Anabhimata*, *a*. (අන් *an* and අභිමත *abhimata* liked) undesired, disliked.

අනභිමුඛ, *Anabhimukha*, *a*. (අන් *an* and අභිමුඛ *abhimukha* present) absent.

අනභිමුඛය, *Anabhimukhaya*, *s*. absence.

අනභිරතිය, *Anabhiratiya*, *s*. (අන් *an* and අභිරතිය *abhiratiya* wish) freedom from the influence of passion, having no longing for a thing. [Colloq. නොඇල්ම *noelma*.]

අනභිෂික්ත, *Anabhishikta*, *a*. (අන් *an* and අභිෂික්ත *abhishikta* anointed) not anointed, not regularly appointed to the office of king.

අනය, *Anaya*, } *s*. (අන් *an* neg. අය *aya* good fortune) ill-luck, fate, bad fortune; calamity; sometimes vice, transgression.
අනයවාසන, *Anayawásana*, }

අනයුරු, *Anayuru*, *s*. sea. [Colloquial: සාගරය *ságaraya*.]

අනර්ග, *Anarga*, *a*. corrupt form of අනර්ඝ *anargha*, which see.

අනර්ගල, *Anargala*, *a*. (අන් *an* and අර්ගල *argala* bolt or bar) self willed, unrestrained. [Colloq. නොහික්මුන *nohikmuna*.]

අනර්ඝ, *Anargha*, *a*. (අන් *an* and අර්ඝ *argha* price) invaluable, priceless, precious.

අනර්, *Anartha,* } a. (අන් *an* and අර්‍ථ *arttha*
අනර්‍ථ, *Anarttha,* } meaning or use) without meaning, unmeaning, unjust.

අනර්‍ථය, *Anartthaya,* s. loss, injustice, that which is without meaning or profit.

අනල්ප, *Analpa,* } a. අන් *an* neg. අල්ප *alpa*
අනල්පවූ, *Analpawú,* } few) many, not a few.

අනල, *Anala,* s. fire; bile; name of a plant, රත් නෙටුල් *ratneṭul, (plumbago zeylanica* and *rosea);* also the third constellation.

අනලස, *Analasa,* a. (අන් *an* and අලස *alasa* idle) industrious.

අනව, *Anawa,* s. the ocean; (Námávali. 81.) [Colloq. සාගරය *ságaraya*].

අනවකාශ, *Anawakása,* a. (අන් *an* and අවකාශ *awakása* rest) without rest or leisure, without space, occupied.

අනවතත්ත විල, *Anawatatta vila,* s. name of a lake in the Himálaya mountains, the dark lake; *i. e.* on which the beams of the sun never shine.

අනවද්‍ය, *Anawadya,* a. (අන් *an* not, අවද්‍ය *awadya* guilt) guiltless, innocent.

අනවධාන, *Anawadhána,* s. (අන් *an* and අවධාන *awadhána* attention) carelessness, inattention, inadvertence, mistake.

අනවරණ, *Anawaraṇa,* s. freedom from obstruction. [Colloq. නොවැලකීම *nowęlakíma*]; see අනාවරණ *anáwaraṇa.*

අනවරත, *Anawarata,* a. (අන් *an* neg. අවරත *awarata* ceased, stopped) continual, constant, unremitting, eternal. [Colloq. නිරන්තර *nirantara.*]

අනවරතය, *Anawarataya,* s. constancy. [Colloq. නිරන්තරය *nirantaraya.*]

අනවරතයෙන්, *Anawaratayen,* ad. constantly, continually.

අනවරාග්‍ර, *Anawarágra,* a. (අන් *an* not, අවර *awara* the hinder part or bottom, අග්‍ර *agra* end) without beginning or ending, endless, infinite. [Colloq. අක්මුල්නැති *akmulneti.*]

අනවලොක, *Anawaloka,* } a. (අන් *an* and අව
අනවලොකන, *Anawalokana,* } *awa* and ලොක to see) imperceptible.

අනවින, *Anavina,* s. witchcraft, incantations practised upon persons who have been poisoned, or bitten by a serpent.

අනවිනකාරයා, *Anavinakárayá,* s. juggler, one who practises incantations upon persons who have been poisoned or bitten by a serpent.

අනවුරු, *Anawuru,* s. (අන් *an* and අවුරු *awuru* to cover) the sea. [Colloq. මුහුද *muhuda,*]

අනසක, *Anasaka,* s. order, command, jurisdiction: more correctly අණසක *aṇasaka.*

අනාකුල, *Anákula,* a. (අන් *an* and ආකුල *ákula* confused) clear, unconfused, simple, composed, unperplexed.

අනාගත, *Anágata,* a. (අන් *an* and ආගත *ágata* come) future, not arrived.

අනාගත කාලය, *Anágata kálaya,* s. (අනාගත future, කාලය time) future time; grammatical term for future tense.

අනාගතවක්තෘ, *Anágatawaktṛi,* s. one that foretells, prophet. pl. අනාගතවක්තෘවරු *anágatawaktṛiwaru.*

අනාගතවාක්‍යය, *Anágatawákyaya,* s. a prophecy.

අනාගාමි, *Anágámi,* s. (අන් *an* and ආගාමි *ágámi* one who comes) one who has entered the third of the four paths to Nirváṇa, so called because he cannot be born again in the world of men or of gods, but only in a Brahma world from which he may attain Nirváṇa; the future.

අනාගාමි මාර්ගය, *Anágámi márgaya,* s. (අන් *an* and ආගාමි *ágámi* returning, මාර්ග way) the third of the four paths to Nirváṇa.

අනාගැමි, *Anágęmi,* see අනාගාමි *anágámi.*

අනාචාර, *Anáchára,* a, (අන් *an* and ආචාර *áchára,* established rule of conduct) uncivil, unpolite, rude, immoral, illbehaved; ugly; s. impropriety, violation of moral or civil rule or institute.

අනාචාරිය, *Anácháriya,* a. immoral, indecorous illbehaved, wicked.

අනාචාරියා, *Anáchári yá,* s. vulgar, rude person; adulterer.

අනාත්මය, *Anátmaya,* a. (අන් *an* not, ආත්මය *átmaya* body or soul) bodiless, soul-less.

අනාථ, *Anátha,* a. (අ and නාථ lord) lordless; s. forlorn and destitute person, beggar.

අනාථපිඩකයා, *Anáthapinḍakayá,* } s. charitable
අනාථපිණ්ඩකයා, *Anáthapiṇḍakayá,* } person, phi-
අනාථපිණ්ඩික, *Anáthapinḍika,* } lanthropist; name of a votary of Buddha.

අනාදර, *Anádara,* s. (අන් *an* not, ආදර *ádara* respect) disrespect.

අනාදාන, *Anádána,* s. (අන් *an* and ආදාන *ádána* taking) not taking.

අනාදි, *Anádi,* a. (අන් *an* and ආදි *ádi* beginning) without any beginning, eternal, uncreate, unborn.

අනාදිමත්, *Anádimat,* a. without beginning.

අනාදිය, *Anádiya,* s. eternity. [Colloq. සදාකාලය *sadákálaya.*]

අනාදෘශ, *Anádrisa*, *a.* (අන් *an* and ආදෘශ *ádrisa* shape) without pattern or model.

අනාධාර, *Anádhára*, *a.* (අන් *an* and ආධාර *ádhára* help) without a support, helpless, destitute, distressed, friendless.

අනාපත්තිය, *Anápattiya*, *s.* (අන් *an* and ආපත්ති *ápatti* fault) state of being faultless, innocent; but it is used chiefly of fitness for the office of the Buddhist priesthood.

අනාපු, *Anápu*, *a.* pret. of අනනවා *ananawá*.

අනාමය, *Anámaya*, *s.* (අන් *an* and ආමය *ámaya* sickness) health.

අනාමිකා, *Anámiká*, *s.* the ring finger. [Colloq. මුදුඟිල්ල *mudengilla*.]

අනායාසය, *Anáyásaya*, *s.* (අන් *an* and ආයාස *áyása* effort) facility.

අනායාසයෙන්, *Anáyásayen*, *ad.* easily, with facility. [Colloq. ලේසියෙන් *lésiyen*.]

අනාර්ය, *Anárya*, } *a.* (අන් *an* and ආර්ය *árya*
අනාර්යක, *Anáryaka*, } respectable, ක *ka* aff.) unworthy, disreputable, not noble, of mean origin; belonging to the country of the Mlechchhas, or barbarians; name of a kind of wood, the agallochum or aloe wood *(aquilaria agallochum)*.

අනාරම්භය, *Anárambhaya*, *s.* (අන් *an* and ආරම්භ *árambha* beginning) want of a beginning, non commencement.

අනාවරණ, *Anáwarana*, *a.* (අන් *an* and ආවරණ *áwarana* covering) open, unclosed, uncovered, exposed, unobstructed.

අනාවරණ ඤාණය, *Anáwarana ñánaya*, } *s.* (අන්
අනාවරණ ඥානය, *Anáwarana jñánaya*, } *an* and ආවරණ *áwarana* screen, ඥාන *jñána* knowledge) known wisdom, evident knowledge, omniscience, all seeing.

අනාවරණ නැන, *Anáwarana nena*, see above.

අනාවිල, *Anávila*, *a.* (අන් *an* and ආවිල *ávila* turbid) clear, clean, pure.

අනාවෘත්ත, *Anávritta*, *a.* (අන් *an* neg. ආවෘත්ත *ávritta* round) not circular.

අනාවෘත, *Anávrita*, *a.* (අන් *an* and ආවෘත *ávrita* covered) uncovered, open.

අනාශ්‍රය, *Anáṣraya*, *s.* (අන් *an* and ආශ්‍රය *áṣraya* asylum) absence of attachment or dependence.

අනාශ්‍රව, *Anáṣrawa*, *a.* (අන් *an* and ආශ්‍රව *áṣrawa* lust) free from human passion; *s.* name of Nirvána.

අනාසවය, *Anásawaya*, *s.* Páli form of the preceding.

අනාඥා කරණවා, *Anájñá-karanawá*, corruption of ආඥාකරණවා *ájñákaranawá*.

අනාඥාව, *Anájñáwa*, corruption of ආඥාව *ájñáwa*.

අනික්, *Anik*, *a.* other.

අනික්දා, *Anikdá*, *s.* the day after tomorrow.

අනික, *Anika*, *s.* the other thing,

අනිකක්, *Anikak*, *s.* another one.

අනිකකු, *Anikaku*, *s.* another man.

අනිකා, *Aniká*, *s.* the other one.

අනිකිනි, *Anikini*, *s.* army, host, forces; force consisting of a certain number that is one tenth of an akshauhiṇí; 2187 elephants, and as many chariots, 6561 horse, and 10,935 foot.

අනිකුත්, *Anikut*, *a.* other, the other one also.

අනිකුඩු, *Anikudu*, *s.* the other one; *a.* other.

අනිකෙක්, *Anikek*, *s.* an other person.

අනිච්චං, *Anichchan*, } (Páli). *a.* not lasting, transi-
අනිච්චා, *Anichchá*, } tory, perishable.

අනිච්චෙ, *Anichche*, Páli form of අනිත්‍ය *anitya*.

අනිච්චේ, *Anichché*, *interj.* expressing surprise, as dear me!

අනිටු, *Anitu*, *a.* inauspicious, ominous; *s.* misery, suffering, sin, poison, ingratitude.

අනිත්, *Anit*, *a.* the other.

අනිත්ත, *Anitta*, *s.* plant, *Rhinacanthus communis*, *(Acanthaceæ.)*

අනිත්‍ය, *Anitya*, *a.* (අ neg. නිත්‍ය constant) transient, perishable, changeable, not always abiding,

අනිද්දා, *Aniddá*, *ad.* the day after tomorrow.

අනින්ද්‍රිය, *Anindriya*, *a.* (අන් *an* not, ඉන්ද්‍රිය *indriya* an organ of sense) imperceptible, void of the senses.

අනින්දිත, *Anindita*, *a.* (අ and නින්දිත reproached) honourable, respectable, but its more general meaning is that of beauty or freedom from any deformity; in Sanskrit books it conveys the idea of pious, virtuous.

අනිනවා, *Aninawá*, *v.* to spear, to pierce, to stab, to gore; to punch, to beat with the fist or with a stick. pret. ඇන්නා *enná*.

අනිමිෂ, *Animisha*, } *s.* (අ and නිමිෂ that twinkles)
අනිමිස, *Animisa*, } that which always keeps its eyes open; a god, a deity.

අනිමිසලොචන, *Animisalochana*, *s.* unblenching gaze; *a.* sleepless, *lit.* never closing the eyes.

අනියත, *Aniyata*, *a.* (අ and නියත proper) improper, mistaken; undefined, unprescribed.

අනියම්, *Aniyam*, } *a.* (අ and නියම appointed) un-
අනියම, *Aniyama*, } fixed, unsettled, not appointed, undetermined, indefinite, irregular.

අනිරුඞ, } Aniruddha, *s.* the son of Pradyumna,
අනිරුද්ධ, } a form of Káma and husband of Ushá.

අනිල, *Anila, s.* air or wind, considered also as a deity who has the command of the wind; a subordinate kind of deity 49 of whom form a class called *anilas;* the 15th *nakshatra* or lunar mansion. *a.* airy, windy.

අනිෂ්ට, *Anishṭa, a.* (අන් *an* neg. ඉෂ්ට *ishṭa* wished) bad, unlucky, undesirable; see අනිටු *anitu.*

අනිෂ්ටවෙනවා, *Anishṭawenawá, v.* not to happen, not to accomplish.

අනිස්ස, *Anissa, s.* (අ and නිස්ස that which is proper) an improper act, a duty which a man is not obliged to do.

අනිස, *Anisa, a.* perishable, not always abiding.

අනීක, *Aníka,* see අනික *anika.*

අනීකිනී, *Aníkini,* see අනිකිනි *anikini.*

අනීශ්වර, *Aníṣwara, a.* (අන් *an* neg. ඊශ්වර *íṣwara* lord) lordless, having no authority.

අනු, *Anu,* preposition and prefix implying after, like, in the same manner; under, inferior to: along, lengthwise; with, together with, in part of; severally, each by each, near to; in regard to.

අනු, *Anu, a.* small, minute, subtle, confirming; *s.* atom, well watered place, measure equal to thirty six paramáṇus: more correctly අණු *aṇu.*

අනුක්ත, *Anukta, past. part.* (අන් *an* not, උක්ත *ukta* said) not said, not related.

අනුක්‍රම, *Anukrama, s.* (අනු methodically, ක්‍රම to go) order, method; *a.* very regular, strictly according to rule.

අනුක්‍රමයෙන්, *Anukramayen, ad.* gradually by degrees.

අනුක්ෂුද්‍ර, *Anukshudra, a.* (අනු very, ක්ෂුද්‍ර little) very little, very small, not of importance, insignificant. [Colloq. ඉතා කුඩා *itá kuḍá.*

අනුකම්පා, *Anukampá, s.* (අනු very or intense, කම්පා shaking) great agitation; but the word is invariably used to express an affection of the mind, namely, great compassion, great tenderness of heart, extreme commiseration, pity, compassion.

අනුකම්පා කරණවා, *Anukampá karaṇawá, a.* to compassionate, to shew pity.

අනුකම්පාව, *Anukampáwa, s.* compassion, tenderness.

අනුකම්පාවෙනවා, *Anukampáwenawá, v.* to commiserate, to be kindly affectionate, to feel compassionate.

අනුකර්ෂණ, *Anukarshaṇa, s.* (අනු and කෘෂ *krisha* to draw, ණ aff,) invoking, summoning by incantations.

අනුකූල, *Anukúla, a.* (අනු together with, කූල bank or shore) friendly, favourable or conformable to, agreeable.

අනුකූලව, *Anukúlawa, adv.* according to, in accordance with, conformably to.

අනුග්‍රහය, *Anugrahaya, s.* (අනු afterwards, ග්‍රහ to take) grace, favour, help, assistance, conferring benefits by promoting good and preventing ill.

අනුගත, *Anugata, a.* (අනු and ගත gone) followed, following, relating to, concerning.

අනුගමන, *Anugamana, s.* (අනු together with, ගමන going) a following; follower, companion.

අනුගාමික, *Anugámika, a.* (අනු with, ගාමික going) accompanying, following; *s.* follower.

අනුගායනා, *Anugáyaná, s.* (අනු and ගායනා singing) singing together with another, performing on musical instruments with others.

අනුච්ච, *Anuchcha, a.* (අන් *an* neg. උච්ච *uchcha* high) low, not high, humble.

අනුච්චාරණ, *Anuchchárana, s.* (අන් *an* not, උච්චාරණ *uchcháraṇa* saying) non utterance.

අනුචර, *Anuchara, s.* (අනු with, චර going) companion, follower.

අනුජ, *Anuja, a.* (අනු after, ජ born) born after, younger, junior; *s.* younger brother or sister; brother.

අනුජාත, *Anujáta, a.* (අනු like, ජාත born) similar in nature, used of children who are perfect models of their father; born after, younger.

අනුජීවක, *Anujíwaka, s.* (අනු with, ජීවක who lives) soldier, companion.

අනුඥා, *Anujñá, a.* (අනු according to, ඥා to know) order or command, assent, permission, sanction.

අනුත්තම, *Anuttama, a.* (අන් *an* neg. උත්තම *uttama* best) chief, principal, best.

අනුත්තර, *Anuttara, a.* (අන් *an* and උත්තර *uttara* answer or subsequent) unable to answer, silent; best, chief, principal, excellent.

අනුත්තාප, *Anuttápa,* see අනුතාප *anutápa.*

අනුත්පාද, *Anutpáda. a.* (අන් *an* and උත්පාද *utpáda* birth) without birth.

අනුත්පාදන, *Anutpádana, s.* (අන් *an* and උත්පාදන *utpádana* birth) that which is without birth. *i. e.* Nirváṇa.

අනුතර්ෂ, *Anutarsha*, *s.* (අනු and තර්ෂ from තෘෂ *trisha* to thirst) thirst, wish, desire; [Colloquial: පිපාසය *pipásaya*.] drinking vessel, one used for drinking spirituous liquors.

අනුතර්ෂණ, *Anutarshaṇa*, *s.* a vessel used for drinking spirituous liquors.

අනුතර, *Anutara*, *a.* very little, very small; fare, freight.

අනුතර පාපය, *Anutara-pápaya*, *s.* very small or trifling sin.

අනුතාප, *Anutápa*, *s.* (අනු afterwards, තාප pain) repentance.

අනුතාව, *Anutáwa*, *s.* littleness, smallness.

අනුදත්, *Anudat*, } *a.* permitted, consented,
අනුදන්නා, *Anudanná*, } allowed.

අනුදන්නාලද්දේ, *Anudannáladdé*, *s.* a thing sanctioned.

අනුදන්වනවා, *Anudanwanawá*, *v*, to cause to consent or permit.

අනුදිග, *Anudiga*, *s.* (අනු secondary, දිග direction) any intermediate point, intermediate point of the compass.

අනුදින, *Anudina*, *ad.* daily.

අනුදිව්, *Anudiw*, *s.* general name for any small island; a disease of the tongue in which a small protuberance of flesh appears under the tongue, resembling a small tongue.

අනුදිසා, *Anudisá*, see අනුදිග *anudiga.*

අනුද්‍රුත, *Anudrita*, *s.* half of a druta or one fourth of a *mátrá*, or the time taken to articulate a short vowel.

අනුදෙන්ම, *Anudeṇma*, see අනුදෙනීම, *anudeníma.*

අනුදෙන, *Anudeṇa*, *past. part.* having permitted or consented.

අනුදෙනීම, *Anudeníma*, *s.* permission, consent.

අනුද්ධෘත, *Anuddhrita*, *a*, (අන් *an* neg. උද්ධෘත *uddhṛita* proud) humble, unassuming; not lifted. [Colloq. යටත් *yaṭat.*]

අනුන්, *Anun*, *pron.* others.

අනුනය, *Anunaya*, *s.* salutation, courtesy, civility; shewing extreme respect to a guest or deity.

අනුනවූ, *Anunawú*, *a.* (corrupt form of *anúna*) (අන් *an* neg. ඌන *úna* less) entire, complete, without deficiency. [Colloq. සම්පූර්ණවූ *sampúrṇṇawú.*]

අනුනායක, *Anunáyaka*, *s.* (අනු and නායක chief) sub-chief, vice-president.

අනුනායකයා, *Anunáyakayá*, *s.* second high priest of the Buddhists.

අනුනාසික, *Anunásika*, *a.* (අනු and නාසිකා nose) nasal.

අනුප්‍රඥප්ති, *Anuprajñapti*, *s.* law, order or a command added afterwards, chiefly used in matters of religion.

අනුප්ලව, *Anuplawa*, *s.* follower, companion.

අනුප, *Anupa*, see අනූප *anúpa.*

අනුපක්ලිෂ්ට, *Anupaklishṭa*, *a.* (අන් *an* not, උප ක්ලිෂ්ට *upaklishṭa* sin producing) free from sin, saintly, holy.

අනුපකාරි *Anupakári*, *a.* (අන් *an* neg. උපකාරින් *upakárin* assisting) not assisting, helpless.

අනුපම, *Anupama*, *a*, (අන් *an* and උපමා *upamá* resemblance) best, excellent.

අනුපමෙය, *Anupameya*, *a.* (අන් *an* and උපමෙය *upameya* comparable) incomparable, shapeless.

අනුපලිප්ත, *Anupalipta*, *a.* (අන් *an* and උපලිප්ත *upalipta* tainted) untainted, unpolluted; firm, unshaking.

අනුපසම්පන්න, *Anupasampanna*, *a.* (අන් *an* and උපසම්පන්න *upasampanna* ordained) not ordained; *s.* one not yet ordained; a sámanéra or novice who has no appointment to any temple, being out of the priesthood. [Colloq. සාමණේර *sámaṇéra.*]

අනුපහත, *Anupahata*, *a.* not killed.

අනුපාදිසෙස, *Anupádisesa*, *s.* (අන් *an* and උපාදි *upádi* cleaving, සෙස remainder) that which puts an end to transmigration, that which leads to Nirváṇa.

අනුපාන, *Anupána*, *s.* (අනු with or after, පාන drink) a fluid vehicle in medicine; drink taken with or after medicine.

අනුපූර්ව, *Anupúrwa*, *s.* (අනු after, පූර්ව prior) order, regular, succession, series, degree; *a.* regular, orderly. [Colloq. පිළිවෙළ *piḷiweḷa.*]

අනුපෙර, *Anupera*, *s.* order, succession.

අනුප්‍රාස, *Anuprása*, *s.* (අනු and ප්‍ර *pra* before, අස *asa* to be) alliteration.

අනුබ්‍යජන, *Anub'yanjana*, } *s.* subordinate aus-
අනුබ්‍යඤ්ජන, *Anub'yañjana*, } picious marks on the person of Buddha; signs of beauty, see අනුව්‍යඤ්ජන *anuvyanjana.*

අනුබද, *Anubaṇda*, *ad.* always, continual, ever, unceasing, constant. [Colloq. නිරන්තරය *nirantaraya.*]

අනුබඩ, } *Anubaddha*, *a.* (අනු and බද්ධ bound)
අනුබද්ධ } connected with, attached to; see the next word.

අනුබන්ධ, *Anubandha*, *s.* (අනු after, බන්ධ to bind or confine) an inseparable adjunct or sign of any thing, indication of guilt or symptom of disease, an element of language, as a root or affix; binding, confining.

අනුබල, *Anubala*, *s.* help, reinforcement; additional power, delegated power.

අනුබල දෙනවා, *Anubala denawá*, *v.* to assist, to support, to encourage, to aid.

අනුබුඩ, අනුබුද්ධ, } *Anubuddha*, *s.* (අනු with or after, බුද්ධ known) an inferior Buddha, lesser Buddha, apostle, one who has attained Nirváṇa after Buddha.

අනුබැඳගැණිම, *Anubeṇdageṇíma*, *s.* driving before.

අනුභව, *Anubhawa*, *s.* understanding, enjoyment, eating, partaking.

අනුභවකරණවා, *Anubhawakaraṇawá*, *v.* to enjoy, to partake of, to eat.

අනුභාව, *Anubháwa*, *s.* dignity, authority, power, might, glory, efficacy.

අනුමජ්ජිත, *Anumajjita*, (Páli) *part. a.* cleaned by rubbing, stroked.

අනුමතිය, *Anumatiya*, *s.* thought, opinion, sentiment, consent, assent, sanction, command; fifteenth day of the moon's age on which she rises one digit less than full.

අනුමර්ජ, *Anumarjja*, අනුමර්ජන, *Anumarjjana*, } see අනුමජ්ජිත *anumajjita*.

අනුමරණ, *Anumaraṇa*, *s.* (අනු with, මරණ death) dying with, the voluntary death of a Hindu widow with her husband.

අනුමාත්‍ර, *Anumátra*, *s.* small quantity, little. [Colloq. ස්වල්පය *swalpaya.*]

අනුමාන, *Anumána*, *s.* (අනු after or according to, මා to measure, න aff.) inference; (in logic) drawing a conclusion from given premises, (in common use) doubt, uncertainty.

අනුමෙවෙණි, *Anumeweni*, *s.* satisfaction, approval, thanks; the words which the priests pronounce when they receive the offerings of food from the people expressive of their own gratitude and also of benediction.

අනුමෝදන්, *Anumódan*, අනුමෝදනා, *Anumódaná*, } *s.* see the preceding word.

අනුමැතිය, *Anumeṭiya*, *s.* see අනුමතිය *anumatiya*.

අනුයාත, *Anuyáta*, *a.* (අනු after, යාත gone) followed, accompanied; *s.* a follower.

අනුයුක්ත, *Anuyukta*, *a.* (අනු and යුක්ත joined) complied with; asked; *s.* question.

අනුයොගය, *Anuyogaya*. *s.* (අනු with, යොග union) joining with, compliance with, question; repeating.

අනුර, *Anura*, *s.* seventeenth nakshatra or lunar mansion designated by a row of oblations; stars in Libra.

අනුරති, *Anurati*, *s.* love, passion, one of the eight sentiments expressed by the drama.

අනුරජන, *Anuraṉjana*, අනුරඤ්ජන, *Anurañjana*, } *a.* (අනු and රඤ්ජන to desire, to adhere) sticking, adhering, fixed in or upon; faithful.

අනුරජිත, *Anuraṉjita*, අනුරඤ්ජිත, *Anurañjita*, } *a.* adhered, fastened to.

අනුරා, *Anurá*, අනුරාග, *Anurága*, } *s.* love, passion, attachment, delight.

අනුරාධා, *Anurádhá*, see අනුර *anura*.

අනුරු, *Anuru*, අනුරූ, *Anurú*, } *s.* Elu form of the next word.

අනුරූප, *Anurúpa*, *s.* (අනු similar, රූප form) likeness, similarity; fitness, propriety.

අනුරෙ නැකත, *Anure neḳata*, see අනුර *anura*.

අනුලාප, *Anulápa*, *s.* (අනු again, ලාප saying) repeating, saying again and again; beseeching.

අනුලොම්, *Anulom*, අනුලොම, *Anuloma*, } *s.* (අනු with, ලොම going or hair) natural order, descent, succession.

අනුව්‍යජන, *Anuryaṉjana*, අනුව්‍යඤ්ජන, *Anuvyañjana*, } *s.* (අනු and ව්‍යඤ්ජන a characteristic) the minor marks which accompany the thirty two principal marks in the body of Buddha indicative of his being a great man, such as a well rounded form, well proportioned members, etc. [Colloq. අනුලකුණු *anulakuṇu.*]

අනුව, *Anuwa*, *ad.* with, together with, following.

අනුවන, *Anuwana*, *a.* (අ neg. නුවන wisdom) ignorant, unwise, injudicious, foolish.

අනුව යනවා, *Anuwa-yanawá*, *v.* (අනුව together, යනවා to go) to follow.

අනුවර්තන, *Anuwartana*, *s.* obliging, conferring favours on others.

අනුවාද, *Anuwáda*, *s.* (අනු low, වාද speaking) reviling, abuse, censure; tautology; argumentative contest.

අනුවාදේ, *Anuwádé*, *ad.* by accident, nearly, near, almost; by or on account of evil. [Provincial.]

අනුවාසන, *Anuwásana*, *s.* (අනු after, වාස to fumigate) perfuming the clothes, scenting in general.

අනුවාසන කරණවා, *Anuwásana karaṇawá*, *v.* to perfume the clothes, to perfume or scent, to smoke a place or object.

අනුවිචරිත, *Anuvicharita*, *a.* (අනු with, වි intensive, චරිත walked) walked through, much travelled.

අනුවියදුන්, *Anuviyadun*, Elu form of අනුව්‍යඤ්ජන *anuryañjana*.

අනුවිසි, *Anuvisi*, *a.* conquered, subject, subordinate; one less than twenty.

අනුශය, *Anuṣaya*, *s.* hatred, enmity of long standing; [Colloq. ක්‍රෝධය *krodhaya*]; repentence, regret, object of pursuit.

අනුශාසක, *Anuṣásaka*, *s.* counsellor, instructor, one who interprets and enforces law.

අනුශාසනා, *Anuṣásaná*, *s.* (අනු and ශාසනා governing) governing, order, command, precept, instruction, exhortation, informing, counselling.

අනුෂ්ණ, *Anushṇa*, *a.* (අන් *an* neg. උෂ්ණ *ushṇa* warm, alert) lazy, sluggish; [Colloq. කම්මැලි *kammeli*]; cold, chilly.

අනුස්න, *Anusna*, corruption of the foregoing.

අනුස්මරණය, *Anusmaraṇaya*, *s.* (අනු after, ස්මෘ *smṛi* to think, ණ්‍ය *ṇya* aff.) recollection, memory, meditation. [Colloq. සිහිකෙරීම *sihikeríma*.]

අනුස්මෘතිය, *Anusmṛitiya*, *s.* (අනු and ස්මෘති memory) cherished recollection; see foregoing word.

අනුසම්පන්න, *Anusampanna*, see අනුයුක්ත *anuyukta*.

අනුසර, *Anusara*, *s.* recollection, memory.

අනුසරණ, *Anusaraṇa*, *s.* (අනු and සෘ *sṛi* to go, ණ්‍ය *ṇya* aff.) following, going after; habit, custom.

අනුසස, *Anusasa*, *s.* merit, glory, dignity, power, authority. pl. අනුසස් *anusas*.

අනුසාරය, *Anusáraya*, *s.* following, conformity to usage; pattern, example, help, instruction.

අනුසාරයෙන්, *Anusárayen*, *adv.* according to.

අනුසාසනාව, *Anusásanáwa*, see අනුශාසනා, *anuṣásaná*.

අනුහස, *Anuhasa*, *s.* glory, splendour, dignity, merit. pl. අනුහස් *Anuhas*.

අනුහාර, *Anuhára*, *s.* imitation, resemblance.

අනූන, *Anúna*, *a.* (අන් *an* and ඌන *úna* less) whole, entire, complete. [Colloq. සම්පූර්ණ *sampúrṇa*.]

අනූනක, *Anúnaka*, *a.* see the preceeding word.

අනූප, *Anúpa*, *s.* (අනු *anu* near or with, ආප *ápa* water, ඌ *ú* substituted for ආ *á*) watery, locality.

අනූව, *Anúwa*, *s.* ninety.

අනෘජු, *Anṛiju*, *a.* (අන් *an* neg. ඍජු *ṛiju* straight) crooked, perverse, wicked.

අනෘත, *Anṛita*, *s.* (අන් *an* and ඍත *ṛita* truth) falsehood, agriculture.

අනෙක, *Aneka*, *a.* (අන් *an* not, එක *eka* one) various, many. [Colloq. නොයෙක් *noyek*.]

අනෙකජ, *Anekaja*, *s.* (අනෙක more than one, ජ what is born) bird, which is produced first in the shell and the second time when hatched.

අනෙඩමූක, *Aneḍamúka*, *a.* (අනු *anu* implying similarity, එඩ *eḍa* deaf, මූක dumb) deaf and dumb; wicked, perverse, false.

අනේ, *Ané*, *a.* various, many. *interj*, alas, oh!

අනේක, *Anéka*, see අනෙක *aneka*.

අනොපමෙය්‍ය, *Anopameyya*, } see අනුපම *anupama*.
අනොපමෙය, *Anopameya*, }

අනෝතත්ත, *Anótatta*, *s.* (අන් *an* neg. අවතත්ත *awatatta* heated) one of the seven lakes in the Himálaya, so called from its situation being enclosed by lofty mountains.

අනෝදා, *Anódá*, *s.* marsh-mallow; *Abutilon Asiaticum (Malvaceæ)*.

අනෝනා, *Anóná*, *s.* custard apple, *(anona squamosa)*.

අප්, *Ap*, *pron.* we. *s.* water.

අප්පච්චි, *Appachchi*, see next word,

අප්පජ්ජා, *Appajjá*, *s.* word for father, used only amongst the low caste or caste of tom tom beaters.

අප්පල්ලෙ, *Appalle*, *s.* kind of earthern vessel or pan used by the natives to cook with. pl. අප්පල්ලා *appallá*. [Colloq. ලොකු ඇතිලිය *loku etiliya*.]

අප්පා, *Appá*, *s.* father, (not very respectable). pl. අප්පාලා *appálá*.

අප්පු, *Appu*, *s.* head servant.

අප්පුඩිගහනවා, *Appuḍigahanawá*, *v.* to clap the hands.

අප්පුහාමි, *Appuhámi*, *s.* title of respect to persons of high caste and sons of mudaliyars.

අප්පොච්චි, *s.* father, (more respectable word than අප්පා *appá*). pl. අප්පොච්චිලා *appochchilá*.

අප්‍රකට, *Aprakaṭa*, } *a.* (අ neg. ප්‍රකට or ප්‍රකාශ public) secret, unrevealed, not published, not known. [Colloquial: අප්‍රසිද්ධ *aprasiddha*.]
අප්‍රකාශ, *Aprakáṣa*, }

අප්‍රකෘති, *Aprakṛiti*, *s.* (අ and ප්‍රකෘති nature or matter) accidental property or nature; not natural.

අප්‍රත්‍යක්‍ෂ, *Apratyakṣha*, *a.* (අ and ප්‍රත්‍යක්‍ෂ present) imperceptible, not present, invisible.

අප්‍රත්‍යය, *Apratyaya*, *a.* (අ and ප්‍රත්‍යය cause) causeless, without cause, having no producing principle; also (අ *a* vowel *a*, ප්‍රත්‍යය *pratyaya* an affix) the affix *a*.

අප්‍රතිනාථ, *Apratinátha*, *s.* (අ and ප්‍රති second, නාථ chief) one who has not his superior; interregnum; *a.* peerless.

අප්‍රතිපුද්ගල, *Apratipudgala*, *s.* one to whom none can be compared.

අප්‍රතිභාග, *Apratibhága*, *a.* (අ not, ප්‍රතිභාග like) incomparable, matchless. [Colloquial: අසමානවූ *asamánawú*.]

අප්‍රතිසන්ධික, *Apratisandhika*, *s.* (අ and ප්‍රති again, සන්ධි union, birth) freedom from transmigration.

අප්‍රධාන, *Apradhána*, *a.* (අ and ප්‍රධාන chief) secondary, subordinate.

අප්‍රමත්ත, *Apramatta*, see අප්‍රමාද *apramáda*.

අප්‍රමාණ, *Apramáṇa*, *a.* (අ and ප්‍රමාණ quantity) immeasurable, countless, incalculable, infinite, unlimited, boundless.

අප්‍රමාද, *Apramáda*, *a.* (අ and ප්‍රමාද delay) hasty, quick, without delay, not lingering. *s.* diligence.

අප්‍රමෙය, *Aprameya*, *a.* same as අප්‍රමාණ *apramána*.

අප්‍රයෝග, *Aprayóga*, *a.* (අ and ප්‍රයෝග cunning) ingenuous, sincere, candid, open, frank, void of deceit. *s.* sincerity, freedom from deceit.

අප්‍රයෝජන, *Aprayójana*, *a.* (අ and ප්‍රයෝජන profit) unprofitable, fruitless, vain, unproductive.

අප්‍රලම්බ, *Apralamba*, *a.* (අ and ප්‍රලම්බ slow or hanging) not hanging, not suspending; quick, expeditious.

අප්‍රවෘත්ති, *Apravṛitti*, *s.* (අ neg. ප්‍රවෘත්ති *pravṛitti* news) want of news or information on a subject; non-existence.

අප්‍රවේසම, *Aprawésama*, *s.* (අ and ප්‍රවේසම care) carelessness, inattention, negligence; heedlessness, imprudence.

අප්‍රසන්න, *Aprasanna*, *a.* (අ and ප්‍රසන්න clear) turbid, muddy, not clear; (most commonly,) unwilling, displeased.

අප්‍රසාද, *Aprasáda*, see the preceding word.

අප්‍රසිඩ, } *Aprasiddha*, *a.* secret, unrevealed, un-
අප්‍රසිද්ධ, } published. See අප්‍රකාශ *aprakáṣa*.

අප්‍රසූතිකා, *Aprasútiká*, *s.* (අ not, ප්‍රසූතිකා child bearing) barren woman. [Colloq. වඳ ස්ත්‍රිය *waṇda stiriya*.]

අප්‍රහීණ, *Aprahíṇa*, *a.* (අ and ප්‍රහීණ destruction) that which is not destroyed or wasted.

අප්‍රාණි, *Apráṇi*, *a.* (අ and ප්‍රාණ *prána* life) lifeless, inanimate. [Colloq. පණනැති *paṇaṇeti*.]

අප්‍රාප්ත, *Aprápta*, *a.* (අ and ප්‍රාප්ත arrived) not arrived, not come; not obtained.

අප්‍රිය, *Apriya*, *a.* (අ and ප්‍රිය beloved) not dear, not beloved, not pleasant, unfriendly, inimical, unkind; also (අ neg. ප්‍රිය husband) husbandless.

අප්‍රියා, *Apriyá*, *s.* (අ and ප්‍රියා wife) one wifeless, widower. [Colloq. වැන්දඹුවා *wẹndambuwá*.]

අප්‍රියාව, *Apriyáwa*, *s.* disgust, nuisance.

අප්සරා, *Apsará*, *s.* (අප් *ap* water, සෘ *sṛi* to go or, අප්සු in the waters, රස *rasa* flavour) apsara, nymph of swarga; the name alludes either to production of the nymphs at the churning of the ocean or to their frequent bathing.

අප, *Apa*, *pron.* us, the accusative of the *per. pron.* අපි *api*; also a particle or preposition, the reverse of අධි *adhi* up, implying privation, inferiority, down, below, beneath; contrariety, opposition to, difference from, bad, base; *s.* water.

අපක්‍ෂවාදී, *Apakṣhawádi*, *a.* (අ neg. පක්‍ෂ a party, වාදී attached) not faithful, opposed, disloyal, hostile, impartial.

අපක්‍රම, *Apakrama*, *s.* (අප from ක්‍රම going) flight, retreat.

අපක්‍රෂ්ට, *Apakṛashṭa*, see අපකෘෂ්ට *apakṛishṭa*.

අපක්‍රියා, *Apakriyá*, *s.* (අප against, ක්‍රියා action) hatred, malice; evil doing, wickedness.

අපක්‍රොශ, *Apakroṣa*, *s.* (අප against, ක්‍රුශ *kruṣa* to call out) abuse, reviling. [Colloq. නින්දාව *nindáwa*.]

අපකාර, *Apakára*, *s.* (අප ill, කාර what does) injury, offence, hatred, enmity; helplessness, the leaving destitute of aid.

අපකීර්ති, *Apakírtti*, *s.* (අප before, කීර්ති fame) infamy, disgrace, reproach.

අපකෘෂ්ට, *Apakṛishṭa*, *a.* low, vile, inferior. [Colloq. අධම *adhama*.]

අප කෙරෙන්, *Apa-keren*, the abl. of අපි *api*.

අප කෙරෙහි, *Apa-kerehi*, the loc. of අපි *api*, sometimes used in the sense of අපට *apaṭa* and අපේ *apẹ*.

අපගත, *Apagata*, *a.* (අප away, ගත gone) lost, deprived of; dead, deceased, departed. [Colloq. පහවූ *pahawú*.]

අපගමන, *Apagamana*, *s*, (අප and ගමන going) departure, separation.

අපගේ, *Apagé*, the gen. of අපි *api*.

අපචය, *Apachaya*, *s.* loss, decay, wearing away; [Colloq. ගෙවීයාම *geviyáma;*] respect, obeisance.

අපට, *Apaṭa*, the dat. of අපි *api*.

අපත්උනා, *Apatuná*, see අපත්වුනා *apatwuná*.

අපත්‍ය, *Apatya*, *s.* (අ neg. පත්‍ය falling) that which fails not, offspring male or female.

අපත්‍ය, *Apatya*, *a.* unsuitable, not agreeing with, applied chiefly, medically, with respect to diet, regimen etc; not digesting: more properly අපථ්‍ය *apathya*.

අපත්‍ය ශත්‍රු, *Apatya-ṣatru*, *s.* (අපත්‍ය offspring, ශත්‍රු an enemy) the crab, being said to perish on producing its young. [Colloq. කකුළුවා *kakuḷuwá.*]

අපත්‍රපා, *Apatrapá*, *s.* (අප and ත්‍රපා shame) bashfulness.

අපත්වුනා. *Apatwuná*, *pret.* of following word.

අපත්වෙනවා, *Apathwenawá*, *v.* to die.

අපතර්පණ, *Apatarpaṇa*, *s.* (අප bad, තර්පණ satisfaction) fasting, (chiefly in sickness); [Colloquial: නිරාහාරය *niráháraya.*]

අපතිලෝගුරු, *Apatilóguru*, *s.* (අප our, තිලෝගුරු which see) name of Buddha.

අපද, *Apada*, *a.* (අ neg. පද foot) footless, having no feet.

අපදන්, *Apadan*, *s.* removal, taking away, a term for the Ablative case, අපාදාන විභක්තිය *apádána vibhaktiya*.

අපදන්වෙනවා, *Apadanwenawá*, *v.* to lose. [Colloq. නැතිවෙනවා *nẹtiwenawá.*]

අපදාන, *Apadána*, *s.* approved occupation, work well or completely done, deed, heroic action, tale or legend; thirteenth book of the Khuddakanikáya.

අපදාර්ථය, *Apadárthaya*, *s.* calamity.

අපදිශ, *Apadiṣa*, *s.* (අප and දිශ to show) intermediate space, half of a point of the compass.

අපදෙශ, *Apadeṣa*, *s.* (අප ill, badly, දිශ *diṣa* to shew) contrivance, disguise by dress &c, pretence. [Colloq. උපාය *upáya.*]

අපන්නක, *Apannaka*, *a.* (අ prohibitive, පන්න gone, ක aff.) used of such as deviate from the right road in religion, heretical, erroneous; also certain, true; without leaves; *s.* one of the incarnations of Buddha, first in order.

අපභ්‍රංශ, *Apabhransa*, *s.* (අප and භ්‍රංශ fall) language so called, ungrammatical language.

අපමණ, *Apamaṇa*, *a.* (අ and පමණ quantity) countless, infinite; endless.

අපමානය, *Apamánaya*, *s.* (අප reverse, මාන respect) disrespect, disgrace.

අපයාන, *Apayána*, *s.* (අප from, යාන going) retreat, flight. [Colloq. පලායෑම *paláyẹma.*]

අපර්‍යන්ත, *Aparyanta*, *a.* (අ neg. පර්‍යන්ත end) endless, immeasurable, boundless, unlimited, indefinite. [Colloq. කෙළවරක් නැති *keḷawarak nẹti.*]

අපර, *Apara*, *s.* west; also, other, opposite, contrary. [Colloq. බටහිර *baṭahira.*]

අපරගොයානය, *Aparagoyánaya*, *s.* an imaginary island or continent so called in the west, some say it is America.

අපර පක්ෂය, *Apara-pakṣhaya*, *s.* the wane of the moon.

අපර පර්වතය, *Apara-parwataya*, *s.* (අපර west, පර්වතය rock) the western mountain behind which the sun sets.

අපරභාගය, *Aparabhágaya*, *s.* time just past, afternoon.

අපරා, *Apará*, *a.* other, opposite. [Colloq. අනික් *anik.*]

අපරාජිත, *Aparájita*, *a.* (අ and පරාජිත conquered) unconquered; name of Vishnu and Siva, name of a plant, *(clitoria ternatea ;)* see නිල්කටරොළු *nilkaṭaroḷu*.

අපරාධය, *Aparádhaya*, *s.* (අප badly, රාධ to accomplish) offence, impropriety, guilt, transgression.

අපරාධික, *Aparádhika*, *s.* offender, transgressor, guilty person.

අපරාපර්‍ය, *Aparáparya*, *s.* transmigration. [Colloq. සසර ඉපදීම *sasara-ipadíma.*]

අපරාහ්න, *Aparáḥna*, *s.* (අපර *apara* after, අහන day) afternoon, evening, the last watch of the day. [Colloq. සවස්වරුව *sawaswaruwa.*]

අපරික්ෂිප්ත, *Aparikṣhipta*, *a.* (අ and පරි round about, ක්ෂිප්ත thrown) not surrounded, un-encircled; [Colloq. වටනොකළ *waṭanokaḷa*].

අපරික්ෂීණ, *Aparikṣhiṇa*, *a.* (අ neg. පරි and ක්ෂීණ emaciate) imperishable, not faded, not wearing away.

අපරිග්‍රහිත, *Aparigrihita*, *a.* not taken or accepted, not assented to.

අපරිච්ඡින්න, *Aparichch'hinna*, *a.* not broken or divided.

අපරිඥාත, *Aparijñáta*,
අපරිඤ්ඤාත, *Apariññáta*, } *a.* (අ and පරි emphatic, ඥාත known) unknown, ignorant.

අපරිතප්ත, *Aparitapta*, *a.* (අ and පරි exceeding, තප්ත warmed) not warmed or heated either by fire or of the sun.

අපරිපූර්ණ, *Aparipúrṇṇa*, *a.* (අ and පරි emphatic, පූර්ණ filled) incomplete, not filled; unprofitable, poor.

අපරිභොග, *Aparibhoga*, *a.* not used, not embraced; compare පරිභොග *paribhoga*.

අපරිමාණ, *Aparimáṇa*, *a.* (අ and පරිමාණ measure) immeasurable, boundless, immense.

අපරිමිත, *Aparimita*. *a.* boundless, immense, infinite; compare පරිමිත *parimita*.

අපරිශුඩ, අපරිශුද්ධ, *Apariṣuddha*, අපරිසුඩ, අපරිසුද්ධ, *Aparisuddha*, *a.* not clean, not pure, unholy; compare පරිශුඩ *pariṣuddha*.

අපරීක්ෂා, *Aparíkshá*, *s.* (අ not, පරීක්ෂා test) thoughtlessness, carelessness.

අපරීක්ෂිත *Aparíkshita*, *a.* (අ and පරීක්ෂිත tried) untried, unproved.

අපරොපක්‍රමය, *Aparopakramaya*, *s.* (අපර *apara* other, උපක්‍රම *upakrama* stratagem) another stratagem.

අපල, *Apala*, Elu form of අඵල *aphala* which see.

අපලය, *Apalaya*, *s.* misfortune, disadvantage, unprofitableness, bad luck; evil influence, (used of the planets.)

අපලාප, *Apalápa*, *s.* (අප away or kindly, ලප *lapa* to speak) denial or concealment of knowledge, secrecy; affection, hiding; *a.* (අ neg. පලාප chaff) not empty, useful.

අපවග, *Apawaga*, Elu form of අපවර්ග *apawarga*, *s.* final happiness, the soul being freed from transmigration and delivered from all further connection with the body; name of Nirváṇa.

අපවත්, *Apawat*, *a.* dead. [Colloq. මැරුණ *męruṇa*.]

අපවත්වෙනවා, *Apawatwenawá*, *v.* to die. [Colloq. මැරෙණවා *męreṇawá*.]

අපවර්ග, *Apawarga*, see අපවග *apawaga*.

අපවර්ජන, *Apawarjjana*, *s.* abandoning, forsaking; a gift or donation; final emancipation or beatitude.

අපවාද, *Apawáda*, *s.* (අප bad, වාද speech) censure, blame; indecent speech.

අපවාරණ, *Apawáraṇa*, *s.* covering, concealment, disappearance.

අපවිත්, *Apavit*, අපවිත්‍ර, *Apavitra*, *a.* (අ neg. පවිත්‍ර clean) impure, unclean, defile, polluted.

අපවිස්ත්‍ර, *Apavistra*, corruption of අපවිත්‍ර *apavitra*.

අප විසින්, *Apa visin*, *pron.* instrumental case of අපි *api*.

අපස්මාර, *Apasmára*, *s.* (අප privation, ස්මෘ *smṛi* to remember) epilepsy, falling sickness; a kind of sickness in which the patient is supposed to be affected by a demoniacal possession and suddenly falls. [Colloq. වස්මර රෝගය *wasmara rógaya*.]

අපස්වාදිය, *Apaswádiya*, *s.* (අ neg. පස්වාදි alliance) enmity, hostility. [Colloq. ද්‍රොහිකම *drohikama*.]

අපසද, *Apasada*, *s.* ungrammatical speech.

අපසර්ජන, *Apasarjana*, *s.* emancipation, abandonment; a gift or donation.

අපසර, *Apasara*, *s.* goddess, (Elu); removal from one place to another, (Sanskrit).

අපසව්‍ය. *Apasavya*, *a.* (අප and සව්‍ය left) the right (as opposite to left); opposite, contrary; the space between the thumb and fore finger.

අපහරණය, *Apaharaṇaya*, *s.* taking away, carrying off, stealing. [Colloq. පහකෙරීම *pahakeríma*.]

අපහස, *Apahasa*, *s.* scorn, contempt.

අපහසුව, *Apahasuwa*, *s.* (අ neg. පහසුව ease) affliction, illness, disorder, sickness: fatigue, inconvenience.

අපහාසය, *Apahásaya*, *s.* disgrace.

අපා, *Apá*, *s.* hell, general name for the infernal regions.

අපා, *Apá*, *adj.* footless. [Colloq. පාද නැති *páda nęti*.]

අපාක, *Apáka*, *s.* (අ and පාක ripeness) unripeness, the state of not being well cooked, or digested, immaturity. [Colloq. නොපැසීම *nopęsíma*.]

අපාඞ්ග, *Apáṅga*, *s.* (අප *apa* before, අඞ්ග *aṅga* limb) outer corner of the eye, corner of the eye next the object when taking a side glance at any thing. [Colloq. අඩ බැල්ම *aḍa bęlma*.]

අපාද, *Apáda*, අපාදක, *Apádaka*, *a.* (අ and පාද feet) footless, applied to serpents &c.

අපාදාන, *Apádána*, *s.* (අප *apa* from, ආදාන *ádána* taking) removal, taking from; it conveys the sense of the fifth or ablative case in Sanskrit and Páli.

අපාදි, *Apádi*, see අපාද *apáda*.

අපා දුක, *Apá duka*, *s.* (අපා hell, දුක sorrow) sorrows of hell, punishments or sufferings of the infernal regions.

අපාන, *Apána*, *s.* (අප *apa* below, අන *ana* to breathe) the anus, breaking wind, one of the five vital airs.

අපාප, *Apápa*, *a*, (අ neg. පාප sin) sinless, virtuous. pure.

අපාම්පති, *Apámpati*, *s.* (අපාම් *apám* the gen. case of අප *apa* water, පති master) the ocean; name of Varuṇa.

අපාමඟ, *Apámaga*, *s.* (අපා hell, මඟ a way) path to hell, sin; Elu form of අපාමාර්ග *apámárga*.

අපාමාර්ග, *Apámárga*, see අපාමඟ *apámaga*.

අපාය, *Apáya*, *s.* (අප *apa* privative, අය *aya* profit) hell, penal infliction, retributive punishment; see සතර අපාය *satara apáya*.

අපාය භය, *Apáya bhaya*, *s.* (අපාය hell. භය fear) fear of hell.

අපාසු, *Apásu*, *s.* affliction, sickness, illness, uneasiness; *a.* hard to cure, very sick.

අපි, *Api*, *pron.* we; also a preposition and particle corresponding to our particles even, though, yet, assuredly; also implying enquiry, interogation, doubt, possibility.

අපිධාන, *Apidhána*, *s.* covering, concealment, disappearance. [Colloq. පියන *piyana.*]

අපිරි, *Apiri*, *a.* (අ neg. පිරි filled) not filled; see අප්‍රිය *apria*.

අපිරිපුන්, *Apiripun*, *a.* not full, incomplete.

අපිරිය, *Apiriya*, Elu form of අප්‍රිය *apriya*.

අපිරියත්, *Apiriyat*, Elu form of අපර්‍යන්ත *aparyanta*, endless, infinite. [Colloq. කෙළවරක් නැති *keḷawarak nęti.*]

අපිරිසිදු, *Apirisidu*, *a.* (අ and පිරිසිදු clean) unclean, foul, stained, polluted.

අපිස්, *Apis*, Elu form of අල්පේච්ඡ *alpéchchha*.

අපිසැස්, *Apisas*, *a.* not haunted by evil spirits or hobgoblins.

අපුණ්‍ය, *Apuṇya*, *a.* (අ and පුණ්‍ය virtuous) bad, wicked; unfortunate, unlucky. [Colloq. පින් නැති *pin nęti.*]

අපුණ්‍යය, *Apuṇyaya*, *s.* demerit, sin.

අපුත්‍රක, *Aputraka*, *a.* (අ and පුත්‍ර son, ක aff.) childless; *s.* man who has no son.

අපුල්ලන්නා, *Apullanná*, *s.* washerman.

අපුල්ලනවා, *Apullanawá*, *v.* to strike, to beat, used of washing clothes which the natives do by beating them against a stone. pret. ඇපුල්ලුවා *ępulluwá*.

අපුල, *Apula*, *a.* loathesome, disgusting; *s.* disgust.

අපූර්වවූ, *Apúrwawú*, *a.* (අ and පූර්ව before) not happened before, strange, wonderful, admired, surpassing.

අපූරුව, *Apúruwa*, *s.* wonder, strange thing, surprise. *a.* unusual, wonderful.

අපෙන්, *Apen*, abl. of අපි *api*.

අපේ, *Apé*, *pron.* our.

අපේක්ෂාව, *Apekshåwa*, *s.* (අප *apa* emphatic, ඊක්ෂ *íksha* seeing) hope, regard, expectation; looking intensely into anything.

අපොයි, *Apoyi*, *interj.* alas! oh!

අපොලනවා, *Apolanawá*, *v.* to clap the hands; [Colloq. අත්පොළසන්දෙනවා *atpoḷasandenawá*]; also to strike; see අපුල්ලනවා *apullanawá*.

අපොහොසත්, *Apohosat*, *a.* (අ and පොහොසත් rich) not rich, poor; unable.

අඵල, *Aphala*, *a.* (අ and ඵල fruit) fruitless, sterile, barren; unprofitable, disadvantageous.

අඵලකම, *Aphalakama*, *s.* barrenness, sterility, unprofitableness.

අඵාසුව, *Aphásuwa*, *s.* see අපහසුව *apahasuwa*.

අබ්ජ, *Abja*, *s.* (අබ් *ab* for, අප් *ap* water, ජ *ja* born) the lotus, [Colloq. නෙළුම් *nelum*]; moon, physician of the gods.

අබ්ජයොනි, *Abjayoni*, *s.* one of the names of Brahma.

අබ්ජිනී, *Abjiní*, *s.* multitude of lotus flowers.

අබ්ජිනීපති, *Abjinípati*, *s.* (අබ්ජිනී and පති lord) the sun. [Colloq. සූර්‍ය්‍යයා *súryayá.*]

අබ්ධි, *Abdhi*, *s.* sea, ocean. [Colloq, මූද *múda.*]

අබ්බාගාත, *Abbágáta*, *a.* cripple, lame; see අබ්භාඝාත *abbhágháta*. [Colloq. කොර *kora.*]

අබ්බාගාතයා, *Abbágátayá*, } *s.* cripple, person hav-
අබ්භාඝාත, *Abbhágháta*, } ing lost a limb.

අබ්භූත ධම්ම, *Abbhúta dhamma*, *s.* (අ not, භූත being or been, ධම්ම event) that which has not happened before, strange event, wonder, miracle; one of the branches of sacred science into which Buddhism is divided, comprehending such sútras or works as describe the miraculous powers of ṣráwakas.

අබ්භොකාසිකාඞ්ගය, *Abbhokáṣikáńgaya*, the Páli form of අභ්‍යවකාශිකාඞ්ගය *abhyawakáṣikáńgaya* which see.

අබ්‍රහ්මචාරි, *Abrahmachári*, see බ්‍රහ්මචාරි *brahmachári*.

අබ්‍රහ්මණ්‍ය, *Abrahmaṇya*. *a.* (අ neg. බ්‍රහ්මණ්‍ය proper for a brahman; *i. e.* death) sacred, not to be killed.

අබ, *Aba*, *s.* mustard, *brassica juncea (Cruciferæ).*

අබතුර, *Abatura*, } Elu form of අභ්‍යන්තර *abhyan-*
අබතුරු, *Abaturu*, } *tara*.

අබන්ධු, *Abandhu*, *a.* (අ and බන්ධු relative) without relations, not related.

අබබ, *Ababa*, *s.* a hell so called; a number.

අබය, *Abaya*, *s.* (අ and බය fear) exemption from fear or danger.

අබර, *Abara*, *a.* (අ not, බර weight) light, not heavy. [Colloq. සැහැල්ලු *sẹhẹllu.*]

අබරණ, *Abaraṇa*, *s.* ornaments, jewels.

අබල, *Abala*, *a.* (අ and බල strength) powerless, weak, old.

අබලා, *Abalá*, *s.* woman. [Colloq. ස්ත්‍රී *strí.*]

අබලි, *Abali*, *a.* old, worn out, damaged.

අබලී, *Abalí*, *s.* see අබලා *abalá*.

අබලුව, *Abaluwa*, *s.* husk of the mustard seed. [Colloq. අබපියල්ල *abapiyalla.*] plural අබලු *abalu.*

අබා, *Abá*. *s.* (අ and බා fortune or fear) misfortune, bad luck; safety, confidence.

අබි, *Abi*, prep. and prefix meaning before, in front of.

අබිං, *Abiṇ*, } *s.* opium.
අබින්, *Abin*, }

අබිප්‍රාව, *Abipráwa*, incorrectly used for අභිප්‍රාය *abhipráya*.

අබිමන්, *Abíman*, Elu form of අභිමාන *abhimána*.

අබිමුව, *Abimuwa*, Elu form of අභිමුඛ *abhimukha*.

අබිය, *Abiya*, see අභය *abhaya*.

අබිය, *Abiya*, } *s.* (අ not, බිය fear, ද what
අබියද, *Abiyada*, } gives) Nirváṇa, freedom from existence.

අබියස, *Abíyasa*, *a.* near, proximate, close on the borders of. [Colloq. ළඟ *laṉga.*]

අබියුත්, *Abiyut*, see අභිජිත් *Abhijit*.

අබියෙස්, *Abiyes*, see අබියස *abiyasa*.

අබියෝග, *Abiyóga*, *a.* silly, foolish, stupid; *s.* insanity.

අබිරු, *Abiru*, *a.* Elu form of අභීරු *abhíru*.

අබිසරු. *Abisaru*, *s.* woman who goes to an assignation.

අබිසෙව්, *Abisew*, *a.* Elu form of අභිසේක *abhiseka*.

අබූත, *Abúta*, *a.* false; *s.* falsehood, folly, idiocy: properly written අභූත *abhúta*.

අබොධ්‍ය, } *Abodhya*, *a.* unintelligible.
අබෝධ්‍ය, }

අභ්‍යග්‍ර, *Abhyagra*, *a.* (අභි *abhi* in the presence of අග්‍ර *agra* the front) near, proximate. [Colloq. ළඟ *laṉga.*]

අභ්‍යඟ, *Abhyaṉga*, } *s.* smearing the body with
අභ්‍යඞ්ග *Abhyańga*. } oil, rubbing the body with any unctuous substance.

අභ්‍යඤ්ජන, *Abhyanjana*, } *s.* (අභි and අඤ්ජ to
අභ්‍යඤ්ජන, *Abhyañjana*, } anoint) ointment, smearing the body with oil in unction; applying collyrium to the eyelashes.

අභ්‍යන්තර, *Abhyantara*, *prep.* within, inside, inner space, the space included. [Colloq. ඇතුළ *ẹtuḷa.*]

අභ්‍යවකාශය, *Abhyawakáṣaya*, *s.* firmament. [Col. අවකාශය *awakáṣaya.*]

අභ්‍යවකාශිකාඞ්ගය, *Abhyawakáṣikáńgaya*, *s.* (අභ්‍යවකාශ *abhyawakáṣa* atmosphere, ඉක *ika* aff. අඞ්ග *ańga* ordinance) institute of the Buddhist code enjoining upon the priests to reside in the open air, and not to employ the slightest covering or defence, whatever may be the weather to which they are exposed. See තෙළෙස් ධුතාඞ්ග *teḷes dhutáńga*.

අභ්‍යාඛ්‍යාන, *Abhyakhyána*, *s.* (අභි *abhi* and ආඛ්‍යාන *ákhyána* saying) groundless demand; false accusation.

අභ්‍යාගාරික, *Abhyágárika*, *s.* (අභි *abhi* and ආගාර *ágára* house, ඉක *ika* aff.) one diligent in supporting the concerns of a house.

අභ්‍යාදාන, *Abhyádána*, *s.* beginning, commencement. [Colloq. පටන්ගැන්ම *paṭangẹnma.*]

අභ්‍යාසය, *Abhyásaya*, *s.* practice, exercise. [Colloq, පුරුද්ද *purudda.*]

අභ්‍යුපගමන, *Abhyupagamana*, *s.* (අභි *abhi* and උප *upa* implying association or vicinity, ගමන going) promise, an agreement. [Colloq. පොරොන්දුව *poronduwa*]; approaching. [Colloq. එළඹීම *elaṃbíma.*]

අභ්‍ර, *Abhra*, *s.* sky, firmament; *a.* cloud; plumbago.

අභ්‍රංලිහ, *Abhraṇliha*, *s.* air, wind. [Colloq. වාතය *wátaya.*]

අභ්‍රක, *Abhraka*, *s.* mineral substance, talc. [Colloq. මිනිරන් *miniran.*]

අභ්‍රමාලා, *Abhramálá*, *s.* (අභ්‍ර and මාලා garland) line or succession of clouds.

අභක්ති, *Abhakti*, *s.* (අ neg. භක්ති faith) unbelief, want of devotion to, impiety. [Colloq. නොඇදහිල්ල *noẹdahilla.*]

අභක්තික, *Abhaktika*, *a.* ungodly.

අභක්තිය, *s.* *Abhaktiya*, impiety, wickedness, ungodliness.

අභය, *Abhaya*, *a.* (අ not, භය fear) fearless, freedom from fear or danger.

අභව්‍ය, *Abhawya*, *a.* (අ and භව්‍ය fit, proper) unfit, improper.

අභාව, *Abháwa*, *s.* (අ and භාව being) non existence, annihilation.

අභාවිත, *Abhávita*, *a.* (අ and භාවිත accustomed) unaccustomed to a thing, not exercised in.

අභි, *Abhi*, *prep.* implying similarity, in the presence of, separation, severally, wish, desire; conjoined, belonging to, with respect to.

අභිගමන, *Abhigamana*, *s.* (අභි near to, ගමන going) approaching.

අභිඝාතී, *Abhigháti*, *s.* (අභිඝාත *abhighâta* what kills, ඊ *í* pers. aff.) enemy.

අභිචාරිකා, *Abhichárikâ*, see අබිසරු *abisaru*.

අභිජ්ඣා, *Abhijjhá*, *s.* Páli form of අභිධ්‍යාව *abhidhyáwa*.

අභිජාත, *Abhijáta*, *a.* (අභි and ජාත born) well born, noble; learned, wise.

අභිජිත්, *Abhijit*, *s.* three stars inserted between the twenty first and twenty second lunar mansions.

අභිඥ, *Abhijña*, } *s.* (අභි very, ඥ, knowledge)
අභිඥා, *Abhijñá*, } profound knowledge, supernatural acquirements, used chiefly to express the five kinds of knowledge acquired by the Rahats or Buddhistical ascetics; viz.—1. The power to assume any shape. 2. Supernatural hearing, by which words or sounds however low can be heard at any distance. 3. The power of knowing the hearts of others. 4. The knowledge of men's condition in a former state of existence. 5. The power of seeing objects at any distance, *a.* having known, become cognizant of.

අභිඤ්ඤා, *Abhiññá*, Páli form of අභිඥා *abhijñá*.

අභිතප්ත, *Abhitapta*, *a.* (අභි and තප්ත burnt) scorched, burnt.

අභිධ්‍යාව, *Abhidhyáwa*, *s.* extreme desire, excessive longing, violent covetousness.

අභිධර්ම, *Abhidharma*, *s.* (අභි profound, ධර්ම sayings of Buddha) those addresses of Buddha which were delivered to the gods; one of the three piṭakas or divisions of Buddhism.

අභිධර්ම පිටකය, *Abhidharma-piṭakaya*, *s.* (අභිධර්ම and පිටකය basket) third of the three piṭakas or collections of the discourses of Buddha. It contains books, which were addressed to gods.

අභිධාන, *Abhidhána*, *s.* name, appellation; vocabulary, dictionary.

අභින්‍යාස, *Abhinyása*, *s.* (අභි very, නි *ni* and අස *asa* to throw) incurable or mortal fever.

අභිනන්දනය, *Abhinandanaya*, *s.* (අභි emphatic, particle, නන්දන joy) extreme joy; in Hindu mythology, name of the fourth Jaina Tirt'hakára, or deified saint.

අභිනව, *Abhinawa*, *a.* new, modern; young. [Coll. අලුත් *alut.*]

අභිනිවේශ, *Abhiniweṣa*, *s.* (අභි and නි before, විශ to enter) intense application to any object, determination to effect a purpose or to attain an object.

අභිනිෂ්ක්‍රමණ, *Abhinishkramaṇa*, *s.* (අභි intensitive, නිෂ්ක්‍රමණ departing) forsaking the world and retiring into solitude for the purposes of asceticism, chiefly used of Buddha.

අභිනීල, *Abhiníla*, *s.* (අභි intensitive, නීල blue) very blue.

අභිනීහාර, *Abhiníhára*, *s.* (අභි very, නි before, the final, ඉ *i* lengthened, හාර what brings) hope, expectation, earnest wish, or aspiration; prayer, request, freedom from all doubt.

අභිප්‍රාය, *Abhipráya*, } *s.* meaning, intention, wish,
අභිප්‍රාව, *Abhipráwa*, } purpose, design, thought; allusion.

අභිභව, *Abhibhawa*, *s.* defeat, subjugation, want of kindness; humiliation. [Colloq. පරාජය *parájaya.*]

අභිභවන, *Abhibhawana*, *s.* overpowering, overcoming, defeat, conquest. [Colloq. මැඩපැවැත්වීම *meḍapewetrima.*]

අභිභවා, *Abhibhawá*, *past. part.* having subjugated, having eclipsed.

අභිභූතව, *Abhibhútawa*, *pass. part.* being defeated or subjugated.

අභිභූත, *Abhibhúta*, *a.* defeated, conquered, subdued, subjugated; humbled.

අභිමඞ්ගල, *Abhimangala*, *s.* (අභි emphatic, මඞ්ගල feast) great feast, high festival, splendid entertainment, solemnity.

අභිමත, *Abhimata*, *a.* (අභි and මත thought) great pleasure, very willing, wished.

අභිමතාර්ථ, *Abhimatártha*, *s.* (අභිමත, wished, අර්ථ object) desired object, favourite pursuit.

අභිමන්, *Abhiman*, } *s.* pride, haughtiness.
අභිමානන, *Abhimánna*, } [Colloq. වැඩි මානනය
අභිමාන, *Abhimána*, } *weḍi-mánnaya.*]

අභිමුඛ, *Abhimukha*, *prep.* (අභි before, මුඛ face) before the face, in the presence of, present.

අභිමුඛය, *Abhimukhaya*, *s.* presence.

අභියුක්ත, *Abhiyukta*, *a.* (අභි and යුක්ත joined) surrounded, encompassed by an enemy, [Colloq. වටකරණලද *waṭakaraṇalada*]; *s.* servant attending a priest.

අභිරති, *Abhirati*, *s.* (අභි emphatic, රති pleasure) excessive desire.

අභිරම්‍ය, *Abhiramya*, *a.* (අභි very, රම්‍ය delightful) very pleasant, delightful, agreeable.

අභිරමණය, *Abhiramaṇaya*, *s.* copulation, adultery.

අභිරාම, *Abhiráma*, *a.* (අභි before, රම to sport) very good, dear, affectionate; beautiful.

අභිරූප, *Abhirúpa*, *a.* (අභි emphatic, රූප beautiful) extremely beautiful; *s.* philosopher, name of Śiva or Vishṇu.

අභිලාෂ, *Abhilásha*, අභිලාස, *Abhilása*, *s.* (අභි and ලෂ *lasha* to like) desire, appetite, sensual desire, lust.

අභිවුඩ්ඩිය, *Abhirraddhiya*, improperly written for අභිවෘද්ධිය *abhivriddhiya*.

අභිවාද, *Abhiwáda*, *s*, (අභි against, වාද speech) opprobrious speech, abuse; see next.

අභිවාදන, *Abhiwádana*, *s.* (අභි in presence of, වාදන speech) worship, salutation, honouring.

අභිවෘඩිය, අභිවෘද්ධිය, *Abhirriddhiya*, *s.* increase, growth, prosperity; superabounding. [Coll. වැඩසිඩිය *wedasiddhiya*.]

අභිෂික්ත, *Abhishikta*, see අභිසෙක *abhiseka*.

අභිසංස්කෘත, *Abhisanskrata*, see අභිසංස්කෘත *abhisanskrita*.

අභිසංස්කාර, *Abhisanskára*, *s.* thought, idea, conception, fancy, forming, perfecting, accumulation, collection. This word is sometimes found written as අභිස(ංකාර *abhisanskára*, in old manuscripts.

අභිසංස්කෘත, *Abhisanskrita*, *a.* (අභි and සංස්කෘත well done) completely or well made, perfected; prepared, formed.

අභිසම්බුධි, අභිසම්බුද්ධි, *Abhisambuddhi*, *s.* (අභි emphatic, සම්බුද්ධි wisdom) great wisdom, universal knowledge, infallible knowledge.

අභිසමනය, *Abhisamanaya*, *s.* check, suppression, that which causes anything to cease. [Colloq. සංසිඳවීම *sansindavíma*.]

අභිසමය, *Abhisamaya*, *s.* penetration, comprehension, clear understanding; fine weather, good or favourable season; good religion.

අභිසාරිකාව, *Abhisárikáwa*, *s.* woman who goes to an assignation.

අභිසික්ත, *Abhisikta*, අභිසෙක, *Abhiseka*, *s.* (අභි before, සික්ත sprinkling) an anointing, royal unction; sprinkling.

අභිහිත, *Abhihita*, *a.* (අභි before, ධා *dhá* to have, ක්ත *kta* aff, හි *hi* substituted for the root) spoken, said, called, named. [Colloq. කියනලද *kiyanalada*.]

අභීත, *Abhíta*, *a.* (අ neg. භීත daunted) fearless, undaunted.

අභීම, *Abhíma*, අභීමක, *Abhímaka*, *s.* (අ and භීම terrific) causing no fear, unterrific; opposite.

අභීරු, *Abhíru*, *a.* (අ and භීරු timid) fearless, undaunted; *s.* name of a plant, *(asparagus racemosus)*.

අභීරුක, *Abhíruka*, *s.* courageous man.

අභූත, *Abhúta*, *s.* (අ and භූත being) that which is not, that which has not been, falsehood; non-existence, annihilation.

අභෙද්‍ය, *Abhedya*, *a.* (අ and භෙද්‍ය to be broken) not to be broken, solid; *s.* diamond.

අඹ, *Amba*, *s.* water, rainy cloud; woman, wife; chaste wife; mother; also a medicinal drug, see හිරිවේරිය *hiriwériya*.

අඹ, *Amba*, *s.* mango, *mangifera indica* or *mangifera zeylanica (Anacardiaceæ)*.

අඹකහ, *Ambakaha*, *s.* tuberous plant, with scarcely any stem, *Kaempferia pandurata (Scimitamineæ)*.

අඹ ගහ, *Amba-gaha*, *s.* mango tree.

අඹගෙඩිය, *Ambagediya*, *s.* mango fruit; kidney.

අඹනවා, *Ambanawá*, *v.* to make, to form; to drive away: pret. ඇඹුවා *embuwá*.

අඹ මල්, *Amba-mal*, *s.* flower of the mango.

අඹර, *Ambara*, *s.* the sky, the atmosphere; apparel, clothes; also a powder applied to the body.

අඹරණවා, *Ambaraṇawá*, *v.* to grind, to twist: pret. ඇඹරුවා *embaruwá*.

අඹ රුක, *Amba-ruka*, *s.* mango tree.

අඹල. *Ambala*, *s.* plant, *Limnanthemum cristatum*, *(Loganiaceæ)*.

අඹලම, *Ambalama*, see අම්බලම *ambalama*.

අඹවනවා, *Ambawanawá*, *v.* to drive, to drive away; to cause to be driven away, to chase after, to mould: pret. ඇඹෙවුවා or ඇඹෙව්වා *embewwá*.

අඹාගණ, *Ambágana*, අඹාගෙණ, *Ambágena*, *a.* chasing, chased, having chased.

අඹු, *Ambu*, *s.* water, [Colloq. ජලය *jalaya*]; wife, (disrespectful).

අඹුජ, *Ambuja*, *s.* (අඹු water, ජ born) lotus. [Colloq. නෙළුම් *nelum*.]

අඹුදරුවෝ, *Ambudaruwó*, *s.* wife and children, the family.

අඹුරා, *Ambura*, *s.* sky, heaven; Elu form of අම්බර *ambara*. [Colloq. අහස *ahasa*.]

අඹුරුනී, *Amburuní*, *s.* (අඹුරු and නී river) the river of swarga or heaven.

අඹුව, *Ambuwa*, *s.* wife.

අඹුස්, *Ambus*, *s.* water. [Colloq. වතුර *watura*.]

අඹේ, *Ambé*, *s.* singular of අඹ *amba*, mango.

අම්බර, *Ambara*, *s.* sky; apparel, clothes; talc.

අම්බරීෂ, *Ambarísha*, *s.* frying pan, war, battle; name of Ṣiva, also of Vishṇu; young animal, colt, boy; division in hell; the sun, repentance, a king so called of the Súriya race; kind of tree, *(spondias mangifera)*, [Colloq. ඇඹරැල්ල *embarella*].

අම්බලම, *Ambalama*, *s.* kind of shed built on the road side for travellers to rest in.

අම්බා, *Ambá*, *s.* mother.

අම්බිකාව, *Ambikáwa*, *s.* mother, wife; plant, *(clypea hernandifolia)*.

අඹු, *Ambu*, *s.* water.

අම්බුජ, *Ambuja*, *s.* (අඹු water, ජ born) lotus, moon, fish, oyster; *a.* aquatic.

අම්බුද, *Ambuda*, *s.* (අඹු and ද what gives) cloud; plant, *(cyperus rotundus)*; [Colloq. කලාඳුරු *kalánduru*].

අම්බුධරී, *Ambudharí*, *s.* (අම්බු and ධර *dhara* which bears) cloud.

අම්බුධි, *Ambudhi*, *s.* (අම්බු and ධි what possesses) the ocean. [Colloq. සමුද්‍රය *samudraya*.]

අම්බු ප්‍රසාදන, *Ambu-prasádana*, *s.* (අම්බු and ප්‍රසද *prasada* to cleanse) clearing nut tree, *(strychnos potatorum)*; the nuts of this plant are used for purifying water, they are rubbed upon the inner surface of the vessel and cause the precipitation of the impurities of the fluid. [Colloq. ඉඟිනි *ingini*.]

අම්බුරුහ, *Amburuha*, *s.* (අම්බු and රුහ what grows in or on) lotus, any aquatic plant.

අම්භෝජ, *Ambhoja*, *s.* (අම්භස් *ambhas* water, ජ born) water born, lotus; moon.

අම්භෝ නිධි, *Ambho-nidhi*, *s.* (අම්භස් *ambhas* and නිධි treasure) ocean. [Colloq. සාගරය *ságaraya*].

අම්භෝරුහ, *Ambhoruha*, *s.* (අම්භස් *ambhas* and රුහ what rises or grows) lotus. [Colloq. පියුම් *piyum*.]

අම්මණ්ඩි, *Ammandi*, *s.* respectful term for mother used in conversation.

අම්මා, *Ammá*, *s.* mother. pl. අම්මාලා *ammálá* or අම්මාවරු *ammáwaru*.

අම්මාපල්ල, *Ammápalla*, } *s.* common asseveration,
අම්මාපා, *Ammápá*, } "by my mother."

අම්‍ර, *Amra*, *s.* mango. [Colloq. අඹ *amba*.]

අම්‍රත, *Amrata*, see අමෘත *amrita*.

අම්ල, *Amla*, *s.* sourness, acidity; [Colloq. ඇඹුල් *embul*]; wood sorrel, *(oxalis monadelpha)*.

අම්ලිකා, *Amliká*, *s.* tamarind tree, [Colloq. සියඹලා *siyambalá*]; wood sorrel.

අම, *Ama*, *s.* water; [Colloquial: ජලය *jalaya*]. ambrosia and nectar. See අමෘත *amrita*.

අමග, *Amaga*, *s.* (අ neg. මග the way) heresy.

අමඞ්ගල, *Amangala*, *s.* (අ and මඞ්ගල auspicious) inauspicious, unlucky; *s.* castor oil plant, the wood of which has no sap and is useless.

අමත්තු, *Amattu*, *s.* cessation. [Provin.]

අමත, *Amata*, *s.* nectar or ambrosia, Nirváṇa, water, see අමෘත *amrita*.

අමතන්නා, *Amatanná*, *s.* thinker, inventor. pl, අමතන්නෝ *amatannó*.

අමතන, *Amatana*, *a.* inviting, thinking, expecting.

අමතනවා, *Amatanawá*, *v.* to think, to ponder, to look for by the mind as for an answer to a question, to invent, invite: pret. ඇමතුවා *ematuwá*.

අමද, *Amada*, *s.* perfume, odour; leprosy; pleasure, delight.

අමද, *Amada*, *a.* (අ neg. මද little) not a little, much, sufficient, plentiful, abundant.

අමදින, *Amadina*, *a.* sweeping.

අමදිනවා, *Amadinawá*, *v.* to sweep, to clean, to rub as with a cloth: pret. ඇමැද්දා *emeddá*. [Colloquial: අතුගානවා *atugánawá*, පිහිනවා *pihinawá*.]

අමදිනී, *Amadíni*, *s.* mother, sweeper, broom,

අමදු, *Amadu*, *s.* eating, feeding.

අමදුර, *Amadura*, } *a.* (අ and මදුර savour) taste-
අමදුරු, *Amaduru*, } less, having no savour. [Coll. රස නැති *rasa-neti*.]

අමධුර, *Amadhura*, Páli form of preceding word.

අමන, *Amana*, *a.* (අ and මන thought) thoughtless, ignorant, stupid, idiotic.

අමනයා, *Amanayá*, *s.* simple-man, stupid-man.

අමනවා, *Amanawá*, *v.* to blow, convey a very good or bad smell.

අමනාප, *Amanápa*, *a.* (අ priv. මනාප content) discontented, dissatisfied, unwilling.

අමනාපය, *Amanápaya*, *s.* dislike, displeasure.

අමනුෂ්‍ය, *Amanushya*, *s.* (අ neg. මනුෂ්‍ය man) not a human being, demon or evil spirit, [Colloq. යක්ෂ *yaksha*]; *a.* devilish.

අමනොඥ, *Amanojña*, *a.* (අ priv. මනොඥ excellent) inferior; not excellent.

අමපා, *Amapá*, *s.* (අම nectar, පා who drinks) deity; god.

අමයිත්‍රී, *Amayitrí*, see අමෛත්‍රී *amaitrí*.

අමයුරු, *Amayuru*, *a.* (අම nectar, අයුර *ayura* like) delicious, resembling ambrosia.

අමයුරු වදන, *Amayuru wadana*, *s.* (අමයුර sweet, වදන word) sweet speech, pleasing words.

අමර්ෂ, *Amarsha*, *s.* anger, passion, wrath. [Colloq. තරහ *taraha.*]

අමර, *Amara*, *s.* (අ and මර dying) immortal; deity; heaven or world of the gods; quicksilver.

අමරණීය, *Amaraniya*, *a.* (අ and මරණීය perishable) that cannot die, undying, immortal.

අමරභාවය, *Amarabháwaya*, *s.* (අමර undying, භාවය state or condition) the undying state.

අමරලා, *Amaralá*, *s.* name of a fish.

අමරා, *Amará*, *s.* deity, god, kind of panic grass *(heterepogon hirtus)*, [Colloq. ඊතණ *ítana*]; kind of creeper, holy basil; banyan tree; city of gods.

අමරුපු, *Amarupu*, *s.* (අම god, රුපු an enemy) name of Buddha.

අමල්, *Amal*, *a.* pure, clean. [Colloq. පිරිසිදු *piri-sidu.*]

අමල, *Amala*, *a.* (අ neg. මල rust) unsullied, clear, pure, as polished brass or steel.

අමළු, *Amalu*, *s.* crystal. [Colloq. පළිඟු *palingu.*]

අමා, *Amá*, *s.* name of Nirvána; ambrosia, day of the new moon.

අමා ඇඳුරු, *Amá-eduru*, *s.* (අමා Nirvána, ඇඳුරු teacher) the teacher that shows the way to Nirvána, Buddha.

අමාත්‍ය, *Amátya*, } *s.* prime minister, counsellor, state officer. [Coll. ඇමතියා *ematiyá.*]
අමාත්‍යයා, *Amátyayá*, }

අමාදිය, *Amádiya*, *s.* (අමා immortal or sweet, දිය water) water of life, nectar; sweet or pure water.

අමාප්ත, *Amápta*, } *s.* incorrectly written for අමාත්‍ය *amátya* which see.
අමාප්ත්‍ය, *Amáptya*, }

අමාපැන්, *Amápen*, *s.* see අමාදිය *amádiya*.

අමාමහ නිවණ, *Amámaha niwana*, *s.* name of Nirvána.

අමායා, *Amáyá*, *a.* (අ priv. මායා deceit) sincere, frank, open. [Colloq. රැවටිලි නැති *rewotili-neti.*]

අමාරණවා, *Amáranawá*, *v.* to flourish a weapon, etc. as if to strike, to strike as with a sword or weapon: pret. ඇමැරුවා *emeruwá*.

අමාරස, *Amárasa*, *s.* (අමා immortal, රස taste) ambrosial taste, such a savour as is pleasing to the gods.

අමාරු, *Amáru*, *a.* difficult.

අමාරැස, *Amáresa*, *s.* (අමා and රැස rays) moon; pl. අමාරැස් *amáres*. [Colloq. චන්ද්‍රයා *chandrayá.*]

අමාලිය, *Amáliya*, *s.* (අමා and ලිය creeper) a sort of creeper, species of the amaranthus.

අමාවක, *Amáwaka*, *s.* the day of the new moon.

අමාවතුර, *Amáwatura*, *s.* (අමා and වතුර water) the water of life; Sinhalese book so called.

අමාවසි, *Amáwasi*, see අමාවාසි *amáwási*.

අමාවහරෙි, *Amá-waharé*, *s.* (අමා ambrosial, වහරෙි rain) Elu form of අමෘත වර්ෂා *amrita warshá*; the fall of ambrosia from heaven; pleasant rain.

අමාවාසි, *Amáwási*, *s.* (අමා with, වස to abide) the day in which the moon is with or in the same quarter as the sun; the day of the new moon.

අමා වැසි, *Amá-wesi*, see අමාවහරෙි *amá-waharé*.

අමාසේ, *Amásé*, *s.* (අමා and සේ shade) ambrosial shade, pleasant shade.

අමිත්, *Amit*, } *a.* (අ and මිත්‍ර friendly) unfriendly, adverse, inimical.
අමිත්‍ර, *Amitra*, }

අමිත, *Amita*, *a.* (අ priv. මිත measure) immeasurable, infinite, boundless. [Colloq. අප්‍රමාණ *apra-mána.*]

අමිතුරා, *Amiturá*, *s.* enemy; pl. අමිතුරෝ *ami-turó*.

අමිතුරු, *Amituru*, *a.* Elu form of අමිත්‍ර *amitra*.

අමිතෝදන, *Amitódana*, *s.* a king so called, brother to Suddhódana the father of Buddha.

අමින්, *Amin*, *s.* multitude, assembly; [Colloquial: සමූහය *samúhaya.*] *a.* immeasurable.

අමියාව, *Amiyáwa*, *s.* see ඇමියාව *emiyáwa*.

අමියු, *Amiyu*, *s.* eating.

අමියුරු, *Amiyuru*, *a.* (අ not, මියුරු savour) tasteless, having no savour, insipid; not pleasing.

අමිශ්‍ර, *Amisra*, *a.* (අ and මිශ්‍ර mixture) unmixed, uncompounded,

අමිස, *Amisa*, *s.* flesh, food, luxury. See ආමිෂ *ámisha*.

අමිසි, *Amisi*, *s.* kind of dill or fennel, *(anethum sowa)* [Colloq. සතකුප්ප *satakuppa*].

අමිහිරි, *Amihiri*, see අමියුරු *amiyuru*.

අමි, *Amí*, *s.* eating. [Colloq. වැලඳුම *welanduma.*]

අමිරස, *Amírasa*, *s.* bad taste, insipidity; *a.* tasteless, disagreeable taste.

අමු, *Amu*, *a.* raw, green, unripe; a kind of paddy; a plant, of which there are five or six species in Ceylon, *paspalum scrobiculatum, (Gramineæ).*

අමුක්කරා, *Amukkará*, *s.* a sort of plant, *(physalis flexuosa)*; *Withania somnifera (Solanaceæ.)*

අමුක්ත, *Amukta*, *a.* (අ neg. මුක්ත released) not loosed, retained; *s.* weapon that is always grasped to be used as a knife.

අමු කපුරු, *Amu-kapuru*, *s.* unprepared camphor.

අමුකැර, *Amukara*, *past. part.* begun, brought into the presence.

අමුඛ්‍ය, *Amukhya*, *a.* (අ not, මුඛ්‍ය chief) secondary, inferior, not chief. [Colloq. අප්‍රධාන *apradhána.*]

අමුඩ, *Amuḍa*, } *s.* piece of cloth used to pass
අමුඩෙ, *Amuḍe*, } between the legs from the front to behind for the purpose of tucking up the lower garments.

අමුණ, *Amuṇa*, *s.* the standard measure of paddy and other grain, containing eight parrahs or 160 measures of paddy, *i. e.* five bushels. It varies in different parts of the Island. In the Colombo district it is equal to about six bushels; a superficial measure containing as much ground as an *amuṇa* of grain will sow, it is reckoned at 2½ acres but in the central province about two acres; a temporary dam for diverting or stopping the water of a stream for the purpose of irrigation; the bank in a paddy field. pl. අමුණු *amuṇu.*

අමුණු බඳිනවා, *Amuṇu bandinawá*, *v.* to construct a dam, to stop up a water course to irrigate the fields.

අමුත්ත, *Amutta*, *s.* a new thing, anything strange.

අමුත්තා, *Amuttá*, *s.* stranger, visitor, guest; pl. අමුත්තෝ *amuttó.*

අමුතු, *Amutu*, *a.* novel, of another kind.

අමුතු, *Amutu*, *s.* procession, miracle, wonder. [Coll. පෙළහර *peḷahara.*]

අමුතු කිම, *Amutu kima*, *s.* poetical invention, (literally) new saying; pl. අමුතු කිම් *amutu kim.*

අමුතු බත, *Amutu bata*, *s.* (අමුතු new, බත boiled rice) food given to strangers, hospitality; food cooked out of the first produce of a harvest.

අමුතුම්, *Amutum*, see ඇමතුම් *ęmatum.*

අමුතු වැඩ, *Amutu węḍa*, *s.* additional work.

අමුතු හැටි, *Amutu hęṭi*, *s.* new or strange forms.

අමුතු හැඩ, *Amutu hęḍa.* *s.* new shapes, other fashions.

අමුනන, *Amunana*, *a.* stringing together; *s.* string of beads, or flowers, or any kind of ornaments that are strung or linked together.

අමුනනවා, *Amunanawá*, *v.* to string beads; to thread (needle), to arrange: pret. ඇමුනුවා *ęmunuwá.*

අමුපාට, *Amupáṭa*, *s.* (අමු unripe or fresh as leaves, පාට colour) green.

අමු රන්, *Amu-ran*, *s.* unwrought gold.

අමුළු, *Amuḷu*, *a.* (අ neg. මුළු multitude) crowdless.

අමුව, *Amuwa*, *s.* unripe, green colour.

අමුසොහොන, *Amusohona*, *s.* ground where dead bodies are cast without a burial.

අමු හොද්ද, *Amu-hodda*, *s.* (අමු raw, හොද්ද soup) soup or condiment prepared without the help of fire; soup that is not well boiled. pl. අමු හොදි *amu-hodi.*

අමූලික, *Amúlika*, *a.* (අ neg. මූල *múla* root, beginning, ඉක *ika* aff.) endless, infinite.

අමෘත, *Amṛita*, *a.* (අ and මෘත dead) immortal, imperishable, unfading; *s.* freedom from death, final emancipation of the soul from the body, according to the Buddhistical philosophy deliverance from transmigration, *i. e.* Nirváṇa; also the food of the gods, ambrosia, nectar.

අමෘත වර්ෂා, *Amṛita warshá*, see අමාවහරේ *amáwaharé.*

අමේධ්‍ය. *Amedhya*, *s.* (අ and මේධ්‍ය pure) fœces, excrement; *a.* impure, foul. [Colloq. අසූචි *asúchi.*]

අමේධස්, *Amedhas*, *s.* fool, idiot. [Colloq. මෝඩයා *móḍayá.*]

අමෛත්‍රී, *Amaitrí*, *s.* unfriendliness.

අමෝඝ, *Amógha*, *v.* (අ priv. මෝඝ vain) productive, fruitful.

අමෝද, *Amóda*. *s.* joy, pleasure, [Colloq. සතුට *satuṭa*]; strong perfume, fragrance.

අමෝරා, *Amórá*, *p. p.* having lifted up as if to strike. [Colloq. උළුක්කොට *uḷukkoṭa.*]

අමෝහ, *Amóha*, *s.* (අ neg. මෝහ folly) absence of ignorance or error, correct knowledge.

අමෝහී, *Amóhi*, *s.* (අ not, මෝහී foolish) wise judicious person. [Colloq. නුවණැත්තා *nuwanęttá.*]

අය, *Aya*, *s.* taxes, produce, gain; person; iron; in Sanskrit writings, good luck, fortune. pl. අය or අයවල් *ayawal.*

අයකරණවා, *Ayakaraṇawá*, *v.* to recover a debt, to collect as a tax, to levy taxes (judicially).

අයකල්, *Ayakal*, *s.* the fourth or the iron age of the world. [Colloq. කලියුගය *kaliyugaya.*]

අයජාමෙන්, *Ayajamen*, *adv.* by the request, on account of the request. [Colloq. ආරාධනාවෙන් *árádhanáwen.*]

අයති, *Ayati*, *a.* belonging to, attached to.

අයද ගන්නවා, *Ayada-gannawá*, *v.* to pray, to entreat, to beseech.

අය දමනවා, *Aya-damanawá*, *v.* to win at games played with cowry or dice, to play at dice.

අයදින, *Ayadina*, *part. a.* praying.

අයදිනවා, *Ayadinawá*, *v.* to pray, to ask, to beseech, to bless: pret. අයදුවා *ayaduwá* or අයැද්දා *ayęddá*. [Colloq: යාච්ඤාකරණවා *yáchñákaraṇawá*.]

අයදුම, *Ayaduma*, *s.* prayer, request. [Colloq. ඉල්ලීම *illíma*.] pl. අයදුම් *ayadum*.

අයදැකුම්, *Ayadękum*, *s.* tribute to a king, revenue; giving to a temple the produce of the lands attached thereto.

අයන්, *Ayan*, *s.* road. [Colloq. මාවත *máwata*.]

අයන, *Ayana*, *s.* way, road, [Colloq. මාර්ගය *márgaya*]; half year, that is the sun's passage north or south; going, motion.

අයනවා, *Ayanawá*, *v.* to gape, to yawn, to open, pret. ඇයුවා *ęyuwá*.

අයනැදුරු, *Ayanęduru*, *s.* (අයන *ayana* Nirvána, ඇදුරු *ęduru* teacher) name of Buddha.

අයපඬුරු, *Ayapaṇḍuru*, *s.* revenue.

අයබද්ද, *Ayabadda*, *s.* tax, impost, revenue; pl. අයබදු *ayabadu*.

අයම්, *Ayam*, *s.* length. [Colloq. දිග *diga*.]

අයම්නොයම්, *Ayamnoyam*, *s.* see අයාම්නොයාම් *ayámnoyám*.

අයම්විතර, *Ayamvitara*, *s.* length and breadth. [Colloq. දිග පලල *diga palaḷa*.]

අයම, *Ayama*, see අයම් *ayam*.

අයමින්, *Ayamin*, abl. of අයම *ayama*.

අයල්, *Ayal*, *s.* a rock, [Colloq. පර්වතය *parwataya*]; yellow fragrant wood.

අයව්‍යය, *Ayavyaya*, } *s.* (අය gain, ව්‍යය loss) profit
අයවැය, *Ayavęya*, } and loss of any concern; incomings and out goings of a family; revenue and expenditure.

අයශ්ශූල, *Ayaśśúla*, } *s.* (අයස් iron, ශූල a pike)
අයස්සූල, *Ayassúla*, } iron pike used as an instrument of punishment in hell; any iron pike. [Colloq. යකඩ උල *yakaḍa ula*.]

අයස්, *Ayas*, *s.* iron. [Colloq. යකඩ *yakaḍa*.]

අයස්කාන්ත, *Ayaskánta*, *s.* (අයස් and කාන්ත stone) loadstone. [Colloq. කාන්දම *kándama*.]

අයස්කාර, *Ayaskára*, *s.* iron smith.

අයස, *Ayasa*, *s.* (අ not, යස fame) dispraise, public odium; weariness.

අයසුන්, *Ayasun*, *s.* (අය iron, සුන් powder) iron filings.

අයහපත්, *Ayahapat*, *a.* (අ not, යහපත් good) bad, unrighteous, improper.

අයහපත, *Ayahapata*, *s.* wickedness, misfortune.

අයාගන්නවා, *Ayágannawá*, *v.* to gape, to yawn.

අයාම් නොයාම්, *Ayám-noyám*, *s.* dearth, need, scarcity, necessity. [Colloq. අගහිගකම් *agahigakam*.]

අයාම, *Ayáma*, *s.* dearth, need, scarcity, want; pl. අයාම් *ayám*. [Colloq. හිඟය *higaya*.]

අයාලයා, *Ayálayá*, *s.* vagrant, wanderer, vagabond.

අයාලෙ යනවා, *Ayále yanawá*, *v.* to go astray, to wander. [Colloquial: පාදඩෙ යනවා *pádaḍe-yanawá*.]

අයාස, *Ayása*, *s.* for ආයාස *áyása* which see.

අයි, *Ayi*, see අයිද *ayida*.

අයිති, *Ayiti*, *a.* belonging to.

අයිතිකාරයා, *Ayitikárayá*, *s.* owner, possessor, inheritor; slave.

අයිද, *Ayida*, *ind.* seldom used, see ඇයි *ęyi* or ඇයිද *ęyida*.

අයින්, *Ayin*, *s.* wealth not given.

අයින, *Ayina*, *s.* side, border, multitude, shoal (of fishes). pl. අයින් *ayin*.

අයිනාදන, *Ayinádana*, *s.* theft.

අයියණ්ඩි, *Ayiyaṇḍi*, *s.* respectful term for an elder brother used in conversation.

අයියා, *Ayiyá*, *s.* elder brother; pl. අයියාලා *ayiyálá*.

අයියෝ, *Ayiyó*, *interj.* ah! oh! alas!

අයිරාවණ, *Ayiráwaṇa*, *s.* Elu form of ඓරාවණ *airáwaṇa*, elephant with tusks; elephant of Śakra.

අයිරා දහස්, *Ayirá dahas*, *a.* (අයිරා more, දහස් thousand) more than a thousand.

අයිශ්වර්‍ය්‍ය, *Ayiśwaryya*, see ඓශ්වර්‍ය්‍ය *aiśwaryya*.

අයුක්ත, *Ayukta*, *s.* injustice, injury; *a.* improper; sometimes written අයුත්ත *ayutta*.

අයුක්තිය, *Ayuktiya*, *s.* (අ neg. යුක්ති justice) injustice, illegality.

අයුකල්, *Ayukal*, *s.* the past, the past time. [Colloq. අතීත කාලය *atíta kálaya*.]

අයුණු, *Ayuṇu*, *s.* fault. [Colloq. අගුණ *aguṇa*.]

අයුතු, *Ayutu*, *a.* (අ and යුතු proper) improper, unjust.

අයුතුකම, *Ayutukama*, *s.* impropriety, injustice.

අයුරු, *Ayuru*, *a.* like, similar. [Colloq. ආකාර *ákára*.]

අයොග්‍ය, *Ayogya*, *a.* (අ and යොග්‍ය proper) improper, unfit, unsuitable. [Colloq. නොනිසි *nonisi*.]

අයොග *Ayoga*, *s.* (අ and යොග union) separation, disjunction; unlike, dissimilar.

අයොධ්‍යා, } *Ayodhyá*, *a.* (අ and යුද්ධ *yuddha* to
අයොද්ධ්‍යා, } make war) not to be warred against; *s.* the capital of Ráma; the modern Oude.

අයෝමය, *Ayómaya*, *a.* made of iron.

අයෝ මල, *Ayó-mala*, *s.* (අයස් *ayas* iron, මල dirt) rust of iron. [Colloq. යකඩ මල *yakaḍa-mala.*]

අයෝමුද්ගර, *Ayómudgara*, *s.* club of iron.

අයඃ පර්වතය, *Ayaḥ parwataya*, *s.* (අයස් *ayas* iron, පර්වතය mountain) mountain of iron; instrument of punishment in hell.

අර්ක, *Arka*, *s.* sun; [Colloq. සූර්යයා *súryayá.*]

අර්කනන්දන, *Arkanandana*, *s.* (අර්ක and නන්දන son) Yama, son of Súrya.

අර්කබන්ධු, *Arkabandhu*, } *s.* (අර්ක sun, බන්ධු
අර්කබාන්ධව, *Arkabándhawa*, } kinsman) name of Buddha expressive of his family origin, viz, Súrya waṃsa or line of the sun.

අර්ගල, *Argala*, *s.* wooden pin or bolt for fastening the door, [Colloq. අගුල *agula*]; a surge or billow. [Colloq. රළ *reḷa.*]

අර්ඝ, *Argha*, *s.* price, cost, value, [Colloq. අගය *agaya*]; reverence or mode of worship.

අර්ජුන, *Arjuna*, *s.* name of a king with a thousand arms; peacock; name of a plant, *terminalia glabra, (Combretaceæ)*, commonly called කුඹුක් *kuṃbuk;* the third of the five Páṇḍavas.

අර්ණව, *Arṇawa*, } *s.* (අර්ණස් *arṇas* water, ව aff.
අර්ණ්ණව, *Arṇṇawa*, } and ස *sa* is dropped) ocean. [Colloq. මුහුද *muhuda.*]

අර්ථ, *Artha*, *s.* meaning, signification, [Colloquial: තේරුම *téruma*]; property, riches, wealth, [Coll. වස්තුව *wastuwa*]; profit, fruit; cause, origin; request, petition; acquisition of wealth by foreign conquests, and by punishment of the wicked with justice.

අර්ථ කියනවා, *Artha-kiyanawá*, *v.* to say the meaning of, to interpret, to explain.

අර්ථ දූෂණ, *Artha-dúshaṇa*, *s.* (අර්ථ and දූෂණ spoiling) waste, prodigality, extravagance.

අර්ථ ප්‍රයෝග, *Artha-prayóga*, *s.* (අර්ථ wealth, ප්‍රයෝග application) the profession of usury.

අර්ථ රසය, *Artha-rasaya*, *s.* elegance, taste.

අර්ථවත්, *Arthawat*, *a.* wealthy, rich; significant, having good sense or meaning.

අර්ථ විඥාන, *Artha-vijñána*, *s.* (අර්ථ meaning, විඥාන knowledge) one of the six sciences contained in the වේදාංග *wédánga* viz, comprehension of meanings.

අර්ථ ශාස්ත්‍රය, *Artha-ṣástraya*, *s.* the science of polity or moral and political government.

අර්ථසිද්ධිය, } *Arthasiddhiya*, *s.* (අර්ථ and සිද්ධි ac-
අර්ථසිද්ධිය, } complishment) fulfilment of purpose, success.

අර්ථ හීන, *Artha-hína*, *a.* (අර්ථ and හීන wanting) poor, failing; unmeaning, nonsensical.

අර්ථාගම, *Arthágama*, *a.* (අර්ථ *artha* and ආගම *ágama* coming) treasury, or depot of wealth; acquisition of wealth.

අර්ථාවගම, *Artháwagama*, *s.* comprehension of meanings.

අර්ධ, *Ardha*, *s.* part, half.

අර්ධ චන්ද්‍රයා, *Ardha chandrayá*, *s.* (අර්ධ half, චන්ද්‍ර moon) half moon, crescent; semicircular scratch of the finger nail; semicircular marks on the peacock's tail. [Colloq. අඩසඳ *aḍasaṇḍa.*]

අර්ධපාල, *Ardhapála*, *s.* kind of fabled Rahat said to clothe only the part of the body from the hips upward to the shoulders.

අර්ධමාත්‍ර, *Ardhamátra*, *s.* half a syllabic instant.

අර්ධ යාම, *Ardha-yáma*, *s.* (අර්ධ and යාම a watch) half a watch, two hours.

අර්ධ රාත්‍ර, *Ardha-rátra*, *s.* midnight. [Colloq. මද්දුම රෑ *maddimaré.*]

අර්ධ වීක්ෂණ, *Ardha-vikshaṇa*, *s.* (අර්ධ half, වීක්ෂණ looking) side look, glance, leer. [Colloq. අඩ බැල්ම *aḍabelma.*]

අර්ධාංග නෘත්‍ය, *Ardhánga-nritya*, *s.* (අර්ධ *ardha* and අංග *anga* body, නෘත්‍ය dance) kind of dance in which only half of the body is in motion.

අර්ධාර්ධය, *Ardhárdhaya*, *s.* quarter, one fourth. [Colloq. පංගුවෙන් පංගුව *panguwen panguwa.*]

අර්ධේන්දු, *Ardendu*, *s.* (අර්ධ *ardha* and ඉන්දු *indu* moon) half moon or crescent; the impression of a finger nail; an arrow with a crescent shaped head. See අර්ධ චන්ද්‍රයා *ardha chandrayá.*

අර්පණ, *Arpaṇa*, *s.* fixing, placing in or upon; delivering.

අර්බ්බුද, *Arbbuda*, *s.* ophthalmia; canker, boil, stain; hundred million.

අර්හත්, *Arhat*, *s.* (අර්හ to worship, ත් aff. or අරි *ari* an enemy; *i. e.* the passions, හත *hata* destroyed) Rahat, one who has completely destroyed kléṣha or passion, and is consequently prepared for Nirváṇa; it is the first of the nine pre-eminent qualities of Buddha; see නවගුණ *nawaguṇa.* [Colloq. රහත් *rahat.*]

අභීත් ඵලය, *Arhat-phalaya*, *s.* fruition of the Rahatship.

අභීත් මාර්ග, *Arhat-márgaya*, *s.* (අභීත් arhat, මාර්ග way, path) the last of the four paths or grades to Nirváṇa, when, the passions which are a source of existence being destroyed, the devotee finally attains Nirváṇa or extinction.

අර්ඝිකාව, *Arghikáwa*, *s.* artificial tree of lamps. [Colloq. පාන්රුක *pánruka.*]

අර, *Ara*, *pron.* that, (at a distance).

අර, *Ara*, *s.* spoke or radius of a wheel. [Colloq. රෝදයේ ග්‍රාදි *ródayé grádi.*]

අරක්, *Arak*, Elu form of ආරක්‍ෂා *árakshá.*

අරක්කු, *Arakku*, *s.* arrack, spirituous liquor.

අරක්කැමියා, *Arakkemiyá*, *s.* cook.

අරක්ගන්නවා, *Arakgannawá*, *v.* to protect, to guard, to inhabit. [Colloquial: ආරක්‍ෂාකරණවා *árakshákaraṇawá.*]

අරක්දෙව්, *Arakdew*, *s.* protecting god, guardian angel.

අරක, *Araka*, *s.* that thing, (masc.); name of an aquatic plant *(vallisneria)*; protection, pl. අරවා *arawá.*

අරකට, *Arakaṭa*, *s.* dat. or acc. of අරක *araka.*

අරකා, *Araká*, *pron.* that one, (disrespectful) commonly used of the lower animals; pl. අරකාලා *arakálá.*

අරකී, *Arakí*, the fem. form of the above. pl. අරකිලා *arakílá.*

අරගන්නවා, *Aragannawá*, *v.* to take, to receive.

අරගණ යනවා, *Aragaṇa-yanawá*, *v.* to carry, to fetch.

අරගල, *Aragala*, *s.* noise, din, tumult, uproar. [Colloq. කෝලාහලය *kóláhalaya.*]

අරඤ්ඤ, *Arañña*, Páli form of අරණ්‍ය *araṇya.*

අරටුව, *Araṭuwa*, *s.* heart or hard part of a tree. pl. අරටු *araṭu.*

අරණ්‍ය, *Araṇya*, *s.* forest. [Colloq. වනාන්තරය *wanántaraya.*]

අරණ්‍ය කදලී, *Araṇya-kadalí*, *s.* (අරණ්‍ය and කදලී plantain) the wood or wild plantain. [Colloq. වන කෙසෙල් *wana- kesel.*]

අරණ්‍ය කාර්පාසී, *Araṇya-kárpásí*, *s.* (අරණ්‍ය and කාර්පාසී cotton) wild cotton. [Colloq. වන කපු *wana-kapu.*]

අරණ්‍ය මක්‍ෂිකා, *Araṇya-makshiká*, *s.* (අරණ්‍ය and මක්‍ෂිකා fly) gad fly. [Colloq. වන මැස්සා *wana-messá.*]

අරණ්‍ය වායස, *Araṇya-wáyasa*, *s.* jungle crow. [Colloq. වන කවුඩා *wana-kawuḍá.*]

අරණ, *Araṇa*, *s.* Elu form of අරණ්‍ය *araṇya.*

අරණි, *Araṇi*, *s.* wood used for kindling a fire exciting it by attrition; plant from which this wood is taken *(premna spinosa).*

අරත්ත, *Aratta*, *s.* ichneumon plant, *(mimosa octandra)*; when the mungoose is wounded by a poisonous snake, it is supposed to prevent the effects of the venom by the use of this plant.

අරති, *Arati*, *s.* (අ not, රති desire) not to be desired, dislike, discontent, abstinence from anger, passion.

අරද, *Arada*, *ind.* always, continuually. [Colloq. නිතර *nitara.*]

අරදඟ, *Aradaṉga*, *s.* mischief.

අරඳ, *Araṉda*, *adv.* corruption of අරද *arada.*

අරන්, *Aran*, *part.* taking, having taken; *s.* preserved wilderness. (Námávali. 110). [Colloq. ඇතිකළ වන *etikaḷa wana.*]

අරන්කහ, *Arankaha*, *s.* (අරන් forest, කහ turmeric) turmeric, *(curcuma longa).*

අරන් ගොසින්, *Aran-gosin*, *p. p.* of the following. having carried.

අරන් යනවා, *Aran-yanawá*, *v.* see අරගණ යනවා *aragaṇa-yanawá.*

අරන, *Arana*, *s.* incorrectly for අරණ *araṇa.*

අරබ, *Araba*, *ad.* therefore, on account of, for; *s.* beginning.

අරබයා, *Arabayá*, *ad.* on account of, for.

අරඹ, *Araṉba*, *s.* beginning, grove, forest.

අරම, *Arama*, see ආරාම *áráma.*

අරමණ, *Aramaṇa*, *s.* kind of leprosy.

අරමණයා *Aramaṇayá*, *s.* kind of small worm or maggot which breeds in sores.

අරමණා, *Aramaná*, *s.* tree, *Cassia siamea* or *C. florida (Leguminosæ)*; also called වා *wá.*

අරමිණිය, *Aramiṇiya*, *s.* being seated cross legged as the images of Buddha are frequently represented in the temples.

අරමුණ, *Aramuṇa*, *s.* thought which is the result of seeing any beautiful or striking object, thought, conception, an idea, beginning; pl. අරමුණු *aramuṇu.*

අරමුණුකරණවා, *Aramuṇukaraṇawá*, *v.* to determine, to resolve, to intend.

අරමුදල, *Aramudala*, *s.* the treasury of the king or government money; pl. අරමුදල් *aramudal.*

අරළු, *Araḷu*, *s.* name of a plant, *terminalia chebula (Combretaceæ).*

අරළුව, *Araḷuwa*, *s.* the radical fibres which hang from the branches of the nugagaha or banyan tree, and which in time penetrate the earth and become fresh stems; an araḷu fruit.

අරවනවා, *Arawanawá*, *v.* to cause to be put away; to cause to be sent; to cause to open: pret. ඇරෙව්වා *ẹrewwá*.

අරවරකම, *Arawarakama*, *s.* mischief. [Colloq. චණ්ඩිකම *chaṇḍikama*.]

අරවරයා, *Arawarayá*, *s.* quarrelsome person.

අරවා, *Arawá*, *s.* those things; pl. of අරක *araka*.

අරවින්ද, *Arawinda*, *s.* lotus, *nymphæa nelumbo*. [Colloq. නෙළුම් *neḷum*.]

අරස, *Arasa*, *a.* (අ not, රස flavour) insipid, tasteless, dull, (as a composition).

අරසර, *Arasara*, see ආචාර *áchára*.

අරහ, *Araha*, *a.* just, proper, fit, worthy, venerable, sanctified.

අරහත්, *Arahat*, *a.* finally sanctified.

අරා, *Ará*, *p. p.* having ascended; commonly; *s.* a fish.

අරාජක, *Arájaka*, *a.* (අ neg. රාජක kingship) interregnum; anarchical, having no king or government.

අරාම, *Aráma*, *s.* (අ and රාම joy) disconsolate state. [Colloq. සැනසිලි නැතිබව *sẹnasili nẹtibawa*.]

අරි, *Ari*, *s.* enemy, [Colloq. සතුරා *saturá*]; wheel; species of mimosa.

අරි අට, *Ari-aṭa*, see අෂ්ටාර්ය *ashṭárya*.

අරිටු, *Ariṭu*, *s.* enemy; [Colloq. සතුරා *saturá*]; *a.* wicked, bad; see අරිෂ්ට *arishṭa*.

අරිටුකම, *Ariṭukama*, *s.* fierceness; pl. අරිටුකම් *ariṭukam*.

අරිණවා, *Ariṇawá*, *v.* to send; to open, to let go the hold; to leave, to abandon: pret. ඇරියා *ẹriyá*.

අරිත්‍ර, *Aritra*, *s.* a ship's rudder. [Colloq. සුක්කානම *sukkánama*.]

අරිද්ද, *Aridda*, *s.* tree, *Campnosperma zeylanicum (Anacardiaceæ)*.

අරිම්බුව, *Arimbuwa*, *s.* carved work on the margin, used of metals only.

අරිය, *Ariya*, *s.* Rahat, one of the highest orders of the Buddhist ascetics; see ආර්ය *árya*.

අරියන. *Ariyana*, *a.* entreating.

අරියර, *Ariyara*, } *ind.* always, constantly, incessantly. [Colloq. නිරන්තර
අරියොර, *Ariyora*, } යෙන් *nirantarayen*.]

අරිෂ්ට, *Arishṭa*, *s.* name of a plant, soap berry plant, *sapindus saponaria*, also garlic; the nimb tree, *melia azadaracta;* evil symptom; sign or symptom of approaching death; asura or infernal spirit; any portent or natural phenomenon indicating calamities; crow, heron; vinous spirit. See අරිටු *ariṭu*.

අරිෂ්ටකම, *Arishṭakama*, *s.* (අරිෂ්ට disagreeable, කම aff.) bitterness, wrath; malice. [Colloq. නපුරුකම *napurukama*.]

අරිෂ්ටයා, *Arishṭayá*, *s.* disobedient man, cruel man.

අරිසස, *Arisasa*, *s.* hemorrhoids, piles; pl. අරිසස් *arisas*.

අරුක්, *Aruk*, *s.* kind of leprosy.

අරුචි, *Aruchi*, *s.* (අ neg. රුචි desire) disgust, loathing of food, antipathy, aversion.

අරුණ, *Aruṇa*, *s.* sun; charioteer of the sun; dawn of day, the colour of dawn, dark red or mixture of red and black, redness of sunset; name of the bitter apple, *(colocynth)*; the plant that yields the red and black berry from which the jeweller's weight, the *retti*, is derived; kind of leprosy.

අරුණප්‍රභා, *Aruṇaprabhá*, *s.* dawn of day.

අරුණවන්ත, *Aruṇawanta*, *a.* (අරුණ and වන්ත poss. aff. having) of a light red colour; of a kind of red colour.

අරුණ සාරථි, *Aruṇa-sárathi*, *s.* sun; charioteer of the sun.

අරුණු, *Aruṇu*, *s.* charioteer of the sun, dawn, morning rays of the sun; *a.* risen, ascended.

අරුණුවන්, *Aruṇuwan*, *s.* (අරුණු and වන් from වර්ණ *warṇa* colour) the colour of the dawn or dark red.

අරුණෝදය, *Aruṇodaya*, *s.* (අරුණ *aruṇa* dawn, උදය *udaya* rise) break of day, dawn.

අරුත, *Aruta*, *s.* see අරුචි *aruchi*.

අරුදුනුහුගේ දුන්න, *Arudunuhugé dunna*, *s.* bow of Arjuna.

අරුන්දේ, *Arundẹ*, *pron.* that endearing person.

අරුන්ධතී, *Arundhatí*, *s.* wife of one of the seven ṛishis named Vaṣishṭha; she is considered as a pattern of conjugal excellence, and is invoked at the marriage ceremony by the bridegroom; one of the Pleiades.

අරුන්ධතී නාථ, *Arundhatí-nátha*, *s.* Vaṣishṭha, one of the stars in the Great Bear.

අරුමය, *Arumaya*, } *s.* wonder, curiosity. [Coll.
අරුමයක්, *Arumayak*, } පුදුමය *pudumaya*.]

අරුමයක්කෙ, *Arumayakke*, *ad.* low word meaning seldom, since a long while, unusually, for the first time.

අරුව, *Aruwa*, *a.* (අ neg. රුව beauty) ugly, ill formed; *s.* potter.

අරූ, *Arú*, *pron.* that fellow; pl. අරුන් *arun.*

අරූතලය, *Arútalaya*, *s.* one of the four heavens the inhabitants of which are immaterial beings.

අරූප, *Arúpa*, *a.* (අ neg. රූප beauty, or image) ugly, deformed; disfigured; bodiless, having no visible form.

අරූපවත්, *Arúpawat*, *a.* ugly, shapeless. [Colloq. රුවනැති *ruwaneti.*]

අරූපවන්ත, *Arúpawanta*, *a.* bodiless, formless.

අරූපවන්තයා, *Arúpawantayá*, *s.* deformed person.

අරූපාවචර, *Arúpáwachara*, *s.* the world or realm of formlessness; *a.* belonging to arúpabrahmalóka.

අරූපි, *Arúpi*, *a.* formless, incorporeal, immaterial.

අරූපි බඹලොව, *Arúpi-bambalowa*, *s.* (අරූපි and බඹ brahma, ලොව world) formless brahma heaven. There are said to be four heavens peopled by formless brahmas.

අරොව, *Arowa*, *s.* dispute.

අරෝකාරයා, *Arókárayá*, *s.* disputant, antagonist.

අරෝගි, *Arógi*, *a.* healthy, free from sickness.

අරෝගිතා, *Arógitá*, *s.* health.

අරෝම, *Aróma*, *a.* (අ neg. රෝම hair) without hair, woolless.

අරෝව, *Arówa*, *s.* contest, dispute, disturbance.

අරෙත්ත, *Aretta*, see අරත්ත *aratta.*

අරේ, *Aré*, *pro.* that one, (fem.)

අල්, *Al*, *s.* a mute letter or the symbol to neutralize the inherent vowel of consonants.

අල්කරණවා, *Alkaraṇawá*, *v.* to put the *Al* mark (් or ්) over a consonant, signifying that the inherent vowel is dropped.

අල්ගේ, *Algé*, *s.* weaving room. [Colloq. රෙදි වියන ගේ *redi viyana gé.*]

අල්ප, *Alpa*, *a.* small, little, inferior, insignificant, low; unaspirated, put in opposition to මහාප්‍රාණ *maháprána* or aspirated.

අල්පගන්ධ, *Alpagandha*, *s.* (අල්ප and ගන්ධ smell) a little smell; the red lotus.

අල්පතනු, *Alpatanu*, *a.* (අල්ප and තනු body) small, thin, short, having a little body.

අල්පශ්‍රුතයා, *Alpaṣrutayá*, *s.* unlearned person, ignorant person.

අල්පායුස, *Alpáyusa*, *s.* (අල්ප *alpa* and ආයුස *áyusa* life) short life.

අල්පෙච්ඡ, *Alpechchha*, *a.* (අල්ප *alpa* little, ඉච්ඡා *ichchhá*, desire) freedom from covetousness, contentment. [Colloq. ටිකින් සතුටු බැව් *ṭikin satuṭu bew.*]

අල්පෙනෙත්තිය, *Alpenettiya*, *s.* pin.

අල්ප ශාක්‍ය, *Alpe-ṣákya*, *s.* (අල්ප *alpa* and ශාක්‍ය power) one of little power or influence.

අල්මාරිය, *Almáriya*, *s.* almirah, (Port.)

අල්ල, *Alla*, *s.* palm of the hand.

අල්ලනවා *Allanawá*, *v.* to contain; to seize, to apprehend, to lay hold of, to take hold of, to catch: pret. ඇල්ලුවා *elluwá*; p. p. අල්ලා *allá.*

අල්ලවනවා, *Allawanawá*, *v.* to cause to seize: pret. ඇල්ලෙව්වා *ellewwá.*

අල්ලස, *Allasa*, *s.* bribe; pl. අල්ලස් *allas.*

අල්ලා, *Allá*, *part.* having seized or laid hold of.

අල්ලාප සල්ලාප, *Allápa-sallápa*, *s.* courtship, conversation.

අල්ලාපු, *Allápu*, *a.* seized, laid hold of; (generally,) near, next to, adjoining; *part.* apprehended, attacked with.

අල්ලාසිටිනවා, *Allásiṭinawá*, } *v.* to bear, to keep
අල්ලාහිටිනවා, *Alláhiṭinawá*, } up, to hold on, to continue: pret. අල්ලාහිටියා *alláhiṭiyá.*

අල්ලිය, *Alliya*, *s.* spot, place, a place or square on a chess board, (sometimes) a small Hindu temple under a tree &c.

අල්වනවා, *Alwanawá*, *v.* to seize or apprehend: pret. ඇල්ලුවා *elluwá.*

අල, *Ala*, *s.* yam; house, fondness, desire.

අලං, *Alaṉ*, *adv.* expletive, conveying the idea of sufficiency and of beauty.

අලංකාර, *Alaṉkára*, see අලඞ්කාර, *Alaṅkára.*

අලංකාරය, *Alaṉkáraya*, see අලඞ්කාරය *alaṅkáraya.*

අලංකෘත, *Alaṉkṛita*, see අලඞ්කෘත *alaṅkṛita.*

අලංඝනිය, *Alaṉghaniya*, see අලඞ්ඝනිය *alaṅghaniya.*

අලංදු, *Alaṉdu*, *s.* tree, *Allœanthus zeylanicus, (Urticaceæ).*

අලංසාටක, *Alaṉsáṭaka*, *s.* class of brahmins, who are so voracious that they untie their girdles previous to eating in order to remove every impediment.

අලක්, *Alak*, *s.* painting, drawing, picture from ආලේඛ්‍ය *álékhya.* [Colloq. සායම *sáyama.*]

අලක්ත, *Alakta*, } *s.* (අ neg. රක්ත *rakta* red,
අලක්තක, *Alaktaka*, } ර *ra* being changed to ල *la*)

kind of red dye made from a sort of resin or wax which is found in its native state in the interior; lac, the red animal dye so called. [Colloq. ලතු දිය *latu-diya*.]

අලක්ෂ්මී, *Alakshmí*, *s.* (අ priv. ලක්ෂ්මී fortune) misery, misfortune, poverty. [Colloq. අවාසනාව *awásanáwa*.]

අලක්ෂණ, *Alakashaṇa*, *a.* (අ and ලක්ෂණ beautiful) not handsome, unfortunate, ill fated.

අලක, *Alaka*, *s.* name of a city, capital of Kuvéra.

අල කන්ද, *Ala kanda*, *s.* ridge of earth raised by planting yams or potatoes; pl. අල කඳු *ala-kaṉdu*.

අලකමඳු, *Alakamaṉdá*, *s.* Kuvéra's city.

අලකලංචිය, *Alakalaṉchiya*, *s.* brawl, noisy quarrel, an uproar; great distress or trouble, [a low word]; vexation, perplexity.

අලකාධිප, *Alakádhipa*, }
අලකාධිපති, *Alakádhipati*, } *s.* (අලකා city, අධිප *adhipa* or අධිපති *adhipati* ruler) name of Kuvéra. [Colloq. වෙසමුණි රජ *wesamuṇi raja*.]

අලකාපුර, *Alakápura*. see අලක *alaka*.

අලග්න, *Alagna*, *a.* (අ not, ලග්න attached to) not joined or connected; not adhering. [Colloq. නොඇලෙනලද *noęlenalada*.]

අලගුව, *Alaguwa*, *s.* mark made to assist the memory in casting up accounts.

අලඟ, *Alaṉga*, *s.* kissing.

අලංකාර, *Alaṅkára*, *a.* beautiful, ornamented, decorated.

අලංකාරය, *Alaṅkáraya*, *s.* beauty, ornament, decoration, ornament (of dress), trinkets, jewels, etc; rhetorical figures, rhetoric.

අලංකෘත, *Alaṅkṛita*, *past. part.* ornamented, decorated, adorned, embellished.

අලංඝනීය, *Alaṅghaníya*, *a.* (අ not, ලංඝනීය to be passed) impassable, inviolable, not to be transgressed.

අලජ්ජිකයා, *Alajjikayá*, *s.* shameless man, glutton.

අලජ්ජිත, *Alajjita*, *a.* (අ priv. ලජ්ජ *lajja* shame, ඉත *ita* aff.) not ashamed, shameless; bold.

අලතා, *Alatá*, *s.* lac, a red animal dye, see අලක්ත *alakta*. [Colloq. ලතුදිය *latudiya*.]

අල්තාව, *Alatáwa*, *s.* gumlac. [Colloq. ලතුදිය *látudiya*.]

අලප්, *Alap*, *s.* word, calling; the vocative relation.

අලපත, *Alapata*, *s.* shoots of the yam.

අලබු, *Alabu*, *s.* gourd, pumpkin; Elu form of අලාබු *alábu*.

අලඹ, *Alaṉba*, *s.* a curer of serpents' venom, kind of stick.

අලමඳු, *Alamaṉdá*, *s.* the city of Wesamuṇi or Kuvéra; Elu form of ආලකමන්දා, *álakamandá*.

අලය, *Alaya*, *s.* yam.

අලරිය, *Alariya*, *s.* kind of tree, *plumeria acuminata*.

අලලනවා, *Alalanawá*, *v.* to put in motion, to stir about as water in a vessel: pret. ඇලලුවා *ęlaluwá*.

අලවංගුව, *Alawaṉguwa*, *s.* crowbar, lever, axletree.

අලවනවා, *Alawanawá*, *v.* to paste or glue together, to cause one thing to adhere to another, to affix: pret. ඇලෙවුවා *ęlewuwá*.

අල වැල, *Ala-węla*, *s.* (අල yam, වැල creeper) a kind of creeper of which the root is edible.

අලස, *Alasa*, *a.* (අ neg. ලස to work) lazy, indolent, idle.

අලසකම, *Alasakama*, *s.* laziness, idleness.

අලසයා, *Alasayá*, *s.* idle person.

අලාබු, *Alábu*, see අලබු *alabu*.

අලාභ, *Alábha*, *a.* (අ neg. ලාභ cheap) dear, expensive; *s.* loss, dearness.

අලාභහානිය, *Alábhahániya*, *s.* loss, damage.

අලාමක, *Alámaka*, *a.* (අ neg. ලාමක mean or childish) honourable, reputable, respectable; wise, prudent, not childish.

අලි, *Ali*, *s.* bee, [Colloq, බඹරා *baṉbará*]; elephants, [Colloq. ඇත්තු *ęttu*]; scorpion; sign of scorpio; plural of අලියා *aliyá*.

අලික්, *Alik*, *s.* picture, painting from ආලේඛ *álékha*. [Colloq. සිතුයම *situyama*.]

අලික්කැමි, *Alikkęmi*, *s.* (අලික් and කැමි who does) painter. [Colloq. සිත්තරා *sittará*.]

අලියම, *Aliyama*, *s.* daybreak, dawn; pl. අලියම් *aliyam*.

අලියා, *Aliyá*, *s.* ***Elephas Indicus***, Indian or Asiatic elephant. pl. අලි *ali*.

අලු, *Alu*, *s.* ray, dawn, morning. [Colloq. රශ්මිය *raṣmiya*.]

අළු, *Aḷu*, *s.* ashes.

අලුක්කාල, *Alukkála*, *s.* one sixteenth of a penny or quarter of a cent or farthing.

අළුකෙසෙල්, *Aḷukesel*, }
අළුකෙහෙල්, *Aḷukehel*, } *s.* ash coloured plantain.

අළුකොබෙය්යා, *Aḷukobeyiyá*, *s.* (අළු ashes, කොබෙය්යා pigeon) ashcoloured pigeon; wild or spotted necked pigeon.

අළු ගස්, *Aḷu-gas*, *s.* plant, ***alpinia alughas (Scitamineæ)***.

අළුගොඩ, *Aḷugoḍa*, *s.* heap of ashes.

අළුගෝමර, *Aḷugómara*, *s.* ash coloured spot.

අලුත්, *Alut*, *a.* new, fresh, novel.

අලුත්කරණවා, *Alutkaraṇawá*, *v.* to repair, to remodel.

අලුත් වත, *Alut-wata*, *s.* a new cloth.

අලුත්වැඩියාකරණවා, *Alutwęḍiyá-karaṇawá*, *v.* to repair, to mend.

අළුදිය, *Aḷudiya*, *s.* ashes mixed with water and used by the washermen when washing clothes.

අළු දෙල්, *Aḷu-del*, *s.* a tree, *artocarpus nobilis.*

අලුප්, *Alup*, *s.* (අ neg. ලුප් cut) not cut off, unchanged, as an affix, etc; fragment, bit, morsel; from අලාප *álápa.*

අළුපාට, *Aḷupáṭa*, *s.* the ash colour.

අළුපිල, *Aḷupila*, *s.* plant, *tephrosia tinctoria (Legum.)*

අලුපු, *Alupu*, *s.* a word. [Colloq. බස *basa.*]

අළුපුසුල්, *Aḷupusul*, } *s.* species of pumpkin cover-
අළුපුහුල්, *Aḷuphul*, } ed with a sort of powder of an ash colour; *benincasa cerifera (Cucurbi.).*

අළුපොඩයා, *Aḷupoḍayá*, *s.* person affected with a cutaneous disease in which the body seems of an ash colour; [a low word.]

අළුපොලඟා, *Aḷupolaṅgá*, *s.* a polongá (a venomous snake) of ash colour.

අළුබෝ, *Aḷubó*, *s.* tree, *eugenia sylvestris (Myrtaceæ.)*

අළුමි පොලඟා, *Aḷumí-polaṅgá*, *s.* a species of polongá, venomus snake.

අලුයම, *Aḷuyama*, *s.* daybreak. pl. අලුයම් *aluyam.*

අලුලිත, *Alulita*, *a.* (අ neg. ලුලිත shaken) unshaken, undisturbed, calm, quiet.

අළුව, *Aḷuwa*. *s.* loom; sides cut in felling a tree.

අළුවා, *Aḷuwá*, *s.* sweet meat made of flour, jaggery, ghee etc.

අළුහම්, *Aḷuham*, *s.* (අළු ash, හම් skin) ash coloured spots on the skin.

අළුහුණු, *Aḷuhuṇu*, *s.* lime (for mortar), chunam.

අලෙන, *Alena*, *a.* (අ neg. ලෙන refuge) destitute, unprotected.

අලෙයිකරණවා, *Aleyikaraṇawá*, } *v.* to spend.
අලෙවිකරණවා, *Alevikaraṇawá*, }

අලෙවු, *Aleıcu*, *s.* picture, painting; anointing.

අලේ, *Alé*, *s.* yam.

අලේසි, *Alési*, *a.* (අ and ලේසි easy) difficult, troublesome; *s.* uneasiness, difficulty, trouble.

අලොප්, *Alop*, *s.* a lump or ball of food; see ආලෝප *álópa.*

අව්‍යක්ත, *Awyakta*, *a.* (අ and ව්‍යක්ත distinct) invisible, imperceptible, indistinct; also not clever, unlearned, illiterate; *s.* the soul; fool.

අව්‍යක්තරාග, *Awyakta-rága*, *s.* (අව්‍යක්ත indistinct, රාග colour) dark red, the colour of the dawn.

අව්‍යභිචාර, *Awyabhichára*, *s.* (අ neg. ව්‍යභිචාර irregularity) constancy, faithfulness, not having committed adultery.

අව්‍යය, *Awyaya*, *s.* (in grammar) the indeclinable words or particles, as adverbs, prepositions etc.

අව්‍යයීභාව, *Awyayíbháwa*, *s.* indeclinable compound.

අව්‍යාධික, *Awyádhika*, *s.* (අ and ව්‍යාධි disease, ක aff.) healthy person. [Colloq. සනීප ඇත්තා *sanípa-ęttá.*]

අවුරා, *Awrá*, } *s.* rampart, entrenchment, breast
අවුරු, *Awru*, } work near the entrance of a city; [Colloq. කොටුතාප්පය *koṭutáppaya*]; mode, manner, from ආකාර *ákára.*

අව්ලන, *Awlana*, *a.* confused; collecting, gathering; shining.

අව්ව, *Awwa*, *s.* sun.

අව්සදය, *Awsadaya*, see ඖෂධ *auskadha.*

අව, *Awa*, *s.* fortnight of the waning moon.

අව, *Awa*, preposition and prefix with the sense of from, down, downwards, down from, away; diminution; disrespect; bad; a negative and privative particle.

අවංක, *Awaṅka*, *a.* see අවඞ්ක *awaṅka.*

අවක්ෂේප, *Awakshepa*, *s.* (අව and ක්ෂේප throwing) insult, reproach. [Colloq. නින්දාව *nindáwa.*]

අවකපනවා, *Awakapanawá*, *v.* to use an illomened expression.

අවකර්ෂණ, *Awakarshaṇa*, *a.* attracting, drawing towards, pulling.

අවකරුණාව, *Awakaruṇáwa*, *s.* (අව priv. කරුණා mercy) unkindness, displeasure.

අවකාශ, *Awakáṣa*, } *s.* (අව between, කාශ to
අවකාස, *Awakása*, } shine) leisure, opportunity, interval; unoccupied space; the atmosphere, sky.

අවකාසකරණවා, *Awakásakaraṇawá*, *v.* to complete, to finish, to vacate, to empty.

අවක්‍රියාව, *Awakriyáwa*, *s.* (අව bad, ක්‍රියාව act.) misdeed, bad conduct.

අවකීර්ණ, *Awakírṇa*, *a.* coarsely pounded, scattered, confused, irregularly thrown together.

අවකැපීම, *Awakępíma*, *s.* saying something inauspicious, contradiction, an ill omen; pl. අව කැපීම් *awakępím.*

අවගඩ, *Awagaḍa*, *s.* boil or pimple on the face. Elu form of අවගණ්ඩ *awa-gaṇḍa.*

අවගණ්ඩ, *Awagaṇḍa*, see අවගඩ *awagaḍa.*

අවගති, *Awagati*, *s.* knowledge; in general bad temper, viciousness, misbehaviour.

අවගාහක, *Awagáhaka*, *s.* bather, one who immerses.

අවගාහන, *Awagáhana*, *s.* (අව before, ගහන *gahana* agitation) bath, bathing. [Colloq. ස්නානය *snánaya.*]

අවගීත, *Awagíta*, *a.* (අව bad. ගීත sounded or sung) detested, reproached, blamed, publicly censured, vile, wicked.

අවගුණ, *Awaguṇa*, *a.* (අව priv. ගුණ virtue) bad, vile, mean; *s.* bad or evil temper, unkindness.

අවඞ්ක, *Awańka*, *a.* (අ priv. වඞ්ක crooked) not crooked, straight, upright, frank, sincere.

අවච්ඡාව, *Awachchháwa*, } *s.* (අව increase, ඡාව
අවච්ඡායා, *Awachchháyá*, } or ඡායා shadow) that part of the sun's shadow which is cut off in reckoning time according to the native custom: vulgarly අවච්චා *awachchá*.

අවචාරිත්‍ර, *Awacháritra*, *s.* (අව bad, චාරිත්‍ර manners) unbecoming behaviour, bad manners, bad course of life.

අව ජලවක, *Awa-jalawaka*, *s.* the 4th day after full moon, reckoned unlucky. [Colloq. පසළොස්වක ගිය හතරවෙනි දින *pasaḷoswaka giya hatarawení dina.*]

අවජාත, *Awajáta*, *a.* (අව implying depreciation, ජාත born) base born, illegitimate.

අවජාතයා, *Awajátayá*, *s.* bastard, adulterine.

අවඤ්චා, *Awaṉchá*, } *a.* (අ priv. වඤ්චා deceit)
අවඤ්චා, *Awañchá*, } sincere, open, frank.

අවඥා, *Awajñá*, } *s.* (අව bad, ඥා to know,
අවඥාන, *Awajñána*, } and ඥාන knowledge) dis-
අවඥාව, *Awajñáwa*, } respect. [Colloq. අනාදරය *anádaraya.*]

අවට, *Awaṭa*, *prep.* around, round about; [Colloq. හාත්පස *hátpasa*] *s.* (from අවාට Páli) hole, vacuity, chasm. [Colloquial: බෙනේ *bené*, වළ *waḷa.*]

අවටු, *Awaṭu*, *s.* hole in the ground; back of the neck.

අවඩ, *Awaḍa*. see අවැඩ *awęḍa*.

අවතංස, *Awatansa*, *s.* earring; crest, crown.

අවතාරය, *Awatáraya*, *s.* (අව down, තර *tara* to cross or pass) descent; this word is used by various oriental nations to express the incarnation of their deities, or their descent from heaven to earth; and in Hindu history it particularly refers to the incarnation of Vishṇu in ten principal forms viz. 1. the fish, 2. the tortoise, 3. the boar, 4. the man lion, 5. the dwarf, 6 and 7. the two Rámas, 8. Kṛishṇa, 9. Buddha, and 10. Kalkí; (in present use) ghost, apparition, generally used in the indefinite form as අවතාරයක් *awatárayak*.

අවතීර්ණ, *Awatírṇna*, *a.* descending, alighting upon. [Colloq. බැස්සාවූ *bęssáwú.*]

අවතීර්ණව, *Awatírṇṇawa*, *part.* having descended. [Colloq. බැස *bęsa.*]

අවතීර්ණවූ, *Awatírṇṇawú*, see අවතීර්ණ *awatírṇṇa*.

අවද්‍ය, *Awadya*, *s.* (අ neg. වද්‍ය to be spoken) fault, sin; [Colloq. වරද *warada*]. *a.* disagreeable, disliked; low.

අවදන, *Awadana*, *s.* thought, meditation, Elu form of ආවර්ජන *áwarjjana*. [Colloq. කල්පනාව *kalpanáwa.*]

අවදාත, *Awadáta*, *a.* white, clean, clear, beautiful: *s.* white (the colour). [Colloq. සුදු *sudu.*]

අවදාරණ, *Awadáraṇa*, *s.* spade or hoe. [Colloq. උදැල්ල *udęlla.*]

අවදි, *Awadi*, Elu form of අවධි *awadhi* which see.

අවදිකරණවා, *Awadikaraṇawá*, *v.* to awaken, to rouse.

අවදිය, *Awadiya*, *s.* period of time, time.

අවදිවෙනවා, *Awadiwenawá*, *v.* to awake.

අවධාරණ, *Awadháraṇa*, *s.* (අව and ධෘ *dhṛi* to hold, ණ්‍ය *ṇya* aff.) ascertainment, affirmation, emphasis; a class of emphatic indeclinables; also see අවධි *awadhi*.

අවධි, *Awadhi*, *s.* limit, division; period of time; agreement; conclusion; ablative case in grammar.

අවධිකළ, *Awadhikaḷa*, *p. p.* appointed, fixed as time.

අවන්, *Awan*, *s.* danger, risk; bazaar, market place.

අවන්ති, *Awanti*, *s.* name of a city, modern Oujein: Avanti is one of the seven sacred cities of the Hindus, to die at which secures eternal happiness; name of a country and its people.

අවන්රජ, *Awanraja*, } *s.* name of Balaráma.
අවන්රද, *Awanradu*, }

අවන්සත්, *Awansat*, *s.* (අවන *awana* came from, ආපන්න *ápanna* and සත් being) a pregnant woman.

අවන්හල, *Awanhala*, *s.* (අවන් drinking together, හල house) tavern, place where spirits are sold.

අවන, *Awana*, *s.* market, shop.

අවනඩු, *Awanaḍu*, *s.* (අව bad, නඩු judgment) perverted judgment, injustice.

අවනඩුකරණවා, *Awanaḍukaraṇawá*, *v.* to judge or deal unjustly.

අවනත, *Awanata*, a. (අව and නත bending) bending, stooping, bowing, humble, respectful. [Coll. නැමුන *nęmuna*.]

අවනම්බු, *Awanambu*, } s. (අව priv. නම්බු honour)
අවනඹු, *Awanambu*, } dishonour, disrespect; a. dishonourable.

අවනවා, *Awanawá*, v. to curse, to imprecate: pret. ඇවුවා *ęwuwá*.

අවනසත්, *Awanasat*, see අවන්සත් *awansat*.

අවනාපය, *Awanápaya*, s. dislike, see අමනාප *amanápa*.

අවනාපවෙනවා, *Awanápawenawá*, v. to dislike.

අවනි, *Awani*, } s. earth. [Colloq. පෘථිවිය *prithiviya*.]
අවනී, *Awaní*, }

අව පය, *Awa-paya*, s. the left foot. [Provincial.]

අවපාත, *Awapáta*, s. (අව down, පත to go or fall) descent, descending; hole or pit in the ground for catching game in.

අවබෝධ, *Awabódha*, s. (අව emphatic, බෝධ knowledge) understanding, full knowledge.

අවබෝධ කරණවා, *Awabódha-karaṇawá*, v. to understand, to know, to comprehend.

අවම්, *Awam*, s. cursing, abusing. See අවනවා *awanawá*.

අවමංගල්‍ය, *Awamangalya*, see අවමඞ්ගල්‍ය *awamańgalya*.

අවමගුල, *Awamagula*, see අවමඞ්ගල්‍යය *awamańgalyaya*.

අවමඞ්ගල්‍ය, *Awamańgalya*, a. (අව bad, මඞ්ගල්‍ය fortunate) unfortunate, inauspicious, calamitous, unhappy.

අවමඞ්ගල්‍යය, *Awamańgalyaya*, s. any calamitous event; funeral ceremony.

අවමත, *Awamata*, a. (අව implying contempt, මත known) despised, contemned. [Colloq. නින්දා කරණලද *nindákaraṇalada*.]

අවමති, *Awamati*, s. (අව bad, මති thought) disregard, contempt.

අවමන්, *Awaman*, see අවමාන්නය *awamánnaya*.

අවමර්දි, *Awamarda*, s. devastation, laying waste a country.

අවමස, *Awamasa*, s. (අව implying depreciation, මස month) the dark fortnight.

අවමාන්න, *Awamánna*, a. disgraceful, shameful. s. disreputableness, disgrace.

අවමාන්නය, *Awamánnaya*, s. (අව bad, මාන්න respect) disrespect, dishonour, disgrace.

අවමානිත, *Awamánita*, a. despised, disrespected.

අවය, *Awaya*, Elu form of අපාය *apáya*.

අවයව, *Awayawa*, s. limb, member of the human body; (vulg.) news, intelligence.

අවර්ණ, *Awarṇa*, } s. (අ neg. වර්ණ praise, colour
අවර්ණ්ණ, *Awarṇṇa*, } etc.) censure, blame; colourless; a. mean, bad, low; the vowels අ *a* and ආ *á*.

අවර, *Awara*, s. (අ and වර preferable) posterior, hinder, last; west; a creeper, *(dolichos tetragonolobus)*.

අවරග, *Awaraga*, } s. (අවර hinder, and අග *aga*
අවරගිර, *Awaragira*, } or ගිර rock) fictitious rock in the west behind which the sun is supposed to set.

අවරජ, *Awaraja*, s. (අවර posterior, after, ජ born) younger brother. [Colloq. මලයා *malayá*.]

අවරණ, *Awaraṇa*. s. covering, wall, door, protection.

අවරදිග, *Awaradiga*, } s. (අවර and දිසාව
අවර දිසාව, *Awaradisáwa*, } direction) west.

අවර පක්ෂය, *Awara-pakshaya*, s. the moon's wane.

අවරි, *Awari*, } s. indigo plant; a small tree
අවරිය, *Awariya*, } *(nerium tinctorium)*; a decoction of the leaves with the addition of a little lime juice makes an indigo of fine quality; see also නිල් අවරි *nil-awari*.

අවරේ, *Awaré*, s. the after part of a vessel.

අවරොධ, *Awarodha*, s. (අව and රුධ *rudha* to inclose or shut up) seraglio of a palace, queen's apartments; covering, obstruction, hindrance.

අවරෝධ ජනයෝ, *Awaródha janayó*, s. females of a harem; attendants of the queen.

අවල් අදිනවා, *Awal adinawá*, v. to pull by oars, to row.

අවල, *Awala*, a. overspread, crowded, replete; confused; [Colloq. ගැවසීගත් *gęwasígat*]. s. cohabitation, confusion; an oar.

අවලක්ෂ, *Awalaksha*, s. (අව and ලක්ෂ to mark) white (the colour).

අවලක්ෂණ, *Awalakshaṇa*, a. (අව priv. ලක්ෂණ beautiful) ugly, not handsome.

අවලකෙළිය, *Awalakeliya*, s. (අවල and කෙළිය an act or sport) cohabitation, copulation, confusion.

අවලග්න, *Awalagna*. a. (අව neg. ලග්න adhered) not firm, not adhering; [Colloq. නොඇලෙන *noęlena*]. s. waist.

අවලඟු, *Awalangu*, } a. (අ neg. වලංගු legal) ille-
අවලංගු, *Awalangu*, } gal, counterfeit; not passable; abrogated, withered, lifeless.

අවලංගුකරණවා, *Awalangukaranawá, v.* to annul, to make void, to render lifeless.

අවලම්බ, *Awalamba*, } *s.* asylum, protection;
අවලම්බන, *Awalambana*, } *part.* depending, suspended, hanging on, or from. [Colloq. එල්ලීම *ellíma.*]

අවලම්බිත, *Awalambita, a.* quick, expeditious; hanging on or from, suspended; protected, cherished. [Colloq, එල්ලෙනලද *ellenalada.*]

අවලමල, *Awalamala, s.* rowlock, lock or hold for rowing. [Colloq. හබල්පාසය *habalpásaya*]

අවලමා, *Awalamá, s.* vagabond; pl. අවලම්මු *awalammu.* also see පාදඩයා *pádadayá.*

අවලාද, *Awaláda, s.* reproach, blame, abuse, remonstrance before the gods.

අවලාද කියනවා, *Awaláda kiyanawá, v.* to reproach, to blame, to censure.

අවලිප්ත, *Awalipta, a.* (අව before, ලිප්ත smeared) plastered, smeared,

අවලිය, *Awaliya, s.* ninetysixth part of a bushel.

අවලෙ, *Awale, s.* oar, paddle, such as those used in the pada boats; pl. අවල් *awal*; [Colloq. හබල *habala*].

අවලේප, *Awalépa, s.* (අව and ලිප *lipa* to smear) pride, anointing, smearing.

අවලේපන, *Awalépana, s.* anointing; daring purpose.

අවලේහ, *Awaléha, s.* licking.

අවලෝකන, *Awalókana, s.* sight, seeing.

අවවාදය, *Awawádaya, s.* (අව and වාද speech) censure, blame, reproach; command, order; advice, warning, admonition.

අවශ්‍ය, *Awaşya, ind.* (අ neg. වශ *waşa* to subdue) certainly, necessarily. [Colloq. ඒකාන්ත *ékánta.*]

අවශ්‍යයෙන්, *Awaşyayen, ad.* certainly.

අවශිෂ්ට, *Awaşishta*, } *a.* (අව and ශිෂ්ට left) left,
අවශෙෂ, *Awaşesha*, } rest, remainder. [Colloq. ඉතුරු *ituru.*]

අවස්, *Awas, s.* see ආවාස *áwása.*

අවස්තාව, *Awastáwa,* corrupt form of the next.

අවස්ථාව, *Awasthátwa, s.* time, season, portion of time, an epoch; state, condition of humanity varying with time, as youth, age. [Colloq. කාලය *kálaya.*]

අවස්ථිත, *Awasthita, a.* (අව before, ස්ථා *sthá* to stay, ක්ත *kta* aff.) occupying place or period, abiding, remaining firm or fixed. [Colloq. සිටියාවූ *sitiyáwú.*]

අවසඟ, *Awasanga*, } *a.* (අ neg. වසඟ submis-
අවසඟව, *Awasangawa*, } sive) not humble, powerless, incapable of making any use. [Colloq. වසඟ නැති *wasanga-neti.*]

අවසන්, *Awasan, s.* end, termination.

අවසන්ධි, *Awasandhi, a.* (අව and සන්ධි joint) disjointed, dislocated.

අවසන්ධි කරණවා, *Awasandhi-karanawá, v.* to disjoint, to dislocate,

අවසන, *Awasana,* see අවසාන *awasána.*

අවසමය, *Awasamaya, s.* (අව and සමය religion) heathenism, heresy. [Colloq. මිථ්‍යාදෘෂ්ටිය *mithyádrishtiya.*]

අවසරය, *Awasaraya, s.* permission, leave.

අවසරගන්නවා, *Awasaragannawá, v.* (අවසර and ගන්නවා to take) to take leave.

අවසාන, *Awasána, s.* (අව and ශෝ *shó* to finish, ඕ *ó* is changed to ආ *á*) end, termination, conclusion, cessation; boundary, limit; death. [Coll. කම්මුත්ත, *kammutta.*]

අවසේ, *Awasé, s.* see අවච්ඡාව *awachchháwa.*

අවසේස. *Awasésa, s.* that which remains, rest, remainder. [Colloq. ඉතුරු *ituru.*]

අවහිත, *Awahita, past. part.* (අව and ධා *dhá* to have or hold) known, celebrated; done with care, attentive.

අවා, *Awá, s.* general name in Elu for hell; house; also past part. of අවම් *awam* to curse.

අවාක්, *Awák, a.* (අ neg. වාක් speech) dumb. [Colloq. ගොළු *golu.*]

අවාච්‍ය, *Awáchya, s.* (අ and වාච්‍ය to be spoken) improper to be uttered. [Colloq. කියනොහැකි *kiyanohęki.*]

අවාචි, *Awáchí, a.* (අ and වාචි speech) dumb; also (අව *awa* down, අඤ්ච *añcha* to go) looking down, headlong; *s.* south, the south quarter which is considered as below.

අවාදිත, *Awádita, a.* not said, not spoken. [Colloq. නොකියනලද *nokiyanalada.*]

අවාන, *Awána, s.* fan; dry, dried (as of fruit) (Port.); more usually පවන්පත *pawanpata.*

අවාබිය, *Awábiya, s.* (අවා hell, බිය fear) fear of hell.

අවාර, *Awára, s.* the near bank of a river. [Colloq. ළඟ ඉවුර *langa iwura.*]

අවාස, *Awása,* see ආවාස *áwása.*

අවාසනා, *Awásaná, a.* (අ neg. වාසනා good fortune) adverse, unfortunate, unhappy, unlucky.

අවාසනාව, *Awásanáwa, s.* misfortune, bad luck.

අවාසනාවන්ත, *Awásanáwanta*, see අවාසනා *awásaná*.

අවාසස්, *Awásas*, *a.* naked. [Colloq. නිර්වස්ත්‍ර *nirwastra.*]

අවාසි, *Awási*, *part.* not obtained, conquered; *a.* not advantageous, indefensible, not supportable.

අවාසිවෙනවා, *Awásiwenawá*, *v.* to be defeated (as in a lawsuit).

අවි, *Avi*, *s.* weapon. [Colloq. ආයුධය *áyudhaya.*]

අවික්ෂිප්ත, *Avikshipta*, *a.* (අ neg. වික්ෂිප්ත trembling) firm, not shaking; unclaimed. [Colloq. චංචලනුවූ *chanchalanuwú.*]

අවිඝ්න, *Avighna*, *a.* (අ and විඝ්න impediment) unobstructed, facile, easy. [Colloq. බාධා නැති *bádhá-neti.*]

අවිච්චියා, *Avichchiyá*, *s.* (අවිච්චි imitative sound, යා aff.) small bird with a red breast, only appearing in October, the red breast.

අවිච්ඡින්න, *Avichchhinna*, } *a.* (අ neg. විච්ඡින්න
අවිච්ඡේද, *Avichchheda*, } cut off.) unbroken, uncut. [Colloq. නොසිඳිනලද *nosindinalada.*]

අවිජ්ජා, *Avijjá*, *s.* (අ priv. විජ්ජා knowledge) Páli form of අවිද්‍යා *avidyá*, ignorance, chiefly of the four great truths of Buddhism.

අවිජහිත, *Avijahita*, *a.* (අ neg. විජහිත put away) not removed, not put away. [Colloq. අත්නොහරිණලද *atnohariṇalada.*]

අවිඤ්ඤාණක, *Aviññáṇaka*, *a.* (අ priv. විඤ්ඤාණ sense, ක aff.) without intelligence or consciousness, inanimate, insensitive. [Colloq. සිත් නැති *sit neti.*]

අවිතර්ක, *Avitarka*, *a.* (අ and විතර්ක thought) thoughtless, destitute of thought, absence of mind. [Colloq. කල්පනා නැති *kalpaná neti.*]

අවිද්‍ය, *Avidya*, *a.* (අ and විද්‍යා knowledge) ignorant, unwise.

අවිද්‍යමාන, *Avidyamána*, *a.* (අ and විද්‍යමාන having) not having, not possessing, not existing, not present.

අවිද්‍යාව, *Avidyáwa*, *s.* ignorance, error. [Colloq. මෝඩකම *módakama.*]

අවිදු, *Avidu*, Elu form of අවිද්‍යා *avidyá*.

අවිදුමන්, *Aviduman*, Elu form of අවිද්‍යමාන *avidyamána*.

අවිනෂ්ට, *Avinashṭa*, *a.* (අ neg. විනෂ්ට destroyed) not destroyed. [Colloq. විනාශනොකරණලද *vináṣa-nókaraṇalada.*]

අවිනීත, *Avinita*, *a.* (අ and විනීත trained) untrained, acting improperly; sometimes applied to acts of infidelity between the sexes.

අවිපර්‍යාස, *Aviparyása*, } *a.* (අ priv. විපරීත dif-
අවිපරීත, *Viparíta*, } ference) steady, firm, the same, not inverted. [Colloq. වෙනස්නොවෙනලද *wenasnowenalada.*]

අවිපාක, *Avipáka*, *a.* (අ and විපාක reward) without reward.

අවිභක්තික, *Avibhaktika*, *a.* indeclinable, without case termination.

අවිමුක්ත, *Avimukta*, *a.* (අ neg. විමුක්ත loosed) unloosed, not separated. [Colloq. නොමිදුන *nomiduna.*]

අවිය, *Aviya*, *s.* implement, tool, weapon. [Colloq. ආයුධය *áyudhaya.*] also, an indeclinable word.

අවියත්, *Aviyat*, Elu form of අව්‍යක්ත *avyakta*.

අවිරත, *Avirata*, *a.* (අ and විරත stopping) eternal, continual. [Colloq. සදාකාලික *sadákálika.*]

අවිරල, *Avirala*, *a.* (අ and විරල fine) gross, coarse, substantial. [Colloq. ඝනවූ *ghanawú.*]

අවිරිදු, *Aviridu*, } *a.* (අ and විරුද්ධ against)
අවිරුද්ධ, *Aviruddha*, } not contrary, unobstructed,
අවිරුදු, *Avirudu*, } without difficulties, certain, at peace, absolute.

අවිලම්බිත, *Avilambita*, *a*, (අ and විලම්බිත slow) quick, expeditious, swift.

අවිවර, *Aviwara*, *a.* (අ priv. විවර opening or chasm) whole, impervious. [Colloq. සිදුරු නැති *siduru neti.*]

අවිවාහක, *Aviwáhaka*, *a.* (අ neg. විවාහක married) unmarried.

අවිවේක, *Aviweka*, *a.* (අ and විවේක discrimination) defective in judgment, indiscriminate, superficial, short sighted; having no rest.

අවිශ්වාස, *Aviṣwása*, *a.* (අ and විශ්වාස trust) mistrusted, unfaithful, unfriendly, unbelieving.

අවිශිෂ්ට, *Aviṣishṭa*, *a.* not distinguished from others.

අවිශේෂ, *Aviṣesha*, *a.* (අ and විශේෂ variation) uniform, alike; *s.* want of distinction.

අවිෂය, *Avishaya*, *a.* (අ and විෂය an object of sense) insensible, not belonging to; unperceived.

අවිසද, *Avisada*, *a.* (අ priv. විසද clean) unclean, polluted, filthy. [Colloq. අපවිත්‍ර *apavitra.*]

අවිසය, *Avisaya*, see අවිෂය *avishaya*; *s.* impossibility.

අවිසිප්, *Avisip*, *s.* the science of using weapons.

අවිහ, *Aviha*, *s.* the twelfth of the Brahma lókas.

අවීචිය, *Avíchiya*, *s.* (අ neg. වීචි shelter, asylum) a hell so called, lowest of the hells.

අවීර, *Avíra*, } *a.* (අ priv. වීර strength) weak,
අවීරිය, *Avíriya*, } impotent, helpless, destitute.

අවු, *Awu*, see අවුව *awuwa.*

අවුත්, *Awut*, *p. p.* having come.

අවුනා, *Awuná*, *past. part.* having strung or linked together as beads. [Colloq. අමුනාලා *amunálá.*]

අවුනු, *Awunu*, *s.* place where fish is sold, meat-market. [Colloq, මස් කඩේ *mas-kaḍé.*]

අවුපත, *Awupata*, *s.* kind of shade or umbrella, usually of a palmyra leaf. pl. අවුපත් *awupat.*

අවුරණවා, *Awuraṇawá*, *v.* to encircle, to enclose, to cover, to shade or screen: pret. ඇවුරුවා *ęwuruwá.*

අවුරම්, *Awuram*, *s.* covering.

අවුරුද්ද, *Awurudda*, *s.* year. pl. අවුරුදු *awurudu.*

අවුරුදුපතා *Awurudupatá*, *ad.* yearly.

අවුරුම්, *Awurum*, *s.* covering; see අවුරණවා *awuraṇawá.*

අවුල්, *Awul*, *a.* confused. *s.* confusion: this form is chiefly used in composition as අවුල්කරණවා *awulkaraṇawá*, to confuse.

අවුල් දැති, *Awul dęti*, *s.* (අවුල *awula* thicket, දැති tooth) an alligator. [Colloq. කිඹුලා *kimbulá.*]

අවුල්හර, *Awulhara*, *s.* kind of necklace, comb.

අවුල, *Awula*, *s.* confusion, perplexity; disturbance. pl. අවුල් *awul.*

අවුලනවා, *Awulanawá*, *v.* to collect, to pick up, to heap up; to shine: pret. ඇවුලුවා *ęwuluwá.*

අවුළු, *Awulu*, *s.* kind of cake.

අවුළුපත්, *Awulupat*, *s.* cakes.

අවුළුවනවා, *Awuluwanawá*, *v.* to cause to take fire, cause to contend, instigate, to contend; to enrage, to catch or fasten by a hook; to cause to gather or collect: pret. ඇවිලෙව්වා *ęvilewwá.*

අවුලේ, *Awulé*, *s.* confusion, perplexity.

අවුව, *Awuwa*, *s.* sun-shine, light or heat of the sun.

අවුස්, *Awus*, *s.* drum in general. [Colloq. බෙරය *beraya.*]

අවුස්සනවා, *Awussanawá*, *v.* to cause to be angry, to vex, to stir up, to irritate; to put into disorder, to confuse: pret. ඇවුස්සුවා *ęwussuwá.*

අවුසධ, *Awusadha*, *s.* medicine, medical drugs. see ඖෂධ *aushadha.*

අවෙක්ෂණ, *Awekshaṇa*, *s.* seeing. [Colloq. දර්ශනය *darṣanaya.*]

අවෙක්ෂා, *Awekshá*, *s.* observation, seeing, looking at.

අවෙද්‍ය, *Awedya*, *a.* (අ priv. වෙද්‍ය to be known) that which cannot be known. [Colloq. නොදත හැකි *nodatahęki.*]

අවෙණි, *Aweni*, Elu form of ආවෙණික *dweṇika.*

අවේලාව, *Awéláwa*, *s.* (අ and වේලාව time) improper time, bad time, unseasonable time.

අවැඩ, *Awęda*, *a.* (අ priv. වැඩ good) evil, bad; *s.* injury, evil.

අශ්මභෙද, *Aṣmabheda*, *s.* (අශ්ම stone, භෙද that breaks) plant *(Æruwa lanata* or *illecebrum lanatum)*, commonly called පොල්කුඩුපලා *pol-kuḍupalá*, said to be good in nephritic complaints.

අශ්මරී, *Aṣmarí*, *s.* disease, stone or gravel.

අශ්‍රද්ධා, *Aṣraddhá*, } *s.* (අ neg. ශ්‍රද්ධා belief)
අශ්‍රද්ධාව, *Aṣraddháwa*, } unbelief.

අශ්‍රමණ, *Aṣramaṇa*, *a.* (අ and ශ්‍රමණ Buddhist priest) unpriestly, unbecoming a priest, acting contrary to the character of a priest.

අශ්‍රු, *Aṣru*, *s.* tear. [Colloq. කඳුලු *kandulu.*]

අශ්‍රුත, *Aṣruta*, *a.* (අ not, ශ්‍රුත heard) unheard. [Colloq. නොඇසනලද *noasanalada.*]

අශ්ලේෂා, *Aṣléshá*, *s.* the ninth Nakshatra or lunar mansion containing five stars.

අශ්ව, *Aṣwa*, *s.* horse.

අශ්වකර්ණ, *Aṣwakarṇa*, *s.* (අශ්ව horse, කර්ණ ear) large timber tree the leaves of which resemble the ears of a horse *(shorea robusta;* Sal in Bengal and Hindi: the Hal tree of the Sinhalese is *Vateria Acuminata* or *V. indica);* also the name of the seventh or outermost of the circular ranges of rocks, surrounding Méru, and forming the boundaries of as many circumambient waters or oceans.

අශ්වගන්ධ, *Aṣwagandha*, *s.* (අශ්ව and ගන්ධ scent) plant, *(hedysarum vaginale).*

අශ්වත්ථ, *Aṣwattha*, *s.* Bó tree, *(ficus religiosa).*

අශ්වතර, *Aṣwatara*, *s.* one of the chief of the nága or serpent race, who inhabit the regions under the earth; mule.

අශ්වපාලයා, *Aṣwapálayá*, *s.* (අශ්ව and පාලයා keeper) horse keeper, groom.

අශ්වමාර, *Aṣwamára*, } *s.* plant, *plumeria*
අශ්වමාරක, *Aṣwamáraka*, } *acuminata.* [Colloq. කනේරු *kanéru.*]

අශ්වමුඛ, *Aṣwamukha*, *s.* (අශ්ව and මුඛ face) kinnara or heavenly chorister; this kind of demigod is represented with a horse's head.

අශ්වමේධ, *Aṣwamédha*, *s.* (අශ්ව horse, මේධ sacrifice) the sacrifice of a horse, actually or emblematically. This sacrifice is one of the highest order among the Hindus, and performed a hundred times entitles the sacrificer to the sovereignty of Swarga: it is sometimes only emblematical, the horse being simply bound during the performance of certain ceremonies, and this appears to have been the original institution.

අශවයා, *Aṣwayá*, *s.* horse.

අශවයුජ්, *Aṣwayuja*, *s.* first lunar mansion; name of a month, September–October. [Colloq. අස්විද නැකත *aṣvida-nękata*]. See අශ්විනී *aṣviní.*

අශවලෙඹ, *Aṣwalemba*, } *s.* mare, pl. අශවලෙම්
අශවලෙම්බ, *Aṣwalemba*, } බියෝ *aṣwalembiyó.*

අශවාචාය්‍ය්‍යා, *Aṣwácháryayá*, } *s.* horse breaker,
අශවාචාරියා, *Aṣwáchàriyá*, } horsekeeper.

අශවාරෝහ, *Aṣwároha*, *s.* (අශව *aṣwa* and ආරෝහ *áróha*, who mounts) horseman. [Colloq. අසරුවා *asaruwá.*]

අශ්විනී, *Aṣviní*, *s.* first of the twenty-seven constellations in the moon's path, hence considered its mansions; the symbol of this nakshatra is a horse's head figured by three stars in the head of Aries. See අශවයුජ *aṣwayuja.*

අශන, *Aṣana*, *s* food, boiled rice; plant, *terminalia alata tomentosa.*

අශනි, *Aṣani*, *s.* Indra's thunderbolt.

අශබ්ද, *Aṣabda*, *a.* (අ neg. ශබ්ද sound) silent.

අශරීර, *Aṣaríra*, *a.* (අ neg. ශරීර body) bodiless, incorporeal. *s.* name of Káma, the god of love.

අශාශවත, *Aṣáṣwata*, *a.* (අ priv. ශාශවත ever) not eternal, temporary.

අශික්ෂිත, *Aṣikshita*, *p. p.* untaught, ill-bred, ignorant.

අශීති, *Aṣiti*, *a.* eighty. [Colloq. අසූව *asúwa.*]

අශුඩ, } *Aṣuddha*, *a.* (අ neg. ශුද්ධ pure) impure,
අශුද්ධ, } unclean.

අශුද්ධාත්මය, *Aṣuddhátmaya*, *s.* (අශුද්ධ and ආත්මය spirit) evil or unclean spirit; impure body or heart.

අශූන්‍ය, *Aṣunya*, *a.* not empty, not void.

අශුභ, *Aṣubha*, *a.* (අ neg. ශුභ good) unlucky, bad, inauspicious. *s.* misfortune, sin.

අශෙෂ, *Aṣésha*, *a.* (අ neg. ශෙෂ remainder) all, entire. [Colloq. සියලු *siyalu.*]

අශෝක, *Aṣóka*, *s.* (අ and ශෝක sorrow) name of a plant or shrub *(jonesia asoca)*; [Colloq. හෝපළු *hópaḷu*]. *a.* free from sorrow.

අශෝභන, *Aṣóbhana*, *a.* unseemly, ugly, uncomely.

අෂ්ට, *Ashṭa*, *s.* eight. [Colloq. අට *aṭa.*]

අෂ්ට උදරය, *Ashṭa udaraya*, *s.* (අෂ්ට and උදර belly) medical term used to express eight kinds of sickness to which the bowels are subject.

අෂ්ටකර්ණ, *Ashṭakarṇa*, *s.* (අෂ්ට and කර්ණ ear) name of Brahma, who is fabled to have four heads and eight ears.

අෂ්ටකර්ම විධිය, *Ashṭakarma vidhiya*, *s.* (අෂ්ට and කර්ම විධිය sorcery) eight supernatural powers, said to be possessed by jugglers.

අෂ්ටගුල්මය, *Ashṭagulmaya*, *s.* eight kinds of diseases caused by worms in the belly.

අෂ්ටදික්පාලයන්, *Ashṭadikpálayan*, } see අටදිග්පා
අෂ්ටදිග්පාලයන්, *Ashṭadigpálayan*, } ලයෝ *aṭadigpálayó.*

අෂ්ට දුෂ්ටක්ෂණය, *Ashṭa dushṭakshaṇaya*, *s.* (අෂ්ට eight, දුෂ්ටක්ෂණය evil time) eight kinds of evil states; according to the doctrines of Buddha, to be born in any one of these is a sore evil: 1. නරකය *narakaya*, in hell; 2. තිරිසන් යෝනිය *tirisan-yóniya*, as an animal; 3. ප්‍රේත යෝනිය *préta-yóniya*, as a kind of ghost or hobgoblin; 4. අරූතලය සහ අසංඥතලය *arútalaya saha asaññátalaya*, in the bodiless world of the Brahmas; 5. ප්‍රත්‍යන්තය *pratyantaya*, in a desert or among savages; 6. පංචෙන්ද්‍රියයන්ගේ විකළබව *pañchéndriyayangé vikaḷabawa*, in a state destitute of the five senses; 7. මිථ්‍යාදෘෂ්ටිය *mithyádrishṭiya*, as a pagan; 8. අබුද්ධොත්පාද කාලය *abuddhotpáda kálaya*, an age in which there is no Buddha.

අෂ්ට ධර්මය, *Ashṭa-dharmaya*, *s.* (අෂ්ට and ධර්ම cause) the eight qualifications necessary to become a Buddha; the candidate must be 1. මනුෂ්‍යබව *manushya bawa*, a man (not a god nor a Brahma); 2. පිරිමිබව *pirimibawa*, a male; 3. හේතු ඇතිබව *hétu ętibawa*, worthy of the character; 4. බුදුන් දුටුබව *budun duṭubawa*, he must have seen a Buddha; 5. මහණබව *mahaṇa bawa*, he must be a priest; 6. ගුණ ඇතිබව *guṇa ętibawa*, virtuous; 7. ප්‍රාර්ථනා ඇතිබව *prártaná ętibawa*, he must possess a hope of becoming a Buddha; 8. වීය්‍ය්‍යසිත් ඇතිබව *víryasit ętibawa*, he must have energy to become such.

අෂ්ට පරිෂ්කාරය, *Ashṭa parishkáraya*, see අටපිරිකර *aṭapirikara.*

අෂ්ටභොගය, *Ashṭabhogaya*, *s.* (අෂ්ට and භොග that which is to be enjoyed) eight things said to constitute human happiness: viz. 1. perfumes,

2. women, 3. robes, 4. beds, 5. betel, 6. food, 7. dancing, 8. modes of conveyance.

අෂ්ටමහා නරකය, *Ashṭamahá narakaya*, see අටමහ නිරය *aṭamaha niraya*.

අෂ්ටමහා රෝගය, *Ashṭamahá rógaya*, see අටමහ රෝගය *aṭamaha rógaya*.

අෂ්ටමී, *Ashṭamí*, *s.* eighth day after the new or full moon. [Colloq. අටවක *aṭawaka*.]

අෂ්ට මූර්ති, *Ashṭa múrti*, *s.* (අෂ්ට and මූර්ති form) name of Ṣiva, referring to the five elements together with the mind, individuality and crude matter.

අෂ්ටලෝක ධර්මය, *Ashṭaloka dharmaya*, *s.* (අෂ්ට and ලෝකධර්ම things of the world) eight things in this life to which mankind are incident: viz. 1. profit, 2. loss, 3. praise, 4. dispraise, 5. disgrace, 6. reputation, 7. health, 8. sickness.

අෂ්ටවිද්‍යා, *Ashṭavidyá*, *s.* (අෂ්ට and විද්‍යා knowledge) eight branches of knowledge peculiar to the rahats: viz. 1. knowledge attained by abstract meditation, 2. power of doing any things desired, 3. ability to assume a variety of shapes, 4. supernatural hearing, 5. knowledge of others' hearts, 6. knowledge of former existence, 7. divine sight, 8. divine knowledge.

අෂ්ටවිධ, *Ashṭavidha*, *a.* (අෂ්ට eight, විධ sort) eightfold, of eight kinds.

අෂ්ටවිධ පානය, *Ashṭavidha pánaya*, *s.* (අෂ්ටවිධ of eight kinds, පාන drink) eight kinds of fruit, the juice of which diluted with water the priests are permitted to drink: viz. mango, jambu, plantain, seedy kind of plaintain, grape, sort of lotus or water lily, jujube, and boraludamnu a sort of *calyptranthes*, or kind of jambu.

අෂ්ටසමාපත්තිය, *Ashṭasamápattiya*, *s.* (අෂ්ට and සමාපත්ති an attainment) eight religious observances practised by one of the religious sects, viz. that of Kapila, as also by the Buddhists, or the four dhyánas and the four duties of the Brahman.

අෂ්ටාඞ්ගමාණික්‍යය, *Ashṭáṅgamáṇikyaya*, see අටඟමිණ *aṭaṇgamiṇa*.

අෂ්ටාඞ්ග ශීලය, *Ashṭáṅga-ṣílaya*, } *s.* (අෂ්ට *ashṭa*
අෂ්ටාඞ්ග සීලය, *Ashṭáṅga-sílaya*, } and අඞ්ග *aṅga* order, ශීලය precept) the eight commands of Buddha: viz. 1. not to take life, 2. not to steal, 3. celibacy, 4. not to lie, 5. to abstain from all intoxicating liquors, 6. not to eat after midday, 7. to avoid all worldly pleasures and luxuries, 8. to avoid lying or sitting on luxurious beds spread with red clothes, or on bedsteads above a certain height. [Colloq. අටසිල් *aṭasil*.]

අෂ්ටාඞ්ගික මාර්ගය, *Ashṭáṅgika márgaya*, *s.* (අෂ්ට *ashṭa* and අඞ්ග *aṅga* limb, ඉක *ika* aff. මාර්ග way) the road to Nirváṇa, consisting of four grades and their four attendant enjoyments, or the eight sacred paths for which see අටඟමග *aṭaṇgamaga*.

අෂ්ටාදශ, *Ashṭádaṣa*, *s.* eighteen. [Colloq. දහඅට *daha-aṭa*.]

අෂ්ටාපද, *Ashṭápada*, *s.* (අෂ්ට *ashṭa* and පද quarter, place etc. අ *a* being made long) a sort of chequered cloth, or board for drafts, dice, etc. [Colloq. දූපෝරුව *dúpóruwa*.]

අෂ්ටාර්‍ය, *Ashṭárya*, *s.* (අෂ්ට *ashṭa* and ආර්‍ය *árya* venerable) those who have attained the four paths to Nirváṇa and the four consequent enjoyments.

අෂ්ථි, *Ashṭhi*, *s.* bone, kernel; [Colloq. ඇටය *eṭaya*]; metre consisting of sixteen syllabic instants in each line.

අෂ්ථි සංඛලික, *Ashṭhi saṇkhalika*, *s.* (අෂ්ථි bone, සංඛලික chain or fetter) skeleton. [Colloq. ඇට සැකිල්ල *eṭasekilla*.]

අෂ්ඨීලා, *Ashṭhílá*, *s.* disease, described as tumours in the viscera, probably an enlargement of the mesentric glands.

අෂාඪ, *Ashádha*, } *s.* a month so called, part
අෂාඪක, *Ashádhaka*, } of June and July, [Colloq. ඇසළමස *esaḷa-masa*.]

අස්, *As*, *s.* horse, seal, signet; angle, corner; bear; half moon; shoulder.

අස් ඔබනවා, *As-obanawá*, *v.* (අස් seal, ඔබනවා to press) to seal, to stamp with a seal. [Colloq. මුද්දර තබනවා *muddara tabanawá*.]

අස්කඩ, *Askaḍa*, *s.* breach or opening in a dam.

අස්කණ්, *Askaṇ*, Elu form of අශ්වකර්ණ *aṣwakarṇa*.

අස්කරණවා, *Askaraṇawá*, *v.* to put in order, to arrange, to put by, to decorate.

අස්කෙඳි, *Askendi*, *s.* (අස් horse, කෙඳි fibres, hairs) long hairs of the horse; fibre obtained from the bark of a creeping plant.

අස්ඛලිත, *Askhalita*, *a.* (අ neg. ඛලිත slipped) firm, permanent, unshaken. [Colloq. නොපැකිලෙනලද *nopekilenalada*.]

අස්ගසනවා, *Asgasanawá*, } *v.* to smooth, as timber
අස්ගහනවා, *Asgahanawá*, } or the ground, to cut the end or edge of anything.

අස්ගොඩු, *Asgodu*, *s.* sort of medicine. [Colloq. අමුක්කරා *amukkará.*]

අස්ගොව්වා, *Asgowuwá*, see අශ්වපාලයා *aśwapálayá.*

අස්ත්‍ර, *Astra*, *s.* weapon, sword, bow, missile weapon.

අස්ත, *Asta*, *s.* the western mountain behind which the sun is supposed to set.

අස්තංගත, *Astangata*, *part.* (අස්තං disappearance, ගත gone) the sun having set.

අස්තංගම, *Astaṇgama*, *s.* (අස්තං and ගම to go) descending, setting (of the sun), disappearance, vanishing, destruction, annihilation.

අස්තම්, *Astam*, *ind.* (අස *asa* to cast, තම් aff.) disappearing, vanishing, setting.

අස්තාචල, *Astáchala*, *s.* the western mountain.

අස්ති, *Asti*, *ind. part.* now being, existent, present, it is. [Colloq. ඇති *ęti.*]

අස්තිකාරයා, *Astikárayá*, *s.* opulent man, wealthy person. [Colloq. ධනවන්තයා *dhanawantayá.*]

අස්ථිර, *Asthira*, *a.* (අ priv. ස්ථිර firm) unsteady, trembling, shaken.

අස්දම්, *Asdam*, *s.* rope to tie a horse in the stable.

අස්න, *Asna*, *s.* news, epistle, seat; pl අසුන් *asun.*

අස්පන්තිය, *Aṣpantiya*, *s.* line or row of horses; stall for horses, stable.

අස්පයා, *Aspayá*, *s.* horse. [vulg.]

අස්පැටවා, *Aspęṭawá*, *s.* foal, colt.

අස්බෙටි, *Asbeṭi*, see අස්වසුර.

අස්මද්, *Asmad*, the first person pronoun; I or we.

අස්මරි, *Asmarí*, see අශ්මරි *aṣmarí.*

අස්මුද්ද, *Asmudda*, *s.* (අස් and මුද්ද the same) seal, signet.

අස්වද්දනවා, *Aswaddanawá*, *v.* improve a paddy field: pret. අස්වැද්දුවා *aswędduwá.*

අස්වද්දවනවා, *Aswaddawanawá*, *v.* to cause to cultivate; pret. අස්වැද්දෙවුවා *aswęddewwá.*

අස්වසනවා, *Aswasanawá*, *v.* to comfort, to console, to cherish: pret. අස්වැසුවා *aswęsuwá.*

අස්වසුර, *Aṣwasura*, *s.* excrements of a horse.

අස්විද, *Asvida*, *s.* the first of the twentyseven constellations in the moon's path.

අස් වෙද, *Aṣ-wedá*, *s.* (අස් horse, වෙද doctor) farrier.

අස්වෙනවා, *Aswenawá*, *v.* to be put aside, to be cleared of, to be arranged.

අස්වෙල්, *Aswel*, *s.* plant, *anodendron paniculatum (Apocynaceæ).*

අස්වැන්න, *Aswęnna*, *s.* crops, (applied to grain): plant, *Alyssicarpus bupleurifolius (Leguminosæ).*

අස්වැසිලිකාරයා, *Aswęsilikárayá*, *s.* comforter.

අස්ස, *Assa*, *s.* corner, angle.

අස්සක, *Assaka*, *loc: indef:* in a corner, inside, amongst.

අස්සට, *Assaṭa*, *lit.* to a corner, acc. or dat of අස්ස *assa;* among.

අස්සෙනග, *Assenaga*, *s.* cavalry.

අස්සේ, *Assé*, locative of අස්ස *assa. part.* between, among.

අස්සේනාව, *Asséndwa*, see අස්සෙනග *assenaga.*

අස්හල, *Ashala*, *s.* stable,

අස, *Asa*. *s.* side, goat; [Colloq. එළුවා *eḷuwá*].

අසංකුල, *Asaṇkula*, see අසඞ්කුල *asańkula.*

අසංඛ්‍ය, *Asaṇkhya*, } *a.* (අ neg. සංඛ්‍ය *saṇkhya*
අසංඛෙය්‍ය, *Asaṇkheyya*, } and සංඛෙය to be numbered) numberless, innumerable; used by native authors to express the highest idea of numbering, beyond which it is impossible to reckon or calculate; *s.* the highest numeral.

අසංගත, *Asaṇgata*, *a.* (අ neg. සංගත connected) unattached, unaccompanied, detached.

අසංවරණ, *Asaṇwaraṇa*, *part.* (අ and සංවරණ covering) uncovering.

අසංවාස, *Asaṇwása*, *a.* (අ neg. සංවාස living together) deprived of co-residence, expelled from the priesthood; not proper to reside with.

අසංවාසික, *Asaṇwásika*, *s.* (අ and සංවාස *saṇwása* living with, ඉක aff.) outcast; applied to persons rejected from society on account of ill behaviour or bad deeds.

අසක්, *Asak*, } *s.* (අ and සක doubt) certainty,
අසක, *Asaka*, } assurance; without eyes, blind; dull; see also අහක *ahaka.* This is the Elu form of අසංඛ්‍ය *asaṇkhya.*

අසඞ්කීර්ණ, *Asańkírṇa*, *a.* (අ and සඞ්කීර්ණ mixed) unmixed, not confused. [Colloq. අමිශ්‍රිත *amiṣrita.*]

අසඞ්කුල, *Asańkula*, *a.* (අ and සඞ්කුල crowded) open, broad.

අසත්, *Asat*, *a.* not existing; not true, not good; wicked.

අසත්දම්, *Asatdam*, *s.* see අසද්ධර්ම *asaddharma.*

අසත්පුරුෂ, *Asatpurusha*, *a.* (අ neg. සත්පුරුෂ virtuous) wicked, unrighteous, base.

අසත්පුරුෂකම, *Asatpurushakama*, *s.* viciousness, wickedness.

අසත්‍ය, *Asatya*, *a.* (අ and සත්‍ය true) untrue, false, deceitful.

අසතුටු, *Asatuṭu*, *a.* not pleasing, not pleased.

අසදිටු, *Asadiṭu*, see අසන්දිටු *asandiṭu*.

අසදිස, *Asadrisa*,
අසදෘශ, *Asadṛiṣa*, } *a.* (අ and සදෘශ likeness) unlike, incomparable.

අසද්ධර්ම, *Asaddharma*, *s.* unrighteousness; used also for the union of the sexes, cohabitation.

අසන්, *Asan*, see ආසන්න *ásanna*.

අසන්තොෂය, *Asantoshaya*, *a.* (අ and සන්තොෂ joy) unwilling, displeasing, discontented; *s.* unwillingness, displeasure, anger.

අසන්දිටු, *Asandiṭu*, *s.* (අ bad, සං *saṇ* with, දිටු sight, or අ neg. සම්දිටු *samdiṭu* orthodoxy) false sight, used only of religion; one who professes an erroneous religion, heretic.

අසන, *Asana*, *s.* name of a tree, *(terminalia alata tomentosa)*.

අසනවා, *Asanawá*, *v.* to hear, to ask, to question: pret. ඇසුවා *esuwá*.

අසනිපාත, *Asanipáta*, *s.* thunderbolt.

අසනියමල්, *Asaniyamal*, *s.* fried grain.

අසනීප, *Asanípa*, *a.* (අ neg. සනීප health) unhealthy, sick, disordered.

අසනීපය, *Asanípaya*, *s.* ill health, sickness.

අසප්පුරිස, *Asappurisa*, Páli form of අසත්පුරුෂ *asatpurusha*.

අසපුව, *Asapuwa*, *s.* house adjoining a Buddhist temple for the priest, residence of a Hindoo priest, pl. අසපු *asapu*.

අසබඩ, *Asabaḍa*, *s.* border, edge, margin.

අසම්දිටු, *Asamdiṭu*, see අසන්දිටු *asandiṭu*.

අසම්පූර්ණ, *Asampúrnna*, *a.* (අ neg. සම්පූර්ණ complete) incomplete, unfulfilled.

අසම්භින්න, *Asambhinna*, *a.* (අ and සම්භින්න broken) unbroken, uninterrupted.

අසම්මත, *Asammata*, *s.* (අ and සං *saṇ* with, මත minded) difference of opinion, dissenting from.

අසම්මුඛය, *Asammukhaya*, *s.* absence.

අසම්මූඪ, *Asammúḍha*, *s.* (අ and සම්මූඪ foolish) cool, calm, wise, judicious.

අසම, *Asama*, *s.* (අ and සම like) the incomparable one, name of Buddha; *a.* incomparable, unlike.

අසමර්ථ, *Asamartha*, *a.* (අ and සමර්ථ clever) unskilful.

අසමර්ථකම, *Asamarthakama*, *s.* unskilfulness.

අසමධුර, *Asamadhura*, *a.* peerless, one who has not his equal.

අසමාන, *Asamána*, *a.* unlike; see අසම *asama*.

අසමාහිත, *Asamáhita*, *a.* (අ and සමාහිත mild in behaviour) rude, morose, ill behaved.

අසමොදගං, *Asamódagaṇ*,
අසමොදගන්, *Asamódagan*, } *s.* parsley, *petroselinum sativum*.

අසර්ධාව, *Asardháwa*, *s.* (අ and සර්ධාව faith) unfaithfulness, unbelief. Corrupt form of අශ්‍රද්ධාව *aṣraddháwa*.

අසර, *Asara*, *s.* goddess; way.

අසරණ, *Asaraṇa*, *a.* (අ and සරණ help) desolate, forlorn, helpless, friendless, distressed, destitute.

අසරු, *Asaru*, *a.* (අ and සරු fertile) sterile.

අසරුවා, *Asaruwá*, *s.* horseman, horse-soldier, pl. අසරුවෝ *asaruvó*.

අසල්, *Asal*, *s.* border, margin, environs, nearness; firmness; sometimes written අසල *asala*.

අසල්වාසියා, *Asalwásiyá*, *s.* (අසල් near, වාසි who dwells) neighbour.

අසල, *Asala*, *s.* rock, mountain; one well acquainted with anything; see අසල් *asal*.

අසව්ව, *Asawwa*, *s.* hinge of a door.

අසවල්, *Asawal*, *s.* such a one, such as any one, some one, pl. අසවල්ලු *asawallu*.

අසවුව, *Asawuwa*, see අසව්ව *asawwa*.

අසහාය, *Asaháya*, *a.* (අ neg. සහාය like) unlike, unequalled, incomparable, solitary.

අසාධ්‍ය,
අසාද්‍ය, } *Asáddhya*, *a.* (අ and සාධ්‍ය curable) incurable, irremediable.

අසාධාරණ, *Asádháraṇa*, *a.* (අ priv. සාධාරණ general) unrighteous, unjust; uncommon, peculiar, unequalled; *s*, partiality, injustice.

අසාර, *Asára*, *a.* (අ neg. සාර sap) sapless, pithless, sterile, fruitless; *s.* castor oil tree.

අසාසවත, *Asáswata*, see අශාශ්වත *aṣáṣwata*.

අසි, *Asi*, *s.* sword, scimitar; female friend.

අසික්කිත, *Asikkita*, *a.* shabby, mean, low; not under proper control, disobedient, not docile.

අසික්කිතයා, *Asikkitayá*, *s.* filthy person.

අසිත, *Asita*, *s.* black (colour), name of the planet Saturn, the dark fortnight of a lunar month; indigo plant.

අසිද්ධ, *Asiddha*, *a.* (අ neg. සිද්ධ perfect) unripe.

අසිධ්‍ය, *Asiddhya*, *a.* (අ and සිධ්‍ය what can occur) impossible, impracticable.

අසිපත්‍රය, *Asipatraya*,
අසිපත, *Asipata*, } *s.* hell paved with swords, blade of a sword.

අසිරි, *Asiri*, *s.* astonishment, surprise; one of the eight graces in dancing.

අසිරිරූ, *Asirirú*, *s.* (අසිරි surprise, රූ form, beauty) name of Káma the Indian cupid.

අසිවිස, *Asivisa*, *s.* (අසි tooth or fang, විස poison) snake. [Colloq. සර්පයා *sarpayá*.]

අසිති, *Asíti*, *a.* eighty.

අසිරු, *Asíru*, *a.* abstruse, difficult, laborious.

අසිරුව, *Asíruwa*, *s.* difficulty.

අසුකරණවා, *Asukaraṇawá*, *v.* to seize, to catch.

අසුඛ, *Asukha*, *s.* (අ neg. සුඛ pleasure) sorrow, pain, affliction. [Colloq. දුක *duka.*]

අසුගහ, *Asugaha*, see අහු *ahu.*

අසුචි, *Asuchi*, *s.* excrement, dirt; *a.* impure.

අසුද්ධ, *Asuddha*, *a.* (අ and සුද්ධ clean) unclean, impure.

අසුන්, *Asun*, *s.* intelligence; horses.

අසුපෑවත, *Asupéwata*, *s.* a rich crop of grain; *adj.* pleasing to the sight, beautiful, plump.

අසුභ, *Asubha*, *a.* (අ and සුභ auspicious) inauspicious, unfortunate, unlucky, unhappy.

අසුර, *Asura*, *s.* (අ priv. සුර deity) a class of demons who are perpetually at war with the gods; Titan. pl. අසුරෝ *asuró.*

අසුරකාය, *Asurakáya*, *s.* (අසුර asura, කාය habitation) the residence or place of confinement allotted to the vanquished Asuras or Titans, after their conflict with the gods, situated beneath Méru, and surrounded by the ocean which prevents all egress; it is one of the four states of punitive infliction: See සතර අපාය *satara apáya.*

අසුරගහනවා, *Asuragahanawá*, *v.* to snap the fingers: pret. අසුරගැහුවා *asuragęhuwá.*

අසුරගුරු, *Asuraguru*, *s.* (අසුර asura, ගුරු teacher) Ṣukra, the regent of Venus, and preceptor of the Titans, sometimes written අසුරරජ *Asura raja.*

අසුරරද, *Asura-rada*, *s.* one of the names of Venus.

අසුරිඳු, *Asurindu*, *s.* chief of the Asuras.

අසුරී, *Asurí*, *s.* black mustard, *(sinapis ramosa).*

අසුරුවනවා, *Asuruwanawá*, *v.* to cause to collect, to put things together, to bring into order, to regulate: pret. ඇසිරෙව්වා *ęsirewwá.*

අසුරුසන්, *Asurusan*, *s.* the sound occasioned by snapping the fingers.

අසුවෙනවා, *Asuwenawá*, *v.* to be caught, to be seized.

අසූචි, *Asúchi*, see අසුචි *asuchi.*

අසූන්‍ය, *Asúnya*, *a.* (අ neg. සූන්‍ය annihilation) undestroyed, existing; corrupt form of අශූන්‍ය *aṣunya.*

අසූව්‍යඤ්ජන ලක්ෂණ, *Asúryañjana lakshaṇa*, *s.* (අසූ and ව්‍යඤ්ජන inherent, ලක්ෂණ mark) the eighty minor tokens inherent in the person of Buddha; see අසීති *asíti* and අනුව්‍යංජන *anuvyaṇjana.*

අසූව, *Asúwa*, *s.* eighty.

අසූවෙනි, *Asúweni*, *a.* eightieth.

අසෙ, *Ase*, *s.* female friend.

අසෙස්, *Ases*, *a.* all, entire, the whole. [Colloq. සියලු *siyalu.*]

අසේ, *Asé*, see අසෙ *ase.*

අසේතුව, *Asétuwa*, *a*, unhappy, miserable; *s.* misfortune; incorrectly for අහේතුව *ahétuwa.*

අසෝ, *Asó*, } *s.* tree, *(jonesia asoca)*; a plant
අසෝක, *Asóka*, } which is used for medicine; *a.* without sorrow; see අශෝක *aṣoka.*

අසෝභන, *Asóbhana*, *a.* (අ neg. සෝභන beautiful) not handsome, ugly.

අසෑක, *Aseka*, *s.* certainty.

අහ, *Aha*, *interj.* oh!

අහංකාරය, *Ahaṇkáraya*, *s.* (අහං I, කාර which makes) self-conceit, pride, arrogance, egotism.

අහක්කරණවා, *Ahakkaraṇawá*. *v.* to put aside, to put away, to dismiss.

අහක, *Ahaka*, *ad.* aside, apart, away; *s.* side, place, little apart from another.

අහත්පහත්, *Ahatpahat*, *a.* humble, submissive.

අහන්කාර, *Ahankára*, see අහංකාරය *ahaṇkáraya.*

අහනවා, *Ahanawá*, *v.* to ask, to enquire, to question; to hear, to listen: pret. ඇහුවා *ęhuwá.*

අහපති, *Ahapati*, *s.* the sun.

අහබඩ, *Ahabaḍa*, *s.* border.

අහම්බය, *Ahambaya*, } *s.* accident, chance, sur-
අහඹය, *Ahaṃbaya*, } prise.

අහම්බෙන්, *Ahamben*, *ad.* accidentally.

අහර, *Ahara*, *s.* food, victuals; road.

අහර කිස, *Ahara kisa*, *pret.* (අහර food, කිස *kisa* deed) the act of taking a meal.

අහරකුක්කා, *Aharakukká*, *s.* kind of a snake not venomous.

අහල, *Ahala*, *s.* border, margin; environ; sometimes written අසල *asala.*

අහලපහල, *Ahalapahala*, *ad.* in the neighbourhood, near-about; *s.* neighbourhood.

අහවර, *Ahawara*, *s.* leisure; termination of a thing.

අහවරකරණවා, *Ahawarakaraṇawá*, *v.* to terminate, to finish.

අහවරවෙනවා, *Ahawarawenawá*, *v.* to be at leisure, to be finished.

අහවල්, *Ahawal*, *a.* such, that, such and such.

අහවලා, *Ahawalá*, *s.* such and such a one, pl. අහවල්ලු *ahawallu*.

අහස් ගඟ, *Ahas ganga*, *s.* (අහස *ahasa* sky, ගඟ river) the celestial river.

අහස්තලය, *Ahastalaya*, *s.* (අහස *ahasa* and තලය plane) visible heaven.

අහස්සන්, *Ahassan*, *s.* (අහස *ahasa* and සන් covering from ඡන්න *chhanna*) canopy, awning, carried canopy.

අහස, *Ahasa*, *s.* sky, firmament, atmosphere.

අහහ, *Ahaha*, *interj.* interjection of surprise or wonder, as, ah, aha.

අහි, *Ahi*, *s.* snake, serpent; the name of Ráhu or the ascending node.

අහිත, *Ahita*, *s.* enemy, adversary; fool.

අහිතු, *Ahitu*, *s.* dung.

අහිතුණ්ඩිකයා, *Ahituṇḍikayá*, *s.* snake catcher, snake exhibitor, juggler who carries snakes with him, the poisonous fangs of the snakes being extracted they are often permitted to bite the exhibitor.

අහිංසක, *Ahiṇsaka*, *a.* (අ neg. හිංසා *hiṇsá* pain) that which gives no pain.

අහිරාවා, *Ahiráwá*, *s.* kind of fish.

අහිවාතක, *Ahiwátaka*, *s.* (අහි snake, වාත wind, breath, ක aff.) pestilence, plague.

අහිවිස. *Ahivisa*, *s.* poison of serpents.

අහිසැව, *Ahiseẉa*, *s.* slough cast off by the serpent.

අහිපාත, *Ahípáta*. *s.* poverty, want.

අහු, *Ahu*, *s.* tree, *Morinda citrifolia* and *M. tinctoria*, *(Rubiaceæ)*.

අහුකරණවා, *Ahukaraṇawá*, *v.* to seize, to catch.

අහුපෑවත, *Ahupẹ́wata*, *a.* flourishing, in a state of perfection, plump (applied principally to vegetable productions); *s.* heap of paddy.

අහුර, *Ahura* *s.* as much as can be held in the closed hand, handful, pl අහුරු *ahuru*.

අහුරණවා, *Ahuraṇawá*, *v.* to set up (as type) to put together, to arrange, to pack up, to enclose as by a fence, to block up, to cork: pret. ඇහුරුවා *ẹhuruwá*.

අහුරුගහනවා, *Ahurugahanawá*, *v.* to snap the fingers.

අහුරුසැනේ, *Ahurusẹné*, *s.* moment, so short a time as the snap of the fingers.

අහුවෙනවා, *Ahuwenawá*, *v.* to be caught (as fish in a net, or a trap) to be seized.

අහේතුව, *Ahétuwa*, *a.* (අ neg. හේතුව producing cause) vain, causeless, unfortunate, unhappy; *s.* misfortune, ill-luck.

අහේනිය, *Aheniya*, *s.* distress, stress, tiresomeness, fatigue, impotency.

අහේනිවෙනවා, *Aheniwenawá*, *v.* to be tired, to be fatigued.

අහෝ, *Ahó*, *interj.* oh! alas!

අහෝ රාත්‍රි, *Ahó-rátri*, *s.* (අහන් *ahan* day, රාත්‍රි night) day and night.

ආ

The second letter in the alphabet; it corresponds in sound with our *a* in charm: in composition where it is non-initial it is written after the consonant:—as කා *ká*.

ආකර්ෂ, *Ákarsha*, *s.* attraction, drawing.

ආකරය, *Ákaraya*, *s.* mine.

ආකල්ප, *Ákalpa*, *s.* ornament, decoration; demeanour.

ආකාර, *Ákára*, *s.* form, manner, mode; hint, sign, token; mine.

ආකාරගුප්ති, *Ákáragupti*, *s.* dissimulation.

ආකාශ, *Ákáṣa*, } *s.* the fifth element, ether; sky,
ආකාස, *Ákása*, } atmosphere.

ආකාස වියන, *Ákása viyana*, *s.* a carried canopy.

ආකාසානඤ්ඤායතන, *Ákásánaññáyatana*, *s.* one of the Brahma lókas, first of the four arútalas, or states of immaterial existence.

ආකීර්ණ, *Ákírṇṇa*, *a.* crowded, confused, impervious.

ආකුල, *Ákula*, *a.* confounded, perplexed, distressed; crowded, confused.

ආකෘති, *Ákṛiti*, *s.* form, figure, body, tribe, species.

ආකෘෂ්ට, *Ákṛishṭa*, *s.* drawn, attracted.

ආක්‍රොශ, *Ákróṣa*, *s.* abuse, curse, censure, an oath.

ආඛ්‍යා, *Ákhyá*, *s*, name, appellation.

ආඛ්‍යාත, *Ákhyáta*, *part.* said, spoken; belonging to a verb.

ආඛ්‍යාතය, *Ákhyátaya*, *s.* a part of grammar, the verb.

ආඛ්‍යායිකා, *Ákhyáyiká*, *s.* tale, story, legend.

ආඛණ්ඩල, *Ákhaṇḍala*, *s.* name of Indra.

ආග්‍රහායණ, *Ágraháyaṇa*, *s.* month so called, first of the Hindu year, part of November and December.

ආග්‍රහායණී, *Ágraháyaṇí*, *s.* name of a constellation consisting of three stars, one of which is λ Orionis figured by an antelope's head; the day of the full moon in the month ආග්‍රහායණ *ágraháyaṇa*.

ආගන්තුක, *Ágantuka*, *a.* (ආ and ගම *gama* to go, තුක aff.) incidental, strange, adventitious.

ආගන්තුක ජ්වරය, *Ágantuka-jwaraya*, *s.* (ආගන්තු incidental, ක aff. ජ්වර fever) slight fever, strange fever, fever brought on by accident, as a fall or the fracture of a limb etc.

ආගන්තුකයා, *Ágantukayá*, *s.* guest, visitor, one who comes by accident or unexpectedly, new-comer, stranger.

ආගම, *Ágama*, *s.* (ආ and ගම to come, to go) an approaching, coming; grammatical augment; science, a work on any of the sacred sciences; the word is universally used in colloquial intercourse to express religion.

ආගමන, *Ágamana*, *s.* arrival, coming.

ආගාර, *Ágára*, *s.* house.

ආඝ්‍රාණ, *Ághráṇa*, *s.* smelling,

ආඝාත, *Ágháta*, } *s.* killing; slaughter-house,
ආඝාතන, *Ághátana*, } place for killing animals or victims.

ආච්චි, *Áchchi*, *s.* grand-mother.

ආච්ඡාදනය, *Áchchhádanaya*, *s.* cloth, clothes; putting on cloth, covering.

ආච්ඡේදන, *Áchchhedana*, *s.* cutting.

ආචරණ, *Ácharaṇa*, *part.* walking.

ආචරිත, *Ácharita*, *a.* trained, used, observed.

ආචාර්‍ය්‍යයා, *Ácháryayá*, see ආචාරීන්වහන්සේ *áchárínwahansé*.

ආචාර, *Áchára*, *s.* established rule of conduct, ordinance, institute; precept; (commonly) a salutation.

ආචාරකරණවා, *Áchárakaraṇawá*, *v.* to bow, to make obeisance.

ආචාරය, *Ácháraya*, *s.* salutation.

ආචාරවන්තයා, *Áchárawantayá*, *s.* well-behaved man.

ආචාරියා, *Áchàriyá*, *s.* blacksmith.

ආචාරියාපළු, *Áchàriyá-paḷu*, *s.* plant, cowitch, *Mucuna pruriens (Legum)*; or අචාරියාපළු *achàriyá-paḷu*.

ආචාරීන්වහන්සේ, *Áchárínwahansé*, *s.* teacher, preceptor.

ආජානෙය, *Ájáneya*, *s.* horse of a good breed.

ආජීව, *Ájíwa*, *s.* livelihood, profession.

ආජීවක, *Ájíwaka*, see අජීවක *ajíwaka*.

ආජීවකයා, *Ájíwakayá*, *s.* religious mendicant of a peculiar class.

ආටොප, *Áṭopa*, *a.* fat, glutinous, thick.

ආටෝප, *Áṭópa*, *s.* pride.

ආඩම්බර, *Áḍambara*, *s.* pride, arrogance; *a.* proud, arrogant.

ආඩාතෝඩා, *Áḍátóḍá*, *s.* plant, *justicia adhenatoda;* [Colloq. අගල්ආදාර *agaládára*].

ආඪ්‍ය, *Áḍhya*, *a.* abounding in, opulent, wealthy, rich.

ආඪක, *Áḍhaka*, *s.* a corn measure containing about 7 lbs. 11 oz. avoirdupois.

ආඪරූඪක, *Áḍharúḍhaka*, see ආඩාතෝඩා *áḍátóḍá*.

ආණ්ඩියා, *Áṇḍiyá*, *s.* religious mendicant, fakir.

ආණ්ඩුව, *Áṇḍuwa*, *s.* government, ruling, reign.

ආත්තා, *Áttá*, *s.* grand-mother, pl. ආත්තාලා *áttálá;* a fruit, bullock's heart; *anona reticulata*.

ආත්තුනෑතිකම, *Áttunetikama*, *s.* poverty, destitution.

ආත්මජ, *Átmaja*, *s.* (ආත්ම and ජ born) son, daughter.

ආත්මභූ, *Átmabhú*, *s.* (ආත්ම and භූ who is born, existent) name of Káma the god of love.

ආත්මය, *Átmaya*, *s.* soul; understanding, intellect; mind or faculty of reason; life, spirit, animated frame, vivifying soul in opposition to the sentient; self, abstract individuality, pl. ආත්මවල් *átmawal*.

ආත්මාර්ථය, *Átmárthaya*, *s.* (ආත්ම *átma* self, අර්ථ *artha* good) self-interest, one's own good.

ආත්මානුදෘෂ්ටිය, *Átmánudṛishṭiya*, *s.* (ආත්ම *átma* and අනුදෘෂ්ටිය *anudṛishṭiya* seeing) experience.

ආතප, *Átapa*, *s.* sunshine. [Colloq. අව්ව *awuwa*.]

ආතපත්‍ර, *Átapatra*, } *s.* (ආතප sunshine,
ආතපවාරණ, *Átapawáraṇa*, } ත්‍ර what preserves, or වාරණ which prevents) umbrella. [Colloquial: කුඩේ *kuḍé*.]

ආතර්පණ, *Átarpaṇa*, *s.* satisfaction.

ආතා, *Átá*, *s.* grandfather, pl. ආතාලා *átálá*.

ආතුර, *Átura*, *a.* diseased.

ආතුර පක්ෂ, *Átura-pakshe*, *s.* the party of the bridegroom or the bride.

ආතුරයා, *Áturayá*, *s.* diseased person, patient.

ආද්‍යන්ත *Ádyanta*, *a.* first and last.

ආදර්ශ, *Ádarṣa*, *s.* mirror; commentary; the original manuscript from which a copy is taken.

ආදර, *Ádara*, *s.* respect, reverence, affection, love.

ආදාන, *Ádána*, *s.* taking, receipt, acceptance.

ආදායම, *Ádáyama*, *s.* revenue.

ආදරය, *Ádáraya*, *s.* favour, help, assistance.

ආදාසතල, *Ádásatala*, *s.* mirror. [Colloq. කැඩපත *kędapata.*]

ආදාහන, *Ádáhana*, *s.* (ආ and දහ to burn) burning, conflagration.

ආදි, *Ádi*, *a.* ancient, first, prior, other; *s.* et-cetera. *adv.* formerly.

ආදිත්‍ය, *Áditya*, *s.* sun; general name for a deity.

ආදිය, *Ádiya*, see ආදි *ádi.*

ආදීනව, *Ádínawa*, *s.* distress, pain, uneasiness, fault, transgression, evil consequence.

ආදීප්ත, *Ádípta*, *a.* enlightened, illuminated.

ආදේශ, *Ádésa*, *s.* (in grammar) substitute.

ආඳා, *Áṇḍá*, *s.* eel.

ආධ්‍යාත්ම, *Áddhyátma*, *s.* (අධි *ádhi* and අන් *an* aff. ආත්ම *átma* self etc.) inner man, soul or seat of intelligence.

ආධ්‍යාත්මික, *Áddhyátmika*, *a.* internal, mental.

ආධ්‍යාස, *Áddhyása*,
ආධ්‍යාස, *Ádhyása*, } *s.* thought, reflection; meaning, intent, purpose.

ආධාර, *Ádhára*, *s.* comprehension, in grammar, the sense of the locative or ablative (7th) case, in or on.

ආධාරය, *Ádháraya*, *s.* help, support.

ආන්ත්‍රාව, *Ántráwa*, *s.* danger; more correctly අන්තරාය *antaráya.*

ආන, *Ána*, *s.* breath inspired, shelf, clothes-line.

ආනන්ද, *Ánanda*, *s.* happiness, joy; fabulous fish, 4000 yoduns in length; see තිමිය *timiya.*

ආනන, *Ánana*, *s.* mouth, and by syncope, face.

ආනනවා, *Ánanawá*, *v.* to gape, to yawn: pret. ඇනුවා *énuwá.*

ආනමානය, *Ánamánaya*, *s.* contrivance, plot, scheme.

ආනවාළු, *Ánawáḷu*, *s.* kind of plantain.

ආනාපාන, *Ánápána*, *s.* (ආන *ána* breath inspired, අපාන *apána* breath respired) inspiration and respiration of the breath.

ආනිසංස, *Ánisaṇsa*, *s.* reward, gain, efficacy, effect,

ආනික, *Ánika*, *s.* army; corrupt form of අනික *anika.*]

ආනුභාව, *Ánubháwa*, *s.* power, glory, influence.

ආප්ත, *Ápta*, *a.* confidential, trusted, gained, obtained; twisted.

ආප්ති, *Ápti*, *s.* gain, acquisition, binding, joining.

ආප්ලව, *Áplawa*, *s.* bathing.

ආප්‍ය, *Ápya*, *a.* (ආප *ápa* water, ය aff.) watery, consisting of water, as froth; plant, kind of costus. [Colloq. තෙබු *tebu.*]

ආප, *Ápa*, *s.* water, [Colloq. වතුර *watura*].

ආපක්ව, *Ápakwa*, *a.* (ආ diminutive, පක්ව dressed, cooked) half baked grain etc. eaten from the hand.

ආපගා, *Ápagá*, *s.* (ආප water, ගා what goes) river, stream. [Colloq. ගංගාව *gangáwa.*]

ආපණ, *Ápaṇa*, *s.* market, shop.

ආපණික, *Ápaṇika*, *s.* merchant, dealer.

ආපත්ති, *Ápatti*,
ආපදා, *Ápadá*, } *s.* misfortune, calamity.

ආපන්න, *Ápanna*, *a.* unfortunate, calamitous, unhappy; gained, obtained; required.

ආපසු, *Ápasu*, *ad.* backwards.

ආපසුමඩු, *Ápasumadu*, *s.* kind of creeper, (*bindweed.*)

ආපාත, *Ápáta*, *a.* descending, falling; *ad.* the same moment, immediately.

ආපාන, *Ápána*, *s.* (ආ together, පාන drinking) place for drinking in society.

ආපෝකසින, *Ápokasina*, *s.* (ආපස් *ápas* water, කසින kasina) power of producing the watery humour of the body in a sensible form from the mouth, eyes, etc. attained by intense abstraction.

ආපෝධාතුව, *Ápodhátuwa*, *s.* (ආපස් *ápas* water, ධාතු *dhátu* an element) water as one of the primary elements.

ආබරණය, *Ábaraṇaya*, *s.* corrupt form of ආභරණය *ábharaṇaya.*

ආබහිකම, *Ábahikama*, *s.* avarice,

ආබාධය, *Ábádhaya*, *s.* sickness, danger, obstacle.

ආභරණය, *Ábharaṇaya*, *s.* any ornaments for wearing, decoration; jewellery, ornament.

ආභාෂණ, *Ábháshaṇa*, *part.* addressing, speaking to.

ආභෝග, *Ábhóga*, *s.* completion, fulness; effort, pains; extended hood of the cobra capella used by Varuṇa as his umbrella.

ආම්බංකරණවා, *Ámbaṇkaraṇawá*, *v.* to train, to manage.

ආම්‍ර, *Ámra*, *s.* mango tree, *magnifera indica.* [Colloq. අඹ *amba.*]

ආම්බලික, *Ámbalika*, see ආම්ල *ámla.*

ආම්ල, *Ámla*,
ආම්ලිකා, *Ámliká*, } *s.* tamarind tree. [Colloq. සියඹලා *siyambalá.*]

ආම්‍රෙඩිත, *Ámredita*, *s.* repetition of a word or sound.

ආම, *Áma*, *a.* raw, unripe, undigested, undressed; *s.* sickness, disease, affection of the bowels arising from indigestion, rawness.

ආමජ්වරය, *Ámajwaraya*, *s.* (ආම and ජ්වර fever) bilious fever, fever arising from indigestion.

ආමන්ත්‍රණ, *Ámantraṇa*, *s.* calling, invitation, salutation.

ආමර්ෂණ, *Ámarshaṇa*, *part.* meditating, thinking; bearing; rubbing; stroking with the hand as an act of fondling.

ආමලක, *Ámalaka*, ආමලකී, *Ámalakí*, } *s.* gem, crystal; tree, *phyllanthus emblica;* [Colloq. නෙල්ලි *Nelli*].

ආමවාතය, *Ámawátaya*, *s.* (ආම and වාත wind) morbid air producing a slight diarrhœa.

ආමා, *Ámá*, *s.* wet nurse, pl. ආමාවරු *ámáwaru*, or ආමාලා *ámálá*.

ආමාශය, *Ámásaya*, *s.* stomach.

ආමිෂ, *Ámisha*, *s.* flesh, hence a bribe, secular gain; enjoyment; pleasing or beautiful object; coveting, longing for, lust, desire; food.

ආමිෂදාන, *Ámishadána*, *s.* (ආමිෂ and දාන gift) bestowing flesh, alms etc., material gifts.

ආමුක්ත, *Ámukta*, *a.* (ආ and මුච *mucha* to release, unbind, ක්ත *kta* aff.) clothed, accoutred; cast, shot.

ආමෝද, *Ámóda*, *s.* fragrancy, perfume, joy, pleasure; *a.* diffusive.

ආයත්ත, *Áyatta*, *a.* (ආ and යම *yama* to restrain, ක්ත *kta* aff.) docile, tractable, dependent.

ආයත, *Áyata*, *a.* long.

ආයතන, *Áyatana*, *s.* (Páli) the five senses; (Sanskrit), altar, shed for sacrificing, abode, cause.

ආයම්, *Áyam*, *s.* government duty on the saltpans.

ආයම්පල, *Áyampala*, *s.* the place where the salt duty is collected.

ආයා, *Áyá*, *s.* nurse, children's nursemaid, pl. ආයාලා *áyálá*, or ආයාවරු *áyáwaru*.

ආයාම, *Áyáma*, *s.* scarcity; length.

ආයාස, *Áyása*, *s.* fatigue, wearisomeness, sometimes written අයාස *ayása*.

ආයිත්තම, *Áyittama*, *s.* dress, uniform, ornament.

ආයු, *Áyu*, *s.* age, duration of life.

ආයුද, *Áyuda*, ආයුධ, *Áyudha*, } *s.* weapon, implement, tool.

ආයුබෝවන්, *Áyubówan*, *interj.* salutation, expressing desire for another's long life and happiness.

ආයුර්වේද, *Áyurweda*, *s.* the science of medicine.

ආයුෂ්මත්, *Áyushmat*, *a.* (ආයුස් *áyus* life, මත් poss. aff.) long lived, venerable.

ආයුස්කල්පය, *Áyuskalpaya*, *s.* age.

ආයුසය, *Áyusaya*, *s.* age, duration.

ආයෙත්, *Áyet*, ආයෙම, *Áyema*, ආයේ, *Áyé*, } *ad.* again, once more.

ආර්ද්‍ර, *Árdra*, *s.* (අද *ada* to go, රක් *rak* aff.) sixth nakshatra or lunar mansion.

ආර්ද්‍රක, *Árdraka*, *s.* ginger in its undried state.

ආර්ය, *Árya*, *a.* term of high respect, of veneration, and applied to persons of high descent, venerable, respectable, proper: *s.* name of Buddha, but particularly applied to the priests of Buddha.

ආර්යරත්නය, *Áryaratnaya*, *s.* (ආර්ය venerable, රතන gem) rahat, saint.

ආරංචිය, *Áranchiya*, *s.* news, intelligence.

ආරක්ෂාව, *Árakshááwa*, *s.* (ආ prefix, රක්ෂා to preserve) preservation, support, protection.

ආරච්චි, *Árachchi*, ආරච්චිරාල, *Árachchirála*, ආරච්චිල, *Árachchila*, } *s.* aratchy, officer in the native militia of the rank of sergeant, a petty village official.

ආරණ්‍ය, *Áraṇya*, *s.* forest, wilderness. [Colloq. වනාන්තරය *wanántaraya*.]

ආරණ්‍යකාංග, *Áraṇyakánga*, *s.* (ආරණ්‍ය forest, ක *ka* aff. අංග *anga* ordinance) institute of the Buddhist priesthood enjoining upon the priests to live in forests or solitary places and not in town or villages; see තෙළෙස් ධූතාංග *teḷesdhutánga*.

ආරණවා, *Áraṇawá*, *v.* to become fat or stout.

ආරබ්ධ, *Árabdha*, *s.* begun, commenced.

ආරම්භකරණවා, *Árambhakaraṇawá*, *v.* to commence, to attempt.

ආරම්භය, *Árambhaya*, *s.* commencement, beginning; [Colloq. පටන්ගැන්ම *paṭangeṇma*].

ආරම්මණ, *Árammaṇa*, *s.* being affected; reflection, thought; subject of thought, that which occupies the mind.

ආරචාර, *Árachára*, *s.* (ආර far, චර *chara* to go) living far from evil ways, leading a virtuous life.

ආරාධනාව, *Árádanáwa*, *s.* invitation.

ආරාධන, *Árádhana*, *s.* accomplishment, worshipping, propitiating, attainment, request, invitation.

ආරාධනාව, *Árádhanáwa*, *s.* entreating, solicitation, request; gratifying.

ආරාම, *Aráma*, *s.* garden, orchard, grove, forest; residence of the disciples of Buddha, monastery.

ආරාවුල, *Árawula*, *s.* dispute, quarrel.

ආරූඪ, *Árúḍha*. *a.* ascending, mounting, rising.

ආරූඪවෙනවා, *Árúḍhawenawá*, *v.* to mount, to take possession, to ascend.

ආරෝග්‍ය, *Árógya*, *s.* (අ *a* neg. රෝග *róga* sickness) health.

ආරෝපණය, *Arópaṇaya*, *s.* planting, fixing.

ආරෝපිත, *Árópita*, *a.* planted, fixed.

ආරෝහ, *Áróha*, *s.* length; ascent; rising, mounting; riding.

ආරෝහණ, *Áróhaṇa*, *s.* (ආ and රුහ *ruha* to ascend, ණ්‍ය *ṇya* aff.) ladder, stair-case, rising, ascending.

අලකමන්ද, *Álakamandá*, *s.* sity of Kuvéra.

ආලඟා, *Álangá*, } *s.* moon-flower; *Ipomæa Bona-*
ආලංගා, *Álangá*, } *nox, (Convolv.);* kind of cake.

ආලපන්නෙ, *Álapanne*, *s.* materials, tools.

ආලම්බනය, *Álambanaya*, } *s.* hanging down, sup-
ආලම්බනය, *Álambanaya*, } porting.

ආලය, *Álaya*, *s.* affection, attachment, inclination; house, place of worship; desire.

ආලවක, *Álawaka*, *s.* demon or yaksha, one of the yaksha chiefs under Kuvera.

ආලස්‍ය, *Álasya*, *s.* idleness, sloth.

ආලාප, *Álápa*, *s.* (ආ and ලප *lapa* to speak) speaking to, addressing.

ආලි, *Áli*, *s.* woman's female friend; row, continuous line; race, family.

ආලිංගන, *Álingana*, *s.* (ආ before, ලිංගන to approach) embracing, an embrace.

ආලේඛ්‍ය, *Álekhya*, *s.* (ආ and ලිඛ *likha* to write, ණ්‍ය *ṇya* aff.) painting.

ආලෙපකරණවා, *Álepakaraṇawá*, *v.* to smear, to plaster, to anoint.

ආලේ, *Álé*, *s.* wish, desire.

ආලේපය, *Álépaya*, *s.* ointment, anointing.

ආලෝක, *Álóka*, *s.* light, sight, seeing, looking.

ආලෝපය, *Álópaya*, *s.* ball of boiled rice.

ආවඩනවා, *Awaḍanawá*, *v.* (ආ life, වඩන increase) to salute, to wish long life to one: pret. ආවැඩුවා *áweḍuwá.*

ආවතේව, *Áwaṭéwa*, *s.* ministrations.

ආවර්ජනා, *Áwarjjaná*, *s.* thought, reflection, considering. [Colloq. කල්පනාව *kalpanáwa.*]

ආවර්ත, *Áwarta*, *s.* whirlpool, revolving, turning round.

ආවර්තන, *Áwartana*, *s.* stirring anything in a state of fusion, melting metals together, alligation.

ආවරණ, *Áwaraṇa*, } *s.* shield, shelter, screen,
ආවරණීය, *Áwaraṇíya*, } covering.

ආවලි, *Áwali*, *s.* row, range, continuous line.

ආවාට, *Áwáṭa*, *s.* very deep hole, pit.

ආවාස, *Áwása*, } *s.* house, residence, one of the
ආවාසය, *Áwásaya*, } names for all kind of drums.

ආවාහ, *Áwáha*, *s.* marriage.

ආවි, *Ávi*, *s.* age, life, period of a person's life.

ආවුද, *Áwuda*, *s.* implement, instrument, tool, weapon.

ආවෘත, *Ávṛita*, *a.* enclosed, surrounded as by a wall or ditch.

ආවෙණික, *Áweṇika*, *adj.* detached, separate.

ආවෙශන, *Áweṣana*, *s.* house in which work is done, manufactory, work shop; demoniacal possession, fury.

ආවේශ, *Áwésa*, *s.* pride, arrogance; demoniac frenzy.

ආශ්චර්‍ය, *Áṣcharya*, *s.* miracle, anything marvellous, wonder.

ආශ්චර්‍යමත්, *Áṣcharyamat*, *a.* wonderful, admirable.

ආශ්‍රම, *Áṣrama*, *s.* hermitage, abode of retired saints or ascetics.

ආශ්‍රය, *Áṣraya*, *s.* (ආ and ශ්‍රි *ṣri* to serve) cheating, fraud, circumvention; asylum, shelter, refuge, protection.

ආශ්‍රව, *Áṣrawa*, *s.* distress, fatigue; fault, transgression.

ආශ්වාස, *Áṣwása*, *s.* inhaled air.

ආශය, *Áṣaya*, *s.* meaning, intention; receptacle.

ආශා, *Áṣá*, *s.* wish, desire, hope; quarter, region.

ආශීර්වාද, *Áṣírwáda*, *s.* blessing, benediction.

ආශීවිෂ, *Áṣívisha*, *s.* (ආශී and විෂ poison) snake.

ආෂාඪ, *Áshádha*, *s.* month so called (June and July); name of the twenty first or twenty second lunar mansion.

ආස්චර්‍ය, *Áscharya*, see ආශ්චර්‍ය *áṣcharya.*

ආස්තරණය, *Ástaraṇaya*, *s.* elephant's housings, painted blanket or cloth worn on his back; covering, sheet.

ආස්පද, *Áspada*, *s.* business, affair; place, situation, dignity, authority.

ආස්මි, *Ásmi*, } *s.* sweetmeat like a pancake,
ආස්වද, *Áswada*, } made of flour, oil and jaggery.

ආස්වාද, *Áswáda*, *s.* health, happiness; the act of tasting, enjoyment.

ආස්විනා, *Ásvina*, see අශ්විනී *aṣvini.*

ආස්‍රව, *Ásrawa*, see ආශ්‍රව *áṣrawa.*

ආසංකා, *Ásanká*, *s.* doubt, uncertainty.

ආසන්න, *Ásanna*, *a.* near, proximate; *s.* end, termination.

ආසනය, *Ásanaya*, *s.* seat, throne.

ආසා, *Ásá*, see ආශා *áṣá.*

ආසාඪ, *Ásádha*, see ආෂාඪ *áshádha.*

ආසාව, *Ásáwa*, see ආශා *áṣá.*

ආසිය, *Ásiya*, *s.* ace in a Sinhalese game.

ආසිර්වාද, *Ásírwáda*, see ආශීර්වාද *áṣírwáda,*

ආහර, *Áhara*, } *s.* food, victuals.
ආහාර, *Áhára*, }

ආහිතුණ්ඩික, *Áhitundika*, see අහිතුණ්ඩික *ahituṇḍika.*

ඉ

The third vowel in the alphabet having the fine, sharp sound of *i* in his or him or pin; where non-initial it is written above the consonant, as කි *ki*.

ඉක්, *Ik*, *s.* sight, looking; sugar cane, passing time.

ඉක්කාමදුල, *Ikkámadula*, *s.* soft part of the jack fruit without stone, pl. ඉක්කාමදුලු *ikkámadulu*.

ඉක්කාව, *Ikkáwa*, *s.* hiccough.

ඉක්බිති, *Ikbiti*, *ad.* thereafter, then.

ඉක්මණ, *Ikmaṇa*, *s.* quickness, expedition,

ඉක්මන්, *Ikman*, *a.* quick, expeditious.

ඉක්මන්කරණවා, *Ikmankaraṇawá*. *v.* to expedite, to hasten.

ඉක්මෙණ, *Ikmeṇa*, *part.* passing away, vanishing, disappearing, expiring.

ඉක්මෙණවා, *Ikmenawá*, *v.* to pass away, to vanish, to disappear: pret. ඉක්මුණා *ikmuṇá*.

ඉක්ෂ්වාකු, *Ikshwáku*, *s.* first monarch in the Súrya-vaṉsa, or line of the sun, commencing in the second yuga, or silver age of the Hindus; in this line Buddha was born.

ඉක්ෂු, *Ikshu*, *s.* sugar cane. [Colloq. උක්ගහ *uk-gaha*.]

ඉක්ෂුකාණ්ඩ, *Ikshukáṇḍa*, *s.* species of the sugar cane, *saccharum munja*.

ඉක්ෂුව, *Ikshuwa*, see ඉක්ෂු *ikshu*.

ඉකිගහනවා, *Ikigahanawá*, *v.* to sob, to weep, to pant.

ඉකිණි, *Ikiṇí*, *s.* female louse.

ඉකිබිඳිනවා, *Ikibiṉdinawá*, *v.* (ඉක්කා *ikká* hiccough, බිඳිනවා to break) to sob, to sigh.

ඉකිරි, *Ikiri*, *s.* plant barleria; [Colloq. කටුකරඬු *kaṭukaruṉḍu*]; shell-fish, sea-urchin, species of echinus.

ඉකිරිකුඩුප්පුවා, *Ikirikuḍuppuwá*, *s.* species of fish.

ඉකිරියා, *Ikiriyá*, *s.* (ඉකිරි and යා aff.) sea-urchin.

ඉකිලි, *Ikili*, *s.* plant, *Acanthus ilicifolus*, *(Acanthaceæ)*; also කටු ඉකිලි *kaṭu-ikili*.

ඉකිලිය, *Ikiliya*, *s.* hip, groin; vessel; floating plant with white flowers, *Trapa bispinosa (Onagraceæ)*.

ඉකුත්, *Ikut*, *a.* past, gone, ancient, after; *part.* ended, finished.

ඉකුත්වෙනවා, *Ikutwenawá*, *v.* to die, to cease to exist, to expire, to pass away.

ඉඟ, *Iṉga*, } *s.* waist, loins, pl. ඉඟවල් *iṉgawal* or ඉං *iṉ*.
ඉඟටිය, *Iṉgaṭiya*, }

ඉඟපටිය, *Iṉgapaṭiya*, *s.* girdle.

ඉඟි, *Iṉgi*, *s.* hint or sign given by the eye, wink; thought, intention.

ඉඟිකරණවා, *Iṉgikaraṇawá*, *v.* to wink significantly.

ඉඟිකරුව, *Iṉgikaruwa*, *part.* looking round about with caution.

ඉඟිත, *Iṉgita*, *s.* (ඉඟ *iṉga* to go, ක්ත *kta* aff.) hint, sign, gesture.

ඉඟිනි, *Iṉgini*, *s.* tree bearing the clearing nut, *strychnos potatorum*, *(Loganiaceæ)*.

ඉඟිමරණවා, *Iṉgimaraṇawá*, *v.* to intimate sentiment by the eye, gesture etc., to hint.

ඉඟිරියාව, *Iṉgiriyáwa*, *s.* ball of the eye.

ඉඟු, *Iṉgu*, *s.* sugar cane.

ඉඟුර, *Iṉgura*, see ඉඟුරු *iṉguru*.

ඉඟුරා, *Iṉgurá*, *s.* small fish used by fishermen as bait.

ඉඟුරු, *Iṉguru*, *s.* ginger.

ඉඟුල්, *Iṉgul*, *s.* vermilion.

ඉගණගන්නවා, *Igaṇagannawá*, *v.* to learn, to be instructed.

ඉගණගැණීම, *Igaṇageṇíma*, *s.* learning, the act of learning.

ඉගණීම, *Igaṇíma*, *s.* learning.

ඉගිලෙනවා, *Igilenawá*, *v.* to fly off; to peel as bark from trees; to be rooted up: pret. ඉගුලුනා *igulunā*.

ඉගැන්වීම, *Igeṉvíma*, *s.* teaching, instruction, pl. ඉගැන්වීම් *igeṉvím*.

ඉච්චාකරණවා, *Ichcháikaraṇawá*, *v.* to flatter.

ඉච්චාව, *Ichcháwa*, *s.* flattery.

ඉච්ඡාව, *Ichchháwa*, *s.* wish, desire.

ඉට්ටන්කරණවා, *Iṭṭankaraṇawá*, *v.* to emancipate.

ඉට්ටන්වීම, *Iṭṭanvíma*, see ඉට්ටම *iṭṭama*.

ඉට්ටන්වෙනවා, *Iṭṭanwenawá*, *v.* to be emancipated.

ඉට්ටම, *Iṭṭama*, *s.* emancipation.

ඉටනවා, *Iṭanawá*, *v.* to exist in a future state; to determine, purpose, resolve.

ඉටමිතුර, *Iṭamitura*, *s.* (ඉට wished, මිතුර friend) a chosen friend.

ඉටි, *Iṭi*, *s.* wax, candle, wax candle.

ඉටිගෙ, *Iṭigé*, *s.* tent, pl. ඉටිගෙවල් *iṭigewal*.

ඉටිපන්දම, *Iṭipandama*, *s.* candlestick; wax candle, pl. ඉටිපන්දම් *iṭipandum*.

ඉටු, *Iṭu*, Elu form of ඉෂ්ට *Ishṭa*.

ඉඩ, *Iḍa*, *s.* place, room, opportunity.

ඉඩ අරිණවා, *Iḍa-ariṇawá, v.* to make room.

ඉඩ දෙනවා, *Iḍa-denawá, v.* to give place, to allow, to permit.

ඉඩප්‍රස්තාව, *Iḍaprastáwa, s.* opportunity.

ඉඩම, *Iḍama, s.* spot, place.

ඉඩෙ, *Iḍe, s.* time.

ඉඩේ, *Iḍé, s.* leisure, occasion.

ඉඩෝරය, *Iḍóraya, s.* dry weather.

ඉණිමඟ, *Iṇimaga, s.* ladder, pl. ඉණිමං *iṇimaṇ.*

ඉත්ත, *Itta, s.* cluster of fruit; plant, *Heptapleurum stellatum (Araliaceæ).*

ඉත්තක්, *Ittak, a.* bridle, bit.

ඉත්තා, *Ittá, s.* game resembling draughts. pl. ඉත්තෝ, *ittó.*

ඉත්තෑකූර, *Ittḗkúra, s.* prickle of the porcupine.

ඉත්තෑවා, *Ittḗwá, s.* hedge-hog, porcupine.

ඉත, *Ita, a.* (from Elu), beloved, desired, wished for; (from Sanskrit) gone, remembered.

ඉතා, *Itá, ad.* much, very.

ඉතාම, *Itáma, ad.* exceedingly.

ඉති, *Iti,* an indeclinable particle (in Siṇhalese composition generally changed into the termination යි) implying cause, (thus, therefore); manifestation, (lo! behold!); something additional (etcetera); conclusion (finis); manner (so, thus, even, in this manner); a grammatical copulative, indicating a preceding sound or sense to be again intended.

ඉතින්, *Itin, ad.* well then, now then, perhaps, henceforth.

ඉතිරි, *Itiri, s.* remainder, woman, wife. *adj.* another, other, remaining.

ඉතිරිවෙනවා, *Itiriwenawá, v.* to remain; to recover from sickness.

ඉතිරීම, *Itiríma, s.* overflowing or boiling over.

ඉතිරෙණවා, *Itireṇawá, v.* to overflow, to boil over, to exceed: pret. ඉතුරුණ *ituruṇá.*

ඉතිවුත්තක, *Itiwuttaka, s.* (ඉති thus, වුත්ත said, ක aff.) one of the nine divisions of sacred science which belong to Buddhism; it comprehends such sútras or works as are written in the catechetical form; see නවඟසාසන *nawaṅgasásana.*

ඉතිහාස, *Itihása, s.* history, traditional accounts; heroic history.

ඉතුරු, *Ituru, a.* remaining, surplus.

ඉතුරුකරණවා, *Iturukaraṇawá, v.* to reserve, to spare.

ඉතුරුවා, *Iturwá, s.* remainder, arrear; also the pret. of උතුරණවා *uturaṇawá.*

ඉතුරුවෙනවා, *Iturụwenawá, v.* to remain, to be in arrear.

ඉද්ද, *Idda, s.* spindle; plant, the flowers of which are offered in temples, *Wrightia zeylanica;* also called සුදු ඉද්ද *sudu-idda* and වල් ඉද්ද *wal-idda.*

ඉද්දර, *Iddara, s.* head of a bed, the upper part of anything.

ඉද්දෙනවා, *Iddenawá, v.* to pain, to give pain; to pain by coming in contact with anything (as a boil or sore): pret. ඉද්දුනා *idduná.*

ඉදල, *Idala, s.* broom; dried branch or plant.

ඉදිකටුව, *Idikaṭuwa, s.* needle.

ඉදිකඩුල්ල, *Idikaḍulla, s.* kind of gate closed by means of bars, pl. ඉදිකඩුලු *idikaḍulu.*

ඉදිකරණවා, *Idikaraṇawá, v.* to make earthern vessels, to build, to do, to form.

ඉදිච්ච, *Idichcha, a.* ripe.

ඉදිමුම, *Idimuma, s.* swelling.

ඉදිමෙනවා, *Idimenawá, v.* to swell: pret. ඉදිමුනා *idimuná.*

ඉදිරි පසු, *Idiri pasu, a.* (ඉදිරි before, පසු last) confused, out of order; first last, and last first.

ඉදිරි පසුව, *Idiri pasuwa, s.* obstacle, hindrance, discrepancy, inconsistency.

ඉදිරිපිට, *Idiripiṭa, prep.* before, in the presence of

ඉදිරිය, *Idiriya, s.* position in front of an object, before, or in the presence of a person or thing.

ඉදිරෙණවා, *Idireṇawá, v.* to fall (as a tree from decay of the roots) to be plucked up by the roots: pret. ඉදුරුණ *iduruṇá.*

ඉදිවැල, *Idiwḗla, s.* (ඉද්ද *idda* spindle, වැල stick) the distaff.

ඉදු, *Idu, s.* name of a tree, *Cratæva religiosa,* or *C. Roxburghii*; [Colloq. ලුණුවරණ *luṇuwaraṇa*]; row (of plants, trees etc).

ඉදුකිල්, *Idukil, s.* threshold.

ඉදුබා, *Idubá,* } *s.* tortoise.
ඉදුබු. *Idubu,* }

ඉදුර, *Idura, s.* semen virile.

ඉදුරු, *Iduru, s.* semen; east; name of Indra.

ඉදුවැල්, *Iduwḗl, s.* creeping plant, *cardiospermum haliacabum, (Sapindaceæ);* [Colloq. පෙනෙල *penela*].

ඉදෙනවා, *Idenawá, v.* to ripen; to suppurate.

ඉඳගන්නවා, *Iṉdagannawá, v,* to sit down, to be seated.

ඉඳි, *Iṉdi, s.* date. see ඉඳිගස *iṉdigasa.*

ඉදිකඩ, *Indikaḍa*, *s.* entrance to a fenced garden, stile.

ඉඳිගස, *Indigasa*, *s.* date tree, *Phœnix zeylanica (Palmæ).*

ඉඳිනවා, *Indinawá*, *v.* to sit: pret. උන්නා *unná*.

ඉඳිර, *Indira*, *s.* bee.

ඉඳිවර, *Indiwara*, } *s.* blue lotus, *nymphæa cærulea.*
ඉඳීවර, *Indíwara*,

ඉඳු, *Indu*, *s.* moon; name of Sakra; chief, eminence.

ඉඳුකාන්තා, *Indukántá*, *s.* (ඉඳු and කාන්තා husband) night.

ඉඳුකිල, *Indukila*, see ඉන්ද්‍රකිල *indrakíla*.

ඉඳුදු, *Induda*, *s.* thunder.

ඉඳුදද, *Indudada*, *s.* rainbow. [Colloq. දේදුන්න *dédunna*.]

ඉඳුන්, *Indun*, *s.* sitting.

ඉඳුනිල්, *Indunil*, *s.* emerald, blue sapphire.

ඉඳුපුත්, *Induput*, *s.* (ඉඳු and පුත් son) planet Mercury.

ඉඳුමිණි, *Indumiṇi* *s.* emerald, blue sapphire.

ඉඳුර, *Indura*, *s.* name of Sakra; Vishṇu; east.

ඉඳුරත්න, *Induratna*, *s.* pearl.

ඉඳුරන්, *Induran*, *s.* the five senses.

ඉඳුරා, *Indurá*, *a.* true. *ad.* in truth, verily, indeed.

ඉඳුරු, *Induru*, *s.* plant; *susum anthelminticum (Flagellaricaæ)*; east, eminence.

ඉඳුරුගජ, *Indurugaja*, *s.* Indra's elephant.

ඉඳුරුදිග, *Indurudiga*, *s.* east.

ඉඳුරුදෑලි, *Indurudęli*, *s.* juggler, deceiver.

ඉඳුරුපති, *Indurupati*, *s.* ruler of the east.

ඉඳුල්, *Indul*, *s.* remainder of a meal.

ඉඳුල්කරණවා, *Indulkaraṇawá*, *s.* to taste first of all.

ඉඳුල්වෙනවා, *Indulwenawá*, *s.* to be polluted by eating off the same plate with another, to have contracted some impurity and rendered unfit for use.

ඉඳුවනවා, *Induwanawá*, *v.* to cause to plant: pret. ඉන්දෙව්වා, *indewwá*.

ඉඳුවර, *Induwara*, Elu form of ඉන්දීවර *indíwara*.

ඉඳුවල්ලි, *Induwalli*, } *s.* (ඉඳු and වල්ලි creeper) moon plant, in Sanskrit Soma lata, *asclepias acida*. It yields, a quantity of milky juice, mild and acid. Roxburgh 252.
ඉඳුවැල්, *Induwęl*,

ඉඳුසල්, *Indusal*, *s.* hal tree, *Shorea robusta* or *Vateria Acuminata*.

ඉඳුසෙන, *Indusena*, *s.* (ඉඳු and සෙන thunder) thunder.

ඉඳුසැව්, *Indusęw*, *s.* rainbow.

ඉන්අනිද්දා, *In-aniddá*, *adv.* two days after to-morrow.

ඉන්ගන්, *Ingan*, *s.* limit, boundary, pl. ඉන්ගම් *ingam* or ඉම්ගම් *imgam*.

ඉන්දනවා, *Indanawá*, *s.* to cause to sit, to plant.

ඉන්ද්‍ර, *Indra*, *s.* organ of sense; the human or animal soul, the portion of spirit residing in the body; name of a Hindu deity presiding over Swarga and the secondary class of divinities; he is more particularly the deity of the atmosphere and regent of the east quarter, and corresponds in many respects with the Grecian Jove; one of the yogas or divisions of a circle on the plane of the ecliptic.

ඉන්ද්‍රකීල, *Indrakíla*, *s.* (ඉන්ද්‍ර and කීල pin or bolt) threshold of a door; the fabulous mountain Mandaar, with which the ocean was churned by the gods.

ඉන්ද්‍රචාප, *Indrachápa*, *s.* (ඉන්ද්‍ර and චාප bow) rain bow. [Colloq, දේදුන්න *dédunna*.]

ඉන්ද්‍රජාල, *Indrajála*, *s.* (ඉන්ද්‍ර and ජාල net) deception, cheating, juggling.

ඉන්ද්‍රනීල, *Indraníla*, *s.* emerald, blue sapphire.

ඉන්ද්‍රවෘක්ෂ, *Indrawriksha*, *s.* kind of fir.

ඉන්ද්‍රායුධ, *Indráyudha*, *s.* rainbow.

ඉන්ද්‍රිය, *Indriya*, *s.* organ of sense.

ඉන්ද්‍රියායතන, *Indriyáyatana*, *s.* (ඉන්ද්‍රිය and ආයතන *áyatana* mansion) body, residence of the senses.

ඉන්ද්‍රියාර්ථ, *Indriyártha*, *s.* object of sense, as sound, smell, taste, etc.

ඉන්දිවර, *Indiwara*, see ඉන්දීවර *indíwara*.

ඉන්දීම, *Indíma*, *s.* act of planting or fixing any thing.

ඉන්දීවර, *Indíwara*, *s.* blue lotus, *nymphœa cærulea.*

ඉන්න, *Inna*, *s.* hedge stake, pl. ඉනි *ini*.

ඉන්නලේ, *Innalé*, *s.* small kind of yam somewhat like a potato, *Plectranthus tuberosus (Labiatæ)*. pl. ඉන්නල *innala*.

ඉන්නවා, *Innawá*, *v.* to sit, to be, to be present: pret. උන්නා *unná*.

ඉන්නහල, *Innahala*, see ඉන්නලේ *innalé*.

ඉන්නා, *Inná*, *s.* wart, verbal form meaning there is (within sight); pl. ඉන්නෝ *innó*.

ඉන්නිසා, *Innisá*, *conj.* therefore, (incorrectly used for ඒ නිසා *énisá* or එය නිසා *eya nisá*).

ඉන්පසු, *Inpasu*, *ad.* after that.

ඉන, *Ina*, *s.* waist.

ඉනංගු, *Inangu, a.* proper, fit, suitable.
ඉනම, *Inama, s.* a general name for any low caste.
ඉනහැඩේ, *Inahedé, s.* girdle used only by toddy drawers.
ඉනහැඳ, *Inahenda, s.* dress worn by devil dancers, supposed to represent the demon they wish to propitiate.
ඉනිකුණ, *Inikuná, s.* white louse found in cloth, pl. ඉනිකුණෝ *inikunó.*
ඉනියා, *Iniyá, interj.* expression of tenderness, used at the loss of a beloved object or the occurrence of a misfortune.
ඉනුම, *Inuma, s.* spring of water; loosening or separation of any thing tied or fastened.
ඉනෙනවා, *Inenawá, v.* to spring up as water; to be loosened or separated: pret, ඉනුවා *inuwá.*
ඉපදින්, *Ipadin,* } *s.* birth.
ඉපදිල්ල, *Ipadilla,* }
ඉපදීම, *Ipadíma,* } *s.* birth.
ඉපදුම, *Ipaduma,* }
ඉපදෙනවා, *Ipadenawá, v.* to be born: pret. ඉපදුනා *ipaduná.*
ඉපනැල්ල, *Ipanella, s.* stalk of grain, stubble, pl. ඉපනැලි *ipaneli.*
ඉපල, *Ipala, s.* rod; leafless branch, pl. ඉපල් *ipal.*
ඉපිට, *Ipita, ad.* distant, far.
ඉපියා, *Ipiyá, s.* mouth of a wind instrument; insect which destroys the inside of the grains of paddy; float used in angling.
ඉපිරෙණවා, *Ipirenawá,* see ඉතිරෙණවා *itirenawá.*
ඉපිල්ල, *Ipilla, s.* float used in angling; buoy or out-rigger of a canoe.
ඉපිල්ලා, *Ipillá, s.* kind of fish.
ඉපිල්ලෙනවා, *Ipillenawá, v.* to spring up, as water; to become vain or proud: pret. ඉපිල්ලුනා *ipilluná,*
ඉපිල, *Ipila, s.* boiling up of water; *a.* elated with.
ඉපුල, *Ipula, s.* blue lotus *(nymphoea cœrulea)*; see උපුල *upula.*
ඉපැද්දීම, *Ipeddíma, s.* creation, the cause of birth or origin of things.
ඉබ්බා, *Ibbá, s.* land tortoise, pl. ඉබ්බෝ *ibbó.*
ඉබ, *Iba, s.* an elephant. [Colloq. අලියා *aliyá.*]
ඉබාගාතෙ, *Ibágáte, s.* sauntering, walking about without any special object.
ඉබු, *Ibu,* see ඉබ *iba.*
ඉබේ, *Ibé,* } *ad.* spontaneously; of itself, of its
ඉබේට, *Ibéta,* } own accord.
ඉභ, *Ibha,* see ඉබ *iba.*

ඉඹිනවා, *Imbinawá, v.* to smell, to kiss: pret. ඉඹ්බා *imbá.*
ඉඹුල්, *Imbul, s.* cotton tree, *Eriodendron anfractuosum (Malvaceæ,) bombax heptaphyllum* of *Roxburgh;* the tree cotton used in stuffing pillows, etc.
ඉඹුල්කිරිබත, *Imbulkiribata, s.* (ඉඹුල් and කිරිබත rice milk) balls of rice milk in the shape of the silk cotton pod. pl. ඉඹුල්කිරිබත් *imbulkiribat.*
ඉඹුල් පුළුන්, *Imbul pulun, s.* the tree cotton used in stuffing pillows, etc.
ඉම් කණුව, *Im kanuwa, s.* boundary pillar or post, landmark.
ඉම්ගහනවා, *Imgahanawá, v.* to mark the limit.
ඉම් ටැඹ, *Im temba,* see ඉම් කණුව *im kanuwa.*
ඉම, *Ima, s.* boundary, limit, pl. ඉම් *im.*
ඉය, *Iya,* see හිය *hiya.*
ඉය උරේ, *Iya uré,* quiver; see හියවුර *hiyawura.*
ඉයොර, *Iyora,* see ඉය උරේ *iya uré.*
ඉර්‍යාපථය, *Iryápathaya,* see ඉරියාපථය *iriyápathaya.*
ඉර්ධි, *Irdhi, s.* superhuman power, power of flying through the air, said to be possessed by the Rahats, (incorrectly for ඍද්ධි *ridhi.*)
ඉර්ධිමත්, *Irdhimat, s.* Rahat, Buddhist saint of the highest order. see ඍද්ධිමත් *ridhimat*
ඉර, *Ira, s.* the sun; line; row (as of trees, shrubs.) pl. ඉරි *iri.*
ඉරට්ටය, *Irattaya, s.* even number, two, double, not odd.
ඉරටිය, *Iratiya, s.* long basket for catching fish.
ඉරටුව, *Iratuwa,* } *s.* central fibre of the cocoanut
ඉරටෙ, *Irate,* } or palmyra leaf, pl. ඉරටු *iratu* or ඉරටා *iratá.*
ඉරත්තය, *Irattaya,* see ඉරට්ටය *irattaya.*
ඉරණ, *Irana, part.* sawing, tearing, splitting.
ඉරණම, *Iranama, s.* fate, decree, predestination; rib, pl. ඉරණම් *iranam.*
ඉරණවා, *Iranawá, v.* to saw, to split, to tear, to rend: pret. ඉරුවා *iruwá.*
ඉරමසු, *Iramasu, s.* sarsaparilla, *hemidesmus indicus (Asclepiadeæ);* the root of which is used as medicine.
ඉරමුදුන, *Iramudun... s.* (ඉර sun, මුදුන summit) mid-day, noon.
ඉරා, *Irá, ad.* exceedingly.
ඉරි, *Iri,* pl. of ඉර *ira.*
ඉරිඋදේ, *Iriudé, s.* sunrise, very early in the morning.

ඉරිඟහනවා, *Irigahanawá*, *v.* to rule, to draw line: pret. ඉරිඟෑහුවා *irigęhuwá*.

ඉරිඟු, *Iringu*, *s.* maize, Indian corn.

ඉරිතු, *Iritu*, *s.* a season. Incorrectly for ඍතු *ṛitu*.

ඉරිදා, *Iridá*, *s.* Sunday.

ඉරිඳු, *Iridu*, *s.* uprightness. *a.* straight.

ඉරිමට්ටම, *Irimaṭṭama*, *s.* (ඉර *ira* line, මට්ටම rule) carpenter's rule.

ඉරිමදය, *Irimadaya*, *s.* defect in the pith of plants.

ඉරිමුසු, *Irimusu*, see ඉරමසු *iramasu*.

ඉරියව්ව, *Iriyawwa*, *s.* general term expressing existence; either sitting, standing, reclining or walking.

ඉරියාපථය, *Iriyápathaya*, see ඉරියව්ව *iriyawwa*.

ඉරිවේරිය, *Iriwériya*, *s.* medicinal plant, *Plectranthus zeylanicus (Labiatæ)*; a drug; vegetable perfume.

ඉරිවැටීම, *Iriwęṭíma*, *s.* act of splitting, cracking, pl. ඉරිවැටුම් *iriwęṭum*.

ඉරු, *Iru*, *s.* sun.

ඉරුතු, *Irutu*, *s.* season; division of two months. See ඍතු *ṛitu*.

ඉරුම, *Iruma*, *s.* split, rent, crack, pl. ඉරුම් *irum*.

ඉරුමඬල, *Irumaṇḍala*, *s.* halo; horizon.

ඉරුරාජ, *Irurája*, *s.* plant, *Zeuxine regia (Burmanniaceæ)*.

ඉරුව, *Iruwa*, *s.* leaf of a book, page; quarter from any point.

ඉරුවාරදය, *Iruwáradaya*, *s.* sun-stroke.

ඉල්, *Il*, *s.* earth; forest; palanquin or dooly, litter.

ඉල්තණ, *Iltaṇa*, *s.* father in law.

ඉල් පණුවා, *Il-paṇuwá*, *s.* a vermin which destroys the leaves of trees principally in November.

ඉල්පෙනවා, *Ilpenawá*, *v.* to float; to become high-minded; to float: pret. ඉල්පුනා *ilpuná*.

ඉල් මස, *Il-masa*. *s.* November.

ඉල්ල, *Illa*, *s.* plant, *Callicarpa lanata (Verben.)*

ඉල්ලනවා, *Illanawá*, *v.* to ask, request, solicit: pret. ඉල්ලුවා *illuwá*.

ඉල්ලම, *Illama*, *s.* a vein of metal.

ඉල්ලාගැන්ම, *Illágęnma*, } *s.* obtainment.
ඉල්ලාගැණීම, *Illágęṇíma*, }

ඉල්ලීම, *Illíma*, *s.* petition, prayer, pl. ඉල්ලීම් *illím*, or ඉල්ලුම් *illum*.

ඉල්ලුම්කාරයා, *Illumkárayá*, *s.* petitioner, applicant.

ඉල්ලුම, *Illuma*, see ඉල්ලීම *illíma*.

ඉල්වනවා, *Ilwanawá*, *v.* to ask, to request, to solicit: pret. ඉල්ලෙව්වා *illewwá*.

ඉල්වීම, *Ilvíma*, see ඉල්ලීම *illíma*.

ඉලංගම, *Ilangama*, *s.* kind of dancing school, where dancing and beating of the tom tom are taught. pl. ඉලංගං *ilangaṇ*.

ඉලඇටය, *Ilaeṭaya*, *s.* rib.

ඉලක්කම, *s.* cypher, figure, number, pl. ඉලක්කම් *ilakkam*.

ඉලක්කය, *Ilakkaya*, } *s.* target, mark for shooting,
ඉලක්කෙ, *Ilakke*, } pl. ඉලක්ක *ilakka*.

ඉලත්තට්ටුව, *Ilattaṭṭuwa*, *s.* betel dish, tray.

ඉලත්තිය, *Ilattiya*, *s.* elephant's dung. [Colloq. ඇත් බෙටි *ęt beṭi*].

ඉලදළුව, *Iladaḷuwa*, *s.* rib.

ඉලන්ද, *Ilanda*, *s.* tree, *zizyphus jujuba (Rhamnaceæ)*. [Colloq. මසන් *masan*.]

ඉලන්දාරියා, *Ilandáriyá*, *s.* youth, young man.

ඉලපත, *Ilapata*, *s.* small broom made of the strong fibres of the coconut leaf, pl. ඉලපත් *ilapat*.

ඉලව්ව, *Ilawwa*, *s.* misfortune, mishap, woe; funeral.

ඉලිත්තියා, *Ilittiyá*, *s.* kind of fish.

ඉලිප්පෙනවා, *Ilippenawá*, *v.* to float, rise to the surface: pret. ඉලිප්පුනා *ilippuná*.

ඉලීම, *Ilíma*, *s.* rubbing.

ඉලෙයා, *Ileyá*, *s.* kind of fish used for curry.

ඉව, *Iwa*, *s.* scent, instinct, power of smelling at a distance after the manner of hounds; *a* so, even, like, as, in the same manner.

ඉවඅල්ලනවා, *Iwaallanawá*, *v.* to search by scent.

ඉවත්කරණවා, *Iwatkaraṇawá*, *v.* to put aside, put out of the way.

ඉවත, *Iwata*, *ad.* aside, aslant, out of the way.

ඉවද, *Iwada*, *s.* medicinal plant.

ඉවර, *Iwara*, *s.* leisure, end, termination, accomplishment.

ඉවරකරණවා, *Iwarakaraṇawá*, *v.* to finish, to terminate.

ඉවරවෙනවා, *Iwarawenawá*, *v.* to be at leisure, to be finished.

ඉවසන, *Iwasana*, *part.* forbearing, enduring, bearing.

ඉවසනවා, *Iwasanawá*, *v.* to bear with, to endure, to support, to accept: pret. ඉවසුවා *iwasuwá*.

ඉවසිල්ල, *Iwasilla*, *s.* patience, forbearance, pl. ඉවසිලි *iwasili*.

ඉවසීම, *Iwasíma*, *s.* endurance, forbearance, acceptance.

ඉවසු, *Iwasu*, *a.* accepted, endured.

ඉවසුම, *Iwasuma*, see ඉවසීම *iwasíma*.

ඉව්ලි, *Irili*, *s.* food cooked: see උයනවා *uyanawá*.

ඉව්ම, *Iríma*, *s.* the act of cooking: see උයනවා

ඉවුර, *Iwura*, *s.* border, margin, bank of a river. pl. ඉවුරු *iwuru*.

ඉෂ්ට, *Ishṭa*, *a.* wished, desired; *s.* worship, reverence; oblation; good fortune; that which happens.

ඉෂ්ටකරණවා, *Ishṭakaraṇawá*, *v.* to cause to happen; to complete, accomplish, fulfil.

ඉෂ්ටගන්ධ, *Ishṭagandha*, *s.* (ඉෂ්ට and ගන්ධ smell) fragrant odour, fragrance, scent of perfumes.

ඉෂ්ට විපාකය, *Ishṭa-ripákaya*, *s.* (ඉෂ්ට and විපාකය reward) good luck, good fortune; reward of merit.

ඉෂ්ටවෙනවා, *Ishṭawenawá*, *v.* to be accomplished.

ඉෂ්ටානිෂ්ට, *Ishṭánishṭa*, *s.* (ඉෂ්ට *ishṭa* and අනිෂ්ට *anishṭa* bad luck) merit and demerit, good and bad fortune, gain and loss.

ඉෂ්ටාර්ථ, *Ishṭártha*, *s.* (ඉෂ්ට *ishṭa* and අර්ථ *artha* profit) good fortune, reward of merit; fortunate undertaking.

ඉෂ්ටාලම්බනය, *Ishṭálambanaya*, *s.* (ඉෂ්ට *ishṭa* and අලම්බන *alambana* thought, mind) pious reflections, good thoughts.

ඉස්කබල, *Iskabala*, *s.* skull, pl. ඉස්කබල් *iskabal*.

ඉස්කර, *Iskara*, *s.* head and part of the neck which is separated from the body by decapitation.

ඉස්කාකරය, *Iskákaraya*, *s.* arrack distillery, distillery house.

ඉස්ටකරණවා, *Isṭakaraṇawá*, *v.* to bring about, to perform: see ඉෂ්ටකරණවා *ishṭakaraṇawá*.

ඉස්ටවෙනවා, *Isṭawenawá*, *v.* to meet with success: see ඉෂ්ටවෙනවා *ishṭawenawá*.

ඉස්ත්‍රික්කය, *Istrikkaya*, *s.* (Portuguese) smoothing iron.

ඉස්තෝප්පුව, *Istóppuwa*, *s.* (Portuguese) outer verandah.

ඉස්ථුල *Isthula*, see ස්ථූල *sthúla*.

ඉස්පයිය, *Ispayiya*, *s.* covering for the head, kind of hood.

ඉස්පාසුව, *Ispásuwa*, *s.* opportunity, leisure.

ඉස්බ, *Isba*, *s.* measure of 140 cubits.

ඉස්බුන්, *Isbun*, } *s.* ease, repose, sleeping.
ඉස්බුම්, *Isbum*, }

ඉස්ම, *Isma*, *s.* juice, sauce.

ඉස්මතුකරණවා, *Ismatukaraṇawá*, *v.* to patronize, to encourage, to show forth prominently, to promote.

ඉස්මන්, *Isman*, *a.* quick, rapid, expeditious.

ඉස්මුදුන, *Ismuduna*, *s.* the crown of the head.

ඉස්වැටිය, *Iswęṭiya*, *s.* (ඉස *isa* head, වැටි what encompasses) turban.

ඉස්සර, *Issara*, *ad.* before, prior, previous, antecedent.

ඉස්සරහ, *Issaraha*, *ad.* (ඉස්සර and අහ *aha* side) before, in front of, in presence of.

ඉස්සා, *Issá*, *s.* shrimp, prawn.

ඉස්සීම, *Issíma*, *s.* act of lifting up; verbal noun from උස්සනවා *ussanawá*.

ඉස්හොරි, *Ishori*, *s.* dandruff, scabbed head.

ඉස, *Isa*, *s.* head; bear.

ඉසකඩ, *Isakaḍa*, *s.* turban.

ඉසකෙයියා, *Isakeyiyá*, } *s.* hair on the head.
ඉසකෙස, *Isakes*, }

ඉසටිය, *Isaṭiya*, *s.* lance used in war.

ඉසා, *Isá*, *ind.* Elu form of ඊර්ෂ්‍යා *írshyá*; a copulative particle = ද *da* and. (Inscription at Mihintalé).

ඉසාන. *Isána*, *s.* north-east.

ඉසි, *Isi*, *s.* jealousy at the prosperity of others, envy; shrimps; Siva; a sage.

ඉසිනවා, *Isinawá*, *v.* to sprinkle, to scatter as seed, to throw out as water from a pond: pret. ඉස්සා *issá*.

ඉසිරෙණවා, *Isireṇawá*, *v.* to spill accidentally: pret. ඉසිරුණ *isiruṇá*.

ඉසිලීම, *Isilíma*, *s.* act of bearing up, carrying, from උසුලනවා *usulanawá*.

ඉසිවතුන්, *Isiwatun*, *s.* Elu form of ඊර්ෂ්‍යාවන්ත *írshyáwanta*.

ඉසිවරයා, *Isiwarayá*, *s.* general name for a saint or holy person, a sage.

ඉසු, *Isu*, *s.* envy.

ඉසුම්, *Isum*, *s.* covetousness, excessive desire, prayer.

ඉසුර, *Isura*, *s.* fame, honour, renown; wealth, prosperity, riches; name of Siva, pl. ඉසුරු *isuru*; *a.* chief, excellent, honourable.

ඉසුරුමත්, *Isurumat*, *a.* having fame, honour, renown; being famous.

ඉසෙනවා, *Isenawá*, *v.* to be sprinkled: pret. ඉසුනා *isuná*.

ඉසේ රදය, *Isé-radaya*, *s.* head-ache.

ඉහ, *Iha*, *s.* head. *adv.* here.

ඉහගහනවා, *Ihagahanawá*, *v.* to be troubled, to knock the head against, to put up with.

ඉහත, *Ihata*, *a.* preceding, foregoing, before mentioned; above.

ඉහඳ, *Ihanda*, *s.* eggs of a blue fly producing maggots in dead bodies.

ඉහල, *Ihala*, *prep.* above.

ඉහාත්මභාවය, *Ihátmabháwaya*, ඉහාත්මය, *Ihátmaya*, } *s.* (ඉහ here, අත්ම existence, භාව state) the present state of existence.

ඉහි, *Ihi*, *prep.* with, in the company of, (සියනිහි, with relations, Sęlalihini Sandésa).

ඉහිදෙල, *Ihidęla*, *a.* coarse, as cloth; *s.* prawn net.

ඉහිනවා, *Ihinawá*, *v.* to sprinkle, to scatter, to bale off, or throw out water as from a large hole or pond: pret. ඉස්සා *issá*.

ඉහිරෙණවා, *Ihireṇawá*, *v.* to be scattered, sprinkled, spilt: pret. ඉහිරුණ *ihiruṇá*.

ඉහිල්, *Ihil*, *s.* kind of cloth of a thin or loose texture; cohabitation; softness. *a.* soft, of a loose texture.

ඉහිලිම, *Ihilíma*, *s.* the act of bearing up: see also ඉසිලිම *isilíma*.

ඉහිලුම, *Ihiluma*, see ඉසිලිම *isilíma*.

ඉහිලැලි, *Ihilęli*, *a.* soft, of a loose texture.

ඉහෙනවා, *Ihenawá*, *v.* to be sprinkled with, to be spattered with.

ඉළු, *Iḷu*, *s.* forest; congregation, multitude.

ඉළුක්, *Iḷuk*, ඉළුක්තණ, *Iḷuktaṇa*, } *s.* kind of reed, *Imperata arundinacea (Gramineæ)*; or *Saccharum cylindricum*.

ඊ

The fourth letter in the alphabet; it is sounded like *ee* in feel; where non-initial it is written above the consonant; as කී *kí*,—said, how many.

ඊඋරය, *Íuraya*, *s.* quiver.

ඊක්ෂණ, *Íkshaṇa*, *s.* sight, seeing; eye.

ඊකාර, *Íkára*, *s.* the letter ඊ *í*.

ඊගස, *Ígasa*, ඊගහ, *Ígaha*, } *s.* an arrow.

ඊගානේ, *Ígáné*, *a.* various, multiplied; *adv.* repeatedly.

ඊගාවා, *Ígáwá*, *a.* proximate, near.

ඊට, *Íṭa*, to that.

ඊටිය, *Íṭiya*, *s.* long hook by which an elephant is guided.

ඊතණ, *Ítaṇa*, *s.* species of the panic grass, *Heteropogon hirtus (Gramineæ)*.

ඊතලය, *Ítalaya*, *s.* the head or blade of an arrow.

ඊපැත්ත, *Ípętta*, *s.* plant, *Cyathocalyx zeylanicus (Anonaceæ)*; also called කැකල *kękala*.

ඊම, *Íma*, *s.* (එනවා *enawá* he comes) coming or approaching.

ඊය, *Íya*, *s.* arrow.

ඊයන්, *Íyan*, ඊයම්, *Íyam*, ඊයම, *Íyama*. } *s.* lead.

ඊයේ, *Íyé*, *ad.* yesterday.

ඊර්ෂ්‍යාව, *Írshyáwa*, *s.* envy, impatience of another's success, jealousy.

ඊර්ෂ්‍යාවන්ත, *Írshyáwanta*, *a.* envious.

ඊරි, *Íri*, *s.* sow, pl. ඊරියෝ *íriyó*.

ඊරිත, *Írita*, *part.* (ඊරති *írati* he sends) sent, despatched.

ඊරිය, *Íriya*, *s.* forest tree, *Myristica Iriya, (Myristicaceæ)*.

ඊල්, *Íl*, *s.* palanquin.

ඊල්ල, *Ílla*, *s.* name of a tree, *callicarpa lanata (Verbeneaceæ)*.

ඊලඟ, *Ílaṅga*, *a.* next.

ඊශ්වරයා, *Íṣwarayá*, *s.* chief, lord, head or master; owner, proprietor; name of Ṣiva or Kámadéva.

ඊශ්වරී, *Íṣwarí*, *s.* wife of Ṣiva, otherwise named Lakshmí, Durgá, or Saraswatí.

ඊශාන, *Íṣána*, north east quarter; name of Ṣiva as regent of that quarter.

ඊෂත්, *Íshat*, *a.* little, some.

ඊස්වරයා, *Íswarayá*, see ඊශ්වරයා *íṣwarayá*.

ඊස්වරී, *Íswarí*, see ඊශ්වරී *íṣwarí*.

ඊසධර, *Ísadhara*, *s.* one of the seven mountains surrounding Mahaméru.

ඊසැරය, *Ísęraya*, *s.* journey or passage of the arrow.

උ

The third short vowel, and fifth in the alphabet; it sounds like *u* in put.

උක්, *Uk*, *s.* sugar cane.

උක්කගන්නවා, *Ukkagannawá*, *v.* to chide, to speak snappishly, to speak in a snarling way.

උක්කුටිකය, *Ukkuṭikaya*, *s.* act of sitting on the heels, as commonly practised by the natives.

උක්කුන්, *Ukkun*, *inter.* expression of fondness used to infants when giving them the breast.

උක්ගස, *Ukgasa*, see උක් *uk*.

උක්ත, *Ukta*, *s, part.* spoken, said.

උක්ති, *Ukti*, *s.* speech, speaking.

උක්දණ්ඩ, *Ukdaṇḍa*, *s.* sugar cane, pl. උක්දඬු *ukdaṇḍu*.

උක්දුනු, *Ukdunu*, *s.* name of Kámadéva the Indian Cupid.

උක්පැණි, *Ukpęṇi*, *s.* (උක් and පැණි juice) juice of the sugar cane.

උක්සකුරු, *Uksakuru*, *s.* sugar.
උකට, *Ukaṭa*, *s.* eminence.
උකටලී, *Ukaṭalí*, *s.* disgust, aversion, weariness.
උකටලීවෙනවා, *Ukaṭalíwenawá*, *v.* to become indolent, to grow lazy, to become dissatisfied.
උකනවා, *Ukanawá*, *v.* to scoop or lade out; to take with the hand, pick up, raise.
උකස්කැරය, *Ukaskęraya*, *s.* mortgage deed.
උකස්ගන්නවා, *Ukasgannawá*, *v.* to take in mortgage.
උකස් තිබනවා, *Ukastibanawá*, *v.* to pledge, to lay down a stake.
උකස, *Ukasa*, } *s.* pledge, pawn, mortgage, secu-
උකහ, *Ukaha*, } rity, pl. උකස් *ukas.*
උකා, *Uká. p. p.* having raised, lifted.
උකාර, *Ukára*, *s.* the letter උ *u.*
උකු, *Uku*, *a.* thick (as applied to liquids).
උකුකම, *Ukukama*, *s.* thickness (as applied to liquids).
උකුණා, *Ukuṇá*, *s.* louse, pl. උකුණෝ *ukuṇó.*
උකුණුවළ, *Ukuṇuwaḷa*, *s.* nape or hollow on the back part of the head.
උකුත්වෙනවා, *Ukutwenawá*, *v.* to die, to expire.
උකුනිල්ල, *Ukunilla*, *s.* hook or stick used by toddy drawers to hang their vessels on.
උකුබානවා, *Ukubánawá*, *v.* to chide, to speak snappishly.
උකුල් ඇටේ, *Ukulęṭé*, *s.* hip.
උකුල, *Ukula*, *s.* hip. lap, pl. උකුල් *ukul.*
උකුස්සා, *Ukussá*, *s.* kite; eagle.
උකුසුවන්, *Ukusuwan*, *s.* one of the six names of the Guruḷas, a race of imaginary birds possessing supernatural powers.
උග්‍ර, *Ugra*, *s.* name of Ṣiva; wrath, anger; a severe affliction; plant said to be *murunga hyperanthum*; *a.* angry, cruel, violent.
උගත්, *Ugat*, *a.* learned.
උගත්කම, *Ugatkama*, *s.* erudition.
උගතා, *Ugatá*, *s.* learned man, pl. උගත්තෝ *ugattó.*
උගන්නවා, *Ugannawá*, *v.* to learn: pret. උගත්තා *ugattá.*
උගන්වනවා, *Uganwanawá*, *v.* to teach, to instruct: pret. ඉගැන්නුවා *igęnnuwá.*
උගහට, *Ugahaṭa*, *a.* difficult, laborious, troublesome.
උගු, *Ugu*, *s*, sugar cane. [Colloq. උක්ගහ *ukgaha.*]
උගුඩුවා, *Uguḍuwá*, *s.* wild cat, ocelet, *Paradoxurus musanga.* pl. උගුඩුවෝ *uguḍuwó.*

උගුර, *Ugura*, *s.* throat, pl. උගුරු *uguru.*
උගුරු ඇටය, *Uguru-ęṭaya*, *s.* Adam's apple, or the prominent part of the throat.
උගුරු දණ්ඩ, *Uguru-daṇḍa*, *s.* wind pipe.
උගුරැස්ස, *Ugurȩssa*, *s.* tree, sweet lovilovi, *Flacourtia Ramontchi (Bixineæ).*
උගුල, *Ugula*, *s.* snare, trap, pl. උගුල් *ugul.*
උගුලනවා, *Ugulanawá*, *v.* to eradicate, to root up, to pluck up, to pull up by the roots: pret. ඉගිල්ලුවා *igilluwá.*
උගුළුවනවා, *Uguḷuwanawá*, *v.* to cause to eradicate: pret. ඉගිලෙව්වා *igilewwá.*
උගේ, *Ugé*, *pron.* his; (not respectful in common speech.)
උච්ච, *Uchcha*, *a.* high, tall, lofty.
උච්චාරණය, *Uchcháraṇaya*, *s.* utterance; pronunciation.
උච්චාරණය කරණවා, *Uchcháraṇaya-karaṇawá*, *v.* to confess, to pronounce.
උච්චිට්ටුව, *Uchchiṭṭuwa*, *s.* quittance or discharge.
උච්චිෂීක, *Uchchirshaka*, *s.* pillow.
උච්ඡින්න, *Uchchhinna*, *part.* eradicated or cut up by the roots.
උච්ඡේද, *Uchchhéda*, *s.* cutting off, destruction.
උච්ඡේද දෘෂ්ටික, *Uchchhéda drishṭika*, *s.* (උච්ඡේද and දෘෂ්ටිය *drishṭiya* sight) a sect who embraced a system of atheism and denied the future existence of the soul.
උච්ඡේදවාදය, *Uchchhadawádaya*, *s.* (උච්ඡේද and වාදය discussion) system of religion denying the transmigration of beings.
උච්ඡේදවාදී, *Uchchhédawádí*, *s.* (උච්ඡේද and වාදී who speaks) atheist, properly one denying transmigration or the future existence of souls.
උඩ, *Uḍa*, *prep.* above, higher up, upwards, over, above the head.
උඩ ඇල්ම, *Uḍa-ęlma*, *s.* difficulty in breathing, asthma.
උඩගන්නවා, *Uḍagannawá*, *v.* to lift up, to take up.
උඩඟු, *Uḍangu*, *a.* high, exalted, haughty, arrogant, proud.
උඩඟුකම, *Uḍangukama*, *s.* pride, haughtiness, arrogance, height.
උඩත්, *Uḍat*, *adv.* above; *s.* the upper end.
උඩන, *Uḍana*, *s.* ignorant foolish persons.
උඩනු, *Uḍanu*, *s.* wicked man, wretch, an ignorant man.
උඩැප්පරන්, *Uḍapparan*, *s.* conceit, puppyism.

උඩලිපත, *Uḍalipata, s.* strong piece of plank laid horizontally over the door or window when building, for the purpose of supporting that part of the wall which does not rest on the frame: pl. උඩලිපත් *uḍalipat.*

උඩහල්ල, *Uḍahalla, s.* something suspended in order to preserve some little things, shelf, hanging wicker safe: pl. උඩහලු *uḍahalu.*

උඩික්කිය, *Uḍikkiya, s.* kind of small drum carried in the hand by the Malabar mendicants, and beaten at the doors of the persons from whom they ask alms.

උඩින්, *Uḍin, ad.* above, higher, over.

උඩු, *Uḍu, s.* a constellation, plough; riches; *a.* high.

උඩුතල්ල, *Uḍutalla, s.* roof of the mouth, palate, pl. උඩුතලු *uḍutalu.*

උඩුතොල, *Uḍutola, s.* upper lip; pl. උඩුතොල් *uḍutol.*

උඩුප, *Uḍupa,* }
උඩුබ, *Uḍuba,* } *s.* raft, float.

උඩුබුරුලනවා, *Uḍuburulanawá, v.* to howl, to yell, to bark (as a dog): pret. උඩුබුරුලෑවා *uḍuburulẹwá.*

උඩුබැල්මෙන්, *Uḍubẹlmen, ad.* (උඩ *uḍa* up බැල්ම *bẹlma* looking) with the face upwards, prone.

උඩුමහල, *Uḍumahale, s.* floor of an upper room, upstair; pl. උඩුමහල් *uḍumahal.*

උඩුමියාවෙනවා, *Uḍumiyáwenawá, v.* to raise the head to look at anything.

උඩුරැවුල, *Uḍurẹwula, s.* mustache.

උඩේ, *Uḍé, s.* breeches (worn under cloth).

උඩෑක්කිය, *Uḍẹkkiya,* see උඩික්කිය *uḍikkiya.*

උණ්ඩිය, *Uṇḍiya, s.* ball.

උණ්ඩෙ, *Uṇḍe, s.* cannon shot, ball to shoot with. pl. උණ්ඩ *uṇḍa.*

උණ, *Uṇa, s.* fever; common bamboo tree, *bambusa vulgaris (Gramin.)*

උණමකුළු, *Uṇamakuḷu, s.* the manna in the trunk of the bamboo tree.

උත්, *Ut, prep.* preposition or prefix, implying up, upwards, much, excessive.

උත්ක්ෂිප්ත, *Utkshipta. a.* thrown up, tossed up; *s.* the thorn apple.

උත්කණ්ඨා, *Utkaṇṭhá, a.* (උත් much, කඨි *kaṭhi* to be sad) regretting, missing any object.

උත්කණ්ඨිත, *Utkaṇṭhita, a.* regretted; discouraged, sorrowful, sad.

උත්කර්ෂ, *Utkarsha, s.* excellence, eminence.

උත්ක්‍රම, *Utkrama, s.* (උත් priv. ක්‍රමි to go in order) irregularity, want of order, perversion.

උත්ක්‍රිෂ්ට, *Utkrishṭa,* incorrectly for උත්කෘෂ්ට *utkrishṭa.*

උත්කෘෂ්ට, *Utkrishṭa, a.* eminent, superior, excellent, much.

උත්කුට, *Utkuṭa, s.* sleeping with the head erect.

උත්කුණ, *Utkuṇa, s.* (උත් loud, කුණ to call. ක *ka* aff.) louse.

උත්ගත, *Utgata, part.* (උත් upwards, ගත gone) ascended; literally gone up.

උත්ත්‍රාස, *Uttrása, s.* (උත් much, ත්‍රාස fear) fear, terror; [Colloq. භය *bhaya*].

උත්තම, *Uttama, a.* best, first, principal.

උත්තමයා, *Uttamayá, s.* (උත්තම and යා aff.) chief.

උත්තමාංග, *Uttamánga, s.* head. [Colloq. හිස *hisa* or ඉස *isa.*]

උත්තර, *Uttara, s.* answer, reply; (in law) defence, rejoinder; the North. *a.* best, highest, most excellent; northern.

උත්තරකුරු, *Uttarakuru, s.* the country about the north pole.

උත්තරතර, *Uttaratara, a.* (උත්තර and තර very) very eminent.

උත්තරණ, *Uttaraṇa, s.* passing over.

උත්තරය, *Uttaraya, s.* answer, reply, defence; see උත්තර *uttara.*

උත්තරඵාල්ගුණී, *Uttaraphálguṇí, s.* (උත්තර subsequent, ඵාල්ගුණ *phálguṇa* asterism) twelfth lunar mansion containing two stars figured by a bed.

උත්තරභාද්‍රපද, *Uttarabhádrapada, s.* (උත්තර and භාද්‍රපද constellation) twentyseventh lunar mansion figured by a couch and comprehending two stars.

උත්තරසාටකය, *Uttarasáṭakaya, s.* upper and outer garment: see උත්තරාසඞ්ග *uttarásanga.*

උත්තරායණය, *Uttaráyaṇaya, s.* sun's northern course.

උත්තරාෂාඪා, *Uttarásháḍhá, s.* twentyfirst of the lunar mansions figured by an elephant's tooth or a bed and containing two stars one of which is β in Sagittarius.

උත්තරාසඞ්ග, *Uttarásanga, s.* upper and outer garment.

උත්තරීය, *Uttaríya,* see උත්තරාසඞ්ග *uttarásanga.*

උත්තාන, *Uttána, a.* shallow; *s.* the act of sleeping supinely, or with the face upwards.

උත්තානසය, *Uttánasaya*, *s.* (උත්තාන and සය who sleeps) one who sleeps with his face upwards; infant.

උත්තුංග, *Uttunga*, *a.* high, lofty, tall.

උත්පත්තිය, *Utpattiya*, *s.* (උත් up, පත to go) birth, nativity, production.

උත්පන්න, *Utpanna*, *a.* born, produced.

උත්පල, *Utpala*, *s.* blue lotus.

උත්පලගන්ධ, *Utpalagandha*, *s.* (උත්පල and ගන්ධ smell) species of sandal wood of the colour of brass and very fragrant.

උත්පාටන, *Utpáṭana*, *s.* (උත් and පට *paṭa* to go, අන aff.) eradicating, pulling up by the roots.

උත්පාටිත, *Utpáṭita*, *a.* eradicated, pulled up by the roots.

උත්පාත, *Utpáta*, *s.* portent, some natural prodigy, phenomenon.

උත්පාද, *Utpáda*, *s.* birth, production.

උත්ප්‍රෙක්ෂා, *Utprekshá*, *s.* (in poetry or rhetoric) illustration or comparison.

උත්සන්න, *Utsanna*, *a.* violent, furious, excessive.

උත්සව, *Utsawa*, } *s.* festival, jubilee. [Colloq. මඞ්ගල්‍යය *mańgalyaya.*]
උත්සව ක්‍රීඩාව, *Utsawa kríḍáwa*, }

උත්සාහ, *Utsáha*, *s.* effort, endeavour, strenuous exertion; desire.

උත්‍රය, *Utraya*, corrupt for උත්තරය *uttaraya.*

උතු, *Utu*, *s.* season; vulva; menstrual discharge.

උතුකටුව, *Utukaṭuwa*, *s.* hard cocoanut shell.

උතුකඩය, *Utukaḍaya*, *s.* cocoanut in a certain tender stage.

උතුනී, *Utuní*, *s.* woman arrived at puberty.

උතුම්, *Utum*, *a.* eminent, excellent, exalted.

උතුම්කම, *Utumkama*, *s.* eminence, excellence, exaltation; supremacy, pl. උතුම්කම් *utumkam.*

උතුමග, *Utumaga*, *s.* head, vulva, pl. උතුමං *utumaṇ.*

උතුමා, *Utumá*, *s.* person of eminence.

උතුමානන්වහන්සේ, *Utumánanwahansé*, *s.* (උතුමානන් and වහන්සේ title of respect) commonly used to signify the Governor; pl. උතුමානන් වහන්සේලා *utumánanwahansélá.*

උතුර, *Utura*, *s.* North; answer.

උතුරණවා, *Uturaṇawá*, *v.* to boil, to run over, to spill from being too full: pret. ඉතිරුවා *itiruwá*, උතුළා *utuḷá.*

උතුරු, *Uturu*, *a.* northern.

උතුරුකුරු, *Uturukuru*, see උත්තරකුරු *uttarakuru.*

උතුරුතෙපුල, *Uturutepula*, *s.* reply.

උතුරුනා, *Uturuná*, *s.* (උතුර *utura* North, නා lord) name of Kuvéra, the regent of the north.

උතුරුසළුව, *Uturusaḷuwa*, *s.* upper garment, cloak.

උද්ගත, *Udgata*, *a.* risen, ascended; vomited, cast up: *part.* gone up, ascended.

උද්ගාර, *Udgára*, *s.* (උත් *ut* up, ගෘ *gṛí* to vomit) vomiting; sound.

උද්ඝොෂණ, *Udghoshaṇa*, *s.* (උද් great, ඝොෂණ noise) loud noise.

උද්දනවා, *Uddanawá*, *v.* to give pain: pret. ඉද්දුවා *idduwá.*

උද්දීප්ත, *Uddípta*, *a.* } exciting, inflaming, as passion.
උද්දීප්තිය, *Uddíptiya*, *s.* }
උද්දීපන, *Uddípana*, *s.* }

උද්දෙස, *Uddesa*, *s.* illustration, exemplification.

උද්දෙසික වස්තුව, *Uddesika wastuwa*, *s.* a thing erected in memory of Buddha, such as the images of his person.

උද්දෙහිකා, *Uddehiká*, *s.* the white ant, termes.

උද්ධත, *Uddhata*, *a.* rude, arrogant, ill-behaved.

උද්භව, *Udbhawa*, *s.* (උද් up, භූ *bhú* to be) birth, production.

උද්භිද්, *Udbhid*, *a.* (උද් and භිද් to break or burst) sprouting, germinating.

උද්භිද, *Udbhida*, *s.* culinary salt; borax.

උද්‍යාන, *Udyána*, *s.* garden. [Colloq. උයන *uyana.*]

උද්‍යානපාලයා, *Udyánapálayá*, *s.* (උද්‍යාන and පාලයා keeper) gardener.

උද, *Uda*, *s.* water.

උදක්, *Udak*, } *a.* much, great deal. *ad.* earnestly.
උදක්ම, *Udakma*, }

උදක, *Udaka*, *s.* water. [Colloq. වතුර *watura.*]

උදකලාව, *Udakaláwa*, *a.* alone, single, by himself.

උදධි, *Udadhi*, *s.* sea, ocean. [Colloq. මූද *múda.*]

උදන් අනනවා, *Udan ananawá*, *v.* to be pleased, to express one's self with joy.

උදපාන, *Udapána*, *s.* (උද and පාන to drink) place where water is drunk, well.

උදම්, *Udam*, *a.* high. [Colloq. උස් *us.*]

උදය, *Udaya*, *s.* (commonly), morning; (in books), rising, ascending; name of a mountain in the east behind which the sun is supposed to rise.

උදයගිර, *Udayagira*, *s.* a mountain so called.

උදරය, *Udaraya*, *s.* belly.

උදරය, *Udaraya*, } *s.* dropsy.
උදර රොගය, *Udara-rógaya*, }

උදළු, *Udalu*, see උදැල්ල *udella.*

උදව්, *Udaw*, } *s.* help, assistance, favour.
උදව්ව, *Udawwa*, }

උදවිය, *Udaviya*, *s.* multitude, people.

උදහස්වෙනවා, *Udahaswenawá*, *v.* to be angry.

උදහස, *Udahasa*, *s.* wrath, anger, indignation.

උදාන, *Udána*, *s.* one of the five vital airs, that which rises up the throat and passes into the head; one of the nine classes of books into which the sacred writings of the Buddhists are divided, such as are written in Páli stanzas with a prose Páli comment; joy, pleasure.

උදාපව්, *Udápaw*, *s.* fabulous rock in the East.

උදාර, *Udára*, *a.* great, generous, liberal, munificent; proud, arrogant.

උදාරම, *Udárama*, *s.* pride, arrogance; pl. උදාරම් *udáram*.

උදාවර්ත, *Udáwarta*, *s.* disease, flatulence and constipation.

උදාවෙනවා, *Udáwenawá*, *v.* to arise, to ascend.

උදාසන, *Udásana*, *s.* (උදය *udaya* morning, සන time) morning, dawn.

උදාසනක්සේ, *Udásanaksé*, *ad.* early dawn, very early.

උදාසීන, *Udásína*, *s.* stranger, common acquaintance, person neither friend nor foe; *a.* indifferent.

උදාහරණය, *Udáharaṇaya*, *s.* an example, illustration, apposite argument; precedent, instance.

උදිත, *Udita*, *part.* said, spoken, risen, born.

උදු, *Udu*, *a.* straight, upright.

උදුන, *Uduna*, *s.* oven.

උදුම්බර, *Udumbara*,
උදුඹර, *Udum̱bara*, } *s.* fig tree, *ficus glomerata*.

උදුර, *Udura*, *s.* rat. [Colloq. මීයා *miyá*.]

උදුරණවා, *Uduraṇawá*, *v.* to pluck up, to eradicate: pret. ඉදුරුවා *iduruwá*.

උදුල්, *Udul*, *a.* shining, glittering, good, excellent.

උදුල්බෑවු, *Udulbęwu*, *s.* gracefulness; name of the forms in dancing.

උදුල, *Udula*, see උදුල් *udul*.

උදෙසනවා, *Udesanawá*, *v.* to enunciate, to say or declare.

උදෙසා, *Udesá*, *prep.* on account of, for that reason, instead of.

උදෑල්ල, *Udęlla*, *s.* kind of hoe, mammoṭi; pl. උදලු *udalu*.

උදේසන, *Udésana*, *s.* morning.

උඳු, *Un̲du*, *s.* plant, species of *flemingia*.

උඳුගොව්වා, *Un̲dugowwá*, *s.* kind of small worm which eats away the roots of the hair, pl. උඳු ගොව්වෝ *un̲dugowwó*.

උඳුන, *Un̲duna*, *s.* oven; kiln.

උඳුපියලි, *Un̲dupiyali*, *s.* medicinal plant, *Desmodium* or *hedysarum*, *(Leguminosæ)*; of which there are many species in Ceylon.

උඳුරු, *Un̲duru*, see උන්දුර *undura*.

උඳුවප් මස, *Un̲duwap masa*, *s.* part of the months of December and January.

උන්, *Un*, *pron.* they, a form generally used when speaking of low classes and animals.

උන්ගේ, *Ungé*, *pron.* their, of them.

උන්ට, *Unṭa*, *pron.* to them.

උන්දුර, *Undura*,
උන්දුරයා, *Undurayá*, } *s.* rat.

උන්නාන්සේ, *Unnánsé*, *pron.* third pers. sing. he (respectfully); *s.* buddhist priest, pl. උන්නාන් සේලා *unnánsélá*.

උන්මත්, *Unmat*,
උන්මද්, *Unmad*, } *a.* insane, mad, frantic; drunk, intoxicated; *s.* name of the plant datura, or thorn apple, of which there are several species and which name is given to them on account of their deleterious properties.

උන්මාද, *Unmáda*, *s.* madness, insanity, extravagance.

උන්මීලන, *Unmílana*, *s.* winking, twinkling the eye.

උන්මීලනය කරණවා, *Unmílanaya karaṇawá*, *v.* to open the eyes.

උන්මුඛ, *Unmukha*, *s.* looking upwards, literally the face up.

උන්මූලිත, *Unmúlita*, *part.* eradicated, plucked up by the roots.

උන්වහන්සේ, *Unwahansé*, *pron.* third pers. sing. applied to God, to kings, and to persons of high rank.

උන්හිස, *Unhisa*, *s.* (more correctly, උණ්හිස *uṇhisa*) crown; cloth wrapped round the head.

උනකිලිල, *Unakilila*, *s.* shoot or tender part of the bamboo.

උනගහ, *Unagaha*, *s.* bamboo tree, pl. උනගස් *unagas*; see උණ *uṇa*.

උනඟ, *Unaṉga*, *s.* name of Ananga the Indian Cupid.

උනන්දුව, *Unanduwa*, *s.* awakening.

උනන්දුවෙනවා, *Unanduwenawá*, *v.* to awake, to get up, to lift up the head after sleep; to delay, to be agitated, to be confused.

උනනවා, *Unanawá*, *v.* to spring as water, to loosen as a string: pret. ඉනුවා *inuwá*.

උනපුපුළුවා, *Unapupuluwá*, *s.* loris.

උනම්බර, *Unambara*, *s.* (උන deficient, අම්බර *ambara* clothing) naked ascetic.

උනලි, *Unalí*, *s.* kind of bamboo.

උනහපුළුවා, *Unahapuḷuwá*, *s.* the loris, kind of monkey, loris gracilis.

උනා, *Uná*, *v.* incorrectly for වුනා *wuná*; pret. of වෙනවා *wenawá*, to be.

උනාදමනවා, *Unádamanawá*, *v.* to loose, to untie, to let loose.

උනු, *Unu*, *a.* (incorrect form of උණු *uṇu*) hot, warm; *s.* earring; decrease.

උනුනු, *Ununu*, *s.* plant, *Pygeum Wightianum (Rosaceæ)*.

උනුහුම, *Unuhuma*, } *s.* warmth, heat.
උනුහුම්, *Unuhum*, }

උප්පත, *Uppata*, *s.* leaf of betel. [Colloq. බුලත් *bulat*].

උප්පල, *Uppala*, *s.* lotus.

උප්පාද, *Uppáda*. *s.* birth, nativity.

උප්පැන්නවෙනවා, *Uppennawenawá*, *v.* to be born.

උප, *Upa*, particle and prefix to verbs, implying excess, over, above; near, by the side of, together with; inferiority, secondary, lower; likeness, resemblance; disease, extinction; ornament; command; reproof; astonishment; giving; diffusion; wish, desire; effort, exertion.

උපක්‍රම, *Upakrama*, *s.* (උප over, ක්‍රම to go) stratagem, overreaching; deliberate commencement or undertaking; providing means and anticipating consequences; beginning in general; valour; trying the fidelity of a friend.

උපක්ලේශය, *Upakleṣaya*, *s.* sinful thought.

උපක්‍රෝශය, *Upakróṣaya*, *s.* censure, reproach.

උපකරණ, *Upakaraṇa*, *s.* implements, materials, means; provisions for a journey; insignia of royalty.

උපකාර්‍ය, *Upakárya*, *a.* deserving assistance or favour.

උපකාරකරණවා, *Upakárakaraṇawá*, *v.* to help, assist, favour.

උපකාරය, *Upakáraya*, *s.* help, assistance, favour, protection, in Sanskrit authors it sometimes means a flower full blown.

උපගත, *Upagata*, *a.* (උප with, ගත gone) come to; promised, agreed.

උපගම, *Upagama*, *s.* approach, approximation; promise, agreement.

උපඝාත, *Upagháta*, *s.* (උප much, ඝාත injuring) touch, contact, especially with an intent to injure; sickness, disease.

උපචර, *Upachara*, see උපචාර *upachára*.

උපචරිත, *Upacharita*, *a.* served, ministered to.

උපචාර, *Upachára*, *s.* (උප well or near, චර *chara* to go) being or living near to; practice, profession, usage, service, assistance; present, bribe; practice of physic; ellipsis.

උපචිත, *Upachita*, *a.* (උප and චිත collected) collected, assembled.

උපජාත, *Upajáta*, *a.* born, brought forth.

උපජිව්හ, *Upajiwha*, *s.* (උප likeness or privation, ජිව්හා tongue) uvula or soft palate; kind of insect; disease, enlargement of the uvula.

උපත, *Upata*, *s.* birth, origin, source.

උපතාප, *Upatápa*, *s.* (උප and තාප heat) burning, heat, heatedness; haste, hurry, disease, sickness.

උපද්දනවා, *Upaddanawá*, *v.* to cause, to produce: pret. ඉපැද්දුවා *ipedduwá*.

උපද්‍රව, *Upadrawa*, *s.* portent, omen, natural phenomenon; danger, risk.

උපද්‍රවය, *Upadrawaya*, *s.* danger, misfortune.

උපදංශය, *Upadanṣaya*, *s.* (උප much, දංශ biting) relish, something to produce an appetite; the venereal disease.

උපදන්, *Upadan*, *s.* pillow. [Colloq. කොට්ටය *koṭṭaya*].

උපදවනවා, *Upadawanawá*, *v.* to produce, to cause: pret, ඉපැද්දුවා *ipedduwá*.

උපදිනවා, *Upadinawá*, *v.* to be produced, to be born, to arise, to originate: pret. ඉපදුනා *ipaduná* or උපන්නා *upanná*.

උපදේශ, *Upadesa*, *s.* advice, instruction, information; stratagem; meat: pl. උපදේස් *upades*.

උපධාන, *Upadhána*, *s.* pillow, kindness, affection; poison; religious observance.

උපධි, *Upadhi*, *s.* fraud, circumvention.

උපන්, *Upan*, *part.* born.

උපන්ලපය, *Upan-lapaya*, *s.* wart, spot, mole or freckle with which a man is born.

උපන, *Upana*, see උපන් *upan*.

උපනගර, *Upanagara*, *s.* suburb, city or town of a secondary class.

උපනයන, *Upanayana*, } *s.* custom of investing the
උපනාය, *Upanáya*, } Brahmins with the cord as the insignia of their office, according to their respective age and rank.

උපනිධි, *Upanidhi*, *s.* deposit, pledge, property put into the care of a friend.

උපනිශ්‍රය, *Upaniṣraya*, *s.* happiness, fortune.

උපනිශ්‍රිත, *Upaniṣrita*, *a.* with, united, joined.

උපනිෂද්, *Upanishad*, s. portion of the religious writings of the Hindús: *i. e.* the theological part and the védanta or argumentative part of the Védas.

උපනිසින්න, *Upanisinna*, a. sat, seated.

උපපති, *Upapati*, s. paramour, gallant.

උපභොග, *Upabhoga*, s. pleasure, satisfaction, enjoyment; wealth, things used for comfort such as furniture.

උපමා, *Upamá*, } s. (උප like, මා to measure)
උපමාන, *Upamána*, } likeness, resemblance as a
උපමාව, *Upamáwa*, } picture, an image etc., parable, simile.

උපයනවා, *Upayanawá*, v. to amass, as money or wealth, to collect, to procure, to earn.

උපයාචිත, *Upayáchita*, a. (උප much, යාචිත to ask or beg) offered, especially to the deities to render them propitious.

උපරක්ත, *Uparakta*, s. (උප implying distress, රක්ත to colour) afflicting with pain or calamity; eclipse of sun or moon; Ráhu, the ascending node.

උපරති, *Uparati*, } a. stopping, ceasing.
උපරම, *Uparama*, }

උපරාග, *Uparága*, see උපරක්ත *uparakta*.

උපරාජ, *Uparája*, s. viceroy.

උපරාම, *Uparáma*, see උපරති *uparati*.

උපල, *Upala*, see උපුල *upula*.

උපලක්ෂණ, *Upalakshaṇa*, s. synecdoche of a part for a whole or of quality for that in which it resides; the characteristic mark by which any thing is distinguished, as සැරදේ නුවන්මිණි පඬුරෙන් *seradé nuwanmiṇi paṇḍuren*, Sidatsangará; live long in the possession of gifts of eye-gems, *i. e.* admired by the world.

උපලක්ෂිත, *Upalakshita*, a. (උප near, ලක්ෂ *laksha* mark, and ක්ත *kta* affix) endued with, contained or inherent.

උපලබ්ධි, *Upalabdhi*, s. (උප and ලභ *labha* to receive) gain, acquisition; mind, understanding, knowledge, especially religious.

උපලිප්ත, *Upalipta*, a. (උප and ලිප *lipa* to smear, ක්ත aff.) smeared, daubed, anointed.

උපවධූ, *Upawadhu*, s. concubine.

උපවන, *Upawana*, s. (උප like, වන wood) kind of garden, grove, wilderness bordering a village.

උපවාද, *Upawáda*, s. abuse. [Colloq. බැණීම් *beṇíma*].

උපවාස, *Upawása*, s. fast, fasting on stated days.

උපශම, *Upaṣama*, see උපශමණය *upasamaṇaya*.

උපස්තම්භ, *Upastambha*, s. service rendered to persons of respectability, support of life.

උපස්ථානය, *Upasthánaya*, s. standing by; rite of hospitality.

උපස්ථායකයා, *Upastháyakayá*, s. attendant, servant, one employed to serve a person of great respectablility.

උපසංක්‍රමණ, *Upasaṇkramaṇa*, s. (උප near, සංක්‍රමණ to go) approaching, going to.

උපසම්පදා, *Upasampadá*, s. (උප again, සම්පද gain) acquirement of office or emolument; order of a Buddhist priest who has passed his novitiate, highest order of Buddhist priests.

උපසම්පදාව, *Upasampadáwa*, s. the admission of a Buddhist priest to the full privileges of the priesthood.

උපසම්පන්න, *Upasampanna*, p. a. perfected, immolated, sacrificed as a victim; attained to.

උපසමණය, *Upasamaṇaya*, s. tranquility, calmness, patience.

උපසර්ග, *Upasarga*, s. (උප near or with, සෘජ *srija* to go) portent, omen, indication of future evil; particle prefixed to roots; preposition.

උපශාන්ත, *Upasánta*, a. very tranquil, very peaceful.

උපසිත්, *Upasit*, s. medicinal plant, *hoya hirsuta.*

උපශොභිත, *Upasobhita*, a. (උප very, ශොභිත beautiful) extremely beautiful, very suitable.

උපහරණ, *Upaharaṇa*, s. illustration. See උදාහරණය *udáharaṇaya.*

උපහසිත, *Upahasita*, s. laughter, laughing.

උපහාර, *Upahára*, s. complimentary gift, present to a superior.

උපහැරණය, *Upaheraṇaya*, s. explanation.

උපාද්‍ය, *Upádya*, s. spiritual preceptor or teacher.

උපාදාන, *Upádána*, s. (උප and ආදාන *ádána* to take) abstraction, restraining the organ of sense or perception; cause, motive; proximate or immediate cause.

උපාධ්‍යාය, *Upádhyáya*, } s. spiritual precep-
උපාධ්‍යායයා, *Upádhyáyayá*, } tor.

උපාධි, *Upádhi*, s. virtuous reflection, great powers of discrimination; respectability.

උපාමාරු, *Upámáru*, s. deception, deceit, disguise.

උපාය, *Upáya*, s. means of success against an enemy: four are usually enumerated; viz. sowing discord, chastisement, conciliation and gifts; an expedient or stratagem.

උපායන, *Upáyana, s.* present, respectful or complimentary gift.

උපායාස, *Upáyása, s.* mental sorrow, great distress of mind. [Colloq. ශෝකය *sókaya*].

උපාලි, *Upáli, s.* name of the compiler and arranger of the Vinaya or the sacred code of the Buddhist priesthood.

උපාසක, *Upásaka, s.* worshipping, serving.

උපාසකයා, *Upásakayá, s.* (උප near, ආස *ása* to be and ක *ka* affix) one devoted to religious exercises, strict Buddhist, lay devotee.

උපාසිකාව, *Upásikáwa, s.* female devotee, see උපාසකයා *upásakayá*.

උපුටනවා, *Upuṭanawá,* } *v.* to pluck, to pluck up,
උපුරණවා, *Upuraṇawá* } to pluck out, to root up:

උපුල්, *Upul, s.* lotus; stone.

උපුල් කොල, *Upul-kola, s.* leaves of the water lilies; plant, *costus speciosus.*

උපුල්වන්, *Upulwan, s,* (උපුල් and වන් colour, blue) name of Vishṇu, from his colour.

උපුල්වනවා, *Upulwanawá, v.* to raise, to lift up.

උපුල, *Upula, s.* piece of stone.

උපෙක්ෂා, *Upekshá, s.* middle state, mediocrity; trick, deceit; indifference.

උපෙත, *Upeta, part.* having, being.

උපෙන්ද්‍ර, *Upendra, s.* name of Vishṇu.

උබ්බෙරිය, *Ubbériya, s.* name of a tree, *Carallia calycina (Rhizophoraceæ.)*

උභය, *Ubhaya, pron.* both.

උභයකුල, *Ubhayakula, s.* (උභය and කුල progeny) both from father and mother, *i. e.* progeny or race coming in equal lines from both parents.

උඹ, *Umba, pron.* you, addressed familiarly to equals or inferiors.

උම්මග්ග, *Ummagga, s.* subterraneous passage.

උම්මාද, *Ummáda, s.* madness; *a.* foolish, silly.

උමග, *Umaga,* see උම්මග්ග *ummagga.*

උමතු, *Umatu, s.* plant, *stramonium*; epilepsy, *a.* foolish, insane.

උමංකනිනවා, *Umankaninawá,* } *v.* to enter a
උමන්කනිනවා, *Umankaninawá,* } house by a hole made in the wall, to break into a house, to rob.

උමන්ලිය, *Umanlíya, s.* stick used as rafter, etc.

උමයංගනා, *Umayanganá, s.* name of the goddess Párvatí or Durgá.

උමා, *Umá, s.* see උමයංගනා *umayanganá* which is sometimes written උමාදේවි *umádévi*; a wave.

උමාකත, *Umákata,* } *s.* name of the goddess
උමාදේවි, *Umádévi,* } Párvatí or Durgá.

උමාපති, *Umápati, s.* (උමා and පති lord, husband) name of Ṣiva, as the husband of Párvatí.

උමාසුත, *Umásuta, s.* name of Kártikéya usually called Kataragama-deviyo.

උමුටු, *Umuṭu, s.* chameleon.

උයන්ගොව්වා, *Uyangowwá,* } *s.* gardener, pl. උ
උයන්පාලයා, *Uyanpálayá,* } යන්ගොව්වෝ *uyangowwó.*

උයන්නා, *Uyanná, s.* cook.

උයන, *Uyana. s.* royal garden; garden, pl. උයන් *uyan.*

උයනගේ, *Uyanagé, s.* kitchen.

උයනවා, *Uyanawá, v.* to dress provisions, to cook: pret. ඉව්වා *iwwá.*

උයමන, *Uyamana, s.* cooking, pl. උයමන් *uyaman.*

උයල, *Uyala, s.* tuberous plant, kind of yam, *Dioscorea tomentosa (Dioscoraceæ).*

උර, *Ura, s.* heart; mind, shoulder, bosom, snake.

උරඉස, *Ura-isa, s.* tip of the shoulder, pl. උරඉස් *ura-is.*

උරඟප්‍රිය, *Urangapriya, s.* sandal wood.

උරඟයා, *Urangayá, s.* snake, serpent. [Colloq. සර්පයා *sarpayá*].

උරග, *Uraga, s.* snake.

උරගල, *Uragala, s.* touch stone for trying gold and other precious metals, pl. උරගල් *uragal.*

උරගානවා, *Uragánawá, v.* to prove the quality of metals by the touch-stone.

උරච්චිකරණවා, *Urachchikaraṇawá, v.* to rub, to polish by rubbing, to rub so as to extract or ascertain the quality of anything.

උරචක්‍රමාලා, *Urachakramálá, s.* (උර neck, චක්‍ර discus, මාලා garland) discus worn as a punishment in one of the infernal regions; it appears to the victim like a splendid necklace, but when he has put it on it cuts him to pieces by its circular motion.

උරණ, *Uraṇa, s.* anger, wrath; species of the cassia.

උරණවා, *Uraṇawá, v.* to imbibe, to suck in, to absorb, to smell, to snuffle: pret. ඉරුවා *iruwá.*

උරණවෙනවා, *Uraṇawenawá, v.* to be angry.

උරද, *Uradá, s.* son, legitimate son.

උරප්පුව, *Urappuwa, a.* haughty; *s.* haughty man.

උරපත්, *Urapat, s.* (උර belly, පත් what goes) snake.

උරපිය, *Urapiya, s.* sandal wood.

උරබාහුව, *Urabáhuwa, s.* (උර breast, බාහුව arm) disease in the arm and shoulder, rheumatism.

උරමාව, *Uramáwa*, s. turban.

උරය, *Uraya*, s. shoulder; pillow-case.

උරරුපු, *Urarupu*, s. (උර snake, රුපු an enemy) garuḍa, the bird of Vishṇu.

උරශ්ඡද, *Uraṣchhada*, s. (උරස් breast, ඡද what covers) armour, mail.

උරස්, *Uras*, s. breast, bosom.

උරස්‍ය, *Urasya*, s. legitimate son or daughter, *i. e.* one born from a married couple of the same tribe or caste.

උරසැද, *Uraṣḍa*, see උරශ්ඡද *uraṣchhada*.

උරහර, *Urahara*, s. (උර snake, හර necklace) necklace reaching down the breast; name of Ṣiva; race of imaginary birds possessing supernatural powers.

උරහිස, *Urahisa*. s. (උර shoulder, හිස head) shoulder blade.

උරා, *Urá*, s. snake, serpent.

උරාබොනවා, *Urábonawá*, v. to drink with great avidity, to suck: pret. උරාබිව්වා *urábiwwá*.

උරිඳු, *Urindu*, s snake. [Colloq. සර්පයා *sarpayá*.]

උරිඳු යහන්, *Urindu yahan*, s. (උරිඳු snake, යහන් who rides) Vishṇu.

උරිරු, *Uriru*, s. blood.

උරිරුපා, *Urirupá*, s. Rákshasa, demon.

උරු, *Uru*, a. large, great.

උරුළි, *Uruli*, ad. truly, verily.

උරුපු, *Urupu*, } s. castor oil plant, *ricinus*
උරුබුක, *Urubuka*, } *communis*. [Colloq. එඬරු *endaru*.]

උරුම, *Uruma*, s. possession, estate, hereditary property, inheritance.

උරුමක්කාරයා, *Urumakkárayá*, s. heir, inheritor.

උරුමකරණවා, *Urumakaraṇawá*, v. to inherit.

උරුලෑවා, *Urulẹwá*, s. sort of wild cat, lesser civet cat, *Viverra malaccensis*.

උරුලෑසත්තම, *Urulẹsattama*, s. musk, procured from the musk rat.

උරෙහිදා, *Urehidá*, s. one born legitimately.

උල්කටුව, *Ulkaṭuwa*, s. stilus, iron pen used by the natives with which they write or engrave their books and manuscripts on the talipot leaf.

උල්කරණවා, *Ulkaraṇawá*, v. to make anything pointed.

උල්කා, *Ulká*, s. (උෂ *usha* to burn, ල *la* sub. for ෂ *sha* and ක *ka* aff) firebrand; meteor, flame.

උල්කාතරුව, *Ulkátaruwa*, } s. (උල්කා flame, පාත
උල්කාපාත, *Ulkápáta*, } which falls) fire falling from heaven, meteor; fire-brand.

උල්පට්ටු, *Ulpaṭṭu*, a. public. [Colloq. ප්‍රසිද්ධ *prasiddha*].

උල්පත, *Ulpata*, s. spring of water; fountain, pl. උල්පත් *ulpat*.

උල් මැස්සා, *Ul-mẹssá*, s. kind of fly with a long pointed beak.

උල්ලංඝ, *Ullangha*, s. (උල් up or beyond, ලඝ *lagha* to go) going beyond, transgressing, leaping, bounding or springing over.

උල්ලෝගං, *Ullógaṇ*, s. the thrush.

උල, *Ula*, s. point of a dart or any sharp instrument; spike, stake, pl. උල් *ul*.

උලඟි, *Ulangi*, s. rising, ascending.

උලතියනවා, *Ulatiyanawá*, v. to impale a person.

උලනවා, *Ulanawá*, v. to rub, to touch: pret. ඉලුවා *iluwá*.

උලමා, *Ulamá*, s. devil bird. pl. උලමෝ *ulamó*.

උලරු, *Ularu*, a. large, great.

උලලිහිණියා, *Ulalihiṇiyá*, s. kind of stork.

උලාර, *Ulára*, a. great; famed; liberal.

උලූක, *Ulúka*, s. owl. [Colloq. බකමූනා *bakamúná*.]

උලෙල, *Ulela*, s. whirling in the water, festival.

උලොල, *Ulola*, s. waves.

උලෑඟි, *Ulẹngí*, s. rising.

උව, *Uwa*, s. bow: a prefix, near.

උවට, *Uwaṭa*, } see උපස්ථාන *upasthána*.
උවටැන්, *Uwaṭẹn*, }

උවතඹ, *Uwatamba*, see උපස්තම්භ *upasthambha*.

උවදුර, *Uwadura*, s. portent, danger, pestilence, pl. උවදුරු *uwaduru*.

උවන, *Uwana*, s. face. pl. උවන් *uwan*. [Colloq. මුහුණ *muhuna*.]

උවම, *Uwama*, s. comparison, simile. See උපමාව *upamáwa*.

උවමනා, *Uwamaná*, a. suitable, proper, fit, consistent, necessary.

උවරණ, *Uwaraṇa*, see උපකරණ *upakaraṇa*.

උවස, *Uwasa*, s. affection, regard. [Colloq. ප්‍රේමය *prémaya*.]

උවසර, *Uwasara*, s. assistance; see උපචාර *upachára*.

උවසු, *Uwasu*, see උපාසකයා *upásakayá*.

උවාරණ, *Uwáraṇa*, see උපකරණ *upakaraṇa*.

උවිඳු, *Uvindu*, s. name of Vishṇu; Elu form of the Sanskrit word උපෙන්ද්‍ර *upendra*.

උවිඳුකත, *Urindukata*, s. wife of Vishṇu, Lakshmí.

උවිඳුබෑ, *Urindubẹ́*, s. elder brother of Vishṇu, Balaráma.

උවිඳුසුත, *Urindusuta*, *s.* (උවිඳු Vishṇu, සුත son) name of Anaṅga.

උවැටන්, *Uweṭan*, see උපස්ථාන *upasthána.*

උෂ්ණ, *Ushṇa*, *s.* heat, warmth; hot season.

උෂ්ණීෂ, *Ushṇísha*, *s.* turban, diadem.

උස්, *Us*, *a.* high, elevated.

උස්මුරුතාවි, *Usmurutáwa*, *s.* sickness, swelling of the belly from indigestion.

උස්‍ර, *Usra*, *s.* ray of light. [Colloq. රශ්මිය *rẹsmiya.*]

උස්සනවා, *Ussanawá*, *v.* to lift up, to raise, to elevate: pret. ඉස්සුවා *issuwá.*

උස්සහ, *Ussaha*, *s.* labour, exertion, diligence.

උස්සා, *Ussá*, *s.* kite, hawk; pl. උස්සෝ *ussó.*

උස්සාහය, *Ussáhaya*, see උස්සහ *ussaha.*

උස, *Usa*, *s.* height, eminence, exaltation. see උස් *us*; *a.* high, tall.

උසබ, *Usaba*, *s.* an ox; in composition, best, excellent, from ඍෂභ *ṛishabha.*

උසවය, *Usawaya*, *s.* eminent or chief person.

උසස්, *Usas*, *a.* high, elevated.

උසසුන්, *Usasun*, *s.* throne, high seat.

උසා, *Usá*, *s.* labour, exertion; from උත්සාහ *utsáha.*

උසායනි, *Usáyaní*, *s.* night.

උසාවි, *Usári*, *s.* contrivance, plot, disguise, deception, stratagem.

උසාවිය, *Usáriya*, *s.* court of justice.

උසි, *Usi*, *s.* inciting, urging as dogs etc. to the chase.

උසිගන්වනවා, *Usiganwanawá*, *v.* to set on, to incite as a dog, to instigate.

උසිත්, *Usit*, *s.* labour, endeavour, exertion.

උසුකාර, *Usukára*, *s.* maker of arrows.

උසුලනවා, *Usulanawá*, } *v.* to bear up, to
උසුලාගන්නවා, *Usulágannawá*, } carry, to support, to be long-suffering: pret. ඉසුලුවා *isuluwá.*

උසුවනවා, *Usuwanawá*, *v.* to lift up, raise, elevate.

උසොලි, *Usoli*, *s.* exertion, effort.

උහ, *Uha*, *a.* high, lofty, applied only to things. *s.* height.

උහල්ලා, *Uhallá*, *s.* tall man, pl. උහල්ලෝ *uhalló.*

උහාගන්නවා, *Uhágannawá*, *v.* to lift up, to raise

උහාදමනවා, *Uhádamanawá*, *v.* to push off, to shove.

උහු, *Uhu*, *pron.* him, his: pl. they.

උළිඳු, *Uḷindu*, *s.* (උළු *uḷu* star, ඉඳු *indu* lord) moon. [Colloq. හඳ *handa.*]

උළු, *Uḷu*, *s.* star: tiles such as are used for covering houses.

උළුඅස්ස, *Uḷuassa*, see උළුවස්ස *uḷuwassa.*

උළුක්කරණවා, *Uḷukkaraṇawá*, *v.* to menace.

උළුක්කුව, *Uḷukkuwa*, *s.* disjointing, dislocation, sprain.

උළුකැටය, *Uḷukeṭaya*, *s.* tile.

උළුකැන්, *Uḷukẹn*, *s.* congee or gruel.

උළුඳු, *Uḷundu*, see උඳු *undu.*

උළුප්පනවා, *Uḷuppanawá*, *v.* to hollow out, to scoop: pret. ඉළිප්පුවා *ilippuwá.*

උළු රජ, *Uḷu-raja*, *s.* (උළු stars, රජ king) moon. [Colloq. හඳ *handa.*]

උළු වඩුවා, *Uḷu-waḍuwá*, *s.* (උළු tiles, වඩුවා workman) bricklayer, mason.

උළුවස්ස, *Uḷuwassa*, *s.* door frame, pl. උළුවහු *uḷuwahu.*

උළුවහාල්, *Uḷuwahál*, } *s.* small grain or seed used
උළුවා, *Uḷuwá*, } by natives to put in to their curries; condiment.

උළුසුන්, *Uḷusun*, *s.* brick dust.

උළුහාල්, *Uḷuhál*, see උළුවහාල් *uḷuwahál.*

උළුළු, *Uḷuḷu*, *s.* tree, *Machilus glaucescens (Lauraceæ).*

ඌ

The sixth vowel of the alphabet: it is sounded like *u* in rule.

ඌ, *Ú*, *pron.* he, (disrespectful) applied to inferiors or animals.

ඌදුවෙනවා, *Úduwenawá*, *v.* to swell, to become large or bloated.

ඌන, *Úna*, *a.* short, deficient, less.

ඌනත්වය, *Únatwaya*, *s.* want, deficiency.

ඌමයා, *Úmaya*, *s.* mute, dumb or silent person.

ඌර්ණ, *Úrṇa*, } *s.* circle of hair between
ඌර්ණරෝම, *Úrṇaróma*, } the eye-brows considered as a token of greatness.

ඌර්ධ්ව, *Úrdhwa*, *a.* high, above, upper, uppermost.

ඌර්ධ්වකාය, *Úrdhwakáya*, *s.* part from the waist upwards.

ඌර්ධ්වශ්වාස, *Úrdhwaṣwása*, *s.* (ඌර්ධ්ව *úrdhwa* up, ශ්වාස breathing) difficulty of breathing; rattling in the throat which precedes death.

ඌර්ධ්වාග්‍ර, *Úrdhwágra*, *a.* (ඌර්ධ්ව *úrdhwa* and අග්‍ර *agra* point) top-end.

ඌර්වශී *Úrwaṣí*, } *s.* nymph of Swarga, goddess.
ඌර්වසී, *Úrwasí*, }

ඌරල, *Úrala*, *s.* plant said to be *cyclamen indicum*, kind of yam, hog's meat.

ඌරා, *Úrá*, *s.* hog, pl. ඌරෝ *úró.*

ඌරකැටය, *Úrákeṭaya*, *s.* circle of burnt clay used in forming the inside of a well.

ඌරු, *Úru*, *a.* big, large; *s.* the thigh.

ඌරුකනු, *Úrukanu*, *s.* *Lasianthera apicalis (Olacineæ).*

ඌරුගෙඳ, *Úrugeṇda*, *s.* kind of herbs, *Portulaca tuberosa.*

ඌරුතෝර, *Úrutóra*, *s.* name of plant, *Cassia Sophera (Leguminosæ).*

ඌරුමියා, *Úrumiyá*, *s.* rat of large size; *Mus giganteus;* bandicoot.

ඌරුමුව, *Úrumuwa*, *s.* (ඌරු large, මුව mouth) owl.

ඌරුයුග, *Úruyuga*, *s.* two thighs.

ඌරුව, *Úruwa*, *s.* thigh; barren ground, sand.

ඌරු වී, *Úru-wí*, *s.* wild paddy, *Oryza sativa. (Gram.)*

ඌරුවෙනවා, *Úruwenawá*, *v.* to spoil, to become bad.

ඌලාව, *Úláwa*, *s.* a fish.

ඌලියක්කාරයා, *Úliyakkárayá*, *s.* palanquin bearer.

ඌලියම, *Úliyama*, *s.* work or service of carrying palanquins; compulsory labour to which strangers are liable; perfunctory discharge of duties, (Colloquial use).

ඌලූක, *Úlúka*, *s.* owl.

ඌලෑවා, *Úlẹwá*, see ඌලාව *úláwa.*

ඌෂ්ණ, *Úshṇa*, *s.* heat, ray; corrupt form of උෂ්ණ *ushṇa.*

ඌෂ්ණ රෝගය, *Úshṇarógaya*, } *s.* venereal disease,
ඌෂ්ණ වාතය, *Úshṇawátaya*, } gonorrhea.

ඌහා, *Úhá*, *s.* reasoning; completing a defective sentence or verse, supplying an ellipsis.

ඍ

A vowel-consonant, the sound of which is in Sanskrit=*ṛi* in English, which sound is retained in some Sanskrit words, naturalized in the Siṇhalese language, while in others it is=*ru.*

ඍ, *Ṛi*, sometimes *ru.*

ඍක්, *Ṛik*, *s.* the Rig Véda.

ඍජු, *Ṛiju*, *a.* straight; metaphorically upright, just.

ඍණ, *Ṛiṇa*, *s.* debt; fort, strong hold.

ඍතු, *Ṛitu*, *s.* season, Siṇhalese divide the year into six seasons each consisting of two months; the menstrual evacuation.

ඍතුමතී, *Ṛitumatí*, *s.* woman during her menstruation.

ඍතුව, *Ṛituwa*, see ඍතු *ṛitu.*

ඍද්ධි, *Ṛiddhi*, *s.* wealth, possession, property; superhuman power of flying in the air.

ඍද්ධිමත්, *Ṛiddhimat.* rich, prosperous, endowed with superhuman power.

ඍෂභ, *Ṛishabha*, *s.* one of the eight chief medicaments of the Indians; bull; *a.* excellent, best.

ඍෂි, *Ṛishi*, *s.* general name for a saint or holy person; but the name is usually applied to seven ancient sages, who in Hindu mythology hold an exalted and mysterious rank, and in astronomy form the asterism of the great bear.

ඎ

ඎ, *Ṛí*, *s.* The long sound of the vowel-consonant ඍ *ṛi* which see.

එ

The seventh vowel of the alphabet, sounds as *a* in hay, or *e* in men; in composition it is written before the consonant after which it is pronounced as කෙ *ke*, මෙ *me.*

එ, *E*, *pron.* he, that (spoken of before).

එක්, *Ek*, *a.* one (indefinitely).

එක්ක, *Ekka*, *prep.* together with, united to.

එක්කරණවා, *Ekkaraṇawá*. *v.* to join, to unite, to collect, to put together.

එක්කලා, *Ekkala*, *ad.* certainly, truly, verily.

එක්කළ, *Ekkaḷa*, *v.* added, joined.

එක්කාසු, *Ekkásu*, *part.* united, collected, gathered together, assembled with.

එක්කාසුකරණවා, *Ekkásukaraṇawá*, *v.* to assemble, to collect, to gather, to join, to put together.

එක්කෙලිපිට, *Ekkelipiṭa*, *prep.* over against, opposite.

එක්කොම, *Ekkoma*, *s.* all, the whole.

එක්කෝ, *Ekkó*, *conj.* either, or.

එක්තරා, *Ektará*, *pron.* one, certain person, applied only to persons.

එක්තල, *Ektala*, *s.* drum beaten only on one end; harmony, unison.

එක්දත්, *Ekdat*, *s.* name of Gaṇa Deviyo the Hindu god of wisdom.

එක්බිජු, *Ekbiju*, *s.* karaṇda tree, *galedupa arborea;* see කරඳ *karaṇda.*

එක්ව, *Ekwa*, *part.* united, collected, gathered, assembled with.

එක්වන්, *Ekwan*, *ad.* always, continually, unremittingly.

එක්වැණි, *Ekweni*, *a.* alone, solitary.

එක්සත්, *Eksat*, *s.* (එක *eka* one, සත් umbrella) universal rule or government.

එක්හෙලි, *Ekheli*, *a.* open, exposed, uncovered.

එක, *Eka*, *a.* one, best.

එකඑකා, *Ekaeká*, *pron.* every one, one by one.

එකක්, *Ekak*, *s.* one thing.

එකකු, *Ekaku*, *s.* person, (acc or gen).

එකඟ, *Ekanga*, *a.* united, peaceful. acquiescing, cementing, amicable.

එකඟකම, *Ekangakama*, } *s.* unity, agreeableness,
එකඟය, *Ekangaya*, } agreement, unanimity.

එකණෙහි, *Ekanehi*, *ad.* at that instant, then, immediately, instantly.

එකත්, *Ekat*, *ad.* (එක one, අත් *at* side) on one side.

එකත්පස්ව, *Ekatpaswa*, } *ad.* (එකත් and පස
එකත්පසෙක, *Ekatpaseka*, } *pasa* side) on one side, on the same side, aside, standing on one side out of respect to a person.

එකතාත්තුව, *Ekatáttuwa*, *s.* harmony in singing or chanting continually.

එකතාල, *Ekatála*, *s.* (එක one, තාල musical measure or tune) harmony, unison, the accurate adjustment of song and dance.

එකතාලෙටම, *Ekatáletama*, *ad.* harmoniously, in a regular train, continually, without intermission.

එකතුකරණවා, *Ekatukaranawá*, *v.* to unite, to join together, to assemble, collect, combine.

එකතුකාරයා, *Ekatukárayá*, *s.* ally, partner.

එකතුව, *Ekatuwa*, *p.* being united.

එකද, *Ekada*, *a.* one, even one.

එකදෙහ, *Ekadeha*, *s.* (එක best, දෙහ body) one of elegant form; the planet Mercury.

එකනින්නාද, *Ekaninnáda*, *s.* (එක one, නින්නාද loud noise) one continued noise, blast.

එකනෙහිම, *Ekanehima*, see එකණෙහි *ekanehi*.

එක පමණ, *Eka-pamana*, *a.* (එක and පමණ size) of the same size, quantity etc., equal.

එකබඳු, *Ekabandu*, *a.* like, similar.

එකම, *Ekama*, *a.* one, one only, alone.

එකමුතු, *Ekamutu*, *a.* collected, gathered, assembled; friendly, united, agreeable.

එකල්, *Ekal*, }
එකල්හි, *Ekalhi*, } *ad.* then, when, at that time.
එකල, *Ekala*, }

එකලස්, *Ekalas*, *a.* collected, gathered, arranged, numbered.

එකලාව, *Ekaláwa*, *a.* alone, solitary.

එකස්, *Ekas*, *a.* (එක one, අස *asa* corner or shoulder) on one side, over one shoulder etc.

එකස්බෙර, *Ekasbera*, *s.* (එකස් one side, බෙර drum) timbrel, tympanum.

එකසත්, *Ekasat*, *a.* (එක one, සත් or ඡත්‍ර *chhatra* umbrella, used here metaphorically for government) under one government, under the same sovereign, unanimous.

එකසමාන, *Ekasamána*, *a.* like, equal, similar.

එකහෙලා, *Ekahelá*, *ad.* at once, all together.

එකා, *Eká*, *pron.* one person, one man or animal, (mas.)

එකාකාර, *Ekákára*, *a.* alike, similar.

එකාවේරිය, *Ekáwériya*, *s.* plant, *Rauwolfia Serpentina (Apocynaceæ)*.

එකාවැල, *Ekáwela*, *s.* necklace of pearls, beads, flowers etc.

එකිඑකින්, *Ekiekin*, *ad.* one by one.

එකින්එක, *Ekineka*, } *ad.* one by one, each one.
එකින්එකා, *Ekineká*, }

එකී, *Ekí*, *pron.* that woman (not respectful); part. aforesaid.

එකුන්, *Ekun*, *a.* less one, one under (as එකුන් සියය *ekun siyaya*, literally one hundred less one, *i. e.* ninety nine).

එකුරුතුපට, *Ekurutupata*, *s.* (එකුරුතු and පට fold) end of the cloth folded and fastened at the waist as a pocket.

එකෙණෙහි, *Ekenehi*, *ad.* at that time, immediately, forthwith.

එකොළහ, *Ekolaha*, *s.* eleven.

එකොළොස්වෙනි, *Ekolosweni*, *a.* eleventh.

එගොඩ, *Egoda*, *s.* other side, as of a river, lake etc.

එච්චර, *Echchara*, *ad.* so much.

එට්ටුව, *Ettuwa*, *s.* loss, risk.

එඬරු, *Endaru*, *s.* castor oil plant, *ricinus communis (Euphorb)*: see එරඬු *Erandu*.

එඬරුතෙල්, *Endarutel*, *s.* castor oil.

එඬේරා, *Endérá*, *s.* herdsman, shepherd, keeper, එඬේරු *Endéru*.

එඩි, *Edi*, *s.* pride, arrogance.

එතකල්, *Etakal*, *ad.* until, till then.

එතකින්, *Etakin*, *ad.* so much, that much.

එතකුදුරුවත්, *Etakudu-uwat*, *conj.* but, however.

එතකොට, *Etakota*, *conj.* then.

එතන, *Etana*, *ad.* there, in that place.

එතනා, *Etaná*, *s.* a term of respect applied to females; as Mrs. etc., in English; used chiefly among Kandyans.

එතනිං, *Etaniṅ*, } *ad.* from thence.
එතනින්, *Etanin*,

එතර, *Etara*, *s.* other side of a river or lake etc; *adv.* beyond.

එතුම, *Etuma*, *s.* involution, wrapping up; he, (respectful term).

එතෙක්, *Etek*, *s.* conclusion, end, finishing; *ad.* till then.

එතෙකින්, *Etekin*, *ad.* by so much.

එතෙම, *Etema*, *pron.* he; sometimes written හෙතෙම *hetema*.

එතෙර, *Etera*, see එතර *etara*.

එදා, *Edá*, *ad.* that day, the other day.

එදිනෙදාට, *Edinedáṭa*, *ad.* day by day.

එදිරි, *Ediri*, *a.* inimical, adverse, against.

එදිරිකාරයා, *Edirikárayá*, *s.* enemy, adversary, opponent.

එදිරිපිට, *Ediripiṭa*, *prep.* before, sometimes written ඉදිරිපිට *idiripiṭa*.

එදිරිපිරිමහනවා, *Ediripirimahanawá*, *v.* to revenge: pret. එදිරිපිරිමැහුවා *ediripirimẹhuwá*.

එදිරිය, *Ediriya*, *s.* aversion, enmity, opposition.

එදිරිවාදු, *Ediriwádu*, *s.* malice, envy.

එන්සාල්, *Ensál*, *s.* Ceylon cardamoms, *elettaria cardamomum (Scitamineæ).*

එනවා, *Enawá*, *v.* to come; pret. ආවා *áwá*.

එපමණ, *Epamaṇa*, *ad.* about, so much.

එපා, *Epá*, *ad.* particle of prohibition, don't want, used after the infinitive mood to form an imperative: as මරන්ට එපා *maranṭa epá*, do not kill.

එපිට, *Epiṭa*, *ad.* distant, far, at a distance.

එබඳු, *Eba̲ndu*, *a.* such, like that.

එබව, *Ebawa*, *s.* that fact.

එබිකන්, *Ebikan*, *s.* peeping, sly look.

එබිකන්කරණවා, *Ebikankaraṇawá*, } *v.* to peep.
එබි බලනවා, *Ebí-balanawá*,

එබුම, *Ebuma*, *s.* pressure; see ඔබනවා *obanawá*,

එබූපිය, *Ebúpiya*, *s.* stamped foot mark.

එබෙනවා, *Ebenawá*, *v.* to peep into, to look in a sly unperceived manner: pret. එබුනා *ebuná*.

එබැවින්, *Ebẹvin*, *conj.* then, therefore.

එම්බල, *Embala*, *s.* interjection of calling, oh! ah!

එම්බා, *Embá*, *interj*, O! oh! woe!

එම, *Ema*, *pron.* same.

එමට, *Emaṭa*, *adv.* much, abundantly.

එමසඳ, *Emasa̲nda*, *s.* same time.

එමෙන්, *Emen*, *ad.* so, thus, in that way or manner.

එයට, *Eyaṭa*, *pron.* dative sing. neut; to that.

එයා, *Eyá*, *pron.* he, that person, (not very respectful.)

එයාවර, *Eyáwara*, *ad.* then.

එයින්, *Eyin*, *ad.* from that, from those, thence.

එයින්පසු, *Eyinpasu*, *ad.* from that time, since.

එරඬු, *Era̲ndu*, *s.* castor oil plant, see එඬරු *e̲ndaru*.

එරබදු, *Erabadu*, *s.* coral tree, *erythrina indica*, *(Legum).*

එරමිණියා, *Eraminiyá*, *s.* plant, the fruit of which is about the size of a pepper corn and is eaten when ripe, *zizyphus napeca (Rhamnaceæ).*

එරවණ, *Erawaṇa*, *s.* Elu form of Sanskrit ඓරාවණ *airáwaṇa*, the elephant of Indra or Ṣakra.

එරවනවා, *Erawanawá*, *v.* to cause to sink in the ground, to fill the udders with milk.

එරහැඬි, *Erahẹ̲ndi*, } *s.* tree, *cathartocarpus fistula.*
එරහැන්ද, *Erahẹnda*,

එරවැටෙනවා, *Eráwẹṭenawá*, *v.* to sink in the mud.

එරිස්සලය, *Erissalaya*, *s.* ill humour, peevishness.

එරෙණවා, *Ereṇawá*, *v.* to sink in the mud, to fill the udder with milk: pret. එරුණා *eruṇá*.

එරෙහිය, *Erehiya*, *s.* anger, wrath.

එල්බැද්ද, *Elbẹdda*, *s.* plant, *Meliosma Wightii (Sabiaceæ).*

එල්ලනවා, *Ellanawá*, *v.* to hang, to suspend.

එල්ලවනවා, *Ellawanawá*, *v.* to cause to be hung, to cause to be suspended.

එල්ලුන්ගහ, *Ellungaha*, *s.* gallows, the erection on which criminals are hung, pl. එල්ලුන්ගස් *ellungas*.

එල්ලෙනවා, *Ellenawá*, *v. a.* to be hanged, to be suspended.

එල්වීම, *Elvíma*, *s.* hanging.

එල, *Ela*, *a.* white; *s.* goat.

එල ඉඹුල්, *Ela-imbul*, *s.* tree, *cochlospermum gossypium (Bixineæ).*

එල ඔලිඳ, *Ela-olinda*, *s.* species of the *abrus* or wild liquorice.

එල කටරොළු, *Ela-kaṭaroḷu*, *s.* medicinal plant, *clitoria ternatea.* See නිල් කටරොළු *nilkaṭaroḷu.*

එලකරණවා, *Elakaraṇawá*, *v.* to bleach, to make white.

එලකිරි, *Elakiri*, *s.* cow's milk, in contradistinction to buffalo's milk.

එලඟිතෙල්, *Ela̲ngitel*, } *s.* cow's butter, in contradistinction to buffalo's butter.
එල ගිතෙල් *Ela-gitel*,

එල ගොකටු, *Ela-gokaṭu*, *s.* tree, *Gaiunia spicata. (Guttiferœ).*

එලදදකිරිය, *Eladadakiriya*, *s.* plant, *Euphhorbia parviflora. (Euphorbiaceœ.)*

එලදෙන්, *Eladen*, *s.* cow, pl. එලදෙන්නු *eladennu.*

එලනවා, *Elanawá*, *v.* to throw down, to cause to fall, to spread: pret. එලුවා *eluwá.*

එල නුග, *Ela-nuga*, *s.* large tree, *Ficus Tsiela.*

එල නෙටුල්, *Ela-neṭul*, *s.* medicinal plant, *plumbago zeylanica (Plumbagineœ).*

එලපනේ, *Elapané*, *s.* the tender part of trees next under the bark.

එලබටු, *Elabaṭu*, *s.* species of night shade, *Solanum Xanthocarpum (Solanaceœ).*

එලඹි, *Elambi*, *s.* arrival, approach.

එලඹෙනවා, *Elambenawá*, *v.* to come, to approach, to come near to: pret. එලඹුනා *elambuná.*

එලමල්, *Elamal*, *s.* flowering plant, *Hedychium coronarium (Scitamineœ).*

එල මිදෙල්ල, *Ela-midella*, *s.* tree, resembling the oak, *Barringtonia acutangula (Myrtaceœ).*

එල රත්මල්, *Ela-ratmal*, *s.* plant, *Knexia zeylanica, (Rubiaceœ).*

එලලනවා, *Elalanawá*, *v.* to darn, to repair, to mend with the needle: pret එලලුවා *elaluwá.*

එල ලූනු, *Ela-luhunu*, *s.* white onions.

එලවරා, *Ela-wará*, see හෙලවරා *helawará.*

එලවලු, *Elawalu*, *s.* vegetables.

එලවුරා, *Elawurá*, *a.* (එල white, වු aff. රා red) light red, pink.

එලවෙනවා, *Elawenawá*, *v.* to drive, to cause to run away, to pursue: pret. එලෙව්වා *elewwá.*

එල වෙවැල්, *Ela-wéwęl*, *s.* kind of rattan, *Calamus Roxburghii (Palmœ).*

එලවොලු, *Elawolu*, see එලවලු *elawalu.*

එලවැල්, *Elawęl*, *s.* kind of ratan, *Calamus rivalis (Palmœ).*

එලහන්, *Elahan*, *prep.* near.

එලහරකා, *Elaharaká*, *s.* ox, cattle, in contradistinction to the buffalo.

එලළු, *Elaḷu*, *s.* complexion, a fair complexion, light red, brown.

එලාදමනවා, *Eládamanawá*, *v.* to put down, to subdue: pret. එලාදැම්මා *eládęmmá.*

එලි, *Eli*, *a.* public, open; plural of එලිය *eliya*, a light.

එලිකරණවා, *Elikaraṇawá*, *v.* to clear the ground from jungle.

එලිදරව්, *Elidaraw*, *a.* published, made known.

එලිපත, *Elipata*, *s.* threshold.

එලිපාන, *Elipána*, *s.* day light.

එලිමහන, *Elimahana*, *s.* open plain.

එලිය, *Eliya*, *s.* light; open space or plain.

එලිලි, *Elilí*, *a.* light red, copper coloured.

එලිවෙනවා, *Eliwenawá*, *v.* to dawn, to become light.

එලෙනවා, *Elenawá*, *v.* to twist round, to entwine; to be fatigued.

එලෙස, *Elesa*, *ad.* so, in that manner.

එලොව, *Elowa*, *s.* other world, future world, futurity, a future state of being.

එව්, *Ew*, *adv.* as, like: come.

එවක්, *Ewak*, *ad.* that time, then.

එවක්පටන්, *Ewakpaṭan*, *ad.* from that time.

එවකට, *Ewakaṭa*, *ad.* then, at that time.

එවනවා, *Ewanawá*, *v.* to send: pret. එවුවා *ewuwá.*

එවර, *Ewara*, *s.* then, at that time, at that day.

එවලෙම, *Ewalema*, *ad.* immediately, instantly.

එවිගස, *Ewigasa*, *ad.* immediatly, forthwith.

එව්චර, *Ewichara*, *ad.* so much.

එවිට, *Ewiṭa*, *ad.* then, on that occasion, at that time.

එවිතර, *Ewitara*, *ad.* so much.

එවු, *Ewu*, see එව් *ew.*

එවෙනි, *Eweni*, *a.* like that, such.

එවේලාව, *Ewéláwa*, } *ad.* then in that time.
එවේලෙහි, *Ewélehi*, }

එවැනි, *Ewęni*, see එවෙනි *eweni.*

එසඳ, *Esanda*, } *ad.* then, at that time.
එසමයෙහි, *Esamayehi*, }

එසවීම, *Esavíma*, *v.* noun of ඔසවනවා *osawanawá.*

එසවු, *Esawu*, see එසෙවු *esewu.*

එසළු, *Esaḷu*, *s.* ascending, elevation.

එසෙත්, *Eset*, *conj.* but, though.

එසෙයින්, *Eseyin*, *conj.* in that manner.

එසෙවු, *Esewu*, *s.* rise, ascent, a rising; *a.* raised, such.

එසේ, *Esé*, *ad.* so, in that manner.

එසේඋවත්, *Eséuwat*, *ad.* although, nevertheless.

එසේනුමුත්, *Esénumut*, *ad.* nevertheless, notwithstanding.

එසේම, *Eséma*, *ad.* in that very manner.

එසේය, *Eséya*, *ad.* yes.

එසේවිනුමුත්, *Esévínumut*, *ad.* yet, although.

එසේහෙයින්, *Eséheyin*, *conj.* therefore.

එහා, *Ehá*, *prep.* there, in that place: *sec: pers: sing:* you; pl. එහාලා *ehálá.* [Colloq. තමුසේ *tamusé.*]

එහි, *Ehi, prep.* there, in it.
එහෙත් *Ehet, conj.* but, though, although.
එහෙනම්, *Ehenam, ad.* then, in that case.
එහෙනුමුත්, *Ehenumut, conj.* but, nevertheless.
එහෙම, *Ehema, ad.* so, in that manner, in that way.
එහෙමපිටින්, *Ehemapiṭin, ad.* wholly.
එහෙයි, *Eheyi, ad.* yes. (honorific form.)
එහෙයින්, *Eheyin, conj.* therefore, by that.
එහේ, *Ehé, ad.* there.
එළු, *Eḷu, s.* species of cassia; goat; sheep, see එළුවා *eḷuvá.*
එළු එඬේරා, *Eḷu eṇḍérá, s.* shepherd, goatherd, pl. එළු එඬේරු *eḷu eṇḍéru.*
එළු ගජ, *Eḷu-gaja, s.* one of the names of the cassia: see තුවර *tuvara.*
එළුදෙන, *Eḷudena, s.* ewe, she goat, pl. එළුදෙන්නු *eḷudennu.*
එළු පට්ටිය, *Eḷu-paṭṭiya, s.* watch-house.
එළුපාලයා, *Eḷupálayá, s.* shepherd.
එළුරැස, *Eḷureṣa, s.* (එළු goat, රැස sign) sign Aries.
එළුව, *Eḷuva, s.* the ancient Sinhalese language.
එළුවා, *Eḷuvá, s.* goat.
එළුසන්, *Elusan, s.* to cry like a goat; in the Kandian provinces this word is used to mean whistling.

ඒ

The eleventh vowel of the alphabet: it sounds like *a* in made.

ඒ, *É, pron.* that or those.
ඒක්ෂණයෙන්, *Ekshaṇayen, ad.* in an instant.
ඒක, *Éka, a.* alone, solitary; other, different; chief, pre-eminent; *pron.* that thing.
ඒකාංස, *Ékaṅsa, s.* (ඒක one, අංස *aṅsa* shoulder) having one shoulder.
ඒකඝන, *Ékaghana, a,* cemented, made strong.
ඒකච්ඡත්‍ර, *Ékachchhatra,* see එකසත් *ekasat.*
ඒකචාරී, *Ékachári, s.* (ඒක alone, චර *chara* which goes) one going alone.
ඒකජ්වාල, *Ékajjwála, s.* flame.
ඒකතාල, *Ékatála, s.* harmony, unison.
ඒකදන්ත, *Ékadanta, s.* (ඒක one, දන්ත tooth) name of Ganésa who lost one of his tusks in a scuffle with Kártikéya.
ඒකදෙහ, *Ékadeha,* see එකදෙහ *ekadeha.*
ඒකපක්ෂ, *Ékapaksha, s.* (ඒක and පක්ෂ side) one of the same side or party, ally, associate, partizan.
ඒකස්වරූප, *Ékaswarúpa, a.* of the same manner, like form.
ඒකා, *Éká, pron.* he, that fellow.
ඒකාංග, *Ékáṅga, s.* (ඒක excellent, අංග *aṅga* body) name of the planet Mercury.
ඒකාක්ෂි, *Ékákshi. s.* (ඒක one, අක්ෂි *akshi* eye) the one eyed one, crow.
ඒකාකාර, *Ékákára, a.* like, equal, of the same kind, similar.
ඒකාග්‍ර, *Ékágra, a.* closely attentive, intent, the mind bent on one object.
ඒකාන්ත, *Ékánta,* / ඒකාන්තයෙන්ම, *Ékántayenma,* } *ad.* verily, truly, indeed.
ඒකාබද්ධ, *Ékábaddha, s.* (ඒක one, ආබද්ධ *ábaddha,* bound to) *a.* joined, united.
ඒකායන, *Ékáyana,* / ඒකායනගත, *Ékáyanagata,* } *s.* (එක *eka* alone, අයන *ayana* road) the way to Nirváṇa, the sole road *(to salvation).* See Childers' Páli Dictionary.
ඒකාවැල, *Ékáwela,* see එකාවැල *ekáwela.*
ඒකාසනික, *Ékásanika, s.* (ඒක one, අසනික *asanika* who eats) religious observance among the Buddhists to eat only once a day; priest.
ඒකාසනිකාංග, *Ékásanikáṅga, s.* (ඒක and ආසන *ásana* seat, ඉක *ika* aff. අඟ *aṅga* and ordinance) an institute of the Buddhist code, enjoining upon the priests always to use the same seat while eating: see තෙළෙස්ධුතාංග *teḷesdhutáṅga.*
ඒකී, *Éki, pron.* fem. she, a term of disrespect; also applied to females of irrational animals.
ඒකේ, *Éké, ad.* there, in that place; in it.
ඒඩ, *Éḍa, a.* deaf.
ඒඩමූක, *Éḍamúka, a.* (ඒඩ and මූක dumb) deaf and dumb; wicked, perverse.
ඒණ, *Éṇa,* / ඒණක, *Éṇaka,* / ඒණී, *Éṇi,* } *s.* (ඉණ *iṇa* to go, ණ aff.) sort of deer or antelope, described as being of a black colour, with beautiful eyes, and short legs.
ඒත්තුගන්නවා, *Éttugannawá, v.* to accept, to approve.
ඒතාක්, *Éták, ad.* so much, till, till then, until.
ඒදණ්ඩ, *Édaṇḍa, s.* plank or beam laid across a river or brook to pass over as a bridge; pl. ඒදඬු *édaṇḍu.*
ඒදනවා, *Édanawá, v.* to prepare or mix a curry, or condiment: pret. ඒදුවා *éduwá.*
ඒධ, *Édha, s.* fuel, as wood, grass, etc.
ඒධිත, *Édhitá, a.* increased, grown.
ඒනම්, *Énam, ad.* that is, that is to say, then, if so.

ඒනිසා, *Énisá, conj.* therefore, on that account.
ඒපමණ, *Épamaṇa, ad.* so much, about.
ඒපවත්, *Épawat,* see එපවත් *epawat.*
ඒපා, *Épá,* see එපා *epá.*
ඒරකඳ, *Érakaṇḍa, s.* pole of a cart or carriage, pl. ඒරකඳන් *érákaṇḍan.*
ඒරකවත්තික, *Érakawattika, s.* a capital punishment, stripping the skin from the neck to the waist, and folding it as a cloth.
ඒරණ්ඩ, *Éraṇḍa,* see එඬරු *eṇḍaru.*
ඒරාකඳ, *Érákaṇḍa, s.* keel of a ship.
ඒරියාකඳ, *Ériyákaṇḍa,* see ඒරකඳ *érakaṇḍa.*
ඒලවාලුක, *Élawáluka, s* (ඒලා *élá* cardamoms, වල to breathe, ක aff.) granular substance apparently vegetable, of a reddish brown colour, and used as a drug or perfume.
ඒලා, *Élá, s.* small cardamoms, *eletaria cardamomum.* [Colloq. එන්සාල් *ensál*].
ඒලාළු, *Éláḷú, s.* species of cucumber, *cucumis madraspatanus.*
ඒ වග, *É-waga, s.* that affair.
ඒවා, *Éwá, pron.* those.
ඒ හැටි, *Éheṭi, s,* that manner.

ඓ

Diphthong: it sounds like *i* in while.

ඓකාගාරික, *Aikágárika, s.* (ඓක *aika* or එක *eka* one, අගාර *agára* house) possessor of one residence.
ඓන්ද්‍රියක, *Aindriyaka, a.* perceptible, perceived; *s.* object of the sense of seeing.
ඓරාවණ, *Airáwaṇa, s.* elephant of Indra.
ඓරාවත, *Airáwata, s.* elephant of the north or Indra's elephant; orange.
ඓරාවතී, *Airáwatí, s.* female of Indra's elephant.
ඓශ්වර්‍ය්‍ය, *Aiṣwarya, s.* (ඊශ්වර *íṣwara* master, a deity, ෂ්‍යන් *shyan* aff.) superhuman power; the divine attributes of omnipresence, omnipotence, invisibility; it may also be used to express supremacy in general; human greatness, such as the power, glory, honour, magnificence and wealth of kings.
ඓශානී, *Aiṣání, s.* quarter of the world so called —north-east.
ඓහ ලෞකික, *Aiha-laukika, s.* (ඉහ *iha* here, ලෞකික wordly) things of this world.

ඔ

The thirteenth vowel of the alphabet: it has nearly the sound of *o* in olive.

ඔක්කාරෙ, *Okkáre, s.* retching at the stomach, vomiting.
ඔක්කොම, *Okkoma, pron.* all, every one.
ඔකඳ, *Okaṇḍa, a.* thick, coagulated; *s.* stream or pillar of light, thickness.
ඔග, *Oga, s.* flood. [Colloq. ගැලීම *geḷíma*].
ඔච්චම, *Ochchama, s.* quizzing, joking, banter, sport, ridicule.
ඔච්චර, *Ochchara, ad.* so much.
ඔජ, *Oja, s.* joy, delight, pleasure, juice flowing from an elephant's temples when in rut; each alternate sign of the zodiac, 1st, 3rd, 5th, etc.
ඔජකරණවා, *Ojakaraṇawá, v.* to allure, to attract.
ඔජරෙ, *Ojare, s.* kind of sickness which causes the swelling of the belly.
ඔජවඩනවා, *Ojawaḍanawá, v.* to overvalue, to make a fuss.
ඔට්ටුකච්චිය, *Oṭṭukachchiya, s.* belt for the waist, girdle.
ඔට්ටුකරණවා, *Oṭṭukaraṇawá, v.* to bet, to wager, to stake a wager.
ඔට්ටුව, *Oṭṭuwa, s.* wager, bet, stake.
ඔට, *Oṭa, s.* the lip, from ඕෂ්ඨ *óshṭha*; regard, affection; plant, *Macaranga digyna, (Euphorb.)*
ඔටු, *Oṭu,* see ඔටුවා *oṭuwá.*
ඔටුන්න, *Oṭunna, s.* crown, diadem; pl. ඔටුනු *oṭunu.*
ඔටුනු පැලඳීම, *Oṭunu-peḷaṇḍíma, s.* coronation.
ඔටුවා, *Oṭuwá, s.* camel.
ඔඩ්ඩිදෙහි, *Oḍḍidehi, s.* lime or lemon of ඔඩ්ඩි country so called.
ඔඩපන, *Oḍapana, s.* pledge, stake.
ඔඩම, *Oḍama, s.* drinking vessel.
ඔඩි, *Oḍi, s.* banner, standard. [Colloq. කොඩිය *koḍiya*].
ඔඩියරුකිම, *Oḍiyarukima, s.* irony, covert praise or censure.
ඔඩුතුලන්, *Oḍutulan, s.* mint, *Mentha javanica* or *M. arvensis (Labiatæ).*
ඔඩුව, *Oḍuwa, s.* something inserted into a boil or cancer.
ඔඩොක්කුව, *Oḍokkuwa, s.* kind of pocket, that is the place in the waist where the natives deposit their betel box and money.
ඔත්, *Ot, a.* reclining, resting.
ඔත්ත, *Otta,* see ඔතු *otu*
ඔත්තු, *Ottu, s.* act of a spy.
ඔත්තුකාරයා, *Ottukárayá, s.* spy, guide to an army, envoy.

ඔත්තුබලනවා, Ottubalanawá, *v.* to watch for an opportunity as a spy.

ඔත්තුව, *Ottuwa*, *s.* information given by a spy.

ඔත්තේ, *Otté*, *a.* odd, uneven.

ඔත, *Ota*, *s.* falsehood, untruth; name of a tree.

ඔතන, *Otana*, *ad.* there (near you).

ඔතනවා, *Otanawá*, *v.* to fold, to lap, to wrap: pret. එතුවා *etuwá*.

ඔතප්, *Otap*, *s.* fear to commit sin, shame.

ඔතු, *Otu*, *s.* tax, tithe, duty; *otu* duty is one tenth of any thing; sing. ඔත්ත *otta*.

ඔතැණි, *Otẹni*, *a.* weak, feeble, emaciated.

ඔද්දල්කරණවා, *Oddalkaraṇawá*, *v.* to hurt, to smash, as a boil or sore.

ඔද, *Oda*, *s.* pride, haughtiness, power, force; nectar; pleasure.

ඔදන, *Odana*, see ඕදන *ódana*.

ඔදබිඳිනවා, *Odabiṇdinawá*, *v.* to humble, to bring down, to break the power of, to weaken: pret. ඔදබින්දා *odabindá*.

ඔඩුතුලන්, *Odutulan*, *s.* kind of mint, *mentha javanica, (Labiatæ)*.

ඔන්චිල්ලාව, *Onchilláwa*, *s.* swing.

ඔන්න, *Onna*, *interj.* of consent; there! 'tis so! even so!

ඔප්, *Op*, *a.* clean, glittering.

ඔප්නගණවා, *Opnagaṇawá*, *v.* to polish, to make bright: pret. ඔප්නැගුවා *opnẹguwá*.

ඔප්පුව, *Oppuwa*, *s.* proof, document, evidence; pl. ඔප්පු *oppu*,

ඔප, *Opa*, see ඔප් *op*.

ඔපේ, *Opé*, see ඔප් *op*.

ඔබ්බ, *Obba*, *ad.* there, off, away.

ඔබ, *Oba*, *ad.* there, yonder; *pron.* you or thou, respectfully.

ඔබනවා, *Obanawá*, *v.* to press, to imprint by pressure.

ඔබමොබ, *Obamoba*, *ad.* here and there, up and down.

ඔබල, *Obala*, } *a.* weak, infirm from age.
ඔබලත්, *Obalat*, }

ඔබවහන්සේ, *Obawahansé*, *pron.* your worship, your honour; thou, (very respectful, applied to God and persons of eminence).

ඔබින, *Obina*, *a.* fit, suitable, worthy, proper.

ඔබිනවා, *Obinawá*, *v.* to be suitable, to become, to be fit.

ඔමරි, *Omari*, *s.* ogling.

ඔය, *Oya*, *s.* rivulet, stream; pl. ඔයවල් *oyawal*. *pron.* that (demonstrative pronoun).

ඔයනවා, *Oyanawá*, *v.* to peel, to strip off the shell or bark.

ඔයා, *Oyá*, } *pron.* that person (familiar and some-
ඔයෑ, *Oyẹ*, } what low); pl. ඔයැලා *oyẹlá*.

ඔරවනවා, *Orawanawá*, *v.* to look fierce, to stare: pret. එරෙව්වා *erewwá*.

ඔරුකහ, *Orukaha*, *s.* the gunwale of a boat, pl. ඔරුකස් *orukas*.

ඔරුව, *Oruwa*, *s.* boat, canoe, pl. ඔරු *oru*.

ඔල්මාද, *Olmáda*, *a.* mad, insane.

ඔල්මාදය, *Olmádaya*, *s.* madness.

ඔල්වරහඬ, *Olwarahaṇḍa*, *s.* loud cry, shout of joy or triumph.

ඔලගම, *Olagama*, *s.* place of refuge or concealment from enemies or disease.

ඔලගුව, *Olaguwa*, *s.* large purse; see ඔලොගුව *ologuwa*.

ඔලයා, *Olayá*, see ඔලෙයියා *oleyiyá*.

ඔලරු, *Olaru*, } *a.* great, large.
ඔලාරි, *Olári*, }

ඔලිඳ වැල්, *Oliṇda-wẹl*, *s.* plant, *abrus precatorius*, wild liquorice.

ඔලි, *Olí*, *s.* caste of tom tom beaters and dancers.

ඔලුපෙත්ත, *Olupetta*, *s.* plant, *Ostodes zeylanica, (Euphorbiaceæ)*: also called වල් කැකුන *walkẹkuna*.

ඔලුව, *Oluwa*, *s.* head.

ඔලෙයියා, *Oleyiyá*, *s.* bird so called; kind of water wag tail.

ඔලොගුව, *Ologuwa*, *s.* two bundles tied and thrown over the shoulder to carry.

ඔව්, *Ow*, *ad.* yes.

ඔවනවා, *Owanawá*. *v.* to pour into, to fill:

ඔවප්, *Owap*, *s.* beam, ray.

ඔවා, *Owá*, *s.* advice.

ඔවිතර, *Ovitara*, *a.* so much.

ඔවිලි, *Ovili*, *s.* palanquin, swing, pain.

ඔවු, *Owu*, see ඔව් *ow*.

ඔවුන්, *Owun*, *pron.* they, (applied only to things animate).

ඔවුනොවුන්, *Owunowun*, *pron.* they, one with another.

ඔවුහු, *Owuhu*, *pron.* they.

ඔස්සේ, *Ossé*, *ad.* along.

ඔසදවටු, *Osadawaṭu*, *s.* druggist.

ඔසන, *Osana*, *s.* perfumes, unguents.

ඔසනවටුවා, *Osanawaṭuwá*, *s.* person who deals in perfumes, perfumer.

ඔසප්, *Osap*, ඔසප, *Osapa*, } *s.* menstrual flux.

ඔසඹිය, *Osambiya*, ඔසබිය, *Osabiya*, } *s.* drug brought from the Himálaya.

ඔසල, *Osala*, *s.* collection, gathering, crowd.

ඔසවනවා, *Osawanawá*, *v.* to raise, to lift up, to elevate: pret. එසෙව්වා *asewwá*.

ඔසු, *Osu*, *s.* medicine.

ඔසුපත්, *Osupat*, *s.* hell so called.

ඔහු, *Ohu*, *pron.* he; they (in ancient writings).

ඔහුන්, *Ohun*, *pron.* see ඔවුන් *owun*.

ඔහුනොහුන්, *Ohunohun*, *pron.* see ඔවුනොවුන් *owunowun*.

ඔහෙ, *Ohe*, *ad.* there.

ඔහොම, *Ohoma*, *ad.* so, in that way or manner.

ඔහොරිය, *Ohoriya*, *s.* kind of female dress, such as is worn by Tamil women.

ඔහෝ, *Ohó*, *interj.* of recollection, aye! oh!

ඕ

The fourteenth letter of the alphabet; it takes the sound of the vowel *o* held long; as in stone.

ඕං, *Ón*, *s.* among the Hindus the mysterious name of the deity, more properly written ඕම් *óm*, which see.

ඕක, *Óka*, *pron.* that; house, asylum, refuge.

ඕකඩ, *Ókaḍa*, *s.* a sheet of water near the sea-shore.

ඕකඳ, *Ókanda*, *s.* the shore or level ground along the banks of a river.

ඕකා, *Óká*, *s.* a person or animal or thing, used in common language, (disrespectful when applied to a person), pl. ඕකාලා *ókálá*.

ඕකාර, *Ókára*, the latter ඕ *ó*.

ඕකී, *Ókí*, *pron.* that woman (disrespectful), pl. ඕකිලා *ókílá*.

ඕකුරු, *Ókuru*, *s.* plant, *Cleidion javanicum*, *(Euphorbiaceæ)*.

ඕකෙයියා, *Ókeyiyá*, *s.* kind of wildpine, *Pandanus zeylanicus*, *(Pandanaceæ)*.

ඕඝ, *Ógha*, *s.* quick time in music; river, flood, stream, torrent, flow of water, multitude.

ඕජස, *Ójasa*, *s.* light, splendour; manifestation, appearance; power; vitality; moisture of the human body or plants. pl. ඕජස් *ójas*.

ඕඩෙ, *Óḍé*, *s.* small lake; water course.

ඕඩ්‍රපුෂ්ප, *Óḍra-pushpa*, *s.* flower, Chinese rose, *Hibiscus mutabilis*; name of a country, the northern part of Orissa.

ඕතෙලියා, *Óteliyá*, *s.* a fish so called.

ඕතොමෝ, *Ótomó*, *pron. fem.* she, respectfully, (used only in books).

ඕදන, *Ódana*, *s.* (උඳ *unda* to be wet, ඤ *nya* aff.) boiled rice.

ඕදස්, *Ódas*, ඕදස, *Ódasa*, ඕදසේ, *Ódasé*, } see ඕජස *ójasa*.

ඕන්, *On*, see ඕම් *óm*.

ඕනා, *Óná*, *part.* pouring into; falling.

ඕනෑ, *Óné*, *ad.* must, ought, want.

ඕනෑකම, *Ónékama*, ඕනෑව, *Ónéwa*, } *s.* need, necessity, want.

ඕපපාතික, *Ópapátika*, *s.* one born by chance; one who appears ready-formed on the earth.

ඕපාදූප, *Ópádúpa*, *s.* insinuation, information, slander, backbiting, detraction.

ඕම්, *Óm*, *s.* mystic name of the Hindu deity; the general opinion is, that it is composed of the following letters: අ *a* name of Vishṇu, උ *u* of Siva, ම *m* of Brahma, which implies the Indian triad, and expresses the three in one. It prefaces most of the writings of the Hindus, and all their prayers. It has the same place in all the books, prayers, charms, and incantations of the Kapuwas, the Yakaduras and the Balikárayas of Ceylon, and in most of the books on astronomy. It is always pronounced with great reverence by the natives in their temples and on all religious occasions: the Hindus are, it is believed, accustomed to pass over the word in silence as the Jews did the word Jehovah.

ඕයි, *Óyi*, *interj.* of calling; as O there, hallo there.

ඕලු, *Ólu*, *s.* species of waterlily, *Nymphæa Lotus*, *(Nymphæaceæ)*; also *Limnanthemum indicum*, *(Gentianaceæ)*.

ඕලුවා, *Óluwá*, *s.* sort of deer; antelope.

ඕවා, *Ówá*, *pron.* those, applied to things.

ඕවිට, *Óvita*, *s.* low ground which may be used for the cultivation of paddy or yams. pl. ඕවිටි *óviṭi*.

ඕවිල්ල, *Óvilla*, *s.* child's swing, cradle; pain.

ඕවිලි, *Óvili*, *plur.* of the above word.

ඕෂ්ඨ, *Óshṭha*, *s.* lip, especially the upper lip.

ඕෂ්ඨජ, *Óshṭhaja*, *s.* (ඕෂ්ඨ and ජ which produces) labial, that which is pronounced by the lip.

ඕෂ්ඨය, *Óshṭhaya*, see ඕෂ්ඨ *óshṭha*.

ඕෂධී, *Óshadhí*, *s.* (ඕෂ heat, ධා *dhá* to have or to bear) star; an annual plant or herb, one that dies after becoming ripe.

ඕසධී තාරකා, *Ósadhí táraká*, s. (ඕසධී medicine, තාරකා star) star that presides over medicine; star that accompanies the moon; morning star.

ඕෂධීශ, *Óshadhíṣa*, s. (ඕෂධී star, ඊශ *iṣa* lord) moon. [Colloq. සඳ *sa̱nda.*]

ඕසේ, *Ósé*, s. protracted sound of the voice after the word or sentence is finished.

ඕහට, *Óhaṭa*, the dative of ඔහු *ohu*, he.

ඖ

The fifteenth letter in the alphabet: it sounds like *ou* in our.

ඖරස, *Aurasa*, s. (උරස් *uras* best and අණ් *aṇ* affix) a legitimate child, *i. e.* a child whose mother is of the same caste as the father.

ඖරුද්ද, *Aurudda*, s. year, see අවුරුද්ද *awurudda*.

ඖෂධ, *Aushadha*, s. drugs, medicine in general.

ඖෂධී, *Aushadhí*, see ඕෂධී *óshadhí*.

ඇ

Not reckoned as a separate letter: it sounds somewhat like *a* in cat, and, when lengthened (ඈ *ẹ́*,) like *a* in jam.

ඇක්ම, *Ẹkma*, s. sixth sign or figure in astronomical reckoning.

ඇක්මෙනවා, *Ẹkmenawá*, v. to be crushed, to be bruized, to be seized: pret. ඇක්මුනා *ẹkmuná*.

ඇක්සුම්, *Ẹksum*, s. curse, imprecation.

ඇක, *Ẹka*, } s. hip, side.
ඇකය, *Ẹkaya*, }

ඇකිල්ල, *Ẹkilla*, s. chain for tying elephants.

ඇකිලෙනවා, *Ẹkilenawá*, v. n. to fold, to close, to shrivel: pret. ඇකුළුනා *ẹkuluná*.

ඇගලදඬුලේනා, *Ẹgaladaṉḍuléná*, s. brown flying squirrel, *pteromys oral*.

ඇගිලිය, *Ẹgiliya*, s. ditch, drain.

ඇගෑව, *Ẹgẹ́wa*, s. festoon work.

ඇඟ, *Ẹ̱nga*, s. body.

ඇඟවීම, *Ẹ̱ngavíma*, } s. information.
ඇඟවුම, *Ẹ̱ngawuma*, }

ඇඟිල්ල, *Ẹ̱ngilla*, s. finger, pl. ඇඟිලි *ẹ̱ngili*.

ඇඟිලිපුරුක, *Ẹ̱ngilipuruka*, s. knuckle.

ඇඟිලිවර, *Ẹ̱ngiliwara*, s. space between the fingers or toes at the bottom.

ඇඟෙනවා, *Ẹ̱ngenawá*. v. to feel; to be convinced; to know; to perceive; to understand, to experience: pret. ඇඟුනා *Ẹ̱nguná*.

ඇජර, *Ẹjara*, s. master, teacher.

ඇට්ටකුනාවෙනවා, *Ẹṭṭakunáwenawá*. v. to be par boiled.

ඇට්ටඹරා, *Ẹṭṭa̱mbará*, s. plant, *solandra oppositifolia.*

ඇට්ටමුරා, *Ẹṭṭamurá*, s. climbing shrub, *cansiera scandens.*

ඇට්ටර, *Ẹṭṭara*, a. hard, obstinate.

ඇට්ටර ගස, *Ẹṭṭara gasa*, s. variety of the *sisu* tree, *dalbergia sisu.*

ඇට්ටරයා, *Ẹṭṭarayá*, s. stubborn man.

ඇට්ටේරිය, *Ẹṭṭériya*, s. small tree, with white fragrant flowers, *murraya exotica (Rutaceæ).*

ඇට, *Ẹṭa*, s. bone, kernel; seed, grain of any thing; hardness.

ඇටකටුගැහෙනවා, *Ẹṭakaṭugẹhenawá*, v. to grow lean, to become a skeleton.

ඇට කිරිඳ්වැල්, *Ẹṭa kiri̱ndawẹl*, s. plant, *strychnos cinnamomifolia, (Loganiaceæ).*

ඇටකිරිල්ල, *Ẹṭakirilla*, s. forest tree, *Turpinia pomifera* or *T. nepalensis (Sapindaceæ);* also called කුන්කුඹලා *kunkumbalá.*

ඇට කුහුඹියා, *Ẹṭa-kuhu̱mbiyá*, s. small ant.

ඇට කෙහෙල්, *Ẹṭa kehel*, s. kind of plaintain or banana, *musa sapientum.*

ඇට ගෙමඩියා, *Ẹṭa gemaḍiyá*. s. kind of toad or frog.

ඇටපන්, *Ẹṭapan*, s. plant, *Lepironia mucronata. (Cyperaceæ).*

ඇටපල, *Ẹṭapala*, s. porcupine.

ඇට බෙලි, *Ẹṭa-beli*, s. tree, *ægle marmelos, (Rutaceæ)* or බෙලි *beli.*

ඇටඹරු, *Ẹṭambaru*, } s. tree, *Fagræa zeylanica*
ඇටඹරු, *Ẹṭa̱mbaru*, } *(Loganiaceæ).*

ඇටඹ, *Ẹṭa̱mba*, s. *mangifera indica* or the common wild mango.

ඇටමදයා, *Ẹṭamadayá*, s. bull.

ඇටමිදුළු, *Ẹṭamidaḷu*, s. marrow.

ඇටමිරිය, *Ẹṭamiriya*, s. plant, *Ericybe Paniculata, (Convolv.).*

ඇටමුල් *Ẹṭamul*, s. (ඇට bone, මුල් root) marrow of the bones.

ඇටමොල, *Ẹṭamola*, see ඇටමිදුළු *ẹṭamidaḷu*.

ඇටමැස්සා, *Ẹṭamẹssá*, s. horse fly, pl. ඇටමැස්සෝ *ẹṭamẹssó*.

ඇටවරා, *Ẹṭawará*, s. river fish so called; also see ඇටෝරා *ẹṭórá*.

ඇටවල්ලා, *Ẹṭawallá*, s. name of a large sea fish.

ඇටවැරැල්ල, *Ẹṭawẹrẹlla*, s. shrub, *dodonæa viscosa, (Sapindaceæ).*

ඇටවැල, *Ẹṭawẹla*, s. necklace, pl. ඇටවැල් *ẹṭawẹl*.

ඇටසැකිල්ල, *Ẹṭasẹkilla*, s. skeleton, pl. ඇටසැකිලි *ẹṭasẹkili*.

ඇටිකිත්තා, *Ėṭikittá*, s. small kind of frog.

ඇටිකුකුලා, *Ėṭikukulá*, s. kind of jungle fowl; red cock.

ඇටිකුල්, *Ėṭikul*, s. Greek partridge.

ඇටිකුලා, *Ėṭikulá*, see ඇටිකුකුලා *ėṭikukulá*.

ඇටුන, *Ėṭuna*, s. plant, *Heritiera littoralis (Sterculiaceæ)*.

ඇටුවන, *Ėṭuwana*, s. holes in the trunk or root of a tree proceeding from decay, pl. ඇටුවන් *ėṭuwan*.

ඇටෝරා, *Ėṭórá*, s. panic grass, *panicum repens*.

ඇඬිම, *Ėnḍíma*, } s. crying, weeping, pl. ඇඬිම් *ėnḍím* or ඇඬුම් *ėnḍum*.
ඇඬුම, *Ėnḍuma*,

ඇත්, *Ėt*, shoulders; elephants, pl. of ඇතා *ėtá*.

ඇත් අඩි, *Ėt-aḍi*, s. plant with hairy leaves chiefly radical, *elephantopus scaber*, *(Compositæ)*.

ඇත් උඳුපියලි, *Ėt unḍupiyali*, s. small plant, food for rabbits, *hedysarum heterocarpon* or *dermodium (Leguminosæ)*.

ඇත් ඕළු, *Ėt óḷu*, s. water lily, *nymphœa*.

ඇත් කටු, *Ėt kaṭu*, s. (ඇතා *ėtá* elephant, කටු prick) an elephant hook.

ඇත්කඳලිහිණියා, *Ėtkanḍalihiṇiyá*, s. kind of eagle fabled to be the destroyer and eater of elephants.

ඇත්කන්, *Ėtkan*, s. plant, *arum macrorhizon*, name of the kėla tree, *butea frondesa*.

ඇත් කුකුරුමාන්, *Ėt kukurumán*, s. plant, *randia uliginosa (Rubiaceæ)*.

ඇත් කොරසවැල්, *Ėt korasawėl*, s. plant, *Petracera lævis (Dilleniaceæ)*.

ඇත්ගොව්වා, *Ėtgowwuwá*, s. elephant keeper.

ඇත්ත, *Ėtta*, s. truth, certainty, fact, that which really is.

ඇත්තණ්ඩල, *Ėttaṇḍala*, s. plant, *arum colocasia*.

ඇත්තා, *Ėttá*, s. possessor, owner, pl. ඇත්තෝ *ėttó* or ඇත්තන් *ėttan*.

ඇත්තාඩිය, *Ėttáḍiya*, s. see ඇත් අඩි *ėt-aḍi*.

ඇත්ති, *Ėttí*, s. female owner, pl. ඇත්තියෝ *ėttó*.

ඇත්තු, *Ėttu*, *pl.* of ඇතා *ėtá*.

ඇත්තුත්තිරි, *Ėttuttiri*, s. kind of grass, *aristida adscensionis*.

ඇත්තො, *Ėtto*, s. people, the natives or residents of a place.

ඇත්තෝර, *Ėt tóra*, s. plant, *Atylosia Candollei (Legum.)*

ඇත් දත, *Ėt data*, s. elephant's tusk, pl. ඇත්දත් *ėtdat*.

ඇත්දන් වැටකොළු, *Ėtdanwėṭakoḷu*, s. plant, *momordica cylindrica*.

ඇත් දම, *Ėt dama*, s. chain for tying elephants.

ඇත් දළ, *Ėt daḷa*, see ඇත් දත *ėt data*.

ඇත් දෙමට, *Ėt demaṭa*, s. timber tree with yellow flowers, *gmelina arborea (Verbenaceæ)*.

ඇත් නෙරෙංචි, *Ėt nerenchi*, s. plant with small stem, long branches and yellow flowers; it renders water or milk mucilaginous, *pedalium murex*, *(Pedaliaceæ)*.

ඇත් පන්තිය, *Ėt pantiya*, s. elephants' stall.

ඇත් පනික්කියා, *Ėt panikkiyá*, s. elephant keeper.

ඇත් පඹ, *Ėt pamba*, s. fern, *Lygodium dichotomum*, *(Filices.)*

ඇත්පල්, *Ėtpal*, s. elephant keeper, pl. ඇත්පල්හු *ėtpalhu*.

ඇත් පිටවක්කා, *Ėt piṭawakká*, s. plant, *Agyneia bacciformis*, *(Euphorb)*.

ඇත් පැටවා, *Ėt pėṭawá*, s. young elephant.

ඇත් බැම්කිරිය, *Ėt bėmikíriya*, s. stemless plant, *phrynium capitatum (Scitamineæ)*.

ඇත්මද, *Ėtmada*, s. a tree, *echites* or *alstima scholaris*.

ඇත්මීවන, *Ėtmíwana*, s. shield-fern, *aspidium arboreum*.

ඇත් මුඩමහන, *Ėt muḍamahana*, s. plant, *sphoeranthus indicus* or මුඩමහන *muḍamahana*.

ඇත්වගපුල්, *Ėtwagapul*, s. climbing plant with an aromatic seed something of the nature of pepper, *pothos officinalis* or පෝටාවැල් *póṭáwėl*.

ඇත්වරණ, *Ėtwaraṇa*, s. (ඇත් *ėt* elephant, වරණ stopping) elephant hook.

ඇත්සොඬ, *Ėtsonḍa*, s. elephant's trunk.

ඇත්සැටිය, *Ėtsėṭiya*, a medicinal plant.

ඇත්හල, *Ėt-hala*, s. elephant's stall.

ඇත් හවරි, *Ėt-hawari*, s. plant, *Psilotum nudum (Lycopodiaceæ)*.

ඇත් හෙරලිය, *Ėt-heraliya*, s. plant, peculiar to Ceylon, *Kurrimia zeylanica (Celastraceæ)*.

ඇත, *Ėta*, *ad.* is it enough, there is.

ඇතම්, *Ėtam*, *a.* some.

ඇතරු, *Ėtarú*, s. (ඇත and රු who mounts) elephant driver.

ඇතා, *Ėtá*, s. elephant, pl. ඇත්තු *ėttu*.

ඇති, *Ėti*, *a.* enough, sufficient, existing; *v.* there is.

ඇතිකරණවා, *Ėtikaraṇawá*, *v.* to bring up, to breed; to adopt; to educate.

ඇතිකළවන, *Ėtikaḷawana*, s. garden, park or pleasure ground.

ඇතින්නි, *Ėtinní*, } s. female elephant, pl. ඇතින්නියෝ *ėtinniyó*.
ඇතිනි, *Ėtini*,

ඇතිරිය, *Ẹtiriya*, see ඇතිරිල්ල, *ẹtirilla*.

ඇතිරිල් පලා, *Ẹtiril palá*, s. plant, *gisekia pharnaceoides, (Ficsideæ)*.

ඇතිරිල්ල, *Ẹtirilla*, s. that which is spread; but generally a piece of cloth spread upon chairs and other seats out of respect to a guest; a sheet, pl. ඇතිරිලි *ẹtirili*.

ඇතිරෙණවා, *Ẹtireṇawá*, v. to be spread: pret. ඇතිරුණ *ẹtiruṇá*.

ඇතිලිය, *Ẹtiliya*, s. large open cooking vessel, pl. ඇතිලි *ẹtili*.

ඇතිවෙනවා, *Ẹtiwenawá*, v. to grow, to spring up as a child, to be brought up, to be satisfied.

ඇතිහැටි කියනවා, *Ẹtihẹti kiyanawá*, v. to confess, to acknowledge.

ඇතු, *Ẹtu*, s. elephant.

ඇතුන්, *Ẹtun*, *plur*. of ඇතු *ẹtu*.

ඇතුම, *Ẹtuma*, s. body with life.

ඇතුල්, *Ẹtul*, ad. inside, inner, within.

ඇතුල්කරණවා, *Ẹtulkaraṇawá*, v. to thrust in.

ඇතුල් නුවර, *Ẹtul nuwara*, s. citadel, the inner-city.

ඇතුල්පුර, *Ẹtulpura*, s. inner city, usually the residence of royalty and courtezans.

ඇතුළ, *Ẹtuḷa*, see ඇතුල් *ẹtul*.

ඇතුළත්, *Ẹtuḷat*, a. belonging to, intimate, connected with, admitted, friendly.

ඇතුළත්වෙනවා, *Ẹtuḷatwenawá*, v. to be admitted, to become intimate.

ඇතුළුව, *Ẹtuḷuwa*, ad. with, including.

ඇතුව, *Ẹtuwa*, *part*. having, with.

ඇතොර, *Ẹtora*, see අන්තඃපුරය *antaḥpuraya*.

ඇද්ද, *Ẹdda*, ad. is it enough? is it?

ඇද්දෙනවා, *Ẹddenawá*, v. to drag or trail itself along the ground, to creep, to crawl.

ඇද, *Ẹda*, a. crooked, bent, unfriendly.

ඇද අරිණවා, *Ẹda-ariṇawá*, v. to make straight, correct.

ඇදගන්නවා, *Ẹdagannawá*, v. to draw, to pull; to attract; to absorb, to convey (as property); to find fault.

ඇදහිල්ල, *Ẹdahilla*, s. faith, belief, religious confidence, pl. ඇදහිලි *ẹdahili*.

ඇදහෙලනවා, *Ẹdahelanawá*, v. to throw down, to drag down with violence.

ඇදිලි, *Ẹdili*, s. putting the palms of the hands together, as the natives do when saluting.

ඇදිම, *Ẹdíma*, s. dragging, attraction; difficulty of breathing.

ඇදුම, *Ẹduma*, s. difficulty in breathing; rattling in the throat as a precursor of death.

ඇදුරා, *Ẹdurá*, } s. expeller of devils, an exorcist;
ඇදුරු, *Ẹduru*, } teacher; messenger; rock, pl. ඇදුරෝ *ẹduró*.

ඇදේ, *Ẹdé*, s. crookedness, bending.

ඇඳ, *Ẹnda*, s. bed, sleeping couch.

ඇඳගන්නවා, *Ẹndagannawá*, v. to put on dress.

ඇඳ මකුණ, *Ẹnda-makuṇá*, s. bug.

ඇඳිනගන්නවා, *Ẹndinagannawá*, v. to obtain knowledge (of persons or things).

ඇඳිනෙනවා, *Ẹndinenawá*, v. to be known, to be come acquainted with: pret. ඇඳිනුනා *ẹndinuná*.

ඇඳිරි, *Ẹndiri*, s. darkness; a. dark, obscure.

ඇඳිම, *Ẹndima*, s. clothes, dress; painting; drawing, pl. ඇඳිම් *ẹndím*.

ඇඳුනුම්වෙනවා, *Ẹndunumwenawá*, v. to know, to be acquainted with.

ඇඳුම, *Ẹnduma*, s. clothes, dress, wearing, pl. ඇඳුම් *ẹndum*.

ඇන්නෑ, *Ẹnnẹ́*, *interj*. expression of anger, mishap, misfortune or sorrow; a. unlawful.

ඇන්නෑව, *Ẹnnẹ́wa*, s. nuisance.

ඇණ, *Ẹna*, s. nail (of iron &c), peg.

ඇණඉන්නවා, *Ẹna-innawá*, v. to squat on the ground.

ඇණගහනවා, *Ẹnagahanawá*, v. to nail.

ඇණවනවා, *Ẹnawanawá*, v. to call.

ඇණිය, *Ẹniya*, s. prow of a dhony or ship.

ඇණීම, *Ẹníma*, } s. kneading, stabbing, pl. ඇණීම්
ඇණුම, *Ẹnuma*, } *ẹním*, ඇණුම් *ẹnum*.

ඇණෙනවා, *Ẹnenawá*, v. to be pierced; to be kneaded: pret. ඇණුනා *ẹnuná*.

ඇණේ, *Ẹné*, s. nail (of iron &c.)

ඇප්, *Ẹp*, Elu *pron*. we.

ඇප, *Ẹpa*, s. security, bail.

ඇපකාරයා, *Ẹpakárayá*, s. surety.

ඇපල, *Ẹpala*, s. plant, *Triumfetta Rhomboidea (Tiliaceæ)*.

ඇපිල්ලීම, *Ẹpillíma*, s. the act of washing, pl. ඇපිල්ලීම් *ẹpillím*.

ඇබ්බැහිවෙනවා, *Ẹbbẹhiwenawá*, v. to become accustomed to, to become acquainted with, to frequent uncourteously.

ඇබය, *Ẹbaya*, s, cork, stopper, plug, prop.

ඇබිත්ත, *Ẹbitta*, s. very little.

ඇබිත්තයා, *Ẹbittayá*, s. the servant of a priest.

ඇබිස්ස, *Ẹbissa*, s. very little quantity.

ඇබිස්සක්, *Ẹbissak*, *s.* short space, little time, very little.

ඇබෙ, *Ẹbé*, see ඇබය *ẹbaya*.

ඇඹරවීම, *Ẹm̲baravíma*, *s.* act of causing to grind, or twist: see අඹරණවා *am̲baraṇawá*.

ඇඹරෙණවා, *Ẹm̲bareṇawá*, *v.* to become twisted or turned, to be ground: pret. ඇඹරුණ *ẹm̲baruṇá*.

ඇඹල, *Ẹm̲bala*, plant, buck bean, *Limnanthemum cristatum* or *L. indicum*: see අඹල *am̲bala*.

ඇඹලයා, *Ẹm̲balayá*, *s.* red ant.

ඇඹිල්ල, *Ẹm̲billa*, *s.* name of plant genus, *antidesma (Euphorbiaceæ)*.

ඇඹුල්, *Ẹm̲bul*, *a.* sour; *s.* sourness, acidity, sour curry of natives; plant, species of the *phyllanthus (Euphorb.)*

ඇඹුල් අනවාළුකෙසෙල්, *Ẹm̲bul ánawáḷukesel*, *s.* wild plaintain tree, *musa paradisiaca* or වල් කෙහෙල් *wal-kehel*.

ඇඹුල් දොඩන්, *Ẹm̲bul doḍan*, *s.* sour variety of the orange tree.

ඇඹුල් පලා, *Ẹm̲bul palá*, *s.* a peculiar curry, made of vegetables; plant, *hedyotis diffusa*.

ඇඹුල් හොනරවාළු, *Ẹm̲bul honarawáḷu*, *s.* variety of the plantain or banana tree, *musa sapientum*,

ඇඹුල, *Ẹm̲bula*, *s.* variety of water lily, *nymphœa*.

ඇඹුළු, *Ẹm̲buḷu*, *s.* plant, species of the *phyllanthus*.

ඇඹුලැඹිලිය, *Ẹm̲bulẹm̲biliya*, *s.* plant, species of the *marsilea*, or දිය ඇඹුල් ඇඹිලිය *diya-ẹmbul ẹm̲biliya*.

ඇම්බරැල්ල, *Ẹmbarẹlla*, *s.* tree, hog-plum, *spondias mangifera*, *(Anacardiaceæ)*.

ඇම්බෙනියා, *Ẹmbeniyá*, *s.* wife; woman.

ඇම්බැට්ටයා, *Ẹmbẹṭṭayá*, *s.* barber.

ඇම්ම, *Ẹmma*, *s.* ache, pain.

ඇම, *Ẹma*, *s.* bait, pl. ඇම් *ẹm*: another form of සෑම *sẹma*, all.

ඇමකල, *Ẹmakala*,
ඇමකලැ, *Ẹmakalẹ*, } *ad.* everlastingly.

ඇමතියා, *Ẹmatiyá*, *s.* minister of state.

ඇමතුම, *Ẹmatuma*, *s.* thought, reflection; calling, invitation, pl. ඇමතුම් *ẹmatum*.

ඇමදීම, *Ẹmadíma*,
ඇමදුම, *Ẹmaduma*, } *s.* sweeping, as with a broom.

ඇමිටිල්ලා, *Ẹmiṭillá*, *s.* kind of small rat, *mus musculus?*

ඇමිනිල්ල, *Ẹminilla*, *s.* stringing (as beads), see අමුනනවා *amunanawá*.

ඇමිනෙනවා, *Ẹminenawá*, *v.* to be caught with a bait, to be stuck in.

ඇමියා, *Ẹmiyá*, *s.* name of a plant, a species of the *dentella*.

ඇමියාව, *Ẹmiyáwa*, *s.* disease in the stomach and bowels, proceeding from indigestion.

ඇයද, *Ẹyada*, *past part*, අයදිනවා *ayadinawá*, to pray.

ඇයි, *Ẹyi*, *interj.* of enquiry, why?

ඇයුම්, *Ẹyum*, *v.* noun of අයනවා *ayanawá*.

ඇර, *Ẹra*, *ad.* besides, except, too, save.

ඇරත්, *Ẹrat*, *ad.* besides, besides that, in addition to what has been said or done.

ඇරඹ, *Ẹram̲ba*, *conj.* for, on account of, instead of, therefore; *s.* beginning.

ඇරයුම්, *Ẹrayum*, *s.* prayer, request.

ඇරලනවා, *Ẹralanawá*, *v.* to conduct, to escort, accompany a person a certain distance on his journey, out of respect: pret. ඇරලුවා *ẹraluwá*.

ඇරිවුන්, *Ẹriwun*, *s.* request.

ඇරීම, *Ẹríma*,
ඇරුම, *Ẹruma*, } *s.* sending, opening or quieting, the verbal noun of අරිණවා *ariṇawá*, which see.

ඇරෙණවා, *Ẹreṇawá*, *v.* to be put away, to be laid aside, to be out of employment: pret. ඇරුණ *ẹruṇá*.

ඇල්, *Ẹl*, *a.* cold, frigid.

ඇල්කරණවා, *Ẹlkaraṇawá*, *v.* to cool, (applied chiefly when cold water is poured into warm).

ඇල් කසාඹිලියා, *Ẹl-kasám̲biliyá*, *s.* a sort of plant, *acalypha*.

ඇල් කෙත, *Ẹl-keta*, *s.* kind of paddy field, *i. e.* ground which has been cleared of jungle, and sown with a particular kind of paddy.

ඇල් ගොවියා, *Ẹl-goviyá*, *s.* cultivator of hill-paddy.

ඇල් පැන්, *Ẹl-pẹn*, *s.* cold water.

ඇල්ම, *Ẹlma*, *s.* love, attachment; slope.

ඇල්මරණවා, *Ẹlmaraṇawá*, *v.* to take off the chill from water, to make water lukewarm, literally to kill the cold, to remove distension of the abdomen.

ඇල්මුවා, *Ẹlmuwá*, *s.* small louse, pl. ඇල්මුවෝ *ẹlmuwó*.

ඇල්මෙලනවා, *Ẹlmélanawá*, *v.* to separate a cow and calf from the flock, to cause the young calf to repose while the mother cow is grazing: pret. ඇල්මෙලැවා *ẹlmélẹwá*.

ඇල්ල, *Ẹlla*, *s.* water fall; rapid.

ඇල් වී, *Ẹl-ví*, *s.* sort of paddy so called.

ඇල, *Ẹla*, *s.* brook, rivulet, channel, canal; *a.* inclined, bent.

ඇලපත, *Ẹlapata*, } *s.* side of the body.
ඇලය, *Ẹlaya*, }

ඇලලනවා, *Ẹlalanawá*, *v.* to open water courses for the irrigation of the paddy or rice fields.

ඇලලීම, *Ẹlalíma*, verbal noun of ඇලලනවා *ẹlalanawá*.

ඇලවනවා, *Ẹlawanawá*, *v.* to stick, to cause to adhere: pret. ඇලෙව්වා *ẹlewwá*.

ඇලවුන්, *Ẹlawun*, *s.* speaking in the presence (from අලපන *álapana*); pillar to which an elephant is tied.

ඇලවෙනවා, *Ẹlawenawá*, *v.* to recline, to lean, to fall on one side.

ඇලි, *Ẹli*, *a.* white.

ඇලි ඇතා, *Ẹli-ẹtá*, *s.* white elephant, pl. ඇලි ඇත්තු *ẹli-ẹttu*.

ඇලික්, *Ẹlik*, *s.* picture.

ඇලිය, *Ẹliya*, *s.* ditch, drain, river; wish, desire.

ඇලි වඳුරා, *Ẹli-wandurá*, *s.* white monkey, *semnapithicus thersites*.

ඇලි සවරම, *Ẹli-sawarama*, *s.* (ඇලි white, සවරම whisk) white whisk.

ඇලීම, *Ẹlíma*, *s.* verbal noun of ඇලෙනවා *ẹlenawá*.

ඇලුන, *Ẹluna*, *a.* adhering, loving.

ඇලුප්, *Ẹlup*, *s.* speech, a word from අලප *álapa*.

ඇලුම්වෙනවා, *Ẹlumwenawá*, *v.* to adhere to, to stick to, to be attached to, to love.

ඇලුම, *Ẹluma*, *s.* desire, longing, attachment.

ඇලෙනවා, *Ẹlenawá*, *v.* to adhere to, to stick to; to be attached to, to love: pret. ඇලුනා *ẹluná*.

ඇලේ, *Ẹlé*, *s.* side of the body.

ඇවත, *Ẹwata*, see ඇවැත්නි *ẹwẹtni*.

ඇවිටි, *Ẹviti*, *a.* teazing, perplexing, vexing, fondling.

ඇවිටියල්, *Ẹvitiyal*, *a.* wild, fierce, not tamed.

ඇවිටිලි, *Ẹvitili*, *s.* perseverance, urgent request. persistency.

ඇවිත්, *Ẹvit*, *part.* having come (from එනවා *enawá*).

ඇවිද්දවනවා, *Ẹviddawanawá*, *v.* to cause to walk: pret. ඇවිද්දෙව්වා *ẹviddewwá*.

ඇවිදිනවා, *Ẹvidinawá*, *v.* to walk: pret. ඇවිද්දා *ẹviddá*.

ඇවිදීම, *Ẹvidíma*, verbal noun of the preceding.

ඇවිදුම, *Ẹviduma*, *s.* journey, walking.

ඇවිනුම්, *Ẹvinum*, s. linking together.

ඇවිරුද්ද, *Ẹviridda*, *s.* year, pl. ඇවිරිදි *ẹviridi*

ඇවිරිලි, *Ẹvirili*, *s.* wall, [Colloq. බිත්තිය *bittiya*].

ඇවිලිල්ල, *Ẹvililla*, } *s.* sharp piercing or shooting
ඇවිලීම, *Ẹvilíma*, } pain, as, a stitch in the side; rheumatism, pl. ඇවිලිලි *ẹvilili*.

ඇවිලෙනවා, *Ẹvilenawá*, *v.* to be affected with rheumatism, to take fire, to catch fire: pret. ඇවිලුනා *ẹviluná*.

ඇවිස්සීම, *Ẹvissíma*, verbal noun of the following word, pl. ඇවිස්සීම් *ẹvissím*.

ඇවිස්සෙනවා, *Ẹvissenawá*, *v.* to become angry, to become roused or stirred up: pret. ඇවිස්සුනා *ẹvissuná*.

ඇවීම, *Ẹvíma*, *s.* cursing, imprecation.

ඇවොම. *Ẹwoma*, *a.* all, the whole.

ඇවැත්, *Ẹwẹt*, *s.* guilt,

ඇවැත්නි, *Ẹwẹtni*, *s.* term of respectful salutation; as when a priest or a person of age is addressed.

ඇවැස්ස, *Ẹwẹssa*, *a.* near, proximate; in relative connection, related either by the father's sister, or mother's brother, direct relation; as ඇවැස්ස මාමා *ẹwẹssa mámá*, uncle, *i. e.* mother's brother.

ඇවෑම, *Ẹwẹ́ma*, } *s.* that which comes next
ඇවෑමෙන්, *Ẹwẹ́men*, } after, in succession, decease, pl. ඇවෑම් *ẹwẹ́m*.

ඇස්, *Ẹs*, *plur.* of ඇස *ẹsa;* also *s.* corner, angle.

ඇස්කුලි, *Ẹskuli*, *s.* reward for restoring or finding lost things, literally the reward of the eyes.

ඇස්ගුල්ලා, *Ẹsgullá*, *s.* snake.

ඇස්ගුලිය, *Ẹsguliya*, *s.* eye-ball.

ඇස් දැල්, *Ẹs-dẹl*, *s.* (ඇස *ẹsa* eye, දැල *dẹla* net, multitude) name of Indra; *a.* having interstices, coarse.

ඇස්පත, *Ẹspata*, *s.* hasp, joint, moveable hinge or fastening, link, that which faces or covers the key hole, pl. ඇස්පත් *ẹspat*.

ඇස්පිය, *Ẹspiya*, *s.* eye lids.

ඇස්පියගහනවා, *Ẹspiyagahanawá*, *v.* to twinkle the eye.

ඇස්පිල්, *Ẹspil*, *s.* (ඇස *ẹsa* eye, පිල *pila* feather) peacock's tail.

ඇස්පිහාට්ට, *Ẹspiháṭṭa*, *s.* (ඇස and පිහාට්ට wing) eyelash, pl. ඇස්පිහාටු *ẹspiháṭu*.

ඇස්පොල, *Ẹspola*, *s.* ophthalmia, cataract.

ඇස්බැන්දුම, *Ẹsbẹnduma*, *s.* juggling, pl. ඇස් බැන්දුම් *ẹsbẹndum*.

ඇස්බැම, *Ẹsbẹma*, *s.* eye brow, pl. ඇස්බැම් *ẹsbẹmi*.

ඇස්මුසු, *Ẹsmusu*, *s.* lamp.

ඇස්වටය, *Ẹswaṭaya*, *s.* ancle bone.

ඇස්වහ, *Ẹswaha, s.* curse supposed to be produced by envious eye, literally eye poison; evil sight.

ඇස්වහගන්නවා, *Ẹswahagannawá, v.* to look with an envious eye.

ඇස, *Ẹsa, s.* eye, tear, from අශ්‍රු *aṣru*, see ඇස් *ẹs.*

ඇසටු, *Ẹsaṭu,* } see ඇහැටු *ẹhẹṭu.*
ඇසතු, *Ẹsatu,* }

ඇසළ, *Ẹsaḷa.* see ඇහැළ *ẹhẹḷa.*

ඇසළ මස, *Ẹsaḷa masa, s.* June-July.

ඇසිකිනි, *Ẹsikiní, s.* pupil of the eye.

ඇසිපිය, *Ẹsipiya, s.* eye lid,

ඇසිරිල්ල, *Ẹsirilla, s.* arrangement, order, pl. ඇසිරිලි *ẹsirili.*

ඇසිරු, *Ẹsiru, a.* joined, connected from ආශ්‍රය *áṣraya*, living with.

ඇසිල්ල, *Ẹsilla, s.* snapping the finger and thumb; twinkling the eyes; instant.

ඇසිල්ලකින්, *Ẹsillakin, ad.* instantly, in the twinkling of an eye.

ඇසීම, *Ẹsíma, s.* hearing, question, pl. ඇසීම් *ẹsím;* verbal noun of අසනවා *asanawá.*

ඇසුන්, *Ẹsun, s.* cursing.

ඇසුම, *Ẹsuma, s.* hearing.

ඇසුරු, *Ẹsuru,* see ඇසිරු *ẹsiru.*

ඇසූ, *Ẹsú, past part.* of අසනවා *asanawá.*

ඇසෙනවා, *Ẹsenawá, v.* to be heard: pret. ඇසුනා *ẹsuná.*

ඇහිඳිනවා, *Ẹhiṇdinawá, v.* to gather up, to pick up, to pick out, to sort as coffee: pret. ඇහින්ද *ẹhindá.*

ඇහිරෙණවා, *Ẹhireṇawá, v.* to assemble, to come together; to become parched.

ඇහීම, *Ẹhíma, s.* hearing, question, verbal noun of අහනවා *ahanawá.*

ඇහුන්කන්දෙනවා, *Ẹhunkandenawá, v,* to hear, to listen attentively.

ඇහුම, *Ẹhuma, s.* hearing, verbal noun of the following.

ඇහෙනවා, *Ẹhenawá, v.* to be heard.

ඇහැ, *Ẹhẹ,* see ඇස් *ẹs.*

ඇහැටු, *Ẹhẹṭu, s.* large tree, *Ficus Tsiela (Urticaceæ).*

ඇහැටුල්ලා, *Ẹhẹṭullá, s.* whip snake, *passerita mycterizans, dryiophidæ* order *ophidia.*

ඇහැමුලා, *Ẹhẹmulá, s.* snake.

ඇහැළ, *Ẹhẹḷa, s,* ornamental and medicinal tree, *Cassia fistula (Leguminosæ).*

ඇහැළ මස, *Ẹhẹḷa masa,* see ඇසළ මස *ẹsaḷa masa.*

ඈ, *Ẹ́, pron,* she, her; *s.* etcetra, Elu form of ආදි *ádi.*

ඈක්, *Ẹ́k, a.* can, possible.

ඈකන්සාව, *Ẹ́kansáwa, s.* induration of the glands of the cheek, mumps.

ඈකි, *Ẹ́kí,* see ඈක් *ẹ́k.*

ඈත්, *Ẹ́t, a.* far, distant; *s.* distance.

ඈත්කරණවා, *Ẹ́tkaraṇawá, v.* to put to a distance.

ඈත්වෙනවා, *Ẹ́twenawá, v.* to be distant.

ඈත, *Ẹ́ta, s.* distance.

ඈනුම, *Ẹ́numa, s.* gaping, yawning, pl. ඈනුම් *ẹ́num;* verbal noun of ආනනවා *ánanawá.*

ඈපොත්ත, *Ẹ́potta, s.* scales of the pangolin.

ඈයා, *Ẹ́yá, s.* pangolin.

ඈලියාව, *Ẹ́liyáwa, s.* disease in which the belly is swelled.

ඈලියාවා, *Ẹ́liyáwá. s.* glutton, a term of reproach, pl. ඈලියාවෝ *ẹ́liyáwó.*

ක

The first consonant of the alphabet and sounds like *k* in kalendar.

කංඨ, *Kaṇtha,* see කණ්ඨ, *kaṇtha.*

කංස, *Kansa, s.* seed, which has lost the power of fructifying; uncle and enemy of Kṛishṇa by whom he was slain; he is generally considered an asur or demon, inhabiting pátála; goblet or drinking vessel; kind of metal called by the natives tuttanágam, *i. e.* white copper; bell metal, or any mixture of zinc and copper.

කංසක, *Kaṇsaka, s.* kind of salt used by the native medical men in mixing some of their medicines.

කංසජිත්, *Kaṇsajit, s.* (කංස and ජිත් who conquers) he that conquered the demon Kaṇsa, *i. e.* Kṛishṇa or Vishṇu.

කංසාරාති, *Kaṇsáráti, s.* (කංස *kaṇsa* and අරාති enemy) the enemy of Kaṇsa, *i. e.* Kṛishṇa or Vishṇu.

කක්කිසය, *Kakkisaya, s.* accident, unpleasant event, troublesome event.

කක්කුස්සිය, *Kakkussiya, s.* necessary, privy, pl. කක්කුස්සි *kakkussi.* (Port.)

කක්කුටු පලා, *Kakkuṭu-palá, s.* water-cress, *Nasturtium officinale, (Cruciferæ).*

කකණ්ටක, *Kakaṇṭaka, s.* lizard.

කකා, *Kaká,* part. of කනවා *kanawa,* eating.

කකාරණවා, *Kakáraṇawá, v.* to stir any boiling liquid with a spoon, to make an infusion or decoction, by boiling etc: pret. කැකෑරුවා *kẹkẹ́ruwá.*

කකියනවා, *Kakiyanawá, v.* to be pained, to ache.

කකියවනවා, *Kakiyawanawá*, *v.* to boil; to cause pain: pret. කැකියෙව්වා *kẹkiyewwá*.

කකිස, *Kakisa*, *a.* fatigued, tired.

කකුධභාණ්ඩය, *Kakudhabháṇḍaya*, *s.* the insignia of royalty.

කකුල් කෙඩෙත්තුව, *Kakul-kedettuwa*, *s.* pain and feebleness in the legs from weariness.

කකුල්ගානවා, *Kakulgánawá*, *v.* to work with the foot: pret. කකුල්ගෑවා *kakulgẹwá*.

කකුල්දඩ, *Kakuldaḍa*, *s.* continual moving, perpetual motion; wandering, vagrancy.

කකුල්දඩයා, *Kakuldaḍayá*, *s.* vagabond.

කකුල, *Kakula*, *s.* foot, calf of the leg, pl. කකුල් *kakul*.

කකුළු රැස, *Kakuḷu-rẹsa*, *s.* fourth sign of the Indian zodiac, Cancer, or the crab.

කකුළුවා, *Kakuḷuwá*, *s.* crab.

කකුළු සුං, *Kakuḷu-suṇ*, *s.* (කකුළු crab, සුං or ශෘඞ්ග *ṣṛiṅga* horn or claw of the crab) a plant, fruit of which is compared to the claw or feeler of a crab.

කගපත, *Kagapata*, *s.* blade of a sword or sabre.

කගමුව, *Kagamuwa*, *s.* edge of the sword; squirrel, unicorn.

කගය, *Kagaya*, *s.* sword.

කගවිස, *Kagavisa*, }
කගවිසණ, *Kagavisaṇa*, } *s.* unicorn.

කඟවේණා, *Kaṅgawẹ́ṇá*, *s.* unicorn, pl. කඟවේන්නු *kaṅgawénnu*.

කඟු, *Kaṅgu*, }
කඞ්ගු, *Kaṅgu*, } *s.* kind of dry grain or millet, which is cultivated as an article of food, *panicum italicum* or *setaria italica*.

කච්චිය, *Kachchiya*, *s.* piece of linen cloth no part of which has been torn off. pl. කච්චි *kachchi*.

කච්ඡප, *Kachchhapa*, *s.* (කච්ඡ armpit, ප which drinks) turtle, tortoise.

කඤ්චන, *Kañchana*. *s.* gold; *a.* golden.

කඤ්චුක, *Kañchuka*, *s.* skin of a snake; armour, mail; bodice or jacket; clothes, dress.

කජ්ජ, *Kajja*, *s.* native cake made with oil, honey and flour, pl. කජ්ජු *kajju;* also a cashew nut.

කජ්ජල, *Kajjala*, *s.* cloud; lamp black, used by the natives as a collyrium, being applied upon the eye brows and eyelashes either as an ornament or medicine.

කජු, *Kaju*, *s.* cashew nut tree, *Anacardium occidentale; (Anaciordiuceæ)*.

කජුපුහුලම, *Kajupuhulama*, *s.* cashew apple, pl. කජුපුහුලම් *kajupuhulam*.

කට්ට, *Kaṭṭa*, *s.* steps cut in wood or stone; detached piece of wood or stone, notch.

කට්ටකුමංචල්, *Kaṭṭakumanchal*, *s.* frankincense.

කට්ට ගහ, *Kaṭṭa-gaha*, *s.* brittle tree.

කට්ටබුද්ධියා, *Kaṭṭabuddhiyá*, *s.* person who misconceives, whose thoughts are crude, shallow fellow.

කට්ටයා, *Kaṭṭayá*, *s.* cheat, rogue; diminutive person.

කට්ටාඩියා, *Kaṭṭádiyá*, *s.* sorcerer, enchanter, magician, expeller of devils, devil priest or dancer.

කට්ටාවා, *Kaṭṭáwá*, *s.* kind of sea fish, pl. කට්ටාවෝ *kaṭṭáwó*.

කට්ටි, *Kaṭṭi*, feminine of කට්ටයා *kaṭṭayá*.

කට්ටිය, *Kaṭṭiya*, *s.* portion of work; pl. කට්ටි *kaṭṭi*.

කට්ටුව, *Kaṭṭuwa*, *s.* bundle, parcel; crowd.

කට, *Kaṭa*, *s.* fuel, throat, corpse; thin piece of wood; plank; mouth.

කටකය, *Kaṭakaya*, }
කටක ලග්නය, *Kaṭaka-lagnaya*, } *s.* fourth sign of the Indian zodiac, Cancer, or the crab.

කටකලියාව, *Kaṭakaliyáwa*, *s.* bit.

කටකලු නයා, *Kaṭakalu-nayá*, *s.* a kind of snake.

කටකලුවා, *Kaṭakaluwá*, *s.* a kind of snake.

කටකොලිය, *Kaṭakoliya*, *s.* spitting vessel.

කටගඳයා, *Kaṭagaṇdayá*, *s.* man with stinking breath.

කටගමුව, *Kaṭagamuwa*, *ad.* up to the mouth.

කටපදන්, *Kaṭapadan*, *ad.* to the mouth, as far as the mouth.

කටපයාදිය, *Kaṭapayádiya*, *s.* a mode of calculation in which figures are represented by letters, thus:

1	2	3	4	5	6	7	8	9	0
ක,	ඛ,	ග,	ඝ,	ඞ,	ච,	ඡ,	ජ,	ඣ,	ඤ,
ට,	ඨ,	ඩ,	ඪ,	ණ,	ත,	ථ,	ද,	ධ,	න,
ප,	ඵ,	බ,	භ,	ම,					
ය,	ර,	ල,	ව,	ශ,	ෂ,	ස,	හ,	ළ,	

and reckoned from right to left. Every letter under each of the above columns represents the respective figure or zero against which the same is placed. Initial vowels and mute consonants are not reckoned. It is permissible to inflect the above numeral consonants with vowels in order to render them euphonious: *e. g.* ගජකුට= 3811 or 1183 reading from right to left.

කටපාඩම, *Kaṭapáḍama*, *s.* lesson committed to memory.

කටපුර, *Kaṭapurá*, *s.* mouthful.

කටබහකාරයා, *Kaṭabahakárayá*, *s.* talkative person.

කටඹරා, *Kaṭambará*, *s.* medicinal plant, *cucumis maderaspatanus.*

කටමිණ, *Kaṭamiṇa*, *a.* neck-jewel.

කටමින්, *Kaṭamin*, see කටමැන් *kaṭamen.*

කටමැතකම, *Kaṭametakama*, *s.* imperious language; egotism.

කටමැන්, *Kaṭamen*, *s.* neck gem of Vishṇu; neck-gem in general. (සහ කටමැණ සපුන්මෙන් *ṣaha kaṭameṇa sapunmen*, Sidatsangará).

කටයුක්ත, *Kaṭayukta*, } *s.* that which is proper to
කටයුත්ත, *Kaṭayutta*, } be done.

කටයුතු, *Kaṭayutu*, *a.* proper, suitable, lawful.

කටරොළු, *Kaṭaroḷu*, *s.* plant; *duriyo zibethinus.*

කටලු කථාව, *Kaṭalu-katháwa*, *s.* fable; story.

කටවහ, *Kaṭawaha*, *s.* evil tongue.

කටවාචාලයා, *Kaṭawáchálayá*, *s.* talkative person.

කටහඬ, *Kaṭahaṇḍa*, *s.* sound of the mouth, used to express a good or sweet voice.

කටා, *Kaṭá*, *s.* elephant's cheek.

කටාක්‍ෂ, *Kaṭáksha*, *s.* leer, glance, side look.

කටාරම, *Kaṭárama*, *s.* vase of stone, or any manufacture of carved stone, caldron, cistern, pl. කටාරම් *kaṭáram.*

කටාහ, *Kaṭáha*, *s.* vessel; shallow vessel for holding oil, butter, &c, turtle shell; hell, infernal regions.

කටි, *Kaṭi*, *s.* hip, buttocks; loins.

කටිගොංගා, *Kaṭigoṇgá*, *s.* a fish.

කටින්බඩින් යනවා, *Kaṭinbaḍin yanawá*, *v.* to be attacked as with the cholera. (vulgar.)

කටින, *Kaṭina*, *a.* difficult; sharp to the taste.

කටිනවා, *Kaṭinawá*, *v.* to spin as thread: pret. කැට්ටා *keṭṭá.*

කටිනෙ, *Kaṭine*, *s.* offering of cloth for a robe made to Buddha or to his priests in the course of a single day and night.

කටිප්‍රදේශ, *Kaṭipradéṣa*, *s.* waist.

කටිය, *Kaṭiya*, see කටි *kaṭi.*

කටිල්ලා, *Kaṭillá*, *s.* a small river fish.

කටිවායුව, *Kaṭiwáyuwa*, *s.* pain in the loins, lumbago.

කටු, *Kaṭu*, *a.* pungent; envious; fierce, impetuous; hot; displeasing, disagreeable; thorny.

කටු අන්දර, *Kaṭu-andara*, *s.* tree, *acacia leucophlœa (Legum.)*; also called මහ අන්දර *maha-andara.*

කටු ඉකිරි, *Kaṭu-ikiri*, *s.* plant, *Hygrophila spinosa (Acanthaceæ).*

කටු ඉකිලි, *Kaṭu-ikili*, *s.* plant, *Acanthus ilicifolius (Acanthaceæ)*; also called ඉකිලි *ikili.*

කටු ඉඹුල්, *Kaṭu-imbul*, *s.* red cotton tree, *bombax malabaricum (Malvaceæ).*

කටු ඉඹුල, *Kaṭu-imbula*, *s.* thorny tree, believed to be in hell.

කටු උණ, *Kaṭu-uṇa*, *s.* spiny bamboo, *bambusa spinosa (Gramineæ).*

කටු ඇඹිල්ල, *Kaṭu-embilla*, *s.* plant, *elæagnus latifolia (Elæagnaceæ).*

කටුක, *Kaṭuka*, *a.* bitter, sharp to the taste, acrid; *s.* plant, the bark and seed of which have an acrid and bitter taste, and used in medicine for worms and dysentery; *echites antidysenterica*; mustard; medicinal compound of three pungent substances, viz. black pepper, long pepper and dried ginger.

කටුකරඬු, *Kaṭukaraṇḍu*, *s.* plant, *barleria prionitis (Acanthaceæ).*

කටුකරඳ, *Kaṭukaraṇda*, *s.* gray bonduc, plant.

කටුකරසය, *Kaṭukarasaya*, *s.* bitter taste, sharp taste.

කටුකරොහිණී, *Kaṭukarohiṇí*, *s.* medicinal plant, used as a sedative and laxative, see කටුරෝහිණී *kaṭuróhiṇí.*

කටුකාලාබු, *Kaṭukálábu*, *s.* bitter gourd.

කටුකිතුල්, *Kaṭu-kitul*, *s.* tree, *Oncosperma fasciculata (Palmæ).*

කටු කිරිඳි, *Kaṭu-kiriṇdi*, *s.* tree, *strychnos recurva.*

කටු කින, *Kaṭu-kína*, *s.* plant, *zanthoxylum tetraspermum (Rutaceæ).*

කටු කිරිය, *Kaṭu-kiriya*, *s.* plant, *alpinia calcarata (Scitamineæ).*

කටු කුකුලල, *Kaṭu-kukulala*, *s.* kind of yam, *dioscorea alata.*

කටු කුරුඳු, *Kaṭu-kuruṇdu*, *s.* prickly plant used for fences, *scolopia crenata (Bixineæ).*

කටුකෙන්ද, *Kaṭukenda*, *s.* see the last word; also name of a timber tree.

කටු කැටකෑල, *Kaṭu-keṭakela*, *s.* tree, *briedelia spinosa.*

කටුගහ, *Kaṭugaha*, *s.* thorn tree.

කටුගානවා, *Kaṭugánawá*, *v.* to blot out, to obliterate, to erase: pret. කටුගෑවා *kaṭugewá.*

කටුගැස්ම, *Kaṭugesma*, *s.* illegible letters, erasure, split.

කටුත්‍රය, *Kaṭutraya*, see කටුරෝහිණී *kaṭuróhiṇí.*

කටු තම්පලා, *Kaṭu-tampalá*, *s.* plant, *amaranthus spinosus (Amarantaceæ).*

කටු තිඹොල්, *Kaṭu-timbol*, *s.* plant, *plecospermum spinosum (Urticaceæ).*

කටුනියද, *Kaṭuniyada*, *s.* plant, *monetia barlerioides.*

කටු නෙළු, *Kaṭu-neḷu*, *s.* plant, *barleria buxifolia (Acanthaceæ).*

කටු පතුක්, *Kaṭu-patuk*, *s.* plant, *opuntia Dillenii (Cactaceæ).*

කටු පඳුර, *Kaṭu-pandura*, *s.* thicket of thorn bushes.

කටු පඹුරු, *Kaṭu-pamburu*, *s.* tree, *scleropyron Wallichianum (Santalaceæ).*

කටුපහණ, *Kaṭupahaṇa*, *s.* gravel, pebbles.

කටුපිල, *Kaṭupila*, *s.* tree, *celastrus emarginatus* staff tree.

කටුපිළිකා, *Kaṭupiḷiká*, *s.* indurated ulcer arising from a wound.

කටුපෙඳ, *Kaṭupenda*, *s.* plant, *caulinia indica.*

කටුපැලැල්ල, *Kaṭupeḷella*, *s.* gate or screen made of thorns, pl. කටුපැලලි *kaṭupeḷali.*

කටුබොඩ, *Kaṭuboḍa*, *s.* tree, wild durian, *cullenia excelsa (Malvaceæ).*

කටුඹරා, *Kaṭumbará*, see කටඹරා *kaṭambará.*

කටුමස්සා, *Kaṭumassá*, *s.* sea and river fish.

කටුමැටි, *Kaṭumeṭi*, *s.* first clay coating of a wall.

කටුරෝහිණී, *Kaṭuróhiní*, *s.* medicinal plant, used as a sedative and laxative, black hellebore.

කටුල්ල, *Kaṭulla*, *s.* sorrow, distress.

කටුලැහැබ, *Kaṭuleheba*, see කටුපඳුර *kaṭupandura.*

කටුව, *Kaṭuwa*, *s.* thorn, any thing with a sharp point, bone, pl. කටු *kaṭu.*

කටුවල්ලා, *Kaṭuwallá*, *s.* garter fish, pl. කටුවල්ලෝ *kaṭuwalló.*

කටුවල, *Kaṭuwala*, *s.* kind of yam, *dioscorea pentaphylla.*

කටුවා, *Kaṭuwá*, *s.* kind of worm.

කටුවාකනවා, *Kaṭuwákanawá*, *v.* to eat by the above named worm, producing leanness etc.

කටුවෙලඟ, *Kaṭuwelanga*, see වෙලඟ *welanga.*

කටුවැල්බටු, *Kaṭuwelbaṭu*, *s.* plant, kind of night shade, used medicinally, *Solanum jacquini (Solanaceæ).*

කටුස්සා, *Kaṭussá*, *s.* chameleon; bloodsucker, pl. කටුස්සෝ *kaṭussó*; name of genus *Calotes.*

කටුසර බෝග, *Kaṭusara-bóga*, *s.* all sorts of grain in general except rice.

කටුසෙවෙල්, *Kaṭusewel*, } *s.* plant, *draxantium*
කටුසෙවෙල, *Kaṭusewela*, } *spinosum.*

කටුසැමිටිය, *Kaṭusemiṭiya*, *s.* (කටු thorn, සැමිටි whip) scourge.

කටේනරිවාදන්, *Kaṭénariwádan*, *s.* bad words, abusive language. (vulgar.)

කටොල්, *Kaṭol*, *s.* sorrow, distress.

කඨින, *Kaṭhina*, *a.* hard, solid; rude, rough.

කඩ, *Kaḍa*, *s.* (from ඛණ්ඩ *khaṇḍa*) piece, part, fragment; half moon, arrow; rag, bit of cloth; boutiques, pl. of කඩය *kaḍaya* which see.

කඩඉම, *Kaḍa-ima*, *s.* limit, boundary of a country, frontier, pl. කඩඉම් *kaḍa-im.*

කඩකපනවා, *Kaḍakapanawá*, *v.* to cut in pieces, to chip.

කඩකරණවා, *Kaḍakaraṇawá*, *v.* to disobey, to transgress; to trade in a boutique.

කඩකාරයා, *Kaḍakárayá*, *s.* shop keeper, market man, man who keeps a bazaar or shop.

කඩකැත්ත, *Kaḍaketta*, *s.* razor, pl. කඩකැති *kaḍaketi.*

කඩතුර, *Kaḍatura*, *s.* canopy.

කඩතුරාව, *Kaḍaturáwa*, *s.* cloth put before the face of those supposed to be possessed by the devil, during the ceremonies performed by an exorcist, screen.

කඩද *Kaḍada*, *s.* half, part.

කඩදත්, *Kaḍadat*, *a.* possessing only one half of the original teeth, the rest having disappeared by age, etc.

කඩදාසිය, *Kaḍadásiya*, *s.* paper.

කඩනවා, *Kaḍanawá*, *v.* to break; to part; to tear; to separate, pluck; to detach: pret. කැඩුවා *keḍuwá.*

කඩපිල, *Kaḍapila*, *s.* small bazaar or shop, pl. කඩපිල් *kaḍapil.*

කඩමරියා, *Kaḍamariyá* *s.* name of a sea fish, Russel's batlu, (horse mackerel tribe) *trachonytis russelii,*

කඩමල්කඩ, *Kaḍamalkaḍa*, ragged cloth.

කඩමලු, *Kaḍamalu*, *a.* ragged, torn; *s.* old rags or clothes.

කඩමාල්ල, *Kaḍamálla*, *s.* rag, ragged or patched cloth.

කඩය, *Kaḍaya*, *s.* shop, bazaar, elevated place or terrace in front of a house, where articles are exposed for sale, pl. කඩ *kaḍa.*

කඩල, *Kaḍala*, *s.* kind of small bean, usually called gram, which is given to horses, *cicer arietinum* or *pisum arvense.*

කඩවත, *Kaḍawata*, *s.* post or station, gravet.

කඩවර, *Kaḍawara*, *s.* channel, ditch, gutter.

කඩවසම, *Kaḍawasama*, *s.* sketch, lineament, outline, well proportioned shape.

කඩාකනවා, *Kaḍákanawá*, *v.* to peck or nibble at, to tear as a bird of prey: pret. කඩාකෑවා *kaḍákéwá*.

කඩාගන්නවා, *Kaḍágannawá*, *v.* to tear off or break off for one's self.

කඩාදමනවා, *Kaḍádamanawá*, *v.* to pull down, to break down: pret. කඩාදැමුවා *kaḍádémuwá*.

කඩාබාදු, *Kaḍábádu*, *a.* vagabond, scampish, vagrant.

කඩාබාදුවෙනවා, *Kaḍábáduwenawá*, *v.* to become disappointed, to scatter.

කඩාර, *Kaḍára*, *s.* variegated colour, mixture of blue and yellow.

කඩින්කඩ, *Kaḍinkaḍa*, *a.* from place to place, scattered; dispersed; piecemeal; in detachments.

කඩිනම්, *Kaḍinam*, *a.* quick, sharp, hasty.

කඩිප්පුව, *Kaḍippuwa*, *s.* drumstick.

කඩියා, *Kaḍiyá*, *s.* black ant.

කඩියාලම, *Kaḍiyálama*, *s.* bridle.

කඩිවේගං, *Kaḍiwégaṇ*, *s.* see කඩුවේගං *kaḍuwégaṇ*.

කඩිසර, *Kaḍisara*, *a.* quick; diligent, active, smart.

කඩුක්කම, *Kaḍukkama*, *s.* large earring, chiefly worn by the Chetty caste; small earing worn by native females, pl. කඩුක්කන් *kaḍukkan*.

කඩුකාරයා, *Kaḍukárayá*, *s.* swordsman, soldier armed with a sword.

කඩුකොපුව, *Kaḍukopuwa*, *s.* scabbard.

කඩුත්තුව, *Kaḍuttuwa*, *s.* flux, diarrhœa.

කඩුතලේ, *Kaḍutalé*, *s.* blade of a sword, pl. කඩුතල *kaḍutala*.

කඩුප්පුව, *Kaḍuppuwa*, see කඩිප්පුව *kaḍippuwa*.

කඩුපහර, *Kaḍupahara*, *s.* blow with a sword.

කඩුපාර, *Kaḍupára*, *s.* plant, *cacalia* or *emilia sonchifolia (Compositæ)*.

කඩුපුල්, *Kaḍupul*, *s.* species of *lotus*.

කඩුම්බේරිය, *Kaḍumbériya*, *s.* bastard ebony, *diospyros Gardneri (Ebenaceæ)*.

කඩුම, *Kaḍuma*, *s.* sign, mark.

කඩුමිට, *Kaḍumiṭa*, *s.* hilt or handle of sword.

කඩුල්ල, *Kaḍulla*, *s.* opening in a fence or enclosure, stile, pl. කඩුලු *kaḍulu*.

කඩුව, *Kaḍuwa*, *s.* sword, sabre.

කඩුවේගං, *Kaḍuwégaṇ*, *s.* scorbutic eruption in the feet of children.

කඩුසිල්ප, *Kaḍusilpa*, *s.* (කඩු and ශිල්ප an art) sword exercise.

කඩුහරඹ, *Kaḍuharamba*, *s.* sword exercise.

කඩේ, *Kaḍé*, *s.* market place, bazaar, pl. කඩ *kaḍa*.

කඩොල්, *Kaḍol*, *s.* tree, mangrove tree, *rhizophora mucronata, (Rhizophoraceæ)*.

කඩොල්ල, *Kaḍolla*, *s.* stile in a fence, see කඩුල්ල *kaḍulla*.

කණ්ටක, *Kaṇṭaka*, *s.* thorn; foe; rudeness; workshop, manufactory; bamboo; fault; point of a pin or needle; sea monster.

කණ්ඨ, *Kaṇṭha*, *s.* throat; sound, especially guttural sound; rope to tie round the neck of a horse; small tree, *vangueria spinosa*.

කණ්ඨපාශ, *Kaṇṭhapáṣa*, *s.* rope passing round an elephant's neck.

කණ්ඨ භූෂා, *Kaṇṭha-bhúshá*, *s.* collar or short necklace, ornament for the neck.

කණ්ඨමණි, *Kaṇṭhamaṇi*, } *s.* (කණ්ඨ
කණ්ඨමාණික්‍යය, *Kaṇṭhamáṇikyaya*, } and මාණික්‍ය gem) jewel worn on the throat, reckoned by the natives to be one of very great value and supposed to be found in the throat of the cobra capella.

කණ්ඩන, *Kaṇḍana*, *s.* dividing, separating; threshing, separating chaff from corn.

කණ්ඩ ලවණ, *Kaṇḍalawaṇa*, *s.* mineral salt; salt dug from the earth.

කණ්ඩායම, *Kaṇḍáyama*, *s.* multitude, company, regiment, pl. කණ්ඩායම් *kaṇḍáyam*.

කණ්ඩූ, *Kaṇḍú*, } *s.* itch, itching.
කණ්ඩූති, *Kaṇḍúti*, }

කණ්ඩූයන, *Kaṇḍúyana*, } *s.* itch.
කණ්ඩූයා, *Kaṇḍúyá*, }

කණ්ඩූර, *Kaṇḍúra*, *s.* (කණ්ඩූ itching, ර *rá* what makes) plant so called, bearing legumes with stinging hairs, the cowach, *carpopogon pruriens*.

කණ, *Kaṇa*, *s.* ear, species of attana, *stramonium*; drop of water; long pepper; *a.* blind; part. eating, pl. කන් *kan*.

කණකරණවා, *Kaṇakaraṇawá*, *v.* to blind.

කණ ගතිය, *Kaṇa-gatiya*, *s.* blindness.

කණවැල, *Kaṇawéla*, *s.* that by which a blind man is led.

කණා, *Kaṇá*, *s.* blind man; gold; long pepper, pl. කන්නු *kannu*.

කණිකාව, *Kaṇikáwa*, *s.* Elu form of කණ්ණිකා *kaṇṇiká*, pistil or female organs of generation in flowers.

කත්, *Kat*, plural of කද *kada* which see; woman.

කත්තරි, *Kattari*, *s*, pair of scissors, see කර්තරී *kartarí*.

කත්තිරිකාව, *Kattirikáwa*, s. two pieces of wood laid across.

කත්‍රු, *Katru*, s. nominative case in grammar, cause or agent; incorrectly for කර්තෘ *kartṛi*.

කත් ලනුව, *Kat-lanuwa*, s. string by which bundles are tied to the pingo, see කත් *kat*.

කත්ලීය, *Katlíya*, } s. piece of wood shaped
කත් ලෑල්ල, *Kat-lęlla*, } like a bow and laid across the shoulders to carry burdens, *i. e.* a pingo.

කත්වැල, *Katwęla*, s. pingo-string, (කද *kada* elastic stick, වැල cord, trap.)

කත්හුස්ම, *Kat-husma*, s. (කද *kada* porter's load, හුස්ම breathing) the distance at which a cooly or carrier usually rests, generally reckoned one mile English.

කත, *Kata*, s. woman; lustre, effulgence, a ray of the sun, pl. කතුන් *katun*.

කතර, *Katara*, s. unfrequented and bad road.

කතරගම, *Kataragama*, s. (කතර desert, ගම village) village in the south East of Ceylon, celebrated for a temple of Kártikéya.

කතරගම දෙවියො, *Kataragama deviyo*, s. (කතර ගම and දෙවි god) name of Kártikéya the god of war, by which he is generally designated in Ceylon.

කතාකරණවා, *Katákaraṇawá*, see කථාකරණවා *kathákaraṇawá*.

කතාන්දර, *Katándara*, } see කථාන්තරය *kathán-*
කතාන්තර, *Katántara*, } *taraya*.

කතාව, *Katáwa*, see කථාව *katháwa*.

කතාවස්තුව, *Katáwastuwa*, see කථාවස්තුව *katháwastuwa*,

කතික, *Katika*, see කථිකයා *kathikayá*.

කතිකාව, *Katikáwa*, see කථිකාව *kathikáwa*.

කතිකාවත, *Katikáwata*, s. regulations or rules, enactments for the Buddhist priests.

කතිරය, *Katiraya*, s. two pieces of wood laid thus ×.

කතු, *Katu*, Elu form of කර්තෘ *kartṛi*.

කතුර, *Katura*, s. scissors, pl. කතුරු *katuru*.

කතුරු, *Katuru*, s. venom-curer, kind of stick, mode of describing.

කතුරුපෑන්නා, *Katurupęnná*, s. fish.

කතුරුමුරුංගා, *Katuru-murungá*, s. tree, *sesbania grandiflora (Legum.)* species of murunga used medicinally.

කතුරුයටි, *Katuruyaṭi*, s. staff.

කතුස්ම, *Katusma*, see කත්හුස්ම *kat-husma*.

කථන, *Kathana*, s. saying, narrating, relating.

කථා, *Kathá*, s. speech, tale or fable; historical narration.

කථාකරණවා, *Kathákaraṇawá*, v. to speak, to talk, to converse, to relate, to narrate.

කථාන්තරය, *Kathántaraya*, s. history, narrative, set discourse, historical narration, tale.

කථාප්‍රසඞ්ග, *Kathá-prasańga*, s. (කථා fable, ප්‍රසඞ්ග who retales) talkative person, one fond of talking much; babbler, silly half witted talker; conjuror, dealer in antidotes.

කථාව, *Katháwa*, s. talk, oration, speech, conversation; history, historical account.

කථාවස්තුව, *Katháwastuwa*, s. history, collection of historical records.

කථාවිච්ඡේදය, *Kathávichchhédaya*, s. refutation of the arguments of another.

කථික, *Kathika*, } s. orator, counsellor.
කථිකයා, *Kathikayá*, }

කථිකාව, *Kathikáwa*, s. oration, set speech.

කද, *Kada*, s. cloud; load or pack, as much as can be carried on a pingo, pl. කත් *kat*.

කදම්, *Kadam*, s. mud from කර්දම *kardama*.

කදම්බ, *Kadamba*, } s. tree, *nauclea cordifolia;*
කදම්බක, *Kadambaka*, } [Colloq කොළොං *kolong*]; mustard seed plant, *sinapis dichotoma;* paḷol tree, *bignonia;* multitude, an assemblage, collection.

කදර්‍ය, *Kadarya*, a. avaricious, miserly.

කදලි, *Kadalí*, s. plantain tree, *musa sapientum;* [Colloq. කෙසෙල් *kesel*].

කදා, *Kadá*, s. silicious earth used in the manufacture of glass, beads, bracelets, &c.; particle signifying, when, at what time.

කදාවළලු, *Kadáwalaḷu*, s. (කදා and වළලු ring) bracelet made from the earth called කදා *kadá*.

කදිමය, *Kadimaya*, } s. interjection of approval,
කදිමයි, *Kadimayi*, } good! well! a. good, fine.

කදුබු, *Kadubu*, } s. ray of light.
කදුම්බු, *Kadumbu*, }

කදුරු, *Kaduru*, s. tree, sometimes called the forbidden tree on account of the poisonous nut it produces, generic name of several species of dogsbane *(Apocynaceæ);* see ගොඩකදුරු *goḍa-kaduru*.

කදුරුකැටිය වැල්, *Kadurukęṭiya-węl*, s. plant, *combretum ovalifolium (Leguminosæ).*

කදුළු, *Kaduḷu*. see කඳුළු *kanduḷu*.

කදො, *Kado*, s. light, reflection; fire-fly.

කදෝකිමි, *Kadókimi*, s. fire-fly.

කඩෝකිමි රුපු, *Kadókimi-rupu*, s. (කඩෝකිමි and රුපු enemy) sun.

කඩෝ පැණි, *Kado-pęṇi*, s. fire-fly; glow worm.

කඳ, *Kanda*, s. stem or trunk of a tree; body of a man, shoulder; one of the names of Kártikéya, pl. කඳන් *kandan*.

කඳකුමරු, *Kandakumaru*, } s. Skanda or Kártikéya, the son of
කඳකුමාරයා, *Kandakumárayá*, } Śiva and military deity of the Hindus, commonly called කතරගම දෙවියෝ *kataragama deviyó*.

කඳකොල, *Kandakola*, s. betel leaves which are not soft or smooth.

කඳදෙස්, *Kandades*, s. withers of an elephant.

කඳප්, *Kandap*, s. name of Anaŋga, the Indian Cupid; see කන්දර්ප *kandarpa*.

කඳප්යුද, *Kandapyuda*, s. copulation.

කඳපණුවා, *Kandapaṇuwá*, s. a grub in the trunk of a tree.

කඳපා, *Kandapá*, s. Cupid or god of love, Anaŋga.

කඳපිළිවෙළ, *Kanda-piḷiweḷa*, s. transmigration.

කඳමල, *Kandamala*, s. (කඳ trunk, මල flower) tree producing a very fragrant flower from its trunk, *horsfieldia odorata*.

කඳයුර, *Kandayura*, s. military encampment; breast work raised outside of a city or town to defend it against an invading enemy; suburb, pl. කඳයුරු *kandayuru*.

කඳල, *Kandala*, s. plant, *colocasia antiquorum* or *arum colocasia (Araceæ)*, kind of yam.

කඳවුර, *Kandawura*, } see කඳයුර *kandayura*.
කඳවුරු, *Kandawuru*, }

කඳවෙලෙප්, *Kandawelep*, s. thicket.

කඳවැට, *Kandawęṭa*, s. railed fence, fence made of thicker wood than common fence sticks, pl. කඳවැටවල් *kandawęṭawal*.

කඳහතු, *Kandahatu*, s. (කඳ trunk of tree, හතු mushroom) kind of mushroom so called, fungus growing on decayed trees.

කඳු, *Kandu*, plural of කන්ද *kanda*.

කඳුපාතාලේ *Kandupátálé*, s. valley.

කඳුබු, *Kandubu*, see කදුබු *kadubu*.

කඳුරු, *Kanduru*, } s. small stream descend-
කඳුරැලිය, *Kandurẹliya*, } ing from the hills.

කඳුලු, *Kandulu*, s. tears.

කඳුලැලි, *Kandulẹli*, s. shedding tears, flood of tears, weeping.

කඳුලැස්ස, *Kandulẹssa*, s. plant, *arosera indica*.

කන්කටුල, *Kankaṭula*, s. extreme suffering, great distress.

කන්කළු, *Kankaḷu*, a. good, pleasing to the ear.

කන්කානම, *Kankánama*, s. officer in the Siŋhalese militia of the rank of a corporal, petty headman, overseer.

කන්කාරිය, *Kankáriya*, s. (කන් and කාරිය business) invocation of devils, etc.

කන්කුන්, *Kankun*, s. plant, *Ipomœa aquatica (Convolv.)*

කන්කුන්ඩා, *Kankuṇḍá*, s. insect resembling the centipede, pl. කන්කුන්ඩෝ *kankuṇḍó*.

කන්කුඹල් කොටියා, *Kankumbal koṭiyá*, s. tree, *pygeum Zeylanicum (Rosaceæ)*, also called ගල් මොර *gal-mora* or ගොළු මොර *goḷu-mora*.

කන්කුඹලා, *Kankumbalá*, s. forest tree, *Turpinia pomifera* or *T. nepalensis (Sapindaceæ)*; also called ඇටකිරිල්ල *ẹṭakirilla*; twining plant, *cynanchum pauciflorum (Asclepiadeæ)*.

කන්කෙඳිරිගානවා, *Kankendirigánawá*, v. to grumble; to beg earnestly.

කන්ගෑටය, *Kangẹṭaya*, s. (කන *kana* ear, ගෑටය knot) lobe of the ear.

කන්ඩ පනිනවා, *Kanḍa-paninawá*, v. to snap or snatch (as a dog): pret. කන්ඩ පැන්නා *kanḍa pẹnná*.

කන්ඩායම, *Kanḍáyama*, see කණ්ඩායම *kaṇḍáyama*.

කන්ද, *Kanda*, s. hill, mountain, hillock, pl. කඳු *kandu*; yam.

කන්ධර, *Kandhara*, s. (කං *kaŋ* water or the head, ධර what supports) cloud; neck.

කන්දර, *Kandara*, s. artificial or natural cave; elephant's hook.

කන්දරාකර, *Kandarákara*, s. (කන්දර *kandara* and ආකර *ákara* having) mountain.

කන්දර්ප, *Kandarpa*, s. name of Cama, Indian god of love.

කන්දුක, *Kanduka*, s. ball of wood or pith for playing with.

කන්නලව්ව, *Kannalawwa*, s. supplication, earnest intreaty.

කන්නාඩි පොලඟා, *Kannádi-polaŋgá*, s. snake.

කන්නාඩිය, *Kannáḍiya*, s. spectacles; mirror; looking glass.

කන්පට, *Kanpaṭa*, s. pendant part of the ear which has been much elongated by weighty ornaments.

කන්පොත්ත, *Kanpotta*, s. (කන *kana* ear පොත්ත bark) outer part of the ear, pl. කන්පොතු, *kanpotu*.

කන්බිබුල, *Kanbibula*, } s. drum or tympanum of
කන්බුබුල, *Kanbubula*, } the ear.

කන්මුල, *Kanmula*, *s.* cheek, pl. කන්මුල් *kanmul.*

කන්‍යා, *Kanyá. s.* virgin; sign of the zodiac *Virgo.*

කන්‍යාකම, *Kanyákama*, *s.* virginity.

කන්‍යාඞ්ගනාව, *Kanyáṅganáwa*, *s.* virgin.

කන්‍යාව, *Kanyáwa*, } *s.* virgin, girl, maiden.
කන්‍යාවි, *Kanyávi*, }

කන්වයින, *Kanwayina*, *s.* pillow.

කන්වායා, *Kanwáyá*, *s.* small red insect or worm, said to cause death by entering the ear.

කන්වැල, *Kanwẹla*, *s.* that by which a blind man is led: pendant ornaments of the ear.

කන්වෑයා, *Kanwẹ̄yá*, *s.* earwig.

කන්සා, *Kansá*, *s.* opium plant.

කන්සාරාති, *Kansaráti*, see කංසාරාති *kaṉsáráti.*

කන්සිදුර, *Kansidura*, *s.* ear hole.

කන්සිල්, *Kansil*, *s.* auditory passage in the ear.

කන්සේ, *Kansé*, *s.* cheek, pl. කන්ස: see කංස *kaṉsa.*

කන්හැන්ද, *Kanhẹnda*, *s.* (කණ *kaṇa* ear, හැන්ද spoon) ear-pick, pl. කන්හැඳි *kanhẹṉdi.*

කනක, *Kanaka*, } *s.* gold, (not used in speak-
කනකම්, *Kanakam*, } ing.)

කනකාචල, *Kanakáchala*, *s.* (කනක and අචල mountain) golden mountain, Mahaméru.

කනකොක්විල, *Kanakokvila*, *s.* species of the hedge-hyssop, *gratiola veronicifolia.*

කනකොකා, *Kanakoká*, *s.* pond-heron, *ardeola grayi* (order *Herodiones.*)

කනගාටු, *Kanagáṭu*, *a.* vexatious, distressing, annoying.

කනගාටුව, *Kanagáṭuwa*, *s.* (කන and ගැහැටු *gẹhẹṭu* teasing) vexation, sorrow, trouble, distress.

කනගොංගා, *Kanagoṉgá*, *s.* fish.

කන ගොන්න, *Kana-gonna*, *s.* small jak, *artocarpus lakoocha (Urticaceæ).*

කන ගොරක, *Kana-goraka*, *s:* gamboge, *garcinia morella (Guttiferæ)*, also called ගොකටු *gokaṭu.*

කනත්ත, *Kanatta*, *s.* elevated ground, hilly ground, field (with a little jungle).

කනදෝ, *Kanadó*, *s.* lightning.

කනප්පුව, *Kanappuwa*, *s.* wooden stand or small table, teapoy.

කනපිට, *Kanapiṭa*, *s.* unprinted side of cloth; wrong side.

කනපැද්දා, *Kanapẹddá. s.* kind of fish.

කනමගුරා, *Kanamagurá*, *s.* kind of river fish.

කනමී, *Kanamí*, *s.* nest or hive of honey flies.

කනමැදිරියා, *Kanamẹdiriyá*, *s.* fire-fly.

කනයා, *Kanayá*, *s.* fish found in fields and ponds.

කනවා, *Kanawá*, *v.* to eat; pret. කෑවා *kẹ̄wá.*

කනවි, *Kanavi*, *s.* spear.

කනවැන්දුම්, *Kanawẹndumi*, *s.* widow, pl. කනවැන්දුම්යෝ *kanawẹndumiyó.*

කනස්සලු, *Kanassalu*, *s.* vexation, sorrow, teasing; *a.* vexatious, tedious, sorrowful.

කනසර, *Kanasara*, *s.* saint so called.

කනාටු, *Kanáṭu*, *a.* old and tall (applied to trees.)

කනාදෙ, *Kanáde*, *s.* measure of capacity equal to two seers, pl. කනාද *kanáda.*

කනාමැදිරියා, *Kanámẹdiriyá*, see කනමැදිරියා *kanamẹdiriyá.*

කනිටු, *Kaniṭu*, Elu form of කනිෂ්ඨ *kanishṭha.*

කනිනවා, *Kaninawá*, *v.* to dig, to excavate: pret. කැන්නා *kẹnná.*

කනිෂ්ඨ, *Kanishṭha*, *a.* small, little, younger, younger born.

කනිෂ්ඨා, *Kanishṭhá*, *s.* little finger.

කනිසම, *Kanisama*, *a.* about, near; *s.* size; period of time, instant, pl. කනිසම් *kanisam.*

කනු, *Kanu*, *plur.* of කනුව *kanuwa.*

කනුපල, *Kanupala*, *s.* enclosure for cattle; marked spot.

කනුමස, *Kanumasa*, *s.* flesh round the nails.

කනුව, *Kanuwa*, *s.* pillar of stone or wood, post.

කනේර, *Kanéra*, } *s.* tree, *plumeria acuminata.*
කනේරු, *Kanéru*, }

කනෑස්, *Kanẹs*, *s.* peacock's tail.

කප්, *Kap*, *s.* pillar.

කප්කෙළවර, *Kapkẹḷawara*, *s.* termination of a Kalpa or age of the world, see කල්පාන්තය *kalpántaya.*

කප්තුරු, *Kapturu*, *s.* celestial tree.

කප්පන්, *Kappan*, *s.* tribute, tax.

කප්පර, *Kappara*, *s.* ship, sloop.

කප්පරවල්ලිය, *Kapparawalliya*, *s.* kind of mint, *coleus aromaticus* or *mentha indica (Labiatæ).*

කප්පාකන්නා, *Kappákanná*, *s.* pimp.

කප්පාඩු, *Kappádu*, *a.* castrated, emasculated.

කප්පාඩු කරණවා, *Kappádu-karaṇawá*, *v.* to castrate, to emasculate.

කප්පාඩුවා, *Kappáduwá*, *s.* (කප්පාඩු with the nom. of. වා) eunuch, capon, gelding, castrated animal &c.

කප්පි, *Kappi*, *s.* grit, bran; last remains of any powdered grain.

කප්පිභාණ්ඩ, *Kappibháṉdha*, see කප්පියභාණ්ඩ *kappiyabháṉdha.*

කප්පිය, *Kappiya*, *s.* pulley.

කප්පිල්, *Kappil*, *s.* an ornamented pillar; the eyes in a peacock's tail.

කප් රුක, *Kap-ruka*, *s.* kalpa tree; fabulous tree which yields to the possessor every thing he desires; sometimes written කප්තුර *kaptura*.

කප්හිටුවනවා, *Kap-hiṭuwanawá*, *v.* (කප් pillar, හිටුවනවා *hiṭuwanawá* to fix) to worship Pattini etc.; a pillar is set up, and the votaries move round muttering invocations, beating drums etc.; to recite a kind of poetical incantation for the cure of the sick, or to procure prosperity, to make a vow to a demon, by setting a stick on the ground, to perform a ceremony as the fulfilment of a vow.

කප, *Kapa*, *s.* see කල්ප *kalpa*.

කපට, *Kapaṭa*, *s.* fraud, deceit, cheating, circumvention; *a.* fraudulent, deceitful, roguish.

කපටිකම, *Kapaṭikama*, *s.* fraud, roguery. pl. කපට කම් *kapaṭakam*; see කපට *kapaṭa*.

කපත්, *Kapat*, *s.* crab.

කපනවා, *Kapanawá*, *v.* to cut, to chop: pret. කැපුවා *kępuwá*.

කපල්දර, *Kapaldara*, *s.* (කපල *kapala* skull, දර who has) name of Ṣiva, who wears a necklace of skulls; beggar.

කපල්ල, *Kapalla*. *s.* an opening in a fence.

කපාල, *Kapála*, *s.* skull, kind of leprosy; cut, break in a dam; gap; head.

කපාලභෘත්, *Kapálabhṛit*, *s.* (කපාල skull, භෘත් *bhṛit* who bears) name of Ṣiva, alluding to his necklace of human skulls.

කපි, *Kapi*, *s.* ape or monkey.

කපිනී, *Kapiní*, *s.* female monkey.

කපිල, *Kapila*, *s.* name of a celebrated saint, founder of the Sáṅkhya philosophy; female elephant of the south east; fabulous car much celebrated in the Puráṇas; *a.* tawny coloured.

කපිලද්‍යුති, *Kapiladyuti*, *s.* (කපිල and ද්‍යුති light) name of Súrya or the sun.

කපිලවන් පැය, *Kapilawan-pęya*, *s.* anything of a tawny colour.

කපිලෝහ, *Kapiloha*, *s.* brass.

කපිවක්ත්‍ර, *Kapiwaktra*, *s.* name of Nárada, saint and friend of Kṛishṇa.

කපිශීර්ෂ, *Kapiśírsha*, *s.* upper part or coping of a wall.

කපිතන, *Kapítana*, *s.* tree, *spondias mangifera*.

කපීන්ද්‍ර, *Kapíndra*, *s.* (කපි and ඉන්ද්‍ර *indra* chief) monkey-chief; Hanumán.

කප්පියභාණ්ඩ, *Kappiyabhánḍha*, *s.* things proper to be offered to a Buddhist priest.

කපු, *Kapu*, *s.* silk cotton tree; cotton.

කපුකිනිස්ස, *Kapukinissa*, *s.* annual hairy plant, *hibiscus angulosus* or *h. abelmoschus (Malvaceæ)*.

කපුටා, *Kapuṭá*, *s.* crow, pl. කපුටෝ *kapuṭó*. see කාක්කා *kákká*.

කපුටුබයා *Kapuṭubayá*, *s.* bird, Ceylonese Drongo, *dissemurus lophorinus*, (order *Passeres;*) also called කවුඩා *kawuḍá*.

කපුටුබෝ, *Kapuṭubó*, see කවුඩුබෝ *kawuḍubó*.

කපුටුවා, *Kapuṭuwá*, *s.* crow, pl. කපුටුවෝ *kapuṭuwó*. see කාක්කා *kákká*.

කපු පිළි, *Kapu-piḷí*, *s.* cotton cloth.

කපු ඵල, *Kapu-phala*, *s.* unwrought cotton, fruit of the cotton tree.

කපුරාල, *Kapurála*, see කපුවා *kapuwá*.

කපුරු, *Kapuru*, *s.* camphor; *goniothalamus walkeri (Anonaceæ)*; *gaultheria fragrantissima (Ericaceæ)*.

කපුවා, *Kapuwá*, *s.* barber; demon priest, pl. කපුවෝ *kapuwó*.

කපුහැන්නැද්දා, *Kapuhęnnęddá*, *s.* kind of fish.

කපෝත, *Kapota*, } *s.* dove or pigeon.
කපෝතක, *Kapotaka*,

කපෝත පාලිකා, *Kapota-pálíká*, *s.* dove-cot or aviary.

කපෝල, *Kapola*, } *s.* cheek, pl. කපොල් *kapol*.
කපෝලය, *Kapólaya*,

කපෝලේ, *Kapólé*, *s.* cancer, imposthume.

කඵ, *Kapha*, *s.* phlegm, one of the three humors of the body.

කබ්බ, *Kabba*, *s.* phosphorescent light seen in waves at night, in the sea, salt water lakes etc.

කබ, *Kaba*, *s.* gum of the eye.

කබඳු, *Kabandu*, } *s.* headless trunk, especially retaining the power of action;
කබන්ධ, *Kabandha*, } water; name of Ráhu.

කබර, *Kabara*, *s.* scrofulous or cutaneous disease, white scab.

කබරගොයා, *Kabaragoyá*, } *s.* large spotted lizard or iguana, *hydrosaurus*
කබරා, *Kabará*, } *salvator* (order *Sauria*), pl. කබරගොයි *kabaragoyi*.

කබරි, *Kabari*, *s.* woman suffering with scrofula; spreading shrub used in tattooing, *eclipta prostrata* or *verbesina scandens*.

කබරොස්ස, *Kabarossa*, *s.* creeping plant resembling *sarsaparilla*, the genus *Smilax (Liliaceæ)*.

කබල් කාරල්ලා *Kabal-kárallá*, *s.* sea fish.

කබල්මාරා, *Kabal-márá*, *s.* tree, *albizzia stipulata (Legum.)*

කබල්ලෑවා, *Kaballéwá*, *s.* five-fingered pangolin. ant eater, *manis pentaductyla.*

කබල්වෙනවා, *Kabalwenawá*, *v.* to decay, to become old and bad, (applied to drums and pots).

කබල, *Kabala*, *s.* shell of the tortoise or any testaceous animal; skull; clay oven; remnant of any thing old or decayed, potsherd; scab, pl. කබල් *kabal.*

කබලක්, *Kabalak*, *s.* mouthful of meal.

කබලිටියා. *Kabaliṭiyá*, *s.* Indian cone goose, *sarcidiornis melanonotus*, (order *Anseres.*)

කබලු, *Kabalu*, *s.* sort of cake; scales; scabs; crust.

කබාය, *Kabáya*, *s.* coat.

කබොල්ල, *Kabolla*, *s.* dry incrustation of a sore.

කඹපිල්, *Kam̲bapil*, *s.* peacock's tail.

කඹය, *Kam̲baya*, *s.* large rope, pl. කඹ *kam̲ba.*

කඹිලියා, *Kam̲biliyá*, *s.* incorrectly for කම්බිලියා *Kambiliyá.*

කඹුරණවා, *Kam̲buraṇawá*, *v.* to serve as a menial or slave.

කඹුරා, *Kam̲burá*, *s.* brazier, smith; from කර්මාර *karmára.*

කඹුරු, *Kam̲buru*, *a.* variegated.

කඹුරුවන් පැය, *Kam̲buruwan-péya*, *s.* variegated colour.

කඹුරු සම, *Kam̲buru-sama*, *s* (කඹුරු and සම hide) bellows.

කම්, *Kam*, *s.* water; desire: Elu form of කර්ම *karma.*

කම්කරුවා, *Kamkaruwá*, *s.* servant, bond servant, one skilled in manufacture.

කම්කිලිය, *Kamkiliya*, *s.* menial servant, female servant of the lowest order.

කම්දද, *Kam-dada*, *s.* name of අනඟ *anan̲ga* or කාම *káma*, Indian god of love; shark.

කම්නැති, *Kamnęti*, *a.* useless, needless, having no occasion for.

කම්පන, *Kampana*, *a.* trembling, unsteady, shaken, agitated.

කම්පස්, *Kampas*, *a.* obedient, manageable.

කම්පස්කරණවා, *Kampas-karaṇawá*, *v.* to punish severely.

කම්පා, *Kampá*, *s.* shaking, trembling, agitation.

කම්පාව, *Kampáwa*, *s.* compassion.

කම්පාවෙනවා, *Kampáwenawá*, *v.* to shake, to be agitated, to be sorry.

කම්පිත, *Kampita*, *part.* shaken, agitated, alarmed.

කම්පිල්ල, *Kampilla*, } *s.* plant used in dyeing
කම්පිලිය, *Kampiliya*, } and as a perfume; sort of *crinum.*

කම්පොත්තා, *Kampottá*, *s.* plant, *aporosa latifolia (Euphorbiaceæ).*

කම්බය, *Kambaya*, *s.* board covering an óla book.

කම්බර, *Kambara*, *s.* variegated (colour).

කම්බල, *Kambala*, *s.* blanket.

කම්බස්, *Kambas*, see කම්පස් *kampas.*

කම්බස්කරණවා, *Kambaskaraṇawá*, *v.* see කම්පස් කරණවා *kampas-karaṇawá.*

කම්බාය, *Kambáya*, *s.* coloured cloth chiefly worn by native women.

කම්බිය, *Kambiya*, *s.* wire, pl. කම්බි *kambi.*

කම්බියා, *Kambiyá*, *s.* kind of worm which breeds in rotten trees or wood.

කම්බිලි, *Kambili*, see කම්මැලි *Kammęli.*

කම්බිලිය, *Kambiliya*, *s.* kind of hair cloth or carpet, blanket, pl. කම්බිලි *kambili.*

කම්බිලියා, *Kambiliyá*, *s.* idle person. see කම්මැලියා *kammęliyá.*

කම්බු, *Kambu*, *s.* gold; conch, shell; bracelet, ring; neck; vein; *a.* speckled, variegated.

කම්බු ග්‍රීවා, *Kambu-gríwá*, *s.* neck marked with three lines like a shell, and considered to be indicative of exalted fortune; sign of great beauty.

කම්මටම, *Kammaṭama*, *s.* smith's shop, smithery.

කම්මල, *Kammala*, *s.* smith's shop, forge, pl. කම්මල් *kammal.*

කම්මුතු, *Kammutu*, *part.* finished, ended, done.

කම්මුතුකරණවා, *Kammutukaraṇawá*, *v.* to finish, to end, to complete.

කම්මුතුවෙනවා, *Kammutuwenawá*, *v.* to be finished.

කම්මුල, *Kammula*, *s.* cheek, pl. කම්මුල් *kammul.*

කම්මැලි, *Kammęli*, *a.* lazy, indolent, idle.

කම්මැලිකම, *Kammęlikama*, *s.* laziness, indolence, idleness.

කම්මැලියා, *Kammęliyá*, *s.* lazy person.

කම්රුපු, *Kam-rupu*, *s.* (කම් god of love, Cupid, රුපු enemy) name of Ṣiva.

කම්හල, *Kamhala*, *s.* work shop, manufactory.

කම, *Kama*, *s.* business, deed, act, matter; need, necessity, occasion, pl. කම් *kam.*

කමක්නැති, *Kamaknęti*, *a.* useless, unnecessary.

කමක්නෑ, *Kamakné*, *ind.* never mind; there is no need of it.

කමටහන්, *Kamaṭahan*, *s.* abstract meditations for the purpose of subjugating the passions of which there are forty varieties.

කමණ්ඩලා, *Kamaṇḍalá*, } *s.* earthen or wooden vessel
කමණ්ඩා, *Kamaṇḍá*, } out of which an ascetic eats his food.

කමත, *Kamata*, *s.* threshing floor, pl. කමත් *kamat*.

කමන, *Kamana*, *a.* libidinous; desirous.

කමනීය, *Kamaníya*, *a.* pleasing, beautiful, desirable.

කමල්, *Kamal*, s. blue lotus, lotus in general.

කමල් අල, *Kamal-ala*, *s.* the edible part of the lotus.

කමල්කල්, *Kamal-kal*, *s.* name of Vishṇu and also wife of Vishṇu.

කමල්දල, *Kamal-dala*, see කමලදල *kamala-dala*.

කමල් නෙත්, *Kamal-net*, *s.* (කමල් lotus, නෙත් eye) name of Vishṇu.

කමල් නැබ, *Kamal-nęba*, s. Vishṇu.

කමල, *Kamala*, *s.* lotus, *nymphæa nelumbo*.

කමලකර, *Kamalakara*, *s.* sun.

කමල දල, *Kamala-dala*, } *s.* leaf of the lotus.
කමල පත්‍ර, *Kamala-patra*, }

කමලා, *Kamalá*, *s.* name of Lakshmi.

කමලාකර, *Kamalákara*, *s.* lake where the lotus abounds.

කමලාසන, *Kamalásana*, *s.* name of Brahma.

කමලිනී, *Kamaliní*, *s.* place abounding with lotus.

කමා, *Kamá*, *s.* woman.

කමාව, *Kamáwa*, *s.* forgiveness, pardon, remission.

කමාවෙනවා, *Kamáwenawá*, *v.* to forgive, to pardon.

කමිස, *Kamisa*, *s.* colour, see කල්මාෂ *kalmásha*.

කමිසය, *Kamisaya*, *s.* shirt, pl. කමිස *kamisa*.

කමිහි, *Kamihi*, *s.* delay, loitering, [Colloq. ප්‍රමාදය *pramádaya*].

කය, *Kaya*, *s.* body, see කාය *káya*.

කයස්ථා, *Kayasthá*, see කායස්ථා *káyasthá*.

කයි කියනවා, *Kayi-kiyanawá*. *v.* to chant songs: pret. කයි කිව්වා *kayi-kiwwá*.

කයිත්තාව, *Kayittáwa*, *s.* unprofitable conversation, pl. කයිත්තා *kayittá*.

කයිතාලම, *Kayitálama*, *s.* cymbal.

කයිප්පු, *Kayippu*, *s.* astringent mixture chewed with betel; plant, *Knoxia corymbosa*.

කයිය, *Kayiya*, *s.* kind of song or chant, sung by a band of labourers.

කයියෙලිය, *Kayiyeliya*, *s.* cloth with coloured border worn by the natives.

කයිලවැල *Kayilawęla*, *s.* creeping plant, *phylanthus reticulatus;* also called වැල් කයිල *węl-kayila*.

කයිල හතු, *Kayila-hatu*, *s.* kind of mushroom, *fungus phalloides*.

කයිවාරු, *Kayiwáru*, *s.* songs, congratulation.

කර්කට, *Karkaṭa*, *s.* crab; sign of the zodiac, *Cancer;* kind of bird, *numidian crane*, long gourd.

කර්කටක රාශිය, *Karkaṭaka-ráṣiya*, *s.* sign of the zodiac, *Cancer*.

කර්කටකශෘංගී, *Karkaṭakaṣṛingi*, *s.* medicinal plant, the fruit of which is said to resemble the claws of the crab.

කර්කශ, *Karkaṣa*, *a.* harsh, rude, violent, unfeeling, unkind, unmerciful.

කර්ණ, *Karṇa*, } *s.* ear; prince so called,
කර්ණය, *Karṇaya*, } sovereign of Aṅgadésa; plant, kind of swallow wort; another plant *cassia fistula* [Colloq. ඇහැළ *ęhęla*].

කර්ණධාර, *Karṇadhára*, *s.* (කර්ණ ear used here metaphorically for helm and ධර *dhara* to hold) pilot, helmsman.

කර්ණ නාද, *Karṇa-náda*, *s.* (කර්ණ and නාද sound) disease of the ear.

කර්ණමුඩ, *Karṇamuḍa*, *s.* one of the seven lakes in the Himálaya.

කර්ණාභරණය, *Karṇábharaṇaya*, *s.* ear-ring.

කර්ණිකා, *Karṇiká*, } *s.* rock rose, *cistus lobatus*;
කර්ණිකාව, *Karṇikáwa*, } pericarp of a lotus.

කර්තරි, *Kartarí*, } *s.* (කෘත *kṛita* to cut) pair of
කර්ත්‍රී, *Kartri*, } scissors.

කර්තෘ *Kartṛi* *s.* nominative case in grammar, cause or agent; author, editor.

කර්දම, *Kardama*, *s.* mud, mire, clay. [Colloq. මඩ *maḍa*].

කර්දමජ, *Karda-maja*, *s.* (කර්දම and ජ born) lotus.

කර්පාස, *Karpása*, *s.* cotton.

කර්පාස ශාටක, *Karpása-ṣáṭaka*, *s.* cotton cloth.

කර්පූර, *Karpúra*, *s.* camphor.

කර්ම, *Karma*, } *s.* merit or demerit of actions
කර්ම්ම, *Karmma*, } performed in a previous state of existence, act, action, object of action; subject of action in grammar; moral duty, religious action or sacrifices to secure a future recompense.

කර්මක්ෂම, *Karmakshama*, *a.* competent to act.

කර්මක්ෂය, *Karmakshaya*, *s.* (කර්ම merit, ක්ෂය consumption) extinction of karma.

කර්මකර, *Karmakara*, *s.* hired labourer, servant,; name of Yama, regent of the dead; slave.

කර්මකාර, *Karmakára*, *s.* hired servant; blacksmith.

කර්මජ, *Karmaja*, *a.* resulting from human actions, principally from those supposed to have been performed in a prior state of existence; *s.* kaliyuga, the fourth or present age of the Hindus; age of sin.

කර්ම ඵල, *Karma-phala*, *s.* pain or pleasure considered as the fruit of human actions in a previous state of existence.

කර්ම වාක්‍යය, *Karma-wákyaya*, *s.* religious discourse, formula prescribed for ecclesiastical proceedings among the priests of Buddha in ordination, deposition, acts of discipline, &c., rubric.

කර්ම විපාකය, *Karma-vipákaya*, see කර්ම ඵල *karma phala*.

කර්ම ශීල, *Karma-ṣíla*, *a.* assiduous, laborious; *s.* one who perseveres in his duty without looking forward to its reward.

කර්මස්ථාන, *Karmasthána*, *s.* instruction necessary to be received prior to the student entering upon abstract meditation for the subjugation of the passions.

කර්මාකාර. *Karmákára*, see කර්මකාර *karmakára*.

කර්මාන්ත, *Karmánta*, *s.* (කර්ම and අන්ත *anta* end) tilled or cultivated land; trade, calling, work.

කර්මාර, *Karmára*, *s.* brazier.

කර්මාර පුත්‍ර, *Karmára-putra*, *s.* people of the brazier employment.

කර්ෂ, *Karsha*, *s.* weight of gold or silver; karsha is equal to 16 máshas or about 280 grains troy; ploughing, husbandry.

කර්ෂණ, *Karshaṇa*, *s.* ploughing, attracting.

කර, *Kara*, *s.* hand, arm; neck; shoulder; palm of the hand; one of the dances which people perform in religious observances; one of the eight castes in dancing; ray of light, sun or moon beam; toll, tax, impost; elephant's trunk; thorny shrub, *canthium parviflorum (Rubiaceæ)*.

කරඅඹනවා, *Kara-ambanawá*, *v.* to geld, the act of crushing the testicles of young bullocks between two pieces of wood to produce the effects of castration.

කර ක්ගෙඩිය, *Karakgediya*, *s.* conical shaped wicker basket, used principally for catching fish in rivers &c., of no great depth; it is of a portable size and open at top and bottom.

කර කතුර, *Kara-katura*, *s.* razor.

කර කණ්ටක, *Kara-kaṇṭaka*, *s.* (කර hand, කණ්ටක thorn) finger nail.

කරකම්, *Karakam*, *s.* act of shaving the head or beard.

කරකරණවා, *Karakaraṇawá*, *v.* to roast too much.

කරකවනවා, *Karakawanawá*, *v.* to turn round as a wheel: pret. කරකැව්වා *karakęwwá*.

කරකාර බඳිනවා, *Karakára bandinawá*, *v.* to marry.

කරකාර බැඳීම, *Karakára bęndíma*, *s.* (කර hand, කාර same, බැඳීම tying) marriage.

කරකොලය, *Karakolaya*, *s.* raw talipot leaf for writing.

කරකැවිල්ල, *Karakęvilla*, *s.* dizziness in the head, giddiness; turning, revolution.

කරකැවෙනවා, *Karakęwenawá*, *v.* to go round as a wheel, to turn, to revolve: pret. කරකැවුනා *karakęwuná*.

කරග්‍රහ, *Karagraha*, *s.* (කර hand, ග්‍රහ taking) marriage; one part of the ceremony being the placing the right hand of the bride, with the palm uppermost, in the right hand of the bridegroom.

කරගන්, *Karagan*, *s.* name of Ganeṣa, Hindu god of wisdom.

කරගල, *Karagala*, *s.* hone, whetstone, pl. කරගල් *karagal*.

කරගේ, *Karagé*, *s.* hair-cutter's shop, place where the hair of a person is cut who is to become a Buddhist priest.

කරගැටේ, *Karagęté*, *s.* hard excrescence or induration of the palm of the hand caused by overwork or unusual work.

කරගැණුම්, *Karagęṇum*, *s.* marriage.

කරච්චල් කරණවා, *Karachchal-karaṇawá*, *v.* to tease, to plague, to vex.

කරටිය, *Karaṭiya*, *s.* neck; part of a tree above the stem from which the branches grow.

කරඬුව, *Karaṇduwa*, *s.* small box or casket of any kind.

කරණ, *Karaṇa*, *v.* body; organ of sense; instrument or means of action; cause, motive; act, action; business; occupation, trade; copulation; plastering anything with the hand; field, foot mark; newness.

කරණකොටගෙණ, *Karaṇakoṭagena*, *s.* *prep.* by, for, on account of, through.

කරණම, *Karaṇama*, *s.* summerset; kind of dance performed by giving the body a rotatory motion, pl. කරණම් *karaṇam*.

කරණවා, *Karaṇawá*, *v.* to do, to act, to make, to perform: pret. කළා *kaḷá*.

කරණි, *Karaṇí*, *a.* proper, right, fit.

කරණු, *Karaṇu*, *s.* doing, *Imp.* let it be done.

කරණෑමියා, *Karaṇẹmiyá*, *s.* barber.

කරත්තෙ, *Karatte*, *s.* any kind of wheeled carriage.

කරතල, *Karatala*, *s.* palm of the hand.

කරතාලෙ, *Karatále*, *s.* act of beating time to music by clapping the hands; musical instrument.

කරදර, *Karadara*, *a.* teasing, plaguing; *s.* troubles.

කරදින්, *Karadin*, *s.* nails on the fingers &c.

කරදිය, *Karadiya*, *s.* sea water, salt water.

කරදු, *Karadu*, *s.* plant, *dracontium*.

කරඳ, *Karaṉda*, *s.* plant, *galidupa arborea*.

කරනෑවෑමියා, *Karanẹwẹmiyá*, *s.* barber.

කරප්පන්, *Karappan*, *s.* cutaneous disease.

කරපටිය, *Karapaṭiya*, *s.* collar, neckband of any kind.

කර පත්‍ර, *Kara-patra*, *s.* saw; splashing the water about when bathing.

කරපත, *Karapata*, *s.* saw.

කරපල, *Kara-pala*, *s.* root of the lotus.

කරපාල, *Karapála*, *s.* sword, scymitar.

කරපාලිකා, *Karapáliká*, *s.* cudgel, wooden sword.

කරපිංච, *Karapiñcha*, *s.* aromatic plant the leaves of which are used in making curry, *murraya Koenigii (Rutaceæ)*.

කරපුට, *Karapuṭa*, *s.* (කර hand, පුට cavity) hands joined as if to receive water.

කරපෙත, *Karapeta*, *s.* palm of the hand.

කරපෙන, *Karapena*, *s.* foam or froth of salt water.

කරබ්, *Karab*, see කරක්ගෙඩිය *karakgeḍiya*.

කරබ, *Karaba*, see කරභ *Karabha*.

කරබටු, *Kara-baṭu*, *s.* sort of night-shade, *solanum sodomeum*.

කරබාගණ ඉන්නවා, *Karabágaṇa innawá*, *v.* to be silent, to hang down the head.

කරබාන, *Karabána*, *a.* silent, sitting in silence with the head hanging down; neck-rope.

කරබිම, *Kara-bima*, *s.* unfruitful ground.

කරබෙඹිය, *Karabeṃbiya*, see කරපිංච *karapiñcha*.

කරභ, *Karabha*, *s.* young camel or elephant; young of any animal; metacarpus; hand from the wrist to the root of the fingers.

කරඹ, *Karaṃba*, *s.* tree, of which there are two species මහ කරඹ *maha-karaṃba*, *carissa carandas*; හින් කරඹ *hín-karaṃba*, *carissa spinarum (Apocynaceæ)*.

කරමර්ද, *Karamarda*, } see the preceding word.
කරමර්දක, *Karamardaka*, }

කරමල, *Karamala*, *s.* crest of a cock; gills of a fish, pl. කරමල් *karamal*.

කරමුක්ත, *Karamukta*, *s.* missile weapon to be thrown by the hand, dart, javelin.

කරමුව, *Karamuwa*, *a.* sharp, as a razor.

කරය, *Karaya*, *s.* razor.

කරරශ්ම, *Kararęsa*, *s.* (කර strong, රශ්ම ray) the sun.

කරල් ඉරිඟු, *Karal iriṉgu*, *s.* plant, *holcus sorghum*.

කරල් තණ, *Karal taṇa*, *s.* common meadow grass.

කරල් තලා, *Karal talá*, *s.* plant, *ocymum polystachymum*.

කරල්සැබෝ, *Karalsẹbó*, *s.* plant, *achyranthes aspera*.

කරල, *Karala*, *s.* ear of corn; pod or seed of any kind; plant, *paspalum kora*; pl. කරල් *karal*.

කරලබු, *Karalabu*, *s.* species of gourd.

කරව්, *Karaw*, *s.* plant, *phyllanthus indicus (Euphorb.)*

කරව්තලා, *Karawtalá*, *s.* species of basil.

කරවටමාන, *Karawaṭamána*, *s.* plant, *anthistiria Cymbaria (Gramineæ)*.

කරවන්, *Karawan*, *s.* saw.

කරවල, *Karawala*, *s.* dried fish.

කරවල කැබෙල්ල, *Karawala-kẹbella*, *s.* small tree, *Antidesma Bunius, variety A. Twaitesianum, (Euphorb.)*

කරවලා, *Karawalá*, *s.* kind of small venomous snake, *Bungarus Ceylonicus* or *B. cæruleus, (Elapidae)*.

කරවිකාරයා, *Karavikárayá*, *s.* horse soldier.

කරවිය, *Karaviya*, *s.* coat of mail.

කරවිර, *Karavira*, } see කරවීර *karavíra* and
කරවිරක, *Karaviraka*, } කරවීරක *karavíraka*.

කරවී, *Karaví*, *s.* leaf of the assafœtida plant.

කරවික, *Karavika*, *s.* kókila or Indian cuckoo.

කරවීර, *Karavíra*, } *s.* fragrant plant, *nerium*
කරවීරක, *Karavíraka*, } *odorum*; sword.

කරවෙනවා, *Karawenawá*, *v.* to dry to excess, to be scorched.

කරවෑල් කොකා, *Karawẹl-koká*, *s.* purple heron, *ardea purpurea*; black bittern, *ardeirella flavicollis* (order *Herodiones*); pl. කරවෑල්කොක්කු *karawẹl-kokku*.

කරශාඛා, *Karaṣákhá*, *s.* (කර hand, ශාඛා branch) finger.

කරසා, *Karasá*, *s.* finger.

කරසාකා, *Karasáká*, see කරශාඛා *karaṣákhá*.

කරහු, *Karahu*, } *a.* hard.
කරහො, *Karaho*, }

කරළු, *Karaḷu*, *a.* hard; *s.* new cloth.

කරා, *Kará*, *ad.* near, proximate; *s.* sun; taxes; articles subject to taxation.

කරා කපුටා, *Kará-kapuṭá*, *s.* kind of crow.

කරාන්ත, *Karánta*, *s.* (කර *kara* hand, අන්ත *anta* end) end of the fingers or hand.

කරාබු, *Karábu*, *s.* clove tree, *Caryophyllus aromaticus:* arabic, *Kerunpul*.

කරාව, *Karáwa*, *s.* a caste so called.

කරි, *Kari*, *s.* elephant.

කරිවිල, *Karivila*, *s.* creeping plant, the fruit of which is used in making curry, *momordica charantia (Cucurbitaceæ)*.

කරී, *Karí*, see කරි *kari*.

කරීන්ද්‍ර, *Karíndra*, *s.* chief of the elephants.

කරීෂ, *Karísha*, s. dry cow dung.

කරුංකා, *Karuṇká*, } *s.* dried areca nut.
කරුංගා, *Karuṇgá*, }

කරුකුරුගානවා, *Karukurugánawá*, *v.* to scratch as a rat; to incise as a person writing on ólas.

කරුගානවා, *Karugánawá*, *v.* (කරුව *karuwa* harrow, ගානවා to rub) to harrow.

කරුණ, *Karuṇa*, *s.* goods, things, effects; event, reason, cause, circumstance. pl. කරුණු *karuṇu*: see කාරණ *káraṇá*.

කරුණා, *Karuṇá*, } *s.* mercy, tenderness, compassion; feeling or sentiment.
කරුණාව, *Karuṇáwa*, }

කරුණාවන්ත, *Karuṇáwanta*, *a.* merciful, kind, compassionate.

කරුමය, *Karumaya*, *s.* merit or demerit of actions, performed in a previous state of existence: commonly used as signifying fate, misfortune, see කර්ම *karma*.

කරුමාන්තය, *Karumántaya*, *s.* labour, work, occupation, employment, see කර්මාන්ත *karmánta*.

කරුව, *Karuwa*, *s.* mould, matrix: share: half: quarter; prop, support, harrow.

කරුවා, *Karuwá*, *s.* artificer.

කරේණු, *Kareṇu*, *s.* female elephant.

කරෝන්, *Karon*, *s.* plant, *Tournefortia argentea (Boragineæ)*.

කල්, *Kal*, *a.* beautiful, pleasant to the sight: plural of කල *kala* time: *s.* goodness; husband; owner: woman.

කල්ක, *Kalka*, *s.* levigated powder.

කල්කය, *Kalkaya*, *s.* sediment, any unctuous substance; dirt, filth, ordure, wax of the ear; collection of medicinal drugs. pl. කල්ක *kalka*.

කල්කරණවා, *Kalkaraṇawá*, *v.* to live, to pass time.

කල්ගිය, *Kalgiya*, *a.* old, ancient; postponed.

කල්දුම, *Kalduma*, *s.* tree, *myrobalans*.

කල්දේරම, *Kaldérama*, *s.* caldron.

කල්ප, *Kalpa*, *s.* in the mythology of the Hindus a kalpa comprehends a day and night of Brahma equal to a period of 432,000,000 years of men, measuring the duration of the world, and as many, the interval of its annihilation. It means also one of six Védáṇgas, or sacred works of the Brahmins, namely the one which contains the description of religious rites. A resolve, a purpose or act of determination.

කල්පද්‍රැම, *Kalpadruma*, *s.* (කල්ප purpose, ද්‍රැම tree) one of the fabulous trees of Indra's heaven; a tree which yields whatever may be desired.

කල්පනාව, *Kalpanáwa*, *s.* thought, reflection, consideration, opinion, pl. කල්පනා *kalpaná*.

කල්පය, *Kalpaya*, see කල්ප *kalpa*.

කල්පලතා, *Kalpalatá*, see කල්පද්‍රැම *kalpadruma*.

කල්පාන්ත, *Kalpánta*, *s.* (කල්ප *kalpa* period, අන්ත *anta* end) end of the Kalpa or the four ages of its existence, namely the destruction of the world (commonly used to signify a long time); see කල්ප *kalpa*.

කල්පාන්ත වර්ෂාව, *Kalpánta warsháwa*, *s.* (කල්පාන්ත and වර්ෂාව rain) according to native mythology the world is to be destroyed three times, the first by rain, කල්පාන්ත වර්ෂාව; second by wind, කල්පාන්ත වාතය *kalpánta wátaya;* third by fire, කල්පාන්ත වහ්නිය *kalpánta wahniya*.

කල්බඳ, *Kalbanda*, *s.* woman.

කල්මස, *Kalmasa*, *s.* sin; kind of hell, division in the internal regions; *a.* dirty, foul.

කල්මාෂ, *Kalmásha*, *s.* variegated colour, mixture of black and white; demon or goblin.

කල්යවනවා, *Kalyawanawá*, *v.* to pass away, to pass the time, used also metaphorically for the mode or manner of life.

කල්ල, *Kalla*, *a.* deaf; healthy, recovered from sickness: trickish, cunning; *s.* person in health: mud, clay.

කල්ලිකුට්ටා, *Kallikuṭṭá*, see කල්ලියා *kalliyá*.

කල්ලි කෙළිය, *Kalli-keḷiya*, *s.* sort of game; game with sticks.

කල්ලියා, *Kalliyá*, *s.* sticks used in playing the aforementioned game.

කල්‍ය, *Kalya*, *s.* health, freedom from sickness; dexterity, cleverness, good fortune, prosperity, happiness, luck.

කල්‍යාණ, *Kalyána*, *s.* good fortune, happiness, prosperity; beauty, mark of beauty; *adj.* prosperous fortunate, virtuous; happy, well, right.

කල්‍යාබ්ද, *Kalyábda*, *s.* see කලියුග *kaliyuga*.

කල්ලෝල, *Kallola*, *s.* surge, billow; joy, happiness, pleasure.

කල්වහාරෙ, *Kalwahare*, *s.* seasonable rain.

කල්හර, *Kalhara*, } *s.* white water lily, white lotus.
කල්හාර, *Kalhára*, }

කල, *Kala*, *s* time, period; dancing girl; threshing floor; vinegar; good; kind of bird, Indian cuckoo; low or soft tone as chirping or buzzing; digit or one sixteenth of the moon's diameter; division of time equal to thirty káshhtás or about eight seconds; part or portion; menstrual discharge; boat; fraud, deceit; goodness; dexterity; semen virile; Yama, the regent of death; crab; woman; poison; mould, matrix.

කලංක, *Kalańka*, *s.* sign, spot, mark; rust of iron; abuse.

කලන්දක, *Kalandaka*, *s.* squirrel.

කලකම, *Kalakama*, *s.* misfortune, unlucky event, pl. කලකම් *kalakam*.

කලකල, *Kalakala*, *s.* confused noise of a crowd, tumult, loud murmuring.

කලකිරිය, *Kalakiriya*, *s.* death.

කලකිරි, *Kalakirí*, *s.* anger.

කලකිරෙණවා, *Kalakirenawá*, *v.* to put off a thing, to lay aside a work, to give up a pursuit; to be pained, to be discouraged, to be disheartened, to be disgusted: pret. කලකිරුණ *kalakíruná*.

කලකුල, *Kalakula*, *s.* war, battle.

කලටි, *Kalati*, *s.* tree, *Polyalthea suberosa (Anonaceæ)*; *a.* unripe, half ripe.

කලටිය, *Kalatiya*, *s.* plant, *Pithecolobium geminatum, (Legum.)*; half ripe cocoa-nut.

කලණ, *Kalana*, *s.* spot, stain, offence, fault, defect; *a.* good, fortunate.

කලත්, *Kalat*, *s.* kind of small bean or gram.

කලත්තනවා, *Kalattanawá*, *v.* to agitate, to stir about as water: pret. කැලැත්තුවා *kelettuwá*.

කලත්‍ර, *Kalatra*, *s.* wife; hip, loins; royal citadel, strong hold or fastness.

කලතනවා, *Kalatanawá*, see කලත්තනවා *kalattanawá*.

කලතුරු, *Kalaturu*, Elu form of කලත්‍ර *kalatra*.

කලද, *Kalada*, *s.* squirrel.

කලදෝ, *Kaladó*, *s.* silver.

කලඳ, *Kalanda*, *s.* kind of jeweller's weight, twenty másha seeds or one twelfth of an ounce; squirrel, pl. කලන් *kalan*.

කලධෞත, *Kaladhauta*, *s.* gold; silver.

කලන්දක, *Kalandaka*, see කලද *kalada*.

කලන්පඩිය, *Kalan-padiya*, *s.* weight equal to a කලඳ *kalanda* which see.

කලන්දා, *Kalandá*, *s.* small kind of fish, the smelt, whiting.

කලප්, *Kalap*, *s.* multitude, assemblage, bundle, see කලාප *kalápa*, sometimes written කලබ *kalaba*.

කලපරන්දෙල්ලා, *Kalaparandellá*, *s.* bird called the Rufus Babbler, *malaco-cercus rufescens (order Passeres)*; also called රතු දෙමලිච්චා *ratu-demalichchá*, පරන්දල් කුරුල්ලා *parandal kurullá*, or පන්දරෙල්ලා *pandarellá*.

කලපුව, *Kalapuwa*, *s.* lake which communicates with the sea, salt water lake.

කලපුව කරවැල්කොකා, *Kalapuwa-karawelkoká*, *s.* grey heron, *ardea cinerea (Herodiones)*; also called ඉඳුරුකොකා *indurukoká*.

කලබ, *Kalaba*, *s.* (කල black, අබ *aba* cloud) rainy cloud.

කලබැගෑනි, *Kalabegéni*, *a.* confused, hurried.

කලබැගෑනි කරණවා, *Kalabegéni-karanawá*, *v.* to confuse, to confound.

කලඹ, *Kalamba*, *s.* young elephant; cluster, bunch, multitude; peacock's tail, an arrow; birds eye view, plant, the cadamba, *nauclea cadamba*.

කලඹනවා, *Kalambanawá*, *v.* to stir, to agitate; to disturb; pret. කැලැඹුවා *kelambuwá*.

කලම්පෙ, *Kalampe*, *s.* back cross plank of a door or of window shutters.

කලමඩල, *Kalamadala*, *s.* threshing floor.

කලමඩුව, *Kalamaduwa*, *s.* tree, *Ficus nervosa (Urticaceæ)*.

කලයිත්ත, *Kalayitta*, *s.* apparatus.

කලරව, *Kalarawa*, *s.* Indian cuckoo; dove, pigeon.

කලරැවු, *Kalarewu*, *s.* Elu form of the foregoing.

කලරැවුලප්, *Kalarewulap*, *s.* wood pecker.

කලල්, *Kalal*, *s.* dirt, mud; time immediately following conception prior to the fœtus being formed.

කලල් ගඩුව, *Kalal-gaḍuwa*, *s.* bubo.

කලල, *Kalala*, *s.* womb, uterus, embryo.

කලව, *Kalawa*, *s.* thigh.

කලවන්, *Kalawan*, *a.* mixed.

කලවන්කරණවා, *Kalawankaraṇawá*, *v.* to mix.

කලවා, *Kalawá*, plural of කලව *kalawa*.

කලවිට, *Kalawiṭa*, *s.* threshing floor, place where the paddy is trodden out of the ear by the bullocks.

කලවැද්දා, *Kalawęddá*, *s.* wild cat, golden musang, (mungoose family) *Paradoxurus zeylanicus*.

කලවැල්, *Kalawęl*, *s.* creeping plant, *Derris Scandens (Leguminosæ)*.

කලශ, *Kalaṣa*, කලස, *Kalasa*, කලසාල, *Kalasála*, } *s.* earthen water pot; it frequently means a water pot containing a quantity of the flowers of the cocoanut tree and placed before the door of a house on festival occasions.

කලහ, *Kalaha*, *s.* tumult, quarrel; war, battle, strife, dissension; water pot; tree, *Ficus infectoria*.

කලහංස, *Kalahansa*, *s.* (කල black, හංස goose) goose with black feet and bill; swan.

කලා, *Kalá*, *s.* art, digit or one-sixteenth of the moon's diameter.

කලාංගෙ, *Kalánge*, *s.* bag or basket made of the leaf of the areca tree.

කලාතුර, *Kalátura*, *ad.* perhaps, sometime or other, uncertain period.

කලාතුරකින්, *Kaláturakin*, *ad.* at times, now and then.

කලාඳුරු, *Kalánduru*, *s.* bulbous plant or grass used medicinally (*cyperus rotundus*), wax of the ear; sort of fly.

කලානි, *Kaláni*, Elu form of the following word.

කලානිධි, *Kalánidhi*, *s.* moon.

කලාප, *Kalápa*, *s.* ornament in general; zone; string of bells worn by women round the waist; peacock's tail; assemblage, multitude; quiver; moon; clever and intelligent man; volume, part.

කලාල, *Kalála*, *s.* kind of carpet or mat.

කලාලේ, *Kalálé*, *s.* kind of mat, pl. කලාල *kalála*.

කලාව, *Kaláwa*, *s.* influence which the moon is supposed to have on the human body, or any of its members, reckoned according to the moon's age.

කලා ශිල්ප *Kalá-ṣilpa*, *s.* any mechanical art or profession.

කලි, *Kali*, see කලියුග *kaliyuga*.

කලිකා, *Kaliká*, *s.* calix of flowers; unblown flower; base or bottom of a lute or Indian *víṇá*.

කලිඟු, *Kalingu*, *s.* country so called which embraces a district on the Coromandel coast, extending from below Cuttack to the vicinity of Madras.

කලින්ද නන්දනි, *Kalinda-nandani*, *s.* (කලින්ද and නන්දනි daughter) the river Jumna, name which it bears in consequence of having its source in the mountain Kalinda.

කලිඳු, *Kalindu*, *s.* name for Yama, regent of the dead; river Yamuná or Jumna.

කලිඳු හිමි, *Kalindu-himi*, *s.* name of Vishṇu.

කලියුග, *Kaliyuga*, *s.* fourth age of the world; according to the Hindús it corresponds with the iron age or age of vice; the commencement of the Kaliyuga age is placed about 3101 years anterior to the Christian era; the number of its years is 432,000 at the expiration of which the world is to be destroyed.

කලුෂ, *Kalusha*, *s.* sin; [Colloq. පාපය *pápaya.*] *adj.* turbid, foul, wicked.

කලේබර, *Kalébara*, කලේවර, *Kaléwara*, } *s.* body (chiefly applied to a dead body).

කලොස්වාරණිය, *Kaloswáraṇiya*, *s.* plant, *justicia gendurussa (Acanthaceæ)*.

කව්, *Kaw*, *s.* poem.

කව, *Kawa*, *s.* circle, *a.* circular.

කවකටුව, *Kawakaṭuwa*, *s.* pair of compasses.

කවගහනවා, *Kawagahanawá*, *s.* to describe a circle.

කවච, *Kawacha*, *s.* armour; mail; drum used in battle, kettle-drum; amulet, charm.

කවචපත්‍ර, *Kawachapatra*, *s.* (කවච and පත්‍ර leaf) pieces of the bark of the tree called bhúrjapatra, inscribed with mystical verses and worn as charms and amulets.

කවටකම්කරණවා, *Kawaṭakamkaraṇawá*, *v.* to joke.

කවටකම, *Kawaṭakama*, *s.* jest, ridicule, banter.

කවටයා, *Kawaṭayá*, *s.* jocose person, wag.

කවඩියා, *Kawaḍiyá*, *s.* small shell commonly called cowri, and used in Bengal as money.

කවද, *Kawada*, *s.* armour.

කවදද, *Kawadáda*, *ad.* on what day, when.

කවදාවත්, *Kawadáwat*, *ad.* ever, at any time.

කවඳ, *Kawanda*, *s.* headless trunk.

කවන්දන්, *Kawandan*, *s.* yoke of a bullock.

කවන්ධ, *Kawandha*, *s.* headless trunk.

කවනවා, *Kawanawá*, *v.* to feed, to cause to eat: pret. කැවුවා *kęwuwá.*

කවනිය, *Kawaniya*, *s.* muslin.

කවය, *Kawaya*, *s*, circle.

කවර, *Kawara*, *s.* braid or fillet of hair; plant, *mimosa octandra*, leaf of the assafœtida tree; *ad.* which? when? what?

කවල, *Kawala*, *s.* mouthful; kind of fish, *lacerta scincus.*

කවලන්කරණවා, *Kawalankaraṇawá*, *v.* to mix. see කලවන්කරණවා *kalawankaraṇawá.*

කවලම, *Kawalama*, *s.* intermixture, pl. කවලන් *kawalan.*

කවාටය, *Kawáṭaya*, *s.* opening in a house for the purpose of letting in light, etc., air hole, window.

කවාළු, *Kawáḷu*, *s.* kind of grass, *Setaria glauca*, *(Gramineæ).*

කවි, *Kavi*, *s.* poetry, song, etc.; covetousness; the planet Venus; also Sukra, the regent of that planet and preceptor of the demons; learned or wise person.

කවික, *Kavika*, *s.* bit of a bridle.

කවිකාරයා, *Kavikárayá*, *s.* poet, writer of songs, ballads, etc.

කවිජන, *Kavijana*, *s.* learned man, wise man.

කවිදන, *Kavidana*, *s.* (කවි poem, දන man) poet.

කවිය, *Kaviya*, *s*, poem, song, verse; pl. කවි *kavi.*

කවිවර, *Kaviwara*, *s.* (කවි and වර best, most excellent) head or chief of the poets.

කවුඩා, *Kawuḍá*, *s.* crow; see කවුඩුවා *kawuḍuwá.*

කවුඩුකැකිරි, *Kawuḍukękiri*, *s.* plant, *bryonia umbellata.*

කවුඩුපණික්කියා, *Kawuḍupanikkiyá*, *s.* (කවුඩු crow, පණික්කියා master) small bird remarkable for its enmity to the crow; see කවුඩුවා *kawuḍuwá.*

කවුඩුබෝ, *Kawuḍubó*, *s.* tree, *Ammotina.*

කවුඩුවා, *Kawuḍuwá*, *s.* crow; Ceylonese white bellied drongo, *buchanga leucopygialis*, also called කවුඩුපණික්කියා, *kawuḍupanikkiyá*; Ceylonese crested drongo, *dissemurus lophorinus*, also called කපුටුබයා *kapuṭubayá;* (order *Passeres.*)

කවුද, *Kawuda*, *pron.* who?

කවුරුන්, *Kawurun*, the plural of කවුද *kawuda.*

කවුළුදොර, *Kawuḷudora*, *s.* window frame or place.

කවුළුව, *Kawuḷuwa*, *s.* window. pl. කවුළු *kawuḷu.*

කවෙළු, *Kawėḷu*, *s.* plant, see කාකොළි *kákoli.*

කවොෂ්ණ, *Kawoshṇa*, *s.* slight warmth.

කශ්මීර ජන්ම, *Kaṣmíra-janma*, *s.* saffron.

කශා, *Kaṣá*, *s.* whip.

කශෙරු, *Kaṣeru*, *s.* back bone; plant, *aponogeton monostachyon.*

කෂ්ට, *Kashṭa*, *s.* bodily pain or uneasiness.

කෂ, *Kasha*, *s.* touch stone.

කෂාය, *Kasháya*, *s.* astringent taste or flavour; anointing; perfuming a person; plant, *bignonia indica;* medical decoction.

කස්, *Kas*, *s.* whip; kind of itch or cutaneous eruption.

කස්තල, *Kastala*, *s.* bell; any piece of metal struck with sticks; thickness.

කස්තානේ, *Kastáné*, *s.* kind of sabre, worn by native headmen, pl. කස්තාන *kastána.*

කස්තුර්‍ය, *Kasturya*, } see කස්තූරි *kastúri.*
කස්තුරි, *Kasturi*, }

කස්තුරි දෙහි, *Kasturi-dehi*, *s.* species of lime, *limonia trifoliata.*

කස්තුරිමුවා, *Kasturi-muwá*. *s.* civet cat.

කස්තූරි, *Kastúri*, *s.* musk.

කස්මල, *Kasmala*, *s.* fainting, syncope.

කස්‍ය, *Kasya*, } *s.* see කාංස්‍යං *káṅsyaṅ.*
කස්‍යන්, *Kasyan*, }

කස, *Kasa*, *s.* touch stone; cocoanut; whip.

කසගහ, *Kasagaha*, *s.* tree, *casuarina equisitifolia.*

කසට, *Kasaṭa*, *a.* astringent, acrid, harsh.

කසටගස, *Kasaṭagasa*, *s.* saffron tree.

කසට්පැය, *Kasaṭpęya*, *s.* yellow, saffron colour.

කසනවා, *Kasanawá*, *v.* to itch, to scratch: pret. කැසුවා *kęsuwá.*

කසපාර, *Kasapára*, *s.* stroke or lash of the whip.

කසපුපුරවනවා, *Kasapupurawanawá*, *v.* to crack or smack a whip.

කසපෑන්, *Kasapęn*, *s.* young, unripe cocoanuts, such as are taken to drink the milk, [Colloq. කුරුම්බා *kurumbá.*]

කසඹිලිය, *Kasambiliya*, see කහඹිලිය *kahambiliya.*

කසල, *Kasala*, *s.* excrement, dung, fœces

කසලමග, *Kasalamaga*, *s.* anus.

කසව්, *Kasaw*, *s.* gold lace, gold fringe.

කසා, *Kasá*, *s.* turmeric, saffron, see කහ *kaha;* shrub, *ixora coccinea;* [Colloquial: රතඹලා *ratambalá*].

කසාක්කාපාන, *Kasákkapána*, see කහ අක්කාපාන *kaha-akkapána.*

කසාදබඳිනවා, *Kasádabandinawá*, *v.* to marry.

කසාදය, *Kasádaya*, *s.* marriage.

කසාය, *Kasáya*, *s.* decoction, see කෂාය *kasháya.*

කසායවස්ත්‍ර, *Kasáyawastra*, *s.* yellow robe of the Buddhist priest.

කසින, *Kasina*, *a.* all, whole, entire.

කසි රට, *Kasi-raṭa*, *s.* Benares.

කසිස්තන, *Kasistana*, *s.* kind of grass.

කසිසන්, *Kasisan*, *s.* pewter.

කසුන්, *Kasun*, *s.* gold, [Colloq. රත්රන් *ratran.*]

කසුබුවා, *Kasubuwá*, *s.* tortoise.

කසේ, *Kasé*, *s.* whip, cat of nine tails.

කහ, *Kaha*, *s.* saffron, turmeric, *curcuma longa (Scitamineæ)*; small tree, the anotta, *Bixa orellana (Bixineæ)*: see කසා *kasá*.

කහ අක්කපාන, *Kaha-akkapána*, *s.* small plant, *bryophyllum calycinum;* see අක්කපාන *akkapána*.

කහ අගමුල්නැති වැල, *Kaha-agamulnẹti wẹla*, *s.* creeping plant, *cuscuta reflexa*.

කහ අඬනහිරිය, *Kaha-aṉḍanahiriya*, *s.* plant, *crotularia retusa (Legum.)*

කහ ඉඳින්නරු, *Kaha-iṉdinnaru*, *s.* hooded milfoil *utricularia bifida*.

කහ උනලි, *Kaha-unalí*, *s.* bamboo cane, *bambusa arundinacea*.

කහ කට්ටාවා, *Kaha-kaṭṭáwá*, *s.* sea fish.

කහකඩ, *Kahakaḍa*, see කහගඩ *kahagaḍa*.

කහ කරවලා, *Kaha-karawalá*, *s.* snake.

කහ කුකුළුකරල් මල්, *Kaha-kukuḷukaral mal*, *s.* cock's comb, *celosia cristata*.

කහ කුරුල්ලා, *Kaha-kurullá*, *s.* bird called black headed oriole, *oriolus melanocephalus;* black headed bulbul, *rubigula melanictera*, (order *Passeres*).

කහ කොරලියා, *Kaha-koraliyá*, *s.* kind of river fish.

කහකොලොඳු, *Kahakolondu*, *s.* tree, *chrysanthemum indicum*.

කහ කැල, *Kaha-kẹla*, *s.* tree, *Diospyros Toposia (Ebenaceæ)*.

කහගඩ, *Kahagaḍa*, *s.* tender husk of the cocoanut.

කහ ගස්මිරිස්, *Kaha-gasmiris*, *s.* pepper plant, *caspicum frutescens*.

කහ ගොනකොල, *Kaha-gonakola*, *s.* creeping plant *Adenosma camphoratum (Scrophulariaceæ)*.

කහ ගැරඬියා, *Kaha-gẹraṉḍiyá*, *s.* snake.

කහට, *Kahaṭa*, *a.* bitter, acrid, astringent; *s.* tree, Patana oak, *Careya arborea (Myrtaceæ)*.

කහට පරාටියා, *Kahaṭa-paráṭiyá*, *s.* kind of fish.

කහ තැල්කොල, *Kaha-tẹlkola*, *s.* plant, *Ipomœa chryseides, (Convolvulaceæ)*.

කහනවා, *Kahanawá*, *v.* to scratch: pret. කැහුවා *kẹhuwá*, see කසනවා *kasanawá*.

කහපන්, *Kahapan*, see කසපැන් *kasapẹn*.

කහ පාට, *Kaha-páṭa*, *s.* yellow colour, saffron colour.

කහ පෙතන්, *Kaha-petan*, *s.* shrub, *Bauhinia tomentosa (Leguminosæ)*.

කහ පෙනෙල, *Kaha-penela*, *s.* tree, *Sapindus laurifolius, (Sapindaceæ.)*

කහ බත්, *Kaha-bat*, *s.* (කහ yellow, බත් boiled rice) rice boiled with a small quantity of turmeric.

කහඹිලියා, *Kahambiliyá*, *s.* nettle, see වල්කහඹිලියා *wal-kahambiliyá* and ගස්කහඹිලියා *gas-kahambileyá*.

කහ මගුරා, *Kaha-magurá*, *s.* kind of fish.

කහමදේ, *Kahamadé*, *s.* yolk of an egg.

කහ මාපිලා, *Kaha-mápilá*, *s.* snake, *dipsas Forsenii (Ophidia.)*

කහ මිරිස්, *Kaha-miris*. *s.* saffron and chilly.

කහමිරිස්ගල, *Kahamirisgala*, *s.* turmeric stone; grinding stone.

කහරම්න, *Kaharamna*, *s.* sort of paddy.

කහලගොඩ, *Kahalagoḍa*, *s.* dung-hill.

කහලමාර්ගය, *Kahalamárgaya*, *s.* anus.

කහලි, *Kahali*, *s.* cheating at play, fraud in gambling.

කහවණුව, *Kahawaṇuwa*, *s.* gerandi, kind of rat snake; weight for weighing gold or silver, equal to about 280 grains troy.

කහල, *Kahala*, *s.* dung, see කසල *kasala*.

කහිනවා, *Kahinawá*, *v.* to cough: pret. කැස්සා *kẹssá*.

කළ, *Kaḷa*, *part.* done.

කළගුණ, *Kaḷaguṇa*, *s.* (කළ done, ගුණ virtue) favour.

කළගුණ දන්නා, *Kaḷaguṇa-danná*, *s.* (කළගුණ and දන්නා who knows) grateful man.

කළගෙඩිය, *Kaḷageḍiya*, *s.* water-pot.

කළමනා, *Kaḷamaná*, *a.* proper, fit, suitable, (applied only to actions) *s. pl.* proper actions.

කළය, *Kaḷaya*, *s.* waterpot.

කළු, *Kaḷu*, *s.* name of Vishṇu; *a.* pleasing, agreeable; black, blue, etc.

කළු අගිල්, *Kaḷu-agil*, *s.* tree, *aquilaria agallochum.*

කළු අත්තන. *Kaḷu-attana*, *s.* species of the thorn apple, *datura fastuosa*.

කළු අලංගා, *Kaḷu-álangá*, *s.* plant, *ipomœa bananox*.

කළුඉඟිරියාව, *Kaḷu-iṉgiriyáwa*, *s.* pupil of the eye.

කළු උක්ගස්, *Kaḷu-ukgas*, *s.* species of the sugar cane.

කළු උණ, *Kaḷu-uṇa*, *s.* common bamboo, ***Bambusa vulgaris.***

කළු ඕරාවා, *Kaḷu-óráwá*, *s.* brown surgeon fish, *Acanthurus maloides.*

කළු කඳ, *Kaḷu-kaṇda*, *s.* tree, *embryapteris glutinifera.*

කළු කඳල, *Kaḷu-kaṇdala*, *s.* plant. *arum colocasia.*

කළු කඩුම්බේරිය, *Kaḷu-kaḍumbériya*, *s.* tree, *diospyros oocarpa (Ebenaceæ).*

කළු කන්මේරිය, *Kaḷu-kanmériya*, *s.* plant, species of night shade, *solanum nigrum.*

කළු කරවලා, *Kaḷu-karawalá*, *s.* kind of snake.

කළු කිහිරි, *Kaḷu-kihiri*, *s*, tree, species of *santalum.*

කළුකුමා, *Kaḷukumá*, *s.* turkey fowl.

කළු කුහුඹි, *Kaḷu-kuhumbi*, *s.* small black ant.

කළු කොකා, *Kaḷu-koká*, *s.* black bittern; see කරවැල් කොකා *karawel-koká.*

කළු කොල්ලු, *Kaḷu-kollu*, *s.* sort of gram, *glycine villosa.*

කළු කැර, *Kaḷu-kẹra*, *s.* plant, *goniothalamus thwaitesii (Anonaceæ).*

කළුගල, *Kaḷugala*, *s.* common black granite, pl. කළුගල් *kaḷugal.*

කළු ගස්මිරිස්, *Kaḷu-gasmiris*, *s.* plant, *capricum futesans.*

කළු ගැරඬියා, *Kaḷu-gẹraṇḍiyá*, *s.* black rat snake.

කළු තල, *Kaḷu-tala*, see තලා *talá.*

කළු තලා, *Kaḷu-talá*, *s.* tree, *nyctanthes arbor tristis.*

කළු තිඹිරි, *Kaḷu-timbiri*, *s.* (කළු black, and තිඹිරි) tree, *diospyros melanoxylon.*

කළු තුඹ, *Kaḷu-tumba*, see තුඹ *tumba.*

කළු දඹල, *Kaḷu-dambala*, *s.* negro kidney bean.

කළු දඬුලේනා, *Kaḷu-daṇḍulẹná*, *s.* black hill-squirrel, *Sciurus Tennentii.*

කළුදුරු, *Kaḷuduru*, *s.* (කළු black, දුරු cummin) black cummin seed, *nigella indica.*

කළුදේවා, *Kaḷudẹwá*, *s.* ass.

කළුන්, *Kaḷun*, *s.* women.

කළු නයා, *Kaḷu-nayá*, *s.* black cobra.

කළු නික, *Kaḷu-nika*, *s.* tree, sort of vitex.

කළු පොල්ලිච්චා, *Kaḷu-pollichchá*, *s.* black robin, *thamnobia fulicata*, (order *Passeres.*)

කළු පොලඟා, *Kaḷu-polangá*, *s.* black viper.

කළු බඩුල්ල, *Kaḷu-badulla*, *s.* species of the marking nut plant, *semecarpus obovatum.*

කළුමදිනවා, *Kaḷumadinawá*, *v.* to blacken the letters written on ólas: pret. කළුමැද්දා *kaḷumẹddá.*

කළු මසුන්, *Kaḷu-masun*, *s.* kind of black fish.

කළු මීමා, *Kaḷu-mímá*, *s.* black buffalo, ***Bubalus arni.***

කළු මීයා, *Kaḷu-míyá*, *s.* black rat, ***Mus rattus.***

කළු මුවා, *Kaḷu-muwá*, *s.* (කළු black, මුවා deer, or mouth) dark kind of deer; monkey.

කළුමැදිරිය, *Kaḷumẹdiriya*, *s.* tree, *diospyros oppositifolia (Ebenaceæ);* commonly called calamander wood.

කළු රත, *Kaḷu-rata*, } *s.* (කළු black, රත red)
කළු රතු, *Kaḷu-ratu*, } mixture of black and red, purple.

කළු රාජාලියා, *Kaḷu-rájáliyá*, *s.* black kite eagle, *neopus malayensis*, (order *Accipitres.*)

කළු රාබු, *Kaḷu-rábu*, *s.* black radish.

කළුරිය, *Kaḷuriya*, *s.* death, [Colloquial: මරණය *maraṇaya*].

කළුරියකරණවා, *Kaḷuriyakaraṇawá*, *v.* to die.

කළු ලුණු, *Kaḷu-luṇu*, *s.* kind of black salt used in the preparation of medicine.

කළුවට, *Kaḷuwaṭa*, *s.* kind of radish, ***raphanus** sativus.*

කළු වඳුරා, *Kaḷu-waṇdurá*, *s.* black monkey, Ceylon laugur, *semnopithicus cephalopterus.*

කළුවර, *Kaḷuwara*, *s.* ebony; *a.* dark.

කළුවර දෙපෝය, *Kaḷuwara-depóya*, *s.* two dark quarters of the moon.

කළු වල්ගහල, *Kaḷu-walgahala*, *s.* plant.

කළු වවුලැටිය, *Kaḷu-wawuleṭiya*, *s.* bonduc or nicker tree, *guilandina bonduc.*

කළුවා, *Kaḷuwá*, } *s.* tuberous plant, kind of
කළුවාල, *Kaḷuwála*, } turmeric; *alpinia galanga (Scitamineœ) great galangal :* medicinal root.

කළුවෙළු, *Kaḷuweḷu*, *s.* venom, poison.

කළු වැටකොළු, *Kaḷu-weṭakoḷu*, *s.* plant, *momordica cylindrica.*

කළු වැරනිය, *Kaḷu-weraniya*, *s.* plant, *justicia gendurassa.*

කළුවැල්, *Kaḷuwel*, *s.* odoriferous creeper.

කළු හබරල, *Kaḷu-habarala*, *s.* species of the wake robin; bulbous plant with very broad leaves.

කළු හබරලිය, *Kaḷu-habaraliya*, *s.* tree, *maba buxifolia (Ebenaceæ).*

කළුහර, *Kaḷuhara*, see කළුවර *kaḷuwara*,

කළුහිස්වලසා, *Kaḷuhis walasá*, *s.* (කළු black, හිස *hisa* head, වලසා bear) hyena.

කළේ, *Kalé*, *s.* water pot, pl. කළු *kaḷa.*

කා, *Ká*, *pron.* who; *s.* heaven; head; body; crow; vessel, water.

කාංසිය, *Káṇsiya*, *s.* lonesomeness, tedium.

කාංසිවෙනවා, *Káṇsiwenawá*, *v.* to become sorrowful, to be distressed.

කාංස්‍ය, *Káṇsya*, *s.* goblet, drinking vessel.

කාංස්‍යං, *Káṇsyaṇ*, *s.* white copper, queen's metal; any amalgam of zinc and copper; sort of musical instrument or *gong* made of bell metal and struck with a stick.

කාක්කා, *Kákká*, *s.* black crow, *corone macrorhynea (order Passeres)*; also called ගොයිගම කාක්කා *goyigama-kákká*.

කාක, *Káka*, *s.* crow, see කාක්කා *kákká;* cripple; measure; heaven; head; body; plant, *ardisia solanacea.*

කාකගුඤ්ජා, *Kákaguṇjá*, *s.* kind of plant, species of the ගුඤ්ජා which see.

කාකජම්බු, *Kákajambu*, *s.* plant, *ardisia solanacea.*

කාකතුණ්ඩිකා, *Kákatuṇḍiká*, see ගුඤ් *gunja.*

කාකපක්ෂ, *Kákapaksha*, *s.* locks left at the tonsure.

කාකපක්ෂි, *Kákapakshi*, *s.* crow.

කාකපුෂ්ට, *Kákapushṭa*, *s.* (කාක crow, පුෂ්ට nourished) Indian cuckoo, name which it has in consequence of leaving its eggs in the nests of crows or other birds, as the same bird in England, for the purpose of being hatched and the young ones brought up by them.

කාකස්වර, *Kákaswara*, *s.* (කාක crow, ස්වර voice) hoarse or harsh voice.

කාකාරි, *Kákári*, *s.* owl.

කාකාල, *Kákála*, *s.* raven.

කාකි, *Káki*, *s.* female crow.

කාකු, *Káku*, *s.* change of the voice in fear, grief, etc.

කාකොත්පල, *Kákotphala*, *s.* kind of lotus.

කාකොදර, *Kákodara*, *s.* snake.

කාකොල, *Kákola*, *s.* raven; snake; boar.

කාකොලි, *Kákoli*, *s.* plant from which is produced a poisonous drug.

කාගෙ, *Káge*, *pron.* whose.

කාචය, *Káchaya*, *s.* disease of the eyes, affection of the optic nerve or gutta serena; kind of siliceous clay or earth from which glass is made.

කාඤ්චන, *Káñchana*, *s.* gold; turmeric; name of several plants and trees which they bear in consequence of the yellow colour of their flower as the champaca, etc.; *a.* golden.

කාඤ්චි, *Káñchi*, *s.* woman's girdle; one of the seven sacred cities of the Hindús: name of a plant, *abrus precatorius.*

කාඤ්චික, *Káñchika*, *s.* sour gruel, see කාඩි *káḍi.*

කාටුව, *Káṭuwa*, *s.* chaff.

කාඩක්කූඩයා, *Káḍakkúḍayá*, } *s.* vagabond: adventurer.
කාඩයා, *Káḍayá*,

කාඩි, *Káḍi*, } *s.* vinegar; toddy or boiled rice water in a state of spontaneous fermentation, used in the preparation of medicine.
කාඩි දිය, *Káḍidiya*,

කාණ්ඩ, *Káṇḍa*, *s.* arrow; part, portion; chapter, section; stalk or stem, the part of the trunk of a tree whence the branches proceed; cluster; opportunity, season; water; kind of sugar cane, *saccharum sara;* implement.

කාණ්ඩකාර, *Káṇḍakára*, *s.* betel nut, fruit of the areca tree.

කාත්, *Kát*, *s.* any one, some one.

කාත්නැති, *Kátneti*, *a.* (කාත් and නැති without) solitary, friendless, destitute.

කාත්‍යායන, *Kátyáyana*, *s.* name of a sage and grammarian.

කාදැති, *Kádeti*, *s.* pin or nail driven into the wall to suspend any thing upon.

කාන්ත, *Kánta*, *a.* pleasing, agreeable, beautiful.

කාන්තගල, *Kántagala*, } *s.* load-stone.
කාන්තපාසාන, *Kántapásána*,

කාන්තා, *Kántá*, *s.* wife, mistress, any beloved object.

කාන්තාර, *Kántára*, *s.* bad or difficult road: wood or forest; wilderness, desert; hole or cavity.

කාන්තාව, *Kántáwa*, *s.* woman: [Colloq. ස්ත්‍රී *strí*]

කාන්තිය, *Kántiya*, *s.* beauty, splendor, light; lustre, effulgence; wish, desire.

කාන්තඃ *Kántaḥ*, *s.* moon; name of Kṛishṇa; iron; gem; husband.

කාන්දං, *Kándaṇ*, } *s.* magnet, loadstone.
කාන්දංගල, *Kándangala*,

කාන්සාව, *Kánsáwa*, *s.* sorrow, grief, distress of mind.

කාන්සිය, *Kánsiya*, *s.* melancholy or depression of spirits occasioned by being in solitude, lonesomeness.

කාන, *Kána*, *s.* crow; *a.* one eyed, monoculous.

කානන, *Kánana*, *s.* forest, grove.

කානුව, *Kánuwa*. *s.* drain. (Portuguese.)

කාපථ, *Kápatha*, *s.* bad road.

කාපිල, *Kápila*, see කපිල *kapila.*

කාබුන්, *Kábun*, *s.* death.

කාම්බල, *Kámbala*, *s.* kind of snake; sort of woollen cloth or blanket; name of a sort of Indian car covered with a blanket.

කාම්පිල්‍ය, *Kámpilya*, *s.* sandal wood; perfume said to be brought from Kampila.

කාම්බෝජ, *Kámbója*, *s.* country so called, situated in the north east of Bengal; name of plant, sort of white mimosa.

කාම, *Káma*, *s.* Hindu cupid or deity of love; wish, desire; lust; semen virile; particle of assent; also, of assertion, as truly, verily; *a.* lustful.

කාමකේලි, *Kámakéli*, *s.* (කාම and කෙළි play) copulation.

කාමච්ඡන්දය, *Kámachchhandaya*, *s.* lechery, libidinousness.

කාම තෘෂ්ණාව, *Káma-tṛishṇáwa*, *s.* (කාම lust, තෘෂ්ණාව the same) lechery, sensual desire.

කාමදූති, *Kámadúti*, *s.* female demon so called.

කාම ධාතු, *Káma-dhátu*, *s.* (කාම and ධාතු source) semen virile.

කාමපාල, *Kámapála*, *s.* one of the names of Balaráma the brother of Kṛishṇa.

කාමභව, *Kámabhawa*, *s.* (කාම passion, භව being) one of the three states of existence, that which includes men and gods.

කාමමිථ්‍යාචාරය, *Káma-mithyácháraya*, *s.* adultery, fornication.

කාමය, *Kámaya*, *s.* lust, desire of corporeal enjoyment.

කාමයා, *Kámayá*, *s.* greedy person.

කාමරංගා, *Kámarangá*, *s.* tree, kind of bilimbi, *averrhoa carambola, (Geraniaceæ).*

කාමරය, *Kámaraya*, *s.* chamber. (Portuguese.)

කාමල, *Kámala*, *s.* disease, *jaundice.*

කාමලෝක, *Kámalóka*, *s.* the world in which bodily pains or pleasures are experienced, including the hells, the world, and the six heavens.

කාමවිකාර, *Kámavikára*, *a.* (කාම lust, විකාර gesture) wanton gesture.

කාමාතුරයා, *Kámáturayá*, *s.* lecher, libidinous man.

කාමාවචර, *Kámáwachara*, *a.* (කාම and අවචර *awachara* going) sensual, subject to passion.

කාමාවචර දිව්‍යලොක, *Kámáwachara divyaloka*, *s.* (කාමාවචර and දිව්‍යලොක heaven) highest or last of the heavens.

කාමාශ්‍රව *Kámáṣrawa*, *s.* sexual pollution.

කාමී, *Kámí*, *s.* libidinous man, lecher.

කාමුක, *Kámuka*, *a.* desirous, cupidinous, lustful, libidinous.

කාය, *Káya*, *s.* body; multitude, assembly; natural temperament; house, habitation.

කායබන්ධන, *Káyabhandana*, *s.* (කාය body, බන්ධන tying) girdle, zone.

කායම, *Káyama*, *s.* dregs of an infusion, a broth or decoction of spices, as pepper etc.

කායස්ථ, *Káyastha*, *s.* one of the castes among the Hindus, the writer caste; name of Brahma the Hindu Supreme Being.

කායික, *Káyika*, *a.* belonging to the body.

කාර්තික, *Kártika*, *s.* the month ඉල් *il* (October and November) when the moon is full near the Pleiades.

කාර්තිකේය, *Kártikéya*, *s.* Indian god of war, generally called in Ceylon Kataragama deviyo, answering to the Grecian Mars.

කාර්පණ්‍ය, *Kárpaṇya*, *s.* poverty, indigence.

කාර්පාස, *Kárpása*, *s.* cotton plant, [Colloquial: කපු *kapu.*]

කාර්ම, *Kárma*, *a.* laborious, industrious, occupied.

කාර්මණ, *Kármaṇa*, *s.* magic.

කාර්මික, *Kármika*. *a.* worked, embroidered, intermixed with coloured thread, cloth, etc.

කාර්මුක, *Kármuka*, *s.* bow; bamboo.

කාර්‍ය්‍ය, *Kárya*, } *s.* cause, origin, motive, object,
කාර්‍ය්‍යා, *Káryá*, } affair, business.

කාශ්මරී, *Kárṣmarí*, *s.* tree, *gmelina arborea.*

කාර්ෂක, *Kárshaka*, *s.* husbandman.

කාර්ෂාපණ, *Kárshápaṇa*, *s.* weight or measure of silver equal to sixteen panas or cowries; weight of copper equal to eighty retis; weight of shells equal to the same number of cowries.

කාර, *Kára*, *s.* killing, slaughter; certainty; effort, exertion, religious austerity; tax, toll, royal revenue; master, lord.

කාරක, *Káraka*, *s.* act, deed, agent especially in grammar; that part of grammar comprising all nouns which imply the agent, object, instrument &c. or any thing except the radical idea; it also includes the application of all the cases; the hal tree, *shorea robusta.*

කාරකකම, *Kárakakama*, *s.* instrumentality.

කාරකය, *Kárakaya*, *s.* horn to put in pills etc.

කාරගෑණුම, *Káragéṇuma*, *s.* marriage.

කාරණවා, *Káraṇawá*, *v.* to hawk, to clear the throat: pret. කෑරුවා *kéruwá.*

කාරණ, *Káraṇá*, *s.* cause, motive, principle, action, agency; organ of sense; instrument, means; pain, agony.

කාරණාව, *Káraṇáwa*, } *s.* the preceding with the
කාරනාව, *Káranáwa*, } affix ව *wa;* affair, circumstance, matter.

කාරම, *Kárama*, *s.* corrosive quality, corrosiveness.

කාරල්ලා, *Káraḷḷá*, *s.* small kind of fish.

කාරව, *Kárawa*, *s.* crow.

කාරවල්ලි, *Kárawalli*, *s.* plant, kind of gourd, *momordica charantia.*

කාරවි කාක්කා, *Káravi kákká*, *s.* common grey crow, *corone splendens*, (order *Passeres.*)

කාරවි, *Káravi*, *s.* kind of paddy or unhusked rice.

කාරවෙල්ලි, *Kárawelli*, see කාරවල්ලි *kárawalli.*

කාරි, *Kári*, *s.* action, act, agency, artist.

කාරිකා, *Káriká*, *s.* kind of actress, dancing girl; action, agency; explanatory verse; art, profession; sharp pain.

කාරිය, *Káriya*, *s.* matter, affair, circumstance, thing.

කාරු, *Káru*, *s.* artist, artificer, agent, maker, doer; name of Viṣwakarma, the architect of the gods.

කාරුණික, *Káruṇika*, *a.* compassionate, merciful, kind.

කාරුපු, *Kárupu*, *s.* owl.

කාල්‍ය, *Kálya*, *s.* dawn, day break.

කාල, *Kála*, *s.* time; quarter; name of Yama regent of the dead; black (colour,) death; form of Ṣiva; iron; black agallochum.

කාලක්‍රියා, *Kálakriyá*, *s.* death.

කාලක්‍රියා කරණවා, *Kálakriyá-karaṇawá*, *v.* to die.

කාලක, *Kálaka*, *s.* freckle, mark; water-snake; liver.

කාලකණ්ඨ, *Kálakaṇṭha*, *s.* (කාල black, කණ්ඨ neck or throat) name of Ṣiva; waterfowl, gallinule; sparrow; peacock; tree, *pentaptera tomentosa.*

කාලකණ්ණි, *Kálakaṇṇi*, *a.* miserable, unfortunate, unlucky, wretched, unhappy.

කාලකණ්ණියා, *Kálakaṇṇiyá*, *s.* miserable person.

කාලකූට, *Kálakúṭa*, *s.* (කාල Yama, කූට to destroy) kind of poison said to be so powerful that it even destroys Yama the regent of death.

කාලකෘත්, *Kálakṛit*, } *s.* (කාල time, කෘත් who
කාලකෘත, *Kálakrata*, } makes) he who makes or measures time, the sun.

කාලඛඤ්ජන, *Kálakhañjana*, } *s.* liver.
කාලඛණ්ඩ, *Kálakhaṇḍa*, }

කාලඤ්ජර, *Kálañjara*, *s.* name of Ṣiva; also of a country, the modern Kallinjer; an assembly or collection of religious mendicants; Kallinjer is one of the places at which such assemblies meet, being enumerated in the Védas amongst the Tapasyasthánas or places adapted to practices of austere devotion.

කාලත්‍රය, *Kálatraya*, *s.* (කාල time, ත්‍රි three) past, present and future time.

කාලතුවක්කුව, *Kálatuwakkuwa*, *s.* cannon.

කාලධර්ම, *Káladharma*, *s.* (කාල and ධර්ම virtue or property) death, dying.

කාලපක්ෂය, *Kálapakshaya*, *s.* (කාල black, පක්ෂය side) the moon's wane.

කාලපන්දම, *Kálapandama*, *s.* kind of large torch used in the temples.

කාලම, *Kálama*, *s.* magic; black art, actions performed by the agency of the devil.

කාලමුඛ, *Kálamukha*, *s.* (කාල black, මුඛ mouth) monkey. [Colloquial: වඳුරා *wandurá* or රිලවා *rilawá*].

කාලය, *Kálaya*, *s.* time, see කාල *kála*.

කාල ලවණ, *Kála-lawaṇa*, *s.* factitious and purgative salt.

කාල ලෝහ, *Kála-loha*, *s.* (කාල and ලෝහ metal) iron.

කාලවර්ණ, *Kálawarṇa*, *s.* black (colour).

කාලව්‍යාපි, *Kálavyápi*, *a.* constant, perpetual, eternal.

කාලසිංහ, *Kálasiṇha*, *s.* (කාල and සිංහ lion) bear, [Colloq. වලසා *walasá*].

කාලසූත්‍රය, *Kálasútraya*, *s.* one of the twenty-one hells mentioned in Hindu mythology; one of the eight principal hells of the Buddhists.

කාලහංස, *Kálahaṇsa*, *s.* black swan.

කාලාගරු, *Kálágaru*, *s.* black kind of aloe wood or agallochum.

කාලායස්, *Káláyas*, *s.* iron.

කාලි, *Káli*, *s.* name of Durgá the wife of Ṣiva.

කාලික, *Kálika*, *s.* curlew; black kind of sandal; multitude of clouds; dark cloud threatening rain; fog or mist; goddess Gauri; form of Chaṇḍí or Durgá; female singer of swarga; blackness; black colour; fault or flaw in gold, etc.; black scorpion; spikenard; line of hair extending to the navel; female crow; ink; in proper time.

කාලිඞ්ග, *Káliṅga*, *s.* country so called; elephant; snake; species of cucumber, *cucumis utilatissimus;* blue dove.

කාලිදාස, *Kálidása*, *s.* celebrated poet, who was one of the nine poets or gems of Vikramáditya's court and is supposed by some to have flourished in the century preceding the Christian era.

කාලි නයා, *Káli-nayá*, *s.* snake.

කාලි පොලඟා, *Káli-polangá*, *s.* snake.

කාව්‍ය, *Kávya*, *s.* name of Sikurá, preceptor of the demons; poetical composition, poem; intelligence, understanding.

කාව්‍ය කර්තෘ *Kávya-kartṛi*, *s.* (කාව්‍ය poem, කර්තෘ who makes) poet.

කාවත්, *Káwat*, *s.* sun. [Colloq. ඉර *ira.*]

කාවයියා, *Káwaiyá*, *s.* kind of fish.

කාවල්, *Káwal* *s.* care, preservation.

කාවළු, *Káwaḷu*, *s.* species of panic grass, *panicum glaucum.*

කාවා, *Káwá*, *s.* moth.

කාවාටියා, *Káwáṭiyá*, *s.* oyster.

කාවියම, *Káviyama*, *s.* poem, poetry, pl. කාවියම් *káviyam.*

කාවුළු, *Káwuḷu*, *s.* kind of grass, *panicum glaucum.*

කාශ්‍යප, *Káṣyapa*, } *s.* name of Aruṇa charioteer
කාශ්‍යපි, *Káṣyapi*, } of the sun; name of Garuḍa the bird of Vishṇu, both of whom were sons of Káṣyapa.

කාශ, *Káṣa*, see කාස *kása.*

කාශ, *Káṣa*, see කාසි *kási.*

කාෂ්ඨක, *Káshṭaka*, *a.* dry.

කාෂ්ඨතක්‍ෂ, *Káshṭatakṣha*, *s.* (කාෂ්ඨ wood, තක්‍ෂ to cut or pare) carpenter. [Colloq. වඩුවා *waḍuwá.*]

කාෂ්ඨ, *Káshṭha*, *s.* wood.

කාෂ්ඨා, *Káshṭhá*, *s.* quarter or region of the world, space, tract; place, site; limit, boundary; measure of time, the 30th part of a kalá or eighteen twinklings of the eye; excellency, superiority; plant, *curcuma zanthorhiza.*

කාශ්මීර, *Káṣmíra*, *s.* noted city or country in the north west of India, Cashmere; plant with a tuberous root, a sort of costus, *costus speciosus.*

කාශ්මීරජ, *Káṣmíraja*, } *s.* (කාශ්මීර and
කාශ්මීරජන්මන්, *Káṣmírajanman*, } ජ born) saffron; costus, see කාශ්මීර *káṣmíra.*

කාස්‍යප *Kásyapa*, see කාශ්‍යප *káṣyapa.*

කාස, *Kása*, *s.* cough, catarrh; tree, kind of reed or long grass, *saccharum spontaneum;* species of the murunga; whip tree, *Casuarina equisetifolia (Casuarineæ);* thin kind of white cloth.

කාසඝ්නී, *Kásaghní*, *s.* (කාස and ඝ්නී a termination from හන් *han* which kills) that which removes a cough; sort of prickly night shade.

කාසමර්ද, *Kásamarda*, *s.* (කාස and මර්ද which destroys) acid preparation, mixture of tamarinds and mustard; shrub producing edible peas, *cytisus cajan.*

කාසය, *Kásaya*, *s.* consumption: see කාස *kása.*

කාසාරි, *Kásári*, see කාසමර්ද *kásamarda.*

කාසාව, *Kásáwa*, *s.* yellow robes worn by the Buddhist priests.

කාසීස, *Kásísa*, *s* (කාස *kása* cough, ඊසණ් *ísaṇ* affix) green vitriol, green sulphate of iron.

කාසි, *Kási*, *s.* city greatly celebrated in the Buddhistical writings, the modern Benares; money.

කාසිවලට ගන්නවා, *Kásiwalaṭa gannawá*, *v.* to purchase.

කාහල, *Káhala*, *s.* sound in general; kind of large drum or tom tom.

කිං, *Kiṇ*, see කිම් *kim.*

කිංකර, *Kiṇkara*, *s.* servant.

කිංකිණික, *Kiṇkiṇika*, } *s.* girdle of small bells or
කිංකිණී, *Kiṇkiṇí*, } any tinkling ornaments.

කිංජල්ක, *Kiṇjalka*, *s.* anther of the lotus.

කිංශුක, *Kiṇṣuka*, *s.* tree bearing beautiful red blossoms, almost every part of which is medicinal, *butea frondosa.* [Colloq. කැල *kẹla.*]

කික්කි, *Kikki*, *s.* bitch whelp.

කිකරු, *Kikaru*, see කීකරු *kíkaru.*

කිකල, *Kikala*, Elu particle signifying what time?

කිකින්දැල, *Kikindẹla*, see කිංකිණී *kiṇkiṇí.*

කිකිණි, *Kikini*, see කිංකිණික *kiṇkiṇika.*

කිකිළි, *Kikiḷi*, *s.* hen, pl. කිකිළියෝ *kikiḷiyó.*

කිකිළිබිජ්ජ, *Kikiḷibijja*, } *s.* egg, pl. කිකිළි
කිකිළිබිත්තරය, *Kikiḷibittaraya*, } බිජු *kikiḷibiju.*

කිකුර, *Kikúra*, *s.* servant of Ṣiva.

කිඤ්ජල්ක, *Kiñjalka*, *s.* filament of a lotus, great numbers of which surround the pericarp.

කිට්ටු, *Kiṭṭu*, *ad.* near to.

කිට්ටුකරණවා, *Kiṭṭukaraṇawá*, *v.* to place near.

කිට්ටුව, *Kiṭṭuwa*, *s.* neighbourhood.

කිට්ටුවෙනවා, *Kiṭṭuwenawá*, *v.* to approach, to approximate.

කිඩ, *Kiḍa*, *s.* Elu form of ක්‍රීඩාව sport, pleasure, dancing; the kneeling of an elephant.

කිඩගහනවා, *Kiḍagahanawá*, *v.* to kneel as an elephant.

කිඩවර, *Kiḍawara*, *s.* worker in straw or rattan, basket maker.

කිඩහකෙළි, *Kiḍahakeḷi*, *s.* little girl, pl. කිඩහ කෙල්ලෝ *kiḍaha-kelló.*

කිඩාරන්, *Kiḍáran*, *s.* plant, *amorphophallus campanulatus (Araceæ).*

කිඩිය, *Kiḍiya*, *s.* dancing; dancing girl.

කිඩියර, *Kiḍiyara*, *s.* conjuror, Elu form of ක්‍රීඩාකාර *kríḍákára.*

කිඩු, *Kiḍu*, see කිඩ *kiḍa.*

කිඩු බිම, *Kiḍu-bima*, *s.* dancing school or assembly room.

කිඩෑහෑකෙලි *Kiḍęhękeli*, see කිඩහකෙලි *kiḍaha kelí.*

කිඩෑ, *Kiḍę*, see කුඩා *kuḍá.*

කිණුකට, *Kiṇukaṭa*, *s.* (කිණු black, කට from කණ්ඨ *kaṇṭha* neck) name of Ṣiva.

කිණුමග, *Kiṇumaga*, *s.* (කිණු black resembling charcoal, මග way) fire.

කිණුමස්, *Kiṇumas*, *s.* fresh water fish of a dark-colour.

කිත්, *Kit*, *s.* fame, see කීර්තිය *kírtiya.*

කිත්තන්, *Kittan*, *s.* marline; tow, hemp.

කිත්ති, *Kitti*, *s.* Pali form of කීර්ති *kírti* which see.

කිතයුග, *Kitayuga*, *s.* golden age.

කිතල, *Kitala*, *s.* sort of plantain, *musa sapientum.*

කිතලා, *Kitalá*, *s.* water cock, *gallicrex cincrea.* also called වලිකුකුළා *walikukuḷá;* Indian blue-coat, *porphyrio polliocephalus*, (order *Grallæ.)*

කිතව, *Kitawa*, *s.* gamester, gambler; cheat, cheating, fraudulent; thorn apple, *datura stramonium.*

කිතිකවනවා, *Kitikawanawá*, *v.* to tickle.

කිතුල්, *Kitul*, *s.* tree from which jaggory is obtained; the pith of old trees resembles sago, *caryota urens (Palmae).*

කිදු, *Kidu*, *s.* pepper.

කිඳ, *Kiṉda*, } *s.* marsh, bog.
කිඳලිය, *Kiṉdaliya*, }

කිඳනවා, *Kiṉdanawá*, *v.* to sink: pret. කිඳුනා *kiṉduná.*

කිඳවනවා, *Kiṉdawanawá*, *v.* to cause to sink, to immerse: pret. කිඳෙව්වා *kiṉdewwá.*

කිඳි, *Kiṉdi*, *s.* pepper, plant, the *túlsi ocymum sanctum;* also *tinospora cordifolia;* see ගළුචි *galúchi.* [Colloq. මදුරුතලා *maduru-talá* or රස කිඳ *rasakiṉda.*]

කිඳු, *Kiṉdu*, *s.* order, arrangement; branch; pepper.

කිඳුරා, *Kiṉdurá*, *s.* kind of fabulous being the upper part said to resemble a man, the lower part a bird; merman; in Hindu mythology it means a kind of demi-god attached to the service of Kuwéra chief of the devils; celestial musician; pl. කිඳුරෝ *kiṉduró.*

කිඳුරි, *Kiṉduri*, *s.* mermaid, pl. කිඳුරියෝ *kiṉduriyó.*

කිඳුරිඳු, *Kiṉdurindu*, *s.* (කිඳුරා *kiṉdurá* demigod or satyr, ඉඳු *iṉdu* chief) Kuvéra.

කිඳුරු, *Kiṉduru*, see කිඳුරා *kiṉdurá.*

කිඳෙනවා, *Kiṉdenawá*, *v.* to sink: pret. කිඳුනා *kiṉduná.*

කින්කිනික, *Kinkinika*, see කිංකිණික *kiṉkiṇika.*

කින්තුල්ලා, *Kintullá*, see කිනිතුලා *kinitulá.*

කින්ද, *Kinda*, *pron.* what?

කින්නරයා, *Kinnarayá*, *s.* low caste man, weaver of mats.

කින්නරා, *Kinnará*, *s.* the mat weaver, see කිඳුරා *kiṉdurá.*

කින්නරේස, *Kinnaresa*, *s.* name of Kuvéra regent of Pátála or hell.

කින්නාරම, *Kinnárama*, *s.* large sort of lute; guitar.

කින්පිය, *Kinpiya*, *s.* logwood.

කින්සුක, *Kinsuka*, see කිංශුක *kiṉṣuka.*

කිනම්, *Kinam*, *pron.* who, what.

කිනි, *Kini*, *s.* sun. [Colloq. ඉර *ira.*]

කිනිඟු, *Kiniṉgu*, *s.* tender fruit.

කිනිඟුල්, *Kiniṉgul*, *s.* unripe fruit.

කිනිටු, *Kiniṭu*, *s.* worthless person, mean person.

කිනිත්ත, *Kinitta*, *s.* end of a bunch, cluster; tender branch, twig, pl. කිනිති *kiniti.*

කිනිතුලා *Kinitulá*, *s.* dog louse, tick, pl. කිනිතුලෝ *kinituló.*

කිනිමග, *Kinimaga*, see කිණුමග *kinumaga.*

කිනිස්ස, *Kinissa*, *s.* dagger, kind of ladle made of the shell of cocoanut, and used to take water from a jar to drink, pl. කිනිසි *kinisi.*

කිනිහිරය, *Kinihiraya*, } *s.* tree, *cochlospermum*
කිනිහිරිය, *Kinihiriya*, } *gossypium*, *(Bixineæ.)*
also called එල ඉඹුල් *ela-iṃbul.*

කිනිහී *Kinihí*, *s.* (කිනි sore, හ *ha* which removes) tree said to be good for wounds which it removes by cicatrizing them, *achyranthes aspera.* [Colloq. කරල්හෑබ *karalhęba.*]

කිනිරේ, *Kiníré*, *s.* anvil, pl. කිනිර *kinira.*

කිනු, *Kinu*, Elu form of කෘෂ්ණ *kṛishṇa* black.

කිනුටු, *Kinuṭu*, see කිනිටු *kiniṭu.*

කිනුදම්, *Kinudam*, *s.* ornamental chain for the neck.

කිනුපුල්, *Kinupul*, *s.* species of the nymphea, *blue lotus.*

කිනුමග, *Kinumaga*, *s.* (කිනු black resembling charcoal, මග way) fire.

කිනුරා, *Kinurá*, *s.* attendants of Kuvéra the king of Pátála or the infernal regions.

කිනුරිඳු, *Kinurindu*, *s.* name of Wesamuni king of Yakas or devils.

කිනුරු, *Kinuru*, *s.* retinue of Wesamuni.

කිපීම, *Kipíma*, *s.* verbal noun of කිපෙනවා *kipenawá.*

කිපෙනවා, *Kipenawá*, *v.* to be in a passion, to be angry: pret. කිපුනා *kipuná*.

කිබිදෙනවා, *Kibidenawá*, *v.* to awake: pret, කිබිදුනා *kibiduná*.

කිබිලි, *Kibili*, *s.* shrimp, prawn, [Colloquial: ඉස්සා *issá*.]

කිබුව, *Kibuwa*, *s* hood of a gig.

කිබුලා, *Kibulá*, *s.* bird, see කිරලා *kiralá*.

කිඹිලි, *Kimbili*, *s.* kind of sprat. *clupea cultrata*.

කිඹිසිනවා, *Kimbisinawá*, } *v.* to sneeze, pret.
කිඹිහිනවා, *Kimbihinawá*, } කිඹිස්සා *kimbissá*.

කිඹිහිල්ල, *Kimbihilla*, *s.* sneezing.

කිඹුල්, *Kimbul*, *s.* plant, *plumbago rosea*, lead wort; tawny colour.

කිඹුල්මුව, *Kimbulmuwa*, *s.* name of a carriage wheel.

කිඹුල්වන්, *Kimbulwan*, *s.* tawny colour.

කිඹුල්වැන්න, *Kimbulwẹnna*, *s.* generic name of *Polygonum*.

කිඹුල් හූනා, *Kimbul-húná*, *s.* kind of lizard.

කිඹුලා, *Kimbulá*, *s.* crocodile, alligator, pl. කිඹුලෝ *kimbuló*.

කිම්, *Kim*, *ind. part.* signifying, what, how; either, or, a particle of doubt or interrogation, also a *rel. pron.* what, who, which, expressing doubt, interrogation, disdain, reproach; as, in English. Who are you, etc.

කිම්ද, *Kimda*, *interrog. pron.* what? what of that?

කිම්පුරුෂ, *Kimpurusha*, see කිඳුරා *kindurá*.

කිම, *Kima*, *interrog. pron.* why, wherefore, which, what? see the preceding.

කිමි, *Kimi*, *s.* small monkey, worms, see ක්‍රිමි *krimi*.

කිමිදිනවා, *Kimidinawá*, *v.* to dive: pret. කිමිද්දා *kimiddá*.

කිමෙක්ද, *Kimekda*, see කිම්ද *kimda*.

කියත, *Kiyata*, *s.* saw, pl. කියත් *kiyat*.

කියනවා, *Kiyanawá*, *v.* to speak, to say, to tell: pret. කිව්වා *kiwwá*.

කියඹු, *Kiyambu*, *s.* hair of the head; hair platted and tucked up behind the head.

කියවනවා, *Kiyawanawá*, *v.* to read, to cause to say: pret. කියෙව්වා *kiyewwá*.

කියළු, *Kiyalu*, *s.* publishing, informing.

කියා, *Kiyá*, *s.* bullock's hump; *par.* having said.

කියාදෙනවා, *Kiyádenawá*, *v.* to inform, to communicate, to expound; to confess, to acknowledge, to dictate, to teach: pret. කියාදුන්නා *kiyádunná*.

කියු, *Kiyu*, *s.* speech.

කියුළු, *Kiyuḷu*, *s.* information, announcement.

කිර, *Kira*, parrot; [Colloq. ගිරවා *girawá*.] milk.

කිරඋල් *Kira-ul*, *s.* properly කිරිවුල් *kiriwul* which see.

කිරඟු, *Kirangu*, *s.* elk, [Colloq. ගෝනා *góná*.]

කිරණ, *Kiraṇa*, *s.* ray, sun-beam; white sea.

කිරණවා, *Kiraṇawá*, *v.* to weigh, to balance: pret. කිරුවා *kiruwá*.

කිරණමාලි, *Kiraṇamáli*, *s.* (කිරණ ray, මාලි collection) sun.

කිරත, *Kirata*, *s.* small plant, *gentiana chirayta*.

කිරලගහ *Kirala-gaha*. species of cork tree.

කිරලා, *Kiralá*, *s.* red wattled lap-wing, *lobivanellus indicus*, also called කිබුලා *kibulá;* yellow wattled lap-wing, *lobipluria malubarica*, (order *Grallæ)*.

කිරලාවා, *Kiraláwá*, *s.* sea fish.

කිරවුල්, *Kirawul*, *s.* body.

කිරාතක, *Kirátaka*, } *s.* barbarians, uncivilized peo-
කිරාතජ, *Kirátaja*, } ple, savages.

කිරාත තික්ත, *Kiráta-tikta*, *s.* (කිරාත and තික්ත bitter) kind of gentian, *gentiana chirayta*, found in the woods.

කිරාවැටෙනවා, *Kiráwẹṭenawá*, *v.* to slumber.

කිරි, *Kiri*, *a.* white; *s.* milk; plant, *clinsene coracana;* learned men; elephants.

කිරිඅඟුණ, *Kiri-anguṇa*, *s.* plant, *dregea volubilis* or *hoya viridiflora (Asclepiadiaceæ)*.

කිරි ඉබ්බා *Kiri-ibbá*, *s.* fresh water burrowing turtle, *emyda Ceylonensis* (order *Chelonia)*.

කිරි කජු, *Kiri-kaju*, *s.* plant, *vissadula zeylanica (Malvaceæ)*.

කිරි කවෙළු, *Kirikawéḷu*, *s.* Elu form of ක්ෂීරකාකෝලි *ikshíra-kákóli*.

කිරි කොටනවා, *Kiri-koṭanawá*, *v.* to churn, pret. කිරි කෙටුවා *kiri-keṭuwá*.

කිරි කෝන්, *Kiri-kón*, *s.* tree, *walsura piscidia*, *(Meliaceæ);* the bark is stated to be thrown into ponds to kill the fish without rendering them unwholesome.

කිරිගඩුව, *Kirigaḍuwa*, *s.* little boil, bubo.

කිරිගරුඬ, *Kirigaruṇḍa*, *s.* sort of white substance which when pulverized is used in medicine, species of alabaster.

කිරිගොටුව, *Kirigoṭuwa*, *s.* milk strainer made of wicker work.

කිරිඟු, *Kiringu*, see කිරඟු *kirangu*.

කිරිච්චය, *Kirichchaya*, *s.* poniard, dagger.

කිරිඳි, *Kirindi*, *s.* tares.

කිරිඳිමානා, *Kirindi-máná*, *s.* kind of grass, *coix lachryma (Gramineæ).*

කිරිඳිවැල්, *Kirindi-wel*, *s.* creeper, *rouria santaloides (Connaraceæ).*

කිරිනගුළුවා, *Kirinaguluwá*, *s.* kind of fish.

කිරිපළු, *Kiripalu*, *s.* tree, *buchanania latifolia.*

කිරිපා, *Kiripá*, *s.* unicorn.

කිරිපිඩු, *Kiripidu*, *s.* rice milk, mixture of boiled rice and milk.

කිරිපොවනවා, *Kiri-powanawá*, *v.* suckle.

කිරිපැල්ල, *Kiripella*, *s.* tree, *ficus Tsjakela (Urticaceæ).*

කිරිබත්, *Kiribat*, *s.* rice boiled with the milk of the cocoa-nut.

කිරිබදු, *Kiribadu*, *s.* plant, *Ipomœa digitata (Convolvulaceæ).*

කිරිබදුල්ල, *Kiribadulla*, *s.* tree, species of the marking nut plant, *semecarpus latifolium.*

කිරිබොන දරුවා, *Kiribona-daruwá*, *s.* suckling.

කිරිබොනවා, *Kiribonawá*, *v.* to drink milk.

කිරිමකුළු, *Kiri-makulu*, *s.* small tree, (juice poisonous, seeds used for intoxicating fish,) *sapium indicum, (Euphorbiaceæ).*

කිරිමඩුවා *Kiri-maduwá*, *s.* sea fish.

කිරි මත්ගාණවා, *Kiri-matgánawá*, *v.* to churn.

කිරිමදු, *Kirimadu*, *s.* plant, *Ipomœa cymosa (Convolv.)*

කිරිමව්, *Kiri-maw*, *s* (කිරි milk, මව් mother) nurse, foster mother, pl. කිරිමවුන් *kirimawun.*

කිරිමෝරා, *Kirimórá*, *s.* white shark.

කිරිමෝරු, *Kirimóru*, *s.* churned milk.

කිරිමැටි, *Kirimeti*, *s.* (කිරි milk, මැටි clay) white clay; pipe clay, marl; Kaolin or China clay.

කිරිය, *Kiriya*, *s.* ground sufficient to sow four මාණිකා *mániká*=64 ලාස් *lás*; a saw; grammatical term for verb.

කිරිල්ල, *Kirilla*, *s.* tree, *Sonneratia acida (Lythraceæ)*; cork tree.

කිරිල්ල, *Kirilla*, } the fem. of කුරුල්ලා *kurullá*,
කිරිල්ලි, *Kirilli*, } pl. කිරිල්ලියෝ *kirilliyó.*

කිරිවඩිනවා, *Kiriwadinawá*, *v.* to be not quite ripe, juicy: pret. කිරිවැදුනා *kiriwedunú.*

කිරිවරල, *Kiriwarala*, *s.* plant, *Isonandra wightiana (Sapotaceæ).*

කිරිවල්ලා, *Kiriwallá*, *s.* tree, *Holarrhena mitis (Apocynaceæ).*

කිරිවව්ලා, *Kiriwawlá*, *s.* small bat, pl. කිරිවව්ලෝ *kiriwawló.*

කිරිවුල් *Kiriwul*, *s.* body.

කිරිවැල්, *Kiriwel*, *s.* creeping plant, *Morinda umbellata (Rubiaceæ)*; also *Ichnocarpus frutescens (Apocynaceæ).*

කිරිසිදු, *Kirisidu*, *s.* (කිරි and සිදු sea) sea of milk.

කිරිහඟුළු, *Kirihangulu*, *s.* plant, *marsdenia asthmatica.*

කිරිහිරිය, *Kirihiriya*, *s.* plant, *exacum zeylanicum (Gentianaceæ)*; also called *Binduru*; see *kirihembiliya.*

කිරිහැන්ද, *Kirihenda*, *s.* plant, *Celocia argentea (Amarantaceæ).*

කිරිහැඹිලිය, *Kirihembiliya*, *s.* tree, *Dichopsis grandis (Sapotaceæ)*; also called *Kirihiriya*, and *Mihiriya.*

කිරීට, *Kiríta*, *s.* crown, diadem.

කිරීම, *Kirima*, verbal noun of කිරණවා *kiranawá* or කරණවා *karanawá.*

කිරුතු, *Kirutu*, see කිරාතක *kirátaka.*

කිරුන්බර, *Kirunbara*, } *s.* weights for scales.
කිරුම්බර, *Kirumbara*, }

කිරුළ, *Kirula*, *s.* crown, diadem.

කිරුළුමිණ, *Kirulumina*, *s.* precious stone on the top of a crown.

කිරෙන්වරණවා, *Kirenwaranawá*, *v.* to wean: pret. කිරෙන්වැරුවා *kirenweruwá.*

කිල්ල, *Killa*, *s.* menstrual flux, impurity. see කිලි *kili.*

කිල්ලොට, *Killoté*, *s.* small box containing the chunam which is eaten by the natives with the betel leaf, pl. කිල්ලොටා *killotá.*

කිල, *Kila*, *s.* small house or cottage.

කිලන්, *Kilan*, *s.* butter milk.

කිලල, *Kilala*, *s.* plant, *sonneratia acida* Ceylon cork tree: [Colloq. කිරිල්ල *kirilla*].

කිලසි, *Kilasi*, *s.* ailment, slight pain.

කිලාස, *Kilása*, *s.* itch, blotch, scab.

කිලි, *Kili*, *s.* menstrual flux; small house or hut.

කිලිටි, *Kiliti*, see කිළුටු *kilutu.*

කිලිදිල්ලා, *Kilidillá*, *s.* kind of fish.

කිලිපොළනවා, *Kilipolanawá*, *v.* to shiver, to startle: pret. කිලිපෙළුවා *kilipeluwá.*

කිලිපැල, *Kilipela*, *s.* kind of small hut connected with the residence of families in which females are forced to reside during the flow of the menses, pl. කිලිපැල් *kilipel.*

කිලිමාලේ, *Kilimálé*, *s.* bloody issue.

කිලිල්, *Kilil*, *s.* edible part of the stem of cocoa-nut tree, *cocoanut cabbage.*

කිලුටු, *Kiluṭu*, *a.* dirty, impure, filthy, defiled, polluted, Elu form of ක්ලිෂ්ට *klishṭa.*

කිව්, *Kiw*, *s.* speech, speaking; *part.* said, mentioned.

කිවි, *Kivi*, *s.* planet Venus; poet; professor of learning; monkey of the black kind.

කිවිදින, *Kividina*, *s.* Friday.

කිවිඳු, *Kivindu*, *s.* name of Venus.

කිවියර, *Kiviyara*, *s.* poet.

කිවුල්, *Kiwul*, *a.* wanting salt, *i. e.* provisions which are deficient in salt; but when used of water, brackish.

කිස්, *Kis*, *pron.* all, anything, whatever; *s.* for කුස් *kus* which see.

කිස්කනවා, *Kiskanawá*, *v.* to smart, (as when whipped): pret. කිස්කෑවා *kiskẹwá.*

කිස්දස්, *Kisdas*, *s.* beggar, mendicant, [Colloquial: හිඟන්නා *hinganná.*]

කිස්දෙවුන්, *Kisdowun*, *s.* last born, youngest brother.

කිස්ණා, *Kisṇá*, Elu form of කෘෂ්ණ *Kṛishṇa.*

කිස, *Kisa*, Elu form of කෘත්‍ය *kṛitya* which see.

කිසඳ, *Kisanda*, *s.* dwelling house.

කිසපිටුකුස්, *Kisapiṭukus*, *s.* man living at another's expense.

කිසල, *Kisala*, *s.* sprout, shoot; extremity of a shoot bearing new leaves.

කිසි, *Kisi*, *a.* any, some; some thing, any thing.

කිසිකවනවා, *Kisikawanawá*, *v.* to smack a whip.

කිසිත්, *Kisit*, *a.* any, some, anything, whatever.

කිසිනු, *Kisinu*, *s.* practice of austerities for the purpose of destroying the passions.

කිසිම්, *Kisim*, *s.* flower, [Colloq. මල *mala*].

කිසිම, *Kisima*, }
කිසියම්, *Kisiyam*, } *a.* any, some.

කිසිල්ල, *Kisilla*, *s.* armpit, pl. කිසිලි *kisili.*

කිසිවක්, *Kisiwak*, *s.* something.

කිසිවෙක්, *Kisiwek*, *s.* some one.

කිසුණු, *Kisuṇu*, *a.* all, see පරිකසිණ *parikasiṇa.*

කිසුම්, *Kisum*, *s.* flower, [Colloq. මල *mala*].

කිසුළු, *Kisuḷu*, *s.* body, [Colloq. ශරීරය *ṣaríraya*].

කිහිරි, *Kihiri*, *s.* tree, *acacia catechu* also called *a. suma* and *a. sundra*, see රත්කිහිරි *rat-kihiri.*

කිහිරැළි, *Kihirẹḷi*, *s.* an epithet of Vishṇu, derived from ඛදිරදේහලි *Khadira-déhalí*, where ඛදිර is equal to කිහිරි *kihiri*, *Mimosa catechu*, and දේහලි the threshold of a door, an image of the deity having, they say, been made of කිහිරි kihiri-wood.

කිහිල්ල, *Kihilla*, *s.* armpit, pl. කිහිලි *kihili.*

කී, *Kí*, prefix to words signifying number or quantity: *part.* said, spoken.

කීකරු, *Kíkaru*, *a.* obedient, docile, tractable.

කීකරුවා, *Kíkaruwá*, *s.* obedient person.

කීකරුවෙනවා, *Kíkaruwenawá*, *v.* to become obedient.

කීකිරිඳිය, *Kíkirindiya*, *s.* shrub, medicinal plant, *eclipta erecta (Compositæ).*

කීට, *Kíṭa*, *s.* general name for worms.

කීන, *Kína*, *s.* tree, *calophyllum tomentosa* and *c. Walkeri; (Gutiferæ);* there are about seven or eight other species in Ceylon.

කීප, *Kípa*, *ad.* many, much, some, several.

කීපවරක්, *Kípawarak*, *ad.* many times, often, frequently.

කීම, *Kíma*, *s.* saying, pl. කීම් *kím*; verbal noun of කියනවා *kiyanawá.*

කීයද, *Kíyada*, *ad.* how much? how many? what o'clock is it?

කීර්ණ, *Kírṇa*, *a.* covered, secreted, hidden; scattered, thrown, cast; injured.

කීර්තන, *Kírtana*, *s.* speech, words.

කීර්ති, *Kírti*, }
කීර්තිය, *Kírtiya*, } *s.* fame, renown, glory, reputation; favour, approbation; sound; light, lustre; diffusion, expansion.

කීර, *Kíra*, *s.* splinter; parrot.

කීල්, *Kíl*, *s.* tar, pitch.

කීළන, *Kíḷana*, }
කීළා, *Kíḷá*, } *s.* play, sport, amusement.
කීළිත, *Kíḷita*, }

කු, *Ku*, *s.* earth; indeclinable particle of deprecation, implying sin, guilt; reproach, contempt, meanness; diminution, littleness; prevention, hinderance.

කුංකුම, *Kunkuma*, *s.* saffron, *crocus sativus.*

කුංචනාද, *Kunchanáda*, *s.* roaring of an elephant.

කුංචිකා *Kunchiká*, *s.* plant bearing seeds which are used as weights, *abrus precatorius;* [Colloq. ඔලිඳවැල් *olinda-wẹl*]; branch or shoot of a bamboo; key.

කුංචිකාච්ඡිද්‍ර, *Kunchikáchchhidra*, *s.* (කුංචිකා key, ඡිද්‍ර hole) keyhole.

කුක්කා, *Kukká*, *s.* young dog, pup, whelp.

කුක්කුට, *Kukkuṭa*, *s.* gallinaceous fowl, cock, wild cock.

කුක්කුටී, *Kukkuṭí*, *s.* feminine of the preceding word.

කුක්කුර, *Kukkura*, *s.* dog, [Colloq. බල්ලා *ballá*].

කුක්ෂි, *Kukshi*, *s.* belly, [Colloq. බඩ *baḍa*].

කුකුරුමාන්, *Kukurumán*, කුකුරුමුවං, *Kukurumuwaṇ*, } *s.* thorny shrub, *randia dumetorum (Rubiaceæ.)*

කුකුල්, *Kukul*, *s.* hair gathered into a bunch at the top or behind the head; *a.* relating to fowls, hard, rough.

කුකුල් පොර, *Kukul-pora*, *s.* (කුකුල් cock, පොර battle) cock fighting.

කුකුල්මස්සා, *Kukulmassá*, *s.* kind of fish.

කුකුලල, *Kukulala*, *s.* sort of yam or country potatoe.

කුකුලු, *Kukulu*, *s.* valuable earring; cocks; kind of creeper.

කුකුලුවැල්, *Kukuluwel*, *s.* kind of ratan, *calamus pachystemonus, (Palmæ.)*

කුකුස්, *Kukus*, *s.* doubt, uncertainty.

කුකුස් උපදිනවා, *Kukus-upadinawá*, *v.* to doubt, to be uncertain, become dubious.

කුකුළා, *Kukuḷá*, *s.* cock, pl. කුකුළෝ *kukuḷó*.

කුච, *Kucha*, *s.* breast, pap.

කුචන්‍දන, *Kuchandana*, *s.* (කු bad, චන්‍දන sandal) red sanders, *pterocarpus santalinus;* kind of log wood; leguminous plant, *adenanthera pavonina;* inferior kind of sandal-wood.

කුජ්ජ, *Kujja*, *s.* man who stoops.

කුජ, *Kuja*, *s.* planet Mars; (කු earth, ජ produced) tree.

කුජදින, *Kujadina*, *s.* Tuesday. [Colloq. අඟහරුවාදා *aṇgaharuwádá*.]

කුජයා, *Kujayá*, see කුජ *kuja*.

කුජවර, *Kujawara*, කුජවාර, *Kujawára*, } see කුජදින *kujadina*.

කුජා, *Kujá*, see කුජ *kuja*.

කුඤ්ජර, *Kuñjara*, *s.* (කු earth, ජර which presses) elephant; (in composition) pre-eminent.

කුට්ටිය, *Kuṭṭiya*, *s.* lump, piece, slip.

කුටි, *Kuṭi*, *s.* house; tree; body.

කුටිකාරක, *Kuṭikáraka*, *s.* (කුටි and කාරක doer) house builder.

කුටිය, *Kuṭiya*, see කුටි *kuṭi*.

කුටිල, *Kuṭila*, *a.* crooked, bent; metaphorically, deceitful.

කුටිලයා, *Kuṭilayá*, *s.* deceitful fellow, idle fellow.

කුටුම්බ, *Kuṭumba*, *s.* family, race; name; kinsman; relation by the mother's side by marriage; offspring, progeny, kindred.

කුටුම්බින්, *Kuṭumbin*, *s.* (කුටුම්බ *kuṭumba* kindred, ඉනි *ini* possessive affix.) householder, paterfamilias.

කුටුම්බිනී, *Kuṭumbini*, *s.* wife of a house-holder and mother of a family, matron.

කුඩ, *Kuḍa*, *s.* umbrella, any pulverized substance, dust.

කුඩප්පා, *Kuḍappá*, *s.* uncle, father's brother; step father, pl. කුඩප්පාලා, *kuḍappálá*.

කුඩම්මා, *Kuḍammá*, *s.* aunt, mother's sister; step mother, pl. කුඩම්මාලා *kuḍammálá*.

කුඩමස්සා, *Kuḍamassá*, *s.* fish, general name for river fish, pl. කුඩමස්සෝ *kuḍamassó*.

කුඩහකොල්ලා, *Kuḍaha-kollá*, *s.* lad, low or very familiar word.

කුඩා, *Kuḍá*, *a.* small, little, diminutive, short.

කුඩාකඩුත්තු, *Kuḍákaḍuttu*, *s.* urine.

කුඩාකඩුත්තු කරණවා, *Kuḍákaḍuttu-karaṇawá*, *v.* to void urine.

කුඩාකම් පානවා, *Kuḍákam-pánawá*, *v.* to disparage or degrade one's-self.

කුඩාකම, *Kuḍákama*, *s.* meanness, dishonour.

කුඩාකරණවා, *Kuḍákaraṇawá*, *v.* to make small or less.

කුඩා කොල්ලා, *Kuḍá-kollá*, see කුඩහ කොල්ලා *kuḍaha-kollá*.

කුඩා ගෙය, *Kuḍá-geya*, *s.* cottage, small house.

කුඩාහැඩයා, *Kuḍáheḍayá*, *s.* plant, *lycopodium hookeri (Lycopodiaceæ.)*

කුඩිගන්නවා, *Kuḍigannawá*, *v.* to marry.

කුඩිච්චිය, *Kuḍichchiya*, *s.* shell of a cocoa-nut made into a cup to drink out of or to measure any liquid.

කුඩිම්බිය, *Kuḍimbiya*, *s.* comb or crest of a fowl; tuft of hair.

කුඩු, *Kuḍu*, *s.* powder, dust, film; any small thing.

කුඩුකේඩුකම, *Kuḍukéḍukama*, *s.* hatred, malice, pl. කුඩුකේඩුකම් *kuḍukéḍukam*.

කුඩු කැකිරි, *Kuḍu-kekiri*, *s.* plant, *zehneria hookeriana, (Cucurbitaceæ.)*

කුඩුගහනවා, *Kuḍugahanawá*, *v.* to winnow.

කුඩුගානවා, *Kuḍugánawá*, *v.* to grate, to reduce to powder.

කුඩුදවුළු, *Kuḍudawuḷu*, *s.* plant, *litsea zeylanica (Lauraceæ.)*

කුඩුප්පුවා, *Kuḍuppuwá*, *s.* fish.

කුඩු පාට, *Kuḍu-páṭa*, *s.* brown colour,

කුඩුපුව, *Kuḍupuwa*, *s.* food or cake made of the refuse of grain.

කුඩු පොලඟා, *Kuḍu-polaṇgá*, *s.* snake.

කුඩුමිරිස්, *Kuḍu-miris*, *s.* plant, *loddalia scopolia* or *aculeata*.

කුඩෙ, *Kuḍé*, *s.* umbrella.

කුණ්ඩල, *Kuṇḍala*, } *s.* earring;
කුණ්ඩලාභරණය, *Kuṇḍalábharaṇaya*, } bracelet; fetter; tie; collar; ornaments for the ear.

කුණ්ඩලිය, *Kuṇḍaliya*, *s.* this sign ⁓ used in native books, it is the same as our full stop.

කුණ්ඩහට්ටිය, *Kuṇḍahaṭṭiya*, *s.* cooking chatty.

කුණප, *Kuṇapa*, *s.* dead body, corpse; stink, foul smell; *a.* foul, filthy, bad, mean.

කුණල්, *Kuṇal*, *s.* kókila or Indian cuckoo, see කුණාල *kuṇála*.

කුණාල, *Kuṇála*, *s.* one of the seven lakes in the Himálaya; kókila or Indian cuckoo.

කුණි, *Kuṇi*, *s.* cripple with a crooked or withered arm.

කුත්තිරම, *Kuttirama*, *s.* deceit, cheating, tricking.

කුත්සා, *Kutsá*, *s.* reproach, contempt, censure.

කුත්සිත, *Kutsita*, *a.* low, vile, contemptible, mean.

කුතුක, *Kutuka*, *s.* eagerness, vehemence, desire, inclination.

කුතුහල, *Kutúhala*, *s.* eagerness, vehemence, impetuosity, desire; *a.* excellent, best, praised, celebrated; surprising, wonderful.

කුද්දටිය, *Kuddaṭiya*, } *s.* boil, swelling of the
කුද්දෙටිය, *Kuddeṭiya*, } glands.

කුද, *Kuda*, *s.* hunch-backed.

කුදා, *Kudá*, *s.* crooked man, male animal, hunch-backed man, pl. කුද්දු *kuddu*.

කුදිකපනවා, *Kudi-kapanawá*, *v.* (කුදිය *kudiya* fetlock joint, කපනවා to cut) to hough, to hamstring.

කුදිටු, *Kudiṭu*, *s.* (කු bad, දිටු from දෘෂ්ටි *dṛishṭi* sight) pagan, one professing a false religion, heretic, heresy.

කුදිය, *Kudiya*, *s.* fetlock joint.

කුදී, *Kudí*, *s.* hunch-backed woman, the fem. of කුදා *kudá*.

කුදු, *Kudu*, *a.* small, little, short, diminutive, hunch-backed; *s.* man who stoops in walking.

කුදුගොත්සඟිය, *Kudugotsangiya*, *s.* last of the five divisions of the sútra piṭaka, comprising fifteen books.

කුදුනි, *Kuduni*, *s.* ditch, brook, canal.

කුදුමුද්ද, *Kudumudda*, *s.* ringlet, small rings.

කුදුවිල, *Kuduvila*, *s.* kind of small lake or pond overgrown with flowers; marsh.

කුදුවැව්, *Kuduwęw*, *s.* (කුදු small, වැව් lakes) tanks, ponds.

කුදෘෂ්ටික, *Kudṛishṭika*, } see කුදිටු *kudiṭu*.
කුදෘෂ්ටිය, *Kudṛishṭiya*, }

කුදේ, *Kudé*. *a.* crooked, bent; *s.* the state of being hunch-backed.

කුන්ද, *Kunda*, *s.* kind of jasmine.

කුන්දුකහිනවා, *Kundukahinawá*, } *v.* to hop, jump
කුන්දුගහනවා, *Kundugahanawá*, } on one leg.

කුන, *Kuna*, *s.* dirt, filth, any decayed substance, pl. කුනු *kunu*.

කුනපය, *Kunapaya*, see කුණප *kuṇapa*.

කුනා, *Kuná*, *s.* filthy man, covetous man, pl. කුන්නු *kunnu*.

කුනාටුව, *Kunáṭuwa*, *s.* tempest, storm.

කුනී, *Kuní*, *s.* filthy or miserly woman.

කුනු, *Kunu*, *s.* dirt, dust, filth; *a.* filthy, dirty.

කුනුකටුවා, *Kunukaṭuwá*, *s.* viperine snake, *hypnale nepa* (order *Ophidia:*) the word is also applied to any one who is uncharitable.

කුනුකන්දල්, *Kunukandal*, *s.* dirt, filth.

කුනුකරවලා, *Kunukarawalá*, *s.* snake, *bungarus*.

කුනුගානවා, *Kunugánawá*, *v.* to besmear, to daub: pret. කුනුගෑවා *kunugęwá*.

කුනුදිය කලුවා, *Kunudiya-kaluwá*, *s.* snake.

කුනුපොලඟා, *Kunupolangá*, *s.* viperine snake.

කුනුමි කරවලා, *Kunumí-karawalá*, *s.* colubrine snake.

කුනුමි පොලඟා, *Kunumí-polangá*, *s.* viperine snake.

කුනුමැල්ලා, *Kunumęllá*, *s.* snail.

කුනුවෙනවා, *Kunuwenawá*, *v.* to putrefy, to become filthy.

කුප්පමේනිය, *Kuppaméniya*, *s.* plant, *acalypha indica (Euphorbiaceæ).*

කුප්පිය, *Kuppiya*, *s.* vial; calyx of a flower.

කුපය, *Kupaya*, see කූපය *kúpaya*.

කුපිත, *Kupita*, *a.* angry, wrathful, enraged.

කුපිතකරණවා, *Kupitakaraṇawá*, *v.* to enrage, to agitate.

කුබ්ජ, *Kubja*, *s.* hump-backed man, crooked man, one who stoops in walking.

කුබුද්දනවා, *Kubuddanawá*, *v.* to cause to awake, to arouse: pret. කිබිද්දුවා *kibidduwá*.

කුබුදිනවා, *Kubudinawá*, *v.* to awake: pret. කිබිදුනා *kibiduná*.

කුබුදු, *Kubudu*, *s.* half blown flower; shame.

කුබෙරැස්, *Kuberęs*, *s.* tree with fragrant flowers, *bignonia suave-olens*.

කුඹ, *Kumba*, *s.* pot, mast of a ship.

කුඹගහ, *Kumbagaha*. *s.* mast of a ship, pl. කුඹගස් *kumbagas*.

කුඹල් සක, *Kumbal-saka*, *s.* potter's wheel.

කුඹලා, *Kumbalá*, s. potter; kind of winged insect, pl. කුඹල්ලු *kumballu*.

කුඹළු, *Kumbaḷu*, s. tree, wild bilimbi, *ailantus malabarica (Simarubaceæ)*; also called වල් බිලිං *wal-biliṇ*.

කුඹුක්, *Kumbuk*, s. tree, *terminalia glabra, (Combretaceæ)*.

කුඹුකරු, *Kumbukaru*, s. potter.

කුඹුදු, *Kumbudu*, see කුබුදු *kubudu*.

කුඹුයොන්, *Kumbuyon*, see අගස්ති *Agasti*.

කුඹුර, *Kumbura*, s. paddy field, pl. කුඹුරු *kumburu*.

කුඹුරුවැල්, *Kumburu-wel*. s. plant, *cæsalpinia bonduc, (Leguminosæ)*.

කුඹුවත්, *Kumbuwat*, s. variegated colour.

කුඹුවරු, *Kumbuwaru*, s. the bonduc or sucker tree.

කුඹේ, *Kumbé*, see කුඹ *kumba*.

කුම්බිල *Kumbili*, see කුම්භිල *kumbhíla*.

කුම්භ, *Kumbha*, s. frontal globe on the upper part of the forehead of an elephant; there are two of these projections which swell in the rutting season; jar, water pot, earthen cooking vessel; mast of a ship; sign of the zodiac (Aquarius): name of a noted demon, nephew of Rávaṇa; fragrant resin, or the plant which bears it; *bdellium*.

කුම්භකාර, *Kumbhakára*, s. (කුම්භ pot, කාර who makes) potter.

කුම්භයොනි, *Kumbha-yoni*, s. (කුම්භ jar, යොනි womb) one of the names of Agasti, alluding to the fable of his being produced from a water jar; name of Vaṣishṭha and of Droṇa military preceptor of the Kurus and Páṇḍus.

කුම්භරාශිය *Kumbha-rásiya*, s. sign of the zodiac *Aquarius*.

කුම්භස්ථලය, *Kumbhastalaya*, s. hollow on the top of an elephant's head, between the frontals.

කුම්භාණ්ඩ, *Kumbháṇḍa*, s. (කුම්භ *kumbha* water-jar, අණ්ඩ *aṇḍa* testicle or semen genitale) sort of demon of enormous size.

කුම්භිර, *Kumbhíra*, } s. crocodile, alligator.
කුම්භිල, *Kumbhíla*, } [Colloq. කිඹුලා *kimbulá*].

කුම්මැහියා, *Kummehiyá*, s miser.

කුම, *Kuma*, see කිම *kima*.

කුමක්, *Kumak*, s something, somewhat.

කුමට, *Kumaṭa*, *ad*. why, wherefore.

කුමටිය, *Kumaṭiya*, s. plant, *allmania nodiflora, (Amarantaceæ:)* also called වෙනිවෙල්ල *weni-wella*.

කුමන, *Kumana*, s. what.

කුමර, *Kumara*, s. little child, see කුමාර *kumára*.

කුමරා, *Kumará*, s. prince, pl. කුමරෝ *kumaró*, see කුමාර *kumára*.

කුමරිය, *Kumariya*, } s. princess, pl. කුමරියෝ, see
කුමරි, *Kumarí*, } කුමාරි *kumári*.

කුමරු, *Kumaru*, s. Kataragama deviyo, a child, prince.

කුමරුවා, *Kumaruwá*, s. child, infant, prince.

කුමාර, *Kumára*, s. son or male child, boy under five years of age; prince, heir, and who is associated to the empire; name of Kártikéya or Kataragama deviyo; parrot; tree, *tapia cratæva;* name of the river Indus or Sindhu.

කුමාරකා, *Kumáraka*, s. boy, lad.

කුමාර දේවතාවා, *Kumára-déwatáwá*, s. devil noxious to women.

කුමාරයා, *Kumárayá*, s. prince.

කුමාරි, *Kumári*, s. princess; girl from ten to twelve years old, virgin; name of Durga the wife of Ṣiva; according to Hindu geography the central part of the universe, usually called Jambudwípa, India proper; the most southern part of the peninsula of India, whence comes the name cape Comorin or Kumári; name of a river flowing from the mountain Saktiman; plant, *clitoria ternatea*, [Colloq. නිල් කටරොළු *nil-kaṭaroḷu;*] double jasmine; aloe tree, *aloes perfoliata*.

කුමාරිකා, *Kumáriká*, s. girl from ten to twelve years of age, or generally a virgin, princess.

කුමු, *Kumu*, s. unblossomed flower.

කුමුකු, *Kumuku*, s. areca tree; [Colloq. පුවක්ගහ *puwak-gaha*.]

කුමුකුළු, *Kumukuḷu*, s. cock; half blown flower.

කුමුටු, *Kumuṭu*, s. swallowing; diving, sinking.

කුමුද, *Kumuda*, s. white esculent water lily, *nymphea esculenta*, red lotus, *nymphea rubra;* silver; elephant of the south west quarter; dánava or infernal deity; camphor.

කුමුදවනවා, *Kumudawanawá*, v. to rinse the mouth.

කුමුදා, *Kumudá*, s. aquatic plant, *pistia stratiotes*, [Colloquial: දියපරඬලා *diyaparaṇḍalá*]; tree, *gmelina arborea*, [Colloq. ඇත්දෙමට *et-demaṭa*].

කුමුදු, *Kumudu*, see කුමුද *kumuda*.

කුමුදුවති, *Kumuduwati*, s. place abounding in water lilies.

කුරක්කන්, *Kurakkan*, s. sort of grain, sometimes called nachchiṇi, millet, *eleusine coracana (Gramineæ)*.

කුරගානවා, *Kuragánawá*, *v.* to walk as quadrupeds, principally used in speaking of hoofed animals.

කුරඟ, *Kuraṅga*, *s.* sort of deer, antelope.

කුරට, *Kuraṭa*, *s.* plant, *gmelina*, of which there are three species in Ceylon.

කුරණ්ඩක, *Kuraṇḍaka*, *s.* plant, *barleria prionites*, [Colloq. කටුකරඬු *kaṭu-karaṇḍu*]; and also *jasminum indicum spinosum.*

කුරය, *Kuraya*, *s.* hoof of animals.

කුරර, *Kurara*, *s.* fish-hawk, sort of eagle.

කුරල්, *Kural*, *s.* ear of corn, paddy.

කුරවිකෙවිල්ලා, *Kuravi-kevillá*, *s.* Indian cuckoo.

කුරවින්දක, *Kuravindaka*, see කුරුවින්ද *kuruvinda.*

කුරවීක, *Kuravíka*, *s.* Indian cuckoo.

කුරහන්, *Kurahan*, see කුරක්කන් *kurakkan.*

කුරහන් තලප, *Kurahan-talapa*, *s.* kañji or porridge made of millet.

කුරා, *Kurá*, *s.* dwarf, pigmy, any male animal stinted in its growth; ant, pl. කුරෝ *kuró.*

කුරාලය, *Kurálaya*, *s.* stage or high altar used in demon ceremonies; bier.

කුරිඤ්ඤං, *Kuriññaṅ*, *s.* creeper, *gymnema lactiferum (Asclepiadaceæ).*

කුරිරයා, *Kuriraya*, *s.* the following word with the nominal affix යා, a cruel man etc.

කුරිරු, *Kuriru*, *a.* harsh, cruel, severe, austere; bad, noxious.

කුරිරුකම, *Kurirukama*, *s.* cruelty, pl. කුරිරුකම් *kurirukam.*

කුරු, *Kuru*, *s.* bud, tender leaves; bow; tortoise; according to Indian geography Kuru or Uttara Kuru is the northern of the four mahá-dwípas or principal divisions of the known world; it evidently means the country beyond the most northern range of mountains and extending to the frozen ocean; *a.* small; cruel; short; a prince so called.

කුරුඟමිග, *Kuruṅga-miga*, see කුරඟ *kuraṅga.*

කුරුටුගානවා, *Kuruṭugánawá*, *v.* to rasp, to scribble.

කුරුණිය, *Kuruṇiya*, *s.* measure, one eighth of a bushel; five of which make one parrah.

කුරුතුඬු, *Kurutuṇḍu*, see කුරා *kurá.*

කුරුඳු, *Kuruṇdu*, *s.* cinnamon, *cinnamomum zeylanicum (Lauraceæ.)*

කුරුඳුගල්, *Kuruṇdu-gal*, *s.* cinnamon stone. a sort of *hyacinth.*

කුරුන්, *Kurun*, plural of කුරා *kurá* or කුරුම *kuruma* which see.

කුරුන්ද කොබෙයියා, *Kuruṇda-kobeyiyá*. *s.* purple wood-pigeon, *alsocomus puniceus*, (order *Columbæ).*

කුරුන්දනවා, *Kurundanawá*, *v.* to scrape the ground with the hoof, as a bull when enraged.

කුරුප්, *Kurup*, *s.* tortoise.

කුරුපාව, *Kurupáwa*, *s.* post, an oblique or upright supporter of a beam or wall plate.

කුරුබිලි, *Kurubili*, *s.* sally-port.

කුරුම්බාව, *Kurumbáwa*, *s.* young cocoa-nut.

කුරුම, *Kuruma*, *s.* Coin=five shillings sterling.

කුරුමානම්, *Kurumánam*, *s.* aim when shooting.

කුරුමානම් බලනවා, *Kurumánam-balanawá*, *v.* to aim.

කුරුමිණි කුරුල්ලා, *Kurumini-kurullá*, *s.* blue-tailed bee eater, *merops phillipensis;* green bee eater, *m. viridis;* chesnut-headed bee eater, *m. swinhoii*, (order *Picariæ).*

කුරුමිණියා, *Kuruminiyá*, *s.* black kind of beetle with an extremely hard snout, by which it perforates wood as if bored with an instrument; it lodges chiefly in the tops of cocoa-nuts and often destroys the tree by its boring to get at the cabbage.

කුරුමුරලා, *Kurumuralá*, *s.* kind of fish.

කුරුල්ලා, *Kurullá*, *s.* the general name for bird.

කුරුළු, *Kuruḷu*, *s.* young children; *a.* young, infantine.

කුරුළුගොයා, *Kuruḷugoyá*, *s.* bird; marsh harrier, *circus aeruginosus;* pied harrier, *c. melanoleucus;* Montagu's harrier, *c. cineraceus*, also called රාජාලියා *rájáliyá;* pale harrier, *c. macrurus;* Indian buzzard, *buteo plumipes;* common kestrel, *cerchneis tinnunculus*, two last also called උකුස්සා *ukussá*, (order *Accipitres);* pl. කුරුළු ගොයි *kuruḷugoyi.*

කුරුලෑව, *Kuruléwa*, *s.* pimple.

කුරුවිටි, *Kuruviṭi*, *a.* round, globular.

කුරුවින්ද, *Kuruvinda*, *s.* fragrant grass, *cyperus rotundus;* ruby.

කුරුවිල්ල, *Kuruvilla*, *s.* ruby.

කුරුසිකරණවා, *Kurusikaraṇawá*, *v.* to peep.

කුරුසිය, *Kurusiya*, *s.* the cross, gibbet consisting of two pieces of timber placed across each other either in form of a T or an ×.

කුරූර, *Kurúra*, corruption of ක්‍රූර *krúra*, cruel, harsh, severe, wicked, bad, vicious.

කුරේ, *Kuré*, *s.* hoof of animals.

කුරෝ, *Kuró*, *s.* kind of ant; pl. of කුරා *kurá.*

කුල්මත්, *Kulmat*, *s.* surprise, wonder; joy ecstasy; *a.* lofty, haughty.

කුල්මත්වෙනවා, *Kulmatwenawá*, *v.* to be astonished, to be surprised or high-minded.

කුල්‍ය, *Kulya*, *s.* bone; kind of measure; winnowing basket; flesh: *a.* of a good family, well born; of high rank; of high descent.

කුල්ල, *Kulla*, *s.* winnowing fan or basket; hawk or kite.

කුල, *Kula*, *s.* pungent taste; large rock; plunder, things stolen; disgrace; family, race, tribe or caste; herd or flock etc. of animals of the same species; inhabited country; house, abode; body.

කුලඟන, *Kulan̲gana*, *s.* (කුල and අඟන *an̲gana* woman) woman of rank, woman of high descent or caste; chaste woman.

කුලජ, *Kulaja*, *s.* (කුල race, ජ born) well born, of good family.

කුලජ්‍යෙෂ්ඨයා, *Kulajyeshṭhayá*, *s.* head of a family.

කුලදරුවා, *Kuladaruwá*, *s.* (කුල family, දරුවා child) legitimate child; man of a good family.

කුලදූ, *Kuladú*, *s.* woman of a good family, chaste woman.

කුලදෙටු, *Kuladeṭu*, Elu form of කුලජ්‍යෙෂ්ඨයා *kulajyeshṭhayá* head of a family.

කුල ධර්ම, *Kula-dharma*, *s.* (කුල family, ධර්ම virtue) practice or observance peculiar to a tribe or caste; peculiar duty of caste or race.

කුලප්පුව, *Kulappuwa*, *s.* agitation, confusion, tumult.

කුලප්පුවෙනවා, *Kulappuwenawá*, *v.* to be agitated, to turn fierce (as a horse).

කුලපතියා, *Kulapatiyá*, *s.* (කුල and පති chief) head of a family or race, chief of a tribe.

කුලපාලි, *Kulapáli*, *s.* (කුල and පාලි who nourishes) chaste woman.

කුල පුත්‍රයා, *Kula-putrayá*, see කුල දරුවා *kula-daruwá*.

කුලපැල්, *Kula-pẹl*, *s.* woman with one husband.

කුලමල, *Kulamala*, *s.* depreciation; abuse of a person's rank.

කුලය, *Kulaya*, *s.* race, tribe, caste; disgrace.

කුලල්, *Kulal*, *s.* kind of wind instrument, sort of horn; plural of the following word.

කුලල, *Kulala*, *s.* neck; scar.

කුලවද්දනවා, *Kulawaddanawá*, *v.* to cause to enter into the caste, to name, to give the family name and title or privileges.

කුලවමි, *Kulawami*, *s.* (කුල and වමි woman) chaste woman, woman of rank.

කුලස්ත්‍රී, *Kulastrí*, *s.* woman of rank, chaste woman

කුලාඞ්ගනාව, *Kuláńganáwa*, *s.* (කුල *kula* and අඞ්ගනාව *ańganáwa* woman) woman of good family, woman of rank.

කුලාව, *Kuláwa*, *s.* vessel, jug, can.

කුලිච්චම, *Kulichchama*, *s.* bolster.

කුලී, *Kulí*, *s.* hire, wages, fare, rent.

කුලීකාරයා, *Kulíkárayá*, *s.* (කුලී wages, කාරයා doer) hired servant, cooly.

කුලීන, *Kulína*, *a.* of good family.

කුලීර, *Kulíra*, *s.* crab; [Coll. කකුළුවා *kakuḷuwá*.]

කුලුඳුල්, *Kulun̲dul*, *s.* first born.

කුලූපග, *Kulupaga*, *s.* (කුල *kula* and උප *upa* near, ග going) faithful friend, familiar acquaintance.

කුලේ, *Kulé*, *s.* caste, rank, race, family, disgrace.

කුවර, *Kuwara*, *s.* an astringent taste; Elu form of කුවේර *kuvera* which see.

කුවිදිනවා, *Kuvidinawá*, see කුඹුදිනවා *kubudinawá*.

කුවින්ද, *Kuvinda*, *s.* weaver.

කුවේණි, *Kuwéni*, *s.* noted female demon, who forms a very prominent character in the mythology of Ceylon; she is the same that was changed into the form of a bitch when Vijaya Raja first arrived in Ceylon.

කුවේර, *Kuwéra*, *s.* (කු bad, evil, වේර body) the Indian Plutus, god of wealth; the name of this deity alludes to his deformity, he being represented as having three legs and only eight teeth; his most common name is වෙසමුණි රජ *wesamuṇi-raja* which see.

කුවේරැස්, *Kuwéręs. s. Casalpinia Bonduc*, [Colloq. කුඹුරුවැල *kum̲buruwẹla*.]

කුශේශය, *Kuṣéṣaya*, *s.* lotus in general.

කුෂ්ඨඝ්නි, *Kushṭhaghni*, *s.* (කුෂ්ඨ leprosy, ඝ්න *ghna* what destroys) medicinal plant used in the cure of leprosy.

කුෂ්ඨ, *Kushṭha*, *s.* plant, kind of costus; cutaneous disorder; leprosy; kind of poison.

කුෂ්ඨරෝගය, *Kushṭha-rógaya*, *s.* any cutaneous disorder; leprosy.

කුෂ්මාණ්ඩ, *Kushmáṇḍa*, *s.* pumpkin gourd, *cucurbita pepo*.

කුස්, *Kus*, *s.* belly, womb, inside.

කුස්දර, *Kusdara*, *s.* man living at another's expense.

කුස්සිය, *Kussiya*, *s.* kitchen.

කුස, *Kusa*, *s.* belly, womb; interior or inside,

breast; a sacrificial grass, *heterepogon hirtus;* water; yoke of a plough; in Hindu history name of the sons of Ráma; also, one of the great dwípas, or divisions of the universe, surrounded by the sea of spirituous liquor, supposed by some to be the land of Kush in Scripture and to comprehend the countries between the Indus, the Persian Gulf and Caspian sea; rope; wrought iron; nose rope of a horse; rein, bridle; *a.* weak; depraved, mad, inebriate.

කුසඔත්තා, *Kusaottá, s.* uterine brother, one born in the same womb.

කුසතණ, *Kusa-taṇa,* } *s.* arrowgrass, *panicum*
කුසතෘණ, *Kusa-triṇa,* } *paniculatum.* It is stated that on a certain occasion a Brahmin gave a handful of this grass to Buddha, who cast it on the ground under a Bó-tree, when it immediately became a seat for him to sit upon; hence it is a sacred grass among the Buddhists.

කුසදරය, *Kusadaraya, s.* state of dependence on others.

කුසපිළිකාව, *Kusapiḷikáwa, s.* (කුස belly, පිළිකාව cancer) cancer in the inside of the belly.

කුස පිළිසිඳීම, *Kusa-piḷisiṉdíma, s.* fœtus in the womb; conception.

කුසපොත්ත, *Kusapotta, s.* omentum, caul.

කුසල, *Kusala, s.* merit, power or virtue of good works, pl. කුසල් *kusal.*

කුසලාන, *Kusalána, s.* cup, drinking vessel, pl. කුසලාන් *kusalán.*

කුසි, *Kusi, s.* part of a priest's dress.

කුසිනාරා, *Kusinárá, s.* city in the district of Mallawa, celebrated among the Buddhists as the death place of Gautama Buddha.

කුසීද, *Kusída, s.* laziness, usury.

කුසුම්දද, *Kusumdada, s.* (කුසුම් flowers, දද ensign) name of අනංගයා *anaṉgayá.*

කුසුම්දල, *Kusumdala, s.* see මල්පැනි *mal-peni.*

කුසුම්දුනු, *Kusumdunu, s.* name of අනංගයා *anaṉgayá,* the Indian cupid.

කුසුම *Kusuma, s.* flower in general; menstrual discharge; disease of the eyes, *ophthalmia;* fruit, pl. කුසුම් *Kusum.*

කුසූල, *Kusúla, s.* granary, cupboard, place or vessel in which grain is kept.

කුහක, *Kuhaka, s.* juggling, deception, sleight of hand; hypocrite, cheat, rogue.

කුහන, *Kuhana,* } *s.* small earthen vessel; rat;
කුහනා, *Kuhaná,* } snake; hypocrisy; false pretensions to sanctity or religion.

කුහුඹියා, *Kuhumbiyá,* } *s.* ant.
කුහුඹුවා, *Kuhumbuwá,* }

කුහුල්, *Kuhul, s.* doubt, deceit, uncertainty.

කුළා, *Kuḷá, a.* wild, disobedient, unmanageable.

කුළු, *Kuḷu, a.* stubborn, disobedient, wild, unruly, ungovernable; hard; *s.* peak of a rock; unblossomed flower.

කුළුගන්වනවා, *Kuḷuganwanawá, v.* (කුළු top, summit, ගන්වනවා causal of ගන්නවා *gannawá* to take) to place or set on the summit, literally or metaphorically.

කුළුගෙඩිය, *Kuḷugeḍiya, s.* sledge-hammer.

කුළුණු, *Kuḷuṇu, s.* mercy, kindness; one of the eight tastes as an object of poetry or composition.

කුළුතුණ, *Kuḷutuṇa, s.* medicament consisting of three spices, pepper, ginger and tippili.

කුළුදෙස්, *Kuḷudes, s.* false witness.

කුළුන, *Kuḷuna, s.* column, cap of a pillar.

කුළුපස, *Kuḷupasa. s.* (කුළු spice, පස five) compound of five spices, viz. ginger, pepper, tippili, cinnamon and cardamoms.

කුළුබඩු, *Kuḷubaḍu, s.* pungent substances, such as, dry ginger, pepper, etc.

කුළුයර, *Kuḷuyara, s.* basket maker, worker in straw, ratans etc.

කුළුරේණ, *Kuḷuréṇa,* see කටුකරොහිණී *kaṭukarohiṇí.*

කුළුවර, *Kuḷuwara,* see කුළුයර *kuḷuyara.*

කුළුවෙනවා, *Kuḷuwenawá, v.* to become disobedient, or unmanageable.

කුළෑටි, *Kuḷéṭi, a.* wild, unruly, unmanageable, ungovernable.

කූට්ටම, *Kúṭṭama, s.* pair, set of any thing, pl. කූට්ටම් *kúṭṭam.*

කූට්ටු, *Kúṭṭu, a.* together, with, joined, united.

කූට, *Kúṭa, s.* upper part of the frame of a circular roof; house, dwelling; peak or summit of a mountain; multitude, assemblage; firmness; uniform and elementary substance; illusion by feats of jugglers; water jar; ham; mallet, large hammer; plough-share; body of a plough; trap for catching deer; fraud, deceit, untruth, falsehood, lie; *a.* counterfeit, untrue.

කූටක, *Kúṭaka, a.* hot.

කූටකේ, *Kúṭaké, s.* heat.

කූට තාපසයා, *Kúṭa-tápasayá. s.* (කූට fraud, තාපසයා ascetic) fraudulent priest, counterfeit hermit.

කූටය, *Kúṭaya*, see කූට *kúṭa*.
කූට යන්ත්‍රය, *Kúṭa-yantraya*, *s.* trap, snare for deer, birds, etc.
කූටශාල්මලි, *Kúṭaṣálmali*, *s.* species of the simul or silk cotton tree.
කූටාගාර, *Kúṭágára*, *s.* (කූට *kúṭa* peak, අගාර *ágára* house) upper room, apartment on the top of a house.
කූඩ්‍ය, *Kúḍya*, *s.* wall.
කූඩලුදෙහි, *Kúḍaludehi*, *s.* leech-lime.
කූඩලුමල්, *Kúḍalu-mal*, *s.* plant, *impatiens flaccida (Geraniaceæ)*.
කූඩාරම, *Kúḍárama*, *s.* tent, pl. කූඩාරම් *kúḍáram*.
කූඩුව, *Kúḍuwa*, *s.* nest, cage.
කූඩේ, *Kúḍé*, *s.* basket, pl. කූඩා *kúḍá*.
කූඩැල්ලා, *Kúḍellá*, *s.* leech, pl. කූඩැල්ලෝ *kúḍelló*.
කූණියා, *Kúṇiyá*, } *s.* very small kind of shrimp,
කූණිස්සා, *Kúṇissá*, } pl. කූණි *kúṇi*, කූණිස්සෝ *kúṇissó*.
කූද්දනවා, *Kúddanawá*, *v.* to awake: pret. කිද්දුවා *kidduwá*.
කූනම, *Kúnama*, *s.* palanquin with a crooked bamboo, pl. කූනම් *kúnam*.
කූප, *Kúpa*, *s.* well, hole, hollow; mast; tree or rock in the midst of a river.
කූපක, *Kúpaka*, *s.* mast of a vessel; stake to which a boat is moored; leathern oil vessel; hollow below the loins; funeral pile.
කූපෝදක, *Kúpódaka*, *s.* (කූප *kúpa* well, උදක *udaka* water) well-water.
කූබර, *Kúbara*, *s.* nave of a wheel, pole of a carriage or wood to which the yoke is fixed.
කූඹියා, *Kúmbiyá*, see කුහුඹියා *kuhumbiyá*.
කූඹු, *Kúmbu*, *s.* elephant; water pot: the proboscis of an elephant; unfruitfulness; more properly කුඹු *kumbu*.
කූර්චශීර්ෂ, *Kúrchaṣírsha*, *s.* drug, commonly called jívaka, one of the eight principal medicaments.
කූර්ම, *Kúrma*, *s.* tortoise, turtle.
කූර්මරාජ, *Kúrmarája*, *s.* (කූර්ම turtle, රාජ king) king of turtles, in the mythology of the Hindus; it is the tortoise on the back of which the world is supposed to rest.
කූර්මෝදර, *Kúrmódara*, *s.* (කූර්ම *kúrma* tortoise, උදර *udara* belly) disease, induration of the mesenteric glands.
කූර, *Kúra*, *s.* boiled rice; hair pin, skewer, pl. කූරු *kúru*.

කූරතම්පලා, *Kúratampalá*, see තම්පලා *tampalá*.
කූරපයිය, *Kúrapayiya*, *s.* wallet, pocket, large kind of purse.
කූරයියා, *Kúrayiyá*, *s.* general name for a fish.
කූරලා, *Kúralá*, *s.* name of a fish.
කූරියා, *Kúriyá*, see කූරයියා *kúrayiyá*.
කූරුගානවා, *Kúrugánawá*, *v.* to stir up with a pin or wire: pret. කූරුගෑවා *kúrugewá*.
කූරැටිය, *Kúreṭiya*, *s.* plant, *memecylon rostratum, (Melastomaceæ)*.
කූල්‍ය, *Kúlya*, see කුල්‍ය *kulya*.
කූල, *Kúla*, *s.* shore, bank; heap, mound; pond, pool.
කූවර, *Kúwara*, see කූබර *kúbara*.
කූෂ්මාණ්ඩ, *Kúshmáṇḍa*, see කුෂ්මාණ්ඩ *kushmáṇḍa*.
කෙංකරණවා, *Keṇkaraṇawá*, *v.* to use a kind of magic.
කෙංකොක් වැරැල්ල, *Keṇkok-weṛella*, *s.* plant, *botrychium zeylanicum*, or moon wort.
කෙංකෑකිරි, *Keṇkekiri*, *s.* plant, *bryonia grandis*.
කෙංවැල, *Keṇwela*, see කෙම්වැල *kemwela*.
කෙක්ක, *Kekka*, *s.* stick with a hooked end for gathering fruit, pl. කෙකි *keki*.
කෙකටිය, *Kekaṭiya*, } *s.* aquatic plant, *Aponogeton*
කෙකතිය, *Kekatiya*, } *Crispum (Naiadaceæ)*.
කෙකරගානවා, *Kekaragánawá*, *v.* to chuck as a hen, when about to lay: pret. කෙකරගෑවා *kekaragewá*.
කෙකා, *Keká*,
කෙකාරාවය, *Kekáráwaya*, } *s.* cry of a peacock.
කෙකාරාව්, *Kekárew*,
කෙකි, *Kekí*, *s.* female crane.
කෙකු, *Keku*, *s.* plant, *Bocagea coriacea (Anonaceæ)*.
කෙඤ්චි, *Keñchi*, *s.* fun, sport, ridicule; *a.* lean, niggard.
කෙඤ්චිකරණවා, *Keñchikaraṇawá*, *v.* to pray, to implore, to supplicate, to entreat, to tease by importunity.
කෙඤ්චිවෙනවා, *Keñchiwenawá*, *v.* to become thin, to grow lean.
කෙඤ්ජිකරණවා, *Keñjikaraṇawá*, see කෙඤ්චිකරණවා *keñchikaraṇawá*.
කෙට්ටු, *Keṭṭu*. *a.* thin, lean, meagre, gaunt.
කෙට, *Keṭa*, *a.* short (not long); *s.* short woman.
කෙටල, *Keṭala*, *s.* plant, *Lagenandra toxicaria (Araceæ)*.
කෙටවිල්ල, *Keṭavilla*, *s.* instigation, setting on, setting people together by the ears, pl. කෙටවිලි *keṭavili*.

කෙටි, *Keṭi*, *a.* short (not tall).

කෙටීම, *Keṭíma*, *s.* pounding; digging.

කෙටුම්පත, *Keṭumpata*, *s.* rough copy, rough draft of a writing, pl. කෙටුම්පත් *keṭumpat*.

කෙටුම, *Keṭuma*, *s.* act of making an incision, of digging, cutting, or beating.

කෙටේරි, *Keṭeri*, } *s.* sort of axe with a long
කෙටේරිය, *Keṭériya*, } handle, used by Sanyásis or mendicant priests.

කෙඩෙත්තු, *Kedettu*, *a.* wearied, fatigued, lean, tired; thin.

කෙණ්ඩය, *Keṇḍaya*, *s.* the calf of the leg, pl. කෙණ්ඩා *keṇḍá*.

කෙණ්ඩිකාව, *Keṇḍikáwa*, } *s.* pitcher or jug with
කෙණ්ඩිය, *Keṇḍiya*, } a lip or spout.

කෙණ්ඩේ, *Keṇḍé*, *s.* calf of the leg, pl. කෙණ්ඩා *keṇḍá*.

කෙණෙර, *Keṇera*, } *s.* female elephant.
කෙණෙරඟන, *Keṇerangana*, }

කෙණෙහි, *Keṇehi*, *ad.* at that time, immediately, forthwith.

කෙත්පලු, *Ket-palu*, *s.* one whose business it is to watch the field, husbandman.

කෙත, *Keta*, *s.* Elu form of ක්ෂෙත්‍ර *kshetra*, field: house, abode, pl. කෙත් *ket*.

කෙතරම්, *Ketaram*, *ad.* how much.

කෙතෙක්, *Ketek*, *ad.* how much, how many, how.

කෙඳි, *Kendi*, *s.* wire; small thread, fibre.

කෙඳිරිගානවා, *Kendirigánawá*, *v.* to groan, to mourn.

කෙන්ඩය, *Kendaya*, see කෙණ්ඩය *keṇḍaya*.

කෙන්ඩයා, *Kendayá*, *s.* kind of fish.

කෙන්ඩිය, *Kendiya*, see කෙණ්ඩිය *keṇḍiya*.

කෙන්ඩෙ, *Kende*, see කෙණ්ඩය *keṇḍaya*.

කෙන්ද, *Kenda*, *s.* wire, small thread, fibre, pl. කෙඳි *kendi*.

කෙන්දගම්, *Kendagam*, *s.* sulphur, brimstone.

කෙන්හෑන්ද, *Kenhęnda*, *s.* plant, *clerodendrum serratum (Verbenaceæ)*.

කෙනම්, *Kenam*, *s.* some one, certain one, what.

කෙනෙක්, *Kenek*, *pron.* one, one person.

කෙනෙස්ස, *Kenessa*, *s.* water ladle.

කෙප්ප, *Keppa*, }
කෙප්ප වාතේ, *Keppa-wáté*, } *s.* disease of the
කෙප්ප වායිය, *Keppa-wáyiya*, } womb.
කෙප්ප වායුව, *Keppa-wáyuwa*, }

කෙපමණ, *Kepamaṇa*, *ad.* how much, how many.

කෙබඳු, *Kebandu*, *ad.* how, in what manner.

කෙම්, *Kem*, *pl.* of කෙම *kema;* in Elu, plant *bryonia grandis;* feast, happiness.

කෙම්වර, *Kemwara*, *s.* capuism, worship of the gods, demons, etc.

කෙම්වැල, *Kemwęla*, *s.* creeping plant, which bears a fruit of the gourd species, *bryonia grandis*.

කෙම, *Kema*, *s.* sort of magic, exercised to avert mischief.

කෙමන, *Kemana*, *s.* sort of long basket used for catching fish in very shallow water.

කෙමි, *Kemi*, *s.* the pedicle or part of the flower when the leaves are fallen off.

කෙමිය, *Kemiya*, *s.* spout of a vessel of any kind; pedicle, pl. කෙමි *kemi*.

කෙමෙන්, *Kemen*, } *s.* Elu form of ක්‍රමයෙන් *kra-*
කෙමෙන, *Kemena*, } *mayen;* basket used for catching fish.

කෙමැලි, *Kemęli*, *s.* froth of the sea.

කෙයියා, *Keyiyá*, *s.* generic name of wild pines, *Pandanus*.

කෙයුර, *Keyura*, see කේයුර *kéyúra*.

කෙර, *Kera*, *s.* lame woman, or any lame female animal, feminine of කොරා *korá*, lame person.

කෙරටිල්ල, *Keraṭilla*, *s.* sprig, small branch, top of a tree, pl. කෙරටිලි *keraṭili*.

කෙරල, *Kerala*, see කේරල *kérala*.

කෙරවල, *Kerawala*, *s.* extremity, point, or end, termination, pl. කෙරවල් *kerawal*.

කෙරී, *Kerí*, *s.* lame woman.

කෙරීම, *Keríma*, } verbal noun of කරණවා *kara-*
කෙරුම, *Keruma*, } *ṇawá*, to do, pl. කෙරීම් *kerím*.

කෙරෙණවා, *Kereṇawá*, *v.* it is being done: pret. කෙරුණ *keruṇá*.

කෙරෙන්, *Keren*, *affix* from.

කෙරෙමින්, *Keremin*, *part.* doing, being done.

කෙරෙවි, *Kerevi*, *s.* small venomous serpent, species of *coluber*.

කෙරෙහි, *Kerehi*, *prep.* in, upon, towards; particle and affix, used for dative and locative.

කෙල්මුව, *Kelmuwa*, *s.* kind of deer.

කෙල්ල, *Kella*, *s.* female slave; little girl, lass (a low word), pl. කෙල්ලෝ *kelló*.

කෙලගහනවා, *Kelagahanawá*, *v.* to spit: pret. කෙලගෑහුවා *kelagęhuwá*.

කෙලතොලු, *Kelatolu*, *s.* stammering, speaking as an idiot.

කෙලසනවා, *Kelasanawá*, } *v.* to defile; to defame,
කෙලහනවා, *Kelahanawá*, } to spoil, to dirty: pret. කෙලහෑව්වා *kelahęwwá*.

කෙලි, *Keli*, *s.* play, sport, pastime, amusement, pleasure; flag, an ensign.

කෙලින්, *Kelin*, *a.* straight, upright, perpendicular.

කෙලිනවා, *Kelinawá*, *v.* to play, to sport as children: pret. කෙලියා *keliyá*.

කෙලිනළු, *Kelinaḷu*, *s.* dancing, sport, play, pleasure, pastime.

කෙලිබඩුව, *Kelibaḍuwa*. *s.* toy, pl. කෙලිබඩු *kelibaḍu*.

කෙලිමඩුල්ල, *Kelimaḍulla*, *s.* dancing room.

කෙලිය, *Keliya*, *s.* play, sport, verbal noun of කෙලිනවා *kelinawá*, pl. කෙලි *keli*,

කෙලිල්ල, *Kelilla*, *s.* knee.

කෙලිවැඩේ, *Keliwęḍé*, *s.* toy, plaything.

කෙලෙන, *Kelena*, *a.* playing, sporting.

කෙලෙස්, *Keles*, *s.* nose; excrement (used for semen); filth; evil in the thoughts, desires, or affections; mountain so called: see කෛලාස *kailása*.

කෙලෙස් නිවෙස්, *Keles-niwes*, *s.* (කෙලෙස් rock so called, නිවෙස් residence) name of Ṣiva so called from the rock on which he is supposed to reside.

කෙලෙස, *Kelesa*, *ad.* how, in what manner.

කෙලෙසීම, *Kelesíma*, verbal noun of කෙලසනවා *kelasanawá*.

කෙලෙසුන්, *Kelesun*, } see කෙලෙස් *keles*.
කෙලෙසුම, *Kelesuma*, }

කෙවිට, *Keviṭa*, *s.* goad, pl. කෙවිටි *keviṭi*.

කෙවිටියකිර, *Keviṭiya-kira*, *s.* plant, *Memecylon exalata (Melastomaceæ)*.

කෙවින්න, *Kevinna*, *s.* part of a ring where the stone is set, pl. කෙවිනි *kevini*.

කෙවිල්ලී, *Kevillí*, } *s.* feminine of කොවුලා *kowulá* Indian cuckoo, multitude, flock, heap.
කෙවිලි, *Kevili*, }

කෙවුල්, *Kewul*, *a.* relating to water.

කෙවුලා, *Kewulá*, *s.* fisherman, pl. කෙවුලන් *kewulan*.

කෙවුලි, *Kewuli*, *s.* fem. of the above, pl. කෙවුලියෝ *kewuliyó*.

කෙවුලී, *Kewulí*, *a.* known, understood.

කෙවෙන්න, *Kewenna*, *s.* handle of a plough, pl. කෙවෙනි *kaweni*.

කෙවෙනවා, *Kewenawá*, *v.* to pain, as the eye, when any thing has fallen into it, as dust or dirt: pret. කෙවුනා *kewuná*.

කෙවෙනි, *Keweni*, *ad.* how, in what manner.

කෙවෙනියා, *Keweniya*, *s.* base born son, illegitimate child, bastard.

කෙස්, *Kes*, *s.* hairs.

කෙස්මඳන්, *Kesmandan*, } *s.* comb for fastening up the hair.
කෙස්මදනේ, *Kesmadané*, }

කෙස, *Kesa*, *s.* hair; urine, pl. කෙස් *kes*.

කෙසකිළිය, *Kesakiḷiya*, *s.* (කෙස urine, කිළිය house) privy.

කෙසග, *Kesaga*, *s.* hair, single hair of the head, tip of the hair.

කෙසඟ, *Kesaṇga*, Elu form of කෘශාඞ්ග *kriṣáṇga*, poor, lean.

කෙසර, *Kesara*, *s.* stamina of flowers; mane; hair on the body, pl. කෙසරු *kesaru*.

කෙසර බැවිල, *Kesara-bęvila*, see බැවිල *bęvila*.

කෙසරා, *Kesará*, *s.* maned lion.

කෙසරිඳු, *Kesarindu*, *s.* lion: [Colloq. සිංහයා *sinhayá*.]

කෙසරු, *Kesaru*, *s.* tree, *mimusops elengi*; lion.

කෙසරු බැලිල, *Kesaru-bęlila*, see බැවිල *bęvila*.

කෙසිමුදු, *Kesimudu*, *s.* key.

කෙසිවිද, *Kesivida*, *s.* key hole.

කෙසුරු, *Kesuru*, *s.* the pollen of flowers; dust.

කෙසෙල්, *Kesel*, *s.* banana or plantain, of which there are according to Mr. Moon about fifty-three species and varieties in Ceylon; for their names and arrangement, reference must be had to his valuable work.

කෙසෙල්මුව, *Keselmuwa*, *s.* flower of the plantain.

කෙසේද, *Keséda*. particle of interrogation, how? in what manner? it is used also as a particle of introduction to a subject under relation; as, that is to say, namely, in the following manner.

කෙසේනම්, *Kesénam*, } particle of introduction to a chapter or section, or a subject under relation, namely, that is, etc., also in this manner, thus, so, as etc.
කෙසේවූ, *Keséwú*, }

කෙහෙ, *Kehe*, *s.* hair, single hair.

කෙහෙතු, *Kehetu*, see කේතු *kétu*.

කෙහෙල්, *Kehel*, *s.* plantains, bananas, see කෙසෙල් *kesel*.

කෙහෙලි, *Keheli*. *s.* flags, or trophies of victory, banner.

කෙහෙලිදුම්, *Kehelidum*, *s.* fire.

කෙළ *Keḷa*, *s.* spittle. saliva; end; numeral of 100 lakhs; bud, sprout.

කෙළක්, *Keḷak*, *s.* 100, lakhs.

කෙළවර, *Keḷawara*, *s.* end, utmost, final, termination, extremity.

කෙළිඳ, *Keḷinda*, *s.* medicinal nut or seed, from the tree, *nerium antidysentericum;* it is used in cases of diarrhœa, dysentery, etc.

කෙළෙඹි, *Keḷembi*, *s.* man of wealth, or rich person.

කේ, *Ké*, *s.* hairs; field; screw pine, *pandanus odoratissimus*; also, who?

කේකා, *Kéká*, *s.* cry of the peacock.

කේකි, *Kéki* *s.* peacock; species of crane, or as it is usually called in Ceylon paddy bird.

කේජු, *Kéju*, *s.* cheese.

කේඩරේ, *Kéḍaré*, } කේඩුව, *Kéḍuwa*, } *s.* lassitude, weariness, fatigue, exhaustion of strength.

කේතක, *Kétaka*, } කේතකී, *Kétakí*, } *s.* screw pine, *pandanus odoratissimus*. [Colloq. දුනුකෙයියා *dunukeyiyá*.]

කේතලේ, *Kétalé*, *s.* kettle, pl. කේතල *kétala*.

කේතු, *Kétu*, *s.* in Indian astronomy the ninth of the planets; the dragon's tail or descending node, see also රාහු *ráhu*; in their mythology a noted demon; banner, flag; mark, sign, symbol; comet; falling star; enemy.

කේතුමාලාව, *Kétumáláwa*, *s.* one of the nine great divisions of the known world, the western part of Jambu-dwípa, or India proper.

කේඳි, *Keṇdi*, *s.* scores or lines drawn upon any thing, but more especially upon fish previously to their being cooked.

කේඳිලනවා, *Keṇdilanawá*, *v.* to make incisions, to score; see the preceding: pret. කේඳිලෑවා *kéṇdiléwá*.

කේන්‍ද්‍ර, *Kéndra*, *s.* squares and diagrams used by astrologers in casting nativities, horoscope.

කේනිපාත, *Kénipáta*, *s.* (ක *ka* water, නිපාත who goes or falls) oar; helm; rudder, large oar used as a rudder.

කේයූර, *Kéyúra*, *s.* bracelet worn on the upper part of the arm.

කේරල, *Kérala*, *s.* large fish, one of the whale tribe? with the addition of දේස *désa* it is an appellation of a country, the modern Malabar.

කේරලි *Kérali*, *s.* an astronomical science; period of time, about an hour.

කේරී, *Kérí*, *s.* cocoa-nut tree. [Colloq. පොල්ගහ *pol-gaha*.]

කේලම් කියනවා, *Kélam-kiyanawá*, *v.* to slander, to backbite, to traduce: pret. කේලම් කිව්වා *kélam-kiwwá*.

කේලම, *Kélama*, *s.* slander, backbiting, pl. කේලම්

කේලමා *Kélamá*, *s.* slanderous, backbiting man, pl. කේලම්මු *kélammu*.

කේවල, *Kéwala*, *ad.* one, only, alone, by itself; all, entire, whole; one of the names of Nirwáṇa; absolute, certain; an envious or selfish man; a kind of knowledge, probably of the unity of God.

කේවල වෛයාකරණ, *Kéwala-vaiyákaraṇa*, *s.* (කේවල only, වෛයාකරණ grammarian) mere grammarian, one not versed in any other science.

කේවලි, *Kéwali*, *s.* sort of religious ascetic; one who lives in retirement.

කේවෙල්කරණවා, *Kéwelkaraṇawá*, *v.* to grieve, to pain, to cause sorrow, to tease, to grumble, to haggle.

කේශ්‍ය, *Késya*, *s.* medicinal plant or tree, which in medical works is usually called ප්‍රියංගු *priyangu* and described as bearing a medicinal and fragrant seed.

කේශකල්‍යාණ, *Késakalyáṇa*, *s.* (කේශ hair, කල්‍යාණ excellent) fine head of hair, both as to colour and length.

කේශමුෂ්ටි, *Késamushṭi*, *s.* large species of the nimba tree.

කේශරජනික, *Késarajanika*, *s.* kind of tree, *barleria prionitis*.

කේශාග්‍රය, *Késágraya*, *s.* end of the hair.

කේසකලාපය. *Késakalápaya*, *s.* well dressed head of hair.

කේසධාතුව, *Késadhátuwa*, *s.* hair of Buddha preserved in one of the temples or dágebas, and ever treated as an object of worship.

කේසපාස, *Késapása*, *s.* much or ornamented hair.

කේසපාසි. *Késapási*, *s.* lock of hair on the top of the head.

කේසර, *Késara*, *s.* iron wood tree, *mesua ferrea;* assafœtida plant; tree bearing a white strong smelling flower *mimusops elengi*, [Colloq. මූනමල් *múna-mal*.]

කේසරාග, *Késarága*, *s.* (කේස hair, රාග adhesion) kind of unctuous substance used by natives as a perfume for the head and to make the hair grow.

කේසරින්, *Késarin*, *s.* lion; horse; citron tree.

කේසරී, *Késarí*, *s.* lion; plant, kind of ginger.

කේසරීන්ද්‍ර, *Késaríndra*, *s.* name of Vishṇu, lordly lion.

කේසව, *Késawa*, *s.* name of Vishṇu or Krisṇa, alluding to his fine hair.

කේසවේස, *Késawésa*, s. (කේශ hair, වේස ornament) tress or fillet of hair.

කෛතව, *Kaitawa*, s, deceit, fraud, cheating, roguery.

කෛපුඩිය, *Kaipuḍiya*, s. handle of a box or trunk.

කෛරව, *Kairawa*, s. white esculent water lily; rogue, cheat; enemy.

කෛරාටක, *Kairáṭaka*, s. poison, one of the fixed kinds.

කෛරාටික, *Kairáṭika*, a. deceitful, fraudulent.

කෛලාස, *Kailása*, s. name of a mountain, stated in the Hindu mythology to be the residence of Kuvéra, the Indian Plutus, and a favourite resort of Ṣiva; it is generally considered to be among the Himálayan mountains.

කෛවර්ත, *Kaiwarta*, s. fisherman, waterman.

කොංකරණවා, *Koṇkaraṇawá*, v. to put aside, to set apart.

කොංගනියා, *Koṇganiyá*, s. small prawn.

කොක්ක, *Kokka*, s. hook, pl. කොකු *koku*.

කොක්කනම්පයිය, *Kokkanam-payiya*, } s. sort of wallet or
කොක්කනම, *Kokkanama*, } bag used by pilgrims or sanyásis, which they hang upon the arm.

කොක්කු, *Kokku*, *pl.* of කොකා *koká*.

කොක්නා පක්ෂියා, *Kokná-pakshiyá*, s. (කොක් fork, නා bill, පක්ෂි bird) bird, *turdus gingianus*.

කොක්නා මුව, *Kokná-muwa*, s. (කොක්නා and මුව deer) wolf.

කොක්මොට, *Kokmoṭa*, s. plant, pipe wort, *eriocaulon quinquangulare (Eriocauloneæ)*.

කොක්සන්, *Koksan*, s. violent laughter.

කොක්හඬලනවා, *Kokhaṇḍalanawá*, v. to call workmen or labourers together by a certain kind of whoop, to shout out in laughter: pret. කොක්හඬලෑවා *kokhaṇḍalǽwá*.

කොකා, *Koka*, s. wolf.

කොකටිය, *Kokaṭiya*, s. tree, *garcinia ternophylla (Guttiferæ)*.

කොකදෙනවා, *Kokadenawá*, v. to hallo or shout, to huzza.

කොකනද, *Kokanada*, s. red lotus, red water lily.

කොකනද වේනාව, *Kokanada wénáwa*, s. sort of fiddle given by Sakra to Buddha when he was Kusa Raja, made of wood which resembled the red lotus.

කොකනදවෑල, *Kokanadawǽla*, s. red lotus.

කොකා, *Koká*, s. crane or heron, of which there are many species in Ceylon; some are named as follows බෙලිකොකා *beli-koká* muscle coloured, සුදුකොකා *sudu-koká* white, කනකොකා *kana-koká* dun coloured; කරවෑල්කොකා *karawǽlkoká* long necked; මානන්කොකා *mánan-koká* spreading; *(order Herodiones)*.

කොකිල, *Kokila*, s. Indian cuckoo, *cuculus micropterus* (order *Picariæ)*.

කොකිස්, *Kokis*, s. kind of food or bread made of rice flour.

කොකුං, *Kokuṇ*, s. saffron; tree, *swietenia febrifugia*.

කොකුංපොතු, *Kokuṇpotu*, s. tree, *kokuna zeylanica (Celastraceæ)*; also called වනපොතු *wana-potu*.

කොකුම්, *Kokum*, see කොකුං *kokuṇ*.

කොච්චර, *Kochchara*, ad. how much, how many.

කොච්චි බතල, *Kochchi-batala*, s. species of bind weed *convolvulus batatas*.

කොච්චියා, *Kochchiyá*, s. kind of fish, a man of Cochin.

කොට්ට, *Koṭṭa*, a. dry, dried; s. pillow, bolster;

කොට්ට උරේ, *Koṭṭa-uré*, s. pillow case, pl. කොට්ට උර *koṭṭa-ura*.

කොට්ටං, *Koṭṭaṇ*, see කොට්ටම් *koṭṭam*.

කොට්ටං ගෙඩිය, *Koṭṭaṇ-geḍiya*, s. medicinal nut, used also in marking cloth.

කොට්ටම්, *Koṭṭam*, s. plant, *costus speciosus*; [Colloq. තෙබු *tebu*.]

කොට්ටම්බා, *Koṭṭambá*, s. Indian almond tree, *terminalia catappa (Combretaceæ)*.

කොට්ටාසය, *Koṭṭásaya*, s. part, portion, division, section, pl. කොට්ටාස *koṭṭása*.

කොට්ටේ, *Koṭṭé*, s. cushion, pillow, pl. කොට්ට *koṭṭa*.

කොට්ටෝරුවා, *Koṭṭóruwá*, s. bird, brown-headed barbet, *megalæma zeylanica*; yellow-pointed barbet, *m. flavifrons*; crimson-breasted barbet, *xantholæma hæmacephala*, also called මල් කොට්ටෝරුවා *mal-koṭṭóruwá*: (order *Picariæ)*.

කොට, *Koṭa*, a. short; little, abridged, curtailed; also, *perf. part.* of කරණවා *karaṇawá* to do; s. jackal.

කොටකන්වවුලා, *Koṭakan-waulá*, s. small fox bat, *Cynopteris marginatus*.

කොටදිඹුලා, *Koṭadimbulá*, s. kind of fig-tree, *ficus oppositifolia, variety of F. hispida (Urticaceæ)*.

කොටන්නා, *Koṭanná*, s. wood cutter.

කොටන්හත්ත, *Koṭan-hatta*, s. fungus which grows on the trunks of trees.

කොටනවා, *Koṭanawá*, *v.* to dig with a spade; to bruise, or beat as paddy, when separating the husk from the grain; to fight, as cocks only; to cut as with an axe: pret. කෙටුවා *keṭuwá*.

කොටලවැල්, *Koṭala-wel*, *s.* creeping plant, *Torenia asiatica (Scrophulariaceæ).*

කොටවනවා, *Koṭawanawá*, *v.* to set on, to instigate a quarrel; to chop, to dig: pret. කෙටෙව්වා *keṭewwá*.

කොටස, *Koṭasa*, *s.* part, portion.

කොටහළු, *Koṭahaḷu*, *s.* present given by a young woman to her dhoby on her puberty.

කොටළුදෙන, *Koṭaḷudena*, *s.* she ass, pl. කොටළුදෙන්නු *koṭaḷudennu*.

කොටළුවා, *Koṭaḷuwá*, s. ass, jackass.

කොටා, *Koṭá*, *s.* short man, pl. කොට්ටු *koṭṭu; perf. part.* of කොටනවා *koṭanawá*, see above.

කොටිකං බැලිල, *Koṭikaŋ-belila*, } *s.* medicinal
කොටිකං බැවිල, *Koṭikaŋ-bevila*, } fibrous plant, *sida rhombifolia (Malvaceæ).*

කොටිකා, *Koṭiká*, *s.* dried arecanut.

කොටිදෙන, *Koṭidena*, *s.* tigress, pl. කොටිදෙන්නු *koṭidennu*.

කොටියා, *Koṭiyá*, *s.* Ceylon tiger or leopard, *felis pardus;* pl. කොටි *koṭi*.

කොටු, *Koṭu*, *a.* surrounded, fenced in.

කොටුඅත්ත, *Koṭu-atta*, *s.* path, by-way.

කොටුතාප්පේ, *Koṭu-táppé*. *s.* rampart, pl. කොටු තාප්ප *koṭu táppa*.

කොටුපත, *Koṭupata*, *s.* see කොටුඅත්ත *koṭu-atta*.

කොටුපවුර, *Koṭupawura*, *s.* walls of a fortress etc. pl. කොටුපවුරු *koṭupawuru*.

කොටුව, *Koṭuwa*, *s.* enclosure; fortress, castle, pl. කොටු *koṭu*.

කොටේ, *Koṭé*, *s.* short thing, stump, pl. කොට *koṭa*.

කොට්ඨක, } *Kotthaka*, *s.* inner apartment; gran-
කොට්ඨක, } ary; fort.

කොට්ඨාස, } *Kotthása*, see කොට්ඨාසය *koṭṭásaya*.
කොට්ඨාස, }

කොඩයා, *Koḍayá*, *s.* black ant, pismire.

කොඩි, *Koḍi*, *plur.* of කොඩිය *koḍiya*.

කොඩිකාරයා, *Koḍikárayá*, *s.* standard bearer.

කොඩිතුවක්කුව, *Koḍituwakkuwa*, *s.* sort of gun used by the Kandians, and placed when fired on a portable tripod; grasshopper gun, jingal.

කොඩිය, *Koḍiya*, *s.* colour, standard, flag, banner.

කොඩිවින, *Koḍivina*, *s.* magical incantations of a mischievous tendency: any other acts done with a view to produce mischief.

කොඬ, *Koṇḍa*, *s.* fruit; pig; socket of the arm where it joins the shoulder; huge hog.

කොඬලිඳු, *Koṇḍalindu*, *s.* king, [Colloq. රජ *raja*].

කොඬොල්, *Koṇḍol*, *s.* snakes; goats; ear ornaments.

කොඬොල, *Koṇḍola*, *s.* kind of yam, pl. කොඬොල් *koṇḍol*.

කොඬොලා, *Koṇḍolá*, *s.* earrings, plant, kind of yam.

කොණ්ඩෙ, *Koṇḍe*, *s.* kind of binder used to tuck up the hair of the head, hair of the head as tied up behind, pl. කොණ්ඩා *koṇḍá*.

කොත්, *Kot*, *s.* sceptre; point of a bow, spear; wife of Vishṇu; banner of Cupid.

කොත්කැරැල්ල, *Kot-kerella*, *s.* spiral lines or wreaths winding round the ornaments on the top of a house.

කොත්තම, *Kottama*, *s.* kind of jacket worn by the Siŋhalese; kind of waistcoat, pl. කොත්තම් *kottam*.

කොත්තමල්ලි, *Kottamalli*, *s.* coriander, *coriandrum sativum.*

කොත්තුකරණවා, *Kottukaraṇawá*, *v.* to prick or pierce with a small puncture.

කොත් මල, *Kot-mala*, see කොත්කැරැල්ල *kot-kerella*.

කොත්විලක්කුව, *Kotvilakkuwa*, *s.* standing lamp of copper etc.

කොත, *Kota*, *s.* spire or other ornament, at the top of a building, pl. කොත් *kot*.

කොතන, *Kotana*, *ad.* where? in, or to, or at what place?

කොතඹු, *Kotambu*, *s.* neck gem of Vishṇu.

කොතලය, *Kotalaya*, *s.* vessel with a spout for drinking out of.

කොතායුද, *Kotáyuda*, *s.* spear, lance; name of Kanda; see කඳකුමරු *kandakumaru*.

කොතු, *Kotu*, *s.* laughter.

කොතුකරණවා, *Kotukaraṇawá*, *v.* to pick, nibble (as a fish at a bait).

කොතුරුබැද්ද, *Koturubedda*, *s.* plant, *psychotria herbacea.*

කොතුව, *Kotuwa*, *s.* one-twentieth part of a parrah

කොතුහල, *Kotuhala*, *s.* tumult, uproar, disturbance.

කොතෙක්, *Kotek*, *ad.* how much, how many.

කොතැන්හිද, *Kotenhida*, *ad.* where? in what place?

කොද, *Koda*, *s.* rancour, grudge; *pron.* who?

කොදෙව්ව, *Kodewwa*, } *s.* island.
කොදෙවුව, *Kodewuwa*,

කොඳ, *Kon̲da*, *s.* white esculent water lily, *nymphæa esculenta.*

කොඳකැකුළු, *Kon̲da-kękuḷu*, *s.* plant, species of *jasmin*; another plant. species of the *nymphæa* or water lily.

කොඳසැර, *Kon̲dasęra*, *s.* bow of flowers; garland.

කොඳු, *Kon̲du*, *s.* things made of goats hair.

කොඳු පලස, *Kon̲du-palasa*. *s.* exceedingly fine cloth, made of goats hair.

කොඳුරණ, *Kon̲duraṇa*, *a.* whispering, murmuring

කොඳුරණවා, *Kon̲duraṇawá*, *v.* to whisper, to murmur, to grumble, to complain: pret. කෙඳුරුවා *ken̲duruwá*.

කොන්, *Kon*, *plur.* of කොන *kona*.

කොන්කරණවා, *Konkaraṇawá*. *v.* to put aside or apart.

කොන්චම්කරණවා, *Koncham-karaṇawá*, } *v.* to mock,
කොන්චිකරණවා, *Konchi-karaṇawá*.
jeer, laugh at, ridicule.

කොන්ඩ, *Konḍa*. *s.* kind of binder or girdle used for tucking up the hair, pl. කොන්ඩෙ *konḍe*.

කොන්ඩ කුරුල්ලා, *Konḍa-kurullá*, *s.* small bird, called Madras bulbul, *pycnonotus hæmorrhois*, (order *Passeres*).

කොන්ඩකොහා, *Konḍa-kohá*, *s.* pied-crested cuckoo, *coccystes jacobinus*; red-winged crested cuckoo, *c. coromandus* (order *Picariæ*).

කොන්ඩකැවුන්, *Konḍakęwun*. } *s.* kind of cake,
කොන්ඩකැවුම්, *Konḍakęwum*. in shape resembling the කොන්ඩෙ *konḍe*.

කොන්ඩ වඳුරා, *Konḍa-wan̲durá*, *s.* Madras laugur, *Semnopithicus priamus*.

කොන්ඩෙ, *Konḍe*, *s.* bunch, or knot, in which the Sin̲halese tie up their hair, pl. කොන්ඩා *konḍá* or කොන්ඩ *konḍa*.

කොන්ත, *Konta*, *s.* kind of spear or lance, rosary.

කොන්තායුධය, *Kontáyudhaya*, *s.* spear, or lance; Indian god of war, see කඳකුමාරයා *kan̲da-kumáraya*.

කොන්තේ, *Konté*, *s.* stick forming one part of a tripod, with a large iron hook at the top, two of which are used for supporting a palanquin when not in motion, and to prevent it from touching the ground.

කොන්ද, *Konda*, *s.* rump.

කොන්දෑටේ, *Kondęṭé*. *s.* spine, pl. කොන්දැට *kondęṭa*.

කොන්වෙනවා, *Konwenawá*, *v.* to go aside, to step out of the way.

කොන, *Kona*, *s.* end, corner, angle; corner of a room, pl. කොන් *kon*.

කොනක, *Konaka*, *ad.* apart, aside.

කොනහනවා, *Konahanawá*, } *v.* to pinch, to nip:
කොනිස්සනවා, *Konissanawá*, pret. කෙනහුවා *kenahuwá*; කෙනිස්සුවා *kenissuwá*.

කොප්පර, *Koppara*, *s.* kernel of the cocoanut cut in pieces and dried in the sun, from which oil is extracted.

කොප්පරා, *Koppará*, *s.* sort of large sea fish.

කොපමණ, *Kopamaṇa*. *ad.* how much, what number.

කොපිල්, *Kopil*, *s.* cheek, [Colloq. කම්මුල *kammula*].

කොපු, *Kopu*, *s.* well, [Colloq. ළිඳ *lin̲da*].

කොපුල් අත, *Kopul-ata*, *s.* cheek.

කොපුල, *Kopula*, *s.* cheek, jaw, pl. කොපුල් *kopul*.

කොපුව, *Kopuwa*, *s.* sheath, scabbard, pl. කොපු *kopu*.

කොපෙ, *Kope*, *s.* anger. see කෝපය *kópaya*.

කොපොල, *Kopola*, *s.* cheek

කොබ්බෑ, *Kobbę*, *s.* tree, *allophylus cobbe (Sapindaceæ)*.

කොබ, *Koba*, *ad.* where.

කොබනිල, *Kobanila*, } *s.* tree, mountain ebony,
කොබලිල, *Kobalila*, *bauhinia purpurea*.

කොබෙයියා, *Kobeyiyá*, *s.* common Indian dove, *turtur risorius*; spotted dove, *t. suratensis*, also called අළුකොබෙයියා *aḷu-kobeyiyá*; (order *Columbæ*).

කොබෝගෙඩිවලල්ල, *Kobógeḍi-walalla*, *s.* pigeon house.

කොබෝගෙඩිවලලු, *Kobógeḍi-walalu*, *s.* projecting ends of beams in houses etc. often ornamented.

කොබෝ නයා, *Kobó-nayá*, *s.* snake.

කොබෝ මල්, *Kobó-mal*, *s.* tree, *Eugenia operculata (Myrtaceæ)*; also called බටදොඹ *baṭa-dom̲ba*.

කොබෝවක්කා, *Kobówakká*, *s.* plant, *ventilago maderaspatana*.

කොඹුව, *Kom̲buwa*, } *s.* musical instrument shaped like a French horn:
කොම්බුව, *Kombuwa*. Sin̲halese character ෙ *kombuwa* representing the vowel එ *e*.

කොමඩා, *Komaḍá*, *s.* name of a fish.

කොමඩු, *Komaḍu*, *s.* water melon, *citrullus vulgaris (Cucurbitaceæ)*.

කොමඩු, *Komandu*, *s.* gourd, *cucurbita citrulla;* [Colloq. යක් කොමඩු *yak-komadu.*]
කොමන්දෙ, *Komande*, *s.* troop, detachment, pl. කොමන්ද *komanda.*
කොමල, *Komala*, *a.* soft, flexible; *s.* things producing love or affection, any thing soft.
කොමලකරණවා, *Komala-karaṇawá*, *v.* to make love, or to court.
කොමාරිකා, *Komáriká*, see කෝමාරිකා *kómáriká.*
කොමු, *Komu*, *s.* fine cloth made of goats hair.
කොමුපිඩු, *Komupiḍu*, *s.* kind of cake or bread made of rice flower.
කොමුපිලි, *Komupili*, see කොමු *komu.*
කොයක, *Koyaka*, *ad.* which?
කොයි, *Koyi*, *ad.* where? which?
කොයින්ද, *Koyinda*, *ad.* whence, from whence.
කොර, *Kora*, *a.* lame; *s.* scales of fishes.
කොරකහ, *Korakaha*, *s.* plant, *memecylon umbellatum (Melastomaceæ).*
කොරකහා, *Korakahá*, *s.* kind of saffron.
කොරගහනවා, *Koragahanawá*, *v.* to limp, to walk lame.
කොරටු, *Koraṭu*, *s.* jackal; enclosure.
කොරටුව, *Koraṭuwa*, *s.* sort of fence in order to prevent cattle trespass.
කොරඬු, *Korandu*, *s.* abridgment, conciseness.
කොරපොත්ත, *Korapotta*, *s.* scale of fish; scab, pl. කොරපොතු *korapotu.*
කොරපොල් ගෙඩිය, *Korapol-geḍiya*, *s.* cocoa-nut for fighting; at pestilential times the natives have a ceremony of throwing cocoa-nuts one against the other, to remove sickness, but at other times for sport, sometimes and more properly written පොරපොල්ගෙඩිය *porapolgeḍiya.*
කොරඹුරුවා, *Koramburuwá*, *s.* fish, char.
කොරල්, *Koral*, *s.* coral.
කොරල, *Korala*, *s.* scaliness.
කොරලන්, *Koralan*, *s.* flat fish, carp.
කොරලාවා, *Koraláwá*, *s.* kind of small sea fish.
කොරලියා, *Koraliyá*, *s*, fresh water fish, species of the carp.
කොරවකා, *Korawaká*, *s.* bird called ruddy rail, *porzana fusca;* blue-breasted rail, *hypotænidia striata;* white-breasted water hen, *erythra phœnicura;* (order *Grallæ.*) pl. කොරවක්කු *korawakku.*
කොරස, *Korasa*, *s.* large pan: *a.* rough.
කොරසවැල්, *Korasa-wel*, see කොරොසවැල *korosa weḷa.*
කොරසැඩි, *Korasędi*, *a.* rough, rugged, hard, severe.
කොරහ, *Koraha*, *s.* large pan, large chatty, see කොරස *korasa.*
කොරහැඩි, *Korahędi*, see කොරසැඩි *korasędi.*
කොරා, *Korá*, *s.* lame man, any male lame animal, pl. කොරු *koru.*
කොරු, *Koru*, *s.* jackal, [Colloq. නරියා *nariyá*].
කොරොස්, *Koros*, *a.* cruel, barbarous, hard hearted; plant, see the following word.
කොරොස වැල, *Korosa-węla*, *s.* creeper, *delima sarmentosa (Dilleniaceæ).*
කොරොස කොල, *Korosa-kola*, *s. pl.* leaves of a creeper, used to clean furniture.
කොල්ලකනවා, *Kollakanawá*, *v.* to rob, to plunder, to pillage.
කොල්ලන්කොල, *Kollankola*, *s.* plant, kind of mint.
කොල්ලන් ගහ, *Kollan-gaha*, *s.* tree, *garcinia* or *xanthocymus pictorius*, [Colloq. රටගොරක *raṭa-goraka*].
කොල්ලය, *Kollaya*, *s.* plunder, pillage, things taken by theft.
කොල්ලා, *Kollá*, *s.* young lad, youngster, (a low word), pl. කොල්ලෝ *kalló.*
කොල්ලු, *Kollu*, *s.* horse gram, Madras gram, *dolichos biflorus (Leguminosæ).*
කොල්ලැව, *Kollęwa*, *s.* outrigger of a fishing canoe.
කොලකුර, *Kolakura*, *s.* bud, young shoots of the leaves.
කොලකැටිය, *Kola-kęṭiya*, *s.* heap or stack of corn.
කොලතු, *Kolatu*, *s.* branches.
කොලතුර, *Kolatura*, *s.* tree.
කොල දිවියා, *Kola-diviyá*, *s.* (කොල and දිවියා ounce) tiger cat, *felis rubiginosa.*
කොල නෙලනවා, *Kola-nelanawá*, *v.* to weed, to pluck out weeds.
කොලපත, *Kolapata*, *s.* leaf of a book or tree, pl. කොලපත් *kolapat.*
කොලපරටියා, *Kola-paráṭiyá*, *s.* kind of fish.
කොල පාට, *Kola-páṭa*, *s.* green (literally leafy colour).
කොලපුව, *Kolapuwa*, *s.* spathe of the flower of the cocoa-nut tree.
කොල මඩිනවා, *Kola-maḍinawá*, *v.* to thrash corn by trampling: pret. කොලමැඩ්ඩා *kola-męddá.*
කොලමුරුවා, *Kolamuruwá*, *s.* kind of small sea fish.

කොලහලය, *Kolahalaya*, *s.* tumultuous noise; noise, uproar, quarrel.

කොල හිඹුල්, *Kola-him̱bul*, *s.* sort of silk cotton, from කූටශාල්මලී *kúṭaṣálmalí.*

කොලි, *Koli*, *s.* tree, *zizyphus jujuba*, [Colloq. මහ ඩෙබර *maha-ḍebara* and මසං *masaṉ*].

කොලිහ, *Koliha*, *s.* extreme point of a tree.

කොලු, *Kolu*, } see කොල්ලා *kollá.*
කොලුවා, *Koluwá*, }

කොලෙ, *Kolé*, *s.* leaf, branch; herbs; raiment; rat snake, Garunḍa; ferry, pl. කොල *kola.*

කොලොඹිය, *Kolom̱biya*, *s.* species of mango tree.

කොලොඹුව, *Kolom̱buwa*, *s.* wooden stool, log of wood to sit upon.

කොවක්කා, *Kowakká*, *s.* plant, *bryonia grandis.*

කොවිචර, *Kovichara*, } *ad.* how much, how many.
කොවිතර, *Kovitara*, }

කොවුල්ලා, *Kowullá*, *s.* kókila or Indian cuckoo.

කොවුල, *Kowula*, *s.* decayed or rotten tree, pl. කොවුල් *kowul.*

කොස්, *Kos*, *s.* jack tree, *artocarpus integrifolia (Urticaceæ).*

කොස් අත්ත, *Kos-atta*, *s.* plant, *Blachia umbellata (Euphorbiaceæ).*

කොස්ඇට මියා, *Koseṭa-miyá*, *s.* common Indian mouse, *mus urbanus.*

කොස්ඇට වව්ලා, *Koseṭa-wawlá*, *s.* Coromandel bat, *Scotophilus coromandelianus.*

කොස් කුරුල්ලා, *Kos-kurullá*, *s.* bird called little minivet, *pericrocotus peregrinus (*order *Passeres).*

කොස්කැටියා, *Koskeṭiyá*, *s.* sort of tree.

කොස්බඩ *Kos-baḍa*, *s.* tree, *Litsea tomentosa (Lauraceæ).*

කොස්ලිහිණියා, *Koslihiṇiyá*, *s.* curlew.

කොස්ස, *Kossa*, *s.* brush, broom, fibre; matter in a boil, pl. කොහු *kohu.*

කොස්සා, *Kossá*, *s.* kind of sea fish or fly.

කොසඹ, *Kosam̱ba*: see කොහොඹ *kohom̱ba.*

කොසඹ පොලඟා *Kosam̱ba-polaṉgá*. *s.* snake.

කොහල, *Kohala*, s. secret things, hidden property; umbrella.

කොහා, *Kohá*, *s.* Indian plaintive cuckoo, *cuculus passerinus (*order *Picariæ).*

කොහිල, *Kohila*, *s.* plant, (both leaves and root edible); *Lasia spinosa (Araceæ).*

කොහු, *Kohu*, *s.* sort of paddy, *oryza sativa;* fibre of the cocoa-nut husk.

කොහු අඹ, *Kohu-am̱ba*, *s.* species of mango, *mangofera indica.*

කොහු කිරිල්ල, *Kohu-kirilla*, *s.* plant, *microcos paniculata.*

කොහු දෙවරැද්දිරි, *Kohu-dewareḍdiri*, *s.* sort of paddy, *oryza sativa.*

කොහුලනුව, *Kohu-lanuwa*, *s.* cord made from the fibres of the husk of the cocoa-nut.

කොහේ, *Kohé*, } *ad.* where, in what place.
කොහේද, *Kohéda*, }

කොහොට, *Kohoṭa*, *s.* share, part, portion, see කොටස *koṭasa.*

කොහොනි, *Kohoni*, *s.* school, place for learning, [Colloq. ස්කෝලය *skólaya.*]

කොහොඹ, *Kohom̱ba*, *s.* margosa tree, *azadirachta indica (Meliaceæ).*

කොහොම, *Kohoma*, } *ad.* how? in what manner?
කොහොමද, *Kohomada*, }

කොහොල්, *Kohol*, *s.* shame facedness, shyness; covered or concealed place, rod, stick.

කොහොල්ලෑ, *Koholle̥*, *s.* gum of the jack tree.

කොහොවිල, *Kohovila*, *s.* plant, *dracontium spinosum.*

කොළොම්, *Koḷom*, *s.* tree, *adina cordifolia* or *nauclea (Rubiaceæ).*

කෝ, *Kó*, *ad.* where; *s.* anger.

කෝක, *Kóka*, *ad.* which; *s.* wolf, see කොක *koka.*

කෝකියා, *Kókiyá*. *s.* cook.

කෝකිලයා, *Kókilayá*, *s.* black Indian cuckoo; this bird has a pleasing and affecting note, and according to Indian poets produces strong emotions in the heart, and makes a prominent figure in their poetry.

කෝට්ටය, *Kóṭṭaya*, *s.* fort.

කෝටි, *Kóṭi*, } *s.* number, 100 lacs or ten millions; end, termination; edge of a sword; end of a bow; point, edge, corner, angle; eminence, excellence; plant *medicago esculenta.*
කෝටිය, *Kóṭiya*, }

කෝටුව, *Kóṭuwa*, small stick, pl. කෝටු *kóṭu.*

කෝද්‍රව, *Kódrawa*, } *s.* species of grain eaten by the common people *paspalum scrobiculatum*, [Colloq. අමු *amu*].
කෝද්‍රවක, *Kódrawaka*, }

කෝදණ්ඩ, *Kódanḍa*, } *s.* bow; the eye brow.
කෝදෝන, *Kódóna*, }

කෝඳුරුවා, *Koṉduruwá*, *s.* eye fly; gnat.

කෝන්, *Kón*, *s.* tree, Ceylon oak, producing a pleasant acid fruit, *schleichera trijuga (Sapindaceæ).*

කෝන, *Kóna*, *s.* general name for the three divisions of the year.

කෝනම, *Kónama*, *s.* general name for cloth, bathing cloth, hence, rag, poor man's cloth.

කෝප, *Kópa*, *a.* angry, wrathful, passionate.

කෝපය, *Kópaya*, *s.* anger, wrath, passion, sorrow, indignation.

කෝපි, *Kópi*, *s.* coffee, *coffea arabica*.

කෝපිවත්ත මීයා, *Kópiwatta-míyá*, *s.* bush or coffee rat, *golunda ellioti*.

කෝමාරිකා, *Kómáriká*, *s.* kind of medicinal plant, aloe, *aloe vulgaris*.

කෝරක, *Kóraka*, *s.* bud, unblown flower; kind of perfume; berry containing a resinous and fragrant substance.

කෝරළේ, *Kóralé*, *s.* part of a province, division, pl. කෝරළ *kórala*.

කෝරාළ, *Kórála*, *s.* the chief of a Kóralé.

කෝල, *Kóla*, *s.* fruit of the jujube tree; kind of pepper, *piper chavya*, [Colloq. සිවිය *siviya*]; hog; raft, float; haunch, hip or flank; embrace; planet Saturn; kind of plumbago *plumbago zeylanica;* a country, Kaliṇga, including the sea coast from Kuttack to Madras; kind of weapon.

කෝලක, *Kólaka*, *s.* kind of pepper, *piper longum;* perfume.

කෝලම්බක, *Kólambaka*, *s.* body of a lute, whole of it except the strings; large water jar.

කෝලම, *Kólama*, *s.* masked dance in which both human and supernatural characters are introduced, masquerade, show, pl. කෝලම් *kólam*.

කෝලවල්ලි, *Kólawalli*, *s.* long pepper.

කෝල සන්නිය, *Kóla-sanniya*, *s.* excess of phlegm in the throat so as to cause suffocation; *cholera morbus*.

කෝලාරුව, *Kóláruwa*, *s.* want, need, necessity.

කෝලාහල, *Koláhala*, *s.* tumult, uproar, loud and confused noise, riot.

කෝලි, *Kóli*, *s* jujube tree.

කෝලිකුට්ටු, *Kólikuṭṭu*, *s.* large sort of plantain, table plantain.

කෝලේ, *Kólé*, *s.* diffidence, shyness, bashfulness; kind of paralytic affection.

කෝව, *Kówa*, *s.* crucible.

කෝවක්කා, *Kówakká*, *s.* plant, *cephalandra indíca*, or *coccinea (Cucurbitaceæ)*.

කෝවි, *Kóvi*, *s.* cabbage, *brasica oleracea*.

කෝවිද, *Kóvida*, *a.* wise, learned.

කෝවිදාර, *Kóvidára*, *s.* species of ebony, *bauhinia variegata*.

කෝවිල, *Kóvila*, *s.* brahminical temple, pl. කෝවිල් *kóvil*.

කෝවේ, *Kówé*, see කෝව *kówa*.

කෝශ, *Kóṣa*, *s.* egg; gold; shoe, sandal.

කෝශල, *Kóṣala*, see කෝසල *kósala*.

කෝෂ්ඨ, *Kóshṭha*, *s.* granary, place in which grain is kept; apartment; stomach.

කෝෂ, *Kósha*, *s.* egg; sheath, scabbard; bud; gold, any of the precious metals; wealth, treasure; treasury; drinking vessel; vulva; womb; testicle; scrotum; penis; ball, globe; nutmeg; dictionary, vocabulary; shoe, sandal; beard of corn.

කෝෂක, *Kóshaka*, *s.* egg, testicle.

කෝෂකාර, *Kóshakára*, *s.* sugar cane; silk worm, or the insect while in its cone, *chrysalis*.

කෝෂ ගර්භය, *Kósha-garbhaya*, *s.* leathern purse or bag of any kind; scrotum.

කෝෂාතක, *Kósháṭaka*, *s.* hair; creeper, *momordica cylindrica*.

කෝෂාතකී, *Kósháṭakí*, *s.* small species of cucumber; cucurbitaceous plant, *luffa acutangula* [Colloq. වැටකොළු *weṭakoḷu*]; night.

කෝස, *Kósa*, see කෝෂ *kósha*.

කෝස ඵල, *Kósa-phala*, *s.* (කෝස egg, ඵල fruit) kind of berry, in shape resembling an egg, containing a waxy and fragrant substance, *bdellium*.

කෝසල, *Kósala*, *s.* name of the city Ayódhyá; country or district south of Ayódhyá, *(Oude)* and one of the great scenes of the public ministry of Buddha; one of the kings of this city was the first who set up an image of Buddha for public worship.

කෝසාතක, *Kósáṭaka*, see කෝෂාතක *kósháṭaka*.

කෝසාතකී *Kósáṭakí*, see කෝෂාතකී *kósháṭakí*.

කෝසේ, *Kósé*, see කෝෂ *kósha*.

කෝසෙය්‍යං, *Kóseyyaṇ*, *s.* silken cloth; carpet inwrought with gold.

කෞකෘත්‍ය, *Kaukritya*, *s.* (කු *ku* bad, කෘත්‍ය action) evil, wicked deed, wickedness.

කෞටික, *Kauṭika*, *s.* (කූට *kúṭa* trap, ඨික් *ṭhak* affix) hypocrite, cheat, deceiver; one who kills animals and sells their flesh for his own subsistence; hunter, poacher, mountaineer.

කෞඩුබෝ, *Kauḍu-bó*, *s.* tree, *Ficus arnottiana (Urticaceæ);* also called කපුටුබෝ *kapuṭu-bó* or කවුඩුබෝ *kawuḍu-bó*.

කෞණ්ඩින්‍ය, *Kauṇḍinya*, *s.* thirteenth lunar asterism designated by a hand containing five stars, one of which is seven or eight Corvi; tree *borago zeylanica?*

කෞතුක, *Kautuka*, *s.* desire to see strange things, curiosity, eagerness; vehemence, impatience; joy, pleasure, happiness; sport, pastime, festival; friendly greeting.

කෞතුකාගාරය, *Kautukágáraya*, *s.* museum.

කෞතුහල, *Kautúhala*, *s.* eagerness, vehemence.

කෞන්තික, *Kauntika*, *s.* spearman, lancer, soldier, armed with a spear.

කෞබේරි, *Kaubéri*, *s.* name of Kuvéra or Wesamuṇi-raja chief of the demon race; the North quarter of which he is regent.

කෞමද, *Kaumada*, *s.* white lotus, from its resemblance to moonlight, or from the circumstance of its always opening in the moonlight.

කෞමද බන්ධු, *Kaumada-bandhu*, *s.* moonlight.

කෞමුද, *Kaumuda*, *s.* month Kartik (October and November).

කෞමුදී, *Kaumudí*, *s.* moonlight; Hindu festival in honour of Kártikéya (commonly called Kataragama deviyo) held on the full moon of the month Kartik; day of the full moon in the months Aṣwiṇi and Kartik.

කෞමුදී වෘක්ෂ, *Kaumudí-wṛiksha*, *s.* (කෞමුදී light, වෘක්ෂ tree) lamp stand.

කෞරව, *Kaurawa*, *s.* descendant of Kuru; see කුරු *kuru*.

කෞල, *Kaula*, *s.* one of a good family, well born.

කෞලීන, *Kaulína*, *s.* high birth, family, descent; rumour, report; combat of animals birds, snakes etc., cock fighting; privity, privy part; improper act; the son of a female beggar.

කෞලේයක, *Kauléyaka*, *a.* of good family, of good parentage.

කෞස්තුභ, *Kaustubha*, *s.* jewel of Kṛishṇa suspended on his breast.

කෞසල්‍ය, *Kausalya*, *s.* good fortune, well being; mother of Ráma.

කෞශික, *Kausika*, *s.* name of Indra; fragrant substance, *bdellium;* owl; snake catcher; ichneumon; title of Wiṣwamitra; one skilled in dictionaries; dictionary compiler; love, passion; marrow; a river in Bahar, the Kosi or Koosa; name of the goddess Durgá.

කෞශේය, *Kauséya*, *a.* silken, of silk.

කැක්, *Kęk*, *s.* sorrow.

කැක්කුම, *Kękkuma*, *s.* pain, ache.

කැකල, *Kękala*, *s.* tree, *Cyathocalyx zeylanicum*, *(Anonaceæ);* also called ඊපැත්ත *ipętta*.

කැකිර, *Kękira*, *s.* generic name for cucumber, pl. කැකිරි *kękiri*.

කැකිරිවරා, *Kękiri-wará*, *s.* name of *Schumacheria castaneæfolia (Dillenaceæ)* and of *axinandra zeylanica (Lythraceæ)*, both plants peculiar to Ceylon.

කැකිල්ල, *Kękilla*, *s.* small thicket, fern, *Gleichania linearis (Filices)*.

කැකුන, *Kękuna*, *s.* tree, *canarium zeylanicum (Burseraceæ)*, peculiar to Ceylon.

කැකුල, *Kękula*, *s.* flower bud; *adj.* hard, pl. කැකුළු *kękuḷu*.

කැකුළු, *Kękuḷu*, s. strong glare; hardness.

කැකෑරෙණවා, *Kękęreṇawá*, *v.* to boil with a gentle heat; neutral form of කකාරණවා *kakáraṇawá*.

කැට්ට, *Kętta*, *a.* spun, see කටිනවා *kaṭinawá*.

කැට්ටවෙනවා, *Kęṭṭawenawá*, *v.* to be disinclined to, proceeding either from fear or disgust.

කැට, *Kęṭa*, *s.* looking glass, mirror; pebble, small stone, bit of stone; lamp; cocoanut shell.

කැටකිරිල්ලි, *Kęṭa-kirilli*, fem. of කැටකුරුල්ලා *kęṭa-kurullá*.

කැටකුරුල්ලා, *Kęṭakurullá*, *s.* small bird found in paddy fields.

කැටකෑල, *Kęṭa-kéla*, *s.* tree, *Bridelia retusa (Euphorbiaceæ)*.

කැට දීම, *Kęṭa-díma*, *s.* giving a solemn pledge or assurance, as truly, verily.

කැටන්, *Kęṭan*, *s.* troubling (as of water.)

කැටපත, *Kęṭapata*, see කැඩපත *kędapata*.

කැට පාගණවා, *Kęṭa-páganawá*, *v.* to tread the ground in the cultivation of fields.

කැටය, *Kęṭaya*, see කැට *kęṭa*.

කැටයම්කරණවා, *Kęṭayamkaraṇawá*, *v.* to engrave, to carve.

කැටයම, *Kęṭayama*, *s.* engraving, carving, pl. කැටයම් *kęṭayam*.

කැටි, *Kęṭi*, *s.* ball, clod, lump, any thing congealed.

කැටිය, *Kęṭiya*, *s.* clod, lump; plant, *Pittosporum zeylanicum (Pittosporaceæ)*, peculiar to Ceylon.

කැටුව, *Kęṭuwa*, *prep.* together with, along with.

කැටේ, *Kęṭé*, *s.* small earthen pot, see කැට *kęṭa*.

කැඩ, *Kęḍa*, *s.* mark, sign.

කැඩපත, *Kęḍapata*, *s.* looking glass, mirror, pl. කැඩපත් *kęḍapat*.

කැඩපන, *Kęḍapana*, *s.* letter addressed to a king, embassy.

කැඩීම, *Kęḍíma*, *s.* act of breaking, pl. කැඩීම් *kęḍím*.

කැඩුං, *Kẹduṇ*, } verbal noun of කඩනවා *kaḍana-*
කැඩුම්, *Kẹdum*, } *wá*, to break or cut.

කැඩෙන, *Kẹdena*, *part.* breaking.

කැඩෙනවා. *Kẹdenawá*, *v.* to break (neut.) *pret.* කැඩුනා *kẹduná.*

කැත්, *Kẹt*, *a.* of noble birth, royal.

කැත් ඇඹිල්ල, *Kẹt-ẹmbilla*, *s.* plant, *aberia gardneri, (Bixiniæ)*, peculiar to Ceylon.

කැත්කත්, *Kẹtkat*, } *s*, (කැත් royal, කත් woman)
කැත්කල, *Kẹtkala*, } queen.

කැත් කුල, *Kẹt-kula*, *s.* (කැත් and කුල family, race or offspring) royalty, of royal descent.

කැත්ත, *Kẹtta*, *s.* bill, large sort of crooked knife, bill hook, chopping knife, pl. කැති *kẹti.*

කැත්ලිය, *Kẹt-liya*, *s.* (කැත් and ලිය woman) queen.

කැත්වග, *Kẹt-waga*, *s.* (කැත් royal, වග or වර්‍ග *warga* sort, kind or race) royalty, of royal descent.

කැත, *Kẹta*, *a.* disgusting, filthy, base, vile, mean, ugly; *s.* dirt, filth.

කැති, *Kẹti*, plural of කැත්ත *kẹtta.*

කැති තලේ, *Kẹti-talé*, *s.* iron part or blade of the bill hook, pl. කැතිතල *kẹti-tala.*

කැතිමල්ල, *Kẹti-malla*, *s.* (කැත්ත *kẹtta* knife, මල්ල bag) toddy drawer's knife case.

කැදුල්ල, *Kẹdẹlla*, *s.* nest, lump (as of flesh); confused assemblage (as of worms or any thing like them), pl. කැදලි *kẹdali.*

කැඳ, *Kẹnda*, *s.* rice gruel, decoction, congee.

කැඳෑටි, *Kẹndaṭi*, *s.* corner of a house.

කැඳත්ත, *Kẹndatta*, *s.* small quantity of gruel.

කැඳලනවා, *Kẹndalanawá*, *v.* to starch, pret. කැඳ ලෑවා *kẹnda-lẹwá.*

කැඳවනවා, *Kẹndawanawá*, *v.* to call, to summon, to invite.

කැඳවාගෙණ එනවා, *Kẹndawágaṇa enawá*, *v.* to bring home (a bride.)

කැඳවීම, *Kẹndavíma*, *v.* invitation, call, verbal noun of කැඳවනවා *kẹndawanawá.*

කැන්ද, *Kẹnda*, *s.* plant, *Macaranga tomentosa, (Euphorbiaceæ).*

කැන්දගහ, *Kẹnda-gaha*, *s.* candle nut tree, *croton moluccanum*, formerly called *aleurites trilboa;* also called තෙල්කැකුන *tel-kẹkuna.*

කැන්දනවා, *Kẹndanawá*, see කැඳවනවා *kẹndawanawá.*

කැන්දවනවා, *Kẹndawanawá*, *v.* to call, to cause to call, to invite, to send for by another.

කැන්දායනවා, *Kẹndá-yanawá*, *v.* go along with (a bride).

කැන්මේරිය, *Kẹnmériya*, } *s.* night shade; *solanum*
කැන්වේරිය, *Kẹnwériya*, } *nigrum.*

කැන්හැන්ද, *Kẹnhẹnda*, *s.* plant, *clerodendrum serratum (Verbenaceæ).*

කැන, *Kẹna*, *s.* assembly, multitude; bunch of fruit; past participle of කනිනවා *kaninawá*, pl. කැන් *kẹn.*

කැනටු, *Kẹnaṭu*, *s.* betel, [Colloq. බුලත් *bulat*].

කැනහිලා, *Kenahilá*, *s.* jackal, fox, pl. කැනහිල්ලු *kẹnahillu*, [Colloq. නරියා *nariyá*].

කැනැත්ත, *Kẹnẹtta*, *s.* cluster, bunch, (as පපු කැනැත්ත *papu-kẹnẹtta* heart, liver and lungs), pl. කැනැති *kẹnati.*

කැප්පිටියා, *Kẹppiṭiyá.* } *s.* species of croton,
කැප්පෙට්ටියා, *Kẹppeṭṭiyá*, } *croton lacciferum (Euphorbiaceæ).*

කැප, *Kẹpa*, *s.* offering to a deity or a devil; *a.* proper, fit, devoted, but particularly that which is offered to a god or demon.

කැපකරුවා, *Kẹpakaruwá*, *s.* priest's attendant.

කැපීම, *Kẹpíma*, *s.* cutting or wounding.

කැපුන, *Kẹpuna*, *a.* cut.

කැපුම, *Kẹpuma*, *s.* scare, trembling, cutting, pl කැපුම් *kẹpum.*

කැබරලා, *Kẹbaralá*, *s.* red woodpecker, *brachypternus ceylonus (Picidæ* order *Picariæ.)*

කැබලි, *Kẹbali*, plural of කැබෙල්ල *kẹbella.*

කැබලිකරණවා, *Kẹbalikaraṇawá*, *v.* to reduce to pieces.

කැබිලි. *Kẹbili*, *s.* half moon; *a.* half.

කැබිලිත්ත, *Kẹbilitta*, *s.* broken piece of earthen pot or vessel, potsherd, pl. කැබිලිති *kẹbiliti.*

කැබෙල්ල, *Kẹbella*, *s.* piece, bit, slice, pl. කැබලි *kẹbali.*

කැබෙල්ල ගහ, *Kẹbella-gaha*, *s.* tree, *aporosa Lindleyana (Euphorbiaceæ).*

කැබැල්ල, *Kẹbẹlla*, see කැබෙල්ල *kẹbella.*

කැම්, *Kẹm*, see කෙංවැල *keṇwẹla.*

කැමති, *Kẹmati*, *a.* contented, pleased, willing.

කැමතිවෙනවා, *Kẹmatiwenawá*, *v.* to be willing or contented; to consent.

කැමි, *Kẹmi*, *s.* writer.

කැමී, *Kẹmí*, *s.* row, arrangement, order; doer, worker from කර්මී *karmi.*

කැමැත්ත, *Kẹmẹtta*, *s.* contentment, will, willingness, consent.

කැර, *Kęra*, *s.* bunch of flowers growing together; nosegay.

කැරපොත්තා, *Kęrapottá*, *s.* sort of small house cricket, cockroach, pl. **කැරපොත්තෝ** *kęrapottó*.

කැරය, *Kęraya*, *s.* writing, deed, contract; voucher, bond.

කැරල්ල, *Kęralla*, see **කැරැල්ල** *kęręlla*.

කැරලි, *Kęrali*, *s.* heap, bundle; assembly, multitude, union or association; mob or company of people assembled for riotous purposes.

කැරලිගහනවා, *Kęraligahanawá*, *v.* to rebel, to assemble for riotous purposes.

කැරේ, *Kęré*, see **කැරය** *kęraya*.

කැරැල්ල, *Kęręlla*, *s.* assembly, multitude, crowd; riotous company; army, company of soldiers or men ready to fight; bundle, skein, pl. **කැරලි** *kęrali*.

කැරැකොකු, *Kęrękoku*, *s.* fern, *acrosticum aureum (Filices)*.

කැල්, *Kęl*, *s.* light; morning.

කැල, *Kęla*, *s.* multitude; wood, jungle etc. in the latter sense written **කැලේ** *kęlé*.

කැලණිය, *Kęlaṇiya*, *s.* name of a village and river; aromatic plant, *alpinia alughas (Scitamineæ)*; also called **අළුගස්** *aḷu-gas*.

කැලත, *Kęlata*, *s.* dregs, lees, sediment, confusion; *a.* muddy, thick, not clear, not pellucid.

කැලති, *Kęlati*, *s.* troubling; sediment, lees.

කැලතෙනවා, *Kęlatenawá*, *v.* to become muddy as when a liquor containing a sediment is shaken; to be agitated: pret. **කැලතුනා** *kęlatuná*.

කැලඹීම, *Kęlambíma*, verbal noun of the following word.

කැලඹෙනවා, *Kęlambenawá*, *v.* to trouble, to stir.

කැලම, *Kęlama*, *ad.* wholly, totally.

කැලය, *Kęlaya*, *s.* jungle, thicket, wood, pl. **කැලෑ** *kęlę*.

කැලල්, *Kęlal*, plural of the following.

කැලල, *Kęlala*, *s.* cicatrice; mark, scar, blemish, wound.

කැලි, *Kęli*, *s.* unblown flower, derived from Sanskrit **කලි** *kali*.

කැලිකසල, *Kęli-kasala*, *s.* filth, or dirt swept away.

කැලිපන, *Kęlipana*, *s.* shadow, sign.

කැලිය, *Kęliya*, *s.* black (the colour); plant, *grewia microcos (Tiliaceæ)*.

කැලුම්, *Kęlum*, *s.* gladness of heart, cheerfulness; brightness, resplendency; solar heat or rays, effulgence.

කැලේ, *Kęlé*, see **කැලය** *kęlaya*.

කැලේ කොන්ඩයා, *Kęlé-koṇḍayá*, *s.* black bulbul, *hypsipetes ganeesa (Brachypodidæ* order *Passeres)*.

කැලෑව, *Kęlęwa*, *s.* a wood, wild uncultivated spot, jungle.

කැවිට, *Kęviṭa*, *s.* goad, pl. **කැවිටි** *kęviṭi*.

කැවිල්ල, *Kęvilla*, *s.* food, anything that can be eaten, pl. **කැවිලි** *kęvili*.

කැවිලි, *Kęvili*, *s.* sweet meats, cakes.

කැවූ, *Kęwu*, *a.* rubbed, smeared.

කැවුත, *Kęwuta*, *s.* liver, pl. **කැවුතු** *kęwutu*.

කැවුම, *Kęwuma*, *s.* sort of cake, made of rice flour honey and cocoa-nut oil, pl. **කැවුම්** *kęwum* or **කැවුන්** *kęwun*.

කැවුලෑහියා, *Kęwulęhiyá*, *s.* gormandizer, glutton.

කැවෙනවා, *Kęwenawá*, *v.* to smart, to pain (in the eye): pret. **කැවුනා** *kęwuná*.

කැස්පාපොතු, *Kęspá-potu*, *s.* shell of a sea tortoise.

කැස්බා, *Kęsbá* } *s.* Indian edible turtle, *chelonia virgata*.
කැස්බෑවා, *Kęsbęwá*, }

කැස්බෑ ලෙල්ල, *Kęsbę-lella*, see **කැස්පා පොතු** *kęspá-potu*.

කැස්වටුවා, *Kęswaṭuwá*, *s.* common snipe, *gallinago scolopacina*; pin-tailed snipe, *g. stenura (Scolopacidæ* order *Grallæ)*.

කැස්ස, *Kęssa*, *s.* cough.

කැස, *Kęsa*, *s.* arm pit, thicket.

කැසපට, *Kęsapaṭa*, *s.* clothes tucked up, (**කක්ෂා** *kakshá* girdle, **පට** *paṭa* cloth) end of the lower garment, which after the cloth is carried round the body is brought up behind and tucked into the waist band.

කැසපටගහනවා, *Kęsapaṭa-gahanawá*, *v.* to gird up the garments for a journey or work.

කැසි, *Kęsi*, plural of **කැස්ස** *kęssa*.

කැසිපිස්සන්, *Kęsipissan*, *s.* plant, *Cyclea Burmanni (Menispermaceæ)*.

කැසීම, *Kęsíma*, *s.* itching, or scratching, verbal noun of **කහිනවා** *kahinawá*.

කැසුප්, *Kęsup*, } *s.* turtle, tortoise. [Colloquial: **කැස්බා** *kęsbá*.]
කැසුබු, *Kęsubu*, }
කැසුඹු, *Kęsumbu*, }

කැසුම, *Kęsuma*, verbal noun of **කසනවා** *kasanawá* or **කහනවා** *kahanawá*.

කැහි, *Kęhi*, *pl.* of **කැස්ස** *kęssa*.

කැහිපිත්තන්, *Kęhipittan*, see **කැසිපිස්සන්** *kęsipissan*.

කැහිබෙල්ලා, *Kęhibellá*, *s.* Ceylonese jay, *cissa ornata (Corvidæ* order *Passeres).*

කැහුම, *Kęhuma*, see කැසුම *kęsuma.*

කැහැපටගහනවා, *Kęhępaṭagahanawá*, see කැසපට ගහනවා *kęsapaṭagahanawá.*

කෑ, *Kę*, *p.* eaten, *past part.* of කනවා *kanawá.*

කෑකෝගහනවා, *Kękógahanawá*, *v.* to make a noise or uproar.

කෑගහනවා, *Kęgahanawá*, } *v.* to cry out, to bawl,
කෑගානවා, *Kęgánawá*, } to squall.

කෑදර, *Kędara*, *a.* gluttonous, ravenous, greedy of food.

කෑදරයා, *Kędarayá*, *s.* glutton.

කෑදැත්තා, *Kędęttá*, } *s.* bird with a peculiarly
කෑඳත්තා, *Kęndattá*, } plaintive or begging cry; it is supposed when crying to be begging water from the clouds, the sole source of the fluid that this bird drinks; Ceylonese hornbill; *tockus gingalensis (Bucerotidæ,* order *Picareæ).*

කැප්පුර, *Kęppura*, *s*, camphor. [Colloq. කපුරු *kapuru.*]

කෑඹලාවා, *Kęmbaláwá*, see කෑදරයා *kędarayá.*

කෑම, *Kęma*, *s.* food, victuals, eatables, provisions.

කෑම අරිණවා, *Kęma-ariṇawá*, *v.* to lay food on tables. to have food ready to be eaten, to serve up meat.

කෑරලා, *Kęralá*, *s.* general name of the woodpecker, viz: Layard's woodpecker, *chrysolaptes stricklandi;* black-backed woodpecker, *c. festious;* Madras rufous woodpecker, *micropternus gularis;* red woodpecker, (see කෑබරලා *kębaralá*); Southern golden-backed woodpecker, *brachypternus puncticollis;* (family *Picidæ*, order *Picarice).* pl. කෑරල්ලු *kęrallu.*

කෑරීම, *Kérima*, *s.* coughing, slight exertion of the lungs to clear away expectoration; hawk.

කෑරැස්සා, *Kęręssá*, *s.* cricket, pl. කෑරැස්සෝ *kęręssó.*

කැල්ල, *Kęlla*, *s.* piece, bit, scrap, crumb, pl. කැලි *kęli.*

කෑල, *Kęla*, *s.* tree bearing beautiful red blossoms, *butea frondosa*, [Colloq. ගස්කෑල *gas kęla*].

කෑලම, *Kęlama*, *adv.* alone, only.

කෑලි, *Kęli*, see කෑල්ල *kęlla.*

ක්‍රන්දන, *Krandana*, *s.* weeping, lamenting, sobbing; crying out, calling; mutual daring or defiance, challenging.

ක්‍රන්දිත, *Krandita*, *a.* lamented, bewailed, challenged; defied; called.

ක්‍රම, *Krama*, *s.* order, method, degree; power, strength; overcoming, subduing; surpassing; sacred precept, religious practice; fort.

ක්‍රමක, *Kramaka*, *s.* (ක්‍රම to go or, order, ක nominal affix) one who goes through a regular course of study; one who goes methodically, student.

ක්‍රමක්‍රමයෙන්, *Kramakramayen*, *ad.* by degrees, gradually.

ක්‍රමණ, *Kramaṇa*, } *s.* foot, [Colloq. කකුල
ක්‍රමණය, *Kramaṇaya*, } *kakula*].

ක්‍රමය, *Kramaya*, see ක්‍රම *krama.*

ක්‍රමික, *Kramika*, *a.* regular, according to order, proceeding by rule.

ක්‍රමු, *Kramu*, *s.* areca nut tree, [Colloq. පුවක් *puwak*].

ක්‍රමුක, *Kramuka*, *s.* areca or betel nut tree; another tree, red species of the tree, bark of which is used in dyeing, *symplocos racemosa;* kind of mulberry tree, *morus indica;* fruit of the cotton tree.

ක්‍රමුමාල, *Kramumála*, *s.* tree, *cathartocarpus fistula.*

ක්‍රමෙ *Krame*, see ක්‍රම *krama.*

ක්‍රමෙලක, *Kramelaka*, *s.* (ක්‍රම *krama* order, ඉල *ila* to go) camel, [Colloq. ඔටුවා *oṭuwá*].

ක්‍රය, *Kraya*, *s.* buying, purchasing.

ක්‍රය වික්‍රය, *Kraya-vikraya*, *s.* (ක්‍රය and වික්‍රය sale) buying and selling, trade, traffic, merchandize.

ක්‍රයාරෝහ, *Krayáróha*, *s.* (ක්‍රය and ආරෝහ *áróha* to rise) market, fair.

ක්‍රයික, *Krayika*, *s.* trader, dealer; purchaser, buyer.

ක්‍රව්‍ය, *Krawya*, *s.* flesh, raw flesh.

ක්‍රව්‍ය ඝාතන, *Krawya-ghátana*, *s.* (ක්‍රව්‍ය and ඝාතන to kill) that which is killed for its flesh, deer, [Colloq. මුවා *muwá*].

ක්‍රව්‍යාත්, *Krawyát*, } *s.* (ක්‍රව්‍ය and අද් *ad* to eat)
ක්‍රව්‍යාද්, *Krawyád*, } that which eats flesh, beast, carnivorous animal; imp, goblin, rákshayá.

ක්‍රාන්ති, *Kránti*, *part.* ascending, surmounting, either in a literal or figurative sense; surpassing, going beyond.

ක්‍රාන්තු, *Krántu*, *s.* bird; bird in general, [Colloq. පක්ෂියා *pakshiyá*].

ක්‍රාබු, *Krábu*, *s.* cloves; earring, properly කරාබු *karábu.*

ක්‍රායක, *Kráyaka*, see ක්‍රයික *krayika.*

ක්‍රිං, *Kriṇ*, *s.* imitative sound, clang of concussion.

ක්‍රිකර, *Krikara*, *s.* name of Ṣiva; that one of the five vital airs which assists digestion.

ක්‍රිමි, *Krimi*, *s.* worm, insect; lac, which is the accumulation of an insect; also කෘමි *kṛimi*.

ක්‍රියා, *Kriyá*, ක්‍රියාව, *Kriyáwa*, } *s.* act, action, deed; acting; means, expedient; beginning, undertaking; atonement; study; worship; disquisition; bodily action; remedying; physical treatment or practice; instrument, implement; religious initiatory ceremony; obsequies, rites preformed immediately after death.

ක්‍රියෙන්ද්‍රිය, *Kriyendriya*, *s.* (ක්‍රිය *kriya* action, ඉන්ද්‍රිය *indriya* organ) organ of action, as the hand, foot, voice etc.; organ of generation, and that of excrement.

ක්‍රීඩන, *Kríḍana*, *s.* play, sport.

ක්‍රීඩා, *Kríḍá*, *s.* sport, pleasure, pastime, play, amusement.

ක්‍රීඩාභාණ්ඩ, *Kríḍábháṇḍa*, *s.* toys or play things for children.

ක්‍රීඩාමඩුල්ල, *Kríḍá-maḍulla*, *s.* place for amusements.

ක්‍රීඩා රථය, *Kríḍá-rathaya*, *s.* (ක්‍රීඩා pleasure, රථය car) car or carriage of pleasure.

ක්‍රීඩාව, *Kríḍáwa*, *s.* sport, pleasure.

ක්‍රීත, *Kríta*, *s.* son, one of the twelve kinds acknowledged by the ancient Hindu law, he who is purchased from his parents; *a.* bought, purchased.

කෘකලාස, *Kṛikalása*, *s.* lizard, chameleon.

කෘච්ඡ්‍ර, *Kṛichchhra*, *s.* bodily pain; religious penance; expiation.

කෘත්තික, *Kṛittika*, *s.* third of the lunar mansions or constellations in the moon's path consisting of six stars, and corresponding to the Pleiades.

කෘත්‍ය, *Kṛitya*, කෘත්‍යය, *Kṛityaya*, } kind of affix in grammar, forming verbal nouns with an active or passive sense; motive, cause.

කෘත්‍යා, *Kṛityá*, *s.* act, action.

කෘත්ස්න, *Kṛitsana*, *a.* all, whole, entire, complete.

කෘත, *Kṛita*, *s.* according to the mythology of the Hindus the first of the four ages of the world, satya-yuga; consequence; fruit; *part.* done, made, finished.

කෘතක, *Kṛitaka*, *s.* that which is artificial; *a.* factitious; made, not produced spontaneously.

කෘතකං, *Kṛitakaṇ*, *s.* artificial salt, produced by boiling and evaporating from saline soils; *part.* done, made, performed.

කෘතකර්ම, *Kṛitakarma*, *s.* skill, dexterity, expertness, cleverness.

කෘතඝ්න, *Kṛitaghna*, *s.* (කෘත done, ඝ්න destroying) ingratitude, ungrateful, not acknowledging former good offices.

කෘතඥ, *Kṛitajña*, *s.* (කෘත and ඥ who knows) one who remembers former aid or favors, properly one that is grateful for kindness.

කෘතපුණ්‍ය, *Kṛita-puṇya*, *s.* (කෘත and පුණ්‍ය happy, fortunate) auspicious events, good deeds, meritorious actions, such works as procure final beatitude.

කෘත ලක්ෂණ, *Kṛita-lakshaṇa*, *s.* (කෘත done, alluding to good deeds, ලක්ෂණ sign, mark) one noted for good deeds, virtuous, excellent or holy man.

කෘතහස්ත, *Kṛita-hasta*, *s.* (කෘත done, exercised, හස්ත hand) clever, skilful, skilled in archery.

කෘතාඤ්ජලි, *Kṛitáñjali*, *s.* act of joining the palms of the hands together in the manner of the natives, as an act of salutation or reverence.

කෘතාධිකාර, *Kṛitádhikára*, *s.* one possessed of great merit, a fortunate person, chiefly referring to religious merit.

කෘතාන්ත, *Kṛitánta*, *s.* (කෘත done, act, අන්ත *anta* end) name of Yáma, the regent of death, alluding to his office of deciding on the final states of departed spirits according to their deeds in this life, answering to the Grecian Pluto; death personified; fate, destiny; sinful or inauspicious actions.

කෘතාන්ත ජනක, *Kṛitánta-janaka*, *s.* (කෘතාන්ත Yama, ජනක progenitor) father of Yama, a name of the sun.

කෘතාවකාශ, *Kṛitáwakása*, *s.* leisure, rest from labour.

කෘති, *Kṛiti*, *s.* act, action, doing etc. injuring, hurting, hurt.

කෘතෝපකාර, *Kṛitópakára*, *s.* (කෘත *kṛita* done, උපකාර *upakára* favor) act of kindness or generosity, but used chiefly to express a sense of kindness, received from another; gratitude, thankfulness.

කෘතෝපකාර සැලකීම, *Kṛitópakára-selakíma*, *s.* gratitude.

කෘපණ, *Kṛipaṇa*, *a.* miserable, avaricious; low, vile.

කෘපා, *Kṛipá*, *s.* tenderness, compassion, kindness, benevolence, [Colloq. කරුණාව *karuṇáwa*].

කෘපාලු, *Kṛipálu*, *a.* kind, tender, compassionate, benevolent.

ක්‍රිමිඝනා, *Krimighaná*, *s.* (ක්‍රිමි worm, ඝන which destroys) anthelmintic shrub, *serratula* or *conyza anthelmintica*, [Colloq. වලඟසාල් *walangasál*].

ක්‍රිමිජ, *Krimija*, *s.* aguru or aloe wood, [Colloq. අගිල් *agil*].

ක්‍රිමිදන්, *Krimidan*, *s.* Elu form of the preceding.

ක්‍රිමිශත්‍රු, *Krimiṣatru*, *s.* (ක්‍රිමි and ශත්‍රු enemy) kind of grass, *Panicus antidotale (Gramineæ).*

ක්‍රිමින්, *Krimín*, *pl.* of ක්‍රිමි *krimi.*

ක්‍රිශ, *Kriṣa*, *a.* small, little, thin, minute; spare, lean, emaciated.

ක්‍රිශාංගය, *Kriṣáńgaya*, *s.* (ක්‍රිශ *kriṣa* thin, අංගය *ańgaya* body) thin or well shaped person.

ක්‍රිශානු *Kriṣánu*, *s.* name of fire; plant *plumbago zeylanica*; [Colloq. එළනෙතුල් *ela-neṭul*].

ක්‍රිෂ්ට, *Krishṭa*, *a.* ploughed, furrowed, tilled, as a field etc.

ක්‍රිෂ්ණ, *Krishṇa*, *s.* in Hindu mythology Krishṇa is considered the most celebrated form of Vishṇu or rather Vishṇu himself; in that form he is however distinct from the ten avatárs or incarnations of Vishṇu, being always identified with the deity himself; one of the names of Arjuna the charioteer of the sun; kókila or Indian cuckoo; crow; kind of fruit, *carissa carandas;* [Colloq. මහකරඹ *maha-karamba*]; black or dark blue; black pepper; blue vitriol; iron; sin.

ක්‍රිෂ්ණ කර්ම, *Krishṇa-karma*, *s.* (ක්‍රිෂ්ණ black, කර්ම action) guilt, sin, criminality.

ක්‍රිෂ්ණ කාක, *Krishṇa-káka*, *s.* raven.

ක්‍රිෂ්ණකාන්ත, *Krishṇa-kánta*, *s.* black (colour) or dark blue.

ක්‍රිෂ්ණ කාම්බෝජි, *Krishṇa-kámbóji*, *s.* blue lotus.

ක්‍රිෂ්ණ ජීරක, *Krishṇa-jíraka*, *s.* (ක්‍රිෂ්ණ and ජීරක cummin seed) plant having a small black seed which is used for medical and culinary purposes, *nigella indica*, [Colloq. කළුදුරු *kaluduru*].

ක්‍රිෂ්ණ පක්ෂ, *Krishṇa-paksha*, *s.* (ක්‍රිෂ්ණ and පක්ෂ half) dark half of a lunar month, fifteen days during which the moon is in the wane.

ක්‍රිෂ්ණ බුමි, *Krishṇa-búmi*, }
ක්‍රිෂ්ණ භූමි, *Krishṇa-bhúmi*, } *s.* ක්‍රිෂ්ණ black, බුමි earth) country with a dark soil, one of mould, blue clay etc.

ක්‍රිෂ්ණභෙදි, *Krishṇa-bhedi*, *s.* (ක්‍රිෂ්ණ dirt, excrement, භෙදි what breaks) medicinal plant.

ක්‍රිෂ්ණ මඤ්ජරි, *Krishṇa-mañjari*, *s.* kind of tree, the wood of which, is usually called calamander wood *diospyros quæsita;* [Colloq. කළුමැදිරිය *kaḷumẹdiriya*].

ක්‍රිෂ්ණ මෝචක, *Krishṇa-móchaka*, *s.* species of the banana or plantain tree.

ක්‍රිෂ්ණරාජි, *Krishṇa-ráji*, *s.* black species of the coriander seed.

ක්‍රිෂ්ණ වෘන්තා, *Krishṇa-wrintá*, *s.* trumpet flower, *datura suave-olens;* [Colloq. රට අත්තන *raṭa-attana*].

ක්‍රිෂ්ණා, *Krishṇá*, *s.* name of Draupadi, wife of the Pándávas; indigo plant; long pepper; kind of grape; sort of drug, *nigella indica;* black mustard; this name is applied to several other vegetable substances, in consequence of their black colour.

ක්‍රිෂ්ණාචල, *Krishṇáchala*, *s.* mountain so called; it is part of the western portion of the Vindhyá chain, it is also one of the nine principal mountains, that separate the same divisions or Varshas of the world inhabited by living beings.

ක්‍රිෂ්ණික, *Krishṇika*, *s.* black mustard.

ක්‍රිෂක, *Krishaka*, *s.* plough share; husbandman, cultivator, thin or spare man.

ක්‍රිෂි, *Krishi*, *s.* husbandry, agriculture; ploughing, cultivating the soil.

ක්‍රූර, *Krúra*, *a.* evil, bad; vicious, cruel, pitiless, harsh; hard, solid; hot; mischievous, destructive; formidable, terrible.

ක්‍රූරලෝචන, *Krúralóchana*, *s.* (ක්‍රූර evil, ලෝචන eye) of an evil or inauspicious aspect, name of the planet Saturn.

ක්‍රූරාකෘති, *Krúrákriti*, *s.* (ක්‍රූර and ආකෘති form) name of Rávaṇa.

ක්‍රෝධය, *Kródhaya*, *s.* anger, wrath, passion, choler.

ක්ලාන්ත, *Klánta*, *a.* weak, faint, fatigued, wearied.

ක්ලිබ, *Klíba*, }
ක්ලිව, *Klíwa*, } *s.* eunuch. [Colloq. නපුංසකයා *napuṇsakayá*].

ක්ලේශ, *Kléṣa*, *s.* pain; affliction or distress; pain from disease, anguish; worldly occupation, care, trouble; wrath, anger; lust, passion, evil, pollution, defilement; the sinful corruption of all the senses and spiritual faculties of man; according to the doctrines of Buddhism kléṣa is the source of all the miseries to which existence in any stage is subject; and so long as it exists in any degree either in man or any sentient being it binds him to existence which is considered a calamity; the destruction of kléṣa is therefore the sole object of a Buddhist's religious life; hence without any reference to a supreme being, all the laws, precepts, rites and ceremonies of

Buddhism have a regard only to the entire destruction of kléṣa; this object accomplished, the soul or sentient faculty in man or any higher order of being escapes from existence and obtains Nirváṇa or annihilation.

ක්‍ෂණ, *Kshaṇa*, *s.* moment; measure of time equal to four minutes; leisure, opportunity; certain day of the fortnight, as the full moon, change etc.

ක්‍ෂණකාස, *Kshaṇakása*, *s.* asthma.

ක්‍ෂණද, *Kshaṇada*. *s.* (ක්‍ෂණ leisure, ද who gives) water; astrologer.

ක්‍ෂණදා, *Kshaṇadá*, *s.* night; turmeric.

ක්‍ෂණ ප්‍රභා, *Kshaṇa-prabhá*, *s.* (ක්‍ෂණ moment, ප්‍රභා light) lightning, [Colloq. විදුලිය *viduliya*].

ක්‍ෂණික, *Kshaṇika*, *a.* momentary.

ක්‍ෂත්‍ර, *Kshatra*, *s.* weapon, sword; man of the royal or military tribe.

ක්‍ෂත්‍රිය, *Kshatriya*, *s.* man or woman of the royal or military race.

ක්‍ෂත්‍රිය කුලය, *Kshatriya-kulaya*, *s.* royal or military family or tribe.

ක්‍ෂත්‍රිය ධර්මය, *Kshatriya-dharmaya*, *s.* royal virtue, or those particular qualities that are supposed to exist in royalty, as honour, fidelity, justice, benignity, kindness, benevolence, mercy etc.

ක්‍ෂත්‍රිය මායා, *Kshatriya-máyá*, *s.* secrets of royalty, those particular secrets that are supposed to be possessed by kings and are hereditary from one generation to another.

ක්‍ෂත, *Kshata*, *s.* wound, hurt, sore; *a.* broken, rent, torn, hurt, wounded.

ක්‍ෂතකාස, *Kshatakása*, *s.* (ක්‍ෂත blood, කාස cough) pulmonary cousumption.

ක්‍ෂතජ, *Kshataja*, *s.* (ක්‍ෂත and ජ which produces) blood, pus, matter.

ක්‍ෂපා, *Kshapá*, *s.* night; [Colloq. රාත්‍රිය *rátriya*].

ක්‍ෂපාකර, *Kshapákara*, *s.* (ක්‍ෂපා and කර who makes) moon; [Colloq. හඳ *haṇda*].

ක්‍ෂම, *Kshama*, *a.* proper, fit; patient, able.

ක්‍ෂමා, *Kshamá*, *s.* resignation; benevolence; night; earth.

ක්‍ෂමාකරණවා, *Kshamákaraṇawá*; *v.* pardon, forgive.

ක්‍ෂමාකරවනවා, *Kshamákarawanawá*, *v.* obtain pardon.

ක්‍ෂමාදංශ, *Kshamádaṇsa*, *s.* horse-radish tree, *moringa pterogosperma*, [Colloquial: මුරුංගා *muruṇgá*].

ක්‍ෂමාව, *Kshamáwa*, *s.* pardon; forgiveness; excuse, apology.

ක්‍ෂමාවෙනවා, *Kshamáwenawá*, *v.* to pardon, to excuse, to remit.

ක්‍ෂය, *Kshaya*, *s.* fourth incarnation of Vishṇu (Narasiṇha avatár); destruction of the world; in algebra, negative quantity or minus, loss; disappearance; decay, decline, consumption.

ක්‍ෂයරොග, *Kshayaroga*, *s.* consumption.

ක්‍ෂර, *Kshara*, *s.* water, cloud, [Colloq. වලාකුළ *walákuḷa*].

ක්‍ෂව, *Kshawa*, *s.* sneezing; cough.

ක්‍ෂවක, *Kshawaka*, *s.* mustard plant, [Colloq. අබ *aba*].

ක්‍ෂවථු, *Kshawathu*, see ක්‍ෂව *kshawa*.

ක්‍ෂාන්ත, *Kshánta*, *a.* patient, enduring.

ක්‍ෂාන්ති, *Kshánti*, } *s.* patience, forbearance;
ක්‍ෂාන්තිය, *Kshántiya*, } endurance.

ක්‍ෂාන්තු, *Kshántu*, see ක්‍ෂාන්ත *kshánta*.

ක්‍ෂාම, *Kshága*, *a.* slender, thin, emaciated, weak.

ක්‍ෂාර, *Kshára*, *s.* factitious or medicinal salt, juice, essence; kind of molasses or treacle; salt; ashes; rogue, cheat; borax, borate of soda; alkali, either soda or potash.

ක්‍ෂාරක, *Kshāraka*, *s.* juice, essence; blossom, new blown flower, [Colloq. කැකුළ *kękuḷa*]; cage, basket; washerman.

ක්‍ෂාරද්‍රු, *Ksháradrú*, *s.* tree with flowers bell shaped, *bignonia indica*. [Colloq. පළොල් *paḷol*.]

ක්‍ෂාරවධ, *Kshára-wadha*, *s.* (ක්‍ෂාර salt, වධ infliction) punishment inflicted on malefactors, cutting the flesh and introducing salt etc. into the wound.

ක්‍ෂාරච්ඡ, *Kshárachchha*, *s.* (ක්‍ෂාර *kshára* and අච්ඡ *achchha* clear, pure) sea salt.

ක්‍ෂාරොදක, *Ksháródaka*, *s.* (ක්‍ෂාර *kshára* salt, උදක *udaka*, water) salt, or brackish water; exceedingly hot or boiling water, which forms the means of punishment in the hell called ක්‍ෂාරොදක නරක *ksháródaka-naraka*.

ක්‍ෂාලන, *Kshálana*, *s.* washing, sprinkling, cleaning with water.

ක්‍ෂිත්‍යදිති, *Kshityaditi*, *s.* (ක්‍ෂිති *kshiti* earth, අදිති *aditi* mother of the gods) mother of Kṛishṇa, the terrestrial parent of the gods.

ක්‍ෂිති, *Kshiti*, *s.* the earth; abode, dwelling, house; loss, destruction; wane; period of the destruction of the universe; kind of perfume.

ක්ෂිප්ත, *Kshipta*, *past part.* thrown, sent, dismissed.

ක්ෂිප්තා, *Kshiptá*, *s.* night, [Colloq. රාත්‍රිය *rátriya*].

ක්ෂිප්‍ර, *Kshipra*, *a.* quick. [Colloq. ඉක්මන් *ikman*].

ක්ෂිප, *Kshipa*, *s.* art of throwing or casting; one who throws.

ක්ෂිපක, *Kshipaka*, *s.* warrior, fighter.

ක්ෂිපණි, *Kshipaṇi*, *s.* missile weapon; oar.

ක්ෂීණ, *Kshíṇa*, *a.* thin, slender, emaciated, feeble.

ක්ෂීබ, *Kshíba*, *a.* drunk, intoxicated. [Colloq. වෙරි *weri*].

ක්ෂීර, *Kshíra*, *s.* water [Colloq. වතුර *watura*]; milk [Colloq. කිරි *kiri*].

ක්ෂීරකණ්ඨ, *Kshírakaṇṭha*, *s.* (ක්ෂීර milk, කණ්ඨ *kaṇṭha* throat) infant, young child.

ක්ෂීරකාකෝලිකා, *Kshírakákólíká*,
ක්ෂීරකාකෝලි, *Kshírakákólí*, } *s.* one of the eight principal medicaments of the Indian medical men, see කාකෝලි *kákoli*.

ක්ෂීරදෝහනය, *Kshíra-dóhanaya*, *s.* a milk pail, milking.

ක්ෂීරධාරාව, *Kshíra-dhárawa*, *s.* stream of milk which flows when milking.

ක්ෂීරපායාස, *Kshíra-páyása*, *s.* rice boiled or cooked in milk.

ක්ෂීරපර්ණී, *Kshíra-parṇṇi*, *s.* medicinal plant; [Colloq. හෙලවරා *hela-wará*].

ක්ෂීරපිණ්ඩ, *Kshíra-piṇḍa*, *s.* ball of rice milk or as much as is taken in the hand at once when eating.

ක්ෂීරාබ්ධි, *Kshírábdhi*, *s.* (ක්ෂීර milk, අබ්ධි *abdhi* ocean) sea of milk, one of the seven seas said to surround as many worlds.

ක්ෂීරභක්තා, *Kshírabhaktá*, *s.* tree, *eugenia operculata*, [Colloq. බටදොඹ *baṭadomba*].

ක්ෂීරවල්ලී, *Kshírawallí*,
ක්ෂීරවිදාරී, *Kshíravidárí*, } *s.* sort of medicinal creeper, *convolvulus paniculatus*.

ක්ෂීරවෘක්ෂ, *Kshíra-wṛiksha*, *s.* species of fig tree, *ficus glomerata;* [Colloq. අට්ටික්කා *aṭṭikká*].

ක්ෂීරශර, *Kshíraṣara*, *s.* cream.

ක්ෂීර සාගරය, *Kshíra-ságaraya*, *s.* sea of milk, one of the seven seas surrounding as many worlds.

ක්ෂීරසාර, *Kshírasára*, *s.* butter, [Colloq. වෙඬරු *weṇḍarú*].

ක්ෂීරී, *Kshírí*, *s.* tree, species of *mimusops;* name of several plants, which yield a milky or juicy sap upon expression or incision, the name being formed from ක්ෂීර milk with ඉනි *ini* affix.

ක්ෂුත්, *Kshut*, *s.* sneezing, the act of sneezing; hunger.

ක්ෂුත් පිපාසා, *Kshut-pipásá*, *s.* (ක්ෂුත් hunger, පිපාසා thirst) hunger and thirst.

ක්ෂුද්‍ර, *Kshudra*, *a.* small, little; mean, low; niggardly, avaricious; cruel; poor, indigent.

ක්ෂුද්‍රපර්ණී, *Kshudra-parṇṇi*, *s.* medicinal plant, [Colloq. මුංවැන්න *muṇwęnna*].

ක්ෂුද්‍රබලා, *Kshudrabalá*, *s.* medicinal plant, [Colloq. සුළු බෑලිල *sulu-bęlila*].

ක්ෂුද්‍රමාග, *Kshudramága*, *s.* medicinal plant, *drymoglossum heterophyllum*, [Colloq. මස්වැන්න *maswęnna*].

ක්ෂුද්‍ර රෝග, *Kshudra-róga*, *s.* minor disease.

ක්ෂුද්‍රවර්ෂාභූ, *Kshudra-warshábhú*, *s.* medicinal plant, [Colloq. සාරණ *sáraṇa*].

ක්ෂුද්‍රවාර්තාකිණී, *Kshudrawártákiṇi*, *s.* medicinal plant, *Solanum indicum*, [Colloq. තිබ්බටු *tibbaṭu*].

ක්ෂුද්‍රා, *Kshudrá*, *s.* woman maimed or crippled, wanting a limb etc., dancing girl; harlot; fly, bee, wasp; gnat; prickly nightshade; egg plant; kind of sorrel; *solanum Jacgnini*, [Colloq. කටු වැල්බටු *kaṭuwęlbaṭu*].

ක්ෂුධා, *Kshudhá*, *s.* hunger, [Colloq. බඩගිනි *badagini*].

ක්ෂුධිත, *Kshudhita*, *a.* hungry, hungered.

ක්ෂුභිත, *Kshubhita*, *a.* frightened, alarmed, agitated.

ක්ෂුමා, *Kshumá*, *s.* linseed, sort of flax.

ක්ෂුර, *Kshura*, *s.* razor; plant *barleria longifolia;* another plant *tribulus lanuginosus;* hoof of a horse or cow; foot of a bedstead.

ක්ෂුරධාරා, *Kshuradhárá*, *a.* sharp, as a razor, knife etc.

ක්ෂුල්ල, *Kshulla*, *a.* little, small; [Colloq. සුළු *sulu*].

ක්ෂුල්ලක, *Kshullaka*, *a.* little, small; hard; poor, indigent; low, vile, mean; wicked; malicious; abandoned; young, youngest; *s.* small shell.

ක්ෂේත්‍ර, *Kshétra*, *s.* field; body; wife; place of pilgrimage; geometrical figure.

ක්ෂේත්‍රජ, *Kshétraja*, *s.* (ක්ෂේත්‍ර wife, ජ born) son; offspring of the wife by a kinsman or person duly appointed to procreate issue to the husband; this is one of the twelve kinds of issue acknowledged by the old Hindu law.

ක්ෂේත්‍රඥ, *Kshétrajña*, *s.* (ක්ෂේත්‍ර body, ඥ who knows) soul.

ක්ෂේප, *Kshépa*,
ක්ෂේපය, *Kshépaya*, } *s.* sending, dismissing, throwing; pride, haughtiness, disrespect, contempt; passing away time; delay, dilatoriness; clump of flowers.

ක්ෂෙම, *Kshéma*, s. happiness, well-being; preservation, protection; keeping what is acquired; final emancipation, or eternal happiness.

ක්ෂොද, *Kshóda*, s. powder, any pulverised substance.

ක්ෂොභ, *Kshóba*, s. agitation, shaking.

ක්ෂොම, *Kshóma*, s. wove silk; room on the top of a house.

ක්ෂෞද්‍ර, *Kshaudra*, s. honey.

ක්ෂෞම, *Kshauma*, s. airy room on the top of a house; apartment on the top of a hall; back of an edifice; fortified place in front of a building; building of a particular form; wove silk; linen cloth.

ක්ෂෞර, *Kshaura*, s. shaving.

ඛ

The second consonant in the Sinhalese alphabet; it is the foregoing letter aspirated and is expressed in English letters by kh and pronounced like k in back-hall, allowing the h to coalesce. s. heaven, sky, or ether; organ of sense; knowledge; happiness, pleasure; vacuity; dot, cipher; city; field; action; auspiciousness.

ඛග්ග, *Khagga*, s. rhinoceros; sword.

ඛග්ගවිසාණ *Khagga-visáṇa*, s. rhinoceros.

ඛග, *Khaga*, s. (ඛ sky, ග who goes) bird; arrow; sun; planet; deity; air, wind; grasshopper.

ඛගෙශ්වර, *Khageṣwara*, s. (ඛග and ඊශ්වර *íṣwara* king) king of birds, garuda the bird of Vishṇu.

ඛගොල, *Khagóla*, s. vault of the heavens.

ඛජ්ජුර, *Khajjura*, s. silver; date tree.

ඛජ්ජොත, *Khajjóta*, s. fire fly, [Colloq. කණාමැදිරියා *kaṇámẹdiriyá*].

ඛඤ්ජ, *Khañja*, a. lame, limping, crippled.

ඛඤ්ජන, *Khañjana*, s. small bird, kind of wagtail.

ඛඤ්ජරීට, *Khañjaríṭa*. s. bird, wagtail.

ඛඤ්ජා, *Khañjá*, s. species of metre, stanza of two lines, one of thirty-two, the other of thirty feet.

ඛට්වා, *Khaṭwá*, s. bed, couch, [Colloq. ඇඳ *ẹnda*].

ඛඩ්ග, *Khaḍga*, s. rhinoceros, rhinoceros' horn; sword; kind of large sacrificial knife; arrow; bird.

ඛණ්ඩ, *Khaṇḍa*, s. flaw in a jewel; treacle or molasses, piece, part, fragment, portion; chapter, section; sugar.

ඛණ්ඩගුඩ, *Khaṇḍaguḍa*, s. (ඛණ්ඩ piece, ගුඩ sugar) sugar candy, [Colloq. සූකිරි *súkiri*].

ඛණ්ඩ, *Khaṇḍa*, s. piece, part, bit, small quantity, [Colloq. කොටස *koṭasa*].

ඛණ්ඩපරශු, *Khaṇḍa-parṣu*, s. (ඛණ්ඩ and පරශු axe) he whose axe cuts every thing to pieces; name of Paraṣuráma; Ṣiva; Ráhu the personified ascending node, see රාහු *Ráhu*.

ඛණ්ඩපරශු, *Khaṇḍa-paraṣu*, s. (ඛණ්ඩ part, පරශු hatchet) name of Ṣiva alluding to his cutting his enemies in pieces by a hatchet.

ඛණ්ඩඵුල්ල, *Khaṇḍaphulla*, a. broken.

ඛණ්ඩලවණ, *Khaṇḍa-lawaṇa*, s. black salt.

ඛණ්ඩශර්කරා, *Khaṇḍa-ṣarkará*, }
ඛණ්ඩසිතා, *Khaṇḍasitá*, } s. (ඛණ්ඩ piece, ශර්කරා *ṣarkará* sugar) sugar candy.

ඛත්තිය, *Khattiya*, Páli form of ක්ෂත්‍රිය *kshatriya*.

ඛදිර, *Khadira*, s. name of Indra; moon; tree, the resin of which is used in medicine, *mimosa catechu;* [Colloq. කිහිරි *kihiri*].

ඛදිරදෙහලී, *Khadiradéhalí*, s. see කිහිරෙළි *kihireḷi*.

ඛදිරී, *Khadirí*, s. sensitive plant, *mimosa pudica;* [Colloq. මිදි *midi*].

ඛද්‍යොත, *Khadyóta*, s. (ඛ sky, ද්‍යොත what is luminous) sun [Colloq. සූරියා *súriyá*]; fire fly, see ඛජ්ජොත *khajjóta*.

ඛන්ධ, *Khandha*, s. multitude; the five constituent parts of the human body, see පඤ්චස්කන්ධ *pañchaskandha*; shoulder; head of the humerus; figure; trunk of a tree; virtue; good quality or disposition; name of Kataragama deviyo; house; juice of the sugar cane.

ඛනක, *Khanaka*, s. (ඛන to dig ක affix) rat; housebreaker; miner.

ඛනි, *Khani*, s. mine, especially of precious stones.

ඛනික, *Khanika*, see ඛනක *khanaka*.

ඛනිත්‍ර, *Khanitra*, s. spade, hoe, [Colloq. බිම කනින හුල *bima-kaninahula*].

ඛපුර, *Khapura*, s. water jar; city in the sky, city of Harischandra, areca tree, *areca catechu*, [Colloq. පුවක් *puwak*]; fragrant grass, *cyperus pertenuis;* garlic.

ඛමණි, *Khamaṇi*, s. (ඛ sky, මණි jewel) sun.

ඛය, *Khaya*, s. pulmonary consumption; loss; expenditure.

ඛර්ජූ, *Kharjú*, s. cutaneous eruption, itch, scab, etc. worm, insect.

ඛර්ජූර, *Kharjúra*, }
ඛර්ජූරී, *Kharjúrí*, } s. fruit of the date, date tree; [Colloquial. ඉඳි *indi*]; yellow orpiment; scorpion.

ඛර්පර, *Kharpara*, s. thief, rogue, cheat; beggar's bowl or dish; crown of the cranium; umbrella or parasol; collyrium or application to the eye lashes.

ඛර්ඛ, *Kharba*, *s.* dwarf, short person; *a.* short, low, of little size or stature; [Colloq. මිටි *miṭi*]. ten million millions; one of the nine treasures of Kuvéra.

ඛර්ව, *Kharwa*, see ඛර්ඛ *kharba*.

ඛර, *Khara*, *a.* hot, sharp, pungent, piercing, sharp-edged, sharp-pointed; cruel, harsh; *s.* ass, heron, crow, kind of grass, *andropogon serratus.*

ඛරගන්ධනිභා, *Kharagandhanibhá*, *s.* plant, *hedysarum lagopodioides.*

ඛරගන්ධා, *Kharagandhá*, *s.* tree, bearing beautiful red blossoms, *butea frondosa;* [Colloq. ගස් කැල *gas-kẹla*].

ඛරධ්වංසින්, *Kharadhwaṇsin*, *s.* (ඛර a Rákshasa, ධ්වංසින් who destroys) name of Ráma alluding to his conquering and destroying a demon called Khar.

ඛරනාද, *Kharanáda*, *s.* braying of an ass.

ඛරපත්‍ර, *Kharapatra*, *s.* red sort of tulasi or basil; teak tree [Colloq. තේක්ක *tékka*].

ඛරපත්‍රක, *Kharapatraka*, *s.* plant bearing an oily seed, oil and seed being much used in oriental cooking *sesamum orientale* [Colloq. තල *tala*].

ඛරපුෂ්ප, *Kharapushpa*, } *s.* kind of tulasi, *ocymum*
ඛරපුෂ්පා, *Kharapushpá*, } *gratissimum.*

ඛරමඤ්ජරී, *Kharamañjarí*, *s.* (ඛර pungent, මඤ්ජරී pedicle) plant, *achyranthes aspera*, [Colloquial: කරල්හැබ *karalhẹba*].

ඛරලොමන්, *Kharalóman*, *s.* (ඛර ass, ලොමන් hair of the body) one having the skin of an ass, that is one of the chiefs of the serpent race inhabiting Pátála or the world of serpents.

ඛරස්කන්ධ, *Kharaskandha*, *s.* date tree, [Colloq. ඉඳි ගහ *iṇdi-gaha*].

ඛරාංශු, *Kharáṇṣu*, *s.* (ඛර hot, අංශු *aṇṣu* ray) sun, [Colloq. සූරියා *súriyá*].

ඛරාශ්වා, *Kharáṣwá*, *s.* plant, *celosia cristata.*

ඛරාසු, *Kharásu*, see ඛරාංශු *Kharáṇṣu.*

ඛරු, *Kharu*, *s.* name of Ṣiva; horse; tooth; pride; love or the god Káma: white colour; fool, idiot; *a.* harsh, cruel.

ඛල්‍යා, *Khalyá*, *s.* multitude of threshing floors; gang of thieves.

ඛල, *Khala*, *s.* earth, mould or soil; sediment, deposit of oil; place, site; granary; threshing floor; low or vile man; cruel man; the sun.

ඛලපූ, *Khalapú*, *s.* sweeper, cleanser, one taking care of and cleaning a threshing floor.

ඛලාධාරා, *Khaládhárá*, *s.* cockroach, [Colloq. කැරපොත්තා *kẹrapottá*].

ඛලිතා, *Khalitá*, *s.* black pepper, *piper nigrum;* [Colloq ගම්මිරිස් *gammiris*].

ඛලින, *Khalina*, *s.* bit of a bridle.

ඛලිනී, *Khaliní*, *s.* thieves, gang of robbers; multitude of threshing floors.

ඛලීන, *Khalína*, see ඛලින *khalina.*

ඛලොක්ති, *Khalókti*, *s.* low or wicked language, formed of ඛල *khala* and උක්ති *ukṭi.*

ඛසා, *Khasá*, *s.* mother of the imps or goblins.

ඛාජික, *Khájika*, *s.* fried grain.

ඛාත, *Kháta*, *s.* large square or oblong pond excavation.

ඛාද්‍ය, *Khádya*, *s.* what is to be or may be eaten, edible; solid or dry food.

ඛාදන, *Khádana*, *s.* eating, food, victuals.

ඛාදිත, *Khádita*, *part*: eaten.

ඛාණ්ඩය, *Khanḍaya*, *s.* part, section, portion.

ඛානි, *Kháni*, *s.* mine. [Colloq. ආකරය, *ákaraya*].

ඛානික, *Khánika*, *s.* hole or breach in a wall; mine.

ඛානිල, *Khánila*, *s.* house-breaker.

ඛාණු, *Khánu*, *s.* trunk of a lopped tree; pillar, post

ඛාර, *Khára*, *s.* salt ground, salt; blossom; measure of three bushels; *a.* saltish.

ඛාරාපතච්ඡික, *Khárápatachchhika*, *s.* punishment inflicted by sawing the flesh of the culprit in the first instance and then applying a mixture of salt and chillies to the wounds.

ඛාරි, *Khári*, *s.* measure of grain containing 16 dróṇas, or about three bushelṣ; scar, wound.

ඛාරික, *Khárika*, *s.* a field sown with three bushels of grain.

ඛිඩ්ඩා, *Khiḍḍá*, *s.* Páli form of ක්‍රීඩා *kríḍá.*

ඛින්නදෙහ *Khinna-déha*, *s.* (ඛින්න suffering, දෙහ body) one who is tired or wearied.

ඛිප්පං, *Khippaṇ*, *a.* quick, Páli form of ක්ෂිප්‍ර *kshipra.*

ඛිල, *Khila*, *s.* unploughed or waste land; *a.* empty, vacant.

ඛිණාසවො, *Khiṇásawo*, *s.* (ඛිණ *khiṇa* destroyed or subdued, ආසව *ásawa* sinful thought) one that has entirely subdued his passions, rahat.

ඛිරං, *Khíraṇ*, Páli form of ක්ෂිර *kshíra*,

ඛුජ්ජ, *Khujja*, *s.* humpbacked man; Páli form of කුබ්ජ *kubja.*

ඛුර, *Khura*, *s.* razor; hoof, horse's hoof; foot of a

bedstead; sort of perfume, apparently dried shell-fish of the shape of a hoof; medicine commonly called සක්නෑබ *saknęba*.

ඛුරක, *Khuraka*, *s*. plant, bearing an oily seed, *sesamum orientale*.

ඛුරණසා, *Khuraṇásá*, *s*. (ඛුර hoof, නාස nose) flat-nosed; one having a nose like a horse's hoof.

ඛුරා, *Khurá*, *s*. creeping plant; durian tree, *durio zebethinus*.

ඛෙචර, *Khéchara*, *s*. (ඛෙ in heaven or atmosphere, චර who goes) name of Ṣiva; kind of demigods; magical pills, by putting one of which into the mouth a person has the power of flying to heaven; sun; wind; moon; general name for a planet, star; arrow; bird; perspiration; cloud.

ඛෙට, *Kheṭa*, *s*. grass; hunting, chase; *a*. vile, bad, low; armed with weapons; shield; village; suburb: phlegm, phlegmatic, or watery humour; club of Balaráma.

ඛෙත්ත, *Khetta*, Páli form of ක්ෂෙත්‍ර *kshétra*.

ඛෙද, *Khéda*, *s*. sorrow, affliction, distress; regret, repentance.

ඛෙම, *Khéma*, *s*. peace, happiness, well being; safety; name of Nirváṇa; *a*. well, right, happy; preserved, guarded.

ඛෙය, *Khéya*, *s*. ditch, moat. [Colloq: අගල *agala*].

ඛෙල, *Khéla*, *a*. decrease; wasting, decay; derision, ridicule, contempt; place of safety, refuge.

ඛෙලන, *Khélana*, } *s*. play, sport, pastime, amuse-
ඛෙලා, *Khélá*, } ment. [Colloquial සෙල්ලම *sellama*].

ඛෙලි, *Khéli*, *s*. song, hymn; arrow; sun; bird; animal.

ඛෙලො, *Khélo*, *s*. spittle, saliva.

ඛොඩ, *Khóḍa*, *a*. lame, or limping.

ඛොර, *Khóra*, *a*. lame.

ඛොල, *Khóla*, *a*. lame, limping. [Colloq: කොරවූ *korawú*].

ඛොලක, *Khólaka*, *s*. shield, armour for the head; pot, sauce pan; ant hill; shell of a betel nut.

ඛ්‍යාත, *Khyáta*, *a*. famous, renowned, celebrated.

ඛ්‍යාති, *Khyáti*, *s*. fame, celebrity.

ග

The third consonant of the Siŋhalese alphabet, corresponding to the letter *G;* it is always pronounced hard.

ග, *Ga*, *a*. who or what goes, used in composition.

ගං, *Gaŋ*, *s*. *plur*. of ගඟ *gaŋga* river, and incorrectly, of ගම *gama* village.

ගංකන්ද, *Gaŋ-kanda*, *s*. small hill lying on the banks of a river; bank of a river.

ගං කොල්ලන්කොල, *Gaŋ-kollankola*, *s*. plant, *Pogostemon Heyneanus (Labiatæ)*; it is from a variety of this plant, viz. *p. patchouli*, that the patchouli leaves of commerce are procured.

ගංගරු, *Gaŋgarú*, *s*. shrimps or prawns, [Colloq. ඉස්සෝ *issó*].

ගංගාධර, *Gaŋgádhara*, see ගඞාධර *gaŋgádhara*.

ගංගාව, *Gaŋgáwa*, *s*. river, more properly written ගඞ්ගාව *gańgáwa* or in Páli ගඞාව *gaŋgáwa*, pl. ගංගා *gaŋgá* or ගඞා *gaŋgá*.

ගංගෙය්‍ය, *Gaŋgeyya*, see ගඞෙය්‍ය *Gaŋgeyya*.

ගංතෙර, *Gaŋtera*, *s*. bank or border of a river; ferry.

ගංපල්ල, *Gaŋpalla*, *s*. bottom of a river.

ගංබඩ, *Gaŋbaḍa*, *s*. border or edge of a river.

ගංමී, *Gaŋ-mí*, *s*. tree peculiar to Ceylon, *bassia nerifolia (Sapotaceæ)*.

ගංවතුර. *Gaŋwatura*. *s*. flood, high-water, river-water.

ගංවතුර ගලනවා, *Gaŋwatura-galanawá*, *v*. to overflow, to inundate with river water.

ගග්ගර, *Gaggara*, *s*. sound, noise, distant rumbling, as of the sea or thunder.

ගගණ, *Gagaṇa*, *s*. sky, atmosphere; sometimes written ගගන *gagana*.

ගගණතලය, *Gagaṇatalaya*, *s*. visible heavens; literally, the plane of the heavens.

ගගනොදර, *Gaganódara*, *s*. (ගගන *gagana* sky, උදර *udara* cavity) concavity of the sky.

ගගා, *Gagá*, *s*. continuing to rub or polish.

ගඟ, *Gaŋga*, *s*. river.

ගඟදර, *Gaŋgadara*, *s*. name of Ṣiva, see ගඞාධර *gaŋgádhara*.

ගඟබඩ, *Gaŋgabaḍa*, *s*. border or brink of a river.

ගඟමීවන, *Gaŋgamíwana*, *s*. species of shield fern, *aspidium viviparum*.

ගඞා, *Gaŋgá*, *s*. river Ganges, personification of that river as a goddess, see ගඞාදේවි *gaŋgádévi*.

ගඞාතීරය, *Gaŋgátíraya*, } see ගංතෙර *gaŋtera*.
ගඞාතෙර, *Gaŋgátera*, }

ගඞාතොට, *Gaŋgá-toṭa*, *s*. ferry, part of a river bank from whence the river is crossed.

ගඞාදේවි, *Gaŋgá-dévi*, *s*. name of the goddess Párvatí wife of Ṣiva as the personification of the Ganges, see ගඞා *gaŋgá*.

ගඟාධර, *Gangádhara*, *s*. (ගඟා Ganges, ධර who holds or receives) ocean; name of Ṣiva, alluding to the legend that the Ganges in its descent first alighted on the head of Ṣiva and continued for some period entangled in his hair.

ගඟාප්‍රවාහ, *Gangáprawáha*, *s*. overflowing of a river, flood, [Colloq. වතුරගැල්ම *waturagẹlma*].

ගඟාව, *Gangáwa*, see ගංගාව *gangáwa*.

ගඟුල, *Gaṉgula*. *s*. rapid, small water fall in a brook, pl. ගඟුල් *gaṉgul*.

ගාංගෙය්‍ය, *gangeyya*, *a*. belonging to the Ganges: *s*. kind of elephant.

ගාංගෙය්‍යකුලේ, *Gangeyya-kulé*, *s*. of the Gangeyya tribe.

ගච්ඡ, *Gachchha*, *s*. tree, small tree, shrub.

ගජ, *Gaja*, *s*. elephant; [Colloq. අලියා *aliyá*.] measure of length, yard, two cubits; mound of earth sloping on both sides, on which a house may be erected.

ගජ අත්, *Gaja-at*, *s*. (ගජ and අත් hand) elephant's trunk.

ගජකණ, *Gajakaṇá*, *s*. long-pepper, *piper longum;* [Colloq. ගජ තිප්පිලි *gajatippili*].

ගජකුම්භ, *Gajakumbha*, *s*. forehead of an elephant.

ගජතා, *Gajatá*, *s*. multitude or herd of elephants.

ගජතිප්පිලි, *Gaja-tippili*, *s*. particular species of long-pepper; see ගජකණ *gajakaṇá*.

ගජදත්, *Gaja-dat*, } *s*. (ගජ elephant, දන්ත *danta* tooth.) elephant's tooth,
ගජදන්ත, *Gajadanta*, } ivory; name of Gaṇéṣa, Hindu god of wisdom, who is figured with an elephant's head.

ගජදන්ත ඵල, *Gajadanta-phala*, *s*. kind of cucumber. [Colloq. කැකිරි *kẹkiri*].

ගජන්, *Gajan*, plur. acc. or gen of ගජ *gaja*.

ගජන්කර, *Gajankara*, see ගජ අත් *gaja-at*.

ගජනාව, *Gajanáwa*, *s*. breech of a gun.

ගජපරක, *Gajaparáka*, *s* leguminous plant bearing red seeds with black mark; *Abrus precatorius*, [Colloq. ඔලිඳ ඇට *olinda-ẹta*].

ගජපිටු, *Gajapiṭu*, *s*. top of the shoulders of elephant.

ගජපොතක, *Gajapótaka*, *s*. (ගජ and පෝතක cub) young elephant.

ගජප්‍රිය, *Gajapriya*, *s*. gum olibanum tree, *boswellia serrata;* plantain or banana tree.

ගජබලා, *Gajabalá*, *s*. lion; plant, species of the *sida*: [Colloq: බැවිල *bẹvila*.]

ගජමද, *Gaja-mada*, *s*. semen of an elephant.

ගජමාචල, *Gajamáchala*, *s*. (ගජ elephant, මා fortune චල which shakes) destroyer of the elephant, lion.

ගජමොටන, *Gajamóṭana*, *s*. (ගජ and මුට *muṭa* to cause to run away) lion. [Colloq. සිංහයා *siṉhayá*].

ගජයා, *Gajayá*, *s*. big fellow, one like an elephant.

ගජලි, *Gajali*, *s*. general name for a river, [Colloq. ගඟාව *gangáwa*].

ගජවත්, *Gajawat*, Elu form of ගජවක්ත්‍ර *gajawaktra*.

ගජවදන, *Gajawadana*, *s*. (ගජ and වදන face) name of Ganéṣa, Hindu god of wisdom, alluding to his being figured with an elephant's head.

ගජ සම, *Gaja-sama*, *s*. (ගජ and සම skin) name of Íṣwara or Ṣiva.

ගජසිව්, *Gaja-siw*, *s*. the earth, [Colloquial: පොළව *poḷawa*].

ගජාරි, *Gajári*, *s*. (ගජ *gaja* and අරි *ari* enemy) lion, [Colloq. සිංහයා *siṉhayá*].

ගජාසන, *Gajásana*, *s*. sacred fig tree, *ficus religiosa*, [Colloq. බෝගහ *bó-gaha*].

ගජේන්ද්‍ර, *Gajéndra*, *s*. leading, or chief elephant in the herd.

ගඤ්ජ, *Gañja*, *s*. disrespect, contempt; mine, jewel mine; cow house; treasury, or jewel room; place where plate etc., is deposited and preserved; tavern; drinking vessel; hut, hovel and abode of low people; plant bearing oliṉda seed, *Abrus precatorius*.

ගඩ, *Gaḍa*, *s*. stone; jaw; kind of fish (sort of gilt head); impediment, obstacle; screen, covering; fence; ditch, moat.

ගඩගෙඩිය, *Gaḍageḍiya*, *s*. boils or pustules on the skin.

ගඩයා, *Gaḍayá*, *s*. kind of fish.

ගඩවියල, *Gaḍa-viyala*, *s*. sort of boil or pustules on the skin.

ගඩාගෙඩි, *Gaḍágedi*, *s*. general name for fruit as oranges, pines etc.

ගඩාදෙහි, *Gaḍádehi*, *s*. sort of rough skinned lime or lemon, sometimes called a Cáffre lime.

ගඩු, *Gaḍu*, *s*. hump on the back, also *pl*. of ගඩුව *gaḍuwa*.

ගඩුල, *Gaḍula*, *a*. (ගඩු hump, ල affix) crooked, hump-backed.

ගඩුව, *Gaḍuwa*, *s*. boil or pustule of any sort, abscess; blister.

ගඩේ, *Gaḍé*, see ගඩ *gaḍa*.

ගඩොල, *Gaḍola*, *s*. brick or flat tile, used for paving houses, pl. ගඩොල් *gaḍol*

ගණ්ඨි, *Ganṭhí*, *s.* knot; snare; joint in a bamboo.

ගණ්ඩ, *Gaṇḍa*, *s.* culture; cheek, whole side of the face including the temples; blister, boil, pimple; mark or spot; hero; rhinoceros; tenth yóga, or one of the twentyseven portions of a circle on the plane of the ecliptic; astronomical period; knot or joint; *v.* infinitive of the verb to take.

ගණ්ඩක, *Gaṇḍaka*, *s.* rhinoceros; mode of reckoning; obstacle or impediment; disjunction, separation; science of astrology; name of a river in the north of India.

ගණ්ඩකාරි, *Gaṇḍakári*, *s.* (ගණ්ඩ boil, කාරි what occasions) sensitive plant, *mimosa pudica*. [Colloq. නිදිකුම්බ *nidikumba*].

ගණ්ඩකුසුම, *Gaṇḍa-kusuma*, *s.* (ගණ්ඩ elephant's temples, කුසුම flower from its supposed fragrance) juice that exudes from the temples of an elephant in time of rut.

ගණ්ඩමාලා, *Gaṇḍamálá*, *s.* (ගණ්ඩ boil, මාලා necklace) inflammation of the glands of the neck.

ගණ්ඩාර, *Gaṇḍára*, see කොබලිල *kobalila*.

ගණ්ඩිර, *Gaṇḍira*, *s.* kind of pot herb, described as growing in watery ground; according to some a species of cucumber; hero, champion.

ගණ්ඩුප්පාද, *Gaṇḍuppáda*, ගණ්ඩූපද *Gaṇḍúpada*, } *s.* earthworm. [Colloq. ගැඩවිල්පණුවා *geḍa-wilpaṇuwá*].

ගණ, *Gaṇa*, *s.* flock, multitude, troop, tribe, class; priest; wickedness; body of troops, comprising twenty-nine chariots, eighty-one horses and one hundred and thirty-five foot; the troops called Gándharwa, kind of inferior deities considered as Ṣiva's attendants and under the especial command of Gaṇéṣa the Hindu god of wisdom; arithmetical number: kind of perfume; name of Gaṇéṣa; attendants of Ṣiva; cloud; plant, *cyperus rotundus*, [Colloq. කලාඳුරු *kaláṇḍuru*].

ගණක, *Gaṇaka*, *s.* astrologer, calculator of nativities.

ගණකුල, *Gaṇakuḷa*, *s.* fabulous mountain Kailása, supposed to be the residence of the Kumára yakshayas, and other classes of demons and subordinate deities, sometimes written ගනකුල *ganakula*.

ගණදෙවියෝ, *Gaṇadeviyó*, *s.* (ගණ multitude, දෙවි god) Gaṇéṣa, the Hindu god of wisdom; this name alludes to his being the chief of the Gándharwa, kind of inferior deities, the immediate attendants of Ṣakra or Ṣiva.

ගණන්, *Gaṇan*, *plur.* of ගණන *gaṇana*.

ගණන්කරණවා, *Gaṇankaraṇawá*, *v.* to count, to reckon.

ගණන්ගන්නවා, *Gaṇangannawá*, *v.* to take account.

ගණන්පථය, *Gaṇanpathaya*, *s.* Arithmetic.

ගණන් චක්‍රය, *Gaṇanchakraya*, ගණන් මණ්ඩලය, *Gaṇan-maṇḍalaya*, } *s.* table in Arithmetic.

ගණන, *Gaṇana*, *s.* counting, enumerating; account; price, value, rate, pl. ගණන් *gaṇan*.

ගණනාව, *Gaṇanáwa*, *s.* account, number, reckoning.

ගණපති, *Gaṇapati*, *s.* name of Gaṇéṣa the Hindu god of wisdom, see ගණදෙවි *gaṇadevi;* name of Ṣiva.

ගණපන්තිය, *Gaṇa-pantiya*, *s.* communion or school of pupils under the care and instruction of the priests of Buddha, resident in any temple.

ගණය, *Gaṇaya*, *s.* poetical measure consisting of three feet; residence or dwelling of the priests of Buddha, always situated close to a temple. [Col: පන්සල *pansala*].

ගණරූප, *Gaṇarúpa*, *s.* swallow-wort or mudar, *gigantea calotropis*. [Colloq. වරා *wará.*]

ගණරූපික, *Gaṇarúpika*, swallow wort, the white sort. [Colloq. එලවරා *elawará.*]

ගණයා, *Gaṇayá*, *s.* assemblage of priests; sometimes, a disrespectful term for a Buddhist priest.

ගණසංගණික, *Gaṇasangaṇika*, *s.* assembly, congregation of priests; one who lives with an assembly of priests.

ගණාධිප, *Gaṇádhipa*, see ගණදෙවි *gaṇadevi*.

ගණි, *Gaṇi*, *s.* harlot.

ගණිකා, *Gaṇiká*, *s.* harlot, courtezan, pl. ගණිකාවෝ *gaṇikáwó*.

ගණිකාව, *Gaṇikáwa*, *s.* harlot, courtezan; elk; female elephant; sort of jasmin *jasminum auriculatum;* [Collq. සේපාලිකා *sépáliká.*] tree, *premna spinosa;* [Colloq. සිහින්මිදි *sihin-midi.*] counting, enumerating.

ගණිත, *Gaṇita*, *a.* numbered, counted, reckoned, calculated.

ගණිතගර්භය, *Gaṇitagarbhaya*, *s.* arithmetical table.

ගණිතය, *Gaṇitaya*, *s.* astrological or astronomical treatise; calculating; computing, arithmetic.

ගණිතයා, *Gaṇitayá*, *s.* framer of horoscopes, astrologer.

ගණිතශාස්ත්‍රය, *Gaṇitaṣástraya*, *s.* science of Arithmetic.

ගණිති, *Gaṇiti*, third person plural of ගණිනවා *gaṇinawá* or ගන්නවා *gannawá*.

ගණිඳු, *Gaṇiṇdu*, *s.* name of Gaṇésa, Hindu god of wisdom. see ගණේශ *gaṇéṣa*.

ගණින්නා, *Gaṇinná*, *s.* arithmetician, one who counts.

ගණින්නාන්සේ, *Gaṇinnánsé*, *s.* (ගණ *gaṇa* multitude or association, referring here to a company of priests, resident in one dwelling or pansala ඉන්නා *inná* being, න්සේ *nsé* for වහන්සේ *wahansé* a term of respect) priest of Buddha, generally applied to one of the lowest order, whose office it is to read the Baṇa or sacred books on public occasions; after which it is interpreted by a higher one: he also presides at the altar, and attends to the cleaning of the temples.

ගණිනවා, *Gaṇinawá*, *v.* to add up, to count, to reckon, to compute, to calculate: pret. ගැන්නා *gęnná*.

ගණිසුරු, *Gaṇisuru*, *s.* (ගණ *gaṇa* ඉසුරු *isuru*) see the following.

ගණේශ, *Gaṇéṣa*, (ගණ *gaṇa* a troop ඊශ *íṣa* lord or chief) the Hindu god of wisdom; he is represented in their temples as a short fat man with the head of an elephant; he is the son of Ṣiva by Párvatí and is considered the remover of obstacles; hence in the commencement of all undertakings and in the opening of all compositions he receives the reverential homage of the Hindus; he is considered as the chief of the various classes of subordinate deities who are regarded as Ṣiva's attendants; Ṣiva himself is sometimes called by this name.

ගත්, *Gat*, *p.* taken; *s.* books, literary compositions.

ගත්ත, *Gatta*, *s.* information of some crime or offence, pl. ගතු *gatu*.

ගත්තා, *Gattá*, *v.* pret. took, got.

ගත, *Gata*, *s.* body; limb, multitude; verse, stanza, book; participial form of verb from the root ගම *gama*, gone; known, understood; obtained; gained, pl. ගත් *gat*.

ගතකුරු, *Gatakuru*, see ගාත්‍රාක්ෂර *gátrákshara*.

ගතයුත්තක්, *Gatayuttak*, *s.* that which is proper to be taken.

ගතවෙනවා, *Gatawenawá*, *v.* to pass away, to be transitory or fleeting.

ගති, *Gati*, *s.* mode, manner, custom; march; procession; species of birth; any of the several modes of obtaining existence according to the tenets of Buddha; establishment, support; end, termination; inclination; wisdom, knowledge; habitation, residence, dwelling; journey, road, way, path; period of life, as youth, age, &c; expedient. means of success; sinus, fistular sore; worldly vanity, wickedness; course of events, fate, fortune; slave.

ගතිය, *Gatiya*, *s.* nature, disposition, temper; quality, state

ගතු, *Gatu*, *s.* evil speech, slander.

ගතුකාරයා, *Gatukárayá*, *s.* informant, a complainant.

ගතුකියනවා, *Gatukiyanawá*, *s* to inform against, to slander.

ගද, *Gada*, s. disease, sickness; speech; weapon; the younger brother of Kṛishṇa; womb.

ගදබඅත්, *gadaba-at*, / ගදඹ, *Gadamba*, } *s. palma christi* or castor-oil tree, *ricinus communis* [Colloq. රට එඬරු *raṭa-eṇḍaru*].

ගදඹා, *Gadambá*, *s.* camel; chorister.

ගදා, *Gadá*, *s.* sickness; weapon, particularly that of the Wessawaṇa, mace, club; plant, trumpet flower, *bignonia suave-olens*. [Col. පලොල් *palol.*]

ගදාගද, *Gadágada*, *s.* physicians of Swarga, the two sons of Aṣwini by Súrya.

ගදාධර, *Gadádhara*, *s.* (ගදා club; ධර who holds) name of Kṛishṇa or Vishṇu who is figured as holding a mace in one of his hands.

ගඳ, *Gaṇda*, *s.* smell, perfume, fragrance; stink, odour, &c. see ගන්ධ *gandha*.

ගඳකලල්, *Gaṇdakalal*, *s.* perfume, made from mixture of fragrant substances.

ගඳකිළිය, *Gaṇdakiḷiya*, *s.* (ගඳ perfume, කිළිය house) the residence of Buddha, a fragrance issuing from every part of his person perfuming his dwelling; sweet scented house.

ගඳකුහුඹි, *Gaṇdakuhumbi*, *s.* small kind of ant.

ගඳගජ, *Gaṇdagaja*, *s.* kind of elephant.

ගඳගහනවා, *Gaṇdagahanawá*, *v.* to stink.

ගඳපාන, *Gaṇdapána*, *s.* plant, lantana, *lantana mixta (Verbenaceæ)*, also called රටහිඟුරු, *raṭa-hiṇguru*; another plant, *mappia ovata (Olacineæ)*.

ගඳපූතික, *Gaṇdapútika*, *s.* stench, offensive smell.

ගඳමල්, *Gaṇdamal*, *pl.* fragrant flowers.

ගඳමහන්, *Gaṇdamahan*, *s.* mountain, see ගන්ධමාදන *gandhamádana*.

ගඳවණ, *Gaṇdawaṇa*, *s.* (ගඳ and වණ a wound) smell from a wound.

ගඳවිලවුන්, *Gandavilawun*, s. perfumes, unguents consisting of sandalwood &c. used for anointing the body.

ගඳසාර, *Gandasára*, s. sandal wood, a sense of perfume.

ගුඳැත්, *Gandet*, s. musk elephant.

ගන්කුකුළා, *Gankukulá*, s. the domestic cock, pl. ගන්කුකුළෝ *gankukuló*.

ගන්ට, *Ganta*, r. to take.

ගඳමාදන, *Gandamádana*, s. see ගන්ධමාදන *Gandhamádana*.

ගන්දිය, *Gandiya*, s. (ගන් river, දිය water) river water, corruptly for ගංදිය *gandiya*.

ගන්ධ, *Gandha*, s. smell, odour, perfume, fragrance; any fragrant substance; sulphur; kind of elephant; tree *moringa pterygosperma;* pride, arrogance; neighbour; aloe-wood; *a.* small, little, diminutive; small in quantity.

ගන්ධක, *Gandhaka*, s. sulphur; tree *moringa pterygosperma* [Colloq. මුරුංගා *murungá.*]

ගන්ධකාෂ්ඨ, *Gandhakáshtha*, s. any fragrant wood, as sandal wood, aloe-wood &c.

ගන්ධකුටිය, *Gandhakutiya*, s. (ගන්ධ perfume, කුටි *kuti* abode) Buddha's residence; kind of perfume.

ගන්ධදාම, *Gandhadáma*, s. (ගන්ධ and දාම string of flowers) string or necklace of flowers.

ගන්ධධූලි, *Gandhadhúli*, s. (ගන්ධ fragrant, ධූලි dust) musk.

ගන්ධන, *Gandhana*, s. continued effort, perseverance; injury; intimation; information; hurting; killing.

ගන්ධනිලයා, *Gandhanilayá*, s. double jasmine; [Colloq. සත්පෙතිදෑසමන් *satpetidésaman.*]

ගන්ධනාකුලි, *Gandhanákulí*, s. medicinal plant, [Colloq. අරත්ත *aratta.*]

ගන්ධපත්‍ර, *Gandhapatra*, s. white sort of basil, *ocimum gratissimum*; [Colloq. මදුරුතලා *madurutalá.*]

ගන්ධපලා, *Gandhapalá*,
ගන්ධපලාශිකා, *Gandhapalásiká*,
ගන්ධපලි, *Gandhapali*, } s. turmeric, saffron, *curcuma longa*; [Colloq. කහ *kaha*].

ගන්ධපලාශි, *Gandhapalásí*, s. a plant, *Kaempferia Galangu* [Colloq. හිඟුරුපියලි *hingurupiyali.*]

ගන්ධපාසාණ, *Gandhapásána*, s. (ගන්ධ and පාසාණ stone) sulphur. [Colloq. කෙන්දගං *kendagan.*]

ගන්ධපිසාචිකා, *Gandhapisáchiká*, s. (ගන්ධ and පිසාචික *pisáchika*, female demon) incense or the smell of incense; diffusive incense; so called from its dark colour or implike appearance, or from its cloudy nature attracting demons by its fragrance.

ගන්ධපුෂ්ප, *Gandhapushpa*, s. kind of cane *(Calamus rotang)*; name of a fragrant reed growing near the water, [Colloq. රුක්අඟුන *ruk-anguna.*] also of several aromatic plants; kind of fragrant offering consisting of flower and sandal presented at the time of worship.

ගන්ධඵල, *Gandhaphala*, s. gum olibanum tree *boswellia serrata;* flowers or blossoms of the champaca tree; *Michaelia champaca;* [Colloq. සපු *sapu.*]

ගන්ධබ්බ, *Gandhabba*, Páli form of ගන්ධර්ව *gandharwa* which see.

ගන්ධමාදන, *Gandhamádana*, s. name of a mountain said to be in the Himálaya range; one of the monkey chiefs, so called; sulphur; large black bee.

ගන්ධමූල, *Gandhamúla*, s. (ගන්ධ and මූල root) plant with a fragrant and tuberous root, *alpinia galanga.* [Colloq. කළුවාල *kaluwála.*]

ගන්ධමූලක, *Gandhamúlaka*, s. sort of *curcuma*; sandal wood; plant *hemidesmus indicus.* [Colloq. ඉරමුසු *iramusu.*]

ගන්ධමූෂිකා, *Gandhamúshiká*, s. musk shrew *sorex moschata.*

ගන්ධමෘග, *Gandhamriga*, s. (ගන්ධ and මෘග deer, musk deer; civet-cat. [Coll: උරුලෑවා *uruléwá.*]

ගන්ධයුක්ත, *Gandhayukta*, a. fragrant, perfumed.

ගන්ධර්ව, *Gandharwa*, s. choristers or musicians that inhabit *Indra's* heaven or the celestial regions; at all the principal banquets of the gods they compose the orchestra; horse, kind of deer; the soul after death and previous to its being born again, a being somewhat like the western notion of a ghost; a singer in general; the kókila or Indian cuckoo.

ගන්ධර්වහස්ත, *Gandharwahasta*, s. (ගන්ධර්ව deer, හස්ත hand) plant, the leaves of which are compared to the foot of the deer; *ricinus communis* or castor oil plant, [Colloq. රටඑඬරු *rataendaru.*]

ගන්ධරස, *Gandharasa*, s. (ගන්ධ and රස essence) myrrh.

ගන්ධරාජ, *Gandharája*, s. sandal; any sweet smelling flower.

ගන්ධවරා, *Gandhawará*, s. (ගන්ධ and වර *wara* excellence) highest degree of fragrance; camphor. [Colloq. කපුරු *kapuru.*]

ගන්ධවල්ලිකා, *Gandhawalliká*, s. (ගන්ධ and වල්ලිකා creeper) species of jasmin.

ගන්ධවහ, *Gandhawaha*, s. (ගන්ධ fragrance, වහ what conveys) air, wind; nose.

ගන්ධවාහ, *Gandhawáha*, s. (derived as ගන්ධවහ *gandhawaha*) wind; musk deer; nose.

ගන්ධසාර, *Gandhasára*, s. (ගන්ධ perfume, සාර essence) essence of perfume, sandal wood. [Coll. හඳුන් *haṇdun*.]

ගන්ධහස්ති, *Gandhahasti*, s. musk elephant.

ගන්ධහාරකා, *Gandhahárakú*, s. female artisan working in another person's house.

ගන්ධාඛු, *Gandhákhu*, s. (ගන්ධ *gandha* and අඛු *ákhu* rat) musk rat. [Colloq. හික්මියා *hikmíyá*.]

ගන්ධාර, *Gandhára*, s. country so called; sound like the cry of a goat.

ගන්ධාශ්මන්, *Gandháṣman*, s. (ගන්ධ *gandha* and අශ්මන් *aṣman* stone) sulphur. [Colloq. කෙන්ද ගන් *kendagan*.]

ගන්ධාරි, *Gandhári*, see ගන්ධාර *gandhára*.

ගන්ධික *Gandhika*, s. sulphur.

ගන්ධොත්තමා, *Gandhóttamá*, s. ගන්ධ *gandha* smell, උත්තම *uttama* highest or best) any spirituous liquor; toddy, the liquid extracted from the cocoa-nut tree. [Colloq. රා *rá*.]

ගන්ධොලි, *Gandhóli*, s. kind of cucumber; eagle; jaw.

ගන්ධොලී, *Gandhólí*, s. wasp; fragrant grass *cyperus rotundus*. [Colloq. කලාඳුරු *kaláṇduru*].

ගන්නවා, *Gannawá*, v. to take; to assume, pret. ගත්තා *gattá*.

ගන්ලද්දා, *Ganladdá*, s. (ගම *gama* and ලද්දා who has received) the grantee of lands or villages from the king, and who exercises an authority over the tenants similar to that of a lord of the manor.

ගන්වනවා, *Ganwanawá*, v. to cause to take or receive; pret. ගැන්නෙව්වා *gennewwá*.

ගනකඩ, *Ganakaḍa*, a. extremely thick, s. thick cloth.

ගනකම, *Ganakama*, s. thickness.

ගනකල්, *Ganakal*, s. rainy season.

ගනකුළ, *Ganakuḷa*, s. a cloud.

ගනකුළු, *Ganakuḷu*, s. line of clouds.

ගනගහනවා, *Ganagahanawá*, v. to twist.

ගනගැජුම්, *Ganagejum*, s. thunder; [Colloq. අහස ගෙරවීම *ahasagerawima*]; modern.

ගනඟ, *Ganaṇga*, s. (ගන thick, අඟ *aṇga* body) name of Gaṇésa, Hindu god of wisdom.

ගනදර, *Ganadara*, see ගනඳර *ganaṇdara*.

ගනඳර, *Ganaṇdara*, s. darkness, thick darkness.

ගනපුෂ්ප, *Ganapushpa*, s. woollen cloth woven with flowers.

ගනබ, *Ganaba*, s. thick cloud, or line of clouds thickly charged with water.

ගනරූපු, *Ganarupu*, s. the sun. [Colloq. ඉර *ira*.]

ගනිච්චි, *Ganichchi*, s. esteem, regard, respect.

ගප්සාවිම, *Gapsárima*, s. for ගස්සාවිම *gassárima* which see.

ගබ්බ, *Gabba*, Páli form of ගර්ව *garwa*.

ගබ්භ, *Gabbha*, Páli form of ගර්භ *garbha*.

ගබ්භිනි, *Gabbhiní*, s. pregnant woman.

ගබ්භ්‍යාන, *Gabbhyána*, s. any complaint or disease in the bowels or womb.

ගබ, *Gaba*, s. belly; womb; inside, or inner part of any thing.

ගබඩාකාරයා, *Gabaḍákárayá*. s. storekeeper.

ගබඩාව, *Gabaḍáwa*, s. store room; pantry; magazine.

ගබමල, *Gabamala*, s. child dead in the womb; abortion.

ගභස්ති, *Gabhasti*, s. ray of light, sun or moon beam; light, splendour.

ගභස්තිමත්, *Gabhastimat*, s. (ගභස්ති and මත් poss. affix) sun, [Colloq. සූය්‍යයා *súryayá*.]

ගම්, *Gam*, *plur.* of ගම *gama*,

ගම්ජේස්ඨයා, *Gamjésṭayá*, s. corruptly, for ග්‍රාම ජ්‍යෙෂ්ඨයා *grámajyéshṭhayá*, which see.

ගම්තොට, *Gamtoṭa*, for ගංතොට *gaṇtoṭa* s. ferry.

ගම්දෙටුවා, *Gamdeṭuwá*, Elu form of ගම්ජේස්ටයා *gamjésṭayá*.

ගම්දොර, *Gamdora*, s. gate or entrance into a village.

ගම්පිලි, *Gampili*, s. plant, *galega purpurea*.

ගම්බාරි, *Gambári*, see ගම්භාරි *gambhári*.

ගම්භාර, *Gambhára*, s. mantra, or magical incantation, written in prose; lotus; citron.

ගම්භාරි, *Gambhári*, s. name of a tree, commonly called by the same name Gambhári, *Gmelina arborea* [Colloq. ඇත්දෙමට *eṭdemaṭa*.]

ගම්භීර, *Gambhíra*, a. deep, as water, but applied metaphorically to sound, intellect &c.

ගම්මලු, *Gammalu*, s. resinons timber tree, *pterocarpus marsupium (Leguminosæ.)*

ගම්මානේ, *Gammáné*, s. cultivated country; inhabited country in the neighbourhood of a village, pl. ගම්මාන් *gammán*.

ගම්මිරිස්, *Gammiris*, s. black pepper.

ගම්මිරිස්වැල්, *Gammiriswęl* s. black pepper plant, *piper nigrum (Piperaceæ).*

ගම්මුදලියා, *Gammudaliyá*, s. the chief of a village.

ගම්‍ය, *Gamya*, a. attainable, accessible; perceptible.

ගම්වාසියා, *Gamwásiyá*, ගම්වැසියා, *Gamwęsiya*, } s. villager.

ගම, *Gama*, s. village; going, moving, marching, journeying, journey, road; kind of game, backgammon; pl. ගම් *gam*.

ගමථ, *Gamatha*, s. road; traveller.

ගමන, *Gamana*, s. journey; gait; going in general, march; march of an assailant, pl. ගමන් *gaman*.

ගමනාශන, *Gamanáṣana*, s. (ගමන *gamana* and අශන *aṣana* victuals), provisions for a journey.

ගමනී, *Gamaní*, s. traveller.

ගමබිම, *Gamabima*, s. landed property, pl. ගම්බිම්, *gambim*.

ගමයා, *Gamayá*, ගමරදල, *Gamaradala*, ගමරාල, *Gamarála*, } s. head man of a village.

ගමික, *Gamika*, s. traveller; going, marching.

ගමිසුරු, *Gamisuru*, s. (ගම *gama* and ඉසුරු *isuru* chief) chief or head man of a village.

ගය, *Gaya*, s. kind of ox; name of a royal or military saint; verse or stanza.

ගයනුකිත්ත, *Gayanukitta*, s. the symbol ෟ as used in the word ගෞරවකරණවා *gaurawakaraṇawá*.

ගයා, *Gayá*, s. Gaya, city in Behar, rendered famous on account of its being the residence of Buddha; according to ancient tradition Buddha was born in a forest which formerly surrounded this city; in Sanskrit authors it is called Buddha Gaya, it is a place of great sanctity among the Hindus.

ගර්ගරී, *Gargarí*, s. (ගර්ග imitative sound, a gurgling, ර *ra* what makes) churn; water vessel, goglet.

ගර්ජ *Garja*, s. roaring of elephants; rumbling of clouds; growling of wild beasts; thunder.

ගර්ජක, *Garjjaka*, s. kind of fish, commonly Gajar.

ගර්ජනාව, *Garjjanáwa*, s. sound, noise; rumbling of the clouds; thunder; war, battle, conflict; passion, wrath, excessive indignation; reproach; menace.

ගර්ජිත, *Garjita*, s. an elephant in rut; rumbling of clouds, rolling of distant thunder.

ගර්ත, *Garta*, s. hole, the hollow of the loins.

ගර්දභ, *Gardabha*, s. white lotus; smell, odour; ass, camel.

ගර්දභී, *Gardabhí*, s. insect, kind of beetle breeding from cowdung; she-ass; cutaneous eruption.

ගර්ධන, *Garddhana*, a. avaricious or covetous.

ගර්භ, *Garbbha*, ගර්භ, *Garbha* } s. womb; fœtus, embryo; belly; the inside; inner apartment; middle; pride; joining, union.

ගර්භක, *Garbhaka*, s. chaplet of flowers worn on the hair; period of a day and two nights.

ගර්භග්‍රහණ, *Garbbhagrahaṇa*, s. (ගර්භ womb, ග්‍රහණ taking) conception.

ගර්භපාතක, *Garbhapátaka*, s. (ගර්භ and පාත *páta* falling) red kind of murunga, supposed to produce abortion.

ගර්භප්‍රතිග්‍රහණය, *Garbbhapratigrahaṇaya*, s. formation of the fœtus, conception.

ගර්භප්‍රතිෂ්ඨානය, *Garbbhapratishṭhánaya*, s. prevention of miscarriage.

ගර්භශය්‍යාව, *Garbbhaṣayyáwa*, s. uterus.

ගර්භශාන්තිය, *Garbbhaṣántiya*, s. period between the birth of a child and conception.

ගර්භස්‍රාව, *Garbhasráwa*, s. (ගර්භ womb, ස්‍රාව expulsion) abortion, miscarriage; the afterbirth.

ගර්භාගාර, *Garbhágára*, s. lying-in chamber.

ගර්භාධාන, *Garbhádhána*, s. conception, ceremony performed prior to conception.

ගර්භාවක්‍රාන්තිය, *Grabbháwakrántiya*, s. conception; formation of the fœtus in womb.

ගර්භිණී, *Garbhiṇí*, s. pregnant woman; twining plant with milky gum and large flowers see ගරබෝ *garabó*, *asclepias rosea.*

ගර්භෝත්ක්‍රමණය, *Garbbhótkramaṇaya*, s. bringing forth from the womb, birth.

ගර්ව, *Garwa*, s. pride, arrogance, haughtiness. [Coll. ආඩම්බරය *ádambaraya*.]

ගර්විත, *Garvita*, a. proud, haughty, arrogant.

ගර්හණ, *Garhaṇa*, s. censure, blame, reproach. [Colloq. ගැරහීම *gęrahíma*.]

ගර්හාව, *Garháwa*, s. censure, contempt.

ගර්හිත, *Garhita*, a. contemptible, despised.

ගර්හ්‍ය, *Garhya*, a. low, vile, contemptible. [Colloq. නීච *nícha*.]

ගර්හ්‍යකරණවා, *Garhyákaraṇawá*. v. to abuse, to censure, to blame; to despise, to contemn, to treat without respect; to disgrace. [Colloq. නින්දාකරණවා *nindákaraṇawá*.]

ගර, *Gara*, s. sickness, disease; poison; house; antidote; sprinkling, wetting.

ගරඩියා, *Garaṇdiyá*, s. rat-snake, pl. ගරඬි *garaṇdi*, *ptyas mucosus (Colubridæ* order *Ophidia.)*

ගරණවා, *Garaṇawá*, s. to cleanse the grain, or separate it from the dirt, to sift.

ගරද, *Garada*, *s.* (ගර poison, ද who gives) poisoner, poison; *a.* unwholesome.

ගරබ්, *Garab*, ගරබෝ, *Garabó*, } *s.* rat snake; plant *ichnocarpus frutescens*, [Colloq. කිරි වැල් *kiriwęl.*]

ගරල, *Garala*, *s.* venom of a snake, venom in general, [Colloq. වච්චනාවි *wachchanávi.*]; bundle of hay or grass; measure in general.

ගරවාසියා, *Garawásiyá*, *s.* (ගර house, වාසි *wási* who lives) the inhabitant of a house, house holder, pl. ගරවාසි *garawási*, incorrectly for ඝර වාසි *gharawási*.

ගරවිල්, *Garavil*, *s.* rat snake; commonly called ගරඬියා *garandiyá*.

ගරවිල *Garavila*, see ගරල *garala*.

ගරවෘන්දක, *Garavrindaka*, *s.* (ගර house, වෘන්දක god) house-hold god, improperly for ඝරවෘන්දාරක *gharavrindáraka*.

ගරහනවා, *Garahanawá*, *s.* to contemn, to despise, to censure, to blame, to reproach, pret. ගැරහුවා *gerahuwá*.

ගරහා, *Garahá*, *s.* contempt, scorn, ridicule; part. having despised.

ගරා, *Gará*, *s.* swallowing. [Colloq. ගිලීම *gilíma.*]

ගරාදිය, *Garádiya*, *s.* railing, meter, spoke of a wheel.

ගරායකුම, *Garáyakuma*, *s.* a particular demon ceremony.

ගරී, *Garí*, *s.* sort of grass *andropogon serratus*.

ගරු, *Garu*, *s.* wing; respect, honour, veneration, esteem, regard; *a.* respectable, estimable, worthy of regard.

ගරුක, *Garuka*, *a.* much, heavy, serious.

ගරුකටයුතු, *Garukatayutu*, honourable, worthy of respect.

ගරුකම, *Garukama*, *s.* respect, honour, grandeur.

ගරුකරණවා, *Garukaranawá*, *v.* to respect, to esteem, to regard.

ගරුකාපත්ති, *Garukápatti*, *s.* (ගරුක *garuka* serious, ආපත්ති *ápatti* guilt) any great crime, but particularly the thirteen sins which are to be avoided by the priests of Buddha.

ගරුකාර, *Garukára*, *s.* respect, honour, veneration.

ගරුඩ, *Garuda*, *s.* bird and vehicle of Vishnu: this is generally represented as being something between a man and a bird and is considered as sovereign of the feathered kind; he is the son of Kásyapa and Vinatá and younger brother of Aruna; alabaster, sometimes written ගරුඬ *garunda*.

ගරුඩධ්වජ, *Garudadhwaja*, *s.* (ගරුඩ and ධ්වජ symbol or ensign) he whose symbol is Garuda, one of the names of Vishnu.

ගරුඩපාෂාණ, *Garudapásána*, *s.* (ගරුඩ and පාෂාණ stone) emerald.

ගරුඩා, *Garudá*, *s.* large centipede.

ගරුත්, *Garut*, *s.* wing.

ගරුත්මාන්, *Garutmán*, *s.* name of Vishnu's bird, see ගරුඩ *garuda*.

ගරුතර, *Garutara*, *a.* very respectable, highly honourable; exceedingly venerable.

ගරුභාණ්ඩ, *Garubhánda*, property common to the priests, as opposed to පරික්ඛාර *parikkhára*, their personal property.

ගරුළා *Garulá*, *s.* see ගුරුළා *gurulá*.

ගල්, *Gal*, pl. of ගල *gala*, stone, rock.

ගල්අන්නාසි, *Galannási*, *s.* kind of pineapple.

ගල්ඇහි, *Galęhi*, *s.* plant, *Cyperus corymbosus (Cyperaceæ)*.

ගල්ඉබ්බා, *Galibbá*, *s.* fresh water tortoise, *Emys trijuga*.

ගල්කටුව, *Galkatuwa*, *s.* pick axe.

ගල්කඩයා *Galkadayá*, *s.* kind of sea fish.

ගල්කණ්ඩු, *Galkandu*, *s.* sugar-candy.

ගල්කප්පරවල්ලිය, *Galkapparawalliya*, *s.* plant, *Anisochilus carnosus (Labiatæ)*.

ගල්කරඳ, *Galkaranda*, *s.* plant, *Humboldtia laurifolia (Leguminosæ)*; small tree, *Canthium didymum (Rubiaceæ)*, also called පොරවමාරා *porawa-mára*.

ගල්කරුවා, *Galkaruwá*, *s.* stone cutter; quarry man.

ගල්කුසුඹා, *Galkusumbá*, *s.* Carey or Indian green turtle, edible, *chelonia virgata* (order *Chelonia.)*

ගල්කුළ, *Galkula*, *s.* rock, pl. ගල්කුළු, *galkulu*,

ගල්කූර, *Galkúra*, *s.* slate pencil; medicinal herb.

ගල්කෙම, *Galkema*, *s.* tank hewn in a rock.

ගල්කැටය, *Galkętaya*, *s.* stone, piece of stone.

ගල්ගාන්නා, *Galgánná*, *s.* lapidary, cutter of precious stones, pl. ගල්ගාන්නෝ *galgánnó*.

ගල්ගුහාව, *Galguháwa*, *s.* cave in a rock.

ගල්ගෙඩිය, *Galgediya*, *s.* stone so cut as to be ready for the mason, stone.

ගල්ටැඹ, *Galtęmba*, *s.* stone pillar.

ගල්තාංගුවෙනවා, *Galtánguwenawá*, *v.* to be astonished.

ගල්තැලුම, *Galtęluma*, *s.* sore foot hurt by stone.

ගල්දෙමට, *Galdemaṭa, s.* plant, kind of balsam peculiar to Ceylon; *Impatiens repens (Geraniaceæ).*

ගල්දොර, *Galdora, s.* stone door.

ගල්නයා, *Galnayá, s.* variety of the cobra; see නයා *nayá.*

ගල්නහර, *Galnahara, s.* gum olibanum.

ගල්පවුර, *Galpawura, s.* stone rampart.

ගල්පහුර, *Galpahura, s.* ledge of rocks.

ගල්පියලි, *Galpiyali,* see ගල්මද *galmada.*

ගල්පුළුන්නා, *Galpuḷunná, s.* fish, Block's sea perch, *priacanthus blockii.*

ගල්බිලය, *Galbilaya, s.* natural cave or hole in a rock or stone.

ගල්මද, *Galmada, s. talc; benzoin* or gum benjamin; medicinal plant.

ගල්මී, *Galmí, s.* kind of gum resin *(styrax?)*

ගල්මොර, *Galmora, s.* tree (Kandian country) *Pometia (nephelium) eximia (Sapindaceæ);* tree (low country) *Cryptocarya Wightiana (Lauraceæ)*

ගල්මැන්ඩෝර, *Galmẹnḍóra, s.* timber tree, *Cynometra ramiflora (Leguminosæ).*

ගල්රුපු, *Galrupu, s.* pigeon; [Colloq. පරවියා *paraviyá.*]

ගල්ලැල්ල, *Gallẹlla, s.* slab or flat piece of stone, slate; pl. ගල්ලැලි *gallẹli.*

ගල්ලෙන, *Gallena, s.* cave in a rock, natural cave.

ගල්වනවා, *Galwanawá, s.* to dye, to daub, to rub or smear on the body; to put, to apply one thing to another; to cause to sink; to cause to swallow, pret. ගෑල්ලෙව්වා *gẹllewwá.*

ගල්වලු, *Galwalu, s.* see ගලවලු *galawalu.*

ගල්වෙරළු, *Galweraḷu, s.* tree, peculiar to Ceylon; *Elæocarpus subvillosus (Tilliaceæ).*

ගල්වෙරෙප්පුව, *Galwereppuwa, s.* kind of cancer.

ගල්සියඹලා, *Galsiyam̱balá, s.* timber and fruit tree peculiar to Ceylon, *Dialium ovoideum (Leguminosæ).*

ගල්සෙවෙල්, *Galsewel, s.* rock moss.

ගල, *Gala, s.* stone, rock; throat, neck; rope; kind of resin; sort of reed, *saccharum cylindricum:* musical instrument; kind of fish, sort of gilt head, pl. ගල් *gal.*

ගලකඩ, *Galakaḍa, s.* flesh that hangs from the throat of oxen which laps or licks the dew in grazing, hence called the dew-lap,

ගලගණ්ඩ, *Galagaṇḍa, s.* inflammation, enlargement of the glands of the neck.

ගලග්‍රහය, *Galagrahaya, s.* (ගල throat, ග්‍රහ *graha* seizure) act of seizing by the throat; disease, inflammation of the glands of the neck; sauce of fish ground up with salt, pepper, ghee &c.

ගලතල, *Galatala, s.* (ගල stone, තල plane) surface of a stone.

ගලතාංගුව, *Galatáṅguwa, s.* recovery from going to fall.

ගලනවා, *Galanawá, v.* to flow, to overflow, to dip pret. ගෑලුවා *gẹluwá.*

ගලපනවා *Galapanawá, v.* to unite, to join, to knot. pret. ගෑලපුවා *gẹlapuwá.*

ගලප්පත්තිකරණවා, *Galappattikaraṇawá, v.* to caulk.

ගලප්පත්තිය, *Galappattiya, s.* overlaying with tar the planks of a ship or boat.

ගලමුවා, *Galamuwá, a.* made of stone; kind of sea fish; kind of deer.

ගලමේඛලා, *Galamékhalá, s.* (ගල neck, මේඛලා girdle) necklace.

ගලරුපු, *Galarupu,* see ගල්රුපු *galrupu.*

ගලරැව්, *Galarẹw, s.* (ගල throat, රැව් sound) cock; pigeon; sound, noise, sounds from the throat of animals, in contradistinction to other sounds.

ගලවනවා, *Galawanawá, v.* to deliver, to set free, to loosen, to save; pret. ගෑලෙව්වා *gẹlewwá.*

ගලවලු, *Galawalu, s.* back part of the neck; head of the humerus.

ගලා, *Galá, part.* having overflowed or dipped, *s.* term used to signify a stubborn fellow.

ගලිත, *Galita, a.* fallen, dropped.

ගලිනවා, *Galinawá, v.* to swallow, pret. ගෑල්ලා *gẹllá.*

ගලිස්, *Galis, s.* tree, *Gardenia latifolia.*

ගව්, *Gaw,* plur. of ගව්ව *gawwa* which see.

ගව්‍ය, *Gawya, a.* of or belonging to a cow; proper or fit for cattle; *s.* cow-butter; bow string; colouring substance, dye, yellow orpiment.

ගව්‍යා, *Gawyá, s.* multitude of cows; measure of 4000 yards; *a.* of or belonging to a cow; proper or fit for cattle.

ගව්ව, *Gawwa, s.* measure of distance of the Siṇhalese mile 5600 yards, or about three and half miles.

ගව, *Gawa, s.* ox; bullock.

ගවඟන, *Gawaṉgana, s.* cow; [Colloq. එළදෙන *eladena.*]

ගවජ, *Gawaja,* } *s.* kind of ox, *bos gavæus.*
ගවද, *Gawada,* }

ගවපල්, *Gawapal*, } *s.* cowherd; cowkeeper;
ගවපාලයා, *Gawapálayá*, } one of the names of Vishṇu.

ගවයහන්, *Gawayahan*, *s.* (ගව ox, යහන් vehicle) name of Íṣwara or Ṣiva.

ගවයා, *Gawayá*, *s.* a species of ox, the *gayal* or *bos gavæus*, bullock; name of a fish.

ගවරවළ, *Gawarawaḷa*, *s.* mud hole, place for the lodgment of dirt or rubbish.

ගවරස, *Gawarasa*, *s.* curdled milk, or coagulated milk.

ගවරා, *Gawará*, *s.* species of buffalo; zebra.

ගවල, *Gawala*, *s.* wild buffalo; buffalo's horn; *bubahis arni.* [Colloq. වල්මීමා *walmímá.*]

ගවසනවා, *Gawasanawá*, *v.* to ornament the head with a chaplet of flowers, to stick, to fasten, pret. ගැවසුවා *gęwasuwá.*

ගවාක්ෂ, *Gawáksha*, *a.* (ගව *gawa* ox, අක්ෂ *aksha* eye) ox-eyed; *s.* window, air-hole, loop-hole; round window; bull's eye; kind of monkey (with eyes like those of an ox).

ගවාක්ෂි, *Gawákshi*, *s.* (ගෝ *gó* earth, අක්ෂ *aksha* to spread) sort of cucumber *cucumis madraspatanus*, [Colloq. ගොන්කැකිරි *gonkękiri;*] plant *clitoria ternatea*, [Colloq. නිල්කටරොළු *nil-kaṭa roḷu.*]

ගවාදන, *Gawádana*, *s.* pasture or meadow grass.

ගවාදනී, *Gawádaní*, *s.* hay-rack, trough for holding grass; plant, see ගවාක්ෂි *gawákshi.*

ගවාලූක, *Gawálúka*, *s.* *gayal*, species of ox found in the upper provinces of India, *bos gavæus.*

ගවි, *Gavi*, *s.* clarified butter, things proper to be offered in sacrifice.

ගවීන, *Gavína*, s. cow-butter.

ගවේරුක, *Gavéruka*, *s.* red chalk. [Colloq. සිවංගුරු *sivanguru.*]

ගවේසන, *Gavésana*, *s.* search.

ගවේසිත, *Gavésita*, sought, from ගවේසති *gavésati* he seeks.

ගවෝදක, *Gawódaka*, *s.* cow's urine.

ගස්, *Gas*, pl. of ගස *gasa.*

ගස්කයිල, *Gaskayila*, *s.* plant, *breynia rhamnoides (Euphorbiaceæ).*

ගස්කරල්හැබ, *Gas-karal-hęba*, *s.* weed, *achyranthes aspera (Amarantaceæ).*

ගස්කහඹිලියා, *Gas-kahambiliyá*, *s.* kind of nettle, *girardinia Zeylanica (Urticaceæ).*

ගස්කැප්පිටියා, *Gas-kęppiṭiyá*, *s.* plant *croton lacciferum (Euphorbiaceæ)*; also called, කැප්පෙටියා *kęppeṭiyá.*

ගස්කැල, *Gas-kęla*, *s.* Pulas tree producing a gum and beautiful flowers, *butea frondosa (Leguminosæ)*; also called ඇත්කන් *ętkan.*

ගස්කැලිය, *Gas-kęliya*, *s.* plant *grewia lævigata.*

ගස්ගෙමඩියා, *Gas-gemaḍiyá*, *s.* kind of frog, said to live on suction from trees; it is frequently found in the tops of the trunks of trees, its bite is said to be poisonous, pl. ගස්ගෙමඩි *gasgemaḍi, polypedates maculatus (order Batrachia Salientia.)*

ගස්දූල්, *Gas-dúl*, *s.* plant, *debregeasia velutina, (Urticaceæ).*

ගස්නිදිකුම්බ, *Gas-nidikumba*, *s.* plant, *biophytum nervifolia (Geraniaceæ)*; aquatic plant *neptunia oleracea* or *mimosa natans (Leguminosæ).*

ගස්නිවිති, *Gas-niviti*, *s.* esculent plant, malabar night shade.

ගස්නෙටුල්, *Gas-neṭul*, *s.* plant, *fiars gibbosa (Urticaceæ).*

ගස්පිච්ච, *Gas-pichcha*, *s.* plant, *Coffea travancorensis (Rubiaceæ).*

ගස්පින්න, *Gas-pinna*, *s.* plant, *clerodendron infortunatum (Verbenaceæ).*

ගස්මදිනවා, *Gas-madinawá*, *v.* to extract toddy from the trees; pret. ගස්මැද්දා *gas-męddá.*

ගස්මියා, *Gas-miyá*, *s.* tree rat, *mus rufescens.*

ගස්සනවා, *Gassanawá*, *v.* to pull the trigger, to fire off, to strike against, to give a violent shock; pret. ගැස්සුවා *gęssuwá.*

ගස්සාවීම, *Gassávíma*, *s.* abortion; miscarriage.

ගස්සාවෙනවා, *Gassáwenawá*, *v.* to miscarry.

ගස, *Gasa*, *s.* tree in general; also called ගහ *gaha.*

ගසනවා, *Gasanawá*, *v.* to beat, to strike; pret. ගැසුවා *gęsuwá* ; see ගහනවා *gahanawá.*

ගසාකනවා, *Gasákanawá*, *v.* to prey on, to seize voraciously; to snatch away for the purpose of eating.

ගසාගන්නවා, *Gaságannawá*, *v.* to snatch, to take by force.

ගසාදමනවා, *Gasádamanawá*, *v.* to shake off, to brush off the dust.

ගහ්වර, *Gahwara*, } *s.* cave, cavern, grotto; recess
ගහ්වරී, *Gahwarí*, } in a rock or mountain, thicket, a wood; pride weeping; crying, but not violently; arbour, bower.

ගහ, *Gaha*, *s.* tree; house; planet; cultivator.

ගහගැමුනු, *Gahagęmunu*, *s.* (ගහ plant, ගාමිනී *gáminí* chief) lord of the planets, sun.

ගහගෙවි, *Gahagevi*, *s.* householder; husbandman.

ගහට, *Gahaṭa*, *s.* suffering; afflictions, sorrow.

ගහණ, *Gahaṇa*, *s.* nose, eclipse.

ගහණී, *Gahaṇí*, *s.* belly; digestive faculty, internal heat producing digestion.

ගහදමනවා, *Gahadamanawá*, *v.* to behead; to do a thing in a hurry; knock down.

ගහන්, *Gahan*, *s.* nose. [Colloq. නාහේ *náhé*].

ගහන්මග, *Gahanmaga*, *s.* (ගහ planet, මග way) sky; circuit made by a planet on the plane of the ecliptic.

ගහන්සිව්, *Gahansiw*, *s.* name of Brahma.

ගහන, *Gahana*, *a.* impervious; beating, nailing, fastening;—*s.* multitude; great quantity; wood, thicket; cave; pain; distress.

ගහනත්, *Gahanat*, *s.* (ගහන් *gahan* nose, අත් *at* hand) name of Gaṇéṣa who is figured with the head of an elephant.

ගහනවා, *Gahanawá*, *v.* to beat, to strike, to knock, to thump, to flog, pret. ගැහුවා *gehuwá*.

ගහපති, *Gahapati*, *s.* householder, head of a family;—cultivator.

ගහමග, *Gahamaga*, *s.* see ගහන්මග *gahanmaga*.

ගහමිණි, *Gahamiṇi*, *s.* (ගහ constellation, මිණි gem) sun. [Colloq. ඉර *ira*]

ගහරද, *Gaharada*, *s.* (ගහ planet, රද king) moon [Colloq. හඳ *haṉda*].

ගහල, *Gahala*, *s.* plant, a yam, *colocasia antiquorum (Araceæ).*

ගහලගම්බඩයා, *Gahala-gambaḍayá*, *s.* scavenger, outcaste who cleans the streets, inters corpses etc.

ගහලයා, *Gahalayá*, person of the caste so called.

ගළුචි, *Gaḷúchi*, *s.* holy basil, *ocimum sanctum;* [Colloq. මදුරුතලා *madurutalá*, also රසකිඳ *rasakiṉda;*] timber tree, *terminalia citrina.*

ගා, *Gá*, *s.* song, singing; bullock; *part.* having smeared rubbed or played on a lute; from ගානවා *gánawá*

ගාඞ්ගායනි, *Gáńgáyani*, } name of Krishṇa; also,
ගාඞ්ගෙය, *Gáńgéya*, } name of Kartakéya;—in the first name it is the river Gaṇges personified as the wife of Santanu, and mother of that celebrated hero; in the latter sense, as the receiver of Kártikéya, the son of Ṣiva from Agni, the god of fire; kind of fish, *clupia alosa;* gold; fragrant grass *cyperus rotundus.* [Colloq. කලාඳුරු *Kaláṉduru*].

ගාඞ්ගෙරි, *Gáńgéri* *s.* fragrant grass, *cyperus rotundus;* species of the *marsebá.*

ගාටනවා, *Gáṭanawá*, *s.* to waddle; pret. ගැටුවා *geṭuwá.*

ගාඩි, *Gáḍi*, *s.* respectful term for a රොඩියා *Roḍiyá*

ගාණ්ඩි, *Gáṇḍi*, *s.* bow of Arjuna; carriage drawn by oxen.

ගාණ්ඩිර, *Gáṇḍira*, *s.* long pepper plant *piper longum* [Colloq. තිප්පිලි *tippili*].

ගාණ්ඩිහෙය, *Gáṇḍiheya*, *a.* golden, made of gold or the quality of gold.

ගාණ්ඩිරික, *Gáṇḍírika*, } see ගාණ්ඩීව *gáṇḍíwa.*
ගාණ්ඩිරිකා, *Gáṇḍíriká*, }

ගාඪ, *Gáḍha*, much, excessive; hard; thick; oppressive.

ගාඪමොහිනි, *Gáḍhamóhini*, *s.* plant said to render those invisible that eat of it.

ගාණ්ඩිව, *Gáṇḍiwa*, } *s.* bow; particularly the
ගාණ්ඩීව, *Gáṇḍíwa*, } bow of Arjuna.

ගාත්‍රය, *Gátrya*, *s.* body; fore quarter of an elephant; limb, member; pl. ගාත්‍රා *gátrá.* ගාත *gáta.*

ගාත්‍රාක්ෂර, *Gátrákshara* *s.* consonant.

ගාත්‍රානුලේපනි, *Gátránulépani* *s.* (ගාත්‍ර *gátra* body, අනු *anu* upon, ලිප *lipa* to smear) fragrant unguents etc. smeared upon the body; perfumes for the person.

ගාතාව, *Gátáwa*, see ගාථාව *gátháwa.*

ගාතු, *Gátu*, *s.* one of the celestial choristers; the Kókila or Indian cuckoo; large black bee; singer; *a.* angry, wrathful.

ගාතේ, *Gáté*, *s.* leg, including the part both above and below the knee, pl. ගාත *gáta.*

ගාථක, *Gáthaka*, *s.* singer, musician, chorister.

ගාථාව, *Gátháwa*, *s.* verse, stanza; metre, rhythm; song, verse or chant to be sung or chanted. pl. ගාථා *gáthá.*

ගාන්දාරි, *Gándári* see ගාන්ධාර *gándhára.*

ගාන්ධර්ව, *Gándharwa*, *s.* heavenly chorister, see ගන්ධර්ව *gandharwa*, song, singing; form of marriage, that which requires only amorous and mutual agreement.

ගාන්ධාර, *Gándhára*, *s* one of the seven primary notes of music; minium or red lead; country so called, lying between the north of India and Persia; gum myrrh.

ගාන්ධාරි, *Gándhári*, mother of Duryódhana; see also ගන්ධාර *gandhára.*

ගාන, *Gána*, *s.* song, singing in general, sound.

ගානවා, *Gánawá*, *v.* to daub, to smear, to plaster, to rub: pret. ගෑවා *gǽwá*.

ගාම්භීර, *Gámbhíra*, *a.* deep, as water, sound &c. profound; proud, lofty, haughty, ostentatious.

ගාය, *Gáya*, *s.* pain, suffering; strength of body.

ගායකයා, *Gáyakayá*, *s.* singer.

ගායත්‍රී, *Gáyatrí*, *s.* stanza of twenty four syllables, or four lines of six syllables each; another measure in prosody containing six feet; in the mythology of the Hindus a gáyatrí means a sacred verse from the Védas, to be recited only mentally; this is usually personified and considered a goddess, the metaphorical mother of the three first classes of the Hindus in their capacity of twice born, investiture with the Brahminical cord, their sacred and distinguishing string, being considered as a new brith.

ගායන, *Gáyana*, *s.* singing, singer, chorister: chatterer.

ගායනා කරණවා, *Gáyaná-karaṇawá*, *v.* to sing, to chant; to perform on a musical instrument.

ගාර්පුව, *Gárpuwa*, *s.* fork.

ගාරුඩ, *Gáruḍa*, *s.* charm against poison; emerald, gold.

ගාරුත්මත්, *Gárutmat*, *s.* emerald; this gem is supposed to be generated from the voided phlegm of Garuḍa the bird of Vishṇu.

ගාල, *Gála*, *s.* enclosure for elephants or cattle; thicket, pl. ගාල් *gál*.

ගාලාගෝට්ටිය, *Gálágóṭṭiya*, *s.* tumultuous noise.

ගාව, *Gáwa*, *s.* border, brim, edge.

ගාවා, *Gáwá*, *par.* near, next, proximate.

ගාවිනාව, *Gáwináwa*, *s.* pain, labour, trouble, travail, affliction.

ගාස්තුව, *Gástuwa*, *s.* (Port.) fees.

ගාහිනවා, *Gáhinawá*, *v.* to shed, to pour out.

ගිගිරි, *Gigiri* *s.* thunder; rings put on the hands of tom-tom beaters to increase the sound when in the act of beating; bells and rings on the feet of dancers and dancing girls.

ගිගිරි වලල්ල, *Gigiri-walalla*, *s.* one of the rings mentioned in the foregoing, pl. ගිගිරි වලලු *gigiri-walalu*.

ගිගිරුම, *Gigiruma*, *s.* noise, sound, roaring of thunder, rumbling of the clouds.

ගිගුම්, *Gigum*,
ගිගුම, *Giguma*,
ගිගුරුම, *Giguruma*, } *s.* thunder.

ගිජ්ඣකූට, *Gijjhakúṭa*, *s.* (ගිජ්ඣ vulture, කූට peak) mountain in the neighbourhood of Rájagáha, so called from its resembling a vulture in shape.

ගිජා, *Gijá*, *s.* name of the goddess Párvatí or Durgá, wife of Ṣiva.

ගිජිඳු, *Gijiṉda*, *s.* elephant, pl. ගිජිඳුන් *gijiṉdun*. [Colloq. අලියා *aliyá*].

ගිජු, *Giju*, *a.* gluttonous, greedy.

ගිජුකුළුපව, *Gijukuḷupawa*, see ගිජ්ඣකූට *gijjhakúṭa*.

ගිජුලිහිණියා, *Gijulihiṇiyá*, *s.* golden eagle, pl. ගිජුලිහිණි *gijulihiṇi*.

ගිණුම, *Giṇuma*, *s.* counting.

ගිතෙල්, *Gitel*, *s.* ghee, or clarified butter.

ගිදු, *Gidu*, *s.* Elu from of ගිජු *giju*.

ගිද්ධ, *Giddha*, *a.* covetous, greedy.

ගින්, *Gin*, *s.* bullock; resemblance; heat.

ගින්නර ගහ, *Ginnara-gaha*,
ගින්නේරිය, *Ginnériya*, } see ගිනිහිරිය *gini hiriya*.

ගින්පොල්, *Ginpol*, *s.* tree, native of salt swamps, *Nipa fruticans (Palmæ).*

ගින, *Gina*, *s.* fire.

ගිනි, *Gini*, *s.* fire; heat; plant *plumbago rosea*.

ගිනි අඟුර, *Gini-aṉgura*, *s.* live coal, pl. ගිනි අඟුරු *gini-aṉguru*.

ගිනි ඇවිළෙනවා, *Gini-ævilenawá*, *v.* to be kindled.

ගිනිකටුව, *Ginikaṭuwa*, *s.* steel for striking fire.

ගිනිකබල, *Ginikabala*, *s.* (ගිනි and කබල a sherd) small furnace, piece of any clay vessel in which fire is placed, pl. ගිනිකබල් *ginikabal*.

ගිනිකරඳ, *Ginikaraṉda*, *s.* defects or flaws in iron, or earthen vessels.

ගිනිකුකුළා, *Ginikukuḷá*, *s.* (ගිනි fire, කුකුළා cock) kind of domestic cock, pl. ගිනිකුකුළෝ *ginikukuḷó*.

ගිනිකුරුල්ලා, *Ginikurullá*, *s.* bird called Ceylonese trogon *harpactes fasciatus (Trogonidæ)*; also called නවනිල කුරුල්ලා *nawanila-kurullá* and රන්වන් කොන්ඩයා, *ranwan-kondayá*. (order *Picariæ)* bird called the orange minivet, *pericrocotus flammeus* (order *Passeres).*

ගිනිකොණ, *Ginikoṇa*, *s.* south-east quarter, pl. ගිනිකොන් *ginikon*.

ගිනිජලාව, *Ginijáláwa*, *s.* (ගිනි fire, ජලාව stream) flame of fire.

ගිනිතියනවා, *Ginitiyanawá*, *v.* to set fire.

ගිනිදණ්ඩ, *Ginidaṇḍa*, *s.* stick used in producing fire by friction, pl. ගිනිදඬු *ginidaṇḍu.*

ගිනිදල්වනවා, *Ginidalwanawá s.* to kindle a fire.

ගිනිදිග, *Ginidiga*, *s.* south east,

ගිනිදිව්, *Ginidiw*, *s.* creeping plant *gloriosa superba* [Colloq. නියඟලා *niyaṉgalá*]

ගිනිදිව, *Ginidiva*, *s.* tongue of fire, pl. ගිනිදිව් *ginidiw.*

ගිනිදුම, *Giniduma*, *s.* smoke, literally fire vapour.

ගිනිදෙවි, *Ginidevi*, *s* Agnidevi, the god of fire; regent of the south east quarter.

ගිනිදෙවොල්, *Ginidewol*, *s.* place where offerings are made to Agnidevi.

ගිනිදැල. *Ginidęla*, *s.* spark of fire; fire, pl. ගිනිදැල් *ginidęl.*

ගිනිපුපුර, *Ginipupura*, *s.* spark of fire. pl. ගිනිපුපුරු *ginipupuru.*

ගිනිපෙනෙල්ල, *Ginipenella*, *s.* fire brand, pl. ගිනිපෙනෙලි *ginipeneli.*

ගිනිමල, *Ginimala*, *s.* large flame, flake of fire; spark.

ගිනිමු, *Ginimu*, *s.* } plant *plumbago zeylanica*;
ගිනිමුව, *Ginimuwa*, } [Colloq. එලනෙටුල් *elanețul.*] another plant *gloriosa superba*; [Colloq. නියඟලා *niyaṉgalá*].

ගිනිමොලවනවා, *Ginimolawanawá*, *v.* to make fire blaze, to blow the fire.

ගිනිමැලය, *Ginimęlaya*, *s.* large flame, flake of fire, bonfire.

ගිනිමැස්ස, *Ginimęssa*, *s.* fire grate; spit; fire kindled in the night on a kind of raised wicker work or platform, by those who watch the corn in the fields, for the purpose of warming themselves and keeping off the elephants, &c. pl. ගිනිමැහි *ginimęhi* or ගිනිමැසි *ginimęsi.*

ගිනියම, *Giniyama*, *s.* heat, pl. ගිනියම් *giniyam.*

ගිනිරොන්, *Giniron*, *s.* spark of fire.

ගිනිරැස, *Ginirẹsa*, *s.* beam, ray

ගිනිලන්නා, *Ginilanná*, *s.* incendiary, pl. ගිනිලන්නෝ *ginilannó.*

ගිනිලනවා, *Ginilanawá*, *v.* to set on fire.

ගිනිසිළු, *Ginisiḷu*, *s.* root of the plant leadwort *plumbago rosea;* plant *gloriosa superba:* see ගිනිමුව *ginimuwa.*

ගිනිසැර, *Ginisęra*, *s.* power of fire; fireworks.

ගිනිහල, *Ginihala*, *s.* fire place, room where a fire is kindled.

ගිනිහිරිය, *Ginihiriya*, *s.* small plant *chinoria myxa.*

ගිනිහුල, *Ginihula*, *s.* torch.

ගිනිහොරා, *Ginihorá*, *s.* bird with a long tail, pl. ගිනිහොරු *ginihoru*, 'paradise flycatcher *tersiphone paradisi (Muscicapidæ* order *Passeres);* also called රෙදිහොරා *redihorá.*

ගිම්, *Gim*, *a.* hot. [Colloq. ග්‍රීෂ්ම *gríshma*].

ගිම්උතු, *Gim-utu*, *s.* } (ගිම් heat, උතු season) hot
ගිම්කල්, *Gimkal*, } season.

ගිම්රැස්. *Gimręs*, *s.* (ගිම් fire or heat, රැස් ray) sun [Colloq. සූරියා *súriyá*]

ගිමන්, *Giman*, *s.* heat.

ගිමන්හරිණවා, *Gimanhariṇawá*, *v.* to cool one's self by resting during or after a journey.

ගිය, *Giya*, *s.* clarified butter.

ගිර, *Gira*, *s.* rock; vomiting.

ගිරඹ, *Giraṃba*, *s.* species of mango tree, *mangifera indica.*

ගිරය, *Giraya*, *s.* instrument for cutting the areca nut, resembling a pair of scissors. pl. ගිරා *girá.*

ගිරවා, *Girawá*, *s.* parrot, pl. ගිරව් *giraw*, *(genus palæornis* order *Psittaci)*

ගිරා, *Girá*, *s.* vomiting; parrot; colour blue; speech.

ගිරා අඹ, *Girá-aṃba*, see ගිරඹ *giraṃba.*

ගිරාකුරුල්ලා, *Girákurullá*, *s.* green bulbul *phyllornis jerdoni*, Malabar green bulbul, *p. mabaricus, (Brachypodidæ* order *Passeres).*

ගිරාපලා *Girápalá s.* creeping plant, *Commelina elevata* or *c. salicifolia (Commelinaceæ).*

ගිරාමලිච්චියා, *Girámalichchiyá*, *s.* Ceylonese lorikeet, *loriculus indicus (Psiitaci).*

ගිරාවන්, *Giráwan*, *s.* (ගිරා green, වන් colour) the colour green, parrot colour.

ගිරාවලයා, *Giráwalayá*, *s.* kind of fish.

ගිරි, *Giri*, *s.* small rat; mouse; act of swallowing; mountain, hill; disease of the eyes: wooden ball for playing with: *a.* venerable, respectable.

ගිරික, *Girika*, *s.* tree *spathodea indica.*

ගිරිකණ්ටක, *Girikaṇṭaka*, *s.* (ගිරි mountain, කණ්ටක thorn) Indra's thunderbolt, referring to its splitting or tearing the rocks.

ගිරිකඳුර, *Girikandara*, *s.* cave, cavern.

ගිරිකර්ණී, *Girikarṇní*, *s.* plant *ipomœa zeylanica;* another plant *clitoria tornatea*, [Colloq. කටරොළු *kaṭaroḷu*].

ගිරිකර්ණිකා, *Girikarṇniká*, *s.* (ගිරි and කර්ණිකා ear) the earth. [Colloq. පොළව *poḷawa.*]

ගිරිකා, *Giriká*, *s.* small rat; mouse.

ගිරිකාණ, *Girikána*, *s.* blind or one-eyed man, one blind from a particular disease.

ගිරිකුල, *Girikula*, *s.* large rock, mountain, rock.

ගිරිගබ්භාර, *Girigabbhára*, *s.* natural or artificial cave in a rock.

ගිරිජ්වර, *Girijwara*, *s.* (ගිරි and ජ්වර heat or what burns) the thunder bolt.

ගිරිජ, *Girija*, *s.* (ගිරි and ජ born) talc; benzoin or gum benjamin; bitumen; iron. [Colloq. ගල් මද *galmada*].

ගිරිජා. *Girijá*, (derived as before) the mountain born, a gum resin, styrax; one of the names of Párvatí, as daughter of the personified Himálaya mountain; pumplemose, *citrus decumana;* plant, a white species of *rásná*. [Colloq. වන මොර *wanamora*].

ගිරිජාමල, *Girijámala*, *s.* (ගිරිජ *girija* mountain born, අමල *amala* clear) talc.

ගිරිණි, *Girini*, *s.* wife.

ගිරිතලා, *Giritalá*, *s.* the summit of a rock; plant, kind of basil.

ගිරිති, *Giriti*, *a.* vexing, tearing.

ගිරිතිල්ල, *Giritilla*, *s.* creeping plant, peculiar to Ceylon, *Argyreia populifolia, (Convolvulaceæ).*

ගිරිදි, *Giridi*, see ගිරිඳු *girindu*.

ගිරිදුන්, *Giridun*, name of Durgá, the wife of Şiva.

ගිරිදුන්හිමි, *Giridunhimi*, *s.* (ගිරිදුන් and හිමි lord) name of Şiva.

ගිරිඳු, *Girindu*, *s.* king or chief of mountains, Mount Méru; one of the names of Şiva.

ගිරිනිල්, *Girinil*, *s.* plant *chinoria myxa*.

ගිරිනිවෙස්, *Giriniwes*, *s.* fabulous mountain Kailása, the residence of Şiva.

ගිරිමල්ලිකා, *Girimallikú*, *s. echites antidysenterica*, [Colloq. කෙළිඳ *kelinda*].

ගිරිමාන, *Girimána*, *s.* (ගිරි mountain, මාන a measure) that which resembles a mountain in bulk, a large and powerful elephant.

ගිරිමාලක, *Girimálaka*, *s.* Coraiya tree; also, *cathartocarpus fistula*. [Colloq. ඇසල *esala*]

ගිරිමාලකා, *Girimálaká*, *s.* see ගිරිමල්ලිකා *girimalliká*, plant *echites antidysenteria*.

ගිරිමෙඛල, *Giriménkhala*, *s.* (formed from the same primitives as ගිරිමාන *girmána)* an elephant resembling a mountain in bulk, *i. e.* the elephant of Márayá, the noted demon and opposer of Buddha in his assumption of the sacred office of Buddhaship.

ගිරිමෙවුල්, *Girimevul*, *s.* Márayá's elephant; see මාර *mára*.

ගිරිය, *Giriya*, *s.* inner part of the throat, the part between the top and the trunk of any palm tree.

ගිරිරද, *Girirada*, *s.* (ගිරි and රද king) one of the six names of Mahá-méru.

ගිරිලෙන, *Girilena*, *s.* natural or artificial cave in a rock.

ගිරිවස්, *Giriwas*, *s.* name of Şiva; lion, see ගිරි නිවෙස් *giriniwes*.

ගිරිශ, *Girişa*, *s.* (ගිරි and ශී *şí* to sleep) name of Şiva, in allusion to his inhabiting the mountain Kailási, or frequenting the Himálaya range of mountains.

ගිරිශෘඞ්ග, *Girişringa*, *s.* (ගිරි mountain, ශෘඞ්ග peak) name of Ganésa alluding to his bulk.

ගිරිස, *Girisa*, see ගිරිශ *Girişa*.

ගිරිසතුරු, *Girisaturu*, *s* (ගිරි and සතුරු an enemy) unicorn, alluding to the fable of his piercing the rocks with his horn. [Colloq. කඟවේණ *Kanga wéná*].

ගිරිසාර, *Girisára*, *s.* (ගිරි and සාර essence) iron; tin; name of the Malaya mountains situated in the south of India.

ගිරිසිඛර, *Girisikhara*, *s.* summit of a rock or mountain; cave in a rock.

ගිරිසුතා, *Girisutá*, *s.* Párvatí, wife of Şiva.

ගිරිහඩු, *Girihadu*, *s.* barren place, wilderness.

ගිරේ, *Giré*, *s.* see ගිරය *giraya*.

ගිල්ම, *Gilma*, *s.* moat.

ගිල්ලවනවා, *Gillawanawá*, *v.* to cause to swallow, to drench, to immerse, to drown: pret. ගිල්ලෙව්වා *gillewwá*.

ගිල, *Gila*, *s.* citron; swallowing

ගිලදමනවා, *Giladamanawá*, *v.* to swallow greedily, to gulp: pret. ගිලදැම්මා *gilademmá*.

ගිලන්, *Gilan*, *a.* sick, diseased, afflicted, decrepit, infirm, emaciated with age, fatigue, or sickness; *s.* whey.

ගිලන්පස, *Gilanpasa*, see ගිලානපච්චය *gilánapachchaya*.

ගිලනා, *Gilaná*, *s.* sick man.

ගිලපු, *Gilapu*, past part. pass, of ගිලිනවා *gilinawá*.

ගිලම්පස. *Gilampasa*, *s.* sick diet? of Buddhist priests; refreshments taken by them in the afternoon and evening: incorrectly for ගිලන්පස *gilanpasa*.

ගිලාන, *Gilána, a.* sick, diseased.

ගිලානප්‍රත්‍යය, *Gilánapratyaya,* } *s.* things proper
ගිලානපච්චය, *Gilánapachchaya,* } to be eaten by
ගිලානපඩය, *Gilánapaḍaya,* } a priest; medicament or medicine in general.

ගිලි, *Gili, s.* falling, swallowing, eating.

ගිලිනවා, *Gilinawá, v.* to swallow: pret. ගිල්ලා *gillá.*

ගිලිහුම *Gilihuma, s.* act of falling to the ground.

ගිලිහෙනවා, *Gilihenawá, v.* to fall to the ground; to drop, as fruit, flowers, etc, from trees: pret. ගිලිහුනා *gilihuná.*

ගිලු, *Gilu, a.* swallowed.

ගිලුන, *Giluna, s.* that which has been swallowed, sunk as in water or mud.

ගිලෙනවා, *Gilenawá, v.* to be swallowed up or absorbed; to sink: pret. ගිලුනා *giluná.*

ගිලේගන්නවා, *Giléganawá, v.* to swallow with difficulty, to be suffocated, to stop in the throat.

ගිව්, *Giw,* Elu form of ග්‍රිව *gríwa* which see.

ගිවිස්සනවා, *Givissanawá, v.* to promise, to convince, to prove: pret. ගිවිස්සුවා *givissuwá.*

ගිවිස, *Givisa, part.* promised, having agreed.

ගිවිසගන්නවා, *Givisagannawá, v.* to promise, to contract.

ගිවිසි, *Givisi, a.* promised, agreed.

ගිවිසිනවා, *Givisinawá, v.* to promise, to agree, to make a contract: pret. ගිවිසුනා *givisuná.*

ගිවිසිම, *Givisíma,* } *s.* agreement, promise, con-
ගිවිසුම, *Givisuma,* } tract, compact, pl. ගිවිසුම් *givisum.*

ගිවුලු, *Giwulu, s.* wood apple, *feronia elephantum,* [Colloq. දිවුල් *diwul*].

ගිහි, *Gihi, a.* not in the priesthood; *s.* householder as opposed to a Buddhist monk.

ගිහිගේ, *Gihigé, s.* household, family.

ගිහිනි, *Gihini, a.* inherent, possessed of.

ගිහිපන්නෙ, *Gihipanne, s.* household furniture.

ගිහිබන්‍ධනය, *Gihibandanaya,* } *s.* married state, lit-
ගිහිබන්ධනං, *Gihibandhanaŋ,* } erally state of a man bound to a family.

ගිහියා, *Gihiyá, s.* householder, family man, laic; opposite to a hermit or Buddhist ascetic or priest, who lives in a state of celibacy; one not in the priesthood.

ගිහිවිනය, *Gihivinaya, s.* book so called, containing directions for the conduct of a householder or family.

ගී, *Gí, s.* clarified cow-butter; singing.

ගී කියනවා, *Gí-kiyanawá, v.* (ගී song, කියනවා to say) to sing, to chant.

ගී කිම, *Gí-kíma, s.* psalmody, song.

ගීගනවා, *Gíganawá, s.* priest of the goddess Pattini, capua who repeats songs while worshipping; singing songs.

ගීත, *Gíta, s.* singing; song, either general or particular.

ගීතා, *Gítá, a.* sung, chanted, sounded, etc., name often applied to books, but particularly such as consist of Gátrás or measured lines.

ගීතිකාව, *Gítikáwa, s.* song, chant, psalm, hymn, ode, singing.

ගීතු, *Gítu, s.* vain or empty talk, old woman's fables.

ගීතු කියනවා, *Gítu-kiyanawá, v.* to murmur, to grumble.

ගීරස, *Gírasa, s.* sweet or musical sound or voice.

ගීෂ්පති, *Gíshpati, s.* name of Vṛihaspati, regent of the planet Jupiter and preceptor of the gods; learned paṇḍit or teacher.

ගුග්ගුල, *Guggula,* Páli form of ගුගුලු *gugulu,* which see.

ගුගුරණවා, *Guguraṇawá, v.* to thunder; to roar as wild beasts; to make a loud noise, as the sea: pret. ගිගුරුවා *giguruwá.*

ගුගුල්, *Gugul, s.* plant, *amyrus agallocha*; balm.

ගුගුළු, *Guguḷu, s.* fragrant gum resin, *bdellium*; murunga tree, *moringa pterygosperma.*

ගුච්ඡ, *Guchchha, s.* cluster of blossoms, as that of the palm or cocoa-nut tree; clump of grass; collection, assemblage; bundle; kind of necklace.

ගුච්ඡපත්‍ර, *Guchchha-patra, s.* (ගුච්ඡ and පත්‍ර leaf) palm tree.

ගුච්ඡි, *Guchchhi, s.* species of bonduc.

ගුජ්ජරය, *Gujjaraya, s.* modern Guzeratta or Gujerat.

ගුජනා, *Gujaná, s.* red onion, *allium cepa,* [Colloq. රතුලූනු *ratulúnu.*]

ගුජුන්, *Gujun,* see ගැජුන් *gejun.*

ගුඤ්ජ, *Gunja, s.* cluster of blossoms, as that on the cocoa-nut tree; nosegay.

ගුඤ්ජා, *Gunjá, s.* small shrub, *abrus precatorius,* [Colloq. ඔලිඳ *olinda*], bearing a red and black seed, which forms the smallest of the jeweller's weights; the seed averages about one five sixteenth gr. troy; kettle drum; low murmuring, sound indistinctly heard as the sound of the sea; reflection, meditation.

ගුටිකා, *Guṭiká*, *s.* pill, bolus; small globe or ball.

ගුටිය, *Guṭiya*, *s.* blow, stroke, lump, handful, ball, sphere.

ගුඩ්ඩයා, *Guḍḍayá*, *s.* stupid man, fool.

ගුඩ, *Guḍa*, *s.* globe, ball; jaggery, coarse sort of sugar, raw sugar, powdered sugar; trappings or armour of an elephant; mouthful.

ගුඩත්වච්, *Guḍatwach*, *s.* aromatic bark of the woody cassia.

ගුඩත්වච, *Guḍatwacha*, *s.* cassia bark; mace.

ගුඩපල, *Guḍapala*, *s.* tree, *careya arborea*, [Colloq. කහට *kahaṭa*].

ගුඩපලා, *Guḍapalá*, *s.* tree, commonly called lovi lovi, *flacourtia inermis*.

ගුඩඵල, *Guḍaphala*, see ගුඩපල *guḍapala*.

ගුඩවෘක්ෂ, *Guḍawṛiksha*, *s.* (ගුඩ sugar, වෘක්ෂ tree) sugar cane. [Colloq. උක්ගහ *ukgaha*.]

ගුඩා, *Guḍá*, *s.* plant called milk hedge, *euphorbia tirucalli;* [Colloq. නවහඳී *nawahandi*], see ගුලා *gulá*; powder, any pounded substance.

ගුඩාකේශ, *Guḍákéṣa*, *s.* (ගුඩා plant *euphorbia*, කේශ hair) he whose hair forms matted locks, resembling in shape the leaves of the plant *euphorbia;* one of the names of Ṣiva and of Arjuna.

ගුඩු, *Guḍu*, *a.* well-dried.

ගුඩුගෙඩිය, *Guḍugeḍiya*, see ගුඩුපොල් *guḍupol*.

ගුඩුචි, *Guḍuchí*, *s.* twining plant, *tinospora cordifolia*, [Collq. රසකිඳ *rasakiṉda*].

ගුඩුපොල්, *Guḍupol*, *s.* dried cocoa-nut.

ගුණ්ඨිත, *Gunṭhita*, *a.* pounded, ground.

ගුණ, *Guṇa*, *s.* virtue; quality, attribute or property in general; property of humanity; film over the eye; multitude; heap; advantage, happy consequence; fastening, securing; means of defence; form, shape etc., property of the body; knowledge, ignorance etc., or quality of the mind; heroism, valour, etc.; colour, white, black etc.; observance of the ordinances of Buddha; an organ of sense; rope, string, bow string; excellency, freedom from fault or blemish: *a.* subordinate, secondary.

ගුණධර්මය, *Guṇadharmaya*, *s.* virtue incident to certain qualities; clemency is the virtue of royalty, holiness that of the priesthood.

ගුණමකු, *Guṇamaku*, *a.* (ගුණ excellence, මකු erasing) detracting, depreciating another's worth, envious.

ගුණරතන, *Guṇaratna*, *s.* (ගුණ and රතන gem) jewel of virtue.

ගුණවත්, *Gaṇawat*, } *a.* (ගුණ and වත් or වන්ත
ගුණවන්ත, *Guṇawanta*, } poss. aff.) humane, virtuous, kind, merciful, benevolent.

ගුණවන්තකම, *Guṇawantakama*, *s.* humanity, amenity, benevolence, pl. ගුණවන්තකම් *guṇawantakam*.

ගුණවෘක්ෂ, *Guṇawṛiksha*, *s.* (ගුණ rope, වෘක්ෂ tree) mast, mast of a ship.

ගුණා, *Guṇá*, *s.* plant of the fibres of which bow strings are made, *sanseviera zeylanica.* [Colloq. නියඳ *niyaṉda*.]

ගුණාකර, *Guṇákara*, *s.* (ගුණ *guṇa* excellence, ආකර *ákara* mine) mine of excellence or merit, name or title of Buddha.

ගුද, *Guda*, *s.* anus.

ගුදකීලක, *Gudakílaka*, *s.* (ගුද and කීලක pin or boll) piles.

ගුදපියස, *Gudapiyasa*, *s.* (ගුද and පියස district) fundament.

ගුදම, *Gudama*, *s.* (Portuguese) store-house, cellar, godown, pl. ගුදම් *gudam*.

ගුදමාර්ගය, *Gudamárgaya*, see ගුද *guda*.

ගුදිරිඤ්ඤ, *Gudiriññe*, } *s.* mattrass, bolster. pl.
ගුදිරිම, *Gudirima*, } ගුදිරිඤ්ඤ *gudiriñña*.

ගුදෙ, *Gudé*, see ගුද *guda*.

ගුන්දිරා පොල්, *Gundirá-pol*, *s.* kind of cocoa nut imported from the Maldive isles.

ගුන්ද්‍ර, *Gundra*, } *s.* kind of grass, *saccharum sara;*
ගුන්ද්‍රා, *Gundrá*, } another species of fragrant grass, *cyperus pertenuis; c. rotundus*, [Colloq. කලාඳුරු *kaláṉduru*].

ගුනය, *Gunaya*, see ගුණ *guṇa*.

ගුනරුක්, *Gunaruk*, see ගුණවෘක්ෂ *guṇawṛiksha*.

ගුප්ත, *Gupta*, *a.* preserved, protected; hidden, concealed; joined, combined; invisible, withdrawn from sight.

ගුප්ති, *Gupti*, *s.* concealment; protection, preserving; cavern; sink, cellar, etc., place of concealment; prison; name of Yama regent of the dead.

ගුබ්බායම, *Gubbáyama*, *s.* hovel, hut of the Roḍiyas; sometimes written කුප්පායම *kuppáyama*.

ගුඹ, *Gumba*, *s.* multitude, collection, heap; thicket.

ගුම්, *Gum*, *s.* sound, noise, roaring.

ගුම, *Guma*, *s.* heat. [Colloq. ග්‍රීෂ්ම *gríshma*.]

ගුමු, *Gumu*, *s.* beating; fence of bushes cut down and placed at the foot of a tree, to give notice by the rustling of the approach of wild beasts; thicket, live hedge, grove.

ගුය්හය, *Guyhaya*, ගුය්හස්ථානේ, *Guyhastáné*, } *s.* virile member.

ගුරණ, *Guraṇa*, *s.* effort, perseverance; great or continued exertion.

ගුරු, *Guru*, *s.* planet Jupiter; teacher, schoolmaster, preceptor; religious teacher, one who explains the law and religion to his pupils and instructs them in the sástras; parent; this person may be either the natural parent or religious preceptor; father, or any venerable male relation; term of respect applied to a man sustaining place in the character of a teacher; among the Hindus a kind of spiritual guardian of youth; name of Vṛihaspati the preceptor of the gods; mixture of red chalk; long vowel; sound equal to two mátras or simple sounds: *a.* heavy, weighty, great, large or eminent; difficult, arduous; best, excellent.

ගුරු අකුරු, *Guru-akuru*, *s.* the letters which are given as models to the scholars to write.

ගුරුකම, *Gurukama*, *s.* office of a teacher, lesson.

ගුරුකීන, *Gurukína*, *s.* tree, *Calophyllum Burmanni (Guttiferæ).*

ගුරුගල, *Gurugala*, *s.* red chalk, or as sometimes applied, red orpiment; gold.

ගුරුගිනි, *Gurugini*, *s.* large or very destructive fire.

ගුරුදින, *Gurudina*, *s.* Thursday.

ගුරුන්නාන්සේ, *Gurunnánsé*, *s.* teacher, preceptor, honorific of ගුරු *guru.*

ගුරුනු, *Gurunu*, *s.* melting, dissolving.

ගුරුපඬුර, *Gurupaṇḍura*, *s.* offerings or gifts to teachers or instructors.

ගුරුල්ල, *Gurulla*, *s.* shrub, *Leea sambucina (Ampelideæ);* also called බුරුල්ල *burulla.*

ගුරුලේත්තුව, *Gurulèttuwa*, *s.* goglet, goblet,

ගුරුවරයා, *Guruwarayá*, *s.* teacher, school-master.

ගුරුවා, *Guruwá*, *s.* juggler, sleight of hand man; name of a sea fish.

ගුරුහිනි, *Guruhini*, *s.* deficiency.

ගුරුහෝරාව, *Guruhóráwa*, *s.* the power or influence which the planet Jupiter is said to have on the affairs of men every Thursday morning during the space of one hour.

ගුරුළා, *Guruḷá*, *s.* imaginary monstrous bird, see ගරුඩ *garuḍa.*

ගුරුළුදද, *Guruḷudada*, *s.* name of Vishṇu; it is the Elu form of ගරුඩධ්වජ *garuḍadhwaja.*

ගුල්ඵ, *Gulpha*, *s.* ankle. [Colloq. වලලුකර *walalukara*].

ගුල්ම, *Gulma*, *s.* spleen; division of an army; body of troops consisting of nine platoons, or nine elephants, nine chariots, twentyseven horse, and fortyfive foot; shrub, bush, clump of grass, etc. fort, intrenchment; disciplining an army, keeping it in a posture of defence; wharf or stairs; disease, chronic enlargement of the spleen, or an induration of the mesenteric glands so as to be perceived externally; according to others an enlargement of the intestines by worms.

ගුල්මමූල, *Gulmamúla*, *s.* ginger.

ගුල්මි, *Gulmi*, *s.* tent; plant, *emblic myrobalan* or *phyllanthus emblica,* [Colloq. නෙල්ලි *nelli*]; small sort of cardamons, [Colloq. එන්සාල් *ensál*]; cluster or clump of trees; multitude of thickets.

ගුල්මිනී, *Gulminí*, *s.* spreading creeper, any creeping plant.

ගුල්‍ය, *Gulya*, *s.* sweetness, saccharine taste.

ගුල්ලා, *Gullá*, *s.* very small insect which perforates timber, rice-worm, pl. ගුල්ලෝ *gulló.*

ගුල, *Gula*, *s.* food; juice of the sugar cane; raw, or unrefined sugar; vent, small cavity; hole; pl. ගුල් *gul.*

ගුලපිණ්ඩය, *Gulapiṇḍaya*, *s.* ball of jaggery or country raw sugar.

ගුලපුෂ්ප, *Gulapushpa*, *s.* Indian tree (not found in Ceylon); its sweet flowers are eaten under the name of mahwa, *bassia latifolia.*

ගුලා, *Gulá*, *s.* plant, *euphorbia tirucalli:* [Colloq. නවහන්දි *nawahandi*].

ගුලාමා, *Gulámá*, *s.* dirty mean fellow, sloven, pl. ගුලම්මු *gulammu.*

ගුලි, *Guli*, *s.* pill, bolus, any small globular substance, ball, lump.

ගුලිගහනවා, *Guligahanawá*, *v.* to make pills, etc.

ගුලු, *Gulu*, *s.* falling, sinking; name of tree.

ගුලුඅරුත්, *Guluarut*, *s.* hidden, (in meaning).

ගුලුගුරුවා, *Guluguruwá*, *s.* bird called white eyebrowed bulbul, *ixos luteolus (Brachypodidæ* order *Passeres).*

ගුවන්, *Guwan*, ගුවන්මග, *Guwanmaga*, ගුවන, *Guwana*, } *s.* sky, firmament, visible heavens. [Colloq. අහස *ahasa.*]

ගුවාක, *Guwáka*, *s.* areca nut tree, [Colloq. පුවක් *puwak*].

ගුහ්‍යක, *Guhyaka*, *s*, kind of demon or demigod attendant upon Kuvéra the deity of wealth, and guardian of his treasures.

ගුහ්‍යකේශ්වර, *Guhyakésẉara*, *s.* name of Kuvéra the Indian Plutus.

ගුහ, *Guha*, *s.* name of Kártikéya or, as he is called in Ceylon, Kataragama deviyo.

ගුහා, *Guhá*, *s.* plant, *hedysarum lagopodioides.* [Colloq. පස්වැන්න *paswẹnna*].

ගුහාරය, *Guháraya*, } *s.* any large cavity, cave,
ගුහාව, *Guháwa*, } natural cave in a rock, place of concealment; cavern, hole, pit, vault.

ගුහාශයෝ, *Guháṣayó*, *s.* (ගුහා cave, ආශය *áṣaya* asylum) lion, [Colloq. සිංහයා *siṇhayá*].

ගූ, *Gú*, *s.* dung, fæces.

ගූඪ, *Gúḍha*, *a.* hidden, concealed, secret.

ගූඪජ, *Gúḍhaja*, *s.* (ගූඪ hidden or secret, ජ born) son of a concealed birth; *a.* born privately of a woman whose husband is absent and the real father unknown.

ගූඪපාද්, *Gúḍhapád*, *s.* (ගූඪ and පාද *páda* foot) snake. [Colloq. සර්පයා *sarpayá*].

ගූඪපුරුෂ, *Gúḍha-purusha*, *s.* (ගූඪ and පුරුෂ man) spy, secret emissary.

ගූථ, *Gútha*, *s.* dung, fæces, ordure.

ගූථ කූපය, *Gútha-kúpaya*, *s.* cess-pool, water-closet.

ගූථ නරකය, *Gútha-narakaya*, *s.* hell of ordure.

ගූන, *Gúna*, *a.* voided as ordure.

ගූරණ, *Gúraṇa*, *s.* effort, exertion.

ගූරේන්ද, *Gúrẹnda*, *s.* tree, *celtis cinnamomea, (Urticaceæ).*

ගෙ, *Ge*, *s.* house, dwelling house, pl. ගෙවල් *gewal.*

ගෙකුස, *Gekusa*, *s.* interior of a house.

ගෙජ්ජ, *Gejja*, *s.* small bell or tinkling ornament used by dancers, pl. ගෙජ්ජි *gejji.*

ගෙඩිගේ, *Geḍigé*, *s.* ornamental wall surrounding a well; ornamented arch fixed up in front of a house on festive occasions.

ගෙඩිය, *Geḍiya*, *s.* fruit; boil, tumour, pl. ගෙඩි *geḍi.*

ගෙඩියතුර, *Geḍiyatura*, *s.* padlock; also ඉබියතුර *ibiyatura.*

ගෙණයනවා, *Geṇayanawá*, *v.* to carry, to carry off, to convey: pret. ගෙණගියා *genagiyá* or ගෙණිච්චා *geṇichchá.*

ගෙණියනවා, *Geṇiyanawá*, *v.* to carry, to convey.

ගෙණෙනවා, *Geṇenawá*, *v.* to bring: pret. ගෙන්නුවා *gennuwá.*

ගෙත්තම්කරණවා, *Gettamkaraṇawá*, *v.* to sew, to stitch, to patch, to embroider.

ගෙතුන, *Getuna*, *p.* woven, knotted.

ගෙතුම, *Getuma*, *s.* any thing knotted, twisted or platted; twisting.

ගෙදර, *Gedara*, *s.* house with the premises, home.

ගෙදර නම, *Gedara-nama*, *s.* house name, family name.

ගෙදිගුවිල්, *Gediguvil*, *s.* a large and long pond near a house

ගෙඳ, *Genda*, *s.* vegetable used in making curry; purslane, *portulaca oleracea (Portuculaceæ);* lean, thin.

ගෙන්, *Gen*, a particle or termination, sign of the ablative case, as මාගෙන් *mágen*, from me.

ගෙන්වනවා, *Genwanawá*, *v.* to cause to bring: pret. ගෙන්නෙව්වා *gennewwá.*

ගෙපල, *Gepala*, *s.* area or site of a house, pl. ගෙපල් *gepal.*

ගෙපිළිවෙළ, *Gepiḷiweḷa*, *s.* row of houses.

ගෙබිම, *Gebima*, see ගෙපල *gepala.*

ගෙම්බා, *Gembá*, } *s.* frog, general name for
ගෙමඩිත්තා, *Gemaḍittá*, } frog or toad, the most
ගෙමඩියා. *Gemaḍiyá*, } common species found under flower pots, *bufo melanostictus* (order *Batrachia salientia).*

ගෙමව්, *Gemaw*, *s.* (ගේ *gé* house, මව් mother) matron.

ගෙමිණ, *Gemiṇa*, } *s.* (ගේ *gé* and මිණ gem,
ගෙමිතුර, *Gemitura*, } මිතුර sun) lamp. [Colloq. පහන *pahana.*]

ගෙමියුරු, *Gemiyuru*, *s.* (ගේ *gé* and මියුරු peacock) tame or domestic peacock.

ගෙය්‍ය, *Geyya*, *s.* (ගී *gí* to sing, to chant, එය්‍ය *eyya* aff.) one of the nine divisions of sacred science, that which is in gáthás or verses.

ගෙය, *Geya*, *s.* house, dwelling place; song, singing a song, chant; couple.

ගෙයි නම, *Geyi-nama*, see ගෙදර නම *gedara-nama.*

ගෙයුම, *Geyuma*, *s.* exertion, attrition.

ගෙරි, *Geri*, *s.* sort of pismire or black ant; also pl. of ගෙරියා *geriyá.*

ගෙරි ඇට, *Geri-ẹta*, *s.* bones of cattle.

ගෙරිඇට ගස්, *Gerieṭa-gas*, *s.* shrub, *Linociera purpurea:* see ඝෙරිඇට ගස් *gherieṭa-gas.*

ගෙරිකුණ, *Gerikuṇa, s.* carcass, pl. ගෙරිකුණු *gerikuṇu.*

ගෙරිකොකා, *Gerikoká, s.* bird called cattle-egret, *babulcus coromandus (Ardeidæ,* order *Herodiones).*

ගෙරිමස්, *Gerimas, s.* beef.

ගෙරියා, *Geriyá, s.* bull, ox; buffalo; middle sized black ant, beef eater, pl. ගෙරි.

ගෙල්, *Gel, s.* beating.

ගෙල, *Gela, s.* neck, throat.

ගෙලෙමුතු, *Gelemutu, s.* necklace of pearls.

ගෙවදිනවා, *Gewadinawá, v.* to enter a new house, ceremony of considerable importance among the Siŋhalese: pret. ගෙවදුනා *gewaduná.*

ගෙවනවා, *Gewanawá, v.* to pay, to discharge a debt; to rub, to polish, to waste by rubbing, to pass as time: pret. ගෙව්වා *gewwá.*

ගෙවරණ, *Gewaraṇa, s.* wall, walls of a house.

ගෙවල්, *Gewal,* plural of ගේ *gé.*

ගෙවල් කුරුල්ලා, *Gewal-kurullá,* see ගේ කුරුල්ලා *gé-kurullá.*

ගෙවල් බද්ද, *Gewal-badda, s.* tax imposed on house property.

ගෙවල් මියා, *Gewal-miyá, s.* brown rat, *mus decumanus.*

ගෙවා, *Gewá, p.* preterite of ගෙවනවා *gewanawá,* which see.

ගෙවාපු, *Gewápu, p.* paid, discharged (as a debt).

ගෙවිටන්, *Geviṭan, s.* waggon; [Colloquial: රථය *rathaya*]; mixture.

ගෙවීම, *Gevíma, s.* payment, reckoning; verbal noun of ගෙවනවා *gewanawá,* which see.

ගෙවුන, *Gewuna, p.* worn, paid; preterite of ගෙවෙනවා *gewenawá.*

ගෙවුයන, *Gewuyana, s.* (ගේ *gé* house, උයන *uyana* garden) grove, garden near a house.

ගෙවෙනවා, *Gewenawá, v.* to be paid, or spent as time; to wear away, to consume, to fritter.

ගෙහ, *Géha, s.* house, dwelling.

ගෙහිමි, *Gehimi, s.* boundary of a house.

ගෙහෙඩියා, *Geheḍiyá, s.* sort of hornet.

ගේ, *Gé,* Elu form of the Sanskrit, ගේහ *géha* house, dwelling; termination or sign of the genitive case in grammar.

ගේකුරුල්ලා, *Gékurullá, s* sparrow, literally house bird, *passer domesticus (Fringillidæ);* Loten's sun bird, *cynnyris lotenius;* also called රන් සූටික්කා *ran-súṭikká* and මොදරේ සූටික්කා *modare-súṭikká;* purple sun bird, *c. asiaticus: (Cynnyridæ* order *Passeres);* also called ගෙවල් කුරුල්ලා *gewal-kurullá.*

ගේ නම, *Gé-nama, s.* house-name, family name.

ගේනවා, *Génawá, v.* to bring: pret. ගෙනාවා *genáwá.*

ගේසරස, *Gésarasa, s.* (ගේ and සරස lake) pond close to a house.

ගේහ, *Géha, s.* house, dwelling; name of Gaṇéṣa the Hindu god of wisdom who is usually invoked on laying the foundation of a house.

ගේහසූර, *Géhasúra, s.* (ගේහ and සූර hero) cotquean, house hero, slothful and trifling man who is unfit for any thing beyond the concerns of a house

ගේහාංගනය, *Géhánganaya, s.* veranda or terrace of a house; court or yard of a house.

ගේහිමියා, *Géhimiyá, s.* (ගේ and හිමි *himi* lord) landlord, head of a house, pater familias.

ගෛරික, *Gairika, s.* red chalk; red orpiment; [Colloq. සිවංගුරු *siwaṇguru*]; gold; dog.

ගෛරෙය, *Gairéya, s.* red chalk; bitumen; rock moss; *a.* mountain born.

ගෛරෙයි, *Gaireyi, s.* fragrant grass *cyperus rotundus.* [Colloq. කලාඳුරු *kalánduru,*]

ගො, *Go, s.* heaven, paradise; bull; cow; ox; cattle; lizard; earth; ray of light; thunderbolt; moon; sun; sacrifice of a cow; speech.

ගොංකටිල්ලා, *Goŋkaṭillá, s.* kind of fish.

ගොක්කොල, *Gokkola, s.* young shoots of the cocoa-nut leaves which are used for tying the ólas when covering houses, constructing bungalows; they are used also in ornamenting the triumphal arches and festooning houses on festival occasions.

ගොක්ෂුර, *Gókshura, s.* (ගො cow, ක්ෂුර hoof) plant, the leaves of which resemble the hoofs of a cow, *ruellia longifolia,* [Colloq. ගොකටු *gokaṭu*].

ගොකටු, *Gokaṭu, s.* thistles, name of several thorny plants; Gamboge tree, *garcinia morella (Guttiferæ);* also called කනගොරක *kanagoraka.*

ගොකණ්ටක, *Gókaṇṭaka, s.* thistle; goraka tree, *garcinia cambogia.*

ගොකර්ණ, *Gókarṇa, s.* object of sense; span from the tip of the thumb to that of the little finger; kind of deer; mule; class of demigods; snake.

ගොකර්ණී, *Gókarṇi, s.* (ගො cow, කර්ණී ear) plant, the leaves of which are said to resemble the ears of a cow, *sanseviera zeylanica,* [Colloq. නියඳ *niyaṇḍa*].

ගොකිල, *Gókila*, } s. plough; pestle.
ගොකිල, *Gókíla*, }

ගොකුර, *Gokura*, s. cow's hoof.

ගොකුල, *Gókula*, s. (ගො and කුල assemblage) multitude of cows; cow house or station, fold for kine.

ගොගණ, *Gógaṇa*, s. herd of cattle,

ගොචර, *Góchara*, s. object of sense; shape; sound; colour, country, district; food, feeding, provender.

ගොජබ්බා, *Gojabbá*, s. plant, *Hygroriza aristata (Gramineæ)*.

ගොජල, *Gójala*, s. cow's urine.

ගොජාගරික, *Gójágarika*, a. happy, fortunate, auspicious.

ගොජිහ්වා, *Gójiḥwá*, s. (ගො cow, ජිහ්වා tongue) kind of wild pot herb, the leaves of which are compared to the tongues of cattle, *trophis aspera*.

ගොජුර, *Gojura*, s. food, feeding, provender, pl. ගොජුරු *gojuru*. see ගොදුර *godura*.

ගොටු, *Goṭu*, s. cup, any thing made in the resemblance of a cup; tree, *gmelina asiatica*, [Colloq. දෙමට *demaṭa*].

ගොටුකොල, *Goṭukola*, s. herb, generic name of *Hydrocotyle*, see මහ *maha* and හීන් ගොටුකොල *hín-goṭukola*.

ගොටු මල්, *Goṭu-mal*, s. flowers of the foregoing.

ගොටුව, *Goṭuwa*, s. cup made of leaves of any kind, any flexible substance rolled to hold liquid, pl. ගොටු *goṭu*.

ගොඩ, *Goḍa*, s. heap, mass; land, (*i. e.* a place without water); village, hamlet.

ගොඩ ඉත්ත, *Goḍa-itta*, s. plant, *Heptapleurum* (or *Hedera) exaltatum*, *(Araliaceæ)*.

ගොඩ කදුරු, *Goḍa-kaduru*, s. tree, *Strychnos nux vomica (Loganiaceæ)*.

ගොඩ කිරිල්ල, *Goḍa-kirilla*, s. timber tree, Ceylon elm, *Holoptelea* (or *ulmus*) *integrifolia (Urticaceæ)*.

ගොඩනගණවා, *Goḍanagaṇawá*, v. to erect, to raise, to build.

ගොඩනගිනවා, *Goḍanaginawá*, v. to ascend, to mount, to come to land.

ගොඩපර, *Goḍapara*, s. timber tree, *dillenia retusa*, *(Dilleneaceæ)*.

ගොඩබානවා, *Goḍabánawá*, v. to land.

ගොඩබානවා, *Goḍabánawá*, v. to unship, to unload, to discharge; to land, to disembark: pret. ගොඩබෑවා *goḍabẹ́wá*.

ගොඩ මහනෙල්, *Goḍa-mahanel*, } s. bulbous stemless plant, *Crinum zeylanicum* or *C. ornatum*, or *Amaryllis zeylanica (Amaryllideæ)*.
ගොඩ මානිල්, *Goḍa-mánil*, }

ගොඩමේරියා, *Goḍaméríyá*, s. shrub, *barleria cristata*.

ගොඩයා, *Goḍayá*, s. kind of fish; rustic, clown.

ගොඩ වවුලැටිය, *Goḍa-wawuleṭiya*, s. plant, *Mezoneurum enneaphyllum (Leguminosæ)*.

ගොඩහිඟුර, *Goḍahiṉgura*, s. tree, *acacia pennata*.

ගොඩිගලා, *Goḍigalá*, s. bungler, blockhead, pl. ගොඩිගල්ලු *goḍigallu*.

ගොඩැල්ල, *Goḍella*, s. hill; mound, rising ground.

ගොණ්ඩ, *Góṇḍa*, s. prominent navel or a lump of flesh on the navel.

ගොණ *Goṇa*, s. nose, [Colloq. නාසය *násaya*].

ගොණා, *Goṇá*, s. bull, ox, bullock.

ගොත්, *Got*, s. Elu form of ගොත්‍ර *gótra* which see.

ගොත්‍ර, *Gótra*, s. family, race, tribe, lineage, kin; name, appellation; forest; field; umbrella; road; knowledge of futurity; kind of inspiration; genus, class, species; increase, wealth, mountain.

ගොත්‍රජ, *Gótraja*, s. (ගොත්‍ර family, ජ born) relation; in law among the Hindus the term is nearly equivalent to the Gentile of Roman law, and is applied to kindred of the same general family who are connected by offerings of food and water, and stands opposed to the bandhu or cognate kin who do not partake in the offerings made to the common ancestors.

ගොත්‍රභිත්, *Gótrabhit*, } s. (ගොත්‍ර mountain, භිද් who splits) name of Indra alluding to his splitting mountains with his thunderbolt.
ගොත්‍රභිද්, *Gótrabhid*, }

ගොත්‍රභූත, *Gótrabhúta*, see ගොත්‍රජ *gótraja*.

ගොත්‍රා, *Gótrá*, s. earth; herd of kine.

ගොත, *Gota*, a. inarticulate, indistinct in speech, stammering.

ගොතනවා, *Gotanawá*, v. to knot, to plait, to knit, to contrive, to fetter, to weave a net: pret. ගෙතුවා *getuwá*.

ගොතම, *Gótama*, s. one of the Gotama family, epithet of the last Buddha.

ගොතමී, *Gotamí*, see ගොරද *gorada*.

ගොදන්ත, *Gódanta*, s. (ගො cow, දන්ත tooth) fossil substance of a white colour, apparently an earthy salt, and so called from its resemblance to a cow's tooth; it is found in great abundance on the sea shore; cow's tooth; yellow orpiment, [Colloq. හිරියල් *hiriyal*].

ගොදුර, *Godura. s.* food; prey, plunder, Elu form of ගෝචර *góchara.*

ගොදුරු, *Goduru, s.* five senses; food, victuals, see the preceding.

ගොදුරු බොක්ක, *Goduru-bokka, s.* stomach.

ගොන්, *Gon, plur.* of ගොණා *goṇá.*

ගොන් කදුරු, *Gon-kaduru, s.* tree, *Cerbera odollum (Apocynaceæ).*

ගොන්කම, *Gonkama, s.* stupidity.

ගොන්කවඩා, *Gonkawaḍá*, ගොන්කවඩිච්චා, *Gonkawaḍichchá*, ගොන්කවඩියා, *Gonkawaḍiyá*, } *s.* Ceylonese myna, *acridotheres melanosternus, (Sturnidæ* order *Passeres).*

ගොන්කැකිරි, *Gonkękiri, s.* kind of cucumber, *Cucumis pubescens (Cucurbitaceæ).*

ගොන්ගා, *Gongá, s.* large cowrie.

ගොන්ගෙය, *Gongeya, s.* (ගොණා *goṇá* ox, ගෙය couple) yoke of oxen.

ගොන්ගෝරිය, *Gongóriya, s.* bullock's hump.

ගොන්ටා *Gonṭá, s.* properly ඝොණ්ටා *ghonṭá*, which see.

ගොන්න, *Gonna, s.* tree, *Diospyros insignis (Ebenaceæ);* also called පොරුවමල්ල *poruwamalla* and වල්මැදිරිය *walmędiriya.*

ගොන්බෙල්ලා, *Gonbellá, s.* snail, sometimes written ගොම්බෙල්ලා *gombellá, helix.*

ගොන්බෙලි කොකා, *Gonbeli-koká, s.* bird called shell ibis, *anastomus oscitans (Plataleidæ* order *Herodiones).*

ගොනගුල්, *Gonagul*, ගොනඟුල්, *Gonangul*, } *s.* black faced monkey.

ගොනටු, *Gonaṭu, s.* benches placed at the distance of a mile from each other, on the high road side, for travellers to rest upon.

ගොප් ඇටය, *Gop-ęṭaya, s.* ankle.

ගොප් මස, *Gop-masa, s.* calf of the leg.

ගොපලංගා, *Gopalangá, s.* plant, *Corallocarpus epigæa (Cucurbitaceæ).*

ගොපලා, *Gopalá. s.* cow-herd, or cow-keeper, pl. ගොපල්ලු *gopallu.*

ගොපසඳුන්, *Gopasandun, s.* white kind of sandal wood, *syrium myrtifolium.*

ගොපු, *Gopu, s.* poison,

ගොපොල්ලා, *Gopollá, s.* cowherd.

ගොබඩු, *Gobaḍu, a.* tender, (as tender cocoa-nut).

ගොබය, *Gobaya. s.* topmost shoot of a plant, bud.

ගොබොල්ල, *Gobolla, s.* tender cocoa-nut.

ගොම්, *Gom, s.* rock, stone, sun-beam; keeper, guard, preserver, protector.

ගොම, *Goma, s.* cow dung.

ගොමඬල, *Gomanḍala, s.* enclosure for cattle, [Colloq. ගාළ *gáḷa*].

ගොමතිල්ලා, *Gomatillá, s.* kind of fish.

ගොමතැම්බ, *Gomatęmba, s.* heap of cow dung, cow clap.

ගොමරිට්ට, *Gomariṭṭa, s.* moss growing on heaps of cow dung, pl. ගොමරිටි *gomariṭi.*

ගොමවැරටි, *Gomawęraṭi, s.* dried cow dung, used in some parts of India as fuel.

ගොමහත්ත, *Gomahatta, s.* mushroom.

ගොමු, *Gomu, s.* cow's urine.

ගොමුඩු, *Gomuḍú, s.* stall, place for keeping cattle.

ගොමුව, *Gomuwa, s.* small room at the end of a house formed by the roof being continued, small outer verandah; thicket.

ගොයම් කපනවා, *Goyam-kapanawá, v.* to reap.

ගොයම, *Goyama, s.* corn, grain in general, harvest, pl. ගොයම් *goyam.*

ගොයා, *Goyá, s.* land lizard, viz. iguana, *varanus dracæna,* [Colloquial: තලගොයා *talagoyá*] and *hydrosaurus salvator,* [Colloq. කබරගොයා *kabaragoyá*]; *(order Sauria).*

ගොයි, *Goyi, plur.* of ගොයියා *goyiyá.*

ගොයි කර්මාන්තය, *Goyi-karmántaya, s.* husbandry, cultivation of the ground.

ගොයිගම, *Goyigama, s.* caste so called, vellála, husbandmen.

ගොයිගම කාක්කා, *Goyigama-kákká. s.* another name for the black crow, commonly called කාක්කා *kákká, corone macrorhynea (Corvidæ* order *Passeres).*

ගොයිතැන, *Goyitena, s.* cultivation.

ගොයිපල, *Goyipala, s.* cultivated or arable ground, field.

ගොයිබිම, *Goyibima, s.* cultivated ground as corn or paddy fields.

ගොයියා, *Goyiyá, s.* husbandman, cultivator of the ground.

ගොයියෝ, *Goyiyó, s.* a term used in friendly conversation in second person singular vocative case.

ගොයි වසම, *Goyi-wasama, s.* occupation of a cultivator, agricultural tribe.

ගොයිවැල්, *Goyiwęl, s.* plant, *Flagellaria indica (Flagellariaceæ).*

ගොයු, *Goyu, s.* freckle; slave.

ගොයුම්, *Goyum, a.* descended from Gotama.

ගොයුම්ගොත්, *Goyumgot, s.* (ගොයුම් Gótama, ගොත් race or caste) family or race from which Gautama Buddha was descended.

ගොර, *Gora*, *a.* white, [Colloq. සුදු *sudu*]; causing fear.

ගොරක, *Goraka*, *s.* acid fruit used in making curries, tree, *garcinia cambogia (Guttiferæ).*

ගොරකයා, *Gorakayá*, *s.* child, infant.

ගොරතර, *Goratara*, *a.* very dreadful, terrible.

ගොරද, *Gorada*, *s.* bezoar stone found in the stomach of cattle; wild fellow; crocodile.

ගොරබා, *Gorabá*, *s.* pigeon, [Colloq. පරවියා *paraviyá*].

ගොරවනවා, *Gorawanawá*, *v.* to snore, to growl, to rumble as thunder; pret. ගෙරෙව්වා *gerewwá*.

ගොරොක්, *Gorok*, *s.* old person; affliction; any hard or heavy substance, assistance; *garcinia cambogia.*

ගොල්ල, *Golla*, *s.* party, relations, grove.

ගොල, *Gola*, *s.* blow; distress; *a.* short.

ගොලගැට, *Golageṭa*, *s.* inside part of an half baked ball or cake.

ගොලහැල, *Golahẹla*, *s.* deep hole, full of mud.

ගොලා, *Golá*, } *s.* snail, *helix.*
ගොලුබෙල්ලා, *Golubellá*, }

ගොලෝව, *Golówa*, *s.* glass globe, globe lamp. (Eng.)

ගොව්වා, *Gowwá*, *s.* keeper of cattle, watcher, protector.

ගොවද, *Gowada*, *s.* enclosure for cattle, cow pen, [Colloq. ගාළ *gáḷa*].

ගොවිකුලය, *Govikulaya*, see ගොයිගම *goyigama;* cultivators of the ground.

ගොවිඳු, *Govindu*, *s.* name of Vishṇu; Elu form of ගෝවින්ද *góvinda*, which see.

ගොවියා, *Goviyá*, see ගොයියා *goyiyá.*

ගොස්, *Gos*, *s.* noise. roaring of thunder; *part.* having gone.

ගොස, *Gosa*, *s.* noise, sound, thunder.

ගොසඳුන්, *Gosandun*, see ගොපසඳුන් *gopasandun.*

ගොසින්, *Gosin*, *part.* having gone.

ගොහොඩු, *Gohodu*, *a.* miry, muddy.

ගොහොරු, *Gohoru*, *s.* mire, muddy place or hole.

ගොළු, *Goḷu*, *a.* dumb, shallow.

ගොළුමූද, *Goḷu-múda*, *s.* the sea not far from the land, the shallow sea.

ගොළුමොර, *Goḷumora*, *s.* plant peculiar to Ceylon, *Pygeum Wightiana (Rosaceæ);* also called කන් කුඹල් කොටියා *kankumbal-koṭiyá.*

ගොළුවා, *Goḷuwá*, *s.* dumb man.

ගෝ අං, *Gó-an*, *s.* bullock's horn.

ගෝකන, *Gókana*, *s.* bull, ox, bullock.

ගෝට්ටිය, *Góṭṭiya*, *s.* noise.

ගෝටවිය, *Góṭaviya*, *s.* helm of a ship or any vessel.

ගෝණ, *Góna*, see ගොණ *goṇá.*

ගෝණිය, *Góṇiya*, *s.* sack, cloth bag.

ගෝදාන, *Gódána*, *s.* presents distributed by the surviving relations of a person at his death, for the benefit of his soul; namely to procure freedom from all liability to be born again; the most valuable gift is that of a cow, from which the word is formed.

ගෝදාරණ, *Gódáraṇa*, *s.* (ගෝ earth, දාරණ what cleaves or splits) plough; spade, hoe.

ගෝධන, *Gódhana*, *s.* (ගෝ cow, ධන wealth) herd of cattle.

ගෝධා, *Gódhá*, *s.* iguana, see ගොයා *goyá;* leather fence worn by archers on the left arm to prevent its being injured by the bow-string; alligator.

ගෝධුම, *Gódhuma*, *s.* wheat.

ගෝධූම, *Gódhúma*, *s.* wheat, orange; name of a drug

ගෝනක, *Gónaka*, *s.* kind of fleecy counterpane.

ගෝනකොල, *Góna-kola*, *s.* generic name of *adenosma*, see කහ ගෝනකොල *kaha-gónakola* and නිල් ගෝනකොල *nil-gónakola.*

ගෝනන්දි, *Gónandí*, *s.* female of the Sáras or Indian crane.

ගෝනමුවා, *Gónamuwá*, *s.* elk of Ceylon, *Rusa aristotelis.*

ගෝනර්දී, *Gónarda*, *s.* Sáras or Indian crane; fragrant grass *cyperus rotundus.* [Colloq. කලාඳුරු *kalándurū.*]

ගෝනල, *Gónala*, *s.* esculent root, sort of yam or country potatoe.

ගෝනවැල්, *Góna-weḷ*, *s.* plant, peculiar to Ceylon *Ancistrocladus Vahlii (Ancistrocladeæ).*

ගෝනස, *Gónasa*, *s.* viper, [Colloq. පොලඟා *polangá*].

ගෝනා, *Góná*, *s.* elk, *rusa aristotelis*, pl. ගෝන්නු *gónnu.*

ගෝනාස, *Gónása*, *s.* (ගො ox, නාස nose) large snake, considered by some the boa constrictor from its nose resembling that of an ox.

ගෝනුන්, *Gónun*, acc. *plur.* of ගෝනා *góná.*

ගෝනුස්සා, *Gónussá*, *s.* scorpion, *Scolopendra.*

ගෝනැස්, *Gónẹs*, *s.* rafter.

ගෝප, *Gópa*, *s.* herdsman; head of a cowpen; cowherd; milk man; superintendent of a district; king; myrrh.

ගෝපක්ෂ්ම, *Gópakshma*, *s.* one of the thirty-two personal beauties of Buddha, namely the beauty of his eyelashes.

ගෝපක, *Gópaka*, *s.* myrrh; herdsman, cow-herd; superintendent of a district.

ගෝපති, *Gópati*, *s.* (ගෝ earth, පති lord of master) name of Ṣiva, Indra; sun; king; bull.

ගෝපනය, *Gópanaya*, *s.* protection, safeguard, preserving.

ගෝපයියා, *Gópayiyá*, *s.* sort of tick or body louse.

ගෝපල්, *Gópal*, *s.* herdsman, cow keeper.

ගෝපා, *Gópá*, *s.* milk-woman, female cowherd.

ගෝපානසි, *Gópánasi*, *s.* wood of a thatch roof, rafter.

ගෝපායිත, *Gópáyita*, *a.* preserved, guarded, saved.

ගෝපාල, *Gópála*, *s.* king, sovereign, cowherd.

ගෝපාලයා, *Gópálayá*, *s.* (ගෝ earth, පාල *pála* who protects) king; sovereign; cow-herd; name of Kṛishṇa.

ගෝපි, *Gópí*, *s.* plant, *echites frutescens*, cowherd's wife; protectoress; nature, natural disposition or property.

ගෝපුර, *Gópura*, *s.* door, town gate, ornamented gateway of a temple; gate in general; kind of grass, *cyperus rotundus*.

ගෝපුරීෂ, *Gópurísha*, *s.* cowdung.

ගෝපෙන්ද්‍ර, *Gópendra*, *s.* (ගෝප *gópa* cow herd, ඉන්ද්‍ර *indra* lord or chief) name of Kṛishṇa or Vishṇu, alluding to his being the chief or lord of the herdsmen or cattle keepers.

ගෝබර, *Góbara*, *s.* spots on the body.

ගෝභව, *Góbhawa*, see ගොරද *gorada*.

ගෝමය, *Gómaya*, *s.* cow-dung; nature or property of a cow.

ගෝමර, *Gómara*, *s.* yellow spot on the skin, spot, freckle, or any cutaneous mark.

ගෝමර පිළිහුඩුවා, *Gómara-piḷihuḍuwá*, *s.* red kingfisher, *Ceryle rudis* (*Alcedinidæ* order *Picarii*), also called වතුරනුවා *waturanuwá*.

ගෝමරිටා, *Gómariṭá*, *s.* wood wagtail, *limonidromus indicus;* Richard's pipit *corydalla Richardi* (*Motacillidæ*); Indian skylark *alauda gulgula;* Madras bush lark, *mirafra affinis* (*Alaudidæ*, order *Passeres*).

ගෝමායු, *Gómáyu*, *s.* jackall; Gándharba or celestial musician; bile or bilious humour of the cow.

ගෝමි, *Gómi*, } in Páli ගොමික, *a.* rich in
ගෝමින්, *Gómin*, } herds, rich in kine; an honourary epithet.

ගෝමුඛ, *Gómukha*, *s.* chasm in the Himálaya mountains, through which the Ganges flows, erroneously conceived by the natives of the East to be of the shape of a cow's mouth.

ගෝමූත්‍ර, *Gómútra*, *s.* cow's urine.

ගෝමේද, *Góméda*, *s.* (ගෝ eye, මේද to anoint) gem of a yellow colour; topaz? kind of poison, (see කාකොල *kákóla*,) smearing the body with unguents.

ගෝමේධ, *Gómédha*, } *s.* (ගෝ cow, මේධ sacri-
ගෝමැඩල, *Gómeḍala*, } fice) sacrifice of a cow.

ගෝයුග, *Góyuga*. *s.* (ගෝ and යුග yoke) yoke of oxen.

ගෝයෝනිය, *Góyóniya*, *s.* state of birth as cattle.

ගෝර්ද, *Górda*, *s.* brain. [Colloq. මොලේ *molé*.]

ගෝරංකු, *Góraṇku*, *s.* water fowl; prisoner; naked man; mendicant etc. wandering about naked.

ගෝරක්ෂා, *Górakshá*, *s.* (ගෝ and රක්ෂා who keeps) cow keeper; preserver of kine; orange.

ගෝරස, *Górasa*, *s.* milk, [Colloq. අමුකිරි *amu-kiri*]; curdled or coagulated milk, [Colloq. මුදවාපු කිරි *mudawápu-kiri*]; buttermilk, [Colloq. මෝරු *móru*].

ගෝරිපු, *Góripu*, *s.* (ගෝ cattle, රිපු enemy) tiger [Colloq. කොටියා *koṭiyá*].

ගෝරෝචන, *Góróchana*, *s.* bezoar stone found in the stomachs of cattle.

ගෝල, *Góla*, *s.* circle, ball, any thing round, or globular; globe, sphere; wooden ball with which children play; woman's female friend; Godáviry river; large water jar; ink; red arsenic; name of the goddess Durga; diminutive person; *a.* relative to disciple or pupil.

ගෝලයා, *Gólayá*, *s.* scholar, disciple.

ගෝලිස, *Gólisa*, } *s.* tree, *bignonia indica*. [Colloq.
ගෝලිහ, *Góliha*, } වල් පලොල් *wal-palol*].

ගෝලෝමි, *Gólómí*, *s.* orris root; arrow grass with white blossoms; root of the plant sweet flag *acorus calamus*, [Colloq. වදකහ *wadakaha*]; harlot.

ගෝවජ, *Gówaja*, *s.* (ගෝ and වජ enclosure) cow-pen.

ගෝවන්. *Gówan*, *s.* dusky red or brown colour.

ගෝවා, *Gówá*, *s.* cabbage, *brassica oleracea*.

ගෝවිට්, *Góviṭ*, *s.* cow dung, [Colloq. ගොම *goma*].

ගෝවින්ද, *Góvinda*, *s.* one who has the principal charge of cattle; one of the most usual appellations of Kṛishṇa or of Vishṇu in that form; name of Vṛihaspati or Jupiter.

ගෝව්‍රජ, *Góvraja*, *s.* station for cattle.

ගෝවෘන්ද, *Góvṛinda*, *s.* property in cattle; herd of cattle.

ගෝශීර්ෂ, *Góṣírsha*, *s.* kind of sandal of the colour of brass and of great fragrance.

ගෝෂ්ඨ, *Góshṭha*, *s.* cowpen; fold for cattle; station of cowherds.

ගෝෂ්ඨී, *Góshṭhí*, *s.* school; assembly, meeting; conversation.

ගෝෂා, *Góshá*, *s.* corruptly for ඝෝෂා *ghóshá*, sound, noise, tumult, uproar.

ගෝස්තන, *Góstana*, *s.* udder of a cow, garland consisting of four or thirty-four strings; cluster of blossoms; nosegay.

ගෝස්තනී, *Góstaní*, *s.* grape, [Colloq. මිදි ගෙඩිය *midigeḍiya*].

ගෝස්තරය, *Góstaraya*, *s.* food, corrupt form of ගෝචර *góchara*.

ගෝස්මෙස, *Gósmesa*, *s.* kind of bird of the gull tribe, *larus* (order *Gaviæ*).

ගෝස, *Gósa*, *s.* gum; myrrh; last watch of the night, day-break.

ගෝසං, *Gósaṉ*, see කළුදුරු *kaḷuduru*.

ගෝසංඛ්‍ය, *Gósaṉkhya*, *s.* herdsman, cow keeper.

ගෝසුව, *Gósuwa*, *ad.* much.

ගෝහිරිපන්, *Góhiri-pan*, *s.* plant, *Cyperus pumilus* (*Cyperaceæ*).

ගෝළුගන්නවා, *Góḷugannawá*, *v.* to shout in anger, to scold.

ගෞ, *Gau*, corrupt form of ගව් *gaw*, which see.

ගෞතම, *Gautama*, *s.* name of Buddha which he took from his teacher a celebrated sage and supposed by some to be the founder of the Náya philosophy: so our first Edition, but Burnouf says, "Gautama was the sacerdotal family name of the Ṣákyas who being Kshatriyas had no ancestor or tutelary saint like the Brahmans, but might as the Hindu law permits have taken the name of the sage to whose family belonged their spiritual guide."

ගෞධාර, *Gaudhára*, } *s.* (ගොධා *godhá* alligator,
ගෞධෙය, *Gaudheya*, } අරක් *arak* aff. of descent) iguana, considered as the offspring of the alligator, [Colloq. තලගොයා *talagoyá*].

ගෞනව්සව, *Gaunawsawa*, *s.* poison, one of the fixed kinds, mineral or vegetable.

ගෞර, *Gaura*, *s.* colour white, yellow, pale, red; [Colloquial: හිරියල් *hiriyal*]; filament of lotus; gold; saffron; tree, *grislea tomentosa; a.* clean, cleansed, pure.

ගෞරව, *Gaurawa*, *s.* honour; respect, veneration; consequence or weight.

ගෞරවකටයුතු, *Gaurawa-kaṭayutu*, *a.* reverend, honourable.

ගෞරවකරණවා, *Gaurawa-karaṇawá*, *v.* to respect, to venerate.

ගෞරවනීය, *Gaurawaníya*, see ගෞරවකටයුතු *gaurawakaṭayutu*.

ගෞර සර්ෂප, *Gaura-sarshapa*, *s.* white mustard, *sinapis alba*.

ගෞරා, *Gaurá*, } *s.* name of the goddess Párvatí;
ගෞරී, *Gaurí*, } young girl, eight years old; any young girl prior to menstruation, maid, virgin; name of a river; wife of the deity Varuṇa; earth; turmeric; yellow dye; plant, see රොචනී *róchaní*; plant bearing fragrant seed, see ප්‍රියඞ්ගු *priyaṅgu*; white kind of durva or bent grass; Arabian jasmine; sacred basil.

ගෞලිකා, *Gaulíká*, *s.* lizard; name of plant, *portulaca oleracea*: purslane.

ගෞව්‍ය, *Gauwya*, *s.* (corruptly for ගව්‍ය *gawya*) curds; butter.

ගෞව, *Gauwa*, *s.* (corruptly for ගව්ව *gawwa*) distance of 5600 yards.

ගැජුන්, *Gejun*, } Elu form of ගර්ජනාව *garjanáwa*,
ගැජුම්, *Gejum*, } which see.

ගැටය, *Geṭaya*, *s.* knot; joint in a reed or bamboo, etc. pl. ගැට *geṭa*.

ගැටඔළුව, *Geṭa oḷuwa*, *s.* plant, *Clinogyne virgata* (*Scitamineæ*).

ගැටකපන්නා, *Geṭa-kapanná*, *s.* pick pocket.

ගැටකරවලා, *Geṭa-karawalá*, *s.* kind of snake.

ගැටකින, *Geṭa-kína*, *s.* sort of tree, *calophyllum calaba*.

ගැටකහඹිලිය, *Geṭa-kahaṃbiliya*, *s.* species of nettle, *urtica heterophylla*.

ගැටකොල, *Geṭakola*, *s.* plant, with short branching stem, *Hedyolis auricularia*, (*Rubiaceæ*).

ගැටගහනවා, *Geṭagahanawá*, *v.* to tie with a knot.

ගැටතුඹ, *Geṭa-tumba*, *s.* plant, *leucas zeylanica* (*Labiatæ*).

ගැටතෝර, *Geṭa-tóra*, *s.* sort of pepper, *piper betle.*

ගැටනිටුල්, *Geṭa-niṭul*, *s.* small tree, *Streblus asper* or *trophis aspera* (*Urticaceæ*).

ගැටනිමුල්, *Geṭanimul*, *s.* ornament.

ගැට දන්, *Geṭa-dan*, *s.* plant, *calyptranthes caryophyllata*.

ගැටපදය, *Geṭapadaya*, *s.* explanation of difficult terms; glossary.

ගැටපන්, *Gęṭa-pan*, *s.* species of club rush, *scirpus lateralis.*

ගැටපහටු, *Gęṭapahaṭu*, *s.* musical instrument.

ගැටපිච්ච, *Gęṭa-pichcha*, *s.* sort of jasmine, *jasminum sambac.*

ගැටපුරුක්විල, *Gęṭapurukvila*, *s.* plant, *bergia verticillata.*

ගැට පොලඟා, *Gęṭa-polan͟gá*, *s.* kind of snake.

ගැටබෙරය, *Gęṭaberaya*, *s.* sort of tom-tom, or native drum.

ගැටඹළුවා, *Gęṭam͟baḷuwá*, *s.* kind of grass, *maranta paniculata.*

ගැටමාමේරු, *Gęṭamáméru*, *s.* species of pepper, *piper betle*, [Colloq. බුලත්වැල් *bulat-węl*].

ගැටමි කරවලා, *Gęṭamí-karawalá*, *s.* kind of snake.

ගැටමි පොලඟා, *Gęṭamí-polan͟gá*, *s.* kind of snake.

ගැටමොන, *Gęṭamona*, *s.* plant, *andropogon caricosus.*

ගැටයා, *Gęṭayá*, *s.* young man not arrived at puberty, not come to maturity, boy.

ගැටලනවා, *Gęṭalanawá*, see ගැටගහනවා *gęṭagahanawá.*

ගැටවටු, *Gęṭawaṭu*, *s.* kind of button or loop in the priest's robes, button.

ගැටවරයා, *Gęṭawarayá*, *s.* young man, youth.

ගැටවරා, *Gęṭawará*, *s.* young fruit.

ගැට වෙනිවැල, *Gęṭa-weniwęla*, *s.* creeper plant, *cissampelos convolvulus.*

ගැටසු, *Gęṭasu*, *s.* thief, robber.

ගැටහූ, *Gęṭahú*, *s.* (ගැට knot or lump, හූ thread) knotted thread.

ගැටිය, *Gęṭiya*, *s.* brim, edge, rim; plant, මහ *maha* or බූගැටිය *búgęṭiya*, *Hugonia mystax (Linaceæ).*

ගැටිස්සි, *Gęṭissi*, *s.* young girl not arrived at puberty.

ගැටේ වැටෙනවා, *Gęṭé-węṭenawá*, *v.* to miscarry.

ගැඩපණුවා, *Gęḍa-paṇuwá*, *s.* kind of long worm, ground worm.

ගැඩඹු, *Gęḍam͟bu*, see ගැඩුඹු *gęḍum͟bu.*

ගැඩලු, *Gęḍalu*, *s.* red worm.

ගැඩවි, *Gęḍavi*, *s.* bow of Arjuna.

ගැඩවිලා, *Gęḍavilá*, *s.* kind of ground worm.

ගැඩු, *Gęḍu*, } *s.* tree, *Trema orientalis (Urticaceæ).*
ගැඩුඹු, *Gęḍum͟bu*, }

ගැණ, *Gęṇa*, *ad.* concerning, respecting, about, etc. *s.* fire.

ගැණිම, *Gęṇíma*, *s.* act of taking, act of counting; *verb.* noun of ගන්නවා *gannawá*, to take.

ගැත්තා, *Gęttá*, }
ගැති, *Gęti*, } *s.* servant.
ගැතියා, *Gętiyá*, }

ගැබ්, *Gęb*, plural of ගැබ *gęba*; *s.* inside of the squares that compose a priest's robe.

ගැබ්ගන්නවා, *Gębgannawá*, *v.* to conceive.

ගැබ, *Gęba*, *s.* water pot; wooden fork; womb, belly, pl. ගැබ් *gęb.*

ගැබදුනු, *Gębadunu*, *s.* conception.

ගැබනි, *Gębaní*, see ගැබිණි *gębiṇi.*

ගැබපෙරහැර, *Gębaperahęra*, *s.* (ගැබ embryo, පෙරහැර ceremony) festive ceremony performed on conception.

ගැබර, *Gębara*, *s.* child in the womb; depth.

ගැබලි, *Gębali*, *s.* juice or sap of trees and fruit.

ගැබසිරි, *Gębasiri*, *s.* pregnancy, considered as a fortunate omen.

ගැබසිරු, *Gębasiru*, *s.* time immediately after conception.

ගැබිණි, *Gębiṇí*, *s.* pregnant woman.

ගැඹුර, *Gęm͟bura*, *s.* depth, profundity.

ගැඹුරු, *Gęm͟buru*, *a.* deep, profound, difficult to be understood.

ගැමි, *Gęmi*, *s.* villager, countryman.

ගැමිඅරුත්, *Gęmiarut*, *s.* clown, plebeian, rustic,

ගැමිදං, *Gęmidan̄*, corrupt form of the following.

ගැමිදම්, *Gęmidam*, *s.* copulation.

ගැමිදුද, *Gęmiduda*, *s.* the words of the populace.

ගැරඬිදුල්, *Gęran͟ḍi-dúl*, *s.* plant, *ichnocarpus frutescens.*

ගැරඬියා, *Gęran͟ḍiyá*, *s.* rat snake, *ptyas mucosus*; see ගරඬියා *garan͟ḍiyá.*

ගැරද්ධ, *Gęraddha*, *s.* plant, *arum colocasia.*

ගැරහුම්, *Gęrahum*, *s.* ridicule, banter, despising.

ගැරහුම්කරණවා, *Gęrahum-karaṇawá*, *v.* to ridicule, to banter, to despise.

ගැරහුම, *Gęrahuma*, *s.* ridiculing.

ගැල්, *Gęl*, plural of ගැළ *gęḷa.*

ගැල් අකුර, *Gęl-akura*, *s.* axle tree of a cart.

ගැල් නාබිය, *Gęl-nábiya*, *s.* nave of a cart wheel.

ගැල් පදිනවා, *Gęl-padinawá*, *v.* to drive a cart, (bullock bandy).

ගැල්ම, *Gęlma*, *s.* sinking; flowing.

ගැල්විය, *Gęlviya*, *s.* yoke of a cart.

ගැල්සක, *Gęl-saka*, *s.* cart wheel.

ගැලවීම, *Gęlavíma*, *s.* escape, deliverance; salvation.

ගැලවුම්කාරයා, *Gęlawumkárayá*, *v.* Saviour.

ගැලවෙනවා, *Gęlawenawá*, *v.* to escape, to be delivered; to be saved.

ගැලීම, *Gélíma*, *s.* sinking: flood, pl. ගැලීම් *gęlím.*

ගැලෙනවා, *Gęlenawá*, *v.* to sink: pret. ගැළුනා *gęluná.*

ගැලොම, *Gęloma*, *s.* gallon, (Eng.) pl. ගැලොම් *gęlom.*

ගැවසීම, *Gęwasíma*, *s.* verbal noun of ගැවසෙනවා *gęwasenawá.*

ගැවසෙනවා, *Gęwasenawá*, *v.* to be covered or overspread, to frequent: pret. ගැවසුනා *gęwasuná.*

ගැවුරු, *Gęwuru*, *s.* affection, esteem, honour.

ගැස්ම, *Gęsma*, *s.* tremulous motion, shivering, shaking, wavering.

ගැස්සීම, *Gęssíma*, *s.* drawing the trigger of a gun, striking against, act of starting.

ගැස්සෙනවා, *Gęssenawá*, *v*, to shake, to quiver, to be affected by a tremulous motion, to strike against or to knock involuntarily: pret. ගැස්සුනා *gęssuná.*

ගැසීම, *Gęsíma*, *s.* stroke, blow, striking.

ගැසෙනවා, *Gęsenawá*, *v.* to knock, to strike against; to crack; to quake, to quiver, to be agitated: pret. ගැසුනා *gęsuná.*

ගැහැටු, *Gęhętu*, *a.* tired, fatigued, wearied; teazed, vexed, troubled, [Colloq. වෙහෙස *wehesa*].

ගැහැණි, *Gęhęni*, *s.* fatigue, wearisomeness; woman.

ගැහැණිවෙනවා, *Gęhęniwenawá*, *v.* to be fatigued, to be wearied.

ගැහුනු, *Gęhunu*, *a.* thick.

ගැළ, *Gęla*, *s.* sort of cart or waggon, [Colloq. කරත්තය *karattaya*]. pl. ගැල් *gęl.*

ගැළපෙනවා, *Gęlapenawá*, *v.* to join, to join together, to unite, to be conjugated, to be joined: pret. ගැළපුනා *gęlapuná.*

ගෑ, *Gę*, *part.* smeared, rubbed over, plastered.

ගෑටෙනවා, *Gętenawá*, *v.* to crowd, to press close together, to waddle: pret. ගෑටුනා *gętuná.*

ගෑණි, *Gęni*, *s.* woman, female.

ගෑණුසතා, *Gęnusatá*, *s.* female animal.

ගෑම, *Géma*, *s.* daubing, smearing, plastering; verb. noun of ගානවා *gánawá.*

ගෑවෙනවා, *Géwenawá*, *v.* to be smeared, to be daubed, to have applied any unctuous substance, to come in contact.

ගෑහුම්, *Géhum*, *s.* thunder.

ග්‍රජන, *Grajana*, *s.* murungá.

ග්‍රන්ථ, *Grantha*, *s.* knot, tying or stringing; book or any composition in verse; poetical stanza; metre or measure of thirty-two syllables; wealth, property.

ග්‍රන්ථකාර, *Granthakára*, *s.* author of a book.

ග්‍රන්ථධුරය, *Granthadhuraya*, *s.* (ග්‍රන්ථ and ධුර *dhura* office) instruction of pupils in temples or houses by priests, not in deserts or as ascetics.

ග්‍රන්ථනයකරණවා, *Granthanaya-karaṇawá*, *v.* to twist, to twine, to plait, to string, to tie; to improve, to edify, to teach.

ග්‍රන්ථි, *Granthi*, *s.* knot or joint of a reed or cane, etc. and figuratively of the body; knot or tie in a cord etc.; distortion; rheumatism; crookedness.

ග්‍රන්ථික, *Granthika*, *s.* astrologer, fortune teller; thorny plant, *capparis aphylla*, described as growing in deserts and fed upon by camels; root of long pepper, [Colloq. තිප්පිලිමුල් *tippili-mul*]; kind of rosin, *bdellium;* perfume.

ග්‍රන්ථිකා, *Granthiká*, see ග්‍රන්ථික *granthika.*

ග්‍රන්ථිමූලා, *Granthi-múlá*, *s.* plant, *hemedesmus indicus.* [Colloq. ඉරමුසු *iramusu.*]

ග්‍රන්ථිලොමක, *Granthilómaka*, see ගෝලෝමි *gólómí.*

ග්‍රන්ථිස්ථාන, *Granthisthána*, *s.* very difficult passage of a book.

ග්‍රහ, *Graha*, *s.* taking by acceptance or seizure; eclipse of the sun or moon, see රාහු *Ráhu;* planet; name of Ráhu or the ascending node; imp, goblin; effort in battle; tenacity; perseverance; favour, patronage.

ග්‍රහණ, *Grahaṇa*, *s.* taking, seizure; receiving, acceptance; assent; agreement; respect; hand; eclipse of the sun or moon, which is fabled to result from the Asura Ráhu seizing and attempting to swallow the sun or moon; comprehension, taking or receiving instruction.

ග්‍රහණි, *Grahaṇi*, *s.* diarrhæa, dysentery.

ග්‍රහණික, *Grahaṇika*, *a.* belonging to diarrhœa.

ග්‍රහණීය, *Grahaṇiya*, *part.* to be taken.

ග්‍රහණෙ, *Grahaṇe* *s.* corruptly for ග්‍රහණය *grahaṇaya.*

ග්‍රහතාරකාව, *Graha-tárakáwa*, *s.* fixed star; asterism, constellation.

ග්‍රහාධාර, *Grahádhára*, *s.* (ග්‍රහ *graha* planet, ආධාර *ádhára* asylum) constellation dhruva or polar star; it has this name in allusion to its remaining fixed amidst the planetary movements.

ග්‍රාම්‍ය, *Grámya*, *s.* rustic or homely speech; rustic (in discourse).

ග්‍රාම්‍ය ධර්ම, *Grámya-dharma*, *s.* (ග්‍රාම්‍ය village, ධර්ම virtue) village virtue, copulation.

ග්‍රාම්‍යාශ්ව, *Grámyáṣwa*, *s.* (ග්‍රාම්‍ය *grámya* and අශ්ව *aṣwa* horse) ass.

ග්‍රාමය, *Grámaya*, *s.* village, hamlet; scale in music; multitude; castle.

ග්‍රාමික, *Grámika*, *a.* resident in a village, rustic, village born.

ග්‍රාමීණ, *Gráminа*, *s.* villager; dog; crow; indigo plant.

ග්‍රාසය, *Grásaya*, *s.* mouthful, lump of rice etc.

ග්‍රාහ, *Gráha*, *s.* taking or seizure; shark; alligator.

ග්‍රීවය, *Gríwaya*, *s.* neck, [Colloq. බෙල්ල *bella*]; back part of the neck, nape; debt.

ග්‍රීවරාව, *Gríwaráwa*, *s.* (ග්‍රීව throat, රාව sound) hoarseness, speaking in the throat.

ග්‍රීවාභරණ, *Griwábharaṇa*, *s.* (ග්‍රීව *gríwa* neck, ආභරණ *ábharaṇa* ornament) neck ornament.

ග්‍රීෂ්ම, *Gríshma*, *s.* heat; warmth, hot season; *a.* hot, warm.

ග්‍රීෂ්ම ඍතුව, *Gríshma-rituwa*, } *s.* hot season,
ග්‍රීෂ්ම කාලය, *Gríshma-kálaya*, } (June-July).

ගෘඤ්ජන, *Gṛiñjana*, *s.* poisoned flesh, flesh of an animal destroyed by poison; garlic, [Colloq. සුදු ලූනු *sudulúnu*].

ගෘධ්‍ර, *Gṛiddhra*, *a.* desirous, greedy; *s.* vulture.

ගෘෂ්ටි, *Gṛishṭi*, *s.* cow that has had one calf; plant, *lycopodium imbricatum;* jujube tree, [Colloq. මසං *masaṇ*]; pig.

ගෘහ, *Gṛiha*, *s.* house, mansion, dwelling, habitation, [Colloq. ගෙ *gé*]; wife; name, appellation.

ගෘහකන්‍යා, *Gṛihakanyá*, *s.* aloe, *aloe perfoliata.*

ගෘහගර්භය, *Gṛiha-garbhya*, *s.* inner part of a house, inner room

ගෘහගෝලිකා, *Gṛihagóliká*, *s.* (ගෘහ house, ගෝලික lizard) small house lizard, [Colloq. හූනා *húná*].

ගෘහද්‍රුම, *Gṛihadruma*, *s* tree, *cordia myxa*, [Coll: ලෝළු *lóḷu*],

ගෘහධූම, *Gṛiha-dhúma*, *s.* (ගෘහ house, ධූම smoke) house smoke.

ගෘහනාශන, *Gṛihanáṣana*, *s.* (ගෘහ and නාශන what destroys or defaces) common house pigeon, so called in consequence of its defacing the house where it builds its nest, [Colloq. පරෙවියා *pareviyá*].

ගෘහපතියා, *Gṛihapatiyá*, *s.* (ගෘහ house, පති *pati* chief) head or lord of a family; householder; householder of particular merit, giving alms and performing all the prescribed duties of religion; virtue, especially of a householder, hospitality; sun, (derived from ගෘහ planet, පති lord.)

ගෘහපතිරත්න, *Gṛihapati-ratna*, *s.* (ගෘහපති and රත්න gem) one of the seven gems of a universal emperor; viz. a man who possesses the faculty of discovering hid treasures.

ගෘහබන්ධනය, *Gṛihabandhanaya*, *s.* (ගෘහ house, බන්ධන bound) family tie, household life.

ගෘහමණි, *Gṛihamaṇi*, *s.* (ගෘහ and මණි jewel) lamp, [Colloq. පාන *pána*].

ගෘහරාජ, *Gṛiharája*, *s.* (ගෘහ planet, රාජ king) sun; moon; planet Jupiter, or its regent.

ගෘහවස්තුව, *Gṛihawastuwa*, *s.* site of a house or dwelling.

ගෘහස්ථ, *Gṛihastha*, *s.* (ගෘහ house, ස්ථ dwelling) householder, master of a house, one performing all the duties of a house and father of a family, laic, the opposite to the Buddhist priesthood.

ගෘහස්ථකම, *Gṛihasthakama*, *a.* dwelling in a house; domestic state; having a house and family.

ගෘහස්ථයා, *Gṛihasthayá*, *s.* householder.

ගෘහාරාම, *Gṛiharáma*, *s.* (ගෘහ house, ආරාම *aráma* grove) garden or grove near a house.

ගෘහිණී, *Gṛihiṇí*, *s.* female housekeeper, wife.

ගෘහිත, *Gṛihíta*, *a.* taken, attached, seized, caught.

ගෘහෝද්‍යානය, *Gṛihódyánaya*, *s.* (ගෘහ *gṛiha* house, උද්‍යාන *udyána* garden) garden attached to a house.

ගෘහෝදරය, *Gṛihódaraya*, *s.* (ගෘහ *gṛiha* house, උදර *udara* inner part) inside of a house.

ගෘඪ, *Gṛiḍha*, corrupt form of ගූඪ *gúḍha*, which see.

ඝ

The fourth consonant in the Siṇhalese alphabet; it is the preceding consonant aspirated and sounds like *gh* in ghastly.

ඝං, *Ghaṇ*, *s.* bell; any tinkling ornament; killing; striking.

ඝට්ට, *Ghaṭṭa*, *s.* quay or landing place.

ඝට්ටනා, *Ghaṭṭaná*, *s.* going, moving; covering; touching, striking.

ඝට, *Ghaṭa*, *s.* earthen water jar, chatty; assembly; among the Hindus a suspending the breath as a religious exercise; grinding; effort or exertion.

ඝටන, *Ghaṭana*, *s.* mixing; effort; assembling, collection, bringing together.

ඝටනවා, *Ghaṭanawá*, *v.* to grind; to twist; to tie; ensnare; to mix.

ඝටනා, *Ghaṭaná*, see ඝටන *ghaṭana*.

ඝටා, *Ghaṭá*, *s.* effort, exertion, endeavour; assemblage; troop of elephants.

ඝටික, *Ghaṭika*, *s.* posteriors, waterman.

ඝටිකා, *Ghaṭiká*, *s.* ancle; period of time, sixtieth part of a day and night, or twenty-four minutes.

ඝටිකාර, *Ghaṭikára*, corruptly for ඝටීකාර *ghaṭíkára*.

ඝටිතෝදනය, *Ghaṭitódanaya*, *s.* food, prepared victuals.

ඝටී, *Ghaṭí*, *s.* plate of iron or mixed metal on which the hours are struck, Indian clock; water jar.

ඝටීකාර, *Ghaṭíkára*, *s.* (ඝටී water jar, කාර who makes) potter.

ඝටියන්ත්‍රය, *Ghaṭi-yantraya*, *s.* rope and bucket of a well, any machine for raising water.

ඝණ්ටා, *Ghaṇṭá*, *s.* bell; plate of iron or mixed metal for the purpose of being struck as a bell.

ඝණ්ටාරය, *Ghaṇṭáraya*, *s.* bell.

ඝණ්ටිකා, *Ghaṇṭiká*, *s.* uvula or soft palate.

ඝණවිට්භිදී, *Ghaṇaviṭbhidí*, *s.* sort of cucumber, [Colloq. තියඹරා *tiyambará*].

ඝත, *Ghata*, *s.* ghee or clarified butter.

ඝතෝදන, *Ghatódana*, *s.* (ඝත *ghata* and ඕදන *ódana* boiled rice) food, victuals prepared from boiled rice and ghee or clarified butter.

ඝන, *Ghana*, *a.* thick, gross, coarse, solid, without interstices; material, auspicious, fortunate; permanent, eternal; *s.* thickness; cloud; iron club; cymbal; bell; gong; any brazen or composite metallic instrument which is struck as a clock etc., iron; skin, rind, bark; body; hardness, solidity, substance, matter; fragrant grass, *cyperus rotundus*.

ඝනකඵ, *Ghanakapha*, *s.* (ඝන cloud, කඵ phlegm) hail.

ඝනකම, *Ghanakama*, *s.* thickness.

ඝනකාල, *Ghanakála*, *s.* (ඝන cloud, කාල time or season) rainy season; wet cloudy weather.

ඝනප්‍රජා, *Ghanaprajá*, *s.* tree, *bassia latifolia;* liquorice, [Colloq. වැල්මී *wẹlmí*].

ඝනප්‍රිය, *Ghanapriya*, *s.* (ඝන wet or moist weather, ප්‍රිය what delights) swallow, [Colloq. වැහිලිහිණියා *wẹhi-lihiṇiyá*].

ඝනමූල, *Ghanamúla*, *s.* cube root.

ඝනමූලිකා, *Ghanamúliká*, *s.* tree, *celastrus emarginatus.*

ඝනරස, *Ghanarasa*, *s.* camphor; water; extract, decoction etc., thick juice; plant, *sanseviera zeylanica*, [Colloq. නියඳ *niyaṉda*].

ඝනසාර, *Ghanasára*, *s.* camphor, [Colloq. කපුරු *kapuru*]; mercury; water.

ඝනාකර, *Ghanákara*. *s.* (ඝන *ghana* rain, අකර *ákara* mine) rainy season.

ඝනෝදධි, *Ghanódadhi*, *s.* (ඝන *ghana* large, උදධි *udadhi* ocean) division of hell.

ඝර්ඝර, *Gharghara*, *s.* door; gate; owl; laughter, mirth; river so called, the Gogra.

ඝර්ඝරා, *Ghargharā*, *s.* one of the tones or notes in music; kind of lute.

ඝර්ඝරිකා, *Gharghariká*, *s.* river so called; musical instrument; small bells; fried grain.

ඝර්ඝරී, *Ghargharí*, *s.* girdle of small bells or any tinkling ornaments worn by women.

ඝර්ම, *Gharma*, *s.* heat; warmth, hot season; sunshine; sweat, perspiration.

ඝර්මාංශු, *Gharmáṇṣu*, *s.* (ඝර්ම *gharma* and අංශු *aṇṣu* ray) sun.

ඝර්මාභිතප්ත, *Gharmábhitapta*, *a.* (ඝර්ම *gharma* and අභිතප්ත *abhitapta* oppressed or fatigued) oppressed with heat, fainting from heat.

ඝර්මික, *Gharmika*, *a.* (ඝර්ම *gharma* heat, ඉක *ika* affix) hot.

ඝර්ෂණය, *Gharshaṇaya*, *s.* grinding, pounding; striking.

ඝර්ෂණී, *Gharshaṇí*, *s.* turmeric, [Colloq. කහ *kaha*].

ඝර, *Ghara*, *s.* house, [Colloq. ගේ *gé*].

ඝරණී, *Gharaṇí*, *s.* wife.

ඝස්මර, *Ghasmara*, *a.* gluttonous, voracious, greedy of food.

ඝාට, *Gháṭa*, *s.* nape or back of the neck.

ඝාත, *Gháta*, *s.* murder, killing, slaughter.

ඝාතක, *Ghátaka*, *s.* murderer, slaughterer, killer.

ඝාතකරණවා, *Ghátakaraṇawá*, *v.* to destroy life, to kill.

ඝාතන, *Ghátana*, *s.* killing, slaughtering, murdering.

ඝාතුක, *Ghátuka*, *a.* mischievous; hurtful; cruel, savage, violent, ferocious.

ඝාස, *Ghása*, *s.* meadow grass; food, eating, enjoyment.

ඝුට, *Ghuṭa*,
ඝුටි, *Ghuṭi*, } *s.* ancle, [Colloq. බොලටය *bolaṭaya*].

ඝුණ්ඩා, *Ghuṇḍá*, *s.* large black bee.

ඝුණ, *Ghuṇa*, *s.* kind of insect found in timber.

ඝුණප්‍රිය, *Ghuṇapriya*, *s.* (ඝුණ and ප්‍රිය what pleases) timber, wood.

ඝුණප්‍රියා, *Ghuṇapriyá*, see අතිවිඩයන් *ativiḍayan*.

ඝෙරිඇට ගස්, *Gherieṭa-gas*, *s.* small tree, peculiar to Ceylon, *Linociera purpurea* or *Chionanthus zeylanica (Oleaceæ)*: corrupt form of ගෙරිඇට ගස් *gerieṭa-gas*,

ඝොණ්ටා, *Ghonṭá*, *s.* jujube tree, *zizyphus jujuba*, [Colloq. මසන් *masan*]; areca nut tree, *areca catechu*, [Colloq. පුවක් *puwak*].

ඝෝටක, *Ghóṭaka*, *s.* horse, [Colloquial: අශ්වයා *aṣwayá*].

ඝෝණ, *Ghóṇá*, *s.* nose, [Colloq. නාහෙ *náhe*]; nose or nostrils of a horse.

ඝෝනස, *Ghónasa*, *s.* polangá or viper; according to others (ඝො for ගො *go* cow, නස nose) boa constrictor.

ඝෝර, *Ghóra*, *s.* name of Ṣiva, alluding to the terror which he inspires into the mind; horror, fear, horribleness; *a.* terrific.

ඝෝරදර්ශන, *Ghóradarṣana*, *a.* (ඝෝර and දර්ශන sight) frightful, horrible, terrific.

ඝෝරනාදය, *Ghóranádaya*, *s.* roaring or growling sound, as of wild beasts etc.

ඝෝරා, *Ghórá*, *s.* night.

ඝෝෂ, *Ghósha*, *s.* village of herdsmen; kind of bell metal, [Colloq. තුත්තනාගන් *tuttanágan*]; sound; low thunder, gnat, musquito.

ඝෝෂක, *Ghóshaka*, *s.* kind of creeping plant, so called, bearing white or yellow flowers. [Colloq. තිත්ත වැටකොළු *titta-weṭakoḷu*].

ඝෝෂණ, *Ghóshaṇa*, *a.* loud sounding, speaking loud, thundering, crying out as a public proclaimer.

ඝෝෂා, *Ghóshá*, *s.* kind of fennel, *anethum sowa*; noise, loud sound, high speaking, proclamation.

ඝෝෂාක්ෂරය, *Ghósháksharaya*, *s.* (ඝෝෂ *ghósha* and අක්ෂර *akshara* letter) sonant letter.

ඝෝසා, *Ghósá*, see ඝෝෂ *ghósha*.

ඝ්‍රාණ, *Ghráṇa*, *s.* nose; smell, sense of smelling.

ඝ්‍රාණරෝග, *Ghráṇa-róga*, *s.* catarrh.

ඝෘණ, *Ghriṇá*, *s.* reproach, blame, censure; kindness, compassion, tenderness.

ඝෘණි, *Ghriṇi*, *s.* ray, beam of the sun or moon; sun.

ඝෘත, *Ghrita*, *s.* ghee, clarified butter, butter; water.

ඝෘතමණ්ඩ, *Ghritamaṇḍa*, *s.* (ඝෘත ghee, මණ්ඩ scum) medicinal plant, so called from the scum of its infusion resembling ghee; it is described as sweet and cooling, allaying fever, removing phlegm etc.

ඝෘෂ්ටි, *Ghrishṭi*, *s.* grinding, pounding; emulation, contest; plant, *lycopodium imbricatum*.

ඝෘෂ්ටික, *Ghrishṭika*, *a.* grinding, pounding.

ච

The sixth consonant of the alphabet, and first of the second or palatal class of consonants; it has the sound of *ch* in champion; it is also a particle and conjunction, copulative or disjunctive, corresponding to and, also, moreover, but.

චංක්‍රම, *Chaṉkrama*, *s.* walking, pacing, going; place for walking, kind of covered walk.

චංක්‍රමණ, *Chaṉkramaṇa*, *part.* going, walking, pacing, proceeding.

චංචු, *Chaṉchu*, *s.* castor oil plant, see එඬරු *eṇḍaru*; beak of a bird.

චංචුව, *Chaṉchuwa*, *s.* beak of a bird.

චක්ක, *Chakka*, Páli form of චක්‍ර *chakra* which see.

චක්කරතන, *Chakkaratana*, Páli form of චක්‍ර රත්නය *chakraratnaya* which see.

චක්කවත්ති, *Chakkawatti*, see චක්‍රවර්ති *chakrawarti*.

චක්ඛු, *Chakkhu*, *s.* Páli form of චක්ෂු *chakshu*, eye, [Colloq. ඇස *ęsa*]; omniscience of Buddha, or the faculty of knowing three things, viz. impermanency of matter, existence of sorrow in all things, annihilation of the spirit; mental perception, that perception of truth which leads to the sówán-márga; eye of the mind.

චක්ඛුන්ද්‍රිය, *Chakkundriya*, *s.* sight of the eye, pupil of the eye.

චක්‍ර, *Chakra*, *s.* wheel, wheel of a carriage; circle; mark or sign; religious code; discus, worn as a punishment in one of the infernal regions (උර චක්‍රමාලා නරක *urachakramálá-naraka*); this appears to the victim like a splendid necklace, but as soon as he puts it on, it cuts him to pieces by its circular motion; four acts, namely, walking, standing, sitting, reposing; complete prosperity; success; the movable palace of Chakrawarti-rája, made of precious stones; region or tract of country; assembly; army, forces; potter's wheel; order, edict; weapon in form of a discus having the outward edge exceedingly sharp; alms giving; heap or multitude; astronomical or mystical figure; anatomical division or portion of the body; six of these are enumerated, viz. pubis, navel, pit of the stomach, root of the nose, hollow between the frontal sinuses, and the union of the frontal and coronal sutures; cycle of years.

චක්‍රකූබර, *Chakrakúbara*, *s.* pole of a carriage.

චක්‍රපාණි, *Chakrapáṇí*, *s.* (චක්‍ර discus, පාණි hand) name of Vishṇu.

චක්‍රපූර්ව, *Chakra-púrwa*, *s.* tree, *eugenia operculata*, [Colloq. කොබුගස් *kobu-gas*].

චක්‍රබීජ, *Chakra-bíja*, see කපුකිනිස්ස *kapukinissa*.

චක්‍රමණ්ඩල, *Chakra-maṇḍala*, *s.* collection of cars or war chariots.

චක්‍රමර්දක, *Chakramardaka*, *s.* (චක්‍ර wheel, here meaning figuratively, a large leprous spot, මර්දක which cleanses) plant, *cassia tora*, [Colloquial: තෝර *tóra*].

චක්‍රමාලා, *Chakra-málá*, *s.* (චක්‍ර wheel, මාලා necklace) discus or sharp circular weapon which is used as an instrument of punishment in one of the hells: see චක්‍ර *chakra*.

චක්‍රමුඛ, *Chakra-mukha*, *s.* (චක්‍ර discus, මුඛ face or snout) hog, [Colloq. ඌරා *úrá*].

චක්‍රයාන, *Chakrayána*, *s.* wheeled carriage.

චක්‍රරත්නය, *Chakraratnaya*, *s.* (චක්‍ර region, empire, රත්න *ratna* excellence) carriage of Chakravarti-rája.

චක්‍රලක්ෂණ, *Chakralakshaṇa*, *s.* twining plant, *tinospora cordifolia*, [Colloq. රසකිඳ *rasakinda*]; lines on the soles of the feet of Buddha which betokened his becoming a Chakrawarti-rája and also a Buddha.

චක්‍රවර්ති, *Chakrawarti*, *s.* (චක්‍ර region, වෘත *wṛita* to abide) emperor, sovereign of the world, universal monarch whose authority is supposed to extend over the large continents situated to the east, west, north and south of Mahámeru; Europe, Asia and Africa forming the southern continent or Jambudvípa.

චක්‍රවාක, *Chakrawáka*, *s.* ruddy goose, commonly called in India the brahmany goose or brahmany kite.

චක්‍රවාටය, *Chakrawáṭaya*, } *s.* (චක්‍ර region, වට
චක්‍රවාල, *Chakrawála*, } *waṭa* to encompass) range of mountains supposed to encircle the Sakwaḷa or system comprising the hells, the four large continents, the visible heavens and the worlds of gods and Brahmans; boundaries of the world; limit of light and darkness; sensible horizon.

චක්‍රවේධන, *Chakra-wédhana*, *s.* car or war chariot armed with instruments like sword blades, that are designed to destroy when the car is in motion.

චක්‍රසේනා, *Chakra-sená*, *s.* creeping plant, see මැඩහඟු *meḍahangu*.

චක්‍රාකාර, *Chakrákára*, *a.* round, circular, [Colloq. වටකුරු *waṭakuru*].

චක්‍රාඞ්ග, *Chakrániga*, *s.* gander; carriage; medicinal plant used as a sedative and laxative.

චක්‍රාඞ්ගී, *Chakrángí*, *s.* goose; drug *echites antidysenterica*; potherb *hilancha repens*.

චක්‍රායුධය, *Chakráyudhaya*, *s.* (චක්‍ර *chakra* circle, ආයුධ *áyudha* instrument) discus used as an instrument of torture in one of the hells, see චක්‍ර *chakra;* it is also the instrument of Márayá by which he attempted in vain to oppose and destroy Buddha when he was a candidate for Buddhaship.

චක්‍රින්, *Chakrin*, *s.* name of Vishṇu; potter; brahmany goose; tumbler, one who exhibits tricks with a discus or wheel; oil grinder; emperor.

චක්‍රේශ්වරී, *Chakréṣwarí*, *s.* (චක්‍ර *chakra* universe, ඊශ්වරී *íṣwarí* mistress) universal empress; queen of Chakrawarti-rája; among one of the Hindu sects it is the name of their goddess of wisdom.

චක්ෂු, *Chakshu*, *s.* eye; sight; sense of seeing.

චක්ෂුද්වාරය, *Chakshuddwáraya*, *s.* (චක්ෂු eye, ද්වාරය door or entrance) the door of the eye.

චක්ෂුපථය, *Chakshu-pathaya*, *s.* (චක්ෂු sight, පථය way) that which is visible, in sight, line of vision.

චක්ෂුඵල, *Chakshu-phala*, *s.* (චක්ෂු and ඵල fruit, profit, gain) beautiful sight, that which is exceedingly agreeable to the eye; missile weapon, kind of discus, fruit of eye-sight.

චක්ෂුරා, *Chakshurá*, *s.* kind of fig tree, [Colloq. දිඹුල් *dimbul*].

චක්ෂුශ්‍රව, *Chakshuṣrawa*, see චක්ෂුඃශ්‍රවස් *chahshuḥ-ṣrawas*.

චක්ෂුෂ්‍ය, *Chakshushya*, *s.* collyrium or application to the eyes extracted from the amomum anthorhiza; agreeable for the eyes.

චක්ෂුසය, *Chakshusaya*, *s.* eye, [Colloq. ඇහැ *ẹhẹ*].

චක්ෂුඃශ්‍රවස්, *Chakshuḥ-ṣrawas*, *s.* (චක්ෂුඃ eye, ශ්‍රවස් ear) one whose eyes are ears; snake.

චකිත, *Chakita*, *a.* fearful, timid; amazed, terrified.

චකෝර, *Chakóra*, *s* bartavelle or Greek partridge *perdix rufa*, [Colloq. ඇටිකුකුළා *ẹtikukuḷá*]; this bird delights in coolness, and is frequently seen and heard on moonlight evenings; hence it is fabulously reported that it lives on the moonbeams.

චඤ්චල, *Chañchala*, *s.* tremor, agitation; telegraph plant, *Desmodium gyrans (Leguminosæ)*; *a.* trembling, shaking, moving, unsteady, fickle.

චඤ්චලකම, *Chañchalakama*, *s.* tremor, agitation, instability.

චඤ්චලවෙනවා, *Chañchalawenawá*, *v.* to be agitated or shaken.

චඤ්චලා, *Chañchalá*, *s.* lightning; name of Lakshmí.

චටක, *Chaṭaka*, *s.* sparrow, [Colloq. ගේකුරුල්ලා *gé-kurullá*].

චටකා, *Chaṭaká*, *s.* hen sparrow; root of the long pepper plant.

චටුල, *Chaṭula*, *a.* trembling, tremulous; beautiful.

චටුලා, *Chaṭulá*, *s.* woman; lightning.

චණ්ඩ, *Chaṇḍa*, *s.* tamarind tree; messenger of Yama, the Indian Pluto; demon, daitya; a mischievous, furious, unruly man, a demon like man; heat, warmth; *a.* hard, severe, furious, violent.

චණ්ඩපරුෂ, *Chaṇḍa-parusha*, *a.* furious, violent, cruel.

චණ්ඩමාරුතය, *Chaṇḍamárutaya*, *s.* hurricane, strong wind.

චණ්ඩා, *Chaṇḍá*, *s.* passion, wrath; kind of perfume; sort of grass, *andropogon aciculatum*; name of a river in the east of Bengal

චණ්ඩාල, *Chaṇḍála*, *s.* chaṇḍála is a kind of generic name for a man of the lowest caste; properly an outcast; sort of mischievous demon like wretch, one ready to execute any vile or mischievous act.

චණ්ඩි, *Chaṇḍi*, *s.* name of the goddess Durgá, alluding especially to her incarnation for the purpose of destroying Mahésásur; passionate, furious or demon like woman; *a.* vile, furious, mischievous.

චණ්ඩියා, *Chaṇḍiyá*, *s.* vile fellow. pl. චණ්ඩි *chaṇḍi*.

චණක, *Chaṇaka*, *s.* chick-pea.

චණකා, *Chaṇaká*, *s.* linseed.

චතු, *Chatu*, *a.* four, [Colloq. හතර *hatara*].

චතුමධුර, *Chatumadhura*, *s.* (චතු and මධුර sweet) food prepared from sugar, honey, fine sort of jaggery and butter and presented to the priests.

චතුර්ගති, *Chaturgati*, *s.* tortoise, [Coll: ඉබ්බා *ibbá*].

චතුර්ගුණය, *Chaturguṇaya*, *a.* four-fold.

චතුර්ජාති ගන්ධ, *Chaturjáti-gandha*, *s.* aggregate of four perfumes used by kings and great persons, consisting of කුංකුම *kuṇkuma*, යවනපුෂ්ප *yawana pushpa*, තගර *tagara* and තුරුක්ඛ *turukkha* which see.

චතුර්ථ, *Chaturtha*, *ad.* fourth, [Colloq. හතරවෙනි *hataraweni*].

චතුර්ථජ්වර, *Chaturthajwara*, *s.* quartan ague.

චතුර්ථධ්‍යානය, *Chaturthadhyánaya*, *s.* (චතුර් *chatur* and ධ්‍යාන mental religious reflection) four kinds of religious meditation or reflection; it is that profound and abstract meditation which brings its object fully and undisturbedly before the mind; it is the favourite religious exercise of the Buddhistical ascetics and is practised chiefly with a view of freeing the soul from all evil propensities.

චතුර්දල, *Chaturdala*, *s.* kind of jasmine, [Colloq. වතුසුද්ද *watusudda*].

චතුර්දශ, *Chaturdaṣa*, *adv.* fourteen, [Colloq. දහ හතර *daha-hatara*].

චතුර්මුඛ, *Chaturmukha*, *s.* (චතුර් four, මුඛ face) name of Brahma, alluding to his having four faces.

චතුර්මූලි, *Chaturmúli*, see අහු *ahu*.

චතුර්වර්ණ, *Chaturwarṇa*, *s.* (චතුර් four, වර්ණ sort or tribe) the four chief divisions of men, or the four chief castes; viz, royal caste, sacerdotal order, merchant caste, cultivators or husbandmen.

චතුර්විද්‍ය, *Chaturvidya*, *s.* Hindu priest who has studied the four Védas.

චතුර්විධ මාර්ගය, *Chaturvidha-márgaya*, *s.* (චතුර් four, විධ sort, මාර්ග *márga* way) four states which precede Nirwáṇa, 1st. ශ්‍රෝතසාපත්ති *ṣrótasápatti* including those persons that have carefully studied and comprehended the චතුස්සත්‍ය *chatussatya*; 2nd. සකෘදාගාමි *ṣakṛidágámi* those who have so far subdued the passions as to have only one more birth in this world; 3rd. අනාගාමි *anágámi* those who have attained exemption from mundane existence; 4th. අර්හත් *arhat* one who has entirely subjugated the passions, saint.

චතුර්වේදය, *Chaturwédaya*, the four chief Védas, see වේද *wéda*.

චතුර්වෛශාරද්‍ය, *Chaturwaiṣárádya*, *s.* (චතුර් and වෛශාරද්‍ය profound knowledge) four degrees of supernatural knowledge said to be possessed by Buddha.

චතුර, *Chatura*, *s.* four, [Colloq. හතර *hatara*]; *a.* dexterous, ingenious, clever; visible, perceptible.

චතුරඞ්ග, *Chaturańga*, *a.* (චතුර් *chatur* four, අඞ්ග *ańga* member) fourfold, four times; as චතුරඞ්ග අන්‍ධකාර *chaturańga-andhakára* four fold darkness, darkness produced by four different causes.

චතුරඞ්ගිනීසේනා, *Chaturańginí-séná*, *s.* army consisting of horsemen, men on elephants, men in cars, and footmen.

චතුරඞ්ගුල, *Chaturańgula*, *e.* (චතුර and අඞ්ගුල *ańgula* finger) plant the leaves of which are said to be four fingers in length, *cassia fistula*, [Colloq. ඇහැළ *ęhęla*]; but another derivation is a tree the leaves of which resemble the four fingers of the hand *catharto carpus fistula*.

චතුරංස, *Chaturansa*, *a.* four sided.

චතුරස්‍ර, *Chaturasra*, *a.* (චතුර් *chatur* and අස්‍ර *asra* corner) four cornered, quadrangular.

චතුරස්‍රා, *Chaturasrá*, *s.* plant, [Colloq. හිරැස්ස *híręssa*], *vitis guadrangularis*.

චතුරාශ්‍රව, *Chaturáṣrawa*, *s.* (චතුර් *chatur* and ආශ්‍රව *áṣrawa* evil thought or passion) four evil propensities to which human nature is naturally subject; viz. lust, improper wish for existence, pride of the eye, ignorance.

චතුරෝඝ, *Chaturóga*, *s.* (චතුර් *chatur* and ඕඝ *ógha* torrent) four torrents, used here metaphorically of the passions by which men are governed, also see චතුරාශ්‍රව *chaturáṣrawa*.

චතුරෝපාය, *Chaturópáya*, *s.* four means used in conquering, viz. force, punishment, treaty, intrigue.

චතුෂ්ටය, *Chatushṭaya*, *s.* four; square.

චතුෂ්පථ, *Chatushpatha*, *s.* (චතුර් *chatur* four, පථ road) place where four roads meet.

චතුෂ්පදික, *Chatushpadika*, see චතුෂ්පාදක *chatushpádaka*.

චතුෂ්පාද, *Chatushpáda*, *s.* verse, metre of stanzas especially consisting of four pádas or lines; quadruped.

චතුෂ්පාදක, *Chatushpádaka*, *a.* (චතුර් *chatur* and පාදක foot) fourfooted.

චතුස්සංග්‍රහවස්තුව, *Chatussangraha wastuwa*, *s.* four chief moral virtues, viz. alms giving, affability, promoting the prosperity of others and loving others as ourselves.

චතුස්සත්‍ය, *Chatussatya*, *s.* (චතුර් *chatur* and සත්‍ය truth) the four chief truths connected with religion; viz. 1, that sorrow is connected with existence in every state: 2, that men are attached to existence only by sensual desires: 3, the means conducing to the complete subjugation of the passions: 4, the state preparatory to Nirváṇa, in which the passions are subjected, and every attachment to a continuance of existence destroyed.

චන්‍දන, *Chandana*, *s.* sandal, *santalum album;* it implies either the tree, wood or the unctuous preparations of the wood, held in high esteem as perfumes, [Colloq. සඳුන් *sandun*]; red sandal wood, *pterocarpus santalinus*.

චන්‍දනඝටිකාව, *Chandana-ghaṭikáwa*, *s.* knot in sandal wood.

චන්‍දනාචල, *Chandanáchala*, *s.* (චන්‍දන *chandana* and අචල *achala* hill or mountain) sandal mountains, or the hills producing sandal; name of the Malaya mountain, part of the southern range of the Gháts where sandal is produced in abundance.

චන්‍දස, *Chandasa*, *s.* science of prosody, corruptly for ඡන්‍දස *chhandasa*.

චන්‍දිමා, *Chandimá*, *s.* moon, [Colloq. හඳ *handa*].

චන්‍ද්‍ර, *Chandra*, *s.* moon; deity so called; gold; water; eye in the peacock's tail; one of the eighteen minor dvípas or divisions of the known world.

චන්‍ද්‍රක, *Chandraka*, *s.* eye in a peacock's tail; finger nail.

චන්‍ද්‍රකලා, *Chandrakalá*, *s.* one sixteenth part of the moon's orb.

චන්‍ද්‍රකාන්ත, *Chandrakánta*, *s.* (චන්‍ද්‍ර and කාන්ත splendid) fabulous gem, supposed to be formed of the congelation of the moon's rays, crystal.

චන්‍ද්‍රකාන්ති, *Chandrakánti*, corruptly for චන්‍ද්‍රකාන්ත *chandrakánta*, which see; moonbeam.

චන්‍ද්‍රග්‍රහණය, *Chandragrahaṇaya*, *s.* (චන්‍ද්‍ර moon, ග්‍රහණ *grahaṇa* seizure) fabulous seizure of the moon, used to signify eclipse of the moon; see රාහු *Ráhu*.

චන්‍ද්‍රගෝල, *Chandragóla*, *s.* orb or sphere of the moon.

චන්‍ද්‍රදාර, *Chandradára*, *s.* (චන්‍ද්‍ර and දාර wife) twenty seven daughters of Daksha who were married to the moon and who in Indian astronomy represent the twenty-seven lunar mansions.

චන්‍ද්‍රප්‍රභා, *Chandraprabhá*, *s.* moon beam.

චන්‍ද්‍රබාලා, *Chandrabálá*, see එන්සාල් *ensál*.

චන්‍ද්‍රමණ්ඩලය, *Chandra-maṇḍalaya*, *s.* circle round the moon in wet weather; lunar sphere.

චන්ද්‍රමණි, *Chandramaṇi*, } see චන්ද්‍රකාන්ත *chan-*
චන්ද්‍රමරීචි, *Chandramaríchi*, } *dra-kánta.*

චන්ද්‍රමෞලි, *Chandra-mauli*, s. (චන්ද්‍ර moon, මෞලි crest) this deity being represented with a half moon; name of Ṣiva.

චන්ද්‍රරේඛා, *Chandrarékhá*, } s. digit of the moon.
චන්ද්‍රලේඛා, *Chandralékhá*, }

චන්ද්‍රවිහඞ්ගම, *Chandravihaṅgama*, s. sort of crane.

චන්ද්‍රශාලා, *Chandra-ṣálá*, s. moonlight, apartment on the house-top.

චන්ද්‍රශේඛර, *Chandraṣékhara*, s. (චන්ද්‍ර and ශේඛර crest) name of Ṣiva, alluding to his being sometimes represented with a half moon on his fore head.

චන්ද්‍රාලෝකය, *Chandrálókaya*, s. moonlight.

චන්ද්‍රිකාව, *Chadrikáwa*, s. moonbeam.

චපල, *Chapala*, a. trembling, tremulous, shaking, wavering; unruly; criminal; swift, expeditious.

චපලප්‍රසූ, *Chapalaprasú*, s. screw pine, *pandanus fascicularis* or *p. odoratissimus*, [Colloq. මූදු කෙයියා *múdukeyiyá*].

චපලා, *Chapalá*, s. Lakshmí the goddess of luck or fortune; lightning; whore; tongue; long pepper, [Colloq. තිප්පිලි *tippili*].

චම්ප, *Champa*, s. capital of Karṇa and the modern Bhágalpúr.

චම්පක, *Champaka*, s. tree bearing a yellow fragrant flower, with which the altars in the temples of Buddha are covered every morning, *michelia champaca*, [Colloq. සපු *sapu*]: division in the jack fruit.

චම්පා, *Champá*, see චම්ප *champa*.

චම්පූ, *Champú*, s. work in which the same subject is continued through alternations in the composition of prose and verse.

චමර, *Chamara*, s. kind of deer, or more properly the yak or *bos grunniens*.

චමරික, *Chamaṛika*, see කොබලිල *kobalila*.

චමූ, *Chamú*, s. army, squadron or division of an army.

චමූප, *Chamúpa*, s. (චමූ army, ප who preserves) general.

චමුරු, *Chamuru*, s. (චම *chama* eat, උරච් *urach* aff.) sort of deer.

චය, *Chaya*, s. assemblage, multitude; heap, collection; rampart, mound of earth raised from the ditch of a fort; gate of a fort; cover, covering.

චයාව, *Chayáwa*, s. shade, shadow, corruptly for ඡායාව *chháyáwa*; [Colloq. හෙවනැල්ල *hewanella*].

චර්ම, *Charma*, s. skin; bark; [Colloq. හම *hama*]; hide; shield; hide used by Hindu students and ascetics as their seat and bed, usually the skin of a tiger or antelope.

චර්මකශා, *Charma-kashá*, s. medicinal plant, [Coll: ලුනුවිල *lunuvila*], *herpestis monniera*.

චර්මකාර, *Charmakára*, s. (චර්ම skin, කාර who does or makes) worker in leather, currier; shoemaker.

චර්මකීල, *Charma-kíla*, s. (චර්ම and කීල pin) severe kind of piles.

චර්මඝාත, *Charmagháta*, s. leather cutter; shoemaker.

චර්මච්ඡේදනය, *Charmachhédanaya*, s. circumcision.

චර්මපත්‍රා, *Charma-patrá*, s. (චර්ම skin, පත්‍ර *patra* wing) bat, small house-bat, [Colloq. කිරි වවුලා *kiri-wawulá*].

චර්මප්‍රසේවිකා, *Charma-prasévikå*, s. bellows.

චර්මය, *Charmaya*, see චර්ම *charma*.

චර්මාග්‍රය, *Charmágraya*, s. foreskin.

චර්මින්, *Charmin*, s. shield bearer, soldier armed with a shield.

චර්යය, *Charyaya*, } s. due and regular observance
චර්යාව, *Charyáwa*, } of all religious rites and ceremonies; perseverance in the practice of religious austerities.

චර්විත, *Charvita*, a. eaten.

චර, *Chara*, s. spy, secret emissary or agent; planet Mars; game similar to back-gammon; wag-tail.

චරක, *Charaka*, s. spy or secret emissary; name of a treatise upon medicine, as well as the name of the author.

චරණ, *Charaṇa*, s. foot; root of a tree; race or family; fixed or instituted observance; peculiarity of condition or conduct implied by the English word hood, as, manhood, priesthood; the fourth part of a stanza; *past. part.* wandering, roaming, going about.

චරණනඛ, *Charaṇa-nakha*, s. toe nail.

චරණයුගලය, *Charaṇa-yugalaya*, s. biped.

චරණාම්බුජ, *Charaṇámbuja*, s. lotus like feet.

චරණායුධ, *Charaṇáyudha*, s. (චරණ *charaṇa* foot, ආයුධ *áyudha* weapon) who fights with his foot, cock.

චරපුරුෂයා, *Charapurushayá*, s. spy, secret emissary; guide.

චරම, *Charama*, a. last, final; west.

චරාචර, *Charáchara*, *part. a.* movable and immovable, shaking, trembling; s. the world.

චරිත්‍ර, *Charitra, s.* instituted and peculiar observance or conduct; observance, custom, mode.

චරිත, *Charita, s.* fixed institute, proper or peculiar observance; mode, manner, condition.

චරිෂ්ණු, *Charishṇu, a.* movable, locomotive.

චල, *Chala, a.* trembling, shaking, tremulous, unsteady, unfixed, rolling, moving, movable.

චලන, *Chalana, a.* wandering, roaming; trembling, shaking; spearing, piercing.

චලපත්‍ර, *Chalapatra, s.* tree, see බෝගහ *bógaha.*

චලාචල, *Chaláchala, s.* crow: *a.* tremulous, unsteady, unfixed; movable and stationary.

චලිත, *Chalita, part. a.* shaking, trembling; *part.* gone, departed.

චව්‍ය, *Chawya, s.* species of pepper, *piper chawya,* [Colloq. සිවිය *siviya*].

චවන, *Chawana, s.* death, [Colloq. මරණය *maraṇaya*].

චවමාන, *Chawamána, past, part.* dead, [Colloq. මළ *maḷa*].

චවික, *Chavika,* see චව්‍ය *chawya.*

චෂක, *Chashaka, s.* vessel for drinking spirits with, wine glass; any drinking vessel.

චාග, *Chága, s.* donation, gift; state of destitution.

චාගධන, *Chága-dhana, s.* things which have been given, presents.

චාට, *Cháṭa, s.* cheat, rogue, peculator, one who makes away with money etc. which has been entrusted to him.

චාටු, *Cháṭu, s.* pleasing or grateful discourse; flattery; *a.* cunning, cheating, deceiving, misleading.

චාටුකරණවා, *Cháṭukaraṇawá, v.* to circumvent; flatter.

චාණ්ඩාල, *Cháṇḍála, s.* name of an impure or degraded tribe; kind of an outcaste or pariah, see චණ්ඩාල *chaṇḍála* and its compounds.

චාණ්ඩාලික, *Cháṇḍálika, s.* name of Durgá, alluding to her mischievous and irascible temper; kind of vulgar lute.

චාතක පක්ෂියා, *Chátaka-pakshiyá, s.* kind of bird usually called කෑදැත්තා *kẹṇdẹttá.*

චාතුද්දසී, *Chátuddasí, s.* new moon.

චාතුර්මහාරාජික, *Cháturmahárájika, s.* (චතුර් *chatur* four, මහ *maha* great, රජ *raja* to shine, ඉක *ika* aff.) the first or lowest of the six worlds of the gods, so named from the four great chiefs who preside over it, see සතරවරම් දෙවියෝ *satarawaram-deviyó*; sky, firmament.

චාතුර්මහාරාජිකය, *Cháturmahárájikaya, s.* visible heavens, firmament.

චාන්, *Chán, a.* plain, not ornamental.

චාන්ද්‍ර, *Chándra, s.* planet Mercury; *a.* lunar.

චාප, *Chápa, s.* bow.

චාම්පෙය්‍ය, *Chámpeyya, s.* champac tree, see චම්පක *champaka;* ironwood tree, *mesua ferrea,* [Colloq. නාගහ *ná-gaha*].

චාමර, *Chámara, s.* sort of large fan made from the root of a fragrant grass and used to fan kings or great men; kind of whisk or brush made from the tail of the Indian Yak, *bos grunniens,* and used to whisk off the flies; species of fire work.

චාමරපුෂ්ප, *Chámara-pushpa, s.* areca nut tree, [Colloq. පුවක් *puwak*]; mango tree, [Colloq. අඹ *amba*]; sort of grass *saccharum cylindricum;* screw pine, *pandanus odoratissimus,* [Colloq. මුදුකෙයියා *múdukeyiyá*].

චාමරවාලධිය, *Chámara-wáladhiya, s.* tail of the Indian yak, *bos grunniens.*

චාමරෙ, *Chámaré,* see චාමර *chámara.*

චාමීකර, *Chámíkara, s.* gold, variety of gold.

චායාව, *Cháyáwa, s.* shade, shadow, see ඡායාව *chháyáwa,*

චාර්වාක, *Chárwáka, s.* (චාරු *cháru* beautiful, වාක discourse) one who enchants or deludes by his beautiful or enticing speeches; sceptic in matters of religion; sophist, philosopher.

චාර, *Chára, s.* going, motion; spy, secret agent or emissary; fetter; prison; tree, *buchannania latifolia;* wandering about, travelling; morality.

චාරකයා, *Chárakaya, s.* groom, horseman, cavalier; binding, fetter; associate, companion.

චාරිකාව, *Chárikáwa, s.* wandering, going about, moving, travelling.

චාරිත්‍රය, *Cháritraya, s.* practice, observance; custom, peculiarity of custom or condition, fit or proper action.

චාරු, *Cháru, s.* name of Vṛihaspati regent of Jupiter and preceptor of the gods; prepared oblation for the gods; gold; *a.* beautiful, pleasing, delightful.

චාරුදර්ශන, *Chárudarṣana, s.* (චාරු beautiful, දර්ශන sight) any beautiful object or pleasing sight; tree පුළිලගහ *pulila-gaha;* long pepper.

චාරුද්‍රක්ෂ, *Chárudraksha, s.* kind of tree, *buchannania latifolia.*

චාරුද්‍රු, *Chárudru*, *s* banyan tree, *ficus bengalensis*, [Colloq. මහනුග *maha-nuga*].

චාරුපලා, *Chárupalá*, see චාරුඵලා *cháruphalá*.

චාරුපුෂ්පි, *Chárupushpí*, *s*. trumpet flower.

චාරුඵලා, *Cháruphalá*, *s*. (චාරු beautiful, ඵල *phala* fruit) grape; name of a tree, *bignonia grandis*.

චාරුබ්‍රාහ්මිකා, *Cháru-brahmíka*, *s*. kind of tree, bark of which is medicinal, *swietenia febrifugia*.

චාරුර්තක, *Chárurtaka*, *s*. blue vitriol; sulphate of copper, especially considered as medicinal; collyrium extracted from the *amomum zanthorrhiza*.

චාරුලෝචන, *Chárulóchana*, *s*. (චාරු and ලෝචන eye) deer; epithet for a woman, considered as the highest mark of beauty.

චාරුශිලා, *Chárușilá*, *s*. (චාරු and ශිලා stone) gem, any precious stone.

චාලන, *Chálana*, *s*. sieve, strainer, [Colloq. පෙනේරේ *penéré*]; causing to move.

චාලිත්‍ර, *Chálitra*, } corruption of චාරිත්‍රය *chári-*
චාලිස්ත්‍ර, *Chálistra*, } *traya*.

චිංචින්, *Chinchin*, *s*. tamarind, [Colloq. සියඹලා *siyambalá*]; *a*. sour, acid.

චිකිත්සක, *Chikitsaka*. *s*. physician, practitioner in medicine.

චිකිත්සාව, *Chikitsáwa*, *s*. practice of medicine, healing, curing, administering or applying remedies.

චිකිල, *Chikila*, *s*, mud, mire, [Colloq. මඩ *maḍa*].

චිකුර, *Chikura*, *s*. hair; mountain; snake; musk rat; kind of bird; *a*. rashly criminal, inconsiderately guilty; punishing or injuring others without consideration.

චිච්චිටා, *Chichchitá*, *s*. sound, sharp or shrill noise; sound like the dropping of water.

චිඤ්චා, *Chiñchá*, *s*. tamarind tree, [Colloq. සියඹලා *siyambalá*].

චිටිචිටා, *Chiṭichiṭá*, see චිච්චිටා *chichchiṭá*.

චිත්, *Chit*, *s*. intellect, understanding; collection, multitude, heap; affix to words giving them an indefinite signification.

චිත්ත, *Chitta*, *s*. mind or faculty of reasoning, heart considered as the seat of intellect; thought, conception.

චිත්තර්ද්ධිය, *Chittardhiya*, *s*. (චිත්ත thought, ඍද්ධිය *ṛiddhiya* supernatural power) faculty of producing anything or event by mere thought.

චිත්තසන්තාන, *Chitta-santána*, *s*. train of thought.

චිත්තා, *Chittá*, *s*. one of the lunar constellations; star in the virgin's spike.

චිත්තාභෝග, *Chittábhóga*, *s*. consciousness, perception, sensibility.

චිත්‍ය, *Chitya*, *s*. memento, monument, remembrancer, mark of the site of a funeral pile.

චිත්‍ර, *Chitra*, *s*. wonder, surprise; painting; delineation, writing etc., sky, heaven; circular ornament; sectarial mark on the forehead of a Hindu; white or spotted leprosy; medicinal plant. [Coll: මීනුග *mí-nuga*]; variegated colour; name of Yama the Indian Pluto; *a*. variegated, spotted; speckled; wonderful, surprising.

චිත්‍රක, *Chitraka*, *s*. mark made with sandal etc., on the forehead of a Hindu to distinguish the religious sect to which he belongs; chíta or small hunting leopard; painter; castor oil plant, [Colloq. එඬරු *eṇḍaru*]; medicinal plant, *plumbago zeylanica*, [Colloq. එලනෙටුල් *ela-neṭul*].

චිත්‍රකථික, *Chitra-kathika*, *s*. (චිත්‍ර ornamented, කථික speech) highly finished speech; clever speaker.

චිත්‍රකර්ම, *Chitrakarma*, *s*. tree, *dalbergia ougeiniensis*; painting, magic.

චිත්‍රකර්මාන්ත, *Chitra-karmánta*, *s*. painting,

චිත්‍රකාය, *Chitrakáya*, *s*. (චිත්‍ර spotted, කාය body) tiger.

චිත්‍රකාරයා, *Chitrakárayá*, *s*. (චිත්‍ර painting, කාර *kára* who does) painter.

චිත්‍රකූටය, *Chitrakúṭaya*, *s*. (චිත්‍ර wonderful, කූට *kúṭa* peak) name of a mountain in Bundelcund, the modern Kompteh and first habitation of Ráma in his exile.

චිත්‍රගුප්ත, *Chitra-gupta*, *s*. (චිත්‍ර writing, ගුප්ත preserving) name of Yama, alluding to his office as regent of the dead and the judge of their actions; Yama's registrar, who records the vices and virtues of mankind.

චිත්‍රතණ්ඩුල, *Chitra-taṇḍúla*, *s*. medicinal plant said to possess anthelmintic virtues, [Colloq. වළඟසාල් *waḷangasál*].

චිත්‍රපර්ණිකා, *Chitraparṇiká*, *s*. plant, *hemionites cordifolia*; Bengal madder *hedyotes umbellata*.

චිත්‍රපලා, *Chitrapalá*, *s*. snake gourd, *trichosanthes anguina*, [Colloq පටෝල *patóla*].

චිත්‍රපාටලී, *Chitrapáṭalí*, *s*. trumpet flower, *bignonia chelonoides*.

චිත්‍රඵලම්, *Chitraphalam*, see චිත්‍රපලා *chitrapalá*.

චිත්‍රභානු, *Chitrabhánu*, *s.* (චිත්‍ර surprising, භානු light) fire; sun; name of Bhairava a form of Ṣiva.

චිත්‍රරථ, *Chitra-ratha*, *s.* (චිත්‍ර painted, රථ car) sun; chief of the choristers of Indra's heaven.

චිත්‍රලතා, *Chitralatá*, *s.* garden of Indra.

චිත්‍රවල්ලිකා, *Chitrawallika*, *s.* sheat fish, *silurus pelorius*.

චිත්‍රශිඛණ්ඩිජ, *Chitraṣikhaṇḍija*, *s.* name of Vṛihaspati or the regent of the planet Jupiter.

චිත්‍රශිඛණ්ඩින, *Chitraṣikhaṇḍina*, *s.* the seven sages so much celebrated in Hindu history, but especially as represented in the seven principal stars of the great bear.

චිත්‍රා, *Chitrá*, *s.* star in the virgin's spike; medicinal plant, [Colloquial: මහගොන්කැකිරි *mahagon-kẹkiri*].

චිත්‍රාඞ්ගතා, *Chitráṅgatá*, *s.* (චිත්‍ර *chitra* spotted, අඞ්ග *aṅga* body) kind of snake; plant, *plumbago zeylanica*, [Colloq. එලනෙටුල් *ela-neṭul*]; yellow orpiment, vermilion; name of Subhadra the sister of Jagannátha; star in the virgin's spike; river so called; illusion; worldly unreality; name of a nymph of Swarga.

චිත්‍රිකා, *Chitrika*, *s.* month called බක්මස *bak-masa* (March–April).

චිත, *Chita*, *a.* covered, veiled, concealed, closed, pressed together.

චිතක, *Chitaka*, *s.* heap of food, funeral pile.

චිතඞ්ගුලිතා, *Chitaṅgulitá*, *s.* fingers so closely pressed together that no opening is seen, one of the beauties of Buddha's hand.

චිතා, *Chitá*, see චිතක *chitaka*.

චිති, *Chiti*, *s.* funeral pile; heap, quantity.

චින්තා, *Chintá*, *s.* reflection, consideration, thought, meditation, contemplation.

චින්තාමාණික්‍යය, *Chintámáṇikyaya*, *s.* (චින්තා thought, මාණික්‍ය *máṇikya* gem) fabulous gem, supposed to give its possessor every thing desired.

චින්නා, *Chinná*, *s.* kind of grain, [Colloq. අමු *amu*].

චිනේලය, *Chinélaya*, *s.* slipper. (Port.)

චිබුක, *Chibuka*, *s.* chin, [Colloq. නිකට *nikaṭa*].

චිර, *Chira*, *a.* ancient, long, protracted, much.

චිරකාල, *Chirakála*, *s.* (චිර long, කාල time) long period.

චිරඤ්ජීවි, *Chirañjívi*, *s.* tree, *oroxylum indicum*, [Colloq. තොටිල *toṭila*].

චිරන්තන, *Chirantana*, *a.* old, very ancient, antiquated, [Colloq. බොහෝකල් පැවති *bohókal-pẹwati*]; long lasting.

චිරපාක, *Chirapáka*, *a.* very old, exceedingly ripe.

චිරරාත්‍ර, *Chirarátra*, *s*, (චිර long, රාත්‍රි *rátri* night) period of very many nights, long period; great bear.

චිරස්, *Chiras*, *a.* ancient, of long continuance, antiquated.

චිරස්ථායී, *Chirasthâyí*, *a.* long enduring.

චිරාත්, *Chirát*, *s.* long period, long time; name of Garuḍa.

චිරාත්කාලය, *Chirát-kálaya*, *s.* long period.

චිරි, *Chiri*, *s.* parrot, [Colloq. ගිරවා *girawá*].

චිරිබිල්ව, *Chiribilwa*, *s.* tree, *dalbergia arborea*, [Colloq. කරඳ *karaṇḍa*].

චිල්ල, *Chilla*, *s.* Bengal kite *falco cheela;* bleared or sore eyes; cricket; cutaneous disease.

චිලිචිම, *Chilichima*, *s.* kind of sprat, *clupea cullrata*; kind of prawn.

චිහ්න, *Chihna*, *s.* mark, spot, sign.

චී, *Chí*, *par.* fy! shame!

චීත්ත, *Chítta*, *s.* (Port.) chintz.

චීන, *Chína*, *s.* country so called, Cochin China; the native geographers divide this country into two parts Cochin China, චීන *chína*, and මහචීන *maha chína*, that is Great China or Proper; kind of deer; sort of banner (made of deer skins); sort of cloth; thread; sort of panic grass, *panicum miliaceum;* tin.

චීනක, *Chínaka*, *s.* *panicum miliaceum*.

චීන කපු, *Chína-kapu*, *s.* brown cotton plant, *gossypium religiosum*.

චීනගුණ්ඩු, *Chína-gunḍu*, *s.* species of firework.

චීනමුල්, *Chína-mul*, *s.* medicinal root, *cacalia cathartica*.

චීර, *Chíra*, *s.* cloth, clothes, [Colloq. රෙදි *redi*]; rag, old torn cloth; bark, rind; crest; kind of garland; lead; line; stroke; writing; dress of the priests.

චීරකවාසික, *Chírakawásika*, *s.* punishment, pouring boiling lead down the throat.

චීරිකා, *Chíriká*, *s.* cricket, [Colloquial: රැහැයියා *rẹhẹyiyá*].

චීරී, *Chírí*, *s.* eye cloth, veil, covering for the eyes; cricket: ends or hem of a garment.

චීලිකා, *Chíliká*, see චීරිකා *chíriká*.

චීවරය, *Chíwaraya*, *s.* dress of the Buddhist priests.

චුංචු, *Chuṇchu*, *s.* musk rat or shrew.

චුංචුරි, *Chuṇchuri*, *s.* game, kind of hazard played with tamarind seeds instead of dice.

චුක්‍ර, *Chukra*, *s*, sourness, acid seasoning; sorrel; tamarind tree; *a*. sour, acid.

චුක්‍රාම්ල, *Chukrámla*, *s*. tamarind tree, *tamarindus indica*, [Colloq. සියඹලා *siyam̱balá*].

චුක්‍රික, *Chukrika*,
චුක්‍රිකා, *Chukriká*,
චුක්‍රිකි, *Chukriki*, } *s*. wood sorrel, *oxalis monadelphia;* another plant, variety of the *marcilea coromandelina?*

චුච්චු, *Chuchchu*,
චුච්චුක, *Chuchchuka*, } *s*. nipple, [Colloq. තනපුඩුව *tanapuḍuwa*].

චුච්චුන්දරි, *Chuchchundari*, *s*. musk rat, *sorex cærulescens*, [Colloq. හික්මියා *hikmíyá*].

චුචුක, *Chuchuka*, see චුච්චුක *chuchchuka*.

චුත, *Chuta*, *s*. anus; mango; that which has fallen; murder, killing, death.

චුතවීම, *Chutavíma*, *s*. death, dying; exit from one state of existence to another.

චුතවෙනවා, *Chutawenawá*, *v*. to die, to depart.

චුතුප්පත්ති, *Chutuppatti*, *s*. (චුත *chuta* dead, උප්පත්ති *uppatti* birth) new or fresh birth, transmigration.

චුම්බක, *Chumbaka*, *s*. one who kisses; lecher; rogue, cheat; loadstone; general scholar, one who knows parts in a variety of books; upper part of middle of a balance.

චුම්බකපාෂාණ, *Chumbakapásána*, *s*. magnet.

චුම්බට, *Chumbaṭa*, *s*. (Páli form of සුඹුල *sum̱bula*).

චුම්බන, *Chumbana*, *part. a*. (from the root චුබි *chubi* to kiss) kissing, [Colloq. සිඹීම *sim̱bíma*].

චුරා, *Churá*, *s*. theft, stealing, [Colloq. හොරකම *horakama*].

චුල්ල, *Chulla*, *s*. blear eye; cutaneous disease; oven; *a*. little, small, diminutive, [Colloq. සුලු *sulu*].

චුල්ලි, *Chulli*,
චුල්ලී, *Chullí*, } *s*. chimney; fire place; funeral pile.

චුලුක, *Chuluka*, *s*. mud, mire; small vessel or pot, gallipot etc., the hand hollowed to hold water; rinsing the mouth with water held in the palm of the hand.

චූඩා, *Chúḍá*, *s*. single lock of hair on the crown of the head; crest, plume, diadem; peacock's crest; top, summit; upper room, one on the top of a house.

චූඩාමණි, *Chúḍámaṇi*, *s*. creeper plant, *abrus precatorius*, [Colloq. ඔලිඳ *oliṉda*].

චූඩාමාණික්‍ය, *Chúḍámáṇikya*, *s*. (චූඩා crest, මණි *maṇi* jewel) jewel worn in crest or diadem.

චූඩාල, *Chúḍála*, *s*. head, [Colloq. හිස *hisa* or ඔලුව *oluwa*].

චූඩාලා, *Chúḍálá*, *s*. kind of grass, *kyllinga monocephala;* *a*. crested, having a lock of hair on the crown of the head.

චූතක, *Chútaka*, *s*. mango, [Colloq. අඹ *am̱ba*]; small or shallow well.

චූර්ණ, *Chúrṇṇa*, *v*. powder, dust, any pulverized substance, applied chiefly to medicinal powder; fossil alkali, [Colloq. කුඩු *kuḍu*].

චූර්ණක, *Chúrṇṇaka*, *s*. grain fried and pounded.

චූර්ණකං, *Chúrṇṇakaṇ*, *s*. sentence in prose expounding the purport of the foregoing Gáthá or verse.

චූර්ණ කරණවා, *Chúrṇṇa-karaṇawá*, *v*. to pulverize.

චූර්ණිකා, *Chúrṇiká*, *s*. toasts proposed at feasts.

චූලා, *Chúlá*, *s*. upper room, one on the top of the house; lock of hair left on the crown of the head, [Colloquial: කුඩුම්බිය *kuḍumbiya*]; crest, diadem; peacock's crest.

චූලිකා, *Chúliká*, *s*. root of an elephant's ear; drama, inferior personages of a drama collectively.

චේටක, *Chéṭaka*, *s*. servant, slave, [Colloq. දාසයා *dásayá*].

චේටි, *Chéṭi*, *s*. female servant or slave, [Colloq දාසි *dási*].

චේත, *Chéta*, see චේතන *Chétana*.

චේතක, *Chétaka*, *s*. dog trained to the chase.

චේතකී, *Chétakí*, *s*. yellow myrobalan, *terminalia chebula*, [Colloq. අරළු *araḷu*].

චේතන, *Chétana*, *s*. mind or faculty of reason; understanding, intelligence; wisdom; reflection; soul.

චේතනාව, *Chétanáwa*, *s*. animal or existent being; rational or sentient being; mind as the seat of thought and reason; understanding.

චේතස්, *Chétas*,
චේතස, *Chétasa*, } *s*. mind, intellect, faculty of reasoning or understanding.

චේතා, *Chétá*, see චේතන *chétana*.

චේල, *Chéla*, *s*. dress, clothes, raiment, cloth, [Colloq. රෙදි *redi*]; *a*. vile, bad, wicked.

චේලාව, *Cheláwa*, *s*. weapon, missile weapon.

චෛත්‍ය, *Chaitya*, *s*. place of sacrifice or religious worship; as a temple, tree, shed or any place where offerings are made and the deity propitiated; Buddhist dágaba; monument, tomb or column erected in memory of some deceased person.

චෛත්‍ර, *Chaitra*, *s*. name of a month usually called බක්මස *bak-masa* (March, April); monument erected to the memory of the dead, column or block of wood etc., being so considered.

චෛත්‍රක, *Chaitraka*, } *s.* month usually call-
චෛත්‍රමාස, *Chaitra-mása*, } ed bak-masa (March, April).

චෛතන්‍ය, *Chaitanya*, *s.* soul, spirit; intellect, source of thought.

චෛතසික, *Chaitasika*, *s.* thought, reflection, intellect.

චෝච, *Chócha*, *s.* bark, rind, [Colloq. පොතු *potu*]; skin; cassia bark; cinnamon, [Colloq. කුරුඳු *kurundu*]; half eaten fruit; fruit of the palm; banana or plantain, [Colloq. කෙසෙල් *kesel*]; cocoa-nut, [Colloq. පොල් *pol*].

චෝචක, *Chóchaka*, *s.* bark, rind.

චෝඩ, *Chóda*, *s.* tank, pond, reservoir, [Colloq. පොකුණ *pokuṇa*].

චෝදනාව, *Chódanáwa*, *s.* precept, sacred ordinance; sending, commanding, directing; fault, flaw.

චෝදනිකා, *Chódaniká*, *s.* plant, species of the *sida*, white leaved.

චෝදිතා, *Chóditá*, *a.* published, made known, proclaimed; guilty.

චෝර, *Chóra*, *s.* thief, robber; kind of tree from which a resinous substance is extracted and in some parts of India a perfume is made from it, *dipterocarpus turbinatus*, see හොරගස් *hora-gas*.

චෝරක, *Chóraka*, *s.* aromatic plant, *kempferia galanga*, [Colloq. හිඟුරුපියලි *hingurupiyali*]

චෝරකර්මය, *Chórakarmaya*, *s.* theft, robbery.

චෝරනාලිකා, *Chóranáliká*, *s.* creeping plant, bind weed *ipomœa turpethum*, [Colloq. ත්‍රස්තවාලු *trastawálu*].

චෝරපුෂ්ප, *Chórapushpa*, *s.* kind of grass, *andropogan aciculatum*; flowering shrub, *crotularia laburnifolia*, [Colloq. යක්බෙරිය *yakberiya*]; see චෝරක *chóraka*.

චෝල, *Chóla*, *s.* short jacket, kind of bodice, stays, (worn by females), [Colloq. චෝලිය *chóliya*]; name of a country, the modern Tanjore.

චෝලක, *Chólaka*, *s.* breast plate; cuirass; bark, rind.

චෝලිය, *Chóliya*, see චෝල *chóla*.

චෞර්‍ය්‍ය, *Chaurya*, *s.* theft, robbing.

චෞර, *Chaura*, *s.* thief, robber, pilferer, [Colloq. හොරා *horá*]; planet, see චෝරපුෂ්ප *chórapushpa*.

චෞල, *Chaula*, *s.* beard; tonsure; single tuft of hair left on the crown of the head after the rest has been shaven.

චෞලකර්ම, *Chaula-karma*, *s.* ceremony of cutting off the hair from the head of a Hindu child at three years old.

චඃ, *Chaḥ*, *part.* fy, shame!

ච්‍යුත, *Chyuta*, *part.* dropped, fallen, lost, departed.

ච්‍යුති, *Chyuti*, *s.* departure, loss.

ඡ

The preceding consonant aspirated; it is expressed by *chha*.

ඡගණ, *Chhagaṇa*, *s.* fœces, dried cowdung.

ඡගල, *Chhagala*, *s.* blue cloth or raiment; goat.

ඡගලක, *Chhagalaka*, *s.* goat, [Colloquial: එළුවා *eḷuwá*].

ඡගලා, *Chhagalá*, } *s.* she goat; kind of plant, *ipo-*
ඡගලී, *Chhagalí*, } *mœa biloba* or *i. pes capræ*, [Colloq. මූදු බින්තඹුරු *múdu-bintamburu*].

ඡචක්‍ර සූත්‍ර, *Chhachakka-sútra*, *s.* (ඡ six, චක්‍ර wheel, *i. e.* the five senses and mind, සූත්‍ර short rule) a sútra so called.

ඡටා, *Chhaṭá*, *s.* light, assemblage, quantity, straight or continuous line.

ඡටාඵල, *Chhaṭá-phala*, *s.* palmyra tree, [Colloq. තල්ගහ *tal-gaha*].

ඡත්ත, *Chhatta*, *s.* Páli form of ඡත්‍ර *chhatra*, with some few additional meanings, as, an ensign of royalty, great rapidity, etc.

ඡත්තිංසය, *Chhattinsaya*, *s.* thirty six.

ඡත්‍ර, *Chhatra*. *s.* umbrella, parasol, [Colloq. කුඩේ *kuḍé*].

ඡත්‍රක, *Chhatraka*, *s.* kingfisher, [Colloq. පිලිහුඩුවා *pilihuḍuwá*]; shrub, *leucas zeylanica*, [Colloq. ගැටතුඹ *gęṭatumba*].

ඡත්‍රධර, *Chhatradhara*, *s.* bearer of an umbrella.

ඡත්‍රපර්ණ, *Chhatraparṇa*, *s.* plant, *alstonia scholaris*, [Colloq. රුක්අත්තන *rukattana*].

ඡත්‍රපර්විකා, *Chhatraparviká*, *s.* creeping plant, *vitis quadrangularis*, [Colloq. හීරැස්ස *hiręssa*].

ඡත්‍රභංග, *Chhatrabhanga*, *s.* widowhood; subversion of dominion.

ඡත්‍රා, *Chhatrá*, *s.* kind of fennel, *anethum sowa*; coriander seed, [Colloq. කොත්තමල්ලි *kottamalli*]; anise; mushroom.

ඡත්‍රාක, *Chhatráka*, *s.* mushroom; plant, *mimosa octandra*.

ඡත්‍රාකි, *Chhatráki*, *s.* plant, *mimosa octandra*.

ඡත්‍රාවහ, *Chhatráwha*, *s.* kind of plant, *leucas zeylanica*, [Colloq. ගැටතුඹ *gęṭatumba*].

ඡත්‍රාසි, *Chhatrási*, *s.* sort of creeper, commonly called හිරැස්ස *hirẹssa;* see ඡත්‍රපර්විකා *chhatra-parviká.*

ඡද්දන්ත, *Chhaddanta*, *s.* kind of elephant; large lake in the Himálaya mountains.

ඡද්ම, *Chhadma*, *s.* fraud, deceit, trick; disguise, masquerade,

ඡද, *Chhada*, *s.* leaf; wing; plant; bark, rind.

ඡදන, *Chhadana*, *s.* leaf; wing; roof; covering; sheath, scabbard.

ඡදි, *Chhadi*, *s.* roof; covering, shade.

ඡන්ද, *Chhanda*, ඡන්දය, *Chhandaya*, *s.* meaning, intention, purport, opinion; subjection; poison; wish, desire.

ඡන්දරාගය, *Chhandarágaya*, *s.* vehement desire, ardent wish.

ඡන්දස, *Chhandasa*, *s.* prosody; poetical metre; peculiar kind of metre such as that of the book Vṛittódaya; meaning, purport; object; intention; wish, desire; independence or uncontrolled desire.

ඡන්දා, *Chhandá*, *s.* wish, desire; *a.* solitary, private, secret.

ඡන්දොවිචිති, *Chhandóvichiti*, *s.* one of the Védáṅgas, prosody.

ඡන්න, *Chhanna*, *s.* ordinance, precept; *a.* fit, proper, convenient; private, secret; concealed, covered; solitary; clothed, accoutred.

ඡර්ද, *Chharda*, *s.* vomiting, sickness, retching, [Colloq. වමනේකෙරිම *wamanékerima*].

ඡර්දන, *Chhardana*, *s.* nimb tree, also called bead tree and Indian Lilac; *melia azedarach;* demon.

ඡර්දි, *Chhardi*, ඡර්දික, *Chhardika*, *s.* vomiting, retching, sickness at the stomach.

ඡව, *Chhawa*, *a.* dead; low, vile.

ඡවක, *Chhawaka*, *s.* dead body, corpse; mean, low, vile person.

ඡවඩාහක, *Chhawaḍáhaka*, *s.* he whose business or place it is to prepare the funeral pile, and burn dead bodies.

ඡවි, *Chhavi*, *s.* moonlight; beauty, splendour, effulgence, brilliance, light, lustre.

ඡවිකල්‍යාණය, *Chhavi-kalyáṇaya*, *s.* one of the five personal beauties, beauty of the skin, particularly the lips.

ඡල්ලි, *Chhalli*, *s.* rind, bark; skin.

ඡල, *Chhala*, *s.* cunning, stumbling; wickedness, fraud, circumvention, stratagem.

ඡාග, *Chhága*, *s.* goat, [Colloq. එළුවා *eḷuwá*].

ඡාගකර්ණ, *Chhágakarṇa*, *s.* (ඡාග and කර්ණ ear) tree, *terminalia alata.*

ඡාගභක්‍ෂ්‍ය, *Chhága-bhakshya*, *s.* kind of hemp or flax.

ඡාගමෝද, *Chhágamóda*, *s.* parsley, [Colloq. අසමෝදගං *asamódagaṇ*].

ඡාගි, *Chhági*, ඡාගිකා, *Chhágiká*, *s.* she goat, [Colloq. එළුදෙන *eḷudena*].

ඡාත්‍ර, *Chhátra*, *s.* scholar, disciple, pupil; weakness.

ඡාත, *Chháta*, *part.* cut, divided, separated; hungry.

ඡාතක, *Chhátaka*, *s.* famine.

ඡාදන, *Chhádana*, *s.* roof; covering, screen, leaf; disappearance.

ඡාදිත, *Chhádita*, *a.* covered, concealed; cut, divided.

ඡායා, *Chháyá*, *s.* shade, shadow; reflected image; any image, statue or picture; wife of the sun; radiance; beauty; splendor, lustre, light; nourishment; bribe; darkness, obscurity.

ඡායාපථ, *Chháyápatha*, *s.* (ඡායා light, පථ road) firmament; ether.

ඡායාපුත්‍ර, *Chháyá-putra*, *s.* (ඡායා wife of the sun, පුත්‍ර son) name of Saturn.

ඡායාරූපය, *Chháyárúpaya*, *s.* shadow; image, likeness.

ඡායාව, *Chháyáwa*, see ඡායා *chháyá.*

ඡායාසුත, *Chháyásuta*, *s.* name of Saturn.

ඡින්න, *Chhinna*, *s.* death; whore, harlot; *a.* cut, divided, broken (as by sorrow).

ඡින්නගන්ධි, *Chhinnagandhi*, *s.* asafœtida, [Colloq. පෙරුංකායම් *peruṇkáyam*].

ඡින්නරුහා, *Chhinnaruhá*, ඡින්නා, *Chhinná*, ඡින්නොද්භව, *Chhinnódbhawa*, *s.* kind of creeping plant, *tinospora cordifolia;* [Colloq. රසකිඳ *rasakiṇdu*].

ඡිද්‍ර, *Chhidra*, *s.* hole, perforation, vacuity, small opening; fault, flaw, defect.

ඡිද්‍රිත, *Chhidrita*, *a.* perforated, pierced, having holes or any small openings.

ඡිල්ලි, *Chhillí*, *s.* plant, *amaranthus polygonoides*, [Colloq. සුළුකූර *sulukúra* or කූරතම්පලා *kúra-tampalá*].

ඡුරිකා, *Chhuriká*, *s.* knife, instrument for cutting.

ඡේක, *Chhéka*, *a.* conversant with; well informed; clever; tame, domesticated, as a bird or beast; citizen, town-bred; rakish; buckish, smart, trained in the acuteness and vice of towns.

ඡේද්‍ය, *Chhédya, past part.* fit to be cut, separated, divided.

ඡේද්‍යකරණවා, *Chhédya-karaṇawá, v.* to cut off.

ඡේදන, *Chhédana, a.* cutting, dividing, breaking, separating.

ඡේදනා, *Chhédaná, s.* that which cuts; breaker.

ඡේදිත, *Chhédita, p. part.* cut, divided.

ජ

The third letter of the second class of consonants and the twenty-first in the alphabet; it sounds like *ja* in jam: *s.* name of Șiva, and of Vishṇu; birth, production; parent, progenitor; *a.* born.

ජංගම, *Jaṅgama,* properly ජඞ්ගම *jaṅgama,* which see.

ජංඝා, *Jaṅghá, s.* calf of the leg.

ජංඝාල, *Jaṅghála, s.* traveller, journeyer, pedestrian, runner, racer, quick marcher, rapid walker.

ජංජාල, *Jaṅjála, s.* error, mistake, injury.

ජක්ෂ්ම, *Jakshma,* / ජක්ෂ්මන්, *Jakshman,* } *s.* consumption, phthisis, [Colloq. ක්‍ෂයරෝගය *kshaya rógaya*].

ජගත්, *Jagat, s.* world, universe, earth; people, mankind; air, wind; *a.* opulent, renowned, celebrated.

ජගත්‍රය, *Jagattraya, s.* three worlds; heaven, earth and hell.

ජගත්පති, *Jagatpati, s.* king, deity.

ජගත්ප්‍රාණ, *Jagat-práṇa, s.* (ජගත් and ප්‍රාණ life) air, wind, [Colloq. හුලඟ *hulaṅga*].

ජගත් සාක්ෂි, *Jagat-sákshi, s.* (ජගත් earth, සාක්ෂි witness) sun, [Colloq. ඉර *ira*].

ජගදීශ්වර, *Jagadíśwara, s.* (ජගත් *jagat* world, ඊශ්වර *íśwara* lord) king, name of Buddha.

ජගන්නාථ, *Jagannátha, s.* (ජගත් *jagat* world, නාථ lord) name or form of Vishṇu; a celebrated idol of this name is worshipped on the Coromandel coast in Orissa and is visited by pilgrims from every part of India.

ජඝන්‍ය, *Jaghanya, a.* last, final, hindmost; low, vile.

ජඝන්‍යජ, *Jaghanyaja, s.* Sudra; younger brother.

ජඝන, *Jaghana, s.* hip and loins.

ජඝනේඵලා, *Jaghanéphalá, s.* opposite leaved fig tree, [Colloq. කොටදිඹුලා *koṭadimbulá*].

ජගර, *Jagara, s.* armour, mail.

ජගල්‍යා, *Jagalyá,* / ජගල, *Jagala,* } *s.* toddy or liquid extracted from the cocoanut tree; any vinous liquor for distillation.

ජඞ්ගම, *Jaṅgama, s.* movable, not stationary, locomotive.

ජඞ්ගමවිෂ, *Jaṅgamavisa, s.* poison which circulates rapidly through the blood.

ජඞ්ගල, *Jaṅgala, s.* desert, jungle, flesh; *a.* wild.

ජඞ්ගාල, *Jaṅgála, s.* landmark, boundary, [Colloq. මායිම *máima*]; dam over a field, [Colloq. නියර *niyara*].

ජඞ්ගාව, *Jaṅgáwa, s.* buttocks.

ජඞ්ගුල, *Jaṅgula, s.* poison, venom, [Colloq. විසය *visaya*].

ජඤ්ජාල, *Jaṅjála, s.* error, mistake.

ජටකාරිකා, *Jaṭakáriká, s.* (ජට clotted hair, කාරික *kárika* doer) one who has long clotted hair brought over the head, so as to project like a horn from the forehead.

ජටර, *Jaṭara, s.* stomach, corruptly for ජඨර *jaṭhara.*

ජටා, *Jaṭá, s.* turban; entangled matted or clotted hair; clotted hair of ascetics; matted hair as worn by Șiva as the regent of the clouds and the giver of rain; cluster of bamboos; entanglement; wish, desire; concupiscence; spikenard.

ජටාධර, *Jaṭádhara, s.* (ජටා entangled hair, ධර who bears) name of Șiva; an ascetic.

ජටාමකුට, *Jaṭámakuṭa, s.* kind of spikenard.

ජටාමාංස, *Jaṭámáṅsa, s.* Indian spikenard.

ජටාමාලාව, *Jaṭámáláwa, s.* tuft of hair on the crown of the head.

ජටායු, *Jaṭáyu, s.* bdellium, [Colloq. ගුගුල් *gugul*].

ජටාලා, *Jaṭálá, s.* spikenard.

ජටි, *Jaṭi,* see ජටී *jaṭí.*

ජටිල, *Jaṭila, s.* lion; ascetic or religious penitent with clotted hair.

ජටිලා, *Jaṭilá, s.* Indian spikenard; long pepper; orris root.

ජටී, *Jaṭí, s.* kind of fig tree, the waved-leaf fig tree, *ficus venosa,* [Colloq. පුලිල *pulila*].

ජඨර, *Jaṭhara, s.* belly, stomach, [Colloq. බඩ *baḍa*]; *a.* hard, firm, bound, tied.

ජඨරාග්නිය, *Jaṭharágniya, s.* (ජඨර *jaṭhara* stomach, අග්නි *agni* fire) fire of the stomach, that is, the bile or digestive faculty.

ජඩ, *Jaḍa, a.* frosty, cold, frigid, chilly; dull, sluggish in mind or body, stupid, idiotic, apathetic; mean, vile; dumb; hard.

ජඩකම, *Jaḍakama*, *s.* meanness, vileness.

ජඩයා, *Jaḍayá*, *s.* paltry pitiful man, mean fellow, low vile contemptible person, blockhead, mean vile fellow.

ජඩා, *Jaḍá*, *s.* cowach. [Colloq. වඳුරුමෑ *wanḍurumẹ*].

ජතු, *Jatu*, *s.* lac, red dye, [Colloq. ලාකඩ *lákaḍa*]. or animal pigment, analogous to cochineal.

ජතුක, *Jatuka*, *s.* bat; see also ජතු *jatu*; asafœtida, [Colloq. පෙරුංකායම් *perunkáyam*].

ජත්‍රු, *Jatru*, *s.* collar bone, clavicle.

ජන්තු, *Jantu*, *s.* any animal, sentient being, any being endowed with animal life; it is however, more usually applied to beings of the lowest organization.

ජන්තුක, *Jantuka*, *s.* animal, animal in general; animated being.

ජන්තුඵල, *Jantuphala*, *s.* (ජන්තු animal (worm), ඵල fruit or leaf) kind of fig tree, *ficus glomerata*, the leaves of which swarm with insects, [Colloq. අට්ටික්කා *aṭṭikká*].

ජන්ම, *Janma*, *s.* nature; birth; nation, race, tribe, lineage; *a.* born.

ජන්මන්, *Janman*, *s.* birth, production.

ජන්මසාඵල්‍ය, *Janmasáphalya*, *s.* attainment of the object of existence.

ජන්මාන්තර, *Janmántara*, *s.* (ජන්ම *janma* birth, අන්තර *antara* other) other world, regeneration, another birth.

ජන්මාන්ධ, *Janmándha*, *s.* blind from birth.

ජන්‍ය, *Janya*, *s.* father; friend, attendant or companion of a bridegroom; war, combat; rumour, report; market, fair; portent, one occurring at a birth.

ජන්‍යා, *Janyá*, *s.* mother; friend of a mother; bridesmaid; pleasure, happiness.

ජන, *Jana*, *s.* man, individually or collectively; mankind, sentient being; festival; birth, production.

ජනක, *Janaka*, *s.* father, progenitor.

ජනගහන, *Janagahana*, *s.* (ජන people, ගහන pressure) crowd of people, multitude.

ජනතා, *Janatá*, *s.* mankind, number of men.

ජනන, *Janana*, *s.* birth, production; family, race, lineage.

ජනනී, *Janani*, *s.* mother; tenderness, compassion; Arabian jasmine, [Colloq. බොලිද්ද *bolidda*].

ජනපදය, *Janapadaya*, *s.* (ජන man, පද *pada* going) an inhabited country; mankind.

ජනපදරෝග, *Janapadaróga*, *s.* pestilence.

ජනපදිකය, *Janapadikaya*, *s.* province.

ජනප්‍රවාද, *Janaprawáda*, *s.* rumour, report.

ජනප්‍රිය, *Janapriya*, *a.* agreeable to mankind.

ජනමූර්ති, *Janamúrti*, *s.* one who is like the soul (literally body) of the people, protector of the people.

ජනයා, *Janayá*, *s.* multitude.

ජනයෝ, *Janayó*, *s.* people, pl. of ජනයා *janayá*.

ජනරඤ්ජනය, *Janarañjanaya*, *s.* (ජන and රඤ්ජන *rañjana* pleasure) national happiness and prosperity arising from an equitable government and a due administration of law.

ජනවාද, *Janawáda*, *s.* news, intelligence.

ජනශූන්‍ය, *Janaşúnya*, *a.* (ජන man, ශූන්‍ය void) uninhabited, solitary, desolate.

ජනශ්‍රුති, *Janaşruti*, *s.* news, report, rumour, tidings, intelligence.

ජනසඞ්ගනිකා, *Janasaṅganiká*, *s.* inhabited, peopled, abounding in inhabitants.

ජනසඤ්චර, *Janasanchara*, *s.* (ජන people, සඤ්චර to walk) inhabited place, populous country.

ජනසම්බාධ, *Janasambádha*, *s.* crowded with people, peopled to excess.

ජනහිතනිරත, *Janahitanirata*, *a.* entertaining good will toward all men, philanthropical.

ජනාර්දන, *Janárdana*, *s.* (ජන *jana* man, අර්දන *ardana* worshipping) he whom man worships, name of Vishṇu.

ජනාශ්‍රය, *Janáşraya*, *s.* (ජන *jana* and ආශ්‍රය *áşraya* asylum) temporary hall, place for meeting or resting.

ජනි, *Jani*, *s.* woman; mother; birth, production.

ජනිත, *Janita*, *past part.* born, produced, brought forth.

ජනිතවිම, *Janitavíma*, *s.* birth, production.

ජනී, *Janí*, see ජනි *jani*.

ජනු, *Janu*, *s.* birth.

ජනේරු, *Janéru*, *s.* January, applied to the new year, (Port.)

ජනේලය, *Janélaya*, *s.* window

ජනේශ්වර, *Janéşwara*, *s.* (ජන *jana* man, ඊශ්වර *íşwara* lord) king.

ජනෝද්දහරණ, *Janóddaharaṇa*, *s.* fame, glory.

ජප, *Japa*, *s.* offering to a demon; muttering of prayers at offering to demons; repeating inaudibly charms, names of gods and demons, on certain religious occasions; practice of Hindu religious mendicants to count in silence the beads of a rosary.

ජපා, *Japá*, *s.* China rose; aquatic plant, *vallisneria.*
ජබාදු, *Jabádu*, *s.* musk, [Colloq. කස්තුරි *kastúri*].
ජබාදුවා, *Jabáduwá*, *s.* civet cat, [Colloq. උරුලේවා *urulẹ́wá*].
ජම්බුර, *Jambura*, *s.* depth, profundity.
ජම්බුරු, *Jamburu*, *a.* deep, profound, either naturally or metaphorically; hard, difficult.
ජම්බුරුකරණවා, *Jamburukaranawá*, *v.* to deepen.
ජම්පති, *Jampatí*, *s.* man and wife.
ජම්බල, *Jambala*, *s.* shaddock: see ජම්බෝල *jambóla.*
ජම්බාල, *Jambála*, *s.* mud, clay, mire, [Colloq. මඩ *maḍa*].
ජම්බිර, *Jambíra*, *s.* lemon; citron; common lime; it may be applied to several species of lime; sort of basil.
ජම්බු, *Jambu*, *s.* fruit tree, rose apple, *Jambosa vulgaris;* fruit of the same.
ජම්බුක, *Jambuka*, *s.* jackal, [Colloq. නරියා *nariyá*].
ජම්බුද්වීපය, *Jambudwípaya*, *s.* (ජම්බු rose apple tree, ද්වීපය Island) country so called from its producing that fruit in abundance; according to the geography of the Hindus the name of the central division of the universe or the known world; but according to the Buddhists it is the continent of India or more strictly India proper, or India within the Ganges, it being generally reckoned by them as the scene of the labours of Buddha.
ජම්බුනද, *Jambunada*, *s.* for ජාම්බුනද *jámbúnada* which see.
ජම්බූල, *Jambúla*, *s.* rose apple, see ජම්බු *jambu.*
ජම්බෝල, *Jambóla*, *s.* tree, shaddock or pumelow, *citrus decumana.*
ජම්භිර, *Jambhíra*, *s.* lime or citron, see ජම්බිර *jambíra.*
ජම්මගතිය, *Jammagatiya*, *s.* nature, natural disposition.
ජම්මය, *Jammaya*, *s.* nature, birth; nation, caste, see ජන්ම *janma.*
ජමනාරං, *Jamanáraṇ*, *s.* mandarin orange. [Colloq. මහනාරං *maha-náraṇ*].
ජය, *Jaya*, *s.* victory, conquest, triumph; name of Yudhishṭhira in allusion to his warlike character and the victories he obtained, particularly over the Kurus in the beginning of the fourth age.
ජයකේතුව, *Jayakétuwa*, } ජයකොඩිය, *Jayakoḍiya*, } *s.* (ජය victory, කේතු *kétu* banner) military flag or banner, banner of victory.
ජයකොන්තය, *Jayakontaya*, *s.* flag; banner; ensign; royal sceptre.
ජයගන්නවා, *Jayagannawá*, *v.* to conquer, to overcome.
ජයගැණීම, *Jayageṇíma*, *s.* conquest, victory, pl. ජයගැණීම් *jayageṇím:* verbal noun of ජයගන්නවා *jayagannawá.*
ජයන්ත, *Jayanta*, *s.* hero and demigod, son of Indra; name of Ṣiva; moon.
ජයන්ති, *Jayantí*, *s.* name of the goddess Durga; flag, banner; plant, *æschynomene sesban.*
ජයපාල, *Jayapála*, *s.* (ජය victory, පාල who nourishes) king, sovereign; it is an appellation of several celebrated Hindu princes; plant, *croton tiglium (Euphorbiaceæ).* sometimes written ජාපාල *jápála.*
ජයශ්‍රියාව, *Jayaṣriyáwa*, } ජයසිරිය, *Jayasiriya*, } *s.* pride or exultation of victory.
ජයසක, *Jayasaka*, *s.* kind of horn or large chank blown on festive occasions, bugle.
ජයා, *Jayá*, *s.* name of the goddess Párvatí the wife of Ṣiva; the third, eighth, and thirteenth lunar day of either half of the moon; yellow myrobalan plant, [Colloq. අරළු *araḷu*].
ජර්ජර, *Jarjara*, *s.* emblem or banner of Ṣakra; aquatic plant, *vallisneria;* *a.* old, infirm.
ජර්ජරික, *Jarjaríka*, *a.* torn, ragged; perforated, full of holes; old, decayed.
ජර, *Jara*, } ජරත්, *Jarat*, } *a.* old, advanced in years; rotten, decayed, hard, solid; cruel, harsh; infirm; decrepit.
ජරණ, *Jaraṇa*, *s.* cummin seed; plant, yielding a pungent seed, *nigella indica;* sort of salt, *bit lobon;* old, decayed; old age, infirmity from decrepitude, asafœtida.
ජරා, *Jará*, *s.* decay; old age; infirmity (from old age) decrepitude; tree, *mimusops kauki;* noted female demon.
ජරාජම්බු, *Jará-jambu*, *s*, plant, see බළුදන් *baḷudan.*
ජරාප්‍රේතවෙනවා, *Jarápréta wenawá*, *v.* to become disfigured.
ජරායු, *Jaráyu*, *s.* womb, uterus; fœtus.
ජරාව, *Jaráwa*, see ජරා *jará.*
ජල්පාක, *Jalpáka*, *s.* singer, chanter; chatterer, prattler, babbler.
ජල, *Jala*, *s.* water, [Colloq. වතුර *watura*]; kind of perfume, [Colloq. ඉරිවේරිය *iriwériya*]; uterus of a cow; *a.* dull, stupid, idiotic; apathetic; cold, frigid.

ජලකඩුත්තුව, *Jalakaḍuttuwa*, *s.* strangury.

ජලකපි, *Jalakapi*, *s.* (ජල water, කපි ape) Gangetic porpoise.

ජලකරංක, *Jalakaraṇka*, *s.* (ජල and කරංක cup) cocoanut; shell, conch; lotus.

ජලකූපී, *Jalakúpí*, *s.* whirlpool; pond; spring, well.

ජලක්‍රීඩාව, *Jalakríḍáwa*, *s.* bathing for amusement.

ජලගුල්ම, *Jalagulma*, *s.* whirlpool.

ජලඝ්නද්‍රුම, *Jalaghnadruma*, *s.* tree, *cassia auriculata*, [Colloq. රණවරා *raṇawará*].

ජලචර, *Jalachara*, *s.* (ජල water, චර what goes) fish; *a.* aquatic.

ජලජ, *Jalaja*, *s.* (ජල and ජ born) fish; shell; lotus; a water-born.

ජලජන්තු, *Jalajantu*, *s.* (ජල and ජන්තු animal) fish or any marine, aquatic, or amphibious animal.

ජලජන්ම, *Jalajanma*, *s.* (ජල and ජන්ම born) lotus.

ජලජාසන, *Jalajásana*, *s.* (ජලජ *jalaja* lotus, ආසන *ásana* seat) name of Brahma alluding to his being born from or resting upon the lotus which sprung from Vishṇu's navel.

ජලතල, *Jalatala*, *s.* (ජල water, තල plain) surface of water; face of the deep.

ජලතලාව, *Jalataláwa*, *s.* (ජල and තලාව surface) place overspread with water; marsh; surface of water; sheet of water.

ජලතාල, *Jalatála*, *s.* hilsa or sable fish, *clupea alora*.

ජලතෘණ, *Jalatṛiṇa*, *s.* (ජල and තෘණ grass) aquatic grass, [Colloq. දිය තණකොළ *diya-taṇakola*].

ජලද, *Jalada*, *s.* (ජල and ද what gives) cloud; plant, *cyperus rotundus*, [Colloq. කලාඳුරු *kalánduru*].

ජලදර, *Jaladara*, *s.* plant, *corchorus acutangulus*.

ජලධර, *Jaladhara*, *s.* (ජල and ධර bearing) cloud, [Colloq. වලාකුළ *walákuḷa*].

ජලධි, *Jaladhi*, *s.* (ජල and ධි from ධා to have) ocean, [Colloq. සාගරය *ságaraya*].

ජලධිජ, *Jaladhija*, *s.* (ජලධි ocean, ජ produced) ocean born, name of the goddess Lakshmí, alluding to the fable that she was amongst the fourteen precious things that were recovered at the churning of the ocean, corresponding to Venus being produced from the froth of the sea.

ජලනිධි, *Jalanidhi*, *s.* sea, ocean, [Colloq. මූද *múda*].

ජලනිර්ගම, *Jalanirgama*, *s.* drain, pipe for carrying off water, water fall.

ජලනීලී, *Jalanílí*, *s.* aquatic plant, *vallisneria;* (ජල water, නීලී *nílí* blue dye or indigo) alluding to its imparting its own tinge to the water or to the stream.

ජලපති, *Jalapati*, *s.* (ජල and පති chief or lord) Varuṇa, the Hindu Neptune; ocean.

ජලඵල, *Jala-phala*, *s.* cocoa-nut, [Colloq. පොල් ගෙඩිය *polgeḍiya*].

ජලපිප්පලී, *Jalapippalí*, *s.* (ජල and පිප්පලී long pepper) aquatic plant, *commelina salicifolia*, or *c. clevata;* [Colloq. ගිරාපලා *girá-palá*].

ජලපොළව, *Jala-poḷawa*, *s.* (ජල and පොළව substratum) one of the three foundations on which this universe is supposed to rest.

ජලප්‍රවාහ, *Jalaprawáha*, *s.* (ජල and ප්‍රවාහ overflow) flood, overflow of water, deluge.

ජලමග, *Jalamaga*, *s.* water course, stream.

ජලමට්ටම, *Jalamattama*, *s.* (ජල and මට්ටම rule) carpenter's rule, so called from its inequalities being discovered by placing it on a surface of water; level of the water.

ජලමල අඩස්සිය, *Jalamala-aḍassiya*, *s.* constipation of bowels and suppression of urine.

ජලමාර්ග, *Jalamárga*, *s.* drain or issue from a pond.

ජලමුච්, *Jalamuch*, *s.* cloud, [Colloquial: වලාකුළ *walákuḷa*].

ජලය, *Jalaya*, *s.* water.

ජල යන්ත්‍රය, *Jala-yantraya*, *s.* (ජල and යන්ත්‍රය machine) water work, machine for raising water, watercan for gardens.

ජලරංක, *Jalaraṇka*, } *s.* ජල water, රංක greedy)
ජලරංකු, *Jalaraṇku*, } bird feeding on fish and therefore frequenting lakes and swamps, kind of crane; gallinule.

ජලව්‍යාල, *Jalawyála*, *s.* watersnake.

ජලවක, *Jalawaka*, *s.* fourth day of the lunar month.

ජලශුක්ති, *Jalaṣukti*, *s.* (ජල and ශුක්ති oyster) bivalve shell.

ජලශූක, *Jalaṣúka*, *s.* aquatic plant, *vallisneria*.

ජලස්තම්භ, *Jalastambha*, *s.* (ජල and ස්තම්භ pillar) waterspout.

ජලසම්බුක, *Jalasambuka*: see ජලශුක්ති *jalaṣukti*.

ජලසාටිකා, *Jalasáṭiká*, *s.* cloth used to tie round the waist when bathing, [Colloq. දියරෙද්ද *diya-redda*].

ජලාටන, *Jaláṭana*, *s.* heron, genus *ardea*.

ජලාටනී, *Jaláṭaní*, *s.* (ජල *jala* and අටන *aṭana* who goes) leech; fish.

ජලාබුජ, *Jalábuja*, *a.* born from the womb, viviparous.

ජලාර්ණවය, *Jalárṇawaya*, *s.* rainy season; sea of fresh water.

ජලාවර්ත, *Jaláwarta*, *s.* eddy, whirlpool.

ජලාශය, *Jaláṣaya*, *s.* (ජල *jala* and ආශය *áṣaya* abode) pond, tank, lake, reservoir, or any piece of water; sea, ocean; fragrant grass, cuscus, *andropogon muricatus*, [Colloq. සැවැන්දරා *sęwęndará*].

ජලුකා, *Jaluká*, *s.* leech, [Colloq. කූඩැල්ලා *kúḍęllá*).

ජලූකා, *Jalúká*, *s.* leech (water).

ජලේ, *Jalé*, *s.* water.

ජලේරුහ, *Jaléruha*, *s.* (ජලේ in water, රුහ growing) lotus; any water flower.

ජලෝකා, *Jalóká*, *s.* (ජල *jala* and ඕක *óka* house) whose house is water, leech.

ජලෝච්ඡ්වාස, *Jalóchchhwása*, *s.* drain or channel made on purpose for carrying off water, or such a channel made naturally by the overflow of water.

ජලෞකා, *Jalawká*, see ජලෝකා *jalóká*.

ජව, *Jawa*, *s.* speed, velocity; racer, runner; express.

ජවන, *Jawana*, *s.* speed, velocity; courser, fleet horse; name of a country; *a.* swift, expeditious, see යවන *yawana*.

ජවනහංස, *Jawana-haṇsa*, *s.* kind of swift moving swans.

ජවනාරං, *Jawanáraṇ*, *s.* mandarin orange, variety of *citrus aurantium*.

ජවනිකා, *Jawaniká*, *s.* curtain; wall or screen of cloth surrounding a tent; outer tent; small tinkling bells such as are sometimes tied to flags.

ජවසම්පන්න, *Jawasampanna*, *a.* swift, speedy.

ජවා, *Jawá*, *s*, China rose, [Colloq. සපත්තු මල *sapattu-mala*].

ජවාධික, *Jawádhika*, *s.* race horse, fleet horse, courser.

ජහානක, *Jahánaka*, *s.* period when the world will be totally destroyed.

ජාගර්‍ය්‍යා, *Jágaryá*, } *s.* wakefulness, vigilance, waking; mail, armour.
ජාගර, *Jágara*, }

ජාගරී, *Jágarí*, *s.* one who sleeps little.

ජාගරූක, *Jágarúka*, *s.* one who sleeps little, watcher.

ජාංගල, *Jáṅgala*, *s.* flesh; painted partridge, *francolinus pictus* (order *Gallinæ*); wood, jungle; *a.* wild, rural, picturesque, diversified with hill and dale, wood and water (country); barbarous, savage.

ජාංගලි, *Jáṅgali*, *s.* (ජාංගල *jáṅgala* wilderness, ඉ *i* aff.) snake catcher.

ජාංගලී, *Jáṅgalí*, *s.* cowach, *carpopogon pruriens.*

ජාංගුල, *Jáṅgula*, *s.* poison, venom, [Colloq. විෂ *visha*].

ජාංගුලි, *Jáṅguli*, *s.* snake-catcher, dealer in antidotes.

ජාංගුලික, *Jáṅgulika*, *s.* snake catcher, snake doctor, one who pretends chiefly by charms to cure the bite of serpents and other venomous animals; dealer in antidotes.

ජාංගුලී, *Jáṅgulí*, *s.* knowledge of poisons; possession of charms or drugs and the employment of them as antidotes; kind of pot herb, *luffa acutangula*, [Colloq. වැටකොළු *węṭakoḷu* or දාරවැටකොළු *dára-węṭakoḷu*].

ජාත්‍ය, *Játya*, *a.* (ජාති *játi* birth, යත් *yat* aff) well born, of good family; best, excellent; pleasing, beautiful.

ජාත්‍යන්ධයා, *Játyandhayá*, *s.* (ජාති *játi* birth, අන්ධ *andha* blind) one born blind.

ජාත, *Játa*, *s.* child, offspring; kind, class, species, sort; description; multitude, collection; individuality; specific condition; birth, production; *a.* born, produced, engendered, generated.

ජාතක, *Játaka*, *s.* birth, production; that which has been born; astrological calculation of a nativity; *a.* born, produced.

ජාතක පොත, *Játaka-pota*, *s.* (ජාතක birth, පොත book) work of great celebrity among the Buddhists; it is usually reckoned a history of the five hundred and fifty births of Buddha, or more properly of Bódhisatwa while a candidate for that high and sacred character; the work however only comprehends a narrative of some one principal event or action in the life of Bódhisatwa in each of the births and is recorded to illustrate his wisdom and the benevolence of his character, and at the same time to impress upon mankind moral and religious sentiments; this book is so sacred among the Buddhists that they will offer to it and worship it.

ජාතකවීම, *Játakavíma*, *s.* being generated.

ජාතමාත්‍ර, *Játamátra*, *s.* (ජාත birth, මාත්‍ර moment) moment of the birth of a child; time from which the nativity is cast.

ජාතය, *Játaya*, *s.* generation, race, sort, tribe, see ජාත *játa*.

ජාතරූප, *Játarúpa*, *s.* (ජාත produced, රූප form) gold, silver; any precious metal; coined gold; *a.* embodied, assuming shape or form.

ජාතවේද, *Játa-wéda*, *s.* (ජාත born, වේද védas) fire; gold; name of Agni the Hindu god of fire, alluding to a certain legend among them that the Védas issued from his mouth.

ජාතාපත්‍යා, *Játápatyá*, *s.* woman who has had children.

ජාති, *Játi*, *s.* plant, *emblic myrobalan*, [Colloq. නෙල්ලි *nelli*]; great flowered jasmin, [Colloq. සමන්පිච්ච *samanpichcha*]; mace; nutmeg; birth, kind.

ජාති කණා, *Játi-kaṇá*, *s.* (ජාති birth, කණා blind) one born blind, man blind from his birth.

ජාති කොරා, *Játi-korá*, *s.* man crippled from his birth,

ජාතිකෝස, *Játikósa*, *s.* (ජාති mace, කෝස sheath or covering) that which has mace for its covering, nutmeg, [Colloq. සාදික්කා *sádikká*]

ජාති ගොළුවා, *Játi-goḷuwá*, *s.* man born dumb.

ජාති ධර්මය, *Játi-dharmaya*, *s.* duty of caste; specific or generic property.

ජාතිපත්‍ර, *Játi-patra*, *s.* (ජාති jasmin, පත්‍ර leaf) leaf of the great flowered jasmine; mace, [Colloq. වසාවාසි *wasáwási*].

ජාතිපල, *Játipala*, } *s.* (ජාති mace, ඵල fruit)
ජාතිඵල, *Játiphala*, } nutmeg.

ජාතිමත්, *Játimat*, *a.* (ජාති race, family, මත් poss. aff.) honourable, high born, of good family.

ජාතිය, *Játiya*, *s.* birth, production; reunion of the soul with some other body; kind, sort, class, species; nation; lineage, race, family, tribe; poetical metre; rhetorical ornament, pl. ජාති *játi*.

ජාතිරංග, *Játiranga*, *s.* kind of gem usually called deranga.

ජාති වදය, *Játi-wadaya*, *s.* (ජාති and වද *wada* affliction) transmigration.

ජාති වාද, *Játi-wáda*, *s.* caste controversy.

ජාති වෛර, *Játi-waira*, *s.* innate hostility.

ජාතිස්මරණඥානය, *Játismaraṇajñánaya*. *s.* (ජාති birth, ස්මරණ recollection, ඥානය knowledge) acquaintance with what transpired in former births the wisdom by which previous states of existence are perceived.

ජාතිසම්පදා, *Játisampadá*, *s.* (ජාති birth, සම්පදා fortunate) auspicious birth.

ජාතිසම්පන්න, *Játisampanna*, *a.* of a good family, well born, of noble birth.

ජාතිසම්භේද, *Játisambhéda*, *s.* (ජාති family or race, සම්භේද, breaking) breaking the breed, interrupting or destroying the lineal descent.

ජාතුක, *Játuka*, *s.* assafætida.

ජාතෝක්ෂ, *Jatóksha*, *s.* (ජාත *játa* born, උක්ෂ *uksha* ox) bullock, [Colloq. ගොණා *goṇá*].

ජානන, *Jánana*, *s.* knowledge, information.

ජානපද, *Jánapada*, *s.* inhabited country; people mankind.

ජානු, *Jánu*, *s.* knee, [Colloq. දණ *daṇa*].

ජානුමණ්ඩලය, *Jánumaṇḍalaya*, *s.* cap of the knee.

ජාප, *Jápa*, *s.* muttering prayers inaudibly, [Colloq. මැතිරීම *metiríma*].

ජාපාල, *Jápála*, *s.* goatherd; sheep fold; kind of plant, corrupt form of ජයපාල *jayapála*, which see.

ජාම්බව, *Jámbawa*, *s.* rose apple, [Colloq. ජම්බු *jambu*].

ජාම්බූනද, *Jámbúnada*, *s.* gold; from ජම්බුනදී *jambunadí*, river flowing from mount Suméru, the Indian Pactolus.

ජාම්බෝනද, *Jámbónada*, *s.* gold; particular kind of gold said to be produced in the jambu nadí river.

ජාම, *Jáma*, *s.* period of time, a watch, four hours, corruptly for යාම *yáma*.

ජාමාතෘ, *Jámátri*, *s.* daughter's husband, son-in-law; husband, lord or master; friend; sunflower.

ජාමි, *Jámi*, *s.* virtuous and respectable woman; woman of high rank or caste; sister.

ජායා, *Jáyá*, *s.* wife, wedded according to the lawful ritual, [Colloq. භාර්‍යාව *bháryáwa*].

ජායාපතී, *Jáyápatí*, *s.* (ජායා wife, පති husband) husband and wife, [Colloq. ස්ත්‍රී පුරුෂ *strí purusha*].

ජාර, *Jára*, *s.* paramour, gallant, [Colloq. හොර පුරුෂයා *hora-purushayá*].

ජාරක, *Járaka*, see කුඹුරුවෑල් *kumburuwel*.

ජාරජ, *Járaja*, *s.* (ජාර paramour, ජ born) bastard, child born of a woman by her gallant, adulterine.

ජාරය, *Járaya*, *s.* yard or two cubits. (Port.)

ජාල්ම, *Jálma*, *s.* low man, one of a mean or degraded caste; *a.* cruel, rash.

ජාල, *Jála*, *s.* net, [Colloq. දැල *dela*]; window; lattice, eyelet, loop hole; multitude, assemblage; unblown flower; pride, arrogance; magic, conjuring, illusion, supernatural deception; kadamba tree, *nauclea;* young fruit of a gourd or cucumber.

ජලක, *Jálaka*, *s.* bud, germ, unblown flower; nest; net; pride; plantain fruit; multitude; assemblage; window shutter; window, lattice; loop-hole or eyelet.

ජල කවුළුව, *Jála-kawuḷuwa*, *s.* window, [Colloq. ජනේලෙ *janéle*].

ජාලකාරක, *Jála-káraka*, *s.* (ජල net, cobweb, කාරක maker) spider, [Colloq. මකුළුවා *makuḷuwá*].

ජලකිනී, *Jálakiní*, *s.* sheep, ewe,

ජලය, *Jálaya*, *s.* net, see ජල *jála*.

ජලයා, *Jálayá*, *s.* name given to a cock of a certain colour.

ජලාව, *Jáláwa*, *s.* flame.

ජලි, *Jáli*, *s.* small kind of cucumber, *trichosanthes diœca;* medicine, drug; trumpet flower, *bignonia chelonoides.*

ජලික, *Jálika*, *s.* one who uses a net, spider; fisherman; hunter using a net; cheat, rogue, vagabond; conjuror; juggler.

ජලිකා, *Jáliká*, *s.* armour, chain armour; kind of cloth or raiment; woollen cloth; leech; window; iron; maker of nest.

ජලිකා වෘක්ෂ, *Jáliká-wṛiksha*, *s.* kind of fig tree, *ficus oppositifolia*, [Colloq. කොටදිඹුලා *koṭa-dimbulá*].

ජලිනී, *Jáliní*, *s.* wish, desire; kind of plant or creeper, *momordica cylindrica*, [Colloq. වැටකොළු *wẹṭakoḷu*]; painting room, room with a particular kind of window or eyelet, so as to throw the light conveniently to the painter.

ජවා, *Jáwá*, *s.* plant, endive, *cichorium endivia;* native of Jáva; Malay.

ජවාලෙ, *Jáwále*, *s.* kind of esculent root.

ජිගීෂා, *Jigíshá*, *s.* emulation, wish to excel or overcome.

ජිඝත්සා, *Jighatsá*, *s.* hunger.

ජිඝත්සු, *Jighatsu*, *a.* hungry, [Colloq. බඩගිනි *bada-gini*].

ජිඞ්ගි, *Jiṅgi*, *s.* species of madder, *rubia manjitha*, [Colloq. වැල්මදට *wẹlmadaṭa*].

ජිඥාසා, *Jijñásá*, *s.* act of asking, inquiring, search.

ජිඥාසු, *Jijñásu*, *a.* inquisitive, desirous of knowing.

ජිත්වර, *Jitwara*, *a.* victorious, triumphant.

ජිත, *Jita*, *past. part.* conquered, vanquished, overcome, subdued, surpassed.

ජිතේන්ද්‍රිය, *Jiténdriya*, *s.* (ජිත *jita* and ඉන්ද්‍රිය *indriya* organ of sense) one who has conquered his passions, ascetic, sage.

ජින, *Jina*, *s.* one that has conquered, conqueror; one that has subdued his passions; sage, teacher; ascetic; in the Mythology of the Hindus it is the name of an eminent sage, the leader and founder of the Jaina sect; name of Buddha as the subduer of sin.

ජිනපුත්‍ර, *Jinaputra*, *s.* name applied to a disciple or priest of Buddha.

ජිනවර, *Jinawara*, *s.* eminent Jina or Buddha.

ජිනේන්ද්‍ර, *Jinéndra*, *s.* (ජින one who has conquered his passions, saint, ඉන්ද්‍ර *indra* lord) epithet of Buddha, alluding to his being the chief of the sect of Buddhist ascetics; an ascetic.

ජිම්හලා, *Jimhalá*, *s.* earthquake, or the subterranious rumbling which accompanies an earthquake, [Colloq. පොළෝකම්පාව *poḷókampáwa*].

ජිව්හා, *Jiwhá*, *s.* tongue, [Colloq. දිව *diwa*].

ජිව්හාප, *Jiwhápa*, *s.* (ජිව්හා and පා *pá* who drinks) dog; cat; tiger; leopard, hunting leopard; bear.

ජිවුල්, *Jiwul*, *s.* elephant or wood apple tree, *feronia elephantum*, sometimes called දිවුල් *diwul*.

ජිවුල් මැලියම්, *Jiwul-mẹliyam*, } ජිවුල් ලාටු, *Jiwul-láṭu*, } *s.* gum or resinous substance which oozes from the foregoing tree, more properly ගිවුල් *giwul*.

ජිෂ්ණු, *Jishṇu*, *s.* name of Vishṇu or Indra.

ජිහ්ම, *Jihma*, *a.* crooked, slow; tortuous.

ජිහ්මග, *Jihmaga*, *s.* (ජිහ්ම and ග which goes) serpent, snake, from its going tortuously; Saturn; plant, [Colloq. වලාවැන්න *waláwẹnna*].

ජිහ්වා, *Jihwá*, *s.* tongue.

ජිජුකා, *Jíjuká*, *s.* plant, *abrus precatorius*, wild liquorice, [Colloq. ඔලිඳ *olinda*].

ජීන, *Jína*, *a.* old, [Colloq. නාකි *náki*].

ජීමූත, *Jímúta*, *s.* cloud; mountain; elephant; kókila or Indian cuckoo; tree; sort of ebony; plant or grass, *andropogon serratum;* sort of fragrant grass, *cyperus rotundus*, [Colloq. කලාඳුරු *kalán-duru*]; name of Indra; nourisher; musk.

ජීර්ණ, *Jírṇa*, *s.* cumin seed; *a.* old, ancient, digested.

ජීර්ණජ්වරය, *Jírṇajjwaraya*, *s.* (ජීර්ණ old, ජ්වර *jwara* fever) fever of some continuance and diminished intensity.

ජීර්ණවෙනවා, *Jírṇawenawá*, *v.* to digest, or be digested, to decay.

ජීර, *Jíra*, *s.* cumin seed; sacrificial knife; sword, scimitar; sort of panic seed.

ජීරක, *Jíraka*, *s.* cumin seed, [Colloq. කළුදුරු *kaḷuduru*].

ජීව, *Jíwa*, *s.* life, existence; sentient soul; that which is incorporated with the animal body and gives it life, motion and sensation; livelihood, profession, occupation; Vṛihaspati, regent of the planet Jupiter; Brahma as the soul of the world

ජීවක, *Jíwaka*, *s.* animal, living being; servant, one who gets his livelihood by his service; snake catcher, mendicant or one who lives by begging; one whose life is prolonged by blessings; any medicinal plant; tree, *pentaptera tomentosa;* medical practitioner; *a.* living, existing, endowed with life.

ජීවඤ්ජීවක, *Jíwañ-jíwaka*, *s.* (ජීව *jíwa* life, ජීවක who lives) one that is long lived, name of a bird and supposed to be a pheasant; Greek partridge, [Colloq ඇටිකුකුළා *eṭikukuḷá*].

ජීවත්, *Jíwat*, *a.* living, having life, existing.

ජීවත්විම, *Jíwatvíma*, *s.* living, existence.

ජීවත්වෙනවා, *Jíwatwenawá*, *v.* to live.

ජීවති, *Jíwati*, *s.* plant, holy basil, *ocimum sanctum*, [Colloq. මදුරුතලා *madurutalá*].

ජීවථ, *Jíwatha*, *s.* life, existence; virtue, piety.

ජීවද, *Jíwada*, *s.* (ජීව life, ද from දා *dá* who gives) physician, medical practitioner, [Colloq. වෙදරාල *wedarála*].

ජීවධන, *Jíwa-dhana*, *s.* (ජීව life, ධන wealth) living property, wealth in flocks and herds.

ජීවන්ත, *Jíwanta*, *s.* life, existence.

ජීවන්තික, *Jíwantika*, *s.* fowler, bird catcher.

ජීවන්තිකා, *Jíwantiká*, *s.* name of several plants which possess either aromatic or medicinal qualities, see ජීවන්ති *jíwantí*.

ජීවන්ති, *Jíwantí*, *s.* name of a tree, *celtis orientalis;* plant, *tinospora cordifolia*, [Colloq. රසකිඳ *rasa-kinda*]; yellow myrobalan, [Colloq. අරළු *araḷu*]; betel plant, [Colloq. බුලත් වැල් *bulat-wel*].

ජීවන, *Jíwana*, *s.* life, existence, living sentient being; water; butter; marrow; plant, *odina wodier;* [Colloq. හික් *hik*]; another plant, *celtis orientalis.*

ජීවනය, *Jíwanaya*, *s.* life, see ජීවන *jíwana*.

ජීවනා, *Jíwaná*, *s.* plant, see ජීවන්ති *jíwantí*.

ජීවනාලිනී, *Jíwanáliní*, *s.* plant, *dregea volubilis* or *hoya viridiflora*, [Colloq. කිරිඅඟුන *kiri-anguna*].

ජීවනී, *Jíwaní*, *s.* jasmine, [Colloq. පිච්ච *pichcha*].

ජීවනීය, *Jíwaníya*, *s.* water, [Colloq. වතුර *watura*].

ජීවනියා, *Jíwaniyá*, *s.* milk of the breast.

ජීවමාන, *Jíwamána*, *a.* living, existent, having life, endowed with life.

ජීවසුමන, *Jíwa-sumana*, *s.* shoe-flower, *hibiscus rosa-sinensis*, [Colloq. සපත්තු මල *sapattu-mala*].

ජීවා, *Jíwá*, *s.* earth; bowstring; tinkling of metallic ornaments; orris root, [Colloq. වදකහ *wadakaha*].

ජීවාත්මන්, *Jíwátman*, *s.* (ජීව *jíwa* life, ආත්ම *átma* soul) vital principle or spirit; that spiritual essence which renders bodies susceptible of motion or sensation; animal soul, that principle of vitality which is alike common to all sentient beings.

ජීවාතු. *Jíwátu*, *s.* drug for reanimating the dead.

ජීවාන්තක, *Jíwántaka*, *s.* (ජීව *jíwa* and අන්තක *antaka* destroyer) bird-catcher, fowler.

ජීවිකා, *Jíviká*, *s.* livelihood; profession or occupation by which a subsistence is obtained.

ජීවිකාව, *Jívikáwa*, *s.* life; livelihood, occupation, any calling by which subsistence is obtained.

ජීවිතය, *Jívitaya*, *s.* life, existence, being.

ජීවිතාන්තය, *Jívitántaya*, *s.* (ජීවිත life, අන්ත *anta* end) end of life, termination of human existence.

ජීවිතේන්ද්‍රිය, *Jíviténdriya*, *s.* heart, considered as the source of life; (ජීවිත *jívita* and ඉන්ද්‍රිය *indriya* organ) principle of life, supposed to be of an oval shape and watery colour, see also ජීවාත්මන් *jíwátman*.

ජීවිතේශ, *Jívitéṣa*, *s.* (ජීවිත *jívita* and ඊශ *íṣa* lord) name of Yama the regent of death; moon; lover; husband.

ජුගුප්සන, *Jugupsana*, } *s.* censure, abuse, reproach,
ජුගුප්සා, *Jugupsá*, } reviling, [Colloq. නින්දාකිරීම *nindákiríma*].

ජුගුප්සිත, *Jugupsita*, *a.* censured, reviled.

ජුඞ්ග, *Juṅga*, *s.* kind of creeping plant, *Ipomea zeylanica.*

ජුඞ්ගිත, *Juṅgita*, *a.* outcast; deserted; injured; abandoned.

ජුණ්හපක්ඛ, *Junha-pakkha*, *s.* (Páli.) bright half of the month.

ජුණ්හා, *Junhá*, *s.* (Páli.) moonlight.

ජුති, *Juti*, *s.* appetite; light, splendour, effulgence; moonlight.

ජුෂ්ට, *Jushṭa*, *a.* gratified, served, obliged, examined, explored.

ජුහූ, *Juhú*, *s.* wooden vessel of the shape of a semicircle or crescent and used at sacrifices.

ජූත, *Júta*, *s.* speed, velocity, expedition, [Colloq. ඉක්මණ *ikmaṇa*].

ජූල් ගහ, *Júl-gaha*, *s.* wood apple tree, commonly called දිවුල් ගහ *diwul-gaha*.

ජූල් ගෙඩිය, *Júl-geḍiya*, *s.* wood apple.

ජේතා, *Jétá*, *s.* conqueror, victor, [Colloq. ජය ගන්නා *jayaganná*].

ජේය, *Jéya*, *a.* conquerable, fit to be conquered.

ජෛන, *Jaina*, *s.* follower of the principles of Jina a noted heretic from Brahminism, and who taught a number of heterodox notions, the chief of which are the supremacy of certain religious pontiffs over the gods of the Hindus, a denial of the divine authority of the Védas, and a disregard of the distinction of caste.

ජෛවාතෘක, *Jaiwátṛika*, *s.* moon; drug; medicament; *a.* long lived, thin, spare.

ජෝංගක, *Jóṅgaka*, *s.* aloe wood, [Colloq. අගිල් *agil*].

ජෝතිසත්ථ, *Jóti-sattha*, *s.* (Páli) astronomy.

ජෝති සිටානෝ, *Jóti-siṭánó*, *s.* eminent person so called, often referred to in the Játakas.

ජෝෂ, *Jósha*, *s.* happiness, felicity, pleasure, enjoyment, satisfaction.

ජෝෂිත්, *Jóshit*, } *s.* woman.
ජෝෂිතා, *Jóshitá*, }

ජෝඩුකරණවා, *Jóḍukaraṇawá*, *v.* to prepare.

ජෝඩුව, *Jóḍuwa*, *s.* pair, couple; preparation.

ජෝති, *Jóti*, *s.* sunshine, light, effulgence; fire; star.

ජෝතිමාලික, *Jótimálika*, *s.* (ජෝති fire, මාලා *málá* garland, ඉක *ika* aff.) capital punishment, wrapping the culprit in cloth saturated with oil, etc. and setting him on fire.

ජෝතියා, *Jótiyá*, *s.* astronomer, astrologer.

ජෘම්භ, *Jṛimbha*, *s.* gaping, yawning, expansion, stretching, swelling.

ජෘම්භණ, *Jṛimbhaṇa*, *s.* yawning, gaping; blowing.

ජෘම්භිත, *Jṛimbhita*, see ජෘම්භ *jṛimbha*.

ජ්‍යා, *Jyá*, *s.* bowstring, chord of an arc.

ජ්‍යෙෂ්ඨ, *Jyéshṭha*, *a.* best, most excellent, pre-eminent, first, highest (in rank); *s.* month so called (May-June), [Colloq. පොසොන් මස *posonmasa*].

ජ්‍යෙෂ්ඨයා, *Jyéshṭhayá*, *s.* chief, leader; person of eminence; elder, one very far advanced in life, man of age; elder born.

ජ්‍යෙෂ්ඨවාස, *Jyéshṭha-wása*, *s.* name of Ṣakra alluding to his residence on Mahámèru.

ජ්‍යෙෂ්ඨා, *Jyéshṭhá*, *s.* one of the asterisms, considered as lunar mansions; the eighteenth, comprising three stars of which one is *a* Scorpionis figured by a ring or earring; the middle finger; misfortune; small house lizard.

ජ්‍යෝත්ස්නා, *Jyótsná*, *s.* moonlight, moonlight night; creeper, *trichosanthes cucumiriana*, [Colloq. දුම්මැල්ල *dummélla*].

ජ්‍යෝත්ස්නාප්‍රිය, *Jyótsnápriya*, *s.* bird called the chakóra or common coucal or Ceylonese coucal, *centropus rufipennis*, and *c. chlorohyncus, (Cuculidæ* order *Picariæ)*. [Colloq. ඇටිකුකුළා *eṭikukuḷá*].

ජ්‍යෝත්ස්නී, *Jyótsní*, *s.* kind of perfume; plant, *luffa acutangula*, [Colloq. වැටකොළු *weṭakoḷu* and දාරවැටකොළු *dára-weṭakoḷu*].

ජ්‍යෝතිර්ඥානය, *Jyótirjñánaya*, *s.* (ජ්‍යෝති star, ඥාන *jñána* knowledge) knowledge of the planetary system.

ජ්‍යෝතිමත්, *Jyótimat*, *a.* light, effulgent; shining, glittering.

ජ්‍යෝතිර්විද්‍යා, *Jyótirvidyá*, *s*, science of computation, from arithmetic to astronomy and astrology.

ජ්‍යෝතිරිංග, *Jyótiriṅga*. *s.* fire-fly, [Colloq. කනමැදිරියා *kanameḍiriyá*].

ජ්‍යෝතිශ්ශාස්ත්‍රය, *Jyótiṣṣástraya*, *s.* astronomy, astrology.

ජ්‍යෝතිෂ්ක, *Jyótishka*, *s.* planetary or heavenly body; generic term for the sun, moon, planet, asterism, star; plant, *plumbago zeylanica*, [Coll: එලනෙටුල් *ela-neṭul*].

ජ්‍යෝතිෂ්මතී, *Jyótishmatí*, *s.* heart pea, *cardiospermum halicacabum*, [Colloq. පෙනෙලවැල් *penelawel*].

ජ්‍යෝතිෂ, *Jyótisha*, *s.* science of astronomy and astrology.

ජ්‍යෝතිෂී, *Jyótishi*. *s.* star, planet, asterism, [Colloq. තාරකාව *tárakáwa*].

ජ්‍යෝතිස්, *Jyótis*, *s.* light; star; pupil of the eye; fire, god of fire.

ජ්‍යෝතිඃශාස්ත්‍රය, *Jyótiḥsástraya*, *s.* science of astronomy,

ජ්‍යෝතිරථ, *Jyóti-ratha*, *s.* polestar.

ජ්වරය, *Jwaraya*, *s.* fever, intermitting or continued, [Colloq. උණ *uṇa*].

ජ්වරාතුරයා, *Jwaráturayá*, *s.* one sick of a fever.

ජ්වල, *Jwala*, *s.* flame, blaze, light, jealousy.

ජ්වලන, *Jwalana*, *s.* agni or fire, [Coll: ගිනි *gini*]; fervency, zeal; inflammation; blazing, burning.

ජ්වලිත, *Jwalita*, *s.* jealousy, burning, blazing, flaming, shining; zeal; *a.* jealous, burning.

ජ්වාල, *Jwála*, *s.* flame, blaze.

ඣ

The ninth consonant of the alphabet; aspirate of the preceeding letter; it is usually expressed by *jha*.

ඣංකාර, *Jhan̥kára*, *s.* tinkling sound; sound as of the voice of birds etc.

ඣටා, *Jhaṭá*, *s.* plant, *flacourtia cataphracta*, [Colloq. රට උගුරැස්ස *raṭa-ugurẹssa*].

ඣම්පා, *Jhampá*, *s.* jumping, springing, plunging; hoping, expecting.

ඣර්ඣර, *Jahrjhara*, *s.* kind of tom-tom or native drum; cymbals; Kaliyuga, or the present age of the world; name of a river.

ඣර, *Jhara*, *s.* cascade, water fall.

ඣරී, *Jharí*, *s.* river, [Colloq. ගඟ *gan̥ga*]; cascade, water fall, [Colloq. ඇල්ල *ẹlla*].

ඣල්ල, *Jhalla*, *s.* prize fighter, cudgel player.

ඣල්ලක, *Jhallaka*, *s.* cymbals.

ඣලා, *Jhalá*, *s.* daughter; sunshine; splendour, brilliancy, light.

ඣෂ, *Jhasha*, *s.* fish, one of the signs of the zodiac, Pisces; heat, warmth; forest, thicket.

ඣෂා, *Jhashá*, *s.* pulas tree, *butea frondosa*, [Coll: ගස්කැලිය *gas-kẹliya*].

ඣාට, *Jháṭa*, *s.* arbour, bower, place over grown with creepers; wood, thicket; jasmine.

ඣාටාල, *Jháṭála*, *s.* kind of flower, trumpet flower, *bignonia indica*.

ඣාන, *Jhána*, *s.* contemplation, reflection, meditation. (Páli.)

ඣාවුක, *Jháwuka*, *s.* tree, *Sterculia balanghas*, [Colloq. පිචුල *pichula* or නාවාගස් *náwá-gas*].

ඣිඞ්ගාක, *Jhińgáka*,
ඣිඞ්ගිනි, *Jhińginí*, } *s.* sort of cucumber, *luffa acutangula*, [Colloq. වැට කොළු *wẹṭakoḷu*].

ඣිණ්ටිනි, *Jhiṇṭiní*, *s.* indigo plant, [Colloq. අවරිය *awariya*],

ඣිණ්ටී, *Jhiṇṭí*, *s.* plant, *barleria prionitis*, [Colloq. කටුකරඬු *kaṭukaran̥ḍu*].

ඣිරිකා, *Jhiriká*,
ඣිරී, *Jhirí*, } *s.* cricket, [Colloq. රැහැයියා *rẹhẹyiyá*].

ඣිරිකා, *Jhiriká*,
ඣිරුකා, *Jhiruká*,
ඣිල්ලිකා, *Jhilliká*, } *s.* cricket; light of sunshine, [Colloq. අව්ව *awwa*]; strong light, splendour; dirt taken off the body in rubbing it with perfumes; wick of a lamp; cloth or rag for applying ungents to the body; cricket's cry.

ඣිල්ලී, *Jhillí*, *s*, cricket, light, wick of a lamp; cymbals.

ඤ

The second nasal of the Sin̥halese and Páli alphabet and is usually expressed by *ña*. N. B: In Sanskrit words, this does not occur as an initial but only as a mute letter joined to a consonant, as චඤ්චල *chañchala*.

ඤත්ති, *Ñatti*, *s.* announcement, declaration.

ඤත්වා, *Ñatwá*, *part.* having known.

ඤාණ, *Ñáṇa*, *s.* wisdom, understanding, intelligence, knowledge in general; religious knowledge, such as is acquired by the reading and study of the sacred books.

ඤාණදස්සන, *Ñáṇadassana*, *s.* (ඤාණ knowledge, දස්සන sight, vision) fruit, or reward of an action of a priest of Buddha; supernatural vision obtained by intense meditation; faculty of knowing things past, present, and future; omniscience, confined to Buddha by his followers; reflection; knowledge obtained by turning the thoughts on the past, the path of Buddha and other purified persons of his religion.

ඤාණවන්තකම, *Ñáṇawantakama*, *s.* wisdom.

ඤාණවන්තයා, *Ñáṇawantayá*, *s.* sage.

ඤාණී, *Ñáṇí*, *s.* sage, one possessing great religious knowledge; fortune-teller: astrologer.

ඤාතකෝ, *Ñátakó*,
ඤාති, *Ñáti*, } *s.* relative, kinsman, [Colloq. නෑයා *nẹyá*].

ඤාතිකුලය, *Ñáti-kulaya*, *s.* race or lineage in a direct line.

ඤාතිධම්මො, *Ñáti-dhammo*, *s.* duty to relations.

ඤාතිමිත්තා, *Ñátimittá*,
ඤාතිමිත්‍රයෝ, *Ñátimitrayó*, } *s.* relations and friends, [Colloq. නෑදෑ මිත්‍රයෝ *nẹdẹ-mitrayó*].

ඤාව්, *Ñáw*, *s.* cry made by a cat.

ඤාවුවා, *Ñáwuwá*, *s.* water-pheasant, *hydrophasianus chiragus*, (*Parridæ*, order *Grallac)*.

ඤෙය්‍යො, *Ñeyyó*, *p. f. p.* that should be known, cognisable.

ඥ

A compound letter which appears to be composed of ජ *ja* and ඤ *ña;* it is difficult to express the sound in Roman letters.

ඥ, *Jña*, *s.* one who knows; name of the planet Mercury; sometimes applied to the planet Mars or its regent; *a.* wise.

ඥප්ත, *Jñapta*, see ඥපිත *jñapita*.

ඥප්ති, *Jñapti*, *s.* understanding, wisdom, comprehension; exercise of the intellectual faculties.

ඥපිත, *Jñapita*, *a.* taught, learned, well informed; expounded, made known.

ඥාත, *Jñáta*, *s.* known.

ඥාති, *Jñáti*, *s.* kinsman, relation, [Colloq. නෑයා *néyá*].

ඥාන, *Jñána*, *s.* wisdom, knowledge in general; specific and religious knowledge.

ඥානගම්‍ය, *Jñánagamya*, *a.* (ඥාන wisdom, ගම්‍ය attainable) attainable by knowledge.

ඥානගර්ජනා, *Jñána-garjaná*, *s.* (ඥාන and ගර්ජනා sound) praise or fame of wisdom or knowledge.

ඥානදර්ශන, *Jñána-darṣana*, *s.* insight by knowledge.

ඥානදීප, *Jñána-dípa*, *s.* lamp of knowledge.

ඥානවන්ත, *Jñánawanta*, *a.* wise, knowing; prudent, cautious.

ඥානවිඥාන, *Jñána-vijñána*, *s.* sacred and profane knowledge.

ඥානී, *Jñání*, *s.* wise or learned man, a literary character; sage, but particularly one skilled in astronomy and the powers of the planetary system over the affairs and destinies of men; astrologer; fortune-teller, man prescient of future events.

ඥානේන්ද්‍රිය, *Jñánéndriya*, *s.* organ of perception.

ඥාප්ති, *Jñápti*, } *s.* making known, informing.
ඥාපන, *Jñápana*,

ඥේය, *Jñéya*, *part.* to be known, what may or ought to be known.

ට

The eleventh consonant of the modern Siṇhalese alphabet and first of the third class or cerebrals; it corresponds in sound to the letter *t*, pronounced far back in the mouth as in true; sign of the accusative, dative or genitive case in grammar.

ටංකණ, *Ṭaṇkaṇa*, *s.* borax, used as a flux for metals etc., [Colloq. පුස්කර *puskara*]; binding, tying.

ටකපෝරුව, *Ṭakapóruwa*, *s.* a piece of board hung up on a tree to scare away birds, squerrels etc. from orchards and fruit trees by pulling it, when it makes the sound tak, tak, hence the name, ටක පෝරුව which literally means the "tak-board."

ටගර, *Ṭagara*, *s.* borax; play, sport; confusion of mind; an object of sense; *a.* squint-eyed, [Coll: වපර *wapara*].

ටඞ්ක, *Ṭaṅka*, *s.* species of the elephant or wood apple, [Colloquial: නිල් දිවුල් *nil-diwul*]; borax; spade or hoe; stone-cutter's chisel, [Colloq. ගල් පළන පෙණුම *galpaḷana peṇuma*]; hatchet; sword; sacrificial knife; scabbard, sheath; anger, wrath; pride, arrogance.

ටඞ්කක, *Ṭaṅkaka*, *s.* stamped coin.

ටඞ්කපති, *Ṭaṅkapati*, *s.* master of a mint.

ටඞ්කශාලා, *Ṭaṅka-ṣálá*, *s.* mint.

ටඞ්කා, *Ṭaṅká*, *s.* edge or side of a mountain.

ටඞ්ග, *Ṭaṅga*, *s.* spade, axe, borax.

ටාං ගානවා, *Ṭáṇ-gánawá*, *v.* to make the sound ṭáṇ.

ටාඞ්කර, *Ṭáṅkara*, *s.* (ටාං *ṭáṇ* oath, කර who makes) blackguard; lecher, libertine.

ටිං ටිං ගානවා, *Ṭiṇ ṭiṇ gánawá*, *v.* to make the sound ṭiṇ ṭiṇ.

ටික, *Ṭika*, *a.* little, small in quantity, few.

ටිකක්, *Ṭikak*, *s.* little, small quantity.

ටිකකින්, *Ṭikakin*, *ad.* in a little while, by and bye, shortly.

ටිකින්ටික, *Ṭikin-ṭika*, *adv.* little by little, gradually.

ටිකිරිපැංචා, *Ṭikiri-peñchá*, *s.* little boy.

ටිකිරියා, *Ṭikiriyá*, *s.* little boy (a term used only in the Kandian Province.)

ටිගිනි, *Ṭigini*, *s.* eyelid, eyeball.

ටිට්ටිභක, *Ṭiṭṭibhaka*, *s.* kind of bird, *parra jacana* or *goensis*.

ටීකා, *Ṭíká*, *s.* commentary.

ටුණ්ටුක, *Ṭunṭuka*, *s.* tree, *bignonia indica* or *spathodea indica*, [Colloq. තොටිල *toṭila*]; name of a bird, *sylvia sutoria*.

ටොක්ක, *Ṭokka*, *s.* blow on the head with the fist, pl. ටොකු *ṭoku*.

ටැබ, *Ṭẹba*, *s.* water-pot.

ටැඹ, *Ṭẹmba*, *s.* pillar, stone pillar, pl. ටැම් *ṭẹm*.

ඨ

The aspirate of the preceding letter; its sound is expressed by *ṭh*.

ඨපනීය, *Ṭhapaníya*, *s.* what should be placed, or set aside.

ඨාන, *Ṭhána*, *s.* place, situation; stay or continuance; post, rank.

ඨානාන්තරය, *Ṭhánántaraya*, *s.* employment, high office, office of responsibility.

ඩ

The third letter of the cerebral class of consonants having the sound of d with the tip of the tongue thrown back on the palate, as in the word dance; it is also a substitute for the ට *ta* of the infinitive mood.

ඩබර, *Ḍabara*, *s.* quarrel, affray, conflict without weapons, tumult, riot, kind of skirmishing warfare; fight.

ඩබරාව, *Ḍabaráwa*, *s.* large spoon made of the shell of a cocoanut or gourd and used by ascetics for the double purpose of straining and conveying water.

ඩබු, *Ḍabu*, } *s.* delay, procrastination; conceal-
ඩඹු, *Ḍambu*, } ment; plunder.

ඩමර, *Ḍamara*, *s.* sound of the ඩමරු *ḍamaru*.

ඩමරු, *Ḍamaru*, *s.* kind of small tom-tom or native drum shaped like an hour glass and held in one hand and beaten by the other; it is chiefly used by the Hindu mendicants.

ඩයන *Ḍayana*, *s.* palanquin or ḍóli, flying in the air.

ඩලක, *Ḍalaka*, *s.* sling; basket; presents of fruit, sweetmeats etc.

ඩවගස්, *Ḍawa-gas*, *s.* tree, *lythrum fructicosum*,

ඩවිනි, *Ḍaviní*, *s.* female imp.

ඩහදිය, *Ḍahadiya*, *s.* sweat, perspiration.

ඩහනවා, *Ḍahanawá*, *v.* to bite: pret. ඩැහුවා *ḍẹhuwá*.

ඩහු, *Ḍahu*, *s.* bread fruit tree, *artocarpus incisa*, [Colloq. රටදෙල් *raṭadel*].

ඩා, *Ḍá*, *s.* kind of female imp or goblin, [Colloq. යකින්නි *yakinní*]; basket carried by a sling; perspiration.

ඩාකිනි, *Ḍákini*, *s.* kind of female demon, imp or evil being, [Colloq. යකින්න *yakinna*].

ඩාදිය, *Ḍádiya*, *s.* (ඩා sweat, දිය moisture) perspiration, moisture from perspiration.

ඩානවා, *Ḍánawá*, *v.* to bite, to seize by the mouth.

ඩාමර, *Ḍámara*, *s.* affray, conflict with weapons, uproar.

ඩාලිම, *Ḍálima*, *s.* pomegranate, [Colloq. දෙළුම් *deḷum*].

ඩාසිදුරු, *Ḍá-siduru*, *s.* (ඩා sweat, සිදුරු perforation) pores of the skin.

ඩිංග, *Ḍiṇga*, *s.* bit, small portion, moderate.

ඩිංගිත්තක්, *Ḍiṇgittak*, *s.* little bit.

ඩිංගිරි, *Ḍiṇgiri*, *a.* small, little.

ඩිංගිස්ස, *Ḍiṇgissa*, *s.* a little.

ඩිංගෙන්, *Ḍiṇgen*, *s.* within a little, almost.

ඩිණ්ඩිම, *Ḍiṇḍima*, *s.* small drum or tabor; plant bearing a small fruit, *carissa carandas*, [Colloq. කරඹ *karamba*].

ඩිණ්ඩිර *Ḍiṇḍira*, *s.* cuttle fish bone, considered to be the foam of the sea.

ඩිණ්ඩිරමෝදක, *Ḍiṇḍiramódaka*, *s.* garlic, [Colloq. සුදුළූනු *sudulúnu*].

ඩිම්බ, *Ḍimba*, *s.* affray, quarrel, fight, assault, defiance. sound or noise occasioned by terror; egg; bladder; spleen; uterus; fear, terror; young animal.

ඩිම්භ, *Ḍimbha*, *s.* young animal; fool, idiot, blockhead.

ඩුණ්ඩුක, *Ḍuṇḍuka*, *s.* tree, *spathodea indica.*

ඩුණ්ඩුභ, *Ḍuṇḍubha*, *s.* water snake, *cerberus rhynchops*, [Colloq. දියබරියා *diyabariyá*].

ඩෙබර, *Ḍebara*, *s.* tree, *zizyphus jujuba*, [Colloq. මසන් *masan*].

ඩෙබරා, *Ḍebará*, *s.* corruptly for දෙබරා *debará*, wasp, bee.

ඩෝලා. *Ḍólá*, *s.* palanquin, corruptly for දෝලා *dólá*, which see.

ඩෝලාඵල, *Ḍólá-phala*, *s.* tree, *bassia longifolia* [Colloq. මී *mi*].

ඩැක්කිය, *Ḍẹkkiya*, *s.* kind of tom-tom or native drum; it is beat only on one end and is chiefly used by the Kapuwas.

ඩැහැගන්නවා, *Ḍẹhẹgannawá*, *v.* to bite, to seize with the mouth, or bill.

ඩැහැගැන්ම, *Ḍẹhẹgẹnma*, verbal noun of the preceding word.

ඩැගන්නවා, *Ḍẹgannawá*, see ඩැහැගන්නවා *ḍẹhẹgannawá*.

ඪ

The preceding letter aspirated.

ඪක්ක, *Ḍhakka*, *s.* city or district; concealment, covering; disappearance.

ඪක්කා, *Ḍhakká*, *s.* large drum, see ඩැක්කිය *ḍẹkkiya*.

ඪෝල, *Ḍhóla*, *s.* dhól or drum.

ණ

The nasal *ṇ* of the third or cerebral class of consonants. It seldom occurs as an intial letter except in roots of verbs.

ත

The first consonant of the fourth or dental class; it sounds like *th* in thin; ත *ta* is sometimes used for තගේ *tagé* genitive case of තෝ *tó*, as in තසිත *tasita*, thy mind.

තක්කඩ, *Takkaḍa*, *s.* shrub, common by the sea side, *scævola koenigii*, *(Goodenoviaceæ)*.

තක්කඩිකම, *Takkaḍikama*, *s.* villany, roguery, knavery.

තක්කඩියා, *Takkaḍiyá*, *s.* rogue, rascal, vile fellow, knave.

තක්කෝල, *Takkóla*, *s.* (Páli) *bdellium;* sort of perfume made from the berry of the kakkóla plant. Siṇhalese තකුල් *takul.*

තක්‍ර, *Takra*, *s.* butter-milk mixed with water, [Colloq. කිරි මෝරු *kiri-móru*].

තක්ෂක, *Takshaka*, *s.* carpenter, [Colloq. වඩුවා *waḍuwá*].

තක්ෂණ, *Takshaṇa*, *s.* chipper, peeler; carpenter; name of Viṣwakarma the architect of the gods.

තක්ෂශිලා, *Taksha-ṣilá*, *s.* name of a city, the Taxilá of Ptolemy, a renowned university town.

තකතිරුවා, *Takatiruwá*, *s.* stupid man, blackguard.

තකනවා, *Takanawá*, *v.* to esteem, to regard, to reverence: pret. තැකුවා *tẹkuwá.*

තකු, *Taku*, Elu form of තර්ක *tarka*, which see.

තකුල්, *Takul*, *s.* nut of the annual hairy plant, කපුකිනිස්ස *kapukinssa.*

තකුල, *Takula*, *s.* plant, *hibiscus abelmoschus.* [Colloq. කපුකිනිස්ස *kapukinissa*].

තකුසත, *Takusata*, see තර්කශාස්ත්‍ර *tarkaṣástra.*

තගණ, *Tagaṇa*, *s.* poetical foot having the two first syllables long and the third short.

තගර, *Tagara*, *s.* tree, *tabernæmontana coronaria*, [Colloq. තුවරලා *tuwaralá*]; myrrh; waves.

තගු, *Tagu*, *s.* delay, loitering; slow travelling.

තචපංචක, *Tachapañchaka*, *s.* five parts of the human body, viz. hair of the head, hair of the body, nails, teeth, and skin.

තට්ට, *Taṭṭa*, *a.* bald.

තට්ට කුරුල්ලා, *Taṭṭa-kurullá*, *s.* common weaver bird, *ploceus philippinus (*order *Passeres)*; also called වඩුකුරුල්ලා *waḍu-kurullá.*

තට්ටම, *Taṭṭama. s.* buttocks, hind part of a man or beast, pl. තට්ටම් *taṭṭam.*

තට්ටයා, *Taṭṭayá*, *s.* bald man.

තට්ටසේරා, *Taṭṭa-sérá*, *s.* Indian whistling teal, *dendrocygna javanica*, *(Anatidæ* order *Anseres)*; also called සේරා *sérá.*

තට්ටු, *Taṭṭu*, *s.* knocking, tapping, slight knock; shelves, layers; ceiling; deck of a ship.

තට්ටුකරණවා, *Taṭṭukaraṇawá*, *v.* to knock.

තට්ටුව, *Taṭṭuwa*, *s.* ceiling of a house; deck of a ship; coating (as of dirt on the body).

තට්ටුවෙනවා, *Taṭṭuwenawá*, *v.* to hit.

තට *Taṭa*, the dative of තෝ *tó* thou; *s.* shore, bank of a river.

තටක, *Taṭaka*, *s.* shore, bank of a river.

තටතට, *Taṭataṭa*, *s.* tremour, shaking; trembling; sound.

තටමනවා, *Taṭamanawá*, *v.* to strain when evacuating by stool; to make a strong attempt, to essay: pret. තැටමුවා *tẹṭamuwá.*

තටාකය, *Taṭákaya*, *s.* pond, deep enough for the lotus and other aquatic plants, tank, [Colloq. පොකුණ *pokuṇa* or විල *vila*], plural තටාක *taṭáka.*

තටුකොකා, *Taṭu-koká*, *s.* black headed white ibis, *Ibis melanocephala (Plataleidæ*, order *Herodiones).*

තටුව, *Taṭuwa*, *s.* brazen vessel for eating; wing of a bird; offering made to a demon, pl. තටු *taṭu.*

තඩ, *Taḍa*, *s.* burden carried by two people on a pole.

තඩිත්, *Taḍit*, *s.* lightning.

තඩිබානවා, *Taḍibánawá*, *v.* to cudgel: pret. තඩිබෑවා *taḍibẹwá.*

තඩිය, *Taḍiya*, *s.* pole used in carrying burdens.

තඩියා, *Taḍiyá*, *s.* fat or corpulent man; any fat animal, louse.

තඩිස්සිය, *Taḍissiya*, *s.* small swelling.

තඩිස්සිවෙනවා, *Taḍissiwenawá*, *v.* to swell.

තඩුත්තුව, *Taḍuttuwa*, *s.* obstruction, impediment; stopping of the breath, panting.

තණ්ඩල්දමනවා, *Taṇḍal-damanawá*, *s.* to place an additional pair of animals in front of a vehicle to carry a heavy load.

තණ්ඩල, *Taṇḍala*, *s.* plant, cultivated variety of *colocasia antiquorum (Araceæ)*; see ගහල *gahala* and කඳල *kaṇḍala.*

තණ්ඩලා, *Taṇḍalá*, *s.* Tindal or master of a vessel,

තණ්ඩුල, *Taṇḍula*, *s.* thrashed and winnowed grain, but especially rice; sort of plant, species of *amaranth.*

තණ්ඩුලී, *Taṇḍulí*, *s.* plant, *amarantus polygonoides*, [Colloq. කූරතම්පලා *kúra-tampalá*].

තණ්හා, *Tanhá*, } *s.* lust, covetousness, longing,
තණ්හාව, *Tanháwa*, } ardent desire; wish, thirst; name of Máraya the great opposer of Buddha.

තණ්හාවෙනවා, *Tanháwenawá*, *v.* to desire, to covet.

තණ කබල, *Tana-kabala*, *s.* (තණ grass, කබල mouthful) mouthful of grass.

තණකොළ, *Tanakola*, *s.* blades of grass, grass.

තණ කැලය, *Tana-kelaya*, *s.* place overgrown with high and thick grass.

තණග, *Tanaga*, *s.* point of a blade of grass.

තණ ගිරවා, *Tana-girawá*, *s.* (තණ grass, ගිරවා parrot) grasshopper, genus *cicada*.

තණපත, *Tanapata*, *s.* blade of grass.

තණ පලා, *Tana-palá*, *s.* plant resembling grass, *commelina diffusa*

තණ රජ, *Tana-raja*, } *s.* (තණ and රජ king) chief
තණ රද, *Tana-rada*, } of the grasses; palmyra tree, [Colloq. තල්ගස *tal-gasa*].

තණ හාල්, *Tana-hál*, *s.* millet, *setaria italica (Gramineæ)*.

තත්, *Tat*, conjunction answering to even if, although, as ඔහු එතත් *ohu etat*, although he come; *s.* string of a musical instrument: *a.* that.

තත් කබල, *Tat-kabala*, *s.* vessel painted red.

තත්කවනවා, *Tatkawanawá*, *v.* to tighten the string of an instrument; to stretch a bow: pret. තත් කැව්වා *tatkewwá*.

තත්ත්ව, *Tattwa*, *s.* (තත් that (divine being), ත්වං *twan* thou, art) name of the Hindu Supreme Being or Brahma which is expressive of his real and essential nature and existence; essential nature, the human soul considered as one and the same with the divine spirit animating the universe; nature, state; truth, reality; substance as opposed to illusion, first principle, elementary property.

තත්ත්වඥාන, *Tattwajñána*, *s.* knowledge of divine truth, or the essence of any thing.

තත්තුව, *Tattuwa*, *s.* manner, mode.

තත්තෙ, *Tatte*, *s.* thirst.

තත්‍ර, *Tatra*, *adv.* there, therein, [Colloq. එහි *ehi*].

තත්පර, *Tatpara*, *s.* one thirtieth part of the time of the twinkling of the eye: *a.* diligent, attached to; careful; addicted to.

තත්පුරුෂ, *Tatpurusha*, *s.* that person; species of compound words usually consisting of two nouns, the first of which was in any case except the Nominative or Vocative; sometimes the case inflexion is retained.

තත්ව, *Tatwa*, see තත්ත්ව *tattwa*.

තත් සවභාව, *Tat-swabháwa*, *s.* its own peculiar nature.

තත්සම, *Tatsama*, see තසම *tasama*.

තත, *Tata*, *s.* string of a violin or lute; sound of the lute: *a.* spread, diffused, expanded.

තතන, *Tatana*, *s.* sickness, disease, disorder, suffering (bodily); shaking.

තතනනවා, *Tatananawá*, *v.* to rave, to storm when in a passion; to shake; to thunder: pret. තැතනුවා *tetanuwá*.

තතු, *Tatu*, *s.* cord, string; nature, disposition, mode, manner; fact, state.

තථා, *Tathá*, *adv* so, thus, in like manner.

තථාගත, *Tathágata*, *s.* (තථා thus, ආගත *ágata* who came) name or epithet of Buddha, given him in allusion to his having come to or obtained the rank of Buddha in the same way as his predecessors.

තද්, *Tad*, adjective pronoun, that.

තද්භව, *Tadbhawa*, see තබව *tabawa*.

තද, *Tada*, *a.* hard, obdurate, firm, strong; great, excessive; resolute; vehement; severe, harsh.

තදකම, *Tadakama*, *s.* severity, hardness.

තදකරණවා, *Tadakaranawá*, *v.* to tighten, to press down or close together.

තදබල, *Tadabala*, *a.* powerful, severe; serious.

තදබලකරණවා, *Tadabala-karanawá*, *v.* to compel, to press on.

තදයා, *Tadayá*, *s.* harsh austere man, hard hearted obdurate one.

තදවෙනවා, *Tadawenawá*, *v.* to be tightened or pressed.

තද්ධිත, *Taddhita*, *s.* term applied to derivative nouns, as patronymics or derivatives of various kinds.

තන්ගුස්, *Tangus*, *s.* sort of weed used in fishing.

තන්ඩල්, *Tandal*, *s.* master of a dhóni.

තන්තවා, *Tantawá*, see බෙරවා *berawá*.

තන්තිරිපට, *Tantiripata*, *s.* kind of musical instrument.

තන්තු, *Tantu*, *s.* thread; offspring, race, descendants.

තන්තුවාය, *Tantuwáya*, *s.* weaver, spider.

තන්ත්‍රය, *Tantraya*, *s.* treatise which teaches the nature and powers of the mantras, a sort of mystical or magical formula much used by astrologers and magicians in their intercourse with demons; medicament, drug, or charm considered as such, much used by natives of every class; thread, cord; cord of a lute; service; dependence; trial, ordeal; oath; heap, multitude; wealth; house; loom; happiness, felicity.

තන්ත්‍රී, *Tantrí*, *s.* string, rope; wire, or string of a lute; any vessel of the body; plant, *menispermum glabrum*, [Colloq. රසකිඳ *rasakiṇda*]; stalk of a bunch of plantains; musician.

තන්දිරම්කාරයා, *Tandiramkáraya*, *s.* artful man, sharper.

තන්දිරම, *Tandirama*, *s.* perfidy.

තන්ද්‍රා, *Tandrá*, } *s.* drowsiness, lassitude, exhaus-
තන්ද්‍රි, *Tandri*, } tion, weariness; sluggishness; syncope.

තන්වෑසි, *Tanwęsi*, *s.* one using speech fit for the occasion: *a.* skilled, refined.

තන්හා, *Tanhá*, } see තණ්හා *taṇhá*.
තන්හාව, *Tanháwa*, }

තන්හි, *Tanhi*, *adv.* there, therein.

තන, *Tana*, *s.* breast; longing; avarice; cocoa-nut tree: *a.* fine, thin; shaking, trembling; it frequently occurs as a corruption of තණ්හා *taṇhá*.

තනකිරි, *Tana-kiri*, *s.* woman's milk.

තනකිහ, *Tanakiha*, *s.* under part of the breast.

තනඟ, *Tananga*, *s.* nipple or teat.

තනතුර, *Tanatura*, *s.* office, service, appointment, employment, pl. තනතුරු *tanaturu*.

තනනවා, *Tananawá*, *v.* to make, to do, to build, to construct, to educate, to rear, to bring up; to shake: pret. තැනුවා *tęnuwá*.

තනපා, *Tanapá*, *s.* (තන breast, පා who drinks) sucking child; breast-milk.

තනපුඩුව, *Tana-puḍuwa*, see තනඟ *tananga*.

තනය, *Tanaya*, *s.* son, male descendant; child, offspring; breast of a female, sometimes written තනේ *tané*.

තනයා, *Tanayá*, *s.* daughter, [Colloq. දුව *duwa*].

තනර, *Tanara*, *s.* eyeball.

තනි, *Tani*, *a.* alone, single, individual.

තනි එලකහ, *Tani-ela-kaha*, *s.* plant, *hibiscus rosa sinensis*, [Colloq. සපත්තුමල් *sapattu-mal*].

තනි දණ්ඩ, *Tani-daṇḍa*, *s.* shin, pl. තනිදඬු *tani-daṇḍu*.

තනිදහස්, *Tani-dahas*, *s.* plant, *tajetes patula*.

තනිය, *Taniya*, see තනි *tani*.

තනි යක්මල්, *Tani-yakmal*, *s.* plant, *tajetes erecta*.

තනිරගු, *Taniragu*, *s.* plant, *hibiscus rosa sinensis*, [Colloq. සපත්තුමල් *sapattu-mal*].

තනිවතුසුද්ද, *Tani-watusudda*, *s.* ornamental shrub, *tabernæmontana coronaria*.

තනිස්නාඩු, *Tanisnáḍu*, *s.* rape.

තනි සූර්‍යකාන්ති, *Tani-súryakánti*, *s.* plant, *helianthus annuus*, sun flower

තනු, *Tanu*, } *s.* body; skin: *a.* small, little,
තනුක, *Tanuka*, } minute, thin, fine, slender, delicate, lean, meagre, emaciated.

තනුජ, *Tanuja*, *s.* (තනු body, ජ born) son; descendant.

තනුත්‍ර, *Tanutra*, *s.* (තනු and ත්‍ර what preserves) mail, armour.

තනුත්‍යාගය, *Tanutyágaya*, *s.* (තනු and ත්‍යාග *tyága* offering) offering of the body either as a religious sacrifice or as an act of charity; it is related of Buddha that while a candidate for that rank he gave his own flesh and blood to feed the poor to satisfy demons and to feed animals, to such an extent that he gave more blood than there is water in the sea and flesh than the earth of which this world is composed.

තනුමධ්‍ය, *Tanu-maddhya*, *s.* (තනු and මධ්‍ය middle) waist.

තනුරුහ, *Tanuruha*, *s.* hair (of the body); wing of a bird; son.

තනුවඟ, *Tanuwanga*, *s.* (තනු fine, soft, අඟ *anga* body) woman, [Colloq. ස්ත්‍රී *strí*].

තනේ, *Tané*, *s.* sternum or breast, see තනය *tanaya*.

තප්, *Tap*, *s.* burning, consuming; destroying.

තප්ත, *Tapta*, *a.* heated, inflamed, burnt with heat, parched.

තප්පණ, *Tappaṇa*, *s.* satisfaction, satiety, fulness; either the act of pleasing or being pleased; religious rite presenting water to the manes of the dead.

තප්පලියා, *Tappaliyá*, *s.* plump short man.

තප, *Tapa*, *s.* austerity, self-denial, penance, subduing the passions, virtue, moral merit; mental or bodily pain; superhuman power; heat, warmth, hot season.

තපන, *Tapana*, *s.* sun, [Colloq. ඉර *ira*]; one of the eight hells; heat, burning; also, marking nut.

තපනිශ්‍රිත, *Tapaniṣrita*, *s*, (තප penance, නිශ්‍රිත accustomed to) one possessing the virtues of an ascetic.

තපනී, *Tapaní*, *s.* the Gódávarí river.

තපනීය, *Tapaníya*, *s.* (තප to burn, අනීයර් *aniyar* affix, what must be melted) gold, [Colloq. රත්රන් *ratran*]; *a.* to be heated.

තපස්, *Tapas, s.* religious austerity, penance, mortification, practice of mental or personal self denial; world, region inhabited by saints or devotees after death; virtue, moral merit, duty; among the Hindus the special observance of certain things; thus, tapas of a Brahman is sacred learning; of a Kshatriya, the protection of subjects; of a Vaiṣya, almsgiving to Bráhmans; of a Ṣudra, the service of the same tribe; and of a ṛishi or saint, feeding upon herbs and roots; name of a month mágha (January–February); cold dewy season; hot season.

තපස්‍ය, *Tapasya, s.* February–March.

තපස්‍යා, *Tapasyá, s.* devout austerity, religious penance.

තපස්රකිණවා, *Tapas-rakiṇawá, v.* to become an ascetic, to perform the duties of an ascetic.

තපස්වරයා, *Tapaswarayá, s.* hermit, ascetic.

තපස්වින්, *Tapasvin, s.* ascetic, hermit, one given up to religious and devout penance; mendicant, pauper.

තපස්විනී, *Tapasviní, s.* female devotee; spikenard.

තපස, *Tapasa, s.* ascetic life.

තපසඞ්ග, *Tapasaṅga, s.* (තපස් *tapas* and අඞ්ග *aṅga* religious ordinance) ordinance to be observed by an ascetic; there are thirteen of these.

තපසුන්, *Tapasun,* corrupt form of තවසුන් *tawasun,* which see.

තපිනවා, *Tapinawá, v.* to warm one's self near the fire or under the sun: pret. තැප්පා *tęppá.*

තපෝධන, *Tapódhana, s.* (තපස් *tapas* religious austerity, ධන wealth) devotee, ascetic; one abounding in devout religious penance.

තපෝවට, *Tapówaṭa, s.* (තපස් *tapas* and වට what surrounds) country so called; part of central India remarkable for the piety of its inhabitants.

තපෝවන, *Tapówana, s.* sacred grove; place frequented by ascetics.

තපෝවෘත්ති, *Tapóvṛitti, s.* practices of an ascetic, mode or manner of life of an ascetic.

තපැල, *Tapęla, s.* post, post mail, also තැපැල *tępęla.*

තබනවා, *Tabanawá, v.* to put, to place, to fix; to preserve, to keep not to use: pret. තැබුවා *tębuwá* or තිබ්බා *tibbá.*

තබව, *Tabawa, s.* (ත that, බව being derived) term in Elu grammar designating the vocables formed from the Sanskrit or mediately from the Páli by the mutation and elision of letters.

තබා, *Tabá, par.* used in the sense of having put, placed; besides, in addition to, except, instead; 'setting aside' putting out of the question' 'not to speak of,' *e. g.* සොරකමෙහි විපාක මතු තබා මේ ජාතියෙහිම ලද්දේවේද, (සද්ධර්මාලංකාර:) He has suffered for his thievish act in this world, not to speak of (his suffering in) the future life. (Saddharmálaṇkára.)

තඹ, *Tam̲ba, s.* copper; kind of copper colour; dewlap of a bullock; red colour.

තඹක්ක, *Tam̲bakka, s.* pinchbeck.

තඹදුළුල්, *Tam̲baduḷul, s.* name of Íṣwara or Ṣiva.

තඹනඛයා, *Tam̲banakhayá, s.* (තඹ copper, නඛ finger nail, යා pers. aff.) one having copper coloured finger nails.

තඹපත, *Tam̲bapata, s.* copper-plate.

තඹපිල්, *Tam̲ba-pil, s.* cocoa-nut tree, [Colloq. පොල්ගහ *pol-gaha*].

තඹර, *Tam̲bara, s.* red (colour); red water lily, [Colloq. නෙළුම් *neḷum*].

තඹරිළු, *Tam̲bariḷu, s.* multitude of lotuses; also *thocymus pictoris;* see කරඳ *karan̲da;* bark of the bamboo.

තඹල, *Tam̲bala, s.* kind of root, *colocasia antiquorum.*

තඹලයා, *Tam̲balayá, s.* kind of fish.

තඹවතුර, *Tam̲ba-watura, s.* river water during the time of a flood.

තඹවන්, *Tam̲báwan, s.* (තඹ copper, වන් colour) copper colour; dark or coppery red.

තඹවලා, *Tam̲bawalá,* see ගෝනා *góná.*

තඹවළු, *Tam̲bawaḷu, s.* bullock, [Colloq. ගොණා *goṇá*].

තඹසල්ලිය, *Tam̲basalliya, s.* one eighth of a penny, (literally) a copper challi.

තඹසිළු, *Tam̲basiḷu, s.* cock, [Colloq. කුකුළා *kukuḷá*]; gallinule.

තඹාක්ක, *Tam̲bákka,* see තඹක්ක *tam̲bakka,*

තඹුරු, *Tam̲buru, s.* generic name of the nymphea or water lily, lotus, [Colloq. නෙළුම් *neḷum*].

තම්පලා, *Tampalá, s.* kind of greens, rhubarb; plant, *nothosœrua brachiata (Amarantaceœ).*

තම්පා, *Tampá, s.* cow, [Colloq. එලදෙන *eladena*].

තම්බනවා, *Tambanawá, v.* to boil as meat: pret. තැම්බුවා *tęmbuwá.*

තම්බපණ්ණි, *Tambapaṇṇi, s.* name of Ceylon.

තම්බි, *Tambi, s.* term used in addressing a Moorman. (Tamil.)

තම්බුටුවැල, *Tambuṭu-wela*, *s.* rattan or cane, peculiar to Ceylon, *calamus ovoideus (Palmæ)*, pl. තම්බුටුවැල් *tambuṭu-wel.*

තම්බෝරුව, *Tambóruwa*, *s.* drum, tamborine, war drum.

තම්මනා, *Tammaná*, *s.* plant, peculiar to Ceylon, *mischodon zeylanicus (Euphorbiaceæ).*

තම්මැට්ටම, *Tammeṭṭama*, *s.* two drums fastened together as kettle drums, pl. තම්මැට්ටම් *tammeṭṭam.*

තම, *Tama*, *pron.* he himself; *s.* darkness; darkness considered metaphorically, as ignorance; quality of darkness incident to humanity; tranquillity of mind; state of an ascetic having subdued passions; error; name of Ráhu.

තමතමන්, *Tamataman*, *pron.* one with another, applied to persons.

තමන්, *Taman*, *s.* themselves; their own.

තමයි, *Tamayi*, *par.* even so.

තමරුපු, *Tamarupu*, *s.* (තම darkness, රුපු enemy) sun, [Colloq. සූර්යයා *súryayá*].

තමල, *Tamala*, *s.* Sal or Saul tree, timber tree, *shorea robusta.*

තමලු, *Tamalu*, *s.* name of a tree bearing black blossoms, [Colloq. කොල්ලම්ගහ *kollam-gaha*].

තමස්, *Tamas*, *s.* religious austerity, penance, mortification, practice of mental or personal self denial; virtue, moral merit; practice of austerities according to the character or caste of the devotee.

තමස්විනි, *Tamasvini*, *s.* (තමස් darkness, විනි aff.) night, [Colloq. රාත්‍රිය *rátriya*].

තමස, *Tamasa*, see තම *tama.*

තමා, *Tamá*, *pron.* him, one's self.

තමාල, *Tamála*, *s.* name of a tree; see තමලු *tamalu.*

තමාලපත්‍ර, *Tamála-patra*, *s.* (තමාල and පත්‍ර leaf) sectarial mark on the forehead of a Hindu made of a compound of ashes and sandal wood, and usually called tilaka; leaf of the *Laurus cassia.*

තමි, *Tami*, *s.* night.

තමිස්‍ර, *Tamisra*, *s.* darkness.

තමිස්‍රා, *Thmisrá*, *s.* night; very dark night; great darkness; night during the wane of the moon.

තමී, *Tamí*, see තමි *tami.*

තමුන්, *Tamun*, *s.* themselves, their own.

තමුන්නාන්සේ, *Tamunnánsé*, *per. pron.* you (respectful).

තමුන්නැහේ, *Tamunnehé*, *s.* you, somewhat respectful.

තමුසේ, *Tamusé*, *per. pron.* you, (politely).

තමෝනුද, *Tamónuda*, *s.* (තමස් *tamas* darkness, නුද to send away, to disperse) sun; moon; fire; lamp; epithet or title of Buddha.

තර්කින්, *Tarkkin*, *s.* logician, disputer.

තර්ක, *Tarka*, *s.* plant, *sesbania* or *chynomene sesban;* logic, science of disputation; reasoning, argumentation, art of discussion or contending; doubt; thought; supplying an ellipsis; cause, motive; reduction to an absurdity.

තර්කශාස්ත්‍රය, *Tarka-śástraya*, *s.* science of logic.

තර්ජනකරණවා, *Tarjanakaraṇawá*, *v.* to rebuke, menace.

තර්ජනය, *Tarjanaya*, *s.* rebuke, chiding, warning, threatening, menacing.

තර්ජනී, *Tarjaní*, *s.* forefinger, so called on account of its being held up as a sign of threatening or rebuking.

තර්පණය, *Tarpaṇaya*, *s.* satisfaction, satiety, fulness; satisfaction given or received; act of pleasing or state of being pleased; perfumes; that which delights in smell or taste; that which gives health and vigour to the body.

තර්ෂ, *Tarsha*, *s.* thirst; wish, desire, [Colloq. අසාව *ásáwa*].

තර, *Tara*, *s.* raft, float; passing over, crossing; road; strength, power; name of Vishṇu; any thing firm or immovable; *a.* great, stout, fat, lusty, strong, hard.

තරංකේ, *Taranké*, *s.* door-bar, door-fastener.

තරක්ෂු, *Tarakshu*, *s.* (තර road, ක්ෂි *kshi* to annoy) hyena.

තරකම, *Tarakama*, *s.* fatness, stoutness.

තරකරණවා, *Tarakaraṇawá*, *v.* to fatten.

තරඟ, *Taranga*, *s.* wave; debate, contest, argument, strife.

තරඟකරණවා, *Tarangakaraṇawá*, *v.* to compete, to rival, dispute, argue.

තරණ, *Taraṇa*, *s.* crossing, going over; passing; raft, float; sharp or cutting instrument, as sword, knife, axe; shrub, *webera corymbosa (Rubiaceæ).*

තරණබටු, *Taraṇabaṭu*, *s.* species of night shade, *solanum sodomeum.*

තරණි, *Taraṇi*, *s.* going across, passing over; sun; ray of light; float, raft, boat; sort of aloe.

තරදෙන, *Tara-dena*, *s.* fat or well fed cow.

තරප්පුව, *Tarappuwa*, *s.* staircase.

තරම, *Tarama, s.* rank, quality, station in life; size, bulk, measure, quantity, pl. තරම් *taram.*

තරමගහනවා, *Taramagahanawá, v.* to decapitate, to behead.

තරල, *Tarala, s.* agitation, trembling, rolling; moving; gruel, rice gruel; liquid, any vinous or spirituous liquor; necklace, central gem in a necklace.

තරවටුකරණවා, *Tarawaṭukaraṇawá, v.* to censure, to reprove, to reprimand.

තරවටුව, *Tarawaṭuwa, s.* censure, menace, reproof, reprimand.

තරවනවා, *Tarawanawá, v.* to rub on, to daub: pret. තැරෙව්වා *tẹrewwá.*

තරස්, *Taras, s.* strength, power, force; speed, velocity; raft; bear, [Colloq. වලසා *walasá*].

තරස, *Tarasa, s.* hyena, Elu form of තරක්‍ෂු *tarakshu.*

තරහ, *Taraha, s.* wrath, rage, anger, choler, passion.

තරහලා, *Tarahalá, s.* goldsmith, [Colloq. බඩාලා *baḍálá*].

තරහවෙනවා, *Tarahawenawá, v.* to become angry.

තරා, *Tará, s.* sunbeam, ray of light, [Colloq. රශ්මි *rẹsmi*].

තරාතිරම, *Tarátirama, s.* rank, station, pl. තරාතිරම් *tarátiram.*

තරාදිය, *Tarádiya, s.* scales, small pair of scales, balance.

තරි, *Tari, s.* crossing, way over a river; boat, float, raft.

තරිඳු, *Tarin͟du, s.* (තර *tara* star, ඉඳු *in͟du* lord) moon, [Colloq. හඳ *han͟da*].

තරු, *Taru, s.* tree; stars.

තරු එළිය, *Taru-eliya, s.* star-light.

තරුණ, *Taruṇa, s.* young man, youth, one of virile age; castor oil plant; *a.* young, youthful, juvenile; new, fresh.

තරුණි, *Taruṇi, s.* young woman, pl. තරුණියෝ *taruṇiyó*; aloe tree, *aloe vulgaris,* [Colloq. කෝමාරිකා *kómáriká*].

තරුණු, *Taruṇu, s.* youth; young man; *a.* young, juvenile.

තරුප්පු, *Taruppu, s.* kind of gem, *rubal.*

තරුපති, *Tarupati, s.* (තරු stars, පති chief) moon, [Colloq. හඳ *han͟da*].

තරුපොන, *Tarupona, s.* cocoa-nut in which the kernel is not quite hardened.

තරුලතා, *Tarulatá, s.* plant, *ipomea quamoclit.*

තරුවැල, *Taruwẹla, s.* constellation, asterism.

තල්, *Tal, s.* palmyra tree, *borassus flabelliformis (Palmae);* nightshade.

තල්කඳ, *Tal-kan͟da, s.* stem of the palmyra tree.

තල්කොල, *Tal-kola, s.* palmyra leaf used for writing on and making baskets.

තල්ගහ, *Tal-gaha, s.* palmyra tree: see තල් *tal.*

තල්දිවියා, *Tal-diviyá, s.* enraged tiger.

තල්පත, *Talpata, s.* letter written on the leaf of the palmyra tree.

තල් පරාලේ, *Tal-parálé, s.* palmyra rafter.

තල්මහ, *Talmaha, s.* whale.

තල් රා, *Tal-rá, s.* toddy or liquor extracted from the palmyra tree.

තල්ල, *Talla, s.* roof of the mouth, palate; part under the tongue; reservoir, large tank or pond.

තල්ලමරණවා, *Tallamaraṇawá,* see තළුමරණවා *taḷumaraṇawá.*

තල්ලිකා, *Tallikà,* key. [Colloq. යතුර *yatura.*]

තල්ලු, *Tallu, s.* push, thrusting, shove.

තල්ලුකරණවා, *Tallukaraṇawá, v.* to push, to thrust, to shove.

තල්වාකර, *Talwákara, s.* arrack of the second distillation.

තල්වැට, *Talwẹṭa, s.* fan used by the priests of Buddha to hide their faces when preaching and to prevent their seeing women when travelling; common fan, [Colloq. පවන්පත *pawanpata*].

තල, *Tala, s.* plain, surface; shelf or layer; bottom or support of any thing; place or firm spot, the ground; essential nature; depth, bottom; inferiority of position, place under the earth; sole of the foot; palm of the hand; quiver; leathern fence worn by archers on the left arm; palmyra tree; span; hole, hollow; sea shore; blades; sesamum, *sesamum indicum;* talipot tree, *corypha umbraculifera (Palmæ).*

තල ඇටේ, *Tala-ẹṭé, s.* sesamum seed, forming the smallest of the doctor's weights, it is about one ninth of a gr. troy.

තලක්කට්ටු, *Talakkaṭṭu, s.* top.

තලකිරිත්තා, *Talakirittá, s.* francoline or painted partridge, *francolinus pictus (Tetrocindæ* order *Gallinæ).*

තලගොයා, *Talagoyá, s.* land lizard called *iguana* (edible) *Varanus dracæna (*order *Sauria).*

තලත්, *Talat, s.* name of Balabhadra or Balaráma.

තලතෙල්, *Tala-tel, s.* sesamum oil, gingely oil.

තලන්, *Talan, s.* beam, rafter.

තලණි, *Talaní, s.* kind of cloth manufactured from the bark of trees.

තලප, *Talapa, s.* kind of porridge.

තලපත, *Talapata, s.* leaf of the palmyra tree, used as a screen for the head against the sun or rain, pl. තලපත් *talapat.*

තලපතා, *Talapatá, s.* sword fish, pl. තලපත්තු *talapattu.*

තලපොට, *Talapoṭa, s.* plant, *hibiscus abelmoschus;* shrub, *cassia awriculata,* [Colloq. රණවරා *raṇawará* or දියබෙරලිය *diyaberaliya*].

තලමල, *Tala-mala, s.* flower of the talipot tree, or of the sesamum plant.

තලමුරුවට, *Tala-muruwaṭa, s.* dregs or refuse of the sesamum grain after the oil has been expressed, used as food when mixed with jaggery.

තලය, *Talaya, s.* the blade of any instrument, see තල *tala.*

තලවඩි, *Tala-waḍi, s.* spirit of arrack.

තලව්ව, *Talawwa, s.* meadow, plain, [Colloq. පිට්ට නිය *piṭṭaniya*]; part of the road frequently gone over by cart-bullocks, wheels etc.

තලා, *Talá, s.* high ground, hill; plant, *basil,* of which according to Siṇhalese botany there are twenty-two species and varieties; see Mr. Moon's work; Dr. Trimen gives six species of the genus *ocimum* as belonging to Ceylon, see හින්තලා *hintalá* and මදුරුතලා *madurutalá;* Roxburgh includes thirteen species in the *Flora Indica;*-large pond covered with flowers; any large sheet of water; tree, *cathartocarpus fistula.*

තලාකොල, *Talákola, s.* leaf of the *holy basil* which is used medicinally; see මදුරුතලා *madurutalá.*

තලාතල, *Talátala, s.* one of the seven divisions of the infernal regions.

තලාඳ, *Taláṇda,* } *s.* beam, not to support the roof
තලාන්, *Talán,* } but to keep the pillars from moving.

තලාව, *Taláwa, s.* open glade, or meadow, table land; open country without jungle in the mountainous districts, sometimes called පතන *patana.*

තලි, *Tali, s.* brazen or metal dish, platter; basin, charger.

තලිය, *Taliya, s.* charger or large metal or brazen dish; bason; plate.

තලිස්, *Talis, s.* tree so called, which is much used as a medicine by the natives, *flacourtia cataphracta,* [Colloq. රට උගුරැස්ස *raṭa-ugurẹssa*]; yellow orpiment.

තලේ, *Talé, s.* blade of a sword or any sharp instrument.

තලෑට, *Taḷeṭa,* see තලඇටේ *tala-ẹṭé.*

තව්ලැබෙනවා, *Taw-lẹbenawá, v.* to fade, to decay, to waste.

තව්ව, *Tawwa, s.* hole to drive a nail in.

තව, *Tawa, s.* ascetic or the state of an ascetic or Tápasayá: *adv.* more, yet, still, moreover.

තවත්, *Tawat, ad.* furthermore, moreover, still more.

තවතව, *Tawatawa, adv.* more and more.

තවද, *Tawada,* particle used to introduce a sentence or paragraph, answering to our moreover, furthermore, and, etc.

තවන්කරණවා, *Tawankaraṇawá, v.* to rear plants, to put in a nursery, form nursery of plants.

තවනවා, *Tawanawá, v.* to foment, to warm, to revive nature by the application of outward stimulants: pret. තැවුවා *tẹwuwá.*

තවපැල, *Tawapẹla, s.* (තව ascetic, පැල house) house occupied by a Buddhist ascetic or hermit, pl. තවපැල් *tawapẹl,* [Colloq. පන්සල *pansala*].

තවම, *Tawama, adv.* still, to this hour, yet.

තවර, *Tawara, s.* daubing, smearing, anointing.

තවරණවා, *Tawaraṇawá, v.* to besmear, to daub, to anoint, to plaster: pret. තැවරුවා *tẹwaruwá.*

තවල්ල, *Tawalla, s.* upper part of a tank cultivated when the water is low.

තවලම, *Tawalama, s.* number of oxen laden with merchandize; mart or station on the frontiers for the sale or exchange of commodities, pl. තවලම් *tawalam.*

තවස්, *Tawas,* } Elu form of තපස් *tapas* the ප *pa*
තවස, *Tawasa,* } being changed for ව *wa* according to a rule in Elu grammar which applies to all the words formed from this primitive.

තවසර, *Tawasara, s.* ascetic; see තවස් *tawas* and තපස් *tapas.*

තවා, *Tawá, p.* having fomented: pret. of තවනවා *tawanawá.*

තවාන, *Tawána, s.* nursery of plants, pl. තවාන් *tawán.*

තවාලු, *Tawálu, s.* kind of paddy.

තවුතිසාභවනය, *Tawutisábhawanaya, s.* (තාව *táwa* three, තිංස *tiṇsa* thirty, භවන *bhawana* place of residence) name of a Swarga, alluding to the thirty three eminently holy persons who, by the power of their devout religious austerities, went direct from this world to heaven, and are now inferior gods, at the head of whom is Ṣakrayá or Indra.

තවුමරණවා, *Tawumaraṇawá, v.* to cause to fade, by holding a leaf and over the fire: pret. තවුමැරුවා *tawumęruwá.*

තවුමැරෙණවා, *Tawumęreṇawá, v.* to pade as a leaf before the fire and sun: pret. තවුමැරුණ *tawumęruṇá.*

තවුර, *Tawura, a.* solid, firm, immovable.

තවුරු, *Tawuru, a.* delay, procrastination.

තවුස්, *Tawus,* see තවස් *tawas.*

තස්කර, *Taskara, s.* thief, robber; spring shrub, *vangueria spinosa.*

තස්කරී, *Taskarí, s.* passionate woman.

තසම, *Tasama, s.* (ත that, සම like, same) appellation, in Elu grammar, of Sanskrit and Páli words retained in the language without any change of form.

තසර, *Tasara, s.* shuttle. see නඩාව *naḍáwa.*

තහඩුව, *Tahaḍuwa, s.* flatness; any beaten metal plate; lock.

තහන්සිය, *Tahansiya,* see තහනම *tahanama.*

තහනම්කරණවා, *Tahanamkaraṇawá, v.* to prohibit, obstruct, confiscate.

තහනම, *Tahanama, s.* attachment of goods; prohibition, obstruction, impediment.

තහවුරු, *Tahawuru, a.* firm, hard, strong.

තළනවා, *Taḷanawá, v.* to flog, to beat, to strike, to scourge: pret. තැළුවා *tęḷuwá.*

තළාකය, *Taḷákaya, s.* tank, pond, [Colloq. පොකුණ *pokuṇa*].

තළුගසනවා, *Taḷugasanawá, v.* to taste; to move the jaws; to smack the lips.

තළුමරණවා, *Taḷumaraṇawá, s.* smack the lips.

තා, *Tá, pron.* thee.

තාක්, *Ták,* a particle or termination answering to until, unto, to that time, till then &c. &c.

තාක්කුව, *Tákkuwa, s.* mitigation or abatement as applied to disease.

තාගේ, *Tágé, pron.* your, thine or thy.

තාච්චිය, *Táchchiya, s.* large earthen vessel, frying pan.

තාඩංක, *Táḍaṅka, s.* (තඩ *taḍa* shine, අඞ්ක *aṅka* aff.) ornament for the ear.

තාඩන, *Táḍana, s.* beating, whipping, [Colloq. තැළීම *tęlíma*].

තාඩනීය, *Táḍaníya, f. p.* to be beaten, punishable.

තාණ්ඩව, *Táṇḍawa, s.* dancing, the act of dancing.

තාණ්ඩි, *Táṇḍi, s.* science of dancing.

තාත්තා, *Tättá, s.* father, in familiar language.

තාත්තුව, *Táttuwa, s.* chant, musical measure; dancing to the beat of the tom-tom.

තාත, *Táta, s.* father; also a son, in familiar language; holy man, sage, a venerable and respectable.

තාදෘශ, *Tádṛiṣa, a.* such like, like him, it, etc.

තාන්, *Tán, a.* new, unbleached.

තාන්තුවාව, *Tántuwáwa, s.* obstacle, difficulty, perplexity.

තාන්ත්‍රික, *Tántṛika, s.* scholar, man completely versed in any science; but it particularly refers to one who has studied and follows the doctrines of the තන්ත්‍ර *tantra* which see.

තාන්නමාන්න, *Tánnamánna, s.* presents and distinctions conferred by the king or Government.

තාන්රෙද්ද, *Tánredda, s.* new unbleached cloth,

තාන, *Tána, s.* tune; expanse, extension; object of sense; protection, refuge, deliverance, salvation.

තානම, *Tánama, s.* tune or kind of chant repeated to the beat of the tom-tom.

තානාන්තරය, *Tánántaraya, s.* high office, office of state, any great or important employment or avocation, corrupt form of ස්ථානාන්තරය *sthánántaraya.*

තානාපතියා, *Tánápatiyá, s.* ambassador.

තානායම, *Tánáyama, s.* rest house, place of accommodation for travellers.

තානේ, *Táné, s.* place, spot.

තාප්පමෝල, *Táppamóla, s.* large wooden hammer for beating or levelling the ground.

තාප්පෙ, *Táppe, s.* wall of a garden, stone or clay fence, pl. තාප්ප *táppa.*

තාප, *Tápa, s.* heat, burning; splendour (reflection of the sun); pain of mind, sorrow. distress of heart.

තාපනය, *Tápanaya, s.* act of heating or burning, inflaming; sun; arrows of Káma, the Indian god of love.

තාපනීය, *Tápaníya, a.* to be heated, glowing as gold.

තාපය, *Tápaya, s.* name of one of the hells, that in which the punishment consists of burning; see තාප *tápa.*

තාපස, *Tápasa,* see තපස් *tapas.*

තාපසයා, *Tápasayá, s.* ascetic, religious devotee; hermit, one living in the practice of devout religious penance.

තාපිඤ්ජ, *Tápiñja,*
තාපිඤ්ජන, *Tápiñjana,* } *s.* tamála tree, *xanthocymus pictorius,* [Colloq. කොල්ලම්ගහ *kollam-gaha*].

තාපින්, *Tápin*, *s*. person oppressed by heat.

තාපේ, *Tápé*, see තාප *tápa*.

තාම්‍ර, *Támbra*, *s*. corrupt form of තාම්‍ර, copper, [Colloq. තඹ *tamba*]; dark red kind of sandal wood, *pterocarpus santalinus*.

තාම්බූල, *Támbúla*, *s*. betel, *piper betel;* areca-nut.

තාම්බූලවල්ලි, *Támbúlawalli*, *s*. betel creeper, see බුලත්වැල *bulatwela*.

තාම, *Táma*, *s*. object of terror; fault, defect, vice; anxiety, distress; desire; thyself, even thee; see තවම *tawama*.

තාමර, *Támara*, *s*. water; ghee or oiled butter.

තාමරස, *Támarasa*, *s*. blue lotus, *nelumbium speciosum*, [Colloq. නෙළුම් *nelnm*]; gold; copper.

තාමලකී, *Támalakí*, *s*. plant, *flacourtia cataphracta*, [Colloq. රට උගුරැස්ස *rata-uguressa*].

තාමස, *Támasa*, *s*. darkness.

තාමසී, *Támasí*, *s*. very dark night; name of the goddess Durga.

තාම්‍ර, *Támra*, see තඹ *tamba*.

තාම්‍රකුට්ටක, *Támrakuttaka*, *s*. tobacco; the word is imitative of the foreign original, [Colloq. දුම්කොළ *dumkola*].

තාම්‍රකුට, *Támrakuta*, *s*. brazier, [Colloq ලෝකුරුවා *lókuruwá*].

තාම්‍රකුලය, *Támra-kulaya*, *s*. brazier caste.

තාම්‍රකුෂ්ඨය, *Támra-kushthaya*, *s*. leprosy.

තාම්‍රචූඩ, *Támrachúda*, *s*. (තාම්‍ර and චූඩ crest) cock.

තාම්‍රපට්ට, *Támrapatta*, *s*. copper plate, such as Hindu grants of land, etc. are frequently inscribed on.

තාම්‍රපත්‍ර, *Támra-patra*, *s*. copper plate.

තාම්‍රපර්ණ, *Támraparna*, see කොල්ලු *kollu*.

තාම්‍රපර්ණී, *Támra-parnní*, *s*. (තාම්‍ර and පර්ණී leaf) name of a river in India and of the district in its vicinity.

තාම්‍රපල්ලව, *Támra-pallawa*, *s*. tree, *alangium hexapetalum*, [Colloq. හෝපළු *hópalu*].

තාම්‍රපුෂ්ප, *Támra-pushpa*, *s*. (තාම්‍ර and පුෂ්ප flower) name of a plant bearing red flowers, *kæmpferia rotunda*, [Colloq. යවකෙන්ද *yawakenda*]; mountain ebony, *bauhinia variegata* or *purpurea;* trumpet flower, *stereospermum suave-olens*.

තාම්‍රපුෂ්පී, *Támra-pushpí*, *s*. (derived as the foregoing), flowering shrub, *woodfordia floribunda;* trumpet flower; red teori.

තාම්‍රඵල, *Támraphala*, *s*. (තාම්‍ර and ඵල fruit) tree, *alangium hexapetalum*, also රුකඟුණ *rukanguna*.

තාම්‍රලෝහ *Támra-lóha*, *s*. copper, [Colloq. තඹ *tamba*].

තාම්‍රවර්ණ, *Támra-warna*, *s*. (තාම්‍ර and වර්ණ colour) copper colour.

තාම්‍රවර්ණී, *Támra-warni*, *s*. blossoms of sesamum.

තාම්‍රවල්ලි, *Támrawalli*, *s*. (තාම්‍ර and වල්ලි creeper) Bengal madder, *rubia manjith* or *oldenlandia umbellata*, [Colloq. වැල්මදට *welmadata*].

තාම්‍රවෘක්ෂ, *Támra-vriksha*, *s*. (තාම්‍ර and වෘක්ෂ tree) kind of sandal wood, *pterocarpus*.

තාම්‍රවෘන්ත, *Támra-vrinta*, *s*. kind of vetch, [Coll: කොල්ලු *kollu*]; a tree, *nyctanthes arbor tristes*, [Colloq. සේපාල *sépála* or සේපාලිකා *sépáliká*].

තාම්‍රශිඛී, *Támrasikhí*, *s*. (තාම්‍ර and ශිඛා *sikhá* crest, ඉනි *ini* affix) cock, [Colloq. කුකුළා *kukulá*].

තාම්‍රසාර, *Támrasára*, *s*. (තාම්‍ර and සාර pith) red kind of sandal wood: see තාම්‍ර *támbra*.

තාර්ක්ෂ්‍ය, *Tárkshya*, *s*. collyrium for the eyes or eyelashes; name of Garuda; see ගරුඩ *garuda;* horse; gold; tree, *vateria indica*, [Coll: හල් *hal*].

තාර්ක්ෂ්‍යධ්වජ, *Tárkshyadhwaja*, see ගරුඩධ්වජ *garudadhwaja*.

තාර්ක්ෂ්‍ය ශෛල, *Tárkshya-saila*, *s*. (තාර්ක්ෂ්‍ය collyrium, ශෛල stone) substance made from the calx of brass, or from the *amomum anthorrhiza* and used as a collyrium or medical application to the eyes, [Colloq. රසාඤ්ජන *rasáñjana*]; red sandal.

තාර්කික, *Tárkika*, *s*. logician; philosopher, sophist.

තාර, *Tára*, *s*. skeleton; silver, [Colloq. රිදී *ridí*]; crossing or passing over; star; planet, asterism; high note or tone in music; pearl; beauty or elegance of a pearl; pupil of the eye; kind of pitch; *a*. radiant, shining, clean, clear; good; wellflavoured; resplendent.

තාරක, *Táraka*, *s*. star in general; crossing, act of passing over; float, raft; eye, pupil of the eye, pilot; helmsman, steersman; name of a noted demon destroyed by Kártikéya or Kataragama deviyó; protector, preserver.

තාරකාධිප, *Tárakádhipa*, *s*. (තාරක *táraka* star etc. අධිප *adhipa* ruler) moon, [Colloq. හඳ *handa*].

තාරකාව, *Tárakáwa*, *s*. star, planet, asterism, constellation.

තාරකේශ්වර, *Tárakéswara*, *s*. (තාරක *táraka* and ඊශ්වර *íswara* chief) moon.

තාරණ, *Tárana*, *s*. crossing, passing over; boat, float, raft.

තාරතම්‍ය, *Táratamya*, *s.* more or less, the state or condition.

තාරනා, *Táraná*, see තාරපති *tárápati*.

තාරා, *Tárá*, *s.* goddess, wife of Vṛihaspati the regent of the planet Jupiter; wife of Sugríva king of the monkeys; name of Durgá the wife of Ṣiva and mother of the Kataragama deviyó; pupil of the eye; star.

තාරාධිප, *Tárádhipa*, *s.* see තාරාපති *tárápati*.

තාරාපති, *Tárápati*, *s.* (තාරා star, පති chief) moon.

තාරාපථ, *Tárápatha*, *s.* (තාරා and පථ road, way) atmosphere, firmament, sky or visible heavens, [Colloq. අකාශ *ákása*].

තාරාවා, *Tárâwá*, *s.* drake.

තාරාවි, *Tárávi*, *s.* duck.

තාරුකා ඉබ්බා, *Táruká-ibbá*, *s.* starred tortoise, *tes tudo elegans (Chelonia)*.

තාරුකාව, *Tárukáwa*, corruptly for තාරකාව *tárakáwa*.

තාරුණ්‍ය, *Táruṇya*, *s.* youth.

තාල, *Tála*, *s.* short span, one measured by the thumb and middle finger; the open hand with the fingers extended; musical time; beating time in music by clapping the hands: sort of cymbal played with a stick; palmyra tree, [Colloq. තල් ගහ *tal-gaha*]; yellow orpiment, [Colloq. හිරියල් *hiriyal*].

තාලංපටය, *Tálaṇpaṭaya*, *s.* accompaniment of the tambourine with dancing.

තාලපත්‍ර, *Tálapatra*, *s.* (තාල palmyra, පත්‍ර leaf) leaf of the palmyra tree, much used in writing; kind of ear-ring made of pieces of the leaf of this tree, being rolled up in an ornamental way and used as a substitute for the following, viz. a hollow cylinder of gold, with or without a ring attached to it, thrust through the lobe of the ear and worn chiefly by the Hindus and higher classes of Malabar women as an ornament.

තාලපත්‍රිකා, *Tálapatriká*, *s.* leaf of the palmyra tree, much used in writing native books.

තාලපන්තිය, *Tálapantiya*, *s.* row of palmyra trees.

තාලබීජ, *Tála-bíja*, *s.* (තාල palmyra, බීජ seed) seed of the palmyra.

තාලම්පට, *Tálampa*[illegible], *s.* sort of cymbal peculiar to the Tamils; accompaniment of the tambourine with dancing.

තාලම, *Tálama*, *s.* beating time in music; kind of measured chant which is repeated when beating the tom-tom, and dancing.

තාලමූලිකා, *Tálamúliká*, } තාලමූලී, *Tálamúlí*, } *s.* tuberous stemless plant with yellow flowers, *curculigo orchioides*, [Çolloq. හීන් බින් තල් *hín-bintal*].

තාලය, *Tálaya*, see තාලම *tálama*.

තාලවෘක්ෂ, *Tála-vṛiksha*, *s.* palmyra tree, *borassus flabelliformis*, [Colloq. තල් *tal*].

තාලවෘන්ත, *Tála-vṛinta*, *s.* (තාල palm of the hand, වෘන්ත root or stalk) fan, alluding to its shape which when made from the young leaf of the palmyra expands from the hand like a leaf from its stem.

තාලාඞ්ක, *Tálánka*, *s.* name of Balabhadra or Balaráma elder brother of Kṛishṇa.

තාලාඞ්කජිත් *Tálánkajit*, *s.* (තාලාඞ්ක and ජිත් who conquers) name of Kártikéya, or as he is called in Ceylon Kataragama deviyó, in allusion to his conquering Balabhadra, being born for that purpose.

තාලි, *Táli*, *s.* sort of key or pin; species of the mountain palm, *corypha taliera*, or talipot *c. umbraculifera*, [Colloq. තල *tala*]; thorny tree, *flacourtia cataphracta*, [Colloq. රට උගුරැස්ස *raṭa-ugurẹssa*]; fragrant kind of earth; spirituous juice of the palm; common toddy extracted from the cocoa-nut tree.

තාලිය, *Táliya*, *s.* large pot or vessel either earthen or metallic, but chiefly the latter; kind of tablet or collar made of gold and worn on the neck of the Moor and Malabar women, [Colloq. තැල්ල *tẹlla*].

තාලී, *Tálí*, *s.* talipot tree, [Colloq. තලගහ *talagaha*]; see තාලි *táli*.

තාලීසපත්‍රං, *Tálísa-patraṇ*, *s.* kind of medical plant or its leaf, *flacourtia cataphracta*, see තාලි *táli*.

තාලුකා, *Táluká*, *s.* palate.

තාලුජාක්ෂර, *Tálujákshara*, *s.* any palatal letter.

තාවකාලික, *Táwakálika*, *s.* time of the day in which it is lawful for the priests of Buddha to eat, viz. at any hour before twelve o'clock or mid-day

තාවතිංසය, *Táwatiṇsaya*, *s.* name of Ṣakraya's heaven on the summit of Mahámẹru: see තවුතිසාභවනය *tawutisábhawanaya*.

තාවර, *Táwara*, *s.* things without life; plant, *arum macrorhizon;* bow-string; *a.* firm, immoveable, the Elu form of ස්ථාවර *stháwara*.

තාවිකා *Táviká*, *s.* Indian tailor bird, *orthotomus sutorius (Timaliidæ* order *Passeres)*.

තාසප්‍රිය, *Tásapriya*, *s.* tree, *nephelium longana*, [Colloq. මොර *mora* or කිරිපළු ගහ *kiripalu-gaha*].

ති, *Ti*, *s.* three, [Colloq. තුණ *tuṇa*].

තිංත්‍රිණික, *Tiṇtrinika*, *s.* corrupt form of තින්තිඩික *tintiḍika*.

තික්, *Tik*, *s.* spot, freckle, mark, spots on tigers or deer; powerful rays of the sun.

තික්ත, *Tikta*, *s.* bitterness, bitter taste; medical plant, *echites antidysenterica*, [Colloq. කෙළිඳ *keḷinda*]; tree, *capparis Roxburghii;* another medical plant, *mollugo pentaphylla*; *a.* bitter, sharp, pungent, tart, keen.

තික්තක, *Tiktaka*, *s.* sort of gourd, [Colloq. දුම් මැල්ල *dummella*]; kind of gentian; dark kind of *mimosa catechu.*

තික්තගන්ධා, *Tikta-gandhá*, *s.* (තික්ත bitter, ගන්ධ fragrance) plant, *lycopodium imbricatum.*

තික්තදුග්ධා, *Tikta-dugdhá*, *s.* medicinal species of moon-plant.

තික්තවල්ලිකා, *Tiktawalliká*, *s.* plant, *sanseviera zeylanica*, [Colloq. නියඳ *niyanda*].

තික්තශාක, *Tiktaṣáka*, *s.* (තික්ත bitter, ශාක vegetable) kind of mimosa; another plant, *capparis Roxburghii.*

තික්තසාර, *Tiktahára*, *s.* plant, species of the mimosa.

තික්තා, *Tiktá*, *s.* febrile medicament, compounded of three pungent substances, viz. black pepper, long pepper, and dried ginger; medicinal plant, කටුකරෝහිණී *káṭukaróhiṇí*, [Colloq. කටුකරෝසන *kaṭukarósana*].

තික්තිකා, *Tiktiká*, *s.* bitter gourd.

තික්පොලඟා, *Tik-polangá*, see තිත්පොලඟා *tit-polangá.*

තික්මෙරද, *Tikmerada*, *s.* sun, [Colloq. සූර්‍ය්‍යයා *súryayá*].

තික්හෙලි, *Tikheli*, *s.* man without feet; cripple.

තිකිත්සාව, *Tikitsáwa*, corrupt form of චිකිත්සාව *chikitsáwa*, which see.

තිකුළ, *Tikuḷa*, *s.* mountain with three peaks.

තිකුළු, *Tikuḷu*, *s.* (ති three, කුළු pungent) medicine compounded of ginger, black and long pepper.

තිග්ම, *Tigma*, *s.* heat, that peculiar kind of heat existing in spices and aromatic plants; *a.* pungent; sharp, keen, bitter, acrid.

තිග්මාංශු, *Tigmáṇṣu*, *s.* (තිග්ම *tigma* heat, අංශු *anṣu* ray) sun, [Colloq. සූර්‍ය්‍යයා *súryayá*]; *a.* cruel, fierce, savage.

තිගැස්සි, *Tigessi*, *s.* startling, startle, fright; hesitation.

තිගැස්සිවෙනවා, *Tigessiwenawá*, *v.* to be startled.

තිඟුරස, *Tingurasa*, Elu form of තිග්ම රශ්මි *tigma-raṣmi*, see තිග්මාංශු *tigmáṇṣu.*

තිට, *Tiṭa*, *pron. fem. dat. singular* to thee.

තිටිංග, *Tiṭinga*, *s.* *Sesbania ægyptiaca*, (Tamil Karum chembai); *ardisia humilis*, [Colloq. බළු දම් *baḷudam* or දියදඹ *diyadamba*].

තිත්, *Tit*, Elu form of තීර්ථක *tírthaka*, which see; *a.* bitter.

තිත්ත, *Titta*, *a.* bitter, pungent, peppery.

තිත්ත අඟුන, *Titta-anguna*, *s.* plant, *leptadenia reticulata.*

තිත්ත කපුරු, *Titta-kapuru*, *s.* bitter kind of camphor.

තිත්ත කිඳ, *Titta-kinda*, *s.* plant, *Tinospora crispa (Menispermaceæ).*

තිත්ත කොමඩු, *Titta-komaḍu*, *s.* bitter gourd, *citrullus colocynthis*, [Colloq. යක්කොමඩු *yak-komaḍu*].

තිත්ත කැකිරි, *Titta-kekiri*, *s.* bitter species of cucumber, *cucumis madaraspatanus.*

තිත්ත ගස්, *Titta-gas*, *s.* plant, *trichadenia zeylanica (Bixineæ);* also called *Tolol.*

තිත්ත දුම්මැල්ල, *Titta-dummella*, *s.* plant, *trichosanthes cucumerina*, see දුම්මැල්ල *dummella.*

තිත්ත ලබු, *Titta-labu*, see තිත්ත කොමඩු *titta-komaḍu.*

තිත්තයා, *Tittayá*, *s*, small river fish.

තිත්ත රස, *Titta-rasa*, *s.* one of the seven tastes, bitter.

තිත්ත ලි, *Titta-li*, *s.* worm-wood.

තිත්ත වෙරළු, *Titta-weraḷu*, *s.* species of wild olive.

තිත්ත වැටකොළු, *Titta-weṭakoḷu*, *s.* creeping plant, genus *luffa:* see දාරවැටකොළු *dára-weṭakoḷu*, and නියන්වැටකොළු *niyan-weṭakoḷu.*

තිත්ත වැල්, *Titta-wel*, *s.* plant, *anamirta paniculata, (Menispermaceæ).*

තිත්ත හල්, *Titta-hal*, *s.* tree, variety of *vateria indica.*

තිත්ත හොඩල, *Titta-honḍala*, *s.* climbing plant, the root said to be poisonous, *trichosanthes palmata (Cucurbitaceæ).*

තිත්තිර, *Tittira*,
තිත්තිරි, *Tittiri*, } *s.* spotted snipe, [Colloq. තිත් වටුවා *tit-waṭuwá*].

තිත් පොලඟා, *Tit-polangá*, *s.* deadly viper, *daboia russellii (Ophidia).*

තිත් මාපිලා, *Tit-mápilá*, *s.* snake, variety of *dipsas forstenii.*

තිත් මුවා, *Tit-muwá*, *s.* spotted deer, *axis maculatus.*

තිත් වටුවා, *Tit-waṭuwá*, *s.* (තිත් spotted, වටුවා snipe) spotted quail or snipe.

තිත, *Tita*, *s.* speck, freckle, spot, mark; mole, spots upon a tiger, deer. etc.; mark in punctuation.

තිති, *Titi*, Elu form of තිථි *tithi*, which see.

තිතික්ෂා, *Titikshá*, *s.* patience, resignation, sufferance, endurance; pardon, forgiving.

තිතික්ෂු, *Titikshu*, *a.* patient, resigned.

තිතිය, *Titiya*, *s.* Elu form of තිථි *tithi* or තිථිය *tithiya*.

තිථි, *Tithi*, } *s.* lunar day; one-thirtieth of a
තිථිය, *Tithiya*, } whole lunation.

තිදස්, *Tidas*, *s.* a god.

තිදස්පති, *Tidaspati*, see තිදසිඳු *tidasiṉdu.*

තිදස්පුර, *Tidaspura*, *s.* name of Swarga or තවුතිසා භවනය *tawutisá-bhawanaya*, which see.

තිදස්රද, *Tidasrada*, *s.* (තිදස් god, රද king) name of Ṣakra or Indra alluding to his being the chief of gods.

තිදස්රදවිය, *Tidasradaviya*, *s.* (තිදස්රද and අවිය *aviya* instrument) rain-bow, in allusion to its being the bow of Ṣakra or Indra the king of Swarga and regent of the skies or visible heavens.

තිදස, *Tidasa*, *s.* a god.

තිදසපුර *Tidasapura*, *s.* (තිදස and පුර city) Swarga, heaven or the region of the gods, situated on the summit of Mahāméru.

තිදසිඳු, *Tidasiṉdu*, *s.* (තිදස *tidasa* god, ඉඳු *iṉdu* chief or lord) name of Ṣakra as lord or chief of the gods of තවුතිසාභවනය *tawutisábhawanaya*, which see.

තිදෙස්රජ, *Tideṣraja*, see තිදසිඳු *tidasiṉdu.*

තින්තිඩ, *Tintiḍa*, } *s.* tamarind tree, [Colloq.
තින්තිඩිකා, *Tintiḍiká*, } සියඹලා *siyaṉbalá*].

තින්තිඩී, *Tintiḍí*, *s.* tamarind tree; also *emblic myrobalan*, [Colloq. නෙල්ලි *nelli*].

තින්තිඩීක, *Tintiḍíka*, *s.* tamarind tree or its fruit.

තිඳු, *Tindu*, } *s.* tree, from the fruit of which
තිඳුක, *Tinduka*, } a kind of resin is obtained, used in India as pitch for caulking vessels, etc., *diospyros embryopteris*, [Colloq. තිඹිරි *tiṉbiri*].

තිඳුකී, *Tindukí*, *s.* fruit of the last mentioned tree.

තිඳුල, *Tindula*, see තිඳු *tindu.*

තිනිය, *Tiniya*, *s.* tree peculiar to Ceylon, *doona congestifolia (Dipterocarpaceæ).*

තිනියුම්, *Tiniyum*, } *s.* shaking, trembling, tremor.
තිනිව, *Tiniwa*, }

තිනිශ, *Tiniṣa*, *s.* fruit tree, *dalbergia ougeinensis*, [Colloq. කොබු *kobu*].

තිනෙත්, *Tinet*, *s.* (ති three, නෙත් eyes) three-eyed one, name of Ṣiva alluding to his having three eyes, [Colloq. ඊශ්වරයා *íṣwarayá*].

තිප්පිලි, *Tippili*, *s.* long pepper, *piper longum (Piperaceæ).*

තිපල්, *Tipal*, *s.* medicine compounded of the three noted myrobalans or medical nuts අරළු *araḷu*, බුළු *buḷu*, නෙල්ලි *nelli*, which are used in almost every native medicinal preparation; see the words in their proper places.

තිපල් කසාය, *Tipal-kasáya*, *s.* (තිපල් and කසාය purge) purgative decoction made from the above mentioned nuts.

තිපාස, *Tipása*, *a.* thirsty, see පිපාස *pipása.*

තිපාසය, *Tipásaya*, *s.* thirst, (corrupt form of පිපාසා *pipásá*).

තිපුටා, *Tipuṭá*, see ත්‍රිපුටා *tripuṭá.*

තිපුස, *Tipusa*, *s.* plant, species of the *sphæranthus.*

තිබ්බටු, *Tibbaṭu*, *s.* spiny shrub, kind of nightshade, *solanum indicum (Solanaceæ).*

තිබ්බනවා, *Tibbanawá*, *v.* to cause to place: pret. තිබ්බෙව්වා *tibbewwá.*

තිබනවා, *Tibanawá*, *v.* to put, to place, to reserve: pret. තිබ්බා *tibbá* or තිබුවා *tibuwá:* see තියනවා *tiyanawá.*

තිබිලි, *Tibili*, see තිවිලි *tivili.*

තිබීම, *Tibíma*, verbal noun of තිබනවා *tibanawá.*

තිබෙනවා, *Tibenawá*, *v.* to be, (applied only to things): pret. තිබුනා *tibuná:* see තියෙනවා *tiyenawá.*

තිඹ, *Tiṉba*, *s.* measure equal to four kurunies or four fifths of a parrah.

තිඹිරි, *Tiṉbiri*, *s.* tree from which exudes a glutinous substance resembling glue which is much used in the country for the seams of boats; from its exceeding acidity, it is not liable to be attacked by ants, worms or insects of any kind, the unripe fruit contains much tannin used to preserve fishing nets, *diospyros embryopteris (Ebenaceæ):* see තිඳුක *tinduka.*

තිඹිරිගේ *Tiṉbirigé*, see තිමිරිගේ *timirigé.*

තිඹිලි, *Tiṉbíli*, see තිවිලි *tivili.*

තිමි, *Timi*, *s.* hole, cavity; fainting.

තිමිංගල, *Timingala*, see තිමිය *timiya.*

තිමිත, *Timita*, *a.* wet. moist, damp; steady, fixed, unmoved, unshaken.

තිමිය, *Timiya*, *s.* ocean, [Colloq. මුහුද *muhuda*]; fabulous fish of an enormous size, said to be five hundred yoduns in length; there are five kinds, all of the same size, තිමිංගල *timingala*, තිමිරපිංගල *timira-pingala*, අජ්ජාරෝහය *ajjáróhaya*, තිමිය *timiya;* මහතිමිය *maha-timiya;* name for any large fish, as the whale, etc.

තිමිර, *Timira*, *s.* darkness, blindness, either physically or morally; *gutta serena*, arising from an affection of the optic nerve; [Colloquial: අඳුර *andura*].

තිමිර කරවලා, *Timira-karawalá*, *s.* snake, genus *bungarus*.

තිමිරපිංගල, *Timirapingala*, see තිමිය *timiya*.

තිමිර පොලඟා, *Timira-polangá*, *s.* viperine snake.

තිමිරරිපු, *Timira-ripu*, } *s.* (තිමිර darkness, රිපු enemy) sun; moon.
තිමිරාරි, *Timirári*, }

තිමිරිගේ, *Timiri-gé*, *s.* small house or apartment, attached to a dwelling house for woman to be confined in; lying in-room.

තිමුව, *Timuwa*, *s.* leech, [Colloq. කූඩැල්ලා *kúḍellá*]: *a.* having three faces.

තිය, *Tiya*, Elu form of ත්‍රි *tri* three.

තියන්, *Tiyan*, *s.* corrupt form of තියම් *tiyam*, which see.

තියනවා, *Tiyanawá*, *v.* to put, to place, (applied only to things): pret. තිබ්බා *tibbá*, තිබුවා *tibuwá:* see තිබනවා *tibanawá*.

තියඹරා, *Tiyambará*, *s.* sort of cucumber.

තියම්, *Tiyam*, } *s.* (ති three, යම් going or watch) three watches or a period of time equal to twelve of our hours; the Sinhalese divide the day and night into sixty peyas or hours, six yámas or watches, and two tiyams or twelve of our hours, either the day or the night.
තියමු, *Tiyamu*, }

තියල, *Tiyala*, *s.* sort of prepared dish of food, the chief ingredient in which is fish.

තියවක, *Tiyawaka*, *s.* the third day after the new or full moon.

තියා, *Tiyá*, *part.* of තියනවා *tiyanawá*, has an idiomatic use: *e. g.* ඒ වැඩේ පස්දෙනෙකුට තියා දහදෙනෙකුටවත් කරන්ට බැ, The work cannot be done by even ten men, putting five men out of the question, *i. e.* much less can five men do it.

තියු, *Tiyu*, *s.* praise, panegyric.

තියුකරු, *Tiyukaru*, see තිවුකරු *tiwukaru*.

තියුගී, *Tiyugí*, *s.* kind of poetical panegyric.

තියුණු, *Tiyuṇu*, *a.* sharp, piercing, pungent; peppery; clever, discerning.

තියුණුකර, *Tiyuṇukara*, *s.* (තියුණු and කර ray) sun, powerful rays of the sun; see වණ්ඩිභට්ටයා *wandibhaṭṭayá*.

තියුණුනුවන, *Tiyuṇu-nuwana*, *s.* keen penetration, discernment, intelligence; wit.

තියුම්, *Tiyum*, *s.* satisfaction, joy, gladness.

තියෙනවා, *Tiyenawá*, *v.* to be (applied to things inanimate): pret. තිබුනා *tibuná*; part. තිබී *tibí*.

තිර්‍යක්, *Tiryak*, *ad.* across, horizontal.

තිර්‍යග්ගතය, *Tiryagagtaya*, *s.* (තිර්‍යක් *tiryak* and ගත *gata* what goes) any animal; quadruped.

තිර, *Tira*, Elu form of ස්ථිර *sthira*, firmness etc. which see; screen, wall of cloth for surrounding a place; curtain, veil, hanging: *a.* certain, fixed.

තිරච්ඡාන, *Tirachchhána*, *s.* quadruped; general name for an animal, [Colloq. තිරිසනා *tirisaná*].

තිරච්ඡාන යෝනිය, *Tirachchhána-yóniya*, *s.* metempsychosis under the form of an animal; animals, including every species except man.

තිරය, *Tiraya*, *s.* curtain, veil; see තිර *tira*; also, ජවනිකාව *jawanikáwa*.

තිරලියා, *Tiraliyá*, *s.* kind of fish.

තිරශ්චීනයා, *Tiraṣchínayá*, *s.* animal, see තිරච්ඡාන *tirachchhána*.

තිරස්, *Tiras*, *ad.* secretly, covertly; horizontally.

තිරස්කරිණී, *Tiraskariṇí*, *s.* (තිරස් secret, කරිණී making) outer tent, wall or screen of cloth surrounding the principal tent: see තිරස්තවාලු *tirastawálu*.

තිරස්තවාලු, *Tirastawálu*, *s.* creeping plant, having stems with three or four angles and large white flowers; the root is a powerful purgative, *ipomœa turpethum;* sometimes written ත්‍රස්තවාලු *trastawálu*.

තිරසර, *Tirasara*, } *a.* true, certain; firm, unmoved.
තිරසාර, *Tirasára*, }

තිරළු, *Tiraḷu*, *s.* ram, [Colloq. බැටළුවා *beṭaḷuwá*].

තිරාකොල, *Tirákola*, *s.* leaves of a plant used as a vegetable.

තිරිඟිය, *Tiringiya*, *s.* tie, binding; any thing firmly bound.

තිරිඟු, *Tiringu*, *s.* wheat.

තිරිත්තම, *Tirittama*, *s.* good manner, proper conduct, respectable and well behaved demeanour.

තිරිසන් අපාය, *Tirisan-apáya*, *s.* place of punishment for sin committed in a former state of existence; punishment by birth under an animal form.

තිරිසනා, *Tirisaná*, *s.* brute animal, beast, irrational being, see තිරච්ඡාන *tirachchhána*.

තිරිටක, *Tiriṭaka*, *s.* bark of a tree worn by ascetics; bark, rind, [Colloq. රිටි සුඹුල *riṭi-sumbula*, පොත්ත *potta*].

තිරු, *Tiru*, *a.* firm, strong, fixed.

තිරුවා, *Tiruwá*, *s.* fool, simpleton, [Colloq. මෝඩයා *móḍayá*].

තිරුවාකන, *Tiruwákana*, *s.* pan or touch-hole of a gun or cannon, pl. තිරුවාකන් *tiruwákan*.

තිරුවානගල, *Tiruwána-gala*, *s.* white stone, quartz.

තිරෙළුවන්, *Tireḷuwan*, *s.* kind of ram.

තිරේ, *Tiré*, *s.* curtain, veil, pl. තිර *tira*.

තිරෝධාන, *Tiródhána*, *s.* (තිරස් *tiras* secret, ධාන holding) covering, concealment; sheath; veil; cloth or cloak; any thing which withholds an other from sight; disappearance, act of disappearing.

තිරෝහිත, *Tiróhita*, *a.* concealed, hidden, escaping privately, absconding.

තිල්ව, *Tilwa*, } *s.* medicinal tree, *excœcaria*
තිල්වක, *Tilwaka*, } *agallocha*, [Colloq. තෙලකිරිය *tela-kíriya*]; *symplocus racemosa*, [Colloq. හෙළ ලොත් *heḷa-lot*].

තිල, *Tila*, *s.* plant bearing an oily seed, the oil and seed being both much used in oriental cooking. *Sesamum indicum*, [Colloq. තල *tala*]; mole or spot compared to the seed of the sesamum, [Colloq. උපන්ලපය *upan-lapaya*].

තිලක, *Tilaka*, *s.* mark or marks made with coloured earth or unguents and sometimes a composition of ashes and sandal wood, made upon the forehead and between the eye-brows of the Hindus either as an ornamental or sectarial distinction; freckle, mole, natural mark on the person; title, especially in composition, implying preeminence, as ශාක්‍යකුල තිලක *ṣákyakula-tilaka*, the chief or head of the race of Ṣákya, one of the names or epithets of Buddha; the bladder; black salt, [Colloq. කළුලුණු *kaḷu-luṇu*], a factitious salt containing sulphur and iron; a disease viz. the appearance of dark spots on the skin, unattended with inflammation; the spleen; small red berry, [Colloq. මදටිය *madaṭiya*]: *a.* spotted, freckled, having moles or spots; chief, principal.

තිලකාලක, *Tilakálaka*, *s.* (තිල sesamum seed, කාලක black) mole, freckle, freckled person.

තිලකුණු, *Ti-lakuṇu*, *s.* (ති three, ලකුණු sign) three subjects which form a principal part of the meditations of religious ascetics, but chiefly of the priests of Buddha: viz. the impermanency of human nature, sorrow in all worldly things, unreality.

තිලජ, *Tilaja*, *s.* (තිල and ජ what is born or produced) sesamum oil: see තලතෙල් *talatel*.

තිලත්, *Tilat*, see තලත් *talat*.

තිලතණ්ඩුලක, *Tilataṇḍúlaka*, *s.* (තිල sesamum, තණ්ඩුල grain and ක affix, that which is as agreeable as rice mixed with sesamum) an embrace, embracing.

තිලතෛල, *Tilataila*, *s.* (තිල and තෛල oil) sesamum oil, [Colloq. තලතෙල් *tala-tel*].

තිලපර්ණී, *Tilaparṇni*, *s.* red sanders, *pterocarpus santolinum*, [Colloq. රත්සඳුන් *rat-sandun*].

තිලපුෂ්පඃ, *Tilapushpaḥ*, *s.* flower of the sesamum plant.

තිලබීජය, *Tila-bíjaya*, *s.* sesamum seed.

තිලරස, *Tilarasa*, *s.* (තිල and රස what is extracted) sesamum oil.

තිලිත්ස, *Tilitsa*, *s.* snake, [Colloq. පොළඟා *polangá*, or පිඹුරා *pimburá*].

තිලින්, *Tilin*, *par.* from that, from this, abl. of තෙලෙ *tele*.

තිලින, *Tilina*, *s.* present, gift, [Colloq. තෑග්ග *tégga*]; kindness, mercy, pity, [Colloq. කරුණාව *karuṇáwa*].

තිලොව, *Tilowa*, *s.* (ති three, ලොව world) three worlds.

තිලෝගුරු, *Tilóguru*, *s.* (ති three, ලෝ world, ගුරු teacher) title of Buddha as teacher of three worlds, viz. brahmas, gods, and men; procumbent hairy plant, *polygala glaucoides*.

තිලෝතලය, *Tilótalaya*, *s.* (ති and ලෝ world, තල *tala* place) the three substrata or foundations upon which this Sakwaḷa or universe is supposed to rest, viz. the first or lowest of air; the second, water; the third, earth.

තිලෝනා, *Tilóná*, *s.* (තිලෝ and නා from නායක *náyaka* chief) name or title of Buddha as chief of three worlds, viz. brahmas, gods, and men.

තිවට, *Tiwaṭa*, *s.* name of Viṣwakarma, the architect of the gods, who constructed Ṣakra's palace; name of Brahma.

තිවන, *Tiwana*, *s.* parrot, [Colloq. ගිරවා *girawá*].

තිවිධ, *Tiridha*, *a.* (ති three, විධ sort) of three kinds, of three forms, three fold.

තිවිලි, *Tivili*, *s.* person with three dents in his belly (from fatness).

තිවු, *Tiwu*, *s.* praise, eulogium, panegyric.

තිවුකර, *Tiwukara*, *s.* class of persons whose business it is to panegyrize, and who are employed by others for that purpose.

තිවුකරු, *Tiwukaru*, *s.* panegyrist, eulogist.

තිවුතා, *Tiwutá*, *s.* creeping plant, *ipomœa turpethum*, [Colloquial: තුස්තාවාලු *trastawálu*]; small cardamums, [Colloq සිහින් එන්සාල් *sihin-ensál*].

තිවුණුනුවන, *Tiwuṇu-nuwana*, *s.* penetration, keen perception. see තියුණුනුවන *tiyuṇu-nuwana*.

තිෂ්‍ය, *Tishya*, *s.* the eighth of the lunar mansions, an asterism figured by an arrow, and containing three stars, of which one is δ Cancri; month දුරුතු *durutu* (January-February); Kaliyuga, the fourth or present age; plant, *phyllanthus emblica*, [Colloq. නෙල්ලි *nelli*].

තිෂ්‍යඵලා *Tishya-phalá*, *s.* plant, *emblic myrobalan*, [Colloq. නෙල්ලි *nelli*].

තිස්, *Tis*, *a.* thirty.

තිස්නම, *Tis-nama*, *s.* an assembly of thirty priests of Buddha, or of thirty respectable persons.

තිස්‍ය, *Tisya*, see තිෂ්‍ය *tishya*.

තිස්වෙනි, *Tisweni*, *a.* thirtieth.

තිස්සේ, *Tissé*, } *ad.* always, continually, constantly.
තිස්සේම, *Tisséma*, }

තිස, *Tisa*, *s.* number thirty.

තිසත්, *Tisat*, *a.* sharp, pungent.

තිසර, *Tisara*, *s.* sort of swan; according to some a large crane, [Colloq. හංසයා *haṇsayá*]; *a.* high; eminent, excellent

තිසරණ, *Tisaraṇa*, *s.* (ති three, සරණ help) the three religious helps or refuges for the world, viz. Buddha, his doctrines, and his priesthood.

තිසරපට, *Tisarapaṭa*, *s.* kind of dress.

තිසරපෙරලි, *Tisara-perali*, *s.* (තිසර swan, පෙරලි involved) creeper, *clitoria ternata*. [Colloq. නිල් කටරොළු *nil-kaṭaroḷu*].

තිසරහර, *Tisarahara*, *s.* pearl necklace, row of pearls, [Colloq. මුතුවැල *mutuwęla*].

තිසරා, *Tisará*, *s.* teal, wild duck, *anas crecca (Anatidæ* order *Anseres)*.

තිසාවැව, *Tisá-węwa*, *s.* lake or tank so called at Anurádhapura an ancient and celebrated city in Ceylon.

තිසුන්, *Tisun*, *s.* joy, gladness, mirth, hilarity.

තිසුම්, *Tisum*, *s.* trembling, [Colloq. වෙව්ලුම *wewluma*].

තිසුලත්, *Tisulat*, } *s.* name of Íswara.
තිසුලවිය, *Tisulaviya*, }

තිහ, *Tiha*, *a.* thirty, see තිස *tisa*.

තිහිරිපිළී, *Tihiri-piḷí*, *s.* linen; garment made of bark.

තිළි, *Tiḷi*, *s.* joy, pleasure, delight: *a.* contented, satisfied.

තිළින, *Tiḷina*, see තිලින *tilina*.

තී, *Tí*, *pr.* thou (feminine).

තීක්ෂ්ණ, *Tíkshṇa*, *s.* heat, warmth; poison; iron; war, battle; plague, pestilence, epidemic destruction; weapon; death; sea salt; nitre; scrotum or testicles; suicide; orris root; trembling, agitation: *a.* keen, piercing, sharp, pungent, peppery; intelligent, clever, discerning; zealous, active; warm; hot, hasty, speedy; devout.

තීක්ෂ්ණගන්ධ, *Tíkshṇa-gandha*, *s.* (තීක්ෂ්ණ sharp, ගන්ධ smell) horse radish tree, *Moringa pterygosperma*, [Colloq. මුරුංගා *muruṇgá*]; gum olibanum tree; small cardamoms; species of *ocimum;* also, see පියල් *piyal*.

තීක්ෂ්ණගන්ධා, *Tíkshṇa-gandhá*, } *s.* mustard seed, [Colloq. අබ *aba*]; orris root, වදකහ *wadakaha*]; screw pine, *pandanus fascicularis*, [Colloq. මුදු කෙයියා *múdu-keyiyá*].
තීක්ෂ්ණගන්ධිනී, *Tíkshṇa-gandhiní*, }

තීක්ෂ්ණධූම, *Tíkshṇa-dhúma*, *s.* small tree, *murraya exotica*, [Colloq. ඇට්ටේරිය *ęttériya*].

තීක්ෂ්ණපත්‍ර, *Tíkshṇa-patra*, } *s.* coriander seed, [Colloq. කොත්තමල්ලි *kottamalli*]; also, see පියල් *piyal*.
තීක්ෂ්ණඵල, *Tíkshṇa-phala*, }

තීක්ෂ්ණය, *Tíkshṇaya*, *s.* sharpness, acuteness, keenness.

තීක්ෂ්ණසාර, *Tíkshṇa-sára*, *s.* wild sapota tree, *bassia longifolia*, [Colloq. මීගස් *mí-gas*].

තීක්ෂ්ණාග්නි, *Tíkshṇágni*, *s.* (තීක්ෂ්ණ *tíkshṇa* and අග්නි *agni* fire) heart-burn, dyspepsia.

තීන්ත, *Tínta*, *s.* ink, paint.

තීන්ත කුප්පිය, *Tínta-kuppiya*, } *s.* inkstand.
තීන්ත කුඩුව, *Tínta-kúḍuwa*, }

තීන්දු, *Tíndu*, *s.* end, finish, termination, completion: *a.* settled.

තීන්දුකරණවා, *Tíndukaraṇawá*, *v.* to finish, to complete, to decide, to pronounce judgment.

තීන්දුවෙනවා, *Tínduwenawá*, *v.* to expire, to be finished.

තීයල, *Tíyala*, *s.* sort of curry.

තීර්ථ, *Tírtha*, *s.* sacred science; religious persuasion; holy place of pilgrimage; teacher; instructor, sacred preceptor; sacrifice; avatára or descent of a deity; school of philosophy; sect, counsellor, adviser; expedient or means of success, contrivance, device; menses; *vulva;* vessel; ford, ferry.

තීර්ථක, *Tírthaka*, *s.* heretic.

තීරණ, *Tírana*, *s.* certain conclusion, undoubted result.

තීරය, *Tíraya*, *s.* shore, bank; border; hem; arrow; tin; column of a page.

තීරස්ථානය, *Tírasthánaya*, *s.* ferry, place for landing on the bank of a river; the opposite shore.

තීරුව, *Tíruwa*, *s.* rent, duty, custom, ship duty.

තීව්‍ර, *Tíwra*, *s.* heat; pungency; shore, bank; tin; black mustard; *a.* much, excessive, endless, unbounded, unlimited; warm; pungent severe.

තීව්‍රා, *Tíwrá*, *s.* name of a river in the east of Bengal.

තු, *Tu*, *adv.* fie, shame.

තුක්, *Tuk*, තුක්පිටි, *Tukpiṭi*, තුකාක්ෂිරි, *Tukákshíri*, *s.* manna of bambus, sort of pith or flour found in the bambu tree and used medicinally, [Colloq. උණමකුළු *uṇamakuḷu*].

තුගාක්ෂිරි, *Tugákshíri*, see තුකාක්ෂිරි *tukákshíri*.

තුඟු, *Tungu*, see තුඞ්ග *tuṅga*.

තුඟුතර, *Tungutara*, *a.* very lofty on high.

තුඞ්ග, *Tuṅga*, *s.* mountain; highest point of a planet's ring; top; *a.* high, elevated, lofty; chief, principal; passionate, hot.

තුඞ්ගද්‍රුම, *Tuṅgadrima*, *s.* (තුඞ්ග and ද්‍රුම tree) Northern monkeyfaced tree, yielding red dye, *mallotus philippinensis* or *rottleria tinctoria*, [Colloq. හම්පරිල්ල *hamparilla*]; kind of basil, *ocimum gratissimum*, see තුඞ්ගි *tuṅgi*; sort of turmeric; cocoa-nut tree, [Colloq. පොල්ගහ *pol-gaha*].

තුඞ්ගනාසිකා, *Tuṅga-násiká*, *s.* (තුඞ්ග and නාසිකා nose) high or prominent nose.

තුඞ්ගා, *Tuṅgá*, *s.* bambu manna, [Colloq. උණමකුළු *uṇamakuḷu*]: see තුක් *tuk*.

තුඞ්ගි *Tuṅgi* *s.* kind of basil, *ocimum gratissimum*, [Colloq. වෙලාගස් *wélá-gas*].

තුච්ඡ, *Tuchchha*, *a.* void, empty; unimportant, trivial; shallow, idiotic; small, little; abandoned, deserted; mean, low, vile; filthy.

තුච්ඡකරණවා, *Tuchchhakaraṇawá*, *v.* to calumniate, to disparage.

තුච්ඡද්‍රු, *Tuchchhadru*, *s.* castor-oil plant, [Colloq. එරඬු *eranḍu*].

තුච්ඡධාන්‍යක, *Tuchchha-dhányaka*, *s.* straw.

තුච්ඡ පත්‍රය, *Tuchchha-patraya*, *s.* castor oil plant, [Colloq. එඬරු *enḍaru*]; mean writing.

තුච්ඡාර්ථ, *Tuchchhártha*, *a.* (තුච්ඡ *tuchchha* void, අර්ථ *artha* meaning, profit) unmeaning, nonsensical; worthless.

තුට්ටුව, *Tuṭṭuwa*, *s.* pice, one and half cent, fourth part of anna or fanam.

තුට, *Tuṭa*, *s.* joy, gladness, delight, pleasure.

තුටු, *Tuṭu*, *s.* joy, pleasure, satisfaction.

තුටුපහටු, *Tuṭupahaṭu*, *a.* joyful, joyous, pleased, delighted.

තුඩ, *Tuḍa*, *s.* mouth, face; beak, bill; snout; point, corner, end.

තුඩකළුවා, *Tuḍa-kaḷuwá*, *s.* species of snake.

තුඩරණ වෙවැල්, *Tuḍaraṇa-wéwel*, *s.* kind of ratan, *calamus rutendum (Palmæ)*.

තුඩු, *Tuḍu*, *plur.* of තුඩ *tuḍa*.

තුඩුකරණවා, *Tuḍukaraṇawá*, *v.* to raise the wick in a lamp.

තුඩුදෙනවා, *Tuḍudenawá*, *v.* to show the head, speaking of worms in a sore.

තුඩුව, *Tuḍuwa*, *s.* cape, promontory.

තුඩැල්ලා, *Tuḍellá*, *s.* kind of fish.

තුණ්ඩ, *Tuṇḍa*, *s.* bill, beak; mouth; face.

තුණ්ඩිකා, *Tuṇḍiká*, *s.* navel; also, see කෙම්වැල, *kemwela*.

තුණ්ඩිකේරි, *Tuṇḍikéri*, *s.* cotton plant, [Colloq. කපුගස් *kapu-gas*]; sort of gourd, *momordica monadelpha* or *bryonia grandis*.

තුණ්ඩිල, *Tuṇḍila*, *s.* one of a prominent or elevated navel; one speaking harshly or severely; parrot.

තුණ්ඩී, *Tuṇḍí*, *s.* beak or bill, mouth, face.

තුණ්ඩීර, *Tuṇḍíra*, *s.* tree, producing a red berry, smallest of the jewellers weights, *albizzia Lebbek*, [Colloq. මාරා *márá*].

තුණ්ඩුව, *Tnṇḍuwa*, *s.* bit, piece of paper, memo:

තුණ, *Tuṇa*, *s.* number three.

තුත්ත, *Tutta*, *s.* elephant pike or goad; dross of metals.

තුත්තනාගන්, *Tuttanágan*, *s.* pewter, tin.

තුත්තිරි, *Tuttiri*, *s.* common kind of grass, called love grass, *crysopogon aciculatus (Graminæ)*.

තුත්ථ, *Tuttha*, *s.* collyrium extracted from the *amomum zanthorrhiza*; blue vitriol; sulphate of copper, especially medicinally considered as an application to the eyes; indigo, [Colloq. නිල් අවරි *nil-awari*]; small cardamoms, [Colloq. එන්සාල් *ensál*].

තුත්ථක, *Tutthaka*, *s.* blue vitriol.

තුත්ථාඤ්ජන, *Tutthánjana*, *s.* (තුත්ථ *tuttha* blue vitriol, අඤ්ජන *añjana* collyrium) blue vitriol, considered as a medicinal application to the eyes.

තුති, *Tuti*, *s.* praise, panegyric, eulogium.

තුතු, *Tutu*, *s.* fragments of a broken vessel, etc.

තුදු, *Tudu*, *s.* laughter. [Colloq. හිනාහව්ම *hinahavima*].

තුදුස්, *Tudus*, *a.* fourteen.

තුදුස්වක, *Tuduswaka*, *s.* (තුදුස් and වක lunar day) fourteenth day of the moon; day before the full or change of the moon.

තුන්, *Tun*, *a.* three.

තුන් ඍතුව, *Tun-rituwa*, *s.* the three seasons of the year; rainy season, hot season, and the season between the two.

තුන්කටුවා, *Tun-katuwá*, *s.* kind of fish.

තුන්කත, *Tun-kata*, *s.* (තුන් three, කත wife) name of Śiva alluding to his having three wives.

තුන්කලල, *Tun-kalala*, see තුන්කැලල *tun-kelala*.

තුන්කිනි, *Tunkiní*, *s.* jasmine, [Colloq. පිච්ච *pichcha*].

තුන්කොණ, *Tun-koṇa*, *s.* triangle, pl. තුන්කොන් *tun-kon*.

තුන්කැලල, *Tun-kelala*, *s.* (තුන් and කැලල mark, sign) name of Íśwara, probably alluding to the three insignia which he is frequently represented as bearing, viz. his trident, crescent, and necklace.

තුන්තරාබෝධිය, *Tuntará-bódhiya*, *s.* three kinds of bódhi or knowledge possessed by a Supreme Buddha, Pratyéka Buddha (a secondary Buddha), or an Arhat (Saint).

තුන්තලය, *Tuntalaya*, see තිලෝතලය *tilótalaya*.

තුණ්ඩ, *Tunda*, *s.* belly, [Colloq. බඩ *bada*].

තුණ්ඩි, *Tundi*, } *s.* belly, navel.
තුණ්ඩී, *Tundí*, }

තුන්දුමාව, *Tundumáwa*, *s.* cluster of three fruits, like three apples on a twig.

තුන්දොර, *Tun-dora*, *s.* (තුන් three, දොර door) three sources or modes of karma, merit or demerit, viz. personal, verbal, and mental.

තුන්දොස, *Tundosa*, *s.* (තුන් and දොස humour) three humours of the human body, bile, phlegm, and wind (literally the three disorders).

තුන්නවාය, *Tunnawáya*, *s.* seamster, tailor.

තුන්පත් කුරුඳු, *Tunpat-kurundu*, *s.* species of the cinnamon plant; see තුම්පත් කුරුඳු *tumpat kurundu*.

තුන්පත් තල, *Tunpat-tala*, *s.* species of the sesamum plant, gingely, *sesamum indicum*, [Colloq. තෙල් තල *tel-tala*].

තුන්පද කවිය, *Tunpada-kaviya*, *s.* triplet.

තුන්පාය, *Tun-páya*, *s.* (තුන් three, පාය palace) a house with three rooms or upper stories, so constructed as to embrace the advantages of the three seasons; such a one as was occupied by Buddha when living in the palace of his father Suddhódana, as prince Siddhárta Kumára; three storied house.

තුන්පිටකය, *Tun-piṭakaya*, *s.* (තුන් and පිටක *piṭaka* basket) used here metaphorically for a receptacle or depository; name of the Buddhist Scriptures in three divisions viz. Vinaya, Sútra, Abhidharmma, containing the sermons and ordinances of Buddha addressed to three classes of beings; see පිටකය *piṭakaya*.

තුන්පුලිල, *Tunpulila*, *s.* trumpet flower, *stereospermum suave-olens* or *bignonia grandiflora*.

තුන්බෝ, *Tunbó*, see අත්තන *attana*.

තුන්භවය, *Tun-bhawaya*, *s.* (තුන් and භව *bhawa* being) three states of existence through which all beings have to pass previous to their obtaining Nirwáṇa; the first is Káma bhawa, a state in which beings are subject to the influence of the passions, and includes both men and gods; the second is the Rúpa bhawa, a state in which the passions have been destroyed by a previous course of religious austerities, and nothing remains but a refined spiritual body which however is free from the influence of the passions; this state includes the ten Brahma lókas; the third is the Arúpa bhawa, in which nothing remains but a pure etherial spirit totally invisible; it is the next state to Nirwáṇa or entire annihilation, which forms the ultimate object at which the pious Buddhist aims.

තුන්මඬුල්ල, *Tun-maṇdulla*, *s.* (තුන් three, මඬුල්ල what surrounds) robe of a priest of Buddha which covers and ornaments three parts of the body; namely, the waist and right arm, the neck and breast, and the legs.

තුන්මද, *Tun-mada*, *s.* (තුන් and මද humour) elephant, [Colloq. අලියා *aliyá*]; elephant in rut, alluding to the three humours which exude from him in the rutting season, namely, from his temples, his eyes, and penis.

තුන් මාලය, *Tun-málaya*, see තුන්පාය *tunpáya*.

තුන්රත්නය, *Tun-ratnaya*, *s.* (තුන් and රත්න *ratna* gem, or treasure) three inestimable gems which have been bestowed on mankind: namely, Buddha, his doctrines and his priests.

තුන් ලෝකය, *Tun-lókaya, s.* three lower or inferior worlds the inhabitants of which are under the influence of the unsubdued passions; namely, world of gods, world of men, and pátála or the lower regions inhabited by demons and asurs.

තුන්වරක්, *Tun-warak,* } *ad.* thrice.
තුන්විටක්, *Tun-viṭak.* }

තුන්වෙනි, *Tunweni, a.* third.

තුන්වෙනිව, *Tunweniwa,* } *ad.* thirdly.
තුන්වෙනුව, *Tunwenuwa,* }

තුන්සරණ, *Tun-saraṇa, s.* three helps, viz. Buddha, his doctrines, and priests.

තුන්හුලස්, *Tun-hulas, a.* three sided.

තුන, *Tuna, s.* number three, sometimes written තුණ *tuṇa*; cord, string.

තුනඟිල්ල, *Tunaṉgilla, s.* climbing plant, *cissus pedata* or *vitis pedata,* [Colloq. මැඩිය වැල් *meḍiya-weḷ*].

තුනටිය, *Tunaṭiya, s.* loins, waist, hips.

තුනටු, *Tunaṭu,* see බුලත් *bulat.*

තුනි, *Tuni,* see තුනී *tuní.*

තුනිංචිය, *Tuniṉchiya, s.* toy, child's play, any sport or amusement of children; encouragement; fortitude, confidence.

තුනී, *Tuní, a.* thin, fine, slender, delicate, soft or fine in texture; lessening, decrease, diminishing, relaxing.

තුනු, *Tunu, s.* body; human form; agitation, tremour, tremulous affection of the body, palsy: *a.* thin, fine, slender, delicate.

තුනු අඟ, *Tunu-aṉga, s.* (තුනු fine, delicate, අඟ body) name of Káma déwa or Anaṅgayá the Indian Cupid.

තුනුතඹා, *Tunutaṃbá, s.* jungle or wild cock, [Colloq. වලිකුකුළා *wali-kukuḷá*]; common coucal, Ceylonese coucal, [Colloq. ඇටිකුකුළා *eti-kukuḷá*].

තුනුයොන්, *Tunuyon, s.* (තුනු and යොන් pudendum muliebre) name of Anaṅgayá or Kámadéwa the Indian Cupid.

තුනුරුවන්, *Tunuruwan, s.* (තුනු for තුන් *tun* three, රුවන් gems) three gems, used metaphorically of Buddha, his doctrines, and his priests.

තුනුවඟ, *Tunuwaṉga, s.* (තුනු fine, slender, delicate, අඟ *aṉga* body) woman, [Colloq. ස්ත්‍රී *strí*]; name of Anaṅgayá or Káma déwa the Indian Cupid.

තුනුවන, *Tunuwana,* } *s.* name of Anaṅgayá, the
තුනුවනා, *Tunuwaná,* } Indian Cupid.

තුනුවිල, *Tunuvila, s.* lake-like body.

තුනුසපුව, *Tunusapuwa, s.* bodily health or vigour.

තුනුහිරු, *Tunuhiru,* see තුනුවනා *tunuwana.*

තුප්පහිකම, *Tuppahikama, s.* interpretation from one language to another.

තුප්පහියා, *Tuppahiyá, s.* interpreter, Burgher (in contempt).

තුප්පොට්ටිය. *Tuppoṭṭiya, s.* waist cloth.

තුබු, *Tubu, s.* tail, tail of any animal, [Colloq. වල්ගේ *walgé*]; any thing of a trifling or unimportant nature.

තුබුනි, *Tubuni, s.* plantation, act of planting trees, labours in a nursery.

තුබූ, *Tubú, s. p. p.* placed, been.

තුඹ, *Tuṃba, s.* long gourd, *momordica;* back-part of a cocoa-nut; lead.

තුඹ කරවිල, *Tuṃba-karavila, s.* tuberous plant, the fruit used for curries, *momordica dioika (Cucurbitaceæ).*

තුඹනි, *Tuṃbaní,* see තුබුනි *tubuni.*

තුඹස, *Tuṃbasa, s.* hills or mounds raised by the white ants, pl. තුඹස් *tuṃbas.*

තුම්පත්කුරුඳු, *Tumpat-kuruṉdu, s.* shrub, *Limonia alata (Rutaceæ).*

තුම්බ, *Tumba,* } *s.* long gourd.
තුම්බී, *Tumbí,* }

තුම්බුරි, *Tumburi,* } *s.* coriander seed, *coriandrum*
තුම්බුරු, *Tumburu,* } *sativum.*

තුම්බ්‍යජ, *Tumbyaja,* see තුම්බ *tumba.*

තුමා, *Tumá, s.* exalted man, one possessing great authority and honour, (contracted form of උතුමා *utumá*).

තුමු, *Tumu,* suffix denoting Nominative Plural.

තුමුටු, *Tumuṭu, s.* speed, velocity, rapidity; style of a flower; joy.

තුමුතුමු, *Tumutumu,* another form of තමතමන් *tamataman* which see.

තුමුල, *Tumula, s.* power, strength; mingled or tumultuous combat; uproar, tumult, tumultuous noise; plant, *beleric myrobalan,* [Colloq. බුළු *buḷu*]: bulk, magnitude: *a.* great, vast, big.

තුමූ, *Tumú,* see තුමු *tumu.*

තුර, *Tura, s.* tree, [Colloq. ගස *gasa*]; *a.* quick, speedy, expeditious.

තුරග, *Turaga,* } *s.* (තුර speedy, ග which goes)
තුරඟ, *Turaṉga,* } horse, [Colloq. අශ්වයා *aṣwayá*]; mind, considered as the seat of feeling as well as intellect; heart; attendants of Kuvéra.

තුරඟ වදන, *Turanga-wadana*, *s.* (තුරඟ horse, වදන face) class of beings inhabiting Swarga or the region of the gods; described as having the bodies of men, and heads of horses; they are the celestial choristers, see also, ගන්ධර්ව *gandharwa* and කින්නරා *kinnará*.

තුරඞ්ගගන්ධා, *Turańga-gandhá*, *s.* name of a medicinal plant, *alyssicarpus vaginalis*.

තුරඞ්ගම, *Turańgama*, see තුරඟ *turanga*.

තුරඞ්ගි, *Turańgi*, *s.* plant, *withania somnifera*, [Colloq. අමුක්කරා *amukkará*].

තුරාෂාට්, *Turásháṭ*, *s.* name of Ṣakra or Indra.

තුරාසාහ, *Turásáha*, *s.* name of Indra.

තුරිත, *Turita*, *s.* express, runner, courier: *ad.* quickly, speedily.

තුරිය, *Turiya*, see තූර්ය *túrya*.

තුරු, *Turu*, *s.* journey; gladness; star, [Colloq. තාරකාව *tárakáwa*]; drum; bird, debt; tree, [Colloq. ගස *gasa*]: *ad.* till, until.

තුරුක්ඛ, *Turukkha*, *s.* (Páli) Indian incense, see the following.

තුරුක් තෙල්, *Turuk-tel*, *s.* very fragrant oil; one of the four perfumes used by kings.

තුරුණ, *Turuṇa*, } *s.* novelty, new thing; youth,
තුරුණු, *Turuṇu*, } *a.* new, novel.

තුරුපති, *Turupati*, *s.* (තුරු stars, පති lord) moon, [Colloq. හඳ *haṉda*].

තුරුපා, *Turupá*, *s.* shed; shade, shadow; covering, concealment.

තුරුල්, *Turul*, *s.* period immediately preceding conception: *a.* near, proximate, contiguous.

තුරුල්කරගන්නවා, *Turulkaragannawá*, *v.* to clasp, to embrace.

තුරුල්කරණවා, *Turulkaraṇawá*, *v.* to bring within the embrace.

තුරුල්ල, *Turulla*, *s.* embrace, embracing; bosom; lap, pl. තුරුළු *turuḷu*.

තුරුලිය, *Turuliya*, *s.* (තුරු tree, ලිය creeper) any parasitic plant, or trees and creepers.

තුරුෂ්ක, *Turushka*, *s.* incense; a very fragrant oil, one of the four perfumes used by kings.

තුරුස්, *Turus*, *s.* debt, [Colloq. ණය *naya*].

තුල්, *Tul*, *s.* Elu form of තුල්‍ය *tulya* which see; *a.* big.

තුල්‍ය, *Tulya*, *a.* like, resembling, similar, equal or analogous.

තුල්‍යපාන, *Tulyapána*, *a.* (තුල්‍ය and පාන drinking) drinking together.

තුල, *Tula*, *a.* great, big, of great magnitude or dimensions; equal, similar, analogous.

තුලකල, *Tulakala*, *s.* ornament of the feet.

තුලදර, *Tuladara*, *s.* gold and silversmith, sun, trader, string of a balance.

තුලසි, *Tulasi*, } *s.* small shrub held in high
තුලසිය, *Tulasiya*, } veneration by the Hindus, holy basil, *ocimum sanctum*, [Colloquial: මදුරුතලා *maduru-talá*].

තුලා, *Tulá*, *s.* weight of hundred palams or about hundred and fifty ounces troy; balance or goldsmith's scales; sign of the zodiac (Libra); resemblance, likeness, equality, similarity; main beam by which the roof of a house is supported.

තුලාකොටි, *Tulákoṭi*, *s.* ring or ornament of the feet or toes; weight; a number, one hundred millions; one end of a scale or balance.

තුලාධාර, *Tuládhára*, *s.* (තුලා and ධාර holding) sign of the zodiac (Libra); string of a balance; trader, trafficker, dealer.

තුලාභාරය, *Tulábháraya*, *s.* gift of valuables equal to the weight of the donor.

තුලාරාසිය, *Tulárásiya*, } see තුලාධාර *tuládhára*.
තුලාරෙස, *Tuláresa*, }

තුලා ලග්නය, *Tulá-lagnaya*, *s.* rising of the sign Libra.

තුලාව, *Tuláwa*, *s.* balance, or scale; see තුලා *tulá*.

තුලාවරු, *Tuláwaru*, *s.* (තුලා balance, වරු for කරු *karu* who uses) goldsmith, [Colloq. බඩාලා *baḍálá*].

තුලි, *Tuli*, } *s.* fibrous stick or brush, used by
තුලී, *Tulí*, } weavers for cleaning the threads of the woof; painter's brush, fibrous stick used for that purpose.

තුලික, *Tulíka*, *a.* painter's brush; small bird said to resemble the wagtail: see ගෝමරිටා *gómaritá*.

තුළු, *Tulu*, *acc.* case of තෙලෙ *tele*=ඕකා *óká* that one, that fellow.

තුවක්කු කානුව, *Tuwakku-kánuwa*, *s.* gun-barrel.

තුවක්කුව, *Tuwakkuwa*, *s.* gun, musket, fowling piece.

තුවක්කු වල්ල, *Tuwakku-walla*, *s.* breech or lower end of a gun.

තුවටුව, *Tuwaṭuwa*, *s.* stalk; footstalk of a leaf or fruit, [Colloq. නැට්ට *neṭṭa*].

තුවර, *Tuwara*, *s.* astringent taste; frankincense tree; species of cassia, see තෝර *tóra*: *a.* astringent, acrid; beardless.

තුවරක, *Tuwaraka*, *s.* fragrant earth; kind of lentil, *cytisus cajan.*

තුවරලා, *Tuwalalá*, *s.* frankincense, incense, [Coll: කට්ටකුමංචල් *kaṭṭakumañchal*].

තුවාජය, *Tuwájaya*, } *s.* towel, napkin.
තුවාය, *Tuwáya*, }

තුවාල, *Tuwála*, *s.* lameness, defect arising from an injury or accident; wound.

තුවාලකරණවා, *Tuwálakaraṇawá*, *v.* to wound.

තුෂ්ට, *Tushṭa*, *a.* pleased, satisfied, glad, joyful, delighted.

තුෂ්ටවරය, *Tushṭawaraya*. *s.* (තුෂ්ට joyful, වරය request) boon, boon that is greatly to be desired, request of the highest value.

තුෂ්ටි, *Tushṭi*, *s.* joy, pleasure, gladness.

තුෂ්ටිමත්, *Tushṭimat*, *a.* joyful, glad.

තුෂ, *Tusha*, *s.* tree, *terminalia belerica*, [Colloq. බුළු *bulu*].

තුෂාර, *Tushára*, *s.* ice, frost, snow; cold; thin rain, mist, dew; tree; see භොජපත්‍ර *bhojapatra*.

තුස්, *Tus*, Elu form of තුෂ්ට *tushṭa*, which see.

තුස, *Tusa*, *s.* husk of rice, or any grain chaff.

තුසර, *Tusara*, see තුෂාර *tushára*.

තුසරකර, *Tusarakara*, *s.* (තුසර dew, කර what makes) moon, [Colloq. චන්ද්‍රයා *chandrayá*].

තුසාර *Tusára*, see තුෂාර *tushára*.

තුසිත, *Tusita*, *s.* (තුස *tusa* joy, gladness, ඉත poss. aff.) one of the six heavens or regions of the gods; it is the fourth heaven and next above the යාම *yáma* (see this word); it has its name from the happiness of the place, which is obtained by previous works of religious merit; joy, pleasure, happiness, felicity, paradisaical pleasures.

තුසිතකාය, *Tusitakáya*, *s.* (තුසිත joy, කාය body) pleasing forms assumed by the inhabitants of තුසිත *tusita*, which see.

තුසිතපුරය, *Tusita-puraya*, *s.* one of the six heavens or regions of gods.

තුසිතභවනය, *Tusita-bhawanaya*, see above.

තුසීපුරය, *Tusí-puraya*, Elu form of තුසිතපුර *tusitapura*.

තුහින, *Tuhina*, *s.* dew; frost; moonlight, moonshine: ray of light; camphor; white sandal, [Colloq. සඳුන් *sandun*].

තුළ, *Tuḷa*, *s.* inside; *adv.* within.

තූණ, *Túṇa*, *s.* quiver.

තූණී, *Túṇí*, *s.* indigo plant, [Colloq. අවරි *awari*]; quiver.

තූණීර, *Túṇíra*, *s.* quiver.

තූම්බය, *Túmbaya*, *s.* bier.

තූර්ණ, *Túrṇa*, *a.* quick, speedy, swift, [Colloq. ඉක්මන් *ikman*].

තූර්‍ය්‍ය, *Túrya*, *s.* musical instrument, either wind or stringed instrument; music; tone or sound in music.

තූර්‍ය්‍යනාදය, *Túrya-nádaya*, *s.* (තූර්‍ය්‍ය and නාද *náda* sound) sound of a musical instrument, music in general.

තූර්‍ය්‍යභාණ්ඩය, *Túrya-bháṇḍaya*, *s.* any musical instrument.

තූර්‍ය්‍යරාව, *Túryaráwa*, *s.* music, sound of musical instruments of any kind.

තූල, *Túla*, } *s.* mulberry tree, *morus indica*
තූලක, *Túlaka*, } or *m. nigra;* cotton, [Colloq. පුළුන් *puḷun*]; white lead, [Colloq. සුදු ඊයම් *sudu-íyam*].

තූලඵලා, *Túla-phalá*, *s.* (තූල and ඵල *phala* fruit) mulberry; silk cotton tree.

තූලිකා, *Túliká*, *s.* pencil, painter's brush; kind of stick with a fibrous point used by painters; cotton mattress; ingot mould; anointing or perfuming the body.

තූවර, *Túwara*, *s.* beardless man; eunuch; astringency.

තූවරී, *Túwarí*, *s.* fragrant earth.

තූෂ්ණීක, *Túshṇíka*, *s.* silent man, one given to taciturnity: *a.* silent, taciturn.

තූෂ්ණීම්, *Túshṇím*, *a.* silent, taciturn, [Colloq. නිශ්ශබ්දවූ *nisṣebdawú*].

තූෂ්ණීම්භූත, *Túshnímbhúta*, *a.* (තූෂ්ණීම් silent, භූත being) silent, taciturn.

තූෂ්ණීම්භූතවීම, *Túshṇímbhútaríma*, *s.* being silent.

තූෂ්ණීම්ශීල, *Túshṇímṣíla*, see තූෂ්ණීම්භූත *túshṇímbhúta*.

තෙ, *Te*, *a.* three, [Colloq. තුණ *tuṇa*].

තෙක්, *Tek*, *ad.* till, until, as far as.

තෙකරාජ, *Tékarája*, *s.* shrub, medicinal plant used in tattooing, *eclipta erecta*, [Colloq. කිකිරිඳි *kikirindi*]; see බ්‍රහ්මමූලි *brahmamúli*.

තෙකල, *Tekala*, *s.* (තෙ three, කල time) the past, present and future time; applicable either to the omniscience of Buddha or to the three tenses in grammar.

තෙචීවරිකාඞ්ගය, *Techíwarikáṅgaya*, see තේචීවරිකාඞ්ග *téchíwarikáṅga*.

තෙත්, *Tet*, *a.* wet, moist, damp; cold, frigid.

තෙත්කනවා, *Tetkanawá*, *v.* to soak, to steep, to become moist; to mould.

තෙත්තියන් තියනවා, *Tettiyan-tiyanawá*, *v.* to set the teeth of a saw-erect.

තෙත්තු, *Tettu*, *s.* small child, pet; disobedience.

තෙත, *Teta*, } *s.* moisture, dampness. wet.
තෙතමන, *Tetamana*, }

තෙද, *Teda*, Elu form of තේජස් *téjas*.

තෙදියත, *Tediyata*, *s.* (තෙ three, දියත world) the three worlds.

තෙන්කෙළිනවා, *Ten-kelinawá*, *v.* to skip, to jump, to frisk.

තෙන, *Tena*, *s.* son; place, situation, locality.

තෙනුත්, *Tenut*, *s.* theft, robbery.

තෙනෙ, *Tene*, *s.* son, [Colloq. පුතා *putá*].

තෙනෙත්, *Tenet*, *s.* (තෙ three, නෙත් eye) name of Şiva, alluding to his having three eyes, similar to the Grecian Jupiter, one of which is in his forehead.

තෙප්, *Tep*, *s.* large kind of spear used for spearing elephants; any large wooden spear, stake, pointed stick; *pers. pron.* ye or you.

තෙප් ඉන්න, *Tep-inna*, *s.* stake, pointed stick.

තෙප් උල, *Tep-ula*, see තෙප්පුල *teppula*.

තෙප්පම, *Teppama*, *s.* raft.

තෙප්පුල, *Teppula*, *s.* spike,=තෙප් උල *tep-ula*.

තෙපලු, *Tepalu*, see තෙපුල *tepula*.

තෙපි, *Tepi*. *pers. pron.* ye, you.

තෙපුල, *Tepula*, *s.* word, speech; conversation; composition of the medicine for the eye, pl. තෙපුල් *tepul*.

තෙබ, *Teba*, *s.* large wooden dart or spear; see තෙප් *tep*.

තෙබු, *Tebu*, *s.* plant with spirally arranged leaves, *costus speciosus (Scitamineæ)*.

තෙම්, *Tem*, *s.* wetting, soaking.

තෙම්පරාදුකරණවා, *Temparádu-karanawá*, *v.* to season a curry after it has once been cooked.

තෙම්පරාදුව, *Temparáduwa*, *s.* seasoning, tempering.

තෙම, *Tema*, *s.* nominal affix *mas. sing.* and sign of the nominative case: wetting, moistening.

තෙමන, *Temana*, *s.* cooked food, stewed or boiled flesh.

තෙමනල, *Temanala*, *s.* plant, *dracunculus esculentus*.

තෙමනවා, *Temanawá*, *v.* to wet, to moisten, to make damp: pret. තෙමුවා *temuwá*.

තෙමීම, *Temíma*. verbal noun of the preceding word, wetting, moistening.

තෙමුම්, *Temum*, *s.* praise, eulogium, panegyrism; wetting etc.

තෙමුව, *Temuwa*, *s.* leech, [Colloq. කුඩැල්ලා *kúdellá*].

තෙමෙනවා, *Temenawá*, *v. n.* to become wet, damp or moist: pret. තෙමුනා *tamuná*.

තෙමේ, *Temé*, } suffix indicating nominative
තෙමේම, *Teméma*, } singular.

තෙයුම්, *Teyum*, see තෙසුම් *tesum*.

තෙර, *Tera*, *s.* bank or border of a river, [Colloq. ගංඉවුර *gaṉ-iwura*]; priest who has been twenty years in the priesthood and has attained to the rank of උපසම්පදා *upasampa-dá*, which see.

තෙරපනවා,, *Terapanawá*, *v.* to press, to throng: pret. තෙරපුවා *terapuwá*.

තෙරි, *Teri*, *s.* female priest of Buddha.

තෙරිඳු, *Terindu*, *s.* (තෙර *tera* and ඉඳු *indu* chief) chief priest.

තෙරුන්නාන්සේ, *Terunnánsé*, *s.* elderly Buddhist priest.

තෙල්, *Tel*, *s.* oil, see තෙල *tela*.

තෙල් ඔලු, *Tel-olu*, *s.* species of the lotus, *nymphæa Lotus*.

තෙල් කරවලා, *Tel-karawalá*, *s.* snake, variety of *bangarus ceylonicus*.

තෙල්කා, *Telká*, *s.* sediment of oil.

තෙල් කුහුඹි, *Tel-kuhumbi*, *s.* very small kind of ant.

තෙල් කොහොඹ, *Tel-kohomba*, *s.* bead tree, Indian lilac, *melia azidaracta*.

තෙල් කැකුන, *Tel-kekuna*, *s.* candle nut tree, *aleurites trilboa (Euphorbiaceæ)*.

තෙල් කැස්බෑවා, *Tel-kesbewá*, *s.* thin skinned turtle, see දාර කැස්බෑවා *dára-kesbewá*. (order *chelonia)*.

තෙල් තල, *Tel-tala*, *s.* sesamum, gingely, *sesamum indicum (Pedaliaceæ)*,

තෙල් දොඹ, *Tel-domba*, *s.* a tree from the fruit of which an oil is extracted, *calophyllum inophyllum:* see දොඹ *domba*.

තෙල් නුග, *Tel-nuga*, *s.* tree, *ficus Trimeni (Urticaceæ)*.

තෙල් පොලඟා, *Tel-polangá*, *s.* snake.

තෙල් මී, *Tel-mí*, *s.* tree, *bassia longifolia*, [Colloq. මී *mí*].

තෙල්ල, *Tella*, see තෙලිකුර *telikúra*.

තෙල්හිරිය, *Telhiriya*, *s.* tree, *colubrina asiatica (Rhamnaceæ)*.

තෙල, *Tela*, *s.* oil, grease, fat; any unctuous substance; pron. (used only in books)=ඔය *oya*.

තෙලකාන්ත, *Telakánta*, *s.* mango tree, [Colloq. අඹගහ *amba-gaha*].

තෙලකාන්තා, *Telakántá*, *s.* oil woman, female oil vendor.

තෙලකිරිය, *Telakiriya*, *s.* tree with acrid juice, *excæcaria agallocha (Euphorbiaceæ)*.

තෙලඹු, *Telambu*, *s.* large timber tree with edible seeds, yielding oil, *Sterculia fœtida*, *(Sterculiaceæ)*.

තෙලිකාපලා, *Teliká-palá*, *s.* plant, *mollugo pentaphylla*.

තෙලිකූර, *Telikúra*, *s.* fibrous stick used by painters, kind of painting brush or pencil.

තෙලිජ්ජ, *Telijja*, *s.* sweet toddy.

තෙලියා, *Teliyá*, *s.* fish resembling a snake in appearance, the electric eel, river fish.

තෙලිස් පොලඟා, *Telis-polangá*, *s.* largish snake, *hypnale nepa (Crotalidæ* order *Ophidia)*.

තෙලිස්සා, *Telissá*. *s.* sort of venomous snake, small species of the viper.

තෙලිසම්, *Teli-sam*, } *s.* leather.
තෙලිහම්, *Teli-ham*, }

තෙලෙ, *Tele*, *pro.* this, these.

තෙලෙස, *Telesa*, *s.* thirteen, [Colloquial: දහතුණ *dahatuna*].

තෙවළා, *Tewalá*, *s.* name of the book called තුන් පිටක *tunpitaka*, which see.

තෙවිකුන්, *Tevikun*, } *s.* name of Vishnu, Elu form
තෙවිකුම්, *Tevikum*, } of ත්‍රිවික්‍රම *trivikrama*, which see.

තෙවිට, *Tevita*, *ad.* three times, thrice.

තෙවිදු, *Tevidu*, see ත්‍රිවිද්‍යාව *trividyáwa*.

තෙවුන්, *Tewun*, *s.* praise, adulation, panegyrism.

තෙවුනා, *Tewuná*, *s.* praise, adulation: *a.* surrounded as by a fence; shining.

තෙස්තමේන්තුව, *Testaméntuwa*, *s.* Testament. (English).

තෙසත්, *Tesat*, Elu form of ත්‍රිශක්තිය *trisaktiya*, which see.

තෙසරණ, *Tesarana*, *s.* (තෙ three, සරණ help or favour) three religious helps, viz. Buddha, his doctrines, and his priests.

තෙසු, *Tesu*, *s.* words, speech; others, the rest: *a* remaining.

තෙසුම්, *Tesum*, *s.* theft, robbery, [Colloq. හොර කම *horakama*].

තෙහෙට්ටුවෙනවා, *Teheṭṭuwenawá*, *v.* to be wearied, to be fatigued, to be tired.

තෙළෙස්, *Teles*, *a.* thirteen (used in writing).

තෙළෙස්ධුතාඞ්ග, *Telesdhutánga*, *s.* (තෙළෙස් and ධුත *dhuta* shaken, අඞ්ග *anga* religious ordinance) thirteen religious ordinances which are to be observed by the Buddhist priests; they are the following viz. පංසුකූලිකාඞ්ගය *Pansukúlikangaya*, තේචීවරිකාඞ්ගය *Téchíwarikángaya*, පිණ්ඩපාතිකාඞ්ගය *Pindapátikángaya*, සපදානචාරිකාඞ්ගය *Sapadánachárikángaya*, ඒකාසනිකාඞ්ගය *Ékásanikángaya*, පත්තපිණ්ඩිකාඞ්ගය *Pattapindikángaya*, පච්ඡාභත්තිකාඞ්ගය *Pachchhábhattikángaya*, ආරඤ්ඤකාඞ්ගය *Áraññakángaya*, රුක්ඛමූලිකාඞ්ගය *Rukkhamúlikángaya*, අබ්භොකාසිකාඞ්ගය *Abbhokásikángaya*, සෝසානිකාඞ්ගය *Sósánikángaya*, යථාසන්තිකාඞ්ගය *Yathásanthatikángaya*, නේසජ්ජිකාඞ්ගය *Nesajjikángaya*; for further explanation see the words in their alphabetical order in the dictionary; these preposterous ordinances seem to have been given, as most others, only to exhibit the extravagant claims of the religion of Buddha, and not to be kept; for according to the confessions of the Buddhists themselves, these ordinances were never all kept by any one priest except one called Mahá Kásyapa.

තේ, *Té*, *s.* tea; number three.

තේක්ක, *Tékka*, *s.* teak tree or indian oak, *tectona grandis (Verbenaceæ)*.

තේචීවරිකාඞ්ග, *Téchíwarikánga*, *s.* (තේ three, චීවර *chíwara* robe, අඞ්ග *anga* ordinance) one of the thirteen ordinances of the Buddhist priesthood, viz. that which enjoins the priest invariably to dress in one particular kind of robe, consisting of three parts, see තෙළෙස්ධුතාඞ්ග *telesdhutánga*.

තේජ, *Téja*, *s.* power. energy; honour, dignity; splendour, enlightening; effulgence; fire; pungency; heat.

තේජකා, *Téjaká*, *s.* febrile medical compound, the aggregate of three spices, black pepper, long pepper, and dried ginger.

තේජකිසිනු, *Téjakisinu*, *s.* (තේජ fire, කිසිනු religious austerity) the power which Buddha possessed of emitting from his body a fiery splendour and glory so as to be able, without the aid of the sun, to illuminate at any hour a space around him of several yoduns; this supernatural faculty has its name from the mode in which it was acquired by Buddha, viz. the practice, to an infinite extent, of devout religious austerities.

තේජන, *Téjana*, *s.* bambu, [Colloq. උණගස් *unagas*]; bow, arrow: *a.* enlightening; making splendid, illuminating; polishing, sharpening.

තේජනා, *Téjaná*, s. medical compound of three pungent substances, namely, black pepper, long pepper, and ginger, prescribed in cases of fever.

තේජනි, *Téjani*, s. plant, *sansiviera zeylanica* or *aletris hyacinthoides*, [Colloq. නියඳ *niyaṇda*].

තේජවතී, *Téjawatí*, s. aromatic plant, *pothos officinale.*

තේජස, *Téjasa*, s. splendour, effulgence, light, lustre, dazzling; dignity, honour; fame, glory, renown; heat; sunbeams; consequence, strength, power, influence; impatience; gold; bile; marrow; brains; sharpness; brightness; energy, might, authority; metallic pungency, pl. තේජස් *téjas.*

තේජාවහා, *Téjáwhá*, see තේජෝවතී *téjówatí.*

තේජෝකසින, *Téjókasina*, see තේජකසිණු *téjakisinu.*

තේජෝධාතුව, *Téjódhátuwa*, s. (තේජස් *téjas* heat, fire, ධාතුව root, source) the element of fire, caloric, source of animal heat, bile; digestive faculty.

තේජෝවතී, *Téjówatí*, s. kind of pepper plant, *piper chavya*, [Colloq. සිවියවැල් *siviya-wẹl*]; another plant bearing a seed resembling pepper, *pothos officinale*, and considered as a large species of pepper.

තේපේ, *Tépé*, s. name of the banyan tree, *ficus bengalensis*, [Colloq. නුගගහ *nuga-gaha*].

තේරවිල්ල, *Téravilla*, s. explication, interpretation; enigma, riddle, puzzle, pl. තේරවිලි *téaavili.*

තේරී, *Térí*, s. priestess.

තේරුම, *Téruma*, s. meaning, explication; also, the verbal noun of තෝරණවා *tóraṇawá.*

තේරෙණවා, *Téreṇawá*, v. to be understood; to be singled out or withdrawn for some fault or imperfection: pret. තේරුණ *téruṇá.*

තේවකරණවා, *Téwakaraṇawá*, v. to serve, to attend on, to offer.

තේවතුර, *Té-watura*, s. tea as a beverage.

තේවය, *Téwaya*, s. religious service, or offering.

තෛල, *Taila*, s. oil, oil expressed from the cocoa-nut tree, etc. name of a plant, *barleria prionitis*, [Colloq. කටුකරඬු *kaṭukaraṇḍu*]; storax; gum benzoin, incense; see also the following word.

තෛලක, *Tailaka*, s. plant, *musa rosacea;* small quantity of oil.

තෛලකාර, *Tailakára*, s. oil-manufacturer.

තෛලපර්ණික, *Tailaparṇṇika*, s. white sandal-wood, *santalum album*, [Colloq. සුදුහඳුන් *sudu haṇdun*].

තෛලපර්ණී, *Tailaparṇṇí*, s. sandal; incense; turpentine.

තෛලපා, *Tailapá*,
තෛලපායිකා, *Tailapáyiká*, } s. (තෛල oil, පායිකා who drinks) cockroach, [Colloq. කැරපොත්තා *kẹrapottá*].

තෛලපිණ්ඩි, *Tailapiṇḍi*,
තෛලපිණ්ඩිත, *Tailapiṇḍita*, } s. plant, *barleria prionitis*, see තෛල *taila;* also *jasminimundicum spinosum.*

තෛලපින, *Tailapina*, see තෛලපායිකා *tailapáyiká.*

තෛලප්‍රභව, *Tailaprabhawa*. s. (තෛල sesamum, ප්‍රභව producing) flower of the sesamum, [Coll: තලමල *tala-mala*].

තෛල ඵල, *Taila-phala*, s. (තෛල sesamum, ඵල fruit) sesamum seed from which the sesamum oil is expressed.

තෛලම, *Tailama*, s. oil possessing medicinal properties; of these medical oils the native practitioners have a very large variety, extracted from various plants, roots, barks, leaves and seeds; they are much used as emollients to sores, bruises, and wounds, and as unguents to parts affected by local or acute pains; opium, pl. තෛලම් *tailam.*

තෛලය, *Tailaya*, s. oil, see තෛල *tayila.*

තෛලසාවර්තනී, *Tailasáwarthaní*, s. gold; any of the precious metals.

තෛලීන, *Tailína*, s. land for sowing the sesamum seed, field of sesamum.

තොක්කුව, *Tokkuwa*, s. place, situation, site, [Colloq. ස්ථානය *sthánaya*].

තොක, *Toka*, s. bark of a tree, [Colloq. පොත්ත *potta*].

තොංගල, *Toṅgala*, s. end, point.

තොට, *Toṭa*, s. ford, ferry; dative of තෝ *tó* thou.

තොටකුලී, *Toṭakúlí*, s. (තොට ferry, කුලී hire) fare, ferriage.

තොටපල *Toṭapala*, see තොටුපල *toṭupala.*

තොටපියල්ල, *Toṭapiyalla*, s. small shreds of cloth beat off in the act of washing linen and which are used in certain medical prescriptions and as charms in magical incantations; clothes which have been left at a religious bathing place after the ablutions have been performed.

තොටමුනය, *Toṭamunaya*, s. sea-port; place for landing, site of a ferry, quay; district, province.

තොටියා, *Toṭiyá*, s. man that steers or rows a ferry boat.

තොටිල්ල, *Toṭilla*, *s.* child's cot or swinging cradle; swing; tree, *spathodea indica;* another tree, *bignonia indica.*

තොටිල, *Toṭila*, *s.* plant, *oroxylum indicum (Bignoniaceæ).*

තොටු, *Toṭu*, *s.* path over a river, ford; one who has adopted false views of religion, heathen.

තොටුපල, *Toṭupala*, *s.* ferry, ford, site of a ferry, place for landing, quay.

තොඩොත්තුව, *Todottuwa*, *s.* rope or rein by which a bullock is guided, passing through the cartilage of the nostrils; stop or hindrance.

තොණ්ඩුව, *Toṇḍuwa*, *s.* snare or noose for catching birds, deer, etc.

තොත්තුව, *Tottuwa*, *s.* kiss.

තොතනි, *Totani*, *s.* sheet of water, basin for water: *a.* round; the root of a tree.

තොප්පිය, *Toppiaya*, *s.* hat, bonnet, cap. (Port.)

තොප, *Topa*, *per. pron.* you, in the accusative: see තෝ *tó.*

තොපගේ, *Topagé*, genitive case of the preceding.

තොපි, *Topi*, *per. pron.* ye, or you.

තොම, *Toma*, *s.* clump or spot of growing corn, wheat or barley.

තොමෝ, *Tomó*, *pr.* feminine of තෙම *tema*, which see.

තොයිල්කරණවා, *Toyil-karaṇawá*, *v.* to perform demon ceremonies, see තොවිල්කරණවා *tovil-karaṇawá.*

තොර, *Tora*, *s.* interval, cessation.

තොරකිරීම, *Torakiríma*, *s.* removing, separating.

තොරතුර, *Toratura*, *s.* affair; matter; circumstance, concern, news, intelligence, pl. තොරතුරු *toraturu.*

තොරණ, *Toraṇa*, *s.* arch erected on festival occasions and decorated with the young shoots of the cocoa-nut leaves, ferns, flags etc. pandal; outer door, porch; hairy shrub, *canthium parviflorum*, [Colloq. කර *kara*].

තොරනෑතුව, *Toranẹtuwa*, *ad.* always, continually, unceasingly.

තොරපනේ, *Torapané*, *s.* gimlet, bow-wimble.

තොරවෙනවා, *Torawenawá*, *v.* to fail, to be separated from.

තොල, *Tola*, *s.* lip, pl. තොල් *tol.*

තොලබෝ, *Tolabó*, *s.* bulbous plant with umbels of large white flowers, *crinum Asiaticum (Amaryllideæ).*

තොලිනාථ, *Tolinátha*, see තෝලිනාථ *tólinátha.*

තොලොල්, *Tolol*, *s.* plant, peculiar to Ceylon, *Trichadenia zeylanica (Bixiniæ);* also called අත්තාගස් *áttá-gas.*

තොවිල්කරණවා, *Tovilkaraṇawá*, *v.* to expel demons, to destroy demoniacal possessions; to cure diseases by dislodging devils from the patient; all diseases are supposed to be inflicted by some evil demon; hence it is that in almost all cases of severe sickness natives depend more upon the power of the demon priest than upon medicine; the last means used with dying persons is the rejection of all medicine and the sole use of the yantras and mantras of the capuwa.

තොවිලේ, *Tovilé*, *s.* devil ceremony, pl. තොවිල් *tovil.*

තොසය, *Tosaya*, *s.* joy, pleasure, gladness.

තොසියොත්, *Tosiyot*, see කෑඳෑත්තා *kẹ̄ndẹttá.*

තොහල්, *Tohal*, *s.* umbrella, [Colloq. කුඩේ *kuḍé*].

තොළුගානවා, *Toḷugánawá*, *v.* to crop, to graze as cattle, (literally to rub on the lip).

තෝ, *Tó*, *pron.* thou, applied, in modern usage, to persons of great inferiority and of low and degraded caste, or as a term of abuse.

තෝං, *Tóṇ*, *s.* fee charged by one who keeps a gambling house.

තෝක, *Tóka*, *a*, less, short, deficient.

තෝඤ්චිය, *Tóñchiya*, *s.* ceasing, [Colloq. නැවතීම *nẹwatíma*].

තෝඩුව, *Tóḍuwa*, *s.* Malabar ear-ring or ornament, hollow cylinder of gold thrust through the lobe of the ear.

තෝත්‍ර, *Tótra*, *s.* hook used for guiding an elephant; goad or pike for driving cattle.

තෝදන, *Tódana*, *s.* goad; pain; anguish, torture, uneasiness.

තෝන්තුව, *Tóntuwa*, *s.* giddiness.

තෝම්බුව, *Tómbuwa*, *s.* register.

තෝමර, *Tómara*, *s.* iron crow; elephant hook; any weapon for piercing, spear; instrument for perforating, javelin.

තෝය, *Tóya*, තෝයක, *Tóyaka*, } *s.* water, [Colloq. වතුර *watura*].

තෝයද, *Tóyada*, *s.* (තෝය water, ද which gives) cloud; kind of fragrant grass, *cyperus rotundus*, [Colloq. කලාඳුරු *kalánduru*].

තෝයඳ, *Tóyadá*, *s.* tree, *elæagnus latifolia*, [Coll: වෑල් ඇඹිල්ල *wẹl-ẹmbilla* or කටු ඇඹිල්ල *kaṭu-ẹmbilla*].

තෝයධර, *Tóyadhara*, *s.* (තෝය and ධර what holds) cloud.

තෝයපිප්පලි, *Tóya-pippalí*, *s.* plant, *Jussiœa repens.*

තෝයප්‍රසාදන, *Tóyaprasádana*, *s.* (තෝය and ප්‍රසාදන cleansing) clearing nut plant, *strychnos potatorum*, [Colloquial: ඉඟිනි *ingini*]; the seeds of which being rubbed on the inside of a jar or water pot, cause the precipitation of the impurities of water.

තෝයවල්ලි, *Tóyawalli*, *s.* kind of gourd, *momordica charantia*, [Colloq. කරවිල *karavila*].

තෝර, *Tóra*, *s.* cassia plant of which there are many species in Ceylon; for an account of which see Moon's Catalogue of the plants of Ceylon, and Trimen's Systematic Catalogue 257.

තෝරණවා, *Tóraṇawá*, *v.* to explain, to interpret, to expound; to choose, to select, to pick out, to separate: pret. තේරුවා *téruwá*.

තෝරමල්ලි, *Tóramalli*, *s.* general name for the cornelian.

තෝරා, *Tórá*, *s.* seer fish, most valuable fish in these seas; it may be termed the salmon of Ceylon, *cybium* (or *scomber) guttatum*, pl. තෝරු *tóru.*

තෝල්කකම, *Tólkakama*, *s.* interpretation.

තෝලි, *Tólí*, *s.* sign of the zodiac (Libra); name of Ṣukra.

තෝලිනාථ, *Tólínátha*, *s.* Ṣukra the regent of the planet Venus.

තෝවැල්, *Tó-wel*, *s.* creeping plant with numerous small greenish purple flowers; *Vitis erioclada* or *V. indica (Ampelideœ).*

තෞර්‍ය්‍ය, *Taurya*, *s.* harmony, see තූර්‍ය්‍ය *túrya.*

තෞර්‍ය්‍යත්‍රික, *Tauryatrika*, *s.* (තෞර්‍ය්‍ය and ත්‍රික three) the triple or threefold melody, viz. the union of song, dance and instrumental music; symphony.

තෞලි, *Taulí*, *s.* balance; sign of the zodiac (Libra); see තුලා *tulá.*

තෞලින, *Taulína*, *s.* balance; one of the signs of the zodiac (Libra); planet Venus.

තෞලිනාථ, *Taulí-nátha*, *s.* (තෞලි and නාථ chief or lord) name of Ṣukra, regent of the planet Venus.

තැක්, *Tęk*, *s.* whey.

තැටි, *Tęti*, *s.* kind of brazen dish, charger; porringer.

තැඩැල්ලා, *Tędęllá*, *s.* kind of fish.

තැත්කවනවා, *Tętkawanawá*, *v.* to string an instrument; to string a bow, to bend a bow; to strive.

තැත, *Tęta*, *s.* string of a víṇá or native violin; the wire-string of any instrument; labour, endeavour, pains.

තැතන, *Tętana*, *s.* thunder, [Colloq. හෙන *hena*].

තැතනුම, *Tętanuma*, *s.* thunder; roaring, bellowing.

තැති, *Tęti*, *s.* fear, tremour or trembling from fear.

තැතිගන්නවා, *Tętigannawá*, *v.* to be afraid.

තැතිගන්වනවා, *Tętiganwanawá*, *v.* to frighten, alarm.

තැතිල්ල, *Tętilla*, *s.* spoon or head of a working implement, as a spade, hoe, iron part of a spade or hoe, pl. තැතිලි *tętili.*

තැදි, *Tędi*, *s.* bond, covenant.

තැන්, *Tęn*, *plur.* of තැන *tęna*: also any sharp cutting instrument.

තැන්පත්කරණවා, *Tęnpatkaraṇawá*, *v.* to bury, to inter.

තැන, *Tęna*, *s.* place, spot, site, situation.

තැනන්වහන්සේ, *Tęnanwahansé*, *s.* eminent person.

තැනන, *Tęnana*, *s.* thunder, [Colloq. හෙන *hena*].

තැනිතලාව, *Tęnitaláwa*, *s.* level open space.

තැනින්තැන, *Tęnintęna*, *s.* from place to place, here and there.

තැනිවරය, *Tęniwaraya*, *s.* level ground, level plot.

තැනීම, *Tęníma*, *s.* formation, construction, pl. තැනුම් *tęnum*; verbal noun of තනනවා *tananawá*, which see.

තැනුම, *Tęnuma*, *s.* verbal noun of තනනවා *tananawá*, which see; trembling, state of being agitated, tremor.

තැනැත්තා, *Tęnettá*, *s.* person.

තැප්පෙනවා, *Tęppenawá*, *v.* to spoil victuals in the dressing by a deficiency of heat.

තැප්ලනවා, *Tęplanawá*, *v.* to bellow, to low as oxen: pret. තැප්ලැවා *tęplęwá.*

තැපැල, *Tępęla*, *s.* post (for letters), mail.

තැබීම, *Tębíma*, *s.* act of putting or placing, verbal noun of තබනවා *tabanawá*, which see.

තැබුවා, *Tębuwá*, *pret.* of තබනවා *tabanawá.*

තැඹිලි, *Tęmbili*, *s.* species of cocoa-nut tree which produces a nut of a light yellow colour, and is commonly called king cocoa-nut.

තැඹිලිපුවක්, *Tęmbili-puwak*, *s.* sort of areca nut palm, *areca catechu.*

තැඹිලිය, *Tęmbiliya*, *s.* shrub, *Eugenia bracteata, (Myrtaceœ),*

තැම්බීම, *Tęmbíma*, *s*. the act of boiling.
තැම්බුවා, *Tęmbuwá*, past tense of තම්බනවා *tambanawá*.
තැරලි, *Tęrali*, *s*. kind of food.
තැරෘවනවා, *Tęrawenawá*, *v*. to wear away by attrition; to be soiled or besmeared, to touch.
තැරිය, *Tęriya*, *s*. calyx of flowers, pedicle, face of a nut.
තැල්, *Tęl*, *s*. creeping plant, bind-weed, *convolvulus flavus*: *a*. sweet; soft, tender, delicate, weak; slack.
තැල්ම, *Tęlma*, *s*. wound or scar caused by beating or flogging.
තැල්ල, *Tęlla*, *s*. kind of ornament or gold collar worn on the neck or breast of women, particularly on the day of marriage; plate of wrought gold worn as a sign of office; dewlap of an ox; any protuberance of flesh under the chin.
තැල්වැල, *Tęl-węla*, see තැල් *tęl*.
තැලිපිළි, *Tęlipiḷi*, *s*. clothes given by a bridegroom to his bride on the day of their marriage.
තැලිපොල, *Tęlipola*, *s*. dewlap of oxen: see තැල්ල *tęlla*.
තැලිඹුව, *Tęlimbuwa*, *s*. contusion, wound made by a blunt instrument.
තැලිය, *Tęliya*, *s*. culinary utensil, cooking pot or pan, sometimes written, තලිය *taliya*, තැටිය *tęṭiya*, and සැලි *sęli*.
තැවරීම, *Tęwaríma*, verbal noun of තැවරෙණවා *tęwareṇawá*.
තැවරෙණවා, *Tęwareṇawá*, *v*. to be touched; to be daubed, to be smeared: pret. තැවරුණ *tęwaruṇá*.
තැවිල්ල, *Tęvilla*, *s*. fomentation or outward stimulant, decrease, diminishing, but applied chiefly to the abatement of a disease or to the decrease of a swelling, pl. තැවිලි *tęvili*.
තැවීම, *Tęvíma*, *s*. tepefaction, fomentation; inflammation; sorrow of mind; repentance.
තැවුම, *Tęwuma*, *s*. warmth, heat, fomentation, tepefaction, pl. තැවුම් *tęwum*, or තැවුන් *tęwun*.
තැවුරු, *Tęwuru*, *a*. soiled, sullied, spoiled; firm, solid, strong.
තැවුල, *Tęwula*, / තැවුලි, *Tęwuli*, } *s*. heating, sorrow, grief, affliction, pain of mind, repentance.
තැවුව, *Tęwuwa*, *s*. surface of a file; roughness of a leaf used for polishing.
තැවෙනවා, *Tęwenawá*, *v*. to become sorrowful; to be worn away by affliction; to be heated: pret. තැවුනා *tęwuná*.

තැස්, *Tęs*, *s*. bran, powder, any pulverized substance; long gourd; lead; measure of capacity, about four quarts.
තැළීම, *Tęḷíma*, *s*. beating, flogging, verbal noun of තළනවා *taḷanawá*.
තැළුඹුව, *Tęḷumbuwa*, *s*. contusion.
තැළුම්කනවා, *Tęḷumkanawá*, *v*. to be beaten or flogged.
තැළුම, *Tęḷuma*, *s*. blow, stroke, bruising, beating.
තැළෙනවා, *Tęḷenawá*, *v*. to be crushed or bruised: pret. තැළුනා *tęḷuná*.
තෑග්ග, *Tégga*, *s*. gift, donation, present, pl. තෑගි *tégi*.
තෑගිකැරය, *Tégikęraya*, *s*. deed of gift.
තෑන්දේ, *Téndé*, *s*. bedstead.
ත්‍යාග, *Tyága*, *s*. gift, donation; abandonment, deserting; separation, parting from.
ත්‍යාගිවන්ත, *Tyágiwanta*, *a*. disposed to give, generous, liberal.
ත්‍යාගී, *Tyágí*, *s*. donor, giver; abandoner, applied chiefly to the religious ascetic, who abandons all worldly objects, thoughts and passions for the purpose of giving himself up entirely to religious meditation.
ත්‍රංකය, *Traṅkaya*, *s*. bar, bolt. sometimes written තරංකෙ *taraṅke*.
ත්‍රප, *Trapa*, / ත්‍රපා, *Trapá*, } *s*. shame, modesty, bashfulness, [Colloq. ලජ්ජාව *lajjáwa*].
ත්‍රපුෂ, *Trapusha*, *s*. sort of cucumber; tin.
ත්‍රය, *Traya*, *s*. number three.
ත්‍රයත්‍රිංශත්, *Traya-triṇṣat*, see තවුතිසාභවනය *tawutisá-bhawanaya*.
ත්‍රයී, *Trayí*, *s*. three principal Védas of the Hindus; the fourth or Atharwan not being considered a text-book in their religious rites; it is viewed more as an appendix to the others.
ත්‍රයෝදශ, *Trayódaṣa*, *s*. thirteen.
ත්‍රස්ත, *Trasta*, *a*. timid, fearful.
ත්‍රස්තවාලු, *Trastawálu*, *s*. creeping plant with large white flowers and medicinal root, bind-weed, *Ipomœa turpethum*, *(Convolvulaceæ)*.
ත්‍රසර, *Trasara*, *s*. weaving; shuttle.
ත්‍රාණ, *Tráṇa*, *s*. preservation, protection.
ත්‍රායන්ති, *Tráyantí*, *s*. protectress: medical plant, [Colloq. ලුණුවිල *luṇuvila*].
ත්‍රායමාණ, *Tráyamáṇa*, *s*. preserver: preserving: medical plant.
ත්‍රාස, *Trása*, *s*. fear, terror, alarm; flaw or defect in a jewel.

ත්‍රි, *Tri*, *s.* three, [Colloq. තුණ *tuṇa*]; *ad.* thrice.

ත්‍රිංශක, *Trinṣaka*, *s.* thirty; collectively, multitude of thirty.

ත්‍රිංශත්, *Trinṣat*, *a.* thirty, [Colloq. තිහ *tiha*].

ත්‍රිකටුක, *Trikaṭuka*, *s.* (ත්‍රි three, කටුක pungency) aggregate of three pungent spices, viz. black and long pepper and dry ginger.

ත්‍රිකණ්ටක, *Trikaṇṭaka*, *s.* plant, *stalagmites cambogioides;* a fish, *silurus.*

ත්‍රිකාලඥ, *Trikálajña*, *s.* (ත්‍රි and කාල time, ඥ who knows) name or epithet of Buddha, alluding to what is usually termed his omniscience, *i. e.* his perfect knowledge of all things, past, present, and future.

ත්‍රිකාලදර්ශී, *Trikáladarṣí*, *s.* (ත්‍රි and කාල times, දර්ශී who sees) name of Buddha, implying that at one look he sees all events of past, present and future time.

ත්‍රිකූටපර්වත, *Trikúṭa-parwata*, *s.* (ත්‍රි and කූට peak, පර්වත mountain) fabulous tripod mountain, which has its base in the second of the තිලෝතල *tilótala* and on its summit supports Ṣakra's paradise; the space between the three peaks forms the world පාතාල *pátála*, which is inhabited by the serpent race and Asuras; from this region came රාහු *Ráhu* to the churning of the sea by the gods; see රාහු *Ráhu*.

ත්‍රිකෝණ, *Trikóṇa*, *s.* triangle, pl. ත්‍රිකොන් *trikon*.

ත්‍රිගන්ධ, *Trigandha*, see ත්‍රිසුගන්ධ *trisugandha*.

ත්‍රිගුණ, *Triguṇa*, *a.* three-fold, three times, triple.

ත්‍රිගුහා, *Triguhá*, *s.* medicinal plant, *Alyssicarpus bupleurifolius*, [Colloq. අස්වැන්න *aswẹnna*].

ත්‍රිජාත, *Trijáta*, } *s.* (ත්‍රි three, ජාති spice) the three
ත්‍රිජාති, *Trijáti*, } principal spices; nutmeg, cloves, and mace.

ත්‍රිත්වය, *Tritwaya*, *s.* triad, trinity.

ත්‍රිදශ, *Tridaṣa*, *s.* (ත්‍රි and දශා *daṣá* state) a god, deity, divinity; the name refers to the gods being subject to the three states connected with existence, viz. birth, being, and death, *i. e.* transmigration; the gods not having attained that state of the subjugation of their passions which entitles them to final emancipation, they are, like other inferior living sentient beings, liable to be born again or reproduced in some other mode of existence.

ත්‍රිදශාචාර්ය, *Tridaṣáchárya*, *s.* (ත්‍රිදශ *tridaṣa* and ආචාර්ය *áchárya* preceptor) name of Vṛihaspati, the regent of the planet Jupiter, referring to his being the preceptor of the gods.

ත්‍රිදශාරි, *Tridaṣári*, *s.* (ත්‍රිදශ *tridaṣa* gods, අරි *ari* enemy) enemy of the gods, Asura or titan.

ත්‍රිදිව, *Tridiwa*, *s.* (ත්‍රි three alluding to Brahma, Vishṇu, and Ṣiva, දිව to sport) Swarga or heaven, the paradise of the Indian gods, the place where the three deities sport; according to oriental mythology the gods or inhabitants of Swarga indulge in every sensual gratification; sky, atmosphere.

ත්‍රිනයන, *Trinayana*, *s.* (ත්‍රි and නයන eye) name of Íṣwara or Ṣiva, alluding to the eye which he is represented as having in his forehead, similar to the Grecian Jupiter.

ත්‍රිපත්‍රක, *Tripatraka*, *s.* tree, *butea frondosa*, [Coll: ගස්කැල *gas-kẹla*].

ත්‍රිපද, *Tripada*, *s.* tripod; verse or stanza consisting of three lines.

ත්‍රිපදී, *Tripadí*, *s.* creeping plant, *vitis (or cissus) pedata*, [Colloq. මැඩිය වැල් *mẹdiya-wẹl*].

ත්‍රිපර්ණ්‍යා, *Triparṇyá*, *s.* medicinal plant, [Colloq. අස්වැන්න *aswẹnna*]: see ත්‍රිගුහා *triguhá*.

ත්‍රිපරිවෘත්ත, *Tripariwṛitta*, *s.* (ත්‍රි three, පරි severally, වෘත්ත being) three objects of pursuit, viz. desire of wealth, sensuous pleasure, continual existence, which are to be rejected by the Buddhist ascetic.

ත්‍රිපිටකය, *Tripiṭakaya*, see තුන්පිටකය *tunpiṭakaya*.

ත්‍රිපුට, *Tripuṭa*, *s.* (ත්‍රි and පුට skin) pease of three kinds; pulse; bank or shore; cubit; kind of vetch, *cicer arietinum;* a hairy plant, *ruellia longifolia*.

ත්‍රිපුටා, *Tripuṭá*, *s.* sort of creeping plant, bind-weed, *ipomœa Turpethum*, [Colloq. තුස්තවාලු *trastawálu*]; small cardamums, *elletaria cardamomum*, [Colloq. සිහින් එන්සාල් *sihin-ensál*]; Arabian jasmin; goddess.

ත්‍රිපුර, *Tripura*, *s.* (ත්‍රි and පුර city) name of Rávaṇa the noted Asura or demon and king of Lanká or Ceylon; the name alludes to his occupying a district containing three strong and famous cities: see රාවණ *Rávaṇa*.

ත්‍රිපුරදහන, *Tripuradahana*, *s.* (ත්‍රි three, පුර city, දහන burning, consuming) name of Ṣiva, who as Mahádéwa destroyed the three famous cities of Rávaṇa.

ත්‍රිපුෂා, *Tripushá*, *s.* black teori, [Colloq. තියඹරා *tiyambará*].

ත්‍රිඵලා, *Triphalá*, *s.* the three myrobalans, [Colloq. අරළු *araḷu*, බුළු *buḷu*, නෙල්ලි *nelli*].

ත්‍රිභණ්ඩි, *Tribhaṇḍi*, *s.* (ත්‍රි and භණ්ඩි to oppose) a long creeping medical plant, which is said to oppose the three elements, or bile, phlegm and wind; it is called teori, in Bengali, *ipomœa turpethum*, [Colloq. ත්‍රස්තවාලු *trastawálu*].

ත්‍රිභුවන, *Tribhuwana*, *s.* the three worlds, viz. the worlds in which beings are under the influence of passions; *i. e.* déva lóka, or world of gods, world of men, and pátála or world of demons; see තුන්ලෝකය *tunlókaya*.

ත්‍රිමණ්ඩල, *Trimaṇḍala*, *s.* the three circles, *i. e.* the two knees and the navel, applied to the mode of wearing the robe of Buddhist priests so as to cover the said parts.

ත්‍රිමද, *Trimada*, see තුන්මද *tunmada*.

ත්‍රිලක්ෂණ, *Trilakshaṇa*, see තිලකුණු *tilakuṇu*.

ත්‍රිවචන, *Triwachana*, *s.* (ත්‍රි three, වචන word) three memorable words or sentences spoken by Buddha, on the day of his birth, the day of his becoming Buddha, and on the day of his death; the first was අග්ගොහමස්මි ලෝකස්ස *aggóhamasmi lókassa*, "I am the chief of the world"; the second අනේකජාති සංසාරං *anékajáti-saṇsáraṇ*, "I have passed through various transmigrations" (alluding to his five hundred and fifty births); අප්පමාදේන සම්පාදේථ *appamádéna sampádétha*, "Attain (to bliss) by non-procrastination"; grammatical term for the three numbers, viz. sing. dual and plural.

ත්‍රිවර්ග, *Triwarga*, *s.* (ත්‍රි and වර්ග class or sort) three objects of human pursuit; as love, duty, and wealth; three conditions of a king or state, as prosperity, evenness and decay; loss, gain, equality etc.; three qualities of nature, as purity, blindness and depravity; the three myrobalans, see ත්‍රිඵලා *triphalá*; three spices, see ත්‍රිකටුක *trikaṭuka*.

ත්‍රිවික්‍රම, *Trivikrama*, *s.* (ත්‍රි and වික්‍රම going) name of Vishṇu, alluding to his crossing over the three worlds by three steps, to the discomfiture of Bali, the noted demon or Asura, whom he vanquished and destroyed.

ත්‍රිවිද්‍යාව, *Trividyáwa*, *s.* (ත්‍රි and විද්‍යා *vidyá* knowledge) three-fold knowledge, more properly the supernatural knowledge of three important facts, viz. the impermanency of matter, the existence of sorrow in all things, and the annihilation of the spirit, or the living principle or sentient faculty in all living beings; this knowledge forms one of the leading and essential doctrines of Buddhism, and was said to be possessed by Buddha in the highest possible degree and to constitute one of the essential attributes of his character; the acquirement of the same forms one of the chief objects of mental study, and of the abstract and devout meditation of the priests, and all religious ascetics.

ත්‍රිවිධ, *Trividha*, *a.* three, three-fold.

ත්‍රිවිධ ධර්මය, *Trividha-dharmaya*, *s.* three kinds of doctrines delivered by Buddha; viz. the සූත්‍ර *sútra* his sermons addressed to the laity, විනය *vinaya* his sermons to the priests, අභිධර්ම *abhidharma* his sermons to the gods.

ත්‍රිවිධද්වාරය, *Trividhadwáraya*, *s.* (ත්‍රිවිධ and ද්වාරය entrance) the three entrances for good and evil which are found in man; bodily senses, his words, and his thoughts.

ත්‍රිවිධ භව, *Trividhabhawa*, see තුන්භවය *tunbhawaya*.

ත්‍රිවිධරත්නය, *Trividharatnaya*, *s.* (ත්‍රි and විධ sort, රත්න *ratna* gems) the three precious gems which have been given to the world, viz. Buddha, his baṇa *i. e.* sermons and doctrines, and his priests.

ත්‍රිවිධශික්ෂාව, *Trividha-ṣikshàwa*, *s.* (ත්‍රිවිධරත්න *trividharatna* implied and ශික්ෂා *ṣikshá* command or ordinance) devout and religious obedience to the trividharatna or Buddha, his doctrines and priests.

ත්‍රිවිධාග්නි, *Trividhágni*, *s.* (ත්‍රි and විධ *vidha* manner, අග්නි *agni* fire) metaphorically the three destructive passions or circumstances of nature, to which mankind are subject, viz. lust or ardent desire, hatred, and ignorance.

ත්‍රිවෘත්, *Triwṛit*, *s.* plant of valuable purgative properties, commonly called Teori, and distinguished into white and black, *convolvulus turpethum* or *ipomœa turpethum*, [Colloq. ත්‍රස්තවාලු *trastawálu*].

ත්‍රිශක්ති, *Triṣakti*, *s.* (ත්‍රි three, ශක්ති power or ability) the three prerogatives of royalty, viz. the power to inflict punishment, great personal energy, and command of council.

ත්‍රිශූල, *Triṣúla*, *s.* trident or three pointed spear, borne in the hand of Kataragama deviyó as the emblem of his character, he being the god of war.

ත්‍රිස්නාව, *Trisnáwa*, *s.* desire, wish, anxious longing, lust, corrupt form of තෘෂ්ණාව *trishṇáwa*.

ත්‍රිසුගන්ධ, *Trisugandha*, } *s.* (ත්‍රි and සුගන්ධ fra-
ත්‍රිසුගන්ධි, *Trisagandhi*, } grance) the aggregate of three vegetable perfumes, viz. cinnamon, mint, and cardamums.

තෘණ, *Tṛiṇa*, *s.* grass, any gramineous plant.

තෘණකේතකී, *Tṛiṇa-kétakí*, *s.* screw pine, *pandanus odoratissimus*, [Colloq. මුදුකෙයියා *múdukeyiyá*].

තෘණකේතු, *Tṛiṇa-kétu*, *s.* (තෘණ and කේතු banner) bambu tree, *bambusa vulgaris*, [Colloq. උණගහ *uṇa-gaha*].

තෘණගෝධා, *Tṛiṇagódhá*, *s.* kind of newt, chameleon.

තෘණද්‍රුම, *Tṛiṇa-drima*, see තෘණ වෘක්ෂ *tṛiṇa-wriksha*,

තෘණපර්ණ, *Tṛiṇa-parṇa*, *s.* plant, *commelina diffusa*.

තෘණපුෂ්ප, *Tṛiṇa-pushpa*, *s.* tree the bark of which is a febrifuge, *swietena febrifugia*.

තෘණරාජ, *Tṛiṇa-rája*, *s.* (තෘණ grass, රාජ king) palmyra tree, [Colloq. තල්ගහ *tal-gaha*]; cocoanut tree, which is considered by the natives as the king among the grasses and gramineous plants.

තෘණවෘක්ෂ, *Tṛiṇa-wriksha*, *s.* (තෘණ and වෘක්ෂ tree) the tree which is preeminent among the grasses or the gramineous plants; any of the various species of the palm; as the palmyra, cocoa-nut tree, etc.

තෘණශූන්‍ය, *Tṛiṇa-śúnya*, *s.* Arabian jasmin.

තෘණශූල, *Tṛiṇaśúla*, *s.* kind of white flower, not identified.

තෘණසංස්තාර, *Tṛiṇa-saṇstára*, *s.* bed or resting place made of grass spread on the ground.

තෘණසම්භව, *Tṛiṇasambhawa*, *s.* wheat.

තෘණෝදක, *Tṛiṇódaka*, *s.* (තෘණ *tṛiṇa* and උදක *udaka* water) dew.

තෘණෝල්කා, *Tṛiṇólká*, *s.* torch made of grass or cocoa-nut leaves, commonly called chúl.

තෘතීය, *Tṛitíya*, *ad.* third, [Col: තුන්වෙනි *tunweni*].

තෘතීයජ්වර, *Tṛitíyajwara*, *s.* intermitting fever that comes on once every three days, *tertian ague*.

තෘතීයධ්‍යානය, *Tṛitíyaddhyánaya*, see ධ්‍යානය *dhyánaya*.

තෘප්ති, *Tṛipti*, *s.* sufficiency, repletion, enough, satisfaction, contentment.

ත්‍රුටි, *Trúṭi*, *s.* opening, expanding as a flower; doubt, uncertainty; cutting, breaking; small cardamums, [Colloq. සිහින් එන්සාල් *sihin ensál*].

ත්‍රුටිත, *Trúṭita*, *a.* cut, hurt, broken.

ත්‍රේතායුගය, *Trétáyugaya*, *s.* second of the four great periods of the world.

ත්‍රෛලෝක්‍ය, *Trilókya*, see තුන්ලෝකය *tun-lókaya*.

ත්වක්, *Twak*, *s.* skin; bark, rind, peel.

ත්වග්ගන්ධ, *Twaggandha*, *s.* orange.

ත්වග්දෝෂ, *Twag-dósha*, *s.* (ත්වග් skin, දෝෂ rheum) any purulent matter exuding from the skin in cutaneous disorders and affections; pus; leprosy; cutaneous disease.

ත්වගාක්ෂීරී, *Twagákshírí*, *s.* manna of the bambu tree, [Colloq. උණමකුළු *uṇamakuḷu*].

ත්වච, *Twacha*, *s.* skin; bark, rind, peel, [Colloq. සුඹුළු *sumbuḷu*]; plant, species of the cassia, [Coll: කුරුඳුපොතු *kurundupotu*].

ත්වරා, *Twará*, *s.* haste, speed.

ත්වරිත, *Twarita*, *a.* quick, swift, [Colloq. ඉක්මන් *ikman*].

ථ

The seventeenth consonant of the alphabet and second of the class of dentals; it is the aspirate of the preceding; and is expressed by tha.

ථද්ධ, *Thaddha*, *a.* firm, hard, stubborn.

ථල, *Thala*, *s.* land, ground; place, firm spot.

ථලජ, *Thalaja*, *s.* (ථල ground, ජ born) land-born, any thing produced from the earth, the opposite of ජලජ *jalaja*, aquatic.

ථේරී, *Thérí*, *s.* female priest, senior Buddhist nun.

ථේරෝ, *Théró*, *s.* senior Buddhist priest.

ද

The third letter of the dental class, and the eighteenth consonant, it sounds nearly like "*th*" in that; it is also an affix to words and has the power of a copulative conjunction; it is the sign of an interrogation.

දංගෙඩිය, *Daṇgeḍiya*, *s.* log of wood used for the purpose of cutting fish, meat etc.

දංශ, *Daṇsa*, *s.* gadfly; tooth; stinging, biting; sting of a serpent; armour, mail.

දංශන, *Daṇsana*, *a.* biting, stinging.

දංෂ්ට්‍රා, *Daṇshṭrá*, *s.* large tooth, tusk of an elephant, wild boar, eye tooth.

දක්කනවා, *Dakkanawá*, *v.* to drive, to force along by goading: pret. දැක්කුවා *dękkuwá*.

දක්ඛිණ, *Dakkhiṇa*, Páli form of දක්ෂිණ *dakshiṇa*.

දක්ඛිණා, *Dakkhiṇá*, *s.* gift, donation, charity.

දක්ඛිණෙය්‍ය, *Dakkhiṇeiya*, Páli form of දක්ෂිණීය *dakshiṇíya*.

දක්නා, *Dakná, part.* of දකිනවා *dakinawá.*

දක්වනවා, *Dakwanawá,* causal form of දකිනවා *dakinawá,* to show, to exhibit: pret. දැක්කෙව්වා *dękkewwá.*

දක්වා, *Dakwá, ad.* until, till, unto, as far as, to the extent of.

දක්ෂ, *Daksha, a.* dextrous, clever, conversant with; able: *s.* in the mythology of the Hindus a noted deity, who was a son of Brahma, born from the thumb of his right hand for the purpose of assisting in peopling the world; this Daksha had sixty daughters; of whom twenty-seven are the nymphs who were married to the moon and form the twenty-seven lunar asterisms; one of his daughters was Sati or Durgá the wife of Ṣiva, and thirteen were married to Káṣyapa; see කාශ්‍යප *káṣyapa.*

දක්ෂිණ, *Dakshiṇa, s.* the right; south, southern; offerings, religious presents: *a.* clever, skilful, dextrous, able; candid, sincere, honest; dependent, subject.

දක්ෂිණවිභඞ්ගය, *Dakshiṇa-vibhańgaya, s.* (දක්ෂිණ offerings, විභඞ්ග *vibhańga* discrimination, decision) religious rite delivered by Buddha to the priests, enjoining upon them a community of goods; viz. that whatsoever is offered religiously is to be considered as common to all, both priests and people.

දක්ෂිණවිශුද්ධිය, *Dakshiṇa-viṣuddhiya, s.* (දක්ෂිණ offering, විශුද්ධි pure) pure offerings, such as can only be offered to the priests on religious occasions.

දක්ෂිණශංඛය, *Dakshiṇa-ṣankaya, s.* (දක්ෂිණ right, ශංඛය shell or chank) chank shell opening to the right hand; such a chank is very valuable, and is used for pouring water on the heads of kings.

දක්ෂිණස්ථ, *Dakshiṇastha, s.* (දක්ෂිණ and ස්ථ who stands) charioteer, coachman: *a.* upon the south side.

දක්ෂිණා, *Dakshiṇá, s.* offerings, presents, things proper or fit to be offered; south.

දක්ෂිණාපථ, *Dakshiṇápatha, s.* south, the southern direction.

දක්ෂිණාර්හ, *Dakshiṇárha, s.* (දක්ෂිණ gift, offering, අර්හ *arha* worthy) one that is worthy of being offered to a priest of Buddha.

දක්ෂිණාවර්ත, *Dakshiṇáwarta, s.* any thing bent to the south, or turned to the right; as a chank which turns to the right is considered exceedingly valuable; the navel of a person that turns to the right is considered a mark of great beauty.

දක්ෂිණීය, *Dakshiṇíya, s.* meriting a reward, one worthy of receiving gifts or presents; priest.

දක්ෂිණෝද, *Dakshiṇóda,*
දක්ෂිණෝදක, *Dakshiṇódaka,* } *s.* (දක්ෂිණ *dakshiṇa* right hand, උදක *udaka* water) water which is poured into the right hand of a priest, as a ratification of an offering of value that either has been made or is yet to be made.

දක, *Daka, s.* water.

දකණ, *Dakaṇa, a.* south, southward.

දකිනවා, *Dakinawá, v.* to see, to look, to perceive, to find out: pret. දුටුවා *duṭuwá.*

දකුණ, *Dakuṇa, s.* right, dexter, south.

දකුණත්පස, *Dakuṇatpasa, s.* right side; south quarter; measure, two cubits.

දකුණත, *Dakuṇata, s.* right hand; south quarter, pl. දකුණත් *dakuṇat.*

දකුණු, *Dakuṇu, s.* right, dexter; south; gift, donation; region of Yama the Indian Pluto; see දකුණු හිමි *dakuṇu-himi.*

දකුණුදිග, *Dakuṇudiga,*
දකුණුදිඟු, *Dakuṇudingu,* } *s.* the south quarter, pl. දකුණුදිග් *dakuṇu-dig.*

දකුණුසක, *Dakuṇusaka,* see දක්ෂිණශංඛය *dakshiṇa ṣankhaya.*

දකුණු හිමි, *Dakuṇu-himi, s.* (දකුණු south, හිමි lord) name of Yama the Indian Pluto, in allusion to his reigning in the south or Pátála, he is the judge of the dead.

දකුණැලය, *Dakuṇęlaya, s.* right side.

දග්ධ, *Dagdha, a.* burnt, scorched, consumed by fire.

දග්ධමාන, *Dagdhamána, s.* any thing burnt or consumed.

දග්ධා, *Dagdhá, s.* the quarter where the sun is observable; fragrant grass.

දග්ධිකා, *Dagdhiká, s.* scorched rice, [Colloq. දම්කුඩ *damkuḍa*].

දග්ධෝදන, *Dagdhódana, s.* scorched, or boiled rice.

දඟ, *Danga, s.* imprisonment; calf of the leg; sprout, young shoot of a leaf or flower, germ, chain for tying elephants; *a.* crafty, subtile, cunning; troublesome, vexatious; treacherous.

දඟකරණවා, *Dangakaraṇawá, v.* to plague, to vex, to tease, to worry; to struggle with, to wrestle; to twist, to coil, to twine.

දඟගෙය, *Danga-geya*, s. prison, [Colloq. හිරගේ *hirage*].

දඟර, *Dangara*, s. the wanton gestures of a lewd woman when walking: *a.* coiled; spiral.

දඟරකරවලා, *Dangara-karawalá*, s. snake, variety of *bungarus Ceylonicus*.

දඟරගහනවා, *Dangaragahanawá*, v. to coil: pret. දඟරගැහුවා *dangaragehuwá*.

දඟරපොලඟා, *Dangara-polangá*, s. kind of viper.

දඟලනවා, *Dangalanawá*, v. to struggle, to writhe, to flutter, to flounder.

දඩ, *Dada*, s. fine, forfeit; wilderness, [Colloq. වනාන්තරය *wanántaraya*]; belly: *a.* tame, obedient.

දඩ එඬරු, *Dada-endaru*, s. wild castor oil plant.

දඩකලත්, *Dadakalat*, s. sort of gram or bean which grows wild in the jungle.

දඩකහ, *Dada-kaha*, s. plant, *curcuma aromatica (Scitamineæ)*: also called වල්කහ *wal-kaha*.

දඩකිරිල්ල, *Dadakirilla*, s. Ceylon elm, *Holoptelea* (or *ulmus*) *integrifolia;* also called ගොඩ කිරිල්ල *goda-kirilla*.

දඩකිරිය, *Dada-kíriya*, s. generic name of *Euphorbia*.

දඩකෙහෙල්, *Dada-kehel*, s. plant, *raphidophora decursiva (Araceæ)*.

දඩගහනවා, *Dadagahanawá*, v. to fine, to inflict a forfeit.

දඩගැහුම, *Dadagehuma*, verbal noun of දඩගහනවා *dadagahanawá*,

දඩමස්, *Dadamas*, s. flesh, the flesh of quadrupeds only.

දඩමීමා, *Dadamímá*, } s. (දඩ tame, මීවා or මීමා
දඩමීවා, *Dadamíwá*, } buffalo) tame buffalo, used as a decoy in catching wild ones.

දඩය, *Dadaya*, s. fine.

දඩයක්කාරයා, *Dadayakkárayá*, s. hunter.

දඩයම්කරණවා, *Dadayamkaranawá*, v. to shoot or hunt game.

දඩයම, *Dadayama*, s. hunting; shooting game, taking game in any way.

දඩයා, *Dadayá*, see දඩමීවා *dadamíwá*.

දඩාවතේ, *Dadáwaté*, a. wandering, going astray.

දඩින්නරු, *Dadinnaru*, s. plant, *buchnera euphrasioides*.

දඩේ, *Dade*, see දඩය *dadaya*.

දඬු, *Dandu*, s. wood, timber; kind of oar.

දඬුඅඬුව, *Danduanduwa*, s. smith's vice.

දඬුකඳ, *Dandu-kanda*, s. stocks, pl. දඬුකඳන් *dandu-kandan*.

දඬුපත්, *Dandupat*, s. timber, planks.

දඬුපන්නේ, *Dandupanné*, s. varieties of timber.

දඬුමුරලා, *Dandumuralá*, s. kind of sea fish.

දඬුලේනා, *Danduléná*, s. long tailed forest squirrel, called *grizzled hill squirrel, sciurus macrourus*.

දඬුවම, *Danduwama*, s. punishment, chastisement, castigation, pl. දඬුවම් *danduwam*.

දඬුවල්ලා, *Danduwallá*, s. kind of sea fish.

දඬුවලුබෑය, *Danduwalubéya*, s. kind of hive.

දඬුවැට, *Dandu-weta*, s. fence of sticks or any kind of wood; candle-stick; large kind of flambean.

දඬුවැල්බෑය, *Danduwelbéya*, see දඬුවලුබෑය *danduwalubéya*.

දඬුහම, *Danduhama*, corruptly for දඬුවම *danduwama*, which see.

දඬුහල, *Dandu-hala*, s. timber-yard.

දණ්ඩ, *Danda*, s. stick, staff; club; punishment, chastisement, castigation; fine, forfeit; subjection, obedience; measure of four cubits; army; stem of a tree; pride, arrogance; measure of time, a Sinhalese hour or twenty four minutes.

දණ්ඩක, *Dandaka*, s. sort of metre, the stanza of which exceeds twenty seven syllables and may be extended to two hundred.

දණ්ඩකර්මය, *Danda-karmaya*, s. punishment, castigation, chastisement.

දණ්ඩකාරණ්‍යය, *Dandakáranyaya*, s. a noted forest, situated in දණ්ඩකා *dandaká*, the peninsula of India from between the Narmadá and Gódávarí rivers.

දණ්ඩනය, *Dandanaya*, see දණ්ඩ *danda*.

දණ්ඩනීති, *Danda-níti*, s. moral philosophy, ethics; name of Vrihaspati, regent of the planet Jupiter and preceptor of the gods.

දණ්ඩපුෂ්පි, *Dandapushpi*, s. stemless plant bearing a beautiful flower, *crinum* (or *amaryllis*) *zeylanica*, [Colloq. ගොඩමානිල් *goda-mánil*]; medicinal plant, [Coll: කෝමාරිකා *kómáriká*].

දණ්ඩාසනය, *Dandásanaya*, s. small or low kind of table or stool on which the natives lay the book they are copying.

දණ්ඩාහත, *Dandáhata*, s. butter-milk, [Colloq. මෝරු *móru*].

දණ්ඩිකඩයා, *Dandikadayá*, see දණ්ඩියා *dandiyá*.

දණ්ඩින්, *Dandin*, s. staff or mace bearer: name of Yama the Indian Pluto.

දණ්ඩිය, *Dandiya*, s. kind of frame work used when threshing or treading corn.

දණ්ඩියා, *Dandiyá*, s. small kind of river fish.

දණ්ඩෝත්පලා, *Dandótpalá,* see ගොඩමානිල් *goda mánil* and දණ්ඩපුෂ්පී *dandapushpí.*

දත්, *Dat, plur.* of දත *data;* known: part. of දන්නවා *dannawá: s.* tusk of an elephant; sharp edge of any cutting instrument.

දත් අඬුව, *Dat-anduwa,* } *s.* tooth pick.
දත්කටුව, *Dat-katuwa,* }

දත්කැක්කුම, *Dat-kekkuma, s.* tooth ache.

දත්කැටියා, *Datketiyá, s.* plant peculiar to Ceylon, *xylopia champonii (Anonaceæ);* plant with long leaves and many flowered corymbs, *ophiorrhiza mungos (Rubiaceæ).*

දත්නියවනවා, *Dat-niyawanawá, v.* to grin, to make grimaces.

දත්මිටිකනවා, *Datmiti-kanawá, v.* to gnash the teeth from pain or anguish.

දත්යුවල, *Dat-yuwala, s.* pair of teeth, two tusks of an elephant.

දත්රුදු, *Datrudu,* } *s.* lion, [Colloq. සිංහයා *sinha-*
දත්රුපු, *Datrupu,* } *yá*].

දත, *Data, s.* tooth.

දතනියවනවා, *Dataniyawanawá,* see දත්නියවනවා *dat-niyawanawá.*

දතමනා, *Datamaná,* } *s.* that which ought to be
දතයුතු, *Datayutu,* } known, that which is proper to be known.

දද, *Dada, s.* star; fool; leprosy; plant, (costus) bird; parts of generation; male organ of generation; tooth; flag, banner; wicked or low man; Brahmin; ring worm; cutaneous disorder, kind of scurvy.

දදපෙල, *Dada-pela, s.* (දද banner, පෙල row) line of flags of various shapes and colours, by which the temples are ornamented on festival occasions; to bestow a suit of these colours on a temple is reckoned a work of great merit.

දදභුජ, *Dada-bhuja, s.* (දද bird, භුජ what eats) bird of the eagle kind; any bird of prey.

දද මුවා. *Dada-muwá, s.* (දද flag, coloured cloth, මුවා covering or screen) screen made of flags, a screen or wall of coloured cloth; curtain; vail surrounding a room or tent.

දදය, *Dadaya, s.* ring-worm, scurvy.

දදර, *Dadara, s.* frog, [Colloq. ගෙම්බා *gembá*]; decay.

දදරද, *Dada-rada, s.* (දද star, රද king) moon, [Colloq. හඳ *handa*]; sandal wood; bird of Vishnu, garuda.

දදවරණ, *Dada-warana, s.* (දද tooth, වරණ what covers) lip, [Colloq. තොල *tola*].

දද්‍රු, *Dadru, s.* cutaneous and herpetic eruptions.

දද්‍රුඝන, *Dadrughna, s.* species of cassia, *cassia tora,* [Colloq. තෝර *tóra*].

දද්‍රුවෛරී, *Dadru-wairí, s.* plant, *plumbago rosea,* [Colloq. රත්නෙටුල් *ratnetul*].

දධි, *Dadhi, s.* milk curdled, either spontaneously or by heat; a kind of food thus made is held in high estimation among the Hindus, and is considered, medicinally, as a remedy or preventative of most disorders.

දධිපුෂ්පී, *Dadhipushpí, s.* kind of flower, *clitorea ternata,* [Colloq. නිල් කටරොළු *nil-kataroḷu*].

දධිඵල, *Dadhiphala, s.* elephant or wood apple, [Colloq. දිවුල් *diwul*].

දධිමණ්ඩ, *Dadhimanda, s.* whey, [Colloq. කිරි මෝරු *kiri-móru*].

දධිමුඛ, *Dadhimukha, s.* (දධි curdled milk (colour), මුඛ face) white-faced monkey.

දධිසක්තු, *Dadhisaktu, s.* (දධි curdled milk, සක්තු barley meal) sort of food consisting of barley meal mixed with curds.

දධිසාර, *Dadhisára, s.* (දධි and සාර essence) fresh butter, [Colloq. වෙඬරු *wendaru*].

දන්, *Dan, s.* gift, donation, offering; paddy; waist clothing of women; name of a tree of which there are several species; it yields a fruit much eaten by the natives: *Eugenia* or *syzygium cargophyllæa, (Myrtaceæ);* also called හීන් දන් *hín-dan;* see මාදන් *mádan* ; බළුදන් *baludan.*

දන් ගෙඩි, *Dan-gedi, s.* fruit of the dan tree.

දන්ඩ, *Danda, s.* large stick, log of wood; corruptly for දණ්ඩ *danda.*

දන්ත, *Danta, s.* tooth, tusk, peak or side of a mountain.

දන්තකාෂ්ඨ, *Dantakáshtha, s.* a piece of stick used as a tooth brush, [Colloq. දැහැටි *deheti*].

දන්තජ, *Dantaja, a.* dental.

දන්තධාවන. *Dantadháwana, s.* tooth brush, cleaning the teeth; tree, *mimusops elengi,* [Colloq. මුහුනමල් ගස *muhunamal-gasa*]: also see කිහිරි *kihiri.*

දන්තශඨ, *Dantasatha, s.* elephant or wood apple, [Colloquial: දිවුල් *diwul*]; common lime, *citrus limetta* or *c. acida,* [Colloq. දෙහි *dehi*]; tree bearing an acid fruit, *averrhoa carambola,* [Coll: කාමරංගා *kámarangá*]; common orange tree, *citrus aurantium,* [Colloq. දොඩම් *dodam*].

දන්තහර්ෂ, *Dantaharsha*, *s.* tenderness of the teeth; intolerance of any rough or acid substance.

දන්තාගද, *Dantágada*, *s.* specific for every disorder of the teeth.

දන්තාබල, *Dantábala*, *s.* tusked elephant.

දන්තාර්බුද, *Dantárbuda*, *s.* gum boil, ulceration of the gums.

දන්තිකා, *Dantiká*, *s.* medicinal plant, described as a gentle stimulant, [Colloq. දෑත්ත *dętta*].

දන්ති, *Dantí*, *s.* medicinal plant, *Croton polyandrum*, [Colloq. දෑත්ත *dętta*].

දන්තිවිජ, *Dantívija*, *s.* plant, *croton tiglium*, [Coll: ජයපාල *jayapála*].

දන්තුර, *Dantura*, *a.* having a large or projecting tooth; waving, undulating.

දන්තෝෂ්ඨාක්ෂර, *Dantóshṭhákshara*, *s.* (දන්ත *danta* tooth, ඕෂ්ඨ *óshṭha* lip, අක්ෂර *akshara* letter) letter which partakes in sound both of the labial and dental; as the semi-vowel ව *wa* which is the only one in the alphabet of this class.

දන්දෙනවා, *Dandenawá*, *v.* to give alms.

දන්නවා, *Dannawá*, *v.* to know, to be acquainted with: pret. දෑනගත්තා *dęnagattá*.

දන්නා, *Danná*, *a.* acquainted with any matter, intelligent.

දන්වනවා, *Danwanawá*, *v.* to make known: pret. දෑන්නුවා *dęnnuwá*.

දන්වා, *Danwá*, *s.* Asura, titan, demon: *p.* having announced, or made known.

දන්වාසතුරු, *Danwá-saturu*, *s.* (දන්වා and සතුරු enemy) name of Vishṇu, alluding to his being the enemy of the Asuras.

දන්වැට, *Danwęṭa*, *s.* (දන් and වැට observance) charity, alms-giving.

දන්වැල, *Danwęla*, corrupt form of දම්වැල *damwęla*.

දන්සල, *Dansala*, *s.* (දන් gift, සල hall) public place for distributing alms, alms house.

දන, *Dana*, *s.* knee; riches, wealth, property, possessions; people, mankind; birth, origin: pl. දන් *dan*.

දනඉස, *Dana-isa*, *s.* cap of the knee.

දනඋතුකටුව, *Danautukaṭuwa*, *s.* bone of the knee, cap of the knee.

දනගහනවා, *Danagahanawá*, *v.* to kneel.

දනද, *Danada*, *s.* (දන wealth, ද who gives) name of Wesamuṇi-raja or Kuvéra; Indian Plutus.

දනන්, *Danan*, *s.* people.

දනන, *Danana*, *s.* birth, production; conquest, victory.

දනනාලිය, *Dana-náliya*, *s.* knee, knee bone.

දනපති, *Danapati*, *s.* (දන wealth, පති chief) name of Kuvéra or Wesamuṇi-raja, the Indian Plutus; (poetically) wealthy man, one very rich or possessing great property.

දනපද, *Danapada*, see ජනපද *janapada*.

දනඹුල්, *Danambul*, *s.* mountain, hill; vinegar; water in which rice has been washed.

දනමඬල, *Danamaṇḍala*, *s.* (දන and මඬල an orb) knee, cap of the knee.

දනවත්, *Danawat*, *a.* rich, wealthy, opulent.

දනවනවා, *Danawanawá*, *v.* to produce: pret. දෑනවි *dęnavi*, he produced.

දනවා, *Danawá*, *v.* to burn, to consume by fire: pret. දෑවා *dęwá*; part. of දනවනවා *danawanawá*, having produced.

දනවුව, *Danawuwa*, *s.* country, province, district; house of a respectable man, pl. දනව් *danaw*.

දනා, *Daná*, *s.* man, mankind.

දනිඳු, *Danindu*, *s.* name of Wesamuṇi, chief of the Yakshas.

දනු, *Danu*, *s.* bow, [Colloq. දුන්න *dunna*]; sign of the Zodiac (Sagittarius); mother of the Daityas, demons, or Asuras; she was one of the daughters of දක්ෂ *daksha* (which see), and wife of Káṣyapa, the celebrated Ṛishi or holy man, the teacher of Paraṣuráma, from whom he received the sovereignty of the world.

දනුජ, *Danuja*, *s.* (දනු and ජ born) titan, Asura, demon.

දනුමැතියා, *Danumętiyá*, *s.* experienced man; man of mature judgment.

දනුලග්න, *Danu-lagna*, } *s.* (දනු bow, ලග්න sign)
දනුව, *Danuwa*, } sign of the Zodiac, (Sagittarius).

දප, *Dapa*. Elu form of දර්ප *darpa*, pride, arrogance; copulation, cohabitation.

දපණ, *Dapaṇa*, *s.* looking glass, mirror.

දපනවා, *Dapanawá*, *v.* to offer to devils, to repeat mantras inaudibly, to mutter a sort of magical incantations or prayers to demons; to charm demons by the power of magical incantations; these are the practices of the Kaṭṭádiyas or demon priests for the purpose of curing diseases, or to cure a disease by expelling the evil demon who has been supposed to inflict the disease; after the prayers and mantras have been repeated audibly for some time, the Kaṭṭádiya stretches himself on his back on the ground and continues to mutter the charms inaudibly, till he becomes inspired by the demon and ascertains whether or not his requests have been complied with: pret. දෑපුවා *dępuwá*.

දබර, *Dabara*, *s.* quarrel, fight without weapons, tumult, uproar.

දබර ඇඟිල්ල, *Dabara-ęngilla*, *s.* (දබර and ඇඟිල්ල finger) forefinger, so called in allusion to its being used when threatening, or menacing or challenging to a fight or quarrel.

දබරකරණවා, *Dabara-karaṇawá*, *v.* to quarrel.

දඹ, *Damba*, *s.* fruit tree, Elu form of ජම්බු *jambu.*

දඹදිව, *Dambadiwa*, *s.* one of the four continents situated south of Mahá méru, Elu form of ජම්බුවිපය *jambudvípaya*, which see.

දඹ රත්රන්, *Damba-ratran*, *s.* fabulous sort of gold.

දඹල, *Dambala*, *s.* kidney bean, *phaseolus vulgaris.*

දඹු, *Dambu*, *s.* jackal, [Colloq. නරියා *nariyá*]: *a.* not well baked or burnt, as දඹු උළු *dambu-uḷu* tiles slightly baked.

දම්, *Dam*, *ind.* wife; doctrine, religious truth: see also දන් *dan.*

දම්කඳ, *Damkanda*, Elu form of ධර්මස්කන්ධය *dharmaskandhaya*, which see.

දම්කුඩ, *Damkuḍa*, *s.* rice left at the bottom of the pot in which rice has been boiled.

දම්ගෙඩිය, *Damgeḍiya*, *s.* tom-tom used for collecting the priests at the time of repeating the baṇa; chopping or decapitating block.

දම්දෙසනවා, *Damdesanawá*, *v.* (දම් baṇa, දෙසනවා to proclaim) to read the bana, to expound the sermons of Buddha; to preach, to address a sermon to a congregation: pret. දම්දෙසුවා *damdesuwá.*

දම්පතිහු, *Dampatihu*, *s.* husband and wife, [Colloq. අඹු සැමියෝ *ambu sęmiyó*].

දම්පාට, *Dam-páṭa*, *s.* (දම් fruit, පාට colour) purple.

දම්රජ, *Damraja*, see ධර්මරාජ *dharmarája*,

දම්රද, *Dam-rada*, Elu form of ධර්මරාජ *dharmarája.*

දම්වැල, *Damwęla*, *s.* chain, fetter, pl. දම්වැල් *damwęl.*

දම්සක්, *Damsak*, Elu form of ධර්මචක්‍ර *dharmachakra.*

දම්සබාව, *Dam-sabáwa*, *s.* congregation assembled to hear a sermon, but particularly applied to those who hear the baṇa or the discourses of Buddha.

දම්සැරි, *Damsęri*, *s.* charioteer or guide of men who require training, epithet of Buddha.

දම්භ, *Damha*, *s.* deceit, fraud, cheating; hypocrisy; lie; sin, wickedness; pride, arrogance.

දම, *Dama*, *s.* chain; punishment, chastisement; self-command; endurance of the most painful austerities; taming, subduing; self restraint, subduing the senses. suppressing the passions.

දමක, *Damaka*, *s.* tamer, subduer; one who endeavours to subdue himself; penitent, one given up to the practice of religious austerities.

දමථ, *Damatha*, *s.* punishment, chastisement, inflicted chiefly for subduing the passions; self control, endurance of rigorous austerities.

දමන, *Damana*, *s.* resignation, mental tranquillity or composure; self command, control over the passions; state of religious austerity; convincing any person of his errors, applied only to religious matters, religious conversion.

දමනය, *Damanaya*, see දමන *damana.*

දමනයකරණවා, *Damanaya-karaṇawá*, *v.* to subdue, to bring into subjection, to render obedient; to convert, to turn from one religion to another.

දමනවා, *Damanawá*, *v.* to tame, to subdue; to place, to put, to fix: pret. දැම්මා *dęmmá*, දැමුවා *dęmuwá.*

දමනීය, *Damaníya*, *p. a.* to be tamed, subjected, or subdued.

දමිත, *Damita*, *p. a.* subjugated, brought under control, (as the passions); converted, turned from bad practices, converted from heresy.

දමිනිය, *Daminiya*, *s.* tree, *grewia tiliæfolia (Tiliaceæ);* this tree is said to have taken its name from the circumstance of a priest having bound to it a devil whom he wished to compel into his service.

දමෝදර, *Damódara*, *s.* name of Kataragama-deviyo the Indian god of war; name of Vishṇu.

දමෝරා, *Damórá*, *s.* name of Vishṇu.

දයා, *Dayá*, *s.* tenderness, compassion, mercy.

දයාබර, *Dayábara*, } *a.* merciful, tender, kind, compassionate.
දයාලු, *Dayálu*,
දයාවන්ත, *Dayáwanta*,

දයාවන්තකම, *Dayáwantakama*, *s.* kindness, tenderness.

දර්දුර, *Dardura*, *s.* frog.

දර්ද්‍රු, *Dardru*, *s.* ring-worm, kind of scurvy, [Coll: දද *dada*].

දර්ප, *Darpa*, see දප *dapa.*

දර්පක, *Darpaka*, *s.* name of Kámadéva the Indian god of love.

දර්පණය, *Darpaṇaya*, *s.* mirror, looking glass; eye; kindling, inflaming.

දර්බි, *Darbi*, *s.* ladle, spoon, [Colloq. හැන්ද *hẹnda*]; expanded hood of the cobra de capello.

දර්භ, *Darbha*, *s.* *kusa-taṇa* or sacrificial grass; kind of reed, *saccharum spontaneum*.

දර්වි, *Darvi*, *s.* spoon, [Colloq. හැන්ද *hẹnda*].

දර්විකා, *Darvika*, *s.* ladle, spoon.

දර්ශ, *Darṣa*, *s.* sight; seeing; day of the new moon, when she rises invisible; sacrifice made on that day.

දර්ශක, *Darṣaka*, *s.* door-keeper; warder; exhibiter; skilful man; one conversant with any art or science.

දර්ශනය, *Darṣanaya*, *s.* sight, seeing, looking; eye; mirror; dream, vision; virtue, moral merit: knowledge, especially religious illumination; intellect; sect of philosophy.

දර්ශනීය, *Darṣaníya*, *a.* beautiful, handsome, agreeable; fit to see, proper to be seen.

දර, *Dara*, *s.* dried wood, firewood; the sharp edge of any cutting instrument; hole in the ground; cavern, grotto; the earth; Elu form of ජරා *jará*, which see.

දරකපනවා, *Dara-kapanawá*, *v.* to fell timber for firewood.

දරකැටියා, *Darakẹṭiyá*, *s.* large testaceous worm which breeds in dry and rotten wood.

දරච්චාව, *Darachcháwa*, *s.* a reparation or atonement made in a subsequent transmigration for debts or obligations contracted in a former state of existence.

දරණ, *Daraṇa*, *s.* creeping things, the serpent tribe.

දරණගහනවා, *Daraṇa-gahanawá*, *v.* to coil as a rope or snake.

දරණවා, *Daraṇawa*, *v.* to bear, to suffer, to support, to carry: pret. දැරුවා *dẹruwá*.

දරණුව, *Daraṇuwa*, *s.* circle of twined canes for placing vessels on.

දරද, *Darada*, *s.* country bordering on Kashmír; vermillion, [Colloq. සාදිලිංගම් *sádilingam*].

දරදඬු, *Daradaṉḍu*, *s.* firewood; coldness and stiffness of a corpse.

දරදඬුගැහෙනවා, *Daradaṉḍugẹhenawá*, *v.* to become stiff as a corpse.

දරදි, *Daradi*, *s.* debt, [Colloq. ණය *naya*].

දරමිටිය, *Dara-miṭiya*, *s.* faggot.

දරසෑය, *Daraséya*, *s.* funeral pile.

දර හාල්පන්, *Dara-hálpan*, *s.* plant, *Fimbristylis tetragona (Cyperaceæ).*

දරා, *Dará*, *s.* earth, [Colloq. පොළව *poḷawa*]; cave.

දාරණ්ඩ, *Dáráṉḍa*, *s.* upper side of a field.

දරි, *Dari*, *s.* natural or artificial excavation in a mountain, cave, grotto, [Colloq. කඳුරැලි *kaṉdu-rẹli*].

දරිද්‍ර, *Daridra*, *a.* poor, needy, indigent, distressed.

දරිම, *Darima*, *s.* kind of pomegranate, [Colloq. දෙළුම් *deḷum*].

දරී, *Darí*, *s.* cave in a rock, natural or artificial: see දරි *dari*.

දරු, *Daru*, *s.* child.

දරුකම, *Darukama*, *s.* state of being a child, sonship, relation of a child.

දරු ගර්භය, *Daru-garbhaya*, *s.* (දරු child, ගර්භ *garbha* womb) pregnancy, fœtus.

දරුගල, *Daru-gala*, *s.* small rolling stone.

දරුගැබ, *Daru-gẹba*, see දරුගර්භය *daru-garbhaya*.

දරුණු, *Daruṇu*, *a.* rough, harsh, boisterous, austere, severe, hard, obdurate.

දරුබර, *Darubara*, *s.* child bearing.

දරුබර කත, *Darabara-kata*, *s.* (දරු and බර weight, කත woman) mother; woman having a large family of children.

දරුම, *Daruma*, Elu form of ධර්ම *dharma*, which see.

දරුමල, *Darumala*, see දලබුව *dalabuwa*.

දරුමා, *Darumá*, *s.* (දරු child, මා mother) mother, [Colloq. මව් *maw*].

දරු මැහැල්ලී, *Daru-mẹhẹllí*, *s.* woman who has children in her old age.

දරුවා, *Daruwá*, *s.* child, infant, pl. දරුවෝ *daruwó*.

දල්වනවා, *Dalwanawá*, *v.* to kindle, to light, to set fire to any thing, to inflame; open as the mouth: pret. දැල්ලුවා *dẹlluwá*.

දල, *Dala*, *s.* leaf; leaves of flowers; tooth, ivory; fire; flame of fire, effulgence, glittering; covetousness; avarice; water; heart; calix; half; part, portion; division; cutting, tearing; heap.

දලක්ෂිරිණී, *Dalakshiriṇi*, *s.* tree, [Colloq. පතුක් *patuk*].

දලකඳ, *Dala-kanda*, *s.* (දල water, කඳ heap) standing water as a pond or lake.

දලකෙළි, *Dala-keḷi*, *s.* (දල and කෙළි sport) bathing, sporting in the water; venereal pleasures.

දලගැබ, *Dala-gẹba*, *s.* (දල and ගැබ womb) cloud, [Colloq. වලාකුළ *walákuḷa*].

දලදන්, *Daladan*, *s.* (දල and දන් gift) cloud; year; sea, ocean.

දලදර, *Daladara*, *s.* (දල and දර bearing) cloud, cloud condensed with rain; sea, ocean.

දලදරවරණ, *Daladara-warana*, *s.* elephant of Ṣakraya.

දලදලු, *Dala-dalu*, *s.* young shoot or sprout of a leaf, leaf-bud.

දලනදන්, *Dalanadan*, *s.* sea, ocean, [Colloq. මුද *múda*].

දලනිදු, *Dalanidu*, *s.* sea, ocean; name of Anantayá, king of the serpent race.

දල බින්දුව, *Dala-binduwa*, *s.* drop of water.

දලබුව, *Dalabuwa*, *s.* womb.

දලබුවා, *Dalabuwá*, *s.* small worm or grub, caterpillar.

දලබෑම, *Dalabęma*, *s.* whirlpool; whirling round of the water.

දලඹු, *Dalambu*, *s.* womb; time immediately following conception prior to the fœtus being formed; small worm or grub; viviparous.

දලමස්, *Dalamas*, *s.* the Pulas, name of tree, *butea frondosa*, [Colloq. ගස්කැල *gas-kęla*].

දලය, *Dalaya*, see දල *dala*.

දලරද, *Dala-rada*, } *s.* (දල water, රද king, රැස් collection) sea, ocean, [Coll: මුද *múda*].
දලරැස්. *Dala-ręs*,

දලසර, *Dalasara*, *s.* (දල and සර which moves) fish in general, [Colloq. මසුන් *masun*]; water-fowl, any fowl or bird going or residing in water; fish.

දලසා, *Dalasá*, *s.* (දල fire, සා branch) flame, [Coll: ගිනිදළුව *ginidaḷuwa*].

දලා, *Dalá*, *s.* kind of fish.

දලාඪක, *Daláḍhaka*, *s.* sesamum; an aquatic plant *pistia stratiotes*, [Colloq. දියපරණලා *diya-paranalá*]; iron wood tree, *mesua ferrea*, [Colloq. නා *ná*]; flowering tree, *mimosa sirissa;* red chalk; cuttle fish bone; moat, ditch; species of jasmine, *jasminum pubescens;* elephant's ear; hurricane.

දලි, *Dali*, *s.* clod of clay or mould; bud, young shoot of the leaf; sort of small house cricket, cockroach.

දලික, *Dalika*, *s.* timber, wood, [Colloq. ලී *lí*].

දලු, *Dalu*, *s.* bow; the bud or young shoots of leaves.

දලුක්, *Daluk*, *s.* tree, *euphorbia antiquorum*, *(Euphorbiaceæ);* the thorns on this tree are so large and piercing that the branches are used for making fences against elephants, wild buffaloes etc. it has "a grotesque appearance with a prickly cactus-like stem without leaves." (Morris.)

දලුකොටුව, *Dalukoṭuwa*, *s.* betel plantation.

දලුබුලත්, *Dalu-bulat*, *s.* species of the betel leaf.

දලුමුර, *Dalumura*, *s.* betel leaf, [Colloq. බුලත් *bulat*].

දලුමුර ඔප්පුකරණවා, *Dalumura-oppukaranawá*, *v.* to offer to devils, to present an offering to a devil, consisting of the betel leaf, sandal wood and the flowers of the areca tree; to present betel to the king by his officer in waiting or the person who is kept for that purpose; see the following word.

දලුමුරකාරයා, *Dalumurakárayá*, *s.* the person who serves the king with betel; the office is one of great importance and confidence, in consequence of the great number of narcotics and stimulants which are mixed up with the betel, and which vary according either to the state of health, or the fancy of the king.

දලුලනවා, *Dalu-lanawá*, *v.* to bud, to germinate.

දලුව, *Daluwa*, *s.* young shoot of the leaf, bud; long pepper plant.

දලුවත්ත, *Dalu-watta*, *s.* garden planted with the betel creeper.

දලුවමුල්, *Daluwa-mul*, *s.* root of the long pepper plant, *piper longum*, [Colloq. තිප්පිලිමුල් *tippili-mul*].

දව්, *Daw*, *ad*, speedily, quickly, swiftly, expeditiously.

දව්වනවා, *Dawwanawá*, *v.* to take slightly hold, as of a corner or extremity: pret. දෑව්වා *dęwwá*.

දව, *Dawa*, *s.* play, sport, amusement; frolic; wood, wilderness, forest; wood on fire; fire in general: *ad.* quickly, speedily: *a.* two.

දවට, *Dawaṭa*, *s.* timber tree with beautiful foliage, *carallia integerrima (Rhizophoraceæ).*

දවටනවා, *Dawaṭanawá*, *v.* to roll; to envelope; to fold up, to wrap, to twist: pret. දෑවටුවා *dęwaṭuwá*.

දවන, *Dawana*, *s.* black monkey, [Colloq. වඳුරා *wandurá*].

දවනවා, *Dawanawá*, *v.* to burn, to consume by fire: pret. දෑව්වා *dęwwá*.

දවනිය ගස, *Dawaniya-gasa*, *s.* tree, see දමනිය *damaniya*.

දවරු, *Dawarę*, *s.* period of time, sixty of the Singhalese hours, making a day and night.

දවල්, *Dawal*, *s.* day-time.

දවල, *Dawala*, *s.* white (the colour), [Colloq. සුදු *sudu*].

දවලු, *Dawalu*, *a.* white, pure.

දවස්කෙරීම, *Dawaskeríma*, *s.* mode of life, living, conduct.

දවස්පතා, *Dawaspatá*, *ad.* daily.

දවස්මැණ, *Dawas-meṇa*, } *s.* (දවස් days, මැණ gem,
දවස්හිමි, *Dawas-himi*, } හිමි lord) sun, [Colloq. සූර්‍ය්‍යයා *súryayá*].

දවස, *Dawasa*, *s.* day.

දවහ, *Dawaha*, *s.* day-time; *adv.* constantly.

දවහත්තරුව, *Dawahat-taruwa*, *s.* star so called.

දවහල, *Dawahala*, *s.* cloth; day-time, time from the rising to the going down of the sun.

දවහෙයියා, *Dawaheyiyá*, *s.* chaff.

දවාග්නි, *Dawágni*, *s.* wood on fire, conflagration of a forest.

දවාල, *Dawála*, *s.* day-time.

දවු, *Dawu*, *s.* rapidity, celerity, velocity, swiftness; timber tree, *anogeissus* (or *conocarpus*) *latifolia (Combretaceæ)*: *a.* large.

දවුල්කුරුඳු, *Dawul-kurundu*, *s.* variety of *cinnamomum zeylanica*.

දවුල් ගහනවා, *Dawul-gahanawá*, *v.* to beat with a drum stick.

දවුල, *Dawula*, *s.* drum stick with which the native drum is beaten at both ends, pl. දවුල් *dawul*.

දශකණ්ඨ, *Daṣakaṇṭha*, *s.* (දශ ten, කණ්ඨ neck) the ten necked one, name of Ráwaṇa, alluding to his having ten heads.

දශධර්මය, *Daṣadharmaya*, see දශරාජධර්මය *daṣarája dharmaya*.

දශන, *Daṣana*, *s.* tooth; peak of a mountain; armour, mail.

දශනඛ, *Daṣanakha*, *s.* ten nails of the fingers.

දශනච්ඡදන, *Daṣanachchhadana*, } *s.* (දශන tooth,
දශනවාසස්, *Daṣanawásas*, } ච්ඡදන or වාස *wása* covering) lip, [Colloq. තොල *tola*].

දශපරමාර්ථ, *Daṣaparamártha*, see පාරමිතාව *páramitáwa*.

දශපුණ්‍ය ක්‍රියාව, *Daṣapuṇya-kriyáwa*, *s.* (දශ ten, පුණ්‍ය virtuous, ක්‍රියා *kriyá* act) ten virtuous works which are enjoined by the religion of Buddha; viz. alms-giving; observance of moral precepts; abstract religious meditation; imputing to others the religious merit we have acquired from our own good works; receiving from others the merit that has been procured by their good works; obedience to Buddha, his doctrines, and his priests; respect to the aged; reading the baṇa; hearing the baṇa; undeviating orthodoxy in religion.

දශරථ, *Daṣaratha*, *s.* (දශ ten, රථ car) proper name, sovereign of Ayódhyá or Oude, and the father of Ráma; the name alludes to his ten cars, which bore him to the ten points of the universe, viz. the eight points of the compass, and the Zenith and Nadir.

දශරාජධර්ම, *Daṣarája-dharma*, *s.* (දශ ten, රාජ royal or kingly, ධර්ම quality) the ten moral virtues belonging to royalty; viz. alms-giving; observance of religious precepts; liberality in presents; uprightness; compassion; addiction to religious austerities; mild or even temper; tenderness; patience; peacefulness.

දශවිධරත්නය, *Daṣavidha-ratnaya*, *s.* (දශ and විධ sort, රත්න gem) the ten jewels, viz. pearl, gem, lapis lazuli, conch, mineral called silá, coral, silver, gold, emerald, and ruby.

දශා, *Daṣá*, *s.* the end of a garment; state, condition; period of age, as youth, manhood, etc.; the mind or faculty of understanding.

දශානන, *Daṣánana*, *s.* (දශ *daṣa* ten, ආනන *ánana* face) name of Rávaṇa, the noted Asura, and king of Lanká or Ceylon; alluding to his ten faces: see රාවණ *Rávaṇa*.

දශාවතාර, *Daṣáwatára*, *s.* (දශ *daṣa* and අවතාර *awatára* incarnation) name or epithet of Vishṇu alluding to his ten incarnations: see අවතාර *awatára*.

දශාශ්ව, *Daṣáṣwa*, *s.* (දශ *daṣa* ten, අශ්ව *aṣwa* horse) moon, alluding to his chariot being drawn by ten horses.

දශේන්ද්‍රිය, *Daṣéndriya*, *s.* (දශ *doṣa* and ඉන්ද්‍රිය organ of sense) the ten organs of sense and action, viz. skin, eye, tongue, nose, ear, speech, hand, foot, arm and pudendum.

දෂ්ට, *Dashṭa*, *s.* biting, as by the teeth; stinging as a snake etc.

දෂ්ටකරණවා, *Dashṭakaraṇawá*, *v.* to sting as a serpent, bite with a venomous fang.

දස්, *Das*, *s.* slave; skill, ability; sight, seeing.

දස්‍ර, *Dasra*, *s.* either of the twin sons of Aṣvini and physicians of Swarga.

දස්‍රදේවතා, *Dasra-déwatá*, *s.* (දස්‍ර and දේවතා god) lunar constellation of Aṣvini, he being the ruling genius of the asterism.

දස, *Dasa*, *s.* number ten; quarter, side; male slave.

දස අකුසල, *Dasa-akusala*, see දසාකුසල *dasákusala.*

දස අට, *Dasa-aṭa*, see දහ අට *daha-aṭa.*

දස උපපාරමිතා, *Dasa-upapáramitá*, see පාරමිතාව *páramitáwa.*

දසඑකඩමස, *Dasaekaḍamasa*, *s.* ten and half months.

දස කුසල, *Dasa-kusala*, see දශපුණ්‍ය ක්‍රියාව *daṣa-puṇya-kriyáwa.*

දසන්, *Dasan*, *s.* tooth, [Colloq. දත *data*].

දසන්පල, *Dasan-pala*, *s.* ox, bullock, [Colloquial. ගොණා *goṇá*].

දසනුදස, *Dasanudasa*, *s.* four quarters of the compass, with their four intermediate points.

දසපාරමිතාව, *Dasapáramitáwa*, } see පාරමිතාව
දසපෙරුමන්, *Dasaperuman*, } *páramitáwa.*

දසබල, *Dasabala*, } *s.* epithet of Buddha allud-
දසඹුල්, *Dasambul*, } ing to his bodily powers or strength; the rate of which is calculated by the power of a fabulous elephant, which possessed the strength of 300,000,000 of men; in addition to which were nine other elephants, each possessing ten times the power of the other; and Buddha is said to have possessed ten times the strength of the last, making a power equal to 300,000,000,000,000,000 men.

දසභාතික, *Dasabhátika*, *s.* (දස ten, භාතික one having a brother) ten sons of the king Ugraséna, whose wife was daughter of Kaṇsarája; their names are, Wásudéva, Baladéva, Chandradéva, Súryadéva, Agnidéva, Arjunadéva, Payunadéva, Ghata-paṇḍita, Aṅkura, Waruṇadéva,

දසම්, *Dasam*, *s.* lip, [Colloq. තොල *tola*].

දසම්පල, *Dasam-pala*, see දසන්පල *dasan-pala.*

දසමුල්, *Dasa-mul*, *s.* (දස ten, මුල් roots) roots of ten plants from which is prepared a decoction which is a powerful purgative.

දසය *Dasaya*, see දස *dasa.*

දසයනරත්රන්, *Dasayana-ratran*, *s.* gold of ten carats or the tenth degree.

දසරු, *Dasaru*, see දසරුව *dasaruwa.*

දසරුන්, *Dasarun*, *s.* walking, moving; *plur.* of the following word.

දසරුව, *Dasaruwa*, *s.* shoulder, [Colloq. උරහිස *urahisa*].

දසසතර, *Dasasatara*, see දහහතර *dahahatara.*

දසසීලය, *Dasa-sílaya*, *s.* (දස ten, සීල *síla* precept) the ten moral precepts enjoined by the religion of Buddha; viz. to abstain from the destruction of life, (the life of any animal); from theft; from all intercourse with women; from falsehood; from all intoxicating liquors; from eating after mid-day; from all amusement, as music, singing, dancing, etc.; from indulgence in luxuries, such as perfumes, unguents, etc; from ornaments, as gold, gems etc.; from use of seats or couches above the prescribed height.

දසාකුසල, *Dasákusala*, *s.* (දස *dasa* and අකුසල demerit, sin) the ten chief sins which are forbidden by the religion of Buddha; viz. murder, (properly the destruction of life, it extends to all living beings): theft; adultery; lying: abuse; slander; vain talk; covetousness; wishing evil to others; heterodoxy.

දසාව, *Dasáwa*, *s.* end or border of a garment or any piece of cloth; quarter, direction; state, condition of life; period during which a person is supposed to be under the influence of any one of the planets.

දසුන්, *Dasun*, } *s.* seeing, perceiving, beholding;
දසුම්, *Dasum*, } attachment; accordance; stumbling; දසුන් *dasun* is also the plural of දෑසි *dési*, servant.

දහ, *Daha*, *s.* lake or pond in which the lotus grows; bud, young sprout; day, [Colloq. දවස *dawasa*].

දහ අට, *Daha-aṭa*, *s.* eighteen.

දහඩිය, *Dahaḍiya*, *s.* sweat, perspiration.

දහතුණ, *Dahatuṇa*, *s.* thirteen.

දහන්, *Dahan*, *s.* fire; meditation; species of paddy.

දහන්සැරි, *Dahanseri*, *s.* (දහන *dahana* fire, සැරි charioteer) wind.

දහන, *Dahana*, *s.* fire; name of Agni, god of fire; burning, combustion; marking nut plant; leadwort, *plumbago zeylanica:* [Colloq. එල නෙටුල් *ela-neṭul*].

දහනග, *Dahanaga*, } *s.* downy substance on the
දහනඟ, *Dahananga*, } grains of paddy beneath the husk.

දහනය, *Dahanaya*, see දහන *dahana.*

දහනල, *Dahanala*, *s.* species of paddy: see වී *ví.*

දහනවය, *Dahanawaya*, *s.* nineteen.

දහම්, *Daham*, *s.* agitation or erection of the hair of the body, considered as a mark of exquisite pleasure or pain; Elu form of ධර්ම *dharma*, which see.

දහම් දෙසනවා, *Daham-desanawá, v.* (දහම් from ධර්ම *dharma* baṇa, දෙසනවා to speak, or read in public) to read baṇa in public, to repeat baṇa extempore, as the priests do in the baṇa maḍuwa: pret. දහම් දෙසුවා *daham-desuwá*.

දහම්දෙසීම, *Daham-desíma*, verbal noun of the above.

දහම්රජ, *Daham-raja, s.* (දහම් from ධර්ම *dharma* and රජ king) name of Buddha, king of righteousness; prince of virtue; royal dispenser of the baṇa.

දහම්සක්, *Dahamsak*, Elu form of ධර්මචක්‍ර *dharma chakra*, which see.

දහම්සරණ, *Dahamsaraṇa, s.* (දහම් from ධර්ම *dharma* baṇa, සරණ refuge, help) baṇa *i. e.* sermons of Buddha, which are esteemed as an inestimable refuge bestowed upon mankind; there are three of these sacred or religious refuges that have been given to the world, viz. බුත්සරණ *butsaraṇa*, දහම්සරණ *daham-saraṇa*, and සඟසරණ *saṇga-saraṇa*, Buddha, his baṇa, and his priests.

දහම්සැරි, *Dahamsẹri*, corrupt form of දම්සැරි *damsẹri*.

දහම, *Dahama, s.* righteousness, justice, equity, holiness; virtue; it is from ධර්ම *dharma*, which see.

දහය, *Dahaya, s.* ten.

දහයියා, *Dahayiyá, s.* chaff.

දහර, *Dahara, s.* mouse; rat; young animal, child, infant; pimburá or rock snake; youth, young man; shower of rain, stream of water: *a.* young, new, fresh, novel.

දහල්, *Dahal, s.* fire fly, [Colloquial: කනමැඳිරියා *kanamẹdiriyá*].

දහවත්තරු, *Dahawattaru, s.* sometimes written දවහත්තරු *dawahattaru*, which see.

දහවල්, *Dahawal, s.* day, day-time.

දහවල්ල, *Dahawalla, s.* end of a garment,

දහස්, *Dahas, a.* thousand; *plur.* of දහස *dahasa.*

දහසය, *Dahasaya, s.* sixteen.

දහසැස්, *Dahasẹs, s.* (දහස *dahasa* and ඇස් eyes) name of Indrá or Ṣakra, alluding to the fable of his having a thousand eyes; in this character he is a personification of the firmament or region of the stars; according to another authority the name refers to his having been covered over with marks resembling the female organ, in consequence of a curse from a noted Ṛishi called Gautama; the saint afterwards relented, and removed the curse, and the marks were changed to eyes.

දහහත, *Dahahata, s.* seventeen.

දහහතර, *Dahahatara, s.* fourteen.

දළ්හ, *Daḷha, a.* hard, solid, firm.

දළ්හිකර්මය, *Daḷhikarmaya, s.* confirmation.

දළ, *Daḷa, s.* snout of hog, tusk of any animal, fang of a serpent, sting; bulk, magnitude, matted hair, as worn by ascetics, that is, the hair clotted together and brought over the forehead: *a.* thick, coarse.

දළකඩ, *Daḷakaḍa, s.* (දළ coarse, කඩ cloth) cloth, coarse cloth; piece of ivory.

දළදත, *Daḷadata, s.* (දළ great, දත tooth) jaw teeth or grinders.

දළදා, *Daḷadá, s.* (දළ tooth, දා relic) tooth of Buddha, supposed to be preserved in the chief temple at Kandy, a festival is celebrated in its honour on the day of full moon in May.

දළපුඩු, *Daḷapuḍu, s.* (දළ ivory, පුඩු socket, or place of uniting) ornamented head of the white or royal umbrella.

දළපුඩුසේසත, *Daḷapuḍusésata, s.* (දළපුඩු and සේ white, සත umbrella) white umbrella, used by kings and men of high rank.

දළමඩල, *Daḷamaḍala, s.* hair matted and tied in the form of a circle on the crown of the head, as worn by Ṣiva, and by ascetics.

දළමුතු, *Daḷamutu, s.* (දළ snout (of hog), මුතු pearl) fabulous pearl said to grow in the snout of the hog.

දළවෙනවා, *Daḷawenawá, v.* to increase, to enlarge.

දළසඳ, *Daḷasaṇda, s.* name of Íṣwara or Ṣiva.

දා, *Dá, s.* day, (used in composition, as අනිත්දා *anitdá*, the day after tomorrow, කවදා *kawadá*, what day); relic.

දාක්ෂායණ, *Dákshàyaṇa, s.* relation of දක්ෂ *daksha*, which see; gold; gold ornament.

දාක්ෂායිණී, *Dákshàyiṇí, s.* the twenty seven lunar mansions, considered mythologically as the daughters of Daksha and the wives of the moon; lunar asterism in general: see දක්ෂ *daksha*.

දාක්ෂායිණී පති, *Dákshàyiṇí-pati, s.* (දාක්ෂායිණී and පති chief) moon, [Colloq. හඳ *haṇda*].

දාක්ෂිණ්‍ය, *Dákshiṇya, s.* concord, harmony, agreement: *a.* meriting a reward or gift.

දාක, *Dáka, s.* donor, giver.

දාගබ, *Dágaba,*
දාගොබ, *Dágoba,*
දාගැබ, *Dágeba,* } *s.* (දා from ධාතු *dhátu* relic ගබ from ගර්භ *garbha,* womb) a large solid building in the form of a cone, raised close to the Buddhist temples and an object of the highest veneration; the erection of these dágabas had its origin in the fable that after the death of Buddha his body, according to the custom of the country where he lived, was burnt; after the conflagration had ceased certain portions of his bones had survived the operation of the fire; these were carefully collected and deposited with great pomp and solemnity by the priests in a building of this kind, raised for the purpose; afterwards, these sacred relics were divided and sent over the world for the purpose of religious veneration; every temple has its dágaba, and every dágaba has a portion of these bones; so that at this rate of calculation Buddha must have had tolerably large bones!

දාඨා, *Dáṭhá, s.* (Páli) canine tooth, tusk, fang.

දාඩිම *Dáḍima, s.* pomegranate tree, [Colloq. දෙළුම් *deḷum*].

දාඩිමපුෂ්පක, *Dáḍima-pushpaka, s.* species of the erythrina or coral tree, [Colloq. එරබදු *erabadu*].

දාඩිය, *Dáḍiya, s.* sweat, perspiration.

දාඩිවෘක්ෂ, *Dáḍi-vṛiksha, s.* tree, [Colloq. කොළොම් *koḷom*].

දාඪා, *Dáḍhá, s.* large tooth, tusk.

දාඪිකා, *Dáḍhiká, s.* beard, [Colloq. රැවුළ *rewuḷa*].

දාත්‍යූහ, *Dátyúha, s.* bird with a black neck, *gallinule,* [Coll: දාතුඩුවා *dátuḍuwá*]; sort of cuckoo: see කෑඳැත්තා *kẹndettá.*

දාත්‍ර, *Dátra, s.* sort of sickle.

දාත, *Dáta, a.* divided, separated, severed, rent.

දාතකී, *Dátakí, s.* tree, corruptly for ධාතකී *dhátakí,* which see.

දාතු, *Dátu,* corruptly for ධාතු *dhátu.*

දාතුඩුවා, *Dátuḍuwá, s.* gallinule, pelican-ibis, *tantalus leucocephalus (Plataleidæ,* order *Herodiones):* also called දටුඩුවා *daṭuḍuwá.*

දාදු, *Dádu. s.* dice.

දාදුදමනවා, *Dádu-damanawá, v.* to cast lots, to throw the dice.

දාදොස, *Dádosa, s.* disease of any of the seven constituent parts of the body: see සප්තධාතු *sapta-dhátu.*

දාන්ත, *Dánṭa, a.* tamed, subdued; daunted, bearing patiently, calm, tranquil.

දාන්ති, *Dánti, s.* subjugation, humiliation; patient endurance of austerities or privations; calmness of mind, tranquillity.

දාන, *Dána, s.* gift; giving, donation; present, special gift; fluid which flows from the temples of an elephant in the rutting season; nourishing, cherishing; purification; cutting, dividing; beating; striking.

දානපති, *Dánapati, s.* (දාන giving. පති chief) liberal and munificent man.

දාන පරිත්‍යාගය, *Dána-parityágaya, s.* (දාන gift, පරිත්‍යාග *parityága* freely giving) the act of presenting a religious offering without any reserve of feeling, offering freely and with all the heart.

දානපාරමිතාව, *Dánapáramitáwa,* see පාරමිතාව *páramitáwa* and දානසේතුව *dánasétuwa.*

දානප්‍රවාහය, *Dánaprawáhaya, s.* (දාන and ප්‍රවාහ *prawáha* flood) overflow of religious offerings; such as is brought to the temple on the great festival days.

දානය, *Dánaya,* see දාන *dána.*

දානව, *Dánawa, s.* demon, titan; giant, Asura.

දානවගුරු, *Dánawaguru, s.* (දානව asura, ගුරු teacher) name of Ṣukra or Sikurá, regent of the planet Venus, and preceptor of the demons or Asuras.

දානවාරි, *Dánawári, s.* (දානව *dánawa* asura, අරි *ari* foe) a god, a deity.

දානශෞණ්ඩ, *Dánaṣaunḍa, a.* liberal, generous, munificent, [Colloq. ත්‍යාගිවන්ත *tyágiwanta*].

දානශීල, *Dánasíla, a.* liberal, munificent, but especially much addicted to make religious offerings.

දානසේතුව, *Dána-sétuwa, s.* (දාන offerings, සේතු *sétu* bridge) metaphorically the road to Nirwáṇa; religious offerings and alms-giving constitute one of the essential principles of Buddhism; no duties contribute more to the final emancipation of the soul; it is fabled of Buddha that while a candidate for the Buddhaship, in the character of Bodhisat, he gave more flesh from his own body to feed the poor than the bulk of this earth, and blood more than there is water in the sea.

දාන හාල්, *Dána-hál, s.* sort of rice.

දානානිසංස, *Dánánisaṇsa, s.* (දාන *dána* and ආනිසංස *ánisaṇsa* reward) that merit which is the reward of religious offerings and charity.

දානාර්හ, *Dánárha, s.* (දාන *dána* and අර්හ *arha* who is worthy) one worthy of receiving religious offerings; priest of Buddha or religious preceptor.

දනු, *Dánu*, *s.* donor, victor.

දනෝපකරණ, *Dánópakaraṇa*, *s.* any thing used in the preparation of religious offerings, as rice, ghee etc.

දම්කෙළිනවා, *Dám-keḷinawá*, *v.* to play at chess.

දම්ලෑල්ල, *Dám-lęlla*, *s.* chess-board.

දම, *Dáma*, *s.* rope, string, cord, thread; ray, sunbeam.

දමය, *Dámaya*, *s.* string, rope, cord, chain or necklace.

දමෝදර, *Dámódara*, *s.* (දම *dáma* and උදර *udara* belly) name of Kṛishṇa, alluding to the fable of his foster-mother, Yasódará, having in vain passed the folds of a rope round his belly, while a child, to keep him in confinement.

දය, *Dáya*, *s.* gift, donation; any special gift, as a nuptial present; portion, inheritance, dowry; loss, destruction; breaking, dividing; place, site; heat, warmth, burning.

දයක, *Dáyaka*, *s.* donor: *a.* liberal, giving, munificient, generous.

දයකයා, *Dáyakayá*, *s.* giver, donor; sharer; one who is liberal in contributing to the support of the priests.

දයාද, *Dáyáda*, *s.* son; kinsman, near or remote; wedding gift.

දයිත, *Dáyita*, *s.* the person to whom any thing is awarded: *a.* condemned, sentenced; awarded, adjudged.

දර්වාඝාට, *Dárwághâṭa*, *s.* woodpecker, bird of a red colour having a long beak by which he perforates and destroys plants and trees; it is usually called කෑරලා *kęralá;* its cry is considered very ominous by the natives.

දර්වි, *Dárvi*, *s.* bulbous plant, *curcuma zanthorrhiza*, [Colloq. වෙනිවැල් *weniwęl*].

දර්විකාථ, *Dárvikwátha*, *s.* decoction of the plant, *curcuma zanthorrhiza*, taken as a purgative; decoction of *coscinium fenestratum*, [Colloquial: වෙනිවැල් කසාය *weniwęl kasáya*].

දර්විකා, *Dárviká*, *s.* sort of collyrium prepared from an infusion of the plant, *curcuma zanthorrhiza;* Indian sarsaparilla, *hemidesmus indicus*, Colloq. ඉරමුසු *iramusu*].

දර්වී, *Dárví*, *s.* plant, *curcuma zanthorrhiza*, see දර්වි *dárvi ;* sort of pine; turmeric; collyrium extracted from an infusion of the *curcuma zanthorrhiza.*

දර, *Dára*, *s.* wife, [Colloq. භාර්‍යාව *bháryáwa*]; edge of any cutting instrument; edge or border.

දරක, *Dáraka*, *s.* son; child, infant or young child; charioteer of Vishṇu.

දරකර්ම, *Dára-karma*, *s.* (දර wife, කර්ම business) marriage.

දරකරවලා, *Dára-karawalá*, *s.* kind of snake, variety of *bungarus Ceylonicus.*

දරකෑස්බෑවා, *Dára-kęsbęwá*, *s.* thin skinned turtle, *dermatochelys coriacea* (order *Chelonia*); also see තෙල් කෑස්බෑවා *tel-kęsbęwá.*

දරගලනවා, *Dára-galanawá*, *v.* to stream, to flow in a stream; to fall voluntarily into water with the arms extended.

දරණය, *Dáraṇaya*, *s.* tearing, rending, splitting; clearing nut plant, *strychnos potatorum*, [Colloq. ඉඟිනි *iṅgini*]; retention of any thing learnt: learning, education, more correctly ධාරණය *dháraṇaya.*

දරද, *Dárada*, *s.* quicksilver, vermillion, [Colloq. සාදිලිංගන් *sádiliṅgan*]; ocean; poison so called, brought from a country called Dárad; poison of serpents.

දරදඹල, *Dára-daṃbala*, *s.* leguminous plant, *dolichos tetragonolobus.*

දරපුරුක්, *Dára-puruk*, *s.* shrub, *ruellia zeylanica.*

දරපොලඟා, *Dára-polaṅgá*, *s.* kind of viper.

දරය, *Dáraya*, *s.* rim, border, edge.

දරවිල, *Dáravila*, *s.* hedge hyssop, *gratiola oppositifolia.*

දරවැටකොළු, *Dára-weṭakoḷu*, *s.* creeping plant, young fruit eaten as vegetable and in curries, *luffa acutangula (Cucurbitaceæ).*

දරහාල්පන්, *Dára-hálpan*, *s.* club rush, *scirpus quadratus.*

දරා, *Dárá*, *s.* wife; water, liquid; rain, soft sprinkling or drizzling rain.

දරාවක්කරණවා, *Dárá-wakkaraṇawá*, *v.* to pour, as water or any liquid; to rain, to sprinkle.

දරාවැටෙනවා, *Dárá-wętenawá*, *v.* to fall as rain, or water from a height; to sprinkle; to ooze, to wet by rain.

දරිකාව, *Dárikáwa*, *s.* daughter, [Colloq දුව *duwa*]; prostitute, strumpet, [Colloq. වෙසඟන *wesaṅgana*].

දරිත, *Dárita*, *a.* torn, divided, separated; rent, split, cloven.

දරිද්‍රකම, *Dáridrakama*, *s.* poverty, indigence.

දාරු, *Dáru*, *s.* wood; fire-wood, fuel, [Colloq. දර *dara*]; timber; large resinous pine, *pinus déwa-dáru;* brass; giver, donor, one inclined to make gifts, liberal and munificent man.

දාරුණ, *Dáruṇa*, *s.* horror, terror, dread; horribleness; plant, leadwort, *plumbago zeylanica*, [Coll: එළ නෙටුල් *ela-neṭul*]: *a.* horrible.

දාරුනිශා, *Dáruniṣá*, *s.* (දාරු wood, නිශා turmeric) plant, *curcuma zanthorrhiza.*

දාරුනීර, *Dárunira*, *s.* banyan tree, *ficus bengalensis*, [Colloq. මහනුග *maha-nuga*].

දාරුපලා, *Dárupalá*, *s.* kind of potherb.

දාරුමය, *Dárumaya*, *a.* made of wood.

දාරුහරිද්‍රා, *Dáruharidrá*, *s.* (දාරු wood, හරිද්‍රා turmeric) bulbous plant, *curcuma zanthorrhiza.*

දාරුහස්ත, *Dáruhasta*, *s.* (දාරු timber, හස්ත hand) ladle, wooden ladle.

දාරේ, *Dáré*, *s.* edge, border, rim.

දාව, *Dáwa*, *s.* fire, fire in general; heat; forest on fire; begotten by: *v. past part.* of දාවෙනවා *dáwenawá.*

දාවන, *Dáwana*, *s.* tree, [Colloq. කිහිරි *kihiri*].

දාවනී, *Dáwaní*, *s.* plant, *alyssicarpus bupleurifolius*, [Colloq. අස්වැන්න *aswẹnna*].

දාවල්, *Dáwal*, *s.* day time, period from the rising to the setting of the sun.

දාවල්ල, *Dáwalla*, *s.* border of a garment, selvage mark in a piece of cloth.

දාවලු, *Dáwalu*, *plur.* of the foregoing. *s.* clothes.

දාවෙනවා, *Dáwenawá*, *v.* to be engendered, to be begotten.

දාස්, *Dás*, *s.* thousand.

දාස්පෙති, *Dás-peti*, } දාස්මල, *Dás-mala*, } *s.* (දාස් and පෙති corolla of a flower) marigold; general name for flowers of the class Compositæ, given in consequence of the great number of florets with which they abound.

දාස්‍ය, *Dásya*, *s.* (දාස *dása* slave) slavery, servitude, dependence, bond service.

දාස, *Dása*, *s.* slave, servant.

දාසකම්, *Dása-karma*, *s.* (දාස slave, කම් work) slavery; menial service; any low or servile work.

දාසත්ව, *Dásatwa*. *s.* slavery, servitude.

දාසභූත, *Dása-bhúta*, *s.* (දාස and භූත being) slavery, bond-service, any low or menial state; one who is a servant: *a.* enslaved.

දාසයා, *Dásayá*, *s.* slave, bond servant.

දාසිකා, *Dásiká*, *s.* female servant, female slave.

දාසිවෘක්ෂ, *Dási-vṛiksha*, *s.* fragrant plant, commonly called කොල්ලන්කොළ *kollankola;* it is said to be one of the ත්‍රිසුගන්ධ *trisugandha*, a sort of mint.

දාසි, *Dásí*, *s.* female servant or slave, pl. දාසියෝ *dásiyó.*

දාසේය, *Dáséya*, } දාසේර, *Dáséra*, } *s.* servant, slave.

දාහ, *Dáha*, *s.* thousand; heat, warmth, animal heat; perspiration.

දාහගතිය, *Dáha-gatiya*, *s.* (දාහ heat, warmth, ගතිය state, being) animal heat; state of perspiration.

දාහනාශිනී, *Dáhanáṣini*, see හෙලදම් *hela-dam.*

දාහය, *Dáhaya*, see දාහ *dáha.*

දාහශෝඵඝ්නී, *Dáha-ṣóphaghní*, *s.* silk cotton tree.

දාහසර, *Dáhasara*, *s.* (දාහ burning, සර to go) place where dead bodies are burnt.

දාහහර, *Dáhahara*, *s.* white sandal wood, *santalum album*, [Colloq. සුදුහඳුන් *sudu-haṇdun*].

දාහහරණ, *Dáha-haraṇa*, *s.* (දාහ heat, හරණ removing) the root of a fragrant grass, cuscus grass, *andropogon muricatus*, [Colloq. සැවැන්දරා *sẹwẹndará*]; this root is woven into screens, and kept for the purpose of excluding or tempering the hot winds.

දික්, *Dik*, *s.* length; extent; side; any one of the four quarters or of the intermediate points and the Zenith and Nadir.

දික්කරණවා, *Dikkaraṇawá*, *v.* to lengthen, to prolong, to stretch out.

දික්දාහය, *Dikdáhaya*, *s.* (දික් quarter, දාහ *dáha* burning, blazing) meteor, fiery meteor passing from one quarter to another and considered as one of the five evil omens of the firmament.

දික්දෙ, *Dikdẹ*, *s.* (දික් long, දෙ genus) serpent tribe in general, [Colloq. සර්පයා *sarpayá*].

දික්පති, *Dikpati*, } දික්පාල, *Dikpála*, } *s.* regent of a quarter of the universe, as Indra of the east, Agni of the south east.

දිග්, *Dig*, *a.* long; cardinal point, quarter.

දිග්ගජ, *Diggaja*, *s.* (දිග් quarter, ගජ elephant) one of the elephants belonging to the eight quarters of the compass and supposed to support the globe.

දිග්ධ, *Digdha*, *s.* poisoned arrow; oil, unguents, any unctuous substance; fire; tale, true or false: *a.* daubed, anointed, smeared.

දිග්විජය, *Digvijaya*, *s.* (දිග් quarter or space, විජය victory) subjugation of an extensive country.

දිග, *Diga*, *s.* length, extent; side, direction, quarter, cardinal point; space.

දිගඅරිණවා, *Diga-ariṇawá*, see දිගාරිණවා *digáriṇawá*.

දිගටි, *Digaṭi*, *a.* oblong, longer than broad.

දිගත, *Digata*, *s.* (දිග long, quarter, අත *ata* hand, side) long handed person; cardinal point.

දිගන්තර, *Digantara*, *s.* (දික් *dik* cardinal point, අන්තර *antara* interval) any one of the intermediate points of the compass; space: *a.* tedious, extremely long, as දිගන්තර කථාව *digantara katháwa* a tedious story.

දිගබර, *Digabara*, } Elu form of දිගම්බර *digam-*
දිගඹර, *Digambara*, } *bara*: see the following word.

දිගම්බර, *Digambara*, *s.* (දිග් *dig* space, අම්බර *ambara* vestment) one whose only garment is the firmament; a sort of religious mendicant, who goes about naked; a Buddhist priest of the lowest or noviciate order, and usually called Sámaṇéra; goddess; sky, atmosphere, firmament.

දිගා, *Digá*, *s.* (දිගු *digu* long, ආ *á* pers. aff.) tall long bodied man; long bodied animal in general; longevity (from දිගු *digu* long, ආ *á* duration of life;) the saint මාකණ්ඩෙය *Márkaṇḍéya*.

දිගාන්තර, *Digántara*, see දිගන්තර *digantara*.

දිගාරිණවා, *Digáriṇawá*, *v.* to unfold: pret. දිගැරියා *digériyá*.

දිගාවෙනවා, *Digáwenawá*, *v.* to lie down.

දිගු, *Digu*, *s.* direction, space, quarter: *a.* long, stretched, extended.

දිගුකරණවා, *Digukaranawá*, *v.* to stretch out, to elongate.

දිගුනෙත්, *Digunet*, *s.* (දිගු and නෙත් eye) woman, female; epithet applied to females as an expression of beauty, [Colloq. ස්ත්‍රී *strí*].

දිගුවිල්, *Diguvil*, *s.* oblong pond, artificial reservoir for the purpose of retaining water for irrigating the rice fields during the dry season, [Colloq. අගල *agala*, විල *vila*].

දිගැසිය, *Digęsiya*, *s.* (දිග long, ඇස *ęsa* eye, ඉය *iya* fem. aff.) woman, [Colloq. ස්ත්‍රී *strí*].

දිජ, *Dija*, *s.* man of the Bráhmin caste, [Colloq. බමුණා *bamuṇá*]. (Páli.)

දිට්ඨාන්ත, *Diṭṭhánta*, Páli form of දෘෂ්ටාන්ත *drishṭánta*, which see.

දිට්ඨි, *Diṭṭhi*, Páli form of දෘෂ්ටි *drishṭi*, which see.

දිට, *Diṭa*, Elu form of දෘෂ්ටි *drishṭi*, which see.

දිටු, *Diṭu*, *s.* (derived as the foregoing word) appearance; sight, vision; mental illumination; it chiefly refers to religious illumination; part. of දකිනවා for දුටු *duṭu*, seen.

දිටුවා, *Diṭuwá*, see දුටුවා *duṭuwá*.

දිත්, *Dit*, *s.* Asura, titan; ghost, goblin.

දිත්‍ය, *Ditya*, *s.* titan, Asura, demon, giant of the Daityas or Asurs.

දිත්රුපු, *Dit-rupu*, *s.* a god.

දිත, *Dita*, see දිත් *dit*.

දිතරුපු, *Dita-rupu*, *s.* (දිත and රුපු enemy) name of Vishṇu.

දිති, *Diti*, *s.* wife of Káṣyapa.

දිතිජ, *Ditija*, *s.* one born of දිති *diti;* Asura, titan, giant.

දිතිය, *Ditiya*, *s.* one of the wives of Káṣyapa the noted Ṛishi; she was mother of the Daityas or Asurs; another form of දිති *diti*.

දිදලේ, *Didálé*, *s.* thimble, pl. දිදල *didála*.

දින්ඩිභ, *Dindibha*, see කිරලා *kiralá*.

දින, *Dina*, *s.* day; producing, production, origin; name of Buddha; acquisition; conquest, winning.

දිනකර, *Dinakara*, *s.* (දින day, කර who makes) sun, [Colloq. සූර්යයා *súryayá*].

දිනනවා, *Dinanawá*, *v.* to conquer, to overcome, to defeat; to prevail, to gain, to win: pret. දිනුවා *dinuwá*.

දිනපතා, *Dinapatá*, *ad.* daily.

දිනපති, *Dinapati*, } *s.* (දින and පති lord, මණි
දිනමණි, *Dinamaṇi*, } jewel, gem) sun.

දිනය, *Dinaya*, see දින *dina*.

දිනාගන්නවා, *Dinágannawá*, *v.* to conquer, to prevail, to win.

දිනිතිය, *Dinitiya*, *s.* mother of Bódhisatwa when he was born as Kusaraja, who afterwards became Buddha; mother, [Colloq. මවු *mawu*].

දිනිඳු, *Dinidu*, *s.* (දින *dina* day, ඉඳු *iṇdu* chief) sun; name of Buddha; name of Balabhadra: see බලභද්‍ර *Balabhadra*.

දිනිම්, *Dinim*, *s.* birth, production, bringing forth; I gave: pret. of දෙනවා *denawá*.

දිනිසුරු, *Dinisuru*, *s.* (දින *dina* and ඉසුරු *isuru* lord) sun, [Colloq. සූර්යයා *súryayá*]; name of Balabhadra, the younger brother of Vishṇu; also a name of Wesamuṇiraja or Kuvéra, the Indian Plutus.

දිනීම, *Diníma*, }
දිනුම, *Dinuma*, } *s.* wininng, gain, conquest.

දිනෙන්දින, *Dinen-dina*, *s.* day by day.

දිප, *Dipa*, *s.* elephant, [Colloq. ඇතා *ętá*].

දිපද, *Dipada*, *s.* man: *a.* biped.

දිපදෝත්තම, *Dipadóttama*, *s.* (දිපද *dipada* and උත්තම *uttama* chief) epithet of Buddha, alluding to his being chief of the bipeds or men.

දිබ්බ, *Dibba*, *s.* a god, a deity. (Páli.)

දිඹුල්, *Dimbul*, *s.* corrupt form of දිවුල් *diwul*, elephant or wood apple; also a species of the *ficus*, *f. glomerata*, [Colloquial: අට්ටික්කා *aṭṭikká*].

දිමියා, *Dimiyá*, *s.* red ant.

දිමුතු, *Dimutu*, *a.* enlightened, illuminated, splendid, shining.

දිය, *Diya*, *s.* water; world; conquest, victory; bowstring; pepper plant, *piper betel*, [Colloq. බුලත් වැල් *bulat-węl*]: also, give me, used in speaking to servants of low grade, imperative singular of දෙනවා *denawá*.

දිය අගල, *Diya-agala*, *s.* wet ditch, moat.

දිය අඹ, *Diya-amba*, *s.* kind of mango tree, *magnifera indica*.

දිය අළුව, *Diya-aḷuwa*, *s.* (දිය water, අළුව pitcher) bucket, baling vessel.

දිය උදරය, *Diya-udaraya*, *s.* (දිය and උදරය belly) dropsy.

දිය ඇඹුල් ඇඹිලිය, *Diya-ęmbul-ęmbiliya*, *s.* creeping plant on the borders of water, *Marsilea quadrifolia (Rhizocarpeæ)*.

දිය කච්චිය, *Diya-kachchiya*, *s.* bathing dress; small piece of cloth worn round the waist by the cinnamon peelers and cultivators of the ground.

දියකපුටුවා, *Diya-kapuṭuwá*, *s.* (දිය water, කපුටුවා crow) kind of cormorant: see දිය කාවා *diya-káwá*.

දියකරණවා, *Diyakaraṇawá*, *v.* to melt, to dissolve in water.

දියකලඳා, *Diya-kalandá*, *s.* kind of river fish.

දිය කාවා, *Diya-káwá*, *s.* bird called the little cormorant, *phalacrocorax pygmæus*; bird called the darter, *plotus melanogaster (Pelecanidæ*, order *Steganopodes)*.

දිය කිරලා, *Diya-kiralá*, *s.* (දිය water, කිරලා lapwing) kind of water bird.

දිය කිරිඳිවැල්, *Diya-kirindi-węl*, *s.* climbing shrub, with greenish yellow flowers, *hippocratera obtusifolia*, *(Celastraceæ)*.

දිය කිරිල්ල, *Diya-kirilla*, *s.* creeping plant, growing in marshy ground, with blue flowers, *hydrolea zeylanica*, *(Hydrophyllaceæ)*.

දිය කූඩැලු, *Diya-kúḍaḷu*, *s.* plant, *hydrocera triflora (Geraniaceæ)*.

දිය කූඩැල්ලා, *Diya-kúḍęllá*, *s.* water leech.

දියකොන්ත, *Diyakonta*, *s.* flag of victory, banner.

දිය කොමඩු, *Diya-komaḍu*, *s.* water gourd, *cucurbita citrulla*.

දිය කොවුල්ලා, *Diya-kowullá*, *s.* water crane.

දිය කෝනම, *Diya-kónama*, *s.* kind of dress worn by men when bathing.

දියඟ, *Diyanga*, *s.* saffron, [Colloq. කහ *kaha*].

දියත්කරණවා, *Diyatkaraṇawá*, *v.* to launch, to move any thing from the land into the water.

දියත්ත, *Diyatta*, *s.* drop, drop of water.

දියත, *Diyata*, Elu form of ජගත් *jagat*.

දිය තණකොල, *Diya-taṇakola*, *s.* Mauritius grass or water grass, *Panicum molle* or *P. barbinode*, *(Gramineæ)*.

දියතර, *Diyatara*, *s.* fields irrigated by means of tanks and channels and not dependent on rain.

දිය තලිය, *Diya-taliya*, *s.* plant, peculiar to Ceylon, *mastixia tetrandra (Cornaceæ)*.

දියතුණ, *Diyatuṇa*, Elu form of ජගත්‍රය *jagatraya*: see තුන්ලෝකය *tun-lókaya*.

දියදද, *Diyadada*, see ජයකොඩිය *jayakoḍiya*.

දියදහරය, *Diyadaharaya*, see ජලධාරාව *jaladhiráwa*.

දියදංගා, *Diyadángá*, *s.* tree, *Dolichandrone Rheedii* or *Spathodea Rheedii* or *S. longiflora*, *(Bignoniaceæ)*.

දියදෙස්, *Diyades*, *s.* fame, renown; publicity.

දියන්, *Diyan*, *imp.* second pers. sing. of දෙනවා *denawá*, give me.

දියනයා, *Diya-nayá*, *s.* water-cobra.

දියනා, *Diyaná*, *s.* (දිය world, නා lord) name of Buddha; tree, peculiar to Ceylon, *mesua Thwaitesii (Guttiferæ)*.

දියනි, *Diyani*, *s.* daughter.

දියනිල්ල, *Diyanilla*, *s.* plant, with edible stem, *klugia notoniana (Gesneraceæ)*.

දියනෙත්, *Diyanet*, *s.* (දිය world, නෙත් eye) sun, [Colloq. සූර්යයා *súryayá*].

දියපත්තං, *Diyapattaŋ*, *s.* death.

දියපත්‍රිම, *Diyapatríma*, *s.* decease.

දියපණ, *Diyapaṇa*, *s.* (දිය and පණ life) epithet for air, wind considered as the life of the world.

දියපර, *Diyapara*, *s.* timber tree, peculiar to Ceylon, *wormia triquetra (Dilleneaceæ)*.

දියපරඬැල්, *Diyaparaṇḍel*, } *s.* aquatic plant, re-
දියපරණලා, *Diyaparṇalá*, } sembling half grown lettuce with pale yellow flowers, *pistia stratiotes (Araceæ).*

දියපානසි, *Diyapánasi*, *s.* duck weed, *lemna paucicostata* or *l. minor.*

දියපිලිහුඩුවා, *Diya-pilihuḍuwá*, *s.* little Indian kingfisher, *alcedo bengalensis;* also called මල් පිලිහුඩුවා *mal-pilihuḍuwá (Alcedinæ,* order *Picariæ).*

දිය පොළව, *Diya-poḷawa*, *s.* world of water; one of the three bases upon which this universe is supposed to rest; the first or lowest is air, the second water, and the third or highest is earth.

දියබත්, *Diyabat*, *s.* rice mixed with water, and eaten by the poorer classes.

දියබඳ, *Diyabanda*, *s.* (දිය world, බඳ from බන්ධු *bandhu* relation) name of Vishṇu, alluding to his incarnations in this world: see අවතාර *awatára.*

දියබප්, *Diyabap*, *s.* (දිය and බප් father) name of Buddha.

දියබරණ, *Diyabaraṇa*, } *s.* fresh water-snake, *cer-*
දියබරියා, *Diyabariyá*, } *berus rhynchops (Homalopsidæ,* order *Ophidia).*

දියබල්ලා, *Diya-ballá*, *s.* Indian otter, *lutra nair.*

දියබස්නාව, *Diya-basnáwa*, *s.* stream, current.

දියබුබුල, *Diyabubula*, *s.* bubble on the water, spring of water; blister on the skin, pustule, pl. දියබුබුලු *diyabubulu.*

දියබෙත්ම, *Diyabetma*, *s.* division, especially of a water-course, into channels or branches.

දියබෙරලිය, *Diyaberaliya*, *s.* plant, growing in marshy places, with broad leaves and blue flowers: see දියහබරල *diyahabarala.*

දියබේරු, *Diyabéru*, *s.* tree, *agrostistachys* or *sarcoclinium Hookeri (Euphorbiaceæ);* also called මහබේරු *maha-béru.*

දියමන්ති, *Diyamanti*, *s.* diamond.

දියමහා, *Diyamahá*, *s.* kind of snake.

දියමිණි, *Diyamiṇi*, *s.* (දිය world, මිණි gem) sun, [Colloq. සූර්යයා *súryayá*].

දියමිත්ත, *Diyamitta*, *s.* creeping plant, *cissampelos Pareira (Menispermaceæ).*

දියමිත්තා, *Diyamittá*, *s.* kind of fish.

දියමිදෙල්ල, *Diyamidella*, *s.* timber tree, with large leaves and pink flowers, *barringtonia racesmosa (Myrtaceæ).*

දියමෙනේරිය, *Diyamenériya*, *s.* plant, with spathe and blue flowers, *commelina benghalensis (Commelinaceæ).*

දියමෙරලිය, *Diyameraliya*, see දියබෙරලිය *diyaberaliya.*

දියර, *Diyara*, *s.* water.

දියරකුසා, *Diyarakusá*, *s.* fabulous demon said to live in water.

දිය රත්මල්, *Diya-ratmal*, see දිය රතඹලා *diya-ratambalá.*

දියරත්රන්, *Diya-ratran*, *s.* substance resembling gold; pyrites.

දිය රතඹලා, *Diya-ratambalá*, *s.* Asóka tree, with beautiful flowers and foliage, *saraca indica* or *jonesia asoka, (Leguminosæ).*

දියරෙද්ද, *Diyaredda*, *s.* cloth worn when bathing.

දියරේරා, *Diya-rérá*, see දියසේරා *diya-sérá.*

දියල්ලා, *Diyallá*, *imp. pl.* of දියන් *diyan.*

දියලනුව, *Diyalanuwa*, *s.* belt, string or girdle tied round the loins next the skin, to which a cloth is fastened when bathing.

දියලබ්බ, *Diyalabba*, *s.* bottle gourd, *lagenaria vulgaris (Cucurbitaceæ)*, pl. දියලබු *diyalabu.*

දියලිහිණියා, *Diya-lihiṇiyá*, *s.* swallow.

දියවඩන නිලමේ, *Diyawaḍana-nilamé*, *s.* principal lay officer of the palace of the tooth-relic, Kandy.

දියවර, *Diyawara*, *a.* watery.

දියවවුල්ඇටියා, *Diyawawul-eṭiyá*, } *s.* thorny tree,
දියවවුලැටිය, *Diyawawuleṭiya*, } with yellow fragrant flowers, *Cæsalpinia nuga* or *C. paniculata, (Leguminosæ).*

දියවාරය, *Diya-wáraya*, *s.* time for each range of fields to receive water from an ẹla or canal which irrigates fields in rotation.

දියවෙනවා, *Diyawenawá*, *v.* to melt (intransitive).

දියවැඩියාව, *Diyawẹḍiyáwa*, *s.* a disease, eneuresis, incontinency of urine.

දියවැල, *Diyawẹla*, *s.* swell occasioned by the rebounding of the surf on the sea-shore; water course.

දියසලාමුක, *Diyasalámuka*, *s.* whirlpool, vortex; circular openings on the surface of the water in the eddies of a river.

දියසලාව, *Diyasaláwa*, *s.* eddy in a river.

දියසියඹලා, *Diya-siyambalá*, *s.* plant, *æschynomene indica* or *hedysarum neli-tali (Leguminosæ).*

දියසිරාව, *Diyasiráwa*, *s.* humidity, moisture.

දියසෙවෙල්, *Diyasewel*, *s.* stemless, grasslike, diæcious, aquatic plant, growing in stagnant water, *vallisneria octandra.*

දියසේරා, *Diya-sérá*, *s.* bird called little grebe, *podiceps fluviatalis* (order *Pygopodes*).

දියහබරල, *Diya-habarala*, *s.* plant, growing on marshy places, with radical leaves and racemes of blue flowers, *monorchia hastæfolia* or *pontederia hastata (Pontederiaceæ).*

දියහවරිය, *Diya-hawariya*, *s.* (දිය water, හවරිය lock of hair) aquatic plant, *Blyxa Roxburghii* or *vallisneria octandra, (Hydrocharideæ):* see දිය සෙවෙල් *diyasewel.*

දිය හුනුකිරිල්ල, *Diya-hunukirilla*, *s.* plant, *phyllanthus stellatus:* see හුනුකිරිල්ල *hunukirilla.*

දියාළුවා, *Diyáluwá*, *s.* maker of conduits for irrigating rice fields.

දියුණු, *Diyuṇu*, *s.* increasing, prosperity, success: *a.* twofold, twice, [Colloq. දෙගුණ *deguṇa*]; prospered, successful.

දියුණුකරණවා, *Diyuṇukaraṇawá*, *v.* to improve, to advance, to promote.

දියුණුවෙනවා *Diyuṇu-wenawá*, *v.* to improve, to prosper (intransitive).

දියොකස්, *Diyokas*, *s.* (දිය *diya* water, ඔකස් *okas* house) leech.

දිරජ, *Diraja*, *s.* elephant, [Colloq. ඇතා *ętá*].

දිරණවා, *Diraṇawá*, *v.* to rot, to decay: pret. දිරුවා *diruwá.*

දිරි, *Diri*, *a.* leaned, inclined, on one side.

දිරිණි, *Diriṇi*, } *s.* decrepit old woman, [Colloq.
දිරිති, *Diriti*, } මැහැල්ලි *męhelli*].

දිරීම, *Diríma*, *verb.* noun of දිරණවා *diraṇawá.*

දිරුම, *Diruma*, *s.* rottenness.

දිලියෙනවා, *Diliyenawá*, } *v.* to shine, to glitter:
දිලිසෙනවා, *Dilisenawá*, } pret. දිලිසුනා *dilisuná*,
දිලිහෙනවා, *Dilihenawá*, } දිලිහුනා *dilihuná.*

දිලීපය, *Dilípaya*, *s.* name of a king and ancestor of Ráma the conqueror of Rávaṇa.

දිව්, *Diw*, *s.* island; tongue; sky, firmament; Swarga the paradise of the gods: see දිව *diwa:* *p.* run.

දිව්‍ය, *Diwya*, *s.* cloves; sort of sandal; plant, *amyrus agallocha:* *a.* divine, celestial; charming, beautiful, agreeable.

දිව්‍යචක්ෂු, *Diwya-chakshu*, *s.* (දිව්‍ය and චක්ෂු eye) divine perception, knowledge of the past, present and future, attained by devout meditation.

දිව්‍ය පුත්‍රයා, *Diwya-putrayá*, *s.* a god, son of a god.

දිව්‍යමය, *Diwyamaya*, *s.* (දිව්‍ය and මය aff. of origin) divine, of divine origin.

දිව්‍යලෝකය, *Diwya-lókaya*, *s.* heaven, paradise.

දිව්‍යශ්‍රෝත්‍ර, *Diwyaśrótra*, *s.* one of the eight branches of knowledge peculiar to the Rahats, superhuman hearing.

දිව්‍යා, *Diwyá*, *s.* plant, the holy or sacred basil, *ocimum sanctum*, [Colloq. මදුරුතලා *maduru-talá*].

දිව්‍යාංගනාව, *Diwyánganáwa*, } *s.* goddess
දිව්‍යාප්සරාව, *Diwyápsaráwa*, }

දිව, *Diwa*. *s.* tongue; taste; island; sky, firmament, region of the stars; Swarga, the paradise of the gods; a verbal root, which among many other significations, means to play, to sport, to romp, to gambol, to be glad, to rejoice, to be mad or frantic with joy, to be inflated with pride and passion; to wish, to desire, to love; from this root are formed all the words which are used to express that class of beings usually denominated in our language, gods, deities, divinities etc., *i. e.* beings wholly given up to every species of pleasure and the indulgence of every corrupt passion; the Swarga or residence of these beings, which for want of more appropriate terms is called paradise, heaven, etc. signifies a place where every sensual passion is gratified without interruption or restraint: see also දෙවි *devi.*

දිවඉසි, *Diwa-isi*, *s.* (දිව god, ඉසි ṛishi) divine sage.

දිවකුරුමුනි, *Diwakuru-muni*, see දීපංකර *dípankara,*

දිවග, *Diwaga*, *s.* (දිව tongue, අග *aga* end) the tip or point of the tongue.

දිවගුරු, *Diwaguru*, *s.* (දිව god, ගුරු teacher) epithet of Buddha, alluding to his being the religious instructor of the gods; name of Vṛihaspati the regent of the planet Jupiter and the preceptor of the gods.

දිවඟන, *Diwangana*, *s.* (දිව and අඟන *angana* woman) goddess.

දිවත, *Diwata*, *s.* tongue of a lock.

දිවන, *Diwana*, *part.* running.

දිවනවා, *Diwanawá*, see දුවනවා *duwanawá:* [pret. දිව්වා *diwwá.*

දිවනළු, *Diwanaḷu*, *s.* (දිව gods, නළු dancer) one whose business it is to dance for the amusement of the gods, dramatic performer of Swarga, or the paradise of the gods.

දිවනිලමේ, *Diwanilamé*, see දියවඩන නිලමේ *diya-waḍana-nilamé.*

දිවනෙත්, *Diwa-net*, *s.* (දිව divine, නෙත් eye used metaphorically for knowledge) divine knowledge *i. e.* that supernatural knowledge which is supposed to be possessed by the gods and pre-eminently holy men.

දිවබොජුන, *Diwa-bojuna*, *s.* food of the gods, ambrosia.

දිවයින, *Diwayina*, *s.* island, continent, pl. දිවයින් *diwayin*.

දිවයුරු, *Diwayuru*, *s.* the sun, [Colloq. සූර්‍ය්‍යයා *súryayá*].

දිවයොන්, *Diwayon*, *s.* (දිව god, යොන් womb) a god, demi-god, etc.

දිවවස්, *Diwawas*, *s.* (දිව and වස් residence) paradise, [Colloq. දිව්‍යලෝකය *diwyalókaya*].

දිවස්, *Diwas*, *s.* divine eye.

දිවස් උල, *Diwas-ula*, *s.* wood or stake used for the purpose of impaling criminals.

දිවස් කියනවා, *Diwas-kiyanawá*, *v.* to divine.

දිවස්පති, *Diwas-pati*, *s.* (දිවස *diwasa* day, පති lord) sun; name of Indra, Indian Jove.

දිවස, *Diwasa*, *s.* day; divination; divine knowledge.

දිවසභාගය, *Diwasabhágaya*, *s.* (දිවස day, භාගය part) day, day time, from sunrise to sunset.

දිවසර, *Diwasara*, *s.* goddess, female deity, [Colloq. සුරඟනාව *surangandwa*].

දිවසිරි, *Diwasiri*, *s.* (දිව god, සිරි glory) divine happiness.

දිවසැප, *Diwasępa*, *s.* divine happiness.

දිවා, *Diwá*, *s.* day, day time, [Colloq. දවල් *dawal*].

දිවාකර, *Diwákara*, *s.* (දිවා and කර who makes) the sun, [Colloq. සූර්‍ය්‍යයා *súryayá*].

දිවාකීර්ති, *Diwá-kírti*, *s.* owl; barber; man of exceedingly low or base caste: see චණ්ඩාල *chanḍála*.

දිවාටන, *Diwáṭana*, *s.* (දිව day, අටන going) crow, [Colloq. කපුටා *kapuṭá*].

දිවාභාගය, *Diwábhágaya*, *s.* (දිවා day, භාගය part) day, day time.

දිවාභීත, *Diwá-bhíta*, *s.* (දිවා and භීත afraid) owl; nocturnal thief, robber, house-breaker.

දිවාමණි, *Diwá-maṇi*, *s.* (දිවා and මණි jewel) the sun, [Colloq. සූර්‍ය්‍යයා *súryayá*].

දිවාමධ්‍ය, *Diwá-maddhya*, *s.* (දිවා and මධ්‍ය middle) mid-day, noon.

දිවාමාන, *Diwámána*, *s.* equation of time by the adoption of sidereal days, agreeable to the practice of oriental astronomy.

දිවාරාත්‍රි, *Diwá-rátri*, *s.* day and night, [Colloq. රෑ දවල් *rę-dawal*].

දිවි, *Divi*, *s.* life; tiger; leopard; a god, deity; oath, vow; kind of bird, the blue jay; Swarga or the heaven of the gods.

දිවි අඩිය, *Divi-aḍiya*, *s.* twining hairy plant, with white or pink flowers, *ipomœa pes-tigridis (Convolvulaceæ);* also called දිවිපහුරු *divipahuru.*

දිවි කඳුරු, *Divi-kaduru*, *s.* small tree, commonly called forbidden fruit, *tabernæmontana dichotoma (Apocynaceæ).*

දිවිදෙන, *Dividena*, *s.* tigress.

දිවිදොස්, *Dividos*, *s.* evil effects supposed to follow false swearing.

දිවිපසුරු, *Divipasuru*, } දිවිපහුරු, *Divipahuru*, } *s.* creeping plant, *ipomœa pes-tigridis (Convolvulaceæ):* see දිවි අඩිය *divi-aḍiya.*

දිවිමකුණා, *Divi-makuṇá*, *s.* web-spider.

දිවියා, *Diviyá*, *s.* spotted tiger, leopard.

දිවිරීම, *Divirîma*, *s.* vow, oath.

දිවිරැක්ම, *Divi-rękma*, } දිවිවැටුම, *Divi-wętuma*, } *s.* (දිවි life, වැටුම protection) preservation of life; means of supporting life.

දිවිහිම්, *Divihim*, *s.* (දිවි and හිම් boundary) end or extent of life; term of human life; life-time.

දිවිහිමියෙන්, *Divihimiyen*, *ad.* during life.

දිවු, *Diwu*, *s.* lamp, island, tongue.

දිවීම, *Divíma*, *s.* race, running; verbal noun of දුවනවා *duwanawá*.

දිවුණුවෙනවා, *Diwuṇuwenawá*, see දියුණුවෙනවා *diyuṇuwenawá*.

දිවුම, *Diwuma*, *s.* race, career, pl. දිවුම් *diwum*.

දිවුරණවා, *Diwuraṇawá*, *v.* to swear, to attest the truth of any thing by an appeal to some divine or supernatural power: pret. දිවුරුවා *diwuruwá*.

දිවුරුම, *Diwuruma*, *s.* vow, oath.

දිවුල්, *Diwul*, *s.* wood or elephant apple, *feronia elephantum, (Rutaceæ).*

දිවුල් මැලියම්, *Diwul-męliyam*, } දිවුල් ලාටු, *Diwul-láṭu*, } *s.* sort of gum which exudes from the trunk of the *feronia elephantum;* it is used for fixing colours in painting.

දිවෙල, *Diwela*, *s.* pay, hire, wages, land granted by government in lieu of payment for services, pl. දිවෙල් *diwel*.

දිවැස්, *Diwęs*, see දිවනෙත් *diwa-net*.

දිශ්‍ය, *Disya*, *a.* situated, lying in a particular quarter or direction.

දිෂ්ට, *Dishṭa*, *s.* fate, destiny: *a.* shown; seen.

දිස්, *Dis*, see දිස *disa*.

දිස්නය, *Disnaya*, *s.* light, brightness, radiance, gleam, glimpse.

දිස, *Disa*, *s.* the four cardinal and the four intermediate points; region, quarter, space, part.

දිසාව, *Disáwa*, *s.* region, quarter; part, side; one of the cardinal points; direction; Government Agent, chief of a province or tract of land.

දිසාවනේ, *Disáwané*, *s.* province of a Disáwa.

දිසි, *Disi*, *a.* bright, lustrous, illuminated; similar; appearing.

දිහාව, *Diháwa*, *s.* direction: see දිසාව *disáwa*.

දිළිඳා, *Diḷiṇdá*, *s.* poor man, pl. දිළින්දෝ *diḷindó*.

දිළිඳු, *Diḷiṇdu*, *a.* poor, indigent, needy.

දී, *Dí*, an affix and termination, sign of the locative case in grammar, at, in, on, upon; milk coagulated by means of an acid; *p.* having given.

දීක්ෂා, *Díkshá*, *s.* sacrificing, offering, oblations; engaging in a certain course of religious austerities.

දීක්ෂිත, *Díkshita*, *s.* acid juice of the plant, *asclepias acida*, (Sanskrit සෝම ලතා *sóma-latá*) which is drank at the time of sacrificing; sacrificer, the chief or presiding person at a sacrifice; pupil of an ascetic; one by whom the preparatory ceremonies have been observed; initiated.

දීකිරි, *Díkiri*, *s.* incorrectly used for දී *dí*, milk coagulated, curds.

දීග, *Díga*, *s.* marriage; species of marriage among the Kandyans, wherein a woman is given away to live permanently with her husband, opposed to බින්න *binna* where the husband is received into the house of the bride, and abides therein permanently.

දීග ඉන්නවා, *Díga-innawá*, *v.* to live in married life.

දීගණ ඉන්නවා, *Dígana-innawá*, *v.* to allow, to permit, to suffer.

දීගදෙනවා, *Díga-denawá*. *v.* to give in marriage.

දීගයනවා, *Díga-yanawá*, *v.* to go and live with a man as his wife.

දීඝංගුලි, *Díghaṇguli*, Páli form of දීර්ඝාඞ්ගුලි *dírgháṅguli*, which see.

දීධිති, *Dídhiti*, *s.* ray, beam, sun-beam; sunshine.

දීන, *Dína*, *a.* poor, indigent, needy, distressed; afraid, timid.

දීනපුටුව, *Dína-puṭuwa*, *s.* arm chair, [Colloquial: හාන්සි පුටුව *hánsi-puṭuwa*].

දීනබල්ලා, *Dína-ballá*, *s* kind of ferocious dog.

දීනාර, *Dínára*, *s.* gold ornament; seal; weight of gold, thirty two gunjas or about thirty eight grs. troy; coin, dinar.

දීප්ත, *Dípta*, *s.* gold; assafœtida; lime: *a.* flaming, shining.

දීප්තක, *Díptaka*, *s.* gold, [Colloq. රත්රන් *ratran*].

දීප්ත ජිහ්වා, *Dípta-jihwá*, *s.* (දීප්ත fiery, ජිහ්වා tongue) fox, [Colloq. නරියා *nariyá*].

දීප්ත ලෝචන, *Dípta-lóchana*, *s.* (දීප්ත and ලෝචන eye) cat, [Colloq. බළලා *baḷalá*].

දීප්තාක්ෂ, *Díptáksha*, *s.* (දීප්ත *dípta* and අක්ෂ eye) cat; peacock, [Colloq. මොණරා *moṇará*].

දීප්ති, *Dípti*, *s.* splendour; light; lustre; (figuratively) beauty.

දීප්තිමත්, *Díptimat*, *a.* luminous, radiant, splendid; glowing, blazing.

දීප්තිමත්කම, *Díptimatkama*, *s.* lustre, effulgence.

දීප්‍ය, *Dípya*, *s.* plant, cock's comb, *celosia cristata;* aromatic seed, *ligusticum ajwaen*, [Colloq. අසමෝදගං *asamódagaṇ*].

දීප්‍යක, *Dípyaka*, *s.* black cummin seed, [Colloq. කළුදුරු *kaḷuduru*]

දීප, *Dípa*, *s.* lamp; island; light; (metaphorically) mental illumination.

දීපංකර, *Dípaṇkara*, *s.* (දීපං lamp, mental illumination, කර who does) name or epithet of Buddha, in allusion to his enlightening the world by his doctrines.

දීපක, *Dípaka*, *s.* aromatic seed, *ligusticum ajwaen;* small cummin; cock's comb, *celosia cristata;* saffron; lamp; falcon; name of Káma the Indian Cupid; a dog trained to the chase; name of Nirwáṇa; rhetorical beauty, certain elegance of construction; illuminator, enlightener; any thing beautiful: *a.* inflaming, kindling, exciting morally or physically; tonic.

දීපධ්වජ, *Dípaddhwaja*, *s.* (දීප lamp, ධ්වජ symbol) lamp-black, condensed smoke or soot of a lamp.

දීපන්, *Dípan*, *v.* imperative singular of දෙනවා *denawá*, give (to a third person).

දීපන, *Dípana*, *s.* saffron; cock's comb, *celosia cristatá;* species of cassia, *cassia tora* [Colloq. පැනි තෝර *peni-tóra*]; tonic, appetite produced by stimulants: *a.* enlightening, inflaming, exciting.

දීපනී, *Dípaní*, *s.* aromatic seed, *ligusticum ajwaen;* tree, *bignonia indica*.

දීපපුෂ්ප, *Dípa-pushpa*, *s.* champaka tree, *michelia champaca*, which bears a light yellow flower, exceedingly fragrant, and is offered in the temples every morning, [Colloq. සපු *sapu*].

දීපමාලා, *Dípamálá*, *s.* row of lamps.

දීපමූල, *Dípamúla*, *s.* (දීප and මූල root or bottom) bottom or foot of a lamp stand; tree, *celastrus emarginatus*.

දිපය, *Dípaya*, *s.* island.

දිපල්ලා, *Dípallá*, *plur.* of දිපන් *dípan.*

දිප විලෝකනය, *Dípa-vilókanaya*, *s.* (දිප island, විලෝකනය view) one of the five prospective glances taken by Buddha, while he was Bódhisat in the Tusitalókaya respecting his future assumption of the Buddhaship, viz. in what island (or continent) he would suffer himself to be born.

දිපවෘක්ෂ, *Dípa-vṛiksha*, *s.* (දිප and වෘක්ෂ tree) lamp-stand; sort of chandelier or a cluster of lights fixed on a supporter resembling a tree.

දිපි, *Dípi*, *s.* tiger, [Colloq. දිවියා *diviyá*]; car covered with the skins of beasts.

දිපිනි, *Dípiní*, *s.* tigress, [Colloq. දිවිදෙන *divi-dena*].

දිපෙරලිදිය, *Díperalidiya*, *s.* water strained off from curdled milk, whey.

දිබත්, *Dí-bat*, *s.* boiled rice mixed with curdled milk.

දිම, *Díma*, *s.* (from දෙනවා *denawá* to give) gift, donation, pl. දිම් *dím.*

දිමනාව, *Dímanáwa*, *s.* gift, donation, that which is fit to be given.

දි යොදේ, *Dí-yodé*, *s.* serum or cream of curdled milk; coagulum of milk.

දීර්ඝ, *Dírgha*, *a.* long, applied either to space or time.

දීර්ඝකණ්ඨක, *Dírgha-kaṇṭhaka*, *s.* (දීර්ඝ and කණ්ඨ neck, ක added) the crane, [Coll: කොකා *koká*].

දීර්ඝකිල, *Dírgha-kíla*, *s.* tree, *alangium hexapetalum*, [Colloq. රුකඟුන *rukaṉguna*].

දීර්ඝකෝශිකා, *Dírghakóṣiká*, } *s.* cockle.
දීර්ඝකෝෂිකා, *Dírgha-kóshika*, }

දීර්ඝග්‍රීව, *Dírgha-gríwa*, } *s.* (දීර්ඝ long, ග්‍රීවා *gríwá*
දීර්ඝජංඝ, *Dírgha-jaṉgha*, } neck, ජංඝා *jaṉghá* leg) camel, [Colloq. ඔටුවා *oṭuwá*]; crane, [Colloq. කොකා *koká*].

දීර්ඝතරු, *Dírghataru*, *s.* palmyra tree: see තල් *tal.*

දීර්ඝ දර්ශන, *Dírgha-darṣana*, *a.* (derived as the following) seeing; provident; wise; prudent.

දීර්ඝ දර්ශී, *Dírgha-darṣí*, *s.* (දීර්ඝ and දර්ශී seeing) vulture; wise or learned man, pundit.

දීර්ඝද්‍රු, *Dírghadru*, *s.* (දීර්ඝ and ද්‍රු tree) palm tree.

දීර්ඝ නිකාය, *Dírghanikáya*, see නිකාය *nikáya.*

දීර්ඝ පත්‍ර, *Dírgha-patra*, *s.* long-leaved plant, garlic, [Colloq. සුදුලූනු *sululúnu*]; plantain, [Colloq. කෙසෙල් *kesel*]; shrub, *imperata arundinaceæ*, [Colloq. ඉලුක් *iluk*].

දීර්ඝ පත්‍රක, *Dírgha-patraka*, *s.* (දීර්ඝ and පත්‍රක leaf) thorny plant, *capparis aphylla;* tree, growing in marshy places, *bassia longifolia*, [Colloq. මී *mí*]; garlic, *allium sativum;* also, *allium nicum.*

දීර්ඝ පත්‍රිකා, *Dírgha-patriká*, *s.* plant of the genus *hoya*, [Colloquial: රුකඟුන *rukaṉguna*]; herb, [Colloq. සාරණ *sáraṇa*]; garlic, [Colloq. සුදුලූනු *sudu-lúnu*].

දීර්ඝ පර්ණ, *Dírgha-parṇa*, *a.* long-leaved.

දීර්ඝ පාද, *Dírgha-páda*, *s.* (දීර්ඝ and පාද foot) heron.

දීර්ඝ ඵල, *Dírgha-phala*, *s.* tree, *cassia fistula*, [Coll: ඇහැළ *ẹheḷa*].

දීර්ඝ මාරුත, *Dírgha-máruta*, *s.* (දීර්ඝ and මාරුත wind or breath) elephant, [Colloq. අලියා *aliyá*].

දීර්ඝමූල, *Dírgha-múla*, *s.* sort of sensitive plant; kind of *bilwa* or wood-apple: *a.* having a long root.

දීර්ඝ මූලා, *Dírgha-múlá*, *s.* creeping plant, *echites frutescens*; another plant, *hedysarum gangeticum;* small tree, with hard wood, *dichrostachys cinerea*, [Colloq. අන්දර *andara*]; herb, *alyssicarpus bupleurifolius*, [Colloq. අස්වැන්න *as-wẹnan*].

දීර්ඝ මූලී, *Dírgha-múlí*, *s.* (දීර්ඝ and මූල *múla* root) plant, *hedysarum alhagi.*

දීර්ඝ රත, *Dírgha-rata*, } *s.* (දීර්ඝ and රත copulation
දීර්ඝ රද, *Dírgha-rada*, } රද tooth) hog, [Colloq. ඌරා *úrá*].

දීර්ඝ රසනා, *Dírgha-rasana*, *s.* (දීර්ඝ and රසනා *rasaná* tongue) snake, [Colloq. සර්පයා *sarpayá*].

දීර්ඝ රෝමන්, *Dírgha-róman*, *s.* (දීර්ඝ and රෝමන් hair) bear, [Colloq. වලහා *walahá*].

දීර්ඝ වෘක්ෂ, *Dírgha-vṛiksha*, *s.* cocoa-nut tree, *cocus nucifera;* sal or hal tree, *vateria acuminata.*

දීර්ඝ වෘන්ත, *Dírgha-vṛinta*, *s.* plant, *bignonia indica;* another tree, *oroxylum* (or *spathodea*) *indicum*, [Colloq. තොටිල *toṭila*].

දීර්ඝ සූත්‍ර, *Dírgha-sútra*, *a.* lazy, slow, tedious, dilatory.

දීර්ඝාඞ්ගුලි, *Dírgháṅguli*, *s.* (දීර්ඝ *dírgha* and අඞ්ගුලි *aṅguli* finger) epithet of Buddha, expressive of one of his personal beauties, it alludes to the length and beauty of his fingers.

දීර්ඝිකා, *Dírghiká*, *s.* large and oblong pond.

දු, *Du*, Elu form of the prefix දුර් *dur*, which see.

දුඃඛ, *Duḥkha*, *s.* pain, sorrow, trouble: see දුක *duka.*

දුඃඛක්ෂය, *Duḥkhakshaya*, *s.* (දුඃඛ sorrow, ක්ෂය what destroys) name of Nirwáṇa or final emancipation: see the following.

දුඃඛනිරෝධසත්‍ය, *Duḥkhanirôdhasatya*, *s.* (දුඃඛ and නිරෝධ destruction, සත්‍ය truth) one of the four chief truths of Buddhism: see චතුරාර්‍යසත්‍ය *chaturáryasatya;* name of Nirwáṇa alluding to its being the state of the final emancipation of the soul from all existence, before which period sorrow cannot be destroyed, it being inherent in every state of existence: see ක්ලේශ *kléṣa.*

දුඃඛය, *Duḥkhaya*, see දුක *duka.*

දුඃඛසත්‍ය, *Duḥkha-satya*, *s.* (දුඃඛ and සත්‍ය truth) first of the four chief principles or truths in Buddhism, viz. sorrow exists in all things and in all states of existence: see දුඃඛනිරෝධසත්‍ය *duḥkha-nirôdhasatya*, ක්ලේශ *kléṣa*, චතුරාර්‍යසත්‍ය *chaturáryasatya.*

දුඃඛසමුදය, *Duḥkha-samudaya*, *s.* (දුඃඛ sorrow referring here to දුඃඛසත්‍ය *duḥkhasatya*, which see, සමුදය birth or production) one of the four chief truths of Buddhism, that which produces all the sorrow which is inherent in every state of existence, viz. desire or wish: see චතුරාර්‍යසත්‍ය *chaturáryasatya.*

දුඃඛිත, *Duḥkhita*, *a.* sorrowful, mournful, melancholy, suffering pain, miserable; poor, indigent.

දුඃශීල, *Duḥṣíla*, *a.* ill-behaved.

දුඃසාධ්‍ය, *Duḥsádhya*, *a.* incurable or difficult of cure, not easily accomplished.

දුක්, *Duk*, *plur.* of දුක *duka.*

දුක්ඛ, *Dukkha*, *s.* sorrow, distress: see දුක *duka.*

දුක්පත්, *Dukpat*, *a.* distressed, sorrowful; poor, indigent, needy.

දුක්ෂ, *Duksha*, corrupt form of දුක්ඛ *dukkha.*

දුක, *Duka*, *s.* sorrow, pain, unhappiness, misery, distress, affliction; world, pl. දුක් *duk.*

දුකත, *Dukata*, Elu form of දුෂ්කෘත *dushkṛita*, which see.

දුකුළ, *Dukuḷa*, misdeed, from the Páli දුක්කට *dukkaṭa.*

දුකූල, *Dukúla*, *s.* woven silk, very fine cloth or raiment, [Colloq. කපුපිළි *kapu-piḷi*].

දුග්ගති, *Duggati*, *s.* (දු sad, ගති state) hell, [Colloq. නිරය *niraya*].

දුග්ගන්ධ, *Duggandha*, *s.* stench, Páli form of දුර්ගන්ධ *durgandha*, which see.

දුග්ගන්න නිලමේ, *Dugganna-nilamé*, *s.* personal attendant on the king.

දුග්ගන්න පේරුව, *Dugganna-péruwa*, *s.* class from which personal attendants on the king were selected.

දුග්ධ, *Dugdha*, *s.* milk; cow's milk, [Colloq. එලකිරි *ela-kiri*]; plant, *asclepias rosea* or *oxystelma esculentum.*

දුග්ධඵේන, *Dugdhaphéna*, *s.* (දුග්ධ and ඵේන froth) serum of milk, cream of coagulated milk.

දුග්ධිකා, *Dugdhiká*, *s.* plant, *asclepias rosea*, the leaves etc. of which yield a milky sap: see දුග්ධ *dugdha.*

දුග්ධී, *Dugdhí*, *s.* medicinal plant, *euphorbia antiquorum*, [Colloq. දළුක් *daluk*].

දුගතිය, *Dugatiya*, *s.* (දු bad, ගතිය state) hell, place or state in which suffering is endured on account of sins committed in a previous state of existence; vile behaviour, mean disposition.

දුගඳ, *Duganda*, *s.* stench, stink.

දුගියා, *Dugiyá*, *s.* poor, indigent person, beggar, [Colloq. දිළිඳු *diḷindá*]

දුගී, *Dugí*, *a.* poor, indigent, needy.

දුගුල, *Dugúla*, see දුකූල *dukúla.*

දුච්චරිතය, *Duchcharitaya*, *s.* (දු *du* bad, චරිත *charita* manner) bad conduct, sin; evil ways; (Páli form of the Sanskrit දුශ්චරිතය *duṣcharitaya*).

දුජ්ජන, *Dujjana*, Páli form of දුර්ජන *durjana*, which see.

දුජනා, *Dujaná*, *s.* wicked man, pl. දුජනෝ *dujanó.*

දුට, *Duṭa*, *s.* enemy, [Colloq. සතුරා *saturá*].

දුටහට, *Duṭahaṭa*, *a.* carelessly; with eye-service; without due thought or care.

දුටහා, *Duṭahá*, *a.* unimportant; mistaken.

දුටු, *Duṭu*, *p.* seen, perceived; *pret.* of දකිනවා, to see.

දුටුන, *Duṭuna*, *s.* ploughing; harrowing.

දුටුවා, *Duṭuwá*, *v.* saw: pret. of දකිනවා *dakinawá.*

දුටුසතුටු, *Duṭusatuṭu*, *s.* medicinal plant, *centranthera procumbens (Scrophulariaceæ).*

දුත්, *Dut*, *s.* rogue, gamester.

දුතිය, *Dutiya*, *a.* second, [Colloq. දෙවෙනි *deweni*].

දුදන, *Dudana*, Elu form of දුර්ජන *durjana*, which see.

දුදු, *Dudu*, *s.* milk, [Colloq. කිරි *kiri*]; aged person.

දුදුළු, *Duduḷu*, *s.* bad or unfrequented road or path; inaccessible place.

දුන්, *Dun*, *p.* given, bestowed, granted: pret. of දෙනවා *denawá*; see දුන්ගහ *dun-gaha.*

දුන්කවුළුවා, *Dun-kawuḷuwá*, *s.* bird called Indian roller, *Coracias indica (*order *Picariæ).*

දුන්කුඩු, *Dun-kuḍu*, *s.* snuff.

දුන්කොළ, *Dun-kola*, *s.* tobacco, *nicotianum tabacum.*

දුන්ගස, *Dun-gaha*, *s.* large timber tree, resinous, peculiar to Ceylon, *doona zeylanica (Dipterocarpaceæ).*

දුන්තෙල්, *Duntel*, *s.* butter, buffalo ghee.

දුඳුභි, *Dundubhi*, *s.* sort of tom-tom or native drum; it is the one used in war, the kettle drum.

දුඳුමාර, *Dundumára*, *s.* smoke of a house.

දුන්න, *Dunna*, *s.* bow, pl. දුනු *dunu.*

දුන්නා, *Dunná*, *v.* gave: pret. of දෙනවා *denawá.*

දුන්යොන්, *Dunyon*, *s.* (දුන් for දුම් *dum* smoke, යොන් source, origin) fire; line of clouds; dense fog resembling clouds.

දුන, *Duna*, *s.* birth, origin, production.

දුනසුත, *Dunasuta*, *s.* daughter, [Colloq. දුව *duwa*].

දුනු, *Dunu*, *s.* bows; birth, origin; victory, conquest; sharpness.

දුනුකරවලා, *Dunu-karawalá*, *s.* kind of snake.

දුනුකියත, *Dunu-kiyata*, *s.* bow-saw.

දුනුකෙයියා, *Dunukeyiyá*, } *s.* species of the screw
දුනුකේ, *Dunuké*, } pine, *pandanus fœtidus* or *p. humilis, (Pandanaceæ).*

දුනුදිය, *Dunudiya*, *s.* bow-string.

දුනුපිලාව, *Dunupiláwa*, *s.* end of a bow.

දුනුමඩලා, *Dunumadalá*, } *s.* tree of which there
දුනුමඬලා, *Dunumandalá*, } are three species in Ceylon, see Moon's catalogue.

දුනුමුඩාව, *Dunumudáwa*, *s.* point of a bow, the notch upon which the string is fastened.

දුනුමුලාව, *Dunumuláwa*, *s.* quiver.

දුනුවත්, *Dunuwat*, *s.* rag, old or rotten cloth.

දුනුවාය, *Dunuwáya*, *s.* archer, one skilled in the use of the bow, bowyer.

දුනුහිය, *Dunuhiya*, *s.* bow and arrow.

දුප්පත්, *Duppat*, *s.* poor, indigent.

දුප, *Dupa*, *s.* incense: see ධූප *dhúpa.*

දුබල, *Dubala*, Elu form of දුර්බල *durbala*, which see.

දුඹුක්, *Dumbuk*, *a.* nearly ripe, not matured.

දුඹුටු, *Dumbutu*, } *s.* purple, compound of red and
දුඹුරු, *Dumburu.* } black.

දුඹුල්, *Dumbul*, *s.* smoke; soot, grime on the walls of a cook-house; cobweb; aged person, person infirm from age.

දුඹුල්කවනවා, *Dumbulkawanawá.* *v.* to smoke, to smoke any thing by holding it over the fire.

දුඹුල්මැටි, *Dumbul-meti*, *s.* clay on the walls of a cook-house or in the chimney which is so mixed with soot as to resemble it.

දුඹුල්රස, *Dumbul-rasa*, *s.* smoky taste, taste of water that has been boiled in a smoky vessel

දුඹුල්වතුර, *Dumbul-watura*, *s.* water boiled in a smoky vessel.

දුඹුලු, *Dumbulu*, see දුඹුල් *dumbul.*

දුම්, *Dum*, *s.* smoke, steam; Elu form of ද්‍රුම *druma*, a tree.

දුම්කවුළුව, *Dum-kawuluwa*, *s.* (දුම් smoke, කවුළුව outlet) chimney.

දුම්කෙහෙලි, *Dum-keheli*, *s.* (දුම් and කෙහෙලි banner) fire.

දුම්කොල, *Dumkola*, see දුන්කොල *dunkola.*

දුම්ගහනවා, *Dum-gahanawá*, } *v.* to smoke, to as-
දුම්නගිනවා, *Dum-naginawá*, } cend as smoke.

දුම්මල, *Dummala*, *s.* kind of resin; a tree, yielding resin.

දුම්මැල්ල, *Dummella*, } *s.* creeper, *trichosanthes*
දුම්මෑල්ල, *Dummélla*, } *cucumerina (Cucurbitaceæ).*

දුම්යනවා, *Dum-yanawá*, *v.* to smoke, to rise as smoke.

දුම්යොන්, *Dumyon*, *s.* (දුම් smoke, යොන් place of birth) fire, [Colloq. ගින්න *ginna*]; line of clouds.

දුම්වන්, *Dumwan*, *s.* smoke colour; purple.

දුම්සිළු, *Dumsilu*, *s.* flame and smoke emitted from a torch: *a.* inaccessible, impervious, impenetrable; bad, wicked, depraved; unfortunate, unlucky.

දුම, *Duma*, *s.* smoke, steam; a loft or shelf in the kitchen used for keeping chatties etc. pl. දුම් *dum.*

දුමග, *Dumaga*, Elu form of දුර්මාර්ග *durmárga*, which see; also of ද්‍රුමාග්‍ර *drumágra.*

දුමන්, *Duman*, *plur.* of the foregoing, corruptly for දුමං *dumaṅ*, wicked mind, depraved heart.

දුමන, *Dumana*, *s.* bad or depraved heart, vicious mind.

දුමස්, *Dumas*, *s.* (දු bad, මස් flesh) fleshy excrescence on the sole of the foot.

දුමාර, *Dumára*, *s.* smoke, large smoke rising from a fire of rubbish or brushwood, when clearing the ground.

දුමිඳු, *Dumindu*, *s.* (දුම *duma* tree, ඉඳු *indu* chief) bó tree, *ficus religiosa;* tree in Indra's heaven which yields the possessor every thing he desires.

දුර්, *Dur*, *s.* prefix to words implying bad, vicious, vile, contemptible, difficult; ill; painful.

දුර්ග, *Durga*, *s.* (දුර් difficult, ග going or to be gone) difficult road; difficult path leading up a steep or a mountain; road obstructed as by a ditch or intrenchment; fort, stronghold, fastness; name of an Asur slain by the goddess Párvatí, from whom she took the name Durgá: see දුර්ගා *durgá*.

දුර්ගත, *Durgata*, *a.* (දුර් ill, ගත gone, become) poor, indigent, distressed.

දුර්ගති, *Durgati*. *s.* (දුර් and ගති state) poverty, indigence; hell, infernal regions.

දුර්ගන්ධ, *Durgandha*, *s.* (දුර් bad, vile, ගන්ධ smell) stench, any ill smelling substance: *a.* ill-scented.

දුර්ගම, *Durgama*, *s.* (දුර් with pain or difficulty, ගම going) inaccessible, difficult of access or approach; a road impassable or dangerous on account of thieves or the bad state of the road.

දුර්ගය, *Durgaya*, see දුර්ග *durga*.

දුර්ග සඤ්චාර, *Durga-sañchára*, *s.* (දුර්ග defile etc. සඤ්චාර going) progress or passage through an almost inaccessible spot, bridge, etc.; any contrivance for passing a river a defile, etc.; a bye-path leading to a fort built on a hill.

දුර්ගා, *Durgá*, *s.* goddess Durgá, the wife of Şiva and mother of Kártikéya, or, as he is usually called, Kataragama-deviyó, the Indian god of war, and of Gaṇéṣa, the Indian god of wisdom; she is also called Umá and Párvatí etc.; as Durgá she is a goddess of terrific form, and irascible temper; indigo plant; creeping shrub, *clitoria ternata*, [Colloq. නිල්කටරොළු *nil-kaṭaroḷu*].

දුර්ජන, *Durjana*, *a.* vile, bad, wicked, mischievous, malicious.

දුර්ජනයා, *Durjanayá*, *s.* wicked man.

දුර්ජාත, *Durjáta*, *s.* (දුර් and ජාත born) one inauspiciously born or produced; misfortune, calamity; disparity, inconformity; impropriety.

දුර්දර්ශ, *Durdarşa*. *a.* (දුර් and දර්ශ sight) ill-seeing (literally or figuratively); ill-examined, imperfectly investigated; difficult to see.

දුර්දර්ශක, *Durdarşaka*, *s.* person to whom the qualities as given in the foregoing word belong.

දුර්දින, *Durddina*, *s.* dark or cloudy day, day on which the sun is overclouded.

දුර්ධර්ෂ, *Durdharsha*, *a.* difficult of approach, haughty.

දුර්නමා, *Durnamá*, *s.* eel, [Colloq. අඳු *áṇḍá*].

දුර්නාම, *Durnáma*, } *s.* (දුර් and නාම name) *hæmorrhoids*, the piles.
දුර්නාමක, *Durnámaka*,

දුර්බල, *Durbala*, *a.* weak, feeble.

දුර්භග, *Durbbhaga*, *s.* (දුර් bad, භග fortune, luck) unfortunate, unlucky, inauspicious, destitute of any religious merit.

දුර්භාසිත, *Durbhásita*, *s.* abuse, bad word, low language, scurrility: *a.* foul mouthed.

දුර්භික්ෂ, *Durbbhiksha*, *s.* (දුර් bad, භික්ෂා *bhikshá* food) famine, time of great scarcity of provisions.

දුර්මතික, *Durmatika*, *s.* (දුර් and මතික sentient being) fool, ignorant man, simpleton, idiotic fellow, dolt, [Colloq. මෝඩයා *móḍayá*].

දුර්මනා, *Durmaná*, *s.* (දුර් and මනස් *manas* mind) evil minded man.

දුර්මාර්ග, *Durmárga*, *s.* (දුර් difficult, මාර්ග road) bad or difficult road, impassable path.

දුර්මුඛ, *Durmukha*, *s.* (දුර් evil, foul, මුඛ countenance, mouth) displeasure, indignation manifested by the looks, frowns; blackguard; horse; one of the monkey chiefs; one of the nágas or serpent race inhabiting pátála: *a.* foul mouthed, scurrilous.

දුර්ලබ්ධිය, *Durlabdhiya*, *s.* (දුර් evil, false, ලබ්ධිය religious sect) heresy.

දුර්ලභ, *Durlabha*, *s.* (දුර් bad, ලභ receiving) failure, disappointment; difficult to obtain, hard to acquire.

දුර්ලලිත, *Durlalita*, *s.* (දුර් and ලලිත beauty) ugly, deformed.

දුර්වච, *Durwacha*, *s* (දුර් and වච words) evil speech: *a.* disobedient, unruly, unmanageable; speaking ill.

දුර්වර්ණ, *Durwarṇa*, *s.* (දුර් foul, bad, වර්ණ colour) discolouration, bad or imperfect colour, disagreeable colour; (දුර් bad, වර්ණ species) silver; this name it bears in consequence of its being of an inferior species of metal to gold; brass; sort of perfume.

දුර්වල, *Durwala*, properly දුර්බල *durbala*, *a.* (දුර් implying diminution, බල strength) feeble, weak, impotent; thin, emaciated.

දුර්වලකම, *Durwalakama*, *s.* weakness, feebleness, imbecility, pl. දුර්වලකම් *durwalakam*.

දුර්වා, *Durwá*, *s*, kind of grass, [Colloq. හෙල ඊතණ *hela-ítaṇa*].

දුර්වාක්, *Durwák*, *s.* (දුර් bad, වාක් speech) ill speaker; abuse, bad language, scurrility; scurrilous, foul mouthed fellow, blackguard.

දුර්වාච, *Durwácha*, *s.* (දුර් and වාචා *wáchá* word) abuse; bad language, scurrility.

දුර්වාරමේඝ, *Durwára-mégha*, *s.* (දුර් bad, වාර day, මේඝ cloud) rainy day, cloudy dark damp day.

දුර්විඥෙය, *Durvijñéya*, *s.* (දුර් and විඥෙය knowledge) fool, stupid ignorant man; idiotic fellow, [Colloq. මෝඩයා *móḍayá*].

දුර්විධ, *Durvidha*, *a.* (දුර් and විධ manner) poor, indigent; wicked, malevolent; foolish, stupid.

දුර්හෘදය, *Durhṛidaya*, *a.* bad hearted.

දුර, *Dura*, *s.* distance: *a.* far, distant, off, remote.

දුරදිග, *Duradiga*, *s.* due consideration.

දුරධිගම, *Duradhigama*, *a.* difficult to be studied or overcome.

දුරනුබෝධ, *Duranubódha*, *s.* (දුර් *dur* bad or difficult, අනුබෝධ *anubódha* comprehension) hard to be comprehended, abstruse.

දුරයා, *Durayá*, *s.* chief of the Paduwas, a caste whose business is to carry palanquins and provide grass for elephants.

දුරලූ, *Duralú*, *a.* removed from, put away from, put at a distance.

දුරස්තර, *Durastara*, *a.* far, distant.

දුරාරූහ, *Duráruha*, see ඉඹුල් *imbul*.

දුරාලභා, *Durálabhá*, *s.* plant, *acalypha*; [Colloq. කහඹිලියා *kahambiliyá*]; species of prickly night-shade, *solanum jacquini*: *a.* difficult of attainment.

දුරාවා, *Duráwá*, *s.* man of the chando or toddy drawer caste.

දුරාවාරේ, *Duráwáre*, *s.* at distant intervals, now and then; occasionally.

දුරිත, *Durita*, *s.* moral demerit; misfortune, but particularly applied to persons labouring under any deformity or misfortune, in consequence of misdeeds in a former state of existence, and considered as retributive inflictions, [Colloq. අකුසල *akusala*].

දුරින්, *Durin*, *ad.* from far, from a distance; remotely.

දුරු, *Duru*, *s.* cummin seed: *a.* far, distant, off.

දුරුකතර, *Durukatara*, *s.* unfrequented and difficult road.

දුරුකරණවා, *Durukaraṇawá*, *v.* to put at a distance, to remove.

දුරුත්ත, *Durutta*, } *s.* month so called
දුරුතු මාසේ, *Durutu-másé*, } (January–February.

දුරෝදර, *Duródara*, *s.* game, sort of play, dice.

දුල්ලභ, *Dullabha*, Páli form of දුර්ලභ *durlabha*, which see.

දුල, *Dula*, *a.* glittering, shining; effulgent, splendid.

දුලද, *Dulada*, Elu form of දුර්ලබ්ධි *durlabdhi*, which see.

දුලබ, *Dulaba*, Elu form of දුර්ලභ *durlabha*, which see.

දුව, *Duwa*, *s.* daughter, pl. දූවරු *dúwaru*.

දුවඟ, *Duwanga*, see තෙලෙස්ධුතාඟ *teḷesdhutánga*.

දුවණ, *Duwaṇa*, Elu form of දුර්වර්ණ *durwarṇa*, which see.

දුවද, *Duwada*, Elu form of දුර්වාච *durwácha*, which see.

දුවන්, *Duwan*, *s.* hip.

දුවන කරවලා, *Duwana-karawalá*, *s.* kind of snake.

දුවන නයා, *Duwana-nayá*, *s.* kind of cobra.

දුවන පොලඟා, *Duwana-polangá*, *s.* kind of viper.

දුවනවා, *Duwanawá*, *v.* to run, to flee, to speed, to haste away: pret. දිව්වා *diwwá*.

දුවනි, *Duwani*, *s.* daughter, pl. දුවනියෝ *duwaniyó*.

දුවනියන්, *Duwaniyan*, *plur. acc.* of දුවනි *duwani*, daughter, used as a respectful and affectionate mode of expression.

දුශ්චර, *Duṣchara*, *s.* (දුශ් for දුර් *dur* bad, චර going) going with trouble or difficulty; bivalve shell; sin, bad or vicious conduct, vile ways, wicked life.

දුශ්චරිත, *Duṣcharita*, *s.* (දුශ් for දුර් *dur* bad, චරිත mode of life) sin, wickedness; evil conduct.

දුශ්ශබ්ද, *Duṣṣabda*, *s.* (දුර් *dur* bad, ශබ්ද sound) disagreeable or harsh sound; bad voice.

දුශ්ශීල, *Duṣṣíla*, *a.* ill-behaved.

දුෂ්කර, *Dushkara*, *a.* (දුර් *dur* bad, difficult, කර doing, or what does) difficult to be done, hard to be accomplished; ill behaving, rude, doing wrong, wickedly, or badly etc.

දුෂ්ක්‍රීත, *Dushkríta*, *s.* (දුර් *dur* bad, ක්‍රීත bought) bad bargain, any thing dear bought, or purchased at too high a rate.

දුෂ්කෘත, *Dushkṛita*, *s.* (දුර් *dur* bad, vile, කෘත done) wicked action, vile deed; moral demerit, the result of wicked action.

දුෂ්ට, *Dushṭa*, *s.* plant, species of *costus*: *a.* low, vile, wicked, depraved, bad, vicious.

දුෂ්ටාත්ම, *Dushṭátma*, *s.* (දුෂ්ට *dushṭa* evil, malicious, ආත්ම *átma* individual self) evil spirit, demon, devil.

දුෂ්ටාත්මජ, *Dushṭátmaja*, *s.* (දුෂ්ට *dushṭa* bad, ආත්මජ *átmaja* son) undutiful child, wicked disobedient son.

දුෂ්ටි, *Dushṭi*, *s.* wanton woman, harlot, [Colloq. වෙසඟන *wesangana*].

දුෂ්පූරය, *Dushpuraya*, *s.* (දුර් *dur* difficult, පූර *pura* full, complete) any thing difficult to fill; metaphorically, a little or mean contemptible understanding; weak mind, shallow intellect; orientalists use such words when speaking of the intellect of a woman or child.

දුෂ්ප්‍රතිපන්න, *Dushpratipanna*, *s.* (දුර් *dur* evil, ප්‍රතිපන්න observant of religious ordinances) neglect of religious ordinances; one who pretends to religion, but disregards its laws, and ordinances; false pretender to religion; hireling priest.

දුෂ්ප්‍රතිවේධ, *Dushpratiwédha*, *a.* (දුර් *dur* difficult, ප්‍රතිවේධ understanding) difficult to be comprehended, hard to be understood; misunderstood, misapprehended.

දුෂ්ප්‍රදර්ශක, *Dushpradarṣaka*, *s.* (දුර් *dur* evil, ප්‍රදර්ශක who overlooks or investigates judicially) unfaithful overseer; one mistaken in his researches and investigations; perverted judge; mustard, [Coll: අබ *aba*].

දුෂ්ප්‍රධර්ෂිණී, *Dushpradharshaṇi*, *s.* the egg plant, or night shade, *solannm melongena*, [Colloq. වම්බටු *wambaṭu*].

දුෂ්ප්‍රධර්ෂා, *Dushpradharshá*, *s.* plant, *hedysarum alhagi*.

දුස්පර්ශ, *Dussparṣa*, *s.* plant, *hedysarum alhagi*.

දුස්කෘත, *Duskrita*, corrupt form of දුෂ්කෘත *dushkṛita*, which see.

දුස්ස්වප්නය, *Dusswapnaya*, *s.* (දුර් *dur* bad, ස්වප්න dream) horrid or frightful dream, nightmare.

දුස්සංස්ථාන, *Dussaṇsthána*, } *s.* (දුස් evil, සංස්ථාන
දුස්සංස්ථිත, *Dussaṇsthita*, } construction) misformation; deformity, ugliness: *a.* ill constructed; misshapen.

දුස්සීල, *Dussíla*, *a.* (දුස් bad, සීල religious rite or ordinance) irreligious, not performing religious duties, regardless of religious ordinances.

දුස්සීලයා, *Dussílayá*, *s.* vicious, irreligious person.

දුසස්, *Dusas*, *s.* (දු bad, සස් grain) bad harvest, one in which the grain is blasted or mildewed.

දුසිත, *Dusita*, *a.* (දු and සිත mind) evil minded, ill disposed, bad.

දුසිරි, *Dusiri*, } *s.* (දු with සිරි and සිරිත mode,
දුසිරිත, *Dusirita*, } manner) sin, evil; ill conduct, bad ways, wicked practices.

දුහද, *Duhada*, *s.* (දු and හද heart) bad disposition, unfeeling heart, hard heart.

දුහිණී, *Duhiṇi*, Elu form of ද්‍රෝහිණී *dróhiṇí*, which see.

දුහිත, *Duhita*, *s.* woman who hurts or is malicious: *a.* wicked minded, malevolent.

දුහිතෘ, *Duhitṛi*, *s.* daughter, from දුහ *duha*, to milk.

දුහු, *Duhu*, *s.* enemy, [Colloq. සතුරා *saturá*].

දුහුදු, *Duhudu*, *s.* oil so called; climbing shrub, *celastrus paniculata (Celastraceæ)*.

දුහුල්, *Duhul*, *s.* wove silk; fine thin cloth; cobweb.

දුළු, *Duḷu*, see දුල *dula*.

දුළුල්, *Duḷul*, *s.* jaṭá or clotted hair of the follower of Ṣiva, [Colloq. ජටාව *jaṭáwa*].

දුළුලු, *Duḷulu*, *s.* ascetic wearing clotted hair.

දූ, *Dú*, *s.* daughter; kind of game or play, dice, pl. දූලා *dúlá*, දූවරු *dúwaru*, daughters.

දූකෙළිය, *Dúkeḷiya*, *s.* game of dice, [Colloq. දාදු කෙළිය *dádukeḷiya*].

දූත, *Dúta*, *s.* dispatching, sending by an express; messenger, courier, express.

දූතයා, *Dútayá*, *s.* messenger, envoy; one carrying news; angel.

දූතලක්ෂණ, *Dúta-lakshaṇa*, *s.* (දූත messenger, ලක්ෂණ sign, token) tokens in a messenger by which the nature of his message is known; an impression prevails among the natives, that when a messenger is sent to call a doctor, the latter will at once determine the state and the fate of the patient, by the appearance of the messenger or more properly by certain indications in his looks, and from them will be able to augur the future progress of the disease.

දූතවාක්‍යය, *Dúta-wákyaya*, *s.* (දූත and වාක්‍යය word) message.

දූති, *Dúti*, *s.* female messenger; procuress, go-between; confidant.

දූදු, *Dúdu*, *s.* heart pea, *cardiospermum halicacabum*, used in Ceylon for culinary and medicinal purposes, [Colloq. පෙනෙලවැල් *penela-weḷ*].

දූන්, *Dún*, *acc. plur.* of දූ *dú*.

දූන්තෙල්, *Dúutel*, *s.* ghee, or clarified butter: see දුන්තෙල් *duntel*.

දූන, *Dúna*, *a.* suffering from pain or fatigue; going, moving; shaken, agitated.

දූපත, *Dúpata*, *s.* islet.

දූර, *Dúra*, *a.* far, distant, remote.

දූරග, *Dúraga*, *a.* going far, remote.

දූරදර්ශක, *Dúradarṣaka*, *a.* far-seeing.

දූරදර්ශන, *Dúradarṣana*, *s.* vulture, *nephron ginginianus (Falcones*, order *Accipitres)*: *a.* far-seeing, long-sighted.

දුරදර්ශී, *Dúradarṣí*, *a.* (දුර distant, දර්ශී who sees) long sighted, far seeing, literally or metaphorically: *s.* learned man, pandit; vulture; distant view.

දුරදෘක්, *Dúradṛik*, *s.* (දුර distant, far, දෘක් who sees) pandit, learned man, scholar in general.

දුරමුලා, *Dúramúlá*, *s.* plant, *sanseviera zeylanica*, from which a kind of cord is manufactured and is used as bow-strings, [Colloq. නියද *niyanda*].

දුරස්ථ, *Dúrastha*, *a.* (දුර remote, ස්ථ standing, being) distant, remote, removed far off, far away.

දූල්, *Dúl*, *s.* tow, flax; fibrous plant, *anodendron paniculatum, (Apocynaceæ)*; also called අස්වැල් *as-wel*.

දූලි, *Dúli*, *s.* dust.

දූව, *Dúwa*, *s.* island; any small spot of ground or bank surrounded by water.

දූෂ්‍ය, *Dúshya*, *s.* pus, matter; fœces or ordure; clothes; tent; elephant's leather girth: *a.* filthy, dirty; vile, bad, mean; reprehensible; contemptible.

දූෂ්‍යකරණවා, *Dúshya-karaṇawá*, *v.* to corrupt, to defile; to violate female chastity, to ravish; to spoil.

දූෂක, *Dúshaka*, *a.* mean, low, contemptible, infamous.

දූෂණ, *Dúshaṇa*, *s.* blame; fault, defect, error; offence, guilt, crime.

දූෂි, *Dúshi*, } *s.* the rheum of the eye; pencil
දූෂිකා, *Dúshiká*, } or painter's brush.

දූෂිත, *Dúshita*, *a.* calumniated, falsely accused; guilty; impure, filthy, nasty, dirty.

දූසාව, *Dúsáwa*, *s.* calumniation, false accusation; flying rumour.

දූසිත, *Dúsita*, see දූෂිත *dúshita*.

දෙ, *De*, *a.* two, both; as a prefix to nouns it has a dual signification, and is generally used to express two of a pair, or things of which there are only two, as දෙපා *depá* both feet etc.: in native vocabularies and lists of words, it is usual to insert all the words that are formed by this prefix, of which there is a considerable number; but they are here omitted as unnecessary, as the student will easily perceive that when he meets with a word thus formed, it is only to drop the දෙ, and the word immediately following the prefix, beginning with a vowel or consonant, will be found.

දෙඅත, *Deata*, *s.* more commonly දෑත *dẹta*, two hands.

දෙඋර, *Deura*, *s.* the two shoulders.

දෙඇස, *Deẹsa*, *s.* more commonly දෑස *dẹsa*, the two eyes.

දෙක, *Deka*, *a.* two; both, twain.

දෙකක්, *Dekak*, *s.* two (indefinitely).

දෙකට, *Dekaṭa*, *adv.* in two, as in දෙකට කපනවා *dekaṭa kapanawá*, to cut in two; at 2 o'clock, as in දෙකට වරෙන් *dekaṭa waren*.

දෙකටම නැති, *Dekaṭama-nẹti*, *a.* neutral, belonging to neither party; worthless fellow.

දෙකම, *Dekama*, *ad.* both, applied to things.

දෙකසා, *Dekasá*, *s.* (දෙ two, කසා saffron) saffron, [Colloq. කහ *kaha*]; creeping plant which resembles saffron, *coscinium fenestratum*, [Colloq. වෙනිවැල් *weniwẹl*].

දෙකින්දෙක, *Dekindeka*, *ad.* two by two.

දෙකේම, *Dekéma*, *ad.* of or in both.

දෙකොණ, *Dekona*, *s.* two corners, the two ends.

දෙගිඩියා, *Degiḍiyá*, *a.* wavering, undecided between two things.

දෙගුණ, *Deguṇa*, *a.* twofold, twice.

දෙගුරු, *Deguru*, *s.* parents.

දෙගොඩ, *Degoḍa*, *s.* two banks, sides of a river, canal etc.; two heaps.

දෙට්ටා *Deṭṭá*, *s.* kind of fish.

දෙට, *Deṭa*, Elu form of ජ්‍යෙෂ්ඨ *jyéshṭha*, and ජ්‍යෙෂ්ඨා *jyéshṭhá*, both of which see.

දෙටුවන්, *Deṭuwan*, *plur.* of the foregoing word,

දෙඩවිල්ල, *Deḍavilla*, *s.* idle talk, prating.

දෙඩීම, *Deḍíma*, *s.* conversation, talk, speech; verbal noun of දොඩනවා *doḍanawá*, to speak.

දෙඩුබ, *Deḍuba*, see දියබරියා *diyabariyá*.

දෙඩුම, *Deḍuma*, *s.* talking, prating.

දෙණිතණ, *Deṇi-taṇa*, *s.* panic grass, *panicum trigonum*.

දෙණිය, *Deṇiya*, *s.* a level spot of cultivated ground, an irrigated field, open field.

දෙත, *Deta*, *a.* best, excellent.

දෙතන, *Detana*, *s.* the two breasts.

දෙතිස්, *Detis*, } *ad.* thirty-two, [Colloq. තිස්දෙක
දෙතිස, *Detisa*, } *tisdeka*].

දෙදන, *Dedana*, *s.* the two knees.

දෙදරණවා, *Dedaraṇawá*, *v.* to shake, to tremble, to quake (as the earth), to perforate, to split, to rend: pret. දෙදරුවා *dedaruwá*.

දෙදරීම, *Dedaríma*, *s.* verbal noun of the former.

දෙදිය, *Dediya*, *s.* (දෙ two, දිය water) mixed water, salt and fresh water united.

දෙදිවු, *Dediwu*, *s.* (දෙ and දිවු tongue) serpent, snake, alluding to its having a forked tongue, [Colloq. සර්පයා *sarpayá*]: *a.* double tongued.

දෙදුමාව, *Dedumáwa*, *s.* the twin-fruit.

දෙදුරු, *Deduru*, *s.* (දෙ both, දුරු cummin seed) black and white cummin seed, the two species in most common use, කළුදුරු *kaḷuduru* and සුදුදුරු *sududuru*; frog, [Colloq. මැඩියා *mẹḍiyá*].

දෙන්නා, *Denná*, *s.* the two persons.

දෙන, *Dena*, *s.* bier; person; cow; the female of any animal: part. giving.

දෙනවා, *Denawá*, *v.* to give, to bestow, to impart: pret. දුන්නා *dunná*.

දෙනා, *Dená*, *s.* cow; the female of any animal.

දෙනු, *Denu*, *v. n.* of දෙනවා *denawá*, act of giving.

දෙපට, *Depaṭa*, *a.* double, two-fold.

දෙපත්නයා, *Depat-nayá*, *s.* red and yellow spotted short tailed snake, *Cylindrophis maculatus* (*Tortricidæ*); name of genera *rhinophis* and *uropellis* (*Uropeltidæ* order *Ophidia*).

දෙපය, *Depaya*, }
දෙපා, *Depá*, } *s.* the two feet.

දෙපාඇල, *Depá-ẹla*, *s.* the channel or water-course running between two dams or ridges in a tract of fields.

දෙපාට, *Depáṭa*, *s.* the two colours.

දෙපාර, *Depára*, *s.* two blows, two roads.

දෙපාව, *Depáwa*, *s.* two ridges or dams on each side of a water-course in a field.

දෙපාවෙල්ල, *Depá-wella*, *s.* dam on each side of a water-course in a field.

දෙපිල, *Depila*, *s.* both parties.

දෙපෝය, *Depóya*, *s.* two quarters of a lunar month: see පෝය *póya*.

දෙපෑල, *Depẹla*, *s.* two pẹlas or twenty kuruṇies of grain.

දෙබරය, *Debaraya*, *s.* nest of the hornet; it is usually built of clay and attached to the branches of trees, and as large as a common basket or beehive; the sting of the hornet is so exceedingly poisonous, that the natives will sooner forfeit the fruit of a tree where this nest is built than attempt to destroy it; see the following word.

දෙබරා, *Debará*, *s.* a large species of the wasp or hornet, its sting is exceedingly poisonous, *spex ferruginea* (order *Hymenoptera.*), pl. දෙබරු *debaru*.

දෙබලිය, *Debaliya*, *s.* that part of the trunk of a tree, where it parts in two.

දෙබලේ, *Debalé*, *s.* any thing with a double prong, fork, scissors.

දෙබැම, *Debẹma*, *s.* the two eye-brows.

දෙබෑ, *Debẹ*, *s.* two halves, two brothers; division into two.

දෙමංසන්ධිය, *Demaṇsandhiya*, }
දෙමංසල, *Demaṇsala*, } *s.* junction of two roads; place where two roads meet.

දෙමට, *Demaṭa*, *s.* shrub of which there are three species in Ceylon, the root and bark are used medicinally and the nut chewed with betel, *gmelina asiatica* (*Verbenaceæ*).

දෙමව්පිය. *Demawpiya*, *s.* (දෙ both, මව් mother, පිය father) parents.

දෙමලිච්චා, *Demalichchá*, *s.* bird called the common babbler, it is of a grey colour with a yellow bill, *malacho-cercus striatus* (*Timalidiidæ*, order *Passeres*).

දෙමහල්ලෝ, *Demahalló*, *s.* (දෙ two, මහල්ලෝ old ones or those who have attained maturity) husband and wife, couple.

දෙමළ, *Demaḷa*, *a.* Tamil.

දෙමළා, *Demaḷá*, *s.* Tamil man, native of the Coromandel coast.

දෙමුනුබුරා, *Demunuburá*, *s.* great grandson.

දෙය, *Deya*, *s.* thing, article of any kind: see ද්‍රව්‍ය *drawya*.

දෙරණ, *Deraṇa*, *s.* earth, ground, pátála, the nága lóka or world of serpents; an earring.

දෙරණතෙනේ, *Deraṇa-tené*, *s.* (දෙරණ ground, තෙනේ son) regent of the planet Mars; the name alludes to his terrene birth, being turned up from the earth by a plough; in astronomy he is identified with the planet.

දෙරණිඳු, *Deraṇiṇdu*, }
දෙරණිසුරු, *Deraṇisuru*, } *s.* (දෙරණ *deraṇa* earth, ඉඳු *iṇdu* and ඉසුරු *isuru* chief) king, sovereign, monarch, [Colloq. රජ *raja*].

දෙරණි, *Deraṇí*, see දෙරණ *deraṇa*.

දෙල්, *Del*, *s.* wild bread fruit, peculiar to Ceylon, *artocarpus nobilis* (*Urticaceæ*).

දෙලෙහෙනවා, *Delehenawá*, *v.* to blush, to be desparate; to hesitate: pret. දෙලෙහුනා *delehuná*.

දෙලොව, *Delowa*, *s.* the two worlds.

දෙව්, *Dew*, *s.* cloud; rain; king; in mythology a god, deity, divinity.

දෙව්තල, *Dewtala*, *s.* any high mountain; sky, visible heavens.

දෙව්තුර, *Dewtura*, }
දෙව්තුරු, *Dewturu*, } *s.* (දෙව් *dew* god, තුර or තුරු tree) fabulous tree of Swarga or paradise said to yield every thing that is desired: see කල්ප වෘක්ෂ *kalpa-vṛiksha*, and

කල්පද්‍රැම kalpa-druma; plant yielding a fragrant resin, bdellium; tree, alstonia scholaris, [Colloq. රුක් අත්තන ruk-attana]; bó tree, ficus religiosa.

දෙව්දත්, Dewdat, see දෙව්දත් devidat.

දෙව්දුනු, Dewdunu, see දෙව්දුනු devidunu.

දෙව්දුරු, Dewduru, s. large species of cummin; sort of pine, [Colloq. දේවදුර déwadára].

දෙව්දූත, Dewdúta, see දේවදූත déwadúta.

දෙව්නළු, Dewnaḷu, s. (දෙව් divine, නළු dancer) person who dances for the amusement of the gods, dancing girl of Swarga; they are used by the gods both as dramatic performers and prostitutes.

දෙව්නිවෙස්, Dew-niwes, s. (දෙව් and නිවෙස් dwelling) Swarga, paradise of the gods.

දෙව්පිරිස්, Dew-piris, s. attendants of the gods; inferior class of beings inhabiting Swarga, who are employed as messengers etc. by the gods.

දෙව්පුරය, Dewpuraya, s. heaven.

දෙව්රජ, Dewraja, } s. (දෙව් gods, රජ king)
දෙව්රදුන්, Dewradun, } name of Indra or Ṣakra, alluding to his being the ruler of Swarga.

දෙව්රම, Dewrama, s. a famous Vihára so called, [Colloq. ජේතවනාරාමය jétawanárámaya].

දෙව්රුපු, Dew-rupu, s. (දෙව් and රුපු enemy) Asura who is the implacable enemy of the gods.

දෙව්ලොව, Dewlowa, } s. (දෙව් and ලොව world)
දෙව්ලෝ, Dewló, } world or residence of the gods.

දෙව්සැපු, Dew-sapu, s. (දෙව් divine, සැපු pleasure) the pleasures of Swarga or the oriental mythological paradise: see ස්වර්ග swarga and දිව diwa.

දෙව්සර, Dewsara, s. (දෙව් god, සර woman) goddess, female deity.

දෙව්සෙනෙවි, Dew-senevi, s. (දෙව් god, සෙනෙවි army) name of Skandakumára or Kataragama-deviyó, alluding to his being the god of war and commander of the armies of the gods.

දෙවගෙම, Dewagema, s. (දෙ two, වගෙ kind, sort, ම intensive suffix) both kinds.

දෙවඟන, Dewaṉgana, s. (දෙව god, අඟන aṉgana woman) goddess, female deity.

දෙවට, Dewaṭa, s. lane.

දෙවන, Dewana, a. second.

දෙවනවා, Dewanawá, v. to cause to give, causal form of the verb දෙනවා denawá: pret. දෙව්වා dewwá.

දෙවනු, Dewanu, ad. again; secondly.

දෙවර, Dewara, ad. twice.

දෙවරුව, Dewaruwa, s. the forenoon and afternoon; two portions of the day.

දෙවලයක්, Dewalayak, s. two coils of a rope; doubt, (literally two minds).

දෙවලිය, Dewaliya, s. two days.

දෙවි, Devi, s. a god, deity, divinity, pl. දෙවියෝ deviyó.

දෙවිකිරි, Devi-kiri, s. (දෙවි past part of දොවනවා dowanawá, කිරි milk) milk drawn out.

දෙවිට, Deviṭa, } s. two times, twice.
දෙවිඩ, Deviḍa, }

දෙව්දත්, Devidat, s. name of the brother-in-law and rival of Buddha; he was a priest of Buddha and of considerable eminence; assuming the character of a reformer. he required Buddha to insist on a rigid adherence to the ascetical rules of the order, which the latter had in several instances mitigated; not succeeding in this, he created a schism among the priests, formed a separate community, became its superior, and was ever afterwards the determined opponent of Buddha.

දෙවිදුනු, Devi-dunu, s. (දෙවි god, දුනු bow) rainbow, [Colloq. දේදුන්න dédunna].

දෙවිඳු, Deviṉdu, s. (දෙවි and ඉඳු iṉdu chief) a god, one of the chiefs of the gods, Ṣakra.

දෙවියන්, Deviyan, s. a god, deity, divine being; this word, although in the accusative plural, is universally used in the singular number as a respectful mode of expressing that character.

දෙවියන්වහන්සේ, Deviyanwahansé, s. (දෙවියන් deity), respectfully; see last word (වහන්සේ honorific) God, Deity, Supreme Being as revealed in the Christian scriptures; the word is seldom or never met with in this form in heathen authors; Buddhism rejects the doctrine of a Supreme Being as understood by Christians; the words දෙවි devi, දෙවියා deviyá, දෙවියන් deviyan, දෙවියෝ deviyó etc. which are of such frequent occurrence in the writings of the natives, usually translated a god, a deity, a divinity etc. indicate a class of beings inhabiting Swarga or the six worlds of the gods; these words are derived from a root which signifies to shine, to be resplendent, to be beautiful; to play, to sport, to romp, to gambol; to wish, to desire, to love; they are accordingly represented as enjoying to the utmost every sensual pleasure, being attended by troops of the most beautiful females, and possessing every thing for the gratification of the senses; term applied by Christians to designate the Supreme God.

දෙවියා, *Deviyá*, *s.* a god, a deity.

දෙවිවූ, *Deviwú*, *a.* divine, possessing the attributes of deity.

දෙවි සෙනෙවි, *Devi-senevi*, properly දෙව් සෙනෙවි *dew-senevi*, which see.

දෙවු, *Dewu*, properly දෙව් *dew*, which see.

දෙවෙනි, *Deweni*, *ad.* second.

දෙවෙල්යකා, *Dewel-yaká*, corruptly for දෙවොල් යකා *dewol-yaká*, which see.

දෙවෙල, *Dewela*, corruptly for දෙවොල *dewola*, which see.

දෙවෙස්, *Dewes*, *s.* enemy, opponent, adversary; two forms.

දෙවේල, *Dewéla*, *s.* the two times, the two meals in a day.

දෙවොල්, *Dewol*, *s.* (දෙව් *dew* god, demon, අලය *álaya* hall, temple) temple dedicated to a god.

දෙවොල්යකා, *Dewol-yaká*, *s.* foreign devil who is supposed to infest Ceylon; he excites great fear among the natives and is frequently offered to and worshipped.

දෙවොල, *Dewola*, *s.* temple where offerings and worship are made to a Hindu god.

දෙස්, *Des*, *s.* land, country; place, direction; side; curse, imprecation.

දෙස්කියනවා, *Des-kiyanawá*, } *v.* to curse, to im-
දෙස්තිබනවා, *Des-tibanawá*, } precate.

දෙස්ස, *Dessa*, *s.* lime: see දෙසි *desi* or දෙහි *dehi*.

දෙස, *Desa*, *s.* country, in the direction of.

දෙසතර, *Desatara*, *s.* twice four.

දෙසඳුන්, *Desandun*, *s.* the two species of sandal wood, red and white.

දෙසනවා, *Desanawá*, *v.* to preach, to declare: see දේසනාකරණවා *désanákaranawá*.

දෙසනුදෙස, *Desanudesa*, *s.* the four cardinal points and the four intermediate points of the compass, [Colloquial: හතරදිග *hatara-diga*, හතරකොණ *hatara-koṇa*].

දෙසි, *Desi*, *s.* lime, usually written දෙහි *dehi*, which see.

දෙසිත්, *Desit*, *a.* double-minded.

දෙසිය, *Desiya*, *s.* two hundred.

දෙසීම, *Desíma*, *s.* preaching; verbal noun of දෙසනවා *desanawá*.

දෙසීය, *Desíya*, *s.* two hundred.

දෙසුවා, *Desuwá*, *pret.* of දෙසනවා *desanawá*.

දෙසූ, *Desú*, *past part.* of දෙසනවා *desanawá*.

දෙසැට, *Deseṭa*, *s.* number sixty-two, [Colloq. හැට දෙක *heṭadeka*].

දෙසැරයක්, *Deserayak*, *s.* twice.

දෙහි, *Dehi*, *s.* lime, of which there are several species in Ceylon, *citrus limetta*.

දෙහි අල, *Dehi-ala*, *s.* a root, *colocasia antiquorum.*

දෙහිකපනවා, *Dehi-kapanawá*, *v.* to perform the ceremony of "cutting lime" to avert the evil effects of the evil eye or evil tongue.

දෙහි නුග, *Dehi-nuga*, *s.* species of fig tree, *ficus benjamina.*

දෙළුම්, *Deḷum*, *s.* pomegranate tree, *punica granatum.*

දේ, *Dé*, *s.* things, articles, goods, property, furniture: see ද්‍රව්‍ය *drawya*.

දේදුන්න, *Dédunna*, *s.* rain-bow, pl. දේදුනු *dédunu*.

දේය, *Déya*, *s.* that which is proper to be given, what is fit to be offered, any thing suitable for an offering or charitable donation.

දේයධර්ම, *Déya-dharma*, *s.* offerings; gifts; charity, [Colloq. දානය *dánaya*].

දේව, *Déwa*, *s.* deity, a god, divine being; organ of sense; cloud; king.

දේවකාෂ්ඨ, *Déwakáshṭha*, *s.* (දේව divine, කාෂ්ඨ wood) tree, sort of pine, *pinus dévadáru.*

දේවකී, *Déwakí*, *s.* goddess. daughter of Déwaka, wife of Vasudéva and mother of Kṛishṇa.

දේවකී නන්දන, *Déwakí-nandana*, *s.* (දේවකී and නන්දන son) son of Dévakí, name of Kṛishṇa: see the foregoing word.

දේවකුසුම, *Déwa-kusuma*, *s.* (දේව deity, කුසුම flower) cloves, [Colloq. කරාබු *karábu*].

දේවඛාතක, *Déwa-khátaka*, *s.* (දේව deity, ඛාත dug, කන් *kan* aff.) cave or hollow in mountains supposed to have been dug by divine hands; one dug in honour of a god: natural cavern, grotto; according to another authority (දේව cloud, rain, ඛාත dug) lạke or pond made by the rain; natural pond or tank.

දේවගන්ධිකා, *Déwa-gandhiká*, *s.* kind of resin, *sandarac.*

දේවචාරික, *Déwa-chárika*, *s.* (දේව and චාරික who moves or walks) inhabitant of Swarga the paradise of the gods.

දේවජීව, *Déwa-jíwa*, *s.* (දේව and ජීව who lives) officiating priest in a Hindu temple.

දේවතා, *Déwatá*, *s.* a god, a deity, any divine person; divinity.

දේවතාඩ, *Déwatáḍa*, *s.* (දේව deity, තාඩ *taḍa* torment) Ráhu, the personified ascending mode; fire; kind of grass, *andropogon serratum.*

දේවතාවා, *Déwatáwá*, *s.* deity.

දේවදත්ත, *Déwadatta*, *s.* proper name, the cousin of Buddha, who was his enemy and rival: see දෙව්දත් *devidat*; the conch of Arjuna; one of the five vital airs, that which is inhaled in yawning: *a.* given by the gods.

දේවදාර, *Déwadára*, } *s.* (දේව and දාර from දාරු
දේවදාරු, *Déwadáru*, } wood) tree, *uvaria longifolia;* sort of pine, *pinus dévadáru;* tree, *erythroxylum monogynum.*

දේවදලි, *Déwadáli*, *s.* plant described variously as a creeper, plant etc.

දේවදාසී, *Déwa-dásí*, *s.* (දේව and දාසී female servant) courtezan, harlot, one of the strumpets of Swarga or the residence of the gods.

දේවදුන්දුභි, *Déwa-dundubhi*, *s.* (දේව and දුන්දුභි drum) tom-tom or drum used by the Gándharwas or choristers of Swarga.

දේවදුරු, *Déwa-duru*, *s.* (දේව and දුරු cumin) large species of cumin seed.

දේවදූතයා, *Déwa-dútayá*, *s.* angel, messenger of the gods.

දේවදූප, *Déwa-dúpa*, incorrectly for දේවධූප *déwa-dhúpa*, which see.

දේවදේව, *Déwadéwa*, *s.* the god of gods, name of Brahma, and of Şiva; name of Buddha, alluding to his being the chief of the rahats who are sometimes stiled Dévatá, *i. e.* beings of a divine or supernatural nature.

දේවද්‍රු, *Déwadru*, see කල්පවෘක්ෂ *kalpa-vṛiksha.*

දේවද්‍රෝණි, *Déwadróṇí*, *s.* procession of a deity or an idol.

දේවධර්ම, *Déwa-dharma*, *s.* (දේව god, ධර්ම natural state) circumstances of nature or the moral qualities which are inseparable from the state of the gods, viz. the fear of sin, shame of sin, inclination to good works, and love of virtue.

දේවධූප, *Déwa-dhúpa*, *s.* (දේව divine, ධූප incense) fragrant resin, *bdellium*, much used in offering incense to the gods and demons.

දේවනිර්මිතා, *Déwanirmitá*, *s.* plant, *tinospora cordifolia*, [Colloq. රසකිඳ *rasakinda*].

දේවපත්නී, *Déwa-patní*, *s.* (දේව and පත්නී wife) wife of a deity; sweet potato.

දේවපථ, *Déwapatha*, *s.* (දේව and පථ way) sky, visible heavens, firmament.

දේවපුත්‍ර, *Déwa-putra*, *s.* (දේව god, පුත්‍ර son) name by which the gods are frequently designated.

දේවපුත්‍රී, *Déwa-putrí*, *s.* (දේව and පුත්‍රී daughter) name of a plant, *trigonella corniculata.*

දේවපූජක, *Déwa-pújaka*, *s.* offerer to the gods; gods' priest; commonly called කපුරාල *kapurála.*

දේවප්‍රශ්න, *Déwa-praşna*, *s.* (දේව and ප්‍රශ්න question, asking) consulting the stars or gods, astrology.

දේවයන්වහන්සේ, *Déwayanwahansé*, *voc.* දේවයන් වහන්ස, *déwayanwahansa*, respectful form used by Kandyans and other Buddhists in speaking of or to their King.

දේවරාජ, *Déwarája*, *s.* (දේව and රාජ king) name of Indra alluding to his being the chief of the gods.

දේව ලතා, *Déwa-latá*, *s.* double jasmine, [Colloq. ගැටපිච්ච *geṭa-pichcha*].

දේවලෝක, *Déwalóka*, *s.* Swarga or heaven, habitation of the gods: see ස්වර්ග *swarga.*

දේව වක්ත්‍ර, *Déwa-waktra*, *s.* (දේව and වක්ත්‍ර mouth, face) mouth of the gods alluding to the supposition that they eat or consume the oblations made to them; fire, Agni the deity of fire.

දේව වල්ලභ, *Déwa-wallabha*, *s.* (දේව and වල්ලභ friend) tree used in dyeing red, *rottleria tinctoria*, [Colloq. කින දොඹ *kína-domba*].

දේව වෘක්ෂ, *Déwa-vṛiksha*, *s.* tree, *alstonia scholaris*, [Colloq. රුක් අත්තන *ruk-attana*]; the tree of Swarga, see කල්පවෘක්ෂ *kalpa-vṛiksha*, and කල්පද්‍රුම *kalpa-druma;* according to some, the *ficus religiosa*, or bó tree; tree yielding a fragrant resin, *bdellium.*

දේව ශිල්පී, *Déwa-şilpí*, *s.* (දේව and ශිල්ප *şilpa* an art, ඊ *í* aff.) the celestial artizan, name of Vişwakarma the architect and artizan of the gods.

දේවශ්‍රුත, *Déwaşruta*, *s.* (දේව divine, ශ්‍රුත heard) any sacred treatise; any part of the sacred writings of the heathens; any divine or supernatural revelation.

දේවස්ථානය, *Déwasthánaya*, *s.* Church, divine residence, place of divine worship.

දේවසභා, *Déwa-sabhá*, *s.* (දේව and සභා assembly) assembly of the gods.

දේවසහා, *Déwasahá*, *s.* small shrub bearing a beautiful flower, *crinum zeylanicum* or *amaryllis zeylanica*, [Colloq. ගොඩමානිල් *goḍa-mánil*].

දේවසේනාපති, *Déwa-sénápati*, *s.* (දේව celestial, සේනා army, පති chief) name of Skandakumára or as he is commonly called Kataragama-deviyó alluding to his being the commander in chief of the troops of Swarga or the armies of the gods; he is the Indian Mars and is figured in the temples as having twelve hands in each of which he holds a warlike weapon.

දේවාග්නික, *Déwágnika*, *s.* (දේව *déwa* and අග්නි *agni* fire, ක nom. aff.) one who offers burnt sacrifices to the gods.

දේවාත්මය, *Déwátmaya*, *s.* divine Spirit.

දේවාතිදේව, *Déwáti-déwa*, *s.* god of gods.

දේවානමින්ද, *Déwánaminda*, *s.* (දේවානම් *déwánam* of the gods, ඉන්ද *inda* chief) name of Indra as ruler of the gods.

දේවානුභාව, *Déwánubháwa*, *s.* (දේව *déwa* and අනුභාව *ánubháwa* power) divine power, influence of a god or deity.

දේවාලය, *Déwálaya*, *s.* (දේව *déwa* and ආලය *álaya* house) residence of the gods, temple; Hindu temple, place where offerings are made to gods; these places are totally distinct from the viháras or temples of Buddha.

දේවාව්හ, *Déwáwha*, see දේවදාරු *déwadáru*.

දේවාවාස, *Déwáwása*, *s.* (දේව *déwa* and ආවාස *áwása* dwelling) residence of a god, temple; the bó tree, supposed to be particularly the dwelling of the gods.

දේවාශ්ව, *Déwáṣwa*, *s.* (දේව *déwa* and අශ්ව *aṣwa* horse) the horse of Indra, metaphorically, the wind.

දේවි, *Dévi*, }
දේවී, *Déví*, } *s.* goddess, queen; fem. of දේව *déwa*, which see; plant, *marsdenia tennacissima*, [Colloq. මුරුවා *muruwá*].

දේවින්නාන්සේ, *Dévinnánsé*, *s.* queen, [Colloq. බිසවුන්නාන්සේ *bisawunnánsé*].

දේවීලතා, *Déví-latá*, *s.* plant, *trigonella corniculata*, [Colloq. පික් මල් *pik-mal*].

දේවේන්ද්‍ර, *Déwéndra*, *s.* (දේව *déwa* and ඉන්ද්‍ර *indra* ruler) name of Ṣakra or Indra as ruler of the gods.

දේශ, *Désa*, *s.* country, region whether inhabited or uninhabited.

දේශක, *Désaka*, *s.* (දේශ to command, ක affix) ruler, governor; (දේශ to preach, ක nom. aff.) preacher.

දේශගුණය, *Désaguṇaya*, *s.* climate.

දේශනාකරණවා, *Désaná-karaṇawá*, *v.* (දේශනා lecture, sermon, කරණවා to do) to preach, to expound in public, to exhort, to admonish.

දේශනාකාරයා, *Désanákáraya*, *s.* preacher.

දේශනාව, *Désanáwa*, *s.* sermon, address, exhortation.

දේශය, *Désaya*, *s.* country: see දේශ *désa*.

දේශවිලෝකනය, *Désa-vilókanaya*, *s.* (දේශ country, විලෝකනය seeing) one of the five prospective glances which Buddha took when living in the heaven called තුසිතභවන *tusitabhawana*, respecting his future assumption of the Buddhaship, viz. a look of enquiry as to what country or region would be the most suitable in which to suffer himself to be incarnated.

දේශාන්තර, *Désántara*, *s.* (දේශ *désa* and අන්තර *antara* intermediate, intervening) in astronomy the distance east or west of Laṇká or Ceylon which forms the first meridian of longitude on the earth's surface, and from which all astronomical calculations are made; longitude; a foreign country.

දේශික, *Désika*, *s.* traveller; stranger; sojourner.

දේහ, *Déha*, *s.* body, [Colloq. ශරීරය *ṣaríraya*].

දේහක්ෂය, *Déhakshaya*, *s.* (දේහ and ක්ෂය wasting) sickness, disease.

දේහත්‍යාග, *Déhatyága*, *s.* voluntary death; death in general.

දේහධාරක, *Déha-dháraka*, *s.* (දේහ body, ධාරක sustainer) bone.

දේහයාත්‍රා, *Déha-yátrá*, *s.* (දේහ and යාත්‍රා going) death, dying, exit, [Colloq. මරණය *maraṇaya*].

දේහලක්ෂණ, *Déha-lakshaṇa*, *s.* physiognomy, marks on the body.

දේහලා, *Déhalá*, *s.* spirituous liquor.

දේහලි, *Déhali*, *s.* threshold of a door, lower part of a wooden frame of a door; raised terrace in front of a door, [Colloq. එලිපත්ත *elipatta*].

දේහි, *Déhi*, *s.* corporeal, embodied, having a body.

දෛත්‍ය, *Daitya*, *s.* demon, Asura, titan or giant of oriental mythology.

දෛත්‍යගුරු, *Daitya-guru*, *s.* (දෛත්‍ය demon, asura, ගුරු teacher) preceptor of the daityas or Asuras, name of Ṣukra the regent of the planet Venus.

දෛත්‍යයුග, *Daitya-yuga*, *s.* an age of the demons, consisting of twelve thousand divine years or the sum of the four yugas or ages of men equal to 4,320,000 years.

දෛත්‍යාරි, *Daityári*, *s.* (දෛත්‍ය *daitya* and අරි *ari* foe) enemy of the daityas or demons, name of Vishṇu; a deity, a god, so called on account of the gods being the avowed and implacable enemies of the Asuras.

දෛන්‍ය, *Dainya*, *s.* meanness; covetousness; poverty; humbleness.

දෛර්ඝ්‍ය, *Dairghya*, *s.* length.

දෛව, *Daiwa*, *s.* destiny, fate; fortune, luck: *a.* divine.

දෛවඥ, *Daiwajña*, *s.* (දෛව fortune, luck, fate, ඥ who knows) fortune-teller; writer of nativities; astrologer: *a.* acquainted with fate.

දෛවත, *Daiwata*, *s.* a god, deity, divinity: *a.* divine.

දෛවදීප, *Daiwadípa*, *s.* (දේව *déwa* organ of sense, දීප lamp) the eye, considered as the brightest of the sentient organs.

දෛවලේඛයා, *Daiwalékhayá*, *s.* (දෛව fortune, ලේඛ writing, යා nom. aff.) astrologer, fortune teller, one who writes nativities.

දොට්ට ගියා, *Doṭṭa-giyá*, *v.* went out, corrupt form of දොරට ගියා *doraṭa-giyá*.

දොඩ, *Doḍa*, *s.* word, speech, saying.

දොඩං, *Doḍaŋ*, corruptly for දොඩම් *doḍam*.

දොඩන්කහ, *Doḍan-kaha*, *s.* plant, peculiar to Ceylon, *memecylon fuscescens;* another plant, *m. capitellatum (Melastomaceæ)*, the latter, also called වැලිකහ *węli-kaha*.

දොඩන්පනා, *Doḍan-paná*, *s.* plant, *glycosmis pentaphylla (Rutaceæ).*

දොඩන්වැන්න, *Doḍanwęnna*, *s.* small tree, *memecylon grande* or *edule (Melastomaceæ).*

දොඩනවා, *Doḍanawá*, *v.* to speak, to talk, to prate: pret. දෙඩුවා *deḍuwá*.

දොඩම, *Doḍama*, *s.* orange, *citrus aurantium.* pl. දොඩම් *doḍam*, or more commonly දොඩං *doḍaŋ*.

දොඩමළු, *Doḍamaḷu*, *a.* talkative.

දොඩවනවා, *Doḍawanawá*, *v.* to jabber, to prate, to talk foolishly: pret. දෙඩෙව්වා *deḍewwá*.

දොඹ, *Domba*, *s.* timber tree, called Alexandrian laurel, from the seeds of which lamp oil, (poon seed oil) is obtained; *calophyllum inophyllum, (Guttiferæ);* there are several species in Ceylon, as තෙල්දොඹ *tel-domba* and බටදොඹ *baṭa-domba*: water flower.

දොඹකින, *Domba-kína*, *s.* tree, *calophyllum spectabile (Guttiferæ).*

දොම්නස්, *Domnas*, *a.* sorrowful, depressed in mind, low spirited, gloomy, melancholy.

දොම්නස, *Domnasa*, *s.* sorrow.

දොයිතුව, *Doyituwa*, *s.* quarter of a farthing.

දොයියනවා, *Doyiyanawá*, *v.* to sleep, chiefly used of the repose of infants: pret. දොයියාගත්තා *doyiyágattá*.

දොයිරාදුකරණවා, *Doyirádu-karaṇawá*, *v.* to gild.

දොර, *Dora*, *s.* door, gate, entrance.

දොර අරිණවා, *Dora-ariṇawá*, *v.* to open the door.

දොරකඩ, *Dorakaḍa*, *s.* door-way, about the door, near the door.

දොරටුව, *Doraṭuwa*, *s.* gate, portal, gate-way.

දොරටුපාලයා, *Doraṭupálayá*, *s.* door-keeper, porter.

දොරණ, *Doraṇa*, see දොරල *dorala*.

දොරණතෙල්, *Doraṇa-tel*, *s.* oil used in the composition of paint, wood oil.

දොරල, *Dorala*, *s.* tree, (peculiar to Ceylon,) which yields an oil used in the preparation of paint; it is a large tree, with leaves changing from yellow to red and black, and gives a balsamic oil, *dipterocarpus glandulosus (Dipterocarpaceæ).*

දොරවහනවා, *Dora-wahanawá*, *v.* to lock up the door.

දොල, *Dola*, *s.* offering to demons or to any departed spirit or manes; covetousness; desire, wish, longing, whim; rill, small brook, streamlet which has its source in a mountain.

දොලඋපත, *Dola-upata*, } *s.* longing of a pregnant
දොලදුක, *Doladuka*, } woman.

දොලදෙනවා, *Dola-denawá*, *v.* to offer to devils, to offer to demons.

දොලනවා, *Dolanawá*, *v.* to become fat or stout; to desire, to wish: pret. දෙලුවා *deluwá*.

දොලපාර, *Dolapára*, *s.* rill, small brook etc., proceeding from a hill.

දොලමන, *Dola-mana*, *a.* covetous, longing, ardently desiring.

දොලො, *Dolo*, *s.* sorrow, affliction, distress, grief.

දොවිනවා, *Dovinawá*. *v.* to milk a cow: pret. දෙව්වා *dewwá*.

දොවුන්දිය, *Dowundiya*, *s.* water in which rice has been washed.

දොවුනේ, *Dowuné*, *s.* act of taking milk from a cow; act. of washing.

දොස් *Dos*, *s.* fault; hatred; indifference to pleasure or pain, stoicism; the humors of the body, such as bile, wind, and phlegm; displeasure, crime.

දොස්තබනවා, *Dos-tabanawá*, *v.* to impute crime, to criminate, to impeach.

දොස්තර, *Dostara*. *s.* medical man, (corruption of doctor.)

දොස, *Dosa*, *s.* transgression, fault, crime, guilt, sin, offence; defect, blemish; the humours of the body or the functions of bile, phlegm, circulation or wind; sickness, disease; misfortune, mishap, fate, ill-luck, pl. දොස් *dos*.

දොහොත, *Dohota*, *s.* (දොහො for දෙක *deka* two, and අත *ata* hand) both hands; the two hands joined and the palms opened as for receiving two handfuls.

දොහොන, *Dohona*, see දෝහන *dóhana*.

දොළස, *Doḷasa*, *s.* number twelve.

දොළසත්, *Doḷasat*, *s.* (දොළස twelve, අත් *at* hand) name of Skandakumára or the Kataragamadeviyó the Indian god of war, alluding to his twelve hands; he is figured in the temples as having twelve hands, in each of which he holds a warlike instrument.

දොළහ, *Doḷaha*, *s.* number twelve.

දොළුවරය, *Doḷuwaraya*, *s.* country so called; not ascertained.

දොළොස්වෙනි, *Doḷosweni*, *ad.* twelfth.

දොළොස, *Doḷosa*, *s.* number twelve.

දෝ, *Dó*, *s.* star, [Colloq. තාරකාව *tárakáwa*]: also an affix expressing doubt, uncertainty.

දෝංකාරය, *Dóṇkáraya*, *s.* an echo.

දෝණි, *Dóṇi*, *s.* boat, (Tamil.)

දෝත, *Dóta*, *s.* the two hands.

දෝතලු, *Dótalu*, *s.* tree peculiar to Ceylon: it produces a very small species of areca nut, *loxococcus rupicola, (Palmæ)*.

දෝනවා, *Dónawá*, *v.* to milk: see දොවිනවා *dovinawá*.

දෝනියන්දෑ, *Dóniyandẹ*, } *s.* daughter.
දෝනියෝ, *Dóniyó*, }

දෝමනස්ස, *Dómanassa*, *s.* (දු *du* bad, මනස් *manas* mind) sorrow, distress of mind, melancholy, [Colloq. ශෝකය *sókaya*].

දෝරද, *Dó-rada*, *s.* (දෝ star, රද king) moon.

දෝලා, *Dólá*, *s.* indigo plant, [Colloq. අවරි *awari*].

දෝලාව, *Dóláwa*, } *s.* swing, swinging cot or hammock for travelling or diversion; dooly, lighter sort of palanquin usually made of canvas, pl. දෝලා *dólá*.
දෝලි, *Dóli*, }

දෝව, *Dówa*, *s.* field or place between rising grounds, and into which water flows during rain.

දෝෂ, *Dósha*, *s.* wrath, anger; fault, crime, guilt, offence, sin; blemish, defect: see දොස *dosa*.

දෝෂඥ, *Dóshajña*, *s.* (දෝෂ fault, defect, disease, ඥ who knows) pundit, learned man, teacher, sage; physician.

දෝෂාරෝපණය, *Dóshárópaṇaya*, *s.* (දෝෂ *dósha* guilt, crime, ආරෝපණය *árópaṇaya* fixing upon) accusing, imputing guilt; censure, blame.

දෝස, *Dósa*, *s.* sickness, disease; the humours of the body: see දොස *dosa*.

දෝහ, *Dóha*, *s.* milk, milking; milk vessel.

දෝහද, *Dóhada*, *s.* wish, desire; longing of a pregnant woman.

දෝහන, *Dóhana*, *part. a.* milking; *s.* milk-pail.

දෝහල, *Dóhala*, *s.* wish, desire; longing of a pregnant woman.

දෝහලවතී, *Dóhalawatí*, *s.* pregnant woman longing for any thing.

දෝහෝ, *Dóhó*, } *ad.* whether, if, particle expressive of uncertainty.
දෝහෝයි, *Dóhóyi*, }

දෞර්භාග්‍යය, *Daurbhágyaya*, *s.* (දෞර් *daur* from දුර් *dur* bad, භාග්‍ය *bhágya* portion) ill luck, ill fate.

දෞර්මනස්‍ය, *Daurmanasya*, *s.* (දුර් *dur* bad, මනස් *manas* mind) sorrow, pain or distress of mind; gloom, melancholy, depression of spirits: *a.* sorrowful, dejected, depressed in mind, low spirited, [Colloq. ශෝකවූ *sókawú*].

දෞර්වල්‍යක, *Daurwalyaka*, *s.* creeping plant, bearing fruit used as vegetable, *momordica charantia*, [Colloq. කරවිල *karivila*].

දෞර්හෘද, *Daurhṛida*, see දෝහද *dóhada*.

දෞර්හෘදවතී, *Daurhṛidawatí*, see දෝහලවතී *dóhalawatí*.

දෞසලෙය, *Dausaleya*, *s.* small aromatic plant, *kaempferia galanga*, [Coll: හිඟුරුපියලි *hinguru-piyali*].

දැක්කඩි, *Dẹkkadí*, *ad.* with, together with, before, in the presence of.

දැක්කා, *Dẹkká*, *v.* saw, pret. of දකිනවා *dakinawá*, to see; also දුටුවා *duṭuwá*.

දැක්කුවා, *Dẹkkuwá*, *v.* drove, pret. of දක්කනවා *dakkanawá*, to drive.

දැක්ම, *Dẹkma*, *s.* appearance, sight, view; tax, tribute.

දැක්මදෙනවා, *Dẹkma-denawá*, *v.* to pay tax or tribute.

දැක්වීම, *Dẹkvíma*, *s.* showing, presentation: *v.* noun from දක්වනවා *dakwanawá*, which see.

දැක, *Dęka*, *p.* having seen: *part.* of දකිනවා *dakinawá*, to see.

දැකීම, *Dękíma*, *s.* seeing, sight: *v.* noun of දකිනවා *dakinawá*, to see.

දැකුන්, *Dękun*, *s.* incorrectly for දැකුම් *dękum*, cloth worn round the middle; knot, tie, string.

දැකුම, *Dękuma*, *s.* appearance; offering, present, gift, present to a king, bribe, pl. දැකුම් *dękum*.

දැඟුම්, *Dęngum*, *s.* motion, locomotion.

දැට්ට, *Dętta*, *s.* edge, border, pl. දැටි *deṭi*.

දැඩකෙහෙල්, *Dęḍa-kehel*, *s.* plant, *dracontium pinnatifolia*.

දැඩි, *Dęḍi*, *s.* bulk; growth: *a.* hard, strong, firm; resolute.

දැඩිකරණවා, *Dęḍikaraṇawá*, *v.* to harden; to bring up as a child.

දැඩිකහ, *Dęḍi-kaha*, *s.* small tree, leaves used for dyeing, *memecylon tinctoria (Melastomaceæ)*.

දැඩිතර, *Dęḍitara*, *a.* very strong or hard, [Colloq. බොහෝ සවිඇති *bohó savi-ęti*].

දැඩින්නරු, *Dęḍinnaru*, *s.* variety of the sensitive plant, *mimosa pudica*, [Colloq. නිදිකුම්බ *nidi-kumba*].

දැඩියාව, *Dęḍiyáwa*, *s.* sunshine, [Colloq. අව්ව *awwa*].

දැඩිවෙනවා, *Dęḍiwenawá*, *v.* to grow, to increase (in bulk, strength etc.); to coagulate; to become hard, firm etc.

දැතත, *Dętta*, *s.* tooth of a saw or any cutting instrument, pl. දැති *dęti*; tree, called දන්ති *danti*.

දැතන, *Dętana*, *s.* instrument used to rasp the cocoa-nut; tooth of a saw; comb or any thing indented, instrument used in husking the paddy; medicinal shrub, species of the *zapania*.

දැති කිඹුලා, *Dęti-kimbulá*, *s.* sort of alligator.

දැතිගොයියා, *Dętigoyiyá*, *s.* instrument used for removing staw or raking up the stalks of paddy on the threshing floor.

දැති පිර, *Dęti-píra*, *s.* large file, rasp.

දැති මෝරා, *Dęti-mórá*, *s.* the saw fish.

දැතිවිල, *Dętivila*, *s.* hedge hyssop, *gratiola ciliata*: see දැමිතිරිය *dęmitiriya*.

දැදුරු, *Dęduru*, *s.* frog, [Colloq. මැඩියා *męḍiyá*]; splitting, crack, act of splitting or cleaving, [Colloq. පැළීම *pęlíma*]; rumbling noise as of distant thunder, [Colloq. ගිගුරුම *giguruma*]; noise of any thing splitting or cleaving.

දැන්, *Dęn*, *ad.* now, at this present time.

දැන්ම, *Dęnma*, *ad.* immediately, even now, at this instant.

දැන්වනාහි, *Dęn-wanáhi*, *adv*, now, වනාහි being a mere expletive.

දැන්වීම, *Dęnvíma*, *s.* information: *v.* noun of දන්වනවා *danwanawá*, to inform or to cause to know.

දැන්වූකලී, *Dęn-wúkalí*, *ad.* now, at this time, at the present period.

දැන, *Dęna*, *p. part.* of දන්නවා *dannawá* to know.

දැනගත්තා, *Dęnagattá*, *pret.* of දැනගන්නවා *dęnagannawá*, to know, to ascertain, find out.

දැනගැන්ම, *Dęnagęnma*, *s.* knowledge; *v.* noun of the preceding.

දැනට, *Dęnaṭa*, *ad.* at present, at this time, now.

දැනදැන, *Dęna-dęna*, *ad.* consciously, knowingly.

දැනමිති, *Dęnamiti*, *a.* well informed, able to give advice.

දැනමිතිකම් දෙනවා, *Dęnamitikam-denawá*, *v.* to give advice, to reprove.

දැනමිතිකම, *Dęnamitikama*, *s.* advice, warning.

දැනමුතු, *Dęnamutu*, see දැනමිති *dęnamiti*.

දැනීම, *Dęníma*, *s.* knowledge; sensation, perception, feeling, touch, sense of feeling.

දැනුදු, *Dęnudu*, *ad.* even now, now also.

දැනුම්දීම, *Dęnum-díma*, *s.* the act of giving notice.

දැනුම්දෙනවා, *Dęnum-denawá*, *v.* to give information.

දැනුවත්ත, *Dęnuwatta*, *ind.* knowingly, intentionally, designedly, with the knowledge of.

දැනෙනවා, *Dęnenawá*, *v.* to feel, to know by the touch, to perceive: pret. දැනුනා *dęnuná*.

දැප, *Dępa*, *p. part.* of දපනවා *dapanawá*, to mutter as a charmer.

දැපනෙ, *Dępane*, *s.* inablity to move as if under the influence of magic or spell-bound.

දැපී, *Dępí*, *s.* name of Ananga the Indian Cupid; pride, haughtiness, arrogance, [Colloq. ආඩම්බරය *áḍambaraya*]; muttering as prayers: see දපනවා *dapanawá*.

දැපුණු, *Dępuṇu*, *s.* mirror, [Colloq. කැඩපත *kęḍapata*].

දැම්මා, *Dęmmá*, *pret.* of දමනවා *damanawá*, to put or place, corruptly for දැමුවා *dęmuwá*.

දැමිටු, *Dęmiṭu*, *a.* charitable; good natured; Elu form of ධර්මිෂ්ඨ *dharmmishṭha*, which see.

දැමිතිරිය, *Dęmitiriya*, *s.* small creeping plant, with blue flowers, hedge hyssop, *gratiola monnieria*: see දැතිවිල *dętivila*.

දැමු, *Dęmu*, *part.* of දමනවා *damanawá*, to put, place, subdue.

දැමුනා, *Dęmuna, part.* subjugated.

දැරි ඇති, *Dęri-ęti, s.* (දැරි child, ඇති fem. poss. affix) pregnant; with young.

දැරියා, *Dęriya, s.* young girl, child, infant.

දැල්, *Dęl, plur.* of දැල *dęla.*

දැල් අදිනවා, *Dęl-adinawá, v.* to cast or haul up nets in fishing or catching game.

දැල්කත්, *Dęlkat, s.* pole or stick used by fishermen for the purpose of carrying their nets, each end being placed on the shoulders of a man.

දැල්කා, *Dęlká, s.* leech, [Colloq. කුඩැල්ලා *kúdęllá*].

දැල් ගොතනවා, *Dęl-gotanawá, v.* to make nets.

දැල් දමනවා, *Dęl-damanawá, v.* to cast nets.

දැල්පෙලි, *Dél-peli, s.* buoys used to keep nets, afloat, or on the surface of the water.

දැල්ල, *Dęlla, s.* flame of fire, spark, wick of a lamp or candle.

දැල්ලා, *Dęllá, s.* kind of sea fish.

දැල, *Dęla, s.* net; company, congregation, multitude, pl. දැල් *dęl.*

දැලි, *Dęli, s.* beard, [Colloq. රැවුළ *ręwuḷa*]; root; charcoal; net; root of the lotus; half moon; bud, germ, young sprout: *a.* black, charcoal colour.

දැලිකා, *Dęliká,* see ජාලිකා *jáliká.*

දැලිකුණු, *Dęlikuṇu, s.* filth or dirt of soot, grime.

දැලිනූල, *Dęli-núla, s.* (දැලි charcoal, නූල thread) carpenter's marking thread, pl. දැලිනූල් *dęli-núl.*

දැලිපිහිය, *Dęlipihiya, s.* razor.

දැලිපොත්ත, *Dęlipotta, s.* shell of a fish called දැල්ලා *dęllá.*

දැලියා, *Dęliyá, s.* moth that lodges in books, kitchens, etc. young cockroach.

දැලිරොද, *Dęliroda, s.* beard, [Coll: රැවුළ *ręwuḷa*].

දැලි සෙමෙර, *Dęli-semera, s.* (දැලි black, සෙමෙර whisk) kind of whisk or brush, made from the tail of the Indian Yak, *bos grunniens,* and used to whisk off the flies etc.; there are two sorts, the black and white; this is the black one.

දැලී, *Dęlí, s.* bud, germ, young sprout or shoot of a leaf or flower.

දැලැස්, *Dęlęs, s.* (දැල *dęla* net, ඇස් *ęs* eye) meshes or interstices of a net.

දැව, *Dęwa, s.* trunk of a felled tree; timber, wood.

දැව තට්ටුව, *Dęwa-taṭṭuwa, s.* wooden floor; floor of a second story.

දැවදඬු, *Dęwadanḍu, s.* beam, log of timber.

දැවපන්නේ, *Dęwapanné, s.* saw-pit; any place where wood or timber is cut and prepared for the carpenters; sawyer or wood cutter.

දැවාන, *Dęwána, s.* crystal, [Colloq. පළිඟු *paḷingu*].

දැවි, *Dęvi, s.* burning, consuming, conflagration; spoke of a wheel.

දැවිටු, *Dęviṭu, s.* short stick of the root of the *dalbergia arborea,* used for cleaning the teeth.

දැවිල්ල, *Dęvilla, s.* burning; burning sensation over the body.

දැවිලි, *Dęvili, a.* pungent, acrid; hot.

දැවිවට, *Dęvi-waṭa, s.* (දැවි spoke, වට surrounding) rim of a wheel.

දැවීම, *Dęvíma, s.* burning: verbal noun of දවනවා *dawanawá.*

දැවු, *Dęwu, s.* burning, conflagration: *p.* burned.

දැසි, *Dęsi, s.* female slave.

දැසිදසුන්, *Dęsi-dasun, s.* slaves male and female.

දැහැ, *Dęhę, s.* removal to a distance, driving away: part. of දහනවා *dahanawá,* to remove.

දැහැටි දඬු, *Dęheṭi-danḍu, s.* the root used for cleaning the teeth: see දැවිටු *dęviṭu.*

දැහැන, *Dęhęna, s.* short incantation, or magical invocation.

දැහැම, *Dęhęma, s.* justice, righteousness, fitness, propriety; this word is from ධම්ම *dhamma.*

දැහැමිටු, *Dęhęmiṭu,* Elu form of ධර්මිෂ්ඨ *dharmmishṭha,* which see.

දැහැවිල්ල, *Dęhęvilla, s.* anger, wrath, [Colloq. තරහ *taraha*].

දෑ, *Dę,* Elu form of ද්‍රව්‍ය *drawya,* and ජාති *játi; s.* thing, jasmine, [Colloq. පිච්ච *pichcha*]; sort, class, genus; number two.

දෑකැත්ත, *Dékętta, s.* sickle, pl. දෑකැති *dékęti.*

දෑගසව්, *Dégasaw, s.* (දෙ *de* two, අග *aga* chief, සව් pupil, hearer) two chief disciples of Buddha: see අගසව් *agasaw.*

දෑත, *Déta, s.* (දෙ *de* both, අත *ata* hand) both hands; two handsful, as බුලත් දෑත *bulat-déta,* two handsful of betel.

දෑතුලේ, *Dé-tulé, ad.* between two.

දෑරඟ, *Déranga,* } *s.* gem, commonly call-
දෑරඟමිණ, *Dérangamiṇa,* } ed ජාතිරංග *játiranga;* it is not ascertained; some say the ruby; others, the crystals.

දෑලය, *Délaya, s.* both sides.

දෑවා, *Déwá, pret.* of දනවා *danawá,* to be burnt, or be on fire.

දෑවැද්ද, *Déwędda, s.* dowry.

දෑස්, *Dés,* } *s.* both eyes.
දෑස, *Désa,* }

දෙස අල, *Désa-ala, s.* plant with small edible tubers, *alocasia indica, (Araceæ);* also called රට අල *raṭa-ala.*

දෙසමන්, *Désaman, s.* arabian jasmine, *jasminum sambac,* [Colloq. පිච්ච *pichcha*].

දෙහත, *Déhata, s.* present of betel given to a priest, pl. දෙහත් *déhat.*

දෙහිඟුල්, *Déhiṅgul, s.* vermilion, [Colloq. සාදිලිංගං *sádiliṅgaṅ*].

ද්‍යු, *Dyu, s.* day.

ද්‍යුත්, *Dyut, s.* ray of light.

ද්‍යුති, *Dguti, s.* light, beauty or splendour; ray of light.

ද්‍යුතිකර, *Dyutikara, s.* (ද්‍යුති light, කර who makes) sun, [Colloq. සූර්‍ය්‍යයා *súryayá*]; dispeller of darkness, enlightener; also, polar star.

ද්‍යුපති, *Dyupati,* } *s.* (ද්‍යු day, පති lord, මණි
ද්‍යුමණි, *Dyumaṇi,* } jewel) sun, [Colloq. සූර්‍ය්‍යයා *súryayá*].

ද්‍යූත, *Dyúta, s.* gaming, playing with dice, etc.

ද්‍රව්‍ය, *Drawya, s.* wealth, property; substance, thing; the receptacle or substratum of properties; elementary substance, nine sorts of which are reckoned, viz. earth, water, fire, air, ether, time, space, soul and intellect; brass; stake, wager; drug, medicament, any thing used in medicine; anointing, plastering; lac, the animal dye; extract; gum, resin, etc, derived from vegetables; modesty, propriety; spirituous liquor.

ද්‍රව, *Drawa, s.* flight, retreat; going, motion; juice, essence; exudation; fusion, liquefaction; decoction; dropping, distilling, trickling.

ද්‍රවණ, *Drawaṇa, s.* going; dropping, trickling, exuding.

ද්‍රවන්ති, *Drawantí, s.* a river in general, [Colloq. ගඟ *gaṅga*]; tree, variety of the *banyan* or *ficus bengaliensis,* [Colloq. මීනුග *mí-nuga*].

ද්‍රව විනාශිනී, *Drawa-vináṣiní, s.* species of murunga tree, *hyperanthera moringa* or *moringa pterygosperma,* [Colloq. මුරුංගා *muruṅgá*].

ද්‍රවිණ, *Draviṇa, s.* wealth, property; substance, thing; strength, power.

ද්‍රාක්ෂා, *Drákshá, s.* grape, [Colloq. මිදි ගෙඩි *midi-geḍi*].

ද්‍රාවක, *Dráwaka, s.* wit, wag, sharp or clever man; thief: libertine, lecher; pursuer, chaser, one who causes to fly.

ද්‍රාවන, *Dráwana, s.* causing to fly or retreat; fusing; distilling.

ද්‍රාවිඩ, *Dráviḍa, s.* a Tamil or Malabar man: *a.* Dravidian or Tamil.

ද්‍රාවිඩක, *Dráviḍaka, s.* zedoary, *curcuma zerumbet,* [Colloq. හරංකහ *haraṅkaha*]; also *kaempferia galanga,* [Colloq. හිඟුරුපියලි *hiṅgurupiyali*].

ද්‍රාවිඩී, *Dráviḍí, s.* small cardamoms, [Colloq. සිහින් එන්සාල් *sihin-ensál*].

දෘක්, *Dṛik, s.* sight, view, vision, seeing; eye; knowledge, wisdom; learning, information; skill; seer, looker; wise man, one possessed of knowledge.

දෘඪ, *Dṛiḍha,* } *a.* much, exceeding; hard,
දෘඪතර, *Dṛiḍhatara,* } firm; great, powerful, able; bulky, massy.

දෘඪතරු, *Dṛiḍhataru, s.* timber tree, any tree which grows sufficiently large for timber.

දෘඪදාරු, *Dṛiḍhadáru, s.* tree, *nephelium longanum,* [Colloq. මොර *mora*].

දෘඪපාදප, *Dṛiḍhapádapa, s.* plant, *cortulana laburnifolia.*

දෘඪවෘන්ද, *Dṛiḍhavṛinda, s.* nutmeg tree, *myristica fragrans,* [Colloq. සාදික්කා *sádikká*].

දෘඪාංඝ්‍රික, *Dṛiḍháṅghrika, s.* tree, *acacia* of which there are several species and varieties in Ceylon, [Colloq. සිනිය *síniya,* රත්කිහිරි *rat-kihiri*].

දෘශ්, *Dṛiṣ,* see දෘක් *dṛik.*

දෘශ්‍ය, *Dṛiṣya, a.* appearing, visible.

දෘශ්‍යමාන, *Dṛiṣyamána, p.* being seen, apparent, visible.

දෘශද්, *Dṛiṣad, s.* stone, rock, [Colloq. ගල *gala*].

දෘශා, *Dṛiṣá,* see දෘක් *dṛik.*

දෘෂ්ට, *Dṛishṭa, part.* seen, visible, apparent.

දෘෂ්ටකූට, *Dṛishṭa-kúṭa, s.* riddle, enigma.

දෘෂ්ටගතික, *Dṛishṭa-gatika, s.* (දෘෂ්ට seeing or vision, used here metaphorically for religious illumination of a false kind, heresy, ගති from ගත *gata* gone, ක nominal affix) heretic.

දෘෂ්ට ධර්ම්ම, *Dṛishṭa-dharmma, s.* (දෘෂ්ට visible, ධර්ම්ම nature) materiality, corporeality; present state of being; manhood.

දෘෂ්ටාන්ත, *Dṛishṭánta, s.* (දෘෂ්ට *dṛishṭa* seen, අන්ත *anta* end) an apposite argument, illustration, but especially the apologues introduced in the *artha kathás,* or commentaries on the professed original writings of Buddha, as the experienced result of the doctrine or moral laid down in the text; [Colloq. උදාහරණය *udáharaṇaya*]; death, dying, [Colloquial: මරණය *maraṇaya*]; science, [Colloq. ශාස්ත්‍රය *ṣástraya*].

දෘෂ්ටි, *Drishṭi*, s. eye; sight, seeing; wisdom, knowledge; mental, perception; religious illumination; it is usually applied to scepticism as to the established faith.

දෘෂ්ටිජාල, *Drishṭijála*, s. (දෘෂ්ටි and ජාල net or web) the various religious and philosophical sects which existed in the days of Buddha and which were combated by him.

දෘෂ්ටෞඝය, *Drishṭaughaya*, s. (දෘෂ්ට *drishṭa* visible, ඕඝ *ógha* torrent, used here metaphorically for passion) one of the four chief passions by which human nature is governed; it means the passions which are produced by objects that are seen, viz. the lust of the eye; heresy.

දෘෂ්ට්‍යනුගතික, *Drishṭyanugatika*, s. (දෘෂ්ටි *drishṭi* vision, sight, used here metaphorically for heresy, අනු *anu* with, ගති going, ක nominal affix) heretic.

දෘෂ්ට්‍යාශ්‍රවය, *Drisṭyáṣrawaya*, s, (දෘෂ්ටි *drishṭi* sight seeing. ආශ්‍රව *áṣrawa* evil propensity) one of the four evil passions which adhere to human nature, viz. the evil which enters by the eye or sight, the lust of the eye; heresy.

ද්‍රුත, *Druta*, a. quick, swift.

ද්‍රුම, *Druma*, s. tree in general, [Colloq. ගහ *gaha*]; name of Kuvéra the Indian Plutus.

ද්‍රුමනඛ, *Druma-nakha*. s. (ද්‍රුම tree, නඛ finger nail) thorn, [Colloq. කටුව *kaṭuwa*].

ද්‍රුමව්‍යාධි, *Druma-wyádhi*,
ද්‍රුමාමය, *Drumámaya*, } s. (ද්‍රුම tree, ව්‍යාධි disease, ආමය *ámaya* sickness) lac, animal dye.

ද්‍රුමොත්පල, *Drumotpala*, s. rock-rose plant, *cistus labatus;* also *cochlospermum gossypium*, [Colloq. කිණිහිරිය *kiṇihiriya*].

ද්‍රුහණ, *Druhaṇa*,
ද්‍රුහිණ, *Druhiṇa*, } s. name of Brahma.

ද්‍රෙක්කාණ, *Drekkáṇa*, s. regent of one-third of a planetary sign, the *Decanus* of European astrology.

ද්‍රෝණ, *Dróṇa*, s. corn measure, containing about seven pounds eleven ounces avoirdupois; proper name, military preceptor of the Páṇḍawas; raven, carrion crow; scorpion; any oval vessel made of wood. stone, etc., in the shape of a boat, and used for holding or pouring out water; bathing tub, bathing vessel; basket; watering pot, etc.; a trough or rack for feeding cattle; country so called; river so called; name of a noted warrior, the enemy of Vishṇu.

ද්‍රෝණපුෂ්පි, *Dróṇa-pushpí*, s. plant, *leucas zeylanica*, [Colloq. ගැටතුඹ *geṭa-tumba*].

ද්‍රෝණමුඛය, *Dróṇa-mukhaya*, s. harbour, place for landing goods; capital of a district; chief of four hundred villages.

ද්‍රෝණිකා, *Dróṇiká*, s. indigo plant, [Colloq. අවරි *awari*].

ද්‍රෝහ, *Dróha*, s. mischief, malice; trespass, injury; treachery.

ද්‍රෝහචින්තන, *Dróha-chintana*, s. (ද්‍රෝහ and චින්තන thinking) injurious design, malice prepense.

ද්‍රෝහී, *Dróhí*, a. malicious, rebellious, hurting, ungrateful.

ද්වන්ද්ව, *Dwandwa*,
ද්වන්ද, *Dwanda*, } s. pair, brace, couple of animals, male and female; union of the sexes or coupling; strife, dispute; secret; form of grammatical combination, uniting two or more words in the same case; sign of the zodiac Gemini; sort of disease, complication of two disorders.

ද්වය, *Dwaya*, s. pair, couple, two.

ද්වා, *Dwá*, ad. two, [Colloq. දෙක *deka*].

ද්වාකාර, *Dwákára*, a. double, twofold, in a twofold manner.

ද්වාත්‍රිංශත්, *Dwátrinṣat*, ad. thirtytwo, [Colloq. තිස් දෙක *tisdeka*].

ද්වාදශ, *Dwádaṣa*, a. twelve, [Colloq. දොළහ *doḷaha*].

ද්වාදශකර, *Dwádaṣa-kara*,
ද්වාදශලෝචන, *Dwádaṣa-lóchana*, } s. (ද්වාදශ and කර hand, ලෝචන eye) name of Kártikéya, usually called Kataragama-deviyó, the Indian Mars, alluding to his having twelve hands which holds twelve weapons of war; also, name of Vṛihaspati.

ද්වාදශාක්ෂ, *Dwádaṣáksha*, s. (ද්වාදශ *dwádaṣa* twelve, අක්ෂ *aksha* eye) the above, alluding to his having six hands and twelve eyes; name of Buddha, alluding probably to his twelve names or epithets expressive of his twelve chief attributes.

ද්වාදශාඞ්ගය, *Dwádaṣáńgaya*,
ද්වාදශාත්මය, *Dwádaṣátmaya*, } s. (ද්වාදශ *dwádaṣa* twelve, අඞ්ග *ańga* mode, manner, ආත්ම *átma* soul or identity) the sun; probably alluding to his being indentified with the twelve months of the year, in each of which periods he is supposed to undergo some change: *a.* ද්වාදශාත්මක *dwádaṣátmaka*.

ද්වාපර, *Dwápara*, *s.* (ද්වා for ද්වි *dwi* two, පර after, subsequent) third of the four Yugas or great periods of the world, comprising 864,000 years; doubt, uncertainty.

ද්වාර, *Dwára*, *s.* door, gate, entrance, passage; gateway; way, means, medium.

ද්වාරපාලයා, *Dwára-pálayá*, *s.* (ද්වාර and පාල who keeps, යා pers. aff.) doorkeeper, warder, porter

ද්වාරයන්ත්‍ර, *Dwára-yantra*, *s.* (ද්වාර and යන්ත්‍ර instrument) lock, bolt.

ද්වි, *Dwi*, *a.* two, dual.

ද්විගුණ, *Dwiguṇa*, *a.* (ද්වි two, ගුණ form) two-fold.

ද්විජ, *Dwija*, *s.* (ද්වි twice, ජ born) among the Hindus a man of the Brahmin caste, or more properly a Brahmin, alluding to his second birth at the time of his investiture with the sacred string; any oviparous animal, as a bird, snake, fish, etc. tooth; coriander seed, [Colloq. කොත්තමල්ලි *kottamalli*]: *a.* twice born, oviparous, born first in the shell and in the second instance produced from the shell.

ද්විජප්‍රිය, *Dwijapriya*, *s.* creeping plant, *sarcostemma Brunonianum*, [Colloq. මුවකිරිය *muwakíriya*].

ද්විජමාංසය, *Dwijamáṇsaya*, *s.* (ද්විජ tooth, මාංසය flesh) gums.

ද්විජවෘක්ෂ, *Dwija-vṛiksha*, *s.* tree: see කැල *kḛla*.

ද්විජිහ්ව, *Dwijihwa*, *s.* (ද්වි two, ජිහ්ව tongue) serpent, snake in general, [Colloq. සර්පයා *sarpayá*]; slanderer, backbiter; informer, whisperer, [Coll: කේලාම්කියන්නා *kélámkiyanná*].

ද්විත්වරූප, *Dwitwa-rúpa*. *s.* In Sandhi doubling final letter instead of initial vowel of next word.

ද්විතීය, *Dwitíya*, *a.* second, secondary, [Colloq. දෙවෙනි *deweni*].

ද්විතීයධ්‍යානය, *Dwitíyadhyánaya*, *s.* (ද්විතීය second, ධ්‍යාන *dhyána* devout meditation) the second of the four degrees or stages into which dhyána is divided as practised by religious devotees with the view of obtaining Nirváṇa or the final emancipation of the soul: according to the principles laid down for the performance of this stage of dhyána, the devotee having fully accomplished the ප්‍රථමධ්‍යාන *prathama-dhyána*, or first dhyána, and remaining still in a state of abstract and undisturbed meditation, with the single object of his consideration, namely Nirváṇa, fully in view, and being freed from all mental discussions on the nature and qualities of things and all doubt respecting their real or relative properties, and having so far subdued the passions as to be free from wish and desire, the mind must be filled with calm undisturbed tranquillity and joy at the certain prospect of Nirváṇa or final emancipation.

ද්විතීයවාක්‍යය, *Dwitíya-wákyaya*, *s.* Deuteronomy.

ද්විධා, *Dwidhá*, *ad.* of two kinds; in two ways,

ද්විධාගති, *Dwidhágati*, *s.* (ද්විධා and ගති going) crocodile, [Colloq. කිඹුලා *kimbulá*]; any amphibious animal.

ද්විප, *Dwipa*, *s.* (ද්වි two, ප who drinks) elephant, so called in allusion to his manner of drinking, viz. imbibing fluids in the first instance by his trunk, and thence conveying them to his mouth, [Colloq. ඇතා *ḛtá*]; iron-wood tree, *mesua ferrea*, [Colloq. නාගහ *ná-gaha*].

ද්විපද, *Dwipada*, } *s.* (ද්වි and පාද foot) man; any
ද්විපාද, *Dwipáda*, } biped.

ද්විපාදෝත්තම, *Dwipádóttama*, *s.* (ද්විපාද *dwipáda* man, උත්තම pre-eminent, chief) epithet of Buddha, alluding to his being the chief of mankind, in respect both to his physical, moral and religious properties. (Páli form, දිපදුත්තම *dipaduttama.*)

ද්විප්‍රකාර, *Dwiprakára*, *a.* two-fold, in a two fold manner.

ද්විමාතෘජ, *Dwimátraja*, *s.* (ද්වි two, මාතෘ mother, ජ born) name of Ganésa, the god of wisdom, alluding to the fable of his being born of the goddess Párvati, but not in the usual way, being produced from the scurf of her body.

ද්විමුඛ, *Dwimukha*, *s.* (ද්වි and මුඛ mouth) snake, serpent, [Colloq. සර්පයා *sarpayá*].

ද්විරද, *Dwirada*, *s.* (ද්වි and රද tooth) elephant, [Colloq. ඇතා *ḛtá*].

ද්විරදකර, *Dwiradakara*, *s.* (ද්විරද elephant, කර arm) elephant's trunk, [Colloq. ඇතාගේ හොඬ *ḛtágé hoṇḍa*].

ද්විරසනා, *Dwirasaná*, *s.* (ද්වි two, රසනා tongue) snake, serpent, alluding to its having a double or forked tongue.

ද්විරේඵ, *Dwirepha*, *s.* large black bee, *apis terrestris*, [Colloq. බමරා *bamará*].

ද්විවිධ, *Dwividha*, see ද්විප්‍රකාර *dwiprakára*.

ද්විවිධශීල, *Dwividha-ṣíla*, *s.* (ද්විවිධ two sorts, ශීල religious ordinance) the two divisions of religious ordinances, viz. චාරිත්ත *cháritta* and වාරිත්ත *wáritta*: see ශීල *ṣíla*.

ද්විශීර්ෂක, *Dwiṣírshaka*, *s.* (ද්වි two, ශීර්ෂ head, ක pers. aff.) a god or deity in general, name of Agni the god of fire, who is supposed to have two faces or mouths, viz. that of the priest and that of fire, by which the sacrifices are consumed.

ද්විෂත්, *Dwishat*, *s.* enemy, [Colloq. සතුරා *saturá*]: *a.* hostile, inimical, hating, detesting.

ද්විසහස්‍රාක්ෂ, *Dwisahasráksha*, *s.* (ද්විසහස්‍ර two thousand, අක්ෂ eye) name of Ṣakra or Indra the regent of the skies or visible heavens, or this deity considered as a personification of the firmament or region of the stars; or the name may allude to the fable of his being covered by obscene marks, in consequence of a curse from Gautama a noted ascetic, but the saint relenting, they were subsequently changed to eyes; name of Anantayá king of Nága-lóka and regent of the serpent race.

ද්වීපය, *Dwípaya*, *s.* island, any land surrounded by water; the word is hence applied to the seven grand divisions of the terrestrial world, each of these being separated from the rest by a peculiar and circumambient ocean; the seven dwípas, reckoning from the centre one, are Jambu, Kusa, Plaksha, Sálmalí, Krauncha, Sáka and Pushkara; the central dwípa or the known continent is again portioned into ten divisions likewise termed dwípas, viz. Kuru, Chandra, Varuṇa, Saumya, Nága, Kumáriká, Gabhastimán, Támraparṇí, Kaséru and Indra; tiger's skin.

ද්වීපිශත්‍රු, *Dwípi-ṣatru*, *s.* creeping plant, *asparagus falcatus*, [Colloq. හාතාවාරිය *hátáwáriya*].

ද්වීපී, *Dwípi*, *s.* islander, tiger, panther.

ද්වේගති, *Dwégati*, *s.* (ද්වි *dwi* two, ගති who goes) any amphibious animal; crocodile, [Colloq. කිඹුලා *kimbulá*].

ද්වේෂ, *Dwésha*, *s.* hate, enmity; impatience at another's success, envy.

ද්වේෂකරණවා, *Dwéshakaraṇawá*, *v.* to hate.

ද්වේෂී, *Dwéshí*, *s.* enemy, adversary, opponent, [Colloq. සතුරා *saturá*].

ද්වෛධීකරණ, *Dwaidhíkaraṇa*, *s.* making two, separating.

ධ

The foregoing letter aspirated; it is generally expressed by dh.

ධජ, *Dhaja*, see ධජය *dhajaya*.

ධජපතාකය, *Dhajapatákaya*, *s.* flag, banner, weather cock.

ධජය, *Dhajaya*, *s.* flag, banner, colour, standard, [Colloq. කොඩිය *koḍiya*].

ධට, *Dhaṭa*, *s.* pair of scales, balance; sign of Zodiac (Libra).

ධටී, *Dhaṭí*, *s.* piece of old cloth worn round the middle.

ධන්‍ය, *Dhanya*, *a.* fortunate, lucky, good; virtuous, well fated.

ධන්‍යා, *Dhanyá*, } *s.* plant, *emblic myrobalan*,
ධන්‍යාක, *Dhanyáka*, } *phyllanthus emblica*, [Colloq. නෙල්ලි *nelli*]; coriander, *coriandrum sativum*, [Colloq. කොත්තමල්ලි *kottamalli*]; nurse.

ධන්ව, *Dhanwa*, *s.* bow, [Colloq. දුන්න *dunna*].

ධන්වයවාස, *Dhanwayawása*, } *s.* twining plant,
ධන්වයාස, *Dhanwayása*, } *tragia involucrata*, [Colloq. වැල්කහඹිලියා *wel-kahambiliyá*].

ධන්වී, *Dhanví*, *s.* name of Arjuna alluding to his use of the bow; archer, bow-man, man armed with a bow.

ධන, *Dhana*, *s.* property of any description, thing, substance, wealth; a term of endearment.

ධනක, *Dhanaka*, see අගිල් *agil*.

ධනකේලි, *Dhanakéli*, *s.* (ධන wealth, කේලි who sports) name of Kuvéra the Indian Plutus.

ධනගර්විත, *Dhanagarvita*, *a.* purse-proud.

ධනඤ්ජය, *Dhanañjaya*, *s.* (ධන and ජය *jaya* victory) fire; deity of fire; name of Arjuna; one of the nágas or serpents of Pátála; one of the five vital airs, that which is supposed to fatten; tree, *pentaptera arjuna;* according to others *terminalia glabra*, [Colloq. කුඹුක් *kumbuk*]; plant, screw pine, *pandanus fascicularis*, [Colloq. මූදුකෙයියා *múdukeyiyá*].

ධනද, *Dhanada*, *s.* (ධන and දා *dá* to give) beneficent liberal person, one who gives much in charity; name of Kuvéra the Indian Plutus or god of wealth.

ධනදණ්ඩනය, *Dhana-daṇḍanaya*, *s.* (ධන property, දණ්ඩනය punishment) fine, confiscation of goods.

ධනදර්ප, *Dhana-darpa*, *s.* pride of wealth.

ධනදාක්ෂි, *Dhanadákshi*, *s.* (ධනද *dhanada* Kuvéra, අක්ෂි *akshi*, eye) the seed of the creeping plant, *cæsalpinia bonduc*, [Colloq. කුඹුරුවැල් *kumburuwel*], which is said to resemble the eye of Kuvéra or any demon.

ධනදානුජ, *Dhanadánuja*, *s.* (ධනද *dhanada* and අනුජ *anuja* younger brother) younger brother of Kuvéra, name of Rávaṇa.

ධනධාරි, *Dhanadhári*, *s.* (ධන wealth, ධාරි what bears) the earth, [Colloq. පොළව *poḷawa*].

ධනපති, *Dhanapati*, *s.* (ධන riches, පති master or lord) name of Kuvéra, the god of wealth.

ධනපිශාචිකා, *Dhana-piṣáchiká*, *s.* (ධන wealth, පිශාචි *piṣáchí* female demon, කන් *kan* affix) avarice, thirst of wealth.

ධනවත්, *Dhanawat*, } *a.* rich, wealthy, opulent.
ධනවන්ත, *Dhanawanta*, }

ධනවන්තකම, *Dhanawantakama*, *s.* wealth, opulence.

ධනහරී, *Dhanaharí*, *s.* sort of perfume made from the plant *kaempferia galanga*, [Colloq. හිඟුරු පියලි *hiṇgurupiyali*].

ධනාධිප, *Dhanádhipa*, *s.* (ධන *dhana* wealth, අධිප *adhipa* lord) name of Kuvéra the god of wealth.

ධනාශා, *Dhanáṣá*, *s.* (ධන *dhana* and ආශා *áṣá* wish) avarice, thirst of riches, covetousness.

ධනික, *Dhanika*, *s.* coriander, [Colloq. කොත්තමල්ලි *kottamalli*]; husband: *a.* pious. virtuous, excellent; rich, opulent.

ධනිකා, *Dhaniká*, *s.* virtuous or excellent woman; wife, young woman; tree, *echites antidysenterica*, [Colloq. කෙළිඳ *kelinda*].

ධනිෂ්ඨා, *Dhanishthá*, *s.* the twenty-fourth lunar mansion, [Colloq. දෙනට *denaṭa*]; it comprises four stars, apparently, *alpha*, *beta*, *gamma*, *delta*, Delphini, and is figured by a native drum usually called a tom tom.

ධනී, *Dhaní*, *s.* rich or opulent man.

ධනිය, *Dhaniya*, } *s.* coriander seed, *coriandrum*
ධනියක, *Dhaníyaka*, } *sativum*, [Colloq. කොත්තමල්ලි *kottamalli*].

ධනු, *Dhanu*, *s.* bow, [Colloq. දුන්න *dunna*]; sign of the Zodiac Sagittarius; tree, *Nephelium Longana*, [Colloq. මොර *mora*]: marking nut plant, *semicarpus anacardium*.

ධනුධර, *Dhanudhara*, Páli form of ධනුර්ධර *dhanurdhara*, which see.

ධනුර්ධර, *Dhanurdhara*, *s.* (ධනුස් *dhanus* bow, ධර *dhara* who possesses) archer, one armed with a bow, Vẹddá.

ධනුර්වෘක්ෂ, *Dhanurvṛiksha*, *s.* plant, *hoya reticulata;* bambu, *bambusa vulgaris*, [Colloq. උණගස් *unagas*].

ධනුශ්ශිල්පය, *Dhanuṣṣilpaya*, *s.* (ධනුස් *dhanus* bow, ශිල්ප *ṣilpa* art) archery.

ධනුශ්‍රේණි, *Dhanuṣréṇi*, *s.* plant, *sanseviera zeylanica*, [Colloq. නියඳ *niyandu*].

ධනුස්, *Dhanus*, see ධනු *dhanu*.

ධනේශ්වර, *Dhanéṣwara*, *s.* (ධන *dhana* riches ඊශ්වර *íṣwara* chief) name of Kuvéra, the Indian god of wealth.

ධනේශ, *Dhanéṣa*, see ධනේශ්වර *dhanéṣwara*.

ධනේශදික්, *Dhanéṣadik*, *s.* (ධන *dhana* and ඊශ *íṣa* chief or lord, දික් quarter or region) north; the name alludes to this quarter being under the government of Kuvéra the Indian Plutus.

ධම්ම, *Dhamma*, Páli form of ධර්ම *dharma*.

ධම්ම සභා, *Dhamma-sabhá*, *s.* (ධම්ම baṇa, සභා assembly) assembly in which the baṇa is read, a baṇa maḍuwa.

ධම්මිල්ල, *Dhammilla*, *s.* braided hair.

ධම්සක්, *Dhamsak*, corrupt form of දම්සක් *damsak*, which see.

ධම් සෙනෙවි, *Dham-senevi*, *s.* corrupt form of දම් සෙනෙවි *dam-senevi*, priest, but the word chiefly refers to the priest who accompanied Buddha and was always on his right hand.

ධමන්‍ය, *Dhamanya*, *s.* coral tree, *erythrina indica*, [Colloq. එරබදු *erabadu*]; vein, artery.

ධමන, *Dhamana*, *s.* reed, *arundo tibialis;* blowing (a wind instrument); one who blows a bellows, trumpet etc.: *a.* cruel, harsh,

ධමනී, *Dhamaní*, *s.* any tubular vessel of the body, as a vein, nerve, etc.; neck; turmeric; sort of perfume.

ධර්ම, *Dharma*, } *s.* righteousness; justice, equity;
ධර්ම්ම, *Dharmma*, } virtue, moral and religious merit; fitness, propriety; nature, proper or natural state or disposition; innocence, innoxiousness; any peculiar or prescribed practice or duty, thus giving alms etc. is the dharma of a house holder, administering justice the dharma of a king, attention to the study and practice of religion, is the dharma of a priest; baṇa including all the instructions, sermons and addresses of Buddha whether addressed to gods, Brahmas, or men; name of Yama, regent of the dead; virtue personified; bull of Ṣiva as a personification of virtue.

ධර්ම කථාව, *Dharma-katháwa*, *s.* (ධර්ම baṇa, කථාව history) sacred history, but chiefly the historical narratives delivered by Buddha.

ධර්මකථික, *Dharma-kathika*, *s.* (ධර්ම and කථික orator) priest very clever in reading or pronouncing the baṇa.

ධර්මගුණය, *Dharma-guṇaya*, *s.* virtue, moral worth, excellency, merit.

ධර්මචක්‍රය, *Dharma-chakraya*, *s.* (ධර්ම and චක්‍රය law) laws contained in the whole of the sacred and moral discourses delivered by Buddha; also, name of a Játaka which was delivered by Buddha to a noted Ṛishi or holy person.

ධර්මතාවය, *Dharmatáwaya*, *s.* righteousness; equity, justice; religious merit; effect, result, consequence; the natural result of any state or process of events.

ධර්මදේශනාව, *Dharma-déṣanáwa*, *s.* (ධර්ම and දේශනාව discourse) sermons delivered by Buddha to gods, Brahmas, and men.

ධර්මධ්වජ, *Dharmadhwaja*, *s.* (ධර්ම piety, ධ්වජ emblem) one having every mark of oriental piety, viz. the practices of an ascetic; a religious hypocrite or impostor, one who makes a livelihood by assumed devotion.

ධර්මපත්තන, *Dharma-pattana*, *s.* pepper, [Colloq. ගම්මිරිස් *gammiris*]; name of an Indian district, celebrated for the growth of pepper.

ධර්මය, *Dharmaya*, see plural ධර්ම *dharma*.

ධර්මරත්නය, *Dharmaratnaya*, *s.* (ධර්ම sacred, රත්න *ratna* gem) the baṇa or sermons of Buddha which he delivered to gods, Brahmas, and men; the word applies to them in their collective form and is synonymous with the term scripture.

ධර්මරාජ, *Dharmarája*, *s.* (ධර්ම justice, equity, රාජ king) name of Yama, regent of the dead and the final judge of the actions of men; deified saint; king in general; name of Buddha, as the author and fulfiller of the baṇa.

ධර්මවිනය, *Dharma-vinaya*, *s.* doctrinal portions of the Tripiṭaka and rules of discipline for the priesthood.

ධර්මශාස්ත්‍රය, *Dharma-ṣástraya*, *s.* (ධර්ම and ශාස්ත්‍රය treatise) code of laws; study of the baṇa so as to be able to read and expound it.

ධර්මශාලාව, *Dharma-ṣáláwa*, *s*, (ධර්ම and ශාලාව hall) court of justice; tribunal; baṇa maḍuwa, place where the baṇa is read and expounded.

ධර්මශීල, *Dharma-ṣíla*, *a.* (ධර්ම and ශීල *ṣíla* attached to) virtuous, just, pious.

ධර්මශ්‍රවණය, *Dharmaṣrawaṇaya*, *s.* the hearing of baṇa.

ධර්මස්කන්ධය, *Dharmaskandhaya*, *s.* the whole collection of Buddha's doctrines, discourses and precepts; division of the Dharma.

ධර්මසංහිතාව, *Dharma-saṇhitáwa*, *s.* code of laws.

ධර්මසම්මර්ෂණය, *Dharma-sammarshaṇaya*, *s.* study of the baṇa; or gaining a thorough knowledge of it.

ධර්මාභිසමය, *Dharmábhisamaya*, *s.* (ධර්ම *dharma* baṇa, අභිසමය *abhisamaya* great gain) advantages of hearing the baṇa, the obtaining Nirwáṇa by hearing the baṇa. In his Páli Dictionary Childers explains, ධම්මාභිසමය *dhammábhisamaya*, as "Comprehension of truth, conversion."

ධර්මාමෘත, *Dharmámṛita*, *s.* (ධර්ම *dharma* baṇa, අමෘත *amṛita* nectar) epithet of the baṇa, expressive of its excellencies.

ධර්මිෂ්ඨ, *Dharmmishṭha*, *a.* righteous, holy, virtuous, pious, just.

ධර්මිෂ්ඨකම, *Dharmmishṭhakama*, *s.* righteousness, holiness, justice.

ධර්මිෂ්ඨයා, *Dharmmishṭhayá*, *s.* righteous man.

ධර්ම්‍ය, *Dharmya*, *s.* conformable or according to justice or morality, obtainable by virtue or justice.

ධර්ෂණ, *Dharshaṇa*, *s.* contumely, contempt; copulation.

ධර්ෂිණී, *Dharshiṇí*, *s.* dishonest or unchaste woman.

ධර්ෂිත, *Dharshita*, *s.* cohabitation.

ධර්ෂිතා, *Dharshitá*, *s.* unchaste woman.

ධරණ, *Dharaṇa*, *a.* bearing, upholding, sustaining, possessing.

ධරණවා, *Dharaṇawá*, *v.* corruptly for දරණවා *daraṇawá*, to bear, to hold, to contain, to support.

ධරණී, *Dharaṇí*, *s.* the earth, [Colloq. පොළව *poḷawa*].

ධරණීකීලක, *Dharaṇí-kílaka*, *s.* (ධරණී and කීලක bolt or pin) mountain, [Colloq. කන්ද *kanda*].

ධරණීධර, *Dharaṇídhara*, *s.* (ධරණී and ධර who sustains) name of Vishṇu; mountain.

ධරණීප්ලව, *Dharaṇí-plawa*, *s.* (ධරණී and ප්ලව what swims) that in which the earth floats, the ocean.

ධරණීපූර, *Dharṇí-púra*, *s.* (ධරණී and පූර to surround) sea, ocean, [Colloq. මුහුද *muhuda*].

ධරණීශ්වර, *Dharaṇíṣwara*, *s.* (ධරණී earth, ඊශ්වර lord) lord of the earth, king, monarch, [Colloq. රජ *raja*].

ධරණීසුතා, *Dharaṇí-sutá*, *s.* (ධරණී and සුතා daughter) the earth-born, name of Sítá the wife of Ráma, alluding to her being turned up from the soil by a plough as Janaka was ploughing a spot to prepare it for a sacrifice.

ධරා, *Dhará*, *s.* earth; mountain.

ධරාත්මජ, *Dharátmaja*, *s.* (ධරා earth, ආත්මජ *átmaja* son) planet Mars or its regent.

ධරාධර, *Dharádhara*, see ධරණීධර *dharaṇídhara*.

ධරාසූනු, *Dhará-súnu*, *s.* (ධරා and සූනු son) name of the regent of the planet Mars, alluding to his being turned up from the earth by a plough.

ධරිත්‍රී, *Dharitrí*, *s.* the earth, [Colloq. පොළව *polawa*].

ධරුණ, *Dharuṇa*, *s.* name of Brahma; Swarga the paradise of the gods; water; opinion; conception.

ධව, *Dhawa*, *s.* man, husband; rogue; cheat; small flowering tree, *Woodfordia floribunda*, [Colloq. මලිත *malita*]; another tree, *bauhinia racemosa*, [Colloq. මයිල *mayila*].

ධවල, *Dhawala*, *s.* white, [Colloq. සුදු *suda*]; conch shell; white pepper: *a.* white, handsome, beautiful.

ධවලච්ඡත්‍රය, *Dhawalachchhatraya*, *s.* (ධවල white, ඡත්‍රය umbrella) white umbrella used only by kings and the sacredotal order.

ධවලා, *Dhawalá*, *s.* white cow.

ධවලාතපත්‍රය, *Dhawaláta-patraya*, see ධවලච්ඡත්‍රය *dhawalachchhatraya*.

ධාතකී, *Dhátakí*, *s.* tree, [Colloq. මයිල *mayila*]: see ධව *dhawa*.

ධාතා, *Dhátá*, *s.* name of Brahma; bearer, carrier.

ධාතු, *Dhátu*, *s.* Budhistical relic; grammatical root; principle or humour of the body, as phlegm wind and bile; any constituent part of the body, as blood, flesh etc.; primary or elementary substance, viz. earth, water, fire, air and ákáṣa or atmosphere; the property of a primary element, as odour, colour, flavour, touch, and sound; an organ of sense; a mineral or fossil; metal.

ධාතුක, *Dhátuka*, *s.* mineral, fossil, metal.

ධාතුකාශීශ, *Dhátukáṣíṣa*, *s.* (ධාතු mineral කාශීශ green sulphate) red sulphate of iron.

ධාතුගර්භ, *Dhátu-garbha*, see දාගැබ *dágeba*.

ධාතුප, *Dhátupa*, *s.* (ධාතු essential constituent of the body, ප what nourishes) the elementary juice or chyle.

ධාතුපුෂ්පිකා, *Dhátu-pushpiká*, *s.* tree, [Colloq. මයිල *mayila*]: see ධව *dhawa*.

ධාත්‍රී, *Dhátri*, *s.* mother, foster mother; tree, *emblic myrobalan*, [Colloq. නෙල්ලි *nelli*]: *a.* fostering, nourishing; having, containing, possessing.

ධාතෘ, *Dhátṛi*, *s.* name of Brahma; title of Vishṇu; father, parent.

ධාන්‍ය, *Dhánya*, *s.* corn in general, but especially rice, *oryza sativa*, of which an endless variety is cultivated in India; coriander.

ධාන්‍යක, *Dhányaka*, *s.* coriander, *coriandrum sativum*, [Colloq. කොත්තමල්ලි *kottamalli*].

ධාන්‍යකෝෂ්ඨක, *Dhánya-kóshṭhaka*, *s.* granary, [Colloq. අටුව *aṭuwa*].

ධාන්‍යගන්ධ, *Dhánya-gandha*, *s.* coriander seed, [Colloq. කොත්තමල්ලි *kottamalli*].

ධාන්‍යමාය. *Dhányamáya*, *s.* (ධාන්‍ය corn, මා *má* to measure) corn seller or merchant.

ධාන්‍යමාෂ, *Dhányamásha*, *s.* plant yielding beans, *dolichos* or *vigna catjang*, [Colloq. ලිමෑ *límẹ*].

ධාන්‍යශීර්ෂක, *Dhánya-ṣírshaka*, *s.* (ධාන්‍ය corn, ශීර්ෂක top or head) ear or spike of corn.

ධාන්‍යාම්ල, *Dhányámla*, *s.* sour gruel made of the fermentation of rice water.

ධානා, *Dháná*, *s.* fried barley or rice, [Colloq. බැදි යව *bẹdi-yawa*]; coriander, *coriandrum sativum*, [Colloq. කොත්තමල්ලි *kottamalli*]; grain fried or reduced to powder.

ධානී, *Dhání*, *s.* coriander; granary, receptacle; site of a habitation; what has or contains, as රාජධානී *rájadhání*, royal capital, having the king's presence.

ධාම, *Dháma*, *s.* body; house, dwelling; dignity, consequence; light; ray of light.

ධාමනිධි, *Dháma-nidhi*, *s.* (ධාම ray of light, නිධි what contains, treasure) sun, [Colloq. සූර්යයා *súryaya*].

ධාමාර්ගව, *Dhámárgawa*, *s.* common weed, *achyranthes aspera*, [Colloq. ගස් කරල්හැබ *gas-karalhẹba*]; plant, kind of Ghosa with white flowers, [Colloq. වැටකොළු *wẹṭakoḷu*].

ධාය්‍යා, *Dháyyá*, *s.* a magical invocation to be repeated when lighting a fire.

ධාර්‍ය, *Dhárya*, *part.* borne, upheld or contained.

ධාර, *Dhára*, *s.* sort of stone; debt; slight sprinkling rain; frost; end, bound, line or limit; deep place, depth.

ධාරණ, *Dhárana*, *s.* holding, having, supporting, upholding, keeping, maintaining; retention of memory.

ධාරණයකරගන්නවා, *Dháraṇaya-karagannawá*, *v.* to hold; to maintain, to retain in memory.

ධාරා, *Dhárá*, *s.* horse's pace, as a trot or canter etc.; van of an army; sharp edge of a sword or of any cutting instrument; distillation, dripping, oozing or issuing of any substance by drops;

offspring; leak or flaw, hole in a pitcher; excellence; wheel of a carriage; garden wall or fence; hedge; edge of a mountain; quantity; multitude; heavy shower; plant, *tinospora cordifolia*, [Colloq. රසකිඳ *rasakinda*].

ධාරාධර, *Dhárádhara*, *s.* (ධාරා rain, edge, ධර what has) cloud; sword.

ධාරානිපාත, *Dháránipáta*, *s.* raining, streaming as rain, dropping as rain; heavy fall of rain.

ධාරාව, *Dhárawa*, *s.* issue, flow, current: see ධාරා *dhárá*.

ධාරි, *Dhári*, *s.* bearer, holder, sustainer, container.

ධාවන්ති, *Dháwantí*, *s.* plant, [Colloq. පුස්වැන්න *puswenna*].

ධාවන, *Dháwana*, *s.* nutmeg tree, *myristica fragrans*, [Colloq. සාදික්කා *sádikká*].

ධාවනය, *Dháwanaya*, *s.* going, motion; running; cleansing, purifying.

ධාවනයකරණවා, *Dháwanaya-karanawá*, *v.* to run.

ධාවනි, *Dháwani*, *s.* creeping plant, *hedysarum lagopodioides*; prickly night shade, *solanum jacquini*, [Colloq. කටුවැල්බටු *katuwelbatu*].

ධික්, *Dhik*, *ind.* prefix, implying contempt, disgrace; fie, shame etc.

ධික්කාර, *Dhikkára*, *s.* (ධික් fie, කාර making) disrespect, reproach, censure, contempt.

ධික්කෘත, *Dhikkrita*, *s.* (ධික් and කෘත done, made) cursed, reproached, reviled, censured, condemned.

ධිෂ්ණ්‍යපති, *Dhishnyapati*, *s.* moon, [Colloq. හඳ *handa*].

ධිෂණ, *Dhishana*, *s.* name of Vrihaspati the regent of the planet Jupiter and teacher of the gods; any ácharya or preceptor, pandit.

ධිෂණා *Dhishaná*, *s.* understanding, intellect, [Coll: ඥානය *jñánaya*].

ධී, *Dhí*, *s.* understanding, intellect, knowledge.

ධීත්‍රුව, *Dhítruwa*, *s.* daughter, corrupt form of දුහිතෘ *duhitri*.

ධීන්ද්‍රිය, *Dhíndriya*, *s.* (ධී intellect, ඉන්ද්‍රිය *indriya* organ of sense in general) intellectual organ, as the mind, eye, ear, nose, tongue, and skin.

ධීමත්, *Dhímat*, *a.* sensible, wise, learned.

ධීමාන්, *Dhímán*, *s.* (ධී knowledge, මාන් possessive personal aff.) name of Vrihaspati the preceptor of the gods.

ධීර, *Dhíra*, *s.* pandit, learned man, scholar; saffron; tree, *kokoona zeylanica*, [Coll: කොකුං *kokun*]; green sulphate of iron: *a.* wise, sensible, learned; firm, steady, consistent; determined, headstrong, selfwilled; uncontrollable; lazy, dull, slow; strong, powerful; courageous.

ධීරත්ව, *Dhíratwa*, *s.* firmness, fortitude; feminine property of suppressing an excess of jealousy.

ධීවර, *Dhíwara*, *s.* fisherman, [Colloq. මසුන් අල්ලන්නා *masun allanná*].

ධීවරී, *Dhíwarí*, *s.* fisherman's wife; sort of harpoon for catching fish with.

ධීසචිව, *Dhísachiwa*, *s*, (ධී and සචිව friend) counsellor, minister; friendly or prudent adviser.

ධුත්තුර, *Duttura*, *s.* plant, *datura fastuosa*. [Colloq. අත්තන *attana*].

ධුත, *Dhuta*, *a.* abandoned, left, deserted, forsaken; shaken, agitated (as leaves by wind).

ධුතාංග, *Dhutanga*, see තෙළෙස්ධුතාඞ්ග *telesdhutánga*.

ධුතගුණය, *Dhuta-gunaya*, see තෙළෙස්ධුතාඞ්ග *telesdhutánga*.

ධුනි, *Dhuni*, *s.* river, [Colloq. ගඟ *ganga*].

ධුර්‍ය්‍ය, *Dhurya*, *s.* bearer of burdens; beast of burden.

ධුර්වහ, *Durwaha*, *s.* (ධුර් burden, වහ who bears) beast of burden; carrier.

ධුරන්ධර, *Dhurandara*, *s.* (ධුර් *dhur* burden, ධර to have or bear) beast of burden; flowering shrub, *woodfordia floribunda* or *grislea tomentosa*, [Colloq. මලිත *malita*].

ධුරය, *Dhuraya*, *s.* load, burden, office.

ධුරීණ, *Dhurína*, *s.* beast of burden, bearer of burden.

ධුස්තුර, *Dhustura*, ධුස්තූරි, *Dhusturí*, ධුස්තූර, *Dhustúra*, } *s.* plant, *datura fastuosa*, [Colloq. අත්තන *attana*].

ධූත, *Dhúta*, *a.* shaken, agitated; reproached, reviled; abandoned, deserted; judged, discriminated.

ධූතනං, *Dhútanan*, *s.* shaking, trembling, agitation, [Colloq. වෙව්ලීම *wewlíma*].

ධූප, *Dhúpa*, *s.* incense.

ධූප වෘක්ෂ, *Dhúpa-vriksha*, *s.* species of pine, *pinus longifolia*.

ධූම්‍යා, *Dhúmyá*, *s.* (ධූම *dhúma* smoke, ය *ya* implying aggregation) quantity of smoke.

ධූම්‍යාට, *Dhúmyáta*, *s.* bronze-winged dove, [Colloq. නිලකොබෙයියා *nílakobeyiyá*].

ධූම, *Dhúma*, *s.* smoke, [Colloq. දුම් *dum*].

ධූමකේතන, *Dhúma-kétana*, *s.* (ධූම and කේතන symbol) fire or its deity; Kétu personified descending node.

ධූමකේතු, *Dhúma-kétu*, *s.* (ධූම and කේතු symbol) comet or falling star; personified descending node.

ධූමධ්වජ, *Dhúmadhwaja*, *s.* (ධූම and ධ්වජ symbol) fire, [Colloq. ගිනි *gini*].

ධූමප්‍රභා, *Dhúmaprabhá*, *s.* (ධූම and ප්‍රභා what shines) division of hell, hell of smoke.

ධූමමහිෂී, *Dhúma-mahishí*, *s.* (ධූම smoke, මහිෂී buffalo) fog, mist.

ධූමයෝනි, *Dhúma-yóni*, *s.* (ධූම and යෝනි womb) what is engendered from smoke or vapour, cloud, [Colloq. වලාකුළ *walákuḷa*].

ධූමල, *Dhúmala*, *s.* (ධූම and ල what is) purple, colour compounded of black and red.

ධූමශිඛා, *Dhúmaṣikhá*, *s.* (ධූම and ශිඛා crest) flame, fire.

ධූමෝර්ණා, *Dhúmorṇá*, *s.* (ධූම *dhúma* smoke, ඌර්ණ *úrṇa* hair or wool) wife of Yama the regent of death, alluding to her smoky hue and woolly hair.

ධූම්‍ර, *Dhúmra*, *s.* (ධූම *dhúma* and ර *rá* to have or get) purple, smoky red colour.

ධූර්, *Dhúr*, *s.* forepart of a carriage, pole where the yoke is fixed; agitation, trembling; reflection; recollection; spark of fire; burden, load; part or portion; wealth; office, employment, charge.

ධූර්ත, *Dhúrta*, *s.* libertine, vicious man, drunkard, gambler, rogue, cheat, knave, rake, gamester; jackal; plant, *datura fastuosa*, [Colloq. අත්තන *attana*]; medicinal salt, [Colloq. බලල් ලුණු *balal-luṇu*]: *a.* wicked, vile, fraudulent, crafty.

ධූර්තජන්තු, *Dhúrta-jantu*, *s.* (ධූර්ත crafty, ජන්තු animal) crafty man.

ධූර්තමණ්ඩල, *Dhúrta-manḍala*, *s.* (ධූර්ත cheat, මණ්ඩල circle) party of rogues or gamblers.

ධූර්ධර, *Dhúrdhara*, *s.* (ධූර් burden, ධර bearing) beast of burden.

ධූරය, *Dhúraya*, *s.* office, employment; charge, trust, [Colloq. තනතුර *tanatura*].

ධූලි, *Dhúli*, *s.* dust.

ධූලි කදම්බ, *Dhúli-kadamba*, *s.* species of the kadamba tree, *adina* or *nauclea cordifolia*, [Colloq. කොලොං *kolon̥*]; another tree, *cratæva Roxburghii*, [Colloq. ලුණුවරණ *luṇuwaraṇa*].

ධේනු, *Dhénu*, *s.* milch cow, one that has lately calved

ධේනුකා, *Dhénuká*, *s.* she elephant; milch cow; cow that has lately calved.

ධේනුව, *Dhénuwa*, *s.* female of any quadruped.

ධෛනුක, *Dhainuka*, *s.* herd of milch cows.

ධෛර්‍ය, *Dhairya*, *s.* steadiness, firmness; strength; courage, boldness, intrepidity; nutmeg.

ධෛවත, *Dhaiwata*, *s.* sixth note of the Indian gamut.

ධෝත, *Dhóta*, *a.* washed, cleansed, purified.

ධෝරණ, *Dhóraṇa*, *s.* vehicle, any mode of conveyance; elephant keeper.

ධෝවනය, *Dhówanaya*, *s.* washing, cleansing, purifying.

ධෝවනයකරණවා, *Dhówanaya-karaṇawá*, *v.* to wash, to cleanse.

ධෞතකෞශේය, *Dhauta-kauṣéya*, *s.* (ධෞත washed, කෞශේය silken) bleached or wild silk.

ධෞරිතක, *Dhauritaka*, *s.* horse's trot.

ධෞරෙය, *Dhaureya*, *s.* beast of burden, carrier, any bearer of burdens.

ධැරීම, *Dheríma*, *s.* bearing, supporting, possessing, corruptly for දැරීම *deríma*; verbal noun of ධරණවා *dharaṇawá*.

ධ්‍යානය, *Dhyánaya*, *s.* meditation, reflection; but especially that profound consideration, which brings its object fully and undisturbedly before the mind; as a religious exercise dhyána is divided into four degrees or stages, to each of which belong certain duties, states and attainments, performed with the view of obtaining Nirwáṇa or the final emancipation of the soul; the following are the four divisions of dhyána, ප්‍රථම ධ්‍යානය *prathama-dhyánaya*, ද්විතීය ධ්‍යානය *dwitíya-dhyánaya*, තෘතීය ධ්‍යානය *tṛitíya-dhyánaya*, චතුර්ථ ධ්‍යානය *chaturtha-dhyánaya*, see these words.

ධෘත, *Dṛita*, *a.* possessed, held, contained; cherished, supported.

ධෘතරාෂ්ට්‍ර, *Dhṛitaráshṭra*, *s.* Nága or serpent of the lower regions; sort of goose; chief of the Gandharwas or choristers of Swarga.

ධෘති, *Dṛiti*, *s.* sort of metre, stanza of four lines of eighteen syllables each; firmness, strength, courage; holding, having, containing.

ධෘෂ්ට, *Dhṛishṭa*, *a.* impudent, confident, bold, shameless.

ධෘෂ්ටා, *Dhṛishṭá*, *s.* unfaithful or unchaste woman.

ධ්‍රුව, *Druwa*, *s.* polar star or north pole itself; trunk of a lopped tree; ascertainment, certainty; logic, reasoning, discussion; Swarga; introductory stanza of a song; ray, sun-beam: *a.* eternal, continual, perpetual; permanent, fixed.

ධ්‍රුවක, *Dhruwaka*, *s.* trunk of a lopped tree; longitude.

ධ්වජය, *Dhwajaya*, *s.* pride; hypocrisy, fraud; flag or banner; mark, sign, symbol; the penis; (In Prosody) Iambic.

ධ්වනි, *Dhwani*, *s.* sound, the sound of a drum or other instrument; figurative or poetical style.

ධ්වාංසමාචි, *Dhwáṇsamáchí*, *s.* plant, *solanum nigrum*, [Colloq. කළුකැම්මේරිය *kaḷu-kęmmériya*].

න

The twentieth consonant of the Siṇhalese alphabet; it corresponds in sound to the letter *n*; it is also a negative and privative particle answering to our, no, not, particle of prohibition.

නංගි, *Naṇgi*, *s.* younger sister.

නංවනවා, *Naṇwanawá*, *v.* to cause to elevate, to raise, to cause to hoist up: pret. නැංගුවා *nęṇguwá.*

නක්ත, *Nakta*, *s.* night, [Colloq. රෑ *rę*].

නක්තක, *Naktaka*, *s.* dirty or ragged cloth; towel, wiper, handkerchief, etc.

නක්තභෝජන, *Naktabhójaṇa*, *s.* (නක්ත by night, භෝජන food) supper.

නක්තමාල, *Naktamála*, *s.* (නක්තම් *naktam* by night, අල *ála* to ornament) tree, *pongamia glabra*, [Colloq මගුල්කරඳ *magul-karaṇda*].

නක්තවාර, *Naktawára*, *s.* (නක්ත night, වාර day) day and night, [Colloq. රෑ දවල් *ré-dawal*].

නක්‍ර, *Nakra*, *s.* (න not, ක්‍රම *krama* to go) upper timber of a door-frame; nose; string of bees or wasps; crocodile, alligator.

නක්ෂත්‍ර, *Nakshatra*, *s.* astrology, astronomy; star in general; asterism in the moon's path, lunar mansion, of which twenty-eight, distinct in name, figure and number of stars, are enumerated.

නක්ෂත්‍රකාරයා, *Nakshatrakárayá*, *s.* astronomer; astrologer.

නක්ෂත්‍ර ක්‍රීඩාව, *Nakshatra-kríḍáwa*, see නකත්කෙළි *nakatkeḷi.*

නක්ෂත්‍ර ඝෝෂණය, *Nakshatra-ghóshaṇaya*, *s.* announcement of the appearance of a planet which is to be celebrated by great festivity.

නක්ෂත්‍ර මාලාව, *Nakshatra-máláwa*, *s.* (නක්ෂත්‍ර constellation, මාලා *málá* garland) necklace containing twenty-seven pearls; table of the twenty-eight asterisms in the moon's path, exhibiting their names, positions and the signs by which they are figured.

නක්ෂත්‍ර යෝගය, *Nakshatra-yógaya*, *s.* art of consulting stars or planets for astrological purposes, such as finding lucky days, etc.; leading star of a lunar mansion, conjunction of stars.

නක්ෂත්‍රේශ, *Nakshatrésa*, *s.* (නක්ෂත්‍ර *nakshatra* star, ඊශ *ísa* lord) moon, [Colloq. හඳ *haṇda*].

නක්ෂමාරෝහ, *Nakshamáróha*, *s*, date tree, *Phœnix zeylanica*, [Colloq. ඉඳිගහ *iṇdi-gaha*].

නක, *Naka*, *s.* nail of the finger or toe.

නකත්, *Nakat*, *s.* star, planet; asterism, lunar mansion.

නකත්කෙළිය, *Nakat-keḷiya*, *s.* (නකත් asterism, කෙළිය play, sport) festival, chiefly celebrated among the Hindus, when the moon is full near the Pleiades in the month ඉල් මස *il-masa*, (October–November).

නකත් ගෘහය, *Nakat-grihaya*, *s.* (නකත් star, ගෘහය house, mansion) asterism, lunar mansion; of which, according to Siṇhalese astronomy, there are twenty-eight in the moon's path: see නක්ෂත්‍ර *nakshatra.*

නකත්තා, *Nakattá*, *s.* astronomer.

නකු, *Naku*, *s.* crocodile, alligator, [Colloq. කිඹුලා *kimbulá*]; ichneumon.

නකුට, *Nakuṭa*, *s.* nose; tail.

නකුල, *Nakula*, *s.* Bengal mungoose, *viverra ichneumon*, [Colloq. මුගටියා *mugaṭiyá*]; fourth of the five Páṇḍu princes: *a.* rejected from a family, outcast.

නකුලි, *Nakuli*, *s.* (න not, කුල race or heap with feminine affix ඊ *i*) silk cotton tree, *eriodendron anfractuosum*, [Colloq. ඉඹුල් *imbul*]; Indian spikenard; sort of perfume.

නකුලේෂ්ටා, *Nakuléshṭá*, *s.* (නකුල *nakula* ichneumon, ඉෂ්ට *ishṭa* wished) plant, *mimosa octandra*, [Colloq. අරත්ත *aratta*]; the mungoose, when wounded in a conflict with a poisonous snake, is supposed to prevent the effects of the venom by the use of this plant.

නඛ, *Nakha*, *s.* finger nail; toe nail, [Colloq. නියපොත්ත *niyapotta*]; claw, perfume, dried substance of a brown colour, and of the shape of a finger nail, apparently dried shell fish used as a perfume.

නඛර, *Nakhara*, *s.* finger nail, toe nail, claw.

නඛරායුධ, *Nakharáyudha*, *s.* (නඛර *nakhara* claw, ආයුධ *áyudha* weapon) lion, beast of prey, any animal that defends himself in a conflict by his claws.

නඛාග්‍රය, *Nakhágraya*, *s.* end or tip of the finger nail.

නඛී, *Nakhí*, *s.* vegetable perfume. (Siŋh. වක්නිය *wakniya.*)

නග්න, *Nagna*, *a.* naked.

නග්නජිත්, *Nagnajit*, *s.* (නග්න nakedness, ජිත් what conquers) cotton tree, in allusion to clothes being made from its produce, *gossypium indicum*, [Colloq. කපු *kapu*].

නග්නයා, *Nagnayá*, } *s.* (නග්න naked, අට *aṭa* who
නග්නාට, *Nagnáṭa*, } goes) naked man, especially a kind of Hindu religious mendicant who wanders about without clothes.

නග්නිකා, *Nagniká*, *s.* naked woman; young girl before menstruation or about ten years old.

නග, *Naga*, *s.* (න not, ග going) mountain; tree; fixed star; stone, rock.

නගජ, *Nagaja*, *s.* (නග mountain, ජ born) elephant, [Colloq. අලියා *aliyá*]; mountaineer.

නගනන්දිනී, *Nagnandiní*, *s.* (නග *naga* and නන්දිනී daughter) name of Durgá, the wife of Ṣiva, alluding to her being in one of her characters the daughter of Himálaya the snowy Imaus personified, and hence also frequently called Párwatí.

නගනවා, *Naganawá*, *v.* to raise, to lift up; to build, translate: pret. නැගුවා *neguwá.*

නගනි, *Nagani*, *s.* younger sister, (a word of endearment,) pl. නගනියෝ *naganiyó.*

නගනේ, *Nagané*, *s.* sty.

නගපති, *Nagapati*, *s.* (නග mountain, පති lord) the personified range of snowy mountains dividing India from Tartary, usually termed the Himálayan range.

නගර, *Nagara*, *s.* town, city, [Colloq. නුවර *nuwara*].

නගරඝාත, *Nagaragháta*, *s.* (නගර city, ඝාත who destroys or subverts) elephant; invading army.

නගරමා, *Nagaramá*, *s.* man of a low caste.

නගරය, *Nagaraya*, see නගර *nagara.*

නගරයා, *Nagarayá*, *s.* kind of fish.

නගරා, *Nagará*, *s.* citizen.

නගරී, *Nagarí*, see නගර *nagara.*

නගරෝපාන්ත, *Nagarópánta*, *s.* suburb, skirts of the town.

නගරෞෂධි, *Nagaraushadhi*, *s.* (නගර *nagara* and ඖෂධි medicament) plantain, banana, [Colloq. කෙහෙල් *kehel*].

නගල්, *Nagal*, *s*, tail,]Colloq. වල්ගේ *walgé*].

නගල, *Nagala*, *s.* plough.

නගා, *Nagá*, *s.* younger sister.

නගාටන, *Nagáṭana*, *s.* (නග *naga* mountain, අට *aṭa* to go) monkey.

නගාධිපති, *Nagádhipati*, *s.* (නග *naga* and අධිපති chief) Himálaya mountain: see නගපති *nagapati.*

නගාපියා, *Nagápiyá*, *p.* having vomited.

නගිනවා, *Naginawá*, *v.* to mount, to rise, to ascend: pret. නැගුනා *neguná.*

නගුට, *Naguṭa*, *s.* tail, [Colloq. වල්ගේ *walgé*].

නගුන්, *Nagun*, *acc. plur.* of නගා *nagá.*

නගුර, *Nagura*, *a.* (න neg. ගුර long) short, [Colloq. කොට *koṭa*].

නගුල්, *Nagul*, *plur.* of නගුල *nagula;* also a tail, tail of any animal.

නගුල, *Nagula*, *s.* plough.

නගුලත්, *Nagulat*, *s.* name of Balabhadra the elder brother of Kṛishṇa.

නගුලිස, *Nagulisa*, *s.* head of a plough.

නච්ච, *Nachcha*, *s.* dance, dancing, pantomime.

නට්ටිය, *Naṭṭiya*, *s.* knee.

නට, *Naṭa*, *s.* dancer, actor; tree, *oroxylum indicum*, [Colloq. තොටිල *toṭila*]; tree, *saraca indica* or *jonesia asoca*, [Colloq. දිය රතඹලා *diya-ratambalá*]; precipice; destroyed, Elu form of නෂ්ට *nashṭa.*

නටන, *Naṭana*, *s.* art or act of dancing, pantomime.

නටනවා, *Naṭanawá*, *v.* to dance, to dance as an actor, to perform as a dramatist; to bubble as boiling water: pret. නැටුවා *neṭuwá.*

නටනු, *Naṭanu*, *s.* dance, dancing, pantomime, dramatical exhibitions.

නටබුන්, *Naṭabun*, *a.* (නට destroyed, බුන් broken) desolate, destroyed, demolished, waste, devastated.

නටබුන්කරණවා, *Naṭabun-karaṇawá*, *v.* to destroy, to lay waste, to threaten.

නටබුන්වෙනවා, *Naṭabunwenawá*, *v.* to be destroyed or devastated, to become waste or desolate.

නටභූෂණ, *Naṭa-bhúshaṇa*, *s.* (නට actor, භූෂණ ornament) yellow orpiment, [Colloq. හිරියල් *hiriyal*].

නටමණ්ඩන, *Naṭamanḍana*, *s.* (නට actor, මණ්ඩන adorning) sort of dye, (yellow orpiment), so called in consequence of its being used in dyeing the robes of dancers, actors, or dramatic performers.

නටා, *Naṭá*, *past. part.* of නටනවා *naṭanawá*, which see: *s.* shrub, *cæsalpina bonducella.*

නටි, *Naṭi*, } *s.* dancing girl; actress; prostitute;
නටී, *Naṭí*, } red arsenic.

නටුව, *Naṭuwa*, *s.* stalk of a leaf or fruit, petiole, pedicel; pl. නටු *naṭu*.

නඩ, *Naḍa*, *s.* filth, dirt, any filthy or impure thing; sort of small reed, *arundo tibialis*, [Colloq. කුලල්බට *kulalbaṭa*]; verandah, outer verandah in an upper story.

නඩත්තු, *Naḍattu*, *s.* sustenance, subsistence, maintenance.

නඩත්තුකරණවා, *Naḍattu-karaṇawá*, } *v.* to
නඩමාඩුකරණවා, *Naḍamáḍu-karaṇawá*, } maintain, to support, to afford subsistence.

නඩමින, *Naḍamina*, see නලමින *nalamina*.

නඩලන්, *Naḍalan*, *plur.* of නඩලම *naḍalama*.

නඩලම, *Naḍalama*, *s.* vexation, teasing, plaguing; confusion, foolery.

නඩාව, *Naḍáwa*, *s.* weaver's shuttle.

නඩි, *Naḍi*, *a.* large, stout, bulky, fat.

නඩියා, *Naḍiyá*, *s.* (නඩි stout, යා mas. aff.) large bulky man, or male animal.

නඩු, *Naḍu*, *plur.* of නඩුව *naḍuwa*.

නඩු අහනවා, *Naḍu-ahanawá*, *v.* to investigate judicially.

නඩුකාරයා, *Naḍukárayá*, *s.* (නඩු justice, කාර doer, යා aff.) judge, magistrate.

නඩුකියනවා, *Naḍu-kiyanawá*, *v.* institute a lawsuit.

නඩුතනනවා, *Naḍu-tananawá*, *v.* to make or get up a case at law, to judge: pret. නඩු තැනුවා *naḍu-tenuwá*.

නඩුතීන්දුව, *Naḍutínduwa*, *s.* (නඩු and තීන්දුව finishing) sentence, judicial decree.

නඩුමග, *Naḍumaga*, } *s.* law, course of law,
නඩුමාර්ගය, *Naḍumárgaya*, } legal practice.

නඩු යනවා, *Naḍu-yanawá*, *v.* to go to law.

නඩුව, *Naḍuwa*, *s.* justice, equity; lawsuit; decision or judgment of a court of justice.

නඩුවටනැති, *Naḍuwaṭa-neti*, *a.* lawless, illegal.

නඩුවිචාරණවා, *Naḍu-vicháraṇawá*, *v.* to sit in judgment, to investigate a matter judicially.

නඩුවිසඳනවා, *Naḍu-visadanawá*, *v.* (නඩු and විසඳනවා to interpret or explain) to investigate a case; to explain a matter judicially.

නත්, *Nat*, *s.* (න neg. අත් *at* for අනත *anta* end) name of Ananta, chief of the serpent race and regent of Pátála: *ad.* endless, innumerable, infinite.

නත්තල්, *Nattal*, } *s.* Christmas.
නත්තල, *Nattala*, }

නත්තිරම, *Nattirama*, *s.* patch in a net.

නත්නාරං, *Natnáraṇ*, *s.* common citron, *citrus medica.*

නත, *Nata*, *s.* name of Ananta, king of the Nágas or serpent race and regent of Nága lóka, or Pátála; Elu form of අනනත *ananta*: *a.* bent, bowed, reclining; curved, crooked.

නතනා, *Nataná*, Elu form of අනන්තනාග *ananta-nága*, see the foregoing.

නතනාසික, *Natanásika*, *s.* (නත bent, නාසික nose) one having a flat nose.

නතර, *Natara*, *s.* casual support or livelihood; support, prop.

නතරකරණවා, *Natarakaraṇawá*, *v.* to support, to prop, to sustain, to uphold; to detain, to impede.

නතු, *Natu*, *s.* estate, inheritance; legacy: *a.* bent, brought under power or into possession.

නතුකරණවා, *Natukaraṇawá*, *v.* bend, [Colloq. නවනවා *nawanawá*].

නතුවා, *Natuwá*, *s.* heir, [Colloq. උරුමක්කාරයා *urumakkárayá*].

නද, *Nada*, *s.* sound, noise; tone; joy, gladness; pleasure, delight; river.

නදන්, *Nadan*, *s.* joy, gladness; cause, motive, reason; in common language, circumstance, occurrence, event.

නදන, *Nadana*, *s.* hidden treasure, Elu form of නිධාන *nidhána*, which see; son.

නදවට, *Nadawaṭa*, *s.* flowering shrub, *tabernæmontana coronaria*, [Colloq. තුවරලා *tuwaralá*].

නදිගු, *Nadigu*, } *a.* (න neg, දිගු long) short.
නදිඟු, *Nadingu*, }

නදිය, *Nadiya*, } *s.* river in general, [Colloq. ගඟ
නදී, *Nadí*, } *ganga*]; the common personification of rivers being female.

නදීකාන්ත, *Nadíkánta*, *s.* medicinal plant, *spilanthes acmella*, [Colloq. අක්මැල්ල *akmella*]; tree, *barringtonia acutangula*, [Colloq. එල මිදෙල්ල *ela-midella*].

නදීජ, *Nadíja*, *s.* (නදී river, ජ born) antimony; lotus; fish.

නදීතීරය, *Nadí-tíraya*, *s.* (නදී and තීර *tíra* bank) border or shore of a river, [Colloq. ඉවුර *iwura*].

නදීන, *Nadína*, *s.* (නදී and ඉන *ina* lord) ocean: name of Varuṇa the god of water: *a.* (න neg. දීන poor) wealthy, rich, opulent.

නදීසර්ජ, *Nadísarja*, *s.* tree, *terminalia glabra*, [Colloq. කුඹුක් *kumbuk*].

නඳුන්, *Nadun*, *s.* garden of Ṣakra or Indra situated in Swarga.
නන්, *Nan*, *ad.* various, several, of different kinds.
නන්කරණවා, *Nankaraṇawá*, *v.* to erect, to construct, to build.
නන්ද, *Nanda*, *s.* any one of the nine inestimable gems or treasures of Kuvéra, the god of wealth; cowherd Nanda, who was the foster-father of Kṛishṇa; happiness, joy, pleasure.
නන්දන, *Nandana*, *s.* twenty-fifth year of the Indian cycle of sixty; joy, gladness, pleasure, delight; son; pleasure ground of Indra in Swarga, the elysium of the gods.
නන්දනා, *Nandaná*, *s.* daughter.
නන්දනී, *Nandaní*, *s.* daughter, only used in letters of invitation, [Colloq. දුව *duwa*].
නන්දනෝද්‍යානය, *Nandanódyánaya*, *s.* (නන්දන *nandana* joy, pleasure, උද්‍යාන *udyána* garden) pleasure garden; the garden of Swarga, elysium.
නන්දපාල, *Nandapála*, *s.* (නන්ද treasures of Kuvéra, පාල keeper) name of Varuṇa, alluding to his being the keeper or protector of the treasures of Kuvéra the god of wealth.
නන්දපුත්‍රී, *Nanda-putrí*, (නන්ද cowherd Nanda, පුත්‍රී daughter) name of the goddess Durgá who became incarnate as the infant daughter of Nanda.
නන්දා, *Nandá*, *s.* tank of Ṣakra, in the garden of Swarga or the region of the gods, in which that god is accustomed to bathe.
නන්දි, *Nandi*, *s.* gambling; sloth, drowsiness, listlessness; joy, happiness, pleasure; the speaker of the prelude or prologue to a drama.
නන්දික, *Nandika*, *s.* tree peculiar to Ceylon, the wood of which resembles mahogany and is used for furniture etc. *Pericopsis Mooniana*, [Colloq. නැඳුන් *nẹndun*].
නන්දිකා, *Nandiká*, *s.* garden of Swarga, region of the gods, or Ṣakra's pleasure ground; earthen water pot.
නන්දිනී, *Nandiní*, *s.* name of the goddess Párwati; Gangá the river goddess; husband's sister; the Alakanandá river.
නන්දොඩනවා, *Nandoḍanawá*, *v.* to prate much and foolishly, to prate, to talk without meaning.
නන්ද්‍යාවර්ත, *Nandyáwarta*, *s.* sort of temple; peculiar diagram; shrub: see නදවට *nadawaṭa*.
නන්විසිතුරු, *Nanvisituru*, *a.* (නන් several, විසිතුරු ornamented) variegated, of diversified beauties, of various colours.

නනරුත්, *Nanarut*, *a.* having various meanings.
නනු, *Nanu*, *ind.* particle implying certainty, verity, truth; particle of interrogation or assent.
නපුංසක, *Napuṇsaka*, *s.* (න neg. පුංසක male) eunuch; neuter gender in grammar.
නපුර, *Napura*, *s.* wickedness, vice, mischief.
නපුරා, *Napurá*, *s.* wicked man.
නපුරී, *Napurí*, *s.* wicked woman.
නපුරු, *Napuru*. *a.* wicked, bad, vile, evil; mischievous.
නබය, *Nabaya*, } *a.* (න neg. බය fear) fearless,
නබිය, *Nabiya*, } courageous, bold, intrepid.
නභ, *Nabha*, *s.* ether; atmosphere, sky, [Colloq. අහස *ahasa*]; month Nikini, (July–August.)
නභස්, *Nabhas*, *s.* month Nikini, (July–August); cloud; rains; smell; fibres of the lotus; bird; grey headed man.
නභස්තල, *Nabhastala*, *s.* (නභස් heaven, තල plane) visible heavens, firmament.
නභස, *Nabhasa*, *s.* sky, [Colloq. අහස *ahasa*]; atmosphere; ether; visible heavens.
නභසඞ්ගම, *Nabha-saṅgama*, *s.* (නභස heaven, ගම what goes) bird in general, [Colloq. කුරුල්ලා *kurullá*].
නභෝ මණ්ඩල, *Nabhó-maṇḍala*, *s.* (නභස් *nabhas* cloud, මණ්ඩල circuit) atmosphere; ether, [Coll: ආකාස *ákása*].
නභෝ රජස්, *Nabhó rajas*, *s.* (නභස් *nabhas* sky, රජස් dust) darkness.
නඹුව, *Nambuwa*, corruptly for නම්බුව *nambuwa*, which see.
නම්, *Nam*, an affix implying possibility, as if, though, etc., also, of certainty, that is, etc.; the plural of නම *nama*.
නම්කරණවා, *Nam-karaṇawá*, } *v.* to name, to give
නම් තබනවා, *Nam-tabanawá*, } names.
නම්නම්, *Namnam*, *s.* tree, *cynometra cauliflora*, Malay niam-niam.
නම්නැති, *Namnẹti*, *a.* anonymous; nameless.
නම්බුකාරයා, *Nambukárayá*, *s.* respectable man.
නම්බුව, *Nambuwa*, *s.* honour, respect.
නම්‍ර, *Namra*, *a.* bent, crooked, curved, doubled, [Colloq. නැමුණු *nẹmunu*].
නම, *Nama*, *s.* name, epithet; (in composition) the numeral nine, which is however a corruption of නව *nawa;* a verbal root, to bend, to salute, to worship, to reverence.
නමකර, *Namakara*, Elu form of නමස්කාර *namaskára*, which see: *part.* having bowed to, or saluted.

නමකළ, *Namakaḷa*, *part.* worshipped, [Colloq. නමස්කාරකළාවූ *namaskára-kaḷáwú*].

නමඩි, *Namaḍi*, *s.* tree, *cratæva Roxburghii*, or *c. religiosa*, [Colloq. ලුනුවරණ *lunuwaraṇa*]: see නමුඩු *namuḍu*.

නමදිනවා, *Namadinawá*, *v.* to bow, to bend, to curve: pret. නැමදුනා *nęmaduná*, [Colloq. වඳිනවා *wan̲dinawá*].

නමන, *Namana*, *a.* bending, bowing; curving; saluting, adoring.

නමනවා, *Namanawá*, *v.* to bow, to bend; to curve, to double; to salute with reverence or respect, to bow or bend down in homage or worship; to salute, to worship: pret. නැමුවා *nęmuwá*.

නමරත්න, *Namaratna*, *s.* (නම nine, රතන gem) the nine principal gems peculiar to Ceylon; name of a celebrated treatise in verse, on Ethics and moral subjects, comprehending nine slókas or stanzas; corrupt form of නවරතන *nawaratna*.

නමය, *Namaya*, see නවය *nawaya*.

නමවක, *Namawaka*, *s.* (නම and වක lunar day) ninth day of the new or full moon, which is considered unlucky.

නමවෙනි, *Namaweni*, *ad.* ninthly.

නමස්කාර, *Namaskára*, *s.* (නමස් worship, කාර doing) reverence, respect, salutation; adoration, worship, veneration; address.

නමස්කාර කරණවා, *Namaskára-karaṇawá*, *v.* to adore, to worship.

නමස්‍ය, *Namasyá*, *s.* reverence, respect; worship, adoration.

නමස්‍යිත, *Namasyita*, *a.* reverenced, respected; worshipped, adored; saluted.

නමාමේ, *Namámé*, *s.* crowd, multitude, throng, [Colloq. සමූහය *samúhaya*].

නමුඩි, *Namuḍi*, } *s.* tree, *cratæva Roxburghii* or
නමුඩු, *Namuḍu*, } *c. religiosa*, [Colloq. ලුනුවරණ *lunuwaraṇa*]: see නමඩි *namaḍi*.

නමුදු, *Namudu*, an affix meaning though, however, notwithstanding, generally written නුමුත් *numut*.

නමෝ, *Namó*, *s.* salutation, worship, reverence; Páli form of නමඃ *namaḥ*.

නමඃ, *Namaḥ*, indeclinable particle, much used in native compositions, the beginning of නමඃ සර්වඥය *namaḥ-sarwajñáya*, let the omniscient (Buddha) be worshipped, literally, adoration (be) to the Omniscient one, *i. e.* Buddha.

නය, *Naya*, *s.* debt; mode, manner.

නයකාරයා, *Nayakárayá*, *s.* (නය debt, කාර who does, යා aff.) debtor.

නයකැරේ, *Nayakęré*, *s.* (නය and කැර *kęra* letter) bond or obligation for money, promissory note.

නයගන්නවා, *Naya-gannawá*, } *v.* to borrow; to
නයටගන්නවා, *Nayaṭa-gannawá*, } take a loan.

නයටදෙනවා, *Nayaṭa-denawá*, *v.* to lend, to give on loan, to give on credit.

නයන, *Nayana*, *s.* eye, [Colloq. ඇස *ęsa*]; leading, guiding, (literally or figuratively).

නයනභූෂණ, *Nayana-bhúshaṇa*, *s.* (නයන and භූෂණ ornament) collyrium, made from a preparation of antimony, and used to anoint the eye brows for the purpose of darkening and adding to their beauty.

නයනරසායන, *Nayana-rasáyana*, *s.* (නයන and රසායන imparting delight) any thing grateful to the sight.

නයනාමෘත, *Nayanámṛita*, *s.* (නයන *nayana* eye, අමෘත *amṛita* nectar) any specific for the eyes; collyrium; any thing agreeable or grateful to the sight.

නයනායුධ, *Nayanáyudha*, *s.* (නයන *nayana* and ආයුධ *áyudha* weapon) name or epithet of Yama the Indian Pluto, alluding to his terrific aspect which is said by one glance to drive the soul out of the body.

නයනෞෂධ, *Nayanawshadha*, *s.* (නයන *nayana* and ඖෂධ *aushadha* medicament) any specific for the eyes; collyrium; green sulphate of iron or the salt in a state of partial decomposition by exposure to the atmosphere.

නයා, *Nayá*, *s.* cobra capella, deadly snake with spectacle marks on hood, *naga tripudians*, *(Elapidæ* order *ophidia)*.

නයාස, *Nayása*, corruptly for න්‍යාස *nyása*, which see.

නයිකාරයා, *Nayikárayá*, *s.* snake charmer.

නයිගල, *Nayi-gala*, *s.* (නයා *nayá* cobra capella, ගල stone) gem fabled to be produced in the throat of the cobra capella, ruby? stone used to cure the bite of serpents by rubbing the part wounded.

නයිදේ, *Nayidé*, *s.* workman, artificer, tradesman; term applied to certain labourers who held land in lieu of services rendered to government.

නයිනටවන්නා, *Nayi-naṭawnná*, *s.* snake charmer.

නයිපනික්කියා, *Nayi-panikkiyá*, *s.* snake catcher.

නයිපෙනේ, *Nayi-pené*, *s.* hood of a cobra capella.

නයිමිරිස්, *Nayimiris*, s. (නයා *nayá* and මිරිස් chili) small sort of chili, exceedingly pungent, called bird-pepper, *capsicum fastigiatum (Solanaceæ)*.

නයිරුති, *Nayiruti*, s. demon, fiend, [Colloq. රකුසන් *rakusan*]; south-west quarter.

නයිහත්ත, *Nayi-hatta*, s. (නයා *nayá* and හත්ත mushroom) toad-stool.

නයිහබරල, *Nayi-habarala*, s. plant, *alocasia cucullata, (Araceæ)*: also called පනුහබරල *panu-habarala*.

නයිහුඹහ, *Nayi-hum̱baha*, s. (නයා *nayá* and හුඹහ ant hill) white-ant hill taken possession of by a cobra capella.

නර, *Nara*, s. man, individually or generally; grey hair; according to the Brahminical system of theology the anima munḍi or the spirit pervading the universe: *a.* grey (as to hair).

නරඉසුරු, *Nara-isuru*, s. king, [Colloq. රජ *raja*].

නරක්කරණවා, *Narakkaraṇawá*. v. to make bad.

නරක, *Naraka*, s. hell, infernal regions; name of a noted daitya or demon slain by Vishṇu: *a.* bad, wicked, vile.

නරකගින්න, *Naraka-ginna*, s. hell-fire: see නරකාග්නි *narakágni*.

නරකදුක්ඛය, *Naraka-dukkhaya*, s. (නරක and දුක්ඛ *dukkha* suffering) pains of hell, torments of the infernal regions.

නරකපුරය, *Naraka-puraya*, s. (නරක bad පුර *pura* city) city of Yama the regent of death and judge of the infernal regions.

නරකප්‍රපාත, *Naraka-prapáta*, s. (නරක hell, ප්‍රපාත precipice) tartarus: abyss, chasm or pit of immense depth.

නරකරිපු, *Naraka-ripu*, s. (නරක demon, රිපු enemy) name of Vishṇu, alluding to his subduing the demon Naraka.

නරකාග්නි, *Narakágni*, s. (නරක *naraka* and අග්නි *agni* fire) hell-fire: see නරකගින්න *naraka-ginna*.

නරකාදිය, *Narakádiya*, s. hell, more correctly නරක *naraka* etc. *i. e.* hell and other states of suffering, such as irrational animals, hobgoblins, Asuras etc.

නරකාමය, *Narakámaya*, s. (නරක *naraka* hell, ආමය *ámaya* sickness) soul after death.

නරකාවාටය, *Narakáwáṭaya*, s. hole formed at the root of a decayed tree.

නරකෙන්ද, *Narakenda*, s. (නර grey, කෙන්ද wire) grey hair, hair become grey through old age.

නරකෙස්, *Nara-kes*, s. (නර and කෙස් hairs) hair become grey by age.

නරඟ, *Naraṉga*, s. pimples on the face; name of Káma, gode of love; penis.

නරඟනෝ, *Naraṉganó*, s. female of the human species.

නරජල, *Nara-jala*, s. (නර man, ජල water) urine.

නරණ, *Naraṇá*, see නරනා *naraná*.

නරතුරු, *Naraturu*, *ad.* (න negative, අතුරු *aturu* interval, with ර *ra* argument) unceasingly, continually, always: *a.* coarse, gross, without interstices; Elu form of නිරන්තර *nirantara*.

නරද, *Narada*, s. plough, [Colloq. නගුල *nagula*]; arrow, [Colloq. ඊගහ *ígaha*].

නරදම්, *Naradam*, s. (නර man, දම් to be subjugated) men whose passions have to be quelled; slough of a snake.

නරදම්සැරි, *Naradam-seri*, s. name of Buddha; පුරිසදම්මසාරථි *purisadammasárathi*, epithet of Buddha, guide of "the human steer, *i. e.* of unconverted men." Childers.

නරදිය, *Nara-diya*, see නරජල *narajala*.

නරදෙටු, *Naradeṭu*, s. monarch, king.

නරදෙව්, *Naradew*, s. (නර man, දෙව් deity) king, sovereign, monarch, [Colloq. රජ *raja*].

නරනා, *Naraná*, s. (නර and නා leader or master) king, sovereign; name of Vishṇu.

නරනිඳු, *Naranidu*, s. (නරන් *naran* men, ඉඳු *iṉdu* chief) monarch, king, prince, pl. නරනිඳුන් *naraniṉdun*.

නරපති, *Narapati*, s. (නර and පති lord) king, sovereign.

නරප්‍රවර, *Naraprawara*, s. (නර man, ප්‍රවර eminent) monarch, king; lord, chief, master.

නරඹ, *Naram̱ba*, s. valley, [Colloq. පාතාලය *pátálaya*].

නරඹනවා, *Naram̱banawá*, v. to see, to look, to behold: pret. නැරඹී *nerambí*, he saw.

නරඹා, *Naram̱bá*, p. having looked, [Colloq. බලා *balá*].

නරයන්, *Narayan*, the *acc. plur.* of නරයා *narayá*.

නරයහන්, *Narayahan*, / නරයහන, *Narayahana*, } s. (නර man, යහන vehicle) name of Wesamuṇi or Kuvéra the god of riches.

නරයා, *Narayá*, s, (නර and යා masculine affix) man, [Colloq. මිනිහා *minihá*].

නරලොව, *Nara-lowa*, s. (නර man, ලොව world) the world of men, in contradistinction to the worlds of gods and demons.

නරවර, *Narawara*, *s.* (නර mankind, වර pre-eminent) king, sovereign, prince; name of Buddha, as chief of the human race.

නර වළ, *Nara-waḷa*, see නරාවළ *nará-waḷa*.

නරවාහන, *Nara-wáhana*, *s.* (නර and වාහන vehicle) name of Wesamuṇi or Kuvéra, the deity of wealth.

නරවැල, *Nara-wela*, *s.* plant, *clematis smilacifolia* (or *naravelia zeylanica*) (*Ranunculaceæ*).

නරසිංහ, *Narasiṇha*, *s.* (නර man, සිංහ lion) Vishṇu, in his fourth Avatára or incarnation, in which he appeared as a man-lion, for the purpose of destroying the two noted giants Hiraṇyakáśyapa, and Hiraṇyáksha; chief, man of eminence or power; name of Buddha.

නරසිරි, *Narasiri*, *s.* (නර and සිරි glory, riches) human glory or happiness.

නරසි, *Narasí* see නරසිංහ *narasiṇha*.

නරසීහ, *Narasíha*, *s.* name of Buddha; Páli form of නරසිංහ *narasiṇha*.

නරා, *Nará*, see නරාවළ *nará-waḷa*.

නරාතුරු, *Naráturu*, see නරතුරු *naraturu*.

නරාධම, *Narádhama*, *s.* (නර *nara* and අධම *adhama* low) low or vile man, wretch.

නරාධාරා, *Narádhárá*, *s.* (නර *nara* man, අධාර *ádhára* receptacle) earth, [Colloq. පොළව *poḷawa*].

නරාධිප, *Narádhipa*, *s.* (නර *nara* and අධිප *adhipa* lord or chief) king, sovereign, monarch.

නරාවළ, *Naráwaḷa*, *s.* abyss; deep pit; large deep hole in the ground occasioned by the decay of the roots of a large tree.

නරි, *Nari*, plur. of නරියා *nariyá*.

නරිතන්තු, *Naritantu*, *s.* thread, fibre.

නරිනාටක, *Narináṭaka*, *s.* fatuity; conceit.

නරියා, *Nariyá*, *s.* jackal, fox, *canis aureus*.

නරුව, *Naruwa*, *s.* fold of the waist cloth of the natives which is used as a pocket; plaits or folds of cloth, pl. නරු *naru*.

නරේන්ද්‍රභෝග්‍ය, *Naréndrabhógya*, *s.* species of sandal wood, *santalum album*, [Colloq. සඳුන් *saṇdun*].

නරේන්ද්‍රයා, *Naréndrayá*, *s.* (නර *nara* and ඉන්ද්‍ර *indra* chief) king, anointed sovereign.

නරේශ්වර, *Naréśwara*, see නරේන්ද්‍ර *naréndra*.

නල, *Nala*, *s.* delay; dancing girl; life; crab; tube, or the aperture of a tube; bamboo cane, *bambusa vulgaris*, [Colloq. උණ *uṇa*]; reed, *Phragmites Roxburghii*, see නල ගස් *nala-gas*; reed in general; wind; fire; fiftieth year of the Indian cycle of sixty; hindrance.

නලංගුව, *Nalaṇguwa*, *s.* sorrow, trouble, dejection of mind.

නලංගුවෙනවා, *Nalaṇguwenawá*, *v.* to be dejected.

නලකරු, *Nalakaru*, *s.* tat-maker: see නලගස් *nala-gas*.

නලකාරයා, *Nalakárayá*, *s.* (නල and කාර who does, යා aff.) basket maker, tat-maker.

නලකුමුදු, *Nala-kumudu*, *s.* lotus or water lily, *nelumbium speciosum*, [Colloq. නෙළුම් *neḷum*].

නලකුවේර, *Nala-kuwéra*, *s.* son of Kuwéra.

නලගස්, *Nala-gas*, *s.* reed, *Phragmites Roxburghii* (*Gramineæ*).

නලගොදුරු, *Nalagoduru*, *s.* bear, [Colloq. වලහා *walahá*].

නලදත්, *Nala-dat*, *s. pl.* disordered teeth.

නලඳ, *Nalaṇda*, *s.* thief, [Colloq. හොරා *horá*].

නලදු, *Naladu*, } *s.* hindrance, obstacle, impediment, [Colloq. වැළැක්ම *weḷahima*].
නලනු, *Nalanu*, }

නලමසුන්, *Nalamasun*, } *s.* (නල reed, මීන fish) prawn, [Colloq. ඉස්සෝ *issó*]; crab, sort of sprat, *clupea cultrata*.
නලමින්, *Nalamin*, }
නලමීන, *Nalamína*, }

නලය, *Nalaya*, *s.* claw of a crab, head of a shrimp, tube, reed.

නලයා, *Nalayá*, *s.* one of a tribe of palanquin bearers so called; crab.

නලවනවා, *Nalawanawá*, *v.* to appease, to pacify, to lull, to soothe, to quell: pret. නැළෙව්වා *neḷewwá*.

නලවර, *Nalawara*, *s.* piper, one that plays on a reed or flute.

නලවරු, *Nalawaru*, *s.* makers of mats from bamboos and reeds.

නලසහ, *Nalasaha*, *s.* fire, [Colloq. ගිනි *gini*].

නලා, *Nalá*, plur. of නලාව *naláwa*.

නලාගහ, *Nalá-gaha*, *s.* panic grass, *panicum arborescens*; and see නලගස් *nala-gas*.

නලාතණ, *Nalá-taṇa*, *s.* (නලා and තණ grass) wild sugar cane, *saccharum spontaneum*.

නලාව, *Naláwa*, *s.* reed (for playing), flute, wind instrument; trumpet, horn.

නලි, *Nali*, *s.* bamboo cane, *bambusa vulgaris*; [Colloq. උණ *uṇa*]; lotus, *nelumbium speciosum*, [Colloq. නෙළුම් *neḷum*]; crab; dancing girl.

නලිඟු, *Naliṇgu*, *s.* vermilion.

නලින, *Nalina*, *s.* lotus, *nelumbium speciosum*, [Colloq. නෙළුම් *neḷum*]; water; indigo.

නලිනී, *Naliní*, *s.* assemblage of lotus flowers, place abounding in the lotus; flexible stalk of a water lily; pond in which the lotus grows; fermented and intoxicating liquor of the cocoanut tree.

නලියනවා, *Naliyanawá*, *v.* to shake, to have a tremulous motion, to wriggle, to move, to creep (as worms in a wound): pret. නලියෙව්වා *naliyewwá*.

නලී, *Nalí*, *s.* red arsenic.

නලේ, *Naḷé*, *s.* claw of a crab, etc. see නල *nala:* many persons or animals (in contempt).

නව්‍ය, *Nawya*, *a.* new, recent, young.

නව, *Nawa*, *s.* praise, panegyric, eulogium; any thing new or novel; number nine: *a.* new, novel, fresh, [Colloq. අලුත් *alut*].

නවක, *Nawaka*, *a.* new.

නවගුණ, *Nawaguṇa*, *s.* (නව nine, ගුණ virtue, moral quality) nine pre-eminent qualities, which are possesed exclusively by Buddha, viz. අරහං *arahaṉ*, perfectly holy and free from concupiscence, සම්මාසම්බුද්ධො *sammá-sambuddho*, the true and perfect Buddha, විජ්ජාචරණ සම්පන්නො *vijjácharaṇa-sampanno*, versed in all science and wisdom, සුගතො *sugato*, righteous and amiable in conduct, ලොකවිදූ *lokavidú*, acquainted with all worlds and every state of being, අනුත්තරො පුරිසදම්මසාරථි *anuttaro-purisadammasárathi*, he who subjects men and controls their morals by his irrefutable wisdom, සත්ථා දේවමනුස්සානං *satthá-déwamanussánaṉ*, the teacher of gods and men, බුද්ධො *buddho*, the wise one, භගවා *bhagawá*, blessed, fortunate or happy one: for more particular explanations see the words in their proper place.

නවත්වනවා, *Nawatwanawá*, *v.* to stop, to hinder; to cause to leave off: pret. නැවැත්තෙව්වා *nẹwẹttewwá:* causal form of නවතිනවා *nawatinawá*.

නවත, *Nawata*, *s.* elephant's painted or variegated housings; small watercourse cut for the purpose of letting off the water in paddy fields.

නවතනවා, *Nawatanawá*, *v.* to stop, to put a stop to, to hinder: pret. නැවැත්තුවා, *nẹwẹttuwá*.

නවතිනවා, *Nawatinawá*, *v.* to leave off, to cease, to desist: pret. නැවතුනා *nẹwatuná*.

නවදල, *Nawadala*, *s.* (නව new, දල germ) young shoot of a leaf; new leaf of a lotus, [Colloq. ලා දළු *lá-daḷu*].

නවදිලි, *Nawadili*, *s.* maiden crop.

නවදොර, *Nawadora*, නවද්වාර, *Nawadwára*, } *s.* (නව nine, දොර door, inlet) the nine openings of the human body, viz. eyes, ears, nostrils, mouth, anus, and the urinary passage.

නවන්, *Nawan*, *s.* number nine, [Colloq. නවය *nawaya*]; any new thing, novelty.

නවන්දන්නා, *Nawandanná*, *s.* man of the gold or silversmith caste.

නවන්මස, *Nawan-masa*, *s.* month so called, eleventh of the Siṉhalese year, (February—March), some times written නවම් මස *nawam-masa*.

නවනවා, *Nawanawá*, *v.* to bend, to curve, to double, to fold: pret. නැව්වා *nẹwwá*.

නවනීත, *Nawaníta*, *s.* fresh butter, [Colloq. අලුත් වෙඬරු *alut-weṉdaru*].

නවනීල කුරුල්ලා, *Nawaníla-kurullá*, *s.* bird called the Ceylon Trogon, *Harpactes fasciatus (*order *Picariæ);* also called රන්වන් කොණ්ඩයා *ranwan-koṇḍayá*, ගිනිකුරුල්ලා *gini-kurullá*.

නවනෑබිලිය, *Nawanẹbiliya*, *s.* plant, *agyreia bacciforma* or *phyllanthus urinaria*, [Colloq. පිටවක්කා *piṭawakká*].

නවභූෂණ, *Nawabhúshaṇa*, *s.* new ornaments, fresh dress or accoutrements.

නවම, *Nawama*, *a.* ninth.

නවමල්ලිකා, *Nawamalliká*, නවමලි, *Nawamali*, } *s.* jasmine: see නව මාලිකා *nawamáliká*.

නවමහල්, *Nawamahal*, *s.* house having nine floors or stories.

නවමාල, *Nawamála*, *s.* house with nine stories, one having nine floors.

නවමාලිකා, *Nawamáliká*, *s.* Arabian jasmine, *jasminum zambac*, [Colloq. පිච්ච *pichcha* or දෑසමන් *dẹsaman*].

නවමු, *Nawamu*, *s.* any thing fresh or new, novelty

නවය, *Nawaya*, *s.* number nine.

නවයෞවන, *Nawayauwana*, *s.* (නව and යෞවන youth) youth, puberty.

නවයෞවනා, *Nawayauwaná*, *s.* young woman.

නවරත්න, *Nawaratna*, *s.* name of a moral treatise; nine principal gems, *i. e.* ruby, pearl, topaz, diamond, emerald, lapis lazuli, coral, sapphire, and a yellow stone called góméda.

නවවත්, *Nawawat*, Elu form of නවවස්ත්‍ර *nawawastra*.

නවවන, *Nawawana*, *s.* (නව new, nine, වන being) new: *ad.* ninth.

නවවස්ත්‍ර, *Nawa-wastra*, *s.* (නව and වස්ත්‍ර cloth) new cloth.

නවසඳ *Nawasanda*, *s.* new moon, [Colloq. අලුත් හඳ *alut-handa*].

නවසාර, *Nawasára*, *s.* (නව and සාර essence) muriate of ammonia or sal ammoniac.

නවසි, *Nawasi*, *s.* variety of cocoa-nut, *cocos nucifera*, the husk of which is edible.

නවසිය, *Nawasíya*, *s.* nine hundred.

නවහඬි, *Nawahandi*, *s.* (නව and හඬි joints) plant, called milkhedge, *euphorbia Tirucalli (Euphorbiaceæ)*.

නවා, *Nawá*, *s.* rest: *part.* having bent, corrupt form of නමා *namá*.

නවාංගශාස්ත්‍ර, *Nawánga-şástri*, *s.* (නව *nawa* nine, අංග *anga* limb, member, ශාස්ත්‍ර religious teacher) name or epithet of Buddha, alluding to his being the founder of a religion consisting of nine Angas, or divisions of sacred science, viz. සුත්ත *sutta*, ගෙය්‍ය *geyya*, වෙය්‍යාකරණ *weyyákaraṇa*, ගාථා *gáthá*, උදාන *udána*, ඉතිවුත්තක *itiwuttaka*, ජාතක *játaka*, අබ්භුතධම්ම *abbhutadhamma*, වෙදල්ල *wédalla:* for a more paticular explanation see each separately.

නවාතැන, *Nawátęna*, *s.* (නවා rest, තැන place) lodging house, rest house, place for a temporary abode, pl. නවාතැන් *nawátęn*.

නවාම්, *Nawám*, *s.* new work: *a.* new, fresh, [Colloq. අලුත් *alut*].

නවීන, *Navína*, *a.* new, fresh, [Colloq. අලුත් *alut*].

නෂ්ට, *Nashṭa*, *a.* lost; removed; destroyed, annihilated.

නෂ්ටකාම, *Nasṭakáma*, *s.* (නෂ්ට destroyed, කාම lust) state in which all carnal desire and passion are destroyed.

නෂ්ටස්වර, *Nashṭaswara*, *s.* (නෂ්ට lost, ස්වර voice) loss of voice by disease or any other cause.

නස්, *Nas*, *s.* nose, [Colloq. නහය *nahaya*].

නස්න, *Nasna*, *s.* any medicine inhaled by the nostrils, sternutatory.

නස්නකරණවා, *Nasna-karaṇawá*, *v.* to inhale a medicine by the nostrils.

නස්නා, *Nasná*, *a.* killing, destroying; mischievous, perishing.

නස්නාපහණ, *Nasnápahaṇa*, *s.* touchstone, [Colloq. උරගල *uragala*].

නස්නාරන්, *Nasnáran*, *s.* species of wild lime, citron.

නසනවා, *Nasanawá*, *v.* to destroy, to annihilate, to kill: pret. නැසුවා *nęsuwá*.

නසිනවා, *Nasinawá*, *v.* to die, to expire, to become extinct: pret. නැසුනා *nęsuná*.

නහ, *Naha*, *s.* plant, *Lasiosiphon eriocephalus, (Thymelæaceæ)*.

නහගන්නවා, *Nahagannawá*, *v.* to commit suicide.

නහනවා, *Nahanawá*, *v.* to destroy, to make an end of, to kill, to annihilate, to subdue as the passions: pret. නැහුවා *nęhuwá*.

නහබ, *Nahaba*,
නහබා, *Nahabá*,
නහබු, *Nahabu*, } *a.* young, (as an animal) not full grown.

නහඹර, *Nahambara*, *a.* half grown, not arrived at maturity.

නහඹු, *Nahambu*, see නහබ *nahaba*.

නහම, *Nahama*, *s.* seeing, looking, beholding, [Colloq. බැලීම *bęlíma*]; forbidding, prohibiting, [Colloq. තහනම්කෙරීම *tahanamkeríma*].

නහමන, *Nahamana*, *a.* (න not, හමන blowing) calm.

නහය, *Nahaya*, *s.* nose.

නහරය, *Naharaya*, *s.* vein, nerve, tendon, pl. නහර *nahara*.

නහරි, *Nahari*, *s.* zedoary, *curcuma zedoaria*; plant, *kaempferia galanga*, [Colloq. හිඟුරුපියලි *hingurupiyali*].

නහවනවා, *Nahawanawá*, *v.* to bathe another, to wash: pret. නැවුවා *nęuwá*.

නහස්, *Nahas*, *s.* rubbing.

නහස්නාපාණ, *Nahasnápáṇa*,
නහස්නාපාසාණ, *Nahasnápásáṇa*, } *s.* (නහස්නා rubbing, පාණ stone) touchstone, [Colloq. උරගල *uragala*].

නහස, *Nahasa*, *s.* nose.

නහාපිත, *Nahápita*, *s.* barber, [Colloq. පනික්කියා *panikkiyá*]; Páli form of නාපිත *nápita*.

නහිනවා, *Nahinawá*, *v.* to die, to expire: pret. නැහුනා *nęhuná*.

නහුත, *Nahuta*, *s.* number, 10,000; also, number equal to 1 followed by 28 ciphers.

නහෙතු, *Nahetu*, *a.* (න neg. හෙතු cause) causeless, sourceless.

නළඟන, *Naḷangana*, *s.* (නළ dancing, අඟන *angana* woman) actress, female performer; dancing girl.

නළුඹ, *Nalamba*, *s.* dancing girl, actress.

නළල් *Naḷal*, *plur.* of නළල *naḷala*.

නළල්කෙළ, *Naḷalkeḷa*, *s.* the temples.

නළල්තලය, *Naḷaltalaya*, *s.* (නළල් and තලය surface) forehead, temples.

නළල්පටය, *Naḷalpaṭaya*, *s.* (නළල් and පට *paṭa* cloth) cloth for the head, turban, one of a superior kind, that worn by kings etc.

නළල, *Naḷala*, *s.* forehead.

නළු, *Naḷu*, *s.* dancer, pantomime, an actor.

නළුගණ, *Naḷugana*, *s.* (නළු and ගණ multitude) company of actors, set of dramatic performers.

නළුනාටක, *Naḷunáṭaka*, *s.* dancing, acting, pantomime.

නළුලිය, *Naḷuliya*, *s.* actress; dancing girl.

නළුවා, *Naḷuwá*, *s.* actor, dancer, dramatic performer; mime.

නා, *Ná*, *s.* snake, cobra capella, see නයා *nayá*; chief, ruler; sound; elephant; iron-wood tree: see නාගහ *ná-gaha*: *ad.* no, not.

නා ඉඹුල්, *Ná-imbul*. *s.* small tree with small yellow flowers, *Harpullia eupanoides (Sapindaceæ).* N. B. Harpulli is the vernacular name at Chittagong of which this tree is a native.

නාක, *Náka*, *s.* Swarga, the region of the gods, [Colloq. දිව්‍යලෝකය *diwya-lókaya*]; sky, atmosphere, ether, [Colloq. ආකාශය *ákásaya*].

නාකි, *Náki*, *a.* old, (advanced in years).

නාකියා, *Nákiyá*, *s.* (නාකි and යා pers. aff.) old man.

නාකුල, *Nákula*, *s.* ichneumon, mungoose, [Colloq. මුගටියා *mugaṭiyá*].

නාකුලී, *Nákulí*, *s.* ichneumon plant, herb supposed to furnish the mungoose with an antidote when bitten in a conflict with a snake, *rauwolfia* or *ophiaxylon serpentinum;* it is also used by native practitioners for the bite of serpents, [Colloq. ඒකාවේරිය *ekáwériya* or අරත්ත *aratta*].

නාකෙසුරු, *Nákesuru*, see නාමල් රේණු *námal-réṇu.*

නාග, *Nága*, *s.* hooded snake or cobra capella, [Colloq. නයා *nayá*]; serpent in general; elephant; demigod so called, having a human face and the tail of a serpent; this class of beings inhabits Pátála or the infernal regions; Ráhu or the ascending node; cloud; pin, nail in the wall for hanging things upon; lead, black lead, [Colloq. කළු ඊයම් *kaḷu-íyam*]; tin; iron-wood tree, *mesua ferrea*, [Colloq. නාගහ *ná-gaha*]; betel; one of the airs of the human body, that which is expelled by belching.

නාගකිඤ්ජල්ක, *Nága-kiñjalka*, } *s.* iron-wood tree,
නාගකේසර, *Nága-késara*, } bearing a white fragrant flower, *mesua ferrea*, [Colloq. නාගහ *ná-gaha*]; the stamina of its flowers, [Colloq. නාමල්රේණු *námal-réṇu*], used medicinally in coughs, catarrhs, etc.

නාගගන්ධ, *Nága-gandha*, *s.* (නාග and ගන්ධ scent) fragrance of the flower of the ná-gaha or iron-wood tree.

නාගජිහ්වා, *Nága-jiḥwá*, *s.* (නාග snake, ජිහ්වා tongue) plant, the leaves of which resemble the tongue of a snake, *hemidesmus indicus* or *asclepias pseudosara*, [Colloq. ඉරමුසු *iramasu*].

නාගත, *Nágata*, *s.* Ráhu, the ascending node, [Colloq. කෙහෙතු *kehetu*].

නාගතාර්තවා, *Nágatártawá*, *s.* young girl, one that has not menstruated.

නාගදණ්ඩ, *Nága-daṇḍa*, *s.* (නාග and දණ්ඩ wood) wood of the *nágaha* or *mesua ferrea.*

නාගදන්ත, *Nága-danta*, *s.* (නාග elephant, දන්ත tooth) tooth of an elephant; ivory; wooden pin in the wall for hanging things upon.

නාගදන්තක, *Nága-dantaka*, *s.* (derived as last) a wooden pin projecting from a wall to hang things upon.

නාගදන්ති, *Nága-danti*, *s.* flower, *heliotropium indicum.*

නාගදරණ, *Nágadaraṇa*, *s.* creeping or winding of a snake; circular path of a snake; medicinal root efficacious in the bite of snakes.

නාගදිවයින, *Nága-diwayina*, *s.* (නාග snake, දිවයින island) island near Ceylon.

නාගද්‍රැ, *Nága-dru*, *s.* (නාග and ද්‍රැ tree) iron-wood tree, *mesua ferrea*: see නාගහ *ná-gaha.*

නාගන්නවා, *Nágannawá*, *v.* to bathe one's self, to wash.

නාගපර්ෂද, *Nága-parshada*, *s.* (නාග snake, පර්ෂද multitude) collection or multitude of snakes.

නාගපාශ, *Nága-pása*, *s.* weapon of Varuṇa the regent of water; sort of noose or running knot.

නාගපාෂාණං, *Nága-pásánaŋ*, *s.* arsenic.

නාගපුෂ්ප, *Nága-pushpa*, *s.* (නාග mesua ferrea, පුෂ්ප flower) flower of the *mesua ferrea* or iron-wood tree, which is presented in the morning offerings at the Buddhist temples; tree used in dyeing, *mallotus philippensis* or *rottlera tinctoria*, [Colloq. හම්පරිල *hamparila*]; the champaka tree, [Colloq. සපු *sapu*].

නාගබන්ධු, *Nága-bandhu*, *s.* (නාග elephant, බන්ධු friendly) bó tree or holy fig tree, so named on account of the extensive shade it affords.

නාගබලා, *Nágabalá*, *s.* plant, *grewia lævigata*, [Colloq. ගස්කෑලිය *gas-kęliya*]: see the following word.

නාගබෑබිල, *Nágabębila*, නාගබෑවිල, *Nágabęvila*, } *s.* creeping plant, *hedysarum lagopodioides.*

නාගභවනය, *Nága-bhawanaya*, *s.* (නාග cobra, භවන residence) Pátála, the world inhabited by the serpent race.

නාගමල්ල, *Nága-malla*, *s.* (නාග elephant, මල්ල boxer) name of Indra's elephant.

නාගමාතා, *Nága-mátá*, *s.* (නාග cobra, මාතා mother) name of Manasá, a goddess supposed to preside over snakes.

නාගමාණවිකා, *Nága-mánavika*, *s.* female cobra capella.

නාගමාණික්‍ය, *Nága-mánikya*, *s.* (නාග snake, මාණික්‍ය gem) the ruby, a name which it has from a fable that that stone is found in the throat of the cobra capella.

නාගමාලිකා, *Nága-máliká*, *s.* (නාග and මාලිකා garland) garland or necklace of the flowers of the iron-wood tree.

නාගයා, *Nágayá*, *s.* cobra capella: see නාග *nága*.

නාගර, *Nágara*, *s.* form of writing, Déwa-nágara alphabet; citizen, resident in a city; dried ginger, [Colloq. වෙලිච්ච ඉඟුරු *wélichcha-inguru*]; sort of grass, *cyperus pertenuis*: *a.* clever, knowing; town-born or bred; bad, vile.

නාගරක, *Nágaraka*, *s.* orange.

නාගරඞ්ග, *Nágaranga*, *s.* sort of orange; mandarin orange, *citrus nobilis*, [Colloq. හින්නාරන් *hinnáran*]; another variety of the *citrus aurantium.*

නාගරාජයා, *Nágarájayá*, *s.* (නාග and රාජ king, යා pers. aff.) name of Ananta king of Pátála and regent of the serpent race, which, according to Buddhism, possessed of superhuman powers, can assume the human form and intermarry with mankind; their serpentine form is that of a cobra capella.

නාගරික, *Nágarika*, *s.* citizen, one resident in a city, [Colloq. නුවර වාසයකරණ *nuwara-wásaya-karana*].

නාගරුක්, *Nága-ruk*, *s.* (නාග and රුක් tree) iron-wood, tree, *mesua ferrea*, [Colloq. නාගහ *nágaha*].

නාගරේයක, *Nágaréyaka*, see නාගරික *nágarika*.

නාගලතා, *Nága-latá*, *s.* penis: see නාගවල්ලි *nágawalli*].

නාගලෝකය, *Nága-lókaya*, *s.* the world of snakes: see නාගභවන *nága-bhawana*.

නාගවඩම්, *Nágawadam*, *s.* earrings with the figure of a serpent worn by females.

නාගවදන, *Nága-wadana*, *s.* (නාග elephant, snake, වදන face) name of Ganésa the god of wisdom, alluding to his having the face of an elephant; name of Ráhu, the ascending node, in allusion to his having the head of a snake.

නාගවල්ලි, *Nágawalli*, නාගවල්ලිකා, *Nágawalliká*, } *s.* (නාග infernal nága, වල්ලි creeper) creeper betel, which has variegated leaves, [Colloq. බුලත් *bulat*].

නාගවාරික, *Nágawárika*, *s.* bird Garuda or vehicle of Vishnu; peacock; royal elephant.

නාගවික්කන්ත, *Nága-vikkanta*, Páli form of the next.

නාගවික්‍රාන්ත, *Nága-vikránta*, *s.* (නාග elephant, වික්‍රාන්ත going) gait or pace of an elephant.

නාගවීථි, *Nága-víthi*, *s.* path of Airavata, the milky way.

නාගසම්භව, *Nága-sambhawa*, *s.* (නාග lead, සම්භව production) red lead.

නාගසුගන්ධා, *Nága-sugandhá*, *s.* ichneumon plant: see නාකුලී *nákulí*.

නාගහ, *Ná-gaha*, *s.* iron-wood tree, *mesua ferrea*, *(Guttiferæ).*

නාගාන්තක, *Nágántaka*, *s.* (නාග *nága* snake, අන්තක who destroys) bird Garuda, the vehicle of Vishnu; it is also applied to many other birds, as the peacock etc, being enemies of the snake.

නාගාවෘත්ත, *Nágávritta*, *s.* (නාග *nága* snake, අවෘත්ත *árritta* surrounded) coiled as a snake, or a snake twisted round any thing.

නාගාශන, *Nágásana*, *s.* (නාග *nága* and අශන *asana* food) bird Garuda: see නාගාන්තක *nágántaka*,

නාගේන්ද්‍ර, *Nágéndra*, *s.* (නාග *nága* snake, elephant, ඉන්ද්‍ර *indra* chief) name of Ananta regent of Pátála and king of the serpent race; king of the elephants.

නාඟන, *Nángana*, *s.* female nága; female of the cobra capella.

නාඟවල්ලි, *Nángawalli*, *s.* betel plant, *piper betel*, [Colloq. බුලත් වැල් *bulat-węl*]: see නාගවල්ලි *nágawalli*.

නාඟිනි, *Nángini*, *s.* dewlap, [Colloq. තැල්ල *tęlla*].

නාට්‍ය, *Nátya*, *s.* science or art of dancing or acting, the union of song and dance accompanied with instrumental music.

නාට්‍යධර්මික, *Nátya-dharmika*, *s.* rules of dramatic representation.

නාට, *Náṭa*, *s.* dancing, acting, performing, exhibiting as a dramatist.

නාටක, *Náṭaka*, *s.* dancer, actor; mime; play, dramatic exhibition.

නාටකයා, *Náṭakayá*, *s.* (නාටක play, යා pers. aff.) dancer, dramatic performer; mimic.

නාටක ස්ත්‍රී, *Náṭaka-strí*, } *s.* (නාටක and ස්ත්‍රී woman) actress, female dancer.
නාටිකා *Náṭiká*,

නාඩගම, *Náḍagama*, *s.* native comedy or farce.

නාඩි, *Náḍi*, *s.* the stalk or culm of any plant; pulse; any tubular vessel of the body, as a vein, artery, intestine, etc; any pipe or tube; minute.

නාඩිකා, *Náḍiká*, *s.* stalk or culm of any plant, hollow stock of plants; Indian hour, or twenty-four minutes.

නාඩිවණය, *Náḍiwaṇaya*, } *s.* (නාඩි artery etc. ව්‍රණ wound) any disease affecting the blood; cutaneous disorder, fistulous or sinuous sore.
නාඩිව්‍රණ, *Náḍiwraṇa*,

නාඩිශාස්ත්‍ර, *Náḍi-ṣástra*, *s.* (නාඩි and ශාස්ත්‍ර science) branch of pathology, that which relates to the arteries etc.

නාඩුකරණවා, *Náḍukaraṇawá*, *v.* to threaten, to make afraid.

නාඩුව, *Náḍuwa*, *s.* anger, wrath, choler.

නාඩුවෙනවා, *Náḍuwenawá*, *v.* to roar, to threaten violently.

නාථ, *Nátha*, *s.* master, chief, lord; name of Buddha.

නාථවත්, *Náthawat*, *a.* (නාථ master, වත් poss. aff.) dependent, subject; subservient.

නාද, *Náda*, *s.* sound in general; tone, voice.

නාදකරණවා, *Náda-karaṇawá*, *v.* to sound, to make melody, to roar.

නාදළ, *Ná-daḷa*, *s.* (නා elephant, දළ tooth) tusk of an elephant, [Colloq. ඇත්දත *ętdata*].

නාදේ, *Nádé*, *s.* sound, tune, pl. නාද *náda*.

නාදේය, *Nádéya*, *s.* sea salt, [Colloq. සෛන්ධව ලුණු *saindhawa-luṇu*]: *a.* ocean or river born, aquatic.

නාදේයී, *Nádéyí*, *s.* sort of reed usually growing in watery places, *calamus fasciculatus;* plant, *premna herbacea;* tree, *æschynomene sesban*, [Colloq. දියදඹ *diya-da̲mba*]; orange.

නාදෙත්ත, *Nádętta*, *s.* wooden pin, bracket.

නාඳුනනවා, *Nán̲dunanawá*, *v.* (න *na* neg. අඳුනනවා *an̲dunanawá* to know) not to know, to be unacquainted with.

නානකාමරේ, *Nána-kámaré*, } *s.* bathing room.
නානගේ, *Nána-gé*,

නානත්වය, *Nánatwaya*, *a.* (නානා *nána* various, ත්ව *twa* affix denoting essense or quality) variety.

නානවා, *Nánawá*, *v.* to bathe: pret. නෑවා *nęwá*.

නානළුවා, *Nánaḷuwá*, *s.* (නා nága, නළුවා dancer) dancer of Pátála.

නානා, *Náná*, *ad.* various, several, many, manifold, [Colloq. නොයෙක් *noyek*]; *p.* bathing.

නානාගේ, *Náná-gé*, *s.* bath, bathing house.

නානාප්‍රකාර, *Nánáprakára*, *a.* various, several; of several kinds, of different sorts.

නානාරූප, *Náná-rúpa*, *a.* (නානා many, රූප form) multiform, various.

නානාවර්ණ, *Náná-warṇa*, *s.* bind-weed, *convolvulus paniculatus:* *a.* (නානා and වර්ණ colour) variegated, of many colours.

නානාවිධ, *Nánávidha*, see නානාප්‍රකාර *nánáprakára*.

නානු, *Nánu*, *s.* perfumed powder scattered on the guests at feasts etc.; kind of ointment for anointing the heads of kings on great feast days; composition for cleansing the hair.

නාපිත, *Nápita*, *s.* barber, written also නහාපිත *nahápita*.

නාපිරිත්ත, *Nápiritta*, *s.* hairy, thorny shrub, with large yellow flowers having dark crimson bottom, *hibiscus furcatus (Malvaceæ).*

නාබරණ, *Nábaraṇa*, *s.* Ṣiva, [Colloq. ඊශ්වරයා *íṣwarayá*].

නාබි, *Nábi*, *s.* navel: see නාභි *nábhi*.

නාබිමණ්ඩල, *Nábi-manḍala*, see නාභිමණ්ඩල *nábhi-manḍala*.

නාබුල්, *Nábul*, *a.* first begotten, first born (of animals); first produced (of fruits).

නාභ්‍ය, *Nábhya*, *a.* umbilical, relating to the navel.

නාභි, *Nábhi*, *s.* navel; musk; nave of a wheel.

නාභිජ, *Nábhija*, *s.* (නාභි navel, ජ born) name of Brahma, alluding to his being produced from the lotus, which sprung from Vishṇu's navel.

නාභිනාලා, *Nábhinálá*, *s.* (නාභි and නාලා string) umbilical cord.

නාභිමණ්ඩල, *Nábhi-manḍala*, *s.* (නාභි and මණ්ඩල circle) hollow round the navel.

නාභිය, *Nábhiya*, *s.* navel.

නාභිල, *Nábhila*, *s.* prominent or ruptured navel; hollow of the navel.

නාඹර, *Nám̆bara*, *a.* half ripe, partly matured.

නාම්බා, *Námbá*, *s.* young bull, one of three or four years and ready for castrating; half grown animal.

නාම, *Náma*, *s.* name, appellation; (in grammar) a noun, substantive.

නාමකරණ, *Námakaraṇa*, *s.* giving a name.

නාමපදය, *Náma-padaya*, *s.* a division of grammar which treats of nouns, adjectives and pronouns, grammatical term for noun, substantive.

නාමමාලා, *Náma-málá*, *s.* declensions of nouns.

නාමය, *Námaya*, *s.* name, appellation in grammar, noun: see නාම *náma*.

නාමල්, *Ná-mal*, *s.* (නා mesua ferrea, මල් flower) flower of the iron-wood tree, very fragrant white flower, which is offered in the Buddhist temples.

නාමල් රේණු, *Námal-réṇu*, *s.* (නාමල් and රේණු dust) stamina of the flower of the iron-wood tree, which is taken in medicinal preparations for catarrhs, etc.

නාම වචන, *Náma-wachana*, *s.* substantive, noun.

නායක, *Náyaka*, *a.* chief, principal, head, pre-eminent; guiding, directing.

නායකයා, *Náyakayá*, *s.* chief, leader, commander, person of eminence, guide.

නායන්, *Náyan*, *s.* annual plant, *vernonia anthelmintica (Compositæ)*, also called සන්නිනායන් *sannindruyan*.

නායහන්, *Ná-yahan*, *s.* (නා nága, යහන් couch) name of Vishṇu.

නාර, *Nára*, *s.* water, [Colloq. වතුර *watura*].

නාරං, *Náraṇ*, *s.* mandarin orange.

නාරංගහ, *Náraṇ-gaha*, *s.* (නාරං and ගහ tree) mandarin orange tree, *citrus nobilis*.

නාරක, *Náraka*, *s.* hell, infernal regions: *a.* hellish, infernal.

නාරකික, *Nárakika*, *s.* (නාරක *náraka* hell, ඉක aff.) inhabitant of hell.

නාරඞ්ග, *Náraṅga*, *s.* juice of the pepper plant; animal, but one of twins; catamite; orange tree.

නාරජ, *Ná-raja*, Elu form of නාගරජයා *nága-rájayá*.

නාරටිය, *Náraṭiya*, } *s.* fibres of the branches of
නාරටුව, *Náraṭuwa*, } the cocoanut tree.

නාරණ, *Naraṇa*, *s.* name of Vishṇu: see නාරායණ *nárúyaṇa*.

නාරද, *Nárada*, *s.* in Hindu mythology Nárada the son of Brahma, and one of the original Ṛishis or Muṇis, he was the inventor of the víṇá or Indian lute.

නාරන්ගහ, *Náran-gaha*, see නාරංගහ *náraṇ-gaha*.

නාරසිංහ, *Nárasiṇha*, *s.* name of Vishṇu, in his character of Narasiṇha or the man lion: see අව තාර *awatára*.

නාරාච, *Nárácha*, *s.* iron arrow.

නාරාචි, *Nárāchi*, *s.* goldsmith's scales, balance, [Colloq. තරාදිය *tarádiya*].

නාරායණ, *Náráyaṇa*, *s.* name of Vishṇu, alluding especially to his being considered as the deity before all worlds.

නාරායණප්‍රිය, *Náráyaṇapriya*, *s.* red sandal wood, variety of *santalum album*, [Colloquial: රන්වන් සඳුන් *ranwan-sandun* or රත්කිහිරිය *rat-kihiriya*].

නාරායණී, *Naráyaṇí*, *s.* name or the goddess Durgá, the wife of Ṣiva; name of Lakshmí the goddess of beauty; plant, *asparagus racemosa*, [Colloq. හාතාවාරිය *hátáwáriya*].

නාරිකේල, *Nárikéla*, *s.* cocoa-nut.

නාරි, *Nári*, *s.* woman.

නාරු, *Náru*, *s.* filaments in the pulp of some fruits.

නාරුක, *Ná-ruka*, *s.* (නා and රුක tree) iron-wood tree, *mesua ferrea*, pl. නාරුක් *ná-ruk*.

නාරුපු, *Ná-rupu*, *s.* (නා snake, රුපු enemy) Garuḍa or bird of Vishṇu so called on account of his destroying and feeding on serpents; ichneumon, mungoose, [Colloq. මුගටියා *mugaṭiyá*].

නාරොන්, *Ná-ron*, *s.* (නා tree nágaha, රොන් dust) pollen of the flower of the iron-wood, which is taken in catarrhs, coughs etc.

නාල, *Nála*, *s.* hollow or tubular stalk; the stalk of the water lily; yellow orpiment; tube, pipe.

නාලය, *Nálaya*, see නාල *nála*.

නාලාගිරි, *Nálágiri*, *s.* elephant so called, sent by Ajásat-raja to destroy Buddha.

නාලි, *Náli*, *s.* any tubular vessel of the body, as a vein, artery, intestine etc.; stalk of a water lily; measure.

නාලික, *Nálika*, *s.* buffalo; lotus.

නාලිකා, *Nálikā*, *s.* tubular stalk of plants; stalk of a lotus; any tubular stalk; instrument for piercing elephant's ear; plant, *hibiscus cannabinus*.

නාලිකේර, *Nálikéra*, *s.* cocoa-nut tree, [Colloq. පොල්ගහ *pol-gaha*].

නාලිය, *Náliya, s.* female elephant; betel, [Colloq. බුලත්වැල *bulat-węla*].

නාලික, *Nálíka, s.* arrow; dart, javelin, pike; lotus.

නාලොව, *Nálowa,* see නාගභවන *nága-bhawana.*

නාව්‍ය, *Náwya, a.* navigable, belonging to ships.

නාව, *Náwa,* see නාවා *náwá.*

නාවනවා, *Náwanawá, v.* to wash another, the causal form of නානවා *nánawá,* to bathe, to wash: pret. නැව්වා *nęwwá*].

නාවා, *Náwá, s.* ship, [Colloq. නැව *nęwa*]; tree with small flowers in pendulous panicles and edible seeds, *sterculia Balanghas (Sterculiaceæ)*

නාවි, *Návi, s.* root of a plant, *gloriosa superba,* which is reckoned a very subtile poison, [Colloq නියඟලා *niyangalá*].

නාවික, *Návika, s.* rower or steersman of a vessel, helmsman, pilot.

නාවුකා, *Náwuká* corruptly for නෞකා *nawuká,* which see.

නාවැසි, *Náwęsi, s.* (නා elephant, වැසි who dwells) elephant keeper, [Colloquial: ඇත්ගොවුවා *ęt-gowuwá*].

නාස්ති, *Násti, s.* non-existence, annihilation; destruction, loss, ruin: *ind.* particle implying not, is not.

නාස්තික්‍ය, *Nástikya, s.* atheism.

නාස්තික, *Nástika, s.* atheist, one who denies the divine authority of the Vedas.

නාස්තිකතා, *Násti-katá, s.* term used by the Hindus to designate the Buddhistical heresy, atheism.

නාස්තිකරණවා, *Nástikaranawá, v.* to destroy, to ruin.

නාස්තිය, *Nástiya, s.* destruction, ruin.

නාස්පුඩුව, *Náspuduwa, s.* (නාස *násа* nose, පුඩුව aperture) nostril.

නාස්පොල්ල, *Náspolla, s.* (නාස *nása* and පොල්ල bar) bridge of the nose.

නාස්සිදුර, *Nás-sidura, s.* (නාස *nása* and සිදුර aperture) nostril.

නාස, *Nása, s.* death, destruction, loss, annihilation; flight, retreat, abandonment, desertion; nose.

නාසනය, *Násanaya, s.* death, destruction, annihilation.

නාසය, *Násaya, s.* nose, [Colloq. නහය *nahaya*]: see නාස *nása.*

නාසාපුටය, *Násápuṭaya, s.* entrance of the nose, nostrils.

නාසික්‍ය, *Násikya, s.* the two sons of Asvini: see අශ්විනී *asvini.*

නාසිකාමල, *Násikámala, s.* (නාසිකා nose, මල excrement) mucus of the nose.

නාසිකාව, *Násikáwa, s.* nose.

නාසේ, *Násé, s.* nose, pl. නාසා *násá.*

නාහන, *Náhana, a.* (න *na* not, අහන *ahana* hearing) inexorable; disinclined to hear.

නාහෙ, *Náhe, s.* nose.

නි, *Ni, s.* a river in general, [Colloq. ගංගාව *gangáwa*]: *ind.* prefix to words, implying negation, privation, etc.

නිඃක්ෂිප්ත, *Niḥkshipta, a.* rejected, abandoned; foregone, given or thrown away.

නිඃක්ෂේප, *Niḥkshépa, s.* pledge, deposit; rejecting, leaving, forsaking, abandoning.

නික්, *Nik, s.* goldsmith's weight.

නික්කුජ්ජිත, *Nikkujjita, s.* upsetting, overturning: *a.* upset, turned over.

නික්ම, *Nikma, part.* going out, departing, proceeding from; Elu form of නිෂ්ක්‍රම්‍ය *nishkramya.*

නික්මයාම, *Nikmayáma, s.* departure, Exodus.

නික්මුණ, *Nikmuna, part.* gone, departed, left.

නික්මෙණවා, *Nikmeṇawá, v.* to depart, to leave, to proceed from, to set out: pret. නික්මුණ *nikmuṇá.*

නික, *Nika,* } නිකගහ *Nika-gaha,* } *s.* tree, species of the vitex; medicinal shrub so called: weight of 15 kalandas, or 2 oz. 13 dwt. 20 gr. troy.

නිකට, *Nikaṭa, s.* chin: *a.* near, proximate, [Coll: ලඟ *langa*].

නිකන්, *Nikan,* corruptly for නිකම් *nikam.*

නිකම්, *Nikam, a.* (නි neg. කම් work etc.) useless, unemployed; empty, nothing; simple, mere.

නිකම් ඉන්නවා, *Nikam-innawá, v.* to be unemployed.

නිකර, *Nikara, s.* flock, multitude, [Colloq. සමූහය *samúhaya*]; large quantity, abundance; pith, sap, essence; suitable or proper gift; treasure.

නිකරණ, *Nikaraṇa,* } නිකරුණ, *Nikaruṇa,* } *s.* (නි neg. කරණ doing) causeless; without motive.

නිකෂ, *Nikasha,* } නිකස, *Nikasa,* } *ad.* touchstone, [Colloq. උරගල *uragala*].

නිකසල, *Nikasala, a.* (නි neg. කසල filth) pure, clean, purified.

නිකා, *Niká, s.* house; multitude, quantity, heap.

නිකාම, *Nikáma, s.* (නි neg. කාම lust) freedom from lust or desire; the state of an ascetic who has completely subjugated his passions.

නිකාය, *Nikáya*, *s.* multitude, congregation, assemblage of persons performing like duties; flock; house, habitation.

නිකාර, *Nikára*, *s.* helplessness, destitution; malice, revenge; abuse, reproach, disrespect; injury; offence.

නිකාරණ, *Nikárana*, *s.* killing, slaughter.

නිකාස, *Nikása*, *a.* like, similar, resembling.

නිකිණි මස, *Nikiṇi-masa*, } *s.* fifth month of the
නිකින්නිය, *Nikinniya*, } Siṇhalese year, (July-August).

නිකුඤ්චක, *Nikuñchaka*, *s.* measure of capacity, equal to about as much as the palm of the hand will hold.

නිකුඤ්ජ, *Nikuñja*, *s.* arbour, bower, place overgrown with shrubs.

නිකුටු, *Nikuṭu*, *s.* reproach, scorn, abuse, slander.

නිකුත්, *Nikut*, *a.* gone, departed; dead.

නිකුත්කරණවා, *Nikutkaraṇawá*, *v.* to bring out or forth.

නිකුත්වෙනවා, *Nikutwenawá*, *v.* to depart, to go away, to set off.

නිකුම්භ, *Nikumbha*, *s.* son of Kumbhakarṇa, the brother of Ráwaṇa; medicinal plant, *croton polyandrum*, [Colloq. දැත්ත *detta*], and described as a gentle stimulant.

නිකේත, *Nikéta*, } *s.* house, habitation, dwell-
නිකේතන, *Nikétana*, } ing, residence, [Colloquial: වාසස්ථානය *wásasthánaya*].

නිකෘත, *Nikṛita*, *past. part.* tricked, cheated, deceived; dishonest; removed; dismissed.

නිකෘති, *Nikṛiti*, *s.* rejection, abuse, dishonesty.

නිකෘෂ්ට *Nikṛishṭa*, *a.* low, mean, despised, vile, outcast, degraded.

නිඛිල, *Nikhila*, *pron.* all, entire, complete, whole.

නිග්‍රහ, *Nigraha*, *s.* scorn, mockery, insult, derision; aversion, disfavour; discouragement; dislike; deviation from rectitude, impropriety; binding, confinement.

නිග්‍රහකරණවා, *Nigrahakaraṇawá*, *v.* to scorn, to mock, to deride; to treat with contempt.

නිග්‍රෝධ, *Nigródha*, *s.* banyan tree, *ficus bengalensis*, [Colloquial: මහනුග *maha-nuga*]; fathom, measured by the extended arms.

නිගණ්ඨ, *Niganṭha*, *s.* naked mendicant.

නිගද, *Nigada*, *s.* speech, discourse; audible recitation of prayers, charms; tone or sound of voice.

නිගම, *Nigama*, *s.* market, fair; town, city; holy writ; road, way; trade, traffic.

නිගමන, *Nigamana*, *s.* logical conclusion.

නිගමවාසයා, *Nigama-wásayá*, *s.* (නිගම city, වාස who dwells, යා aff.) inhabitant of a town or city, resident in a town, citizen.

නිගරණ, *Nigaraṇa*, *s.* throat; eating; swallowing.

නිගල, *Nigala*, *s.* elephant's foot chain; throat, gullet; collar, fetter.

නිගා, *Nigá*, *s.* scorn, mockery, insult, derision, contempt.

නිගාද, *Nigáda*, see නිගද *nigada*.

නිගු, *Nigu*, *s.* mind, faculty of reason and of feeling.

නිගුළ්හ, *Niguḷha*, *a.* (නි emphatic, ගුළ්හ hidden) concealed, profound; obscure, mysterious.

නිඝෝස්, *Nigos*, *s.* sound in chorus, echo; weeping, moaning, lamenting; cry of birds etc.

නිඝ්න, *Nighna*, *a.* menial, dependent.

නිඝණ්ටුව, *Nighanṭuwa*, } *s.* vocabulary; collection
නිඝණ්ඩුව, *Nighanḍuwa*, } of words or names.

නිචය, *Nichaya*, *s.* heap, assembly, collection, [Colloq. රාසිය *rásiya*].

නිචිත, *Nichita*, *a.* full, complete; collected.

නිචුල, *Nichula*, *s.* tree, *barringtonia speciosa*, [Colloq. මිදෙල්ල *midella* or මූදිල්ල *múdilla*].

නිජ්ඣර, *Nijjhara*, *s.* cascade, waterfall.

නිජ්ඣාමතණ්හික, *Nijjhámatanhika*, *s.* (නි intense, ඣාම burning, තණ්හික who desires) sprite or damned spirit, doomed to excruciating hunger and thirst, until his crimes are atoned for.

නිජ, *Nija*, *pron.* own, perpetual, eternal.

නිජබල, *Nijabala*, *s.* (නිජ own, බල strength) party influence, power of a partizan or confederacy; individual or peculiar strength.

නිට්ටාවෙනවා, *Niṭṭáwenawá*, *v.* to perish totally, to disappear finally, to be ended.

නිට්ඨා, *Niṭṭhá*, *s.* accomplishment of any action or purpose, finish, conclusion; disappearance; destruction; Páli form of නිෂ්ඨා *nishṭhá*.

නිටල, *Niṭala*, *s.* forehead, [Colloq. නළල *naḷala*].

නිත්ත, *Nitta*, } *a.* unceasing, continual, perpetual,
නිත්‍ය, *Nitya*, } constant, [Colloq. නිතර පවතින *nitara-pawatina*].

නිත්‍යගති, *Nitya-gati*, *s.* (නිත්‍ය constant, ගති going) air, wind.

නිත්‍යතාවය, *Nityatáwaya*, *s.* (නිත්‍ය and තාව *táwa* state) perpetuity.

නිත්‍යඵල, *Nitya-phala*, *a.* fruitful, abundant, always fruitful.

නිතම්බ, *Nitamba*, *s.* hips of a woman, buttocks or posteriors.

නිතර, *Nitara, ad.* always, continually.

නිතරම, *Nitarama, ad.* always, unceasingly, ever, continually.

නිතල, *Nitala, s.* (නි not, තල place or bottom) one of the seven divisions of hell, tartarus or the bottomless pit.

නිති, *Niti, ad.* continually, constantly, without ceasing, endless.

නිතිනින්ද, *Nitininda, a.* alone, single, sole, [Coll: තනියම *taniyama*].

නිතිපතා, *Nitipatá, ad.* always, ever, unceasingly, perpetually, [Colloq. නිතරම *nitarama*].

නිතොර, *Nitora,* see නිතර *nitara.*

නිතැතින්, *Niteṭin, ad.* easily, with facility, without trouble or difficulty.

නිද්‍රව, *Nidrawa, s.* dryness, want of moisture.

නිද්‍රා, *Nidrá,* } නිද්‍රාව, *Nidráwa,* } *s.* sleep, sleeping, drowsiness, [Colloq. නිදාගැන්ම *nidágeṇma*]; sloth, indolence, [Colloq. කම්මැලිකම *kammeli-kama*].

නිද්‍රෝපගත, *Nidrópagata, a.* (නිද්‍රා *nidrá* sleep, උපගත *upagata* gone) asleep, sleeping, in a state of sleep.

නිදන්, *Nidan,* } නිදන, *Nidana,* } *s.* mine, hidden treasure; treasury, depository for riches; beggar, mendicant; poverty, penury; Elu form of නිධාන *nidhána:* see නිදානය *nidánaya.*

නිදනවා, *Nidanawá, v.* to sleep.

නිදර්ශන, *Nidarṣana, s.* (නි emphatic, දර්ශන seeing) example, illustration, injunction, purport, authority.

නිදහස්කරණවා, *Nidahaskaraṇawá, v.* to set free, release.

නිදහස, *Nidahasa, s.* (නි priv. දාස slave) freedom, liberty, exemption.

නිදා, *Nidá, part.* having slept.

නිදාගන්නවා, *Nidágannawá, v.* to sleep, to take repose.

නිදාඝ, *Nidágha, s.* (නි always, දහ *daha* to burn, ඝ sub. for හ *ha*) heat, warmth; hot season, summer, [Colloq. ග්‍රීෂ්ම කාලය *gríshma-kálaya*].

නිදානය, *Nidánaya, s.* Elu form of නිධානය *nidhánaya,* in the sense of hidden wealth; cause, first cause, primary or remote cause; ascertaining the cause or symptoms of disease.

නිදා නැගී, *Nidá-negí, p.* having reposed and risen.

නිදාවැටෙනවා, *Nidáweṭenawá, v.* to fall asleep, to doze, to slumber.

නිදි, *Nidi, s.* sleep, disposition to sleep; hidden treasure: *a.* in a state of sleep, sleeping.

නිදිකුම්බ, *Nidikumba, s.* species of the sensitive plant, *mimosa pudica*; name of a snake.

නිදිග්ධ, *Nidigdha, a.* smeared, anointed, daubed with unguents, plastered.

නිදිග්ධා, *Nidigdhá, s.* small cardamoms, *elettaria cardamomum (Minor)*, [Colloq. හින් එන්සාල් *hín-ensál*].

නිදිග්ධිකා, *Nidigdhiká, s.* sort of prickly night shade, *solanum jacquini*, [Colloq. කටුවැල්බටු *kaṭuweḷ-baṭu*].

නිදිපොලඟා, *Nidi-polangá, s.* kind of viper.

නිදි බෙහෙත, *Nidi-beheta, s.* (නිදි and බෙහෙත medicine) opiate, narcotic.

නිදිමත, *Nidimata, s.* (නිදි sleep, මත stupor) sleepiness, drowsiness.

නිදි මීපොලඟා, *Nidi-mípolangá, s.* kind of viper.

නිදිෂ්ට, *Nidishṭa, p. p.* directed, pointed out; advised.

නිදු, *Nidu, s.* sleep, repose; outcast; sea, ocean, [Colloq. මුහුද *muhuda*].

නිදු අවර, *Nidu-awara, s.* (නිදු sleep, අවර last) thief, robber.

නිදුක්, *Niduk, a.* (නි neg. දුක් sorrow) at ease, exempt from pain or sorrow, happy, healthy.

නිදුකා, *Niduká, s.* (නිදුක් *niduk* and ආ *á* pers. aff.) a person at ease, one free from pain or grief, any one exempt from affliction.

නිදොස්, *Nidos, a.* blameless, faultless; Elu form of නිර්දෝෂ *nirdósha,* which see.

නිදෑස්, *Nideṣ,* } නිදෑස්දිවු, *Nideṣ-diwu,* } *s.* elephant, tusked elephant, [Colloq. අලියා *aliyá,* ඇතා *eṭá*].

නිධ්‍යාන, *Nidḍhyána, s.* sight, seeing: see ධ්‍යාන *dhyána.*

නිධන, *Nidhana, s.* death, dying; loss, disappearance, annihilation; race, family; seventh asterism of the lunar mansions, reckoning from that under which a person is born, and generally considered as the place of death.

නිධාන, *Nidhána,* } නිධානය, *Nidhánaya,* } *s.* hidden treasure, receptacle or depository for riches, hoard or subterraneous place for the concealment of riches.

නිධි, *Nidhi, s.* one of the divine treasures belonging to Waiṣrawaṇa the Indian god of wealth; there are nine of these enumerated in the Amarasiṇha kósha or vocabulary, viz. Padma, Mahápadma, Sankha, Makara, Kachchhapa, Mukunda, Nanda, Níla and Kharba; treasure in general, any depository of wealth.

නිඳු, *Nindu*, *s.* sleep, repose.

නින්දන, *Nindana*, *s.* reproach, blame; censure.

නින්දා, *Nindá*, *s.* censure, reproach, blame; abuse, scurrility; disgrace, shame; meanness, vileness.

නින්දාකරණවා, *Nindákaraṇawá*, *v.* to abuse, to scorn, to treat with contempt.

නින්දාව, *Nindáwa*, *s.* scorn, disgrace.

නින්දිත, *Nindita*, *a.* reviled, blamed, censured; mean, low, despicable, worthy of being despised.

නිනද, *Ninada*, *s.* sound in general, [Colloq. නාදය *nádaya*].

නිනව්, *Ninaw*, *s.* memory, sense, recollection.

නිප, *Nipa*, *s.* tree, *anthocephalus* or *nauclea cadamba*, [Colloq. බක්මී *bakmí*].

නිපද්, *Nipad*, } *s.* birth, production, bringing
නිපද, *Nipada*, } forth.

නිපදවනවා, *Nipadawanawá*, *v.* to produce, to cause to be born, to cause to bring forth.

නිපදවිය, *Nipadaviya*, preterite of නිපදවනවා *nipadawanawá*.

නිපන්, *Nipan*, *s.* birth, production, from නිෂ්පන්න *nishpanna;* term in Elu grammar denoting the primitive or peculiar vocables of the language, which cannot be traced to Páli or Sanskrit origin.

නිපන, *Nipana*, *s.* fish, fish in general.

නිපස්, *Nipas*, *s.* birth, origin, [Colloq. ඉපදීම *ipadíma*].

නිපා, *Nipá*, } *s.* falling, descending; affix to
නිපාත, *Nipáta*, } words, indeclinable particles, irregularity (in grammar).

නිපාන, *Nipána*, *s.* (නි emphatic, පාන drinking) trough or ditch near a well for watering cattle; milk-pail; well.

නිපුණ, *Nipuṇa*, *a.* (නි and පුණ to be pure) clever, skilful, conversant with, learned, wise, knowing.

නිපුස්, *Nipus*, *s.* female arrived at puberty.

නිපොල්, *Nipol*, *s.* (නි neg. පොල් coconut) coconut not fully matured and prior to the shell becoming hard; also part of a gun where the cap is placed.

නිබඳ *Nibanda*, *ad.* always, continually, unceasingly, endlessly.

නිබන්ධ, *Nibandha*, } *s.* constipation; attach-
නිබන්ධන, *Nibandhana*, } ment to; binding; grant of property; commentary.

නිබොරු, *Niboru*, *a.* not false, true, certain.

නිබෝ, *Nibó*, *a.* like, similar, resembling: *adv.* exactly, naturally.

නිඹ, *Nimba*, *s.* margosa tree, [Colloq. කොහොඹ *kohomba*]: see නිම්බ *nimba*.

නිඹුල්ලු, *Nimbullu*, *s.* twins.

නිඹුළු, *Nimbuḷu*, *s.* lotus; twins.

නිඹෝ, *Nimbo*, *ad.* all, every.

නිභ, *Nibha*, *s.* fraud, trick, deceit; pole to which the bullock is fastened in the plough, or cart: *a.* like, resembling, similar.

නිම්, *Nim*, *s.* iron rim of a wheel, pl. of නිම *nima*.

නිම්න, *Nimna*, *a.* low; deep, profound (literally or figuratively).

නිම්නස්ථාන, *Nimnasthána*, *s.* (නිම්න deep, ස්ථාන place) valley, place of refuge.

නිම්බ, *Nimba*, *s.* nimba or margosa tree, *azadarachta indica*, [Colloq. කොහොඹ *kohomba*].

නිම්බතරු, *Nimbataru*, *s.* coral tree, *erythrina indica*, [Colloq. එරබදු *erabadu*]; nimba or *azadaracta indica*, [Colloq. කොහොඹ *kohomba*].

නිම්ම, *Nimma*, *s.* end, conclusion, finish, [Colloq. අන්තිමය *antimaya*].

නිම්මාව, *Nimmáwa*, *s.* conclusion, end; boundary, limit.

නිම්වලල්ල, *Nim-walalla*, *s.* (නිම් circumference, වලල්ල ring) iron rim of a wheel.

නිම, *Nima*, *s.* end, completion, finish; boundary, circumference of a wheel.

නිමකරණවා, *Nimakaraṇawá*, *v.* to end, to complete.

නිමකළ, *Nimakaḷa*, *a.* completed, finished.

නිමග්න, *Nimagna*, *s.* plunged in, immersed.

නිමජ්ජන, *Nimajjana*, *s.* bathing, immersion.

නිමන්ත්‍රණය, *Nimantraṇaya*, *s.* conversation, speech; counsel, advice; invitation, calling.

නිමන්ත්‍රණය කරණවා, *Nimantraṇaya-karaṇawá*, *v.* to invite, convoke.

නිමන්ත්‍රිත, *Nimantrita*, *s.* (නි before, මන්ත්‍ර *mantra* invite, ඉත *ita* aff.) guest: *a.* invited, called.

නිමන, *Nimana*, *a.* what is collected as revenue, used for the net revenue.

නිමනවා, *Nimanawá*, *v.* to end; to extinguish, to quench, to put out: pret. නිමුවා *nimuwá*.

නිමිනැති, *Nímanęti*, *a.* endless, unlimited.

නිමය, *Nimaya*, *s.* barter, exchange.

නිමල, *Nimala*, *s.* (නි neg. මල dirt) pure, spotless, undefiled, unpolluted, unstained, [Colloq. පිරිසිදු *pirisidu*].

නිමවනවා, *Nimawanawá*, *v.* to finish, to end, to complete, to cause to extinguish or quench: pret. නිමෙව්වා *nimewwá*.

නිමවූ, *Nimawú*, *a.* finished, ended.

නිමාව, *Nimáwa*, *s.* end; bound, limit, line or boundary.

නිමි, *Nimi*, *a.* ended, finished.

නිමිත්, *Nimit*, *s.* cause, motive, reason; circumstance, event, occurrence.

නිමිත්ත, *Nimitta*, *s.* mark, sign, spot; trace, token; omen; prognostic; cause, motive; organ of generation; prognostic of approaching childbirth.

නිමිත්තකාරණ, *Nimitta-kárana*, *s.* instrumental cause, the material or agent.

නිමිත්තකොටගෙණ, *Nimittakoṭa-geṇa*, *adv.* by the instrumentality of, for the sake of, [Colloq. කරණකොටගෙණ *karaṇakoṭageṇa*, උදෙසා *udesá*].

නිමිත්තග්‍රහණ, *Nimitta-grahana*, *s.* (නිමිත්ත token, cause, ග්‍රහණ seizure) affected by personal beauty, falling in love.

නිමිත්තපාඨක, *Nimitta-páthaka*, *s.* (නිමිත්ත omen, පාඨක teller) fortune-teller, necromancer, astrologer, explainer of omens.

නිමිත්තමාත්‍ර, *Nimitta-mátra*, *s.* mere agent or instrument.

නිමිති, *Nimiti*, *s.* omens..

නිමිති අල්ලනවා, *Nimiti-allanawá*, *v.* to draw a lot, in order to ascertain one's fate by divination, to soothsay, to tell fortunes by marks or omens.

නිමිති අහනවා, *Nimiti-ahanawá*, *v*, to consult a sooth-sayer or one who pretends to predict an event by omens, with a view to find out a lost article, etc.

නිමිය, *Nimiya*, *s.* end, termination; completion, finish.

නිමිස, *Nimisa*, *s.* twinkling of an eye, twinkling of an eye considered as a division of time.

නිමීලන, *Nimílana*, *s.* twinkling of an eye, winking, blinking.

නිමීලනය, *Nimílanaya*, *s.* twinkling of an eye, closing of the eye,

නිමීලිත, *Nimílita*, *s.* closed, twinkled.

නිමුජ්ජන, *Nimujjana*, *s.* sinking.

නිමුන්මිට, *Nimun-miṭa*, } *s.* handle of a plough.
නිමුන, *Nimuna*, }

නිමුනුන්, *Nimunun*, *s.* twins.

නිමුනුන, *Nimununa*, see නිමුන්මිට *nimunmiṭa*.

නිමුලා, *Nimulá*, *s.* twins, two born at the same birth.

නිමෙනවා, *Nimenawá*, *v.* to be finished, to be completed, to be extinguished: pret. නිමුනා *nimuná*.

නිමේෂ, *Nimésha*, *s.* twinkling of the eye.

නිමොක්, *Nimok*, *s.* (නි forth, මුච *mucha* to let loose) slough of a serpent, [Colloq. සැවය *sẹwaya*].

නිය, *Niya*, *s.* wisdom, judgment, understanding, intellect, [Colloq. නුවන *nuwana*]; frankincense tree; finger-nail.

නියංකරණවා, *Niyaṇkaraṇawá*, *v.* to dry, to remain a dry season.

නියංසාය, *Niyaṇsáya*, *s.* dearth or famine produced by a dry season.

නියකටුව, *Niya-kaṭuwa*, *s.* (නිය finger-nail, කටුව prick) finger-nail pick.

නියග, *Niyaga*, *s.* drought, dryness, aridity; heat.

නියගලා, *Niyagalá*, *s.* creeping plant with handsome flowers, *gloriosa superba (Liliaceæ).*

නියඟ, *Niyaṇga*, see නියග *niyaga*.

නියත, *Niyata*, *a.* ascertained, certain, true; fixed, appointed.

නියතවිවරණ, *Niyata-viwaraṇa*, *s.* (නියත certain, විවරණ proclaiming, assurance) certainty of becoming Buddha, derived from the predictions of former Buddhas.

නියද, *Niyada*, *s.* stemless plant with long leaves, from the fibres of which cord and bow strings are made, called bow-string hemp, *sanseviera zeylanica, (Hæmodoraceæ).*

නියද ලනුව, *Niyada-lanuwa*, *s.* cord manufactured from the plant *sanseviera zeylanica.*

නියඳ, *Niyaṇḍa*, see නියද *niyada*.

නියන්, *Niyan*, plural of නියන *niyana;* corrupt form of නියං *niyaṇ*, hot or dry season, [Colloq. ඉඩෝර කාලය *iḍóra-kálaya*]; corrupt form of නිගම *nigama*, wich see.

නියන්කොබෙයියා, *Niyan-kobeyiyá*, *s.* purple wood pigeon, *alsocomus puniceus (Columbidæ* order *Columbæ).*

නියන්ගම, *Niyangama*, *s.* large village or town, market town.

නියන් වැටකොළු, *Niyan-wẹṭakoḷu*, *s.* creeping plant, monæcious, *luffa ægyptiaca* or *pentandra (Cucurbitaceæ).*

නියන, *Niyana*, *s.* chisel, pl. නියන් *niyan*.

නියපඬුර, *Niya-paṇḍura*, *s.* finger-nails, claws of a bird or animal considered collectively.

නියපිරිත්තා, *Niyapirittá*, *s.* kind of worm which eats the finger-nails.

නියපොත්ත, *Niyapotta*, *s.* finger-nail, toe-nail, pl. නියපොතු *niyapotu*.

නියබලා, *Niyabalá*, } s. (නි neg. ඇබලා *ębalá* for
නියඹලා, *Niyambalá*, } ඇඹුල *ęmbula* acid) curry prepared without the addition of acid, kind of curry, curry made of jack.

නියම්ගම, *Niyamgama*, see නියන්ගම *niyangama*.

නියම, *Niyama*, s. appointment, fixing, settlement: ordinance, religious observance, as fasting, watching, pilgrimage; voluntary penance, meritorious piety; any meritorious act; voluntary duty; name of Nirwáṇa or final emancipation; agreement, contract, engagement; assent, promise: *a.* right, fit, proper, just, suitable, fixed.

නියමකරණවා, *Niyamakaraṇawá*, *v.* to appoint, to fix, to settle, to determine.

නියමල, *Niya-mala*, s. white spot on the nails, pl. නියමල් *niya-mal*.

නියමවෙනවා, *Niyamawenawá*, *v.* to be appointed.

නියර, *Niyara*, s. dike, dam; narrow embankments raised in paddy fields, which serve to dam in the water and as pathways through the fields.

නියරි, *Niyari*, s. city, town, [Colloq. නුවර *nuwara*].

නියරී, *Niyarí*, s. citizen, one town bred.

නියලුන්, *Niyalun*, } s. sorrow, affliction, distress.
නියලුම්, *Niyalum*, }

නියවත්, *Niyawat*, } s. (නිය wisdom, වතා poss.
නියවතා, *Niyawatá*, } aff.) wise man, pandit, scholar, [Colloq. පණ්ඩිතයා *paṇḍitayá*].

නියවනවා, *Niyawanawá*, *v.* to grin, to make grimaces: pret. නියෙව්වා *niyewwá*.

නියසැත්, *Niyasęt*, s. (නිය and සැත් instrument) finger-nail or claw of a beast or bird, considered as a weapon to fight with.

නියහත්ත, *Niya-hatta*, s. (නිය finger nail, හත්ත fungus) white spot on the nails.

නියාය, *Niyáya*, } s. mode. manner, form, [Colloq.
නියාව, *Niyáwa*, } අන්දම *andama*].

නියුක්ත, *Niyukta*, *a.* (නි before, යුජ *yuja* to join) engaged in, attached to; authorized, called, appointed.

නියුක්තිය, *Niyuktiya*, s. authority.

නියුලු, *Niyulu*, s. distress, sorrow, pain.

නියෝග, *Niyóga*, s. (නි before, යුජ *yuja* to join) order, command, appointment, authority.

නියෝගකරණවා, *Niyógakaraṇawá*, *v.* to appoint, ordain, command.

නියෝජන, *Niyójana*, s. (නි before. යුජ *yuja* to join) order, command, appointment.

නිර්, *Nir*, *ind.* particle and prefix implying negation, privation; out, certainty.

නිර්ගත, *Nirgata*, *a.* (නිර් forth, ගම *gama* to go, ක්ත *kta* aff.) gone out, proceeded, departed.

නිර්ගම, *Nirgama*, s. going forth, [Colloq. පිටත්වයාම *piṭatwa-yáma*].

නිර්ගුණ්ඨි, *Nirgunthí*, s. shrub, *vitex negundo*, [Coll: නිල්නික *nil-nika*, සුදුනික *sudu-nika*]; root of the lotus.

නිර්ගුණ, *Nirguṇa*, *a.* (නිර් priv. ගුණ virtue, quality) worthless; bad, vile; void of all good qualities.

නිර්ග්‍රන්ථ, *Nirgrantha*, s. (නිර් not, ග්‍රන්ථ tie or connexion with the world) ascetic, devotee, one who has withdrawn from the world and lives as a mendicant or hermit.

නිර්ජර, *Nirjara*, s. (නිර් neg. ජරා *jará* decay) deity, a god, immortal being; food of the gods, ambrosia: *a.* immortal, imperishable.

නිර්ජරා, *Nirjará*, s. (නිර් and ජරා decay) exemption from the infirmities of age; plant, [Colloq. රසකිඳ *rasakiṇda*].

නිර්ජල, *Nirjala*, *a.* (නිර් and ජල water) destitute of water, desert, waste.

නිර්ඣර, *Nirjhara*, } s. cascade, waterfall, river.
නිර්ඣරී, *Nirjharí*, }

නිර්ණය, *Nirṇaya*, s. complete ascertainment, sentence, decision, positive conclusion.

නිර්ණේජක, *Nirṇéjaka*, s. washerman, [Colloq. රදවා *radawá*].

නිර්දය, *Nirdaya*, *a.* (නිර් priv. දයා kindness) unkind, unfeeling, cruel, hard, unmerciful.

නිර්දිෂ්ට, *Nirdishṭa*, *a.* described, depicted, pointed out, shown.

නිර්දේශ, *Nirdéṣa*, s. order, command, description, depicting, pointing out, exhibiting.

නිර්දෝෂ, *Nirdósha*, *a.* (නිර් neg. දෝෂ guilt) faultless, guiltless, blameless, without defect or flaw.

නිර්ධන, *Nirdhana*, *a.* (නිර් neg. ධන wealth) poor, indigent, needy.

නිර්ධර්ම, *Nirdharma*, s. (නිර් neg. ධර්ම righteousness, equity) unrighteousness: *a.* impious; unjust, wicked; irreligious, void of law or religion.

නිර්බන්ධන, *Nirbandhana*, s. (නිර් and බන්ධන to bind) intent and earnest pursuit of any thing; seizing, laying hold of any thing.

නිර්භය, *Nirbhaya*, s. (නිර් and භය fear) fearlessness, courage: *a.* fearless, bold, undaunted.

නිර්භව, *Nirbhawa*, s. (නිර් and භව being) impediment, hindrance, obstruction; delay.

නිර්භීත, *Nirbhíta*, see නිර්භය *nirbhaya*.

නිර්මල, *Nirmala*, *s.* (නිර් neg. මල dirt) clean, pure, free from filth or impurities (literally or figuratively).

නිර්මාණරති, *Nirmáṇa-rati*, *s.* (නිර්මාණ making, රති pleasure) name of the fifth divine world, so called because "when the inhabitants of this heaven wish to enjoy themselves in a greater degree than the enjoyments originally prepared for them admit of, they create ad libitum new sources of pleasure and enjoy themselves." Childers.

නිර්මාල්‍ය, *Nirmálya*, *s.* cleanness, purity, clearness, remains of an offering presented to a deity.

නිර්මිතකරණවා, *Nirmmita-karaṇawá*, *v.* to make, form, creat.

නිර්මුක්ත, *Nirmmukta*, *s.* snake that has lately cast his skin: *a.* liberated, loosed, freed.

නිර්මූල, *Nirmmúla*, *a.* baseless, unfounded, eradicated.

නිර්මෝක, *Nirmóka*, *s.* slough of a snake; setting free; armour.

නිර්යාස, *Niryása*, *s.* extract, decoction, infusion.

නිර්යූහ, *Niryúha*, *s.* extracted juice or decoction; crest, ornament for the head; door, gate; pin in the wall.

නිර්ලජ්ජ, *Nirlajja*, *a.* (නිර් neg. ලජ්ජා *lajjá* shame) shameless, impudent, immodest.

නිර්ව්‍යක්ත, *Nirwyakta*, *a.* (නිර් neg. ව්‍යක්ත oratorical, wise) stammering, having imperfect powers of speech; unlearned, ignorant.

නිර්වචන, *Nirwachana*, *s.* explanation, vocabulary, index: *a.* silent.

නිර්වර්ණ, *Nirwarṇa*, *a.* (නිර් neg. වර්ණ colour) colourless.

නිර්වර්තන, *Nirwartana*, *s.* leaving off, desisting from; completing, ending.

නිර්වස්ත්‍ර, *Nirwastra*, *a.* (නිර් priv. වස්ත්‍ර clothes) naked, in a state of nudity.

නිර්වාණ, *Nirwáṇa*, *s.* (නිර් out, වාණ *waṇa* to sound or go; or from the Páli නි neg. වාණ desire, extinction of desire) the summum bonum of Buddhism, viz. entire destruction of all the passions, total cessation of all the animal functions, extinction of every particle of the vivifying principle, final emancipation of the soul or sentient faculty, exemption from further transmigration, escape from every state of existence, annihilation! "The word Nirvaṇa is used to designate two different things, the state of blissful sanctification called Arhatship, and the annihilation of existence in which Arhatship ends.... Since Arhats die Arhatship is not an eternal state.... The Arhat does not live again but ceases to exist....there being no annihilation without Arhatship and no Arhatship that does not end in annihilation." Childers, confirming Hardy and Jas. De Alwis.

නිර්විකාර, *Nirvikára*, *a.* (නිර් neg. විකාර change) uniform, immutable.

නිර්වේදය, *Nirwédaya*, *s.* (නිර් and වේද *wéda* knowledge) humility, self disparagement: *a.* not having the Védas, infidel, unscriptural.

නිර්වේධ, *Nirwédha*, *a.* (නිර් and වේධ piercing) unpierced, impervious.

නිර්වේශ, *Nirwéṣa*, *s.* wages, hire, enjoyment, attaining, entering in.

නිර්වේෂ්ටනය, *Nirwéshṭanaya*, *s.* (නිර් and වේෂ්ටන *wéshṭana* folding, coiling) unfolding, loosening (literally or metaphorically).

නිර්හරණ, *Nirharaṇa*, } *s.* removing entirely, evac-
නිර්හාර, *Nirhára*, } uation of any of the natural excrements of the body, fæces, urine, sweat etc.; drawing out, rooting up, extracting; burning, combustion.

නිරග්ගල, *Niraggala*, *s.* one of the four great sacrifices of the Hindus: *a.* unimpeded, unobstructed.

නිරත, *Nirata*, *a.* engaged in, attached to: *ad.* always, perpetually, continually.

නිරතු, *Niratu*, *a.* empty, vacant, void.

නිරතුර, *Niratura*, } *ad.* always, ever, unceasingly,
නිරතුරු, *Niraturu*, } perpetually, continually.

නිරතුරූ, *Niraturú*, *s.* growling, making a noise in the throat.

නිරද, *Nirada*, *s.* (නීර water, ද what gives) sea, ocean, [Colloq. මුහුද *muhuda*].

නිරන්තර, *Nirantara*, *a.* (නිර් *nir* neg. අන්තර *antara* intermission, interstices) continuous, perpetual, constant; coarse, gross, without interstices.

නිරපරාධ, *Niraparádha*, *a.* (නිර් *nir* and අපරාධ *aparádha* guilt) faultless, guiltless, blameless, innocent.

නිරපේක්ෂ, *Nirapéksha*, *s.* (නිර් *nir* and අපේක්ෂා *apekshá* care) independent of, indifferent, without hope; disregarding, used of such as give up all for religious pursuits.

නිරය, *Niraya*, *s.* (නිර් *nir* neg. අය *aya* good fortune, welfare) hell, infernal regions; there are eight chief hells, each surrounded by four smaller ones, in which punishments are inflicted according to the nature and extent of the guilt of the culprit.

නිරර්ගල, *Nirargala*, *s.* (නිර් *nir* and අර්ගල *argala* bolt, bar) unbolted, insecure; unobstructed, unimpeded.

නිරර්ථක, *Nirarthaka*, *a.* (නිර් *nir* not, අර්ථ *artha* meaning, good) unmeaning, vain, fruitless, unprofitable.

නිරවග්‍රහ, *Nirawagraha*, *a.* (නිර් *nir* neg. අවග්‍රහ *awagraha* control) selfwilled, uncontrolled, headstrong, independent.

නිරවද්‍ය, *Nirawadya*, *a.* (නිර් *nir* and අවද්‍ය *awadya* guilt) guiltless, blameless, innocent, unobjectionable, unexceptionable.

නිරවශේෂ, *Nirawaṣésha*, *a.* (නිර් *nir* and අවශේෂ *awaṣésha* remainder) finished, ended, completed, concluded, nothing remaining; all, whole, entire.

නිරවුල්, *Nirawul*, *a.* (නිර් *nir* and අවුල් *awul* confused) unconfused, clear, undisturbed; unmixed.

නිරස්ත, *Nirasta*, *a.* (නිර් *nir* out, අස්ත *asta* thrown) sent, thrown, cast away, shot or sent as an arrow; rejected, left, abandoned, [Colloq. අත් ඇරුණු *at-ẹruṇu*].

නිරසන, *Nirasana*, *s.* (නිර් *nir* out, අස *asa* to throw) rejecting, casting away; denying, disallowing; killing, destroying.

නිරා, *Nirá*, *s.* hell, the infernal regions: see නිරය *niraya*.

නිරාකරණ, *Nirákaraṇa*, *a.* obstructing, opposing, rejecting, contradicting, [Colloq. වැලකීම *wẹlakíma*, නැතිකෙරීම *nẹtikeríma*].

නිරාකරිෂ්ණු, *Nirákarishṇu*, *a.* obstructing, impeding; sending, casting away, sending off, rejecting.

නිරාකාර, *Nirákára*, *s.* (නිර් *nir* neg. අකාර *akára* shape or mode) a god, invisible being; name of Vishṇu and of Ṣiva: *a.* devoid of form or figure.

නිරාකෘති, *Nirákṛiti*, *a.* rejected, sent, thrown, shot or sent as an arrow.

නිරාග්නි, *Irágni*, *s.* (නිර *nira* hell, අග්නි *agni* fire) hell-fire, flames of the infernal regions.

නිරාචාර, *Niráchára*, *s.* (නිර් *nir* neg. ආචාර *áchára* moral ordinance) lawless, wicked; corrupt, barbarous.

නිරාතපා, *Nirátapá*, *s.* (නිර් *nir* and ආතප *átapa* sunshine) night, [Colloq. රෑ *rẹ*].

නිරාදරව, *Nirádarawa*, *a.* (නිර් *nir* and ආදරව *ádarawa* having affection) unloving, unkind, unmerciful; cruel, hard hearted.

නිරාදුක්, *Nirá-duk*, *s.* (නිරා hell, දුක් sorrow) pains of hell, punishments of hell: see නිරය *niraya*.

නිරාබාධ, *Nirábádha*, *a.* (නිර් *nir* neg. ආබාධ *ábádha* pain) free from pain, healthy; frivolously or unreally vexatious, having no real cause to complain.

නිරාමය, *Nirámaya*, *a.* recovered from sickness, well, hale.

නිරායාස, *Niráyása*, *s.* (නිර් *nir* neg. ආයාස *áyása* fatigue, exhaustion from pain or mental suffering) unwearied, vigorous, active; not giving trouble; easily attainable.

නිරාර්ථක, *Nirárthaka*, corrupt form of නිරර්ථක *nirarthaka*, which see.

නිරාලම්බනය, *Nirálambanaya*, *s.* (නිර් *nir* and ආලම්බන *álambana* adhering, hanging) unoccupied space, vacuum, region of space: *a.* unstable, loose, inconstant.

නිරාශ, *Niráṣa*, *a.* (නිර් *nir* priv. ආශා *áṣá* hope) hopeless, disappointed.

නිරාශා, *Niráṣá*, (නිර් *nir* neg. ආශා *áṣá* hope) despair, despondency.

නිරාහාර, *Niráhára*, *s.* (නිර් *nir* and ආහාර *áhára* food) fasting, abstinence; hunger, want of food.

නිරි, *Niri*, *s.* second crop, second and inferior crop of grain, grass etc.

නිරිඟි, *Niringi*, *s.* veil.

නිරිත, *Nirita*, *s.* one of the intermediate points of the compass (South-west).

නිරිඳු, *Nirindu*, *s.* (නිර *nira* for නර *nara* man, ඉඳු *indu* chief) king, sovereign, monarch, [Colloq. රජ *raja*].

නිරින්ද්‍රිය, *Nirindriya*, *a.* (නිර් *nir* neg. ඉන්ද්‍රිය *indriya* organ of sense) imperfect, mutilated, maimed.

නිරිවස්ත්‍ර, *Niriwastra*, corrupt form of නිර්වස්ත්‍ර *nirwastra*, which see.

නිරිවැල්, *Niri-wẹl*, *s.* plant, *limacia cuspidata*, (*Menispermiaceæ*).

නිරිසතා, *Niri-satá*, *s.* (නිර *nira* hell, සතා being) inhabitant of hell, any infernal being, pl. නිරි සත්තු *niri-sattu*.

නිරීක්ෂණ, *Nirîkshaṇa*, *s.* sight, seeing, vision, [Colloq. බැලීම *bẹlíma*].

නිරු, *Niru*, plural of නිර *nira*.

නිරුක්ත, *Nirukta*, *s.* (නිර් *nir* implying certainty, or privation, උක්ත *ukta* spoken) glossary, explanation of obscure terms: *a.* obscure, obsolete, unexplained.

නිරුක්ති, *Nirukti, s.* one of the Védáṅgas, explanation of obscure and difficult terms, verbal analysis, use or expression of a language.

නිරුත්තර, *Niruttara, a.* (නිර් *nir* neg, උත්තර *uttara* answer) unanswered, unanswerable, silenced.

නිරුද්ධ, *Niruddha, a.* destroyed, stopped, restrained.

නිරුදක, *Nirudaka, a.* (නිර් *nir* and උදක *udaka* water) dry, having no water.

නිරුපද්‍රව, *Nirupadrawa, a.* (නිර් *nir* and උපද්‍රව *upadrawa* danger) dangerless, safe, secure, free from alarm.

නිරුපම, *Nirupama,* } *a.* unequalled, having
නිරුපමාන, *Nirupamána,* } no resemblance or likeness.

නිරුපාදිශේෂ, *Nirupádisésa, s.* (නිර් *nir* priv. උපාදි *upádi* five elements of existence, ශේෂ remaining) freedom from transmigration, final emancipation of the soul, annihilation of the five Skandhas or elements of existence; name of Nirwáṇa.

නිරුවන්, *Niruwan, s.* (නිර *nira* hell, වන් arrived) doomed to the infernal regions, appointed to suffer the torments of hell.

නිරූප, *Nirúpa, a.* (නි priv. රූප form, beauty) incorporeal, immaterial; ugly, deformed.

නිරූපණ, *Nirúpaṇa. s.* sight; seeing; doubt; discussion; investigation; ascertaining; determining.

නිරෙහි කෙළිනවා, *Nirehi-keḷinawá,* see නිරෝහි කෙළිනවා *niróhi-keḷinawá.*

නිරෝග, *Niróga,* } *a.* (නි neg. රෝග disease)
නිරෝගී, *Nirógi,* } healthy, well, hale, free
නිරෝගිව, *Nirógiwa,* } from disease.

නිරෝධ, *Niródha, s* (නි neg. රුධ *rudha* obstruct) annihilation, Nirwáṇa, final emancipation of the soul; that state in which the passions have been so far subdued that there is no further obstruction to the obtaining of Nirwáṇa: see ක්ලේශ *kléṣa;* death, destruction; confinement; dislike, disfavour.

නිරෝධ මාර්ගය, *Niródha-márgaya, s.* (නිරෝධ and මාර්ගය way) entire subjugation or destruction of the passions, see the last.

නිරෝධ සත්‍ය, *Niródha-satya, s.* (නිරෝධ and සත්‍ය truth) one of the four chief truths of Buddhism, viz. doctrine of final emancipation of the soul, considered as the result of the destruction of ක්ලේශ *kléṣa* or the entire subjugation of the passions, Nirwáṇa: see ක්ලේශ *kléṣa.*

නිරෝධ සමාපත්තිය, *Niródha-samápattiya, s.* (නි රෝධ and සං *saṇ* complete, ආපත්ති *ápatti* arrival) practice of religious duties and austerities for the purpose of obtaining Nirwáṇa; that state of devout and abstract meditation in which the senses and passions have been so far destroyed, that all wish, all desire, and all the mental faculties have ceased to operate.

නිරෝෂණ, *Niróshaṇa, a.* (නි priv. රෝෂණ anger) calm, mild, placid, placable.

නිරෝහි කෙළිනවා, *Niróhi-keḷinawá, v.* to rejoice publicly for any great event.

නිල්, *Nil, s.* substance in standing water, plant, *blyxa Roxburghii* or *vallisneria octandra,* [Coll: දියහවරි *diyahawari*]; tender fruit, මැලෙස්ස *mẹlẹssa* (Námáwaliya); *a.* blue; green.

නිල් අඬනහිරිය, *Nil-aṇdanahiriya, s.* annual plant, *crotalaria verrucosa (Leguminosæ).*

නිල් අවරි, *Nil-awari, s.* East Indian indigo plant, *indigofera tinctoria (Leguminosæ).*

නිල් ඉඳින්නරු, *Nil-iṇdinnaru, s.* hooded milfoil, *utricularia uliginosa.*

නිල් උණලී, *Nil-uṇalí, s.* bamboo cane, *bambusa arundinacea.*

නිල්කට, *Nilkaṭa, s.* (නිල් blue, කට neck) name of Íṣwara or Ṣiva, alluding to his having a blue neck; peacock, [Colloq. මොණරා *moṇará*].

නිල් කටරොඩු, *Nil-kaṭaroḍu,* } *s.* creeping plant,
නිල් කටරොළු, *Nil-kaṭaroḷu,* } bearing a beautiful blue flower, *clitoria Terneata (Leguminosæ).*

නිල් කටුස්සා, *Nil-kaṭussá, s.* lizard in green colour (common about Colombo) *Calotes ophiomachus (Agamidæ* order *Sauria).*

නිල් කවුඩුදල, *Nil-kawuḍudala, s.* plant, *hedyotis graminifolia.*

නිල් කාපිරි, *Nil-kápiri, s.* endive, *cichorium endivia.*

නිල්කැට, *Nil-kẹta, s.* (නිල් and කැට stone) blue sapphire.

නිල්ගෙල, *Nil-gela, s.* (නිල් and ගෙල neck) peacock, [Colloq. මොණරා *moṇará*].

නිල් ගෝනකොල, *Nil-gónakola, s.* shrub, *Adenosma capitatum* or *stemodia camphorata (Scrophulariaceæ).*

නිල් තණ, *Nil-taṇa, s.* general name for grass.

නිල් තම්පලා, *Nil-tampalá, s.* plant, amaranth with crimson flowers and concave leaves, *amaranthus cruentus.*

නිල් තලා, *Nil-talá, s.* species of basil.

නිල් දුරදඹල, *Nil-dáradaṃbala, s.* leguminous cultivated plant, *dolichos tetragonolobus.*

නිල් දිවිපහුරු, *Nil-diripahuru*, *s.* plant, *ipomœa hepaticifolia.*

නිල් දිවුල්, *Nil-diwul*, *s.* variety of the elephant or wood apple, *feronia elephantum.*

නිල් නකුට, *Nil-nakuṭa*, *s.* bastard vervain, *stachytarpheta indica*; also called බලුනකුට *baḷu-nakuṭa.*

නිල් නවසි, *Nil-nawasi*, *s.* sort of coconut, the husk of which is eatable.

නිල් නික, *Nil-nika*, *s.* small tree with small purplish flowers, leaves medicinal, *vitex Negundo (Verbenaceæ).*

නිල් පාට, *Nil-páṭa*, *s.* (නිල් and පාට colour) blue, dark blue; green.

නිල් පුරුක්, *Nil-puruk*, *s.* plant, *ruellia ringens.*

නිල් පොල්, *Nil-pol*, *s.* (නිල් green, පොල් coconut) common coconut, *cocos nucifera.*

නිල්පැහැ, *Nilpęhę*, *s.* blue or green (colour).

නිල් බොල්හිඳ, *Nil-bolhinda*, *s.* spider wort, *tradescantia tristata.*

නිල් මහනෙල්, *Nil-mahanel*, } *s.* variety of the
නිල් මානෙල්, *Nil-mánel*, } *nymphæa stellata*, species of water lily.

නිල්මිණ, *Nilmiṇa*, } *s.* (නිල් blue, මිණ gem) blue
නිල්මිණි, *Nilmiṇi*, } sapphire.

නිල්මේ, *Nilmé*, *s.* thick cloud, cloud condensed with rain.

නිල් මොනරැස්ස, *Nil-monaręssa*, *s.* hooded milfoil, plant with large purple flowers, common in rice-fields, *utricularia reticulata (Lentibulariaceæ).*

නිල්මැලි, *Nilmęli*, *s.* Bengal quince, *ægle marmelos:* see බෙලි *beli.*

නිල්රාජකුරුල්ලා, *Nil-rája-kurullá*, *s.* fairy blue bird, *Irena puella (Brachypodidæ* order *Passeres).*

නිල් රාබු, *Nil-rábu*, *s.* radish, *raphanus sativa.*

නිල්රැස්, *Nilręs*, *s.* one of the colours of the prism, azure.

නිල්ල, *Nilla*, *s.* verdure.

නිල් ලනවා, *Nil-lanawá*, *v.* to dye blue, to add a little blue to the clothes, as is done by washermen: pret. නිල් ලෑවා *nil-léwá.*

නිල්වන්, *Nilwan*, *s.* the colour blue: *a.* bluish.

නිල් වම්බටු, *Nil-wambaṭu*, *s.* sort of nightshade, brinjal, *solanum melongena.*

නිල් වලාව, *Nil-waláwa*, *s.* (නිල් dark-blue, වලාව cloud) dense cloud, one heavily impregnated with rain.

නිල්වසන, *Nil-wasana*, *s.* (නිල් blue, වසන covering) name of Balabhadra, alluding to his being generally represented in the temples as clothed in blue garments.

නිල්වැල්ල, *Nil-węlla*, *s.* plant, sub-parasitical, *dracontium pertusum.*

නිල් වැලිවැන්න, *Nil-węliwęnna*, *s.* plant, *hedyotis octacea*: see වැලිවැන්න *węliwęnna.*

නිල, *Nila*, *s.* colours blue and green; house, [Coll: ගෙය *geya*]; blue sapphire.

නිලංකාර, *Nilaṅkára*, *s.* blue eye, person having blue eyes, considered a mark of great beauty, green colour.

නිලගල, *Nilagala*, *s.* (නිල black, ගල neck) peacock, [Colloq. මොණරා *moṇará*]: see නිලග්‍රීව *níla-griwa.*

නිලගුරු, *Nilaguru*, *s.* (නිල් *nil* for නිර් *nir* neg. අගුරු *aguru* for අකුරු *akuru* letter) illiterate person, ignorant man; tusked elephant.

නිලඟ, *Nilanga*, *s.* name of the planet Saturn; name of Vishṇu; fetter.

නිලඟ දින, *Nilanga-dina*, *s.* (නිලඟ Saturn, දින day) Saturday, [Colloq. සෙනසුරාදා *senasurádá*].

නිලතල, *Nilatala*, *s.* high office, one of great revenue.

නිලතුර, *Nilatura*, *ad.* (නිල් *nil* for නිර් *nir* neg. අතුර *atura* interval) always, ever, perpetually.

නිලන්කාර, *Nilankára*, *a.* dazzled, unable to see through excessive light.

නිලන්තර, *Nilantara*, *ad.* always, propetual.

නිලපලා, *Nilapalá*, } *s.* any land which has
නිලපාළුව, *Nilapáḷuwa*, } devolved to government, from the death of persons who held it on the tenure of doing government service.

නිලබ, *Nilaba*, Elu form of නිලාභ්‍ර *níl**á**bhra.*

නිලබර, *Nilabara*, } *s.* (නිල් *nil* blue, අඹර *am-*
නිලඹර, *Nilambara*, } *bara*, atmosphere; dress) visible heavens, sky, [Colloq. අහස *ahasa*]; name of Balaráma, alluding to his warlike character and being figured in the temples in a dark blue garment; planet Saturn, dark blue garment.

නිලමේ, *Nilamé*, } *s.* high office, office of state,
නිලමය, *Nilamaya*, } office, nobleman.

නිලමැස්සා, *Nilamęssá*, *s.* (නිල and මැස්සා fly) blue fly; flesh fly.

නිලය, *Nilaya*, *s.* house, habitation, [Colloq. ගේ *gé*]; office, appointment.

නිලයා, *Nilayá*, see නිලමැස්සා *nilamęssá.*

නිලාව, *Niláwa*, *s.* blue light.

නිලි, *Nili*, *s.* slime or mucus, substance in standing waters; darkness produced by a cloud.

නිලිගත් පත්‍ර, *Niligat-patra*, *s.* green or fresh leaf.

නිලිපුල්, *Nilipul*, *s.* (නිල් *nil* blue, ඉපුල් *ipul* for උපුල් *upul* lotus) blue lotus, *nymphœa stellata*, [Colloq. නිල් මානෙල් *nil-mánel*].

නිලිපුල්වන්, *Nilipulwan*, *s.* (නිල් *nil* and උපුල් *upul* lotus, වන් colour) epithet of Vishṇu, he being always figured in the temples of a dark blue colour.

නිලිපුලැසි, *Nilipulęsi*, *s.* woman having dark-blue eyes.

නිලිය, *Niliya*, *s.* Lakshmí, wife of Vishṇu.

නිලිහි, *Nilihi*, *s.* tree, *bridelia spinosa*.

නිලීන, *Nilína*, *a.* encompassed, surrounded, shut up, wrapt up; embraced; concealed, hidden, clandestine.

නිලුපුල්, *Nílupul*, Elu form of නීලෝත්පල *nílótpala*: see නිලිපුල් *nilipul*.

නිලැස්, *Nilęs*, *s.* (නිල් *nil* blue, ඇස් *ęs* eye) name of Waiṣrawaṇa, alluding to the blue mark on his forehead, which stands in the place of any eye.

නිවට, *Niwaṭa*, *a.* poor, needy, indigent; inexpert, unskilful, ignorant.

නිවටු, *Niwaṭu*, *s.* religious mendicant, devotee who has renounced the world and lives by begging or as an ascetic, [Colloquial: මිථ්‍යාදෘෂ්ටින් *mithyádṛishṭín*]; goat.

නිවත්, *Niwat*, *s.* birth, production: *a.* poor, needy, indigent.

නිවතා, *Niwatá*, *s.* (නිවත් *niwat* poor, ආ *á* pers. aff.) indigent man, person of great poverty.

නිවණ, *Niwaṇa*, Elu form of නිර්වාණ *nirwáṇa*, which see.

නිවනවා, *Niwanawá*, *v.* to extinguish, to put out, to quench; to annihilate: pret. නිව්වා *niwwá*.

නිවරණ, *Niwaraṇa*, *s.* (නි and වරණ supporting) hindrance, impediment, obstacle, brand-marks.

නිවරදි, *Niwaradi*, *a.* (නි neg. වැරදි *węradi* faulty) blameless, faultless, guiltless, irreproachable, innocent.

නිවරා, *Niwará*, *s.* (නි and වර husband) virgin, unmarried woman.

නිවාඩු, *Niwáḍu*, *s.* rest: *a.* unocupied, easy.

නිවාඩුව, *Niwáḍuwa* *s.* leisure, ease, rest.

නිවාත, *Niwáta*, *s.* (නි and වාත wind) asylum: *a.* calm; not windy, safe, secure, excluded from the wind.

නිවාතැන, *Niwátęna*, *s.* place from which the wind is excluded, screened place, asylum; rest.

නිවාප, *Niwápa*, *s.* gifts in honour of a deceased parent or relative, offering water at the seasons of absolution to the manes.

නිවාපන, *Niwápana*, *s.* gift, donation, [Colloq. දිමනාව *dímanáwa*].

නිවාරණ, *Niwáraṇa*, *s.* (නි emphatic, වාරණ opposition) obstacle, impediment, hindrance; finish; extermination, extripation, annihilation.

නිවාරණ කරණවා, *Niwáraṇa-karaṇawá*, *v.* to put an end to, to close; to hinder, to exterminate.

නිවාස, *Niwása*, *s.* (නි and වාස dwelling) house, habitation; dwelling, residence, place of staying or abiding, abode.

නිවාසන, *Niwásana*, *s.* (නි and වාසන clothes) inner or under garment.

නිවාසය, *Niwásaya*, see නිවාස *niwása*.

නිවාසස්ථාන, *Niwásasthána*, *s.* (නිවාස house, ස්ථාන place) dwelling, place of staying or abiding; resting place.

නිවාසි, *Niwási*, *s.* living in, residing.

නිවි, *Nivi*, *s.* husbandman, cultivator, [Colloq. ගොවියා *goviyá*]; star.

නිවිත්ත, *Nivitta*, corruptly for නිමිත්ත *nimitta*, pl. නිවිති *niviti*.

නිවිති, *Niviti*, *s.* Malabar nightshade, plant with leaves resembling spinage, *basella alba*, *(Chenopodiaceœ)*.

නිවිතිකාරයා, *Nivitikárayá*, *s.* fortune-teller, soothsayer, prognosticator.

නිවිෂ්ට, *Nivishṭa*, *a.* entered, placed in or upon.

නිවිහැනහි, *Nivihęnahi*, *ad.* slowly, leisurely.

නිවී, *Niví*, *s.* merchandise, traffic, commerce.

නිවීම, *Nivíma*, *s.* quenching, extinguishing, verbal noun of නිවනවා *niwanawá*, which see.

නිවුම, *Niwuma*, *s.* extinction, annihilation, cooling.

නිවෙනවා, *Niwenawá*, *v.* to become cold, to cool; to be extinguished: pret. නිවුනා *niwuná*.

නිවෙස්, *Niwes*, Elu form of නිවාස *niwása*, which see.

නිවෙස, *Niwesa*, *s.* (නි emphatic, වස *wasa* dwelling) house, [Colloq. ගෙදර *gedara*]; camp; entrance.

නිවේශනය, *Niwéṣanaya*, *s.* house, dwelling, habitation, [Colloq. වාසස්ථානය *wásasthánaya*].

නිවේශාන්තරය, *Niwéṣántaraya*, *s.* (නිවේශ camp, palace, dwelling, අන්තර *antara* inside) inner apartment of a house, camp or palace.

නිවෘත්ත, *Nivṛitta*, *a.* ceased, stopped.

නිවෘත්ති, *Nivṛitti*, *s.* cessation, stoppage.

නිවෘත, *Nivṛita*, *s.* (නි emphatic, වෘත surrounding) veil, mantle, wrapper: *a.* surrounded, encompassed, encircled, enclosed; concealed, hidden.

නිශ්, *Niṣ*, particle and prefix of privation and negation, being another form of නිර් *nir*.

නිශ්චය, *Niṣchaya*, *s.* certainty, ascertainment, positive conclusion.

නිශ්චල, *Niṣchala*, *a.* (නිශ් priv. චල shaking) immovable, still, fixed, unshaken, firm, steady.

නිශ්ශ්වාස, *Niṣṣwása*, *s.* breath, breath expired.

නිශ්ශබ්ද, *Niṣṣabda*, *a.* (නිශ් neg. ශබ්ද sound, voice) silent, taciturn.

නිශ්ශේෂ, *Niṣṣésha*, *a.* complete, entire.

නිශ්ශ්‍රිත, *Niṣṣrita*, *s.* plant, commonly teori, *ipomœa Turpethum*, [Colloq. ත්‍රස්තවාලු *trastawálu*]: *a.* contained in; unemployed.

නිශමන, *Niṣamana*, *s.* sight, seeing, looking; hearing.

නිශා, *Niṣá*, *s.* night, [Colloq. රෑ *ṛé*]; turmeric, *curcuma longa*, [Colloq. කහ *kaha*]; plant, [Colloq. වෙනිවැල් *weniwẹl*].

නිශාචර, *Niṣáchara*, *s.* plant, *kaempferia galanga*, [Colloq. හිඟුරුපියලි *hingurupiyali*]; evil spirit, fiend, thief, owl; zedoary.

නිශාමණි, *Niṣámaṇi*, *s.* (නිශා night, මණි gem) moon, [Colloq. හඳ *haṇda*].

නිශාරණ, *Niṣáraṇa*, *s.* killing, slaying.

නිශාරත්න, *Niṣáratna*, *s.* (නිශා night, රත්න jewel) moon, [Colloq. හඳ *haṇda*].

නිෂ්ක්වාථ, *Nishkwátha*, *s.* decoction, broth, soup.

නිෂ්ක, *Nishka*, *s.* kalanda, goldsmith's weight, weighing forty gunja seeds, each of which is one grain five-sixteenths troy.

නිෂ්කල, *Nishkala*, *a.* impotent, seedless, barren; diminished, waned.

නිෂ්කලංක, *Nishkalaṇka*, *s.* (නිෂ් for නිර් *nir* priv. කලංක spot) tranquillity, rest, quiescence: *a.* spotless, undefiled, without blemish, pure.

නිෂ්කාරණ, *Nishkáraṇa*, *a.* (නිර් *nir* priv. කාරණ cause, motive) causeless, vain, groundless, fruitless.

නිෂ්කාශිත, *Nishkáṣita*, }
නිෂ්කාසිත, *Nishkásita*, } *a.* expelled, dismissed, turned out, gone forth, issued; opened, blown, expanded; reviled, reproached.

නිෂ්කුට, *Nishkuṭa*, *s.* grove near a house; private apartments, the zenana.

නිෂ්කුටා, *Nishkuṭá*, }
නිෂ්කුටි, *Nishkuṭi*, }
නිෂ්කුටී, *Nishkuṭí*, } *s.* large cardamums, *elettaria cardamomum, major*, [Colloq. එන්සාල් *ensál*].

නිෂ්ක්‍රමණය, *Nishkramaṇaya*, *s.* (නිෂ් for නිර් *nir* forth, ක්‍රමණ *kramaṇa* going) going out, exit, departure; degradation, baseness.

නිෂ්ක්‍රාන්ත, *Nishkránta*, *a.* (නිෂ් for නිර් *nir* forth, ක්‍රාන්ත gone) gone out, departed, gone.

නිෂ්ඨා, *Nishṭhá*, *s.* (නි completely, assuredly, ඨා to stay, to stop) catastrophe of a drama; end, conclusion, termination, completion; disappearance; loss; ordinary and uniform practice or profession; good conduct, excellence; religious practice, devout and austere exercise; trouble, distress, anxiety.

නිෂ්ඨීව, *Nishṭhíwa* }
නිෂ්ඨීවන, *Nishṭhíwana*, } *s.* spitting out, ejecting any thing from the mouth.

නිෂ්ඨුර, *Nishṭhura*, *a.* harsh, contumelious (speech); hard, solid.

නිෂ්ඨ්‍යූති, *Nishṭhyúti*, *s.* spitting out.

නිෂ්ඨේව, *Nishṭhéwa*, *s.* spitting out, ejecting from the mouth.

නිෂ්පක්ව, *Nishpakwa*, *a.* decocted, infused, boiled.

නිෂ්පත්තිය, *Nishpattiya*, *s.* completion, conclusion, termination; birth.

නිෂ්පන්න, *Nishpanna*, *a.* born, produced; done, finished, ended, concluded, completed; happened.

නිෂ්පාදනය, *Nishpádanaya*, *s.* end, finish, completion; birth, production.

නිෂ්පාප, *Nishpápa*, *a.* (නිෂ් for නිර් *nir* neg. පාප sin) sinless, faultless, blameless.

නිෂ්පාව, *Nishpáwa*, *s.* winnowing, cleaning corn etc. straw, chaff; legume, pod, sort of pulse, *phaseolus radiatus*, [Colloq. ලිමෑ, *límẹ*].

නිෂ්ප්‍රපඤ්ච, *Nishprapañcha*, *a.* (නිර් *nir* priv. ප්‍රපඤ්ච delay) quick, swift, expeditious.

නිෂ්ප්‍රභා, *Nishprabhá*, *a.* (නිර් *nir* priv. ප්‍රභා light) dark, caliginous, gloomy, obscure, [Colloq. අඳුරු *aṇduru*].

නිෂ්ඵල, *Nishphala*, *a.* (නිර් *nir* and ඵල fruit) barren, impotent, fruitless, seedless; vain, unprofitable, unfruitful.

නිෂණ්ණ, *Nishaṇṇa*, *a* rested, reclined; seated, placed in or on.

නිෂද්‍යා, *Nishadyá*, *s.* (නි and ෂද *shada* to go) sitting, reclining, market; small bed.

නිෂද්‍යාදොෂ, *Nishadyá-dósha*, *s.* (නිෂද්‍යා and දොෂ fault) indecencies or improprieties to be avoided when sitting down in the presence of a superior, not before, not behind, not above nor below, not in actual contact, not very distant, etc.

නිස්කාරණේ, *Niskárané*, *ad.* without a cause, corruptly for නිෂ්කාරණයේ *nishkáranayé*.

නිස්තාරණය, *Nistaranaya*, *s.* going out, departure; crossing over, passing over; means of success, an expedient.

නිස්තල, *Nistala*, *a.* (නිර් *nir* priv. තල support or stay, depth) round, spherical, globular; trembling, shaking, moving; low, below.

නිස්පර්‍ය්‍යාය, *Nisparyáya*, *a.* (නිර් *nir* neg. පර්‍ය්‍යාය order) out of order, irregular, not according to the arrangement of the synonyms of a vocabulary.

නිස්ස, *Nissa*, *s.* fitness, propriety.

නිස්සඞ්ග, *Nissańga*, *a.* free from attachment or desire.

නිස්සරණ, *Nissarana*, *s.* (නිර් *nir* forth, out, සරණ going) name of Nirwána or annihilation, escape; entrance of a house, passage in or out of a house; entrance through the door; departure: *a.* helpless, destitute.

නිස්සහ, *Nissaha*, *a.* (නිර් *nir* neg. සහ together) disunited, disjoined, parted, separated.

නිස්සා, *Nissá*, *s.* correct or right man, deserving man; agreeable person, one of engaging demeanour.

නිස්සාර, *Nissára*, *a.* (නිර් *nir* and සාර essence) barren, pithless.

නිස්සිත, *Nissita*, *a.* living with, dwelling with; connected with.

නිස්සේවනය, *Nisséwanaya*, *s.* (නිර් *nir* priv. සේවනය servitude) freedom, independence, liberty.

නිස්සේස, *Nissésa*, *a.* (නිර් *nir* neg. සේස remaining) all, whole, entire, complete.

නිස්සෝභන, *Nissóbhana*, *a.* (නිර් *nir* priv. සෝභන beautiful) ugly, deformed, unhandsome, misshapen.

නිස්සැබ්ද, *Nissębda*, corruptly for නිශ්ශබ්ද *nisșabda*.

නිස, *Nisa*, *s.* night, [Coll: රෑ *rę*]; sound in chorus.

නිසක්, *Nisak*, *s.* cord for binding an elephant.

නිසක, *Nisaka*, *a.* undoubted, certain, sure, indubitable.

නිසග, *Nisaga*, *s.* truth, certainty, nature, giving up.

නිසඟ, *Nisanga*, *s.* union, meeting, association.

නිසදි, *Nisadi*, } *ad.* continually, constantly.
නිසදී, *Nisadí*, }

නිසන්, *Nisan*, *a.* near, [Colloq. ළඟ *langa*].

නිසන, *Nisana*, *a.* error, mistake, fault, blunder.

නිසපති, *Nisapati*, } *s.* (නිස night, පිය delighted)
නිසපිය, *Nisapiya*, } moon, [Colloq. හඳ *handa*].

නිසම්, *Nisam*, see නිසන් *nisan*.

නිසයුරු, *Nisayuru*, *s.* (නිස and යුරු for කරු *karu* who makes) moon, [Colloq. හඳ *handa*].

නිසර්ග, *Nisarga*, *s.* natural state, peculiar character or condition; form, abandonment.

නිසර, *Nisara*, *s.* sound; village near a royal city; *a.* unfruitful.

නිසරු, *Nisaru*, *a.* empty, void, unfruitful, unprosperous.

නිසරුකරණවා, *Nisarukaranawá*, *v.* to despise, to scorn; to render unfruitful, to render unprosperous.

නිසල්, *Nisal*, *a.* near, proximate; firm.

නිසල, *Nisala*, *s.* (නි neg. සල shaken) stone, rock, [Colloq. ගල *gala*]; harp, firmness.

නිසවර, *Nisawara*, *s.* mud, mire, [Colloq. මඩ *mada*].

නිසසර, *Nisasara*, *s.* (නිස night, සර who walks) thief, [Colloq. හොරා *horá*]; ghost; Elu form of නිශාචර *nișáchara*, which see.

නිසා, *Nisá*, *s.* night, turmeric, see නිශා *nișá*; particle and affix, answering to for, on account of, since, because of; lying near.

නිසාකර, *Nisákara*, } *s.* (නිසා night, කර who
නිසාකේතු, *Nisákétu*, } makes, කේතු symbol) moon, [Colloq. හඳ *handa*].

නිසාචර, *Nisáchara*, *s.* (නිසා and චර who walks) Rákshayá, fiend, imp, goblin; jackal; owl; snake; ghost; thief.

නිසාචාරී, *Nisáchárí*, *s.* (නිසා and චාර *chára* who goes, ඊ *í* fem. aff.) harlot; she-devil, female fiend.

නිසාත, *Nisáta*, *a.* sharpened, polished, whetted, burnished.

නිසාද, *Nisáda*, *s.* man of a low caste, man of a degraded tribe, outcast; first of the seven musical notes.

නිසානාථ, *Nisánátha*, } *s.* (නිසා and නාථ or පති
නිසාපති, *Nisápati*, } lord) moon, [Colloq. හඳ *handa*].

නිසාරණ, *Nisárana*, *s.* killing, slaying, slaughter.

නිසාරතන, *Nisáratana*, *s.* (නිසා and රතන gem) moon, [Colloq. හඳ *haṇda*].

නිසාල්, *Nisál*, see නිසල් *nisal*.

නිසි, *Nisi*, *a.* fit, proper, suitable, agreeable; incidental.

නිසිණි, *Nisiṇi*, *s.* ladder, [Colloq. ඉණිමග *iṇimaga*], staircase.

නිසිත, *Nisita*, *a.* sharpened, whetted.

නිසිරි, *Nisiri*, *s.* (නි neg. සිරි prosperity) reproach, scandal, abuse; poverty, indigence; misfortune.

නිසුළු, *Nisuḷu*, *s.* tree, *Barringtoṇia acutangula*, [Colloq. එල මිදෙල්ල *ela-midella*].

නිසේධය, *Nisédhaya*, *s.* prohibition, negation.

නිශෝක, *Nisóka*, *a.* (නි priv. ශෝක sorrow) joyous, joyful, pleased, delighted, free from sorrow.

නිසැක, *Niseka*, *a.* (නි and සැක doubt) indubitable, certain, true, undoubted.

නිසැකව, *Nisekawa*, *ad.* undoubtedly, unhesitatingly.

නිසැදි, *Nisedi*, *ad.* continually, constantly.

නිහඬුරු, *Nihaṇḍuru*, *s.* sighing, heaving, throbbing.

නිහත, *Nihata*, *a.* slain, killed, destroyed.

නිහතමාන, *Nihatamána*, *s.* (නිහත destroyed, මාන pride) humility, lowliness, unassuming demeanour: *a.* humbled.

නිහනන, *Nihanana*, *s.* slaying, killing, destroying.

නිහර, *Nihara*, } *s.* dew, [Colloq. පිනි *pini*]; frost.
නිහාර, *Nihára*,

නිහාලුව, *Niháluwa*, *s.* poverty, indigence, want.

නිහුනුගා, *Nihunugá*, *s.* sharpening, whetting.

නිළි, *Niḷi*, *s.* female dancer.

නී, *Ní*, *s.* water; river in general; mine, hoard, subterraneous place of concealment for riches; penetration, judgment; finger-nail.

නික්කුනිල, *Nikku-nila*, *s.* non-employment, out of office, expression used jeeringly to persons out of office.

නීකසා, *Níkasá*, *s.* mother of the Rákshas or goblins, more correctly නිකෂා *nikashá*.

නීකසාත්මජ, *Níkasátmaja*, *s.* (නිකසා and ආත්මජ *átmaja* son) sort of Rákshayá or demon.

නීකා, *Niká*, *s.* water hen, *gallinula chloropus*, *(Rallidæ* order *Grallæ)*.

නීකාර, *Níkára*, *s.* disrespect, contempt, vilifying.

නීකාශ, *Níkáṣa*, *s.* ascertainment, certainty, assurance: *a.* like, similar, resembling.

නීගොස, *Nígosa*, *s.* rumbling of clouds, corruptly for නිගොස *nigosa*.

නීච, *Nícha*, *a.* low, base, mean, vile, contemptible, worthless.

නීචකම, *Níchakama*, *s.* vileness.

නීචකුල, *Nícha-kula*, *a.* (නීච vile, කුල race) base born, of a low and degraded tribe, outcast.

නීචයා, *Níchayá*, *s.* mean fellow, vile man.

නීත, *Níta*, *a.* gained, obtained; led, conducted; well-behaved, modest, humble, obedient.

නීති, *Níti*, *s.* ordinance, statute; moral philosophy, ethics, it comprises all works whose object is moral instruction: *a.* guiding, directing, leading.

නීතිඥ, *Nítijña*, *s.* statesman, politician: *a.* knowing what is right, politic.

නීතිදායකයා, *Nítidáyakayá*, *s.* legislator.

නීතිය, *Nítiya*, see නීති *níti*.

නීතිවිද්‍යා, *Níti-vidyá*, *s.* political science; knowledge of ethics.

නීතිවේදි, *Nítiwédi*, *s.* (නීති and වේදි who knows) moral philosopher, one skilled in ethics.

නීති ශාස්ත්‍ර, *Níti-ṣástra*, *s.* (නීති statute, ethics, ශාස්ත්‍ර scripture) institute, law, code of law; code of moral philosophy.

නීඬු, *Níṇḍu*, *s.* name of Wesamuṇi the king of devils and god of wealth; ocean.

නීප්පාණ්ඩුව, *Nippáṇḍuwa*, *s.* a disease, *cholera morbus*, [Colloq. කොලරා රෝගය *kolará-rógaya*].

නීප, *Nípa*, *s.* tree, *Barringtonia speciosa*, [Colloq. මූදිල්ල *múdilla*, or මිදෙල්ල *midella*]; another tree, *sarcocephalus cordatus* or *nauclea coadunata*, [Colloq. බක්මී *bakmí*]; kadamba tree, *anthocephalus* (or *nauclea*) *cadamba*, [Colloq. කොළොම් *koḷom* or හලඹ *halaṃba*].

නීය, *Níya*, *s.* approach, advance.

නීර, *Níra*, *s.* water, [Colloq. වතුර *watura*]; juice, [Colloq. ඉස්ම *isma*], liquor.

නීරජ, *Níraja*, *s.* (නීර water, ජ born) lotus in general; otter; plant, *costus speciosus*, [Colloq. තෙබු *tebu*].

නීරද, *Nírada*, *s.* (නී river, රද king) sea, ocean; the celestial river; according to another (නීර water, ද what gives) cloud.

නීරධි, *Níradhi*, *s.* (නීර and ධි having) sea, ocean, [Colloq. මූද *múda*].

නීරවංජුල, *Nírawanjula*, *s.* common cane, *calamus rotang* or *c. Roxburghii*, [Colloq. වේවැල් *wéwel*].

නීරා, *Nírá*, *s.* small species of fig tree, *ficus oppositifolia*, [Colloq. කොටදිඹුලා *koṭa-dimbulá*].

නීල, *Níla*, *s.* blue, black, or dark blue; gem, sapphire; indigo (the dye); blue vitriol; characteristic mark on the skin.

නීලකණ්ඨ, *Nílakaṇtha*, *s.* (නීල blue or black, කණ්ඨ neck) name of Íṣwara or Ṣiva, alluding to the dark blue or black colour of his neck; peacock, [Colloq. මොණරා *moṇará*]; gallinule; blue jay: see නීලග්‍රීව *nílagríva.*

නීලකසින, *Nílakasina*, *s.* name of a celebrated Arhat or Rahatan; one of the forty Karmasthána, religious exercises or meditations.

නීලකොබෙයියා, *Níla-kobeyiyá*, *s.* bronze-winged dove, *chalcophaps indica*, *(Gouridæ* order *Columbæ).*

නීලග්‍රීව, *Nílagríva*, *s.* (නීල and ග්‍රීව neck) peacock, [Colloq. මොණරා *moṇará*]; name of Mahádéva or Ṣiva, alluding to the colour of his neck, which was stained black by the acrimony of the poison that he swallowed, produced at the churning of the ocean.

නීලපත්‍ර, *Níla-patra*, see නියඳ *niyaṉda.*

නීලපුෂ්පි, *Níla-pushpí*, *s.* plant, *evolvulus alsinoides*, [Colloq. විෂ්ණුක්‍රාන්ති *vishṇukránti*].

නීලමල්ලිකා, *Nílamalliká*, *s.* bael tree or Bengal quince, *ægle marmelos*, [Coll: බෙලිගස් *beli-gas*].

නීලි, *Níli*, *a.* cunning.

නීලිකා, *Níliká*, *s.* plant, *nyctanthes arbor tristis*, species with blue flowers, [Colloq. සේපාලිකා *sépáliká*].

නීලී, *Nílí*, *s.* indigo plant, *indigofera tinctoria*, [Colloq. අවරිය *awariya*].

නුකම්, *Nukam*, *s.* order, arrangement, [Colloq. පිළිවෙළ *piḷiweḷa*].

නුකුල, *Nukula*, *a.* of no caste.

නුකුසීදව, *Nukusídawa*, *s.* not lazy, industrious, [Colloq. නොකම්මැළිව *nokammeliwa*].

නුග, *Nuga*, *s.* milky fig tree, *ficus altissima*, var. *laccifera* [N. B. the banyan, *ficus bengalensis*, is මහනුග *maha-nuga*], *(Urticaceæ).*

නුග අරළු, *Nuga-araḷu*, *s.* pendant shoots or branches of the banyan.

නුගතම්පලා, *Nuga-tampalá*, *s.* variety of plant, called තම්පලා *tampalá*, *nothosærua brachiata (Amarantaceæ).*

නුගපත් ඇල්වී, *Nugapat-ẹlví*, *s.* kind of ඇල්වී *ẹlví*, hill paddy, variety of *oryza sativa.*

නුදුටුවිරූ, *Nuduṭu-virú*, *a.* not seen before.

නුදුරු, *Nuduru*, *a.* (නු neg. දුරු far) not distant.

නුනුවන, *Nunuwana*, *s.* foolishness, [Colloq. මෝඩකම *módakama*].

නුපු, *Nupu*, *s.* order, arrangement.

නුපුරුදු, *Nupurudu*, *a.* unaccustomed, unpractised.

නුපුළුල්, *Nupuḷul*, *a.* (නු neg. පුළුල් broad) narrow, strait.

නුපුළුවන්, *Nupuḷuwan*, *a.* unable, impossible.

නුබ, *Nuba*, *s.* sky, [Colloq. අහස *ahasa*]: *pr.* you (slightly respectful), equivalent to උඹ *um̲ba* and නුඹ *num̲ba*, pl. නුබලා *nubalá.*

නුබතල, *Nubatala*, *s.* sky, firmament, [Colloq. අහස් තල *ahastala*].

නුබමිණි, *Nuba-miṇi*, *s.* (නුබ sky, මිණි gem) the sun, [Colloq. ඉර *ira*].

නුඹ, *Num̲ba*, *s.* sky, [Colloq. අහස *ahasa*]; *per. pron.* another form of නුබ *nuba*, the second pers. sing. (slightly respectful).

නුඹකුස්, *Num̲bakus*, *s.* (නුඹ sky, කුස් belly) cavity of the sky, space or expanse of heaven.

නුමුත්, *Numut*, *ind.* but, although, if, notwithstanding, though.

නුමුහුකළ, *Numuhukaḷa*, *a.* unripe, not matured; fresh; not mixed.

නුමුළාව, *Numuḷáwa*, *a.* (නු neg. මුළා *muḷá* error) not having erred; without fail.

නුමුළාසිව, *Numuḷásiwa*, *adv.* without fail.

නුරා, *Nurá*, *s.* love, affection, [Colloq. ප්‍රේමය *prémaya*].

නුරු, *Nuru*, *s.* parable; simile, figure of speech, [Colloq. උපමාව *upamáwa*].

නුරුප්, *Nurup*, / නුරුපා, *Nurupá*, } *s.* kind of tinkling ornament or bracelets, large hollow rings used by Kapurálas when invoking demons.

නුරුව, *Nuruwa*, *s.* kind of tinkling bracelets or rings worn on the ankles and wrists.

නුරුවලා, *Nuruwalá*, *s.* ornaments for the feet worn by women.

නුරුස්ස, *Nurussa*, *s.* (නු priv. රුස්ස wish) dislike, antipathy; hatred.

නුරුස්සනවා, *Nurussanawá*, *v.* to detest, to loathe, to abhor: pret. නිරිස්සුවා *nirissuwá.*

නුවට, *Nuwaṭa*, *s.* devotee, religious ascetic, one who has withdrawn from the world and lives either as a beggar or a hermit; some of these devotees wander about naked as mendicants; one who has subdued his passions by the practice of religious austerities.

නුවන්, *Nuwan*, *s.* eye, [Colloq. ඇස *ẹsa*].

නුවන් කඳුළු, *Nuwan-kaṉduḷu*, *s.* (නුවන් and කඳුළු tear) tear.

නුවන්බර, *Nuwan-bara*, *s.* (නුවන් and බර twelve) name of Kataragama-deviyó or Skandakumára the god of war, alluding to his having six heads and twelve eyes.

නුවන් වර, *Nuwan-wara*, } *s.* (නුවන් eye, වළ pit)
නුවන් වළ, *Nuwan-waḷa*, } socket of the eye.

නුවන, *Nuwana*, *s.* eye; wisdom, understanding, judgment, intellect; skill, ability.

නුවන අහනවා, *Nuwana-ahanawá*, *v.* to consult, to ask advice.

නුවනක්කාරයා, *Nuwanakkárayá*, *s.* wise man.

නුවනග බැලුම, *Nuwanaga-bęluma*, *s.* (නුවන eye, අග *aga* extremity, බැලුම looking) leering.

නුවන දීම, *Nuwana-díma*, *s.* (නුවන wisdom, දීම giving) advice, admonition.

නුවන පෙරුම්, *Nuwana-perum*, *s.* highest knowledge.

නුවනබා, *Nuwanabá*, *s.* tear, [Colloq. කඳුළු *kaṇḍuḷu*].

නුවන වැඩු, *Nuwana-węḍu*, *s.* adult, one of mature judgment.

නුවනැත්තා, *Nuwanęttá*, *s.* wise man, intelligent person.

නුවර, *Nuwara*, *s.* town, city, royal city, native name for Kandy.

නුවරු, *Nuwaru*, *s.* (නුවර *nuwara* city, උ *u* pers. aff.) inhabitant of a city, citizen, one resident in a town.

නුවාව, *Nuwáwa*, *s.* hem of a garment, but used chiefly in speaking of the siwura or garment worn by the priests.

නුවූ, *Nuwú*, *ind.* formed from the preterite of the verb වෙනවා *wenawá* and the neg. particle නු *nu*, relative participle implying who or which has not been.

නුසර, *Nusara*, *s.* thought, act of thinking, [Colloq. සිහිකෙරීම *sihikeríma*]; conformity to usage, established authority.

නුසුදුසු, *Nusudusu*, *a.* (නු neg. සුදුසු fit) unbecoming, improper, unfit.

නුසුන්, *Nusun*, *a.* (නු neg. සුන් broken) whole, unbroken, not pulverised.

නුහුනු, *Nuhunu*, *a.* (නු neg. හුනු fallen) stopped, hindered, prevented; not happened, not occurred.

නුහුරු, *Nuhuru*, *s.* (නු neg. හුරු dexterous) clumsy, awkward, unskilful, unaccustomed; left handed.

නුහුව, *Nuhuwa*, *s.* ten thousand, [Colloq. දසදහස *dasa-dahasa*].

නුහුස, *Nuhusa*, *s.* scorpion, [Colloq. ගෝනුස්සා *gónussa*].

නුළුද, *Nuḷuda*, *s.* thief. [Colloq. හොරා *horá*].

නූ, *Nú*, see නුවූ *nuwú*.

නූගත්, *Núgat*, *a.* (නූ neg. උගත් *ugat* learned) unlearned, ignorant, illiterate; foolish, stupid.

නූත්න, *Nútna*, } *a.* new, fresh, recent, [Colloq.
නූතන, *Nútana*, } අලුත් *alut*], young.

නූද, *Núda*, *s.* mulberry tree, *morus indica.*

නූදම්, *Núdam*, *s.* woman's girdle, chain worn round the loins.

නූන, *Núna*, *s.* thought, reflection; mind: *ad.* certainly, truly, verily, indubitably: *part.* not happened.

නූනු, *Núnu*, *a.* unprecedented; not been or become.

නූපන්, *Núpan*, *a.* (නු *nu* neg. උපන් *upan* birth) unborn, non-existent.

නූපුර, *Núpura*, *s.* bracelets; ornament for the toes and feet.

නූල්, *Núl*, plural of නූල *núla*.

නූල් අදිනවා, *Núl-adinawá*, *v.* to stitch roughly.

නූල් කටිනවා, *Núl-kaṭinawá*, *v.* to spin thread.

නූල් කොහිල, *Núl-kohila*, *s.* plant, *Lasia spinosa.*

නූල් බඳිනවා, *Núl-baṇḍinawá*, *v.* to tie thread for a charm.

නූල් මතුරණවා, *Núl-maturaṇawá*, *v.* to charm thread.

නූල, *Núla*, *s.* thread, string; fibre, pl. නූල් *núl.*

නෙ, *Ne*, *ind.* no, not.

නෙක්, *Nek*, *a.* much, many, various.

නෙක, *Neka*, *a.* many (poetical term).

නෙකදාමය, *Nekadámaya*, *s.* bracelets.

නෙත්, *Net*, plural of නෙත *neta.*

නෙත්තිය, *Nettiya*, *s.* forehead; ends or tips of the fingers; corner, point, end.

නෙත්තොලියා, *Nettoliyá*, *s.* kind of sea fish.

නෙත්මල, *Net-mala*, *s.* (නෙත් eye, මල excrement) gum or rheum of the eye.

නෙත්සිලිල්, *Net-silil*, *s.* tear, [Colloq. කඳුළු *kaṇḍuḷu*].

නෙත, *Neta*, *s.* eye, Elu form of නේත්‍ර *nétra*, which see.

නෙදැනුම, *Nedanuma*, *s.* (නෙ not, දැනුම *dęnuma* knowledge) ignorance, stupidity.

නෙදිගින්, *Nedigin*, *s.* from many sides.

නෙපෙණෙනවා, *Nepaṇenawá*, *v.* to disappear, to be invisible, to vanish.

නෙබණ, *Nebaṇa*, *a.* (නෙ not, බණ word) silent, taciturn.

නෙබැද්ද, *Nebędda*, *s.* tree with digitate leaves and panicles of whitish flowers, *vitex Leucoxylon (Verbenaceæ).*

නෙයදස්ස, *Neyadassa*, *s.* wild tea, *eurya japonica, (Ternstrœmiaceæ).*

නෙයියාඩම, *Neyiyáḍama*, *s.* play, sport, amusement, dancing.

නෙර, *Nera*, *s.* road rendered impassable by the jungle or by trees cut down and thrown across.

නෙරණවා, *Neraṇawá*, *v.* to become fat or bloated, to puff up; to set aside, to put out of the way: pret. නෙරුවා *neruwá*.

නෙරතල මීයා, *Neratala-míyá*, *s.* species of field rat.

නෙරපනවා, *Nerapanawá*, *v.* to persecute; to put away, to set aside, to do away with; to expel: pret. නෙරපුවා *nerapuwá*.

නෙරළු, *Neraḷu*, *s.* tree, *elæodendrum glaucum*, var. *e. montanum (Celastraceæ)*; coconut tree, [Colloq. පොල් ගහ *pol-gaha*].

නෙරිය, *Neriya*, *s.* selvage or ornamented edge of dress.

නෙරියනවා, *Neriyanawá*, *v.* to grow large with fatness or disease, to protuberate: pret. නෙරුවා *neruwá*.

නෙරිවිෂ, *Nerivisha*, *s.* medicine, antidote for the poison of serpents.

නෙරෙක්කුකරණවා, *Nerekku-karaṇawá*, *v.* to persecute.

නෙරෙක්කුව, *Nerekkuwa*, *s.* persecution, vexation, oppression, hardship, tyranny.

නෙල්ලි, *Nelli*, *s.* tree with wood hard, bark astringent, fruit acid, *phyllanthus emblica* or *Myrobalana emblica* of the Materia Medica, *(Euphorbiaceæ)*..

නෙලනවා, *Nelanawá*, *v.* to break, to pluck, to gather (fruit), to root up weeds: pret. නෙලුවා *neluwá*.

නෙලීම, *Nelíma*, *s.* plucking, picking, rooting up; verbal noun of නෙලනවා *nelanawá*.

නෙවරදී, *Newaradí*, *part.* not failing, without fail.

නෙවෙනවා, *Newenawá*, (the verb වෙනවා *wenawá* to be, with the neg. particle නෙ *ne*) not to be.

නෙළු, *Neḷu*, *s.* small tree abundant in the jungles of Ceylon, name applied to the whole genus *Strobilanthes*, of which *S. viscosus* and many other species are peculiar to Ceylon, *(Acanthaceæ)*; male calf; decay, fading.

නෙළුන්, *Neḷun*, see නෙළුම් *neḷum*.

නෙළුපබලා, *Neḷu-pabalá*, *s.* lotus.

නෙළුඹල, *Neḷumbala*, *s.* (නෙළුම් *neḷum* lotus, අල *ala* root) edible root of the nelumbium or sacred bean of India.

නෙළුඹු, *Neḷumbu*, see නෙළුම් *neḷum*.

නෙළුඹුදෙලි, *Neḷumbudeḷi*, *s.* bud or young sprout of the lotus, [Colloq නෙළුම්දළු *neḷum-dalu*]; root of the lotus.

නෙළුඹෑස, *Neḷumbęsa*, *s.* film or fibres attached to the stalk of the lotus; small fibre in the water lily.

නෙළුම්, *Neḷum*, *s.* lotus, water lily, *nelumbium speciosum, (Nymphæaceæ)*, or the sacred flower of India.

නෙළුම් අල, *Neḷum-ala*, *s.* edible root of the lotus.

නේ, *Né*, *a.* many; Elu form of ඥෙය *jñéya*, what should be learned or known, fit or proper to be known.

නේක, *Néka*, *a.* much, many, various.

නේත්‍ර, *Nétra*, *s.* leader, guide, [Colloq. මඟ පෙන්වන්නා *maga-penwanná*]; eye; root of a tree; car, carriage; tubular vessel.

නේත්‍ර තාරකාව, *Nétra-tárakáwa*, *s.* (නේත්‍ර and තාරකා *táraká* pupil) pupil of the eye.

නේත්‍රධාර, *Nétra-dhára*, *s.* (නේත්‍ර and ධාර having) tear, [Colloq. කඳුළු *kaṇḍuḷu*].

නේත්‍රභේෂජ, *Nétra-bhéshaja*, } නේත්‍රභෛෂජ, *Nétra-bhaishaja*, } *s.* (නේත්‍ර eye, භේෂජ medicament) green sulphate of iron, considered as a collyrium; any specific for the eyes.

නේත්‍රය, *Nétraya*, see නේත්‍ර *nétra*.

නේත්‍රාමය, *Nétrámaya*, *s.* (නේත්‍ර and ආමය *ámaya* sickness) any disease of the eyes.

නේතා, *Nétá*, *s.* master, owner, chief, [Colloquial: ස්වාමියා *swámiyá*]; bread fruit tree, [Colloq. රටදෙල් ගහ *raṭadel-gaha*].

නේපාලය, *Népálaya*, *s.* country so called, Nepal; tree, having a disagreeable smell and producing a nut powerfully purgative, *croton tiglium*, [Colloq. ජයපාල *jayapála*].

නේමි, *Némi*, *s.* tree, *dalbergia Oujeiniensis*, [Colloq. කොබුගස් *kobu-gas*]; circumference of a wheel.

නේමින්ධර, *Némindhara*, *s.* the fifth, reckoning from the centre, of the seven circular rocks which surround Mahaméru, and which form the boundaries of so many seas or circumambient waters, encircling that mountain.

නේරංජරා, *Néranjará*, *s.* river so called.

නේවාසික, *Néwásika*, *s.* one who resides always in the same place.

නේසජ්ජිකාඞ, *Nésajjikánga*, *s.* (නිසජ්ජා *nisajjá* sitting, අඞ *anga* ordinance) ordinance of the Buddhist priesthood, enjoining it upon the priests to sleep in a sitting posture: see තෙළෙස්ධුතාඞ *teḷes-dhutánga*.

නේසාද, *Nésáda*, *s.* archer, bowman, forester, veddá.

නෛක, *Naika*, *a.* various, multiform, manifold; several, many.

නෛකභේද, *Naika-bhéda*, *a.* (නෛක many, භේද division) various, multiform.

නෛකශ්‍රීන්, *Naikasrín*, *s.* with manifold splendour or prosperity.

නෛගම, *Naigama*, *s.* trader, merchant; citizen, townsman; road, way; leading, guiding, directing; portion of the Hindu Védas, an Upanishad.

නෛපාල, *Naipála*, *s.* copper, [Colloq. තඹ *tamba*].

නෛපාලි, *Naipálí*, *s.* double jasmine; red arsenic, [Colloq. රත්හිරියල් *rat-hiriyal*]; plant, *nyctanthes arbor-tristis*, [Colloq. සේපාලිකා *sépáliká*]; indigo, *indigofera tinctoria*, [Coll: අවරි *awari*].

නෛමිත්තක, *Naimittaka*, *s.* (නෛමිත්ත from නිමිත්ත *nimitta* omen, ක pers. aff.) necromancer, fortune teller, astrologer.

නෛඍත, *Nairṛita*, *s.* demon, fiend, ruler of the south-west quarter.

නෛඍති, *Nairṛití*, *s.* south west quarter.

නෛර්‍යාණික, *Nairyáṇika*, *a.* leading to final emancipation.

නෛෂ්කික, *Naishkika*, *s.* mint-master.

නෛෂ්ක්‍රම්‍ය, *Naishkramya*, *s.* (from නිෂ්ක්‍රම *nishkrama*) departure, forsaking, leaving, abandonment; act of abandoning the world and all worldly pursuits for the purpose of religious devotion.

නෛෂ්ක්‍රම්‍ය පාරමිතාව, *Naishkramya-páramitáwa*, *s.* (නෛෂ්ක්‍රම්‍ය abandonment of the world, පාරමිතාව páramitáwa) the last great Páramitá performed by Bódhisat previous to his becoming Buddha; it is fabled that when living in the palace of his father king, Suddhódana, as prince Siddhártha Kumára, on a certain occasion he saw four objects, viz., a sick man, a decrepit man, a corpse, and a priest, which so deeply impressed his mind with the vanity and misery of life in any state, and the desirableness of attaining Nirwáṇa or final emancipation, that he immediately formed the resolution of abandoning the world and becoming a Buddha; this resolution was opposed by Máraya and all his infernal hosts; yet he left his palace, his princess, his court and kingdom and assuming the garb and habits of a priest, retired into solitude and after performing every species of devout religious austerities and meditations for a period of six years, he obtained the Buddhaship; see පාරමිතාව *páramitáwa*.

නෛෂධ, *Naishadha*, *s.* celebrated Sanskrit poem. also, name of Nala the hero of the poem.

නෛස්ත්‍රිංශික, *Naistriṇṣika*, *s.* swordsman, soldier armed with a sword.

නෛසර්ගික, *Naisarggika*. *a.* innate, natural.

නො, *No*, *ind.* prefix, implying negation, privation, it is used in combination with many words; some of these forms most commonly used are given below.

නොඅඩු, *Noaḍu*, *a.* (නො neg. අඩු *aḍu* less) abounding, not decreasing.

නොඑක්, *Noek*, *a.* not one, *i. e.* more than one, many.

නොකටයුතු, *Nokaṭayutu*, *a.* not expedient, improper to be done.

නොකඩ, *Nokaḍa*, *a.* (නො neg. කඩ broken) unbroken, whole; uninterrupted; constant.

නොකඩව, *Nokaḍawa*, *ad.* incessantly; always, ever.

නොකළ, *Nokaḷa*, *a.* not done, unperformed, unfinished.

නොකළෙමි, *Nokaḷemi*, *v.* I did not do, I have not done.

නොකා, *Noká*, *v.* not having eaten, without eating; *past. part.* of කනවා *kanawá* with the neg. prefix නො *no*.

නොකී, *Noki*, *s.* (නො not, කී said) not said, not mentioned.

නොකැමති, *Nokẹmati*, *a.* unwilling, involuntary.

නොණ්ඩිච්චි, *Noṇḍichchi*, *s.* lame woman.

නොණ්ඩියා, *Noṇḍiyá*, *s.* cripple, lame man.

නොතකා, *Notaká*, *part.* (නො not, තකා having regarded) disregarding.

නොතනි, *Notani*, *a.* not solitary, not alone.

නොතාරිස්, *Notáris*, *s.* Notary. (English.)

නොතිර, *Notira*, *a.* (නො neg. තිර fixed) movable, impermanent; shaking, tossing.

නොතේරීම, *Notérima*, *s.* not selecting or explaining.

නොතේරුම්කම, *Notérumkama, s.* want of understanding, ignorance.

නොතේරෙණ, *Notéreṇa, a.* unintelligible, not understandible.

නොදන්නා, *Nodanná, a.* not knowing, not acquainted with.

නොදූදු, *Nodá-dú, s.* step-daughter.

නොදූ පුතා, *Nodá-putá, s.* step-son.

නොදිසි, *Nodisi, a.* (නො neg. දිසි visible) invisible, not apparent.

නොදිරණ, *Nodiraṇa, a.* undecaying.

නොදිරූ, *Nodirú, a.* not rotten or decayed,

නොදැමි, *Nodẹmi, a.* unsubdued, [Colloq. නොහික්මුනාවූ *nohikmunáwú*].

නොනගතේ, *Nonagaté, s.* the period of time when it is considered improper to go out on business.

නොනස්නා, *Nonasná*, නොනහින, *Nonahina*, } *a.* (නො neg. නස්නා or නහින dying) immortal, imperishable, not liable to decay.

නොපමණ, *Nopamaṇa, a.* (නො neg. පමණ measure) infinite, innumerable, beyond measure.

නොපමාව, *Nopamáwa, part.* not delaying.

නොපරක්කුව, *Noparakkuwa, part.* without losing time.

නොපවතින, *Nopawatina, a.* (නො neg. පවතින continuing) transient; uncertain, impermanent, frail; not existing.

නොපහන්, *Nopahan*, නොපහන, *Nopahana*, } *a.* not clear, not pleased.

නොපෙළා, *Nopẹlá, part.* not having harassed.

නොපැකිලි, *Nopẹkili, a.* not stumbling, [Colloq. නොහැපි *nohẹpi*].

නොබලා, *Nobalá part.* not looking at.

නොබා, *Nobá, part.* (නො neg. බා fearing) without fearing, [Colloq. භයනැතිව *bhaya-nẹtiwa*].

නොබොන, *Nobona, a.* temperate, sober; not drinking, unfit to be drunk, abstaining from intoxicating drink.

නොබෝ, *Nobó, a.* little, not much, few (quantity),

නොබෝදා, *Nobódá, ad.* not many days since, recently, lately.

නොමද, *Nomada, a.* not little, much, [Colloq ටිකනොවූ *ṭika-nowú*].

නොමනාවූ, *Nomanáwú, a.* discontented, disagreeable.

නොමල්, *Nomal, s.* tree, *ficus glomerata*, [Colloq. අට්ටික්කා *aṭṭikká*].

නොමින්, *Nomin, s.* multitude, assembly, collection, [Colloq. සමූහය *samúhaya*]: *ad.* without measure; abundantly.

නොයාම, *Noyáma, s.* necessity; not going.

නොයික්මවා, *Noyikmawá, part.* without transgressing or overstepping the limits.

නොයිවසිලි, *Noyiwasili, a.* (නො neg. ඉවසිලි *iwasili* patience) impatient.

නොයෙක්, *Noyek, a.* (නො neg. එක් *ek* one) manifold, various, multiform; many.

නොයෙක් වෙස්, *Noyek-wes, s.* (නොයෙක් various, වෙස් form, covering or appearance) name of Vishṇu alluding to his ten Avatáras, or incarnations: see අවතාර *awatára*.

නොයෙකුත්, *Noyekut, a.* various, multiform, multifarious; many.

නොරබුරු, *Noraburu*, නොරඹුරු, *Noraṃburu*, } *s.* secret, mystery, [Coll: රහස *rahasa*].

නොලප, *Nolapa, s.* snake, serpent in general, [Colloq. සර්පයා *sarpayá*].

නොලස්, *Nolas, s.* speed, velocity, dispatch, quickness, [Colloq නොපමාව *nopamáwa*, ඉක්මන්කම *ikmankama*].

නොව, *Nowa, part.* not, not being.

නොවකා, *Nowaká, a.* not joined, disunited, unmixed, not adhering.

නොවටිනා, *Nowaṭiná, a.* undeserving, unworthy; worthless, vile.

නොවන, *Nowana, a.* not happening, not occurring.

නොවරදින, *Nowaradina, a.* unfailing, infallible, unerring.

නොවලහා, *Nowalahá, part.* not concealing, [Coll: නොසඟවා *nosangawá*].

නොවිතර, *Novitara, a.* much, many, [Colloq. බොහෝ *bohó*]; infinite=අප්‍රමාණ *apramáṇa*.

නොවීම, *Novíma, s.* non-occurrence; not being, not happening.

නොවුනු, *Nowunu, a.* not been, not occurred.

නොවෙනස්, *Nowenas, a.* similar, like; same, not different; united, amicable, friendly; immutable, unchangeable.

නොවැලකීම, *Nowẹlakíma, s.* non-hindrance, non-interruption.

නොසඟවා, *Nosangawá, part.* not concealing.

නොසතුටු, *Nosatuṭu, a.* dissatisfied, discontented, displeased, joyless.

නොසඳ, *Nosanda, s.* the sun, (literally) not the moon.

නොසමර, *Nosamara, part.* not calling to mind, not taking notice of, [Colloq. නොතකා *notaká*].

නොසරස්, *Nosaras*, *s.* speed, haste, velocity: *ad.* always, ever, continually, eternally, [Colloq. නිතරම *nitarama*].

නොසරු, *Nosaru*, *a.* unfruitful, not flourishing, barren, sterile.

නොසරු ක්‍රියාව, *Nosaru-kriyáwa*, *s.* vain or fruitless act, unproductive proceeding.

නොසල, *Nosala*, *a.* (නො neg. සල shaking) firm, solid; immovable, motionless; Elu form of නිශ්චල *niṣchala*, which see.

නොසහන, *Nosahana*, *a.* unbearable, impatient, unforgiving.

නොසෙවු, *Nosewu*, *a.* unexplored; unexamined.

නොසොයා, *Nosoyá*, *part.* not having sought.

නොසැලකීම, *Noselakíma*, *s.* disregard, carelessness.

නොසෑහෙණ, *Noséheṇa*, *a.* unfit, unsuitable; inadequate.

නොහසල, *Nohasala*, *a.* unpractised, not familiar with; not conversant with.

නොහළ, *Nohaḷa*, *a.* confined, detained, not released; not opened.

නොහික්මුනු, *Nohikmunu*, *a.* (නො neg. හික්මුනු tamed) perverse, incorrigible.

නොහිට, *Nohiṭa*, *part.* not stopping or standing.

නොහිරු, *Nohiru*, *s.* moon, (literally) not the sun, [Colloq. හඳ *haṇda*].

නොහී, *Nohí*, *a.* unable, impossible, [Colloq. නුපුළුවන් *nupuḷuwan*].

නොහෙති, *Noheti*, *v.* they are unable.

නොහෙන, *Nohena*, *a.* impossible, unable.

නොහොත්, *Nohot*, *conj.* or, if not.

නොහොඳ, *Nohoṇda*, *a.* bad, evil.

නොහොබිනා, *Nohobiná*, *a.* indecent, improper, unsuitable; not decorous.

නොහැකි, *Noheki*, *a.* unable, impossible.

නෝංජල, *Nóṇjala*, *a.* sluggish, slothful, lazy, indolent, unskilful, silly.

නෝක්කඩුව, *Nókkaḍuwa*, *s.* displeasure.

නෝට්ටුව, *Nóṭṭuwa*, *s.* note, paper promising payment.

නෝනා, *Nóná*, *s.* lady, applied only to one in European costume, pl. නෝනාලා *nónálá*, නෝනාවරු *nónáwaru*.

නෝම්බි අල්ලනවා, *Nómbi-allanawá*, *v.* to fast, as used by Moormen and applied only to them.

නෝස්, *Nós*, *s.* nutmeg, *myristica fragrans.*

නෞ, *Nau*, } *s.* ship, boat, vessel in general,
නෞකා, *Nauká*, } [Colloq. නැව *neẉa*].

නෞකා දණ්ඩ, *Nauká-daṇḍa*, *s.* (නෞකා boat, දණ්ඩ stick) oar, paddle; helm, rudder of a ship.

නෞතාර්‍ය්‍ය, *Nautárya*, *a.* navigable.

නැ, *Nẹ*, *ind.* particle of negation, privation, etc., equivalent to න *na*, නෑ *né*, නැහැ *nẹhẹ*.

නැඅත්, *Nẹat*, *s.* (නැ nose, අත් trunk) name of Gaṇésa, alluding to his being represented as one furnished with the trunk of an elephant.

නැංගුරම, *Nẹṇgurama*, *s.* anchor, pl. නැංගුරම් *neṇguram.*

නැකත්, *Nẹkat*, *plur.* of the following word.

නැකත, *Nẹkata*, *s.* star in general, planet; asterism in the moon's path or lunar mansion, of which twenty eight distinct in name, figure, and number, are enumerated in Siṇhalese astronomy.

නැකතියා, *Nẹkatiyá*, *s.* tom tom beater, astrologer.

නැකිටිනවා, *Nẹkiṭinawá*, corruptly for නැගිටිනවා *nẹgiṭinawá.*

නැකැත්කාරයා, *Nẹkẹtkárayá*, *s.* astrologer, astronomer.

නැකැත් කෙළිය, *Nẹkẹt-keliya*, *s.* (නැකත් *nẹkat* and කෙළිය play, sport) festival which is celebrated in the Siṇhalese month called ඉල් මස *il-masa*, (October–November), when the moon is full near the Pleiades.

නැකැත්තරු, *Nẹkẹt-taru*, *s.* (නැකත් *nẹkat* asterism, තරු star) planet.

නැකැත් යෝගය, *Nẹkẹt-yógaya*, *s.* (නැකත් *nẹkat* star, යෝග yóga) act of consulting the movements of the planets for astrological purposes, as ascertaining lucky or unlucky days; conjunction of planets or stars.

නැගනි, *Nẹgani*, *s.* younger sister, [Colloq. නංගි *naṇgi*].

නැගනෙ, *Nẹgane*, *s.* boil or tubercle on the eye-lid.

නැගිටිනවා, *Nẹgiṭinawá*, *v.* to arise, to get up as from a seat or sleep, to stand up: pret. නැගිට්ටා *nẹgiṭṭá.*

නැගීම, *Nẹgíma*, *s.* ascending, ascension; verbal noun of නගිනවා *naginawá.*

නැගෙණවා, *Negeṇawá*, *v.* to climb, to mount, to ascend, to rise: pret. නැගුණ *nẹguṇá.*

නැගෙණහිර, *Nẹgeṇahira*, *s.* (නැගෙණ ascending, හිර sun) east.

නැගුටුවනවා, *Nẹguṭuwanawá*, *v.* to raise, to cause to rise: pret. නැගිටෙව්වා *nẹgiṭewwá.*

නැගුරුවන්, *Nẹguruwan*, *s.* gold, purified or burnished gold.

නැට්ට, *Nẹṭṭa*, *s.* culm of a plant, stalk of a flower.

නැටීම, *Neṭíma*, *s.* dancing, ebullition; verbal noun from නටනවා *naṭanawá*, to dance.

නැටුම්, *Neṭum*, *s.* pantomime, acting, dancing.

නැටුම්කරු, *Neṭumkaru*, *s.* (නැටුම් and කරු doer) dancer, actor, dramatic performer.

නැටුම්කාරයා, *Neṭumkárayá*, *s.* dancer.

නැටුම, *Neṭuma*, see නැටීම *neṭíma*.

නැටෑව්, *Neṭęw*, *s.* large tree, peculiar to Ceylon, *xylopia parviflora (Anonaceæ)*.

නැත්, *Net*, *ind.* no, not.

නැත්ත, *Netta*, *s.* denial, contradiction, untruth.

නැත්මය, *Netmaya*, *ind.* not, no; emphatically, certainly not.

නැත, *Neta*, *ind.* nay, not, no: *v.* is not, are not; used in denying the subject, නෙවේ *newé* or නොවේ *nowé* being used to deny the predicate.

නැතක්, *Netak*, *a.* many, endless.

නැතහොත්, *Netahot*, *ind.* not, if not.

නැති, *Neti*, *a.* (න *na* neg. ඇති *eti* having) without, not having; not being: *v.* is not.

නැතිකම, *Netikama*, *s.* indigence.

නැතිකරණවා, *Netikaraṇawá*, *v.* to destroy, to extirpate, to annihilate.

නැතිවුනා, *Netiwuná*, past tense of the following word.

නැතිවෙනවා, *Netiwenawá*, *v.* to be lost, to perish.

නැතුව, *Netuwa*, *ind.* not being, without.

නැද්ද, *Nedda*, *ind.* used in interrogation, no? not? is not?

නැදි, *Nedi*, *s.* binding; wife's mother; paternal aunt.

නැදිමයිලන්, *Nedimayilan*, *s.* wife's parents.

නැදුන්, *Nedun*, *s.* large timber tree, the wood of which is used for furniture, peculiar to Ceylon, *pericopsis Mooniana (Leguminosæ)*.

නැදුන්හිරි, *Nedunhiri*, *s.* fresh water plant, *cyperus umbellatus*.

නැදුප්, *Nedup*, *a*, small, little, minute, atomic.

නැඳුන්, *Neṇdun*, see නැදුන් *nedun*.

නැඳුන්හිරි, *Neṇdunhiri*, see නැදුන්හිරි *nedunhiri*.

නැන්දනියන්, *Nendaniyan*, see නැන්දා *nendá*.

නැන්දම්මා, *Nendammá*, *s.* mother in law, mother's sister in law.

නැන්දා, *Nendá*, *s.* paternal aunt; mother in law, or wife's mother; mother's brother's wife.

නැන, *Nena*, *s.* wisdom, knowledge, intellect, understanding; intelligence; Elu form of ඥාන *jñána*.

නැනවත්, *Nenawat*, *a.* (නැන wisdom, වත් poss. aff.) wise, knowing, prudent.

නැනසර, *Nenasara*, *s.* (නැන and සර vigour) wisdom, knowledge, great wisdom; scholar, pandit, learned man, [Colloq. පණ්ඩිතයා *paḍitayá*].

නැබ, *Neba*, *s.* navel; Elu form of නාභි *nábhi*.

නැබපියුම, *Neba-piyuma*, *s.* (නැබ and පියුම lotus) lotus which sprang from the navel of Vishṇu and gave birth to Brahma.

නැබමඩුළු, *Neba-maḍuḷu*, *s.* orifice of the navel; nave of a wheel; central spot of a spider's web.

නැබල, *Nebala*, *a.* great, large, [Colloq. මහත් *mahat*].

නෑබුරු, *Néburu*, *a.* inclined, bent, leaning.

නැබුරුවෙනවා, *Neburuwenawá*, *v.* to bend, to lean.

නැබුලු, *Nebulu*, *s.* greatness, bigness, magnitude, bulk, vastness; also, noted demon so called on account of his enormous size.

නැඹමඩුළු, *Nembamaḍuḷu*, incorrectly for නැබමඩුළු *nebamaḍuḷu*.

නැම්ම, *Nemma*, *s.* bend, curve, turn in a road or river.

නැමති, *Nemati*, *ind.* particle, implying like, resembling, figuring, having the name of, named; an abbrevation for නම ඇති *nama-eti*.

නැමද, *Nemada*, *part.* having worshipped, [Colloq. වැඳ *wenda*].

නැමි, *Nemi*, *a.* bent, crooked, curved, reclined.

නැමිපනාව, *Nemipanáwa*, *s.* (නැමි curved, පනාව comb) small semi-circular comb.

නැමීම, *Nemíma*, *s.* bending, bowing.

නැමුඩු, *Nemuḍu*, see නමඩි *namaḍi*.

නැමූ, *Nemú*, *a.* worshipped, adored, saluted, with the hands joined on the breast or on the head and the body bent.

නැමෙනවා, *Nemenawá*, *v.* to bend, to become crooked: pret. නැමුනා *nemuná*.

නැරඹීම, *Nerambíma*, } *s.* sight, seeing, appearance,
නැරඹුන්, *Nerambun*, } vision, [Colloq. දැකීම *dekíma*]; perceiving, viewing, beholding.

නැලවිල්ල, *Nelavilla*, *s.* stopping, refraining, checking; coaxing, soothing.

නැලවිලිවන්ත, *Nelaviliwanta*, *a.* (නැලවිල්ල *nelavilla* restraining, වන්ත poss. aff.) placid, peaceable, gentle, mild, pacific.

නැලවෙනවා, *Nelawenawá*, *v.* to be quiet or appeased, to cease crying, as a child.

නැලිතෙල්, *Neli-tel*, *s.* coconut oil, [Colloq. පොල් තෙල් *pol-tel*].

නැලිය, *Nęliya, s.* measure of capacity, about three pints wine measure; the twenty-fourth part of a parrah or the thirty-second part of a bushel heaped up.

නැව, *Nęwa, s.* ship, boat, vessel in general, pl. නැව් *nęw.*

නැවත, *Nęwata,* } *ad.* again, afresh, once more.
නැවතත්, *Nęwatat,* }

නැවතිල්ල, *Nęwatilla, s.* impediment, hindrance, obstruction.

නැවතීම, *Nęwatíma, s.* stop, suspension, verbal noun of නවතිනවා *nawatinawá.*

නැවතුනු, *Nęwatunu, a.* stopped, ceased, calmed.

නැවි, *Nęvi, s.* sailor, commander of a ship.

නැවියා, *Nęviyá, s.* (නැව *nęwa* ship, ඉයා *iyá* pers. aff.) one that teaches the art of sailing or managing a vessel, sailor, navigator.

නැවිම, *Nęvíma,* corrupt form of නැමීම *nęmíma.*

නැවුනගිනවා, *Nęwu-naginawá, v.* to embark, to go on board: pret. නැවුනැග්ගා *nęwu-nęggá,* or නැවුනැංගා *nęwu-nęngá.*

නැවැත්, *Nęwęt, v.* stopped: pret. of නවතිනවා *nawatinawá,* to stop or cease.

නැවැත්තීම, *Nęwęttíma, s.* stopping, checking; obstacle, impediment.

නැසී, *Nęsí, part.* having hid one's self, having died, having been destroyed.

නැසීගිය, *Nęsígiya, a.* deceased, late, as the late Governor, නැසීගිය උතුමානන්වහන්සේ *nęsígiya utumánanwahansé.*

නැසීම, *Nęsíma, s.* loss, destruction, death, act of killing.

නැසුම, *Nęsum, s.* covering, hiding, dancing.

නැසෙනවා, *Nęsenawá, v.* to be destroyed, to be annihilated, to die: pret. නැසුනා *nęsuná.*

නැහැ, *Nęhę, ind.* no, not: *v.* is not, are not.

නැහැරෙණවා, *Nęhęreṇawá, v.* (නැ not, හැරෙණවා to be turned) to be inflexible; to adhere, to hold fast.

නෑ, *Nę́, s.* relation, relative, kindred; nose: *ind.* nay, no, not; equivalent to නැහැ *nęhę* or නැත *nęta.*

නෑ අත්, *Nę́-at, s.* (නෑ nose, අත් trunk) name of Gaṇésa, alluding to his character as remover of obstacles, as an elephant; hence he is worshipped by the Hindus at the beginning of a composition or at the commencement of an undertaking.

නෑකම, *Nę́kama, s.* relationship, kindred; connection.

නෑකුලය, *Nę́kulaya, s.* family, relation, tribe, race.

නෑදෑයා, *Nę́dę́yá, s.* relation, kinsman.

නෑනා, *Nę́ná, s.* female cousin; father's sister's daughter, mother's brother's daughter, wife's sister, pl. නෑනාවරු *nę́náwaru.*

නෑඹිලිය, *Nę́mbiliya, s.* chatty for cleaning rice.

නෑඹ, *Nę́mba,* } *s.* young female animal, heifer,
නෑඹි, *Nę́mbi,* } pl. නෑඹියෝ *nę́mbiyó.*

නෑය, *Nę́ya, s.* rope passed through the nose of a bullock for the purpose of guiding him.

නෑයන්, *Nę́yan,* plural of the following word.

නෑයා, *Nę́yá, s.* relative, relation, male relation.

නෑර, *Nę́ra, part.* (නෑ *nę* not, ඇර *ęra* having left) not giving up, not leaving.

නෑරකරණවා, *Nę́ra-karaṇawá, v.* to persevere.

නෑලනුව, *Nę́-lanuwa, s.* (නෑ nose, ලනුව cord) string passed through the nostrils of an ox.

නෑසියෝ, *Nę́siyó, s.* relations, kindred.

න්‍යග්‍රෝධ, *Nyagródha, s.* banyan tree, *ficus bengalensis,* [Colloq. මහනුග *maha-nuga*]; species of mimosa, *mimosa albida;* fathom measured by the extended arms.

න්‍යාය, *Nyáya, s.* propriety, fitness; system of philosophy so called; logic.

න්‍යාස, *Nyása, s.* deposit, pledge, delivering; abandoning, deserting, forsaking.

නෘ, *Nṛi, s.* man, mankind.

නෘත්‍ය, *Nṛitya, s.* dancing, pastime.

නෘත්‍ය ස්ථාන, *Nṛitya-sthána, s.* (නෘත්‍ය and ස්ථාන place) theatre, dancing place.

නෘති, *Nṛiti, s.* dancing, science or practice of dancing.

නෘප, *Nṛipa, s.* (නෘ man, ප who preserves) king, sovereign, monarch, [Colloq. රජ *raja*].

නෘපති, *Nṛipati, s.* (නෘ and පති lord) name of Kuvéra, Indian god of riches; king, sovereign.

නෘපද්‍රුම, *Nṛipa-druma, s.* tree, *cassia fistula,* [Colloq. ඇහැළ *ęhęla*].

නෘපමන්දිර, *Nṛipa-mandira, s.* (නෘප king, මන්දිර house) palace, royal mansion, [Colloq. මාලිගාව *máligáwa*].

නෘප ස්ත්‍රී, *Nṛipa-strí, s.* (නෘප king, ස්ත්‍රී woman) queen, princess, [Colloq. බිසව *bisawa*].

නෘපාම්බු, *Nṛipámbu, s.* species of murunga, *moringa pterygosperma.*

නෘපාසන, *Nṛipásaṇa, s.* (නෘප king, ආසන *ásana* seat) throne, [Colloq. සිංහාසනය *sinhásanaya*].

නෘමාන, *Nṛimána, s.* (නෘ man, මාන measure) human stature, four cubits.

නෘශංස, *Nṛiṣaṇsa, a.* malicious, wicked; hurtful, injurious, mischievous, destructive.

නෘසිංහ, *Nṛisiṇha, s.* (නෘ man, සිංහ lion) fourth Avatára of Vishṇu in the form of a man with the head and claws of a lion; chief, noble, great or illustrious man.

ප

The twenty first consonant of the Siṇhalese alphabet, corresponding to the letter *p;—s.* prince, ruler; drinking.

පංගං, *Paṇgaṇ, s.* creeping plant, bearing an exceedingly bitter nut eaten with the betel; abuse, scurrility, insult.

පංගාඩම්කරණවා, *Paṇgáḍam-karaṇawá, v.* to raise, to elevate as a seat; to make, to order or arrange, to overseer or manage any undertaking.

පංගාඩම, *Paṇgáḍama, s.* preparation, provision.

පංගාර්තුකරණවා, *Paṇgártukaraṇawá, v.* to prepare, to provide, to arrange.

පංගාර්තුව, *Paṇgártuwa, s.* preparation, provision.

පංගුකරණවා, *Paṇgukaraṇawá, v.* to separate, to divide, to share.

පංගුකාරයා, *Paṇgukárayá, s.* partner, shareholder.

පංගුව, *Paṇguwa, s.* part, share; half, pl. පංගු *paṇgu.* (Tamil.)

පංගුස්ස, *Paṇgussa, s.* snare, trap, gin, pitfall, noose for catching wild animals, [Colloq. උගුල *ugula*].

පංසු, *Paṇsu, s.* earth, mud, clay, mire.

පංසුකූලිකංග, *Paṇsukúlikaṇga, s.* (පංසුකූලික old cast off clothes, අංග *aṇga* religious ordinance) ordinance of the Buddhist priesthood, which enjoins that the robes of the priests be made from old cast off clothes which are found on dunghills, on burial grounds or in any place which testifies them to be the property of no other person but to have been cast away as useless: see තෙලෙස්ධුතාංග *telesdhutáṇga.*

පංසුජ, *Paṇsuja, s.* (පංසු mud, ජ born produced) lotus, [Colloq නෙළුම් *neḷum*].

පක්, *Pak, s.* bird; fruit, ripe fruit, [Colloq. ගෙඩි *geḍi*].

පක්ව, *Pakwa, a.* cooked, ripe, matured, perfect, able.

පක්වාශය, *Pakwáṣaya, s.* stomach, [Colloq. අහර බොක්ක *ahara-bokka*].

පක්ෂ්මන්, *Pakshman, s.* eyelash; filament of a flower; point of a thread.

පක්ෂ, *Paksha, s.* wing, feather; partisan, friend; party influence or power; side, flank; half of a lunar month, or fortnight comprising fifteen days; taking, accepting, thesis, argument, position advanced; tribe, class; royal elephant: *a.* alternative, partial.

පක්ෂක, *Pakshaka, s.* private or concealed backdoor; side; sidesman; associate, confederate, partisan.

පක්ෂකම, *Pakshakama, s.* partiality; loyalty, allegiance; party spirit.

පක්ෂගත, *Pakshagata, a.* partial; loyal.

පක්ෂග්‍රහණය, *Paksha-grahaṇaya, s.* (පක්ෂ side, ග්‍රහණ *grahaṇa* seizing) partiality; taking to one side of a cause or contest, confederating, using party influence.

පක්ෂ පත්‍ර, *Paksha-patra, s.* (පක්ෂ wing, පත්‍ර feather) wing of a bird.

පක්ෂපාත, *Pakshapáta, s.* partisan, adherent: *a.* loyal; faithful, confederate with, partial to; obedient; courteous, complaisant, civil.

පක්ෂපිරමාණ, *Pakshapiramáṇa, s.* allegiance; fidelity, loyalty.

පක්ෂප්‍රසාරණ, *Paksha-prasáraṇa,* } *s.* flapping of the
පක්ෂප්‍රහාරය, *Paksha-prahárya,* } wings of a bird; flying.

පක්ෂබලය, *Paksha-balaya, s.* confederacy, power of a party, party influence.

පක්ෂය, *Pakshaya,* see පක්ෂ *paksha.*

පක්ෂවාදී, *Pakshawádi, a.* loyal.

පක්ෂවාදීකම, *Pakshawádikama, s.* partisanship, party attachment; partiality, loyalty.

පක්ෂවාදියා, *Pakshawadiyá, a.* partisan, confederate, ally.

පක්ෂාඝාත, *Pakshágháta, s.* (පක්ෂ *paksha* side, අඝාත *ágháta* killing) refutation of an argument; palsy: *a.* palsied.

පක්ෂාන්ත, *Pakshánta,* } *s.* (පක්ෂ *paksha* fort-
පක්ෂාවසර, *Pakshávasara,* } night, අන්ත *anta* or අවසර *awasara* end) fifteenth or last day of either half of a month, day of the new or full moon.

පක්ෂි, *Pakshi, s.* bird.

පක්ෂි කූඩුව, *Pakshi-kúḍuwa, s.* (පක්ෂි bird, කූඩුව nest) bird's nest, bird-cage, aviary.

පක්ෂිධේනුව, *Pakshi-dhénuwa, s.* (පක්ෂි and ධේනුව female) female bird.

පක්ෂියා, *Pakshiyá, s.* bird, pl. පක්ෂි *pakshi.*

පක්ෂිවැද්දා, *Pakshi-weddá, s.* (පක්ෂි fowl, වැද්දා hunter) fowler.

පක්ෂි ස්වාමින්, *Pakshi-swámin, s.* (පක්ෂි and ස්වාමින් lord) Garuḍa or bird of Vishṇu, considered as lord of the feathered tribe.

පක්‍ෂි, *Pakshí*, *s.* arrow, [Colloq. ඊගහ *ígaha*].

පගතිය, *Pagatiya*, *s.* family; part, portion.

පගෝඩිය, *Pagódiya*, *s.* gold coin worth about four rupees.

පඝන, *Paghana*, *s.* veranda or terrace before a house.

පඞ්ක්ති, *Pańkti*, *s.* line, row, range, company, society; metre, stanza of four lines, each line consisting of ten syllables.

පඞ්ක, *Pańka*, *s.* mud, clay, mire; any thing mixed with water so as to form consistence; sin, demerit.

පඞ්කජ, *Pańkaja*, *s.* (පඞ්ක mud, ජ born, produced) lotus, *nelumbium speciosum:* see පඞ්කේරුහ *pańkéruha*, [Colloq. නෙළුම් *neḷum*].

පඞ්කජිනි, *Pańkajiní*, *s.* (පංකජ *pańkaja* and ඉනි *iní* aff.) pool or pond where the lotus grows.

පඞ්කාර, *Pańkára*, *s.* bridge, or raised bank, forming a path amidst inundated fields; stemless aquatic plant, *blyxa Roxbughii* or *vallisneria octandra.*

පඞ්කිල, *Pańkila*, *a.* muddy, clayey, marshy.

පඞ්කේරුහ, *Pańkéruha*, *s.* (පඞ්කේ in mud, රුහ produced) lotus, [Colloq. නෙළුම් *neḷum*]: see පඞ්කජ *pańkaja.*

පඞ්ගු, *Pangu*, *s.* cripple, one who has lost his legs; planet Saturn; part, share.

පච්ච, *Pachcha*, *s.* green.

පච්ච කුරුල්ලා, *Pachcha-kurullá*, *s.* southern yellow-naped woodpecker, *chrysophlegma chlorigaster (Picidæ* order *Picariæ).*

පච්ඡාභත්තිකාඞ්ග, *Pachchhábhattikáṅga*, *s.* (පච්ඡා after, භත්තික *bhattika* relating to food or meals, අඞ්ග *aṅga* ordinance) ordinance of the Buddhist priesthood, enjoining it upon the priests to live on one meal a day, which meal must not be eaten before or after midday: see තෙළෙස්ධුතාඞ්ග *teḷesdhutáṅga*. According to Hardy, the priest who keeps this ordinance cannot eat any more after he has met with that which is අකැප *akęp*a, improper.

පච්ඡිම, *Pachchhima*, *s.* end, conclusion; west: *a.* behind, after.

පච, *Pacha*, *s.* cooking, ripening, maturing, etc.

පචක, *Pachaka*, *s.* cook, [Colloquial: කෝකියා *kókiyá*].

පචම්පචා, *Pachampachá*, *s.* climbing shrub, *coscinium fenestratum* [Colloq. වෙනිවැල් *weniwęl* or වනුවැල් *wanuwęl*].

පචමාන, *Pachamána*, *s.* cooking, dressing food.

පජ්ජ, *Pajja*, *s.* (පද් *pad* foot, ජ born) road, path; Páli form of පථ *patha;* also, low caste man, Sudra, in allusion to the fable of this caste being born from the feet of Brahma; verse; things agreeable to the feet, as water for ablution; shoe flower plant, *hibiscus rosa-sinenis*, [Colloquial: සපත්තු මල් *sapattu-mal*].

පජ්ජෝත, *Pajjota*, *s.* lamp, [Colloq. පාණ *páṇa* or ලාම්පුව *lámpuwa*].

පජ, *Paja*, *s.* (ප foot, ජ born) Sudra, man of a low and degraded tribe, alluding to the fable of the Sudras being sprung from the feet of Brahma.

පජයා, *Pajayá*, *s.* (පජ and යා pers. aff.) low and wicked man, one of a degraded tribe, mischievous fellow: see the last.

පජා, *Pajá*, *s.* sentient being; multitude; progeny, offspring; people, subjects.

පජානනං, *Pajánanaṅ*, *s.* knowledge, learning, information.

පජාපති, *Pajápati*, *s.* (පජා and පති lord) name of Brahma, alluding to his being the chief of all created beings, [Colloq. මහාබ්‍රහ්මයා *mahá-brahmayá*].

පඤ්ජරය, *Pañjaraya*, *s.* cage, aviary, dove-cot.

පඤ්ච, *Pañcha*, *a.* five, [Colloq. පහ *paha*].

පඤ්ච ඉන්ද්‍රිය, *Pañcha-indriya*, *s.* (පඤ්ච five, ඉන්ද්‍රිය organ of sense) the five senses: seeing, hearing, feeling, smelling, tasting, commonly written පඤ්චෙන්ද්‍රිය *pañchendriya.*

පඤ්චක, *Pañchaka*, *s.* collection or aggregation of five: *a.* five, relating to five.

පඤ්ච කකුධභාණ්ඩය, *Pañcha-kakudhabhánḍaya*, *s.* (පඤ්ච and කකුධ royal insignia, භාණ්ඩ treasure) five chief insignia of royalty: sword, white umbrella, plate of gold for the forehead, gold shoes, and chámara or white fan or whisk made from the tail of the Indian Yac or bos grunniens.

පඤ්ච කර්ම, *Pañcha-karma*, *s.* (පඤ්ච and කර්ම act) five operations of the human body: vomiting, evacuating by stool, bloodletting, blowing the nose, and diseased excretion of the fæces.

පඤ්චකල්‍යාණ, *Pañcha-kalyáṇa*, *s.* (පඤ්ච and කල්‍යාණ beauty) five marks of beauty, peculiar to the female ideal: red lips, long soft hair, white regular teeth, soft and blooming skin, and youth.

පඤ්චකාමය, *Pañcha-kámaya*, *s.* (පඤ්ච five, කාම *káma* object of sense) five objects of sense: form, sound, smell, taste and touch.

පඤ්චක්ලේශය, *Pañcha-kléṣaya*, *s.* (පඤ්ච and ක්ලේශ *kléṣa* moral defilement, human passion) five internal evils to which men are most subject: lust, anger, ignorance, self-confidence and pride.

පඤ්චකෙළිය, *Pañcha-keḷiya*, see පඤ්චිකෙළිය *pañchi-keḷiyo.*

පඤ්චකෝලය, *Pañcha-kólaya*, *s.* (පඤ්ච and කෝල *kóla* spice) medical preparation or compound, consisting of the aggregate of five spices: long pepper, its root, *piper chavya*, plumbago or leadwort and dry ginger.

පඤ්චගව්‍ය, *Pañcha-gawya*, *s.* (පඤ්ච and ගව්‍ය belonging to a cow) five articles derived from the cow: milk, curds, clarified butter, cow's urine and cow's dung.

පඤ්චගීතනාදය, *Pañcha-gítanádaya*, *s.* (පඤ්චගීත five-fold singing, නාද sound) five sounds or musical tones that are produced from five different sorts of tom-toms: see පඤ්චතූර්ය්‍යය *pañcha túryaya.*

පඤ්චචණ්ඩාල, *Pañcha-chaṇḍála*, *s.* (පඤ්ච five, චණ්ඩාල man of a degraded caste) five of the supposed inferior castes: those of the washerman, potter, barber, silversmith and tailor.

පඤ්චතූර්ය්‍යය, *Pañcha-túryaya*, *s.* (පඤ්ච and තූර්ය්‍ය *túrya* musical instrument) five different kinds of tom-tom or native drum, each producing a different sound: they are used as an accompaniment to singing and performance on wind instruments.

පඤ්චධර්මය, *Pañcha-dharmaya*, *s.* (පඤ්ච and ධර්ම *dharma* virtue) five chief virtues: faith, obedience, study (of religion), benevolence, and knowledge.

පඤ්චනවුති, *Pañch-nawuti*, *ad.* ninety-five, [Coll: අනූපහ *anú-paha*]; this refers to ninety-five erroneous religions which existed when Buddha came into this world, the whole of which he destroyed by the power of his doctrines: see සකස්කඩ *sakaskaḍa.*

පඤ්චපක්ෂියා, *Pañcha-pakshiyá*, *s.* (පඤ්ච and පක්ෂි *pakshi* bird) five ominous birds from which prognostics are drawn in the science of augury: Garuḍa, (Vishṇu's bird) owl, crow, cock and the peacock.

පඤ්චපද්මය, *Pañcha-padmaya*, *s.* (පඤ්ච five, පද්ම *padma* lotus) five sorts of lotus.

පඤ්චපාණ්ඩවයෝ, *Pañcha-páṇḍawayó*, *s.* (පඤ්ච and පාණ්ඩව *páṇḍawa* descendant of Páṇḍu sovereign of ancient Delhi) the five Páṇḍawa princes so much celebrated in Hindu history, one of whom was the famous Yudhishṭhira.

පඤ්චපාපය, *Pañcha-pápaya*, *s.* (පඤ්ච and පාප *pápa* sin) five chief sins prohibited by the laws of Buddha: not to take away life, not to thieve, not to commit adultery, not to drink any intoxicating liquor, not to lie.

පඤ්චපෙත, *Pañcha-peta*, see පඤ්චිපෙත *pañchi-peta.*

පඤ්චප්‍රසාද, *Pañcha-prasáda*, *s.* (පඤ්ච five, ප්‍රසාද joy) joy in five stages, reckoning from the common feeling of satisfaction until complete ecstasy takes place.

පඤ්චබලය, *Pañcha-balaya*, *s.* (පඤ්ච and බල *bala* power) five powers: faith, innocence, fear (of sin), effort (religious), wisdom (religious).

පඤ්චබාණ, *Pañcha-báṇa*, *s.* (පඤ්ච and බාණ arrow) name of Anaṅga the Indian Cupid alluding to his being armed with five arrows.

පඤ්චභූම, *Pañcha-bhúma*, *s.* (පඤ්ච and භූම ground) five storied house.

පඤ්චම, *Pañchama*, *s.* the fifth, [Colloq. පස්වෙනි *pasweni*]; one of the seven musical notes, seventh in the Indian gamut.

පඤ්චමධුරමාංස, *Pañcha-madhura-máṇsa*, *s.* (පඤ්ච and මධුර flavour, මාංස flesh) five constituents of the body: blood, flesh, bones, marrow and adeps.

පඤ්චමහාගංගාව, *Pañchamahá-gaṅgáwa*, *s.* (පඤ්ච and මහා chief, ගංගා *gaṅgá* river) five principal rivers of Jambudwípa or India proper: Gaṅgá, Yamuná (Jumná), Achirawatí, Sarabhú and Mahí.

පඤ්චමහාපරිත්‍යාග, *Pañchmahá-parityága*, *s.* (පඤ්ච five, මහා great, පරිත්‍යාග sacrifice) among the Hindus, the five chief sacrifices: worship (by offerings) of spirits, progenitors, gods, Védas and mankind; among the Buddhists, five supreme offerings, which none but Buddha himself can offer: eyes, flesh, blood, head, wife and children.

පඤ්චමහාපූර්වනිමිත්ත, *Pañchamahá-púrwa-nimitta*, *s.* (පඤ්ච five, මහා great, පූර්ව before, නිමිත්ත token) five objects which Bódhisat saw when sporting in the garden of Lumbini, and which led him to resolve upon renouncing the world, becoming an ascetic and attaining the Buddhaship: *i. e.* a decrepit man, an old man, a corpse, a funeral procession and a priest.

පඤ්චමහා ස්වප්න, *Pañchamahá-swapna*, *s.* (පඤ්ච five, මහා great, ස්වප්න dream) five dreams which Bódhisat saw when Siddhárta Kumára; these were among the causes of his determining to embrace the life of an ascetic and to obtain the Buddhaship.

පඤ්චමුඛ, *Pañcha-mukha*, see පඤ්චානන *pañchánana.*

පඤ්චමූල, *Pañcha-múla*, *s.* (පඤ්ච and මූල root) the aggregate of the roots of five plants: *premna lalifolia*, [Colloq. මහ මිදි *maha-midi*]; *oroxylum indicum* or *colosanthes indica*, [Colloq. තොටිල *toṭila*]; *gmelina arborea*, [Colloq, ඇත් දෙමට *ęt-demaṭa*]; *ægle marmelos*, [Colloq. බෙලි *beli*], and the trumpet flower, *stereospermum suaveolens*, [Colloq. පළොල් *paḷol*].

පඤ්චරසා, *Pañchrasá*, *s.* plant, *phyllanthus emblica* or *myrobalana emblica*, [Colloq. නෙල්ලි *nelli*].

පඤ්ච ලවණ, *Pañcha-lawaṇa*, *s.* (පඤ්ච five, ලවණ salt) five kinds of salt found in the east: rock salt, sea salt, factitious salt or bit-loben, salt petre, and *sal ammoniac.*

පඤ්චලෝහ, *Pañcha-lóha*, *s.* (පඤ්ච and ලෝහ metal) five chief or most common metals: copper, brass, tin, lead and iron, or a metalic alloy compounded of the aggregate of these metals.

පඤ්ච වක්ත්‍ර, *Pañcha-waktra*, *s.* (පඤ්ච and වක්ත්‍ර face) name of Ṣiva: see පඤ්චානන *pañckánana.*

පඤ්ච වර්ණ, *Pañcha-warṇa*, *s.* (පඤ්ච and වර්ණ colour) five colours which are reflected from the body of Buddha: blue, gold colour, red, white, and black.

පඤ්ච වල්කල, *Pañcha-walkala*, *s.* (පඤ්ච and වල්කල bark) collection of the bark of five different trees: banyan tree, *ficus bengalensis*, [Colloq. මහ නුග *maha-nuga*]; bó-tree, *f. religiosa;* opposite leaved fig, *f. oppositifolia*, [Colloq. කොටදිඹුලා *koṭadimbulá*]; wave-leaved fig, [Colloq. පුළිල *pulila*]; *f. Tsjakela*, [Colloq. කිරිපැල්ල *kiripęlla*].

පඤ්ච වස්තුව, *Pañcha-wastuwa*, *s.* (පඤ්ච and වස්තුව treasure) five treasures of Kuvéra the Indian god of wealth.

පඤ්චශර, *Pañchaṣara*, *s.* (පඤ්ච and ශර arrow) name of Káma, the Hindu deity of love.

පඤ්ච ශික්ෂාපදය, *Pañcha-ṣikshápadaya*, see පඤ්චසීල *pañcha-síla.*

පඤ්චශිඛ, *Pañchaṣikha*, *s.* (පඤ්ච spreading, five, ශිඛා *ṣikhá* crest) lion; chorister of Swarga the oriental paradise.

පඤ්චශිඛ දිව්‍යපුත්‍රය, *Pañchaṣikha-diwyaputra*, *s.* (පඤ්චශිඛ chorister, දිව්‍ය divine, පුත්‍ර *putra* son) chorister of Swarga, said to have five faces; it is also an epithet of several of the gods, who are said to have five faces, as Ṣiva, Viṣwakarma etc. see පඤ්චානන *pañchánana.*

පඤ්චස්කන්ධ, *Pañchaskandha*, *s.* (පඤ්ච five, ස්කන්ධ portion, division) in metaphysics, five branches of human knowledge or objects of understanding: රූප *rúpa* five bodily senses; වේදනා *wédaná* sensation; සඤ්ඤා *saññá* perception; සංඛාර *saṇkhára* memory or the faculty of recollection, mental condition; විඤ්ඤාණ *viññáṇa* comprehension or understanding.

පඤ්ච සාඛා, *Pañcha-sákhá*, *s.* (පඤ්ච and සාඛා branch) hand, [Colloq. අත *ata*].

පඤ්චසීලය, *Pañchasílaya*, *s.* (පඤ්ච five, සීල *síla* religious obedience or observance of law) subordinate code of moral law in Buddhism applicable to all men: not to kill, this extends to all animals; not to steal; not to commit adultery; not to lie; not to drink intoxicating liquors.

පඤ්චාක්ෂිය, *Pañchákshiya*, *s.* (පඤ්ච *pañcha* and අක්ෂි *akshi* eye) name of Buddha alluding to his five faculties of perception: his divine eye, his human eye, his mental eye, his omniscient eye, the eye of a Buddha, *i. e.* knowledge of Nirwáṇa.

පඤ්චාංග, *Pañcháṅga*, *s.* (පඤ්ච *pañcha* and අංග *aṅga* part, limb) five parts of the body which must be bent and touch the ground when in the act of worshipping Buddha: waist, elbows, knees, head and toes; five parts of a plant used for medicinal purposes: bark, leaf, flower, root, and leaf stalk; almanac describing solar days, lunar days, periods of asterisms, යෝග, Yógas, (or $\frac{1}{27}$ part of 360° of a great circle measured on the plane of the ecliptic and used in calculating the longitudes and latitudes of the sun and moon; also twenty-eight divisions of the moon's path, corresponding with the twenty-eight nakshatras or lunar mansions) and කරණ, Karaṇas of which there are eleven, two of these being equal to one lunar day.

පඤ්චාංග ගුප්ත, *Pañcháṅga-gupta*, *s.* (පඤ්ච *pañcha* five, අංග *aṅga* limb, ගුප්ත concealed) animal concealing his head and four legs beneath his shell; tortoise, or turtle, [Colloq. කැස්බෑවා *kęsbęwá*, or ඉබ්බා *ibbá*].

පඤ්චාඞ්ගික, *Pañcháṅgika*, a. (පඤ්ච *pañcha* five, අඞ්ග *aṅga* limb, part, ඉක *ika* aff.) five limbed, having five parts or members, composed of five portions.

පඤ්චාඞ්ගුල, *Pañcháṅgula*, s. (පඤ්ච *pañcha* and අඞ්ගුලි *aṅguli* finger) measure of five fingers; castor oil plant, *ricinus communis*, [Colloq. එඬරු *eṇḍaru*], the (palmate) leaf of which has five lobes resembling the five fingers of the open hand.

පඤ්චානන්තරියකර්මය, *Pañchánantariya-karmaya*, s. (පඤ්ච *pañcha* and අනන්තරිය *anantariya* immediate, කර්ම *karma* act, deed) five great sins for which there is no pardon: murder of mother, murder of father, murder of a Rahat, shedding the blood of Buddha, (it is not possible to take away his life), schism in religion; five sins that bring with them immediate retribution.

පඤ්චානන, *Pañchánana*, } s. (පඤ්ච *pañcha*
පඤ්චානනාත්මක, *Pañchánanátmaka*, } spreading, five, ආනන *ánana* face) lion, [Colloq. සිංහයා *siṅhayá*]; name of Ṣiva, in allusion to his being sometimes represented in the temples, in the form of meditation used daily by the Bramins, as a silver coloured man with five faces.

පඤ්චාභිඥා, *Pañchábhijñá*, s. (පඤ්ච *pañcha* five, අභිඥා *abhijñá* profound knowledge) five supernatural acquirements possessed by the Rahats or highest order of Buddhist ascetics: the power of assuming any form; supernatural hearing by which sounds may be heard at any distance; the faculty of knowing the hearts of others; the knowledge of men's condition in former states of existence; the power of seeing objects at any distance.

පඤ්චාමෘත, *Pañchámṛita*, s. (පඤ්ච *pañcha* and අමෘත *amṛita* nectar) mixture of sugar, milk, curds, honey, and ghee or clarified butter.

පඤ්චායුධ, *Pañcháyudha*, s. (පඤ්ච *pañcha* and ආයුධ *áyudha* weapon) five warlike weapons: sword, spear, bow, battle-axe and shield.

පඤ්චාල, *Pañchála*, s. country so called in the north of India.

පඤ්චාශුචි, *Pañcháṣuchi*, s. (පඤ්ච *pañcha* five, අශුචි *aṣuchi* filth) five excrements of the human body: saliva, phlegm, mucus of the nose, fœces, and urine.

පඤ්චාස්‍ය, *Pañchásya*, s. (පඤ්ච *pañcha* spreading, ආස්‍ය *ásya* face) lion, alluding to his spreading mane.

පඤ්චිකෙළිය, *Pañchi-keḷiya*, s. (පඤ්චි five, කෙළි *keḷi* game) game, kind of drafts played with five shells.

පඤ්චිපෙත, *Pañchi-peta*, s. board used for playing the game mentioned in the last.

පඤ්චින්ද්‍රිය, *Pañchindriya*, } see පඤ්ච ඉන්ද්‍රිය *pañ-*
පඤ්චේන්ද්‍රිය, *Pañchéndriya*, } *cha-indriya*.

පඤ්චෝපක්ලේශ, *Pañchópa-kléṣa*, see පඤ්චක්ලේශ *pañchakléṣa*.

පඤ්ජි, *Pañji*, s. ball or whisp of cotton from which thread is spun; journal, register; almanac, [Colloq. ලිත *lita*].

පඤ්ජිකා, *Pañjiká*, s. (පංජි register, ක aff.) the register of Yama (Pluto) or record of human actions; perpetual commentary.

පඤ්ඤා, *Paññá*, s. god-father, (Port); wisdom; Páli form of ප්‍රඥා, *prajñá*.

පට්ට, *Paṭṭa*, s. cloth; coloured cloth; silk; wove silk; bandage, ligature; upper garment; waist cloth; turban, any cloth used for that purpose; bark of a plant, *corchorus olitorius* from the fibres of which a coarse kind of sackcloth and cordage is made; chair, seat, stool; place where four roads meet; grinding stone; city, town, village.

පට්ටන, *Paṭṭana*, s. sea port, trading town.

පට්ටම, *Paṭṭama*, s. side of any solid body.

පට්ටය, *Paṭṭaya*, s. bark of a tree, pl. පට්ටා *paṭṭá*.

පට්ටයා, *Paṭṭayá*, s. vile or worthless man, wicked mischievous fellow, rascal.

පට්ටල, *Paṭṭala*, s. work shop, forge.

පට්ටා, *Paṭṭá*, s. red lódh, or a bark used for dyeing, obtained from the *symplocos racemosa;* ornament for the head; horse girth.

පට්ටා ඇපල, *Paṭṭá-ẹpala*, s. bushy tree, *urena lobata (Malvaceæ)*.

පට්ටා ගහනවා, *Paṭṭá-gahanawá*, v. to strip the bark of a tree.

පට්ටාබඹර, *Paṭṭá-bambara*, s. plant, not identified.

පට්ටා වල්ලා, *Paṭṭá-wallá*, s. bastard mangeneel, peculiar to Ceylon, *Gyrinops Walla, (Thymeleaceæ);* also called වල්ලා *wallá*.

පට්ටික්කා, *Paṭṭikká*, s. creeping plant, not identified.

පට්ටිය, *Paṭṭiya*, s. stall for cattle, crib; herd of cattle.

පට්ටිලෝද්‍ර, *Paṭṭilódhra*, s. tree, the bark of which is used as an astringent; red species of the lódh *symplocos racemosa*.

පට්ටේ, *Paṭṭé*, *s.* bark of a tree, pl. පට්ටා *paṭṭá*.

පට, *Paṭa*, *s.* wove silk; fine cloth; coloured cloth; single fold.

පටකඩ, *Paṭakaḍa*, *s.* (පට and කඩ cloth) silk cloth, [Colloq. පටරෙද්ද *paṭa-redda*].

පටකාර, *Paṭakára*, *s.* (පට and කාර who does) weaver.

පට කුඩේ, *Paṭa-kuḍé*, *s.* silk umbrella.

පටන්, *Paṭan*, *s.* first, beginning, commencement: particle used in the sense of from, commencing, beginning from.

පටන්ගන්නවා, *Paṭangannawá*, *v.* (පටන් beginning, ගන්නවා to take) to begin, to commence.

පටපඹ, *Paṭa-pamba*, *s.* plant, not identified.

පටපිට පට, *Paṭapiṭa-paṭa*, *ad.* fold upon fold, lying in layers.

පටපිළි, *Paṭapiḷi*, *s.* silk, wove silk.

පටපැඹුරා, *Paṭa-pęmburá*, *s.* plant, not identified.

පටබඳිනවා, *Paṭabandinawá*, *v.* to confer a title or office by putting on the forehead a metal plate, on which is engraven the name, title etc., or a piece of embroidered silk on it.

පටබැන්ද, *Paṭabęndá*, *s.* chief who has been appointed to an office or title, by applying a piece of gold to the forehead, see above; but this word in the maritime provinces is almost invariably used as the title of a chief of the fisher caste: *part.* conferred a title.

පටම්පටි, *Paṭampaṭí*, *s.* cotton plant, [Colloq. කපුගස් *kapu-gas*].

පටල, *Paṭala*, see පටලය *paṭalaya*.

පටලනවා, *Paṭalanawá*, *v.* to tie round, to wrap, to fold, to double: pret. පටලෑවා *paṭalęwá*.

පටලය, *Paṭalaya*, *s.* multitude; cataract, film over the eyes; mark on the forehead with sandalwood; cover, roof, thatch.

පටලී, *Paṭalí*, *s.* stalk.

පටව, *Paṭawa*, *s.* sort of drum or tom-tom.

පටවනවා, *Paṭawanawá*, *v.* to load, to freight: pret. පැටෙව්වා *pęṭewwá*.

පටහ, *Paṭaha*, *s.* kind of tom-tom, drum used in battle, kettle drum.

පටහළ, *Paṭahaḷa*, *s.* kind of long tom-tom; sort of shield or buckler.

පටහැනි, *Paṭa-hęni*, *s.* (පට for පටි *paṭi*=ප්‍රති *prati* against + අනීක *aníka* army = ප්‍රත්‍යනීක *pratyaníka*) one of the opposite force or army, or of the hostile party: *a.* opposed, hostile.

පටි, *Paṭi*, *s.* curtain; screen of cloth surrounding a tent; girdle or cloth binder for the waist, belt, girdle.

පටිකා, *Paṭiká*, *s.* coarse thick cloth, canvas; white woollen cloth for covering.

පටිග්ගහ, *Paṭiggaha*, පටිග්ගහණය, *Paṭiggahaṇaya*, } *s.* acceptance; reserve of troops 400 yards in rear of the line; vessel shaped like a bowl; sun near the moon's node.

පටිච්ඡන්න, *Paṭichchhanna*, *a.* covered, concealed, hidden.

පටිජග්ගනය, *Paṭijagganaya*, *s.* nourishing, watching over, fostering, bringing up.

පටිජග්ගනදානය, *Paṭijaggana-dánaya*, *s.* (පටිජග්ගන nourishing, දාන *dána* gift) nourishment, support preservation.

පටිධාතුව, *Paṭidhátuwa*, see පටිධාතුව *paṭidhátuwa*.

පටිපන්න, *Paṭipanna*, *a.* known, understood; determined; engaged, agreed, assented to; walking, entered upon.

පටිපාටිය, *Paṭipáṭiya*, *s.* order, arrangement, method.

පටිබෙඳුරු, *Paṭibéndurn*, *s.* fern, species of adder's tongue, *ophioglossum pendulum*.

පටිභාන, *Paṭibhána*, *s.* wisdom; understanding, intellect; presence of mind, readiness in replying to what is advanced.

පටිය, *Paṭiya*, *s.* ribbon, band, girdle, binder for the waist or loins.

පටිලාභ, *Paṭilábha*, *s.* (පටි again, ලාභ receiving) receiving, obtaining, reward, return; mutual profit or advantage.

පටිවිරත, *Paṭivirata*, *s.* (පටි before විරත stopped, ceased) preventing, stopping; impediment, hindrance, obstacle, stoppage: *a.* separate, sundered, abandoned, relinquished.

පටිවුත්ත, *Paṭiwutta*, *a.* (පටි again, වුත්ත said) answered, replied, the Páli form of ප්‍රත්‍යුක්ත *pratyukta*.

පටිසංඛරණය, *Paṭisaṇkharaṇaya*, *s.* (පටි and සංඛරණ *saṇkharaṇa* repairing) purifying, cleansing, renovating, renewal.

පටිසන්ථාර, *Paṭisanthára*, *s.* (පටි and සන්ථාර couch) love, affection, kindness, reciprocal esteem, friendly greeting.

පටිසම්භිදාය, *Paṭisambhidáya*, *s.* (පටි before සම්භිදා *sambhidá* discrimination) universal knowledge, ability to explain terms respecting all subjects of art or science.

පටිසල්ලාණ, *Paṭisallána*, *s.* (පටි emphatic, සල්ලාණ concealed) solitude, privacy: *a.* secluded, retired, solitary.

පටිසෝතගාමි, *Paṭisóta-gámi*, *s.* (පටි against, සෝත rapid stream, ගාමිනී *gáminí* going) going against the current of a river, metaphorically, against the flood of human passions, dfficult.

පටිහාර, *Paṭihára*, *s.* door-way, [Colloq. දොරකඩ *dorakaḍa*]; door-keeper.

පටි, *Paṭi*, *s.* girdle, belt, binder for the waist.

පටිධාතුව, *Paṭidhátuwa*, *s.* (පටි girdle, ධාතු *dhátu* relic) girdle-relic, *i. e.* girdle of Buddha, which he used when in this world, and which is supposed to be preserved by the gods as a sacred relic.

පටිර, *Paṭira*, *s.* sandal wood, *santalum album*, [Colloq. සඳුන් *saṇdun*].

පටු, *Paṭu*, *s.* rock salt, [Colloquial: සෛන්ධව ලුණු *saindhawa-luṇu*]; small kind of cucumber, *trichosanthes cucumerina*, [Colloq. දුම්මැල්ල *dummęlla*]: *a.* narrow, strait; dextrous, skilful, clever; diligent, smart, sharp; hale, healthy; cruel, ferocious, unfeeling; harsh, contumelious (speech); fraudulent, crafty, roguish; loquacious, talkative.

පටුත්ව, *Paṭutwa*, *s.* skill, cleverness.

පටුන, *Paṭuna*, *s.* seaport, town; list of the contents of a book, index; fame, renown, pl. පටුනු *paṭunu:* *a.* large, bulky, massive, great.

පටුනක්කාර, *Paṭunakkára*, *s.* (පටුන town, කාර possessor) egotist, boaster.

පටුනක්කාරි, *Paṭunakkárí*, *s.* female boaster.

පටුනු, *Paṭunu*, *a.* large, extensive, great; also, pl. of පටුන *paṭuna*.

පටුපර්ණී, *Paṭuparṇṇí*, *s.* (පටු narrow, පර්ණ *parṇa* leaf, ඊ *í* fem. aff.) medicinal kind of moon-plant.

පටුමා, *Paṭumá*, *a.* clever, dextrous, skilful.

පටෝල, *Paṭóla*, } *s.* creeper, *trichosanthes*
පටෝලක, *Paṭólaka*, } *cucumerina*, [Colloq. දුම්මැල්ල *dummęlla*].

පටෝලා, *Paṭólá*, *s.* plant, [Colloq. තිත්ත වැටකොළු *titta-wętakoḷu*].

පඨම, *Paṭhama*, *a.* first, prior, [Colloq. පළමුවෙනි *paḷamuweni*].

පඨමජ්ඣාන, *Paṭhamajjhána*, Páli form of ප්‍රථම ධ්‍යාන *prathama-dhyána*, which see.

පඨමසංගීති කථා, *Paṭhama-sangíti-kathá*, *s.* (පඨම first, සංගීති rehearsal, කථා history) history of the first rehearsal of the text of the Buddhist canon.

පඨමා, *Paṭhamá*, *s.* the first or the nominative case in Páli grammar.

පඨවි, *Paṭhavi*, *s.* earth, Páli form of පෘථිවි *prithivi*.

පඨවිධාතුව, *Paṭhavidhátuwa*, *s.* (පඨවි earth, ධාතුව element) one of the four primary elements that constitute the essence of things; earth, [Colloq. පොළව *poḷawa*].

පඩ, *Paḍa*, *s.* breaking wind behind.

පඩ අරිණවා, *Paḍa-ariṇawá*, *v.* to break wind behind.

පඩත්තලයා, *Paḍattalayá*, *s.* warrior, man skilled in martial affairs, hero; captain or commander of an army.

පඩව්ව, *Paḍawwa*, *s.* boat, lighter.

පඩි, *Paḍi*, *s.* pay, hire, wages; income, salary; steps, stairs.

පඩික්කම, *Paḍikkama*, *s.* spitting pot, pl. පඩික්කං *paḍikkaṇ*.

පඩිකනවා, *Paḍikanawá*, *v.* to receive wages.

පඩිකාර නිලේ, *Paḍikára-nilé*, *s.* office of Paḍikára whose duty is to provide accommodation for the Maldive Ambassador and purchase presents for the Sultan at the cost of the Ceylon government.

පඩිදෙනවා, *Paḍi-denawá*, *v.* to pay wages.

පඩිනවා, *Paḍinawá*, *v.* to break wind behind: pret. පැඩ්ඩා *pęḍḍá*.

පඩිය, *Paḍiya*, *s.* step.

පඩියන්, *Paḍiyan*, *s.* blue sapphire.

පඬර, *Paṇḍara*, *s.* white (colour); kind of elephant, white lotus.

පඬි, *Paṇḍi*, see පණ්ඩිත *paṇḍita*.

පඬි, *Paṇḍí*, *s.* liquid dye of a saffron colour.

පඬු, *Paṇḍu*, *a.* pale or yellowish colour.

පඬු ඇඹුල්, *Paṇḍu-ęmbul*, } *s.* throne of Ṣakra or
පඬුපුල්, *Paṇḍupul*, } Indra, commonly called පාණ්ඩුකම්බල ශෛලාසනය *páṇḍukambala-sailásanaya*.

පඬුර, *Paṇḍura*, *s.* tax, custom, tribute; revenue, income; present, gift.

පඬුරු, *Paṇḍuru*, *s.* white lotus, *nymphæa lotus*, [Colloq. ඕලු *ólu*]; gift, present; offering to a deity; tribute to a king; incense; scent, perfume, odour.

පඬුරු මිල, *Paṇḍuru-mila*, *s.* Kandyan term for a fine.

පඬු රෙද්ද, *Paṇḍu-redda*, *s.* (පඬු saffron (dye), රෙද්ද cloth) yellow robe worn by the Buddhist priests, [Colloq. සිවුර *siwura*].

පඬුවන්, *Paṇḍuwan*, *a.* saffron coloured, yellow; pale or whitish colour.

පඬෙර, *Pan̤dera*, *s.* colour white; white lotus, variety of *nelumbium speciosum*, [Colloq. එල නෙළුම් *ela-neḷum*]: see පඬුරු *pan̤duru*.

පඬෙරඟ, *Pan̤deranga*, *s.* (පඬෙර white, අඟ *an̤ga* body) name of Íṣwara or Ṣiva alluding to the colour of his body, which resembles a white lotus or is of a pale yellow colour.

පණ්ඩ, *Paṇḍa*, } *s.* eunuch, [Colloq නපුංසක
පණ්ඩක, *Paṇḍaka*, } යා *napuṇsakayá*]; catamite.

පණ්ඩා, *Paṇḍá*, *s.* wisdom, understanding; science, learning.

පණ්ඩිත, *Paṇḍita*, *a.* learned, erudite, well informed in scholastic and theological study.

පණ්ඩිතංමන්‍ය, *Paṇḍitaṇmanya*, } *s.* (පණ්ඩිතං
පණ්ඩිතමානි, *Paṇḍitamáni*, } learned, මන *mana* to think) pedant, one who thinks himself a scholar, an arrogant and ignorant man.

පණ්ඩිතයා, *Paṇḍitayá*, *s.* pandit, learned man, one possessing general knowledge.

පණ්‍ය, *Paṇya*, *a.* to be sold, saleable, vendible.

පණ්‍ය මූල්‍ය, *Paṇya-múlya*, *s.* price of a commodity.

පණ්‍ය විථිකා, *Paṇya-víthiká*, *s.* (පණ්‍ය commodity, විථි *víthi* street, with කන් *kan* added) market place, stall, shop, any place of sale, [Colloq. කඩේ *kaḍé*].

පණ්‍ය ශාලාව, *Paṇya-ṣáláwa*, *s.* පණ්‍ය article of sale, hire, ශාලා *ṣálá* house) wareroom, market shop.

පණ්‍යස්ත්‍රී, *Paṇyastrí*, *s.* prostitute, [Modern වෙස ඟන *wesan̤gana*].

පණ්‍යා, *Paṇyá*. *s.* heart-pea.

පණ්‍යාඞ්ගනා, *Paṇyáṅganá*, *s.* prostitute.

පණ්‍යාජීව, *Paṇyá-jíwa*, *s.* trader, [Colloq. වෙ ළෙන්දා *weḷendá*].

පණ, *Paṇa*, *s.* measure of account in cowries or small shells, viz. eighty cowries; wages, hire; bet, wager; gaming, playing with dice; price, wealth, property; commodity for sale; business; distiller; house, dwelling; snare, trap; life, vitality, being, existence; dove; pigeon; love, affection; hood of the cobra capella; yoke; hand; bulrush; carpenter stone.

පණ අදිනවා, *Paṇa-adinawá*, *v.* to draw the last breath, to expire.

පණකුර, *Paṇakura*, *s.* (පණ life, අකුර *akura* letter) vowel, Elu form of ප්‍රාණාක්ෂර *práṇákshara*.

පණගබ, *Paṇagaba*, *s.* (පණ hood, ගබ cavity) concave of the hood of the cobra capella when raised.

පණගාත, *Paṇagáta*, Elu form of ප්‍රාණඝාත *práṇa-gháta*.

පණත, *Paṇata*, *s.* law, ordinance, command, statute, institute; wing: pl. පණත් *paṇat*: *a.* bowed, inclined, fallen.

පණතියනවා, *Paṇa-tiyanawá*, *v.* (පණ life, තියන වා to put) to temper iron.

පණදර, *Paṇadara*, *s.* cobra capella, [Colloq. නයා *nayá*].

පණනල, *Paṇanala*, *s.* (පණ and නල wind) life; animation, breath of life.

පණම්පෙති, *Paṇampeti*, *s.* kind of creepers.

පණම, *Paṇama*, *s.* coin, value three halfpence, a fanam, six and quarter cents.

පණපොවනවා, *Paṇapowanawá*, *v.* to temper iron, etc.

පණයනවා, *Paṇa-yanawá*, *v.* (පණ life, යනවා to go) to die, to expire, to become extinct.

පණයම්, *Paṇayam*, *s.* wages of a harlot, piece of any article of merchandise.

පණයම, *Paṇayama*, *s.* wages or hire of a prostitute.

පණර, *Paṇara*, *s.* (from Páli පණ්ණරස *paṇṇarasa* fifteen) fifteenth day of a lunar month, day of the full or change of the moon.

පණරද, *Paṇarada*, *s.* (පණ snake, රද king) name of Ananta, king of the serpent race and regent of the infernal regions; name of Ráhu.

පණව, *Paṇawa*, small drum or tabor.

පණවනවා, *Paṇawanawá*, *v.* to appoint, to fix, to settle as a law or statute; to make, to cause to be; to raise, to elevate as a seat: pret. පැණෙව්වා *pẹnewwá*.

පණවම්, *Paṇawami*, *s.* strumpet, prostitute, harlot, courtezan; [Modern: වෙසඟන *wesan̤gana*.]

පණස්වෙනි, *Paṇas-weni*, *s.* fiftieth.

පණස, *Paṇasa*, *s.* number fifty.

පණහ, *Paṇaha*, *s.* fifty.

පණාඞ්ගනා, *Paṇáṅganá*, *s.* (පණ hire, අඞ්ගනා *aṅganá* woman) prostitute, strumpet.

පණායා, *Paṇáyá*, *s.* business, merchandise, traffic.

පණිඳු, *Paṇin̤du*, *s.* (පණි serpent, ඉඳු *in̤du* chief or lord) cobra capella; name of Ananta, chief of the serpent race and regent of Pátála; name of Ráhu, ascending node: see රාහු *Ráhu*.

පණිවාය, *Paṇiwáya*, *s.* (පණි life, වා *wá* destruction) murder, killing, taking away life; slander, scandal.

පණිවිඩය, *Paṇiviḍaya*, *s.* message, order, command, pl. පණිවිඩ *paṇiviḍa*.

පණිවිඩකාරයා, *Paṇiviḍakárayá*, *s.* (පණිවිඩ message, කාර *kára* who does) messenger, courier, herald; envoy; Kandyan term for headman of inferior rank.

පණිවිඩපන්න, *Paṇiviḍa-panna*, *s.* (පණිවිඩ and පන්න business, service) government order, royal edict, conveying a message.

පණිවිඩපණත්, *Paṇiviḍa-paṇat*, *s.* proclaimed law, edict, order.

පණිවුඩ, *Paṇiwuḍa*, see පණිවිඩ *paṇiviḍa*.

පණු, *Paṇu*, *a.* living, existing, animated: see පණුවා *paṇuwá*.

පණු අඹ, *Puṇu-am̱ba*, *s.* variety of the *mangifera indica*, or common mango.

පණු අල, *Paṇu-ala*, *s.* stemless, tuberous plant, *trifonium arum* or *trilobatum (Araceæ)*.

පණු කහ, *Paṇu-kaha*, *s.* plant,

පණු කොඩොල්, *Paṇu-koṉdol*, *s.* creeping plant, *dioscorea bulbifera (Dioscoreaceæ)*.

පණු කෝන්, *Paṇu-kón*, *s.* variety of the *schleichera trijuga:* see කෝන් *kón*.

පණුකැවිල්ල, *Paṇukẹvilla*, *s.* (පණු worm, කැවිල්ල eating) disease in the skin occasioned by worms, ring-worm.

පණුකැර, *Paṇukẹra*, *s*, tree, peculiar to Ceylon, *eugenia Neesiana (Myrtaceæ)*.

පණු ගිරවා, *Paṇu-girawá*, *s.* small species of parrot, the paroquet.

පණු දන්, *Paṇu-dan*, *s.* tree, variety of *eugenia caryophyllæa*.

පණුදිය, *Paṇu-diya*, *s.* excessive saliva in children, supposed to arise from worms.

පණු නුග, *Paṇu-nuga*, *s.* species of fig-tree, *ficus nitida*.

පණුපලඟ, *Paṇu-palaṉga*, *s.* sort of grass hopper.

පණු පිල, *Paṇu-pila*, *s.* plant, variety of *tephrosia purpurea*.

පණු බඹර, *Paṇu-bambara*, *s.* tree, *unona esculenta*.

පණුර, *Paṇura*, *s.* obscurity; small shrine, casket.

පණුවා, *Paṇuwá*, *s.* worm, maggot, an insect in general.

පණුවො දමනවා, *Paṇuwo-damanawá*, *v.* to generate worms in a sore, to produce worms.

පණුවැල, *Paṇu-wẹla*, *s.* creeper, not identified.

පණු හබරල, *Paṇu-habarala*, *s.* tuberous plant, *alocasia (or colocasia) cuculata, (Araceæ);* also called නයි හබරල *nayi-habarala*.

පණැති, *Paṇẹti*, *a.* living, having life, existing.

පත්, *Pat*, *s.* leaf, leaves, wing, feather: *part. a.* arrived at, attained to.

පත් අංකුට්ටා, *Pat-aṉkuṭṭá*, *s.* kind of river fish.

පත්අඬුව, *Pat-aṉḍuwa*, *s.* nippers, small pincers.

පත් අඹ, *Pat-am̱ba*, *s.* (පත් or පත *pata* leaf, අඹ mango) variety of the common mango, *mangifera indica*.

පත් ඉර, *Pat-ira*, *s.* lines or scores on the jack fruit.

පත් ඉරුව, *Pat-iruwa*, *s.* leaf of an ola book, pl. පත් ඉරු *pat-iru*.

පත් කටිල්ලා, *Pat-kaṭillá*, *s.* kind of river fish.

පත්කට්ටුව, *Pat-kaṭṭuwa*, *s.* (පත් leaves, කට්ටුව bundle) set of palm leaves, blank or written, arranged alphabetically and consisting of sixteen, sometimes eight leaves, beginning with ක *ka*, කා *ká*, කි *ki*, කී *kí*, කු *ku*, කූ *kú*, කෘ *kṛi*, කෲ *kṛí*, කෟ *klu*, කෳ *klú*, කෙ *ke*, කෛ *kai*, කො *ko*, කෞ *kaw*, කං *kan̤*, කඃ *kaḥ*.

පත්කඩ, *Patkaḍa*, *s.* (පත් approaching, කඩ cloth) cloth on which the priests of Buddha prostrate themselves in the temple.

පත්කරණවා, *Patkaraṇawá*, *v.* to appoint, to ordain, to decree; to inflict; to confer, to bestow.

පත්කඩොල්, *Patkaḍol*, *s.* tree, *rhizophora mangle*.

පත්කිණ, *Pat-kíṇa*, *s.* tree, species of *calophyllum*.

පත්කුරුඳු, *Pat-kuruṉdu*, *s.* tree, variety of cinnamon, *cinnamomum zeylanicum*,

පත්කෙරීම, *Patkeríma*, *s.* appointment.

පත්කොල, *Patkola*, *s.* leaves, plantain leaves.

පත්කැඳ, *Pat-kẹnda*, *s.* tree, *macaranga tomentosa (Euphorbiaceæ);* also called කැඳ *kẹnda*.

පත්කැල, *Pat-kẹla*, *s.* tree, peculiar to Ceylon, *bridelia Moonii (Euphorbiaceæ)*.

පත්ගහනවා, *Pat-gahanawá*, *v.* (පත් leaf, fan, ගහනවා to beat) to fan.

පත්ත, *Patta*, *s.* bowl, dish, beggar's dish, serving the purpose both of begging and eating; Páli form of පාත්‍ර *pátra*.

පත්තන, *Pattana*, *s.* town, city, seaport town; sort of drum.

පත්තපිණ්ඩිකාඞ්ගය, *Pattapiṇḍikáṅgaya*, *s.* (පත්ත bowl, පිණ්ඩික *piṇḍika* who eats cooked rice, අඞ්ග *aṉga* ordinance) ordinance of the Buddhist priesthood which enjoins the eating out of one dish only.

පත්තායම, *Pattáyama*, *s.* granary, pl. පත්තායම් *pattáyam*.

පත්ති, *Patti*, *s.* foot soldier; hero; going, moving, walking.

පත්තිනි, *Pattini*, *s.* wife, corrupt form of පත්නි *patní*, which see.

පත්තිනි දේවි, *Pattini-dévi*, *s.* (පත්නි *patní* wife, දේවි goddess) goddess of great celebrity; she is said to have come originally from the Coromandel coast and is chiefly invoked in cases of small pox.

පත්තියම, *Pattiyama*, *s.* regimen, diet.

පත්තිරිප්පුව, *Pattirippuwa*, *s.* royal residence; elevated place from which the king gives audience.

පත්තු, *Pattu*, *s.* light, flame, blaze, blazing; also, pl. of පත්තුව *pattuwa*, which see.

පත්තුකරණවා, *Pattukaraṇawá*, *v.* to light.

පත්තුව, *Pattuwa*, *s.* division of a Kórale; medicament, healing application.

පත්තුවෙනවා, *Pattuwenawá*, *v.* to blaze, to burn, to be on fire, to light.

පත්තූර, *Pattúra*, *s.* creeping plant, the leaf of which is used as a vegetable, *achyranthes triandra*, [Colloq. මුගුණුවැන්න *mugunuwẹnna*].

පත්තෑ බතල, *Pattẹ-batala*, *s.* bind-weed, creeping plant yielding a bulbous root or yam, variety of sweet potato, *ipomœa (*or *Convolvulus) batatas*.

පත්තෑයා, *Pattẹyá*, *s.* centipede, *(Myriapoda)*.

පත්නි, *Patní*, *s.* wife; virtuous woman, one who performs her marriage vow.

පත්පට, *Patpaṭa*,
පත්පාඩගං, *Patpáḍagaṇ*,
පත්පාඩගම්, *Patpáḍagam*, } *s.* plant, *mollugo Cerviana (Ficoideæ)*. (Trimen.)

පත්බානවා, *Patbánawá*, *v.* to mend mats and straw roofs.

පත්බේරිය, *Patbériya*, *s.* tree, variety of *lumnitzera racemosa*.

පත්‍ය, *Patya*, corruptly for පථ්‍ය *pathya*, which see.

පත්‍ර, *Patra*, *s.* leaf, wing of a bird, feather, feather of an arrow; vehicle in general, as a car, horse, elephant, etc.; leaf of a book, any thin sheet or plate of metal.

පත්‍රඞ්ග, *Patraṅga*, *s.* red sandal wood, *pterocarpus santalinus*.

පත්‍රච්ඡේදනය, *Patrachchhédanaya*, *s.* (පත්‍ර leaf, ඡේදන *chchhédana* what cuts) saw, [Colloq. කියත *kiyata*].

පත්‍රපාශ්‍යා, *Patrapáṣyá*, *s.* ornament of the forehead, gold leaf situate on it, or painted mark on it.

පත්‍රපුටය, *Patrapuṭaya*, *s.* cup or concavity made of a leaf folded or donbled, [Colloq. කොළ ගොටුව *kola-goṭuwa*.

පත්‍රභඞ්ග, *Patra-bhanga*, *s.* decorating the person by staining with fragrant pigments of sandal, musk, etc.; mace.

පත්‍රමකා, *Patramaká*, *s.* mace, [Colloq. වසාවාසි *wasáwási*].

පත්‍රමජ්ජකා, *Patra-majjaká*, *s.* medicinal plant, aloe, *aloe vulgaris*, [Colloq. කෝමාරිකා *kómáriká*].

පත්‍රය, *Patraya*, *s.* epistle, leaf of a tree, wing: see පත්‍ර *patra*.

පත්‍රයාන, *Patrayána*, *s.* (පත්‍ර wing, යාන vehicle) bird, bird in general.

පත්‍රලා, *Patralá*, *s.* plant, [Colloq. කූර පලා *kúra-palá*].

පත්‍රලේඛා, *Patralékhá*, see පත්‍රභඞ්ග *patra-bhaṅga*.

පත්‍රස්නුහා, *Patrasnuhá*, see පතුක් *patuk*.

පත්‍රහලාව, *Patra-haláwa*, *s.* space between the shoulders.

පත්‍රහීන, *Patrahína*, *s.* tree, *calophyllum spectabile*, [Colloq. දොඹ කින *domba-kina*].

පත්‍රාඞ්ග, *Patráṅga*, *s.* sandal-wood tree or red sanders, *pterocarpus santalinus;* sappan tree, *Cæsalpina sappan*, [Colloq. පතඞ්ගි *pataṅgi*].

පත්‍රාඞ්ගුලි, *Patráṅguli*, *s.* painting the forehead, neck, throat etc. with coloured sandal, saffron, or any other fragrant substance.

පත්‍රාඤ්ජන, *Patráñjana*, (පත්‍ර leaf of a book, අඤ්ජන anointing) ink, or a kind of resinous oil prepared from sandarac and used by the natives for blacking the writing of their books after it has been engraved by the style on palm leaves called Puskola, [Colloq. දුම්මල තෙල් *dummala-tel*].

පත්‍රිකා, *Patriká*, *s.* leaf, written leaf or page, letter; also a medicinal plant, [Colloq. උඩත්ත *uḍatta*].

පත්‍රී, *Patrí*, *s.* tree, *euphorbia antiquorum*, [Colloq. දළුක් *daḷuk*].

පත්‍රෝර්ණ, *Patrórṇa*, *s.* wove silk; tree, *oroxylum indicum* (or *colosanthes indica*), [Colloq. තොටිල *toṭila*].

පත්ල, *Patla*. *s.* sole of the foot: *par.* underneath, the place below.

පත්ව, *Patwa*, *part.* coming to, approaching, approximating; condemned (to punishment).

පත් වී, *Pat-ví*, *s.* kind of paddy, *oryza sativa*.

පත්සලනවා, *Pat-salanawá*, *v.* (පත් leaf, සලනවා to shake) to fan; to winnow.

පත, *Pata*, *s.* leaf; wing of a bird, feather; leaf of a book; writing on a leaf, letter; small measure of grain or liquids, four of which make a seer or Nẹliya, pl. පත් *pat*.

පතක, *Pataka*, *s.* astronomical table; who or what falls.

පතකඩේ, *Patakaḍé*, *s.* stick with a sharp point for digging, pl. පතකඩ *patakaḍa*.

පතඟ, *Patañga*, *s.* (පත wing, ග what goes) bird in general, [Colloq. කුරුල්ලා *kurullá*]; Saturn (planet.)

පතඟි, *Patangi*, *s.* sappan tree, *Cæsalpinia sappan, (Leguminosæ).*

පතඞ්ග, *Pataṅga*, *s.* grasshopper; bird; sort of rice; sun, [Colloq. සූර්යයා *súryayá*]; quicksilver.

පතඞ්ගම, *Pataṅgama*, *s.* bird, grass-hopper.

පතාඤ්ජලි, *Patañjali*, *s.* (පත *pata* fallen, අඤ්ජලි *añjali* hands joined as a mark of respect) name of a saint or Muni and teacher of the yóga philosophy, thence called after him the Pátáñjala; the name alludes to the fable of Patañjali's having fallen from heaven into the hands of Páṇini while performing the above mentioned act of devotion; also, the author of the Mahábháshya or commentary on Páṇini, and of the Charaka a famous medical work; name of the poet Wararuchi.

පතන, *Patana*, *s.* falling; small hill covered with grass, and, in some cases, overgrown with low shrubs: this word is commonly applied to open country without jungle in the mountainous districts; but the more correct word for this is තලාව *taláwa*, open glade.

පතනය, *Patanaya*, *s.* falling, latitude of a planet.

පතනවා, *Patanawá*, *v.* to hope, to wish, to expect, to look for: pret. පැතුවා *pętuwá*.

පතබුළු, *Pata-buḷu*, *s.* tree, variety of *terminalia belerica.*

පතඹ, *Patamba*, *s.* variety of the common mango, *mangifera indica.*

පතයා, *Patayá*, *s.* stout fat man, any bulky male animal.

පතයාලු, *Patayálu*, *a.* falling, liable or accustomed to fall.

පතර, *Patara*, *s.* liquid; diffusive, spreading; any thing that diffuses itself, as water etc.; powder, any pulverised substance; circle, zone; stem of the sugar-cane; assembly; publicity, notoriety; greatness; multitude.

පතරතුරු, *Pataraturu*, *s.* slave, bond servant, menial, dependant, [Colloq. දාසයා *dásayá*].

පතස, *Patasa*, } *s.* bird; large ditch, deep hole,
පතහ, *Pataha*, } pit.

පතළ, *Patala*, *a.* public, notorious, spread abroad, diffused; famed.

පතළකරණවා, *Patalakaraṇawá*, *v.* to publish, to make known, to spread.

පතා, *Patá*, *par.* particle indicating recurrence, as දවස්පතා *dawaspatá* daily, නිතිපතා *nitipatá* constantly; also the perfect participle of පතනවා *patanawá*, which see.

පතාක, *Patáka*, } *s.* flag, banner, [Colloquial:
පතාකය, *Patákaya*, } කොඩිය *koḍiya*]; flagstaff;
පතාකා, *Patáká*, } emblem carried as an ensign, flag carried on a lance as a banner; sign, symbol, mark; episode; good fortune, auspiciousness.

පතාකින්, *Patákin*, *s.* standard bearer.

පතාගය, *Patágaya*, *s.* rixdollar, one shilling and six pence, seventy-five cents.

පතාප, *Patápa*, *s.* dignity, majesty, splendour.

පතාපණ, *Patápaṇa*, *s.* blazing, shining, one of the eight chief hells, that the punishment of which consists in being constantly in fire.

පතාරණගහ, *Patáraṇa-gaha*, *s.* tree, not identified.

පති, *Pati*, *s.* lord, master, owner, husband; root; going, proceeding, motion; another form of ප්‍රති *prati.*

පතිඇමිය, *Patięmiya*, *s.* plant, *dentella repens.*

පතිකුලය, *Patikulaya*, *s.* (පති husband, කුල *kula* family) husband's family or kindred.

පතිට්ඨා, *Patiṭṭhá*, *s.* (පති lord, near, ඨා to be) attendance; assistance, help; favour.

පතිත, *Patita*, *a.* fallen, [Colloq. වැටුන *węṭuna*]; overcome, subdued, conquered; alighted; fallen (from virtue), abandoned, wicked.

පතිදම්, *Patidam*, *s.* (පති husband, දම් virtue) duty of a wife to her husband, conjugal fidelity.

පතිනි, *Patiní*, *s.* virtuous woman, one who never violates her marriage vow, woman of inviolable chastity.

පතිබද්ධ, *Patibaddha*, *s.* (පති again, mutual, බද්ධ bound) love, affection, attachment: *a.* bound, connected with.

පතිම්වරා, *Patimwará*, *s.* (පති husband, වෘ *wri* to choose) bride choosing her husband.

පතිමණ්ඩිත, *Patimaṇḍita*, *a.* (පති before, මණ්ඩිත adorned) beautiful, adorned, decorated; fit, suitable, becoming, proper.

පතිරජ, *Patiraja*, *s.* minister so called; sub-king.

පතිරණ, *Patiraṇa*, *s.* chief of the lascorins who are attached to a native headman.

පතිරන්නැහේ, *Patirannęhé*, *s.* headman or chief of a village.

පතිරාජ, *Patirája*, *s.* plant, not identified; sub-king.

පතිරිල්ල, *Pati-rilla*, *s.* plant, not identified.

පතිවරා, *Patiwará*, Páli form of පතිම්වරා *patimwará*.

පතිව්‍රතා, *Patiwratá*, *s.* (පති husband, ව්‍රත *wrata* religious obligation; who never violates her marriage vow) good and virtuous wife.

පතිව්‍රතා ධර්මය, *Patiwratá-dharmaya*, duty of conjugal fidelity.

පතිසල්ලාණ, *Patisalláṇa*, *a.* (පති before, සල්ලාණ concealed) alone, solitary; secluded.

පතු, *Patu*, *s.* small board, small piece of wood.

පතුක්, *Patuk*, *s.* small thorny tree, *euphorbia neriifolia (Euphorbiaceæ).*

පතුක් තණ, *Patuk-taṇa*, *s.* plant, not identified.

පතුන්, *Patun*, *s.* asking, beseeching, begging.

පතුර, *Patura*, *s.* splinter; board, planed piece of wood, wedge, pl. පතුරු *paturu*: *a.* public, published, known, spread abroad.

පතුරුවනවා, *Paturuwanawá*, *v.* to publish, to proclaim, to make known; to spread abroad: pret. පැතිරෙව්වා *pętirewwá*.

පතුරු තඹුරු, *Paturu-tamburu*, *s.* species of lotus.

පතුරු තලය, *Paturu-talaya*, *s.* (පතුරු and තල *tala* plane) boarded or wooden floor.

පතුල්වැන්න, *Patulwęnna*, *s.* persicaria or buck wheat, *polygonum recurvum*.

පතුල, *Patula*, *s.* sole of the foot, bottom of a well, vessel, etc., pl. පතුල් *patul*.

පතුවගළ, *Patuwagaḷa*, *a.* of which the branches have fallen, [Coll: පිතිගැලවුන *piti-gęlawuna*].

පතෝල, *Patóla*, *s.* annual plant, producing the snake gourd, much used as a vegetable, *trichosanthes anguina (Cucurbitaceæ):* see පටෝල *paṭóla*.

පතැඟි, *Patęngi*, Elu form of පත්‍රාඞ්ග *patrángа*, which see.

පථ්‍ය, *Pathya*, *s.* road, path, way: *a.* suitable or proper, applied chiefly medically with respect to diet, regimen, etc.

පථ්‍යා, *Pathyá*, *s.* tree, yellow myrobalan, *terminalia chebula*, [Colloq. අරළු *araḷu*]; creeping plant, *tinospora cordifolia*, [Colloq. රසකිඳ *rasakinda*].

පථ, *Patha*, } *s.* road, path, way, [Colloq. පාර
පථය, *Pathaya*, } *pára*].

පථික, *Pathika*, *s.* (පථ *patha* way, ඉක *ika* pers. termination) traveller, wayfarer, [Colloq. ගමන් යන්නා *gaman-yanná*]; guide.

පථිද්‍රැම, *Pathi-druma*, *s.* (පථි way, ද්‍රැම tree) tree, *mimosa alba*.

පද්දා, *Paddá*, see පදුවා *paduwá*.

පද්ම, *Padma*, *s.* lotus, *nelumbium speciosum*, [Coll: නෙළුම් *neḷum*]; one of Kuvéra's treasures or gems; numeral, ten billions; coloured marks on the face and trunk of an elephant; name of Ráma.

පද්මක, *Padmaka*, *s.* coloured marks on the face and trunk of an elephant.

පද්ම කණ්ටනිකා, *Padma-kanṭaniká*, *s.* plant, *solanum jacquini*, [Colloq. කටුවැල්බටු *kaṭuwęlbaṭu*].

පද්මකර්ණී, *Padma-karṇní*, *s.* (පද්ම lotus, කර්ණ *karṇa* ear, ඊ *í* aff.) pericarp of lotus.

පද්මකා, *Padmaká*, *s.* sort of drug, [Colloq. වැල්මදට *węlmadaṭa*].

පද්මකාෂ්ඨ, *Padma-káshṭha*, *s.* fragrant wood used in medicine, and described as cooling and tonic.

පද්ම කේශර, *Padma-késara*, *s.* tree, *calophyllum inophyllum*, [Colloq. දොඹ *domba*]; filaments of a lotus.

පද්මගන්ධ, *Padmagandha*, *a.* (පද්ම and ගන්ධ *gandha* scent) lotus scented, smelling like a lotus.

පද්ම ගර්භය, *Padma-garbhaya*, *s.* (පද්ම and ගර්භ *garbha* womb) name of Brahma, alluding to his being born from the lotus, which sprang from Vishṇu's navel.

පද්මචාරිණී, *Padmacháriṇí*, *s.* (පද්ම and චර *chara* to resemble, ඉණී *iṇí* aff.) small tree, with whitish flowers which turn red at night, *hibiscus mutabilis*.

පද්මනාභි, *Padma-nábhi*, *s.* (පද්ම lotus, නාභි navel) name of Vishṇu, alluding to the fable of the lotus containing Brahma springing from Vishṇu's navel.

පද්මනාල, *Padma-nála*, *s.* stalk of a lotus.

පද්මපාණී, *Padma-páni*, *s.* name of Brahma; sun, [Colloq. සූර්යයා *súryayá*].

පද්මබන්ධ, *Padma-bandha*, *s.* arrangement of the words of a verse in a figure representing the leaves of a lotus.

පද්මබන්ධු, *Padma-bandhu*, *s.* bee, sun.

පද්මභූ, *Padmabhú*, *s.* (පද්ම and භූ being) name of Brahma: see පද්මගර්භය *padma-garbhaya*.

පද්මය, *Padmaya*, *s.* lotus: see පද්ම *padma*.

පදුමයෝනි, *Padma-yóni*, *s.* (පදුම lotus, යෝනි place of production) name of Brahmá.

පදුමරාග, *Padmarága*, *s.* (පදුම and රාග colour) ruby, [Colloq. රතුකැටය *ratukeṭaya*].

පදුම රේඛා, *Padma-rékhá*, *s.* (පදුම and රේඛා line) line on the palm of the hand indicating the possession of great wealth.

පදුම රේණු, *Padma-réṇu*, *s.* (පදුම and රේණු pollen) stamen or pollen of the lotus.

පදුමලාඤ්ඡන, *Padmaláñchhana*, *s.* (පදුම and ලාඤ්ඡන mark, designation) king, sovereign, monarch; sun; Kuvéra, god of wealth; Brahmá.

පදුමසම්බෝධ, *Padma-sambódha*, *s.* (පදුම lotus, සං *saṇ* implying intensity, බෝධ what causes to expand) sun, [Colloq. ඉර *ira*].

පදුමා, *Padmá*, *s.* name of the goddess Lakshmí the Indian goddess of beauty; tree, *hibiscus mutabilis*, see පදුමචාරිණී *padmachárinī*; female serpent; goddess Manasá; flower of the carthamus, or safflower.

පදුමාකර, *Padmákara*, *s.* (පදුම *padma* lotus, ආකර *akara* pond) large deep pond, one in which the lotus grows.

පදුමාචර, *Padmáchara*, *s.* (පදුම *padma* and ආචර *áchara* what goes) bee, honey bee, [Colloq. මී මැස්සා *mí-meṣsá*].

පදුමාලයා, *Padmálayá*, *s.* (පදුම *padma* and ආලය *álaya* asylum) name of Lakshmí.

පදුමාවතී, *Padmáwatí*, *s.* name of river; snake-goddess Manasá.

පදුමාසන, *Padmásana*, *s.* (පදුම *padma* and ආසන *ásana* sitting, seat) name of Brahma, probably alluding to his resting on the lotus which sprang from the navel of Vishṇu; posture of religious ascetics when occupied in devout meditation.

පද්මිනී, *Padminí*, *s.* (පදුම *padma* lotus, ඉනී *iní* aff.) multitude of lotuses or a place abounding in them; woman of the first and most excellent class; lotus.

පද්මිනී වල්ලභ, *Padminí-wallabha*, *s.* (පද්මිනී pond of lotuses, වල්ලභ friend) the sun, [Colloq. ඉර *ira*].

පද්මී, *Padmí*, *s.* elephant, [Colloq. අලියා *aliyá*].

පද්මෝත්තර, *Padmóttara*, *s.* (පදුම *padma* lotus, උත්තර *uttara* excellent) name of Buddha who made his appearance in one of the first Kalpas; safflower.

පද්‍ය, *Padya*, *s.* metre; verse; wickedness, infamy: *a.* relating to the feet.

පද, *Pada*, *s.* foot; footstep, mark or print of a foot; word, sentence; foot or rather line of a stanza; cause; place, site; protection, defence; thing; rank, station, degree; mark, spot; name of Nirwáṇa; ray of light, [Colloq. රැස්මිය *reṣmiya*].

පදක්කම, *Padakkama*, *s.* medal.

පදක්ඛිණ, *Padakkhiṇa*, *s.* (ප before, දක්ඛිණ right hand) reverential salutation by circumambulating a person or object, keeping the right side towards it; Páli form of ප්‍රදක්ෂිණ *pradakshiṇá*.

පදඟිලි, *Padaṇgili*, *s.* (පද foot, අඟිලි *aṇgili* for ඇඟිලි *eṇgili* finger) toe.

පදච්ඡේදය, *Padachchhédaya*, see පදභඤ්ජන *padabhañjana*.

පදන්, *Padan*, *s.* gift; due mixture of different substances, state of a metal or other substance as to its hardness.

පදනම, *Padanama*, *s.* foundation; commencement; buttress, pl. පදනම් *padanam*.

පදපරමයා, *Padaparamayá*, *s.* man incapable of sacred or religious studies, through moral demerit, etc.

පදබන්ධනය, *Padabandhanaya*, *s.* (පද verse, බන්ධන *bandhana* binding) any poetical composition, composing verse.

පදබරණ, *Padabaraṇa*, *s.* (පද foot, අබරණ *abaraṇa* ornament) ornaments for the feet, toes or ancles.

පදබැඳිම, *Pada-bendíma*, *s.* composition of verses: see පදබන්ධනය *padabandhanaya*.

පදභඤ්ජන, *Padabhañjana*, *s.* (පද word, භඤ්ජන breaking) explanation of obscure or obsolete terms, etymology.

පදම, *Padama*, *s.* quantity, heap: measure, proportion.

පදය, *Padaya*, *s.* verse, foot, footstep: see පද *pada*.

පදර, *Padara*, *s.* shed; plank or slab; breaking, separating; cavern, any large chasm in the earth.

පදලස, *Padalasa*, *s.* (පද foot, ලස mark) footmark.

පදවාර, *Padawára*, *s.* stop or rest in reading; measuring or reckoning by the feet, pacing.

පදවි, *Padavi*, *s.* road, path, way; family; office, rank.

පදවි දෙනවා, *Padavi-denawá*, *v.* to marry, to give in marriage; to confer rank.

පදවිතිහාර, *Padavitihára*, see පදවිතිහාරය *padavitiháraya*.

පදවිය, *Padaviya*, *s.* office, rank, degree; station.

පදවිතිහාරය, *Padavítiháraya*, *s.* (පද foot, විතිහා ර exchange) long footstep, stride, pace, distance between two feet marks when walking.

පදහර, *Padahara*, *s.* foot ornament.

පදාන්තරය, *Padántaraya*, see පදවිතිහාරය *padavítiháraya.*

පදාන, *Padána*, *s.* (ප before, දාන giving) gift, donation, food procured by begging; giving.

පදාර්ථය, *Padárthaya*, *s.* (පද *pada* word, thing, අර්ථ meaning) meaning of a word or sentence, etymology; category or predicament in logic, of which seven are enumerated, viz. substance, quality, action, identity, variety, relation, and annihilation; thing, substantial or material form of being.

පදාසන, *Padásana*, *s.* (පද *pada* foot, ආසන *ásana* seat) footstool.

පදිංචිය, *Padinchiya*, *s.* residence.

පදිංචිවෙනවා, *Padinchiwenawá*. *v.* to inhabit, to reside; to settle.

පදිනවා, *Padinawá*, *v.* to row, to pull: pret. පැද්දා *peddá.*

පදියම්කරණවා, *Padiyamkaranawá*, *v.* to cause to take up a residence.

පදියම, *Padiyama*, *s.* transplantation; residence, place of being.

පදිරිඤ්ඤා, *Padiriññá*, *s.* godfather, (Port.) pl. පදිරිඤ්ඤාවරු *padiriññáwaru.*

පදුම, *Paduma*, *s.* lotus, [Colloq. නෙළුම් *nelum*]; numeral, 1 followed by 119 ciphers; one of the hells; Páli form of පද්ම *padma.*

පදුමරාග, *Padumarága*, see පද්මරාග *padmarága.*

පදුවා, *Paduwá*, *v.* man of the Paduwa caste, whose business it is to provide food for elephants, and carry palanquins; they are also employed as scavengers, smelters of iron, and in other servile business.

පඳුර, *Pandura*, *s.* bush, shrub in general, thicket.

පඳුරු වටුවා, *Panduru-watuwá*, *s.* Chinese quail, *coturnix chinensis (Tetrocindæ)*, also called වෙනැල්ල වටුවා *wenella-watuwá;* black-breasted bustard quail, *turnix taigoor (Tinamidæ*, order *Gallinæ)*, also called වටුවා *watuwá* and බෝල වටුවා *bóla-watuwá.*

පධාන, *Padhána*, *s.* king's companion, chief minister or minister of state; nature, supreme subsistence; energetic effort, perseverance: *a.* chief, principal.

පන්, *Pan*, *s.* leaf, leaves, [Colloq. කොළ *kola*]; rush, bulrush; strength, muscular power.

පන් අදිනවා, *Pan-adinawá*, *v.* to draw an extended rope on the water on which white strips of coconut leaflets are suspended, for the purpose of driving fish into nets; to mend or decorate rush mats.

පන්තිය, *Pantiya*, *s.* multitude, flock, herd; row of trees; procession; stall, stable, cattle stand.

පන්දම, *Pandama*, *s.* torch, flambeau, row of lights; firebrand, candle, as ඉටිපන්දම *itipandama* waxcandle, light: see පහන්දමය *pahandamaya.*

පන්දල, *Pandala*, *s.* bower, scaffold of sticks for the betel creeper, vine, etc.

පන්දලම, *Pandalama*, *s.* shed made on funeral occasions; scaffolding over a plantation intended to give shade.

පන්දුගහනවා, *Pandu-gahanawá*, *v.* to toss a ball.

පන්දුව, *Panduwa*, *s.* ball, small wooden or other ball for playing with; coil of rattan coir or thread.

පන්නග, *Pannaga*, *s.* (පන්න fallen, or පද් *pad* foot, න *na* not, ග who goes; *i. e.* moving without feet) snake, serpent in general, [Colloq. සර්පයා *sarpayá*].

පන්නනවා, *Pannanawá*, *v.* to drive away, to fray: pret. පැන්නුවා *pennuwá.*

පන්නම්, *Pannam*, *s.* weaving, plaiting, weaving mats; preparing cotton for the purpose of making thread.

පන්නය, *Pannaya*, *s.* article, thing, apparatus; any set of articles, as the tools of a carpenter, etc.; handicraft.

පන්නයා, *Pannayá*, *s.* (පන් leaf, න pleonasm, යා pers. aff.) one of a tribe or caste whose duty it is to procure food for elephants; elephant driver; grass cutter.

පන්නරය, *Pannaraya*, *s.* temper of iron.

පන්නාවා, *Pannáwá*, *s.* kind of sea fish.

පන්නෙටි වී, *Panneti-ví*, *s.* kind of paddy, variety of *oryza sativa.*

පන්නේ, *Panné*, see පන්නය *pannaya.*

පන්වා, *Panwá*, *s.* snake, nága or inhabitant of Nága-lóka, [Colloq. සර්පයා *sarpayá*].

පන් විල, *Pan-vila*, *s.* field of bulrushes.

පන්සල, *Pansala*, *s.* (පන් leaf, සල hall, house) residence of a Buddhist priest; the name alludes to the directions given in reference to the abodes of the sacerdotal order, who are commanded to live as ascetics in the woods and jungles; if they build houses, they are to be constructed of the boughs of trees, bent and interwoven so as to form a mere covering; but the name is now used of the house, generally permament and substantial enough, which is attached to their temples, pl. පන්සල් *pansal*.

පන්සාලිස, *Pansálisa*, *s.* (පන් five, සාලිස forty) forty-five, [Colloq. හතලිස්පහ *hatalis-paha*].

පන්සිල්, *Pansil*, *s.* five precepts of Buddha: see පඤ්චසීලය *pañchasílaya*.

පන්සිළු, *Pansiḷu*, *s.* one of the celestial choristers, or a musician of Swarga; name of Ṣiva; name of Viṣwakarma; commonly පඤ්චශිඛ *pañchaṣikha*.

පන්සැර, *Pansęra*, *s.* (පන් five, සැර arrow) name of Anańgayá or Káma the Indian Cupid; being armed with five arrows.

පන්හිඳ, *Panhiṇda*, *s.* (පන් leaves, හිඳ for සිඳ *siṇda* what cuts) iron pen or stylus, used by the natives in writing or engraving their books, pl. පන්හිත් *panhit*.

පන, *Pana*, *s.* carpenter, [Colloq. වඩුවා *waḍuwá*]; froth: *adv.* again.

පනතු, *Panatu*, *s.* way, road; path, foot-path, [Colloq. පාර *pára*].

පනතුරු, *Panaturu*, *s.* (පන and තුරු tree) a tree, *terminalia belerica*, [Colloq. බුළු *buḷu*].

පනදා, *Panadá*, *s.* second of a month, or second day of the moon; the following day.

පනපල, *Panapala*, *s.* love, kindness, [Colloq. කරුණාව *karuṇáwa*].

පනගර, *Panayara*, *s.* weaver of mats.

පනර, *Panara*, *s.* gift, [Colloq. තෑග්ග *tęgga*].

පනවරු, *Panawaru*, *s.* carpenter, [Colloq. වඩුවා *waḍuwá*].

පනස, *Panasa*, } *s.* jack fruit tree, *artocarpus*
පනා, *Paná*, } *integrifolia*, [Colloq. කොස් *kos*].

පනාකටුව, *Panákaṭuwa*, *s.* old comb of which teeth portion is broken.

පනාකැවුම්, *Panákęwum*, *s.* kind of native cake.

පනාගහනවා, *Paná-gahanawá*, *v.* to fasten the hair with a comb, to stick a comb in the hair.

පනාදැත්ත, *Panádętta*, *s.* plant, not identified; tooth of a comb.

පනාබෙර, *Paná-bera*, *s.* sort of tom-tom or drum.

පනාමල, *Panámala*, *s.* bud of jack fruits.

පනාමැඩියා, *Paná-mędiyá*, *s.* the sole, (fish) *psettodes erumei*.

පනායව, *Panáyawa*, *s.* toddy, intoxicating liquor extracted from the flower of the coconut tree.

පනාව, *Panáwa*, *s.* general name for comb, of which there are four kinds, viz. නැම්පනාව *nemipanáwa* and රැල්පනාව *ręl-panáwa* worn by native males, and අඩහඳ පනාව *aḍahaṇda-panáwa* by native females, and පීරණ පනාව *píraṇa-panáwa* combing comb.

පනික්කියා, *Panikkiyá*, *s.* barber; elephant keeper; headman of low caste.

පනික්කිල, *Panikkila*, *s.* term applied to a tom-tom beater.

පනිජ්ජක, *Panijjaka*, *s.* plant, apparently a species of basil, *ocimum*.

පනින කරවලා, *Panina-karawalá*, *s.* snake, variety of *bungarus Ceylonicus*.

පනින පොලඟා, *Panina-polaṇgá*, *s.* variety of *trimeresurus trigonocephalus*.

පනිනවා, *Paninawá*, *v* to jump, to leap, to spring, to bound: pret. පැන්නා *pęnná*.

පනුගාය, *Panugáya*, *s.* worm complaint, more correctly පණුගාය *paṇugáya*.

පනුහොරි, *Panu-hori*, *s.* itch, more correctly පණුහොරි *paṇu-hori*.

පනේ, *Pané*, *s.* term of affection as darling, love, corrupt form of පණ *paṇa*, life.

පනේලය, *Panélaya*, *s.* panel, (from the English.)

පපටිකා, *Papaṭiká*, *s.* splinter of stone, any splinter.

පපන්, *Papan*, *s.* nose of a horse, [Colloq අශ්ව නාහෙ *aṣwa-náhe*].

පපාත, *Papáta*, *s.* (ප before, පාත falling, descent) precipice; cliff; cascade.

පපාතන, *Papátana*, *s.* fall, falling, descent, declivity.

පපු, *Papu*, *s.* nurse, foster mother; breast; plur. of පපුව *papuwa*.

පපුකැනැත්ත, *Papukęnętta*, *s.* (පපු breast, කැනැත්ත cluster) heart, liver, and lungs.

පපුව, *Papuwa*, *s.* heart, liver and lungs; breast, bosom.

පබ්බජිත, *Pabbajita*, *s.* (ප implying intensity, බජිත roaming) ascetic, one who has renounced the world for religious purposes; priest of Buddha.

පබ, *Paba*, *s.* (ප intensive, බා *bá* to shine) light, shining, brightness, [Colloq. රශ්මිය *reṣmiya*]; heat; Elu form of ප්‍රභා *prabhá*.

පබඳ, *Pabaṇda*, *s.* (ප before, බඳ bound) connected discourse, narrative; quality, attribute.

පබල, *Pabala*, *s.* (ප implying intensity, බල strength) power, strength, might; bud, sprout, germ, young shoot of a leaf.

පබසර, *Pabasara, s.* (පබ light, සර essence) brightness, effulgence, splendour, lustre.

පබළු, *Pabaḷu, s.* bud, germ, sprout, young shoot of leaves or flowers; coral: necklace of coral; the buds or young sprouts of the echites antidysenterica.

පබළු ඇට, *Pabaḷu-ęṭa, s. pl.* beads.

පබළුදම්, *Pabaḷu-dam, s.* (පබළු coral, දම් chain) necklace of coral.

පබළුවැල, *Pabaḷuwęla, s.* necklace, string of beads.

පබළුසිඳු, *Pabaḷu-sin̆du, s.* (පබළු and සිඳු sea) coral sea, sea abounding in coral.

පබා, *Pabá,* Elu form of ප්‍රභා *prabhá,* which see.

පබාව, *Pabáwa,* Elu form of ප්‍රභාව *prabháwa,* which see.

පභංකර, *Pabhaṅkara, s.* (පභා *pabhá* light, කර who makes) sun, [Colloq. සූර්යයා *súryayá*].

පභව, *Pabhawa, s.* (ප before, භව being) generative cause, cause, source; place where any thing is first perceived, place of origin.

පභා, *Pabhá, s.* light, radiance, effulgence; ray; Páli form of ප්‍රභා *prabhá.*

පභාව, *Pabháwa, s.* majesty; light, splendour, effulgence.

පඹ, *Pamba, s.* kind of weed; kind of brush wood; name of a genus of ferns, ඇත් පඹ *ęt-pam̆ba,* මහ පඹ *maha-pam̆ba* and හින් පඹ *hín-pam̆ba, Lygodium (Filices).*

පඹයා, *Pam̆bayá, s.* bugbear, scarecrow, the figure of a man made of the pam̆ba.

පඹුරු, *Pam̆buru, s.* plant, *atalantia missionis, (Rutaceæ).*

පම, *Pama, s.* love, affection; woman; delay.

පමණ, *Pamaṇa, s.* measure, quantity, sufficiency: *ad,* about, much, many, (as කොපමණද *kopamaṇada* how much, කොපමණ දෙනෙක්ද *kopamaṇa-denekda* how many persons).

පමණක්, *Pamanak, par.* only, merely.

පමණදැනීම, *Pamaṇa-dęníma, s.* moderation, temperance.

පමදා, *Pamadá, s.* (ප intensive, මද *mada* to delight) woman, young woman; joy.

පමා, *Pamá, s.* dancing girl, woman; delay, procrastination; love, dalliance.

පමාණ, *Pamáṇa, s.* quantity; cause; law; speaker of truth; authority; measure; limit, boundary.

පමාද, *Pamáda, s.* delay, hesitancy, dilatoriness; Páli form of ප්‍රමාද *pramáda.*

පමාව, *Pamáwa, s.* delay, hesitancy, procrastination, dilatoriness.

පමාවන, *Pamáwana, s.* (පමා dalliance, වන garden) royal pleasure garden.

පමාවෙනවා, *Pamáwenawá, v.* to tarry, to delay.

පමුණුවනවා, *Pamuṇuwanawá, v.* to cause to come up or to arrive at; to appoint to; to introduce, to produce before, to bring forward: pret. පැමිණෙවුවා *pęmiṇewwá.*

පමෝද, *Pamóda, s.* joy, happiness, [Colloquial: සන්තෝසය *santósaya*].

පය, *Paya, s.* (පා *pá* to drink, ය aff.) water, milk; vessel; foot.

පයකුරු වී, *Payakúru-ví, s.* plant, variety of paddy.

පයවදිනවා, *Paya-wadinawá, v.* to strike or touch with the foot.

පයස්, *Payas, s.* water, [Colloq. වතුර *watura*]; milk.

පයස්‍ය, *Payasya, a.* made from milk, (cheese, butter, curds).

පයස, *Payasa,* see පයස් *payas.*

පයින්, *Payin, ad.* on foot.

පයින් ගහනවා, *Payin-gahanawá, v.* to kick.

පයිය, *Payiya, s.* small bag or wallet, purse, pocket.

පයෝධරපට්ට, *Payódhara-paṭṭa, s.* woman's bathing cloth.

පයෝධරය, *Payódharaya, s.* (පයස් *payas* water, milk, ධර *dhara* which bears) woman's breast; cloud; coconut; sugar cane.

පයෝධස්, *Payódhas, s.* sea, ocean, [Colloq. මුහුද *muhuda*]; cloud.

පර්ණ, *Parṇa, s.* leaf; betel leaf; tree, *butea frondosa,* [Colloq. ගස්කැල *gas-kęla*].

පර්ණභෝජන, *Parṇa-bhójana, s.* (පර්ණ leaf, භෝජන eating) goat, [Colloq. එළුවා *eḷuwá*].

පර්ණශාලාව, *Parṇa-śáláwa,* see පන්සල *pansala.*

පර්ණහින, *Parṇa-hína, s.* plant, peculiar to Ceylon, *munronia pumila,* [Colloq. බිංකොහොඹ *biṅkohom̆ba*].

පර්ණාස, *Parṇása,* see තලා *talá.*

පර්ණාසි, *Parṇási,* see අඳුනලා *an̆du-talá.*

පර්ණිකා, *Parṇṇiká, s.* plant, [Colloq. පුස්වැන්න *puswęnna*].

පර්ණී, *Parṇṇí, s.* aquatic plant, *pistia stratiotes,* [Colloq. දියපරණලා *diyaparaṇalá*].

පර්ප, *Parpa, s.* wheelchair, or one on which a cripple can move about.

පප්ට, *Parpaṭa*, } *s.* small medicinal plant,
පප්ටක, *Parpaṭaka*, } *mollugo Cerviana*, [Colloq. පත්පාඩගං *patpáḍagaṇ*].

පර්‍ය්‍යංක, *Paryaṇka*, *s.* seat, chair, [Colloq. පුටුව *puṭuwa*], couch.

පර්‍ය්‍යටන, *Paryaṭana*, *s.* (පරි *pari* about, අට *aṭa* to go) wandering about, roaming.

පර්‍ය්‍යන්ත, *Paryanta*, *s.* (පරි *pari* complete, අන්ත *anta* end) end, termination, finish, completion: *a.* last, ultimate.

පර්‍ය්‍යන්ත ප්‍රාප්ත, *Paryanta-prápta*, *a.* (පර්‍ය්‍යන්ත and ප්‍රාප්ත arrived) ended, finished, terminated, completed.

පර්‍ය්‍යය, *Paryaya*, *s.* (පරි *pari* improperly, අය *aya* to go) irregularity, neglect of enjoined duty.

පර්‍ය්‍යවසාන, *Paryawasána*, *s.* (පරි *pari* complete, අවසාන end) end, termination, conclusion.

පර්‍ය්‍යාප්ත, *Paryápta*, *a.* obtained, gained; able, complete.

පර්‍ය්‍යාප්ති, *Paryápti*, *s.* willingness, readiness; obtaining, acquiring; preserving, guarding, warding off a blow; satisfaction, repletion, satiety; baṇa of Buddha, including the whole of his sermons, addresses and directions to the priests, gods and men.

පර්‍ය්‍යාය, *Paryáya*, *s.* figure, metaphor, figure of speech; name, epithet expressing the qualities of things; vocabulary or the order of synonyms for any term; order, arrangement, regularity, method: see පරියාය *pariyáya*.

පර්‍ය්‍යාය වචන, *Paryáya-wachana*, *s.* text of a vocabulary, order of the synonyms of any term.

පර්‍ය්‍යාස, *Paryása*, *s.* inverted order, change of position.

පර්‍ය්‍යුදඤ්ච, *Paryudañcha*, *s.* debt, [Colloq. ණය *naya*].

පර්‍ය්‍යුපාසන, *Paryupásana*, *s.* (පරි *pari* intensitive prefix, උපාසන *upásana* serving) service, attendance, adoration.

පර්‍ය්‍යුපාසින, *Paryupásina*, *a.* seated or sitting upon.

පර්‍ය්‍යුෂිත, *Paryushita*, *a.* (from පරි *pari* about, and වස *wasa* to abide) stale, not fresh.

පර්‍ය්‍යෙෂණ, *Paryéshaṇá*, *s.* (පරි *pari* before, ඉෂ *isha* to go) research, search, enquiry.

පර්ව, *Parwa*, *s.* knot, joint; chapter, division in a book.

පර්වත, *Parwata*, *s.* mountain, rock, hill.

පර්වත ගුහාව, *Parwata-guháwa*, *s.* (පර්වත and ගුහා *guhá* cave) cave in a rock or mountain, either natural or artificial.

පර්වත විවර, *Parwata-viwara*, *s.* cleft or fissure in a rock.

පර්වත ශිඛර, *Parwata-şikhara*, *s.* (පර්වත and ශිඛර top) peak or summit of a mountain.

පර්වතාන්තර, *Parwatántara*, *s.* (පර්වත *parwata* mountain, අන්තර *antara* interval) passage between two rocks, narrow road between two mountains, pass, defile.

පර්වයෝනි, *Parwa-yóni*, *s.* (පර්ව knot, joint, යෝනි place of birth) cane; reed, sugar cane.

පර්ශු, *Parşu*, *s.* axe, hatchet, [Colloq. පොරොව *porowa*].

පර්ශුකා, *Parşuká*, *s.* rib, [Colloq. ඉළඇටේ *ila-ęṭé*].

පර්ෂ, *Parsha*, corruptly for පරුෂ *parusha*, which see.

පර්ෂත්, *Parshat*, } *s.* retinue, train, company of at-
පර්ෂද්, *Parshad*, } tendants, multitude, [Colloq. පිරිස *pirisa*]; assembly, audience; followers.

පර, *Para*, *s.* enemy, adversary; timber tree, *dillenia dentata*: *a.* inimical; other, different, foreign; remote, distant; subsequent; superior, high, best, pre-eminent; low, vile, mean, worthless, outcast.

පරං, *Paraṇ*, *s.* pre-eminence; final beatitue, Nirwáṇa.

පරංගි, *Parangi*, } *s.* syphilis, venereal
පරංගි ලෙඩ, *Parangi-leḍa*, } sickness.

පරංගිවනස්ස, *Parangi-wanassa*, *s.* plant, not identified.

පරක්කු, *Parakku*, *s.* delay, dilatoriness; covering.

පරක්කුකරණවා, *Parakku-karaṇawá*, *v.* to delay another, to quiet as a child; to spend too much time on any work.

පරක්කුවෙනවා, *Parakkuwenawá*, *v.* to loiter, to be quieted.

පරකට, *Parakaṭa*, *s.* publicity, excellence, [Colloq. ප්‍රසිද්ධ *prasiddha*]; eminence, pre-eminence.

පරකුල, *Para-kula*, *s.* (පර other, කුල tribe) foreign breed, different race; fetter, band.

පරගාම්, *Paragám*, *s.* to roar as sea.

පරඬල් කුරුල්ලා, *Paraṇḍal-kurullá*, *s.* bird called rufus babbler, *malaco-cercus rufescens (Timaliidæ* order *Passeres)*; also called රතුදෙමලිච්චා *ratu-demalichchá*, පන්දරෙල්ලා *pandarellá*, and කලපරන්ඳෙල්ලා *kalaparandellá*.

පරඬල, *Paraṇḍala*, *s.* dried or withered leaf.

පරණ, *Paraṇa*, *s.* small stones, pebbles; slave; strange servant: *a.* old; ancient.

පරණ බිජු, *Paraṇa-biju*, *s.* beating, flogging, punishing.

පරතීරය, *Paratíraya*, } *s.* (පර other, තීර or තෙර
පරතෙර, *Paratera*, } shore, border) opposite shore, other side, [Colloq. එගොඩ *egoḍa*].

පරදර, *Paradara*, see පරදූර *paradára*.

පරදවනවා, *Paradawanawá*, *v.* to conquer, to beat, to subdue, to defeat, to overcome: pret. පැරදෙව්වා *peradewwá*.

පරදූර, *Paradára*, *s.* (පර other, foreign, දූර wife) another's wife; adultery, fornication.

පරදිනවා, *Paradinawá*, *v.* to be overcome, to lose: pret. පැරදුනා *peraduná*.

පරදු, *Paradu*, *s.* prize, stake at a game.

පරදේශ, *Paradésa*, *s.* (පර other, දේශ country) foreign country, abroad.

පරදේශිකයා, *Paradésikayá*, } *s.* foreigner, stranger.
පරදේශියා, *Paradésiyá*, }

පරන්තප, *Parantapa*, *a.* subduing a foe, annoying another.

පරනිර්මිතය, *Paranirmitaya*, }
පරනිර්මිත වසවර්තිය, *Paranirmita-wasawartiya*, } *s.* (පර other (person), නිර්මිත made) sixth or highest of the divine worlds or worlds of the gods, usually called Swarga: see සදෙව්ලොව *sadewlowa*.

පරපුටු, *Paraputu*, *s.* (පර another, පුටු nourished) kókila or Indian cuckoo, *cuculus micropterus:* see පරපුෂ්ට *parapushṭa*.

පරපුර, *Parapura*, *s.* (පර another (repeated) race, lineage; generation, etc.; Elu form of පරම්පරාව *paramparáwa*.

පරපුරුෂ, *Parapurusha*, *s.* (පර other, පුරුෂ husband) paramour, adulterer.

පරපුෂ්ට, *Parapushṭa*, *s.* (පර another, පුෂ්ට nourished) kókila or Indian cuckoo, name which it has from its leaving its eggs in the nests of other birds, as the same bird does in Europe, to be hatched and brought up by them: see පරපුටු *paraputu*.

පරභාග, *Parabhága*, *s.* (පර and භාග portion) excellence, superior merit; supremacy; good fortune, luck, prosperity.

පරම්පරාව, *Paramparáwa*, *s.* (පර subsequent, repeated, and the nasal augment) race, lineage, general order, succession, generation.

පරම, *Parama*, *a.* much, exceeding, exalted, preeminent, best, [Colloq. උතුම් *utum*]; chief, principal, preceding, superior.

පරමණ්ඩල, *Paramaṇḍala*, *s.* (පර other, මණ්ඩල region) foreign region, but applied more especially to those countries to which the religion of Buddha does not extend; heaven.

පර මල, *Para-mala*, *s.* faded flower; flower of the tree so called.

පරමාණු, *Paramáṇu*, *s.* (පරම *parama* first, අණු *aṇu* atom) atom, invisible base of all aggregate bodies, thirty of them are supposed to form a mote in a sun-beam; the lowest measure of weight.

පරමාත්ම, *Paramátma*, *s.* (පරම *parama* and ආත්ම soul) Supreme Being who, according to the Hindus, is considered as the first and last spirit, *i. e.* one from which all other spirits originally emanated and to which in lapse of time they will be reunited.

පරමාන්න, *Paramánna*, *s.* (පරම *parama* excellent, අන්න *anna* food) oblation of rice mixed with milk.

පරමාර්ථය, *Paramártaya*, *s.* (පරම *parama* and අර්ථ *artha* profit) barter, traffic, mutual advantage, principal or highest sense of a word or expression.

පරමු, *Paramu*, *a.* other, another, different.

පරමුඟ, *Paramulga*, *s.* plant, wheat, [Colloq. තිරිඟු *tiringu*].

පරමුන, *Paramuna*, *s.* front of an army or of a distinguished visitor, corruptly for පෙරමුන *peramuna*.

පරමේශ්වර, *Paraméswara*, *s.* (පරම *parama* and ඊශ්වර *íśwara* lord) name of Ṣiva, Vishṇu; Supreme being.

පරමේෂ්ඨ, *Paraméshṭha*, *s.* (පරමෙ in the most exalted place, ෂ්ඨ to be) name of Brahma or Mahá Brahma; deity: *a.* supreme.

පරය, *Paraya*, *s.* rock, range, as ගල් පරය *gal-paraya*, මුතු පරය *mutu-paraya*.

පරයන, *Parayana*, *a.* (පර another, ය substituted for ද *da* to overcome) conquering, subduing, overcoming.

පරයා, *Parayá*, *s.* (පර vile, යා aff.) slave, outcast: *part.* having defeated or surpassed.

පරරුපු, *Para-rupu*, *s.* enemy, opponent, adversary.

පරලවෙනවා, *Paralawenawá*, *v.* to become subject to a sort of fainting or a trance.

පරලොව, *Paralowa*, *s.* (පර other, ලොව world) another world, future state; heaven, paradise.

පරලොව යාම, *Paralowa-yáma*, s. (පරලොව future state, යාම going) death, dying.

පරලෝ, *Paraló*, } see පරලොව *para-*
පරලෝකය, *Paralókaya*, } *lowa*.

පරව, *Parawa*, s. (පර excellent, ව to speak) bard, panegyrist, poet who sings the praises of a prince in his presence: *part.* having faded.

පරවත්, *Parawat*, s. (another, වත් property) another's property.

පරවර, *Parawara*, a. (පර superior, වර noble) eminent, great, mighty, illustrious.

පරවරයා, *Parawarayá*, s. shoemaker, [Colloq. සපත්තු හදන්නා *sapattu-hadanná*]; immigrant from Tuticoreen.

පරවරා, *Parawará*, s. Malabar huckster of cloth, draper.

පරවශ, *Parawaṣa*, a. (පර another, වශ subjection) subservient, dependant, subject.

පරවසන්, *Para-wasan*, s. disguise, [Colloq. අන් වෙස් *an-wes*].

පරවාදය, *Para-wádaya*, s. (පර and වාද *wáda* speaking) discussion, arguing.

පරවිටිලි, *Paraviṭili*, s. death, dying, [Colloq. මරණය *maraṇaya*].

පරවියා, *Paraviyá*, s. dove, pigeon, (order *Columbæ*): see කොබෙයියා *kobeyiyá*.

පරවෙණිය, *Paraweṇiya*, s. landed property, possessions, inheritance.

පරවෙනවා, *Parawenawá*, v. to fade.

පරවැඩ, *Parawęḍa*, s. another's good, public good; work of a slave.

පරශුරාම, *Paraṣuráma*, s. (පරශු axe, රාම Ráma) in Hindu mythology the sixth Avatára or descent of the god Vishṇu, who appeared in the world as the son of a noted saint called Jamadagni, for the purpose of repressing the tyranny and punishing the violence of the military tribe or caste.

පරශුව, *Paraṣuwa*, s. axe, hatchet, [Colloq. පොරොව *porowa*].

පරස්ත්‍රීසේවන, *Parastrí-séwana*, s. (පර other, ස්ත්‍රී woman, සේවන serving) adultery, fornication.

පරස්පර, *Paraspara*, s. (පර another, repeated) mutual, interchanging.

පරසත්වයා, *Parasatwayá*, s. (පර another, සත්ව *satwa* being) stranger, foreigner; one of a different species.

පරසතු, *Parasatu*, s. Kalpa-vṛiksha or divine tree in Indrá's heaven, furnishing everything which may be desired.

පරසතුරා, *Para-saturá*, s. (පර implying intensity, සතුරා enemy) adversary, opponent.

පරසතු රුක, *Parasatu-ruka*, s. tree in Indrá's heaven which yields the possessor every thing desired.

පරසමය, *Parasamaya*, } s. (පර another, සමය
පරසමයම, *Parasamayama*, } religious obligation) heresy; *i. e.* any other religion than that of Buddha.

පරසුම, *Parasuma*, s. heavy work.

පරහ, *Paraha*, s. defect, fault: a. not straight, not level.

පරහට, *Parahaṭa*, *ad.* towards others.

පරහන, *Parahana*, s. straining water etc. through a cloth.

පරහස්, *Parahas*, a. (ප implying intensity, රහස් secret) secret, hidden, concealed.

පරහිතඥානී, *Parahitajñání*, s. (පර another, හිත mind, ඥාන *jñána* knowledge, ඊ *í* pers. aff.) epithet of Buddha; Rahat, or one of the highest order of Buddhist ascetics; a god, deity.

පරළු, *Paraḷu*, s. bran.

පරා, *Pará*, *ind.* particle and prefix implying inverted order, encounter, overcoming, surpassing; excess, exceeding; pride, contumacy; killing, destroying, injuring; going, motion etc.

පරාක්‍රමය, *Parákramaya*, s. (පරා supremacy, ක්‍රම *krama* going, order) power, strength; heroism, valour, prowess; exertion; renown.

පරාග, *Parága*, s. farina of a flower; dust, [Colloq. රේණු *réṇu*].

පරාඞ්මුඛ, *Paráṅmukha*, a. having the face averted, turning away.

පරාජය, *Parájaya*, s. (පරා implying inverted order, reverse, ජය victory) defeat, complete victory.

පරාජිතව, *Parájitawa*, *part.* being defeated or overcome.

පරාටියා, *Paráṭiyá*, s. name of a small fish.

පරාද, *Paráda*, s. (පරා encounter, ද substituted for ජය *jaya* victory) loss, defeat: *p.* defeated, conquered, overcome.

පරාදවෙනවා, *Parádawenawá*, v. to be defeated, to be overcome.

පරාධි, *Parádhi*, s. hunting, chase.

පරාධීන, *Parádhína*, a. (පර *para* another, අධීන *adhína*, humble) dependent, subject, subservient.

පරාධීන වෘත්ති, *Parádhína-vṛitti*, s. (පරාධීන subject to others, වෘත්ති means of living) dependence, subservience.

පරාන්න, *Paránna*, s. (පර *para* and අන්න *anna* food) living at another's expence.

පරානුවාද, *Paránuwáda*, s. (පර *para* and අනුවාද *anuwáda* abuse) abuse, scurrility; slander, calumny.

පරාප, *Parápa*, s. (පර *para* away, අප් *ap* water) place from which water has retired etc.

පරාපවාදය, *Parápawádaya*, see පරානුවාද *paránuwáda*.

පරාභව, *Parábhawa*, s. (පරා disgrace, භව being) discomfiting, overcoming; fortieth year of the Indian cycle; contempt, disrespect; destruction; a Sútra of Buddha so called.

පරාභූත, *Parábhúta*, a. defeated, discomfited, degraded.

පරාම්මුඛ, *Parámmukha*, more correctly පරාඞ්මුඛ *paráṅmukha*, which see.

පරාමර්ශ, *Parámarṣa*, පරාමර්ශණ, *Parámarṣaṇa*, } s. discrimination, judgement, drawing conclusions from analogy or experience.

පරාමර්ෂ, *Parámarsha*, පරාමර්ෂණය, *Parámarshaṇaya*, } s. forbearance, endurance, patience, resignation.

පරායණ, *Paráyaṇa*, s. (පර *para* one only object, අයන *ayana* going) name of Vishṇu; attending, waiting on for protection or support: adherence to any pursuit, attachment to any object; name of Nirwáṇa: a. zealous, diligent, active; attached to; connected with, depending upon.

පරාර්ථ, *Parártha*, s. (පර *para* another, අර්ථ *artha* profit) barter, exchange, mutual traffic; other's welfare, the good of others.

පරාලය, *Parálaya*, s. rafter, pl. පරාල *parála*.

පරාශ්‍රය, *Paráṣraya*, s. (පර *para* another, ආශ්‍රය *áṣraya* asylum) dependence on another: a. dependent or relying upon another.

පරාශ්‍රයා, *Paráṣrayá*, s. parasite plant, *loranthus*, [Colloq. පිල්ල *pilla*, or පිලිල *pilila*].

පරාස්කන්දි, *Paráskandi*, s. (පර *para* another's (property), ස්කන්ද *skanda* to steal, with ආ *á* prefix) thief, robber, [Colloq. හොරා *horá*].

පරාසු, *Parásu*, a. (පර *para* away, from අසු *asu* breath) dead, expired, extinct.

පරි, *Pari*, *ind.* a particle and prefix, implying ubiquity, (around, on every side); abandonment, (away); end, termination; enforcement, stress, (even, very great); separateness, several, distribution, (each, by each); encircling, embracing; depreciation; homage, respect; rejection, turning off or away; ornament; diffusion, extension.

පරික්ඛාර, *Parikkhára*, පරික්ඛාරට්ඨ, *Parikkháraṭṭhá*, } s. articles required by a priest of Buddha, viz. bowl to receive alms, three yellow cloths, girdle, razor, needle, and a water strainer, [Colloq. අටපිරිකර *aṭa-pirikara*].

පරික්ෂක, *Parikshaka*, corruptly for පරීක්ෂක *paríkshaka*, which see.

පරික්ෂය, *Parikshaya*, s. (පරි emphatic, ක්ෂි *kshi* to decay) the act of growing less or wearing away, decay, decrease.

පරික්ෂාව, *Pariksháwa*, corruptly for පරීක්ෂාව *paríkshávwa*, which see.

පරික්ෂිප්ත, *Parikshipta*, a. (පරි round, ක්ෂිප්ත thrown) surrounded, encircled, intrenched, enclosed.

පරික්ෂේප, *Parikshépa*, s. scattering, spreading, surrounding, leaving.

පරික්ෂේප කරණවා, *Parikshépa-karaṇawá*, v. to surround, encircle.

පරිකථා, *Pari-kathá*, s. (පරි ornament, කථා tale) interesting narrative or history; work of fiction, tale, story, history or adventures of any fabulous person.

පරිකම්ප, *Pari-kampa*, s. (පරි great, කම්ප trembling) trembling; fear, terror.

පරිකර්ම, *Pari-karma*, s. (පරි ornament, කර්ම business) personal decoration, dressing, painting or perfuming the body; purifying.

පරිකල්පන, *Parikalpana*, s. (පරි intense, කෲප *klupa* to be able) making, inventing, dividing, setting, providing.

පරිකල්පිත, *Parikalpita*, a. made, invented; divided; settled.

පරිකසින, *Parikasina*, s. (පරි around, කසින all, entire) initiatory rite of religious ascetics which must be completed preparatory to their entrance upon the performance of dhyána: the devotee having abandoned the world and retired into solitude, must fix his mind upon some one of the four elements viz. earth, air, fire or water; to aid him in this duty some portion of the element, must be placed in a chatty or earthen vessel, the outsides of the vessel being so marked as to powerfully impress the mind of the devotee with the reality of the substance which he contemplates; fixing his attention on this single object, he must continue to address the element, repeating its name, until the mind attains that degree of absorption into the element itself that no other object or appearance is observable to the sentient faculties; this religious rite is divided into තේජෝකසින *téjókasina*, ආපෝකසින *ápókasina*, ආකාශෝකසින *ákásókasina* and පඨවිකසින *paṭharikasina*.

පරිකීර්ණ, *Parikírṇa*, *a.* scattered, diffused.

පරිකීර්තන, *Parikírtana*, *s.* boasting, talking of, saying, telling of.

පරිකීර්ත්ත, *Parikírttita*, *a.* said, declared, vaunted or boasted.

පරික්‍රම, *Parikrama*, *s.* (පරි about, ක්‍රම going) walking for amusement; going round or about.

පරික්ලේශ, *Pariklésa*, *s.* vexation, trouble.

පරිඛා, *Parikhá*, *s.* (පරි round, ඛන *khana* to dig) moat, trench, ditch round a fort, [Colloq. අගල *agala*].

පරිගත, *Parigata*, *a.* (පරි round, ගත gone) known, understood; sought, inquired after; obtained, gained; encircled, encompassed.

පරිගම, *Parigama*, *s.* (පරි about, round etc. ගමු *gamu* to go) surrounding, encompassing; knowing; enquiring after; obtaining, spreading.

පරිගලිත, *Parigalita*, *a.* fallen, dropped off, fallen off.

පරිග්‍රහ, *Parigraha*, *s.* (පරි intensitive prefix, or round about, ග්‍රහ to take) seizure, taking, laying hold of; assent, acceptance; train, retinue; wife; family; reserve of an army in the rear of the line; sun near the moon's node.

පරිග්‍රහණය, *Parigrahaṇaya*, *s.* (පරි intensitive prefix, ග්‍රහණ *grahaṇa* taking) acceptance, taking, seizing: see the last.

පරිගෘහිත, *Parigṛihíta*, *s.* accepted, assented, consented to, obeyed.

පරිඝ, *Parigha*, *s.* bludgeon, stick mounted with iron, iron club; spike; spear; pin or bolt of a door; glass vessel; water jar; outer door or gate of a palace; destroying, killing.

පරිච්ඡින්න, *Parichchhinna*, *a.* (පරි emphatic, ඡිද් *chhid* to cut) broken, divided, rent, separated; destroyed.

පරිච්ඡේදය, *Parichchhédaya*, *s.* (පරි successively, ඡේද *chchhéda* division) division of a book, section, chapter, paragraph; cutting; limit; remedying.

පරිචර්‍යා, *Paricharyá*, *s.* service, dependence, veneration, worship.

පරිචර, *Parichara*, } *s.* (පරි about, චර to walk, චා
පරිචාර, *Parichára*, } ර who walks) guard; attendant, companion; slave, servant.

පරිචාරක, *Paricháraka*, } *s.* servant, attendant: *a.*
පරිචාරික, *Paricharika*, } dependent, subject, subservient, attending.

පරිචාරිකාව, *Paricharikáwa*, *s.* (පරි and චාරිකාව walking) encircling, encompassing; female attendant.

පරිචාර්‍ය, *Paricharya*, *part.* to be served, obeyed or worshipped, [Colloq. සේවනය කළයුතු *séwanaya-kalayutu*].

පරිචිත, *Parichita*, *a.* acquainted with; heaped up.

පරිචුම්බ, *Parichumba*, *s.* kiss, caress, embrace, [Colloq. සිඹීම *simbíma*].

පරිජනයා, *Pari-janayá*, *s.* (පරි about, ජන *jana* man) attendants, train, retinue, suite, [Colloq. පිරිස *pirisa*].

පරිඥාන, *Parijñána*, *s.* (පරි emphatic, ඥාන knowledge) universal knowledge; comprehending, understanding.

පරිණත, *Pariṇata*, *a.* ripe, mature, bowed, bent.

පරිණය, *Pariṇaya*, } *s.* marriage, [Colloq. කසා
පරිණයන, *Pariṇayana*, } දය *kasádaya*].

පරිණාම, *Pariṇáma*, *s.* change of form or state; maturity; last stage.

පරිණාමශූල, *Pariṇámaśúla*, *s.* flatulence with pain or vomiting after eating, dyspepsia.

පරිණායක, *Pariṇáyaka*, *s.* husband, [Colloq. ස්වාමි පුරුෂයා *swámi-purushayá*].

පරිණාහ, *Pariṇáha*, *s.* width, breadth, [Colloq. පළල *palala*]; circumference of a circle, [Colloq. වටය *waṭaya*].

පරිණීත, *Pariṇíta*, *a.* married.

පරිත්ත, *Paritta*, *s.* (ප exceeding, රිත්ත small or පරි intensitive prefix, ත්ත *tta* for ත්‍රා *trá* to defend) atom, particle; defence, protection, means of defence or protection: see also පිරිත *pirita*.

පරිත්තාභය, *Parittábhaya*, *s.* (පරිත්ත *paritta* small, ආභා *ábhá* splendour) one of the inferior Brahma lókas so called.

පරිත්‍යක්ත, *Parityakta*, *a.* (පරි intensitive prefix, ත්‍යක්ත left) expelled, driven away; abandoned, resigned, deserted, [Colloq. අත්හැරිය *ateriya*].

පරිත්‍යජ්‍ය, *Parityajya*, *part.* (පරි and ත්‍යජ *tyaja* to leave, to quit) having abandoned.

පරිත්‍යාග, *Parityága*, *s.* (පරි away, or intensive prefix, ත්‍යාග quitting, gift) abandonment, desertion, giving away, gift; offering; sacrifice.

පරිත්‍රාණ, *Paritrána*, *s.* (පරි exceeding, ත්‍රාණ preserving) self preservation, self defence; protecting.

පරිතාප, *Paritápa, s.* (පරි intensitive prefix, තාප burning) pain, anguish, sorrow; heat, warmth; one of the divisions of hell, that in which punishment is inflicted by burning.

පරිතුෂ්ට, *Paritushṭa, a.* (පරි intensive, තුෂ්ට pleased) pleased, rejoiced.

පරිතෝ, *Parító, adv.* round, every way, all round.

පරිද්දෙන්, *Paridden,* auxiliary or ablative case of පරිදි *paridi,* used in the sense of 'according to', 'in the manner of'.

පරිදාන, *Paridána, s.* (පරි reciprocally, දාන giving) exchange, barter, returning any thing for its equivalent.

පරිදාහ, *Paridáha, s.* (පරි intensitive prefix, දාහ burning) heat, warmth.

පරිදි, *Paridi, s.* mode, manner.

පරිදේවනා, *Paridéwaná, s.* lamentation, weeping.

පරිධාන, *Paridhána, s.* (පරි round, over, ධාන holding) garment, clothes; trituration of perfume; lower garment, under garment.

පරිධාවි, *Paridhávi, s.* forty-sixth year of the Indian cycle of sixty.

පරිධි, *Paridhi, s.* (පරි around, ධා *dhá* to have) disc of the sun or moon, [Colloquial: ඉරමඬල *ira-manḍala*]; circumference of a circle, [Colloq. නිම්වලල්ල *nim-walalla*].

පරිනිබ්බාන, *Parinibbána,* } පරිනිර්වාණය, *Parinirwáṇaya,* } *s.* (පරි emphatic, නිබ්බාන, nirwáṇa) complete and final emancipation of the soul from all existence, that attainment of Nirwáṇa or annihilation which is peculiar to a Buddha or Rahat, life in all its forms being regarded as in a greater or less degree inseparably connected with suffering.

පරිපක්ව, *Paripakwa, a.* (පරි intensitive prefix, පක්ව matured) fully matured, completely ripened; shrewd; digested.

පරිපණ, *Paripaṇa, s.* (පරි severally, පණ price) capital, principal, stock.

පරිපාක, *Paripáka, s.* maturity, cleverness; digestion; being cooked or dressed.

පරිපාලනය, *Paripálanaya, s.* defence, protection, support, [Colloquial: ආරක්ෂාකෙරීම *árakshá-keríma*].

පරිපීඩිත, *Paripíḍita,* } පරිපීළිත, *Paripíḷita,* } *a.* (පරි exceeding, පීඩිත afflicted) greatly afflicted, distressed.

පරිපූර්ණ, *Paripúrṇa,* } පරිපූරිත, *Paripúrita,* } *a.* (පරි complete, පූර්ණ full) complete, full, satisfied.

පරිපේල, *Paripéla,* } පරිපේලව, *Paripélawa,* } *s.* fragrant grass, *cyperus rotundus,* [Colloq. කලාඳුරු *kalánduru*].

පරිප්ලව, *Pariplawa, s.* shaking, trembling; immersing; oppression.

පරිබ්‍රාජ, *Paribrája,* } පරිබ්‍රාජක, *Paribrájaka,* } see පරිව්‍රාජක *pariwrájaka.*

පරිභව, *Paribhawa,* } පරිභාව, *Paribháwa,* } *s.* abuse, contempt; disrespect, disregard, defeat.

පරිභාවිත, *Paribhárita, a.* accustomed to, well trained; mixed with, infused.

පරිභාෂණ, *Paribháshaṇa,* see පරිභාසන *paribhásana.*

පරිභාෂා, *Paribháshá,* see පරිභාසා *paribhásá.*

පරිභාසන, *Paribhásana, s.* (පරි implying depreciation, or mutually, භාසන speaking) abuse, scurrility; reproof; ridicule, expression of censure or contempt; addressing; rule, precept.

පරිභාසා, *Paribhásá, s.* appointment, engagement; grammatical maxim given as a summary explanation of certain rules in grammar; (in medicine) prognosis; conventional term in any science.

පරිභූත, *Paribhúta, a.* treated with contempt, disrespect, or disregard.

පරිභෝග, *Paribhóga, s.* (පරි intensitive prefix, භෝග enjoyment) riches, wealth, property, possession or enjoyment.

පරිභෝගික, *Paribhógika, a.* rich, abounding in property, wealthy.

පරිභ්‍රම, *Paribhrama, s.* (පරි round, භ්‍රම roaming) walking about, perambulating, wandering about, going to and fro, error.

පරිභෘත, *Paribṛita, a.* nourished, brought up, educated.

පරිමණ්ඩලය, *Parimanḍalaya, s.* (පරි and මණ්ඩල ball) ball, globe, circle.

පරිමර්ජන, *Parimarjana, s.* (පරි completely, මෘජ *mṛija* to clean) cleansing, clearing; moderating, stopping.

පරිමර්ද, *Parimarda, s.* plant, pigeon pea, *cajanus indicus,* [Colloq. රටතෝර *raṭa-tóra*], another pea, *cytisus cajan.*

පරිමර්දනය, *Parimardanaya, s.* trampling, moderating, rubbing, grinding, embracing.

පරිමල, *Parimala, s.* exquisite scent, especially arising from the trituration of fragrant substantumes; copulation; meeting of learned men.

පරිමාණ, *Parimáṇa, s.* (පරි complete, මාණ measure) complete measure of any kind, [Colloq. සම්පූර්ණ මිම්ම *sampúrṇa mimma*].

පරිමිත, *Parimita, a.* measured, regulated.

පරිමිතාහාර, *Parimitáhára, a.* eating moderately.

පරිමුක්ත, *Parimukta, a.* (පරි completely, මුච *mucha* to untie) loosened, freed, emancipated, liberated.

පරිමෝචන, *Parimóchana, s.* release, emancipation.

පරිමෘජ්‍ය, *Parimṛijya, part. a.* to be touched or cleaned.

පරියන්ත, *Pariyanta,* Páli form of Sanskrit පර්‍ය්‍යන්ත *paryanta,* which see.

පරියාපන්න, *Pariyápanna, a.* included, contained, belonging to.

පරියාය, *Pariyáya, s.* (පරි successively, අය *aya* to go) figure, metaphor, figure of speech; epithet which expressess the properties of substances or things; vocabulary or order of the synonyms for any term; order, method; religious discourse; time for doing any work, opportunity, occasion; surrounding wall; Páli form of Sanskrit පර්‍ය්‍යාය *paryáya,* which see.

පරියේසනා, *Pariyésaná, s.* (පරි exceeding, ඉස *isa* to go) research, inquiry, investigation; Páli form of Sanskrit පර්‍ය්‍යේෂණ *paryéshaṇá.*

පරියෝසානය, *Pariyósánaya, s.* (පරි complete, ඕසාන *ósána* end) conclusion, end, termination; Páli form of Sanskrit පර්‍ය්‍යවසානය *paryawasánaya.*

පරිරම්භ, *Parirambha,* } *s.* (පරි before රම්භ
පරිරම්භන, *Parirambhana,* } to begin) embrace, embracing.

පරිලාභ, *Parilábha, s.* (පරි complete, ලාභ receiving) obtaining, gaining; mutual profit.

පරිලිප්ත, *Parilipta, a.* (පරි intensive prefix, ලිප *lipa* to smear) daubed, smeared, anointed, rubbed with any unctuous substance.

පරිව්‍යය, *Pariwyaya, s.* rice, [Colloq. සාල් *sál*].

පරිව්‍යාධ, *Pariwyádha, s.* tree, *cochlospermum gossypium,* [Colloq. කිණිහිරිය *kiṇihiriya*]; sort of reed growing in water.

පරිවත්ත, *Pariwatta,* Páli form of පරිවෘත්ත *parivṛitta,* which see.

පරිවත්සර, *Pariwatsara, s.* (පරි end, වත්සර year) complete year.

පරිවර්ජනය, *Pariwarjanaya, s.* killing, slaughter, abandoning, quitting.

පරිවර්ත, *Pariwarta, s.* (පරි severally, round, වෘත *vṛita* to be) act of turning or inverting; changing, or exchanging one thing for another; substitution of one word for another, transmutation of a word; exchange, barter; flight, retreat; desertion; tortoise incarnation (see අවතාර *awatára*); end of the period of four ages or the destruction of the world; book, chapter, canto.

පරිවර්තන, *Pariwartana, s.* (පරි mutually, වර්තන being) barter, exchange, traffic; turning round; inverting.

පරිවාද, *Pariwáda, s.* (පරි censure, වාද speech) abuse, reproach; accusation; reproof; censure, blame.

පරිවාදක, *Pariwádaka, s.* (derived as the last) abuser, calumniator; accuser, plaintiff, complainant, [Colloq. පැමිණිලිකාරයා *pemiṇilikárayá*].

පරිවාප, *Pariwápa, s.* pool, pond, [Colloq. පොකුණ *pokuṇa*], any sheet of water; shaving, shearing; train, retinue.

පරිවාපන, *Pariwápana, s.* shaving, shearing.

පරිවාපිත, *Pariwápita, a.* shaven, shorn.

පරිවාර, *Pariwára, s.* (පරි around, වෘ *vṛi* to be) dependant; retinue, followers; sheath, scabbard; insignia of dignity.

පරිවාරජන, *Pariwára-jana, s.* (පරිවාර and ජන man) train, retinue, attendants; guard.

පරිවාරිත, *Pariwárita, part. a.* surrounded, enclosed by.

පරිවාහ, *Pariwáha, s.* (පරි about, වහ *waha* to carry) inundation, overflowing; water-course, drain for carrying off water.

පරිවිතර්කය, *Parivitarkaya, s.* (පරි implying abandonment, විතර්ක *vitarka* thinking) change of mind, change of sentiment or opinion.

පරිවුතෝ, *Pariwutó, a.* (පරි round, වෘ *vṛi* to be) train, retinue; encompassed, surrounded.

පරිවෙණ, *Pariwéṇa, s.* hermitage, cell or hut forming a monk's private chamber; college attached to a monastery.

පරිවේදන, *Pariwédana, s.* (පරි exceeding, වේදන feeling) severe pain, anguish.

පරිවේදනා, *Pariwédaná, s.* shrewdness, wit, foresight.

පරිවේශ, *Pariwéṣa, s.* (පරි round, විශ *viṣa* to pervade) disc of the sun or moon; surrounding, encompassing.

පරිවේෂ්ටන, *Pariwéshṭana, s.* (පරි before, වේෂ්ට *wéshṭa* to surround) surrounding, encompassing.

පරිවේෂ්ටිත, *Pariwéshṭita, part. a.* surrounded, enclosed.

පරිවේෂ, *Pariwésha,* } *s.* (පරි round, වේෂණ
පරිවේෂණ, *Pariwéshaṇa,* } covering) surrounding enclosing; serving, serving up a dinner, etc.: see පරිවේශ *pariwéṣa.*

පරිව්‍රජ්‍යා, *Pariwrajyá*, *s.* ascetic devotion; religious austerities, abandonment of the world.

පරිව්‍රාජ්, *Pariwráj*, *s.* (පරි about, ව්‍රජ *wraja* to wander) mendicant ascetic.

පරිව්‍රාජ්‍ය, *Pariwrájya*, *s.* (derived as the last) state of an ascetic.

පරිව්‍රාජ, *Pariwrája*, *s.* mendicant devotee, ascetic.

පරිව්‍රාජක, *Pariwrájaka*, *s.* ascetic, religious hermit, mendicant.

පරිවෘත්ති, *Parivṛitti*, *s.* exchange, barter; encircling, surrounding, encompassing.

පරිවෘත, *Parivṛita*, *a.* encompassed, encircled, surrounded, gained, acquired, known.

පරිශුද්ධ, *Pariṣuddha*, *a.* (පරි intensive prefix, ශුද්ධ clean) clean, cleansed, purified; holy.

පරිශෝධ, *Pariṣódha*, *s.* cleansing, purifying.

පරිශ්‍රම, *Pariṣrama*, *s.* labour, weariness, fatigue.

පරිශ්‍රාන්ත, *Pariṣránta*, *a.* wearied, exhausted.

පරිශ්‍රාන්ති, *Pariṣránti*, *s.* trouble, fatigue.

පරිෂ්කාර, *Parishkára*, *s.* (පරි before, කර *kara* with, ස *sa* inserted) decoration, finishing, cooking, surrounding.

පරිෂද්, *Parishad*, *s.* assembly, audience, congregation, [Colloq. රැස්වීම *rẹsvíma*].

පරිෂද්‍ය, *Parishadya*, *s.* spectator at a play, guest, one of a party or assembly.

පරිෂද, *Parishada*, see පරිෂද්‍ය *parishadya*.

පරිස්කන්ද, *Pariskanda*, *s.* foster child, one nourished by a stranger.

පරිස්කන්න, *Pariskanna*, *s.* foster child.

පරිස්කාර, *Pariskára*, *s.* (පරි completely or ornament, කාර making) the articles allowed to a Buddhist priest as his private property, viz. a bowl in which to receive food, three yellow cloths (forming one suit of apparel) girdle, needle, razor and a water strainer; all other property should belong to the community of priests: see පරිෂ්කාර *parishkára*.

පරිෂ්කෘත, *Parishkṛita*, *a.* adorned, decorated, embellished; highly finished; surrounded, encompassed.

පරිස්තෝම, *Paristóma*, *s.* elephant's coloured cloth or trappings.

පරිස්පන්ද, *Parispanda*, *s.* beating, throbbing; train, retinue; decorating the hair with flowers, etc.

පරිස්පන්දන, *Parispandana*, *s.* beating, throbbing.

පරිස්‍යන්ද, *Parisyanda*, *s.* oozing, dropping, decoration of the hair.

පරිස, *Parisa*, *s.* train, retinue: *a.* clear, clean, pure.

පරිසම්බාධ, *Parisambádha*. *a.* squeezed; imprisoned, confined, straitened.

පරිසමාප්ත, *Parisamápta*, *a.* (පරි intensive prefix, සමාප්ත done) ended, completed, finished, terminated, performed.

පරිසමාප්තිය, *Parisamáptiya*, *s.* entire completion.

පරිසර්ප, *Parisarpa*, *s.* (පරි around, සර්ප going) encompassing, encircling, surrounding; going, proceeding.

පරිසර්‍යා, *Parisaryá*, *s.* perambulation, wandering about.

පරිසර, *Parisara*, *s.* cow-house; dying, death; fate, destiny; ground on the skirts of a river or mountain or contiguous to a town; border, neighbourhood.

පරිහරණය, *Pariharaṇaya*, *s.* preservation, protection, safeguard, seizing, leaving, avoiding.

පරිහානය, *Pariháṇaya*, } *s.* (පරි implying intensity,
පරිහානිය, *Pariháṇiya*, } හා *há* to be destroyed) decay, decrease, wearing away, wane.

පරිහාර, *Parihára*, *s.* contempt, disrespect; leaving, abandoning, forsaking, dismissing; courtesy; benefit; protection; figure of speech; example or illustration, apposite argument; precedent, instance; honour, pomp, state.

පරිහාර යෝග, *Parihára-yóga*, see the last explanation of the preceding word.

පරිහාස, *Parihása*, *s.* (පරි exceeding, හස *hasa* to laugh) mirth, sport, pastime; contempt, ridicule, banter.

පරිහීණ, *Parihíṇa*, see පරිහානය *pariháṇaya*.

පරිහෘත, *Parihṛita*, *a.* avoided, expelled; taken.

පරීක්ෂක, *Paríkshaka*, *s.* (පරි before, ඊක්ෂ *íksha* to look) investigator, assayer, judge, tempter; investigating acutely.

පරීක්ෂණ, *Paríkshaṇa*, *s.* trial, experiment, temptation.

පරීක්ෂා, *Paríkshá*, *s.* trial, experiment, investigation.

පරීක්ෂාකරණවා, *Paríkshákaraṇawá*, *v.* to tempt, to try, to prove, to test, to examine.

පරීක්ෂාව, *Paríksháwa*, see පරීක්ෂා *paríkshá*.

පරීවාර, *Paríwára*, see පරිවාර *pariwára*.

පරීවෘත්ත, *Parívṛitta*, see පරිවෘත්ත *parivṛitta*.

පරීසාර, *Parísára*, see පරිසර *parisara*.

පරීහාර, *Paríhára*, see පරිහාර *parihára*.

පරීහාස, *Paríhása*, *s.* mirth, sport, amusement.

පරුවත, *Paruwata*, see පර්වත *parwata*.

පරුෂ, *Parusha*, *s.* plant, *barleria prionitis*, [Colloq. කටුකරඬු *kaṭukarṇḍu*]; tree, *carapa moluccensis* or *xylocarpus granatum:* *a.* rough, harsh.

පරුස, *Parusa*, Elu form of පරුෂ *parusha.*

පරුසත්, *Parusat*, corruptly for පර්ෂත් *parshat.*

පරුසබස්, *Parusa-bas*, } *s.* (පරුස rough, බස් or වචන speech) scurrility, abuse.
පරුසවචන, *Parusa-wachana*,

පරුසු, *Parusu*, *s.* hatchet, chopper, [Colloq. අත් පොරොව *at-porowa*].

පරූෂ, *Parúsha*, } see පරුෂ *parusha.*
පරූෂක, *Parúshaka*,

පරෙයිමල්, *Pareyi-mal*, *s.* plant, orchid with small white flowers like pigeons, often cultivated on the trunks of coconut trees, *dendrobium crumenatum;* also called සුදු පරෙයියාමල් *sudu-pareyiyá-mal*].

පරෙයියා, *Pareyiyá*, corruptly for පරවියා *paraviyá*, which see.

පරෝක්ෂ, *Paróksha*, *s.* ascetic, religious hermit: *a.* invisible, past tense (in grammar).

පරෝක්ෂාර්ථ, *Parókshártha*, *s.* absent or invisible object.

පරෝපකාර, *Parópakára*, *s.* (පර another, උපකාර *upakára* help) help, assistance rendered to others.

පරෝපකාරිත්වය, *Parópakáritwaya*, *s.* state of being a helper of others.

පරෝපක්‍රමය, *Parópakramaya*, *s.* (පර and උපක්‍රම *upakrama* cunning) foreign intrigue, being killed or betrayed by another.

පරෝපකෘත, *Parópakṛita*, *a.* helped by another.

පරෝපදේශ, *Parópadéṣa*, *s.* instruction received from others.

පල්, *Pal*, *s.* mud, mire; support, protection, preservation: *a.* old, corrupt, rotten.

පල්කම, *Palkama*, *s.* mud, sediment, fetid sediment, staleness, stagnation.

පල්කරණවා, *Palkaraṇawá*, *v.* to make stale or fetid.

පල් ගඳ, *Pal-ganda*, *s.* stench from any fetid sediment, stale smell.

පල්දොරුව, *Paldoruwa*, *s.* sewer.

පල්මාණික්කං, *Palmánikkan*, *s.* blue vitriol; copperas.

පල්ල, *Palla*, *s.* large basket or matted shed for keeping corn; underneath, ground below, bottom; kind of oar used to direct boats.

පල්ලක්කිය, *Pallakkiya*, *s.* kind of palanquin.

පල්ලම, *Pallama*, *s.* low place, hollow, valley, descent of a hill, declivity, pl. පල්ලම් *pallam.*

පල්ලරු, *Palluru*, *s.* subdivision of පලී *palí* a term applied to washers for low castes.

පල්ලල, *Pallala*, *s.* small lake, pond, tank.

පල්ලව, *Pallawa*, *s.* sprout, shoot, extremity of a branch bearing new leaves; branch; expansion; wood; red dye, lac; bracelet; unsteadiness.

පල්ලවාංකුරය, *Pallawáṅkuraya*, *s.* (පල්ලව *pallawa* and අංකුර *aṅkura* bud) sprout, germ, young shoot of leaves.

පල්ලවාද, *Pallawáda*, *s.* (පල්ලව *pallawa* leaf, අද what eats) goat, [Colloq. එළුවා *eḷuwá*]; deer, [Colloq. මුවා *muwá*],

පල්ලවෝද්ගම, *Pallawódgama*, *s.* (පල්ලව *pallawa* shoot, උද්ගම ascending, coming up) budding, sprouting, shooting of the sprouts or buds of leaves or flowers.

පල්ලි, *Palli*, *s.* small village, city, or rather an affix to words forming the name of a town, as Trichinopoly or palli; small house-lizard; school, place of Christian worship; low caste woman.

පල්ලිය, *Palliya*, *s.* chapel, church, school room.

පල්ලෙයි ඇල් වී, *Pálleyi-ẹl-ví*, *s.* kind of hill paddy which ripens in three months.

පල්වන්, *Palwan*, *s.* air, wind, [Colloq. හුළඟ *hulanga*].

පල්සොරා, *Palsorá*, } *s.* (පල් corrupt, සොරා thief) thief of the most depraved kind, highwayman.
පල්හොරා, *Palhorá*,

පල, *Pala*, *s.* fruit; flesh; straw; weight of gold or silver, equal to four කර්ෂ *karshas;* proclamation, spreading abroad; cotton cloth; affliction, sorrow: roof; imperative of the verb යනවා *yanawá*, to go; (not respectful as තෝ පල *tó-pala*, go away, be off); place; spot.

පලංගාන, *Palangána*, *s.* dish, platter, large plate.

පලක්කට්ටුව, *Palakkaṭṭuwa*, *s.* placard, poster.

පලක්බැඳ, *Palak-bẹnda*, *s.* sitting cross legged.

පලක්ෂාර, *Palakshára*, *s.* (පල flesh, ක්ෂාර what oozes) blood, [Colloq. ලේ *lé*].

පලඟ, *Palanga*, *s.* name of Ráhu, ascending node; similitude, resemblance; shield; locust, grass-hopper; seat, sitting on one's legs in the oriental manner.

පලඟැටියා, *Palangẹṭiyá*, *s.* locust, grass-hopper, *cicada.*

පලඞ්කට, *Palaṅkaṭa*, *a.* timid, fearful, frightened.

පලඞ්කර, *Palaṅkara*, *s.* bile, [Colloq. පිත *pita*].

පලඞ්කෂ, *Palaṅkasha*, *s.* Rákshayá, imp, goblin.

පලඞ්කෂා, *Palaṅkashá*, *s.* bdellium tree, [Colloq. ගුගුල් *gugul*]; ichneumon plant, *mimosa octandra*, [Colloq. අරත්ත *aratta*]; lac, animal dye, [Coll: ලාකඩ *lákaḍa*]; plant, *acanthus ilicifolus*, [Colloq. ඉකිරි *ikiri*]: see නකුලේෂ්ඨා *nakuléshṭá.*

පලටු, *Palaṭu*, *s.* tree, jack in a box, *hernandia peltata.*

පලතුරු, *Palaturu*, *s.* (පල fruit, තුරු tree or difference) any tree bearing fruit; also, fruits of different kinds.

පලදරණවා, *Paladaraṇawá*, *v.* to bear fruit, to be fruitful.

පලදල, *Paladala*, *a.* very stout, fat, bulky, gross, sluggish.

පලදුව, *Paladuwa*, *s.* wound, scar; flaw, fault, defect.

පලදෙනවා, *Paladenawá*, *v.* to flourish, to be fruitful, to be rewarded or punished.

පලඳන, *Palan̲dana*, *s.* jewel; ornament, decoration.

පලඳනවා, *Palan̲danawá*, *v.* to dress, to ornament, to decorate, to adorn, to arm another: pret. පැලැන්දුවා *pęlęnduwá*,

පලඳනාව, *Palan̲danáwa*, *s.* ornament for dress, trinket.

පලඳිනවා, *Palan̲dinawá*, *v.* to dress, to adorn, to decorate, to wear, put on: pret. පැලැන්ද *pęlęndá.*

පලනාසන, *Palanásana*, *s.* (පල fruit, නාසන what destroys) misfortune, mishap.

පලපුරුද්ද, *Palapurudda*, *s.* practice, experience.

පලපුරුදු, *Palapurudu*, *a.* familiar, accustomed.

පලම්, *Palam*, plural of පලම *palama;* scale or balance for weighing, [Colloq. තරාදිය *tarádiya*].

පලම්දණ්ඩ, *Palam-daṇḍa*, *s.* (පලම් and දණ්ඩ beam) beam of a balance.

පලම, *Palama*, *s.* weight equal to twelve kalan̲das: see කලඳ *kalan̲da.*

පලරුක, *Pala-ruka*, see ඵලවෘක්‍ෂ *phala-vriksha.*

පලල්, *Palal*, *a.* wide, broad, extended, diffused.

පලල් අතට, *Palal-ataṭa*, *ad.* crosswise, transversely.

පලල්කරණවා, *Palalkaraṇawá*, *v.* to widen, to make broad.

පලල, *Palala*, *s.* breadth, width; mud, mire, clay; pounded sesamum; flesh; Ráksha, imp, goblin: see පලඞ්කෂ *palaṅkasha.*

පලවත, *Palawata*, see පස්පලවත *paspalawata.*

පලවනවා, *Palawanawá*, *v.* to drive, to expel, to cause to run.

පලවැල, *Palawęla*, *s.* ripe fruit; fruit matured by nature or art; ripe (වැල *węla*) and unripe (පල *pala*) fruit.

පලස, *Palasa*, *s.* woollen cloth; cloth thrown loosely over the shoulders, cloak, mantle; carpet; trappings, housings of an elephant; tree, bearing beautiful blossoms, *butea frondosa*, [Colloq. ගස් කෑල *gas-kęla*].

පලහනවා, *Palahanawá*, *v.* to burn, to roast, to toast, to cook: pret. පැලහුවා *pęlahuwá.*

පලා, *Palá*, *s.* greens, vegetables, herbs in general.

පලා උල්ලා, *Palá-ullá*, *s.* slug.

පලා කරවලා, *Palá-karawalá*, *s.* snake, variety of *bungarus Ceylonicus.*

පලා ගැරඬියා, *Palá-gęraṇḍiyá*, *s.* variety of rat snake, *ptyas mocusus.*

පලාණ්ඩව, *Paláṇḍawa*, } *s.* eschalot, species of
පලාණ්ඩු, *Paláṇḍu*, } garlic, *allium ascalonicum*, [Colloq. රතුලූනු *ratu-lúnu*].

පලාත, *Paláta*, *s.* district, province, circuit.

පලා පණුවා, *Palá-paṇuwá*, *s.* slug, caterpillar.

පලාපිළිහුඩුවා, *Palá-piḷihuḍuwá*, *s.* variety of kingfisher (family *Alcedinidæ*, order *Picariæ*).

පලා පොලඟා, *Palá-polangá*, *s.* viperine snake, *trimeresurus trigonocephalus* (*Crotalidæ*, order *Ophidia*).

පලාබරියා, *Palábariyá*, *s.* snake of a green colour inhabiting green trees.

පලායන, *Palá-yana*, *s.* flight, retreat: *a.* fleeing.

පලායනවා, *Paláyanawá*, *v.* to flee, to run away, to abscond, to retreat.

පලායාම, *Paláyáma*, *s.* flight, retreat, absconding, running away.

පලාල, *Palála*, *s.* straw, chaff, stalk of paddy.

පලාල පීඨක, *Palála-píṭhaka*, *s.* (පලාල straw, පීඨක footstool) truss or mat of straw for cleaning the feet; capital punishment, beating the culprit until he resembles a truss of straw.

පලාවන්, *Paláwan*, *s.* (පලා herb, වන් colour) green (colour); blue.

පලාශ, *Paláṣa*, *s.* green (colour); leaf; tree bearing red blossoms, *butea frondosa*, [Colloq. ගස්කෑල *gas-kęla*]: see පලස *palasa.*

පලාශක, *Paláṣaka*, *s.* plant, *curcuma reclinata.*

පලාශින්, *Paláṣin*, *s.* tree in general, [Colloq, ගහ *gaha*]; goblin, imp.

පලාස, *Palása*, see පලාශ *paláṣa.*

පලිග, *Paliga*, *s.* nineteenth of the astronomical Yógas: see යෝග *yóga.*

පලිඝ, *Paligha*, *s.* glass vessel, water-pot, gateway of a building, window, air-hole; bludgeon; stick mounted with iron, or an iron club: see පලිග *paliga.*

පලිඝ පරිවර්ත, *Paligha-pariwarta*, *s.* (පලිඝ iron club, පරිවර්ත revolving) capital punishment, fastening the culprit to a block of wood by driving an iron club through his head and whirling the body round.

පලිත, *Palita*, *s.* greyness of the hair; much or ornamental hair; heat, burning; mud, mire; benzoin, [Colloq. ගල්මද *gal-mada*]: *a.* grey haired, old.

පලිතා, *Palitá*, *s.* old, grey-haired woman.

පලිප්පුව, *Palippuwa*, *s.* polishing gold and silver; burnishment of metals.

පලිස, *Palisa*, } *s.* shield, buckler.
පලිහ, *Paliha*, }

පලිහ පානවා, *Paliha-pánawá*, *v.* to shield, to defend with a buckler, to parry a blow.

පලි හරඹ, *Pali-haramba*, *s.* defending with a shield, parrying a blow.

පලී, *Palí*, *s.* washers for low castes.

පලෙළු, *Paleḷu*, *s.* large kind of goat or ram.

පව්, *Paw*, plur. of පව *pawa*.

පව්ර, *Pawra*, *s.* fortification; walls of a fort or city; breast-work, pl. පව්රු *pawru*.

පව්රුණු, *Pawruṇu*, see පවාරණ *pawárana*.

පව්ල, *Pawla*, *s.* family, household; robe, dress, mantle.

පව්ව, *Pawwa*, *s.* rock, large stone.

පව, *Pawa*, *s.* sin, demerit; mountain, stone; air, wind, gentle breeze; winnowing corn; purification, purity; cow dung; rock, hill.

පවග, *Pawaga*, } *s.* (පව mountain, ග who goes)
පවඟු, *Pawangu*, } black monkey, *Presbytes cephalopterus*, [Colloq. වඳුරා *wandurá*]; also name of plant commonly known by the term ප්‍රියඞ්ගු *priyangu*.

පවත්, *Pawat*, *s.* news, tidings, intelligence; continuance, being: see ප්‍රවෘත්ති *prawṛitti*.

පවත්වනවා, *Pawatwanawá*, *v.* to cause to exist, remain, to endure, to keep, to preserve, to observe in practice as a command or usage: pret. පැවැත්වූවා *pewetwuwá*.

පවත, *Pawata*, *s.* (ප implying intensity, වත being) being, existence; continuance.

පවතඹල, *Pawatambala*, see තඹල *tambala*.

පවතිනවා, *Pawatinawá*, *v.* to be, to exist; to continue, to endure, to last; to obey: pret. පැවතුනා *pewatuná*.

පවතු, *Pawatu*, *Imp. Mood* of පවතී *pawatí*. is, be thou, let it be, may it continue.

පවන්, *Pawan*, *s.* air, wind, [Colloquial: හුලඟ *hulanga*].

පවන්ගසනවා, *Pawangasanawá*, } *v.* (පවන් air,
පවන්ගහනවා, *Pawangahanawá*, } ගසනවා to beat) to fan, to winnow.

පවන්පත, *Pawanpata*, *s.* (පවන් air, පත leaf) fan, fan in general; peculiar kind of fan which the priests carry in their hand when walking abroad to hide their faces and prevent their seeing females; it is also used by them when reading the baṇa in public both for the foregoing purpose, and to prevent the distortions of their countenance being seen by the congregation.

පවන්මග, *Pawanmaga*, *s.* (පවන් wind, මග way) sky, atmosphere, [Colloq. අකාශය *ákáṣaya*].

පවන් වේගය, *Pawan-wégaya*, } *s.* (පවන් and වේග
පවන් සැරය, *Pawan-seraya*, } *wéga* or සැර *sera* strength) storm of wind, gale, [Colloq. හුලන් සැරේ *hulan-seré*, කුනාටුව *kunáṭuwa*].

පවන, *Pawana*, *s.* air, wind; winnowing; gently blowing; purifying.

පවර, *Pawara*, *s.* (ප intensitive prefix, වර noble) chief, principal, noble, superior, pre-eminent, [Colloq. උත්තම *uttama*].

පවරණවා, *Pawaraṇawá*, *v.* to call, to invite, to request; to invite a priest to take up his residence in a house during the rainy season; to give in charge, to give over; to impute; see also පවාරණය *pawáraṇaya*: pret. පැවරුවා *pewaruwá*.

පවස, *Pawasa*, *s.* thirst, [Colloq. පිපාසය *pipásaya*].

පවසනවා, *Pawasanawá*, *v.* to speak, to talk, to utter, to declare; to publish, to make known, to inform, to communicate: pret. පැවසුවා *pewasuwá;* [Colloq. දැනුම්දෙනවා *denum-denawá*].

පවළ, *Pawaḷa*, *s.* red coral, [Colloq. පබළු *pabaḷu*].

පවළ සිඳු, *Pawaḷa-sindu*, *s.* (පවළ and සිඳු sea) ocean of red coral.

පවළු, *Pawaḷu*, see පබළු *pabaḷu*.

පවා, *Pawá*, *s.* valley: *adv.* even.

පවාරණ, *Pawáraṇa*, } *s.* rejection, throwing
පවාරණය, *Pawáraṇaya*, } aside, discontinuance; finishing, ending, completing; leaving, abandoning; prayer, entreaty, request, prohibition, injunction, invitation.

පවාරු, *Pawáru*, *s.* creeping plant, *momordica charantia*, [Colloq. කරවිල *karirila*].

පවි, *Pavi*, *s.* thunderbolt of Indra, [Colloq වජ්‍රායුධය *wajráyudhaya*, හෙන *hena*].

පවිටු, *Paviṭu*, *a.* guilty, sinful, depraved, impure; heretical, heterodox.

පවිත්‍ර, *Pavitra*, *s.* sacrificial grass, *poa cynosuroides*, kusa grass, [Colloq. කුසතණ *kusatana*]; copper; water: *a.* pure, clean, cleansed; purified, sanctified, holy.

පවිත්‍රකම, *Pavitrakama*, *s.* purity.

පවිත්‍රා, *Pavitrá*, *s.* holy basil, *ocimum sanctum*, [Colloq. මදුරුතලා *maduru-talá*].

පවිස්ත්‍ර, *Pavistra*, corrupt form of පවිත්‍ර *pavitra*, which see.

පවු, *Pawu*, see පව් *paw*.

පවුර, *Pawura*, see පව්ර *pawra*.

පවුල, *Pawula*, *s.* family, household, pl. පවුල් *pawul*.

පශ්චාත්, *Paschát*, *adv.* after, afterwards.

පශ්චාත්තාප, *Pascháttápa*, *s.* repentance.

පශ්චිම, *Paschima*, *a.* west, behind, after.

පශ්චිම චක්‍රවාටය, *Paschima-chakrawátaya*, *s.* western division of this Sakwala: see සක්වළ *sakwala*.

පශ්චිමතරු, *Paschima-taru*, *s.* evening star.

පශ්චිමදිග, *Paschima-diga*, *s.* (පශ්චිම west, දිග quarter) the west.

පශ්චිමභාගය, *Paschima-bhágaya*, *s.* (පශ්චිම and භාග *bhága* side) the west, western side.

පශ්චිමයාමය, *Paschima-yámaya*, *s.* (පශ්චිම afterward, යාම *yáma* watch of four hours) last of the three watches of the night.

පශු, *Pasu*, *s.* animal in general, beast, any living being; screw pine, *pandanus fascicularis*, [Coll: මුදුකෙයියා *múdukeyiyá*]; fig tree, *ficus glomerata*, [Colloq. අට්ටික්කා *attikká*].

පශුගන්ධා, *Pasugandhá*, *s.* plant, root of which is highly medicinal, *physalis flexuosa;* plant, *gynandropsis pentaphylla*, [Colloq. වේලා *wélá*].

පශුපති, *Pasupati*, *s.* name of Siva, [Colloq. ඊශ්වරයා *íswarayá*].

පශුපාල, *Pasupála*, *s.* herdsman.

පශුපාලන, *Pasupálana*, *s.* tending or rearing cattle.

පස්, *Pas*, *s.* earth, mould, soil; side; touch, feeling: *a.* five; after.

පස්ඇස්, *Pas-es*, *s.* (පස් five, ඇස් eye) epithet of Buddha, alluding to his five mental attributes: see පඤ්චාක්ෂිය *pañchákshiya*.

පස් ඉඳුරන්, *Pas-induran*, Elu form of පඤ්ච ඉන්ද්‍රිය *pañcha-indriya*, which see.

පස් ඉරණම, *Pas-iranama*, *s.* (පස් earth, ඉරණම fate, destiny) place or ground intended for a grave.

පස්කම්, *Paskam*, } *s.* five objects of sense, පස්කම්රස, *Paskamrasa*, } sensual gratification (poetical term); Elu form of පඤ්චකාමය *pañchakámaya*,

පස්කලණ, *Paskalana*, see පඤ්චකල්‍යාණ *pañchakalyána*.

පස්කිරි වක්කරණවා, *Paskiri-wakkaranawá*, *v.* to perform a ceremony called sprinkling the five kinds of milk when the blossoming season of the crops is over.

පස්කුල, *Pas-kula*, *s.* (පස් five, කුල tribe) the five handicraft castes or trades, viz. carpenter, weaver, washerman, barber and shoe or sandal maker.

පස්කුළු, *Paskulu*, *s.* (පස් and කුළු spice) the aggregate of five spices, viz. pepper, ගම්මිරිස් *gammiris*, dill, උළුවා *uluwá*, coriander, කොත්තමල්ලි *kottamalli*, and two varieties of cummin seed, called සුදුදුරු *sududuru* and මහදුරු *mahaduru*.

පස්කෙළි, *Paskeli*, *s.* pleasure derived from the indulgence of the five senses.

පස්කොල, *Paskola*, *s.* (පස් and කොල spice) the aggregate of five spices, viz. long pepper, [Coll: තිප්පිලි *tippili*], its root, [Colloq. තිප්පිලි මුල් *tippili-mul*], piper chavya, [Colloq. සිවියවැල් *siviya-wel*]; *plumbago zeylanica*, [Colloq. රත්නෙතුල් *ratnetul*], and dry ginger, [Colloquial: සිද්දිඟුරු *siddinguru*].

පස්කැටිය, *Pas-ketiya*, *s.* clod of earth, ball or lump of clay.

පස්කැන්, *Pasken*, *s.* ear-ring.

පස්ගතිය, *Pasgatiya*, *s.* (පස් and ගති *gati* being, state) five states of existence, into one of which man must pass after death, viz. he becomes a god, man again, a sprite or goblin, an animal, or goes into hell.

පස්ගෝරස, *Pasgórasa*, *s.* (පස් five, ගෝ belonging to a cow, රස taste, flavour) the five articles derived from the cow, viz. milk, කිරි *kiri*, ghee, or clarified butter, ගිතෙල් *gitel*, curds, දී *dí*, butter-milk, මෝරු *móru*, and butter වෙඬරු *wendaru*.

පස්තෙල්, *Pas-tel*, *s.* (පස් and තෙල් oil) five common medicinal oils: castor oil, [Colloq. එඬරු තෙල් *endaru-tel*], sesamum, [Colloq. තලතෙල් *tala-tel*], ghee, [Colloq. ගිතෙල් *gitel*], oil of the nimba tree, [Colloq. කොහොඹ තෙල් *kohomba-tel*], and the oil or spirit distilled from the *bassia longifolia*, [Colloq. මීතෙල් *mí-tel*].

පස්ධාතුව, *Pasdhátuwa*, *s.* (පස් five, ධාතු *dhátu* elements, primary or elementary substances) earth, fire, water, wind, and ákása or atmosphere.

පස්නා, *Pasná*, *a.* scorched, burnt, heated, fried.

පස්පන, *Paspana*, *s.* name of Varuṇa regent of the west and deity of the waters, god of rain.

පස්පල, *Paspala*, } *s.* five ingredients used
පස්පලවත, *Paspalawata*, } with the betel, viz. camphor, bdellium, cinnamon, cardamums, and ginger.

පස්පවු, *Paspawu*, see පඤ්චපාපය *pañchapápaya*.

පස්පිඩැල්ල, *Paspiḍella*, *s.* (පස් earth, පිඩැල්ල clod) lump of earth, clod.

පස්පියුම්, *Paspiyum*, *s.* (පස් five, පියුම් nymphæa) five varieties of the nymphæa or water lily.

පස්පොළව, *Pas-poḷawa*, *s.* (පස් earth, පොළව ground) ground or land, one of the three structures of which this world is supposed to consist.

පස්පැහැය, *Paspęhęya*, } *s.* (පස් five, පැහැ *pęhę*
පස්පෑ, *Paspé*, } or පෑ *pé* colour) five primitive colours, viz. white, black, blue or green, yellow, and red.

පස්බිඩැල්ල, *Pasbiḍella*, } *s.* small quantity of earth
පස්බුද, *Pasbuda*, } or clay, clod.

පස්බැලුම්, *Pas-bęlum*, *s.* (පස් five, බැලුම *bęluma* looking) five prospective views which Bódhisat took when living in the Tusita-bhawana respecting his approaching assumption of the Buddhaship, viz. to ascertain the proper time to be born, the world in which to be born, in what Dwípa or country, in what race or family, and who was to be his mother.

පස්මර, *Pasmara*, } *s.* (පස් and මර enemy)
පස්මරුන්, *Pasmarun*, } five great obstructions or enemies in the road to Nirwáṇa, viz. පඤ්චක්ලේශ *pañchaklésa*, පඤ්චස්කන්ධ *pañchaskandha*, මෘත්‍යු *mrityu*, වසවර්ති *wasawartti*, and අභිසංස්කාර *abhi-sanskára*, which see.

පස්මස්, *Pasmas*, *s.* grain grown on dry soil, *eleusine coracana*, [Colloq. කුරක්කන් *kurakkan*].

පස්මහ ගඟ, *Pasmaha-ganga*, see පඤ්චමහා ගඞ්ගාව *pañchamahá-gañgáwa*.

පස්මුල්, *Pas-mul*, see පඤ්චමූල *pañcha-múla*.

පස්මේන්තුව, *Pasméntuwa*, *s.* fringe, gold lace.

පස්රස, *Pasrasa*, see පඤ්චරසා *pañcha-rasá*.

පස්ලුණු, *Pas-luṇu*, see පඤ්චලවණ *pañcha-lawaṇa*.

පස්ලෝ, *Pasló*, *s.* five metals, compound of copper, brass, tin, lead, and iron: see පඤ්චලෝහ *pañcha-lóha*.

පස්වග, *Paswaga*, *s.* (පස් five, වග sort) five sorts, five kinds.

පස්වග මහණ, *Paswaga-mahaṇa*, *s.* (පස්වග belonging to a group of five, මහණ ascetic) five brahmins that accompanied Buddha when he embraced asceticism.

පස්වණක් ප්‍රිති, *Paswaṇak-priti*, *s.* five degrees of joy, viz. ඛුද්දකාපිති *khuddaká-píti*, slight joy, ඛණිකාපිති *khaṇiká-píti*, momentary joy, ඔක්කන්තිකාපිති *okkantiká-píti*, joy that comes like a sudden shock (like a wave breaking upon the shore) උබ්බෙගපිති *ubbega-píti*, transporting joy, (that will make you leap into the air) and ඵරණපිති *pharaṇa-píti*, all pervading joy. Childers.

පස්වත්, *Paswat*, *s.* Ṣiva; lion, [Colloq. සිංහයා *sinhayá*].

පස්වන, *Paswana*, *s.* (පස් five, වන corruptly for වණ *waṇa* colour, or වන being) five colours, see පස්පැහැය *paspęhęya*: *a.* fifth.

පස්වරු, *Paswaru*, *s.* (පස් after, වරු time) afternoon.

පස්වලලු, *Pas-walalu*, *s.* ornament.

පස්වාදහස, *Paswádahasa*, *s.* (පස් five, වා year, දහස thousand) five thousand years, the period between the death of Buddha and the birth of his successor.

පස්විස්ස, *Pasvissa*, *s.* twenty-five, [Colloq. විසිපහ *visipaha*].

පස්විසි, *Pasvisi*, *a.* twenty-five, [Colloq. විසිපස් *visi pas*.

පස්විසි මහභය, *Pasvisi-maha-bhaya*, *s.* (පස්විසි twenty-five, මහ great, භය fear) twenty-five circumstances connected with existence which are sources of great fear, viz. birth, old age, sickness, death, and sorrow; these being alike incident to living beings in past and future states of existence as well as in the present are accordingly reckoned threefold, or fifteen in all; to which are added ten more, viz. fear of thieves, enmity, oppression, water, fire, conscience, persecution, punishment, wild animals, and incurable affliction.

පස්වෙනි, *Pasweni*, *a.* fifth.

පස්වැන්න, *Paswęnna*, *s.* fifth year, fifth one in order.

පස්ස, *Passa*, *s.* hinder part, the after, posterior or latter part.

පස්සය, *Passaya*, see කහඹිලියා *kahambiliyá*.

පස්සෙන්, *Passen*, *ad.* behind, from behind.

පස්සේ, *adv.* afterwards.

පස්හි, *Pashí*, *s.* (පස් five, හී arrow) name of Anańgayá the Indian Cupid alluding to his holding five arrows in his hand: (loc. case of පස් *pas* side) by the side of.

පස, *Pasa*, *s.* article; number five; side; Elu form of ප්‍රත්‍යය *pratyaya*, which see.

පසඇට, *Pasa-ęta*, *s.* die, dice.

පසක්, *Pasak*, *a.* perceivable by the senses; experienced, known by experience: see ප්‍රත්‍යක්‍ෂ *pratyaksha*.

පසඟ, *Pasanga*, *s.* (පස් *pas* five, අඟ *anga* limb) five parts of the body which must be bent and touch the ground when saluting Buddha, viz. waist, elbows, knees, head, and toes; tortoise; aggregate of five parts or things.

පසඟතුරු, *Pasangaturu*, *s.* (පස් *pas* five, අඟ *anga* limb, තුරු musical instrument) five sorts of musical instruments, [Colloq. පඤ්චාඞ්ගිකතූර්‍ය *pañcháńgika-túrya*]; viz. ආතත *átata*, විතත *vitata*, ආතතවිතත *átata-vitata*, ඝන *ghana*, සුසිර *susira*; see each in its place.

පසඟුල්, *Pasangul*, see පඤ්චාඞ්ගුල *pañcháńgula*.

පසඟුල් රුක, *Pasangul-ruka*, *s.* castor-oil tree, [Colloq. එරඬු *erandu*].

පසඩ, *Pasaḍa*, *s.* game, kind of dice.

පසඩ මස, *Pasaḍa-masa*, *s.* third and fourth quarters of the moon, the dark fortnight, [Colloq. කළුවර දෙපෝය *kaḷuwara-depóya*].

පසතුරු, *Pasaturu*, see පඤ්චතූර්‍යය *pañchatúryaya*.

පසන, *Pasana*, *s.* joy, gladness, pleasure, delight: see ප්‍රසන්න *prasanna*.

පසපන, *Pasapana*, *s.* name of Wesamuṇi or Kuvéra god of riches.

පසම, *Pasama*, *s.* gold stone.

පසමිතුරා, *Pasa-miturá*, *s.* enemy, adversary, opponent, [Colloq. හතුරා *haturá*].

පසය, *Pasaya*, *s.* gift, favour received: articles given to a priest of Buddha.

පසරණ, *Pasaraṇa*, *s.* (ප before, සරණ going) cloth spread on the ground, carpet; lacker work, enamel; going forth, spreading.

පසල්, *Pasal*, *s.* (ප before, අසල් near) near, proximate, adjoining, neighbouring.

පසල, *Pasala*, *s.* extremities of a kingdom, or part distant from the capital.

පසව, *Pasawa*, *s.* (ප and සව to bring forth) bringing forth, [Colloq. වැදීම *wędíma*].

පසවත්, *Pasawat*, *s.* lion, [Colloq. සිංහයා *sinhayá*]; *a.* attaching a grammatical affix.

පසවිය, *Pasariya*, *s.* (පස් *pas* five, අවිය *aviya* weapon) name of Anańgayá alluding to his being armed with five arrows; five warlike instruments, viz. sword, helmet, bow, shield and battle axe.

පසැස්, *Pasas*, *s.* (පස් *pas* and ඇස් *ęs* eye) five-eyed one, name of Buddha, alluding to his five attributes: see පඤ්චාක්‍ෂිය *pañchákshiya*.

පසස්නා, *Pasasná*, *a.* good, excellent, comely.

පසස, *Pasasa*, *s.* joy, gladness; praise, fame, renown.

පසළොස්වක, *Pasaḷoswaka*, see පහළොස්වක *pahaḷoswaka*.

පසළොස, *Pasaḷosa*, *s.* (පස five, ළොස substituted for දස *dasa* ten) number fifteen.

පසාර, *Pasára*, *s.* hindrance, obstacle, impediment, [Colloq. වැළැක්වීම *węḷękvíma*]; extending; stretching forth; pretence.

පසාරුකරණවා, *Pasárukaraṇawá*, *v.* to put through as thread through a needle: to pass as a document through an office.

පසිදු, *Pasidu*, *a.* celebrated, famous.

පසිඳ, *Pasinda*, *a.* (ප intensitive prefix, සිඳ to cut, to divide) *part.* having destroyed, exterminated; judged, investigated, discriminated.

පසිඳිනවා, *Pasindinawá*, *v.* to investigate, to judge: to examine; to destroy, to extirpate, to root out.

පසිලින්, *Pasilin*, *s.* religious hermit, ascetic.

පසු, *Pasu*, *ad.* after, behind; see also පශු *pasu*.

පසුකරණවා, *Pasukaraṇawá*, *v.* to delay, to postpone; to pass.

පසුගමන්යනවා, *Pasugaman-yanawá*, *v.* to accompany as on a journey.

පසුගමන, *Pasu-gamana*, *s.* accompanying, conducting, escorting.

පසුගිය, *Pasugiya*, *a.* past, former, ancient, last.

පසුඝාතය, *Pasughátaya*, *s.* (පසු animal, ඝාත *gháta* killing) taking away life, slaughtering animals.

පසුජාති, *Pasujáti*, *s.* animal in general, [Colloq. සත්වයා *satwayá*].

පසුතැවි, *Pasutęvi*, } *s.* (පසු after, තැවි or තැ
පසුතැවිලි, *Pasutęvili*, } විලි sorrow) repentance, contrition, remorse.

පසුතැවිලිවෙනවා, *Pasutęvili-wenawá*, *v.* to repent.

පසුන්, *Pasun*, *a.* (ප exceeding, සුන් broken, discriminated) cut, decided; judged, examined, investigated, explained.

පසුනු, *Pasunu*, *s.* master, lord; husband: *a.* near, proximate, adjoining.

පසුපති, *Pasupati*, *s.* name of Ṣiva, [Colloq. ඊශ්වර යා *íṣwarayá*].

පසුපස්සේ, *Pasupassé*, *ad.* behind, backward, hindmost; afterwards, by and bye.

පසුපාලක, *Pasupálaka*, *s.* (පසු and පාල who preserves, ක aff.) herdsman.

පසුපෙර, *Pasupera*, *ad.* behind and before.

පසුබට, *Pasubaṭa*, *s.* (පසු behind, බට descending) retrograding; deteriorating; neglect, dilatoriness, delay; obstruction, impediment.

පසුබටවෙනවා, *Pusubaṭawenawá*, *v.* to retrograde, to backslide; to be disheartened.

පසුබසිනවා, *Pasubasinawá*, } *v.* to lag; to retreat,
පසුබහිනවා, *Pasubahinawá*, } to retire backward, to flee away.

පසුම්බිය, *Pasumbiya*, *s.* small wallet or purse.

පසුර, *Pasura*, *s.* foot; batch of wood, float of wood on a river, raft.

පසුරු, *Pasuru*, *s.* plur. of the preceding; tortoise; boat, ship, vessel of any kind; claws or finger nails.

පසුව, *Pasuwa*, *ad.* after, afterward; behind, backward.

පසුවුනු, *Pasuwunu*, *a.* elapsed; passed, gone by.

පසුවෙනවා, *Pasuwenawá*, *v.* to be behind, to be after; to be delayed, to be postponed; to be passed; to remain.

පසූත, *Pasúta*, *a.* brought forth, born.

පසේබුදුන්, *Pasébudun*, *s.* (පස් *pas* from පති *pati* severally, ඒ *é* for එක *eka* one, one by one, බුදුන් Buddha) inferior class of Buddhas who frequently appeared in the world previous to the birth of Gautama Buddha; although they assumed the habits of Buddhist ascetics and practised the austerities which lead to Nirwáṇa or final emancipation, yet they obtained this state without any legislative power or other prerogatives peculiar to a supreme Buddha, and rendered no assistance to others.

පසැඹුල, *Pasẹmbula*, *s.* (පස් *pas* five, ඇඹුල *ẹmbula* acid) juice of five acid plants, viz. pomegranate, citron, jujube, spondias or hog plum, and sorrel.

පසැස්, *Pasẹs*, see පඤ්චාක්ෂිය *pañchákshiya*.

පහ, *Paha*, *s.* fire, house, mansion, palace, residence of a king or nobleman, [Colloq. මාලිගාව *máligáwa*]; five: *ad.* aside, away.

පහකරණවා, *Pahakaraṇawá*, *v.* (පහ aside, කරණවා to do) to drive away, to put out of the way, to set aside, to cast off, to reject; to retaliate.

පහකුම්භ, *Pahakumbha*, *s.* hinder parts of an elephant or of any animal.

පහට්ටුකරණවා, *Pahaṭṭukaraṇamá*, *v.* to play tricks, to deal cunningly.

පහටු, *Pahaṭu*, *a.* pleased, delighted.

පහණ, *Pahaṇa*, *s.* stone. gravel.

පහණබෙය, *Pahaṇabeya*, *s.* plant, *plectranthus scutellaroides*, [Colloq. පොල්පලා *polpalá*].

පහත්, *Pahat*, *a.* low, under.

පහත්කරණවා, *Pahatkaraṇawá*, *v.* to lower, to degrade, to abase, to let down.

පහත්වෙනවා, *Pahatwenawá*, *v.* to be lowered, to be abased.

පහත, *Pahata*, *ad.* below, under, underneath.

පහදන, *Pahadana*, see පැහැදීම *pẹhẹdíma*.

පහදනවා, *Pahadanawá*, *v.* to praise, to celebrate, to eulogise, to make clear: pret. පැහැදුවා *pẹhẹduwá*.

පහදවනවා, *Pahadawanawá*, the foregoing verb in the causal form, to cause to be pleased, to convert to a religion: pret. පැහැදෙව්වා *pẹhẹdewwá*.

පහදිනවා, *Pahadinawá*, *v.* to be pleased or favorable, to become clear: pret. පැහැදුනා *pẹhẹduná*.

පහදෙවිය, *Pahadeviya*, *s.* palace, royal residence, mansion.

පහන්, *Pahan*, *s.* morning; light; lamps: *a.* pleased, glad.

පහන්කඩය, *Pahankaḍaya*, *s.* (පහන් and කඩ *kaḍa* cloth) wick of a lamp or candle.

පහන්දම, *Puhandáma*, *s.* (පහන් lamp, දම cord, string) number of lamps hung on a rope, row of lights, chandelier.

පහන්දැල්ල, *Pahandẹlla*, *s.* flame of a lamp, blaze of a candle, pl. පහන්දැලි *pahandẹli*.

පහන්රුක, *Pahan-ruka*, *s.* (පහන් and රුක tree) candlestick.

පහන්වෙනවා, *Pahanweṇawá*, *v.* to become morning, to dawn.

පහන, *Pahana*, *s.* lamp, pl. පහන් *pahan*.

පහනවා, *Pahanawá*, *v.* to solder, to weld, to fasten: pret. පැහැව්වා *pẹhẹwwá*.

පහය, *Pahaya*, *s.* temple, any building consecrated to a deity; palace, royal residence, mansion; means, way; dwelling house; Elu form of ප්‍රාසාද *prásáda*.

පහර, *Pahara*, *s.* knock, blow, stroke, slap.

පහරණවා, *Paharaṇawá*, *v.* to strike, to fist, to cuff; to evacuate by stool: pret. පැහැරුවා *pęhęruwá*.

පහරස්, *Paharas*, *a.* hard, solid, firm, strong, [Colloq. දැඩි *dędi*].

පහස, *Pahasa*, *s.* touch, feeling; sense of feeling, sensibility: pl. පහස් *pahas*.

පහසු, *Pahasu*, *a.* hale, sound, healthy; easy, light, convenient.

පහසුවෙනවා, *Pahasuwenawá*, *v.* to recover from sickness; to become easy or convenient.

පහළ, *Pahaḷa*, *s.* publicity, notoriety: *a.* public, published, made known: *ad.* below, beneath, underneath; under, deficient, (less than.)

පහළව, *Pahaḷawa*, see පහළහ *pahaḷaha*.

පහළවෙනවා, *Pahaḷawenawá*, *v.* to come into existence without an apparent cause, to be manifest, to spring into being, as එළිය පහළවුනා *eliya pahaḷawuná*, light commenced to be; to come down as from heaven.

පහළහ, *Pahaḷaha*, *s.* (පහ five, ළහ for දස *dasa* ten) number fifteen.

පහළොස්වක, *Pahaḷoswaka*, *s.* (පහළොස් fifteen, වක lunar day) fifteenth day or day of full moon.

පහළොස, *Pahaḷosa*, see පසළොස *pasaḷosa*.

පහා, *Pahá*, *part.* having left or rejected.

පහාර, *Pahára*, *s.* beating, scratching; watch of four hours.

පහිලස්, *Pahilas*, *s.* sandals, kind of wooden slippers.

පහුපස්සේ, *Pahupassé*, see පසුපස්සේ *pasupassé*.

පහුබහිනවා, *Pahubahinawá*, *v.* to retreat, to flee, to run away.

පහුර, *Pahura*, *s.* raft; rope made of the stalk of a creeping plant, *sanseviera zeylanica*, [Colloq. නියඳ *niyanda*]; large number of bamboos together to float as a boat to carry timber etc. in canals or rivers, pl. පහුරු *pahuru*.

පහුරු, *Pahuru*, *s.* finger nails, claws, [Colloq. නියපොතු *niyapotu*.

පහුරුගානවා, *Pahurugánawá*, *v.* (පහුරු and ගානවා to apply) to scratch, to dig with the nails.

පහුව, *Pahuwa*, *ad.* after, behind, afterward, subsequent, by and by, presently.

පහූත, *Pahúta*, *a.* much, many, very, large.

පහූතජිව්හා, *Pahúta-jivhá*, *s.* (පහූත large, ජිව්හා tongue) name or epithet of Buddha, alluding to the largeness of his tongue, which is considered as one of his personal beauties.

පළකරණවා, *Paḷakaraṇawá*, *v.* to reveal, to discover, to disclose; to publish, to spread abroad; to commence a work.

පළන, *Paḷana*, *s.* yoke of a cart; cleaving, rending, splitting.

පළනවා, *Paḷanawá*, *v.* to split, to cleave, to rend, to tear asunder: pret. පැළුවා *pęluwá*.

පළමු, *Paḷamu*, *a.* first, former, prior, previous, before; past, gone by.

පළමුදා, *Paḷamudá*, *s.* two days before yesterday.

පළමුවෙනි, *Paḷamuweni*, *a.* (පළමු former, වෙනි being) first, principal, chief, head.

පළය, *Paḷaya*, *s.* roof, covering.

පළසෙවෙනි, *Paḷa-seweni*, *s.* shade, the shade of a roof.

පළි, *Paḷi*, *s.* revenge; retaliation, satisfaction for an injury.

පළිගන්නවා, *Paḷigannawá*, *v.* to retaliate, to take revenge, to avenge.

පළිගහනවා, *Paḷigahanawá*, *v.* (පළි revenge, ගහනවා to strike) to seek redress by prostrating in presence of the king to attract his attention to the cause of complaint; to make a complaint, as insufficient, desiring more; to murmur; to state one's grievance before a deity in a heathen temple.

පළිඟු, *Paḷingu*, *s.* crystal, common rock crystal.

පළිබෝධය, *Paḷibódhaya*, *s.* (පළි for පරි *pari*, බෝධ *bódha* substituted for රුධ *rudha* obstruct) guilt, crime, accusation.

පළිය, *Paḷiya*, *s.* revenge, retaliation; redress, satisfaction for an injury.

පළිරෝධය, *Paḷiródhaya*, *s.* (පළි for පරි *pari* රුධ *rudha* to oppose) crime, fault, guilt, accusation.

පළු, *Paḷu*, *s.* knot, joint, joint in bamboo etc. sprout, germ; timber tree, *mimusops hexandra* or *m. indica*, *(Sapotaceæ)*.

පළුඅණේ, *Paḷu-ęné*, *s.* (පළුව *paḷuwa* and අණේ nail) joint, fastening.

පළුකන්, *Paḷukan*, } *s*, plant, *uvaria zeylanica*,
පළුකැන්, *Paḷukęn*, } *(Anonaceæ)*.

පළුටු, *Paḷuṭu*, *s.* tree, *hernandia peltata* or *h. sonora*, *(Lauraceæ)*.

පළුතණ, *Paḷu-taṇa*, *s.* club rush, *scirpus cibaris*.

පළුදුව, *Paḷuduwa*, *s.* defect, flaw; wound, scar.

පළුදෙල, *Paḷudela*, see පලදල *paladala*.

පළුපත, *Paḷupata*, *s.* oar; leaf of the *mimusops hexandra*; leaf of the palm tree.

පළුපළන, *Paḷupaḷana*, s. name of Kataragama-deviyó, the Indian god of war; splitting, breaking.

පළුපළනවා, *Paḷupaḷanawá*, v. to split, to cleave.

පළුමුදුව, *Paḷu-muduwa*, s. key-ring.

පළුව, *Paḷuwa*, s. the part cut off.

පළුවිර, *Paḷuvíra*, s. tree, *guatteria dulcis.*

පළේ, *Paḷé*, s. roof, thatch of a house: pl. පළ *paḷa.*

පළේ ලනවා, *Paḷé-lanawá*, v. to put the roof on a building.

පළොල්, *Paḷol*, s. tree bearing the trumpet flower, *stereospermum suaveolens: a.* brown.

පළොල්වන්, *Paḷolwan*, s. brown; pale red, [Colloq. මදක්රතු *madak-ratu*].

පා, *Pá*, s. (පා to drink etc.) water; foot; sin, moral demerit; lust, passion; wooden fork; bowl; the residence of Ṣakra; cup, drinking cup; tree in general; declaring, making known; root of a tree; milk, rice-milk; mansion, palace, royal residence.

පාං, *Páṇ*, s. bread. (Port.)

පාංගෙඩිය, *Páṇ-gediya*, s. loaf.

පාංශු, *Páṇṣu*, s. dust; dirt, filth; earth, clay; manure: see පාංසු *páṇsu.*

පාංශුකූල, *Páṇṣukúla*, s. (පාංශු dust, කූල heap) old cast off clothes, such as may be picked up on dunghills or in cemeteries, which had been taken from the dead previous to the bodies being burnt.

පාංශුකූල චීවරය, *Paṇṣukúla-chíwaraya*, s. (පාංශු කූල and චීවරය priest's robe) robes or dress of a priest which must be made from the páṇṣukúla according to one of the ordinances of the priesthood: see තෙලෙස්ධුතාංග *teḷesdhutánga.*

පාංශුජ, *Páṇṣuja*, s. kind of salt.

පාංශුපිශාච, *Páṇṣu-piṣácha*, s. (පාංශු dirt, filth, පිශාච sprite, goblin) class of sprites or goblins who are said to frequent dunghills and the cemeteries of the dead, and live on ordure and the remains of dead carcases.

පාංශුල, *Páṇṣula*, s. name of Ṣiva; one of Ṣiva's weapons: *a.* dusty, covered with dust.

පාංශුලා, *Páṇṣulá*, s. unchaste woman, one who has broken her marriage vow; a woman during menstruation.

පාංසු, *Páṇsu*, s. dust. [Colloquial: දූවිලි *dúvili*], manure, [Colloq. පොර *póra*].

පා ඇලුව, *Pá-aḷuwa*, s. that which supports the bedstead.

පා ඇට, *Pá-ęta*, s. bones of the foot.

පාක්කුඩම, *Pákkuḍama*, s. curiosity, valuable as a present for a king; gift, [Colloq. තෑග්ග *tęgga*].

පාක්‍ය, *Pákya*, s. medicinal salt impregnated with iron, *bit loben;* nitre, saltpetre, [Colloq. බළල්ලුණු *baḷal-luṇu*, යවකාරලුණු *yawakára-luṇu*].

පාක්ෂායණ, *Pákshâyaṇa*, a. (පක්ෂ *paksha* half a month) belonging to or occurring in a fortnight.

පාක්ෂික, *Pákshika*, s. (පක්ෂි bird, or පක්ෂ *paksha* party, ඉක *ika* pers. aff.) fowler, bird-catcher; partizan: *a.* factious, belonging to a party.

පාක, *Páka*, s. maturity, natural or artificial; state of being ripened or cooked; digestion, assimilation of food; vessel in which any thing is dressed, as boiler, sauce-pan etc.; greyness of hair; general panic or the subversion of a country; name of a demon who was conquered by Indra; young of any animal, bird etc.

පාක ඵල, *Páka-phala*, s. tree, *carissa carandas.* [Colloq. මහ කරඹ *maha-karaṃba*].

පාකය, *Pákaya*, see පාක *páka.*

පාකරණවා, *Pákaraṇawá*, v. to push off, to launch, to let a thing float (as a boat in the water); to retaliate, to take revenge.

පාකල, *Pákala*, s. plant, *costus speciosus*, [Colloq. තෙබු *tebu* and සෙංකොට්ටම් *seṇkoṭṭam*]; fever in an elephant.

පාකලි, *Pákali*, s. tree, *bauhinia candida.*

පාකලී, *Pákalí*, s. common cucumber, *cucumis utilatissimus* or *c. satirus*, [Colloq. රටකැකිරි *raṭa-kękiri* or පිපිඤ්ඤ *pipiñña*].

පාකශාසන, *Páka-ṣásana*, s. (පාක demon Páka, ශාසන ruling, overcoming) name of Indra, alluding to his conquering the demon Páka.

පාකශාසනි, *Páka-ṣásaní*, s. (පාකශාසන *páka-ṣásana* Indra, ඊ *í* aff. of descent) son of Indra.

පාකස්ථාන, *Pákasthána*, s. (පාක cooking, ස්ථාන place) kitchen, cooking room, [Colloq. කුස්සිය *kussiya*].

පාකිම, *Pákima*, a. cooked; matured, ripened.

පාකේයුරු, *Pákéyuru*, s. (පා foot, කේයුරු ornament) foot ornament.

පාඛණ්ඩ, *Pákhaṇḍa*, s. (පා for පාල *pila* what nourishes (mankind, virtue), ඛණ්ඩ to subvert) heretic.

පාගණවා, *Págaṇawá*, v. to trample, to tread, to tread out corn by the feet of oxen or men: pret පෑගුවා *pęguwá.*

පාච්චලෙ, *Páchchale*, s. opportunity, occasion.

පාචන, *Páchana*, *s.* medicinal preparation, infusion, decoction of various simples together: *a.* cooking; ripening.

පාචනක, *Páchanaka*, *s.* borax, [Colloq. පුස්කර *puskara*].

පාචන රෝගය, *Páchana-rógaya*, *s.* dysentery.

පාචනවෙනවා *Páchanawenawá*, *v.* to have frequent evacuations from the intestines.

පාචනී, *Páchaní*, *s.* one of the myrobalans, *terminalia chebula*, [Colloq. අරළු *aralu*].

පාචල, *Páchala*, *s.* cooking, maturing; fire, air, wind; thing dressed without the aid of fire; whatever causes digestion.

පාචිත්තිය, *Páchittiya*, } *s.* sin, culpability, slight
පාචිත්‍ය, *Páchitya*, } crime: *a.* requiring expiation, expiatory. There are ninety two priestly offences requiring confession and absolution, enumerated in the Vinaya Piṭaka. Childers.

පාඤ්චාල, *Páñchála*, *s.* sovereign of Pañchála; association of five trades, viz. carpenter, weaver, barber, washerman and shoemaker: *a.* belonging to Pañchála.

පාට, *Páṭa*, *s.* colour; breadth, width, extension, expansion.

පාටක, *Páṭaka*, *s.* half of a village; shore, bank; casting dice, musical instrument; large span; expense or loss of capital or stock.

පාටකරණවා, *Páṭakaraṇawá*, *v.* to colour, to dye.

පාටගානවා, *Páṭa-gánawá*, *v.* to paint; to daub or anoint with coloured unguents, to colour, to tinge.

පාටල, *Páṭala*, *s.* pale red, rose colour; rice ripening in the rains.

පාටලා, *Páṭalá*, } *s.* trumpet flower, *sterospermum*
පාටලි, *Páṭali*, } *suaveolens*, [Colloquial: පලොල් *paḷol*]; lódh, a red dye derived from the bank of the *symplocos racemosa*.

පාටලිපුත්‍ර, *Páṭali-putra*, see පැළලුප් නුවර *pęlalup nuwara*.

පාටව, *Páṭawa*, *s.* cleverness, talent, eloquence.

පාටවැටෙනවා, *Páṭawęṭenawá*, *v.* to colour, to blush, to become coloured, become pale.

පාටිකා, *Páṭiká*, *s.* crystal stone, [Colloq. පළිඟු *paḷingu*].

පාටිපද, *Páṭipada*, *s.* first day after the new or full moon.

පාටිර, *Páṭira*, *s.* field; pungent root, sort of radish; pith or manna of the bamboo; cloud; sieve or cribble; tin; disease arising from wind; sandal.

පාඨ, *Páṭha*, *s.* among the Hindus one of the five great sacraments, viz. the study of the Védas; reading, perusing in general; text.

පාඨක, *Páṭhaka*, *s.* lecturer, public reader of the baṇa or sacred works, religious preceptor.

පාඨය, *Páṭhaya*, see පාඨ *páṭha*.

පාඨශාලා, *Páṭha-ṣálá*, *s.* (පාඨ reading, ශාලා hall) college, school.

පාඨා, *Páṭhá*, *s.* creeping plant, *cissampelos pareira*, [Colloq. දියමිත්ත *diyamitta*].

පාඨීන, *Páṭhína*, *s.* sheat fish, *silurus pelorius*, [Colloq. පෙටියා *peṭiyá*]; public reader or lecturer: see පාඨක *páṭhaka*.

පාඩ, *Páḍa*, *s.* piebald (colour), mixture of black and white.

පාඩගම්, *Páḍagam*, *s.* ankle ring worn by women; foot ornament: see පාදකටක *páda-kaṭaka*.

පාඩම්කරණවා, *Páḍamkaraṇawá*, *v.* to learn, to study a lesson, to learn a lesson by heart, to commit to memory.

පාඩම, *Páḍama*, *s.* lesson, task at school; reading, perusal in general, study of books, pl. පාඩම් *páḍam*.

පාඩසු, *Páḍasu*, *s.* dust, [Colloq. දූවිලි *dúvili*].

පාඩාවාරිය, *Páḍáwáriya*, *s.* mistake, error, [Colloq. වැරැද්ද *węręddla*].

පාඩුකරණවා, *Páḍukaraṇawá*, *v.* to cause deficiency or loss.

පාඩුව, *Páḍuwa*, *s.* deficiency, insufficiency.

පාණ්ඩි, *Páṇḍi*, *v.* yellowish colour; kind of fish.

පාණ්ඩි රට, *Páṇḍi-raṭa*, *s.* name of the ancient Madura kingdom.

පාණ්ඩු, *Páṇḍu*, see පාණ්ඩු *páṇḍu*.

පාණ්ඩර, *Páṇḍara*, *s.* white (colour), yellow orpiment, [Colloq. හිරියල් *hiriyal*].

පාණ්ඩර භූරුහ, *Páṇḍara-bhúruha*, *s.* tree, *echites antidysenterica*, [Colloq. කෙළිඳගස් *keḷinda-gas*].

පාණ්ඩව, *Páṇḍawa*, *s.* yellow (colour); descendant of Páṇḍu.

පාණ්ඩු, *Páṇḍu*, *s.* pale or yellowish white; name of a sovereign of ancient Delhi, nominal father Yudhishṭhira and the other four Páṇḍawa princes; jaundice, [Coll: සෙංගමාලය *sengamálaya*].

පාණ්ඩුකම්බල, *Páṇḍukambala*, *s.* (පාණ්ඩු yellow, කම්බල blanket) sort of blanket, or warm upper garment; housings of a royal elephant; Ṣakra's throne made of an ornamental stone.

පාණ්ඩුකම්බලී, *Páṇḍukambalí*, s. (පාණ්ඩු pale, කම්බල *kambala* blanket, ඊ *í* aff.) coloured or dyed dress; white carriage, conveyance in the construction of which white cloth is used instead of boards; carriage covered with a sort of blanket; housings of a royal elephant.

පාණ්ඩුනාග, *Páṇḍu-nága*, s. tree, *calophyllum inophyllum*, [Colloq. දොඹ *domba*].

පාණ්ඩුර, *Páṇḍura*, s. yellow (colour); white or pale yellow colour; jaundice of a yellowish white colour; white leprosy.

පාණ්ඩුරාකාර, *Páṇḍurákára*, s. (පාණ්ඩුර *páṇḍura* and ආකාර *ákára* manner) yellowish or pale appearance.

පාණ්ඩු රෝග, *Páṇḍu-róga*, s. (පාණ්ඩු and රෝග disease) jaundice.

පාණක, *Páṇaka*, s. worm; insect; any sentient being, one possessing animation, [Colloq. පණුවා *paṇuwá*; සත්වයා *satwayá*].

පාණද, *Páṇadá*, s. (පාණ life, ද what gives) tree which bears the yellow myrobalan, *terminalia chebula*, [Colloq. අරළු *araḷu*].

පාණපාලක, *Páṇapálaka*, s. (පාණ and පාල what preserves, ක aff.) food, aliment, [Colloq. කෑම *kėma*].

පාණාතිපාතය, *Páṇátipátaya*, s. (පාණ *páṇa* and අතිපාත *atipáta* transgression) killing, slaughter, destruction of life, [Colloq. මැරීම *mėríma*].

පාණි, *Páṇi*, s. hand, [Colloq. අත *ata*]; sentient being, one possessing animation; instrument for smoothing the ground; trowel.

පාණිග්‍රහණ, *Páṇigrahaṇa*, } s. marriage, [Colloq. කසාදය *kasádaya*]; laying hold of the hand.
පාණිග්‍රාහ, *Páṇigráha*, }

පාණීත, *Páṇíta*, corruptly for පණීත *paṇíta*, a. soft, delicate; sweet, delicious, saccharine; Páli form of ප්‍රණීත *praṇíta*.

පාණිතල, *Páṇitala*, s. (පාණි hand, තල surface) palm of the hand, [Colloq. අල්ල *alla*].

පාණිනි, *Páṇini*, s. name of a celebrated Sanskrit grammarian.

පාණිපීඩන, *Páṇi-píḍana*, s. marriage, [Colloq. විවාහය *viwáhaya*, කසාදය *kasádaya*].

පාණිප්‍රහාර, *Páṇipraháras*, s. (පාණි hand, ප්‍රහාර beating) blow inflicted by the hand, stroke with the fist, cuff.

පාණිමුක්ත, *Páṇimukta*, s. missile weapon.

පාණිවාද, *Páṇiwáda*, s. (පාණි being, hand, වාද destruction, sounding) killing, slaughter; musician who plays, striking with the hand only.

පාත්, *Pát*, s. falling, descending, alighting: a. down, low, below; beneath, under.

පාත්අහර, *Pát-ahara*, s. (පාත් and අහර way, mode) subjection, submission, humility.

පාත්කරණවා, *Pátkaraṇawá*, v. to lower.

පාත්තයා, *Páttayá*, s. goose.

පාත්තිය, *Páttiya*, s. plot of ground where edible roots are planted, bed of yams etc.

පාත්බහිනවා, *Pátbahinawá*, v. to submit, to yield, to become subject or subservient, to go down.

පාත්‍ර, *Pátra*, s. vessel in general, plate, cup, jar, etc.; vessel or bowl in which the priests beg their food, and from which they eat; fit or competent person; receptacle of any kind, what holds or supports, pl. පාත්‍රා *pátrá*.

පාත්‍රධාතුව, *Pátra-dhátuwa*, s. (පාත්‍ර ascetic's begging bowl, ධාතුව relic) one of the four bowls which were brought to Buddha by the guardian deities of the four quarters of the world, presented to him in the eighth week after his assumption of the Buddhaship; it is said to be made of the clay of blue sapphire, and was brought from the continent of India and preserved as a sacred relic in a Dágaba on the banks of the Mahawėli-ganga near the city of Kandy.

පාත්‍රභූත, *Pátrabhúta*, a. deserving of a present or respectful treatment.

පාත්‍රවැරැල්ල, *Pátra-wėrėlla*, s. fern, *blechnum orientale*.

පාත්‍රා, *Pátrá*, plur. of පාත්‍ර *pátra*.

පාත, *Páta*, see පාත් *pát*.

පාතක, *Pátaka*, s. sin, crime; cause of falling literally or figuratively.

පාතඞ්ගි, *Pátańgi*, s. regent of Saturn.

පාතව්‍යතා, *Pátawyatá*, s. being in the act of falling or descending; state of being worthy of protection.

පාතාලමූලිකා, *Pátála-múliká*, s. plant, *sanseviera zeylanica*. [Colloq. නියඳ *niyaṇḍa*].

පාතාලය, *Pátálaya*, s. regions below; abode of the Nágas or serpent race, the infernal regions under the earth, hell; abyss; valley, dale, low place.

පාතාලවාසී, *Pátála-wási*, s. (පාතාල and වස *wasa* to dwell, ඉ *i* aff.) inhabitant of the regions below, snake or asura; inhabitant of hell; betel creeper, *piper betel*, [Colloq. බුලත් *bulat*].

පාති, *Páti*, s. master, lord, husband; cup, bowl; in the latter sense it is the Páli form of පාත්‍රි *pátri*.

පාතික, *Pátika*, *s.* (පාති bowl, ක pers. aff.) one who carries a bowl, beggar, religious mendicant, priest of Buddha; the Gangetic porpoise.

පාතිමොක්ඛ, *Pátimokkha*, *s.* Páli form of ප්‍රාති මෝක්ෂ *práti-móksha*, which see.

පාතිලි, *Pátilí*, *s.* trap or snare for catching wild animals; priest's begging bowl.

පාතුක, *Pátuka*, *s.* declivity of a mountain, precipice; falling, descending.

පාතුභූත, *Pátubhúta*, *s.* falling, descending, descent.

පාථ, *Pátha*, *s.* sun; fire; water.

පාථස්, *Páthas*, *s.* water: see පාථෝ *páthó*.

පාථෙය, *Pátheya*, *s.* provender, provisions for a journey.

පාථෝ, *Páthó*, *s.* water, [Colloq. වතුර *watura*].

පාථෝද, *Páthóda*, *s.* (පාථෝ and ද what gives) cloud, [Colloq. වලාකුළ *walákuḷa*].

පාථෝධර, *Pátódhara*, *s.* (පාථෝ and ධර what bears) cloud.

පාථෝධි, *Páthódhi*, *s.* (පාථෝ and ධි receptacle) sea, ocean, [Colloq. මුහුද *muhuda*].

පාද්‍ය, *Pádya*, *s.* that which relates to the feet, as water etc. for cleansing.

පාද, *Páda*, *s.* foot, [Colloq. කකුල *kakula*]; foot or root of a tree; ray of light: foot or line of a stanza.

පාදකටක, *Páda-kaṭaka*, *s.* foot ornament or an ornament for the toes: see පාඩගම් *páḍagam* and පාදාභරණය *pádábharaṇaya*.

පාදකිංකිණික, *Páda-kiṅkiṇika*, *s.* tinkling ornaments for the feet or toes.

පාදගුල්ඵ, *Pádagulpha*, *s.* (පාද foot, ගුල්ඵ ankle) ankle bone.

පාදග්‍රහණය, *Páda-grahaṇaya*, *s.* (පාද and ග්‍රහණ *grahaṇa* laying hold of) respectful mode of obeisance by touching the foot of a superior.

පාදචරණ, *Páda-charaṇa*, *s.* (පාද and චරණ who goes) footman; foot-soldier.

පාදජාල, *Páda-jála*, *s.* (පාද and ජාල net) stockings of net work, literally net for the feet, [Colloq. මේස් *més*].

පාදඩයා, *Pádaḍayá*, *s.* vagabond, vagrant, mean low fellow.

පාදඬුව, *Pádanḍuwa*, *s.* (පා foot, දඬු *danḍu* stick) horizontal bar which the people lay hold of when treading out corn.

පාදතල, *Pádatala*, *s.* (පාද and තල plane) sole of the foot.

පාදත්‍රාණ, *Pádatráṇa*, *s.* (පාද foot, ත්‍රාණ protection) boot, shoe.

පාදනවා, *Pádanawá*, *v.* to cleanse, to clear; to elucidate, to explain, to unfold: pret. පෑදුවා *pḗduwá*.

පාදප, *Pádapa*, *s.* tree in general; footstool; cushion for the feet.

පාදපද්ම, *Páda-padma*, *s.* (පාද foot, පද්ම lotus) lotus like foot or feet, epithet used when addressing a king or a nobleman, also when speaking of Buddha.

පාදපරිචාරි, *Pádaparichári*, }
පාදපරිචාරිකා, *Pádaparichárikú*, } *s.* (පාද foot, පරිචාරි servant) wife, [Colloq. භාර්‍යාව *bháryáwa*].

පාදපා, *Pádapá*, *s.* shoe, slipper.

පාදපීඨය, *Páda-píṭhaya*, }
පාදපෝරුව, *Páda-póruwa*, } *s.* (පාද and පීඨ *píṭha* stool, or පෝරුව board) footstool, [Colloq. පාපුටුව *pápuṭuwa*].

පාදප්‍රසාරණ, *Páda-prasáraṇa*, *s.* stretching out the foot on the ground at a salutation.

පාදප්‍රහාරණ, *Páda-prahúraṇa*, *s.* (පාද and ප්‍රහාරණ blow) kick, blow with the foot.

පාදමර්ෂණය, *Páda-marshaṇaya*, see පාදග්‍රහණය *páda-grahaṇaya*.

පාදමූලය, *Pádamúlaya*, *s.* (පාද and මූල *múla* root) heel, [Colloq. විළුඹ *viḷumba*].

පාදය, *Pádaya*, *s.* foot, also a flat boat so called; quarter, part: see පාද *páda*.

පාදර, *Pádara*, *s.* foot of a bed.

පාදරථ, *Páda-ratha*, *s.* (පාද foot, රථ car) shoe, slipper, sandal, [Colloq. සපත්තුව *sapattuwa*, සෙරෙප්පුව *sereppuwa*].

පාදලක්ෂණ, *Páda-lakshaṇa*, *s.* (පාද and ලක්ෂණ mark, token) lines on the foot which denote good or bad fortune.

පාදලාඤ්ඡන, *Páda-láñchhana*, *s.* (පාද and ලාඤ්ඡන impress) impression of the foot.

පාදසංඛලා, *Páda-saṅkhalá*, *s.* (පාද feet, සංඛලා fetter) fetter for the foot, trammel.

පාදසටහන, *Páda-saṭahana*, *s.* (පාද and සටහන mark) footmark, impression of the foot.

පාදසේවන, *Pádaséwana*, *s.* (පාද and සේවන waiting upon) service, duty.

පාදාඞ්ගුලි, *Pádáṅguli*, *s.* (පාද *páda* foot, අඞ්ගුලි *aṅguli* finger) toe.

පාදාඞ්ගුෂ්ඨ, *Pádáṅgushṭha*, *s.* (පාද *páda* and අඞ්ගුෂ්ඨ *aṅgushṭha* thumb) great toe.

පාදාත, *Pádáta*, }
පාදාති, *Pádáti*, } *s.* (පාද *páda* and අත *ata* to go) footman or a man on foot (travelling); foot soldier; infantry.

පාදුන්තය, *Pádántaya*, *s.* (පාද *páda* foot, අන්ත *anta* end) sole of the foot; tip or end of the foot.

පාදාභරණය, *Pádábharaṇaya*, *s.* (පාද *páda* foot, ආභරණ ornament) ornament for the feet or toes: see පාදකටක *páda-kaṭaka*.

පාදාර්ධ, *Pádárdha*, *s.* (පාද *páda* quarter, අර්ධ *ardha* half) eighth; half a line of a stanza.

පාදින, *Pádina*, *s.* quarter, fourth part, [Colloq. හතාරෙන් පංගුව *hataren panguwa*].

පාදිරි උන්නාන්සේ, *Pádiri-unnánsé*, see පාදිලි උන්නාන්සේ *pádili-unnánsé*.

පාදිරි කොකා, *Pádiri-koká*, *s.* white-necked stork, *dissura episcopa*, (*Ciconiidæ* order *Herodiones*).

පාදිලි උන්නාන්සේ, *Pádili-unnánsé*, *s.* Christian clergyman.

පාදුකා, *Páduká*, *s.* (පාදු shoe, කා aff.) shoe, slipper, sandal, [Colloq. සපත්තුව *sapattuwa*].

පාදුකාකාර, *Pádukákára*, *s.* (පාදුකා and කාර who makes) shoe or sandal maker.

පාදුකාව, *Pádukáwa*, *s.* shoe, slipper, sandal; kind of magical incantation repeated over a sick person.

පාදුකෘත්, *Pádukṛit*, *s.* shoemaker, [Colloq. සපත්තු මහන්නා *sapattu-mahanná*].

පාදුපේන, *Pádupéna*, *s.* foresight, caution; preservation, defence.

පාදුප්‍රවේසම, *Pádu-prawésama*, *s.* foresight, caution, vigilance; defence, protection.

පාදූ, *Pádú*, see පාදුකා *páduká*.

පාදේ, *Pádé*, *s.* flat bottomed boat; part, portion, quarter, pl. පාද *páda*.

පාදෝන, *Pádóna*, } *s.* (පා foot, ධෝහන washing) place for washing the feet near the entrance of a temple.
පාදෝහන, *Pádóhana*, }

පාන්, *Pán*, *s.* bread: see පාං *pán̤*; also plur. of පාන *pána*, lamp.

පාන්කඩය, *Pánkaḍaya*, *s.* lamp-wick, piece of rag.

පාන් කඳ, *Pán-kanda*, *s.* (පාන් lamp, කඳ supporter) candlestick.

පාන්චිවෙනවා, *Pánchiwenawá*, see පාන්සිවෙනවා *pánsiwenawá*.

පාන් තාරකාව, *Pán-tárakáwa*, *s.* (පාන් light, තාරකාව star) morning star.

පාන්තිරය, *Pán-tiraya*, *s.* lamp-wick.

පාන්තුඩ, *Pán-tuḍa*, *s.* notch in a lamp.

පාන්ථ, *Pántha*, *s.* traveller, [Colloq. ගමන්යන්නා *gaman-yanná*].

පාන්දර, *Pándara*, *s.* (පාන් light, දර what has) morning, day break.

පාන් පූජාව, *Pán-pújáwa*, *s.* (පාන් and පූජාව offering) offerings of lights to demons: see the next.

පාන් මඩුව, *Pán-maḍuwa*, *s.* (පාන් lamp. මඩුව shed) temporary shed erected for the purpose of offering to and invoking demons; these sheds are so called in consequence of the devil or demon worship being performed by night when the use of lamps is necessary.

පාන්වෙනවා, *Pánwenawá*, *v.* to become morning, to dawn.

පාන්වැටිය, *Pánweṭiya*, *s.* lamp-wick.

පාන්සිය, *Pánsiya*, *s.* shrinking, startling; scolding; rough speech.

පාන්සිවෙනවා, *Pánsiwenawá*, *v.* to scold, to speak roughly.

පාන්සිළ, *Pánsiḷa*, *s.* (පාන් lamp, සිළ crest) flame of a lamp or candle.

පාන, *Pána*, *s.* lamp, light of any kind; drink, drinking; drinking cup or vessel, pl. පාන් *pán*.

පාන පාත්‍රය, *Pána-pátraya*, *s.* (පාන drinking, පාත්‍ර *pátra* vessel) drinking cup, vessel of any kind for drinking.

පාන භාජනය, *Pána-bhájana*, *s.* (පාන and භාජන cup, vessel) drinking vessel, drinking cup.

පානය, *Pánaya*, *s.* drink; any kind of beverage, drinking, [Colloq බීම *bíma*].

පානයකරණවා, *Pánayakaraṇawá*, *v.* to drink.

පානවා, *Pánawá*, *v.* to show, to display; pret. පෑවා *péwá*.

පානාගාරය, *Pánágáraya*, *s.* (පාන *pána* lamp, drinking, අගාර *ágára* house) inhabited house; house for refreshment, tavern, place where spirits or fermented liquors of any kind are sold.

පානිලතා, *Páni-latá*, *s.* rope, or dried stalk of a creeping plant used for that purpose, passed from one end of a foot bridge to the other, to hold on by the hand when crossing; corruption of ඵනිලතා *phani-latá*.

පානීය, *Pániya*, *s.* (පා to drink, අනීයර් *aníyar* participial affix) water, [Colloq. වතුර *watura*]: *a.* drinking, drinkable.

පානුදියර, *Pánu-diyara*, *s.* water in which rice has been cleaned.

පාප්ප, *Páppa*, *s.* child's food, or food prepared for infants, poultice. (Port.)

පාප, *Pápa*, *s.* sin, crime, wickedness, vice, demerit; according to the tenets of Buddhism the guilt or bad effects of pápa will pursue men through every stage of being till a full equivalent has been made so as to neutralize its effects; traitor: *a.* wicked, mischievous, vicious, abandoned, sinful.

පාපක, *Pápaka, s.* (පාප sin, with ක aff.) sin: *a.* sinful.

පාප කර්මය, *Pápa-karmaya, s.* (පාප sin, කර්ම *karma* act) sinful act, wicked deed.

පාපකාරයා, *Pápakáráyá, s.* (පාප and කාර *kára* who does) sinner, depraved man, [Colloq. පව් කාරයා *paukáráyá*].

පාප ක්‍රියාව, *Pápa-kriyáwa, s.* (පාප sinful, ක්‍රියා *kriyá* act) wicked act; vicious proceeding.

පාපගත, *Pápagata, s.* (පාප sin, ගත gone) sinful, wicked, depraved, vicious.

පාපචරිත, *Pápacharita, s.* (පාප and චරිත manner, mode) sinful act, living in sin.

පාපචේතනාව, *Pápa-chétanáwa, s.* (පාප sinful, චේතනාව thought) wicked desire, sinful thought.

පාපචේලි, *Pápachéli, s.* creeping plant, *cissampelos pareira,* [Colloq. දියමිත්ත *diyamitta*].

පාප ධර්මය, *Pápa-dharmaya, s.* (පාප sinful, ධර්ම *dharma* act) demerit, sinful deed.

පාපය, *Pápaya,* see පාප *pápa.*

පාපයා, *Pápayá, s.* (පාප and යා pers. aff.) wicked man, sinner.

පාපානුසය, *Pápánusaya, s.* (පාප *pápa* sinful, අනුසය *anusaya* inclination, thought) retributive inflictions, or according to the tenets of Buddhism the final effects of unvirtuous actions; pápa is an act of demerit that any sentient being, including every class from a god down to a sprite, an animal or reptile, is capable of committing, and its effects will be experienced till a full equivalent has been made; sinful thought, evil desire.

පාපියුම්, *Pápiyum, s.* lotus-like feet.

පාපිෂ්ඨ, *Pápishṭha, s.* (පාප *pápa* sinful, ඉෂ්ඨන් *ishṭhan* aff.) very sinful, wicked, vicious, depraved.

පාපිසුන්, *Pápisun, s.* mat or bundle of straw for wiping the feet.

පාපුච්චාරණය, *Pápuchcháraṇaya, s.* (පාප *pápa* sin, උච්චාරණ *uchcháraṇa* saying) confession, acknowledging guilt.

පාපුටුව, *Páputuwa, s.* footstool.

පාපුස්, *Pápus, s.* slippers. (Port.)

පාබල, *Pábala, s.* (පා foot, බල warrior) infantry, foot soldiers.

පාබලසෙනඟ *Pábala-senanga,* }
පාබලසේනාව, *Pábala-sénáwa,* } *s.* (පාබල foot soldier, සෙනඟ or සේනා *séná* host) army of infantry, one of the four divisions constituting a complete army.

පාබිස්ස, *Pá-bissa, s.* (පා foot, බිස්ස wiping) mat for wiping the feet, bundle of straw used for that purpose.

පාම, *Páma, s.* leprosy, leprous scab, cutaneous disorder, [Colloq. කුෂ්ඨය *kushṭhaya*].

පාමන්, *Páman, s.* cutaneous eruption, herpes, scab.

පාමර, *Pámara, s.* idiot, fool, man following a degrading profession: *a.* wicked, low, vile, base, stupid.

පාමුදු, *Pámudu, s.* bangles for the feet, rings worn by women on the toes.

පාමුල, *Pámula, s.* (පා foot, මුල root) that part of a bed or couch where the feet lie; foot of a bed: *ad.* near the feet, at the feet.

පාමොක්, *Pámok,* Elu form of ප්‍රාතිමෝක්ෂ *prátimóksha,* which see: *a.* chief, principal.

පාය, *Páya, s.* water; milk; plenty, abundance; palace, mansion, residence of a king or nobleman; temple.

පායනවා, *Páyanawá, v.* to clear, to become clear, to shine; to cease; to rise as the sun: pret. පෑව්වා *pẹwwá.*

පායස, *Páyasa, s.* milk, oblation of rice, milk and sugar: *a.* made of milk.

පායාස, *Páyása, s.* (පයස් *payas* milk, අණ් *aṇ* aff.) rice boiled in milk, or rice boiled and mixed with milk; oblation of milk, rice and sugar.

පායු, *Páyu, s.* anus.

පායුග, *Pá-yuga, s.* (පායු anus, ග what goes; or පා foot, යුග couple) ordure, fæces, excrement; breaking wind behind; two feet.

පාර්ථ, *Párttha, s.* king, sovereign, prince, [Colloq. රජ *raja*].

පාර්ථකී, *Pártthakí, s.* tree, *terminalia glabra,* [Colloq. කුඹුක් *kumbuk*].

පාර්ථව, *Pártthawa, s.* greatness, immensity; the eighteenth year of the Indian cycle of sixty.

පාර්ථිව, *Pártthiwa, s.* king, prince, one holding the reins of government, [Colloq. රජ *raja*].

පාර්වත, *Párwata, s.* (පර්වත *parwata* mountain, අණ් *aṇ* aff.) hilly, mountainous.

පාර්වතී, *Párwatí, s.* name of Durgá, in her capacity of daughter of Himálaya, sovereign of the snowy-mountains.

පාර්වතේය, *Párwatéya, s.* antimony: *a.* mountain-born.

පාර්ශ්වගත, *Párṣwagata, a.* partial.

පාර්ශ්වය, *Párṣwaya, s.* side, part.

පාර්ශ්වශූල, *Párṣwa-ṣúla*, *s.* side-pain, spasm of the chest, stitch.

පාර්ශ්වික, *Párṣvika*, *s.* partisan: *a.* lateral.

පාර්ෂ්ණි, *Párshṇi*, *s.* heel; back; rear of an army; violent woman.

පාර, *Pára*, *s.* way, road, path; blow, stroke; the further or opposite bank of a river; end, termination, extremity, boundary, limit; time, as එක පාර *ekapára*, one time, once.

පාර අරිණවා, *Pára-ariṇawá*, *v.* to open or construct a road; to get out of the way.

පාරග, *Páraga*, *s.* act of crossing, crossing over.

පාරගත, *Páragata*, *a.* crossed, gone over; metaphorically, taught, learned, fully instructed.

පාරට්ටු, *Páraṭṭu*, *a.* excellent, superior, surpassing.

පාරට්ටුකරණවා, *Páraṭṭukaraṇawá*, *v.* to praise, to extol, to eulogize; to flatter, to boast.

පාරට්ටුව, *Páraṭṭuwa*, *s.* praise, panegyric; excellence, superiority, boasting.

පාරත, *Párata*, *s.* quicksilver.

පාරතොට, *Páratoṭa*, *s.* whereabouts of a journey.

පාරද, *Párada*, *s.* quicksilver, [Colloq. රසදිය *rasadiya*].

පාරදාර්‍ය, *Páradárya*, *s.* (පර *para* another, දාර *dára* wife) adultery, fornication.

පාරදාරික, *Páradárika*, *s.* (පරදාර *paradára* other's wife, ඉක *ika* pers. aff.) adulterer, fornicator.

පාරප්‍රාප්ත, *Paráprápta*, *a.* (පාර termination, ප්‍රාප්ත come) ended, terminated, finished, concluded, completed; (metaphorically,) learned, taught, instructed.

පාරමිතාව, *Páramitáwa*, *s.* (පාරං *páraṇ* opposite bank, ඉත gone, or පාරමි *párami* the feminine form of පරම *parama* chief or highest, and තා *tá* affix of abstract nouns); highest state of perfection gone over, crossed, as a river; metaphorically, any thing completely done or fully accomplished; in this sense it is chiefly used in reference to the religious ordinances, duties and works of merit which must be completely performed as a pre-requisite to the Buddhaship. The following are the ten chief páramitáwas, viz. දානපාරමිතා *dána-páramitá*, almsgiving, ශීලපාරමිතා *síla-páramitá*, moral virtue, නිෂ්ක්‍රමපාරමිතා *nishkrama-páramitá*, religious retirement from the world, ප්‍රඥාපාරමිතා *prajñá-páramitá*, wisdom, වීර්‍යපාරමිතා *vírya-páramitá*, perseverance, ක්ෂාන්තිපාරමිතා *kshánti-páramitá*, mildness, tranquility, සත්‍යපාරමිතා *satya-páramitá*, truth, අධිෂ්ඨානපාරමිතා *adhishṭhána-páramitá*, powerful or strong volition, මෛත්‍රීපාරමිතා *maitrí-páramitá*, friendliness or kind feeling towards all beings, උපෙක්ෂාපාරමිතා *upekshá-páramitá*, freedom from attachment to the objects of sense; each of these is again subdivided, by inserting the two particles උප *upa* and පරමාර්ථ *paramárttha* between the name and the පාරමිතාව *páramitáwa*, and make what are termed the සම ත්‍රිංශත්පාරමිතාව *sama-triṇṣat-páramitáwa* or full thirty páramitáwas; the former of these particles is equivalent to the word secondary, and expresses the duty as performed only in a subordinate degree; the latter is equivalent to the word pre-eminent, and conveys the idea of the duty being carried to the highest possible degree; *e. g.* දානපාරමිතා *dána-páramitá* (දාන gift or giving, පාරමිතා completely done) expresses the duty in general terms, and signifies acts of charity or making offerings without any reference to their nature or value; දානුපපාරමිතා *dánupa-páramitá*, signifies presenting gifts of an inferior kind, as, gold, silver, robes, treasures, etc.; දානපරමාර්ථපාරමිතා *dána-paramárttha-páramitá*, expresses religious offerings or gifts of the highest order, the gift of wife and children, the gift of one's own body, flesh, bones, blood and sinews, as well as the soul or principle of life, when required: see the words as found in alphabetical order in the dictionary.

පාරමිධර්ම, *Párami-dharma*, see පාරමිතාව *páramitáwa*.

පාරලිවන, *Páralí-wana*, *s.* (පාරලි elephant so called, වන wilderness) wilderness to which Buddha retired after making frequent efforts to quell a dispute and quarrel among his priests but in vain; in this wilderness he resided for a length of time, during which period he was attended to and all his wants supplied by an elephant.

පාරවත, *Párawata*, *s.* pigeon, [Colloq. පරවියා *paraviyá*].

පාරවනවා, *Párawanawá*, *v.* to squeeze or hit against a boil.

පාරශව, *Páraṣawa*, *s.* (පර *para* another, ශව to go) adulterine, bastard; iron; weapon.

පාරශීක, *Páraṣíka*, *s.* the kingdom of Persia; inhabitant of Persia.

පාරසික, *Párasika*, } see පාරශීක *páraṣíka*.
පාරසීක, *Párasíka*, }

පාරජිකා, *Párájiká*, s. (පරජී overcome with ක *ka* aff, or අජ *aja* to go, with පරා prefixed, meaning inverted order, back, overcoming) unpardonable sin committed by a Buddhist priest; there are four of these sins which not only exclude him from the priesthood but for which there is no pardon in this life, viz. sexual intercourse, theft or robbery, murder, and the false assumption of the name and character of a rahat; the particulars of these transgressions and the ordinances relating to this department of the priesthood are given in a book of which this word is the name, and is the first in the class called ප්‍රකරණ *prakaraṇa* in the collection of විනයපිටක *vinaya-piṭaka*, which see.

පාරපත, *Párápata*, s. dove, pigeon, [Colloq. පරවියා *paraviyá*].

පාරපාර, *Párápára*, s. (පාර *pára* further, bank, අපාර *apára* near bank) ocean, two banks of a river.

පාරයණ, *Páráyaṇa*, s. (පාර *pára* boundary, අයන *ayana* going) totality, entireness, completeness; going across.

පාරයණී, *Páráyaṇí*, s. action, act; light; meditating, considering; name of the goddess Saraswatí.

පාරරුක, *Párá-ruka*, s. rock.

පාරවත, *Páráwata*, s. monkey, dove, pigeon; kind of ebony, *diospyros glutinosa*, probably *d. embryopteris*, [Colloq. තිඹිරි *timbiri*]; mountain, so called in the Indian peninsula.

පාරවතී, *Páráwatí*, s. river; fruit of the *anona reticulata*, [Colloq. ආත්තා *áttá*].

පාරවලල්ල, *Páráwalalla*, s. short curved cudgel.

පාරවාර, *Páráwára*, s. near and opposite banks of a stream; ocean, sea, [Colloq. මූද *múda*].

පාරශර, *Páráṣara*, s. name of the poet Vyása.

පාරිකා, *Páriká*, s. noted ascetic so called.

පාරිච්ඡත්තක, *Párichchhattaka*, s. tree, mountain ebony, *bauhinia purpurea*; nimba tree, *azadirachta indica*, [Colloq. කොහොඹ *kohomba*].

පාරිජත, *Párijáta*, } පාරිජාතක, *Párijátaka*, } s. (පරි *pari* emphatic, ජාත production) kalpa tree, or one of the five trees of Swarga, which is said to produce every thing desired; coral tree, *erythrina indica*, [Colloq. එරබදු *erabadu*].

පාරිණවා, *Páriṇawá*, v. to burst, to split, to crack, to rend, [Colloq. ඉරණවා *iraṇawá*].

පාරිදර්ශක, *Páridarṣaka*, s. overseer.

පාරිප්ලව, *Páriplawa*, s. (පරි *pari* exceeding, ප්ලව to move) shaking, trembling, moving: *a.* unsteady, perturbed, troubled in mind; tremulous.

පාරිපාට්‍ය, *Páripáṭya*, } පාරිපාටි, *Páripáṭi*, } s. orderly course, regularity, methodicalness, succession.

පාරිපුල්ල, *Páripulla*, a. opened, expanded, blown as a flower.

පාරිභද්‍ර, *Páribhdra*, } පාරිභද්‍රක, *Páribhdraka*, } s. (පරි *pari* completely, භද්‍ර auspicious) coral tree, *erythrina indica*, [Colloq. එරබදු *erabadu*]; nimba tree, *azadirachta indica*, [Colloq. කොහොඹ *kohomba*]; bead tree, *melia azedarach;* sort of pine, *pinus devadáru*, [Colloq. දේවදාර *déwadára*]; another sort, *pinus longifolia*.

පාරිභාව්‍ය, *Páribháwya*, s. plant, *costus speciosus*, [Colloq. තෙබු *tebu* or කොට්ටම් *koṭṭam*].

පාරිෂද්‍ය, *Párishadya*, } පාරිෂද, *Párishada*, } s. spectator, person present at an assembly or congregation; train, retinue; assembly.

පාරිහාර්‍ය, *Párihárya*, s. bracelet, any ornament for the wrist: golden or conch bracelet; taking.

පාරී, *Párí*, s. quantity of water; water jar; rope for tying the feet of an elephant.

පාරුත, *Páruta*, a. covering with clothes, wrapping round.

පාරු තැල්ල, *Páru-tella*, s. forepart or hind part of a páda boat.

පාරුපත්ත, *Páru-patta*, s. side of barge.

පාරුව, *Páruwa*, s. flat bottomed boat, páda boat, barge.

පාරුෂ්‍ය, *Párushya*, s. abuse, reproach, opprobrious speech; harshness in speaking; the forest of Indra; aloe wood; severity, violence, either in word වාක්පාරුෂ්‍ය *wák-párushya*, abuse, or දණ්ඩපාරුෂ්‍ය *daṇḍa-párushya*, assault.

පාරේ යනවා, *Páré-yanawá*, v. to follow, to pursue, to track.

පාල, *Pála*, s. nourisher, protector, keeper, fosterer.

පාලංකඩ, *Pálaṅkaḍa*, s. (පාලම *pálama* bridge, කඩ piece) small bridge, trunk of a tree or a plank laid across a brook or small stream.

පාලක, *Pálaka*, s. keeper, protector, nourisher, guardian.

පාලනය, *Pálanaya*, s. protection, preserving, guarding, nourishing, keeping.

පාලනයකරණවා, *Pálanaya-karaṇawá*, v. to preserve, keep.

පාලම, *Pálama*, s. bridge, pl. පාලම් *pálam*.

පාලයා, *Pálayá*, s. keeper, fosterer.

පාලස, *Pálasa*. *s.* tree, *butea frondosa*, [Colloq. ගස් කැල *gas-kęla*].

පාලාශ, *Páláṣa*, *s.* green (the colour), alluding to the beautiful green of the páláṣa tree.

පාලි, *Páli*, *s.* row, line, range, [Colloq. පේලිය *péliya*]; name of the Magadha-bháshâwa, *i. e.* the ancient language of South Behar or India within the Ganges; it bears this epithet in consequence of the perfection of its grammatical construction: see මගධභාෂා *magadha-bháshá*; lobe or pendant part of the ear; sharp edge of a sword; house; pot, boiler; sign, token; mark, spot, stain.

පාලිකා, *Páliká*, *s.* sharp edge of a cutting instrument, sort of ladle or knife for skimming milk etc., lobe of the ear.

පාලිගා, *Páligá*, *s.* row, terrace, raised border or bank in the walks of a garden; unoccupied spot.

පාලිත, *Pálita*, *s.* small tree: see ගැටනිටුල් *gęta-niṭul*]: *a.* nourished.

පාලින්ද, *Pálinda*, *s.* species of jasmine, *jasminum sambac*, [Colloq. පිච්ච *pichcha*].

පාලින්දි, *Pálindí*, *s.* plant, *cardiospermum halicacabum*, [Colloq. පෙනෙලවැල් *penela-węl*].

පාලින්ධි, *Pálindhí*, *s.* plant, black species of teori, *Ipomœa turpethum*, [Colloq. කළු තුස්තවාලු *kaḷu-trastawálu*].

පාලිනී, *Páliní*, *s.* (පාල *pála* to preserve, ඉනී *iní* fem. aff.) protectress, any female nourisher, or preserver.

පාලිය, *Páliya*, see පාලි *páli*.

පාවක, *Páwaka*, *s.* fire; name of Agni the god of fire; tree, the wood of which is used to procure fire by attrition, *premna serratifolia*, [Colloq. සිහින්මිදි *sihin-midi*]; lead wort, *plumbago zeylanica*, [Colloq. එලනෙටුල් *ela-neṭul*]; the marking nut tree, *semcearpus anacardium*, or *semecarpus gardneri*, [Colloq. බඩුල්ල *badulla*].

පාවට්ටා, *Páwaṭṭá*, *s.* shrub, *adhatoda vasica* or *justicia adhenatoda*, [Colloq. අගල්අඳර *agal-ádára*]; name of another shrub with white flowers, *pavetta indica*, variety of which *p. montana* is peculiar to Ceylon, *(Rubiaceæ)*.

පාවඩය, *Páwaḍaya*, *s.* cloth spread on the ground, out of great respect, to walk upon.

පාවර, *Páwara*, *s.* threshing floor, place where oxen tread out the corn.

පාවාගන්නවා, *Páwágannawá*, *v.* to receive, to take in charge, to take in, to surrender.

පාවාඩය, *Páwáḍaya*, *s.* cloth spread on the ground for distinguished persons to walk upon, carpet: see පාවඩය *páwaḍaya*.

පාවාදෙනවා, *Páwádenawá*, *v.* to give, to give in charge, to surrender up; to betray.

පාවිච්චිකරණවා, *Pávichchikaraṇawá*, *v.* to use.

පාවිච්චිය, *Pávichchiya*, *s.* use, custom, practice, usage.

පාවී, *Páví*, *s.* drift; wicked woman: *part.* having floated: see පාවෙනවා *páwenawá*.

පාවුල, *Páwula*, *s.* lower portion of land.

පාවුල ලනවා, *Páwula-lanawá*, *v.* to clear the lower portion of land.

පාවෙනවා, *Páwenawá*, *v.* to drift, to float, to float on shore.

පාශ, *Páṣa*, *s.* fetter, chain, noose. This means *quantity*, when used in composition with words signifying hair, කේශපාශ *kéṣapáṣa*, "much or flowing hair," and *beauty* with කර්ණ *karṇa*, the ear, as කර්ණපාශ *karṇapáṣa*, "handsome ear." In composition with ඡත්‍ර *chhatra*, it implies depreciation, as ඡත්‍රපාශ *chhatrapáṣa*, "inelegant or shabby umbrella."

පාශක, *Páṣaka*, *s.* dice, particularly the long sort used in playing chaupai.

පාශනිබන්ධජීව, *Páṣanibandha-jíwa*, *s.* (පාශ fetter, snare, නිබන්ධ binding, ජීව who lives) forester, one who lives by catching wild animals.

පාශින්, *Páṣin*, *s.* (පාශ *páṣa* noose or snare, ඉන් *in* aff.) name of Varuṇa the regent of water, who is frequently figured in the temples holding a cord in one hand shaped like a noose.

පාෂණ්ඩ, *Páshaṇḍa*, *s.* heretic, any sect not Hindu.

පාෂාණ, *Pásháṇa*, *s.* stone in general, [Colloq. ගල *gala*]; small stone used as a weight.

පාෂාණභේදක, *Pásháṇabhédaka*, *s.* plant, *plectranthus scutellaroides*, [Colloq. පොල්පලා *polpalá*].

පාස්කුව, *Páskuwa*, *s.* Easter. (Port.)

පාස්සනවා, *Pássanawá*, *v.* to solder, to fasten, to weld: pret. පෑස්සුවා *pęssuwá*.

පාස, *Pása*, see පාශ *páṣa* above.

පාස කියනවා, *Pása-kiyanawá*, *v.* to threaten, to menace, to complain of bad treatment.

පාසය, *Pásaya*, *s.* snare, fetter: see පාශ *páṣa*.

පාසලඹ, *Pá-salamba*, *s.* (පා and සලඹ ring) bracelets or rings for the feet and ankles covering the instep.

පාසා, *Pásá*, *ad.* alternately, successively, in order, by turns, from one to the other.

පාසාණාසන, *Pásáṇásana*, *s.* (පාසාණ *pásáṇa* stone, අසන *asana* food, or ආසන *ásana* seat) peacock; stone seat.

පාසාදික, *Pásádika*, *a.* joyful, pleasing, delightful; agreeable.

පාසානං, *Pásánaṇ*, *s.* arsenic.

පාසිනවා, *Pásinawá*, *v.* to pound, to cleanse by pounding as rice; to cut branches of trees: pret. පෑස්සා *pęssá*.

පාසු, *Pásu*, *a.* facile, easy; convalescent, recovered.

පාසුව, *Pásuwa*, *s.* ease, facility, convalescence.

පාසේ, *Pásé*, *s.* tie, string, cord, snare, noose, fetter.

පාහනවා, *Páhanawá*, see පහනවා *pahanawá*.

පාහාත, *Páháta*, *s.* mulberry tree, *morus indica*.

පාහිනවා, *Páhinawá*, *v.* to pound, to grind, to bruise; to cut: pret. පෑස්සා *pęssá*.

පාහුණ, *Páhuṇa*, *s.* inmate, guest.

පාළු, *Páḷu*, *a.* unoccupied, unemployed; unprepared, uncultivated, waste; devastated, destroyed, desolate.

පාළු ඉඩම, *Páḷu-idama*, *s.* (පාළු and ඉඩම place) vacant or waste spot.

පාළුකරණවා, *Páḷukaraṇawá*, *v.* to lay desolate, lay waste.

පාළුව, *Páḷuwa*, *s.* waste, desolation, devastation.

පික්මල්, *Pik-mal*, *s.* plant, *trigonella corniculata*.

පික, *Pika*, *s.* kókila or Indian cuckoo, *cuculus micropterus*, [Colloq. කොවුලා *kowulá*].

පිකදප්, *Pikadap*, *s.* (පික kókila, දප් influence) name of Káma the Indian Cupid, alluding to the power of inspiring love which the note of the kókila is supposed to possess.

පිකබන්ධු, *Pika-bandhu*, *s.* (පික Indian cuckoo, බන්ධු friend) mango tree, the favorite haunt of that bird.

පිකම, *Pikama*, *s.* pick-axe; sort of hoe, pl. පිකම් *pikam*.

පිකවල්ලභ, *Pika-wallabha*, *s.* (පික and වල්ලභ beloved) mango tree, [Colloq. අඹ *amba*].

පිකී, *Pikí*, *s.* female Indian cuckoo.

පිගුර, *Pigura*, *s.* figure (Eng.), plan of a garden, etc.

පිඟන්කෝප්ප, *Pinganköppa*, *s.* crockery.

පිඟන්මැටි, *Pingan-męṭi*, *s.* pipe clay.

පිඟල්, *Pingal*, *s.* palm of the hand, [Colloq, අල්ල *alla*].

පිඟාන, *Pingána*, *s.* plate, pl. පිඟන් *pingan*.

පිඟිහි, *Pingihi*, *a.* squinting, squint-eyed.

පිඟු, *Pingu*, *s.* tawny.

පිඟුනෙත්, *Pingu-net*, *s.* (පිඟු tawny, නෙත් eye) name of Ṣiva: see පිඞ්ගාක්ෂ *pińgáksha*.

පිඟුල්, *Pingul*, } see පිඞ්ගල *pińgala*.
පිඟුල, *Pingula*, }

පිඟුවන්, *Pinguwan*, *s.* (පිඟු tawny, වන් colour) tawny colour.

පිඞ්ග, *Pińga*, *s.* tawny (colour).

පිඞ්ගල, *Pińgala*, *s.* tawny; sun, bezoar stone found in the stomach of cattle, [Colloq. ගෝරෝචන *góróchana*]; planet Saturn; elephant; drug, vegetable perfume; fifty-first year of the Indian cycle; owl.

පිඞ්ගලක, *Pińgalaka*, *s.* owl; sort of crane; drug; vegetable perfume.

පිඞ්ගා, *Pińgá*, *s.* name of the goddess Durga, wife of Ṣiva; assafœtida; turmeric: *a.* tawny.

පිඞ්ගාක්ෂ, *Pińgáksha*, *s.* (පිඞ්ග *pińga* tawny, අක්ෂ *aksha* eye) name of Ṣiva, alluding to the colour of his eye, reddish brown.

පිඞ්ගාශ, *Pińgáṣa*, *s.* (පිඞ්ග *pińga* and ආශ *áṣa* flesh) sort of fish, *silurus sagittarius;* headman or proprietor of a village; virgin gold.

පිඞ්ගී, *Pińgí*, *s.* indigo plant, *indigofera tinctoria*, [Colloq. නිල් අවරි *nil-awari*]; also, *acacia suma* or *a. catechu*.

පිච්ච, *Pichcha*, *s.* species of jessamine, *jasminum sambac, (Oleaceœ).*

පිච්චට, *Pichchaṭa*, *s.* tin; lead; inflammation of the eyes, ophthalmia.

පිච්ච වැල, *Pichcha-wela*, *s.* (පිච්ච jasmine, වැල creeper): see පිච්ච *pichcha*.

පිච්චීම, *Pichchíma*, *s.* burning, verbal noun of පුච්චනවා *puchchanawá*.

පිච්ඡ, *Pichchha*, *s.* tail of a peacock; crest; tail in general.

පිච්ඡා, *Pichchhá*, *s.* gum of the silk cotton tree, line, row, range; diseased affection of a horse's feet; areca nut, betel nut; plantain; scum of boiled rice; sort of body dress or jacket; venomous saliva of a snake; timber tree, *dalbergia sisu;* sheath, coat, cover.

පිච්ඡි, *Pickchhi*, } *s.* sauce mixed with rice
පිච්ඡිල, *Pichchhila*, } gruel; sauce, gravy, or condiments with water or ghee; moist and split pulse; bark of trees; silk cotton tree, *eriodendron anfractuosum*, [Colloq. ඉඹුල් *imbul*]; orange.

පිච්ඡිලත්වච, *Pichchhilatwacha*, *s.* (පිච්ඡිල orange, ත්වච skin) orange, *citrus aurantium*, [Colloq. පැණිදොඩම් *pęnidodam*]; peel of an orange.

පිච්ඡිලපත්‍රය, *Pichchhila-patraya,* } *s.* silk cotton tree,
පිච්ඡිලා, *Pichchhilá,* } *eriodendron anfractuosum;* large timber tree, *dalbergia sisu;* river so called; esculent root, *alocasia indica;* [Colloq. රට අල *raṭa-ala* or දේස අල *désa-ala*]; pot herb, *basella rubra* and *lucida,* allied to නිවිති *niviti;* Indian tamarisk, *tamarix indica.*

පිචව්‍ය, *Pichawya, s.* cotton plant, *gossypium indicum,* [Colloq. කපු *kapu*].

පිචු, *Pichu, s.* cotton; sort of cutaneous eruption; leprosy.

පිචුක, *Pichuka, s.* small tree, *randia dumetorum,* [Colloq. කුකුරුමාන් *kukurumán* or කුකුරුමුවං *kukurumuwaŋ*].

පිචුපර්ණී, *Pichuparṇṇí, s.* (පිචු and පර්ණ *parṇa* leaf, ඊ *i* aff.) silk cotton tree: see පිච්ඡිලා *pichchhilá.*

පිචුමන්ද, *Pichumanda,* } *s.* margosa or nimba
පිචුමන්දක, *Pichumandaka,* } tree, *azadirachta indica,* [Colloq. කොහොඹ *kohomba*].

පිචුල, *Pichula, s.* cotton; tamarisk, see පිච්ඡිලා *pichchhilá;* diver or water crow; plant, *barringtonia acutangula,* [Colloq. මිදෙල්ල *midella* or මූදිල්ල *múdilla*].

පිඤ්ච, *Piñcha, s.* little thing.

පිඤ්ජ, *Piñja, s.* stooping, bending, folding; killing, slaughter; strength, power; the crest or tail of a peacock, peacock's wing or feather; injury, hurting, injuring; cotton; turmeric; switch.

පිඤ්ජකලාපය, *Piñja-kalápaya, s.* tail of a peacock.

පිඤ්ජනය, *Piñjanaya, s.* bow used for cleaning cotton.

පිඤ්ජභාර, *Piñjabhára,* see පිඤ්ජකලාපය *piñjakalápaya.*

පිඤ්ජර, *Piñjara, s.* sort of tawny reddish yellow or a mixture of red and yellow; gold; yellow orpiment; cage; ribs or cavity formed by them, thorax: *a.* tawny, reddish yellow.

පිඤ්ජල, *Piñjala, s.* army panic-struck or in great disorder; leaf of the kusa grass; yellow orpiment: *a.* confounded, overcome with terror or grief.

පිට්ටනිය, *Piṭṭaniya, s.* meadow, field, lawn.

පිට්ටුව, *Piṭṭuwa, s.* loaf, made of any kind of flour except wheat, pl. පිට්ටු *piṭṭu.*

පිට්ටුවැල, *Piṭṭu-wẹla, s.* plant, not identified.

පිට්ඨි, *Piṭṭhi, s.* back, [Colloq. පිට *piṭa*].

පිට, *Piṭa, s.* back; page, basket for holding grain, sort of cupboard or granary made of bamboo or canes; mat: *ad.* out, outward; upon, outside.

පිට ඇට, *Piṭa-ẹta, s.* (පිට back, ඇට bone) spine.

පිට ඇල, *Piṭa-ẹla, s.* narrow canal round a field.

පිටංගන, *Piṭaŋgana, ind.* outside, outside the compound, out of doors.

පිටක, *Piṭaka,* } *s.* basket; trunk; granary
පිටකත්‍රය, *Piṭakatraya,* } made of basket work; receptacle, depository; collection of books including all that go under the general name of baṇa; it comprehends all the works which are attributed to Buddha, and is divided into three classes, viz. විනයපිටක *vinaya-piṭaka* or those which relate entirely to the priests; සූත්‍රපිටක *sútra-piṭaka* or those which were addressed to mankind in general; අභිධර්මපිටක *abhidharma-piṭaka* or those which were addressed to the gods; this last class of the piṭaka is written in so difficult a style of Páli that only a few of even the learned are able to read them; the consequence is they are but little studied and not much known; to be able to understand the abhidharma is generally regarded as one of the highest scholastic qualifications of the priesthood; this class contains seven prakaraṇas; viz. ධම්මසංගණි *dhamma-sangani,* විභඞ්ග *vibhanga,* කථාවත්‍ථු *katháwatthu,* පුග්ගලපඤ්ඤත්ති *puggala-paññatti,* ධාතුකථා *dhátu-kathá,* යමක කථා *yamaka-kathá,* පට්ඨාන කථා *patthána-kathá,* these comprehend 293,680 granthas or poetical stanzas of 32 syllables each; for an account of the other two classes see විනයපිටක *vinaya-piṭaka* and සූත්‍රපිටක *sútra-piṭaka.*

පිටකොටුව, *Piṭa-koṭuwa, s.* (පිට out, කොටුව fort) suburb, Pettah.

පිටකොන්ද, *Piṭakonda, s.* back shoulder; spine.

පිටගම, *Piṭa-gama, s.* (පිට outside, ගම village) village other than one's own.

පිටත්, *Piṭat, ind.* outside, out, outward.

පිටත්කරණවා, *Piṭatkaraṇawá, v.* to set off another on a journey.

පිටත්වයාම, *Piṭatwa-yáma, s.* going forth.

පිටත්වෙනවා, *Piṭatwenawá, v.* to depart, to set off (on a journey).

පිටත, *Piṭata, s.* outside, out, forth, abroad.

පිටදමනවා, *Piṭa-damanawá, v.* to throw out.

පිටනුවර, *Piṭa-nuwara, s.* (පිට out, නුවර city) suburbs of a city.

පිටපටය, *Piṭapaṭaya, s.* cloth or lower garment of a native tucked up behind when at work etc.

පිටපත්කරණවා, *Piṭapatkaraṇawá*, v. to banish, to exile; to transcribe; to copy, to translate.

පිටපත, *Piṭapata*, s. translation, version, copy.

පිටපය, *Piṭa-paya*, s. giving way; foot outside.

පිටපාර, *Piṭa-pára*, s. outside way.

පිටපිට, *Piṭapiṭa*, a. repeatedly, over and over, again and again.

පිටපෙරලනවා, *Piṭa-peralanawá*, v. to turn over, to turn topsy turvy.

පිටපෙරළු, *Piṭaperaḷu*, a. turned over, topsy turvy.

පිටමංකරණවා, *Piṭamaṇkaraṇawá*, v. to cast out, to turn out.

පිටමංවෙනවා, *Piṭamaṇwenawá*, v. to go out of a place.

පිටමුල, *Piṭamula*, s. hip.

පිටරට, *Piṭa-raṭa*, s. (පිට out, රට country) distant country or foreign country.

පිටරටයා, *Piṭaraṭayá*, s. (පිටරට and යා pers. aff.) foreigner.

පිට ලිවීම, *Piṭa-livíma*, s. superscription, address.

පිටවක්කා, *Piṭawakká*, s. plant, common weed, root said to be a remedy for jaundice, *phyllanthus niruri (Euphorbiaceæ)*: see ඇත් පිටවක්කා *ęt-piṭawakká*, and රත් පිටවක්කා *rat-piṭawakká*.

පිටවක, *Piṭawaka*, s. outside of bend or curve.

පිටවගුර, *Piṭawagura*, s. muddy place.

පිටවත, *Piṭawata*, s. outside, back part.

පිටවහල්කරණවා, *Piṭawahal-karaṇawá*, v. to banish a culprit out of town to an uninhabited place.

පිටවානේ, *Piṭawáné*, see පිටඇල *piṭa-ęla*.

පිටස්තර, *Piṭastara*, s. external part, outward part.

පිටසක්වළ, *Piṭa-sakwaḷa*, s. (පිට and සක්වළ world) exterior of the universe, out-lying world.

පිටසුදු පලා, *Piṭasudu-palá*, s. plant, *hedyotis nitida*, *(Rubiaceæ)*; another plant with minute flowers in heads, *boerhaavia diffusa (Nyctagineæ)*.

පිටසැලි, *Piṭaseli*, s. parsley, (Dutch.) [Colloq. අසමෝදගං *asamódagaṇ*].

පිටාතර, *Piṭátara*, s. outward part: see පිටස්තර *piṭastara*.

පිටාරි, *Piṭári*, s. ditch or channel outside a field or garden for the purpose of carrying off the water.

පිටාරෙ, *Piṭáre*, s. overflowing of a stream, abundance of rain-water.

පිටි, *Piṭi*, s. meal, flour, rice flour, any ground grain, powder, dust, any pulverised substance.

පිටිඅත්ල, *Piṭi-atla*, } s. back of the hand.
පිටිඅල්ල, *Piṭi-alla*, }

පිටිකර, *Piṭikara*, s. nape, hind part of the neck.

පිටිකරණවා, *Piṭikaraṇawá*, v. to grind or pound into meal.

පිටිගොටුවා, *Piṭigoṭuwá*, s. kind of fish.

පිටිතලාව, *Piṭitaláwa*, } s. arms bound, behind, as criminals.
පිටිතොල, *Piṭitola*, }

පිටින්, *Piṭin*. ad. from without; with, having, possessing, as පණපිටින් *paṇapiṭin*, alive.

පිටිපතුල, *Piṭipatula*. s. the instep.

පිටිපස්ස, *Piṭipassa*, s. behind the back.

පිටිපස, *Piṭipasa*, s. back part, behind.

පිටිපානවා, *Piṭipánawá*, v. (පිටි back, පානවා to show) to turn the back.

පිටිමන්, *Piṭiman*, see පිටිපස්ස *piṭipassa*.

පිටිය, *Piṭiya*, s. plain tract of ground; place of game as අං පිටිය *aṇ-piṭiya*, පොරපොල් පිටිය *porapol-piṭiya*.

පිටියවැල, *Piṭiyawęla*, s. plant, not identified.

පිටිවහල්, *Piṭiwahal*, s. help, favour, assistance, [Colloq. පිහිට *pihiṭa*].

පිටිසර, *Piṭisara*, s. (පිටි outside, සර to go) distance, place in the country; rural district, distant place or abroad.

පිටු, *Piṭu*, s. multitude, [Colloq. සමූහය *samúhaya*]; pages.

පිටුකර, *Piṭukara*, see පිටිකර *piṭikara*.

පිටුපස්ස, *Piṭupassa*, see පිටිපස්ස *piṭipassa*.

පිටුවහල්, *Piṭuwahal*, see පිටිවහල් *piṭiwahal*.

පිටොස්, *Piṭos*, s. outside of the jack fruit after the prickly crust is taken away.

පිටෝත, *Piṭóta*, s. back part, outside.

පිඨර, *Piṭhara*, s. vessel, tub, pot; pan; churning stick; fragrant grass, *cyperus rotundus*, [Colloq. කලාඳුරු *kaláṇduru*]; sort of building, apparently a hut or watch-box made of bamboos and mats.

පිඩ, *Piḍa*, s. small quantity, ball, as of dough, lump, pl. පිඩු *piḍu*.

පිඩක, *Piḍaka*, s. small boil, pimple.

පිඩු, *Piḍu*, plur. of පිඩ *piḍa*.

පිඩැල්ල, *Piḍella*, s. turf, sod; clod, pl. පිඩලි *piḍali*.

පිඬා, *Piṇḍá*, s. sediment of salt after being dissolved in water.

පිණ්ඩ, *Piṇḍa*, s. iron; lump, heap, cluster, quantity, collection; ball, globe; mouthful or roundish lump of food, considered as equivalent to a mouthful; oblation to deceased ancestors, as a ball or lump of meat or rice mixed up with milk, curds, flowers, etc. and offered to the manes by the nearest surviving relations; body; side, the part immediately below the arm-pit; part of a house; sort of portico or shed in front of the door; strength, power; myrrh, frankincense; Chinese rose; food, flesh, meat; projection of an elephant's frontal sinus; embryo or fœtus in an early state of gestation; sum (in arithmetic).

පිණ්ඩක, *Piṇḍaka*, *s.* goblin, demon; incense.

පිණ්ඩගෝස, *Piṇḍa-gósa*, *s.* (පිණ්ඩ and ගෝස both meaning myrrh) dross of iron; gum myrrh.

පිණ්ඩද, *Piṇḍada*, *s.* one who gives the funeral cake to deceased ancestors; one who supports or feeds another; nearest male relation; patron, master.

පිණ්ඩදාන, *Piṇḍadána*, *s.* presentation of the funeral cake.

පිණ්ඩපාත, *Piṇḍapáta*, *s.* (පිණ්ඩ ball of boiled rice, පාත fall, cast) food received in vessel or bowl used by the priests, when asking alms.

පිණ්ඩපාතකරණවා, *Piṇḍapáta-karaṇawá*, *v.* to beg from door to door: the word is only applied to the ordinance as exercised by the Buddhist priests.

පිණ්ඩපාතික, *Piṇḍapátika*, *s.* (පිණ්ඩපාත *piṇḍa-páta* begging bowl, ඉක *ika* pers. aff.) religious mendicant, a priest of Buddha.

පිණ්ඩපාතිකාඞ්ග, *Piṇḍapátikáṅga*, *s*, (පිණ්ඩපාතික *piṇḍapátika* one who carries a begging bowl, අඞ්ග *aṅga* religious ordinance) ordinance of the Buddhist priesthood, enjoining it upon the priests to procure their food by begging with a bowl: see තෙළෙස්ධුතාඞ්ග *teḷesdhutáṅga*.

පිණ්ඩපුෂ්ප, *Piṇḍa-pushpa*, *s.* flower of the asóka tree, *saraca indica* or *jonesia asoca*, [Colloq. දිය රතඹලා *diya-ratambalá* or හෝපලු මල් *hópalu-mal*].

පිණ්ඩල, *Piṇḍala*, *s.* bridge, causeway, passage over a stream or ravine etc., mound raised to form a path across inundated fields.

පිණ්ඩාලු, *Piṇḍálu*, *s.* sand, gravel; esculent and medical root described as sweet, cooling, and diuretic; spear, lance.

පිණ්ඩාලුක, *Piṇḍáluka*, *s.* preparation of milk and ghee; medical preparation of ghee.

පිණ්ඩිකා, *Piṇḍiká*, *s.* nave of a wheel; instep.

පිණ්ඩිත, *Piṇḍita*, *a.* mutiplied, added; numbered, counted; thick, massy; lumpish, collected and heaped together.

පිණ්ඩිඵල, *Piṇḍiphala*, *s.* mango, *mangifera indica*, [Colloq. අඹ *amba*].

පිණ්ඩිඵලා, *Piṇḍiphalá*, *s.* bitter gourd, *trichosanthes palmata*, [Colloq. තිත්ත හොඬල *titta-hoṇḍala* or තිත්ත ලබු *titta-labu*].

පිණ්ඩිල, *Piṇḍila*, *s.* bridge; mound, causeway; astrologer, caster of nativities.

පිණ්ඩිලා, *Piṇḍilá*, *s.* cucumber, *cucumis utilatissimus*, or *c. sativus*, [Colloq. පිපිඤ්ඤා *pipiñña*].

පිණ්ඩී, *Piṇḍí*, *s.* flower of the asóka tree, *saraca indica* or *jonesia asoca*, [Colloq. දියරතඹලා *diya-ratambalá*]; Chinese rose or shoe flower, *hibiscus rosa sinensis*, [Coll: සපත්තුමල් *sapattu-mal*]; nave of a wheel.

පිණ්‍යා, *Piṇyá*, *s.* heart-pea, *cardiospermum halicacabum*, [Colloq. පෙනෙලවැල *penela-weḷa*].

පිණ්‍යාක, *Piṇyáka*, *s.* sediments of seeds etc. ground for oil; cil-cake, or the seeds after expression; saffron; assafœtida, incense.

පිණ, *Piṇa*, *s.* charity, religious charity, distribution of alms, etc., virtue, religious or moral merit; fulness; Elu form of පුණ්‍ය *puṇya*.

පිණන, *Piṇana*, *s.* act of filling, satisfaction; see the next.

පිණනවා, *Piṇanawá*, *v.* to rejoice, to be glad or joyful, to be satisfied with: pret. පිණුවා *piṇuwá*.

පිණවනවා, *Piṇawanawá*, the causal form of the foregoing: pret. පිණෙව්වා *piṇewwá*.

පිණවීම, *Piṇavíma*, verbal noun of පිණවනවා *piṇawanawá*.

පිණවුම, *Piṇawum*, *s.* joy, gladness, satisfying.

පිණහැඹිලි, *Piṇahembili*, *s.* species of ant.

පිණා, *Piṇá*, *part.* being pleased, glad, contented, being filled.

පිණිස, *Piṇisa*, *ind.* particle and affix, meaning for the purpose of, in order to, for, on account of.

පිණු, *Piṇu*, from පුණු *puṇu*, *a.* full, complete, fulfilled.

පිණුපොහොය, *Piṇu-pohoya*, *s.* (පිණු full, පොහො *poho* Buddhist fast-day, which occurs four times in the month) day of full moon, fortunate or lucky day, on which the chief festivals of the Buddhist are celebrated.

පිණැති, *Piṇeti*, *a.* (පින් *pin* religious merit, charity, ඇති *eti* having) charitable, meritorious, virtuous by the exercise of charity, fortunate.

පිත්, *Pit*, *s.* son; bile.

පිත්ත, *Pitta*, *s.* bile; bilious humour, stalk of a branch of the palm kind, pl. පිති *piti*.

පිත්තකාමලා, *Pitta-kámalá*, *s.* (පිත්ත bile, කාම desire, ලා to get) jaundice, [Colloq. සෙංගමාලය *sengamálaya*].

පිත්තඝ්න, *Pittaghna*, *a.* antibilious.

පිත්තඝ්නී, *Pittaghní*, *s.* plant, *tinospora cordifolia* or *menispermum glabrum*, [Colloq. රසකිඳ *rasa-kinda*].

පිත්තජ්වර, *Pittajwara*, *s.* (පිත්ත bile, ජ්වර fever) bilious fever.

පිත්තල, *Pittala*, *s.* (පිත්ත bile, ලා *lá* to receive) brass: *a.* bilious.

පිත්තල මල, *Pittala-mala*, *s.* (පිත්තල brass, මල excrement) verdigris.

පිත්තලවැල, *Pittala-węla*, *s.* brass wire.

පිත්තලා, *Pittalá*, *s.* floating plant, *jussiœa repens*, [Colloq. බෙරුදියනිල්ල *béru-diyanilla*].

පිත, *Pita*, *s.* bile, bilious humour; choler: pl. පිත් *pit*.

පිතා, *Pitá*, *s.* father.

පිතාමහ, *Pitá-maha*, *s.* (පිතා and මහ great) grandfather, paternal grandfather; name of Brahma, alluding to his being the father of all.

පිතෘ, *Pitri*, *s.* father; paternal ancestor; manes of a deceased ancestor.

පිතෘක, *Pitṛika*, *a.* paternal, relating or belonging to a parent or progenitor.

පිතෘකානන, *Pitṛikánana*, *s.* (පිතෘ father, කානන wood) cemetery.

පිතෘඝාතක, *Pitṛighátaka*, *s.* (පිතෘ and ඝාතක slayer) parricide.

පිතෘතර්පණ, *Pitṛi-tarpaṇa*, *s.* (පිතෘ manes of deceased ancestors, තර්පණ satisfaction) offering to or in honour of deceased ancestors.

පිතෘදාන, *Pitṛi-dána*, *s.* (පිතෘ and දාන gift) offerings to the manes of deceased ancestors.

පිතෘපති, *Pitṛi-pati*, *s.* (පිතෘ deceased ancestors, පති lord) name of Yama, regent of the dead.

පිතෘපිතෘ, *Pitṛi-pitṛi*, *s.* (පිතෘ father, පිතෘ father) paternal grandfather.

පිතෘව්‍ය, *Pitṛiwya*, *s.* paternal uncle.

පිතෘවධ, *Pitṛi-wadha*, *s.* (පිතෘ and වධ to destroy) one of the five heinous crimes, parricide.

පිතෘවන, *Pitṛi-wana*, *s.* (පිතෘ father, වන wood) cemetery, place where dead bodies are buried or burnt.

පිදවින්න, *Pidavinna*, } *s.* offering to a deity or
පිදවිල්ල, *Pidavilla*, } demon.

පිදිම, *Pidíma*, *s.* an offering (religious), a sacrifice, pl. පිදිම් *pidím*; verbal noun of පුදනවා *pudanawá*.

පිදුම, *Piduma*, *s.* worship, adoration, obeisance, offering, prostration: pl. පිදුම් *pidum*.

පිදුරු, *Piduru*, *s.* straw, stalk of the paddy.

පිදුරු හතු, *Piduru-hatu*, *s.* straw mushroom.

පිදූ, *Pidú*, *part.* of පුදනවා *pudanawá*.

පිදෙනවා, *Pidenawá*, *v.* to offer one's self, to sacrifice one's self: pret. පිදුනා *piduná*.

පිදේන්න, *Pidénna*, *s.* offering made to demons.

පිධාන, *Pidhána*, *s.* cover, covering, lid, concealment; sheath, wrapper, cloak, mantle.

පින්, *Pin*, *plur.* of පිණ *piṇa*.

පින්කම, *Pinkama*, *s.* (පින් moral or religious merit, කම from කර්ම *karma* doing, act) act of making religious offerings, distribution of religious charities among the priests, almsgiving to the poor, literally a meritorious act; Buddhist festival.

පින්කරණවා, *Pinkaraṇawá*, *v.* to give alms; to do meritorious acts.

පින්න, *Pinna*, *s.* name of a plant, *clerodendron infortunatum*; dew.

පින්න ඇල්වී, *Pinna-ęlví*, *s.* kind of paddy.

පින්තාලිය, *Pintáliya*, *s.* water-pot set on the road side: corruptly for පැන්තලිය *pęn-taliya*.

පින්පෙත්, *Pinpet*, *s.* (පින් merit, පෙත් for පත්ති *patti* attainment, here meaning the act of imparting) offerings to the manes, offerings to deceased ancestors, or the manes of virtuous people; transference to another of the merit acquired by one's self.

පින්රැස, *Pin-ręsa*, *s.* stock of merit, accumulation of religious or moral merit.

පින්වත්, *Pinwat*, *a.* (පින් merit obtained by religious charity, වත් poss. aff.) fortunate; religiously charitable, happy, possessed of merit arising from charity,

පිනාක, *Pináka*. *s.* bow of Ṣiva; trident or three-pronged spear; trident of Ṣiva; shower of dust.

පිනාකී, *Pinákí*, *s.* musical instrument, sort of viol; name of Ṣiva.

පිනි, *Pini*, *s.* dew.

පිනිතුත්තිරි, *Pini-tuttiri*, *s.* species of grass, peculiar to Ceylon, *eriachne triseta (Gramineœ)*.

පිනිදිය, *Pinidiya*, *s.* nectar of flowers; dew; water distilled from the Beli or wood apple flower.

පිනිපා, *Pinipá*, } *s.* (පිනි dew, water, පා to drink)
පිනිපු, *Pinipu*, } fish, fish in general; (ප *pa* and නි before, පා for පාත *páta* falling) worship, obeisance, [Colloq. නමස්කාරය *namaskáraya*]; salutation, prostration; moon, [Coll: හඳ *handa*];

serpent, snake; hare, [Colloq. හාවා *háwá*]; elephant (පන *pana* again, a second time, පා to drink,) the elephant imbibing fluids by his trunk and thence conveying them into his mouth.

පිනිබරු, *Pinibaru*, *s.* tree, *eugenia Mooniana*, (*Myrtaceæ*).

පිනිබරුතණ, *Pinibaru-taṇa*, *s.* vernal grass, *anthisteria tremula* (*Gramineæ*).

පිනිබානවා, *Pinibánawá*, *v.* to fall as dew.

පිනිබිඳ, *Pinibiṇda*, } *s.* drop of dew.
පිනිබිඳුව, *Pinibinduwa*, }

පිනිමුවා, *Pinimuwá*, *s.* kind of deer, raindeer.

පිනිහිරිය, *Pinihiriya*, *s.* plant, not identified.

පිනුම් පනිනවා, *Pinum-paninawá*, *v.* to take leaps, to leap or spring.

පිනුම, *Pinuma*, *s.* somersault; gambol: pl. පිනුම් *pinum*.

පිප්පපාණ්ඩුව, *Pippa-páṇḍuwa*, *s.* jaundice.

පිප්පයා, *Pippayá*, *s.* one who has jaundice or a pale colour.

පිප්පල, *Pippala*, *s.* holy fig tree, *ficus religiosa*, [Colloq. බෝගහ *bó-gaha*]; bird; sleeve of a jacket or coat.

පිප්පලි, *Pippali*, } *s.* long pepper, [Colloq. තිප්පිලි
පිප්පලී, *Pippalí*, } *tippili*].

පිප්පලීමූල, *Pippalí-múla*, *s.* (පිප්පලී and මූල root) root of the long pepper plant, [Colloq. තිප්පිලි මුල් *tippili-mul*].

පිප්පිකා, *Pippiká*, *s.* tartar of the teeth, [Colloq දත් මැලියම් *dat-meliyam*].

පිප්පීම, *Pippíma*, verbal noun of පිප්පෙනවා *pippenawá*.

පිප්පෙනවා, *Pippenawá*, *v.* to be puffed, used of bladders, frogs, snakes etc.; also called පිම්බෙන වා *pimbenawá*.

පිප්ලු, *Piplu*, *s.* freckle, mark or spot on the skin, mole, [Colloq. ලපය *lapaya*].

පිපාසය, *Pipásaya*, } *s.* (පා *pá* to drink in the
පිපාසා, *Pipásá*, } desiderative form, to wish to drink) thirst, desire to drink.

පිපාසාතුර, *Pipásátura*, *a.* (පිපාසා thirst, අතුර *átura* suffering from) oppressed with thirst.

පිපාසික, *Pipásika*, *s.* (පිපාසා *pipásá* and ඉක *ika* pers. aff.) thirsty person.

පිපාසිත, *Pipásita*, *a.* (පිපාසා *pipásá* and ඉත *ita* aff.) athirst, thirsty, dry.

පිපි, *Pipi*, *s.* expanding, opening, blowing as a flower; cobra; snake; small black ant: past part. of පිපෙනවා *pipenawá*.

පිපිච්ච, *Pipichcha*, *p. part.* of පිපෙනවා *pipenawá*: opened, expanded (applied to flowers).

පිපිඤ්ඤ, *Pipiñña*, *s.* common garden cucumber, *cucumis sativus*.

පිපිපත්, *Pipi-pat*, *s.* enemy, adversary.

පිපිරීම, *Pipiríma*, verbal noun of පිපිරෙණවා *pipireṇawá*.

පිපිරෙණවා, *Pipireṇawá*, *v.* to crack, to burst; to rave, to become furious through passion: pret. පිපුරුණ *pipuruṇá*.

පිපිහළු, *Pipihaḷu*, *a.* swollen, pale.

පිපී, *Pipí*, *past part.* of පිපෙනවා *pipenawá*.

පිපීම, *Pipíma*, verbal noun of පිපෙනවා *pipenawá*.

පිපීලක, *Pipílaka*, *s.* large black ant; common red ant.

පිපීලිකා, *Pipíliká*, *s.* common small red ant.

පිපු, *Pipu*, *s.* hare, [Colloq. හාවා *háwá*].

පිපුන, *Pipuna*, *a.* expanded, blown, as a flower; risen as bread, leavened.

පිපෙනවා, *Pipenawá*, *v.* to open, to expand, to blow (as a flower), to blossom; to rise as bread: pret. පිපුනා *pipuná*.

පිබිදීම, *Pibidíma*, *s.* awaking.

පිබිදෙනවා, *Pibidenawá*, *v.* to awake: pret. පිබිදුනා *pibiduná*.

පිඹිනවා, *Pimbinawá*, *v.* to blow, to blow a wind instrument; to hiss as a serpent: pret. පිම්බා *pimbá*.

පිඹීම, *Pimbíma*, } *s.* blowing, verbal noun of the
පිඹුම, *Pimbuma*, } foregoing.

පිඹුරා, *Pimburá*, *s.* rock snake, *python molurus*; this snake is sometimes said to grow to eighteen feet in length and twenty-seven inches in circumference: pl. පිඹුරෝ *pimburó*.

පිම්බෙනවා, *Pimbenawá*, see පිප්පෙනවා *pippenawá*.

පිම්ම, *Pimma*, *s.* somersault, leap.

පිම්මේයනවා, *Pimmé-yanawá*, *v.* to gallop.

පිය, *Piya*, *s.* father; husband, lord; woman; foot; foot-mark; stanza; birth, being, existence: *a.* pleasing, paternal, agreeable, beautiful; beloved; in the latter senses it is the Elu form of ප්‍රිය *priya*.

පියඋරුම, *Piya-uruma*, *s.* paternal inheritance.

පියකරණ, *Piyakaraṇa*, *s.* (පිය foot, කරණ what makes) footstep, footmark.

පියකරු, *Piyakaru*, *s.* making joyful, [Colloq. ප්‍රීති කරන්නාවූ *prítikarannáwú*].

පියකිරිල්ල, *Piya-kirilla*, *s.* plant, *hydrolea zeylanica*; also called දියකිරිල්ල *diya-kirilla*.

පියගඳ, *Piyaganda*, *s.* (පිය pleasant, ගඳ smell) perfume, fragrance, any agreeable smell, [Colloq. සුවඳ *suwanda*].

පියගැට, *Piyageṭa*, *s.* ladder, steps, stairs, [Colloq. ඉණිමග *iṇimaga*].

පියඟු, *Piyangu*, Elu form of ප්‍රියඞ්ගු *priyańgu*.

පියතම, *Piyatama*, *s.* husband.

පියතමා, *Piyatamá*, *s.* woman who goes to an assignation.

පියදමනවා, *Piyadamanawá*, see පිහදමනවා *pihadamanawá*.

පියන්, *Piyan*, *s.* rice field; lid; feathers.

පියන්පත, *Piyanpata*, *s.* lid, cover.

පියන, *Piyana*, *s.* cover, lid; one side of a folding door or window shutter: pl. පියන් *piyan*.

පියනවා, *Piyanawá*, *v.* to shut, to cover, to balance up, to close: pret. පිව්වා *piwwá*.

පියපතර, *Piyapatara*, *s.* wing of a bird.

පියපස්, *Piyapas*, *s.* (පිය foot, පස් earth) dust or mire which adheres to the feet in walking.

පියපස, *Piyapasa*, *s.* pudendum muliebre.

පියපාර්ශ්වය, *Piya-párṣwaya*, *s.* paternal side (as to relations.)

පියපෝරුව, *Piyapóruwa*, *s.* (පිය foot, පෝරුව stool) footstool, foot-board.

පියබන්ධු, *Piyabandu*, *s.* paternal relatives.

පියබඳ, *Piyabanda*, *s.* (පිය pleasing, බඳ body) woman, agreeable woman, [Colloq. ස්ත්‍රී *strí*].

පියඹ, *Piyamba*, } පියඹා, *Piyambá*, } *s.* copulation; thick set man; agreeable woman: *a.* active, industrious.

පියයුර, *Piyayura*, *s.* breast of a woman: pl. පියයුරු *piyayuru*.

පියයුරු, *Piyayuru*, *s.* thick cloud, cloud condensed with rain; breasts of a woman.

පියරි, *Piyari*, *s.* tree, *pleurostylia Wightii*, (*Celastraceæ*).

පියරුක, *Piya-ruka*, see පියාගස *piyá-gasa*.

පියරැව්, *Piyarew*, *s.* (පිය delightful, රැව් sound) delightful tone, agreeable voice, pleasing sound.

පියරැව්දෙනවා, *Piyarew-denawá*, *v.* to sing delightfully as a bird.

පියල්, *Piyal*, *s.* worn out clothes, rags.

පියල්ගහ, *Piyal-gaha*. *s.* tree, *nephelium longana*, [Colloq. මොරගහ *mora-gaha*].

පියල්ල, *Piyalla*, *s.* rag, piece of old cloth, half of a coconut shell, half of any thing globular, pl. පියලි *piyali*.

පියලි, *Piyali*, *s.* piece of cloth; any grain that divides in two as a bean, pea, etc; split pease, name of a tree: see පියාල *piyála*.

පියලිකරණවා, *Piyalikaraṇawá*, *v.* to reduce any globular seed into halves.

පියවනවා, *Piyawanawá*, *v.* to cause to be shut: pret. පියෙව්වා *piyewwá*.

පියවර, *Piyawara*, *s.* footstep, impression of the foot.

පියවරල, *Piyawarala*, *s.* fish, fish in general, [Coll: මත්‍ස්‍යයා *matsyayá*].

පියවි, *Piyavi*, *s.* nature; natural form; uninflected word, radical form of a word before the affixes forming the cases are subjoined.

පියවීම, *Piyavíma*, verbal noun of පියවනවා *piyawanawá*.

පියවුර, *Piyawura*, see පියයුර *piyayura*.

පියවුරු, *Piyawuru*, see පියයුරු *piyayuru*.

පියවෙනවා, *Piyawenawá*, *v.* to be closed (as a door), to balance (as an account), to have the eyes shut.

පියස්, *Piyas*, } පියස්ස, *Piyassa*, } *s.* court yard; roof of a house; projecting roof of a house. (Port.)

පියස, *Piyasa*, *s.* house or hut made of leaves; neighbourhood: *a.* near, proximate.

පියසි, *Piyasi*, *s.* woollen cloth; also, plur. of පියස්ස *piyassa*, roof.

පියසිත්, *Piyasit*, *a.* (පිය delightful, සිත් mind) agreeable, cheerful, pleasant.

පියසිය, *Piyasiya*, *a.* uninterrupted, constant.

පියහසර, *Piyahasara*, *s.* foot-path, [Colloq. අඩිපාර *aḍipára*].

පියා, *Piyá*, *s.* father; wing or feather of a bird.

පියාගස, *Piyá-gasa*, *s.* tree, *sarcocephalus cordatus*; also, *buchanania latifolia*.

පියාගැබ, *Piyá-geba*, *s.* (පියා wing, ගැබ womb) space under the wings of a fowl where the young are brooded.

පියානන්දෑ, *Piyánandé*, } පියානෝ, *Piyánó*, } *s.* father; (terms of more respect than පියා *piyá*.)

පියාපත, *Piyápata*, *s.* (පියා wing, පත leaf) feather; wing, pl. පියාපත් *piyápat*.

පියාඹනවා, *Piyámbanawá*, *v.* (පියා and අඹනවා *ambanawá* to exert) to fly: pret. පියෑඹුවා *piyémbuwá*.

පියාල, *Piyála*, *s.* tree, *Nephelium longana*. [Coll: මොරගහ *mora-ga*].

පියාසර, *Piyásara*, *s.* (පියා wing, සර to go) flying.

පියාසරකරණවා, *Piyásara-karaṇawá*, *v.* to fly.

පියු, *Piyu*, *s.* hiding, concealment.

පියුන්කල්, *Piyunkal*, corruptly for පියුම්කල් *piyum-kal*, which see.

පියුම්, *Piyum*, *s.* name of Ṣrí Kántáwa, or Lakshmí the goddess of prosperity and wife of Vishṇu: see also පද්ම *padma*.

පියුම්කල්, *Piyum-kal*, *s.* (පියුම් lotus, කල් woman) name of Lakshmí, wife of Vishṇu.

පියුම්කෙමි, *Piyum-kemi*, *s.* (පියුම් and කෙමි pistil) pistil of the lotus.

පියුම්ගැබ, *Piyum-gęba*, *s.* (පියුම් and ගැබ womb) name of Brahma, alluding to the fable of his being produced from the lotus that sprang from Vishṇu's navel.

පියුම්තඹ, *Piyumtamba*, *s.* name of Vishṇu.

පියුම්තෙනෙ, *Piyum-tené*, *s.* (පියුම් and තෙනෙ son) name of Káma the god of love.

පියුම්දම්, *Piyumdam*, *s.* (පියුම් lotus, දම් string) necklace of lotuses.

පියුම්නෙත්, *Piyum-net*, *s.* (පියුම් and නෙත් eye) name of Vishṇu, in allusion to his having eyes resembling the blue lotus.

පියුම්නැබ, *Piyum-nęba*, *s.* (පියුම් and නැබ navel) name of Vishṇu, alluding to the fable of the lotus which sprang from his navel, and from which Brahma was produced.

පියුම්පත, *Piyum-pata*, *s.* (පියුම් and පත leaf) leaf of the lotus.

පියුම්පණ, *Piyumpaṇa*, *s.* (පියුම් and පණ hand) name of Brahma, alluding to his holding a lotus in one hand; name of the sun.

පියුම්පෙත්ත, *Piyum-petta*, *s.* petal of the lotus.

පියුම්යොන්, *Piyumyon*, see පියුම්ගැබ *piyumgęba*.

පියුම්රා, *Piyumrá*, *s.* (පියුම් and රා colour) ruby; lotus-pond.

පියුම්රාමිණි, *Piyumrá-miṇi*, *s.* ruby, [Colloq. පද්මරාග *padmarága*].

පියුම්වනය, *Piyum-wanaya*, *s.* (පියුම් and වනය grove) place abounding with lotus flowers.

පියුම්විල, *Piyum-vila*, *s.* (පියුම් lotus, විල lake) lake or any standing water in which the lotus grows.

පියුම, *Piyuma*, *s.* lotus, *nelumbium speciosum:* see පද්ම *padma* and නෙළුම් *nęlum*.

පියුමකර, *Piyumakara*, see පියුම්විල *piyum-vila*.

පියුමරා, *Piyumará*, see පියුම්රා *piyumrá*.

පියුමසන, *Piyumasana*, *s.* (පියුම් *piyum* lotus, අසන *asana* seat) posture of religious meditation; name of Brahma, alluding to the fable of his being born from the lotus that sprang from Vishṇu's navel.

පියෙව්, *Piyew*, *s.* putting away, rejecting, casting off or away, driving from.

පියෙවි, *Piyevi*, corrupt form of පියවි *piyavi*.

පියෙස, *Piyesa*, *s.* enclosed, or purified spot; place, country, district.

පියෝ, *Piyó*, *s.* effort, exertion; dissimulation, deceit, cunning, trick; application, employment, usage, construction; also plur. of පියා *piyá*.

පිරට්ටිය, *Piraṭṭiya*, *s.* dislocation, crookedness; confused state.

පිරවිල්ල, *Piravilla*, } *s.* filling up, swelling.
පිරවීම, *Piravíma*, }

පිරි, *Piri*, *s.* ditch: *a*, filled, full: *ind.* around, surrounding, on every side; embracing, encircling; ornament; enforcement, stress; completion, fulfilling.

පිරිකම්, *Pirikam*, *s.* dressing, decoration; complete work, [Colloq. සැරසුම *sęrasuma*].

පිරිකර, *Pirikara*, *s.* (පිරි ornament, කර to make) jewel, ornament; decoration, embellishment; retinue, train; thing, article.

පිරිකෙව්, *Pirikew*, *s.* surrounding, encircling.

පිරිත, *Pirita*, *s.* (from පරිත්තා *parittá* (Páli.) protection) defence, protection, preservation; work so called comprising nine Sútras, complied from the Sútra Piṭaka, by the disciples of Buddha after his death; it consists chiefly of instructions for the expelling of demons and curing diseases.

පිරිතැස්ලි, *Piritęsli*, } *s.* prayer, request, [Colloq.
පිරිතැසුම්, *Piritęsum*, } ඉල්ලීම *illíma*].

පිරිදෙව්, *Piridew*, *s.* weeping, crying, mourning, [Colloq. වැලපීම *węlapíma*]; Elu form of පරිදේවනා *paridéwaná*.

පිරිනිවන්පානවා, *Piriniwanpánawá*, see the following word.

පිරිනිවනවා, *Piriniwanawá*, *v.* (පිරි completely, නිවනවා to extinguish) to die, to expire, to become extinct, as a Buddha, *i.e.* to be free from future transmigration: pret. පිරිනිවුනා *piriniwuná*, (uncommon).

පිරිනිවීම, *Pirinivíma*, verbal noun of the foregoing.

පිරිනැමු, *Pirinęmu*, *s.* right, due, claim: *a.* set apart.

පිරිපත, *Piripata*, *s.* danger, calamity: stickness, disease, pl. පිරිපත් *piripat*, [Colloq. උවදුර *uwadura*].

පිරිබඩ, *Piribaḍa*, *s.* sweeping; cleaning, cleansing.

පිරිබඩලනවා, *Piribaḍa-lanawá*, *v.* to cleanse, to rub.

පිරිබුන්, *Piribun*, *a.* (පිරි completely, බුන් breaking) destroyed, exterminated, rooted up, extirpated.

පිරිමඩිනවා, *Pirimaḍinawá*, see පිරිමදිනවා *pirimadinawá*.

පිරිමද, *Pirimada*, *s.* (පිරි and මද to cleanse) rubbing, polishing, cleaning.

පිරිමදිනවා, *Pirimadinawá*, *v.* to rub, to stroke; to caress, to fondle.

පිරිමසනවා, *Pirimasanawá*, } *v.* to distribute, to
පිරිමහනවා, *Pirimahanawá*, } give in small portions; to allow one's self a bare sufficiency, to economize: pret. පිරිමැහුවා *pirimẹhuwá*.

පිරිමි, *Pirimi*, *a.* masculine; also plur. of the next.

පිරිමියා, *Pirimiyá*, *s.* male, man.

පිරිමැස්ම, *Pirimẹsma*, } *s.* bare sufficiency,
පිරිමැසිල්ල, *Pirimẹsilla*, } economy; avarice.

පිරිමැහිල්ල, *Pirimẹhilla*, } see above.
පිරිමැහීම, *Pirimẹhíma*, }

පිරියත, *Piriyata*, *a.* (පිරි completely, යත to endeavour, to strive) finished, completed, done.

පිරියම්, *Piriyam*, *s.* (පිරි ornament, යම් substituted for කම් *kam* act) any beautiful or well finished piece of work.

පිරියස්, *Piriyas*, } *s.* seeking, searching, explor-
පිරියසුන්, *Piriyasun*, } ing, [Colloq. සෙවීම *sevíma*].

පිරිරු, *Piriru*, *a.* distant, far, [Coll: දුරවූ *durawú*].

පිරිවනවා, *Piriwanawá*, *v.* to read, to say, to repeat, to mutter, to repeat inaudibly, as mantras or kind of mystical formula.

පිරිවනු, *Piriwanu*, *past part.* of preceding verb.

පිරිවය, *Piṛiwaya*, *s.* disgrace, [Colloq. ලජ්ජාව *lajjáwa*].

පිරිවර, *Piriwara*, *s.* (පිරි around, වෘ *vṛi* to be) retinue, train, suite, attendants, followers.

පිරිවරණවා, *Piriwaraṇawá*, *v.* (පිරි and වෘ *vṛi* to be) to congregate, to surround as followers, attendants etc.: pret. පිරිවැරුවා *piriwẹruwá*.

පිරිවෙණ, *Piriweṇa*, *s.* building, house; priest's residence; hermit's cell; cell or hut forming a monk's private chamber in a Buddhist monastery; (Childers). This word is sometimes applied to a college attached to a Buddhist monastery.

පිරිවෙස්, *Piriwes*, *s.* (පිරි surrounding, encircling, වෙස් covering) disc of the sun or moon; halo round the sun or moon.

පිරිවැණි, *Piriwẹni*, *s.* contortions of the body through pain.

පිරිවැස්ස, *Piriwẹssa*, *s.* basket made by interweaving the leaves of the coconut tree: pl. පිරිවැසි *piriwẹsi* or පිරිවැහි *piriwẹhi*.

පිරිස්, *Piris*, *s.* attendants, followers.

පිරිස, *Pirisa*, *s.* train, retinue, suite.

පිරිසඳ, *Piri-saṉda*, *s.* full moon.

පිරිසිදු, *Pirisidu*, *a.* (පිරි completely, සිදු clean) pure, clean, spotless.

පිරිසිඳ, *Pirisiṉda*, *part.* (පිරි and සිඳ to investigate) having ascertained; having cleared up doubts.

පිරිහීම, *Pirihíma*, *s.* destruction, annihilation; verbal noun of පිරිහෙනවා *pirihenawá*.

පිරිහුන්, *Pirihun*, *part.* wasted; lost.

පිරිහෙනවා, *Pirihenawá*, *v.* (පිරි implying intensity, හා *há* to quit) to consume, to waste away, to be destroyed or annihilated, to decline.

පිරිහෙළනවා, *Pirihelanawá*, *v.* to scorn, to contemn: pret. පිරිහෙළුවා *piriheḷuwá*: [Colloq. නින්දාකරණවා *nindákaraṇawá*].

පිරි, *Pirí*, *a.* full, filled.

පිරුණු, *Piruṇu*, *a.* filled, fulfilled, completed; vanished.

පිරුමිණි, *Pirumiṇi*, *part.* filling, being filled.

පිරුවට, *Piruwaṭa*, *s.* cloth or dress lent by a washerman to a person to wear while his own is being washed; lending clothes for a marriage; fitting up a place for festival occasions.

පිරුළු, *Piruḷu*, *s.* answer, reply, [Colloq. උත්තරය *uttaraya*].

පිරෙණවා, *Pireṇawá*, *v.* to be filled, or become full: pret. පිරුණා *piruṇá*.

පිල්, *Pil*, *s.* flower; cripple, man born lame; peacock's feathers.

පිල් ඇස්, *Pil-ẹs*, *s.* (පිල් tail, ඇස් eye) peacock, [Colloq. මොණරා *moṇará*].

පිල්කලප්, *Pil-kalap*, *s.* pot filled with water and flowers on festival occasions: see පුන්කලස *punkalasa*; cluster of peacock's feathers, peacock's tail.

පිල්කලඹ, *Pilkalaṃba*, *s.* peacock's tail.

පිල්බර, *Pilbara*, *s.* (පිල් feather, බර multitude) peacock's tail, [Colloq. මොණර පෙඳේ *moṇara-peṉdé*].

පිල්ල, *Pilla*, *s.* blear-eye; branch; wing of a peacock; testicles, pl. පිලි *pili*.

පිල්ලං, *Pillaṇ*, *s.* rheum of the eye; art of teaching children how to unite the vowels with a consonant; symbol of a vowel; twig, sprout: *a.* blear-eyed.

පිල්ලංකියනවා, *Pillaŋ-kiyanawá*, *v.* to repeat each letter with all the symbols of the vowels successively.

පිල්ලම, *Pillama*, *s.* attaching vowel-symbols to consonants.

පිල්ලි, *Pilli*, *s.* destruction or injury of an enemy by magical or demoniacal incantations, witchcraft, spell.

පිල්ලෑව, *Pillẹ́wa*, *s.* little mounds in a swamp.

පිල්වල්ල, *Pil-walla*, *s.* spreading tale of a bird, plumage; meadow land attached to a field.

පිල්සෙවෙල, *Pil-sewela*, *s.* plant, variety of *blyxa Roxburghii* or *vallisneria octandra.*

පිල, *Pila*, *s.* verandah of a house, portico or vestibule; plant, *nerium.*

පිලක, *Pilaka*, *s.* spear, lance, javelin, dart.

පිලගෙඩිය, *Pila-geḍiya*, *s.* very thin line used by anglers.

පිලන්ධන, *Pilandhana*, *s.* ornament, decoration for the person; putting on a garment.

පිලවා, *Pilawá*, *s.* young of any animal, grub, maggot: pl. පිලව් *pilaw.*

පිලාඔරුව, *Pilá-oruwa*. *s.* very small boat.

පිලිකන්න, *Pilikanna*, *s.* back of the house: pl. පිලිකනු *pilikanu.*

පිලිදු, *Pilidu*, *s.* multitude, [Colloq. සමූහය *samúhaya*].

පිලින්වෙනවා, *Pilinwenawá*, *v.* to become stale, putrified (as rice when left for a day or two).

පිලිස්සෙනවා, *Pilissenawá*, *v.* to burn, to be on fire, to be scorched: pret. පිලිස්සුනා *pilissuná.*

පිලීමෝල, *Pilí-móla*, *s.* iron-ringed pestle.

පිවිටු, *Piviṭu*, *s.* approaching, arriving, coming near; entering; Elu form of ප්‍රවිෂ්ට *pravishṭa*: *p.* entered.

පිවිතුරු, *Pivituru*, *s.* joy, gladness, pleasure; gracefulness in dancing; sentiment of love, as a poetical taste; mind; arrow grass, *heteropogon hirtus*, [Colloq. ඊතණ *ítaṇa*]; purity, cleanness; ornament, trinket: *a.* pure, clean (poetical term).

පිවිස, *Pivisa*, *s.* entering, approaching, coming near, [Colloq. පැමිණ *pẹmina*].

පිවිසෙනවා, *Pivisenawá*, *v.* to enter: pret. පිවිසුනා *pivisuná.*

පිවු, *Piwu*, *s.* removing afar off, separating from: *a.* shut, closed; sometimes written පියු *piyú.*

පිශාච, *Piṣácha*, see පිසස් *pisas.*

පිශුන, *Piṣuna*, see පිසුන *pisuna.*

පිෂ්ට, *Pishṭa*, *s.* flour, meal, any ground corn, rice etc.: *a.* ground, bruised, pounded, pulverized.

පිෂ්ටක, *Pishṭaka*, *s.* (පිෂ්ට and ක aff.) cake made of the flour or meal of any grain; disease of the eyes, film or opacity of the cornea.

පිෂ්ට පචන, *Pishṭa-pachana*, *s.* (පිෂ්ට flour, meal, පචන cooking) seething pot, large chatty or earthen pot for cooking.

පිෂ්ටාත, *Pishṭáta*, *s.* (පිෂ්ට *pishṭa* pounded (saffron) etc. අත *ata* to go, to be) powder, dust, but especially perfumed powder.

පිස්තෝලෙ, *Pistóle*, *s.* pistol. (Port.)

පිස්නාකඩේ, *Pisnákaḍé*, *s.* wiping cloth, napkin, towel.

පිස්සන්කොටුව, *Pissan-koṭuwa*, *s.* lunatic asylum.

පිස්සා, *Pissá*, *s.* mad man, maniac; fool: pl. පිස්සෝ *pissó*: *v.* pret. of පිසනවා *pisanawá.*

පිස්සි, *Pissi*, *s.* mad woman.

පිස්සි කෙසෙල්, *Pissi-kesel*, *s.* variety of plantain, *musa sapientum.*

පිස්සු, *Pissu*, *a.* mad, insane.

පිස්සුකම, *Pissukama*, } *s.* insanity.
පිස්සුව, *Pissuwa*, }

පිස්සුවැටෙනවා, *Pissuwẹṭenawá*, } *v.* to become
පිස්සුවැහෙනවා, *Pissuwẹhenawá*, } mad, to turn maniac, to be seized with fury.

පිස, *Pisa*, *part* of පිසිනවා *pisinawá;* having cleaned, rubbed; cooked.

පිසදමනවා, *Pisadamanawá*, *v.* to sweep, to clean; to rub, to wipe.

පිසන්, *Pisan*, *s.* disappearance, concealment, covering.

පිසන්නා, *Pisanná*, *s.* (පිස cooking, අන්නා *anná* pers. aff.) cook, [Colloq. කෝකියා *kókiyá*].

පිසන, *Pisana*, *s.* cooking, preparing food; maturing, ripening; wiping, cleaning.

පිසනගේ, *Pisana-gé*, *s.* (පිසන cooking, ගේ house) kitchen, cook-house.

පිසනවා, *Pisanawá*, *v.* to cook, to prepare food; to ripen, to mature: pret. පිසුවා *pisuwá* or පිස්සා *pissá.*

පිසස්, *Pisas*, *s.* demon, [Colloq. යකා *yaká*].

පිසාචද්‍රු, *Pisáchadru*, *s.* (පිසාච goblin, ද්‍රු tree) tree, *streblus asper* or *trophis aspera;* this name alludes to the supposition that this tree is the favourite haunt of these beings, [Colloq. ගැට නිටුල් *gẹṭaniṭul*].

පිසාචි, *Pisáchi*, *s.* sprite, fiend, malevolent being, infernal being, ghost, but always described as fierce and malignant.

පිසාචිකා, *Pisáchiká*, *s.* Indian spikenard, [Colloq. ජටාමාංස *jaṭámáṇsa*].

පිසාචි, *Pisáchi*, *s.* (පිසාච *pisácha* goblin, ඊ *í* fem. aff.) female imp, she goblin.

පිසි, *Pisi*, *s.* cleansing, sweeping.

පිසිත, *Pisita*, *s.* flesh, meat.

පිසිතා, *Pisitá*, *s.* spikenard: see පිසාචිකා *pisáchicá*.

පිසින, *Pisina*, *a.* cleaning, rubbing, wiping.

පිසිනවා, *Pisinawá*, *pret.* පිස්සා *pissá*: see පිසදමන වා *pisadamanawá*.

පිසිඹ, *Pisimba*, *s.* nimba or margosa tree, *azadirachta indica*, [Colloq. කොහොඹ *kohomba*].

පිසීම, *Pisíma*, verbal noun of පිසනවා *pisanawá*.

පිසුන, *Pisuna*, *s.* saffron; cotton; crow; spy, informer, tale bearer: *a.* vile, low, contemptible; stupid, foolish; cruel, wicked: *p.* cooked.

පිසුනා, *Pisuná*, *s.* leguminous plant, *trigonella corniculata*: *v.* cooked.

පිසුනාවාචා, *Pisunáwáchá*, *s.* (පිසුනා and වාචා speech) abuse, slander.

පිසුනු, *Pisunu*, *s.* slander, calumny, tale-bearing, backbiting: *a.* cooked; matured, ripe.

පිහදමනවා, *Pihadamanawá*, see පිසදමනවා *pisadamanawá*.

පිහන්නා, *Pihanná*, see පිසන්නා *pisanná*.

පිහනගේ, *Pihana-gé*, see පිසනගේ *pisana-gé*.

පිහනවා, *Pihanawá*, see පිසනවා *pisanawá*.

පිහා *Pihá*, *s.* wing.

පිහාට්ට, *Piháṭṭa*, *s.* feather, quill, wing of a bird, pl. පිහාටු *piháṭu*.

පිහාඹනවා, *Pihámbanawá*, corruptly for පියාඹනවා *piyámbanawá*, which see.

පිහාමැස්සා, *Pihá-messá*, *s.* flying-fish; general name for species of *gar pikes*.

පිහාසර, *Pihásara*, corruptly for පියාසර *piyásara*, which see.

පිහි, *Pihi*, *s.* wiping, cleansing, scouring; sweeping.

පිහිකල, *Pihikala*, *s.* when shut or closed.

පිහිකුල්, *Pihikul*, } *a.* covered, closed, shutted up,
පිහිකුළු, *Pihikuḷu*, } [Colloq. වැසුනු *wesunu*].

පිහිට, *Pihiṭa*, *a.* help, favour, assistance.

පිහිටනවා, *Pihiṭanawá*, *v.* to operate, to be effectual as a medicine; to be established: pret. පිහිටුනා *pihiṭuná*.

පිහිටවනවා, *Pihiṭawanawá*, *pret.* පිහිටෙව්වා *pihiṭewwá*: see පිහිටුවනවා *pihiṭu-wanawá*.

පිහිටවෙනවා, *Pihiṭawenawá*, *v.* to help, to assist.

පිහිටාධාරය, *Pihiṭádháraya*, *s.* help, assistance.

පිහිටි, *Pihiṭi*, *a.* fixed, placed, planted, settled, established; situated.

පිහිටුවනවා, *Pihiṭuwanawá*, *v.* to fix, to plant, to establish, to settle in a place: pret. පිහිටෙව්වා *pihiṭewwá*.

පිහිත, *Pihita*, *a.* covered, concealed.

පිහිනනවා, *Pihinanawá*, *v.* to swim, to float: pret. පිහිනුවා *pihinuwá*: also, see පීනනවා *pínanawá*.

පිහිනවා, *Pihinawá*, *v.* to rub, to wipe: pret. පිස්සා *pissá*.

පිහිනුම, *Pihinuma*, *s.* act of swimming.

පිහිය, *Pihiya*, } *s.* knife, chopper, pl. පිහියා *pi-*
පිහියේ, *Pihiyé*, } *hiyá*: see පිහය *píhaya*.

පිහිර, *Pihira*, *s.* file, rasp; also, see පීර *píra*.

පිහිරණවා, *Pihiraṇawá*, *v.* to comb, to dress the hair with a comb: pret. පිහිරුවා *pihiruwá*: see පීරණවා *píraṇawá*.

පිහිල්ල, *Pihilla*, *s.* spout, gutter; also, see පීල්ල *pílla*.

පිළා, *Piḷá*, *s*, cripple.

පිළි, *Piḷi*, *s.* cloth; fruit; tree; wing of a bird, feather; demon: *ind.* particle and prefix implying substitution, exchange, return etc., order, arrangement, severally: see ප්‍රති *prati*; around, on every side; encompassing: see පරි *pari*.

පිළිඇදුරන්, *Piḷi-eduran*, *s.* rival teachers.

පිළිකාව, *Piḷikáwa*, *s.* abscess; cancer.

පිළිකාවනස්ස, *Piḷiká-wanassa*, *s.* plant of the *genus lycopodium*.

පිළිකුල්, *Piḷikul*, *a.* (පිළි completely, කුල් filthy) unclean, filthy, dirty, nasty: *a.* disgusting, abominable.

පිළිකුල, *Piḷikula*, *s.* disgust, loathing; filth, uncleanness, abomination.

පිළිකේ, *Piḷiké*, see පිළිකාව *piḷikáwa*.

පිළිගත්, *Piḷigat*, *s.* accepted.

පිළිගඳ, *Piḷiganda*, *s.* smell of fishes.

පිළිගන්නවා, *Piḷigannawá*, *v.* (පිළි and ගන්නවා to take) to accept, to receive, to approve.

පිළිගැනීම, *Piḷigeníma*, *s.* acceptance.

පිළිණ, *Piḷiṇa*, *s.* promise, agreement, covenant, pledge, [Colloq. ගිවිසුම *givisuma*].

පිළිතුර, *Piḷitura*, } *s.* (පිළි implying return, තුරු
පිළිතුරු, *Piḷituru*, } for උත්තර *uttara* answer) rejoinder, reply, answer.

පිළිතොරණ, *Piḷitoraṇa*, see පිළිතොරණ *piḷitoraṇa*.

පිළිදගින්, *Piḷidagin*, *s.* favour, protection, care.

පිළිපදිනවා, *Piḷipadinawá*, *v.* to preserve, to keep, to observe as directions or commands.

පිළිපන්, *Piḷipan*, s. knowledge: p. come to, attained.

පිළිපෙට්ටිය, *Piḷipeṭṭiya*, s. rattan basket.

පිළිපැදීම, *Piḷipędíma*, s. observance; verbal noun of පිළිපදිනවා *piḷipadinawá*.

පිළිබඳ, *Piḷibaṉda*, a. (පිළි implying intensity, බඳ bound) attached, connected with.

පිළිබිඹු, *Piḷibimbu*, s. likeness, image, painting; face as shown or reflected in a mirror, [Colloq. රූපය *rúpaya*].

පිළිමය, *Piḷimaya*, s. likeness, picture, image, counterpart of any thing, the face when reflected in a mirror, idol.

පිළිමල්, *Piḷimal*, s. (පිළි against, මල් boxer) enemy, adversary, opponent, [Colloq. සතුරා *saturá*].

පිළිමසත්, *Piḷimasat*, s. covering, screen, defence.

පිළිමිණ, *Piḷimiṇa*, } s. crystal, [Colloquial: පළිඟු
පිළිමිණි, *Piḷimiṇi*, } *paḷiṉgu*].

පිළිය, *Piḷiya*, see පිළි *piḷi*.

පිළියන, *Piḷiyana*, s. slave, dependant, servant, menial, [Colloq. දාසයා *dásayá*].

පිළියම්කරණවා, *Piḷiyamkaraṇawá*, v. to heal, to cure, to practice medicine; to piece, to make whole; to mend, to refit.

පිළියම, *Piḷiyama*, s. refitting, mending: see පිළියම් කරණවා *piḷiyamkaraṇawá*.

පිළියෙළ, *Piḷiyeḷa*, s. preparation, readiness.

පිළියෙළකරණවා, *Piḷiyeḷa-karaṇawá*, v. to make ready, to prepare.

පිළිරූ, *Piḷiru*, s. likeness, counterpart, image, reflection of the face in a mirror; similitude; metaphor, simile: see පිළිමය *piḷimaya*.

පිළිරැව්, *Piḷiręw*, s. (පිළි return, instead, රැව් sound) noise, sound, sound in general, [Colloq. හඬ *haṉḍa*]; resonance, echo, reiterated sound.

පිළිල, *Piḷila*, s. wave; parasite, *loranthus longiflorus*, growing on trees, the name is applied to the whole genus, *(Loranthaceæ)*.

පිළිවක්, *Piḷiwak*, s. resemblance, likeness, similarity.

පිළිවදන්, *Piḷiwadan*, s. answer, [Colloq. උත්තරය *uttaraya*].

පිළිවන්, *Piḷiwan*, a. able, possible.

පිළිවිස්සාහ, *Piḷivissáha*, p. questioned, [Colloq. ඇසූවාය *ęsuwáya*].

පිළිවිස, *Piḷivisa*, *past part.* of the following.

පිළිවිසිනවා, *Piḷivisinawá*, v. (පිළි and විසනවා to judge) to inquire, to investigate, to ask, to search into, to investigate thoroughly: pret. පිළිවිස්සා *piḷivissá*.

පිළිවෙත්කරණවා, *Piḷiwet-karaṇawá*, v. to observe a religious rite, to perform a ceremony, to order, to arrange; to accomplish, to practise; to obey.

පිළිවෙත, *Piḷiweta*, s. religious obedience; practice, use, performance; attainment, acquirement; tidings, intelligence.

පිළිවෙළ, *Piḷiweḷa*, s. order, method, degree.

පිළිසඳර, *Piḷisaṉdara*, s. salutation, friendly conversation.

පිළිසඳර කථාව, *Piḷisaṉdara-katháwa*, s. (පිළිසඳර and කථාව talk) mutual intercourse, conversing together, pleasing or interesting conversation.

පිළිසන්, *Piḷisan*, s. invisibility; loss, disappearance, vanishing; concealment, hiding, [Colloq. සැඟවීම *sęṉgavíma*]: a. covered, hidden.

පිළිසර, *Piḷisara*, s. (පිළි successively, සර thought) doubt, perplexity, uncertainty; sorrow of mind.

පිළිසරණ, *Piḷisaraṇa*, s. (පිළි exceeding, සරණ help) help, assistance, favour; patronage.

පිළිසිඳින, *Piḷisiṉdina*, *part.* conceiving.

පිළිසිඳීම, *Piḷisiṉdíma*, s. conception.

පිළිසිඳෙනවා, *Piḷisiṉdenawá*, v. to be produced, to conceive, to be generated: pret. පිළිසිඳුනා *piḷisiṉduná*.

පිළිසිඹියාව, *Piḷisiṃbiyáwa*, s. perfect knowledge; Elu form of පටිසම්භිදා *paṭisambhidá*: see සිවුපිළිසිඹියාව *siwupiḷisiṃbiyáwa*.

පිළිසුන්, *Piḷisun*, a. covered, conceived.

පිළිසුන්දසාව, *Piḷisun-dasáwa*, s. the asterism under which one is conceived in the mother's womb.

පිළිහුඩුපලා, *Piḷihuḍu-palá*, s. braken, *pteris thalictroides*,

පිළිහුඩුවා, *Piḷihuḍuwá*, s. red kingfisher, *ceryle rudis (Alcedinidæ)*; white-breasted kingfisher, *halcyon smyrnensis*, *(Halcyoninæ*, order *Pecariæ)*.

පිළී, *Piḷí*, s. cloth; filth, dirt.

පිළීකඩ, *Piḷíkaḍa*, s. piece of cloth, handkerchief.

පිළීතොරණ, *Piḷí-toraṇa*, s. (පිළී cloth, තොරණ triumphal arch) ornamented with cloth, fruit, flowers etc. and erected on festival occasions.

පිළු, *Piḷu*, s. cloth; cripple, lame man.

පිළුන්වෙනවා, *Piḷunwenawá*, v. to become unfit for use, as meat when it gets stale.

පීඨ, *Pítha*, s. stool, seat, chair; wooden platform on which things are exposed for sale, shop.

පීඨසප්පි, *Pítha-sarppí*, s. (පීඨ stool, සප් *sarpa* to go, ඉ *i* aff.) cripple who moves about on a wheeled chair.

පීඩන, *Píḍana*, *s.* oppression, affliction.

පීඩාකරණවා, *Píḍákaraṇawá*, *v.* to persecute, to afflict.

පීඩාකෙරීම, *Píḍákeríma*, verbal noun of පීඩාකරණවා *píḍákaraṇawá*.

පීඩාව, *Píḍáwa*, *s.* pain, anguish, suffering, affliction; devastation, laying waste.

පීඩිත, *Píḍita*, *a.* pained, suffering distress or pain; devastated, laid waste, destroyed.

පීත්ත, *Pítta*, *s.* ribbon. (Port.)

පීත, *Píta*, *s.* yellow (colour); safflower; topaz; yellow pigment prepared from the urine of kine; yellow orpiment; drinking; turmeric; medicinal plant, *betula*: *a.* yellow, of a yellow colour; drank, quaffed.

පීතක, *Pítaka*, *s.* yellow orpiment, saffron; aloe-wood; brass; honey; sort of gentian.

පීතකරෝහිණී, *Pítakaróhiṇí*, *s.* yellow orpiment.

පීතකසිණ, *Píta-kasiṇa*, *s.* (පීත and කසිණ kasiṇa) powers of vision so affected by the performance of this part of the kasiṇa, (*i. e.* process by means of which mystic meditation may be induced), viz. the eyes having been for a length of time immovably fixed on some yellow substance, as clay, earth, etc. that every other object appears to be of a yellow colour.

පීතචන්දන, *Píta-chandana*, *s.* (පීත yellow, චන්දන sandal) yellow fragrant wood, considered as a yellow species of sandal; turmeric, saffron, *curcuma longa*.

පීතතෛලා, *Píta-tailá*, *s.* creeper, species of the heart-pea, *cardiospermum halicacabum*, [Colloq. පෙනෙලවැල් *penela-węl*].

පීතදාරු, *Pítadáru*, *s.* (පීත and දාරු wood) sort of pine, *pinus dévadáru;* also, *pinus longifolia*.

පීතද්‍රු, *Pítadru*, *s.* (පීත and ද්‍රු tree) tree, *pinus longifolia;* sort of *curcuma*, *c. zanthorrhiza;* also, *coscinium fenestratum*, [Colloq. වෙනිවැල් *weni-węl*].

පීතන, *Pítana*, *s.* hog plum, *spondias mangifera*, [Colloq. ඇඹරැල්ල *ęmbaręlla*]; tree, *pentaptera tomentosa;* waved-leaf fig; saffron; sort of pine, *pinus dévadáru;* yellow orpiment.

පීතපුෂ්පක, *Píta-pushpaka*, *s.* (පීත and පුෂ්ප *pushpa* flower) plant, yellow *barleria prionitis*, [Colloq. කටුකරඬු *kaṭukaranḍu*]; it may also be applied to any plant bearing yellow flowers.

පීතපුෂ්පි, *Pítapushpi*, *s.* (පීත yellow, පුෂ්ප *pushpa*, flower, ඉ *i* aff. of comparison) yellow barleria; saffron.

පීතපුෂ්පිකා, *Píta-pushpiká*, *s.* ash pumpkin, *benincasa cerifera*, [Colloq. අළුපුහුල් *aḷu-puhul*].

පීතඵල, *Píta-phala*, *s.* (පීත yellow, ඵල fruit) tree, *trophis aspera:* see පිසාචද්‍රු *pisáchadru*.

පීතමණි, *Píta-maṇi*, *s.* (පීත yellow, මණි gem) topaz, [Colloq. පුෂ්පරාග *pushparága*].

පීතමර්කට, *Píta-markaṭa*, *s.* (පීත and මර්කට monkey) species of ape or monkey.

පීතමූල, *Píta-múla*, *s.* (පීත and මූල root) saffron, turmeric, *curcuma longa*, [Colloq. කහ *kaha*].

පීතරත්න, *Pítaratna*, *s.* yellow gem, [Colloq. ගෝමේද *góméda*].

පීතලෝහ, *Pítalóha*, *s.* yellow brass; queen's metal, or a mixed metal resembling gold.

පීතවර්ණ, *Píta-warṇa*, *s.* (පීත yellow, වර්ණ colour) yellow colour.

පීතවාසස්, *Píta-wásas*, *s.* (පීත and වාසස් vesture) name of Kṛishṇa, alluding to the colour of his dress.

පීතසාර, *Pítasára*, } *s.* (පීත and සාර essence)
පීතසාරක, *Pítasáraka*, } sandal; yellow gem, topaz; tree, *alangium hexapetalum*, [Colloq. රුක් අඟුන *ruk-anguna*]; *morinda citrifolia* or *m. tinctoria*, [Colloq. අහුගස් *ahu-gas*].

පීතාම්බර, *Pítámbara*, *s.* (පීත *píta* yellow, අම්බර vesture) religious mendicant wearing a yellow dress; name of Kṛishṇa or Vishṇu in that form; actor, dancer, they being so dressed.

පීතාශ්මන්, *Pítáṣman*, *s.* (පීත *píta* yellow, අශ්මන් *aṣman* stone) yellow gem, topaz, [Colloq. පුෂ්පරාග *pushparága*].

පීති, *Píti*, *s.* joy, gladness, Páli form of ප්‍රීති *príti*, dram shop; drinking.

පීථ, *Pítha*, *s.* sun; fire; time; water.

පීදෙනවා, *Pídenawá*, *v.* to form ears, as corn; to bear fruit: pret. පිදුනා *piduná*.

පීන, *Pína*, *a.* fat, bulky, large, corpulent; full, complete.

පීනනවා, *Pínanawá*, *v.* to float, to swim: pret. පීනුවා *pínuwá*.

පීනස, *Pínasa*, *s.* cold affecting the nose, catarrh.

පීනීම, *Piníma*, } verbal noun of පීනනවා *pínana-*
පීනුම, *Pínuma*. } *wá*.

පීනෝධ්නී, *Pínódhní*, *s.* (පීන *pína* full, උධ්නී *udhní* from උධස් *udhas* udder, ඊ *í* aff. and අනඞ් *anań* augment) full udder; cow having udders full of milk.

පීප්පවලලු, *Píppa-walalu*, *s.* hoop-iron.

පීප්පෙ, *Píppe*, *s.* cask, pl. පීප්ප *píppa*.

පීම, *Píma*, *s.* (පා *pá* to drink) drink, drinking.

පිය, *Píya*, *s.* sun, [Colloq. සූර්‍ය්‍යයා *súryayá*].

පියු, *Píyu*, *s.* sun; time; owl; crow.

පියූෂ, *Piyúsha*, } *s.* food of the gods, ambrosia, nectar; milk.
පියූෂරුචි, *Piyúsha-ruchi*, }

පිර, *Píra*, *s.* file, rasp, pl. පිරි *píri*.

පිරණවා, *Píraṇawá*, *v.* to comb, to dress the hair with a comb: pret. පිරුවා *píruwá*.

පිරා, *Pírá*, *past part.* of the foregoing.

පිරිගානවා, *Pírigánawá*, *v.* to file.

පිරිතලේ, *Píri-talé*, *s.* file without the handle.

පිරිස්කෝප්පය *Pírisḱóppaya*, *s.* cup of a saucer.

පිරිසිය, *Pírisiya*, *s.* saucer.

පිල්ල, *Pílla*, *s.* spout, aqueduct, conduit; gutter, sewer.

පිලක, *Pílaka*, *s.* large black ant, [Colloq. කඩියා *kaḍiyá*].

පිලු, *Pílu*, *s.* name of a tree applied in some places to the patana oak, *careya arborea*, [Colloq. කහට *kahaṭa*], and in others to the mustard, *salvadora persica*, [Colloq. අබ *aba*]; tree, *nephelium longana*, [Colloq. මොර *mora*]; flower; atom; blossom of the *saccharum sara;* insect; metacarpus, central part of the hand; stem of the palm tree.

පිලුක, *Píluka*, *s.* tree, *nephelium longana*, [Colloq. මොර *mora*].

පිලුපර්ණී, *Pílu-parṇṇi*, *s.* plant, *marsdenia tennacissima*, [Colloq. මුරුවාදුල් *muruwá-dúl*]; also, *momordica monadelpha*, [Colloq. කෙම්වැල් *kemwel*].

පීවර, *Píwara*, *a.* fat, large, bulky.

පීවරස්තනී, *Píwarastaní*, *s.* (පීවර large, ස්තන *stana* breast, ඉ *i* fem. aff.) cow with large udders or a woman with large breasts.

පීවරී, *Píwarí*, *s.* plant, *asparagus falcatus*, [Colloq. හාතාවාරිය *hátáwáriya*].

පිහය, *Píhaya*, *s.* knife.

පීළනය, *Píḷanaya*, *s.* pain, infliction of sufferings.

පුං, *Puṇ*, *a.* male, masculine.

පුංචි, *Puṇchi*, *a.* little, small, diminutive: also written පුඤ්චි *puñchi*.

පුංචිය, *Puṇchiya*, *s.* small tenon in carpentry.

පුංචිදිව, *Puṇchi-diwa*, *s.* uvula or soft palate.

පුංලිංග, *Puṇ-liṅga*, *s.* male organ, masculine gender, (in grammar).

පුංසවන, *Puṇ-sawana*, *s.* (පුං male, සවන bearing as children, bringing forth) religious and domestic festival held among the Hindus on the mother's observing the first signs of a living conception.

පුක්කුස, *Pukkusa*, *s.* chanḍála or man of the caste or tribe so called; one of a low or base occupation; scavenger.

පුක්කුසී, *Pukkusí*, *s.* indigo, *indigofera tinctoria*, [Colloq. අවරි *awari*]; bud or blossom; also the fem. of the last word.

පුක් පනිනවා, *Puk-paninawá*, *v.* to start from the socket (the eye): see පුප්පැලෙනවා *pup-pęlenawá*.

පුක, *Puka*, *s.* ball of the eye; posteriors; anus.

පුකිරි, *Pukiri*, *s.* goglet, [Colloq. ගුරුලේත්තුව *guruléttuwa*].

පුග්ගල, *Puggala*, *s.* man; any sentient being; Páli form of පුද්ගල *pudgala*, which see.

පුඟුල, *Puṉgula*, } see the following, pl, පුඟුල් *puṉgul*.
පුඟුලා, *Puṉgulá*, }

පුඞ්ඛ, *Puṅkha*, *s.* (පුං man, ඛන *khana* to destroy) feathered part of an arrow; tree, *nerium*, or *tephrosia*, [Colloq. පිල *pila* and කටුපිල *kaṭu-pila*].

පුඞ්ගල, *Puṅgala*, *s.* soul: see පුග්ගල *puggala* and පුද්ගල *pudgala*.

පුඞ්ගව, *Puṅgawa*, *s.* bull, [Colloq. ගොණා *goṇá*]; (in composition,) *a.* excellent, pre-eminent.

පුච්චනවා, *Puchchanawá*, *v.* to bake, burn, scald: pret. පිච්චුවා *pichchuwá*.

පුච්ඡ, *Puchchha*, *s.* tail; tail or hinder part; horse's tail; tail of a peacock.

පුච්ඡා, *Puchchhá*, *s.* question (for investigation), enquiry, demand.

පුච්ඡිකා, *Puchchhiká*, *s.* medicinal plant, fern, *drymoglossum heterophyllum*, [Colloq. මස්වැන්න *maswęnna*].

පුඤ්චා, *Puñchá*, *s.* little one.

පුඤ්චාවි, *Puñchávi*, *a.* young girl.

පුඤ්චි, *Puñchi*, *s.* small in size: also written පුංචි *puṇchi*.

පුඤ්චිකම, *Puñchikama*, *s.* disgrace, literally smallness.

පුඤ්චිකරණවා, *Puñchikaraṇawá*, *v.* to reduce in size, to disparage, to disgrace.

පුඤ්චි කොහා, *Puñchi-kohá*, *s.* small cuckoo or Sonnerat's cuckoo, *cuculus sonnerati*, *(Cuculidæ* order *Picariæ)*.

පුඤ්චි බස්සා, *Puñchi-bassá*, *s.* Forster's scops owl, *scops bakkamuna;* Rufous scops owl, *s. sunia;* little scops owl, *s. minatus;* brown hawk owl, *nicox scutulata;* chesnut-backed owlet, *glaucidium custanotum; (Bubonidæ*, sub-order *Striges*, order *Acciptres)*.

පුඤ්චි මල්පිළිහුඩුවා, *Puñchi-malpiḷihuḍuwá*, *s.* Indian three-toed kingfisher, *Ceyx tridactyla* (sub-order *Halcyoninæ*, order *Picariæ*).

පුඤ්ජ, *Puñja*, *s.* heap, quantity, collection, multitude, [Colloq. හුඟක් *hungak*, සමූහය *samúhaya*].

පුඤ්ජන, *Puñjana*, *s.* wiping, cleansing.

පුඤ්ඤ, *Puñña*, *a.* blessed, happy, fortunate, lucky; meritorious.

පුඤ්ඤකිරිය, *Puññakiriya*, *s.* good action, virtue, merit, moral or religious merit.

පුඤ්ඤවන්ත, *Puññawanta*, see පුඤ්ඤ *puñña*.

පුට, *Puṭa*, *s.* placing the palms of the hands together, closing or shutting the hands so as to hold any thing; narrowing or folding any thing so as to form a cup or concavity; small flame or blaze; cloth worn to cover the privities.

පුටක, *Puṭaka*, *s.* cup or concavity made of a leaf doubled into the shape of a funnel, [Colloq. ගොටුව *goṭuwa*].

පුටකෝෂ, *Puṭakósha*, *s.* garlic, *allium sativum*, [Colloq. සුදුළූනු *sudulúnu*].

පුටදෙනවා, *Puṭadenawá*, *v.* (පුට fire, දෙනවා to give) to calcine metals; to prepare medicines by the operation of fire.

පුටපාකය, *Puṭapákaya*, *s.* (පුට flame, පාක *páka* cooking) preparing food, condiments or any medicine made by the operation of fire; digesting, subliming; burning, conflagration.

පුටභේද, *Puṭabhéda*, } *s.* (පුට contraction, භේ
පුටභේදන, *Puṭabhédana*, } ද breaking) bend of a river, city, town; musical instrument.

පුටු, *Puṭu*, the plur. of පුටුව *puṭuwa*.

පුටුතණ, *Puṭu-taṇa*, *s.* kind of grass, creeping at the base, *eleusine ægyptiaca*, (*Gramineæ*).

පුටුලේල්ල, *Puṭu-lḗlla*, *s.* board of a barge on which oar-men sit.

පුටුව, *Puṭuwa*, *s.* seat, chair, stool.

පුඩුව, *Puḍuwa*, *s.* loop of a snare, gin; aperture of the nose; nipple; tip or point of any thing.

පුණ්ඩ්‍ර, *Puṇḍra*, *s.* plant, *gaertnera racemosa*, [Coll: පොඩරු *poṇḍaru*]; worm.

පුණ්ඩ්‍රක, *Puṇḍraka*, *s.* creeping plant, *borago zeylanica*, [Colloq. යොහොඹු *yohombu*]; sort of sugar cane.

පුණ්ඩරීක, *Puṇḍaríka*, *s.* elephant of the south east quarter; fever affecting an elephant; leopard; sort of snake, *amphisbæna;* fragrant kind of mango, variety of *mangifera indica;* sort of sugar cane, *saccharum officinarum;* silk worm; student's water pot; white; numeral; religious ascetic of the highest order; white lotus, variety of *nelumbium speciosum*, [Colloq. සුදු නෙළුම් *sudu-neḷum*]; white umbrella; species of *costus speciosus*, [Colloq. තෙබු *tebu*]; lotus in general.

පුණ්ඩරීකමුඛී, *Puṇḍaríka-mukhí*, *s.* (පුණ්ඩරීක white lotus. මුඛ *mukha* face) epithet expressive of female beauty.

පුණ්ඩරීකා, *Puṇḍaríká*, *s.* courtezan of the gods.

පුණ්ඩරීකාක්‍ෂ, *Puṇḍaríkáksha*, *s.* (පුණ්ඩරීක *puṇḍaríka* lotus, අක්‍ෂ *aksha* eye) name of Vishṇu; name of Buddha.

පුණ්ණ, *Puṇṇa*, *a.* full, complete.

පුණ්‍ය, *Puṇya*, *a*, happy, blessed; fortunate, lucky, possessing religious merit, virtuous; pure, purified. righteous; pleasing, beautiful.

පුණ්‍යජන, *Puṇya-jana*, *s.* (පුණ්‍ය and ජන man) pious or virtuous man.

පුණ්‍යවන්ත, *Puṇyawanta*, *a.* (පුණ්‍ය virtue, වන්ත possessed of) happy, blessed, fortunate, virtuous.

පුණු, *Puṇu* from පූර්ණ *púrṇa*, *a.* full, filled, complete.

පුණුපොහොය, *Puṇu-pohoya*, *s.* (පුණු full, පොහොය phase of the moon) day of full moon, lucky or fortunate day, on which the chief religious festivals of the Buddhists are celebrated, [Colloq. පහළොස්වක *pahaḷoswaka*].

පුත්, *Put*, *s.* son.

පුත්ගලයා, *Putgalayá*, corruption of පුද්ගල *pudgala*, which see.

පුත්‍ර, *Putra*, } *s.* son; child.
පුත්‍රක, *Putraka*, }

පුත්‍රජනනී, *Putrajananí*, *s* medicinal plant, *ipomœa sepiaria*, [Colloq. රසතැල් *rasateḷ*].

පුත්‍රජීව, *Putrajíwa*, } *s.* (පුත්‍ර son, ජීව life)
පුත්‍රජීවක, *Putrajíwaka*, } tree from the fruit of which necklaces are made of supposed prolific efficacy, *putranjiva Roxburghii*, [Colloq. බුත්සරණ *butsaraṇa*].

පුත්‍රදාර, *Putradárá*, *s.* children and wife.

පුත්‍රප්‍රජාතනී, *Putra-prajátani*, *s.* (පුත්‍ර son, ප්‍රජාතනී who has produced, ඊ *i* fem. aff.) woman that has borne children.

පුත්‍රයා, *Putrayá*, *s.* son: see පුත්‍ර *putra*.

පුත්‍රිකා, *Putriká*, *s.* (පුත්‍රී *putrí* daughter, කන් *kan* aff.) daughter, [Colloq. දුව *duwa*].

පුත, *Puta*, *s.* son.

පුතණ්ඩ, *Putaṇḍa*, *s.* son in the voc. case.

පුතණුවෙෝ, *Putanuwó*, } *s.* son, (a term of endear-
පුතේ, *Puté*, } ment).

පුථුජ්ජන, *Puthujjana*, *s.* (පුථු *puthu* away from, (virtue), ජන *jana* man) vile person, fool, man subject to his passions.

පුථුපඤ්ඤ, *Puthu-pañña*, *s.* (පුථු extensive, පඤ්ඤ knowledge) professed scholar, one famed for his learning.

පුථුල, *Puthula*, *a.* great, large, extensive.

පුද්ගල, *Pudgala*, *s.* soul; individual; body; sentient being: *a.* beautiful, handsome, of a handsome form or figure; having a form or property.

පුද්ගලික, *Pudgalika*, *s.* (පුද්ගල *pudgala* man, ඉක *ika* aff.) human, appertaining to man, that which belongs to man, that which belongs to one person, personal property.

පුද, *Puda*, *s.* worship, adoration; offering; obeisance, salutation; Elu form of පූජා *pújá*.

පුදකරණවා, *Pudakaranawá*, *v.* to consecrate, to set apart.

පුදනවා, *Pudanawá*, *v.* to offer, to present gifts in the temple, to make offerings on any religious occasion: pret. පිදුවා *piduwá*.

පුදුම, *Puduma*, *s.* surprise, amazement, astonishment; wonder, unusual occurrence, strange event, prodigy: *a.* surprising, wonderful, miraculous.

පුදුමවෙනවා, *Pudumawenawá*, *v.* to be surprised, to wonder.

පුන්, *Pun*, from පූර්ණ *púrṇa*, *a.* full, complete, fulfilled; also, male, masculine from පුමා *pumá*.

පුන්කලස, *Pun-kalasa*, *s.* (පුන් full, කලස water pot) water jar or vessel filled with water used at the consecration of a king; vessel with water and flowers placed at the door on festival occasions.

පුන්නාග, *Punnága*, *s.* (පුං *puṇ* male, නාග elephant) white elephant; white lotus; tree, from the fruit of which an oil is extracted, used for medicinal and domestic purposes, *calophyllum inophyllum*, [Colloq. දොඹ *domba*]; nutmeg, *myristica fragrans*, [Colloq. සාදික්කා *sádikká*]; chief, preeminent man.

පුන්සඳ, *Punsaṇda*, Elu form of පූර්ණචන්ද්‍ර *púrṇa-chandra*.

පුන, *Puna*, *s.* in Elu tree, *calophyllum inophyllum*, [Colloq. දොඹ *domba*]; pomegranate, *punica granatum*, [Colloquial: දෙළුම් *delum*]; particle signifying again, over again.

පුනක්කු, *Punakku*, *s.* oil cake, refuse of the coconut after the oil has been expressed, poonac.

පුනබ්භව, *Punabbhawa*, *s.* (පුන again, repeatedly, භව birth, production) nail of the finger or toe; second birth.

පුනර්, *Punar*, *ind.* particle implying again, but, on the contrary; assuredly, certainly.

පුනර්නව, *Punarnawa*, *s.* (පුනර් *punar* again, නව *nawa* new) finger nail.

පුනර්නවා, *Punarnawá*, *s.* hogweed, *boerhaavia diffusa*, [Colloq. පිටසුදුපලා *piṭasudu-palá*, සාරණ *sáraṇa*].

පුනර්භව, *Punarbhawa*, *s.* (පුනර් *punar* again, භව *bhawa* being) new birth, re-existence; transmigration; finger nail.

පුනර්භවින්, *Punarbhavin*, *s.* (පුනර් and භව *bhawa*, ඉන් *in* poss. aff.) sentient soul alluding to its existing again after the dissolution of one body in another form.

පුනර්භූ, *Punarbhú*, *s.* (පුනර් and භූ being) re-existence, virgin widow remarried.

පුනර්වසු, *Punarwasu*, *s.* (පුනර් *punar* and වස *wasa* to dwell) seventh lunar asterism, containing according to some authorities two, and according to others four stars, [Colloq. පුනාවස *punáwasa*].

පුනරුක්ත, *Punarukta*, *a.* (පුනර් *punar* again, උක්ත *ukta* said) repeated.

පුනරුක්ත ජන්මන්, *Punarukta-janman*, *s.* (පුනර් *punar* again, උක්ත *ukta* said, ජන්මන් birth) Brahmin, alluding to the saying, at the time of his investiture with the sacred thread, that he is born again.

පුනරුක්ති, *Punarukti*, *s.* repetition, tautology.

පුනරුත්, *Punarut*, see පුනරුක්ත *punarukta*.

පුනරුත්පත්තිය, *Punarutpattiya*, *s.* (පුනර් *punar* and උත්පත්තිය *utpattiya* birth) second birth, being born again in another state, transmigration.

පුනාවස, *Punáwasa*, *s.* seventh lunar asterism; Elu form of පුනර්වසු *punarwasu*.

පුප්, *Pup*, *s.* flower, Elu form of පුෂ්ප *pushpa*.

පුප්තෙලි, *Pup-teli*, see මල්තෙලිස්සා *mal-telissá*.

පුප්පනවා, *Puppanawá*, *v.* to bloat, to leaven, to inflate: pret. පිප්පුවා *pippuwá*: causal of පිපෙනවා *pipenawá*.

පුප්පාකනවා, *Puppákanawá*, *v.* to eat at another's expense; to spunge, to hang on others for maintenance.

පුප්පි, *Puppi*, *s.* tree, *bauhinia racemosa*. [Colloq. මයිල *mayila*].

පුප්පෑලෙනවා, *Pup-pęlenawá*, *v.* to be afflicted with a certain incurable cutaneous disorder: it is more dreaded than the leprosy and is considered as the effects of the parangi-leḍa or venereal.

පුප්ඵ, *Puppha*, *s.* flower; menses; Páli form of පුෂ්ප *pushpa*.

පුප්ඵඡඩ්ඩක, *Puppha-chhaḍḍaka*, *s.* caster away of withered flowers; one employed in sweeping the room and the altar where flowers are offered to Buddha.

පුප්ඵුස, *Pupphusa*, *s.* lungs, [Colloq. පපුව *papuwa*, පෙනහල්ල *penahalla*].

පුපුදු, *Pupudu*, corruptly for පුබුදු *pubudu*, which see.

පුපුර, *Pupura*, *s.* spark, grain, particle of anything: pl. පුපුරු *pupuru*.

පුපුරණවා, *Pupuraṇawá*, *v.* to burst: pret. පිපුරුණ *pipuruṇá*, පිපුරුවා *pipuruwá*.

පුපුරුගහනවා, *Pupurugahanawá*, *v.* to smart, to give pain, to ache.

පුපුල, *Pupula*, *s.* creeping plant, peculiar to Ceylon, it abounds in the underwood or jungles of the country, *vernonia zeylanica (Compositæ)*.

පුබ්බ, *Pubba*, Páli form of පූර්ව *púrwa*.

පුබ්බර, *Pubbara*, *a.* callow, unfledged.

පුබ්බරා, *Pubbará*, *s.* unfledged bird, young bird, grub.

පුබුදිනවා, *Pubudinawá*, *v.* to be awakened, to be aroused: pret. පිබිදුනා *pibidunú*.

පුබුදු, *Pubudu*, *a.* expanded, blossomed, blown (as a flower).

පුබුදුවනවා, *Pubuduwanawá*, *v.* to awake, to waken.

පුම්බනවා, *Pumbanawá*, *v.* to puff: pret. පිම්බුවා *pimbuwá*.

පුම, *Puma*, *a.* masculine, (gender).

පුමන්, *Puman*, *s.* man.

පුමලිඟු, *Puma-lingu*, *s.* (පුම man, ලිඟු gender) masculine gender in grammar.

පුයර්, *Puyar*, *s.* hair powder. (Port.)

පුයරිය, *Puyariya*, *s.* festal chariot, car used only on festival occasions.

පුෂ, *Pursha*, corrupt form of පුරුෂ *purusha*, which see.

පුර, *Pura*, *s.* city, town, market town; any large village or collection of houses; house or cluster of houses walled in; body; calyx of a flower; any receptacle or cup formed of leaves; fragrant grass, *cyperus*; the increasing moon, first half of the lunar month; beginning, commencement: *bdellium*, [Colloq. ගුගුල් *gugul*]: *prep.* before, in presence of, in front of.

පුරක්ඛත, *Purakkhata*, *a.* anointed or consecrated to some office by having a liquid poured on the head; worshipped, reverenced; placed before, or in front of.

පුරඟන, *Purangana*, *s.* (පුර city, අඟන *angana* woman) female citizen; beautiful woman.

පුර ජලවක, *Pura-jalawaka*, *s.* fourth day of the first lunar fortnight, reckoned unlucky.

පුරණ, *Puraṇa*, *s.* fallow or waste land; land where the crop has been reaped: see the next.

පුරණවා, *Puraṇawá*, *v.* to begin, to commence, to undertake, to swell: pret. පිරුවා *piruwá*.

පුරදියවක, *Puradiyawaka*, *s.* second day of the first lunar fortnight.

පුරදොර, *Pura-dora*, *s.* (පුර city, දොර door) city gate, principal entrance to a town, [Colloq. නුවර දොර *nuwara-dora*].

පුරඳර, *Purandara*, } *s.* name of Ṣakra or Indra;
පුරඳුරු, *Puranduru*, } Elu form of පුරන්දර *purandara*.

පුරන්දර, *Purandara*, *s.* (පුර city, දෘ *drú* to tear) name of Ṣakra or Indra; sort of pepper, *piper chawya*, [Colloq. සිවියවැල් *siviya-węl*].

පුරප්පට්ටුව, *Purappaṭṭuwa*, *s.* sound of a signal drum.

පුරප්පාඩුව, *Purappáduwa*, *s.* vacancy.

පුර පහළොස්වක, *Pura-pahaḷoswaka*, *s.* (පුර beginning, පහළොස් fifteen, වක day of the lunar month) full moon day of the first half of a lunar month.

පුරපෑලවිය, *Purapęlaviya*, *s.* first day of the first lunar fortnight.

පුරය, *Puraya*, *s.* city (used chiefly in composition): see පුර *pura*.

පුරවනවා, *Purawanawá*, *v.* to fill, to fill up: pret. පිරෙව්වා *pirewwá*.

පුරවරය, *Purawaraya*, *s.* eminent city.

පුරවාදමනවා, *Purawádamanawá*, *v.* to fill up.

පුරවිකොවුල්ලා, *Puravi-kowullá*, *s.* kókila or Indian cuckoo, *cuculus micropterus*, [Colloq. කොහා *kohá*].

පුරස්, *Puras*, *adv.* in front, before, eastward, formerly, first.

පුරස්ත්‍රී, *Purastrí*, see පුරඟන *purangana*.

පුරස්සර, *Purassara, s.* (පුරස් before, සර to go) leader, one who goes before, [Colloq. මග පෙන් වන්නා *maga-penwanná*]: *a.* preceded by, attended with.

පුරසඳ, *Purasanda, s.* moon in the first half of the lunar month.

පුරා, *Purá, a.* full, filled; also the past part. of පුරණවා *puraṇawá.*

පුරාණ, *Puráṇa, s.* in Hindu mythology, a sacred and poetical work, supposed to be compiled or composed by the poet Vyása; and comprising the whole body of Hindu theology: each Puráṇa treats of five topics especially, the creation, destruction, and renovation of worlds, the genealogy of gods and heroes, the reigns of the Manus and the transactions of their descendants; there are eighteen acknowledged Puráṇas, which are reckoned to contain four hundred thousand stanzas; there are also eighteen Upapuráṇas, or similar poems of inferior sanctity and different appellations; the whole constitute the popular or poetical creed of the Hindus, and some of them or particular parts of them, are very generally read, and studied: *a.* old, ancient, former.

පුරාතන, *Purátana, a.* old, ancient, former.

පුරාතනයන්, *Purátanayan, s.* men of old.

පුරාම, *Purâma, s.* abundance, fulness, completion: *adv.* in full.

පුරාරම්භය, *Purárambhaya, s.* preface, corruptly for ප්‍රාරම්භය *prárambhaya.*

පුරා සිටිම, *Purá-siṭima, s.* (පුරා full, සිටිම being) fulness, overflowing.

පුරි, *Puri, s.* town, city; king, sovereign; river.

පුරිපු, *Puripu, s.* lie, falsehood, [Colloq. බොරුව *boruwa*].

පුරිම, *Purima, a.* first, prior, former.

පුරිස්, *Puris,* } *s.* man, soul, sentient faculty.
පුරිස, *Purisa,* }

පුරිසදම්ම, *Purisadamma, s.* (පුරිස man, දම්ම to be subdued or a steer) man whose passions have to be overcome; the human steer; the unconverted man being compared to a refractory bullock. Childers.

පුරී, *Purí,* see පුරි *puri.*

පුරීතත්, *Purítat, s.* (පුරී for පුර *pura* body, තන *tana* to pervade) gut, entrail, intestine.

පුරීමෝහ, *Purímóha, s.* thorn apple, *datura fastuosa,* [Colloq. අත්තන *attana*].

පුරීෂ, *Purísha,* see පුරීස *purísa.*

පුරීෂම, *Puríshama, s.* red gram, *dolichos catjang,* [Colloq. ලිමෑ *límẹ́*]; also, black kidney bean, *phaseolus radiatus,* [Colloq. මුංඇට *muṇẹṭa*].

පුරීස, *Purísa, s.* fæces, excrement, ordure, [Colloq. අසුචි *asuchi*].

පුරු, *Puru, s.* heaven, residence of immortals; farina of a flower; name of a king of the lunar dynasty.

පුරුක්, *Puruk, s.* plant, *asystasia coromandeliana (Acanthaceæ):* also see පුරුක *puruka.*

පුරුක්ගැහෙනවා, *Purukgẹhenawá, v.* to drop off at the joint, as bones through cariosity.

පුරුක්තණ, *Puruk-taṇa, s.* hard grass, *rottboellia tinctoria.*

පුරුක්නෙළු, *Puruk-neḷu, s.* plant, species of *strobilanthes.*

පුරුක්විල, *Puruk-vila, s.* plant, *diccros paniculatus.*

පුරුක, *Puruka,* } *s.* joint, knot in a bamboo etc.;
පුරුකු, *Puruku,* } angle, corner; knob, link.

පුරුද්ද, *Purudda, s.* custom, habit, usage: pl. පුරුදු *purudu.*

පුරුද්දනවා, *Puruddanawá, v.* to entwine; to dovetail; to set a dislocated joint: pret. පිරිද්දුවා *piridduwá.*

පුරුද, *Puruda, s.* gold, [Colloq. රත්රන් *ratran*].

පුරුදු, *Purudu, a.* accustomed, used, practised.

පුරුදුකරණවා, *Purudukaraṇawá, v.* to train.

පුරුදුපට්ටු, *Purudupaṭṭu, s.* well experienced.

පුරුදුව, *Puruduwa, s.* habit, custom, usage; practice, exercise.

පුරුදුවෙනවා, *Puruduwenawá, v.* to be accustomed to.

පුරුෂ, *Purusha, s.* man, soul, sentient faculty; life; mankind; friend: *a.* male, masculine.

පුරුෂත්ව, *Purushatwa, s.* manhood; manly nature; valour.

පුරුෂපශු, *Purusha-paṣu, s.* human animal, brute of a man.

පුරුෂ පුඞ්ගව, *Purusha-puṅgawa,* } see පුරුෂර්ෂභ
පුරුෂ පුණ්ඩරීක, *Purusha-puṇḍaríka,* } *purusharshabha.*

පුරුෂයා, *Purushayá, s.* husband: see පුරුෂ *purusha.*

පුරුෂර්ෂභ, *Purusharshabha,* } *s.* (පුරුෂ + ඍෂභ
පුරුෂ ව්‍යාඝ්‍ර, *Purusha-vyághra,* } *ṛishabha,*
පුරුෂ ශාර්දූල, *Purusha-ṣárdúla,* } ව්‍යාඝ්‍ර and ශාර්දූල affixes implying eminence) excellent or eminent person.

පුරුෂසිංහ, *Pusura-siṅha, s.* eminent man.

පුරුෂාධම, *Purushádhama*, *s.* low man, outcast.

පුරුෂාධිකාර, *Purushádhikára*, *s.* manly office or duty.

පුරුෂාර්ථ, *Purushártha*, *s.* human object; as the gratification of desire, acquirement of wealth, discharge of duty and final emancipation.

පුරුෂෝත්තම, *Purushóttama*, *s.* (පුරුෂ *purusha* mankind, උත්තම *uttama* best) name of Vishṇu; one of the generic terms for a teacher of the Jainas.

පුරුස, *Purusa*, *s.* name of a tree from the fruit of which an oil is extracted, *calophyllum inophyllum*, [Colloq. දොඹ *domba*]: see පුරුෂ *purusha*.

පුරු, *Puru*, } පුරුහ, *Puruha*, } පුරුහු, *Puruhu*, } *a.* much, many, exceeding, [Colloq. බොහෝ *bohó*].

පුරුහූත, *Puruhúta*, *s.* (පුරු much, හූත worshipped) name of Ṣakra or Indra, alluding to his being much worshipped among the Hindus.

පුරෙ, *Pure*, *prep.* before, in presence of, in front of; also, පුර *pura* city, in the seventh or locative case.

පුරේ, *Puré*, see පුරය *puraya*.

පුරෝග, *Puróga*, *s.* (පුරස් *puras* before, ග who goes) leader: *a.* chief, principal, pre-eminent; going before, preceding.

පුරෝධා, *Puródhá*, } පුරෝහිත, *Puróhita*, } *s.* (පුරස් *puras* first, ධා to hold, or හිත held, revered) amongest the Brahmans, the family priest conducting all the ceremonials and sacrifices of a house or family; chief; minister; counsellor; planet Jupiter, or Vṛihaspati, the regent of that planet, and preceptor of the gods.

පුල්, *Pul*, *s.* sort of stone; flower: *a.* expanded, blown, as a flower, [Colloq. පිපුන *pipuna*]; Páli form of පුං *puṇ* male, masculine.

පුල්කොල, *Pulkola*, *s.* drug, *costus speciosus*, [Colloq. තෙබු *tebu*].

පුල් මහනෙල්, *Pul-mahanel*, *s.* (පුල් blown, මහනෙල් blue lotus) blue lotus full blown, *nymphæa stellata*.

පුල්ල, *Pulla*, see ඵුල්ල *Phulla*.

පුල්ලිය, *Pulliya*, *s.* spot on the body, mark, freckle.

පුල්ලියා, *Pulliyá*, *s.* remarkable fellow.

පුල්ලෝරම, *Pullórama*, *s.* rasp.

පුල, *Pula*, *s.* erection of the hairs of the body, considered as a proof of exquisite delight.

පුලක, *Pulaka*, *s.* see the preceding word; an insect of any class, sort of stone; flaw or defect in a gem; ball of bread or sweetmeats with which elephants are fed; yellow orpiment; gándharwa or heavenly chorister; wine goblet or glass; sort of mustard,

පුලන්නා, *Pulanná*, *s.* poor person of a respectable family.

පුලපුලා, *Pulapulá*, *p.* extending, expanding; said of a person anxiously waiting for the arrival of a friend or relation.

පුලවුල්, *Pulawul*, *s.* lotus, *nelumbium speciosum*, [Colloq. නෙළුම් *neḷum*].

පුලා, *Pulá*, *s.* one of the paces of a horse, canter or gallop; soft palate or uvula: *a.* vast, great, extensive.

පුලාක, *Puláka*, *s.* shrivelled grain; lump of boiled rice; rice water; brevity; compendium, abbreviation; dispatch, celerity.

පුලා යනවා, *Pulá-yanawá*, *v.* (පුලා galloping, යනවා to go) to gallop (as a horse); to spring, to bound, as an animal.

පුලිඟු, *Puḷingu*, *s.* (පුං masculine, ලිඟු gender) masculine gender in grammar; Elu form of පුල්ලිඞ්ග *pulliṅga*; spark, [Colloq ගිනිපුපුර *ginipupura*].

පුලිඳු, *Pulindu*, } පුලිඳ, *Pulinda*, } *s.* barbarian, savage; mountaineer, Vẹddá or one who lives by hunting; one who uses an uncultivated and unintelligible dialect.

පුලින, *Pulina*, *s.* sand, [Colloq. වැලි *wẹli*]; sediment; island, island of alluvial formation or one from which the water has recently withdrawn, small island or rock left in the middle of a river upon the falling of the waters.

පුලිල, *Pulila*, *s.* tree, *ficus arnottiana (Urticaceæ)*; also called කවුඩුබෝ *kawuḍu-bó* (and කපුටුබෝ *kapuṭu-bó*).

පුලිමුකම්, *Pulímukam*, *s.* in architecture, an ornamental work representing the face of a tiger.

පුලුටු, *Puluṭu*, *a.* burnt, fried, grilled, roasted.

පුලුටුමුහුණ, *Puluṭu-muhuna*, *s.* long face, angry look.

පුලුටුවෙනවා, *Puluṭuwenawá*, *v.* to be burnt or roasted.

පුලුන්නා, *Pulunná*, *s.* kind of sea fish.

පුලුල්, *Pulul*, *a.* broad, wide, extensive, large; spread abroad, published.

පුලුස්සනවා, *Pulussanawá*, *v.* to burn, to set on fire; to scorch, to fry, to roast, to scald: pret. පිලිස්සුවා *pilissuwá*.

පුලෝමජා, *Pulómajá. s.* (පුලෝමන් pulóman, ජ *ja* born, ආ *á* fem. aff.) wife of Indra, and daughter of Puloman a celebrated saint, destroyed by Indra to prevent his curse for having violated his daughter.

පුව, *Puwa, s.* sort of cake: *a.* former, prior, ancient; Elu form of පූර්ව *púrwa.*

පුවක්, *Puwak, s.* areca-nut palm, *areca catechu (Palmæ).*

පුවක්ගෙඩිය, *Puwak-geḍiya, s.* arecanut.

පුවක්ගෙඩියාවැල, *Puwakgediyáwęla, s.* creeping plant, with beautiful fragrant flowers, *hiptage madablota,* formerly called *gaertnera racemosa (Malpighiaceæ).*

පුවක්බඩිල්ලා, *Puwakbaḍillá, s.* kind of fish.

පුවක් මල, *Puwak-mala, s.* arecanut flower.

පුවඟු, *Puwangu, s.* lofty tree which produces fragrant flowers, *myristica horsfieldia,* [Colloq. රුක් ගස *ruk-gasa*].

පුවටා, *Puwaṭá, s.* creeping plant, bearing a red berry, *pothos officinalis.*

පුවටු, *Puwaṭu, s.* approaching, coming to, arriving; happening, coming to pass.

පුවත, *Puwata, s.* continuance, being, existence; race, lineage, descent, generation; narration, news (used in poetry).

පුවතර, *Puwatara, s.* publicity; fame, renown, celebrity.

පුවතැස්, *Puwatęs, s.* publicity, publication.

පුවපල්, *Puwapal,* Elu form of පූර්වඵල්ගුනී *púrwa-phálguní,* eleventh lunar asterism.

පුවපුටුපේ, *Puwapuṭupé, s.* twenty-fifth nękata or constellation in the moon's path; Elu form of පූර්වප්‍රෝෂ්ඨපද *púrwa-próshṭhapadá,* which see.

පුවරු, *Puwaru,* } *s.* board, piece of plank,
පුවරුව, *Puwaruwa,* } [Colloq. ලෑල්ල *lęlla*].

පුවසළ, *Puwasaḷa, s.* twentieth lunar asterism; Elu form of පූර්වාෂාඪා *púrwáshádhá,* which see.

පුවසා, *Puwasá, s.* greediness, avarice, covetousness, miserliness.

පුවළ, *Puwaḷa, a.* hard, firm, solid; proud, haughty, overbearing; Elu form of ප්‍රෞඪ *prauḍha.*

පුවාලු, *Puwálu, s.* variety of plantain; sort of paddy.

පුෂ්කර, *Pushkara, s.* sky, atmosphere, heaven; water; lotus, *nelumbium speciosum,* [Colloq. නෙළුම් *neḷum*], or *nymphæa nelumba;* tip of an elephant's trunk; head of a drum, or place where any musical instrument is struck; drug, *costus speciosus,* [Colloq. කොට්ටං *koṭṭan,* තෙබු *tebu*]; sword, the blade or edge of a sword, sheath of a sword; tom-tom or drum; arrow; body; pillow or bolster; bow of the víṇá or Indian fiddle; palace of Waiṣrawaṇa.

පුෂ්කර පර්ණිකා, *Pushkara-parṇṇiká, s.* medicinal plant, *alternanthera triandra* or *illecebrum sessile,* [Colloq. මුගුනුවැන්න *mugunuwęnna*].

පුෂ්කරාහ්ව, *Pushkaráhwa, s.* Indian crane, [Colloq. කොකා *koká*].

පුෂ්කරිණී, *Pushkariṇi, s.* pond, piece of water, lake, pool where the lotus does or may grow, [Colloq. පොකුණ *pokuṇa*]; female elephant.

පුෂ්කල, *Pushkala, a.* beautiful, agreeable; excellent, eminent, chief, best; much, many; complete, filled.

පුෂ්ට, *Pushṭa, a.* nourished, fed, brought up (as a tame animal).

පුෂ්ටි, *Pushṭi, s.* cherishing, nourishing, feeding; increase, advance, thriving, prosperity.

පුෂ්ටිමත්, *Pushṭimat, s.* healthy, fat, stout.

පුෂ්ප, *Pushpa, s.* flower, flower in general; menses; disease of the eyes, specks on the eyes, albugo; car of Kuvéra the Indian Plutus.

පුෂ්පක, *Pushpaka, s.* calx of brass; chariot of Kuvéra; disease of the eyes, albugo; bracelet of diamonds or jewels; cup or vessel of iron; small earthen fireplace or furnace; sort of collyrium; blue vitriol.

පුෂ්ප කදලී, *Pushpa-kadalí, s.* sort of plantain.

පුෂ්ප කර්ණිකා, *Pushpa-karṇṇiká, s.* (පුෂ්ප and කර්ණි *karṇni* pistil) pistil of a flower.

පුෂ්පකේතන, *Pushpakétana, s.* (පුෂ්ප flower, කේතන banner) name of Káma the Indian Cupid.

පුෂ්පගිරි, *Pushpa-giri, s.* (පුෂ්ප and ගිරි mountain) fabulous mountain, favourite resort of Varuṇa.

පුෂ්පචාප, *Pushpa-chápa, s.* (පුෂ්ප and චාප bow) name of Anańgayá or Káma, the Indian god of love.

පුෂ්පද, *Pushpada, s.* (පුෂ්ප and ද what gives) tree, [Colloq. ගහ *gaha*].

පුෂ්පදන්ත, *Pushpa-danta, s.* elephant of the north-west quarter; chief of the Gándharwas, choristers of Swarga, an attendant upon Ṣiva; Nága, or serpent of the infernal regions.

පුෂ්පද්‍රව, *Pushpa-drawa, s.* (පුෂ්ප flower, ද්‍රව oozing, distributing) nectar of flowers; infusion of flowers, as rose water etc.

පුෂ්පපථ, *Pushpa-patha*, *s.* (පුෂ්ප menses, පථ road) vulva.

පුෂ්පඵල, *Pushpa-phala*, *s.* elephant or wood apple, *feronia elephantum*, [Colloq. දිවුල් *diwul*]; pumpkin gourd.

පුෂ්පමඤ්ජරී, *Pushpa-mañjarí*, *s.* (පුෂ්ප flower, මඤ්ජරී cluster) bunch of flowers, nosegay; mango tree, *mangifera indica*, [Colloq. අඹ *amba*].

පුෂ්පරක්ත, *Pushpa-rakta*, *s.* (පුෂ්ප and රක්ත red) shrub, *hibiscus phœniceus*.

පුෂ්පරථ, *Pushpa-ratha*, *s.* (පුෂ්ප and රථ car) carriage for pleasure or amusement.

පුෂ්පරස, *Pushpa-rasa*, *s.* (පුෂ්ප and රස taste) nectar or honey of flowers, [Colloq. මල්පැණි *malpęni*].

පුෂ්පරාග, *Pushparága*, *s.* (පුෂ්ප and රාග colour) topaz.

පුෂ්පරේණු, *Pushpa-rénu*, *s.* (පුෂ්ප flower, රේණු dust) farina of a flower.

පුෂ්පරෝචන, *Pushpa-róchana*, *s.* (පුෂ්ප and රෝචන pleasing) iron-wood tree, *mesua ferrea*, [Coll: නාගහ *ná-gaha*].

පුෂ්පසමය, *Pushpa-samaya*, *s.* (පුෂ්ප and සමය season) spring.

පුෂ්පාම්ල, *Pushpámla*, *s.* tamarind tree, *tamarindus indica*, [Colloq. සියඹලා *siyambalá*].

පුෂ්පාරාම, *Pushpáráma*, *s.* (පුෂ්ප and ආරාම *áráma* garden) flower garden, [Colloq. මල්වත්ත *malwatta*].

පුෂ්පාසන, *Pushpásana*, *s.* (පුෂ්ප flower, ආසන *ásana* seat) name of Brahma.

පුෂ්පෝදක, *Pushpódaka*, *s.* (පුෂ්ප and උදක *udaka* water) nectar of flowers; infusion of flowers, rose water etc.

පුෂ්‍ය, *Pushya*, *s.* eighth lunar asterism, comprising three stars, of which one is δ canceri; month දුරුතු *durutta* (December and January); Kaliyuga or fourth age.

පුෂ්‍යරථ, *Pushya-ratha*, *s.* (පුෂ්‍ය and රථ car) carriage for pleasure or for any other purpose than war.

පුස්, *Pus*, *s.* mould, fungus forming on things in a damp place, mildew: *a.* blank, empty, barren, vacant; blighted as fruit etc.

පුස්කනවා, *Puskanawá*, *v.* (පුස් mould, කනවා to eat) to become mouldy or mildewed.

පුස්කර, *Puskara*, *s.* borax, used as a flux: see also පුෂ්කර *pushkara*.

පුස්කොල, *Puskola*, *s.* (පුස් blank, කොල leaf) blank leaf of the talipot tree prepared for being written or engraved upon.

පුස්ත, *Pusta*, පුස්තක, *Pustaka*, } *s.* book, [Colloq. පොත *pota*], manuscript: *a.* smeared, anointed, plastered.

පුස්තකාලය, *Pustakálaya*, *s.* library.

පුස්නා, *Pusná*, *s.* nourishing, preserving; defending, protecting; worth, valued.

පුස්ප, *Puspa*, *a.* fragrant, sweet smelling, odoriferous: see also පුෂ්ප *pushpa*.

පුස්පස්, *Puspas*, *s.* medley, fuss, bustle, (Dutch).

පුස්බඳිනවා, *Pusbandinawá*, *v.* to become mouldy, to mould, to soil.

පුස්ඹ, *Pusmba*, *s.* fragrance, agreeable odour.

පුස්ඹගහනවා, *Pusmba-gahanawá*, *v.* to emit fragrance etc.

පුස්ම, *Pusma*, see පුස්ඹ *pusmba*.

පුස්මින්, *Pusmin*, *part.* preserving, protecting, screening, supporting.

පුස්රට, *Pus-rața*, *s.* (පුස් empty, vacant, රට country) country without king, interregnum.

පුස්රහ, *Pus-raha*, *s.* mouldy taste.

පුස්රිය, *Pus-riya*, *s.* (පුස් empty, also, පුෂ්‍ය *pushya* asterism, රිය car) empty carriage, festal car, royal chariot.

පුස්වැන්න, *Puswęnna*, *s.* small plant possessing medical properties, and used as a diuretic, *plectranthus scutellaroides*, [Colloq. පොල්පලා *polpalá*].

පුස්වැල, *Puswęla*, *s.* sort of hollow creeper, producing the bat-bur, *entada scandens*, *(Leguminosæ)*.

පුස්ස, *Pussa*, *s.* that which is empty, vacant, hollow, unproductive, barren; blighted; fruit without kernel.

පුස්සා, *Pussá*, *s.* animal born without testicles or castrated when very young: see පුසියා *pusiyá*.

පුස්සී, *Pussí*, *s.* (පුස්ස barren, ඊ *í* fem. aff.) barren cow.

පුසිකරණවා, *Pusikaranawá*, *v.* to castrate: see also කරඅඹනවා *karaambanawá*.

පුසිත, *Pusita*, *a.* nourished, cherished, fed.

පුසිඹ, *Pusimba*, *s.* margosa tree, *azadirachta indica*. [Colloq. කොහොඹ *kohomba*].

පුසියා, *Pusiyá*, *s.* an old or decrepit ox.

පුසුල, *Pusula*, *s.* pumpkin, gourd in general, [Coll: පුහුල *puhula*, ලබු *labu*].

පුසේනැකත, *Pusé-nękata*, *s.* (පුසේ and නැකත lunar asterism): see පුෂ්‍ය *pushya*.

පුහු, *Puhu*, *a.* hollow (applied to fruits without kernel).

පුහු අඹ, *Puhu-amba*, *s.* kind of mango, *mangifera indica;* nutless mango fruits.

පුහුණුකරගන්නවා, *Puhuṇukaragannawá*, *v.* to improve one's self, to acquire learning by one's self.

පුහුණුකරණවා, *Puhuṇukaraṇawá*, *v.* to improve, to educate.

පුහුණුව, *Puhuṇuwa*, } *s.* improvement of the
පුහුණුවීම, *Puhuṇuvima*, } mind, training.

පුහුදුනා, *Puhuduná*, *s.* wicked man, one under the influence of his passions, sinner; fool.

පුහුම, *Puhuma*, *s.* decay, affecting the pulp of fruit and pith of trees.

පුහුල්, *Puhul*, *s.* pumpkin gourd; ash-pumpkin.

පුහුල් කපනවා, *Puhul-kapanawá*, *v.* to cut gourds when offering to demons: see සූනියම *súniyama.*

පුහුල්ගෙඩිය, *Puhul-gediya*, *s.* ash pumpkin, *benincasa cerifesa.*

පුළුගෑටයා, *Pulugeṭayá*, *s.* man with a prominent navel.

පුළුන්, *Puḷun*, *s.* cotton used in stuffing pillows.

පුළුන් ඉඹුල්, *Puḷun-imbul*, *s.* silk cotton tree, *eriodendron anfractuosum.*

පුළුපු, *Puḷupu*, *s.* coconut, [Colloq. පොල් *pol.*]

පුළුල්, *Puḷul*, } see පුළුල් *pulul.*
පුළුලු, *Puḷulu*, }

පුළුවන්, *Puḷuwan*, *a.* possible, able, possessing the means of doing any thing.

පුළුවන්කම, *Puḷuwankama*, *s.* power, strength, ability, possibility.

පුළුවනි, *Puḷuwani*, *par.* can, is able.

පුළුවුත්, *Puḷuwut*, *part.* enquired: part. of පිළිවිසිනවා *piḷivisinawá.*

පුළුවුස්නා, *Puḷuwusná*, *part.* enquiring.

පූ, *Pú*, *s.* cake; winnowing: past part. of පානවා *pánawá.*

පූකරණවා, *Púkaraṇawá*, *v.* to winnow; to thresh.

පූකුරුව, *Púkuruwa*, *s.* small earthen water jar, jug with two handles.

පූග, *Púga*, *s.* areca nut tree, *areca catechu*, [Colloq. පුවක් *puwak*]; heap, quantity, multitude; disposition, property, nature; jack tree, *artocarpus integrifolia*, [Colloq. කොස් *kos*].

පූගපාත්‍ර, *Púga-pátra*, *s.* (පූග betel, පාත්‍ර vessel) betel box.

පූග පුෂ්පිකා, *Púga-pushpiká*, *s.* (පූග and පුෂ්ප *pushpa* flower, ඉකා *iká* aff.) flowers and betel presented to the principal guests at a marriage feast.

පූජ්‍ය, *Pújya*, *a.* worshipful, venerable, deserving admiration.

පූජකයා, *Pújakayá*, *s.* priest, worshipper.

පූජනය, *Pújanaya*, *s.* offerings, presents; worship, adoration.

පූජනීය, *Pújaníya*, *a.* (පූජ *púja* to worship, අනියර් *aníyar* affix, suitable) fit to receive offerings, suitable or fit to be offered to.

පූජා, *Pújá*, *s.* offering, sacrifice, worship, homage, adoration; respect.

පූජාකරණවා, *Pújákaraṇawá*, *v.* to sacrifice, to offer.

පූජාර්හ, *Pújárha*, *s.* (පූජා worship, අර්හ *arha* deserving) worshipful, venerable, respectable, sacred.

පූජාව, *Pújáwa*, *s.* sacrifice, offering: see පූජා *pújá.*

පූජාසනය, *Pújásanaya*, *s.* altar.

පූජිත, *Pújita*, *a.* (පූජ *púja* to worship, ක්ත *kta* affix) worshipped, adored, reverenced, respected, esteemed; celebrated, famous, notorious.

පූජෝත්සවය, *Pújótsawaya*, *s.* (පූජා *pújá* offering, උත්සව *utsawa* festival) sacred and religious festival; sports and amusements which take place at such festivals.

පූට්ටුකරණවා, *Púṭṭukaraṇawá*, *v.* to join as wood.

පූට්ටු කෙළිය, *Púṭṭu-keliya*, *s.* game of children with small kinds of nuts.

පූට්ටුව, *Púṭṭuwa*, *s.* joint, flexion; union, joining, annexing.

පූඩාවා, *Púḍáwá*, *s.* leech, *hemadipsa Ceylanica*, [Colloq. කූඩැල්ලා *kúḍellá*].

පූත්‍යණ්ඩ, *Pútyaṇda*, *s.* (පූති *púti* stinking, අණ්ඩ *aṇda* testicle or egg) musk deer; insect with a fetid smell; winged bug.

පූත, *Púta*, *a.* pure, purified, cleansed; threshed, winnowed; foul, smelling, stinking.

පූතනා, *Pútaná*, *s.* yellow myrobalan, *terminalia chebula*, [Colloq. අරළු *araḷu*]; name of a female demon killed by Kṛishṇa; disease, atrophy and wasting in a child, ascribed to the malignant operations of the female fiend Pútaná.

පූති, *Púti*, *s.* purity, purification; stench, stink.

පූතිකා, *Pútika*, } *s.* grey bonduc, *cæsalpinia*
පූතිකරජ, *Pútikaraja*, } *bonduc*, [Colloq. කුඹුරු වැල් *kumburu-wel*; also, සිරිල *sirila*].

පූතිකාෂ්ඨ, *Pútikáshṭha*, *s.* (පූති purity, කාෂ්ඨ wood) sort of pine, *pinus devadáru*, [Colloq. දේවදර *déwadára*].

පූතිකුල්මාෂ, *Pútikulmásha*, *s.* (පූති stinking, කුල්මාෂ forced rice, with pulse etc.) food called kulmásha, the day after it is made.

පූතිගන්ධ, *Pútigandha*, *s.* (පූති and ගන්ධ smell) ill-smell, stench, insufferable stink; sulphur; creeper, borago, *borago zeylanica*, [Colloq. යොන්තුඹ *yontumba*].

පූතිතෛලා, *Púti-tailá*, *s.* (පූති and තෛල *taila* oil) heart pea or heart seed, *cardiospermum haliacacabum*, [Coll: පෙනෙලවැල් *penela-węl*].

පූතිදන්ත, *Púti-danta*, *s.* (පූති and දන්ත tooth) filthy teeth.

පූතිදර්භ, *Pútidarbha*, *s.* kind of reed, *imperata arundinaceæ*, [Colloq. ඉළුක් *iļuk*].

පූතිදාරු, *Pútidáru*, see පූතිකාෂ්ඨ *pútikáshṭha*.

පූතිපර්ණී, *Pútiparṇí*, see පූතික *pútika*.

පූතිපුෂ්පිකා, *Púti-pushpiká*, *s.* (පූති stinking, පුෂ්ප *pushpa* flower, ඉකා *iká* aff.) variety of the common citron, *citrus medica.*

පූතිඵලී, *Púti-phalí*, *s.* plant, [Colloq. බෝඩි ඇට *bódi-ęta*].

පූතිබීජ, *Púti-bíja*, *s.* (පූති stink, බීජ seed) heart seed: see පූතිතෛලා *púti-tailá*.

පූතිභාවය, *Púti-bháwaya*, *s.* (පූති and භාව *bháwa* state, being) dirtiness, filthiness, uncleanness, pollution.

පූතිමාරුත, *Pútimáruta*, *s.* bael tree, *ægle marmelos*, [Colloq. බෙලිගස් *beli-gas*].

පූතිවෘක්ෂ, *Púti-vṛiksha*, *s.* (පූති foul smell, වෘක්ෂ tree) tree, *oroxylum indicum* or *calosanthes indica*, [Colloq. තොටිල *toṭila*].

පූතික, *Pútika*, *s.* plant, *cæsalpinia bonduc*, [Colloq. කුඹුරුවැල් *kumburu-węl*]; see පූතික *pútika*; pole or civet cat; a pot herb, *basella rubra* or *lucida*, allied to නිවිති *niviti*.

පූදිනවා, *Púdinawá*, *v.* to be in the ear, to blossom, to bear fruit for the first time: pret. පිදුනා *piduná*.

පුන්නාග, *Púnnága*, *s.* tree yielding a red dye, *rottleria tinctoria*.

පූනක්කං, *Púnakkaṇ*, *s.* gem, cat's eye.

පූනනූල, *Púna-núla*, *s.* (පූන destroyed (dangers), නූල thread) sacred string or cord of the Brahmans; the ring round the neck of a parrot: pl. පූනනූල් *púnanúl*.

පූනාව, *Púnáwa*, *s.* vessel with many spouts for pouring out water, and used by the Kapuwas in the déváła, in the service of the demons; this vessel is considered so sacred, that in cases of great difficulty or importance people are compelled to swear upon it.

පූනිල්, *Pú-nil*, *s.* beautiful blue colour.

පූනුව, *Púnuwa*, *s.* nave of a wheel.

පූප, *Púpa*, *s.* bread, cake.

පූපලා, *Púpalá*, *s.* sort of cake fried with ghee or oil.

පූපාලිකා, *Púpáliká*, } *s.* sort of cake half baked or
පූපාලී, *Púpálí*, } fried in oil or ghee.

පූය, *Púya*, } *s.* pus, matter, discharge from an
පූයන, *Púyana*, } ulcer, [Colloq. හැරව *hęrawa*].

පූයරක්ත, *Púyarakta*, } *s.* (පූය and රක්ත or
පූයශෝණිත, *Púyaṣóṇita*, } ශෝණිත blood) ichor, sanies.

පූයාරි, *Púyári*, *s.* (පූය *púya* pus, අරි *ari* enemy) nimb tree, *azadirachta indica*, [Colloq. කොහොඹ *kohomba*].

පූර්ණ, *Púrṇa*, *a.* full, complete, filled; all, entire; strong, powerful, able.

පූර්ණකලශ, *Púrṇa-kalasa*, } *s.* (පූර්ණ full, කලස
පූර්ණකුම්භය, *Púrṇa-kumbhaya*, } or කුම්භ *kumbha* water jar) water vessel, one filled with holy water, used at the consecration of a king; full cup or jar; flower pot placed at the door on festival occasions.

පූර්ණචන්ද්‍ර, *Púrṇa-chandra*, *s.* (පූර්ණ and චන්ද්‍ර moon) full moon, [Colloq. පහළොස්වක *pahaḷoswaka*].

පූර්ණමා, *Púrṇamá*, *s.* (පූර්ණ and මා moon) day of full moon.

පූර්ණමාස, *Púrṇa-mása*, } *s.* (පූර්ණ and මාස month)
පූර්ණමාසි, *Púrṇa-mási*, } day of full moon; monthly sacrifice performed on the day of full moon.

පූර්ව, *Púrwa*, *a.* first, prior, former, preceding, initial: eastern; before, in front of.

පූර්වක, *Púrwaka*, *a.* prior, before, preceding.

පූර්වකර්මය, *Púrwa-karmaya*, *s.* (පූර්ව former, කර්ම *karma* act) actions performed in a former state of existence.

පූර්වකාල, *Púrwa-kála*, *s.* former time.

පූර්වකෘත, *Púrwa-krita*, *a.* done formerly, or in a previous existence.

පූර්වගඞ්ගා, *Púrwa-gaṅgá*, *s.* (පූර්ව formerly, (called) ගඞ්ගා Ganges) name of the Narmadá river.

පූර්වඞ්ගම, *Púrwaṅgama*, *a.* going before, preceded by.

පූර්වජ, *Púrwaja*, *s.* (පූර්ව formerly, first, ජ born) elder brother; deified progenitors of mankind; ancestors, forefathers in general.

පූර්වජන්මය, *Púrwa-janmaya*, *s.* (පූර්ව former, ජන්ම *janma* birth) former state of existence.

පූර්වජාතිය, *Púrwa-játiya*, *s.* former birth.

පූර්වදිග්භාගය, *Púrwa-digbhágaya*, *s.* eastern direction, the east.

පූර්වදිශා, *Púrwa-diṣá*, s. (පූර්ව eastern, දිශා side) east quarter.

පූර්වදිශාපති, *Púrwadiṣá-pati*, s. (පූර්වදිශා east quarter, පති lord) name of Ṣakra as regent of the east.

පූර්වදෙව, *Púrwa-dewa*, s. (පූර්ව formerly, දෙව god) Asura or demon, being the elder offspring of Káṣyapa the parent of both gods and demons; parents, fathers, ancestors.

පූර්වදෙශ, *Púrwa-deṣa*, s. (පූර්ව eastern, දෙශ country) eastern country or eastern part of India.

පූර්වනිමිත්ත, *Púrwa-nimitta*, s. පූර්ව before, නිමිත්ත sign) presage, prognostic, omen.

පූර්වපක්ෂ, *Púrwa-paksha*, s. (පූර්ව first, පක්ෂ argument, fortnight) proposition, assertion; first part of an argument, to which an assent or refutation is necessary; first half of a lunar month.

පූර්වපද, *Púrwa-pada*, s. first member of a compounded word, of a sentence, verse etc.

පූර්වපර්වත, *Púrwa-parwata*, s. (පූර්ව eastern, පර්වත mountain) eastern mountain behind which the sun is supposed to rise.

පූර්වප්‍රෝෂ්ඨපද *Púrwa-próshṭhapadá*, s. one of the constellations, twenty-fifth or twenty-sixth, containing stars in the wing of Pegasus.

පූර්වඵල්ගුනි, *Púrwa-phalguní*, s. (පූර්ව first, ඵල්ගුනි name of the two asterisms) eleventh lunar asterism; the first phalguní, the twelfth nakshatra being termed uttara or subsequent; asterism figured by a couch, contains two stars, one of which is δ leonis.

පූර්වඵල්ගුනිභව, *Púrwaphalguní-bhawa*, s. (පූර්වඵල්ගුනි and භව being, born) planet Jupiter.

පූර්වඵල, *Púrwa-phala*, s. first fruits.

පූර්වභද්‍ර, *Púrwa-bhadra*, see පූර්වභාද්‍රපද *púrwa-bhádrapadá*.

පූර්වභාග, *Púrwa-bhága*, s. (පූර්ව former, භාග part, of time or place) ante-meridian; front; east: *a.* previous, before.

පූර්වභාද්‍රපද, *Púrwa-bhádrapadá*, s. (පූර්ව first, භාද්‍රපද asterism so named) first of the two lunar asterisms called Bhádrapadá, and twenty-sixth of the whole, containing two stars.

පූර්වරාත්‍ර, *Púrwa-rátra*, s. first part of the night.

පූර්වරූප, *Púrwa-rúpa*,
පූර්වලක්ෂණ, *Púrwa-lakshaṇa*, } s. indication of some approaching change; symptom of disease, etc.

පූර්වවත්, *Púrwawat*, adv. as before, as aforesaid.

පූර්වවිදේහය, *Púrwa-vidéhaya*, s. (පූර්ව former or eastern, විදේහ *vidéha* country) one of the four great Dwípas.

පූර්වශෛල, *Púrwa-ṣaila*, see පූර්වපර්වත *púrwa-parwata.*

පූර්වසන්ධ්‍යා, *Púrwa-sandhyá*, s. (පූර්ව prior, සන්ධ්‍යා junction of the day, twilight) dawn, day-break.

පූර්වාචාරි, *Púrwáchári*, s. (පූර්ව *púrwa* first, ආචාරි instructor) parents; ancient teachers.

පූර්වාද්‍රි, *Púrwádri*, see පූර්වපර්වත *púrwa-parwata.*

පූර්වාපර, *Púrwápara*, s. (පූර්ව *púrwa* first, අපර *apara* last or opposite) first and last, beginning and end.

පූර්වාර්ධය, *Púrwárdhaya*, s. (පූර්ව *púrwa* and අර්ධ *ardha* part) first half.

පූර්වාෂාඪා, *Púrwáshádḥá*, s. (පූර්ව *púrwa* and ආෂාඪා *áshádḥá* áshádhá) first of the two constellations called áshádḥá, and twentieth of the lunar asterisms, containing two stars of which one is δ sagittarii.

පූර්වාහ්න, *Púrwáhna*, s. (පූර්ව *púrwa* first, අහන් *ahan* day) first part of the day, forenoon.

පූර්වේනිවාසය, *Púrwé-niwásaya*, s. (පූර්වේ former, නිවාසය residence) former state of existence.

පූර්වෝක්ත, *Púrwókta*, s. (පූර්ව *púrwa* first, උක්ත *ukta* said) before-mentioned, aforesaid.

පූර්වෝත්තර, *Púrwóttara*, s. (පූර්ව *púrwa* eastern, උත්තර *uttara* north) north-east quarter.

පූර්වෝදිත, *Púrwódita*, a. (පූර්ව *púrwa* first, උදිත *udita* said) aforesaid, afore-mentioned.

පූර, *Púra*, s. piece of water, large quantity of water.

පූරණ, *Púraṇa*, s. filling, completing; sort of cake or biscuit; rain, raining; fragrant grass, *cyperus rotundus*, [Colloq. කලාඳුරු *kaláṇduru*]; cross-threads in weaving a piece of cloth; bridge; causeway; medicinal oil or embrocation.

පූරණා, *Púraṇá*, s. silk cotton tree, *eriodendron anfractuosum*, [Colloq. ඉඹුල් ගහ *imbul-gaha*].

පූරානිතෙ, *Púránite*, s. boasting, egotism.

පූලි, *Púli*, s. mace, spice, [Colloq. වසාවාසි *wasá-wási*]; thin plate placed under a gem to increase its brilliancy.

පූව, *Púwa*, s. sort of cake.

පූවාළු කෙසෙල්, *Púwáḷu-kesel*, s. kind of plantain.

පූවාළු වී, *Púwáḷu-ví*, s. kind of paddy.

පූෂ, *Púsha*, s. mulberry, *morus indica*.

පූෂා, *Púshá*, s. sort of reed, *saccharum cylindricum;* sun.

පෙං, *Peṇ*, corrupt form of පෙම *pema*, love, affection.

පෙංකෙළිනවා, *Peṇkeḷinawá*, *v.* to skip, to frisk, to sport, to bound: pret. පෙංකෙළියා *peṇkeḷiyá*.

පෙකනිය, *Pekaniya*, *s.* navel; nave of a wheel.

පෙකනිවැල, *Pekaniwęla*, *s.* (පෙකනි navel, වැල creeper) umbilical cord.

පෙච්ච, *Pechcha*, *adv.* in the next world, hereafter.

පෙට්ටගම, *Peṭṭagama*, *s.* trunk, coffin: pl. පෙට්ටගම් *peṭṭagam*.

පෙට්ටිමල්ල, *Peṭṭi-malla*, *s.* bag of four corners.

පෙට්ටිය, *Peṭṭiya*, *s.* basket, box, trunk; coffer.

පෙටියා, *Peṭiyá*, *s.* sheat fish, *silurus pelorius*, flat river fish, crab.

පෙණය, *Peṇaya*, *s.* expanded hood of a snake.

පෙණගොබ, *Peṇagoba*, පෙණගැබ, *Peṇageba*, *s.* (පෙණ and ගැබ womb) inside of the extended hood of the cobra capella.

පෙණීම, *Peṇima*, *s.* appearance, sight, scene, prospect, aspect; verbal noun of පෙණෙනවා *peṇenawá*.

පෙණුම, *Peṇuma*, *s.* present to a superior, serving as an introduction; wedge of a carpenters plane.

පෙණෙනවා, *Peṇenawá*, *v.* to appear, to be visible: pret. පෙණුනා *peṇuná*.

පෙත්, *Pet*, *s.* disembodied spirit, manes of the deceased; sprite, goblin; Elu form of ප්‍රේත *préta;* also, row or line; acquirement.

පෙතත, *Petta*, *s.* slice, piece, bit. any thin piece of wood, brass etc.

පෙතතප්පු, *Pettappu*, *s.* pet name for a parrot.

පෙතතා, *Pettá*, *s.* word used in calling a parrot.

පෙතං, *Petaṇ*, *s.* St. Thomas' tree, the dried buds and leaves being a remedy for dysentery, *bauhinia tomentosa, (Leguminosæ)*.

පෙතන්කින, *Petaṇ-kína*, *s.* tree, variety of *calophyllum*.

පෙතන් මාරා, *Petan-márá*, *s.* tree, variety of *albizzia* or *pithecolobium*.

පෙතන් මැඩිය, *Petan-męḍiya*, *s.* tree, variety of *hunteria corymbosa*.

පෙතලි, *Petali*, *a.* flat.

පෙති, *Peti*, *plur.* of පෙතත *petta*.

පෙතිකඩ, *Petikaḍa*, *s.* (පෙති and කඩ cloth) piece of cloth on which an image of Buddha is painted.

පෙතිකඩයා, *Petikaḍayá*, *s.* kind of fish.

පෙති කපුරු, *Peti-kapuru*, *s.* water parsnip, *sium lobatum*.

පෙතිකාවැල්, *Petiká-węl*, *s.* creeping plant, *artabotrys zeylanicus (Anonaceæ)*.

පෙතිගහනවා, *Petigahanawá*, *v.* to slice, to cut into small pieces; to grind, to pound.

පෙතිගොමු නයා, *Petigomu-nayá*, *s.* snake, variety of *naja tripudians*.

පෙතිගොමුවා, *Petigomuwá*, *s.* snake.

පෙති තෝර, *Peti-tóra*, *s.* sort of cassia or senna with offensive smell, *cassia occidentalis (Leguminosæ)*.

පෙති දඹල, *Peti-dambala*, *s.* plant, producing beans, variety of *phaseolus vulgaris*.

පෙතිපියුම්, *Peti-piyum*, *s.* plant, kind of lotus.

පෙතිමල්, *Peti-mal*, *s.* plant, not identified.

පෙතිලිය, *Peti-líya*, *s.* cross sticks of a ladder.

පෙතිවල, *Peti-wala*, *s.* pitfall, hole dug in the ground and slightly covered, for the purpose of ensnaring animals.

පෙතිවිල, *Petivila*, *s.* plant, *lobelia zeylanica* or *l. trigona*.

පෙතෙල, *Petela*, *s.* gutter, conduit.

පෙතැල්ල, *Peteḷla*, *s.* doll, puppet: pl. පෙතැලි *peteḷi*.

පෙද්දි මේල, *Peddi-méla*, *s.* plant, *timonius jambosella (Rubiaceæ)*; also called අංගණ *angana*.

පෙද, *Peda*, *s.* valuable ear-ring or jewel; connected sentence; foot or rather line of stanza.

පෙදරේරුවා, *Pedaréruwá*, *s.* mason.

පෙදෙස, *Pedesa*, *s.* country, province, district; Elu form of ප්‍රදේශ *pradésa*.

පෙඳ, *Peṇda*, *s.* froth, foam, lather; bubble; tail of a bird; ball, small wooden or other ball for playing with; moss.

පෙඳ කොක්මොට, *Peṇda-kokmoṭa*, *s.* pipe-wort, *eriocaulon setaceum*.

පෙඳවල්ල, *Peṇdawalla*, පෙඳේ, *Peṇdé*, *s.* tail of a bird: pl. පෙඳවලු *peṇdawalu* and පෙඳ *peṇda*.

පෙන් වතුර, *Pen-watura*, corruptly for පෙම් වතුර *pem-watura*.

පෙන්වනවා, *Penwanawá*, *v.* to show, to exhibit, to cause to appear, to make visible: pret. පෙන්නුවා *pennuwá*.

පෙන්හෙලි, *Penheli*, *s.* firebrand.

පෙන, *Pena*, *s.* lather, froth, foam, surf; bubble.

පෙනදමනවා, *Penadamanawá*, *v.* to foam, to froth at the mouth.

පෙනපුපුව, *Penapapuwa*, *s.* lungs.

පෙනපිඩු, *Pena-piḍu*, *s.* scum or froth lying on the surface of a river or the sea.

පෙනලි, *Penali*, *s.* firebrand, [Colloq. ගිනිපෙනෙල්ල *ginipenella*].

පෙනහල්ල, *Penahalla*, } *s.* lungs: pl. පෙනහැලි
පෙනහැල්ල, *Penahęlla*, } *penahęli*,

පෙනෙල්ල, *Penella*, *s.* firebrand, lighted stick: pl. පෙනෙලි *peneli*.

පෙනෙල, *Penela*, *s.* hole, pit; drain, gutter; spout: soap-berry plant, *sapindus emarginatus*, *(Sapindaceæ)*.

පෙනෙලවැල, *Penela-węla*, *s.* heart-seed creeper. *cardiospermum halicacabam (Sapindaceæ)*.

පෙනේ, *Pené*, *s.* hood of a cobra, corruptly for පෙණය *peṇaya*.

පෙනේරය, *Penéraya*, } *s.* sieve, riddle: pl. පෙනේර *penéra*.
පෙනේරේ, *Penéré*, }

පෙම්, *Pem*, Elu form of the Páli පේම *péma*, love, affection.

පෙම්බර, *Pembara*, *s.* (පෙම් love affection, බර weight, load) extreme affection.

පෙම්වඩන, *Pem-waḍana*, *s.* (පෙම් love, වඩන increasing) pleasant, agreeable, delightful, lovely.

පෙම්වතුර, *Pem-watura*, *s.* (පෙම් pleasant, වතුර water) water of affection (poetical).

පෙම, *Pema*, *s.* love, affection, attachment.

පෙය්‍ය, *Peyya*, *s.* water; milk; rice gruel; decoction of any thing after straining; drink in general.

පෙය්‍යාලම, *Peyyálama*, *s.* symbol, පෙ *pe*, signifying "and so on."

පෙර, *Pera*, *a.* former, ancient; eastern; before, in presence of, in front of.

පෙරංගානවා, *Perangánawá*, *v.* to scrape off.

පෙරකදෝරුවා, *Perakadóruwá*, *s.* proctor.

පෙරකිරිය, *Pera-kiriya*, "adverbial participle" which is a new coined word and which means "a participle joined to a verb:" the word literally means the preceding act; this however is very vague.

පෙරකුඹ, *Perakumba*, *s.* (පෙර in front, කුඹ head of an elephant) frontal globes of an elephant.

පෙරකුල්, *Perakul*, *s.* chain for tying elephants.

පෙරගිර, *Peragira*, *s.* (පෙර eastern, ගිර mountain) eastern mountain behind which the sun is supposed to rise.

පෙරඟුරු, *Peranguru*, *s.* deception, cheating, juggling.

පෙරටු, *Peraṭu*, *ind.* (පෙර before, ටු for ස්ථ *stha* being) in front, in presence of.

පෙරඩමස, *Peraḍamasa*, } *s.* (පෙර former, අඩ *aḍa* half, මස month
පෙරඩහඳ, *Peraḍahanda*, } and හඳ moon) light half of a lunar month, fifteen days from the new to the full moon.

පෙරණවා, *Peraṇawá*, *v.* to strain, to filter: pret. පෙරුවා *peruwá*.

පෙරතු, *Peratu*, } *adv.* foremost, in front,
පෙරතුව, *Peratuwa*, } before, in presence of.
පෙරතුරුව, *Peraturuwa*, }

පෙරදිග, *Peradiga*, *s.* (පෙර eastern, දිග quarter) east, east quarter.

පෙරදිගපති, *Peradiga-pati*, } *s.* (පෙරදිග east, පති chief, හිමි lord) name
පෙරදිගහිමි, *Peradiga-himi*, } of Ṣakra or Indra as regent of the east.

පෙරදිගු, *Peradigu*, } *s.* eastern direction, east.
පෙරදිඟු, *Peradingu*, }

පෙරදුරු, *Peraduru*, *s.* (පෙර ancient, first, ඇදුරු *ęduru* teacher) literati of antiquity; parents.

පෙර දෙපෝය, *Pera-depóya*, *s.* (පෙර first, දෙ two, පෝය change of the moon) the first two quarters of the moon.

පෙරදෙව්, *Pera-dew*, *s.* (පෙර prior, දෙව් god) an Asura; Elu form of පූර්වදේව *púrwa-déwa*.

පෙරදෙරි, *Peradęri*, *a.* former, prior, ancient; borne or held in front.

පෙරනම, *Pera-nama*, *s.* banns of marriage: pl. පෙරනම් *peranam*; incorrectly called පෙරගම *peragama*, and පෙරකම *perakama*.

පෙර නියමය, *Pera-niyamaya*, *s.* predestination.

පෙර පුරුද්ද, *Pera-purudda*, *s.* old habit.

පෙරඹර, *Perambara*, *s.* (පෙර eastern, අඹර *ambara* sky) eastern sky, east quarter of the firmament.

පෙරමග, *Peramaga*, *s.* (පෙර before, මග way) confronting road, front, meeting, encountering.

පෙරමුන, *Peramuna*, } *s.* van of an army, ad-
පෙරමුනේ, *Peramuné*, } vanced part of a suite of attendants; going to meet a visitor.

පෙර යම, *Pera-yama*, *s.* (පෙර and යම watch) first night watch, from 6 to 10 o'clock.

පෙරවනවා, *Perawanawá*, *v.* to fold, to wrap round, to cover; to double: pret. පෙරෙව්වා *perewwá*.

පෙරවරු, *Perawaru*, *s.* (පෙර first, වරු time) morning, former part of the day, forenoon, antemeridian.

පෙරවි, *Peravi*, *s.* pigeon; family priest, prime minister, premier: see පෙරවියා *peraviya*.

පෙරවි බමුණා, *Peravi-bamuṇá*, } *s.* domestic priest
පෙරවියා, *Peraviyá*, } who performs all the religious ceremonials of a family.

පෙර විබත්, *Pera-vibat*, *s.* the first or nominative case in grammar.

පෙරවිල්ල, *Peravilla,* } *s.* putting on a robe, cover-
පෙරවීම, *Peravíma,* } ing one's self with a garment or cloak.

පෙරසර, *Perasara, s.* (පෙර former, before, සර vowel) preceding vowel.

පෙරසරලොප්, *Perasaralop, s.* elision of the final vowel of the preceding word and the coalition of the initial vowel of the next word with the last vowelless consonant of the preceding word.

පෙරසිට *Pera-siṭa, par.* from the beginning or commencement.

පෙරහන්කඩ, *Perahankaḍa, s.* (පෙරහන් straining, water, කඩ cloth) cloth used for straining water.

පෙරහන, *Perahana, s.* straining, filtering.

පෙරහර, *Perahara, s.* (from the Páli පරිහාර *parihára* honour, pomp, state, ceremony) procession, accompanied by dancing and music; festival, time of public rejoicing.

පෙරළනවා, *Peraḷanawá, v.* to overturn, to upset: pret. පෙරළුවා *peraḷuwá.*

පෙරළි, *Perali, s.* kind of game; change; war: *a.* rebellious, factious, seditious; quarrelsome; warlike, martial.

පෙරළු, *Peraḷu, part.* of පෙරළනවා *peraḷanawá.*

පෙරළෙනවා, *Peraḷenawá, v.* to upset, to overturn, to reverse: (neuter.) Pret. පෙරළුනා *peraḷuná.*

පෙරාගන්නවා, *Perágannawá, v.* to filter or strain one's self.

පෙරුංකායම්, *Peruṇkáyam, s.* assafætida.

පෙරුම්, *Perum,* Elu form of පාරමිතා *páramitá,* which see.

පෙරුම්පුරණවා, *Perum-puraṇawá, v.* to make preparations slowly, to carry out an intention; the poetical form of පාරමිතා පුරණවා *páramitá-puraṇawá.*

පෙරුම, *Peruma, s.* hope, wish; aim, endeavour, aspiring; straining.

පෙරෙණවා, *Pereṇawá, v.* to flow: pret. පෙරුණ *peruṇá.*

පෙරෙයිදා, *Pereyidá,* } *s.* day before yesterday.
පෙරේදා, *Perédá,* }

පෙරෙත්තය, *Perettaya, s.* urgent request; excuse for declining a request.

පෙරෙත්තකරණවා, *Perettakaraṇawá, v.* to importune, to repeat a request earnestly; to press.

පෙල්ල, *Pella, s.* testicle; business, duty, service; turn, pole tied to the neck of cattle to prevent them entering enclosures; small sticks or pieces of light wood tied to nets to make them float: pl. පෙලි *peli.*

පෙල්ලටයනවා, *Pellaṭa-yanawá, s.* to work by rotation, applied chiefly to the work of cinnamon peelers.

පෙල්ගැහෙනවා, *Pellugẹhenawá, s.* to assemble as a company of artizans or workmen.

පෙල, *Pela, s.* line, family name, row, rank; text as opposed to a commentary, as ජාතක පෙල *játaka-pela,* the original Páli or text of the Játaka or birth stories of Buddha.

පෙලං, *Pelaṇ, s.* plant, peculiar to Ceylon, *kurrimia zeylanica, (Celastraceæ),* also called හුරුකන්ඩු *hurukandu,* and ඇත්හෙරලිය *ẹt-heraliya;* another plant, peculiar to Ceylon, *putranjiva* (or *pelenga*) *zeylanica, (Euphorbiaceæ).*

පෙලක්, *Pelak, s.* line, row: *a.* some.

පෙලක්දාට, *Pelakdáṭa, s.* on some days.

පෙලගැහෙනවා, *Pelagẹhenawá, v.* to be habituated or accustomed to.

පෙලන්තිය, *Pelantiya, s.* family line: see the following.

පෙලපත, *Pelapata, s.* (පෙල continuous line, උපත birth) generation, tribe, race, descent, lineage.

පෙලපාලිය, *Pelapáliya, s.* (පෙල line, පාලිය row) order, arrangement, successive rows; sacred texts of Buddhist Scripture.

පෙලඹුම, *Pelambuma, s.* love, affection, regard, enticement.

පෙලඹුවා, *Pelambuwá, v.* enticed.

පෙලරස්නය, *Pelarasnaya, s.* ray of the sun, sunbeam.

පෙලවස්, *Pelawas, s.* (පෙල family or tribe, වස් dwell) marriage.

පෙලවස්කරණවා, *Pelawas-karaṇawá, v.* to marry.

පෙලවහ, *Pelawaha,* see පෙලවස් *pelawas.*

පෙලි, *Peli, s.* trunk, box, chest: plur. of පෙල්ල *pella.*

පෙලිදඬු, *Peli-daṇḍu, s.* (පෙලි testicles, දඬු wood) two pieces of wood used in squeezing the testicles of young bullocks, to produce the same effects as castration.

පෙලි පාරණවා, *Peli-páraṇawá, v.* to squeeze the testicles of young bullocks between two pieces of wood, for the purpose of producing the same effects as castration.

පෙව්, *Pew, s.* rising, ascending, going up: *a.* soaked, imbibed.

පෙව්වා, *Pewwá, pret.* of පොවනවා *powanawá.*

පෙවෙනවා, *Pewenawá, v.* to soak, to steep, to imbibe, to saturate: pret. පෙවුනා *pewuná.*

පෙස්ස, *Pessa*, *s.* servant, slave, [Coll: වාළා *wáḷá*].

පෙහු, *Pehu*, *s.* seeing, [Colloq. බැලුම *beḷuma*].

පෙහෙ, *Pehe*, *s.* one of the phases of the moon, quarter, [Colloq. පෝය *póya*], sacred day of the Buddhists, of which there are four in a month.

පෙහෙකර, *Pehekara*, *s.* tom-tom beater, [Colloq. බෙරවායා *berawáyá*].

පෙහෙඹිය, *Pehembiya*, *s.* elegant fern-leaved timber tree, *felicium decipiens, (Burseraceæ).*

පෙහෙරා, *Peherá*, *s.* weaver, one of the weaver caste or tribe, Elu form of පේසකාර *pésakára.*

පෙහෙවස්, *Pehewas*, *s.* (පෙහෙ any phase of the moon, වස් observance) religious fast among the Buddhists on any of the four quarters of the moon.

පෙහෙවෙනවා, *Pehewenawá*, *v.* to fast, to keep holy the පෝය *póya* days.

පෙහෙසුන්, *Pehesun*, *s.* slander.

පෙළහර, *Peḷahara*, *s.* (පෙළ substituted for පෙර හර *perahara*) procession, religious procession; also, a miracle.

පෙළාව, *Peḷáwa*, *s.* basket, box.

පෙළිපෙළි, *Peḷipeḷi*, *s.* being stricken.

පෙළිම, *Peḷíma*, verbal noun of පෙළෙනවා *peḷenawá.*

පෙළු, *Peḷu*, *a.* winnowed, threshed, cleaned, (as corn); sorted, cleaned, (as cotton).

පෙළුම්, *Peḷum*, *s.* grief, sorrow, affliction, distress. pain, [Colloq. දුක *duka*].

පෙළෙනවා, *Peḷenawá*, *v.* to be afflicted, to be oppressed or tormented.

පේ, *Pé*, *s.* devil, demon; sprite, goblin; but in the latter senses it chiefly refers to the manes of departed persons; quarter of the moon; also, tree or grove as in හල්පේ *halpé*, grove of හල් *hal* trees, දොම්පේ *dompé*, grove of දොඹ *domba* trees. මාදම්පේ *mádampé*, etc.

පේකඩය, *Pékaḍaya*, *s.* piece of wood inserted in the wall of a house and supporting the beam; the cap of a pillar, chapiter: pl. පේකඩ *pékaḍa.*

පේකරණවා, *Pékaraṇawá*, *v.* to make offerings to a devil, to hallow, to set apart for gods: pret. පේකළා *pékaḷá*,

පේට, *Péṭa*, *s.* basket.

පේටක, *Péṭaka*, *s.* basket for holding clothes, books, etc., chest, trunk; multitude.

පේටා, *Péṭá*, පේටිකා, *Péṭiká*, පේටි, *Péṭi*, } *s.* basket.

පේඩියා, *Péḍiyá*, *s.* washerman, head or chief among the washermen.

පේත්තයා, *Péttayá*, *s.* species of fish.

පේත, *Péta*, *s.* sprite, goblin, ghost, manes of a departed person: *a.* dead, extinct, expired.

පේතසෙය්‍යා, *Péta-seyyá*, *s.* posture in which specters, goblins, and the manes of the deceased sleep, viz. on the back, it being impossible for them to lie on either side, as the bones would pierce through the skin.

පේන, *Péna*, *s.* demoniacal possession, soothsaying.

පේන කියනවා, *Péna-kiyanawá*, *v.* to speak under the supposed inspiration of a demon.

පේන කීම, *Péna-kíma*, *s.* (පේන and කීම saying) saying uttered by a Kapuwá under the pretended inspiration of a demon; these declarations are generally of very ambiguous import, are spoken when the priest is in a state of demonical phrensy, and are supposed to be the sayings of the demon; verbal noun of පේන කියනවා *péna-kiyanawá.*

පේනවා, *Pénawá*, *v.* to appear, to be visible or apparent: pret. පෙණුනා *peṇuná:* see පෙණෙනවා *peṇenawá.*

පේනිල, *Pénila*, *s.* soap-berry plant, *sapindus emargenatus*, [Colloq. පෙනෙල *penela*].

පේනිවෙනවා, *Péniwenawá*, *v.* to expect, to take care.

පේනුකරණවා, *Pénukaraṇawá*, *v.* to cherish, to watch, to preserve.

පේනුව, *Pénuwa*, *s.* stopper, plug.

පේය, *Péya*, *s.* (පා *pá* to drink) water; milk; any thing drinkable.

පේයා, *Péyá*, *s.* rice gruel, decoction of any thing after straining.

පේයාව, *Péyáwa*, *s.* drink, beverage: see the last.

පේයූෂ, *Péyúsha*, *s.* milk of a newly calved cow; fresh ghee; nectar.

පේර, *Péra*, *s.* guava tree, *psidium guyava, (Myrtaceæ)*, (from the Portuguese.)

පේරතඹල, *Péra-tambala*, *s.* plant, *Gaertnera Kœnigii, (Loganiaceæ).*

පේරදොඹ, *Péra-domba*, *s.* variety of *calophyllum inophyllum.*

පේරුකරණවා, *Pérukaraṇawá*, *v.* to distribute; to allot service.

පේරුව, *Péruwa*, *s.* race, tribe, caste, [Colloq. ජාතිය *játiya*]; division of a district; setting apart, devoting to some particular purpose, share.

පේරුවැටෙනවා, *Péruwețenawá*, *v.* to come to by turn.

පේරෝස, *Pérósa*, *s.* gem of blue or greenish blue colour, turquoise.

පේරුස්මුද්ද, *Pérẹsmulda*, පේරුස්මුන්ද, *Pérẹsmunda*, පේරුස, *Pérẹsa*, } *s.* ring studded with jewels and worn by headmen; signet ring.

පේරුහැ, *Pérẹhẹ*, *s.* thick rope used to fasten a stag's horn to a post, to which is hooked another horn, when they are pulled in game till one of them is broken which loses the game.

පේලව, *Pélawa*, *s.* fragrant grass or weed, *cyperus rotundus*, [Colloq. කලාඳුරු *kaláṇduru*]: *a.* delicate, fine, thin, slender, slim, soft.

පේලිය, *Péliya*, *s.* rule; line, row, rank.

පේවස්, *Péwas*, see පෙහෙවස් *pehewas*.

පේවෙනවා, *Péwenawá*, *v.* to prepare for any religious ceremony or festival.

පේශල, *Péșala*, *a.* dexterous, clever; beautiful; agreeable; crafty; smooth, fraudulent.

පේශි, *Péși*, *s.* thunderbolt; egg; split pease.

පේශී, *Péșí*, *s.* egg of a bird; blown bud; spikenard, *valeriana jaṭámansi;* ball of flesh or meat; muscle; sheath or scabbard; name of a river.

පේෂණ, *Péshaṇa*, *s.* grinding, hand mill; stone and muller; sending, forwarding, dismissing, letting loose.

පේෂණි, *Péshaṇi*, *s.* stone slab on which condiments are ground with a muller or roller.

පේස, *Pésa*, *s.* wove-silk.

පේසකාර, *Pésakára*, *s.* (පේස and කාර who makes) weaver, man of the weaver caste.

පේසනක, *Pésanaka*, *s.* kind of highway robber, highway man, one of a banditti.

පේසිකා, *Pésiká*, *s.* rind, shell.

පේසිකෝස, *Pési-kósa*, *s.* (පේසි egg, කෝස sheath) egg shell.

පේසිත, *Pésita*, *a.* sent, forwarded, dismissed, let loose.

පේහිමි, *Péhimi*, *s.* (පේ demon, හිමි lord) name of Kuvéra or Wesamuṇi king of the devils.

පේළා, *Pélá*, පේළාව, *Péláwa*, } *s.* testicle; egg; basket, box, trunk.

පෛත්තික, *Paittika*, *s.* (පිත්ත *pitta* bile, ඉක *ika* aff. or relation) creeping plant, *cocculus orbiculatus:* *a.* having a great deal of bile; bilious, of or belonging to the bile.

පෛත්‍ර, *Paitra*, *s.* (පිතෘ *pitṛi* father, etc.) part of the hand between the thumb and fingers, or the root of the finger: *a.* paternal, ancestral, relating or belonging to a parent or progenitor.

පෛශාච, *Paiśácha*, *a.* (පිශාච *piśácha* demon, etc.) infernal, demoniacal, relating to the piśáchas.

පොක්කරම, *Pokkarama*, *s.* mass, crowd, multitude; bunch, cluster, purse: pl. පොක්කරම් *pokkaram*.

පොක්ඛර, *Pokkhara*, *s.* lotus, *nelumbium speciosum*, [Colloq. නෙළුම් *neḷum*]; rain water; comeliness, beauty; tip of an elephant's trunk; belly of a lute; upper surface of a sort of drum.

පොක්ඛරණි, *Pokkharaṇí*, *s.* lotus pond, tank, reservoir.

පොක්ඛරසාතක, *Pokkharasátaka*, *s.* sort of teal or wild duck; name of a celebrated Brahman, of whom it is fabled that previous to his being born in this world he requested that he might not be born of a woman; his prayer was heard, and he was produced from a lotus.

පොකිරිස්සා, *Pokirissá*, *s.* lobster.

පොකුටු, *Pokuṭu*, *s.* curls, locks of hair.

පොකුණ, *Pokuṇa*, *s.* lake, pond, natural or artificial cistern, reservoir: pl. පොකුණු *pokuṇu*.

පොකුර, *Pokura*, *s.* lotus, [Colloq. නෙළුම් *neḷum*]; tip of an elephant's trunk; bunch, cluster, branch: pl. පොකුරු *pokuru*.

පොකුරුණි, *Pokuruṇi*, *s.* pond, lake, reservoir, [Colloq. විල *vila*].

පොකුරුදෙලි, *Pokurudẹli*, *s.* (පොකුරු and දෙලි root) edible root of the lotus; the bud or germ of the lotus.

පොකුරුපත, *Pokurupata*, *s.* leaf of the lotus.

පොකුරුමුල, *Pokuru-mula*, *s.* root of the lotus, [Colloq. නෙළුම් අල *neḷum-ala*].

පොකුරුසර, *Pokurusara*, *s.* (පොකුර *pokura* and සර pond) pond where the lotus grows.

පොඟනවා, *Poṇganawá*, *v.* to soak: pret. පෙඟුවා *peṇguwá*.

පොඟවනවා, *Poṇgawanawá*, *v.* to steep, to saturate: පෙඟෙව්වා *peṇgewwá*.

පොට්ඇල් වී, *Poṭel-ví*, *s.* kind of paddy, variety of *oryza sativa*.

පොට්ටනිය, *Poṭṭaniya*, *s.* bundle, parcel, pack, bale.

පොට්ටයා, *Poṭṭayá*, *s.* man blind of one eye, blind man, man with a defective eye.

පොටතල, *Poṭatala*, *s.* plant, variety of *doona cordifolia*, [Colloq. දියබෙරලිය *diyaberaliya*].

පොඩ්ඩ, *Poḍḍa*, see පොඩිස්ස *poḍissa*.

පොඩ්ඩා, *Poḍḍá*, *s.* lad, pl. පොඩ්ඩෝ *poḍḍó*.

පොඩ්ඩී, *Poḍḍí*, *s.* lass, pl. පොඩ්ඩියෝ *poḍḍiyó*.

පොඩි, *Poḍi*, *s.* very thin piece of metal mixed with borax for the purpose of fastening metals: *a.* broken, crushed, broken by squeezing; small, as පොඩි ළමයා *poḍi-lamayá*, small child, පොඩි කෑල්ල *poḍi-kėlla*, small bit.

පොඩිකරණවා, *Poḍikaraṇawá*, *v.* (පොඩි fragments, කරණවා to make) to crush, to bruise, to break into small fragments or bits.

පොඩිකිර, *Poḍikíra*, *s.* splinter, chip: pl. පොඩිකිරි *poḍikíri*.

පොඩි පැරෑටියා, *Poḍi-perėṭiyá*, *s.* kind of sea fish.

පොඩිය, *Poḍiya*, *s.* small bit, fragment, crumb, particle.

පොඩිවිලාංගු, *Poḍiviláṅgu*, *s.* plant, snake gourd, *trichosanthes anguina*, [Colloq. පතෝල *patóla*].

පොඩි වී, *Poḍi-ví*, *s.* kind of paddy, variety of *oryza sativa*.

පොඩිවෙට්ටුව, *Poḍiweṭṭuwa*, *s.* silversmith's large scissors or clippers.

පොඩිස්ස, *Poḍissa*, *s.* fragment, bit, atom, minute piece.

පොඩිස්සී, *Poḍissí*, see පොඩොස්සී *poḍossí*.

පොඩිහාතලි වී, *Poḍi-hátali-ví*, *s.* kind of paddy.

පොඩිහිනටි වී, *Poḍi-hínaṭi-vi*. *s.* kind of paddy.

පොඩොස්සී, *Poḍossí*, *s.* girl, maid, girl under thirteen years of age.

පොඩරු, *Ponḍaru*, *s.* creeping plant of the *genus piper*, [Colloq. වල්ගා මිරිස් *walgá-miris*].

පොත්, *Pot*, *plur.* of පොත *pota*.

පොත්කම්බය, *Pot-kambaya*, *s.* wooden cover or frame of a native book.

පොත්ගෙඩිය, *Potgeḍiya*, *s.* bundle or packet of the puskola or leaf of the talipot tree prepared for being written or engraved upon.

පොත්ත, *Potta*, *s.* bark of a tree; husk of fruit; shell of testaceous animals: pl. පොතු *potu*.

පොත් පටුන, *Pot-paṭuna*, *s.* (පොත් books, පටුන index) index or list of the contents of a book.

පොත් ලනුව, *Pot-lanuwa*, *s.* (පොත් and ලනුව string) string which is passed through a hole in the centre of the leaves and wooden covers of the native books or manuscripts, and serves both to keep the leaves in their places when being read and also of tying up the books.

පොත්සකිය, *Potsakiya*, *s.* (පොත් and සකිය button) button which is fastened to the end of the string used in tying up and connecting together the leaves and wooden covers of the native books or manuscripts.

පොත, *Pota*, *s.* book, manuscript.

පොතත, *Potata*, *s.* (පොත් *pot* books, අත *ata* hand) epithet of Brahma, [Colloq. මහාබ්‍රහ්මයා *mahá brahmayá*].

පොතරිල්ල, *Potarilla*, *s.* plant, not ascertained.

පොතල්, *Potal*, *s.* jackal, *canis aureus*, [Colloq. නරියා *nariyá*].

පොතු, *Potu*, *plur.* of පොත්ත *potta*: *a.* flat, thin.

පොතුකොල, *Potukola*, *s.* species of rush, used in making coarse mats, *scleria oryzoides (Cyperaceæ)*; also called පොතුපන් *potupan*.

පොතුගහනවා, *Potugahanawá*, *v.* to decorticate, to strip off bark.

පොතුපන්, *Potupan*, see පොතුකොල *potukola*.

පොතුපලා, *Potupalá*, *s.* plant, *Ipomœa uniflora*, *(Convolvulaceæ)*.

පොතුබරා, *Potubará*, *s.* kind of sea fish.

පොතුමගුරා, *Potumagurá*, *s.* kind of fish.

පොතුමසා, *Potumasá*, *s.* (පොතු and මසා fish) shell-fish in general.

පොතුවැල, *Potuwela*, *s.* creeping plant, not ascertained.

පොතුහොඩ, *Potuhonḍa*, *s.* passion flower, *modecca palmata (Passifloraceæ)*; also called හොඩල *honḍala*.

පොද, *Poda*, *s.* drop.

පොදගහනවා, *Podagahanawá*, *v.* to drizzle, to be dripping.

පොදවැහෙනවා, *Podawėhenawá*, *v.* (පොද drop, වැහෙනවා to fall) to drop, to fall in drops, as rain.

පොදිය, *Podiya*, *s.* bundle, bale, parcel.

පොදු, *Podu*, *a.* universal, general, common to more than one; equal, impartial.

පොදුවේ, *Poduwé*, *ad.* commonly, generally, universally.

පොන්ස, *Ponsa*, *s.* punch, (Dutch.)

පොනි, *Poni*, *s.* flower, [Colloq. මල් *mal*].

පොනේ, *Poné*, *ad.* before, prior, preceding.

පොපි, *Popi*, *s.* trembling, tremor, agitation, [Coll: වෙවුළුම *wewuḷuma*]: *a.* wavering, unfixed, unsteady.

පොපිය, *Popiya*, *s.* shaking or involuntary motion of part of the body.

පොපියනවා, *Popiyanawá*, *v.* to shake, to tremble, to be agitated, to quiver, to feel a tickling sensation.

පොබ, *Poba, s.* expanding, blowing, opening as a flower, Elu form of ප්‍රබෝධ *prabódha.*

පොබයනවා, *Pobayanawá, v.* to open, to blow, to expand as flower.

පොබලිමාරා, *Pobali-márá, s.* tree, not ascertained.

පොම, *Poma, s.* superiority.

පොර, *Pora, s.* boxing, fighting, seizing, wrestling; counters used in games; innings; match, as හොඳ ගොන්පොර *honda-gon-pora,* well matched pair of bullocks.

පොරඅන්නවා, *Pora-annawá,* } *v.* (පොර fighting,
පොරඅනිනවා, *Pora-aninawá,* } අනිනවා or අන්නවා to pierce with horns) to butt, to fight as bulls, sheep, goats etc.

පොර අල්ලනවා, *Pora-allanawá, v.* (පොර and අල්ලනවා to seize) to grip, to wrestle, to grasp in wrestling.

පොරකටුව, *Pora-katuwa, s.* (පොර fighting, කටුව thorn) cock's spur.

පොරකනවා, *Porakanawá, v.* (පොර and කනවා to bite) to contend, to fight as dogs or animals biting each other.

පොරකාරයා, *Porakárayá, s.* (පොර and කාර *kára* who does) fighter, boxer, champion.

පොරකුකුළා, *Pora-kukulá, s.* fighting cock.

පොරකෙළිනවා, *Pora-kelinawá, v.* to fight as cocks.

පොරකේරු, *Porakéru, s.* mischievous, wild.

පොරකොටනවා, *Pora-kotanawá, v.* to fight, as cocks, turkeys etc.

පොරඩාව, *Poradáwa, s.* deceit.

පොරණ, *Porana, a.* ancient, old, former.

පොරඩස්, *Poraddhas, s.* gum or rheum of the eye.

පොරපොල්, *Porapol, s.* (පොර fighting, පොල් coconut) sort of native game, in which two persons place themselves at a measured distance from each other, and each having a ripe peeled coconut in his hand, the one is thrown at the other until one of them is broken when the hardest wins the game.

පොරපොල් ගහනවා, *Porapol-gahanawá, v.* to throw coconuts at games: see the preceding word.

පොරබදනවා, *Porabadanawá, v.* to wrestle in conflict, to grasp.

පොරව, *Porawa, s.* hatchet, axe; name of a playing card, queen, (Dutch vrou).

පොරව කෑඳත්තා, *Porawa-kendattá, s.* crowned hornbill, *anthracocerus coronatus, (Bucerotidæ,* order *Picariæ).*

පොරවනකඩ, *Porawanakada, s.* piece of a garment; cloak.

පොරවන රෙද්ද, *Parawana-redda, s.* cloak.

පොරවනවා, *Porawanawá, v.* to put on, to wrap round, to robe, to cover with clothes: pret. පෙරෙව්වා *perewwá.*

පොරවමාරා, *Porawa-márá, s.* small tree, *canthium didymum (Rubiaceæ):* also called ගල් කරඳ *galkaranda.*

පොරි, *Pori, s.* fried or parched grain used as food, [Colloq. විලඳ *vilanda*].

පොරුවමල්ල, *Poruwamalla, s.* tree, *diospyros insignis (Ebenaceæ):* also called ගොන්න *gonna* and වල්මැදිරිය *walmediriya.*

පොරොත්තු, *Porottu, s.* dwelling, residing; staying, awaiting, tarrying.

පොරොත්තුකරණවා, *Porottukaranawá, v.* to detain.

පොරොත්තුවෙනවා, *Porottuwenawá, v.* to wait.

පොරොන්දුව, *Poronduwa, s.* agreement, engagement, promise, condition.

පොරොන්දුවෙනවා, *Poronduwenawá, v.* to promise, to engage.

පොරොයි, *Poroyi, s.* bubbles caused by pouring.

පොරොවනවා, *Porowanawá,* see පොරවනවා *porawanawá.*

පොරෝකෙටිය, *Poróketiya,* see පොරව *porawa.*

පොරෝණය, *Porónaya, s.* robe, vesture.

පොරෝ තලේ, *Poró-talé, s.* blade of a hatchet or axe.

පොරෝහිත, *Poróhita,* corrupt form of පුරෝහිත *puróhita,* which see.

පොල්, *Pol, s.* coconut full grown, or in its last state and ready for culinary purposes; plant, *paspalum kora.*

පොල් අඹ, *Pol-amba, s.* variety of the *mangifera indica,* or common mango.

පොල්අත්ත, *Pol-atta, s.* cadjan, dried and plaited coconut leaf, coconut branch.

පොල් අමු, *Pol-amu, s.* plant, variety of *paspalum scrobiculatum.*

පොල් ඇල්වී, *Polel-ví, s.* kind of paddy, variety of *oryza sativa.*

පොල්උල, *Pol-ula, s.* pointed stick for peeling coconut.

පොල්කටුව, *Polkatuwa, s.* shell of a coconut.

පොල්කටුවා වැල, *Polkatuwá-wela, s.* plant,

පොල්කිරි, *Polkiri, s.* juice of coconut.

පොල්කුඩු, *Polkudu, s.* (පොල් coconut, කුඩු dust) refuse of the coconut after it has been rasped and the milk expressed; sort of grass: see the next.

පොල්කුඩුපලා, *Polkuḍupalá*, *s.* knot-grass, *ærua lanata* or *illecebrum lanatnm*, *(Amarantaceæ)*.

පොල්කූර, *Polkúra*, *s.* pointed stick or iron used for peeling coconuts.

පොල්කොහු, *Pol-kohu*, *s.* coconut fibre.

පොල් කෝම්බෙ, *Pol-kómbe*, *s.* shell of the coconut.

පොල්ගහ, *Polgaha*, *s.* coconut palm, *cocos nucifera (Palmæ)*.

පොල්ගහනවා, *Pol-gahanawá*, see පොරපොල් ගහනවා *porapol-gahanawá*.

පොල්ගිරවා, *Pol-girawá*, *s.* Ceylonese lorikeet, *loriculus indicus;* also called ගිරාමලිච්චියා *girámalichchiyá: (Trichoglossidæ*, order *Psittaci.)*

පොල්ගුටිය, *Polguṭiya*, *s.* punishment among the Kandyans, which consists of pelting the culprit with coconuts.

පොල්ගෙඩිය, *Pol-geḍiya*, *s.* coconut, sweet-bread, pancreas.

පොල්තෙල්, *Pol-tel*, *s.* coconut oil.

පොල්පලා, *Polpalá*, see පොල්කුඩුපලා *polkuḍupalá*.

පොල්පිත්ත, *Polpitta*, *s.* stem of a coconut branch.

පොල්මල්කරවලා, *Polmal-karawalá*, *s.* beautiful tree snake, *chrysopelea ornata (Dendrophidæ* order *Ophidia)*.

පොල්මැල්lුම, *Pol-mælluma*, *s.* condiment made of coconut, saffron, chilli and salt; sweet sauce made of coconut juice.

පොල්ල, *Polla*, *s.* stick, pole, club, staff, stave; size, measure: pl. පොලු *polu*.

පොල්ලා, *Pollá*, *s.* young of any animal, [Colloq. පැටවා *peṭawá*].

පොල්ලිච්චා, *Pollichchá*, *s.* magpie robin, *copsychus saularis, (Saxicolidæ* order *Passeres)*.

පොල්ලෙල්ල, *Pollella*, *s.* husk or rind of a coconut.

පොල්වල්ල, *Pol-walla*, *s.* coconut bunch.

පොල්වාකර, *Polwákara*, *s.* arrack of the first distillation.

පොල්හොද්ද, *Pol-hodda*, *s.* sort of curry made of coconuts.

පොල, *Pola*, *s.* pupil of the eye.

පොලඟා, *Polaṅgá*, *s.* general name for the viper: see තිත්පොලඟා *titpolaṅgá*, පලාපොලඟා *palápolaṅgá*, and පොලොංතෙලිස්සා *poloṅtelissá*: pl. පොලොංගු *poloṅgu*.

පොලඟැටියා, *Polaṅgæṭiyá*, *s.* locust, grasshopper, (order *Homoptera)*.

පොලබිජු, *Pola-biju*, *s.* gold, wrought or unwrought gold.

පොලබුං, *Polabuṅ*, *s.* separation, [Colloq. වෙන්වීම *wenvíma*].

පොලඹ, *Polamba*, *s.* variety of the common mango, *mangifera indica*.

පොලඹනවා, *Polambanawá*, *v.* to desire, to lust after; to decoy, to coax, to entice; to cheat, to deceive, to pursuade, to induce.

පොලවී, *Pola-ví*, *s.* kind of paddy, *oryza sativa*.

පොලහ, *Polaha*, *s.* young jack fruit, *artocarpus integrifolia*: pl. පොලොස් *polos*.

පොලු, *Polu*, *plur.* of පොල්ල *polla*.

පොලුකූර, *Polukúra*, *s.* headless hairpin in a set of four, two having heads.

පොලුගහනවා, *Polu-gahanawá*, *v.* to cut in pieces; to throw at with a stick.

පොලොං අල, *Poloṅ-ala*, *s.* tuberous stemless plant, *typhonium divaricatum* (or *arum Roxburghii) (Araceæ)*.

පොලොං ගහල, *Poloṅ-gahala*, *s.* tuberous plant, variety of *colocasia antiquorum*.

පොලොං තෙලිස්සා, *Poloṅ-telissá*, *s.* viperine snake, *hypnale nepa (Crotalidæ* order *Ophidia);* also called කුනුකටුවා *kunukaṭuwá*.

පොලොං ලබු, *Poloṅ-labu*, *s.* plant, kind of pumpkin: also see පැලමද *pęla-máda*.

පොලොත්ත, *Polotta*, *s.* coconut shell.

පොලොව, *Polowa*, see පොළව *poḷawa*.

පොලොස්, *Polos*, *s.* young jack fruit: see පොලහ *polaha*.

පොලෝ උල්ලා, *Poló-ullá*, }
පොලෝගුල්ලා, *Poló-gullá*, } *s.* snake.

පොව්, *Paw*, *s.* young of any animal.

පොව්වනවා, *Powwanawá*, *v.* to be in one's depth in water.

පොවනවා, *Powanawá*, *v.* to soak, to wet, to cause to drink or imbibe, to dip; to ford, to wade: pret. පෙව්වා *pewwá*.

පොවුවා, *Powuwá*, see පොව් *pow*.

පොස, *Posa*, *s.* man, [Colloq. මිනිහා *miniha*].

පොසොන්, *Poson*, *s.* month Poson (June—July); flower.

පොසොන් ඇල්වී, *Poson-ælví*, *s.* variety of paddy, *oryza sativa*.

පොසොන් වී, *Poson-ví*, *s.* variety of paddy, *oryza sativa*.

පොහොට්ටු, *Pohoṭṭu*, *s.* plant, *gomphrena;* knob.

පොහොට්ටුව, *Pohoṭṭuwa*, *s.* ornamental knot attached to native girdles, unblown flower.

පොහොදින, *Pohodina*, *s.* (පොහො phase of the moon, දින day) day of any of the changes of the moon and that on which the religious festivals of the Buddhists are usually celebrated.

පොහොනා, *Pohoná*, *a.* able, competent, sufficient.

පොහොනි, *Pohoni*, *s.* nourishment: *a.* stout, fat, healthy.

පොහොය, *Pohoya*, *s.* any one of the phases of the moon, or a quarter of a lunar month.

පොහොසත්, *Pohosat*, *a.* rich, opulent, wealthy; able, capable, possessed of the power of performing any thing,

පොහොසත්කම, *Pohosatkama*, *s.* wealth, opulence.

පොහොසතා, *Pohosatá*, *s.* rich man.

පොළ, *Poḷa*, *s.* calf; cataract in the eye; boil, tumour.

පොළ නඟිනවා, *Poḷa-naginawá*, *v.* to have a cataract in the eye.

පොළනවා, *Poḷanawá*, *v.* to winnow, to separate the grain from the chaff by tossing it up in an open basket, to sift; to fan; to sort, to clean (as cotton): pret. පෙළුවා *peḷuwá*.

පොළව, *Poḷawa*, *s.* earth.

පොළාදමනවා, *Poḷádamanawá*, *v.* to winnow, to sift; to fan etc.: see පොළනවා *poḷanawá*.

පොළි, *Poḷi*, *s.* interest, usury.

පොළෝ, *Poḷó*, *s.* the earth.

පොළෝකම්පාව, *Poḷókampáwa*, *s.* earthquake.

පොළෝතලය, *Poḷótalaya*, } *s.* (පොළෝ and තල
පොළෝතෙල, *Poḷótela*, } *tala* plane etc.) surface of the earth, *terra firma*.

පෝ, *Pó*, *s.* young of any animal: see පොව් *pow:* phase of the moon: see පොහොය *pohoya*.

පෝක්කරුට්ටම, *Pókkareṭṭama*, *s.* frugality.

පෝංගුව, *Pónguwa*, *s.* double hook for the purpose of catching alligators; bamboo or any hollow trunk used for catching fishes in rivers.

පෝච්චිය, *Póchchiya*, *s.* jug, (from Dutch potji).

පෝටගල, *Póṭagala*, *s.* sort of reed, *arundo tibialis*, [Colloq. වැලුක් *weḷuk*].

පෝටලිකා, *Póṭaliká*, *s.* bundle or packet.

පෝටා, *Póṭá*, *s.* woman with a beard; creeping plant, *pothos scandens:* see පෝටාවැල් *póṭá-weḷ*.

පෝටාව, *Póṭáwa*, *s.* dam, mound of earth, or a bank raised in the rice fields to dam in the water and to serve as a foot path when the fields are inundated; spill water, usually in the earth-bank of an eḷa, collection of water from a bank, retained by a bund, for use below after it has passsd the upper fields, [Colloq. නියර *niyara*].

පෝටාවැල්, *Póṭá-weḷ*, *s.* creeping plant, *pothos scandens*, (*Araceæ*).

පෝටෑ, *Póṭẹ*, see පෝටාවැල් *póṭá-weḷ*.

පෝත, *Póta*, *s.* young of any animal; boat, vessel; site of a dwelling house; cloth; value, worth.

පෝතක, *Pótaka*, } *s.* young of any animal:
පෝතකයා, *Pótakayá*, } see පොව් *pow*.

පෝතකී, *Pótakí*, *s.* fem. of පෝතක *pótaka*; name of plant, *basella lucida*, allied to නිවිති *niviti*.

පෝතවනික්, *Pótawanik*, } *s.* (පෝත ship, වනික්
පෝතවනිජ්, *Pótawanij*, } merchant) voyaging merchant.

පෝතවාහ, *Pótawáha*, *s.* (පෝත vessel, වහ *waha* to carry) rower, boatman, steersman, tow-man, one of the crew who keeps watch at the mast-head.

පෝතාධාන, *Pótádhána*, *s.* (පෝත *póta* young of an animal, vessel, අධාන *ádhána* having, holding) small fry; shoal of young fish, shoal of fish so large as to impede the course of a ship.

පෝතේ, *Póté*, *s.* value, worth, (speaking depreciatingly).

පෝථන, *Póthana*, *s.* beating, squeezing, crushing, [Colloq. මිරිකීම *mirikíma*].

පෝථිත, *Póthita*, *a.* crushed, squeezed.

පෝදා, *Pódá*, *s.* any quarter of the moon: see පොහොදින *pohodina*.

පෝනියා, *Póniyá*, *s.* pony, (Eng.)

පෝනේ, *Póné*, *s.* sufficiency, enough.

පෝය, *Póya*, *s.* quarters of the moon observed sacred by the Buddhists: see පොහොය *pohoya*.

පෝයකෙරුම, *Póyakeruma*, *s.* private confession among the priests on póya days: see පොහොය *pohoya*.

පෝය හේවිසි, *Póya-hérisi*, *s.* beating tom toms at the temples on the day of the change of the moon.

පෝර්කේ, *Pórké*, *s.* gibbet, gallows: pl. පෝර්ක *pórka*.

පෝර්ණුව, *Pórṇuwa*, *s.* an oven.

පෝර, *Póra*, *s.* dung, manure.

පෝරපස්, *Póra-pas*, *s.* manured soil, rich soil.

පෝරු, *Póru*, lining.

පෝරුගානවා, *Pórugánawá*, *v.* to harrow.

පෝරුව, *Póruwa*, *s.* agricultural implement, kind of roller made of wood and used for levelling or smoothing the rice fields after ploughing and previous to the sowing of the grain; a place where the bride and the bridegroom stand during part of the mariage ceremony according to native usage, board; rake; living.

පෝල, *Póla*, *s.* bulk, magnitude, quantity.

පෝලිකරණවා, *Pólikaranawá*, *v.* to abash, to confound, to embarrass.

පෝලිංගහනවා, *Pólingahanawá*, *v.* to arrange in line.

පෝෂ්‍ය, *Póshya*, *s.* nourishment, aliment; food, feeding.

පෝෂ්‍යකරණවා, *Póshyakaranawá*, *v.* to nourish.

පෝෂණ, *Póshana*, *s.* nourishing, cherishing; maintaining, supporting.

පෝසක, *Pósaka*, *s.* cherisher, nourisher.

පෞණ්ඩර්‍ය, *Paundarya*, *s.* drug so called, made from the root of a medicinal creeping plant and used as a remedy for sore eyes.

පෞතව, *Pautawa*, *s.* sort of scale or balance, steel yard; measure.

පෞත්‍ර, *Pautra*, *s.* (පුත්‍ර *putra* son, අණ් *an* aff. of descent) son's son, grandson: *a.* relating to a son.

පෞත්‍රි, *Pautri*, *s.* (පුත්‍ර *putra* son, අණ් *an* aff. & *i* fem. aff.) grand-daughter, either in the male or female line, though more usually confined to a son's daughter.

පෞර්ණමාස, *Paurna-mása*, *s.* (පූර්ණ මාස *púrna-mása* and අණ් *an* affix) ceremony performed at the full of the moon by persons maintaining a perpetual fire.

පෞර්ණමාසි, *Paurnamási*, *s.* day of full moon.

පෞර, *Paura*. *s.* (පුර *pura* city, අණ් *an* affix of relation) castle, city, tower, fortification; citizen: *a.* relating to or produced in a town.

පෞරජන, *Paurajana*, *s.* citizen.

පෞරස්ත්‍ය, *Paurastya*, *s.* (පුරස් *puras* before, formerly, අණ් *an* aff. of relation) prior, first, initial, former, preceding.

පෞරුෂ, *Paurusha*, *s.* (පුරුෂ *purusha* man, අණ් *an* aff. of relation) measure of a man, equal to the height to which he reaches with both arms elevated and the fingers extended; property of manhood, virility; semen virile; action incidental to the state of humanity; manliness, strength, power, vigour: *a.* manly, of or belonging to man.

පෞරෝගව, *Paurógawa*, *s.* overseer or superintendent of the kitchen.

පෞලස්ත්‍ය, *Paulastya*, *s.* (පුලස්ත්‍ය *pulastya* saint so called, අණ් *an* aff. of descent) name of Wesamuni or Kuvéra the god of wealth and chief of the demons.

පෞෂ්‍ය, *Paushya*, see පුෂ්‍ය *pushya*.

පෞෂ, *Pausha*, *s.* (පුෂ්‍ය *pushya* asterism in which the moon is full in this month and අඤ් *añ* aff.) month so called (December—January).

පෞෂී, *Paushí*, *s.* day of the full moon in the month පෞෂ *pausha*.

පැ, *Pę*, Elu form of ප්‍ර *pra*, which see.

පැකන්, *Pękan*, *s.* mire, mud, [Colloq. මඩ *mada*].

පැකිරීම, *Pękiríma*, *s.* yawning, stretching.

පැකිලීම, *Pękilíma*, *s.* stumbling; verbal noun of පැකිලෙනවා *pękilenawá*.

පැකිලෙනවා, *Pękilenawá*, *v.* to stumble, to fall; to start through fear; to be obstructed or impeded: pret. පැකිලුනා *pękiluná*.

පැකුන්, *Pękun*, } *s.* circle; girdle, zone; mud,
පැකුම්, *Pękum*, } mire.

පැකුලුම, *Pękuluma*, verbal noun of පැකිලෙනවා *pękilenawá*.

පැඟිරා, *Pęngirá*, *s.* young animal.

පැඟිරි, *Pęngiri*, *s.* zest (applied to the expressed juice of the rind of oranges etc.): *a.* sour, harshly sour, acid.

පැඟිරි කුරුඳු, *Pęngiri-kurundu*, *s.* kind of cinnamon, peculiar to Ceylon, the bark has the fragrance of cinnamon and citronella, *cinnamomum citriodorum*, *(Lauraceæ)*.

පැඟිරිතෙල්, *Pęngiri-tel*, *s.* citronella oil.

පැඟිරිමාන්, *Pęngirimán*, *s.* (පැඟිරි acid, මාන් having) citronella grass, cultivated variety of *andropogon nardus*, *(Gramineæ)*.

පැඤ්චා, *Pęñchá*, *s.* little one, child, infant, little boy.

පැඤ්චි, *Pęñchi*, fem. of the foregoing.

පැට්ටුන්, *Pęttun*, *s.* vanishing, disappearance.

පැටංගා, *Pętangá*, see පැටියා *pętiyá*.

පැටවා, *Pętawá*, *s.* young of any animal, young person: pl. පැටව් *pętaw*.

පැටවිල්ල, *Pętawilla*, *s.* load, burden, cargo, charge.

පැටවීම, *Pętawíma*, *s.* loading, freighting; verbal noun of පටවනවා *patawanawá*.

පැටවුම්, *Pętawum*, *s.* loss, disappearance, concealment, vanishing.

පැටි, *Pęti*, *s.* concealment, hiding; commencement, beginning; also see පැටියා *pętiyá*.

පැටික්කි, *Pętikki*, *s.* girl, maiden, young woman.

පැටිකාවැල්, *Pętiká-węl*, *s.* climbing plant, *artabotrys zeylanicus*: see පෙතිකාවැල් *petiká-węl*.

පැටියා, *Pętiyá*, *s.* young of any animal; sometimes applied to a young person.

පැටිහුන්, *Pętihun*, *s.* concealment, [Colloq. සැඟවීම *sęngavíma*].

පැඩ්ඩා, *Pęḍḍá*, *s.* small domestic insect: also pret. of පඩිනවා *paḍinawá*.

පැඩිලි, *Pęḍili*, *s.* colour white.

පැණ, *Pęṇa*, *s.* question, demand, Elu form of ප්‍රශ්න *prașna;* intricate question, puzzle; Elu form of ප්‍රඥා *prajñá;* wisdom, knowledge, cleverness, ability, skill, discernment, judgement.

පැණඇස, *Pęṇa-ęsa*, *s.* (පැණ wisdom, ඇස eye) understanding, intellect, skill, ability.

පැණපිළිවිසිනවා, *Pęṇa-piḷivisinawá*, *v.* to propose an intricate question or enigma.

පැණවත්, *Pęṇawat*, *a.* (පැණ knowledge, වත් poss. aff.) wise, learned, well informed, [Colloq. පණ්ඩිත *paṇḍita*].

පැණවිසඳනවා, *Pęṇa-visaṉdanawá*, *v.* (පැණ question, විසඳනවා to explain) to solve an enigma.

පැණවිම, *Pęṇavima*, *s.* causing to skip over, applied to the intentional neglect of the hour of any engagement; erecting, enacting; the verbal noun of පණවනවා *paṇawanawá*, which see.

පැණසර, *Pęṇasara*, *s.* (පැණ and සර essence) great learning, extensive or profound knowledge, wisdom; wise man, scholar, sage: *a.* wise, extensively intelligent.

පැණෙනවා, *Pęṇenawá*, *v.* to appear, to be visible; to spring as an elastic substance: pret. පැණුනා *pęṇuná*.

පැතත, *Pętta*, *s.* side, side of the body; quarter, direction; slice cut: pl. පැති *pęti*.

පැත්ම, *Pętma*, *s.* wish, hope, expectation, opportunity, chance.

පැතලි, *Pętali*, *a.* flat, even, smooth.

පැති, *Pęti*, *s.* sides; plural of පැතත *pętta*.

පැතිර, *Pętira*, *part.* having been spread, expanded, published, promulgated.

පැතිරෙණවා, *Pętireṇawá*, *v.* to spread, to be expanded, to be diffused: pret. පැතුරුණ *pęturuṇá*.

පැතිම, *Pętíma*, *s.* hope, expectation.

පැතුම, *Pętuma*, *s.* request, petition; begging, beseeching; expectation, hope: pl, පැතුම් *pętum*.

පැතුරුම, *Pęturuma*, *s.* diffusion (as news etc.); verbal noun of පැතිරෙණවා *pętireṇawá*.

පැද්දී, *Pęddí*, *s.* female of the Paduwá caste.

පැද්දීම, *Pęddíma*, *s.* causing to row, as a boat, or to move forwards and backwards as a swing.

පැදකුණ, *Pędakuṇu*, *s.* (පැ for ප්‍ර *pra* before, දකුණ *dakuṇa* right side) circumambulating any one with the right side towards the person, as a mark of homage or a reverential salutation.

පැදකුණුකරණවා, *Pędakuṇu-karaṇawá*, *v.* to circumambulate any one with the right side towards the person, being a mark of great respect.

පැදීම, *Pędíma*, *s.* rowing, swinging; verbal noun of පදිනවා *padinawá*.

පැදුම්, *Pędum*, *s.* east, [Colloq. නැගෙණහිර *negeṇa-ira*]; mountain behind which the sun is supposed to rise; morning, sunrise; cloud; rain.

පැදුම්දිසාව, *Pędum-disáwa*, *s.* (පැදුම් east, දිසා *disá* side) east quarter, [Colloq. නැගෙණහිර *negeṇa-ira*].

පැදුම්සක්වළ, *Pędum-sakwaḷa*, *s.* (පැදුම් and සක්වළ sakwaḷa) eastern Sakwaḷa.

පැදුම, *Pęduma*, *s.* rowing, swinging.

පැදුර, *Pędura*, *s.* mat: pl. පැදුරු *pęduru*.

පැදුරුඅන, *Pęduru-ána*, *s.* loft containing mats.

පැන්, *Pęn*, *s.* water, drink, drinking: see also පැණ *pęṇa*.

පැන්තලිය, *Pęn-taliya*, *s.* water-pot set on the road side.

පැන් තිබාස, *Pęn-tibása*, *s.* (පැන් water, තිබාස substituted for පිපාසා *pipásá* thirst) thirst.

පැන්තුරු, *Pęnturu*, *s.* young or unripe areca-nut.

පැන්තොට, *Pęn-toṭa*, *s.* (පැන් and තොට ferry) ford over a river, ferry.

පැන්නා, *Pęnná*, *s.* small fish, sort of sheat fish: pl. පැන්නෝ *pennó*; also pret. of පණිනවා *paṇinawá*.

පැන්නුවා, *Pęnnuwá*, *pret.* of verb පන්නනවා *pannanawá*.

පැන්පම, *Pęnpama*, *s.* thirst.

පැන්පල, *Pęnpala*, *s.* (පැන් and පල place) place of ablution for priests.

පැන් පවස, *Pęn-pawasa*, } *s.* (පැන් and පවස or
පැන් පිපාස, *Pęn-pipása*, } පිපාස thirst) thirst.

පැන් පොද, *Pęn-poda*, } *s.* (පැන් water, පොද
පැන් බිඳුව, *Pęn-binduwa*, } or බිඳුව drop) drop of water.

පැන්මල්, *Pęn-mal*, } *s.* cup or drinking vessel,
පැන්මල, *Pęn-mala*, } [Colloq. කෝප්පේ *kóppé*].

පැන්මෝරු, *Pęn-móru*, *s.* watery part of milk, whey.

පැන්සය, *Pęnsaya*, *s.* penny. (English.)

පැන්සලය, *Pęnsalaya*, *s.* pencil, (English).

පැනලා, *Pęnalá*, *s.* black monkey, [Colloq. වඳුරා *waṉdurá*]; also part. of පනිනවා *paninawá*, to leap or jump.

පැණි, *Pęṇi*, *s.* treacle, spume of coconut toddy; juice of ripe fruit; juice, sweetness, syrup: *a.* sweet.

පැණි කුරුඳු, *Pęni-kurundu*, *s.* (පැණි sweet, කුරුඳු cinnamon) sweet or cultivated cinnamon.

පැණි කොමඩු, *Pęni-komaḍu*, *s.* (පැණි sweetness or juicy, කොමඩු melon) species of melon, *cucumis citrullus:* see යක් කොමඩු *yak-komaḍu.*

පැණි කෝන්, *Pęni-kón*, *s.* variety of the Ceylon oak, *schleichera trijuga.*

පැණිත්ත, *Pęnitta*, *s.* (පැන් *pęn* sweet, ඉත්ත *itta* particle) drop of water.

පැණි තෝර, *Pęni-tóra*, *s.* (පැණි and තෝර cassia) sort of cassia or senna, *cassia tora, (Leguminosæ).*

පැණිදොඩන්, *Pęnidoḍan*, *s.* (පැණි sweet, දොඩන් orange) common orange, *citrus aurantium.*

පැණින්, *Pęnin*, *s.* joy, gladness, merriment.

පැණි පොල්, *Pęni-pol*, *s.* (පැණි and පොල් coconut) sweet coconut; sort of marmalade made of coconut treacle and scraped coconut.

පැණිරස, *Pęnirasa*, *s.* (පැණි and රස taste, flavour) sweetness, saccharine flavour.

පැණිවරකා, *Pęni-waraká*, *s.* sweet hard ripe jack.

පැනීම, *Pęníma*, *s.* jumping, leaping: verbal noun of පනිනවා *paninawá.*

පැපිළිය, *Pępiḷiya*, *s.* plant, peculiar to Ceylon, *aperosa latifolia, (Euphorbiaceæ)*, also called මාපත් කැබෙල්ල *mápat-kębella* and කම්පොත්තා *kampottá;* another plant, *mollugo Cerriana,* [Colloq. පත්පාඩගං *patpáḍagan̤*].

පැපොල්, *Pępol*, *s.* papaw tree, *carica papaya. (Passifloreaceæ)*; name of a cutaneous disorder. chicken pox.

පැමිණ, *Pęmiṇa*, *part.* of පැමිණෙනවා *pęmiṇenawá.*

පැමිණි, *Pęmiṇi*, *part.* arrived, approached; happened, come to pass, fulfilled, accomplished. effected, finished, done, concluded.

පැමිණිතැන, *Pęmiṇitęna*, *s.* (පැමිණි arrived or received, තැන office) lord, master, chief, headman, very respectful term used in addressing superiors, corresponding with 'your honour.'

පැමිණිල්ල, *Pęmiṇilla*, *s.* complaint, claim, law suit: pl. පැමිණිලි *pęmiṇili.*

පැමිණිලිකරණවා, *Pęmiṇilikaraṇawá*, *v.* (පැමිණිලි complaints, කරණවා make) to complain to a magistrate, to prosecute.

පැමිණිලිකාරයා, *Pęmiṇilikárayá*, *s.* prosecutor, plaintiff.

පැමිණීම, *Pęmiṇíma*, *s.* coming, approach; happening, coming to pass.

පැමිණෙනවා, *Pęmiṇenawá*, *v.* to come, to arrive, to approach, to happen, to come to pass: pret. පැමිණුනා *pęmiṇuná.*

පැය, *Pęya*, *s.* an hour; Sin̤halese measure of time consisting of twenty-four minutes.

පැයකටුව, *Pęya-kaṭuwa*, *s.* hour-hand.

පැරකුන්, *Pęrakun*, } *s.* power, strength, might,
පැරකුම්, *Pęrakum*, } heroism; dignity, majesty; (poetical term); Elu form of පරාක්‍රම *parákrama.*

පැරණි, *Pęraṇi*, *a.* old, ancient, former, antique, decayed.

පැරද, *Pęrada*, *part.* of පරදිනවා *paradinawá*, being defeated, lost (as a battle). conquered, overcome, subdued; Elu form of පරාජය *parájaya.*

පැරදීම, *Pęradíma*, *s.* loss in battle etc. verbal noun of පරදිනවා *paradinawá.*

පැරදෙනවා, *Pęradenawá*, *v.* to lose, to be overcome or subdued, to sustain a defeat: pret. පැරදුනා *peraduná.*

පැරප්, *Pęrap*, *s.* basket for catching fish in brooks and shallow water.

පැරුම්, *Pęrum*, *s.* wish, hope, expectation: see පාරමිතාව *páramitáwa.*

පැරුද්දුවා, *Pęręddúwá*, *pret.* of පරද්දනවා *paraddanawá.*

පැල්දොර, *Pęldora*, *s.* wages in paddy for the man who takes care of the harvest; door of hut.

පැලීම, *Pęlma*, *s.* bursting, cleft; verbal noun of පැළෙනවා *pęlenawá.*

පැල්ලගිනවා, *Pęl-laginawá*, *v.* (පැල් hut, ලගිනවා to sleep) to watch the rice fields.

පැල්ලම, *Pęllama*, *s.* mark, spot, flaw, blot, stain: pl. පැල්ලම් *pęllam.*

පැල්වති, *Pęlwati*, *s.* permanence, lasting; uncleanness, filthiness, abomination.

පැල්වාඩිය, *Pęlwáḍiya*, *s.* small hut or shed, tent, temporary residence; name of village.

පැල, *Pęla*, *s.* plant, shrub; small hut, kind of raised platform used when watching the rice fields, hut, shed, hovel; the west: pl. පැල් *pęl.*

පැලකරණවා, *Pęlakaraṇawá*, *v.* to plant, to cultivate trees; to cause to germinate.

පැලකිඹුලා, *Pęla-kimbulá*, *s.* marsh crocodile, *crocodilus palastris,* (order *Sauria*): also called හැලකිඹුලා *hęla-kimbulá.*

පැලඟැටියා, *Pęlangęṭiyá*, see පලඟැටියා *palangęṭiyá.*

පැලටකහඬුව, *Pęlaṭakahan̤ḍuwa*, *s.* name of Íṣwara or Ṣiva.

පැලදිගු, *Pęla-digu*, *s.* (පැල west, දිග *diga* quarter) west quarter, [Colloq. බස්නාඉර *basná-ira*].

පැලදිගුහිමි, *Pęladigu-himi*, *s.* (පැලදිගු and හිමි lord) name of Varuṇa regent of the west.

පැලඳගන්නවා, *Pęlandagannawá*, *v.* to dress one's self, to put on ornaments.

පැලඳගැන්ම, *Pęlandagęnma*, *s.* ornamenting, decorating one's own person.

පැලඳීම, *Pęlandíma*, *s.* ornamenting, decorating: verbal noun of පලඳිනවා *palandinawá*.

පැලඳුම්, *Pęlandum*, *s.* ornaments; dresses.

පැලපත, *Pęlapata*, *s.* young plant, seedling.

පැලපොල්, *Pęlapol*, *s.* sprouting coconut.

පැලඹීම, *Pęlambíma*, verbal noun of the following.

පැලඹෙනවා, *Pęlambenawá*, *v.* to behave proudly, to be haughty, to act in an overbearing manner, to appear gay: pret. පැලඹුනා *pęlambuná*.

පැලමදය, *Pęlamadaya*, *s.* (පැල plant, මද *mada* pith) round ball or pulp inside the coconut which forms the seed from which the young plant grows.

පැලය, *Pęlaya*, *s.* plant, shrub, plant in general.

පැලවාඩිය, *Pęlawáḍiya*, see පැල්වාඩිය *pęlwáḍiya*.

පැලහා, *Pęlahá*, *part.* of පලහනවා *palahanawá*.

පැලහීම, *Pęlahíma*, verbal noun of පලහනවා *palahanawá*, to burn.

පැලහුනු, *Pęlahunu*, *p.* burnt.

පැලැල්ල, *Pęlęlla*, *s.* blinds of open wicker work, door, or tat serving that purpose: pl. පැලලි *pęlali*.

පැලැටිය, *Pęlęṭiya*, *s.* small plant: pl. පැලැටි *pęlęṭi*.

පැවතෙනවා, *Pęwatenawá*, *v.* to last, to endure, to remain, to continue: pret. පැවතුනා *pęwatuná*.

පැවරීම, *Pęwaríma*, *s.* distribution of service, shares, alms; invitation; verbal noun of පවරණවා *pawaraṇawá*, which see.

පැවසීම, *Pęwasíma*, *s.* saying; verbal noun of පවසනවා *pawasanawá*, which see.

පැවසු, *Pęwasu*, *s.* information: *p.* said, spoken; pret. of පවසනවා *pawasanawá*.

පැවිජි, *Pęviji*, } Elu form of ප්‍රව්‍රජ්‍යාව *pravrajyáwa*, which see.
පැවිදි, *Pęvidi*, }

පැවැත්ත, *Pęwętta*, *s.* custom, habit, practice.

පැවැත්ම, *Pęwętma*, *s.* being, remaining, continuing, permanency, existence, mode of life.

පැවැත්වීම, *Pęwętvíma*, *s.* observance, as of rites etc; causing to continue or exist.

පැවැදි, *Pęwędi*, another form of පැවිජි *pęviji*.

පැස්බරා, *Pęsbará*, *s.* unfledged bird.

පැස, *Pęsa*, *s.* basket, [Colloq. පෙට්ටිය *peṭṭiya*]; small instrument made of cane for expressing the juice of the sugar cane: pl. පැස් *pęs*.

පැසවනවා, *Pęsawanawá*, *v.* to cook, to ripen, to mature artificially, causal form of පැසෙනවා *pęsenawá*: pret. පැසෙව්වා *pęsewwá*.

පැසවෙනවා, *Pęsawenawá*, *v.* to ripen, to suppurate, to come to a head.

පැසසුම්, *Pęsasum*, *s.* praise, [Colloquial: ප්‍රශංසාව *praṣansáwa*].

පැසිගිනියා, *Pęsiginiyá*, *s.* avaricious or greedy man, miser.

පැසීම, *Pęsíma*, verbal noun of පැසෙනවා *pęsenawá*.

පැසුන්, *Pęsun*, *s.* any thing future, something yet to come or happen; nearly ripe, almost matured.

පැසුනු, *Pęsunu*, see පැසෙනවා *pęsenawá*.

පැසුළු, *Pęsuḷu*, *ad.* behind, in the rear, after, [Colloq. පසු *pasu*].

පැසෙනවා, *Pęsenawá*, *v.* to ripen, to mature, as fruit; to be cooked or cooking; to suppurate; to decay; to digest: pret. පැසුනා *pęsuná*.

පැහි, *Pęhi*, *s.* curry of pungent spices.

පැහිච්ච, *Pęhichcha*, *a.* ripe, mature, fit for plucking (applied to fruits), cooked.

පැහැ, *Pęhę*, *s.* colour; rattan basket used for putting in the fishing bait, or for squeezing oil: see also පැස *pęsa*.

පැහැද, *Pęhęda*, see පැහැදෙනවා *pęhędenawá*.

පැහැදිලි, *Pęhędili*, *a.* limpid, transparent; perspicuous, plain, easy.

පැහැදීම, *Pęhędíma*, } *s.* joy, gladness, rejoicing; transparency.
පැහැදුම, *Pęhęduma*, }

පැහැදෙනවා, *Pęhędenawá*, *v.* to be cleared, to confide in, to trust in, to be convinced: pret. පැහැදුනා *pęhęduná*.

පැහැන්, *Pęhęn*, *s.* ray, sunbeam, sunshine.

පැහැපත්, *Pęhępat*, *a.* shining, bright.

පැහැය, *Pęhęya*, *s.* colour, colour in general.

පැහැර, *Pęhęra*, *s.* forbearance, endurance; discontinuance, leaving off, desisting; plunder, pillage.

පැහැරඅරිණවා, *Pęhęra-ariṇawá*, *v.* to forego, evade, neglect.

පැහැරගන්නවා, *Pęhęragannawá*, *v.* to plunder, to pillage, to take from.

පැහැරපියනවා, *Pęhęrapiyanawá*, *v.* to cast away.

පැහැරයනවා, *Pęhęra-yanawá*, *v.* to forbear, to discontinue; to flee from, to forsake.

පැහැරයාම, *Pęhera-yáma*, *s.* forsaking, flight; flinching as from a blow, forbearance.
පැහැරුම, *Pęhęruma*, *s.* evacuation by stool.
පැහැල, *Pęhęla*, see පහළ *pahaḷa*.
පැහැසීම, *Pęhesím*, *s.* dressing.
පැළලුප් නුවර, *Pęḷalup-nuwara*, *s.* (පැළලුප් pęḷalup, නුවර city) name of a city on the continent of India, supposed to be the ancient Palibothra and the modern Patna.
පැළවීම, *Pęḷavíma*, verbal noun of පැළවෙනවා *pęḷawenawá*.
පැළවෙනවා, *Pęḷawenawá*, *v.* to sprout, to shoot out, to grow, to spring up, as plants.
පැළි, *Pęḷi*, *a.* cleft, split, rent.
පැළිවළ, *Pęḷiwaḷa*, *s.* (පැළි cleft, වළ hole) crack as in dried mud or clay, furrow, rut.
පැළීම, *Pęḷíma*, *s.* splitting, cleaving; verbal noun of පැළෙනවා *pęḷenawá*.
පැළෙනවා, *Pęḷenawá*, *v.* to burst, to crack, to split of itself: pret. පැළුනා *pęḷuná*.
පැළෙනු, *Pęḷenu*, *s.* dividing, cleaving, splitting.
පෑ, *Pé*, *s.* colour; also, plur. of පැය *peya*, hour.
පෑගෙණවා, *Pégeṇawá*, *v.* to be trampled on: pret. පෑගුණා *péguṇá*.
පෑතැටිය, *Pé-tęṭiya*, *s.* clepsydra, water-clock, a contrivance to measure time by the flow of water.
පෑදෙනවා, *Pédenawá*, *v.* to become clear, as water or any other liquid substance: pret. පෑදුනා *péduná*.
පෑනමස් පිහිය, *Pénamas-pihiya*, *s.* pocket knife (from Dutch pennemes).
පෑන, *Péna*, } *s.* pen. (English.)
පෑනේ, *Péné*, }
පෑමැටි, *Pémęṭi*, *s.* (පෑ colour, මැටි clay) the last and coloured coating of a wall.
පෑය, *Péya*, *s.* colour; also native time-piece.
පෑරෙණවා, *Péreṇawá*, *v.* to be hurt or touched, as a sore or boil: pret. පෑරුණා *péruṇá*.
පෑල, *Péla*, *s.* measure equal to ten kuruṇis: see කුරුණිය *kuruṇiya;* the west.
පෑලදිග, *Péla-diga*, } *s.* (පෑල west, දිග or දෙස
පෑලදෙස, *Péla-desa*, } quarter) west quarter.
පෑලදොර, *Péla-dora*, *s.* door opening to the west; back-door.
පෑලවිය, *Pélaviya*, *s.* first day of a lunar fortnight, first day after the new or full moon.
ප්‍ර, *Pra*, *ind.* particle and prefix, implying excess, much, very, exceeding; excellence; away; forth, forward.

ප්‍රක්වණ, *Prakwaṇa*, } *s.* sound of the víṇá, or In-
ප්‍රක්වාණ, *Prakwáṇa*, } dian lute.
ප්‍රක්වථිත, *Prakwathita*, *s.* powerfully purgative decoction prepared from the leaves or roots of plants.
ප්‍රක්ෂර, *Prakshara*, *s.* iron armour for the defence of a horse or elephant.
ප්‍රක්ෂාලන, *Prakshálana*, *s.* cleansing, cleaning, washing.
ප්‍රක්ෂිප්ත, *Prakshipta*, *a.* (ප්‍ර before, ක්ෂිප *kshipa* to throw) thrown, cast, hurled; determined.
ප්‍රක්ෂේප, *Prakshépa*, *s.* (ප්‍ර before, ක්ෂි *kshi* to throw) throwing, casting.
ප්‍රක්ෂේපණ, *Prakshépaṇa*, see the foregoing.
ප්‍රකට *Prakaṭa*, *a.* displayed, unfolded, manifest, apparent, published.
ප්‍රකම්ප, *Prakampa*, *s.* shaking.
ප්‍රකම්පන, *Prakampana*, *s.* violent motion, great trembling: *a.* trembling violently.
ප්‍රකර්ෂ, *Prakarsha*, *s.* excellence, eminence; speciality, intensity (in grammar), effect of the prefix ප්‍ර *pra* upon verbal roots.
ප්‍රකර, *Prakara*, *s.* heap, quantity; bundle of flowers, nosegay; aid, assistance; friendship; usage, custom, continuance of a similar practice; aloe wood.
ප්‍රකරණය, *Prakaraṇaya*, *s.* introduction, prologue, prelude; poetical fiction or poem in which the story and principal persons are wholly imaginary; chapter, section, place for pause or stopping; book.
ප්‍රකරි, *Prakari*, *s.* theatrical dress or disguise, as wearing a woman's garb etc; open space of ground; the meeting of four roads, or the proper site of any magical operations.
ප්‍රකල්පනා, *Prakalpaná*, *s.* (ප්‍ර intense, කල්පනා thought) decoration; study, intense thought.
ප්‍රකල්පිත, *Prakalpita*, *a.* made, done.
ප්‍රකාණ්ඩ, *Prakáṇḍa*, *s.* stem of a tree; branch, shoot; excellence; happiness: *a.* best, excellent happy.
ප්‍රකාමං *Prakámaṇ*, *ad.* (ප්‍ර intense, කාම *káma* wish) voluntarily, willingly.
ප්‍රකාර, *Prakára*, } *s.* mode, manner; sort, kind,
ප්‍රකාරය, *Prakáraya*, } species; similitude; difference.
ප්‍රකාශ, *Prakáṡa*, *s.* (ප්‍ර eminent, කාශ to shine) publicity of an event, manifestation of a truth; white or bell metal; declaration: *a.* like,

resembling; famous, famed, celebrated; open, public, manifest; expanded, diffused; published, manifested.

ප්‍රකාශක, *Prakáṣaka*, s. (ප්‍රකාශ manifest, ක pers. aff.) expounder, publisher, illustrator.

ප්‍රකාශකරණවා, *Prakáṣakaraṇawá*, v. to publish, to proclaim, to announce.

ප්‍රකාශිත, *Prakáṣita*, a. (ප්‍රකාශ *prakáṣa* and ඉත *ita* affix) visible, apparent, manifest, evident.

ප්‍රකාස, *Prakása*, incorrectly for ප්‍රකාශ *prakáṣa*, which see.

ප්‍රකීර්ණ, *Prakírṇa*, s. the Indian chowri, or the tail of the yak or *bos grunniens* used as a whisk or fan: a. crowded, heaped together, miscellaneous.

ප්‍රකීර්ණක, *Prakírṇaka*, s. chapter, section of a book; extent, length, especially of a stanza; decree, decision at law not provided for by the standing codes; miscellany: a. spread abroad, expanded promulgated, published: see the last.

ප්‍රකීර්‍ය, *Prakírya*, s. plant, *galedupa arborea*, [Coll: සිරිල *sirila*]; according to another authority, *cæsalpinia bonduc*, [Colloq. කුඹුරුවැල් *kumburu-wel*]: a. spread abroad, diffused, promulgated, expanded, extended.

ප්‍රකුපිත, *Prakupita*, a. (ප්‍ර implying intensity, කුප *kupa* to be angry) angry, wrathful; enraged, incensed.

ප්‍රකෝටි, *Prakóṭi*, s. (ප්‍ර and කෝටි kóṭi) number, kóṭi is ten millions, prakóṭi is ten million kóṭis, or a number equal to 100,000,000,000,000.

ප්‍රකෝප, *Prakópa*, ප්‍රකෝපන, *Prakópana*, } s. irritation, provocation, enraging.

ප්‍රකෝෂ්ඨ, *Prakóshṭha*, s. fore-arm; part of the frame of a door or window.

ප්‍රකෝෂ්ඨක, *Prakóshṭhaka*, s. cubit; part of a door or window frame: a. belonging to the arm, or measured by the fore-arm.

ප්‍රක්‍රම, *Prakrama*, s. (ප්‍ර before or first, ක්‍රම to go) beginning, commencement, introduction; proceeding, going.

ප්‍රකෘත, *Prakṛita*, a. (ප්‍ර before, කෘත done) made, done, completed, accomplished.

ප්‍රකෘති, *Prakṛiti*, s. nature, natural state of any thing; male and female organs of generation; uninflected word; radical form of a word, before the affixes forming cases etc. are subjoined; woman, woman-kind; according to the Hindus, divine power, as liable to be exerted by the operation of the divine will and personified in the peculiar goddess of each divinity, the term is hence an appellation of Lakshmí, Durgá etc; cause, origin; mother; animal; radical form or predicament of being, of which eight sorts are reckoned, viz. illusion, magnitude, pride of independent existence or egotism, and the five elements *i. e.* ákása, fire, air, earth, water.

ප්‍රකෘතිවත්, *Prakṛitiwat*, a. (ප්‍රකෘති nature, වත් aff.) natural; restored, renewed.

ප්‍රකෘෂ්ට, *Prakṛishṭa*, a. (ප්‍ර implying intensity, කෘෂ *kṛisha* to attract) eminent, chief, principal, remote.

ප්‍රඛ්‍යාත, *Prakhyáta*, a. celebrated, famed, famous; pleased, happy; forestalled.

ප්‍රඛ්‍යාති, *Prakhyáti*, s. pubilicity, notoriety; praise; happiness.

ප්‍රඛර, *Prakhara*, s. iron armour for the defence of a horse or elephant; dog; mule: a. very hot, or acrid.

ප්‍රගණ්ඩ, *Pragaṇḍa*, s. (ප්‍ර principal, much, ගණ්ඩ part) upper arm from the elbow to the shoulder.

ප්‍රගල්භ, *Pragalbha*, s. (ප්‍ර intense, much, ගල්භ to be proud) man, scholar, pandit: a. bold, confident; audacious, shameless, impudent; robust, strong, able; illustrious, eminent.

ප්‍රගාඪ, *Pragáḍa*, a. much, hard: *adv.* exceedingly, tightly, firmly.

ප්‍රගුණ, *Praguṇa*, a. (ප්‍ර excellent, ගුණ quality) honest, upright; straight; accustomed, habituated, trained or used to.

ප්‍රග්‍රහ, *Pragraha*, ප්‍රග්‍රහණ, *Pragrahaṇa*, ප්‍රග්‍රාහ, *Pragráha*, } s. string suspending a balance; rein, rope or halter for horses or cattle; prisoner, captive, either man or beast in confinement; restriction, restraint, captivity; ray of light; tree, *cassia fistula*, [Colloq. ඇහැළ *ẹhẹla*].

ප්‍රග්‍රීව, *Pragríwa*, s. window, lattice, balcony; summer house; pleasure house, building on the top of a palace; painted turret; wooden balustrade or fence on the edge of a building; stable; top of a tree.

ප්‍රගෘහිත, *Pragṛihíta*, a. accepted.

ප්‍රඝණ, *Praghaṇa*, ප්‍රඝාණ, *Pragháṇa*, } s. terrace before a house; green gram, *phaseolus mungo*, [Colloq. මුංඇට *muṇẹṭa*].

ප්‍රච්ඡන්න, *Prachchhanna*, s. (ප්‍ර completely, ඡන්න covered) back-door, private door within a house, any private door; lattice, loophole: a. private, covered, concealed.

ප්‍රච්ඡාදන, *Prchchhádana*, s. (ප්‍ර and ඡද *chchhada* to cover) upper or outer garment, cloak, mantle; covering, concealing.

ප්‍රච්ඡින්න, *Prachchhinna*, a. broken, [Colloq. කැඩුන *keḍuna*].

ප්‍රච්‍යුත, *Prachyuta*, a. fallen from, deviated from, loosened, liberated, freed.

ප්‍රචණ්ඩ, *Prachanḍa*, s. (ප්‍ර very, චණ්ඩ hot etc.) sort of nerium with white flowers: *a.* intolerable, insupportable, excessively hot or burning; bold, confident, wrathful, passionate, fierce.

ප්‍රචය, *Prachaya*, s. heap, quantity, number.

ප්‍රචර, *Prachara*, s. (ප්‍ර much, චර to walk) road, path.

ප්‍රචල, *Prachala*, } s. moving much or widely
ප්‍රචලන, *Prachalana*, } current, customary.

ප්‍රචලායිත, *Prachaláyita*, s. (ප්‍ර much, චල to shake) shaking, rolling about, tossing; turning, going round, whirling, nodding, dropping from sleepiness; tumbling (as in sleep).

ප්‍රචාල, *Prachála*, s. stick or body of the Víṇá or Indian lute.

ප්‍රචුර, *Prachura*, a. much, many, [Colloq. බොහෝ *bohó*].

ප්‍රචේතස්, *Prachétas*, s. (ප්‍ර first, best, චේතස් heart) name of Varuṇa, the regent of water: *a.* happy, pleased, delighted.

ප්‍රචෝදිනී, *Prachódiní*, s. plant, kind of nightshade, *solanum jacquini*, [Colloq. කටුවැල්බටු *kaṭuwel-baṭu*].

ප්‍රජන, *Prajana*, s. first impregnation of cows or any other animal, impregnation in general.

ප්‍රජනන, *Prajanana*, s. birth, production.

ප්‍රජව, *Prajawa*, s. (ප්‍ර much, ජව quickness) festival, holiday; great speed, velocity.

ප්‍රජවී, *Prajaví*, s. (ප්‍ර and ජව *jawa* quickness, ඊ *i* aff.) runner, courier, express; racer, any one possessing great speed in running.

ප්‍රජා, *Prajá*, s. progeny, offspring; people, subjects.

ප්‍රජාගර, *Prajágara*, s. (ප්‍ර before, ජාගර vigilance) waking, watching.

ප්‍රජාතා, *Prajátá*, s. (ප්‍ර and ජාත *játa* born) woman who has borne children.

ප්‍රජාප, *Prajápa*, s. (ප්‍රජා people, ප who preserves) king, sovereign, [Colloq. රජ *raja*].

ප්‍රජාපති, *Prajápati*, s. (ප්‍රජා people, or the world, පති master) king, sovereign; name of Brahma; according to the Hindus the epithet common to the ten divine personages, who were first created by the Brahmá; they are also termed Brahmádaikas, and their names are Marichi, Atri, Angiras, Pulastya, Pulaha. Kratu, Daksha, Vasishṭha, Bhṛigu, and Nárada; some authorities make the Prajápatis only seven in number, and others reduce them to three, or Daksha, Nárada and Bhrigu; father; son in law, daughter's husband; sun; fire; name of Viṣwakarma; the fifth year of the Indian cycle of sixty.

ප්‍රජානායක, *Prajánáyaka*, s. (ප්‍රජා people, නායක chief) king, sovereign, ruler, [Colloquial: රජ *raja*].

ප්‍රජාහිත, *Prajáhita*, s. (ප්‍රජා and හිත friendly, useful) water, [Colloq. වතුර *watura*]: *a.* favourable or good for children or subjects, kind to them, useful to them.

ප්‍රජේශ්වර, *Prajéṣwara*, s. (ප්‍රජා *prajá* and ඊශ්වර *íṣwara* lord) king.

ප්‍රජ්වලිත, *Prajwalita*, a. (ප්‍ර before, or much, ජ්වලිත shining) glittering, resplendent, intensely illuminated.

ප්‍රඥප්ත, *Prajñapta*, a. (ප්‍ර before, ඥප *jñapa* make known) appointed, fixed, determined, settled, as a low or statute.

ප්‍රඥප්තිය, *Prajñaptiya*, s. appointment, engagement, to meet etc., at a fixed time; sermons, discourses and institutes of Buddha; institutes.

ප්‍රඥා, *Prajñá*, s. (ප්‍ර before or much, ඥා to know) wisdom, knowledge, understanding.

ප්‍රඥා චක්ෂුසය, *Prajñá-chaksusaya*, s. (ප්‍රඥා intelligence, චක්ෂුස් *chakshus* eye) name of a wise and celebrated king, also called Dhṛitaráshṭra, who was the uncle of the Páṇḍu princes: also see ප්‍රඥානේත්‍ර *prajñá-nétra*.

ප්‍රඥාන, *Prajñána*, s. (ප්‍ර before or much, ඥාන knowledge) wisdom, skill, cleverness, learning, knowledge: *a.* wise, learned.

ප්‍රඥා නේත්‍ර, *Prajñá-nétra*, s. (ප්‍රඥා knowledge, නේත්‍ර eye) understanding, intellect; quick apprehension, discernment, or discrimination of mind.

ප්‍රඥා පාරමිතාව, *Prajñá-páramitáwa*, see පාරමිතාව *páramitáwa*.

ප්‍රඥාව, *Prajñáwa*, s. wisdom, skill, cleverness, learning, knowledge.

ප්‍රඥාවන්ත, *Prajñáwanta*, a. (ප්‍රඥා and වන්ත poss. aff.) wise, learned, skilful, clever, knowing.

ප්‍රඥාහීන, *Prajñá-hína*, a. (ප්‍රඥා wisdom, හීන void of) unwise, silly, ignorant.

ප්‍රඥින්, *Prajñin*, s. (ප්‍රඥා, *prajñá* and ඉන් *ín* aff.) sage, scholar, pandit, learned man, [Colloq. පණ්ඩිතයා *paṇḍitayá*].

ප්‍රඥු, *Prajñu*, a. (ප්‍ර separate, ජානු *jánu* knee, ඥු *ñu* substituted) bandy-legged, having the knees far apart.

ප්‍රඩීන, *Praḍína*, s. flying rapidly or flying in every direction.

ප්‍රණත, *Praṇata*, a. (ප්‍ර before, ණම *nama* to bend) bending, bowed, stooping, inclined, [Colloq. නැමුණු *nęmuṇu*].

ප්‍රණති, *Praṇati*, s. salutation, reverence.

ප්‍රණමිත, *Praṇamita*, a. bending, bowing.

ප්‍රණය, *Praṇaya*, s. affection, trust, reverence; asking, begging.

ප්‍රණයන, *Praṇayana*, s. leading, conducting; dispensing, distributing; sentencing, awarding.

ප්‍රණව, *Praṇawa*, s. small kind of drum or tabor.

ප්‍රණාද, *Praṇáda*, s. (ප්‍ර before, නද *nada* to sound) loud sound.

ප්‍රණාම, *Praṇáma*, s. (ප්‍ර and ණම *ṇama* to bend) respectful salutation, bending, worshipping, [Colloq. වැඳීම *węndíma*].

ප්‍රණිධාන, *Praṇidhána*, s. (ප්‍ර and නි before, ධා *dhá* to have) great effort, energy.

ප්‍රණිධි, *Praṇidhi*, s. (ප්‍ර and නි before, ධා *dhá* to have) spy, secret emissary; asking, solicitation.

ප්‍රණිපාත, *Praṇipáta*, see ප්‍රණාම *praṇáma*.

ප්‍රණිහිත, *Praṇihita*, a. entrusted, placed, obtained, careful, admitted.

ප්‍රණීත, *Praṇíta*, s. fire, consecrated by prayers or mystical formulæ: *a.* dressed, cooked; ripened; made, done, constructed, composed; thrown, cast, sent; entertained; proper, fit; savoury, highly flavoured; delicious, excellent.

ප්‍රණීතාමෘත, *Praṇítámṛita*, s. (ප්‍රණීත *praṇíta* and අමෘත *amṛita* ambrosia) ambrosia, food of the gods: *a.* sweet, saccharine.

ප්‍රණුත, *Praṇuta*, a. praised, eulogized, celebrated, applauded, commended, [Colloquial: ප්‍රශංසාකළ *praṣaṇsákaḷa*].

ප්‍රත්න, *Pratna*, a. former, prior, preceding; old, ancient, [Colloq. පුරාණ *puráṇa*].

ප්‍රත්‍යක්, *Pratyak*, a. subsequent, behind, following in time or place, [Colloq. පස්සේ *passé*].

ප්‍රත්‍යක්පර්ණී, *Pratyakparṇṇí*, } s. (ප්‍රත්‍යක් uniform, පර්ණී leaf,
ප්‍රත්‍යක්පුෂ්පී, *Pratyak-pushpí*, } and පුෂ්පී flower) plant, *achyranthes aspera*, [Colloq. ගස් කරල්හැබ *gas-karalhęba*].

ප්‍රත්‍යක්ශ්‍රේණි, *Pratyakṣréṇi*, s. tree, species of *ficus*, [Colloq. මිනුග *mí-nuga*].

ප්‍රත්‍යක්‍ෂ, *Pratyaksha*, a. (ප්‍රති *prati* indicative prefix, අක්‍ෂ *aksha* organ of sense) perceptible, preceivable, present as cognizable by any of the organs of sense; experienced.

ප්‍රත්‍යක්‍ෂ දර්ශන, *Pratyaksha-darṣana*, s. (ප්‍රත්‍යක්‍ෂ and දර්ශන seeing) witness, eye witness, [Colloq. සාක්‍ෂිකාරයා *sákshikárayá*].

ප්‍රත්‍යක්‍ෂින්, *Pratyakshin*, a. (ප්‍රත්‍යක්‍ෂ *pratyaksha* and ඉන් *in* aff.) seeing, perceiving, conscious of what is present or perceptible.

ප්‍රත්‍යක්‍ෂීකරණ, *Pratyakshíkaraṇa*, s. making manifest or apparent.

ප්‍රත්‍යක්‍ෂීකෘත, *Pratyakshíkṛita*, a. made manifest or apparent.

ප්‍රත්‍යග්‍ර, *Pratyaggra*, s. (ප්‍රති *prati* before, අග්‍ර *agra* chief) new, fresh, recent, novel; best, excellent.

ප්‍රත්‍යඞ්ග, *Pratyaṅga*, s. (ප්‍රති *prati* belonging to, අඞ්ග *aṅga* body) organ of perception; any member of the body.

ප්‍රත්‍යදන, *Pratya-dana*, s. (ප්‍රති *prati* before, අද *ada* to eat) eating food, [Colloq. කෑම *kęma*].

ප්‍රත්‍යන්ත, *Pratyanta*, a. (ප්‍රති *prati* about, අන්ත end) barbarous, savage, uncivilized; bordering on a town, skirting, contiguous.

ප්‍රත්‍යන්ත දේශය, *Pratyanta-déṣaya*, s. (ප්‍රත්‍යන්ත barbarous, දේශ *déṣa* country) country inhabited by barbarians or savages; any country where the religion of Buddha is not professed.

ප්‍රත්‍යනීක, *Pratyaníka*, s. (ප්‍රති *prati* against, අනීක *aníka* army) an enemy, [Colloq. සතුරා *saturá*].

ප්‍රත්‍යය, *Pratyaya*, s. knowledge, apprehension; trust, faith, belief, confidence; oath, ordeal; cause, motive; usage, custom, practice; fame, celebrity; certainty, ascertainment; affix to roots and words forming derivatives and inflections; dependant, subject; source, productive cause, instrument, means of agency, helpmate or associate, applicable to either persons or things; householder who keeps a sacred fire; religious contemplation.

ප්‍රත්‍යයලාභ, *Pratyaya-lábha*, s. receiving food, clothing, and other necessaries for the maintenance of a priest.

ප්‍රත්‍යය සමුත්පන්න, *Pratyaya-samutpanna*, s. (ප්‍රත්‍යය cause, සං *saṇ* with, උත්පන්න *utpanna* born) cause, producing or originating cause, [Colloq. හේතුව *hétuwa*]: see ප්‍රතීත්‍යසමුත්පාද *pratítya-samutpáda*.

ප්‍රත්‍යවසාන, *Pratyawasána*, *s.* eating food.

ප්‍රත්‍යවසිත, *Pratyawasita*, *a.* eaten.

ප්‍රත්‍යවාට්‍යාලක, *Pratya-wáṭyálaka*, *s.* medicinal plant, species of *sida*, [Colloq. සුළුබෑවිල *suḷu bęvila*].

ප්‍රත්‍යවේක්ෂණ, *Pratya-wékshaṇa*, *s.* knowledge, understanding, ascertaining, information, [Colloq. දැනගැන්ම *dęnagęnma*].

ප්‍රත්‍යවේක්ෂා, *Pratya-wékshá*, *s.* thought, meditation, study, revolving a thing in the mind, [Colloq. කල්පනාව *kalpanáwa*].

ප්‍රත්‍යහන්, *Pratyahan*, *adv.* (ප්‍රති *prati* before or implying succession, අහන් *ahan* day) in the morning; day by day, every day, daily, [Colloq. දවස්පතා *dawaspatá*].

ප්‍රත්‍යාදේශ, *Pratyádéṣa*, *s.* (ප්‍රති *prati* before, දිශ *diṣa* to show) rejection, disallowance; sending away, dismissal; information, apprising.

ප්‍රත්‍යාසන්න, *Pratyásanna*, *a.* (ප්‍රති *prati* and ආසන්න near) near, proximate, contiguous, [Colloq. ළඟ *laṉga*].

ප්‍රත්‍යාහරණ, *Pratyáharaṇa*, *s.* (ප්‍රති *prati* and ආ *á* before, හර *hara* to take) restraining the organs of sense, taking back.

ප්‍රත්‍යාහාර, *Pratyáhára*, *s.* abstraction, insensibility, restraining the organs so as to be indifferent to agreeable or disagreeable excitement; abridgement, compendium; combination of two or more letters to form a group of letters.

ප්‍රත්‍යුට්ඨාන, *Pratyuṭṭhána*, another form of ප්‍රත්‍යුත්ථාන *pratyutthána*.

ප්‍රත්‍යුත්තර, *Pratyuttara*, *s.* (ප්‍රති *prati* again, උත්තර *uttara* answer) rejoinder, reply to an answer.

ප්‍රත්‍යුත්ථාන, *Pratyutthána*, *s.* (ප්‍රති *prati* before, උත්ථාන *utthána* rising) polite reception of a guest, rising to welcome him.

ප්‍රත්‍යුත්පන්න, *Pratyutpanna*, *a.* (ප්‍රති *prati* again, උත්පන්න *utpanna* born, produced) reproduced, regenerated; prompt, ready.

ප්‍රත්‍යුපකාර, *Pratyupakára*, *s.* (ප්‍රති *prati* again, උපකාර *upakáda* favour) repaying, rewarding, adding favour to favour.

ප්‍රත්‍යූෂ, *Pratyúsha*, *s.* sun, [Colloq. ඉර *ira*]; morning, [Colloq. උදය *udaya*]; one of the demigods called Vasus.

ප්‍රත්‍යූහ, *Prtyúha*, *s.* hindrance, obstacle, impediment, [Colloq. බාධාව *bádháwa*].

ප්‍රත්‍යේක, *Pratyéka*, *adv.* singly, one by one, one at time.

ප්‍රතන, *Pratana*, *a.* old, ancient, former, [Colloq. පුරාණ *puráṇa*]

ප්‍රතති, *Pratati*, *s.* (ප්‍ර before, තන *tana* to spread) spreading, expansion; creeping plant (in general).

ප්‍රතම, *Pratama*, corruptly for ප්‍රථම *prathama*, which see.

ප්‍රතර්කණ, *Pratarkaṇa*, *s.* (ප්‍ර before, තර්ක *tarka* to reason) reasoning, discussion, doubt.

ප්‍රතල, *Pratala*, *s.* (ප්‍ර exceeding, තල lowness) one of the seven principal divisions of the lower regions; the open hand with the fingers extended.

ප්‍රතාන, *Pratána*, *s.* (ප්‍ර before, තන *tana* to spread) spreading, expanding; low spreading creeping plant.

ප්‍රතානිනී, *Pratánini*, *s.* low spreading creeper.

ප්‍රතාප, *Pratápa*, *s.* (ප්‍ර much, තප *tapa* to burn) heat, warmth; majesty, dignity; the high spirit arising from the possession of rank and power.

ප්‍රතාපන, *Pratápana*, *s.* (ප්‍ර much, තප *tapa* to be hot, to burn) hell, that division of the infernal regions in which the punishments are inflicted by burning; burning, consuming.

ප්‍රතාපවාන්, *Pratápawán*, *s.* (ප්‍රතාප heat, වාන් poss. aff.) hot, warm; glorious, majestic, dignified.

ප්‍රති, *Prati*, *ind.* particle and prefix, implying substitution (in lieu, instead); severally, (each by each); direction, designation (to, towards, upon); belonging to (as a part, a portion); exchange, return (again, back again); a little etc.

ප්‍රතික්ෂිප්ත, *Pratikshipta*, *a.* (ප්‍රති against, ක්ෂිප්ත thrown, sent) dismissed, rejected, turned away; sent, dispatched; calumniated, falsely accused; opposed, repelled, resisted.

ප්‍රතික්ෂේප, *Pratikshépa*, *s.* rejecting, dismissing, turning away; sending, dispatching.

ප්‍රතිකර්ම, *Prati-karma*, *s.* dress, decoration, ornament, personal embellishment; retaliation, remedy.

ප්‍රතිකාය, *Pratikáya*, *s.* (ප්‍රති again, කාය body) effigy, image, picture; butt, mark, probably the effigy of a man for archers to practise at.

ප්‍රතිකාර, *Pratikára*, *s.* (ප්‍රති again, against, කාර doing) revenge, retaliation; healing, curing, practice of medicine.

ප්‍රතිකාශ, *Pratikáṣa*, } *a.* (ප්‍රති again, කාශ to shine)
ප්‍රතිකාස, *Pratikása*, } like, resembling, [Colloq. සමාන *samána*].

ප්‍රතිකූල, *Pratikúla*, *a.* (ප්‍රති for ප්‍රතිප *pratípa* averted, කූල bank or shore) contrary, adverse, cross-grained; reverse, inverted; displeasing, offensive; disagreeable, unpleasant.

ප්‍රතික්‍රම, *Pratikrama*, *s.* (ප්‍රති back, ක්‍රම to go) return, retreat.

ප්‍රති ක්‍රියාව, *Prati-kriyáwa*, *s.* (ප්‍රති again, against, ක්‍රියා act) revenge, retaliation; image, counterpart of any thing, reflection of a figure in a mirror; remedying, counteracting.

ප්‍රතිකෘත, *Pratikṛita*, *s.* (ප්‍රති again, කෘත done) effigy, image, figure, [Colloq. රූපය *rúpaya*].

ප්‍රතිකෘති, *Pratikṛiti*, *a.* reflected image, effigy; retaliation, revenge.

ප්‍රතිගත, *Pratigata*, *s.* flying backwards and forwards, wheeling in flight.

ප්‍රතිග්‍රහණ, *Pratigrahaṇa*, *s.* (ප්‍රති again ග්‍රහණ taking) taking, acceptance, assent, acceptance of a gift or donation; sun near the moon's node.

ප්‍රතිග්‍රාහ, *Pratigráha*, *s.* acceptance, taking, [Coll: ගැණිම *geṇima*]; spitting pot, [Colloq. පඩික්කම *paḍikkama*].

ප්‍රතිගෘහ්‍ය, *Pratigṛihya*, *a.* fit to be taken, proper to be accepted.

ප්‍රතිගෘහිත, *Pratigṛihíta*, *a.* taken, accepted.

ප්‍රතිඝ්න, *Pratighna*, *s.* (ප්‍රති again, ඝ්න what destroys) body, [Colloq. ශරීරය *ṣaríraya*].

ප්‍රතිඝ, *Pratigha*, *s.* (ප්‍රති again, severally, ඝ striking) anger, wrath, rage, fury; fighting, conflict, combat; fainting.

ප්‍රතිඝටන, *Pratighaṭana*, *s.* (ප්‍රති and ඝටන striking) bruising, crushing. fighting, striking.

ප්‍රතිඝාත, *Pratigháta*, *s.* (ප්‍රති before, හන *hana* to strike) return blow, warding off a blow; preventing.

ප්‍රතිඝාතන, *Pratighátana*, *s.* (ප්‍රති and හන *hana* to kill) killing, slaughter.

ප්‍රතිච්ඡන්ද, *Pratichchhanda*, *s.* reflected image, any image, picture, statue.

ප්‍රතිච්ඡන්න, *Pratichchhanna*, *s.* (ප්‍රති and ඡන්න covered) hid, concealed, covered, hidden, [Coll: වසනලද *wasanalada*].

ප්‍රතිඡායා, *Pratichháyá*, *s.* (ප්‍රති again, ඡායා shadow) image, statue, bas relief; picture; reflected image, shade or shadow.

ප්‍රතිජග්ගන, *Pratijaggana*, *s.* (corruptly for පටිජග්ගන *paṭijaggana* nourishing) nourishment, support, protection, [Colloq. ආරක්ෂාව *árakshá-wa*].

ප්‍රතිජඞ්ඝා, *Pratijaṅghá*, *s.* (ප්‍රති before, ජඞ්ඝා leg) fore part of the leg.

ප්‍රතිඥා, *Pratijñá*, *s.* (ප්‍රති mutually, ඥා to know) assent, promise, agreement, engagement; admission; acknowledgment; (in logic,) proposition, the assertion to be proved.

ප්‍රතිඥාත, *Pratijñáta*, *s.* (ප්‍රති mutually, ඥාත known) propounded: *a.* promised, agreed.

ප්‍රතිඥාන, *Pratijñána*, *s.* (ප්‍රති mutually, before, ඥාන knowledge) promise, agreement, engagement; perception, conception.

ප්‍රතිඥාපත්‍ර, *Pratijñá-patra*, *s.* (ප්‍රතිඥා promise, පත්‍ර writing) bond, written contract, [Colloq. ඔප්පුව *oppuwa*].

ප්‍රතිඥාව, *Pratijñáwa*, see ප්‍රතිඥා *pratijñá*.

ප්‍රතිඥෙය, *Pratijñéya*, *s.* reciter or pronouncer of a panegyric, proclaimer of rank and titles, herald, bard, panegyrist: *a.* to be promised or propounded.

ප්‍රතිත්‍ය, *Pratitya*, *s.* cause, origin, producing cause, motive.

ප්‍රතිත්‍ය සමුත්පාද, *Pratitya-samutpáda*, *s.* (ප්‍රතිත්‍ය cause, origin, සං *saṇ* with, උත්පාද birth) source of animation, origin of life, which gave birth to sentient beings; this enquiry engaged the profound meditations of Buddha on the first day of his attaining the Buddhaship. "I exist" said he, "others existed before me: there was a period when no living being existed." Hence he imagined that the whole animated world came into existence according to the following process; from ignorance proceeded the faculty of reflection, from the faculty of reflection proceeded knowledge, from knowledge proceeded the union of mind and matter, or body and spirit, from this proceeded the six senses, from the six senses proceeded the faculty of perception, from perception proceeded enjoyment, from enjoyment wish or ardent desire, from desire came the generative faculty, from the generative faculty proceeded all the various states of being from the gods to the minutest reptiles, from this proceed all the incidents of life and circumstances of nature, as decay, sorrow, sickness, death, transmigration etc.

ප්‍රතිදාන, *Pratidána*, *s.* (ප්‍රති again, දාන giving) giving back, returning, returning a pledge or deposit.

ප්‍රතිධ්වනි, *Pratidhwani*, } *s.* (ප්‍රති and ධ්වනි or
ප්‍රතිධ්වාන, *Pratidhwána*, } ධ්වාන, sound) echo, reiterated or repeated sound.

ප්‍රතිපක්‍ෂ, *Pratipaksha*, *s.* (ප්‍රති against, පක්‍ෂ part, party) enemy, opponent, defendant, respondent, [Colloq. විත්තිකාරයා *vittikárayá*]: *a.* envious, opposed, disagreeable.

ප්‍රතිපත්, *Pratipat*, see ප්‍රතිපද් *pratipad*.

ප්‍රතිපත්තිය, *Pratipattiya*, *s.* gaining, acquiring; action; worldliness; arrogance; knowledge; ascertainment; elevation, exaltation; acknowledgment; assent; religious obedience, observance of all the laws sacred ordinances and institutions of Buddha with a view to the acquirement of Nirváṇa.

ප්‍රතිපද්, *Pratipad*, *s.* first day of a lunar fortnight, first of the moon's increase or wane; understanding, intellect; rank, consequence: *ad.* step by step, repeatedly.

ප්‍රතිපන්න, *Pratipanna*, *a.* known, ascertained; appointed, fixed, determined; promised, engaged, assented to, accepted; subdued, overcome, conquered; see also ප්‍රතිපත්තිය *pratipattiya*.

ප්‍රතිපාදක, *Pratipádaka*, *s.* (ප්‍රති before, පද *pada* to go) nourisher; giver, donor; benefactor, cause which produces effects; explanatory.

ප්‍රතිපාදන, *Pratipádana*, *s.* gift, donation; nourishment, support; ascertaining, determining, rendering clear or intelligible; action, worldly conduct or interest.

ප්‍රතිපාදිත, *Pratipádita*, *a.* delivered, given, caused.

ප්‍රතිපාලක, *Pratipálaka*, *s.* protector, king.

ප්‍රතිපාලන, *Pratipálana*, *s.* nourishment, protection, support.

ප්‍රතිපුරුෂ, *Pratipurusha*, *s.* deputy, substitute.

ප්‍රතිපූජන, *Pratipújana*, *s.* exchange of civilities.

ප්‍රතිපෘච්ඡා, *Pratipṛichchhá*, *s.* (ප්‍රති repeatedly or severally, පෘච්ඡ *pṛichchha* to ask) enquiry, investigation, examining into a subject by questions; third part of vyákaraṇa or grammar.

ප්‍රතිඵල, *Pratiphala*, *s.* return, requital.

ප්‍රතිබද්ධ, *Pratibaddha*, *a.* dependent, belonging to: wishful, desirous, attached to by affection; stopped, impeded, obstructed; disappointed; set, inlaid; bound, connected with.

ප්‍රතිබන්ධ, *Pratibandha*, *s.* (ප්‍රති against, බන්ධ bound) obstacle, impediment, disappointment; connection.

ප්‍රතිබන්ධක, *Pratibandhaka*, *s.* (ප්‍රති before, බන්ධ bound, ක aff.) branch, shoot, [Colloq. රිකිල්ල *rikilla*].

ප්‍රතිබාහනය, *Pratibáhanaya*, *s.* (ප්‍රති completely, බහ *baha* for වහ *waha* to carry) dismissing, sending, removing away.

ප්‍රතිබිම්බ, *Pratibimba*, *s.* (ප්‍රති again, බිම්බ image) image, likeness, reflected image, shadow; idol, [Colloq. රූපය *rúpaya*].

ප්‍රතිභය, *Pratibhaya*, *s.* (ප්‍රති complete, භය fear) fear: *a.* fearful, formidable, frightful.

ප්‍රතිභා, *Pratibhá*, *s.* (ප්‍රති before, භා to shine) understanding, intellect; light, splendour; boldness, audacity; consequence.

ප්‍රතිභාග, *Pratibhága*, *a.* like, similar, resembling.

ප්‍රතිභාන, *Pratibhána*, *s.* understanding, boldness; wisdom, knowledge; brilliancy.

ප්‍රතිභූ, *Pratibhú*, *s.* surety, pledge, stake at play.

ප්‍රතිම, *Pratima*, *a.* like, resembling, similar.

ප්‍රතිමණ්ඩිත, *Pratimaṇḍita*, *a.* (ප්‍රති before, මණ්ඩිත adorned) ornamented, beautified, adorned, [Coll: අලංකාරවූ *alaṅkárawú*].

ප්‍රතිමා, *Pratimá*, *s.* image, picture, resemblance, likeness, shadow: see ප්‍රතිබිම්බ *pratibimba*.

ප්‍රතිමාන, *Pratimána*, *s.* likeness, resemblance, [Colloq. සමානකම *samánakama*].

ප්‍රතිමාලා, *Pratimálá*, *s.* exercise analogous to capping verses, reciting verse for verse, as a trial of memory or skill.

ප්‍රතිමුක්ත, *Pratimukta*, *a.* loosed or liberated repeatedly; thrown mutually or at one another.

ප්‍රතියත්න, *Pratiyatna*, *a.* (ප්‍රති intensitive, යත්න effort) active, vigorous, diligent, making effort or exertion.

ප්‍රතියෝග, *Pratiyóga*, *s.* (ප්‍රති against, යුජ් *yuja* to join) opposition, enmity, [Colloq. සතුරුකම *saturukama*].

ප්‍රතිරම්භ, *Pratirambha*, *s.* rage, violent or passionate abuse.

ප්‍රතිරාවය, *Pratiráwaya*, *s.* (ප්‍රති again, රාව *ráwa* sound) echo, reiterated or responded sound.

ප්‍රතිරූඪ, *Pratirúḍha*, *a.* (ප්‍රති before, රුහ *ruha* to ascend) ascended, mounted, gone up, [Colloq. නැඟුණ *nẹguṇa*].

ප්‍රතිරූප, *Pratirúpa*, *s.* (ප්‍රති against, රූප form) picture, image, counterpart of any thing, [Colloq. රූපය *rúpaya*].

ප්‍රතිලබ්ධ, *Pratilabdha*, *a.* received, obtained, gained, acquired.

ප්‍රතිලම්භ, *Pratilambha*, ප්‍රතිලාභ, *Pratilábha*, s. abuse, censure, reviling, [Colloquial: බැණීම *bęníma*]; obtaining.

ප්‍රතිලෝම, *Pratilóma*, a. (ප්‍රති reverting, ලෝම hair) left, not right; reverse, inverted, contrary to the natural course or order, against the hair or grain.

ප්‍රතිවචන, *Pratiwachana*, ප්‍රතිවචස්, *Pratiwachas*, ප්‍රතිවාක්, *Pratiwák*, ප්‍රතිවාක්‍ය, *Pratiwákya*, s. (ප්‍රති again, වචන *wachana*, වචස් *wachas*, වාක් *wák*, වාක්‍ය *wákya*, word) answer, reply, rejoinder.

ප්‍රතිවාතය, *Prati-wátaya*, s. (ප්‍රති against, වාත *wáta* wind) against the wind, contrary to the wind.

ප්‍රතිවාදින්, *Pratiwádin*, s. (ප්‍රති and වාදින් who speaks) defendant, respondent, [Colloq. විත්තිකාරයා *vittikárayá*].

ප්‍රතිවාප, *Pratiwápa*, s. any thing added to a decoction to render it more easy to take, as salt, sugar etc.

ප්‍රතිවේධ, *Pratiwédha*, s. (ප්‍රති before, විධ *vidha* to pierce) knowledge, understanding, information, learning.

ප්‍රතිශ්‍යා, *Pratiṣyá*, s. cold in the head, catarrh.

ප්‍රතිශාසන, *Pratiṣásana*, s. (ප්‍රති again, ශස *ṣasa* to speak or rule) answer, rejoinder; calling, inviting, questioning; sending a servant on a message.

ප්‍රතිශුද්ධ, *Pratiṣuddha*, a. (ප්‍රති completely, ශුධ *ṣudha* to be or make pure) cleansed, purified, holy.

ප්‍රතිශ්‍රුත, *Pratiṣruta*, a. promised, assented.

ප්‍රතිෂ්ඨා, *Pratishṭhá*, s. (ප්‍රති before, ස්ථා *sthá* to be) fame, celebrity; the earth; accomplishment of a religious ceremony or any set of rites, especially those instituted for the attainment of supernatural and magical powers; form of metre, consisting of a stanza of four lines, of four syllables each; it is also applied to a form of Gáyatrí, being a triplet of eight, seven and six syllable lines, making altogether twenty-one syllables; place, site; standing, fixing; staying; accomplishment, completion in general; consecration of a monument erected in honour of a deity, or of the image of a deity; endowment of a temple; portioning or marrying a daughter; favour, help, assistance; charity, almsgiving.

ප්‍රතිෂ්ඨාධාර, *Pratishṭhádhára*, s. (ප්‍රතිෂ්ඨා favour, ආධාර *ádhára* support) charity, help, assistance, [Colloq. උපකාරය *upakáraya*].

ප්‍රතිෂ්ඨිත, *Pratishṭhita*, a. (ප්‍රතිෂ්ඨා *pratishṭhá* fame, etc., ඉත *ita* affix) famous, celebrated; completed, finished; consecrated, endowed; portioned, established in life, married.

ප්‍රතිෂේධය, *Pratishédhaya*, s. obstruction, impediment, prohibition.

ප්‍රතිස්‍යාය, *Pratisyáya*, s. a cold affecting the head or nose, catarrh: see ප්‍රතිශ්‍යා *pratiṣyá*,

ප්‍රතිසංක්‍රමණය, *Pratisaṇkramaṇaya*, s. (ප්‍රති successively, සංක්‍රමණ *saṇkramaṇa* walking) walking, perambulating, walking for pleasure, health or amusement.

ප්‍රතිසංචිත, *Pratisaṇchita*, a. (ප්‍රති before, සංචිත collected) collected, gathered together, assembled.

ප්‍රතිසංයුක්ත, *Pratisaṇyukta*, a. (ප්‍රති and සංයුක්ත united) joined, united.

ප්‍රතිසන්ධි, *Pratisandhi*, s. (ප්‍රති again, සන්ධි union) re-union of the soul with a body, birth, conception in the womb, transmigration.

ප්‍රතිසිරා, *Prtisirá*, s. outer tent, screen or wall of cloth; stoppage, hindrance, impediment, obstacle.

ප්‍රතිහාර, *Pratihára*, s. door; door keeper; juggler; trick, disguise.

ප්‍රතිහාරක, *Pratiháraka*, s. (ප්‍රතිහාර trick, ක pers. aff,) juggler; one who practises sleight of hand.

ප්‍රතිහාස, *Pratihása*, s. (ප්‍රති much, හස *hasa* to laugh) temple tree, *plumeria acutifolia*, [Colloq. අලරිය *alariya*]; sport, mockery, ridicule, banter, disgrace.

ප්‍රතීචී, *Pratíchí*, s. west quarter, [Colloq. බස්නාහිර *basnáira*].

ප්‍රතීත, *Pratíta*, a. famous, celebrated; known; glad, delighted; respected.

ප්‍රතීප, *Pratípa*, a. turned away, having the face averted; backwards, against the grain, against the natural order.

ප්‍රතීපදර්ශිනී, *Pratípa-darṣiní*, s. (ප්‍රතීප and දර්ශිනී who looks) a woman, alluding to the custom of Indian women looking with the face turned backward.

ප්‍රතීර, *Pratíra*, s. (ප්‍ර and තීර bank) shore, bank; bank of river, ferry, ford.

ප්‍රතීවාප, *Pratíwápa*, s. throwing one substance into another to alter its form or state; adding any thing to a medicine either during or after decoction.

ප්‍රතෝද, *Pratóda*, s. (ප්‍ර much, තුද *tuda* to torment) goad.

ප්‍රතෝදකණ්ටක, *Pratóda-kaṇṭaka*, s. (ප්‍රතෝද and කණ්ටක thorn) prong or iron point of a goad.

ප්‍රථම, *Prathama*, *a.* first, prior, initial; chief, principal.

ප්‍රථමධ්‍යානය, *Prathamaddhyánaya*, *s.* (ප්‍රථම first, ධ්‍යාන *dhyánaya* devout meditation) first of the four degrees of dhyána as practised by religious devotees with the view of obtaining Nirváṇa or final emancipation; according to the principles laid down for the performance of this stage of the dhyána, the devotee must go into solitude; his mind abstracted from worldly pursuits and objects must retire into itself and investigate or discuss only the properties and qualities of things; after due discrimination, all other thoughts and desires being rejected, the mind must fix upon one object, viz. the acquirement of Nirváṇa or the final emancipation of the soul; upon this object the thoughts must be undisturbedly fixed until the prospect of its attainment fills the mind with ecstasy.

ප්‍රථම පාදය, *Prathama-pádaya*, *s.* first quarter, one fourth, [Colloquial: හතරෙන් පංගුව *hataren-panguwa*].

ප්‍රථමාලින්දය, *Prathamálindaya*, *s.* (ප්‍රථම *prathama* first, අලින්ද *álinda* terrace etc.) veranda on the first floor of a house.

ප්‍රථවිකා, *Prathaviká*, *s.* corruptly for පෘථ්විකා *prithviká*, plant, *ruellia longifolia*, [Colloq. ගොකටු *gokaṭu*].

ප්‍රථා, *Prathá*, *s.* fame, celebrity, renown; notoriety, [Colloq කීර්තිය *kírtiya*].

ප්‍රථිත, *Prathita*, *a.* famous, renowned, celebrated; declared, published, promulgated.

ප්‍රථුවි, *Prathuvi*, *s.* the earth, [Colloq. පොළව *polawa*], corruptly for පෘථිවි *prithivi*.

ප්‍රද, *Prada*, *s.* (ප්‍ර before, දා *dá* to give) giver; giving, donation.

ප්‍රදක්ෂිණා, *Pradakshiṇá*, *s.* (ප්‍ර and දක්ෂිණ *dakshiṇa* right) reverential salutation, by circumambulating a person keeping the right side towards him.

ප්‍රදර්ශන, *Pradarṣana*, *s.* exhibition, explaining generally, prophesying.

ප්‍රදර, *Pradara*, *s.* (ප්‍ර intensitive, දෘ *dri* to tear) splitting, rending, tearing; fracture, breaking; disease of women, *mænorrhagia;* arrow.

ප්‍රදාන, *Pradána*, *s.* (ප්‍ර before, දාන giving) gift, donation; goad.

ප්‍රදිග්ධ, *Pradigdha*, *a.* smeared, anointed.

ප්‍රදිශ, *Pradiṣa*, *s.* intermediate point of the compass, as south-east, north-east etc.

ප්‍රදිෂ්ට, *Pradishṭa*, *a.* showed, directed.

ප්‍රදීප්ත, *Pradípta*, *a.* kindled, inflamed, excited.

ප්‍රදීප, *Pradípa*, *plur.* of ප්‍රදීපය *pradípaya.*

ප්‍රදීපන, *Pradípana*, *s.* (ප්‍ර intensitive, දීපන inflaming) sort of mineral poison of red colour and caustic operation; poison of a snake.

ප්‍රදීපය, *Pradépaya*, *s.* (ප්‍ර before, දීප to shine) a lamp, light.

ප්‍රදූෂක, *Pradúshaka*, *s.* filth, dirt, nastiness, [Coll: කිලුටුකම *kiluṭukama*].

ප්‍රදේශන, *Pradéṣana*, *s.* (ප්‍ර and දිශ *diṣa* to show) gift, present or offering, bribe; any thing given to any of the gods, to superiors or friends; tribute.

ප්‍රදේශය, *Pradéṣaya*, *s.* (ප්‍ර before, දේශ *désa* place) place in general, country, district, province; foreign country, abroad; short span measured from the tip of the thumb to that of the forefinger: pl. ප්‍රදේශ *pradéṣa.*

ප්‍රදේශිනී, *Pradéṣiní*, *s.* (ප්‍ර and දිශ *diṣa* to show) forefinger; according to another authority, the third finger.

ප්‍රදොෂ, *Pradósha*, *s.* (ප්‍ර much, දොෂ guilt) fault, offence, transgression; defect; evening, first part of the night.

ප්‍රද්‍රාව, *Pradráwa*, *s.* (ප්‍ර before, ද්‍රු *dru* to go) flight. retreat, running away; abandoning, forsaking, leaving, quitting.

ප්‍රධාන, *Pradhána*, *s.* (ප්‍ර and ධා *dhá* to have) nature, natural state of any thing or the cause of the material world; intellect, understanding; first companion of a king, his minister, his eunuch or confidant etc; chief counsellor; courtier or noble; elephant driver: *a.* chief, principal, first in excellence.

ප්‍රධානයා, *Pradhánayá*, *s.* (ප්‍රධාන chief, යා pers. aff.) chief ruler, principal person.

ප්‍රධි, *Pradhi*, *s.* (ප්‍ර before, ධා *dhá* to have) iron rim or periphery of a wheel.

ප්‍රනලී, *Pranalí*, *s.* water pot, earthen jar; water course, drain.

ප්‍රනාල, *Pranála*, *s.* canal, water-course.

ප්‍රපඤ්ච, *Prapañcha*, *s.* (ප්‍ර before, පඤ්චි *pañchi* to spread) delay, loitering, procrastination; reverse, opposition, reversion or inversion; diffusion, extent, expanse; heap, abundance, quantity; delusion, deceit, trick or fraud; prolixity, copiousness in style or composition; error, illusion.

ප්‍රපතන, *Prapatana*, *s.* falling forwards, alighting.

ප්‍රපතිත, *Prapatita*, *a.* (ප්‍ර and පත *pata* to descend) fallen, inclined.

ප්‍රපද, *Prapada*, *s.* (ප්‍ර projecting, පද foot) point of the foot, tip of the toes.

ප්‍රපාත, *Prapáta*, *s.* (ප්‍ර before, පත *pata* to descend) cliff, precipice, descent; summit, highest peak of a mountain; cascade or waterfall; bank, shore; facing an enemy.

ප්‍රපිතාමහ, *Pra-pitámaha*, *s.* (ප්‍ර preceding, පිතාමහ grandfather) paternal great grandfather; name of Brahma.

ප්‍රපුන්නාඩ, *Prapunnáḍa*, *s.* plant, *cassia tora*, [Colloq. පැනිතෝර *pęni-tóra*].

ප්‍රපෞණ්ඩරීක, *Prapaunḍaríka*, *s.* (ප්‍ර excllent, පුණ්ඩරීක *punḍaríka* and අණ් *aṇ* aff.) small herbaceous plant used in medicine and as a perfume; in medicine it forms the basis of applications to ulcers and sore eyes.

ප්‍රපෞත්‍ර, *Prapautra*, *s.* great grandson.

ප්‍රඵුල්ල, *Praphulla*, *a.* (ප්‍ර before, ඵුල්ල blown) blown, expanded as a flower.

ප්‍රබන්ධ, *Prabandha*, *s.* (ප්‍ර and බන්ධි *bandhi* to bind) connected discussion or narrative, a tale, invention, versification: *ad.* always, uninterruptedly, ever.

ප්‍රබන්ධකල්පනා, *Prabandha-kalpaná*, *s.* feigned story, work of imagination, whether founded on fact or not.

ප්‍රබල, *Prabala*, *s.* (ප්‍ර and බල strength) strength; power, great strength; shoot, sprout: *a.* powerful.

ප්‍රබාහිකාව, *Prabáhikáwa*, *s.* (ප්‍ර much, බහ *baha* for වහ *waha* to carry, ඉකා *iká* aff.) diarrhœa; also written ප්‍රවාහිකාව *prawáhikáwa*.

ප්‍රබුද්ධ, *Prabuddha*, *a.* (ප්‍ර before, බුධ *budha* to be wise) wise, learned; blown, expanded as a flower; awake, wakened, roused.

ප්‍රබෝධ, *Prabódha*, *s.* (ප්‍ර and බුධ *budha* to understand) vigilance, wakefulness, active or vigilant state of being; intellect, understanding; knowledge, wisdom.

ප්‍රබෝධ කරණවා, *Prabódha-karaṇawá*, *v.* to open, to illumine.

ප්‍රබෝධන, *Prabódhana*, *s.* reviving the fragrance of a perfume which had lost its scent; awakening, arousing, reviving, exciting.

ප්‍රභඤ්ජන, *Prabhañjana*, *s.* (ප්‍ර and භඤ්ජ *bhañja* to break) air or wind; breaking, destroying.

ප්‍රභද්‍රක, *Prabhadraka*, *s.* margosa tree, *azadirachta indica*, [Colloq. කොහොඹ *kohomba*].

ප්‍රභව, *Prabhawa*, *s.* (ප්‍ර superiority or manifestation, භව being) generative cause, basis or root of being or existence; operative cause or immediate origin of being, as the father or mother, etc; the place of receiving existence or the place where an object is first perceived; birth, production; the basis or origin of water, that is, light; strength, superiority, power; the first year of the Indian cycle of sixty.

ප්‍රභා, *Prabhá*, *s.* (ප්‍ර intense, භා to shine) light, radiance, splendour; movable palace of Kuvéra.

ප්‍රභාකර, *Prabhákara*, *s.* (ප්‍රභා light, කර what makes) sun, [Colloq. ඉර *ira*].

ප්‍රභාත, *Prabháta*, *s.* (ප්‍ර before, භා *bhá* to shine) morning, dawn, daybreak, [Colloq. පාන්දර *pándara*].

ප්‍රභාධර, *Prabhádhara*, *s.* (ප්‍රභා light, ධර what bears) sun, [Colloq. ඉර *ira*].

ප්‍රභාමණ්ඩල, *Prabhá-manḍala*, *s.* (ප්‍රභා light, මණ්ඩල circle) radiancy that encircles the sun.

ප්‍රභාව, *Prabháwa*, *s.* (ප්‍ර pre-eminence, භාව quality) light, splendour, effulgence; radiance, majesty, dignity; magnanimity, high spirit; power, strength; tranquility, conciliation.

ප්‍රභාස්වරය, *Prabháswaraya*, *s.* radiance that encircles the sun or any other object.

ප්‍රභින්න, *Prabhinna*, *a.* (ප්‍ර much, භින්න broken, seized with fury) furious elephant, one in rut or from whose temples the juice is exuding; broken, shivered.

ප්‍රභූ, *Prabhú*, *s.* (ප්‍ර pre-eminent, භූ to be) master, chief, lord; quicksilver: *a.* strong, able.

ප්‍රභූත, *Prabhúta*, *a.* (ප්‍ර principal, භූත been) much, many; gone up or upwards; been, become, produced; high, lofty; governed, presided over.

ප්‍රභෘති, *Prabhṛiti*, *s.* the rest, etcætera, [Colloq. යනාදි *yanádi*]: *a.* like, resembling, similar.

ප්‍රභේද, *Prabhéda*, *s.* (ප්‍ර before, භේද kind) kind, sort; separation; difference, dissimilarity, schism, contradiction, division.

ප්‍රභේදන, *Prabhédana*, *s.* (ප්‍ර and භේදන breaking) breaking, separation.

ප්‍රමථ, *Pramatha*, *s.* attendant or follower of Ṣiva.

ප්‍රමථන, *Pramathana*, *s.* (ප්‍ර and මථ *matha* to churn) killing, slaughter; churning.

ප්‍රමථාධිප, *Pramathádhipa*, *s.* (ප්‍රමථ *pramatha* a follower of Ṣiva, අධිප *adhipa* chief) name of Ṣiva.

ප්‍රමද, *Pramada*, *s.* (ප්‍ර before, මද mad, drunk) joy, pleasure, delight, rapture; fruit of *datura metel*: *a.* mad, intoxicated.

ප්‍රමදා, *Pramadá*, *s.* woman, handsome woman.

ප්‍රමදී, *Pramadí*, *s.* forty seventh year of the Indian cycle of sixty.

ප්‍රමාණ, *Pramáṇa*, *s.* (ප්‍ර before, මා *má* to measure) size, standard, proportion, limit, measure, quantity; cause, motive, proof, authority.

ප්‍රමාණපුරුෂ, *Pramáṇa-purusha*, *s.* umpire, arbitrator.

ප්‍රමාණ, *Pramáṇá*, *a.* (ප්‍ර implying pleasure, මණස් *maṇas* the mind, අණ් *aṇ* aff. of relation) pleased, glad, delighted, joyous, cheerful, of an even temper.

ප්‍රමාණාතික්‍රාන්ත, *Pramáṇátikránta*, *a.* (ප්‍රමාණ *pramáṇa* measure, අතික්‍රාන්ත *atikránta* going beyond) infinite, boundless; exceeding, beyond measure.

ප්‍රමාතාමහ, *Pramátá-maha*, *s.* (ප්‍ර before, මාතාමහ maternal grandfather) maternal great grandfather.

ප්‍රමාතා මහී, *Pramátá-mahí*, *s.* (ප්‍රමාතාමහ *pramátá-maha* maternal grandfather, ඊ *í* fem. aff.) maternal great grandmother.

ප්‍රමාථී, *Pramáthi*, *s.* (ප්‍ර before, මථ *matha* to pain) afflicting; killing, destroying; twelfth year of the Indian cycle of sixty.

ප්‍රමාද, *Pramáda*, *s.* (ප්‍ර and මද *mada* to be mad) inadvertence, carelessness, error, inaccuracy; delay, dilatoriness, procrastination, religious indifference.

ප්‍රමාදකරණවා, *Pramáda-karaṇawá*, *v.* to delay, to put back, to impede.

ප්‍රමාදවෙනවා, *Pramádawenawá*, *v.* to delay, to loiter.

ප්‍රමාපන, *Pramápana*, *s.* slaughter, killing.

ප්‍රමිත, *Pramita*, *s.* (ප්‍ර before, මා *má* to measure, ක්ත *kta* aff.) limit, measure, quantity: *a.* known, understood, established, measured.

ප්‍රමිති, *Pramiti*, *s.* (ප්‍රමිත *pramita* and ඉ *i* aff.) true knowledge, or knowledge resulting from positive fact; measuring.

ප්‍රමීත, *Pramíta*, *a.* (ප්‍ර before මී *mí* to hurt, to kill) dead, deceased; immolated, sacrificed.

ප්‍රමීල, *Pramíla*, } ප්‍රමීලා, *Pramílá*, } *s.* (ප්‍ර and මීල to twinkle) shutting the eyes, winking; lassitude, enervation, exhaustion from indolence or fatigue.

ප්‍රමුක්ත, *Pramukta*, *a.* (ප්‍ර and මුක්ත loosed) freed, liberated, emancipated, [Colloquial: නිදහස්කළ *nidahaskaḷa*].

ප්‍රමුඛ, *Pramukha*, *s.* (ප්‍ර and මුඛ face) chief, sage, any respectable man; heap, multitude; plant used in dyeing, *mallotus philippensis* or *rottleria tinctoria*, [Colloq. හම්පරිල *hamparila*]: *a.* before, in presence of; present, the time being; first, chief, principal, best, most excellent.

ප්‍රමුදිත, *Pramudita*, *a.* (ප්‍ර intense, මුද *muda* to be pleased) pleased, glad, contented, happy, joyous, [Colloq. ප්‍රීතිවූ *prítiwú*].

ප්‍රමේය, *Praméya*, *a.* (ප්‍ර before, මා *má* to measure) what may or ought to be bounded, limited, measured; proved.

ප්‍රමේහ, *Praméha*, *s.* (ප්‍ර implying change, මිහ *miha* to pass urine) urinary affection, as change in the colour, quality or consistence of the urine; twenty one varieties are enumerated, including diabetes, gonorrhœa, etc; rheumatism.

ප්‍රමෝද්‍ය, *Pramódya*, } ප්‍රමෝද, *Pramóda*, } *s.* (ප්‍ර intense, මුද *muda* to be glad) pleasure, happiness, delight; the fourth year of the Indian cycle of sixty.

ප්‍රමෝදනී, *Pramódani*, *s.* plant, *solanum jacquini*, [Colloq. කටුවැල්බටු *kaṭuwęlbaṭu*].

ප්‍රයත, *Prayata*, *s.* (ප්‍ර intensely, යත to endeavour) one purified by austerity and mortification, [Colloq. තාපසයා *tápasayá*]: *a.* restrained, self-subdued.

ප්‍රයස්ත, *Prayasta*, *a.* cooked, seasoned, dressed with sauces and condiments.

ප්‍රයාග, *Prayága*, } ප්‍රයාජ, *Prayája*, } *s.* (ප්‍ර principal, යජ *yaja* to worship) principal ceremony, chief sacrifice; celebrated place of pilgrimage, place where worship is considered peculiarly efficacious.

ප්‍රයාණ, *Prayáṇa*, *s.* going forth, [Colloq. යාම *yáma*]; attack, invasion.

ප්‍රයුක්ත, *Prayukta*, *a.* (ප්‍ර before, යුජ *yuja* to join) endowed with, possessing as an attribute, etc; resulting from, appointed, nominated.

ප්‍රයෝග, *Prayóga*, *s.* (ප්‍ර and යුජ *yuja* to join) trick, deceit, cunning, cheating, fraud, the operation of magical or mysterious rites; example, comparison; consequence, result: *a.* deceitful, cunning, designing, fraudulent.

ප්‍රයෝගකාරයා, *Prayógakárayá*, *s.* crafty man.

ප්‍රයෝග විපත්තිය, *Prayóga-vipattiya*, *s.* (ප්‍රයෝග fraud, විපත්ති *vipatti* danger) calamitous consequence of fraud, the results or effects of deceit.

ප්‍රයෝග සම්පත්, *Prayóga-sampat*, *s.* (ප්‍රයෝග and සම්පත් wealth) wealth accumulated by fraudulent means.

ප්‍රයෝජක, *Prayójaka*, *s.* instigator, original cause of any act, author, principal.

ප්‍රයෝජන, *Prayójana*, *s.* (ප්‍ර before, යුජ *yuja* to join) profit, gain, advantage; cause, occasion; motive, origin.

ප්‍රරෝහ, *Praróha*, *s.* (ප්‍ර and රුහ *ruha* to grow) bud, sprout.

ප්‍රලම්බ, *Pralamba*, *s.* branch; breast of a female; bud of a creeping plant; garland of flowers; delay, procrastination; tin: in the mythology of the Hindus a noted demon or Daitya slain by Bala Ráma: *a.* hanging down; slow.

ප්‍රලම්භන, *Pralambhana*, *s.* enticing, coaxing.

ප්‍රලය, *Pralaya*, *s.* (ප්‍ර intensely, ලී *lí* to destroy) the end of time, properly the end of a kalpa or destruction of the world; death, dying; loss, destruction, dissolution, annihilation; fainting, syncope, loss of sense.

ප්‍රලයකරණවා, *Pralayakaraṇawá*, *v.* to destroy, to drive away as evil spirits.

ප්‍රලාප, *Pralápa*, *s.* (ප්‍ර much, ලප *lapa* to speak) unmeaning or unconnected speech, gibberish.

ප්‍රවචන, *Prawachana*, *s.* (ප්‍ර principal, වචන word or speech) excellent speech or language; the reverse of ප්‍රලාප *pralápa;* scripture, any sacred writing.

ප්‍රවචනීය, *Prawachaníya*, *s.* good or excellent speaker: *a.* expressing, to be well or elegantly spoken.

ප්‍රවණ, *Prawaṇa*, *s.* declivity, descent, steep: *a.* bent, bowed; crooked, curved, stooping; humble, modest, virtuous.

ප්‍රවයස්, *Prawayas*, *s.* (ප්‍ර much, වයස් life or age) old man, [Colloq. මහලු අය *mahalu-aya*].

ප්‍රවර, *Prawara*, *s.* offspring, descendants; family, race, kindred; covering, screening: *a.* best, most excellent; pre-eminent.

ප්‍රවරා, *Prawará*, *s.* tree, variety of *Eugenia*, [Colloq. එලදම් *ela-dam*].

ප්‍රවහ, *Prawaha*, *s.* (ප්‍ර forth, වහ to bear) departure, going forth from a town; air, wind.

ප්‍රවහණ, *Prawahaṇa*, *s.* (ප්‍ර and වහණ carrying) sort of covered car, litter or carriage for women; car or carriage fitted up and ornamented for festivals.

ප්‍රවාන, *Prawána*, *s.* belly of the víṇá or Indian lute; also the bow with which the víṇá is played.

ප්‍රවාර, *Prawára*, *s.* (ප්‍ර before, වෘ *vṛi* to cover) covering, upper garment; concealment, screening.

ප්‍රවාරණය, *Prawáraṇaya*, *s.* rejection, throwing aside; discontinuance; prohibition, objection, opposition; injunction, [Colloq. වැලකිම *wẹlakíma*, නියෝගය *niyógaya*].

ප්‍රවාල, *Prawála*, *s.* coral, [Colloq. පබළු *pabaḷu*]; bud or young shoot of a leaf, sprout, germ.

ප්‍රවාලඵලිකා, *Prawála-phaliká*, *s.* climbing plant, *vitis quadrangularis*, [Colloq. හිරැස්ස *hírẹssa*].

ප්‍රවාලමධ්‍ය, *Prawála-madhya*, *s.* tree, *calophyllum inophyllum*, [Colloq. දොම්බ *domba*].

ප්‍රවාල සාගර, *Prawála-ságara*, (ප්‍රවාල coral, සාගර ocean) sea of coral.

ප්‍රවාලාභඵලා, *Prawálábha-phalá*, *s.* creeping plant, *bryonia grandis*, [Colloq. කෙම්වැල් *kemwẹl*].

ප්‍රවාස, *Prawása*, *s.* (ප්‍ර far, distant, වාස abode) separation, living in a temporary or foreign residence, habitation away from home.

ප්‍රවාසන, *Prawásana*, *s.* (ප්‍ර removed, වස *wasa* to dwell) exile, killing, slaughter; dwelling abroad, sojourning.

ප්‍රවාසින්, *Prawásin*, *s.* (ප්‍රවාස *prawása* and ඉන් pers. aff.) traveller, sojourner.

ප්‍රවාහ, *Prawáha*, *s.* (ප්‍ර much, වහ *waha* to bear, to carry) stream, flow, flood; action, occupation.

ප්‍රවාහක, *Prawáhaka*, *s.* (ප්‍රවාහ and ක aff.) travelling merchant; carman; imp, goblin.

ප්‍රවාහිකා, *Prawáhiká*, *s.* (ප්‍ර much, වහ *waha* to bear, ඉක *ika* aff.) diarrhœa.

ප්‍රවිදාරණ, *Pravidárana*, *s.* (ප්‍ර before, විදාරණ tearing) rending, tearing, breaking; war, battle, combat; tumult, crowd, confusion.

ප්‍රවිෂ්ට, *Pravishṭa*, *a.* (ප්‍ර and විශ *viṣa* to enter) entered (literally or metaphorically).

ප්‍රවිෂ්ටවෙනවා, *Pravishṭawenawá*, *v.* to enter, [Colloq. ඇතුල්වෙනවා *ẹtulwenawá*].

ප්‍රවීණ, *Pravíṇa*, *a.* (ප්‍ර implying excellence, වීණා *viṇá* lute) skilful, clever, conversant with; quick, expeditious.

ප්‍රවීර, *Pravíra*, *s.* (ප්‍ර pre-eminent, වීර hero) hero, warrior; chief, person of rank.

ප්‍රවේණි, *Prawéṇi*, *s.* hair twisted and undecorated; elephant's housings; custom, practice.

ප්‍රවේණිය, *Prawéṇiya*, *s.* landed property long possessed by any family, inheritance, possession; cloth or trappings of an elephant; superiority, eminence.

ප්‍රවේශ, *Prawéṣa*, *s.* entrance.

ප්‍රවේශක, *Prawéṣaka*, *s.* one who enters; inferior actor.

ප්‍රවේශන, *Prawéṣana*, *s.* (ප්‍ර before, විශ *viṣa* to enter) entrance to a house, entering, entrance.

ප්‍රවේෂ්ට, *Prawéshṭa*, *s.* (ප්‍ර and වේෂ්ට to encompass) arm; forearm or wrist; elephant's gums; elephant's housings.

ප්‍රවේසම්කරණවා, *Prawésam-karaṇawá*, *v.* to take care, to preserve,

ප්‍රවේසම, *Prawésama*, *s.* care, caution, circumspection; preservation, protection, safe guard.

ප්‍රව්‍යක්ත, *Prawyakta*, *a.* (ප්‍ර and වි *vi* before, අඤ් *añja* to spread) evident, apparent, manifest, explicit; burst; blown, opened, expanded as a flower.

ප්‍රව්‍රජ්‍යා, *Prawrajyá*, *s.* (ප්‍ර emphatic, ව්‍රජ *wraja* to go) state of a religious ascetic, renunciation of the world for religious purposes; the Buddhist priesthood, [Colloq. සංඝයා *sanghayá*].

ප්‍රව්‍රජිත, *Prawrajita*, *s.* (ප්‍ර and ව්‍රජිත gone) religious ascetic, priest, pupil or attendant on a priest.

ප්‍රව්‍රජිතා, *Prawrajitá*, *s.* (ප්‍රව්‍රජිත *prawrajita* and ආ *á* fem. aff.) female ascetic; spikenard, *valeriana jatamansi*.

ප්‍රවෘත්ත, *Pravṛitta*, *a.* (ප්‍ර emphatic, වෘත *vṛita* to be) done, fixed, settled, determined; continuing, being.

ප්‍රවෘත්ති, *Pravṛitti*, *s.* (ප්‍ර and වෘත *vṛita* to be) tidings, intelligence; activity, occupation, active life as opposed to contemplative devotions, stream, current; addiction, inclination, partiality or predilection; news, account.

ප්‍රවෘද්ධ, *Pravṛiddha*, *s.* (ප්‍ර much, වෘධ *vṛidha* to grow) increased, multiplied, grown, full grown; expanded, diffused, spread abroad, or dispersed.

ප්‍රවෘෂායනි, *Pravṛisháyaní*, *s.* plant, *vigna sinensis*, [Colloq. වඳුරුමෑ *wanduru-mẹ*].

ප්‍රශ්නදූති, *Praṣna-dúti*, *s.* (ප්‍රශ්න and දූති who plays) riddle, enigma, intricate or enigmatical question.

ප්‍රශ්නය, *Praṣnaya*, *s.* (ප්‍රච්ඡ *prachchha* to ask) question, enquiry, demand; incorrectly written ප්‍රශ්ණය *prashṇaya*.

ප්‍රශ්නව්‍යාකරණ, *Praṣna-wyákaraṇa*, *s.* (ප්‍රශ්න question, ව්‍යාකරණ explanation) solving an intricate question.

ප්‍රශ්නි, *Praṣni*, *s.* aquatic plant, *pistia stratiotes*, [Colloq. දියපරණලා *diyaparaṇalá*].

ප්‍රශංසන, *Praṣansana*, *s.* praising, eulogising.

ප්‍රශංසනීය, *Praṣansaniya*, *a.* to be praised, praiseworthy.

ප්‍රශංසා, *Praṣansá*, *s.* (ප්‍ර before,ශංස *ṣansa* to praise) praise, applause, eulogy; commendation; flattery.

ප්‍රශංසාකරණවා, *Praṣansá-karaṇawá*, *v.* to praise, to laud.

ප්‍රශංසිත, *Praṣansita*, *a.* praised, eulogised.

ප්‍රශමන, *Praṣamana*, *s.* pacifying, killing, reposing.

ප්‍රශස්ත, *Praṣasta*, *a.* (ප්‍ර much, ශංස *ṣansa* to praise or commend) good, happy, well, right, excellent, best; praised, applauded, flattered.

ප්‍රශ්‍රවණ, *Praṣrawaṇa*, *s.* (ප්‍ර before, ශ්‍රු *ṣru* to ooze) spring, source, fountain, [Colloq. උල්පත *ulpata*]; cascade.

ප්‍රශ්‍රිත, *Praṣrita*, *a.* (ප්‍ර and ශ්‍රි *ṣri* to serve) modest, humble, unassuming, [Colloq. යටත්වූ *yaṭatwú*].

ප්‍රෂ්ටපානිකර, *Prashṭapánikara*, *s.* corruptly for පිෂ්ටපාන්තකරී *pishṭapántakarí*, fruit of *zizyphus jujuba*, [Colloq. මසන් *masan*].

ප්‍රෂ්ඨ, *Prashṭha*, *s.* (ප්‍ර pre-eminent, ස්ථා *sthá* to stay) leader, conductor, preceder, one who goes before: *a.* chief, principal, best.

ප්‍රෂත, *Prashata*, *s.* spotted deer, *axis maculata* [Colloq. මුවා *muwá*].

ප්‍රස්තර, *Prastara*, *s.* rock, low hill; stone; bed; tabular form of representing the long and short vowels of poetical metre.

ප්‍රස්තාර, *Prastára*, *s.* thicket overgrown with grass; bed made with blossoms, leaves, etc; any bed or couch.

ප්‍රස්තාව, *Prastáwa*, *s.* time, season, occasion, opportunity; subject matter.

ප්‍රස්තාවනා, *Prastáwaná*, *s.* introduction; prelude to a drama.

ප්‍රස්තාවසදෘශ, *Prastáwa-sadṛiṣa*, *a.* suited to the occasion, appropriate.

ප්‍රස්තුත, *Prastuta*, *a.* (ප්‍ර before, ස්තු to praise, ක්ත *kta* aff.) said, revealed, propounded; declared, praised, panegyrized.

ප්‍රස්ථ, *Prastha*, *s.* kind of measure, making about forty-eight double handfuls; table-land, or land on the top of a mountain.

ප්‍රස්ථපුෂ්ප, *Prastha-pushpa*, *s.* (ප්‍රස්ථ top of a mountain, පුෂ්ප flower) sort of tulasi or basil, *ocimum.*

ප්‍රස්ථාන, *Prastháṇa*, *s.* (ප්‍ර away from, ස්ථා *sthá* to stay) going, going forth, proceeding, journey, march.

ප්‍රස්ථාව, *Prastháwa*, incorrectly for ප්‍රස්තාව *prastáwa*, which see.

ප්‍රස්ඵුට, *Prasphuṭa*, *a.* (ප්‍ර before, ස්ඵුට to blossom) blown. expanded.

ප්‍රස්ඵෝටන, *Prasphóṭana*, *s.* winnow, small open basket for the purpose of cleaning grain; blowing, expanding; budding; opening; winnowing corn; striking, beating.

ප්‍රසංසා *Prasaṇsá*, corruptly for ප්‍රශංසා *praṣaṇsá*, which see.

ප්‍රසන්න, *Prasanna*, *a.* (ප්‍ර principally, සද *sada* to go) pleasing, pleased, glad, delightful, delighted; complacent; gracious, favourable; clear, clean, bright, pellucid.

ප්‍රසන්නතා, *Prasannatá*, *s.* (ප්‍රසන්න bright, තා aff. of the abstract) brightness, clearness, pellucidness.

ප්‍රසන්නය, *Prasannaya*, *s.* pleasure, gladness, delight.

ප්‍රසන්නේරා, *Prasannérá*, *s.* (ප්‍රසන්න *prasanna* clear, ඊරා *írá* wine) spirituous liquor.

ප්‍රසර, *Prasara*, *s.* (ප්‍ර before, සෘ *sri* to go) boil, swelling in a state of suppuration, *i. e.* spreading, extending; affectionate solicitation; speed, velocity; war, battle; multitude, assemblage; an iron arrow.

ප්‍රසරණ, *Prasaraṇa*, *s.* (ප්‍ර and සරණ going) surrounding an enemy; spreading over a country to forage; army in motion.

ප්‍රසව්‍ය, *Prasawya*, *a.* (ප්‍ර inclined towards, සව්‍ය the left or wrong side) contrary, reverse, inverted, reverted.

ප්‍රසව, *Prasawa*, *s.* (ප්‍ර before, සූ *sú* to bring forth) birth, bringing forth, bearing (as young); production, offspring: *a.* travailing, bearing.

ප්‍රසව රුජාව, *Prasawa-rujáwa*, *s.* (ප්‍රසව birth, රුජ *ruja* to ache) the pain or travail of childbirth.

ප්‍රසවාඞ්කුරා, *Prasawáṅkurá*, *s.* (ප්‍රසව *prasawa* and අඞ්කුර *aṅkura* bud) blossom, flower bud.

ප්‍රසහ, *Prasaha*, *s.* (ප්‍ර before, සහ to be able) beast or bird of prey.

ප්‍රසාද, *Prasáda*, *s.* (ප්‍ර principally, සද *sada* to go) favour, kindness, help; joy, pleasure; welfare, elegance of style; perspicuity: *a.* clear, clean, bright, pleasing, excellent.

ප්‍රසාදන, *Prasádana*, *s.* clearing, cleansing, cleaning; boiled rice; servitude, dependence; dress, decoration; ornament, embellishment.

ප්‍රසාදය, *Prasádaya*, *s.* clearness, brightness: see ප්‍රසාද *prasáda.*

ප්‍රසාදික, *Prasádika*, *a.* (ප්‍ර before, සද *sada* with, ක්ත *kta* aff.) brightened, cleansed, polished.

ප්‍රසාධ, *Prasádha*, } *s.* (ප්‍ර before, සාධ *sádha*
ප්‍රසාධන, *Prasádhana*, } to accomplish) ornament, decoration, embellishment.

ප්‍රසාධනී, *Prasádhaní*, *s.* comb; kind of drug.

ප්‍රසාර, *Prasára*, *s.* spreading, extending, spreading over the country; foraging, going forth in search of provender.

ප්‍රසාරණ, *Prasáraṇa*, *s.* spreading over a country for collecting forage; surrounding an enemy.

ප්‍රසාරණී, *Prasáraṇí*, *s.* plant, *pæderia fœtida;* foraging, etc.

ප්‍රසාරි, *Prasári*, *s.* spreading abroad, extending over a country.

ප්‍රසාරිණී, *Prasáriṇí*, *s.* creeping plant, *ipomæa tridentata* or *i. angustifolia*, [Colloq. අපසුමදු *ápasu-madu*].

ප්‍රසාරිත, *Prasárita*, *s.* stretched, extended, [Colloq. දිඟුකළ *diṅgukaḷa*].

ප්‍රසිත, *Prasita*, *s.* exertion, diligence, attentive adherence to any thing: *a.* attached to.

ප්‍රසිද්ධ, *Prasiddha*, *a.* (ප්‍ර before, සිද්ධ accomplished) published, public, known, noised abroad; famous, celebrated, notorious.

ප්‍රසිද්ධකරණවා, *Prasiddha-karaṇawá*, *v.* to publish, to blaze abroad.

ප්‍රසූත, *Prasúta*, *a.* (ප්‍ර before, සූ *sú* to bear) born, engendered, brought forth, delivered of a child.

ප්‍රසූතා, *Prasútá*, *s.* (ප්‍රසූත *prasúta* and ආ *á* fem. aff.) a woman who has borne children.

ප්‍රසූති, *Prasúti*, *s.* (ප්‍ර before, සූ *sú* to bear) bearing, bringing forth, childbirth.

ප්‍රසූතිකා, *Prasútiká*, *s.* one who has been recently delivered of a child.

ප්‍රසූතිකාව, *Prasútikáwa*, see ප්‍රසූතා *prasútá.*

ප්‍රසූන, *Prasúna*, *s.* flower, bud, [Colloq. මල් *mal*]; *a.* born, produced.

ප්‍රස්‍රබ්ධි, *Prasrabdhi*, *s.* (ප්‍ර before, ස්‍රබ්ධි tranquility) one of the Buddháṅgas, state of mental tranquillity, state of freedom from all agitation with the thoughts enjoying undisturbed repose.

ප්‍රසෘත, *Prasṛita*, *s.* palm of the hand hollowed as if to hold any thing; a weight equal to about

4 ozs. 12⅘ dwts: *a.* extended, spread abroad, dispersed, stretched; modest, humble; swift, quick; attached to, engaged in, occupied.

ප්‍රසෘතා, *Prasṛitá, s.* leg, [Colloq. කකුල *kakula*].

ප්‍රහර්ෂ, *Praharsha,* } *s.* (ප්‍ර much, හෘෂ *hṛisha* to rejoice) great joy;
ප්‍රහර්ෂණ, *Praharshaṇa,* } planet Mercury.

ප්‍රහර, *Prahara, s.* watch, eighth part of the day or a division comprising about three hours, [Colloq. යාමය *yámaya*].

ප්‍රහරණ, *Praharaṇa, s.* weapon; covered car; litter for women, or any litter or small covered car for pleasure or diversion.

ප්‍රහස්ත, *Prahasta, s.* (ප්‍ර before, හස්ත hand) open hand with the fingers extended.

ප්‍රහසන, *Prahasana, s.* (ප්‍ර much, හස *hasa* to laugh) loud, violent or hearty laughter, mirth, merriment; sarcasm, banter, ridicule; irony, reproof.

ප්‍රහාණි, *Praháṇi, s.* (ප්‍ර before, හා *há* to leave) declining, wasting, lessening, decreasing.

ප්‍රහාරය, *Prahâraya, s.* (ප්‍ර and හර *hara* to take) stroke, blow, wound inflicted by a blow; smiting, killing.

ප්‍රහාස, *Prahása, s.* laughter, blowing as a flower.

ප්‍රහිත, *Prahita, a.* (ප්‍ර and හිත proper) sent, dismissed; learned; suitable, proper, fit to be used.

ප්‍රහීණ, *Prahína, a.* (ප්‍ර intense, හීන *hína* left) decayed, diminished, lessened, reduced, decreased; forsaking, leaving, abandoning.

ප්‍රහේලිකා, *Prahéliká, s.* (ප්‍ර before, හිල *hila* to play) riddle, enigma, puzzling or enigmatical question.

ප්‍රාංශු, *Práṅṣu, a.* (ප්‍ර and අංශු *aṅṣu* a ray) high, tall, lofty; famous, famed, celebrated.

ප්‍රාක්, *Prák, ind.* before, prior, preceding in time or place; east, eastern; past, gone, [Colloq. පූර්ව *púrwa*]: see ප්‍රාච් *prách* and ප්‍රාච්‍ය *práchya*.

ප්‍රාක්තන, *Práktana, a.* (ප්‍රාක් formerly, and තන aff.) old, ancient, anterior, [Colloq. පුරාණ *purána*].

ප්‍රාක්ඵල්ගුණී, *Prákphalguṇí, s.* (ප්‍රාක් preceding, ඵල්ගුණී asterism) eleventh of the lunar asterisms.

ප්‍රාකාම්‍ය, *Prákámya, s.* (ප්‍ර *pra* before, අණ් *aṇ* aff. කාම්‍ය will) one of Ṣiva's eight attributes, irresistible will or fiat.

ප්‍රාකාරය, *Prákáraya, s.* fence, inclosure; walled rampart: see ප්‍රාචීර *práchíra*.

ප්‍රාක්‍රම, *Prákrama,* corruptly for පරාක්‍රම *parákrama*.

ප්‍රාකෘත, *Prákṛita, s.* (ප්‍ර *pra* pre-eminently, අකෘත *akṛita* not made) any low or degraded language; it is the provincial and peculiar dialect of the Sanskrit language, it is especially spoken by the female characters and inferior personages of plays: *a.* natural.

ප්‍රාග්භාර, *Prágbhára, s.* stone building; cave in a rock; top or peak of a mountain.

ප්‍රාග්භාරශීර්ෂ, *Prágbhára-ṣírsha, s.* (ප්‍රාග්භාර cave, ශීර්ෂ head) top of a cave.

ප්‍රාගල්භ්‍ය, *Prágalbhya, s.* ප්‍රගල්භ *pragalbha* confident, යඤ් *yañ* aff.) confidence, boldness, arrogance; importance, rank; ability, skill.

ප්‍රාච්, *Prách, ind.* (ප්‍ර *pra* before, අඤ්ච *añja* to go) east, eastern; prior, preceding; before, in presence of; above, on the top: see ප්‍රාක් *prák*.

ප්‍රාච්‍ය, *Práchya, a.* east, eastern; first, prior, former.

ප්‍රාචී, *Práchí, s.* east.

ප්‍රාචීන, *Práchína, a.* (ප්‍රාච් *prách* east, with ඛ *kha* aff.) eastern, east; prior, former, old, ancient.

ප්‍රාචීන පනස, *Práchína-panasa, s.* bael tree, *ægle marmelos*, [Colloq. බෙලි *beli*].

ප්‍රාචීනා, *Práchíná, s.* creeping plant, *cissampelos pareira*, [Colloquial: දියමිත්ත *diyamitta*]: also, ichneumon plant, අරත්ත *aratta*.

ප්‍රාචීනාමලක, *Práchínámalaka, s.* fruit, *flacourtia cataphracta*, [Coll: රට උගුරැස්ස *raṭa-ugurẹssa*].

ප්‍රාචීපති, *Práchípati, s.* (ප්‍රාචී east, පති chief, lord) name of Indra.

ප්‍රාචීඵල, *Práchíphala, s.* medicinal plant, *spilanthes acmella*, [Colloq. අක්මැල්ල *akmẹlla*].

ප්‍රාචීර, *Práchíra, s.* (ප්‍ර *pra* before, අණ් *aṇ* aff. චි *chí* to collect) fence, enclosure, wall.

ප්‍රාජක, *Prájaka, s.* (ප්‍ර *pra* and අජ *aja* to go, in the causal form) shepherd, herdsman; driver.

ප්‍රාජාපත්‍ය, *Prájápatya,* see ප්‍රජාපති *prajápati*.

ප්‍රාඤ්ජලි, *Práñjali, s.* putting the hands together to the forehead, a mark of respect.

ප්‍රාඥ, *Prájña, a.* (ප්‍ර *pra* and අ *á* aff. ඥා *jñá* to know) learned, wise, skilful, clever, intelligent, sensible; patient in investigation.

ප්‍රාඥභාව, *Prájñabháwa, s.* wisdom.

ප්‍රාණ, *Práṇa, s.* air inhaled, life, vital breath, poetical inspiration, aspiration in the articulation of letters.

ප්‍රාණඝාත, *Práṇaghâta, s.* (ප්‍රාණ life, ඝාත destroying) killing, destroying animal life.

ප්‍රාණඝාතකරණවා, *Práṇaghâta-karaṇawá, v.* to kill, to take away life.

ප්‍රාණද, *Práṇada, s.* (ප්‍රාණ life, ද what gives) one of the three noted myrobalans, the yellow species, *terminalia chebula,* [Colloq. අරළු *araḷu*].

ප්‍රාණනාථ, *Práṇa-nátha, s.* (ප්‍රාණ life, නාථ lord) husband, [Colloq. පුරුෂයා *purushayá*].

ප්‍රාණය, *Práṇaya, s.* life: see ප්‍රාණ *práṇa.*

ප්‍රාණවධ, *Práṇa-wadha,* see ප්‍රාණඝාත *práṇagháta.*

ප්‍රාණින්, *Práṇin, s.* living being.

ප්‍රාණී, *Práṇí, s.* (ප්‍රාණ *práṇa* vital air, ඊ *í* aff.) animal, sentient being.

ප්‍රාණේශ, *Práṇéṣa, s.* (ප්‍රාණ *práṇa* and ඊශ *íṣa* lord) husband, [Colloq. පුරුෂයා *purúshayá*].

ප්‍රාතර්, *Prátar, ind.* (ප්‍ර *pra* before, අත *ata* to go, අර් *ar* aff.) morning, dawn, daybreak, [Colloq පාන්දර *pándara*].

ප්‍රාතර්ගේය, *Prátargéya, s.* (ප්‍රාතර් morning, ගේය to be sung) a minstrel or bard employed to wake the sovereign by his morning chant.

ප්‍රාතිමෝක්ෂ, *Prátimóksha, s.* book included in the Vinaya piṭaka, and containing the first discourse addressed by Buddha to the priests; it is read by them in private twice a month on the days of the new and full moon.

ප්‍රාතිහාර්ය, *Prátihárya, s.* wonder, supernatural preformance.

ප්‍රාතිහාර, *Prátihára,* } *s.* (ප්‍රතිහාර juggler,
ප්‍රාතිහාරක, *Prátiháraka,* } අණ් *aṇ* aff.) juggler, one practising sleight of hand, conjuror.

ප්‍රාදුර්භූත, *Prádurbhúta, a.* (ප්‍රාදුර් evidently, visible, භූත been) become visible, manifest, apparent.

ප්‍රාධාන්‍ය, *Prádhánya, s.* supremacy.

ප්‍රාන්ත, *Pránta, s.* (ප්‍ර *pra* before, අන්ත *anta* end) margin, border.

ප්‍රාප්ත, *Prápta, a.* (ප්‍ර *pra* and අප *ápa* to gain) obtained, gained, received, procured; arrived, approached; fixed, placed; proper, right.

ප්‍රාප්තිය, *Práptiya, s.* gain, profit, acquiring; success; rise, ascent; collection, assemblage, assembly; one of the eight superhuman faculties, power of obtaining every thing.

ප්‍රාමාණ්‍ය, *Prámáṇya, s.* proof, authority.

ප්‍රාමාණික, *Prámáṇika, s.* chief or head of a trade, etc; learned man, one who supports his arguments by reference to books etc: *a.* having authority.

ප්‍රාර්ථන, *Prártthana,* } *s.* (ප්‍ර *pra* before, අර්ථ *arttha*
ප්‍රාර්ථනා, *Prártthaná,* } to request) asking, begging.

ප්‍රාර්ථනාව, *Prártthanáwa, s.* request, prayer, petition; hope; wish, desire.

ප්‍රාර්ථනීය, *Prártthaníya, s.* (ප්‍ර *pra* before, අර්ථ *arttha* to ask, අනීයර් *aníyar* aff.) alms; name of the Dwápara or third age of the world: *a.* fit to be asked, proper to be begged.

ප්‍රාර්ථිත, *Prártthita, a.* (ප්‍ර *pra* and අර්ථ *arttha* to ask, with ක්ත *kta* aff.) begged, requested, solicited; hoped; wished.

ප්‍රාරබ්ධ, *Prárabdha, a.* (ප්‍ර *pra* and ආඞ් *áṅ* aff. before, රභ *rabha* to begin) begun, beginning.

ප්‍රාරබ්ධි, *Prárabdhi,* } *s.* commencement, begin-
ප්‍රාරම්භය, *Prárambhaya,* } ning.

ප්‍රාලම්බ, *Prálamba. s.* (ප්‍ර *pra* and අණ් *aṇ* aff. ලබි *labi* to hang or fall) garland hanging round the neck and reaching to the breast.

ප්‍රාලේය, *Praléya, s.* frost, dew, [Colloq. පිනි *pini*]: camphor, [Colloq. කපුරු *kapuru*].

ප්‍රාවාරණ, *Práwáraṇa, s.* cloak, upper garment. covering.

ප්‍රාශ්වාසය, *Práṣwásaya, s.* (ප්‍ර *pra* and ආශ්වාස *áṣwása* inspiration) expirated breath.

ප්‍රාස, *Prása, s.* (ප්‍ර *pra* and අස *asa* to throw) bearded dart.

ප්‍රාසඞ්ග, *Prásaṅga, s.* (ප්‍ර *pra* before, අණ් *aṇ* aff. සඤ්ජ *sañja* to join) yoke for cattle.

ප්‍රාසඞ්ගික, *Prásaṅgika, a.* inseparably connected with, incidental; inherent, innate, relevant, belonging to any topic.

ප්‍රාසාදය, *Prásádaya, s.* (ප්‍ර *pra* and අණ් *aṇ* aff. සද *sada* to go) temple, building consecrated to a deity; palace or the residence of a prince, mansion, storied house.

ප්‍රාසාරණ, *Prásáraṇa,* see ප්‍රසාරණ *prasáraṇa.*

ප්‍රිය, *Priya, s.* (ප්‍රී *prí* to please) love, affection; joy, pleasure, delight; husband: *a.* beloved.

ප්‍රියක, *Priyaka, s.* tree, *anthocephalus (or nauclea) cadamba,* [Colloq. කොළොම්ගස් *koḷom-gas*]: timber tree, *pentaptera tomentosa;* spotted deer, *axis maculata,* [Colloquial: තිත්මුවා *titmuwá*]: bee, (Family *apidæ,*) [Colloq. මීමැස්සා *mímessá*].

ප්‍රියකරණවා, *Priyakaraṇawá, v.* to please, to delight, to conciliate; to take a pleasure in.

ප්‍රියඞ්ගු, *Priyaṅgu, s.* (ප්‍රිය desired, ගම *gama* to go panic seed, millet, *setaria italicum,* [Colloq. තණහාල් *taṇa-hál*]; black mustard seed; long pepper, *piper longum,* [Colloq. තිප්පිලි *tippili*]; tree which produces fragrant flowers. (Sinhalese පුවඟු *puwaṅgu.*)

ප්‍රියතම, *Priyatama*, *s.* plant, *nothosœrua brachiata*, [Colloq. තම්පලා *tampalá*]: *a.* most dear, most beloved.

ප්‍රියතර, *Priyatara*, *a.* dearer, more beloved.

ප්‍රියතා, *Priyatá*, *s.* (ප්‍රිය beloved, තා aff. of the abstract) love, affection.

ප්‍රියදර්ශන, *Priyadarṣana*, *a.* (ප්‍රිය and දර්ශන appearance) handsome, beautiful, lovely, good or agreeable looking.

ප්‍රියවන්ත, *Priyawanta*, *a.* pleasing or pleasant.

ප්‍රියවර්ණ, *Priyawarṇa*, *s.* (ප්‍රිය pleasant, වර්ණ class,) creeping plant, *echites frutescens*.

ප්‍රියවාදී, *Priyawádí*, *a.* sweet-spoken, flattering.

ප්‍රියසඞ්ගම, *Priyasaṇgama*, *s.* (ප්‍රිය desired, සඞ්ගම union) friendship, union formed on principles of mutual delight.

ප්‍රියා, *Priyá*, *s.* wife, mistress; news, information; small cardamoms; Árabian jasmine; spirituous or vinous liquor.

ප්‍රියාල, *Priyála*, *s.* tree, *nephelium longana*, [Colloq. මොර *mora*].

ප්‍රියාව, *Priyáwa*, *s.* epithet for a wife expressive of fondness, equivalent to dear, beloved.

ප්‍රිෂ්ටපාසාන්තක, *Prishṭapásántaka*, *s.* tree, *zizyphus jujuba*, [Colloq. ඩෙබර *ḍebara* or මසන් *masan*]; corruptly for පිෂ්ටපාන්තකාරි *pishṭapántakarí*.

ප්‍රීණ, *Príṇa*, *a.* (ප්‍රී to please) pleased, satisfied; old, ancient.

ප්‍රීණන, *Príṇana*, *s.* satisfaction, satisfying, satiety.

ප්‍රීත, *Príta*, *a.* pleased, satisfied.

ප්‍රීති, *Príti*, *s.* joy, pleasure, gladness, happiness; love, affection, regard, attachment.

ප්‍රීතිද, *Prítida*, *s.* (ප්‍රීති joy, ද who gives) jester, buffoon, mimic: *a.* affectionate; inspiring joy or regard.

ප්‍රීතිපූර්වක, *Príti-púrwaka*, *adv.* through favour or kindness.

ප්‍රීතිමත්, *Prítimat*, *a.* (ප්‍රීති and මත් poss. aff.) glad, joyful, pleased, happy.

ප්‍රීතිමාලි, *Prítimálí*, *s.* tree, variety of *eugenia carophyllœa*, [Colloq. හෙලදම් *hela-dam*].

ප්‍රීතිය, *Prítiya*, *s.* joy.

ප්‍රීතිවාක්‍යය, *Príti-wákyaya*, *s.* (ප්‍රීති and වාක්‍යය speech) exclamation of joy uttered by Buddha on the day of his birth in his last incarnation during which he attained the sacred character: viz. "I am the chief of the world; I am the most excellent (being) of the world; I am the pre-eminent (being) of the world; this is my last birth, I shall no more transmigrate."

පෘථක්, *Pṛithak*, *ind.* again, other, different, [Coll: වෙන *wena*].

පෘථක්පර්ණී, *Pṛithakparṇni*, *s.* plant, *entada scandens*, [Colloq. පුස්වැන්න *puswẹnna*]; medicinal plant or shrub, *hydrocarpus venenata*, [Colloq. මකුළුවැන්න *makuḷuwẹnna*]; creeping plant, *ipomœa tridentata* or *angustifolia*, [Colloq. ආපසුමදු *ápasu-madu*].

පෘථක්ඵල, *Pṛithakphala*, *s.* (පෘථක් and ඵල fruit) plant, *gardenia*.

පෘථක්විධ, *Pṛithakvidha*, *a.* (පෘථක් again, විධ sort) various, multiform, of many sorts, [Colloq. නොයෙක් ආකාර *noyek-ákára*].

පෘථග්ජන, *Pṛithagjana*, *s.* (පෘථග් and ජන born) one subject to be born again, one not having subdued his passions and therefore liable to transmigration, one with natural passions; low man, mean vile wicked fellow, one following a degrading profession.

පෘථිවි, *Pṛithivi*, *s.* the earth, [Colloq. පොළව *poḷawa*].

පෘථිවීශ්වර, *Pṛithivíṣwara*, *s.* (පෘථිවි *pṛithavi*, and ඊශ්වර *íṣwara* a lord) king, monarch, sovereign, [Colloq. රජ *raja*].

පෘථු, *Pṛithu*, *s.* black cumin seed; opium: *a.* wide, extensive, broad spacious; great large.

පෘථුල, *Pṛithula*, *a.* (පෘථු extensive, ල to have) wide, broad, spacious, extensive, expanded, [Colloq. විසාල *visála*].

පෘථුවාර්තාකී *Pṛithuwártákí*, *s.* brinjal, *solanum melongena*, [Colloq. වම්බටු *wambaṭu*].

පෘථුවිකා, *Pṛithuviká*, *s.* Ceylon cardamoms, *elettaria cardamomum*, [Colloq. එන්සාල් *ensál*].

පෘථුවිකාලා, *Pṛithuvikálá*, *s.* black cummin seed, *nigella indica*, [Colloq. කළුදුරු *kaḷuduru*].

පෘථුවීජක, *Pṛithuvíjaka*, *s.* plant, *oroxylum indicum*, [Colloq. තොටිල *toṭila*].

පෘථුශෘඞ්ගී, *Pṣithuṣriṅgí*, *s.* tree, not ascertained, [Colloq. මහරි *mahari*].

පෘශ්නි, *Pṛiṣni*, *a.* small or diminutive, delicate, short, thin.

පෘෂ්ඨා, *Prishṭhá*, *s.* plant, peculiar to Ceylon, *wrightia zeylanica*, [Colloq. ඉද්ද *idda*].

ප්‍රේක්ෂණ, *Prékshaṇa*, *s.* (ප්‍ර *pra* before, ඊක්ෂ *iksha* to see) the eye, [Colloq. ඇහැ *ẹhẹ*]; looking, beholding.

ප්‍රේක්ෂණීය, *Prékshaṇíya*, *a.* (ප්‍ර *pra* and ඊක්ෂ *iksha* අනීයර් *aníyar* aff.) to be looked at, visible, apparent.

ප්‍රේක්‍ෂා, *Prékshá*, *s.* (ප්‍ර *pra* and ඊක්‍ෂ *íksha* to see) intellect, understanding; viewing, looking, observing, seeing.

ප්‍රේක්‍ෂිත, *Prékshita*, *a.* seen, beheld, looked at.

ප්‍රේත්‍ය, *Prétya*, *adv.* in the next world: *part.* having died.

ප්‍රේත, *Préta*, *s.* (ප්‍ර *pra* before, ඉත *ita* gone) ghost, goblin, sprite, an evil being especially animating the carcases of the dead; manes of deceased ancestors: *a.* dead, extinct, expired; disembodied.

ප්‍රේතකම, *Prétakama*, *s.* (ප්‍රේත sprite, කම an act) nature or disposition of a sprite, but especially applied to the actions of any low, vile wretch.

ප්‍රේතකර්ම, *Prétakarma*, ප්‍රේතකාර්‍ය, *Prétakárya*, ප්‍රේතකෘත්‍ය, *Prétakṛitya*, *s.* funeral or obsequial rites.

ප්‍රේතපති, *Prétapati*, *s.* (ප්‍රේත disembodied spirits, පති chief) name of Yama, regent of the dead.

ප්‍රේතයා, *Prétayá*, *s.* evil spirit, hobgoblin, applied also to filthy persons: see ප්‍රේත *préta*.

ප්‍රේතලෝක, *Pretalóka*, *s.* region of disembodied spirits.

ප්‍රේතවන, *Prétawana*, *s.* (ප්‍රේත and වන wood) burying ground, cemetery, place where bodies are burnt or buried, [Colloq. සොහොන *sohona*].

ප්‍රේත වස්තුව, *Préta-wastuwa*, *s.* (ප්‍රේත disembodied spirit, sprite, වස්තු history) name of a sútra of Buddha, included in the කුදුගොත්සඟිය *kudugot-sangiya*, the fifth division of the Sútra piṭaka: see පිටක *piṭaka*.

ප්‍රේතාන්න, *Prétánna*, *s.* (ප්‍රේත *préta* ghost, අන්න *anna* food) food offered to the manes.

ප්‍රේම, *Préma*, *s.* love, affection, esteem, regard, attachment.

ප්‍රේමවන්ත, *Prémawanta*, *a.* (ප්‍රේම love, වන්ත poss. aff.) loving, affectionate.

ප්‍රේමවන්තයා, *Prémawantayá*, *s.* beloved one, friend.

ප්‍රේයස්, *Préyas*, *a.* (ප්‍රිය *priya* affection) dearest, most dear, most beloved.

ප්‍රේරණ, *Préraṇa*, *s.* (ප්‍ර *pra* before, ඊර *íra* to go) sending, directing; passion, operation of the organs of sense.

ප්‍රේරිත, *Prérita*, *a*, sent, dispatched, directed.

ප්‍රේරිතයා, *Préritayá*, *s.* (ප්‍රේරිත sent, යා pers, aff.) apostle, messenger.

ප්‍රේෂණ, *Préshaṇa*, *s.* (ප්‍ර *pra* before, ඉෂ *isha* to go) sending, dispatching.

ප්‍රේෂිත, *Préshita*, *a.* sent, dispatched.

ප්‍රෛශුන්‍ය, *Praiśúnya*, *s.* (ප්‍රිය *priya* attachment, ශුන්‍ය breaking, destroying) slander; tale bearing, backbiting, calumny, [Colloq. කේලාම් *kélám*]; corrupt form of පෛශුන්‍ය *paiṣunya*.

ප්‍රෝක්ත, *Prókta*, *a.* (ප්‍ර *pra* before, උක්ත said) said, uttered, declared, [Colloq. කිවු *kiwu*].

ප්‍රෝෂ්ඨපදා, *Próshṭhapadá*, *s.* (ප්‍රෝෂ්ඨ here said to mean an ox, පද *pada* foot) one of the constellations; according to one system it is the twenty-sixth, but according to another it is the twenty-seventh; it contains stars in the wing of Pegasus.

ප්‍රෝහිත, *Próhita*, corruption of පුරෝහිත *puróhita*.

ප්ලක්‍ෂ, *Plaksha*, *s.* the waved-leaf fig tree, *ficus arnottiana*, [Colloq. පුළිල *pulila* and කවුඩුබෝ *kawuḍubó*]; holy fig tree, *ficus religiosa*, [Coll: බෝ ගහ *bó-gaha*]; tulip tree, *thespesia populnea*, [Colloq. සූරිය *súriya*].

ප්ලව, *Plawa*, *s.* (ප්ලව to go) jumping, leaping, going by leaps or plunging; swimming, diving; raft, float; frog; monkey; bird, sort of diver; continuous protracted accent, lengthened sound of vowels in poetry; protracting a sentence through several stanzas; declivity, shelving ground; thirty-sixth year of the Indian cycle.

ප්ලවක, *Plawaka*, *s.* (ප්ලව *plawa* to tumble etc.) tumbler, dancer, rope dancer, one who walks on the edge of a sword; plant, [Colloq. රුක්අඟුන *ruk-anguna*].

ප්ලවග, *Plawaga*, ප්ලවඞ්ග, *Plawaṅga*, *s.* (ප්ලව tumbling, ග who goes) monkey, ape; frog.

ප්ලවඞ්ගම, *Plawaṅgama*, *s.* forty-first year of the Indian cycle of sixty; see also ප්ලවග *plawaga*.

ප්ලවාකා, *Plawáká*, *s.* ප්ලව *plawa* tossing, අක *aka* what goes) float, raft.

ප්ලාවින්, *Plávin*, *s.* (ප්ලව *plawa* going, ඉන් *in* aff.) bird, bird in general, [Colloq. කුරුල්ලා *kurullá*].

ප්ලිහන්, *Plihan*, *s.* (ප්ලිහ to enlarge) the spleen, [Colloq. බඩදිව *baḍadiwa*].

ප්ලිහනාශන, *Plihanáśana*, ප්ලිහනාශිනී, *Plihanáśiní*, *s.* coral tree, *erythrina indica*, [Colloq. එරබදු *erabadu*].

ප්ලීහඝ්න, *Plíhaghna*, ප්ලීහාරි, *Plihári*, *s.* (ප්ලීහ *plíha* spleen, ඝ්න what destroys, or අරි *ari* enemy) medicinal plant, *andersonia rohituka Rox.*; bó-tree, *ficus religiosa*, [Colloq. බෝ *bó*].

ප්ලුත, *Pluta*, *s.* (ප්ලු to go by leaps, ක්ත *kta* aff.) third sound given to vowels, the protracted or continuous sound, being three times the length of the short vowel and occupying three moments in its utterance.

ප්ලුෂ්ට, *Plushṭa, a.* burnt.

ප්ලුෂ, *Plusha, s.* (ප්ලුෂ to burn) burning, consuming, conflagration.

ඵ

The twenty-second consonant of the Siṇhalese alphabet, the aspirate of the preceding letter and usually expressed in English characters by *ph*, (not as sounded in physic, but as heard in up-hill).

ඵ *Pha, s.* wind expelled in yawning; increasing, swelling, enlarging.

ඵට, *Phaṭa, s.* expanded hood of the cobra de capello.

ඵණ්ඩ, *Phaṇḍa, s.* belly, [Colloq. බඩ *baḍa*].

ඵණ, *Phaṇa*, see ඵට *phaṭa*.

ඵණකර, *Phaṇakara, s.* (ඵණ hood, කර what makes) snake, especially, the cobra de capello, *naja tripudians*, [Colloq. නයා *nayá*].

ඵණී, *Phaṇi, s.* serpent; expanded hood of the cobra de capello; name of plant priyaṅgu: see ප්‍රියඞ්ගු *priyaṅgu*.

ඵණිජිහ්වා, *Phaṇijihwá, s.* creeping plant, *asparagus falcatus*, [Colloq. හාතාවාරිය *hátáwáriya*].

ඵණිජිහ්විකා, *Phaṇijihviká, s.* sarsaparilla, *hemidesmus indicus*, [Colloq. ඉරමුසු *iramusu*].

ඵණිලතා, *Phaṇilatá*, } s. plant, *piper betel*, [Coll:
ඵණිවල්ලී, *Phaṇiwallí*, } බුලත්වැල් *bulat-wel*].

ඵණීන්ද්‍ර, *Phaṇíndra, s.* (ඵණී *phaṇi* snake, ඉන්ද්‍ර *indra* chief) name of Ráhu the ascending node; also of Ananta king of the Nágalóka.

ඵරශුව, *Pharasuwa, s.* axe, hatchet, [Colloq. පොරොව *porowa*].

ඵල්ගු, *Phalgu, s.* falsehood; sort of fig tree, *ficus hispida* var. *oppositifolia*, [Colloq. කොටදිඹුලා *koṭadimbulá*]; spring season: *a.* pithless, sapless; vain, unmeaning, unprofitable; useless; false, of lying speech.

ඵල්ගුණ, *Phalguṇa, s.* mace, spice, [Colloq. වසාවාසි *wasáwási*].

ඵල්ගුන, *Phalguna, s.* the eleventh and twelfth constellations or lunar asterisms; month so called (March–April); large tree chiefly growing on the banks of rivers, *terminalia alata*.

ඵල්ලවය, *Phallawaya, s.* leaf, leaf of any plant or tree; properly written පල්ලව *pallawa*.

ඵල, *Phala, s.* fruit, fruit in general; fruit (metaphorically), result, produce, consequence; prosperity; gain, profit, acquisition; shield; blade of a sword; ploughshare; furrow made by a plough; nutmeg; menstrual discharge; knowledge of the source of rewards and punishments, *i. e.* the tracing of good received or evil suffered to particular actions performed in a former birth; anything enjoyed or suffered as the effect of some predisposing cause; parts of generation; cotton.

ඵලංකසා, *Phalaṅkasá, s.* plant, species of *barleria*; black variety of the *aquilaria agallocha* or aloe-wood; gum or gum resin; sealing-wax; plant, *acanthus ilicifolius*, [Colloq. ගොකටු *gokaṭu*].

ඵලක්ෂීරි, *Phalakshíri, s.* (ඵල *phala* fruit, ක්ෂීර *kshira* milk) plant called mudar, kind of swallow wort, *calotropis (*or *asclepias) gigantea*, [Colloq. වරා *wará*].

ඵලක, *Phalaka, s.* (ඵල to split or divide) shield; bone, the *os frontis* or bone of the forehead; iron-wood tree, *mesua ferrea*, [Colloq. නාගහ *ná-gaha*]; leaf or page for writing on, small table, bench, plank; buttocks.

ඵලකපාණී, *Phalakapáṇi, s.* (ඵලක shield, පාණී hand) soldier armed with a shield.

ඵලකය, *Phalakaya*, see ඵලක *phalaka*.

ඵලකේශර, *Phalakéśara, s.* (ඵල fruit, කේශර hair) coconut tree, fruit being covered with a fibrous coat like hair, [Colloq. පොල්ගහ *pol-gaha*].

ඵලගණ්ඩ, *Phalagaṇḍa, s.* carpenter, [Colloq. වඩුවා *waḍuwá*].

ඵලඞ්ගු, *Phalaṅgu, a.* unfruitful, unprofitable, vain, unproductive; corruptly for ඵල්ගු *phalgu*].

ඵලත්‍රය, *Phalatraya, s.* (ඵල fruit, ත්‍රය three) three sorts of fruit collectively, as fruit of the vine, *parush*, and *gmelina arborea*, [Colloq. ඇත්දෙමට *et-demaṭa*]; three myrobalans, viz. අරළු *araḷu*, බුළු *buḷu*, නෙල්ලි *nelli*.

ඵලත්‍රික, *Phalatrika, s.* (ඵල and ත්‍රික threefold) the three myrobalans collectively, [Colloquial: තිපල් *tipal*], *i. e. terminalia chebula*, [Colloq. අරළු *araḷu*]; *t. belerica*, [Colloq. බුළු *buḷu*]; *phyllanthus emblica*, [Colloq. නෙල්ලි *nelli*].

ඵලතර, *Phalatara, a.* (ඵල and තර abounding) abounding in fruit, exceedingly fruitful or productive.

ඵලද, *Phalada, s.* (ඵල fruit, ද what gives) tree, [Colloq. ගහ *gaha*]: *a.* fruitful, yielding fruit.

ඵලදර, *Phaladara, a.* (ඵල and දර having) fruitful, yielding fruit in due season, bearing fruit.

ඵලදෙන, *Phaladena, a.* (ඵල and දෙන giving) fruitful, productive, successful.

ඵලනාසන, *Phalanásana*, *s.* common medicinal plant, *acanthus ilicifolius;* also called *ikiri* and *gokaṭu*.

ඵලනි, *Phalaní*, *s.* beleric myrobalan, *terminalia belerica*, [Colloq. බුළු *buḷu*].

ඵලපාක, *Phalapáka*, *s.* ripening of fruit.

ඵලපාකාන්තා, *Phalapákántá*, *s.* (ඵල fruit, පාක *páka* ripening, අන්ත *anta* end; dying after bearing fruit) any annual plant.

ඵලපූර, *Phalapúra*, ඵලපූරක, *Phalapúraka*, } *s.* (ඵල and පූර full) common citron, *citrus medica*, [Colloq. ලප්නාරං *lapnáraṇ*]; pomegranate, *punica granatum*, [Colloq. දෙළුම් *deḷum*].

ඵලප්‍රාප්ති, *Phalaprápti*, *s.* (ඵල and ප්‍රාප්ති attainment) acquirement of rank or dignity: *a.* obtaining the desired result.

ඵලය, *Phalaya*, see ඵල *phala*.

ඵලවත්, *Phalawat*, see ඵලවාන් *phalawán*.

ඵලවල්ලී, *Phalawallí*, *s.* ash-pumpkin, *benincasa cerifera*, [Colloq. පුහුල් *puhul*].

ඵලවාන්, *Phalawán*, *a.* (ඵල and වාන් poss. aff.) fruitful, yielding or giving fruit.

ඵලවිනාශිනි, *Phala-vináṣiní*, *s.* (ඵල and විනාශිනි who destroys) parrot, *palæornis eupatrius*, [Coll: ගිරවා *girawá*].

ඵලවෘක්ෂ, *Phala-vṛiksha*, *s.* (ඵල and වෘක්ෂ tree) any tree yielding fruit.

ඵලස්‍යක, *Phalasyáka*, *s.* tree, *adhatoda vasica* or *justicia adhatoda*, [Colloquial: අගල් අඩුර *agal-ádára*]: see ඵාලි *pháli*.

ඵලස, *Phalasa*, *s.* (ඵල and සහ *saha* to bear) the bread fruit tree, *artocarpus incisa*, [Colloq. රට දෙල් *raṭa-del*]; jack fruit tree, *a. integrifolia*, [Colloq. කොස් *kos*].

ඵලසමාධි, *Phala-samádhi*, *s.* (ඵල fruit, gain, සමාධි tranquillity) state of mental tranquillity resulting from the performance of religious duties and the acquirement of religious attainments.

ඵලාධ්‍යක්ෂ, *Phaládhyaksha*, *s.* (ඵල *phala* and අධ්‍යක්ෂ *adhyaksha* superintendant) according to one authority a species of *mimosa;* according to another *mimusops kauki;* but also applied to several plants yielding a milky or juicy sap upon expression or incision.

ඵලාඵල, *Phaláphala*, *s.* fruit in general, the whole genera of fruits.

ඵලාරඪ, *Phaláraḍha*, ඵලාරාඪ, *Phaláráḍha*, } *s.* (ඵල *phala* and රාඪ beauty) plant, the *gardenia*.

ඵලාරාම, *Phalaráma*, *s.* (ඵල *phala* and ආරාම *aráma* garden) orchard, fruit garden.

ඵලාශන, *Phaláṣana*, *s.* (ඵල *phala* fruit, අශන *aṣana* food) parrot: see ඵලවිනාශිනි *phala-vináṣiní*.

ඵලාස, *Phalása*, *s.* palas tree, *butea frondosa*, [Colloq. ගස්කැල *gas-kẹla*]; sometimes written පලාශ *paláṣa*.

ඵලාහාර, *Phaláhára*, *s.* (ඵල *phala* and ආහාර *áhára* food) parrot; edible fruit.

ඵලි, *Phali*, *s.* (ඵල *phala* and ඉනි *ini* aff,) fruit tree, any tree bearing fruit.

ඵලික, *Phalika*, *a.* (ඵල *phala* and ඉක *ika* aff.) belonging to fruit trees, possessing the qualities of fruit trees.

ඵලිත, *Phalita*, *s.* small tree, *streblus asper* or *trophis aspera*, [Colloq. ගැටනිටුල් *gẹtaniṭul*].

ඵලින්, *Phalin*, *a.* (ඵල *phala* and ඉනි *ini* aff.) bearing fruit, fruitful.

ඵලිනි, *Phaliní*, *s.* tree, *myristica horsfieldia*, [Coll: රුක්ගස *ruk-gasa*].

ඵලෙරුහා, *Phaleruhá*, *s.* (ඵල *phala* fruit, in the seventh or locative case, රුහ *ruha* to grow) trumpet flower, *stereospermum suaveolens*, [Colloq. පළොල් *paḷol*].

ඵලෝත්කට, *Phalótkaṭa*, *s.* plant, *phyllanthus niruri*, [Colloq. පිටවක්කා *piṭawakká*].

ඵලෝදය, *Phalódaya*, *s.* (ඵල *phala* fruit, උදය *udaya* rising) gain, profit; heaven, paradise; joy, happiness.

ඵස්ස, *Phassa*, *s.* feeling, touch. (Páli.)

ඵාණිත, *Pháṇita*, *s.* sugar candy; kind of candied jaggery or raw sugar; juice of the sugar cane, [Colloq. උක්පැණි *ukpẹni*].

ඵාණ්ට, *Pháṇṭa*, *a.* (ඵණ *phaṇa* to prepare easily) readily prepared, made by an extemporaneous easy process, (decoctions etc.)

ඵාල්ගුනික, *Phálgunika*, *s.* (ඵල්ගුනි *phalguni* asterism in this month, ඉක *ika* aff.) month so called; also Mẹdindina, (March–April), and the last of the Siṇhalese year.

ඵාල, *Phála*, *s.* name of Ṣiva; name of Balaráma; share of a plough: *a.* made of cotton, (a vesture etc.)

ඵාලි, *Pháli*, *s.* that which is made of cotton, vesture, cotton cloth; small tree, *justicia adhatoda:* see ඵලස්‍යක *phalasyáka*.

ඵාලින්දි, *Phálindi*, *s.* large Barbadoes or Bourbon cotton tree, *gossypium barbadense;* plant, *ipomœa* or *convolvulus turpethum*, [Colloq. ත්‍රස්තවාලු *trastawálu*]; creeping plant, *cardiospermum halicacabum*, [Colloq. පෙනෙලවැල් *penela-węl*].

ඵාසු, *Phásu*, see පාසු *pásu*.

ඵි, *Phi*, *s.* rage, wrath, anger, [Colloq. තරහ *taraha*, උදහස *udahasa*].

ඵුල්ල, *Phulla*, *a.* expanded, blown, opened as a flower.

ඵුල්ලි, *Phulli*, *s.* blowing, blossoming.

ඵේන, *Phéna*, *s.* froth, foam; cuttle-fish bone, supposed to be the indurated foam of the sea, [Colloq. මුහුදු පෙණ *muhudu-peṇa*].

ඵේනක, *Phénaka*, *s.* (ඵේන froth, ක aff.) cuttle-fish bone.

ඵේනල, *Phénala*, *s.* (ඵේන and ලා *lá* to have) soap-berry plant, *sapindus emarginatus*, [Colloq. පෙනෙල *penela*]; fruit of the *zizyphus jujuba*, [Colloq. මසන් *masan*]; also, fruit of the *vangueria spinosa*: *a.* frothy, foamy.

ඵේනමාලා, *Phéna-málá*, *s.* (ඵේන foam, මාලා garland) foam of the extended breaker on the sea shore.

ඵේනිල, *Phéníla*, *s.* soap-berry plant, *sapindus emarginatus*: see ඵේනල *phénala*.

ඵේර, *Phéra*, ඵේරව, *Phérawa*, ඵේරු, *Phéru*, } *s.* (ඵේ imitative sound, රු to utter) jackal, *canis aureus*, [Colloq. නරියා *nariyá*].

ඵේලක, *Phélaka*, ඵේලා, *Phélá*, ඵේලි, *Phéli*, } *s.* orts, leavings of a meal or droppings of the mouth, leavings.

බ

The twenty-third consonant of the Siŋhalese alphabet, corresponding to the letter *b*; considerable difficulties arise from a custom which has gained both among authors and copyists substituting the බ *ba* for ව *wa* and vice versa.

බ, *Ba*, *s.* water jar; name of Varuṇa, the regent of water.

බක්, *Bak*, *s.* father (corruptly for බප් *bap*); month so called, first of the Siŋhalese year, (April–May).

බක්ක, *Bakka*, *s.* that which is big, bulky, large, vast.

බක්කන්, *Bakkan*, *a.* large, plump, clumsy.

බක්කා, *Bakká*, *s.* (බක්ක *bakka* big, ආ *á* masculine aff.) big man or any enormous animal.

බක්කිය, *Bakkiya*, *s.* box (from Dutch bakji).

බක්ත, *Bakta*, *s.* boiled rice, properly written භක්ත *bhakta*.

බක් මස, *Bak-masa*, see බක් *bak*.

බක්මි, *Bakmí*, *s.* tree, *sarcocephalus cordatus* (or *nauclea coadunata*) (*Rubiaceæ*).

බක, *Baka*, *s.* crane, Indian crane, or paddy bird, [Colloq. කොකා *koká*]; sort of stork; noted Asura or demon so called.

බකබඹ, *Bakabamba*, බකබ්‍රාහ්ම, *Bakabráhma*, } *s.* noted Bráhma whom Buddha encountered in his preaching mission to the Brahma lóka.

බකමුහුනා, *Bakamuhuná*, බකමූනා, *Bakamúná*, } *s.* general name of the owl, especially the brown fish owl, *ketupa Ceylonesis* (*Striges*, order *Accipitres*).

බකමූනු තණ, *Bakamúnu-taṇa*, *s.* plant, peculiar to Ceylon, *scleria Neesii*, (*Cyperaceæ*).

බකල, *Bakala*, *a.* distorted, disfigured; bow-legged, bandy-legged.

බකලගහනවා, *Bokalagahanawá*, *v.* to limp; to walk distortedly.

බකලයා, *Bakalayá*, *s.* man or any animal with distorted or disfigured limbs.

බකාඞ්ගනාව, *Bakáṅganáwa*, *s.* (බක *baka* crane, අඞ්ගනාව *aṅganáwa* female) female crane.

බකාරාදේසය, *Bakárádésaya*, *s.* substitution of the letter බ "*ba*."

බකෝට, *Bakóṭa*, *s.* Indian crane, commonly called the paddy bird; stork: see බක *baka*.

බග, *Baga*, *s.* pudendum muliebre; month called බක්මස *bak-masa*, (March–April.)

බගන්තරාව, *Bagantaráwa*, බගන්දරාව, *Bagandaráwa*, } *s.* disease, inflamed tumour, between the anus and the testicles; fistula in ano.

බගවත්, *Bagawat*, *s.* name of Buddha, [Colloq. බුදුන් *budun*], incorrectly for භගවත් *bhagawat*.

බඟය, *Baŋgaya*, *s.* spreading shrub, *eclipta* (or *verbesina*) *erecta*, [Colloq. කිකිරිඳිය *kíkiriŋdiya*].

බඟහර, *Baŋgahara*, *s.* kind of toddy or vinous preparation; intoxicating liquor; arrack, [Colloq. රා *rá*, අරක්කු *arakku*].

බජනය, *Bajanaya*, *s.* association, union; embracing, an embrace.

බට්ටා, *Baṭṭá*, *s.* seeds of the creeper, *cæsalpinia memosoides*, in English *brasiletto*; they are used in playing a certain game.

බට්ටිච්චියා, *Baṭṭichchiyá*, *s.* name of several species of bird, Ceylonese scimitar babbler, *pomatorhinus melanurus;* white-throated wren babbler. *dumetia albogularis;* Ceylon wren babbler, *alcippe nigrifrons;* whistling quaker babbler, *pellorneum fuscicapillum;* black-billed babbler, *pyctorhis nasalis (Timaliidæ,* order *Passeres).*

බට, *Baṭa, s.* plant, small species of bamboo: see බටලී *baṭa-lí;* an army; descent, going down, descent from a height; the west: *a.* sunk as in mud, descended.

බට කපුරු, *Baṭa-kapuru, s.* manna of the small bambu or reed.

බට කිරිල්ල, *Baṭa-kirilla, s.* plant peculiar to Ceylon, *erythroxylon lucidum (Linaceæ).*

බටගොයා, *Baṭugoyá, s.* Imperial green pigeon, *carpophaga ænea,* also called මහනිලගොයා *maha-nílagoyá;* orange-breasted green pigeon, *osmotreron bicincta;* pompadour green pigeon, *o. pompadoura, (Threronidæ,* order *Columbæ):* pl. බටගොයි *baṭagoy.*

බට තණ, *Baṭa-taṇa, s.* plant of the order *Gramineæ.*

බටදණ්ඩ, *Baṭadaṇḍa, s.* (බට bamboo, දණ්ඩ stick) the bamboo cane cut away and ready for use as to build fences etc: pl බටදඬු *baṭadanḍu;* sometimes written, බටලීය *baṭalíya.*

බටදොඹ, *Baṭadomba, s.* tree, *eugenia operculata* or *syzygium nervosum (Myrtaceæ):* also called කොබෝමල් *kobó-mal.*

බටදෙල් තණ, *Baṭadeḷ-taṇa, s.* plant of the order *Gramineæ.*

බටදෙල්ල, *Baṭadeḷla, s.* panic grass, *panicum repens.*

බටනිල, *Baṭanila, s.* privy, [Colloq. කක්කුස්සිය *kakkussiya*].

බටපොතුපීර, *Baṭapotu-píra, s.* kind of file.

බටයා, *Baṭayá, s.* kind of fish.

බටලී, *Baṭalí, s.* small species of bamboo or bamboo cane, peculiar to Ceylon, *ochlandra stridula (Gramineæ).*

බටහිර, *Baṭahira, s.* (බට descending, හිර sun) setting sun; also, quarter in which the sun sets, the west.

බටු, *Baṭu, s.* plant, small kind of brinjal used in making curry; the night shade, of which there are about twenty-four species and varieties in Ceylon, genus *solanum.*

බටු ඇල්වී, *Baṭu-eḷví, s.* variety of paddy, *oriza sativa.*

බටු කරවිල, *Baṭu-karavila, s.* plant, *momordica muricata.*

බටුකිරියල්වී, *Baṭukiriyal-ví, s.* kind of paddy.

බටුගහ, *Baṭu-gaha, s.* brinjal plant, prickly nightshade, *solanum.*

බටුගිනිකුරුල්ලා, *Baṭu-ginikurullá, s.* bird called little minevet, *pericrocotus peregrinus, (Campophagidæ,* order *Passeres);* also called කොස් කුරුල්ලා *kos-kurullá.*

බටුගිරවා, *Baṭugirawá, s.* blossom-headed parakeet. *palæornis cyanocephalus* (order *Psittaci):* pl. බටුගිරව් *baṭugiraw.*

බඩ, *Baḍa, s.* belly, abdomen; womb.

බඩ අමු, *Baḍa-amu, s.* kind of amu or *paspalum.*

බඩ ඇරෙණවා, *Baḍa-ęreṇawá,* see බඩ උගුලනවා *baḍa-ugulanawá.*

බඩ ඇවිලෙනවා, *Baḍa-ęvilenawá, v.* to be subject to a shooting pain in the belly.

බඩ ඉගිලීම, *Baḍa-igilíma, s.* looseness, diarrhœa.

බඩ ඉරිඟු, *Baḍa-iringu, s.* species of maize.

බඩ උගුලනවා, *Baḍa-ugulanawá, v.* (බඩ belly, උගුලනවා to root up) to purge, to suffer from diarrhœa or looseness: pret. බඩඉගුලුවා *baḍa-iguluwá.* (Vulgar.)

බඩකඩහුව, *Baḍakaḍahuwa,* }
බඩකඩුත්තුව, *Baḍakaḍuttuwa,* } *s.* (බඩ and කඩුත්තුව flux) dysentry, diarrhœa. (Vulgar.)

බඩ ගසායනවා, *Baḍa-gasáyanawá, v.* to suffer from dysentery, diarrhœa or copious purging.

බඩගානවා, *Baḍagánawá, v.* to go on the belly, to creep.

බඩගා යනවා, *Baḍagá-yanawá, v.* to go or move on the belly, to creep as serpents, reptiles etc.

බඩගින්න, *Baḍaginna, s.* (බඩ belly (stomach), ගින්න fire for bilious humour) hunger.

බඩගිනි, *Baḍagini, a.* hungry, suffering from hunger.

බඩජාරි, *Baḍa-jári, a.* greedy, gluttonous, voracious, ravenous.

බඩජහරියා, *Baḍajahariyá, s.* greedy man, glutton, gormandizer, one of a gluttonous appetite.

බඩතුර, *Baḍatura, s.* front part of the waist, bend of the belly; place between the waist and the cloth of a native which he uses as a pocket or purse: pl. බඩතුරු *baḍaturu.*

බඩදරු, *Baḍadaru, a.* (බඩ and දරු child) pregnant, having the fœtus formed.

බඩදිව, *Baḍa-diwa, s.* (බඩ belly, දිව tongue) the spleen.

බඩදෙල් කොකා, *Baḍadeḷ-koká, s.* large white egret, *Herodius alba, (Ardeidæ,* order *Herodiones).*

බඩදූවිල්ල, *Baḍa-devilla*, *s.* (බඩ and දූවිල්ල burning) inflammation of the bowels, severe belly ache, colic, excessive hunger.

බඩපණුවා, *Baḍa-paṇuwá*, *s.* worm produced within the bowels of man.

බඩපතු, *Baḍapatu*, *s.* side of the belly; part of the body between the ribs and the hip.

බඩපිස්සා, *Baḍapissá*, *s.* (බඩ womb, පිස්සා who sweeps) last child, or the last born of any animal.

බඩපුතු, *Baḍaputu*, *s.* (බඩ and පුතු child) embryo, fœtus.

බඩපුප්පන්නා, *Baḍapuppanná*. *s.* one who puffs up or bloats his belly.

බඩපුරාම, *Baḍapuráma*, *adv.* bellyful.

බඩබන්කඩ, *Baḍabankaḍa*, *s.* cloth tied round the belly or waist.

බඩබැඳගණ ඉනනවා, *Baḍabendagaṇa-innawá*, *v.* to show the most tender affection, to be clasped in an embrace.

බඩබැඳිම, *Baḍabendíma*, *s.* (බඩ and බැඳිම binding) verbal noun of the foregoing; also, waistband.

බඩමද, *Baḍamada*, *s.* (බඩ and මද pith) pith of a tree or plant; pulp of fruit.

බඩමාළු, *Baḍamálu*, *s.* (බඩ and මාළු fish) inside of a fish, the edible part of the entrails of fish.

බඩයනවා, *Baḍayanawá*, see බඩඋගුලනවා *baḍa-ugulanawá*.

බඩයාම, *Baḍayáma*, verbal noun of the foregoing.

බඩරලා, *Baḍaralá*, *s.* kind of fish.

බඩරුජාව, *Baḍarujáwa*, } *s.* (බඩ and රුජ to ache)
බඩරුදාව, *Baḍarudáwa*, } pain in the belly, gripes; colic; pains of labour.

බඩල්වනස්ස, *Baḍalwanassa*, *s.* club moss, *lycopodium cernuum, (Lycopodiaceæ);* also called වනස්ස *wanassa*.

බඩල්වැඩ, *Baḍal-weḍa*, *s.* trade of a gold and silver smith.

බඩලෙඩ, *Baḍa-leḍa*, *s.* (බඩ bowels, ලෙඩ disease) dysentery; diarrhœa; any disease of the bowels.

බඩව්, *Baḍaw*, *s.* kind of sea fish.

බඩවත, *Baḍawata*, *s.* front part of the abdomen; the external part of a tree.

බඩවරා, *Baḍawará*, *s.* kind of fish.

බඩවිම, *Baḍavíma*, *s.* pregnancy. (Vulgar.)

බඩවෙටිය, *Baḍaweṭiya*, *s.* fence or line of bushes, (especially thorn bushes) or small plants thickly set, and serving as a protection for a field or garden.

බඩවෙළිම, *Baḍa-wélima*, *s.* (බඩ and වෙළිම drying) costiveness, constipated bowels.

බඩවැටිය, *Baḍaweṭiya*, *s.* bush, thicket, fence or boundary consisting of impermeable bushes or thickets.

බඩවැල, *Baḍawela*, *s.* (බඩ belly, වැල creeper) intestines, entrails.

බඩසාය, *Baḍasáya*, *s.* hunger.

බඩහැර, *Baḍahera*, *s.* store keeper, man who takes care of a treasury, etc.

බඩහැලයා, *Baḍahelayá*, *s.* potter, man who makes chatties or earthen cooking vessels.

බඩාලා, *Báḍálá*, *s.* gold or silver smith, or a man of that caste: pl. බඩල්ලු *baḍallu*.

බඩින්යනවා, *Baḍinyanawá*, *v.* (බඩින් belly, in the ablative, යනවා to go) to have an involuntary motion.

බඩිල, *Baḍila*, *s.* tamarind tree, *tamarindus indica*, [Colloq. සියඹලා *siyambalá*].

බඩු, *Baḍu*, } *s.* movables, goods, effects,
බඩුමුට්ටු, *Baḍumúṭṭu*, } property; baggage.

බඩුව, *Baḍuwa*, *s.* article, thing: see the last.

බඩේ, *Baḍé*. *s.* pith of a tree or plant.

බඩේ ඇම්ම, *Baḍé-emma*, *s.* colic.

බණ්ඩක්කා, *Banḍakká*, *s.* plant with mucilaginous edible capsules, *hibiscus esculentus*.

බණ්ඩා, *Banḍá*, *s.* son, boy, youth; son of a chief.

බණ්ඩාර, *Banḍára*, *s.* son of a chief or nobleman, prince, a term used only in the Kandian provinces.

බණ, *Baṇa*, *s.* arrow; sound, noise; sacred writings of the Buddhists; the word of Buddha.

බණසු, *Baṇásu*, *s.* (බණ *baṇa* arrow, අසු *asu* to throw) bow, [Colloq. දුන්න *dunna*].

බත්, *Bat*, *s.* boiled or cooked rice.

බත්උල, *Batula*, *s.* (බත් and උල grain) grain of boiled rice.

බත් උයනවා, *Bat-uyanawá*, *v.* to cook or boil rice.

බත් කනවා, *Bat-kanawá*, *v.* (බත් and කනවා to eat) to eat rice, to dine.

බත්කිතුල, *Bat-kitula*, *s.* variety of the Malabar sago palm, *caryota urens*, [Colloq. කිතුල් *kitul*].

බත්කෙණ්ඩ, *Batkenḍa*, *s.* calf of the leg: pl. බත්කෙණ්ඩා *batkenḍá*.

බත්තනරාල, *Battanarála*, *s.* (බත්තන and රාල master) superintendent or overseer of the kitchen.

බත්දෙනවා, *Bat-denawá*, *v.* to give boiled rice.

බත්පිඩු, *Batpiḍu*, *s.* (බත් and පිඩු ball) ball of boiled rice, mouthful, as much as can be put in the mouth at once.

* බණකියනවා, *Baṇa-kiyanawá*, *v.* to read the Buddhist scriptures; to preach the Baṇa; to speak unintelligibly.

* බණකොත, *Baṇa-kota*, *s.* (බණ and කොත cupola) tower or cupola of the baṇa maḍuwa or temporary building where the baṇa is read.

* බණනවා, *Baṇanawá*, *v.* to speak, to say, to deliver an oration.

* බණපොත, *Baṇapota*, see බණ *baṇa*.

* බණමඩුව, *Baṇa-maḍuwa*, *s.* (බණ and මඩුව bungalow) temporary building for reading the baṇa or sacred books of Buddhism, on which occasion offerings are made to the priests, great numbers of whom generally attend and receive presents according to their rank in the priesthood.

* බණරුපු, *Baṇarupu*, *s.* name of Vishṇu.

* බණවරය, *Baṇa-waraya*, *s.* (බණ and වර *wara* turn) a turn at reading the baṇa; it is usual when the baṇa is read to continue the exercise through the night, when the priests take it in turns; the time employed by one priest in reading or repeating is called baṇawara.

* බණවසුන්, *Baṇawasun*, *s.* (බණ and වසුන් covering, a cover) bag made of silk or any painted cloth in which to keep the books of the baṇa: any cloth wrapper or cover for books.

* බණිනවා, *Baṇinawá*, *v.* to abuse, to revile; to rail, to cavil; to insult: pret. බැණනා *beṇná*.

බත්මඟුල, *Bat-magula*, *s.* feast on the occasion of feeding babies with rice for the first time.

බත්මෙවඩනවා, *Batméwaḍanawá*, *v.* to eat rice, said only of persons of rank.

බත්හික්, *Bat-hik*, *s.* small tree with astringent leaves, *elæodendrum glaucum*, variety *e. montanum*, peculiar to Ceylon, [Colloq. නෙරළු *neraḷu*].

බත, *Bata*, *s.* boiled or cooked rice; daily hire or ration of a soldier or cooly.

බතක, *Bataka*, *s.* servant, [Colloq. වැඩකාරයා *weḍakárayá*].

බතල, *Batala*, *s.* plant, sort of bindweed, *edulis batatas*, the root of which is the sweet potato: sweet potatoes.

බද්ද, *Badda*, *s.* tax, revenue, tribute; rent, hire: pl. බදු *badu*.

බද්දිය, *Baddiya*, *s.* coral tree, *erythrina indica*, [Colloq. එරබදු *erabadu*].

බද්දිවෙල, *Baddiwela*, *s.* paddy field.

බද, *Bada*, *s.* kind of grass, *paspalum kora*: *a.* united, joined, fastened, belonging to.

බද අදර, *Bada-adara*, *s.* (බද and අදර love) affection, cordial regard.

බද එලකහ, *Bada-elakaha*, *s.* shoe-flower plant, *hibiscus rosa sinensis*, [Colloq. සපත්තුමල් *sapattu-mal*].

බදදහස්, *Badadahas*, *s.* spreading annual plant, *tajetes patula*.

බදන, *Badana*, *s.* vessel of any kind, either metal, wood, or clay.

බදනවා, *Badanawá*, *v.* to seize, to wrestle: pret. බැදුවා *beduwá*.

බදපැපොල, *Badapepola*, *s.* variety of papaw, *carica papaya*.

බදමල් තණ, *Badamal-taṇa*, *s.* kind of grass, *ischæmum muticum*.

බදයක්මල, *Bada-yakmala*, *s.* annual ramous plant, *tajetes erecta*.

බදර, *Badara*, *s.* jujube tree, *zizyphus jujuba*, [Colloquial: ඩෙබර *ḍebara* and මසන් *masan*]; berry or seed of the cotton plant; seed of the cotton pod.

බදරත්කුඩළු, *Badarat-kúḍaḷu*, *s.* balsam, *impatiens balsamina*.

බදරතු, *Badaratu*, *s.* shoe-flower plant: see බද එල කහ *bada-elakaha*.

බදරා, *Badará*, *s.* plant, *mimosa octandra*; another kind of plant or moss, *lycopodium imbricatum*.

බදරී, *Badarí*, see බදර *badara*.

බදව, *Badawa*, *a.* (බඳ *baṉda* to tie etc.) belonging to, attached to, connected with.

බද වතුසුද්ද, *Bada-watusudda*, *s.* shrub, *tabernæ montana dichotoma*, [Colloquial: දිවිකදුරු *divikaduru*].

බදසුදුකුඩළු, *Badasudu-kúḍaḷu*, see බදරත් කුඩළු *badarat-kúḍaḷu*.

බද සූර්යකාන්ති, *Bada-súryakánti*, *s.* sun-flower, *helianthus annuus*.

බදා, *Badá*, *s.* planet Mercury: *part.* having seized, grasped, clasped in the arms, or embraced.

බදාගන්නවා, *Badágannawá*, *v.* (බදා and ගන්නවා to take) to seize, to grasp, to clasp, to embrace.

බදාදා, *Badádá*, *s.* (බදා Mercury, දා day) Wednesday.

බදාම, *Badáma*, *s.* cement, plaster of lime; gum or glue.

බදිනවා, *Badinawá*, *v.* to fry, to grill, to roast, to parch: pret. බැද්දා *beddá*.

බදිර, *Badira*, *s.* pulas tree, *butea frondosa*, [Colloq. ගස්කැල *gas-kela*].

* These nine words should have been inserted after බණ baṇa on page 408.

බදිරෝ, *Badiró*, *s.* tree, *cochlospermum gossypium*, [Colloq. කිණිහිරිය *kiṇihiriya* and එළ ඉඹුල් *ela-imbul*].

බදු, *Badu*, *s.* buffalo, [Colloq. මීහරකා *míharaká*]; deception; also, plur. of බද්ද *badda*.

බදුකම, *Badukama*, *s.* deception, delusion, misleading.

බදුකරණවා, *Badukaraṇawá*, *v.* to rent, to hold in rent, to farm taxes.

බදුකාරයා, *Badukárayá*, *s.* (බදු rent, කාර who does, යා masculine aff.) renter, one who holds a rent, farmer of taxes.

බදුකැරේ, *Badukęré*, *s.* written contract leasing any property.

බදුගන්නවා, *Badu-gannawá*, *v.* (බදු and ගන්නවා to take to take and hold by lease.

බදුදෙනවා, *Badu-denawá*, *v.* (බදු and දෙනවා to give) to let out, to rent.

බඳුන, *Baduna*, *s.* vessel of any kind, either of wood or clay; Elu form of භාජන *bhájana*.

බදුරු, *Baduru*, *a.* good, excellent, [Colloq. හොඳ *honda*]; Elu form of භද්‍ර *bhadra*.

බදුල්ල, *Badulla*, } බදුලුරුක්, *Badulu-ruk*, } *s.* the marking nut tree, *semicarpus Gardneri*, formerly called *s. anacardium (Anacardiaceæ)*; of this genus there are thirteen species peculiar to Ceylon.

බදුවද, *Baduwada*, see බදඑලකහ *bada-elakaha*.

බඳ, *Banda*, *s.* body, [Colloq. ඇඟ *ęnga*]; breast, chest: *a.* bound, [Colloq. බැන්ද *bęnda*].

බඳපටිය, *Bandapaṭiya*, *s.* (බඳ and පටිය tie) band worn round the loins, girdle, girth, zone.

බඳිනවා, *Bandinawá*, *v.* to bind, to tie, to brace: pret. බැන්ද *bęndá*.

බඳුජීව, *Bandujíwa*, *s.* (බඳු friend, ජීව to live) shoe-flower, *hibiscus rosa sinensis:* corruptly for බන්‍ධුජීව *bandhujíwa*.

බඳුරු, *Banduru*, see බදුරු *baduru*.

බධ, *Badha*, *s.* (බධ to kill) killing, slaughter, slaying, murder; killer, murderer.

බධක, *Badhaka*, *s.* (බධ to kill, ක aff.) murderer, killer, [Colloq. මිනිමරුවා *minimaruwá*].

බධස්ථාන, *Badhasthána*, *s.* (බධ killing, ස්ථාන place) place of execution.

බධාඞ්ගක, *Badháṅgaka*, *s.* (බධ *badha* to kill, අඞ්ග *aṅga* body, ක aff.) poison, [Colloq. වහ *waha*].

බධිර, *Badhira*, *a.* (බන්‍ධ *bandha* to bind (the hearing) deaf, [Colloq. බිහිරි *bihiri*].

බධිරයා, *Badhirayá*, } බධිරා, *Badhirá*, } *s.* (බධිර deaf, ආ *á* aff.) deaf man, [Colloq. බිහිරා *bihirá*].

බධූ, *Badhu*, *s.* wife, [Colloq. භාර්‍යාව *bháryáwa*].

බද්ධ, *Baddha*, *a.* (බන්‍ධ *bandha* to bind) bound, secured by fetters, seized, secured, clasped.

බද්ධ පර්‍යඞ්ක, *Baddha-paryaṅka*, *s.* (බද්ධ bound, පර්‍යඞ්ක seat) sitting with the legs crossed under, posture of sitting often adopted by persons given up to religious meditation; posture assumed by a religious recluse and one in which the images of Buddha are frequently represented in the temples.

බද්ධරව, *Baddharawa*, *s.* (බද්ධ bound, රව sound) unceasing sound, perpetual cry, as the noise of birds, etc.; cry of any animal in danger or distress.

බද්ධවෛරය, *Baddha-wairaya*, *s.* (බද්ධ bound, වෛර *waira* anger) malice, hatred.

බන්, *Ban*, *a.* bound, tied; fastened.

බන්කුව, *Bankuwa*, *s.* bench. (Port. or Dutch.)

බන්ගලාව, *Bangaláwa*, *s.* bungalow.

බන්ඳනය, *Bandanaya*, *s.* binding, ligament, fetter, snare, trap: pl. බන්ඳන *bandana*, corruptly for බන්‍ධන *bandhana*.

බන්ඳනා, *Bandaná*, *a.* binding, securing.

බන්දේසිය, *Bandésiya*, *s.* tray, trencher.

බන්‍ධ, *Bandha*, *s.* pledge, deposit; binding, tie, fetter; body.

බන්‍ධකී, *Bandhakí*, *s.* (බන්‍ධ to bind, කී fem. aff.) woman who has broken her marriage vow, unchaste woman, harlot, wanton; barren woman.

බන්‍ධන, *Bandhana*, *s.* binding, tying, fastening; rope for tying cattle; killing; hurting, injuring.

බන්‍ධනය, *Bandhanaya*, *s.* binding, ligament, fetter, bond; snare, trap.

බන්‍ධනාගාරය, *Bandhanágáraya*, } බන්‍ධනාලය, *Bandhanálaya*, } *s.* (බන්‍ධන *bandhana* binding, confining, අගාර *ágára* house, ආලය residence) prison, [Colloq. හිරගේ *hiragé*].

බන්‍ධනි, *Bandhaní*, *s.* (බන්‍ධ to bind) the implement of tying or binding, rope, chain, fetter, cord for catching animals.

බන්‍ධු, *Bandhu*, *s.* (බන්‍ධ *bandha* to bind) kinsman, relation but especially of the distant or cognate kind; friend; brother; flower, *pentapetes phœnicea*.

බන්‍ධුක, *Bandhuka*, } බන්‍ධුකුසුම, *Bandhu-kusuma*, } *s.* shoe-flower plant, see බඳුජීව *bandjíwa*, etc. [Colloq. සපත්තුමල් *sapattu-mal*]

බන්ධුත්ව, *Bandhutwa*, } s. (බන්ධු friend, ත්ව or තා
බන්ධුතා, *Bandhutá*, } aff. of the abstract) kindred, kin, relationship; friendship.

බන්ධුමතී, *Bandhumatí*, s. city so called on the continent of India.

බන්ධුර, *Bandhura*, s. diadem, crest; dregs of oil or oil cake; goose; flower, *pentapetes phœnicea:* see බන්ධු *bandhu*, බන්ධූලි *bandhúli;* drug; crane; bird; dregs of oil, oil cake: *a.* high, exalted, chief; uneven, undulating, waving; wavy, partially even and depressed; bowed, bent; pleasing, delightful; handsome, beautiful; deaf; injurious, mischievous.

බන්ධුරා, *Bandhurá*, s. prostitute, [Colloq. වෙසඟන *wesangana*]; meal of parched corn.

බන්ධූලි, *Bandhúli*, s. (බන්ධ *bandha* to bind) son of an unchaste wife, bastard; flower, *pentapetes phœnicea.*

බන්ධූලික, *Bandhúlika*, s. tree, *pentaptera tomentosa;* also the plant bearing the flower *pentapetes phœnicea:* see last word.

බන්ධ්‍ය, *Bandhya*, a. (බන්ධ *bandha* to bind) seized, detained, arrested; barren, unfruitful.

බන්ධ්‍යා, *Bandhyá*, s. (බන්ධ්‍ය *bandhya* barren, ආ *á* aff.) barren woman, [Colloq. වඳ ස්ත්‍රී *wanda-strí*].

බනු, *Banu*, s. sun, also written භානු *bhánu*, [Coll: ඉර *ira*].

බප්, *Bap*, see බප *bapa.*

බප්පුව, *Bappuwa*, s. panic, horror, sudden fear.

බප, *Bapa*, s. name of Buddha; tears; father, [Colloq. පියා *piyá*].

බපු, *Bapu*, s. arrow, [Colloq. ඊගහ *ígaha*].

බබලනවා, *Babalanawá*, v. to shine, to glitter, to be resplendent: pret. බැබලුවා *bębaluwá.*

බබලවනවා, *Babalawanawá*, v. (causal form of the above) to enlighten, to illumine, to cause to shine: pret. බැබලෙව්වා *bębalewwá.*

බබා, *Babá*, s. baby: pl. බබ්බු *babbu.*

බභ්‍රිෂ්ට, *Babhrishta*, s. tree, *tabernœmontana coronaria*, [Colloq. තුවරලා *tuwaralá*].

බඹ, *Bamba*, s. god Brahma; Brahmin: *a.* good, best, excellent, pre-eminent; Elu form of බ්‍රහ්ම *brahma.*

බඹකත්, *Bambakat*, s. (බඹ Brahma, කත් woman) goddess Saraswatí who was born from the head of Brahma.

බඹගුරු, *Bambaguru*, s. (බඹ and ගුරු teacher) planet Jupiter, or the regent of that planet and preceptor of the gods, [Colloq. වෘහස්පති *vrihaspati*].

බඹගොස්, *Bamba-gos*, s. (බඹ and ගොස් voice) voice of Buddha, so called on account of its resemblance to that of Mahá Brahma; glorious voice.

බඹතලය, *Bambatalaya*, s. the world of Brahma: see බ්‍රහ්මලෝකය *brahmalókaya.*

බඹතැන්, *Bambaten*, s. (බඹ best, තැන් place) middle of a house, inner apartment.

බඹදූ, *Bambadę*, s. (බඹ brahman, දූ tribe, kind) caste or tribe of Brahmins.

බඹපුත්, *Bamba-put*, s. in Indian astronomy the ninth of the planets, [Colloq. කේතු *kétu*].

බඹය, *Bambaya*, s. measure, the extent of both arms stretched out and about equal to a fathom: pl. බඹ *bamba.*

බඹර, *Bambara*, s. large black bee; beehive; wasp; top, child's play-thing; corruptly for බමර *bamara.*

බඹර ඉටි, *Bambara-iti*, s. (බඹර and ඉටි wax) large black bee's wax.

බඹර ගහනවා, *Bambara-gahanawá*, v. to play at tops.

බඹර මිය, *Bambara-míya*, s. (බඹර and මිය *míya* bee-hive) hive of the large black bee.

බඹර වදේ, *Bambara-wadé*, s. honey-comb of the large black bee.

බඹරවැල්, *Bambara-wel*, s. climbing plant, *dalbergia Champonii, (Leguminosœ).*

බඹරා, *Bambará*, s. large black bee, *Apidœ;* wasp, *Sphegidœ*, order *Hymenoptera.*

බඹරු, *Bambaru*, s. purple (the colour); cock: pl. බඹරා *bambará.*

බඹරුක්, *Bamba-ruk*, s. (බඹ and රුක් tree) a cock; tree bearing beautiful red blossoms, *butea frondosa*, [Colloq. ගස්කැල *gas-kęla*].

බඹලොව, *Bamba-lowa*, see බ්‍රහ්මලෝක *brahmalóka.*

බඹසර, *Bambasara*, s. (බඹ brahman, සර duty) religious ascetic whose chief virtue is continence; residence of a tápasayá or religious ascetic; dwelling of a Buddhist priest contiguous to a temple; Elu form of බ්‍රහ්මචාරී *brahmachárí.*

බඹසරවස්, *Bambasara-was*, s. observance of the law enjoining continence on religious ascetics.

බඹසරා, *Bambasará*, s. (බඹසර *bambasara* and ආ *á* pers. aff.) one who observes the laws of Bambasara, or abstains from intercourse with women.

බඹා, *Bambá*, see බඹ *bamba.*

බඹුරු, *Bamburu*, *s.* top; child's play thing; twirling, whirling; tawny colour; large black bee.

බඹුරු කෙස්, *Bamburu-kes*, *s.* (බඹුරු twisted, කෙස් hair) lock of hair, plaited hair, curled lock of hair.

බඹේ, *Bambé*, *s.* a fathom measured by the extended arms.

බම්බිගහ, *Bambi-gaha*, corruptly for බක්මී ගහ *bakmí-gaha.*

බම්බුව, *Bambuwa*, *s.* piece cut out of the stem of bamboo, *bambusa vulgaris*, [Colloq. උණලි කැබෙල්ල *unalí-kębella*].

බමකරු, *Bamakaru*, *s.* worker in wood, carver, [Colloq. ලියන වඩුවා *liyana-waḍuwá*],

බමණ, *Bamaṇa*, *s.* twirling, whirling, going round.

බමණවා, *Bamaṇawá*, *v.* to have a rotatory motion, to whirl or go round; to circumambulate.

බමර, *Bamara*, *s.* bee, large black bee; wasp: see බඹරා *bambará.*

බමරකුල, *Bamara-kula*, *s.* (බමර bee, කුල tribe, family) swarm of bees, hive.

බමර පතර, *Bamara-patara*, *s.* small species of cardamums, Madras cardamums, *elettaria cardomum (minor)*, [Colloq. රට එන්සාල් *raṭa-ensál*]; *verbesina prostrata* or *v. scandens.*

බමර පිය, *Bamara-piya*, *s.* (බමර and පිය desired) mace, spice, [Colloq. වසාවාසි *wasáwási*].

බමරමිය, *Bamara-miya*, see බඹරමිය *bambara-míya.*

බමර වැල, *Bamara-węla*, *s.* (බමර and වැල line or row) swarm or hive of bees.

බමරු, *Bamaru*, see බඹරු *bambaru.*

බමරේ, *Bamaré*, *s.* hive of the large black bee; whipping or humming top.

බමුණා, *Bamuṇá*, *s.* Brahmin, man of the Brahmin caste.

බය, *Baya*, *s.* fear, terror, alarm.

බයකරණවා, *Bayakaraṇawá*, *v.* to terrify, to make afraid.

බයකාරයා, *Bayakáraya*, }
බයගුල්ලා, *Bayagullá*, } *s.* (බය fear, කාර who possesses) coward, poltroon, spiritless fellow, dastard.

බයානික, *Bayánika*, *a.* dreadful, fearful, terrific: corruptly for භයානක *bhayánaka.*

බර්බට, *Barbaṭa*, *s.* sort of bean, *dolichos biflorus*, [Colloq. කොල්ලු *kollu*].

බර්බරා, *Barbará*, }
බර්බරිකා, *Barbariká*, } *s.* plant believed to be a cure for ring-worm, *xyris indica*, [Colloq. රංමනිස්ස *raṇmanissa* or රංමොටු *raṇmoṭu*].

බර්ව, *Barwa*, *s.* opium plant, *papaver somnifera* [Colloq. කන්සා *kansá*].

බර්හ, *Barha*, *s.* peacock's tail; dependants, train, retinue; leaf.

බර්හි, *Barhi*, *s.* (බර්හ and ඉන් *in* aff.) peacock, [Colloq. මොණරා *moṇará*]; peacock's tail; crest of a peacock; fire.

බර්හිණ, *Barhiṇa*, *s.* (බර්හ *barha* peacock, ඉනච් *inach* aff.) peacock, [Colloq. මොණරා *moṇará*].

බර්හිර්මුඛ, *Barhirmukha*, *s.* (බර්හිර් fire, මුඛ mouth) a god, deity, demon; name given to them in allusion to most offerings passing through fire.

බර්හිෂ්ඨ, *Barhishṭha*, *s.* plant, *plectranthus zeylanicus*, [Colloq. ඉරිවේරිය *iriwériya*].

බර, *Bara*, *s.* number twelve, [Colloq. දොළහ *doḷaha*]; weight; load; saffron, *curcuma longa*, [Colloq. කහ *kaha*]: *a.* heavy, weighty, cumbersome; important, of consequence; best, excellent; slightly desired, preferable.

බර අත්, *Bara-at*, *s.* (බර twelve, අත් hands) name of Kataragama deviyó or Skanda kumára the Indian god of war, alluding to his having twelve hands, each armed with a missile weapon, [Coll: කඳකුමරු *kaṇḍakumaru*].

බර අදිනවා, *Bara-adinawá*, *v.* to carry a load.

බර අරිණවා, *Bara-ariṇawá*, }
බරකපනවා, *Bara-kapanawá*, } *v.* to lighten a load; take off a weight placed on any thing.

බරකම, *Barakama*, *s.* weight, heaviness, preponderance.

බරකරත්තය, *Barakarattaya*, *s.* double bullock cart.

බරගෙණියනවා, *Bara-geṇiyanawá*, *v.* to carry a load.

බරණ, *Baraṇa*, *s.* (from ආභරණ *ábharaṇa* the initial vowel being dropped, and the aspirate භ *bha* changed into its corresponding soft letter) ornament, jewel; serpent, snake, [Colloq. සර්පයා *sarpayá*]; name of Íṣwara or Ṣiva.

බරණිය, *Baraṇiya*, *s.* jar, pot; gallipot.

බරණැස්, *Baraṇęs*, *s.* city of Varáṇasí or Benares; Elu form of වරාණසී *waráṇasí.*

බරත්තු, *Barattu*, *s.* tax from gamblers.

බරත, *Barata*, *s.* music, the science of music; drama.

බරත සත, *Barata-sata*, *s.* (බරත and සත science) science of music, histrionic or theatric art.

බරතිබීම, *Bara-tibima*, *s.* (බර weight, තිබීම placing) pressing, squeezing by a weight, but especially the act of pressing the paddy after it has been steeped in water and previous to its being sown.

බරදියපාසි, *Bara-diyapási*, *s.* hooded milfoil, *utricularia stellaris.*

බරනුවන්, *Bara-nuwan*, } *s.* (බර twelve, නුවන් or
බරනෙත්, *Bara-net*, } නෙත් eyes) name of Kataragama deviyó or Skanda kumára the Indian god of war, alluding to his being figured in the temples with six heads and twelve eyes.

බර පටවනවා, *Bara-paṭawanawá*, *v.* to load, to freight; to press, to squeeze with weight.

බරපතළ, *Barapataḷa*, *a.* (බර weight, පතළ spread) exceedingly weighty, important; serious, terrible, horrible, cruel.

බරපොට් ඇල්වී, *Barapot-ęlví*, *s.* kind of paddy, *oryza sativa.*

බරබද්දර, *Barabaddara*, *s.* heavy loads of a traveller.

බරම්, *Baram*, *s.* name of Brahma: see බ්‍රහ්ම *brahma.*

බරමා, *Baramá*, *s.* stout one, applied chiefly to uncastrated pigs, steer.

බරලිය, *Baraliya*, *s.* tree peculiar to Ceylon, *doona cordifolia, (Dipterocarpaceæ).*

බරවය, *Barawaya*, *s.* (බර heavy, ව *wa* aff. of the abstract) the elephantiasis or cochin leg.

බරවාවැල, *Barawá-węla*, *s.* creeping plant, not ascertained.

බරවා හික්, *Barawá-hik*, *s.* tree, variety of *odina Woodier.*

බරවේ, *Barawé*, see බරවය *barawaya.*

බරසැහැල්ලු, *Barasęhellu*, *s.* light and heavy work; responsibilities, misfortunes, distress.

බරා, *Bará*, *s.* the three noted myrobalans, viz. *terminalia chebula*, [Colloq. අරළු *araḷu*]; *t. belerica*, [Colloq. බුළු *bulu*]; *phyllanthus emblica*, [Coll: නෙල්ලි *nelli*]; creeping plant, *asparagus racemosus*, [Colloq. හාතාවාරිය *hátáwáriya*].

බරාඳය, *Baráṇḍaya*, *s.* verandah: pl. බරාඳ *baráṇḍa.*

බරිත, *Barita*, *s.* full.

බරින්, *Barin*, *s.* (බර *bara* weight, ඉන් *in* aff.) porter, carrier of burdens, cooly, corruptly for භාරින් *bhárin.*

බරී, *Barí*, *s.* plant, *asparagus racemosus*, [Colloq. හාතාවාරිය *hátáwáriya*]: see බරා *bará.*

බරු ඇල්වී, *Baru-ęlví*, *s.* kind of paddy.

බරු කොටැල්වී, *Baru-koṭęlví*, *s.* kind of paddy.

බරුදැල, *Barudęla*, *s.* net with lead balls attached.

බරුව, *Baruwa*, *s.* pieces of lead fastened to the bottoms of the fishing nets or lines, for the purpose of sinking them and causing them to drag while in the act of fishing: pl. බරු *baru.*

බරුවා කොස්සා, *Baruwá-kossá*, *s.* small sea fish.

බල්ගැහෙනවා, *Balgęhenawá*, *v.* to cleave, to crack, to rend, to split.

බල්‍ය, *Balya*, *s.* semen virile: *a.* strong, powerful, mighty, vigorous.

බල්‍යඵල, *Balya-phala*, *s.* tender fruit, [Colloq. ලා පල *lá-pala*].

බල්ලා, *Ballá*, *s.* stopper of wheels; kind of sea fish; dog: pl. බල්ලෝ *balló.*

බල්ලාත, *Balláta*, *s.* tree, *semicarpus anacardium* or *s. gardneri*, [Colloq. බදුල්ල *badulla*]; corruptly for භල්ලාතක *bhallátaka.*

බල, *Bala*, *s.* (බල to live) strength, power, might, ability, courage; bulkiness; form, figure; army, forces; gum myrrh; leaf of a tree; blood; body; rigour, severity; cave, natural or artificial; crow; name of Baladéwa; Daitya, demon; tree, *nothopegia Colebrookiana (Anacardiaceæ)*: *interj.* behold, look, lo!

බලක්‍ෂ, *Balaksha*, *s.* (බල power, ක්‍ෂෛ *kshai* to destroy) white (colour).

බලකඩදාසිය, *Bala-kaḍadásiya*, *s.* license, permit.

බලකනුව, *Balakanuwa*, see බලකරුව *balakaruwa.*

බලකරණවා, *Balakaraṇawá*, *v.* to compel, to force.

බලකරුව, *Balakaruwa*, *s.* anything with two prongs at the end, prop or supporter of wood.

බලකාරයා, *Balakárayá*, *s.* one who has authority.

බලකොටුව, *Balakoṭuwa*, *s.* fortress.

බලකේතු, *Balakétu*, *s.* symbol of power.

බලගතු, *Balagatu*, *a.* (බල strength, ගත *gata* gone, acquired) strong, powerful, robust, having authority, important, serious.

බලජ, *Balaja*, *s.* (බල and ජ born) field; city gate; fruit; war; pith, marrow: *a.* produced by power.

බලජා, *Balajá*, *s.* beautiful woman; earth; Arabian jasmine, [Colloq. පිච්ච *pichcha*].

බලතර, *Balatara*, *s.* (බල and තර much) great strength, prowess: *a.* very strong, powerful.

බලදෙව්මල්, *Baladewmal*, *s.* (බලදෙව් Baladew, මල් younger brother) name of Kṛishṇa, who was the younger brother of Baladéwa or Balabhadra: see බලදේව *baladéwa.*

බලදේව, *Baladéwa*, *s.* (බල Bala, දේව divine) deity so called; air, wind: see බලරාම *balaráma.*

බලධාරි, *Baladhári*, *s.* (බල strength, power, ධාර *dhára* who bears, ඉ *i* aff.) strong or powerful man; one possessing great influence and authority.

බලනවා, *Balanawá*, v. to look, to see, to behold, to superintend, to overlook: pret. බැලුවා *bęluwá*.

බලනහරේ, *Bala-naharé*, s. strong tendon or muscle; artery.

බල නිලම්බර, *Bala-nilambara*, s. (බල baladéwa, නිලම්බර having blue garments) name of Balabhadra or Baladéwa: see බලදෙව්මල් *baladewmal*.

බලප්පට්ටුව, *Balappattuwa*, s. great strength; mightiness, power, influence, authority.

බලභද්‍ර, *Balabhadra*, s. (බල strength, භද්‍ර auspicious, excellent) name of a god or deity; it sometimes refers to බලදේව *baladéwa* which see, also to Anantayá the chief of the serpent race; strong or robust man; tree, *symplocos racemosa*.

බලභද්‍රා, *Balabhadrá*, s. young girl, maiden, [Coll: ලමිස්සි *lamissi*].

බලම, *Balama*, s. canoe.

බලමැඩියා, *Balamędiyá*, s. frog, *bufo melanostictus*, (order *Batrachia salientia*), [Colloq. ගෙමඩියා *gemadiyá*].

බලය, *Balaya*, s. power, chiefly indicating political or legal power.

බලයා, *Balayá*, s. sea-fish.

බලරාම, *Balaráma*, s. (බල strength, රම *rama* to sport) demigod so called, half brother of Krishṇa and third of the Rámas and supposed by some to be the eighth avatára of Vishṇu.

බලරුපු, *Balarupu*, s. (බල demon, රුපු enemy) name of Indra, alluding to his overcoming the Daityas or demons: see also බලිරුපු *bali-rupu*.

බලල්, *Balal*, a. young, immature, infantine.

බලල්කාව, *Balalkáwa*, see බලල්ලෑව *balallęwa*.

බලල් තණ, *Balal-taṇa*, s. kind of grass.

බලල්පහුරු, *Balalpahuru*, s. club moss, *lycopodium ornithopedioides*.

බලල්මරුවා, *Balalmaruwá*, s. a beautiful small sea fish.

බලල්ලෑව, *Balallęwa*, s. space between the roof and wall of a house, literally a cat hole.

බලල්වාණේ වී, *Balalwáné-ví*, s. kind of paddy, *oryza sativa*.

බල ලත්, *Bala-lat*, a. (බල authority, ලත් received) empowered, authorized.

බලව, *Balawa*, *imp. sing.* of බලනවා *balanawá*, to see, to look behold.

බලවත්, *Balawat*, a. (බල strength, වත් poss. aff.) strong, powerful, stout, lusty.

බලවතා, *Balawatá*, s. (බලවත් strong, ආ *á* pers. aff.) athletic or powerful man, one possessing great muscular power.

බලවතුර, *Bala-watura*, s. (බල strong, වතුර water) torrent, mountain stream, strong current.

බලවන්ත, *Balawanta*, a. (බල strength, වන්ත poss. aff.) strong, powerful, athletic, muscular; mighty.

බලවන්තයා, *Balawantayá*, s. (බලවන්ත strong, යා pers. aff.) strong man, man of great might or power, one in authority.

බලවාන්, *Balawán*, a. (බල strength, වාන් poss. aff.) strong, powerful.

බලස, *Balasa*, s. fish-hook.

බලසම්පන්න, *Balasampanna*, a. (බල and සම්පන්න possessing) mighty, strong, powerful.

බලසූදන, *Bala-súdana*, s. (බල demon, සූදන destroyer) name of Indra; see බලිරුපු *balirupu*.

බලසෙන්, *Balasen*,
බලසේනග, *Balasenaga*, } s. (බල strength, සේනග army) efficient or powerful army, one ready to take the field.

බලහීනතා, *Bala-hínatá*, s. (බල and හීනතා abandonment) exhaustion, weakness, prostration of strength, infirmity from fatigue or age.

බලා, *Balá*, s. hairy plant, *sida humilis*, [Colloq. බෑවිල *bęrila*]; bird of the crane kind, usually called the paddy bird: see කොකා *koká*: part. of බලනවා *balanawá*.

බලාක, *Baláka*, s. small species of crane which frequents the paddy or rice fields and is usually called the paddy bird: see කොකා *koká*.

බලාගන්නවා, *Balágannawá*, v. (බලා looking, ගන්නවා to take) to beware, to act with caution or circumspection; to look out or seek for.

බලාත්කාර, *Balátkára*, s. (බලාත් with strength, කාර doing) violence, force, compulsion, coercion, exaction.

බලාත්කාර කරණවා, *Balátkára-karaṇawá*, v. to force, to use compulsion.

බලානුජ, *Balánuja*, s. (බල *bala* Bala ráma, අනුජ *anuja* younger brother) name of Krishṇa: see බලරාම *balaráma*.

බලාපොරොත්තුව, *Báláporottuwa*, s. hope, expectation.

බලාපොරොත්තුවෙනවා, *Báláporottu-wenawá*, v. to hope, to expect.

බලාරාති, *Balaráti*, s. (බල *bala* demon, අරාති *aráti* enemy) name of Indra: see බලිරුපු *balirupu*.

බලාවැල, *Balá-węla*, s. (බලා crane, වැල row or flock) flock of birds of the crane kind: see කොකා *koká*.

බලාසනි, *Balásaní*, *s.* (බල *bala* demon, ආසන *ásana* seat, ඊ *í* aff.) Pátála, infernal regions or world of serpents.

බලා සිටිනවා, *Balá-sitinawá*, *v.* (බලා looking, සිටිනවා to be, to stay) to wait, to expect, to look out for, to hope.

බලාහක, *Baláhaka*, *s.* cloud; mountain.

බලි, *Bali*, *s.* (බල *bala* power, force, exaction) tax, royal revenue; claim, due, right, obligation; propitiatory offerings, religious gifts or sacrifice: whole system of sidereal worship or the adoration of the heavenly bodies as practised in Ceylon; according to the Hindus, the name of a celebrated king and Daitya, the virtuous sovereign of Mahábalipura; he was tricked out of the dominion he had obtained over earth and heaven by Vishṇu in the Vámana or dwarf incarnation; yet in consequence of his great merit he was left in the sovereignty of Pátála or the infernal regions; orts, fragments, the remainder of a meal or sacrifice; a wrinkle.

බලි අඹනවා, *Bali-ambanawá*, *v.* (බලි and අඹනවා to make) to make an image of clay representing any one of the planets.

බලි අරිණවා, *Bali-ariṇawá*, *v.* to perform incantatory services before clay images to avert the evil influences of the planets.

බලිකර්මය, *Bali-karmaya*, *s.* (බලි and කර්ම *karma* act) sidereal worship: see බලි *bali*.

බලිපුටු, *Baliputu*, Elu form of the following.

බලිපුෂ්ට, *Balipushṭa*, *s.* (බලි crumbs or fragments of food, පුෂ්ට nourished) crow.

බලිබිලි, *Balibili*, *s.* demonical ceremonies and sacrifices; offerings to planets and demons.

බලිභ, *Balibha*, *a.* (බලි wrinkle, භ aff.) shrivelled, withered, flaccid, wrinkled.

බලිභුක්, *Balibhuk*, } *s.* (බලි the orts of a meal or
බලිභුජ්, *Balibhuj*, } sacrifice, භුජ් who eats) crow; sparrow; crane.

බලිමර්ද, *Bali-marda*, see බලිවර්ද *bali-warda*.

බලිමුඛ, *Balimukha*, *s.* (බලි wrinkle, මුඛ face) monkey, *macatus pileatus*, or *presbytes*, [Colloq. රිළවා *rilawá*, වඳුරා *wandurá*].

බලිය, *Baliya*, *s.* planetary sacrifice, effigy, image of clay representing the planet under which any one is born; it is made and worshipped by a person in a fit of sickness: see බලි *bali*.

බලිරුපු, *Bali-rupu*, *s.* (බලි demon, රුපු enemy) name of Vishṇu alluding to his wars and conquests of the demons or Asuras; it may also allude to his depriving the king or Daitya Bali of the sovereignty of earth and heaven: see බලි *bali*.

බලිවර්ද, *Baliwarda*, *s.* bull, ox, bullock, [Colloq. ගොණා *goṇá*].

බලිශ, *Balisa*, *s.* fish-hook.

බලිශ මංසික, *Baliṣa-mansika*, *s.* (බලිශ fish-hook, මංසික hooking or seizing with a hook) capital punishment, punishment inflicted upon culprits who are hooked as fish.

බලිසතුර, *Bali-satura*, *s.* (බලි and සතුර enemy) name of Vishṇu: see බලිරුපු *bali-rupu*.

බලිසද්මන්, *Bali-sadman*, *s.* (බලි demon, සද්මන් abode) Pátála, infernal regions, or Nága lóka, the world of serpents.

බලිහන්, *Balihan*, *s.* (බලි and හන් to injure, to destroy) name of Vishṇu.

බලී, *Balí*, *s.* wrinkle; Balaráma; strong man; person of power or influence; sort of pulse green gram, *phaseolus mungo*, [Colloq. මුංඇට *muneta*].

බලීමුඛ, *Balí-mukha*, see බලිමුඛ *bali-mukha*.

බලීවර්ද්ධ, *Balí-wardda*, *s.* (බලී for බල *bala* strength, වර්ද්ධ *warddha* increasing) bull, ox: see බලිවර්ද *bali-warda*.

බලේ, *Balé*, *s.* might, power, authority.

බව්ම, *Bawma*, *s.* planet Mars, [Colloq. අඟහරුවා *angaharuwá*]; corruptly for භෞම *bhawuma*.

බව්හාදීනව, *Bawhádínawa*, *s.* (බහු *bahu* much, ආදීනව *ádínawa* crime) great guilt or culpability; badness, wickedness, depravity; many evil consequences.

බව, *Bawa*, *s.* being, existing; birth; the state of being; fact, as ඔහු ගිය බව මට කිව්වා *ohu giya bawa mata kiwwá*, "he told me that he went;" Elu form of භව *bhawa*.

බවකිල, *Bawa-kila*, *s.* (බව being, කිල stake) one of the eight great hells, in which punishment is inflicted by transfixing the culprit with a stake, corruptly for භවකිල *bhawakíla*.

බවතුරු, *Bawaturu*, see බවන්තර *bawantara*.

බවදුකු, *Bawaduku*, *s.* (බව being, existence, දුකු sorrow) metempsychosis, transmigration; according to the Buddhist system, existence in any state is considered a curse, and sorrow is inevitably connected with it: see ක්ලේශ *kléṣa*.

බවන්තර, *Bawantara*, *s.* (බව existence, අන්තර other) another existence, either a previous or subsequent one.

බවන, *Bawana*, *s.* being, existing; dwelling; residence; corruptly for භවන *bhawana*.

බවුල, *Bawula*, *s.* trunk or chest with an arched top.

බෂ්කයණි, *Bashkayaṇi*, *s.* cow bearing many calves.

බස්ත, *Basta*, *s.* goat, he-goat; ram.

බස්තගන්ධකා, *Bastagandaká*, } *s.* (බස්ත ram, ගන්ධ
බස්තගන්ධා, *Bastagandhá*, } smell) plant, *gynandropsis pentaphylla*, [Colloq. වේලා *wélá*]: *a.* strong smelling, fetid.

බස්තම, *Bastama*, *s.* walking stick: pl. බස්තම් *bastam*.

බස්තශෘඞ්ගි, *Bastasṛińgi*, *s.* (බස්ත ram, ශෘඞ්ග *sṛińga* horn) horn of a goat or ram; plant, *dœmia extensa*, [Colloq. මැඩහඟු *meḍahangu*].

බස්නකරණවා, *Basnakaraṇawá*, *v.* to prepare a medicine by laying it under earth for days.

බස්නය, *Basnaya*, *s.* medicine prepared in a young coconut, etc.

බස්නා, *Basná*, *a.* descending; setting as the sun.

බස්නාඉර, *Basná-ira*, *s.* (බස්නා and ඉර sun) setting sun; west.

බස්නායක, *Basnáyaka*, *s.* Principal, or lay incumbent of a Hindu temple.

බස්නාව, *Basnáwa*, *s.* ebbing or reflux of the tide, descent, running or flowing down.

බස්නාහිර, *Basnáhira*, see බස්නාඉර *basná-ira*.

බස් පෙරලා කීම, *Bas-peralá-kíma*, *s.* (බස් and පෙරලා inverting, කීම saying) retort; interpreting, expounding.

බස්මානං, *Basmánaŋ*, *s.* unprepared camphor, [Colloq. අමු කපුරු *amu-kapuru*].

බස්සනවා, *Bassanawá*, *v.* to cause to descend or to be abated; the causal form of බසිනවා *basinawá*, which see.

බස්සල්, *Bassal*, *s.* articles, things.

බස්සා, *Bassá*, *s.* small owl, rufous scops owl, *scops sunia;* brow hawk owl, *nicos scutulata*, both of these also called පුංචි බස්සා *puñchi-bassá;* Ceylon bay owl, *phodilus assimilis*, (Sub-order *Striges*, order *Acciptres)*.

බස, *Basa*, *s.* word, speech, language: pl. බස් *bas*.

බසපත, *Basapata*, *s.* order, command, edict, [Coll: ආඥාව *ájñáwa*].

බසිනවා, *Basinawá*, *v.* to descend, to go down, to set as the sun: pret. බැස්සා *bessá*.

බහ, *Baha*, *s.* word, speech, saying.

බහති, *Bahati*, *s.* species of night shade, *solanum xanthocarpum*, [Colloq. එලබටු *ela-baṭu*].

බහදීම, *Bahadíma*, *s.* (බහ and දීම giving) act of pledging one's word, promise: pl. බහදීම් *bahadím*.

බහදුරු, *Bahaduru*, *a.* good, excellent, best, supreme; Elu form of භද්‍ර *bhadra*.

බහදෙනවා, *Bahadenawá*, *v.* to give one's word, to contract verbally.

බහන, *Bahana*, *s.* strong rope or cord used for tying cattle; rope, cord: pl. බහන් *bahan*.

බහනවා, *Bahanawá*, *v.* to put in, to introduce.

බහපත, *Bahapata*, see බසපත *basapata*.

බහමචරී, *Bahamacharí*, *a.* chaste, pure, continent; corrupt form of බ්‍රහ්මචාරී *brahmachárí*, which see.

බහරී, *Baharí*, *s.* arrowgrass, *panicum paniculatum* or *poa cynosuroides*, [Colloq. කුසතණ *kusataṇa*].

බහල, *Bahala*, *ad.* much, many, great, abounding; hard, solid; firm, compact.

බහලත්වච්, *Bahalatwach*, *s.* tree, *ægle marmelos*, [Colloq. බෙලිගස් *beli-gas*]; tree, *nephelium longana*, [Colloq. මොරගස් *mora-gas*].

බහලතර, *Bahalatara*, *a.* (බහල much, තර intensive) exceeding, excessive, very much.

බහලන්ධකාර, *Bahalandhakára*, *s.* (බහල much, අන්ධකාර *andhakára* darkness) great or thick darkness.

බහා, *Bahá*, *part.* having placed, fixed, put, settled.

බහාලනවා, *Bahálanawá*, *v.* (බහා and ලනවා to put) to place, to fix, to settle, to insert.

බහාලීම, *Bahálíma*, *s.* placing, putting, [Colloq. දැමීම *demíma*].

බහි, *Bahi*, *ad.* out, outside; outer, outward.

බහිද්ධා, *Bahiddhá*, *ad.* out, outside.

බහිද්වාර, *Bahidwára*, see බහිර්ද්වාර *bahirdwára*.

බහින්බස්වෙනවා, *Bahinbas-wenawá*, *v.* to contradict each other, to pass angry words.

බහිනවා, *Bahinawá*, *v.* to descend, to come down, to set, (as the sun), to alight.

බහිර්, *Bahir*, *ad.* out, outer, outside, outward.

බහිර්ද්වාර, *Bahirdwára*, *s.* (බහිර් out, ද්වාර door) outer gate of a house or city; door of a back yard or premises: *a.* out of doors, forth from the house.

බහිර්නිෂ්ක්‍රමණ, *Bahir-nishkramaṇa*, *s.* (බහිර් out, නිෂ්ක්‍රමණ departing) setting off, departure.

බහිරවයා, *Bahirawayá*, *s.* demon of that name; corruptly for භෛරවයා *bhayrawayá*.

බහු, *Bahu*, *a.* much, many; large, great, numerous, [Colloq. බොහෝ *bohó*].

බහුක, *Bahuka*, *s.* crab; gallinule; shrub called mudar, *calotropis* or *asclepias gigantea*, [Colloq. වරා *wará*]; tank digger.

බහුකණ්ටක, *Bahukanṭaka*, *s.* (බහු many, කණ්ටක thorn) prickly plant, *hedysarum alhagi*; marshy date tree.

බහුකර, *Bahukara*, s. (බහු much, කර what does) camel; sweeper: *a.* industrious, labouring.

බහුකරා, *Bahukará*, *s.* sweeper: *a.* industrious, labouring.

බහුකරී, *Bahukarí*, *s.* broom.

බහුගන්ධ, *Bahugandha*, *s.* (බහු much, ගන්ධ odour) Arabian jasmine, [Colloq. පිච්ච *pichcha*]; *olibanum*; bud or flower of the *michelia champaka* tree, [Colloq. සපු *sapu*]: *a.* strong scented.

බහුච්ඡද, *Bahuchchhada*, *s.* tree, *ficus arnottiana*, [Colloq. කවුඩුබෝ *kawudu-bó* or පුලිල *pulila*].

බහුච්ඡිද්‍රා, *Bahuchchhidrá*, *s.* plant, *tinospora cordifolia*, [Colloq. රසකිඳ *rasakinda*].

බහුජන, *Bahujana*, *s.* (බහු many, ජන man) multitude, company of people, [Colloq. සමූහය *samúhaya*].

බහුතස්, *Bahutas*, *ind.* (බහු much, තසි *tasi* aff.) from or by much or many.

බහුද, *Bahuda*, *s.* kind of dill or fennel, *anethum sowa*, [Colloq. ශතපුෂ්ප *ṣatapushpa*]: *a.* liberal, giving much.

බහුධන, *Bahu-dhana*, *s.* (බහු and ධන wealth) great wealth, much or valuable property: *a.* wealthy, rich.

බහුධා, *Bahudhá*, *adv.* in many ways-sorts, etc.

බහුධාන්‍ය, *Bahu-dhánya*, *s.* (බහු and ධාන්‍ය corn) eleventh year of the Indian cycle.

බහුනාද, *Bahu-náda*, *s.* (බහු and නාද sound) conch shell.

බහුපත්‍ර, *Bahu-patra*, *s.* (බහු many, පත්‍ර leaf) onion; talc: *a.* many leaved.

බහුපත්‍රී, *Bahupatrí*, *s.* (බහුපත්‍ර *bahupatra* and ඊ *í* aff.) medicinal plant, *trigonella fœnum græcum*.

බහුපතී, *Bahupatí*, *s.* tree, *ficus arnottiana*, [Colloq. පුලිල *pulila*].

බහුපන්, *Bahupan*, see බහුපර්ණිනී *bahuparṇní*.

බහුපර්ණික, *Bahuparṇnika*, *s.* bó-tree, *ficus religiosa*, [Colloq. බෝ *bó*].

බහුපර්ණිනී, *Bahuparṇní*, *s.* (බහු many, පර්ණ *parṇa* leaf, ඉනි *ini* aff.) medicinal plant or drug, *trigonella fœnum græcum*.

බහුපල, *Bahupala*, see බහුඵල *bahuphala*.

බහුපාද්, *Bahupád*, *s.* (බහු many, පාද් foot) banyan tree, *ficus indica*, alluding to the fibrous branches which grow down wards and take root again, [Colloq. මහනුග *maha-nuga*].

බහුපුත්‍ර, *Bahu-putra*, *s.* tree, *alstonia scholaris*, [Colloq. රුක්අත්තන *ruk-attana*]: *a.* having many children.

බහුපුත්‍රා, *Bahu-putrá*, *s.* plant, *phyllanthus niruri*, [Colloq. පිටවක්කා *piṭawakká*].

බහුපුත්‍රිකා, *Bahu-putriká*, *s.* spiny shrub, *solanum indicum*, [Colloq. තිබ්බටු *tibbaṭu*].

බහුපුත්‍රී, *Bahu-putrí*, *s.* medicinal plant, *asparagus falcatus*, [Colloq. හාතාවාරිය *hátáwáriya*].

බහුඵල, *Bahu-phala*, *s.* (බහු much, ඵල fruit) cadamba tree, *anthocephalus* or *nauclea cadamba*, [Colloq. බක්මී *bakmí*]: *a.* fruitful.

බහුඵලී, *Bahuphalí*, *s.* opposite leaved fig tree, *ficus oppositifolia*, [Coll: කොටදිඹුලා *koṭadimbulá*]; plant, species of night-shade, *solanum nigrum*, [Colloq. කළුකන්වෙරිය *kaḷu-kanmériya*].

බහුබීජ, *Bahubíja*, } *s.* (බහු and බීජ seed)
බහුබීජක, *Bahubíjaka*, } pomegranate tree, *punica granatum*, [Colloq. දෙළුම් *deḷum*]; sweet sop, a kind of custard apple, *anona squamosa*, [Colloq. අනෝනා *anóná*].

බහුභාර්‍ය්‍ය, *Bahubhárya*, *a.* having many wives.

බහුභාස, *Bahubhása*, *s.* (බහු and භාසා *bhásá* speech) verbosity, loquacity, prattling, talking much to little purpose.

බහුමඤ්ජරී, *Bahumañjari*, see තලා *talá*.

බහුමත, *Bahumata*, *a.* thought much off; having many different opinions.

බහුමාන, *Bahumána*, *s.* (බහු much, මාන reverence) reverence, much respect, adoration.

බහුමූල්‍ය, *Bahu-múlya*, *a.* (බහු much, මූල්‍ය price) costly, of high price.

බහුමූල, *Bahu-múla*, *s.* (බහු many, මූල root) kind of reed or grass, *andropogon muricatus*, [Colloq. සැවැන්දරා *sẹwẹndará*]: see සාතාවාරිය *sátáwáriya*.

බහුමැතියා, *Bahumẹtiyá*, *s.* one who talks in a pompous and affected manner, braggadocio.

බහුර, *Bahura*, *s.* low or vile man, one who subsists on the gleanings of the rice fields, or on gathering the fragments of the thrashing floor.

බහුරි, *Bahuri*, *s.* sort of dance performed by giving the body a rotatory motion; summerset.

බහුරු, *Bahuru*, *s.* hole, [Colloq. සිදුර *sidura*].

බහුරූප, *Bahu-rúpa, s.* (බහු many, රූප shape, form) chameleon; love, Cupid; dummala or resin; name or epithet of Brahma, Şiva or Vishṇu: *a.* various, multiform.

බහුරේණුක, *Bahuréṇuka, s.* (බහු much, රේණු dust, ක aff.) kind of orange.

බහුරෝමන්, *Bahu-róman, s.* (බහු and රෝමන් hair) sheep, [Colloq. බැටළුවා *beṭaḷuwá*].

බහුල, *Bahula, s.* (බහු and ලා *lá* to get) sky; dark half of a lunar month; name of Agni the regent of fire; fire: *a.* much, many, abundant, black.

බහුලත්ව, *Bahulatwa, s.* (බහුල much, ත්ව aff. abstract) abundance, comprehensiveness.

බහුලා, *Bahulá, s.* indigo, *indigofera tinctoria,* [Colloq. නිල්අවරි *nil-awari*]; cardamoms, *elettaria cardamomum,* [Colloq, එන්සාල් *ensál*]; Pleiades; cow.

බහුලීකත, *Bahulíkata,* } *part.* (බහුල *bahula* and
බහුලීකෘත, *Bahulíkṛita,* } කත or කෘත made)
thrashed and winnowed, cooked, dressed, cleaned or prepared, (used of rice etc.)

බහු වචනය, *Bahu-wachanaya, s.* the plural number, (in grammar.)

බහුවාතක, *Bahu-wátaka,* } *s.* tree, the wood of
බහුවාහක, *Bahuwáhaka,* } which is used for boat
building and fuel, the bark for ropes and the fruit as a vegetable, *cordia myxa,* [Colloq. ලෝළු *lóḷu*].

බහුවිධ, *Bahuvidha, a.* (බහු many, විධ sort) various, multiform, of various sorts of kinds.

බහුවින්නා, *Bahuvinná, s.* plant, *tinospora cordifolia,* [Colloq. රසකිඳ *rasakinda*].

බහුවීජ, *Bahuvíja,* see බහුබීජ *bahubíja.*

බහුවීර්‍ය, *Bahu-vírya, s.* tree, *terminalia belerica,* [Colloq. බුළු *buḷu*]; also *morinda citrifolia,* [Colloq. අහු *ahu*]; much strength.

බහුව්‍රීහි, *Bahuvríhi, s.* (බහු and ව්‍රීහි grain, paddy) form of grammatical composition, *i. e.* compounding two or more words to furnish an epithet or attributive.

බහුශ්‍රුත, *Bahuṣruta, s.* (බහු much, ශ්‍රුත *ṣruta* heard) learned man, pandit: *a.* learned, having heard much and being consequently well-informed.

බහුසුතා, *Bahusutá, s.* creeping plant, *asparagus falcatus,* [Colloq. හාතාවාරිය *hátáwáriya*].

බළල් ඇස්, *Baḷal-ęs, s.* (one having) eyes like those of a cat.

බළල් ලුණු, *Baḷal-luṇu, s.* nitre, saltpetre.

බළලා, *Baḷalá, s.* cat: pl. බළල්ලු *baḷallu.*

බළු, *Baḷu, s.* dog.

බළුකම, *Baḷukama, s.* mean act, low vulgarity.

බළුකික්කි, *Baḷu-kikkí,* the feminine form of the next.

බළුකුක්කා, *Baḷu-kukká, s.* (බළු and කුක්කා pup) pup, whelp: pl. බළුකුක්කෝ *baḷukukkó.*

බළුතණ, *Baḷu-taṇa, s.* panic grass, *panicum polystachyon.*

බළුදන්, *Baḷudan, s.* shrub with rose coloured flowers, *ardisea humilis* or *a. elliptica (Myrsineæ).*

බළුනකුට, *Baḷunakuṭa, s.* tree, *chailletia gelonioides (Chailletiaceæ);* plant, *stachytarpheta indica (Verbenaceæ).*

බළුනියඳඬු, *Baḷu-niyadaṇḍu, s.* plant, not identified.

බළුමක්කා, *Baḷumakká,* } *s.* (බළු and මැක්කා fly)
බළුමැක්කා, *Baḷumękká,* } flea: pl. බළුමැක්කෝ
baḷumękkó.

බළුව, *Baḷuwa, s.* the hook of a stick, supporter.

බළුහැල්ම, *Baḷuhęlma, s.* the gait or way in which a dog runs, trot.

බා, *Bá, s.* arm; hand; half, share, portion; happiness, prosperity, auspiciousness; wise man, rays; the participle of බානවා *bánawá.*

බාකුචි, *Bákuchí, s.* plant producing beans, *serratula anthelmintica,* [Colloq. බෝදි ඇට *bódi-ęṭa*].

බාග්‍ය, *Bágya, s.* good luck, more properly written භාග්‍ය *bhágya,* which see.

බාග්‍යවන්ත, *Bágyawanta, a.* (බාග්‍ය and වන්ත poss. aff.) sharing, possessing; happy, fortunate, prosperous, lucky; corruptly for භාග්‍යවන්ත *bhágyawanta.*

බාග, *Bága, s.* part, portion, moiety, half; some.

බාගදා, *Bágadá, s.* (බාග some, දා day) some time: *adv.* perhaps.

බාගන්නවා, *Bágannawá, v.* to take down or unload goods.

බාගය, *Bágaya, s.* part, portion, half: pl. බාගා *bágá.*

බාගවිට, *Bágaviṭa,* } *ad.* (බාග some, විට
බාගවේලාවට, *Bágawéláwaṭa,* } or වේලාව time)
perhaps; sometimes.

බාගි, *Bági, s.* (බාග *bága* part, ඉ *i* aff.) possessor, partner, sharer.

බාච්චිය, *Báchchiya, s.* jacket worn by men.

බාජ්ජ, *Bájja, s.* ebb-tide; corrupt form of බාදිය *bádiya.*

බාජන, *Bájana, s.* vessel, vessel in general, see භාජන *bhájana.*

බාඩ, *Báḍa*, *a.* hard, solid, firm, resisting.

බාඪ, *Bádha*, *s.* promise, engagement, agreement, confederation; approaching, coming near or to: *a.* exceeding, much, excessive.

බාණ්ඩාරෙ, *Báṇḍáre*, *s.* pantry, treasury.

බාණ, *Báṇa*, *s.* arrow, [Colloq. ඊගහ *ígaha*].

බාණබලි, *Báṇabali*, } *s.* child or offspring of an
බාණබලී, *Báṇabalí*, } Asura or demon, an imp; arrow.

බාණා, *Báṇá*, *s.* creeping plant, *ipomœa zeylanica;* black species; number or value of money, equivalent to six pence; arrow; blue kind of *barleria prionitis*, [Colloq. කටුකරඬු *kaṭukaranḍu*].

බාණාසන, *Báṇásana*, *s.* (බාණ *báṇa* arrow, අසන *asana* throwing or seat) bow, [Colloq. දුනන *dunna*].

බාණි, *Báṇi*, *s.* (බණ *baṇa* to speak) speech; goddess of speech.

බාණිජ්, *Báṇij*, see වණිජ් *waṇij*.

බාදර, *Bádara*, *s.* (බදර *badara* cotton, අන් *an* aff.) cotton plant; cotton cloth.

බාදා, *Bádá*, *s.* hindrance; impediment, obstruction; evil omen, unlucky sign.

බාදිය, *Bádiya*, *s.* (බා and දිය water) ebb or reflux of the tide.

බාදුර, *Bádura*, } *s.* pitcher plant, the
බාඳුරා, *Bánḍurá*, } stems of which are used
බාඳුරාවැල්, *Bánḍurá-węl*, } for tying fences, peculiar to Ceylon, *nepenthes distillatoria (Nepenthaceæ)*.

බාධ, *Bádha*, see බාධා *bádhá*.

බාධක, *Bádhaka*, *a.* what hinders, impedes or obstructs.

බාධන, *Bádhana*, *s.* opposing, resisting, hindering, impeding; pain.

බාධය, *Bádhaya*, } *s.* hindrance, impediment;
බාධා, *Bádhá*, } opposition; contradiction; evil omen; pain, affliction.

බාධාකරණවා, *Bádhákaraṇawá*, *v.* to hinder, impede.

බාධාවෙනවා, *Bádháwenawá*, *v.* to be hindered.

බාධිත, *Bádhita*, *a.* (බාධ *bádha* to oppose, ක්ත *kta* aff.) stopped, opposed, hindered, obstructed.

බාන්, *Bán*, *ind.* word used in addressing equals or inferiors, not respectful, as වරෙන් බාන් *waren-bán*, "come"; මොකද බාන් *mokada-bán*, "What?"; answer to "you there."

බාන්ධකිනේය, *Bándhakinéya*, *s.* (බාන්ධකී and ඪක් *ḍhak* aff. and ඉනඞ් *inań* augment) bastard, son of a disloyal wife, offspring of an unchaste woman.

බාන්ධකී, *Bándhakí*, *s.* a wanton.

බාන්ධව, *Bándhawa*, *s.* (බන්ධු *bandhu* kinsman, අණ් pleonastic aff.) relation, kinsman; friend, acquaintance: see බන්ධු *bandhu*.

බාන, *Bána*, *s.* bow; thick cord or rope; couple, pair, yoke, used only of cattle: pl. බාන් *bán*.

බානද, *Bánada*, *s.* stone, small stone, pebble; rock.

බානවා, *Bánawá*, *v.* to lower, to let down, to unload; to descend. to mend mats, to take out of the hearth or oven, to shave (when compounded with රැවුල් *rẹwul* and ඉසකෙස් *isakes*); to angle, to fish: pret. බැවා *bẹwá*.

බානාදාසි, *Bánádási*, *s.* medicinal plant, [Colloq. නිල් ගිරිනිල්ල *nil-girinilla*].

බානි, *Báni*, *s.* cloth; according to another authority, silk stuff.

බානු, *Bánu*, *s.* sun; also written භානු *bhánu*, [Coll: ඉර *ira*].

බාප්පා, *Báppá*, } *s.* uncle, father's youn-
බාප්පොච්චි, *Báppochchi*, } ger brother; mother's younger sister's husband: pl. බාප්පාලා *báppálá*.

බාපත, *Bápata*, see බාව *báwa*.

බාර්ලි, *Bárli*, *s.* barley, (Eng.)

බාරය, *Báraya*, *s.* charge, custody.

බාර ඔරුව, *Bára-oruwa*, *s.* small fishing boat.

බාරකරණවා, *Bárakaraṇawá*, *v.* to give in charge, to give in custody, to entrust.

බාරගන්නවා, *Báragannawá*, *v.* (බාර and ගන්නවා to take) to take in charge, to receive into custody.

බාරදුන්නා, *Báradunná*, *pret.* of the verb බාරදෙනවා *báradenawá*.

බාරදූර, *Báradúra*, *a.* large, bulky, heavy, important.

බාරදෙනවා, *Báradenawá*, *v.* (බාර charge, දෙනවා to give) to give in charge, to deliver up, to capitulate; to commit, to entrust.

බාරියා, *Báriyá*, *s.* wife, another form of භාර්‍යා *bhárya*.

බාරුසිගඟ, *Bárusi-gaṉga*, *s.* celestial river.

බාරේ, *Báré*, *s.* charge, custody.

බාල්කේ, *Bálké*, *s.* beam. (Dutch,)

බාල්දිය, *Báldiya*, *s.* tub.

බාල්දුව, *Bálduwa*, *s.* low, degradation.

බාල්‍ය, *Bálya*, *s.* childhood.

බාල, *Bála*, *s.* child, infant; stupidity, ignorance; perfume, or a sort of fragrant grass, *andropogon schœnanthus;* plant, *plectranthus zeylanicus*, [Colloq. ඉරිවේරිය *iriwériya*]; simpleton, dolt; hair, hair of the head: *a.* young, infantine, immature; unwise, foolish, uninstructed, ignorant.

බාලක, *Bálaka*, *s.* infant, boy under sixteen years of age; fool, blockhead; tail; finger ring; bracelet; perfume; small cardamoms, *elettaria cardamomum (minor)*; plant, *hibiscus mutablis.*

බාල කපු, *Bála-kapu*, *s.* sort of cotton.

බාලකාලය, *Bála-kálaya*, *s.* period of youth, minority.

බාලකුරක්කන්, *Bála-kurakkan*, *s.* sort of grain, *eleusine coracana.*

බාලකෝවි, *Bála-kóvi*, *s.* cabbage, *brasica oleracia.*

බාලගර්භිණී, *Bála-garbhiṇí*, *s.* (බාල and ගර්භිණී pregnant female) pregnant woman or any female animal: cow with calf for the first time.

බාලගොරඩිය, *Bála-goraḍiya*, *s.* pea plant, *pisum sativum;* also called බෝල කඩල *bóla-kaḍala.*

බාලග්‍රහී, *Bálagrahí*, } *s.* (බාල child, ග්‍රහ *graha*
බාලග්‍රී, *Báligrí*, } seizing, ඊ *í* fem. aff.) disease, atrophy and wasting in a child, ascribed to the malignant operation of the female fiend Pútaná.

බාලග්‍රිදෝෂය, *Bálagridóshaya*, *s.* unusual crying of infants within the first three months, assigned by natives to effect of demons.

බාලත්ව, *Bálatwa*, *s.* childhood.

බාලතන්ත්‍ර, *Bálatantra*, *s.* midwifery; care of a lying-in-woman, and her child.

බාලතනය, *Bálatanaya*, *s.* young son: see also කිහිරි *kihiri.*

බාලදේව, *Báladéwa*, see බලදේව *baladéwa.*

බාලප්පා, *Bálappá*, *s.* (බාල younger, අප්පා *appá* father) paternal uncle, father's younger brother, mother's younger sister's husband.

බාලපාශ්‍යා, *Bálapáṣyá*, *s.* (බාල hair, පාශ *páṣa* tie, binding) ornament of gold or silver etc., worn between the hair and divided on the forehead; string of pearls binding the hair.

බාලපුෂ්පිකා, *Bála-pushpiká*, *s.* (බාල hair, පුෂ්ප *pushpa* flower) species of jasmine, *jasminum sambac*, [Colloq. පිච්ච *pichcha* and බොලිද්ද *bolidda*]; the name alludes to a custom of oriental women wearing fillets of jasmine in the hair.

බාලම්මා, *Bálammá*, *s.* mother's younger sister, father's younger brother's wife.

බාල මාවි, *Bála-mávi*, *s.* kind of paddy, *oriza sativa.*

බාල මිපත් ඇල්වි, *Bála-mipat-ęlvi*, *s.* kind of hill paddy.

බාල මිපත් වි, *Bála-mipat-ví*, *s.* kind of paddy.

බාලමූෂිකා, *Bála-múshiká*, *s.* (බාල small, මූෂිකා rat) small rat or mouse, *mus musculus*, (order *Rodentia*); small kind of bat, variety of *scotophilus coromandelicus*, (order *Cheiroptera*).

බාලමෙනේරි, *Bála-menéri*, *s.* kind of panic grass, variety of *panicum miliare* or *p. psilopodium.*

බාලයා, *Bálayá*, *s.* (බාල young, ignorant, යා mas. aff.) child, youth, minor; stupid fellow, dolt, fool.

බාල වයස්කාරයා, *Bála-wayaskárayá*, *s.* minor.

බාල වයස, *Bála-wayasa*, *s.* childhood, young age.

බාලවාසස්, *Bála-wásas*, *s.* (බාල hair, of cows, goats etc. වාසස් vesture) woollen cloth or garments.

බාලසූදන, *Bálasúdana*, see බලසූදන *balasudana.*

බාලා, *Bálá*, *s.* woman, female; small cardamoms: see බාලක *bálaka;* aloes; coconut tree, [Colloq. පොල්ගහ *pol-gaha*]; turmeric, *curcuma longa*, [Colloq. කහ *kaha*]; sort of jasmine: see බාල පුෂ්පිකා *bála-pushpiká;* flower, *hibiscus tortuosus:* *a.* pure, clean, free from blemish or defilement, fit to be offered; ignorant, unwise, uninstructed; infantine, young, childish.

බාලාතප, *Bálátapa*, *s.* (බාල *bála* young, ආතප *átapa* ray of the sun) cool of the morning; heat of the sun in the morning.

බාලාර්කමණ්ඩල, *Bálárka-manḍala*, *s.* (බාල early or young, අර්ක *arka* the sun, මණ්ඩල circle) daybreak, circular reflection caused by the sun's rays on the horizon before his rise.

බාලාරාති, *Báláráti*, *s.* (බාල *bála* incorrectly for බල *bala* Asura, demon, අරාති *áráti* enemy) name of Indra, alluding to his being the enemy and vanquisher of Bala a demon.

බාලි, *Báli*, *s.* (බාල *bála* hair, ඉන් *in* aff.) name of a monkey, son of Indra: it alludes to his production from his mother's hair; small cardamoms.

බාලිකා, *Báliká*, *s.* female infant; sand; the knot or flower of an earring; rustling of leaves; small cardamoms, *elettaria cardamomum (minor)*, [Colloq. සිහින් එන්සාල් *sihin-ensál*]; plant, small species of hibiscus, *hibiscus mutabilis.*

බාලිය, *Báliya*, *s.* tub, (Tamil.) wooden vessel; vessel.

බාලිශ, *Báliṣa*, *a.* ignorant, stupid, dull; young, infantine; careless.

බාලී, *Bálí*, *s.* younger female.

බාලු, *Bálu*, } *s.* drug, perfume.
බාලුක, *Báluka*, }

බාලුකා, *Báluka*, *s.* sand, gravel; camphor; sort of cucumber.

බාලේය, *Báléya*, *s.* ass; Daitya, demon; plant, *siphonanthus indica;* black cumin seed, *nigella indica*, [Colloq. කළුදුරු *kaḷuduru*]; name of Kártikéya or Kataragama deviyó: *a.* soft; fit or proper for a child; fit or proper for sacrifice, etc.

බාලොලියා, *Báloliyá*, *s.* plant, *desmodium triquetrum (Leguminosæ).*

බාව, *Báwa*, *s.* alligator's or crocodile's tail.

බාවනවා, *Báwanawá*, *v.* to lay or put down; to cause to lie down: pret. බෑව්වා *bęwwá*.

බාවනාව, *Báwanáwa*, *s.* meditation, pious reflection, religious meditation, the act of bringing an object undisturbedly before the mind; corruptly for භාවනා *bháwaná*.

බාවය, *Báwaya*, *s.* (බව *bawa* being, අණ් *aṇ* aff.) state, manner, the quality of being; also written භාව *bháwa*, which see.

බාවිතාකරණවා, *Bávitákaraṇawá*, *v.* to use, to habituate.

බාවිතාව, *Bávitáwa*, *s.* usage, custom, habit: see භාවිතා *bhávitá*.

බාස්, *Bás*, *s.* foreman. (Dutch.)

බාස, *Bása*, *s.* speech, language, speaking.

බාසාව, *Básáwa*, *s.* speech, language: pl. බාසා *básá*.

බාසිත, *Básita*, *s.* conversation, intercourse; speech, saying: *a.* spoken, said, uttered, declared; corruptly for භාසිත *bhásita*.

බාසුරු, *Básuru*, *s.* (බා arm, බාස *bása* to shine, සුරු hero) sun, [Colloq. ඉර *ira*]; lion.

බාහලික, *Báhlika*, *s.* horse; assafœtida; plant, *monochoria hastæfolia*, or *pontederia hastata*, [Colloquial: දියහබරල *diya-habarala*]; another plant, *plumbago rosea*, [Colloq. රත්නෙටුල් *ratneṭul*]; *swietenia febrifugia.*

බාහ, *Báha*, *s.* (බාහ to endeavour) arm.

බාහිත්ථ, *Báhittha*, *s.* frontal of an elephant.

බාහිත, *Báhita*, *a.* placed or driven out, outward, external.

බාහිර, *Báhira*, *a.* outer; outward; external, outside.

බාහිරා, *Báhirá*, *a.* outside, outward; put out; disgraced, despised.

බාහිරාකම, *Báhirákama*, *s.* defamation, disgrace, meanness.

බාහිරාකරණවා, *Báhirákaraṇawá*, *v.* to defame, to disgrace, to insult, to ridicule.

බාහිරාව, *Báhiráwa*, see බාහිරාකම *báhirákama*.

බාහු, *Báhu*, *s.* arm; hand, [Colloq. අත *ata*]; side of any angular geometrical figure: *a.* many, much.

බාහුජ, *Báhuja*, *s.* (බාහු and ජ born) man of the kshatriya or warrior caste, alluding to the fable of that caste being born from the arm of Brahma; parrot; sesamum plant, *sesamum indicum*, [Colloq. තෙල් තල *tel-tala*].

බාහුදණ්ඩිය, *Báhu-daṇḍiya*, *s.* bracelet.

බාහුභූෂා, *Báhu-bhúshá*, *s.* (බාහු and භූෂා ornament) armlet, ornament worn round the upper arm.

බාහුමූල, *Báhu-múla*, *s.* (බාහු and මූල root) armpit, [Colloq. කිහිල්ල *kihilla*].

බාහුයුග්මය, *Báhu-yugmaya*, *s.* (බාහු and යුග්ම *yugma* couple) both arms.

බාහුයුද්ධය, *Báhu-yuddhaya*, *s.* (බාහු arm, යුද්ධ *yuddha* war) close fight, personal struggle, conflict, boxing, wrestling.

බාහුල්‍ය, *Báhulya*, *s.* plenty, abundance, large quantity.

බාහුල, *Báhula*, *s.* (බහුල *bahula* fire, with අණ් *aṇ* aff.) much, many, various; plural; grammatical term implying various or irregular formation; fire; Agni the regent of fire; black (the colour); month Kártika (October–November).

බාහුලේය, *Báhuléya*, *s.* (බහුලා *bahulá* Pleiades) name of Kártikéya or Kataragama deviyo, the Indian god of war; month (October–November).

බාහුව, *Báhuwa*, *s.* arm; hand, [Colloq. අත *ata*].

බාහුවල්ලී, *Báhu-wallí*, *s.* creeping plant, *momordica charantia*, [Colloq. කරවිල *karivila*].

බාහුවීර්‍ය, *Báhuvírya*, *s.* personal prowess.

බාහ්‍ය, *Báhya*, *ind.* out, outer, outside, without, extraneous.

බික්, *Bik*, *s.* house adjoining a temple where the priest usually resides; religious mendicant; ascetic; priest of Buddha; begging, asking, soliciting or demanding alms: see බික *bika*.

බික්තිය, *Biktiya*, *s.* wall of a building; corruptly for භිත්තිය *bhittiya*.

බික, *Bika*, *s.* any one of the natural segments or carpels of an orange or any similar fruit.

බිඟ, *Biṉga*, } *s.* wasp, large black bee, [Colloq.
බිඟු, *Biṉgu*, } බඹරා *bambará*]; plant, low spreading creeper or shrub possessing medicinal qualities, *eclipta* or *verbesina prostrata*, [Colloq. කිකිරිඳිය *kikiriṉdiya*]; according to another authority, *verbesina scandens.*

බිඟුදිය, *Biṉgudiya*, *s.* (බිඟු wasp, දිය bow-string) Ananga whose bow is strung with wasps o. bees.

බිඟුපිය, *Bingupiya, s.* (බිඟු bee, පිය loved) mace, spice, [Colloq. වසාවාසි *wasáwási*].

බිඟුපෙල, *Bingupelá*, } *s.* (බිඟු bee, පෙල line or
බිඟුමුළු, *Bingumulu*, } මුළු multitude) swarm or hive of bees.

බිච්චිය, *Bichchiya*, more properly written භිත්තිය *bhittiya*, බිත්තිය *bittiya* and බික්තිය *biktiya*, which see.

බිජ, *Bijja, s.* egg; pl. බිජු *biju*: corrupt form of බිජුව *bijuwa*.

බිජ්ජුරු, *Bijjuru*, see බිජුරු *bijuru*.

බිජපුර, *Bijapura, s.* common citron, *citrus medica*, [Colloq. ලප්නාරන් *lapnáran*].

බිජු, *Biju, s.* cause, origin in general; seed; seed of any animal; semen virile; testicles; egg; seed of plants etc; receptacle, place of deposit or prepartion; marrow.

බිජුත, *Bijuta, s.* wall, [Colloq. බික්තිය *biktiya*].

බිජු රකිනවා, *Biju-rakinawá, v.* (බිජු egg, රකිනවා preserve) to sit, to hatch eggs as a hen.

බිජුරු, *Bijuru, s.* (බිජු seed, රු to grow) corn, wheat.

බිජුව, *Bijuwa*, } see බිජු *biju*.
බිජුවට, *Bijuwata*, }

බිටි, *Biti, s.* water melon, *citrullus vulgaris* [Colloq. කොමඩු *komadu*].

බිඩ, *Bida, s.* factitious salt, salt produced from boiling the soil found near the sea shore or any earth impregnated with saline particles; particular kind of salt used as a tonic aperient, commonly called black salt or *bit loben*, prepared by fusing rock salt with a small portion of *emblic myrobalan*, the produce of which is muriate of soda with small quantities of muriate of lime, sulphur and oxide of iron.

බිඩංග, *Bidanga, s.* main part of coconut branch.

බිඩාල, *Bidála, s.* cat, [Colloq. බළලා *balalá*].

බිඩාලක, *Bidálaka, s.* yellow orpiment, application of ointment to the external part of the eye, especially to the eye-lids of which the lashes have fallen off or been ulcerated.

බිඩැල්ල, *Bidella, s.* sod.

බිඩැල, *Bidela*, see බිඩාල *bidála*.

බිණිම, *Biníma, s.* talk, speech; scolding, abuse.

බිණු, *Binu*, } *s.* speech, saying, speaking. [Coll:
බිණුම, *Binuma*, } කථාව *katháwa*].

බිත්තටය, *Bittataya, s.* seed; seed corn, seed of plants etc.

බිත්තර, *Bittara, s.* seed, seed corn; egg.

බිත්තිය, *Bittiya, s.* wall.

බිත, *Bita, s.* wall; wall of a house: pl. බිත් *bit*: see බිජු *biju*.

බිතක්කණ, *Bitakkana, s.* end or top of a wall.

බිතු, *Bitu*, see බිත *bita*.

බිදලා, *Bidalá, s.* any grain which divides in two, as peas, beans etc; dicotyledon: see බියල් *biyal*.

බිදුර, *Bidárá, s.* assafætida, [Colloq. පෙරුංකායම් *perunkáyam*]; small species of *jujube*.

බිදුරගන්ධ, *Bidáragandha, s.* (බිදුර and ගන්ධ smell) smell of assafætida.

බිදුරිකා, *Bidáriká, s.* plant, *Ipomæa digitata*, [Colloq. කිරිබඳු *kiribadu*]; bubo.

බිදුරී, *Bidárí, s.* kind of yam, hog's meat, *cyclamea indicum*, [Coll: ඌරල *úrala*]; *Ipomæa digitata*, [Colloq. කිරිබඳු *kiribadu*].

බිදි, *Bidi, s.* eating (of priests); breaking, tearing, rending.

බිඳ, *Binda, s.* drop: *part.* having broken, shivered, or smashed.

බිඳ එලනවා, *Binda-elanawá, v.* to break down, to destroy, to extirpate, to smash, to shiver.

බිඳපු, *Bindapu, p.* broken.

බිඳිනවා, *Bindinawá, v.* to break: pret. බිඳ, *bindá*.

බිඳීම, *Bindíma, s.* breaking, shivering.

බිඳුවනවා, *Binduwanawá, v.* to cause to break, to cause to flow.

බිඳෙනවා, *Bindenawá, v.* to break, to break of it self, to crack, to part asunder, to separate: pret. බිඳුනා *binduná*.

බින්, *Bin, s.* ground, spot, site, place; the earth, corruptly for බිම් *bim;* eating (of priests).

බින් අමු, *Bin-amu, s.* grain, variety of *paspalum scrobiculatum*.

බින් අවරි, *Bin-awari, s.* plant, *indigofera enneaphylla*.

බින් ඇතිරිල්ලපලා, *Bin-ẹtirilla-palá, s.* plant, not ascertained.

බින් ඇපල, *Bin-ẹpala, s.* plant, variety of *triumfetta*.

බින් ඕළු, *Bin-ólu, s.* plant, *Limnanthemum parvifolium (Gentianaceæ)*.

බින් කරල්තණ, *Bin-karal-tana, s.* kind of grass.

බින් කරල්සැබෝ, *Bin-karalsẹbó*, } *s.* plant, *cyathu-*
බින් කරල්හැබ, *Bin-karalhẹba*, } *la geniculata*, or *c. prostrata, (Amarantaceæ)*.

බින් කහ, *Bin-kaha, s.* variety of *curcuma longa*.

බින් කිතුල්, *Bin-kitul, s.* plant, *curculigo orchioides*; also called හින් බින්තල් *hin-bintal*.

බින් කුරටිය, *Bin-kúraṭiya*, *s.* plant, variety of *memecylon rostratum.*

බින් කොහොඹ, *Bin-kohomba*, *s.* plant, peculiar to Ceylon, *munronia pumila, (Meliaceæ).*

බින්ගේ, *Bin-gé*, *s.* (බින් and ගේ house) cave, cavern, subterraneous apartment, natural or artificial.

බින්තඹුරු, *Bintamburu*. *s.* bindweed, bearing a red flower, *ipomæa Beladamboe* or *i. rugosa (Convolvulaceæ).*

බින් තල්, *Bin-tal*, *s.* name of two species of *curculigo*: see මහ බින්තල් *maha-bin-tal* and හින් බින් තල් *hín-bin-tal.*

බින් තල, *Bin-tala*, *s.* general name for river fish.

බින් දදකිරිය, *Bin-dadakiriya*, *s.* spurge with branches pressing flat on the earth, *euphorbia thymifolia, (Euphorbiaceæ)*: see එල *ela*–බූ *bú*–and මුදු දදකිරිය *múdu-dadakiriya.*

බින් දර, *Bin-dara*, *s.* herb with violet flowers, peculiar to Ceylon, *exacum zeylanicum (Gentianaceæ)*: also called කිරිහිරිය *kirihiriya.*

බින් දිවුල්, *Bin-diwul*, *s.* variety of *feronia elephantum* or wood apple.

බින්දිම, *Bindima*, *s.* hemorrhage.

බිඳු, *Bindu*, *s.* drop, spot or speck; sign ං which is the nasal mark used in connection with the miscellaneous letters.

බිඳුජලක, *Bindujálaka*, *s.* (බිඳු marks, ජල *jála* multitude) coloured spots or freckles on an elephant.

බින් දුම්මල, *Bin-dummala*, *s.* (බින් ground, දුම්මල resin) resinous oil, prepared by boiling and evaporation from earth mixed with bitumen or petroleum.

බිඳුව, *Binduwa*, see බිඳු *bindu.*

බින්නානු, *Bin-nánu*, *s.* plant, not ascertained,

බින්නිඹ, *Binnimba*, *s.* (බිම් *bim* ground, නිඹ nimba) plant, according to Sinhalese authority the kiráta or *gentiana cherayta*, but named by Mr. Moon *melia pumila;* the name alludes to its bitter taste; *munronia pumila*, [Colloq. බිංකොහොඹ *bin-kohomba*].

බින්නුග, *Bin-nuga*, *s.* Indian ipecacuanha, *tylophora asthmatica (Asclepidiaceæ).*

බින් නෙල්ලි, *Bin-nelli*, *s.* plant, *phyllanthus urinaria*, [Colloq. රත්පිටවක්කා *rat-piṭawakká*].

බින් නෙළු, *Bin-neḷu*, *s.* small tree, variety of *strobilanthes.*

බින් පුරුක්තණ, *Bin-puruk-taṇa*, *s.* hard grass, *rottboellia thomæa.*

බින් පේරදොඹ, *Bin-péradomba*, *s.* tree, species of *calophyllum.*

බින් බෙඳුරා, *Bin-béndurá*, *s.* plant, not ascertained.

බින්ම, *Binma*, see බිණුම *biṇuma.*

බින්මෑ, *Bin-mẹ*, *s.* kind of green gram, *phaseolus trilobus, (Leguminosæ).*

බින් රටතණ, *Bin-raṭataṇa*, *s.* kind of guinea grass, *panicum maximum.*

බින්විල, *Bin-vila*, *s.* hedge hyssop, *gratiola parvifolia.*

බින්සවන්, *Bin-sawan*, *s.* species of the hedge hyssop, *gratiola juncea.*

බින් සියඹලා, *Bin-siyambalá*, *s.* plant, *æschynomene pumila.*

බින් හකඹලා, *Bin-hakambalá*, *s.* plant, *begonia tenera.*

බින් හෑඩයා, *Bin-hẹḍayá*, *s.* club moss, *lycopodium repens.*

බිනර මස, *Binara-masa*, *s.* month so called (September–October).

බිනිසා, *Binisá*, *s.* opium plant, *papaver somnifera*, [Colloq. කන්සා *kansá*].

බිබිල, *Bibila*, *s.* bubble; pimple, pustule.

බිබුල, *Bibula*, *s.* bubble; blister, pustule; fountain, spring or place where water oozes.

බිඹු, *Bimbu*, *s.* (බිම්බ *bimba* halo etc. උ *u* aff.) the orb of the sun or moon; plant, *bryonia grandis*: see බිඹ *bimba.*

බිඹුරු, *Bimburu*, *s.* image, picture; statue, [Colloq. රූපය *rúpaya*]: see පෙන *pena.*

බිඹුල, *Bimbula*, *s.* bubble; spring, fountain; pimple, pustule, boil, blister: pl. බිඹුල් *bimbul.*

බිම්, *Bim*, *plur.* of බිම *bima*, landed property, ground.

බිම් ඌරා, *Bim-úrá*, *s.* (බිම් and ඌරා hog) sort of large grasshopper or locust.

බිම් පලා, *Bim-palá*, *s.* vegetable, plant in general; greens, vegetables etc.

බිම් පුහුල්, *Bim-puhul*, *s.* medicinal creeping plant, not ascertained.

බිම් පොල්, *Bim-pol*, *s.* small medicinal plant, the root of which is taken in powders, *trichopus zeylanicus (Dioscoreaceæ).*

බිම්පොලඟා, *Bim-polangá*, *s.* viperine snake.

බිම්බ, *Bimba*, *s.* rim or halo round the moon in cloudy weather; disc of the sun or moon; picture, likeness or representation, image, statue;

cucurbitaceous plant, *bryonia grandis* or *momordica monadelphia*, [Coll: කෙම්වැල් *kemwęl*]; *cephalandra indica*, [Coll: කෝවක්කා *kówakká*].

බිම් බටු, *Bim-baṭu*, *s.* plant of the genus *solanum.*

බිම්බඵල, *Bimba-phala*, *s.* (බිම්බ and ඵල fruit) creeping plant, *bryonia grandis*, [Colloq. කෙම්වැල් *kemwęl*]: see the preceding word.

බිම්බර, *Bimbara*, *s.* multitude, [Colloq. සමූහය *samúhaya*].

බිම්බස්සා, *Bim-bassá*, *s.* bird called Kelaart's night jar, *caprimulgus Kalaartii;* jungle night jar, *c. atripennis*, also called රෑබස්සා *rę-bassá* and බමර බස්සා *bamara-bassá;* common Indian night-jar, *c. asiaticus*, also called රෑබස්සා *rę-bassá:* (*Caprimulgidæ*, order *Picariæ).*

බිම්බා, *Bimbá*, *s.* queen Yasódhará and wife of Buddha.

බිම්බාදක, *Bimbádaka*, *s.* tree, *leea sambucina;* marking nut plant, *semecarpus anacardium.*

බිම්බිකා, *Bimbiká*, } *s.* creeping plant, *bryonia*
බිම්බි, *Bimbí*, } *grandis*, or *momordica monadelpha* [Colloq. කෙම්වැල් *kemwęl*].

බිම්බෝහනය, *Bimbóhanaya*, *s.* pillow, mattress, bolster.

බිම් මොණරමල්, *Bim-moṇara-mal*, *s.* variety of *dianella ensifolia.*

බිම්ලිය, *Bim-liya*, *s.* (බිම් *bim* ground, ලිය creeper) long earth worm.

බිම් සපු, *Bim-sapu*, *s.* tree, variety of *Michelia.*

බිම, *Bima*, *s.* ground, place, site; earth, land, soil.

බිම අනනවා, *Bima-annawá*, *v.* to strike or beat the ground, (as a vessel,) to run on shore or aground.

බිම එලනවා, *Bima-elanawá*, *v.* to throw down, to drop down.

බිය, *Biya*, *s.* fear, terror, alarm, dread.

බියකරණවා, *Biyakaraṇawá*, see බයකරණවා *baya-karaṇawá.*

බියපත්, *Biyapat*, *a.* (බිය fear, පත් come, arrived) fearful, horrible; frightened, alarmed, horror-struck.

බියල්, *Biyal*, } *s.* half, division; splitting, rending
බියලි, *Biyali*, } or separating; dividing any grain that has two or more lobes, as beans, peas, etc.; dicotyledon: see බිදලා *bidalá.*

බියලිකරණවා, *Biyalikaraṇawá*, *v.* to slice seeds (as mustard.)

බියලි දොර, *Biyali-dora*, *s.* (බියලි dividing, separating, දොර door) folding door; door dividing and opening in the centre.

බියෙස්, *Biyes*, *a.* nigh, near, proximate, neighbouring.

බිරම්, *Biram*, *a.* fearful, dreadful, terrific.

බිරාන්ත, *Biránta*, *s.* fear, terror, panic, astonishment, corrupt form of භ්‍රාන්ත *bhránta*, revolved, blundering, wandering.

බිරාන්තවෙනවා, *Biránṭawenawá*, *v.* to be surprised with fear.

බිරි, *Biri*, *s.* woman, wife: *a.* fearful, terrific, horrifying.

බිරිඳ, *Birinda*, *s.* woman, wife, [Colloq. භාර්‍යාව *bháryáwa*].

බිරීම, *Biríma*, *s.* barking, bark of a dog etc.

බිරු, *Biru*, see බිරි *biri.*

බිරුම, *Biruma*, *s.* barking; verbal noun of බුරණවා *buraṇawá.*

බිරුසර, *Birusara*, *s.* (බිරු fearful, සර voice, sound) bear, [Colloq. වලහා *walahá*].

බිරෝව, *Birówa*, *s.* bureau, (Dutch).

බිල්ල, *Billa*, *s.* sacrifice of animals to demons, or offerings made in honor of deceased ancestors; bait for fishing or catching birds etc.; bell; tax, revenue; fragments: pl. බිලි *bili.*

බිල්ලා, *Billá*, *s.* kidnapper, ghost talked of to fighten children: pl. බිල්ලෝ *billó.*

බිල්ව, *Bilwa*, *s.* fruit tree, *ægle marmelos*, [Colloq. බෙලි *beli*]; weight: see පල *pala.*

බිල්වජ, *Bilwajá*, *s.* (බිල්ව and ජ born) tree, commonly වැලුක්ගහ *węluk-gaha.*

බිල, *Bila*, *s.* cave, natural or artificial hollow in a rock; fissure, rent, perforation; a term used by elephant keepers for lifting up the leg of elephant.

බිලඟ, *Bilaṅga*, *s.* sour gruel; vinegar.

බිලඟථාලික, *Bilaṅgathálika*, *s.* punishment inflicted by taking off the scalp of the person, and pouring boiling gruel upon the head.

බිලාල, *Bilála*, *s.* (බිඩාල *biḍála* with the lingual changed into the semivowel ල) cat, the Páli form of බිඩාල *biḍála.* [Colloq. බළලා *baḷalá*]; a factitious salt, *bit loben*: see බිඩ *biḍa.*

බිලි, *Bili*, *s.* thing sacrificed; value.

බිලිකටුව, *Bilikaṭuwa*, *s.* (බිලි and කටුව hook) fish-hook.

බිලිඳා, *Bilindá*, *s.* child, male infant: pl. බිලිඳෝ *bilindó.*

බිලින්, *Bilin*, *s.* country gooseberry, blimbing or bilimbi with acid fruit used in preserves etc; *averrhoa bilimbi (Geraniaceæ).*

බිලිපිත්ත, *Bilipitta*, *s.* fishing or angling rod.

බිලිපුටු, *Biliputu*, *s.* (බිලි fragments of food, or what is offered to demons, පුටු who is nourished) crow, so called in allusion to its eating or feeding on the offerings or the remains of the sacrifices made to demons, [Colloq. කපුටා *kaputá*].

බිලිපූජාව, *Bili-pújáwa*, *s.* sacrifice to demons: see බිල්ල *billa*.

බිලිය, *Biliya*, *s.* fish-hook; large species of earth worm.

බිලියම, *Biliyama*, *s.* plummet, or mason's lead; ceremony of making offerings to propitiate planets or demons.

බිලි ලනුව, *Bili-lanuwa*, *s.* (බිලි bait, ලනුව line) fishing line.

බිලී, *Bilí*, see බිල්ල *billa*.

බිලීබානවා, *Bilí-bánawá*, *v.* (බිලී bait, බානවා to cast) to angle, to fish.

බිලීමස්, *Bilí-mas*, *s.* red kind of fish, *cyprinus denticulatus: (Malacopterygii)*.

බිලේ, *Bilé*, *s.* hollow in a trunk.

බිලේශය, *Bileśaya*, *s.* snake, serpent; nága or inhabitant of Nága-lóka or Pátála.

බිස්ස, *Bissa*, *s.* large oval basket for holding corn or grain of any kind; mat or bundle of straw placed at the door for wiping the feet; clod thickly overgrown with grass.

බිස, *Bisa*, *s.* film or fibres attached to the stalk of the lotus or the water lily; stalk of the lotus.

බිසකණ්ඨිකා, *Bisakaṇṭhiká*, *s.* (බිස fibres of the lotus, කණ්ඨ *kaṇtha* throat, කන් *kan* aff.) small crane.

බිසගුත්තමයා, *Bisaguttamayá*, see භිෂගුත්තම *bhishaguttama*.

බිසපුෂ්ප, *Bisapushpa*, *s.* (බිස and පුෂ්ප flower) blue lotus, *nymphœa stellata*, [Coll. මානෙල් *mánel*]; flower of the lotus or the water lily.

බිසව්, *Bisaw*,
බිසව, *Bisawa*,
බිසවුන්නාන්සේ, *Bisawunnánsé*, } *s.* (අභිෂේක *abhiséka* royal unction, dropping the initial vowel, and changing the aspirate into its corresponding soft letter) queen, one who has been anointed and crowned.

බිසි, *Bisi*, *s.* ascetic's seat.

බිසිනී, *Bisiní*, *s.* tank or pond producing the lotus; assemblage of lotus flowers.

බිසෙව්, *Bisew*, *s.* anointing, royal unction.

බිසෝ, *Bisó*, *s.* queen, empress: see බිසව *bisawa*.

බිහි, *Bihi*, *s.* demon, devil; mat for wiping the feet: *ad.* out, extraneous; outward, outer, outside.

බිහිදොර, *Bihidora*, *s.* (බිහි outer, දොර door, gate) outer door or gate of a house; portico in front of a house or mansion.

බිහිරා, *Bihirá*, *s.* deaf man: pl. බිහිරෝ *bihiró*.

බිහිරි, *Bihiri*, *s.* deaf woman: *a.* deaf, Elu form of බධිර *badhira*.

බිහිවීම, *Bihivíma*, *s.* birth, bringing forth, producing.

බිහිවෙනවා, *Bihiwenawá*, *v.* to be born, to be brought forth, [Colloq. උපදිනවා *upadinawá*].

බිහිස, *Bihisa*, *a.* good, best, excellent, virtuous.

බිහිසු, *Bihisu*, *a.* good, auspicious, virtuous, excellent, best, preeminent.

බිහිසුණු, *Bihisuṇu*, *a.* terrible, fearful, alarming, dreadful.

බීජ, *Bíja*, *s.* egg; seed of plants, etc; semen of any animal; semen virile; germ of any thing; penis; cause, originating principle; any one of the senses.

බීජ කදලි, *Bíja-kadali*, *s.* kind of plantain or banana, *musa sapientum*, [Colloq. ඇට කෙහෙල් *eṭa-kehel*].

බීජකෝෂ, *Bíjakósa*, *s.* (බීජ seed, කෝෂ purse) scrotum; pericarp or seed vessel of the lotus; capsule of flowers.

බීජතර, *Bíjatara*, *s.* (බීජ and තර much) pomegranate, *punica granatum*, [Coll. දෙළුම් *delum*].

බීජපුෂ්ප, *Bíja-pushpa*, *s.* (බීජ and පුෂ්ප flower) common citron; thorny plant, *vangueria spinosa*.

බීජපූර, *Bíjapúra*, *s.* (බීජ seed, පූර what is full) common citron, *citrus medica*, [Colloq. ලප්නාරං *lapnáraṇ*]; pomegranate, *punica granatum*, [Colloq. දෙළුම් *deḷum*].

බීජපූරක, *Bíjapúraka*, *s.* (බීජ and පූර full, ක aff.) pomegranate: see බීජතර *bíjatara*.

බීජඵල, *Bíja-phala*, *s.* (බීජ and ඵල fruit) long pepper plant, *piper longum*, [Colloq. තිප්පිලි *tippili*].

බීජමොච, *Bíjamocha*, *s.* species of plantain, *musa sapientum*.

බීජය, *Bíjaya*, see බීජ *bíja*.

බීජාකෘත, *Bíjákṛita*, *a.* (බීජ *bíja* seed, කෘත *kṛita* prepared, with ආ *á* added to the first) ploughed, the ground prepared for receiving the seed.

බීජාහ්ව, *Bíjáhwa*, *s.* (බීජ *bíja* and ආහ්වා *áhwá* name, appellation) common citron: see බීජපූර *bíjapúra;* citron gourd.

බිත, *Bíta*, *s.* fear, terror, alarm, fright.

බිතාක්ෂ, *Bitáksha*, *s.* tree, *terminalia belerica.* [Coll: බුළු *bulu*].

බිභත්ස, *Bíbhatsa*, *s.* (බධ *badha* to bind, to hate) disgust produced on the mind by the actions and performances of dancing women; abhorrence.

බිම, *Bíma*, *s.* drink, drinking, draught, beverage.

බිමත්, *Bímat*, *a.* (බි drinking, මත් intoxicated) drunk, intoxicated with spirituous liquor.

බිමත්කම, *Bímatkama*, *s.* drunkenness, intoxication.

බිරණකාල, *Bíranakála*, *s.* (බිරණ *bírana* and කාල time) foggy weather; dark and obscure weather.

බිරණය, *Bíranaya*, *s.* fog, mist, [Colloq. මීදුම *míduma*]; darkness proceeding from the sun being overcast.

බිරළුව, *Bíraluwa*, *s.* bobbin for making lace.

බිරා, *Birá*, see බිහිරා *bihirá.*

බිරානි, *Biráni*, *a.* cloudy, foggy.

බිරි, *Bíri*, *s.* deaf woman: see බිහිරි *bihiri.*

බිරිතට්ටුව, *Bíritattuwa*, *s.* deafness occasioned by a loud noise.

බිරිම, *Bírima*, } *s.* gloomy, misty weather.
බිරුම, *Bíruma*,

බුංක, *Bunka*, *s.* castor oil plant, *ricinus comunis*, [Colloq. රත් එඬරු *rat-endaru*].

බුක්ක, *Bukka*, *s.* heart; goat.

බුක්කන, *Bukkana*, *s.* barking (as a dog).

බුක්කාර, *Bukkára*, *s.* (බුක්ක *bukka* to bark, ආර *ára* aff.) roaring or barking of a lion.

බුක්තිය, *Buktiya*, *s.* possession, an inheritance.

බුකවාගණ ඉන්නවා, *Bukawágana-innawá*, *v.* to be sulky or peevish.

බුකුල් අනිනවා, *Bukul-aninawá*, *v.* to beat with the fist, to box.

බුකුල, *Bukula*, *s.* blow from the fist on the side.

බුජ, *Buja*, *s.* hand, arm, [Colloq. අත *ata*]; snake.

බුජඟ, *Bujanga*, *s.* serpent, [Colloq. සර්පයා *sarpayá*]; gamester, [Colloq. සූදුකාරයා *súdukárayá*].

බුජඟය, *Bujangaya*, *s.* tree, *moringa pterygosperma*, [Colloq. මුරුංගා *murungá*].

බුජම, *Bujama*, *s.* jar: pl. බුජම් *bujam.*

බුජමුල්, *Bujamul*, *s.* (බුජ arm, මුල් root) arm-pit, [Colloq. කිහිල්ල *kihilla*].

බුඩ්ඩයා, *Buddayá*, *s.* stupid man.

බුත්, *But*, *s.* for බුදු *budu* Buddha, as බුත්සරණ *butsarana* refuge in Buddha, or the feet of Buddha.

බුත්තිය, *Buttiya*, *s.* possession.

බුත්තිවිඳිනවා, *Buttivindinawá*, *v.* to enjoy, to possess, to occupy; to eat.

බුත්සරණ, *Butsarana*, *s.* plant called Indian shot, *canna indica (Scitamineæ)*; refuge in Buddha, or Buddha's feet.

බුද්දාලය, *Buddálaya*, *s.* (බුද්ද *budda* corrupt form of බුඩ *buddha*, Buddha, ආලය *álaya* residence, hall, saloon) temple of Buddha.

බුද්බුද, *Budbuda*, *s.* (බුද් imitative sound, බුද to perceive) bubble.

බුද, *Buda*, *s.* planet Mercury, the regent of that planet.

බුද දින, *Buda-dina*, *s.* (බුද and දින day) Wednesday, used in writing, බදාදා *badádá* in speaking.

බුදහු, *Budahu*, *s.* planet Mercury.

බුදිනවා, *Budinawá*, *v.* to eat.

බුදිමත, *Budimata*, *s.* drowsiness, sleepiness.

බුදියනවා, *Budiyanawá*, } *v.* to sleep, to take repose, to nap.
බුදියාගන්නවා, *Budiyágannawá*,

බුදීම, *Budíma*, *s.* eating, verbal noun of බුදිනවා *budinawá.*

බුදු, *Budu*, *s.* Elu form of බුඩ Buddha; knowledge, understanding.

බුදුන්, *Budun*, *plur.* of the last, but used as a respectful term for Buddha.

බුධ, *Budha*, *s.* regent of the planet Mercury and son of the moon.

බුධාන, *Budhána*, *s.* wise man, sage, holy teacher.

බුධිත, *Budhita*, *a.* known, understood, instructed.

බුඩ, *Buddha*, *s.* (බුධ *budha* to know) name of the founder of Buddhism, the religion which is professed by the Sinhalese part of the population of Ceylon, the Burman empire and several other nations in the East; sage, wise or learned man; philosopher; any eminent or deified teacher: great confusion has taken place among Sanskrit writers and the Europeans who have followed them, by confounding Buddha, which is a generic name for a wise man or philosopher, with Buddha (Gautama) the son of Suddhódana and the founder of the religion which goes by his name.

බුඩක්ෂේත්‍රය, *Buddhakshétraya*, *s.* (බුඩ and ක්ෂේත්‍ර *kshétra* field) any country where either the power or religion of Buddha prevails, or where the knowledge of him exists.

බුඩකාරක, *Buddhakáraka*, *a.* (බුඩ and කාර doing; doer, ක aff.) making one a Buddha, *i. e.* (actions) necessary for the attainment of the Buddhahood.

බුඩකෝලාහල, *Buddha-kóláhala*, *s.* (බුඩ and කෝලාහල noise, rejoicing) the festive rejoicings at the birth of Buddha.

බුඩඝෝෂ, *Buddhaghósha*, *s.* (බුඩ and ඝුෂ *ghusha* to proclaim) name of a celebrated Buddhist sage and saint, the author of the Artha-kathás or perpetual comments on the orations of Buddha; these, as the author was a rahat possessed of superhuman endowments, are of equal authority with the text; he came from the continent of India and is supposed to have flourished early in the fifth century A. D.

බුඩත්වය, *Buddhatwaya*, *s.* Buddhaship.

බුඩරාජ කල්කය, *Buddharája-kalkaya*, *s.* medicinal drug; levigated powder, so called.

බුඩරාජ ගුලිය, *Buddharája-guliya*, *s.* medicinal pill, so called.

බුඩරාජ තෛලය, *Buddharája-tailaya*, *s.* name of a medicinal oil.

බුඩවර්ෂ *Buḍdha-warsha*, *s.* (බුඩ and වර්ෂ year) the era of Buddha, commencing about 543 years before Christ.

බුඩාගම, *Buddhágama*, *s.* Buddhist religion.

බුඩාඞ්කුරය, *Buddháńkuraya*, *s.* (බුඩ *buddha* and අඞ්කුර *ańkura* bud or young shoot) embryo Buddha, candidate for the Buddhaship.

බුඩාන්තර, *Buddhántara*, *s.* (බුඩ *buddha* and අන්තර between, intervening) time which elapses between the death of one Buddha and the birth of another.

බුඩානුභාව, *Bnddhánubháwa*, *s.* (බුඩ *buddha* and අනුභාව power, dignity etc.) dignity or the supreme power and authority of Buddha.

බුඩාසන, *Buddhásana*, *s.* (බුඩ *buddha* and ආසන *ásana* sitting, a seat) Buddha's seat or throne.

බුඩි, *Buddhi*, *s.* (බුධ *budha* to know) wisdom, intellect, understanding.

බුඩිමත්, *Buddhimat*, } *a.* (බුඩි understanding, මත්
බුඩිමාන්, *Buddhimán*, } poss. aff.) wise, learned, skilled; famed, known; humble, docile.

බුඩිවන්ත, *Buddhiwanta*, *a.* (බුඩි and වන්ත poss. aff.) learned, wise, well informed; sensible, clever.

බුඩීන්ද්‍රිය, *Buddhíndriya*, *s.* (බුඩි and ඉන්ද්‍රිය organ) organ of intellect, as the mind, eye, ear, nose, tongue, and skin.

බුන්, *Bun*, *a.* eaten; opened, blown, expanded, as a flower; broken, fractured, torn, rent.

බුන්න, *Bunna*, *s.* that which is eaten or broken.

බුන්හුළු, *Bunhuḷu*, *s.* expansion, as of flowers etc.

බුන, *Buna*, *a.* crooked, bent, tortuous.

බුපවු, *Bupawu*, see බූපවු *búpawu.*

බුපැල්, *Bupẹl*, see බූපැල *Búpẹla.*

බුබුන්, *Bubuin*, *s.* root of a tree or plant of any kind.

බුබුල, *Bubula*, *s.* bubble; blister, pustule; spring of water for purposes of irrigation: pl. බුබුල් *bubul.*

බුබුස්තණ, *Bubus-taṇa*, *s.* cuscus grass, *andropogon muricatus*, [Colloq. සැවැන්දරා *sẹwẹndará*].

බුභුක්ෂා, *Bubhukshá*, *s.* (භුජ *bhuja* to eat, in the desiderative form) hunger.

බුභුක්ෂිත, *Bubhukshita*, *a.* (බුභුක්ෂා *bubhukshá* hunger, ඉත *ita* aff.) hungry, [Colloq. බඩගිනි *baḍagini*].

බුම්මනවා, *Bummanawá*, } *v.* to sit
බුම්මාගණඉන්නවා, *Bummágaṇa-innawá*, } silent and unoccupied, either through grief or anger, to look sullen.

බුරණවා, *Buraṇawá*, *v.* to bark, (as a dog): pret බිරුවා *biruwá.*

බුරල්, *Bural*, *s.* an aged person, one upwards of seventy.

බුරිකැවුම්, *Buri-kẹwum*, *s.* kind of sweet cakes.

බුරිය, *Buriya*, *s.* navel.

බුරියා, *Buriyá*, *s.* man with a prominent navel.

බුරුත්ත, *Burutta*, *s.* cluster as of fruits.

බුරුත, *Buruta*, *s.* satin wood, *chloroxylon Swietenia (Meliaceæ).*

බුරුමය, *Burumaya*, } *s.* wimble; gimlet, auger: pl.
බුරුමේ, *Burumé*, } බුරුම *buruma.*

බුරුල්, *Burul*, *s.* old or aged person; person weak from age: *a.* slack, loose, soft, flaccid.

බුරුල්කරණවා, *Burulkaraṇawá*, *v.* to loosen.

බුරුල්බානවා, *Burulbánawá*, *v.* to have the udder heavy with milk before giving brith to a calf.

බුරුල්ල, *Burulla*, *s.* udder; small tree, *leea sambucina (Ampelideæ);* also called ගුරුල්ල *gurulla.*

බුරුල, *Burula*, *s.* leniency, state of being loose.

බුරුලදෙනවා, *Burula-denawá*, *v.* to render slack, used to signify to connive at or shew indulgence.

බුරුලනවා, *Burulanawá*, *s.* long barking of dogs.

බුරුසුව, *Burusuwa*, *s.* rocket, sky rocket; brush.

බුලත්, *Bulat*, *s.* creeping plant bearing a pungent leaf, called betel pepper, *piper (or chavica) betle, (Piperaceæ);* the leaf with the arecanut, a small quantity of caustic lime or chunam, with catechu, and occasionally cloves, cardamoms, etc. forms the pan or betel of the Asiatics.

බුලත් අත, *Bulat-ata, s.* forty betel leaves.

බුලත්තට්ටුව, *Bulat-taṭṭuwa, s.* betel stand.

බුලත් තලා, *Bulat-talá, s.* plant, not ascertained.

බුලත් නෙළු, *Bulat-neḷu, s.* plant, not ascertained.

බුලත්මල්ල, *Bulat-malla, s.* small bag of betel worn by native women in their waist.

බුලත්විට, *Bulatviṭa, s.* chew of betel.

බුලත්වැල, *Bulat-weḷa, s.* (බුලත් and වැල creeper) betel creeper: see බුලත් *bulat.*

බුලත්හුරුල්ල, *Bulat-hurulla, s.* bundle of forty betel leaves and a leaf of tobacco.

බුවන, *Buwana, s.* sky, firmament: see also භුවන *bhuwana.*

බුස්ස, *Bussa, s.* a ball used for play.

බුස, *Busa, s.* chaff; wealth; dry cow dung; sour curds.

බුසල, *Busala, s.* bushel. (English.)

බුසුන්, *Busun, s.* foot or root of a tree, [Colloq. ගහ මුල *gaha-mula*].

බුසේරු, *Buséru,* see බූසේරු *búséru.*

බුහු, *Buhu, a.* much, many.

බුහුගහනවා, *Buhu-gahanawá, v.* to play at ball.

බුහුගෙඩිය, *Buhugeḍiya, s.* small unripe pomplemose or pumelow, *citras decumana,* used as a ball to play with.

බුහුටියා, *Buhuṭiyá, s.* clever or skilful man.

බුහුන්, *Buhun,*
බුහුනනි, *Buhunani,*
බුහුනනියන්, *Buhunaniyan,* } s. sister, but invariably used for an elder sister.

බුහුමන්, *Buhuman, s.* (බුහු much, මන් from මාන *mána* to honor) love, affection, attachment, regard, great esteem, respect, reverence.

බුහුමන්කරණවා, *Buhumankaraṇawá, v.* to reverence, to respect.

බුහුරු, *Buhuru, s.* hole, pit.

බුළු, *Buḷu, s.* one of the three myrobalans, tree with small grey flowers, kernels reckoned intoxicating, *terminalia belerica (Combretaceæ).*

බුළුකොට්ටම්බා, *Buḷu-koṭṭambá, s.* variety of the country almond, *terminalia Catappa.*

බුළුපැත්ත, *Buḷupętta, s.* tree, not identified.

බූ, *Bú, s.* earth, world; demon, etc.; see භූත *bhuta*: *a.* (as applied to plants) hairy.

බූ අනෝදා, *Bú-anódá, s.* plant, variety of *abutilon asiaticum.*

බූ අවරි, *Bú-awari, s.* species of indigo, *indigofera hirsuta.*

බූ ඇඹිල්ල, *Bú-ęmbilla, s.* small tree, *antidesma ghæsembilla* or *a. paniculatum (Euphorbiaceæ)*; see හින් ඇඹිල්ල *hín-ęmbilla.*

බූ උඩුපියලි, *Bú-uṇḍupiyali, s.* plant, variety of *desmodium* (or *hedysarum*) *heterophyllum.*

බූ කඩුපාර, *Bú-kaḍupára, s.* plant, *cacalia sonchifolia.*

බූ කටුගඳ, *Bú-katugaṇḍa,*
බූ කටුහැඳ, *Bu-katuhęnda,* } s. hound's tongue, *cynoglossum furcatum (Boragineæ).*

බූ කපරුතලා, *Bú-kaparutalá, s.* wild mint, *mentha sylvestris.*

බූ කරවු, *Bú-karawu, s.* plant, peculiar to Ceylon, *scleria hirsuta.*

බූ කවනවා, *Bú-kawanawá, v.* to slouch.

බූ කිඳ, *Bú-kiṇda, s.* plant, *tinospora malabarica (Menispermaceæ)*: also called වල්කිඳ *wal-kiṇda.*

බූ කිනිතුල්, *Bú-kinitul, s.* plant, not identified.

බූ කිරිය, *Bú-kíriya, s.* plant, *amomum echinatum.*

බූකෙටියා, *Búkeṭiyá, s.* creeper.

බූ කොබ්බෑ, *Bú-kobbę, s.* plant, variety of *allophyllus* (or *schmidelia* or *ornithrope*) *cobbe.*

බූ කොල්ලු, *Bú-kollu, s.* variety of kollu, *dolichos uniflorus.*

බූ කැඳ, *Bú-kęnda, s.* plant, *Mallotus albus* or *Rottlera tetracocca (Euphorbiaceæ).*

බූ කැලිය, *Bú-kęliya, s.* plant, variety of *grewia Microcos.*

බූගානවා, *Búgánawá, v.* to shave the head.

බූ ගිරිතිල්ල, *Bú-giritilla, s.* plant, variety of *argyreia populipolia* or *rivea zeylanica.*

බූ ගැටකොල, *Bú-gęṭakola, s.* plant, variety of *hedyotis auricularia.*

බූගැටියා, *Búgęṭiyá, s.* plant, *hugonia Mystax (Linaceæ)*; also called හින්ගැටියා *hín-gęṭiyá.*

බූතයා, *Bútayá,* see භූත *bhúta.*

බූ තරණ, *Bú-taraṇa, s.* plant, variety of *webera corymbosa.*

බූ තුත්තිරි, *Bú-tuttiri, s.* variety of grass, *chrysopogon aciculatus.*

බූ තෝර, *Bú-tóra, s.* species of cassia or senna, *cassia absus (Leguminosæ).*

බූ තැල්කොල, *Bú-tęlkola, s.* bind weed, *convolvulus obscurus.*

බූ දදකිරිය, *Bú-dadakíriya, s.* spurge, hairy plant, *euphorbia hirta (Euphorbiaceæ)*: see එල *ela*—බින් *bin*—මුදු දදකිරිය *múdu-dadakíriya.*

බූදලය, *Búdalaya, s.* estate (as of a deceased person.) (Dutch.)

බූ දුම්මැල්ල, *Bú-dummęlla, s.* plant, variety of *trichosanthes cucumerina.*

බූ දෙනිතණ, *Bú-denitaṇa, s.* panic grass, *panicum cimicinum.*

බුන්දරේ, *Búndaré*, } *s.* brush for cleaning shoes,
බුන්දලේ, *Búndalé*, } furniture, broom. (Dutch.)

බූනනියන්, *Búnaniyan*, *s.* sister, elder sister.

බූනා, *Búná*, } *s.* (බූ earth, නායක lord)
බූනායක, *Búnáyaka*, } name of Íṣwara or Ṣiva, alluding to his character as ruler or chief of the world.

බූනික්කා, *Búnikká*, *s.* doll, pl. බූනික්කෝ *búnikkó*; more commonly බෝනික්කා *bónikká*.

බූ නුග, *Bú-nuga*, *s.* species of fig tree, *ficus mysorensis (Urticeæ).*

බූ නෙළු, *Bú-neḷu*, *s.* jungle tree, *stenosiphonium Russellianum (Acanthaceæ)*: see නෙළු *neḷu*.

බූපට්ටා ඇපල, *Búpaṭṭá-ẹpala*, *s.* plant, variety of *urena lobata.*

බූපති, *Búpati*, *s.* (බූ earth, පති chief) name of Ṣiva; king, monarch, sovereign, emperor.

බූ පවු, *Bú-pawu*, *s.* (බූ and පවු mountain) eastern mountain, from behind which the sun is supposed to rise, [Colloq. උදයගිරි පර්වතය *udayagiri-parwataya*].

බූපා, *Búpá*, *s.* king, protector of the world.

බූ පිච්ච, *Bú-pichcha*, *s.* (බූ earth, පිච්ච jasmine) species of jasmine, *jasminum pubescens.*

බූ පිල, *Bú-pila*, *s.* goat's rue, *tephrosia villosa (Leguminosæ).*

බූ පැල, *Bú-pẹla*, *s.* (බූ demon, පැල hut or shed) small temple appropriated to the worship of demons.

බූ බටදැල්ල, *Bú-baṭadella*, *s.* panic grass, *panicum hirsutum.*

බූ බටු, *Bú-baṭu*, *s.* thorny plant, *solanum ferox*, also called මලබටු *malabaṭu*.

බූ බළුතණ, *Bú-baḷutaṇa*, *s.* bent grass, *agrostis penicea.*

බූ බින්තල්, *Bú-bintal*, *s.* plant, *cucurligo angustifolia.*

බූ බින්පොල්, *Bú-binpol*, *s.* plant, variety of *tricopus zeylanicus.*

බූ මඩු, *Bú-maḍu*, *s.* variety of *cycas circinalis.*

බූමදන, *Búmadána*, *s.* burying, burial, interment.

බූමදනකරණවා, *Búmadána-karaṇawá*, *v.* to inter, to bury.

බූමිශාස්ත්‍රය, *Búmiṣástraya*, corruptly for භූමිශාස්ත්‍ර *bhúmiṣástra*.

බූ මෙනේරි, *Bú-menéri*, *s.* variety of *panicum miliare* or *p. psilopodium.*

බූ මොට්ටු, *Bú-moṭṭu*, *s.* winter cherry, *physalis pubesceus.*

බූ මෑ, *Bú-mẹ*, *s.* kidney bean, *phaseolus max*, [Colloq. දඹල *dam̱bala*].

බූ රටයක්බෙරිය, *Bú-raṭa-yakbériya*, *s.* plant, *crotularia capensis.*

බූරුවා, *Búruwá*, *s.* ass; name of a playing card, knave (from Dutch boer).

බූරෙණ්ඩ, *Búrẹnda*, *s.* tree, not ascertained.

බූ රැවුල, *Bú-rẹwula*, *s.* young beard.

බූලිය, *Búliya*, *s.* large earthen vessel, stone bottle.

බූව, *Búwa*, *s.* down on leaves, fruits, or insects; the texture of leaves or fruits; the soft sting of some leaves.

බූ වල්අඟුන, *Bú-wal-aṉguna*, *s.* plant, *echites fragrans.*

බූ වල්අබ, *Bú-wal-aba*, *s.* plant, *cleome isocandra.*

බූ වල්අවර, *Bú-wal-awara*, *s.* plant, variety of *canavalia ensiformis.*

බූ වල්මෙනේරි, *Bú-wal-menéri*, *s.* variety of panic grass, *panicum miliare.*

බූවල්ල, *Búwalla*, *s.* dried coconut flower.

බූවල්ලා, *Búwallá*, *s.* kind of small sea fish.

බූ වල්වැල්මිදි, *Bú-walwẹlmidi*, *s.* plant, *cissus villosa.*

බූවලුනැට්ට, *Búwalu-neṭṭa*, *s.* culm of coconut flower.

බූ වසතැල්කොල, *Bú-wasatẹlkola*, *s.* bindwort, *convolvulus malabaricus.*

බූසනාව, *Búsanáwa*, *s.* extirpation, destruction.

බූසනාවෙනවා, *Búsanáwenawá*, *v.* to be extirpated, to be destroyed.

බූසිය, *Búsiya*, *s.* wadding used in charging guns.

බූ සුළුනයි, *Bú-suḷunayi*, *s.* plant, *rungia longifolia.*

බූසේරු, *Búséru*, *s.* tree with small greenish yellow flower, *premna tomentosa (Verbenaceæ).*

බූ හකඹලා, *Bú-hakam̱balá*, *s.* plant, *bignonia rupestris.*

බූ හකුළු, *Bú-hakuḷu*, *s.* plant, *marsdenia asthmatica.*

බූ හවරි, *Bú-hawari*, *s.* plant, variety of *convolvulus.*

බූ හුනුකිරිල්ල, *Bú-hunukirilla*, *s.* plant, peculiar to Ceylon, *Phyllanthus pubescens (Euphorbiaceæ).*

බූ හොර, *Bú-hora*, *s.* wood-oil tree, peculiar to Ceylon, *dipterocarpus hispidus (Dipterocarpaceæ).*

බෙක, *Beka*, *s.* frog, *bufo melanostictus*, (order *Batrachia salientia*), [Colloq. ගෙමඩියා *gemaḍiyá*].

බෙට්ට, *Beṭṭa*, *s.* dung, ordure, the dung of animals and birds etc: pl. බෙටි *beṭi*.

බෙටි, *Beṭi*, *s.* lake, pond; any small round substance; ball, lump, ball of dung etc.: *a.* round, plump.

බෙටිගහනවා, *Beṭigahanawá*, *v.* to dung, as an animal.

බෙටුව, *Beṭuwa*, *s.* neck, throat, [Colloq. බෙල්ල *bella*].

බෙටුවමිරිකනවා, *Beṭuwa-mirikanawá*, *v.* (බෙටුව throat, මිරිකනවා to squeeze) to throttle, to seize by the neck.

බෙඬුවල, *Beṇḍuwala*, *s.* razor used by the priests of Buddha for shaving the head; spear.

බෙදනවා, *Bedanawá*, *v.* to separate, to divide, to part, to apportion, to distribute: pret. බෙදුවා *beduwá*.

බෙදාදෙනවා, *Bedádenawá*, *v.* to distribute, to allot, to assign.

බෙණු, *Benu*, *s.* stone; fear, alarm.

බෙණුදස, *Benudasa*, *s.* stones, pebbles.

බෙණෙනවා, *Benenawá*, *v.* to speak; to abuse, to use opprobrious language.

බෙනේ, *Bené*, *s.* hole, hollow in a tree etc: pl. බෙන *bena*.

බෙයද, *Beyada*, *s.* rock.

බෙරකඳ, *Bera-kaṇda*, *s.* (බෙර tom-tom, කඳ trunk) wooden frame of a tom-tom.

බෙරකාරයා, *Berakárayá*, *s.* (බෙර and කාර who does, යා aff.) tom-tom beater, drummer.

බෙරගහනවා, *Beragahanawá*, *v.* to beat the tom-tom.

බෙරණ, *Beraṇa*, } *s.* second lunar mansion or
බෙරණී, *Beraṇi*, } constellation in the moon's path: see භරණී *bharaṇi*.

බෙරය, *Beraya*, *s.* tom-tom, drum; corn measure; parrah containing twenty-four neliyas, ⅞ of a bushel: pl. බෙර *bera*.

බෙරලිය, *Beraliya*, *s.* tree, peculiar to Ceylon, seeds edible, *doona cordifolia, (Dipterocarpaceæ)*.

බෙරවා, *Berawá*, } *s.* (බෙර and වා from වද
බෙරවායා, *Berawáyá*, } *wada* to sound) man of the tom-tom beater caste.

බෙරි, *Beri*, *s.* roaring or growling of wild beasts: *a.* overdone, overcooked, over ripe.

බෙරිබෙරි, *Bere-berí*, *s.* disease: see බැරිබැරි *bęri-bęri*.

බෙරිවෙනවා, *Beriwenawá*, *v.* to be overcooked as rice, to be ripened to excess as fruits.

බෙරිහන්දෙනවා, *Berihandenawá*, *v.* to roar as a lion.

බෙරු, *Beru*, *a.* mellow, ripe, mature.

බෙරුගහ, *Beru-gaha*, } *s.* panic grass, *panicum*
බෙරුතණ, *Beru-taṇa*, } *elatius;* fragrant grass, *andropogon muricatus*, [Coll: සැවැන්දරා *sęwęndará*].

බෙරේ, *Berę*, see බෙරය *beraya*.

බෙල්ල, *Bella*, *s.* neck, throat: pl. බෙලි *beli*.

බෙල්ලං කෙළිය, *Bellaṇ-keḷiya*, *s.* game with cowries.

බෙල්ලා, *Bellá*, *s.* oyster, shell fish in general: pl. බෙල්ලෝ *belló*.

බෙල, *Bela*, *s.* wood apple tree, *ægle marmelos;* power, strength, force, might; dignity, authority.

බෙලසුල්, *Belasul*, *s.* slime, mucus; saliva, spittle.

බෙලහීන, *Belahína*, *a.* (බෙල strength, හීන abandoned) exhausted, weak, powerless, infirm; frail.

බෙලහීනතා, *Belahínatá*, *s.* (බෙලහීන exhausted, තා aff.) prostration of strength, exhaustion.

බෙලි, *Beli*, *s.* the plur. of බෙල්ල *bella*, neck; tree nearly every part of which is used medicinally, the fruit, a kind of wood apple, is called bel, marmel or Bengal quince and is a remedy for dysentery, *ægle marmelos (Rutaceæ);* oysters: *a.* belonging to.

බෙලිකටු, *Belikaṭu*, *s.* (බෙලි and කටු shell) shell of the muscle or oyster.

බෙලිතෝර, *Belitóra*, *s.* plant, not ascertained.

බෙලිපට්ටා, *Beli-paṭṭá*, *s.* shrub found on the borders of brooks or running water; the inner bark is used for cordage, *hibiscus tiliacus (Malvaceæ)*.

බෙලිමුල, *Beli-mula*, *s.* hall, saloon, any spacious room; root of the beli tree or *ægle marmelos*.

බෙලියත්, *Beliyat*, *s.* notice of sale.

බෙලි සිප්පිය, *Beli-sippiya*, *s.* (බෙලි and සිප්පි *sippi* shell) shell of the muscle, oyster etc.

බෙලෙක්, *Belek*, *s.* tin, (from Dutch blik).

බෙලේ, *Belé*, *s.* force, strength, power, might.

බෙහෙත, *Beheta*, } *s.* remedy, drug, medicament;
බෙහෙද, *Beheda*, } medicine, physic: pl. බෙහෙත් *behet*.

බෙහෙරු, *Beheru*, *s.* species of the night shade, of which there are twenty four species and varieties in Ceylon, [Colloq. බටු *baṭu*].

බෙළේ, *Beḷé*, *s.* warrior, soldier.

බේ, *Bé*, *s.* part, division, distinction.

බේගල, *Bégala*, *s.* lying, falsehood, prevarication, (vulgar); small silver or gold box hung at the side as an ornament; the end or bent part of a cart spring: pl. බේගල් *bégal*.

බේද, *Béda*, *s.* (භිද *bhida* to separate) distinction, disagreement, disunion; opposition; kind, sort.

බේඳුර, *Béṇdura*, *s.* the thin cutting part of a tool.

බේඳුරු, *Béṇduru*, *s.* large leaved parasitical plant, *polypodium folislatissimus.*

බෙබද්ද, *Bébaddá*, බෙබදුවා, *Bébaduwá*, } *s.* drunkard, tippler, sot.

බෙරණවා, *Béraṇawá*, *v.* to filter, to sift; to sift out, to inquire into, to scrutinize, to settle a dispute, to sort, to release: pret. බෙරුවා *béruwá*.

බෙරිය, *Bériya*, *s.* small tree growing in salt marshes, timber durable, *lumnitzera racemosa (Combretaceæ)*.

බෙරු, *Béru*, *s.* plant, *agrostistachys indica (Euphorbiaceæ)*.

බෙරුදියනිල්ල, *Bérudiyanilla*, *s.* water plant, *jussiæa repens (Onagraceæ)*.

බොක්ක, *Bokka*, *s.* stomach; corner of a house, back of a hearth; gulf; creek: pl. බොකු *boku*.

බොකටු, *Bokaṭu*, *s.* medicinal plant.

බොකල, *Bokala*, *s.* pericarp of a plant; paroquet.

බොකලවැල, *Bokala-węla*, *s.* creeping plant, *dalbergia filiformis*.

බොකු, *Boku*, *s.* secret, mystery; hand bent as if to receive water; piece of cloth or any thing that is pliable, as a leaf or piece of paper, bent into a hollow shape, *e.g.* a sugar paper; intestines: *a.* oval, hollow.

බොකුගහනවා, *Bokugahanawá*, *v.* to bend or fold into a hollow shape: see the foregoing.

බොකුට, *Bokuṭa*, *s.* curl, lock of hair.

බොකු නියන, *Boku-niyana*, *s.* curved chisel.

බොකුර, *Bokura*, *s.* plant, *ochna sqarrosa*.

බොජ්ඣඞ්ග, *Bojjhańga*, see බෝධ්‍යඞ්ග *bódhyańga*.

බොජුන, *Bojuna*, *s.* food, provisions, victuals, provender: pl. බොජුන් *bojun*.

බොටුව, *Boṭuwa*, *s.* neck; gullet, throat, [Colloq. බෙල්ල *bella*.

බොත්තම, *Bottama*, *s.* button. (Eng.)

බොතලේරුවා, *Botaléruwá*, *s.* butler. (Eng.)

බොදන, *Bodana*, *s.* food, victuals, provisions, Elu form of භෝජන *bhójana;* knowledge, planet Mercury, Elu form of බෝධන *bódhana*.

බොදු, *Bodu*, *s.* boiled or cooked rice.

බොදුන්, *Bodun*, *s.* food, victuals, eatables.

බොදුන්පා, *Bodunpá*, *s.* cup, basin, bowl, dish for eating out of.

බොදුම, *Boduma*, see බෝදුම *bóduma*.

බොන බදන, *Bona-badana*, *s.* drinking-vessel.

බොනවා, *Bonawá*, *v.* to drink: pret. බිව්වා *bíwá*.

බොම්බිලියා, *Bombiliyá*, *s.* small sea fish, bombay duck.

බොර, *Bora*, *s.* mud, clay, mire; sediment, dregs, lees; dross, refuse.

බොරළු, *Boraḷu*, *s.* gravel, pebbles, a gravelly or gritty soil; chaff.

බොරළුදමුනු, *Boraḷudamunu*, *s.* plant, sort of *calyptranthes*.

බොරළුවා, *Boraḷuwá*, *s.* kind of sea fish.

බොරු, *Boru*, *a.* false, untrue; also plur. of බොරුව *boruwa*, which see.

බොරුකාරයා, *Borukárayá*, *s.* (බොරු and කාර who does, යා aff.) liar, utterer of falsehoods.

බොරුකියනවා, *Borukiyanawá*, *v.* to lie, to utter falsehoods.

බොරුකීම, *Borukíma*, *s.* lying, falsehood, prevarication.

බොරුපන්, *Borupan*, *s.* kind of sedge used for weaving mats; club-rush, *Heleocharis plantaginea (Cyperaceæ)*.

බොරුපය, *Borupaya*, බොරුපාව, *Borupáwa*, } *s.* (බොරු false, පය or පා *pá* foot) wooden leg; stilt.

බොරුව, *Boruwa*, *s.* lie, falsehood, untruth.

බොරු වළ, *Boru-waḷa*, *s.* (බොරු false, වළ hole) pit-fall, trap for catching animals, made by digging a deep hole in the bottom of which sharp pointed instruments are planted, the hole being covered with sticks and earth.

බොල්, *Bol*, *s.* chaff: *a.* thick or solid.

බොල්පොළව, *Bolpoḷawa*, *s.* (බොල් solid, පොළව world or earth) third or highest of the three strata of this earth, the first or lowest is air, the second water, the third the division we inhabit.

බොල්ල, *Bolla*, *s.* skull; shell, cowri.

බොල්ලෑවා, *Bellęwá*, *s.* man with long and large teeth and projecting gums.

බොල්ලෑවි, *Bollęvi*, *s.* feminine form of the above.

බොල්විල, *Bolvila*, plant, not ascertained.

බොල්හිඳ, *Bolhiṇda*, *s.* spiderwort, *tradescantia cristata*.

බොල, *Bola*, *s.* thickness, grossness; name or epithet used in calling to persons of low caste, as coolies, slaves; as බොල පාදඩයා *bola pádaḍayá*, you vagabond.

බොලට, *Bolaṭa*, *s.* ancle.

බොලඳ, *Bolaṇda*, *s.* child, [Colloq. ළදරුවා *ladaruwá*], male child or infant: *a.* childish, puerile.

බොලඳකම, *Bolaṇdakama*, *s.* puerility, childishness.

බොලඳ කථාව, *Bolaṇda-katháwa*, *s.* (බොලඳ and කථාව speech, discourse) infantine discourse or the repetition of a story in a manner suited to the capacity of children; it is used also of friendly and agreeable conversation.

බොලන්, *Bolan*, *a.* term used in a friendly way in addressing any one.

බොලරසා, *Bolarasá*, *s.* the dross of iron which falls while in the act of being forged.

බොලිද්ද, *Bolidda*, *s.* plant, *oleander*.

බොලෝ, *Boló*, *s.* familiar term of address: see බොල *bola*.

බොස්ගෙඩිය, *Bosgeḍiya*, *s.* hub or nave, central part of a wheel in which spokes are fixed.

බොස්තොරොක්කේ, *Bostorokké*, *s.* stays. (Dutch.)

බොසෝ, *Bosó*, corruptly for බොහෝ *bohó*.

බොහොඩා, *Bohoṇḍá*, *s.* chameleon, [Colloq. කටුස්සා *kaṭussá*], genus *calotes*, sub order *Agamidæ*.

බොහෝ, *Bohó*, } *a.* many, much, abounding,
බොහෝම, *Bohóma*, } excessive, various.

බොහෝසෙයින්, *Bohóseyin*, *ad.* exceedingly.

බොළු, *Boḷu*, *s.* male calf.

බොළුපයිය, *Boḷu-payiya*, *s.* purse used by astronomers to keep their counting shells in.

බෝ, *Bó*, *s.* tree, *ficus religiosa*, see බෝගහ *bó-gaha*: *a.* many, much, abounding, excessive.

බෝක්කුව, *Bókkuwa*, *s.* arch. (Dutch.)

බෝකරණවා, *Bókaraṇawá*, *v.* to multiply, to increase, to cause to abound.

බෝකැර, *Bókéra*, *s.* plant, *gomphia angustifolia (Ochnaceæ).*

බෝග, *Bóga*, *s.* grain, corn, grain in general; pleasure, enjoyment: see භෝග *bhóga*.

බෝගහ, *Bó-gaha*, *s.* sacred fig tree, which is held in the highest veneration by the Buddhists, who believe that the day on which Buddha attained his sacred character he went and seated himself on a miraculous throne which had instantly sprung up for him under this tree, *ficus religiosa (Urticaceæ)*; the Indian pípul.

බෝජන, *Bójana*, *s.* food, eating; victuals, provisions, (corruptly for භෝජන *bhójana*.)

බෝංචි, *Bóñchi*, *s.* French or kidney bean, *phaseolus vulgaris*. (Dutch.)

බෝට්ටුව, *Bóṭṭuwa*, *s.* boat. (Eng.)

බෝතලේ, *Bótalé*, *s.* bottle. (Dutch.)

බෝද, *Bóda*, *s.* awakening, rousing; properly written බෝධ *bódha*.

බෝදකර, *Bódakara*, *s.* (බෝද and කර making) opening, expanding, blowing as a flower; awakening, rousing.

බෝදා, *Bódá*, *s.* (Dutch,) auctioneer: pl. බෝදාවරු *bódawaru*.

බෝදි, *Bódi*, see බෝධි *bódhi*.

බෝදි ඇට, *Bódi-eṭa*, *s*, plant, *vernonia* or *serratula anthelmintica*.

බෝදිරිමවු, *Bódirimawu*, *s.* female elf.

බෝදුම, *Bóduma*, *s.* tree, *ficus religiosa:* see බෝ ගහ *bó-gaha*.

බෝධ්‍යඞ්ග, *Bódhyańga*, *s.* (බෝධි *bódhi* knowledge, අඞ්ග *ańga* requisite) the seven requisites for attaining the supreme knowledge of a Buddha, viz. ස්මෘතිය *smṛitiya* intense thought, ධර්මවිචය *dharmavichaya*, investigation of the truth, වීර්‍ය *vírya*, effort, perseverance, ප්‍රීතිය *prítiya*, joy, ප්‍රශ්‍රබ්ධි *praṣrabdhi*, mental tranquillity, සමාධි *samádhi*, complete command of the passions, උපෙක්ෂා *upekshá*, equanimity.

බෝධ, *Bódha*, *e.* wisdom, intellect; waking, rousing.

බෝධක, *Bódhaka*, *s.* teacher, instructor; spy, informer.

බෝධකර, *Bódha-kara*, *s.* (බෝධ rousing, කර who does) awakener, sort of minstrel who awakens the prince or chief in the morning by his music.

බෝධන, *Bódhana*, *s.* teaching, instructing; awakening, arousing; planet Mercury; knowledge, information; act of burning incense.

බෝධනීය, *Bódhaníya*, *s.* (බුධ *budha* to know, අනීයර් *aníyar* aff.) kind of turmeric, [Colloq. කහ *kaha*]: *a.* to be explained, or expounded, to be rendered intelligible.

බෝධනෙය්‍ය, *Bódhaneyya*, *a.* studious, acquiring knowledge, attentive to the particular study of the sacred knowledge of Buddhism.

බෝධය, *Bódhaya*, see බෝධ *bódha*.

බෝධි, *Bódhi*, *s.* knowledge, intellect, understanding; omniscience, the state of being a Buddha; particular kind of holy study, that which must be attended to by the followers of Buddha; sacred precept, religious ordinance; holy fig tree, *ficus religiosa:* see බෝගහ *bó-gaha*.

බෝධිඥාන, *Bódhijñána*, *s.* (බෝධි Buddha, ඥාන knowledge) knowledge necessary to be acquired in order to the attainment of the character of Buddha; omniscience; hence one of the most common epithets of Buddha is සර්වඥ *Sarwajña*, all-wise, the omniscient one.

බෝධිතරු, *Bódhitaru*, } *s.* holy fig tree: see බෝ
බෝධිද්‍රුම, *Bódhidruma*, } ගස *bó-gaha*.

බෝධිපර්‍ය්‍යඞ්ක, *Bódhiparyańka*, *s.* (බෝධි and පර්‍ය්‍යඞ්ක seat) diamond throne which sprung up at the foot of the Bó-tree when the Brahmin threw down eight handfuls of Kusa grass, for Buddha to sit on, the day he became Buddha.

බෝධිපාක්ෂික, *Bódhi-pákshika*, *s.* pertaining to the Bódhi or supreme knowledge.

බෝධිසත්තෝ, *Bódhisattó*, see බෝධිසත්වයෝ *bódhisatwayó*.

බෝධිසත්ව තෛලය, *Bódhisatwa-tailaya*, *s.* sort of medicinal oil.

බෝධිසත්වයෝ, *Bódhisatwayó*, *s.* (බෝධි intellect, සත්ව *satwa* being) one who discovers the truth, or one who uses every lawful and prescribed means for the acquirement of all sacred knowledge; it is usually applied to Buddha in his various states of existence previous to his attaining the Buddhaship.

බෝධිසම්භාර, *Bódhi-sambhára*, *s.* (බෝධි and සම්භාර elements, materials) works necessary to be done for the acquirement of the Buddhaship.

බෝන්කර, *Bón-kara*, *s.* neck pole of a hackery.

බෝන්ලිය, *Bónlíya*, *s.* shaft of a hackery or waggon.

බෝබිජු, *Bóbiju*, *s.* pomegranate tree, *punica granatum*, [Colloq. දෙළුම් *deḷum*].

බෝඹු, *Bómbu*, *s.* tree, with small white or yellow flowers in spikes, *symplocos spicata (Styraceæ)*.

බෝම්බෙ, *Bómbe*, *s.* bomb, fire-work. (Eng.)

බෝමි, *Bómí*, *s.* tree, *Litsea sebifera* or *Tetranthera Roxburghii*, *(Lauraceæ)*.

බෝය, *Bóya*, *s.* buoy. (Eng.)

බෝරගහනවා, *Bóragahanawá*, *v.* to bore stones. (Eng.)

බෝල්ලා, *Bóllá*, *s.* kind of sea fish.

බෝලය, *Bólaya*, *s.* ball. (Eng.)

බෝල වටුවා, *Bóla-waṭuwá*, *s.* black-breasted bustard quail, *turnix taigoor*, *(tinamidæ* order *Gallinæ)*, also called වටුවා *waṭuwá* and පඩුරු වටුවා *paṇḍuru-waṭuwá*; lesser ringed plover, *ægialitis curonica*, *(charadridæ* order *Grallæ)*.

බෝවාකල්, *Bówákal*, *s.* (බෝ many, වා years, කල් period) term of many years, meaning long life.

බෝවිටියා, *Bóviṭiyá*, *s.* plant with purplish flowers, bearing a black edible fruit, *Osbeckia aspera*, *(Melastomaceæ)*: see මහබෝවිටියා *maha-bóviṭiyá* and හින්බෝවිටියා *hín-bóviṭiyá*.

බෝවෙනවා, *Bówenawá*, *v.* to multiply, to increase, to be fruitful, to become many.

බෝසතාණෝ, *Bósatánó*, see බෝධිසත්වයෝ *bódhisatwayó*.

බෞද්ධ්‍යාඞ්ගය, *Baudhyáńgaya*, corrupt form of බෝධ්‍යඞ්ග *bódhyańga*.

බැගින්, *Bẹgin*, *ad.* in order, by course, according to order, severally, at the rate of.

බැගෑ, *Bẹgẹ́*, } *a.* humble, submissive, sup-
බැගෑපත්, *Bẹgẹ́pat*, } pliant.

බැට්ටයා, *Bẹṭṭayá*, *s.* bard, panegyrist.

බැටදෙනවා, *Bẹṭadenawá*, *v.* to box; strike.

බැටය, *Bẹṭaya*, *s.* blow, stroke, [Colloq. පහර *pahara*]; flogging, punishing, inflicting blows.

බැටළු එඬේරා, *Bẹṭaḷu-eṇḍérá*, *s.* (බැටළු sheep, එඬේරා keeper) shepherd.

බැටළු නාම්බා, *Bẹṭaḷu-námbá*, *s.* lamb.

බැටළුවා, *Bẹṭaḷuwá*, *s.* sheep.

බැණගන්නවා, *Bẹṇagannawá*, *v.* to abuse each other.

බැණගැණිම, *Bẹṇagẹṇíma*, *s.* abuse, reviling, scurrility.

බැණිම, *Bẹṇíma*, *s.* abuse, scurrility.

බැතියෙන්, *Bẹtiyen*, *adv.* with devotion or piety.

බැද්ද, *Bẹdda*, *s.* forest, wood, thicket or jungle: *a.* fried, parched, grilled, roasted.

බැද, *Bẹda*, *part.* having burnt, fried or cooked, from බදිනවා *badinawá*.

බැදි, *Bẹdi*, *plur.* of බැද්ද *bẹdda*, which see.

බැදිවදිනවා, *Bẹdiwadinawá*, *v.* to traverse a jungle, to enter into a jungle.

බැදීම, *Bẹdíma*, *s.* frying; verbal noun of බදිනවා *badinawá*; also of බදනවා *badanawá*, to wrestle.

බැදුම, *Bẹduma*, *s.* that which has been burnt, cooked, or fried; embrace: pl. බැදුම් *bẹdum*.

බැඳුනියන්, *Bẹḍẹniyan*, *s.* female cousin on the mother's side.

බැඳ, *Bẹnda*, *part.* having bound, tied, or fastened.

බැඳි, *Bẹndi*, *a.* tied, bound.

බැඳීම, *Bẹndíma*, *s.* binding, tying, fastening; bond.

බැඳුම, *Bẹnduma*, *s.* bond, tie, obligation: pl. බැඳුම් *bẹndum*.

බැඳෙනවා, *Bẹndenawá*, *v.* to become united or bound together; passive form of බඳිනවා *bandinawá*.

බැනවුම, *Bẹnawuma*, *s.* calling, addressing.

බැබලීම, *Bẹbalíma*, *s.* light, shining, glittering.

බැබිලෙන, *Bẹbilena*, *a.* bright, lucid, transparent.

බැබිලෙනවා, *Bẹbilenawá*, *v.* to shine, to glitter: pret. බැබුලුනා *bẹbuluná*.

බැම්ම, *Bęmma*, *s.* binding, ligament; building, structure.

බැම, *Bęma*, *s.* eye-brow.

බැමබිඳුන, *Bęma-binduna*, *s.* (බැම and බිඳුන moving) act of lifting the eye-brows; sign, indication of sentiment by the eye.

බැමමඩුළු, *Bęma-maḍuḷu*, *s.* (බැම and මඩුළු circle) circle formed by the eye-brows, or the region of the eye-brows.

බැමය, *Bęmaya*, *s.* eye-brow.

බැම සඟල, *Bęma-sangala*, *s.* (බැම and සඟල pair) the two eye-brows.

බැමසිරිය, *Bęmasiriya*, *s.* plant, species of hedge hyssop, *herpestis* or *gratiola monniera.*

බැමිණි, *Bęmiṇí*, *s.* wife of a Brahman, a woman of the Brahman caste.

බැමිතිරිය, *Bęmitiriya*, see බැමසිරිය *bęmasiriya.*

බැමීම, *Bęmíma*, *s.* whirling round, [Colloq. කර කැවීම *karakęvíma*].

බැර, *Bęra*, *a.* heavy, weighty, gross.

බැරපන්, *Bęrapan*, *s.* charges or fees for copying a Buddhist book.

බැරි, *Bęri*, *s.* inability, incapability, impossibility: *a.* impossible, impracticable.

බැරිණි, *Bęriṇi*, *s.* pregnant woman, [Colloq. ගර්භිණී *garbhiṇí*].

බැරිබැරි, *Bęribęri*, *s.* (derived from බැරි *bęri* expressive of debility, or from Malay word signifying *sheep*) a disease, *anæmia*, of which there are two forms: (1) that resulting from malarial poisoning; (2) that caused by parasite worms (mainly *anchylostoma duodendale*) in the intestines; in the latter form the disease is called *anchylostomiasis.*

බැරිවෙනවා, *Bęriwenawá*, *v.* to be unable.

බැරුව, *Bęruwa*, *a.* ill; being unable.

බැරැඬි, *Bęręṇḍi*, *s.* hoarseness, loss of voice.

බැරෑරුම්, *Bęręrum*, *a.* proud, haughty, ambitious; disrespectful.

බැරෑරුම, *Bęręruma*, *s.* responsibility; importance.

බැල්ම, *Bęlma*, *s.* look: see බැලීම *bęlíma.*

බැල්ලි, *Bęlli*, *s.* bitch.

බැලගෙඩිය, *Bęlageḍiya*, *s.* coconut fruit which a plucker gets for his hire.

බැලතණ, *Bęlataṇa*, *s.* (බැල dog, තණ grass) grass eaten by dogs to induce vomiting, *eleusine indica (Gramineæ);* also called වල් කුරක්කන් *walkurakkan.*

බැලමෙහෙ, *Bęlamehe*, *s.* (බැල hire, මෙහෙ work) hired service, work done for wages.

බැලමෙහෙකරණවා, *Bęlamehe-karaṇawá*, *v.* to work for wages.

බැලය, *Bęlaya*, *s.* hire, wages, pay: pl. බැල *bęla.*

බැලිකික්කි, *Bęlikikkí*, *s.* female whelp.

බැලිමක්කා, *Bęlimakká*, *s.* (බැලි and මක්කා fly) flea.

බැලීම, *Bęlíma*, *s.* sight, seeing, vision; appearance: pl. බැලුම් *bęlum.*

බැව, *Bęwa*, *s.* being, existing, Elu form of භව *bhawa;* also written බව *bawa.*

බැවහාර, *Bęwahára*, *s.* custom, habit.

බැවින්, *Bęvin*, *ind.* (බැව *bęwa* being, ඉන් *in* aff.) particle and affix: because, therefore, on account of, in consequence of, etc.

බැවිල, *Bęvila*, *s.* medicinal plant, *sida humilis (Malvaceæ).*

බැවුල, *Bęwula*, *s.* hilly ground, [Colloq. ගොඩලි බිම *goḍali-bima*].

බැවුලි, *Bęwulí*, *s.* dancing girl, [Colloq. නැටුම්කාරි *nęṭumkári*].

බැස්ස, *Bęssa*, *s.* descended, gone down.

බැස, *Bęsa*, *s. past part.* of බසිනවා *basinawá.*

බැසීම, *Bęsíma*, *s.* descent, the act of alighting, descending, coming down.

බැහෙනවා, *Bęhenawá*, *v.* to subside as water or disease, to grow down as the root of yams etc.

බැහැ, *Bęhę*, *par.* impossible, as මට බැහැ *maṭa bęhę*, I cannot: see බැරි *bęri.*

බැහැටි, *Bęhęṭi*, *s.* young woman, [Colloq. යෞවනී *yauwaní*].

බැහැදකිනවා, *Bęhędakinawá*, *v.* to adore, to worship, [Colloq. නමස්කාරකරණවා *namaskára-karaṇawá*].

බැහැනා, *Bęhęná*, *s.* elder brother; nephew, sister's son.

බැහැපත්වීම, *Bęhępatvíma*, verbal noun of බැහැපත්වෙනවා *bęhępatwenawá.*

බැහැපත්වෙනවා, *Bęhępatwenawá*, *v.* to submit, to give in, to yield.

බැහැර, *Bęhera*, *ad.* out, forth, outside, external; aside, away.

බැහැරයනවා, *Bęherayanawá*, *v.* to go off.

බැළලි, *Bęḷalí*, *s.* cat (female one).

බෑ, *Bę́*, *s.* brother, [Coll: සහෝදරයා *sahódarayá*].

බෑනා, *Bę́ná*, *s.* nephew, sister's son, son in law.

බෑම, *Bę́ma*, *s.* descent, alighting, letting down.

බෑය, *Bę́ya*, *s.* half, equal share or part, [Colloq. බාගය *bágaya*].

බෑයා, *Bę́yá*, see බෑනා *bę́ná.*

බැරක්, *Bẹrak*, *s.* what place, polite form of putting a question as to where one is going.

බැවුම, *Bẹwuma*, *s.* descent, slope, declivity.

බැවුවා, *Bẹwuwá*, *v.* caused to recline.

බැවෙනවා, *Bẹwenawá*, *v.* to lie down (involuntarily).

බැසනය, *Bẹsanaya*, *s.* corrupt form of ව්‍යසනය *vyasanaya*, pain, anguish, suffering, affliction, [Colloq. පීඩාව *píḍáwa*]; custom, habit, usage, [Colloq. පුරුද්ද *purudda*].

 බ්‍යඤ්ජන, *Byañjana*, see ව්‍යඤ්ජන *vyañjana*.

බ්‍රඟ, *Branga*, *s.* kind of large black bee, humble bee; wasp; bird, the fork-tailed shrike; plant, *eclipta prostrata*, more properly written භෘඞ්ග *bhṛinga*.

බ්‍රඟරිකා, *Brangariká*, *s.* (බ්‍රඟ bee, අරි *ari* enemy) corrupt form of භෘඞ්ගාරිකා *bhṛingáriká*, cricket, [Colloq. රැහැයියා *rẹhẹyiyá*].

බ්‍රමණ, *Bramaṇa*, *s.* turning, whirling, going round; perambulating, corruptly for භ්‍රමණ *bhramaṇa*.

බ්‍රහ්ම, *Brahma*, *s.* (වෘහ *vṛiha* or බෘහ *bṛiha* to increase [mankind]) according to the Védas and doctrines of the Hindus, the divine cause and essence of the world, from which all created things are supposed to emanate and to which they return, the unknown God; a celebrated Hindu deity; Brahma is generally reckoned the chief of the gods and ranks first in the Hindu triad, and is the operative creator of the world; hence he is frequently styled the grandfather of both gods and men; he is represented in their temples as having four faces of a golden colour, dressed in white garments, and riding on a goose; in one hand he holds a stick, and in the other a pátra or alms dish; a Brahman or man of the sacerdotal or first Hindu tribe.

බ්‍රහ්මචර්‍ය්‍යා, *Brahmacharyá*, *s.* (බ්‍රහ්ම Véda, චර්‍ය්‍යා observance) religious observance of the Hindu Védas; the state or condition of a Hindu student.

බ්‍රහ්මචාරි, *Brahmachári*, *s.* (බ්‍රහ්ම and චර *chara* to go or follow) kind of religious ascetic, one whose chief virtue is the observance of continence.

බ්‍රහ්මජාල, *Brahmajála*, *s.* (බ්‍රහ්ම Brahman, ජාල net) name of one of the Sútras of Buddha, and the first of that class of books; this Sútra professes to be an exposure of the weakness and falsehood of the Braḥminical system.

බ්‍රහ්මත්ව, *Brahmatwa*, *s.* (බ්‍රහ්ම and ත්ව aff. of the abstract) identification with Brahma or the supreme god.

බ්‍රහ්මදණ්ඩි, *Brahmadaṇḍi*, *s.* (බ්‍රහ්ම and දණ්ඩ stick) plant, *siphonanthus indica;* curse, anathema.

බ්‍රහ්මදණ්ඩින්, *Brahmadaṇḍin*, *s.* plant, *borago zeylanica*, [Colloq. යොන්තුඹ *yontumba*].

බ්‍රහ්මදත්ත, *Brahmadatta*, *s.* (බ්‍රහ්ම by or to, දත්ත given) one of the sovereigns of the Ikshwáku race, frequently referred to in the Játakas and other Buddhistical records.

බ්‍රහ්මදර්භා, *Brahma-darbhá*, *s.* parsley, *petroselinum sativum*, [Colloq. අසමෝදගන් *asamódagan*].

බ්‍රහ්මදාරු, *Brahmadáru*, *s.* (බ්‍රහ්ම and දාරු wood) mulberry tree, *morus indica*.

බ්‍රහ්මන්, *Brahman*, see බ්‍රහ්ම *brahma*.

බ්‍රහ්මනාද, *Brahma-náda*, *s.* (බ්‍රහ්ම and නාද sound) voice of Brahma, but applied as an epithet to Buddha, alluding to the sweetness of his voice, that of Brahma being supposed to surpass that of all the other gods.

බ්‍රහ්මපුත්‍ර, *Brahma-putra*, *s.* (බ්‍රහ්ම and පුත්‍ර offspring) name of a river, flowing through Bengal and joining the Ganges below Luckipoor, sometimes called the Burampooter; sort of poison; venom of snakes.

බ්‍රහ්මපුත්‍රී, *Brahma-putrí*, *s.* (බ්‍රහ්මපුත්‍ර *brahma-putra* with the fem. ඊ *í* aff.) Ṣaraswatí river; goddess Saraswatí, wife of Brahma.

බ්‍රහ්මපුරී, *Brahma-purí*, *s.* (බ්‍රහ්ම and පුර *pura* city) the capital of Brahma on the mountain Kailása.

බ්‍රහ්මභූය, *Brahma-bhúya*, *s.* (බ්‍රහ්ම and භූය being) identification with Brahma, absorption into the supreme being.

බ්‍රහ්මයා, *Brahmayá*, *s.* Brahma; sometimes incorrectly written බ්‍රඃමයා *braḥmayá*; see බ්‍රහ්ම *brahma*.

බ්‍රහ්මරාජයා, *Brahmarájayá*, *s.* prince or chief among the Brahmas.

බ්‍රහ්මලතා, *Brahma-latá*, *s.* creeper, *tinospora cordifolia*, [Colloq. රසකිඳ *rasakinda*].

බ්‍රහ්මලෝක, *Brahma-lóka*, *s.* (බ්‍රහ්ම and ලෝක world) that division of the universe supposed to be the residence of Brahma, and the highest of the celestial regions next to Nirváṇa or state of final emancipation; there are sixteen Brahma lókas, or rather perhaps divisions of the Brahma lóka; the highest five are called Suddháwása or the residence of the purified after death, in the last Nirváṇa is attained; sometimes incorrectly written බ්‍රඃමලෝක *braḥmalóka*.

බ්‍රහ්මවෘක්ෂ, *Brahma-vṛiksha*, s. (බ්‍රහ්ම and වෘක්ෂ tree) Pulas tree, *butea frondosa*, [Colloq. ගස් කැල *gas-kẹla*]; glomerous fig-tree, *ficus glomerata*, [Colloq. අට්ටික්කා *aṭṭikká*].

බ්‍රහ්මස්තාල, *Brahmastála*, } see බ්‍රහ්මලෝක *brah-*
බ්‍රහ්මස්ථාල, *Brahmasthála*, } *ma lóka*.

බ්‍රහ්මසායුජ්‍ය, *Brahmasáyujya*, s. (බ්‍රහ්ම and සායුජ්‍ය intimate union) identification with Brahma, or essential union with the supreme being.

බ්‍රහ්මසූ, *Brahmasú*, s. (බ්‍රහ්ම and සූ the son) name of Kámadéva the Indian god of love; also, Aniruddha the son of Káma.

බ්‍රහ්ම ස්වර, *Brahma-swara*, s. mellifluous voice: see බ්‍රහ්මනාද *brahma-náda*.

බ්‍රහ්මා, *Brahmá*, s. the divine cause and essence of the world, from which all created things are supposed to emanate and to which they return.

බ්‍රහ්මාණ්ඩය, *Brahmáṇḍaya*, s. (බ්‍රහ්ම *brahma* and අණ්ඩ egg) the globe, the world, so called from its being compared to an egg.

බ්‍රහ්මාද්‍ය, *Brahmádya*, s. cow's urine, [Colloq. ගෝ මූත්‍ර *gó-mútra*].

බ්‍රහ්මාසන, *Brahmásana*, s. (බ්‍රහ්ම *brahma* and ආසන sitting) posture in which the Brahmas place themselves, one suited to devout and religious meditation.

බ්‍රහ්මී, *Brahmí*, s. (වෘහ *vṛiha* to grow, to increase) shrub, *herpestis monniera*, [Colloq. බෙමිතිරිය *bẹmitiriya*, ලුනුවිල *lunuvila*].

බ්‍රහ්මෝත්පත්තිය, *Brahmótpattiya*, s. (බ්‍රහ්ම Brahma, උත්පත්ති *utpatti* birth) birth into the Bráhmin tribe.

බ්‍රාහ්ම, *Bráhma*, s. (බ්‍රහ්ම *brahma* and අණ් *aṇ* aff.) part of the hand under the root of the thumb; mode of marriage, the presentation of the bride elegantly adorned by the father to the bridegroom whom he has invited; name of Nárada the sage and son of Bráhma.

බ්‍රාහ්මණ, *Bráhmaṇa*, s. man of the first Hindu tribe, or the sacredotal caste, Bráhmin.

බ්‍රාහ්මණී, *Bráhmaṇí*, s. (බ්‍රාහ්මණ *bráhmaṇa* with the fem. aff.) wife of a Bráhman or Hindu priest, a woman of the Bráhman caste; shrub, *siphonanthus indica*; plant, *trigonella corniculata*; wasp; ant; pot herb, *ruta grave-olens*.

බ්‍රාහ්මිකා, *Bráhmiká*, s. plant or shrub, *siphonanthus indica*.

බ්‍රාහ්මී, *Bráhmí*, s. wife of a Bráhman; according to the Hindu mythology, one of the eight divine mothers of created beings or the personified energies of the gods; name of Saraswatí the goddess of speech; constellation: see රෝහිණී *róhiṇí*; frog; yellow coloured ant; plant, *alternanthera triandra*, [Colloq. මුගුණුවැන්න *muguṇuwẹnna*].

බෘංහණ, *Bṛiṇhaṇa*, a. nutritious, fat, stout, lusty.

බෘංහිත, *Bṛiṇhita*, p. cherished, increased.

බෘන්ද, *Bṛinda*, s. multitude, assembly, collection.

බෘන්දාරක, *Bṛindáraka*, s. a god, deity; chief, ruler: a. pleasing, agreeable.

බෘහත්, *Bṛihat*, a. (බෘහ to increase) large, great, bulky, vast.

බෘහතිකා, *Bṛihatiká*, s. upper garment, cloak, gown; small sort of egg-plant.

බෘහතී, *Bṛihatí*, s. plant, species of night-shade, *solanum xanthocarpum*, [Colloq. එළබටු *elabaṭu*].

බෘහස්පති, *Bṛihaspati*, s. (බෘහත් *bṛihat* great, illustrious, as the deities, පති master) regent of the planet Jupiter and preceptor of the gods, identified astronomically with the planet.

බෘහස්පති තරුව, *Bṛihaspati-taruwa*, s. (බෘහස්පති and තරුව star, planet) planet Jupiter.

බෘහස්පතින්දා, *Bṛihaspatindá*, s. Thursday.

භ

The twenty-fourth letter of the Siṇhalese alphabet; it is the foregoing letter aspirated, usually expressed by *bh*.

භක්ත, *Bhakta*, s. (භජ් *bhaja* to serve, ක්ත *kta* aff.) boiled rice; food: a. devout, faithful, devoted to, attached or attentive to, engrossed by; served; worshipped.

භක්ති, *Bhakti*, s. faith, fidelity, devotion, adherence; worship, adoration, culture.

භක්තිවන්ත, *Bhaktiwanta*, a. devout, pious.

භක්ෂක, *Bhakshaka*, a. gluttonous, voracious, gourmand.

භක්ෂකාර, *Bhakshakára*, s. (භක්ෂ food, කාර who does or makes) cook, confectioner.

භක්ෂණ, *Bhakshaṇa*, s. eating, feeding.

භක්ෂණයකරණවා, *Bhakshaṇaya-karaṇawá*, v. to eat, to feed, to devour.

භක්ෂිත, *Bhakshita*, a. eaten.

භග්න, *Bhagna*, a. (භඤ්ජ *bhañja* to break) conquered, defeated, overcome, subdued; torn, broken; disregarded, despised.

භග, *Bhaga*, s. vulva, *pudendum muliebre*; sun; fortune, prosperity, happiness; excellence, greatness; beauty, splendour; desire, wish, love;

strength, vigour; fame, glory; knowledge; absence of passion, tranquillity of the religious man who has divested himself of all worldly excitability; omnipotence or supreme power; virtue, moral merit; final emancipation.

භගන්දර, *Bhagandara*, *s.* (භග vulva, දෘ *dri* to tear) fistula in ano.

භගවත්, *Bhagawat*, *a.* (භග fortune, supremacy, වත් poss. aff.) generic title of a Buddha; also of a Jina or Jaina deified saint; virtuous, fortunate, prosperous, happy; worshipful, adorable.

භගවතා, *Bhagawatá*, } *s.* (භගවත් *bhagawat* with
භගවා, *Bhagawá*, } an aff.) name or generic title of a Buddha.

භගිනී, *Bhaginí*, *s.* (භග *bhaga* prosperity, desire, ඉනි *ini* aff.) sister, woman in general.

භගීරථ, *Bhagíratha*, *s.* name of a king, whose austerities, according to Hindu fable, brought the Ganges down from heaven.

භඞ්ග, *Bhańga*, *s.* (භඤ්ජ *bhañja* to break) breaking, splitting; fissure, division, chasm; defeat, discomfiture; disease, *hemiplegia* or palsy; fear; dishonesty, fraud, circumvention, cheating; wave; water course, canal; disease in general.

භජනය, *Bhajanaya*, *s.* (භජ *bhaja* to serve) worship, adoration; service, attendance upon for favour or assistance, intimacy.

භජනයකරණවා, *Bhajanaya-karaṇawá*, *v.* to attend upon, to associate with.

භජමාන, *Bhajamána*, *a.* (භජ to serve) right, fit, proper; serving, waiting; enjoying; dividing.

භඤ්ජන, *Bhañjana*, } *s.* (භඤ්ජ *bhañja* to
භඤ්ජනක, *Bhañjanaka*, } break) breaking; rending, tearing; disease of the mouth, contortion of the lips and decay of the teeth.

භට, *Bhaṭa*, *s.* (භට to maintain) warrior, soldier, combatant.

භටිත්‍ර, *Bhaṭitra*, *a.* (භට *bhaṭa* to nourish, ඉත්‍ර *itra* aff.) roasted on a spit, (as meat etc.)

භණ්ටාකී, *Bhaṇṭákí*, *s.* brinjal or egg plant, *solanum melongena*, [Colloq, වම්බටු *wambaṭu*].

භණ්ඩන, *Bhaṇḍana*, *s.* quarrel, contention, strife, war, battle; armour, mail.

භණ්ඩාර, *Bhaṇḍára*, see බණ්ඩාර *baṇḍára*.

භණ්ඩි, *Bhaṇḍi*, *s.* tree from the wood of which a red dye is prepared; Bengal madder, *rubia manjith* or *oldenlandia umbellata;* wave.

භණ්ඩිල, *Bhaṇḍila*, *s.* tree, *albizzia lebbek*, [Colloq. මහරි *mahari* or මාරා *márá*].

භණිත, *Bhaṇita*, *a.* (භණ *bhaṇa* to sound) sounded, spoken, uttered.

භත්ත, *Bhatta*, *s.* boiled rice, [Colloq. බත් *bat*]; cooked food.

භත්තකාර, *Bhattakára*, *s.* (භත්ත and කාර who does or makes) rice boiler, cook; pastry cook or confectioner.

භද්‍ර, *Bhadra*, *s.* (භදි *bhadi* to be happy) prosperity, fortune, happiness, propitiousness; excellence: *a.* fortunate, happy, prosperous, lucky; pure, pious, virtuous; best, excellent; good, right; pleasing, beautiful.

භද්‍රක, *Bhadraka*, *s.* species of grass, *cyperus pertenuis;* species of pine, *pinus devadáru*: *a.* beautiful, pleasing, agreeable.

භද්‍රකල්ප, *Bhadrakalpa*, *s.* (භද්‍ර happy, auspicious, කල්ප kalpa or period of time) present age of the world; period in which the religion of Buddha prevails; the Buddhists reckon four kalpas, three of which have elapsed; the present is the fourth or most auspicious kalpa, for in it five Buddhas are to exist, of whom four have already come and one called Maitrí Buddha has yet to make his appearance.

භද්‍රකාලි, *Bhadrakáli*, *s.* one of the forms of the goddess Durgá; fragrant grass, *cyperus pertenuis* or *rotundus*.

භද්‍රකුම්භ, *Bhadrakumbha*, } (භද්‍ර auspicious, කුම්භ
භද්‍රඝට, *Bhadraghaṭa*, } or ඝට water jar) golden jar filled with water from a holy place, or with water of the Ganges, and used especially at the consecration of a king; jar filled with water and flowers and placed before the door of a house on festival occasions.

භද්‍රදාරු, *Bhadradáru*, *s.* (භද්‍ර and දාරු wood) sort of pine, *pinus devadáru*, [Colloq. දේවදාර *déwadára*].

භද්‍රපද, *Bhadrapada*, *s.* month so called (September–October), also called බිනර *binara*.

භද්‍රපදා, *Bhadrapadá*, *s.* name given to the twenty-sixth and twenty-seventh lunar asterisms.

භද්‍රපර්ණා, *Bhadraparṇá*, *s.* shrub, *pæderia fœtida*.

භද්‍රපර්ණී, *Bhadraparṇní*, *s.* (භද්‍ර auspicious, පර්ණ leaf) tree, *gmelina arborea*, [Colloq. ඇත්දෙමට *ęt-demaṭa*].

භද්‍රපීඨ, *Bhadrapítha*, } *s.* (භද්‍ර excellence, පීඨ
භද්‍රපීඨක, *Bhadrapíṭhaka*, } chair) chair of superior beauty and worth, royal couch.

භද්‍රබලන, *Bhadrabalana*, *s.* (භද්‍ර conferring happiness, බල to live) name of Balaráma, the demigod and half brother to Krishṇa: see බලරාම *balaráma*.

භද්‍රබලා, *Bhadrabalá*, *s.* creeping plant, *ipomœa tridentata* or *angustifolia*, [Colloquial. ආපසුමඩු *ápasu-madu*].

භද්‍රමුස්ත, *Bhadramusta*, භද්‍රමුස්තක, *Bhadramustaka*, *s.* (භද්‍ර lucky, මුස්ත cyperus) fragrant grass, *cyperus rotundus*, [Colloq. කලාඳුරු *kaláṉduru*].

භද්‍රයව, *Bhadra-yawa*, *s.* medicinal nut or seed, *nerium antidysentericum*, [Colloq. කෙළිඳ ඇට *keḷiṉda-ęṭa*].

භද්‍රවල්ලී, *Bhadrawallí*, *s.* (භද්‍ර lucky, වල්ලී creeper) Arabian jasmine, *jasminum sambac*, [Coll: පිච්ච *pichcha*]; large Bengal creeper, *gaertnera racemosa*.

භද්‍රශ්‍රී, *Bhadraṣrí*, *s.* (භද්‍ර auspicious, ශ්‍රී excellence) sandal wood, or the sandal wood tree, *santalum album*, [Colloq. සඳුන් *saṉdun*].

භද්‍රා, *Bhadrá*, *s.* astrological period so called, also called Vishṭi, regarded as an unlucky period; the Ganges of heaven; the ichneumon plant, *mimosa octandra*, [Colloq. අරත්ත *aratta*]; indigo, *indigofera tinctoria*, [Coll: නිල් අවරි *nil-awari*]; *sarsaparilla*, *hemidesmus indica;* shrub, *pœderia fœtida;* name of the second, seventh, and twelfth days of the lunar fortnight; tree, *gmelina arborea*, [Colloq. ඇත්දෙමට *ęt-demaṭa*]; cow; turmeric, *curcuma longa*, [Colloq. කහ *kaha*]; sort of grass, *digitaria linearis*.

භද්‍රාලි, *Bhadráli*, *s.* plant, *ipomœa tridentata* or *angustifolia*, [Colloq. ආපසුමඩු *ápasu-madu*].

භද්‍රාව, *Bhadráwa*, *s.* woman, wife; term of endearment used in addressing a woman.

භද්‍රාශ්ව, *Bhadráṣwa*, *s.* (භද්‍ර *bhadra* auspicious, අශ්ව horse) one of the four Mahá-dwípas, according to some systems, into which the world is divided; or according to another system, one of the nine khandas, or smaller divisions of the continent; in either case it is the east division; it has its name from one of the nine sons of Agnídhra, to whom it was originally assigned.

භද්‍රාසන, *Bhadrásana*, *s.* (භද්‍ර *bhadra* auspicious or beautiful, ආසන *ásana* seat) throne; peculiar posture in which abstract meditation is performed by the devotee, the legs bent and crossed underneath and turned so as to bring the ankles in contact with the perineum, whilst the soles of the feet are held close to the sides.

භද්‍රෝදනී, *Bhadródani*, *s.* plant, *sida humilis*, [Colloq. බෑවිල *bęvila*].

භමු, *Bhamu*, *s.* the eye brow.

භය, *Bhaya*, *s.* (භී *bhí* to fear) fear, alarm, fright, horror, dread; flower of the *trapa bispinosa*, [Colloq. ඉකිලිය *ikiliya*]: *a.* frightful, horrible, dreadful.

භයඞ්කාර, *Bhayaṅkára*, *s.* (භය *bhaya* fear, කර *kara* to make) fearful, formidable, frightful; terrible, horrible.

භයද්‍රැත, *Bhayadruta*, *s.* (භය and ද්‍රැත flown, fled) routed, put to flight; terrified, frightened.

භයපත්, *Bhayapat*, *a.* (භය fear, පත් come etc.) afraid, dismayed.

භයානක, *Bhayánaka*, *a.* (භී *bhí* to fear, ආනක *ánaka* aff.) fearful, alarming, formidable.

භර්තා, *Bhartá*, *s.* husband; lord, master, owner; cherisher, supporter, one who sustains or upholds.

භර, *Bhara*, *a.* (භෘ *bhṛi* to cherish) who or what cherishes, upholds, supports, etc. heavy; much, excessive.

භරණ, *Bharaṇa*, *s.* cherishing, maintaining, nourishing, supporting; wages, hire: constellation bharaṇi, which see.

භරණී, *Bharaṇi*, *s.* name of the second lunar asterism, containing two stars *(musca)*.

භරත, *Bharata*, *s.* son of Dushymanta by Ṣakmitalá; name of a celebrated writer on dramatic composition.

භරතය, *Bharataya*, *s.* celebrated treatise on the Nṛitya ṣástra, including every branch of dramatic performance.

භරතවර්ෂ, *Bharata-warsha*, *s.* India.

භල්ල, *Bhalla*, *s.* (භල්ල to hurt or kill) bear; arrow with a crescent shaped head.

භල්ලක, *Bhaḷḷaka*, *s.* bear, [Colloq. වළහා *waḷahá*].

භල්ලාතක, *Bhallátaka*, *s.* marking nut tree, *semicarpus anacardium*, [Colloq. කිරි බඩුල්ල *kiri-badulla*].

භල්ලුක, *Bhalluka*, භල්ලූක, *Bhallúka*, *s.* bear; name of a famous warrior who lived in the time of Duṭugęmuṇu king of Ceylon, about seven centuries previous to the arrival of the Portuguese, and who distinguished himself against the Malabars in their invasion of the kingdom of Kandy.

භව්‍ය, *Bhawya*, *a.* happy, auspicious, prosperous; well, proper, fit, right; true; to be or become, what is to be; being, what is or exists; small fruit, *averrhoa carambola*, [Colloq. කාමරංගා *kámarangá*]; name of Umá or Durgá the wife of Ṣiva; large sort of pepper; bone; fruit; result; being, existence.

භව, *Bhawa*, *s.* (භූ *bhú* to be, to exist) being, existing, the self-support of something already produced; birth; obtaining, acquiring; world; name of Íṣwara or Ṣiva; excellence, superiority; welfare, prosperity; place, means or state of being; deity, a god; being or becoming possessed of any thing, as family, cattle etc.

භවකාන්තාරය, *Bhawa-kántáraya*, *s.* (භව being, කාන්තාර *kántára* bad road or forest) transmigration; in this form the word has a figurative meaning, alluding to the dangers and difficulties attending transmigration or the miseries that persons are doomed to endure in that state.

භවගතිය, *Bhawagatiya*, *s.* (භව existence, ගති *gati* going, state) transmigration, continued existence.

භවත්, *Bhawat*, *s.* (භා *bhá* to shine) being, existing: in Sanskrit, *pron.* thou, but used as a respectful term of address, as Sir, or Lord.

භවත්‍රය, *Bhawatraya*, *s.* (භව existence, ත්‍රය three) the three states of existence through which living beings have to pass previous to obtaining Nirwáṇa or final emancipation: see තුන්භවය *tunbhawaya*.

භවතණ්හාව, *Bhawa-taṇháwa*, *s.* (භව and තණ්හා *taṇhá* wish, desire) wish for existence, the opposite of භවකාන්තාර *bhawa-kántára:* the first, according to Buddhists, is the feeling of a fool, the latter of a wise man.

භවදුක්ඛය, *Bhawa-dukkhaya*, *s.* (භව and දුක්ඛ *dukkha* sorrow) transmigration, the misery of existence, in opposition to Nirwáṇa.

භවන, *Bhawana*, } *s.* existence; visibility; the
භවනය, *Bhawanaya*, } place of abiding or being, house, dwelling, site, field, spot; nature, quality; bow.

භවනීය, *Bhawaníya*, *a.* (භූ *bhú* to be, අනීයර් *aníyar* aff.) been or become, what is or ought to be.

භවභෝග, *Bhawa-bhóga*, *s.* (භව existence, භෝග enjoyment) worldly goods, riches, wealth; vain pleasure or enjoyment.

භවය, *Bhawaya*, see භව *bhawa*.

භවයෝනි, *Bhawa-yóni*, *s.* (භව and යෝනි birth) state of existence, still subject to transmigration.

භවරාග, *Bhawarága*, *s.* (භව and රාග love, adherence) cleaving to existence, desiring transmigration.

භවාග්‍ර, *Bhawágra*, *s.* (භව *bhawa* and අග්‍ර *agra* end, termination) boundless or unoccupied space; according to oriental ideas, that part of the universe beyond the limit of any of the worlds either of men or gods, the extremity of the universe.

භවාන්තර, *Bhawántara*, *s.* (භව *bhawa* being, existence, අන්තර *antara* among, amidst) the term of existence; repeated births, metempsychosis.

භවානී, *Bhawání*, *s.* (භව *bhawa* Ṣiva, with a fem. aff.) name of the goddess Párwatí or Durgá in her pacific or amiable form.

භවාලය, *Bhawálaya*, *s.* (භව *bhawa* and ආලය *álaya* desire) adherence to life; state of existence in this world: *a.* subject to transmigration; liable to be born etc.

භවික, *Bhavika*, *s.* prosperity, welfare; festival, an auspicious or festival occasion: *a.* prosperous, happy, faring well.

භවිත, *Bhavita*, *a.* been, become.

භවිෂ්‍යත්, *Bhavishyat*, *s.* (භූ *bhú* to be, with ශතෘ *ṣatṛi* aff. and ස්‍ය *sya* augment) what is to be, what will be, that which is future.

භස්ත්‍රා, *Bhastrá*, } *s.* bellows, large hide with valves
භස්ත්‍රී, *Bhastrí*, } and a clay nozzle, which is used for this purpose.

භස්ම, *Bhasma*, *s.* (භස *bhasa* to shine) ashes, [Coll: අළු *aḷu*].

භස්මගන්ධිකා, *Bhasmagandhiká*, } *s.* (භස්ම ashes,
භස්මගන්ධිනි, *Bhasmagandhini*, } ගන්ධ *gandha* smell, ඉනි *ini* aff.) kind of perfume and drug: see රේණුක *réṇuka*.

භස්මගර්භා, *Bhasma-garbhá*, *s.* (භස්ම and ගර්භ *garbha* place of production) *sisu* tree or a variety of it, *dalbergia sisu;* also a sort of perfume: see රේණුක *réṇuka*.

භස්මභාස්කර, *Bhasma-bháskara*, *s.* camphor, [Coll: කපුරු *kapuru*].

භා, *Bhá*, *s.* light; beauty, splendour, effulgence; ray of light, [Colloq. එළිය *eliya*].

භාක්ත, *Bhákta*, *s.* (භක්ත *bhakta* food, අණ් *aṇ* aff.) follower, dependant, one to whom food is regularly supplied; rice, boiled rice; etc.

භාග්‍ය, *Bhágya*, *s.* (භජ් *bhaja* to divide) destiny, fortune, luck; religious merit.

භාග්‍යපති, *Bhágya-pati*, *s.* (භාග්‍ය and පති lord) married couple, pair, man and wife.

භාග්‍යවත්, *Bhágyawat*, *a.* (භාග්‍ය good luck, වත් poss. aff.) happy, fortunate, lucky, meritorious, deserving.

භාග්‍යවන්තයා, *Bhágyawantayá*, *s.* fortunate person.

භාග, *Bhága*, *s.* part, portion, share; fortune, luck; half rupee; part of any thing given as interest; division of time, the thirtieth part of a Rási or zodiacal sign; fraction; 360th part of the circumference of a great circle.

භාගධේය, *Bhágadhéya*, *s.* (භාග part, ධේය to be taken) heir, co-heir; royal revenue; fate, destiny, luck.

භාගිනේය, *Bhágineya*, *s.* (භගිනී *bhaginí* sister, with an aff.) sister's son.

භාගී, *Bhágí*, *s.* co-heir; *a.* who or what shares; having parts.

භාගීරථී, *Bhágírathí*, *s.* (භගීරථ *bhagíratha* king so called, අණ් *an* aff.) the river Ganges in Bengal, so called in allusion to the fable, that this river first descended from heaven in answer to the prayers and intercessions of භගීරථ *bhagíratha*.

භාජන, *Bhájana*, } *s.* (භජ් *bhaja* to serve or
භාජනය, *Bhájanaya*, } share) any vessel, as a pot or cup; plate etc: *a.* clever, capable, fit.

භාටක, *Bháṭaka*, *s.* wages, hire, price, etc.

භාඩාරය, *Bháṇḍáraya*, more correctly භාණ්ඩාරය *bháṇḍáraya*, contracted form of භාණ්ඩාගාරය *bháṇḍágáraya*, which see.

භාණ්ඩ, *Bháṇḍa*, *s.* any vessel as a cup, pot or dish; instrument or utensil of any kind; ornament for the neck and breast of a horse; ornament in general; mimicry, buffoonery.

භාණ්ඩක, *Bháṇḍaka*, see භාණ්ඩික *bháṇḍika*.

භාණ්ඩාගාරය, *Bháṇḍágáraya*, *s.* (භාණ්ඩ *bháṇḍa* vessel, cup, etc. අගාර *ágára* house) store room, place where household goods and utensils are kept, treasury.

භාණ්ඩාගාරික, *Bháṇḍágárika*, *s.* (භාණ්ඩාගාර *bháṇḍágára* store room etc. ඉක *ika* aff.) store keeper, a man who has charge of a treasury, etc.

භාණ්ඩි, *Bháṇḍi*, *s.* shrub bearing the mára seed, *albizzia Lebbek*: see මාරගහ *mára-gaha*.

භාණ්ඩික, *Bháṇḍika*, *s.* musician, one especially whose business it is to awaken the prince or chief in the morning by his vocal or instrumental music.

භාත, *Bháta*, *s.* (භා *bhá* to shine) morning, dawn, day break, [Colloq. පාන්දර *pándara*]: *a.* shone, bright, glittering, resplendent.

භාතු, *Bhátu*, *s.* (භා to shine, තු aff.) sun.

භාද්‍රපද, *Bhádrapada*, *s.* name of a month (August-September), when the moon is full near the wing of Pegasus.

භානු, *Bhánu*, *s.* (භා to shine, නු aff.) sun; light, ray of light; master; sovereign, prince.

භානුභක්තා, *Bhánubhaktá*, *s.* (භානු ray of light, භක්ත *bhakta* which eats) medicinal plant, *bryonia umbellata*, or *cephalandra indica*, [Colloq. කොබෝවක්කා *kobówakká* or කෝවක්කා *kówakká*].

භානුමත්, *Bhánumat*, *s.* (භානු light, මත් poss. aff.) sun, [Colloq. ඉර *ira*]: *a.* luminous, resplendent; handsome, beautiful.

භාම, *Bháma*, *s.* (භා *bhá* to shine, or භාම to be passionate) passion, wrath, anger, [Colloq. උදහස *udahasa*]; light, lustre, [Coll: එලිය *eliya*].

භාමින්, *Bhámin*, *a.* (භාම *bháma* passion, ඉනි *ini* aff.) passionate, wrathful, angry.

භාමිනී, *Bháminí*, *s.* wrathful or passionate woman.

භාර්ගව, *Bhárgawa*, *s.* name of Paraṣuráma; name of Ṣukra or Sikurá regent of the planet Venus and preceptor of the Titans or Asurs; an archer; elephant.

භාර්ගවී, *Bhárgaví*, *s.* name of the goddess Párwatí wife of Ṣiva; name of the goddess Lakshmí wife of Vishṇu; bent grass, *panicum dactylon* or *agrostis linearis*, [Colloq. හෙළ ඊතණ *heḷa-ítaṇa*].

භාර්ගී, *Bhárgí*, *s.* shrub, *siphonanthus indica;* it is sacred to Brahma.

භාර්‍යා, *Bháryá*, } *s.* (භෘ *bhṛi* to nourish) wife,
භාර්‍යාව, *Bháryáwa*, } one espoused according to established forms and ritual.

භාර, *Bhára*, *s.* (භෘ *bhṛi* nourish) charge, care, custody; weight, burden, load; yoke for carrying burdens; name of Vishṇu.

භාරත, *Bhárata*, *s.* (භරත *bharata* inventor of the Indian drama, අණ් *an* aff. or භෘ *bhṛi* to nourish) celebrated epic poem of the Hindus; see මහා භාරත *mahá-bhárata*: it is also supposed to be the name of a great prince, who wrote a celebrated work on dramatic performances, and this opinion is defended on the ground that the wars which are celebrated in the Bhárata occurred among the descendants of this prince: see භරත *bharata*.

භාරතවර්ෂ, *Bhárata-warsha*, *s.* (භාරත and වර්ෂ continent or division of a continent) name of India proper, so called from the prince Bharata who received it as a patrimony from his father Dushmanta.

භාරති, *Bhárati*, *s.* name of Saraswatí the goddess of speech; speech, word; talipot tree, the leaves of which are used for writing books, *corypha umbraculifera*, [Colloq. තල *tala*].

භාරදාරු, *Bháradáru*, *s.* (භාර weight or much, දාරු wood) sal tree, *vateria acuminata*. [Colloq. හල් ගහ *hal-gaha*].

භාරදෙනවා, *Bháradenawá*, *v.* to give in charge, to deliver over, to surrender.

භාරද්වාජ, *Bháradwája*, *s.* (භරද්වාජ *bharadwája* lark, අණ් *aṇ* pleonastic or derivative aff.) name of Dróṇa, the military preceptor of the Kurus and Páṇḍus; one of the seven Ṛishis who it is said was abandoned by his parents at his birth, and nursed by a lark; name of the Muni Agastya; son of Vṛihaspati or Jupiter; sky lark: see භාරය *bháraya*.

භාරද්වාජි, *Bháradwájí*, *s.* wild cotton.

භාරය, *Bháraya*, *s.* charge, custody, etc: see භාර *bhára*; lark, *alauda gulgula*, [Colloq. ගෝමරිටා *gómariṭá*].

භාරයෂ්ටි, *Bhárayashṭi*, *s.* (භාර load, යෂ්ටි stick) pole or yoke for carrying burdens; stick carried over the shoulder with the burden suspended at both ends by strings, usually called a pingo, [Colloq. කත්ලිය *katlíya*].

භාරවාහ, *Bhárawáha*, *s.* (භාර burden, වහ *waha* to bear, අණ් *aṇ* aff.) porter, bearer of burdens.

භාරවාහි, *Bhárawáhi*, *s.* (භාර load, වාහි what bears) indigo plant, *indigofera indica*, [Colloq. නිල්අවරි *nil-awari*]; capila plant, *rottlera tinctoria*, [Colloq. හම්පිරිල *hampirila*].

භාරින්, *Bhárin*, *s.* (භාර *bhára* burden, ඉන් aff.) porter, bearer of burdens.

භාල, *Bhála*, *s.* forehead; light; lustre; excellence, worth.

භාව, *Bháwa*, *s.* (භූ *bhú* to be) state or condition of being; natural state of being, innate property, disposition, nature; state or affection of mind, emotion or passion; birth; thing, substance; being, living thing; the place of birth or pudendum muliebre; abstract idea conveyed by any word; the simple idea derived from the root.

භාවන, *Bháwana*, } *s.* (භූ *bhú* to be, in the causal form) mental perception,
භාවනා, *Bháwaná*, } recollection, the present consciousness of past ideas or perceptions; religious and abstract meditation; thinking, reflecting, mental investigation; looking about, (literally or figuratively), observing, investigating; abstract meditation.

භාවය, *Bháwaya*, *s.* state or condition, state of existence: see භාව *bháwa*.

භාවික, *Bhárika*, see භවික *bharika*.

භාවිත, *Bhárita*, *a.* (භූ *bhú* to be, in the causative passive form) accustomed to, practised, habituated, used to; mixed with any thing as an ingredient, as sesamum and other fragrant substances with curry, etc.; obtained, got.

භාවිතාව, *Bháritáwa*, *s.* custom, practice, use: pl. භාවිතා *bhávitá*.

භාවුක, *Bháwuka*, *s.* happiness, auspiciousness; festival, joyous or auspicious occasion: *a.* happy, well, right; actually, being or disposed to be; (in composition with other nouns), becoming what it was not before.

භාෂ්‍ය, *Bháshya*, *s*, commentary, but particularly the explanation and application of a technical sútra or aphorism; hence applied to many of the annotations on the grammatical aphorisms of Páṇini, to comments on the Vedas, etc.

භාෂා, *Báshá*, *s.* language, speech; name of Saraswatí the goddess of speech.

භාෂාමාර්ගය, *Bháshá-márgaya*, *s.* the analogy or idiom of language.

භාෂාරීතිය, *Bháshá-rítiya*, *s.* (භාෂා language, රීති *ríti* custom, usage) the (established) usage or idiom of language.

භාෂාව, *Bháshấwa*, *s.* speech, language: see භාෂා *bháshá*.

භාෂිත, *Bháshita*, *s.* (භාෂ *bhásha* to speak, ක්ත *kta* aff.) speech: *a.* spoken, said, uttered.

භාස්, *Bhás*, *s.* light, ray of light; wish, desire.

භාස්කර, *Bháskura*, *s.* (භාස් and කර what makes) sun; fire; hero; name of a celebrated astronomer; gold.

භාස්වත්, *Bháswat*, *s.* (භාස් and වත් poss. aff.) sun; light; hero: *a.* shining, resplendent, brilliant.

භාස, *Bhása*, *s.* (භාස to shine) light, lustre, shining; vulture; sort of bird described as a water fowl.

භාසමාර්ග, *Bhása-márga*, *s.* (භාස light, මාර්ග path) sky, atmosphere, [Colloq. අහස *ahasa*].

භාසාව, *Bhásáwa*, *s.* language, speech.

භාසිත, *Bhásita*, s. (භාස to shine or to speak, ක්ත *kta* aff.) light, lustre, shining; speech, language, written composition: *a.* shining, bright, splendid; spoken, said, uttered.

භිංකාර, *Bhinkára*, s. (භිං imitative sound, කාර what makes) golden vase, [Colloq. රන්කෙණ්ඩිය *ran-kendiya*].

භික්ඛු, *Bhikkhu*, Páli form of භික්ෂු *bhikshu*.

භික්ති, *Bhikti*, s. wall of earth or stone; wall of a house as opposed to a mere wall or enclosure; incorrectly for භිත්ති *bhitti*.

භික්ෂා, *Bhikshá*, s. (භික්ෂ *bhiksha* to beg) service; hire, wages; begging, asking; thing obtained by begging, alms; mouthful or handful of food given as alms.

භික්ෂාචර, *Bhikshá́chara*, s. (භික්ෂා food, චර to go) mendicant, beggar, Buddhist priest.

භික්ෂාචාර, *Bhikshá́chára*, s. (භික්ෂා and ආචාර *áchára* going) begging, asking alms, practice of a mendicant Buddhist priest, going about to ask alms for his support.

භික්ෂාචාරවේලා, *Bhikshá́chára-wélá*, s. (භික්ෂාචාර alms begging, වේලා time) forepart of the day, before meridian when it is lawful for the priests to beg their food.

භික්ෂාටනය, *Bhikshá́tanaya*, s. (භික්ෂා alms, අටන *aṭana* going about for) begging, mendicancy: see භික්ෂාචාර *bhikshá́chára*.

භික්ෂාභාජනය, *Bhikshá-bhájanaya*, s. alms-bowl.

භික්ෂාව, *Bhiksháwa*, see භික්ෂා *bhikshá*.

භික්ෂු, *Bhikshu*, s. (භික්ෂ *bhiksha* to beg, with an aff.) beggar, mendicant, Buddhist priest who supports himself by begging, being the way in which he must procure a livelihood according to the established ordinances of the priesthood: pl. භික්ෂූන් *bhikshun* or භික්ෂූහු *bhikshuhu*.

භික්ෂුක, *Bhikshuka*, s. beggar, religious mendicant; tree, *Woodfordia floribunda* or *grislea tomentosa*, [Colloq. මලිත *malita*]; tree, *bauhinia racemosa*, [Colloq. මයිල *mayila*].

භික්ෂුණී, *Bhikshuní*, s. priestess, woman who has entered the Buddhist priesthood: see භික්ෂු *bhikshu*.

භික්ෂුභාව, *Bhikskubháwa*, s. (භික්ෂු and භාව being) mendicancy, alms begging.

භිඞ්ගා, *Bhińgá*, s. heart-pea, *cardiospermum halicacabum*, [Coll. පෙනෙලවැල් *penela-wel*]; shrub, *celastrus paniculata*, [Colloq. දුදු *dúdu*].

භිණ්ඩිවාල, *Bhiṇḍiwála*, s. kind of weapon, short arrow thrown from the hand or shot through a tube.

භිත්ත, *Bhitta*, s. (භිද *bhida* to divide, ක්ත *kta* aff.) part, portion, share, [Colloq. පංගුව *panguwa*].

භිත්ති, *Bhitti*, s. (භිද *bhida* to divide) wall of earth or masonry; thing broken or divided; rent, fissure; fragment, bit, broken piece or part; breaking, rending.

භිද්, *Bhid*, } s. (භිද *bhida* to divide or break) kind,
භිද, *Bhida*, } sort, difference; breaking, dividing.

භිදා, *Bhidá*, s. tearing, rending; coriander.

භින්දපාල, *Bhindapála*, see භිණ්ඩිවාල *bhiṇḍiwála*.

භින්න, *Bhinna*, s. (භිද *bhida* to break) flaw in a jewel, bit, fraction: *a.* split, broken, rent, torn; divided, distinguished; other, different; blown, budded, opened; connected, joined.

භින්නගුණන, *Bhinna-guṇana*, s. multiplication of fractions.

භින්නඝන, *Bhinna-ghana*, s. cube of a fraction.

භින්නන්දර, *Bhinnandara*, s. plant, *cyperus rotundus*, [Colloq. කලාඳුරු *kalanduru*].

භින්නවර්ග, *Bhinna-warga*, s. square of a fraction.

භින්න ව්‍යවකලන, *Bhinna-wyawakalana*, s. subtraction of fractions.

භිෂග්ජිත, *Bhishagjita*, s. (භිෂග් physician, ජිත subdued (by which) overcoming) tulasi plant, holy basil, *ocimum sanctum*, [Colloq. මදුරුතලා *maduru-talá*]; drug, medicament.

භිෂජ්, *Bhishaj*, s. physician, [Colloq. වෙදා *wedá*].

භිස්සටා, *Bhissaṭá*, s. scorched rice, [Colloq. දම්කුඩ *damkuḍa* or දඹුබත් *dambu-bat*].

භිස්සා, *Bhissá*, s. boiled rice, [Colloq. බත් *bat*].

භිසක්, *Bhisak*, see භිෂජ් *bhishaj*.

භිසක්මාතා, *Bhisakmátá*, s. medicinal plant, *adhatoda Vasica* or *justicia adhatoda*, [Colloq. අගල් අඩදර *agaládára*].

භී, *Bhí*, s. (භී to fear, dread) fear, dread, alarm.

භීත, *Bhíta*, s. fear, alarm, apprehension: *a.* afraid, frightened, fearful, timid.

භීතවෙනවා, *Bhítawenawá*, v. to be terrified.

භීති, *Bhíti*, s. fear, apprehension; trembling, shaking.

භීතිකර, *Bhítikara*, a. creating fear, alarming; terrific.

භීම, *Bhíma*, s. (භී *bhí* to fear etc.) horror, terror; name of Śiva; one of the five Páṇḍu princes; kind of sorrel, *rumex vesicarius*: *a.* fearful, horrible, alarming; pitiless, cruel, hard, stern.

භීමතා, *Bhímatá*, s. (භීම fearful, තා aff. of the abstract) fear, terror, dread.

භීමනාද, *Bhímanáda*, *s.* (භීම fearful, නාද voice) lion, fearful sound.

භීමනේත්‍ර, *Bhíma-nétra*, *s.* (භීම terrific, නේත්‍ර eye) name of Íṣwara or Ṣiva, alluding to the terror inspired by the large circular eye in his forehead.

භීමා, *Bhímá*, *s.* (භී to fear etc.) name of Durgá, wife of Ṣiva; whip; sort of perfume.

භීරු, *Bhíru*, *s.* (භී to fear etc.) woman, name expressive of her natural timidity, a quality much admired by orientals; tree, *gmelina arborea*, [Colloq. ඇත්දෙමට *ęt-demaṭa*]; creeping plant, *asparagus falcatus*, [Colloq. හාතාවාරිය *hátáwáriya*]: *a.* fearful, timid.

භීරුක, *Bhíruka*, *s.* wood, forest; owl; bear: *a.* fearful, timid.

භීරුහෘදය, *Bhíru-hridaya*, *r.* (භීරු timid, හෘදය heart) deer, [Colloq. මුවා *muwá*].

භීෂ්ම, *Bhíshma*, *a.* (භී to fear etc.) timid, fearful.

භීෂණ, *Bhíshaṇa*, } *s.* horror, dread, terror; any
භීසන, *Bhísana*, } thing that excites horror or terrific ideas; name of Ṣiva; see the next: *a.* terrific, horrible.

භීසනාග, *Bhísanága*, *s.* gum olibanum tree, *boswellia thurifera*, [Colloq. කනන්ග *kananga*].

භුක්ත, *Bhukta*, *s.* (භුජ් *bhuja* to eat,) eaten, either that which is eaten or the person who has eaten; eating, food.

භුක්තානුමෝදනා, *Bhuktánumódaná*, *s.* (භුක්ත *bhukta* eaten, අනුමෝදනා *anumódaná* thanks) expression of thanks or praise after a meal.

භුක්ති, *Bhukti*, *s.* (භුජ් *bhuja* to eat, ක්තින් *ktin* aff.) eating; possession, fruition, usufruct.

භුක්තිවිඳිනවා, *Bhuktivindinawá*, *v.* to possess, to enjoy.

භුග්න, *Bhugna*, *a.* (භුජ *bhuja* to curve) bent, crooked, curved.

භුජ, *Bhuja*, *s.* (භුජ to bend) hand; arm; bending, curve; arm of a geometrical figure, as a square or triangle.

භුජග, *Bhujaga*, *s.* (භුජ crooked, ග who goes) serpent, snake, [Colloq. සර්පයා *sarpayá*].

භුජඞ්ග, *Bhujańga*, *s.* black lead, [Colloq. කළු ඊයම් *kaḷu-íyam*]; snake; catamite.

භුජඞ්ගභුක්, *Bhujańga-bhuk*, } *s.* (භුජඞ්ග snake,
භුජඞ්ගභුජ්, *Bhujańga-bhuj*, } භුජ් who eats) Garuḍa the bird and vehicle of Vishṇu.

භුජඞ්ගම, *Bhujańgama*, *s.* snake, serpent, [Colloq. සර්පයා *sarpayá*].

භුජඞ්ගාක්ෂි, *Bhujańgákshi*, *s.* (භුජඞ්ග *bhujanga* snake, අක්ෂ *aksha* to pervade, or අක්ෂි *akshi* eye, the flowers being compared to the eye of the snake) ichneumon plant, *mimosa octandra*, [Coll: අරත්ත *aratta*]; variety of the saffron plant, *curcuma longa*, [Colloq. කහ *kaha*].

භුජපත්‍ර, *Bhuja-patra*, *s.* tree, භෝජපත්‍ර *bhója-patra*, which see.

භුත්ත, *Bhutta*, *a.* eaten, enjoyed.

භුවන, *Bhuwana*, *s.* (භූ *bhú* to be) world; water; heaven; man, mankind.

භූ, *Bhú*, *s.* (භූ to be) earth, [Colloq. පොළව *poḷuwa*]; place, site, place of being or abiding; sacrificial fire; seventh hell.

භූකම්පා, *Bhúkampá*, *s.* (භූ and කම්පා trembling) earthquake: see භූමිකම්පාව *bhúmikampáva*.

භූකේශ, *Bhúkéṣa*, *s.* (භූ and කේශ hair) aquatic plant, *blyxa Roxburghii* or *vallisneria octandra;* the Indian fig or banyan tree, *ficus bengalensis*, [Colloq. මහනුග *maha-nuga*]: plant, with composite flowers *vernonia* or *serratula anthelmintica*, [Colloq. නායන් *náyan* and සන්නි නායන් *sanni-náyan*].

භූගෝලය, *Bhúgólaya*, *s.* the terrestrial globe, the earth.

භූගෝලශාස්ත්‍රය, *Bhúgóla-sástraya*, *s.* geography.

භූත, *Bhúta*, *s.* goblin, ghost, malignant spirit haunting cemeteries, lurking in trees, animating carcases and deluding or devouring human beings; demigod of a particular class; tree, plant, shrub, creeper, etc.; son, child; name of Ṣiva; fourteenth day of the dark half of a lunar month; element, five bhútas are enumerated, earth, fire, water, air and ákása or ether; living being; figure, identity; thought, perception; fact, matter of fact, the real state of the case, or what has actually been: *a.* evident, apparent, known; been, become; gone, past; (in composition) like, resembling; obtained, got; proper, right; true.

භූතකේශ, *Bhútakéṣa*, *s.* (භූත spirit, කේශ hair) root of sweet flag, *acorus calamus*, [Colloq. වදකහ *wadakaha*].

භූතකේශි, *Bhútakéṣí*, *s.* tree, *vitex negundo*, [Coll: නිකගහ *nika-gaha*]: see නිල්නික *nil-nika* and සුදුනික *sudu-nika*.

භූතගන්ධා, *Bhútagandhá*, *s.* (භූත goblin, ගන්ධ *gandha* perfume) kind of perfume or resin, used, perhaps, in the ceremonies with which those beings are worshipped and propitiated.

භූතඝන, *Bhútaghna*, *s.* (භූත sprite, ඝන what destroys or removes) camel, [Colloq. ඔටුවා *oṭuwá*]; garlic, *allium sativum*, [Colloq. සුදුළූනු *sudu-lúnu*].

භූතඝ්නී, *Bhútaghní*, *s.* plant, Muṇḍírí; holy basil, *ocimum sanctum*, [Colloq. මදුරුතලා *maduru-talá*].

භූතජටා, *Bhútajaṭá*, *s.* (භූත goblin, ජටා clustered locks) Indian spikenard, *valeriana jatamansi*, [Colloq. ජටාමාංස *jaṭámáṇsa*].

භූතධරා, *Bhútadhará*, *s.* (භූත living being, ධර *dhara* what bears) the earth, [Colloq. පොළව *poḷawa*].

භූතනාථ, *Bhútanátha*, *s.* (භූත spirit or element, නාථ lord) name of Ṣiva; see the next.

භූතනායක, *Bhútanáyaka*, *s.* (භූත spirit or goblin, නායක leader) name of Ṣiva; also of Wesamuṇi-raja or Kuvéra the prince of demons.

භූතනාශන, *Bhúta-náṣana*, *s.* marking nut plant, *semicarpus anacardium*, [Colloq. කිරි බඩුල්ල *kiri-badulla*]; mustard, *brassica juncea* or *sinapis alba*, [Colloq. අබ *aba*]; the seed of the wild olive, *elæocarpus cuneatus*, [Colloq. වෙරළු *weraḷu*].

භූතපති, *Bhúta-pati*, *s.* (භූත demon, පති lord) name of Ṣakra, alluding to his overcoming the demons.

භූතපුෂ්ප, *Bhúta-pushpa*, *s.* (භූත sprite, පුෂ්ප flower) tree, *oroxylum indicum* or *bignonia indica*, [Colloq. තොටිල *toṭila*].

භූතප්‍රිය, *Bhúta-priya*, *s.* (භූත and ප්‍රිය agreeable) offerings and sacrifices to demons.

භූතයඥ, *Bhútayajña*, *s.* (භූත and යඥ sacrifice) offering viands, flowers etc., to demons.

භූතල, *Bhútala*, *s.* face of the earth.

භූතවාස, *Bhúta-wása*, *s.* (භූත goblin, වාස abode) beleric myrobalan, *terminalia belerica*, [Colloq. බුළු *buḷu*], this tree being supposed a favourite residence of sprites.

භූතවේශී, *Bhútawéṣi*, *s*, (භූත and විශ *viṣa* to pervade) plant bearing white flowers, *nyctanthes arbor-tristis*, [Colloq. සේපාල *sépála* and සේපාලිකා *sépáliká*].

භූතවෘක්ෂ, *Bhúta-vriksha*, *s.* (භූත and වෘක්ෂ tree) tree, *streblus aspera*, this tree being supposed a favourite haunt of sprites, [Colloq. ගැටනෙටුල් *géṭa-neṭul*]; tree, *bignonia indica*: see also භූතපුෂ්ප *bhúta-pushpa* and භූතවාස *bhúta-wása*.

භූතස්ථාන, *Bhútasthána*, see භූතසංචාර *bhúta-sançhára*.

භූතසංචාර, *Bhúta-sançhára*, *s.* (භූත goblin, සම් *sam* with, චර *chara* to go) possession by evil spirits.

භූතසංඥාව, *Bhúta-sañjñáwa*, *s.* apparition.

භූතාලය, *Bhútálaya*, *s.* (භූත *bhúta* demon or sprite, ආලය *álaya* residence) any place supposed to be the residence of demons, as a tree, mountain, etc; place haunted by a ghost or sprite; déwála or demon temple.

භූතාවිෂ්ට, *Bhútávishṭa*, *a.* (භූත *bhúta* goblin, ආවිෂ්ට *ávishṭa* entered) occupied or possessed by a devil.

භූතාවේශ, *Bhútáwéṣa*, *s.* (භූත *bhúta* sprite, ආවේශ *áwéṣa* entrance) demoniacal possession.

භූතාවෘත්ත, *Bhútávritta*, *s.* superhuman power, the power of performing miracles by the influence of demons.

භූති, *Bhúti*, *s.* superhuman power, attainable by the performance of austere and magical rites; production; state of being.

භූතික, *Bhútika*, *s.* plant, yielding tonic and febrifuge, *gentiana cherayta;* fragrant grass, *andropogon schœnanthus;* plant, *ligusticum ajwaen.*

භූතිනිධාන, *Bhúti-nidhána*, *s.* (භූති prosperity, නිධාන receptacle) twenty fourth lunar mansion, Dhanishṭha.

භූතීක, *Bhútíka*, see භූතික *bhútika*.

භූතේශ, *Bhútéṣa*, } *s.* name of Ṣiva as lord of all
භූතේස, *Bhútésa*, } created beings; name of Kuvéra or Wesamuṇi-raja, the chief of the demon race and god of wealth.

භූදාර, *Bhúdára*, *s.* (භූ earth, දෘ *dri* to tear) hog, [Colloq. ඌරා *úrá*].

භූදේව, *Bhúdéwa*, *s.* (භූ and දේව divinity) Brahman; any terrestrial god or demon.

භූධර, *Bhúdhara*, *s.* (භූ and ධර to support) mountain, [Colloq. කන්ද *kanda*].

භූධාත්‍රී, *Bhúdhátrí*, *s.* plant, *phyllanthus niruri*, [Colloq. පිටවක්කා *piṭawakká*].

භූනිම්බ, *Bhúnimba*, *s.* plant, peculiar to Ceylon, *munronia pumila*, [Colloq. බිංකොහොඹ *binkohomba*].

භූපදී, *Bhúpadí*, *s.* plant, peculiar to Ceylon, *wrightia zeylanica*, [Colloq. ඉද්ද *idda*].

භූපරිධි, *Bhú-paridhi*, *s.* (භූ and පරිධි circle) circumference of the earth.

භූපාල, *Bhúpála*, *s.* (භූ earth, පාල who preserves) king, sovereign, [Colloq. රජ *raja*].

භූපුත්‍ර, *Bhú-putra*, *s.* (භූ and පුත්‍ර son) regent of the planet Mars, who is said to have been turned up out of the ground by a plough.

භූපුත්‍රී, *Bhú-putrí*, *s.* (භූ and පුත්‍රී daughter) name of Sitá the wife of Ráma.

භූම්‍යන්තර, *Bhúmyantara*, *s.* භූමි *bhúmi* earth, අන්තර *antara* midst or interval) kind of demon or imaginary being, supposed to dwell in the air and sometimes to alight on the highest mountains where they are worshipped: *a.* earthly, terrestrial, produced in; relating or belonging to the earth.

භූම්‍යන්තරික, *Bhúmyantarika*, *a.* (භූම්‍යන්තර and ඉක *ika* aff.) terrestrial; produced in or belonging to the earth.

භූමණ්ඩලය, *Bhúmandalaya*, *s.* surface of the earth.

භූමදාන, *Bhúmadána*, see භූමධාන *bhúmadhána*.

භූමදානකරණවා, *Bhúmadána-karanawá*, *v.* to bury, to inter.

භූමධාන, *Bhúmadhána*, *s.* (භූම corruptly for භූමි earth, ධාන inclosing) burying, interment.

භූමය, *Bhúmaya*, *a.* made or consisting of earth, earthly.

භූමි, *Bhúmi*, *s.* earth; land, place. site in general.

භූමික, *Bhúmika*, *a.* (භූමි and ක aff.) terrestrial, earthly, belonging to the earth.

භූමිකන්දක, *Bhúmi-kandaka*, *s.* (භූමි and කන්දක root) yam, potato, any edible root.

භූමිකම්පාව, *Bhúmi-kampáwa*, *s.* (භූමි earth, කම්ප *kampa* shaking) earthquake.

භූමිගුහා, *Bhúmi-guhá*, *s.* (භූමි and ගුහා cave) cavern, cave natural or artificial, one used as a house.

භූමිචම්පක, *Bhúmi-champaka*, *s.* (භූමි and චම්පක michelia) plant, *kaempferia rotunda*, [Colloq. යවකෙන්ද *yawakenda*].

භූමිජ, *Bhúmija*, *s.* (භූමි and ජ born) regent of the planet Mars: see භූ පුත්‍ර *bhú-putra*.

භූමි ජම්බු, *Bhúmi-jambu*, *s.* (භූමි and ජම්බු eugenia) plant with small flowers in corymbs, *premna herbacea*.

භූමිතලය, *Bhúmitalaya*, *s.* (භූමි and තල *tala* site) surface or region of the earth.

භූමිදේව, *Bhúmidéwa*, *s.* (භූමි and දේව divinity) a Brahman; any terrestrial god or demon.

භූමිනාද, *Bhúminada*, *s.* (භූමි earth, නාද sound) subterranean rumbling accompanying an earthquake.

භූමිනාරඞ්ග, *Bhúminâranga*, *s.* Mandarin orange, *citrus nobilis*, [Colloq. හින්නාරන් *hin-náran*].

භූමිප, *Bhúmipa*, } *s.* (භූමි and පාල who pre-
භූමිපාල, *Bhúmipála*, } serves) king, sovereign, [Colloq. රජ *raja*].

භූමිපිශාච, *Bhúmi-pisácha*, *s.* (භූමි and පිශාච goblin) palmyra tree, *borassus flabelliformis*, [Colloq. තල්ගහ *tal-gaha*].

භූමිබලා, *Bhúmibalá*, *s.* plant, variety of *sida humilis*, [Colloq. බිම්බෑවිල *bim-bevila*].

භූමි මණ්ඩා, *Bhúmi-mandá*, *s.* (භූමි earth, මඩි *madi* to ornament) Arabian jasmine, *jasminum sambac*, [Colloq. පිච්ච *pichcha*].

භූමිශාස්ත්‍රය, *Bhúmi-sástraya*, *s.* description of the earth; geography.

භූමීන්ද්‍ර, *Bhúmíndra*, *s.* (භූමි and ඉන්ද්‍ර *indra* chief) king, sovereign, [Colloq. රජ *raja*].

භූයෝ, *Bhúyó*, *ad.* much, repeatedly.

භූර්ජ, *Bhúrjja*, *s.* the bhój or bhój-patra, a tree growing in the snowy mountains, kind of birch; the bark is used for writing on.

භූර්ජසාර, *Bhúrjjasára*, *s.* waved leaf fig tree, *ficus arnottiana*, [Colloq. පුලිල *pulila*].

භූර්ලෝක, *Bhúrlóka*, *s.* (භූඃ *bhúh* earth, ලෝක *lóka* world) earth, residence of mortals, [Colloq. ලෝකය *lókaya*].

භූරි, *Bhúri*, *a.* much, many.

භූරිඵේනා, *Bhúriphéná*, *s.* plant, species of hedge-hyssop, *herpestis* or *gratiola monniera*, [Colloq. බෑමිතිරිය *bemitiriya*, or ලුණුවිල *lunuvila*].

භූරිමේධ, *Bhúrimédha*, *s.* (භූරි much, මේධා *médhá* wisdom) name of Buddha; great wisdom; wise man.

භූරිරස, *Bhúri-rasa*, *s.* sugar-cane, *saccharum officinarum*, [Colloq. උක්ගස් *ukgas*].

භූරිශස්, *Bhúrisas*, *ad.* manifold, many, by many.

භූරුහ, *Bhúruha*, *s.* (භූ earth, රුහ what grows) tree, [Colloq. ගහ *gaha*].

භූලතා, *Bhú-latá*, *e.* (භූ and ලතා creeper) worm, earth-worm, [Colloq. පණුවා *panuwá*].

භූශක්‍රය, *Bhú-sakraya*, *s.* (භූ and ශක්‍ර *sakra* Indra) king, [Colloq. රජ *raja*].

භූෂණ, *Bhúshana*, *s.* (භූෂ *bhúsha* to adorn) ornament, embellishment.

භූෂා, *Bhúshá*, *s.* (භූෂ *bhúsha* to adorn) adorning, decorating with trinkets, jewels, etc.

භූෂිත, *Bhúshita*, *a.* (භූෂ *bhúsha* and ක්ත *kta* aff.) adorned, decorated, dressed.

භූස්තෘණ, *Bhústrina*, *s.* (භූ earth, තෘණ *trina* grass with සුට් *sut* augment) fragrant grass, *andropogon schœnanthus:* see භූතික *bhútika*.

භූස්ඵෝට, *Bhúsphóṭa*, *s.* (භූ and ස්ඵෝට fungus) species of mushroom, not ascertained.

භූස්වර්ග *Bhúswarga*, *s.* (භූ earth, ස්වර්ග paradise) mountain Mahámeru, on the summit of which, according to oriental fable, Swarga is situated.

භූසා, *Bhúsá*, see භූෂා *bhúshá*.

භූසිත, *Bhúsita*, see භූෂිත *bhúshita*.

භූසුත, *Bhúsuta*, *s*, (භූ and සුත offspring) name of the regent of the planet Mars: see භූපුත්‍ර *bhúputra*.

භේකි, *Bhékí*, *s.* female frog, small frog; kind of creeper, *hydrocotyle asiataca*, [Colloq. හීන් ගොටුකොල *hín-goṭukola*].

භේද්‍ය, *Bhédya*, *a.* to be broken, rent, divided, etc.

භේද, *Bhéda*, *s.* (භිද *bhida* to divide) dividing, separating; tearing, rending, breaking etc.; distinction, kind, sort, species, difference; disunion, disagreement; sowing dissension, breaking the unanimity of confederates, one of the means of success against an opponent.

භේදකරණවා, *Bhédakaraṇawá*, *v.* to divide.

භේදචිත්ත, *Bhéda-chitta*, *a.* (භේද breaking, චිත්ත mind) broken-hearted, penitent, contrite.

භේදන, *Bhédana*, *s.* dividing, separating, (literally or figuratively,) tearing, breaking; specifying, discriminating.

භේදප්‍රත්‍යය, *Bhéda-pratyaya*, *s.* (භේද difference, ප්‍රත්‍යය faith) dissent from the established religion, heterodoxy; belief in the reality of the multiform appearances of the world, in opposition to the doctrine that every thing is God.

භේදය, *Bhédaya*, *s.* dispute, disagreement.

භේදිත, *Bhédita*, *a.* (භිද *bhida* to break, ක්ත *kta* aff.) divided, separated: see භේද *bhéda*.

භේරි, *Bhéri*, *s.* drum, tom-tom; kettle drum.

භේරිතල, *Bhéritala*, *s.* (භේරි drum, තල surface) end or flat part of the tom-tom which is struck when beating.

භේරිනාද, *Bhérináda*, *s.* (භේරි and නාද sound) sound of the drum.

භේරුණ්ඩ, *Bhéruṇḍa*, *s.* (භී *bhí* to fear etc.) bird so called, not ascertained, it forms a prominent object in the native astronomy and astrology; one of the yakshaṇís or female attendants on Durgá: *a.* fearful, formidable.

භේෂජ, *Bhéshaja*, } *s.* remedy, drug, medicament;
භේසජ, *Bhésaja*, } kind of fennel, *nigella indica.*

භෛරව, *Bhairawa*, *s.* (භීරු *bhíru* fearful, අණ් *aṇ* aff.) horror, property of exciting terror; name of Ṣiva, in one of his inferior manifestations, of which there are eight called by this name; name of river: *a.* horrible.

භෛරවී, *Bhairaví*, *s.* (භෛරව *bhairawa* Ṣiva, ඊ *í* fem. aff.) name of Durgá, as wife of Ṣiva in his manifestations under the name Bhairawa.

භෛෂජ්‍ය, *Bhaishajya*, *s.* drug, medicament; dry ginger.

භෛෂජ, *Bhaishaja*, *s*, (භිෂජ *bhishaja* physician, අණ් *aṇ* aff.) drug, medicament; sort of quail.

භෝග, *Bhóga*, *s.* (භුජ *bhuja* to eat etc.) snake's body; expanded hood of a snake; food, eating; pleasure, enjoyment; wealth, riches; numerator of a fraction; hire; army in column; yard, the court yard of a house; crookedness, curvedness.

භෝගසම්පත්, *Bhóga-sampat*, *s.* (භෝග riches, සම්පත් increase, enjoyment) wealth, enjoyments.

භෝගී, *Bhógí*, *s.* snake; king, prince; barber; headman of a village; one who enjoys.

භෝගීන්ද්‍ර, *Bhógíndra*, *s.* (භෝගී snake, ඉන්ද්‍ර *indra* lord) name of Anantayá, chief of the serpent race; Ráhu, the ascending node.

භෝජ්‍ය, *Bhójya*, *s.* (භුජ *bhuja* to eat, ණ්‍යත් *ṇyat* aff.) to be eaten, proper or suitable for food, edible.

භෝජ, *Bhója*, *s.* name of a country, the present Patna; celebrated king, sovereign of Ougein, who lived about the end of the tenth century, and was a great encourager of learned men; cowherd.

භෝජන, *Bhójana*, *s.* (භුජ *bhuja* to eat) food, eating.

භෝජපත්‍ර, *Bhója-patra*, *s.* tree, Adam's needle, *yucca gloriosa*.

භෝජාජානේය, *Bhójá-jánéya*, *s.* (භෝජ *bhója* Patna, අජානේය *ajánéya* horse of a good breed) horse of a particular breed; horse bred in Bhója or Patna, and said to be exceedingly swift.

භෞතික, *Bhautika*, *a.* (භූත *bhúta* plant, sprite, අණ් *aṇ* aff.) botanical; relating or pertaining to evil spirits, etc.

භෞතිකශාස්ත්‍ර, *Bhautika-ṣástra*, *s.* (භෞතික and ශාස්ත්‍ර science) botany.

භෞම, *Bhauma*, *s.* (භූමි *bhúmi* earth, අණ් *aṇ* aff.) name of the regent of the planet Mars, in allusion to the fable of his being turned up from the earth by the plough of a husbandman.

භ්‍යාම ප්‍රභා, *Bhyáma-prabhá*, s. halo or lustre which extended for a fathom (ව්‍යාම *vyáma*) around Buddha; corrupt form of ව්‍යාමප්‍රභා *vyáma-prabhá*.

භ්‍රංකාර, *Bhraṇkára*, s. (භ්‍රං imitative sound, කාර making) sound, noise; hum, buzz.

භ්‍රංශ, *Bhraṇṣa*, s. (භ්‍රංශ to fall) falling, declining from height or propriety.

භ්‍රම, *Bhrama*, s. (භ්‍රම් to go round etc.) whirling, going round; error, ignorance, mistake, misapprehension; eddy, whirlpool; roaming, wandering; lathe, potter's wheel.

භ්‍රමණ, *Bramaṇa*, s. (භ්‍රම *bhrama* to go round etc.) whirling, going round; wandering, walking about.

භ්‍රමණකණ්ටක, *Bhramaṇa-kaṇṭaka*, s. (භ්‍රමණ whirling, කණ්ටක thorn) gimlet, auger.

භ්‍රමණය කරණවා, *Bhramaṇaya-karaṇawá*, v. to whirl, to perambulate.

භ්‍රමර, *Bhramara*, s. large black bee; lecher; lover; vertigo, epilepsy.

භ්‍රමරගණය, *Bhramaragaṇaya*, s. (භ්‍රමර bee, ගණ *gaṇa* multitude) swarm or hive of bees.

භ්‍රමර ප්‍රිය, *Bhramara-priya*, s. (භ්‍රමර and ප්‍රිය beloved) species of කදම්බ *kadamba*, which see; clove tree, *caryophyllus aromaticus*, [Colloq. කරාබු *karábu*].

භ්‍රමරේෂ්ට, *Bhramaréshṭa*, s. (භ්‍රමර *bhramara* bee, ඉෂ්ට *ishṭa* wished) red lotus, *nymphæa rubra*, [Colloq. රත්නෙළුම් *rat-neḷum*].

භ්‍රමි, *Bhrami*, s. (භ්‍රම *bhrama* to go round, ඉන් *in* aff.) whirling, turning or going round; error, mistake; lathe, potter's wheel; whirlpool.

භ්‍රෂ්ට, *Bhrashṭa*, a. (භ්‍රංශ *bhraṇṣa* to fall, ක්ත *kta* aff.) fallen; vicious, depraved, fallen from virtue; fried; parched.

භ්‍රාතෘ, *Bhrátṛi*, s. brother, uterine brother.

භ්‍රාත්‍රීය, *Bhrátṛiya*, s. (භ්‍රාතෘ *bhrátṛi* brother, ඡ *chha* aff.) brother's son: a. fraternal, belonging or relating to a brother.

භ්‍රාන්ත, *Bhránta*, a. (භ්‍රම *bhramá* to go round, ක්ත *kta* aff.) whirled, revolved; blundering, mistaken.

භ්‍රාන්තවෙනවා, *Bhrántawenawá*, v. to be alarmed.

භ්‍රාන්තිය, *Bhrántiya*, s. whirling, going round, revolving; error, mistake; unsteadiness, locomotion; wandering, roaming.

භෘගු *Bhṛigu*, s. in Hindu mythology, name of a celebrated Muni and one of the ten Brahmádikas or Prajápatis, the sons of Brahma and first created of beings; name of Ṣiva.

භෘගුජ, *Bhṛiguja*, s. (භෘගු and ජ born) name of Sukra, regent of the planet Venus, son of Bhṛigu, and preceptor of the demons.

භෘංග, *Bhṛiṅga*, s. large black bee, humble bee, [Colloq. බඹරා *bambará*]; wasp, common kind or *vespa solitaria;* fork tailed shrike, *lanius cærulescens;* libertine; plant, *eclipta prostrata*: see භෘංගරාජ *bhṛiṅga-rája;* woody cassia, *litsea zeylanica*, [Colloq. දවුල් කුරුඳු *dawul-kurundu*]; golden vase; talc.

භෘංගප්‍රිය, *Bhṛiṅga-priya*, s. (භෘංග and ප්‍රිය beloved) flower of the screw pine, *pandanus fascicularis* or *odoratissimus*, [Colloq. වැටකෙයියා *weṭakeyiyá*]; mace; tree, *bassia latifolia*.

භෘංගප්‍රියංකර, *Bhṛiṅga-priyaṇkara*, s. shrub with rose coloured flowers, *ardisea humilis* or *a. elliptica*, [Colloq. බළුදං *baḷudaṇ*].

භෘංගරාජ, *Bhṛiṅga-rája*, s. (භෘංග bee, රාජ to shine) spreading shrub, *eclipta prostrata* or *erecta*, [Colloq. කිකිරිඳිය *kíkirindiya*], or *verbesina scandens;* bird called Malabar shrike, *lanius malabaricus;* humble bee.

භෘංගාර, *Bhṛiṅgára*, s. (භෘංග *bhṛiṅga* bee, අරි *ari* enemy, or භෘ to contain, water etc. අරන් *áran* affix, and ගුක් *guk* augment) golden vase, especially used at royal ceremonials; shrub, see භෘංගරාජ *bhṛṅgarája:* cloves, [Colloq. කරාබු *karábu*]; gold.

භෘංගාරි, *Bhṛiṅgári*,
භෘංගාරිකා, *Bhṛiṅgáriká*, } s. (භෘංග *bhṛiṅga* and අරි *ari* enemy) cricket, [Colloq. රැහැයියා *reheyiyá*].

භෘංගාවලි, *Bhṛiṅgáwali*, s. (භෘංග *bhṛiṅga* and ආවලි *áwali*, multitude) swarm or flight of bees.

භෘත්‍ය, *Bhṛitya*, s. (භෘ *bhṛi* to nourish, with ක්‍යප් *kyap* aff.) servant, slave.

භෘත්‍යා, *Bhṛityá*, s. hire, wages, money paid for work performed.

භෘත, *Bhṛita*, a. (භෘ to nourish, ක්ත *kta* aff.) hired, paid, maintained; endowed with, having.

භෘතක, *Bhṛitaka*, s. (භෘත and කන් *kan* added) hired labourer, servant; slave.

භෘති, *Bhṛiti*, s. (භෘ to nourish, ක්තින් *ktin* aff.) hire, wages, pay; nourishment, maintenance.

භෘතිභුජ්, *Bhṛitibhuj*, s. (භෘති wages, භුජ් who eats or enjoys) hired servant or labourer.

භෘෂ්ට, *Bhṛishṭa*, p. (භ්‍රස්ජ *bhrasja* to fry) fried.

භෘෂ්ට තණ්ඩුල, *Bhṛishṭa-tanḍula*,
භෘෂ්ටාන්න, *Bhṛishṭánna*, } s. rice boiled and then fried, [Colloq. බැදිසාල් *bedi-sál*].

භෘෂ්ටි, *Bhrishti*, s. (භ්‍රස්ජ *bhrasja* to fry) frying.

භ්‍රෑ, *Bhrú*, s. (භ්‍රම *bhrama*, to turn round) eye brow, [Colloq. ඇස් බැම *ęs-bęma*].

භ්‍රෑකුටි, *Bhrúkuti*, s. (භ්‍රෑ eye brow, කුටි contraction) frown; side look, the leer of a woman.

භ්‍රෑභඞ්ග, *Bhrú-bhańga*, s. (භ්‍රෑ *bhrú* eye brow, භඞ්ග breaking, bending) a frown.

ම

The twenty-fifth consonant of the Sinhalese alphabet, corresponding to the letter *m*; personal pronoun, first person: *ad.* even; emphatic.

මං, *Man*, *plur.* of මඟ *maga*, road; an abreviation of මම *mama*.

මංගල්‍ය, *Mangalya*, see මඞ්ගල්‍ය *mańgalya*.

මංගල, *Mangala*, see මඞ්ගල *mańgala*.

මංජුල, *Manjula*, see මඤ්ජුල *mañjula*.

මංජුස, *Manjusa*, see මඤ්ජුස *mañjusa*.

මංඩල, *Mandala*, see මණ්ඩල *mandala*.

මංඩුර, *Mandura*, see මණ්ඩුර *mandura*.

මංස, *Mansa*, s. flesh.

මංසචක්ඛු, *Mansa-chakkhu*, s. (මංස flesh, චක්ඛු eye) eye of the body, in opposition to the eye of the mind.

මංසන්ධි, *Mansandhi*, } s. (මං roads, සන්ධි union)
මංසල, *Mansala*, } place where two or more
මංහන්දිය, *Manhandiya*, } roads meet; the corner of a street.

මක්, *Mak*, *par.* what.

මක්කල, *Makkala*, } s. chalk, mineral substance
මක්කෝල, *Makkóla*, } considered variously to be chalk or benzoin.

මක්ඛලි, *Makkhali*, s. (මක්‍ෂ *maksha* hypocrisy, ලා *lá* to have) name of a man, head of a religious sect.

මක්නිසා, *Maknisá*, *ind.* (මක් what or which, නිසා because) for, because, wherefore.

මක්නිසාද, *Maknisáda*, *ind.* (මක්නිසා because, ද interrogative aff.) for, because; why? wherefore? on what account?

මක්නිසාද කිව්වොත්, *Maknisáda-kiwot*, *par.* because, for this reason; if it be asked, why? (literally) if (I) should say, why?

මක්‍ෂි, *Makshi*, } s. (මක්‍ෂ *maksha* to be angry)
මක්‍ෂිකා, *Makshiká*, } fly; bee.

මක්‍ෂිකාලය, *Makshikálaya*, s. (මක්‍ෂිකා and ආලය *álaya* abode) web or net of a fly; hive of a bee; honey.

මක්‍ෂිතුත්ථ, *Makshituttha*, s. (මක්‍ෂි bee, තුත්ථ mineral) dark coloured mineral substance used medicinally, apparently the common pyritic iron ore; the name is applied to the ore from its honey-like colour; blue vitriol.

මකනවා, *Makanawá*, *v.* to erase, to obliterate, to deface; to destroy or extirpate; to melt, to smelt: pret. මැකුවා *mękuwá*.

මකර, *Makara*, s. marine monster, properly a fabulous animal; it is often drawn, as in the pictured signs of the zodiac, with the head and fore legs of an antelope and the tail and body of a fish; it is the emblem of the god of love; in astronomy it is one of the signs of the zodiac, corresponding with Capricorn, and like the Greek representation of that sign being an animal in the foreparts and ending in the tail of a fish; one of Kuvéra's treasures.

මකර කට, *Makara-kata*, s. (මකර and කට mouth) entrance of the hell called Avíchi-maha-naraka.

මකරකේතන, *Makara-kétana*, s. (මකර and කේතන banner) name of Káma the Hindu Cupid.

මකරතොරණ, *Makara-torana*, s. (මකර and තොරණ ornamental arch or outer door) painted representation of two makaras facing each other, for ornamenting the arch or entrance to a temple.

මකරන්ද, *Makaranda*, s. (මකර and දෙ *do* to destroy) nectar or honey of a flower, [Colloq. මල් පැණි *mal-pęni*]; kókila or Indian cuckoo, said to surpass the banner of Káma as an incentive to love, *cuculus micropterus*; fragrant kind of mango; plant, *jasminum pubescens*; filament of a lotus.

මකරරාසිය, *Makara-rásiya*, } s. (මකර and රාසිය
මකරරැස, *Makara-ręsa*, } or රැස sign of the zodiac) Capricorn.

මකරලග්නය, *makara-lagnaya*, s. (මකර and ලග්න *lagna* sign of the zodiac) sign of the zodiac, Capricorn.

මකරේ, *Makaré*, s. imaginary whirlpool in the ocean connected with hell.

මකා, *Makú*, *past. part.* of මකනවා *makanawá*.

මකු, *Maku*, s. defacing, obliterating; calumniating.

මකුට, *Makuta*, s. (මකි *maki* to adorn) crown, head dress, tiara, [Colloq. ඔටුන්න *otunna*]; parsley, *petroselinum sativum*, [Colloq. අසමෝදගං *asu-módagan*].

මකුණා, *Makuná*, s. spider; bug: pl. මකුණෝ *ma kunó*.

මකුණුදැල, *Makuṇudęla*, *s.* (මකුණු and දැල net) cobweb, spider's web.

මකුල්, *Makul*, *s.* spider; monkey, ape; sort of white siliceous earth used by the natives for paint, sort of pipe clay.

මකුල, *Makula*, *s.* (මකි *maki* to adorn) tree, *mimusops elengi*, [Colloq. මූනමල *múnamala*]; opening bud.

මකුෂ්ඨක, *Makushṭaka*, *s.* (මකි *maki* to adorn ෂ්ඨක to impede) kind of kidney bean, wild variety perhaps of the *phaseolus mungo*, [Colloq. මුංඇට *muṇęṭa*].

මකුළු, *Makuḷu*, *s.* monkey, [Colloq. රිළවා *riḷawá*]; kind of white pipe clay: see මකුල් *makul;* plant peculiar to Ceylon, *hydnocarpus venenata (Bixineæ)*.

මකුළුදැල, *Makuḷudęla*, see මකුණුදැල *makuṇudęla*.

මකුළුවා, *Makuḷuwá*, *s.* spider.

මකුළුවැන්න, *Makuḷuwęnna*, *s.* (මකුළු and වැන්න class) medicinal plant, *hydrocotyle asiatica*, [Colloq, හින් ගොටුකොල *hín-goṭukola*].

මකුළුහුය, *Makuḷuhuya*, *s.* (මකුළු and හුය thread) spider's web, cobweb.

මග, *Maga*, *s.* way, road, path; Elu form of මාර්ග *márga*.

මග අරිණවා, *Maga-ariṇawá*, *r.* (මග road, අරිණවා to leave) to abscond, to run away or escape; to turn aside, to get out of the way, to avoid a blow.

මගට, *Magaṭa*, *s.* sweeping, [Colloquial. අතුගෑම *atugéma*].

මගද, *Magada*, *a.* panegyrist; cumin seed, *nigella indica*: see the next.

මගධ, *Magadha*, *s.* country, South Behár; the chief scene of Buddha's labours; hence the original name of Páli, Magadha bháshá, which was Buddha's native tongue; inhabitant of that country; bard, whose duty it is to sing the praises of a chief's ancestry in his presence, family bard, minstrel.

මගධා, *Magadhá*, *s.* long pepper, *piper longum*, [Colloq. තිප්පිලි *tippili*].

මගධේශ්වර, *Magadhéśwara*, *s.* (මගධ *magadha* and ඊශ්වර *íśwara* lord or king) name of Bimbisára king of Magadha at the time of Buddha's appearance on earth.

මගධෝද්භව, *Magadhódbhawa*, *s.* (මගධ *magadha* and උද්භව *udbhawa* birth) native of Magadha; birth in Magadha.

මගපෙන්වන්නා, *Maga-penwanná*, *s.* leader, guide.

මගයන එකා, *Maga-yana-eká*, *s.* (මග way, යන going, එකා person) (term of compassion), poor fellow.

මගවියදම, *Maga-viyadama*, *s.* (මග way or journey, වියදම spending) travelling expenses.

මගින්මගට, *Maginmagaṭa*, *s.* from path to path.

මගී, *Magí*, *s.* (මග *maga* way, ඉන් *in* aff.) traveller, journeyer; travelling, going, journeying.

මගී පුරුෂ, *Magí-purusha*, *s.* (මගී and පුරුෂ man) traveller, pilgrim, one who travels into distant countries for the purpose of visiting holy places or offering to some particular idol or demon.

මගුරා, *Magurá*, *s.* river fish.

මඟුල්, *Magul*, *plur.* of මඟුල *magula*; name of planet Mars, [Colloq. අඟහරුවා *aṇgaharuwá*]: *a.* auspicious, happy, fortunate.

මඟුල් අහනවා, *Magul-ahanawá*, *r.* (මඟුල් marriage, අහනවා to request) to ask in marriage, to solicit.

මඟුල් ඇතා, *Magul-ętá*, *s.* (මඟුල් auspicious, ඇතා tusked elephant) royal elephant appropriated to the king's use on festival occasions.

මඟුල්කඩමල්, *Magul-kaḍámal*, *s.* (මඟුල් and කඩා මල් crown of flowers) garlands and head dress made of flowers, with which the bride and bridegroom are adorned by their relations and friends on the day of marriage.

මඟුල්කඩුව, *Magul-kaḍuwa*, *s.* (මඟුල් and කඩුව sword) royal sword, sword worn by the king on state occasions.

මඟුල්කපුවා, *Magul-kapuwá*, *s.* (මඟුල් and කපුවා barber) one who dresses the hair and beard of a king; messenger sent about to invite to a marriage; match-maker.

මඟුල් කරඳ, *Magul-karaṇda*, *s.* (මඟුල් auspicious, කරඳ genus galedupa) tree, formerly called *galedupa indica* or *dalbergia arborea*, now *pongamia glabra (Leguminosæ)*.

මඟුල්පෝරුව, *Magulpóruwa*, *s.* (මඟුල් and පෝරුව board) raised board or platform on which the bride and bridegroom stand while their hands are tied with a string, which completes the marriage ceremony.

මඟුල්මාරා, *Magul-márá*, *s.* tree, genus *albizzia*.

මඟුල් ලකුණ, *Magul-lakuṇa*, *s.* (මඟුල් auspicious, ලකුණ mark) mark or feature of the body indicating good fortune.

මඟුල්සක්වළ, *Magulsakwaḷa*, *s.* (මඟුල් fortunate, සක්වළ universe) an epithet applied to this world, in consequence of its being favoured with the religion of Buddha.

මඟුල්සල්, *Magulsal*, *s.* (මඟුල් auspicious, සල් sal tree) tree probably a species of *shorea robusta* or *vateria acuminata.*

මඟුල් සල්වට, *Magul-salwaṭa*, *s.* round stone kept in a royal park.

මඟුල, *Magula*, *s.* happiness, good fortune; marriage, marriage ceremony; feast, festival, auspicious occasion, the Elu form of මඞ්ගල *mańgala.*

මගේ, *Magé*, *pers. pron. gen.* of මම *mama*, my, mine.

මගෝඩියා, *Magóḍiyá*, *s.* contemptuous term equivalent to sweep, scamp.

මඞ්ගල, *Mangala*, see මඞ්ගල *mańgala.*

මඝා, *Maghá*, *s.* tenth lunar asterism, containing five stars figured by a house, apparently Alpha, Gamma, Zeta, Eta, and Nu, leonis; sort of grain.

මඞ්ගල්‍ය, *Mańgalya*, *s.* (මඞ්ගල *mańgala* and යත් *yat* aff.) bó tree, *ficus religiosa*, [Colloq. බෝගහ *bó-gaha*]; bael tree, *ægle marmelos*, [Colloq. බෙලි *beli*]: *a.* auspicious, propitious, conferring happiness, prosperity, etc; beautiful, agreeable, pleasing; pure, pious.

මඞ්ගල්‍යා, *Mańgalyá*, *s.* bezoar stone found in the stomachs of cattle, [Colloq. ගෝරෝචන *góróchana*]; small plant, *evolvulus alsinoides*, [Colloq. විෂ්ණුක්‍රාන්ති *vishṇukránti*]; species of agallochum with the fragrance of jasmin flowers, [Colloq. සමන්මල් වගේ සුවඳ ඇති අගිල් *samanmal wagé suwanda-ęti agil*].

මඞ්ගල, *Mańgala*, *s.* (මගි *magi* to go) feast, banquet, marriage, marriage feast; happiness, good fortune; name of the planet Mars; name of Umá the wife of Śiva; bent grass with white blossoms, *panicum dactylon;* white lotus, *nelumbium speciosum*, [Colloq. එලනෙළුම් *ela-neḷum*]; caution, prudence: *a.* lucky, fortunate, etc.

මඞ්ගලා, *Mańgalá*, *s.* bent grass, *panicum dactylon*, with white blossoms.

මඞ්ගලී, *Mańgalí*, *s.* bulbous stemless plant, *Crinum zeylanicum* or *C. ornatum*, or *Amaryllis zeylanica*, [Colloq. ගොඩමානිල් *goḍa-mánil*].

මච්ඡ, *Machchha*, *s.* fish in general, [Colloq. මාළුකූරියා *máḷukúriyá*].

මච්ඡගන්ධා, *Machchha-gandhá*, see මත්‍ස්‍යගන්ධා *matsya-gandhá.*

මච්ඡාරි, *Machchhári*, } *s.* (මච්ඡ *machchha* fish, අරි *ari* enemy, ඉක *ika* aff.) fisherman, [Colloq. මස්මරන්නා *mas-maranná*].
මච්ඡිකා, *Machchhiká*,

මජ්ජ, *Majja*, *s.* marrow of bones; pith, sap; spirituous liquor.

මජ්ජන්, *Majjan*, } *s.* marrow; pith, sap.
මජ්ජා, *Majjá*,

මජ්ඣ, *Majjha*, *s.* middle, centre; waist; Páli form of මධ්‍ය *madhya.*

මජ්ඣිම, *Majjhima*, *s.* waist; middle finger; meditation, reflection; India proper, or India within the Ganges; musical sounds: *a.* middle, centrical, [Colloq. මැද *męda*].

මජ්ඣිමනිපාත, *Majjhima-nipáta*, *s.* second grand division of the sútra-piṭaka: see මැදුම් සඟිය *mędum-sangiya.*

මජරයා, *Majarayá*, *s.* gluttonous person.

මඤ්ච, *Mañcha*, } *s.* (මචි *machi* to be high or tall, අච් *ach* aff.) bed, bedstead; platform, scaffold; elevated shed raised on bamboos in a cornfield etc., where a watch man is stationed to protect the corn from cattle, birds, wild beasts etc.; sort of throne, or chair of state, or the platform on which it is raised.
මඤ්චක, *Mañchaka*,

මඤ්ජර, *Mañjara*, } *s.* (මඤ්ජු *mañju* beautiful, ඍ *ṛi* to go or be) pearl, [Colloq. මුතු *mutu*]; compound pedicle; plant: see තිලක *tilaka.*
මඤ්ජරි, *Mañjarí*,

මඤ්ජරි පුෂ්පක, *Mañjari-pushpaka*, *s.* (මඤ්ජරි and පුෂ්ප *pushpa* flower) compound pedicle; fruit or flower stalk; flower of the මඤ්ජර *mañjara:* see also මඟුල්කරඳ *magul-karanda.*

මඤ්ජිෂ්ඨා, *Mañjishṭhá*, *s.* species of madder, *rubia manjith*, [Colloq. වැල්මදට *węlmadaṭa*].

මඤ්ජු, *Mañju*, *a.* beautiful, pleasing, agreeable.

මඤ්ජුල, *Mañjula*, *s.* water-course; arbour, bower: *a.* beautiful, agreeable, pleasing.

මඤ්ජූෂා, *Mañjúshá*, } *s.* box, basket, purse; collection, list (of words); stone; plant, chay-root, *oldenlandia* (or *hedyotis*) *umbellata*, [Colloq. සයමුල් *saya-mul.*
මඤ්ජූසා, *Mañjúsá*,

මඤ්ඤා, *Maññá*, *s.* god-mother, (Dutch.)

මඤ්ඤොක්කා, *Maññokká*, *s.* plant, cassava yam, *manihot cassava.*

මට්ට, *Maṭṭa*, *s.* round ornament for the ear: *a.* shining, glittering.

මට්ටන්කරණවා, *Maṭṭankaraṇawá*, *v.* to smooth,

මට්ටන්පෝරුව, *Maṭṭan-póruwa*, *s.* (මට්ටම *maṭṭama* smooth, පෝරුව board) carpenter's or bricklayer's level.

මට්ටන් යත්ත, *Maṭṭan-yatta*, *s.* carpenters' smoothing plane,

මට්ටන්ලෙල්ල, *Maṭṭan-lęlla*, see මට්ටන්පෝරුව *maṭṭan-póruwa.*

මට්ටම, *Maṭṭama*, *s.* level: *a.* polished, shining, bright.

මට්ටි, *Maṭṭi*, *s.* cockle, shell fish in general.

මට්ටුකරණවා, *Maṭṭukaraṇawá*, *v.* to correct, to set right, to subdue.

මට්ටුපඩත්තුව, *Maṭṭupaḍattuwa*, *a.* well-conducted and obedient.

මට, *Maṭa*, *pron.* to me, dative of මම *mama*: *a.* polished, bright, shining.

මට බිම්බිය, *Maṭa-bimbiya*, *s.* plant, *mœsa indica (Myrsineœ).*

මටසිළුටු, *Maṭasiḷuṭu*, *a.* polished and smooth; glittering, bright, shining.

මටහුගහ, *Maṭahu-gaha*, *s.* tree, not ascertained.

මටුල්ල, *Maṭulla*, *s.* fibrous wrapper that covers the pedicle of the young branch of the coconut tree: pl. මටුළු *maṭuḷu.*

මඨර, *Maṭhara*, *s.* name of a Muṇi or saint.

මඩ, *Maḍa*, *s.* mud, slime; scum, froth, etc.; in this sense Elu form of මණ්ඩ *maṅḍa;* beauty, ornament, adorning, from මඩි *maḍi*, to adorn.

මඩ අංකුට්ටා, *Maḍa-aṇkuṭṭá*, *s.* kind of river fish.

මඩ ඇල්වි, *Maḍa-ęlvi*, *s.* kind of paddy, variety of *oryza sativa.*

මඩක්කුව, *Maḍakkuwa*, *s.* little, small quantity; earthern plate or dish, [Colloq. බත්වලඳ *batwalaṇḍa*].

මඩ කානයා, *Maḍa-kanayá*, *s.* kind of river fish.

මඩකරියා, *Maḍakariyá*, *s.* small kind of fresh water fish.

මඩගොහොරුව, *Maḍagohoruwa*, *s.* muddy place.

මඩන, *Maḍana*, *s.* (from මර්දන *marddana*) crushing, squeezing, treading; form of මණ්ඩන *maṇḍana*, ornamenting, adorning; arming, accoutring.

මඩනවා, *Maḍanawá*, *v.* to crush, to squeeze, to press.

මඩනා, *Maḍaná*, *s.* one that squeezes or crushes; an oppressor.

මඩප්පුලිරාල, *Maḍappulirála*, *s.* officer in the Náta-Déwálé, Kandy, who sweeps the sanctuary, cleans and tends its lamps.

මඩබද්ද, *Maḍa-badda*, *s.* tax on paddy land.

මඩ බිම, *Maḍa-bima*, *s.* muddy place, sink; bog, swamp; place prepared for the sowing of paddy by trampling it with oxen.

මඩල, *Maḍala*, *s.* hall, the ring round the moon: orb, disk: see මණ්ඩල *maṇḍala.*

මඩලග, *Maḍalaga*, see මණ්ඩලාග්‍ර *maṇḍalágra.*

මඩලපත්, *Maḍala-pat*, *s.* bó tree, *ficus religiosa*, [Colloq. බෝ *bó*].

මඩවනවා, *Maḍawanawá*, *v.* to make the ground soft and muddy by trampling it with oxen, prior to the sowing of the rice: pret. මැඩෙව්වා *męḍewwá.*

මඩාරා, *Maḍárá*, *s.* sort of river fish.

මඩිගේ, *Maḍi-gé*, *s.* carriage department of the Kandyan kings; it generally consisted of Moors or Mahommedans.

මඩිත්ත, *Maḍitta*, *s.* muddy ground, slough, bog.

මඩිනවා, *Maḍinawá*, *v.* to bruise, to crush, to clean, (rice from the husk); to squeeze, to press, to rub or brush: pret. මැඩ්ඩා *męḍḍá.*

මඩිපල්ල, *Maḍi-palla*, *s.* bottom part of a net bag.

මඩිය, *Maḍiya*, *s.* bag of a net.

මඩිසූරිය, *Maḍisúriya*, *s.* corner of a net bag.

මඩිහුංගං, *Maḍihuṇgaṇ*, *s.* taxes levied at kaḍawata or gravets, *i. e.* the boundary of a town.

මඩු, *Maḍu*, *s.* tree called the false sago palm, *cycas circinalis (Cycadeœ).*

මඩු පියලි, *Maḍu-piyali*, *s.* nuts of the maḍu tree, broken into pieces, dried and converted into flour for food.

මඩුපුරයා, *Maḍupurayá*, *s.* devil dancer's assistant.

මඩුල්ල, *Maḍulla*, *s.* circle, ring; orb, circumference in general; district, province: pl. මඩුළු *maḍuḷu;* Elu form of මණ්ඩල *manḍala.*

මඩුව, *Maḍuwa*, *s.* shed, temporary building, bungalow: pl. මඩු *maḍu.*

මඩුවා, *Maḍuwá*, *s.* fish, the skate.

මඩොරපිය, *Maḍorapiya*, *s.* name of Ṣakra or Indra.

මඩොල්, *Maḍol*, *s.* tree, peculiar to Ceylon, allied to the goraka, *garcinia echinocarpa (Guttiferœ).*

මඩොල්වෙනවා, *Maḍolwenawa*, *v.* to become muddy (as when jaggery is spoiled).

මඬු, *Maṇḍu*, see මඩු *maḍu.*

මඬුල, *Maṇḍula*, see මණ්ඩල *maṇḍala.*

මණ්ඩ, *Maṇḍa*, *s.* plate, deep plate of metal, brazen dish or charger; scum, skimmings; froth, foam, barm, etc; dregs, dross, lees; ornament, decoration; castor oil plant, *ricinus communis*, [Colloq. එඬරු *eṇḍaru*]; spirituous or vinous liquor; pith, marrow.

මණ්ඩ කල්ප, *Maṇḍa-kalpa*, *s.* (මණ්ඩ ornament, කල්ප kalpa) second of the four kalpas or the grand divisions of time, which, according to the Buddhists, measure the period of duration from the production to the annihilation of the universe; these kalpas are denominated from the number of Buddhas that make their appearance in them; in the maṇḍa kalpa two were born; in the present or bhadra kalpa five are to be born, four of whom have already appeared and one called Maitrí Buddha has yet to come.

මණ්ඩන, *Maṇḍana*, *s.* ornament, decoration; jewels, trinkets etc; adorning, decorating, dressing: *a.* fond of or putting on ornaments.

මණ්ඩප, *Maṇḍapa*, *s.* temporary building, open shed or hall, adorned with flowers, and erected on festival occasions, as marriages etc; tabernacle, an open building or temple consecrated to a deity.

මණ්ඩල, *Maṇḍala*, *s.* (මඩි *maḍi* to adorn) disk of the sun or moon; orb, circumference in general, the circle bounding the view, sensible horizon; ball, globe; wheel; province, region, district; heap, quantity, multitude, assemblage; sort of mystical diagram; audience hall.

මණ්ඩලත්‍රය, *Maṇḍalatraya*, *s.* (මණ්ඩල region, ත්‍රය three) three parts of the body covered by the priestly robe, breast, privities and the knees.

මණ්ඩලපත්‍ර, *Maṇḍala-patra*, *s.* (මණ්ඩල and පත්‍ර leaf) bó-tree, *ficus religiosa:* see බෝගහ *bó-gaha.*

මණ්ඩලාග්‍ර, *Maṇḍalágra*, *s.* (මණ්ඩල *maṇḍala* and අග්‍ර top, point) sword, scimitar, [Colloq. කඩුව *kaḍuwa*].

මණ්ඩලින්, *Maṇḍalin*, *s.* (මණ්ඩල *maṇḍala* circle, ඉනි *ini* aff.) large species of snake; ruler of a district; sun.

මණ්ඩලේශ්වර, *Maṇḍaléśwara*, *s.* (මණ්ඩල *maṇḍala* and ඊශ්වර *íśwara* king) emperor, supreme monarch, one possessed of universal empire.

මණ්ඩා, *Maṇḍá*, *s.* any vinous or spirituous liquor.

මණ්ඩාගාර, *Maṇḍágára*, *s.* (මණ්ඩ *maṇḍa* liquor, අගාර *ágára* house) tavern, place where liquors are vended, [Colloq. තැබෑරුම *tębęruma*].

මණ්ඩාව, *Maṇḍáwa*, *s.* zigzag; sort of dart or harpoon for striking fish.

මණ්ඩාමදිනවැල, *Maṇḍámadinawęla*, *s.* madder: see මඤ්ජුෂා *mañjúshá.*

මණ්ඩි, *Maṇḍi*, *s.* scum, skimmings, upper part of any infusion in a state of boiling or ferment.

මණ්ඩිය, *Maṇḍiya*, *s.* place, spot, locality.

මණ්ඩූක, *Maṇḍúka*, *s.* frog, [Colloq. ගෙමඩියා *gemaḍiyá*]; flower tree, *oroxylum indicum* or *calosanthes* (or *bignonia*) *indica*, [Coll: තොටිල *toṭila*]; Bengal madder, see මඤ්ජුෂා *mañjúshá*; female or small frog; shrub, *siphonanthus indica;* creeping plant, *hydrocotyle asiatica;* unchaste or abandoned woman.

මණ්ඩූකපත්‍ර, *Maṇḍúkapatra*, see මණ්ඩූකපර්ණ *maṇḍúkaparṇa.*

මණ්ඩූකපත්‍රී, *Maṇḍúkapatrí*, *s.* creeping plant, *hydrocotyle asiatica*, [Colloquial. හීන් ගොටුකොල *hín-goṭukola*].

මණ්ඩූකපර්ණ, *Maṇḍúkaparṇa*, *s.* (මණ්ඩූක frog, පර්ණ leaf) tree, *bignonia indica*, [Colloq. තොටිල *toṭila*]

මණ්ඩූකපර්ණී, *Maṇḍúka-parṇṇi*, *s.* Bengal madder: see මඤ්ජුෂා *mañjúshá:* shrub, *siphonanthus indica;* creeping plant: see මණ්ඩූකපත්‍රී *maṇḍúkapatrí.*

මණි, *Maṇi*, *s.* (මණ *maṇa* to sound, ඉන් *in* aff.) gem, jewel, precious stone; pearl; wrist.

මණිකාර, *Maṇikára*, *s.* (මණි jewel, කාර who does) jeweller, lapidary, any worker in precious stones.

මණිපුංඛික, *Maṇipuṅkhika*, *s.* plant, *tephrosia purpurea*, [Colloq. පිලගස් *pila-gas* or අළුපිල *aḷupila*].

මණිබන්ධ, *Maṇibandha*, *s.* wrist, [Colloq. මැණික් කටුව *męṇikkaṭuwa*].

මණිභූමි, *Maṇi-bhúmi*, *s.* (මණි jewel, භූමි ground) jewel mine, place where precious stones are found.

මණිමාලා, *Maṇimálá*, *s.* (මණි and මාලා garland) necklace, zone, fillet, etc. of precious stones; Lakshmí goddess of beauty; light, lustre.

මත්, *Mat*, *ind.* an affix implying possession: *s.* top, summit, head: *a.* drunk, intoxicated; stupefied.

මත් අමු, *Mat-amu*, *s.* plant, *paspalum scrobiculatum*; also called අමු *amu.*

මත් කංසා, *Mat-kansá*, *s.* hemp, dried portions called bhang used for intoxicating purposes, *cannabis sativa.*

මත්කුණ, *Mat-kuṇa*, *s.* bug; elephant without tusks; beardless man; coconut; armour for the thighs or legs; buffalo.

මත්ගතිය, *Mat-gatiya*, *s.* (මත් drunk, ගති *gati* going, state) drunkenness, intoxication.

මත්ගා, *Matgá*, see මතගානවා *matagánawá.*

මත්ත, *Matta*, *s.* furious elephant, one in rut; top, summit, pinnacle; little or small quantity; future time; prosperity; buffalo; the kókila or Indian cuckoo, *cuculus micropterus*; thorn apple, *datura stramonium;* vinous liquor: *a.* pleased, delighted; drunk, intoxicated, literally or figuratively; furious, insane, mad; small, little.

මත්තට, *Mattaṭa*, *ind.* in future, for the future, henceforward.

මත්තභාවය, *Mattabháwaya*, *s.* (මත්ත drunk, භාවය state) drunkenness, intoxication; lust, passion; lewdness.

මත්තහස්ති, *Matta-hasti*, *s.* (මත්ත furious, හස්ති elephant) furious elephant, one in rut.

මත්තාලම, *Mattálama*, *s.* large kind of tom-tom or long drum beaten at both ends: pl. මත්තාලම් *mattálam.*

මත්තිකා, *Mattiká*, *s.* clay, earth.

මත්තෙහි, *Mattehi*, } *s.* on the head or top of:
මත්තේ, *Matté*, } *ad.* in future, in the time to come, hence.

මත්තේ පණදෙනවා, *Matté-paṇadenawá*, } *v.* to
මත්තේ හැපෙනවා *Matté-hẹpenawá*, } die at the feet of, to fall in the presence of.

මත් බෙහෙත, *Mat-beheta*, *s.* (මත් intoxicating, බෙහෙත drug) soporific.

මත්ව, *Matwa*, *part.* being drunk, intoxicated (with liquor, pride, passion etc.)

මත්වෙනවා, *Matwenawá*, *v.* to be intoxicated, to be drunk; to be in a state of stupor, either as the effects of drunkenness or want of sleep, to be under the powerful excitement of pride, lust etc: pret. මත්වුනා *matwuná.*

මත්ස්‍ය, *Matsya*, *s.* fish in general; name of Vishṇu in his avatára under the character of a fish.

මත්ස්‍යගන්ධා, *Matsyagandhá*, *s.* (මත්ස්‍ය and ගන්ධ *gandha* smell) stemless plant, *hydrolea zeylanica*, [Colloq. දියකිරිල්ල *diya-kirilla*]; creeping three-leaved plant, *commelina clavata* or *c. salisifolia*, [Colloq. ගිරපලා *girá-palá*].

මත්ස්‍යණ්ඩි, *Matsyaṇḍí*, *s.* (මන්ද *manda* slowly, ස්‍යන්ද *syanda* to trickle or ooze) coarse or unrefined sugar, juice of the sugar cane previous to its being refined or after it has been partially freed from impurities.

මත්ස්‍යාක්ෂි, *Matsyákshi*, *s.* (මත්ස්‍ය *matsya* fish, අක්ෂ eye) moon-plant or sóma-latá (Sanskrit), *asclepias acida* or *cynanchum pauciflora*, [Colloq. කංකුඹලා *kaṇkumbalá*]; plant, *alternanthera triandra*, [Colloq. මුගුණුවැන්න *muguṇuwẹnna*], the flowers being compared to the eye of a fish.

මත්ස්‍යාධානි, *Matsyádhání*, *s.* (මත්ස්‍ය *matsya* fish, ආධාන *ádháṇa* that which holds) fish-hook; fish basket; fishing kraal.

මත්සර, *Matsara*, *s.* envy, passion: *a.* envious, covetous, niggardly.

මත, *Mata*, *s.* (මන *mana* to mind, ක්ත *kta* aff.) motive, purpose, doctrine, tenet, belief, opinion, death, dying; intoxication; stupor, arising either from intoxication or want of sleep: *a.* known, understood; admitted; believed, held or retained (as an opinion etc.); dead, extinct.

මතක්කරණවා, *Matakkaraṇawá*, *v.* to recollect, to call to mind; to remind; to inform, to state, to lay down a subject for consideration; also to remind a superior of any circumstance.

මතක, *Mataka*, *s.* (මන *mana* to mind) memory, recollection, remembrance: *a.* dead, extinct, deceased.

මතක දානය, *Mataka-dánaya*, *s.* almsgiving in behalf of deceased persons.

මතකභත්ත, *Mataka-bhatta*, *s.* (මතක dead, deceased, භත්ත boiled rice, food) funeral obsequies, rites in honour of the dead; offerings of food to the manes of deceased ancestors.

මතකනැති, *Mataka-nẹti*, *a.* forgetful, forgotten.

මතගානවා, *Matagánawá*, *v.* to stir, to churn, to purify, as butter etc; to perform lustrations.

මතගැම, *Matagẹma*, verbal noun of the foregoing.

මතඟ, *Mataṇga*, *s.* cloud; elephant.

මතඞ්ග, *Mataṅga*, } *s.* elephant [Colloq. අලියා
මතඞ්ගජ, *Mataṅgaja*, } *aliyá*].

මතල්ලිකා, *Matalliká*, *s.* chaste and elegant language; excellence, happiness: *a.* best, excellent.

මති, *Mati*, } *s.* understanding, intellect; wish,
මතිය, *Matiya*, } desire, inclination; memory, recollection; motive, intention.

මතිශ, *Matiṣa*, *s.* (මති *mati* wisdom or knowledge, ඊශ *íṣa* lord) Vṛihaspati, the regent of the planet Jupiter, alluding to his character as preceptor of the gods,

මතු, *Matu*, *s.* branch of a tree: *a.* future: *ad.* formerly, prior, heretofore; only.

මතුකරණවා, *Matukaraṇawá*, *v.* to raise, to elevate, to promote, to bring to light or notice.

මතුගල, *Matu-gala*, *s.* (මතු and ගල stone) upper grinding stone.

මතුදේ කියනවා, *Matudé-kiyanawá*, *v.* (මතු future, දේ an event, කියනවා to tell, to declare) to prophesy, to foretell future events.

මතුපිට, *Matupiṭa, s.* upperside, top.

මතුබිඹිය, *Matubimbiya, s.* tree, not ascertained.

මතුමහල, *Matu-mahala,* } *s.* (මතු and මහල room)
මතුමාල, *Matumála,* } upper room, room in an upper story.

මතුරණවා, *Maturanawá, v.* to repeat or mutter magical charms or incantations; to exorcise; to conjure: pret. මැතුරුවා *meturuwá.*

මතුරු, *Maturu, s.* mystical verse or incantation, magical formula used in exorcising and conjuring; Elu form of මන්ත්‍ර *mantra.*

මතු ලෙස, *Matu-lesa, ad.* as in future, or hereafter.

මතුවෙනවා, *Matuwenawá, v.* to come to the surface.

මතේ, *Maté,* see මත *mata.*

මතැත්, *Matet, s.* furious elephant, elephant in rut.

මථන, *Mathana, s.* (මථ to stir or agitate) mixing, stirring about butter milk; tree, the wood of which is used to produce fire by attrition, *premna latifolia,* [Colloq. මහමිදි *maha-midi*]; churning.

මථි, *Mathi, s.* (මථ *matha* to churn, ඉන් *in* aff,) a churn stick.

මථිත, *Mathita, s.* (මථ *matha* and ක්ත *kta* aff.) butter-milk, without any watery admixture, [Colloq. මෝරු *móru*]: *a.* churned, stirred, agitated.

මද්ගු, *Madgu, s.* an aquatic bird, the shag or water hen, *gallinula chloropus.*

මද්ගුර, *Madgura, s.* a fish, *macropteronatus magur,* [Colloq. මගුරා *magurá*].

මද්දල, *Maddala, s.* cymbal.

මද්දහන, *Maddahana,* } *s.* mid-day, noon: pl. මද්දැන්
මද්දැන, *Maddána,* } *maddán.*

මද්දාරම්, *Maddáram, a.* cloudy, overcast, gloomy.

මද්දාරම, *Maddárama, s.* cloudiness, gloominess, sometimes written මංඩාරම *maṇḍárama.*

මද්දිලිය, *Maddiliya, s.* sort of drum used by the Tamils.

මද්ධිම, *Maddhima,* corruptly for මධ්‍යම.

මද්‍ය, *Madya, s.* wine, vinous or spirituous liquor, arrack: *a.* centrical, middle: in this sense, corruptly for මධ්‍ය *madhya.*

මද්‍යපාන, *Madyapána, s.* (මද්‍ය and පාන drink) spirituous or intoxicating liquor.

මද, *Mada, s.* (මද to be pleased etc.) joy, pleasure, delight; juice that flows from an elephant's temples when in rut; spirituous or vinous liquor; inebriety, intoxication; pride, arrogance; insainity, madness; semen virile; passion, desire; name of Káma, the Hindu Cupid; core or kernel of a fruit etc.

මදක්, *Madak, ind.* little, small quantity; a few: as මදක් දුර *madak dura,* a little distance.

මදකල, *Mada-kala, a.* speaking inarticulately.

මදකලී, *Madakali,* see මදඝ්නී *madaghní.*

මදකාරී, *Madakárí, s.* (මද and කාර *kára* what makes) any thing that intoxicates, that which inflames the passions; harlot, [Colloq. වෙසඟන *wesaṇgana*]; opium plant, [Colloq. කන්සා *kansá*].

මදඝ්නී, *Madaghní, s.* (මද inebriety, ඝ්නී what destroys) pot herb, *basella alba,* [Colloq. නිතිවැල් *níti-wel* or නිවිතිවැල් *niviti-wel*].

මදට, *Madaṭa, s.* small red berry, used as a jeweller's weight, and averaging about $1\frac{1}{12}$ grs. troy.

මදටිය, *Madaṭiya, s.* tree, interior wood red, called red sanders or false red sandal wood, seeds worn as beads, *adenanthera pavonina (Leguminosæ).*

මදන, *Madana, s.* love; name of Káma, the Indian Cupid; season of spring; plant, *randia dumetorum,* [Colloq. කුකුරුමුවන් *kukurumuwan*]; thorn apple, *datura fastuosa,* [Colloq. අත්තන *attana*]: sort of bean, *phaseolus mungo,* [Colloq. මුංඇට *muṇeṭa*]; bee's wax; tree, *acacia catechu;* spirituous or vinous liquor; plant, *gardenia.*

මදනක, *Madanaka, s.* bee's wax, [Colloq. මී ඉටි *mí-iṭi*].

මදනයකා, *Madana-yaká, s.* demon of love.

මදන ශාස්ත්‍ර, *Madana-śástra, s.* (මදන love, ශාස්ත්‍ර science) works on erotic subjects, consisting of incantations for ensnaring the affections of women.

මදනීය, *Madaníya, a.* fit to inflame the passions; to be enamoured.

මදමත, *Mada-mata, s.* (මද semen virile, මත influence) wantonness; sensual desire.

මදමද, *Mada-mada, ad.* by little and little, by degrees.

මදමරු, *Madamaru, s.* name of Anańgayá the Indian Cupid; gentle breeze.

මදමැදිරි, *Mada-mediri, s.* vulva.

මදය, *Madaya, s.* kernel: see මද *mada.*

මදයා, *Madayá, s.* (මද pride etc. යා aff.) bull (uncastrated),

මදර, *Madara,* } *s.* coral tree, see මදරරුක
මදරගිර, *Madaragira,* } *madara-ruka;* name of Maha-méru: see මේරු *méru.*

මදරත, *Mada-rata*, *s.* (මද little, රත red) light red, pink.

මදරරුක, *Madara-ruka*, *s.* coral tree, *erythrina indica*, [Colloq. එරබදු *erabadu*].

මදරා, *Madará*, *s.* plant, *cleistanthus collina (Euphorbiaceæ)*.

මදරාග, *Madarága*, *s.* (මද passion or desire, රාග propensity, inclination) name of Káma, the Hindu Cupid; cock.

මදවි ලතා, *Madavi-latá*, *s.* creeping plant, liquorice, properly මාධවී ලතා *mádhaví-latá*.

මදවෙනවා *Madawenawá*, *v.* to diminish, to decrease, to wane or lessen, to become scarce or insufficient.

මදවැටෙනවා, *Madawęṭenawá*, *v.* to lust, to be inflamed with desire.

මදස්ථල, *Madasthala*, } *s.* (මද intoxication, ස්ථල, මදස්ථාන, *Madasthána*, } ස්ථාන place) tavern, arrack shop, dram shop, [Colloq. තැබෑරුම *tęběruma*].

මදහස, *Madahasa*, *s.* (මද little, හස laughter) smile, smiling.

මදහේතු *Madahétu*, *s.* tree, *bauhinia racemosa*, [Colloq. මයිලා *mayila*],

මදාඩුව, *Madáḍuwa*, *ind.* insufficiency, not enough.

මදාත්‍යය, *Madátyaya*, *s.* (මද *mada* intoxication, අත්‍යය *atyaya* consequence) disorder induced by drunkenness, viz. headache, sickness, loss of appetite, etc.

මදායුස, *Madáyusa*, *s.* (මද *mada* little, ආයුස *áyusa* term of life) short lived.

මදාර, *Madára*, *s.* (මද *mada* to be intoxicated) tree, mountain ebony, *bauhinia purpurea;* elephant; libertine; elephant in rut.

මදාරා, *Madárá*, *s.* tree, *cluytia collina;* another tree, *erythrina corallodendron*.

මදි, *Madi*, *a.* insufficient, defective, not enough; low, base, vile.

මදිංචිකරණවා, *Madiṇchikaraṇawá*, *v.* to daub, to smear, to plaster; to play a game at even and odds.

මදිකම්කරණවා, *Madikam-karaṇawá*, *v.* to defile a woman, outrage on a woman.

මදිකම, *Madikama*, *s.* insufficiency; baseness, vileness; insult, affront; disgrace.

මදිච්චිකෙළිය, *Madichchi-keḷiya*, *s.* game with red sander nuts: see මදැටිය *madaṭiya*.

මදින්නා, *Madinná*, *s.* toddy drawer.

මදින්මද, *Madinmada*, *ad.* gradually, by degrees, by little and little.

මදිනවා, *Madinawá*, *v.* to smooth, to polish; to sharpen, to whet; to extract the toddy or spirituous liquor from the coconut tree: pret. මැද්දා *męddá*.

මදිපාඩු, *Madipáḍu*, *a.* insufficient, defective, deficient, contumelious.

මදිර, *Madira*, } *s.* tree, *acacia suma* or *a. catechu;* මදිරා, *Madirá*, } wine, spirits, vinous or spirituous liquor, arrack; wag tail.

මදිරාගෘහ, *Madirágriha*, *s.* (මදිර liquor, ගෘහ house) tavern, dram shop: see මදස්ථාන *madasthána*.

මදිරෝදක, *Madiródaka*, *s.* (මදිර *madira* and උදක *udaka* water) name of a sea, so called from its being supposed to be an ocean of spirituous or intoxicating liquor.

මදු, *Madu*, *s.* eatable creeper, *ipomœa obscura;* rope for seizing cattle, etc.

මදුකරවලා, *Madu-karawalá*, *s.* kind of small venomous snake, *bungarus*.

මදුරු, *Maduru*, } *s.* name of Maha Méru; මදුරුගිර, *Madurugira*, } Elu form of මන්දර *mandara;* musquito, gnat.

මදුරුතණ, *Maduru-tana*, *s.* plant, not ascertained of the order *gramineæ*.

මදුරුතලා, *Madurutalá*, *s.* small shrub, species of basil, hairy with purple flowers in racemes, called *tulasi*, by the Hindus with whom it is sacred, *ocimum sanctum (Labiatæ):* see තලා *talá*.

මදුරුවා, *Maduruwá*, *s.* musquito, gnat.

මදුල, *Madula*, *s.* the part in the inside of the jack fruit inclosing the seed or nut, and the part chiefly eaten: pl. මදුලු *madulu*.

මදුවැල, *Madu-węla*, *s.* (මදු sweet, වැල creeper) liquorice; creeper, *ipomœa*.

මදූරිකා, *Madúriká*, see මධූරිකා *madhúriká*.

මදේ, *Madé*, see මදය *madaya*.

මදොස්, *Mados*, *s.* a sort of box or chest, trunk.

මධ්‍ය, *Madhya*, *s.* middle, centre; waist; west; mean or common time in music: *a.* middle, intermediate.

මධ්‍යදේශය, *Madhya-déṣaya*, *s.* (මධ්‍ය and දේශ *déṣa* country) the middle region; according to Hindu authorities a part of India, bounded by Kurukshétra, Allahabad, the Himálaya mountains, and the Vindhyá mountains, comprising therefore the modern provinces of Allahabad, Agra, Delhi, Oude, etc. but according to the Buddhists, south Behár: see මධ්‍ය මණ්ඩලය *madhya-maṇḍalaya*.

මධ්‍යම, *Madhyama*, *s.* the waist; middle of the body; the middle country: see මධ්‍යදේශය *madhya-déṣaya*; girl arrived at puberty, or one in whom menstruation has commenced; middle finger; form of metre, verse of four lines or of three syllables each: *a.* middle, centrical, intervening.

මධ්‍යමණ්ඩලය, *Madhya-maṇḍalaya*, *s.* (මධ්‍ය and මණ්ඩල *maṇḍala* country, province) according to Hindu authority, the middle region: see මධ්‍යදේශය *madhya-déṣaya;* according to Buddhists the centre of the universe; the middle of Jambudwípa, namely India within the Ganges, or south Behár; this country is peculiarly sacred to the Buddhists in consequence of its being the place where Buddha stood when he assumed the Buddhaship, where the bó-gaha or sacred tree spontaneously sprang up to shelter him, where the kusa grass became a throne and seat for his repose, and whence also he commenced his career of proclaiming his doctrines to the world.

මධ්‍යමලෝක, *Madhyma-lóka*, *s.* (මධ්‍යම and ලෝක world) the earth, the world of mortals, situated between heaven and hell.

මධ්‍යම යාමය, *Madhyama-yámaya*, } *s.* (මධ්‍යම and
මධ්‍යම රාත්‍රිය, *Madhyama-rátriya*, } යාමය watch, රාත්‍රිය night) middle watch, midnight.

මධ්‍යස්ථ, *Madhyastha*, *s.* (මධ්‍ය middle, ස්ථ what or who stays) middle man, umpire, arbitrator, mediator: *a.* middle, centrical, intervening, mediating.

මධ්‍යාහ්න, *Madhyáhna*, *s.* (මධ්‍ය and අහන් day) midday, noon.

මධු, *Madhu*, *s.* honey, [Colloq. මීපැණි *mí-peṇi*]; honey or nectar of flowers; spirituous liquor, distilled from the blossoms of the *bassia latifolia;* water; milk; sugar; sweetness in flavour, sound or disposition; demon slain by Vishṇu; tree, *bassia latifolia;* asóka tree, *saraca indica* or *Jonesia asoka*, [Colloq, දියරතඹලා *diya-ratambalá*]; liquorice; tree, *celtis orientalis: a.* sweet, saccharine.

මධුක්ෂීර, *Madhukshíra*, *s.* (මධු honey, ක්ෂීර milk) date tree, peculiar to Ceylon, *phœnix zeylanica* or *p. sylvesttris*, [Colloq. ඉඳි *indi*].

මධුක, *Madhuka*, *s.* (මධු sweet, කෛ *kai* to sound) bard, panegyrist, minstrel who recites the lineage and praises of sovereigns in their presence; tree, *bassia latifolia;* honey; liquorice; tin.

මධුකණ්ඨ, *Madhukaṇtha*, *s.* (මධු and කණ්ඨ throat) kókila or Indian cuckoo, *cuculus micropterus.*

මධුකප්‍රිය, *Madhukapriya*, *s.* (මධුක honey, ප්‍රිය what pleases or delights) bee, [Colloq. මීමැස්සා *mí-meṣsá*].

මධුකර, *Madhukara*, *s.* (මධු sweet, කර what makes) bee; lover; plant, *achyranthes aspera*, [Colloq. ගස් කරල්හැබ *gas-karalheba*]; round, sweet lime.

මධුකා, *Madhuká*, *s.* plant, *tinospora cordifolia* or *menispermum glabrum*, [Coll: රසකිඳ *rasakinda*]; sweet lime; kind of panic seed; liquorice plant, [Colloq. වැල්මී *welmi*].

මධුකෝෂ, *Madhukósha*, *s*, (මධු honey, කෝෂ receptacle) beehive, honey comb, [Colloq. මීවදය *mí-wadaya*].

මධුකෘත්, *Madhukrit*, see මධුකර *madhukara.*

මධුජිත්, *Madhujit*, *s.* (මධු demon, ජිත් who conquered) name of Vishṇu or Krishṇa.

මධුතෘණ, *Madhu-triṇa*, *s.* (මධු sweet, තෘණ grass) sugar cane, *saccharum officinarum*, [Colloq. උක්ගහ *uk-gaha*].

මධුද්‍රැම, *Madhu-druma*, *s.* (මධු and ද්‍රැම tree) *bassia latifolia*, from the blossoms of which a spirituous liquor is distilled: see මධුක *madhuka.*

මධුධූලි, *Madhu-dhúli*, *s.* (මධු and ධූලි dust) molasses, sugar before it is quite purified.

මධුප, *Madhupa*, *s.* (මධු honey, ප who drinks) bee, honey bee, [Colloq. මීමැස්සා *mí-meṣsá*].

මධුපත්‍රක, *Madhupatraka*, see මධුපර්ණී *madhuparṇní.*

මධුපර්ණී, *Madhuparṇni*, *s.* plant, *tinospora cordifolia*, [Colloq. රසකිඳ *rasakinda*].

මධුපර්ණික, *Madhuparṇnika*, } *s.* (මධු honey,
මධුපර්ණිකා, *Madhuparṇniká*, } ප ර්ණී leaf, කන් *kan* aff.) indigo plant, *indigofera tinctoria*, [Colloq. නිල් අවරි *nil-awari*]; tree, *gmelina arborea*, [Colloq. ඇත්දෙමට, *et-demaṭa*]; moon plant, *asclepias acida* or *cynanchum pauciflora*, [Colloq. කංකුඹලා *kankumbalá*]; creeper, *lycopodium imbricatum*; shrub, *tinospora cordifolia* or *menispermum glabrum.*

මධුපර්ණී, *Madhuparṇní*, *s.* creeper, *menispermum glabrum;* tree, *gmelina arborea*; indigo plant, *indigofera tinctoria*, [Coll: නිල් අවරි *nil-awari*]; the sweet lime: see the last word.

මධුපායාස, *Madhupáyása*, *s.* (මධු honey, පායාස milk) sort of food prepared from honey, curdled milk and flour etc.

මධුපායින්, *Madhupáyin*, see මධුප *madhupa*.

මධුපිණ්ඩික, *Madhu-piṇḍika*, *s.* (මධු and පිණ්ඩික ball of dough for food) sort of food prepared from honey and flour.

මධුපුෂ්ප, *Madhu-pushpa*, *s.* (මධු honey or wine, පුෂ්ප flower) tree, *bassia latifolia; mimosa sirisha;* tree, *mimusops elengi*, [Colloq. මූනමල් *múnamal*].

මධුපුෂ්පිකා, *Madhu-pushpiká*, *s.* kind of dill or fennel, [Colloq. ශතපුෂ්ප *ṣatapushpa*].

මධුප්‍රිය, *Madhu-priya*, *s.* (මධු honey, wine etc. ප්‍රිය fond of) bee; shrub, *ardisia solanacea:* see බලරාම *bala-ráma*.

මධුඵල, *Madhu-phala*, *s.* (මධු and ඵල fruit) tree, *flacourtia cataphracta*, [Colloq. රට උගුරැස්ස *raṭa-ugurẹssa*]; sweet kind of coconut.

මධුමක්ෂිකා, *Madhu-makshiká*, *s.* (මධු and මක්ෂිකා fly) bee, honey bee, [Colloq. මීමැස්සා *mímẹssá*].

මධුමක්ෂිප්‍රිය, *Madhumakshi-priya*, *s.* tree, *pogamia glabra:* see මගුල්කරඳ *magul-karanda*.

මධුමේහ, *Madhuméha*, *s.* (මධු and මේහ urinary disease) disease, sort of diabetes, *diabetes mellitus*.

මධුයෂ්ටි, *Madhuyashṭi*, *s.* (මධු sweet, යෂ්ටි cane) sugar cane, *saccharum officinarum*, [Colloq. උක් ගහ *uk-gaha*].

මධුයෂ්ටිකා, *Madhuyashṭiká*, } *s.* (මධුයෂ්ටි and කා
මධුයෂ්ටි, *Madhuyashṭi*, } aff.) liquorice, *glycirrhiza glabrum*, [Colloq. වැල්මී *wẹlmí*]; Indian liquorice, *abrus precatorius*, [Colloq. ඕලිඳවැල් *olinda-wẹl*].

මධුයෝනි, *Madhu-yóni*, *s.* (මධු honey, යෝනි place of production) honey bee; grape vine, *vitis vinifera*, [Colloq. මිදිවැල් *midi-wẹl*].

මධුර, *Madhura*, *s.* (මධු honey, ර *rá* to have or get) sweetness, sweet taste; treacle; syrup; tin: *a.* sweet; pleasing, agreeable, liked.

මධුරඵල, *Madhura-phala*, see මධුඵල *madhu-phala*.

මධුරමාර්ජික, *Madhuramárjika*, *s.* date tree, *phœnix zeylanica*, [Colloq. ඉඳිගහ *indi-gaha*].

මධුරස්වර, *Madhuraswara*, *s.* sweet voice; the Indian cuckoo, *cuculus micropterus*.

මධුරස, *Madhu-rasa*, *s.* (මධු wine, honey etc. රස juice, flavour) sugar cane, [Colloq. උක්ගහ *uk-gaha*]; palm tree; sweetness.

මධුරසා, *Madhurasá*, *s.* shrub, *sanseviera zeylanica*, [Colloquial: නියඳ *niyanda*]; plant, *cynanchum pauciflorum* or *asclepias acida*, [Colloq. කංකුඹලා *kankumbalá*]; plant, *marsdenia tenacissima*, [Colloq. මුරුවාදූල් *muruwá-dúl*].

මධුරා, *Madhurá*, *s.* (මධු sweetness, රා to have or get) sort of fennel *anethum sowa* or *pammorium;* anise, *pimpinella anisum;* plant, *sanseviera zeylanica*, [Colloq. නියඳ *niyanda*]; liquorice, see මධුයෂ්ටිකා *madhuyashṭiká*; sweet lime.

මධුරිකා, *Madhuriká*, *s.* kind of dill or fennel, *anethum sowa*, [Colloq. ශතපුෂ්ප *ṣatapushpa*].

මධුරෝදක, *Madhuródaka*, *s.* (මධුර *madhura* sweet, උදක *udaka* water) sea of fresh or sweet water, surrounding Pushkara dwípa and being the outermost of the seven seas incircling Méru: see මේරු *méru*.

මධුලේහ, *Madhuléha*, *s.* (මධු and ලිහ *liha* to lick) honey bee, [Colloq. මීමැස්සා *mí-mẹssá*].

මධුවන, *Madhu-wana*, *s.* (මධු and වන who sounds or cries) the kókila or Indian cuckoo, *cuculus micropterus*.

මධුව්‍රත, *Madhu-wrata*, *s.* (මධු honey, ව්‍රත observance) bee, [Colloq. මීමැස්සා *mí-mẹssá*].

මධුශර්කරා, *Madhu-ṣarkará*, *s.* (මධු and ශර්කරා sugar) sort of sugar, congealed honey used as such.

මධුශාඛ, *Madhuṣáka*, *s.* tree, *bassia latifolia*.

මධුශිග්‍රු, *Madhuṣigru*, *s.* (මධු and ශිග්‍රු hyperanthera etc.) red variety of the *moringa pterogosperma*, [Colloq. වැල්මුරුංගා *wẹl-murungá*].

මධුස්‍රවස්, *Madhuṣrawas*, *s.* tree, *bassia longifolia*, [Colloq. මීගහ *mí-gaha*]; shrub, *clitoria ternata*, [Colloq, වලාවැන්න *waláwẹnna*, නිල්කටරොළු *nil-kaṭaroḷu*].

මධුශ්‍රේණි, *Madhuṣréṇi*, *s.* (මධු and ශ්‍රේණි row or line) plant, bowstring hemp, *sanseviera zeylanica*, [Colloq. මුරුවා *muruwá*, නියඳ *niyanda*].

මධුෂ්ඨීල, *Madhushṭhíla*, *s.* (මධු spirit, ෂ්ඨීව *shṭhíwa* to eject) tree, *bassia longifolia*, [Colloq. මී ගහ *mí-gaha*].

මධුස්වර, *Madhu-swara*, *s.* (මධු sweet, ස්වර note, song) kókila or Indian cuckoo: see මධුවන *mabhu-wana*.

මධුස්‍රවස්, *Madhusrawas*, *s.* (මධු spirituous liquor, ස්‍රු *sru* to drop or distil) tree, from the blossoms of which a spirituous liquor is distilled, *bassia longifolia*.

මධුස්‍රවා, *Madhusrawá*, *s.* plant, *celtis orientalis;* liquorice: see මධුකා *madhuká*.

මධූක, *Madhúka*, *s.* tree, *bassia longifolia*, [Colloq. මීගහ *mí-gaha*].

මධූච්ඡිෂ්ට, *Madhúchchhishṭa*, *s.* bee's wax, [Colloq. මී ඉටි *mí-iṭi*].

මධූලක, *Madhúlaka*, } s. (මධු honey or spirit, ලා
මධූලිකා, *Madhúliká*, } *lá* to be or get) *bassia latifolia*, growing in watery and mountanous sites in India; plant, *sanseviera zeylanica*, [Colloq. නියඳ *niyanda*]; sweetness; plant, *marsdenia tenacissima* [Colloq. මුරුවා-දුල් *muruwá-dúl*].

මන්, *Man*, s. heart; pride, haughtiness, from මාන *mána;* road.

මන්ත්‍ර, *Mantra*, s. mystical verse or incantation; formula sacred to any individual deity; secret consultation, private advice; among the Hindus, a division of the Védas, including hymns and prayers, addressed to particular deities, and used at peculiar sacrifices.

මන්ත්‍රකාරයා, *Mantrakárayá*, s. one who performs incantation.

මන්ත්‍රකෘත්, *Mantrakrit*, s. (මන්ත්‍ර advice, කෘත් who makes or gives) counsellor, minister.

මන්ත්‍රඥ, *Mantrajña*, s. (මන්ත්‍ර and ඥ, who knows) spy, secret emissary or agent; counsellor, adviser; sacred teacher.

මන්ත්‍රණකරණවා, *Mantraṇa-karaṇawá*, v. to counsel, to talk together.

මන්ත්‍රණය, *Mantraṇaya*, s. counsel, conspiracy, charm, counsel: see මන්ත්‍ර *mantra*.

මන්ත්‍රණශාලාව, *Mantraṇa-ṣáláwa*, s. (මන්ත්‍ර *mantra* consultation, ශාලාව hall) counsel room, place for secret or private consultation.

මන්ත්‍රණසභාව, *Mantraṇa-sabháwa*, s. (legislative,) council, conference.

මන්ත්‍රවක්තෘ, *Mantra-waktṛi*, s. (මන්ත්‍ර and වක්තෘ who speaks) a repeater of mystical texts for evil purposes, sorcerer: this may also mean a reciter of the Veda formulas.

මන්ත්‍රවිත්, *Mantravit*, } see මන්ත්‍රඥ *mantrajña*.
මන්ත්‍රවිද්, *Mantravid*, }

මන්ත්‍රී, *Mantri*, s. (මන්ත්‍ර counsel, advice, ඉන් *in* aff.) minister, counsellor, adviser, king's minister, privy counsellor; also name of Vṛihaspati, tutor of the gods.

මන්ත්‍රීමණ්ඩලය, *Mantri-maṇḍalaya*, s. council of ministers.

මන්ත්‍රීශ්වරයා, *Mantríṣwarayá*, s. supreme counsellor, also honorific epithet of Mudaliyars and other high officials.

මන්ථන, *Manthana*, s. (මන්ථ *mantha* to churn) agitating, stirring, churning; killing, injuring.

මන්ද, *Manda*, s. yoke; name of the planet Saturn; name of Yama: *a.* slow, tardy, dull, stupid, heavy, foolish; sick, diseased; idle, lazy; cold, phlegmatic: *adv.* why, for what reason, on what account?

මන්දගාමින්, *Mandagámin*, } s. (මන්ද slowly ගම *gama*
මන්දගාමී, *Mandagámí*, } to go) going slowly or gently, a slow march or pace; planet Saturn,

මන්දජනනී, *Manda-jananí*, s. (මන්ද Saturn, ජනනී mother) wife of Súryá.

මන්දබුද්ධි, *Mandabuddhi*, *a.* imprudent, foolish.

මන්දභාග්‍ය, *Manda-bhágya*, *a.* (මන්ද and භාග්‍ය fortune) unfortunate, unlucky.

මන්දමති, *Mandamati*, *a.* (මන්ද slow, dull, මති intellect) dull, stupid, foolish.

මන්දමතිත්ව, *Mandamatitwa*, s. (මන්දමති stupid, ත්ව aff. of the abstract) stupidity, dulness, deficiency in intellect.

මන්දමදිනි වැල, *Mandamadini-wæla*, s. creeping plant yielding a red dye, *rubia cordifolia (Rubiaceæ).*

මන්දමාරුත, *Mandamáruta*, s. (මන්ද and මාරුත wind) gentle wind or breeze, zephyr.

මන්දයා, *Mandayá*, s. (මන්ද dull, යා pers. aff.) idiot, stupid or silly fellow.

මන්දර, *Mandara*, s. (මදි *madi* to please) mountain Mandara, with which the ocean was churned by the Suras and Asuras after the deluge, for the purpose of recovering the sacred things lost in it during that period; one of the trees of Swarga or paradise.

මන්දස්මිත, *Mandasmita*, s. (මන්ද gently, ස්මිත laughing) smile, gentle laugh.

මන්දහාස්‍ය, *Mandahásya*, s. smile, gentle laugh.

මන්දාක්ෂ, *Mandáksha*, s. (මන්ද *manda* gentle, retiring, අක්ෂ *aksha* organ of sense) modesty, bashfulness.

මන්දාකිනී, *Mandákiní*, s. (මන්ද *manda* slowly, අක *aka* to go, ඉනී *ini* aff.) large lake in the Himálayan mountains; the Ganges of Swarga.

මන්දාග්නිය, *Mandágniya*, s. (මන්ද *manda* slow, අග්නි *agni* fire) want of appetite.

මන්දාර, *Mandára*, s. one of the five trees of Swarga; coral tree, *erythrina indica*, [Colloq. එරබදු *erabadu*]; swallow-wort, *calotropis gigantea*, [Coll: වරා *wará*]; the western mountain behind which the sun is supposed to set.

මන්දාරම්, *Mandáram*, *a.* cloudy, overcast with clouds, obscure, gloomy.

මන්දාරම, *Mandárama*, s. cloudiness, gloominess.

මන්දාරි, *Mandárí*, s. plant, *acalypha indica*, [Colloq. කුප්පමේනිය *kuppaméniya*].

මන්දිරය, *Mandiraya*, s. royal palace; the residence of a nobleman; house, mansion; temple; any place dedicated to a deity; sea; town.

මන්ද්‍ර, *Mandra*, s. base or low tone, such as the grumbling of clouds etc. a drum.

මන්නේ, *Manné*, s. toddy drawer's knife.

මන්බිඳීම, *Manbindíma*, s. (මන් mind, බිඳීම breaking) subduing, humbling; conquering, taming.

මන්මථ, *Manmatha*, s. (මන් mind, මථ to agitate) name of Káma, the Hindu Cupid; elephant or wood apple, *feronia elephantum*, [Colloq. දිවුල් *diwul*]; love, amorous passion or desire; twenty-eighth year of the Indian cycle of sixty.

මන්මද, *Manmada*, } s. name of Káma, god of love;
මන්මදා, *Manmadá*, } see the last.

මන්මාවත්, *Manmáwat*. s. highways and byways.

මන්මින්නා, *Manminná*, s. kind of snake.

මන්මිනි, *Manmini*, s. salutation, obeisance.

මන්මුළා, *Manmulá*, a. more correctly මංමුළා *manmulá*, (මන් (මං) way, මුළා strayed) gone astray, wandered out of the way; erred, in error.

මන්මුළාවෙනවා, *Manmuláwenawá*, v. to go astray.

මන්යොන්, *Manyon*, s. (මන් mind, යොන් place of production) name of Káma, the deity of love.

මන්වන්තර, *Manwantara*, s. in Hindu mythology, the reign of a Manu, a period equal to 306,720,000 years of mortals, or seventy one ages of the gods; fourteen of these periods constitute a Kalpa.

මන්සන්ධි, *Mansandhi*, s. (මන් roads, සන්ධි junction) place where two or more roads meet.

මනඃකර්ම, *Manah-karma*, s. (මනඃ mind, කර්ම act) subject of thought or reflection; operation of the mind.

මන, *Mana*, s. (මන to know, to understand) the mind considered as the seat of thought or reflection; Indian spikenard; name of Yama, regent of death; heart.

මනආප, *Manaápa*. a. pleasing, agreeable, beautiful.

මනකර, *Manakara*, s. (මන mind, කර what does) thought, reflection, [Coll: කල්පනාව *kalpanáwa*].

මනකල්, *Manakal*, a. (මන and කල් pleasing) desirable, agreeable, pleasing.

මනකල, *Manakala*, s. woman, wife, [Colloq. ස්ත්‍රී *strí*]; that which is good: *a*. good, pleasing, [Colloq. යහපත් *yahapat*].

මනදීම, *Mana-díma*, s. (මන and දීම giving) assent, agreeing to any proposition.

මනදොළ, *Manadola*, s. (මන and දොළ wish) wish, desire, hope, [Colloq. ආසාව *ásáwa*].

මනන්නා, *Mananá*, s. a low caste man, employed by respectable Kandyans to be in charge of paddy.

මනන, *Manana*, s. (මන to know) minding, understanding.

මනනද, *Mananada*, a. good, pleasing to the mind, [Colloq. යහපත් *yahapat*].

මනබැඳි, *Manabendi*, a. attached, [Colloq. සිත බැඳුනාවූ *sita-bendunáwú*].

මනමාලයා, *Manamálayá*, s. bridegroom, lover.

මනමාලි, *Manamáli*, s. bride.

මනයොන්, *Manayon*, s. (මන mind, යොන් place of production) name of Anangayá the Indian Cupid.

මනරම්, *Manaram*, a. (මන mind, රම් to sport or please) beautiful, pleasant, agreeable, delightful.

මනවඩනවා, *Manawadanawá*, v. to raise the passions, to excite affection, to fall in love.

මනස්කාර, *Manaskára*, s. (මනස් mind, කාර operation) attention of the mind to its own sensations, consciousness of pleasure or pain.

මනස්තාප, *Manastápa*, s. (මනස් and තාප burning) grief, sorrow, vexation.

මනස, *Manasa*, s. mind: see මන *mana*.

මනසා, *Manasá*, s. goddess of the serpent race and the particular protectress against their venom; hence the name, object of love.

මනසිකර, *Manasikara*, s. (මනසි in the mind, කර operation) thought, reflection, meditation: see මනස්කාර *manaskára*.

මනහර, *Manahara*, a. pleasing, agreeable, delightful; lovely.

මනා, *Maná*, a. good, excellent; delightful, pleasing.

මනාප, *Manápa*, a. (මන *mana* mind, ආප *ápa* to go or attract) pleasing, beautiful, agreeable; contented, willing, satisfied or inclined.

මනාපය, *Manápaya*, s. wish, inclination, propensity.

මනාපවෙනවා, *Manápawenawá*, v. to wish, to consent.

මනාව, *Manáwa*, s. a measure, fortieth part of a parrah, or as much as can be held in the open hand with the fingers joined and hollowed a little: *adv*. well, correctly.

මනාවූ, *Manáwú*, a. good, pleasing, [Colloq. යහපත්වූ *yahapatwú*].

මණි, *Mani*, *s.* plant with many jointed stems and small rose coloured flowers, *justicia procumbens (Acanthaceæ)*.

මණිත, *Manita*, *a.* (මන *mana* to know, ක්ත *kta* aff.) known, understood.

මිණිනවා, *Maninawá*, *v.* to mete, to measure: pret. මැන්නා *menná*.

මණිස්ස, *Manissa*, *s.* plant, not ascertained.

මනීෂා, *Manishá*, *s.* (මනස් *manas* mind, ඊෂ *ísha* to go) intellect, understanding; wisdom, knowledge, information.

මනු, *Manu*, *s.* (මන *mana* to know, the Védas or scripture) among the Hindus, name of a celebrated legislator and saint, son of Brahma or a personification of Brahma himself, the creator of the world and progenitor of mankind; the name is however a generic term, and in every kalpa or interval from creation to creation, there are fourteen successive Manus, presiding over the universe for the period of a Manwantara, respectively; man in general.

මනුජ, *Manuja*, *s.* (මනු legislator and progenitor of mankind, ජ born, descended) man in general.

මනුෂ්‍ය, *Manushya*, *s.* (මනු manu, යත් *yat* aff. of descent) man, mankind.

මනුෂ්‍යජාතිය, *Manushya-játiya*, *s.* mankind, human kind.

මනුෂ්‍යත්ව, *Manushyatwa*, *s.* state or condition of man, manhood.

මනුෂ්‍යධර්ම, *Manushya-dharma*, *s.* (මනුෂ්‍ය man ධර්ම piety) name of Kuvéra, the Indian god of wealth, he being the idol of mankind; duty of man.

මනුෂ්‍යනාරකික, *Manushya-nárakika*, *s.* a demon like man.

මනුෂ්‍යපථය, *Manushya-pathaya*, *s.* (මනුෂ්‍ය and පථ *patha* way) habits, customs.

මනුෂ්‍යසභා, *Manushya-sabhá*, *s.* (මනුෂ්‍ය and සභා an assembly) multitude, crowd, meeting, [Colloq. සමූහය *samúhaya*].

මනෝ, *Manó*, see මන *mana*.

මනෝගුප්තා, *Manóguptá*, *s.* red arsenic, [Colloq. රත්හිරියල් *rat-hiriyal*].

මනෝජ, *Manója*, } *s.* (මනස් *manas* mind, ජ born, or ජන්ම birth)
මනෝජන්ම, *Manójanma*, } name of Káma, the Hindu Cupid.

මනෝජව, *Manójawa*, *s.* (මනස් *manas* and ජව speed, quickness) quickness of thought or apprehension: *a.* parental, fatherly; quick in thought.

මනෝඥ, *Manójña*, *a.* (මනස් *manas* and ඥා *jñá* to know or get) beautiful, handsome; lovely, pleasing.

මනෝඥා, *Manójñá*, *s.* princess, red arsenic.

මනෝනුකූල, *Manónukúla*, *a.* (මනස් *manas* mind, අනුකූල *anukúla* agreeable to) wishful, desirous.

මනෝනන්දනීය, *Manónandaníya*, *a.* (මනස් *manas* and නන්දනීය pleasant) agreeable, delightful, affording gratification.

මනෝප්‍රණිධාන, *Manópranidhána*, *s.* (මනස් *manas* and ප්‍රණිධාන prayer) mental request or petition.

මනෝබල, *Manóbala*, *a.* wise, [Colloq. ප්‍රඥාවන්ත *prajñáwanta*].

මනෝභව, *Manóbhawa*, *s*, (මනස් *manas* and භව being) name of Káma god of love.

මනෝමය, *Manómaya*, *a.* (මනස් *manas* and මය aff.) produced or originating in the mind.

මනෝමය ඍද්ධිය, *Manómaya-riddhiya*, *s.* (මනෝමය mental ඍද්ධි *riddhi* superhuman power) faculty of doing whatsoever is desired by the mere exertion of thought.

මනෝමය ගණිතය, *Manómaya-ganitaya*, *s.* mental arithmetic, or calculation.

මනෝරථ, *Manóratha*, *s.* (මනස් *manas* and රථ vehicle) wish, desire.

මනෝරම්‍ය, *Manóramya*, } *a.* (මනස් *manas* mind, රම to sport or delight)
මනෝරම, *Manórama*, } beautiful, pleasing, agreeable, delightful.

මනෝරමා, *Manóramá*, *s.* shrub with rose coloured flowers, *ardisea humilis* or *a. elliptica*, [Colloq. බළුදන් *baludan*].

මනෝශිල, *Manósila*, *s.* red arsenic.

මනෝහර්ම, *Manóharma*, *s.* sort of orange, *citrus nobilis*, [Colloq. හින්නාරං *hinnáran*].

මනෝහර, *Manóhara*, *s.* (මනස් *manas* mind or heart, හර to take, to steal) moon, [Colloq. හඳ *handa*]: *a.* beautiful, lovely, agreeable, pleasing.

මනෝහරී, *Manóharí*, *s.* (මනෝහර *manóhara* lovely, ඊ *í* aff.) beautiful woman.

මම්ම, *Mamma*, *pron.* I myself.

මම, *Mama*, *pron.* I.

මමංකාර, *Mamankára*, *s.* (මම *mama* and කාර doing) pride, haughtiness, [Colloquial: ආඩම්බරය *ádambaraya*].

මමත්ව, *Mamatwa*, } *s.* (මම of me, ත්ව and තා affixes
මමතා, *Mamatá*, } of the abstract quality) pride, arrogance, self sufficiency; interest or affection entertained for other objects from considering them as belonging to or connected with one's self.

මමන, *Mamana*, s. pouring, shedding, pouring out.

මයාසුත, *Mayásuta*, s. planet Saturn, [Colloq. සෙනසුරා *senasurá*].

මයිනහම, *Mayinahama*, s. smith's bellows.

මයියම, *Mayiyama*, s. model, pattern, example, [Colloq. ආදර්ශය *ádrişaya*].

මයිල්, *Mayil*, s. hair, hair of the body, either of men or animals; maternal uncle, father-in-law.

මයිල, *Mayila*, s. tree; large creeper with large leaves and white flowers turning to yellow, *bauhinia racemosa (Leguminosæ)*.

මයිලක්කණ්ඩි, *Mayilakkandi*, s. a female demon.

මයිලක්කණ්ඩියා, *Mayilakkandiyá*, s. a large sea fish said to be of about twenty yards in length.

මයිලනුවන්, *Mayilanuwan*, s. maternal uncle; father-in-law..

මයු, *Mayu*, s. (මි *mi* to scatter, sweet sounds, etc.) chorister of Swarga; see ගන්ධර්ව *gandharwa*; deer.

මයුරා, *Mayurá*, s. peacock, *pavo cristatus:* pl. මයුරෝ *mayuró*, [Colloq. මොණරා *monará*].

මයුරාජ, *Mayurája*, s. (මයු and රාජ king) name of Kuvéra, he having the kinnaras attached to his court and capital: see කිඳුරා *kindurá*,

මයුරුතණ, *Mayuru-tana*, s. sort of grass, *chloris barbata (Gramineæ)*.

මයූඛ, *Mayúkha*, s. light, lustre, brightness; ray of light; flame; beauty; pin or gnomon of a sun dial.

මයූර, *Mayúra*, s. peacock, [Colloq. මොණරා *monará*], see මයුරා *mayurá*; flower, coxcomb, *celosia cristata;* plant, *achyranthes aspera*, [Colloq. ගස් කරල්හැබ *gas-karalheba*].

මයූරක, *Mayúraka*, s. plant, *achyranthes aspera;* see the last; also, blue vitriol; flower, *celosia cristata*.

මයූරගල, *Mayúra-gala*, s. (මයූර peacock, ගල stone) gem said to be found in the throat of the peacock, emerald, [Colloq. ඉන්ද්‍රනීල *indraníla*].

මයූරචූඩා, *Mayúra-chúdá*, s. (මයූර and චූඩා crest) coxcomb, *celosia cristata*.

මයූරජංඝ, *Mayúra-jangha*, s. tree, *oroxylum indicum* or *bignonia indica*, [Colloq. තොටිල *totila*].

මර්කට, *Markata*, s. monkey or ape; spider; large crane, called in India the adjutant, *ardea argala* or *a. goliath;* kind of venom.

මර්කටී, *Markatí*, s. variety of the grey bonduc, *cæsalpinia bonduc* or *guilandina bonducella*, [Colloq. කුඹුරුවැල් *kumburuwel*]; cowatch, *mucuna dolichos* or *carpopogon pruriens*, [Colloq. ආචාරියාපළු *áchdriyápalu*]; small or female monkey; plant, *vigna sinensis*, [Colloq. වඳුරුමෑ *wandurumé*].

මර්ජාර, *Marjára*, s. (මෘජ *mrija* to cleanse) cat, [Colloq. බළලා *balalá*].

මර්ජාරමෝහනී, *Marjára-móhaní*, s. (මර්ජාර cat, මෝහන *móhana* fascinating) small plant, *acalypha indica*, said to have fascinating effects on cats when they smell or eat it, [Colloq. කුප්පමේනිය *kuppaméniya*].

මර්ත්‍ය, *Martya*, s. man, mortal; earth, world, considered as the habitation of mortals.

මර්තවාලු කෙසෙල්, *Martawálu-kesel*, s. kind of plantain, *musa sapientum*.

මර්තුමාන් කෙසෙල්, *Martumán-kesel*, s. kind of plantain.

මර්දන, *Mardana*, s. (මෘද *mrida* to rub or grind) rubbing, grinding, pounding; squeezing, crushing, pressing; rubbing the body.

මර්ම, *Marma*, s. joint, articulation of the body, [Colloq. හන්දිය *handiya*]; vital member or organ, secret meaning or purpose, any thing hidden or recondite.

මර්මක්‍රම, *Marmakrama*, s. articulation of the joints of the human body.

මර්මර, *Marmara*, s. sort of pine, *pinus déradáru;* gentle wind; rustling of cloth or dry leaves.

මර්මස්ථාන, *Marmasthána*, s. (මර්ම joint, ස්ථාන place) articulation of the joints of body.

මර්යාදා, *Maryádá*, s. boundary, limit; steadiness, rectitude; bank, shore, [Colloq. සීමාව *símáwa*].

මර්ෂණ, *Marshna*, s. patience, enduring, resignation; stroking, robbing, polishing.

මර්ෂ, *Marsha*, s. (මෘෂ *mrisha* to bear with) patience, endurance.

මර, *Mara*, s. (මෘ *mri* to die) name of Káma the Hindu Cupid; death.

මරක්කලයා, *Marakkalayá*, s. moorman, *i.e.* Mohammedan of Ceylon.

මරක, *Maraka*, s. epidemic or pestilential desease.

මරකත, *Marakata*, s. emerald, [Colloq. පච්ච *pachcha*, පේරෝස *pérósa*].

මරගත, *Maragata*, } s. (මර death, ගත gone)
මරගාත, *Maragáta*, } struggles of a dying person, agonies of death.

මරගාතකරණවා, *Maragátakaranawá*, v. to struggle as at the point of death, to agonise.

මරඟනා, *Maranganá*, s. (මර Káma, අඟනා *anganá* woman) wife of Káma.

මරණ, *Maraṇa*, *s.* death, dying; name of Yamaraja, the Indian Pluto.

මරණවා, *Maraṇawá*, *v.* to slay, to kill, to destroy: pret. මැරුවා *męruwá*.

මරණාතුරයා, *Maraṇáturayá*, *s.* (මරණ *maraṇa* death, ආතුර *átura* diseased) dying man, one labouring under a mortal disease.

මරණාසන්නය, *Maraṇásannaya*, *s.* nearness to death.

මරණාසන, *Maraṇásana*, *s.* (මරණ *maraṇa* and ආසන *ásana* seat) deathbed; Yama's throne or judgment seat.

මරදන, *Maradána*, *s.* sandy region or soil, sandy plain.

මරදෙව්, *Maradew*, *s.* (මර and දෙව් a god) name of Káma, the Hindu Cupid.

මරඳ, *Maraṉda*, } *s.* tree, *eugenia zeylanica*,
මරන්ද, *Maranda*, } *(Myrtaceæ)*.

මරපියෝ, *Marapiyó*, *s.* name of Sakra or Indra.

මරයෝගය, *Marayógaya*, *s.* an astronomical term, conjunction of planets indicative of death.

මරරුපු, *Mararupu*, *s.* (මර form of මාරයා *márayá* and රුපු enemy) name of Buddha: see මාරයා *márayá*.

මරවනවා, *Marawanawá*, *v.* to cause to kill: pret. මැරෙව්වා *męrewwá*.

මරවැඩි, *Marawęḍi*, *s.* sort of slipper or sandals, sometimes written මිරිවැඩි *miriwęḍi*.

මරසුවහස්, *Marasuwahas*, } *s.* (මර Márayá, සුවහස්
මරසෙනග, *Marasenaga*, } 100,000 සෙනග *senaga* army) army of Márayá who opposed Bódhisat in his assumption of the Buddhaship: see මාරයා *márayá*.

මරහඬ, *Marahaṉḍa*, *s.* death-cry.

මරහන්දි, *Marahandi*, *s.* fatal parts of the body.

මරහු, *Marahu*, see මාරයා *márayá*.

මරා, *Mará*, *s.* emerald, [Colloq. පච්ච *pachcha*, පේරෝස *pérósa*]: *a.* green.

මරාමිණි, *Marámiṇi*, *s.* (මරා and මිණි gem) emerald.

මරාල, *Marála*, *s.* (මෘ *mṛi* to die, ආලච් *álach* aff.) lamp-black; rogue: *a.* soft, mild.

මරාවන්, *Maráwan*, *s.* (මරා and වන් colour) emerald colour, green; according to another authority, blue.

මරිච, *Maricha*, *s.* (මෘ *mṛi* to die, venom, ඉච *icha* aff.) pepper, considered as an antidote.

මරිචි, *Marichi*, see මරීචි *maríchi*.

මරිචිමඤ්ජරී, *Marichi-mañjarí*, *s.* (මරිචි ray, මඤ්ජරී collection) corona, circle of light surrounding the heads of celestial beings.

මරිතොණ්ඩි, *Maritoṇḍi*, *s.* shrub or small tree, called tree Mignonette, (Persian henna) *Lawsonia alba* or *inermis Lawsonia*. (Tamil.)

මරින්දා, *Marindá*, *s.* small sea fish.

මරියාදාව, *Mariyádáwa*, *s.* good conduct or behaviour; limit, boundary.

මරීච, *Maricha*, *s.* (මෘ *mṛi* to die) black pepper, *piper nigrum*, [Colloq. ගම්මිරිස් *gammiris*].

මරීචි, *Maríchi*, *s.* ray of light; mirage, or sultry vapour which, in hot and sandy countries especially, appears at a distance like a sheet of water; niggard, miser; name of one of the Prajápatis; flower, *wrightia zeylanica*, [Colloq. ඉද්ද *idda*].

මරීචිකා, *Maríchiká*, *s.* (මරීචි and කත් *kat* aff. implying resemblance) mirage: see the last.

මරු, *Maru*, *s.* (මෘ *mṛi* to die, උ *u* aff.) region or soil destitute of water, sandy desert etc.; name of Anaṅga the Indian Cupid, name of the god of wind; the north-west.

මරුකතර, *Marukatara*, *s.* (මරු and කතර wild) region destitute of water, desert, wilderness: see මරුබිම *maru-bima*.

මරුත්, *Marut*, *s.* wind, air, or its deified personification; deity, an immortal; plant, *trigonella corniculata*, [Colloq. පික්මල් *pik-mal*].

මරුත්කර, *Marutkara*, *s.* (මරුත් wind, eructation, කර making) sort of bean, *dolichos catjang*, [Colloq. ලිමෑ *limę*].

මරුත්පථ, *Marutpatha*, *s.* (මරුත් and පථ way) atmosphere, sky, heaven, [Colloq. අහස *ahasa*].

මරුතැන්, *Marutęn*, see මරහන්දි *mara-handi*.

මරුද්භවා, *Marudbhawá*, *s.* plant, *sanseviera zeylanica*, [Colloq. නියඳ *niyaṉda*].

මරුන්මාලා, *Marun-málá*, *s.* (මරුත් *marut* and මාලා necklace) plant, *trigonella corniculata:* see මරුත් *marut*.

මරුපහර, *Maru-pahara*, *s.* fatal blow.

මරුපෙණෙනවා, *Maru-penenawá*, *v.* to be in deadly terror.

මරුප්‍රිය, *Marupriya*, *s.* (මරු sandy soil, ප්‍රිය fond of) camel, [Colloq. ඔටුවා *oṭuwá*].

මරුබිම, *Maru-bima*, *s.* desert, wilderness, region destitute of water, [Colloq. කාන්තාරය *kántáraya*].

මරුමුඛය, *Marumukhaya*, *s.* the mouth of death.

මරුවක, *Maruwaka*, *s.* (මරු sandy soil, වා *wá* to grow) large thorny shrub, *vangueria spinosa;* species of basil, *ocimum*, with small leaves and red flowers; variety of the citron or lime, said to be a thorny plant bearing a small fruit; plant, *artemisia vulgaris*, [Colloq. වල්කොලොන්දු *walkolondu*]; ascending node; tiger; crane.

මරුවා, *Maruwá*, *s.* death personified; see also මාරයා *máraya*.

මල්, *Mal*, *plur.* of මල *mala*, flower; in Elu, brother, younger brother; rock, row; little child; carpet; plate; Veddás or savages; drinking cup.

මල්අම්මා, *Mal-ammá*, *s.* flower woman.

මල් ඇටෝරතණ, *Mal-ętóra-taṇa*, *s.* meadow grass, *poa reclinata*.

මල් උයන, *Mal-uyana*, *s.* (මල් flower, උයන garden) flower garden.

මල් කරවලා, *Mal-karawalá*, *s.* kind of small snake, *bungarus*.

මල්කරු, *Malkaru*, *s.* (මල් and කරු who makes) florist, one who makes wreaths and necklaces of flowers for people of rank.

මල්කලඹ, *Malkalamba*, *s.* bunch of flowers, nosegay.

මල්කලාඳුරු, *Mal-kalánduru*, *s.* plant, variety of *cyperus rotundus*.

මල්කවුඩා, *Mal-kawuḍá*, *s.* Ceylon myna, *eulabes ptilogenys (Sturnidæ*, order *Passeres)*.

මල්කිනිත්ත, *Malkinitta*, *s.* (මල් flowers, කිනිත්ත cluster) bunch of flowers, cluster or collection of flowers; stalk or compound pedicle of flowers.

මල් කෙකටිය, *Mal-kekaṭiya*, *s.* pond weed, *potamogeton lateralis*.

මල් කොට්ටෝරුවා, *Mal-koṭṭóruwá*, *s.* little Ceylon barbet, *xantholæma rubricapilla*; crimson breasted barbet, *x. hæmacephala (Capitonidæ* order *Picarii)*.

මල්කොන්ද, *Malkonda*, *s.* anther of a flower: pl. මල්කොඳු *malkoṇdu*.

මල්කැකුන, *Mal-kękuna*, *s.* tree, *canarium balsamiferum*.

මල්කැකුල, *Malkękula*, *s.* unblown flower, flower bud: pl. මල්කැකුලු *mal-kękulu*.

මල්කැන, *Malkęna*, *s.* flower stalk, compound pedicel; bunch of flowers: pl. මල්කැන් *mal-kęn*.

මල්කැඳැත්තා, *Mal-kęndattá*, *s.* a bird called red faced malkoha, *phœnicophaes pyrrhocephalus*; also green-billed malkoha, *zanclostomus viridirostris (Cuculidæ*, order *Picariæ)*.

මල්කැර, *Malkęra*, *s.* small tree with fragrant flowers, *ochna squarrosa (Ochnaceæ)*.

මල්කෑරලා, *Mal-kęralá*, *s.* the pigmy woodpecker, *yungipicus gymnophthalmus (Picidæ*, order *Picariæ)*.

මල්ගිය, *Malgiya*, *s.* plant, oleander; according to another authority, species of jasmine.

මල්ගොම, *Malgom*, *s.* florist, one who sells flowers etc.

මල්ගොමු, *Malgomu*, *s.* bed of flowers, large collection of flowers, flower bush.

මල්ගොව්වා, *Malgowwá*, *s.* (මල් and ගොව්වා keeper) florist, flower gardener.

මල්ගැරඬියා, *Mal-gęraṇdiyá*, *s.* rat snake, variety of *ptyas mucosus*.

මල්තුඹ, *Mal-tumba*, *s.* plant, species of *momordica*.

මල්තෙලිස්සා, *Maltelissá*, *s.* small species of the viper, *hypnale nepa*.

මල්තැළුම, *Maltęluma*, *s.* heavy piece of wood with which the flowers of the coconut tree are bruised before extracting toddy.

මල්තැළුමා, *Maltęlumá*, *s.* kind of fish.

මල්දම, *Maldama*, *s.* (මල් flowers, දම chain) string of flowers, garland, wreath or necklace of flowers.

මල්දර, *Maldara*, *s.* paddy, rice in the husk.

මල්දිව, *Maldiwa*, *s.* (මල් or මල *mala* veddá, forrester, දිව island) the Maldive islands, so called, according to Sinhalese authorities, from their being inhabited by a race of savages or an uncivilized people living by the bow; but according to Hindu authorities the word is derived from මලයද්වීප *malayadwípa* or the Malaya islands: see මලය *malaya;* both refer to the same group lying to the westward of Ceylon, and the Malabar coast.

මල්ධරා *Maldhará*, see මල්දර *maldara*.

මල්පිළිහුඩුවා, *Mal-piḷihuḍuwá*, *s.* little Indian kingfisher, *alcedo bengalensis (Alcedinidæ* order *Picariæ)*; also called දියපිළිහුඩුවා *diya-piḷihuḍuwá*.

මල්පෙත්ත, *Malpetta*, *s.* corolla or inner covering of a flower: pl. මල්පෙති *malpeti*.

මල්පොකුර, *Mal-pokura*, *s.* bunch or cluster of flowers, nosegay.

මල්පොල, *Malpola*, *s.* cataract of the eye.

මල්පොලඟා, *Mal-polangá*, *s.* kind of viper, variety of *trimeresurus* or *hypmale*.

මල්පැණි, *Mal-pęni*, *s.* nectar or honey of a flower.

මල්පැපොල, *Mal-pępola*, *s.* variety of the papaw, *carica papaya*.

මල්පැල, *Mal-pęla*, *s.* flower plants; shed used for offering flowers.

මල්බෑයා, *Malbẹyá*, s. brother, [Colloq. සහෝදරයා *sahódarayá*].

මල්මද, *Malmada*, } s. name of Anaṅgayá the In-
මල්මදා, *Malmadá*, } dian Cupid.

මල්මාලා, *Malmálá*, s. garland, fillet, wreath of flowers.

මල්මී, *Malmí*, s. (මල් and මී honey) nectar of flowers.

මල්‍යගන්ධික, *Malyagandhika*, s. timber tree, *dalbergia sissu*.

මල්රජ, *Malraja*, } s. (මල් and රජ or රදු pollen of
මල්රදු, *Malrada*, } flowers) honey or nectar of flowers, so called from its resting on the flowers in small drops resembling the pollen.

මල්ල, *Malla*, s. sack, bag made of any thing but cloth; war, fighting; wrestler, boxer; cup, vessel; cheek and temples, hemicranium.

මල්ලභූ, *Mallabhú*, s. (මල්ල boxer, etc. භූ earth, place) palæstrum or arena; place for athletic contests; site of any contest, as a field of battle.

මල්ලයුද්ධය, *Malla-yuddhaya*, s. wrestling, boxing.

මල්ලව, *Mallawa*, s. boxer, wrestler, fighter.

මල්ලව දේශය, *Mallawa-dẹsaya*, s. country so called, modern Malwa, large province of Hindustan; to the north bounded by Ajmeer and Agra, on the south by Kandesha and Berar, to the east it has Allahabad and Gunduwana, on the west Ajmeer and Guzerat; it was in Kusinárá a city of this district that Buddha died or attained Nirváṇa: see කුසිනාරා *kusinárá*.

මල්ලවයා, *Mallawayá*, see මල්ලව *mallawa*.

මල්ලි, *Malli*, s. younger brother; Arabian jasmin, *jasminum sambac*, [Colloq. පිච්ච *pichcha*].

මල්ලික, *Mallika*, s. bird, said to be a sort of goose with brown legs and bill; shuttle; month nawam (February–March).

මල්ලිකා, *Malliká*, s. Arabian jasmine, see මල්ලි *malli*; plant, the flowers of which are offered in temples, *wrightia zeylanica*, [Colloq. ඉද්ද *idda*]; vessel made of the shell of a coconut for holding oil, etc.; goblet, cup, drinking vessel, [Colloq. කෝප්පය *kóppaya*].

මල්ලිගන්ධි, *Malligandhi*, s, (මල්ලි jasmine, ගන්ධි smelling) fragrant aloe wood.

මල්ලිපත්‍ර, *Malli-patra*, s. mushroom, [Colloq. හතු *hatta*].

මල්ලී, *Mallí*, s. Arabian jasmine, *jasminum sambac*, [Colloq. පිච්ච *pichcha*]; younger brother: pl. මල්ලිලා *mallilá*.

මල්වඩම, *Malwaḍama*, s. chaplet of flowers, garland.

මල්වත්ත, *Mal-watta*, s. flower garden.

මල්වදේශ, *Malwadésa*, see මල්ලවදේශය *mallawadẹsaya*.

මල්වර, *Malwara*, s. first menstrual discharge.

මල්වරවෙනවා, *Malwarawenawá*, v. for a female to arrive at the age of puberty.

මල්වරු, *Malwaru*, s. weaver of flower wreaths and garlands.

මල්වැල, *Malwẹla*, s. flower creeper, row of flowers painted or drawn.

මල්සර, *Malsara*, s. name of Anaṅgayá the Hindu Cupid.

මල්සරා, *Malsará*, s. kind of snake.

මල්සූටික්කා, *Mal-súṭikká*, s. Ceylonese sun bird, *cynnyris zeylanicus (Cynnyridæ*, order *Passeres)*.

මල්සේරා, *Mal-sérá*, s. green-backed goose-teal, *nettapus coromandelianus (Anatidæ* order *Anseres)*.

මල්සැද, *Malsẹda*, s. coverlet, stuffed with flowers

මල්සැර, *Malsẹra*, see මල්සර *malsara*.

මල්හි, *Malhí*, s. monkey: see also, මල්සර *malsara*.

මල, *Mala*, s. according to Elu authorities, vẹddá, forester, one who lives by his bow; bow; net or noose; flower; (according to Sanskrit authorities it is derived from මල to hold or contain, in the body) any excretion of the body, as serum, semen, blood, marrow, urine, fœces, ear wax, nails, phlegm, tears, rheum, and sweat; sin; dirt, filth; dreg sediment; rust: *a.* miserly, niggardly; dead, in this sense more correctly written මළ *maḷa*.

මලකඩ, *Malakaḍa*, s. rust, any concretion formed on metals: see the preceding.

මලගල්, *Malagal*, s. Himálayan range of mountains, formed from හිමාලය *himálaya* by dropping the initial.

මලගස්, *Mala-gas*, see මලරුක් *malaruk*.

මලගහනවා, *Malagahanawá*, v. to burn a bon-fire.

මලඟ, *Malaṅga*, s. name of Káma, the Indian Cupid.

මලණ්ඩ, *Malaṇḍa*, s. voc. O younger brother.

මලදර, *Maladara*, s. (මල bow, net. දර who carries) bowman, archer, one who lives by his bow or by catching animals with a net, barbarian, mountaineer.

මලනුවන්, *Malanuwan*, } s. younger brother (res-
මලනුවෝ, *Malanuwó*, } pectful form).

මලපත, *Malapata*, s. noose, net, snare for catching wild animals.

මලබටු, *Malabaṭu*, s. small hairy species of night shade, *solanum ferox (Solanaceæ)*.

මලබද්ධ, *Malabaddha*, s. (මල fœces, බද්ධ bound) constipation, costiveness.

මල බඳිනවා, *Mala-bandinawá*, v. (මල rust, බඳිනවා to bind) to rust, to become rusty.

මලබුලත්, *Mala-bulat*, s. kind of betel.

මලබොඩ, *Malaboḍa*, s. species of nutmeg tree, peculiar to Ceylon, *myristica laurifolia (Myristaceæ)*.

මලමඩුල්ල, *Malamaḍulla*, } s. (මල an archer, මඩුල්ල
මලමඩුව, *Malamaḍuwa*, } a district or country) site of a veddá village, country inhabited by foresters.

මලමාර්ග, *Malamárga*, s. (මල fœces etc. මාර්ග way) anus; rectum.

මලමිරිස්, *Mala-miris*, s. species of pepper, *piper silvestre (Piperaceæ)*: also called වල් ගම්මිරිස් වැල් *wal-gammiris-wẹl*.

මලමූත්‍ර, *Malamútra*, s. (මල fæces, මූත්‍ර urine) excrement, fæces and urine.

මලය, *Malaya*, s. mountain or mountainous range that runs along the western side of the peninsula of India, from which the country of Malayálam or Malabar takes its name; by modern writers the term is often erroneously applied to the whole country from Cape Comorin to Bombay, whereas it extends no farther than from the southern extremity of the peninsula to the river Chandra-giri in lat. 12° 27 north; garden of Indra.

මලයජ, *Malayaja*, s. (මලය mountain Malaya, ජ produced) sandal wood, large quantities being produced in that country.

මලයා, *Malayá*, s. younger brother.

මලයු, *Malayu*, } s. opposite leaved fig-tree, *ficus*
මලයූ, *Malayú*, } *oppositifolia*, [Colloq. කොටදිඹුලා *koṭadimbulá*].

මලරට, *Mala-raṭa*, s. (මල and රට inhabited country) country so called; country that lies along the Malaya range of mountains on the west coast of the peninsula of India usually called Malabar: see මලය *malaya*.

මලරුක්, *Mala-ruk*, s. worm, worm in general, [Colloq පණුවා *paṇuwá*]; tree bearing a large and beautiful flower, *lagerstrœmia flos-reginæ*, [Colloq. මුරුත *muruta*].

මලරෝධ, *Malaródha*, s. (මල excrement, රෝධ impediment) constipation.

මලලබු, *Mala-labu*, s. species of pepper, *piper subpeltanum (Piperaceæ)*.

මලවනවා, *Malawanawá*, v. to stir about when cooking, to cook herbs for curry or medicine: pret. මැලෙව්වා *mẹlewwá*.

මලවාරිය වී, *Malawáriya-ví*, s. kind of paddy, *oryza sativa*.

මලවිය, *Malaviya*, s. (මල් *mal* flower, අවි *ari* weapon, යා *yá* personal aff.) one whose shafts are tipped with flowers; name of Anaṅgayá, the Hindu Cupid.

මලසන, *Malasana*, s. (මල් *mal* flowers, අසන seat) table or altar in the temples of Buddha on which the flowers are placed when offered to his image; plate, small chatty, cover or lid made of clay for cooking utensils.

මලසා, *Malasá*, s. small cardamoms, *elettaria cardamomum (minor)*, [Colloq. සිහින් එන්සාල් *sihin-ensál*].

මලසුන්, *Malasun*, s. (මල් *mal* flower, අසුන් *asun* seat) altar on which flowers are offered.

මලා, *Malá*, s. noose, snare; plate, lid: pret. of මැරෙණවා *mẹreṇawá*; when it is more correctly written මළා *maḷá*.

මලාමැලි, *Malámẹli*, s. (මල *mala* flower, camphor etc. මැලි gum) fragrance, the fragrance of flowers etc.; perfumes, as camphor, sandal.

මලාය, *Maláya*, s. ornamented or painted cloth folded round the waist and loins, reaching down to the ankles, and worn by the natives.

මලාරුක්, *Maláruk*, see මලරුක් *malaruk*.

මලාව, *Maláwa*, s, plate, lid, cover.

මලිගිය, *Maligiya*, s. jasmine creeper or shrub, *jasminum*, plant, *Wrightia zeylanica*, [Colloq. ඉද්ද *idda*].

මලිත්ත, *Malitta*, s. very small species of parrot, paroquet, *palæornis*.

මලිත, *Malita*, s. beautiful flowering shrub with permanent red calyx, *Woodfordia floribunda* or *grislea tomentosa*, *(Lythraceæ)*, [Colloq. මයිල *mayila*].

මලිති, *Maliti*, see මලිත්ත *malitta*.

මලින, *Malina*, s. (මල *mala* dirt, filth etc. ඉනච් *inach* aff.) fault, defect; borax: *a*. dirty, filthy, foul; black; vile, bad; (figuratively) soiled with crime or vice, sinful, depraved.

මලිනත්ව, *Malinatwa*, *s.* (මලින black etc. ත්ව aff. of the abstract) blackness etc.; filthiness, dirtiness; foulness; depravity.

මලිනමුඛ, *Malinamukha*, *s.* (මලින and මුඛ countenance) name of Agni, the god of fire; fire; ghost, goblin; black faced monkey: *a.* cruel, fierce, savage.

මලිනාම්බු, *Malinámbu*, *s.* (මලින dirty, අම්බු water) ink; foul or impure water in which any thing has been washed.

මලිස්සා, *Malissá*, *s.* small kind of fresh water shrimps.

මලීමස, *Malímasa*, *s.* iron; green vitriol: *a.* dirty, foul; wicked.

මලුපු, *Malupu*, *s.* cluster of blossoms, nosegay.

මලේ, *Malé*, *s.* hole, opening, perforation, perforation or eye of a needle, [Colloq. සිල *hila*].

මලෝලඹු, *Malólambu*, *s*, (මල් *mal* flowers, ලබි *labi* to sound) shaking or tremulous motion of an unplucked flower.

මව්, *Maw*, *s.* mother, [Colloq, අම්මා *amma*].

මව්තනතුර, *Mawtanatura*, *s.* woman supplying the place of mother in a family.

මව්හත්කම, *Mawhatkama*, *s.* (මව් and හත්කම affection) maternal affection, regard felt by a mother for her young.

මව, *Mawa*, *s.* mother.

මවනවා, *Mawanawá*, *v.* to make, to form, to create: pret. මැව්වා *mẹwwá*.

මවාපානවා, *Mawápánawá*, *v.* to bring into existence.

මවිත, *Mavita*, *a.* strung, tied; wonderful, surprising; astonished.

මවිතය, *Mavitaya*, *s.* wonder, prodigy; surprise, astonishment.

මවිතවෙනවා, *Mavitawenawá*, *v.* to be astonished or amazed.

මවුල්, *Mawul*, *s.* crown.

මවෙනිකම, *Mawenikama*, see මව්හත්කම *mawhatkama*.

මශක, *Maṣaka*, *s.* gnat, musquito.

මෂ්ටක, *Mashṭaka*, } *s.* fish in general.
මෂ්ටකයා, *Mashṭakayá*, }

මස්, *Mas*, *s.* fish; flesh; small stone, pebble; beard; plant, species of the *flemingia*, [Colloq. උඳු *uṉdu*]; part, portion: *a.* blind.

මස්අරළු, *Mas-araḷu*, *s.* tree, variety of *terminalia chebula*.

මස්කටුව, *Maskaṭuwa*, *s.* fork; prong; fish bone.

මස්කඩේ, *Mas-kaḍé*, *s.* butcher's shop.

මස්කර, *Maskara*, *s.* bamboo, *bambusa vulgaris*, [Colloq. උණගස් *uṇagas*].

මස්කරණවා, *Maskaraṇawá*, *v.* to cut up the flesh of an animal.

මස්කාරයා, *Maskárayá*, *s.* butcher.

මස්ත, *Masta*, } *s.* summit, pinnacle, top of any
මස්තක, *Mastaka*, } thing, head, skull, [Colloq. මුදුන *muduna*].

මස්තකඵල, *Masthaka-phala*, *s.* (මස්තක top, summit, ඵල fruit) any fruit produced from the head of the tree, as the plantain etc.

මස්තකය, *Mastakaya*, see මස්තක *mastaka*.

මස්තු, *Mastu*, *s.* watery part of curds, the whey.

මස්තුලුංග, *Mastuluṅga*, *s.* brain, [Colloq. මොලේ *molé*].

මස්තෙල්, *Mas-tel*, *s.* fish oil; fat or marrow of flesh.

මස්දිව්, *Masdiw*, *s.* fisher, man of the fisher caste.

මස්පැන්නා, *Maspẹnná*, *s.* small sea fish.

මස්බානවා, *Masbánawá*, *v.* to angle, to fish.

මස්බුළු, *Mas-buḷu*, *s.* tree, variety of *terminalia belerica*.

මස්බැද්ද, *Mas-bẹdda*, *s.* creeping plant, not ascertained.

මස්මරන්නා, *Mas-maranná*, *s.* fisherman.

මස්මොර, *Masmora*, *s.* plant, *adenanthera bicolor*, *(Leguminosæ)*.

මස්රද, *Masrada*, *s.* eel, [Colloq. අඳ *áṉdá*].

මස්රොද, *Masroda*, *s.* red lump chiefly in the eye.

මස්ලොඹුව, *Maslombuwa*, *s.* a block of wood on which meat is cut.

මස්වලපොත්තා, *Maswalapottá*, *s.* small sea fish.

මස්වලු, *Maswalu*, *s.* bundle or burden carried in the hand.

මස්වැඩිම, *Maswẹḍima*, *s.* proud flesh.

මස්වැන්න, *Maswẹnna*, *s.* fern, *drymoglossum heterophyllum (Filices)*.

මස්ස, *Massa*, *s.* coin, anciently nineteen pice or six pence three farthings, or about eight pence: pl. මසු *masu*.

මස්සපාඩුව, *Massapáḍuwa*, *s.* rape.

මස්සිනා, *Massiná*, *s.* cousin, cognate cousin; brother in law.

මස, *Masa*, *s.* a fish; month.

මසක, *Masaka*, *s.* species of amaranth, *amaranthus cruentus*, [Colloquial: රත්තම්පලා *rat-tampalá*]; gnat, [Colloq. මදුරුවා *maduruwá*].

මසන්, *Masan*, *s.* tree, bearing a yellow edible fruit like a cherry, *zizyphus jujuba (Rhamnaceæ)*; also called මහදෙබර *maha-ḍebara*.

මසනවා, *Masanawá*, *v.* to sew, to fetter, to enchain: pret. මැසුවා *mẹsuwá*.

මසා, *Masá*, *s.* fish.

මසාර, *Masára*, *s.* emerald, [Colloq. පේරෝස *pérósa*]; in some places it seems to be confounded with another gem of a blue colour, perhaps the sapphire.

මසාරගල්ල, *Masáragalla*, *s.* coral; see also the foregoing.

මසි, *Masi*, *s.* ink; stalk of the *nyctanthes arbortristis*, [Colloq. සේපාල *sépála*].

මසිකූපි, *Masikúpi*, }
මසිධාන, *Masidhána*, } *s.* (මසි ink, කූපි well, ධාන stand) inkstand, [Colloq. තින්තකුප්පිය *tínta-kuppiya*].

මසු, *Masu*, *s.* gem; fish; coin, equal to eight pence: pl. මසුන් *masun*: see මස්ස *massa*.

මසුගන්ධා, *Masugandhá*, see මත්ස්‍යගන්ධා *matsyagandhá*.

මසුන්, *Masun*, *plur.* of මසු *masu*, which see.

මසුර, *Masura*, *s.* sort of lentil or pulse, *ervum hirsutum*.

මසුරන්, *Masuran*, *s.* (මසු and රන් gold) gold coin (not now extant); *sing.* මසුරම *masurama*: see මස්ස *massa*.

මසුරා, *Masurá*, *s.* courtesan; covetous man, miser.

මසුරු, *Masuru*, *a.* covetous, avaricious; stingy.

මසුරුමල, *Masurumala*, *s.* covetousness, extreme avarice.

මසූරවිදලප්‍රභා, *Masúravi-dalaprabhá*, *s.* heart-seed creeper, *cardiospermum halicacabum*, [Colloq. වැල්පෙනෙල *wẹl-penela*].

මසූරවිදලා, *Masúravidalá*, *s.* black variety of the plant, commonly called teori, *ipomœa turpethum*, [Colloq. ත්‍රස්තවාලු *trastawálu*]; twining shrub, *ichnocarpus frutescens*, [Colloq. කිරිවැල් *kiri-wẹl*].

මසූරිකා, *Masúriká*, *s.* (මසුරා *masurá* courtesan, කන් *kan* aff.) bawd, procuress; small pox.

මසූරී, *Masúrí*, *s.* small-pox.

මසැස, *Masẹsa*, *s.* (මස් *mas* flesh, ඇස *ẹsa* eye) eye of the body, in opposition to දිවැස *diwẹsa* or divine perception; worldliness, sensuality.

මහ, *Maha*, *s.* (මහ to increase, to worship) fish; festival: light, lustre; buffalo; sacrifice, oblation: *a.* great, large, big, bulky; harvest.

මහ අක්මැල්ල, *Maha-akmẹlla*, *s.* plant, *spilanthus acmella*; also called අක්මැල්ල *akmẹlla*.

මහ අඳුර, *Maha-andara*, *s.* tree, *acacia leucophlæa (Leguminosæ)*; also called කටු අඳුර *kaṭu-andara*.

මහ අනෝද, *Maha-anódá*, *s.* plant, *sida populifolia*, or *abutilon asiaticum*.

මහ අවරි, *Maha-awari*, *s.* variety of the indigo plant, *indigofera tinctoria*.

මහ අසමෝදගම්, *Maha-asamódagam*, *s.* variety of *pimpinella Heyneana*.

මහ ඇත්අඩිය, *Maha-ẹtaḍiya*, *s.* plant, variety of *elephantopus scaber*.

මහ ඇදුරු, *Maha-ẹduru*, *s.* (මහ great, ඇදුරු teacher) head of a company of artists.

මහ ඇපල, *Maha-ẹpala*, *s.* plant, *hibiscus retifolius*, or species of *urena*.

මහ ඇඹල, *Maha-ẹmbala*, *s.* buck bean, *menyanthes indica*.

මහ ඉඟිනි, *Maha-ingini*, *s.* large variety of the clearing nut plant, *strychnos potatorum*.

මහ ඉත්තවැල, *Maha-itta-wẹla*, ivy creeper, *hedera terebinthinacea*, or species of *heptapleurum*.

මහ ඉඳි, *Maha-indi*, *s.* variety of date-palm tree, *phœnix sylvestris*.

මහ ඉඳුරු, *Maha-induru*, *s.* plant, variety of *susum anthelminticum*.

මහ ඉරමුසු, *Maha-iramusu*, *s.* creeper, variety of *hemidesmus indicus*.

මහඉසි, *Mahaisi*, *s.* name of Buddha, [Colloq. බුදුන් *budun*].

මහ ඊරිය, *Maha-íriya*, *s.* variety of nutmeg tree, *myristica íriya*.

මහ උක්, *Maha-uk*, *s.* large kind of sugar cane, *saccharum officinalis*.

මහ උඳුපියලි, *Maha-undupiyali*, *s.* plant, *desmodium heterophyllum (Leguminosæ)*.

මහ එන්සාල, *Maha-ensála*, *s.* large kind of cardamums, *elettaria cardamomum, major*.

මහ එරමිණියා, *Maha-eramiṇiyá*, *s.* thorny plant, *zizyphus rugosa*.

මහ ඔලෙයියා, *Maha-oleyiyá*, *s.* bird called green shank, *totarns glottis*, *(Scolopacidæ* order *Grallæ)*.

මහ ඔසු, *Maha-osu*, *s.* (මහ great, ඔසු medicament) dry ginger, [Colloq. ඉඟුරු *inguru*]; garlic, [Colloq. සුදුළූණු *sudulúnu*]; Elu form of මහෞෂධ *mahaushadha*.

මහ කඩුත්තු, *Maha-kaḍuttu*, *s.* fæces.

මහ කපු, *Maha-kapu*, *s.* (මහ great, කපු cotton) Bahados or Bourbon cotton tree, *gossypium barbadense.*

මහ කබරස, *Maha-kabarasa*, *s.* plant with flowers in compound umbels, *smilax ovalifolia (Liliaceæ).*

මහ කරඹ, *Maha-karamba*, *s.* thorny shrub, *carissa carandas.*

මහ කරව්, *Maha-karaw*, *s.* kind of large grass, *scleria elata.*

මහ කලාඳුරු, *Maha-kalánduru*, *s.* large variety of the *cyperus rotundus.*

මහ කවුඩා, *Maha-kawuḍá*, *s.* bird called rocket-tailed drongo, *dissemurus paradiseus (Laniidæ* order *Passeres).*

මහ කවුඩුදල, *Maha-kawuḍudala*, *s.* plant, *oldenlandia (or hedyotis) stricta.*

මහ කහඹිලියා, *Maha-kahambiliyá*, *s.* kind of nettle, species of *fleurya* or *girardinia*: see ගස් *gas-* and වල් කහඹිලියා *wal-kahambiliyá.*

මහ කළුවාල, *Maha-kaḷuwála*, *s.* variety of plant called great galanga, *alpinia galanga.*

මහ කිඹු, *Maha-kimbu*, *s.* plant, *cotula bicolor.*

මහ කිරිඳි, *Maha-kirindi*, *s.* plant, variety of *rourea santaloides.*

මහ කිරියල් වී, *Maha-kiriyal-ví*, *s.* kind of paddy, *oryza sativa.*

මහ කිරිවැල්, *Maha-kiriwęl*, *s.* climbing plant, *morinda umbellata* or *m. scandens (Rubiaceæ);* also called කිරිවැල් *kiri-węl.*

මහ කිහිඹිය, *Maha-kihimbiya*, *s.* plant, *micania volubilis.*

මහ කුකුරුමාන්, *Maha-kukurumán*, *s.* thorny shrub, variety of *randia dumetarum.*

මහ කුඩුමැට්ට, *Maha-kuḍumętta*, *s.* plant, *ischæmum barbatum:* see හින් කුඩුමැට්ට *hín-kuḍumętta.*

මහ කූඩළු, *Maha-kúḍaḷu*, *s.* plant, species of *impatiens* or *hydrocera.*

මහ කූරපලා, *Maha-kúrapalá*, *s.* plant, *amaranthus polygonoides*, [Coll: කූරතම්පලා *kúratampalá*].

මහකූරුවී, *Maha-kúru-ví*, *s.* kind of paddy, *oryza sativa.*

මහ කෙටලඅල, *Maha-keṭala-ala*, *s.* plant, variety of *lagenandra toxicaria.*

මහකේතල, *Maha-kétala*, *s.* plant, *caladium ovatum.*

මහ කොක්මොට, *Maha-kokmoṭa*, *s.* plant, variety of *eriocaulon quinquangulare.*

මහ කොහිල, *Maha-kohila*, *s.* thorny plant, *Lasia spinosa (Araceæ);* also called කොහිල *kohila.*

මහ කැබෙල්ල, *Maha-kębella*, *s.* plant, species of *aporosa* or *agyreia obliqua.*

මහකැරැව්, *Maha-kęręw*. *s.* plant, *schleria elata (Cyperaceæ).*

මහ ගම, *Maha-gama*, *s.* (මහ large, ගම village) large village.

මහ ගල්කප්පරවල්ලිය, *Maha-galkapparawalliya*, *s.* catmint, variety of *anisochilus carnosus* or *nepeta indica.*

මහ ගල්කූර, *Maha-galkúra*, *s.* plant, *melochia concatenata.*

මහගහල, *Maha-gahala*, *s.* plant, variety of *colocasia antiquorum.*

මහ ගිම්, *Maha-gim*, *s.* (මහ great, ගිම් warmth) heat; sultry weather.

මහ ගිරාපලා, *Maha-girápalá*, *s.* plant, variety of *commelina clavata.*

මහ ගෙරිඇට, *Maha-gerieṭa*, *s.* variety of tree peculiar to Ceylon, *linociera purpurea.*

මහ ගොකටු, *Maha-gokaṭu*, *s.* tree, species of *garcinia.*

මහ ගොටුකොළ, *Maha-goṭukola*, *s.* creeping plant, pennywort, *hydrocotyle javanica (Umbelliferæ).*

මහ ගොන්කැකිරි, *Maha-gonkękiri*, *s.* kind of cucumber, large variety of the *cucumis pubescens.*

මහ ගොයිවැල්, *Maha-goyiwęl*, *s.* plant, *flagellaria indica:* see ගොයිවැල් *goyi-węl.*

මහ ගොරඩිය, *Maha-goraḍiya*, *s.* plant, *cylista esculenta.*

මහ ගැටකුළු, *Maha-gęṭakuḷu*, *s.* plant, *gardenia fragrans.*

මහ ගැටපන්, *Maha-gęṭapan*, *s.* club rush, *scirpus articulatus (Cyperaceæ).*

මහගැටියා, *Maha-gęṭiyá*, *s.* plant, *hugonia mystax (Linaceæ);* also called බූගැටියා *búgęṭiyá.*

මහගු, *Mahagu*, *a.* very precious, [Colloq. අනර්ඝ *anargha*].

මහච්ඡද, *Mahacchhada*, *s.* tree, *alstonia scholaris*, the wood of which is very light and porous and much used in making the images of Buddha, [Colloq. රුක්අත්තන *rukattana*].

මහජනයා, *Maha-janayá*, *s.* (මහ great, ජනයා men) the public, multitude, crowd, collection of people.

මහ ඩෙබර, *Maha-ḍebara*, *s.* jujube tree yielding good dessert fruit, *zizyphus jujuba (Rhamnaceæ);* also called මසං *masaṇ.*

මහණ, *Mahaṇa*, *s.* (formed from ශ්‍රමණ *sramaṇa* by interchanging the two first letters, dropping the semivowel ර *ra*, and substituting හ *ha* for the sibilant) Buddhist priest, religious ascetic.

මහණවෙනවා, *Makaṇawenawá*, *v.* to become a Buddhist priest.

මහණුන්නාන්සේ, *Mahaṇunnánsé*, *s.* Buddhist priest.

මහත්, *Mahat*, *a.* (මහ *maha* to increase) large, great, bulky; best, excellent, illustrious.

මහත්කරණවා, *Mahatkaraṇawá*, *v.* to expand, to enlarge.

මහත්ත්ව, *Mahattwa*, *s.* (මහත් great, ත්ව, aff. of the abstract quality) greatness, either in bulk or rank.

මහත්මයා, *Mahatmayá*, *s.* (මහ and ආත්ම *átma* soul or mind, යා pers. aff.) one of great soul, the noble minded one, one who is magnanimous: term of respect, equivalent to the English Mr.

මහත්වෙනවා, *Mahatwenawá*, *v.* to become great: pret. මහත්වුනා *mahatwuná*.

මහත, *Mahata*, *s.* bulk, size, dimension, magnitude, greatness.

මහ තක්කඩ, *Maha-takkaḍa*, *s.* plant, variety of *scævola koenigii*: see තක්කඩ *takkaḍa* and හින් තක්කඩ *hín-takkaḍa*.

මහ තක්කඩියා, *Maha-takkḍiyá*, *s.* great vagabond.

මහ තරණ, *Maha-taraṇa*, *s.* plant, *webera corymbosa:* see තරණ *taraṇa*.

මහතා, *Mahatá*, *s.* (මහත් *mahat* great, ආ *á* aff.) chief, lord, great man, gentleman.

මහ තිඹිරි, *Maha-timbiri*, *s.* tree, variety of *diospyros embryopteris:* see තිඹිරි *timbiri*.

මහති, *Mahatí*, *s.* the Víṇá or Indian lute; egg plant, commonly called brinjal, *solanum melongena*, [Colloq. වම්බටු *wambaṭu*].

මහතුන්, *Mahatun*, *plur.* of මහතා *mahatá*, applied to persons of respectability.

මහ තුඹ, *Maha-tumba*, *s.* plant, *borago zeylanica.*

මහ තුඹිලය, *Maha-tumbilaya*, *s.* species of jambu, *eugenia zeylanica:* see මරන්ද *maranda*.

මහතෙර, *Maha-tera*, *s.* (මහ and තෙර priest) chief priest or priest of rank.

මහ තෙලඹු, *Maha-telambu*, *s.* silk cotton tree, *eriodendron anfractuosum*, [Colloq. ඉඹුල් *imbul*]; tree, variety of *sterculia fœtida*.

මහ තෙලිකාපලා, *Maha-teliká-palá*, *s.* pellitary, *parietaria indica.*

මහ තොලබෝ, *Maha-tolabó*, *s.* plant, variety of *crinum asiaticum:* see තොලබෝ *tolabó*.

මහ තෝවැල්ල, *Maha-tówella*, *s.* climbing plant, variety of *vitis erioclada*.

මහ තැඹිලිය, *Maha-tembiliya*, *s.* tree, variety of *eugenia bracteata*.

මහදං, *Maha-daṅ*, *s.* tree with panicles of small white flowers, *eugenia (or syzygium) jambolana (Myrtaceæ)*.

මහ දඩකලත්, *Maha-daḍakalat*, *s.* large kind of gram, Bengal gram.

මහ දඩකිරිය, *Maha-daḍakiriya*, *s.* plant, species of *euphorbia*.

මහ දඹ, *Maha-damba*, *s.* large kind of jambu, *eugenia* or Malay apple.

මහ දුරකෙසෙල්, *Maha-dárakesel*, *s.* kind of plantain, variety of *musa sapientum*.

මහ දියජාවාල, *Maha-diya-jáwála*, *s.* plant, variety of *burmannia disticha*, [Colloq. මැඩියජාවාල *meḍiya-jáwála*].

මහ දියදූල්, *Maha-diyadúl*, *s.* nettle, *Boehmeria malabarica (Urticaceæ)*.

මහ දියසියඹලා, *Maha-diyasiyambalá*, *s.* floating spongy plant, *æschynomene aspera (Leguminosæ)*.

මහදිව්, *Mahadiw*, *s.* any one of the four continents which are situated in front of the four faces of මේරු *méru*.

මහ දිවිඅඩිය, *Maha-diviaḍiya*, *s.* plant, variety of *ipomæa pes-tigridis*.

මහ දුම්මැල්ල, *Maha-dummella*, *s.* plant, variety of the snake gourd, *trichosanthes anguina*, [Colloq. පතෝල *patóla*].

මහ දුමුදු, *Maha-dumudu*, *s.* plant, *argyreia speciosa (Convolvulaceæ)*.

මහදෙවි, *Maha-devi*, *s.* (මහ great, දෙවි god) name of Ṣiva; Elu form of මහාදේව *mahá-déwa*.

මහ දොඩන්පනා, *Maha-doḍanpaná*, *s.* tree, *glycosmis longifolia*.

මහදොඹ, *Maha-domba*, see දොඹ *domba*.

මහදොර, *Maha-dora*, *s.* palace, residence of a king.

මහන්තත්වය, *Mahantatwaya*, *s.* (මහන්ත great, ත්ව *twa* aff. of the abstract) glory, power, dignity, honour, greatness, magnificence, grandure.

මහන්නා, *Mahanná*. *s.* tailor: pl. මහන්නෝ *mahannó*.

මහන්සිය, *Mahansiya*, *s.* wages for labour, short breath, weariness.

මහන්සිවෙනවා, *Mahansiwenawá*, *v.* to become tired.

මහනවා, *Mahanawá*, *v.* to sew, to stitch: pret. මැහුවා *mẹhuwá*.

මහ නහර, *Maha-nahara*, *s.* (මහ great, නහර tendon) nerve described as a hollow tube resembling a string, attached to the bones and supposed to be the passage for the vital air.

මහ නාපිරිත්ත, *Maha-nápiritta*, *s.* plant, *hibiscus surrattensis:* see හින්නාපිරිත්ත *hín-nápiritta*.

මහ නාරන්, *Maha-náran*, *s.* shaddock or pumelow tree, *citrus decumana*.

මහනිදිකුම්බ, *Maha-nidikumba*, *s.* species of the sensitive plant, *mimosa pudica*.

මහනියද, *Maha-niyanda*, *s.* plant, from the fibres of which bow strings are made, *sanseviera zeylanica:* see නියද *niyanda*.

මහ නිල්, *Maha-nil*, *s.* (මහ and නිල් blue) sapphire.

මහ නිලගොයා, *Maha-nílagoyá*, *s.* Imperial green pigeon, *carpophaga ænea*, (*Treronidæ*, order *Columbæ*); also called බටගොයා *batagoyá*.

මහ නුග, *Maha-nuga*, *s.* banyan tree, *ficus bengalensis* (*Urticaceæ*).

මහනෙල්, *Mahanel*, *s.* blue lotus, water lily: see මානෙල් *mánel*.

මහ නෙළු, *Maha-neḷu*, *s.* road side with red flowers in threes, see නෙළු *neḷu;* trees of genus, *strobelanthes*; plant, *justicia bycalyculata*.

මහප්පා, *Mahappá*, *s.* (මහ great, අප්පා *appá* father) uncle, father's elder brother.

මහපට ඇඟිල්ල, *Mahapaṭa-ẹngilla*, *s.* thumb or the great toe.

මහ පනාදූත්ත, *Maha-panádẹtta*, *s.* club moss, *lycopodium caniculatum*.

මහ පඹ, *Maha-pamba*, *s.* fern, *lygodium scandens* (*Filices*).

මහ පරාටියා, *Maha-paráṭiyá*, *s.* kind of sea fish.

මහපාය, *Mahapáya*, *s.* large palace.

මහපාර, *Mahapára*, *s.* main road.

මහ පිනිබරුතණ, *Maha-pinibaru-taṇa*, *s.* kind of grass, variety of *anthistiria tremula*.

මහපියුම්, *Mahapiyum*, *s.* lotus, species of *nymphæa* or *nelumbium*.

මහ පිළිහුඩුවා, *Maha-piḷihuḍuwá*, *s.* Indian stork-billed kingfisher, *pelargopsis gurial* (*Halcyoninæ* order *Psittaci*); also called වතුරනුවා *waturanuwá*.

මහ පුස්වැල, *Maha-puswẹla*, *s.* climbing plant, variety of *entada scandens:* see පුස්වැල *puswẹla*.

මහ පොතුපන්, *Maha-potupan*, *s.* plant, *scleria latifolia:* see පොතුපන් *potupan*.

මහපොළව, *Maha-polawa*, *s.* the earth.

මහබටු, *Maha-baṭu*, see බටු *baṭu*.

මහ බදුල්ල, *Maha-badulla*, *s.* tree, peculiar to Ceylon, *semicarpus subpeltata* (*Anacardiaceæ*).

මහබඹ, *Mahabamba*, see බ්‍රහ්ම *brahma*.

මහබඹර, *Maha-bambara*, see බඹර *bambara*.

මහ බළුදන්, *Maha-baḷudan*, see බළුදන් *baḷudan*.

මහ බින්තල්, *Maha-bintal*, *s.* plant, *cucurligo Finlaysonia:* see මාබින්තල් *má-bintal*.

මහ බින්පොල්, *Maha-binpol*, *s.* plant, variety of *tricopus zeylanicus*.

මහ බින්සියඹලා, *Maha-binsiyambalá*, *s.* plant, variety of *cassia Klenii*.

මහබුරුද, *Maha-buruda*, *s.* creeping plant, *marsilea quadrifolia*, [Colloq. දිය ඇඹුල් ඇඹිලිය *diya-ẹmbul-ẹmbiliya*].

මහ බුළුමොර, *Maha-buḷumora*, *s.* tree yielding resinous gum, peculiar to Ceylon, *Canarium zeylanicum* (*Burseraceæ*).

මහ බූගැටකොල, *Maha-búgẹṭakola*, *s.* plant, variety of *hedyotis auricularias:* see ගැටකොල *gẹṭakola*.

මහ බේරු, *Maha-béru*, *s.* plant, peculiar to Ceylon, *agrostistachys Hookeri* (*Euphorbiaceæ*); also called දියබේරු *diya-béru*.

මහ බොරුපන්, *Maha-borupan*, *s.* club-rush, variety of *heleocaris plantaginea*.

මහබෝ, *Maha-bó*, see බෝගහ *bó-gaha*.

මහ බෝවිටියා, *Maha-bóviṭiyá*, *s.* plant with handsome purplish flowers, *melastoma malabathricum* (*Melastomaceæ*).

මහ බැලිල, *Maha-bẹlila*, see බැවිල *bẹvila*.

මහභාරත, *Maha-bhárata*, *s.* (මහ great, භාරත poem so called) name of the great epic poem so much celebrated among the Hindus, so called in allusion to the fable of the ṛishis putting it in a scale and weighing it against the four Védas, when it was found to outweigh them.

මහම්මා, *Mahammá*, *s.* (මහ and අම්මා *ammá* mother) aunt, mother's elder sister, father's elder brother's wife.

මහ මකුළු, *Maha-makuḷu*, see මකුළු *makuḷu*.

මහ මඩු, *Maha-madu*, *s.* sort of bind-weed, *Ipomœa obscura* (*Convolvulaceæ*).

මහමායා, *Mahamáyá*, *s.* (මහ great, මායා Máyá) mother of Buddha: see මායා *máyá*.

මහමායා තෙනේ, *Mahamáyá-tené*, *s.* (මහමායා and තෙනේ son) name of Buddha as the son of මායා; which see, [Colloq. බුදුන් *budun*].

මහමාවත, *Mahamáwata*, see මහපාර *mahapára*.

මහ මාවී, *Maha-máví*, *s.* (මහ and මාවී paddy) large kind of paddy or rice in the husk, variety of *oryza sativa*: see වී *ví*.

මහ මිදි, *Maha-midi*, *s.* small tree, *premna latifolia (Verbenaceæ)*.

මහ මුඩමහන, *Maha-muḍamahana*, *s.* plant with small white flowers growing in watery places, *sphenoclea zeylanica*.

මහ මුත්තෑස්වී, *Maha-muttęs-ví*, *s.* kind of paddy, *oryza sativa*.

මහ මුහුද, *Maha-muhuda*, *s.* (මහ and මුහුද sea) sea, ocean; that part of the ocean distant from land.

මහමෙර, *Mahamera*, *s.* fabulous mountain round which the sun is supposed to revolve, and on the summit of which the heaven of Indra is situated: see මේරු *méru*.

මහමේවන්, *Mahaméwan*, *s.* fragrant grass, *cyperus rotundus*, [Colloq. කලාඳුරු *kalánduru*].

මහමොට්ටු, *Maha-moṭṭu*, *s.* winter cherry, variety of *physalis angulata*: see මොට්ටු *moṭṭu*.

මහ මොණරකුඩිම්බිය, *Maha-moṇarakuḍimbiya*, *s.* plant, variety of *vernonia cinerea*.

මහ මැඩහඟු, *Maha-męḍahangu*, see මැඩහඟු *męḍa-hangu*.

මහමැඩිල්ල, *Maha-męḍilla*, *s.* plant, not ascertained.

මහ යක්මල්, *Maha-yakmal*, *s.* flower tree, *tajetes erecta*.

මහ යක්වනස්ස, *Maha-yakwanassa*, *s.* plant, *leonotis nepetifolia (Labiatæ)*.

මහ යොතුවැන්න, *Maha-yotuwęnna*, *s.* the violet, *viola suffcuticosa*.

මහරජ, *Maha-raja*, *s.* (මහ and රජ king) sovereign, emperor.

මහරජත, *Maharajata*, *s.* (මහ and රජත silver) gold, [Colloq. රත්රන් *ratran*].

මහ රට, *Maha-raṭa*, see මහාරාෂ්ට්‍ර *mahárâshṭra*.

මහ රටඅසමෝදගම්, *Maha-raṭa-asamódagam*, *s.* plant, celery, *apium graveolens*.

මහ රටතාමට්ටි, *Maha-raṭatámaṭṭi*, *s.* species of night shade, *solanum copersicum*.

මහ රටදෙහි, *Maha-raṭadehi*, *s.* species of citron, *citrus medica*.

මහ රටබටු, *Maha-raṭabaṭu*, see මහ රටතාමට්ටි *maha-raṭatámaṭṭi*.

මහ රත්මල්, *Maha-ratmal*, *s.* shrub, *rhododendron arboreum*: see මාරත්මල් *má-ratmal*.

මහ රතඹලා, *Maha-ratambalá*, *s.* small tree, *ixora parviflora (Rubiaceæ)*.

මහ රවනරැවුල, *Maha-rawana-ręwula*, *s.* plant, *spinifex sqarrosus (Gramineæ)*.

මහරහත්, *Maha-rahat*, *s.* one of the chiefs of the rahats: see රහත් *rahat*.

මහරි, *Mahari*, } *s.* shrub, *adenanthera*
මහරිරුක, *Mahari-ruka*, } *pavonina*, bearing a red berry, used as a jeweller's weight, averaging one and 5–16 grs. troy, [Colloq. මදටිය *madaṭiya*]; tree, *albizzia Lebbek*; *a. odoratissima*, [Colloq. මාරා *márá* and සූරියමාරා *súriya-márá*].

මහරු, *Maharu*, *a.* good, best, excellent; precious, [Colloq. යහපත් *yahapat*, අගේ ඇති *agé-ęti*].

මහරුක්, *Maharuk*, *s.* (මහ eminent, රුක් tree) coconut tree, [Colloq. පොල්ගහ *pol-gaha*].

මහරෑ, *Maharé*, *s.* (මහ great, රෑ night) midnight.

මහල්, *Mahal*, see මහල *mahala*.

මහල්තලය, *Mahaltalaya*, *s.* garret, upstair room.

මහල්ලා, *Mahallá*, *s.* old man, man advanced in years: pl. මහල්ලෝ *mahalló*.

මහල, *Mahala*, } *s.* palace, mansion, [Colloq.
මහලය, *Mahalaya*, } මාලිගාව *máligáwa*]; upper room, inner apartment; pillow, bolster; archer, bowman.

මහලෙඩ, *Maha-leḍa*, *s.* (මහ and ලෙඩ disease) small-pox.

මහලේ, *Mahalé*, } *s.* menses; bloody
මහලේරෝගය, *Mahalé-rógaya*, } flux: see කිලිමාලේ *kilimálé*.

මහවග, *Mahawaga*, *s.* class of books so called, the fourth of the grand divisions of Vinaya the third of the three Piṭakas: see පිටක *piṭaka*.

මහ වටුවා, *Maha-waṭuwá*, *s.* bird called common red shank, *totarns calidris (Scolopacidæ*, order *Grallæ)*.

මහවත්, *Mahawat*, *s.* (මහ great, වත් face) an owl, [Colloq. බස්සා *bassá*, බකමූනා *bakamúná*]: see the next.

මහවත, *Mahawata*, *s.* main road, high way; also written මාවත *máwata*.

මහ වඳුරා, *Maha-wanḍurá*, *s.* large grey monkey with black face and white beard *presbytes ursinus*.

මහ වනස්ස, *Maha-wanassa*, *s.* plant, variety of *lycopodium cernuum*.

මහ වල්කොල්ලු, *Maha-walkollu*, *s.* plant, variety of *atylosia rugosa*.

මහවාසල, *Mahawásala*, *s.* (මහ great, වාසල gate) king's audience chamber, which is generally at the entrance of the royal residence or palace; king.

මහවිලගොයා, *Mahavilagoyá*, *s.* Ceylon wood pigeon, *palumbus Torringtonia (Columbæ).*

මහ වී, *Maha-ví*, *s.* (මහ and වී paddy) large sort of paddy, *oryza sativa*: see වී *ví.*

මහවීථිය, *Maha-víthiya*, *s.* main street.

මහවෙලඟ, *Mahawelanga*, *s.* tree, variety of *pterospermum suberifolium:* see වෙලඟ *welanga.*

මහවේ, *Mahawé*, *s.* high road, main way.

මහ වේවැල, *Maha-wéwela*, *s. calamus rudentum;* also called මාවේවැල *máwéwela* and තුඩරණ වේවැල *tudarana-wéwela.*

මහ වැටකොළු, *Maha-wetakolu*, *s.* creeping plant, bearing a kind of pumpkin, variety of *luffa acutangula.*

මහසංඝයා, *Mahasanghayá*, see the following.

මහසඟ, *Mahasanga*, *s.* (මහ illustrious, සඟ company) assembly of the priests of Buddha; association of priests, possessing the power to control and direct the affairs of the priesthood.

මහසත්, *Mahasat*, see බෝධිසත්ව *bódhisatwa.*

මහසල්, *Mahasal*, *s.* (මහ great, සල් house or sal tree) palace, mansion, residence of a nobleman; name of a tree, *vateria acuminata* or *v. indica:* හල් *hal.*

මහ සාරණ, *Maha-sárana*, *s.* plant, *trianthema decandra (Ficoidæ).*

මහ සියඹලා, *Maha-siyambalá*, *s.* variety of the tamarind, or *tamarindus indica:* see සියඹලා *siyambalá.*

මහසුදන, *Mahasudana*, *s.* plant, species of everlasting, *gnaphalium indicum.*

මහසුන්, *Mahasun*, *s.* (මහ and අසුන් *asun* seat) chair of state, throne.

මහසුප්, *Mahasup*, see මහාකාශ්‍යප *Mahákásyapa.*

මහසෙන්, *Maha-sen*, *s.* (මහ and සෙන් army) name of Kataragama deviyó or Skanda kumára, alluding to his character as god of war, and leader of the celestial hosts.

මහසෙරු, *Mahaseru*, *s.* tree, *webera lanceolata.*

මහ හකඹලා, *Maha-hakambalá*, *s.* plant with pinkish fragrant flowers, *begonia malabarica (Begoniaceæ).*

මහ හබරොස්ස, *Maha-habarossa*, *s.* thorny plant, *similax ovalifolia, (Liliaceæ).*

මහ හවරි, *Maha-hawari*, *s.* plant, *ipomæa.*

මහ හිඹුටු, *Maha-himbutu*, *s.* creeper, *salacia diandra:* see හිඹුටුවැල් *himbutu-wel.*

මහ හෙරලිය, *Maha-heraliya*, *s.* plant, see ඇත් හෙරලිය *et-heraliya.*

මහහැඩයා, *Maha-hedayá*, *s.* club-moss, *lycopodium phlegmaria (Lycopodiaceæ).*

මහ හැඩවක, *Maha-hedawaka*, *s.* tree, variety of *chætocarpus castanocarpus.*

මහළු, *Mahalu*, *s.* curry or compound of various species: *a.* old, aged, advanced in years.

මහා, *Mahá*, *a.* great, large; best, excellent.

මහාකණ්හ, *Mahákanha*, *s.* (මහා great, කණ්හ blackness, crime) name of a Játaka (or birth-story) of Gautama, in the character of Bódhisat and under the form of Indra; so called from the universal depravity which prevailed during that incarnation.

මහා කන්ද, *Mahá-kanda*, *s.* (මහා great, කන්ද root) red onion, *allium cepa*, [Colloq. රතු ලූනු *ratu-lúnu*]; very large esculent root, sort of yam; hairy plant growing in moist places with composite flowers, *hingtsha repens;* garlic, *allium sativum*, [Colloq. සුදුලූනු *sudu-lúnu*].

මහාකපිත්ථ, *Mahákapittha*, *s.* (මහා and කපිත්ථ wood apple) tree, *ægle marmelos*, [Colloq. බෙලි *beli*].

මහා කහඹිලිය, *Maha-kasámbiliya*, *s.* large species of *fleurya* or *girardinia:* see වල් *wal* and ගස් කහඹිලියා *gas-kahambiliyá.*

මහාකාල, *Mahákála*, *s.* (මහා excessively, කාල black) a form of Şiva in his character of the destroyer, being then represented of a black colour and terrific aspect; name of Nandi, the door keeper and attendant of Şiva.

මහාකාශ්‍යප, *Mahákásyapa*, *s.* name of a famous disciple of Buddha.

මහාගුල්ම, *Mahágulma*, *s.* disease, chronic enlargement of the spleen, or induration of the mesenteric gland so as to be perceived externally; creeping plant, *sarcostemma brunonianum*, [Coll: මුවකිරියවැල් *muwakiriya-wel*].

මහාගෝවින්ද, *Mahágóvinda*, *s.* (මහා great, ගෝවින්ද Vishnu) name of Vishnu or Krishna.

මහාග්‍රීව, *Mahágriwa*, *s.* (මහා and ග්‍රීව neck) camel, [Colloq. ඔටුවා *otuwá*].

මහාජම්බු, *Mahájambu*, *s.* (මහා and ජම්බු rose apple) large species of *eugenia* or *jambosa vulgaris*, [Colloq. මාදං *mádan*].

මහාජන, *Mahájana*, s. (මහා and ජන man) multitude, man collectively; illustrious man; merchant.

මහාදරු, *Mahádáru*, s. (මහා and දරු wood) sort of pine, *pinus dévadáru*.

මහාදුරාලභා, *Mahádurálabhá*, s. large species of *fleurya* or *girardinia*: see මහ කහඹිලියා *maha-kahambiliyá*.

මහාදේව, *Mahádéva*, s. (මහා and දේව god) name of Śiva.

මහාදේවී, *Mahádévi*, s. (මහාදේව *mahádéva* Śiva, ඊ *í* fem. aff.) Durgá the wife of Śiva.

මහාද්‍රුම, *Mahádruma*, s. (මහා and ද්‍රුම tree) bó tree, *ficus religiosa*, [Colloq. බෝගහ *bó-gaha*].

මහාධන, *Mahádhana*, s. (මහා and ධන wealth) any thing costly or precious; gold; incense; costly raiment: *a*. rich, opulent; costly.

මහානයා, *Mahá-nayá*, s. variety of cobra, *nága tripudians*.

මහානිම්බ, *Mahánimba*, s. (මහා and නිම්බ nimba) large kind of nimba tree, *azadirachta indica*, [Colloq. කොහොඹ *kohomba*]; *oroxylum indicum* [Colloq. තොටිල *totila*].

මහානීල, *Mahánila*, s. (මහා and නීල blue) emerald, [Colloq. පච්චගල *pachcha-gala*]; plant, native of uncultivated places with straggling stem, *verbesina scandens*; medicinal plant, *eclipta erecta*, [Colloq. කිකිරිඳිය *kikirindiya*].

මහානුභාව, *Mahánubháwa*, s. (මහා and අනුභාව *anubháwa* dignity or disposition) power, authority: *a*. magnanimous, liberal.

මහාපත්‍ර, *Mahápatra*, s. (මහා and පත්‍ර leaf) pot herb.

මහාපත්‍රා, *Mahápatrá*, s. tree, kind of *eugenia*.

මහාපථ, *Mahápatha*, s. (මහා great, පථ path) principal path or entrance to a town or house, etc.; main road, high way; end of life, way of all flesh.

මහාපථගම, *Mahápatha-gama*, s. (මහා and පථ way, ගම going) death, dying, [Colloq. මරණය *maranaya*].

මහාපුරුෂ, *Mahá-purusha*, s. (මහා and පුරුෂ man) name of Buddha, alluding to his height, which is said to have been four of his own cubits, measured from the tip of his middle finger to his elbow, and equal to twelve cubits of common measure; besides which, a Kétu or flame of glory emanated from his head to the height of six cubits, which is also reckoned, making him eighteen cubits high; great man.

මහාපුෂ්පා, *Mahá-pushpá*, s. (මහා and පුෂ්ප *pushpa* flower) flowering plant, *clitoria ternatea*, [Colloq. නිල් කටරොළු *nil-kataroḷu*].

මහාප්‍රලය, *Mahá-pralaya*, s. (මහා great, ප්‍රලය destruction) destruction of the world; annihilation of the universe, including every class of beings, both gods and men; according to the mythology of the Hindus, a destruction of the world takes place at the expiration of each day of Brahma, or 4,320,000,000 years; he then reposes a night, which is a period of the same duration; at the expiration of 100 of his years, himself with the whole universe, is annihilated.

මහාපෘථිවිය, *Mahá-prithiviya*, s. earth, world.

මහාඵල, *Mahá-phala*, s. (මහා and ඵල fruit) fruit tree, *ægle marmelos*, [Colloq. බෙලි *beli*]; also, *eugenia jambolana*, [Colloq. මාදං *mádan*]; coconut, [Colloq. පොල් *pol*].

මහාඵලා, *Mahaphalá*, s. brinjal or egg plant, *solanum melongena*, [Colloquial. වම්බටු *wambatu*]; ash-pumpkin, *luffa benincasa cerifera*, [Colloq. පුහුල් *puhul*]; bitter gourd, [Colloq. කැකිරි *kekiri*].

මහාබල, *Mahábala*, s. (මහා and බල strength) name of Buddha; see දසබල *dasabala*: lead; air, wind: *a*. strong, robust, powerful.

මහාබලා, *Mahábalá*, s. plant with yellow flowers, *sida rhombifolia*, [Colloq. කොටිකංබෑවිල *koti-kan-bevila*]: see මහබල *mahabala*.

මහාබ්‍රහ්ම, *Mahábrahma*, s. (මහා great, illustrious, බ්‍රහ්ම Brahma) name of Brahma, as the supreme god; the epithet mahá is frequently prefixed to proper names as an appellation to designate the chief of a class.

මහාභද්‍ර, *Mahábhadra*. s. (මහා much, භද්‍ර auspicious) name of a Kalpa; see භද්‍රකල්ප *bhadra-kalpa*: *a*. happy, fortunate.

මහාභද්‍රකල්පය, *Mahábhadra-kalpaya*, see භද්‍රකල්ප *bhadra-kalpa*.

මහාභද්‍රා, *Mahábhadrá*, s. name of the river Ganges.

මහාභිඥා, *Mahábhijñá*, see අභිඥා *abhijñá*.

මහාභිනිෂ්ක්‍රමණ, *Mahábhinishkramana*, s. (මහා great, අභි *abhi* emphatic, නිෂ්ක්‍රමණ departure) forsaking the world, sacrificing every earthly pleasure and comfort, the means used to destroy the sensual passions; it is applied particularly to Buddha: see නෛෂ්ක්‍රම්‍ය *naishkramya* and පාරමිතාව *páramitáwa*.

මහාභූත, *Mahá-bhúta*, s. (මහා principal, භූත element) primary element, as air, fire, water, earth, and ákása or ether.

මහාභෝග, *Mahábhóga*, s. great wealth, abundance of riches.

මහාමල්ලි, *Mahámallí*, s. (මහා great, මල්ලි jasmine) variety of Arabian jasmine, *jasminum sambac*, [Colloq. පිච්ච *pichcha*].

මහාමාෂ, *Mahámásha*, }
මහාමාස, *Mahámása*, } s. (මහා and මාෂ or මාස grain) kidney bean or green gram, *phaseolus mungo radiatus*; red gram, *dolichos catjang* or *phaseolus erectus*.

මහාමුඛ, *Mahá-mukha*, s. (මහා and මුඛ mouth) crocodile, alligator, *crocodilus palustris* or *c. porosus*, [Colloq. කිඹුලා *kimbulá*].

මහාමුනි, *Mahámuni*, s. (මහා and මුනි saint) name of Buddha; name of the saint Agastya; coriander.

මහාමෛත්‍රි, *Mahá-maitrí*, s. (මහා and මෛත්‍රි friendliness or benevolence) name of Buddha.

මහාමෘග, *Mahá-mriga*, s. (මහා and මෘග animal) elephant, [Colloq. අලියා *aliyá*].

මහායුග, *Maháyuga*, s. (මහා and යුග age) a great yuga, aggregate of the four ages, or a period of 4,320,000 years.

මහාර්ඝ, *Mahárgha*, a. (මහා and අර්ඝ *argha* cost) costly, precious, of great value.

මහාරජත, *Mahárajata*, s. (මහා and රජත silver) gold, [Colloq. රත්රන් *ratran*).

මහාරජන, *Mahárajana*, s. gold; safflower, [Colloq. වනුප් *wanup*].

මහාරස, *Mahárasa*, s. (මහා great, රස juice) date tree, *phœnix sylvestris*, [Colloq. ඉඳි *indi*]; species of club rush, *scirpus kysoor*; gruel, made from the fermentation of rice water; sugar cane, [Colloq. උක්ගස් *uk-gas*].

මහාරාජ, *Mahárája*, s. (මහා and රාජ king) emperor, sovereign.

මහාරාත්‍රි, *Mahárátra*, s. (මහා and රාත්‍රි night) midnight.

මහාරාෂ්ට්‍ර, *Maháráshṭra*, s. (මහා and රාෂ්ට්‍ර country) country, usually called Mahratta; although this country is distinctly noted in ancient geographical works, it has not been minutely defined by the modern writers of India; the Buddhist authorities place it in the western and north western parts of Jambudvípa, and bound it on the north by Guzarat, and the Nerbudda river.

මහාලය, *Mahálaya*, s. (මහා and ආලය *álaya* asylum) place of refuge, asylum, sanctuary; temple: according to the Brahminical system, God, the Supreme Being; place of pilgrimage; tree etc., sacred to a deity; the lóka or world of Brahma.

මහාවංශ, *Mahávaṇsa*, s. (මහා and වංශ race, lineage) high rank, race of nobility; celebrated historical work, giving the chronology and dynasties of the kings of Lanká.

මහාවාර්තාකිනී, *Mahávártákiní*, s. brinjal, *solanum melongena*, [Colloq. වම්බටු *wambaṭu*].

මහාවිල, *Mahávila*, s. (මහා great, විල chasm) sky, atmosphere; cave, hole.

මහාවිෂුව, *Mahávishuwa*, s. (මහා and විෂුව equinox) the sankránti or moment of the sun's entering Aries; vernal equinox, but varying several days from the European computation.

මහාවිස්තාර, *Mahá-vistra*, s. (මහා great or much, විස්තර spreading) extreme prolixity, great extention or diffusion.

මහාවීර්‍ය, *Mahávírya*, s. (මහා great, වීර්‍ය exertion) name of Brahma; strenuous or continued endeavour, fortitude, firmness, resolute determination; quicksilver, [Colloq. රසදිය *rahadiya*].

මහාවීර්‍යා, *Mahávíryá*, s. name of Sajñá wife of the sun; wild cotton.

මහාවීර, *Mahá-víra*, s. (මහා and වීර hero) name of Bódhisat, alluding to his performing the Páramitáwas with a view to acquiring the Buddhaship: see පාරමිතාව *páramitáwa*; hero; religious ascetic, one performing the Páramitáwas.

මහාවේග, *Mahávéga*, s. (මහා and වේග speed) monkey; rapidity, velocity.

මහාව්‍රතින්, *Mahávratin*, s. (මහා and ව්‍රත *vrata* religious penance or observance, ඉනි *ini* aff.) name of Ṣiva; devotee, ascetic.

මහාවෘක්ෂ, *Mahá-wriksha*, s. (මහා and වෘක්ෂ tree) name of several species of *euphorbia*, [Colloq. දළුක්ගස් *daluk-gas*].

මහාශ්‍යාමා, *Maháṣyámá*, s. (මහා great, ශ්‍යාම black) creeping hedge plant, *echites frutescens*.

මහාශ්වේතා, *Maháṣwétá*, s. (මහා much, ශ්වේත *ṣwéta* white) name of Saraswati; a white variety of the *ipomœa digitata* or *batatas paniculata*, [Colloq. කිරිබදු *kiribadu*]; clayed or candied sugar; sort of *clitoria* with white flowers.

මහාශ්‍රමණ, *Mahá-ṣramaṇa*, s. (මහා great, illustrious, ශ්‍රමණ Buddhist ascetic) appellation of Buddha, alluding to his being the chief of the Ṣramaṇas or religious ascetics.

මහාස්කන්ධ, *Maháskándha*, *s.* tree, *eugenia jambolana*, [Colloq. මහදං *mahadaṇ*]; camel.

මහාස්ථවිර, *Mahásthavira*, *s.* (මහා great, ස්ථවිර of long continuance) epithet applied to any of the elderly priests of Buddha.

මහාසම්මත, *Mahásammata*, *s.* (මහා great, universal, සම්මත consent, agreement) name of the first sovereign of the Súrya race, who according to Siṇhalese tradition was elected by the general consent of the people.

මහාසමුද්‍රය, *Mahásamudraya*, *s.* (මහා and සමුද්‍ර *samudra* sea) sea, ocean.

මහාසාර, *Mahására*, *s.* (මහා and සාර wealth) epithet used to express the wealth of the three highest castes of tha Hindus; the Mahására of the royal or military caste, at the lowest rate, is one hundred kóṭis of kaháрaṇas, which, if of gold, is equal, according to the ancient mode of reckoning, to about £ 1,181,200,000; the mahásárá of the sacerdotal order or caste is one half of the above, or £ 590,600,000; the mahásárá of the vellála or cultivator caste is one half of the last mentioned, or £ 295,300,000.

මහාසුගන්ධ, *Mahá-sugandha*, *s.* (මහා and සුගන්ධ perfume) sandal wood, *santalum album*, [Colloq. සඳුන් *saṇdun* or රත්කිහිරි *rat-kihiriya*].

මහාසෙන, *Mahásena*, *s.* (මහා and සෙන an army) name of Kártikéya, or Kataragama deviyó the Indian Mars; general, the commander of a large force.

මහි, *Mahi*, *s.* the earth.

මහිකා, *Mahiká*, *s.* fog, mist, vapour; frost.

මහිත, *Mahita*, *s.* (මහ *maha* to worship, ක්ත *kta* aff.) trident of Ṣiva: *a.* proper, fit, right; worshipped, reverenced.

මහිමතාව, *Mahimatáwa*, *s.* (මහිම greatness, තා *tá* aff. of the abstract) glory, greatness, majesty; magnificence, grandeur.

මහිමා, *Mahimá*, *s.* (මහත් *mahat* great, ඉමනිච් *imanich* aff.) magnitude, as one of Ṣiva's attributes, illimitability; greatness in general, literal or figurative.

මහියා, *Mahiyá*, *s.* the earth personified.

මහිර, *Mahira*, *s.* sun, [Colloq. ඉර *ira*].

මහිලා, *Mahilá*, *s.* woman; plant, bearing a fragrant seed, commonly, ප්‍රියඞ්ගු *priyaṅgu*, [Colloq. පුවඟු *puwangu*].

මහිලාවහයා, *Mahiláwhayá*, *s.* plant: see ප්‍රියඞ්ගු *priyaṅgu*.

මහිෂ, *Mahisha*, *s.* (මහ *maha* to worship or be worshipped) buffalo, *bubalus buffelus*, [Colloq. මීමා *mímá*]; emblem and vehicle of Yama; the name of an Asura or demon slain by Durgá.

මහිෂි, *Mahishí*, *s.* female buffalo, [Colloq. මීදෙන *mídena*]; wife of a king, but especially the one who has been consecrated or crowned, a queen.

මහිස, *Mahisa*,
මහිසා, *Mahisá*, } see මහිෂ *mahisha*.

මහිසුත, *Mahisuta*, *s.* (මහි earth, සුත son) the regent of the planet Mars, alluding to the fable that he sprang from the soil, near Oujein, which was sprinkled with the perspiration from Ṣiva's body.

මහී, *Mahí*, *s.* the earth, [Colloq. පොළව *poḷawa*]; black faced monkey, *presbytes cephalopterus*, [Colloq. වඳුරා *waṇdurá*]; river rising in the province of Malwa and falling into the gulf of Cambay; cow, [Colloq. එළදෙන *eladena*]; pot herb, *hingtsha repens*.

මහීකම්පා, *Mahíkampá*, *s.* (මහී and කම්පා trembling) earthquake.

මහීකාන්තාව, *Mahíkántáwa*, *s.* (මහී and කාන්තාව woman) female personification of the earth, called the protectress of the world from her affording corn etc. to mankind.

මහීගර්ජනාව, *Mahí-garjanáwa*, *s.* (මහී and ගර්ජනාව thunder) earthquake, subterraneous rumbling that accompanies the shock, [Colloq, භූමිකම්පාව *bhúmi-kampáwa*].

මහීතලය, *Mahítalaya*, *s.* (මහී and තල *tala* plane) the earth, surface of the earth, plane of the horizon.

මහීධර, *Mahídhara*, *s.* (මහී and ධර what upholds) mountain: name of Vishṇu in his character of preserver.

මහීධූම, *Mahí-dhuma*, *s.* (මහී and ධූම smoke) vapour, sultry vapour exhaled from the earth, [Colloq. මීදුම *míduma*].

මහීරුහ, *Mahíruha*, *s.* (මහී earth, රුහ to grow) tree or plant in general.

මහීලතා, *Mahí-latá*, *s.* earthworm.

මහීෂාක්ෂ, *Mahísháksha*, *s.* kind of gum, *bdellium*, [Colloq. ගුගුල් *gugul*].

මහීසුත, *Mahísuta*, see මහිසුත *mahisuta*.

මහෙච්ඡ, *Mahechchha*, *a.* (මහා *mahá* great, ඉච්ඡා *ichchhá* wish or design) liberal, magnanimous, high minded.

මහේන්ද්‍ර, *Mahéndra*, s. (මහා *mahá* chief, great, ඉන්ද්‍ර the deity) name of Indra the ruler of Swarga; one of the seven principal ranges of mountains in India, apparently the northern part of the Ghats of the peninsula.

මහේන්ද්‍රනගරී, *Mahéndra-nagarí*, s. (මහේන්ද්‍ර and නගරී city) Amarávati the capital of Indra.

මහේශ්වර, *Mahéṣwara*, } s. (මහා *mahá* great, ඊශ *íṣa* lord, or god) appellation of Ṣiva.
මහේශ, *Mahéṣa*,

මහේසි, *Mahési*, s. (මහා *mahá* and ඉසි *isi* ṛishi) name of Buddha.

මහේසිකාව, *Mahésikáwa*, s. (මහිෂී *mahishí* queen etc.)queen that has been anointed or crowned, empress.

මහෞඝය, *Mahóghaya*, s. (මහා *mahá* great, ඕඝ *ógha* flood) overwhelming torrent, rushing great stream, deluge.

මහෝත්තම, *Mahóttama*, a. (මහා *mahá* and උත්තම chief) very high or great; one of the highest terms of address, used only in addressing God and kings or governors.

මහෝත්පල, *Mahótpala*, s. (මහා *mahá* and උත්පල *utpala* lotus) lotus, *nelumbium speciosum*, [Coll: නෙළුම් *neḷum*].

මහෝදධි, *Mahódadhi*, s. (මහා *mahá* and උදධි *udadhi* sea) ocean; name of Indra.

මහෝදය, *Mahódaya*, s. (මහා *mahá* and උදය *udaya* rising, splendour) final beatitude, emancipation from vitality or the attainment of Nirváṇa; abandoning, relinquishment.

මහෝරග, *Mahóraga*, s. (මහා *mahá* and උරග snake) sort of demigod of the serpent genus, and forming one of the classes inhabiting Pátála; the root of a plant: see තගර *tagara*.

මහෝසධ, *Mahósadha*, s. dry ginger, Páli form of the next.

මහෞෂධ, *Mahaushadha*, s. (මහා *mahá* great, ඖෂධ *aushadha* drug) garlic, [Colloq. සුදුළූනු *sudulúnu*]; plant, *betula;* long pepper, [Colloq. තිප්පිලි *tippili*]; dry ginger, [Colloq. වෙලිච්ච ඉඟුරු *wélichcha-inguru*]; pot herb, *hingtsha repens;* it is also applicable to many other plants and medicinal substances.

මළකඳ, *Maḷakanda*, s. (මළ dead, කඳ trunk) corpse, dead body.

මළකුණ, *Maḷakuṇa*, s. carcase: pl. මළකුණු *maḷakuṇu*.

මළදඬු, *Maḷadaṇḍu*, s. (මළ dead, දඬු wood) rotten or decayed wood, fire wood; snake, serpent.

මළපලාව, *Maḷapaláwa*, } s. land which has devolved to government through the failure of heirs.
මළපාළුව, *Maḷapáḷuwa*,

මළ මිනිය, *Maḷaminiya*, } s. (මළ dead, මිනිහා man) corpse, dead body.
මළ මිනිහා, *Maḷaminihá*,

මළසුන, *Maḷasuna*, s. (මළ death, අසුන *asuna* announcement) information of the death of any person: pl. මළසුන් *maḷasun*.

මලානික, *Malánika*, a. (මල *mala* and අනික *anika* aff. of comparison) exhausted, depressed in spirits, low, spirited; withered, decayed.

මළු, *Maḷu*, *plur.* of මළුව *maḷuwa;* in Elu, younger brother, more commonly written මලු *malu*.

මළුපු, *Maḷupu*, s. bunch or cluster of flowers; plant bearing a small white flower, species of oleander.

මළුමණ්ඩප, *Maḷumaṇḍapa*, } s. court (applied to the outer part of ancient building) yard, fold, enclosure; shed, tent.
මළුව, *Maḷuwa*,

මා, *Má*, the *acc.* of the *pron.* මම *mama;* in Páli a prohibitive and negative particle; moon; name of Lakshmi, the goddess of beauty and wife of Vishṇu; fraud, trick, delusion; see මායා *máyá*: *a.* great, large etc: see මහා *mahá*.

මා ඇල්වී, *Má-eḷví*, s. kind of paddy, *oryza sativa*.

මාඉම, *Máima*, s. limit, boundary: pl. මාඉම් *máim*.

මාඋදේ, *Má-udé*, s. morning before dawn.

මාඋස්සා, *Má-ussá*, s. nettle, *Laportea crenulata (Urticaceæ)*.

මාංජිෂ්ඨ, *Mánjishṭha*, s. (මංජිෂ්ඨා *mánjishṭhá* madder, used as a red dye) red, the colour: *a.* red, of a red colour.

මාංස, *Máṇsa*, s. flesh; time; worm.

මාංස චක්ෂුව, *Máṇsa-chakshuwa*, s. (මාංස flesh, body, චක්ෂුව eye) eye of the body, in contradistinction to the දිව්‍ය චක්ෂු *divya-chakshu*, which see.

මාංස සාර, *Máṇsa-sára*, s. (මාංස flesh, සාර essence) adeps, fat, serum of the flesh.

මාංසාපණ, *Máṇsápaṇa*, s. (මාංස *máṇsa* and ආපණ *ápaṇa* shop) flesh market, shambles.

මාංසි, *Máṇsi*, s. labour, toil, fatigue.

මාංසික, *Máṇsika*, s. (මාංස *máṇsa* and ඉක *ika* aff.) vendor of flesh or meat, a butcher, reckoned by the Buddhists as the vilest of characters: *a.* fleshly, not spiritual, carnal.

මාංසී, *Máṇsí*, s. Indian spikenard, *valeriana jatamansi*, [Colloq. ජටාමාංස *jaṭámáṇsa*]; also a drung called kákóli.

මාක්ෂික, *Mákshika*, *s.* honey, [Colloq. මීපැනි *mí-pęni*]; also see මක්ෂි තුත්ථ *makshi-tuttha*.

මාක්ෂිකා, *Mákshiká*, *s.* bee, [Colloq. මී මැස්සා *mí-męssá*].

මාක්ෂිකාශ්‍රය, *Mákshikáśraya*, *s.* (මාක්ෂික *mákshika* honey, ආශ්‍රය *áśraya* receptacle) bee's wax, [Colloq. මී ඉටි *mí-iṭi*]; honey comb.

මාකන්ද, *Mákanda*, *s.* mango tree, *mangifera indica* or *m. zeylanica*, [Colloq. අඹගහ *amba-gaha*].

මාකරඹ, *Mákaramba*, see මහකරඹ *maha-karamba*.

මාකරු, *Mákaru*, *s.* (මා trick, කරු who does) juggler, sorcerer; mime, actor.

මාකරුවා, *Mákaruwá*, *s.* small sea fish.

මාගධ, *Mágadha*, *s.* bard, minstrel, whose duty it is to sing the praises of sovereigns, their genealogy, and the deeds of their ancestors, in their presence; country in which Buddha was born, and the birth place of his religion, in modern geography called South Behár; ancient name of the Páli or the sacred language of the Buddhists: see පාලි *páli;* an inhabitant of Magadha.

මාගධී, *Mágadhi*, *s.* Páli language: see මාගධ *mágadha:* jasmin, *jasminum auriculatum;* long pepper, *piper longum*, [Colloq. තිප්පිලි *tippili*]; cardamoms, *elettaria cardamomum*, [Colloq. එන්සාල් *ensál*]; refined sugar.

මාගම්, *Mágam*, *s.* woman, [Colloq. ස්ත්‍රී *strí*].

මාගල, *Mágala*, *s.* large mat: pl, මාගල් *mágal*,

මාගුරුවා, *Máguruwá*, *s.* large sea fish.

මාගුවරු, *Máguwaru*, *s.* the Mági; astronomers.

මාගේ, *Mágé*, *pron.* poss. of මම *mama* I; my, mine.

මාචිකා, *Máchiká*, *s.* fly, [Colloq. මැස්සා *męssá*].

මාඩා, *Máḍá*, *s.* bhang, intoxicating preparation of hemp.

මාණව, *Máṇawa*, *s.* (මනු *manu* man, අණ් *aṇ* aff.) youth; man, (in a contemptuous sense), manikin; see also මානව *mánawa*.

මාණික්‍යය, *Máṇikyaya*, *s.* (මණි *maṇi* gem, කෛ *kai* to call, යත් *yat* aff.) gem, jewel, any precious stone; ruby.

මාණික්‍යරත්නය, *Máṇikya-ratnaya*, *s.* (මාණික්‍ය and රත්න *ratna* jewel or treasure) one of the seven treasures possessed by a Chakrawarti, viz. the gem or precious stone as large as a pumpkin gourd, and which emits light and effulgence to the distance of four miles on every side; by its power he could visit any world.

මාණිමත්ථ, *Máṇimattha*, *s.* mountain of rock-salt in the Sindh country, [Colloq. සහින්ද ලුණු *sahinda-luṇu*].

මාත්තුකරණවා, *Máttukaraṇawá*, *v.* to mix a baser metal with a finer.

මාත්තුව, *Máttuwa*, *s.* essay of metals, proving of spirits etc; compound of two or more metals; alloy.

මාත්‍ර, *Mátra*, *s.* whole: *adv.* only, solely (exlusive and identical).

මාත්‍රඥ, *Mátrajña*, *a.* (මාත්‍ර quantity, ඥ who knows) temperate, moderate.

මාත්‍රය, *Mátraya*, see මාත්‍රාව *mátráwa*.

මාත්‍රාංශය, *Mátranṣaya*, *s.* part of a මාත්‍ර *mátra*, as ු, ් attached to a letter, *e. g.* ඍ ෘ, ක්‍ර *kra*.

මාත්‍රාව, *Mátráwa*, *s.* requisite, material; quantity, measure; little; short vowel: moment; quantity in measure or prosody; syllabic foot.

මාතෘ, *Mátṛi*, *s.* mother; cow; female of the Brahman tribe; the earth; space, ether; name of Lakshmí: pl. *nom.* මාතෘහු *mátṛihu*, *acc.* මාතෘන් *mátṛin*.

මාතෘකාව, *Mátṛikáwa*, *s.* alphabet; signature, autograph; simple sound, note, vowel; heading, motto; subject of a discourse.

මාතෘපිතෘ, *Mátṛi-pitṛi*, *s.* (මාතෘ mother, පිතෘ father) parents, mother and father.

මාතෘවධ, *Mátṛi-wadha*, *s.* (මාතෘ mother, වධ to kill) matricide, [Coll: මවුමැරීම *mawu-męrima*].

මාත්සර්‍ය්‍ය, *Mátsarya*, *s.* covetousness, envy, impatience of anothers' success.

මාත්සර, *Matsara*, *a.* (මත්සර envy, අණ් *aṇ* aff.), envious, impatient of another's success.

මාතඞ්ග, *Mátaṅga*, *s.* (මතඞ්ග *mataṅga* elephant etc. අණ් *aṇ* aff. of descent) elephant; man of a low caste, chaṇḍála, an outcaste: see චණ්ඩාල *chaṇḍála;* bó-tree, *ficus religiosa;* mountaineer, barbarian.

මාතඹල, *Má-tambala*, *s.* tree, perhaps variety of *gaertnera Kœnigii*.

මාතා, *Mátá*, *s.* mother, female progenitor.

මාතාපිතෘ, *Mátá-pitṛi*, *s.* mother and father.

මාතාමහ, *Mátámaha*, *s.* (මාතා mother etc.) maternal grand-father.

මාතාමහී, *Mátá-mahí*, *s.* maternal grand mother.

මාතු, *Mátu*, *s.* mother, [Colloq. මව් *maw*].

මාතුගාම, *Mátugáma*, *s.* woman, female, [Colloq. ස්ත්‍රී *strí*].

මාතුමරණ, *Mátu-maraṇa*, *s.* (මාතු mother, මරණ killing) matricide.

මාතුල, *Mátula*, *s.* (මාතෘ *mátri* mother etc.) father-in-law; maternal uncle; thorn apple, *datura stramonium*, [Colloq. අත්තන *attana*]; variegated snake.

මාතුල පුත්‍රක, *Mátula-putraka*, *s.* මාතුල and පුත්‍ර *putra* son) son of a maternal uncle; fruit of the datura, [Colloq. අත්තනගෙඩි *attana-geḍi*].

මාතුලා, *Mátulá*, *s.* wife of a maternal uncle; hemp, *cannabis sativa*. [Colloq. මත්කංසා *mat-kaṇsá*]; san hemp, *crotolaria juncea*, [Colloq. හණ *haṇa*]; generic name for pulas trees of various kinds, especially *butea frondosa* [Colloq. ගස්කැල *gas-kẹla*].

මාතුලාහි, *Mátuláhi*, *s.* (මාතුල *mátula* and අහි *ahi* snake) variegated snake.

මාතුලුංග, *Mátuluṅga*, } *s.* common citron,
මාතුලුංගක, *Mátuluṅgaka* } *citrus medica*, [Colloq. ලප්නාරං *lapnáraṇ*].

මාතු විලෝකන, *Mátu-vilókana*, *s.* (මාතු mother, විලෝකන looking for) one of the five prospective views taken by Buddha, previous to his appearance in the world, viz. the mother in whose womb he would be born.

මාදං, *Mádaṇ*, *s.* tree bearing a small fruit, *calyptranthes cumini*.

මාදන, *Mádana*, *s.* (මද *mada* to be pleased etc.) cloves, *caryophyllus aromaticus*, [Colloq. කරාබු *karábu*]; delighting, inebriating; tree, *eugenia calophyllifolia* or *calyptranthus cumini*.

මාදම්, *Mádam*, *s.* tree, *eugenia jambolana;* also called මහදං *maha-daṇ*.

මාදුරු, *Máduru*, *s.* (මා great, දුරු cumin) large cumin, *nigella indica*, [Colloq. කළුදුරු *kaḷu-duru*]; caraway seed, *carum carui*.

මාදොළුවා වී, *Mádoḷuwá-ví*, *s.* kind of paddy, *oryza sativa*.

මාදැල, *Mádẹla*, *s.* large net: pl. මාදැල් *mádẹl*.

මාධව, *Mádhawa*, *s.* (මධු *madhu* honey etc. අණ් *aṇ* aff. of derivation) name of Kṛishṇa or Vishṇu, the month waiṣákha or wesak, and the first of the Siṇhalese year (April–May), spring.

මාධවී, *Mádhavi*, *s.* sugar clayed or candied; large creeper, *gaertnera racemosa;* spirituous liquor; sacred basil, *ocimum sanctum*, [Colloq. මදුරුතලා *madurutalá*]; sweetness.

මාඤම, *Mándama*, *s.* disease, swelling of the belly attended with pain and slight purging: pl. මාන්දම් *mándam*.

මාන්න, *Mánna*, *s.* honor, respect: see මාන *mána*.

මාන්නක්කාරයා, *Mánnakkárayá*, *s.* respected man; man who lives an honorable life.

මාන්නක්කාරී, *Mánnakkárí*, *s.* respected woman; woman who etc.

මාන්නක්‍රෝධය, *Mánna-kródhaya*, *s.* caste jealousy.

මාන්නෙ, *Mánne*, *s.* honor.

මාන්‍ය, *Mánya*, *a.* (මන *mana* to worship etc.) venerable, respectable; proud, ambitious, tenacious.

මාන්වෙනවා, *Mánwenawá*, *v.* to split, to burst.

මාන, *Mána*, *s.* (මා to measure or මන *mana* to revere oneself) pride, haughtiness, arrogance; tenacity; measure in general, whether of weight, length, or capacity; means, way.

මානනවා, *Mánanawá*, *v.* to point, as a gun, to aim at: pret. මැනුවා *mẹnuwá*.

මානබලනවා, *Mána-balanawá*, *v.* to spy, to aim at.

මානභංග, *Mánabhaṅga*. *s.* (මාන pride, භංග what breaks or destroys) humility, lowliness; humiliation.

මානය, *Mánaya*, see මාන *mána*.

මානයි, *Mánayi*, *s.* plant, *justicia procumbens:* see මනි *mani*.

මානව, *Mánawa*, *s.* (මනු *manu* progenitor of mankind, අණ් *aṇ* aff. of descent) boy, youth not more than sixteen; man.

මානවක, *Mánawaka*, *s.* boy, lad not arrived at puberty.

මානවිකා, *Mánavika*, *s.* young girl, one not more than sixteen years of age.

මානස, *Mánasa*, *s.* (මනස *manasa* mind, අණ් *aṇ* aff.) mind, seat or faculty of reasoning and feeling; the lake Mánasaróvara in the Himálayan mountains: *a.* mental.

මානසෞකස, *Mánasaukasa*, *s.* (මානස *mánasa* lake so called, ඕකස් *ókas* dwelling) wild swan or goose, it being supposed to migrate yearly from Hindustán to the banks of the lake Mánasa.

මානා, *Máná*, *s.* lake called Mánasaróvara; hair crested stork, *leptoptilus javanicus (Ciconiidæ* order *Herodiones);* long aromatic grass, *andropogon nardus* or *a. martini* so called, from General Martin who collected the seeds during the war with Tippu Sultan *(Gramineæ)*; a cultivated variety is citronella grass called පැඟිරිමාන් *pẹngiri-mán*.

මානාංශය, *Mánáṇsaya*, *s.* large bird of the stork tribe, usually called the adjutant bird or the giant heron: see කලපුව කරවැල්කොකා *kalapuwa-karawẹlkoká* and ඉදුරුකොකා *indurukoká*.

මානිල්, *Mánil*, *s.* lotus, *nymphœa stellata:* see මානෙල් *mánel.*

මානුග, *Mánuga*, *s.* (මා great, නුග fig-tree) banyan tree, *ficus bengalensis:* see මහනුග *maha-nuga.*

මානුෂ්‍ය, *Mánushya*, *s.* (මනුෂ manusha man ෂ්‍යඤ් *shyañ* aff.) manhood, manliness; the state or quality of a man.

මානුෂ, *Mánusha*, *s.* man, mankind: *a.* human.

මානුෂී, *Mánushí*, *s.* (මානුෂ *mánusha* man, ඉන් *in* aff.) woman.

මානුසික, *Mánusika*, *s.* (මානුස *mánusa* man, ඉක *ika* aff.) belonging or relating to man, human.

මානෙල්, *Mánel*, *s.* lotus, water lily; Indian species with small blue flowers, *nymphea stellata (Nympheaceæ).*

මානෝඥක, *Manójñaka*, *s.* (මනෝඥ *manójña* agreeable) beauty, comeliness, agreeableness, [Colloq. ලක්ෂණ *lakshaṇa*].

මානැකත්, *Má-nękat*, *s.* (මා and නැකත් asterism) tenth lunar asterism; Elu form of මඝා *maghá*, which see.

මාප්‍රාණ, *Mápráṇa*, *s.* (මා great, ප්‍රාණ life, force) aspirated letter.

මාපට, *Mápaṭa*, *a.* large, great.

මාපට ඇඟිල්ල, *Mápaṭa-ęngilla*, *s.* (මාපට and ඇඟිල්ල finger) thumb or great toe.

මාපත් අඟුන, *Mápat-anguna*, *s.* plant, swallow wort or mudar, *calotropis* (or *asclepias) gigantea.*

මාපත් ඇල්වී, *Mápat-ęlví*, *s.* kind of paddy, *oryza sativa.*

මාපත් එලරතඹලා, *Mápat-ela-ratambalá*, *s.* plant, variety of *Knoxia zeylanica* or එළරත්මල් *elu ratmal.*

මාපත් කුරුඳු, *Mápat-kurundu*, *s.* laurel, variety of *laurus cinnamomum.*

මාපත්කැටකාල, *Mápat-kętakála*, *s.* tree, *brydelia retusa.*

මාපත්කැබෙල්ල, *Mápat-kębella*, *s.* tree peculiar to Ceylon, *aporosa latifolia (Euphorbiaceæ)*; also called පැපිළිය *pępiḷiya* and කම්පොත්තා *kampottá.*

මාපත්කැලිය, *Mápatkęliya*, *s.* small tree, *grewia tiliæfolia*, [Colloq. දමිනිය *daminiya*].

මාපත් නිවිති, *Mápat-niviti*, *s.* Malabar night shade, *basella cordifolia* or *b. alba.*

මාපත්පිහිඹිය, *Mápat-pihimbiya*, *s.* tree, not ascertained.

මාපන, *Mápana*, *s.* balance, pair of scales; measure, measuring; small bazaar, shop, raised bank in front of a house where articles are exposed for sale.

මාපිල්සබරලා, *Mápil-sabaralá*, *s.* kind of snake.

මාපිල්සබිලා, *Mápil-sabilá*, *s.* kind of snake.

මාපිලා, *Mápilá*, *s.* snake, believed by the natives to be deadly: pl. මාපිල්ලු *mápillu; dipsas forstenii* or *d. Ceylonensis* (order *Ophidia).*

මාබණ්ඩා, *Mábanḍá*, *s.* plant, *argyreia tiliæfolia (Convolvulaceæ).*

මාබින්තල්, *Má-bintal*, *s.* plant, *curculigo Finlaysoniana (Amaryllidæ).*

මාමා, *Mámá*, *s.* maternal uncle; father-in-law; father's sister's husband.

මාමෙරු, *Máméru*, *s.* pepper, *piper betel*, [Colloq. බුලත් *bulat*]; also see මෙරු *méru.*

මාය, *Máya*, *s.* mime, juggler; asura or evil spirit.

මායම, *Máyama*, *s.* artifice, subtlety, craft, cunning, device: pl. මායම් *máyam.*

මායා, *Máyá*, *s.* fraud, trick, deceit, illusion, juggling; female juggler; wickedness, villany, villanous deception; according to the Hindus, philosophical illusion, idealism, unreality of all worldly existence.

මායාකාර, *Máyákára*, *s.* (මායා illusion etc. කාර who does) juggler, mime, actor.

මායාදේවි, *Máyádéri*, *s.* (මායා illusion by beauty, දේවි queen) mother of Buddha and wife of Suddhódana king of Kapila who is said to have been the Chakrawarti or the lord paramount of India.

මායාදේවිසුත, *Máyá-dérisuta*, *s.* (මායාදේවි and සුත son) name of Gautama, in allusion to his being the son of Máyádévi: see the preceding.

මායාව, *Máyáwa*, *s.* illusion, idealism; deception, trick: see මායා *máyá.*

මායාවිත්, *Máyávit*, *s.* (මායා and විත් or විද් *vid* who knows) juggler, conjuror; mime, actor.

මායාසුත, *Máyásuta*, see මායාදේවිසුත *máyádévisuta.*

මායාහාරි, *Máyáhári*, *s.* (මායා and හාරි who practises) juggler, actor etc.: see මායාවිත් *máyávit.*

මායික, *Máyika*, } *s.* (මායා *máyá* and ඉක *ika* aff.)
මායින්, *Máyin*, } juggler, conjurer: *a.* illusory, deceptive.

මායිම, *Máyima*, *s.* boundary, limit: pl. මායිම් *máyim.*

මායියා *Máyiyá*, *s.* old woman; wife, (disrespectful).

මායු, *Máyu*, *s.* (මි *mi* to scatter or diffuse) bile, the bilious humour.

මායූර, *Máyúra*, s. flock of peacocks, [Colloq. මොනර රංචුව *monara-ranchuwa*]: *a*. belonging to a peacock.

මාකව, *Márkawa*, s. plant, kind of swallow wort, *calotropis* (or *asclepias*) *gigantea*, [Colloq. වරා *wará*]; medicinal plant, *eclipta erecta*, [Colloq. කිකිරිඳිය *kikirindiya*].

මාර්ග, *Márga*, s. (මෘග *mriga* to enquire, or a deer, අණ් *an* aff.) road, path, way; way to Nirwána used metaphorically of the four states preparatory to Nirwána: see නිර්වාණ *nirwána;* musk; month උඳුවප් *unduwap* (November-December); search, seeking, enquiring; constellation මෘගශිරස් *mriga-siras*.

මාර්ගඥාන, *Márgajñána*, s. (මාර්ග and ඥාන knowledge) knowledge of the four states preparatory to Nirwána: see නිර්වාණ *nirwána*.

මාර්ගය, *Márgaya*, see මාර්ග *márga*.

මාර්ගශිර, *Márgasira*, } s. month, usually called
මාර්ගශීර්ෂ, *Márgasírsha*, } උඳුවප් *unduwap* (November-December): see also මෘගශිරස් *mriga-siras*.

මාර්ගසත්‍ය, *Márgasatya*, s. one of the four great truths or axioms of Buddhism: see චතුස්සත්‍ය *chatussatya*.

මාර්ගිත, *Márggita*, *a*. (මෘග *mriga* to seek, ක්ත *kta* aff.) sought, enquired after, pursued.

මාර්ගෝපකරණ, *Márgópakarana*, s. (මාර්ග *márga* and උපකරණ *upakarana* help) provisions, etc. for a journey.

මාර්ජන, *Márjana*, s. (මෘජ *mrija* to clean) cleansing, cleaning; tree, bark of which is used in dyeing, *symplocos racemosa;* cleaning the person by wiping, bathing, or rubbing it with oil, or fragrant unguents; tree, *cratæva Roxburghii*, [Colloq. ලුණුවරණ *lunuwarana*].

මාර්ජනී, *Márjaní*, s. brush, broom, [Colloq. කොස්ස *kossa*].

මාර්ජාර, *Márjára*, s. common cat, [Colloq. බළලා *balalá*]; wild or pole cat, [Colloq. උගුඩුවා *ugu-duwá*].

මාර්ජාරගන්ධිකා, *Márjára-gandhiká*, s. medicinal plant, [Colloq. මුංවැන්න *munwenna*].

මාර්ජාරමෝහිනී, *Márjára-móhiní*, s. medicinal plant, *acalypha indica*, [Colloq. කුප්පමේනිය *kuppa-méniya*].

මාර්ජාරී, *Márjári*, s. musk, [Colloq. කස්තුරි *kasturi*]; medicinal plant, *acalypha indica*, [Colloq. කුප්පමේනිය *kuppaméniya*]; female cat, [Colloq. බැළලී *belali*].

මාර්තණ්ඩ, *Mártanda*, s. (මෘතණ්ඩ *mritanda* progenitor of the sun, අණ් *an* aff.) sun, [Colloq. ඉර *ira*].

මාර්දඞ්ග, *Márdanga*, s. (මෘදඞ්ග *mridanga* tom tom, අණ් *an* aff.) drummer.

මාර්දඞ්ගික, *Márdangika*, s. (මෘදඞ්ග *mridanga* drum, ඨක් *thak* aff.) drummer, player on the tom-tom, [Colloq. බෙරගහන්නා *bera-gahanná*].

මාර, *Mára*, s. (මෘ *mri* to die etc.) death, dying; name of Káma or Anangayá the Indian Cupid; obstruction, opposition, impediment; thorn apple, *datura fastuosa*, [Colloquial: අත්තන *attana*]; killing, destroying, slaying; half, as එකහමාර *ekahamára* one and a half: see මාරයා *márayá*.

මාරක, *Máraka*, s. (මාර death, killing, අක *aka* aff.) epidemic disease, plague; slayer, destroyer; falcon, hawk.

මාරකේශකය, *Mára-késakaya*, s. opium plant, [Colloq. කන්ෂා *kanshá*].

මාරජිත්, *Márajit*, s. (මාර Káma, ජිත් who overcomes) name of Buddha: see මාරයා *márayá*.

මාරත්මල්, *Má-ratmal*, s. rhododendron, shrub with deep red flowers, *rhododendron arboreum (Ericaceæ)*.

මාරපාශ, *Márapása*, s. (මාර and පාශ net, snare) temptations and wiles used by Káma to seduce men into sin.

මාරම, *Márama*, s. a term used by carpenters for unsmoothness.

මාරයා, *Márayá*, s. chief of demons, the great enemy and opposer of Buddha; on the day of Buddha's attaining to this high character Márayá attacked him with an innumerable host of the fiercest demons, all of whom excited the most infernal rage against him and the most determined opposition to his assuming the sacred character; Buddha, however, speedily vanquished the whole; this is evidently an allegory; the word seems to be a personification of මර *mara* or cupidity and lust, and by such enemies was Buddha opposed.

මාරවිජය, *Mára-vijaya*, s. (මාර and විජය conquest) Buddha's victory over මාරයා *márayá:* see the last.

මාරා, *Márá*, s. tree, *albizzia Lebbec (Leguminoceæ);* also see සූරියමාරා *súriyamárá*.

මාරාගස, *Márá-gasa*, s. tree, seed of the *adenanthera pavonina*, [Colloq. මදටිය *madatiya*].

මාරවා, *Máráwá*, *s.* bird called the Ceylonese azure flycatcher, *Hypothymus Ceylonensis;* whitefronted ferntail *rhipidura albifrontata;* blue redbreast, *siphia tickelliæ*, *(Muscicapidæ* order *Passeres)*.

මාරිත, *Márita*, *a.* killed, slaughtered, slain.

මාරියාව, *Máriyáwa*, *s.* waves.

මාරිෂ, *Márisha*, *s.* friendly term of address, auspicious one, etc.; venerable person; potherb, *amarantus gangeticus* or *a. oleraceus*, [Colloq. සුළු කූර *sulu-kúra*, also, සුදුතම්පලා *sudu-tampalá*].

මාරුක්, *Máruk*, *s.* (මා chief, රුක් tree) coconut tree, *cocos nucifera*, [Colloq. පොල්ගහ *pol-gaha*]; tree, *caryota urens*, [Colloq. කිතුල් *kitul-gaha*].

මාරුකරණ මුද්ද, *Márukaraṇa-mudda*, *s.* wedding ring.

මාරුකරණවා, *Márukaraṇawá*, *v.* to change, to exchange, to barter.

මාරුකු, *Máruku*, *s.* panic grass, *panicum staginum*.

මාරුත, *Máruta*, *s.* air, wind; vital air, one of the three humours of the body.

මාරුව, *Máruwa*, *s.* expedient, means, remedy; artifice, trick; changing, substituting, exchanging, bartering.

මාරුවෙනවා, *Máruwenawá*, *s.* to be changed: pret. මාරුවුනා *máruwuná*.

මාල්‍ය, *Málya*, *s.* flower, garland, wreath; chaplet, garland for the forehead; perfumed chaplet: *a.* fit for a garland.

මාල්‍යා, *Málya*, } *s.* potherb, *trigonella cornicu-*
මාල්‍යාව, *Málydwa*, } *lata*.

මාල්ලා, *Máll*á, *s.* old man or animal.

මාල්ලි, *Málli*, *s.* (මාල්ල *málla* and ඊ *í* aff.) old woman or animal.

මාල, *Mála*, *plur.* of මාලේ *málé*, which see.

මාලක, *Málaka*, *s.* (මාලා *málá* garland, අක *aka* aff.) flower; nimba tree, *azadirachta indica*, [Colloq. කොහොඹ *kohomba*]; flower, *hibiscus mutabilis*.

මාලකා, *Málaká*, *s.* garland.

මාලතී, *Málatí*, *s.* great flowered jasmine, [Colloq. දේසමන් *désaman*]; bud, blossom; moon light; river; flower, *stereospermum* (or *bignonia) suaveolens*, [Colloq. පළොල් *paḷol*]; shrub, *echites caryophyllata; weightia zeylanica*, [Colloq. ඉද්ද *idda*].

මාලතීතිර, *Málatí-tíra*, *s.* (මාලතී and තීර border) bank of a river.

මාලතීතිරජ, *Málatí-tíraja*, *s.* (මාලතීතිර and ජ produced) borax, used as a flux, [Colloq. පුස්කර *puskara*].

මාලතීඵල, *Málatí-phala*, *s.* nutmeg tree, *myristica fragrans*, [Colloq. සාදික්කා *sádikká*].

මාලය, *Málaya*, *s.* ornamental chain; story of a building.

මාලා, *Málá*, *s.* garland, string or wreath of flowers; chaplet of flowers; necklace, bracelet; string of beads, rosary; line, row; declension of nouns, conjugation of verbs.

මාලාකාර, *Málákára*, *s.* (මාලා garland, කාර who makes) flower seller, florist; man who makes and sells garlands; gardener.

මාලාදම, *Máládáma*, *s.* garland of flowers.

මාලාව, *Máláwa*, *s.* string or wreath of flowers; chain, necklace, bracelet.

මාලාස්‍රක්, *Málásrak*, *s.* wreath, chaplet of flowers.

මාලික, *Málika*, *s.* (මාලා *málá* and ඉක *ika* aff.) florist, gatherer and vendor of flowers.

මාලිකා, *Máliká*, *s.* double jasmine, *jasminum sambac*, [Colloq. පිච්ච *pichcha*]; necklace, ornament of the neck, garland of flowers; daughter; spirituous or vinous liquor; linseed, *linum utilatissimum;* palace.

මාලිගය, *Máligaya*, } *s.* palace, residence of a
මාලිගාව, *Máligáwa*, } king.

මාලින්, *Málin*, *s.* (මාලා *málá* flower, ඉනි *ini* aff.) florist, gardener, vendor of flower wreaths.

මාලිනී, *Máliní*, *s.* (මාලා *málá* and ඉනි *ini* aff. with ඊ *í* fem. aff.) wife of a flower vendor, woman who sells wreaths, garlands etc; poetical stanza each line consisting of two *tribrachs*, one *molossus*, and two *bacchics*, with a pause after the eighth and fifteenth syllable.

මාලිම, *Málima*, *s.* science of navigation. (Tamil, captain of a vessel.)

මාලිමයා, *Málimayá*, *s.* one skilled in navigation, navigator; pilot.

මාලිමශාස්ත්‍රය, *Málima-śástraya*, *s.* science of navigation.

මාලී, *Málí*, *s.* (මාලා *málá*, and ඉන් *in* aff. florist; tree, *alangium hexapetalum*, [Colloq. හෝපළු *hópaḷu*]; Asóka tree, *jonesia asoka*, [Colloq. දිය රතඹලා *diya-ratambalá*].

මාලු, *Málu*, *s.* fish, fish in general; curry: *a.* old, aged, advanced in years.

මාලුත, *Máluta*, *s.* wind, air; also written මාරුත *máruta*.

මාලූර, *Málúra*, *s.* tree, *ægle marmelos*, [Colloq. බෙලි *beli*].

මාලේ, *Málé*, *s.* an ornamental chain; menses, in which sense, it is another form of මහලේ *mahalé*.

මාලේයා, *Máléyá*, *s.* large cardamoms.

මාවත්, *Máwat*, *s.* (මා great, වත් face) owl; see the next.

මාවත, *Máwata*, *s.* (from මහා *mahá* chief, පථ *patha* road) high way, road, path; owl, [Colloq. බකමූනා *bakamúná*].

මාවර, *Máwara*, *s.* horizontal sticks of a fence.

මා වවුලා, *Má-wawulá*, *s.* large bat.

මාවී, *Máví*, *s.* (මා and වී grain) large kind of paddy or rice, *oryza sativa*.

මාවුලා, *Máwulá*, *s.* pillow, bolster.

මාවේවැල්, *Máwéwel*, *s.* rattan growing to a great length, *calamus rudentum (Palmæ)*; also called තුඩරණවේවැල් *tuḍaraṇa-wéwel*.

මාවැටියා, *Máweṭiyá*, *s.* kind of sea fish.

මාවැලි, *Máweli*, *s.* (මා and වැලි sand) gravel, gravelly or sandy soil.

මාෂ, *Másha*, *s.* sort of kidney bean, variety of *phaseolus mungo*, [Colloquial: මුංඇට *mun-eṭa*]; jeweller's weight, the seed of the *abrus precatorius*, [Colloq. ඔලිඳුවැල් *olinda-wel*], weighing about seventeen grains troy; cutaneous disease; red gram, plant yielding beans, *dolichos* or *vigna catjang*, [Colloq. ලිමෑ *limé*].

මාෂපර්ණ, *Máshaparṇa*, *s.* (මාෂ kidney bean, පර්ණ leaf) leguminous shrub, *glycine debilis*.

මාෂපර්ණී, *Másha-parṇní*, } *s.* medicinal plant,
මාෂපත්‍රී, *Másha-patrí*, } *drymoglossum heterophyllum*, [Colloq. මස්වැන්න *masweṇna*].

මාස් කල, *Más-kala*, *s.* seasons in months.

මාස, *Mása*, *s.* (මස *masa* to measure), (the year by it) month; there are two kinds of months, chandra mása or the lunar month, reckoned from one new moon or from one full moon to another, and by which all religious festivals and ceremonies are governed; the other is the súrya-mása or solar month, being equal to the sun's passage through a sign of the zodiac, all reckonings in the common affairs of life are calculated by this month: see also මාෂ *másha*.

මාසක්කා, *Másakká*, *s.* medicinal plant.

මාසර, *Másara*, *s.* scum of boiled rice, [Colloq. බතින්පෙරූ කැඳ *batin-perú-keṇda*].

මාසික, *Másika*, *a.* (මාස *mása* month, ඉක *ika* aff.) monthly, relating or belonging to a month.

මාසේ, *Másé*, see මාස *mása*.

මාසේවීම, *Másévíma*, *s.* menstrual flux.

මාසොන්, *Máson*, *s.* kind of boys' play.

මාහ, *Máha*, *s.* one of the two harvests; the larger or that in which the most grain is cultivated; the seed is sown in August, and the corn cut in January.

මාහේය, *Máhéya*, *s*, (මහී *mahí* earth, අණ් *aṇ* aff.) coral; regent of the planet Márs: *a.* made of or from earth.

මාහේශ්වරී, *Máhéṣwarí*, } *s.* (මහේශ්වර *mahéṣwara*
මාහේෂී, *Máhéṣí*, } and මහේශ *mahéṣa* Ṣiva with අණ් *aṇ* aff. and ඊ *í* fem. aff.) name of Durgá; according to the Hindu system, one of the divine mothers or energies of the gods, the sakti of Ṣiva.

මාහැඟි, *Máheṇgi*, *a.* (මා great, ඇඟි *eṇgi* for ඇගි *egi* value) costly, precious, invaluable; Elu form of මහාර්ඝ *mahárgha*.

මාළුකූරියා, *Máḷukúriyá*, *s.* fish of any kind.

මාළුධාන, *Máḷudhána*, *s.* variegated snake; a scare crow.

මාළුපිනි, *Máḷupini*, *s.* curry: see මාලු *málu*.

මාළුබිජු, *Máḷu-biju*, *s.* (මාළු fish, බිජු egg) roe of a fish.

මාළුව, *Máḷuwa*, *s.* curry, compound of various spices.

මාළුවා, *Máḷuwá*, *s.* fish.

මාළූර, *Máḷúra*, *s.* fruit tree, *ægle marmelos*, [Coll: බෙලි *beli*].

මිග, *Miga*, *s.* deer, antelope; animal in general; Páli form of මෘග *mriga*; brag, boast, bravado.

මිග කියනවා, *Miga-kiyanawá*, *v.* to pronounce a curse, to defy, to challenge.

මිගපවර, *Miga-pawara*, *s.* (මිග and පවර chief) lion, [Colloq. සිංහයා *siṇhayá*].

මිගව, *Migawa*, *s.* (මිග animal, වා *wá* to injure, to kill) hunting, deerstalking, the chase.

මිගිඳු, *Migiṇdu*, *s.* (මිග *miga* animal, ඉඳු *iṇdu* chief, lord) lion: see මිගපවර *miga-pawara*.

මිගිනි, *Migini*, *s.* pupil of the eye; sterile or imperfectly matured seed of jack fruit.

මිච්ඡාදිට්ඨි, *Michchháḍiṭṭhi*, *s.* Páli form of මිථ්‍යා දෘෂ්ටි *mithyádrishṭi*.

මිට්ටා, *Miṭṭá*, *s.* short or low man, dwarf.

මිට, *Miṭa*, *s.* fist, closed hand; handful, as much as can be held in the fist; handle of any instrument; Elu form of මුෂ්ටි *mushṭi*: pl. මිටි *miṭi*.

මිටමොලවනවා, *Miṭamolawanawá*, *v.* to clench the fist, to double the fist.

මිටි, *Miṭi*, *s.* heart: *a.* short, dwarfish; low, deep; also plur. of මිටිය *miṭiya* and මිට *miṭa*.

මිටිය, *Miṭiya*, *s.* hammer; bundle, number of things tied together: pl. මිටි *miṭi*.

මිටියා, *Miṭiyá*, *s.* dwarf.

මිටියාව, *Miṭiyáwa*, } *s.* low place, any low
මිටියාවත, *Miṭiyáwata*, } ground, valley.

මිටු, *Miṭu*, *s.* the fist.

මිඩංගුකරණවා, *Midangukaraṇawá*, *v.* to delay, procrastinate, defer.

මිඩංගුව, *Miḍanguwa*, *s.* delay, procrastination.

මිඩංගුවෙනවා, *Miḍanguwenawá*, *v.* to delay.

මිඩි, *Miḍi*, *s.* woman with her head shaven, slave; it being a custom formerly when a female slave was taken into a family to shave her head.

මිඩිය, *Miḍiya*, *s.* female slave.

මිණ, *Miṇa*, *s.* gem, jewel, any precious or costly stone, from මණි *maṇi*; imitative sound.

මිණ ගොටු, *Miṇa-goṭu*, *s.* (මිණ imitative sound, ගොටු hollow substance) bell, handbell, [Colloq. මිණිගෙඩිය *miṇigeḍiya*].

මිණි, *Miṇi*, *s.* crown, gem; imitative sound: plur. of මිණ *miṇa*.

මිණි කිකිණි, *Miṇi-kikiṇi*, *s.* (මිණි and කිකිණි bell) girdle of small bells or tinkling ornaments set with gems.

මිණිගෙඩිය, *Miṇigeḍiya*, *s.* (මිණි bell, from Tamil maṇi, ගෙඩිය fruit, [in form]) bell, gong, any piece of metal struck with a stick.

මිණිගොව්, *Miṇigow*, *s.* (මිණි jewels etc, ගොව් keeper) treasurer, jewel keeper.

මිණි දඬුවැට, *Miṇi-danḍuweṭa*, *s.* (මිණි gems, දඬු වැට row) enclosure ornamented with gems, one that surrounds the palace of Ṣakra in Swarga.

මිණිදම්, *Miṇi-dam*, *s.* (මිණි and දම් chain) necklace of gems, bracelet of precious stones.

මිණිඳු, *Miṇidu*, *s.* large sort of creeper or gourd.

මිණි දැදිරි, *Miṇi-ḍediri*, *a.* opened, expanded, blown as a flower, [Colloq. පිපුණු *pipunu*].

මිණි දැල්, *Miṇi-del*, *s.* (මිණි gems, දැල *ḍela* net) network ornamented with gems for a screen or curtain.

මිණි පලඟ, *Miṇi-palaṅga*, *s.* (මිණි and පලඟ seat) the throne made of gems brought for Buddha to repose upon by the Nága Máṇi-akkhika, on his third journey to Ceylon, for the purpose of quelling the rebellion among the Nágas of Pátála.

මිණි බිම, *Miṇi-bima*, *s.* (මිණි and බිම ground) jewel mine; floor set with gems.

මිණිමුතු, *Miṇimutu*, *a.* opened, as a flower.

මිණි රැස, *Miṇi-resa*, *s.* (මිණි and රැස ray) water in gems; heap of gems.

මිණි ලෙන, *Miṇi-lena*, *s.* (මිණි gems, ලෙන cave) gem mine, place where gems are found; jewelled cave.

මිත්, *Mit*, *s.* Elu form of මිත්‍ර *mitra*, friend.

මිත්‍ර, *Mitra*, *s.* friend, ally, companion, associate; sun: *a.* friendly, amicable.

මිත්‍රක, *Mitraka*, *a.* (මිත්‍ර and අක *aka* aff.) friendly, social.

මිත්‍රකම, *Mitrakama*, *s.* friendship, sociality.

මිත්‍රද්‍රෝහියා, *Mitradróhiyá*, *s.* (මිත්‍ර and ද්‍රෝහි treacherous, යා pers. aff.) traitor, one who betrays his friend.

මිත්‍රධර්ම, *Mitradharma*, *s.* (මිත්‍ර and ධර්ම duty) friendship.

මිත්‍රයා, *Mitrayá*, *s.* friend, associate.

මිත්‍ර සන්ථව, *Mitra-santhawa*, } *s.* (මිත්‍ර and සන්ථව
මිත්‍රසම්බන්ධ, *Mitra-sambandha*, } union) friendship.

මිත, *Mita*, *a.* (මා *má* to measure) measured, literally or figuratively; known, understood.

මිතම්පච, *Mitampacha*, *s.* (මිතම් measured, පච who cooks) beggar, mendicant; miser: *a.* miserly, niggardly.

මිති, *Miti*, *a.* measuring, measure, etc.

මිතුරා, *Miturá*, *s.* friend; ally: see මිත්‍ර *mitra*.

මිතුරු, *Mituru*, *s.* sun, [Colloq. ඉර *ira*]: see also මිත්‍ර *mitra*.

මිතුරුකම, *Miturukama*, *s.* friendship, sociability.

මිථ්‍යා, *Mithyá*, *ad.* falsely, untruly: *a.* false, untrue, erroneous.

මිථ්‍යාග්‍රහය, *Mithyá-grahaya*, *s.* (මිථ්‍යා and ග්‍රහ *graha* seizure) reception of heretical or sceptical ideas of religion.

මිථ්‍යාචාර, *Mithyáchára*, *s.* (මිථ්‍යා and චාර conduct) adultery, fornication; sensuality; acting falsely.

මිථ්‍යාදෘෂ්ටි, *Mithyádrishṭi*, *s.* (මිථ්‍යා falsely, දෘෂ්ටි vision, knowledge) scepticism in religion, heresy, paganism.

මිථ්‍යාදෘෂ්ටියා, *Mithyádrishṭiyá*, *s.* (මිථ්‍යාදෘෂ්ටි and යා pers. aff.) sceptic in religion, heretic, gentile, one who professes a false religion.

මිථ්‍යාභිශංසන, *Mithyábhiṣaṇsana*, *s.* (මිථ්‍යා false, අභිශංසන *abhiṣaṇsana* accusing) false accusation; filth, foulness, impurity.

මිථ්‍යාව, *Mithyáwa*, *s.* falsehood, error, delusion or scepticism.

මිථිලා, *Mithilá*, *s.* city which gives name to a kingdom, lying N. E. of Bengal: see විදේහ *vidéha.*

මිථුන, *Mithuna*, *s.* (මිථ *mitha* to unite) couple, pair, brace, male and female; copulation; union, junction; sign of the zodiac, Gemini.

මිථුනරාශිය, *Mithuna-rásiya*, } *s.* (මිථුන and රාශිය sign) sign of
මිථුනලග්නය, *Mithuna-lagnaya*, } the zodiac; Gemini.

මිද්ධ, *Middha*, *s.* sleep, slumber, sleep accompanied with dreams; sleepiness, torpor, dullness etc.

මිදි, *Midi*, *s.* vine creeper, *vitis vinifera;* shrub or small tree with small greenish white flowers and unpleasant smell, *premna serratifolia (Verbenaceæ);* humble or sensitive plant, *mimosa pudica (Leguminosæ);* also called නිදිකුම්බ *nidikumba.*

මිදිච්ච වතුර, *Midichcha-watura*, *s.* ice.

මිදිඹු, *Midimbu*, see මිදුඹු *midumbu.*

මිදියුස, *Midi-yusa*, } *s.* juice of grape.
මිදිරස, *Midi-rasa*, }

මිදීම, *Midíma*, *s.* release, redemption; verbal noun of මිදෙනවා *midenawá*, which see.

මිදුඹු, *Midumbu*, *s.* (මිද *mida* to understand) thought, reflection; mind as the seat of reason.

මිදුල, *Midula*, *s.* yard, court yard of a house, compound: pl. මිදුල් *midul.*

මිදුළු, *Midulu*, *s.* marrow, the marrow of the bones.

මිදෙනවා, *Midenawá*, *v.* (මුද *muda* to set loose or free) to be loosened, or released, set free, to be redeemed or emancipated; to congeal, to coagulate, to be curdled, frozen.

මිදෙල්ල, *Midella*, *s.* name of certain trees of the genus, *Barringtonia*, namely දියමිදෙල්ල *diya-midella*, *B. racemosa* and ඇලමිදෙල්ල *ela-midella B. acutangula:* and see මූදිල්ල *múdilla.*

මින්, *Min*, *s.* wisdom, knowledge; light, effulgence; lamp; fish, from මීන *mína;* sort of gem, said to be found in the throat of the cobra capella; star; measure; word; heart; multitude, assemblage; ship.

මින්කෙහෙළි, *Min-keheli*, } *s.* (මින් fish, කෙහෙළි or
මින්දද, *Min-dada*, } දද banner) name of Anańgayá the Indian Cupid.

මින්නඹු, *Minnambu*, *s.* midwife, more commonly written වින්නඹු *vinnambu.*

මින්පසු, *Minpasu*, *ad.* hereafter, afterward.

මින්පිටු, *Min-pitu*, *s.* (මින් fish, පිටු multitude) sea, ocean, [Colloq. මූද *múda*].

මින්පුටු, *Minputu*, *s.* water hen.

මින්මඩුලු, *Min-madulu*, see මින්පිටු *min-pitu.*

මින්මත්තට, *Min-mattata*, } *ad.* hereafter, after-
මින්මතු, *Min-matu*, } ward, henceforward.

මින්යන්, *Minyan*, *s.* name of Anańgayá the Indian Cupid.

මින්හල්, *Min-hal*, *s.* (මින් fish, හල් residence) sea, ocean, [Colloq. මූද *múda*].

මිනන්, *Minan*, *s.* flesh market.

මිනිත ශාස්ත්‍රය, *Minita-śástraya*, *s.* incorrectly for මැනුම් ශාස්ත්‍රය *menum-śástraya*, science of measuring, surveying; geometry.

මිනිපිරි, *Minipiri*, } *s.* grand-daughter.
මිනි බිරි, *Minibiri*, }

මිනිය, *Miniya*, *s.* dead carcase, corpse; gong or bell; gem.

මිනිරන්, *Miniran*, *s.* talc; plumbago.

මිනිස්, *Minis*, *s.* (මනුෂ්‍ය *manushya* man) man: *a.* human, belonging or relating to man; manly, manlike.

මිනිස්පථය, *Minispathaya*, *s.* (මිනිස් and පථ *patha* way, road) inhabited country, place frequented by man.

මිනිස්පිය, *Minispiya*, *s.* inhabited country; humanity; manhood.

මිනිස් පියස, *Minis-piyasa*, *s.* (මිනිස් man, පියස from ප්‍රදේශ *pradésa* district) inhabited country.

මිනිස්ලොව, *Minis-lowa*, *s.* (මිනිස් and ලොව world) world of men, residence of mortals, as distinguished from දෙව්ලොව *dew-lowa*, heaven, the world of gods etc.

මිනිස්සු, *Minissu*, *s.* men.

මිනිස, *Minisa*, } *s.* (මනුෂ්‍ය *manushya* man) man,
මිනිසා, *Minisá*, } Elu form of මනුෂ්‍ය *manushya.*

මිනිසත්බව, *Minisat-bawa*, *s.* (මිනිස් *minis* man, අත් *at* soul or self, බව being) manhood, state of man, human nature.

මිනිහා, *Minihá*, *s.* man, mankind.

* මිනී, *Miní*, *s.* dead body, corpse.

* මිනී අඳනවා, *Miní-andanawá*, *v.* to shroud, to prepare a corpse for burial.

* මිනී ගඳ, *Miní-ganda*, *s.* (මිනී and ගඳ smell) cadaverous smell.

* මිනීපිට්ටනිය, *Miní-pittaniya*, } *s.* burying ground,
* මිනී පිටිය, *Miní-pitiya*, } grave yard.

* මිනී පෙට්ටගම, *Miní-pettagama*, } *s.* coffin.
* මිනී පෙට්ටිය, *Miní-pettiya*, }

* In this and the 12 following words, මිනී miní is often written, මිනි mini.

* මිනි මරුවා, *Mini-maruwá*, *s.* (මිනි and මරුවා who kills) murderer; executioner.
* මිනිමලගම, *Mini-malagama*, *s.* funeral, funeral procession.
* මිනිමස් කෑම, *Minimas-kéma*, *s.* cannibalism.
* මිනිමැරීම, *Mini-merima*, *s.* murdering.
* මිනි වළ, *Mini-wala*, *s.* (මිනි corpse, වළ pit) grave.
* මිනි වළලනවා, *Mini-walalanawá*, *v.* to bury, to inter.
මිනුම, *Minuma*, *s.* measure, measuring.
මිනුවන්පං, *Minuwan-pan*, *s.* plant of the genus *cyperus*.
මිම්ම, *Mimma*, *s.* measure, measuring.
මිය, *Miya*, *s.* the earth; mouth: *part.* having died, become extinct.
මියනවා, *Miyanawá*, *v.* to die, to expire: pret. මිවුනා *miwuná* or මැරුණ *meruná*.
මියයාම, *Miyayáma*, *s.* (මිය dead, යාම goin) death, dying.
මියර, *Miyara*, *s.* border, bank; dam, dam or embankment raised in the rice fields to dam in the water and to serve as a foot path when the fields are overflowed, [Colloq. නියර *niyara*].
මියු, *Miyu*, *s.* buffalo.
මියුනු, *Miyunu*, *a.* dead, extinct, expired.
මියුරු, *Miyuru*, *s.* peacock; liquorice; frog: *a.* soft, delicate, agreeable, pleasing, sweet, mellifluous.
මියු රුපු, *Miyu-rupu*, *s.* horse, [Colloq. අශ්වයා *aswayá*].
මියුල්, *Miyul*, *s.* deer, [Colloq. මුවා *muwá*].
මියුලේස, *Miyulesa*, } *s.* woman with eyes similar
මියුලේසී, *Miyulesí*, } to a deer's eyes.
මිර, *Mira*, *s.* coition.
මිරි, *Miri*, see මිහිරි *mihiri*.
මිරිකනවා, *Mirikanawá*, *v.* to crush, to squeeze, to express by pressure; pret. මිරිකුවා *mirikuwá*.
මිරිකීම, *Mirikima*, } *s.* squeezing, crushing, verbal
මිරිකුම, *Mirikuma*, } noun of the foregoing.
මිරිකුළු, *Mirikulu*, *s.* murunga or horse radish tree, *moringa pterygosperma*, [Colloq. මුරුංගා *murungá*]; the pods of this tree furnish a very fine vegetable and the root exactly resembles horse radish.
මිරිකෙනවා, *Mirikenawá*, *v.* to be crushed or squeezed.
මිරිඟු, *Miringu*, } *s.* mirage, sultry va-
මිරිඟුජලය, *Miringu-jalaya*, } pour, floating over
මිරිඟුපැන්, *Miringu-pen*, } sands and deserts during the hottest hours of the day, and appearing at a distance like water.

මිරිජ, *Mirijja*, } *s.* (මිරි sweet, දිය water) fresh
මිරිදිය, *Miridiya*, } water.
මිරිවැඩි, *Miriwedi*, *s.* sandals, shoes.
මිරිස්, *Miris*, *s.* chillies, pepper, pepper in general; there are in Ceylon about eighteen sorts.
මිරිස් කරල, *Miris-karala*, *s.* pod of chilly.
මිරිස්ගල, *Miris-gala*, *s.* chillie grinder.
මිරිස්සා, *Mirissá*, *s.* species of cockle.
මිරිසියානු, *Mirisiyánu*, see මිලිසියානු *milisiyánu*.
මිල, *Mila*, *s.* money, cash; price, rate, value.
මිලකරණවා, *Mila-karanawá*, *v.* to value, to appreciate, to appraise.
මිලගොයා, *Milagoyá*, *s.* Ceylon wood pigeon, *palumbus Torringtonia (Columbidæ*, order *Columbæ)*; also called මහවිලගොයා *maharilagoyá*.
මිලය, *Milaya*, see මිල *mila*.
මිලාත, *Miláta*, *a.* dead, expired, faded, withered.
මිලි, *Mili*, *s.* (from මල dirt etc.) filthiness, dirt; the earth; name of Mahíkántáwa, a personification of the earth: *a.* black, dark, or dark blue; blue; filthy, foul, dirty.
මිලිත, *Milita*, *a.* (මිල *mila* and ක්ත *kta* aff.) mixed, united, combined.
මිලිදු, *Milidu*, *s.* archer, bowman, [Colloq. වැද්දා *weddá*].
මිලින, *Milina*, *a.* corruptly for මලින *malina*, filthy, dirty, foul; corrupting, defiling.
මිලිඹි, *Milimbi*, *s.* act of eating, applied to the priests.
මිලිල, *Milila*, *s.* the chaste tree from which is obtained a valuable and durable timber for buildings, *vitex altissima (Verbenaceæ)*; also called මිල්ල *milla*, සපු මිලිල *sapu-milila*, and මිඅං මිලිල *mian-milila*.
මිලිස්, *Milis*, *s.* savage, barbarian, mountaineer, Elu form of ම්ලේච්ඡ *mlechchha*.
මිලිස්වස්, *Miliswas*, *s.* (මිලිස් savage, වස් residence) wilderness, forest; country of barbarians.
මිලිසියානු, *Milisiyánu*, *s.* excellent gold; this is sometimes called මිරිසියානු *mirisiyánu* and විලිසියානු *wilisiyánu*.
මිලිහස, *Milihasa*, *s.* (මිලි and හස goose) brown goose.
මිලේට ගන්නවා, *Miléta-gannawá*, *v.* to buy.
මිලේට දෙනවා, *Miléta-denawá*, *v.* to sell.
මිවන, *Miwana*, *s.* species of fern: see මිවනකොල *miwanakola*.
මිවු, *Miwu*, *s.* buffalo: see මීස *misa*.

මිවුයත්, *Miwuyat*, *s.* Yama the Indian Pluto, [Coll: යම රජ *yama-raja*].

මිශ්‍ර, *Misra*, *s.* mixing; honorific affix to proper names: *a.* mixed, blended, mingled.

මිශ්‍රකරණවා, *Misra-karanawá*, *v.* to mix, to join, to blend, to combine.

මිශ්‍රණ, *Misrana*, *s.* mixing, uniting.

මිශ්‍රාගන්ධක, *Misrágandhaka*, *s.* yellow orpiment.

මිශ්‍රිත, *Misrita*, *a.* mixed, blended, mingled.

මිස්‍ර, *Misra*, corruptly for මිශ්‍ර *misra*.

මිස්සකේසි, *Missakési*, *s.* goddess, [Colloq. දිව්‍යාඞ්ගනාව *diwyánganáwa*].

මිස, *Misa*, *s.* buffalo, [Colloq. මීහරකා *míharaká*]: *a.* false, erroneous, untrue: *ad.* unless, except.

මිසදිටු, *Misaditu*, } *s.* (මිස false, දිටු or දුටු sight,
මිසදුටු, *Misadutu*, } knowledge) heresy; heathenism.

මිසරය, *Misaraya*, *s.* Egypt.

මිසි, *Misi*, } *s.* plant resembling fennel, *anethum*
මිසී, *Misí*, } *panmori*, and *a. sowa*, [Colloq. ශතපුෂ්ප *satapushpa*]; spikenard, *valeriana jatamansi*, [Colloq. ජටාමාංස *jatámánsa*]; sort of lovage *ligusticum ajowan;* common anise, *pimpinella anisum;* these are sometimes written, මිෂි *mishi* මිෂී *mishí*, මිෂි *misi* මිෂී *misí*.

මිහි, *Mihi*, *s.* the earth, [Colloq. පොළව *polawa*]; honey; lotus; any aquatic flower; semen virile; juice that exudes from the temple of an elephant in the rutting season.

මිහිකත්, *Mihikat*, *s.* (මිහි and කත් woman) female personification of the earth, Elu form of මහී කාන්තාව *mahíkántáwa*, which see.

මිහිකා, *Mihiká*, *s.* (මිහ *miha* to sprinkle, ක *ka* aff.) frost; dew.

මිහිකෙරීම, *Mihikeríma*, *s.* maturing, ripening.

මිහිඟු, *Mihingu*, *s.* tree from the blossoms or flowers of which a spirit is distilled, *bassia longifolia*, [Colloq. මීගහ *mi-gaha*].

මිහිඟුබෙරය, *Mihingu-beraya*, *s.* sort of tabour or drum chiefly used by the Malabars; the drum which is in the Sakra-bhawana or paradise of Indra, and is only beaten at the end of every antah kalpa.

මිහිත, *Mihita*, *s.* laughter, laughing.

මිහිතලය, *Mihitalaya*, *s.* (මිහි earth, තල *tala* plane) the earth, world, plane or surface of the earth.

මිහිදුම්, *Mihidum*, *s.* (මිහි and දුම් smoke) fog, mist, vapour.

මිහිදුරු, *Mihiduru*, *s.* rock, [Colloq. කඳු *kanda*].

මිහිදුල්, *Mihidul*, *s.* stone, stone in general, [Colloq. ගල *gala*].

මිහිඳු, *Mihindu*, *s.* (මිහි and ඉඳු *indu* lord) king, monarch; name of Sakraya.

මිහිප, *Mihipa*, } *s.* (මිහි and පල් who preserves)
මිහිපල්, *Mihipal*, } king, sovereign, [Colloq. රජ *raja*].

මිහිපා, *Mihipá*, *s.* (මිහි honey, පා who drinks) bee, [Colloq. මීමැස්සා *mímessá*].

මිහිපුත්, *Mihi-put*, *s.* (මිහි earth, පුත් son) name of the planet Mars, [Coll: අඟහරුවා *angaharuwá*].

මිහිර, *Mihira*, *s.* softness, delicacy; delight, pleasure, agreeableness; sun; sage; cloud; air, wind; moon.

මිහිරි, *Mihiri*, *a.* soft, sweet, harmonious; sweet literally or figuratively.

මිහිරිදිය, *Mihiri-diya*, *s.* (මිහිරි and දිය water) fresh water.

මිහිරිය, *Mihiriya*, *s.* name of Ganésa, the Indian god of wisdom; sweetness in sound, flavour, or disposition.

මිහිලොල්, *Mihilol*, } *s.* (මිහි honey, ලොල් desir
මිහිලොස්, *Mihilos*, } ing) bee, honey bee: see මිහිපා *mihipá*.

මිහිහල්, *Mihi-hal*, *s.* sea, ocean, [Colloq. මුහුද *múda*].

මී, *Mi*, *s.* from මහී *mahí*, the earth; pollen, toddy, spirituous liquor; honey; rat; buffalo; death: see මීගස *mi-gasa*.

මීඅං, *Mí-an*, *s.* the horn of the buffalos.

මීඅංබදර, *Mían-badara*, *s.* tree, not ascertained.

මීඅංමාරා, *Mían-márá*, *s.* tree, species of *albizzia*.

මීඅංමිලිල, *Mían-milila*, *s.* valuable timber tree, *vitex altissima:* see මිලිල *milila*.

මීඅංවැල, *Mían-wela*, *s.* persicaria or buck wheat, *polygonum chinense*.

මීඅඹ, *Mí-amba*, *s.* small species of mango very sweet.

මීඅරටුගහ, *Míaratu-gaha*, *s.* tree, not ascertained.

මීඅච්චි, *Mí-áchchi*, } *s.* great grand mother.
මීඅත්තා, *Mí-áttá*, }

මීඉටි, *Mí-iti*, *s.* bees wax.

මීකත, *Mí-kata*, see මිහිකත් *mihikat*.

මීකඳනාවැල, *Míkandaná-wela*, *s.* creeping plant, not ascertained.

මීකන්පලා, *Míkan-palá*, *s.* medicinal plant or shrub, *alternanthera triandra* or *a. sessile*, [Colloq. මුකුණුවැන්න *mukunuwenna:* see මීනලෝචන *mínalóchana*.

මී කපල්, *Mí-kapal*, *s.* (මී honey, කපල් depository) honey comb.

මී කල්, *Mí-kal*, *s.* bee hive.

මී කිරි, *Mí-kiri*, *s.* (මී buffalo, කිරි milk) buffalo's milk.

මීකෙළින වේලාව, *Míkelina-wéláwa*, *s.* (මී and කෙළින sport, වේලාව time) evening, the time when the bees collect together, preparatory to their returning to the hive.

මීගස, *Mí-gasa*, *s.* wild sapota tree, the wood of which is used for timber, and the seeds yield the oil, called මීතෙල් *mí-tel*, *bassia longifolia (Sapotaceæ)*.

මීගොණා, *Mí-goṇá*, *s.* male buffalo.

මීගොන් කරපිංච, *Mígon-karapincha*, *s.* tree, *clausena indica*.

මීට, *Míṭa*, *ad.* to this (time); to or for this.

මීඪ, *Mídha*, *a.* passed as urine.

මී තෙල්, (මී and තෙල් oil) oil made from the seeds of the *bassia longifolia*; ghee.

මීදුම, *Míduma*, *s.* (මී earth දුම smoke) mist, fog, vapour.

මීදෙන, *Mídena*, *s.* (මී buffalo, දෙන cow) female buffalo.

මීන, *Mína*, *s.* fish; sign of the zodiac, Pisces.

මීනක්‍ෂ, *Mínaksha*, *s.* shrub called *tabernæ montana dichotoma*, or forbidden fruit, [Colloq. දිවිකදුරු *divikaduru*].

මීනකේතන, *Mína-kétana*, *s.* (මීන fish, කේතන banner) name of Anaṅgayá or Káma the Indian Cupid.

මීනර, *Mínara*, *s.* marine monster, sometimes applied to the shark and alligator: see මකර *makara*.

මීනරාසිය, *Mína-rásiya*, } *s.* (මීන and රාසිය or රැස
මීනරැස, *Mína-ṛesa*, } sign of the zodiac) sign, Pisces.

මීනලෝචන, *Mínalóchana*, *s.* (මීන fish, ලෝචන eye) plant, with a flower resembling the eye of a fish, *illecebrum sessile*: see මීකන්පලා *míkanpalá*.

මීනුග, *Mí-nuga*, *s.* medicinal plant, *hoya hirsuta*.

මීප, *Mípa*, *s.* (මී earth, ප who nourishes, or මී honey, ප who drinks) king; honey bee; see මීපුප් *mí-pup*.

මීපත් ඇල්වී, *Mípat-ęlri*, *s.* kind of paddy, *oryza sativa*.

මීපත්‍රී, *Mípatrí*, *s.* kind of paddy.

මීපති, *Mípati*, *s.* (මී and පති chief) king, sovereign, [Colloq. රජ *raja*].

මීපල්, *Mipal*, see මිහිපල් *mihipal*.

මීපල, *Mí-pala*, *s.* (මී and පල fruit) fruit of the *bassia longifolia*.

මීපා, *Mípá*, *s.* (මී and පා who nourishes or මී honey, පා who drinks) king; honey bee.

මී පිඩු, *Mí-piḍu*, *s.* (මී honey, පිඩු ball) honeycomb, honey in the comb.

මීපුප්, *Mípup*, *s.* flower or blossoms of the *bassia longifolia*, from which a spirituous liquor is distilled.

මීපේ, *Mípé*, *s.* salt.

මීපැණි, *Mí-pęni*, *s.* (මී and පැණි juice) honey, liquid honey.

මී බඳිනවා, *Mí-baṇdinawá*, *v.* to make honey, to collect honey, to construct the hive.

මී මල, *Mí-mala*, *s.* (මී and මල flower) flower of the *bassia longifolia*.

මීමස්මර ලෙඩ, *Mímasmara-leḍa*, *s.* falling sickness, epilepsy.

මීමස, *Mí-masa*, *s.* (මී and මස month) vernal month (April–May).

මීමා, *Mímá*, *s.* buffalo.

මීමින්නා, *Míminná*, *s.* Indian moose deer, *moschus miminna*.

මීමිනිබිරි, *Míminibiri*, *s.* great grand daughter.

මීමිනිබුරා, *Míminiburá*, *s.* great grandson.

මීමිනිමාරා, *Mímini-márá*, *s.* plant, *pithecolobium subcoriaceum (Leguminosæ)*.

මීමුත්තා, *Mímuttá*, *s.* great grand father.

මීමුරුවට, *Mímuruwaṭa*, *s.* medicine prepared from the refuse of the seeds of the *bassia longifolia*, after the oil has been expressed.

මීමැස්සා, *Mí-męssá*, *s.* (මී honey, මැස්සා fly) honey bee.

මීය, *Miya*, *s.* beehive.

මීයන්, *Miyan*, *plur.* of මීයා *miyá*.

මී යහන්, *Mí-yahan*, *s.* (මී rat; buffalo, යහන් vehicle) name of Gaṇéṣa, the Indian god of wisdom, who is usually figured sitting on a rat, [Colloq. ගණදෙවියෝ *gaṇadeviyó*]; name of Yama regent and judge of the dead, alluding to his riding on a buffalo.

මීයා, *Miyá*, *s.* rat, general name for the whole rat tribe.

මීර, *Míra*, *s.* sea, ocean, [Colloq. මූද *múda*].

මීරන්, *Míran*, *s.* tale, more commonly written මිනිරන් *miniran*.

මීරස, *Mí-rasa*, *s.* flavour of the honey.

මිරා, *Mírá*, s. (මී honey, රා toddy) sweet toddy, or a saccharine liquor extracted from the coconut tree and from which a raw sugar is manufactured.

මිරිත, *Mírita*, a. sweet, saccharine.

මිරිය, *Míriya*, see මිහිරිය *míhiriya*.

මීරුපු, *Mí-rupu*, s. (මී rat, රුපු enemy) cat, [Colloq. බළලා *baḷalá*].

මිල්ල, *Milla*, see මිලිල *milila*.

මිල්හ, *Milha*, s. ordure, fæces.

මිලන, *Milana*, s. twinkling, blinking, winking.

මිලිත, *Milita*, s. indirect allusion or description, (in rhetoric): a. twinkled, partly opened as a young bud, etc.

මීලොල්, *Milol*. s. honey bee, [Coll: බමරු *bamaru*].

මීවද, *Mí-wada*, } s. (මී honey, වද receptacle)
මීවදේ, *Mí-wadé*, } honeycomb; sweet cakes.

මීවන, *Míwana*, s. grove of මී *mí* trees.

මීවනකොල, *Míwana-kola*, s. fern called spleenwort, *diplazium (or asplenium) esculentum (Filices)*.

මී වස්සා, *Mí-wassá*, s. calf of a buffalo: pl. මීවස්සෝ *míwassó*.

මීවා, *Míwá*, s. buffalo; worm of the intestines, ascarides.

මීවින්නා, *Mírinná*, s. jungle or field rat: pl. මීවින්නෝ *mírinnó*.

මීවැටියා, *Míweṭiyá*, s. fish, long nosed sea bream, *lethrinus rostatus*.

මීවැන්න, *Míweṇna*, s. plant, *polyalthia (or guateria) tiorinti*.

මීහං, *Mí-haṇ*, s. buffalo's skin; also, buffalo's horn.

මීහරකා, *Míharaká*, s. buffalo.

මිහිරිය, *Míhiriya*, s. large tree seeds of which yield oil similar to මීතෙල් *mí-tel*, *dichopsis (or isonandra) grandis (Sapotaceæ)*; also called කිරිහැඹිලිය *kirihembiliya* and කිරිහිරිය *kirihiriya*.

මුං, *Muṇ*, } s. sort of small green grain
මුං ඇට, *Muṇ-eṭa*, } used for food, green peas, *phaseolus mungo (Leguminosæ)*.

මුං කරල, *Muṇ-karala*, s. the pod of the above grain, *phaselous mungo*.

මුං කැවුම, *Muṇ-kewuma*, s. cake make of pulse.

මුං පියලි, *Muṇ-piyali*, s. (මුං and පියලි division) two lobes of the muṇ grain.

මුංවැන්න, *Muṇweṇna*, s. kind of kidney bean, *phaseolus trilobus*: see බින්මෑ *bin-mé*.

මුක්, *Muk*, s. demon: a. dumb.

මුක්කමා, *Mukkamá*, } s. one who has a disfigur-
මුක්කරයා, *Mukkarayá*, } ed nose, one who speaks with the nose, one who has no nose.

මුක්කාල, *Mukkála*, s. three fourths of any thing. (Tamil.)

මුක්ත, *Mukta*, s. (මුච *mucha* to set free, ක්ත *kta* aff.) the spirit released from mundane existence, and exempted from further transmigration, Nirwáṇa: a. released, liberated, loosed, let go; liberated from corporeal existence, finally happy; discharged, loosed as a weapon.

මුක්තක, *Muktaka*, s. (මුක්ත loosed, අක *aka* aff.) any missile weapon; stanza or sentence completing the sense of a passage.

මුක්ත කංචුක, *Mukta-kaṇchuka*, s. (මුක්ත and කංචුක the slough of a snake) serpent that has cast his slough.

මුක්තකරණවා, *Mukta-karaṇawá*, v. to dart, to emit, to shoot as an arrow, to send out.

මුක්තඵල, *Mukta-phala*, see මුක්තාඵල *muktá-phala*.

මුක්ත රෝග, *Mukta-róga*, s. one cured of his disease.

මුක්තා, *Muktá*, s. pearl, [Colloq. මුතු *mutu*]; see also මුක්ත *mukta*.

මුක්තාකලාප, *Mutá-kalápa*, s. (මුක්තා and කලාප ornament, assemblage) pearl necklace, string of pearls.

මුක්තාගාර, *Muktágára*, s. (මුක්තා and අගාර *ágára* abode) pearl oyster.

මුක්තාඵල, *Muktá-phala*, s. (මුක්තා and ඵල fruit) pearl, [Colloq. මුතු *mutu*]; camphor; custard apple, being comparable to a pearl in whiteness.

මුක්තාමුක්ත, *Muktámukta*, a. (මුක්ත *mukta* loosed, අමුක්ත *amukta* not loosed) loosed and not loosed, applied especially to weapons which may be wielded or hurled, as a club, a javelin, etc.

මුක්ත ලතා, *Muktálatá*, } s. (මුක්තා and ලතා cree-
මුක්තාවලි, *Muktáwali*, } per or අවලි *áwalí* a line or row) pearl necklace.

මුක්තාස්ඵෝට, *Muktásphóṭa*, s. (මුක්තා and ස්ඵුට *sphuṭa* to burst) pearl oyster.

මුක්තාහාරය, *Muktáháraya*, s. pearl necklace.

මුක්ති, *Mukti*, s. (මුච *mucha* to set free, ක්ති aff.) final beatitude, delivery of the soul from the body, exemption from further transmigration, Nirwáṇa; loosing, liberating, setting free.

මුක, *Muka*, s. mouth: see මුඛ *mukha*.

මුකබැඳිම, *Muka-beṇdima*, s. (මුක and බැඳීම binding) mode of enchanting snakes, crocodiles, and other noxious animals, rendering them unable to open their mouths.

මුකරාගකරි, *Mukarágakarí*, see මුඛාලංකාර *mukhálaṅkára*.

මුකවඩම, *Mukawadama*, *s.* (මුක and වඩම covering) cloth tied over the mouth of the person who carries victuals to the king, to prevent his breathing upon them.

මුකාවෙටියා, *Mukaweṭiyá*, *s.* secretary, clerk, writer, office of writer, [Colloq. ලියන්නා *liyanná*].

මුකුණුවැන්න, *Mukuṇuwenna*, *s.* plant, *alternanthera triandra (Amarantaceæ).*

මුකුත්, *Mukut*, *ad.* anything, something.

මුකුන්ද, *Mukunda*, *s.* name of Vishṇu; gum olibanum; precious gem; quicksilver; one of Kuvéras divine treasures.

මුකුන්දක, *Mukundaka*, *s.* onion, [Colloq. ලූනු *lúnu*].

මුකුර, *Mukura*, *s.* (මක *maka* to adorn) mirror; tree, *mimusops elengi*, [Colloq. මූනමල් *múna-mal*].

මුකුරු, *Mukuru*, *s.* dumb person or one having an impediment in his speech: *a.* foul-mouthed, Elu form of මුඛර *mukhara.*

මුකුල, *Mukula*, *s.* opening bud, [Colloq. කැකුළ *kekuḷa*]; body; soul or spirit: pl. මුකුලු *mukulu.*

මුකුලිත, *Mukulita*, *a.* half-shut, winking.

මුකුළු, *Mukuḷu*, *s.* bud, young shoot of a leaf; unblown flower; joke, wanton laughter.

මුකුළුකරණවා, *Mukuḷukaraṇawá*, *v.* to joke.

මුකුෂ්ඨක, *Mukushṭhaka*, *s.* sort of kidney bean, *phaseolus lobatus.*

මුඛ්‍ය, *Mukhya*, *s.* chief, principal person: *a.* chief, primary, principal.

මුඛ්‍යක, *Mukhyaka*, *s.* chief, headman.

මුඛ, *Mukha*, *s.* mouth; face, countenance; entrance to a house; commencement, origin, first cause; means, device, expedient; sound; beak of a bird: *a.* first, initial; chief, principal, pre-eminent.

මුඛධෞතා, *Mukhadhautá*, *s.* (මුඛ mouth, ධෞත *dhauta* washing) plant, *siphonanthus indica.*

මුඛපද්ම, *Mukha-padma*, *s.* (මුඛ mouth, පද්ම lotus) lotus mouth, expression of beauty.

මුඛය, *Mukhaya*, see මුඛ *mukha.*

මුඛර, *Mukhara*, *a.* (මුඛ and ර aff. of depreciation) having an impediment in the speech; foul-mouthed, speaking scurrilously or harshly.

මුඛශෝධන, *Mukha-sódhana*, *s.* (මුඛ and ශෝධන washing) pungency, sharp or pungent flavour; washing or rincing the mouth.

මුඛස්නේහ, *Mukhasnéha*, *s.* cinnamon bark, *cinnamomum zeylanicum*, [Colloq. කුරුඳුපොතු *kuruṇdu-potu*].

මුඛාලංකාර, *Mukhálaṅkára*, *s.* (මුඛ *mukha* and අලංකාර *alaṅkára* ornament) betel, quantity of betel leaf, areca nut, and chunam or caustic lime, eaten together; the constant use of these gives the mouth of the natives a blood-like colour, hence its name.

මුග්ධ, *Mugdha*, *s.* (මුහ *muha* to be foolish, ක්ත *kta* aff.) idiot, fool, stupid fellow: *a.* stupid, foolish, ignorant; lovely, beautiful.

මුගටියා, *Mugaṭiyá*, *s.* ichneumon or mungoose, kind of weasel, *herpestes grisens.*

මුගලන්, *Mugalan*, *s.* one of the two chief priests that attended Gautama Buddha in his personal ministrations.

මුගිංචිය, *Muginchiya*, *s.* decree, decision, award; judicial sentence.

මුගුනගස, *Muguna-gasa*, *s.* tree, *mimusops elengi*, producing a very fragrant flower, [Colloq. මූන මල් *múna-mal*]: see මුකුර *mukura.*

මුගුනුවැන්න, *Mugunuwenna*, *s.* creeper bearing a flower resembling the eye of a fish, *illecebrum sessile:* see මීකන්පලා *míkan-palá.*

මුගුර, *Mugura*, } *s.* club, heart of the top of any
මුගුරු, *Muguru*, } tree, crow-bar, mallet, mace; carpenter's hammer; Elu form of මුද්ගර *mudgara.*

මුච්ඡනා, *Muchchhaná*, *s.* tone or semitone as placed in its scale, seventh part of a gráma or scale.

මුචලින්ද, *Muchalinda*, *s.* name of a snake; tree, [Colloq. මිදෙල්ල *midella*].

මුට්ටිය, *Muṭṭiya*, *s.* earthen cooking pot with a small mouth.

මුට්ටුව, *Muṭṭuwa*, *s.* arrear, deficiency, necessity. (Tamil.)

මුටගත්, *Muṭagat*, } *s.* mirage, sultry vapour, va-
මුටතත්, *Muṭatat*, } pour floating over sands and deserts, and when acted upon by the sun's rays appearing at a distance like water or undulating waves.

මුටද, *Muṭada*, *s.* arrow.

මුඩ, *Muḍa*, see මුණ්ඩ *muṇḍa.*

මුඩමහණ, *Muḍamahaṇa*, *s.* medicinal plant, *sphæranthus indicus* or *s. hirtus (Compositæ).*

මුඩාව, *Muḍáwa*, *s.* slit in the end of the arrow, where it rests on the bow string; point of a bow to which the string is tied: pl. මුඩා *muḍá.*

මුඩු, *Muḍu*, *a.* rancid, rank, fetid; polled, shaved, bald.

මුඩුක්කුව, *Muḍukkuwa*, *s.* lane. (Tamil.)

මුඩුක, *Muḍuka*, *a.* having no hair on the head, bald.

මුඩුකරණවා, *Muḍukaraṇawá*, *v.* to shave.

මුඩුක වාදය, *Muḍuka-wádaya*, *s.* (මුඩුක bald, වාද *wáda* speech) term of abuse, bald head.

මුඩුව, *Muḍuwa*, *s.* fibre at the end of a coconut.

මුඩේ, *Muḍé*, *s.* ladder or flight of steps erected in the rice fields, on which persons are stationed to frighten away the birds, etc. from the grain.

මුණ්ඩ, *Muṇḍa*, *s.* head, forehead; barber; trunk of a lopped tree; name of Ráhu the ascending node: *a.* shaven, bald.

මුණ්ඩක, *Muṇḍaka*, *s.* (මුණ්ඩ and ක aff.) bow; barber; head.

මුණ්ඩන, *Muṇḍana*, *s.* shaving, shearing, cutting.

මුණ්ඩය, *Muṇḍaya*, *s.* leaden bullet.

මුණ්ඩලියා, *Muṇḍaliyá*, *s.* small sea fish.

මුණ්ඩා, *Muṇḍá*, *s.* Bengal madder.

මුණ්ඩාසන, *Muṇḍásana*, *s.* (මුණ්ඩ *muṇḍa* head, අසන *ásana* seat) turban, Malabar head dress.

මුණ්ඩිත, *Muṇḍita*, *a.* (මුණ්ඩ *muṇḍa* bald, ඉතච් *itach* aff.) bald, shorn, shaven.

මුණ්ඩීරි, *Muṇḍírí*, see මුඩමහණ *muḍamahaṇa*.

මුණ්ඩෙ, *Muṇḍe*, *s.* leaden ball, bullet.

මුත්, *Mut*, *s.* (මුද *muda* to be pleased) joy, pleasure, delight: *ad.* except, besides.

මුත්තනියෝ, *Muttaniyó*, *s.* paternal grand mother.

මුත්තා, *Muttá*, *s.* paternal grandfather.

මුත්ති, *Mutti*, *s.* redemption, deliverance; name of Nirwáṇa; Páli form of මුක්ති *mukti*.

මුත්තික, *Muttika*, *s.* pearl, [Colloq. මුතු *mutu*].

මුත්තැස්වී, *Muttęs-ví*, *s.* kind of paddy, *oryza sativa*.

මුත්නා, *Mutná*, *s.* grandfather.

මුත්පත්, *Mut-pat*, } *s.* (මුත් and පත් or පර්ණ leaf) sort of kidney bean,
මුත්පර්ණ, *Mut-parṇa*, } *phaseolus trilobus*, [Colloq. බින්මෑ *bin-mę*]; see මුද්ගපර්ණි *mudgaparṇṇi*.

මුත්පල, *Mutpala*, } *s.* blue lotus, *nymphœa stellata*,
මුත්ඵල, *Mutphala*, } [Colloq. මානෙල් *mánel*].

මුත්‍ය, *Mutya*, *s.* pearl, [Colloq. මුතු *mutu*].

මුතමුත්, *Mutamut*, *a.* (මුත loosened, අමුත් *amut* not loosened) loosened and not loosened, applied to weapons which may be hurled or wielded, as a club, javelin; Elu form of මුක්තාමුක්ත *muktá-mukta*.

මුතු, *Mutu*, *s.* pearl.

මුතුකැල, *Mutukęla*, *s.* (මුතු and කැල multitude) collection or assemblage of pearls, pearl bank.

මුතුදම්, *Mutu-dam*, *s.* (මුතු and දම් chain) pearl necklace, string of pearls.

මුතුදැල්, *Mutudęl*, *s.* assemblage or net-work of pearls.

මුතුන්, *Mutun*, } *s.* forefathers,
මුතුන්මුත්තෝ, *Mutunmuttó*, } ancestors.

මුතුබෙල්ලං, *Mutu-bellaṅ*, *s.* (මුතු and බෙල්ලං oyster) pearl oyster, *margaritifera fugata*.

මුතුවැල, *Mutu-węla*, *s.* (මුතු and වැල row) string of pearls, pearl necklace.

මුතුසුණු, *Mutu-suṇu*, *s.* (මුතු pearl, සුණු powder) pearl reduced to a state of calcination, said to be eaten by eastern monarchs with their betel, instead of chunam a kind of caustic lime.

මුතුහර, *Mutuhara*, see මුතුදම් *mutudam*.

මුද්ග, *Mudga*, *s.* kind of kidney bean, *phaseolus mungo*, [Colloq, මුං *muṅ*].

මුද්ගපත්‍ර, *Mudgapatra*, *s.* plant, *cordia myxa*, [Colloq. ලෝලු *lólu*].

මුද්ගපර්ණි, *Mudgaparṇṇi*, *s.* (මුද්ග and පර්ණ *parṇa* leaf) sort of kidney bean, *phaseolus trilobus*, [Colloq. මුංවැන්න *muṅwęnna*].

මුද්ගපුෂ්පි, *Mudga-pushpí*, *s.* tree, *euphorbia antiquorum*, [Colloq. දලුක්ගහ *daluk-gaha*].

මුද්ගර, *Mudgara*, *s.* mallet, carpenter's hammer; sort of club, staff armed with iron for breaking clods of earth.

මුද්ද, *Mudda*, *s.* ring: pl. මුදු *mudu*.

මුද්දරය, *Muddaraya*, } *s.* stamp: pl. මුද්දර *mud-*
මුද්දරේ, *Muddaré*, } *dara*.

මුද්දිරප්පලම්, *Muddirappalam*, *s.* grapes.

මුද්‍රනයකරණවා, *Mudraṇaya-karaṇawá*, see මුද්‍රාඞ්කණයකරණවා *mudráṅkaṇaya-karaṇawá*.

මුද්‍රා, *Mudrá*, *s.* seal, signet, seal ring, stamp or impression of a seal.

මුද්‍රාඞ්කණයකරණවා, *Mudráṅkaṇaya-karaṇawá*, *v.* to print.

මුද්‍රාඞ්කණ ශාලාව, *Mudráṅkaṇa-ṣáláwa*, *s.* printing office.

මුද්‍රාඞ්කිත, *Mudráṅkita*, *a.* stamped, sealed, printed.

මුද්‍රික, *Mudrika*, see the following.

මුද්‍රිකපාන, *Mudrikhpána*, *s.* corruptly for මෘද්වීක පාන *mridvíkapána*, (මෘද්වීක grape, පාන drink) expressed juice of the grape, wine.

මුද්‍රිකවැල, *Mudrika-węla*, *s.* vine creeper, *vitis vinifera*, corruptly for මෘද්වීකවැල *mridvíka-węla*.

මුද්‍රිකා, *Mudriká*, *s.* (මුද්‍ර *mudra* seal, කන් *kan* aff.) sealed or signed paper; stamp.

මුද්‍රිත, *Mudrita*, *s.* (මුද්‍රා *mudrá* seal, ඉතච් *itach* aff.) stamped, sealed, printed.

මුදඟ, *Mudanga*, *s.* tabor, small drum; Páli form of මෘදඟ *mridanga*.

මුදඟිල්ල, *Mudangilla*, *s.* ring-finger: pl. මුදඟිලි *mudangili*.

මුදනවා, *Mudanawá*, *v.* to release, to set free, to loose; to untie, to unlock; to set at liberty, to manumit, to emancipate: pret. මිදුවා *miduwá*.

මුදරු කිරලා, *Mudaru-kiralá*, *s.* black-bellied marsh tern, *Hydrochelida hybrida (Laridæ,* order *Gaviæ);* also called ලිහිණියා *lihiṇiyá* or ලිණියා *líṇiyá*.

මුදල, *Mudala*, *s.* money, coin, price: pl. මුදල් *mudal*.

මුදලි, *Mudali*, *s.* (මුදල *mudala* money, ඉන් *in* aff.) treasurer, cash keeper, relating to Mudaliyars.

මුදලිඳු, *Mudalindu*, *s.* (මුදල *mudala* and ඉඳු *indu* name of Mahá méru; treasurer, Mudaliyár, chieftain.

මුදවනවා, *Mudawanawá*, *v.* to curdle, to cause to release, to save; causal form of මුදනවා *mudanawá*, which see.

මුදා, *Mudá*, *s.* (මුද *muda* to be pleased) happiness, joy; also, *past part.* of මුදනවා *mudanawá*.

මුදිත, *Mudita*, *a.* (මුද *muda* to be pleased) pleased, delighted; gentle, meek.

මුදිතා, *Muditá*, *s.* (මුද *muda* to be pleased) gentleness, meekness, equanimity of mind, [Colloq. සන්තෝෂය *santóshaya*].

මුදියන්සේ, *Muidyansé*, *s.* Mudaliyár, chief native Revenue officer of a Kóralé.

මුදිහිරුව, *Mudihiruwa*, *s.* ring: see මුද්ද *mudda*.

මුදු, *Mudu*, *a.* soft, delicate, tender; Páli form of මෘදු *mridu*.

මුදුන් ඇටේ, *Mudun-ęté*, } *s.* spine, back bone.
මුදුන් කටුව, *Mudun-katuwa*, }

මුදුන් කනුව, *Mudun-kanuwa*, *s.* king-post in a building.

මුදුන්කරණවා, *Mudunkaraṇawá*, *v.* to heap up.

මුදුන්පත්, *Mudunpat*, *a.* (මුදුන් and පත් arrived) arrived at the head, literally or metaphorically, attained the highest branches of learning, obtained the highest place in office, etc.

මුදුන්පත්කරණවා, *Mudunpat-karaṇawá*, *v.* to extol, reverence in the highest manner, to esteem one as pre-eminently superior.

මුදුන් යටලිය, *Mudun-yaṭaliya*, *s.* ridge beam of a house.

මුදුන් වහල, *Mudun-wahala*, *s* upper roof.

මුදුන, *Muduna*, *s.* the head, top, summit, peak; literally or metaphorically; the meridian: pl. මුදුන් *mudun*.

මුදුනා, *Muduná*, *s.* the leading buffalo in thrashing corn: *a.* soft, flexible, supple.

මුදුව, *Muduwa*, *s.* ring: pl. මුදු *mudu*.

මුදෞවිල්, *Mudowvil*, *s.* (මුදෞව් and විල් lake) Ganges or river of heaven; Elu form of මන්දාකිනී *mandákiní*.

මුන්, *Mun*, *s.* kidney bean, green gram, *phaseolus mungo radiatus, (Leguminosæ);* Elu form of මුද්ග *mudga;* in which sense it is more correctly written මුං *muṅ: pronoun* these (persons), contraction of මොවුන් *mowun*.

මුන්නිලයා, *Munnilayá*, *s.* ancestor.

මුන, *Muna*, *s.* end, top, extremity, tip, point.

මුනගැහෙනවා, *Munagęhenawá*, *v.* to come in contact.

මුනි, *Muni*, *s.* (මන *mana* to reverence) holy sage, pious and learned person endowed with more or less of a divine nature or having attained it by rigid abstraction and mortification; devotee, ascetic; name of a Buddha; also a Rahat or highest order of Buddhist saint; name of the Agastya; tree, *butea frondosa,* [Colloq. ගස්කැල *gas-kéla*]; another tree, *buchanania latifolia;* heart, as the seat of reason.

මුනිද්‍රුම, *Munidruma*, *s.* tree, *æschynomene grandiflora;* another tree, *sesbania grandiflora,* [Colloq. කතුරුමුරුංගා *katuru-murungá*].

මුනිඳු, *Munindu*, *s.* (මුනි and ඉඳු *indu* chief) generic name of a Buddha; sage, wise and holy man.

මුනි නිවෙස්, *Muni-nives*, *s.* (මුනි saint, නිවෙස් residence) wihára.

මුනිප්‍රිය, *Muni-priya*, see මහරි *mahari*.

මුනිශාඛ, *Muni-sákha*, see මුනිද්‍රුම *muni-druma*.

මුනිසව්, *Munisaw*, *s.* (මුනි Buddha, සව් disciple) disciple of Buddha.

මුනිසිද්ධිකෘත්, *Muni-siddhikrit*, *s.* plant, Indian shot, *canna indica,* [Colloq. බුත්සරණ *butsaraṇa*].

මුනින්ද්‍ර, *Munindra*, (මුනි and ඉන්ද්‍ර *indra* chief) generic title of a Buddha.

මුනුපුරා, *Munupurá*, } *s.* grandson.
මුනුබුරා, *Munuburá*, }

මුනේ, *Muné*, *s.* point of any sharp instrument; tip, point; front.

මුමන, *Mumana*, s. thunder; tremour, shaking, tremulous motion.

මුය, *Muya*, s. mouth; Elu form of මුඛ *mukha*.

* මූර්ඡා, *Murchchhá* s. fainting, loss of consciousness or perception.

* මූර්ඡාල, *Murchchhála*, a. fainted, insensible.

* මූර්ඡාව, *Murchchháwa*, s. fainting, loss of consciousness.

* මූර්ඡාවෙනවා, *Murchchhá-wenawá*, v. to swoon, to faint away.

මූර්තා, *Murtá*, corruptly for මූර්ඡා *múrchchhá*.

මුර, *Mura*, s. surrounding, encircling; watching, guarding.

මුරකරණවා, *Murakaraṇawá*, v. to watch, to keep guard.

මුරකාරයා, *Murakárayá*, s. (මුර guarding, කාර *kára* who does) sentry, guard, watchman.

මුරජ, *Muraja*, s. (මුර encircling, with wood etc., ජ born) tomtom, drum, tabor.

මුරජඵල, *Muraja-phala*, s. jack tree. [Colloq. කොස්ගහ *kos-gaha*].

මුරණ්ඩු, *Muraṇḍu*, a. obstinate, stubborn.

මුරණ්ඩුකම, *Muraṇḍukama*, s. obstinacy.

මුරපල, *Murapala*, s. (මුර guarding, පල place) watch post, sentinel's post.

මුරමඩුව, *Mura-maḍuwa*, s. (මුර and මඩුව house) watch house, guard room.

මුරය, *Muraya*, s. season of plucking as of coconuts: pl. මුර *mura*.

මුරල්ලා, *Murallá*, s. kind of sea fish.

මුරහිටිනවා, *Mura-hiṭinawá*, v. to keep watch.

මුරු, *Muru*, s. a god, deity, an immortal; also see මුරුවට *muruwaṭa*.

මුරුංගා, *Murungá*, s. horse radish tree, *moringa pterygosperma (Moringeæ)*.

මුරුංගි, *Murungi*, s. variety of the above, [Colloq. වැල් මුරුංගා *wel-murungá*].

මුරුංගුශ්වේතා, *Murungu-ṣwétá*, s. (මුරුංගු and ශ්වේතා white) white species of murungá

මුරුක්කු, *Murukku*, s. kind of native sweetmeat.

මුරුක්කු වැටෙනවා, *Murukku-weṭenawá*, v. to twist as in a string. (Tamil.)

මුරුත්තාව, *Muruttáwa*, s. epilepsy swoon.

මුරුත, *Muruta*, s. timber tree, bearing a beautiful flower, *lagerstræmia flos-reginæ (Lythraceæ)*.

මුරුතමල්, *Muruta-mal*, s. (මුරුත and මල් flower) flower of the *lagerstræmia regina*; ruby.

* In these words මු mu is corruptly written for මූ mú.

මුරුන්වී, *Murun-ví*, s. kind of paddy, *oryza sativa*.

මුරුබෙර, *Muru-bera*, s. sort of large tom-tom used in the amusements of Swarga.

මුරුවට, *Muruwaṭa*, s. refuse of grain (such as the sesamum) after the oil has been expressed.

මුරුවා, *Muruwá*, } s. plant, *marsdenia tenacissima (Asclepiadeæ)*.
මුරුවා දුල්, *Muruwá-dúl*,

මුරේ, *Muré*, see මුරය *muraya*.

මුල්, *Mul*, s. cause, root, orgin: a. first, chief, primary; essential: see also මූල *mula*.

මුල් අල්ලනවා, *Mul-allanawá*, v. to take root.

මුල්කාරයා, *Mulkárayá*, s. chief mover in an undertaking, an originator.

මුල්කොඩු, *Mulkoṇḍu*, s. pangolin.

මුල් පුටුව, *Mul-puṭuwa*, s. seat of Chairman at a meeting.

මුල්බට්ටා, *Mulbaṭṭá*, s. kind of fish.

මුල්බිජු, *Mul-biju*, s. the quantity of seed to be sown in a field.

මුල්ල, *Mulla*, s. corner, angle.

මුල්ලා, *Mullá*, s. kind of sea fish.

මුල්ව, *Mulwa*, a. being chief, or principal.

මූල, *Mula*, s. root of a tree or any plant; origin; commencement; nineteenth lunar asterism.

මූලාචාරියා, *Mulácháriyá*, s. (මුල් *mul* and ආචාරියා blacksmith) head or chief of the blacksmith caste; chief teacher.

මූලාදෑනියා, *Muládéniyá*, s. chief, headman.

මූලාල, *Mulála*, s. edible root of the lotus.

මුලුසුන්, *Mulusun*, a. (මුල් *mul* and උසුන් *usun* utterly destroyed) completely destroyed, ruined, extripated.

මුව, *Muwa*, s. deer, *axis maculata*; Elu form of මෘග *mṛiga*; mouth from මුඛ *mukha*; bow; covering, shutting.

මුවඉරිඟු, *Muwa-iringu*, s. Indian corn or maize, *zea mays*.

මුවකිරියවැල, *Muwakiriya-weļa*, } s. creeping plant, *sarcostemma brunonianum*.
මුවකිරිය, *Muwakiriya*,

මුවග, *Muwaga*, s. (මුව and ග going) escaping, fleeing away.

මුවගණ, *Muwagaṇa*, s. (මුව deer, ගණ multitude) herd of deer.

මුවත්, *Muwat*, see මුවත *muwata*.

මුවත්තියනවා, *Muwat-tiyanawá*, v. to sharpen.

මුවත, *Muwata*, s. edge, the edge of a knife.

මුව තණ, *Muwa-taṇa*, Elu form of මෘග තෘෂ්ණා *mṛiga-tṛishṇá*, which see.

මුවතඹර, *Muwatambara*, *s.* (මුව and තඹර lotus) lotus mouth, an expression of beauty.

මුවද, *Muwada*, *s.* arrow, [Colloq. ඊගහ *ígaha*].

මුවදුන්, *Muwadun*, } *s.* jackal, [Colloq. නරියා
මුවදුන, *Muwaduna*, } *nariyá*].

මුවදෙන්, *Muwa-den*, *s.* (මුව and දෙන් female) female deer, hind.

මුවන්, *Muwan*, *s.* tree in general, [Colloq. ගහ *gaha*].

මුවන, *Muwana*, *s.* thunder, [Colloq. හෙණ *heṇa*].

මුවනවන්, *Muwanawan*, *s.* principal jewel in a crown or mitre.

මුවනැබ, *Muwanęba*, *s.* (මුව deer, නැබ navel) musk, musk being contained in a bag near the navel of the animal, [Colloq. කස්තුරි *kasturi*].

මුවපියුම් *Muwapiyum*, see මුවතඹර *muwatambara*.

මුවපොල්ල, *Muwa-polla*, *s.* (මුව and පොල්ල young animal) young deer, one not full grown, [Colloq. මුවපැටවා *muwa-pętawá*].

මුවපැටවා, *Muwa-pętawá*, see the preceding.

මුවමස්, *Muwa-mas*, *s.* (මුව and මස් flesh) venison.

මුවමායම්, *Muwa-máyam*, *s.* (මුව and මායම් deception) animal instinct, but applied particularly to the deer, which is remarkable for its cunning in eluding its pursuers.

මුවර, *Muwara*, *s.* shark.

මුවරද, *Muwa-rada*, *s.* (මුව animal, රද king) lion, [Colloq. සිංහයා *sinhayá*]; pollen of flowers; nectar of flowers.

මුවරදද, *Muwara-dada*, *s.* (මුවර and දද banner) name of Anańgayá, the Indian Cupid.

මුවරිට, *Muwariṭa*, } *s.* (මුව mouth, විට or විටිය
මුවවිටිය, *Muwaviṭiya*, } circumference) mouth or brim of any vessel; edge.

මුවවැද්දා, *Muwa-węddá*, *s.* (මුව deer, වැද්දා hunter) deer hunter.

මුවසිරස, *Muwa-sirasa*, *s.* (මුව and සිරස head) fifth lunar asterism, figured by the head of a deer; Elu form of මෘගශිරස් *mriga-ṣiras*, which see.

මුවහත්, *Muwahat*, *a.* sharp.

මුවහත, *Muwahata*, *s.* sharp edge of a knife, sword, etc.

මුවහතවනවා, *Muwahatawanawá*, *v.* to screen, to shade, to hide, to conceal.

මුවා, *Muwá*, *s.* screen, covering, concealment; male deer; animal in general.

මුවාකරණවා, *Muwákaraṇawá*, *v.* to hide, to screen, to conceal.

මුවාත, *Muwáta*, *s.* edge.

මුවාවෙනවා, *Muwáwenawá*, *v.* to be shaded, to hide one's self.

මුවිඳු, *Muvindu*, *s.* (මුව *muwa* animal, ඉඳු lord) lion, [Colloq. සිංහයා *sinhayá*].

මුෂ්ක, *Mushka*, *s.* scrotum, testicles.

මුෂ්කක, *Mushkaka*, *s.* medicinal plant, bearing a flower resembling that of the *bignonia indica* or trumpet flower, and called දේවදාලි *déwadáli*.

මුෂ්ටි, *Mushṭi*, *s.* fist, closed hand; hilt or handle of a sword; handful; filching, stealing.

මුෂ්ටික, *Mushṭika*, *s.* tree, not ascertained, [Colloq. රේරුගස් *réru-gas*]; goldsmith, [Colloq. බඩාලා *baḍálá*].

මුෂ්ටිය, *Mushṭiya*, *s.* fist, closed hand; applied also to the act of a guru or preceptor who withholds some branches of knowledge from his pupils through fear of their surpassing himself.

මුෂල, *Mushala*, *s.* a pestle for cleaning the husks from the rice, [Colloq. මෝල්ගහ *mólgaha*].

මුෂලි, *Mushali*, see මුසලි *musali*.

මුෂා, *Mushá*, *s.* crucible; also see මුසා *musá*.

මුස්තා, *Mustá*, *s.* fragrant plant, *cyperus rotundus*, [Colloq. කලාඳුරු *kaláṉduru*].

මුස්න *Musna*, *s.* broom, brush.

මුස්ස, *Mussa*, *s.* erection of the hairs of the body considered as a mark of exquisite pleasure or pain.

මුස්සැඳ, *Mussęnda*, *s.* plant, one calyx lobe of which developes into a white leaf, *mussænda frondosa*, *(Rubiaceæ)*; also called වැල්බුත්සරණ *węl-butsaraṇa*.

මුස, *Musa*, *s.* error, delusion; straying, wandering; fainting, loss of consciousness or perception; lie, falsehood; asthma.

මුසපත්, *Musapat*, *s.* (මුස fainting, පත් came) fainting, unconsciousness.

මුසල, *Musala*, see මුෂල *mushala*.

මුසලත්, *Musalat*, see මුසලින් *musalin*.

මුසලින්, *Musalin*, *s.* (මුසල *musala* pestle, ඉන් *in* aff.) name of Balabhadrayá alluding to his weapon or club resembling a pestle.

මුසලි, *Musalí*, *s.* small medicinal plant, *cucurligo orchioides* [Colloquial: හින් බින්තල් *hín-bintal*]; house lizard or gecko, *hemidactylus maculatus* or *peripia peronii (Geckotidæ*, order *Sauria)*, [Colloq. හූනා *húná*].

මුසලේ, *Musalé*, see මුෂල *mushala*.

මුසා, *Musá*, *s.* crucible; lie.

මුසාවාද, *Musáwáda*, *s.* (මුසා and වාද speaking) lie, falsehood, untruth, [Colloq. බොරුව *boruwa*].

මුසාවාදී, *Musáwádi*, *s.* (මුසාවාද *musáwáda* lie, ඉන් *in* aff.) liar.

මුසු, *Musu*, *a.* mixed, mingled, combined; Elu form of මිශ්‍ර *miṣra*.

මුසුප්පුව, *Musuppuwa*, *s.* fainting.

මුහ, *Muha*, *s.* asthma.

මුහන්දිරම, *Muhandirama*, *s.* Muhandiram, rank next to a Mudaliyar.

මුහය, *Muhaya*, *s.* flower of plantain.

මුහු, *Muhu*, *s.* ripening, maturing; mixing, mingling.

මුහුකරණවා, *Muhukaraṇawá*, *v.* to mix, to mingle; to mature, to ripen,

මුහුකළ, *Muhukaḷa*, *a.* ripe, mature.

මුහුකුළු, *Muhukuḷu*, *s.* pedicle of a flower.

මුහුද, *Muhuda*, *s.* sea, ocean: pl. මුහුදු *muhudu*.

මුහුදග, *Muhudaga*, *s.* (මුහුද sea, අග *aga* fire) fire of the great hell called Avíchi, supposed to be in the middle of the ocean, and navel or centre of Jambudvípa or the great southern continent.

මුහුදු, *Muhudu*, *s.* seas.

මුහුදුදූ, *Muhudu-dú*, *s.* (මුහුදු sea, දූ *dú* daughter) name of Lakshmí, the Indian goddess of beauty, and in many respects similar to the Grecian Venus.

මුහුදුබඩ, *Muhudubaḍa*, *s.* sea coast.

මුහුදු ලිහිණියා, *Muhudu-lihiṇiyá*, *s.* (මුහුදු and ලිහිණියා bird) sea gull.

මුහුදු ලුණු, *Muhudu-luṇu*, *s.* (මුහුදු and ලුණු salt) sea salt.

මුහුදුවන්, *Muhudu-wan*, *s.* (මුහුදු and වන් colour) black or dark blue.

මුහුදු වෙරළ, *Muhudu-weraḷa*, *s.* sea shore, beach.

මුහුදුසෙම්, *Muhudu-sem*, *s.* (මුහුදු and සෙම් phlegm) surf or foam of the sea.

මුහුන්, *Muhun*, *s.* leaven; compound, mixture.

මුහුන, *Muhuna*, *s*, face, countenance: pl. මුහුනු *muhunu*.

මුහුනගස්, *Muhuna-gas*, *s.* tree, yielding a very fragrant yellow flower, *mimusops elengi*, [Colloq. මූනමල් *múnamal*].

මුහුනත්, *Muhunat*, *s.* (මුහුන *muhuna* face, අත් *at* hand or end) name of Gaṇéṣa, the Indian god of wisdom, alluding to his face which is that of an elephant; tip, point, surface.

මුහුනු, *Muhunu*, *s.* face, countenance.

මුහුනුවර, *Muhunuwara*, *s.* features, cast of the face.

මුහුල, *Muhula*, *s.* hair of the head, lock of hair; crest, diadem; hair tied on the top of the head and ornamented.

මුහුලස, *Muhulasa*, *s.* lock of hair; crest.

මුහුළු, *Muhuḷu*, *s.* bond, fetter; hair of the head; tree, see the next.

මුහුළුමල්, *Muhuḷu-mal*, see මුහුනගස් *muhuna-gas* and මූනමල් *múna-mal*.

මුහුළුමිණි, *Muhuḷu-miṇi*, *s.* (මුහුළු and මිණි gem) crest, jewel, diadem.

මුහුර්ත, *Muhúrta*, *s.* division of time, the thirtieth part of a day and night, or an hour of forty-eight minutes; astrologer; moment, instant.

මුහොටිකා, *Muhoṭiká*, *s.* plant, *solanum jacquini*, [Colloq. කටුවැල්බටු *kaṭuwelbaṭu*].

මුළාව, *Muḷáwa* *s.* error, delusion, infatuation; straying, wandering; want, need, necessity, exigence, expediency.

මුළාව යනවා, *Muḷáwa-yanawá*, } *v.* to go astray,
මුළාවෙනවා, *Muḷáwenawá* } to fall into error.

මුළාසිය, *Muḷásiya*, see මුළාව *muḷáwa*.

මුළු, *Muḷu*, *s.* angle, corner, extremity of a room; boiled rice; multitude: *a.* all, whole, entire.

මුළු ඉරු, *Muḷu-iru*, *s.* day, [Colloq. දවස *dawasa*],

මුළුතැන්, *Muḷuten*, *s.* cook house, kitchen; royal kitchen, [Colloq. කුස්සිය *kussiya*].

මුළුදිව, *Muḷudiwa*, *s.* name of Venus; day-time, [Colloq. දවාල *dawála*].

මුළුමනෙම්ම, *Muḷumanemma*, *ad.* wholly, totally; altogether, entirely.

මුළුල්ල, *Muḷulla*, } *s.* whole.
මුළුළු, *Muḷuḷu*, }

මූ, *Mú*, *s.* urine, Elu form of මූත්‍ර *mútra;* binding, tying: *pron.* he, it, this one, spoken of animals or inferiors.

මූක, *Múka*, *s.* dumb man: *a.* dumb.

මූකරණවා, *Múkaraṇawá*, *v.* to be matured.

මූකළ, *Múkaḷa*, *s.* rice in the husk, paddy: *a.* ripened, matured.

මූකළ කපු, *Múkaḷa-kapu*, *s.* kind of cotton, *gossypium*.

මූකළ කුරක්කන්, *Múkaḷa-kurakkan*, *s.* sort of grain, variety of *eleusine*.

මූකළ කෝව්, *Múkaḷa-kówi*, *s.* sort of cabbage, *brasica oleracea*.

මූකළමා, *Múkaḷamá*, *s.* calf between one and two years old, weaned calf: pl. මූකළම්මු *múkaḷammu*.

මූකළ වී, *Múkaḷa-ví*, *s.* kind of paddy, *oryza sativa*.

මූකලාන, *Múkaḷána*, *s.* large jungle, forest: pl. මූකලන් *múkaḷan*.

මූකොලන්, *Múkolan*, *s.* plant bearing grain, *eleusine coracana*. [Colloq. කුරක්කන් *kurakkan*].

මූට්ටුකරණවා, *Múṭṭukaraṇawá*, *v.* to stitch together, as two pieces of cloth.

මූට්ටුව, *Múṭṭuwa*, *s.* joining, joint, in two planks. seam in cloth, junction.

මූඩ, *Múḍu*, *s.* fool, idiot; corruptly for මූඪ *múḍha*.

මූඩ ගර්භ, *Múḍa-garbha*, corruptly for මූඪ ගර්භ *múḍha-garbha*.

මූඩිය, *Múḍiya*, *s.* lid, cover of a vessel, cork.

මූඪ, *Múḍha*, *s.* (මුහ to be foolish) fool, idiot; sluggard: *a.* foolish, ignorant; cold, apathetic, stupid.

මූඪ ගර්භ, *Múḍha-garbha*, *s.* (මූඪ and ගර්භ womb) bad presentation of the child at birth, causing difficult delivery; dead fœtus.

මූඪ ස්මෘති, *Múḍha-smṛiti*, *s.* (මූඪ and ස්මෘති memory, understanding) stupidity, foolishness. error, mistake in judgment or memory.

මූත්‍ර, *Mútra*, *s.* (මූත්‍ර to urine, etc.) urine, evacuated urine.

මූත්‍ර කෘච්ඡ්‍ර, *Mútra-kṛichchhrá*, මූත්‍ර ඝාත, *Mútra-ghâta*, *s.* (මූත්‍ර urine, කෘච්ඡ්‍ර or ඝාත pain) strangury; urinary affection in general, as gravel, etc.

මූත්‍ර දෝෂ, *Mútra-dósha*, *s.* (මූත්‍ර and දෝෂ fault) gonorrhea, considered as an urinary complaint.

මූත්‍ර බද්ධ, *Mútra-baddha*, *s.* (මූත්‍ර and බද්ධ bound) obstruction of urine, ischury.

මූත්‍ර මාර්ග, *Mútra-márga*, *s.* urethera.

මූත්‍රල, *Mútrala*, *a.* diuritic.

මූත්‍රලා, *Mútralá*, *s.* cucumber, *cucumis pubescens*, [Colloq. කැකිරි *kẹkiri*].

මූත්‍ර සඞ්ග, *Mútra-saṅga*, *s.* urinary obstruction.

මූත්‍රාශය, *Mútráṣaya*, *s.* bladder.

මූත, *Múta*, *a.* (මූ to bind, ක්ත *kta* aff.) bound, tied, fastened, secured.

මූද, *Múda*, sea, ocean; also written මුහුද *muhuda*: pl. මූදු *múdu*.

මූදිල්ල, *Múdilla*, *s.* handsome tree with large leaves and thorny flowers, *barringtonia speciosa (Myrtaceæ)*.

මූදිල්ලා, *Múdillá*, *s.* kind of sea fish.

මූදු, *Múdu*, plural of මූද *múda*, pertaining to sea.

මූදු අවර, *Múdu-awara*, *s.* plant, *dolichos virosa*.

මූදු ඌරා, *Múdu-úrá*, *s.* the dugong (supposed original of the mermiad) *halicor dugong (Mammalia)*.

මූදු කඩුපාර, *Múdu-kaḍupára*, *s.* plant, *cacalia maritima*.

මූදු කදුරු, *Múdu-kaduru*, *s.* shrub, *ochrosia borbonica (Apocynaceæ)*.

මූදු කලාඳුරු, *Múdu-kalán̆duru*, *s.* plant, *cyperus arenarias (Cyperaceæ)*.

මූදුකෙයියා, *Múdukeyiyá*, *s.* screw-pine, *pandanus fascicularis* or *p. odoratissimus (Pandanaceæ)*.

මූදු කොබ්බෑ, *Múdu-kobbẹ*, *s.* medicinal plant with astringent root, *allophyllus (*or *ornithrope) serrata*.

මූදු කැඳ, *Múdu-kẹnda*, *s.* plant, variety of *macaranga tomentosa*.

මූදු ගම්පාළු, *Múdu-gampáḷu*, *s.* plant, not ascertained.

මූදු ගල්පාසි, *Múdu-galpási*, *s.* moss, not ascertained.

මූදු ගල්පෙඳ, *Múdu-galpen̆da*, *s.* moss, not ascertained.

මූදු ගොනිකා, *Múdu-goniká*, *s.* plant, not ascertained.

මූදුගැටකොල, *Múdu-gẹṭakola*, *s.* stemless plant with small pinkish flowers, *hydrophylax maritima (Rubiaceæ)*.

මූදුගැටපන්, *Múdu-gẹṭapan*, *s.* species of club rush, *scirpus supinus*.

මූදු දදකිරිය, *Múdu-dadakiriya*, *s.* spurge, *euphorbia rosea (Euphorbiaceæ)*.

මූදු පෙන, *Múdu-pena*, *s.* (මූදු and පෙන froth) the froth or foam of the sea; also, bone of the cuttle fish, which is supposed to be produced from the froth of the sea.

මූදු බින්තඹුරු, *Múdu-bintam̆buru*, *s.* sort of bindweed with creeping stem and large red-purple flowers, *ipomeœa biloba* or *i. pes capræ (Convoloulaceæ)*.

මූදු බින්නුග, *Mudu-binnuga*, *s.* plant, peculiar to Ceylon, *tylophora flara (Asclepiadeæ)*; see බින් නුග *bin-nuga*.

මූදු බැමිතිරිය, *Múdu-bẹmitiriya*, *s.* plant or shrub, *hedyotis maritima*.

මූදු මුරුංගා, *Múdu-murungá*, *s.* shrub with racemes of bright yellow flowers, *sephora tomentosa (Leguminosæ)*.

මූදු මෑ, *Múdu-mẹ*, *s.* sort of kidney bean, *phaseolus caracalla*.

මූදු වරා, *Múdu-wará*, *s.* plant, variety of *calatropis gigantea*: see වරා *wárá*.

මූදුහතු, *Múdu-hatu*, *s.* sea sponge.

මූදු හම්පලා, *Múdu-hampalá*, *s.* plant, *verbesina biflora*.

මූදු හාල්පන්, *Múdu-hálpan*, *s.* sort of club rush, *fimbristylis miliacea (Cyperaceæ)*.

මූදු හිරිඇල්වී, *Múdu-hiriẹl-ví*, *s.* kind of hill paddy.

මූදු හිරිගල්පාසි, *Múdu-hirigal-pási*, *s.* species of moss.

මූන, *Múna*, *s.* face, countenance.

මූනත්, *Múnat*, see මුහුනත් *muhnnat*.

මූනත්තහඩුව, *Múnat-tahaḍuwa*, *s.* metallic mouth of a key hole.

මූනත, *Múnata*, *s.* (මූන face, අත *ata* top) top, point, upper extremity.

මූනඵල, *Múna-phala*, *s.* jack tree, *artocarpus integrifolia*, [Colloq. කොස් *kos*].

මූනමල්, *Múnamal*, *s.* timber tree, producing a very fragrant yellow or white flower, *mimusops elengi (Sapotaceæ)*.

මූනමෑ, *Múnamẹ*, *s.* kidney bean, *phaseolus mungo*, [Colloq. මුංඇට *muṇ-ẹṭa*].

මූනිස්සම, *Múnissama*, *s.* shot, small shot, (Port.): pl. මූනිස්සන් *múnissan*.

මූනුවර, *Múnuwara*, *s.* the features of the face.

මූර්ඛ, *Múrkha*, *s.* (මුහ *muha* to be foolish) rayed kidney bean, green gram, *phaseolus mungo radiatus*, [Colloq. උළුන්දු මෑ *uḷundu mẹ*]: *a.* foolish, ignorant, stupid, idiotic.

මූර්ඡන, *Múrchchhana*, *s.* fainting, syncope; a tone or semitone as placed in its scale, the seventh part of a gráma or scale.

මූර්ඡා, *Múrchchhá*, *s.* fainting, swooning, loss of consciousness or sense.

මූර්ත, *Múrta*, *a.* fainting, fainted, losing consciousness; solid, material.

මූර්ති, *Múrti*, *s.* matter, substance; solidity; body; form, figure, definite shape or image.

මූර්ධජ, *Múrdhaja*, *s.* (මූර්ධ top, of the mouth, ජ produced) cerebral, the ṭa-warga or hard class of consonants.

මූර්ධන්, *Múrdhan*, *s.* top, summit.

මූර්ධය, *Múrdhaya*, see මූර්ධන් *múrdhan*.

මූර්වා, *Múrwá*, *s.* sort of creeping plant, from the fibres of which bow strings are made, *sanseviera zeylanica*, [Colloq. නියඳ *niyanda*].

මූල්‍ය, *Múlya*, *s.* price; wages, hire, money, coin, etc. see the next.

මූල, *Múla*, *s.* root, root of a tree; origin, commencement; capital, principal; root of the *arum campanulatum*, [Colloq. කිඩාරන් *kiḍáran*]; price, money, wages, hire; rectum.

මූලක, *Múlaka*, *s.* (මූල root, අක *aka* aff.) radish, *raphanus sativus*; red gram, *dolichos* or *vigna catjang*, [Colloq. ලීමෑ *límẹ*]; sort of cucumber, [Colloq. තියඹරා *tiyambará*]: see මූලික *múlika*.

මූලකාරණය, *Múlakáraṇaya*, *s.* (මූල and කාරණ *káraṇa* cause) first cause, origin, producing or efficient principle.

මූලගන්ධ, *Múla-gandha*, *s.* (මූල and ගන්ධ scent) fragrant root.

මූලජ, *Múlaja*, see මූලබීජ *múla-bíja*.

මූල පත්‍රිකා, *Múla-patriká*, *s.* tree, *moringa pterygosperma*, [Colloq. මුරුංගා *muruṇgá*].

මූලපලා, *Múla-palá*, *s.* (මූල root, පලා vegetable) any edible root.

මූලඵල, *Múla-phala*, *s.* jack tree, [Colloq. කොස් ගහ *kos-gaha*].

මූලබීජ, *Múla-bíja*, *s.* (මූල and බීජ seed) any plant growing from the root as the lotus, etc.

මූලරෝග, *Múla-róga*, *s.* (මූල rectum, රෝග disease) piles.

මූලවායිය, *Múlawáyiya*, } *s.* (මූල anus, වායිය or
මූලවායු, *Múlawáyu*, } වායු wind) fistula in ano.

මූලවෑදිය, *Múla-wẹdiya*, *s.* (මූල and වෑදිය disease) piles.

මූල සාධන, *Múla-sádhana*, *s.* medicinal drug, commonly called පොඩරු *poṇḍaru*.

මූලික, *Múlika*, *a.* (මූල *múla* chief, ඉක *ika* aff.) chief, primary, principal, radical, literally or figuratively.

මූලිකයා, *Múlikayá*, *s.* chief, commencer, originator, principal, chairman.

මූලී, *Múlí*, *s.* (මූල *múla* root, ඉනි *ini* aff.) tree in general, [Colloq. ගහ *gaha*].

මූෂ, *Músha*, *s.* crucible, [Colloq. කෝව *kówa*].

මූෂා, *Múshá*, *s.* sort of grass, *andropogon serratus*.

මූෂික, *Múshika*, *s.* (මූෂ *músha* steal, ඉක *ika* aff.) rat, mouse; tree, *mimosa sirisha*; crucible.

මූෂිකකර්ණී, *Múshika-karṇa*, *s.* (මූෂික rat, කර්ණ ear, ඊ *í* aff.) aquatic plant of the *cryptogamia* class, *salvinia cucullata*.

මූෂිකපර්ණී, *Múshika-parṇṇi*, *s.* medicinal plant, *hoya hirsuta*, [Colloq. මිනුග *mínuga*].

මූෂික ශ්‍රවණ, *Múshika-srawaṇa*, see මූෂික කර්ණී *múshika-karṇa*.

මූසලයා, *Músalayá*, *s.* ill-looking fellow (whose very appearance is a bad omen).

මූසිකවපු, *Músika-wapu*, *s.* medicinal plant, *hoya hirsuta*.

මෙච්චර, *Mechchara*, *ad.* so much, as this.

මෙත්, *Met*, *s.* friendliness, benevolence; Elu form of මෛත්‍රී *maitrí*.

මෙත්තය, *Mettaya*, *s.* pillow, cushion. (Tamil.)

මෙත්තිස්ස, *Mettissa*, *s.* (corrupt form of the Portuguese word *Mestiso*), of mixed European and Indian birth; a term applied to one sprung from a European father and Indian mother; one who adopts the female costume of a Mestiso, viz. a jacket and skirt with the native comb and hair-pin, and a pair of slippers.

මෙත්‍රෙක, *Metreka*, *s.* kind of measure; firkin.

මෙතන, *Metana*, *s.* this place.

මේතුවක්, *Metuwak*, *ad.* so long, so much, so many.

මෙතුවක් කල්, *Metuwak-kal*, *s.* so long time.

මෙතෙ, *Mete*, see මෙත් *met*.

මෙතෙක්, *Metek*, *ad.* so much, up to this place or time.

මෙතෙම, *Metema*, *s.* this person (nom. sing.).

මෙතෙර, *Metera*, *s.* this side of a river or sea; rock in general; mirage.

මෙතැන්, *Metẹn*, *s.* this place; this time, the present.

මෙද, *Meda*, *s.* rogue, villain.

මෙදා, *Medá*, *s.* to-day, this day, this time: *ad.* at this season.

මෙන්, *Men*, *ad.* like, resembling; as, so.

මෙන්න, *Menna*, *interj.* lo! behold! look here.

මෙන්ම, *Menma*, *ad.* even thus, even so.

මෙන, *Mena*, *s.* (මන *mana* to know, to understand) mind, reasoning faculty, seat of reason; lamp.

මෙනම්, *Menam*, *a.* of this name, so called.

මෙනෙහි, *Menehi*, *s.* (මෙන *mena* mind, in the locative case.) thought, reflection, meditation.

මෙනෙහිකරණවා, *Menehi-karaṇawá*, *v.* to meditate, to reflect, to consider.

මෙනේරි, *Menéri*, *s.* kind of grass, *panicum psilo podium (Gramineæ)*; grain used as food.

මෙපමණ, *Mepamaṇa*, *s.* this much.

මෙපවත්, *Mepawat*, } *s.* this news or tidings; affair,
මෙපුවත්, *Mepuwat*, } matter under consideration.

මෙබඳු, *Mebandu*, *a.* like this, such, such like.

මෙබව, *Mebawa*, *s.* this fact.

මෙම, *Mema*, *ad.* even this, the same.

මෙයින්, *Meyin*, *s.* from hence.

මෙර්සෙ, *Merse*, *s.* (Portuguese *Mersé*), courtesy, favour, kindness, used in common conversation for 'thanks' as, බොහොම මෙර්සෙසි *bohoma merseyi*, many thanks.

මෙර, *Meru*, *s.* any vinous or spirituous liquor; mountain Maha Méru, rock in general; mirage: see මේරු *méru*.

මෙරගල, *Mera-gala*, *s.* mountain Méru: see මේරු *méru*.

මෙරජ, *Meraja*, *s.* ray, [Colloq. රශ්මිය *rẹsmiya*].

මෙරද, *Merada*, *s.* mountain Méru, [Colloq. මහ මෙර *maha-mera*].

මෙරමා, *Meramá*, *s.* others.

මෙරය, *Meraya*, *s.* toddy or the spirituous liquor, extracted from the coconut tree for distillation, [Colloq. රා *rá*].

මෙරු, *Meru*, *s.* winged white ants.

මෙල්ලකරණවා, *Mellakaraṇawá*, *v.* to tame, to train, to subdue.

මෙල්ලය, *Mellaya*, *s.* submission.

මෙල්ලවෙනවා, *Mellawenawá*, *v.* to be trained, to be subdued.

මෙල, *Mela*, see මේල *méla*.

මෙලක, *Melaka*, *s.* this Laṇká, Ceylon: see මේලක *mélaka*.

මෙලන් කටු, *Melan-kaṭu*, *s.* tools or instruments of a gold or silversmith.

මෙලන, *Melana*, see මේලන *mélana*.

මෙලහකට, *Melahakaṭa*, *s.* by this time.

මෙලා, *Melá*, see මේලා *méla*.

මෙලි, *Meli*, *a.* rich, wealthy.

මෙලෙක්, *Melek*, *a.* soft, fine, bland, literally or figuratively, not hard.

මෙලෙක්කරණවා, *Melek-karaṇawá*, *v.* to soften.

මෙලෙස, *Melesa*, *ad.* thus, so, in this manner.

මෙව්වා, *Mewwá*, *s.* corruptly for මේවා *méwá*, these.

මෙවන්, *Mewan*, *s.* (මෙ cloud, වන් colour) indigo plant, *indigofera tinctoria*, [Colloq. නිල්අවරි *nil-awari*]: see මේඝවර්ණ *méghawarṇa*: *a.* such as these.

මෙවලම, *Mewalama*, *s.* tool, instrument in general, [Colloq. ආයුධය *áyudhaya*]: pl. මෙවලම් *mewalam*.

මෙවිචර, *Merichara*, *s.* as much as this, this quantity.

මෙවුන්, *Mewun*, *s.* pair, couple; copulation; Elu form of මෛථුන *maithuna*.

මෙවුන්දම්, *Mewundam*, *s.* cohabitation.

මෙවුල්, *Mewul*, *s.* zone, girdle; sword belt; neck gem or chain; Elu form of මේඛලා *mékhalá*.

මෙවුල් දම්, *Mewul-dam*, *s.* (මෙවුල් and දම් chain) woman's ornamented girdle, zone; sword belt.

මෙවුල, *Mewula*, *s.* neckchain, girdle.

මෙවුලා, *Mewulá*, *s.* cover, sheath.
මෙවෙනි, *Meweni*, } *a.* of this form, like this,
මෙවැනි, *Mewęni*, } such like.
මෙසඳ, *Mesandu*, } *s.* at present, at this time.
මෙසමය, *Mesamaya*, }
මෙසිඳුරු, *Mesinduru*, *s.* (මෙ cloud, සිඳුරු elephant) name of Ṣakra or Indra, who has a cloud for his elephant.
මෙසුරු, *Mesuru*, *s.* covetousness, avarice.
මෙසුරුසහ, *Mesuru-saha*, *s.* (මෙසුරු and සහ who has) Kuvéra the Indian god of riches.
මෙසේ, *Mesé*, *ad.* so, thus.
මෙහා, *Mehá*, *s.* respectable term for pronoun you: pl. මෙහාලා *mehálá*: *ad.* here, this side or place.
මෙහි, *Mehi*, *ad.* here, in this place.
මෙහෙ, *Mehe*, *s.* work, service: *ad.* here, hither.
මෙහෙකරණවා, *Mehekaraṇawá*, *v.* to work, to minister, to serve, to labour.
මෙහෙකරුවා, *Mehekaruwá*, *s.* (මෙහෙ work, කරුවා who does) servant; artificer, workman.
මෙහෙණින්, *Meheṇin*, *s.* female ascetic or priest.
මෙහෙ නිමවනවා, *Mehe-nimawanawá*, *v.* to eat, used of superiors.
මෙහෙය, *Meheya*, *s.* work, service, labour.
මෙහෙයනවා, *Meheyanawá*, *v.* to appoint, to portion, to send, to employ.
මෙහෙලි, *Meheli*, *s.* old woman.
මෙහෙවඩනවා, *Mehewaḍanawá*, *v.* to eat, used only of a king.
මෙහෙවර, *Mehewara*, *s.* work, trade, business; service, employ.
මෙහෙසි, *Mehesi*, *s.* queen, one of the wives of a king, but especially the one who has been anointed or crowned: pl. මෙහෙසුන් *mehesun*.
මෙහෙසුරු, *Mehesuru*, *s.* name of Íṣwara or Ṣiva; Elu form of මහේශ්වර *maheṣwara*.
මේ, *Mé*, *s.* Elu form of මේඝ *mégha*, which see; sultry season; also food: *pron.* this; this (pointing to something near).
මේක, *Méka*, *s.* this thing; treasure.
මේකල, *Mékala*, *s.* (මේ this, කල time or මේ rain, කල time) this time; present; rainy season, [Colloq. වර්ෂා කාලය *warshá-kálaya*]; mountain in the Vindhyá range, where the Nermadá river has its source.
මේකල කන්‍යකා, *Mékala-kanyaká*, *s.* (මේකල and කන්‍යකා daughter) Nermadá river, having its source in the Mékala mountain; name of Agni the god of fire.

මේකලා, *Mékalá*, corruptly for මේඛලා *Mékhalá*.
මේකා, *Méká*, *pron. mas.* this fellow, this animal, this one.
මේකී, *Mékí*, *pron. fem.* this (female) one; applied only to female servants and slaves or women of the lowest classes: pl. මේකිලා *mékilá*.
මේකුල, *Mékula*, Elu form of මේඝකූට *mégha-kúṭa*.
මේඛලා, *Mékhalá*, *s.* woman's girdle or zone; sword belt: see මෙවුල් *mewul*.
මේඛලාදාමය, *Mékhaládámaya*, *s.* (මේඛලා and දාම *dáma* chain) woman's ornamented girdle or zone; belt round the waist to which the sword is fastened.
මේග, *Méga*, *s.* cloud.
මේඝ, *Mégha*, *s.* (මිහ *miha* to sprinkle) cloud; rain; fragrant grass, *cyperus rotundus*, [Colloq. කලාඳුරු *kalánduru*].
මේඝ අඳුර, *Mégha-andura*, *s.* darkness produced by a cloud.
මේඝ කාලය, *Mégha-kálaya*, *s.* (මේඝ and කාල *kála* time) rainy season, [Colloq. වර්ෂා කාලය *warshá-kálaya*].
මේඝ කූටය, *Mégha-kúṭaya*, *s.* (මේඝ and කූට *kúṭa* peak) condensed cloud heavily charged with rain and portending a storm.
මේඝ ගිගුම්, *Mégha-gigum*, *s.* roaring of thunder, [Colloq. අහස ගෙරවීම *ahasa-geravíma*].
මේඝ චින්තක, *Mégha-chintaka*, *s.* (මේඝ and චින්තක who thinks) Indian cuckoo, *cuculus melanoleucus;* the name alludes to its being supposed to drink nothing but rain and therefore naturally anxious for cloudy and rainy weather.
මේඝ ධ්වනිය, *Mégha-dhwaniya*, *s.* (මේඝ cloud, ධ්වනිය sound) thunder; rumbling of clouds.
මේඝනාද, *Méghanáda*, *s.* (මේඝ and නාද sound) noise or rumbling of a cloud; tree, *butea frondosa*, [Colloq. ගස්කැල *gas-kęla*]; plant, *amarantus polygonoides*, [Colloq. සුළුකූර *suḷukúra* or කූරතම්පලා *kúra-tampalá*].
මේඝ පුෂ්ප, *Mégha-pushpa*, *s.* (මේඝ and පුෂ්ප flower) drop of rain, rain; river water; hail.
මේඝය, *Méghaya*, see මේඝ *mégha*.
මේඝරාව, *Mégha-ráwa*, *s.* (මේඝ and රාව sound) thunder.
මේඝවර්ණ, *Méghawarṇa*, *s.* (මේඝ and වර්ණ colour) indigo plant, *indigofera tinctoria*, නිල් අවරි *nil-awari*]; shrub, *ardisia humilis*, or *a. elliptica*, [Colloq. බළුදං *baḷudaṇ*].

මේචක, *Méchaka*, *s.* black or dark blue (colour): darkness; sulphuret of antimony; eye in the peacock's tail.

මේඪ්‍ර, *Méḍhra*, *s.* (මිහ *miha* to urine) sheep; goat; penis.

මේඪ්‍රශෘංගී, *Méḍhra-ṣriṅgí*, *s.* milky plant, the fruit of which is crooked and therefore compared to a ram's horn, *dæmia extensa*, [Colloq. මැඩහඟු *meḍahangu*].

මෙණ්ඩක, *Méṇḍaka*, *s.* (මිහ *miha* to urine) goat, ram, [Colloq. එළුවා *eḷuwá*].

මේණ්ඩකයුද්ධය, *Méṇḍaka-yuddhaya*, *s.* (මේණ්ඩක and යුද්ධ *yuddha* fight) fight between two rams, [Colloq. එළුපොර *eḷu-pora*].

මේතුටු, *Méṭuṭu*, *s.* (මේ rain, තුටු delighted by) peacock, [Colloq. මොණරා *moṇará*].

මේථි, *Méthí*, *s.* small grain or seed used by natives to put in to their curries, [Colloq. උළුවාහාල් *uḷuwáhál*].

මේථුන, *Méthuna*, see මෛථුන *maithuna*.

මේද්‍ය, *Médya*, see මේධ්‍ය *médhya*.

මේද, *Méda*, *s.* (මිද *mida* to be greasy or unctuous) marrow, either of the bones or flesh; fat, [Coll: තෙල්ධාතුව *tel-dhátuwa*].

මේදක, *Médaka*, *s.* dregs or sediment of toddy, spirituous liquor extracted from the coconut tree; vinous or spirituous liquor for distillation.

මේදතෙල, *Méda-tela*, see මේදස් *médas*.

මේදනී, *Médaní*, see මේදිනී *médiní*.

මේදස්, *Médas*, *s.* marrow, or more properly the serous secretion that spreads amongst the muscular fibres, and which is considered as performing the same functions to the flesh that the marrow of the bones does to them.

මේදා, *Médá*, *s.* drug, drug described as a sort of root resembling ginger; it is one of the eight principal medicaments and is said to be of cooling and emollient properties, and of particular use in fever and consumption.

මේදිනී, *Médiní*, *s.* earth, [Colloq. පොළව *poḷawa*].

මේදුර, *Médura*, *a.* (මිද *mida* to be unctuous) smooth, soft, bland, unctuous.

මේධ්‍ය, *Médhya*, *a.* pure, purified, duly prepared or made fit to be offered.

මේධ්‍යමුඛ, *Médhya-mukha*, *s.* musk, [Colloq. කස්තූරි *kastúri*].

මේධ්‍යා, *Médhyá*, *s.* kind of orris root.

මේධ, *Médha*, *s.* sacrifice, offering, oblation; comprehension, understanding.

මේධග, *Médhaga*, *s.* (මේධා *médhá* wisdom, ග *ga* who goes or possesses) wise man, one who has perceived or understands the advantages of religion.

මේධා, *Médhá*, *s.* wisdom, knowledge; apprehension understanding, [Colloq. නුවණ *nuwana*].

මේධාජනනී, *Médhá-jananí*, *s.* medicinal plant, *herpestis monniera*, [Colloq. ලුණුවිල *luṇuvila*].

මේධි, *Médhi*, *s.* post in the centre of a threshing floor to which the cattle are attached when they turn round to tread out the corn.

මේයන්, *Méyan*, *s.* (මේ cloud, යන් vehicle) name of Indra or Ṣakra.

මේරු, *Méru*, / මේරුපර්වතය, *Méru-parwataya*, *s.* sacred mountain Méru in the centre of the four great continents, compared by the Siṇhalese to the tabor, and encircled by the seven seas called Sídantas, which are separated from each other by seven circular rocks, the residences of various demigods, demons, sprites, Guruḷas, etc. and are under the sway of the four waran deviyó or regents of the four points of the compass; the height of Méru is said to be 168,000 yoduns or yójanas 84,000 of which are below the surface of the earth; on its top Ṣakra holds his court surrounded by the gods of Swarga and underneath its base is the residence of the Asuras.

මේල, *Méla*, *s.* meeting, union, assemblage.

මේලක, *Mélaka*, *s.* meeting, assemblage.

මේලන, *Mélana*, *s.* union, assemblage, meeting.

මේලා, *Mélá*, *s.* ink; antimony or any collyrium.

මේලේ, *Mélé* *s.* loft or garret: pl. මේල *méla*.

මේවඩනවා, *Méwaḍanawá*, *v.* to eat, used only of kings.

මේවර, *Méwara*, *s.* message; work, service, time allotted for work; variegated colour.

මේවා, *Méwá*, *pron.* these.

මේවැඩුම, *Méweḍuma*, *s.* verbal noun of මේවඩනවා *Méwaḍanawá*

මේෂ, *Mésha*, *s.* ram, [Colloq: බැටළුවා *beṭaḷuwá*]; sign of the zodiac, Aries.

මේෂශෘංග, *Mésha-ṣriṅga*, *s.* (මේෂ and ශෘංග horn) ram's horn, [Colloq. බැටළු අං *beṭaḷu-aṅ*]: sort poison, commonly වච්චනාවී *wachchanávi*.

මේෂශෘංගී, *Mésha-ṣriṅgi*, *s.* plant, *gomphocarpus volubilis*; plant, *calotropis gigantia*, [Colloq. වරා *wará*]; creeping plant, *dæmia extensa*, [Colloq. මැඩහඟු *meḍahangu*].

මේෂාක්‍ෂ, *Méshákṣha*, *s.* medicinal plant, *eclipta erecta*, [Colloq. කිකිරිඳිය *kikirindiya*].

මේෂාක්‍ෂි, *Méshákshi*, *s.* (මේෂ *mésha* ram, අක්‍ෂ *aksha* eye) sort of cassia, the flower of which resembles the eye of a ram, [Colloq තෝර *tóra*].

මේස්, *Més*, *s.* stockings. (Port.)

මේසය, *Mésaya*, *s.* table, sign Aries.

මේසා, *Mésá*, *a.* so much, like this.

මේසේ, *Mésé*, *s.* table: pl. මේස *mésa*.

මේහ, *Méha*, *s.* (මිහ *miha* to urine) urinary disease, especially inflammatory affection of the urethra, including gonorrhea, etc.

මේහරිපු, *Méha-ripu*, *s.* tree, *cassia auriculata*, [Colloq. රණවරා *raṇawará*].

මෛත්‍රී, *Maitrí*, *s.* (මිත්‍ර *mitra* friend) friendship; the seventeenth lunar asterism, commonly called අනුරෙ නැකත *anure-nękata;* the name of next Buddha: *a.* friendly, amicable.

මෛත්‍රීබල, *Maitrí-bala*, *s.* (මෛත්‍රී and බල strength) name of Buddha, alluding to his gentle or pacific character.

මෛත්‍රී බුදුන්, *Maitrí-budun*, *s.* name of the next Buddha.

මෛත්‍රෙය, *Maitreya*, *s.* (මිත්‍ර *mitra* friend, එය *eya* aff.) name of Maitrí Buddha.

මෛථුන, *Maithuna*, *s.* (මිථුන *mithuna* couple, අණ් aff.) copulation; union, association.

මෛල, *Maila*, *s.* shrub; mountain ebony, *bauhinia purpurea*: corruptly for මයිල *mayila*, which see.

මෛලමල්, *Maila-mal*, *s.* flower of the මලිත *malita:* corruptly for මයිල මල් *maila-mal*.

මොක්, *Mok*, *s.* freedom from transmigration, eternal emancipation, Nirwáṇa; Elu form of මෝක්‍ෂ *móksha:* *a.* high, honorable, best; chief, preeminent, from මුඛ්‍ය *mukhya*.

මොක්‍ෂ, *Moksha*, see මෝක්‍ෂ *móksha*.

මොක, *Moka*, }
මොකක්, *Mokak*, } *ind.* what, which.

මොකට, *Mokaṭa*, *ind.* what for.

මොකද, *Mokada*, *ind.* an interrogative, what? how?

මොකදුරු, *Mokaduru*, *s.* (මොක් *mok* final emancipation, ඇදුරු *ęduru* teacher) name of Buddha, alluding to his character as the instructor in the doctrine of Nirwáṇa; spiritual preceptor.

මොකවත්, *Mokawat*, *s.* something, any thing.

මොග්ගල්ලාන, *Moggallána*, *s.* name of one of Buddha's two chief Ṣráwakas or disciples, commonly called Mugalan, and who was famed for his ṛiddhi-bala or supernatural powers, acquired by the most intense performance of devout meditation; but particularly of the dhyána, he being the only person that ever performed the pañcha dhyána.

මොට්ට, *Moṭṭa*, *s.* blunt, not sharp.

මොට්ටයා, *Moṭṭayá*, *s.* bald headed man; idiot; blunt fellow.

මොට්ටවෙනවා, *Moṭṭawenawá*, *v.* to become blunt.

මොට්ටු, *Moṭṭu*, *s.* plant, *physalis angulata (Solanaceæ)*: plur. of මොට්ටුව *moṭṭuwa*.

මොට්ටුව, *Moṭṭuwa*, *s.* bud of a flower.

මොට, *Moṭa*, *a.* blunt: *ind.* what for.

මොටද, *Moṭada*, *ind.* why, what for.

මොටියා, *Moṭiyá*, *s.* shoot of a plantain tree.

මොණරගණ, *Moṇaragaṇa*, *s.* (මොණර peacock, ගණ assemblage) flock of peacocks.

මොණරපිලි, *Moṇara-pili*, *s.* (මොණර and පිලි feather) peacock's tail or the feathers of his tail.

මොණරා, *Moṇará*, *s.* peacock, *pavo cristatus (Phasianidæ* order *Gallinæ)*.

මොද, *Moda*, *s.* (මුද *muda* to be glad) joy, gladness, delight; sweet smell.

මොදර සූටික්කා, *Modara-súṭikká*, *s.* Loten's sun bird, *cynniris lotenius (Cynnyridæ*, order *Passeres)*; also called රන් සූටික්කා *ran-súṭikká* and ගෙවල් කුරුල්ලා *gewal-kurullá*.

මොදා, *Modá*, *s.* the tamarind fish, *lates calcarifer*.

මොන්දන් කෙසෙල්, *Mondan-kesel*, *s.* sort of plantain.

මොන, *Mona*, *a.* an interrogative, what?

මොනර ඇල්වී, *Monara-ęlví*, *s.* kind of hill paddy.

මොනර කුඩිම්බිය, *Monara-kuḍimbiya*, *s.* small plant with purple flowers, *vernonia* (or *serratula) cinerea, (Compositæ);* the feathers on the head of peacock.

මොනර පතන්, *Monara-patan*, *s.* plant with panicles of small pale flowers, *dianella ensifolia (Liliaceæ)*.

මොනරපහුරු, *Monara-pahuru*, *s.* plant.

මොනර මල්, *Monara-mal*, *s.* peacock flower, *poinciana pulcherrima*.

මොනර යන්ත්‍ර, *Monara-yantra*, *s.* (මොනර and යන්ත්‍ර machine) sort of balloon or flying apparatus; also called දඬුමොනර යන්ත්‍රය *daṇḍu-monara-yantraya*.

මොනරැස්ස, *Monaręssa*, *s.* plant, *urticularia reticulata:* see නිල් මොනරැස්ස *nil-monaręssa*.

මොනවට, *Monawaṭa, ad.* beautifully, excellently, well.

මොනවා, *Monawá,* | *s.* what (things): plur. of
මොනවාද, *Monawáda,* | මොකද *mokada.*

මොනොවට, *Monowaṭa, ad.* another form of මො නවට *monawaṭa,* which see.

මොර, *Mora, s.* tree. producing fruit of sweet or subacid flowers, *nephelium longanum (Sapindaceæ).*

මොරගහනවා, *Moragahanawá, v.* to cry out, to shout.

මොරගෑසීම, *Moragẹsíma, s.* noise, the noise of tumult, loud cry or scream.

මොරට, *Moraṭa,* see මෝරට *móraṭa.*

මොරටා, *Moraṭá,* see මෝරටා *móraṭá.*

මොරල්ලා, *Morallá, s.* kind of fish.

මොරෙසියා, *s.* shoot of a tree, etc.: see මොටියා *moṭiyá.*

මොල්ලිය, *Molliya, s.* hump on the back of the Indian bullock.

මොල, *Mola, s.* arrow; brains; marrow.

මොලකටුව, *Mola-kaṭuwa, s.* (මොල brains, කටුව shell) skull.

මොලගහ, *Mola-gaha, s.* tree, not ascertained.

මොලබෑගහ, *Molabẹ-gaha, s.* tree, not ascertained.

මොලය, *Molaya,* see මොලේ *molé.*

මොලවනවා, *Molawanawá, v.* to blow the fire; to clinch the hand or fist: pret. මෙලෙව්වා *melewwá.*

මොලේ, *Molé, s.* brain.

මොලොක්, *Molok, a.* soft, tender, delicate; supple, flexible; smooth, unctuous.

මොව්හු, *Mowhu, pron.* these persons: nom. plur. of මේ *mé,* this.

මොවුදු, *Mowudu, s.* feast, festival.

මොවුන්, *Mowun, pron.* they, these, speaking of persons present.

මොවුන්ගේ, *Mowungé, pron.* of these.

මොහු, *Mohu, sing.* of මොවුන් *mowun.*

මොහො, *Moho, s.* (මුහ *muha* to be foolish) error, ignorance, folly; seeing every thing through a false medium; fainting.

මොහොට්ටාල, *Mohaṭṭála, s.* Kandian officer so called.

මොහොත, *Mohota, s.* division of time, the thirtieth part of a day and night, or an hour of forty-eight minutes; moment, instant.

මොහොරු, *Mohoru, s.* mat for wiping the feet.

මොහොල්, *Mohol,* see මෝල *móla.*

මොහොල, *Mohola, s.* pestle for cleaning the husk from the rice; Elu form of මුසල *mushala.*

මෝ, *Mó, s.* mother (not respectful), this woman; ignorance.

මෝක්ෂඥාන, *Móksha-jñána, s.* (මෝක්ෂ emancipation of the soul, ඥාන knowledge) knowledge of the means for the attainment of Nirwáṇa as revealed by Buddha: see the next.

මෝක්ෂය, *Mókshaya, s.* (මෝක්ෂ *móksha* to free, to discharge, to let go) Nirwáṇa or final emancipation; final and eternal happiness; liberation of the soul from the body and its exemption from further transmigration; death, liberation, freedom.

මෝක්ෂෝපාය, *Mókshópáya, s.* (මෝක්ෂ *móksha* emancipation, උපාය *upáya* means) religious ascetic, devotee; means of attaining final release.

මෝඝ, *Mógha, s.* (මුහ *muha* to be foolish trumpet flower: *a.* vain, foolish, fruitless, useless; left, abandoned.

මෝඝපුරුෂයා, *Mógha-purushayá, s.* (මෝඝ and පුරුෂයා man) vain empty person, useless man; term of reproof, the strongest ever used by Buddha in addressing man.

මෝච, *Mócha, s.* tree, *moringa pterygosperma,* [Colloq. මුරුංගා *murungá*].

මෝචක, *Móchaka, s.* devotee, ascetic freed from all passion; anthelmintic shrub, *serratula* or *conyza anthelmintica* [Colloq. වලංගසාල් *walangasál*]: tree, see මෝච *mócha;* plantain tree; silk cotton tree.

මෝචනය, *Móchanaya, s.* remission.

මෝචරස, *Mócha-rasa, s.* gum of the silk cotton tree, [Colloq. ඉඹුල් ලාටු *imbul-láṭu*].

මෝචා, *Móchá, s.* silk cotton tree, *eriodendron anfractuosum* or *bombax heptaphyllum,* [Colloq. ඉඹුල් *imbul*]; jack tree, *artocarpus integrifolia,* [Colloq. කොස් *kos*]; plantain tree, *musa sapientium,* [Colloq. කෙසෙල් *kesel*].

මෝඩකම, *Móḍakama, s.* foolishness, stupidity.

මෝඩයා, *Móḍayá, s.* blockhead, ignorant fellow, fool.

මෝඩී, *Móḍi, s.* foolish woman.

මෝද, *Móda, s.* (මුද *muda* to rejoice) joy, delight, happiness.

මෝදක, *Módaka, s.* a sort of sweet meat, [Colloq. අග්ගලා *aggalá*].

මෝදන, *Módana, s.* pleasing, delighting, causing joy or happiness.

මෝදර, *Módura*, *s.* mouth of a river, place where a river disembogues.

මෝදිමියා, *Módimiyá*, *s.* sacrificer, applied to a Moorish priest.

මෝදුවෙනවා, *Móduwenawá*, *v.* to come up, to shoot out.

මෝය, *Móya*, *s.* mouth of a river.

මෝරට, *Móraṭa*, *s.* sort of cassia, *cassia articulata;* root of the sugar cane.

මෝරටා, *Móraṭá*, *s.* creeping plant, *sanseviera zeylanica*, [Colloq. නියඳ *niyan̲da*].

මෝරණවා, *Móraṇawá*, *v.* to ripen, to become ripe or mature: pret. මේරුවා *méruwá*.

මෝරා, *Mórá*, *s.* shark, generic name for any fish of the shark tribe as *rhinodon typicus;* also a peacock: pl. මෝරු *móru*,

මෝරු, *Móru*, *s.* whey.

මෝල්ගහ, *Mólgaha*, *s.* pestle for cleaning the husk from the rice, etc.

මෝල්පැද්ද, *Mólpędda*, *s.* tree, not ascertained.

මෝල, *Móla*, *s.* pestle for cleaning the husk from the rice; mill. (Dutch.)

මෝවිට, *Móviṭa*, *s.* (මෝ for මුව *muwa* mouth, විට circumference) the rim or circular mouth of any vessel, margin, edge.

මෝවිත (ලිහෙනවා), *Mórita (lihenawá)*, *v.* the rupture of the bag of water, preceding the delivery of a child; the term is used by midwives.

මෝෂක, *Móshaka*, *s.* (මුෂ *musha* to steal) thief, pilferer.

මෝස්තරෙ, *Móstare*, *s.* (Portuguese *Mostra*), pattern.

මෝහය, *Móhaya*. *s.* (මුහ *muha* to be foolish) ignorance, folly, foolishness; fainting, loss of consciousness or sense; stupidity: pl. මෝහ *móha*.

මෝහන, *Móhana*, *s.* arrow of Kámadéva; temptation, seduction, the overpowering of reason and reflection by worldly or sensual allurements; thorn apple, *datura stramonium*, [Colloq. අත්තන *attana*]; fascinating; stupefying, depriving of sense or understanding.

මෝහි, *Móhi*, *a.* (මෝහ *móha* ignorance, ඉන් *in* aff.) illusive, beguiling.

මෝහිනි, *Móhini*, *s.* (මෝහන *móhana* fascinating, ඉනි *ini* fem. aff.) female devil or rather a personification of lust, supposed to overpower reason and reflection by worldly or sensual allurements.

මෝහි, *Móhí*, *s.* hemp or bhang plant, *cannabis sativa*, [Colloq. කංසා *kaṇsá*].

මෞක්තික, *Mauktika*, *s.* (මුක්තා *muktá* pearl, ඨක් *ṭhak* pleonastic aff.) pearl, [Colloq. මුතු *mutu*].

මෞද්ගල්‍ය, *Maudgalya*, see මුගලන් *mugalan*.

මෞන, *Mauna*, *s.* (මුනි *muni* sage who practises silence, අණ් *aṇ* aff.) silence, taciturnity.

මෞනින්, *Maunin*, *s.* (මෞන *mauna* and ඉන් *in* aff.) ascetic, hermit, religious sage.

මෞර්වි, *Maurri*, *s.* (මූර්වා *múrwá* sanseviera zeylanica, etc. අණ් *aṇ* aff.) bow-string, [Colloq. දුනුදිය *dunudiya*].

මෞලි, *Mauli*, *s.* lock of hair on the crown of the head; hair ornamented and braided round head; diadem, tiara; head; the earth.

මෞහූර්ත, *Mauhúrta*, *s.* (මුහූර්ත *muhúrta* hour, අණ් *aṇ* aff.) astrologer, [Colloq. නක්ෂත්‍රකාරයා *nakshatrakárayá*].

මෞහූර්තික, *Mauhúrttika*, *s.* (මුහූර්ත *muhúrta* and ඨක් *ṭhak* aff.) astrologer.

මැ, *Mę*, *s.* juggling, practising the tricks of a juggler.

මැකරු, *Mękaru*, *s.* (මැ juggling, කරු who does) juggler, one who practises sleight of hand.

මැකිලිය, *Mękiliya*, *s.* plant, *sapium indicum*, [Colloq. කිරිමකුළු *kiri-makuḷu*]; the top piece of a wimble.

මැකුර, *Mękura*, } *s.* juggler.
මැකුරු, *Mękuru*, }

මැකුවා, *Mękuwá*, *v.* wiped off, blotted.

මැකෙනවා, *Mękenawá*, *v.* to become effaced or blotted; neuter form of the verb මකනවා *makanawá*.

මැගු, *Męgu*, *past part.* of මග *maga*, to see.

මැගුම, *Męguma*, *s.* perceiving, looking, beholding; sight, seeing: pl. මැගුම් *męgum*.

මැට්ට, *Męṭṭa*, *s.* clay.

මැටි, *Męṭi*, *s.* clay, mould, earth.

මැටිකරු, *Męṭikaru*, *s.* (මැටි clay, කරු who works) potter, [Colloq. බඩහැලයා *baḍahęlayá*].

මැටිකොරවකා, *Męṭi-korawaká*, *s.* eastern little bittern, *ardetta sinensis;* chesnut bittern, *ardeirella cinnamonea*, *(Arcleidæ* order *Herodiones)*.

මැඩ, *Męḍa*, *s.* ram, goat, from මෙඪ්‍ර *méḍhra;* rubbing, grinding, from මර්දන *mardana*.

මැඩපවත්වනවා, *Męḍapawatwanawá*, *v.* to humble, to subdue, to bring into subjection.

මැඩවිරු, *Męḍariru*, *a.* conquered, subdued, reduced under subjection.

මැඩවිළු, *Męḍariḷu*, *s.* small lake, pond, tank.

මැඩවීම, *Mędavíma*, *s.* preparation of a paddy field, by driving buffaloes to loosen the mud; verbal noun of මඩවනවා *maḍawanawá*.

මැඩහගු, *Mędahangu*, *s.* creeping plant, *dæmia extensa (Asclepiadeæ)*.

මැඩි, *Mędi*, *a.* crushed, squeezed: see also මැඩියා *mędiyá*.

මැඩිතලා, *Mędi-talá*, *s.* plant, not ascertained.

මැඩිය, *Mędiya*, *s.* tree with small white flowers, *Hunteria corymbosa (Apocinaceæ)*.

මැඩිය ජවාල, *Mędiya-jáwála*, *s.* plant with sword-shaped leaves and pale blue flowers on spike, *burmannia disticha (Burmanniaceæ)*.

මැඩියවැල්, *Mędiya-węl*, *s.* climbing plant with tendrils and white berries, *vitis (or cissus) pedata (Ampelideæ)*.

මැඩියා, *Mędiyá*, *s.* frog.

මැඩිල්ල, *Mędilla*, *s.* jungle, thicket; ring, circle; disc of the sun or moon; Elu form of මණ්ඩල *maṇḍala*.

මැඩිල්ලා, *Mędillá*, *s.* serpent, the eye snake.

මැඩිලිපත, *Mędilipata*, *s.* basket or any article made of leaves, bark, etc. serving that purpose.

මැඩිසුණු, *Mędi-sunu*, *s.* (මැඩි squeezed, සුණු particles) refuse of the coconut after the milk has been expressed, [Colloq. පොල්කුඩු, පුන්නක්කු *polkuḍu*, *punnakku*].

මැඩීම, *Mędíma*, *s.* crushing, squeezing.

මැණ, *Męna*, *s.* gem, jewel; Elu form of මිණි *maṇi*.

මැණික්, *Męnik*, see මැණික *męṇika*.

මැණික්කටුව, *Męnik-kaṭuwa*, *s.* wrist.

මැණික්වැන්න, *Męnik-węnna*, *s.* small medicinal plant, not ascertained.

මැණික, *Męṇika*, *s.* gem, jewel, any precious stone or costly ornament, from මාණික්‍ය *máṇikya*.

මැණිකේ, *Męniké*, *s.* a respectable term for Kandian women.

මැත්ත, *Mętta*, *s.* in front of, at feet.

මැත, *Męta*, *s.* counsel, advice.

මැති, *Męti*, *s.* kindness, benevolence; counsellor, adviser, king's minister.

මැතිතුම, *Męti-tuma*, } *s*, (මැති and උතුම *utuma*
මැතිතුමා, *Męti-tumá*, } chief) chief counsellor, prime minister of state.

මැතිඳු, *Męṭindá*, }
මැතිඳු, *Męṭindu*, } see the preceding.

මැතිබෙඹිය, *Mętibémbiya*, *s.* shrub producing a sort of currant, *embelia ribes*, [Colloq. වල් ඇඹිල්ල *wal-ęmbilla*].

මැතිරීම, *Mętiríma*, *s.* charming; muttering.

මැද්ද, *Mędda*, } *s.* middle, centre; Elu form of
මැද *Męda*, } මධ්‍ය *madhya*.

මැදඟිල්ල, *Mędaṇgilla*, *s.* (මැද middle, ඇඟිල්ල *ęṇgilla* finger) middle finger, large finger.

මැදදෙස, *Męda-desa*, *s.* middle of the body, waist: see මධ්‍යදේශය *madhya-déṣaya*.

මැදහත්, *Mędahat*, *a.* (මැද middle, between, හත් from ස්ථා *sthá* what stands) interposing, advocating, reconciling, mediating, coming in between two parties to procure peace; middle, central; impartial.

මැදහත්කාරයා, *Mędahatkárayá*, *s.* (මැදහත් reconciling, කාර who does) judge; umpire, arbitrator, mediator.

මැදි, *Mędi*, *a.* middle.

මැදින්දින, *Mędindina*, } *s.* month so called (March,
මැදින, *Mędina*, } April), the last of the Siṇhalese year.

මැදිම, *Mędima*, *s.* neighbourhood.

මැදිර, *Mędira*, *s.* cat; birdcage, aviary; house; temple; Elu form of මන්දිර *mandira*.

මැදිරිය, *Męriya*, *s.* tree; house; cage, temple.

මැදිවයස, *Mędi-wayasa*, *s.* (මැදි middle, වයස time of life) middle age, manhood, prime of life.

මැදිවීම, *Mędiríma*, *s.* interfering.

මැදිවෙනවා, *Mędiwenawá*, *v.* to be surrounded or encircled; to meddle, to interfere.

මැදීම, *Mędíma*, *s.* extracting of toddy, smoothing.

මැදුම්, *Mędum*, *a.* middle, centrical, intervening.

මැදුම්පොල්ල, *Mędum-polla*, *s.* small piece of wood used by the toddy drawers, men who extract the liquor from the coconut tree, to beat the flower and make the liquor exude more freely: see also මල්තැළුම *maltęluma*.

මැදුම්සඟිය, *Mędum-sangiya*, *s.* (මැදුම් and සඟිය collection or compilation) second of the five divisions of Sútra-piṭaka, comprizing fifteen books or 152 Sútras.

මැදුර, *Mędura*, *s.* house, dwelling; birdcage: pl. මැදුරු *męduru*.

මැන්ඩෝර, *Męndóra*, *s.* timber tree, *vatica Roxburghiana* or *v. chinensis (Dipterocarpaceæ)*.

මැනව, *Męnawa*, } *ad.* affix to verbs generally used
මැනවි, *Męnavi*, } in a precative sense, answering to good, well, if you please, etc. and used only in addressing superiors.

මැනවු, *Męnawu*, *s.* feast, festival, auspicious or joyful occasion.

මැනිල්ල, *Męnilla*, see මැනිම *męníma*.

මැනිම, *Męníma*, *s.* measuring, surveying.

මැනො, *Męno*, see මැනවා *męnawa*.

මැර, *Męra*, *s.* ray of light, sunbeam; fence, limit, boundary: *a.* stubborn, hard-hearted.

මැරකම, *Męrakama*, *s.* stubbornness, roughness.

මැරයා, *Męrayá*, *s.* rough fellow, rowdy.

මැරිම, *Męríma*, *s.* killing.

මැරෙණවා, *Męrenawá*, *v.* to die, to expire: pret. මැරුණ *męruṇá*.

මැරෙව්වා, *Męrewwá*, *v.* caused to be slain.

මැරුවා, *Męruwá*, *v.* killed, slain.

මැල්ල, *Męlla*, *s.* plant, peculiar to Ceylon, *olax zeylanica, (Olacineæ).*

මැල්ලි, *Męlli*, } *s.* younger brother.
මැල්ලියා, *Męllyá*, }

මැල්ලුම, *Męlluma*, *s.* dry curry made of minced leaves or fruit mixed with coconut kernel; also, embrocation: pl. මැල්ලුම් *męllum*.

මැල, *Męla*, *s.* maternal uncle.

මැලකි, *Męlaki*, *a.* soft, liquid; supple.

මැලගහනවා, *Męlagahanawá*, *v.* to gather bonfires, to gather sticks to set fire to.

මැලගෑහිම, *Męlagęhíma*, *s.* burning of a thicket, conflagration of a forest.

මැලය, *Męlaya*, *s.* large fire, conflagration.

මැලවෙනවා, *Męlawenawá*, *v.* to wither, to droop, to die as a flower.

මැලසි, *Męlasi*, *s.* young unripe fruit: *a.* soft, tender, delicate.

මැලා, *Męlá*, *s.* laziness, indolence; antimony; also, younger brother.

මැලි, *Męli*, *a.* lazy, indolent.

මැලිකරණවා, *Męlikaraṇawá*, *v.* to become lazy, to neglect, to be reluctant.

මැලියම්, *Męliyam*, *s.* gum, glue, any glutinous substance exuding from trees or plants on incision.

මැලැස්ස, *Męlęssa*, *s.* tender fruit.

මැවිල්ල, *Męvilla*, *s.* creature, created being or substance.

මැවිම, *Męvíma*, *s.* creation, verbal noun of මවනවා *mawanawá*.

මැවුම්කාරයා, *Męwumkárayá*, *s.* (මැවුම *węuvma* and කාර who does) Creator.

මැවුම, *Męwuma*, *s.* creation, creating.

මැවෙනවා, *Męwenawá*, *v.* to be created, passive form of මවනවා *mawanawá*.

මැස්ස, *Męssa*, *s.* small erection made of sticks; place to sit or sleep upon; raised floor or platform in the rice fields, on which a person is stationed to watch the grain; water stand made of sticks; hurdle; hen coop made of wicker work, etc: pl. මැහි *męhi*.

මැස්සා, *Męssá*, *s.* fly, fly in general: pl. මැස්සෝ *męssó*: *a.* of flies.

මැසි, *Męsi*, *s.* anger; bed; also the plural of මැස්ස *męssa*.

මැසිගෙය, *Męsi-geya*, *s.* tower, [Colloq. අට්ටාලය *aṭṭálaya*].

මැසිදෑ, *Męsidę*, *s.* mineral substance of a dark colour, used medicinally, it is apparently the common pyritic iron ore.

මැසිපිලවා, *Męsi-pilawá*, *s.* small or young fly.

මැසිරි, *Męsiri*, } *s.* species of stone or
මැසිරි ගල, *Męsiri-gala*, } cat's eye, [Colloq. වයිරෝඩි *wayiróḍi*].

මැසිල්ල, *Męsilla*, *s.* stitching, sewing, any thing to be stitched.

මැසිවිල්ල, *Męsivilla*, *s.* complaint, prayer in affliction or sorrow, asking for a blessing after a misfortune.

මැසි සමාගම, *Męsi-samágama*, *s.* (මැසි and සමාගම assemblage) swarm of bees.

මැසි සුණු, *Męsi-sunu*, see මැසිදෑ *męsidę*.

මැසිසේ, *Męsisé*, *s.* palm of the hand; platform.

මැසිම, *Męsíma*, see මැහිම *męhíma*.

මැසෙනවා, *Męsenawá*, *v.* to be stitched; to be closed or shut; metaphorically, to be unable to answer.

මැහි තුස, *Męhi-tusa*, *s.* a string.

මැහි පොදිය, *Męhi-podiya*, *s.* swarm of flies or bees.

මැහිල්ල, *Męhilla*, *s.* stitch.

මැහිම, *Męhíma*, *s.* stitching, sewing.

මැහුම්කාරයා, *Męhumkárayá*, *s.* (මැහුම් sewing, කාර *kára* who does) tailor, seamster.

මැහුම, *Męhuma*, *s.* stitching, sewing, work to be sewed.

මැහැණියන්, *Męhęniyan*, } *s.* mother.
මැහැණියෝ, *Męhęniyó*, }

මැහැල්ල, *Męhęlla*, } *s.* old woman, a matron or
මැහැලි, *Męhęli*, } elderly woman, from මහල්ලා *mahallá*, masc.

මෑ, *Mę*, *s.* general name for beans or pulse; mother: *pron.* this (woman), used only of inferiors.

මෑකරල, *Mękarala*, *s.* bean pod: pl. මෑකරල් *mękaral*.

මැත්, *Mėt*, see මැත *mėta*.

මැත්කරණවා, *Mėtkaraṇawá*, *v.* to bring near.

මැත්වෙනවා, *Mėtwenawá*, *v.* to approach, jut out.

මැත, *Mėta*, *s.* this side; this way; recent time.

මැතදී, *Mėtadí*, *s.* lately.

මැනියන්, *Mėniyan*, මැනියන්දෑ, *Mėniyandė*, මැනියෝ, *Mėniyó*, } *s.* mother.

මැනුවා, *Mėnuwá*, *v.* set a trap, from මානනවා *mánanawá*, to aim at, as with a gun.

මෘග, *Mṛiga*, *s.* deer; antelope; animal in general; research, inquiry, investigation; asking, soliciting, begging; the fifth lunar constellation: see මෘග ශිරස් *mṛiga-ṣiras;* month in which the moon is full in mṛiga-ṣiras; musk; hunting, chase.

මෘගකම, *Mṛigakama*, *s.* brutality.

මෘගජාති, *Mṛiga-játi*, *s.* animal kind.

මෘග තෘෂ්ණා, *Mṛiga-tṛishṇá*, see මෘග ප්‍රිය *mṛiga-priya.*

මෘග ධේනුව, *Mṛiga-dhénuwa*, *s.* hind.

මෘග නාභි, *Mṛiga-nábhi*, මෘග නාභිජ, *Mṛiga-nábhija*, } *s.* (මෘග deer, නාභි navel, ජ born) musk, it being formed in a bag attached to the belly of the animal about the navel. [Colloq. කස්තුරි *kastúri*].

මෘගනේත්‍රි, *Mṛiga-nétri*, *s.* (මෘග and නේත්‍ර *nétra* eye, ඉ *i* aff. fem.) epithet applied to women expressive of beauty, deer-eyed one.

මෘග පති, *Mṛiga-pati*, *s.* (මෘග animal, පති chief) lion, [Colloq. සිංහයා *sinhayá*].

මෘග පර්ෂද, *Mṛiga-parshada*, *s.* (මෘග deer, පර්ෂද assemblage) flock of deer.

මෘග ප්‍රිය, *Mṛiga-priya*, *s.* (මෘග deer, ප්‍රිය what delights) sultry vapour which floats over lands and deserts in the hot seasons and has the appearance of water and waves; by it the deer are deceived when in search of water.

මෘග මද, *Mṛiga-mada*, *s.* (මෘග and මද secretion) musk: see මෘග නාභි *mṛiga-nábhi*.

මෘග මායම්, *Mṛiga-máyam*, *s.* (මෘග and මායම් deception) animal instinct, but particularly applied to the deer which is remarkable for its cunning in eluding its pursuers.

මෘගයා, *Mṛigayá*, *s.* animal, beast: see මෘග *mṛiga*.

මෘග රජ, *Mṛiga-rája*, *s.* (මෘග animal, රජ king) lion: see මෘගපති *mṛiga-pati*.

මෘග ශිරස්, *Mṛiga-ṣiras*, මෘග ශීර්ෂ, *Mṛiga-ṣírsha*, } *s.* (මෘග deer, ශිරස් or ශීර්ෂ head) the fifth lunar mansion containing Delta stars, one of which is Lambda Orionis and figured by an antelope's head.

මෘගාක්ෂි, *Mṛigákshi*, *s.* (මෘග *mṛiga* deer, අක්ෂි *akshi* eye) bitter apple, *cucumis coloquintida;* see මෘගාදනි *mṛigádaní*: woman with an eye like that of the deer, considered a mark of great beauty.

මෘගාණ්ඩජ, *Mṛigáṇḍaja*, *s.* (මෘග *mṛiga* and අණ්ඩ *aṇḍa* testicle, ජ produced) musk, [Colloq. කස්තුරි *kastúri*].

මෘගාදන, *Mṛigádana*, *s.* (මෘග *mṛiga* and අදන *adana* eating) hyena; leopard, [Colloq. කොටියා *koṭiyá*].

මෘගාදනි, *Mṛigádani*, *s.* (මෘග *mṛiga* and අදන *adana* eating) plant, colocynth, *citrullus colocynthus*, [Colloq. යක්කොමඩු *yak-komaḍu*].

මෘගාරි, *Mṛigári*, *s.* (මෘග *mṛiga* deer, අරි *ari* enemy) lion, [Colloq. සිංහයා *sinhayá*].

මෘගාව්‍යධ, *Mṛigávidh*, *s.* (මෘග *mṛiga* and ව්‍යධ *vyadha* to destroy with ආ *á* prefix) hunter, deer killer.

මෘගේන්ද්‍ර, *Mṛigéndra*, *s.* (මෘග *mṛiga* animal, ඉන්ද්‍ර *indra* lord, master) lion, [Coll: සිංහයා *sinhayá*].

මෘජා, *Mṛijá*, *s.* act of cleaning the body by washing and anointing it with ashes of sandal wood, etc.

මෘඩ, *Mṛiḍa*, *s.* (මෘඩ to be pleased) name of Ṣiva.

මෘඩානි, *Mṛiḍáni*, *s.* the wife of Ṣiva.

මෘඪා, *Mṛidhá*, *s.* kind of cucumber, *cucumis pubescens*, [Colloq. මහගොන්කැකිරි *maha-gonkėkiri*].

මෘණාල, *Mṛiṇála*, *s.* film or fibres attached to the stalk of the lotus; root of a fragrant grass, *andropogon muricatus*, [Colloq. සැවැන්දරා *sėwėndará*].

මෘණාලිකා, *Mṛiṇálaká*, *s.* plant, *ipomœa digitata*, [Colloq. කිරිබඩු *kiribaḍu*].

මෘත්, *Mṛit*, මෘත්තිකා, *Mṛittiká*, } *s.* earth, clay, soil.

මෘත්තිකා පාණ්ඩු, *Mṛittiká-páṇḍu*, *s.* (මෘත්තිකා and පාණ්ඩු jaundice) jaundice, supposed to arise from eating clay or earth.

මෘත්‍යුංජය, *Mṛityunjaya*, *s.* name of Ṣiva.

මෘත්‍යුරජ, *Mṛityu-rája*, *s.* (මෘත්‍යු death, රජ king) name of Yama alluding to his being the regent of death and sovereign of the final destinies of men.

මෘත්සනා, *Mṛitsná*, *s.* good soil.

මෘත්සා, *Mṛitsá*, *s.* good or rich soil.

මෘත, *Mṛita*, *a.* dead, expired, extinct.

මෘතක, *Mṛitaka*, *s.* dead body, corpse.

මෘතකාන්තක, *Mṛita-kántaka*, *s.* (මෘත and කාන්තක fond of) jackal, [Colloq. නරියා *nariyá*].

මෘතලතා, *Mṛita-latá*, *s.* plant, called tulasi or holy basil, *ocimum sanctum*, [Colloq. මදුරුතලා *ma-duru-talá*].

මෘද්භාජන, *Mṛid-bhájana*, *s.* (මෘත් *mṛit* clay, භාජන vessel) any earthen vessel.

මෘද්වී, *Mṛidví*, *s.* brown grape.

මෘද්වීකා, *Mṛidvíká*, *s.* vine, *vitis vinifera*, [Colloq. මිදිවැල *midi-węla*].

මෘදඞ්ග, *Mṛidańga*, *s.* tomtom or native drum. tabor; sound, noise.

මෘදඞ්ග ධ්වනි, *Mṛidańga-dhwani*, *s.* sound of the tabor.

මෘදු, *Mṛidu*, *a.* soft; blunt, not sharp; gentle, mild.

මෘදුකණ්ටක, *Mṛidu-kaṇṭaka*, *s.* plant, *barleria prionites*, [Colloq. කටුකරඬු *kaṭukaranḍu*].

මෘදුකම, *Mṛidukama*, *s.* gentleness, meekness.

මෘදුත්වච, *Mṛidut-wacha*, *s.* (මෘදු soft, ත්වච skin) the bhója-patra tree, the bark of which peels off like that of the birch and is used in making hooka snakes, etc.; kind of resin, [Colloq. දුම්මල *dummala*].

මෘදුපුෂ්ප, *Mṛidu-pushpa*, *s.* (මෘදු and පුෂ්ප flower) the sirisha tree, *mimosa sirisha*.

මෘදුල, *Mṛidula*, *s.* water: *a.* soft.

මෘදු ලෝහ, *Mṛidu-lóha*, *s.* black lead, [Colloq. කළු ඊයම් *kaḷu-íyam*].

මෘදු විරේචනී, *Mṛidu-viréchaní*, *s.* small thorny tree, *euphorbia neriifolia*, [Colloq. පතුක් *patuk*].

මෘදූත්වක්, *Mṛidúkatwak*, *s.* the bhója-patra tree.

මෘදූත්පල, *Mṛidútpala*, *s.* (මෘදු *mṛidu* and උත්පල *utpala* lotus) blue lotus, *nymphæa cyanea* or *n. stellata*, [Colloq. මානෙල් *mánel*].

මෘෂ්ට, *Mrishṭa*, *a.* cleaned, cleansed.

මෘෂා, *Mṛishá*, *ind.* falsely; uselessly, in vain.

මෘෂාර්ථක, *Mṛishárthaka*, *s.* (මෘෂා falsely, අර්ථ *artha* meaning) impossibility, absurdity, (in speech or composition).

මෘෂාවාද, *Mṛisháwáda*, *s.* (මෘෂා and වාද speech, praise) irony, ironical praise; speaking falsely, lying.

මෘෂාවාදී, *Mṛisháwádi*, *s.* (මෘෂා false, වාදී who speaks) speaking falsely, lying; liar, false accuser, one who brings forward an unjust accusation.

ම්ලාන, *Mlána*, *a.* (ම්ලෛ *mlai* to be languid) weary, languid.

ම්ලේච්ඡ, *Mlechchha*, *s.* (ම්ලේඡ *mlechha* to speak incorrectly or in a barbarous dialect) generic term for a barbarian or foreigner, savage, one of an uncivilized race; barbarous speech.

ම්ලේච්ඡකන්ද, *Mlechchha-kanda*, *s.* garlic, *allium sativum*, [Colloq. සුදුළූනු *sudulúnu*].

ම්ලේච්ඡිත, *Mlechchhita*, *s.* (ම්ලේඡ *mlechha* to speak incorrectly, etc.) barbarous language.

ය

The twenty sixth consonant of the Siṇhalese alphabet; it is the first of the miscellaneous class of letters and may be considered a semivowel, expressed by *ya* in *yarn*.

ය, *Ya*, *s.* iron, [Colloq. යකඩ *yakaḍa*]; also, union.

යං, *Yaṇ*, properly යම් *yam*.

යක්, *Yak*, *s.* demigod, demon, devil.

යක් එරබදු, *Yak-erabadu*, *s.* tree with prickles and red flowers, *erythrina ovafolia (Leguminosæ)*.

යක් කටුස්සා, *Yak-kaṭussá*, *s.* lizard with five toes on the hind legs (common near Galle), *Otocryptis bivittata (Agamidæ* order *Sauria)*.

යක් කහ, *Yak-kaha*, *s.* kind of saffron, species of *curcuma*.

යක් කොමඩු, *Yak-komaḍu*, *s.* plant, colocynth, *citrullus colocynthes (Cucurbitaceæ)*.

යක් දර, *Yak-dara*, *s.* (යක් demon, දර who has) demoniac, one possessed.

යක් දෙස්සා, *Yak-dessá*, *s.* (යක් devil, දෙස්සා who calls to witness) exorcist, devil priest.

යක්න, *Yakna*, *s.* liver, [Colloq. කැවුත්ත *kęwutta*].

යක්බේරිය, *Yakbériya*, *s.* shrub with yellow flowers, *crotalaria laburnifolia, (Leguminosæ)*.

යක් මල්, *Yak-mal*, *s.* African marigold, *tajetes erecta*.

යක් රද, *Yak-rada*, *s.* (යක් devil, රද king) name of Kuvéra or Wesamuṇi, regent of the North and king of the demon race, [Colloq. වෙසමුණි *wesamuṇi*].

යක්වනස්ස, *Yak-wanassa*, *s.* plant, *anisomeles ovata (Labiatæ)*.

යක්ෂ්මන්, *Yashman*, *s.* pulmonary consumption.

යක්ෂ, *Yaksha*, *s.* (යක්ෂ to offer, to worship) demon, good or bad, considered as an object of worship; infernal spirit, devil; the latter meanings are most common, hence the worship of devils almost universally prevails amongst the Siṇhalese inhabitants, see යක්ෂ ධූප *yaksha-dhúpa;* in the mythology of the Hindus, kind of fiend or demigod, especially those who are attendant on Kuvéra, the Indian god of wealth, and employed as guardians of his treasures and gardens.

යක්ෂද්‍රක්, *Yakshadrik*, } s. creeper, *cæsalpinia bonduc*,
යක්ෂද්‍රශ්, *Yakshadriṣ*, } [Colloq. කුඹුරුවැල් *kumburuwel*].

යක්ෂ ධූප, *Yaksha-dhúpa*, s. (යක්ෂ demigod or demon, ධූප perfume, incense) resin in general, [Colloq. දුම්මල *dummala*]; turpentine; the resinous exudation of the pine; this substance is much used in the worship of devils and at the invocation of demons; during the performance of the ceremonies, the officiating priest holds a lighted torch in one hand and with the other throws the resin, pulverized and mixed with a small quantity of nitre, into the flame, which produces a considerable flash and a strong perfume, supposed to be agreeable to the demon and tending to propitiate him.

යක්ෂ පුරය, *Yaksha-puraya*, s. (යක්ෂ and පුර *pura* city) city of Kuvéra or Wesamuṇi, the regent of the north quarter and king of the demon race.

යක්ෂයා, *Yakshayá*, see යක්ෂ *yaksha*.

යක්ෂ රජ, *Yaksha-rája*, s. (යක්ෂ demon, රජ king) name of Kuvéra or Wesamuṇi, king of the yaksha or demon race.

යක්ෂවෘක්ෂ, *Yaksha-vṛiksha*, s. (යක්ෂ and වෘක්ෂ tree) tree supposed to be the favourite haunt of sprites and demons, *terminalia belerica*, [Colloq. බුළු *buḷu*].

යක්ෂාක්ෂි, *Yakshákshi*, s. creeper, *cæsalptnia bonduc*, [Colloq. කුඹුරුවැල් *kumburu-wel*].

යක්ෂාවාස, *Yaksháwása*, s. (යක්ෂ *yaksha* demigod, අවාස *áwása* abode) banyan or Indian fig tree, *ficus bengalensis* or *f. indica*.

යක්ෂිණී, *Yakshiṇí*, s. (යක්ෂ *yaksha* and ඉණී *iṇí* aff.) female devil, a fury; wife of Kuvéra; wife of a yaksha; female fiend attached to the service of Durgá, and frequently maintaining like a sylph or fairy an intercourse with mortals.

යක්ස, *Yaksa*, properly යක්ෂ *yaksha*, which see.

යක් සෙන්, *Yak-sen*, s. (යක් and සෙන් army) multitude or company of devils.

යක, *Yaka*, see යකා *yaká*.

යකඩ, *Yakaḍa*, s. iron.

යකඩ අඩුවැඩිය, *Yakaḍa-aḍuwęḍiya*, s. ironwork or tools, iron-wares.

යකඩමල, *Yakaḍa-mala*, s. (යකඩ and මල excrescence) rust which collects on iron.

යකඩේ, *Yakaḍé*, s. iron: pl. යකඩ *yakaḍa*.

යකදුරා, *Yakadurá*, s. (යක demon, ඇදුරා *ędurá* teacher) person skilled in the invocation and worship of demons; exorcist, expeller of demons.

යකදුරුකම, *Yakadurukama*, s. devil ceremony.

යකහළු, *Yakahaḷu*, s. forest tree, *doona trapezifolia (Dipterocarpaceæ)*.

යකා, *Yaká*, s. devil, Elu form of යක්ෂ *yaksha*, which see: pl. යක්කු *yakku*.

යකාබැඳිවැල, *Yakábęndi-węla*, s. plant, not ascertained.

යකිණි, *Yakiṇi*, s. female devil: see යක්ෂිණී *yakshiṇí*.

යකින්න, *Yakinna*, s. she-demon, a female imp.

යකිනාරන්, *Yakináran*, s. thorny shrub, *atalantia zeylanica*, or *limonia monophylla (Rutaceæ)*.

යකුතලා, *Yakutalá*, s. bulbous plant with ornamental leaves, *colocasia nymphæifolia*, variety of *c. antiquorum* (ගහල *gahala*); also called වැල් අල *węl-ala*: *(Araceæ)*.

යකුන්, *Yakun*, *plur.* of යකා *yaká*.

යකුළ, *Yakuḷa*, s. smith's sledge hammer, [Colloq. කුළුගෙඩිය *kuḷugeḍiya*].

යකෘත්, *Yakṛit*, s. (ය union, of the parts of the body, කෘත් maker of) liver.

යගණ, *Yagaṇa*, s. poetical foot, having the first syllable short and the two last long.

යගදා, *Yagadá*, s. (ය iron, ගදා mace or club) fabulous staff; iron club.

යගුල, *Yagula*, s. bar of iron: pl. යගුල් *yagul*.

යඟ, *Yaṉga*, s. pleasure, joy, happiness, enjoyment.

යජ, *Yaja*, s. a verbal root, signifying to offer, to worship; to present, to endow; to associate with.

යජමාන, *Yajamána*, s. (යජ to worship, මාන aff. of the present participle) a person who institutes a sacrifice, employs the priests, and pays all the expenses attending it.

යජුර්වේද, *Yajurvéda*, s. (යජුස් *yajus* and වේද *véda*) one of the four Védas of the Hindus; it is divided into two parts, the black and the white; both portions of this Véda are chiefly on religious rites, and the prayers peculiar to it are chiefly in measured and poetical prose.

යජුස්, *Yajus*, s. (යජ *yaja* to worship), see the last.

යඥ, *Yajña*, s. (යජ *yaja* to offer, to worship) sacrifice, ceremony in which oblations are presented.

යඥයෝග්‍ය, *Yajña-yógya*, *s.* (යඥ sacrifice, යෝග්‍ය fit) that which is fit to be offered, prepared by purification, etc.; species of fig tree, *ficus glomerata*, [Colloq. අට්ටික්කා *aṭṭikká*].

යඥාඞ්ග, *Yajñáńga*, *s.* (යඥ *yajña* and අඞ්ග *ańga* member) glomerous fig, see the preceding; plant, *siphonanthus indica;* part of any sacrifice.

යට, *Yaṭa*, *ad.* under, below, beneath.

යටකරණවා, *Yaṭakaraṇawá*, *v.* to conceal, suppress.

යටග, *Yaṭaga*, *s.* (යටි *yaṭi* staff, අග *aga* top) top of a pole or flag-staff.

යටගිය, *Yaṭagiya*, *a.* ancient, former; past, bygone.

යටත්, *Yaṭat*, *a.* (යට below, අත් *at* end) humble, obedient, submissive; mean, low, servile.

යටත්කම, *Yaṭatkama*, *s.* humility.

යටත්කරණවා, *Yaṭatkaraṇawá*, *v.* to subdue.

යටත්පිරිසෙයින්, *Yaṭatpiriseyin*, *ad.* at the lowest point, at the least, [Colloq. අඩුතරමින් *aḍutaramin*].

යටත්වෙනවා, *Yaṭatwenawá*, *v.* to be humble, submissive, to submit.

යටත්වැසියා, *Yaṭat-wæsiyá*, *s.* subject, vassal.

යටමිලාව, *Yaṭamiláwa*, *s.* beneath, place below, the under part, underneath.

යටලීය, *Yaṭalíya*, *s.* (යට and ලීය staff, etc.) beam, under beam of a house upon which the rafters are nailed: wall-plate.

යටහත්, *Yaṭahat*, see යටත් *yaṭat*.

යටි, *Yaṭi*, *s.* any creeping plant; staff, stick; Elu form of යෂ්ටි *yashṭi*; also=යට *yaṭa* under.

යටිකුරු, *Yaṭikuru*, *a.* turned downwards.

යටිපතුල, *Yaṭi-patula*, *s.* (යටි and පතුල sole of the foot) sole of the foot.

යටිබඩ, *Yaṭi-baḍa*, *s.* (යටි and බඩ belly) abdomen.

යටිහුලඟ, *Yaṭi-hulaṉga*, *s.* (යටි under, හුලඟ wind) leeward.

යත්ත, *Yatta*, *s.* carpenter's plane: pl. යතු *yatu*.

යත්න, *Yatna*, *s.* effort, exertion, perseverance, energy.

යත්යත්, *Yatyat*, *s.* passing, going, as time rolls on: *a.* any whatever.

යතලබ, *Yataluba*, *s.* whatever is received.

යතහොත්, *Yatahot*, *ind. particle* equivalent to if, if so, that is to say, if it be asked why.

යති, *Yati*,
යතින්, *Yatin*, } *s.* (යම *yama* to restrain or යත *yata* to endeavour, ඉන් *in* aff.) ascetic, one whose passions are completely under subjection; religious mendicant; Buddhist ascetic, a priest; restraining, controlling; stopping, ceasing, rest, term; pause in poetry or metre; stop, a rest.

යතිඳු, *Yatiṉdu*,
යතිඳුන්, *Yatiṉdun*, } *s.* eminent priest or ascetic.

යතීන්ද්‍ර, *Yatíndra*, *s.* (යති *yati* ascetic, priest, ඉන්ද්‍ර *indra* chief) chief or high priest; tree yielding resin, *vateria indica*, [Colloq. හල් *hal*].

යතු, *Yatu*, *s.* going, journey; planing, smoothing; plur. of යත්ත *yatta*.

යතුකඳ, *Yatu-kaṉda*,
යතුකෑටය, *Yatukeṭaya*, } *s.* carpenter's plane.

යතුගානවා, *Yatugánawá*, *v.* to smooth, to plane.

යතුතලේ, *Yatu-talé*,
යතුනියන, *Yatu-niyana*, } *s.* chisel or steel part of a plane.

යතුර, *Yatura*, *s.* key; lock; machine, instrument in general: pl. යතුරු *yaturu;* Elu form of යන්ත්‍ර *yantra*.

යතුරා, *Yaturá*, *s.* going, journey, voyage; way, road, path, from යාත්‍රා *yátrá*.

යතුරු කට, *Yaturu-kaṭa*,
යතුරු කපොල්ල, *Yaturu-kapolla*, } *s.* key-hole.

යතුරු තහඩුව, *Yaturu-tahaḍuwa*, *s.* lock.

යතුරු දුන්න, *Yaturu-dunna*, *s.* (යතුරු and දුන්න bow) spring of a lock.

යතුරු මුදුව, *Yaturu-muduwa*, *s.* key.

යතුරුසර, *Yaturusara*, *s.* elephant keeper; path, road, frequented path.

යථා, *Yathá*, *ind.* as, according to, correlative to තථා *tathá* so.

යථාක්‍රමය, *Yathákramaya*, *s.* order, method, degree, [Colloq. පිළිවෙළ *piḷiweḷa*].

යථාජාත, *Yathájáta*, *a.* (යථා as, ජාත born) foolish, stupid, as simple as at birth; barbarous, outcast; naked.

යථානුරූප, *Yathánurúpa*, *a.* (යථා as, අනුරූප *anurúpa* fit) suitable, proper, consistent, fit.

යථාපි, *Yathápi*, *ad.* somehow.

යථාබල, *Yathá-bala*, *ad.* according to ability.

යථාභූත, *Yathábhúta*, *a.* (යථා as, භූත being) exact, true, real; like, resembling; so, in that manner.

යථාර්හ, *Yathárha*, *ad.* (යථා as, අර්හ *arha* properly) properly, suitably.

යථාශක්ති, *Yathá-ṣakti*, *ad.* (යථා as, ශක්ති strength) extent of capability; as much as possible.

යථාස්වරූප, *Yathá-swarúpa*, *ad.* (යථා as, ස්වරූප form) properly, consistently, according to form or nature.

යථාසන්තතිකාඞ්ග, *Yathá-santatikánga, s.* (යථා as, සන්තතික *santatika* spread, අඞ්ග *anga* ordinance) ordinance of the Buddhist priesthood enjoining it upon the priests never to change or alter the mat or bed which they first spread out to repose upon, as it is first laid down so it must remain: see තෙලෙස්ධූතාඞ්ගය *teḷesdhutángaya*.

යථෝක්ත, *Yathókta, a.* (යථා *yathá* as, උක්ත *ukta* said) as mentioned or said (above).

යද්දෙස්සා *Yaddessá, s.* a long-limbed insect: see also, යක්දෙස්සා *yakdessá*.

යදණ්ඩ, *Yadaṇḍa, s.* (ය iron, දණ්ඩ bar) bar or pig of iron.

යදම, *Yadama,* }
යදූම, *Yadáma,* } *s.* iron chain, fetter: pl. යදම් *yadam*.

යදි, *Yadi, s.* beggar, mendicant: *ind.* particle of suspicion or doubt; if.

යදිනවා, *Yadinawá, v.* to pray, to beseech, to entreat; to ask alms; to curse, to imprecate, to execrate: pret. යැද්දා *yeddá*.

යදුම, *Yaduma, s.* prayer, request, [Colloq. ඉල්ලීම *illíma*]: pl. යදුම් *yadum*.

යන්, *Yan*, see යම් *yam*.

යන්තම්, *Yantam, ad.* little, somewhat; narrowly, at the least.

යන්තුරු, *Yanturu*, see the following.

යන්ත්‍ර, *Yantra, s.* machine in general, implement or apparatus; diagram of a mystical nature or astrological character; sort of vessel; controlling, checking, restraining; charioteer, elephant driver.

යන්ත්‍රිත, *Yantrita, a.* bound, tied; restrained, checked.

යන්නා, *Yanná, s.* goer, traveller, journeyer.

යන්සය, *Yansaya, s.* the sign (ය)=ය *ya*.

යන, *Yana, a.* going, journeying; *affix*, answering to that is, so called.

යනවා, *Yanawá, v.* to go, to walk, to proceed, to journey: pret. ගියා *giyá*.

යනාදිය, *Yanádiya, ad.* and so forth, such like, etcetera.

යනු, *Yanu, s.* that which is (so) called; the expression or word: *ind.* a *continuative particle*, corresponding to that is, that is to say, as the forementioned, etc.

යපත, *Yapata, s.* (ය iron, පත leaf) plate of iron, sheet iron.

යපම්මු, *Yapammu, s.* smelters of iron.

යපල, *Yapala, s.* lie, untruth, falsehood, [Colloq. බොරුව *boruwa*].

යපළුව, *Yapaḷuwa, s.* piece of iron, pig of iron.

යපීම, *Yapíma,* }
යපෙන, *Yapena,* } *s.* satisfaction, support, sustenance, livelihood, means of support, [Colloq. රක්ෂාව *rakshâwa*].

යබර, *Yabara,* }
යබොර, *Yabora,* } *s.* (ය iron, බොර dross) scoria of iron, iron rust.

යම්, *Yam, particle* or *prefix*, signifying some, any, it is variously written; as, යං *yaṇ*, යන් *yan*, etc.

යම් කිසි, *Yam-kisi, pron.* (යම් any, කිසි the same) aught, any (thing), some.

යම්තාක්, *Yamták, ad.* so much, how long, etc.

යම්සේ, *Yamsé, ad.* in any manner.

යම්හෙයකින්, *Yamheyakin, ad.* by any cause or means.

යම, *Yama, s.* regent of death and the final judge of the actions of men; he corresponds in many particulars with the Grecian god Pluto, and the judge of hell Minos; he holds his court in pátála but decides only on doubtful characters; for according to the Buddhist system, evil and virtue reward themselves, so that a decidedly vicious character at the hour of death goes direct to narakádi and a virtuous one to Swarga, without any reference to Yama, his office being only to determine the fate of cases where both vice and virtue have prevailed; name of the planet Saturn; the performance of religious rites for the purposes of purification, religious restraint; forbearance, restraint, cessation, stop, conclusion; let us go in speaking to a low person, යමව් *yamaw*, in speaking to many.

යමක්, *Yamak, adv.* something, any thing, aught.

යමක, *Yamaka, s.* religious obligation or observance; alliteration; rhyme; repetition of similar sounds, either in the course of a sentence or line or at the end of two corresponding stanzas; repetition of a line; pair; twins; one of a pair, twin.

යමක ප්‍රාතිහාර්‍ය, *Yamaka-prátihárya, s.* (යමක two, couple, ප්‍රාතිහාර්‍ය wonder, feat) miracle said to have been performed by Buddha, for the purpose of confounding the Niganṭhayás or naked religious mendicants, and of exhibiting to them a proof that he possessed the power of performing supernatural acts; the alleged miracle performed on this occasion consisted in his causing two streams one as of fire, and the other as of water, to issue at the same moment from his eyes, his ears, and his nostrils,; this supernatural power was the result of his having performed the තේජෝ *téjó* and ආපෝ කසින *ápó-kasina:* see කසින *kasina.*

යමදිග, *Yama-diga, s.* (යම and දිග quarter) south, [Colloq. දකුණුදිග *dakuṇudiga*].

යමදූත, *Yama-dúta, s.* (යම yama, දූත messenger) infernal spirit; messenger or minister of Yama, employed to bring the souls of the dead to Yama's judgment seat and thence conduct them to their final destination.

යමන, *Yamana, s.* name of Yama; binding, confining; term; cessation, rest; controlling, restraining.

යමපල්ලා, *Yamapallá, s.* one of Yama's agents whose business is to inflict the punishments of hell; infernal tormentor, a fury: pl. යමපල්ලෝ *yamapalló.*

යමප්‍රිය, *Yama-priya, s.* (යම Yama, ප්‍රිය beloved) banyan or Indian fig tree, *ficus bengalensis* or *f. indica.*

යමයා, *Yamayá, s.* imaginary being supposed to decide on the punishments to be inflicted in a future state of being, tormentor in hell; judge of the infernal regions.

යමරජ, *Yamaraja,* see යමරාජ *yamarája.*

යමරථ, *Yama-ratha, s.* (යම and රථ car) buffalo, [Colloq. මිහරකා *miharaká*].

යමරද, *Yamarada,* Elu form of the following.

යමරාජ, *Yama-rája, s.* (යම and රාජ ruler) Yama, the Indian Pluto: see යම *yama.*

යමල, *Yamala, s.* pair, brace, couple; contraction of යකඩ මල *yakaḍa-mala,* the rust of iron.

යමල පුෂ්පක, *Yamala-pushpaka, s.* (යමල and පුෂ්ප *pushpa* flower) tree, mountain ebony, *bauhinia purpurea,* [Colloq. කොබලිල *kobalila*].

යම වාහන, *Yama-wáhana, s.* (යම and වාහන vehicle) buffalo, [Colloq. මිහරකා *miharaká*].

යමාමහ පෙළහර, *Yamámaha-peḷahara,* see යමක ප්‍රාතිහාර්‍ය *yamaka-prátihárya.*

යමාන්නු, *Yamánnu, s.* iron manufacturers in the days of Kandyan Kings.

යමානිකා, *Yamániká,* }
යමානි, *Yamáni,* } *s.* sort of lovage, [Colloq. අසමෝදගම් *asamódagam*].

යමුනා, *Yamuná,* }
යමුනාගඟ, *Yamuná-gaṇga,* } *s.* Jumna river which rises on the south side of the Himálaya range, at a short distance to the Northwest of the source of the Ganges, and which after a course of about 378 miles falls into that river immediately below Allahabad; in Hindu mythology the personified river is considered as the daughter of Súrya and sister of Yama.

යමෙක්, *Yamek, pron.* any one, someone (used only of persons).

යයි, *Yayi, ind.* a continuative particle generally connecting two or more subordinate propositions dependent on the principal verb.

යල, *Yala, s.* one of the Siṇhalese harvests, the lesser one in September; time, as in තුන් යලක් *tun-yalak,* three times: *ad.* again, moreover, furthermore.

යලහි, *Yalahi, ad.* again, moreover.

යලි, *Yali,* }
යලිත්, *Yalit,* }
යලිදු, *Yalidu,* } *ad.* again, furthermore, [Colloq. නැවතත් *nęwatat*].

යව්, *Yaw, adv.* as far as, *e. g.* යව් දිව් *yaw-diw,* to the end of life, for life.

යව් අමත්, *Yaw-amat, ind.* (යව් as many as, අමත් invited) as many as have been invited.

යව්‍ය, *Yawya, a.* fit for barley, sown with barley.

යව්ල, *Yawla,* see යවුල *yawula.*

යව, *Yawa, s.* barley, *hordeum hexastichon;* water; tree, *oroxylum indicum* or *bignonia indica,* [Colloq. තොටිල *toṭila*]; speed, velocity; coriander, *coriandrum sativum.*

යවක්ෂාර, *Yawakshára,* }
යවකාර, *Yawakára,* }
යවකාරලුණු, *Yawakára-luṇu,* } *s.* (යව barley, ක්ෂාර ashes or salt) salt petre, nitre, nitrate of potash, prepared from burnt barley, the potash being thus procured.

යවකෙන්ද, *Yawakenda, s.* plant with tuberous root and spikes of beautiful and fragrant flowers, *Kaempferia rotunda (Scitamineæ).*

යවගු, *Yawagu,* see යවාගු *yawágú.*

යවතික්ත, *Yawa-tikta, s.* (යව and තික්ත bitter) sort of barley: see යව *yawa;* sort of paddy, *oryza sativa.*

යව ධාන්‍යක, *Yawa-dhányaka, s.* parsley, *petroselinum sativum,* [Colloq. අසමෝදගම් *asamódagam*].

යවන්‍ය, *Yawanya, s.* black cumin seed, *nigella indica,* [Colloq. කළුදුරු *kaḷuduru*].

යවන, *Yawana, s.* country, most probably Bactria, or it may be extended from that colony to Ionia (to which word it bears some resemblance), or still further to Greece; by late Hindu writers, it is most commonly applied to Arabia; speed, velocity; a swift horse; a Yawana, Greek; a term applied to Mohammedan and European Invaders of India; foreigner.

යවනපුෂ්ප, *Yawana-pushpa*, *s.* (යවන and පුෂ්ප flower) fragrant gum or incense brought from the country of the Yawanas.

යවනවා, *Yawanawá*, *v.* (යනවා *yanawá* in the causal form) to send, to dismiss, to dispatch: pret. යැව්වා *yęwwá*.

යවනාචාර්ය, *Yawanáchárya*, *s.* (යවන *yawana* yawana, ආචාර්ය *áchárya* teacher) astronomical writer, often quoted by Hindu astronomers; perhaps Ptolemy or the Greek astronomers collectively.

යවනිකා, *Yawaniká*, *s.* outer tent, screen of cloth surrounding a tent: see ජවනිකා *jawaniká*.

යවනේෂ්ට, *Yawanéshṭa*, *s.* (යවන *yawana* barbarian, ඉෂ්ට *ishṭa* wished, desired) lead; garlic, *allium sativum*, [Colloq, සුදුලූනු *sudu-lúnu*]; species of onion, *allium cepa;* margosa tree, *azadirachta indica*, [Colloq. කොහොඹ *kohomba*].

යවපත්‍රිකා, *Yawa-patriká*, *s.* plant, not ascertained, [Colloq. උඩත්ත *uḍatta*].

යව පෙත්ත, *Yawa-petta*, *s.* (යව barley, පෙත්ත slice) piece of barley bread.

යව ප්‍රවර, *Yawa-prawara*, *s.* (යව and ප්‍රවර best) a fine species of barley.

යවඵල, *Yawa-phala*, *s.* (යව and ඵල fruit) bamboo, *bambusa vulgaris*, [Colloq. උණගස් *uṇagas*]; Indian spikenard; medicinal plant, *wrightea antidysenterica;* onion, *allium cepa*.

යවබදු, *Yawabadu*, *s.* nut or seed of the *wrightea antidysentrica* used in cases of diarrhœa, dysentery, etc.

යවමය, *Yawamaya*, *a.* (යව barley, මයට් *mayaṭ* aff.) made of or from barley.

යව ලුණු, *Yawa-luṇu*, *s.* (යව and ලුණු salt) salt petre, nitre: see යවක්ෂාර *yawakshára*.

යව වී, *Yawa-ví*, *s.* (යව and වී rice) barley.

යවශූක, *Yawa-ṣúka*, *s.* (යව barley, ශූක beard of corn) nitre, saltpetre, [Colloq. යවකරලුණු *yawa-kara-luṇu*].

යවස, *Yawasa*, *s.* meadow or pasture grass.

යවහන්, *Yawahan*, *s.* final letters ය *ya*, ව *wa*, හ *ha*, and න් *n*, in stanzas; it is laid down as a rule of versification that it is objectionable to rhyme a stanza with any of the above letters unless the penultimate letters be also the same in all the four lines of the stanza.

යවාක්‍ය, *Yawákya*, *s.* corn field, any land fit for sowing corn.

යවාගු, *Yawágú*, *s.* (යු *yu* to mix, ආගුච් *águch* aff.) canjee, rice gruel; sour gruel prepared from the spontaneous fermentation of water in which rice has been boiled, [Colloq. කැඳ *kęnda*].

යවාග්‍රජ, *Yawágraja*, *s.* (යව *yawa* barley, අග්‍ර *agra* top or ear, ජ born) salt petre, nitre: see යවක්ෂාර *yawakshára*.

යවානික, *Yawánika*, *a.* swift, fleet.

යවානි, *Yawání*, *s.* (යව *yawa* swift, නි possessing) umbelliferous plant, with aromatic seeds, *ligusticum ajowan;* parsley, *petroselinum sativum*, [Colloq. අසමෝදගම් *asamódagam*]: *a.* swift, fleet.

යවාස, *Yawása*, *s.* plant from which manna exudes, *hedysarum alhagi;* twining plant, *tragia involucrata*, [Colloq. වැල් කහඹිලියා *wel-kahambiliyá*].

යවිෂ්ඨ, *Yavishṭha*, *s.* younger brother, [Colloq. මලයා *malayá*]: *a.* youngest, very young.

යවීම, *Yavíma*, verbal noun of යවනවා *yawanawá*.

යවුල, *Yawula*, *s.* iron crow, iron bar; spade, any iron implement for digging: pl. යවුල් *yawul*.

යශස්ශ්‍රිය, *Yaṣassriya*, } *s.* (යශස් *yaṣas* fame, ශ්‍රිය
යශස්ශ්‍රී, *Yaṣassrí*, } *ṣriya* the same) great renown, celebrity.

යෂ්ටි, *Yashṭi*, *s.* staff, stick; staff armed with iron, etc. used as a weapon, club, mace; necklace; any creeping plant; liquorice, [Colloq. වැල්මී *wẹlmí*]; shrub, *siphonanthus indica;* string, thread, especially as strung with pearls, thread in general; flag staff; arm and fore arm.

යස, *Yasa*, *s.* fame, glory, celebrity, renown, reputation: *a.* good, excellent. worthy; well, brave.

යසට, *Yasaṭa*, *ad.* excellently, cleverly, well.

යසන, *Yasana*, see යහන *yahana*.

යසස, *Yasasa*, *s.* fame, renown, celebrity; splendour, lustre.

යසි, *Yasí*, *s.* term of commendation applied to females, as excellent, well, bravo.

යහ, *Yaha*, *a.* good, excellent, etc.: see යස *yasa*.

යහඬුව, *Yahaṇḍuwa*, *s.* (ය iron, හඬුව pincers) smith's tongs.

යහද, *Yahada*, *s.* iron ore; heart of iron: *a.* iron hearted.

යහ දසන, *Yaha-dasana*, *s.* (යහ good, දසන appearance) comeliness, beauty: *a.* pleasing to the sight.

යහන්තල, *Yahantala*, *s.* top of a bed or couch.

යහන, *Yahaṇa*, *s.* bed, couch; mode of conveyance, vehicle: pl. යහන් *yahan*.

යහනාව, *Yahanáwa*, *s.* carriage, vehicle, any mode of conveyance.

යහපත්, *Yahapat*, *a.* (යහ good, පත් arrived) good, excellent; suitable; kind; virtuous.

යහපත්කම, *Yahapatkama*, } *s.* goodness, benevolence.
යහපත, *Yahapata*,

යහල, *Yahala*, *s.* forge, fire place in a smith's shop, [Colloq. කම්මල *kammala*].

යහලඟුරු, *Yahalanguru*, *s.* (යහල and අඟුරු *anguru* charcoal) charcoal in a smith's forge.

යහලුකම, *Yahalukama*, *s.* friendship.

යහලුවා, *Yahaluwá*, *s.* friend, companion, associate.

යහලුවෙනවා, *Yahaluwenawá*, *v.* to contract friendship.

යහුණු, *Yahuṇu*, *s.* iron-filings.

යා, *Yá*, *v.* to go, to proceed; personal affix.

යාග, *Yága*, } *s.* (යජ *yaja* to offer, etc.) sacrifice,
යාගය, *Yágaya*, } any ceremony in which offerings and oblations are presented.

යාගකරණවා, *Yágakaraṇawá*, *v.* to offer sacrifice.

යාගකාර, *Yágakára*. *s.* (යාග offering, කාර who does) sacrificer, one accustomed to sacrifice.

යාගස්තම්භ, *Yágastambha*, *s.* (යාග sacrifice, ස්තම්භ *stambha* pillar) pillar to which the animals are bound which are about to be offered in sacrifice.

යාගස්ථක, *Yágasthaka*, *s.* (යාග and ස්ථක who stays or does) sacrificer, one accustomed to make offerings.

යාගස්ථාන, *Yágasthána*, *s.* (යාග offering, ස්ථාන place) place where offerings or sacrifices are made.

යාගාවාටය, *Yágáwáṭaya*, *s.* (යාග *yága* sacrifice, අවාට *áwáṭa* pit) place where sacrifices are burnt; such places are somewhat hollowed and slightly fenced in.

යාච්ඤාකරණවා, *Yáchñákaraṇawá*, *v.* to pray, to implore.

යාච්ඤාව, *Yáchñáwa*, *s.* prayer, supplication, entreaty.

යාච්ඤාවෙනවා, *Yáchñáwenawá*, *v.* to pray.

යාචක, *Yáchaka*, } *s.* (යාච to ask, to beg, ක
යාචකයා, *Yáchakayá*, } aff.) beggar, mendicant, one who asks or solicits alms, [Colloq. හිඟන්නා *hinganná*].

යාචන, *Yáchana*, *s.* begging, soliciting, asking alms, etc.

යාචනක, *Yáchanaka*, *s.* beggar, mendicant.

යාචනා, *Yáchaná*, *s.* asking, begging.

යාචිත, *Yáchita*, *a.* asked, begged, solicited.

යාජ, *Yája*, *s.* boiled rice or food generally.

යාජක, *Yájaka*, *s.* officiating priest, one who conducts any part of a sacrifice; royal elephant, furious elephant.

යාඥික, *Yájñika*, *s.* (යඥ *yajña* sacrifice, ඉක *ika* aff.) sacrificer, institutor of a sacrifice; officiating priest; kusa or sacrificial grass; tree, *butea frondosa*, [Colloquial: ගස්කැල *gas-kéla*]; *mimosa catechu*.

යාඥිය, *Yájñiya*, *a.* fit to be offered or sacrificed.

යාඥෙය, *Yájñéya*, *s.* kusa-taṇa or sacrificial grass: see කුසතණ *kusa-taṇa*.

යාත්‍රා, *Yátrá*, *s.* (යා to go, ත්‍රන් *tran* aff.) going, moving, proceeding, marching, travelling; passing away time; sailing, voyaging.

යාත්‍රා ඔරුව, *Yátrá-oruwa*, *s.* (යාත්‍රා voyage, ඔරුව boat) vessel, largest kind of Sinhalese boat, commonly called dhoney.

යාත්‍රාකරණවා, *Yátrákaraṇawá*, *v.* to sail, to navigate, to make a voyage.

යාත්‍රාව, *Yátráwa*, see යාත්‍රා *yátrá*.

යාතනා, *Yátaná*, *s.* pain, agony, sharp, or acute pain; pain or punishment inflicted by Yama or his ministers, pains of hell.

යාතු, *Yátu*, *s.* (යා to go, තු aff.) demon, goblin, imp or evil spirit; time; traveller, wayfarer, goer.

යාතුධාන, *Yátudhána*, *s.* (යාතු evil spirit, ධාන having) evil spirit, goblin.

යාදව, *Yádawa*, *s.* descendant of යදු *yadu;* stock of cattle.

යාදවී, *Yádaví*, *s.* name of Durgá the wife of Ṣiva.

යාදස්, *Yádas*, *s.* (යා to go with speed) aquatic or amphibious animal.

යාදස්පති, *Yádaspati*, *s.* (යාදස් and පති lord) ocean, [Colloq. මුහුද *muhuda*]; name of Varuṇa the deity of water.

යාදසාංනාථ, *Yádasáṅnátha*, } *s.* (යාදසාං of aquatic
යාදසාම්පති, *Yádasámpati*, } animals, නාථ and පති lord) name of Varuṇa regent of the ocean.

යාන්තන්, *Yántan*, *ad.* scarcely, nearly, slightly.

යාන, *Yána*, *s.* (යා to go) any vehicle or form of conveyance, as a carriage, litter, horse, elephant, etc; going, marching.

යානපාත්‍ර, *Yána-pátra*, *s.* vessel, ship, boat.

යානමුඛ, *Yána-mukha*, *s.* fore part of a carriage, the pole where the yoke is fixed.

යානවා, *Yánawá*, *v.* to anchor a ship or vessel: pret. යෑවා *yéwá*.

යානවාහන, *Yána-wáhana*, *s.* (යාන and වාහන vehicle) travelling carriage, vehicles of various kinds.

යානාව, *Yánáwa*, *s.* vehicle, conveyance.

යානි, *Yáni*, *s.* (යාන *yána* vehicle etc. ඉන් *in* aff.) rider, one conveyed in any vehicle.

යාප්පුව, *Yáppuwa*, *s.* entreaty; submission; conciliatory speech.

යාප්‍ය, *Yápya*, *a.* low, vile, contemptible; to be passed or spent (as time); in medicine, uncertain as to cure, possibly curable; to be alleviated or relieved, though not cured.

යාපන, *Yápana*, *s.* (යා to go, causal form) spending or passing away time; abiding, staying, being, rejection, ejection, expulsion; sufficiency, enough, adequate quantity; allaying pain or sickness.

යාපනු, *Yápanu*, } *s.* fowl, cock, [Colloq. කුකුළා
යාපානු, *Yápánu*, } *kukulá*].

යාපුර, *Yápura*, *s.* medicinal plant, not ascertained.

යාබ, *Yába*, *s.* wax, [Colloq. ලාකඩ *lákaḍa*].

යාම්‍ය, *Yámya*, *s.* sandal; name of the saint Agastya.

යාම්‍යද්‍රුම, *Yámya-druma*, *s.* silk cotton tree, *eriodendron anfractuosum*, [Colloq. ඉඹුල් *imbul*].

යාම්‍යා, *Yámyá*, } *s.* (යම *yama* Yama, ඤ්‍යත්
යාම්‍යාදිග, *Yámyádiga*, } *ṇyat* aff.) the south, which is sacred to or governed by that deity; night; the lunar asterism Bharaṇi, commonly beraṇe, containing three stars (musca).

යාම, *Yáma*, *s.* (යා to go, මන් *man* aff.) sixth part of a day and night, or a watch of ten Siṇhalese hours, equal to four English; forbearance; cessation, term.

යාමදෙව්, *Yámadew*, see යම *yama*.

යාමනාලි, *Yámanálí*, *s.* metal plate on which the hours are struck, or a drum used for that purpose.

යාමය, *Yámaya*, *s.* one of the worlds of the gods, the third heaven, in which a day is equal to two hundred years of mortals.

යාමල, *Yámala*, *s.* (යමල *yamala* couple, අණ් *aṇ* pleonastic affix) pair, couple, brace.

යාමිනි, *Yámini*, *s.* (යාම *yáma* watch, ඉනි *ini* aff.) night.

යාමුන, *Yámuna*, *s.* antimony or rather the sulphuret of antimony, generally used as an application to darken the eye-lashes and strengthen the eyes, [Colloq. හොයඳුන් *hoyandun*].

යාය, *Yáya*, *s.* open champaign country.

යාරය, *Yáraya*, *s.* measure of a yard, or three feet. (English.)

යාල, *Yála*, *s.* measure of capacity, cart-load; twenty amunams of grain; twenty head of cattle.

යාලමැඩියා, *Yála-mędiyá*, *s.* kind of frog.

යාළු, *Yálu*, *s.* friend, acquaintance, companion.

යාළුකම, *Yálukama*, *s.* friendship.

යාළුවා, *Yáḷuwá*, *s.* friend, acquaintance.

යාළුවෙනවා, *Yáḷuwenawá*, *v.* to make friends with.

යාව, *Yáwa*, *s.* (යු *yu* to join or යව *yawa* barley, අණ් *aṇ* aff.) lac, red dye, the grains of which are compared to barley: *a.* adjoining, adjacent: *ad.* until, as long as, as far as, unto, the correlative of තාව *táwa*.

යාවජ්ජීවං, *Yáwaj-jíwaṇ*, *s.* (යාව *yáwa* and ජීවං life) for life, as long as life.

යාවත්, *Yáwat*, *ad.* as long as, as much as, as far as, unto, until, the correlative of තාවත් *táwat*.

යාවන, *Yáwana*, *s.* (යවන *yawana* Yavana, the country so called, අණ් *aṇ* aff.) incense, which is brought from Yavana or Arabia: *a.* relating to Yavana, Ionian, Mohammedan, etc.

යාවශූක, *Yáwaṣúka*, see යවශූක *yawaṣúka*.

යාෂ්ටික, *Yáshṭika*, *s.* (යෂ්ටි *yashṭi* club, අණ් *aṇ* aff.) warrior armed with a club; any one bearing a club as a mark of authority.

යාස, *Yása*, *s.* twining plant, *tragia involucrata*, [Colloq. වැල්කහඹිලියා *wel-kahambiliyá*].

යුක්ත, *Yukta*, } *a.* (යුජ් *yuja* to join or mix, ක්ත
යුක්තා, *Yuktá*, } aff.) right, fit, proper; joined, combined, united, identified; possessing, endowed with, as virtues, qualities, etc. intent on, attached to, as a study or pursuit.

යුක්ති, *Yukti*, } *s.* (යුජ් *yuja* to join, etc. ක්ති *kti*
යුක්තිය, *Yuktiya*, } aff.) propriety, fitness; union, connection, joining; usage, custom; civil right, complaint in law; inference, supplying an ellipsis.

යුග්ම, *Yugma*, *s.* (යුජ් *yuja* to join) pair, brace, couple; mixing, uniting; couple of verses.

යුග්මපත්‍ර, *Yugma-patra*, *s.* tree, *alstonia scholaris*, [Colloq. රුක්අත්තන *ruk-attana*]; also mountain ebony, [Colloq. කොබලිල *kobalila*].

යුග්‍ය, *Yugya*, *s.* (යුජ් *yuja* to join, යත් *yat* aff.) any vehicle or conveyance; any animal yoked.

යුග, *Yuga*, *s.* (යුජ් *yuja* to join) pair, couple, brace; yoke; age of the world, as the Kaitṛ, Tréta, Dwápara and Kali; measure of four cubits.

යුගත්, *Yugat*, } see යුගාන්ත *yugánta*.
යුගත, *Yugata*, }

යුගතගිනි, *Yugata-gini*, *s.* (යුග age, අත *ata* end, ගිනි fire) fire by which the world is destroyed at the end of a Yuga.

යුගදුරු, *Yugaduru*, see යුගන්ධර *yugandhara*.

යුගන්ත, *Yuganta*, see යුගාන්ත *yugánta*.

යුගන්දර, *Yugandara*, } *s.* (යුග *yuga* yoke, ධර
යුගන්ධර, *Yugandhara*, } *dhara* what holds or supports) pole of a carriage or the wood to which the yoke is fixed, [Colloq. ඊරියාකඳ *ériyákanda*]; first or innermost of the seven circular ranges of rocks said to surround Maha Méru, and to form the boundaries to so many circumambient waters or oceans.

යුගපත්, *Yuga-pat*, *s.* mountain ebony, *bauhinia purpurea:* see the next.

යුගපත්‍රක, *Yuga-patráka*, *s.* (යුග pair, පත්‍ර *patra* leaf) mountain ebony, *bauhinia purpurea* or *variegata*, [Colloq. කොබලිල *kobalila*]; tree, *alstonia scholaris*, [Colloq රුක් අත්තන *rukattana*].

යුගපත්‍රිකා, *Yuga-patriká*, *s.* (යුග and පත්‍ර *patra* leaf, ඉකා *iká* aff.) sisu tree, *dalbergia sisu*.

යුගමාත්‍ර දර්ශනය, *Yugamátra-darṣanaya*, *s.* (යුග yoke, මාත්‍ර *mátra* as much as, දර්ශනය sight) an ordinance of the Buddhist priesthood, which enjoins it upon the priests not to look beyond the length of a yoke when travelling or in public.

යුගය, *Yugaya*, see යුග *yuga*.

යුගයෝත්‍ර, *Yugayótra*, *s.* rope that ties the yoke to the bullock.

යුගල, *Yugala*, *s.* (යුග pair, ල aff.) pair, couple, brace, [Colloq. ජෝඩුව *jóduwa*].

යුගසවන්, *Yuga-sawan*, *s.* the two ears, [Colloq. කන්දෙක *kan-deka*].

යුගාන්ත, *Yugánta*, *s.* (යුග *yuga* age or duration of the world, අන්ත *anta* end) destruction of the universe; end of an age.

යුගාන්ත මාරුත, *Yugánta-máruta*, } *s* (යුගාන්ත and
යුගාන්ත වාතය, *Yugánta-wátaya*, } මාරුත or වාත *wáta* wind) the wind or hurricane by which the universe is destroyed at the end of a Yuga or age.

යුජ්, *Yuj*, *s.* (යුජ *yuja* to join) pair, couple, brace; joiner, one who joins or unites.

යුත්, *Yut*, *a.* endowed with, possessed of.

යුත්ත, *Yutta*, see යුක්ත *yukta*.

යුත, *Yuta*, *s.* multitude; measure of four cubits: *a.* joined, united, connected, combined.

යුතු, *Yutu*, *a.* proper, fit, suitable, becoming, just.

යුතුකම, *Yutukama*, *s.* propriety; duty, justice.

යුද්ධ, *Yuddha*, *s.* (යුධ *yudha* to fight, ක්ත *kta* aff.) war, battle, conflict, contest.

යුද්ධසේනාව, *Yuddha-sénáwa*, *s.* (යුද්ධ war, සේනාව army) army.

යුද, *Yuda*, *s.* fighting, contest, war: see යුද්ධ *yuddha*.

යුධිෂ්ඨිර, *Yudhisṭhira*, *s.* (යුධි in war or battle, ෂ්ඨිර for ස්ථිර *sthira* who stands firm) eldest of the five Pánḍawa princes and leader in the great war between them and the Kurus, in the beginning of the fourth age; the nominal son of Pánḍu, whom he succeeded in the sovereignty of India, but according to the legend, begotten on Kunti by the deity Yama.

යුරු, *Yuru*, *s.* resemblance, likeness, similarity, [Colloq. සමානකම *samánakama*].

යුව, *Yuwa*, see යුවන් *yuwan*.

යුවති, *Yuwati*, *s.* young woman from sixteen to thirty.

යුවන්, *Yuwan*, *a.* young, youthful; best, excellent; endowed with native or natural strength.

යුවරජ, *Yuwa-raja*, } *s.* (යුව young, රජ or රාජ
යුවරාජ *Yuwa-rája*, } king) young prince, especially the heir apparent, associated to the throne; sub-king.

යුවල, *Yuwala*, *s.* (යුගල *yugala* having the guttural softened into the semi vowel) brace, couple, pair, two.

යුවලපත්, *Yuwala-pat*, *s.* (යුවල pair, පත් leaves) tree, *bauhinia purpurea:* see යුගපත්‍රක *yugapatraka*.

යුවලෑස, *Yuwalesa*, *s.* the two eyes, [Colloq. ඇස් දෙක *es-deka*].

යුවාධාත, *Yuwádháta*, *s.* ninth year of the Indian cycle.

යුෂ්මත් ශබ්ද, *Yushmat-ṣabda*, *s.* word expressing the second personal pronoun, thou, you, etc.

යුෂ්මද්වාච්‍ය, *Yushmadwáchya*, *s.* (in grammar) second person.

යුෂ, *Yusa*, *s.* juice; essence, sap; plant, *cocculus orbiculatus;* mulberry tree, *morus indica;* pease soup, pease porridge.

යුහු, *Yuhu*, *s.* haste, speed, quickness, celerity.

යුහුව, *Yuhuwa*, *ad.* hastily, speedily, etc.

යුහුසුලු, *Yuhusulu*, *a.* hasty.

යූක, *Yúka*, *s.* louse, [Colloq. උකුණ *ukuná*].

යූති, *Yúti*, *s.* joining, mixing.

යූථ, *Yútha, s.* multitude, assemblage, [Colloq. සමූහය *samúhaya*].

යූථ නාථ, *Yútha-nátha, s.* (යූථ multitude, of elephants, නාථ lord) large elephant, leader of a wild herd.

යූථිකා, *Yúthiká,* } *s.* twining species of jasmine,
යූථි, *Yúthi,* } *jasminum auriculatum,* [Colloq. බොලිද්ද *bolidda*].

යූනි, *Yúni, s.* young woman.

යූප, *Yúpa, s.* sacrificial post, pillar usually made of bamboo, or the wood of *acacia sundra* or *mimosa catechu,* [Colloq. කිහිරි *kihiri*], to which the victim at a sacrifice is bound; trophy, column erected in honor of a victory.

යූපදාරු, *Yúpadáru, s.* species of fir: see දේවදාරු *déwadáru;* sacrificial post; see the foregoing word.

යෙදීම, *Yedíma, s.* contrivance, invention, application, mixture; verbal noun of යොදනවා *yodanawá.*

යෙදුන, *Yeduna, p. p.* of යොදනවා *yodanawá,* serves to form passive verbs when added to the Infinitive mood of an active verb, as, කරන්ට යෙදුන *karanta-yeduna,* made, done.

යෙදෙනවා, *Yedenawá, v.* to be fit or proper; also, to be united, to be consistent.

යෙල, *Yela, s.* one and a half, [Colloq. එකහමාර *ekahamára*], as in යෙල සියයක් *yela-siyayak*=150.

යෙහි, *Yehi, ind.* in grammar, an affix forming the අධාර *ádhára* or locative case singular, as මාර්ගයෙහි *márgayehi,* in the way.

යෙහෙක, *Yeheka,* } *ind.* it is good, well, excellent,
යෙහෙකි, *Yeheki,* } [Colloq. හොඳයි *hondayi*].

යෙහෙන්, *Yehen, ad.* safely, prosperously, well, [Colloq. සුවසේ *suwasé*].

යෙහෙඹි, *Yehembi, s.* young woman, [Colloq. යෞවනි *yauwáni*].

යෙහෙලනියෝ, *Yehelaniyó, s.* niece, daughter-in-law.

යෙහෙලි, *Yeheli, s.* niece, daughter-in-law; female friend.

යේලනියෝ, *Yélaniyó, s.* niece, daughter-in-law.

යොත්න, *Yotna,* see යොදුන *yoduna.*

යොත, *Yota, s.* cord, line, rope, long fishing line, from යෝත්‍ර *yótra*: pl. යොත් *yot.*

යොතුවැන්න, *Yotuwęnna, s.* plant. not ascertained.

යොදන, *Yodana,* see යොදුන *yoduna*: *a.* contriving, mixing.

යොදනවා, *Yodanawá, v.* (යුජ *yuja* to unite, combine) to make, to concert, to construct, to form; to combine, to unite: pret. යෙදුවා *yeduwá.*

යොදුන, *Yoduna, s.* measure of distance, equal to four gaws or about fifteen miles English: pl. යොදුන් *yodun;* some make it equal to thirteen and others to nine miles.

යොදේ, *Yodé, s.* cream of milk: pl. යොද *yoda.*

යොන්, *Yon, s.* vulva; place of birth, nature, state of existence; origin; Elu form of යෝනි *yóni,* and යවන *yawana* or Arabia.

යොන් ඉඳි, *Yon-indi, s.* (යොන් Arabia, ඉඳි date) date, *phœnix zeylanica.*

යොන්තුඹ, *Yon-tumba, s.* creeper, borago, *borago zeylanica:* see යොහොඹුවැල *yohombu-węla.*

යොන් දෙහි, *Yon-dehi, s.* (යොන් and දෙහි lime) species of lime, *citrus,* supposed to have been brought originally from Arabia.

යොන්පුප්, *Yon-pup,* see යවනපුෂ්ප *yawana-pushpa.*

යොන්මග, *Yon-maga, s.* (යොන් and මග way) vulva.

යොන, *Yona, s.* woman, young woman.

යොනා, *Yoná, s.* Moorman (disrespectful), also used for a barbarian in general: pl. යොන්නු *yonnu:* see යොන් *yon.*

යොනි, *Yoni,* see යෝනි *yóni.*

යොබ්බන, *Yobbana,* Páli form of යෞවන *yawwana.*

යොබළ, *Yobaḷa, s.* warrior, hero.

යොම්මග, *Yom-maga,* incorrectly for යොන්මග *yon-maga,* which see.

යොමුකරණවා, *Yomukaraṇawá, v.* to appoint, to allot, determine, to resolve; to direct, to commence.

යොමුල්, *Yomul, s.* time immediately following conception and prior to the formation of the fœtus.

යොර, *Yora, adv.* constantly, repeatedly.

යොලිය, *Yoliya,* see යෝලිය *yóliya.*

යොවුන්, *Yowun, s.* youth.

යොහොඹුවැල, *Yohombu-węla, s.* (යොහොඹු and වැල creeper) creeper, *borago zeylanica,* [Colloq. යොන්තුඹ *yon-tumba*]; twining species of jasmine, *jasminum auriculatum,* [Colloq. බොලිද්ද *bolidda*].

යෝ, *Yó, s.* warrior, union.

යෝග්‍ය, *Yógya, s.* calculator of expedients; vehicle or any conveyance; sandal: *a.* suitable, fit, proper, becoming.

යෝග්‍යා, *Yógyá, s.* military exercise; medical practice.

යෝග, *Yóga*, *s.* junction, joining, union; combination, association, meeting, conflux; religious and abstract meditation, refraining the mind from external objects and fixing it in profound absorption; fitness, propriety; lucky conjuncture; in astronomy, the twenty-seventh part of 360° of a great circle measured on the plane of the ecliptic and used in calculating the longitudes of the sun and moon; each Yóga has a distinct name; astrologers also enumerate twenty-eight yógas differently named from the foregoing, and corresponding with the twenty-eight Nakshatras or the divisions of the moon's path, but varying according to the day of the week; consequence, result; drug, medicament; profit; magic, or the acquisition of supernatural powers by the mystical and magical worship of Ṣiva, Durgá and Kártikéya, etc.; conveyance, carriage; joining, literally or figuratively.

යෝගක්ඛෙම, *Yógakkhéma*, } *s.* (යෝග religious
යෝගක්ෂේම, *Yógakshéma*, } meditation, profit, ඛෙම or ක්ෂේම safety, patience) Nirwáṇa, state of final emancipation obtained by devout and abstract meditation; charge of property for another; insurance or charge for secure conveyance of goods, and the profit on their sale; national prosperity.

යෝගය, *Yógaya*, see යෝග *yóga*.

යෝගවාන්, *Yógawán*, *s.* (යෝග meditation, වාන් poss. aff.) devotee, ascetic practising devout meditation; rock moss.

යෝගවාහි, *Yógawáhi*, *s.* (යෝග joining of metals, වාහි conveyer; effecting) alkali, [Colloq. යවකර ලුණු *yawakara-luṇu*]; quicksilver, [Colloq. රසදිය *rasadiya*]; menstruum or medium for mixing medicines.

යෝගාවචර, *Yógáwachara*, *s.* (යෝග *yóga* religious meditation, අවචර *áwachara* who performs) one who abandons worldly pursuits for the purpose of giving up his mind to religious and abstract meditation.

යෝගිනි, *Yógini*, *s.* female fiend or sprite attendant on and created by Durgá.

යෝගී, *Yógí*, *s.* (යෝග *yóga* meditation, ඉන් *in* aff.) devotee, ascetic in general; religious or devout man who performs worldly actions and ceremonies without regard to their results, and keeps his mind fixed on Brahma alone; the performer of Yóga.

යෝගේෂ්ට, *Yógéshṭa*, *s.* (යෝග *yóga* affinity, of metals, or amalgamation, ඉෂ්ට *ishṭa* desired) lead, [Colloq. ඊයම් *íyam*].

යෝජන, *Yójana*, *s.* (යුජ *yuja* to join) in the Hindu mythology, God, the soul of the world; a measure of distance equal to four gaws or fifteen miles; union, joining; some computations make the Yójana thirteen or nine miles, others make it but about five miles.

යෝජන ගන්ධා, *Yójana-gandhá*, *s.* musk, [Colloq. කස්තූරි *kastúri*].

යෝජනපර්ණී, *Yójana-parṇní*, } *s.* (යෝජන join-
යෝජන වල්ලී, *Yójana-wallí*, } ing, වල්ලී pedicle) Indian madder, *rubia manjith* or *hedyotis umbellata*.

යෝජනාව, *Yójanáwa*, *s.* preparation, provision, scheme; proposal, resolution; composition of medicine, etc.: pl. යෝජනා *yójaná*.

යෝජනාකරණවා, *Yójaná-karaṇawá*, *v.* to prepare; to plan.

යෝජනීය, *Yójaníya*, *a.* to be united, added or applied.

යෝජිත, *Yójita*, *a.* (යුජ *yuja* to join, etc. ක්ත *kta* aff.) mixed, joined.

යෝත්‍ර, *Yótra*, *s.* (යු *yu* to join, ත්‍ර aff.) tie that fastens the yoke of a plough to the neck of the ox.

යෝද මුලක්, *Yóda-mulak*, *s.* company of warriors, [Colloq. යෝධ සමූහයක් *yódha-samúhayak*].

යෝදයා, *Yódayá*, see යෝධයා *yódhayá*.

යෝදි, *Yódi*, *s.* female giant, dexterous woman: pl. යෝදියෝ *yódiyó*.

යෝධයා, *Yódhayá*, *s.* warrior, soldier, combatant; giant, one of unusual strength: pl. යෝධයෝ *yódhayó*.

යෝබළ, *Yóbaḷa*, *s.* warrior, hero, skilful and brave soldier; army.

යෝනන්, *Yónan*, plural of යොන් *yon*.

යෝනි, *Yóni*, *s.* vulva; mine; cause, origin; water; place or site of birth or production in general.

යෝනි මාර්ගය, *Yóni-márgaya*, *s.* vulva.

යෝනිය, *Yóniya*, *s.* birth, production; caste, race.

යෝනිසෝ, *Yónisó*, *ad.* sensibly, prudently; wisely.

යෝනිසෝමනස්කාරය, *Yónisómanaskáraya*, *s.* careful consideration, close attention.

යෝනී, *Yóní*, *s.* young woman, [Colloq. යෞවනී *yauwani*].

යෝලිය, *Yóliya*, *s.* woman, wife.

යෝෂා, *Yóshá*, *s.* woman; maid, damsel.

යෝෂිත්, *Yóshit*, } *s.* woman in general, [Colloq.
යෝෂිතා, *Yóshitá*, } ස්ත්‍රී *strí*].

යෞගන්ධර, *Yaugandhara*, *s.* (යුගන්ධර *yugandhara* mountain, අණ් *aṇ* aff.) mountain Yugandhara.

යෞතක, *Yautaka*, *s.* nuptial gift, [Colloq. දෑවැද්ද *dǽwędda*].

යෞවන, *Yauwana*, *s.* youth, manhood; assemblage of young women.

යෞවනයා, *Yauwanayá*, *s.* young man.

යෞවනී, *Yauwaní*, *s.* young woman.

යැටිය, *Yęṭiya*, *s.* stick, walking stick; Elu form of යෂ්ටි *yashṭi*.

යැදීම, *Yędíma*, verbal noun of යදිනවා *yadinawá*, praying, cursing.

යැවීම, *Yęvíma*, verbal noun of යවනවා *yawanawá*, causing to go, sending.

ර

The twenty seventh consonant of the Siṇhalese alphabet, corresponding to the letter *R*.

රං, *Raṇ*, incorrectly for රන් *ran*, which see.

රක්, *Rak*, *s.* preservation; red arsenic.

රක්ඛා, *Rakkhá*, Páli form of රක්ෂා *rakshá*.

රක්ඛාවරණ, *Rakkháwaraṇa*, *s.* (රක්ඛා and ආවරණ *áwaraṇa* enclosure) place of defence; place defended or guarded, entrenchment.

රක්ත, *Rakta*, *s.* (රඤ්ජ *rañja* to colour, ක්ත *kta* aff.) red, the colour; blood, [Colloq. ලේ *le*]; minium; vermilion, [Colloq. සාදිලිංගම් *sádiliṇgam*]; pearl, [Colloq. මුතු *mutu*]; fruit of the *flacourtia cataphracta*, [Colloq. රට උගුරැස්ස *raṭa-uguręssa*]; gunja plant, *abrus precatorius*, [Colloq. ඔලිඳ වැල් *oliṇda-węl*]; lac; Indian madder, *oldenlandia* or *hedyotis umbellata;* banyan tree, *ficus bengalensis*, [Colloq. නුග *nuga*]: *a.* dyed, tinged, colored, stained; red, of a red colour; fond of, attached to; pure, purified; sporting, engaged in play or pastime.

රක්තක, *Raktaka*, *s.* plant inhabiting wet rice fields and bearing a red blossom, *pentapetes phœnicea*, (Siṇhalese බඳුවද *baṇduwada*); flowering shrub resembling the රතඹලා *rataṃbalá*, *ixora bandhuca;* red variety of globe-amaranth, *gomphrœna globosa;* red garments or cloth; man affected with passion or fondness; gamboller, player, sporter; safflower; kind of pulse, *dolichos biflorus*, commonly called horse gram or Indian gram, [Colloq. කොල්ලු *kollu*].

රක්ත කම්බල, *Rakta-kambala*, *s.* (රක්ත red, කම්බල woollen cloth) red woollen cloth.

රක්ත කමල, *Rakta-kamala*, *s.* (රක්ත and කමල lotus) red lotus, *nymphœa rubra*, [Colloq. රත් නෙළුම් *rat-neḷum*].

රක්ත කුමුද, *Rakta-kumuda*, *s*, red lotus, (Siṇhalese රතෑඹුල *rtęmbula*).

රක්ත කුසුම, *Rakta-kusuma*, *s.* pomegranate tree, *punica granatum*, [Colloq. දෙළුම් *deḷum*].

රක්ත කෙසරු, *Rakta-kesaru*, *s.* flower of the ironwood tree, *mesua ferrea*, [Colloq. නාමල් *ná-mal*].

රක්ත කෛරව, *Rakta-kairawa*, see රක්ත කුමුද *rakta-kumuda*.

රක්ත ගුල්ම, *Rakta-gulma*, *s.* (රක්ත and ගුල්ම disease) enlargement of the intestines by worms, accompanied with the voiding of blood: see ගුල්ම *gulma;* hard lump in the abdomen of a female after conception; clot of blood.

රක්ත ගෝමේද, *Rakta-góméda*, *s.* (රක්ත and ගෝමේද gem so called) gem of a blood red colour; ruby; garnet.

රක්ත චන්දන, *Rakta-chandana*, *s.* (රක්ත red, චන්දන sandal) red wood, either red sandal. *pterocarpus santalinus* or sappan wood, *cœsalpinia sappan;* saffron, *curcuma longa*, [Colloq. කහ *kaha*].

රක්ත චන්දනා, *Rakta-chandaná*, *s.* species of madder, *rubia manjitha*, [Colloq. වැල්මදට *węlmadaṭa*].

රක්තජිහ්ව, *Raktajihwa*, *s.* lion, [Colloq. සිංහයා *siṇhayá*].

රක්තනාලී, *Raktanálí*, *s.* red lotus, [Colloq. රතුපුල් *ratupul*].

රක්තප, *Raktapa*, *s.* (රක්ත blood, ප what drinks) imp, goblin.

රක්ත පද්ම, *Rakta-padma*, *s.* (රක්ත red, පද්ම lotus) red lotus, *nymphœa rubra*, [Colloq. රත් නෙළුම් *rat-neḷum*].

රක්තපා, *Raktapá*, *s.* leech; female goblin.

රක්තපාද, *Rakta-páda*, *s.* (රක්ත and පාද *páda* foot) parrot, *palœornis*, [Coll: ගිරවා *girawá*]; pigeon, [Colloq. කොබෙයියා *kobeyiyá*]: *a.* red-footed.

රක්තපාදී, *Raktapádí*, *s.* plant, [Colloq. වලාවැන්න *waláwęnna*].

රක්ත පාෂාණ, *Rakta-páshána*, *s.* (රක්ත and පාෂාණ stone) red arsenic, [Colloq. සිවංගුරු *siwaṇguru*].

රක්තපිත්ත, *Rakta-pitta*, *s.* (රක්ත red, or blood, පිත්ත bile) plethora, spontaneous hæmorrhages from the mouth, nose, rectum and cuticle, accompanied with fever and headache, vomiting, purging, etc.; the word alludes to the bile being of a red colour or to its being supposed to be an affection of both fluids or humours.

රක්ත පුෂ්ප, *Rakta-puspa*, *s.* (රක්ත red, පුෂ්ප flower) red variety of *nerium odorum*, [Colloq. අලරිගස් *alari-gas*]; small tree, *andersonia rohitaca;* silk cotton tree, *eriodendron anfractuosum*, [Colloq. ඉඹුල් *imbul*]; trumpet flower, *stereospermum* (or *bignonia*) *suave-olens;* the name may be applied to any plant bearing red blossoms.

රක්ත පුෂ්පක, *Rakta-pushpaka*, *s.* (රක්තපුෂ්ප and ක aff.) Palas tree, *butea frondosa*, [Colloq. ගස්කැල *gas-kęla*]; small tree, *andersonia rohitaca;* red flower, *ixora bhanduca* or *pentapetes phœnicea;* silk cotton tree, *eriodendron anfractuosum*, [Coll: ඉඹුල් *imbul*]; tree from which a red dye is prepared *mallotus philippensis* or *rottleria tinctoria.*

රක්ත පුෂ්පිකා, *Rakta-pushpiká*, *s.* (රක්තපුෂ්ප *rakta-puspa* and ඉක *ika* aff.) species of sensitive plant, *mimosa pudica;* species of *lycopodium;* also, silk cotton, *eriodendron anfractuosum*, [Colloq. ඉඹුල් *imbul*].

රක්ත පුෂ්පී, *Rakta-pushpí*, *s.* coral tree, *erythrina indica*, [Colloq. එරබදු *erabadu*]; also, trumpet flower, *stereospermúm suaveolens*, [Coll: පළොල් *palol*].

රක්ත පූරක, *Rakta-púraka*, *s.* tamarind tree, *tamarindus indica*, [Colloq. සියඹලා *siyambalá*].

රක්ත ඵල, *Rakta-phala*, *s.* (රක්ත red, ඵල fruit) species of banyan or Indian fig tree, *ficus altissima*, [Colloq. නුග *nuga*].

රක්ත ඵලා, *Rakta-phalá*, *s.* creeping plant, *momordica monadelpha* or *bryonia grandis*, (Sinhalese කෙම්වැල *kemwęla*), [Colloq. කෝවක්කා *kówakká*].

රක්ත ඵලිකා, *Rakta-phaliká*, *s.* plant, *abrus precatorius*, [Colloq. ඔලිඳ *olinda*].

රක්ත බිංදු, *Rakta-bindu*, *s.* (රක්ත red, බිංදු drop) red spot forming flaw in a gem.

රක්ත බීජ, *Rakta-bíja*, *s.* tree, *adenanthera paronina*, [Colloq. මදටිය ගස් *madatiya-gas*].

රක්ත මඤ්ජරී, *Rakta-mañjarí*, *s.* (රක්ත and මඤ්ජරී pedicle) plant, *barringtonia acutangula*, [Colloq. ඇල මිදෙල්ල *ela-midella*]; medicinal plant, *spilanthes acmella*, [Colloq. අක්මැල්ල *akmęlla*].

රක්තමාලී, *Raktamálí*, *s.* species of jasmine, *jasminum nyctanthes arbor-tristis*, [Colloq. සේපාලිකා *sépáliká*].

රක්තය, *Raktaya*, see රක්ත *rakta.*

රක්තරේණු, *Rakta-rénu*, *s.* (රක්ත red, රේණු dust) red lead, [Colloq. සින්දූරං *sindúran*]; blossom of the Palas, *butea frondosa*, [Colloq. කැල මල් *kęla-mal*]; sort of cloth.

රක්ත ලෝහ, *Rakta-lóha*, *s.* (රක්ත and ලෝහ metal) copper, [Colloq, තඹ *tamba*]; minium.

රක්තවටී, *Raktawatí*, *s.* (රක්ත and වටී pustule) small pox.

රක්ත වර්ණ, *Rakta-warna*, *s.* (රක්ත and වර්ණ colour) earth worm; red (the colour): *a.* red, of a red colour.

රක්ත වර්ධන, *Rakta-wardhana*, *s.* egg plant, *solanum*, [Colloq. බටු *batu*].

රක්තවරටී, *Raktawaratí*, see රක්තවටී *raktawatí.*

රක්ත වාස්තුක, *Rakta-wástuka*, *s.* species of amaranth, *amaranthus cruentus*, [Colloq. රත් තම්පලා *rat-tampalá*].

රක්ත විංදු, *Rakta-vindu*, *s.* drop of blood, red flaw in a gem.

රක්ත විංදුච්ඡදා, *Rakta-vinduchchhadá*, *s.* medicinal plant, *ipomœa sepiaria*, [Colloq. රසතැල් *rasa-tel*].

රක්ත වෘන්තක, *Rakta-wrintaka*, *s.* pot herb, *marsilea quadrifolia*, [Colloq. දිය ඇඹුල් ඇඹිලිය *diya-ęmbul-ęmbilia*]; medicinal plant, hog-weed, *boerhaavia diffusa alata*, [Colloq. සාරණ *sárana*].

රක්ත වෘන්තා, *Rakta-wrintá*, *s.* sort of jasmin, *jasminum auriculatum*, [Coll: සේපාලිකා *sépáliká*].

රක්ත වෛදූර්ය, *Rakta-waidúrya*, *s.* lapis lazuli. [Colloq. වයිරෝඩි *wayiródi*].

රක්ත සංකෝච, *Rakta-sankócha*, *s.* tree, *kokoona zeylanica*, [Colloq. වනපොතු *wana-potu* and කොකුම් පොතු *kokum-potu*].

රක්ත සන්ධ්‍යක, *Rakta-sandhyáka*, *s.* (රක්ත and සන්ධ්‍යා twilight, කන් *kan* aff. of comparison) red lotus, *nymphœa rubra.*

රක්තසාර, *Rakta-sára*, *s.* red sandal wood, *pterocarpus santalinus*, [Coll: රත්හඳුන් *rat-handun*].

රක්තා, *Raktá*, *s.* creeper, *gloriosa superba*, [Colloq. ලියනගලා *liyanangalá* or නියඟලා *niyangalá*]; plant, *abrus precatorius*, [Colloq. ඔලිඳ *olinda*]; Bengal madder, *rubia manjith*, [Colloq. වැල් මදට *wẹlmadata*].

රක්තාක්ෂ, *Raktáksha*, } රක්තාක්ෂි, *Raktákshi*, } *s.* (රක්ත red, අක්ෂ or අක්ෂි eye) buffalo; pigeon; demon, sprite, ogre; barbarous or savage man; Greek partridge; the fifty-eighth year of the Indian cycle: *a.* red eyed.

රක්තාංග, *Raktánga*, *s.* (රක්ත and අංග body) planet Mars; plant, species of *crinum;* bug; coral; saffron.

රක්තාංගී, *Raktángi*, *s.* tree, *trema orientalis*, [Coll: ගැඩුඹ *gędumba*]; also, Bengal madder, *rubia manjith*, [Colloq. වැල්මදට *wẹlmadata*].

රක්තාම්බර, *Raktámbara*, s. (රක්ත red, අම්බර *ambara* verture) any vagrant devotee wearing red garments: *a.* dressed in red.

රක්තාර්ශස්, *Raktárṣas*, s. (රක්ත *rakta* and අර්ශස් *arṣas* pile) bleeding piles.

රක්ති, *Rakti*, s. (රඤ්ජ් *rañja* to be affected, ක්ති *kti* aff.) affection, attachment.

රක්තිකා, *Raktiká*, s. plant, the gunja, *abrus precatorius*, [Colloq. ඔලිඳවැල් *olinda-wel*], the seed of which is used as a weight, and weighs about 1 and 5-16 grains troy.

රක්තොත්පල, *Raktótpala*, s. (රක්ත *rakta* red, උත්පල *utpala* lotus) red lotus, *nymphæa rubra*.

රක්නා, *Rakná*, } s. preserving, guarding, keep-
රක්ෂණ, *Rakshana*, } ing, supporting, protecting, defending.

රක්ෂස්, *Rakshas*, see රකුස් *rakus*.

රක්ෂස්ථානය, *Rakshastháнaya*, s. place of safety, refuge.

රක්ෂසි, *Rakshasí*, s. plant, *curcuma zerumbet*, [Coll: හරන්කහ *haran-kaha*].

රක්ෂා, *Rakshá*, s. (රක්ෂ *raksha* to preserve) preserving, protecting; ashes; sort of bracelet; twist of thread or tinsel with a small packet containing a few carminative seeds bound round the wrist at particular periods.

රක්ෂාකරණවා, *Rakshákaranawá*, v. to preserve, to support, to sustain, to protect, to maintain.

රක්ෂාපේක්ෂක, *Rakshápékshaka*, s. (රක්ෂා preserving, අප *apa* before, ඊක්ෂ *íksha* to see and ක *ka* aff.) door keeper; guard of the women's apartments; catamite; actor, mime.

රක්ෂාව, *Rakshâwa*, s. support, maintenance, livelihood; protection, preservation, defence.

රක්ෂාවරණ, *Rakshâwarana*, s. (රක්ෂා protecting, ආවරණ *áwarana* enclosure) fortified place, entrenchment.

රක්ෂිත, *Rakshita*, a. (රක්ෂ *raksha* to preserve, ක්ත *kta* aff.) preserved, protected, defended.

රක්ෂොඝ්න, *Rakshóghna*, s. (රක්ෂස් *rakshas* goblin, ඝ්න *ghna* what destroys) marking nut tree, [Colloq. බඩුල්ල *badulla*]; sour gruel, made from the fermentation of rice wa-ter; assafætida, [Colloq. පෙරුන්කායම් *perun-káyam*].

රක, *Raka*, v. to protect.

රකණ, *Rakaṇa*, s. preservation, protection, from රක *raka*, to protect.

රකවල, *Rakawaḷa*, s. guard, watch, protection.

රකිණවා, *Rakiṇawá*, v. to watch, to guard, to protect; to sit (as a hen upon eggs): pret. රැක්කා *rękká*.

රකුස්, *Rakus*, s. demon, fiend, hobgoblin, sprite, evil spirit, imp or ogre haunting cemeteries, animating dead bodies, and ensnaring and devouring human beings; Titan, who may be considered the relentless and powerful enemy of the gods.

රකුස්සා, *Rakussá*, } s. harsh or morose man, de-
රකුසා, *Rakusá*, } mon, fiend, sprite, hobgoblin, vampire.

රකුසි, *Rakusí*, s. female demon: pl. රකුස්සියෝ *rakussiyó*.

රකුසු, *Rakusu*, see රකුසා *rakusá*.

රඝු, *Raghu*, s. name of a sovereign of Oude, the great grand father of Ráma Chandra; the family or descendant of Raghu.

රඝුවංශය, *Raghu-waṇṣaya*, s. (රඝු Raghu, වංශ *waṇṣa* race) race or family of Raghu, hence also the name of a celebrated poem by Kálidása, which treats of the ancestors of Ráma, the great Indian warrior, who invaded Lanká or Ceylon, for the purpose of destroying Ráwaṇa; one half of this poem relates to Raghu, and as much to that of Ráma.

රඟ, *Ranga*, s. (රඤ්ජ *rañja* to colour) paint, colour, tint, dye; dancing, acting, singing, etc.; field of battle; tin; resemblance, likeness; ray of the sun.

රඟදිවු, *Rangadiwu*, s. painter.

රඟබිම්, *Ranga-bim*, s. (රඟ war, බිම් ground, spot) dancing room; place for acting, theatre, stage any place where the Indian drama is exhibited; battle-field.

රඟමඩල, *Rangamaḍala*, s. theatre, stage: pl. රඟමඩුලු *rangamaḍulu*.

රඞ්ග, *Raṅga*, s. tin, white lead, [Colloq. සුදු ඊයම් *sudu-iyam*].

රඞ්ග භූමි, *Raṅga-bhúmi*, s. field of battle; theatre.

රඞ්ගිණි, *Raṅgiṇi*, s. (රඞ්ග *raṅga* colour, ඉනි *ini* aff.) plant, *asparagus racemosus*, [Colloq. හාතාවාරිය *hátáwáriya*]; tree, *ficus glomerata*, [Colloq. අට්ටික්කා *aṭṭikká*]: *a.* colouring, dyeing; impassioned, having propensity or passion.

රචනා, *Rachaná*, s. (රච to make, etc.) discourse, spoken narrative or relation; literary composition either in verse or prose; oration; military array; decorating with flowers, chaplets, etc.

රචිත, *Rachita*, *a.* made, written, composed.

රජ්ජු, *Rajju*, *s.* rope, cord.

රජ්ජුරුවෝ, *Rajjuruwó*, *s.* king, sovereign, reigning prince: pl. රජවරු *rajawaru*.

රජ, *Raja*, *s.* (රඤ්ජ *rañja* to colour) dust; pollen of flowers; menstrual excretion; passion, that which produces sensual desire; also (from රාජ *rája*,) king; moon; ray of the sun; lime, row; water; name of Vishṇu; eminent person.

රජක, *Rajaka*, *s.* (රඤ්ජ *rañja* to colour clothes, ක aff.) washerman, man of the washer caste, [Colloq. රදවා *radawá*].

රජගුරු, *Raja-guru*, *s.* (රජ king, ගුරු teacher) royal preceptor: see රාජගුරු *rája-guru*.

රජ ගෙදර, *Raja-gedara*, *s.* king's house, palace.

රජත, *Rajata*, *s.* (රඤ්ජ *rañja* to colour, etc.) silver, [Colloq. රිදී *ridí*]; colour white; elephant's teeth, ivory; asterism, constellation: *a.* white, of a white colour.

රජදහන්, *Raja-dahan*, *s.* town, city, [Colloq. නුවර *nuwara*].

රජදහම, *Raja-dahama*, see රාජධර්ම *rája-dharma*.

රජන, *Rajana*, *s.* (රඤ්ජ *rañja* to colour) colouring, dyeing, painting.

රජනද්‍රුම, *Rajana-druma*, *s.* tree, *adenanthera pavonina*, [Colloq. මදටගස් *madaṭa-gas*].

රජනා, *Rajaná*, see රජන *rajana*.

රජනී, *Rajaní*, *s.* night; indigo plant, *indigofera tinctotia*, [Colloq. නිල්අවරි *nil-awari*]; turmeric, *curcuma longa*, [Colloq. කහ *kaha*]; lac.

රජනීකර, *Rajaníkara*, *s.* moon, [Colloquial. හඳ *haṇda*].

රජනීචර, *Rajaníchara*, *s.* (රජනී night, චර who goes) Ráksha, fiend, goblin, ghost; watchman; thief.

රජනීමුඛ, *Rajaní-mukha*, *s.* (රජනී and මුඛ entrance, commencement) evening, beginning of the night.

රජනීය, *Rajaníya*, *s.* that which delights or fascinates, any object exciting pleasurable sensations.

රජපිරිස, *Raja-pirisa*, *s.* (රජ king, පිරිස attendants) royal attendants; royal guard or escort.

රජ පුත්‍ර, *Raja-putra*, *s.* (රජ king, moon, පුත්‍ර son) king's son, prince; soldier, man of the military caste; planet Mercury.

රජ පෙරහර, *Raja-perahara*, *s.* (රජ and පෙරහර suite) attendants of a king; royal procession.

රජ පොහොට්ටු, *Raja-pohoṭṭu*, *s.* globe amaranth, *gomphræna globosa*.

රජ භවනය, *Raja-bhawanaya*, *s.* (රජ and භවන *bhawana* residence) palace, royal residence.

රජ මැඳුර, *Raja-mẹdura*, see the preceding.

රජ රජ, *Raja-raja*, *s.* (රජ king, රජ king) name of Kuwéra; name of Yama, the regent of the infernal world and judge of the final destinies of men; emperor, universal monarch or king of kings.

රජ රුක්, *Raja-ruk*, *s.* (රජ and රුක් tree) tree, *cassia fistula*, [Colloq. ඇහැළ *ẹhẹla*].

රජලිය, *Raja-liya*, *s.* queen, [Colloq. බිසව *bisawa*].

රජ වංශ, *Raja-waṇṣa*, see රාජ වංශ *rája-waṇṣa*.

රජ වාසල, *Raja-wásala*, *s.* (රජ and වාසල gate) king's gate, hence palace, royal residence.

රජවිල්, *Raja-vil*, *s.* play at chess. (Námáwali.)

රජස්, *Rajas*, *s.* (රඤ්ජ *rañja* to colour) quality or property of passion, that which produces sensual desire, worldly coveting, pride and falsehood, and is the cause of pain; dust; pollen of a flower; menstrual evacuation.

රජස්වලා, *Rajaswalá*, *s.* women in her courses.

රජස, *Rajasa*, *s.* dust.

රජ සභා, *Raja-sabhá*, *s.* (රජ and සභා assembly) king's council.

රජසානු, *Rajasánu*, *s.* cloud; heart or mind.

රජෝ, *Rajó*, see රජස් *rajas*.

රජෝහර, *Rajó-hara*, *s.* (රජස් *rajas* dust, හර who removes) washerman, [Colloq. රදවා *radawá*].

රජෝහරණ, *Rajó-haraṇa*, *s.* (රජස් *rajas* and හරණ what removes) water; cleaning, cleansing, purifying from dust, filth, etc.

රඤ්ජන, *Rañjana*, *s.* (රඤ්ජ *rañja* to colour, etc.) colouring, dyeing, painting; affecting the heart, exciting passion; pleasing, delighting; being, remaining, staying; red sandal or sappan wood: see the next.

රඤ්ජන ද්‍රුම, *Rañjana-druma*, *s.* (රඤ්ජන dyeing, ද්‍රුම tree) red sandal, *pterocarpus santalinus;* or sappan wood, *cæsalpinia sappan;* Bengal madder, see the next.

රඤ්ජනී, *Rañjaní*, *s.* indigo plant, *indigofera tinctoria*, [Colloq. නිල් අවරි *nil-awari*]; Indian madder, *oldenlandia* or *hedyotis umbellata;* another plant, species of *crinum;* flower, *nyctanthes arbor-tristis*, [Colloq. සේපාලිකා *sépáliká*].

රඤ්ජිත, *Rañjita*, *a.* (රඤ්ජ *rañja* to colour, ඉත *ita* aff.) painted, coloured, dyed; moved, affected; attached to.

රට, *Raṭa*, *s.* country, district, inhabited country: *a.* foreign, unindigenous, exotic.

රට අත්තන, *Raṭa-attana*, *s.* thorn apple, *datura suaveolens, (Solanaceæ).*

රට අත්තික්කා, *Raṭa-attikká*, *s.* species of fig, *ficus carica.*

රට අන්නාසි, *Raṭa-annási*, *s.* foreign pineapple, *ananas sativa.*

රට අනෝනා, *Raṭa-anóná*, *s.* soursop, *anona muricata.*

රට අබ, *Raṭa-aba*, *s.* mustard, *sinapis alba.*

රට අඹ, *Raṭa-am̆ba*, *s.* foreign mango, *mangifera indica.*

රට අල, *Raṭa-ala*, *s.* yam, *alocasia indica;* also called දේශ අල *déṣa-ala; (Araceæ).*

රට අසමෝදගන්, *Raṭa-asamódagan*, *s.* parsley. *petroselinum sativum.*

රට අත්තා, *Raṭa-áttá*, *s.* fruit called custard apple or bullock's heart, *anona reticulata.*

රට ඇටඹුරු, *Raṭa-ẹṭam̆buru*, *s.* tree, variety of *fagræa zeylanica.*

රට ඇත් බෑම්කිරිය, *Raṭa-ẹt-bẹmikiriya*, *s.* plant, variety of *phrynium capitatum.*

රට ඇඹිල්ල, *Raṭa-ẹmbilla*, *s.* tree, species of *antidesma.*

රට ඇඳුරු, *Raṭa-ẹnduru*, *s.* plant, not ascertained.

රට ඉඟුරු, *Raṭa-in̆guru*, *s.* ginger, species of *ginger zingiber.*

රට ඉඳි, *Raṭa-in̆di*, *s.* (රට foreign, ඉඳි date) foreign date tree, *phœnix sylvestris.*

රට ඉන්නල, *Raṭa-innala*, *s.* potato, *solanum tuberosum.*

රට උගුරැස්ස, *Raṭa-ugurẹssa*, *s.* thorny shrub, *flacourtia cataphracta (Bixinæ).*

රට එඬරු, *Raṭa-en̆daru*, *s.* physic nut, *jatropha curcas, (Euphorbiaceæ).*

රට එන්සාල්, *Raṭa-ensál*, *s.* short or Madras cardamums, *elettaria cardamomum* (minor).

රට එලමල්, *Raṭa-elamal*, *s.* flowering plant, variety of *hedychium coronarium.*

රට කපු, *Raṭa-kapu*, *s.* silk cotton tree, variety of *eriodendron anfractuosum.*

රට කරපිංච, *Raṭa-karapin̆cha*, *s.* tree, variety of *bergera kœnigii.*

රට කහ, *Raṭa-kaha*, *s.* saffron, turmeric, *curcuma longa.*

රට කිතුල්, *Raṭa-kitul*, *s.* palm tree, variety of *caryota urens.*

රට කුඩලු, *Raṭa-kúḍalu*, *s.* plant, species of *impatiens.*

රට කෙහෙල්, *Raṭa-kehel*, *s.* foreign kind of plantain, banana, *musa sapientum.*

රට කොඬොල්, *Raṭa-kon̆dol*, *s.* cultivated variety of yam, *colocasia antiquorum.*

රට කොමඩු, *Raṭa-komaḍu*, *s.* foreign water melon, *citrullus vulgaris.*

රට කොහොඹ, *Raṭa-kohom̆ba*, *s.* foreign margosa tree, *azadirachta indica.*

රට කෝප්පගහ, *Raṭa-kóppa-gaha*, *s.* plant, not ascertained.

රට කෝපි, *Raṭa-kópi*, *s.* foreign coffee, *coffea arabica.*

රට කැකිරි, *Raṭa-kẹkiri*, *s.* kind of cucumber, *cucumis sativus.*

රට කැකුන, *Raṭa-kẹkuna*, *s.* tree, variety of *canarium zeylanicum.*

රට ගොරක, *Raṭa-goraka*, *s.* tree, Cochin goraka, *garcinia* or *xanthocymus pictoria;* also called කොල්ලන්ගහ *kollan-gaha.*

රට ගෝවා, *Raṭa-góvá*, *s.* plant, species of cabbage, *bryophyllum calycinum (Crassulaceæ);* also called අක්කපාන *akkapána.*

රට ජම්බු, *Raṭa-jambu*, *s.* rose apple, variety of *eugenia* or *jambosa.*

රට තණ, *Raṭa-taṇa*, *s.* Guinea grass, *panicum maximum* or *p. jumentorum, (Gramineæ).*

රට තම්පලා, *Raṭa-tampalá*, *s.* plant, species of *amarantus.*

රට තිබ්බටු, *Raṭa-tibbaṭu*, *s.* species of *solanum.*

රට තුවර, *Raṭa-tuwara*, *s.* plant, cultivated for its leguminous seeds, *cytisus cajan.*

රට තෝර, *Raṭa-tóra*, *s.* pigeon pea, *cajanus indicus;* plant, *cassia alata (Leguminosæ):* see the last.

රට දන්, *Raṭa-ḍan*, *s.* tree, species of *eugenia.*

රට දෙල්, *Raṭa-del*, *s.* (රට foreign, දෙල් bread fruit) species of the bread fruit tree, said to be introduced into Ceylon from the Maldives, *artocarpus incisa (Urticaceæ).*

රට දෙහි, *Raṭa-dehi*, *s.* lime, variety of *citrus limetta.*

රට නාගවල්ලිය, *Raṭa-nágawalliya*, *s.* plant, kind of Croton.

රට නියඳ, *Raṭa-niyan̆da*, *s.* bow-string hemp, kind of *sanseviera zeylanica.*

රට නුග, *Raṭa-nuga*, *s.* fig tree, species of *ficus.*

රට නෙල්ලි, *Raṭa-nelli*, *s.* tree, variety of *phyllanthus emblica.*

රට පඹ, *Raṭa-pamba*, *s.* species of fern, *lygodium.*

රට පුවක් *Raṭa-puwak*, *s.* variety of areca-nut palm, *areca catechu (Palmæ).*

රට බටු, *Raṭa-baṭu*, *s.* potato-tree, *solanum macranthum.*

රට බුත්සරණ, *Raṭa-butsaraṇa*, *s.* plant, variety of Indian shot, *canna indica.*

රට බුලත්වැල්, *Raṭa-bulat-wel*, *s.* species of pepper, *piper (or chavica) siriboa*, variety of *p. betel (Piperaceæ);* also called සිරිබෝ *siribó.*

රට මරඳ, *Raṭa-maranda*, *s.* tree, species of *eugenia.*

රට මිරිස්, *Raṭa-miris*, *s.* plant, species of pepper, *piper.*

රට මොර, *Raṭa-mora*, *s.* tree, variety of *nephelium Longana.*

රට යක්බෙරිය, *Raṭa-yakbériya*, *s.* plant, species of *crotalaria.*

රට යොන්තුඹ, *Raṭa-yontumba*, *s.* creeper, *borago zeylanica.*

රට රත්කිරිය, *Raṭa-ratkíriya*, *s.* tree, variety of *acacia sundra.*

රට රත්කැලිය, *Raṭa-ratkéliya*, *s.* tree, species of *litsea.*

රට ලබු, *Raṭa-labu*, *s.* pumpkin, *cucurbita moschata (Cucurbitaceæ).*

රට ලූනු, *Raṭa-lúnu*, *s.* plant, species of *onion allium.*

රට වදමල්, *Raṭa-wadamal*, *s.* shoe flower, *hibiscus rosa sinensis.*

රට වී, *Raṭa-ví*, *s.* kind of paddy, *oryza sativa.*

රට වැටකොළු, *Raṭa-weṭakoḷu*, *s.* plant, species of pepo or gourd, *luffa.*

රට වැල්මල්, *Raṭa-welmal*, *s.* species of the betel creeper: see රට බුලත්වැල් *raṭa-bulatwel.*

රට වැසියා, *Raṭa-wesiyá*, *s.* inhabitant of the country, native.

රට සපු, *Raṭa-sapu*, *s.* tree, species of champaca, *michelia.*

රට හන්දිරන්වී, *Raṭa-handiran-ví*, *s.* kind of paddy, *oryza sativa.*

රට හිඟුරු, *Raṭa-hinguru*, *s.* lantana, *lantana mixta* or *l. camara (Verbenaceæ);* also called ගඳපාන *gandapána.*

රට හුලංකිරිය, *Raṭa-hulankíriya*, *s.* plant, variety of *phrynium zeylanicum.*

රට හොනරවාළුකෙසෙල්, *Raṭa-honarawáḷu-kesel*, *s.* variety of plantain, banana, *musa sapientum.*

රඩුව, *Raḍuwa*, *s.* chaff, [Colloq. බොල් *bol*, දහයියා *dahayiyá*].

රණ්ඩා, *Raṇḍá*, *s.* floating cryptogamous plant, *salrinia cucullata;* widow.

රණ, *Raṇa*, *s.* (රණ to sound) war, battle; sound, noise; forest; quill or bow of a lute, etc. bambu tree, *bambusa vulgaris.* [Colloq. උණගහ *uṇagaha*].

රණඋණ, *Raṇa-uṇa*, *s.* the red or golden bambu tree.

රණගී, *Raṇagí*, *s.* traces or reins of a horse; war cry, song of battle.

රණඟිල්ල, *Raṇangilla*, *s.* the fourth finger.

රණ තම්පලා, *Raṇa-tampalá*, *s.* plant, the seed of which yields edible flour, *amarantus paniculatus* or *a. frumentaceus (Amarantaceæ).*

රණ දෙරණ, *Raṇa-deraṇa*, *s.* camp, [Colloq. යුද්ධ භූමිය *yuddha-bhúmiya*].

රණ බටලී, *Raṇa-baṭalí*, *s.* cane, *teinostackyum maculatum (Gramineæ).*

රණ මණ්ඩල, *Raṇa-maṇḍala*, see රණදෙරණ *raṇa-deraṇa.*

රණවරා, *Raṇawará*, *s.* shrub, the leaves of which are used as tea and the bark as a buff dye, *cassia auriculata (Leguminosæ).*

රණසෙන, *Raṇa-sena*, *s.* army, hostile army, enemy.

රණිල, *Raṇila*, *s.* flock of geese or swans.

රණෙල්, *Raṇel*, *s.* variety of plantain, *musa sapientum.*

රත්, *Rat*, *s.* name of Balabhadrayá; fire; tree, *calophyllum inophyllum*, [Colloq. දොඹ *domba*]; zone, girdle, belt; blood: *a.* red, of a red colour.

රත් ඇල්වී, *Rat-el-ví*, *s.* (රත් red) kind of paddy, *oryza sativa.*

රත් එඬරු, *Rat-enḍaru*, *s.* (රත් red, එඬරු castor oil) red variety of the castor oil plant, *ricinus communis.*

රත් කතුරුමුරුංගා, *Rat-katuru-murungá*, *s.* tree, variety of *sesbana grandiflora.*

රත් කණෙර, *Rat-kaṇera*, *s.* (රත් and කණෙර nerium odorum) red species of oleander, *nerium odorum.*

රත්කර ඇල්වී, *Ratkara-elví*, *s.* kind of paddy, *oryza sativa.*

රත්කරණවා, *Ratkaraṇawá*, *v.* to heat, to make red hot.

රත් කරව්, *Rat-karaw*, *s.* plant, *phyllanthus indicus:* see කරව් *karaw.*

රත් කිහිරි, *Rat-kihiri*, *s.* (රත් red, කිහිරි mimosa catechu) catechu tree; the catechu formerly known as *Terra Japonica* is obtained from the wood *acacia sundra*, formerly called *a. catechu* or *mimosa catechu*, *(Leguminosæ)*.

රත්කුණ්ඩ මාවී, *Ratkuṇḍa-mávi*, *s.* kind of paddy, *oryza sativa*.

රත්කුණ්ඩවී, *Ratkuṇḍa-ví*, *s.* kind of paddy, *oryza sativa*.

රත් කොහොඹ, *Rat-kohomba*, *s.* margosa tree.

රත්කැලිය, *Ratkęliya*, *s.* tree, *litsea longifolia (Lauraceæ)*.

රත් ගස්කරල්සැබෝ, *Rat-gas-karalsębo*, *s.* plant, variety of *achyranthes aspera*.

රත් ගොකටු, *Rat-gokaṭu*, *s.* variety of the gamboge tree, *garcinia morella*.

රක්ත ජිව්හ, *Ratta-jivha*, *s.* (රක්ත red, ජිව්හ tongue) lion, [Colloq. සිංහයා *sinhayá*].

රත්තටු ඇල්වී, *Rattaṭu-ęlví*, *s.* kind of paddy, *oryza sativa*.

රත්තණ, *Rattaṇa*, *s.* (රත් and තණ grass) red grass, *mimosa octandra*.

රත් තඹර, *Rat-tambara*, *s.* red lotus, *nymphæa rubra*, [Colloq. රත්නෙළුම් *rat-neḷum*].

රත් තම්පලා, *Rat-tampalá*, see රතු තම්පලා *ratu-tampalá*.

රත්තරන්, *Rattaran*, *s.* gold; corruptly for රත්රන් *ratran*, which see.

රත් තලා, *Rat-talá*, *s.* plant, species of *ocimum*.

රත්තා, *Rattá*, *s.* red ant.

රත් තිඹිරි, *Rat-timbiri*, *s.* variety of the gab tree, *diospyros embryopteris*.

රත් දොඹ, *Rat-domba*, *s.* timber tree, variety of *calophyllum inophyllum*.

රත්න ගර්භ, *Ratna-garbbha*, *s.* (රත්න jewel, ගර්භ embryo) god of wealth, Kuvéra; the earth; ocean.

රත්නත්‍රය, *Ratnatraya*, see ත්‍රිවිධරත්නය *trividha-ratnaya*.

රත්න මඤ්ජූෂා, *Ratna-mañjúshá*, *s.* (රත්න gem, මඤ්ජූෂා basket) casket of gems.

රත්නමය, *Ratnamaya*, *a.* gemmed, full or made of gems.

රත්න මුඛ්‍ය, *Ratna-mukhya*, *s.* (රත්න and මුඛ්‍ය chief) diamond, [Colloq. දියමන්ති *diyamanti*].

රත්නය, *Ratnaya*, *s.* jewel, gem, any thing figuratively the best of its species, [Colloq. මැණික *męnika*].

රත්නාවතී, *Ratnáwati*, *s.* (රත්න gem, වත් *wat* poss. aff.) the earth, [Colloq. පොළව *poḷawa*].

රත්නවාළු කෙසෙල්, *Ratnawáḷu-kesel*, *s.* plantain, variety of *musa sapientum*.

රත්නාකර, *Ratnákara*, *s.* (රත්න *ratna* jewel, ආකර *ákara* mine) ocean, [Colloq. මුහුද *muhuda*]; jewel mine.

රත්නාභරණ, *Ratnábharaṇa*, *s.* (රත්න *ratna* gem, ආභරණ *ábharaṇa* ornament) ornament of gems.

රත්නි, *Ratni*, *s.* cubit, measured from the elbow to the closed fist; closed hand, fist.

රත් නිවිති, *Rat-niviti*, *s.* Malabar nightshade, *basella rubra*: see නිවිති *niviti*.

රත් නෙටුල්, *Rat-neṭul*, *s.* plant, lead-wort, *plumbago rosea*.

රත් නෙළු, *Rat-neḷu*, *s.* small tree, species of *strobilanthes*.

රත් නෙළුම්, *Rat-neḷum*, *s.* red lotus, *nymphæa rubra*.

රත්පත් ඇල්වී, *Ratpat-ęlví*, *s.* kind of paddy, *oryza sativa*.

රත් පල, *Rat-pala*, *s.* fig tree: see නුග *nuga*.

රත් පලස, *Rat-palasa*, *s.* scarlet cloth.

රත් පළොල්, *Rat-paḷol*, *s.* tree, variety of *stercospermum suaveolens*.

රත්පා, *Ratpá*, *s.* (රත් blood, පා who drinks) leech, [Colloq. කූඩැල්ලා *kúḍęllá*]; horse leech; goblin, sprite, ogre.

රත් පිටවක්කා, *Rat-piṭawakká*, *s.* plant, eaten by cattle, *phyllanthus urinarea*; another plant, *Sebastiana (or mycrostachys) chamælea*; both *(Euphorbiaceæ)*.

රත් පිත, *Rat-pita*, see රක්ත පිත්ත *rakta-pitta*.

රත් පියුම්, *Rat-piyum*, *s.* red lotus, *nymphæa rubra*, [Colloq. රත්නෙළුම් *rat-neḷum*].

රත් මල්, *Rat-mal*, *s.* shrub, *ixora coccinea*; also called රතඹලා *ratambalá*.

රත් මහනෙල්, *Rat-mahanel*, *s.* red lotus, *nymphæa stellata*.

රත්මිණි, *Rat-miṇi*, *s.* (රත් red, මිණි gem) ruby, red topaz.

රත්‍යඞ්ග, *Ratyańga*, *s.* (රති *rati* and අඞ්ග *ańga* member) male or female organ.

රත්රන්, *Ratran*, *s.* gold; wrought gold.

රත් වල්කවාළු, *Rat-wal-kawáḷu*, *s.* kind of grass, variety of *setaria glauca*.

රත් විල, *Rat-vila*, *s.* plant, variety of *bonnaya ueronicæfolia*.

රත් සඳුන්, *Rat-saṇdun*, *s.* (රත් red, සඳුන් sandal) red sandal wood, *pterocarpus santalinus*.

රත් සිරියල්, *Rat-siriyal*, *s.* (රත් and සිරියල් arsenic) red arsenic.

රත් සැබෝ, *Rat-sębó*, *s.* (රත් red) plant, variety of *achyranthes aspera*, [Colloq. ගස් කරල්හැබ *gas-karalhęba*].

රත් හිරියල්, *Rat-hiriyal*, see රත්සිරියල් *rat-siriyal.*

රත්හිරිය, *Rathiriya*, *s.* sandal wood tree: see සඳුන් *sandun*, and රත්සඳුන් *rat-sandun.*

රත් හැල්, *Rat-hęl*, *s.* (රත් red, හැල් rice or paddy) sort of rice sown on dry ground.

රත, *Rata*, *s.* (රම *rama* to sport) coition; desire, lust, longing; blood, the vital humour; redness, red colour; red hot iron, from රක්ත *rakta.*

රතඟ, *Ratanga*, *s.* (රත් *rat* red, අඟ *anga* limb) name of the planet Mars: see රක්තාඞ්ග *raktáṅga.*

රතන, *Ratana*, *s.* jewel, gem: see රත්නය *ratnaya;* cubit, measured from the elbow to the closed hand.

රතන සූත්‍රය, *Ratana-sútraya*, *s.* name of one of the discourses of Buddha.

රතනාකර, *Ratanákara*, *s.* (රතන *ratana* gem, ආකර *ákara* what produce, mine) sea, ocean; jewel mine.

රත නුවන, *Rata-nuwana*, *s.* (රත red, නුවන eye) name of the kókila or Indian cuckoo; pigeon.

රතඹලා, *Ratambalá*, *s.* shrub with clusters of scarlet flowers, *ixora coccinea* [*Rubiaceæ*); also called රත්මල් *rat-mal.*

රතඹුල, *Ratambula*, *s.* red lotus, *nymphæa rubra.*

රතය, *Rataya*, *s.* redness, bloody inflammation.

රති, *Rati*, *s.* (රම *rama* to sport) wife of Káma-déwa the Indian Cupid; passion, desire; coition; privity.

රති කුහර, *Rati-kuhara*, *s.* (රති and කුහර cavity) vulva.

රති ක්‍රියා, *Rati-kriyá*, } *s.* (රති and ක්‍රියා act or ක්‍රීඩා
රති ක්‍රීඩා, *Rati-krídá*, } sport) copulation.

රතිඳු, *Ratindu*, *s.* (රති and ඉඳු *indu* lord or chief) name of Anańgayá the Indian Cupid.

රතිඳුගොව් *Ratindugow*, } *s.* species of red
රතිඳුගොව්වා, *Ratindu-gowwá*, } beetle.

රතිපති, *Ratipati*, see රතිඳු *ratindu.*

රතිමුක්තක, *Rati-muktaka*, *s.* (රති lust, passion, මුක්ත loosed, freed, ක aff.) one freed from all passion, ascetic who has subdued his passions.

රතිය, *Ratiya*, see රති *rati.*

රතිල, *Ratila*, *s.* plant, *clitoria ternatea*, [Colloq. නිල්කටරොළු *nil-kațaroļu*].

රතිසත්වරා, *Ratisatwará*, *s.* plant, *trigonella corniculata.*

රතු, *Ratu*, *s.* red, the colour: *a.* red, of a red colour.

රතු අක්කපාන, *Ratu-akkapána*, *s.* plant, variety of *bryophyllum calycinum:* see අක්කපාන *akkapána.*

රතු අන්නාසි, *Ratu-annási*, *s.* variety of pineapple, *ananas sativa.*

රතු අරලිය, *Ratu-araliya*, *s.* plant, not ascertained.

රතු අවර, *Ratu-awara*, *s.* creeper, not ascertained: see අවර *awara.*

රතු අවරිය, *Ratu-awariya*, *s.* small tree, species of *indigofera.*

රතු ඔලිඳ, *Ratu-olinda*, *s.* plant, gunja: see ඔලිඳ වැල් *olinda-węl.*

රතු කතුරුමුරුංගා, *Ratu-katurumurungá*, *s.* plant, *sesbana grandiflora;* also called කතුරුමුරුංගා *katurumurungá.*

රතු කඳහතු, *Ratu-kanda-hatu*, *s.* species of mushroom.

රතු කහගහ, *Ratu-kaha-gaha*, *s.* plant, *bixa orellana;* also called කහ *kaha.*

රතු කිඹුල්වැන්න, *Ratu-kimbulwęnna*, *s.* persicarum or buck wheat, *polygonum barbatum (Polygonaceæ).*

රතු කිරිඳිය, *Ratu-kirindiya*, *s.* tares, variety of *coix lacryma.*

රතු කුකුළුකරමල්, *Ratu-kukuļukaramal*, *s.* cock's comb, *celosia cristata.*

රතු කූඩලු, *Ratu-kúḍalu*, *s.* balsam, variety of *impatiens latifolia;* also called කූඩලුමල් *kúḍalu-mal,*

රතු කෙහෙල්, *Ratu-kehel*, *s.* plantain, variety of *musa sapientum.*

රතු කොච්චි, *Ratu-kochchi*, *s.* plant, *musa rosacea.*

රතු කොට්ටම්බා, *Ratu-koṭṭambá*, *s.* tree, variety of *terminalia catappa.*

රතු කොබලිල, *Ratu-kobalila*, *s.* variety of mountain ebony, *bauhinea purpurea.*

රතු කොලොඳු, *Ratu-kolondu*, *s.* plant, *chrysanthemum indicum.*

රතු කෝවි, *Ratu-kóvi*, *s.* variety of cabbage, *brasica oleracea.*

රතුකැටය, *Ratukęṭaya*, *s.* ruby.

රතු කැම්මෙරිය, *Ratu-kęmmériya*, *s.* night shade, species of *solanum;* also called කන්වෙරිය *kanwériya.*

රතුගල්, *Ratu-gal*, see රතුකැටය, *ratukęṭaya.*

රතු ගස්මිරිස්, *Ratu-gas-miris*, *s.* plant, *capsicum frutescens* or *c. rubra.*

රතු ගෙඳකොල, *Ratu-gendakola*, *s.* variety of purslane, *portulaca oleracea:* see ගෙඳ *genda.*

රතු ගොරක, *Ratu-goraka*, *s.* (රතු red) variety of the goraka tree, *garcinia cambogia.*

රතු ගෝවාකොල, *Ratu-gówákola*, *s.* red cabbage, *brassica rubra.*

රතු ජම්බු, *Ratu-jambu*, *s.* rose apple, *Jambosa vulgaris.*

රතු ජම්බෝල, *Ratu-jambóla*, *s.* kind of pumelow, *citrus decumana.*

රතු තම්පලා, *Ratu-tampalá*, *s.* species of amaranth, *amaranthus cruentus.*

රතු තුත්තිරි, *Ratu-tuttiri*, *s.* love grass, variety of *chrysopogon aciculatus.*

රතු තෙල් ඕලු, *Ratu-tel-óḷu*, *s.* variety of water lily, *nymphæa lotus.*

රතු තැඹිලි, *Ratu-tẹmbili*, *s.* variety of coconut tree, *cocos nucifera.*

රතු දඩිනනාරු, *Ratu-daḍinnaru*, *s.* four-sided bristly plant, *buchnera euphrasioides.*

රතු දණ්ඩ, *Ratu-daṇḍa*, *s.* parsley, *petroselinum sativum.*

රතු දාතුඩුවා, *Ratu-dátuḍuwá*, *s.* glossy ibis, *plegadis falcinellus (Plataleidæ* order *Herodiones).*

රතු නවසි, *Ratu-nawasi*, *s.* variety of the coconut, *cocos nucifera.*

රතු නෙළුම්, *Ratu-neḷum*, *s.* sort of lotus, *nelumbium speciosum.*

රතු පතගි, *Ratu-patangi*, *s.* variety of brasiletto or sappan tree, *cæsalpinia sappan.*

රතු පුරුක්, *Ratu-puruk*, *s.* spreading shrub with large flowers, variety of *asystasia coromandeliana:* see පුරුක් *puruk.*

රතු පෙතිදඹල, *Ratu-petidambala*, *s.* plant, *dolichos purpureus*, variety of *dolichos lablab*, cultivated legume.

රතු පේර, *Ratu-péra*, *s.* tree, variety of guava, *psidium pomiferum* or *p. guyava.*

රතු පොල්, *Ratu-pol*, *s.* variety of the common coconut, *cocos nucifera.*

රතු බටතණ, *Ratu-baṭataṇa*, *s.* kind of panic grass, *panicum aristatum.*

රතු බතල, *Ratu-batala*, *s.* bind-weed with edible tuberous root, variety of *ipomæa batatas.*

රතු බාලොලිය, *Ratu-báloliya*, *s.* many-stemmed leguminous plant, variety of *hedysarum triquetrum:* see බාලොලිය *báloliya.*

රතු බින්තඹුරු, *Ratu-bintamburu*, *s.* floating plant with edible leaves, variety of *ipomœa aquatica* or *convolvulus repens.*

රතු බුත්සරණ, *Ratu-butsaraṇa*, *s.* plant, variety of Indian shot, *canna indica.*

රතු මුගටියා, *Ratu-mugaṭiyá*, *s.* ruddy mungoose, *herpestes Smithii.*

රතු මුවඉරිඟු, *Ratu-muwairingu*, *s*, plant, variety of *zea mays.*

රතු මොනරමල්, *Ratu-monaramal*, *s.* shrub, peacock tree, *poinciana pulcherrima.*

රතු යක්වනස්ස, *Ratu-yakwanassa*, *s.* plant, variety of *anisomeles ovata.*

රතු රටඉඟුරු, *Ratu-raṭa-inguru*, *s.* sort of ginger, *zingiber rubens.*

රතු රටපඹ, *Ratu-raṭa-pamba*, *s.* fern, species of *lygodium.*

රතු රටවදමල්, *Ratu-raṭa-wadamal*, *s.* shoe flower, variety of *hibiscus rosa sinensis.*

රතු රතඹලා, *Ratu-ratambalá*, *s.* shrub, *ixora coccinea:* see රතඹලා *ratambalá.*

රතු රදලිය, *Ratu-radaliya*, *s.* tree, variety of *cannarus monocarpus:* see රදලිය *radaliya.*

රතු රාජපොහොට්ටු, *Ratu-rája-pohoṭṭu*, *s.* globe amaranth, *gomphræna globosa.*

රතු රාබු, *Ratu-rábu*, *s.* radish, *raphanus sativus.*

රතු ලූනු, *Ratu-lúnu*, *s.* species of garlic or onion, *allium ascalohicum.*

රතු වදමල්, *Ratu-wadamal*, *s.* shoe flower, *hibiscus rosa sinensis.*

රතු වල්ඉඟුරු, *Ratu-wal-inguru*, *s.* sort of ginger, *zingiber officinale.*

රතුවා, *Ratuwá*, *s.* tree, with leaflets in from ten to twenty pairs, pink flowers, *cassia marginata* or *c. Roxburghii, (Leguminosæ).*

රතුවෙනවා, *Ratuwenawá*, *v.* to become red.

රතු සෙන්දිරික්කා, *Ratu-sendirikká*, *s.* plant, *mirabilis jalapa.*

රතු සෙවුවන්දිමල්, *Ratu-sewuwandimal*, *s.* the rose, *rosa semperflorens:* see සෙවුවන්දිමල් *sewuwandimal.*

රතු හමස්මෑ, *Ratu-hamasmẹ*, *s.* sort of kidney bean, red variety of *dolichos sesquipedalis.*

රතු හාතලිවී, *Ratu-hátali-ví*, *s.* kind of paddy, *oryza sativa.*

රතු හීන්බෝවිටියා, *Ratu-hínbóviṭiyá*, *s.* plant, variety of *osbeckia octandra.*

රතෑස්, *Ratẹs*, *s.* (රත් *rat* red, ඇස් *ẹs* eye) pigeon; buffalo, [Colloq. මිහරකා *miharaká*]; Indian cuckoo: see කෝකිලයා *kókilayá.*

රථ්‍ය, *Rathya*, *s.* car or carriage horse; multitude of cars; high street; main or carriage road; place where several roads meet; wheel.

රථ, *Ratha*, s. car, war chariot; carriage in general, bandy, any vehicle or mode of conveyance; limb, member; body; foot; sort of cane, *calamus rotang*,

රථකට්‍යා, *Rathakaṭyá*, s. (රථ car, කට්‍යච් *kaṭyach* affix of multitude) multitude of cars.

රථකර, *Rathakara*, } s. (රථ and කර or කාර who
රථකාර, *Rathakára*, } makes) carpenter; coach maker, one by profession a car maker.

රථකාරක, *Rathakáraka*, s, one of the seven lakes in the Himálaya range.

රථක්‍රාන්තා, *Rathakrántá*, s. plant, *evolvulus alsinoides*, [Colloq. විෂ්ණුක්‍රාන්ති *vishṇukránti*],

රථචක්‍ර, *Ratha-chakra*, s. wheel of a carriage.

රථත්තරණ, *Rathattharaṇa*, see රථාස්තරණ *rathástaraṇa*.

රථද්‍රු, *Rathadru*, s. (රථ car, ද්‍රු tree) timber tree, *dalbergia ougeinensis*, the wood being used for wheels, [Colloq. කොබුගස් *kobu-gas*].

රථ පන්තිය, *Ratha-pantiya*, s. (රථ car, පන්තිය row) row of carriages, procession of vehicles; carriage house.

රථය, *Rathaya*, see රථ *ratha*.

රථරුවා, *Ratharuwá*, s. (රථ and අරුවා *aruwá* who mounts) charioteer, coachman.

රථසක, *Ratha-saka*, s. wheel of a carriage.

රථාඞ්ග, *Rathánga*, s. (රථ *ratha* and අඞ්ග *anga* limb) wheel, any part of a carriage; the ruddy goose, *anas casarca*.

රථාචාර්‍ය්‍ය, *Rathácharya*, s. (රථ *ratha* and ආචාර්‍ය්‍ය *áchárya* master) charioteer; master of a car.

රථාරෝහින්, *Rathárôhin*, see රථරුවා *ratharuwá*.

රථාලඞ්කාර, *Rathálankára*, s. ornaments and trappings of a chariot or travelling car.

රථාස්තරණ, *Rathástaraṇa*, s. (රථ *ratha* and ආස්තරණ *ástaraṇa* covering) cloth spread over a carriage as a defence against dirt, etc.

රථික, *Rathika*, } s. owner of or rider in a car.
රථින්, *Rathin*, }

රථෝත්තම, *Rathóttama*, s. (රථ *ratha* and උත්තම *uttama* chief, highest) king, [Colloq. රජ *raja*].

රද, *Rada*, s. (රද to tear) tooth; king, sovereign, from රජ *rája*; pain; ache; dust; blood; cord, line, rope; tearing, splitting, dividing.

රදදූ, *Rada-dú*, s. (රද king, දූ daughter) princess, [Colloq. කුමාරිකාව *kumárikáwa*].

රදන, *Radana*, s. tooth; tearing, rending.

රදනච්ඡද, *Radanachchhada*, s. (රදන tooth; ඡද covering) lip, [Colloq. තොල *tola*].

රදනා, *Radaná*, s. tooth, [Colloq. දත *data*].

රදල, *Radala*, s. husband; headman, chief, (a Kandian term).

රදලිය, *Radaliya*, s. creeper tree, *connarus monocarpus*, (*Connaraceæ*).

රදවා, *Radawá*, s. (රඤ් *rañja* to colour or clean) washerman, man of the washer caste: pl. රදව *radaw*.

රදවි, *Radaví*, s. laundress.

රදා, *Radá*, a. belonging to a man or woman of the washer caste.

රදා ඇල්වී, *Radá-ęlví*, s. kind of paddy, *oryza sativa*.

රදාතොට, *Radá-toṭa*, s. place in a river or lake where clothes are washed, laundry.

රදු, *Radu*, s. king, Elu form of රජ *rája*.

රදූ, *Radú*, s. (රද *rada* king, දූ daughter) princess; the inferior wives or concubines of a king; string.

රඳන, *Randana*, s. painting, dyeing, colouring, staying, being, remaining, fixed; Elu form of රඤ්ජන *rañjana*, which see.

රඳනවා, *Randanawá*, v. to tarry, to stay, to remain, to rest; to dye, to paint, to colour, to break a fall: pret. රැඳුවා *ręnduwá*.

රන්, *Ran*, s. gold.

රන් අකුස, *Ran-akusa*, s. golden hook used to guide an elephant.

රන් අවි, *Ran-avi*, s. golden weapon.

රන් ඕවිලි, *Ran-óvili*, s. golden swing.

රන්කරුවා, *Rankaruwá*, s. goldsmith, [Colloq. බඩාල *baḍála*].

රන්කිරි, *Rankiri*, s. first milk given to an infant in which gold is rubbed.

රන්කිරිය, *Rankíriya*, s. shrub with beautiful flowers, (bracts white, petals pink) *alpenia nutans* (*Scitamineæ*).

රන්කෙණ්ඩිය, *Ran-keṇḍiya*, s. golden goglet or jug.

රන්කෙසරු, *Rankesaru*, s. timber tree, *calophyllum inophyllum*: see දොඹ *domba*,

රන්කොතලේ, *Ran-kotalé*, see රන්කෙණ්ඩිය *rankeṇḍiya*.

රන්කැට, *Rankęṭa*, s. gold mirror, mirror of polished gold.

රන්ගිරි, *Rangiri*, s. mountain Maha Méru, [Colloq. මහමෙර *mahamera*].

රන්ගැබ, *Rangęba*, s. (රන් gold, ගැබ womb) name of Brahma; gold mine.

රන්තරු, *Ran-taru*, s. (රන් and තරු star) artificial stars of gold used as ornaments.

රන්තෝඩු, *Ran-tóḍu*, s. gold earings.

රන්තැඹිලි, *Ran-tẹmbili*, s. variety of the coconut tree, *cocos nucifera*.

රන්ධ්‍ර, *Randhra*, s. hole, fissure, cavity, chasm, [Colloq. සිදුර *sidura*]; fault, defect.

රන්නල, *Ran-nala*, s. (රන් gold, නල tube) golden ewer.

රන්නා, *Ranná*, s. kind of fish.

රන් පුහුල්, *Ran-puhul*, s. sort of pumpkin gourd, of the genus, *benincasa* or *cucurbita*.

රන් පොරෝඩු, *Ran-poróḍu*, s. golden trappings or girth.

රන් බෑවිල, *Ran-bẹvila*, s. plant of the genus *sida*.

රන්මනිස්ස, *Ranmanissa*, s. plant with pale pink petals and blue stamens, considered a cure for ringworm, *xyris indica (Xyrideæ):* also called රන්මොටු *ranmoṭu*.

රන් මුගටියා, *Ran-mugaṭiyá*, s. golden spotted mungoose, *herpestes nipalensis (Carnivrra)*.

රන්මොටු, *Ranmoṭu*, see රන්මනිස්ස *ranmanissa*.

රන්රස, *Ran-rasa*, s. (රන් gold, රස quicksilver) gold and quicksilver.

රන් ලිය, *Ran-liya*, s. (රන් and ලිය creeper) golden border of a picture or ornament.

රන්වන්, *Ranwan*, a. of a gold colour.

රන්වන් අත්තන, *Ranwan-attana*, s. species of the datura: see අත්තන *attana*.

රන්වන් කටුකරඬු, *Ranwan-kaṭukaranḍu*, s, plant, variety of *barleria prionitis:* see කටුකරඬු *kaṭukaranḍu*.

රන්වන් කිරිඳි, *Ranwan-kirindi*, s. sort of tares, variety of *coix lacryma*.

රන්වන් කිකිරිඳි, *Ranwan-kikirindi*, s. hairy plant with yellow flowers, *wedelia (or verbisina) calendulacea) (Compositæ)*.

රන්වන් කොණ්ඩයා, *Ranwan-konḍayá*, s. Ceylonese Trogon, *Trogonidæ* order *Picariæ;* also called නවනිල කුරුල්ලා *nawaníla-kurullá*.

රන්වන් සඳුන්, *Ranwan-sanḍun*, s. (රන්වන් and සඳුන් sandal) red sandal wood, variety of *santalum album*.

රන්වලා, *Ran-walá*, s. (රන් gold, වලා chain) golden bracelet.

රන් සිවිගෙය, *Ran-sivigeya*, s. (රන් and සිවිගෙය palanquin, litter) sort of palanquin or litter, carried on the back of an elephant and highly decorated with golden and gold trappings.

රන්සුණු, *Ran-suṇu*, s. gold dust.

රන් සූටික්කා, *Ran-súṭikká*, s. Loten's sun bird, *cynnyris lotenius (Cinnyridæ* order *Passerus);* also called මොදර සූටික්කා *modara-súṭikká* and ගෙවල් කුරුල්ලා *gewal-kurullá*.

රන් සෝල, *Ran-sóla*, } s. (රන් gold, සෝල or
රන් සෝලුව, *Ran-sóluwa*, } සෝලුව stick) gold mace or club.

රබ්බඩ, *Rabbaḍa*, a. light red.

රබන් රෝදය, *Raban-ródaya*, s. wooden frame of a timbrel.

රබාන, *Rabána*, s. tambourine, timbrel: pl. රබන් *raban*.

රඹ, *Ramba*, s. plantain or banana: see රම්භා *rambhá*, [Colloq. කෙසෙල් *kesel*].

රඹකැන, *Rambakẹna*, s. bunch or cluster of plantains.

රඹුක්, *Rambuk*, s. cane resembling but more elegant than the sugar cane, *saccharum procerum (Gramineæ)*.

රඹුටන්, *Rambutan*, s. tree, native of the Malay islands; it bears a red fruit with acidulous pulp, *nephelium lappaceum*.

රම්, *Ram*, s. name of Balabhadrayá, brother of Vishṇu; agreeableness.

රම්දම්, *Ramdam*, s, (රම් for රන් *ran* and දම් chain) gold chain.

රම්භා, *Rambhá*, s. plantain, [Colloq. කෙසෙල් *kesel*]; one of the apsaras or courtezans of Swarga; harlot; lowing, as of a cow.

රම්මනිස්ස, *Rammanissa*, see රන්මනිස්ස *ranmanissa*.

රම්‍ය, *Ramya*, s. champaca tree, *michelia champaca*, [Colloq. සපු *sapu*]; root of a species of cucumber; semen virile: *a.* pleasing, delightful, agreeable, charming.

රම, *Rama*, s. (රම to please) husband, lover; name of Káma the Indian Cupid: *a.* dear, beloved; delighting, charming.

රමණ, *Ramaṇa*, s. name of Káma the Indian Cupid; coition; sporting, playing; dalliance.

රමණී, *Ramaṇí*, s. woman, agreeable woman; wife, mistress.

රමණීය, *Ramaṇíya*, a. pleasing, charming, agreeable, joyful, delightful; delicious; good, excellent.

රමති, *Ramati*, s. love; lover, gallant; name of Káma the Indian Cupid.

රමඹුන්, *Ramambun*, s. (රම Rama, අඹු *ambu* wife) name of Sríkántáwa or Lakshmí, the goddess of beauty.

රමා, *Ramá*, *s.* name of Lakshmí the goddess of beauty; wife, mistress.

රමිඳු, *Ramiṇdu*, *s.* name of Vishṇu.

රමුක්, *Ramuk*, see රඹුක් *rambuk*.

රමුස්, *Ramus*, *s.* thunder, [Colloq. හෙන *hena*].

රල්, *Ral*, *s.* waving, undulating: *a.* hard, firm, strong, solid.

රල්ලක, *Rallaka*, *s.* blanket; eye lash.

රල්ලියා, *Ralliyá*, *s.* kind of fish.

රළ, *Raḷa*, *s.* wave.

රව, *Rawa*, *s.* (රු *ru* to sound, etc.) sound, noise in general.

රවකැර, *Rawakęra*, *s.* plant, *ochna grandiflora*: see මල්කැර *malkęra*.

රවටනවා, *Rawaṭanawá*, *v.* to cheat, to deceive, to defraud, to trick: pret. රැවටුවා *ręwaṭuwá*.

රවණ, *Rawaṇa*, *s.* camel; kókila or Indian cuckoo; bell metal; sound, noise, sound in general.

රවන් ඉදල, *Rawan-idala*, *s.* tree, *Wenlandia Notoria (Rubiaceæ)*.

රවනවා, *Dawanawá*, *v.* to sound, to cry or make a noise; to scowl, to frown, to stare at: pret. රැවුවා *ręwuwá*.

රවය, *Rawaya*, *s.* sound, noise, sound in general.

රවි, *Ravi*, *s.* (රු *ru* to sound, passive form, to be praised, etc.) sun, [Colloq. ඉර *ira*].

රවිකාන්ත, *Ravikánta*, *s.* (රවි and කාන්ත stone) sun stone, sort of crystal.

රවිනාථ, *Ravi-nátha*, *s.* (රවි sun, නාථ a lord) lotus; plant, native of paddy fields with red short-lived flowers, *pentapetes phœnicea*.

රවිප්‍රිය, *Ravi-priya*, *s.* (රවි and ප්‍රිය beloved) copper, [Colloq. තඹ *taṃba*]; red lotus; tree, acid and yielding yellow dye, *artocarpus lakoocha*, [Colloq. කනගොන්න *kanagonna*]; kind of basil, *ocimum gratissimum*; plant, *gynandropsis pentaphylla*, [Colloq. වෙලා *wélá*]; name of Ráwaṇa ancient king of Ceylon.

රවුල, *Rawula*, *s.* beard; name of Ráwaṇa: see රාවණ *ráwaṇa*.

රවුළු, *Rawuḷu*, *s.* beard.

රශ්මි, *Raşmi*, *s.* cord, string, rein; eye-lash; ray, ray of the sun or moon.

රසාණ, *Rasáṇa*, *s.* clarified butter, [Colloq. ගිතෙල් *gitel*].

රස්, *Ras*, *s.* sun beam, ray of the sun, ray of light.

රස්නය, *Rasnaya*, see රස්නේ *rasné*.

රස්නි, *Rasni*, *s.* plant, *lobelia excelsa (Campanulaceæ)*.

රස්නේ, *Rasné*, *s.* solar or animal heat.

රස, *Rasa*, *s.* (රස to taste, to love, etc.) flavour, taste, as sweet, salt, pungent, bitter, sour and astringent; taste, sentiment, emotion, as an object of poetry or composition, nine such are usually enumerated; affection of the mind, passion; juice, exudation; liquid, fluid or liquefied substance; semen virile; water; the primary or essential juice or fluid of the body, whence blood, serum, sweat, etc. are supposed to be engendered; it corresponds best with chyle, but is probably of an fanciful nature; gum myrrh; quicksilver, from its being a semi-fluid metal; mineral or metallic salt, as sulphur, borax, talc, blue or green vitriol.

රස අජීර්ණ, *Rasa-ajírṇa*, *s.* (රස sweetness, අජීර්ණ indigestion) indigestion caused by eating any saccharine substance.

රස කපුරු, *Rasa-kapuru*, } *s.* (රස mercury, කපුරු or කර්පූර camphor)
රස කර්පූර, *Rasa-karpúra*, } medicine or drug so called from its resemblance to mercury; it is a white sublimate or a muriate of mercury, made in close vessels with sulphur, mercury, and common salt; the crystals formed in the first operation are sublimed a second time.

රසකාරක, *Rasakáraka*, *s.* (රස taste, flavour, කාර who makes, ක aff.) cook, [Colloq. කෝකියා *kókiyá*].

රසකිඳ, *Rasakiṇda*, *s.* climbing plant with warted bark and small yellow flowers, *tinospora cordifolia (Menispermaceæ)*; holy basil, *ocimum sanctum*, [Colloq. මදුරුතලා *madurutalá*].

රස ගන්ධ, *Rasa-gandha*, *s.* gum myrrh, [Colloq. ගන්ධරස *gandha-rasa*].

රස ගර්භ, *Rasa-garbha*, *s.* (රස quicksilver, ගර්භ embryo) native antimony or a preparation of antimony used as a stibium, [Colloq. රසාඤ්ජන *rasáñjana*]; vermillion, [Colloq. සාදිලිංගම් *sádiliṇgam*].

රසඥ, *Rasajña*, *s.* (රස taste, etc. ඥ who knows) physician, medicinal preparer and administerer of mercurial and chemical compounds; poet, writer who understands the different *rasas* or sentiments to be described.

රසඥතා, *Rasajñatá*, *s.* alchemy, poetical skill.

රසඥා, *Rasajñá*, *s.* (රස taste, flavor, ඥා, what knows) tongue, [Colloq. දිව *diwa*]: see the last.

රසතැල්කොල, *Rasatęlkola*, } *s.* sort of bind-weed
රසතැල්ල, *Rasatęlla*, } with twining stem, large pointed leaves, and pale rose-coloured flowers, *ipomœa sepiaria (Convolvulaceæ)*.

රසදිය, *Rasadiya*, *s.* (රස mercury, දිය water) quicksilver.

රසදිව, *Rasa-diva*, *s.* uvula.

රසධාතු, *Rasa-dhátu*, *s.* (රස juice, or liquefied substance of the body, ධාතු metal) one of the primary or essential juices of the body, seven of which are enumerated; from the rasa dhátu blood, serum, etc. are engendered; also, quicksilver.

රසධාරා, *Rasa-dhárá*, see රසාධාර *rasádhára*.

රසන්වැල, *Rasanwęla*, *s.* girdle, zone, chain worn round the loins.

රසන, *Rasana*, *s.* (රස to sound or taste) tasting, taste; sound, noise.

රසනා, *Rasaná*, *s.* woman's girdle, chain worn round the loins; rare plant with twining, pink flowers, and root used as an emetic, *pœderia fœtida*.

රසනාථ, *Rasanátha*, *s.* (රස juice, fluid, නාථ chief) quicksilver, [Colloq. රසදිය *rasadiya*].

රසනාදම, *Rasanádáma*, *s.* රසනා girdle, දම string) zone, girdle worn round the loins.

රසබලනවා, *Rasabalanawá*, *v.* to taste: pret. රස බැලුවා *rasabęluwá*.

රසභව, *Rasabhawa*, *s.* (රස chyle, භව produced) blood, [Colloq. ලේ *lé*].

රසමොර, *Rasa-mora*, *s.* tree, *dimocarpus pupilla*, or species of *nephelium*.

රසවත්, *Rasawat*, *a.* (රස taste, වත් poss. aff.) tasty, sapid, savoury.

රසවැල්, *Rasa-węl*, *s.* rings, etc. used by dancers.

රසසය, *Rasa-saya*, *s.* (රස and සය six) the six flavours, sweet, sour, salt, bitter, pungent, astringent.

රසහර, *Rasahara*, *s.* vein, nerve, tendon, [Colloq. නහරය *naharaya*].

රසහල්, *Rasahal*, *s.* Pátála or the Nágalóka: see රසාතල *rasátala;* alligator, [Colloq. කිඹුලා *kim̱bulá*].

රසා, *Rasá*, *s.* the earth, [Colloq. පොළව *poława*]; tongue, [Colloq. දිව *diva*]; twining plant with flowers in compound umbels, *cissampelos hexandra* or *stephania rotunda; cissampelos pareira*, [Colloq. දියමිත්ත *diyamitta*]; millet, *setaria* or *panicum italica*, [Colloq. තණහාල් *tanahál*]; the frankincense tree, *boswellia thurifera* or *canarium odoriferum;* grape; drug: see කාකෝලි *kákóli*.

රසාඤ්ජන, *Rasáñjana*, *s.* (රස *rasa* juice, etc. අඤ්ජන *añjana* collyrium) sort of collyrium prepared with the calx of brass or with the *amomum anthorrhiza*.

රසාණ, *Rasáṇa*, *s.* ghee, or clarified butter, [Colloq. ගිතෙල් *gitel*].

රසාතල, *Rasátala*, *s.* (රසා earth, තල below, underneath) name of Pátála, the infernal regions, and the residence of the Nágas, Asuras, Daityas, and other races of monstrous and demoniacal beings; this is not to be confounded with naraka or tartarus, the proper hell or abode of guilty mortals after death.

රසාධාර, *Rasádhára*, *s.* (රස *rasa* water, ආධාර *ádhára* receptacle) sun, [Colloq. ඉර *ira*].

රසායන, *Rasáyana*, *s.* (රස *rasa* juice, quicksilver, අයන *ayana* road, going) medicine preventing old age and prolonging life, the elixir vitæ of the alchymists; butter milk; alchymy, chemistry; anthelmintic drug, [Colloquial: වලගසාල් *walan̲gasál*]; *embelia ribes*, [Colloq. වැල්ඇඹිල්ල *wel-em̱billa*]; alchymist.

රසාල, *Rasála*, *s.* (රස *rasa* juice, ආ *á* before, ලා *lá* to yield) sugar cane, *saccharum officinarum*, [Colloq. උක්ගස් *uk-gas*]; mango tree, *mangifera indica*, [Colloq. අඹ *am̱ba*]; jak tree, *artocarpus integrifolia*, [Colloq. කොස් *kos*]; olibanum tree, *boswellia thurifera;* see රසා *rasá:* wheat; frankincense; gum myrrh.

රසාලසා, *Rasálasá*, *s.* tubular vessel of the body, tendon, nerve.

රසාලා, *Rasálá*, *s.* tongue; grape; curds mixed up with sugar and spices; bent grass, *panicum dactylon;* flower, *hedysarum gangeticum*.

රසාහර, *Rasáhara*, *s.* (රස *rasa* taste, flavour, අහර *ahara* food) savoury food.

රසු, *Rasu*, *s.* small bells.

රසුවන්, *Rasuwan*, *s.* gold, [Colloq. රත්රන් *ratran*].

රසුවැල, *Rasuwęla*, *s.* girdle of small bells.

රසේන්ද්‍ර, *Raséndra*, *s.* (රස *rasa* mineral, ඉන්ද්‍ර *indra* best) quicksilver; philosopher's stone, the touch of which turns iron into gold.

රසෝන, *Rasóna*, } *s.* garlic, *allium sativum*,
රසෝනක, *Rasónaka*, } [Colloq. හෙලලූනු *helaluhunu* or සුදුලූනු *sudu-lúnu*].

රහ, *Raha*, *s.* solitariness, privacy; sweetness; taste, flavour; toddy; spirituous liquor.

රහත්, *Rahat*, *s.* Elu form of **අර්හත්** *arhát*, order of Buddhistical saints, such as have so far subdued kléṣa or passion, as to be delivered from further transmigration: see **ක්ලේශ** *kléṣa*: *a.* venerable respected, fit or worthy of being worshipped.

රහත්ගුණය, *Rahat-guṇaya*, *s.* (රහත් and ගුණ *guṇa* property) state or quality of a Rahat.

රහත්භාවය, *Rahat-bháwaya*, *s.* state of an Arhat or Buddhist saint.

රහත්වෙනවා, *Rahatwenawá*, *v.* to attain sanctification; to disappear.

රහතුන්, *Rahatun*, *plur. acc.* of රහත් *rahat*.

රහදිය, *Rahadiya*, *s.* quicksilver, mercury.

රහදිව, *Rahadiwa*, *s.* (රහ taste, දිව tongue) uvula, small tongue at the top of the throat, tonsil.

රහස්, *Rahas*, *s.* (රහ *raha* to abandon society,) solitariness, privacy; copulation; privity; religious or mystic truth: *a.* secret, hidden, concealed, unknown, not public, private: *ad.* solitary, private, in private, secretly, privily.

රහස්‍ය, *Rahasya*, *s.* secret, mystery, any thing hidden, recondite, or mysterious: *a.* private, secret, either fit to be concealed or occurring in secret.

රහස, *Rahasa*, *s.* secret, mystery, any thing hidden or recondite; ocean; heaven: pl. රහස් *rahas*.

රහසිගත, *Rahasigata*, *a.* (රහසි in secret, ගත gone) secret, private, alone.

රහසොඬ, *Rahasoṇḍa*, *s.* (රහ liquor, සොඬ addicted to) drunkard, [Colloq. බේබද්ද *bébaddá*].

රහිත, *Rahita*, *s.* (රහ *raha* to quit, to lose) left, quit, abandoned; without, free from, not possessed of, [Colloq. නැති *neti*].

රහුගෙඩි, *Rahugeḍi*, *s.* small bell or tinkling ornament used by dancers: see ගෙජ්ජි *gejja*.

රහෝගත, *Rahógata*, see රහසිගත *rahasigata*.

රළු, *Raḷu*, *a.* mischievous, harsh, vile; rough, cruel.

රළුකම, *Raḷukama*, *s.* roughness.

රා, *Rá*, *s.* (රු *ru* to sound) toddy, liquor extracted from the coconut tree prior to distillation; sound, noise, [Colloq. ශබ්දය *ṣabdaya*]; ray of the sun, [Colloq. රශ්මිය *raṣmiya*]; love, affection, [Colloq. ආදරය *ádaraya*]; passion, desire, [Colloq. ආශාව *áṣáwa*]; name of Káma the Indian Cupid; name of Ráhu the ascending node; sprite, demon, goblin, [Colloq. රාක්ෂයා *rákshayá*].

රාඔඩම, *Ráoḍama*, *s.* (රා liquor, ඔඩම vessel) drinking vessel, cup for drinking liquor out of: pl. රාඔඩම් *ráoḍam*.

රාක්කෙ, *Rákke*, *s.* cupboard, shelf: pl. රාක්ක *rákka*.

රාක්ෂයා, *Rákshayá*, corruptly for රාක්ෂසයා *rákshasayá*.

රාක්ෂස, *Rákshasa*, *s.* (රක්ෂ් *rakshas* demon, අන් *an* aff.) evil spirit, demon, vampire: fiend, but who appears to be of various descriptions and is either a powerful Titan or an enemy of the gods in a superhuman or incarnate form, as Rávaṇa and others; mischievous and cruel goblin or ogre, haunting cemeteries, animating dead bodies, and devouring human beings; surgery, cure by the knife or cautery; forty-ninth year of the Indian cycle: *a.* infernal, demoniacal.

රාක්ෂසයා, *Rákshasayá*, *s.* goblin, etc: see the last.

රාක්ෂසේන්ද්‍ර, *Rákshaséndra*, *s.* (රාක්ෂස *rákshasa* demon, ඉන්ද්‍ර *indra* chief) name of Rávaṇa; Kuwéra.

රාක්ෂා, *Ráksha*, *s.* wax, glue, any glutinous or gummy substance exuding from trees, [Colloq. ලාකඩ *lákaḍa*]; lac, red, animal dye.

රාග, *Rága*, *s.* (රඤ්ජ *rañja* to be attached to, to colour, etc.) affection, love, desire; lust, passion; quality or property of passion; mental affection in general, as sorrow, joy; mode of music, six of which are enumerated; colour, hue, tint, dye.

රාගචරිතය, *Rága-charitaya*, *s.* (රාග passion, චරිත *charita* pursuing) worldliness, sensuality, giving free scope to the passions.

රාගචූර්ණ, *Rága-chúrṇa*, *s.* (රාග colour, චූර්ණ powder) kind of red or yellow powder, which is used to rub the body after bathing; red powder thrown over one another by the Hindus at the vernal festival.

රාගචේතනාව, *Rága-chétanáwa*, *s.* (රාග lust, චේතනාව thought) evil passion, unholy or sinful desire.

රාගද, *Rágadá*, *s.* (රාග colour, ද what gives) crystal.

රාගම, *Rágama*, *s.* (රඤ්ජ *rañja* to please, to delight) mode of music, six of which are enumerated; song ballad: play-ball made of rattan: pl. රාගම් *rágam*.

රාගය, *Rágaya*, see රාග *rága*.

රාගාස්වාදය, *Rágáswádaya*, *s.* (රාග *rága* passion, ආස්වාද *áswáda* enjoying) voluptuousness, sensuality; gratification of sensual desire.

රාගිණී, *Rágiṇí*, *s.* modification of a musical mode, of which five are assigned to each mode.

රාගින්, *Rágin*, *a.* (රාග *rúga* passion, etc. ඉනි *ini* aff.) passionate, impassioned; coloring, dyeing, painting.

රාගී, *Rágí*, *s.* lover, gallant, libertine; dyer, painter.

රාඞ්කව, *Ráṅkawa*, *s.* (රඞ්කු *raṅku* kind of deer, අණ් *aṇ* aff.) woollen cloth made of the hair of a deer or any other animal.

රාජ්‍ය, *Rájya*, *s.* government, country, principality, kingdom; administration or exercise of sovereignty or government.

රාජ්‍යාඞ්ග, *Rájyáṅga*, *s.* (රාජ්‍ය *rájya* royalty, අඞ්ග *aṅga* limb or member) requisite of royal administration, eight of which are enumerated; namely, 1. the monarch, 2. the prime minister, 3. a friend or ally, 4. treasure, 5. territory, 6. a stronghold, 7. an army, 8. population.

රාජ්‍යාධිකාර, *Rájyádhikára*, *s.* government of a kingdom; title to sovereignty.

රාජ, *Rája*, *s.* (රාජ to shine) king, sovereign, monarch; moon: *a.* monarchial; (In composition) royal, eminent, excellent.

රාජක, *Rájaka*, *s.* (රාජ prince, ක aff.) plant, [Colloq. කරඹ *karamba*]: *a.* ruling, splendid, irradiating.

රාජකාරිය, *Rájakáriya*, *s.* king's service, official duty, compulsory labour.

රාජකීය, *Rájakíya*, *s.* royal, kingly.

රාජකුමාරයා, *Rája-kumárayá*, *s.* (රාජ and කුමාර *kumára* child) son of a king, prince royal.

රාජ කුමාරී, *Rája-kumárí*, *s.* princess.

රාජකුල, *Rája-kula*, see රාජවංශය *rája-wanṣaya.*

රාජ කෝෂාතකී, *Rája-kósháṭakí*, *s.* creeper, *luffa acutangula*, [Colloq. වැටකොළු *weṭakoḷu*].

රාජ කැස්වටුවා. *Rája-keswaṭuwá*, *s.* the painted snipe, *rhynchæa capensis (Scolopacidæ* order *Grallæ).*

රාජගුරු, *Rája-guru*, see රජගුරු *raja-guru.*

රාජගෘහ, *Rája-gṛiha*, *s.* (රාජ king, ගෘහ house or ග්‍රහ *graha* to seize) palace, royal residence; city so called, commonly Rajagaha, said to be in the vicinity of Benares, and anciently the seat of various kings, as its name implies.

රාජ ජම්බු, *Rája-jambu*, *s.* tree, *eugenia jambolana*, [Colloq. මාදම් *mádam* or මහදම් *maha-dam*].

රාජතේජස්, *Rája-téjas*, *s.* majesty, kingly dignity.

රාජ දන්ත, *Rája-danta*, *s.* (රාජ royal, දන්ත tooth) upper and fore tooth, applied to the two middle teeth.

රාජදර්ශන, *Rája-darṣana*, *s.* levee, audience.

රාජදේශිය, *Rájadéṣiya*, *s.* petty prince.

රාජද්‍රෝහ, *Rája-dróha*, *s.* (රාජ and ද්‍රෝහ violence) rebellion, treason.

රාජද්‍රෝහී, *Rája-dróhi*, *s.* traitor, rebel.

රාජධන, *Rája-dhana*, *s.* royal revenue or wealth.

රාජ ධර්මය, *Rája-dharmaya*, see දශරාජධර්ම *daṣarája-dharma.*

රාජ ධාන්‍ය, *Rája-dhánya*, *s.* (රාජ and ධාන්‍ය grain) sort of grain, *panicum frumentaceum.*

රාජධාන, *Rájadhána*, } *s.* (රාජ king, ධාන or ධානි
රාජධානි, *Rájadháni*, } holding, containing) royal city, capital, metropolis.

රාජන්, *Rájan*, *s.* king, sovereign, prince; soldier by birth, man of the regal and military tribe; master; moon; name of Indra: *a.* (in composition) royal, denoting pre-eminence or excellence.

රාජනයා, *Rája-nayá*, *s.* cobra capella, *naga tripudians.*

රාජනිර්යාස, *Raja-niryása*, *s.* (රාජ royal, නිර්යාස gum) sort of gum, frankincense; tree, *vateria acuminata*, [Colloq. හල්ගස් *hal-gas*].

රාජනීති, *Rája-níti*, *s.* regal polity, civil and military government.

රාජනීල, *Rája-níla*, *s.* (රාජ and නීල green) emerald.

රාජපුත්‍ර, *Rája-putra*, *s.* (රාජ king or moon, පුත්‍ර son) planet Mercury; name of the military tribe, soldier by profession; son of a king, prince.

රාජපුත්‍රී, *Rája-putrí*, *s.* bitter gourd, variety of *cucurbita* or *lagenaria*, [Colloq. තිත්ත ලබු *titta-labu*].

රාජපුරුෂ, *Rája-purusha*, *s.* (රාජ king, පුරුෂ man) king's messenger; one in the service of a king.

රාජපුෂ්ප, *Rája-pushpa*, *s.* (රාජ royal, පුෂ්ප flower) flower of the iron wood tree, *mesua ferrea*, [Colloq. නා *ná*].

රාජබලා, *Rája-balá*, *s.* creeping plant, *ipomœa tridentata* or *angustifolia*, [Colloq. අපසුමදු *ápasu-madu*].

රාජභෘත්‍ය, *Rája-bhṛitya*, *s.* (රාජ king, භෘත්‍ය servant) servant of a king; any public officer, courtier.

රාජභවනය, *Rája-bhawanaya*, *s.* (රාජ royal, භවන *bhawana* residence) palace, royal residence.

රාජභාණ්ඩය, *Rája-bháṇḍaya*, *s.* (රාජ king, භාණ්ඩ *bháṇḍa* an article) insignia or paraphernalia of royalty, *i. e.* sword, white umbrella, golden diadem, golden slippers and the chámara or white whisk made from the tail of the *bos grunniens.*

රජමාර්ග, *Rája-márga*, *s.* (රජ royal, මාර්ග road) royal road passable for elephants and horses, and forty cubits broad.

රජමාෂ, *Rája-másha*, *s.* (රජ and මාෂ kidney bean) kind of bean, variety of *dolichos* or *phaseolus*, [Colloq. උඳු *un̥du*].

රජමුද්ග, *Rája-mudga*, *s.* (රජ and මුද්ග phaseolus mungo) sort of kidney bean, *phaseolus*.

රජයක්ෂ්ම, *Rája-yakshma*, *s.* (රජ chief, යක්ෂ්ම phthisis) pulmonary consumption.

රජර්ෂි, *Rájarshi*, *s.* (රජ + ඍෂි) royal or eminent saint or sage.

රජරජ, *Rája-rája*, *s.* (රජ yaksha or king) name of Kuvéra; emperor, universal monarch or king of kings; moon.

රජලමයා, *Rája-lamayá*, *s.* the blue and yellow sea perch, *Serranus fuscoguttatus*.

රජවංශය, *Rája-wan̥saya*, *s.* (රජ royal, වංශ *wan̥sa* race) royal race, princely descent.

රජවටුවා, *Rája-waṭuwá*, see රජ කෑස්වටුවා *rája kẹswaṭuwá*.

රජවල්ලි, *Rájawallí*, *s.* creeping plant, *momordica charantia*, [Colloq. කරවිල *karivila*].

රජවලා, *Rája-walá*, see රජබලා *rája-balá*.

රජවලිය, *Rájawaliya*, *s.* chronicles of kings; cor rupt form of රජාවලිය *rájáwaliya*.

රජවාහ, *Rája-wáha*, *s.* (රජ king, වාහ vehicle) horse, [Colloq. අශ්වයා *aṣwayá*].

රජවිධාන, *Rája-vidhána*, *s.* (රජ and විධාන injunction) royal decree; king's message.

රජවිල, *Rája-vila*, *s.* game of chess.

රජවී, *Rája-ví*, *s.* kind of paddy, variety of *oryza sativa*.

රජවෘක්ෂ, *Rája-wṛiksha*, *s.* (රජ and වෘක්ෂ tree) tree, *buchanania latifolia*, [Colloq. කිරිපළු *kiri-paḷu*]; another tree, *cassia fistula*, [Colloq. ඇහැළ *ẹhẹḷa*]; plant, pigeon pea, *cajanus indicus*, [Colloq. රටතෝර *raṭa-tóra*]; *euphorbia* of various sorts.

රජශ්‍රිය, *Rájaṣriya*, *s.* royalty, majesty, the splendour of a king.

රජශාසන, *Rája-ṣásana*, *s.* (රජ and ශාසන edict) royal edict, royal badge.

රජශෘඞ්ග, *Rája-ṣṛiṅga*, *s.* (රජ and ශෘඞ්ග horn) royal chhatra or umbrella, sort of sheat fish *silurus batachus*.

රජසභා, *Rája-sabhá*, *s.* (රජ and සභා assembly) royal assembly or council, the king's court.

රජසර්ප, *Rája-sarpa*, *s.* (රජ and සර්ප snake) large sort of snake.

රජසාරස, *Rája-sárasa*, *s.* (රජ and සාරස Indian crane) peacock, [Colloq. මොණරා *moṇará*].

රජසූය, *Rája-súya*, *s.* (රජ king, සූ *shú* to be produced or effected) sacrifice performed only by a universal monarch, attended by his tributary princes, as in the case of Yudhishṭhira and others; lotus; mountain.

රජහංස, *Rája-han̥sa*, *s.* (රජ royal, හංස goose) white goose with red legs and bill, or more properly perhaps the flamingo; drake; an excellent king.

රජා, *Rájá*, *s.* king, sovereign, prince.

රජාඞ්ගනය, *Rájáṅganaya*, *s.* (රජ *rája* king, අඞ්ගනය court yard) palace yard; court yard of a royal residence.

රජාඞ්ගය, *Rájáṅgaya*, *s.* attribute of a king.

රජාතන, *Rájátana*, *s.* tree, *buchanania latifolia*: see රජවෘක්ෂ *raja-wṛiksha*.

රජාතිරජා, *Rájátirája*, *s.* king of kings, paramount sovereign.

රජාදන, *Rájádana*, *s.* (රජ *rája* king, අදන *adana* eating) tree, *buchanania latifolia*, [Colloq. කිරිපළු *kiripaḷu*]; fruit tree, *mimusops kauki*; ornamental tree, *butea frondosa*, [Colloq. ගස්කෑල *gas-kẹla*].

රජාධිරජ, *Rájádhirája*, *s.* paramount sovereign.

රජාභරණ, *Rájábharaṇa*, *s.* regal attire, royal ornaments.

රජාභිෂේකය, *Rájábhisékaya*, *s.* (රජ *rája* king, අභිෂේක *abhiséka* anointing) the crowning and anointing of a king.

රජාර්ක, *Rájárka*, *s.* tree, white *asclepias*, [Colloq. එලවරා *ela-wará*].

රජාර්හ, *Rájárha*, *s.* (රජ *rája* and අර්හ *arha* proper) royal, noble, fit, or proper for a king; aloe wood, *aquilaria agallocha*, [Colloq. අගිල් *agil*]; also, white lead, [Colloq. සුදුඊයම් *sudu-íyam*].

රජාලියා, *Rájáliyá*, *s.* kite; eagle, name for various species of *aquilinæ* of the *falconidæ* family order *Accipitres*: viz. booted eagle, *nisaetus pennatus*; Ceylon mountain hawk eagle, *spizaetus kelaarti*; Ceylon hawk eagle, *s. ceylonesis*; Ceylonese serpent eagle, *spilornis spilogaster*; bas-tailed fish eagle, *polioaetus ichthyaetus*; Brahminy kite, *haliastur indus*; Indian pariah kite, *milons govinda*; Indian honey buzzard, *pernis ptilonorhyncus*.

රජාවලිය, *Rájáwaliya*, *s.* (රජ *rája* king, ආවලි *áwali* line) a book so called, history of the Siṇhalese kings descended from Vijaya; line of kings, royal dynasty or genealogy.

රජි, *Ráji*, *s.* row, line; unbroken row, continuous line; mustard, *brassica juncea*, [Colloq. අබ *aba*].

රජික, *Rájika*, } *s.* black mustard, *sinapis nigra*,
රජිකා, *Rájiká*, } [Colloq. අබ *aba*]; field; line, row, range.

රජිල, *Rájila*, *s.* fresh water-snake, *cerberus rhynchops*, [Colloq. දියබරියා *diyabariyá*].

රජීව, *Rájíwa*, *s.* large fish, *cyprinus niloticus;* kind of deer; elephant; lotus, *nelumbium speciosum*, [නෙළුම් *neḷum*]: *a.* attending on or living about a prince.

රජේන්ද්‍ර, *Rájéndra*, *s.* emperor.

රජෝත්තම, *Rájóttama*, *s.* emperor, universal king.

රජෝද්‍යානය, *Rájódyánaya*, *s.* (රජ and උද්‍යාන *udyána* garden) royal garden.

රට්, *Rát*, *s.* king, monarch, prince.

රාධ, *Rádha*, *s.* thorny shrub, *randia dumetorum*, [Colloq. කුකුරුමුවං *kukurumuwaṇ* or කුකුරුමාන් *kukurumán*].

රාඪා, *Ráḍhá*, *s.* country or district, part of Bengal.

රාත්තල, *Ráttala*, *s.* a pound weight: pl. රාත්තල් *ráttal*.

රාත්‍රි, *Rátri*, *s.* (රා *rá* to give pleasure or rest) night.

රාත්‍රිචර, *Rátri-chara*, *s.* (රාත්‍රි night, චර who goes) goblin, fiend, ghost or evil spirit; thief, robber; guard, patrole.

රාත්‍රිජ, *Rátrija*, *s.* (රාත්‍රි and ජ born) star, [Colloq. තාරකාව *tárakáwa*], constellation: *a.* produced at night.

රාත්‍රිජල, *Rátri-jala*, *s.* (රාත්‍රි and ජල water) dew, mist, fog.

රාත්‍රිජාගර, *Rátri-jágara*, *s.* (රාත්‍රි and ජාගර waking) keeping watch at night, sitting up at night.

රාත්‍රිංචර, *Rátriñchara*, *s.* (රාත්‍රිං *rátriṇ* and චර who goes) ghost, goblin, evil spirit.

රාත්‍රිනාථ, *Rátri-nátha*, *s.* (රාත්‍රි and නාථ lord) moon, [Colloq. හඳ *haṇda*].

රාත්‍රිභාගය, *Rátribhágaya*, *s.* night.

රාත්‍රිමණි, *Rátri-maṇi*, *s.* (රාත්‍රි and මණි jewel) moon, [Colloq. හඳ *haṇda*].

රාත්‍රිය, *Rátriya*, see රාත්‍රි *rátri*.

රාත්‍රිවේද, *Rátri-wéda*, *s.* (රාත්‍රි night, වේද who knows) cock, [Colloq. කුකුළා *kukuḷá*].

රාත්‍රිස්ථාන, *Rátristhána*, *s.* dark place, place from which the light is shut out; place where night is spent.

රාත්‍රිහාස, *Rátrihása*, *s.* (රාත්‍රි and හාස what smiles) white lotus, which blossoms at night.

රාද්ධාන්ත, *Ráddhanta*, *s.* (රාද්ධ established, අන්ත *anta* end, result) demonstrated truth, proved and established fact and conclusion.

රාධා, *Rádhá*, *s.* asterism in which the moon is full in the month wesak; the sixteenth of the nakshatras containing four stars in the shape of a festoon, favorite mistress of Kṛishṇa during his residence among the cowherds; lightning; tree, *phyllanthus emblica*, [Colloquial: නෙල්ලි *nelli*]; flowering plant, *clitoria terneata*, [Colloq. නිල් කටරොළු *nil-kaṭaroḷu*].

රාබු, *Rábu*, *s.* radish, *raphanus sativus.*

රාම, *Ráma*, *s.* name common to the three incarnations of Vishṇu, namely, first Paraṣuráma; second Ráma Chandra, in which incarnation he slew the demon race but particularly රාවණ *Ráwaṇa;* third Balaráma, which names see: name of Varuṇa, regent of the waters; a horse; sort of deer; potherb, *chenopodium album;* plant, *costus speciosus*, [Colloq. තෙබු *tebu*]; *xyris indica*, [Colloq. රන්මොටු *ranmoṭu* and රන්මනිස්ස *ranmanissa*]: *a.* black; white, beautiful, pleasing.

රාමඤ්ඤ නිකාය, *Rámañña-nikáya*, *s.* (from රාමඤ්ඤ part of Burmah near Rangoon, නිකාය a sect) a term applied to designate a sect of Buddhist priests; this sect was introduced to Ceylon about fifteen years ago by Aṃbagahawatte priest, a pupil of Atthadassi Terunnánse of the Siamese sect who resided in the Vanawása Viháre of Bentoṭa. The religious observances of the Rámañña sect are identical with those of the Amarapura sect; the only difference consists in their using talipot leaves instead of umbrellas.

රාමචන්ද්‍ර, *Rámachandra*, *s.* (රාම and චන්ද්‍ර moon, moon like Ráma) second incarnation of Vishṇu under the name of Ráma, the son of Daṣaratha king of Oude, born at the close of the second age for the purpose of destroying the demons who infested the earth, and who according to fable built Adam's bridge for the purpose of bringing his army over from the continent of India, to make war upon Ráwaṇa who by stealth had carried off his wife Sítá: see රාවණ *Ráwaṇa*.

රමඨ, *Rámaṭha*, *s.* assafætida, [Colloq. පෙරුංකායම් *peruŋkáyam*].

රමණ්ඩි, *Rá-maṇḍi*, *s.* dregs or sediments of toddy.

රමණීයක, *Rámaṇíyaka*, *a.* pleasing, delightful, beautiful.

රමතෙල්, *Rámatel*, *s.* belch.

රමදූත, *Ráma-dúta*, *s.* (රම and දූත messenger) chief of the monkey race, called Hanumán, the friend and messenger of Ráma, and who on several occasions assisted him in his wars with the demons, but especially aided him with his whole army of monkeys in building the bridge, usually calld Adam's bridge, to enable Ráma to take his army from the continent to invade Laŋká or Ceylon, for the purpose of destroying Ráwaṇa.

රමපූග, *Ráma-púga*, *s.* (රම and පූග areca) small species of the areca or betel-nut tree.

රමසේතක, *Rámasétaka*, *s.* plant, peculiar to Ceylon, *munronia pumila*, [Colloq. බිං කොහොඹ *biŋ-kohomba*].

රමා, *Rámá*, *s.* woman, beautiful or pleasing female; assafætida; river.

රමායණ, *Rámáyaṇa*, *s.* among the Hindus a celebrated epic poem recording the adventures of රම *Ráma*, which see.

රල, *Rála*, *s.* husband, master, lord; term affixed to names of titles implying respect: pl. රලලා *rálalá*.

රලබ්බ, *Rá-labba*, *s.* toddy drawer's hollowed pumpkin.

රලහාමි, *Rálahámi*, *s.* (රල and හාමි lord) title of honour, term applied to headmen: pl. රලහාමිලා *rálahámilá*.

රව, *Ráwa*, *s.* (රු *ru* to cry or sound) sound, noise in general.

රවක, *Ráwaka*, *a.* (රව sound, ක aff.) sounding, making a noise.

රවණ, *Ráwaṇa*, *s.* the celebrated giant king of Laŋká or Ceylon, at the time it was inhabited by the giant race; Ráwaṇa was slain by Ráma, in the wars which he waged for the recovery of his wife Sítá, whom Ráwaṇa had surreptitiously carried off to his capital Laŋká; he is figured in the temples as a ferocious monster with ten heads and twenty arms in each of which he holds an instrument of war.

රවණ ඇල්වි, *Ráwaṇa-ęlví*, *s.* kind of paddy, *oryza sativa*.

රවණ රැවුල, *Ráwaṇa-ręwula*, *s.* sort of grass.

රවණවි, *Ráwaṇa-ví*, *s.* kind of paddy, *oryza sativa*.

රවණරි, *Ráwaṇári*, *s.* (රවණ *ráwaṇa* and අරි *ari* enemy) the hero Ráma.

රවයකරණවා, *Ráwayakaraṇawá*, *v.* to make a sound.

රශි, *Ráṣi*, *s.* heap, collection, quantity; sign of the zodiac; arithmetical or algebraical quantity; part and its divisor, or numerator and denominator.

රශි ගෘහය, *Ráṣi-gṛihaya*, *s.* (රශි and ගෘහ *gṛiha* house) sign of the zodiac.

රශි චක්‍රය, *Ráṣi-chakraya*, *s.* (රශි and චක්‍ර *chakra* wheel, circle) zodiac.

රශිභාග, *Ráṣibhága*, *s.* (රශි and භාග part) fraction, part of a sign of the zodiac.

රශිකරණ, *Ráṣí-karaṇa*, *s.* heaping, gathering, piling up.

රෂ්ට්‍ර, *Ráshṭra*, *s.* (රජ් *rája* shine or govern, ෂ්ට්‍රන් *shṭran* aff.) country, region, inhabited or uninhabited; any public calamity, as plague, famine, etc.

රෂ්ට්‍රකා, *Ráshṭraká*, *s.* kind of night shade, *solanum indicum*, [Colloq. තිබ්බටු *tibbaṭu*].

රෂ්ට්‍රකි, *Ráshṭrakí*, *s.* species of night shade, *solanum xanthocarpum*, [Colloq. එලබටු *elabaṭu*].

රෂ්ට්‍රිකා, *Ráshṭriká*, *s.* kind of night shade, *solanum jacquini*, [Colloq. කටුවැල්බටු *kaṭuwęlbaṭu*].

රෂ්ණඵලා, *Ráshṇa-phalá*, *s.* tree, *buchanania latifolia*, [Colloq. කිරිපළු *kiripaḷu*].

රස්නා, *Rásná*, *s.* shrub, *mimosa octandra*, [Colloq. අරත්ත *aratta*]; twining plant, *rauwolfia serpentina*, or *ophioxylon*, [Colloq. එකාවේරිය *ekáwériya*].

රස්සයා, *Rássayá*, *s.* corruptly for රාක්ෂසයා *rákshasayá*, which see.

රස, *Rása*, *s.* confused noise, uproar, hubbub; secret, more correctly written රහස *rahasa*: pl. රස් *rás*.

රසල, *Rásala*, *s.* (රා liquor, සල house, or රස from රස *rasa* juice, ලා *lá* to yield) any place where spirituous or vinous liquor is sold; sugar cane.

රසි, *Rási*, see රශි *ráṣi*.

රසිභූත, *Rásibhúta*, *a.* (රසි heap, භූත become) collected, gathered together.

රසිය, *Rásiya*, *s.* great number of any thing; sign of the zodiac: see රශි *ráṣi*.

රසොඬ, *Rásoṇḍa*, *s.* (රා liquor, සොඬ attached) drunkard, tippler, [Colloq. බේබද්දා *bébaddá*].

රහල, *Rá-hala*, *s.* (රා and හල hall) place where toddy is sold; tavern.

රාහු, *Ráhu*, *s.* the ascending node; according to the mythology of the Hindus, the son of Sinhiká, a Daitya with the tail of a dragon, whose head Vishṇu severed from his body in his wars with the demons or Daityas whom he came to destroy in his incarnation of Rámachandra; but Ráhu being immortal, the head and tail retained their separate existence, and being transferred to the stellar sphere, became the authors of eclipses; the first especially, by endeavouring at various times to swallow the sun and moon. According to the mythology of the Buddhists, Ráhu was a noted Asura inhabiting Pátála or the Nágalóka; when the gods assembled to churn the sea, and produce the nectar or water of life, Ráhu secretly conveyed himself to the spot and surreptitiously obtained a draught by which he became immortal: the sun and the moon who where present on this occasion as overlookers and guards of the nectar reported this to Vishṇu, who severed Ráhu's body in two; but he having become immortal by the draught of the nectar, his head and trunk retained their separate existence, and being transferred, the head to the north, and the tail, Kétu, to the south, they became the ascending and descending nodes; but retaining their feelings of revenge towards the sun and moon for the discovery they made to Vishṇu, they attempt, especially Ráhu, at certain seasons, to destroy them, and the seizure of them in his mouth is the cause of eclipses.

රාහු අසුරේන්ද්‍රයා, *Ráhu-asuréndrayá*, see රාහු *ráhu.*

රාහු අල්ලනවා, *Ráhu-allanawá*, *v.* to be seized by Ráhu, to eclipse.

රාහුග්‍රහ. *Ráhu-graha*, *s.* (රාහු and ග්‍රහ to seize) eclipse of the sun or moon: see රාහු *ráhu.*

රාහු මුඛය, *Ráhu-mukhaya*, *s.* (රාහු *Ráhu* like, මුඛ *mukha* mouth) punishment inflicted on criminals, in which the tongue is forced out and wrapped in cloth soaked in oil and set on fire.

රාහු සංස්පර්ශ, *Ráhu-sansparṣa*, *s.* (රාහු and සංස්පර්ශ seizure, contact) eclipse: see රාහු *ráhu.*

රිංගනවා, *Ringanawá*, *v.* to creep, to move on all fours: pret. රිංගුවා *ringuwá.*

රික්ත, *Rikta*, *a.* (රිච *richa* to void, by stool, ක්ත aff.) void, empty; poor, indigent.

රික්තා, *Riktá*, *s.* fourth, ninth, or fourteenth days of a lunar fortnight: see රිට්ටා *riṭṭá.*

රික්ථ, *Riktha*, *s.* substance, property, wealth.

රික්ෂා, *Rikshá*, *s.* nit; mote in a sunbeam.

රික, *Rika*, *s.* (for රුක *ruka*) tree in general, [Colloq. ගහ *gaha*]; star, constellation; heart, mind; law, litigation.

රිකිල්ල, *Rikilla*, *s.* small branch, sprig, twig; grain in wood: pl. රිකිලි *rikili.*

රිඞ්ගණ, *Riṅgaṇa*, *s.* (රිගි *rigi* to go) creeping (as a child on all fours); slipping, sliding, stumbling; figuratively, deviating from rectitude or virtue.

රිට්ටාව, *Riṭṭáwa*, *s.* first and the fourth day after each quarter of the moon considered to be unlucky: the 4th and 19th days in a lunar month are called ජලවක රිට්ටා *jalawaka-riṭṭá;* the 9th and 24th නවවක රිට්ටා *nawawaka-riṭṭá;* the 14th and 29th තුදුස්වක රිට්ටා *tuduswaka-riṭṭá;* also written රික්තා *riktá.*

රිට්ටාහතු, *Riṭṭá-hatu*, *s.* mushroom.

රිට, *Riṭa*, *s.* long pole used instead of an oar in boats; horizontal sticks in a fence.

රිට බුලත්වැල්, *Riṭa-bulatwel*, *s.* climbing plant, with tendrils and small greenish-purple flowers, black leaves, *vitis (*or *cissus) erioclada* or *indica (Ampeli-deæ);* also called තෝවැල් *tówel.*

රිටි, *Riṭi*, *s.* crackling or roaring of flame; musical instrument; black salt; long pole used instead of an oar; tree allied to the Upas of Java, sacks are made from the inner bark, *antiaris innoxia (Urticaceæ).*

රිටිගහ, *Riṭi-gaha*, *s.* Upas tree.

රිටු, *Riṭu*, *s.* crow, [Colloq. කපුටා *kapuṭá*].

රිත්, *Rit*, *s.* vacuity, vacuum: *a.* empty, void.

රිද්දනවා, *Riddanawá*, *v.* to hurt: pret. රිද්දුවා *ridduwá.*

රිදී, *Ridí*, *s.* silver.

රිදුම, *Riduma*, *s.* pain, aching, smarting.

රිදෙනවා, *Ridenawá*, *v.* (රුජ *ruja* to ache) to feel pain, to hurt, to ache: pret. රිදුනා *riduná.*

රිපු, *Ripu*, *s.* enemy, adversary, [Colloq. සතුරා *saturá*].

රිය, *Riya*, *s.* car, chariot; waggon, any four-wheeled vehicle: wife of Anaṅgayá the Indian Cupid; bird.

රිය ඉස, *Riya-isa*, *s.* head covering or hood of a car.

රියග, *Riyaga*, } *s.* (රිය and අඞ්ග *aṅga* limb, member) wheel of a chariot; ruddy goose, commonly called in India, the Brahmany duck or goose, *Anas casaca.*
රියඟ, *Riyaṅga*, }

රියදර, *Riyadara*, } *s.* (රිය chariot, ඇදුරු *eduru*
රියදුරු, *Riyaduru*, } master) charioteer, coachman; name of Ṣiva.

රියන, *Riyana*, *s.* cubit: see රතන *ratana*: pl. රියන් *riyan*.

රියමඬල, *Riya-maṇḍala*, *s.* (රිය carriage, මඬල circle) circle or enclosure formed of carriages.

රියසම, *Riya-sam*, *s.* (රිය car, සම skin) any part of a carriage, hide or leather placed on.

රියසරි, *Riya-sari*, *s.* (රිය and සරි who goes) coachman.

රියහිමි, *Riya-himi*, *s.* (රිය wife of Anańga, හිමි lord) name of Anańgayá the Indian Cupid.

රිරි, *Rirí*, *s.* pale brass, or prince's metal.

රිල්ල, *Rilla*, *s.* plant, not ascertained; shoal of fish.

රිල්ලවැරැල්ල, *Rilla-węręlla*, *s.* shield fern, *aspidium unitum*.

රිවි, *Riri*, *s.* sun, [Colloq. ඉර *ira*]: see රවි *ravi*.

රිවිගොත්, *Rivigot*, *s.* (රිවි and ගොත් race) solar race or dynasty.

රිවිදූ, *Rividú*, *s.* (රිවි sun, දූ daughter) river Jumná which rises in the south of the Himálaya range of mountains at a short distance to the north west of the source of the Ganges, and which after a course of about 878 miles falls into that river immediately below Allahabad.

රිවිපිත්, *Rivi-pit*, *s.* (රිවි and පිත් son) Saturn; name of the Indian Pluto, judge of hell; he is often identified with Death and Time, [Colloq. යමරජ *yama-raja*].

රිවිපුත්, *Rivi-put*, *s.* (රිවි and පුත් son) regent of the planet Saturn, [Colloq. සෙනසුරා *senasurá*]: see රිවිපිත් *rivi-pit*.

රිවිමග, *Rivi-maga*, *s.* (රිවි and මග path) firmament, visible heavens, [Colloq. අහස *ahasa*]; sun's path.

රිවි මඬල, *Rivi-maṇḍala*, *s.* (රිවි and මඬල disc) disc of the sun.

රිවිමුදුන්, *Rivi-mudun*, *s.* (රිවි and මුදුන් summit) midday, meridian, [Colloq. ඉරමුදුන් වේලාව *iramudun-wéláwa*].

රිවිරියසැරි, *Rivi-riyasęri*, *s.* (රිවි and රියසැරි charioteer) name of Aruṇa; sun's charioteer.

රිවිවත්, *Riviwat*, *s.* sky, [Colloq. අහස *ahasa*].

රිවිවස්, *Rivi-was*, *s.* (රිවි and වස් residence) Súrya's palace.

රිවිහිමි, *Rivi-himi*, *s.* (රිවි and හිමි master) lotus; flower, *pentapetes phœnicea*.

රිෂ්ට, *Rishṭa*, *s.* happiness, prosperity; good luck, fortune; bad luck, ill fortune; destruction, loss, privation; sin; sword; soap plant; demon destroyed by Vishṇu: *a.* hurt, injured, unlucky; lucky.

රිෂ්ටි, *Rishṭi*, *s.* sword; prosperity, good luck, good fortune.

රිෂ්‍ය, *Rishya*, *s.* deer, [Colloq. මුවා *muwá*].

රිෂ්‍යකේතු, *Rishya-ketu*, *s.* (රිෂ්‍ය and කේතු banner) name of Anańgayá the Indian Cupid.

රිෂ්‍යගන්ධා, *Rishyagandhá*, *s.* potherb, *convolvulus argenteus*, from ඍෂ්‍යගන්ධා *ṛishyagandhá*.

රිෂි, *Rishi*, *s.* saint; shrub, screw pine, *pandanus fascicularis* or *p. odoratissimus*, [Colloq. මුදු කෙයියා *múdu-keyiyá*].

රිස්ස, *Rissa*, *s.* strength; desire: pl. රිස්සුන් *rissun*.

රිස්සුන්, *Rissun*, *s.* wish, desire; avarice.

රිසභ, *Risabha*, commonly written ඍෂභ *ṛishabha*, *s.* bull, [Colloq. ගොණා *goṇá*]; drug described as a root resembling the horn of a bull, produced on the Himálaya mountains, of cooling and tonic properties, and serviceable in catarrh and consumption: *a.* best, excellent, preeminent.

රිසි, *Risi*, *s.* wish, desire; covetousness, avariciousness: *a.* desirous.

රිසිවුම, *Risiwum*, *s.* desire.

රිලවා, *Rilawá*, *s.* common brown monkey of Ceylon, *macacus pileatus*: pl. රිළව් *riḷaw*.

රිළා නියදඬු, *Riḷá-niyadaṇḍu*, *s.* plant, not ascertained.

රිළා පුරුක්, *Riḷá-puruk*, *s.* plant, variety of *asystasia coromandeliana*.

රිළා රත්තණ, *Riḷá-rattaṇa*, *s.* species of hill grass.

රීති, *Ríti*, *s.* usage, custom, practice; brass, rust of iron, calx of brass.

රීතිපුෂ්ප, *Ríti-pushpa*, *s.* (රීති and පුෂ්ප flower) clax of brass.

රීප්ප, *Ríppa*, *s.* laths.

රීප්ප වැට, *Ríppa-węṭa*, *s.* railed fence of a garden.

රීරියකා, *Ríri-yaká*, *s.* a devil, so called.

රීස්කා, *Ríska*, *s.* striped cloth.

රුඅරු, *Ruaru*, *s.* festal car, chariot used only on great occasions.

රුක්, *Ruk*, *s.* trees in general, [Colloq. ගස් *gas*]; sorrow, affliction; pain disease.

රුක් අත්තන, *Ruk-attana*, *s.* tree, *alstonia (or echites) scholaris, (Apocynaceæ)*.

රුක් කෙසෙල්, *Ruk-kesel*, *s.* kind of plantain, *musa sapientum*.

රුක්ඛමූලිකාඞ්ග, *Rukkha-múlikanga*, *s.* (රුක්ඛ tree, මූල *múla* root with ඉක *ika* aff. අඞ්ග *anga* ordinance) ordinance of the Buddhist priesthood which enjoins it upon the priests to reside under trees or at the roots of trees in forests; they are neither to build houses nor to use any artificial covering, whatever the weather may be to which they are exposed: see තෙලෙස්ධුතාඞ්ග *teḷesdhutánga*.

රුක්ගස, *Ruk-gasa*, *s.* tree, peculiar to Ceylon, it produces a very fragrant flower from its trunk, *myristica horsfieldia* or *horsfieldia odorata (Myristicaceæ)*.

රුක්දෙවි, *Ruk-devi*, *s.* sort of demon or goblin residing in trees; sylvan deity.

රුක්පෙනෙල, *Ruk-penela*, *s.* soap-berry plant, *sapindus emarginatus*: see පෙනෙල *penela*.

රුක්ම, *Rukma*, *s.* gold; iron.

රුක්ෂ, *Ruksha*, *a.* rough, harsh, unkind; hard; rugged, uneven.

රුක්සිදුර, *Ruk-sidura*, *s.* hollow in a tree.

රුක, *Ruka*, *s.* tree in general, [Colloq. ගහ *gaha*]; liberal man.

රුකඟුන, *Rukanguna*, *s.* plant, *hoya* of which there are several species and varieties in Ceylon.

රුකු, *Ruku*, *s.* tree in general: see රුක් *ruk*.

රුකුල, *Rukula*, *s.* prop, stay, support, exertion, made to swing: pl. රුකුල් *rukul*.

රුග්න, *Rugna*, *a.* diseased, sick, infirm, bent, broken, crooked.

රුචක, *Ruchaka*, *s.* citron, *citrus medica*, [Colloq. ලප්නාරං *lapnáran*]; ornament of the neck or breast; tooth; salt, natron, alkali, [Colloq. පුස්කර *puskara*]; borax, [Colloq. සුවස ලුණු *suwasa-luṇu*]; garland, chaplet; woody-cassia; auspicious or fortunate object; anthelmintic medicine, *embelia ribes*, [Colloq. වල් අඹිල්ල *wel-embilla*]; castor oil plant, *ricinus communis*, [Colloq. එඬරු *endaru*]; marking nut tree, *semecarpus gardneri*, [Colloq. බදුල්ල *badulla*]; sort of temple; stomachic: *a.* agreeable, pleasing; sharp, acrid; tonic, stomachic.

රුචි, *Ruchi*, *s.* light, lustre; beauty; passion; wish, desire; ray of light; intent application to any object or undertaking; hunger, appetite: *a.* wishful, desirous, having appetite.

රුචිර, *Ruchira*, *a.* beautiful, charming, pleasing; sweet; stomachic, restorative.

රුජ්, *Ruj*, *s.* sickness, disease.

රුජාකර, *Rujákara*, *s.* (රුජා sickness, කර what makes) acid fruit, *averrhoa carambola*, [Colloq. කාමරංගා *kámarangá*]: *a.* making sick or ill.

රුජාව, *Rujáwa*, *s.* (රුජ *ruja* to hurt or make sick) pain, ache; sickness, disease; overthrow, destruction, [Colloq. රිදුම *riduma*, වේදනාව *wédanáwa*]: රුජා *rujá*.

රුණ්ඩ, *Runḍa*, *s.* headless body retaining life and mixing in combat.

රුත, *Ruta*, *s.* cry, noise, sound, cry of birds.

රුතඟ, *Rutanga*, *s.* sea, ocean, [Colloq. මූද *múda*].

රුති, *Ruti*, *s.* wish, desire, [Colloq. කැමැත්ත *kemetta*].

රුද්ධ, *Ruddha*, *a.* (රුධ *rudha* to enclose) surrounded, begirt as with a fence or river; secured, protected from access; obstructed, stopped, shut up; opposed, impeded.

රුද්‍යමාන, *Rudyamána*, *s.* weeping or wailing.

රුද්‍ර, *Rudra*, *s.* (රුද *ruda* to weep) sixth lunar mansion; name or form of Ṣiva; demigod, inferior manifestation of Ṣiva, or according to one legend, a being sprung from the forehead of Brahma; the Rudras are eleven in number; also, tree, *ægle marmelos*, [Colloq. බෙලි *beli*].

රුද්‍රපුෂ්ප, *Rudra-pushpa*, *s.* linseed; shoe flower, *hibiscus rosa-sinensis*, [Colloq. වදමල් *wadamal*].

රුද්‍රවල්ලි, *Rudra-walli*, *s.* (රුද්‍ර Ṣiva, වල්ලි creeper) sort of creeping plant, not ascertained.

රුද්‍රාක්ෂ, *Rudráksha*, *s.* tree, *elæocarpus serratus*, [Colloq. වෙරළු *weraḷu*].

රුද්‍රාණි, *Rudráni*, *s.* name of the goddess Párwatí, the wife of Ṣiva.

රුද්‍රාරි, *Rudrári*, *s.* Káma, the deity of love.

රුදා, *Rudá*, *s.* pain, ache; disease, affliction; sorrow.

රුදාරූපා, *Rudárupá*, *s.* plantain or banana tree, [Colloq. කෙසෙල් *kesel*].

රුදාව, *Rudáwa*, see රුදා *rudá*.

රුදිත, *Rudita*, *s.* (රුද *ruda* to cry, ඉත *ita* aff.) weeping, crying, wept.

රුදු, *Rudu*, *s.* name of Kuvéra, the Indian Pluto: *a.* great, big, bulky; cruel, fierce, severe; old.

රුදුමග, *Rudu-maga*, *s.* rough road.

රුදුරු, *Ruduru*, *s.* name of Íṣwara or Ṣiva: see රුද්‍ර *rudra*: *a.* cruel, rough, harsh.

රුධිර, *Rudhira*, *s.* blood; saffron; planet Mars.

රුධිරනාමක, *Rudhira-námaka*, *s.* (රුධිර blood, නාම name, ක aff.) saffron, *curcuma longa*, [Colloq. කහ *kaha*]; tree, *swietenia febrefuga*, [Colloq. කොකුම් *kokum*].

රුපියල, *Rupiyala*, s. rupee: pl. රුපියල් *rupiyal.*

රුපු, *Rupu*, s. enemy, adversary, [Colloq. සතුරා *saturá*].

රුචුක, *Rucuka*, } s. castor oil plant, *ricinus communis*, [Colloq. එඩරු *eṇḍaru*].
රුබූක, *Rubúka*, }

රුයිත, *Ruyita*, s. name of a playing card, diamonds. (Dutch.)

රුරු, *Ruru*, s. sort of deer.

රුලං, *Rulan*, s. coarse flour of wheat. (Portuguese.)

රුව, *Ruwa*, s. image; beauty, comeliness.

රුවන්, *Ruwan*, s. gems or gold.

රුවන් ඇල්වී, *Ruwan-elví*, s. kind of hill paddy, *oryza sativa.*

රුවන් රැස, *Ruwan-resa*, s. heap of gems or gold.

රුවන්වී, *Ruwan-ví*, s. kind of paddy.

රුවන් සෝලු, *Ruwan-sólu*, s. staff set with gems, golden wand; wreath of gold.

රුවන, *Ruwana*, s. gem, jewel in general; gold: pl. රුවන් *ruwan.*

රුවනකර, *Ruwanakara*, s. (රුවන් *ruwan* gem, අකර *akara* mine) sea, ocean, [Colloq. මූද *múda*]: mine.

රුවනවා, *Ruwanawá*, v. to thrust in.

රුවල්ගහනවා, *Ruwalgahanawá*, v. to sail, to spread sail.

රුවල, *Ruwala*, s. sail: pl. රුවල් *ruwal.*

රුවාරූ, *Ruwárú*, s. (රූ *rú* form and අරූ *arú* no form, with ව *wa* inserted, and the first vowel made short) beauty and deformity: *a.* corporeal and incorporeal; with form and without form.

රුවූ, *Ruwú*, see රුබූක *rubúka.*

රුවැති, *Ruweti*, a. comely.

රුෂ්, *Rush*, s. (රුෂ *rusha* to be angry) anger, wrath, passion, [Colloq. කෝපය *kópaya*].

රුස්සනවා, *Russanawá*, v. to relish, to bear, to enjoy, to delight in, to like: pret. රිස්සුවා *rissuwá.*

රුස, *Rusa*, s. quiver.

රුසි, *Rusi*, s. holy or religious person, ascetic, from ඍෂි *rishi.*

රුසියා, *Rusiyá*, s. ascetic, religious ascetic.

රුසිරු, *Rusiru*, a. beautiful, handsome, elegant, agreeable.

රුහ, *Ruha*, a. growing, springing up from seed, as a tree; mounted, ascended; produced.

රුහා, *Ruhá*, s. bent grass, *panicum dactylon.*

රුහිර, *Ruhira*, s. blood, [Colloq. ලේ *lé*].

රූ, *Rú*, s. gold; image; likeness, representation; form, figure; hair of the head; colour; ornament, decoration: silver.

රූක්ෂ, *Rúksha*, s. (රූක්ෂ to be hard or rough) any large tree, tree in general: *a.* harsh, unkindly, unfriendly; rough, not smooth or soft; rough to the taste, not bland or sapid.

රූක්ෂ ගුණය, *Rúksha-guṇaya*, s. (රූක්ෂ and ගුණ *guṇa* quality) harsh temper, ferocious disposition.

රූකඩය, *Rúkaḍaya*, s. (රූ and කඩ *kaḍa* miniature) puppet, image, dancing doll: pl. රූකඩ *rúkaḍa.*

රූකඩ නටනවා, *Rúkaḍa-naṭanawá*, v. to shew puppets.

රූඪ, *Rúḍha*, a. (රුහ *ruha* to be born, ක්ත *kta* aff.) born, produced; famous, notorious; certain, ascertained; budded, blown; traditional, conventional, or known, applied especially to words of foreign and unknown origin, but of which the employment and application are familiar.

රූඪි, *Rúḍhi*, s. traditional or customary meaning of words, as opposed to their etymological signification. It is applied to words of foreign or uncertain origin, and incapable of etymological analysis.

රූණ තම්පලා, *Rúṇa-tampalá*, s. plant, *amaranthus paniculatus* or *frumentaceus:* see රණතම්පලා *raṇa-tampalá.*

රූතලය, *Rútalaya*, s. (රූ form තලය world) the Brahma Lóka or the world where the inhabitants have bodies: see තුන්භවය *tunbhawaya.*

රූප්‍ය, *Rúpya*, s. gold, wrought gold; silver, wrought silver: *a.* handsome, beautiful.

රූපය, *Rúpaya*, s. natural property or disposition, nature; beauty, form, figure; appearance, semblance; declension, conjugation, inflection of verbs and nouns; verse; learning by heart or rote; image, idol, figure, reflection or resemblance of any real object; colour, form, any object of vision: pl. රූප *rúpa*: *a.* like, resembling.

රූපක, *Rúpaka*, s. drama, dramatic poem; form, shape; figure of rhetoric in general; a particular class of rhetorical or poetical figures, including various modes of poetical description.

රූපජීව්, *Rúpajiv*, see රූපාජීවා *rúpájívá.*

රූපත්, *Rúpat*, a. beautiful, elegant; having a form or figure.

රූපධ්‍යාන, *Rúpadhyána*, s. (රූප and ධ්‍යාන meditation) abstract meditation performed in the material Brahma worlds.

රූපලක්ෂණ, *Rúpalakshana*, see රූපශ්‍රියාව *rúpa-śriyáwa.*

රූපවත්, *Rúpawat*, *s.* (රූප form etc. වත් poss. aff.) having shape, or colour, well shaped, beautiful, handsome.

රූපශ්‍රියාව, *Rúpaṣriyáwa*, *s.* personal beauty.

රූපසම්පත, *Rúpa-sampata*, *s.* beauty, elegance; personal accomplishments.

රූපාජීවා, *Rúpájívá*, *s.* (රූප *rúpa* beauty, ආජීව *ájíva* who lives by) harlot, prostitute, [Colloq. වෙසඟන *wesangana*].

රූපාරි, *Rúpári*, *s.* nimb or margosa tree, *azadirachta indica*, [Colloq. කොහොඹ *kohomba*].

රූපාවචර, *Rúpáwachara*, *s.* (රූප *rúpa* form, අවචර *awachara* what possesses) state of existence having a form or figure: see තුන්භවය *tunbhawaya*.

රූපෛශ්වර්‍ය්‍ය, *Rúpaiṣwarya*, *s.* (රූප *rúpa* and ඓශ්වර්‍ය්‍ය *aiṣwarya* supremacy) exquisite beauty, elegance of form.

රූබර, *Rúbara*, *a.* (රූ beauty, බර weight) very beautiful, handsome, elegant.

රූරණවා, *Rúraṇawá*, *v.* to fall or glide off.

රූරු, *Rúrú*, } *s.* sort of deer, incorrectly
රූරුමුවා, *Rúrúmuwá*, } for රුරු *ruru*.

රූසිරු, *Rúsiru*, *a.* beautiful, handsome, elegant, having a fine figure or form, [Colloq. ලක්ෂණ ඇති *laksaṇa-ęti*].

රූළහ, *Rúḷha*, *a.* rough, harsh, severe; hard; ascended, mounted up: see රූඪ *rúḍha*.

රෙට්ටෙ, *Reṭṭe*, *a.* double, two-fold, [Colloq. දෙක *deka*].

රෙණවා, *Reṇawá*, *v.* to evacuate, by stool: pret. රුන්නා *runná*, රිව්වා *riwwá*. (vulgar.)

රෙත්, *Ret*, *s.* body, [Colloq. ශරීරය *ṣaríraya*].

රෙද්ද, *Redda*, *s.* cloth, garment: pl. රෙදි *redi*.

රෙදිකඩ, *Redikaḍa*, *s.* piece of cloth.

රෙදිනැන්ද, *Redinęndá*, *s.* laundress, washer woman; sometimes called රිදිනැන්ද *ridinęndá*.

රෙදි හොරා, *Redi-horá*, *s.* bird called the Paradise flycatcher, *Tersiphone paradisi (Lanidæ order Passeres)*.

රෙවෙර, *Rewera*, *s.* root of the white esculent water lily, *nymphæa stellata*, [Colloq. මානෙල් අල *mánel-ala*; also, ඕලු අල *ólu-ala*].

රෙහෙණ, *Rehena*, *s.* fourth lunar asterism figured by a wheeled carriage and containing five stars, probably Alpha, Beta, Gamma, Delta, Epsilon, Tauri.

රෙහෙණතෙන, *Rehenatena*, *s.* name of Balabhadrayá; planet Mercury, [Colloq. බුදහු *budahu*].

රෙහෙණිසුරු, *Reheṇisuru*, *s.* moon, [Colloq. හඳ *haṇḍa*].

රෙහෙමස්, *Rehemas*, see රේමස් *rémas*,

රෙහෙර, *Rehera*, see රේරා *rérá*.

රෙහෙරල, *Reherala*, *s.* edible root of the lotus, [Colloq නෙළුම් අල *neḷum-ala*].

රේ, *Ré*, *ind.* vocative particle, expressive of contempt, disrespect, etc.

රේඛා, *Rékhá*, *s.* line, continuous line; fulness, satisfaction.

රේචක, *Réchaka*, *s.* (රිච් *rich* to evacuate, by stool) nitre, salt petre; plant, seeds used as purgative, *croton tiglium*, [Colloquial: ජයපාල *jayapála*]; purge; purgative stool; tree, *cassia fistula*, [Colloq. ඇහැළ *ęheḷa*]: *a.* aperient.

රේචන, *Réchana*, } *s.* purging, looseness; twining
රේචනි, *Réchani*, } plant root used as a purgative, *ipomœa turpethum*, [Colloq. ත්‍රස්තවාලු, *trastawálu*].

රේණු, *Réṇu*, *s.* dust; pollen of flowers.

රේණු ඕලු, *Réṇu-ólu*, *s.* aquatic plant, *limnanthemum aurantiacum (Gentianaceæ)*.

රේණුකා, *Réṇuká*, *s.* wild species of pepper, *piper sylvestre*, [Coll: වල් ගම්මිරිස්වැල් *wal-gammiris-węl*]; sort of perfume and medicine of a bitter and slightly pungent taste and greyish colour; it is procured in grains about the size of pepper; also, sort of pulse, *ervum* or *cicer lens*.

රේණු නාමක, *Réṇu-námaka*, *s.* plant, *mollugo cerviana*, [Colloq. පත්පාඩගම් *patpáḍagam* or පැපිලිය *pępiliya*].

රේණු හැඩිල්ල, *Réṇu-hęḍilla*, *s.* plant, *guardia delphinifolia*.

රේතස්, *Rétas*, *s.* seminal fluid; quicksilver.

රේන්ද, *Rénda*, *s.* lease, rent, toll. (Dutch.)

රේන්දකරණවා, *Réndakaraṇawá*, *v.* to farm government rents.

රේන්දකාරයා, *Réndakárayá*, *s.* renter, one who farms the revenue.

රේන්ද කොට්ටේ, *Rénda-koṭṭé*, *s.* lace cushion.

රේන්ද පටිය, *Rénda-paṭiya*, *s.* lace.

රේන්දපල, *Réndapala*, *s.* place where toll is levied.

රේන්දරාල, *Réndarála*, see රේන්දකාරයා *réndakárayá*.

රේඵ, *Repha*, *s.* (රිඵ *ripha* to reproach) the letter ර *ra* in the form "ර්" over a consonant: *a.* low, mean, vile, contemptible.

රේමස්, *Rémas*, *s.* kind of fish, *cyprinus denticulatus*, [Colloq. මගුරෝ *maguró*].

රේරා, *Rérá*, *s.* wild duck; teal: pl. රේරු *réru;* also called සේරා *sérá*, (order *Anseres).*

රේවත, *Réwata*, *s.* prince, father of the wife of Balaráma.

රේවතී, *Réwatí*, *s.* river so called; wife of Balaráma, the brother of Kṛishṇa; last of the lunar asterisms, contains thirty-two stars formed by a tabor, one of the stars is Zeta, Piscium; bow.

රේවතීභව, *Réwatí-bhawa*, *s.* (රේවතී and භව birth, born) Saturn.

රේවතීරමණ, *Réwatí-ramaṇa*, *s.* (රේවතී and රමණ husband) name of Balaráma, the brother of Kṛishṇa.

රේවා, *Réwá*, *s.* Nerbadda or Nermadá river, which rises in the mountain Ámrakúṭa, in the province of Gundwana, and runs nearly due west about 750 miles, when it falls into the sea, below Baroach; Rati, the wife of Káma; indigo plant, *indigofera tinctoria*, [Colloquial; නිල් අවරි *nil-awari*].

රෛ, *Rai*, *s.* wealth, property; substance; gold; sound, noise.

රො, *Ro*, *s.* teal: see රේරා *rérá* and සේරා *sérá*.

රොක්කරණවා, *Rokkaraṇawá*, *v.* to gather, to collect.

රොටි, *Roṭi*, *s.* unleavened bread made of rice flour, crisped rice cake, dry cake.

රොඩ්ඩ, *Roḍḍa*, *s.* saw dust, refuse, sediment, rubbish, chaff: pl. රොඩු *roḍu*.

රොඩියා, *Roḍiyá*, *s.* man of the Roḍiyá or lowest caste: pl. රොඩී *roḍi*.

රොත්ත, *Rotta*, *s.* swarm or flock.

රොද්ද, *Rodda*, *s.* bow used in cleaning cotton.

රොද, *Roda*, *s.* row; hair on the proud flesh of a wound, lock of hair; strip of cotton; curtain, screen.

රොදමාන, *Rodamána*, *a.* weeping, crying, shedding tears.

රොදු, *Rodu*, *s.* string, cord, rope; bow used in cleaning cotton.

රොඳුකැටඹිල්ල, *Rondu-keṭambilla*, *s.* bramble, *rubus parviflorus*.

රොන්, *Ron*, *s.* pollen or dust of flowers; anther of flowers; dust.

රොඹු, *Rombu*, *s.* row, line, [Colloq. පේලිය *péliya*].

රොස්, *Ros*, *s.* anger: *a.* roasted.

රොස්කරණවා, *Roskaraṇawá*, *v.* to roast. (Eng.)

රොස්වෙනවා, *Roswenawá*, *v.* to be angry.

රොස, *Rosa*, *s.* anger, wrath.

රෝ, *Ró*, *s.* sickness, disease.

රෝග, *Róga*, *s.* sickness, disease, disease in general: pl. of රෝගය *rógaya*; tree, *costus speciosus*, [Colloq. තෙබු *tebu*].

රෝගකාරයා, *Rógakárayá*, *s.* sick person.

රෝගය, *Rógaya*, see රෝග *róga*.

රෝගරාජ, *Róga-rája*, *s.* (රෝග disease, රාජ principal) consumption, [Colloquial: සයරෝගය *saya-rógaya*].

රෝගලක්ෂණ, *Róga-lakshana*, *s.* symptoms of a disease.

රෝගහ, *Rógaha*, *s.* (රෝග and හා *há* to leave, to abandon) drug, medicament.

රෝගහාරින්, *Rógahárin*, *s.* (රෝග and හාරින් to remove, to take away) physician, medical practitioner, [Colloq. වෙදරාල *wedarála*].

රෝගාතුරයා, *Rógáturayá*, }
රෝගාර්ත, *Rógárta*, } *s.* (රෝග *roga* and ආතුර *átura* diseased, or
රෝගින්, *Rógin*, } ආර්ත *árta* pained) sick person, one labouring under any disease.

රෝගේ, *Rógé*, see රෝගය *rógaya*.

රෝචක, *Róchaka*, *s.* hunger, appetite; kind of salt, borax; plantain; sort of onion; stomachic, carminative, any medicine, fruit or fossil, supposed to strengthen the tone of the stomach and restore lost appetite.

රෝචන, *Róchana*, *s.* species of the silk cotton tree, *eriodendron anfractuosum*, [Colloq. ඉඹුල් *imbul*]; onion, *allium cepa*, [Colloq. රතුළූනු *ratulúnu*]; small tree, seeds yielding oil, *andersonia rohituca;* tree, *cassia fistula*, [Colloq. ඇහැළ *eheḷa*]; pomegranate, *punica granatum*, [Colloq. දෙළුම් *deḷum*]; citron, *citrus medica*; stomachic, carminative: *a.* beautiful, splendid, irradiating, illumining, beautifying; whetting, sharpening, (the appetite).

රෝචනා, *Róchaná*, }
රෝචනී, *Róchaní*, } *s.* yellow pigment supposed to be the concrete bile of the cow, or according to some authorities to be found in the head of this animal, used as a medicine, dye and perfume, [Colloq. ගෝරෝචන *góróchana*]; plant, sort of *crinum;* white variety of *ipomœa turpethum*, see රේචන *réchana;* red arsenic.

රෝචී, *Róchí*, *s.* potherb, *hingtsha repens*.

රෝදන, *Ródana*, *s.* tear, tears; weeping, crying.

රෝදනි, *Ródani*, *s.* plant, *tragia involucrata*, [Colloq. වැල් කහඹිලියා *weḷ-kahambiliyá*].

රෝදය, *Ródaya*, *s.* wheel, rim or discus of a wheel: pl. රෝද *róda*.

රෝධ්‍ර, *Ródhra*, *s.* tree, commonly ලෝධ්‍ර *lódhra*.

රෝධ, *Ródha*, *s.* (රුධ *rudha* to obstruct) bank, shore.

රෝපණය, *Rópaṇaya*, *s.* planting, fixing, placing, [Colloq. සිටවීම *siṭavíma*]; also, healing application to sores or wounds.

රෝපල යත්ත, *Rópala-yatta*, *s.* carpenter's plane.

රෝපිත, *Rópita*, *a.* placed, planted.

රෝම්බු, *Rómbu*, } *s.* hair on the body, wool; water;
රෝම, *Róma*, } hole; sort of salt.

රෝමක, *Rómaka*, *s.* kind of salt.

රෝමකූපය, *Rómakúpaya*, *s.* (රෝම and කූප *kúpa* well, pit) pore of the skin.

රෝමකෘත, *Róma-kṛita*, *s.* (රෝම and කෘත made or done) hair cloth, woollen cloth.

රෝම භූමි, *Róma-bhúmi*, *s.* (රෝම hair, භූමි soil) skin, [Colloq. හම *hama*].

රෝමය, *Rómaya*, see රෝම *róma*.

රෝම ලුණු, *Róma-luṇu*, *s.* kind of medicinal salt brought from the continent of India.

රෝමවත්, *Rómawat*, *a.* (රෝම hair, වත් poss. aff.) hairy, woolly.

රෝමවික්‍රියා, *Róma-vikriyá*, } *s.* (රෝම hair of the
රෝමවිකාර, *Róma-vikára*, } body, වික්‍රියා or විකාර change of state) horripilation.

රෝමහංස, *Rómahaṇsa*, *s.* sort of red dye or paint.

රෝමහර්ෂ, *Rómaharsha*, *s.* (රෝම hair, හර්ෂ pleasure) horripilation; vermilion, [Colloquial. සාදිලිංගම් *sádiliṅgam*].

රෝමහර්ෂණ, *Rómaharshaṇa*, *s.* horripilation, erection of the hairs of the body.

රෝමානු ආගම, *Rómánu-ágama*, *s.* Romanism.

රෝමානුකාරයා, *Rómánukárayá*, *s.* Romanist.

රෝමානුව, *Rómánuwa*, see රෝමානු ආගම *rómánu-ágama*.

රෝමාලි, *Rómáli*, *s.* (රෝම *róma* and ආලි *áli* line, row) line of hair extending across the navel.

රෝමාවලි, *Rómáwalí*, *s.* line of hair across the middle of the belly or navel.

රෝමෝද්ගම, *Rómódgama*, *s.* (රෝම *róma* and උද්ගම rising) horripilation.

රෝෂ, *Rósha*, *s.* anger, wrath, [Colloq. තරහ *taraha*].

රෝහිණී, *Róhiṇi*, *s.* fourth lunar asterism, figured by a wheeled carriage and containing five stars, probably, Alpha, Beta, Gamma, Delta, Epsilon, Tauri; in mythology, the asterism is personified as one of the daughters of Daksha, and wives of the moon; mother of Balaráma; cow; inflammatory affection of the throat; lightning; medicinal plant, called කටුකරෝසන *kaṭukarósana;* moon plant, *asclepias acida;* yellow myrobalan, *terminalia chebula*, [Colloq. අරළු *araḷu*]; Indian madder, *oldenlandia* or *hedyotis umbellata*]; creeping plant, *surcostemma brunonianum*, [Coll: මුවකිරියවැල් *muwakíriya-węl*]; tree, *adenanthera pavonina*, [Colloq. මදටගස් *madaṭa-gas*].

රෝහිණී පති, *Róhiṇi-pati*, } *s.* (රෝහිණී
රෝහිණී වල්ලභ, *Róhiṇí-wallabha*, } nymph, පති or වල්ලභ lover) moon, [Colloq. හඳ *haṇḍa*].

රෝහිණීශ, *Róhiṇiṣa*, *s.* moon.

රෝහිණේය, *Róhiṇéya*, *s.* name of Balaráma; the planet Mercury; emerald; calf.

රෝහිත, *Róhita*, *s.* red (the colour); fish, *cyprinus denticulatus;* kind of deer; tree, *andersonia rohitaka*, see රෝචන *róchana;* Indra's bow unbent and invisible to mortals; safflower, *carthamus tinctorius;* blood, [Colloq. ලේ *lé*]; coral tree, *erythrina indica*, [Colloq. එරබදු *erabadu*].

රෝහින්, *Róhin*, *s.* the Indian fig-tree; the holy fig-tree; the *andersonia rohitaka*, *(Roxb.)*.

රෝහිෂ, *Róhisha*, *s.* tree, *morinda citrifolia* and *m. tinctoria*, [Colloq. අහු *ahu*]; sort of grass; the Róhi, a kind of fish; a deer said to resemble an ass.

රෞද්‍ර, *Raudra*, *s.* wrath, rage, sentiment as an object of poetical description; warmth, heat; name of Yama; the fifty-fourth year of the Indian cycle: *a.* formidable, fearful, terrific, sharp, acute; relating to Rudra or Ṣiva; violent, irascible, wrathful; harsh, rough.

රෞම, *Rauma*, } *s.* (රුම *ruma* district so call-
රෞමක, *Raumaka*, } ed, අණ් *aṇ* and කණ් *kan* aff.) kind of salt, according to some authorities, brought from a mountain in Ajmere, but in fact procured from a salt lake near the town of Sambher, about twenty miles west of Jayanagara.

රෞරව, *Raurawa*, *s.* division of Naraka or Tartarus; savage, monster: *a.* formidable, horrible, terrific.

රෞහිණේය, *Rauhinéya*, see රෝහිණේය *róhiṇéya*.

රැක, *Ręka*, *part.* (of රකිනවා *rakinawá* to keep) having guarded, watched, preserved.

රැකබලාගන්නවා, *Rękabalágannawá*, *v.* to watch, to protect, to guard.

රැකවරණ, *Rękawarana*, *s.* guard, preservation: a place of defence, an entrenchment.

රැකවල්කරණවා, *Rękawal-karaṇawá*, *v.* to guard, to watch.

රැකවලා, *Rękawalá*, *s.* guard, watchman, keeper.

රැකිම, *Rękíma*, *s.* guarding, protecting, watching. sustenance, means of living, from රකිණවා *rakiṇawá*.

රැකෙණවා, *Rękeṇawá*, *v.* to be maintained or supported: pret. රැකුණා *rękuṇá*.

රැගෙණ, *Ręgeṇa*, *part.* (ඇරගෙණ *ęrageṇa* dropping the initial vowel) taking.

රැඟුම, *Ręnguma*, *s.* dance practised in religious performances: pl. රැඟුම් *ręngum*, [Colloq. නැටුම *nęṭuma*].

රැඟුවන්, *Rę̆nguwan*, *s.* dancer, performer, dramatic performer.

රැත්ත *Rętta*, *s.* species of saffron, from අරැත්ත *arętta*.

රැඳිම, *Ręndíma*, verbal noun of රැඳෙනවා *ręndenawá*.

රැඳෙනවා, *Ręndenawá*, *v.* to stop, to remain, to be fixed: pret. රැඳුනා *ręnduná*.

රැමුවස, *Ręmuwasa*, *s.* evening, after part of the day, [Colloq. සවස *sawasa*].

රැය, *Ręya*, *s.* night.

රැල්පනාව, *Ręl-panáwa*, *s.* large comb, high comb.

රැල්බුරුල් අරිණවා, *Ręlburul-ariṇawá*, *v.* to clear the throat.

රැල්ල, *Ręlla*, *s.* fold, yard, waves.

රැව්, *Ręw*, *s.* sound, noise in general, [Colloq. ශබ්දය *śabdaya*].

රැව්දෙනවා, *Ręwdenawá*, *v.* to sound, to utter sounds, to make a noise.

රැව්පිළිරැව්, *Ręwpiḷiręw*, *s.* sound and echo.

රැවටිල්ල, *Ręwaṭilla*, *s.* (රවටනවා *rawaṭanawá* to deceive) deception, illusion, cheating, guile: pl. රැවටිලි *ręwaṭili*.

රැවටෙනවා, *Ręwaṭenawá*, *v.* to be deceived: pret. රැවටුනා *ręwaṭuná*.

රැවිම, *Ręvíma*, *s.* the act of staring at.

රැවු පුරුක්විල, *Ręwu-purukvila*, *s.* plant, *diceros aquaticus*.

රැවුළ, *Ręwuḷa*, *s.* beard: pl. රැවුල් *ręwul*.

රැවුළ කපනවා, *Ręwuḷa-kapanawá*, *v.* to shave the beard.

රැස් කඳ, *Ręs-kanda*, *s.* collection of rays.

රැස්කනවා, *Ręskanawá*, *v.* to flock, to throng, to come together in large numbers.

රැස්කරණවා, *Ręskaraṇawá*, *v.* to collect together, gather together.

රැස්මඩල, *Ręsmaḍala*, *s.* the orb of the sun or moon; circle of rays.

රැස්මිය, *Ręsmiya*, *s.* ray, sun or moon beam, gleam of light; corrupt form of රශ්මිය *raśmiya*.

රැස්හිමි, *Ręs-himi*, *s.* (රැස් rays, හිමි possessor) sun, [Colloq. ඉර *ira*].

රැස, *Ręsa*, *s.* multitude, company, collection; ray, sun or moon beam; sign of the zodiac: pl. රැස් *ręs*.

රැහණ, *Ręhaṇa*, see රැහැණ *ręhęṇa*.

රැහිම, *Ręhim*, *s.* rent, fissure, cleft.

රැහැ, *Ręhę*, *s.* caste: *a.* of low caste, mean, vile.

රැහැණ, *Ręhęṇa*, *s.* cord, rope, string, line.

රැහැණිය, *Ręhęṇiya*, *s.* anger, wrath, [Colloq. තරහ *taraha*]; bush, thicket, place overgrown with jungle.

රැහැණිව, *Ręhęṇiwa*, *a.* being angry, wrathful.

රැළ, *Ręḷa*, *s.* wave, billow; flock (of birds), flock (of sheep); herd.

රැළි, *Ręḷi*, *s.* wrinkle, folds in a dress: *a.* crooked, curved, tortuous; wrinkled.

රැළිතණ, *Ręḷi-taṇa*, *s.* panic grass, *panicum plicatum*.

රෑ, *Rę̄*, *s.* night; name of Káma, the Indian Cupid.

රෑ කනකොකා, *Rę̄-kanakoká*, *s.* common night heron, *nycticorax griseus (Ardeidæ*, order *Herodiones)*.

රෑ කොකා, *Rę̄-koká*, *s.* Malay bittern, *goisachius melanolophus (Ardeidæ*, order *Herodiones)*.

රෑණ, *Rę̄ṇa*, *s.* rein, long cord, rope, string, withe, twig; cluster, flock, herd: pl. රෑන් *rę̄n*.

රෑණ කරවිල, *Rę̄ṇa-karavila*, *s.* creeping, plant, *momordica charantia*: see කරිවිල *karivila*.

රෑණ ගිරවා, *Rę̄ṇa-girawá*, *s.* rose ringed parrakeet, *palæornis torquatus (Psittacidæ*, order *Psittaci)*.

රෑණමුවා, *Rę̄ṇa-muwá*, *s.* kind of deer.

රෑණ වටුවා, *Rę̄ṇa-waṭuwá*, *s.* bird called the Asiatic golden plover, *charadrius fulvus*, *(Charadridæ*, order *Grallæ)*; also called ඔලෙයියා *oleyiyá* and මහ ඔලෙයියා *maha-oleyiyá*.

රෑණ වැටකොළු, *Rę̄ṇa-węṭakoḷu*, *s.* creeping plant, *momordica cylindrica*.

රෑණවා, *Rę̄ṇáwá*, *s.* kind of sea fish.

රෑ දවස, *Rę̄-dawasa*, *s.* the night time.

රෑන් අඳිනවා, *Rę̄n-adinawá*, *v.* to pass a string over standing corn to whisk off flies and other vermin.

රෙන්ගහනවා, *Rẹngahanawá*, *v.* to pass strings at the ends of a cart, etc. as a protection; to put brand marks on cattle.

රෙ බදුල්ලා, *Rẹ-badullá*, *s.* glow worm.

රෙබස්සා, *Rẹ-bassá*, *s.* bird called jungle night jar, *caprimulgus atripennis*, also called බමරලියා *bamaraliyá;* common Indian night jar, *c. asiaticus;* both the above, also called බිම් බස්සා *bim-bassá (Caprimulgidæ* order *Picariæ).*

රෙයාමය, *Rẹ-yámaya*, *s.* watch of the night.

රෙයියා, *Rẹyiyá*, see රෙහියා *rẹhiyá*

රෙවෙනවා, *Rẹwenawá*, *v.* to become dark at the approach of night, to be late in the day, towards evening.

රෙසියා, *Rẹsiyá*,
රෙහියා, *Rẹhiyá*, } *s.* cricket.

ල

The twenty-eighth consonant of the Siṇhalese alphabet, expressed by the letter *L.*

ල, *La*, *s.* mind, seat of reason; breast, heart: *a.* young, tender.

* ලං, *Laṇ*, *ad.* near, proximate.

* ලංකා, *Laṇká*,
* ලංකාද්වීපය, *Laṇkádvípaya*, } *s.* the ancient name of Ceylon, much celebrated in Hindu history, as being the place where the famous Ráwaṇa had his capital.

* ලංකාධිපති, *Laṇkádhipati*, *s.* (ලංකා and අධිපති *adhipati* over-lord) supreme lord of Laṇká.

* ලංකාපති, *Laṇkápati*, *s.* (ලංකා and පති ruler) name of Ráwaṇa; ruler of Laṇká.

* ලංකේශ්වර, *Laṇkéṣwara*, *s.* (ලංකා *laṇká* and ඊශ්වර *íṣwara* master, lord) ruler of Laṇká.

* ලංඝනය, *Langhanaya*, *s.* hunger; fasting, abstinence; leaping, bounding; going beyond proper bounds.

* ලංඝනයකරණවා, *Langhanaya-karaṇawá*, *v.* to fast, to abstain from food.

ලංවෙනවා, *Laṇwenawá*, *v.* to approach: pret. ලංවුනා *laṇwuná.*

ලක්, *Lak*, *s.* Laṇká or Ceylon; cypher, figure; mark, sign; target, [Colloq. ඉලක්කය *ilakkaya*].

ලක්තක, *Laktaka*, *s.* old and tattered cloth, a rag or rags; lac, the animal dye.

ලක්දිව, *Lakdiwa*, *s.* Elu form of ලංකාද්වීපය *laṇkádvípaya*, which see.

* These words are sometimes spelt with ඞ *ń* instead of ං *ṇ*.

ලක්වැලිය, *Lakwẹliya*, *s.* string of beads or rosary used by Hindu ascetics while repeating in silence their prayers or mental recitations; it is also used by astrologers and soothsayers when practising their arts.

ලක්වැසියා, *Lakwẹsiyá*, *s.* inhabitant of Ceylon.

ලක්ෂ්මණ, *Lakshmaṇa*, *s.* name, appellation; spot, sign, mark; the half brother of Rámachandra: *a.* prosperous, fortunate.

ලක්ෂ්මණා, *Lakshmaṇá*, *s.* sort of drug, *ipomœa sepiaria*, [Colloq. රසතැල් *rasatẹl*].

ලක්ෂ්මී, *Lakshmí*, *s.* one of the three principal female deities of the Hindus, the wife of Vishṇu, and goddess of wealth and prosperity; the name by which she is most generally known in Ceylon, is Sriyákántáwa; fortune, success, prosperity; beauty, splendour; plant: see ප්‍රියංගු *priyańgu;* the wife of a hero; turmeric, *curcuma longa*, [Colloq. කහ *kaha*]; pearl.

ලක්ෂ්මීපති, *Laksmí-pati*, *s.* Vishṇu; clove tree, *caryophyllus aromaticus*, [Colloq. කරාබු *karábu*]: betel nut tree.

ලක්ෂ්මීඵල, *Lakshmí-phala*, *s.* fruit tree, *ægle marmelos*, [Colloq. බෙලි *beli*].

ලක්ෂ්‍ය, *Lakshya*, *s.* example; illustration of a grammatical rule: mark, sign; butt: *a.* to be seen, noted, defined, or described.

ලක්ෂ, *Laksha*, *s.* lac, 100,000; fraud, disguise; mark, butt.

ලක්ෂණ, *Lakshaṇa*, *s.* indication, predicate, any thing by which an object is designated or distinguished; mark, spot; the younger brother of Ráma; Indian crane; name, appellation; grammatical rule or aphorism: *a.* beautiful, pleasing, charming, delightful, agreeable.

ලක්ෂණශාස්ත්‍රය, *Lakshaṇa-ṣástraya*, *s.* (ලක්ෂණ mark, sign, ornament, ශාස්ත්‍ර *ṣástra* science) science which teaches the knowledge of human destinies, by tracing out certain lines and marks in the body which indicate future fortune; it is a species of fortune-telling and is practised by every juggler and native doctor.

ලක්ෂය, *Lakshaya*, see its plural form ලක්ෂ *laksha.*

ලක, *Laka*, *s.* mark, sign; forehead; ear or spike of wild rice; island of Ceylon, Elu form of ලංකා *Laṇká.*

ලකර, *Lakara*, *s.* ornament; rhetoric, beauties of style in composition.

ලකළ, *Lakaḷa*, *a.* good, excellent; auspicious; ornamented, decorated.

ලකුච, *Lakucha*, *s.* species of the bread fruit tree, *artocarpus nobilis*, [Colloq. දෙල් *del*].

ලකුණ්ට, *Lakunṭa*, *s.* short, dwarfish.

ලකුණ්ටකයා, *Lakunṭakayá*, *s.* dwarf.

ලකුණ, *Lakuṇa*, *s.* mark, spot, sign, token, badge: pl. ලකුණු *lakuṇu*.

ලකුණුකරණවා, *Lakuṇu-karaṇawá*, *v.* to make a mark or sign.

ලකේ, *Laké*, *s.* manner, mode, fashion.

ලග්න, *Lagna*, *s.* the rising of a sign, its appearance above the horizon; oblique ascension or the divisions of the equator which rise in succession with each sign in an oblique sphere; in popular acceptation, it is the moment of the sun's entrance into a zodiacal sign; bard, panegyrist: *a.* attached to, intent on; ashamed; joined to, connected with.

ලග්නක, *Lagnaka*, *s.* pledge, security; stake at gaming.

ලග්නය, *Lagnaya*, see ලග්න *lagna*.

ලගිණවා, *Lagiṇawá*, *v.* to repose, to remain at a place for a short time on a journey, to abide, to lodge: to roost; to lie down as beasts: pret. ලැග්ගා *lęggá*.

ලඝු, *Lagu*, *a.* short; light, soft, easy; swift, speedy: see ලඝු *laghu*.

ලගුඩ, *Laguḍa*, *s.* staff, club.

ලඟ, *Lan̲ga*, *s.* (ලගි *lagi* to be near) union, association, proximate connection: *a.* near, proximate; with, together with.

ලඟාවෙනවා, *Lan̲gáwenawá*, *v.* to approach, arrive at.

ලඝු, *Laghu*, *s.* plant, *trigonella corniculata*, [Colloq. පික් මල් *pik-mal*]; fried grain, [Colloq. විලඳ *vilan̲da*]; black kind of aloe wood or agallochum, [Colloq. කළු අගිල් *kaḷu-agil*]; root of the *andropogon muricatus*, [Colloq. සැවැන්දරා මුල් *sęwęndará-mul*]: *a.* short; light, not heavy; swift, quick; sapless, pithless; insignificant; small, little; short (as a vowel).

ලඝු අක්ෂර, *Laghu-akshara*, *s.* (ලඝු short, අක්ෂර letter) short vowel.

ලඝු පුෂ්ප, *Laghu-pushpa*, *s.* areca-nut palm, *areca catechu*, [Colloq. පුවක්ගහ *puwak-gaha*].

ලඝුලය, *Laghulaya*, *s.* root of cuscus grass, *andropogon muricatus*, [Colloq. සැවැන්දරා මුල් *sęwęndará-mul*].

ලඝුවිරේචනී, *Laghu-viréchaní*, *s.* medicinal plant, *croton polyandrum*, [Colloq. දැත්ත *dętta*].

ලඝුහස්ත, *Laghu-hasta*, *s.* (ලඝු quick, හස්ත hand) good archer, expert bow man; *a.* ready or light-handed.

ලඞ්කාද්වීපය, *Laṅkádwípaya*, see ලංකා *Lan̲ká*.

ලඞ්කාධිපති, *Laṅkádhipati*, see ලංකාධිපති *lan̲kádhipati*.

ලඞ්කාපති, *Laṅkápati*, see ලංකාපති *lan̲kápati*.

ලඞ්කාව, *Laṅkáwa*, see ලංකා *lan̲ká*.

ලඞ්කාස්ථායිනී, *Laṅkásthấyiní*, *s.* plant, *euphorbia tirucalli*, [Colloq. නවහන්දි *nawahandi*].

ලඞ්ඝනය, *Laṅghanaya*, see ලංඝනය *lan̲ghanaya*.

ලඞ්ඝනීය, *Laṅghaníya*, *a.* to be fasted; transgressible.

ලජ්ජා, *Lajjá*, *s.* shame, modesty. bashfulness.

ලජ්ජාන්විත, *Lajjánvita*, *a.* (ලජ්ජා and අන්විත *anvita* possessed) ashamed, bashful.

ලජ්ජාලු, *Lajjálu*, *s.* sensitive plant, *mimosa pudica*, [Colloq. මිදි *midi* or නිදිකුම්බා *nidikumba*].

ලජ්ජාහීන, *Lajjá-hína*, *a.* (ලජ්ජා and හීන void of) shameless, impudent.

ලජ්ජිත, *Lajjita*, *a.* (ලජ්ජා *lajjá* and ඉත *ita* aff.) ashamed, modest, bashful.

ලඤ්ජ, *Lañja*, *s.* foot; end of the lower garment tucked into the waist band; tail.

ලටපට, *Laṭapaṭa*, *s.* medley, articles in confusion; incoherent talk.

ලටු, *Laṭu*, *s.* liquorice creeper, *abrus precatorius*, [Colloq. ඔලිඳවැල් *olin̲da-węl*].

ලඩු, *Laḍu*, *s.* native sweetmeat prepared by mixing roasted jack nuts, scraped coconut, and treacle.

ලත්, *Lat*, *pret.* of ලබනවා *labanawá*.

ලතණ, *Lataṇa*, *s.* (ල young, තණ grass) tender grass.

ලතඹ, *Latamba*, *s.* bud, sprout, germ, young shoot of a leaf or flower.

ලතර, *Latara*, *s.* (ල and අතර *atara* inside) in the heart.

ලතවෙනවා, *Latawenawá*, *v.* to be grieved, to be melancholy, to lament.

ලතා, *Latá*, *s.* (ලත *lata* to enfold) creeper, creeping or winding plant in general, [Colloq. වැල *węla*]; branch; manner, sort, form; leguminous plant, *trigonella corniculata*; heart pea, *cardiospermum haliacacabum*, [Colloq. පෙනෙලවැල් *penela-węl*]; creeping plant with fragrant beautiful blossoms, *hiptage madablota*, formerly called *gaertnera racemosa*, [Colloq. පුවක්ගෙඩියාවැල *puwakgediyá-wela*]; species of grass, *panicum dactylon;* thread; tune.

ලතාකර්ම, *Latákarma*, *s.* (ලතා and කර්ම act) sort of encaustic painting, such as is used in adorning the inner walls of temples, and ornamenting the covers of native books.

ලතාන්ත, *Latánta*, *s.* (ලතා creeper, අන්ත *anta* end) flower, [Colloq. මල *mala*].

ලතා ප්‍රතානිනී, *Latá-pratániní*, *s.* (ලතා and ප්‍රතානිනී spreading) spreading creeper.

ලතාමණි, *Latá-mani*, *s.* coral, [Colloquial: පබළු *pabalu*].

ලතා යෂ්ටි, *Latá-yashti*, *s.* (ලතා and යෂ්ටි stem) Bengal madder, *rubia manjitha*, [Colloq. වැල් මදට *wel-madata*].

ලතාලෑල්ල, *Latá-lella*, *s.* plank on the upper part of the frame of a door or window.

ලතාව, *Latáwa*, *s.* tone; creeper.

ලතිකා, *Latiká*, *s.* twining plant.

ලතු, *Latu*, *s.* gumlac; red animal dye: see ලාක්ෂා *lákshá*.

ලතුවන්, *Latuwan*, *s.* light red colour procured from the lac or red dye: see ලාක්ෂා *lákshá;* infusion prepared from the bark of the lódh tree, *phyllanthus longifolius*, and used in dyeing: see ලා *lá*.

ලතෝනිය, *Latóniya*, *s.* lamentation, bewailing.

ලද, *Lada*, *s.* shame; faith, religious; woman; young child; young man; fried grain; tree, *gardenia;* thorny shrub, *randia dumetorum*, [Colloq. කුකුරුමුවන් *kukurumuwan*]; Elu form of ලජ්ජා *lajjá* and ලබ්ධි *labdhi*, which see: *past. part.* received; finished, done, completed: *a.* young, tender.

ලදපල්ලව, *Lada-pallawa*, *s.* (ලද tender, පල්ලව sprout or shoot) young bud, [Colloq. දළුව *daluwa*].

ලදපස්මල්, *Lada-pasmal*, *s.* fried grain, mustard, broken rice, jessamine, and *heteropogon hirtus*.

ලදබොළඳ, *Lada-bolanda*, *s.* (ලද tender, බො for බොහෝ *bohó* very, ළද tender) very tender, childish, infantile, characteristic of little children, as their speech.

ලදරි, *Ladari*, *s.* little girl, young woman; woman in general.

ළදරු, *Ladaru*, *s.* infant, sucking child.

ළඳ, *Landa*, *s.* woman, young woman, tender maid: pl. ළඳුන් *landun*.

ළඳගන, *Landagana*, *s.* young woman.

ලන්තෑරුම, *Lanteruma*, *s.* lantern. (from Portuguese, lanterna.)

ලන්ද, *Landa*, *s.* high ground with low jungle: pl. ලඳු *landu*.

ලන්දේසි, *Landési*, } *s.* Dutch, Hollanders
ලන්සි, *Lansi*, }

ලන්සේ, *Lansé*, *s.* lance, spear: pl. ලන්ස *lansa*.

ලන්සෝළුව, *Lansóluwa*, *s.* coloured sheet, blanket.

ලනවා, *Lanawá*, *v.* to put, to place, to lay as eggs, to fix: pret. ලෑවා *lewá*.

ලනුව, *Lanuwa*, *s.* string, cord, line, rope: pl. ලනු *lanu*.

ළප්නාරන්, *Lapnáran*, *s.* citron, *citrus medica;* species of lemon.

ලප්පාවෙනවා, *Lappáwenawá*, *v.* to be reeling.

ලප්පිය, *Lappiya*, *s.* patch. (Dutch, lap.)

ලපක්, *Lapak*, *s.* unripe fruit, tender fruit.

ලපටි, *Lapati*, *a.* tender, immature, young, (as fruit), unripe, (applied to the youth of any thing.)

ලපතෑල්කොල, *Lapa-telkola*, *s.* plant, not ascertained.

ලපය, *Lapaya*, *s.* spot, freckle, sign, mark: pl. ලප *lapa*.

ලපලු, *Lapalu*, *s.* bud, shoot, sprout.

ලපා, *Lapá*, *s.* word, speech, [Colloq. වචනය *wachanaya*, කථාව *katháwa*].

ලපිරුණු, *Lapirunu*, *s.* (ල heart, පිරුණු full) heart filled with (sorrow, etc.)

ලපුස්, *Lapus*, *s.* species of the bread fruit tree, *artocarpus nobilis*, [Colloq දෙල් *del*].

ලබ්ධ, *Labdha*, *a.* (ලභ *labha* to get) gained, acquired, obtained, received, got.

ලබ්ධ වර්ණ, *Labdha-warna*, *s.* (ලබ්ධ got, වර්ණ praise, celebrity) sage, learned man.

ලබ්ධිය, *Labdhiya*, *s.* (ලබ්ධ *labdha* gained, ඉ *i* pers. aff.) religious belief: heresy, sect, schism in the prevailing Religion: pl. ලබ්ධි *labdhi*.

ලබ්බ, *Labba*, *s.* pumpkin gourd, long gourd: see ලබු ගෙඩිය *labugediya*: pl. ලබු *labu*.

ලබනවා, *Labanawá*, *v.* (ලභ *labha* to get) to obtain, to gain, to receive: pret. ලැබුවා *lebuwá*.

ලබු අඳුර, *Labu-andara*, *s.* sort of tree.

ලබු කිරිබත්, *Labu-kiribat*, *s.* rice milk boiled with pumpkin, etc.

ලබු ගිරවා, *Labu-girawá*, *s.* Alexandrine parrakeet, *palæornis eupatris (Psittacidæ*, order *Psittaci)*.

ලබුගෙඩිය, *Labugediya*, *s.* pumpkin gourd fruit, *cucurbita pepo;* long gourd.

ලබුජ, *Labuja*, *s.* tree, *artocarpus nobilis*, [Colloq. දෙල් *del*].

ලබු මිරිස්, *Labu-miris*, *s.* plant, species of *piper*.

ලබු වෙල්ලංගිරිය, *Labu-wellangiriya*, *s.* plant, variety of *capparis zeylanica* or of *paramignya monophylla*.

ලභ්‍ය, *Labhya*, *a.* (ලභ *labha* to get, යන් *yan* aff.) attainable; procurable.

ලම්බකැටේ, *Lambakeṭé*, *s.* plummet, plumb-line: pl. ලම්බකැට *lambakeṭa*.

ලම්බෝරා, *Lambórá*, *s.* (ලම්බ *lamba* large, උර *ura* for උදර *udara* belly, ආ *á* personal aff.) name of Ganésa, Hindu god of wisdom.

ලම්බ, *Lamba*, *s.* (ලබි *labi* to fall, to sound) perpendicular (in geometry): *a.* spacious, capacious; great, large, broad, long, expanded, either in breadth or length or both; pendulous, depending.

ලම්බක, *Lambaka*, *s.* perpendicular.

ලම්බ කර්ණ, *Lamba-karṇa*, *s.* (ලම්බ large, pendulous, කර්ණ ear) goat; elephant; goblin, Rákshasa; tree, *alangium hexapetalum;* hare; name of Ganéṣa.

ලම්බන, *Lambana*, *s.* long necklace, one which hangs from the neck to the navel; descending, depending, falling; phlegm, the phlegmatic humour.

ලම්බා, *Lambá*, *s.* bitter gourd.

ලම්බෝදර, *Lambódara*, *s.* (ලම්බ *lamba* large, උදර *udara* belly) name of Ganéṣa, the Hindu god of wisdom, alluding to his large belly.

ලමක, *Lamaka*, *s.* lover, gallant.

ලමග, *Lamaga*, } *s.* cinnamon plant, *cinnamomum*
ලමඟ, *Lamanga*, } *zeylanicum*, [Colloq. කුරුඳු *kurundu*].

ලමද, *Lamada*, *s.* the breast, heart.

ලමයා, *Lamayá*, *s.* child, little one; boy: pl. ලමයි *lamayi*.

ලමා, *Lamá*, *a.* childish, infantile.

ලමාඑතනි, *Lamáetani*, *s.* a respectful term applied to the wife of a Mudaliyar.

ලමාකම, *Lamákama*, *s.* childhood, childishness.

ලමාතැනි, *Lamáteni*, see ලමාඑතනි *lamáetani*.

ලමිස්සි, *Lamissi*, *s.* girl, one who has attained the age of puberty: pl. ලමිස්සියෝ *lamissiyó*.

ලමු, *Lamu*, *s.* desire.

ලය, *Laya*, *s.* breast, heart; equal time in music and dancing: adhering, or clinging to, embracing, uniting; sport, pastime; root of the *andropogon muricatus*, [Colloq. සැවැන්දරා මුල් *sewendará-mul*]; loss, destruction; fusion, melting.

ලයාන්විත, *Layánvita*, *a.* having equal time in music and dancing.

ලයින් ඇල්වී, *Layin-elví*, *s.* kind of hill paddy.

ලල, *Lala*, *a.* sporting, lolling, wishing, desirous.

ලලන, *Lalana*, *s.* (ලල to desire) shaking, tremulous; licking, lapping; stirring, touching with the tongue, lolling the tongue, etc.: wantoning, dallying; tree, *vateria acuminata*, [Colloq. හල් *hal*].

ලලනා, *Lalaná*, *s.* woman; tongue; pleasure, sport, pastime.

ලලාටය, *Laláṭaya*, *s.* forehead, temples. [Colloq. නලල *nalala*].

ලලාම, *Lalàma*, *s.* mark, sign; banner; mark on the forehead; tail; horn; horse; ornament, decoration; majesty, dignity, eminence, excellence; line, row.

ලලිත, *Lalita*, *s.* (ලල *lala* to desire, ක්ත *kta* aff.) shaking, moving tremulously; branch of feminine action, arising from the passion or sentiment of love; lolling, languishing; languid signs and gestures indicative of passion: *a.* wished, desired; beautiful, lovely: wanton, dallying: shaken, tremulous.

ලලිතා, *Lalitá*, *s.* musk: woman in general; wanton.

ලව, *Lawa*, *s.* (ලූ *lú* to cut) cutting; loss, destruction; reaping; smallness, littleness; minute division of time, the sixtieth part of the twinkling of an eye; also another division of time thirty twinklings of an eye, about half a second; hair, wool cut from domestic animals; drop of water; numerator of a fraction; nutmeg; cloves: *a.* small, little.

ලවක, *Lawaka*, *s.* (ලූ *lú* to cut) ක aff.) reaper, mower.

ලවඞ්ග, *Lawaṅga*, *s.* clove tree, *caryophyllus aromaticus*, [Colloq. කරාබු *karábu*].

ලවඞ්ගපුෂ්පි, *Lawaṅga-pushpi*, *s.* (ලවඞ්ග cloves, පුෂ්ප *pushpa* flower, ඉන් *in* aff.) mace, [Colloq. වසාවාසි *wasáwási*].

ලවණ, *Lawaṇa*, *s.* (ලූ *lú* to cut, assist digestion) general name for salt; for an account of the principal salts: see ලවණාෂ්ටක *lawaṇáshṭaka;* saltness, saline taste; lip; sea of salt water: *a.* salt, saline; handsome, beautiful; cutting, reaping.

ලවණත්‍රය, *Lawaṇatraya*, *s.* the three common salts, namely, sea salt, rock salt or fossil salt, factitious salt: see the following word.

ලවණ, *Lawaná*, s. plant, *celastrus paniculata*, [Colloq. දුහුදු *duhudu*]; light, lustre, beauty.

ලවණාෂ්ටක *Lawanáshtaka*, s. (ලවණ *lawana* salt, අෂ්ට *ashta* eight) the eight principal salts as enumerated by native practitioners, namely, මුදුලුණු *múdu-lunu*, sea salt; සෛන්ධව ලුණු *saindhawa-lunu*, rock or fossil salt; කළු ලුණු *kalu-lunu*, black salt, factitious salt obtained by boiling the soil found near the sea shore or any earth impregnated with saline particles; උද්භිද ලුණු *udbhida-lunu*, sub-borate or common borax; culinary salt; බළල් ලුණු *balal-lunu*, salt obtained by fusing fossil salt with a small portion of emblic myrobalan, *phyllanthus emblica*; සුවස ලුණු *suwasa-lunu*, natron; යවකාරලුණු *yawakara-lunu*, nitre, saltpetre; රෝම ලුණු *róma-lunu*, particular kind of salt procured from a salt lake near the town of Sámbher, about twenty miles west of Jayanagara on the continent of India.

ලවණෝත්තම, *Lawanóttama*, s. (ලවණ *lawana* salt, උත්තම *uttama* best) nitre; rock or river salt, [Colloq. සෛන්ධව ලුණු *saindhawa-lunu*].

ලවණෝද, *Lawanóda*, s. (ලවණ *lawana* and උද *uda* water) sea of salt water.

ලවන්, *Lawan*, s. forest, wood, grove; jungle.

ලවන, *Lawana*, s. cutting, reaping.

ලවනවා, *Lawanawá*, v. causal form of ලනවා *lanawá*: pret. ලෑව්වා *lewwá*.

ලවනි, *Lawani*, s. coarse kind of custard apple, *anona reticulata*.

ලවයා, *Lawayá*, s. kind of sea fish.

ලවල, *Lawala*, s. bud, plantation of young betel vines.

ලවලාල, *Lawalála*, s. (ලවල *lawala* and අල *ála* what desires) deer; goat.

ලවා, *Lawá*, ind. an affix to nouns answering to by, through, with, etc., denoting agency or instrumentality.

ලවිත්‍ර, *Lavitra*, s. (ලූ *lu* to cut, ත්‍ර aff.) sickle, small reaping hook.

ලශුන, *Lasuna*, s. garlic, *allium sativum*, [Colloq. සුදුලූනු *sudulúnu*].

ලස්, *Las*, s. delay: *a.* lazy, slow.

ලස්තක, *Lastaka*, s. resin, [Colloq. දුම්මල *dummala*]; middle of a bow.

ලස, *Lasa*, s. contracted from අලස *alasa*, slowness, delay: *a.* slow, idle.

ලසුන, *Lasuna*, s. garlic, *allium sativum*, [Colloq. සුදුලූනු *sudulúnu*].

ලසෝ, *Lasó*, s. (ල and සෝ sorrow) distress, grief, [Colloq. කණගාටුව *kanagátuwa*].

ලහ, *Laha*, s. small piece of board, used in the temples to invite the priests to perform services on special occasions; when the person has fixed upon the number of priests he intends to invite, he goes to the temple and places so many pieces of these boards in a corner, which when seen so many proceed to his house.

ලහටු, *Lahatu*, s. gum, [Colloq. මැලියම *meliyam*]; resin, any resinous substance, [Colloq. දුම්මල *dummala*].

ලහරි, *Lahari*, s. large wave of the sea.

ලහස, *Lahasa*, s. measure of capacity, five of which make a parrah.

ලහි, *Lahi*, a. quick, expeditious, [Colloq. ඉක්මන් *ikman*].

ලහිරු, *Lahiru*, s. (ල young or early, හිරු sun) sun when rising, or just after he has risen above the horizon.

ලහිරුමඬල, *Lahiru-mandala*, s. disc of the sun when just above the horizon; see the foregoing word.

ලහුකය, *Lahukaya*, s. ease, softness, lightness, speed, activity.

ලහුන, *Lahuna*, see ලසුන *lasuna*.

ලා, *Lá*, s. an infusion of the bark of the red lódhra tree, *phyllanthus longifolius*: see ලතුවන් *latuwan*; and used in dyeing to fix the colours: *a.* unripe, young, immature.

ලාක්ක, *Lákka*, s. broad cloth. (Dutch, laken.)

ලාක්ෂා, *Lákshá*, s. (ලක්ෂ *laksha* to dye or stain) lac, red dye, [Colloq. ලාකඩ *lákada*]; an insect which is analogous to the cochineal insect, and like it forms, when dried and prepared, a dye of a red colour; the nest is formed of a resinous substance which is used as sealing wax.

ලාක්ෂාප්‍රසාද, *Lákshá-prasáda*, s. red lódh, a tree from the bark of which an astringant infusion is prepared, which is used to fix colour in dyeing, [Colloq. ලොත් *lot*].

ලාක්ෂාරස, *Lákshá-rasa*, s. infusion of the lac or red dye used in dyeing for fixing colours and painting certain parts of the body.

ලාක්ෂාවෘක්ෂ, *Lákshá-wriksha*, s. (ලාක්ෂා and වෘක්ෂ tree) tree, *butea frondosa*. [Colloq. ගස්කෑල *gas-kela*].

ලාක්ෂික, *Lákshika*, a. relating to a lac or ලක්ෂ *laksha*.

ලාක්ෂිකා, *Lákshiká*, *s.* kind of turmeric, *curcuma zerumbet*, [Colloq. හරන්කහ *harankaha*].

ලාකඩ, *Lákaḍa*, *s.* sealing wax.

ලාකඩ තරණ, *Lákaḍa-taraṇa*, *s.* shrub, *webera corymbosa*: see තරණ *taraṇa*.

ලාග්ගා, *Lággá*, *s.* small sea fish, kind of sprat: pl. ලාග්ගෝ *lággó*.

ලාඟු, *Lágu*, *s.* arising, ascending, [Colloq. නගින *nagina*].

ලාඝව, *Lághawa*, *s.* lightness, meanness.

ලාඞ්ගල, *Láṅgala*, *s.* (ලගි *lagi* to go, to limp) plough; penis; palm tree; main beam of a house.

ලාඞ්ගලි, *Láṅgali*, *s.* plant, *gomphocarpus volubilis.*

ලාඞ්ගලිකා, *Láṅgaliká*, *s.* plant, *gloriosa superba*, [Colloq. නියඟලා *niyangalá*].

ලාඞ්ගලී, *Láṅgalí*, *s.* name for certain plants: viz. *jussiæa repens*, [Colloq. බෙරු දියනිල්ල *béru-diyanilla*]; plant, *commelina elevata* or *c. ṣalicifolia*, [Colloq. ගිරාපලා *girá-palá*]; *hydrolea zeylanica*, [Colloq. දියකිරිල්ල *diya-kirilla*]; also *gloriosa superba*: see ලාඞ්ගලිකා *láṅgaliká.*

ලාඞ්ගුල, *Láṅgula*, see ලාඞ්ගල *láṅgala.*

ලාඞ්ගුලිකා, *Láṅguliká*, *s.* medicinal plant, *plectranthus scutellaroides.*

ලාඞ්ගූල, *Láṅgúla*, *s.* hairy tail.

ලාච්චුව, *Láchchuwa*, *s.* drawer to a table. (Dutch, laadje.)

ලාචන, *Láchana*, *s.* resin, [Colloq. දුම්මල *dummala*].

ලාජ, *Lája*, *s.* grain, wetted or sprinkled; root of the *andropogon muricatus*, [Colloq. සැවැන්දරා මුල් *sęwęndará-mul*].

ලාජපුෂ්පි, *Lája-pushpi*, *s.* timber tree, with beautiful flowers, *pongamia glabra*, [Colloq. මගුල් කරඳ *magul-karaṇḍa*].

ලාජා, *Lájá*, *s.* fried grain, [Colloq. විලඳ *vilaṇḍa*].

ලාඤ්ඡන, *Láñchhana*, *s.* (ලාච්ජි *láchji* to mark) mark; sign; name, appellation.

ලාට, *Láṭa*, *s.* name of a country; idle or inebriate language: *adj.* old or worn, spoiled, shabby.

ලාටු, *Láṭu*, *s.* resin, any resinous substance; gum, any glutinous matter.

ලාඩම, *Láḍama*, *s.* horse shoe: pl. ලාඩම් *láḍam*. (Tamil, iladam.)

ලාඩම්ගහනවා, *Láḍam-gahanawá*, *v.* to have a horse or bull shod.

ලාදලු, *Lá-dalu*, *s.* young shoot of a leaf.

ලාඳු, *Ládá*, *s.* betel creeper, *piper betel*, [Colloq. බුලත්වැල් *bulat-węl*].

ලාදුරු, *Láduru*, *s.* leprosy.

ලාපල, *Lá-pala*, *s.* tender fruit.

ලාබ, *Lába*, *s.* gain; profit; gain in general; acquirement, acquisition: *a.* cheap.

ලාබත්, *Lábat*, *s.* food given by a householder to the priests whom he has invited to his house on some special occasion by the laha boards: see ලහ *laha.*

ලාබවෙනවා, *Lábawenawá*, *v.* to become cheap.

ලාභ, *Lábha*, *s.* (ලභ *labha* to get) profit, gain; acquisition, acquirement; gain in general; measure of capacity: see ලහ *laha.*

ලාභකාම, *Lábha-káma*, *s.* (ලාභ gain, කාම wish) desire of gain, avarice.

ලාභමාත්සර්ය, *Lábhamátsarya*, *s.* gain and niggardliness; love of gain and envy; mean, avarice.

ලාභි, *Lábhi*, *s.* person who has acquired gain or profit.

ලාම්පුව, *Lámpuwa*, *s.* lamp. (Eng.)

ලාමක, *Lámaka*, *a.* childish; foolish, idiotic; base, wicked.

ලාමච්ඡ, *Lámachchha*, } *s.* root of the fragrant
ලාමජ්ජක, *Lámajjaka*, } grass, *andropogon muricatus*, [Colloq. සැවැන්දරා මුල් *sęwęndará-mul*].

ලාර්ස්, *Lárs*, *s.* boots. (Duch, laars.)

ලාරසය, *Lárasaya*, *s.* infusion of the bark of the red lódh tree, used in dyeing to fix the colours.

ලාල, *Lála*, *s.* betel creeper: see ලාඳු *ládá.*

ලාලසා, *Lálasá*, *s.* ardent, desire, longing, the longing of pregnant women.

ලාලා, *Lálá*, *s.* saliva, spittle, [Colloq. කෙල *kela*].

ලාලාවිෂ, *Lálávisha*, *s.* (ලාලා spittle, විෂ venom) insect whose spittle is venomous, or acrid, as a spider.

ලාලිත්‍ය, *Lálitya*, *s.* loveliness, gracefulness.

ලාව, *Láwa*, } *s.* sort of quail, *predix*
ලාවටුවෝ *Láwaṭuwó*, } *chinensis.*

ලාවණ්‍ය, *Láwanya*, *s.* beauty, loveliness; saltness.

ලාවා, *Láwá*, *s.* leech, [Colloq. කුඩැල්ලා *kúdęllá*].

ලාවාග්නි, *Láwágni*, *s.* another form of දවාග්නි *dawágni* which see.

ලාවුළු, *Láwuḷu*, *s.* timber tree, with edible fruit, *chrysophyllum Roxburghii (Sapotaceæ).*

ලාස්‍ය, *Lásya*, *s.* dancing; symphony.

ලාසක, *Lásaka*, *s.* (ලස *lasa* to sport) dancer, actor, mime; embracing, enfolding.

ලාසන, *Lásana*, *s.* dancing in general; symphony, or union of song, dance and instrumental music; a mode of dancing confined to attitude and gesticulation, with a shuffling motion of the feet seldom lifted from the ground.

ලාසිකා, *Lásiká*, *s.* female dancer; wanton, harlot.

ලාසුරුව, *Lásuruwa*, *s.* last (measure of fifty-six bushels of chunam).

ලාහෙ, *Láhe*, *s.* measure of quantity, equal to four neli's.

ලි, *Li*, *s.* weariness, fatigue; loss, destruction; end, termination; equality, sameness; bracelet.

ලික්කා, *Likká*, *s.* net; young louse, [Colloq. ඇල්මා *ęlmá*].

ලිකුච, *Likucha*, *s.* species of bread fruit tree, *artocarpus lakoocha*, [Colloq. කනගොන්න *kanagonna*]; lime plant, *citrus limitta*, [Colloq. දෙහි *dehi*]; bread fruit tree, *artocarpus nobilis*, [Coll: දෙල් *del*].

ලිකෝච, *Likócha*, see රුකඟුණ *rukanguna*.

ලිඛිත, *Likhita*, *s.* (ලිඛ *likha* to write, ක්ත *kta* aff.) scripture, writing; manuscript, written book or paper: *a.* written, drawn, delineated (painting being considered a sort of writing).

ලිග්ගල, *Liggala*, *s.* hearth stone: pl. ලිග්ගල් *liggal.*

ලිඟුව, *Linguwa*, *s.* gender in grammar.

ලිඞ්ග, *Linga*, *s.* mark, spot, sign, stain, token; sex; penis; phallus or Şiva under that emblem; according to Hindu philosophy, the androgynal symbol of the creative power Brahma, to whom, as not being the living God but an agent or emanation of the supreme being, no temples are erected or dedicated; gender in grammar.

ලිඞ්ගවාරිණි *Lingawáriṇi*, *s.* tree, bearing a sort of glue, *diospyros embryopteris*, [Colloq. තිඹිරි *timbiri*].

ලිච්ඡවි, *Lichchhavi*, *s.* soft leather; name of a royal dynasty.

ලිත, *Lita*, *s.* almanac, calendar: pl. ලිත් *lit*.

ලිඳ, *Linda*, *s.* well: pl. ලින් *lin*.

ලින්ගුස්, *Lingus*, *s.* sausages. (Port.)

ලින් පඩිය, *Lin-padiya*, *s.* stone or beam laid across a well to serve as a stand for the water-drawer.

ලිප්කෑටය, *Lipkęṭaya*, } *s.* stone used to build a
ලිප්ගල, *Lipgala*, } fire place: see ලිප *lipa*.

ලිප්ත, *Lipta*, *a.* (ලිප *lipa* to smear, ක්ත *kta* aff.) smeared, anointed, plastered, spread.

ලිප්සා, *Lipsá*, *s.* wish, desire.

ලිප, *Lipa*, *s.* (ලිප to smear) smearing, plastering; oven, hearth, fire place where cooking is done.

ලිපි, *Lipi*, *s.* writing in general, hand writing, writing; painting, drawing; smearing.

ලිපිකරුවා, *Lipikaruwá*, *s.* writer, clerk.

ලිම්පනය, *Limpanaya*, *s.* smearing, anointing, plastering.

ලිය, *Liya*, *s.* dwelling house; musk; woman; creeper, any creeping plant.

ලියකතුරු, *Liyakaturu*, *s.* plant, *hibiscus angulosus* or *h. abelmoschus*, [Colloq. කපුකිනිස්ස *kapukinissa*].

ලියන්, *Liyan*, *s.* tree, *homalium zeylanicum (Samydaceæ)*: also, pl. of ලිය *liya*.

ලියන්නා, *Liyanná*, *s.* writer, clerk: pl. ලියන්නෝ *liyannó*.

ලියන අප්පු, *Liyana-appu*, *s.* clerk, writer.

ලියනකටුව, *Liyanakaṭuwa*, *s.* tool used in turning lathes: pl. ලියනකටු *liyanakaṭu*.

ලියන කඳ, *Liyana-kanda*, *s.* turning lathe.

ලියනඟලා, *Liyanangalá*, *s.* plant, *gloriosa superba*, [Colloq. නියඟලා *niyangalá*].

ලියන පට්ටලය, *Liyana-paṭṭalaya*, *s.* turning lathe.

ලියන පෙට්ටිය, *Liyana-peṭṭiya*, *s.* writing box.

ලියන රෝදය, *Liyana-ródaya*, *s.* wheel of a turning lathe.

ලියන වඩුවා, *Liyana-waḍuwá*, *s.* worker in wood, turner.

ලියනවා, *Liyanawá*, *v.* to write, to inscribe, to engrave with an iron pen on the leaves of the palmyra or talipot; to mince or chop into small pieces, as meat or vegetables: pret. ලිව්වා *liwwá*.

ලියමන, *Liyamana*, *s.* writing, an epistle.

ලියලනවා, *Liyalanawá*, *v.* to bud, to sprout: pret. ලියලුවා *liyaluwá*.

ලියවනවා, *Liyawanawá*, *v.* to cause to write or engrave: pret. ලියෙව්වා *liyewwá*.

ලියවැල, *Liyawęla*, *s.* painting, the ornamental or festoon painting of a house or temple.

ලියසැව්, *Liyasęw*, *s.* name of Ananga, the Indian Cupid, [Colloq. අනඞ්ගයා *anangayá*].

ලියු, *Liyu*, *a.* cut into small pieces; written or inscribed.

ලියුම, *Liyuma*, *s.* cutting, mincing; writing: pl. ලියුම් *liyum*.

ලියැද්ද, *Liyędda*, *s.* division or bed of a paddy field: pl. ලියැදි *liyędi* or ලියදි *liyadi*.

ලිවුම, *Liwuma*, *s.* writing, letter, epistle: pl. ලිවුම් *liwum*.

ලිස්සනවා, *Lissanawá*, *s.* to slide, to cause to untie: pret. ලිස්සුවා *lissuwá*.

ලිහනවා, *Lihanawá*, *v.* to unloose, to untie, to unfasten: pret. ලිහුවා *lihuwá*.

ලිහිණියා, *Lihiṇiyá*, *s.* Indian swift, *Cypselus affinis (Cypselidæ*, order *Picariæ)*, also called වැහි ලිහිණියා *wẹhi-lihiṇiyá:* the tern, as the black-bellied marsh tern, *hydrochelidu hybrida*, also called මුදරුකිරලා *mudaru-kiralá;* the Caspian tern, *Sterna caspia;* gull-billed tern, *S. anglica;* large crested, *S. bezgii;* brown winged, *S. anæstheta, (Laridæ*, order *Gaviæ)*.

ලිහිල්, *Lihil*, *a.* soft, tender; slack, loose; easy to be understood, as style.

ලී, *Lí*, *s.* wood, timber; anger.

ලික්ෂා, *Líkshá*, *s.* nit, [Colloq. ලේඩියා *léṇḍiyá*].

ලීකොලපලා, *Likola-palá*, *s.* plant, peculiar to Ceylon, *premna procumbens (Verbenaceæ)*.

ලීඪ, *Líḍha*, *a.* (ලිහ *liha* to lick) licked, eaten.

ලීදඬු, *Lídaṇḍu*, *s.* pieces of timber.

ලීන, *Lína*, *a.* hidden, concealed; adhering.

ලීනාර්ථසංග්‍රහ, *Línártha-saṅgraha*, *s.* (ලීන *lína* hidden, අර්ථ *artha* meaning, සංග්‍රහ compilation) comments on obscure passages in the piṭakas.

ලීනිය, *Líniya*, *s.* small, thinly branched, forest tree, called the screw tree, *helicteres isora (Sterculiaceæ)*.

ලීනියා, *Líniyá*, see ලිහිණියා *lihiṇiyá*.

ලීමදෙහි, *Líma-dehi*, *s.* variety of lime tree, *citrus limetta*.

ලීමෑ, *Límẹ*, *s.* species of bean, *vigna (or dolichos) catiang*.

ලීය, *Líya*, *s.* wood, timber, stick, spar: pl. ලී *lí*.

ලීල්ලා, *Líllá*, *s.* kind of fish.

ලීලා, *Lílá*, *s.* likeness, similarity; manner, gait; branch of feminine action proceeding from love; play, sport, pastime in general; amorous or wanton sport.

ලීලාව, *Líláwa*, *s.* mode, manner, action, deportment: see ලීලා *lílá*.

ලීලෝද්‍යාන, *Lílódyána*, *s.* (ලීලා *lílá* sport, උද්‍යාන *udyána* garden) pleasure ground, garden.

ලීලෝපේත, *Lílópéta*, *s.* (ලීලා *lílá* and උපේත *upéta* endowed with, having) possessed of ලීලා *lílá*, which see; also, shaking, tremulous, playful.

ලිස්තරය, *Listaraya*, } *s.* raised edging, moulding:
ලිස්තරේ, *Listaré*, } pl. ලිස්තර *listara*. (Portuguese, lustre.)

ලුඨන, *Luṭhana*, *s.* (ලුඨ *luṭha* to roll, on the ground) rolling as a horse; rolling on the ground with sorrow.

ලුණු, *Luṇu*, *s.* salt; the saline taste.

ලුණු අන්කෙන්ද, *Luṇu-ankenda*, *s.* shrub with numerous minute white flowers, *evodia Roxburghiana* or *fagara triphylla (Rutaceæ)*.

ලුණු අඳුර, *Luṇu-andara*, see අඳුර *andara*.

ලුණු අලුකෙන්ද, *Luṇu-alukenda*, *s.* tree, not ascertained.

ලුණුකර, *Luṇukara*, *s.* (ලුණු and කර mine) salt mine.

ලුණුකර බිම, *Luṇukara-bima*, *s.* saline soil.

ලුණුකැටිය වැල්, *Luṇukẹṭiya-wẹl*, *s.* creeping plant, *Stephania hernendifolia (Meṇispermaceæ)*.

ලුණුගානවා, *Luṇu-gánawá*, *v.* to salt.

ලුණු දන්, *Luṇu-dan*, *s.* shrub, *ardisia subsessilis* or *humilis (Myrsineæ)*.

ලුණු දමනවා, *Luṇu-damanawá*, *v.* to salt.

ලුණු දෙහි, *Luṇu-dehi*, *s.* salt-lime.

ලුණුබින්ද, *Luṇubinda*, *s.* plant, not ascertained.

ලුණුබි ගහ, *Luṇu-bí-gaha*, *s.* tree, not ascertained.

ලුණුමඩලා, *Luṇumaḍalá*, *s.* tree, with large yellow flowers, *stereospermum (*or *bignonia) chelonioides (Bignoneaceæ)*.

ලුණු මාළු, *Luṇu-máḷu*, *s.* salt-fish.

ලුණු මිදෙල්ල, *Luṇu-midella*, *s.* quick growing timber tree, *melia dubea* or *m. composita (Meliaceæ)*.

ලුණුවරණ, *Luṇuwaraṇa*, *s.* small tree, *cratæva Roxburghii* or *c. religiosa, (Capparideæ)*.

ලුණුවිල, *Luṇuwila*, *s.* hedge hyssop, blue flowers, juice mixed with petroleum used to cure rheumatism, *herpestis (*or *gratiola) Monniera (Scrophulariaceæ)*.

ලුද්දක, *Luddaka*, *s.* hunter.

ලුප්ත, *Lupta*, *s.* (ලුප *lupa* to rob, ක්ත *kta* aff.) booty, plunder; (in grammar) cut off, elided.

ලුප, *Lupa*, *s.* love, affection.

ලුබ්ධ, *Lubdha*, *s.* (ලුභ *lubha* to desire, to covet) hunter; lecher, libertine, covetous or greedy man: *a.* covetous, greedy, desirous, cupidinous.

ලුම්බිනි, *Lumbini*, *s.* wilderness or desert rendered famous in consequence of its being the place in which Buddha was born.

ලුලාප, *Lulápa*, } *s.* (ලුල *lula* to shake, stirring in
ලුලාය, *Luláya*, } the mud) buffalo, [Colloq. මීහරකා *míharaká*].

ලුලිත, *Lulita*, *a.* (ලුල *lula* to agitate, ක්ත *kta* aff.) shaken, trembling, tremulous, agitated, stirred.

ලුව, *Luva*, *s.* largeness (applied to nuts): *a.* large, great, bulky.

ලුහු, *Luhu*, *s.* haste, speed, quickness, celerity. [Colloq. ඉක්මන්කම *ikmankama*]: *a.* short, easy, light; little, small.

ලුහුඩු, *Luhundu*, *a.* short, brief, abridged.

ලුහුඩු කරණවා, *Luhundu-karanawá*, *v.* to abbreviate, to abridge, to curtail.

ලුහුදන, *Luhudana*, *s.* (ලුහු little, දන man) poor man, beggar.

ලුහුබඳිනවා, *Luhubandinawá*, *v.* (ලුහු speed, බඳිනවා to brace) to pursue, to follow after, to chase.

ලුහුල්, *Luhul*, *s.* kind of river fish of a dark colour, [Colloq. ලූලා *lúlá*].

ලූ, *Lú*, *s.* cutting; placing.

ලූතා, *Lútá*, *s.* spider, [Colloq. මකුළුවා *makuluwá*]: local inflammation said to be produced by the urine or spittle of a spider.

ලූතිකා, *Lútiká*, *s.* spider.

ලූන, *Lúna*, *a.* (ලූ *lú* to cut) cut.

ලූනු, *Lúnu*, *s.* onion, garlic.

ලූම, *Lúma*, *s.* tail, hairy tail.

ලූල, *Lúla*, *s.* gin, trap; snare; wicker basket used for catching fish.

ලූලා, *Lúlá*, *s.* fresh water fish, so called *ophiocephalus striatus*.

ලෙංගතු, *Lengatu*, *s.* affection, compassion; kindness, kind disposition.

ලෙඛ්‍යච්ඡද, *Lekhyachchhada*, *s.* palmyra tree, *borassus flabelliformis*, [Colloq. තල් *tal*].

ලෙඩ්ඩුල, *Leddula*, *s.* stone chisel.

ලෙඩ, *Leda*, *s.* sickness, disease: *a.* sick, diseased.

ලෙඩා, *Ledá*, *s.* sick or diseased person: pl. ලෙඩ්ඩු *leddu*.

ලෙඩති තණ, *Lendati-tana*, *s.* club rush, *scirpus fluitans*.

ලෙදමන, *Ledamana*, *s.* livelihood, means of support.

ලෙන, *Lena*, *s.* cave, den, subterraneous dwelling: pl. ලෙන් *len*.

ලෙපෙද, *Lepeda*, *s.* row, line, [Colloq. පෙල *pela*].

ලෙයිගුණය, *Leyigunaya*, *s.* natural temper; compassion, sympathy.

ලෙල්ල, *Lella*, *s.* husk: pl. ලෙලි *leli*.

ලෙල්ලම්කරණවා, *Lellamkaranawá*, *v.* to tease, to worry.

ලෙල්ලම්වෙනවා, *Lellamwenawá*, *v.* to be teased, to be worried.

ලෙල්ලම, *Lellama*, *s.* worrying, teasing.

ලෙල්ලම්පල, *Lellampala*, *s.* place where fishes are sold by auction.

ලෙල, *Lela*, *s.* unfixed, unsteady, wavering.

ලෙලදෙනවා, *Leladenawá*, *v.* to shake, to move, to have a tremulous motion.

ලෙලවනවා, *Lelawanawá*, *v.* to shake, to cause to move, to agitate, to brandish, to vibrate the voice: pret. ලෙලෙව්වා *leleuwá*.

ලෙලිගහනවා, *Leligahanawá*, *v.* to peel, to bark off, to skin.

ලෙලියනවා, *Leliyanawá*, *v.* to wriggle: pret. ලෙලිහුවා *leliyuwá*.

ලෙව්, *Lew*, *s.* the world, inhabitants of the world; aquatic plant, *leersia hexandra (Graminea)*.

ලෙව්තණ, *Lew-tana*, *s.* kind of grass.

ලෙවකනවා, *Lewakanawá*, *v.* to lick.

ලෙවන්, *Lewan*, *s.* (ලෙ blood, වන් colour) red (the colour); planet Mars, [Colloq. අඟහරුවා *angaharuwá*]; (අන් *an* affix to ලෙව් *lew*) inhabitants of the world, mankind.

ලෙවරිය, *Lewariya*, *s.* kind of native sweet-meat.

ලෙස්, *Les*, *s.* hiding, concealment.

ලෙස්සනවා, *Lessanawá*, *v.* to slide: pret. ලෙස්සුවා *lessuwá*.

ලෙස, *Lesa*, *s.* manner: *adv.* so, as; for the purpose of, in order that.

ලෙහිගුණය, *Lehigunaya*, *s.* (ලෙහි in the heart, in or on the breast, ගුණ *guna* good, quality, virtue) tender disposition, a kind and compassionate nature, philanthrophy.

ලෙහෙටු, *Lehetu*, *s.* eating.

ලෙහෙඩ, *Leheda*, *s.* a nit.

ලෙහෙඩියා, *Lehendiyá*, *s.* nit, egg of a louse.

ලෙහෙනා, *Lehená*, *s.* squirrel: see ලේනා *léná*.

ලේ, *Lé*, *s.* blood; line, row.

ලේ අතිසාරය, *Lé-atisáraya*, *s.* dysentery.

ලේකම, *Lékama*, *s.* manuscript, record, writing; writer, scribe, amanuensis.

ලේ කරවලා, *Lé-karawalá*, *s.* kind of small venomous snake.

ලේ කොඩොල්, *Lé-kondol*, *s.* kind of yam.

ලේඛ්‍ය, *Lékhya*, *s.* letter, epistle; manuscript; drawing, delineation; written accusation or defence.

ලේඛ, *Lékha*, *s.* (ලිඛ *likha* to write) letter, epistle, [Colloq. ලියුම *liyuma*].

ලේඛනය, *Lékhanaya*, *s.* writing, scripture; bark of the bhójapatra tree, used for writing on; leaf of the palm tree; vomiting; scraping or cleaning the tongue; scratching; thinning sort of grass or reed of which pens are made, *saccharum spontaneum*.

ලේඛනී, *Lékhaní*, *s.* pen, [Colloq. පෑන *pęna*. English].

ලේඛා, *Lékhá*, *s.* line, mark, row; writing; delineation, painting.

ලේඛිත, *Lékhita*, *a.* written, inscribed.

ලේගලනවා, *Lé-galanawá*, *v.* to bleed.

ලේඩිත්තා, *Léṇḍittá*, } ලේඩියා, *Léṇḍiyá*, } *s.* nit, the egg of a louse.

ලේන්කූඩුව, *Lén-kúḍuwa*, *s.* squirrel's nest.

ලේන්තැරි, *Lénteri*, } ලේන්තැරි පුවක්, *Lénteri-puwak*, } *s.* small areca palm, peculiar to Ceylon, *areca concinna (Palmæ)*.

ලේන්පහුරු, *Lén-pahuru*, *s.* club moss, *lycopodium rupestre*.

ලේන්සුව, *Lénsuwa*, *s.* handkerchief: pl. ලේන්සු *lénsu*]. (Portuguese).

ලේන ඇල්වී, *Léna-ęlví*, *s.* kind of paddy, *oryza sativa*.

ලේනවී, *Léna-ví*, *s.* kind of paddy.

ලේන හතු, *Léna-hatu*, *s.* mushroom.

ලේනා, *Léná*, *s.* squirrel, generic names *sciurus* and *sciuropterus*: pl. ලේන්නු *lénnu*.

ලේනිය පලා, *Léniya-palá*, *s.* plant, *heliuteris isora*.

ලේනුන්, *Lénun*, *acc. plur.* of ලේනා *léná*.

ලේප, *Lépa*, *s.* (ලිප *lipa* to smear) smearing, anointing, plastering; mortar, plaster, lime.

ලේපකරණවා, *Lépa-karaṇawá*, *v.* to smear, to anoint.

ලේපන, *Lépana*, *s.* smearing, plastering, daubing; anointing.

ලේපලු, *Lé-palu*, *s.* eruptions of blood.

ලේපින්, *Lépin*, *s.* (ලිප *lipa* to plaster) ඉනි *ini* aff.) bricklayer, plasterer.

ලේ පොලඟා, *Lé-polangá*, *s.* viper, variety of *trimeresurus*, *hypnale* or *daboia*.

ලේමඩුළු, *Lémaḍuḷu*, *s.* blood spots, [Colloq. ලේ පැල්ලම් *lé-pęllam*].

ලේමාලය, *Lémálaya*, *s.* (ලේ blood, මාල *mála* chain, stream) flow of blood from the womb, bloody issue.

ලේමි පොලඟා, *Lémi-polangá*, *s.* viper: see the preceding word.

ලේමැඩිල්ලා, *Lémedillá*, *s.* olive coloured dwarf snake, *aspidura bracchyorrhos (Calamaridæ*, order *ophidia)*.

ලේලි, *Léli*, *s.* daughter-in-law; niece: pl. ලේලියෝ *léliyó*.

ලේලු, *Lélu*, *s.* fish of the carp tribe, found in mountain streams supposed to be the mahseer, *burbus tor*.

ලේවන්, *Léwan*, *s.* planet Mars; red: see ලෙවන් *lewan*.

ලේවාය, *Léwáya*, *s.* salt pan; saltern.

ලේවා ලුණු, *Léwá-luṇu*, *s.* (ලේවා and ලුණු salt) sea salt made in a saltern.

ලේ වැරැල්ල, *Lé-werella*, *s.* shrub, flea bane, *conyza balsamifera*.

ලේශ, *Lésa*, *s.* smallness, littleness; a little: *a.* small, little.

ලේසි, *Lési*, *a.* easy, convenient. (Tamil, ilésu.)

ලේසිකරණවා, *Lési-karaṇawá*, *v.* to facilitate.

ලේසිය, *Lésiya*, *s.* ease, facility, convenience: *a.* easy, convenient.

ලේ සොල්වනවා, *Lé-solwanawá*, *v.* to shed blood.

ලේහකරණවා, *Léha-karaṇawá*, *v.* to taste, to taste with the tongue, to lick; to excite saliva by a medical process.

ලේහන, *Léhana*, *s.* act of licking, tasting with the tongue.

ලේහය, *Léhaya*, *s.* licking with the tongue; any mucilaginous mixture taken medicinally.

ලොක්වත්, *Lokwat*, *s.* loquat or Japanese medlar, *japonica eriobotrya*.

ලොකරු, *Lokaru*, *s.* (ලො for ලෝ *ló* metal, කරු who does) blacksmith, iron founder, worker on metal; more commonly written ලෝකුරු *lókuru*.

ලොකු, *Loku*, *a.* large, big, bulky; great, exalted.

ලොකු අක්කා, *Loku-akká*, *s.* elder sister.

ලොකු අප්පොච්චි, *Loku-appochchi*, *s.* father's elder brother, literally, great-father.

ලොකු අම්මා, *Loku-ammá*, *s.* mother's elder sister, father's elder brother's wife, literally great-mother.

ලොකුකම, *Lokukama*, *s.* greatness, pride, haughtiness.

ලොකුකරණවා, *Lokukaraṇawá*, *v.* to enlarge, to bring up.

ලොකු තාත්තා, *Loku-táttá*, see ලොකු අප්පොච්චි *loku-appochchi*.

ලොකු බකමූනා, *Loku-bakamúná*, *s.* forest eagle owl, *bubo nipalensis* (sub order *Striges*, order *Accipitres)*.

ලොකු මුගටියා, *Loku-mugaṭiyá*, *s.* furry mungoose, called the Ceylon badger, *herpestes vitticollis*.

ලොකු රාජාලියා, *Loku-rájáliyá*, *s.* white bellied sea eagle, *haliaetus leucogaster*, *(Falconidæ*, order *Accipitres)*.

ලොකු වව්ලා, *Loku-wawlá*, *s.* large bat, called russet or flying fox, *pteropus Edwardsii*.

ලොට, *Loṭa*, *a.* tender, immature, [Colloq. ලපටි *lapaṭi*]; also, ලාට *láṭa*, *a.* old, worn, spoiled, shabby.

ලොඩි, *Loḍi*, *s.* kind of sea jelly-fish.

ලොඩිය, *Loḍiya*, *s.* pulp, (applied to the substance within the fruit of the goraka): pl. ලොඩි *loḍi*.

ලොත්සුඹුළ, *Lotsumbuḷa*, *s.* tree, lódhra, the bark of which is used in dyeing, *symplocos racemosa:* see ලෝධ්‍ර *lódhra*.

ලොතරැයිය, *Lotaręyiya*, *s.* lottery. (Eng.)

ලොඳ, *Loṇda*, *s.* kernel of the young coconut; pulp, soft, succulent part of fruit.

ලොප්කරණවා, *Lopkaraṇawá*, *v.* to suppress (chiefly used in grammar for elision or dropping of letters).

ලොප්කෙරීම, *Lopkeríma*, verbal noun of the above: see ලෝප *lópa*.

ලොබ, *Loba*, *s.* covetousness, avariciousness.

ලොඹුකරණවා, *Lombukaraṇawá*, *v.* to chew, to mumble.

ලොම්, *Lom*, *s.* hair, wool, hair of the body.

ලොම්කොල, *Lomkola*, *s.* single hair of the body.

ලොම්බා, *Lombá*, *s.* toothless man.

ලොම්රොද, *Lomroda*, *s.* (ලොම් and රොද line) row or ringlet of hair.

ලොම, *Loma*, *s.* carpet, mat for the ground.

ලොමුදැහැ, *Lomudęhę*, } *s.* (ලොම් *lom* and උදැහැ
ලොමුදැහැගැම්ම, *Lomudęhęgęmma*, } from උද්ග්‍රහ *udgraha*, and උදැහැගැම්ම *udęhęgęmma* from උද්ග්‍රහණ *udgrahaṇa*, taking up, lifting, raising) horripilation, erection of the hair of the body, supposed to be occasioned by exquisite pleasure or pain.

ලොයිබංකුව, *Loyibaṇkuwa*, *s.* platform, wooden couch, bench.

ලොල්, *Lol*, *a.* (ලොඩ *loḍa* to be frantic) lascivious; covetous, avaricious; lustful, desirous; unsteady, wavering.

ලොව්, *Low*, *s.* uninflected crude form of ලොව *lowa*.

ලොව, *Lowa*, *s.* the world; Elu form of ලෝක

ලොවග, *Lowaga*, *s.* (ලොව් *low* and අග *aga* chief) name of Buddha; chief of the world.

ලොවදුරු, *Lowaduru*, see ලොවැදුරු *lowęduru*.

ලොවනා, *Lowaná*, *s.* (ලොව world, නා chief) name of Buddha; chief of the world.

ලොවාග්‍ර, *Lowágra*, see ලොවග *lowaga*.

ලොවිච්චි කොට්ටේ, *Lovichchi-koṭṭé*, *s.* fringed cushion.

ලොවිච්චිය, *Lovichchiya*, *s.* fringes.

ලොවිඳු, *Loviṇdu*, *s.* (ලොව and ඉඳු lord) name of Buddha, in allusion to his being the lord of the world or the chief of the human race.

ලොවිනවා, *Lovinawá*, *v.* to lap, to lick with the tongue: pret. ලෙව්වා *lewwá*.

ලොවිලොවි, *Lovilovi*, *s.* fruit tree so called, lovilovi. *flacourtia inermis (Bixineæ)*.

ලොවිසුරු, *Lovisuru*, see ලොවිඳු *loviṇdu*.

ලොවැදුරු, *Lowęduru*, *s.* (ලොව *lowa* and ඇදුරු *ęduru* teacher) name of Brahma; name of Buddha.

ලොහො, *Loho*, *s.* iron; metal, either in a crude or wrought state.

ලොහොකරුවා, *Lohokaruwá*, *s.* (ලොහො metal, කරුවා who does) iron founder, blacksmith, worker in metal.

ලොහොතුඩුවා, *Lohotuḍuwá*, *s.* heron, [Colloq. කොස්ලිහිණියා *kos-lihiṇiyá*]; hornbill, [Colloq. කෑඳත්තා *kęṇdattá*].

ලොහොදකය, *Lohodakaya*, *s.* (ලොහ *loha* metal, උදක *udaka* water) water in which hot iron has been cooled.

ලෝ, *Ló*, *s.* world; iron, metal in general, either in a crude or wrought state.

ලෝ අජර, *Ló-ajara*, *s.* (ලෝ world, අජර teacher) name of Brahma; name of Buddha: see ලෝකගුරු *lóka-guru*.

ලෝ ඉසුරු, *Ló-isuru*, *s.* (ලෝ and ඉසුරු chief) name of Buddha; name of Ṣiva.

ලෝක, *Lóka*, *s.* (ලෝක to see) man, mankind; a world, division of the universe; in general three Lókas are enumerated, namely, heaven, earth and hell.

ලෝකග්ගෝ, *Lókaggó*, *s.* (ලෝක and අග්ගෝ *aggó* chief) name of Buddha, as the lord of mankind.

ලෝකගුරු, *Lóka-guru*, *s.* (ලෝක and ගුරු teacher) name of Buddha, alluding to his character as religious preceptor of the three worlds.

ලෝකචක්ඛුස්, *Lóka-chakshus*, *s.* (ලෝක and චක්ඛුස් eye) sun, [Colloq. ඉර *ira*].

ලෝක චූඩාමණි, *Lóka-chúḍámaṇi*, *s.* (ලෝක world, චූඩාමණි gem in the crest) crest-jewel of the world, one occupying the most conspicuous place in the world.

ලෝකජිත්, *Lókajit*, *s.* (ලෝක world, ජිත් who conquers) name of Buddha, he who conquered all.

ලෝකඩ, *Lókaḍa*, *s.* bell metal, bronze.

ලෝකධර්මය, *Lóka-dharmaya*, see ලෝක ව්‍යවහාරය *lóka-vyawaháraya*.

ලෝකධාතුව, *Lóka-dhátuwa*, s. (ලෝක world, ධාතු *dhátu* principle or element) one of the constituent elements of the world, as earth, air, fire, water.

ලෝකනාථ, *Lóka-nátha*, s. (ලෝක and නාථ chief) name of Buddha; sovereign of the world.

ලෝකපාල, *Lóka-pála*, s. (ලෝක and පාල who nourishes) king, sovereign, [Colloq. රජ *raja*].

ලෝකප්‍රවාද, *Lókaprawáda*, s. common or current report or saying.

ලෝක ප්‍රසිද්ධ, *Lóka-prasiddha*, a. notorious, well-known.

ලෝකමාතා, *Lóka-mátá*, s. (ලෝක and මාතා mother) name of Lakshmí the wife of Vishṇu, and goddess of wealth and fortune.

ලෝකය, *Lókaya*, see its plural form ලෝක *lóka*.

ලෝකයාත්‍රා, *Lóka-yátrá*, s. (ලෝක and යාත්‍රා going) worldly affairs, civil conduct, resort of men, traffic, intercourse.

ලෝකරඤ්ජන, *Lóka-rañjana*, s. (ලෝක and රඤ්ජන pleasing) popularity, gaining public confidence.

ලෝකරුවා, *Lókaruwá*, s. (ලෝ metal, කරුවා who does or makes) worker in metal, smith, founder.

ලෝකවාද, *Lóka-wáda*, s. (ලෝක and වාද speech) rumour, report.

ලෝකවාසී, *Lóka-wási*, s. (ලෝක and වාසී who inhabits) men, mankind.

ලෝකවිෂය, *Lókavisaya*, s. sphere of the world.

ලෝක ව්‍යවහාරය, *Lóka-wyawaháraya*, s. (ලෝක and ව්‍යවහාරය custom) custom, habit, worldly maxims or practices, worldliness.

ලෝකස්වාමි, *Lóka-swámi*, s. (ලෝක world, ස්වාමි lord) name of Buddha.

ලෝකාධිපති, *Lókádhipati*, s. (ලෝක *lóka* and අධිපති *adhipati*, chief) king, sovereign, [Colloq. රජ *raja*].

ලෝකාන්තර, *Lókántara*, s. (ලෝක *lóka* and අන්තර *antara* intervening) space between one world and another; another world.

ලෝකාන්තරිකය, *Lókántarikaya*, s. (ලෝකාන්තර *lókántara* and ඉක *ika* aff.) a hell, so called from its being situated in the space between this world and the next below it.

ලෝකායත, *Lókáyata*, s. system of atheistical philosophy taught by Charwáka.

ලෝකාර්ථ, *Lókártha*, s. (ලෝක *lóka* and අර්ථ *artha* profit) any thing calculated for general benefit.

ලෝකාලෝක, *Lóká-lóka*, s. (ලෝක *lóka* seeing, අලෝක *alóka* not seeing; causing light and darkness, as interposed between the Dwípas [continents] and the sun), mountainous belt surrounding the outermost of the seven seas and bounding the world, commonly called Sakwaḷagala or Chakrawáṭaya.

ලෝකාස්වාද රතිය, *Lókáswáda-ratiya*, s. (ලෝක *lóka* man, ආස්වාද *áswáda* enjoyment, රති *rati* desire) copulation, intercourse of the sexes.

ලෝකික, *Lókika*, á. (ලෝක *lóka* and ඉක *ika* aff.) worldly: see ලෞකික *laukika*.

ලෝකුත්තර, *Lókuttara*, s. (ලෝක *lóka* and උත්තර *uttara* chief) king. sovereign, [Colloq. රජ *raja*]; the next world: *a*. relating to the next world; pre-eminent in the world.

ලෝකුරුවා, *Lókuruwá*, s. (ලෝ metal, කුරුවා who does) see ලෝකරුවා *lókaruwá*.

ලෝකේ, *Lóké*, see ලෝකය *lókaya*.

ලෝකේශ, *Lókéṣa*, s. (ලෝක *lóka* world, ඊශ *íṣa* chief) name of Brahma; name of Buddha.

ලෝකෝත්තම, *Lókóttama*, s. (ලෝක and උත්තම *uttama* chief) chief of the world; an epithet of Buddha.

ලෝකෝත්තර, *Lókóttara*, s. (ලෝක *lóka* man, උත්තර *uttara* eminent) king, prince; the next world: *a*. best, excellent, eminent, pre-eminent.

ලෝචක, *Lóchaka*, s. pupil of the eye; stibium, or lamp black, etc. so used.

ලෝචන, *Lóchana*, s. (ලෝච *lócha* to see) eye, [Colloq. ඇහැ *ẹhẹ*].

ලෝණ, *Lóṇa*, Páli form of ලවණ *lawaṇa*.

ලෝණික, *Lóṇika*, a. (ලෝණ *lóṇa* and ඉක *ika* aff.) saltish, of or relating to salt.

ලෝදා, *Lódá*, see ලෝකධාතුව *lókadhátuwa*.

ලෝදිය, *Lódiya*, s. melted brass, melted metal.

ලෝද්‍ර, *Lódhra*, s. (රුධ *rudha* to hinder, ල *la* substituted for ර *ra*, and රන් *ran* aff.) tree, the bark of which is used in dyeing, *cymplocos racemosa:* see ලොත්සුඹුළ *lotsumbuḷa*.

ලෝද්‍රවෘක්ෂ, *Lódhra-wṛiksha*, s. tree, *cratæva Roxburghii*, [Colloq. ලුණුවරණ *luṇuwaraṇa*].

ලෝධ, *Lódha*, see ලෝද්‍ර *lódhra*.

ලෝනවා, *Lónawá*, v. to lap, to lick with the tongue, to taste: pret. ලෙව්වා *lewwá*.

ලෝනිසල, *Lónisala*, s. (ලෝ and නිසල firm) the earth, [Colloq. පොළව *poḷawa*].

ලෝප්ත්‍ර, *Lóptra*, s. (ලුප *lupa* to cut off, ත්‍ර aff.) plunder, booty, stolen goods.

ලෝප, *Lópa, s.* (ලුප *lupa* to cut) rejection, cutting off in general, especially used as a grammatical term for dropping letters, syllables, etc; disappearance, destruction.

ලෝපාශක, *Lópásaka, s.* (ලෝප *lópa* rejection, අශ *aṣa* to eat) jackal, [Colloq. නරියා *nariyá*].

ලෝප්‍රසිද්ධ, *Ló-prasiddha*, see ලෝකප්‍රසිද්ධ *lóka-prasiddha*.

ලෝභ, *Lóbha, s.* (ලුභ *lubha* to desire or covet) covetousness, cupidity, intense or greedy desire.

ලෝභකම, *Lóbhakama, s.* greediness, niggardliness, stinginess.

ලෝභයා, *Lóbhayá, s.* covetous or penurious person.

ලෝම, *Lóma, s.* hair, hair of the body; wool; tail, hairy tail.

ලෝමකූපය, *Lómakúpaya, s.* (ලෝම hair, කූප *kúpa* well) pore of the skin.

ලෝමන්, *Lóman*, see ලෝම *lóma*.

ලෝමමය, *Lómamaya, a.* (ලෝම and මය aff.) woollen.

ලෝමශ, *Lómaṣa, s.* (ලෝම hair, ශ aff.) plant, [Colloq. කොල්ලන්කොල *kollankola*]; woollen: *a.* hairy, covered with or made with hair.

ලෝමශා, *Lómaṣá, s.* fox; sort of bonduc; shrub, *leea hirta;* Indian spikenard, *valeriana jatamansi*, [Colloq. ජටාමාංස *jaṭámáṇsa*]; cowach, *carpopogon pruriens;* hairy plant, *sida cordifolia;* green vitriol, [Colloq. පල්මානික්කං *palmánikkaṇ*]; orris root, [Colloq. වදකහ *wadakaha*].

ලෝමහර්ෂණ, *Lómaharshaṇa, s.* (ලෝම and හර්ෂණ rejoicing) horripilation, erection of the hair of the body, supposed to be an indication of great pleasure.

ලෝමික, *Lómika, a.* (ලෝම *lóma* hair, ඉක *ika* aff.) hairy, woolly.

ලෝල, *Lóla, s.* (ලෝඩ *lóḍa* to be frantic) tree, *cordia myxa:* see ලෝළු *lólu: a.* greedy, avaricious; shaking, tremulous; desiring, wishing, cupidinous.

ලෝලා, *Lólá, s.* tongue; goddess Lakshmí, the goddess of wealth and fortune.

ලෝලිත, *Lólita, a.* (ලුල *lula* to agitate, ක්ත *kta* aff.) shaken, agitated, tremulous.

ලෝවරු, *Lówaru, s.* founder, brazier.

ලෝවැඩ, *Lówęḍa, s.* good of the world, public good.

ලෝවැසි, *Lówęsi*, see ලෝකවාසි *lókawási*.

ලෝහ, *Lóha, s.* (ලූ *lu* to cut) iron, either crude or wrought; any metal; weapon; aloe wood or agallochum, [Colloq. අගිල් *agil*]; steel; blood.

ලෝහක, *Lóhaka, s.* aloe wood.

ලෝහකාන්ත, *Lóha-kánta, s.* (ලෝහ iron, කාන්ත in this compound a gem) loadstone, [Colloq. කාන්දම් *kándam*].

ලෝහකාර, *Lóhakára, s.* (ලෝහ iron, කාර who works in) blacksmith, iron-smith.

ලෝහජ, *Lóhaja, s.* (ලෝහ and ජ produced from) bell metal; rust of iron, iron filings.

ලෝහපෘෂ්ඨ, *Lóha-pṛishtha, s.* (ලෝහ and පෘෂ්ඨ back) heron, [Colloquial. කොස් ලිහිණියා *kos-lihiṇiyá*].

ලෝහරාජක, *Lóharájaka, s.* (ලෝහ metal, රාජ *rája* shining) silver, [Colloq. රිදී *ridí*].

ලෝහල, *Lóhala, s.* (ලෝ and හල house) foundery, or smith's shop, [Colloq. කම්මල *kammala*].

ලෝහවර, *Lóhawara, s.* (ලෝහ and වර best) gold, [Colloq. රත්රන් *ratran*].

ලෝහාභිසාර, *Lóhábhisára*, } *s.* (ලෝහ *lóha* weapon, අභි *abhi* about,
ලෝහාභිහාර, *Lóhábhihára*, } සෘ *ṣri* to go) lustration of arms, formerly a celebration observed by princes before opening a campaign, but now usually confined to the domestic decoration and worship of the soldier's weapons.

ලෝහිත, *Lóhita, s.* red, (the colour); blood; red kind of agallochum; saffron, *curcuma longa*, [Colloq. කහ *kaha*]; red sanders or red sandal wood, *pterocarpus santalinus;* war, battle; planet Mars, [Colloq. අඟහරුවා *angaharuwá*]; kind of fish, *cyprinus denticulatus*, sort of deer; snake; a deity, demigod; sort of bean, *ervum hirsutum* or *e. lenis;* form of array; tree, *andersonia Rohituka.*

ලෝහිතක්‍ය, *Lóhitakya*, see ලෝහිතඞ්කය *lóhitaṅkaya.*

ලෝහිතක, *Lóhitaka, s.* (ලෝහිත red, ක aff.) ruby; planet Mars; calx of brass.

ලෝහිතඞ්කය, *Lóhitaṅkaya, s.* ruby, [Colloq. රතුකැට *ratukęṭa*].

ලෝහිත චන්දන, *Lóhita-chandana, s.* (ලෝහිත red, චන්දන sandal) saffron, *curcuma longa* [Colloq. කහ *kaha*]; tree, *swietenia febrifugia*, [Colloq. කොකුම් *kokum*]; red sandal wood, *pterocarpus santalinus*, [Colloq. රත්සඳුන් *rat-saṇdun*].

ලෝහිත ධාතු, *Lóhita-dhátu, s.* (ලෝහිත and ධාතු element) blood considered as one of the primitive and component elements of the body.

ලෝහිත පක්ඛන්දික, *Lóhita-pakkhandika*, *s.* (ලෝහිත blood, ප intensely, ඛදි *khadi* to go) diarrhæa; dysentery.

ලෝහිත පුෂ්ප, *Lóhita-pushpa*, *s.* (ලෝහිත and පුෂ්ප flower) shoe flower, *hibiscus rosa-sinensis*, [Coll: සපත්තුමල *sapattu-mala*].

ලෝහිතාඞ්ග, *Lóhitáńga*, *s.* (ලෝහිත *lóhita* red, අඞ්ග *ańga* body) planet Mars, [Colloq. අඟහරුවා *angaharuwá*].

ලෝහිමි, *Lóhimi*, *s.* (ලෝ and හිමි lord) name of Buddha: see ලොවිඳු *lovindu*.

ලෝහෝත්තම, *Lóhóttama*, *s.* (ලෝහ *lóha* metal, උත්තම *uttama* best) gold, [Colloq. රත්රන් *rat-ran*].

ලෝළු, *Lólu*, *s.* low tree with edible roots, *cordia myxa (Boragineæ)*.

ලෞකික, *Laukika*, *a.* (ලෝක *lóka* the world, අණ් *aṇ* aff.) mundane, worldly, human, what prevails among mankind.

ලෞහ, *Lauha*, *a.* (ලෝහ *lóha* iron, අණ් *aṇ* aff.) iron, made of iron.

ලැ, *Lę*, *s.* (another form of ල *la*) mind, seat of reason.

ලැගිම, *Lęgíma*, } *s.* roosting, act of lying down as
ලැගුම්, *Lęgum*, } animals: see ලගිනවා *laginawá*.

ලැගුම්ගෙය, *Lęgum-geya*, *s.* (ලැගුම් resting, ගෙය house) priest's sleeping room.

ලැජ්ජාකරණවා, *Lęjjákaraṇawá*, *v.* incorrectly for ලජ්ජාකරණවා *lajjákaraṇawá*, to make ashamed, to abash.

ලැජ්ජාව, *Lęjjáwa*, *s.* incorrectly for ලජ්ජාව *lajjáwa*, shame, shame-facedness, modesty, bashfulness.

ලැතැවිල්ල, *Lętęvilla*, *s.* (ලැ mind, තැවිල්ල burning) emotion, agitation; grief, sorrow.

ලැදි, *Lędi*, *a.* devoted, entirely given up to an object, attached, affectionate.

ලැදිකම, *Lędikama*, *s.* faith, love, attachment.

ලැදිවෙනවා, *Lędiwenawá*, *v.* to be or become attached.

ලැපැත්ත, *Lępętta*, *s.* (ලැ mind, පැත්ත side) breast; heart.

ලැබීම, *Lębíma*, verbal noun of ලැබෙනවා *lębenawá*.

ලැබෙනවා, *Lębenawá*, *v.* to get, to obtain, to receive, to acquire: pret. ලැබුනා *lębuná*.

ලැමඩිය, *Lęmaḍiya*, *s.* breast; mind or heart as the seat of reason; the bosom, pit of the stomach: pl. ලැමඩි *lęmaḍi*.

ලැය, *Lęya*, incorrectly for ලය *laya*.

ලැයින්, *Lęyin*, *s.* glue.

ලැයිම, *Lęyima*, *s.* hut for dwelling.

ලැව්ගිනි, *Lęw-gini*, *s.* conflagration, wood on fire.

ලැවි, *Levi*, *s.* archer, bowyer, bowman.

ලැවිදුනු, *Lęvidunu*, *s.* reconciling, making peace.

ලැවීම, *Lęvíma*, verbal noun of ලවනවා *lawanawá*.

ලැවැන්න, *Lęwęnna*, *s.* distress, productive matter, cause.

ලැස්, *Lęs*, *s.* delay, loitering.

ලැහැබ, *Lęhęba*, } *s.* thicket, bushy place, jun-
ලැහැඹ, *Lęhęmba*, } gle, [Colloq. කැලය *kęlaya*].
ලැහැප්, *Lęhęp*, }

ලැතිගානවා, *Lętigánawá*, *v.* to teeth.

ලෑල්ල, *Lélla*, *s.* plank, board: pl. ලෑලි *léli*.

ලෑවිරේකය, *Lévirékaya*, } *s.* emetic.
ලෑවිරේකේ, *Lévirékē*, }

ලෑස්ති, *Lésti*, *a.* ready. (Portuguese.)

ලෑස්තිකරණවා, *Léstikaraṇawá*, *v.* to make ready, to prepare.

ලෑස්තිය, *Lęstiya*, *s.* preparation, readiness.

ලෑස්තිවෙනවා, *Léstiwennwá*, *v.* to get ready, to prepare one's self.

ව

The twenty-ninth consonant of the Sinhalese alphabet; it is expressed by the letters *w* and *v*.

වංඇපල, *Waṇ-ępala*, *s.* small tree or shrub with large flowers, *adhatoda vasica*, [Colloq. අගල්ආදර *agl-ádára*].

වංක, *Wanka*, *s.* (වකි *waki* to be crooked) bend of a river, winding course of a stream, curve or bend in general: *a.* crooked, curved, bent; deceitful, dishonest; fraudulent.

වංකකම, *Wankakama*, *s.* crookedness, dishonesty.

වංකනාලය, *Wankanálaya*, *s.* (වංක and නාල *nála* tube) clay nozzle of the bellows used by gold and silver smiths.

වංකයා, *Wankayá*, *s.* dishonest or untruthful person.

වංක්‍ය, *Wankya*, *a.* crooked, curved, bent.

වංග, *Wanga*, see වඞ්ග *wańga*.

වංගි, *Wangi*, see වඞ්ගි *wańgi*.

වංගෙඩිය, *Wangeḍiya*, see වන්ගෙඩිය *wangeḍiya*.

වංචාකාරයා, *Wanchákárayá*, see වඤ්චාකාරයා *wañchákárayá*.

වංචාව, *Wancháwa*, see වඤ්චාව *wañcháwa*.

වංපර, *Waṇ-para*, *s.* tree, species of *dillenia:* see වම්පර *wampara*.

වංශ, *Wansa*, *s.* race, lineage, family; bamboo tree, [Colloq. උණගහ *una-gaha*]; assemblage, multitude; backbone, spine.

වංශක්ෂිරි, *Wansakshiri*, see වංශරෝචනා *wansa-róchaná*.

වංශජ, *Wansaja*, *s.* (වංශ and ජ born) bamboo manna, [Colloquial. උණමකුළු *una-makulu*]: *a.* sprung from a good family, well-born.

වංශරෝචනා, *Wansa-róchaná*, *s.* (වංශ and රුච් *ruch* to shine) earthy concretion of a milk white colour formed in the hollow of a bamboo, and called bamboo manna, [Colloq. උණමකුළු *una-makulu*].

වංශභවා, *Wansa-bhawá*, *s.* bamboo manna: see the preceding.

වංශික, *Wansika*, *s.* (වංශ *wansa* bamboo, ඪක් *dhak* aff.) aloe wood, [Colloq. අගිල් *agil*].

වංසය, *Wansaya*, see වංශ *wansa*.

වංශාගත, *Wanságata*, see වංශජ *wansaja*.

වක්, *Wak*, *s.* time: *a.* crooked, bent, curved: see වංක *wanka*.

වක් අත්ත, *Wak-atta*, *s.* pole of a plough; curved timber or rib of a boat or vessel; the felloe of a wheel: pl. වක්අතු *wak-atu*.

වක් අඟ, *Wak-anga*, *s.* powder horn; horn of an ox used by medical practitioners in an operation resembling cupping: see වක්කං *wakkan*.

වක්ක, *Wakka*, *a.* (වකි *waki* to be crooked) crooked, bent, curved.

වක්කං, *Wakkan*, *s.* part, portion, share; sort of cupping instrument made of horn: see වක් අඟ *wak-anga*.

වක්කං ඇවිලීම, *Wakkan-evilíma*, *s.* (වක්කං and ඇවිලීම causing to adhere) operation similar to that of cupping practised by native doctors: see වක්කං *wakkan*.

වක්කඩ, *Wakkada*, *s.* hole or opening in a dam to let off the water from the paddy fields.

වක්කර, *Wakkara*, *s.* piper, one who plays on a flute.

වක්කරණවා, *Wakkaranawá*, *v.* to pour, to pour out, to shed: pret. වැක්කෙරුවා *wekkeruwá*.

වක්කලම, *Wakkalama*, *s.* whirlpool, eddy; deep place in a river where the water is nearly stagnant, and bends to another direction: pl. වක්කලම් *wakkalam*.

වක්කැට, *Wakketa*, *s.* cold of earth.

වක්ත්‍ර, *Waktra*, *s.* (වච *wacha* to speak, ත්‍රච් *trach* aff.) face; mouth; speaking, speaker, an orator: *a.* loquacious or talkative; speaking eloquently or sensibly; wise, learned.

වක්ත්‍රභූෂණ, *Waktra-bhúshana*, *s.* species of madder, *rubia manjitha*, [Colloq. වැල්මදට *wel-madata*].

වක්දිය, *Wakdiya*, *s.* water in rice or paddy fields.

වක්නිය, *Wakniya*, *s.* plant from the fibres of which bow strings are made, *sanseviera zeylanica*, [Colloq. නියද *niyanda*].

වක් මස, *Wak-masa*, properly වප් මස *wap-masa*, which see.

වක් මේවර, *Wak-méwara*, *s.* preparing ground for the sowing of grain.

වක්‍ර, *Wakra*, *s.* (වකි *waki* to go crookedly, රන් *ran* aff.) winding course of a river or waterfall; the arm or bend of a stream; name of Saturn, [Coll: සෙනසුරා *senasurá*]; name of Mars, [Colloq. අඟහරුවා *angaharuwá*]: *a.* crooked, curved, bowed, bent; dishonest, fraudulent.

වක්‍රඛඩ්ග, *Wakra-khadga*, *s.* (වක්‍ර crooked, ඛඩ්ග sword) sabre, scimitar, [Colloq. කඩුව *kaduwa*].

වක්‍රග්‍රීව, *Wakra-gríwa*, *s.* (වක්‍ර and ග්‍රීව neck) camel, [Colloq. ඔටුවා *otuwá*].

වක්‍රපුෂ්ප, *Wakra-pushpa*, *s.* (වක්‍ර and පුෂ්ප flower) tree, *æschynomene grandiflora:* see වකපුෂ්ප *waka-pushpa*.

වක්ෂස්, *Wakshas*, *s.* (වච *wacha* to speak) breast, bosom, chest.

වක්ෂි, *Wakshi*, *s.* small aromatic plant, *kaemferia galanga*, [Colloq. හිඟුරුපියලි *hingurupiyali*].

වක, *Waka*, *s.* (වක to be crooked) crane, white crane, stork or heron, [Colloq. කොකා *koká*]; lunar day, the thirtieth part of a lunar month; tree, *æschynomene grandiflora:* see වකපුෂ්ප *waka-pushpa;* bend, curve.

වකාඞ්ග, *Wakanga*, *s.* (වක් *wak* crooked, අඞ්ග *anga* body) loris or Ceylon sloth, small animal peculiar to Ceylon, *loris graciles (Quadrumana*, [Colloq. උනහපුළුවා *unahapuluwá*].

වකනවා, *Wakanawá*, *v.* to daub, to smear, to stain.

වකපුෂ්ප, *Waka-pushpa*, *s.* (වක curving, පුෂ්ප flower) tree with large flowers and edible legumes, *æschynomene grandiflora*.

වකවනුව, *Wakawanuwa*, *s.* date, time, period.

වකුගඩුව, *Wakugaduwa*, *s.* kidney.

වකුටු, *Wakutu*, *a.* crooked, bowed, bent, curved.

වකුටුකරණවා, *Wakutukaranawá*, *v.* to coil, to bend.

වකුටුවෙනවා, *Wakuṭuwenawá*, *v.* to be curved.

වකුල, *Wakula*, } *s.* timber tree bearing a fragrant
වකුලු, *Wakulu*, } flower, *mimusops elengi*, [Colloq. මූනමල් *múnamal*].

වග්, *Wag*, *s.* tiger, Bengal tiger.

වග, *Waga*, *s.* matter, affair, cause; tail; tiger, royal tiger, from ව්‍යාඝ්‍ර *wyághra;* sort, species, kind, from වර්ග *warga;* excellence, pre-eminence; chapter, section.

වග කියනවා, *Waga-kiyanawá*, *v.* to state a case, to plead, to be responsible, to grumble, to blame, to scold.

වගන්තිය, *Wagantiya*, *s.* matter, subject of writing, sentence (in composition); clause of an Ordinance: pl. වගන්ති *waganti.*

වගපල කියනවා, *Wagapala-kiyanawá*, *v.* to scold, to blame.

වගපුල්, *Wagapul*, *s.* plant, *cucurligo recurvata:* see වයපොල් *wayapol;* long pepper plant, *piper longum*, [Colloq. තිප්පිලි *tippili*].

වගල්යටි, *Wagalyaṭi*, *s.* staff, crook; walking stick.

වගළ, *Wagaḷa*, *a.* fallen, loosened.

වගු ඇල්වී, *Wagu-ęlví*, *s.* kind of paddy, *oryza sativa.*

වගුර, *Wagura*, *s.* slough, marsh; the deep part of a paddy field: pl. වගුරු *waguru.*

වගුරජ, *Wagu-raja*, *s.* king of Wagu (part of Bengal).

වගුරණවා, *Waguraṇawá*, *v.* to shed, to pour, to scatter: pret. වගුළා *waguḷá* or වැගුරුවා *węguruwá.*

වගුරුවනවා, *Waguruwanawá*, *v.* to shed, to spill, to pour, to cause to pour.

වගුළ, *Waguḷa*, see වගළ *wagaḷa.*

වඟුළු, *Waṉguḷu*, *s.* mode of music.

වඞ්ග, *Wańga*, *s.* white lead, [Colloq. ඊයම් *íyam*]; tin; Bengal cotton; brinjal, egg plant, *solanum melongena*, [Colloq. වම්බටු *wambaṭu*].

වඞ්ගාරි, *Wańgári*, *s.* (වඞ්ග *wańga* lead, අරි *ari* foe) yellow orpiment.

වඞ්ගි, *Wańgi*, } *a.* crooked, curved, bent.
වඞ්ගිය, *Wańgiya*, }

වඞ්ගුව, *Wańguwa*, *s.* curve, bend, turn.

වච්චක, *Wachchaka*, *s.* tree bearing a seed used in cases of diarrhœa, *nirium* or *wrightea antidysenterica:* see වත්සක *watsaka.*

වච්චකුටිය, *Wachcha-kuṭiya*. *s.* privy; Páli form of වර්චස්කුටිය *warchaskuṭiya.*

වච්චනාවි, *Wachchanávi*, *s.* active poison, arsenic, apparently the root of a vegetable; it is brought from the continent: see වත්සනාභ *watsanábha.*

වච්චසාලා, *Wachcha-sálá*, *s.* (වච්ච and සාලා house) privy, [Colloq. වැසිකිළිය *węsikiḷiya*].

වච, *Wacha*, see වචස් *wachas.*

වචනය, *Wachanaya*, *s.* (වච to speak) word; sentence, dictum; aphorism, rule; speech: pl. වචන *wachana.*

වචනපොත, *Wachana-pota*, *s.* word book, vocabulary.

වචනානුකූල, *Wachanánukúla*, *s.* (වචන *wachana* and අනුකූල *anukúla* suitable) fit to be spoken, proper to be uttered or declared; conformable to speech.

වචස්, *Wachas*, *s.* (වච *wacha* to speak) speech, voice.

වචා, *Wachá*, *s.* orris root, *acorus calamus*, [Colloq. වදකහ *wadakaha*].

වඤ්චකයා, *Wañchakayá*, *s.* deceiver.

වජ්ජ, *Wajja*, Páli form of වද්‍ය *wadya.*

වජ්ජපුත්ත, *Wajjaputta*, *s.* (වජ්ජ from වධ *wadha* to kill, පුත්ත son) man of the fisher caste; Vęddá, hunter, or one who procures a livelihood by killing animals and selling the flesh.

වජ්‍ර *Wajra*, *s.* (වජ *waja* to go, රක් *rak* aff,) thunderbolt in general, thunderbolt of Indra; diamond, (the thunderbolt being considered analogous to the diamond in hardness or in fact the same substance), [Colloq. විදුර *vidura*, and දියමන්ති *diyamanti*]; *emblic myrobalan*, [Colloq. නෙල්ලි *nelli*]; sour gruel; blossom of the sesamum; kusa grass: *a.* hard, impenetrable, adamantine.

වජ්‍රකණ්ටක, *Wajra-kanṭaka*, see වජ්‍රවෘක්ෂ *wajra-wṛiksha.*

වජ්‍රකන්ද, *Wajra-kanda*, *s.* medicinal root, *amorphophallus campanulatus*, [Colloq. කිඩාරන් අල *kiḍáran-ala*].

වජ්‍රකාන්තිය, *Wajrakántiya*, *s.* medicinal oil so called; a corrupt form of වජ්‍රකන්ද *wajra-kanda.*

වජ්‍රජිත්, *Wajra-jit*, *s.* name of Garuḍa, bird and vehicle of Vishṇu.

වජ්‍රද්‍රැ, *Wajradru*, } *s.* (වජ්‍ර thunderbolt, as
වජ්‍රද්‍රැම, *Wajradruma*, } hard as, ද්‍රැ or ද්‍රැම tree) euphorbia of various species.

වජ්‍රධර, *Wajradhara*, *s.* (වජ්‍ර thunderbolt, ධර who has) Indra the Jupiter tonans of the Hindus.

වජ්‍රපාණි, *Wajra-páṇi*, *s.* (වජ්‍ර and පාණි hand) name of Indra: see the last.

වජ්‍රමණි, *Wajra-maṇi*, *s.* diamond.

වජ්‍රමති, *Wajramati*, *s.* (වජ්‍ර diamond, as sharp as, මති intellect) deep penetration, sharp intellect or clear conception.

වජ්‍රමාණික්‍යය, *Wajra-mánikyaya*, see වජ්‍රමණි *wajra-maṇi*.

වජ්‍රවල්ලි, *Wajra-walli*, *s.* (වජ්‍ර and වල්ලි creeper) species of sun flower, *helianthus annuus*, [Colloq. සූර්යකාන්ති මල් *súryakánti-mal*]; plant, *vitis quadrangularis*, [Colloq. හීරැස්ස *híressa*].

වජ්‍රවෘක්ෂ, *Wajra-wriksha*, *s.* tree, *euphorbia antiquorum*, [Colloq. දලුක් *daluk*].

වජ්‍රා, *Wajrá*, *s.* species of *euphorbia*; plant, *tinospora cordifolia*, [Colloq. රසකිඳ *rasakinda*]: shrub, *siphonanthus indica*.

වජ්‍රාංකුශය, *Wajráńkuṣaya*, *s.* (වජ්‍ර *wajra* diamond, අංකුශ *ańkuṣa* elephant's hook) diamond hook used in guiding a royal elephant.

වජ්‍රාග්‍ර, *Wajrágra*, *s.* (වජ්‍ර *wajra* and අග්‍ර *agra* chief) superior diamond, one of the most brilliant water.

වජ්‍රායුධ, *Wajráyudha*, *s.* (වජ්‍ර *wajra* and ආයුධ *áyudha* weapon) diamond, sword used by Ṣakra or Indra in his wars with the Asuras.

වජ්‍රාසනය, *Wajrásanaya*, *s.* (වජ්‍ර *wajra* and ආසන *ásana* seat) diamond throne of Buddha, which sprang up at the root of the bó-gaha or *ficus religiosa*, when Gautama threw down the eight handfuls of kusa grass.

වජිර, *Wajira*, Páli form of වජ්‍ර *wajra*, which see.

වඤ්චක, *Wañchaka*, *s.* (වඤ්ච to trick, ක aff.) rogue, cheat; jackal, [Colloq. නරියා *nariyá*]; tame or house ichneumon; low or vile man: *a.* crafty, fraudulent.

වඤ්චාකරණවා, *Wañchákaraṇawá*, *v.* to deceive, to impose upon.

වඤ්චාකාරයා, *Wañchákárayá*, *s.* deceiver, cheat, impostor.

වඤ්චාව, *Wañcháwa*, *s.* deceit, cheat, imposture, imposition, cheating, trick, deception, fraud: pl. වඤ්චා *wañchá*.

වඤ්චිත, *Wañchita*, *a.* (වඤ්ච *wañcha* to deceive, ක්ත *kta* aff.) deceived, cheated, tricked, deluded.

වඤ්ජුල, *Wañjula*, *s.* (වඤ්ච *wañcha* to go, උලච් *ulach* affix, with change of ච *cha* into ජ *ja*) Indian timber tree, *dalbergia ougeinensis*; asóka tree, *saraca indica*, [Colloq. හෝපලු *hópalu* or දිය රතඹලා *diya-ratambalá*]; jack fruit tree, *artocarpus integrifolia*, [Colloq. කොස් *kos*]; common cane, *calamus rotang*, [Colloq. වේවැල් *wéwel*]; flower, *hibiscus mutablis*.

වට්ටක්කා, *Waṭṭakká*, *s.* pumpkin, Indian pumpkin, *cucurbita moschata*: see රටලබු *raṭa-labu*.

වට්ටාඩියා, *Waṭṭáḍiyá*, *s.* impostor, an impertinent fellow, clever fellow: pl. වට්ටාඩි *waṭṭáḍi*.

වට්ටිය, *Waṭṭiya*, *s.* lid of a basket; sort of tray made of the fibres of the bamboo: pl. වට්ටි *waṭṭi*.

වට්ටුව, *Waṭṭuwa*, *s.* inclosure, fence surrounding any thing; circle: pl. වට්ටු *waṭṭu*.

වට්ටෝරුව, *Waṭṭóruwa*, *s.* list, catalogue, inventory: pl. වට්ටෝරු *waṭṭóru*.

වට, *Waṭa*, *s.* round figure, circle, girth, circumference; the large Indian fig-tree, *ficus bengalensis*, [Colloq. මහනුග *maha-nuga*]; small shell, cowrie; rain; time; equality in size or dimensions; order, arrangement; tiger, Bengal tiger; rheum of the eye: *a.* round, circular, spherical.

වට ඇස්, *Waṭa-es*, *s.* (වට and ඇස් eyes) moose deer, *moscha meminna*, [Colloq. මීමින්නා *míminná*].

වටකර, *Waṭakara*, *ad.* surrounding, encircling, around.

වටකරණවා, *Waṭakaraṇawá*, *v.* to encompass, to surround.

වටකුරු, *Waṭakuru*, *s.* globular; round.

වටන්, *Waṭan*, *s.* order, arrangement.

වටප්‍රරෝහ, *Waṭapraróha*, *s.* (වට Indian fig tree, ප්‍රරෝහ shoot) spreading roots of the Banyan or Indian fig tree, which rise out of the earth, and form a kind of seat, on which to rest under the shade of the branches, *ficus bengalensis*, [Colloq. මහනුග *maha-nuga*]; also, pendant shoots of the banyan tree.

වටපිට, *Waṭapiṭa*, *s.* hereabout or thereabout, vicinity, neighbourhood.

වටමිදෙල්ල, *Waṭamidella*, *s.* tree, species of *barringtonia*.

වටමුව, *Waṭamuwa*, *s.* moose deer.

වටය, *Waṭaya*, *s.* circumference, chiefly used of trees.

වටයා, *Waṭayá*, *s.* flaw in the body of a timber.

වටරැස්ස, *Waṭaṛessa*, *s.* plant called sun dew, with radical leaves in a circle, *drosera Burmanni (Droseraceæ)*.

වටලනවා, *Waṭalanawá*, *v.* to surround, to inclose, to encircle; to set at bay: pret. වටලෑවා *waṭaléwá*.

වටලබ්බ, *Waṭalabba, s.* (වට round, ලබ්බ gourd) bottle gourd, *lagenaria vulgaris.*

වටවාසින්, *Waṭawásin, s.* (වට Indian fig, වාසින් who dwells) sort of demigod, Yaksha or Yakshiní, *i. e,* male or female demon, Kuvéra's special attendants who are supposed to be fond of abiding in this tree.

වටසක්, *Waṭasak, s.* earring, ear ornament, [Coll: කුණ්ඩලාභරණය *kuṇḍlábharaṇaya*].

වටාකර, *Waṭákara, s.* (වට *waṭa* round, ආකර *ákara* what makes) cord, rope, string, [Colloq. ලනුව *lanuwa*].

වටාපත, *Waṭápata, s.* fan: pl. වටාපත් *waṭápat.*

වටින්, *Waṭin, ad.* around; also see වටි *waṭi.*

වටින්පිටින්, *Waṭinpiṭin, s.* from round about.

වටිනවා, *Waṭinawá, v.* to deserve, to merit, to be worth.

වටිනා, *Waṭiná, a.* worth.

වටිනාකම, *Waṭinákama, s.* desert, merit, worth, value.

වටි, *Waṭí, s.* cord, rope; ball of medicine, pill, bolus.

වටුම, *Waṭuma, s.* road.

වටුමුව, *Waṭumuwa, s.* hare; moose deer: see වට ඈස් *waṭa-ęs.*

වටුවා, *Waṭuwá, s.* snipe in general; green sandpiper, *totarns ochropus;* common sand-piper, *tringoides hypoleucus;* curlew stint, *tringa subar: quata; (Scopolacidæ:)* Mongolian sand plover, *ægialitis mongolia;* Kentish plover, *æ. cantiana; (Charadridæ,* order *Gralliæ);* see also ඔසවටුවා *osa-waṭuwá,* පඬුරු වටුවා *paṇḍuru-waṭuwá,* වෙනැල්ල වටුවා *wenęlla-waṭuwá,* කැස්වටුවා *kęs-waṭuwá,* රාජ වටුවා *rája-waṭawá,* මහ වටුවා *maha-waṭuwá,* සිල වටුවා *sila-waṭuwá,* ඕල වටුවා *óla-waṭuwá,* රේණ වටුවා *réṇa-waṭuwá* and බෝල වටුවා *bóla-waṭuwá.*

වටුවා ඇල්වී, *Waṭuwá-ęlví, s.* kind of paddy, *oryza sativa.*

වටේ, *Waṭé,* see වටය *waṭaya.*

වටේට, *Waṭéṭa, ind.* around, surrounding, encompassing, inclosing.

වටෝර, *Waṭora, s.* thigh, [Colloq. කලව *kalawa*].

වඨර, *Wathara, s.* (වච *wacha* to speak) fool, blockhead: *a.* stupid, foolish; vile, abandoned.

වඩ, *Waḍa, s.* headless trunk; cutting, incision.

වඩදිය, *Waḍadiya, s.* flood tide.

වඩනවා, *Waḍanawá, v.* to take in the arms, to carry a child; to hold, to bear or carry in the hand; to increase, to augment: pret. වැඩුවා *węḍuwá.*

වඩනාතලපත, *Waḍaná-talapata, s.* (වඩනා and තලපත talipot) large section of the talipot leaf, highly ornamented with talc, gilt, etc. and used only by the king.

වඩාපණ, *Waḍapaṇa, s.* stake at a game, wager; pledge, [Colloq. උකස *ukasa*].

වඩබාග්නි, *Waḍabágni,* } *s.* (වඩබ *waḍaba* and
වඩබානල, *Waḍabánala,* } අග්නි *agni* or අනල *anala* fire) submarine fire, also written බඩවාග්නි *baḍawágni.*

වඩභි, *Waḍabhi, s.* (වල *wala* to cover, to inclose) wooden frame of a house or thatch.

වඩම්බ, *Waḍamba,* } *s.* horse merchant, horse
වඩම්බක, *Waḍambaka,* } dealer.

වඩම, *Waḍama, s.* garland, chaplet, string of flowers: pl. වඩම් *waḍam.*

වඩවඩා, *Waḍawaḍá, s.* more and more.

වඩවාගන්නවා, *Waḍawágannawá, v.* to cause to be taken in the arms.

වඩා, *Waḍá, ind.* particle of comparison, more, (and following a noun in the dative case,) more than.

වඩාගන්නවා, *Waḍágannawá,* see වඩනවා *waḍanawá.*

වඩිග, *Waḍiga, s.* the Telugu country or name of the nation, speaking the Telugu language.

වඩිච්චි, *Waḍichchi, s.* wooden frame of a house or thatch, from වඩභි *waḍabhi.*

වඩිජ්ජ, *Waḍijja, s.* flowing tide.

වඩිනවා, *Waḍinawá, v.* to go, to proceed, used respectfully; to increase, to augment: pret. වැඩියා *węḍiyá.*

වඩිම්බුව, *Waḍimbuwa, s.* the border or edge of a roof; board under the eaves of a roof.

වඩිය, *Waḍiya, s.* quantity put in at one time for distillation of oil, arrack, etc.; pledge,

වඩිශ, *Waḍiṣa, s.* (වට *waṭa* line, ශෝ *ṣó* to destroy) fish hook.

වඩු, *Waḍu, a.* pertaining to carpentery: also see වඩුවා *waḍuwá.*

වඩු කුරුල්ලා, *Waḍu-kurullá,* see තට්ට කුරුල්ලා *taṭṭa-kurullá.*

වඩුපට්ටලය, *Waḍu-paṭṭalaya, s.* carpenter's workshop.

වඩුපන්නෙ, *Waḍupanne, s.* set of carpenter's tools.

වඩුමඩුව, *Waḍumaḍuwa, s.* carpenter's work shed.

වඩුරාල, *Waḍurála, s.* carpenter: pl. වඩුරාල්ලා *waḍurállá.*

වඩු රියන, *Waḍu-riyana, s.* (වඩු and රියන cubit) carpenter's cubit, measuring about thirty-six inches or one yard.

වඩුලීය, *Waḍulíya, s.* carpenter's rule, generally reckoned about two cubits.

වඩුවා, *Waḍuwá, s.* (වඪ *wardha* to cut) carpenter; not respectful: pl. වඩුවෝ *waḍuwó.*

වඩුවැඩ, *Waduweḍa, s.* carpenter's work, trade of a carpenter.

වඩුහැඩයා, *Waduheḍayá, s.* chief of outcastes.

වණ්ඩ, *Wanṭa, s.* (වණ්ඩ to partition) part, portion, share.

වණ්ඩ, *Wanda, s.* man who is circumcised or has no prepuce.

වණ්ඩුපිට්ටු *Wanḍu-piṭṭu, s.* kind of native cake.

වණ්ඩුව, *Wanḍuwa, s.* a cloth covering the mouth of an earthen vessel; particular kind of earthen vessel in which medical decoctions are boiled: pl. වණ්ඩු *wanḍu.*

වණකරණවා, *Waṇakaraṇawá, v.* to make sore.

වණනවා, *Waṇanawá, v.* to praise. to panegyrize, to extol or eulogize; to move, to shake, to wag; to say, to tell; to spread, to extend, as cloth in the sun, to dry: pret. වැණුවා *weṇuwá.*

වණය, *Waṇaya, s.* sore, ulcer, etc.: pl. වණ *waṇa.*

වණවෙනවා, *Waṇawenawá, v.* to become sore; to fester as a sore or wound.

වණික්, *Waṇik, s.* measure by weight; trading, traffic, merchandize.

වණිජ, *Waṇij, s.* tradesman, merchant, trafficker, [Colloq. වෙළෙන්ද *weḷendá*].

වණිජ කර්මය, *Waṇija-karmaya, s.* merchandise; business of a merchant.

වණේ, *Waṇé,* see වණය *waṇaya.*

වත්, *Wat, s.* any meritorious act of devotion, imposition of any penance, austerity or privation, as fasting, continence; Elu form of ව්‍රත *wrata;* cloth, dress, robes, from වස්ත්‍ර *wastra;* history, story; wealth, riches, from වස්තු *wastu;* face, countenance, from වක්ත්‍ර *waktra;* figure of speech, simile; calf, from වත්සා *watsá:* affix implying possession,, having; particle of option and doubt, or, either, whether; as, like.

වත් අත්, *Wat-at, s.* Gaṇéṣa, [Colloq. ගණදෙවියෝ *gaṇadeviyó*].

වත්කම, *Watkama, s.* value, worth.

වත්කෙරීම, *Watkeríma, s.* performance of religious duties: see වත් *wat;* pouring.

වත්ත, *Watta, s.* garden; see its plural form වතු *watu.*

වත්තම්, *Wattam, s.* (වත් cloth, කම් *kam* act) cloth making.

වත්තම්කරණවා, *Wattamkaraṇawá, v.* to support, to uphold; to assist a man who is unable to walk by himself.

වත්ථ, *Wattha, s.* clothes, dress; Páli form of වස්ත්‍ර *wastra.*

වත්ථගුහ්‍ය, *Wattaguiha, s.* (වත්ථ dress, ගුහ්‍ය hidden, concealed) privity, either male or female.

වත්දෙසනවා, *Wat-desanawá, v.* (වත් observance, දෙසනවා to repeat) to consecrate, to perform certain ceremonies on the site chosen for a temple.

වත්පිරිම, *Wat-pirima, s.* religious ordinance, abstinence or fasting.

වත්පිළිවෙත්, *Watpiḷiwet, s.* (වත් any act of devotion, පිළිවෙත් *piḷiwet* the same) duties of a priest, strict observance of the ordinances of the priesthood.

වත්ස, *Watsa, s.* breast, chest; calf; year: see වත්සර *watsara;* term of endearment used to children, scholars, etc.

වත්සක, *Watsaka, s.* medicinal plant, *nerium antidysentericum,* [Colloquial: කෙළිඳගස් *keḷindagas*].

වත්සනාභ, *Watsanábha, s.* (වත්ස calf, නභ *nabha* to injure) an active poison, apparently the root of a vegetable, and said to be brought from Népál.

වත්සර, *Watsara, s.* (වද *wada* to abide, and සරන් *saran* aff.) year, [Colloq. අවුරුද්ද *awurudda*].

වත්සල, *Watsala, s.* (වත්ස endearment, ලා *lá* to have) affection, fondness: *a.* affectionate, kind.

වත්සාදනී, *Watsádani, s.* (වත්ස *watsa* calf, අදන *adana* food) plant, *menispermum glabrum;* tree, *buchanania latifolia,* [Colloq. කිරිපළු *kiripaḷu*]; plant, *tinospora cordifolia,* [Colloq. රසකිඳ *rasakinda*].

වත, *Wata, s.* cloth, clothes, dress, robes; face; history, account; the edge.

වතංස, *Watansa, s.* earring; crest.

වතන, *Watana, s.* face, [Colloq. මුහුන *muhuna*].

වතළ, *Wataḷa, a.* large, great; spread, expanded.

වතාව, *Watáwa, s.* time, occasion.

වතාවත්, *Watáwat, s.* serving, attending, waiting upon, nursing, as a sick person.

වතාවෙන්වතාව, *Watáwen-watáwa*, *s.* from time to time, occasionally.

වතිපාකාර, *Wati-pákára*, *s.* (වති and පාකාර fence) hedge, fence, boundary.

වතී *Watí*, *s.* affix attached to nouns to express a female endowed with any quality, as ගුණවතී *guṇawatí*, woman possessed of virtue.

වතු, *Watu*, *s.* plur. of වත්ත *watta*, place or residence consisting of a garden or grove of coconut and other fruit trees.

වතු ඉඟුරු, *Watu-iṇguru*, *s.* species of ginger.

වතු කජු, *Watu-kaju*, *s.* variety of cashew or kaju, *anacardium occidentale.*

වතු කරපිංච, *Watu-karapiṇcha*, *s.* small tree, leaves used in curry, *bergera kœnigii.*

වතු කහ, *Watu-kaha*, *s.* variety of turmeric, *curcuma longa.*

වතු කහඹිලියා, *Watu-kahambiliyá*, *s.* nettle, species of *fleurya.*

වතු කුඹුරු, *Watu-kumburu*, *s.* landed property; gardens and fields.

වතු කූර, *Watu-kúra*, *s.* plant, variety of *amaranthus polygonoides.*

වතු කෝපි, *Watu-kópi*, *s.* coffee tree, *coffea arabica.*

වතු කැකිරි, *Watu-kẹkiri*, *s.* species of cucumber, *cucumis madraspatanus.*

වතුකැන, *Watukẹna*, *s.* bunch or cluster of plantain: pl. වතුකැන් *watukẹn.*

වතු ගෙඩිය, *Watu-geḍiya*, *s.* plantain. *musa sapientum;* also called කෙහෙල්ගෙඩිය *kehelgeḍiya.*

වතු ජම්බු, *Watu-jambu*, *s.* variety of the *eugenia*, the Malay apple, *eugenia* or *jambosa malaccensis.*

වතුපාළු කෙසෙල්, *Watupáḷu-kesel*, *s.* variety of plantain, *musa sapientum.*

වතුපිටි, *Watupiṭi*, *s.* landed property.

වතුමුව, *Watu-muwa*, *s.* plantain flower.

වතුර, *waṭura*, *s.* water.

වතුරගලනවා, *Watura-galanawá*, *v.* to overflow.

වතුරගැලීම, *Watura-gẹlíma*, *s.* flood, overflow of water.

වතුරන් කොවුල්, *Waturan-kowul*, *s.* timber found under ground in fields and marshes.

වතුරනුවා, *Waturanuwá*, *s.* red king-fisher, *ceryle rudis;* also called පිළිහුඩුවා *piḷihuḍuwá* and ගෝමර පිළිහුඩුවා *gómara-piḷihuḍuwá;* Indian stork-billed king-fisher: see මහ පිළිහුඩුවා *maha-piḷihuḍuwá, (Alcedinidœ,* order *Picariœ).*

වතුරපස්ස, *Watura-passa*, *s.* water-level, instrument containing water, formerly used as a level in laying out irrigation works, etc.; now used to ascertain the level of the site of a house or of any plot of ground cleared of jungle for the erection of a building.

වතුරපාර, *Waturapára*, *s.* stream, current of water.

වතුරාන් මරඳ, *Waturán-maranda*, *s.* tree, variety of *eugenia zeylanica.*

වතුරාව, *Waturáwa*, *s.* cultivated ground having abundance of water, farm.

වතුරු, *Waturu*, *s.* flood, flow of water; rainy cloud; squall; cloth, clothes, dress, from වස්ත්‍ර *wastra.*

වතු වැරැල්ල, *Watu-wẹrẹlla*, *s.* shield fern, *aspidium splendens;* species of grass, *andropogon Nardus,* [Colloq. මානා *máná*].

වතුසුද්ද, *Watusudda*, *s.* flowering shrub, *tabernœmontana coronaria;* also called බද වතුසුද්ද *bada-watusudda.*

වතු සැවැන්දරා, *Watu-sẹwẹndará*, *s.* fragrant grass, *andropogon nardus.*

වද්‍ය, *Wadya*, *s.* crime, guilt, sin. [Colloq. පාපය *pápaya*].

වද, *Wada*, *s.* speech; word, sentence, saying; punishment, torture; cattle pen, sheepfold; leathern reins or traces; shoe flower, *hibiscus rosa-sinensis,* [Colloq. සපත්තු මල් *sapattu-mal*]; fault, crime; bringing forth; entering, entrance; weariness, exhaustion: *a.* speaking: *ind.* particle signifying surprise, concession, disappointment.

වදකයා, *Wadakayá*, see වදකරුවා *wadakaruwá.*

වදකරණවා, *Wadakaraṇawá*, *v.* to torture, to tease.

වදකරුවා, *Wadakaruwá*, *s.* (වද punishment, කරුවා who does or inflicts) executioner, tormentor.

වදකසා, *Wadakasá*, } *s.* plant, sweet flag, *acorus*
වදකහ, *Wadakaha*, } *calamus, (Araceœ);* orris root.

වදකාරයා, *Wadakárayá*, see වදකරුවා *wadakaruwá.*

වදන්, *Wadan*, *s.* tree bearing a fragrant flower, *mimusops elengi,* [Colloq. මූනමල් *múnamal*]: see වකුල *wakula;* face, see වදන *wadana.*

වදන්මග, *Wadan-maga*, *s.* (වදන *wadana* word, මග way) the ear, [Colloq. කණ *kaṇa*].

වදන්‍ය, *Wadanya*, *a.* munificent, bountiful.

වදන, *Wadana*, *s.* mouth; face, countenance; birth, bringing forth; speech, speaking, word, saying: pl. වදන් *wadan.*

වදනගේ, *Wadana-gé*, *s.* (වදන and ගේ house) room or small hut apart from the dwelling house where women are delivered in childbirth and remain till they are restored.

වදනවා, *Wadanawá*, *v.* to bear, to bring forth: pret. වැදුවා *wẹduwá*.

වදන වේදනාව, *Wadana-wédanáwa*, *s.* pain of labour; pangs of childbirth.

වදනිඳු, *Wadanin̲du*, } *s.* (වදන *wadana* speech,
වදනිසුරු, *Wadanisuru*, } ඉඳු *in̲du* chief) regent of the planet Jupiter, Bṛihaspati, and preceptor of the gods.

වදබෙරය, *Wada-beraya*, } *s.* drum announcing an
වදබෙරේ, *Wada-beré*, } execution.

වදමල, *Wada-mala*, *s.* shoe flower, *hibiscus rosa-sinensis*, [Colloq. සපත්තුමල *sapattu-mala*].

වදවිඳිනවා, *Wada-vin̲dinawá*, *v.* to suffer punishment.

වදහළ, *Wadahaḷa*, *a.* said, spoken, declared, or uttered.

වදාන්‍ය, *Wadánya*, *a.* (වද *wada* to speak, අන්‍ය *anya* aff.) liberal, munificent; speaking kindly or agreeably.

වදාරණවා, *Wadáraṇawá*, *v.* to speak, to tell, to declare, used of a superior: pret. වැදෑරුවා *wẹdẹruwá*.

වදාවද, *Wadáwada*, *a.* speaking, able to speak, speaking well, eloquent.

වදාළසේක, *Wadáḷaséka*, *s.* said, respectful term.

වදිනවා, *Wadinawá*, *a.* to strike, to hit, to touch, to come in contact; to enter, to go in: pret. වැදුනා *wẹduná*.

වදු, *Wadu*, *s.* wife, woman.

වදුර, *Wadura*, *s.* diamond; Elu form of වජ්‍ර *wajra*.

වදුරවිය, *Waduraviya*, *s.* (වදුර diamond, අවිය *aviya* weapon) name of Ṣakra or Indra in his character as the thunderer: see වජ්‍ර *wajra*.

වදුරු, *Waduru*, *s.* diamond; the creeper, *heliotropium;* creeper, *vitis quadrangularis*, [Colloq. හිරැස්ස *híressa*]; small pox.

වදුරුදන්, *Wadurudan*, *s.* gaming, gambling.

වදුරුවැල්, *Waduru-wel*, *s.* (වදුරු and වැල් creeper) species of sun flower: see වජ්‍රවල්ලි *wajra-walli*.

වදුල, *Wadula*, *s.* thief, robber, [Colloq. හොරා *horá*]; arbour, bower, place overgrown with creepers; natural arbour or bower.

වඳ, *Wan̲da*, *a.* barren.

වඳ කිලිල, *Wan̲da-kilila*, *s.* tree, not ascertained.

වඳිනවා, *wan̲dinawá*, *v.* to bow, to courtesy, to make obeisance, to worship: pret. වැන්ඳ *wẹndá*.

වඳි, *Wan̲dí*, *s.* barren woman, etc.: pl. වඳියෝ *wan̲diyó*.

වඳුරා, *Wan̲durá*, *s.* generic name for the black monkey of which there are four species in Ceylon, 1. *presbytes cephalopterus* (or *leucoprymnus nestor*, common in the low country and called කළු වඳුරා *kaḷu-wan̲durá*; 2. *p. ursinus*, found in the hill country and called මහ වඳුරා *maha-wan̲durá*, or large monkey; 3. *p. thersites*, distinguished by wanting the head tuft; 4. *p. piramus* in the North and East provinces, (*Quadrumana*).

වඳුරු අල, *Wan̲duru-ala*, *s.* plant, species of yam *typhonium* or *dioscorea*.

වඳුරු ආනවාළුකෙසෙල්, *Wan̲duru-ánawáḷu-kesel*, *s.* kind of plantain, *musa sapientum*.

වඳුරුකෙසෙල්, *Wan̲duru-kesel*, *s.* kind of plantain, *musa sapientum*.

වඳුරු තණ, *Wan̲duru-taṇa*, *s.* kind of grass, not ascertained.

වඳුරු තණහාල්, *Wan̲duru-taṇahál*, *s.* sort of millet; sort of paddy, *oryza sativa*.

වඳුරුමෑ, *Wan̲duru-mẹ*, *s.* (වඳුරා *wan̲durá* and මෑ bean) cowach, *carpopogon pruriens*; plant producing black beans, *vigna sinensis*.

වඳුරු වේවැල. *Wan̲duru-wéwẹla*, *s.* species of cane, *calamus*.

වඳුලෑස්ස, *Wan̲dulẹssa*, *s.* plant, not ascertained.

වධ, *Wadha*, *s.* punishment, capital punishment; killing, slaughter.

වධකරණවා, *Wadhakaraṇawá*, see වදකරණවා *wadakaraṇawá*.

වධකරුවා, *Wadhakaruwá*, *s.* (වධ punishment, කරුවා who inflicts) executioner.

වධ දණ්ඩ, *Wadha-daṇḍa*, *s.* infliction of punishment.

වධබෙරය, *Wadha-beraya*, *s.* (වධ and බෙර *bera* tom tom) tom tom or drum beaten before a person going to execution.

වධය, *Wadhaya*, see its plural form වධ *wadha*.

වධු, *Wadhu*, } *s.* wife, woman, [Colloq. ස්ත්‍රී *strí*];
වධූ, *Wadhú*, } maid, damsel; young wife, bride.

වන්, *Wan*, *p.* struck; entered, hit: *a.* like, resembling.

වන්කරණත්, *Wankaraṇat*, *s.* plant, *plumbago zeylanica*, [Colloq. එළ නෙටුල් *ela-neṭul*].

වන්කුරු, *Wankuru*, *s.* fiddler.

වන්කොස්, *Wankos*, *s.* young jack fruit.

වන්ගනාව, *Wanganáwa*, see වංකනාලය *waṅkanálaya.*

වන්ගෙඩිය, *Wangeḍiya*, *s.* large wooden mortar used to clean the husk from the rice.

වන්චාව, *Wancháwa*, see වඤ්චාව *wañcháwa.*

වන්ටා, *Wantá*, *s.* plant: see බැවිල *bęvila.*

වන්ත, *Wanta*, *s.* mark, spot, freckle; mark for a full stop; also, possessive aff, as in ධනවන්ත *dhanawanta*, (ධන wealth, වන්ත possessed of) wealthy.

වන්දන, *Wandana*, *s.* (වදි *wadi* to praise) reverence, worship, adoration; obeisance to a superior by touching the feet, etc.

වන්දනමාලා, *Wandanamálá*, *s.* (වන්දන and මාලා garland) ornamented arch of a gateway, which is decorated with the leaves of the coconut tree and garlands of flowers, on marriages and festival occasions.

වන්දනා, *Wandaná*, *s.* praise, praising, especially the gods or great men; pilgrimage.

වන්දනාකාරයා, *Wandanákárayá*, *s.* (වන්දනා and කාර *kára* who does) religious devotee, pilgrim, one who travels about for the purpose of worshipping the gods.

වන්දනීය, *Wandaníya*, *a.* praiseworthy, to be eulogized or praised.

වන්දාරු, *Wandáru*, *a.* (වදි *wadi* to praise, අරු *aru* aff.) civil, complimentary, polite.

වන්දිගන්නවා, *Wandigannawá*, *v.* to take revenge.

වන්දින්, *Wandin*, *s.* (වදි *wadi* to praise, ඉන් *in* aff.) panegyrist, bard, herald, one whose duty it is to proclaim the titles of a great man as he passes along, or a poet who sings the praises of a prince in his presence, or accompanies an army to chaunt martial songs; praiser, flatterer.

වන්දිපාඨ, *Wandi-páṭha*, *s.* complimentary stanza; eulogium.

වන්දිභට්ටයා, *Wandibhaṭṭayá*, *s.* (වන්දි panegyrist, භට්ට *bhaṭṭa* learned man) eloquent panegyrist or encomiast.

වන්දිය, *Wandiya*, *s.* recompense, satisfaction, revenge.

වන්නම, *Wannama*, *s.* kind, sort, class; race, tribe, [Colloquial: ජාතිය *játiya*]; recital of a song; rehearsal: pl. වන්නම් *wannam.*

වන්‍ය, *Wanya*, *a.* forest, savage, wild, produced in a wood.

වන්හැපල, *Wanhępala*, see වංඇපල *waṅępala.*

වන, *Wana*, *s.* forest, wood, grove; water; (incorrectly for වණ *waṇa*) sore, wound, ulcer; colour; class, sort; mortar, pounder; letter, character; cascade, fountain: *a.* being, occurring, happening: see also වෙනි *weni.*

වනඉදල, *Wanaidala*, *s.* timber tree.

වනකපි, *Wanakapi*, *s.* white faced monkey, *macacus piliatus*, [Colloq. රිළවා *riḷawá*].

වනකර, *Wanakara*, *s.* plant, lead wort, *plumbago zeylanica:* see වන්කරණත් *wankaraṇat.*

වනකස්, *Wanakas*, *s.* the brown monkey, *macacus pileatus (Quadrumana)*, [Colloq. රිළවා *riḷawá*].

වනගු, *Wanagu*, } *s.* (වන and ගු or ගෞ cow)
වනගෞ, *Wanagau*, } kind of ox usually called the gáyal or yak *bos gavæus.*

වනචර, *Wanachara*, *s.* (වන forest, චර who goes) wild man, Vęddá, one living in a forest, hunter; savage, barbarian; robber, highway man: *a.* savage, uncivilized.

වනචරයා, *Wanacharayá*, *s.* savage man, barbarian, forester.

වනජ, *Wanaja*, *s.* (වන and ජ born) lotus; fragrant grass, *cyperus rotundus*, [Colloq. කලාඳුරු *kaláṇduru*]; elephant; the name is applicable to any wild plants or animals.

වනතික්ත, *Wanatikta*, *s.* (වන wood, තික්ත bitter) sort of myrobalan, *terminalia chebula*, [Colloq. අරළු *araḷu*].

වනතික්තා, *Wanatiktá*, } *s.* shrub, *cissampelos*
වනතික්තිකා, *Wanatiktiká*, } *pareira*, [Colloq. දියමිත්ත *diyamitta*].

වනතුරු, *Wanaturu*, *s.* forest tree, any wild tree; forest.

වනද, *Wanada*, *s.* (වන water, ද what gives) cloud, [Colloq. වලාකුළ *walákuḷa*].

වනදීප, *Wana-dípa*, *s.* (වන and දීප lamp or illuminator) timber tree, called champaka, *michelia champaca*, [Colloq. සපු *sapu*].

වනපති, *Wana-pati*, *s.* (වන and පති lord) banyan tree, *ficus bengalensis*, [Colloq. මහනුග *mahanuga*]; lion: see වනස්පති *wanaspati.*

වනපිය, *Wanapiya*, see වනප්‍රිය, *wanapriya.*

වනපුරුක්, *Wana-puruk*, *s.* plant, variety of *asystasia coromandeliana.*

වනපොතු, *Wana-potu*, *s.* tree, the seed oil is used for burning, *kokoona zeylanica, (Celastraceæ)*; also called කොකුම්පොතු *kokum-potu.*

වනප්‍රිය, *Wana-priya*, *s.* (වන wood, ප්‍රිය fond of) kókila or Indian cuckoo, *cuculus micropterus (order Picariæ).*

වනම, *Wanama, s.* caste: pl. වනම් *wanam.*

වනමල්ලි, *Wana-malli, s.* (වන and මල්ලි jasmine) wild jasmine, *jasminum angustifolium*, [Colloq. වල් පිච්ච *wal-pichcha*].

වන මාක්ෂිකා, *Wana-mákshiká, s.* (වන and මාක්ෂිකා fly) gad fly.

වනමාලිකා, *Wanamáliká, s.* plant, *borago zeylanica*, [Colloquial. යොන්තුඹ *yon-tumba*]; plant, *oleander*, [Colloq. බොලිද්ද *bolidda*].

වනමි, *Wanamí, s.* tree, peculiar to Ceylon, *bassia fulva (Myrsineæ)*; wild honey.

වනමුච්, *Wanamuch, s.* (වන water, මුච් to let loose) cloud, [Colloq. වලාකුළ *walákuḷa*].

වනමොර, *Wana-mora, s.* plant, white species of *rásná.*

වනය, *Wanaya*, see its plural form වන *wana.*

වනර, *Wanarà, s.* (වන wood, රම *rama* to play) monkey, [Colloq. වඳුරා *waṉdurá*, රිළවා *riḷawá*].

වනරාජ, *Wanarája, s.* (වන the forest or colour, රාජ king) lion, [Colloq. සිංහයා *siṉhayá*]; small plant, so called from the brilliant colour of its leaves, *anæctochilus setaceus (Orchideæ).*

වනරාජින්, *Wanarájin, s.* (වන wood, රාජි *ráji* row) line or forests.

වනලැහැබ, *Wanaleheba, s.* thicket, [Colloq. කැලෑව *kelëwa* or කැලෑරොද *kelëroda*].

වනවාස, *Wanawása, s.* forest-life; dwelling in a forest, as a hermit.

වනවාසන, *Wanawásana, s.* (වන and වාසන dwelling) civet or pole cat, *viverra Indica (*order *Carnioora).*

වනවාසික, *Wanawásika, a.* living in a forest (as a hermit).

වනවාසින්, *Wanawásin, s.* (වන wood, වාසින් who dwells) anchorite, hermit.

වන ශෘංගාට, *Wana-ṣringáṭa, s.* plant, *acanthus ilicifolus*, [Colloq. ඉකිරි *ikiri*].

වනස්පති, *Wanas-pati, s.* (වන *wana* forest, පති lord) tree that bears fruit but no apparent blossoms, as several species of the fig, the jack, etc.; tree, in general; banyan tree, *ficus bengalensis.* [Colloq. මහ නුග *maha-nuga*].

වනස්ස, *Wanassa, s.* shrubby plant, *lycopodium cernuum (Lycopodiaceæ)*; also called බඩල්වනස්ස *baḍal-wanassa.*

වනස, *Wanasa, s.* loss, ruin, destruction.

වනසනවා, *Wanasanawá, v.* to destroy, to ruin, to extirpate, to annihilate: pret. වැනසුවා *wenasuwá.*

වන සපු, *Wana-sapu, s.* timber tree, *michelia liligirica*; also called වල් සපු *wal-sapu.*

වනසර, *Wanasara, s.* Veddá, savage.

වනසු, *Wanasu, s.* tree, *adenanthera pavonina*, [Colloq මදටිය *madaṭiya.*]

වන සෝභන, *Wana-sóbhana, s.* (වන water, සෝභන adorning) lotus, *nymphea stellata*, [Colloq. මානෙල් *mánel*].

වන සැවුලා, *Wana-sewulá, s.* wild or jungle cock, *gallus lafaytti*, [Colloq. වලිකුකුළා *walikukuḷá*].

වනහළුකරනවා, *Wanahaḷu-karaṇawá, v.* to destroy, to reduce a forest to ashes, burn up.

වනාජ, *Wanája, s.* (වන *wana* and අජ *aja* goat) wild goat.

වනාන්තරය, *Wanántaraya, s.* wood, forest, large or extensive forest, jungle, wilderness.

වනාස, *Wanása, s.* loss, destruction, ruin, [Colloq. විනාසය *vinásaya*].

වනාහි, *Wanáhi, ind.* particle and affix, corresponding to, thus, and, as for, as regards; it is sometimes a mere expletive.

වණික්, *Wanik, Wanik,* } *s.* merchant, trader,
වණිග, *Waniga, Waniga,* } trafficker, [Colloq. වෙළෙන්දා *weḷendá*].

වනිතා, *Wanitá,* } *s.* (වන *wana* to ask, ක්ත *kta*
වනිති, *Waniti,* } aff.) woman, wife, mistress.

වනීක, *Waníka,*
වනීපක, *Waṇípaka,* } *s.* beggar, mendicant, [Coll:
වනීයක, *Waníyaka,* } හිඟන්නා *hiṉganná*].

වනුක්, *Wanuk,* } *s.* plant, the Marvel of Peru,
වනුප්, *Wanup,* } called also the four o'clock flower, *mirablis jalapa*, [Colloq. හෙන්ද්‍රික්කා *hendrikká*].

වනුලරුක්, *Wanularuk, s.* tree, *buchanania latifolia.*

වනුවැල්, *Wanuwel, s.* creeping plant, *coscinium fenestratum:* see වෙනිවැල් *weniwel.*

වනෙචර, *Wanechara, s.* (වනෙ in forest, චර who goes) forester, one of a savage tribe inhabiting woods, satyr, imp, demon; robber.

වනෝකස්, *Wanokas, s.* (වන *wana* and ඔකස් *okas* residence) monkey, [Colloq. වඳුරා *waṉdurá*, and රිළවා *riḷawá*].

වප්, *Wap, s.* rampart; sowing seed.

වප් මගුල, *Wap-magula, s.* (වප් sowing, මගුල feast) feast given to the husbandmen on the day they commence sowing the ground.

වප් මස, *Wap-masa, s.* (වප් and මස month) month so called (September–October) it is the time of sowing for the chief harvest.

වප්‍ර, *Wapra*, *s.* (වප *wapa* to sow, රන් *ran* aff.) field, rampart, mud wall; foundation of a building.

වප, *Wapa*, *s.* sowing seed; shaving; levelling the ground after sowing, in order to cover the seed.

වපර, *Wapara*, *s.* squinting, *strabismus*, (Dutch.)

වපරයා, *Waparayá*, *s.* one who squints.

වපා, *Wapá*, *s.* the mucous or glutinous secretion of the flesh or bones; according to some also the marrow of the bones.

වපු, *Wapu*, *s.* body; handsome figure.

වපුට, *Wapuṭa*, *past part.* of වපුරණවා *wapuraṇawá*

වපුරන්නා, *Wapuranná*, *s.* sower.

වපුරණවා, *Wapuraṇawá*. *v.* to sow seed: pret. වැපුරුවා *wępuruwá*.

වපුව, *Wapuwa*, } see වපු *wapu*.
වපුස්, *Wapus*, }

වම්, *Wam*, *s.* coat of mail, armour, from වර්ම *warma*: *a.* left, sinister.

වම් අත, *Wam-ata*, *s.* left hand.

වම්පර, *Wampara*, *s.* timber tree, *dillenia indica (Dilleniaceæ)*; also called හොඬපර *hoṇḍapara*.

වම්පස, *Wampasa*, } *s.* the left side.
වම්පාර්ශ්වය, *Wampárṣwaya*, }

වම්බටු, *Wambaṭu*, *s.* brinjal or egg plant, *solanum melongena*.

වම්බු, *Wambu*, *a.* bold, saucy, impudent, disrespectful.

වම්බුකම, *Wambukama*, *s.* impudence, roguery.

වම්බුවා, *Wambuwá*, *s.* saucy or impudent man, cheater, swindler.

වම්මික, *Wammika*, *s.* white ant hill, hillock; Páli form of වල්මීක *walmika*.

වම්මුතු, *Wammutu*, *s.* fragrant plant, *cyperus rotundus*, [Colloq. කලාඳුරු *kaláṇduru*].

වම, *Wama*, *s.* vomiting; the left.

වමත්කාරයා, *Wamatkárayá*, *s.* (වමත් and කාර *kára* who use) a left-handed man.

වමත, *Wamata*, *s.* (වම් *wam* left, අත *ata* hand) left hand.

වමථු, *Wamathu*, *s.* (වම to vomit) vomiting, ejecting any thing from the mouth; water ejected from an elephant's trunk.

වමන්, *Waman*, *s.* disrepute, dishonour, from අව මන් *awaman*, dropping the initial.

වමන, *Wamana*, *s.* (වම to vomit) vomiting, ejecting any thing from the mouth; emetic, causing to vomit.

වමනේකරණවා, *Wamanékaraṇawá*, *v.* to vomit, to retch.

වමාරණවා, *Wamáraṇawá*, *v.* to chew the cud; to emit any thing from the mouth: pret. වමෑරුවා *waméruwá*.

වමි, *Wami*, *s.* vomiting, sickness; tree, *adenanthera pavonina*, [Colloq. මදටිය *madaṭiya*]; white ant hill; woman, female.

වමිස, *Wamisa*, *s.* goddess Mahíkántáwa: see මහිකාන්තාව *mahíkántáwa*.

වමී, *Wamí*, *s.* white ant hill: see වමි *wami*.

වමැලය, *Wamęlaya*, *s.* (වම් *wam* left, ඇලය *ęlaya* side) left side.

වමැස, *Wamęsa*, *s.* (වම් *wam* and ඇස *ęsa* eye) left eye.

වය, *Waya*, *s.* age, time of life; disappearance; destruction.

වයකල්‍යාණය, *Waya-kalyáṇaya*, *s.* (වය age, කල්‍යාණ *kalyáṇa* excellence) the bloom of youth, one of the five perfections of personal beauty.

වයනවා, *Wayanawá*, *s.* to beat, to strike; to play on an instrument by striking: pret. වැයුවා *węyuwá*.

වයපොල්, *Waya-pol*, *s.* cultivated plant with yellow flowers, *cucurligo recurvata (Amaryllideæ)*.

වයබ්‍යා. *Wayabyá*, } *s.* region, north west quarter.
වයඹ, *Wayaba*, }

වයඹකොණ, *Wayamba-kona*, *s.* north west quarter.

වයස්, *Wayas*, see වයස *wayasa*.

වයස්කාරයා, *Wayaskárayá*, *s.* old man.

වයස්ථ, *Wayastha*, *s.* (වයස් life, ස්ථා *sthá* to be or stay) young man, friend, associate, contemporary: *a.* young, in the prime of life, youthful.

වයස්ථා, *Wayasthá*, *s.* moon plant, *asclepias acida*; emblic myrobalan, *phyllanthus emblica*, [Colloq. නෙල්ලි *nelli*]; yellow myrobalan, *terminalia chebula*, [Colloq. අරළු *araḷu*]; plant, *alternanthera triandra*, [Colloq. මුකුණුවැන්න *mukuṇuwęnna*]; woman's female friend, confidante.

වයස්‍යයා, *Wayasyayá*, *s.* (වයස් *wayas* life, යත් *yat* aff.) friend, associate; contemporary.

වයස්‍යා, *Wayasyá*, *s.* woman's female friend.

වයස, *Wayasa*, *s.* (වය *waya* to go) age, time of life; bird; youth: pl. වයස් *wayas*.

වයිරෝඩි, *Wayiróḍi*, *s.* lapis lazuli.

වයිල්කොල ඇල්වී, *Wayilkola-ęlví*, *s.* kind of hill paddy, *oryza sativa*.

වයිල්දඩි, *Wayil-dadí*, *s.* moon, [Colloq. හඳ *haṇda*].

වයෝ, *Wayó*, *s.* age, time of life.

වයෝවෘද්ධ, *Wayówṛiddha*, *a.* (වයස් life, වෘද්ධ increased) old, aged, advanced in years.

වයෝවෘද්ධයා, *Wayówṛiddhayá*, *s.* old man, [Coll: නාකියා *nákiyá*].

වර්ග, *Warga*, *s.* class, tribe, sort, multitude of similar things whether animate or inanimate, as the five wargas or classes of letters; triwarga, class of three objects, as, love, duty, and wealth; tribe, nation or class of people; chapter, book, section; square number (in Arithmetic).

වර්ගය, *Wargaya*, see its plural form වර්ග *warga*.

වර්චස්, *Warchas*, *s.* fæces, ordure, excrement; light, lustre; form, figure.

වර්චස් කුටිය, *Warchas-kuṭiya*, *s.* (වර්චස් and කුටිය tent) privy, [Colloq. කක්කුස්සිය *kakkussiya*].

වර්ජන, *Warjana*, *s.* (වෘජ *wṛija* to abandon) quitting, forsaking, abandonment, shunning, avoiding.

වර්ජනීය, *Warjaníya a.* (වෘජ *wṛija* to quite, අනීයර් *aníyar* aff of the future participle) to be avoided or excepted; irregular.

වර්ජිත, *Warjita*, *a.* (වෘජ *wṛija* and ක්ත *kta* aff.) abandoned, forsaken, avoided; excluded, excepted.

වර්ණ, *Warṇa*, *s.* (වර්ණ to paint. etc.) tribe; class, caste, order; colour, hue, tint; coloured cloth thrown over an elephant; quality, property; fame, celebrity; praise; gold; beauty, lustre; letter of the alphabet; form, figure, construction; sort, kind. In Arithmetic, a co-efficient.

වර්ණක, *Warṇaka*, *s.* perfume for the person, especially pounded or ground; paint, pigment; panegyrist.

වර්ණ චාරක, *Warṇa-cháraka*, *s.* (වර්ණ colour, චාර *chára* who goes) painter.

වර්ණතුලි, *Warṇatúli*, } *s.* pen.
වර්ණතුලිකා, *Warṇatúliká*, }

වර්ණදූත, *Warṇa-dúta*, *s.* (වර්ණ letter of the alphabet, දූත messenger) letter; epistle.

වර්ණන, *Warṇana*, *s.* (වර්ණ to paint) describing, expatiating, explaining; colouring, painting; writing.

වර්ණනාව, *Warṇanáwa*, *s.* praise, panegyric: pl. වර්ණනා *warṇaná*.

වර්ණනාකරණවා, *Warṇanákaraṇawá*, *v.* to magnify, to laud; to describe; to eulogise.

වර්ණනි, *Warṇaní*, *s.* crucible, [Colloq. කෝවෙ *kówé*]; touchstone of gold, [Colloq. උරගල *uragala*].

වර්ණ මාතෘ, *Warṇa-mátṛi*, *s.* (වර්ණ letter, මාතෘ mother) pen.

වර්ණමාලා, *Warṇamálá*, *s.* (වර්ණ and මාලා garland) alphabet.

වර්ණය, *Warṇaya*, see its plural form වර්ණ *warṇa*.

වර්ණ රීතිය, *Warṇa-rítiya*, *s.* (වර්ණ letter, රීති *ríti* use, practice) a book so called; Siṇhalese Primer.

වර්ණ විකාර, *Warṇa-vikára*, *s.* (වර්ණ and විකාර change, inversion) grammatical term, substitution or inversion of consonant.

වර්ණ සඞ්කර, *Warṇa-saṅkara*, *s.* (වර්ණ caste, සඞ්කර mixture) mixture or confusion of castes.

වර්ණා, *Warṇá*, *s.* leguminous shrub, called pigeon pea, *cajanus indicus*, [Colloq. රටතෝර *raṭatóra*].

වර්ණාංකා, *Warṇáṅká*, *s.* (වර්ණ *warṇa* letter, අකි *aki* to go) pen, [Colloq. පෑන *péna*].

වර්ණිනී, *Warṇní*, *s.* gold; mould or matrix for casting golden ornaments; painter.

වර්ණිත, *Warṇṇita*, *a.* praised, extolled, eulogized.

වර්ත්මන්, *Wartman*, *s.* road, way, [Colloq. පාර *pára*].

වර්තක, *Wartaka*, *s.* species of quail, *perdicula asiatica*, [Colloq. වටුවා *waṭuwá*]; horse's hoof.

වර්තන, *Wartana*, *s.* (වෘත *wṛita* to be) staying, abiding, property of a fixed presence; road, way; grinding; livelihood, profession, occupation; ball, globe: *a.* fixed, stationary, stable.

වර්තනි, *Wartani*, *s.* road, way, path: see the last.

වර්තමාන, *Wartamána*, *s.* (වෘත *wṛita* being, මාන participial or poss. aff.) grammatical term for the present tense: *a.* present, now being.

වර්ති, *Warti*, *s.* perfume for the person; wick of a lamp; collyrium prepared from various substances and dried in a lozenge form.

වර්තිකා, *Wartiká*, } *s.* wick of a lamp, [Colloq.
වර්තිකාව , *Wartikáwa*, } පාන් තිරය *pán-tiraya*]; ball, pill, bolus; medicinal pill, so called, quail.

වර්තුල, *Wartula*, *s.* kind of jasmine, [Colloq. වටු සුද්ද *watusudda*]; pea; ball: *a.* round, circular, globular, spherical.

වර්ධ, *Wardha*, *s.* (වෘධ *wṛidha* to grow, to increase) increase, augmentation; cutting.

වර්ධකි, *Wardhaki*, *s.* (වර්ධ to cut, to pierce) carpenter, [Colloq. වඩුවා *waḍuwá*].

වර්ධන, *Wardhana*, *s.* increasing, growing, thriving; cutting, dividing.

වර්ධනය කරණවා, *Wardhanaya-karaṇawá*, *v.* to increase, to grow, to improve.

වර්ධනවෙනවා, *Wardhana-wenawá*, *v.* to be increased; to thrive.

වර්ධමාන, *Wardhamána*, *s.* (වෘධ *wṛidha* to increase) castor oil plant, *ricinus communis*, [Colloq. එඬරු *eṇdaru*]; lid, cover, [Colloq. මූඩිය *múḍiya*]: *a.* increasing, thriving, prosperous.

වර්ධමානක, *Wardhamánaka*, *s.* cover, see the last.

වර්ද්ධිත, *Warddhita*, *s.* increased, grown.

වර්මන්, *Warman*, *s.* (වෘ *wṛi* to cover, මනින් *manin* aff.) armour, mail.

වර්‍ය්‍ය, *Warya*, *a.* chief, principal; best, excellent.

වර්වර, *Warwara*, *s.* outcast, barbarian; country inhabited by barbarians; wooly or curly hair, as that of an African; country, Barbary; also written බර්බර *barbara*.

වර්ෂ, *Warsha*, *s.* year; rain, raining; cloud.

වර්ෂකේතු, *Warshakétu*, *s.* name of Ṣiva; pot herb: see සාරණ *sáraṇa*].

වර්ෂණ, *Warshaṇa*, *s.* raining, sprinkling, [Colloq. වැස්ස *wẹssa*]: see වර්ෂ *warsha*.

වර්ෂණඍතුව, *Warshaṇa-ṛituwa*, *s.* (වර්ෂණ rain, ඍතුව season) rainy season.

වර්ෂධර, *Warshadhara*, *s.* eunuch or attendant on the women's apartment; cloud.

වර්ෂප්‍රිය, *Warsha-priya*, *s.* (වර්ෂ rain, ප්‍රිය fond of) Ceylon hornbill: see කෑඳැත්තා *kẹ́ṇdattá*.

වර්ෂවර, *Warsha-wara*, *s.* (වර්ෂ seminal sprinkling, වර free from) eunuch, [Colloq. නපුංසකයා *napunsakayá*].

වර්ෂශත, *Warshaṣata*, *s.* century.

වර්ෂ සහස්‍ර, *Warsha-sahasra*, *s.* thousand years.

වර්ෂා, *Warshá*, *s.* rain, rainy season containing two months; gramineous plant, *trigonella corniculata*.

වර්ෂාකාල, *Warshá-kála*, *s.* rainy season.

වර්ෂාභූ, *Warshábhú*, *s.* (වර්ෂා rain, භූ to be) frog, [Colloq. ගෙමඩියා *gemaḍiyá*]; hogweed; earth worm, *iulus;* herb, *trianthema monogyna* or *t. obcordata*, [Colloq. හීන්සාරණ *hín-sáraṇa*]; *trianthema decandra*, [Colloq. මහසාරණ *maha-sáraṇa*].

වර්ෂික, *Warshika*, *s.* aloe wood or agallochum, [Colloq. අගිල් *agil*]: *a.* relating to the rains.

වර්හ, *Warha*, *s.* peacock's tail; train, retinue; leaf.

වර්හිණ, *Warhiṇa*, *s.* (වර්හ *warha* and ඉන් *in* aff.) peacock, *pavo cristatus*, [Colloquial. මොණරා *moṇará*].

වර්හිර්මුඛ, *Warhirmukha*, *s.* (වර්හිස් *warhis* fire, මුඛ mouth) deity, divinity.

වර්හිස්, *Warhis*, *s.* fire; light, lustre, splendour.

වර, *Wara*, *s.* day time; time in general; saffron; boon, blessing; requesting, soliciting, prevailing on a person by intreaty to undertake any business; engaging, selecting, appointing; surrounding: *a.* best, excellent; valuable.

වරං, *Waraṇ*, *s.* better, preferable: see the last.

වරක්. *Warak*, *s.* one time.

වරක්කලේ, *Warakkalé*, *s.* carpenter's instrument for lining.

වරක්තා, *Waraktá*, *s.* elephant's leather girth: see වරත්‍රා *waratrá*.

වරක, *Waraka*, *s.* cover or awning of a boat; towel, wiper; wild kidney bean.

වරකමඩුලා, *Warakamadulá*, *s.* a beautiful yellow bird.

වරකල්ප, *Warakalpa*, *s.* (වර excellent, කල්ප kalpa) the third of four kalpas in which a Buddha was born, the present is the fourth: see භද්‍රකල්ප *bhadrakalpa*.

වරකා, *Waraká*, *s.* variety of jack in its ripe state.

වරකාහතු, *Waraká-hatu*, *s* mushroom on jack trees.

වරචන්දන, *Wara-chandana*, *s.* (වර best, චන්දන sandal) dark sort of sandal or agallochum; sort of pine, *pinus devadaru*.

වරට, *Waraṭa*, *s.* gander; man of a barbarous or foreign race; many-flowered jasmine; at one time.

වරටා, *Waraṭá*, *s.* goose.

වරණ, *Waraṇa*, *s.* (වෘ *wṛi* to choose or වර *wara* to restrain) appointing, selecting; surrounding, inclosing; screening, covering; restraining, control, preservation; guard; interception; an inclosure, a wall of masonry; protection; setting sun or the place where he sets, west; tusked elephant; small tree, *cratæra Roxburghii*, [Colloq ලුණුවරණ *luṇuwaraṇa*]: *a.* best, excellent, pre-eminent.

වරණ කර්ණික, *Waraṇa-karṇṇika*, *s.* (වරණ elephant, කර්ණ *karṇa* ear, ඉක *ika* affix of resemblance) plant with a bulbous root, the leaves of which resemble the ear of an elephant, *alocasia macrorrhiza* or *arum macrorhizon*, [Colloq. හබරල *habarala*].

වරණවා, *Waraṇawá*, *v.* to be out of season: pret. වැරුවා *wẹruwá*.

වරණා, *Waraṇá*, *s.* rivulet running past the north of Benares into the Ganges, now called the Berná.

වරණසි, *Waraṇusí*, s. (වරණ rivulet, see the preceding, අසි *así* another on the south side of the city) the city Benares, Elu form, බරණැස් *Baraṇęs.*

වරත්තුවා, *Warattuwá*, s. vulgar term for a mean fellow.

වරත්‍රා, *Waratrá*, s. (වෘ *wṛi* to cover or surround) elephant's or horse's leather girth; thong, strip of leather.

වරතික්ත, *Waratikta*, s. (වර best, තික්ත bitter or pungent) medicinal plant with bitter leaves, apparently the *oldenlandia corimbosa*, [Colloq. පත්පාඩගම් *patpáḍagam*]; though the Hindi name Tapar is also applied to the *gardenia latifolia*, [Colloq. ගලිස් *galis*]; also, medical compound, consisting of three pungent substances, viz. black pepper, long pepper, and dried ginger, [Colloq. ඉඟුරු *inguru*, මිරිස් *miris*, තිප්පිලි *tippili*].

වරද්දනවා, *Waraddanawá*, v. to err; to fail, to neglect wilfully, to disappoint: pret. වැරැද්දුවා *węręddúwá.*

වරද, *Warada*, s. fault, error; guilt, crime, offence; hair, hair of the head; the heir apparent and associated with the throne; benefactor; fire for burnt-offerings of a propitiatory; granting a prayer, conferring a boon.

වරදකරණවා, *Waradakaraṇawá*, v. to do wrong, to commit a fault.

වරදකාරයා, *Waradakárayá*, s. (වරද crime, කාර *kára* who does) offender, criminal, one convicted of any crime.

වරදකාරී, *Waradakári*, s. feminine of the above.

වරද තබනවා, *Warada-tabanawá*, }
වරද නගනවා, *Warada-naganawá*, } v. to accuse, to criminate, to inculpate.

වරද ප්‍රාප්ත, *Warada-prápta*, a. (වරද and ප්‍රාප්ත come, arrived) guilty, criminal.

වරදවනවා, *Waradawanawá*, v. to cause to err, to render any thing faulty: pret. වැරැදෙව්වා *węradewwá.*

වරදා, *Waradá*, s. (වර boon, දා who gives) plant, *cephalandra indica*, [Colloq. කෝවක්කා *kówakká*]; tree, species of the vitex, [Coll: නික *nika*].

වරදාන, *Waradána*, s. (වර best or boon, දාන giving, gift) granting a boon; place of pilgrimage; excellent gift.

වරදිනවා, *Waradinawá*, v. to err; to mistake, to blunder, to fail or neglect inadvertently: pret. වැරදුනා *węraduná.*

වරදු, *Waradu*, s. diamond thunderbolt of Indra: see වජ්‍ර *wajra* and වරද *warada.*

වරන්ගන්නවා, *Warangannawá*, v. to accept or receive a boon; to obtain permission.

වරපටය, *Warapaṭa*, s. leather head of a drum, the traces of a drum; strip of leather, thong: pl. වරපට *warapaṭa.*

වරප්‍රදාන, *Warapradána*, s. conferring a boon.

වරප්‍රසාද, *Waraprasáda*, s. permission, leave, [Coll: අවසර *awasara*]; special favour.

වරප්‍රිය, *Warapriya*, s. cinnamon bark, [Colloq. කුරුඳුපොතු *kurundu-potu*].

වරඵල, *Waraphala*, s. (වර best, ඵල fruit) coconut, [Colloq. පොල්ගෙඩිය *polgeḍiya*]; lime, *citrus limetta*, [Colloq. දෙහි *dehi*].

වරම්, *Waram*, a. better, sooner, rather, preferable; guarding, protecting; also, see වරම *warama.*

වරම්දෙවියෝ, *Waram-deviyó*, s. (වරම් guarding, දෙවියෝ gods) four regents of the four points of the compass, viz. Dhṛitaráshtra, Wirúḷha, Wirúpáksha, and Waiṣrawaṇa; see හතරවරම් දෙවියෝ *hatarawaram-deviyó.*

වරම, *Warama*, s. boon, gift from a superior; permission; possession by a devil, assumed supernatural power, inspiration: pl. වරම් *waram.*

වරමඬ, *Waramanda*, s. rope made of the skin of elk for catching wild beasts.

වරය, *Waraya*, s. boon, blessing; gift; permission, leave, authority from a god.

වරරුචි, *Wararuchi*, s. (වර pre-eminent, රුචි light, renown) poet and philosopher, one of the ornaments of the court of Bhója, or one of the nine gems usually ascribed to Vikramáditya's court.

වරල්, *Waral*, s. hair on the head: pl. of වරල *warala.*

වරල, *Warala*, s. fins and tail of a fish: pl. වරල් *waral.*

වරලබ්ධ, *Waralabdha*, s. tree, *mimusops elengi*, [Colloq. මූනමල් *múnamal*].

වරලස, *Waralasa*, s. hair on the head.

වරලු, *Waralu*, }
වරලුන්, *Waralun*, } s. thief, robber; company, multitude, flock, herd; row, line: *a.* bent, crooked, curved.

වරවර්ණිනී, *Warawarṇṇiní*, s. (වර best, වර්ණ *warṇa* class, ඉනී *iní* aff.) excellent or virtuous woman; woman in general; turmeric, *curcuma longa*, [Colloq. කහ *kaha*]; name of Lakshmí: see ප්‍රියඞ්ගු *priyańgu.*

වරවාරණ, *Warawárana*, *s.* (වර best, වාරණ elephant) royal elephant.

වරා, *Wará*, *s.* hog; the three myrobalans, *terminalia chebula*, *t. belerica*, and *phyllanthus emblica*, [Colloquial: අරළු *aralu*, බුළු *bulu*, and නෙල්ලි *nelli*]; swallow-wort or mudar, a common shrub with flowers in umbels, the juice is medicinal, *calotropis (or asclepias) gigantea (Asclepiadeæ)*; twining plant, *cissampelos hexandra*: *v.* being out of season.

වරාගහ, *Wará-gaha*, *s.* swallow-wort or mudar: see වරා *wará*.

වරාඞ්ග, *Waránga*, *s.* (වර *wara* best, excellent, අඞ්ග *anga* body or member) head; privity, male or female; cassia bark, [Colloq. කුරුඳු පොතු *kurundu-potu*]; elegant form or body; elephant.

වරාට, *Waráta*, *s.* cord, rope, string; small shell called a cowrie, used as a coin, [Colloq. කවඩි *kawadi*]; seed vessel or the lotus.

වරාණසී, *Waránasí*, *s.* (වර *wara* best, අනස් *anas* water, ඊ *í* aff. *i. e.* the Ganges on whose bank the city is situated) Benares.

වරාභිෂක්, *Warábhishak*, *s.* tree, *morinda citrifolia* and *m. tinctoria*, [Colloq. අහු *ahu*].

වරාය, *Waráya*, see වරාව *waráwa*.

වරාල, *Warála*, *s.* cloves, *caryophyllus aromaticus*, [Colloq. කරාබු *karábu*]; hog, pig, boar, [Colloq. ඌරා *úrá*].

වරාලක, *Warálaka*, *s.* shrub or small tree bearing caronda fruit, *carissa carandas*, [Colloq. මහ කරඹ *maha-karamba*]; cloves, *caryophyllus aromaticus*, [Colloq. කරාබු *karábu*].

වරාව, *Waráwa*, *s.* harbour, port.

වරාශි, *Waráṡi*, } *s.* coarse cloth; dirty or ragged
වරාසි, *Warási*, } clothes.

වරාහ, *Waráha*, *s.* hog, [Colloq. ඌරා *úrá*]; name of Vishṇu in his third avatára or descent, in which he assumed the shape of a boar; fragrant grass, *cyperus*; plant, *withania somnifera*, [Colloq. අමුක්කරා *amukkará*].

වරාහක, *Waráhaka*, *s.* boar, hog, [Colloq. ඌරා *úrá*].

වරාහකර්ණී, *Waráha-karṇní*, *s.* plant, *withania somnifera*, [Colloq. අමුක්කරා *amukkará*].

වරාහකාන්තා, *Waráha-kántá*, *s.* (වරාහ hog, කාන්ත *kánta* beloved by) sort of yam, [Colloq. ඌරල *úrala*].

වරි, *Wari*, *s.* row, line, [Colloq. පේළිය *péliya*]. (Tamil.)

වරිග, *Wariga*, *s.* caste, race, tribe; generation, descent; sort, species, [Colloq. ජාතිය *játiya*]; from වර්ග *warga*.

වරිගක්කාරයා, *Warigakkáraya*, *s.* man of noble pedigree. one of illustrious descent.

වරිගක්කාරි, *Warigakkári*, *s.* feminine of the above.

වරිගය, *Warigaya*, } see its plural form වරිග *wa-*
වරිගේ, *Warigé*, } *riga*.

වරිච්චි, *Warichchi*, more correctly written වරිච්චු *warichchu*. (Tamil.)

වරිච්චු, *Warichchu*, *s.* wooden frame of a house.

වරින්වර, *Warinwara*, *ad.* by turns, alternately, from time to time.

වරිපනම්, *Waripuṇam*, *s.* tax in property.

වරිෂ්ඨ, *Warishṭha*, *s.* copper, [Colloq. තඹ *tamba*]; pepper, [Colloq. ගම්මිරිස් *gammiris*]; francoline partridge: *a.* largest, greatest; heaviest, mightiest: best, dearest.

වරී, *Warí*, *s.* creeping plant, *asparagus falcatus*, [Colloq. හාතාවාරිය *hátáwáriya*].

වරීවර්ද, *Warí-warda*, *s.* ox, [Colloq. ගොණා *goṇá*]: see බලීවර්ද *balíwarda*.

වරුණ, *Waruṇa*, *s.* Varuṇa, the deity of the waters and regent of the west; water or the ocean; tree, *crateva Roxburghii*, [Colloq. ලුණුවරණ *luṇu-waraṇa*.

වරුණදිග, *Waruṇadiga*, *s.* (වරුණ god so called, දිග direction, in which he is regent) west.

වරුණදෙව්, *Waruṇa-dew*, see වරුණ *waruṇa*.

වරුණයා, *Waruṇayá*, see වරුණ *waruṇa*.

වරුණු, *Waruṇu*, *s.* west.

වරුණේ, *Waruṇé*, *s.* beauty, grandeur, corruptly for වර්ණය *warṇaya*.

වරුන්, *Warun*, *s.* tusked elephant, from වාරණ *wárana*.

වරුව, *Waruwa*, *s.* period of time; time of the day, half-a-day; stack or heap of paddy: pl. වරු *waru*.

වරුසාව, *Warusáwa*, *s.* incorrectly for වර්ෂාව *war-sháwa*, rain.

වරුසෙ, *Waruse*, *s.* incorrectly for වර්ෂය *warshaya*, year.

වරුළු, *Warulu*, *s.* earth, [Colloq. පොළව *polawa*].

වරූථ, *Warútha*, *s.* (වෘ *wri* to surround, ඌථන් *úthan* aff.) wooden fender round a carriage as a defence from collision; armour. mail; leather, skin.

වරූථිනි, *Warúthini*, *s.* (වරූථ *warútha* part of a car, ඉනි *ini* aff.) army, [Colloq: යුද්ධ සේනාව *yuddha-sénáwa*].

වරේණ්‍ය, *Wareṇya*, *a.* chief, principal, pre-eminent, [Colloq. ප්‍රධාන *pradhána*].

වරෙන්, *Waren*, *v.* come: *imper. sing.* of එනවා *enawá.*

වරෙන්තුව, *Warentuwa*, *s.* warrant. (English.)

වරෙල්ලා, *Wareḷḷá*, *v.* come: *imp. pl.* of එනවා *enawá.*

වරේ, *Waré*, *s.* time, also see වර *wara.*

වරෞෂධී, *Waraushadhí*, *s.* plant, medicinal plant, *hydrocotyle asiatica*, [Colloq. මකුළුවැන්න *makuluwenna* or හින්ගොටුකොල *hín-goṭukola*].

වල්, *Wal*, *s.* jungle, wood, thicket; grass; tail: *a.* wild, savage; also, affix forming the plural of nouns.

වල් අඟුන, *Wal-anguna*, *s.* plant, *hoya reticulata.*

වල් අඩ, *Wal-aḍa*, *s.* coverlet.

වල් අනිත්ත, *Wal-anitta*, *s.* plant, variety of *rhinacanthus communis.*

වල් අනෝදා, *Wal-anódá*, *s.* plant, variety of *abutilon asiaticum* or *sida hirta.*

වල් අබ, *Wal-aba*, *s.* (වල් wild, අබ mustard) plant bearing single yellow flowers, *cleome viscosa (Capparidiæ).*

වල් අඹ, *Wal-amba*, *s.* wild mango, *mangifera zeylanica (Anacardiaceæ).*

වල් අමු, *Wal-amu*, *s.* plant, variety of *paspalum scrobiculatum.*

වල් අවර, *Wal-awara*, *s.* twining, biennial plant with flowers in pairs, *canavalia (*or *dolichos), ensiformis (Leguminosæ).*

වල් අවරි, *Wal-awari*, *s.* small tree, species of *indigofera.*

වල් අවිච්චියා, *Wal-awichchiyá*, *s.* spotted thrush, *turdus spiloptera (Saxicolidæ,* order *Passeres).*

වල් අසමෝදගම්, *Wal-asamódagam*, *s.* water parsley, *pimpinella Heyneana (Umbelliferæ).*

වල් ඇලංගා, *Wal-álangá*, *s.* creeper, variety of *ipomœa bona-nox.*

වල් ඇටෝරා, *Wal-ẹṭórá*, *s.* kind of grass, variety of *panicum repens.*

වල් ඇණේ, *Wal-ẹṇé*, *s.* wooden peg.

වල් ඇත්අඩිය, *Wal-ẹtaḍiya*, *s.* plant, variety of *elytraria crenata.*

වල් ඇඹිල්ල, *Wal-ẹmbilla*, *s.* plant, species of *antidesma:* see හින් ඇඹිල්ල *hín-ẹmbilla.*

වල් ඇහැටු, *Wal-ẹheṭu*, *s.* straggling shrub, bark and root bitter, *ficus heterophylla, (Urticaceæ).*

වල් ඇහැළ, *Wal-ẹheḷa*, *s.* species of cassia, *cassia glauca.*

වල් ඉඟුරු, *Wal-inguru*, *s.* (වල් wild, ඉඟුරු ginger) species of ginger, peculiar to Ceylon, *zingiber cylindricum (Scitamineæ).*

වල් ඉද්ද, *Wal-idda*, *s.* plant, peculiar to Ceylon, *Wrightia zeylanica (Apocynaceæ);* also called සුදු ඉද්ද *sudu-idda.*

වල් උඳු, *Wal-undu*, *s.* plant, *flemingia semialata.*

වල් ඌරා, *Wal-úrá*, *s.* (වල් wild, ඌරා hog) wild boar, *sus indicus.*

වල් එකාවේරිය, *Wal-ekáwériya*, *s.* plant, snake root, variety of *rauwolfia (*or *ophioxylon) serpentina.*

වල් එඬරු, *Wal-enḍaru*, *s.* (වල් *wal* wild) plant, *bupleurum mucornatum;* another plant, peculiar to Ceylon, *peucedanum zeylanicum, (Umbelliferæ).*

වල් එන්සාල්, *Wal-ensál*, *s.* kind of cardamoms, variety of *elettaria cardamomum.*

වල් එරබදු, *Wal-erabadu*, *s.* (වල් wild, එරබදු erythrina) species of the *erythrina indica* or coral tree.

වල් ඔලිඳ, *Wal-olinda*, *s.* (වල් and ඔලිඳ abrus) precatorius) wild variety of the *abrus precatorius,* or liquorice creeper.

වල්ක, *Walka*, *s.* bark of a tree; scales of a fish.

වල් කජු, *Wal-kaju*, *s.* kind of cashew, variety of *anacardium occidentale.*

වල් කඩුපාර, *Wal-kaḍupára*, *s.* plant, *cacalia sagittata.*

වල් කදුරු, *Wal-kaduru*, *s.* tree of the order *apocynaceæ.*

වල් කප්පරවල්ලිය, *Wal-kapparawalliya*, *s.* plant, variety of *coleus aromaticus.*

වල් කපු, *Wal-kapu*, *s.* (වල් wild, කපු cotton) species of the cotton tree, *gossypium.*

වල් කපුරු, *Wal-kapuru*, *s.* kind of camphor, *cinnamom camphora.*

වල්කම, *Walkama*, *s.* rusticity, clownishness, incivility, wildness, mischief.

වල් කයිල, *Wal-kayila*, *s.* plant, *phyllanthus multiflorens.*

වල්කරණවා, *Walkaraṇawá*, *v.* to make wild; to mismanage; to treat a subject unskilfully.

වල් කරපිංච, *Wal-karapincha*, *s.* plant, *micromelum pubescens (Rutaceæ).*

වල් කරල්සැබෝ, *Wal-karalsẹbó*, *s.* plant, variety of *cyathula geniculata.*

වල්කල, *Walkala*, *s.* bark of a tree, [Colloq. පොතු *potu*]; garment made of bark.

වල් කහ, *Wal-kaha*, s. (වල් wild, කහ saffron) wild turmeric, *curcuma aromatica (Scitamineæ)*; also called දඩකහ *dada-kaha*.

වල් කහඹිලියා, *Wal-kahambiliyá*, s. plant, *fleurya interrupta (Urticaceæ)*.

වල් කාවුළු, *Wal-káwuḷu*, s. kind of grass, variety of *setaria glauca*.

වල් කිකිළි, *Wal-kikiḷi*, feminine of වල් කුකුළා *wal-kukuḷá*.

වල් කිඩාරන්, *Wal-kiḍáran*, s. plant, *arisæma Leschenaultii (Araceæ)*.

වල් කිඳ, *Wal-kinda*, s. (වල් *wal* wild) plant, *tinospora tomentosa (Menispermaceæ)*.

වල් කිරිමදු, *Wal-kirimadu*, s. plant, variety of *Ipomæa cymosa*: see කිරිමදු *kirimadu*.

වල් කිරිලබු, *Wal-kirilabu*, s. plant, species of *cucurbita*.

වල් කුකුළා, *Wal-kukuḷá*, s. wild or jungle cock, *gallus lafayetti, (Ppasianidæ*, order *Gallinæ)*: see වලිකුකුළා *walikukuḷá*.

වල් කුප්පමේනිය, *Wal-kuppaméniya*, s. plant, variety of *acalypha indica*.

වල් කුරක්කන්, *Wal-kurakkan*, s. plant, *eleusine indica (Gramineæ)*; also called බැලතණ *bęlataṇa*.

වල් කුරුඳු, *Wal-kurundu*, s. (වල් wild, කුරුඳු cinnamon) sort of laurel, variety of *cinnamomum zeylanicum*.

වල් කෙහෙල්, *Wal-kehel*, s. wild plantain, *musa paradisiaca, (Scitamineæ)*.

වල් කොඩොල්, *Wal-kondol*, s. kind of yam, not ascertained.

වල් කොරකහ, *Wal-korakaha*, s. plant, variety of *memecylon umbellatum*.

වල් කොල්ලන්කොල, *Wal-kollankola*, s. annual hairy plant, *Mentha perilloides*.

වල් කොල්ලු, *Wal-kollu*, s. plant, *atylosia rugosa (Leguminosæ)*.

වල් කොලොන්ඳු, *Wal-kolondu*, s. sort of wormwood, *artemisia vulgaris (Compositæ)*.

වල් කොහොඹ, *Wal-kohomba*, s. variety of the margosa tree, *azadirachta indica*.

වල් කෝන්, *Wal-kón*, s. tree, variety of *schleichera trijuga*.

වල් කෝපි, *Wal-kópi*, s. wild coffee plant, peculiar to Ceylon, *scyphostachys coffæoides (Rubiaceæ)*.

වල් කැකුන, *Wal-kękuna*, s. tree, *ostodes (or desmostemon) zeylanica (Euphorbiaceæ)*; also called ඔලුපැතත *olupętta*.

වල් කැප්පිටියා, *Wal-kęppiṭiyá*, s. (වල් *wal* wild) plant, *croton rhombifolium*.

වල් ගම්මිරිස් වැල්, *Wal-gammiris-węl*, s. (වල් wild, ගම්මිරිස් pepper, වැල් creeper) wild pepper, *piper sylvestre (Piperaceæ)*: see මළමිරිස් *maḷamiris*.

වල්ගය, *Walgaya*, s. tail: pl. වල්ගා *walgá*.

වල් ගහල, *Wal-gahala*, s. plant, variety of *colocasia antiquorum*.

වල්ගා තාරකාව, *Walgá-tárakáwa*, s. comet.

වල්ගා මිරිස්, *Walgá-miris*, s. creeping plant of the genus *piper*.

වල් ගුරුළුරාජ, *Wal-guruḷurája*, s. (වල් *wal* wild) plant, not ascertained.

වල් ගුරුඬ, *Wal-gúrenda*, s. shrub, *clerodendrum inerme (Verbinaceæ)*.

වල් ගෙවදිනවා, *Wal-gewadinawá*, v. to clear jungle.

වල් ගෙවදීම, *Wal-gewadíma*, verbal noun of above.

වල් ගොන්න, *Wal-gonna*, s. plant, *ficus callosa (Urticaceæ)*.

වල් ගොනිකා, *Wal-goniká*, s. plant, *psychotria sarmentosa (Rubiaceæ)*.

වල් ගැටපිච්ච, *Wal-gęṭapichcha*, s. (වල් wild, ගැට පිච්ච jasmine) variety of jasmine, *jasminum sambac* or *j. undulatum*.

වල් ජම්බු, *Wal-jambu*, s. (වල් and ජම්බු eugenia) jambu, *eugenia (or jambosa) aquea (Myrtaceæ)*.

වල් ජයපාල, *Wal-jayapála*, s. plant, peculiar to Ceylon, *ostodes (or desmostemon) minor, (Euphorbiaceæ)*.

වල් තණ, *Wal-taṇa*, s. (වල් wild, තණ grass) sort of panic grass, *panicum patens*.

වල් තල, *Wal-tala*, s. plant, variety of *sesamum indicum*.

වල් තිප්පිලි, *Wal-tippili*, s. variety of the long pepper plant, *piper diffusum*.

වල් තිබ්බටු, *Wal-tibbaṭu*, s. plant, *solanum trilobatum (Solanaceæ)*.

වල් තිඹිරි, *Wal-timbiri*, s. tree, variety of *diospyros Embryopteris*.

වල් තෙලඹු, *Wal-telambu*, s. large timber tree, variety of *sterculia fœtida*.

වල් තේකොල, *Wal-tékola*, s. bur marigold or Spanish needle, *bidens decomposita (Compositæ)*.

වල් තෝර, *Wal-tóra*, s. plant, species of *cassia*.

වල් තෝවැල්ල, *Wal-tówęlla*, s. creeper, *cissus suberosa*, or variety of *vitis erioclada*.

වල් ත්‍රස්තවාලු, *Wal-trastawálu*, s. (වල් *mal* wild) twining hairy plant with yellow flowers, purple at bottom of bell, *hewittia bicolor (Convolvulaceæ)*.

වල් දත්කැටියා, *Wal-datkeṭiyá*, s. plant, variety of *xylopia Championii* or of *ophiorrhiza mungos*.

වල් දියමෙනේරි, *Wal-diyamenéri*, s. spider-wort, *tradescantia paniculata* or variety of *commelina bengalensis*.

වල් දියලබු, *Wal-diyalabu*, s. ligneous plant climbing over trees, *vitis (or cissus) adnata (Ampelideæ)*.

වල් දිවිඇඩියා, *Wal-diriadiya*, s. twining hairy plant, variety of *Ipomœa Pestigridis*.

වල් දෙල්, *Wal-del*, s. wild bread fruit tree, yielding good timber, peculiar to Ceylon, *artocarpus nobilis (Urticaceæ)*.

වල්නා, *Walná*, s. fox, jackal, [Colloq. නරියා

වල් පත්පාඩගම්, *Wal-patpáḍagam*, s. plant, *oldenlandia corymbosa* or *hedyotis Barmanniana*, *(Rubiaceæ)*.

වල්පත, *Walpata*, s. the tail of a fish.

වල් පළොල්, *Wal-paḷol*, s. tree, *bignonia indica*.

වල් පිච්ච, *Wal-pichcha*, s. small tree with large white fragrant flowers, *guettarda speciosa (Rubiaceæ)*; also, sort of jasmine, *jasminum angustifolium (Oleaceæ)*.

වල් පිත්තන්, *Wal-pittan*, s. plant, not ascertained.

වල් පොල්ලිච්චා, *Wal-pollichchá*, s. long-tailed robin, *cittacincla mucrura (Saxicolidæ* order *Passeres)*.

වල් පෝටේ, *Wal-póṭé*, s. creeping plant, not ascertained.

වල් බඩ අමු, *Wal-baḍa-amu*, s. species of panic grass, *panicum fluitans*.

වල් බින් අමු, *Wal-bin-amu*, s. species of panic grass, variety of *panicum paspaloides* or *paspalum scrobiculatum*.

වල් බිලින්, *Wal-bilin*, s. tree, *ailantus malabarica (Simarubaceæ)*; also called කුඹළු *kumbaḷu*.

වල් බුත්සරණ, *Wal-butsaraṇa*, s. plant, variety of *canna indica*.

වල් බුරුත, *Wal-buruta*, see වල් සපු *wal-sapu*.

වල් බූමේ, *Wal-búmé*, s. kidney bean, variety of *phaseolus max*.

වල් බෝඹු, *Wal-bómbu*, s. tree, *symplocos spicata (Styraceæ)*; also called බෝඹු *bómbu*.

වල් මකුළු, *Wal-makuḷu*, s. tree, variety of *hydnocarpus venerata*.

වල් මල්කුරක්කන්, *Wal-mal-kurakkan*, s. (වල් *wal* wild) plant, variety of *eleusine indica*.

වල්මික, *Walmika*, s. white ant hill.

වල් මිදෙල්ල, *Wal-midella*, s. tree, species of *Barringtonia*.

වල් මිරිස්, *Wal-miris*, s. plant, variety of *piper silvestre*.

වල්මී, *Walmí*, s. white ant's hill.

වල්මීක, *Walmíka*, s. (වල *wala* to cover, කීකච් *kíkach* aff.) ant hill, or the large accumulations of soil made by the white ant; elephantiasis; poet Wálmíki.

වල් මීමා, *Wal-mímá*, s. wild buffalo, *bos gavæus*.

වල්මීයා, *Walmíyá*, s. (වල් wild, මීයා deer or rat) moose deer, *moschus miminna*.

වල් මුරුංගා, *Wal-murungá*, s. plant, *breynia patens (Euphorbiaceæ)*.

වල් මුරුවාදුල්, *Wal-muruwádúl*, s. plant, variety of *Marsdenia tenacissima*.

වල් මූදුමේ, *Wal-múdumé*, s. plant, variety of *phaseolus caracalla*.

වල් මූනමල්, *Wal-múnamal*, s. (වල් wild, මූනමල් *mimusops elengi*) tree, variety of *mimusops elengi*.

වල් මෙනේරි, *Wal-menéri*, s. grain, variety of *panicum miliare* or *p. miliaceum*.

වල් මැදිරිය, *Wal-mediriya*, s. tree, *diospyros insignis (Ebenaceæ)*; also called ගොන *gona*, and පොරුවමල්ල *poruwa-malla*.

වල් මෑ, *Wal-mé*, s. plant, *phaseolus adenanthus (Leguminosæ)*.

වල් රත්දියලබු, *Wal-rat-diyalabu*, s. plant with flat climbing stem, *vitis (or cissus) carnosa (Ampelideæ)*.

වල් රසකිඳ, *Wal-rasakinda*, s. plant, *zanonia indica (Cucurbitaceæ)*.

වල්රොද, *Wal-roda*, s. (වල් forest, රොද row) line of forests.

වල්ල, *Walla*, s. bunch, cluster (applied to coconuts or grapes etc.) skein of cotton: pl. වලු *walu*.

වල්ලකී, *Wallaki*, s. Indian lute; one of the signs of the zodiac, *gemini*.

වල්ලභ, *Wallabha*, s. lover, husband, friend: superintendent, overseer: *a.* desired, beloved, peer; supreme, superintending.

වල්ලභයා, *Wallabhayá*, s. lover, husband, superintendent.

වල්ලරි, *Wallari*, } s. compound pedicle; creeping
වල්ලරී, *Wallarí*, } or twining plant.

වලලව, *Wallava*, *s.* cook, [Colloq. කෝකියා *kókiyá*]; herdsman, [Colloq. එඬේරා *eṇḍérá*].

වල්ලා, *Wallá*, *s.* tree, bearing a seed used in cases of diarrhœa, dysentery, etc. *nerium antidysentericum*, [Colloq. කිරිවල්ලා *kiri-wallá*]; fibrous plant, peculiar to Ceylon, *gyrinops walla (Thymelœaceœ)*; also called පට්ටා වල්ලා *paṭṭá-wallá*.

වල්ලා, *Wallá*, *s.* kind of small sea fish: pl. වල්ලෝ *walló*.

වල්ලි, *Walli*, *s.* creeper, creeping or climbing plant; grey tailed, as of a bull.

වල්ලිකා, *Wallikâ*, *s.* plant, *vitis quadrangularis*, [Colloq. හිරැස්ස *hiręssa*]; pumpkin, [Colloq. පුහුල් *puhul*].

වල්ලියා, *Walliyá*, *s.* bull with a grey tail.

වල්ලී, *Wallí*, *s.* creeper; aromatic plant, *ligusticum ajowan*.

වල්ලීජ, *Wallíja*, *s.* pepper.

වල්ලී මධුකර, *Wallí-madhukara*, *s.* liquorice plant, *glycyrrhiza glabra*, [Colloq. වැල්මී *wẹlmí*].

වල් ලිමෑ, *Wal-límẹ*, *s.* plant, variety of *dolichos catjang*.

වල්ලුර, *Wallura*, see වල්ලූර *wallúra*.

වල් ලූනු, *Wal-lúnu*, *s.* plant, bearing a single large white flower, *pancratium zeylanicum (Amaryllideœ)*.

වල්ලූර, *Wallúra*, *s.* dried flesh; the flesh of the wild boar; solitude, wild; thicket, arbour, place overgrown with creepers.

වල් වඳුරු කෙසෙල්, *Wal-wandurukesel*, *s.* variety of plantain, *musa sapientum*.

වල් වඳුරුමෑ, *Wal-wandurumẹ*, *s.* plant: see වඳුරු මෑ *wandurumẹ*.

වල් වරකා, *Wal-waraká*, *s.* shrub, the leaves of which when boiled are edible and the roots purgative, *casearia esculenta (Samydaceœ)*.

වල් වහුන්, *Wal-wahun*, *s.* plant, *alocasia macrorrhiza:* see හබරල *habarala* and වහුන් *wahun*.

වල්විදුනා, *Walviduná*, *s.* (වල් tail of the bos grunniens, විදුනා from ව්‍යජන *wyajana* fan) large fan made of the tail of the *bos grunniens*, used by kings and great men; cowri, or a whisk, fly-flapper.

වල්විහි, *Walvihi*, *s.* fallow or uncultivated ground: *a.* overgrown with jungle.

වල් වූරුවා, *Wal-wúruwá*, *s.* Indian vulture.

වල් වෙලා, *Wal-wélá*, *s.* plant, variety of *gynandropsis pentaphylla*.

වල් වැල්මිදි, *Wal-wẹlmidi*, *s.* plant, variety of *mimosa pudica* or of *premna serratifolia*.

වල් සපු, *Wal-sapu*, *s.* forest tree, timber of which is good for furniture, etc. *michelia nilagirica (Magnoliaceœ)*.

වල් සමන්පිච්ච, *Wal-samanpichcha*, *s.* narrow-leaved jasmine, *jasminum angustifolium*.

වල්සර, *Walsara*, *s.* (වල් wild, සර who goes) Vẹddá, wild man, savage, barbarian.

වල් සූරිය, *Wal-súriya*, *s.* tree, variety of *thespesia populnea*.

වල් සැවැන්දරා, *Wal-sęwęndará*, *s.* variety of *andropogon zeylanicus*.

වල, *Wala*, *s.* forest, jungle; carpet; hair; rings or bracelets used by dancers and tom tom beaters; army, forces.

වලංගු. *Walangu*, *a.* passable, current, valid, acceptable.

වලංගුකරණවා, *Walangukaraṇawá*, *v.* to observe as a law; to obey.

වලංගුව, *Walanguwa*, *s.* subjection, obedience to commands, docility.

වලංගුවෙනවා, *Walanguwenawá*, *v.* to be current, to be valid; to be in use; to pass current, as money.

වලක්කනවා, *Walakkanawá*, *v.* to hinder, to suppress: pret. වැලැක්කුවා *wẹlẹkkuwá*.

වලක්වනවා, *Walakwanawá*, *v.* to cause to stop, the causal form of වලකනවා *walakanawá:* pret. වැලැක්වූවා *wẹlẹkwuwá*.

වලකඩ, *Walakaḍa*, *s.* valley.

වලකන්, *Walakan*, *s.* robbery, plunder.

වලකනවා, *Walakanawá*, *v.* to stop, to prevent, to hinder, to impede; to circumvent, to defraud: pret. වැලකුවා *wẹlakuwá*.

වලකිඳු, *Walakidú*, *s.* back; spine.

වලකිනවා, *Walakinawá*, *v.* to stop, to hinder, to prevent: pret. වැලකුනා *wẹlakuná*.

වල කුරුල්ලා, *Wala-kurullá*, *s.* common weaver bird, *Ploceus philippinus;* also called තට්ට කුරුල්ලා *taṭṭa-kurullá*.

වලග, *Walaga*, *s.* tip of the tail; top of the hips, waist, loins, [Colloq. ඉඟ *inga*, ඉඟටිය *ingaṭiya*].

වලගසාල්, *Walagasál*, *s.* climbing anthelmintic shrub, *erycibe paniculata*.

වලඟ, *Walanga*, *s.* submission, obedience; also, see වලග *walaga*.

වලඟසාල්, *Walangasál*, see වලගසාල් *walagasál*.

වලතඩිය, *Walatadiya*, *s.* club, mace, [Colloquial: පොල්ල *polla*]; dislocation of a bone: pl. වලතඩි *walatadi*.

වලඳ, *Walanda*, *s.* sign, mark, spot, token; pot, pan, earthen cooking vessel: pl. වලන් *walan*.

වලඳනවා, *Walandanawá*, *v.* to eat, used only of priests or men of rank; also, to enjoy: pret. වැළඳුවා *welanduwá*.

වලඳිනවා, *Walandinawá*, *v.* to embrace.

වලඳු, *Walandu*, *s.* thief; breaking, rending.

වලන්, *Walan*, plural of වලඳ *walanda*.

වලප්, *Walap*, *s.* weeping.

වලප්නා, *Walapná*, *a.* weeping, crying, lamenting.

වලපනවා, *Walapanawá*, *v.* to cause, to weep; to fatigue, to harass, [Colloq. වෙහෙසනවා *wehesanawá*].

වලපිනවා, *Walapinawá*, *v.* to cry, to lament, to bewail, to weep: pret. වැලපුනා *welapuná*.

වලපොත්තා, *Walapottá*, *s.* kind of fish.

වලබවාය, *Walabawáya*, *s.* Bengal tiger, [Colloq. ව්‍යාඝ්‍රයා *wyághrayá*].

වලභි, *Walabhi*, *s.* (වල to cover) wooden frame of thatch, turret or temporary building on the roof of a house.

වලය, *Walaya*, *s.* (වල to surround) bracelet, armlet; sore throat, inflammation of the larynx; boundary, inclosure.

වලයා, *Walayá*, *s.* kind of fish.

වලයිත, *Walayita*, *a.* surrounded, inclosed.

වලල්ල, *Walalla*, *s.* bracelet, armlet; rings used for ornamenting the arms and ankles; ring, hoop, circle: pl. වලලු *walalu*.

වලලුකර, *Walalukara*, *s.* small of the leg, the ankle.

වලලුපල, *Walalupala*, *s.* name of Kataragama deviyó, Indian Mars.

වලව්ව, *Walawuwa*, *s.* the house of a headman or person of distinction.

වලසා, *Walasá*, *s.* bear: pl. වලස්සු *walassu*.

වලහන්, *Walahan*, *s.* one-seventh of the produce of a paddy field given to those who are employed in reaping and threshing corn. This word is sometimes written වාලහන් *wálahan*.

වලහනවා, *Walahanawá*, *v.* to baffle, to perplex; to hinder, to oppose, to obstruct: pret. වැලහුවා *welahuwá*.

වලහා, *Walahá*, *s.* bear.

වලා, *Walá*, *s.* cloud; bracelet; wild fellow.

වලාකා, *Waláká*, *s.* paddy bird or Indian crane.

වලාකුළ, *Walákula*, *s.* (වලා cloud, කුළ top) cloud: pl. වලාකුල් *walákul*.

වලාදන, *Waládana*, } *s.* thunderbolt, electric
වලාදල, *Waládala*, } shock, [Colloquial: හෙන *hena*].

වලාන්, *Walán*, *s.* grove, forest.

වලාපටලය, *Walápatalaya*, *s.* cloud, long line of clouds.

වලාම, *Waláma*, *s.* misfortune, ill-luck, destruction: *a.* inauspicious, unfortunate, unlucky.

වලාමග, *Walá-maga*, *s.* (වලා cloud, මග path) sky, atmosphere, [Colloq. අහස *ahasa*].

වලාල, *Walála*, *a.* calm, still, unruffled.

වලාව, *Waláwa*, *s.* shower of rain.

වලාවන්, *Waláwan*, see වරණ *warana*.

වලාවැන්න, *Waláwenna*, *s.* kind of medicinal plant.

වලාහක, *Waláhaka*, *s.* cloud; mountain.

වලි, *Wali*, *s.* wrinkle, furrow; line or streak made with fragrant unguents on the person; twig, stalk: *a.* wild, living in a wood.

වලිකවනවා, *Walikawanawá*, *v.* to twist, to twine.

වලිකිකිළි, *Wali-kikili*, *s.* (wild) water hen: see the next.

වලිකුකුළා, *Wali-kukulá*, *s.* (wild) water cock, *gallicrex cincrea, (Rallidæ* order *Grallæ)*; also called කිතලා *kitalá*.

වලිගය, *Waligaya*, *s.* tail, tail of any animal: pl. වලිගා *waligá*.

වලිගහනවා, *Waligahanawá*, *v.* to attempt, to strive.

වලිගේ, *Waligé*, see වලිගය *waligaya*.

වලිප්පුව, *Walippuwa*, *s.* convulsive fit.

වලිමුඛ, *Walimukha*, *s.* (වලි wrinkle, මුඛ countenance) ape, monkey, [Colloq. වඳුරා *wandurá*, and රිළවා *rilawá*].

වලිය, *Waliya*, *s.* given day, portion of a day.

වලියක්දා, *Waliyakdá*, *s.* on a certain day.

වලීමුඛ, *Walímukha*, see වලිමුඛ *walimukha*.

වලීර, *Walíra*, *a.* squint eyed.

වලු, *Walu*, *s.* bunch, cluster.

වලුකින, *Walu-kína*, *s.* tree, peculiar to Ceylon, *calophyllum bracteatum (Guttiferæ)*.

වලු තම්පලා, *Walu-tampalá*, *s.* plant, *amarantus polygamus (Amarantaceæ)*.

වලු පැපොල, *Walu-pepola*, *s.* papaw or pepol tree, *carica papaya*.

වලුහොරා, *Walu-horá*, *s.* (වලු bunch, skein of cotton, හොරා thief) small bird with a white body and tail, hence the name: see රෙදිහොරා *redi-horá.*

වවනවා, *Wawanawá, v.* to cultivate the ground, to plant, to propagate by cuttings: pret. වැවුවා *wewuwá.*

වවුන්න, *Wawunna, s.* spindle: pl. වවුනු *wawunu.*

වවුලා, *Wawulá, s.* bat, flying fox, *pteropus Edwardsii (Cheiroptera)*: pl. වවුලෝ *wawuló.*

වවුලැටිය, *Wawuleṭiya, s.* name of ligneous climbing plants, viz. දිය වවුලැටිය *diya-wawuleṭiya (genus cæsalpinia),* and ගොඩ වවුලැටිය *goda-wawuleṭiya (genus mezorneurum,) (Leguminosæ).*

වශ්‍ය, *Waṣya, a.* (වශ *waṣa* subjection, යත් *yat* aff.) docile, tame, humble.

වශ, *Waṣa, s.* wish, desire; authority, mastership; subjection, submission: *a.* humbled, subdued, tamed; enthralled, subdued by charms and incantations, fascinated, enchanted.

වශග, *Waṣaga, s.* obedient; subject.

වශී, *Waṣi, s.* (වශ *waṣa* to desire, supremacy, ඉන් *in* aff.) one of the eight superhuman attributes of Ṣiva, supposed to be attainable by the performance of mystical rites.

වශිර, *Waṣira, s.* sea salt, [Colloq. මුදු ලුණු *mudu-luṇu*]; tree, *achyranthes aspera,* [Colloq. ගස් කරල්හැබ *gas-karalheba*]; orris root.

වශිරජ, *Waṣi-rája, s.* (වශී and රජ king) name of Ṣiva.

වශීකරණ, *Waṣíkaraṇa, s.* (වශ *waṣa* subduing, කරණ making) subduing, overcoming by charms, poison; drugs, etc. enchanting, charming.

වස්, *Was, s.* year, from වත්සර *watsara;* house; dwelling, residing; bamboo from වංශ *wanṣa;* age, time of life, from වයස *wayasa;* rain, raining from වර්ෂ *warsha;* vice, depravity: see වස්වසනවා *was-wasanawá.*

වස් කවිය, *Was-kaviya, s.* piece of poetry of four lines to bring evil on any man or other thing.

වස් කුලල්, *Was-kulal, s.* (වස් bamboo, කුලල *kulala* tube) sort of pipe or flute made from the reeds of the bamboo cane.

වස්ගහනවා, *Wasgahanawá, s.* calamity as the punishment for an arrogant assumption of high rank.

වස්ති, *Wasti, s.* abdomen, lower belly or part below the navel; bladder; anus; an injection, syringe.

වස්තිකරණවා, *Wastikaraṇawá, v.* to administer an injection.

වස්ති කූඩුව, *Wasti-kúḍuwa, s.* syringe.

වස්ති මල, *Wasti-mala, s.* (වස්ති belly, මල secretion) urine, [Colloq. මූත්‍රා *mútrá*].

වස්තු, *Wastu, s.* thing, matter, substance; property, wealth, riches; natural disposition, essential property, nature, essence.

වස්තුකාම, *Wastu-káma, s.* desire of riches or worldly goods, one of the two chief passions that excite the minds of men.

වස්තුකාරයා, *Wastukárayá, s.* rich man.

වස්තුලෝභී, *Wastulóbhi, a.* greedy for riches.

වස්තුව, *Wastuwa,* see its plural form වස්තු *wastu.*

වස්ත්‍ර, *Wastra, s.* clothes, raiment; covering, cover.

වස්ත්‍රකුට, *Wastra-kúṭa, s.* (වස්ත්‍ර and කුට small house) tent, [Colloq. කූඩාරම *kúḍárama*].

වස්ත්‍ර ගුහ්‍ය, *Wastra-guyhaya, s.* (වස්ත්‍ර dress, ගුහ්‍ය *guyha* hidden) privity, private part, either male or female.

වස්ත්‍ර ගෘහ, *Wastra-griha, s.* (වස්ත්‍ර cloth, ගෘහ house) tent, [Colloq. කූඩාරම *kúḍárama*].

වස්ත්‍ර භූෂණ, *Wastra-bhúshṇa, s.* ornaments of dress or clothing.

වස්ත්‍රය, *Wastraya,* see its plural form වස්ත්‍ර *wastra.*

වස්ත්‍ර යෝනි, *Wastra-yóni, s.* (වස්ත්‍ර cloth, යෝනි place of production) basis or material of cloth, as cotton, silk, wool, etc.

වස්ත්‍රාභරණ, *Wastrábharaṇa,* see වස්ත්‍රභූෂණ *wastra-bhúshṇa.*

වස්දඬු, *Was-danḍu, s.* (වස් bamboo, දඬු stick) whistle, used in demon worship for the purpose of summoning the demon; flute.

වස්දෙව්, *Wasdew, s.* name of Vishṇu.

වස්න, *Wasna, s.* cover, covering; cloth, clothes; price, wages, hire; wealth; thing, substance; abiding, dwelling; death; also see වසන් *wasan.*

වස්මර, *Wasmara, s.* sickness, epilepsy.

වස්‍ය, *Wasya, s.* house, dwelling: see වශ්‍ය *waṣya.*

වස්වසනවා, *Was-wasanawá, s.* (වස් rainy season, වසනවා to abide) to remain in one place during the rainy season, a religious ordinance among the Buddhists; according to whose institutions the priests are not to be house-holders, but constant itinerants among the people, begging food or living in deserts; but they have the privilege of a fixed residence during the rains; in modern times a practice prevails among the priests of going to reside in the house of a person for a given period during which he imparts religious instruction to the family and all they invite.

වස්වාසික, *Waswásika*, *s.* (වස්සාවාසං *wassáwásaṇ* and ඉක *ika* aff.) presents given to the priests at the end of the Was ceremony: see the last.

වස්විසිම, *Wasvisíma*, } *s.* observance of a religious ordinance amongst the Buddhist priests in keeping a fixed residence during the rainy seasons; verbal noun of වස් වසනවා *waswasanawá*.
වස්වැසීම, *Waswęsíma*, }

වස්ස වලාහක, *Wassa-waláhaka*, *s.* the god of rain, [Colloq. වරුණදෙව් *waruṇadew*].

වස්සා, *Wassá*, *s.* calf, young of cattle; Elu form of වත්ස *watsa*: pl. වස්සෝ *wassó*.

වස්සාන, *Wassána*, *s.* rainy season (July-August), time appointed for Buddhist priests to take up a fixed residence.

වස්සාවාසං, *Wassáwásṇ*, see වස්වසනවා *waswasanawá*.

වස්සික, *Wassika*, } *s.* (වස්ස *wassa* the rains, ඉක *ika* aff.) species of jasmine.
වස්සිකා, *Wassiká*, }

වස, *Wasa*, *s.* venom, poison; evening, after part of the day, from සවස *sawasa*; race, lineage; word, speech, from වච *wacha*; year; dwelling, residing; also, see වසා *wasá* and වශ *waṣa*: *a.* poisonous, destructive; bad, mischievous, wicked.

වසංගතය, *Wasaṇgataya*, *s.* (වසං and ගත *gata* what goes) pestilence, the plague.

වසක්කේඩුව, *Wasakkéḍuwa*, *s.* infirmity, languor, or debility, caused by starvation or want of food.

වසක්කේඩුවෙනවා, *Wasakkéḍu-wenawá*, *v.* to be weak or exhausted from want of food.

වස කදුරු, *Wasa-kaduru*, *s.* shrub, peculiar to Ceylon, *alyxia zeylanica (Apocinaceæ)*.

වශග, *Wasaga*, } *a.* (වශ obedience, ග what goes or is) obedient, subject.
වශඟ, *Wasaṇga*, }

වශඟකරණවා, *Wasaṇgakaraṇawá*, *v.* to hold in possession unlawfully, to hold in subjection.

වශඟත්වය, *Wasaṇgatwaya*, *s.* obedience. subjection, control.

වශඟා, *Wasaṇgá*, *s.* (වශ subject, ග *ga* who goes or is) obedient wife.

වසට, *Wasaṭa*, *s.* lower part of the loins, groin.

වසත්, *Wasat*, *s.* spring or sultry season.

වසත්සැර, *Wasatsęra*, *s.* name of the Indian Cupid අනඞ්ගයා *anańgayá*, which see.

වසති, *Wasati*, *s.* (වස to dwell, අති *ati* aff.) house, dwelling; abiding, abode.

වසතෙල, *Wasatela*, see වසා *wasá*.

වසදීම, *Wasadíma*, *s.* poisoning.

වසදෙනවා, *Wasadenawá*, *v.* to poison.

වසන්, *Wasan*, *s.* name of Yama, judge of the dead; cloth; clothes; spring; covering: see වසන්ත *wasanta*, and වසම *wasama*.

වසන්ගතය, *Wasangataya*, see වසංගතය *wasaṇgataya*.

වසන්ත, *Wasanta*, *s.* (වස *wasa* to dwell) season of spring or its deified personification; sultry season; dysentery, diarrhæa; small pox; tree, *terminalia belerica*, [Colloq. බුළු *bulu* .

වසන්ත ඍතුව, *Wasanta-ṛituwa*, } *s.* (වසන්ත and ඍතුව or කාලය season) spring.
වසන්ත කාලය, *Wasanta-kálaya*, }

වසන්ත කුසුම, *Wasanta-kusuma*, *s.* tree, *cordia myxa*, [Colloq. ලෝලු *lólu*].

වසන්ත දූත, *Wasanta-dúta*, *s.* (වසන්ත spring, දූත messenger) kókila or Indian cuckoo, *cuculus micropterus*; month bak (March–April); mango tree, *mangifera indica*, [Colloq. අඹගහ *aṃbagaha*].

වසන්ත දූති, *Wasanta-dúti*, *s.* (වසන්ත and දූත *dúta* messenger, ඉනි *ini* aff.) trumpet flower, *stereospermum suaveolens*, [Colloquial: පලොල් *palol*]; large and beautiful creeper, *hiptage madablota* or *gærtnera racemosa*, [Colloq. පුවක්ගෙඩියා වැල *puwakgeḍiyá-węla*].

වසන්තද්‍රැ, *Wasantadru*, } *s.* (වසන්ත and ද්‍රැ or ද්‍රැම tree) mango tree, which blossoms in March or April, and is then an object of great beauty.
වසන්තද්‍රැම, *Wasantadruma*, }

වසන්ත පුෂ්ප, *Wasanta-pushpa*, *s.* trumpet flower: see the last word.

වසන්තරාව, *Wasantaráwa*, *s.* covering, veil, screen: pl. වසන්තරා *wasantará*.

වසන්තසඛ, *Wasanta-sakha*, *s.* (වසන්ත and සඛි *sakhi* friend) Kámadéwa or Cupid.

වසන්දලු, *Wasandalu*, *s.* (වසන් spring, දලු bud) tree, *echites scholaris*, [Colloq. රුක්අත්තන *rukattana*].

වසන්නෙත්, *Wasan-net*, *s.* name of Íṣwara or Ṣiva.

වසන්සැර, *Wasansęra*, *s.* (වසන් from වශ *waṣa* fascinating, overpowering, සැර arrow) name of Káma, Indian Cupid.

වසන, *Wasana*, *s.* (වස *wasa* to be clothed) cloth, clothes; covering, clothing; dwelling, house.

වසනවා, *Wasanawá*, *v.* to dwell, to abide, to inhabit, to reside; to cover, to dress; to shut, to close: pret. වැසුවා *węsuwá*.

වසම, *Wasama*, *s.* service, profession, employment, office; rank, condition; power, possession; district: pl. වසම් *wasam*.

වසයා, *Wasayá*, *s.* (වස depraved, යා aff.) wicked man, mischievous person, any vicious animal.

වසයෙන්, *Wasayen*, *s.* by way of, in the manner of, as in ගෞරවවසයෙන් *gauravawasayen*, by way of honor or respect.

වසර, *Wasara*, *s.* year, Elu form of වත්සර *watsara*.

වසල්, *Wasal*, *s.* bear, also written වලසා *walasá*: *a.* large, broad, spreading, from විසාල *visála*: *ind.* above, on, upon.

වසල, *Wasala*, *s.* man of the lowest caste, outcaste.

වසලල්, *Wasalal*, *s.* *cobra capella*, [Colloq. නයා *nayá*].

වසවත්මරු, *Wasawat-maru*, Elu form of වසවර්ති මාරයා *wasawarti-máraya*.

* වසවර්ති, *Wasawarti*, *s.* (වස supremacy, වර්තින් *wartin* who abides) one who acts under subjection, or according to the pleasure of another: also, name of the great enemy and opposer of Buddha: see මාරයා *máraya*.

* වසවර්තිමාරයා, *Wasawarti-máraya*, } see the last.
* වසවර්තියා, *Wasawartiyá*,

වසවාසි, *Wasawási*, *s.* more commonly written වසාවාසි *wasáwási*, which see.

වසවිස, *Wasa-visa*, *s.* venom, poison.

වසවෙද, *Wasa-weda*, *s.* (වස poison, වෙද physician) medical practitioner who professes to cure the bite of snakes.

වසා, *Wasá*, *s.* river; piece of cloth used for covering chairs, couches, etc. sheet; serum or marrow of the flesh, considered by some authorities as distinct from the marrow of the bones, though regarded by others as the same substance; adeps, fat, suet.

වසාතෙල, *Wasá-tela*, *s.* serum of the flesh: see the last.

වසාර, *Wasára*, *s.* house, residence, dwelling: wish, purpose, desire.

වසාරාජිය, *Wasárájiya*, } *s.* (වසා and රාජිය or වසාරොද, *Wasároda*, } රොද line) row of hair extending from the breast to the navel, and considered a mark of great beauty.

වසාලනවා, *Wasálanawá*, *v.* to shut, to cover.

වසාලීම, *Wasálíma*, *s.* act of shutting or covering.

වසාවාසි, *Wasáwási*, *s.* mace.

* වසි, *Wasi*, *s.* (වස *wasa* to dwell, ඉන් *in* aff.) dwelling, abode; subjugating.

වසික, *Wasika*, *a.* empty, void.

වසිත, *Wasita*, *s.* dwelling, inhabiting, abiding, residence.

වසිනවා, *Wasinawá*, *v.* to sprinkle, to rain: pret. වැස්සා *wessá*.

* වසිප්‍රාප්ත, *Wasiprápta*, *a.* (වසි dwelling, ප්‍රාප්ත arrived, finished) completed, fulfilled, as penance or religious austerities.

* වසිර, *Wasira*, *s.* sea salt, [Colloq. මුදු ලුණු *múdu-lunu*]; pungent fruit considered as a sort of pepper, *pothos officinalis*.

* වසිෂ්ඨ, *Wasishtha*, *s.* celebrated Muni, and one of the seven stars of Ursa Major.

* වසිභාව, *Wasibháwa*, *s.* (වසි subjection, භාව state) submission, obedience.

වසු, *Wasu*, *s.* wealth; thing, substance; tree, *ficus glomerata*, [Colloq. අට්ටික්කා *attikká*]; small tree, *æschynomene grandiflora*; shrub, *streblus aspera*, [Colloq. ගැට නෙටුල් *geta-netul*]; male calf; thirty-ninth year of the Indian cycle; name of Siva.

වසුදර, *Wasudara*, *s.* (වසු wealth, දර what contains) earth, [Colloq. පොළව *polawa*].

වසුදා, *Wasudá*, } *s.* (වසු wealth, දා give, ධා to
වසුධා, *Wasudhá*, } have or contain) the earth, [Colloq. පොළව *polawa*].

වසුන්, *Wasun*, *s.* pile of chatties or earthen vessels carried in a sling.

වසුන්කද, *Wasun-kada*, *s.* pingo load of chatties containing boiled rice, and other eatables.

වසුන්ධරා, *Wasundhará*, *s.* (වසු wealth, ධර *dhara* bearing) the earth, [Colloq. පොළව *polawa*].

වසුපුත්, *Wasu-put*, *s.* (වසු earth, පුත් son) name of the regent of the planet Mars, in allusion to his being turned up from the earth by a plough.

වසුරු, *Wasuru*, *s.* fæces, dung, excrement; filth, dirt.

වසුරුක්, *Wasu-ruk*, *s.* glomerous fig-tree, *ficus glomerata*, [Colloq. අට්ටික්කා *attikká*].

වසූරි, *Wasúri*, } *s.* small pox.
වසූරිය, *Wasúriya*, }

වහ්නි, *Wahni*, *s.* fire or its deity, agni; leadwort, *plumbago zeylanica*, [Colloq. එළ නෙටුල්, *ela-netul*]; marking nut plant, *semicarpus anacardium*, [Colloq. කිරිබඩුල්ල *kiri-badulla*]; appetite, digestion; metaphorical fire of the stomach.

* Sometimes found with the palatal "ශ" *sa*.

වහනිගර්භ, *Wahni-garbbha*, *s.* (වහනි and ගර්භ embryo) bamboo, *bambusa vulgaris*, [Colloq. උණගහ *uṇa-gaha*]; sort of mimosa, *acacia suma*, the name alludes to the wood taking or producing fire, by friction.

වහනිමාරක, *Wahni-máraka*, *s.* (වහනි fire, මාරක destroyer) water, [Colloq. වතුර *watura*].

වහනිමිත්‍ර, *Wahni-mitra*, *s.* (වහනි and මිත්‍ර friend) wind, air, [Colloq. හුලඟ *hulanga*].

වහනිවර්ණ, *Wahni-warṇa*, *s.* (වහනි and වර්ණ colour) red water lily, *nymphæa rubra*, variety of *n. lotus*, [Colloq. ඕලු *ólu*].

වහනිවල්ලභ, *Wahni-wallabha*, *s.* (වහනි and වල්ලභ friend) resin, [Colloq. දුම්මල *dummala*].

වහනිශිඛ, *Wahni-ṣikha*, *s.* (වහනි and ශිඛා *ṣikhá* crest) safflower, *carthamus tinctorius;* saffron, *curcuma longa*, [Colloq. කහ *kaha*]; potherb. *echites dichotoma;* flame.

වහනිස්කන්ධය, *Wahniskandhaya*, *s.* pillar of fire, large flame of fire rising like a pillar.

වහ, *Waha*, *s.* (වහ to bear) shoulder of an ox; any vehicle or means of conveyance, as a horse, car, etc.; air, wind; road, way; bearing, conveying; poison, venom, from වස *wasa*.

වහගි, *Wahagi*, *a.* clever, dexterous; rich, wealthy.

වහගිකම, *Wahagikama*, *s.* cleverness, dexterity, expertness; wealth.

වහගිකරණවා, *Wahagi-karaṇawá*, *v.* to make rich.

වහගියා, *Wahagiyá*, *s.* wealthy man.

වහගිවෙනවා, *Wahagi-wenawá*, *v.* to become rich.

වහන්, *Wahan*, *s.* sandals, shoes.

වහනතරාව, *Wahantaráwa*, *s.* covering, screen.

වහන්සඟල, *Wahansangala*, *s.* the two shoes, pair of sandals.

වහන්සේ, *Wahansé*, *s.* an affix to names as a term of respect.

වහන, *Wahana*, *s.* pouring out; flowing, bearing, raft, float.

වහනයවෙනවා, *Wahanaya-wenawá*, *v.* to flow, to drop or distil.

වහනවා, *Wahanawá*, *v.* to shut, to cover, to close: pret. වැහුවා *wẹhuwá*.

වහය, *Wahaya*, / වහයේ, *Wahayé*, } *s.* husband, (a disrespectful term).

වහර, *Wahara*, *s.* usage, practice, [Colloq. ව්‍යවහාරය *wyawaháraya*].

වහරේ, *Wahaŕé*, *s.* rain, raining, [Colloq. වැස්ස *wẹssa*]; rainy season; rain.

වහල්, *Wahal*, *s.* favour, help, assistance, [Colloq. උපකාරය *upakáraya*]; slave.

වහල්කම, *Wahalkama*, *s.* slavery; help, assistance.

වහල්යටි, *Wahalyaṭi*, *s.* (වහල් support, යටි stick) staff, walking stick, [Colloq. සැරමිටිය *sẹramiṭiya*]; crutch.

වහල්ල, *Wahalla*, *s.* core of the jack fruit; tegument of fruit: pl. වහලු *wahalu*.

වහල, *Wahala*, *s.* raft, float; roof, cover: *a.* hard, firm, compact.

වහලා, *Wahalá*, *s.* slave: pl. වහල්ලු *wahallu*: *p.* having covered, closed, shut.

වහලේ, *Wahalé*, *s.* the roof of a house.

වහස්, *Wahas*, *s.* side look, leer, [Colloq. අඩබැල්ම *aḍa-bẹlma*]; laughter, smile.

වහස, *Wahasa*, *s.* advantage; favour; axe, chopper; skill, ability; the extent or field of view; the sensible horizon.

වහසල, *Wahasala*, *s.* gate, [Colloq. දොරකඩ *dora-kaḍa*].

වහා, *Wahá*, *s.* river in general: *ad.* quickly, rapidly, speedily, hastily, soon, [Colloq. ඉක්මණට *ikmaṇaṭa*].

වහිනවා, *Wahinawá*, *v.* to rain: pret. වැස්සා *wẹssá*.

වහුන්, *Wahun*, *s.* plant, *alocasia macrorrhiza;* large earthen vessel; covering, lid.

වහුම්පුරයා, *Wahumpurayá*, *s.* man of the jaggery caste.

වළ, *Waḷa*, *s.* pit, hole.

වළබගිනි, *Waḷabagini*, *s.* submarine fire, Elu form of වඩබාග්නි *waḍabágni*.

වළලනවා, *Waḷalanawá*, *v.* to bury, to inter: pret. වැළලුවා *wẹlaluwá*.

වා, *Wá*, *s.* wind, breeze; word, speech, speaking; rain; year; tree, *cassia siamea (Leguminosæ)*, also called අරමණ *aramaṇá;* particle expressive of doubt, consideration, exception, *conjunction* and; or, whether, only, no other; *particle* of comparison, as, like, so; alternative or option, or, either, else, sometimes: *a.* airy, windy.

වාංගු, *Wángu*, *a.* inclining, leaning.

වාක්, *Wák*, *s.* speech; saying, a word, [Colloq. වචනය *wachanaya*].

වාක්දුශ්චරිතය, *Wák-duṣcharitaya*, *s.* (වාක් speech. දුශ්චරිත *duṣcharita* evil conduct) improper government of the conversation: see වාක්සුචරිත *wák-sucharita*.

වාක්පටුත්වය, *Wákpaṭutwaya*, *s.* (වාක් and පටුත්ව *paṭutwa* skill) eloquence.

වාක්පති, *Wák-pati, s.* (වාක් and පති master) name of Bṛihaspati, teacher of the gods and regent of the planet Jupiter; eloquence.

වාක්පාරුෂ්‍ය, *Wák-párushya, s.* (වාක් and පාරුෂ්‍ය violence) abuse, scurrility; defamation, wordy violence or assault.

වාක්ප්‍රණිධාන, *Wákpraṇidhána, s.* (වාක් and ප්‍රණිධාන request or desire) verbal expression of the wishes.

වාක්ප්‍රයෝග, *Wák-prayóga, s.* application or employment of speech, construction of a sentence.

වාක්‍යය, *Wákyaya, s.* sentence; word, speech, dictum; rule or aphorism: pl. වාක්‍ය *wákya.*

වාක්සමාචාර, *Wák-samáchára, s.* (වාක් speech, සම් *sam* and ආචාර *áchára* rule of conduct) respectful salutation, speaking respectfully.

වාක්සුචරිත, *Wák-sucharita, s.* (වාක් and සුචරිත excellence) proper government of the conversation, viz. abstaining from lying, slander, abuse, and gossiping.

වාක්සුද්ධිය, *Wák-suddhiya, s.* (වාක් and සුද්ධි *suddhi* clearness) distinct articulation, see the last.

වාග්මි, *Wágmi, s.* (වාක් *wák* speech, etc.) name of Bṛihaspati preceptor of the gods: *a.* speaking well, eloquent, loquacious, talkative.

වාගණ ඉන්නවා, *Wágaṇa-innawá, v.* to suffer, to endure patiently.

වාගහ, **Wá-gaha**, *s.* tree, *cathartocarpus rosea.*

වාගීශ, *Wágiṣa,* } *s.* (වාක් *wák* speech, ඊස *ísa* master) name of Bṛihaspati preceptor of the gods: *a.* eloquent, well-spoken.
වාගීස, *Wágísa,* }

වාගුරා, *Wágurá, s.* (වා to hurt, උර *ura* aff.) net for catching deer.

වාගුරික, *Wágurika, s.* hunter, deer catcher.

වාගේ, *Wágé, ad.* like, resembling, similar.

වාඞ්මය, *Wáṅmaya, s.* rhetoric, eloquence, belles lettres.

වාච්චිය, *Wáchchiya, s.* success, prosperity; a successful remedy.

වාච්‍ය, *Wáchya, s.* predicate, that which may be said of any thing. (In grammar) the voice or mood of a verb; කර්තෘවාච්‍ය *kartṛi-wáchya* Active Voice, කර්මණිවාච්‍ය *karmmaṇi-wáchya* Passive Voice, භාවවාච්‍ය *bháwa-wáchya* Voice expressive of mere state of being, sometimes called the Substantive Voice: *a.* vile, bad, contemptible; low, outcast; fit or proper to be spoken.

වාච, *Wácha, s.* (වච *wacha* to speak) speech, speaking; name of Saraswatí, goddess of speech.

වාචක, *Wáchaka, s.* word, significant sound, that which expresses: *a.* declaratory, verbal.

වාචස්පති, *Wáchaspati,* see වාක්පති *wákpati.*

වාචා, *Wáchá, s.* speech: see වාච *wácha.*

වාචාට, *Wácháṭa, a.* talkative, chattering, talking nonsense.

වාචාඩම්බර, *Wácháḍambara, s.* (වාච *wácha* speech, ආඩම්බර *áḍambara* pride) talking haughtily, boasting, bragging.

වාචාල, *Wáchála, a.* talkative, gabbling.

වාචාලකම, *Wáchálakama, s.* loquacity.

වාචාලයා, *Wáchálayá, s.* talkative fellow, boaster: pl. වාචාලයෝ *wáchálayó.*

වාචාලි, *Wácháli, s.* feminine of the above.

වාචික, *Wáchika, s.* news, tidings, intelligence.

වාචිකපත්‍ර, *Wáchika-patra, s.* letter, newspaper, gazette.

වාජ්ජම, *Wájjam, s.* bragging, boasting; kind of tom toms.

වාජ, *Wája, s.* sound, as the sound of the tabour, etc.; speed; wing; feather of an arrow; sacrifice, offering of rice, etc. at a funeral ceremony; mantra or prayer at the close of a sacrifice; acidulous mixture of ground meal and water; left to ferment.

වාජපේය, *Wájapéya, s.* (වාජ sour gruel, පේය to be drank, by the gods) one of the four great sacrifices.

වාජි, *Wáji,* see වාජින් *wájin.*

වාජිගන්ධ, *Wájigandha, s.* (වාජි horse, ගන්ධ smell) shrub, *physalis flexuosa;* plant, *Withania somnifera,* [Colloq. අමුක්කරා *amukkará*].

වාජින්, *Wájin, s.* (වාජ *wája* speed, ඉනි *ini* aff.) horse; arrow; bird; flowering shrub, *vasica adhatoda,* [Colloq. අගල්ආදර *agal-ádára*].

වාඤ්ඡා, *Wáñchchhá, s.* (වාඡි *wáchhi* to wish) wish, desire, [Colloq. ආසාව *ásáwa*].

වාට්‍යපුෂ්පි, *Wáṭya-pushpí, s.* medicinal plant, *sida humilis,* [Colloq. මහබෑලිල *maha-bẹlila*].

වාට්‍යා, *Wáṭyá,* } *s.* (වාට *wáṭa* garden, යත් *yat* aff.) herbaceous shrub, *sida cordifolia,* [Colloq. සුළුබෑලිල *suḷu-bẹlila*].
වාට්‍යාල, *Wáṭyála,* }

වාට, *Wáṭa, s.* (වට *waṭa* to surround) enclosure, any enclosed ground, as a court yard, an orchard, etc. wall surrounding a village or town; sort of grain, *panicum spicatum;* ground.

වාටිමහනවා, *Wáṭi-mahanawá, v.* to hem.

වාටිය, *Wáṭiya, s.* edge, border, extremity; border of a garment: pl. වාටි *wáṭi.*

වාටි, *Wáṭi*, s. site of a house or building.

වාඩබ, *Wáḍaba*, s. (වඩබ *waḍaba* and අණ් *aṇ* pleonasm) hell, submarine fire; Brahman.

වාඩබා, *Wáḍabá*, s. stud or collection of mares.

වාඩි පැල, *Wáḍi-pęla*, s. (වාඩිය *wáḍiya* and පැල hut) temporary dwelling.

වාඩිය, *Wáḍiya*, s. rest house, any temporary building.

වාඩිලනවා, *Wáḍilanawá*, v. to take lodging, to lodge, to sit down: pret. වාඩිලෑවා *wáḍilęwá*.

වාඩිවෙනවා, *Wáḍiwenawá*, see the last.

වාඩුව, *Wáḍuwa*, s. deficiency; adjacency, vicinity; revenge.

වාණ, *Wáṇa*, s. arrow.

වාණවාර, *Wáṇawára*, s. (වාණ and වෘ *wṛi* to screen) armour, breastplate.

වාණී, *Wáṇi*, s. word, speech, saying, [Colloq. කථාව *katháwa*]; sound; name of Saraṣwatí the goddess of speech.

වාණිජ්‍ය, *Wáṇijya*, s. (වාණිජ *wáṇija* merchant, යත් *yat* aff.) trade, traffic: see the next.

වාණිජ, *Wáṇija*, s. trader, merchant, [Colloq. වෙළෙන්ඳා, *weḷendá*].

වාණියා, *Wáṇiyá*, s. man who makes oil, or one of the caste whose business it is to manufacture oil: pl. වාණි *wáṇi*.

වාණේ, *Wáṇé*, s. steel, tempered iron.

වාත්තුකරණවා, *Wáttukaraṇawá*, v. to cast metals, to found.

වාත්තුව, *Wáttuwa*, s. casting metals, founding.

වාත, *Wáta*, s. (වා to go, තන් *tan* aff.) air, wind; wind as one of the humours of the body; rheumatism, gout, inflammation of the joints; flatulence.

වාතකුණ්ඩලිකා, *Wáta-kuṇḍaliká*, s. scanty and painful flow of urine.

වාතකේතු, *Wátakętu*, s. (වාත wind, කේතු banner) dust, [Colloq. දූවිලි *dúvili*].

වාතකෝප, *Wáta-kópa*, s. (වාත and කෝප anger) excitement of wind, or flatulence.

වාතගුල්ම, *Wáta-gulma*, s. acute gout or rheumatism.

වාතඝ්න, *Wátaghna*, s. (වාත wind, ඝ්න *hana* what destroys) tree, *cassia fistula*, [Colloq. ඇහැළ *ęhęla*]; senna, *senna officinalis;* plant, *dolichos* or *vigna catjang*, [Colloq. ලිමෑ *límę*].

වාතඝ්නී, *Wátaghni*, s. creeping plant, *ipomœa tridentata* or *angustifolia*, [Colloq. අපසු මදු *ápasu-madu*]

වාතජ්වර, *Wátajwara*, s. (වාත wind, ජ්වර fever) fever, ascribed to the vitiated state of the aerial humour.

වාතධ්වජ, *Wátadhwaja*, s. (වාත and ධ්වජ banner) cloud, [Colloq. වලාකුළ *walákuḷa*.

වාතපෝථ, *Wátapótha*, } s. tree, *butea frondosa*, [Colloq. කැලගස් *kęla-gas*].
වාතපෝථක, *Wátapóthaka*,

වාතමණ්ඩලී, *Wáta-maṇḍalí*, s. (වාත and මණ්ඩල *maṇḍala* region) whirlwind, [Colloq. සුළිහුළඟ *suḷi-hulaṇga*].

වාතමෘග, *Wáta-mṛiga*, s. (වාත and මෘග deer) swift antelope.

වාතමේඝය, *Wátaméghaya*, s. wind and cloud.

වාතමේහ, *Wátaméha*, s. (වාත and මේහ urinary disease) urinary disease caused by morbid wind.

වාතරක්ත, *Wáta-rakta*, s. (වාත wind, රක්ත blood) acute gout or rheumatism, supposed to arise from a vitiated state of the blood, and the aerial humour.

වාතරෝග, *Wáta-róga*, s. (වාත and රෝග disease) rheumatism, gout; flatulence; any disease arising from the aerial humour.

වාතවලාහක, *Wáta-waláhaka*, s. (වාත and වලාහක demon) god of the wind, Indian Æolus.

වාතවස්ති, *Wáta-wasti*, s. suppression of urine.

වාතවෘද්ධි, *Wáta-wriddhi*, s. swelled testicles.

වාතශීර්ෂ, *Wáta-ṣírsha*, s. (වාත wind, ශීර්ෂ head, source) lower belly.

වාතසමන, *Wáta-samana*, s. remedy for flatulence.

වාතසමුට්ඨාන, *Wáta-samuṭṭhána*, s. (වාත and සමුට්ඨාන what is produced) fever, inflammation or sickness brought on by a vitiated state of the aerial humour.

වාතහර, *Wáta-hara*, s. plant, species of *doona*, [Colloq. දියබෙරලිය *diyaberaliya*].

වාතාබාධය, *Wátábádhaya*, s. windy disease.

වාතාය, *Wátáya*, s. (වාත *wáta* and අය *aya* to go) leaf, [Colloq. කොලය *kolaya*].

වාතායන, *Wátáyana*, s. (වාත *wáta* and අයන *ayana* going) window, an eye-let.

වාතාරි, *Wátári*, s. (වාත *wáta* and අරි *ari* enemy) castor oil plant, *ricinus communis*, [Colloq. එඬරු *eṇḍaru*]; another plant, *asparagus racemosus*, [Colloq. හාතාවාරිය *hátáwáriya*].

වාතාශ්ව, *Wátáṣwa*, s. (වාත *wáta* and අශ්ව *aṣwa* horse) swift horse, one of a good breed.

වාති, *Wáti*, s. air, wind, [Colloq. හුළඟ *hulaṇga*].

වාතිග, *Wátiga*, } *s.* (වාත *wáta* wind, ගණ
වාතිඞ්ගණ, *Wátiṅgaṇa*, } to count) brinjal or egg plant, *solanum melongena*, [Colloq. වම්බටු *wambaṭu*].

වාද්‍ය, *Wádya*, *s.* musical instrument.

වාද, *Wáda*, *s.* (වද *wada* to speak, to sound) discourse, discussion; sounding; the sound of musical instruments; controversy, disputation, contest, word.

වාදකරණවා, *Wádakaraṇawá*, *v.* to dispute, to argue.

වාදකාරයා, *Wádakárayá*, *s.* (වාද dispute, කාර *kára* who does) disputant, polemic.

වාදන, *Wádana*, *s.* sounding (as musical instruments).

වාද පඤ්ච, *Wáda-pañcha*, *s.* (වාද sound, පඤ්ච five) five species of musical instruments.

වාදම, *Wádama*, *s.* gout: pl. වාදම් *wádam*.

වාදය, *Wádaya*, *s.* controversy, disputation: see වාද *wáda*.

වාදානුවාද, *Wádánuwáda*, *s.* (වාද *wáda* and අනු වාද *anuwáda* answer) plaint and reply.

වාදි, *Wádi*, *a.* (වද *wada* to speak wisely, etc. ඉන් *in* aff.) wise, learned, skilful, sage.

වාදින්, *Wádin*, *a.* speaking, discoursing: see the last.

වාදී, *Wádí*, *s.* disputant, polemic, controversialist; plaintiff, accuser.

වාදීභසිංහ, *Wádíbha-sinha*, *s.* (වාදී disputants, ඉභ *ibha* elephants, සිංහ lion) epithet of Buddha expressive of his superior skill in argumentation.

වාදු, *Wádu*, *s.* hatred, anger, malice, wrath.

වාදුකාරයා, *Wádukárayá*, *s.* (වාදු hatred, කාර *kára* who does) vindictive or revengeful man.

වාදුඵල, *Wádu-phala*, *s.* (වාදු anger, ඵල fruit) revenge, retaliation.

වාදුව, *Wáduwa*, *s.* anger: see වාදු *wádu*.

වාන්ත, *Wánta*, *a.* (වම *wama* to vomit, ක්ත *kta* aff.) vomited, ejected from the mouth.

වාන්දුකරණවා, *Wándukaraṇawá*, *v.* to pare the sides of palmyra leaves for writing.

වාන, *Wána*, *s.* dry fruit; spill-water; wish, desire; artificial channel; hole in the wall of a house, perfume, fragrance: *a.* relating to a wood; dry, dried.

වානප්‍රස්ථ, *Wána-prastha*, *s.* (වන *wana* wood, අණ් *aṇ* pleonasm, ප්‍රස්ථ who abides) hermit, anchorite, one who has renounced the world, and resides in forests or solitude for the purpose of devoting himself solely to religious and abstract meditation.

වානර, *Wánara*, *s.* (වා implying resemblance, නර man, also වන wood, අණ් *aṇ* pleonasm, රම *rama* to sport) ape, monkey, [Colloq. රිළවා *riḷawá*, වඳුරා *wan̲durá*],

වානරපිය, *Wánara-piya*, *s.* tree, *buchanania latifolia*, [Colloq. කිරිපළු *kiripaḷu*].

වානරප්‍රිය, *Wánara-priya*, *s.* (වානර monkey, ප්‍රිය fond of) tree, *mimusops kauki*.

වානරයා, *Wánarayá*, *s.* ape, monkey: see වානර *wánara*.

වානරී, *Wánarí*, *s.* cowatch or cowitch, *carpopogon pruriens*, [Colloq. වඳුරුමෑ *wan̲durumẹ*].

වානල, *Wánala*, *s.* black kind of holy basil, *ocimum sanctum*, [Colloq. මදුරුතලා *madurutalá*].

වානවා, *Wánawá*, *a.* to bear, to endure, to suffer.

වානවාසි, *Wánawási*, see වානප්‍රස්ථ *wána-prastha*.

වානස්පත්‍ය, *Wánaspatya*, *s.* (වනස්පති *wanaspati* tree bearing fruits without blossoms, අන්‍ය *aṇya* aff.) tree bearing fruits from blossoms, as the mango, eugenia, etc.

වානහම, *Wána-hama*, *s.* (වාන relating to forest, හම leather) sort of shoe worn by a wood cutter or a person who clears away a jungle.

වානාත, *Wánáta*. *s.* bow.

වානේය, *Wáneya*, *s.* (වන *wana* water, අණ් *aṇ* aff.) fragrant grass, *cyperus rotundus*, [Colloq. කලාඳුරු *kalán̲duru*].

වාප්‍ය, *Wápya*, *s.* plant growing in moist shady places, *costus speciosus*, [Colloq. තෙබු *tebu*].

වාප, *Wápa*, *s.* sowing seed; shaving; weaving.

වාපන, *Wápana*, *s.* (වප *wapa* to sow) sowing; the plate on a lascoreen's or peon's belt, breast plate of a belt, more commonly බාපනේ *bápané*, in the latter sense.

වාපි, *Wápi*, *s.* (වප *wapa* to sow seed, of the lotus, etc.) large oblong pond, pool, lake.

වාපිටු, *Wápiṭu*, *s.* (වා air, ටු from පෘෂ්ඨ *prishṭha* back) surface, that which serves as a support; sky, firmament, visible heavens, [Colloq. අහසය *ákásaya*].

වාපුන්, *Wápun*, *s.* cobra capella, [Colloq. නයා *nayá*].

වාපොළව, *Wá-poḷawa*, *s.* (වා air, පොළව ground) lowest of the three bases which constitute the foundation of this Sakwaḷa or universe; first or highest is the පස් පොළව *pas-poḷawa* the earth; this rests upon the ජල පොළව *jala-poḷawa* or water foundation; and these two are supported by the වා පොළව *wá-poḷawa* or region of air which forms the base of the whole.

වාබොජුන්, *Wá-bojun*, *s.* (වා and බොජුන් food) snake, [Colloq. සර්පයා *sarpayá*].

වාම, *Wáma*, *s.* name of Ṣiva; pot-herb, *chenopodium album;* udder, breast; wealth; sentient being: *a.* left, not right, reverse, contrary, inverted; beautiful, pleasing; vile, base, wicked; short, crooked.

වාමදේව, *Wámadéwa*, *s.* (වාම contrary, to human institutions, දේව who sports) name of Ṣiva.

වාමන, *Wámana*, *s.* dwarf; Vishṇu in his character of the dwarf, in which he appeared, on his fifth descent from heaven, to prevent Bali from obtaining dominion of the three worlds; the elephant that supports the south quarter; tree with beautiful wood, *alangium hexapetalum: a.* short, dwarfish; low. vile, base.

වාමනේත්‍ර, *Wáma-nétra*, *a.* fine-eyed.

වාමපාර්ශ්වය, *Wáma-párṣwaya*, } *s.* the left side.
වාමභාගය, *Wáma-bhágaya*, }

වාමලෝචනා, *Wáma-lóchaná*, *s.* (වාම beautiful, ලෝචන *lóchana* eye) handsome woman.

වාමා, *Wámá*, *s.* woman; Gaurí; Lakshmí; Saraswatí.

වාමාක්ෂි, *Wámákshí*, *s.* (වාම beautiful, අක්ෂි *akshi* eye) handsome woman.

වාමිග, *Wá-miga*, *s.* (වා wind, මිග deer) swift antelope.

වාමී, *Wámí*, *s.* she-ass; mare; young female elephant.

වාය, *Wáya*, } *s.* weaving, [Colloq. විවීම *vi-*
වායන, *Wáyana*, } *víma*].

වායනදණ්ඩ, *Wáyana-daṇḍa*, *s.* weaver's loom.

වායව්‍ය, *Wáyawya*, *a.* relating to the wind, sacred to the deity of wind: see the next.

වායවී, *Wáyaví*, *s.* quarter or region of the wind; north west.

වායස, *Wáyasa*, *s.* crow, [Colloq. කපුටා *kaputá*]; agallochum; turpentine.

වායසාරි, *Wáyasári*, *s.* (වායස *wáyasa* crow, අරි *ari* enemy) owl, [Colloq. බස්සා *bassá*].

වායසි, *Wáyasi*, *s.* small species of fig, *ficus oppositifolia*, [Colloq. කොටදිඹුලා *koṭadimbulá*]; egg plant or brinjal, *solanum melongena*, [Colloq. තරණබටු *taraṇa-baṭu*, වම්බටු *wambaṭu*]; bindweed, *convolvulus flavus*, [Colloq. තැල්වැල් *tel-weḷ*].

වායාම, *Wáyáma*, *s.* corruptly for ව්‍යායාම *wyáyáma*, which see.

වායිගෙඩිය, *Wáyi-geḍiya*, *s.* wen.

වායිය, *Wáyiya*, *s.* air, wind; see also වායෝධාතුව *wáyódhátuwa*.

වායු, *Wáyu*, *s.* (වා to go, අණ් *aṇ* aff.) air, wind; air of the body: *a.* airy.

වායුකේතු, *Wáyu-kétu*, *s.* dust: see වාතකේතු *wáta-kétu*.

වායුගුල්ම, *Wáyu-gulma*, *s.* (වායු wind, ගුල්ම cluster) whirlpool, eddy; whirlwind, hurricane.

වායුදිග්, *Wáyu-dig*, *s.* (වායු wind, දිග් quarter) quarter or region of the wind, north west.

වායුපලු, *Wáyu-palu*, *s.* plant, *naravelia zeylanica* or *clematis smilacifolia*, [Colloq. නරවැල් *nara-weḷ*].

වායුවාහ, *Wáyu-wáha*, *s.* (වායු wind, වාහ vehicle) smoke, vapour, [Colloq. දුම *duma*].

වායුවාහිනී, *Wáyu-wáhiní*, *s.* (වායු wind, of the body, වාහ *wáha* vehicle, ඉන් *in* aff.) vessel of the body, supposed, as the arteries were once imagined, to convey the aerial humour.

වායුසඛ, *Wáyu-sakha*, *s.* (වායු wind, සඛි *sakhi* friend) fire, [Colloq. ගිනි *gini*].

වායෝධාතුව, *Wáyódhátuwa*, *s.* (වායු *wáyu* wind, ධාතුව principle, element) one of the principles or humours of the body, the aerial humour.

වාර්, *Wár*, *s.* water, [Colloq. වතුර *watura*].

වාර්ණව, *Wárṇáwa*, *s.* bill of lading.

වාර්ත, *Wárta*, *s.* chaff.

වාර්තා, *Wártá*, *s.* tidings, intelligence; rumour, report; livelihood; trade; egg plant.

වාර්තාක, *Wártáka*, } *s.* brinjal or egg plant, *sola-*
වාර්තාකි, *Wártáki*, } *num melongena*, [Colloq. වම්
වාර්තාකී, *Wártákí*, } බටු *wambaṭu*]; species of
වාර්තාකු, *Wártáku*, } night shade, *solanum xanthocarpum*, [Colloq. එළබටු *ela-baṭu*]; also, තිබ්බටු *tibbaṭu*, තරණබටු *taraṇabaṭu*.

වාර්තික, *Wárttika*, *s.* (වෘත්ති *writti* news, comment, ක *ka* pleonasm, අණ් *aṇ* aff.) intelligencer, agent or envoy; gloss, commentary, especially a supplementary explanation added to a grammatical or philosophical aphorism, and its immediate elucidation, supplying or illustrating both text and comment; *a.* relating to news, belonging to a comment or gloss.

වාර්ද්ධක්‍ය, *Wárddhakya*, *s.* (වෘද්ධ *wriddha* old, ෂ්‍ය *shya* aff.) old age.

වාර්ධක, *Wárdhaka, s.* (වෘද්ධ *wṛiddha* old, අණ් *aṇ* aff.) number of old men; old age; the infirmity of old age.

වාර්භට, *Wárbhaṭa, s.* (වාර් *wár* water, භට to maintain) alligator, [Colloq. කිඹුලා *kimbulá*].

වාර, *Wára, s.* time, occasion, opportunity; multitude; troop; permission; day of the week.

වාරකන්, *Wárakan, s.* south west wind, gale, hurricane.

වාරණ, *Wáraṇa, s.* (වෘ *wṛi* to screen, to defend) defence, resistance, opposition, prohibition, obstacle or impediment; armour, a cuirass, mail for the body; elephant; vulture with a bill said to resemble the trunk of an elephant.

වාරණ කර්ණිකා, *Wáraṇa-karṇṇiká, s.* plant, *alocasia macrorrhiza,* [Colloq. හබරල *habarala*].

වාරණාව, *Wáraṇáwa, s.* bill of lading. (Arabic.)

වාරන්න, *Wáranna, a.* various, of different kinds or sorts.

වාරබාණ, *Wárabáṇa, s.* (වාර opposing, බාණ arrow) armour for the body or breast, iron cuirass or a thick quilted jacket worn for the same purpose.

වාරබූෂා, *Wárabushá, s.* plantain or banana.

වාරමුඛ්‍ය, *Wára-mukhyá, s.* (වාර troop, මුඛ්‍ය chief) head of a set of harlots.

වාරමුඛ, *Wára-mukha, s.* (වාර day, මුඛ commencement) dawn, morning, twilight.

වාරය, *Wáraya, s.* time, occasion, opportunity; day of the week; door, gate; plant, *achyranthes aspera,* [Colloq. ගස්කරල්හැබ *gas-karalhęba*].

වාරවල්ලභා, *Wárawallabhá, s.* plantain or banana.

වාරවාණ, *Wárawáṇa,* see වාරබාණ *wárabáṇa.*

වාරලියා, *Wáraliyá, s.* kind of small sea fish.

වාරස්ත්‍රී, *Warastrí, s.* (වාර many, ස්ත්‍රී woman) harlot, [Colloq. වෙසඟන *wesaṅgana*].

වාරාණසී, *Wáráṇasí, s.* holy city Benares: see වරණසී *waraṇasí.*

වාරාවෙනවා, *Wáráwenawá, v.* to overturn, to subvert; to miss a mark or aim; to fail.

වාරාහී, *Wáráhí, s.* (වරාහ *waráha* hog, අණ් *aṇ* aff.) esculent root, genus, *dioscorea;* hog's meat, *cyclamen indica,* [Colloq. ඌරල *úrala*]; creeper, *borago zeylanica.* [Colloq. යොන්තුඹ *yontumba*]; the earth; sow.

වාරි, *Wári, s.* water, [Colloq. වතුර *watura*]; name of Saraswati the goddess of speech; medical drug, commonly බාල *bála.* [Colloq. ඉරිවේරිය *iriwériya*].

වාරිකණ්ටක, *Wári-kaṇṭaka, s.* (වාරි water, කණ්ටක thorn) aquatic plant, *pistia stratiotes,* [Colloq. දියපරණලා *diya-paraṇalá*]; another aquatic plant, *trapa bispinosa,* [Colloq. ඉකිලිය *ikiliya*].

වාරිකෙන්ද, *Wári-kenda,* }
වාරිකොන්ද, *Wári-konda,* } *s.* slip of the talipot leaf.

වාරික්‍රිමි, *Wári-krimi, s.* (වාරි water, ක්‍රිමි insect) leech, [Colloq. කූඩැල්ලා *kúḍellá*].

වාරිචර, *Wárichara, s.* (වාරි and චර what goes) fish, [Colloq. මත්ස්‍යයා *matsyayá*].

වාරිචාමර, *Wárichámara, s.* (වාරි and චාමර chámara or whisk) aquatic plant, *vallisneria.*

වාරිජ, *Wárija, s.* (වාරි water, ජ born) conch; any bivalve shell; lotus; salt.

වාරිත්‍ර, *Wáritra, s.* (වාර *wára* to prevent, ත්‍ර aff. or වාරි water, ත්‍ර to preserve) the negative precepts of Buddha; umbrella or portable shed of leaves carried on the head as one.

වාරිධි, *Wáridhi, s.* (වාරි water, ධි what contains) ocean, [Colloq. මූද *múda*].

වාරිනිධි, *Wári-nidhi, s.* sea, ocean.

වාරිපර්ණි, *Wári-parṇi,* }
වාරිප්‍රශ්නි, *Wári-prașní,* } *s.* (වාරි and පර්ණ *parṇa* leaf, ඊ *í* aff.) aquatic plant, *pistia stratiotes:* see වාරිකණ්ටක *wári-kaṇṭaka.*

වාරිමාර්ගය, *Wári-márgaya, s.* drain, [Colloq. කානුව *kánuwa*].

වාරිමූලි, *Wári-múli, s.* (වාරි water, මූල *múla* root) aquatic plant, *pistia stratiotes.*

වාරියන්ත්‍ර, *Wári-yantra, s.* (වාරි and යන්ත්‍ර machine) machine for raising water, sort of pump.

වාරිවාහ, *Wári-wáha,* }
වාරිවාහන, *Wári-wáhana,* } *s.* (වාරි and වාහ what bears) cloud, [Colloq. වලාකුළ *walákuḷa*].

වාරුකරණවා, *Wárukaraṇawá, v.* to support, to keep from falling, to bear, to sustain.

වාරුණික, *Wáruṇika, s.* (වාරුණ *wáruṇa* liquor, ඉක *ika* aff.) distiller, spirit maker, or vendor.

වාරුණී, *Wáruṇí, s.* any distilled liquor, or more properly a particular kind prepared from hog weed, ground with the juice of the date or palm tree, and then distilled; the twenty-fifth lunar asterism, of which Varuṇa is the ruling deity; the west, region of Varuṇa.

වාරුව, *Wáruwa, s.* bodily strength, muscular power; support.

වාල්කල, *Wálkala, s.* bark, bark of trees, dress made of the bark of trees, worn by ascetics: *a.* made of bark.

වාල්මීක ඍෂි, *Wálmika-ṛishi*, } *s.* poet Wálmíka,
වාල්මීකි, *Wálmiki*, } author of the Rá-
වාල්මීක, *Wálmíka*, } máyaṇa.

වාල, *Wála*, *s.* hair, [Colloq. කෙස් *kes*]; tail, [Colloq. වල්ගේ *walgé*]; drug, commonly Bála, ඉරිවේරිය *iriwériya*, from හ්‍රීවේර *hriwéra*.

වාලක්කඩියා, *Wálakkaḍiyá*, *s.* sort of venomous reptile found in the sea and certain lakes; water snake.

වාලක, *Wálaka*, *s.* bracelet, finger ring; drug and perfume, commonly ඉරිවේරිය *iriwériya*, from හ්‍රීවේර *hriwéra*, also called බාල *bála*.

වාලදිය, *Wáladiya*, } *s.* වාල hair, ධි what has) tail,
වාලධි, *Wáladhi*, } hairy tail, the tail of any animal.

වාලවිජනි, *Wálavijaní*, *s.* fan made of a yak's tail, a chowri.

වාලවේධි, *Wála-wédhi*, *s.* (වාල hair, වේධි who pierces) skilful archer, one who can split a hair, also, metaphorically an acute arguer, hair-splitter.

වාලව්‍යජන, *Wála-wyajana*, *s.* (වාල tail, ව්‍යජන fan) chámara or chowri, particular kind of whisk made from the tail of the Indian yak, *bos grunniens*, and forming one of the ensigns of royalty.

වාලහන්, *Wálahan*, *s.* fees paid in kind for reaping and threshing corn.

වාලහස්ත, *Wálahasta*, *s.* tail of a horse or any animal.

වාලුක, *Wáluka*, *s.* sort of drug and perfume.

වාලුකා, *Wáluká*, *s.* sand, gravel, [Colloq. වැලි *weli*]; camphor.

වාලුකා කාන්තාරය, *Wáluká-kántáraya*, *s.* (වාලුකා and කාන්තාරය desert) sandy desert.

වාලුකී. *Wálukí*, *s.* sort of cucumber, *cucumis pubescens*, [Colloq. කැකිරි *kekiri*].

වාවදූක, *Wáwadúka*, *s.* name of Vrihaspati the regent of Jupiter: *a.* talking much, gabbling, prattling.

වාවය, *Wáwaya*, *s.* plant, peculiar to Ceylon, *Hortonia floribunda (Monimiaceæ)*; sort of basil, *ocimum sanctum*, [Coll: මදුරුතලා *madurutalá*].

වාශා, *Wáṣá*, *s.* garden shrub, *justicia adhatoda*, [Colloq. වංඇපල *wanępala*, අගල්ඇඳුර *agaládára*].

වාෂ්ප, *Wáshpa*, *s.* vapour, tear.

වාස්තුක, *Wástuka*, *s.* plant, variety of *amaranthus* or of *nothosœrua brachiata*, [Colloq. නිල්තම්පලා *nil-tampalá*].

වාස, *Wása*, *s.* (වස *wasa* to dwell) house, habitation; site, situation; cloth, clothing; perfuming; medicinal plant, *justicia adhatodha*, [Colloq. අගල්ඇඳුර *agaládára*].

වාසක, *Wásaka*, *s.* medicinal plant, *justicia adhatoda*, [Colloq. වංඇපල *wan-ępala*, or අගල්ඇඳුර *agaládára*].

වාසගම, *Wásagama*, *s.* style, manner of writing; sentence; idiom in language; prose: pl. වාසගම් *wásagam*.

වාසගෘහ, *Wása-griha*, *s.* (වාස clothes or abiding, ගෘහ house) store room, wardrobe; inner room, bed chamber; dwelling house.

වාසන්ත, *Wásanta*, *s.* (වසන්ත *wasanta* spring, අණ් *aṇ* aff.) camel, [Colloq. ඔටුවා *oṭuwá*]; Indian cuckoo, *cucullus micropterus;* green gram, *phaseolus mungo*, [Colloq. මුංඇට *muṇeṭa*]; large creeper, *hiptage madablota*, [Colloq. පුවක්ගෙඩියාවැල *puwakgeḍiyá-węla*].

වාසන්ති, *Wásanti*, *s.* species of jasmine, *jasminum auriculatum*, [Colloq. බොලිද්ද *bolidda*]; festival in honour of Kámadéva, the Indian Cupid; long pepper; trumpet flower.

වාසන, *Wásana*, *s.* (වාස *wása* to fumigate) perfuming, fumigating, perfuming with fragrant vapour, incense, etc.; cloth, clothes; abiding, abode.

වාසනා, *Wásaná*, *s.* knowledge of any thing derived from memory, present consciousness of past perceptions, fancy, imagination; trust, confidence: see the next.

වාසනාව, *Wásanáwa*, *s.* chance, luck, lot, fortune; happiness, luckiness.

වාසනාවන්ත, *Wásanáwanta*, *a.* (වාසනා luck, වන්ත poss. aff.) lucky, fortunate, auspicious.

වාසභවන, *Wásabhawana*, } *s.* (වාස residing, භවන
වාසය, *Wásaya*, } abode) house, habitation; abode, place of staying or abiding: see වාස *wása*.

වාසයකරණවා, *Wásayakaraṇawá*, *v.* to inhabit, to reside.

වාසයෝග, *Wása-yóga*, *s.* (වාස perfume, යෝග joining) powdered sandal, or any fragrant powder scattered on the clothes, person, etc.

වාසර, *Wásara*, *s.* (වස *wasa* to abide, අර aff.) day, [Colloq. දවස *dawasa*]; drug, one of the eight principal medicaments.

වාසල්කඩ, *Wásalkaḍa*, } *s.* gate of a city; the
වාසල්දොර, *Wásaldora*, } vestibule of a royal residence, door, gate, entrance.

වාසල, *Wásala*, *s.* door, gate, gate or entrance to a city; royal gate, entrance or antechamber of a palace.

වාසව, *Wásawa*, *s.* (වසු *wasu* Wasu, අණ් *aṇ* aff.) name of Indra: the twenty-fourth lunar asterism figured by a tabor.

වාසවානුජ, *Wásawánuja*, *s.* (වාසව *wásawa* Indra, අනුජ younger brother) younger brother of Indra.

වාසස්ථාන, *Wásasthána*, *s.* (වාස dwelling, ස්ථාන place) dwelling place, an abode, residence, mansion,

වාසා, *Wásá*, *s.* plant, *adhatoda vasica* or *justicia adhatoda*, [Colloq. අඩාතෝඩා *áḍátóḍá* or අගල් අඬුර *agaládára*].

වාසි, *Wási*, *s.* small hatchet, chopper, adze; gain, prize, winning at play; abiding, dwelling.

වාසිකරණවා, *Wásikaraṇawá*, *v.* to give one an advantage over another.

වාසිකියනවා, *Wási-kiyanawá*, *v.* to boast, to brag.

වාසිත, *Wásita*, *a.* (වාස *wása* to perfume, ක්ත *kta* aff.) perfumed, scented, fumigated; clothed, dressed; steeped, infused; spiced, seasoned; knowledge: see වාසනා *Wásaná*; sound.

වාසිතා, *Wásitá*, *s.* woman; female elephant.

වාසිනවා, *Wásinawá*, see වාහිනවා *wáhinawá*.

වාසී, *Wásí*, *s.* (වාස *wása* dwelling, ඊ *í* aff.) dweller, resident, inhabitant.

වාසුදේව, *Wásu-déwa*, *s.* (වසුදේව *wasudéwa* the father of Kṛishṇa, අණ් *aṇ* patronymic) name of Kṛishṇa.

වාසේකරණවා, *Wásékaraṇawá*, *v.* to dwell.

වාහලික, *Wáhlíka*, *s.* assafætida, [Colloq. පෙරුංකායම් *peruṇkáyam*].

වාහලිකපිටාණ, *Wáhlíkapitaṇa*, *s.* tree, *swietenia febrifugia*, [Colloq. කොකුං *kokuṇ*].

වාහ, *Wáha*, *s.* (වහ *waha* to bear) vehicle, carriage, conveyance of any kind; bearer, porter, carrier of burdens; horse; air, wind; bull; buffalo; arm.

වාහනය, *Wáhanaya*, *s.* vehicle, conveyance of any kind, as a horse, elephant, carriage: pl. වාහන *wáhana*.

වාහනවාස, *Wáhanawása*, *s.* sports of the gods in Swarga.

වාහල, *Wáhala*, see වාසල *wásala*.

වාහස, *Wáhasa*, *s.* rock snake or boa constrictor, *python molurus*, [Colloq. පිඹුරා *pimburá*].

වාහිනවා, *Wáhinawá*, *s.* to pour, to shed, to drip: pret. වැහුනා *wéhuná*.

වාහිනී, *Wáhiní*, *s.* army; body of forces consisting of eighty-one elephants, eighty-one cars, 243 horse, and 405 foot, cohort, battalion; river.

වාහිනීපති, *Wáhiní-pati*, *s.* (වාහිනී army or river, පති chief) general, commanding-officer, [Colloq. සේනාපතියා *sénápatiyá*]; ocean.

වාහෙ, *Wáhe*, *s.* husband (low word): see also වාහ *wáha*.

වාළමිග, *Wáḷa-miga*, *s.* (වාළ beast of prey, මිග animal) wild animal; tiger species.

වාළා, *Wáḷá*, *s.* slave, dependant: pl. වාල්ලු *wállu*.

වාළි, *Wáḷi*, *s.* female slave: pl. වාළියෝ *wáliyó*.

වි, *Vi*, *ind.* particle, and prefix, implying variety, difference; certainty, ascertainment; privation; motion, progress; intensity; excellence; separation, disjunction; aversion, repugnance; impatience, intolerance; joy, gladness; defectiveness, deterioration; distance; presence, ignorance; it generally corresponds to the English adjuncts, a, ex, de, dis, in, un, and is frequently an expletive.

විංශ, *Viṇsa*, *a.* twentieth, [Colloq. විසිවෙනි *visiweni*].

විංශති, *Viṇsati*, *s.* twenty, score, [Colloq. විස්ස *vissa*].

වික්කල්, *Vikkal*, } *s.* stammering.
වික්කල, *Vikkala*, }

වික්කා, *Vikká*, *v.* sold, past tense of විකුණනවා *vikuṇanawá*.

වික්‍රම, *Vikrama*, *s.* (වි before, ක්‍රම to go) heroism, courage, prowess, heroic valour; great power or strength; walking, going, proceeding.

වික්‍රමාදිත්‍ය, *Vikramáditya*, *s.* (වික්‍රම *vikrama* strength, ආදිත්‍ය *áditya* sun) name of a celebrated prince, sovereign of Ougein and reputed founder of the era still in use amongst the Hindus, commencing fifty-two years before the Christian era.

වික්‍රය, *Vikraya*, *s.* (වි before, ක්‍රී *kri* to buy) sale, selling, vending.

වික්‍රයික, *Vikrayika*, *s.* vender, salesman, dealer.

වික්‍රාන්ති, *Vikránti*, *s.* (වි before, ක්‍රම *krama* to go) prowess, heroic strength and valour; great power or strength.

වික්‍රියා, *Vikriyá*, *s.* (වි implying reverse, ක්‍රියා action) change of mind, form, purpose.

විකෘත, *Vikṛita*, *s.* (වි implying reverse, කෘත done) disgust, aversion: *a.* imperfect, unfinished, incompleted; sick, diseased: see the next.

විකෘති, *Vikṛiti, s.* change of any kind, as of purpose, mind, form, nature, etc. either permanent or temporary; spirituous liquor.

වික්ෂිප්ත, *Vikshipta, a.* (වි implying distance, ක්ෂිප්ත thrown) scattered, dispersed; thrown, sent.

වික්ෂිප්තවෙනවා, *Vikshiptawenawá, v.* to be agitated, to be perplexed.

වික්ෂේප, *Vikshépa, s.* (වි before, ක්ෂිප *kshipa* to throw) casting; throwing away; confusion, perplexity, fear proceeding from ignorance or error.

වික්ෂෝප, *Vikshópa, s.* fear, perplexity; trouble, sorrow, sadness, grief, melancholy.

වික්ෂෝපවෙනවා, *Vikshópawenawá, v.* to be grieved; to feel grief.

විකච, *Vikacha, s.* (වි apart, separate, කච to go, or වි privative, කච hair) Buddhist priest or mendicant: *a.* bald, having no hair on the head; blown, opened, expanded, spread (as a flower).

විකට, *Vikaṭa, a.* (වි implying separation or expansion, කට to go) formidable, frightful, hideous, horrible; large, great; large toothed; changed in form or appearance.

විකණ්ටක, *Vikaṇṭaka, s.* (වි expansion, කණ්ට thorn, ක aff.) thorny shrub, *hedysarum alhagi.*

විකත්ථන, *Vikatthana, s.* (වි difference or extension, කත්ථන praise) irony, ironical or unmerited praise; praise in general.

විකති, *Vikati, s.* inversion, change of natural order, Páli form of විකෘති *vikṛiti.*

විකනවා, *Vikanawá, v.* to bite, to gnaw, to seize with the teeth, to chew: pret. විකුවා *vikuwá.*

විකප්, *Vikap, s.* alternative, option; doubt; (In Grammar) admission of more than one rule.

විකර්තන, *Vikartana, s.* sun, [Colloq. ඉර *ira*].

විකර්ම්මික, *Vikarmmika, s.* (වි variety, කර්ම *karma* work, ඉක *ika* aff.) clerk or superintendent of markets or fairs; *a.* doing forbidden acts.

විකර්ෂ, *Vikarsha, s.* (වි separate, කෘෂ *kṛisha* to attract) pulling, pulling a part; arrow, [Colloq. ඊගස *igasa*].

විකර, *Vikara, s.* (වි difference, කර making) disease, sickness; making gestures, indication of sentiment by gesture.

විකල්ප, *Vikalpa, s.* (වි implying distinction, කල්ප thought) error, ignorance, mistake; doubt, indecision; alternative, option.

විකල, *Vikala, a.* (වි privative, කලා *kalá* digit of the moon) confused, confounded, agitated; defective, imperfect, decayed, impaired, withered, waned.

විකලය, *Vikalaya, s.* perplexity, perturbation, confusion, derangement: see විකල *vikala.*

විකලවෙනවා, *Vikalawenawá, v.* to be confused, to be confounded.

විකලාඞ්ග, *Vikalánga, a.* (විකල *vikala* defective, අඞ්ග *anga* body) deformed, crippled, maimed.

විකලී, *Vikalí, s.* woman in whom menstruation has ceased.

විකශ්වර, *Vikaṣwara,*
විකෂ්වර, *Vikashwara,*
විකස්වර, *Vikaswara,* } *s.* (වි apart, කස *kasa* to go) opening, expanding.

විකස, *Vikasa, s.* moon, [Colloq. හඳ *haṇda*].

විකසා, *Vikasá, s.* species of madder, *rubia manjitha,* [Colloq. වැල්මදට *węlmadaṭa*].

විකසිත, *Vikasita, a.* (වි apart, කස *kasa* to go, ඉත *ita* aff.) blown as a flower, opened, expanded, [Colloq. පිපුනු *pipunu*].

විකාර, *Vikára, s.* (වි implying alteration, කර *kara* to make) change of form or nature, alteration, or deviation from the natural state; sickness, disease, change from the state of health; passion, feeling, emotion; madness.

විකාරකරණවා, *Vikárakaraṇawá, v.* to make gestures, to make mad or frantic.

විකාරතා, *Vikáratá, s.* (විකාර and තා aff. of the abstract) nature changed or inverted from its natural course, madness, fury.

විකාරය, *Vikáraya, s.* delirium, change: see විකාර *vikára.*

විකාරී, *Vikárí, s.* thirty-third year of the Indian cycle of sixty.

විකාල, *Vikála. s.* (වි implying prohibition, කාල time) any period after midday, the time in which it is unlawful for the priests to take food; twilight.

විකාලභෝජන, *Vikála-bhójana, s.* (විකාල prohibited time, භෝජන food) food taken after midday, which is a breach of the ordinances of the Buddhist priesthood: see the last.

විකාශ, *Vikása, s.* (වි before or apart, කාශ *kása* to shine) display, manifestation, open or splendid appearance; opening, expanding; budding, blowing (as a flower); æther, heaven; solitude, loneliness, privacy.

විකිණීම, *Vikiṇíma, s.* selling, vending, sale, verbal noun of විකුණනවා *vikuṇanawá.*

විකිණෙනවා, *Vikiṇenawá, v.* to be sold: pret. විකුණුනා *vikuṇuná.*

විකිර, *Vikira*, *s.* (වි apart, කෘ *krí* to scatter) bird in general, [Colloq. කුරුල්ලා *kurullá*]; scattering; fallen fragment.

විකිරණ, *Vikiraṇa*, *s.* swallow-wort, *calotropis gigantea*, [Colloq. වරා *wará*]; scattering, spreading about.

විකිරණඵල, *Vikiraṇa-phala*, *s.* plant, variety of *calotropis gigantea*, [Colloq. එලවරා *ela-wará*].

විකිම, *Vikíma*, *s.* biting, gnawing.

විකීර්ණ, *Vikírṇa*, *a.* scattered, spread abroad, extended, diffused.

විකුණනවා, *Vikuṇanawá*, *v.* to sell, to vend, to dispose of: pret. වික්කා *vikká*.

විකුණුම්කාරයා, *Vikuṇumkárayá*, *s.* vender, seller.

විකුණුම, *Vikuṇuma*, *s.* sale; verbal noun of විකුණනවා *vikuṇanawá*.

විකුන්, *Vikun*, see විකුම *vikuma*.

විකුම, *Vikuma*, *s.* biting, gnawing, from විකනවා *vikanawá;* might, power, strength, courage, from වික්‍රම *vikrama*: pl. විකුම් *vikum*.

විකුමැතියා, *Vikumẹtiyá*, *s.* (විකුම *vikuma* and ඇතියා *ẹtiyá* who has) hero, powerful or intrepid man.

විකෙනවා, *Vikenawá*, *v.* to be chewed: pret. විකුනා *vikuná*.

විකේටයනවා, *Vikéṭayanawá*, *v.* to be pardoned, or passed over, as a fault, to be hushed up.

විකොට, *Vikoṭa*, *a.* having sold or disposed of; *past part.* of විකුණනවා *vikuṇanawá*.

විකෝපන, *Vikópana*, *s.* (වි part, කුප *kupa* to be angry) injuring, destruction of trees, etc.

විකෝෂ, *Vikósha*, *a.* (වි privative, කෝෂ sheath) uncovered, denuded, unsheathed.

විග්ගුස්ස, *Viggussa*, *s.* sort of span measured from the tip of the thumb to the second joint of the forefinger.

විග්‍රහ, *Vigraha*, *s.* body; war, battle, conflict; extension, diffusion.

විග්‍රහකරණවා, *Vigrahakaraṇawá*, *v.* to analyze.

විගඩම, *Vigaḍama*, *s.* giddiness, unsteady conduct: pl. විගඩම් *vigaḍam*.

විගත, *Vigata*, *a.* (වි implying separation, ගත gone) gone, departed, disappeared; separated, severed, parted; free from, without; gloomy, dark, obscure.

විගතාර්තවා, *Vigatártawá*, *s.* woman in whom menstrual discharge has ceased; woman past child-bearing.

විගඳ, *Vigada*, } විගඳ, *Viganda*, } *s.* (වි implying depreciation, ගඳ smell) stench, disagreeable smell.

විගන්ධිකා, *Vigandhiká*, *s.* medicinal plant, *sphæranthus indicus* or *s. hirtus*, [Colloq. මුඩමහණ *muḍamahaṇa*]: see විජ්‍රා *vijrá*.

විගම, *Vigama*, *s.* (වි separation, ගම going) separation, parting.

විගල, *Vigala*, *a.* (වි before, ගල to ooze) falling, dropping, oozing.

විගස, *Vigasa*, } විගහ, *Vigaha*, } *s.* speed, haste, expedition.

විගහට, *Vigahaṭa*, *ad.* quickly, speedily.

විගාත, *Vigáta*, *s.* punishment: see විඝාත *vigháta*.

විගු, *Vigu*, Elu form of විඝ්න *vighna*.

විගුරජ, *Viguraja*, *s.* name of Gaṇéṣa: see විඝ්න නාශන *vighna-náṣana*.

විඝ්න, *Vighna*, *s.* (වි before, හන *hana* to injure) obstacle, impediment; shrub used for fences, with edible fruit, *carissa carondas*, [Colloq. මහ කරඹ *maha-karamba*].

විඝ්න නාශන, *Vighna-náṣana*, } විඝ්න රාජ, *Vighna-rája* } *s.* (විඝ්න impediment, නාශන the remover) name of Gaṇéṣa, who is supposed to be capable of either causing or removing difficulties and impediments, and therefore especially worshipped at the commencement of any undertaking.

විඝස, *Vighasa*, *s.* (වි before, අද *ada* to eat, ඝස being substituted for the root) orts, leavings of a meal; food in general.

විඝාත, *Vighátа*, *s.* (වි and හන *hana* to kill or hurt) obstacle, impediment, [Colloq. බාධාව *bádháwa*]; prohibition, destruction.

විඝාතන, *Vighátana*, *s.* killing, destruction, extermination.

විච්චීර්ණ, *Vichchírṇa*, *a.* decorated, ornamented.

විච්ඡේද, *Víchchhéda*, *s.* (වි and ඡිද *chhida* to cut) separation, disjunction, removal; prohibition, prevention; cutting, dividing; division of a book, chapter, section.

විචක්ෂණ, *Vichakshaṇa*, *s.* (වි implying excellence, චක්ෂ *chaksha* to see or speak) pandit, learned man, scholar: *a.* clever, able, wise, sensible; proficient, skilful.

විචය, *Vichaya*, *s.* search, research.

විචර, *Vichara*, *s.* quantity, about, as much as.

විචරණ, *Vicharaṇa*, *s.* (වි before, චර *chara* to go) going, walking, proceeding.

විචාර, *Vichára*, *s.* (වි severally, චර *chara* to go) exercise of judgment or reason on a present object, investigation, consideration, deliberation.

විචාරණ, *Vichárana*, *s.* exercise of judgment or decision after due examination and discussion.

විචාරණවා, *Vichárananawá*, *v.* to discuss, to investigate, to inquire into: pret. විචාළා *vichálá* or විචෑරුවා *vichẹruwá*.

විචාරිම, *Vichárima*, *s.* investigation, research; verbal noun of විචාරණවා *vichárananawá*.

විචිකිච්ඡා, *Vichikichchhá*, Páli form of next.

විචිකිත්සා, *Vichikitsá*, *s.* (වි and කිත *kita* to doubt) doubt, uncertainty, error, mistake.

විචිත්‍ර, *Vichitra*, *a.* (වි before, චිත්‍ර to paint) variegated, spotless; handsome, beautiful; wonderful, surprizing.

විචිත්‍රකර්මාන්තය, *Vichitrakarmántaya*, *s.* ornamented work.

විචිත්‍රතා, *Vichitratá*, *s.* wonder, state of being variegated.

විචිත්‍රාඞ්ග, *Vichitránga*, *s.* peacock; tiger: *a.* elegant, well-formed.

විචිත්‍රාඞ්ගි, *Vichitrángi*, *s.* creeper, *trichosanthes cucumerina*, [Colloq. දුම්මැල්ල *dummẹlla*].

විචූර්ණ, *Vichúrna*, *a.* (වි and චූර්ණ pounded) crushed, pulverized.

විචේතස්, *Vichétas*, *a.* (වි implying privation, චේතස් mind) sad, perplexed, unhappy; ignorant, stupid.

විජ්ජමාන, *Vijjamána*, *a.* being, present or existing.

විජ්ජා, *Vijjá*, *s.* juggling, artifice, knowledge; Páli form of විද්‍යා *vidya*.

විජ්ජාකරණවා, *Vijjá-karanawá*, *v.* to practise jugglery.

විජ්ජාකාරයා,, *Vijjákárayá*, *s.* (විජ්ජා and කාර *kára* who does) sorcerer, magician, juggler.

විජ්ජාධර, *Vijjádhara*, see විද්‍යාධර *vidyádhara*.

විජ්ජාව, *Vijjáwa*, *s.* knowledge, learning; magic, necromancy, from විද්‍යා *vidya*.

විජ්ජු, *Vijju*, *s.* lightning, Páli form of විද්‍යුත් *vidyut*.

විජ්ජුල්ලතා, *Vijjullatá*, *s.* (විජ්ජු and ලතා *latá* creeper) forked lightning.

විජ්‍රා, *Vijrá*, *s.* medicinal plant, *sphæranthus indicus* or *s. hirtus*. [Coll: මුඩමහණ *mudamahana*]: see විගන්ධිකා *vigandhiká*.

විජෘම්භ, *Vijrimbha*, } *s.* (වි before, ජෘම්භි *jribhi*
විජෘම්භණ, *Vijrimbhana*, } to yawn) springing, bounding, leaping; pastime, sport, especially amorous; sporting, wantoning; budding, blossoming.

විජෘම්භිත, *Vijrimbhita*, *s.* wish, desire; pastime, sport: *a.* blossomed, expanded, opened, unfolded; yawning, gaping.

විජටන, *Vijatana*, *s.* (වි privation, ජට *jata* knot, intricacy) disentangling, unfolding, separation, especially by reason; discrimination; untying, disclosing.

විජම්, *Vijam*, *s.* the Abhidhamma or Buddhist metaphysics.

විජය, *Vijaya*, *s.* (වි implying intensity, ජි *ji* to conquer) victory, triumph, conquest; species of spear; name of Arjuna; divine car or chariot of the gods; the god of Hades, Yama; one of the three myrobalans, *terminalia chebula*, [Colloq. අරළු *aralu*]; twenty-sixth year of the Indian cycle of sixty years; sovereign of the Śákya race, and cousin german to Gautama Buddha, who first landed in Ceylon with 700 followers, expelled the Rákshasas or demons, peopled the island from the continent, and established the Sinhalese monarchy.

විජයශ්‍රී, *Vijayaśri*, *s.* name of Lakshmí; victory and prosperity.

විජයා, *Vijayá*, *s.* name of Durgá; hemp, *cannabis sativa*, [Colloq. කංසා *kansá*]; yellow myrobalan, *terminalia chebula*, [Colloq. අරළු *aralu*]; orris root; flower, [Colloq. ඉද්ද *idda*]

විජයොත්, *Vijayot*, *s.* Indra's palace, supposed to be constructed with the diamond.

විජල, *Vijala*, *s.* (විජ *vija* to shake) sauce, etc. mixed with rice water or gruel.

විජාතා, *Vijátá*, *s.* (වි severally, ජාතා born [from whom]) woman who has borne children, mother, matron.

විජාති, *Vijáti*, *s.* a different species or tribe.

විජාතිය, *Vijátiya*, *a.* of a different class or caste or tribe; dissimilar.

විජානන, *Vijánana*, *s.* (වි implying certainty, ඥා *jñá* to know) practical knowledge, experience, [Colloq. අත්දැකීම *atdẹkima*].

විජායන, *Vijáyana*, *s.* (වි and ජායන producing) bringing forth, bearing, as children, [Colloq. වදනවා *wadanawá*].

විජිත, *Vijita*, *s.* (වි implying completely, ජිත conquered) country, realm, kingdom, [Colloq. රාජ්‍යය *rájyaya*: *a.* conquered; defeated.

විජිනි, *Vijini*, corruptly for විජනි *vijani*.

විජිනිපත, *Vijinipata*, *s.* (විජිනි and පත leaf) fan, fan made from the leaf of the Palmyra tree, [Colloq. වටාපත *waṭápata*].

විඥප්ති, *Vijñapti*, *s.* (වි before, ඥා *jñá* to know, causal form) information; representation, respectful communication of information or opinion on any subject.

විඥාන, *Vijñána*, *s.* (වි implying variety, ඥාන knowledge) knowledge, science, learning, general acquaintance with science and literature.

විඥෙය, *Vijñéya*, *a.* cognizable, comprehensible, what is or may be known or understood.

විඤ්ඤත්ති, *Viññatti*, *s.* asking, entreating, solicitation; intimation, whether by signs or speech: Páli form of විඥප්ති *vijñapti*.

විඤ්ඤාණ, *Viññáṇa*, *s.* understanding; mind, intellect, the faculty of reason; Páli form of විඥාන *vijñána*.

විඤ්ඤාත, *Viññáta*, *a.* known, comprehended, understood; learned, acquired.

විඤ්ඤූ, *Viññu*, *s.* learned man, pandit, scholar.

විඤ්ඤෙය, *Niññéya*, see විඥෙය *vijñéya*.

විට්ටම, *Viṭṭama*, *s.* frame of a bed or chair; the back board of a door: pl. විට්ටම් *viṭṭam*.

විට, *Viṭa*, *s.* time, period, occasion, opportunity, [Colloquial: වෙලාව *weláwa*]; catamite, pathic: drunkard, rogue, cheat; mountain; tree, *acacia suma* or *a. catechu;* orange tree, *citrus aurantium*, [Colloq. පැනිදොඩන් *pęnidoḍan*]; branch and its shoot; medicinal salt, *bit loben:* see බිඩ *biḍa;* chew of betel: pl. විටි *viṭi*.

විටංක, *Viṭanka*, *s.* (වි variously, ටකි *ṭaki* to bind) dovecot, aviary.

විටත, *Viṭata*, *s.* house, abode, [Colloq. ගෙදර *gedara*].

විටප, *Viṭapa*, *s.* (විට and පා *pá* to cherish) tree, [Colloq. ගහ *gaha*]; branch of a tree, [Colloq. අත්ත *atta*]; new shoot, sprout, germ; clump, cluster; bush, thicket.

විටපි, *Viṭapi*, *s.* (විටප *viṭapa* branch, ඊ *í* aff.) tree in general; banyan tree, *ficus bengalensis*, [Coll: මහනුග *maha-nuga*].

විටි, *Viṭi*, *s.* yellow saunders; rain, [Colloq. වැස්ස *węssa*].

විටින්විට, *Viṭinviṭa*, *adv.* every now and then, from time to time.

විඩ්භිද්, *Viḍbhid*, *s.* cucumber, *cucumis pubescens*, [Colloq. කැකිරි *kękiri*, තියඹරා *tiyambará*].

විඩ, *Viḍa*, see බිඩ *biḍa* and විට *viṭa*.

විඩඞ්ග, *Viḍanga*, *s.* anthelmintic shrub, *ericybe paniculata*, [Colloq. ඇටමිරිය *ętamiriya* or වලඟ සාල් *walangasál*]; vegetable substance considered of great efficacy as a vermifuge, embelia ribes.

විඩයක්, *Viḍayak*, *s.* one time, (another form of විටක් *viṭak*.)

විඩාදුරුකරණවා, *Viḍá-durukaraṇawá*, *v.* to repose, to take rest.

විඩාල, *Viḍála*, *s.* cat, [Colloq. බළලා *baḷalá*], also written බිඩාල *biḍála*.

විඩාලපාද, *Viḍálapáda*, *s.* a measure of weight, the same as the karsha or weight of sixteen máshas.

විඩාව, *Viḍáwa*, *s* fatigue, exhaustion, weariness, [Colloq. පිපාසය *pipásaya*].

විඩෞජස්, *Viḍójas*, *s.* (විඩ *viḍa* fragment) name of Indra, who splits mountains, etc. with his thunderbolt.

විත්, *Vit*, *s.* knowledge, wisdom, understanding, from විද් *vid;* perforation; shooting, archery; cup, drinking vessel: *v.* having come.

විත්ත, *Vitta*, *s.* thing, substance, wealth, riches, property; gain, acquirement.

විත්තකාරයා, *Vittakárayá*, see විජ්ජාකාරයා *vijjákárayá*.

විත්තිකාරයා, *Vittikárayá*, *s.* (විත්ති and කාර *kára* who does) defendant in a law suit.

විත්තිකියනවා, *Vitti-kiyanawá*, *v.* to state in defence

විත්තිය, *Vittiya*, *s.* judgment, investigation, enquiry; that which one has to state in defence of his conduct: pl. විත්ති *vitti*.

විත්තිවසම, *Vitti-wasama*, *s.* law suit.

විත්ථාර, *Vitthára*, Páli form of විස්තාර *vistára*.

විත, *Vita*, *s.* hole, perforation; drinking vessel.

විතක්, *Vitak*, *s.* thought, reflection, opinion, [Coll: කල්පනාව *kalpanáwa*].

විතණ්ඩ, *Vitaṇḍa*, *s.* reputation; criticism, the subversion of another's opinion or interpretation and establishment of one's own.

විතත, *Vitata*, *s.* (වි and තත spread) any stringed instrument: *a.* stretched, spread, expanded; pervaded, diffused.

විතති, *Vitati*, *s.* clump, cluster of trees, etc; spreading, expansion.

විතථ, *Vitatha*, *a.* false, untrue, [Colloq. බොරු *boru*].

විතන්, *Vitan*, *s.* canopy, awning, from විතාන *vitána*, [Colloq. වියන *viyana*].

විතර්ක, *Vitarka*, *s.* (වි implying discrimination, තර්ක to reason or doubt) reasoning, discussion; doubt, deliberation; consideration of probabilities, mental anticipation of alternatives, conjecture.

විතර්කණ, *Vitarkaṇa*, *s.* reasoning, revolving, ruminating, discussing.

විතර, *Vitara*, *s.* breadth, width, extent; Elu form of විස්තාර *vistára*: *ind.* particle signifying, about, so much; only, merely, alone.

විතරණ, *Vitaraṇa*, *s.* gift, donation; crossing, going over.

විතස්ති, *Vitasti*, *s.* (වි part, තස *tasa* to throw) long span, measured by the extended thumb and little finger, considered equal to twelve fingers or seven inches.

✓විතාන, *Vitána*, *s.* (වි before, තන *tana* to spread) awning, canopy; spreading, expansion; form of metre, consisting of a verse of four lines of eight syllables each; each line of the stanza consists of two Iambics, one Trochee, and one Spondee.

විතානක, *Vitánaka*, *s.* awning: see the last.

විතාරන්න, *Vitáranna*, *s.* Vidán of a village: see විදාන *vidána*.

විතුන්න, *Vitunna*, *s.* medicinal plant, [Colloq. කිඹුල්වැන්න *kimbulwenna*].

විතුන්නක, *Vitunnaka*, *s.* (වි privative, තුන්න *tunna* pained, tortured) thorny shrub, *flacourtia cataphracta*, [Colloq. රටඋගුරැස්ස *raṭa-uguressa*]; coriander seed; blue vitriol.

විද්ධ, *Viddha*, *s.* (විධ *vidha* to pierce) tree, *alstonia scholaris*, [Colloq. රුක්අත්තන *rukattana*]: *a.* pierced, perforated; thrown, directed, cast, sent.

විද්‍යමාන, *Vidyamána*, *s.* (විද *vida* to be, මාන participial aff.) being, being present or in existence; actual, real.

විද්‍යා, *Vidyá*, *s.* (විද *vida* to know) knowledge, learning, science; tree, *premna spinosa*; magical pill or bolus, by putting which into the mouth a person has the power of ascending to heaven.

විද්‍යාචරණ, *Vidyácharaṇa*, *s.* (විද්‍යා knowledge, චරණ going) acting according to reason, one of the ✓nine attributes of Buddha.

විද්‍යාධර, *Vidyádhara*, *s.* (විද්‍යා magical pill, ධර who holds) demigod of a particular order, supposed to be attainable by magical rites and incantations.

විද්‍යුත්, *Vidyut*, } *s.* (වි intense, ද්‍යුත් light,
✓විද්‍යුල්ලතා, *Vidyullatá*, } ලතා creeper) lightning, the electric flash, [Colloq. විදුලිය *viduliya*].

විද්‍රධි, *Vidradhi*, *s.* (විද්‍ර piercing, ධා *dhá* to have) phlegmonoid inflammation, especially deep seated or internal abscess.

විද්‍රුම, *Vidruma*, *s.* (වි sort, ද්‍රුම tree) coral, [Colloq. පබළු *pabaḷu*]; tree said to bear precious gems; ✓young sprout or shoot.

විද, *Vida*, *s.* learning, knowledge, science; understanding.

විදග්ධ, *Vidagdha*, *s.* (වි intensity, දහ *daha* to burn) libertine, lecher, intriguer; learned or clever man, scholar, paṇḍit: *a.* learned, clever, sharp, shrewd, witty, knowing; excellent, eminent.

විදත්, *Vidat*, } *s.* wise or learned man, scholar.
විදද, *Vidada*, }

විදනවා, *Vidanawá*, *v.* to spread: pret. විදුවා *viduwá*; another form of විදහනවා *vidahanawá*.

විදමන, *Vidamana*, *s.* hole, perforation; boring, piercing; archery, practice of archery: pl. විදමන් *vidaman*.

විදර්භ, *Vidarbha*, *s.* (වි privative, දර්භ sacred grass) district and city to the south west of Bengal, considered to be the same as Bara Nagara or Berar proper; the name alludes to a fable that the sacred grass does not grow in that country from the curse of a saint whose son had died of a wound from a blade of the grass.

විදර්ශක, *Vidarṣaka*, *s.* (වි before or ascertainment, දර්ශක who sees) wise man, intelligent person, one of keen penetration, or one possessed of extensive and varied knowledge.

විදර්ශන, *Vidarṣana*, *s.* (වි and දර්ශන seeing) discerning, distinguishing, penetrating, devout abstract meditation.

විදර්ශනධූරය, *Vidarṣana-dhúraya*, see විපස්සනාධූර *vipassaná-dhúra*.

විදර්ශන මාර්ගය, *Vidarṣana-márgaya*, *s.* (විදර්ශන and මාර්ග *márga* way, path) practice of religious and abstract meditation: see විපස්සනාධූර *vipassaná-dhúra*.

විදර්ශනාඥාන, *Vidarṣaná-jñána*, *s.* (විදර්ශනා and ඥාන knowledge) wisdom attained by abstract meditation.

විදර, *Vidara*, *s.* tearing, rending; the Indian prickly pear, *cactus Indicus*.

විදල, *Vidala*, *s.* dividing, splitting; split pease; mountain ebony; shallow basket made of split bambus; pomegranate bark: *a.* opened, rent, split.

විදහනවා, *Vidahanawá*, *v.* to open, to unfold, to expose, to spread out.

විදහා, *Vidahá, past part.* of විදහනවා *vidahanawá.*

විදා, *Vidá, s.* knowledge, intellect, understanding.

විදාන, *Vidána, s.* the Vidán or headman of a village, person who conveys the orders of government to the people.

විදාන ආරච්චිල, *Vidána-árachchila, s.* Native headman so called, next in rank to a Mohandiram.

විදාන මුහන්දිරම, *Vidána-muhandirama, s.* Native headman so called.

විදානරාල, *Vidánarála, s.* Vidane or a village headman.

විදානේ, *Vidáné,* see විදාන *vidána.*

විදාරණ, *Vidárana, s.* (වි before, දෘ *dru* to tear) tearing, breaking, splitting, severing, dividing; killing, slaughter; war, battle; small tree with peltate leaves, *pterospermum acerifolium.*

විදාරිගන්ධා, *Vidárigandhá, s.* plant, *alyssicarpus bupleurifolius,* [Colloq. අස්වැන්න *aswenna*].

විදි, *Vidi, s.* name of Brahma; destiny, fortune.

විදික්, *Vidik, s.* (වි various, දික් side, quarter) intermediate points of the compass.

විදිත, *Vidita, s.* (විද *vida* to know) sage, learned man, scholar, [Colloq. පණ්ඩිතයා *panditayá*]: *a.* known, understood; promised, agreed, assented.

විදිනකටුව, *Vidinakatuwa, s.* (විදින piercing, කටුව awl) fleam; an awl, steel part of a wimble.

විදිනවා, *Vidinawá, v.* to bore, to pierce, to perforate; to spear, to shoot with an arrow; to bleed, to open a vein: pret. විද්දා *viddá.*

විදිනි, *Vidini, s.* fan, [Colloq. පවන්පත *pawanpata*].

විදිය, *Vidiya, s.* rule, form; method, order: see විධිය *vidhiya.*

විදිලි, *Vidili,* see විදුලි *viduli.*

විදිලිකොටනවා, *Vidilikotanawá, v.* (විදිලි and කොටනවා to flash) to lighten as the electric fluid.

විදීම, *Vidíma, s.* piercing, boring, bleeding; vaccination; verbal noun of විදිනවා *vidinawá,* which see.

විදු, *Vidu, s.* lightning, Elu form of විද්‍යුත් *vidyut;* name of Vishnu; coral; diamond; Indra's thunderbolt, from වජ්‍ර *wajra;* old man from වෘද්ධ *wriddha: a.* knowing, wise, learned, from විද *vida,* to know; the hollow between the frontal globes of an elephant.

විදුප, *Vidupa, s.* slave, servant, menial, [Colloq. වැඩකාරයා *wedakárayá*]; fanning.

විදුපන, *Vidupana, s.* cooking vessel, any earthen cooking vessel; fanning.

විදුම, *Viduma, s.* piercing, boring; hole.

විදුර, *Vidura, s.* (විද *vida* to know) clever or learned man; glass, diamond; diamond thunderbolt of Indra; kusa grass from වජ්‍ර *wajra: a.* wise, knowing, intelligent.

විදුරත්, *Vidurat,* }
විදුරදර, *Viduradara,* } *s.* (විදුර and අත් hand, දර who has) name of Indra, alluding to his diamond club or thunderbolt: see වජ්‍ර *wajra.*

විදුරවි, *Viduravi,* }
විදුරවිය, *Viduraviya,* } *s.* (විදුර thunderbolt, අවි *avi* weapon) Indra's diamond thunderbolt; Elu form of වජ්‍රායුධ *wajráyudha;* name of Indra.

විදුරස්න, *Vidurasna,* }
විදුරසුන්, *Vidurasun.* } *s.* (විදුර and අසුන් *asun* seat) throne of Buddha which sprung up from the eight handfuls of kusa grass: see වජ්‍රාසන *wajrásana.*

විදුරු, *Viduru, s.* diamond; thunderbolt of Indra; pomegranate, *punica granatum,* [Colloq. දෙළුම් *delum*].

විදුරුදරු, *Vidurudaru,* see විදුරදර *viduradara.*

විදුරුමහ, *Vidurumaha, s.* (විදුරු diamond, shining like, මහ or මස *masa* flesh) the gums.

විදුරුමිටි, *Viduru-miti, s.* (විදුරු and මිටි handle) bell with a glass handle.

විදුරුමුව, *Viduru-muwa, s.* (විදුරු diamond, as sharp as, මුව mouth) leech, [Colloquial: කූඩැල්ලා *kúdellá*].

විදුලතා, *Vidulatá,* }
විදුලිය, *Viduliya,* } *s.* (විදු lightning, ලතා or ලිය creeper) lightning, forked lightning; Elu form of විද්‍යුල්ලතා *vidyullatá.*

විදූර, *Vidúra, a.* (වි intervening, දූර distant) very far or remote.

විදූෂණ, *Vidúshana, s.* (වි before, දූෂ *dúsha* to make bad) censuring, reviling, abuse, satire.

විදේශී, *Vidési, s.* (වි implying strange, දේශ *désa* country, ඊ *í* aff.) foreigner, stranger.

විදේහ, *Vidéha, s.* district in the province of Behar, same as the ancient Mithilá or the modern Tirhut; name of a king of the family of Janaka, whose prime minister Buddha was, in one of his transmigrations as Bódhisatwa, and the history of whose exploits forms a large volume called Ummagga Játaka.

විඳිනවා, *Vindinawá, v.* to feel, to perceive; to endure, to suffer; to enjoy, to have, to possess: pret. වින්දා *vindá.*

විඳීම, *Vindíma,* verbal noun of විඳිනවා *vindinawá.*

විඳුම, *Vinduma, s.* enduring, suffering.

විඳුවනවා, *Vinduwanawá*, *v.* to cause to suffer pain: pret. විඳෙව්වා *vindewwá*.

විධ්වංස, *Vidhwansa*, *s.* (වි before, ධ්වංස to fall) aversion, disrespect; enmity, dislike; destruction, killing, ruin.

විධ්වංසන, *Vidhwansana*, *s.* destroying, ruining, extirpating.

විධ්වංසනයකරණවා, *Vidhwansanaya-karanawá*, *v.* to destroy, to ruin.

විධ, *Vidha*, *s.* form, formula, rule; manner, kind, sort; piercing.

විධකර්ණි, *Vidha-karni*, *s.* (විධ pierced, කර්ණි ear) shrub, *cissampelos pareira*, [Colloq. දියමිත්ත *diyamitta*]; one whose ears are pierced.

විධවා, *Vidhawá*, *s.* (වි privative, ධව *dhawa* husband) widow, [Colloq. කණවැන්දුම් *kanawendumi*].

විධාතා, *Vidhátá*, } *s.* (වි entirely, ධා to have, to
විධාතෘ, *Vidhátri*, } hold, තෘච් *trich* aff.) name of Brahma, the all pervading spirit; fate.

විධාන, *Vidhána*, *s.* (වි before ධා *dhá* to have) sending, ordering, commanding; rule, precept, ordinance, injunction; form, mode, manner; gaining, getting, taking; in grammar, prefixing, affixing, taking as an affix, etc.; an inferior headman, the Vidán of a village who conveys government orders, etc. to the people.

විධිපූර්වක, *Vidhi-púrwaka*, *a.* after or according to rule.

විධිය, *Vidhiya*, *s.* usage, custom, fashion, rule, form, formula; order, injunction, command; act, action, general or particular; fate, luck, destiny; Brahma.

විධියෝග, *Vidhi-yóga*, *s.* occurrence of predoomed events.

විධිවත්, *Vidhiwat*, *ind.* agreeably to rule.

විධු, *Vidhu*, *s.* moon, [Colloq. හඳ *handa*]. name of Vishnu, of Brahma; Rákshasa, fiend, goblin; camphor.

විධූති, *Vidhuti*, *s.* (වි and ධූ *dhú* to tremble) shaking, trembling, [Colloq. චංචල *chanchala*].

විධුන්තුද, *Vidhuntuda*, *s.* (විධුං *vidhun* moon, තුද to torment) name of Ráhu, personified ascending node, alluding to his attempts at certain periods to swallow the moon: see රාහු *ráhu*.

විධූනන, *Vidhunana*, see විධූති *vidhuti*.

විධුර, *Vidhura*, *s.* separation, agitation of mind from terror: *a.* agitated, separated, perplexed.

විධුවන, *Vidhuwana*, *s.* (වි and ධු *dhú* shake) shaking, trembling.

විධූත, *Vidhúta*, *a.* (වි and ධූ to shake, ක්ත *kta* aff.) shaken, trembling, tremulous: see විධූති *vidhúti*.

විධූනන, *Vidhúnana*, see විධූති *vidhuti*.

විධේය, *Vidhéya*, *a.* (වි before, ධා *dhá* to have) compliant, tractable, governable; to be done, what is or ought to be practised.

විඳෑතය, *Vindátaya*, *s.* sickle, [Colloq. දෑකැත්ත *dékętta*].

විඳු, *Vindu*, *a.* knowing, intelligent, from විද *vida* to know: see බිඳු *bindu*.

වින්ධ්‍ය, *Vindhya*, *s.* the Vindhya or Bindh mountain, the mountainous range which runs across India from the province of Behar, nearly to Guzerat, and properly divides Hindustan from the Dekhin.

වින්ධ්‍යාචල, *Vindhyáchala*, *s.* (වින්ධ්‍ය *vindhya* and අචල *achala* mountain) the Vindhya range of mountains.

වින්ධ්‍යාටවි, *Vindhyátavi*, *s.* (වින්ධ්‍ය and අටවි *atavi* forest) the Vindhya forest.

වින්න, *Vinna*, *a.* (විද *vida* to know, ක්ත *kta* aff.) judged, discussed; gained, obtained; fixed, placed; known.

වින්නඹුවා, *Vinnambuwá*, *s.* midwife, sometimes called මින්නඹුවා *minnambuwá*.

වින්‍යාස, *Vinyása*, *s.* (වි and නි *ni* prefixed to, අස *asa* to take, to throw or place) assemblage, collection; site, place, receptacle; orderly arrangement; deposit.

වින, *Vina*, *s.* obedience, submission; attention to abstract meditation: see විනය *vinaya*; Garula; enchantment, sorcery, witchcraft; any evil act.

විනකරණවා, *Vinakaranawá*, *v.* to enchant, to bewitch; to act wickedly.

විනකාරයා, *Vinakárayá*, *s.* (වින sorcery, කාර *kára* who practises) enchanter, sorcerer, magician.

විනත, *Vinata*, *a.* (වි and නම *nama* to bow, ක්ත *kta* aff.) bent, bowed, stooping; crooked, curved; humble, modest.

විනතක, *Vinataka*, *s.* the sixth from the centre of the seven circular rocks surrounding Maha Méru, and forming the boundaries of so many circumambient waters or oceans.

විනදර, *Vinadara*, *s.* (වින and දර who has or bears) one who has a complete acquaintance with the Vinaya: see විනයපිටක *vinaya-pitaka* and පිටක *pitaka*.

විනය, *Vinaya*, *s.* (වි and නි *ni* to obtain or guide, අය *aya* aff.) modesty, affability, humility, mildness; reverence, obeisance; decorum, decency, propriety of conduct; religious obedience, enchantment, sorcery. subjection; submission to all the prescribed ordinances and duties of the priesthood; name of one of the classes of books called Piṭaka: see තුන්පිටක *tun-piṭaka* and විනය පිටක *vinaya-piṭaka.*

විනයධර, *Vinayadhara, s.* one well-versed in the Vinaya Piṭaka which treats of the Discipline of the Buddhist Priesthood.

විනයපිටක, *Vinaya-piṭaka, s.* (විනය propriety of conduct, පිටක basket, receptacle) second of the three piṭakas, comprizing five principal divisions, viz. පාරාජිකා *párájiká,* පචිති *pachiti,* සුළුවග *suḷu-waga,* මහවග *maha-waga,* and පරිවාර *pariwára,* the last of which is a digest of the leading doctrines of the other four.

විනා, *Viná, s.* name of Buddha alluding to his character as chief of chiefs; name of Gaṇésa the Hindu god of wisdom, Elu form of විනායක *vináyaka: ind.* without, except, but, unless.

විනාකිරි, *Vinákiri, s.* vinegar. (English.)

විනාඩිය, *Vináḍiya, s.* minute, the sixtieth part of a Siṇhalese hour or twenty-four English seconds: pl. විනාඩි *vináḍi.*

විනායක, *Vináyaka, s.* (වි privative, නායක chief) name of Buddha; name of Gaṇésa; obstacle, impediment: see විනා *viná.*

* විනාශ, *Vináṣa, s.* (වි before, නශ *naṣa* to perish) destruction, loss, annihilation, disappearance.

* විනාශක, *Vináṣaka, s.* destroying; destroyer.

* විනාශකරණවා, *Vináṣakaraṇawá, v.* to destroy.

* විනාශකෙරීම, *Vináṣakeríma, s.* destruction.

* විනාශිත, *Vináṣita, a.* destroyed.

විනාසක, *Vinásaka, a.* (වි privative, and නාසිකා *násiká* or නාසා *násá* nose) noseless.

විනි, *Vini, s.* word, [Colloq. වචනය *wachanaya*]; dictum; speech, saying; wood, forest; three-peaked mountain.

විනිගත, *Vinigata, a.* gone, left: see the next.

විනිපාත, *Vinipáta,* / විනිපාතනය, *Vinipátanaya,* } *a.* (වි and නි prefixed to පත *pata* to fall) falling, falling down, literally or figuratively, as from a height or dignity; calamity, unavoidable evil, infliction of gods or fate; pain, distress; hell, infernal regions.

* These words are written with ස *sa* when they are derived from the Páli which has no "ශ *ṣa*".

විනිමය, *Vinimaya, s.* (වි and නි, prefixed to මී *mí* to go) barter, exchange; pledge, deposit, security.

විනිර්ගත, *Vinirgata, a.* (වි and නිර් forth, ගත gone) gone out, left, departed, abandoned.

විනිර්මුක්ත, *Vinirmukta, a.* (වි and නිර් forth, මුක්ත sent) discharged, loosened, freed, exempt, liberated.

විනිවිද, *Vinivida, s.* piercing, perforating, penetrating, passing through.

විනිශ්චය, *Viniṣchaya, s.* (වි implying severally, නිශ්චය ascertainment) judicial process, trial, judgment.

විනිශ්චයකරණවා, *Viniṣchaya-karaṇawá, v.* to judge.

විනිශ්චයකාරයා, *Viniṣchayakárayá, s.* judge.

විනිස, *Vinisa, s.* certainty, ascertainment, freedom from doubt: see also විනිශ්චය *viniṣchaya.*

විනී, *Viní, s.* the three-peaked mountain: see ත්‍රිකූට පර්වත *trikúṭa-parwata.*

විනීත, *Vinita, a.* (වි completely, නීත guided) modest, humble, unassuming, unpretending; pliant, governable, tractable; placid, meek, virtuous, gentle, having the passions restrained and the senses under subjection; well-behaved, decent, decorous, trained, as a horse.

විනේ, *Viné,* see වින *vina* and විනය *vinaya.*

විනේජන, *Vinéjana, s.* people who devote themselves entirely to the study and practice of the විනය *vinaya.*

විනෝද, *Vinóda, s.* (වි before, නුද *nuda* to order) expelling, dismissing; abandoning; eagerness, vehemence; play, sport, pastime; interesting pursuit or occupation.

විනෝදන, *Vinódana, s.* (වි and නුද *nuda* to order) dismissing, abandoning, sending away, putting aside.

විනෝදනයකරණවා, *Vinódanaya-karaṇawá, v.* to dismiss, to remove (doubt or sorrow).

විප්, *Vip, s.* Brahman, Elu form of විප්‍ර *vipra.*

විප්පයෝග, *Vippayóga, s.* separation, absence, disunion, disjunction; difference, disagreement; Páli form of විප්‍රයෝග *viprayóga.*

විප්පවාස, *Vippawása, s.* (වි implying, separation. ප *pa* euphoniæ gratia, පවාස dwelling) living apart; residence in a foreign country; Páli form of විප්‍ර වාස *viprawása.*

විප්‍ර, *Vipra, s.* (වි and ප්‍රා *prá* to fill, to complete, essential observances) Brahman.

විප්‍රකාර, *Viprakára*, s. (වි and ප්‍ර depreciative particle, කාර making) injury, contumely, abuse; wickedness; opposition; retaliation.

විප්‍රකෘති, *Viprakṛiti*, s. retaliation, retort: see also the last.

විප්‍රතිසාර, *Vipratisára*, s. (වි reverse, ප්‍රති to or towards, සාර going, conduct) repentance; hatred, enmity; rage, wrath; evil, wickedness.

විප්‍රයුක්ත, *Viprayukta*, s. (වි implying separation, යුක්ත joined) separated, disjoined, sundered, away or absent from.

විප්‍රයෝග, *Viprayóga*, s. (වි privative, ප්‍රයෝග union, contiguity) separation, absence; disunion, disjunction; quarrel, disagreement.

විප්‍රලබ්ධ, *Vipralabdha*, a. (වි and ප්‍ර prefixed to ලබ්ධ gained) tricked, cheated, deceived; disappointed.

විප්‍රලාප, *Vipralápa*, s. (වි and ප්‍ර contradiction, or reciprocity, ලාප talk) quarrel, wrangling, mutual contradiction; idle or unmeaning discourse, nonsense.

විප්‍රවාස, *Viprawása*, s. (වි and ප්‍ර implying separation, වස *wasa* to abide) residence in a foreign country.

විප්‍රසන්න, *Viprasanna*, a. (වි intense, ප්‍රසන්න pleased) pleased, delighted, gratified.

විප්‍රුෂ්, *Viprush*, s. drop of water; spot, mark, dot.

විප්ලව, *Viplawa*, s. (වි before, ප්ලු *plu* to go) affray, assault, tumultuary contest without weapons; predatory warfare, plundering, devastation; rapine, extortion; evil, calamity.

විප, *Vipa*, s. thought, consideration; Brahman.

විපක්, *Vipak*, s. (වි contrary, opposite, පක් part, side) enemy, adversary, [Colloq. සතුරු *saturá*]; bird in general.

විපක්‍ෂ, *Vipaksha*, s. (වි implying opposite, පක්‍ෂ side, part) enemy, adversary; disputant, opponent; exception, in grammar.

විපක්‍ෂකම, *Vipakshakama*, } s. partizanship, hostility, contradiction.
විපක්‍ෂය, *Vipakshaya*, }

විපඤ්චිකා, *Vipañchiká*, s. a lute.

විපණ, *Vipaṇa*, s. (වි before, පණ to be of value) sale, contract of sale.

විපණි, *Vipaṇi*, } s. place where things are sold,
විපණී, *Vipaṇí*, } shop, stall; fair, market, market place; article or commodity for sale; dealer, trafficker, shopkeeper, [Colloq. වෙළෙන්දා *weḷendá*].

විපත්, *Vipat*, s. calamity, misfortune.

විපත්තිය, *Vipattiya*, s. (වි implying reverse, පත *pata* to go) adversity, calamity, misfortune; distress, misery; pain, agony.

විපත, *Vipata*, s. calamity: see විපත්තිය *vipattiya*

විපතගාමි, *Vipatagámi*, s. (විපත misfortune, ගාමි who goes or is) unfortunate man, ill-fated or wretched person.

විපථ, *Vipatha*, s. (වි depreciative, පථ road) bad road.

විපද්, *Vipad*, see විපත් *vipat*.

විපර්ණක, *Viparṇaka*, s. (වි separate, පර්ණ *parṇa* leaf) Pulas tree, *butea frondosa*, [Colloq. ගස් කැල *gas-kḙla*].

විපර්යය, *Viparyaya*, s. (වි and පරි *pari* implying reverse, ඊ *í* to go) contrariety, opposition; reverse in general, and thence applied to that of which reverse is predicated, as misfortune, calamity, reverse of fortune; inverted order or succession, the reverse of that which is usual or prescribed.

විපර්යාස, *Viparyása*, s. (වි and පරි *pari* prefixed to, අස *asa* to be) contrariety, opposition; imagining what is unreal or false to be real or true.

විපරම්කරණවා, *Viparamkaraṇawá*, v. to exercise thought, to look about, to search.

විපරම, *Viparama*, s. trial, probation, inquiry, search; thought, recollection, remembrance: pl. විපරම් *viparam*.

විපරාවෘත්ත, *Viparáwritta*, see විපර්යාස *viparyása*.

විපරීත, *Viparíta*, a. (වි and පරි *pari* implying reverse, ඉත *ita* gone) reverse, inverse; opposite, contrary; distracted, confused, perplexed.

විපශ්චිත්, *Vipaṣchit*, s. paṇḍit, scholar, learned man.

විපස්සනා, *Vipassaná*, s. (වි implying intensity, පස්ස *passa* substituted for දස්ස *dassa* to see, to perceive) abstract devout meditation.

විපස්සනාධුර, *Vipassanádhúra*, s. (විපස්සනා and ධුර office, employment) duty of devout abstract meditation; every kind of meditation, in contradistinction to the ගන්ථධුර *ganthadhúra* or knowledge of the Buddhistical writings.

විපා, *Vipá*, s. the senses.

විපාක, *Vipáka*, s. reward, recompence, return for any favour; investigation, remembrance; cooking, dressing; flavour, taste; ripening, maturing; consequences of action; change of form or state; assimilation of food, digestion.

විපාකදෙනවා, *Vipákadenawá*, v. to reward, to remunerate.

විපාකඵල, *Vipáka-phala*, *s.* (විපාක act, action, ඵල fruit) reward of meritorious actions performed in a former state of existence.

විපාකය, *Vipákaya*, *s.* reward, remuneration: see විපාක *vipáka.*

විපාදිකා, *Vipádiká*, *s.* kibe, sore or blister on the foot; riddle, enigma.

විපින, *Vipina*, *s.* (වේප *wépa* to shake, ඉනන් *inan* aff.) forest, wood, [Colloq. මුකළාන *múkaḷána*].

විපියා, *Vipiya*, *s.* Bengal tiger.

විපිළිසර, *Vipiḷisara*, *s.* rejecting, refusing; rage, wrath; repentance, contrition.

විපුල්, *Vipul*, } *a.* වි and පුල to be large or lofty)
විපුල, *Vipula*, } large, [Colloquial. මහත් *mahat*]; broad; deep, profound.

විපුලා, *Vipulá*, *s.* the earth, [Colloq. පොළව *poḷawa*]; form of metre, having the line irregularly divided by the cæsura or pause; plant, see මුඩමහණ *muḍamahaṇa.*

විපූය, *Vipúya*, *s.* munja grass, *saccharum munja.*

විපැත්තිය, *Vipettiya*, *s.* misfortune, calamity, corruptly for විපත්තිය *vipattiya.*

විඵල, *Viphala*, *a.* (වි privative, ඵල fruit) vain, useless, unfruitful; idle, unmeaning; barren, unprofitable.

විබන්ධ, *Vibandha*, *s.* (වි intensitive, බන්ධ to bind) ischury, constipation.

විබාග, *Vibága*, corruptly for විභාග *vibháya*, which see.

විබාධා, *Vibádhá*, *s.* (වි various, බාධා affliction) pain, agony, anguish.

විබුධ, *Vibudha*, *s.* (වි and බුධ to know) a god, deity, immortal; learned man, teacher; moon.

විබෝධ, *Vibódha*; *s.* (වි privative or intensive, බුධ *budha* to expand, to know) opening, expanding, blowing; inattention; intelligence; awaking.

විභ්‍රම, *Vibhrama*, *s.* (වි implying variety, භ්‍රම to go round, to err) whirling, going round: error, mistake, blunder; feminine action proceeding from love, youthful caprice, whim, wantonness; doubt, apprehension.

විභ්‍රාන්ත, *Vibhránta*, *a.* (වි and භ්‍රම *bhrama* to err, ක්ත *kta* aff.) hurried, flurried, erring through precipitation.

විභක්ත, *Vibhakta*, *a.* (වි severally, භජ් *bhaja* to divide, ක්ත *kta* aff.) divided, portioned; partitioned, separated, parted.

විභක්තජ, *Vibhaktaja*, *s.* (විභක්ත divided, ජ born) son born after the division of the family property between his parents and brethren.

විභක්තිය, *Vibhaktiya*, *s.* (වි before, භජ් *bhaja* to divide, ක්තින් *ktin* aff.) part, portion, inheritance, or share of inheritance; division, partition; inflexion of nouns, declension.

විභඞ්ග, *Vibhaṅga*, *s.* (වි intensitive, භඞ්ග to break) breaking, bending, contracting; expression or play of features.

විභජ්ජ, *Vibhajja*, *s.* (වි entirely, භජ් *bhaja* to divide) breaking, separating, parting asunder; analysing; the second part of Vyákaraṇa or the solution of difficult questions, viz. separating and arranging all the parts of a subject according to their different properties.

විභජනය, *Vibhajanaya*, *s.* (වි and භජ් *bhaja* to divide) portioning, dividing; partitioning, separating, parting.

විභව, *Vibhawa*, *s.* (වි implying variety, privation, භව being) substance, thing, property, wealth; emancipation from existence, annihilation; supreme or superhuman power; magnanimity or lofty-mindness.

විභව තණ්හා, *Vibhawa-tanhá*, *s.* (විභව annihilation, තණ්හා desire) desire of the immediate and total extinction of the soul at death.

විභා, *Vibhá*, *s.* (වි variously, භා to shine) ray of light, lustre; beauty.

විභාකර, *Vibhákara*, *s.* (විභා light, කර what makes) sun, [Colloq. ඉර *ira*]; fire, [Colloq. ගින්දර *gindara*].

විභාග, *Vibhága*, *s.* (වි variously or intensitively, භජ් *bhaja* to divide, to separate) discussion, examination, search, enquiry, discrimination; part, portion, share, portion of an inheritance; (in arithmetic) numerator of a fraction.

විභාගකරණවා, *Vibhágakaranawá*, *v.* to examine, to search into, to investigate.

විභාත, *Vibháta*, *s.* (වි before, භා to shine, ක්ත *kta* aff.) dawn, day break.

විභාවරී, *Vibháwarí*, *s.* (වි and භා *bhá* to shine with stars) night, [Colloq. රාත්‍රිය *rátriya*]; turmeric, *curcuma longa*, [Colloq. කහ *kaha*]; bawd; harlot, [Colloq. වෙසඟන *wesangana*].

විභාවසු, *Vibháwasu*, *s.* (විභා light, වසු being, substance) sun, [Colloq. ඉර *ira*]; fire, [Colloq. ගින්දර *gindara*]; moon, [Colloq. හඳ *haṇda*]; sort of necklace or garland.

විභාවිත, *Vibhávita*, *s.* perceived, judged, proved.

විභාෂා, *Vibháshá*, *ind.* alternative, either of two ways.

විභින්න, *Vibhinna*, *a.* (වි completely, භින්න divided) mixed, intermixed, mingled; scattered, dispersed; broken, various, different.

විභීත, *Vibhíta*, *a.* (වි privative, භීත fear) fearless.

විභීතක, *Vibhítaka*, *s.* beleric myrobalan, *terminalia belerica*, [Colloq. බුළු *buḷu*].

විභූ, *Vibhu*, *s.* (වි implying superiority or intensity, භූ to be) master, owner; name of Brahma, Vishṇu, and Śiva: *a.* omnipresent, all-pervading; always, eternal; hard, solid, firm.

විභූතිය, *Vibhútiya*, *s.* pomp, splendour; paraphernalia and attributes of royalty, majesty, dignity; superhuman power; eight faculties, especially attributed to Śiva.

විභූෂණ, *Vibhúshaṇa*, *s.* (වි implying variety, භූෂණ adorning) ornament, decoration.

විභූෂා, *Vibhúshá*, *s.* (වි and භූෂ *bhúsha* to adorn) lustre, splendour, beauty; ornament, decoration.

විභූෂිත, *Vibhúshita*, *a.* (වි and භූෂ *bhúsha* to adorn, ත aff.) adorned, ornamented, decorated; shining, splendid.

විභූසන, *Vibhúsana*, see විභූෂණ *vibhúshaṇa*.

විභූසිත, *Vibhúsita*, see විභූෂිත *vibhúshita*.

විම්බ, *Vimba*, }
විම්බජ, *Vimbajá*, } see බිම්බ *bimba*.
විම්බිකා, *Vimbiká*, }
විම්බෝෂ්ඨ, *Vimbóshṭha*, }

විමත, *Vimata*, *s.* (වි adverse, මත disposed) enemy, adversary, [Colloq. සතුරා *saturá*].

විමති, *Vimati*, }
විමතිය, *Vimatiya*, } *s.* (වි privation, මති thought, reflection) confusion, perplexity; doubt, uncertainty; absence, inattention.

විමන්, *Viman*, }
විමන, *Vimana*, } *s.* house, dwelling, residence; mansion, palace: see විමාන *vimána*.

විමනස, *Vimanasa*, *a.* (වි privative, මනස් *manas* mind) perplexed, confused, disordered; heart-broken, sad.

විමර්දන, *Vimardana*, *s.* (වි and මෘද *mrida* to rub) trituration of perfumes; rubbing, pounding, grinding; killing, destroying.

විමර්ශ, *Vimarṣa*, }
විමර්ශන, *Vimarṣana*, } *s.* (වි intensitive, මෘශ *mriṣa* to perceive) discussion, investigation, reasoning, examining, searching.

විමර්ෂ, *Vimarsha*, *s.* (වි before, මෘෂ *mrisha* to endure) irritation, impatience, displeasure, dissatisfaction.

විමල, *Vimala*, *s.* (වි privative, මල dirt) purity, Rahat or highest order of Buddhist ascetic: *a.* clean, pure, literally or figuratively; white; transparent; beautiful.

විමසනවා, *Vimasanawá*, *v.* to try, to prove: to investigate, to search into, from විමර්ශන *vimarṣana:* pret. විමසුවා *vimasuwá*.

විමාන, *Vimána*, *s.* (වි implying excellence, මා *má* to measure or construct) car or chariot of the gods, serving as a seat or throne, and carrying them through the skies, self moved and self directed; palace, residence of a king.

විමානය, *Vimánaya*, *s.* habitation; seat.

විමාර්ග, *Vimárga*, *s.* bad road, wrong road, literally or figuratively.

විමුක්ත, *Vimukta*, *a.* (වි and මුක්ත liberated) loosed, liberated, emancipated; thrown, hurled.

විමුක්ති, *Vimukti*, *s.* (වි intensitive, මුක්ති liberation) emancipation from existence, annihilation, or Nirwáṇa, freedom.

විමුක්තිඥාන, *Vimuktijñána*, *s.* (විමුක්ති final emancipation, ඥාන knowledge) one of the six classes of superhuman knowledge said to be possessed by Buddha and the Rahats, viz. the knowledge of final emancipation from existence, or the acquirement of Nirwáṇa or annihilation.

විමුඛ, *Vimukha*, *a.* (වි reverse, මුඛ countenance) averted, having the face cast down, or turned away.

විමුත්ත, *Vimutta*, Páli form of විමුක්ත *vimukta*.

විමුත්ති, *Vimutti*, Páli form of විමුක්ති *vimukti*.

විමෝහ, *Vimóha*, *s.* (වි and මුහ *muha* to be foolish) seduction, temptation, confounding the mind and exciting the passions.

විමෝහන, *Vimóhana*, *s.* fascinating, seducing, bewitching: see the last.

විමැති, *Vimeti*, corruptly for විමති *vimati*, which see.

විය, *Viya*, *s.* sword, any cutting instrument, weapon in general, from අවිය *aviya*, dropping the initial: past tense of the verb වූ *wú* to be; sickness, disease; yoke; bird in general; lamentation, bewailing: *ind.* as, like; was, has been.

වියකනවා, *Viyakanawá*, *v.* to dissolve, to melt, to liquify; to explain, paraphrase: see the next.

වියකීම, *Viyakíma*, *s.* attrition; melting, dissolving.

වියකෙනවා, *Viyakenawá*, *v.* to wear away, to be destroyed by rubbing or filtering, to be dissolved or melted.

වියගහ, *Viyagaha*, *s.* (විය and ගහ pole) yoke, yoke for oxen.

වියගුරු, *Viyaguru*, *s.* war, battle, [Colloq. යුද්ධය *yuddhaya*].

වියගොන්, *Viyagon*, *s.* (විය yoke, ගොන් oxen) yoke or couple of oxen.

වියච්චාරින්, *Viyachchárín*, *s.* (වියත් *viyat* sky, චාර *chára* who goes, ඉන් *in* aff.) kite.

වියට, *Viyaṭa*, } *s.* (වි paddy, ඇට *ęṭa* grain) grain
වියටේ, *Viyaṭé*, } of paddy.

වියත්, *Viyat*, *s.* paṇḍit, scholar; one who speaks well or distinctly, from ව්‍යක්ත *wyakta;* sky, atmosphere, [Colloq. අහස *ahasa*]; span.

වියත, *Viyata*, *s.* span; orator: pl. වියත් *viyat.*

වියතල, *Viyatala*, *s.* coulter of a plough.

වියතා, *Viyatá*, *s.* scholar, learned or wise man.

වියද් ගඞ්ගා, *Viyat-gańgá*, *s.* (වියද් and ගඞ්ගා river) river of Swarga.

වියදඬු ලබු, *Viyadaṇḍu-labu*, *s.* gourd, *cucurbita lagenaria.*

වියදණ්ඩ, *Viya-daṇḍa*, *s.* (විය yoke, දණ්ඩ pole) yoke, yoke of a plough or bullock cart.

වියදත්, *Viyadat*, *s.* youth, any young person, one arrived at years of discretion.

වියදම්කරණවා, *Viyadamkaraṇawá*, *v.* to expend.

වියදම්වෙනවා, *Viyadamwenawá*, *v.* to be expended.

වියදම, *Viyadama*, *s.* expense; cost, charges, expenditure: pl. වියදම් *viyadam.*

වියන්නා, *Viyanná*, *s.* weaver.

වියන්බඳිනවා, *Viyan-bandinawá*, *v.* to construct an awning of white or coloured cloth on festival occasions.

වියන, *Viyana*, *s.* awning, canopy; spreading, expanding, from විතාන *vitána*, which see.

වියනවා, *Viyanawá*, *v.* to weave, to plait: pret. විව්වා *viwwá.*

වියබාන, *Viyabána*, *s.* (විය yoke, බාන rope) rope that fastens the oxen to the yoke.

වියමන, *Viyamana*, *s.* any thing woven, web, woof; weaving, plaiting: pl. වියමන් *viyaman.*

වියරණ, *Viyaraṇa*, *s.* grammar; Elu form of ව්‍යාකරණ *wyákaraṇa.*

වියරු, *Viyaru*, } *s.* anger, wrath, rage, from
වියරුව, *Viyaruwa*, } වෛර *waira;* change, alteration, from the natural state; insanity, madness; epilepsy; Elu form of විකාර *vikára.*

වියරුවෙනවා, *Viyaruwenawá*, } *v.* to be angry,
වියරුවැටෙනවා, *Viyaruwęṭenawá*, } to be exasperated, to be mad.

වියල්, *Viyal*, *s.* boil, pustule.

වියල, *Viyala*, *s.* tiger; beast of prey; snake; clay prepared for building; frame of a bed or couch; two sticks which keep the outrigger tied to the boat: pl. වියල් *viyal.*

වියලනර, *Viyala-nara*, *s.* old man, [Colloq. නාකියා *nákiyá*].

වියලනවා, *Viyalanawá*, *v.* to dry: pret. වියලුවා *viyaluwá*].

වියලනුව, *Viya-lanuwa*, *s.* (විය yoke, ලනුව rope) the rope that fastens the oxen to the yoke.

වියලා, *Viyalá*, *past. part.* of වියලනවා *viyalanawá.*

වියලි, *Viyali*, *s.* old or emaciated man, [Colloq. මහල්ලා *mahallá*]: *a.* dry, dried.

වියලීම, *Viyalíma*, *s.* drying; drought.

වියලු, *Viyalu*, *s.* old or infirm man: *a.* dry, arid.

වියලුන, *Viyaluna*, *a.* dried, dry.

වියලුම, *Viyaluma*, *s.* drying, verbal noun of වියලනවා *viyalanawá.*

වියලෙනවා, *Viyalenawá*, *v.* to dry, to become arid.

වියවග, *Viyawaga*, *s.* Swarga, divine world in general; name of Káma the Indian Cupid.

වියවනවා, *Viyawanawá*, *v.* to cause to weave, the causal form of වියනවා *viyanawá;* also, to blast, as corn: pret. වියෙව්වා *viyewwá.*

වියවුල්කරණවා, *Viyawulkaraṇawá*, *v.* to confound, to cause a disturbance.

වියවුල්වෙනවා, *Viyawulwenawá*, *v.* to be confused or perplexed, to get into a scrape.

වියවුල, *Viyawula*, *s.* confusion, disorder; perplexity, bewilderment.

වියසිදුරු, *Viyasiduru*, *s.* (විය yoke, සිදුරු perforation) aperture in the yoke through which the rope passes that fastens the oxen.

වියා, *Viyá*, *s.* bird, in general, [Colloq. කුරුල්ලා *kurullá*].

වියාම, *Viyáma*, *s.* fathom, from ව්‍යාම *wyáma.*

වියු, *Viyu*, *s.* saying, speech, talking, [Colloq. කථාව *katháwa*].

වියුක්ත, *Viyukta*, *a.* (වි privative, යුක්ත joined) separated, sundered.

වියෝ, *Viyó*, } *s.* (වි and යෝග union) absence,
වියෝග, *Viyóga*, } separation, especially of lovers; grief arising from the loss of a lover; disunion, disjunction.

වියෝජ, *Viyója*, *s.* separation, disunion, disjunction.

වියෝජිත, *Viyójita*, *s.* separated.

වියෝදුක, *Viyóduka*, *s.* sorrow of separation, but especially the distress of absent lovers.

වියෝව, *Viyówa*, *s.* separation: see වියෝග *viyóga.*

වියෝවග, *Viyówaga*, *s.* name of Káma, the Indian Cupid; Swarga or elysium.

වියෝවගතුර, *Viyówagatura*, *s.* name of Ṣiva.

විර, *Vira*, *s.* plant, *hemicyclia sepiaria (Euphorbiaceæ).*

විරංචි, *Viranchi*, *s.* name of Brahma, also, විරිංච *virincha*, which see,

විරක්ත, *Virakta*, *a.* (වි privation, රක්ත affection) stoical; disgusted, offended, displeased; averse, free from inclination or affection; dejected, sorrowful; impassioned, interested.

විරචිත, *Virachita*, *a.* (වි and රචිත made) made, prepared, effected; written, composed, trimmed, contrived.

විරජස්, *Virajas*, *s.* (වි privative, රජස් menses) woman in whom menstruation has ceased: *a.* free from dust or passion.

විරඤ්ච, *Virañcha*, see විරංචි *viranchi.*

විරත, *Virata*, *a.* (වි and රත stopped) forsaken, abandoned by a lover; stopped, ceased, rested.

විරමණ, *Viramaṇa*, *s.* (වි and රම *rama* to please, or enjoy) abstaining from, aversion, freedom from.

විරල, *Virala*, *a.* (වි apart, රා *rá* to be) fine, delicate, thin, but with interstices; loose, relaxed; apart, wide, separated by an interval; remote, rare.

විරහ, *Viraha*, *s.* (වි and රහ to abandon) separation, parting, absence, especially the separation of lovers; forbearance, cessation, relinquishment.

විරහගින්න, *Viraha-ginna*, *s.* the fire (distress) of separation.

විරහදුක්ඛ, *Viraha-dukkha*, *s.* (විරහ separation, දුක්ඛ sorrow) sorrow occasioned by the absence of friends, but especially the grief of separated lovers.

විරහිත, *Virahita*, *a.* (වි intensitive, රහ *raha* to leave, ක්ත *kta* aff.) left, abandoned, deserted, relinquished; without, free from, exempt, not possessed of.

විරහින්, *Virahín*, *a.* separate, absent or apart from.

විරාග, *Virága*, *s.* (වි privative, රාග passion, desire) absence of desire or passion, indifference, philosophy, disregard of all sensual enjoyment.

විරාජ, *Virája*, *s.* (වි intensitive, රාජ to shine) splendour, beauty, effulgence.

විරාජමාන, *Virájamána*, *a.* (විරාජ splendour, මාන part. aff.) shining, glittering, splendid, irradiant, [Colloq. බබලන *babalana*].

විරාජිත, *Virájita*, *a.* (වි and රාජ *rája* to shine, ක්ත *kta* aff.) splendid, brilliant, gorgeous, [Colloq. දිලියෙන *diliyena*].

විරාටා, *Virátá*, *s.* tree, see තිඹිරි *timbiri.*

විරාම, *Viráma*, *s.* (වි and රම *rama* to stop) end, conclusion; cessation, term; stop, pause; rest from labour.

විරාව, *Viráwa*, *s.* (වි and රු *ru* to sound) sound, noise, [Colloq. අඬ *anda*].

විරි, *Viri*, *a.* thin, fine, delicate.

විරිංච, *Virincha*, විරිංචන, *Virinchana*, විරිංචි, *Virinchi*, } *s.* (වි various, (beings), රච *racha* to make, create) name common to each of the gods of the Hindu triad.

විරික්ත, *Virikta*, *a.* (වි before, රිච *richa* to void by stool and ක්ත *kta* aff.) purged.

විරික්තා, *Viriktá*, *s.* plant, variety of *ilix*, of *polygonum* or of *dimorphocalyx*, [Colloq. වලාවැන්න *waláwenna*].

විරිත, *Virita*, *s.* religious ordinance or observance, from වෘත්ත *writta.*

විරිදු, *Viridu*, *s.* enmity, hostility, from විරුද්ධ *viruddha.*

විරිදුකියනවා, *Viridukiyanawá*, *v.* to recite verses extempore.

විරිදුකීම, *Viridukíma*, *s.* reciting verses extempore, repeating apropos.

විරිය, *Viriya*, *s.* effort, exertion, continued effort; strength, power; valour, intrepidity, from වීර්ය *virya.*

විරී, *Virí*, *a.* thin, fine, delicate, soft, tender.

විරියනවා, *Viríyanawá*, *v.* to melt, to become liquid, to melt as wax.

විරු, *Viru*, *s.* hero, skilful warrior, from වීර *víra*; an expletive derived from පෙර *pera* before, as in නුදුටුවිරු *nudutuviru* not seen before.

විරුණු, *Virunu*, *a.* hot, become hot; liquefied by heat, [Colloq. උණුවුන *unuwuna*].

විරුණුව, *Virunuwa*, *s.* liquefaction by heat; any thing melted or fused, in a state of liquidity.

විරුද්ධ, *Viruddha*, *a.* (වි intensitive, රුධ *rudha* to stop) opposed, hindered; reverse, contrary, opposite; inconsistent; incongruous; hostile, inimical; incompatible.

විරුද්ධකම, *Viruddhakama*, *s.* opposition, resistance.

විරුද්ධකරණවා, *Viruddha-karaṇawá*, *v.* to oppose, to resist.

විරුද්ධකාරයා, *Viruddhakárayá*, *s.* opponent, antagonist.

විරුද්ධවෙනවා, *Viruddha-wenawá*, *v.* to be opposed to.

විරුව, *Viruwa*, *s.* madness, insanity.

විරූඪ, *Virúḍha*, *s.* one of the four Satarawaram deviyó or regents of the cardinal points of the compass, regent of the south and chief of the Kumbháṇḍas.

විරූප, *Virúpa*, *s.* (වි implying variety or privation, රූප form) deformed, monstrous, ugly; incorporeal, immaterial.

විරූපක්ඛ, *Virúpakkha*, Páli form of විරූපාක්ෂ *virúpáksha*.

විරූපතා, *Virúpatá*, *s.* deformity, monstrosity: see විරූප *virúpa*.

විරූපාක්ෂ, *Virúpáksha*, *s.* (වි implying reverse, රූප *rúpa* from අක්ෂ *aksha* eye) name of Ṣiva, alluding to his having three eyes; one of the four waran deviyó or regents of the cardinal points, regent of the west and chief of the Nágas.

විරූළ්හ, *Virúḷha*, *s.* Virúḷha, the regent of the south and king of tke Kumbháṇḍas; Páli form විරූඪ *virúḍha*, which see.

විරේකකරණවා, *Virékakaraṇawá*, *v.* to purge, to give or take a purgative medicine.

විරේකය, *Virékáya*, *s.* (වි and රිච *richa* to purge) opening medicine, purging, evacuation by stool.

විරේචනය, *Viréchanaya*, *s.* (වි and රිච *richa* purge) purging, evacuation.

විරෝචන, *Viróchana*, *s.* (වි intensitive, රුච *rucha* to shine) sun, [Colloq. ඉර *ira*]; moon, [Colloq. හඳ *haṉda*]; fire, [Colloq. ගින්දර *gindara*].

විරෝධ, *Viródha*, *s.* (වි intensitive, රුධ *rudha* to stop) enmity, animosity; restraint, check, constraint, confinement; opposition, contradiction; preventing, hindering; inconsistency; the sixtieth or last year of the Indian cycle.

විරෝධන, *Viródhana*, *s.* opposition, hindering.

විරෝධී, *Viródhí*, *s.* twenty-fourth year of the Indian cycle of sixty.

විල්, *Vil*, *s.* pond, lake; bow, [Colloq. දුන්න *dunna*]; ear; blind man; wrinkle, skin shrivelled by age, from බලි *bali* or වලි *wali*.

විල් කුකුළා, *Vil-kukuḷá*, see විලිකුකුළා *vilikukuḷá*.

විල් කැකිල්ල, *Vil-kękilla*, *s.* plant, *mertensia dichotoma*.

විල්තෙර, *Viltera*, *s.* (විල් lake, තෙර border) bank of a lake.

විල්නකුට *Vil-nakuṭa*, *s.* plant, not ascertained.

විල්නානු, *Vil-nánu*, *s.* plant, not ascertained.

විල්බඩ, *Vilbaḍa*, see විල්තෙර *viltera*.

විල්මුව, *Vilmuwa*, *s.* (විල් wrinkle, මුව countenance) white-faced monkey, variety of *macacus pileatus*, [Colloq. රිළවා *riḷawá*]: see විලිමුව *vilimuwa*.

විල් යක්වනස්ස, *Vil-yakwanassa*, *s.* plant, variety of *anisomeles*.

විල්ල, *Villa*, *s.* border, edge, embossure; ferrule (as of any instrument): pl. විලි *vįli*.

විල් ලිහිණියා, *Vil-lihiṇiyá*, *s.* (විල් pond, ලිහිණියා bird of the falco tribe) species of swift or swallow, bird: see ලිහිණියා *lihiṇiyá*.

විල්ලූද, *Villúda*, *s.* velvet.

විල්ව, *Vilwa*, *s.* fruit, *ægle marmelos*, [Colloq. බෙලි *beli*].

විල් වනස්ස, *Vil-wanassa*, *s.* species of club moss, *lycopodium cernuum*, [Colloq. වනස්ස *wanassa* and බඩල්වනස්ස *baḍal-wanassa*].

විල් වැරණිය, *Vil-węraṇiya*, *s.* shrub, variety of *hedyotis*.

විල්වැර, *Vilwęra*, *s.* shrub, *sida periplocifolia*.

විල් හබරල, *Vil-habarala*, *s.* plant, variety of *alocasia*.

විල් හැඩයා, *Vil-hędayá*, *s.* plant, variety of *lycopodium*.

විල, *Vila*, *s.* hole, chasm, wrinkle, vacuity; pond, marsh, lake overgrown with lotuses; cave, cavern; plant, *bonnaya veronicæfolia (Scrophulariaceæ)*; species of cane, *calamus rotang*.

විලංගජ, *Vilangaja*, *s.* species of aloe wood.

විලංගුව, *Vilanguwa*, *s.* fetter, chain.

විලංඝන, *Vilanghana*, *s.* (වි and ලඝි *laghi* to go, ණ්‍ය *ṇya* aff.) going beyond, transgressing; leaping over; fasting, abstaining from food.

විලක්, *Vilak*, *s.* shame, bashfulness, [Colloq. ලජ්ජාව *lajjáwa*].

විලක්කුව, *Vilakkuwa*, *s.* small torch, firebrand.

විලඳ, *Vilaṉda*, *s.* fried grain, parched corn.

විලඳවැන්න, *Vilaṉdawęnna*, *s.* plant, see විරික්තා *viriktá*.

විලම්බ, *Vilamba*, *s.* (වි and ලබි *labi* to go) falling, hanging down, pendulousness; slowness, tardiness.

විලම්බිත, *Vilambita*, *s.* silliness, foolishness, stupidity: *a.* slow, pendulous, falling.

විලම්බිතකරණවා, *Vilambitakaraṇawá*, *v.* to act foolishly.

විලම්බිතය, *Vilambitaya*, *s.* foolishness, stupidity.

විලම්බි, *Vilambí*, *s.* thirty-second year of the Indian cycle.

විලවුන්, *Vilawun*, *s.* perfume, ointments, unguents for the person; Elu form of විලේපන *vilépana*.

විලස, *Vilasa*, *s.* mode, manner, gait; demeanor, wantoning: see විලාස *vilása.*

විලසි, *Vilasi*, *s.* (වි intensitive, ලස *lasa* to wish) woman, mistress.

විලාප, *Vilápa*, *s.* (වි and ලප *lapa* to speak) lamentation, language of grief and distress.

විලාපකියනවා, *Vilápa-kiyanawá*, *v.* to bewail, to lament, to bemoan.

විලාපය, *Vilápaya*, see its plural form විලාප *vilápa.*

විලාස, *Vilása*, *s.* (වි intensitive, ලස *lasa* to desire) sport, pastime, play, dalliance, wantonness; grace, elegance; likeness, disguise; feminine action, considered as proceeding from and indicative of amorous sentiment, change of gait, look of displeasure, etc.

විලාසකරණවා, *Vilásakaraṇawá*, *v.* to act foolishly, to act awkwardly.

විලාසය, *Vilásaya*, see its plural form විලාස *vilása.*

විලාසිනී, *Vilásini*, *s.* woman; harlot, whore: *a.* wanton, sportive, dallying.

විලි, *Vili*, *s.* shame, modesty, [Colloq. ලජ්ජාව *lajjáwa*]; fruit, bow; wrinkle, from බලි *bali* or වලි *wali;* wild, savage. forest; optionally written වල් *wal*, වලි *wali*, or විල් *vil*, etc.

විලිකුකුළා, *Vilikukuḷá*, *s.* (විලි wild, කුකුළා cock) wild or jungle cock, *gallus lafayetti;* species of pheasant, field fowl: see වැලිකුකුළා *weli-kukuḷá.*

විලිකුන්, *Vilikun*, *a.* ripe, mature, [Colloq. පැසුනු *pesunu*].

විලින්, *Vilin*, *a.* clear, explicit; liquid, liquefied.

විලින, *Vilina*, *a.* mature, ripe; also see the last.

විලිපහරණවා, *Vili-paharaṇawá*, *v.* to travail as in child-birth.

විලිබව, *Vilibawa*, *s.* shame, [Colloq. ලජ්ජාව *lajjáwa*].

විලිඹු, *Vilimbu*, *s.* border, ornamented border of a garment.

විලිමස්, *Vilimas*, *s.* fish, *cyprinus denticulatus.*

විලිමුව, *Vilimuwa*, *s.* (විලි wrinkle, මුව countenance) monkey, white faced monkey: see විල්මුව *vilmuwa*].

විලිය, *Viliya*, *s.* labour of child-birth, travail.

විලිරුජාව, *Vilirujáwa*, *s.* throes of child-bearing.

විලිලනවා, *Vililanawá*, *v.* to travail in child-birth.

විලිස්සනවා, *Vilissanawá*, *v.* to grin, to shew the teeth: pret. විලිස්සුවා *vilissuwá.*

විලිසියානු, *Vilisiyánu*, *s.* excellent gold.

විලී, *Vilí*, *s.* the labcur of child-bearing.

විලීන, *Vilína*, *a.* (වි intensitive, ලී *lí* to melt) liquid, liquefied, semifluid as melted oil or butter; disappeared, perished, hidden, concealed; attached, adhering.

විලු, *Vilu*, *s.* shame, bashfulness, modesty.

විලුම්පන, *Vilumpana*, *s.* (වි intense, ලුප *lupa* to rob) plundering, ravaging.

විලුම්පනයකරණවා, *Vilumpanaya-karaṇawá*, *v.* to plunder, to ravage.

විලේඛන, *Vilékhana*, *s.* (වි before, ලිඛ *likha* to write) digging; dividing, splitting; making marks or furrows.

විලේප, *Vilépa*, } විලේපනය, *Vilépanaya*, } *s.* (වි and ලිප *lipa* to anoint) ointment, unguent, fragrant unguents of sandal or agallochum; mortar, plaster; anointing, plastering.

විලේපනයකරණවා, *Vilépanaya-karaṇawá*, *v.* to anoint.

විලෝකන, *Vilókana*, *s.* (වි and ලෝක *lóka* to see) seeing, perceiving.

විලෝකිත, *Vilókita*, *a.* seen, beheld.

විලෝචන, *Vilóchana*, *s.* (වි and ලෝච *lócha* to see) eye; sight, seeing.

විලෝභ, *Vilóbha*, } විලෝභන, *Vilóbhana*, } *s.* (වි intense, ලුභ *lubha* to delude) allurement, attraction, temptation, seduction.

විලෝභිත, *Vilóbhita*, *a.* allured, deceived.

විලෝම, *Vilóma*, *s.* (වි implying difference, ලෝම hair of the body) reverse, opposite course or order: *a.* reverse, opposite, contrary, backward, against the hair or grain.

විවක්‍ෂා, *Viwakshá*, } විවක්‍ෂාව, *Viwaksháwa*, } *s.* (වච *wacha* to speak, in the desiderative form) wish, desire; wish to speak.

විවක්‍ෂිත, *Viwakshita*, *a.* wished, desired; intended to be spoken or said: see විවක්‍ෂා *viwakshá.*

විවජ්ජිත, *Viwajjita*, Páli form of විවර්ජිත *viwarjita*, which see.

විවට්ට, *Viwaṭṭa*, *s.* (වි privative, වට්ට being, existence) Nirwáṇa, emancipation from existence, annihilation; destruction or end of a kalpa; destruction, end in general; Páli form of විවර්ත *viwarta.*

විවර්ජිකා, *Viwarjiká*, *s.* cutaneous eruption, scab.

විවර්ජිත, *Viwarjita*, *a.* sent, dismissed, dispatched; abandoned.

විවර්ණ, *Viwarṇa*, *s.* (වි privative or implying change, වර්ණ caste, colour) man of low caste, one of degraded race or occupation: *a.* low, colourless, sallow, pale; discoloured, changed in colour; ugly, deformed, uncomely.

විවර්ත, *Viwarta*, *s.* (වි before, වෘත *wṛita* to be, ක්ත *kta* aff.) assemblage, collection, heap or multitude; going or turning round; human error, worldly ignorance, the confounding of truth and falsehood, or the mistaking of unreal objects and taking them for what they are not, as mirage for water, a rope for a snake, etc.

විවර්තන, *Viwartana*, *s.* going round, circumambulating an altar or object of worship; revolving, going round.

විවර, *Viwara*, *s.* hole, chasm, vacuity; perforation; fault, defect, flaw; split, splitting.

විවරණ, *Viwaraṇa*, *s.* (වි and වෘ *wṛi* to select, meaning) gloss, comment, explanation, exposition; interpretation, translation; permission, leave; uncovering, laying bare or open; promise or assurance of becoming Buddha.

විවරය, *Vivaraya*, *s.* vacuity, fissure, a crevice, opening: see විවර *viwara*.

විවස්, *Viwas*, *a.* manifest, evident, apparent; clear, plain, explicit; Elu form of විකාශ *vikáṣa*.

විවස්වත්, *Viwaswat*, විවස්වාන්, *Viwaswán*, *s.* (වි and වස *wasa* to cover, මතුප් *matup* poss. aff.) a god, sun.

විවශ, *Viwasa*, .*a* (වි privative, වශ wish) apprehensive of death, unwilling, thought about death; also, sedate, calm, collected, having the soul free from worldly cares and fears at the time of death.

විවා, *Viwá*, *s.* marriage.

විවාද, *Viwáda*, *s.* (වි intensitive, වද *wada* to speak) contest, contention; contest at law, litigation, contradiction.

විවාදකරණවා, *Viwádakaraṇawá*, *v.* to dispute, to contest.

විවාහ, *Viwáha*, see විවාහය *viwáhaya*.

විවාහබස්දෙනවා, *Viwáha-basdenawá*, *v.* to betroth.

විවාහබස, *Viwáha-basa*, *s.* (විවාහ marriage, බස speech) betrothing, promise or agreement of marriage: pl. විවාහබස් *viwáhabas*.

විවාහය, *Viwáhaya*, *s.* (වි before, වහ *waha* to carry) marriage, matrimony.

විවික්ත, *Vivikta*, *a.* (වි completely, විච *vicha* to be or make separate) lonely, alone, solitary, desert; separated, distinguished, disjoined, detached; discriminative, judicious; discriminated, judged.

විවික්තාසන, *Viviktásana*, *s.* (විවික්ත *vivikta* lonely, ආසන *ásana* seat) residing in solitude for the purposes of devout abstract meditation.

විවිත්ත, *Vivitta*, *a.* (වි intensitive, විත්ත broad) extended, spacious.

විවිධ, *Viridha*, *a.* (වි implying variety, විධ sort) various, multiform, of many sorts.

විවිධාකාරය, *Vividhákáraya*, *s.* diversified manner.

විවුම, *Viwuma*, *s.* weaving, plaiting; verbal noun of වියනවා *viyanawá*.

විවේක, *Viwéka*, *s.* (වි intensely or severally, විච *vicha* to judge) discrimination, judgment, faculty of distinguishing things by their properties and classifying them according to their real not apparent nature; separating truth from untruth, reality from illusion, discussion, investigation; leisure: *a.* solitary, lonely, alone; unemployed.

විවේකජ, *Viwékaja*, *s.* (විවේක discrimination, ජ born) conclusion, result of investigation.

විවේකාභිරත, *Viwékábhirata*, *s.* විවේක *viwéka* solitude, අභිරත *abhirata* ardent wish) asceticism, life or state of an anchorite; earnestly desiring to live a life of solitude.

විවෘක්තා, *Viwṛiktá*, *s.* (වි intensitive, වෘච *wṛicha* to abandon) woman disliked or deserted by her husband.

විවෘත, *Viwṛita*, *a.* (වි intensitive or privative, වෘ to be, ක්ත *kta* aff.) expanded, extended, extensive, large; evident, displayed, made manifest.

විවෘතවෙනවා, *Viwṛitawenawá*, *v.* to expand, to be opened.

විවෘතා, *Viwṛitá*, *s.* disease, ulcer attended with much pain and heat.

විවෘති, *Viwṛiti*, *s.* (වි severally, වෘ to select) explanation, exposition, gloss, comment, interpretation, making clear or manifest.

විවෘද්ධ, *Viwṛiddha*, *s.* tree, *calophyllum spectabile*, [Colloq. කීන දොඹ *kína-domba*].

විවෘද්ධි, *Viwṛiddhi*, *s.* growth, increase, augmentation.

විශ්‍රගන්ධා, *Viṣragandhá*, *s.* plant, *sphæranthus indicus* or *s. hirtus*, [Colloq. මුඩමහණ *mudamahaṇa*].

විශ්‍රබ්ධ, *Viṣrabdha*, see විස්‍රබ්ධ *visrabdha*.

විශ්‍රම්භ, *Viṣrambha*, *s.* (වි and ස්‍රම්භ *srambha* to trust) trust, confidence; affection, regard.

විශ්‍රම, *Viṣrama*, *s.* (වි privative, ශ්‍රම to be weary) rest, repose, cessation from work or labour.

විශ්‍රා, *Viṣrá*, *s.* plant, *sphæranthus indicus* or *s. hirtus*, [Colloq. මුඩමහණ *mudamahaṇa*].

විශ්‍රාන්ති, *Viṣránti*, } *s.* (වි privative, ශ්‍රම *ṣrama* to
විශ්‍රාම, *Viṣráma*, } be wearied) rest, repose, pause, cessation from labour.

විශ්‍රාමගන්නවා, *Viṣrámagannawá*, *v.* to take rest.

විශ්‍රුත, *Viṣruta*, *a.* famous, celebrated; dropped.

විශ්‍රුති, *Viṣruti*, *s.* fame, celebrity; oozing.

විශ්ව, *Viṣwa*, *s.* world, universe; dry ginger; long pepper, [Colloq. තිප්පිලි *tippili*]; class of gods so called; the thirty-eight year of the Hindu cycle of sixty: *a.* all, whole, entire, universal.

විශ්වකර්ම, *Viṣwakarma*, *s.* (විශ්ව universal, කර්ම act, action) son of Brahma, and artist of the gods; the sun.

විශ්වගන්ධා, *Viṣwagandhá*, *s.* (විශ්ව all, ගන්ධ *gandha* fragrance) the earth, [Colloq. පොළව *polawa*]; plant, species of the *ocimum*, [Colloq. අඳුතලා *andutalá*].

විශ්වදේව, *Viṣwadéwa*, *s.* (විශ්ව all, දිව *diwa* to sport) deity of a certain class, of whom ten are enumerated, and are worshipped by the Hindus at funeral obsequies.

විශ්වදේවා, *Viṣwadéwá*, *s.* plant, *grewia lævigata*, [Colloq. ගස්කැලිය *gas-kéliya*].

විශ්වධාරිණී, *Viṣwadhárini*, *s.* (විශ්ව all, ධාරිණී what upholds) the earth, [Colloquial: පොළව *polawa*].

විශ්වභේෂජ, *Viṣwa-bhéshaja*, *s.* (විශ්ව all, diseases, භේෂජ medicament) dry ginger, [Colloq. වෙලිච්ච ඉඟුරු *wélichcha-inguru*].

විශ්වම්භර, *Viṣwambhara*, *s.* (විශ්ව all things, භෘ *bhṛi* to support or nourish) name of Vishṇu, also of Indra.

විශ්වම්භරා, *Viṣwambhará*, *s.* the earth: see the last.

විශ්වරූප, *Viṣwarúpa*, *s.* (විශ්ව all, රූප form) name of Vishṇu; agallochum: *a.* taking all forms, universal, omnipresent.

විශ්වසෘග්, *Viṣwasrig*, } *s.* (විශ්ව all, the universe,
විශ්වසෘජ්, *Viṣwasṛij*, } සෘජ *sṛija* to create) name of Brahma.

විශ්වා, *Viṣwá*, *s.* tree, *lagenandra lancifolia*, [Coll: අතිවිඩයන් *atividayan*].

විශ්වාස, *Viṣwása*, *s.* (වි and ශ්වස *ṣwasa* to breathe or live) trust, faith, confidence, belief.

විශ්වාසකම, *Viṣwásakama*, *s.* confidence, friendship.

විශ්වාසකරණවා, *Viṣwásakaraṇawá*, *v.* to confide, to believe, to trust.

විශ්වාසය, *Viṣwásaya*, see විශ්වාස *viṣwása*.

විශ්වාසයා, *Viṣwásayá*, *s.* (විශ්වාස confidence, යා pers. aff.) friend, companion, associate, confidant.

විශ්වාසී, *Viṣwási*, *a.* trusting; honest, trusty.

විශ, *Viṣa*, *s.* (විශ to enter) film or fibres of the stalk of the water lily, optionally written විස *visa*.

විශද, *Viṣada*, *s.* white, the colour: *a.* white; clear, pellucid, pure.

විශය, *Viṣaya*, *s.* doubt, uncertainty; refuge, asylum.

විශර, *Viṣara*, *s.* (වි and ශෘ *ṣri* to injure or kill) killing, slaying, slaughter.

විශල්‍යකා, *Viṣalyaká*, *s.* plant, *cæsalpinia bonduc*, [Colloq. කුඹුරුවැල් *kumburuwel*].

විශල්‍යා, *Viṣalyá*, *s.* plant, *tinospora cordifolia*, [Colloq. රසකිඳ *rasakinda*]; sort of cucumber, species of *cucumis*, [Colloq. තියඹරා *tiyambará*]; medicinal plant, commonly called *Danti*, [Coll: දැත්ත *detta*]; another, commonly *Teori*, [Colloq. ත්‍රස්තවාලු *trastawálu*].

විශසන, *Viṣasana*, *s.* (වි and ශස *ṣasa* to hurt) killing, slaying, slaughter; sabre, crooked sword.

විශාඛා, *Viṣákhá*, see විසාඛ *visákha*.

විශාරද, *Viṣárada*, see විසාරද *visárada*.

විශාල, *Viṣála*, see විසාල *visála*.

විශිඛ, *Viṣikha*, see විසිඛ *visikha*.

විශිෂ්ට, *Viṣishṭa*, *a.* (වි intensive, ශිෂ *ṣisha* to assign qualities) endowed with, possessed of, having, inherent, or attached to; distinguished, excellent, special, peculiar.

විශුද්ධ, *Viṣuddha*, *a.* (වි intensive, ශුද්ධ pure) very pure, holy, correct.

විශුද්ධි, *Viṣuddhi*, *s.* purity, removal of doubt, correctness.

විශුෂ්ක, *Viṣushka*, *a.* exceedingly dry, parched, arid.

විශේෂ්‍ය, *Viṣéshya*, *s.* object of a predicate: *a.* principal, primary.

විශේෂ, *Viṣésha*, *s.* (වි implying discrimination, ශිෂ *ṣisha* to attribute or distinguish by attributes) sort, kind, manner; difference, individual or specific identity and consequent distinction from every other individual or species; limb, member; figure of rhetoric implying variety of means of effect; in logic, the peculiar attribute; an attribute; predicate.

විශේෂණ, *Viṣéshaṇa*, *s.* adjective, attribute, epithet: *a.* discriminative, attributive, distinguishing, characteristic.

විශේෂ ලක්ෂණ, *Viśésha-lakshaṇa*, s. specific or characteristic mark or sign.

විශේෂ විධි, *Viśésha-vidhi*, s. special rule or observance.

විශෝධන, *Viśódhana*, s. purifying, freeing from defect or sin.

විශෝධිත, *Viśódhita*, a. purified, corrected, cleaned.

විෂ්කම්භ, *Vishkambha*, s. (වි and ෂ්කභි *shkabhi* to stop or hinder) first of the twenty-seven astronomical periods called Yógas; obstacle, hindrance, impediment; bolt or bar of a door; diameter of a circle.

විෂ්කම්භිත, *Vishkambhita*, a. hindered, stopped, obstructed, opposed.

විෂ්කිර, *Vishkira*, s. (වි and කිර *kira* to scatter) bird in general, [Colloq. කුරුල්ලා *kurullá*]; pulling or tearing to pieces.

විෂ්ට, *Vishṭa*, s. (විෂ *visha* to pervade) fæces, excrement: a. entered, penetrated, pervaded.

විෂ්ටම්භ, *Vishṭambha*, s. (වි and ස්තභි *stabhi* to hinder) impediment, hindrance, obstacle; disease, obstruction of urine or fæces, ischury, constipation; paralysis.

විෂ්ටර, *Vishṭara*, s. tree; seat, stool, chair, couch.

විෂ්ටරශවළි, *Vishṭaraṣawaḷi*, } s. (විෂ්ටර and ශ්‍රු
විෂ්ටරශ්‍රවස්, *Vishṭaraṣrawas*, } *ṣru* to hear) name of Kṛishṇa or Vishṇu.

විෂ්ටි, *Vishṭi*, s. seventh of the variable karaṇas or astrological periods so termed, each answering to half a lunar day; hire, wages; sending, dispatching; consigning to torture, casting into hell.

විෂ්ටිරාජ, *Vishṭi-rája*, s. (විෂ්ටි torments of hell, රාජ sovereign) name of Yama, the judge of the final destinies of men.

විෂ්ඨා, *Vishthá*, s. fæces, ordure.

විෂ්ණු, *Vishṇu*, s. (විශ *viṣa* to enter or pervade, the universe) one of the three principal Hindu deities, and the preserver of the world; during the periods of temporary annihilation he is supposed to sleep on the waters, floating on the serpent Ṣésha; Brahmá is fabled to have sprung from a lotus, which grew from the navel of Vishṇu, and the holy river Ganges is said to spring from his foot; the different awatárs are considered as emanations of this deity, and in Kṛishṇa he is supposed to have been really and wholly incarnate; he is usually represented as a mild and benevolent deity.

විෂ්ණුක්‍රාන්තා, *Vishṇukrántá*, s. (විෂ්ණු Vishṇu, ක්‍රාන්ත *kránta* overcome) small flowering plant, *evolvulus alsinoides (Convolvulaceæ)*, which is prized as sacred to the deity.

විෂ්ණුපද, *Vishṇu-pada*, s. (විෂ්ණු and පද foot or abode) sky, heaven, atmosphere, [Colloq. අහස *ahasa*]; sea of milk; lotus.

විෂ්ණුපදී, *Vishṇu-padí*, s. one of the twelve Sankrántis or periods at which the sun enters a sign of the zodiac; Ganges.

විෂ්ණුරථ, *Vishṇu-ratha*, s. (විෂ්ණු and රථ cár or vehicle) Garuḍa, the bird and vehicle of Vishṇu.

විෂ්ණුවල්ලභා, *Vishṇu-wallabhá*, s. (විෂ්ණු and වල්ලභ *wallabha* beloved) twining shrub, *echites caryophyllata;* small fragrant shrub, holy basil, *ocimum sanctum*, [Colloq. මදුරුතලා *maduru-talá*]; plant, *evolvulus alsinoides*, [Colloq. විෂ්ණුක්‍රාන්තා *vishṇukrántá*].

විෂ්ණුවාහන, *Vishṇuwáhana*, s. Garuḍa, bird and vehicle of Vishṇu.

විෂ්ණුශයන, *Vishṇu-ṣayana*, s. milky fig tree, *ficus altissima*, var. *laccifera*, [Colloq. නුග *nuga*].

විෂ්ඵාර, *Vishphára*, s. (වි intensitive, ස්ඵර *sphara* to expand) twang of a bow.

විෂ්වක්සේනප්‍රියා, *Vishwaksénapriyá*, s. sort of yam, *dioscorea*, [Colloq. ඌරල *úrala*].

විෂ්වක්සේනා, *Vishwaksénú*, s. tree, *myristica horsfieldia*, [Colloq. පුවඟු *puwaṇgu*].

විෂ, *Visha*, s. (විෂ to pervade) poison, venom; water; fibres attached to the stalk of the lotus; gum myrrh.

විෂකහ, *Visha-kaha*, s. plant, not ascertained.

විෂගන්ධිනී, *Visha-gandhiní*, s. medicinal drug, *lagenandra lancifolia*, [Colloq. අතිවිඩයන් *ati-viḍayan*].

විෂඝ්න, *Vishaghna*, s. (විෂ poison, ඝ්න what destroys) antidote; tree, *mimossa sirisa;* plant, *hedysarum alhaji;* beleric myrobalan, *terminalia belerica*, [Colloq. බුළු *buḷu*]; tamarind tree, *tamarindus indica*, [Colloq. සියඹලා *siyambalá*];

විෂඝ්නී, *Visaghní*, s. pot herb, *hingtsha repens;* turmeric, *curcuma longa*, [Colloq. කහ *kaha*]; bitter apple or colocynth, *citrullus colocynthis*, [Colloq. යක්කොමඩු *yak-komaḍu*].

විෂඝෝර, *Vishaghóra*, a. (විෂ venom, ඝෝර fearful) possessed of deadly venom; exceedingly poisonous.

විෂද, *Vishada*, s. (විෂ and ද to give) green vitriol, [Colloq. පල්මාණික්කං *palmáṇikkaṇ*].

විෂදන්තක, *Vishadantaka*, *s.* (විෂ and දන්ත tooth, ක aff.) snake.

විෂදාහ, *Vishadáha*, *s.* (විෂ and දාහ burning, consuming) fever attending the bite of a snake.

විෂදූෂණී, *Vishadúshaṇí*, see මුඩමහණ *muḍamahaṇa*.

විෂධර්මා, *Vishadharmá*, *s.* plant, cowach, *carpopogon pruriens*, [Colloq. වඳුරුමෑ *waṉdurumẹ*].

විෂධර, *Vishadhara*, *s.* (විෂ poison, ධර what has) snake: *a.* venomous, poisonous.

විෂධූම, *Vishadhúma*, *s.* (විෂ and ධූම smoke) foam that issues from the mouth of the boa constrictor or of any large snake when in the act of hissing, and which is considered poisonous.

විෂනාශන, *Vishanáṣana*, *s.* (විෂ poison, නාශන destroying) tree, *mimosa sirisa*: see විෂඝ්න *vishaghna*.

විෂපුෂ්ප, *Vishapushpa*, *s.* (විෂ and පුෂ්ප flower) plant, *vangueria spinosa*; blue lotus, *nymphæa stellata*, [Colloq. මානෙල් *mánel*].

විෂපුෂ්පක, *Vishapushpaka*, *s.* thorny shrub, *randia dumatorum*, [Colloq. කුකුරුමුවං *kukurumuwaṉ*].

විෂම, *Vishama*, *s.* (වි privative, සම *sama* smooth, equal) difficulty, pain; unevenness, inequality; oddness, in numeration; an inaccessible place, thicket, precipice: *a.* difficult, painful; troublesome, rough, uneven; odd.

විෂමච්ඡද, *Vishamachchhada*, *s.* (විෂම uneven, odd, ච්ඡද bark or leaf) plant, *alstonia scholaris*, the name alludes to the roughness of its bark, or to its having seven leaves on a stalk, [Colloq. රුක් අත්තන *ruk-attana*].

විෂමජ්වර, *Vishamajwara*, *s.* irregularly intermittent fever.

විෂමත්‍රිභුජ, *Vishama-tribhuja*, *s.* (විෂම unequal, ත්‍රිභුජ triangle) scalene triangle.

විෂමදෝෂක, *Vishama-dóshaka*, *s.* sick person.

විෂමන්ත්‍ර, *Visha-mantra*, *s.* (විෂ poison, මන්ත්‍ර charm) snake catcher, one who by pretended charms, etc. attracts snakes and cures their bite.

විෂමාක්ෂ, *Vishamáksha*, *s.* (විෂම *vishama* odd, අක්ෂ eye) name of Ṣiva, alluding to the eye in his forehead.

විෂමායුධ, *Vishamáyudha*, *s.* (විෂම *vishama* and ආයුධ *áyudha* weapon) name of Káma the Indian Cupid, who is armed with five arrows.

විෂමුෂ්ටි, *Vishamushṭi*, *s.* (විෂ poison, මුෂ්ටි handful) kind of shrub or medicinal plant, [Colloq. රේරු ගස් *réru-gas*].

විෂමේක්ෂණ, *Vishamékshaṇa*, *s.* (විෂම *vishama* and ඊක්ෂණ *íkshaṇa* eye) Ṣiva.

විෂමේෂු, *Vishaméshu*, *s.* (විෂම *vishama* and ඉෂු *ishu* arrow) arrow, [Colloq. ඊගහ *ígaha*].

විෂමැරුම, *Visha-mẹruma*, *s.* (විෂ and මැරුම killing) destroying or counteracting the effects of poison, an antidote.

විෂය, *Vishaya*, *s.* any object of sense, any thing perceivable by the senses, as colour, form, flavour, odour, and sound; object in general, as of affection, desire, etc.; refuge, asylum; department, sphere, province, element, home; country whether inhabited or uninhabited.

විෂවිද්‍යා, *Vishavidyá*, *s.* administration of antidotes.

විෂ විනාශනී, *Visha-vináṣaní*, *s.* bowstring hemp, *sanseviera zeylanica*, [Colloq. නියඳ *niyaṉda*].

විෂවේග, *Vishawéga*, *s.* absorption of venom, as shewn by some bodily effects or changes.

විෂවෛද්‍ය, *Visha-waidya*, *s.* (විෂ poison, වෛද්‍ය physician) dealer in antidotes, one professing by charms, etc. to cure the bite of a snake.

විෂහර, *Vishahara*, *s.* (විෂ and හර to take away) antidote, removing poison.

විෂාණ, *Visháṇa*, *s.* (වි before, අස *asa* to be) horn of an animal; tusk of an elephant; tusk or fang of the boar; plant, *costus speciosus*, [Colloq. තෙබු *tebu*]; the city of Wesamuṇi.

විෂාණී, *Visháṇi*, *s.* (විෂාණ *visháṇa* horn, ඉන් *in* aff.) any animal with horns, or tusks, as a bull, elephant.

විෂාණික, *Visháṇika*, *s.* plant, species of *cassia*, [Colloq. තෝර *tóra*].

විෂාණිකා, *Visháṇiká*, *s.* creeping plant, *dæmia extensa*, [Colloq. මැඩහඟු *mẹdahaṉgu*].

විෂාණී, *Visháṇí*, *s.* plant, the fruit of which is compared to the horn of a ram, etc. commonly මේෂශෘංගී *méshaṣriṅgi*, [Colloq. මැඩහඟු *mẹdahaṉgu*].

විෂාපහා, *Vishápahá*, *s.* (විෂ *visha* poison, අපහා *apahá* removing) kind of birth wort, which is considered as an antidote, *aristolochia indica*, [Colloq. සප්සඳ *sapsaṉda*]; plant producing the durian fruit, *durio zibethinus* [Colloq. කටරොළු *kaṭaroḷu*]; another plant, *citrullus colocynthis*, [Colloq. තිත්තලබු *titta-labu*]

විෂාරී, *Vishárí*, *s.* plant, species of *doona*, [Colloq. දියබෙරලිය *diya-beraliya*].

විෂුව, *Vishuwa*,
විෂුවත්, *Vishuwat*, } *s.* (විෂු equally, මතුප් *matup* poss. aff.) equinox.

විස්කෝත්තු, *Viskóttu*, *s.* biscuit. (Port.)

විස්තර, *Vistara*, *a.* (වි intensitive, ස්තෘ *stṛi* to extend, to diffuse) prolixity; spreading, expansion; affection, affectionate solicitation; number, assemblage; seat, stool; comment, explanation.

විස්තරකරණවා, *Vistarakaraṇawá*, *v.* to explain, to comment.

විස්තාර, *Vistára*, *s.* spreading, extension, diffusion; branch of a tree with its new shoots.

විස්තීර්ණ, *Vistírṇa*, *a.* (වි and ස්තෘ *stṛi* to cover or spread) large, great; spread, expanded.

විස්තීර්ණපර්ණ, *Vistírṇa-parṇa*, *s.* (විස්තීර්ණ large, පර්ණ leaf) esculent root, *arum indicum.*

විස්ඵුලිඞ්ග, *Visphuliṅga*, *s.* (වි and ස්ඵුර් imitative sound, ලිඞ්ග to go) spark of fire.

විස්ඵෝට, *Visphoṭa*, *s.* (වි and ස්ඵුට *sphuṭa* to hurt or break) boil, pustule; small pox, [Colloq. වසූරිය *wasúriya*].

විස්ම, *Visma*, corruptly for විස්මය *vihmaya.*

විස්මකර්ම, *Vismakarma*, corruptly for විශ්වකර්ම *viṣwakarma.*

විස්මපත්, *Vismapat*, *a.* (විස්ම and පත් come, arirved) amazed, astonished, surprized.

විස්මපත්වෙනවා, *Vismapatwenawá*, *v.* to wonder, to be surprised.

විස්මය, *Vismaya*, *s.* wonder, surprize, astonishment.

විස්මයාකුල, *Vismayákula*, *a.* (විස්මය *vismaya* and ආකුල *ákula* perplexed) bewildered, astounded.

විස්මයාන්විත, *Vismayánvita*, *a.* (විස්මය *vismaya* and අන්විත *anvita* affected with) astonished, surprised.

විස්මෘති, *Vismṛiti*, *s.* (වි privative, ස්මෘති recollection) forgetting, forgetfulness.

විස්‍රබ්ධ, *Visrabdha*, *a.* (වි and ස්‍රංභ *sranbha* to trust) trusted, confided; placid, tamed, humble; steady, diligent.

විස්‍රම්භ, *Visrambha*, *s.* (වි and ස්‍රංභ *sranbha* to trust) trust, confidence; affection, regard, affectionate solicitation; acquaintance.

විසෘත, *Visṛita*, *a.* (වි before, සෘ *sṛi* to go) spread, expanded, extended.

විස්වස්, *Viswas*, *s.* trust, confidence, from විශ්වාස *viswáṣa.*

විස්ස, *Vissa*, *ind.* twenty.

විස්සම්, *Vissam*, *s.* name of විශ්වකර්ම *viṣwakarma*, architect of the gods.

විස්සල්, *Vissal*, *adv.* always, ever; quickly.

විස්සහ, *Vissaha*, *s.* trust, confidence, from විශ්වාස *viṣwása.*

විස, *Visa*, *s.* (විශ *viṣa* to pervade) poison, venom: see විෂ *visha;* film or fibres of the stalk of the water lily.

විසකලාව, *Visa-kaláwa*, *s.* (විස and කලා *kalá* digit) space which the vital air is supposed to ascend or descend daily, completing a revolution through the body during a lunation.

විසකුණු, *Visakuṇu*, *s.* publishing, spreading abroad, making known; paṇdit, learned man, from විචක්ෂණ *vichakshaṇa.*

විසකුරු, *Visakuru*, *a.* poisonous, venomous.

විසගහනවා, *Visagahanawá*, *v.* to smart with pain from poisonous bites.

විසඝෝර, *Visagóra*, corruptly for විෂඝෝර *visha-ghóra*, which see.

විසඝ්න, *Visaghna*, see විෂඝ්න *vishaghna.*

විසඝ්නබීජ, *Visaghna-bíja*, *s.* bitter apple or colocynth, *citrullus colocynthis*, [Colloq. යක් කොමඩු *yak-komaḍu*].

විසජ, *Visaja*, *s.* (විස fibres of a lotus, ජ produced) lotus, *nymphœa lotus.*

විසදර, *Visadara*, *s.* (විස poison, දර what has) snake in general.

විසදුරා, *Visadurá*, *s.* (විස and ඇදුරා *ẹdúrá* teacher) curer of snake bites.

විසදූලි, *Visadúli*, *s.* (විස and දූලි pollen) parasitic poisonous plant, peculiar to Ceylon, *cymbidium bicolor (Orchideœ).*

විසඳන්නා, *Visaṉdanná*, *s.* expounder, illustrator.

විසඳනවා, *Visaṉdanawá*, *v.* to reply to a query, to explain a subject under investigation: pret. විසඳුවා *visaṉduwá.*

විසඳා, *Visaṉdá*, *past. part.* of විසඳනවා *visaṉdanawá.*

විසඳීම, *Visaṉdíma*, *s.* explaining, illustrating.

විසඳු, *Visaṉdu*, *past. part. pass.* of විසඳනවා *visaṉdanawá*, explained.

විසප්පුව, *Visappuwa*, *s.* pustule, boil.

විසප්‍රසූන, *Visa-prasúna*, *s.* (විස and ප්‍රසූන flower) lotus, *nelumbium speciosum*, [Colloq. නෙළුම් *neḷum*].

විසභාග, *Visabhága*, *s.* (වි privative or emphatic, සභාග association) separatist, one who lives apart from the world; collection, assemblage.

විසඹ, *Visaṃba*, *s.* trust, confidence; wickedness, injustice: *a.* wicked.

විසඹයා, *Visaṃbayá*, *s.* wicked man, one totally depraved.

විසඹවිම, *Visambavíma*, *s.* malice, deadly hatred, wickedness, depravity, vice.

විසඹි, *Visambí*, *s.* wicked woman.

විසම, *Visama*, *a.* (වි privative, සම even) uneven, rough; difficult of access, etc; irregular, unequal; odd; wicked, mischievous.

විසමච්ඡද, *Visamachchhada*, see විෂමච්ඡද *vishamachchhada.*

විසමජ්වර, *Visamajwara*, *s.* (විසම irregular, ජ්වර fever) irregularly, intermittent fever.

විසමදල, *Visamadala*, *s.* (විසම odd, දල leaf) tree, *alstonia scholaris*: see විෂමච්ඡද *vishamachchhada.*

විසමරණවා, *Visamaraṇawá*, *v.* (විස poison, මරණවා to kill) to counteract or neutralize poison.

විසමරූප, *Visama-rúpa*, *s.* (විසම irregular, රූප form) deformity, ugliness.

විසමැඩියා, *Visameḍiyá*, *s.* (විස venomous, මැඩි *medi* frog) toad.

විසය, *Visaya*, *s.* home, province: see විෂය *vishaya.*

විසර්ග, *Visarga*, *s.* (වි before, සෘජ *sriga* to go) abandoning, relinquishment; evacuation of excrement, voiding by stool; soft aspirate or visarga, marked by two perpendicular dots, ඃ *ḥ*.

විසර්ජන, *Visarjana*, *s.* gift; quitting; sending; dismissing.

විසර්ජනයකරණවා, *Visarjaṇaya-karaṇawá*, *v.* to comment, to explain.

විසර්ප, *Visarpa*, *s.* boil, pustule, any inflamed swelling on the skin: see විසප්පුව *visappúwa.*

විසර්පඝ්න, *Visarpahgna*, *s.* (විසර්ප and ඝ්න what destroys) bees' wax.

විසර, *Visara*, *s.* (වි and සෘ *sri* to go) opening, expanding, extending; multitude, an assemblage; flock, herd.

විසල්, *Visal*, *a.* great, large; wide, extended, extensive, from විසාල *visála.*

විසල් කොක, *Visal-koka*, *s.* tree, *echites scholaris*, [Colloq. රුක්අත්තන *ruk-attana*].

විසවිනාසන, *Visa-vinásana*, see විෂඝ්න *vishaghna.*

විසා, *Visá*, *s.* vegetable poison, commonly wachchanávi: see වත්සනාභ *watsanábha;* also see විෂය *vishaya* and විසාඛා *visákhá.*

විසාඛා, *Visákhá*, *s.* sixteenth lunar asterism, figured by a festoon and containing four or, according to some, two stars, one of which is α or κ Libræ; cucurbitaceous plant, *momordica charantia*, [Colloq. කරිවිල *karivila*]

විසාද, *Visáda*, *s.* lassitude, dejection, lowness of spirits, want of energy; disappointment; distress, affliction.

විසාණ, *Visáṇa*, see විෂාණ *visháṇa.*

විසාන, *Visána*, *s.* city of Kuwéra, god of wealth.

විසානි, *Visáni*, *s.* creeping plant, the fruit of which is said to resemble the horn of a ram, *gomphocarpus rolubilis:* see also විෂාණ *visháṇa.*

විසානැකත, *Visá-nekata*, see විසාඛා *visákhá.*

විසාර, *Visára*, *s.* (වි implying excellence, සර *sara* to go) snake; fish; going smoothly, creeping, gliding; wood, timber.

විසාරද, *Visárada*, *a.* famous celebrated; learned, wise, clever; confident, bold, presuming.

විසාරණ, *Visáraṇa*, *s.* killing, slaughter.

විසාරී, *Visárí*, *s.* region of the winds.

විසාල, *Visála*, *a.* broad, wide, extended; spacious, great, large.

විසාලත්වක්, *Visálatwak*, *s.* tree, *alstonia scholaris*, [Colloq. රුක් අත්තන *ruk-attana*].

විසාලතා, *Visálatá*, *s.* (විසාල broad, තා *tá* affix of the abstract) breadth, expansion.

විසාලා, *Visálá*, *s.* city Oujein; colocynth or bitter apple, *citrullus colocynthis*, [Colloq. යක්කොමඩු *yak-komadu*].

විසි, *Visi*, *s.* word, dictum; speech; body; number twenty; subjection, submission; street; dwelling; changing any one to our interest.

විසිඑක, *Visi-eka*, *s.* twenty-one.

විසිකිස්, *Visikis*, *s.* doubt.

විසිකුල, *Visikula*, *s.* the husbandry caste.

විසිඛ, *Visikha*, *s.* arrow, [Colloq. ඊගහ *ígaha*].

විසිඛා, *Visikhá*, *s.* road; spade, hoe; very minute arrow, sort of needle.

විසිතුරු, *Visituru*, *a.* particolored, variegated in colour; various; curious.

විසින්, *Visin*, *prep.* by, through; an affix to nouns, and the sign of the third or *instrumental* case in grammar.

විසිනි, *Visiní*, *s.* assemblage of lotus flowers.

විසිර, *Visira*, see විසිරී *visirí.*

විසිරයනවා, *Visirayanawá*, *v.* to be spread, to become diffused.

විසිරයාම, *Visirayáma*, *s.* going abroad, spreading about, the act of being scattered, diffusion.

විසිරී, *Visirí*, *part.* of විසිරෙණවා *visireṇawá*; also; *s.* fan, to be scattered.

විසිරෙණවා, *Visireṇawá*, *v.* to be scattered, to be spread or extended: pret. විසිරුණ *visiruṇá.*

විසිම, *Visíma*, *s.* dwelling, residing, continuing in a place.

විසු, *Visu*, *s.* speech, saying.

විසුද්ධ, *Visuddha*, *a.* clean, pure, purified, exceedingly clear; pious, virtuous.

විසුද්ධලවණ, *Visuddha-lawaṇa*, *s.* very white or purified salt.

විසුද්ධිමාර්ගය, *Visuddhi-márgaya*, *s.* "Path of holiness," a book so called, written by Buddhaghósa on the doctrines of B

විසුද්ධිය, *Visuddhiya*, *s.* purity, cleanness, purification; removal of doubt.

විසුදු, *Visudu*, *s.* purity, inward purity, holiness, from විසුද්ධිය *visuddhiya.*

විසුම, *Visuma*, *s.* dwelling, residing.

විසුර, *Visura*, *a.* spread, extended, opened out, stretched out, also විසිරි *visirí.*

විසුරුවනවා, *Visuruwanawá*, *v.* to spread, to expand; to scatter, to disperse: pret. විසිරෙව්වා *visirewwá.*

විසුල, *Visula*, *a.* great, large, extensive; spread, opened, extended; published.

විසුළු, *Visuḷu*, *s.* change, alteration; gesture, grimace: see විහිළුව *vihiḷuwa.*

විසුළුකරණවා, *Visuḷukaraṇawá*, *v.* to ridicule, to jest.

විසූක, *Visúka*, *s.* theatrical amusements, dramatic exhibition.

විසූචිකා, *Visúchiká*, *s.* (වි intensitive, සූචිකා needle) spasmodic cholera; severe species of *urticaria* or nettle rash, accompanied with fever and purging.

විසේ, *Visé*, *s.* poison, venom; heedlessness, giddiness of conduct.

විසේනිය, *Viséniya*, *s.* fifth day, day after the new or full moon.

විසේස, *Visésa*, *s.* details, difference; particulars.

විසේසණ, *Visésaṇa*, *s.* adjective, attribute; discrimination: see විශේෂණ *viséshaṇa.*

විහග, *Vihaga*, } *s.* (විහ for විහායස් *viháyas* in
විහඞ්ග, *Vihaṅga*, } the sky, ග who goes) bird, [Colloq. කුරුල්ලා *kurullá*]; cloud, [Colloq. වලාකුළ *walákuḷa*]; arrow, [Colloq. ඊගහ *ígaha*]; sun, [Colloq. ඉර *ira*]; moon, [Colloq. හඳ *haṇda*]; planet.

විහඞ්ගරාජ, *Vihaṅgarája*, *s.* (විහඞ්ග bird, රාජ king) name of Garuḍa, the bird and vehicle of Vishṇu.

විහත, *Vihata*, *a.* (වි and හත hurt) opposed, impeded, resisted; hurt, killed.

විහර, *Vihara*, *s.* (වි and හර to convey) dwelling. residing, continuance; separation, disunion, absence; see also විසර *visara.*

විහරණ, *Viharaṇa*, *s.* (වි and හර *hara* to go about) roaming, wandering, going about for pleasure or exercise; dwelling, residing, abiding, continuance.

විහාපිත, *Vihápita*, *s.* (වි and හා *há* to abandon, abandoning the thing given) gift, donation.

විහායස, *Viháyasa*, *s.* (වි before, හය *haya* to go) heaven, sky, atmosphere, [Colloq. අහස *ahasa*]; bird.

විහාර, *Vihára*, *s.* (වි and හර *hara* to take) dwelling, residence; Buddhist temple; walking for pleasure or amusement.

විහාරය, *Viháraya*, } *s.* Buddhist temple.
විහාරේ, *Viháré*, }

විහිගුම්, *Vihigum*, *a.* exalted, high, noble.

විහිත, *Vihita*, *a.* (වි priv. and හිත applicable, or වි before, ධා *dhá* to have) improper, unsuitable, unfit; placed, deposited.

විහිද, *Vihida*, *s.* opening, expanding, as a flower; spreading, diffusing, as fragrance, etc.

විහිදයනවා, *Vihidayanawá*, *v.* to overflow, to run over; to spread.

විහිදි, *Vihidi*, *a.* opened, expanded, blown as a flower; spread, diffused.

විහිදීම, *Vihidíma*, *s.* expansion, diffusion, as of flowers or perfumes.

විහිදුවනවා, *Vihiduwanawá*, *v.* to ride, to cause to run or prance as a horse, the causal form of විහිදෙනවා *vihidenawá.*

විහිදෙනවා, *Vihidenawá*, *v.* to open, to expand; to diffuse, to be dilated: pret. විහිදුනා *vihiduná.*

විහින්, *Vihin*, see විසින් *visin.*

විහිළුව, *Vihiḷuwa*, *s.* ridiculous gesture, mimickry, buffoonery; theatrical exhibition, shows of dancers.

විළි, *Viḷi*, *s.* shame, bashfulness.

විළුඹ, *Viḷumba*, *s.* heel.

වී, *Ví*, *s.* paddy, rice in the husk, of which ther is a great variety in Ceylon, *oryza sativa.*

වීකරල, *Ví-karala*, *s.* ear of paddy: pl. වී කරල් *ví-karal.*

වීකාශ, *Víkáśa*, *s.* (වි and කාශ to shine) loneliness, solitude, privacy; display, manifestation.

වීකුරුල්ලා, *Ví-kurullá*, *s.* bird called the hill munia, *munia Kelaarti*, black-bellied, *m. malacca*, spotted, *m. punctulata*, white-backed, *m. striata*, *(Ploceidæ*, order *Passeres).*

විකොටනවා, *Ví-koṭanawá*, *v.* to pound paddy.
විකැන්, *Vikẹn*, *s.* ear of paddy or corn.
විචි, *Víchi*, *s.* wave, small or rippling wave.
විජ, *Víja*, see බීජ *bíja*.
වීණා, *Víṇá*, *s.* the Indian lute.
වීණාව, *Víṇáwa*, see the last.
වීණාවාද, *Víṇáwáda*, *s.* (වීණා and වාද who causes to speak or sound) a player on the lute.
වීත, *Víta*, *a.* (වී to go, ක්ත *kta* aff.) gone, departed; tranquil, quiet, tame.
විතංස, *Vítaṇsa*, *s.* (වි and තසි *tasi* to adorn) cage, chain or net, etc. for confining birds or beasts; enclosure for taming them, aviary, menagerie; place for keeping game, preserve.
වීතතණ්හ, *Víta-taṇha*, *s.* (වීත gone or tamed, තණ්හා *taṇhá* desire) ascetic or sage with subdued passions, rahat.
වීතද්වෙෂි, *Vítadwési*, *s.* (වීත gone, ද්වෙෂ *dwésa* anger, ඉන් *in* aff.) saint, holy or devout personage, rahat; also name of Buddha.
වීතමෝහී, *Vítamóhí*, *s.* one freed from ignorance.
වීතරාගී, *Vítarágí*, *s.* one who has overcome desire, Buddha.
වීතශෝක, *Vítaṣóka*, *s.* asóka tree, *saraca indica* or *jonesia asoka*, [Colloquial: දියරතඹලා *diya-ratam̃balá*, දියරත්මල් *diya-ratmal* or හෝපළු *hópaḷu*]: *a.* freed from care or sorrow.
විති, *Víti*, *s.* going, moving, motion; horse.
විතිහෝත්‍ර, *Vítihótra*, *s.* (විති horse, හෝත්‍ර clarified butter) fire; sun.
විථි, *Víthi*, *s.* (විථ *vitha* to ask or beg) street, road; row, line; terrace in front of a house; stall, shop.
විදිය, *Vídiya*, *s.* road, street: see the last.
වීදුරුකුප්පිය, *Víduru-kuppiya*, *s.* glass vial.
වීදුරුව, *Víduruwa*, *s.* glass: pl. වීදුරු *víduru*.
විනණ්ඩුව, *Vínaṇḍuwa*, *s.* (වී paddy, නණ්ඩුව spike) the spike or beard on a grain of paddy.
විනාහ, *Vínáha*, *s.* (වි and නහ *naha* to bind) top or cover of a well.
වීපොතු, *Ví-potu*, *s.* husk of rice or paddy.
වීබූව, *Vibúwa*, *s.* beard of paddy.
වීර්‍ය, *Vírya*, *s.* (වීර *víra* to be strong) strength, power, vigour; dignity, consequence; fortitude, firmness; heroism, valour; semen virile; splendour, lustre.
වීර්‍යකරණවා, *Víryakaraṇawá*, *v.* to endeavour, to strive.

වීර්‍යවත්, *Víryavat*, *a.* (වීර්‍ය and වත් poss. aff.) strong, stout, robust; overcoming, victorious.
වීර, *Víra*, *s.* (වීර to be valiant) hero, warrior, champion; heroism, heroic feeling; fire, sacrificial fire; actor, mime; flowering plant, *nerium odorum*: *a.* excellent, eminent; heroic; powerful, mighty; strong, robust.
වීරක, *Víraka*, *s.* sort of teal or wild duck, [Colloq. සේරා *sérá*].
වීරකත්. *Vírakat*, *s.* (වීර hero, කත් woman, wife) heroine, wife of a hero.
වීරණ, *Víraṇa*, *s.* fragrant grass, *andropogon muricatus*, [Colloq. සැවැන්දරා *sẹwẹndará*].
වීරත්වය, *Víratwaya*, *s.* (වීර hero, ත්ව affix of the abstract) heroism; labour, exertion, strenuous or heroic effort.
වීරතරු, *Vírataru*, *s.* (වීර and තරු tree) large tree, *pentaptera arjuna*; shrub, *barleria longifolia*; tree, *terminalia glabra*, [Colloq. කුඹුක් *kum̃buk*]; another tree, *dichrostachys cinerea*, [Colloq. අඬර *andara*].
වීරධන්වන්, *Víra-dhanwan*, *s.* (වීර hero, ධන්වන් bow) name of Káma the Indian Cupid.
වීරපාන, *Víra-pána*, *s.* (වීර and පාන drink) drink of warriors taken during the battle for refreshment, or before it, to elevate courage.
වීරමුණ්ඩ, *Víramuṇḍa*, *s.* name of a demon.
වීරයා, *Víraya*, *s.* valiant man, hero, strong muscular man: see වීර *víra*.
වීරරස, *Víra-rasa*, *s.* (වීර and රස sentiment) sentiment of courage.
වීරවෘක්ෂ, *Vírawṛiksha*, *s.* (වීර strong, වෘක්ෂ tree) marking nut tree, *semicarpus gardneri*, [Colloq. බඩුල්ල *badulla*]; large tree, *pentaptera arjuna*; sort of grain, *andropogon* or *holcus sorghum*.
වීරහා, *Víraha*, *s.* (වීර sacrificial fire, හා who destroys) Brahman who has suffered the sacred domestic fire to become extinct, either from carelessness, impiety, or absence.
වීරා, *Virá*, *s.* tree, *flacourtia cataphracta*, [Colloq. රටඋගුරැස්ස *raṭa-uguṛessa*]; twining plant, *asclepias rosea*; opposite-leaved fig tree, *ficus oppositifolia*, [Colloq. කොටදිඹුලා *koṭadim̃bulá*]; white and dark kinds of the *convolvulus paniculatus*; small tree, *gmelina arborea*, [Colloq. ඇත්දෙමට *ẹtdemaṭa*); the aloe, *argave americana*; medicinal plant, commonly called කිරිකෑවිළි *kirikawẹḷu*.
වීරාශංසන, *Víráṣaṇsana*, *s.* (වීර *vira* hero, ආ *á* and ශසි *ṣasi* to wish) the place in which the

battle rages most furiously or which is most exposed, the post of danger.

විරිය, *Viriya, s.* heroism, perseverance, strenuous endeavour, effort, exertion, force: see වීර්‍ය *virya.*

විරියකරණවා, *Viriyakaraṇawá, v.* to endeavour, to strive.

විරියවන්ත, *Viriyawanta, s.* effort, exertion: see වීර්‍යවත් *viryawat.*

විරුත්, *Virut,* } *s.* creeper or spreading creeper;
විරුධ්, *Virudh,* } branch and shoot.

විසති, *Visati, s.* twenty, score, [Colloq. විස්ස *vissa*].

විසිකරණවා *Visikaraṇawá, v.* to throw, to cast: pret. විසිකෙරුවා *visikeruwá.*

විසිදෑල, *Visideḷa, s.* cast net: pl. විසිදැල් *visideḷ.*

විසුකරණවා, *Visukaraṇawá,* corruptly for විසිකරණවා *visikaraṇawá.*

වුනොරු, *Wunoru, s.* charioteer of the sun.

වුරුණුතෙල්, *Wuruṇutel, s.* serum or marrow of the flesh: see වසා *wasá.*

වුහුට, *Wuhuṭa,* } *a.* entered, sent, cast.
වුහුටු, *Wuhuṭu,* }

වූ, *Wú, ind.* affix forming adjectives, from භූ *bhú* to be.

වෙග, *Wega,* see වේග *wéga.*

වෙට්ට, *Weṭṭa, a.* base, as metal.

වෙට්ටයා, *Weṭṭayá, s.* vagabond.

වෙඩ්ඩියා, *Weḍḍiyá, s.* wild ox, [Colloq. කුළුහරකා *kuḷuharaká*].

වෙඩි, *Weḍi,* see වෙඩිල්ල *weḍilla.*

වෙඩිතිබනවා, *Weḍitibanawá,* } *v.* to shoot with a
වෙඩිතියනවා, *Weḍitiyanawá,* } gun.

වෙඩිබෙහෙත්, *Weḍibehet,* } *s.* (වෙඩි shooting, බෙ
වෙඩිබේත්, *Weḍibét,* } හෙත් drug) gunpowder.

වෙඩිල්ල, *Weḍilla, s.* shooting; explosion, gunfire; pl. වෙඩිලි *weḍili.*

වෙඩිලිබඳිනවා, *Weḍili-bandinawá, v.* (වෙඩිල්ල *weḍilla* and බඳිනවා to bind) to make fire works.

වෙඩිලුණු, *Weḍiluṇu, s.* (වෙඩි and ලුණු salt) salt petre, nitre.

වෙඬරු, *Weṇḍaru, s.* ghee, clarified butter.

වෙණකරු, *Weṇakaru, s.* (වෙණ lute, කරු who does or performs) one who plays on the lute.

වෙණතත්, *Weṇatat, s.* (වෙණ and තත *tata* string) strings of the lute.

වෙණද, *Weṇada, s.* merchant, trader, [Colloq. වෙළෙන්ද *weḷendá*].

වෙණනද, *Weṇanada, s.* (වෙණ and නද sound) sound of the lute.

වෙත්‍ර, *Wetra,* see වේත්‍ර *wétra.*

වෙත, *Weta, ind.* near, close to, proximate; also, affixed to nouns, etc. and serving for the locative case.

වෙතවන, *Wetawana, s.* (වෙත near, වන grove) garden or grove near a house, park or pleasure garden.

වෙද, *Weda,* see වේද *wéda;* also a physician, from වෛද්‍ය *waidya.*

වෙදකම්කරණවා, *Wedakamkaraṇawá, v.* to administer medicine.

වෙදකම, *Wedakama, s.* (වෙද and කම action) the pratice of medicine, medical profession, medical treatment: pl. වෙදකම් *wedakam.*

වෙදඟිල්ල, *Wedangilla, s.* forefinger.

වෙදදර, *Wedadara, s.* Brahmin.

වෙදරාල, *Wedarála, s.* doctor, medical practitioner.

වෙදසතර, *Wedasatara, s.* (වෙද and සතර science) science of medicine.

වෙදා, *Wedá, s.* doctor, medical practitioner.

වෙන්, *Wen, s.* Elu form of විෂ්ණු *Vishṇu;* grove, forest, from වන *wana: a.* severed, separated, disunited.

වෙන්කරණවා, *Wenkaraṇawá, v.* to separate, to divide, to disjoin, to disunite.

වෙන්කල්, *Wenkal, s.* (වෙන් Vishṇu, කල් wife) name of Lakshmí; also, වෙනුකල් *wenukal.*

වෙන්දේසිකරණවා, *Wendésikaraṇawá, v.* to sell by public auction.

වෙන්දේසිකාරයා, *Wendésikárayá, s.* auctioneer.

වෙන්දේසිපල, *Wendésipala, s.* place where any thing is sold by public auction.

වෙන්දේසිය, *Wendésiya, s.* public sale, auction.

වෙන්පද, *Wenpada, s.* (වෙන් Vishṇu, පද abode) sky, atmosphere, visible heavens or firmament, [Colloq. අහස *ahasa*].

වෙන්පුත්, *Wenput, s.* (වෙන් and පුත් son) name of Káma; Brahma, alluding to the fable of his birth from the lotus which sprang from Vishṇu's navel.

වෙන්වෙන්ව, *Wenwenwa, ind.* individually, separately.

වෙන්වෙනවා, *Wenwenawá, v.* to be separate or cleft: pret. වෙන්වුනා *wenwuná.*

වෙන, *Wena, s.* name of Vishṇu; víṇá or Indian lute, from වීණා *víṇá: ind.* other, another, different: *pres. part.* of වෙනවා *wenawá,* to be.

වෙනඟන, *Wenangana, s.* (වෙන් *ven* Vishṇu, අඟන *angana* wife) name of Lakshmí, the goddess of prosperity.

වෙනත්, *Wenat, a.* (වෙන with, ත් and) other, and other.

වෙනම, *Wenama, ind.* distinctly, separately; other, another, different.

වෙනවා, *Wenawá, v.* to become, to happen to be: pret. වුනා *wuná.*

වෙනවෙන, *Wenawena, ind.* separately, differently.

වෙනස්කම, *Wenaskama, s.* alteration, change; fickleness, caprice; ill-treatment.

වෙනස්කරණවා, *Wenaskaraṇawá, v.* to alter, change.

වෙනස්වෙනවා, *Wenaswenawá, v.* to be altered, changed.

වෙනස, *Wenasa, s.* change, difference, alteration.

වෙනි, *Weni, ind.* like, resembling; an affix forming ordinal numbers, as, එක්වෙනි *ekweni*, first.

වෙනින්, *Wenin, a.* other, another.

වෙනිය, *Weniya, s.* tail, tail of any animal, [Colloq. වල්ගේ *walgé*].

වෙනිවැල්, *Weniwęl, s.* creeper, *coscinium fenestratum, (Menispermaceæ).*

වෙනිවැල්ල, *Weniwęlla, s.* plant bearing a red flower, cock's comb, *allmania nodiflora (Amarantaceæ);* also called කුමටිය *kumaṭiya.*

වෙනු, *Wenu,* Elu form of විෂ්ණු *Vishṇu.*

වෙනුකල්, *Wenukal, s.* (වෙනු and කල් wife) name of Lakshmi goddess of wealth and prosperity.

වෙනුතණ, *Wenutaṇa, s.* kind of grass, not ascertained.

වෙනුතෙන, *Wenutena, s.* (වෙනු Vishṇu, තෙන son) name of Káma; name of Brahma: see වෙන්පුත් *wenput.*

වෙනුදෙව්, *Wenudew, s.* (වෙනු and දෙව් deity) Vishṇu, Elu form of විෂ්ණුදේව *Vishṇudéwa.*

වෙනුව, *Wenuwa, ind.* instead, in behalf of, for the sake of, on account of.

වෙනුවට, *Wenuwaṭa, ind.* for, for the sake of, on account of.

වෙනුවෙන්, *Wenuwen, par.* on behalf of, instead of.

වෙනේ, *Wené, s.* forest, grove; wound.

වෙනැල්ලවටුවා, *Wenęlla-waṭuwá, s.* Chinese quail, *coturnix chinensis, (Tetrocindæ,* order *Gallinæ);* also called පඬුරුවටුවා *paṇḍuru-waṭuwá.*

වෙය, *Weya, s.* cane or ratan, *calamus Roxburghii:* see වේවැල *wéwęla.*

වෙයග, *Weyaga,* }
වෙයගබඩ, *Weyagabaḍa,* } *s.* top or young shoot of the bamboo cane, used as a vegetable.

වෙර, *Wera, s.* strength, force, muscular power; hate, enmity, from වෛර *waira;* body.

වෙරළ, *Weraḷa, s.* sea shore, shore, coast; beach, wharf, quay.

වෙරළු, *Weraḷu, s.* tree, called wild olive, *elæocarpus serratus,* var. *cuneatus (Tiliaceæ).*

වෙරළුමිණි, *Weraḷumiṇi, s.* gem of a dark colour, lapis lazuli; cat's eye, [Colloq. වයිරෝඩි *wayiróḍi*].

වෙරි, *Weri, a.* inebriated, intoxicated, drunk.

වෙරිකම, *Werikama, s.* drunkenness.

වෙරිකාරයා, *Werikárayá, s.* one who is drunk.

වෙරිවෙනවා, *Weriwenawá, v.* to be drunk.

වෙරේ, *Weré,* see වෙර *wera.*

වෙල්, *Wel, s.* sand-bank, sea-shore, beach, [Colloq. වෙරළ *weraḷa*]; fields: plural of වෙල *wela,* field.

වෙල් ඇත්කලාඳුරු, *Wel-ęt-kaláṇduru, s.* plant, *cyperus dubius* or *c. kyllingæoides.*

වෙල් කරවු, *Wel-karawu, s.* plant, *scleria tesselata.*

වෙල් කලාඳුරු, *Wel-kaláṇduru, s.* plant, species of *cyperus.*

වෙල් කවුඩුදල, *Wel-kawuḍudala, s.* plant, *oldenlandia crystallina* or *hedyotis pumila.*

වෙල්කූඩළු, *Wel-kúḍaḷu, s.* species of balsam, *impatiens biflora.*

වෙල් තුත්තිරි, *Wel-tuttiri, s.* plant, *cyperus santonici.*

වෙල් දහවිය, *Wel-dahaviya, s.* plant, *mikania tomentosa.*

වෙල්බඩ, *Welbaḍa, s.* mounds of earth raised in the paddy fields to dam in the water, and serving as pathways and boundaries.

වෙල් බිම, *Wel-bima, s.* field, cultivated or meadow land.

වෙල් බෙඳුරු, *Wel-beṇduru, s.* plant, see වැල් බෙඳුරු *węl-beṇduru.*

වෙල්ම කලාඳුරු, *Welma-kaláṇduru, s.* plant, *narcissus paniceus.*

වෙල් මාරුකු, *Wel-máruku, s.* species of panic grass, *panicum crus-galli (Gramineæ):* see වැල් මුරුක්කු *węl-murukku.*

වෙල් මොට්ටුතණ, *Wel-moṭṭu-taṇa, s.* plant: see වැල්මොට්ටු *węl-moṭṭu.*

වෙල්ලංගිරිය, *Wellangiriya,* see වැල්ලංගිරිය *węllangiriya.*

වෙල්ලජ, *Wellaja, s.* (වෙල්ල shaking, ජ born) black pepper, *piper nigrum,* [Colloq. ගම්මිරිස් *gammiris*].

වෙල්ලවැහුන්, *Wellawẹhun*, *s.* sort of thin flat cake.

වෙල්ලාව, *Welláwa*, *s.* washerman's pot for boiling clothes.

වෙල්ලිත, *Wellita*, *a.* crooked, shaken, trembling, tremulous.

වෙල්ලිප්පරත්ති, *Wellipparatti*, *s.* creeping plant, *dœmia extensa*, [Colloq. මැඩහඟු *mẹdahangu*].

වෙල්ලිය, *Welliya*, *s.* creeping plant in general; balance, scale, steelyard.

වෙල්හිරි, *Welhíri*, *s.* plant, with culms one to two feet height, growing in moist ground, *cyperus iria (Cyperaceœ)*.

වෙල, *Wela*, *s.* sort of spear; paddy field.

වෙලඟ, *Welanga*, *s.* tree yielding tough wood, *pterospermum suberifolium (Sterculiaceœ)*.

වෙලප, *Welapa*, *s.* lamentation, bewailing, from විලාප *vilápa;* vexation, trouble; tree with its branches.

වෙලපනවා, *Welapanawá*, *v.* to lament, to bewail, to bemoan; to trouble, to vex.

වෙලල, *Welala*, *s.* sea-shore; bank of a river; ferry.

වෙලවි, *Welavi*, *s.* speed, haste, quickness, velocity, [Colloq. ඉක්මණ *ikmaṇa*].

වෙලවිගමන, *Welavigamana*, *s.* speedy march.

වෙලා, *Welá*, *s.* time, occasion, opportunity: see වේලා *wélá*.

වෙලාව, *Weláwa*, *s.* time, opportunity; see the last.

වෙලෙල, *Welela*, *s.* bank of a river.

වෙලෙවි, *Welevi*, *s.* haste, speed, hurry.

වෙවුලනවා, *Wewulanawá*, *v.* to shake, to tremble, to be agitated, to shudder, to quake: pret. වෙවුලුවා *wewuluwá*.

වෙවුලුන්, *Wewulun*, } *s.* trembling, etc. verbal
වෙවුලුම, *Wewuluma*, } noun of වෙවුලනවා *wewulanawá*.

වෙස්, *Wes*, *s.* countenance or form, mask, artificial face; disguise; dresses of dancers or theatrical exhibitors; merchant, trader.

වෙස්කුල, *Weskula*, *s.* (වෙස් merchant, කුල tribe) Vaisya or mercantile and agricultural tribe.

වෙස්පානවා, *Wes-pánawá*, *v.* to act, to perform dramatically; to mimic: pret. වෙස්පෑවා *wes-pẹwá*.

වෙස් පෙරලෙනවා, *Wes-peralenawá*, *v.* to be disguised; to be altered in form.

වෙස්පෑම, *Wespẹma*, *s.* dramatic representation, exhibitions of dancers; mimicry.

වෙස්මූන, *Wesmúna*, *s.* (වෙස් and මූන countenance) artificial face, mask.

වෙස්වණ, *Weswaṇa*, *s.* name of Kuwéra; Elu form of වෛශ්‍රවණ *waiṣrawaṇa*.

වෙස්වළහනවා, *Weswaḷahanawá*, *v.* to disguise one's self; to assume a different form.

වෙස්වළා, *Weswaḷá*, *s.* (for වෙස්වළහා *weswaḷahá* participle of the above) having disguised one's self.

වෙස්ස, *Wessa*, *s.* Páli form of the Sanskrit වෛශ්‍ය *waiṣya;* man of the mercantile and agricultural tribe.

වෙස්සන්තර, *Wessantara*, *s.* name of Buddha in the last birth but one, in which he gave away his treasures, his wife, and children, as religious offerings.

වෙස, *Wesa*, *s.* form, manner.

වෙසක්, *Wesak*, *s.* month in which the moon is full in the constellation විශාඛා *viṣákhá*, (April–May), Elu form of වෛශාඛ *waiṣákha*.

වෙසක්මල්, *Wesak-mal*, *s.* plant, peculiar to Ceylon, *dendrobium Maccarthiœ (Orchideœ)*.

වෙසක්මස, *Wesak-masa*, see වෙසක් *wesak*.

වෙසඟන, *Wesangana*, *s.* (වෙස් *wes* and අඟන *angana* woman) prostitute, courtezan.

වෙසන්න, *Wesanna*, *s.* small lake, pond, tank, reservoir.

වෙසනය, *Wesanaya*, *s.* lust, cupidity, misfortune, calamity, fate: see ව්‍යසන *wyasana*.

වෙසඹු, *Wesambu*, *s.* (වෙස් *wes* and අඹු *ambu* woman) prostitute.

වෙසමුණු, *Wesamuṇu*, *s.* name of Kuvéra regent of the north and chief of the Yakshas; Elu form of වෛශ්‍රවණ *waiṣrawaṇa*.

වෙසෙස්, *Weses*, Elu form of විශේෂ *viṣésha*.

වෙසෙසින්, *Wesesin*, *s.* specially, distinctively.

වෙසේ, *Wesé*, *v.* third person singular of the verb, වස *wasa* to dwell.

වෙහෙර, *Wehera*, *s.* Buddhist temple; priest's residence in or near the temple, Elu form of විහාර *vihára*.

වෙහෙල්, *Wehel*, *s.* deer, [Colloq. මුවා *muwá*].

වෙහෙස්, *Wehes*, } *s.* fatigue, weariness; sorrow,
වෙහෙස, *Wehesa*, } affliction, distress; vexation, trouble; hardship, difficulty.

වෙහෙසනවා, *Wehesanawá*, *v.* to trouble, to vex; to tire, to weary, to distress.

වෙහෙසවෙනවා, *Wehesawenawá*, *v.* to be tired or fatigued.

වෙහෙසි, *Wehesí*, participle of වෙහෙසෙනවා *wehesenawá*, which see.

වෙහෙසිම, *Wehesíma*, s. becoming fatigued or tired, verbal noun of වෙහෙසනවා *wehesanawá* or වෙහෙසෙනවා *wehesenawá*.

වෙහෙසුම, *Wehesuma*, verbal noun of වෙහෙසනවා *wehesanawá* or වෙහෙසෙනවා *wehesenawá*.

වෙහෙසෙනවා, *Wehesenawá*, v. to be tired or fatigued. to vex or trouble one's self.

වෙළඳ, *Weḷanda*, s. merchant, trader, trafficer.

වෙළඳම්කරණවා, *Weḷadamkaranawá*, v. to trade, to traffic.

වෙළඳම්පල, *Weḷadampala*, s. (වෙළඳාම *weḷandáma* and පල place) market, place for trading, mart.

වෙළඳා, *Weḷandá*, s. trader, trafficer, merchant.

වෙළඳාම, *Weḷandáma*, s. traffic, merchandise, trading, commerce.

වෙළනවා, *Weḷanawá*, v. to twist, as cord, etc.; intwine: pret. වෙළුවා *weḷuwá*.

වෙළප්, *Weḷap*, s. tree with its branches; bush.

වෙළඹ, *Weḷamba*, s. mare, from වඩබා *waḍabá*.

වෙළාගන්නවා, *Weḷágannawá*, v. to twist round as a snake or creeper, etc.

වෙළිම, *Weḷima*, s. twisting, twining; drying.

වෙළු, *Weḷu*, s. twisted string, ball; bond, bandage.

වෙළුකවනවා, *Weḷukawanawá*, v. to perform the last process of twisting cord, etc.

වෙළුන, *Weḷuna*, a. twined, twisted.

වෙළුම, *Weḷuma*, s. twisting or tying round, bandage; verbal noun of වෙළනවා *weḷanawá*, to twist.

වෙළුව, *Weḷuwa*, s. twining, twisting: pl. වෙළු *weḷu*.

වෙළෙන, *Weḷena*, a. entangled, twined; *pres. part.* of වෙළෙනවා *weḷenawá*.

වෙළෙනවා, *Weḷenawá*, v. to be twisted or twined, to become entangled.

වෙළෙන්දා, *Weḷendá*, s. merchent, trader: see වෙළඳ *weḷanda*.

වෙළෙප්, *Weḷep*, see වෙළප් *weḷap*.

වෙළෙඹ, *Weḷemba*, s. mare.

වේ, *Wé*, s. way, street; speed; ratan.

වේක්කු, *Wékku*, s. plural of වේකා *wéká;* also, weariness, fainting, fatigue.

වේකා, *Wéká*, s. milk fish belonging to the herring tribe, *chanos salmoneus*.

වේ කුරුඳු, *Wé-kurundu*, s. plant, with small white fragrant flowers, *limonia pentaphylla*.

වේකොලවී, *Wékola-ví*, s. kind of paddy, *oryza sativa*.

වේග, *Wéga*, s. (විජ *vija* to go) speed, dispatch, velocity; stream, current; expulsion or evacuation of the natural excretions; sudden impulse, transition of mind, as from passion to apathy; semen virile; external indication of any internal effect, proceeding from passion, medicine, etc. as, convulsion, horripilation, sweat, etc.

වේගය, *Wégaya*, s. speed, velocity, impatience.

වේගසන්ධාරණ, *Wéga-sandhárana*, s. (වේග and සන්ධාරණ binding) obstruction of the natural evacuations, constipation, ischury.

වේගී, *Wégí*, s. (වේග *wéga* speed, ඉන් *in* aff.) courier, express; hawk: a. swift, fleet, rapid.

වේගුරු, *Wéguru*, s. name of Brahma.

වේඨනය, *Wéṭhanaya*, s. enclosure; encompassing; turban, diadem; twisting, tying.

වේණා, *Wéná*, see වීණා *víná*.

වේණාකාරයා, *Wénákárayá*, s. (වේණා lute, කාර *kára* who does) player on the lute; fiddler.

වේණා ගායනාව, *Wéná-gáyanáwa*, s. (වේණා and ගායනා *gáyaná* playing) performing on the Víṇá or Indian lute, to play the fiddle.

වේණාව, *Wéṇáwa*, see වීණා *víná*.

වේණි, *Wéṇi*, s. braided hair, the hair simply collected on the top of the head, without any ornament, as worn by widows and women whose husbands are absent.

වේණු, *Wéṇu*, s. bamboo, *bambusa vulgaris*, [Colloq. උණගස් *uṇagas*]; flute, pipe or reed for playing with.

වේණුවාද, *Wéṇu-wáda*, s. (වේණු flute, වාද who sounds) player on a flute or reed.

වේත්‍ර, *Wétra*, s. (වි *vi* to go, ත්‍ර aff.) reed, cane, ratan; staff, stick.

වේත්‍රලතා, *Wétra-latá*, s. (වේත්‍ර and ලතා creeper) bamboo cane or ratan, *calamus Roxburghii:* see වේවැල *wéweḷa*.

වේත්‍රවතී, *Wétrawatí*, s. the Betwa river which falls into the Jumna below Calpi; river in the infernal regions.

වේත්‍රී, *Wétrí*, s. (වේත්‍ර *wétra* staff, ඉන් *in* aff.) porter, door keeper.

වේතන, *Wétana*, s. (වි *vi* to go, තන aff.) hire, wages; livelihood, subsistence.

වේතස, *Wétasa*, s. ratan, *calamus rotang* or *c. Roxburghii*, [Colloq. වේවැල් *wéweḷ*].

වේතාල, *Wétála*, *s.* (වේ in the air, තාල habitation, from තල *tala* to fix) sprite or goblin, especially one haunting cemeteries and animating dead bodies; door keeper.

වේද්‍ය, *Wédya*, *a.* to be known, fit or proper to be taught or explained.

වේද, *Wéda*, *s.* (විද *vida* to know) generic term for the sacred writings of the Hindus, supposed to have been revealed by Brahma, and after being preserved by tradition for a considerable time, to have been arranged in the present form by Vyása; the principal Védas are three in number, the Rig, Yajur, and Sáma, to which a fourth, the Atharva, is usually added, and the Itihása and Púráṇas or ancient history and mythology, are sometimes considered as a fifth.

වේදගර්භ, *Wéda-garbha*, *s.* Brahma, a Brahmin.

වේදත්‍රය, *Wédatraya*, *s.* (වේද and ත්‍රය three) three Védas collectively: see වේද *véda*.

වේදනා, *Wédaná*, *s.* (විද *vida* to know, to suffer) sensation, perception, knowledge conveyed by the senses; pain, distress.

වේදනාකරණවා, *Wédanákaraṇawá*, *v.* to pain, to torture.

වේදනාව, *Wédanáwa*, *s.* ache, pain, anguish, torture; affliction, distress.

වේදනාවෙනවා, *Wédanáwenawá*, *v.* to be hurt; to feel pain.

වේදනීය, *Wédaníya*, *a.* fit to be known, proper to be taught or explained.

වේදමන්ත්‍ර, *Wéda-mantra*, *s.* (වේද and මන්ත්‍ර counsel, etc.) study of the Védas, to be able to repeat them at the periods of offering, and for magical purposes.

වේදමුඛ්‍යක, *Wéda-mukhyaka*, *s.* small aromatic plant, *kaempferia galanga*, [Colloq. හිඟුරුපියලි *hiṉgurupiyali*].

වේදය, *Wédaya*, see වේද *wéda*.

වේදල්ල, *Wédalla*, *s.* one of the nine divisions of the Buddhist Scriptures.

වේදස්, *Wédas*, *s.* Védas: see වේද *véda*.

වේදාඞ්ග, *Wédáṅga*, *s.* (වේද *véda* and අඞ්ග *aṅga* member) sacred science, considered as subordinate to, and in some sense, part of the Védas, and comprehending six sciences, viz. ශික්‍ෂා *ṣikshá*, science of pronounciation and articulation; කල්ප *kalpa*, detail of religious ceremonies; ව්‍යාකරණ *vyákaraṇa*, grammar; ඡන්දස් *chhandas*, prosody; ජ්‍යෝතිෂ් *jyótish*, astronomy, and නිරුක්ති *nirukti*, explanation of difficult terms.

වේදාන්ත, *Wédánta*, *s.* (වේද *véda* and අන්ත *unta* end, sum, scope or substance) theological part of the Védas, contained in the many numerous passages or chapters of the Védas termed Upanishads, which inculcate an abstract and speculative monotheistical worship.

වේදී, *Wédi*, *s.* (විද *vida* to know, ඉන් *in* aff.) learned man, teacher: see the next.

වේදිකා, *Wédiká*, } *s.* terrace furnished with
වේදිකාව, *Wédikáwa*, } pillars or lattice work, verandah, balcony; rail surrounding a flight of stairs; ground prepared for sacrificial purposes, rude kind of altars.

වේදිත, *Wédita*, *a.* (විද *vida* to know, causal form, ඉත *ita* aff.) set forth, represented, made known.

වේදින්, *Wédin*, *s.* (විද *vida* to know, ඉන් *in* aff.) paṇdit, learned man, scholar.

වේදු අල්ලනවා, *Wédu-allanawá*, *v.* to fumigate.

වේදුක, *Wéduka*, see වේදිකා *wédiká*.

වේදුව, *Wéduwa*, *s.* sudorific, fumigation.

වේධ, *Wédha*, *s.* (ව්‍යධ *vyadha* to pierce) perforation, piercing; depth (in measurement).

වේධක, *Wédhaka*, *s.* quicksilver, [Colloq. රසදිය *rahadiya*]; camphor; grain, rice in the ear.

වේධන, *Wédhana*, *s.* (ව්‍යධ *vyadha* to perforate) auger, gimlet, or any similar instrument; piercing, perforating.

වේපචිත්ති, *Wépachitti*, *s.* (වේප to tremble, චිත්ත *chitta* mind, ඉන් *in* aff.) chief of the class of Asurs residing beneath Maha Méru.

වේපත, *Wépata*, *s.* (වේ and පත leaf) the ratan split into thin shreds for the purpose of weaving the bottoms of chairs, couches, etc.

වේබඩ, *Wébaḍa*, see වෙයග *weyaga*.

වේම, *Wéma*, *s.* loom.

වේයා, *Wéyá*, *s.* white ant, termites: pl. වේයෝ *wéyó*.

වේර, *Wéra*, *s.* body, egg-plant; saffron.

වේරක, *Wéraka*, *s.* camphor.

වේරජා, *Wé-rajá*, *s.* (වේයා *wéyá* and රජා king) the king (more properly the queen) of the white ant.

වේරුපු, *Wé-rupu*, *s.* (වේයා *wéyá* and රුපු enemy) bear, [Colloq. වළහා *waḷahá*].

වේරෑණ, *Wérẹṇa*, *s.* flower stalk of ratan.

වේල්, *Wél*, *s.* dart, javelin. (Tamil.)

වේල්ල, *Wélla*, *s.* terrace, elevated pathway; raised mound or bank in the paddy fields, which dams in the waters and serves as a pathway.

වේල, *Wéla*, *s.* half a day; any portion of a day.

වේලනවා, *Wélanawá*, *v.* to dry; to drain: pret. වේලුවා *wéluwá*.

වේලා, *Wélá*, *s.* time; boundary, limit; sea shore; plant, *gynandropsis pentaphylla (Capparideæ)*.

වේලාගස්, *Wélá-gas*, *s.* kind of basil, *ocimum gratissimum*.

වේලාන්තර, *Wélántara*, *s.* (වේලා *welá* shore, අන්තර *antara* among) sea shore.

වේලාපස, *Wélápasa*, } *a.* early, betimes.
වේලාපහ, *Wélápaha*, }

වේලායුධ, *Weláyudha*, *s.* (වේල් *wél* dart or javelin, ආයුධ *áyudha* weapon) trident used by Kataragama deviyó, the Hindu god of war.

වේලාව, *Wéláwa*, see වේලා *wélá*.

වේලාවැල, *Wélá-wéla*, *s.* plant, not ascertained.

වේලාසන, *Wélásana*, *a.* betimes, early.

වේලිච්ච ඉඟුරු, *Wélichcha-inguru*, *s.* dry ginger.

වේලෙහි, *Wélehi*, *s.* at that time, in that time, then.

වේවැල, *Wéwela*, *s.* (වේ and වැල creeper) cane or common ratan, *calamus Roxburghii (Palmæ)*.

වේශ්ම, *Wéşma*, *s.* (විශ *vişa* to enter, මනින් *manin* aff.) house, [Colloq. ගෙය *geya*].

වේශ්‍ය, *Wéşya*, *s.* residence of harlots.

වේශ්‍යා, *Wéşyá*, *s.* harlot, prostitute.

වේෂ්ට, *Wéshta*, *s.* fence, enclosure, [Colloq. වැට *weta*]; surrounding, enclosing; twisting, twining; exudation, gum, resin in general.

වේෂ්ටක, *Wéshtaka*, *a.* surrounding, enclosing, encircling.

වේෂ්ටන, *Wéshtana*, *s.* turban, diadem; fence, enclosure; twisting, twining.

වේෂ, *Wésha*, *s.* (විෂ *visha* to invest) ornament, dress, decoration.

වේස, *Wésa*, *s.* disguise, assumed appearance, deception by dress or covering; masquerade dress, mask; place of harlots, brothel.

වේසධාරී, *Wésadhári*, *s.* (වේෂ disguise, ධාරී who bears) hypocrite, deceiver, false devotee.

වේසඹ, *Wésamba*, *s.* dancing girl.

වේසය *Wésaya*, see වේස *wésa*.

වේසා, *Wésá*, *s.* prostitute.

වේසාකම් කරණවා, *Wésákam-karanawá*, *v.* to commit whoredom, to commit adultery.

වේසාකම, *Wésákama*, *s.* prostitution.

වේසාවා, *Wésáwá*, *s.* catamite, libertine, man of immoral character.

වේසාවි, *Wésávi*, *s.* prostitute, whore.

වේසි, *Wési*, *s.* harlot, prostitute.

වේහප්ඵල, *Wéhapphalaya*, *s.* the tenth Brahma lóka.

වේළුරිය, *Wéluriya*, *s.* gem, lapis lazuli, from වෛදූර්‍ය *waidúrya*.

වෛ, *Wai*, *ind.* particle of affirmation, so, indeed; an expletive.

වෛක්‍රාන්ත, *Waikránta*, *s.* (වික්‍රාන්ත *vikránta* hero, අණ් *an* pleonasm) kind of gem, said to resemble the diamond, and to be of similar properties.

වෛකුණ්ඨ, *Waikuntha*, *s.* name of Vishnu, and of Indra; mountain so called, on the summit of which is a paradise or divine region of the same name; its site is so variously described that it is difficult to determine its situation; talc; plant, *leucas zeylanica*, [Colloq. ගැටතුඹ *geta-tumba*].

වෛජයන්ත, *Waijayanta*, *s.* (වි *vi* and ජි *ji* to conquer) palace of Indra: the banner or emblem of Indra.

වෛජයන්තික, *Waijayantika*, *s.* (වෛජයන්ති flag, කන් *kan* aff.) flag bearer.

වෛජයන්තිකා, *Waijayantiká*, *s.* plant, *æschynomene sesban*.

වෛජයන්ති, *Waijayanti*, *s.* flag, banner, ensign; tree, *æschynomene sesban;* small tree with small hairy flowers, *premna spinosa*, [Colloq. සිහින්මිදි *sihin-midi*].

වෛඥානික, *Waijñánika*, *a.* (විඥාන *vijñána* knowledge, science) skilful, clever, dexterous, proficient.

වෛණුක, *Wainuka*, *s.* goad or bamboo pike headed with iron used to drive an elephant, [Colloq. හෙණ්ඩුව *henduwa*].

වෛතනික, *Waitanika*, *s.* (වේතන *wétana* wages) hireling, labourer.

වෛතරණී, *Waitarani*, *s.* (වි *vi* various, තරණී crossing) river of hell.

වෛතාල, *Waitála*, *s.* morning, day-break, [Colloq. පාන්දර *pándara*].

වෛතාලික, *Waitálika*, *s.* bard whose duty it is to awaken a chief or prince at dawn with music and song.

වෛද්‍ය, *Waidya*, *s.* (විද *vida* to know, etc.) physician; shrub, *randia uliginosa (Rubiaceæ);* also called ඇත් කුකුරුමාන් *et-kukurumán;* shrub, *justicia gendurussa:* see the next word.

වෛද්‍ය මාතෘ, *Waidya-mátri*, *s.* (වෛද්‍ය and මාතෘ mother) shrub, *justicia gendurussa*, [Colloq. කළොස්වාරණිය *kaloswáraniya*]; shrub, *justicia adatoda*, [Colloq. වං ඇපල *wan-epala*].

වෛද්‍යශාස්ත්‍රය, *Waidya-ṣástraya*, *s.* science of medicine.

වෛද්‍යාචාර්ය, *Waidyáchárya*, *s.* (වෛද්‍ය *waidya* and ආචාර්ය *áchárya* teacher) physician.

වෛදග්ධ, *Waidagdha*, *s.* cleverness, acuteness, craft, cunning.

වෛදර්භ, *Waidarbha*, *s.* crafty or indirect speech.

වෛදල, *Waidala*, *s.* (වි *vi* and දල to divide) any leguminous vegetable or grain, as peas, beans, etc.

වෛදූර්ය, *Waidúrya*, *s.* gem of a dark colour, lapis lazuli; the word is formed from විදූර *vidúra*, said to be the name of a mountain where the stone is found, or a city where it is polished.

වෛදේහක, *Waidéhaka*, *s.* (විදේහ *vidéha* country, or වි *vi* various, දිහ *diha* to collect goods,) trader by profession, merchant, [Colloq. වෙළෙන්දා *weḷendá*].

වෛදේහි, *Waidéhi*, *s.* long pepper, *piper longum*, [Colloq. තිප්පිලි *tippili*].

වෛනතේය, *Wainatéya*, *s.* (විනතා *vinatá* mother of this being) Garuḍa, the bird and vehicle of Vishṇu.

වෛනීතක, *Wainítaka*, *s.* mediate conveyance, as a porter carrying a letter, horse dragging a chariot, etc.

වෛනේජන, *Wainéjana*, see විනේජන *vinéjana*.

වෛපුල්‍ය, *Waipulya*, *s.* (විපුල *vipula* large, අණ් *aṇ* aff.) greatness, bulk, magnitude; mountain so called.

වෛයාකරණ, *Waiyákaraṇa*, *s.* grammarian: *a.* grammatical.

වෛර, *Waira*, *s.* (වීර *víra* hero, අණ් *aṇ* pleonasm) hate, enmity; heroism, prowess.

වෛරක්කාරයා, *Wairakkárayá*, *s.* enemy, [Colloq. හතුරා *haturá*].

වෛරකරනවා, *Wairakaraṇawá*, *v.* to hate, to cause enmity, to cause hatred.

වෛරබඳිනවා, *Wairabandinawá*, *v.* (වෛර and බඳිනවා to fasten) to hate, to entertain malice; to contract enmity or hostility, to cherish hatred.

වෛරා, *Wairá*, *s.* striped bull, etc.

වෛරාග, *Wairága*, *s.* (විරාග *virága* and අණ් *aṇ* pleonasm) absence of passion.

වෛරී, *Wairí*, *s.* (වෛර *waira* enmity, ඊ *í* aff.) enemy, adversary.

වෛරෝචන, *Wairóchana*, *s.* (විරෝචන *viróchana* sun, අණ් *aṇ* affix of descent) name of Buddha; Bali, sovereign so named; son of Súrya or the sun.

වෛවර්ණ, *Waiwarṇa*, *s.* (වි *vi* privative, වර්ණ colour, tribe) change of colour or complexion; deviation or secession from tribe; heterogeneousness, difference.

වෛවස්වත, *Waiwaswata*, *s.* name of Yama; planet Saturn; the seventh Manu, or Manu of the present period.

වෛශ්‍ය, *Waiṣya*, *s.* man of the agricultural and mercantile tribe.

වෛශ්‍රවණ, *Waiṣrawaṇa*, *s.* (විශ්‍රවස් *viṣrawas* father of the deity, අණ් *aṇ* aff.) name of Kuvéra regent of the north and chief of the Yakshas.

වෛශ්‍රවණවාස, *Waiṣra-waṇawása*, *s.* fig tree, *ficus altissima*, var. *laccifera*, [Colloq. නුග *nuga*].

වෛශ්වානර, *Waiṣwánara*, *s.* fire, [Colloq. ගින්දර *gindara*].

වෛශ්වී, *Waiṣví*, *s.* second of the constellations called Aásháḍhá, and twenty-first of the whole.

වෛශාඛ, *Waiṣákha*, *s.* (විශාඛා *viṣákhá* constellation) month in which the moon is full near the southern scale (April-May); churning stick; creeper, *pæderia fœtida*, [Colloq. සාරණ *sáraṇa*].

වෛශාරද්‍ය, *Waiṣáradya*, see විශාරද *viṣárada*.

වෛෂ්ණව, *Waishṇawa*, *s.* follower of Vishṇu: *a.* relating or belonging to Vishṇu.

වෛස්‍යාකම්කරණවා, *Waisyákamkaraṇawá*, corruptly for වේසාකම්කරණවා *wésákamkaraṇawá*.

වෛස්‍යාව, *Waisyáwa*, corruptly for වේශ්‍යාව *wéṣyáwa*.

වෛසාරින, *Waisárina*, *s.* (වි *vi* and සෘ *sṛi* to go) fish, [Colloq. මාළු *máḷu*].

වොටු, *Woṭu*, *s.* pistil of flowers; camel.

වොපිරි, *Wopiri*, *s.* head-dress, turban.

වොරජනා, *Worajaná*, *a.* (වි *vi* and රජ *raja* to shine) shining, glittering, splendid.

වොලොගන්නවා, *Wologannawá*, *v.* to rob, to plunder, [Colloq. කොල්ලකනවා *kollakanawá*].

වෝඪ, *Wóḍha*, *s.* large snake, Boa constrictor.

වෝර, *Wóra*, *s.* sort of pulse, *dolichos catjang*.

වෝල, *Wóla*, *s.* gum myrrh.

වැක්කෙරෙණවා, *Wękkereṇawá*, *v.* to fall in drops, to be poured out, to distil.

වැකරිල්ල, *Wękarilla*, *s.* ringlet of hair, tress, braid.

වැකරැලි, *Wękaręli*, *s.* wrinkle, spot, blemish, skin shrivelled by old age; fold of flesh forming a double chain.

වැකි, *Węki*, *a.* daubed, smeared, stained, from වකනවා *wakanawá*.

වැකුම, *Wękuma*, *s.* staining, daubing, smearing.

වැගිරීම, *Węgirima*, *s.* effusion, verbal noun of වැගිරෙණවා *węgirenawá.*

වැගිරෙණවා, *Węgirenawá*, *v.* to shed, to drop, to fall off: pret. වැගිරුණා *węgiruná.*

වැගුරුණු, *Węgurunu*, *a.* dropped, shed.

වැජබෙනවා, *Węjabenawá*, see වැජඹෙනවා *węjambenawá.*

වැජඹීම, *Węjambíma*, verbal noun of වැජඹෙනවා *węjambenawá.*

වැජඹෙන, *Węjambena*, *a.* sporting, living happily: see the next.

වැජඹෙනවා, *Wéjambenawá*, *v.* to sport, to wanton; to live in prosperity, to reside, used only of persons of rank.

වැට, *Węta*, *s.* an enclosure of any kind, hedge, fence, from වට *wata* to surround, to encompass; wages; lamp; protection.

වැට එරබදු, *Węta-erabadu*, *s.* coral tree, *erythrina indica;* also called එරබදු *erabadu.*

වැටකෙයියා, *Węṭakeyiyá*, } *s.* screw-pine, *pandanus fascicularis* or *p. odoratissimus;* also called මුදු කෙයියා *mudu-keyiyá.*
වැටකේ, *Węṭaké*,

වැටකොළු, *Węṭakoḷu*, *s.* cultivated plant, the fruit of which is eaten, *luffa acutangula (Cucurbitaceæ);* also called දුරවැටකොළු *dúra-węṭakoḷu.*

වැටහික්ගහ, *Węta-hik-gaha*, *s.* tree, *amyris zeylanica*, or variety of *odina woodier.*

වැටහිර, *Węṭahira*, *s.* plant, *justicia adhatoda*, [Colloq. අගල්අදර *agal-ádára*].

වැටහීම, *Węṭahíma*, *s.* understanding, comprehending, conception.

වැටහෙනවා, *Węṭahenawá*, *v.* to comprehend, to understand, to perceive: pret. වැටහුනා *węṭahuná.*

වැටිකරණවා, *Węṭikaraṇawá*, *v.* to twine, to twist.

වැටිය, *Węṭiya*, *s.* wick of a lamp; rain; bank of a river, pond, lake, etc.; artificial bank, dam, banks in the rice fields, which dam in the water and serve as pathways: pl. වැටි *węṭi.*

වැටිපානවා, *Węṭipánawá*, *v.* to be reduced in circumstances, to be impoverished.

වැටිපෑම, *Węṭipẹma*, *s.* adversity, declining from affluence to poverty.

වැටීම, *Węṭíma*, *s.* falling, fall; verbal noun of වැටෙනවා *węṭenawá*, which see.

වැටු, *Węṭu*, *s.* road, path.

වැටුප්, *Węṭup*, *s.* livelihood, means of subsistence; wages, hire, paid in kind, as paddy, etc.; lamp.

වැටුපු, *Węṭupu*, *s.* lamp, stand or wooden frame of a lamp.

වැටෙනවා, *Węṭenawá*, *v.* to fall, to drop, to fall down: pret. වැටුනා *węṭuná.*

වැඩ, *Węḍa*, *s.* work, service, labour, business, employment; benefit, advantage, good consequence; increase.

වැඩඉන්නවා, *Węḍainnawá*, *v.* to sit down, to be seated, used only of persons of rank or priests.

වැඩකරණවා, *Węḍakaraṇawá*, *v.* to work.

වැඩකරුවා, *Węḍakaruwá*, } *s.* (වැඩ work, කරුවා or කාරයා who does) servant, menial; labourer, workman.
වැඩකාරයා, *Węḍakárayá*,

වැඩකාරි, *Węḍakári*, *s.* female servant.

වැඩපල, *Wéḍapala*, *s.* message, errand; service, business; place where any business is carried on.

වැඩමවන, *Węḍamawana*, *a.* causing to come, or bringing, used only of persons of rank and Buddhist priests.

වැඩමවනවා, *Węḍamawanawá*, *v.* to cause to come, to bring (spoken of persons of rank and Buddhist priests).

වැඩය, *Węḍaya*, *s.* work, labour, explaining, resolving: see also වැඩ *węḍa.*

වැඩවසනවා, *Węḍawasanawá*, *v.* to dwell, to reside, to stay, to continue, used only of priests and persons of rank.

වැඩවසම, *Węḍawasama*, *s.* service pravéṇi lands, *i. e.* the private property of an individual proprietor granted as a remuneration for public service, especially military service.

වැඩවිඳිනවා, *Węḍarindinawá*, *v.* to possess, to use.

වැඩහිටිනවා, *Węḍahiṭinawá*, *v.* to be present, applied to persons of rank.

වැඩහිඳිනවා, *Węḍahindinawá*, *v.* to sit, to be seated, spoken of priests and persons of rank.

වැඩි, *Węḍi*, *s.* increase. abundance, sufficiency: *ind.* more, more than; large, great.

වැඩිකරණවා, *Węḍikaraṇawá*, *v.* to increase, to multiply.

වැඩිකොක්ගහ, *Węḍikok-gaha*, *s.* tree, *dracæna terminalis.*

වැඩිකොට, *Węḍikoṭa*, *ad.* chiefly, particularly.

වැඩිගොරඩිය, *Węḍigoraḍiya*, *s.* Patna or common white field-pea, *pisum sativum.*

වැඩිතරම, *Węḍitarama*, *s.* consequence, importance; rank, influence.

වැඩිදියුණුකරණවා, *Wẹdidiyuṇukaraṇawá*, *v.* to improve.

වැඩිදියුණුවීම, *Wẹdidiyuṇuvíma*. *s.* prosperity, improvement.

වැඩිදියුණුවෙනවා, *Wẹdidiyuṇuwenawá*, *v.* (වැඩි and දියුණු prosperity, වෙනවා to be) to prosper, to improve, to flourish.

වැඩිදුර, *Wẹdidura*, *a.* farther, as වැඩිදුර කල්පනා කරණවා *wẹdidura-kalpanákaraṇawá*, to consider farther, furthermore.

වැඩිදෙනා, *Wẹdidená*, *s.* the majority; the greater number of persons.

වැඩිපුර, *Wẹdipura*, *s.* 'over and above; exceeding a certain number or quantity; surplus.

වැඩිමනත්, *Wẹdimanat*, *s.* surplus, remainder.

වැඩිමල්, *Wẹdimal*, *a.* elder; more advanced in age.

වැඩිමලා, *Wẹdimalá*, *s.* elder one: pl. වැඩිමල්ලු *wẹdimallu*.

වැඩිමහලු, *Wẹdimahalu*. *s.* (වැඩි and මහලු old) older, senior; first in years and rank, superior.

වැඩිය, *Wẹdiya*, *s.* larger number or quantity: *ad.* more, too much: see වැඩි *wẹdi*.

වැඩියසේක, *Wẹdiyaséka*, *v.* come (honorific).

වැඩිවිය, *Wẹdiviya*, *s.* (වැඩි grown up, විය age) maturity, manhood; mature age.

වැඩිවිය පැමිණෙනවා, *Wẹdiviya-pẹminenawá*, *v.* to grow, applied chiefly to young persons when they have attained the age of puberty, to come to maturity.

වැඩිවීම, *Wẹdivíma*, *s.* increasing, augmentation.

වැඩිවෙනවා, *Wẹdiwenawá*, *v.* to increase.

වැඩිසිටි, *Wẹdisiṭi*, *a.* elderly, senior.

වැඩිසිටියන්, *Wẹdisiṭiyan*, *s.* (වැඩි greater or higher, සිටියන් those who are) persons of years or importance, man respectable either from age, learning, or authority.

වැඩීම, *Wẹḍíma*, *s.* nursing, carrying in arms; increasing; verbal noun of වඩනවා *waḍanawá*.

වැඩු, *Wẹḍu*, *a.* increased, augmented, caused to increase.

වැඩුන්, *Wẹḍun*, *s.* cutting, incision, increase, from වර්ධ *wardha*.

වැඩුනු, *Wẹḍunu*, *a.* increased, multiplied.

වැඩුම්, *Wẹḍum*, verbal noun of වඩනවා *waḍanawá*.

වැඩෙනවා,, *Wẹḍenawá*, *v.* to enlarge, to augment, to increase: pret. වැඩුනා *wẹḍuná*.

වැත්, *Wẹt*, *s.* similitude, figure of speech; resemblance, similarity, likeness.

වැත්ත, *Wẹtta*, *s.* time, occasion, opportunity.

වැතිරීම, *Wẹtiríma*, *s.* falling off, dropping, falling over, as liquids from a full vessel; being unimproved, at a stand; deteriorating; see the next.

වැතිරෙණවා, *Wẹtireṇawá*, *v.* to sprawl on the ground, to lie prone or extended, to overflow, to be at a dead stand: pret. වැතුරුණා *wẹturuṇá*.

වැතුම, *Wẹtuma*. *s.* web in a weaver's loom.

වැද්දගන්නවා, *Wẹddagannawá*, *v.* to receive favourably.

වැද්දදෙනවා, *Wẹddadenawá*, *v.* to give reception, to admit, to receive or take in.

වැද්දා, *Wẹddá*, *s.* archer, bowman, one who lives by his bow; man of the Vẹddá tribe, a race of people living in the interior jungles and forests of Ceylon; their history is but imperfectly known; they appear to be a remnant of the aborigines of the island, who were driven into the jungles first by the Hindu invaders, and subsequently by the Siṇhalese who sprang from that race: pl. වැද්දෝ *wẹddó*.

වැද, *Wẹda*, *part.* having entered.

වැදඔත්, *Wẹdaot*, *a.* laid down; reclined, lain.

වැදගත්, *Wẹdagat*, *a.* important, demanding attention.

වැදගත්කම, *Wẹdagatkama*, *s.* importance, respectability.

වැදගන්නවා, *Wẹdagannawá*, *v.* to concern, to affect, to be important.

වැදගැම්ම, *Wẹdagẹmma*, *s.* importance, interest, concern.

වැදහොවිනවා, *Wẹdahovinawá*, *v.* to sleep, to repose, to fall prostrate, to lie down.

වැදි, *Wẹdi*, plural වැද්දෝ *wẹddó*, archer; panegyrist: see වැඳි *wẹndi*.

වැදිකම, *Wẹdikama*, *s.* archery, practice of archery.

වැදිපුතා, *Wẹdiputá*, *s.* (වැදි archer, පුතා son) archer, bowman, one who lives by the bow: man of the Vẹdda tribe.

වැදිලි, *Wẹdili*, plural of වැදැල්ල *wẹdẹlla*.

වැදී, *Wẹdí*, *s.* widow; *past. part.* of වැදෙනවා *wẹdenawá*.

වැදීම, *Wẹdíma*, *s.* entrance: birth, the act of bringing forth; verbal noun of වදනවා *wadanawá*.

වැදු, *Wẹdu*, *a.* brought forth.

වැදුම, *Wẹduma*, *s.* stroke, the act of being struck; act of bringing forth; verbal noun of වදිනවා *wadinawá*.

වැදෙනවා, *Wędenawá, v.* to affect, to concern, to be interesting, to be important, to be struck by an arrow or mentally: pret. වැදුනා *węduná.*

වැදැල්ල, *Węḍęlla, s.* lump, clump, ball, clod; heap, quantity, cluster, piece of flesh: pl. වැදලි *wędali.*

වැදෑරුම්, *Wędęrum,* } *s.* mode, manner, sort, kind;
වැදෑරුම, *Wędęruma,* } saying; verbal noun of වදාරණවා *wadáraṇawá,* to say.

වැඳ, *Węṇda, p.* having worshipped, bowing: *past. part.* of වඳිනවා *waṉdinawá.*

වැඳි, *Węṉdi, s.* bard, panegyrist forming part of the retinue of an eastern monarch, and employed to sing the praises of the prince or chant martial songs: see වන්දි *wandi.*

වැඳිය, *Węṉdiya, s.* worship, respectful salutation.

වැඳිරි, *Węṉdiri, s.* female monkey of the black species, from වඳුරා *waṉdurá.*

වැඳීම, *Węṉdíma, s.* worship, adoration, bowing; verbal noun of වඳිනවා *waṉdinawá.*

වැඳුම, *Węṉduma, s.* worship, adoration; verbal noun of වඳිනවා *waṉdinawá.*

වැඳඹු, *Węndaṃbu, s.* (වඳි *waṉdi* barren, අඹු *aṃbu* woman) barren womam; one who has neither husband nor children, widow.

වැඳඹු පුරුෂයා, *Węndaṃbu-purushayá, s.* widower.

වැඳඹු ස්ත්‍රී, *Węndaṃbu-strí,* see වැඳඹු *węndaṃbu.*

වැන්ද, *Węndá, v.* worshipped, bowed to; *part. a.* of වඳිනවා *waṉdinawá,* to make obeisance.

වැන්න, *Wenna, s.* class, tribe, sort, order; form, figure, from වර්ණ *warṇa.*

වැනසිල්ල, *Węnasilla, s.* extirpation destruction: see වැනසුම *węnasuma.*

වැනසිලිකරණවා, *Węnasilikaraṇawá, v.* to destroy.

වැනසු, *Węnasu, s.* destruction, subversion, ruin.

වැනසුන්, *Węnasun,* see වැනසුම *węnasuma.*

වැනසුනා, *Węnasuná, v.* perished, preterite of වැනසෙනවා *węnasenawá,* to be destroyed or to perish.

වැනසුනු, *Węnasunu, a.* destroyed, extirpated.

වැනසුම, *Węnasuma, s.* loss, disappearance, destruction, ruin; extirpation, devastation.

වැනි, *Węni, a.* like, similar, resembling: *ind.* particle or affix forming the ordinals; also, written වෙනි *weni* as තුන්වෙනි *tunweni,* third.

වැනිය, *Węniya, s.* being, continuance, similarity: see the last.

වැනීම, *Węníma, s.* shaking, moving, agitation, spreading in the sun to dry; praise, eulogium.

වැනු, *Węnu, s.* declaring, uttering, speaking, saying.

වැනුන, *Węnuna, a.* shaken, moved, agitated.

වැනුම, *Węnuma, s.* praise, panegyric, eulogium: shaking, moving.

වැනෙනවා, *Węnenawá, v.* to shake of itself; to move to and fro; to reel: pret. වැනුනා *węnuná.*

වැපිරීම, *Wępiríma, s.* sowing; verbal noun of වපුරණවා *wapuraṇawá:* to sow.

වැපු, *Wępu, s.* lamentation, weeping, the external expression of grief.

වැමෑරූ, *Węmęrú, p.* vomited, thrown out.

වැය, *Węya, s.* expenditure, expense, cost, from ව්‍යය *wyaya.*

වැයස්ථාන, *Węyasthána, s.* sign of the zodiac, Pisces.

වැයින්, *Wein, s.* wine. (Eng.)

වැයිම, *Węyima,* } see වයනවා *wayanawá.*
වැයුම, *Węyuma,* }

වැර, *Węra, s.* strength, force, muscular power: *a.* strong: see වෙර *wera.*

වැරකාරයා, *Węrakárayá, s.* strong man; able-bodied man.

වැරටිය, *Węraṭiya, s.* dried cow dung: pl. වැරටි *węraṭi.*

වැරණිය, *Węraṇiya, s.* shrub, small sticks used instead of laths, *hedyotis fruticosa (Rubiaceæ).*

වැරද, *Węradu, past part.* of වරදිනවා *waradinawá.*

වැරදිකාරයා, *Węradikárayá, s.* (වැරැද්ද *węredda* and කාර *kára* who does) culprit, offender.

වැරදීම, *Węradíma,* } *s.* fault, mistake; verbal
වැරදුම, *Węraduma,* } noun of වරදිනවා *waradinawá.*

වැරදෙනවා, *Węradenawá, v.* to mistake, to err, to blunder: pret. වැරදුනා *węraduná.*

වැරව, *Werawa, s.* cobra capella, [Colloq. නයා *nayá*].

වැරසන, *Węrasana, s.* bear, [Colloquial: වළහා *waḷahá*].

වැරසැර, *Węrasęra, s.* strength, force, power: *a.* strong, harsh.

වැරහැල්ල, *Węrahęlla, s.* rag: pl. වැරහැලි *węrahęli.*

වැරළි, *Węraḷi,* the plural of වැරැල්ල *węręlla.*

වැරීම, *Węríma, s.* weaning, out of season, ceasing to be (as fruit on a tree).

වැරුණු, *Węruṇu, a.* worn out; ceased to be.

වැරැද්ද, *Węręddа, s.* error, mistake; crime, fault, offence: pl. වැරදි *węradi.*

වැරැල්ල, *Węręlla*, *s.* ragged cloth, rags, tatters; slight rain, drizzling; kind of medicinal plant.

වැල්, *Węl*, *s.* creeper, necklace: *a.* creeping, scandent: see also වැල *węla*.

වැල් අඟුණ, *Węl-anguna*, *s.* plant: see අඟුණ *anguna*.

වැල් අන්දර, *Węl-andara*, *s.* plant, variety of *dichrostachys cinera*.

වැල් අනිත්ත, *Węl-anitta*, *s.* plant, variety of *rhinacanthus communis*.

වැල් අල, *Węl-ala*, *s.* tuberous plant, *colocasia nymphæifolia*, var. or *c. antiquorum (Araceæ)*; also called යකුතලා *yakutalá*.

වැල් ඇටඹරු, *Węl-ętambaru*, *s.* tree, variety of *fagræa zeylanica*.

වැල් ඇපල, *Węl-ępala*, *s.* plant, *triumfetta angulata:* see ඇපල *ępala*.

වැල් ඇඹිල්ල, *Węl-ęmbilla*, *s.* large climbing plant, *embelia ribes (Myrsineæ)*; shrub, *elæagnus latifolia (Elæagnaceæ)*; also called කටු ඇඹිල්ල *kaṭu-ęmbilla*.

වැල් ඇහැටු, *Wal-ęhętu*, *s.* straggling plant, *ficus gibbosa (Urticaceæ)*; also called ගස් නෙටුල් *gas-neṭul*.

වැල් ඉකිරි, *Węl-ikiri*, *s.* plant, variety of *acanthus ilicifolius*.

වැල් ඉද්ද, *Węl-idda*, *s.* (වැල් creeper, ඉද්ද oleander) plant, perhaps a species of *oleander*.

වැල්ඊර, *Welíra*, *s.* dried fish.

වැල් එරමිනියා, *Węl-ęraminiyá*, *s.* plant, species of *zizyphus*.

වැල් කඩුරු, *Węl-kaduru*, *s.* tree of the order *Apocynaceæ*.

වැල් කපු, *Węl-kapu*, *s.* species of cotton plant, *gossypium*.

වැල් කපුරු, *Węl-kapuru*, *s.* plant, *andromeda flexuosa*.

වැල් කයිල, *Węl-kayila*, *s.* plant, *phyllanthus reticulatus (Euphorbiaceæ)*.

වැල් කරල්සැබෝ, *Węl-karalsębó*, *s.* biennial straggling plant. *achyranthes lappacea:* see ගස් කරල් හැබ *gas-karalhęba*.

වැල් කලවිය, *Węl-kalaviya*, *s.* scandent plant, *dalbergia scandens*.

වැල් කහ, *Węl-kaha*, *s.* (වැල් creeper, කහ saffron) creeping plant, turmeric, *curcuma longa*.

වැල් කහඹිලියා, *Węl-kahambiliyá*, *s.* twining plant with stinging hairs, *tragia involucrata*, with several varieties peculiar to Ceylon, *t. intermedia*, *cordata* and *montana*: see also ගස් කහඹිලියා *gas-kahambiliyá* and වල් කහඹිලියා *wal-kahambiliyá*.

වැල් කිනිහිරිය, *Węl-kinihiriya*, *s.* (වැල් creeper) tree, variety of *cochospermum gossypium*.

වැල් කුකුලල, *Węl-kukulala*, *s.* sort of yam, of order *araceæ*.

වැල් කුප්පමේනිය, *Węl-kuppaméniya*, *s.* plant, variety of *acalypha indica*.

වැල් කුඹුරු, *Węl-kumburu*, *s.* bonduc or nicker tree, *cæsalpinia* or *guilandia bonducella;* also called කුඹුරුවැල් *kumburuwęl*.

වැල් කොතලා, *Węl-kotalá*, *s.* plant, *torenia asiatica;* also called කොතලාවැල් *kotalá-węl*.

වැල් කොලොඳු, *Węl-kolondu*, *s.* worm wood, *artemisia maderas-patana;* also called වල්කොලොන්දු *wal-kolondu*.

වැල් කැප්පිටිය, *Węl-kęppiṭiya*, *s.* plant, *croton aromaticum (Euphorbiaciæ)*.

වැල් කැලිය, *Węl-kęliya*, *s.* shrub, *grewia orientalis*, called in Tamil, Thuvattai.

වැල් ගොනිකා, *Węl-goniká*, *s.* plant, not ascertained.

වැල් තඹල, *Węl-tambala*, *s.* plant, not ascertained.

වැල් තිබ්බටු, *Węl-tibbaṭu*, *s.* species of egg plant, *solanum trilobatum:* see වල්තිබ්බටු *wal-tibbaṭu*.

වැල් තිඹොල්, *Węl-timbol*, *s.* plant, not ascertained.

වැල් තුඹ, *Węl-tumba*, *s.* species of *momordica:* see තුඹකරිවිල *tumba-karivila*.

වැල් දමනිය, *Węl-damaniya*, *s.* creeping plant, *stilobium pruriens:* see දමනිය *damaniya*.

වැල් දෙහි, *Węl-dehi*, *s.* plant, *azima tetracantha (Salvadoraceæ)*.

වැල් නවහන්දි, *Węl-nawahandi*, *s.* creeping plant, *cactus pendulus:* see නවහන්දි *nawahandi*.

වැල් නානු, *Węl-nánu*, *s.* small spreading shrub, *stylosanthes mucronata (Leguminosæ)*.

වැල් නිටොල්, *Węl-niṭol*, *s.* creeping shrub with many stems, *ficus repens*.

වැල් නිදිකුම්බ, *Węl-nidikumba*, *s.* sensitive plant, *mimosa pudica*.

වැල් නියගලා, *Węl-niyangalá*, *s.* plant, variety of *gloriosa superba*.

වැල් නිවිති, *Węl-niviti*, see නිවිතිවැල් *niviti-węl*.

වැල් නුග, *Węl-nuga*, *s.* tree, species of *ficus*.

වැල් පඹුරු, *Węl-pamburu*, *s.* plant, variety of *atalantia Missionis*.

වැල් පිනිහිරිය, *Węl-pinihiriya*, *s.* plant, not ascertained.

වැල් පුපුල, *Węl-pupula, s.* hemp agrimony, peculiar to Ceylon, *vernonia zeylanica:* see පුපුල *pupula.*

වැල් පුරුක්, *Węl-puruk, s.* plant, variety of *asystasia coromandeliana.*

වැල් පෙනෙල, *Węl-penela, s.* heart-seed, *cardiospermum haliacacabum;* also called පෙනෙල වැල් *penela-węl.*

වැල් බටු, *Węl-baṭu, s.* plant, species of *solanum.*

වැල් බඹර, *Węl-bam̆bara, s.* climbing plant, *dalbergia Championii;* also called බඹරවැල් *bambara-węl.*

වැල් බරණ්ඩ, *Węl-baranda, s.* scandent plant, *lowaria scandens.*

වැල් බාඳුරා, *Węl-bán̆durá, s.* plant, peculiar to Ceylon, *nepenthes distillatoria;* also called බාඳුරා වැල් *bán̆durá-węl.*

වැල් බුත්සරණ, *Węl-butsaraṇa, s.* plant, with calyx-lobe, enlarged as white leaf, *mussænda frondosa (Rubiaceæ);* also called මුස්සැන්ද *mussęnda.*

වැල් බූටෑ, *Węl-búṭę́, s.* prickly shrub, sort of bramble, *rubus moluccanus (Rosaceæ).*

වැල් බූරුන්ද, *Węl-búręnda, s.* shrub, *clerodendrum inerme:* see වල් ගුරුන්ද *wal-gúręnda.*

වැල් බෙඳුරු, *Węl-bén̆duru, s.* fern, *stenochlæna palustre (Filices).*

වැල් බෝවිටියා, *Węl-bóviṭiyá, s.* plant, *melastoma repens.*

වැල් බැවිල, *Węl-bęvila, s.* plant, variety of *sida humilis:* see බැවිල *bęvila.*

වැල් මදට, *Węl-madaṭa, s.* (වැල් creeper, මදට rubia mangitha) plant used in medicine and in dyeing, variety of *rubia manjitha.*

වැල් මරුක්කු, *Węl-marukku, s.* plant. *panicum Crus-galli (Gramineæ).*

වැල් මිදි, *Węl-midi, s.* (වැල් and මිදි vine) grape vine, *vitis vinifera.*

වැල්මී, *Węlmí, s.* (වැල් and මී honey) liquorice plant, *glycirrhiza glabrum.*

වැල් මුරුංගා, *Węl-murun̆gá, s.* variety of murun̆ga, *moringa pterogosperma.*

වැල් මොට්ටු, *Węl-moṭṭu, s.* creeping plant, *ceropegia biflora (Asclepiadeæ).*

වැල් මැඩිය, *Węl-męḍiya, s.* creeping plant, *cissus verrucosa.*

වැල් රදලිය, *Węl-radaliya, s.* plant, peculiar to Ceylon, *connarus champonii (Connaraceæ).*

වැල් රුක්අත්තන, *Węl-rukattana, s.* plant: see රුක්අත්තන *rukattana.*

වැල්ල, *Węlla, s.* sandy place; sand, sand bank, sea shore.

වැල්ලන්ගිරිය, *Węllangiriya, s.* plant, *paramignya monophylla (Rutaceæ).*

වැල්ලල, *Węllala, s.* esculent root, yam, *dioscorea.*

වැල්ලා, *Węllá,* see වල්ලා *wallá.*

වැල් හිඟුරල, *Węl-hin̆gurala, s.* kind of yam.

වැල් හිරිතල, *Węl-hiritala, s.* kind of yam.

වැල්හිරි, *Węl-híri, s.* plant, *cyperus iria (Cyperaceæ).*

වැල් හිරැස්ස, *Węl-hírę̆ssa, s.* creeping plant, *vitis quadrangularis:* see හිරැස්ස *hírę̆ssa.*

වැල, *Węla, s.* creeper, creeping plant in general; likeness, resemblance; shore, beach, sea shore; vine or its tendrils; ripe or matured jack: see වැල ගෙඩිය *węla-geḍiya;* row, line.

වැලක, *Węlaka, past. part.* of වලකිනවා *walakinawá.*

වැලකිල්ල, *Węlakilla, s.* interception, preventing, hindering; concealment, hiding, from වලකිනවා *walakinawá.*

වැලකීම, *Węlakíma, s.* obstacle, impediment, concealment; verbal noun of වලකිනවා *walakinawá.*

වැලගෙඩිය, *Węlageḍiya, s.* soft sort of jack fruit.

වැලඟුණු, *Węlan̆guṇu, s.* creeping plant, perhaps a sort of *hoya:* see අඟුණ *an̆guṇa.*

වැලඳසුන්, *Węladasun, s.* embrace, [Colloq. වැලඳ ගැනීම *węlan̆dagęníma*].

වැලදෙස්, *Węlades, s.* hindrance, [Colloq. තහනම *tahanama*].

වැලඳගන්නවා, *Węlan̆dagannawá, v.* to embrace, to press to the bosom.

වැලඳි, *Węlan̆di, s.* embracing, an embrace; tying, ligature.

වැලඳීම, *Węlan̆díma,* } *s.* eating; attack of a
වැලඳුම, *Węlan̆duma,* } disease; embrace; verbal noun of වලඳනවා *walan̆danawá.*

වැලඳෙනවා, *Węlan̆denawá, v.* to befal, to become holden by: pret. වැලඳුනා *węlan̆duná.*

වැලනිත්ත, *Węlanitta, s.* twining plant with peltate leaves, *stephania;* also called හුණුකැටිය වැල් *huṇukęṭiya-węl:* and see අනිත්ත *anitta.*

වැලප, *Węlapa, past. part.* of වලපිනවා *walapinawá.*

වැලපීම, *Węlapíma,* } *s.* outward expression of
වැලපුම, *Węlapuma,* } grief, lamentation; verbal noun of වලපනවා *walapanawá.*

වැලපෙ, *Węlape. s.* hair of the head.

වැලපෙනවා, *Wẹlapenawá*, *v.* to lament, to bewail, from විලාප *vilápa:* pret. වැලපුනා *wẹlapuná*.

වැලබරණ, *Wẹlabaraṇa*, *s.* (වැල් *wẹl* and අබරණ *abaraṇa* ornament) necklace; any kind of neck or arm ornament as bracelets, armlets.

වැලමිට, *Wẹlamiṭa*, *s.* elbow: pl. වැලමිටි *wẹlamiṭi*.

වැලමිටිපාත, *Wẹlamiṭipáta*, *s.* (වැලමිට *wẹlamiṭa* and පාත below) forearm.

වැලලීම, *Wẹlalíma*, *s.* burying, interment.

වැලහන්, *Wẹlahan*, *a.* near, proximate; concealed, hidden.

වැලහින්න, *Wẹlahinna*, } *s.* female bear.
වැලහින්නි, *Wẹlahinni*,

වැලහිම්, *Wẹlahimi*, *s.* disappearance, vanishing, invisibility.

වැලහිල්ල, *Wẹlahilla*, } *s.* abstaining, refraining; hindering, opposing, hiding.
වැලහීම, *Wẹlahíma*,

වැලහුම, *Wẹlahuma*, *s.* concealment.

වැලි, *Wẹli*, *s.* sand, gravel; wrinkle, shrivelled flesh: *ind.* particle signifying again, yet, moreover, furthermore.

වැලිකලන්ද, *Wẹli-kalandá*, *s.* kind of fish.

වැලි කහ, *Wẹli-kaha*, *s.* plant, the leaves of which yield a yellow dye, *memecylon capitellatun (Melastomaceæ);* also called දොඩන් කහ *doḍan-kaha*.

වැලිකිකිළි, *Wẹli-kikiḷi*, *s.* jungle hen: see වැලි කුකුළා *wẹli-kukuḷá*.

වැලි කුකුරුමාන්, *Wẹli-kukurumán*, *s.* plant, variety of *randia* or *gardenia dumetorum*.

වැලිකුකුළා, *Wẹli-kukuḷá*, *s.* Ceylon jungle cock, *gallus lafayetti, (Phasianidæ*, order *Gallinæ)*.

වැලි කුරුඳු, *Wẹli-kurundu*, *s.* plant, variety of *cinnamomum zeylanicum*.

වැලි කොස්ඇට, *Wẹli-koseṭa*, *s.* jackseed preserved in a heap of sand.

වැලිගොව්වා, *Wẹligowwá*, *s.* (වැලි sand, ගොව්වා guard, keeper) river fish.

වැලිත්, *Wẹlit*, *ind.* particle; and, moreover.

වැලිතලන්, *Wẹlitalan*, plural of the next.

වැලිතලාව, *Wẹlitaláwa*, *s.* (වැලි sand, තලා *talá* plain) sand bank, bed or plain of sand.

වැලිතෙර, *Wẹli-tera*, *s.* (වැලි and තෙර sand) sandy bank of a river.

වැලි දඹ, *Wẹli-damba*, *s.* (වැලි and දඹ eugenia) fruit, probably a species of the jambu or eugenia.

වැලිදු, *Wẹlidu*, *ind. particle.* and, moreover, but, further.

වැලිපියානා, *Wẹlipiyáná*, see වැලිපැන්නා *wẹli-pẹnná*.

වැලිපිල, *Wẹlipiḷa*, *s.* (වැලි and පිළ table) bench or table of stone, clay, etc. covered with sand for writing on, with a style or pointed stick.

වැලි පොල්ල, *Wẹli-polla*, *s.* (වැලි sand, පොල්ල trunk) part of the coconut or areca tree immediately above the ground, from the softness of its texture.

වැලිපැන්නා, *Wẹlipẹnná*, *s.* plant, peculiar to Ceylon, *anisophyllea zeylanica (Rhizophoraceæ);* also called වැලිපියානා *wẹlipiyáná*.

වැලි බිම, *Wẹli-bima*, *s.* (වැලි and බිම ground) sandy or gravelly soil.

වැලිමීයා, *Wẹlimíyá*, *s.* sort of field rat.

වැලිමුව, *Wẹli-muwa*, *s.* (වැලි wrinkle, මුව face) white-faced monkey.

වැලිමැක්කා, *Wẹlimẹkká*, *s.* (වැලි sand, මැක්කා fly) flea found in unpaved houses, *pulex irritans (Syphonoptera)*.

වැලිවරා, *Wẹliwará*, *s.* periwinkle, *vinca rosea*.

වැලිවැන්න, *Wẹliwẹnna*, *s.* plant, *dimorphocalyx glabellus (Euphorbiaceæ)*.

වැලිහකුරු, *Wẹlihakuru*, *s.* species of jaggery, raw sugar made from the juice of the kitul tree, *caryota urens*.

වැලිහත්ත, *Wẹlihatta*, *s.* mushroom: pl. වැලිහතු *wẹlihatu*.

වැලුක්, *Wẹluk*, *s.* (වැල් *wẹl* creeper, උක් *uk* sugar cane) plant growing on the borders of rivers, marshes, etc. in appearance resembling the sugar cane, *arundo tibialis*.

වැලැක්ම, *Wẹlẹkma*, *s.* stopping, obstructing.

වැලැක්වීම, *Wẹlẹkvíma*, *s.* hindering, obstructing.

වැලැක, *Wẹlẹka*, *past. part.* of වලකිනවා *walakinawá*.

වැව් *Wẹw*, plural of the next.

වැව, *Wẹwa*, *s.* lake, pond, large tank, from වාපි *wápi*.

වැවිර, *Wẹvira*, *s.* wound, scar; mark of a rod or whip on animal flesh: pl. වැවිරි *wẹviri*.

වැවිල්ල, *Wẹvilla*, *s.* sowing, plantation, planting, cultivating; that which is planted, vegetables, herbs, from වවනවා *wawanawá:* pl. වැවිලි *wẹvili*.

වැවීම, *Wẹvíma*, } *s.* planting: see වැවිල්ල *wẹvilla*.
වැවුන්, *Wẹwun*,
වැවුම, *Wẹwuma*,

වැවුමාන්සිය, *Wẹwu-mánsiya*, *s.* planting share.

වැවුසොරොව්ව, *Wẹwsorowwa*, *s.* (වැව *wẹwa* and සොරොව්ව dyke) channel for letting off an excess of water from a tank.

වැවෙනවා, *Wẹwenawá*, *v.* to shoot, to sprout, to grow as vegetables, to thrive; to spring up: pret. වැවුනා *wẹwuná*.

වැස්ම, *Wẹsma*, *s.* covering, lid.

වැස්ස, *Wẹssa*, *s.* rain, raining.

වැස්සා, *Wẹssá*, *v.* it rained, past tense of වසිනවා *wasinawá*, it rains.

වැස්සි, *Wẹssi*, *s.* female calf.

වැස, *Wẹsa*, *past. part.* of වසනවා *wasanawá* or වසිනවා *wasinawá*.

වැසන, *Wẹsana*, *s.* clothes; sorrow, affliction.

වැසි, *Wẹsi*, *s.* rain, raining; cloth, clothes, covering; excrement, fæces, from වර්ච්ස් *warchas*.

වැසිකල, *Wẹsi-kala*, *s.* (වැසි rain, කල time) rainy season.

වැසිකළුව, *Wẹsikaḷuwa*, *s.* (වැසි and කළුව blackness) mist accompanying rain, darkness or cloud threatening rain.

වැසිකිළිය, *Wẹsikiḷiya*, } *s.* (වැසි fæces, කිළිය tent)
වැසිගිලිය, *Wẹsigiliya*, } necessary, privy.

වැසිදරාව, *Wẹsidaráwa*, *s.* stream or shower of rain.

වැසිපොද, *Wẹsipoda*, *s.* drop of rain.

වැසිම්, *Wẹsim*, *s.* covering, concealing, hiding: dwelling, residing, from වස *wasa*, to dwell, to cover.

වැසියා, *Wẹsiyá*, *s.* (වස *wasa* to dwell) dweller, inhabitant, resident.

වැසිවලාව, *Wẹsiwaláwa*, *s.* shower of rain.

වැසිවහිනවා, *Wẹsi-wahinawá*, *v.* to rain.

වැසීම, *Wẹsíma*, *s.* covering; verbal noun of වසනවා *wasanawá*.

වැසු, *Wẹsu*, *s.* covering, concealment.

වැසෙනවා, *Wẹsenawá*, *v.* to dwell, to stay, to abide; to be shut, to be closed, or covered; to be possessed by a demon: pret. වැසුනා *wẹsuná*.

වැහි, *Wẹhi*, see වැසි *wẹsi*.

වැහිලිහිණියා, *Wẹhi-lihiṇiyá*, *s.* general name for the swift, (*Cypselidæ*, order *Picariæ*), and swallow, (*Hirundinidæ*, order *Passeres*).

වැහීම, *Wẹhíma*, *s.* covering: see වැසීම *wẹsíma*.

වැහුම, *Wẹhuma*, *s.* covering, lid: see වැසීම *wẹsíma*.

වැහෙනවා, *Wẹhenawá*, *v.* to be poured out, to drop, to be shed: pret. වැහුනා *wẹhuná*: see වැසෙනවා *wẹsenawá*.

වැහැරුම්, *Wẹhẹrum*, *s.* playing on an instrument; becoming lean.

වෑ, *Wẹ́*, plural of වෑය *wẹ́ya*.

වෑකොඳවැල, *Wẹ́koṇda-wẹla*, *s.* species of jasmine, *jasminum azoricum*.

වෑඤ්ජන, *Wẹ́ñjana*, corruptly for ව්‍යඤ්ජන *wyañjana*.

වෑපාද, *Wẹ́páda*, corruptly for ව්‍යාපාද *wyápáda*.

වෑය, *Wẹ́ya*, *s.* adze: pl. වෑ *wẹ́*.

වෑයම්කරණවා, *Wẹ́yamkaraṇawá*, *v.* to endeavour, to attempt.

වෑයම, *Wẹ́yama*, *s.* effort, striving, persevering attempt, unwearied labour, assiduity: pl. වෑයම් *wẹ́yam*.

වෑරීම, *Wẹ́ríma*, *s.* leanness, meagreness.

වෑල්කොල, *Wẹ́lkola*, *s.* twining shrub, bearing a beautiful flower, *butea superba*.

වෑවරගෙඩිය, *Wẹ́wara-geḍiya*, *s.* young coconut.

වෑවරණි, *Wẹ́waraṇi*, *s.* plant, *persea semecarpifolia*, variety peculiar to Ceylon, *p. angustifolia* (*Lauraceæ*).

වෑවරය, *Wẹ́waraya*, *s.* young coconut.

වෑවීම, *Wẹ́víma*, *s.* comfort, consolation.

ව්‍යක්ත, *Wyakta*, *a.* (වි *vi* intensitive, අඤ් *añja* to make clear) wise, learned; evident, manifest, apparent, absolutely and specifically known or understood; individual, specific.

ව්‍යක්ති, *Wyakti*, *s.* (ව්‍යක්ත *wyakta* and ඉන් *in* aff.) individuality, specific appearance or being; appearance, manifestation.

ව්‍යජන, *Wyajana*, *s.* (වි *vi* before, අජ *aja* to go, to move) fan.

ව්‍යඤ්ජන, *Wyañjana*, *s.* (වි *vi* and අඤ්ජ *añja* to make clear) mark, spot, sign, token; sauce, condiment, curry; a consonant; privity either male or female.

ව්‍යඩම්බක, *Wyaḍumbaka*, *s.* castor oil plant, *ricinus communis*, [Colloq. එඬරු *eṇḍaru*].

ව්‍යතිකර, *Wyatikara*, *s.* (වි *vi* and අති *ati* prefixed to කර to make) misfortune, calamity; reciprocity, reciprocal action or relation.

ව්‍යතික්‍රම, *Wyatikrama*, } *s.* (වි *vi* and අති *ati*
ව්‍යතික්‍රමණ, *Wyatikramaṇa*, } with ක්‍රම to go) inverted or retrograde order, inversion, inverse; contrariety, opposition in general; adultery, fornication.

ව්‍යතිරික්ත, *Wyatirikta*, *a.* (වි *vi* and අති *ati* with රිච *richa* to unite, ක්ත *kta* aff.) different, separate, distinct.

ව්‍යතිරේක, *Wyatiréka*, *s.* (වි *vi* and අති *ati* prefixed to රිච *richa* to unite) difference, separateness, exception.

ව්‍යප්තිය, *Wyaptiya*, *s.* (වි *vi* before, අප *apa* to come) disease, *prolapsus utero*.

ව්‍යපකෘෂ්ට, *Wyapakṛishṭa*, *a.* (වි *vi* privative, අප කෘෂ්ට *apakṛishṭa* low, vile) excellent, best, noble, eminent.

ව්‍යපසමනය, *Wyapasamanaya*, *s.* (වි *vi* and අප *apa* prefixed to සම *sama* to calm) calming, pacifying, tranquilization; rest, cessation; taming, restraining, overcoming, disease, passion, etc.

ව්‍යපසමනයකරණවා, *Wyapasamanaya-karaṇawá*, *v.* to calm, to pacify.

ව්‍යපේත, *Wyapéta*, *a.* shut, closed, got rid of; opposed, contrary.

ව්‍යභිචාර, *Wyabhichára*, *s.* (වි *vi* and අභි *abhi* before, චර *chara* to go) erring, straying, literally or figuratively; following improper courses.

ව්‍යය, *Wyaya*, *s.* (ව්‍යය to expend) expenditure, spending; destruction, disappearance.

ව්‍යයස්ථාන, *Wyayasthána*, *s.* (ව්‍යය and ස්ථාන place) the place of the twelfth or last sign of the zodiac.

ව්‍යර්ථ, *Wyartha*, *a.* (වි *vi* privative, අර්ථ *artha* meaning, object) useless, vain, unprofitable, unmeaning.

ව්‍යවච්ඡින්න, *Wyawachchhinna*, *a.* (වි *vi* and අව *awa* before ඡිද *chhida* to cut, ක්ත *kta* aff.) different, separate, divided; cut in pieces.

ව්‍යවච්ඡේද, *Wyawachchhéda*, *s.* (වි *vi* and අව *awa* before ඡිද *chhida* to cut) dividing, separating, division; letting fly an arrow, shooting.

ව්‍යවධා, *Wyawadhá*, ව්‍යවධාන, *Wyawadhána*, ව්‍යවධි, *Wyawadhi* } *s.* (වි *vi* and අව *awa* before ධා or ධාන to have) covering, screen, anything which holds or conceals from sight; state of being covered, concealment, disappearance.

ව්‍යවස්ථාව, *Wyawastháwa*, *s.* (වි *vi* and අව *awa* before ස්ථා *sthá* to be) law, ordinance, injunction, statute; decree, written declaration of the law, code; sacred code of law.

ව්‍යවස්ථිත, *Wyawasthina*, *a.* (ව්‍යවස්ථා *wyawasthá* and ක්ත *kta* aff.) separated, distant, invariable; fixed; appointed.

ව්‍යවහරණ, *Wyawaharaṇa*, *s.* eating, taking food.

ව්‍යවහාර, *Wyawahára*, *s.* usage, custom, practice; lawsuit; statute, ordinance, institute; trading, traffic; profession, business, employment.

ව්‍යවහාරකරණවා, *Wyawahárakaraṇawá*, *v.* to use, to practice.

ව්‍යවහිත, *Wyawahita*, *a.* (වි *vi* and අව *awa* before, ධා *dhá* to have, ක්ත *kta* aff.) placed or situated contiguously to; intervening; covered, concealed.

ව්‍යස්ත, *Wyasta*, *a.* (වි *vi* severally, etc. අස *asa* to be or pervade) confounded, confused, bewildered; pervaded, penetrated, spread; reverse, opposite, inverted, reversed.

ව්‍යසනය, *Wyasanaya*, *s.* calamity, misfortune, fate; fault, vice, crime, frailty.

ව්‍යාකරණ, *Wyákaraṇa*, *s.* (වි *vi* and ආ *á* with කර *kara* to make) grammar; exposition, explanation, gloss, comment; solution of difficult or abstruse questions.

ව්‍යාකුල, *Wyákula*, *a.* (වි *vi* and ආකුල *ákula* confounded) bewildered, perplexed, overcome with fear, etc.

ව්‍යාකුලකරණවා, *Wyákulakaraṇawá*, *v.* to embarrass, to perplex.

ව්‍යාකොඩ, *Wyákoṇḍa*, see වෑකොඩුවැල *wękoṇḍawęla*.

ව්‍යාඛ්‍යා, *Wyákhyá*, *s.* (වි *vi* and ආ *á* before, ඛ්‍යා to relate) exposition, explanation, gloss, comment.

ව්‍යාඛ්‍යාන, *Wyákhyána*, *s.* explaining, expounding, exposition.

ව්‍යාඝ්‍ර, *Wyághra*, *s.* royal or Bengal tiger; (in composition) best, pre-eminent; variety of the castor oil plant; tree, *galedupa* or *dalbergia arborea*.

ව්‍යාඝ්‍රනඛ, *Wyághra-nakha*, *s.* (ව්‍යාඝ්‍ර tiger, නඛ nail) sort of perfume; scratch or impression of the finger nails.

ව්‍යාඝ්‍රනායක, *Wyághra-náyaka*, *s.* (ව්‍යාඝ්‍ර and නායක leader) jackal, [Colloq. නරියා *nariyá*].

ව්‍යාඝ්‍රී, *Wyághri*, *s.* prickly sort of night shade, *solanum jacquini*, [Colloq. කටුවැල්බටු *kaṭuwęlbaṭu*].

ව්‍යාඝාත, *Wyághata*, ව්‍යාඝාතන, *Wyághátana*, } *s.* (වි *vi* and ආ *á* prefixed to, හන *hana* to strike) obstacle, impediment; striking, beating; tree, *cassia fistula*, [Colloq. ඇහැළ *ęhęla*]; the thirteenth of the astronomical Yógas.

ව්‍යාජ, *Wyája*, *s.* (වි *vi* before, අජ *aja* to go) deceit, fraud, craft, cunning; disguise either of person or purpose; wickedness.

ව්‍යාජස්තුති, *Wyájastuti*, *s.* (ව්‍යාජ disguise, ස්තුති praise) praise or censure conveyed in language that expresses the contrary, affected reproach or ironical commendation.

ව්‍යාජිකරණ, *Wyájikaraṇa*, s. corruptly for වාජිකරණ *wájikaraṇa*, medicine preventing old age, and prolonging life, the *elixir vitæ* of the ancients.

ව්‍යාධ, *Wyádha*, s. (ව්‍යධ *wyadha* to pierce) hunter, one who lives by killing deer, etc.; low or wicked man.

ව්‍යාධි, *Wyádhi*, s. (වි *vi* and ආ *á* with ධා *dhá* to have) sickness, disease in general, [Colloq. ලෙඩ *leḍa*]; leprosy; plant, *costus speciosus*, [Colloq. සෙංකොට්ටම් *seṇkoṭṭam*].

ව්‍යාධිඝාත, *Wyádhighâta*, s. (ව්‍යාධි disease, ඝාත what destroys) tree, *cassia fistula*, [Colloq. ඇහැළ *ẹhẹḷa*].

ව්‍යාධිත, *Wyádhita*, a. (ව්‍යාධි sickness, ඉත *ita* aff.) sick, ill, diseased.

ව්‍යාධිනාශ, *Wyádhi-náṣa*, s. tree, *cassia fistula*, [Colloq. ඇහැළ *ẹhẹḷa*].

ව්‍යාන, *Wyána*, } s. (වි *vi* before, අන *ana*
ව්‍යානවාත, *Wyána-wáta*, } to breathe) one of the five vital airs, that which is diffused throughout the body.

ව්‍යාප්ත, *Wyápta*, a. (වි *vi* before, ආප *ápa* to pervade, ක්ත *kta* aff.) pervaded, occupied or penetrated by; filled, full, obtained; got, procured; encircled, encompassed, surrounded.

ව්‍යාප්ති, *Wyápti*, s. pervading, inherence: see the last.

ව්‍යාප්‍ය, *Wyápya*, s. plant, *costus speciosus;* another plant, not ascertained, [Colloq. කොට්ටම් *koṭ-ṭam*].

ව්‍යාපද්, *Wyápad*, s. (වි *vi* and ආ *á* before, පද *pada* to go) death, decease; calamity.

ව්‍යාපන්න, *Wyápanna*, a. (වි *vi* and ආ *á* before, පද *pada* to go, ක්ත *kta* aff.) dead, deceased, expired; hurt, injured, killed; vitiated.

ව්‍යාපාද, *Wyápáda*, s. (වි *vi* and ආ *á* with පද *pada* to go) evil design, malice prepense, the wish or project to injure another.

ව්‍යාපී, *Wyápi*, a. (වි *vi* and ආප *ápa* to pervade) diffusive, comprehensive.

ව්‍යාම, *Wyáma*, s. (වි *vi* and අම *ama* to go) fathom, or the space between the tips of the fingers of either hand when the arms are extended, [Colloq. බඹේ *bambé*].

ව්‍යායම, *Wyáyama*, corruptly for ව්‍යායාම *wyáyáma*, which see.

ව්‍යායාම, *Wyáyáma*, s. (වි *vi* and ආ *á* and යම *yama* to refrain) fatigue, labour; athletic exercise, as playing with heavy clubs, etc.; business, occupation; see also, ව්‍යාම *wyáma*.

ව්‍යාල, *Wyála*, s. (වි *vi* and ආ *á* before, අල *ala* to adorn) snake; beast of prey; rogue, cheat; vicious elephant: *a*. wicked, villainous, bad.

ව්‍යාලප්‍රහරණ, *Wyála-praharaṇa*, s. sort of perfume or root, [Colloq. වක්නිය *wakniya*].

ව්‍යාවෘත්ත, *Wyáwṛitta*, a. (වි *vi* and ආ *á* before, වෘත *wṛita* to be) chosen, appointed; encompassed, surrounded; excepted, excluded.

ව්‍යාවෘත්තවෙනවා, *Wyáwṛitta-wenawá*, v. to be engaged in.

ව්‍යාස, *Wyása*, s. celebrated saint and author, the supposed original compiler of the Védas and Púráṇas; diffusion, extension; diameter of a circle.

ව්‍යාහත, *Wyáhata*, a. (වි *vi* and ආ *á* with හන *hana* to strike, ක්ත *kta* aff.) confused, alarmed; repelled, repulsed.

ව්‍යුත්ථාන, *Wyutthána*, s. (වි *vi* and උත් *ut* before, ස්ථා *sthá* to stay or be) independance, following one's own inclination; obstruction, prohibition, opposing any one.

ව්‍යුත්පත්ති, *Wyutpatti*, s. science, learning; derivation, etymology.

ව්‍යුත්පන්න, *Wyutpanna*, *part.* learned, completed, derived, begotten.

ව්‍යූහ, *Wyúha*, s. (වි *vi* before, ඌහ *úha* to reason) Military array, multitude, logic, reasoning.

ව්‍යෝම, *Wyóma*, s. sky, heaven, atmosphere, [Colloq. අහස *ahasa*].

ව්‍යෝමංගම, *Wyómaṇgama*, s. (ව්‍යෝම heaven, ගම *gama* to go) bird in general: see the next.

ව්‍යෝමචාරි, *Wyómachári*, s. (ව්‍යෝම and චාරි who goes) a god, saint; Brahman; bird.

ව්‍යෝෂ, *Wyósha*, s. the aggregate of three spices, viz. black pepper, long pepper, and dry ginger.

ව්‍රජ්‍යා, *Wrajyá*, s. (ව්‍රජ *wraja* to go, ක්‍යප් *kyap* aff.) journey, going; wandering about, either as an act of religious austerity or in quest of alms; class, flock, tribe: march of an assailant; march in general.

ව්‍රජ, *Wraja*, s. (ව්‍රජ to go) flock, herd, multitude; wandering, roaming; cow pen, station of cowherds.

ව්‍රණ, *Wraṇa*, s. (ව්‍රණ to wound) sore; wound, ulcer, [Colloq. වණය *waṇaya*].

ව්‍රණකා, *Wraṇaká*, s. tree, *nyctanthes arbor tristis;* plant, variety of basil, *ocimum*, [Colloq. කළුතලා *kaḷu-talá*].

ව්‍රණකාරක, *Wraṇakáraka*, *s.* tree, *semecarpus gardneri*, [Colloq. බඩුල්ල *badulla*].

ව්‍රණඝ්නී, *Wraṇághni*, *s.* plant, *gloriosa superba*, [Colloq. නියඟලා *niyaṉgalá*].

ව්‍රණෝජිත, *Wraṇójita*, *s.* plant, *physalis flexuosa* or *withania somnifera*, [Colloq. අමුක්කරා *amukkará*].

ව්‍රත, *Wrata*, *s.* (ව්‍රජ *wraja* to go, etc.) any meritorious act of devotion, voluntary or vowed observance or imposition of any penance, austerity or privation, as fasting, continence, exposure to heat and cold, etc.

ව්‍රතින්, *Wratin*, *s.* (ව්‍රත *wrata* religious observance, ඉන් *in* aff.) employer of priests or one accustomed to offer sacrifices; ascetic, devotee, one engaged in the observance of religious duties.

ව්‍රීඩ, *Vríḍa*, } *s.* shame, bashfulness, [Colloq. විළි,
ව්‍රීඩා, *Vríḍá*, } ලජ්ජා *viḷi, lajjá*].

ව්‍රීහි, *Vríhi*, *s.* rice in general, [Colloq. වී *ví*].

වෘක්ෂ, *Wṛiksha*, *s.* (වෘක්ෂ to cover, to shade) tree in general, [Colloq. රුක *ruka*].

වෘක්ෂචර, *Wṛikshachara*, *s.* (වෘක්ෂ tree, චර who goes) monkey, [Colloq. රිළවා *riḷawá* or වඳුරා *waṉdurá*].

වෘක්ෂදේවතා, *Wṛiksha-déwatá*, *s.* (වෘක්ෂ and දේවතා deity) sylvan deity, inhabiting trees, groves, etc.

වෘක්ෂධූප, *Wṛikshadhúpa*, *s.* (වෘක්ෂ and ධූප incense) turpentine.

වෘක්ෂනාථ, *Wṛikshanátha*, *s.* (වෘක්ෂ and නාථ lord) banyan tree, *ficus bengalensis*, [Colloq. මහනුග *maha-nuga*].

වෘක්ෂභවන, *Wṛiksha-bhawana*, *s.* (වෘක්ෂ tree, භවන residence) hollow in a tree.

වෘක්ෂභිද්, *Wṛikshabhid*, } *s.* (වෘක්ෂ and භිද් or
වෘක්ෂභේදි, *Wṛikshabhédi*, } භේදි what breaks) carpenter's chisel; hatchet.

වෘක්ෂය, *Wṛikshaya*, see වෘක්ෂ *wriksha*.

වෘක්ෂරුහ, *Wṛiksha-ruha*, *s.* (වෘක්ෂ and රුහ growing) parasite plant, *cymbidium (*or *epidendron) tessaloides*, which has its roots attached to the trunk or branches of another plant or tree.

වෘක්ෂාදන, *Wṛikshádana*, *s.* (වෘක්ෂ *wriksha* and අදන *adana* eating or food) carpenter's chisel or adze; hatchet or chopper.

වෘක්ෂාදනී, *Wṛikshádaní*, *s.* (වෘක්ෂ *wriksha* tree, අදනී *adaní* what eats) fungus; any parasite plant.

වෘක්ෂාම්ල, *Wṛikshámla*, *s.* (වෘක්ෂ *wṛiksha* and අම්ල *amla* sour) hog-plum, *spondias mangifera*, [Colloq. ඇඹරැල්ල *ẹmbarẹlla*]; fruit of the tamarind, [Colloq. සියඹලා *siyaṃbalá*].

වෘක්ෂාලය, *Wṛikshálaya*, *s.* (වෘක්ෂ *wṛiksha* tree, ආලය *álaya* abode) bird.

වෘක්ෂාවාස, *Wṛikshávása*, *s.* (වෘක්ෂ *wriksha* and ආවාස *áwása* abode) ascetic, one who lives in the hollows of trees.

වෘක්ෂෝත්පල, *Wṛikshótpala*, *s.* (වෘක්ෂ *wriksha* and උත්පල *utpala* lotus) large handsome tree, *pterospermum acerifolium;* according to another authority the rock rose, *cistus lobatus*.

වෘක, *Wṛika*, *s.* (වෘක to take or වෘ to hide or screen) wolf; crow, *corone macrorhynea;* tree, *æschynomene grandiflora;* jackal; turpentine.

වෘකධූප, *Wṛika-dhúpa*, *s.* (වෘක and ධූප increase) compounded perfume; turpentine, [Sinhalese, සිරිවටු *siriwaṭu*].

වෘත්ත, *Wṛitta*, *s.* enclosing, encircling, surrounding; verse, metre; conduct, observance of enjoined practice; profession, means of gaining a subsistence, circle; brass: *a.* chosen, selected, appointed; round.

වෘත්ත පුෂ්ප, *Wṛitta-pushpa*, *s.* (වෘත්ත round, පුෂ්ප flower) kadamba tree, *anthocephalus* (or *nauclea) cadamba:* see කදම්බ *kadaṃba*.

වෘත්තඵල, *Wṛitta-phala*, *s.* lime, *citrus limetta*, [Colloq. දෙහි *dehi*]; black pepper, *piper nigrum*, [Colloq. ගම්මිරිස් *gammiris*].

වෘත්තාන්ත, *Wṛittánta*, *s.* (වෘත්ත *wṛitta* observance, අන්ත *anta* end) tidings, rumour, intelligence; topic, subject.

වෘත්ති, *Wṛitti*, *s.* (වෘත *wṛita* to be, ක්ති *kti* aff.) being, abiding, staying; gloss, comment, explanation, exposition; livelihood, profession, means of subsistence; style in general.

වෘත්තිකා, *Wṛittiká*, *s.* tree, variety of *eugenia caryophyllæa*, [Colloq. හෙළදම් *heḷa-dam*].

වෘත්තෙ, *Wṛitte*, *s.* corruptly for වෘත්තය *wṛittaya*, verse, metre.

වෘද්ධ, *Wṛiddha*, *s.* (වෘධ *wṛidha* to increase or grow, ක්ත *kta* aff.) old person; sage, saint; benzoin, styrax symplocos: *a.* old, aged, ancient; full grown, large, expanded to the proper size; increased, augmented.

වෘද්ධත්ව, *Wṛiddhatwa*, *s.* (වෘද්ධ old, ත්ව affix of the abstract) old age.

වෘද්ධ වයස, *Wṛiddha-wayasa*, *s.* old age.

වෘද්ධශ්‍රවස්, *Wṛiddha-ṣrawas*, *s.* (වෘද්ධ large, ශ්‍රව ear) name of Ṣakra.

වෘද්ධාඞ්ගුලි, *Wriddhánguli*, *s.* (වෘද්ධ *wṛiddha* and අඞ්ගුලි *anguli* finger) thumb, [Colloq. මාපටඇඟිල්ල *mápaṭa-ęngilla*].

වෘද්ධි, *Wriddhi*, *s.* (වෘධ *wṛidha* to increase) increase, augmentation; prosperity, success; interest, usury; heap, quantity, multitude.

වෘද්ධි, *Wṛiddhi*, } *s.* enlargement of
වෘද්ධිරෝගය, *Wṛiddhirógaya*, } the scrotum either from swelled testicle or hydrocele or other morbid affections.

වෘන්ත, *Wṛinta*, *s.* foot-stalk of a leaf or fruit, [Colloq. නැට්ට *neṭṭa*].

වෘන්ද, *Wṛinda*, *s.* multitude, [Colloq. සමූහය *samúhaya*].

වෘන්දාරක, *Wṛindáraka*, *s.* deity: *a.* beautiful.

වෘශ්චික, *Wṛiṣchika*, *s.* (වෘශ්ච *wṛiṣcha* to cut, ඉක *ika* aff.) scorpion, *scolopendra*, [Colloq ගෝනුස්සා *gónussá*]; the sign scorpio; crab, *ocypode*, [Colloq. කකුළුවා *kakuḷuwá*]; thorny shrub, *vangueria spinosa* or *canthium parviflorum*, [Colloq. කාර *kára*].

වෘෂ්ටි, *Wṛishṭi*, *s.* rain, [Colloq. වැස්ස *węssa*].

වෘෂ්ණි, *Wṛishṇi*, *s.* ram, [Colloq. බැටළුවා *beṭaḷuwá*].

වෘෂ, *Wṛisha*, *s.* (වෘෂ to sprinkle) bull, [Colloq. ගොණා *goṇá*]; sign of the zodiac, *Taurus;* rat, [Colloq. මීයා *míyá*]; flowering shrub, *justicia gendurussa*, [Colloq. කළොස්වාරණිය *kaḷoswáraṇiya*]; in composition excellent, pre-eminent: virtue, moral merit; the fourteenth year of the Indian cycle.

වෘෂක, *Wṛishaka*, *s.* flowering shrub, *justicia gandurussa:* see the preceding.

වෘෂද, *Wṛishada*, *s.* plant, *dolichos* or *vigna catjang*, [Colloq. ලිමෑ *límẹ́*].

වෘෂධ්වජ, *Wṛishadwaja*, *s.* (වෘෂ bull, rat, virtue, ධ්වජ emblem) name of Ṣiva, or Gaṇéṣa; virtuous man.

වෘෂපුෂ්පිකා, *Wṛisha-pushpiká*, *s.* plant, *crinum zeylanicum*, [Colloq. ගොඩමානිල් *goḍa-mánil*].

වෘෂභ, *Wṛishabha*, *s.* (වෘෂ to sprinkle) bull, [Coll: ගොණා *goṇá*]; sign Taurus; in composition, excellent; drug, described as a root resembling the horn of a bull, brought from the Himálaya mountains, of cooling and tonic properties, and serviceable in catarrh and consumption.

වෘෂභගති, *Wṛishabha-gati*, *s.* (වෘෂභ bull, ගති going) name of Ṣiva.

වෘෂභධ්වජ, *Wṛishabhadhwaja*, *s.* (වෘෂභ and ධ්වජ banner) name of Ṣiva.

වෘෂභාක්ෂි, *Wṛishabhákshi*, *s.* creeping plant, [Coll: කටරොළු *kaṭaroḷu*].

වෘෂභී, *Wṛishabhí*, *s.* widow, [Colloq. කණවැන්දුම් ස්ත්‍රී *kaṇawęndum-strí*]; cowach: see වෘෂා *wṛishá;* Ceylon cardamoms, *elettaria cardamomum*, [Colloq. එන්සාල් *ensál*].

වෘෂල, *Wṛishala*, *s.* horse, [Colloq. අශ්වයා *aṣwayá*]; Sudra or man of the servile tribe; sinner, reprobate.

වෘෂවාහන, *Wṛisha-wáhana*, *s.* (වෘෂ bull, වාහන vehicle) name of Ṣiva.

වෘෂා, *Wṛishá*, *s.* aquatic plant, *salvinia cucullata;* cowach, *dolichos (or carpopogon) pruriens;* plant, *hoya hirsuta* [Colloq. මීනුග *mínuga*]; plant, *justicia adhatoda*, [Colloq. අගල්ආදර *agal-ádára*]; grape vine, *vitis vinifera*, [Colloq. මිදිවැල් *midi-węl*]; plant, *celastrus paniculata*, [Colloq. දුහුදු *duhudu*].

වෘෂාදනි, *Wṛishádaní*, *s.* sort of cucumber, *cucumis sativus*, [Colloq. කැකිරි *kękiri*].

වෘහත්, *Wṛihat*, *a.* (වෘහ to grow, to increase, අති *ati* aff.) large, great.

වෘහතී, *Wṛihatí*, *s.* speech, eloquence; small kind of egg plant, *solanum melongena*, [Colloq. වම්බටු *wambaṭu*]; prickly night shade, *solanum jacquini*, [Colloq. කටුවැල්බටු *kaṭuwęlbaṭu*].

වෘහතීපති, *Wṛihatípati*, } *s.* (වෘහතී speech, and
වෘහස්පති, *Wṛihaspati*, } වෘහත් *wṛihat* illustrious පති master, teacher with සුට් *suṭ* augment and the final of the first member rejected) Vṛihaspati, the regent of the planet Jupiter and preceptor of the gods.

ශ

Neither this nor the second sibilant is inserted in the Páli or Elu alphabets; they appear to have been adopted from the Sanskrit: many Sanskrit words were introduced into the ancient Elu, in consequence of the Sanskrit language and literature, especially Medicine and Astronomy, being extensively cultivated. The use of the ශ as an initial has created in Sinhalese, as in Sanskrit, considerable confusion.

ශක්‍ත, *Ṣakta*, *a.* (ශක *ṣaka* to be able, ක්‍ත *kta* aff.) strong, powerful, robust; able, capable; able to please by the manner of speaking.

ශක්ති, *Ṣakti*, *s.* strength, power, prowess; iron spear or dart; force or signification of words.

ශක්තිඛණ්ඩ, *Ṣakti-khaṇḍa*, *s.* plant, *buchnera euphrasioides*, [Colloq. අඬිනාරු *daḍinnaru*].

ශක්තිධර, *Ṣaktidhara*, *s.* spearman; name of Kártikeya.

ශක්තිපත්‍ර, *Ṣakti-patra*, see ශක්තිඛණ්ඩ *ṣaktikhaṇḍa*.

ශක්තිසම්පන්න, *Ṣaktisampanna*, *a.* (ශක්ති and සම්පන්න having) strong, powerful, robust, able, capable.

ශක්තු, *Ṣaktu*, *s.* ball of flour or meal ground from fried rice.

ශක්තුඵලා, *Ṣaktuphalá*, *s.* Ṣamí tree, *mimosa suma*, *Roxburghii*, [Colloq. සෑමගස් *sẹma-gas*].

ශක්‍ය, *Ṣakya*, *s.* possible, practicable.

ශක්‍ර, *Ṣakra*, *s.* (ශක *ṣaka* to possess power, ර *ra* aff.) Indra, the chief of the inferior gods, and ruler of Swarga or paradise; timber tree, *pentaptera arjuna*; *wrightea antidysenterica*, [Colloq. කෙළිඳ *keḷinda*].

ශක්‍රදේවේන්ද්‍ර, *Ṣakradéwéndra*, see the preceding.

ශක්‍රධනු, *Ṣakra-dhanu*, *s.* (ශක්‍ර and ධනු bow) rainbow, [Colloq. දේදුන්න *dédunna*].

ශක්‍රපාදප, *Ṣakrapádapa*, *s.* (ශක්‍ර and පාදප tree) sort of pine, *pinus deradaru*. [Colloq. දේවදර *déwadára*]; *wrightea antidysenterica*, [Colloq. කෙළිඳ *keḷinda*].

ශක්‍රපුරය, *Ṣakrapuraya*, see තවුතිසාභවනය *tawutisá-bhawanaya*.

ශක්‍රභවන, *Ṣakra-bhawana*, *s.* (ශක්‍ර and භවන abode) sky, heaven, firmament; residence of the gods: see තවුතිසාභවනය *tawutisá-bhawanaya*.

ශකටමාර්ග, *Ṣakaṭa-márga*, *s.* (ශකට cart, මාර්ග road) cart or carriage road, [Colloq. කරත්තපාර *karatta-pára*].

ශකවර්ෂ, *Ṣaka-warsha*, *s.* (ශක saka, වර්ෂ year) era of Saka, period usually commencing with some celebrated prince; as, Yudhishṭhira, Vikramáditya, Ṣáliváhana, etc.; the term in ordinary use is especially applied to the era of Sáliváhana, commencing seventy-eight years after the Christian era.

ශකුනීශ්වර, *Ṣakuniṣwara*, *s.* (ශකුනි *ṣakuni* bird, ඊශ්වර *iṣwara* chief) name of Garuḍa, bird of Vishṇu and king of the feathered tribe.

ශඞ්ඛ, *Ṣaṅkha*, *s.* conch shell, [Colloq. හක් *hak*]; one of Kuvéra's treasures; elephant's cheek.

ශඞ්ඛස්ඵටික, *Ṣaṅkha-sphaṭika*, *s.* white arsenic, [Colloq. සුදුපාසානම් *sudu-pásánam*].

ශඞ්ඛනඛ, *Ṣaṅkhanakha*, *s.* drug, [Colloq. සක්නිය *sakniya*].

ශටි, *Ṣaṭi*, *s.* zedoary, *curcuma zerumbet*, [Colloq. හරංකහ *haraṅkaha*]; small aromatic plant, *kæmpferia galanga*, [Colloq. හිඟුරුපියලි *hiṅguru-piyali*].

ශඨ, *Ṣaṭha*, *s.* (ශඨ to be wicked) rogue, knave; thorn apple, *datura stramonium*: *a.* wicked, depraved, perverse, dishonest.

ශඨප්‍රයෝගය, *Ṣaṭhaprayógaya*, *s.* (ශඨ and ප්‍රයෝග trick) cunning. deceit.

ශණ, *Ṣaṇa*, *s.* hemp, *cannabis sativa*; Bengal san, [Colloq. හණ *haṇa*].

ශත්‍රු, *Ṣatru*, *s.* adversary, enemy, opponent.

ශත, *Ṣata*, *s.* hundred, [Colloq. සියය *siyaya*].

ශතක, *Ṣataka*, *s.* Cento, collection of 100 stanzas.

ශතකුම්භ, *Ṣata-kumbha*, *s.* gold; name of a mountain.

ශතගුණ, *Ṣata-guṇa*, *a.* hundred fold.

ශතපත්‍ර, *Ṣatapatra*, *s.* (ශත hundred, පත්‍ර leaf) lotus in general, *nelumbium speciosum*, [Colloq. නෙළුම් *neḷum*]; peacock, [Colloq. මොණරා *moṇará*]; Indian crane.

ශතපදී, *Ṣatapadí*, *s.* (ශත hundred, පද *pada* foot) centipede, [Colloq. පත්තෑයා *pattẹyá*].

ශතපර්වක, *Ṣataparwaka*, *s.* (ශත and පර්වක joint) bamboo, [Colloq. උණගස් *uṇagas*].

ශතපර්වා, *Ṣata-parwá*, *s.* bent-grass, *panicum dactylon*; orris root.

ශතපර්විකා, *Ṣata-parviká*, *s.* plant, [Colloq. හෙළඊතණ *heḷa-ítaṇa*].

ශතපුණ්‍ය, *Ṣatapuṇya*, *s.* (ශත and පුණ්‍ය virtue) great virtue, extraordinary merit.

ශතපුෂ්පා, *Ṣatapushpá*,
ශතපුෂ්පිකා, *Ṣatapushpiká*, } *s.* (ශත hundred, පුෂ්ප flower, ඉක *ika* aff.) kind of dill or fennel, *anethum sowa*.

ශතප්‍රසූතා, *Ṣata-prasútá*, *s.* kind of dill or fennel, *anethum sowa*, [Colloq. සතපුස්ප *satapuspa*].

ශතප්‍රාස, *Ṣataprása*, *s.* (ශත and ප්‍රාස dart) flower, *nerium odorum*, the leaves of which are compared to a dart; tree, *plumeria acutifolia*, [Colloq. අලරිය *alariya*].

ශතභිෂා, *Ṣatabhishá*, *s.* (ශත and භිෂජ් *bhishaj* to cure) twenty-fifth of the nakshatras or lunar mansions, containing one hundred stars in the form of a circular gem; the name alludes to an opinion that it is impossible to cure any person affected with disease while the moon is in this asterism.

ශතය, *Ṣataya*, s. Cent, a coin, value one-hundredth part of a Rupee: pl. ශත *ṣata*.

ශතමූලී, *Ṣatamúlí*, s. (ශත hundred, මූල *múla* root) plant, *asparagus falcatus*, [Colloq. හාතාවාරිය *hátáwáriya*].

ශතර්විකා, *Ṣatarviká*, s. kind of grass, variety of *heteropogon hirtus*, [Colloq. හෙළඊතණ *heḷa-ítaṇa*].

ශතලක්‍ෂ, *Ṣatalaksha*, s. ten millions.

ශතසහස්‍ර, *Ṣatasahasra*, s. hundred thousand.

ශතාව්හ, *Ṣatáwha*, } s. (ශත *ṣata* hundred, roots,
ශතාවරී, *Ṣatáwarí*, } ආ *á* and වෘ *wra* to choose) shrub, *asparagus falcatus*, [Colloq. හාතාවාරිය *hátáwáriya*].

ශනි, *Ṣani*, } s. planet Saturn, [Colloq.
ශනිග්‍රහ, *Ṣanigraha*, } සෙනසුරා *senasurá*].

ශනිප්‍රිය, *Ṣanipriya*, s. emerald or sapphire.

ශනිවාර, *Ṣaniwára*, s. (ශනි and වාර day) Saturday, [Colloq. සෙනසුරාදා *senasurádá*].

ශනීශ්වර, *Ṣaníṣwara*, s. (ශනි and ඊශ්වර *íṣwara* lord) regent of the planet Saturn.

ශනෛශ්වර, *Ṣanaiṣwara*, s. Saturn.

ශඵ, *Ṣapha*, s. hoof; root of a tree; sort of perfume, commonly නඛී *nakhí*, apparently a dried shell-fish.

ශඵර, *Ṣaphara*, } s. small glistening fish, *cyprinus*
ශඵරී, *Ṣapharí*, } *chrysoparius*, [Colloq. පෙටියා *peṭiyá*].

ශබ්දය, *Ṣabdaya*, s. sound; declinable word: pl. ශබ්ද *ṣabda*.

ශබ්දයෝනි, *Ṣabda-yóni*, s, (ශබ්ද and යෝනි place of origin) root, radical word.

ශබ්දශක්ති, *Ṣabda-ṣakti*, s. force or signification of words.

ශබ්දශාස්ත්‍ර, *Ṣabda-ṣástra*, s. philology, grammar, etc.

ශබ්දසංග්‍රහ, *Ṣabda-sangraha*, s. Vocabulary.

ශබ්දික, *Ṣabdika*, a. sounding, sonant, producing or remitting sound.

ශම්පාක, *Ṣampáka*, s. tree, *cassia fistula*, [Colloq. ඇහැළ *ehela*].

ශම්බර, *Ṣambara*, s. water.

ශම්බරී, *Ṣambarí*, s. plant, *hoya hirsuta*, [Colloq. මිනුග *minugu*]; plant, *asparagus racemosus*; medicinal plant with beautiful white flowers, *anthericum tuberosum*; aquatic plant, *salvinia cucullata*; female juggler.

ශම, *Ṣama*, }
ශමථ, *Ṣamatha*, } s. quiet, tranquillity.
ශමන, *Ṣamana*, }

ශමිර, *Ṣamira*, s. variety of the samí tree.

ශමී, *Ṣmí*, s. tree, *acacia suma*, [Sinhalese, සැමගස් *sẹma-gas*].

ශමීර, *Ṣamíra*, see සමීර *am ira*.

ශය්‍යා, *Ṣayyá*, s. (ශී *ṣí* to sleep, ක්‍යප් *kyap* aff.) bed, couch, sofa.

ශයන, *Ṣayana*, s. sleep; bed, couch.

ශයනයකරණවා, *Ṣayanayakaraṇawá*, v. to sleep.

ශයාලු, *Ṣayálu*, s. (ශී *ṣí* to sleep, ආලු *álu* implying disposition or habit) snake, boa or rock-snake, *python molurus*, [Colloq. පිඹුරා *pimburá*]; a. sleepy, slothful, sluggish.

ශර්කරා, *Ṣarkará*, s. potsherd, fragment of a broken pot; gravel, gravely or gritty fragments; coarse kind of clayed sugar, of which there are three sorts, made from the juice of the coconut palm, and kitul trees.

ශර, *Ṣara*, s. arrow; reed; cream of milk.

ශරණ, *Ṣaraṇa*, s. protector, protection.

ශරත්, *Ṣarat*, see ශරද් *ṣarad*.

ශරත්කාල, *Ṣaratkála*, s. autumnal season.

ශරද්, *Ṣarad*, s. season of autumn.

ශරපුංඛ, *Ṣarapunkha*, s. plant, *nerium* or *tephrosia purpurea*, [Colloq. පිලගස් *pila-gas*].

ශරපුංඛා, *Ṣarapunkhá*, s. (ශර arrow, පුංඛා feather, etc.) feathers of an arrow.

ශරභ, *Ṣarabha*, s. animal supposed to have eight legs; grass-hopper.

ශල්‍ය, *Ṣalya*, s. dart, stake; thorny shrub, *vangueria spinosa*; porcupine, *hystrix leuavrus (Rodentia)*, [Colloq. ඉත්තෑවා *ittẹwá*].

ශල්‍යක, *Ṣalyaka*, s. thorny shrub, *randia dumetorum*, [Colloq. කුකුරුමුවං *kukurumuwan*].

ශල්‍යකර්තෘ, *Ṣalya-kartri*, s. (ශල්‍ය dart, කර්තෘ who does) surgeon; barber.

ශල්‍යශාස්ත්‍ර, *Ṣalya-ṣástra*, s. Surgery.

ශලාකා, *Ṣaláká*, s. dart, arrow; rib of an umbrella; slip of bambu; thorny shrub, *vangueria spinosa*.

ශලිමලි, *Ṣalímali*, s. silk cotton tree: see ශාල්මලි *ṣálmalí*.

ශව, *Ṣawa*, s. corpse, [Colloq. මළකඳ *maḷakanda*].

ශශ, *Ṣaṣa*, s. hare, [Colloq. හාවා *háwá*].

ශශි, *Ṣaṣi*, s. moon, [Colloq. හඳ *handa*].

ශශිප්‍රභා, *Ṣaṣiprabhá*, s. (ශශි moon, ප්‍රභා shining, blossoming) white esculent water lily, *nymphæa esculenta*; moonlight.

ශශිප්‍රිය, *Ṣaṣipriya*, *s.* (ශශි and ප්‍රිය fond of) owl, [Colloq. බකමූනා *bakamúná* or බස්සා *bassá*]; variety of the *nymphæa stellata*, [Colloq. නිල් මානෙල් *nil-mánel*].

ශස්ත, *Ṣasta*, *s.* (ශස *ṣasa* to praise, ක්ත *kta* aff.) happiness, excellence; praised, eulogized; best, excellent.

ශස්ත්‍ර, *Ṣastra*, *s.* weapon; iron, steel.

ශස්ත්‍රි, *Ṣastri*, *s.* (ශස්ත්‍ර *ṣastra* and ඊ *í* aff.) knife, [Colloq. පිහය *píhaya*].

ශස්‍ය, *Ṣasya*, *s.* fruit; corn, grain in general.

ශස්‍යමඤ්ජරී, *Ṣasya-mañjarí*, *s.* ear or spike of corn; fruit stalk.

ශස්‍යශූක, *Ṣasya-ṣúka*, *s.* (ශස්‍ය and ශූක beard) beard of corn,

ශාක්‍ය, *Ṣákya*, ශාක්‍යකුලය, *Ṣákyakulaya*. *s.* (ශක *saka* to be able, skilful, etc.) name of a clan or people from which sprang a race of kings; this had its rise in the four sons of Ikshwáku (Páli Okkáka) the founder of the Súryawaṇṣa dynasty; these princes were banished from the court and kingdom of their father by the evil machinations of their step-mother; they built the city of Kapilawastu which became the capital of that dynasty and the seat of government; from them descended Gautama the founder of Buddhism; name of Buddha.

ශාක්‍යමුනි, *Ṣákyamuni*, *s.* (ශාක්‍ය and මුනි saint) Gautama, the real or supposed founder of the Buddhist religion.

ශාක්‍යවංශය, *Ṣákya-waṇṣaya*, see ශාක්‍ය *ṣákya*.

ශාක්‍යසිංහ, *Ṣákyasiṇha*, *s.* (ශාක්‍ය and සිංහ lion) epithet of Gautama Buddha.

ශාකවාස්තුක, *Ṣákawástuka*, *s.* plant, *amaranthus cruentus*, [Colloq. නිල්තම්පලා *nil-tampalá*].

ශාකවෘක්ෂ, *Ṣákawṛiksha*, *s.* teak tree, *tectona grandis*, [Colloq. තේක්ක *tékka*].

ශාකාම්ල, *Ṣákámla*, *s.* tamarind tree, *tamarindus indica*, [Colloq. සියඹලා *siyambalá*].

ශාකිණී, *Ṣákiṇi*, *s.* plant, species of *amarantus*, [Colloq. කූරතම්පලා *kúra-tampalá*].

ශාකුනික, *Ṣákunika*, *s.* (ශකුන *ṣakuna* bird, අණ් *aṇ* and ඉක *ika* aff.) fowler, bird-catcher, one who procures a livelihood by killing and vending game.

ශාකෝට, *Ṣákóṭa*, *s.* small tree, *streblus asper* or *trophis aspera*, [Colloq. ෑටනිටුල් *gẹtaniṭul*].

ශාඛා, *Ṣákhá*, *s.* branch; sect, subdivision.

ශාඛානගර, *Ṣákhá-nagara*, *s.* suburb.

ශාඛාපුර, *Ṣákhá-pura*, see the last.

ශාඛාමෘග, *Ṣákhá-mṛiga*, *s.* monkey, ape; squirrel.

ශාණ්ඩිල්‍ය, *Ṣáṇḍilya*, *s.* (ශණ්ඩිල *ṣaṇḍila* and යත් *yat* aff.) bael fruit, *ægle marmelos*, [Colloq. බෙලි *beli*].

ශාතකුම්භ, *Ṣátakumbha*, *s.* (ශතකුම්භ *ṣatakumbha* mountain so called, අණ් *aṇ* affix of production) gold, [Colloq. රත්රන් *ratran*]; plant, *nerium odorum*.

ශාද්වලා, *Ṣádwalá*, *s.* (ශාද *ṣáda* young grass, වල *wala* aff.) variety of *heteropogon hirtus*, [Colloq. හෙළ ඊතණ *heḷa-ítaṇa*]: *a.* abounding in fresh grass, verdant.

ශාන්ත, *Ṣánta*, *a.* calm, tranquil, meek, purified.

ශාන්තිකර, *Ṣántikara*, *a.* calming, appeasing.

ශාන්තිධර්මය, *Ṣánti-dharmaya*, ශාන්තිය, *Ṣántiya*, *s.* (ශම *ṣama* to be pacified, ක්ති *kti* aff.) quiet, tranquillity, stoicism, absence of passion and indifference to objects of pleasure or pain, especially the tranquillity of devotion or quietism, by which the mind is wholly fixed on the subject of its meditation or worship and is utterly regardless of external impressions.

ශාන, *Ṣána*, *s.* touchstone; grindstone.

ශාප, *Ṣápa*, *s.* (ශප *ṣapa* to curse, අණ් *aṇ* aff.) oath, affirmation by oath or ordeal; curse, imprecation, malediction.

ශාම, *Ṣáma*, *s.* (ශම *ṣama* to appease, මනින් *manin* aff.) conciliation, appeasing, reconciling.

ශාමදානය, *Ṣámadánaya*, *s.* peace, reconciliation.

ශාමල, *Ṣámala*, *s.* tree, *ficus religiosa*, [Colloq. බෝගහ *bó-gaha*].

ශාමවාස්තුක, *Ṣámawástuka*, *s.* plant, *amaranthus cruentus*, [Colloq. නිල් තම්පලා *nil-tampalá*].

ශාර්ඞ්ගෂ්ටා, *Ṣárṅgashṭá*, *s.* creeping plant, *convolvulus flavus*, [Colloq. තෑල්වෑල් *tẹlwẹl*].

ශාර්දූල, *Ṣárdúla*, *s.* tiger: *a.* (in composition), pre-eminent, excellent.

ශාර්දූල වික්‍රීඩිත, *Ṣárdúla-vikríḍita*, *s.* form of metre, stanza consisting of four lines of nineteen syllables each.

ශාරඞ්ග, *Ṣáraṅga*, *s.* (ශර *ṣara* to go, අඞ්ග *aṅga* aff.) Ceylonese hornbill: කෑඳත්තා *kẹṇdattá:* deer; elephant; tree; jewel; lotus.

ශාරද, *Ṣárada*, *s.* (ශරද *ṣarada* autumn, අණ් *aṇ* aff.) year: *a.* autumnal; modest, diffident.

ශාරදී, *Ṣáradí*, *s.* tree, *alstonia scholaris*, [Colloq. රුක්අත්තන *ruk-attana*]; plant, *jussiæa repens*, [Colloq. බෙරුදියනිල්ල *béru-diyanilla*].

ශාරිකා, *Ṣáriká*, *s.* bird, myna, *acridotheres melanosternus*, *eulabes religiosa*, and *e. ptilogenys*, (*Sturnidæ*, order *Passeres*), [Colloq. ගොන් කවඩියා *gon-kawaḍiyá*, සැළලිහිණියා *sẹḷalihiṇiyá* or මල්කවඩියා *mal-kawaḍiyá*]; small bird of the *genes turdus*, Ceylonese black-bird, *t. kinnisi* or spotted thrush, (*Saxicolidæ*, order *Passeres*), [Colloq. මල් අවිච්චියා *mal-avichchiyá*].

ශාරිවා. *Ṣáriwá*, *s.* plant, *echites frutescens;* Indian sarsaparilla, *hemidesmus indicus*, [Colloq. ඉරමුසු *iramasu*].

ශාල්මලී, *Ṣálmalí*, *s.* cotton tree, *eriodendron anfractuosum*, [Colloq. ඉඹුල් *imbul*].

ශාල්මලිරස, *Ṣálmali-rasa*, *s.* gum of cotton tree, [Colloq. ඉඹුල් මැලියම් *imbul-mẹliyam*].

ශාල, *Ṣála*, *s.* tree, *shorea robusta*, [Colloq. හල් *hal*].

ශාලනිර්‍යාස, *Ṣálaniryása*, *s.* resin, resinous exudation of the sal tree, [Colloq. දුම්මල *dummala*].

ශාලපර්ණී, *Ṣálaparṇní*, *s.* (ශාල sal tree, පර්ණ *parṇa* leaf, ඊ *í* aff.) shrub, *desmodium gangeticum*, the leaves of which resemble those of the hal tree; plant, *alyssicarpus bupleurifolius*, [Colloq. අස්වැන්න *aswẹnna*].

ශාලා, *Ṣálá*, *s.* hall; large branch of a tree.

ශාලි, *Ṣáli*, *s.* rice in general, [Colloq. වී *ví* or හාල් *hál*]; two sorts, one white and growing in deep water, and the other a red sort requiring only a moist soil.

ශාලිවාහන, *Ṣáliwáhana*, *s.* (ශාලි from ශාල *ṣála* sal tree or a cross of that wood, වාහන vehicle) sovereign of India, the enemy of Vikramáditya, and institutor of the era now called Saka, beginning seventy-eight years after Christ; the name alludes, to his being borne on a cross, and thence, and from his birth identified by Wilford with Christ, of whose history and character, as received through the spurious gospels, those of Ṣáliwáhana are probably transcripts.

ශාලී. *Ṣálí*, *a.* possessing, having.

ශාලූක, *Ṣáluka*, } *s.* root of the different kinds of
ශාලූක, *Ṣáluka*, } water lily.

ශාවර, *Ṣáwara*, *s.* tree, [Colloq. ලොත්ගස් *lot-gas*].

ශාශ්වත, *Ṣáṣwata*, *a.* continual, perpetual.

ශාශ්වතදෘෂ්ටිය, *Ṣáṣwata-driṣhṭiya*, *s.* (ශාශ්වත perpetual, දෘෂ්ටි *driṣhṭi* religious belief) sect holding the eternity of matter.

ශාශ්වතික, *Ṣáṣwatika*, *s.* (ශාශ්වත *ṣáṣwata* and ඉක *ika* aff.) one of the Ṣáṣwata sect.

ශාස්ත්‍ර, *Ṣástra*, *s.* scripture; science; institutes of religion, law or letters.

ශාස්ත්‍රඥ, *Ṣástrajña*, *s.* skilled in the knowledge of law, and religion especially.

ශාස්ත්‍රවන්තයා, *Ṣástrawantayá*, *s.* one versed in science.

ශාස්තෘ, *Ṣástṛi*, *s.* name of Buddha; ruler, teacher.

ශාසනහර, *Ṣásanahara*, *s.* (ශාසන and හර who takes) messenger, [Colloq. පණිවිඩකාරයා *paṇividakárayá*].

ශාසන, *Ṣásana*, *s.* order, edict, command; grant of land or privileges; charter; writing, deed; written contract; governing, ruling, government.

ශාසනාන්තර්ධාන, *Ṣáṣanántardhána*, see සද්ධර්මාන්තර්ධාන *ṣaddharmántardhána*.

ශිංශපා, *Ṣinṣapá*, *s.* (ශීර්ෂ *ṣírsha* head, පා to cherish) tree, *dalbergia sisu*.

ශික්ෂණ, *Ṣikshana*, *s.* (ශික්ෂ to learn, ණ්‍ය *ṇya* aff.) learning, studying; taming, disciplining.

ශික්ෂා, *Ṣikshá*, *s.* (ශික්ෂ *siksha* and ආ *á* aff.) learning, study, acquisition of science: see ශික්ෂාපදය *ṣikshápadaya*.

ශික්ෂාකාමී, *Ṣikshákámí*, *s.* (ශික්ෂා and කාමී who desires) zealous or strict observer of religious institutes, devotee.

ශික්ෂාපදය, *Ṣikshápadaya*, *s.* (ශික්ෂා and පද *pada* verse) institute of religion, sacred precept, but especially the peculiar observances of Buddhism embodied in metrical aphorisms.

ශික්ෂාපිත, *Ṣikshápita*, causal form of ශික්ෂිත *sikshita*.

ශික්ෂාව, *Ṣiksháwa*, see ශික්ෂාපදය *ṣikshápadaya*.

ශික්ෂාශීල, *Ṣikshá-ṣíla*, *s.* (ශික්ෂ *ṣiksha* to tame, ශීල disposition) docility.

ශික්ෂිත, *Ṣikshita*, *a.* (ශික්ෂ *ṣiksha* to learn, to tame, etc. ක්ත *kta* aff.) tamed, trained; docile; studied, learned; skilful, clever, conversant.

ශිඛණ්ඩ, *Ṣikanḍa*, *s.* tail of a peacock; lock left on the crown or sides of the head at the period of tonsure in children.

ශිඛර, *Ṣikhara*, *s.* (ශිඛා *ṣikhá* crest, රච් *rach* poss. aff.) peak or summit of a mountain; point, end, top, in general; gem described as of the colour of the ripe pomegranate seed.

ශිඛරී, *Ṣikharí*, *s.* (ශිඛර *ṣikhara* top, etc. ඉනි *ini* aff.) mountain; tree; plant, *achyranthes aspera*, [Colloq. ගස් කරල්හැබ *gas-karalhẹba*]; strong hold, hill fort.

ශිඛා, *Ṣikhá*, *s.* point, top in general; crest; peacock's crest; flame; chief, principal.

ශිඛාධර, *Ṣikhádhara*, *s.* ශිඛා crest, ධර what has) peacock, [Colloq. මොණරා *moṇará*].

ශිඛාවල, *Ṣikháwala*, *s.* (ශිඛා and වල aff.) peacock: *a.* crested, pointed.

ශිඛි, *Ṣikhi*, *s.* fire; peacock; cock; tree; lamp: *a.* crested, pointed.

ශිඛිග්‍රීව, *Ṣikhigríwa*, *s.* (ශිඛි peacock, ග්‍රීව neck) blue vitriol [Colloq. මයුරතුතු *mayúratutu*].

ශිඛිවාහන, *Ṣikhi-wáhana*, *s.* (ශිඛි peacock, වාහන vehicle) name of Kártikéya or Kataragama deviyó, who is mounted on a peacock.

ශිඛී, *Ṣikhí*, see ශිඛි *ṣikhi*.

ශිග්‍රු, *Ṣigru*, *s.* (ශි to sharpen, රු *ru* aff. and ග *ga* augment) tree, *moringa pterygosperma*, [Colloq. මුරුංගා *murungá*].

ශිත, *Ṣita*, *s.* thin, weak, sharpened, whetted.

ශිතද්‍රු, *Ṣitadru*, *s.* river Satadru or Sutlej river.

ශිතශූක, *Ṣitaṣúka*, *s.* (ශිත sharpened, ශූක awn or ear) barley; wheat.

ශිතිසාරක, *Ṣitisáraka*, *s.* (ශිති black, සාර essence, ක aff.) species of ebony. *diospyros embryopteris*, [Colloq. තිඹිරි *timbiri*]; yielding a strong black resin used for caulking boats.

ශිථිල, *Ṣithila*, *a.* loose, relaxed; flaccid, flabby; ineffective.

ශිම්බි, *Ṣimbi*, *s.* legume, pod.

ශිම්බික, *Ṣimbika*, *s.* Madras gram, *dolichos biflorus*, [Colloq. කොල්ලු *kollu*].

ශිර, *Ṣira*, *s.* head; root of the pepper plant.

ශිරච්ඡේද, *Ṣirachchhéda*, *s.* (ශිර head, ඡේද cutting) beheading, decapitation.

ශිරජ, *Ṣiraja*, *s.* (ශිර head, ජ born) hair of the head; cutaneous eruption or scab on the head.

ශිරස්, *Ṣiras*, *s.* head, top; principal.

ශිරස්ක, *Ṣiraska*, *s.* (ශිරස් head, ක aff.) helmet; turban; hat or cap.

ශිරස්ත්‍ර, *Ṣirastra*, } ශිරස්ත්‍රාණ, *Ṣirastráṇa*, } *s.* (ශිරස් and ත්‍රෛ *trai* to protect) helmet; cap, turban.

ශිරස්ස්ථ, *Ṣirasstha*, *s.* (ශිරස් head, ස්ථා *sthá* to stay or be) chief, leader: *a.* standing at the head.

ශිරස, *Ṣirasa*, *s.* (ශ්‍රි *ṣri* to be honoured (by the other members), අසුන් *asun* aff.) head; top of a tree; chief, principal.

ශිරසිජ, *Ṣirasija*, } ශිරසිරුහ, *Ṣirasiruha*, } see ශිරජ *ṣiraja*.

ශිරීෂ, *Ṣirísha*, *s.* tree, *albizzia lebbec*, [Colloq. මාරා *márá*].

ශිරෝධරා, *Ṣiródhará*, *s.* (ශිරස් *ṣiras* head, ධර what upholds) neck, [Colloq. බෙල්ල *bella*].

ශිරෝධාතුව, *Ṣiró-dhátuwa*, *s.* (ශිරස් *ṣiras* and ධාතු *dhátu* element) head-relic of Buddha.

ශිරෝමණි, *Ṣirómaṇi*, } ශිරෝමාණික්‍ය, *Ṣirómáṇikya*, } *s.* (ශිරස් *ṣiras* and මණි and මාණික්‍ය jewel) gem worn in a crest, or on the top of the head.

ශිරෝර්ති, *Ṣirórtti*, see ශිරෝරෝගය *ṣirórógaya*.

ශිරෝරුහ, *Ṣiróruha*, *s.* (ශිරස් *ṣiras* and රුහ to grow) hair of the head.

ශිරෝරෝගය, *Ṣirórógaya*, *s.* (ශිරස් *ṣiras* head, රෝග *róga* or අර්ති *artti* disease) pain of the head, headache.

ශිරෝවේෂ්ට, *Ṣiróweshṭa*, *s.* (ශිරස් *ṣiras* and වේෂ්ට what surrounds) turban.

ශිල්ප, *Ṣilpa*, *s.* (ශිල *ṣila* to be clever or skilled, ප aff.) art, any manual or mechanical art.

ශිල්පකාර, *Ṣilpakára*, *s.* (ශිල්ප art, කාර who does) artisan, mechanic.

ශිල්ප විද්‍යා, *Ṣilpa-vidyá*, *s.* (ශිල්ප and විද්‍යා knowledge) art, mechanical or manual skill.

ශිල්ප ශාලාව, *Ṣilpa-ṣáláwa*, *s.* (ශිල්ප and ශාලා *sálá* house) workshop; a hall of science, a place of tuition.

ශිල්පී, *Ṣilpí*, *s.* (ශිල්ප *ṣilpa* and ඉන් *in* aff.) artist, artificer or artizan.

ශිලා, *Ṣilá*, *s.* stone, rock; arsenic; flat stone on which condiments, etc. are ground with a muller; medicinal plant, see ගල්මද *galmada*.

ශිලා කුට්ටක, *Ṣilá-kuṭṭaka*, *s.* (ශිලා and කුට්ට *kuṭṭa* to cut) stone-cutter's chisel.

ශිලාඝර්ෂණ, *Ṣilá-gharshaṇa*, *s.* (ශිලා and ඝර්ෂණ pounding) pounding, grinding.

ශිලාජ, *Ṣilája*, *s.* (ශිලා rock, ජ born) storax or benzoin, resins of the *styrax benzoinum* or *styrax officinale*, which are supposed to be fossil productions, and to exude from the soil of mountainous places, being confounded with bitumen or petroleum; rock moss, [Colloq. ගල්සෙවෙල් *gal-sewel*]; benzoin, [Colloq. ගල්මද *galmada*].

ශිලාජතු, *Ṣilájatu*, *s.* (ශිලා and ජතු lac) bitumen; red chalk; which are supposed to issue from the stones of mountains in hot weather.

ශිලාතලය, *Ṣilátalaya*, *s.* (ශිලා stone, තල *tala* surface) surface of a rock or stone.

ශිලාදද්‍රු, *Ṣiládadru*, *s.* (ශිලා and දද්‍රු herpes) bitumen: see ශිලාජතු *ṣilájatu*.

ශිලාධාතු, *Ṣiládhátu*, *s.* (ශිලා and ධාතු mineral) chalk; mineral in general.

ශිලාපට්ට, *Ṣilápaṭṭa*, *s.* (ශිලා stone, පට්ට flat surface) flat stone for grinding condiments upon.

ශිලාපහ, *Ṣilápaha*, *s.* horse gram, *dolichos biflorus*, [Colloq. කොල්ලු *kollu*].

ශිලාපුෂ්ප, *Ṣilápushpa*, *s.* (ශිලා stone, rock, පුෂ්ප flower) storax: see ශිලාජතු *ṣilájatu*.

ශිලාභිද්, *Ṣilábhid*, *s.* knot-grass, *ærua lanata* or *illicebrum lanatum*, [Colloq. පොල්පලා *polpalá*].

ශිලාභේද, *Ṣilábhéda*, *s.* (ශිලා stone, භේද what breaks) plant, *plectranthus scutellarioides;* stone cutter's chisel.

ශිලාවෘෂ්ටි, *Ṣiláwrishṭi*, *s.* (ශිලා and වෘෂ්ටි rain) hail, shower of hail.

ශිලාසන, *Ṣilásana*, *s.* (ශිලා rock, අසන *asana* abiding or ආසන *ásana* seat benzion or storax; stone bench or seat.

ශිලී, *Ṣilí*, *s.* dart, spike.

ශිලීපද, *Ṣilípada*, *s.* elephantiasis: see ශ්ලීපද *ṣlípada*.

ශිලීමුඛ, *Ṣilímukha*, *s.* (ශිලී dart, මුඛ mouth) bee, [Colloq. මීමැස්සා *mímęssá*]; arrow, [Colloq. ඊගහ *ígaha*]; fool, blockhead.

ශිලෝච්චය, *Ṣilóchchaya*, *s.* (ශිලා *ṣilá* stone or rock, උත් *ut* up, චි *chi* to collect, අ *a* aff.) mountain.

ශිව, *Ṣiva*, *s.* (ශී *ṣí* to sleep, වන් *wan* aff.) the deity Ṣiva, most formidable of the Hindu triad, the worship of which he is the object, is of a more gloomy nature in general than that of the rest; auspiciousness or good luck, well-being, happiness, pleasure; final emancipation from existence, Nirwáṇa or annihilation.

ශිවංකර, *Ṣivaṇkara*, *s.* (ශිවං well being, කර what makes) propitious, conferring happiness or good fortune.

ශිවප්‍රිය, *Ṣiva-priya*, *s.* (ශිව Ṣiva, ප්‍රිය beloved) small slender tree, *æschynomene grandiflora;* seeds of the wild olive, *elæocarpus serratus*, [Colloq. වෙරළු *weraḷu*]; plant, *amyris* or *aquilaria agallocha*, [Colloq. ගුගුල් *gugul*]; crystal.

ශිවප්‍රියා, *Ṣiva-priyá*, *s.* name of Durgá.

ශිවබීජ, *Ṣiva-bíja*, *s.* (ශිව Ṣiva, බීජ semen) quicksilver, which is supposed to originate in the semen of Ṣiva.

ශිවවාහන, *Ṣiva-wáhana*, *s.* (ශිව and වාහන vehicle) bull, [Colloq. ගොණා *goṇá*].

ශිවා, *Ṣivá*, *s.* goddess Durgá, wife of Ṣiva; yellow myrobalan, *terminalia chebula*, [Colloq. අරළු *araḷu*]; jackal, *canis aureus*, [Colloq. නරියා *nariyá*]; emblic myrobalan, *phyllanthus emblica*, [Colloq. නෙල්ලි *nelli*].

ශිවාක්ෂ, *Ṣiváksha*, *s.* seed of the *elæocarpus*.

ශිවාද්‍රි, *Ṣivádri*, *s.* (ශිව *ṣiva* and අද්‍රි *adri* mountain) mount Kailása: see කෛලාස *kailása*.

ශිවාරාති, *Ṣiváráti*, *s.* (ශිවා jackal, අරාති *aráti* enemy) dog, [Colloq. බල්ලා *ballá*].

ශිවාලය, *Ṣiválaya*, *s.* (ශිව *ṣiva* and ආලය *álaya* abode) cemetery, or place where dead bodies are burnt or buried; any temple dedicated to Ṣiva.

ශිශිර, *Ṣiṣira*, *s.* cold season: *a.* cold, chilly, frigid, freezing.

ශිශිරකර, *Ṣiṣirakara*, *s.* (ශිශිර cold, කර what makes) moon, [Colloq. හඳ *haṉda*].

ශිශිරා, *Ṣiṣirá*, *s.* plant, variety of *heteropogon hirtus*, [Colloq. හෙළ ඊතණ *heḷa-itaṇa*]; sarsaparilla, *hemidesmus indicus*, [Colloq. ඉරමුසු *iramasu*].

ශිශු, *Ṣiṣu*, } *s.* young of man or any animal,
ශිශුක, *Ṣiṣuka*, } as a child, calf, pup, etc. pupil, scholar.

ශිශුපාලක, *Ṣiṣupálaka*, *s.* plant, *nauclea cordifolia*.

ශිශුමාර, *Ṣiṣumára*, *s.* (ශිශු child, මාර what kills) gangetic porpoise, *delphinus gangeticus;* crocodile, [Colloq. කිඹුලා *kiṃbulá*].

ශිෂ්ට, *Ṣishṭa*, *a.* (ශාස *ṣása* to order, ක්ත *kta* aff.) obedient, docile; ordered, commanded; disciplined, trained.

ශිෂ්ටි, *Ṣishṭi*, *s.* order, command; ruling, commanding.

ශිෂ්‍ය, *Ṣishya*, *s.* pupil, scholar.

ශීඝ්‍ර, *Ṣighra*, *s.* parallax: *a.* quick, speedy.

ශීත්කාර, *Ṣítkára*, *s.* (ශීත් imitative sound, කාර making) uttering an inarticulate sound, such as is made with the lips when a person shivers with cold; uttering a sound expressive of pleasurable sensation.

ශීත, *Ṣíta*, *s.* cold, coldness; cold weather; camphor; white sandal, *santalum album*, [Colloq. සඳුන් *saṉdun*]; small tree, *cordia myxa*, [Colloq. ලෝලු *lólu*]; sort of aloe, *aloe vulgaris;* plant, *marsilea quadrifolia*, [Colloq. දිය ඇඹුල් ඇඹිලිය *diya-ęmbul-ęmbiliya*]; nimb or margosa tree, *azadirachta indica*, [Colloq. කොහොඹ *kohomba*]: *a.* cold, chilly, frigid; dull, apathetic, stupid.

ශීතක, *Ṣítaka*, *s.* (ශීත and කන් *kan* aff.) cold weather or the cold season; plant, *marsilea dentata*.

ශීතගන්ධ, *Ṣítagandha*, *s.* (ශීත cold, ගන්ධ smell) white sandal: see ශීත *ṣíta*.

ශීතගු, *Ṣítagu*, *s.* (ශීත and ගු ray of light) moon, [Colloq. හඳ *haṉda*].

ශීතචර, *Ṣíta-chara*, *s.* (ශීත and චර to go) tree, *cordia myxa:* see ශීත *ṣíta*.

ශීතද්‍රැ, *Ṣítadru*, *s.* (ශීත and ද්‍රැ tree) nimba tree: see ශීත *ṣíta*.

ශීතපර්ණී, *Ṣíta-parṇi*, *s.* (ශීත cold, පර්ණ *parṇa* leaf, ඊ *í* aff.) annual plant, *cleome* or *gynandropsis pentaphylla*, [Colloq. වේලා *wélá*].

ශීතපාකිනි, *Ṣítapákini*, *s.* medicinal root, commonly Kákóli.

ශීතපාකී, *Ṣíta-pákí*, *s.* (ශීත and පාක *páka* ripening, ඊ *í* aff.) downy plant, *sida cordifolia*, [Colloq. සුළුබෑලිල *suḷu-bẹlila*].

ශීතපුෂ්ප, *Ṣíta-pushpa*, *s.* (ශීත and පුෂ්ප flower) sirisha tree, *mimosa sirisha;* fragrant grass, *cyperus rotundus*, [Colloq. කලාඳුරු *kalánduru*].

ශීතපුෂ්පක, *Ṣíta-pushpaka*, *s.* storax or benzoin.

ශීතපුෂ්පී, *Ṣíta-pushpí*, *s.* tree, *carissa carandas*, [Colloq. කරඹ *karaṁba*].

ශීතප්‍රිය, *Ṣíta-priya*, *s.* (ශීත and ප්‍රිය beloved) small tree, *gardenia latifolia*. [Colloq. ගලිස් *galis*]: plant, *aperosa latifolia*, or *mollugo cerviana*. [Colloq. පැපිළිය *pẹpiḷiya* or පත්පාඩගං *patpádagaṉ*].

ශීතඵල, *Ṣíta-phala*, *s.* (ශීත and ඵල fruit) emblic myrobalan: see ශිවා *ṣivá*.

ශීතභානු, *Ṣíta-bhánu*, *s.* (ශීත cold, භානු sun) moon, [Colloq. හඳ *haṉda*].

ශීතභීරු, *Ṣíta-bhíru*, *s.* (ශීත and භීරු afraid) Arabian jasmine, *jasminum zambac*, [Colloq. පිච්ච *pichcha*]; plant, *wrightia zeylanica*, [Colloq. ඉද්ද *idda*].

ශීතමූලක, *Ṣíta-múlaka*, *s.* (ශීත cold, මූල *múla* root) the root of the *andropogon muricatus*, [Colloq. සෑවැන්දරාමුල් *sẹwẹndará-mul*].

ශීතල, *Ṣítala*, *s.* (ශීත and ල aff. or ලා *lá* to give or get) sandal; storax; white sandal; lotus; pearl; cold, coldness; root of the *andropogon muricatus;* plant, *marsilea quadrifolia:* see ශීත *ṣíta;* tree, *cordia myxa:* see ශීත *ṣíta;* champaka, *michelia champaca*, [Colloq. සපු *sapu*]; camphor, [Colloq. කපුරු *kapuru*].

ශීතලා, *Ṣítalá*, *s.* plant, perhaps the *phrynium dichotymum;* plant, *sida cordifolia*, [Colloq. සුළු බෑලිල *sulu-bẹlila*]; cucumber, *cucumis pubescens*, [Colloq. කෑකිරි *kẹkiri*].

ශීතලාලය, *Ṣítalálaya*, *s.* (ශීතල *ṣítala* cold, ආලය *álaya* residence) Himálaya mountain.

ශීතලාලයා, *Ṣítalálayá*, *s.* plant, variety of *eugenia*, [Colloq. හෙළදන් *heḷa-dan*].

ශීතවල්ලභ, *Ṣíta-wallabha*, *s.* (ශීත cold, වල්ලභ beloved) plant, *ardisia humilis*, [Colloq. බළුදන් *baḷudan*].

ශීතවලාහක, *Ṣíta-waláhaka*, *s.* god of the winds, Eolus.

ශීතවීර්‍ය්‍ය, *Ṣítavírya*, *s.* blue lotus, [Colloq. මානෙල් *mánel*].

ශීතශිව, *Ṣítaṣiwa*, *s.* (ශීත and ශිව auspicious) sort of resin, *storax benzoin;* rock salt, [Colloq. සහිඳ ලුණු *sahiṉda-luṇu*]; sort of fennel, *anethum sowa*.

ශීතසහා, *Ṣítasahá*, *s.* medicinal plant, *aloe vulgaris*, [Colloq. කෝමාරිකා *kómáriká*].

ශීතසෞගන්ධි, *Ṣíta-saugandhi*, *s.* (ශීත and සෞගන්ධ *saugandha* perfume, ඉන් *in* aff.) red lotus, *nelumbium speciosum*, [Colloq. නෙළුම් *neḷum*].

ශීතාංශු, *Ṣítánṣu*, *s.* (ශීත *ṣíta* cold, අංශු *anṣu* ray) moon, [Colloq. හඳ *haṉda*]; camphor, [Colloq. කපුරු *kapuru*].

ශීතාද්‍රි, *Ṣítádri*, *s.* (ශීත *ṣíta* cold, අද්‍රි *adri* mountain) Himálaya mountains.

ශීතාලු, *Ṣítálu*, *s.* (ශීත *ṣíta* and අලු *alu* aff. implying aversion or impatience) cold, shivering, shrinking from cold.

ශීතාශ්ම, *Ṣítáṣma*, *s.* (ශීත *ṣíta* cold, අශ්ම *aṣma* stone) moon-stone; crystal.

ශීතීභාව, *Ṣítíbháwa*, *s.* (ශීත *ṣíta* and භාව nature) coolness, composure.

ශීධු, *Ṣídhu*, *s.* (ශී to sleep, ධු aff.) rum, distilled from molasses.

ශීධුගන්ධ, *Ṣídhugandha*, *s.* plant, *mimusops elengi*, [Colloq. මුනමල් *múna-mal*].

ශීධුපුෂ්පී, *Ṣídhu-pushpi*, *s.* (ශීධු rum, පුෂ්ප *pushpa* flower, ඉන් *in* aff.) plant, *mimusops elengi*, [Colloq. මුනමල් *múna-mal*].

ශීධුඵල, *Ṣídhu-phala*, *s.* (ශීධු and ඵල fruit) emblic myrobalan, [Colloq. නෙල්ලි *nelli*]; see ශීත *ṣíta*.

ශීර්ෂ, *Ṣírsha*, *s.* head: see ශිරස *ṣirasa*.

ශීර්ෂක, *Ṣírshaka*, *s.* (ශීර්ෂ and කන් *kan* aff.) helmet; skull.

ශීර්ෂණ්‍ය, *Ṣírshaṇya*, *s.* helmet; clean and unentangled hair.

ශීර්ෂය, *Ṣírshaya*, see ශීර්ෂ *ṣírsha*.

ශීර්ෂරක්ෂ, *Ṣírsha-raksha*, *s.* (ශීර්ෂ head, රක්ෂ defending) helmet.

ශිර, *Ṣíra, s.* plough; large snake, *pithon molurus,* [Colloq. පිඹුරා *pimburá*].

ශිරපාණි, *Ṣírapáṇi, s.* (ශිර plough, පාණි hand) name of Baladéwa.

ශිරි, *Ṣíri, s.* (ශිර *ṣíra* and ඉන් *in* aff.) name of Baladéwa, who carries a plough in his hand.

ශීල, *Ṣíla, s.* (ශීල to meditate, or to fix, to establish, or ශල *ṣala* to shake, sin) moral and religious observance or obligation, enjoined duty; also, steady and uniform observance of law and morals; quality, disposition.

ශුක්ත, *Ṣukta, s.* flesh; sour gruel; vinegar; acid or an acid preparation: *a.* pure, clean.

ශුක්ති, *Ṣukti, s.* pearl oyster; conch; cockle.

ශුක්තිජ, *Ṣuktija, s.* (ශුක්ති and ජ born) pearl, [Colloq. මුතු *mutu*].

ශුක්‍ර, *Ṣukra, s.* planet Venus or its regent, preceptor of the Daityas or enemies of the gods; semen virile; morbid affection of the iris, change of colour, ulceration, etc. accompanied by imperfect vision.

ශුක්‍රධාතුව, *Ṣukradhátuwa, s,* semen virile.

ශුක්‍රභුජ්, *Ṣukrabhuj, s.* peacock, [Colloq. මොණරා *moṇará*].

ශුක්‍රභූ, *Ṣukrabhú, s.* marrow of the bones.

ශුක්‍රලා, *Ṣukralá, s.* (ශුක්‍ර semen, ල *la* affix or ලා to get or give) fragrant grass, considered by some as a sort of *cyperus* and by others zedoary: *a.* spermatic, augmenting the seminal secretion.

ශුක්ල, *Ṣukla, s.* (ශුච *ṣucha* to be pure, etc. ල aff.) white, [Colloq. සුදු *sudu*]; silver, [Colloq. රිදී *ridí*]; fresh butter; disease of the cornea, opacity, albugo; light half of a month: see ශුක්ල පක්ෂ *ṣukla-paksha: a.* white; of a white colour.

ශුක්ලක, *Ṣuklaka, s.* garlic, *allium sativum,* [Colloq. සුදුලූනු *sudulúnu*].

ශුක්ලකාණ, *Ṣuklakáṇa, s.* (ශුක්ල and කාණ blind) man blind of albugo.

ශුක්ලගන්ධා, *Ṣukla-gandhá, s.* medicinal drug, *lagenandra lancifolia,* [Colloq. අතිවිඩයන් *ativiḍayan*].

ශුක්ලගන්ධිකා, *Ṣukla-gandhiká, s.* creeping plant: see ත්‍රස්තවාලු *trastawálu.*

ශුක්ල ධාතුව, *Ṣukla-dhátuwa, s.* chalk; also, corruptly for ශුක්‍රධාතු *ṣukradhátu.*

ශුක්ලපක්ෂ, *Ṣukla-paksha, s.* (ශුක්ල white, පක්ෂ part or fortnight) the light half of a month, fifteen days from new to full moon.

ශුක්ලමණ්ඩල, *Ṣukla-maṇḍala, s.* (ශුක්ල white, මණ්ඩල circle) white of the eye, cornea.

ශුක්ලවායස, *Ṣukla-wáyasa, s.* (ශුක්ල and වායස crow) Indian crane.

ශුක්ලා, *Ṣuklá, s.* plant, *ipomœa digitata,* [Colloq. කිරිබදු *kiribadu*].

ශුක, *Ṣuka, s.* parrot, [Colloq. ගිරවා *girawá*]; sirisha tree, *mimosa sirisha;* plant, *oroxylum indicum,* [Colloq. තොටිල *toṭila*].

ශුකතරු, *Ṣuka-taru, s.* (ශුක and තරු tree) sirisha, *mimosa sirisha.*

ශුකතුණ්ඩ, *Ṣukatuṇḍa, s.* vermillion, [Colloq. සාදිලිංගම් *sádilingam*].

ශුකනාස, *Ṣuka-nása, s.* (ශුක and නාස nose) plant, *oroxylum indicum,* [Colloq. තොටිල *toṭila*]; small tree, *æschynomene sesban.*

ශුකප්‍රියා, *Ṣuka-priyá, s.* rose apple, *jambosa vulgaris,* [Colloq. ජම්බු *jambu*].

ශුචි, *Ṣuchi, s.* (ශුච් to purify, ඉන් *in* aff.) colour white; moon; purification by ablution, etc.; mental purity, virtue, goodness; accuracy, correctness; month May–June, or June–July; hot season: *a.* white, pure, clean.

ශුණ්ඨ්‍ය, *Ṣunthya,*
ශුණ්ඨි, *Ṣunthi,* } *s.* dry ginger, [Colloq. සිද්දිඟුරු *siddinguru*].

ශුණ්ඩ, *Ṣuṇḍa, s.* exudation from an elephant's temples in time of rut.

ශුණ්ඩා, *Ṣuṇḍá, s.* tavern; spirituous liquor; elephant's proboscis or trunk.

ශුණ්ඩාපාන, *Ṣuṇḍápána, s.* (ශුණ්ඩා spirit, පාන drinking) place where spirits are sold, tavern, dram shop.

ශුණ්ඩි, *Ṣuṇḍi, s.* distiller, preparer and vender of spirituous liquors; elephant.

ශුද්ධ, *Ṣuddha, s.* (ශුධ *suddha* to be or make pure, ක *ka* aff.) rock salt: *a.* pure, purified, clean, cleansed; faultless, correct; white.

ශුද්ධාන්ත, *Ṣuddhánta, s.* (ශුධ *ṣuddha* pure, අන්ත *anta* end, limit) seraglio, harem; private or women's apartment in the palace of a prince.

ශුද්ධිය, *Ṣuddhiya, s.* (ශුධ *ṣuddha* to be or make pure, ක්ති *kti* aff.) cleaning, cleansing; purity, purification; correction, correctness.

ශුන්‍ය, *Ṣunya, s.* cypher; number of dogs: see ශූන්‍ය *ṣúnya.*

ශුන, *Ṣuna,*
ශුනක, *Ṣunaka,*
ශුනි, *Ṣuni,* } *s.* (ශු to hear, to obey, න and කන් *kan* aff.) dog, [Colloquial: බල්ලා *ballá*].

ශුනී, *Ṣuní, s.* bitch, [Colloq. බැල්ලි *bælli*].

ශුභ්‍ර, *Ṣubhra*, *s.* (ශුභ *ṣubha* to shine, ර *ra* aff.) white sandal, *santalum album*, [Colloq. සුදුහඳුන් *sudu-handun*]; talc; silver, [Colloq. රිදී *ridí*]; green vitriol: *a.* white; shining.

ශුභ්‍රකෘත්, *Ṣubhrakṛit*, *s.* (ශුභ්‍ර white, කෘත් making) thirty-sixth year of the Indian cycle.

ශුභ්‍රදේහභෘත්, *Ṣubhra-déhabhṛit*, *s.* (ශුභ්‍ර and දේහ body, භෘත් who supports) name of Balaráma; Indian crane.

ශුභ්‍රා, *Ṣubhrá*, *s.* crystal; bambu manna.

ශුභ්‍රාංශු, *Ṣubhránṣu*, *s.* (ශුභ්‍ර *ṣubhra* and අංශු *anṣu* ray) moon; camphor: see ශීතාංශු *ṣítánṣu*.

ශුභ්‍රි, *Ṣubhri*, *s.* (ශුභ *ṣubha* to be auspicious, රි *ri* aff.) name of Brahma.

ශුල්ක, *Ṣulka*, *s.* toll, custom, tribute in general.

ශුල්ව, *Ṣulwa*, *s.* copper, [Colloq. තඹ *tamba*].

ශුෂ්ක, *Ṣushka*, *a.* (ශුෂ *ṣusha* to dry, ක aff.) dry, dried; groundless.

ශුෂ්ක ගෝමය, *Ṣushka-gómaya*, *s.* dried cow dung, [Colloq. ගොමවැරටි *gomawẹraṭi*].

ශුෂ්ක පයස්, *Ṣushka-payas*, *s.* foam of the sea, [Colloq. මුදුපෙන *múdupena*].

ශුෂ්ක විදර්ශක, *Ṣushka-vidarṣaka*, *s.* (ශුෂ්ක dry, විදර්ශක who meditates) man unable to perform religious meditations, either through natural incapacity or moral demerit.

ශුෂ්කා, *Ṣushká*, *s.* cuttle fish bone.

ශුෂ්ණ, *Ṣushṇa*, *s.* (ශුෂ *ṣusha* to dry, ණ aff.) sun, [Colloq. ඉර *ira*]; fire.

ශුෂ්ම, *Ṣushma*, *s.* sun, fire.

ශුෂ්මන්, *Ṣushman*, *s.* (ශුෂ *ṣusha* and මනි *mani* aff.) strength, prowess; fire; lustre.

ශුෂි, *Ṣushi*, *s.* (ශුෂ *ṣusha* to dry, කි *ki* aff.) hole, chasm; drying, etc.

ශුෂිර, *Ṣushira*, *s.* (ශුෂ *ṣusha* and කිර *kira* aff.) hole, vacuity, chasm; wind instrument: *a.* perforated, bored, full of holes.

ශූක, *Ṣúka*, *s.* awn of barley.

ශූකා, *Ṣúká*, *s.* cowach.

ශූකර, *Ṣúkara*, *s.* (ශූක awn, bristle, ර aff. or ශූ imitative sound, කර what makes) hog; sort of deer, hog deer.

ශූකරික, *Ṣúkarika*, *s.* (ශූකර *ṣúkara* pig, ඉක *ika* aff.) one who kills and vends the flesh of pigs, butcher.

ශූකරී, *Ṣúkarí*, *s.* sow, [Colloq. ඊරි *írí*].

ශූකශිම්බා, *Ṣúkasimbá*, } *s.* cowach, *carpopogon*
ශූකශිම්බි, *Ṣúkasimbi*, } *pruriens*, [Colloq. වඳුරුමෑ *wandurumẹ*].

ශූද්‍ර, *Ṣúdra*, *s*, man of the fourth or servile tribe, said to have sprung from the feet of Brahma.

ශූන්‍ය, *Ṣúnya*, *s.* heaven, sky, æther; cypher; vacuum: *a.* empty, void, lonely, desert.

ශූන්‍යකා, *Ṣúnyaká*, *s.* annual plant, *borago zeylanica*, [Colloq. යොන්තුඹ *yontumba*].

ශූන්‍යා, *Ṣúnyá*, *s.* hollow reed; prickly pear, *opuntia dillenii*, [Colloq. කටුපතුක් *kaṭu-patuk*].

ශූර්ප, *Ṣúrpa*, *s.* winnowing basket; measure of two Dróṇas.

ශූර්පර්ණ, *Ṣúrparṇa*, *s.* species of bean, *phaseolus trilobus*, [Colloq. බින්මෑ *binmẹ*].

ශූර, *Ṣúra*, *s.* (ශූර to brave, අ *a* aff.) hero; lion; bear; sun: *a.* brave, valiant, powerful; clever, skilful.

ශූරණ, *Ṣúraṇa*, *s.* (ශූර *ṣúra* to hurt,) plant with edible root, *amorphophallu campanulatus*, [Coll: කිඩාරන් *kiḍáran*]; tree, *oroxylum indicum*, [Colloq. තොටිල *toṭila*].

ශූල, *Ṣúla*, *s.* (ශූල to disease or ache, අ *a* aff.) sharp pain in general, especially in the belly, as colic, etc. or in the joints, from rheumatism or gout; weapon, pike, dart; iron pin or spit.

ශූලගුල්ම, *Ṣúla-gulma*, *s.* (ශූල and ගුල්ම disease, so called) an acute species of gulma or induration of the mesenteric glands.

ශූලශත්‍රු, *Ṣúla-satru*, *s.* (ශූල colic, ශත්‍රු hostile) castor oil plant, *ricinus communis*, [Colloq. එඬරු *enḍaru*].

ශූලහෘත්, *Ṣúlahṛit*, *s.* (ශූල colic, etc. හෘත් removing) assafœtida, [Colloq. පෙරුංකායම් *perunkáyam*].

ශූලිනී, *Ṣúliní*, *s.* sort of bind-weed, *ipomœa sepiaria*, [Colloq. රසතෑල් *rasatẹl*].

ශේඛර, *Ṣékhara*, *s.* garland, crest.

ශේමුෂී, *Ṣémushi*, *s.* understanding, intellect.

ශේෂ, *Ṣésha*, *s.* (ශිෂ *ṣisha* to specify) Ananta the king of the serpent race; remainder, leavings, rest, balance, what is left, rejected, or omitted.

ශෛක්ෂ, *Ṣaiksha*, *s.* (ශික්ෂා *ṣikshá* pronunciation of the Védas, අණ් *aṇ* aff.) young Brahman in his noviciate, one who has begun to read the Védas.

ශෛඛරික, *Ṣaikharika*, *s.* plant, *achyranthes aspira*, [Colloq. කරල්සෑබෝ *karalsẹbó*].

ශෛත්‍ය, *Ṣaitya*, *a.* (ශීත *ṣíta* cold, අණ් *aṇ* aff.) cold, coldness.

ශෛථිල්‍ය, *Ṣaithilya*, *u.* (ශිථිල *ṣithila* loose, අණ් *aṇ* aff.) looseness, laxity, flabbiness.

ශෛන්‍ය, *Ṣainya*, *s.* (සේනා *séná* army, ණ්‍ය *ṇya* aff.) army, soldier, under arms; guard, sentinel.

ශෛරික, *Ṣairika*, *s.* (සීර *ṣíra* plough, අණ් *aṇ* and ඉක *ika* affixs) plough-man, plough-ox.

ශෛරිය, *Ṣairiya*. } *s.* plant, *barleria prionitis*,
ශෛරීයක, *Ṣairíyaka*, } [Colloq. කටුකරඬු *kaṭu-karaṇḍu*].

ශෛල, *Ṣaila*, *s.* (ශිලා *ṣilá* rock, stone, අණ් *aṇ* aff.) mountain; bitumen; storax; collyrium prepared with the calx of brass or the *ammomum anthorhizon;* rock moss, [Colloq. ගල්සෙවෙල් *gal-sewel*]: *a.* mountainous, mountaineer; stony, rocky.

ශෛලක, *Ṣailaka*, *s.* (ශෛල and ක pleonasm) storax or benzoin.

ශෛලජ, *Ṣailaja*, *s.* (ශෛල mountain, ජ produced) fragrant resinous substance: see ශිලාජ *ṣilája* and ශිලාජතු *ṣilájatu*.

ශෛලාට, *Ṣailáṭa*. *s.* (ශෛල *ṣaila* mountain, අට *aṭa* to go) lion; mountaineer, savage, barbarian; crystal.

ශෛලූෂ, *Ṣailúsha*, *s.* (ශිලූෂ *ṣilúsha* one of the early teachers of the art of dancing, අණ් *aṇ* aff. of descent) actor, dancer, tumbler, etc.; bael tree, *ægle marmelos*, [Colloq. බෙලි *beli*].

ශෛලේය, *Ṣailéya*, *s.* (ශෛල *ṣaila* and එය *aya* aff.) fragrant resin, storax or benzoin: see ශිලාජ *ṣilája;* rock salt.

ශෛව, *Ṣaiwa*, *s.* (ශිව *ṣiva*, අණ් *aṇ* affix of relation) worshipper of Ṣiva; aquatic plant, *vallisneria octandra:* *a.* relating or appertaining to the god Ṣiva.

ශෛවල, *Ṣaiwala*, *s.* aquatic plant: see ශෛවාල *ṣaiwála*.

ශෛවලිනි, *Ṣaiwalini*, *s.* (ශෛවල *ṣaiwala* vallisneria, ඉනි *ini* aff.) river in general, [Colloq. ගඟ *gaṅga*].

ශෛව සමය, *Ṣaiwa-samaya*, *s.* (ශෛව and සමය religion) worship or sect of Ṣiva.

ශෛවාල, *Ṣaiwála*, *s.* (ශී *ṣí* to sleep on the water, වාලන් *wálan* aff.) aquatic plant, *blyxa* or *vallisneria octandra*, [Colloq. සෙවෙල් *sewel*].

ශෛශව, *Ṣaiṣawa*, *s.* (ශිශු *ṣiṣu* child, අණ් *aṇ* aff.) childhood, pupilage, the period under sixteen.

ශෝක, *Ṣóka*, *s.* (සුච *sucha* to regret, ක්ත *kta* aff.) sorrow, grief.

ශෝක සල්ලාප, *Ṣóka-sallápa*, *s.* (ශෝක sorrow, සල්ලාප speaking) lamentation.

ශෝකාග්නිය, *Ṣókágniya*, *s.* (ශෝක *ṣóka* sorrow, අග්නිය *agniya* fire) intense grief; deep distress.

ශෝකාතුර, *Ṣókátura*, *a.* (ශෝක *ṣóka* and ආතුර *átura* afflicted) grieved, sorrowful, downcast.

ශෝකාරි, *Ṣókári*, *s.* (ශෝක *ṣóka* sorrow, අරි *ari* hostile) kadamba tree, *anthocephalus* or *nauclea cadamba*.

ශෝණ, *Ṣóṇa*, *s.* (ශෝණ to be red, අච් *ach* aff.) crimson, colour of the red lotus; flowering tree, *calotropis gigantea*, [Colloq. වරා *wará*]; blood; fire; red lead; river so called, which after an easterly course of 500 miles falls into the Ganges below Patna: *a.* crimson, of a crimson colour.

ශෝණක, *Ṣóṇaka*, *s.* flowering plant, *oryxilum indicum*, [Colloq. තොටිල *toṭila*].

ශෝණරත්න, *Ṣóṇa-ratna*, *s.* (ශෝණ and රත්න gem) ruby, [Colloq. රතුකැටය *ratukéṭaya*].

ශෝණිත, *Ṣóṇita*, *s.* (ශෝණ *ṣóṇa* crimson, ඉත *ita* aff.) blood, [Colloq. ලේ *lé*]; saffron, [Colloq. කහ *kaha*]: *a.* red, crimson, purple.

ශෝථ, *Ṣótha*, *s.* swelling, intumescence, [Colloq. ඉදිමුම *idimuma*].

ශෝථඝ්නි, *Ṣóthaghni*, *s.* hogweed.

ශෝධන, *Ṣódhana*, *s.* (ශුධ *ṣudha* to be or make pure, ණ්‍ය *nya* aff.) cleaning, cleansing, purifying, refusing of metals; correcting, freeing from faults or errors; fæces, ordure; lime: *a.* cleaning, purifying, that which cleanses or purifies.

ශෝධනී, *Ṣódhaní*, *s.* (ශෝධන *ṣódhana* and ඊ *í* aff.) broom, [Colloq. කොස්ස *kossa*].

ශෝධනීය, *Ṣódhaníya*, *a.* to be corrected, cleaned or refined.

ශෝධිත, *Ṣódhita*, *a.* corrected, cleaned, purified, discharged (as a debt).

ශෝඵකාරක, *Ṣóphakáraka*, *s.* marking nut tree, *semicarpus gardneri*, [Colloq. බඩුල්ල *badulla*].

ශෝභන, *Ṣóbhana*, *a.* (ශුභ *ṣubha* to shine, ණ්‍ය *ṇya* aff.) beautiful, handsome; shining, splendid; propitious, auspicious, virtuous, decorous.

ශෝභනක, *Ṣóbhanaka*, *s.* horse-radish tree, *moringa pterygosperma*, [Colloq. මුරුංගා *muruṅgá*].

ශෝභා, *Ṣóbhá*, *s.* (ශුභ *ṣubha* shine, අච් *ach* aff.) light, lustre, beauty, radiance, splendour.

ශෝභාඤ්ජන, *Ṣóbháñjana*, *s*, (ශෝභා beauty, අඤ්ජ *añja* to pervade, ණ්‍ය *ṇya* aff.) tree, *moringa pterygosperma*, [Colloq. මුරුංගා *muruṅgá*], the legumes blossoms and leaves are esculent, and the root of the young tree is used as a substitute for the horse radish.

ශෝෂ, *Ṣósha*, } *s.* (ශුෂ *ṣusha* to dry, අච් *ach*
ශෝෂක, *Ṣóshaka*, } aff.) pulmonary consumption; drying, swelling, intumescence.

ශෝෂණ, *Ṣóshaṇa*, *s.* suction, sucking; drying up.

ශෞටීර, *Ṣauṭíra*, *s.* (ශෞට *ṣauṭa* to be proud, ඊරන් *íran* aff.) hero; ascetic, one who abandons the world: *a.* proud, haughty.

ශෞණ්ඩ, *Ṣauṇḍa*, *a.* (ශුණ්ඩා *ṣuṇḍá* spirituous liquor, අණ් *aṇ* aff.) drunk, intoxicated.

ශෞණ්ඩය්‍ය, *Ṣauṇḍarya*, *s.* pride, arrogance, [Coll: උදාරම *udárama*].

ශෞණ්ඩී, *Ṣauṇḍí*, *s.* long pepper, *piper longum*, [Colloq. තිප්පිලි *tippili*].

ශෞණ්ඩීර, *Ṣauṇḍíra*, *a.* proud, haughty; see ශෞටීර *ṣauṭíra*.

ශෞය්‍ය, *Ṣaurya*, *s.* heroism, valour.

ශ්‍යාම, *Ṣyáma*, *s.* black or dark blue; green; cloud; kokila or Indian cuckoo, *cuculus micropterus;* pepper; sea salt; sort of grain.

ශ්‍යාමල, *Ṣyámala*, *s.* (ශ්‍යාම black, ලා *lá* to have) black pepper, *piper nigrum*, [Colloq. ගම්මිරිස් *gammiris*]; bó tree, *ficus religiosa: a.* of a black or dark blue colour.

ශ්‍යාමා, *Ṣyámá*, *s.* tree, *myristica horsfieldia*, [Coll: රුක්ගස *ruk-gasa*]; plant, variety of *ipomœa Turpethum*, [Colloq. කළුත්‍රස්තාවාලු *kaḷu-trasta-wálu*]; plant, *cardiospermum haliacacabum*, [Colloq. වැල්පෙනෙල *wel-penela*]; plant, Indian Sarsaparilla, *hemidesmus indicus*, [Colloq. ඉරමසු *iramasu*]; indigo plant, [Colloq. අවරි *awari*]; night, [Colloq. රාත්‍රිය *rátriya*].

ශ්‍යාමාඞ්ග, *Ṣyámáṅga*, *s.* (ශ්‍යාම *ṣyáma* black, අඞ්ග *aṅga* body) planet Mercury, [Colloquial: බුදහු *budahu*].

ශ්‍යාල, *Ṣyála*, *s.* wife's brother.

ශ්‍යාලී, *Ṣyálí*, *s.* wife's sister.

ශ්‍යාව, *Ṣyáwa*, *s.* colour brown.

ශ්‍යෙත, *Ṣyeta*, *s.* hawk, falcon, [Colloq. උකුස්සා *ukussá*, රාජාලියා *rájáliyá*]: *a.* white, of a white colour, [Colloq. සුදු *sudu*].

ශ්‍රත්, *Ṣrat*, *ind.* particle and prefix, implying belief or reverence.

ශ්‍රද්ධා, *Ṣraddhá*, *s.* (ශ්‍රත් *ṣrat* implying belief, etc. ධා *dhá* to have or hold, අඞ් *áṅ* and ටාප් *ṭáp* aff.) respect, reverence; faith, belief; wish, desire; purity.

ශ්‍රද්ධාචරිතය, *Ṣraddhá-charitaya*, *s.* (ශ්‍රද්ධා and චරිත *charita* conduct) piety, religiousness.

ශ්‍රද්ධාව, *Ṣraddháwa*, *s.* (සත් *sat* particle implying reverence, ධා *dhá* to hold, to have) trust, confidence, faith, religious belief; respect, reverence; purity.

ශ්‍රද්ධාවන්ත, *Ṣrddháwanta*, *a.* (ශ්‍රද්ධා and වන්ත poss. aff.) pious, religious, faithful; pure, holy.

ශ්‍රද්ධාලු, *Ṣraddhálu*, *a.* (ශ්‍රද්ධා faith, ආලුච් *áluch* aff.) faithful, believing; wishing, desirous.

ශ්‍රන්ථන, *Ṣranthana*, *s.* stringing flowers, etc. tying, binding.

ශ්‍රපිත, *Ṣrapita*, *a.* (ශ්‍රෛ *ṣrai* to cook or boil, ක්ත *kta* aff.) boiled, [Colloq. පිසූ *pisú*, උයාපු *uyápu*],

ශ්‍රබස්තා, *Ṣrabastá*, *s.* creeping plant, *argyreia populifolia*, [Colloq. ගිරිතිල්ල *giritilla*].

ශ්‍රම, *Ṣrama*, *s.* (ශ්‍රම to be wearied) labour, exertion, toil, [Colloq. උත්සාහය *utsáhaya* ; weariness, fatigue, [Colloq. වෙහෙස *wehesa*].

ශ්‍රමණ, *Ṣramaṇa*, *s.* (ශ්‍රම to perform acts of austere devotion, යුච් *yuch* aff.) ascetic, one devoted to meditation for the purpose of obtaining final emancipation from existence, Buddhist ascetic, beggar, the religious mendicant, Buddhist priest.

ශ්‍රමණා, *Ṣramaṇá*, *s.* Indian spikenard, *valeriana jatamansi;* Indian madder, *oldenlandia umbellata*, [Colloq. සයමුල් *sayamul*]; female mendicant.

ශ්‍රමණී, *Ṣramaṇí*, *s.* plant, *sphœranthus indicus* or *s. hirtus*, [Colloq. මුඩමහණ *muḍamahaṇa*].

ශ්‍රයණ, *Ṣrayaṇa*, *s.* (ශ්‍රි *ṣrí* to serve, ල්‍යුට් *lyuṭ* aff.) asylum, refuge, shelter, protection.

ශ්‍රව, *Ṣrawa*, *s.* (ශ්‍රු *ṣru* to hear, to flow, to drop, අ *a* aff.) ear; oozing, trickling, dripping; fountain.

ශ්‍රවණ, *Ṣrawaṇa*, *s.* (ශ්‍රු *ṣru* to hear, to ooze, or ශ්‍රි *ṣrí* to serve) ear; hearing; dripping, oozing; urine; sweat, perspiration; service.

ශ්‍රවණපථ, *Ṣrawaṇa-patha*, *s.* ear.

ශ්‍රවණා, *Ṣrawaṇá*, *s.* twenty-third of the lunar asterisms, represented by three footsteps, and containing three stars, Alpha, Beta, and Gamma, Aquilæ.

ශ්‍රවස්, *Ṣrawas*, *s.* ear, [Colloq. කණ *kaṇa*]: see ශ්‍රව *ṣrawa*.

ශ්‍රවිෂ්ඨා, *Ṣravishṭhá*, *s.* twenty-fourth lunar asterism, corresponding to the Dolphin.

ශ්‍රාද්ධ, *Ṣráddha*, *s.* (ශ්‍රද්ධා *ṣráddhá* faith, අණ් *aṇ* affix of possession or relation) funeral ceremony consisting of offerings of fire, water, food, etc. to the manes and to the gods: *a.* faithful, believing.

ශ්‍රාධදේව, *Ṣráddha-déwa*, *s.* (ශ්‍රාධ funeral ceremony, දේව deity) Yama, judge and monarch of the dead.

ශ්‍රාන්ත, *Ṣránṭa*, *s.* (ශ්‍රම *ṣrama* to be tranquil or wearied, ක්ත *kta* aff.) ascetic, one with subdued passions: *a.* calm, tranquil; wearied, fatigued.

ශ්‍රාමණේර, *Ṣrámaṇera*, *s.* (ශ්‍රම asatic, ණේර aff.) pupil of a Buddhist priest, novice.

ශ්‍රාමාණ්‍ය, *Ṣrámáṇya*, *s.* asceticism; mendicity.

ශ්‍රාය, *Ṣráya*, *s.* (ශ්‍රි *ṣri* to serve) refuge, reliance, shelter or protection.

ශ්‍රාවක, *Ṣráwaka*, *s.* (ශ්‍රු *ṣru* to hear, religious discourses, ක aff.) pupil or follower of Buddha, Buddhist.

ශ්‍රාවන්ති, *Ṣráwantí*, *s.* a city: see සැවැත් *sewẹt*.

ශ්‍රිත, *Ṣrita*, *a.* (ශ්‍රි to serve, ක්ත *kta* aff.) cherished, protected; served, honored, worshipped.

ශ්‍රියාකාන්තාව, *Ṣriyákántáwa*, see ශ්‍රීකාන්තාව *ṣrí-kántáwa*.

ශ්‍රියාව, *Ṣriyáwa*, *s.* noble appearance, beauty.

ශ්‍රියාවන්තයා, *Ṣriyáwantayá*, *s.* person of a beautiful countenance.

ශ්‍රී, *Ṣrí*, *s.* (ශ්‍රි to serve, to worship, and the vowel made long) goddess Lakshmí, the deity of plenty and prosperity; fortune, prosperity, success, thriving; beauty, splendour, lustre; state, paraphernalia; elevation, consequence; fame, glory; wealth; *pinus longifolia;* also, beli tree: *a.* famous, splendid, illustrious, etc.

ශ්‍රීකර, *Ṣríkara*, *s.* (ශ්‍රී fortune, etc. කර who makes or confers) Vishṇu; red lotus, *nymphæa rubra*, [Colloq. රත්නෙළුම් *rat-neḷum*]; also, blue lotus, *nymphæa stellata*, [Colloq. නිල් මානෙල් *nil-mánel*]; plant, *plectranthus zeylanicus*, [Colloq. ඉරිවේරිය *iriwériya*]: *a.* conferring prosperity.

ශ්‍රීකරී, *Ṣríkarí*, *s.* betel pepper, *piper betle*, [Colloq. බුලත් *bulat*].

ශ්‍රීකාන්තාව, *Ṣríkántáwa*, *s.* (ශ්‍රී and කාන්තා *kántá* mistress) name of Lakshmí.

ශ්‍රීඛණ්ඩ, *Ṣrí-khaṇḍa*, *s.* (ශ්‍රී auspicious, ඛණ්ඩ part) sandal wood, *santalum album*, [Colloq. සඳුන් *sa͟ndun*].

ශ්‍රීඝන, *Ṣríghana*, *s.* (ශ්‍රී prosperity, ඝන heap) name of Buddha; also, sour cords.

ශ්‍රීචක්‍ර, *Ṣrí-chakra*, *s.* magical diagram; astrological division of the body, uterine or pubic region.

ශ්‍රීජ, *Ṣríja*, *s.* (ශ්‍රී Lakshmí, ජ born) Káma, the Indian deity of love.

ශ්‍රීද, *Ṣrída*, *s.* (ශ්‍රී wealth, ද who gives) Kuvéra, the god of riches.

ශ්‍රීදේවතා, *Ṣrí-déwatá*, *s.* (ශ්‍රී and දේවතා deity) Lakshmí, see ශ්‍රී *ṣrí*.

ශ්‍රීද්‍රුම, *Ṣrí-druma*, *s.* bael fruit tree, *ægle marmelos*, [Colloq. බෙලි *beli*].

ශ්‍රීධර, *Ṣrídhara*, *s.* (ශ්‍රී the goddess, etc. ධර who has) name of Vishṇu; plant, species of *basil*, [Colloq. තලා *talá*].

ශ්‍රීනිකේත, *Ṣríniketa*, / ශ්‍රීනිකේතන, *Ṣríniketana*, } *s.* Vishṇu; red lotus, *nymphæa rubra*, [Coll: රත්නෙළුම් *rat-neḷum*].

ශ්‍රීනිර්ගුණ්ඩි, *Ṣrí-nirguṇṭi*, *s.* tree, *nyctanthes arbor tristis*, [Colloq. කළුතලා *kaḷutalá*].

ශ්‍රීනිවාස, *Ṣríniwása*, *s.* Vishṇu.

ශ්‍රීපති, *Ṣrípati*, *s.* Vishṇu.

ශ්‍රීපර්ණ, *Ṣrí-parṇa*, *s.* (ශ්‍රී beauty, පර්ණ leaf) shrub, *gmelina arborea*, [Colloq. ඇත්දෙමට *ẹtdemaṭa*]; silk cotton tree; aquatic plant, *pistia stratiotes*, [Colloq. දියපරණලා *diyaparaṇalá*].

ශ්‍රීපර්ණි, *Ṣrí-parṇi*, *s.* tree, *premna spinosa*, [Coll: සිහින්මිදි *ṣihin-midi*].

ශ්‍රීපර්ණිකා, *Ṣrí-parṇiká*, *s.* aromatic plant, the leaves of which are used in making curry, *murraya Koenigii*, [Colloq. කරපිංච *karapiṇcha*].

ශ්‍රීපර්ණී, *Ṣrí-parṇí*, *s.* shrub, *gmelina arborea*, [Colloq. ඇත්දෙමට *ẹt-demaṭa*]; tree, *premna spenosa*, [Colloq. සිහින්මිදි *sihin-midi*].

ශ්‍රීපාද, *Ṣrípáda*, *s.* (ශ්‍රී fame, පාද foot) foot or feet of Buddha; the epithet refers to the 216 auspicious marks or signs on the soles of his feet, indicative of his character and dignity; mountain in the interior of Ceylon, commonly called Adam's Peak, the name Ṣrípáda alludes to the fable of there being an impression of Buddha's foot on its summit.

ශ්‍රීපුෂ්ප, *Ṣrí-pushpa*, *s.* clove tree, *caryophyllus aromaticus*, [Colloq. කරාබු *karábu*].

ශ්‍රීඵල, *Ṣrí-phala*, *s.* (ශ්‍රී beauty, ඵල fruit) bael fruit tree, *ægle marmelos*, [Colloq. බෙලි *beli*].

ශ්‍රීඵලී, *Ṣrí-phalí*, *s.* emblic myrobalan, *phyllanthus emblica*, [Colloq. නෙල්ලි *nelli*]; indigo plant, *indigofera tinctoria*, [Colloq. අවරිය *awariya*].

ශ්‍රීභද්‍ර, *Ṣrí-bhadra*, *s.* (ශ්‍රී Lakshmí, භද්‍ර auspicious) fragrant grass, *cyperus rotundus*, [Colloq. කලාඳුරු *kaláṇduru*].

ශ්‍රීමත්, *Ṣrímat*, *s.* (ශ්‍රී beauty, මතුප් *matup* aff.) name of Vishṇu, Kuvéra and Ṣiva; tree, *adenanthera pavonina*, [Colloquial: මදටිය ගස්

madaṭiya-gas]; red lead, [Colloq. සින්දූරං *sindú-raṇ*]: *a.* wealthy, opulent; famous, illustrious.

ශ්‍රීමුඛ, *Ṣrí-mukha*, *s.* (ශ්‍රී prosperity, beautiful, මුඛ chief, mouth) seventh year of the Indian cycle; beautiful mouth.

ශ්‍රීයාන, *Ṣríyána*, *s.* (ශ්‍රී auspicious, යාන couch) royal couch or bed.

ශ්‍රීයුක්ත, *Ṣrí-yukta*, *a.* (ශ්‍රී prosperity, යුක්ත possessing) famous, illustrious; fortunate, wealthy.

ශ්‍රීරස, *Ṣrí-rasa*, *s.* (ශ්‍රී pine tree, රස juice) turpentine.

ශ්‍රීලංකාද්වීපය, *Ṣrílaṇkádwípaya*, *s.* (ශ්‍රී famous, ලංකා and ද්වීප *dwípa* island) name of Ceylon.

ශ්‍රීවත්ස, *Ṣríwatsa*, *s.* (ශ්‍රී Lakshmí, වත්ස dear to) name of Vishṇu; particular mark, usually said to be a curl of hair on the breast of Vishṇu or Kṛishṇa.

ශ්‍රීවත්සාඞ්ක, *Ṣríwatsáṅka*, *s.* (ශ්‍රීවත්ස *ṣríwatsa* and අඞ්ක *aṅka* mark) Vishṇu, see the last.

ශ්‍රීවාස, *Ṣríwása*, *s.* (ශ්‍රී pine, etc. වාස abode) turpentine; lotus; Vishṇu.

ශ්‍රීවෘක්ෂ, *Ṣrí-wṛiksha*, *s.* (ශ්‍රී auspicious, වෘක්ෂ tree) bó tree, *ficus religiosa*, [Colloq. බෝගහ *bógaha*].

ශ්‍රීවේෂ්ට, *Ṣríwéshṭa*, see ශ්‍රීරස *ṣrírasa*.

ශ්‍රීවේෂ්ටක, *Ṣrí-wéshṭaka*, *s.* plant, *amyrus agallocha*, [Colloq. ගුඟුල් *gugul*].

ශ්‍රීහස්තිනී, *Ṣrí-hastiní*, *s.* (ශ්‍රී Lakshmí, හස්ත *hasta* hand, ඉනී *ini* aff.) sun flower, *heliotropium indicum*, which the goddess holds in her hand.

සෘකාල, *Ṣrikála*, } *s.* (සෘජ *srija* to create, deceit,
ශෘගාල, *Ṣrigála*, } කාලන් *kálan* affix or ශෘඞ්ග *ṣriṅga* horn, අ *a* neg. ලා *lá* to have) jackal, [Colloq. නරියා *nariyá*]; coward, poltroon; rogue, cheat.

ශෘඞ්ඛල, *Ṣriṅkhala*, *s.* belt or chain worn round a man's body; fetter in general.

ශෘඞ්ඛලිත, *Ṣriṅkhalita*, *a.* (ශෘඞ්ඛල *ṣriṅkhala* chain, ඉත *ita* aff.) bound, chained, fettered, captive.

ශෘඞ්ග, *Ṣriṅga*, *s.* horn; mark, sign; the top of a mountain; sovereignty; dignity, etc.; very sharp; minutely fine.

ශෘඞ්ගවෙර, *Ṣriṅga-wera*, *s.* ginger, [Colloq. ඉඟුරු *inguru*].

ශෘඞ්ගාට, *Ṣriṅgáṭa*, } *s.* (ශෘඞ්ග *ṣriṅga* horn,
ශෘඞ්ගාටක, *Ṣriṅgáṭaka*, } අට *aṭa* to go or be) place where four roads meet; aquatic plant, *trapa bispinosa*, [Colloq. ඉකිලිය *ikiliya*]; shrub, *ruellia* or *barleria longifolia*.

ශෘඞ්ගාර, *Ṣriṅgára*, *s.* (ශෘඞ්ග *ṣriṅga* eminence, ඍ *ṛi* to go or obtain) love, the passion or sentiment as an object of poetical description or dramatic representation; coition; cloves; fragrant perfume for the person.

ශෘඞ්ගාරභූෂණ, *Ṣriṅgára-bhúshaṇa*, *s.* red lead.

ශෘඞ්ගාරයෝනි, *Ṣriṅgára-yóni*, *s.* (ශෘඞ්ගාර and යෝනි origin) Káma the deity of love.

ශෘඞ්ගාරී, *Ṣriṅgári*, *s.* betel nut tree, *areca catechu*, [Colloq. පුවක් *puwak*]; dress; decoration.

ශෘඞ්ගි, *Ṣriṅgi*, *s.* sort of sheat fish, *sitrus pungentissimus*; gold for ornaments.

ශෘඞ්ගික, *Ṣriṅgika*, *s.* sort of poison; plant, *betula*.

ශෘඞ්ගිණ, *Ṣriṅgiṇa*, *s.* (ශෘඞ්ග *ṣriṅga* horn, ඉන *ina* aff.) ram, [Colloq. බැටළුවා *beṭaḷuwá*].

ශෘඞ්ගින්, *Ṣriṅgin*, *s.* (ශෘඞ්ග *ṣriṅga* horn, ඉනි *ini* poss. aff.) elephant; mountain; tree: *a.* horned; crested, peaked.

ශෘඞ්ගිණී, *Ṣriṅginí*, *s.* Arabian jasmine; hart pea; medicinal plant, commonly called kaṭukí.

ශ්‍රුත, *Ṣruta*, *s.* (ශ්‍රු to hear, to flaw, ක්ත *kta* aff.) sacred science, holy writ: that which is heard: *a.* heard; understood.

ශ්‍රුතවන්ත, *Ṣrutawanta*, *a.* (ශ්‍රුත that which is heard, වන්ත poss. aff.) skilled in religious science, well versed in religious instructions, etc.

ශ්‍රුති, *Ṣruti*, *s.* (ශ්‍රු to hear, ක්ති *kti* aff.) ear; hearing; scripture, holy writ; intelligence, news, rumour, report.

ශ්‍රුතිශාස්ත්‍ර, *Ṣrutiṣástra*, *s.* (ශ්‍රුති and ශාස්ත්‍ර science) sacred science, the study of theology aided by oral instructions.

ශ්‍රුතිහීන, *Ṣrutihína*, *a.* (ශ්‍රුති hearing, හීන privation) deaf, [Colloq. බිහිරිවූ *bihiriwú*].

ශ්‍රේණි, *Ṣréṇi*, *s.* (ශ්‍රි *ṣri* to serve, නි *ni* aff.) line, row, range, [Colloq. පේළිය *péliya*]; company, comporation.

ශ්‍රේඪි, *Ṣrédhi*, *s.* arithmetical progression.

ශ්‍රේයස්, *Ṣréyas*, *s.* virtue, moral merit; final happiness or emancipation; good fortune, auspiciousness, prosperity: *a.* best, most excellent.

ශ්‍රේයසී, *Ṣréyasí*, *s.* plant, resembling pepper, *piper longum*, [Colloq ගජතිප්පිලි *gaja-tippili*]; yellow or chelubic myrobalan, *terminalia chebula*, [Coll: අරළු *araḷu*]; creeping plant, *cissampelos pareira*, [Colloq. දියමිත්ත *diyamitta*].

ශ්‍රේෂ්ඨ, *Ṣréshṭha*, *a.* best, excellent, most excellent; oldest, senior.

ශ්‍රෙෂ්ඨා, *Ṣréshṭhá*, *s.* tree, *terminalia chebula*, [Colloq. අරළු *araḷu*]; also, the three myrobalans, [Colloq. තිපල *tipala*].

ශ්‍රෙෂ්ඨාධිකරණ, *Ṣréshṭhádhikaraṇa*, *s.* supreme court of justice.

ශ්‍රෙෂ්ඨෝදක, *Ṣréshṭhódaka*, *s.* water in which rice has been cleansed, [Colloq. පානුදියර *pánu-diyara*].

ශ්‍රෝණි, *Ṣróṇi*, *s.* hip and loins.

ශ්‍රෝත්‍ර, *Ṣrótra*, *s.* (ශ්‍රු *ṣru* to hear, ත්‍ර aff.) ear, [Colloq. කණ *kaṇa*].

ශ්‍රෝතස්, *Ṣrótas*, *s.* ear, current of a stream; organ of sense.

ශ්මශාන, *Ṣmaṣána*, *s.* (ශ්ම substituted for ශව *ṣawa* corpse, ශාන *ṣána* for ශයන *ṣayana* place of repose) cemetery, place where dead bodies are burnt or buried, [Colloq. මිනි පිට්ටනිය *mini-pittaniya*].

ශ්මශ්‍රු, *Ṣmaṣru*, *s.* beard, [Colloq. රැවුල *rewula*].

ශ්ලාඝා, *Ṣlághá*, *s.* (ශ්ලාඝ *ṣlágha* to praise, etc. අඞ් *aṅ* and ටාප් *ṭáp* affixes.) praise, panegyric, eulogium.

ශ්ලිෂා, *Ṣlishá*, *s.* (ශ්ලිෂ *ṣlisha* to adhere to, etc. අඞ් *aṅ* and ටාප් *ṭáp* affixes) embracing, an embrace.

ශ්ලිපද, *Ṣlípada*, *s.* elephantiasis, enlargement of the legs.

ශ්ලෙෂ්ම, *Ṣléshma*, see ශ්ලෙෂ්මා *ṣléshmá*.

ශ්ලෙෂ්මක, *Ṣléshmaka*, *s.* tree, *buchanania latifolia*, [Colloq. කිරිපළු *kiripaḷu*].

ශ්ලෙෂ්මඝ්න, *Ṣléshmaghna*, *a.* removing phlegm.

ශ්ලෙෂ්මඝ්නා, *Ṣléshmaghná*, *s.* Arabian jasmine; plant, *odoratissimus pandanus*, [Colloq. වැටකේ *weṭaké*].

ශ්ලෙෂ්මඵල, *Ṣléshma-phala*, *s.* plant, *cordia myxa*, [Colloq. ලෝලු *lólu*]: *a.* phlegmatic, abounding or affected with phlegm.

ශ්ලෙෂ්මා, *Ṣléshmá*, *s.* (ශ්ලිෂ *ṣlisha* to embrace, adhere to, the body, මනින් *manin* aff.) phlegmatic humour, one of the three chief humours of the body.

ශ්ලෙෂ්මාතක, *Ṣléshmátaka*, *s.* plant, *cordia myxa*, [Colloq. ලෝලු *lólu*].

ශ්ලෙෂ, *Ṣlésha*, *s.* (ශ්ලිෂ *ṣlisha* to embrace, adhere to, ඝඤ *ṇa* aff.) union, junction; adhering, clinging to; figure of rhetoric, choice or connection of words so as to admit of a double interpretation, species of paronomasia or pun.

ශ්ලෝක, *Ṣlóka*, *s.* (ශ්ලෝක to compose, as verses, අච් *ach* aff.) verse, stanza; fame, celebrity.

ශ්වදංෂ්ට්‍රා, *Ṣwadanshṭrá*, *s.* dog's tooth; thorny tree, bearing edible fruit, *flacourtia cataphracta*, [Colloq. රට උගුරැස්ස *raṭa-ugurэssa*]; plant, *garcinia morella*, [Colloq. ගොකටු *gokaṭu*].

ශ්වන්, *Ṣwan*, *s.* dog, [Colloq. බල්ලා *ballá*].

ශ්වපච, *Ṣwapacha*, } *s.* (ශ්වන් *ṣwan* and පච *pacha*
ශ්වපාක, *Ṣwapáka*, } to cooks (for his food, අණ් *aṇ* aff.) man of a degraded and outcast tribe, living on the refuse of the other tribes and only employed in the meanest capacities, as public executioners, etc.

ශ්වභ්‍ර, *Ṣwabhra*, *s.* hole, gap, chasm.

ශ්වර්භූ, *Ṣwarbhú*, *s.* tree, *bauhinia purpurea*, [Coll: කොබලිල *kobalila*].

ශ්වවෘත්ති, *Ṣwawritti*, *s.* (ශ්වන් *ṣwan* dog, වෘත්ති practice) service, servitude.

ශ්වශ්‍රූ, *Ṣwaṣrú*, *s.* mother-in-law.

ශ්වශුර්‍ය, *Ṣwaṣurya*, *s.* brother-in-law.

ශ්වශුර, *Ṣwaṣura*, *s.* father-in-law.

ශ්වස්, *Ṣwas*, *ind.* to-morrow, [Colloq. හෙට *heṭa*]; also, particle, implying auspiciousness.

ශ්වස්තන, *Ṣwastana*, } *s.* (ශ්වස් to-morrow, ට්‍යුල්
ශ්වස්ත්‍ය, *Ṣwastya*, } *ṭyul* aff.) future, what will be to-morrow, etc.

ශ්වසද, *Ṣwasada*, *s.* borax. [Colloq. පුස්කර *pus-kara*].

ශ්වසන, *Ṣwasana*, *s.* (ශ්වස to breathe, ල්‍යුට් *lyuṭ* aff.) air, wind; breathing, breath; sighing; plant, thorny shrub, *randia dumetorum*, [Colloq. කුකුරුමුවං *kukurumuwaṅ*].

ශ්වාන, *Ṣwána*, *s.* dog, [Colloq. බල්ලා *ballá*].

ශ්වාස, *Ṣwása*, *s.* (ශ්වස *ṣwasa* to breathe, ඝඤ *ṇa* aff.) breath, breathing; air, wind; sighing, sigh.

ශ්වාස ප්‍රාශ්වාස, *Ṣwása-práswása*, *s.* (ශ්වාස inspiration, ප්‍රාශ්වාස expiration) respiration, breathing.

ශ්වාසින්, *Ṣwásin*, *s.* air, wind, [Colloquial: හුළඟ *huḷanga*].

ශ්විත්‍ර, *Ṣvitra*, *s.* (ශ්විත *ṣvita* to be white, රක් *rak* aff.) leprosy, [Colloq. ලාදුරුලෙඩ *láduru-leḍa*].

ශ්විත්‍රඝ්නී, *Ṣvitraghní*, *s.* (ශ්විත්‍ර leprosy, ඝ්නී what destroys) plant, *trangia involucrata*.

ශ්වෙත්‍ර, *Ṣwétra*, see ශ්විත්‍ර *ṣvitra*.

ශ්වෙත, *Ṣwéta*, *s.* (ශ්විත *ṣvita* to be white, අ *a* aff.) white, [Colloq. සුදු *suda*]; planet Venus or its regent Ṣukra; silver; cummin seed; conch; cowri; one of the minor divisions of the world identified by Wilford with Britain.

ශ්වෙතක, *Ṣwétaka*, *s.* (ශ්වෙත and කන් *kan* aff.) cowri; silver, [Colloq. රිදී *ridí*].

ශ්වේතකුෂ්ඨය, *Ṣwéta-kushṭhaya*, *s.* leprosy.

ශ්වේතඛදිර, *Ṣwéta-khadira*, *s.* (ශ්වේත and ඛදිර mimosa) white sort of *acacia suma* or *a. catechu.*

ශ්වේත ගජ, *Ṣwéta-gaja*, *s.* (ශ්වේත white, ගජ elephant) elephant of Indra.

ශ්වේතච්ඡත්‍ර, *Ṣwétachchhatra*, *s.* (ශ්වේත and ඡත්‍ර umbrella) white umbrella as one of the emblems of royalty.

ශ්වේත චන්දන, *Ṣwéta-chandana*, *s.* white sandal wood, *santalum album*, [Colloq. සුදුහඳුන් *sudu-haṇḍun*].

ශ්වේතජම්බු, *Ṣwéta-jambu*, *s.* (ශ්වේත and ජම්බු eugenia) white species of *eugenia*, [Colloq. හෙළ දඹ *heḷa-dam*].

ශ්වේත ටංකණ *Ṣwéta-ṭaṇkaṇa*, *s.* (ශ්වේත and ටංකණ borax) refined borax.

ශ්වේතදර්භ, *Ṣwéta-darbha*, *s.* kind of reed, *imperata arundinacea*, [Colloq. ඉලුක් *iluk*].

ශ්වේත ධාමන්, *Ṣwéta-dháman*, *s.* (ශ්වේත and ධාමන් ray) moon, [Colloq. හඳ *haṇḍa*]; camphor.

ශ්වේතනීය, *Ṣwétaníya*, *s.* tree, *strychnos potatorum*, [Colloq. ඉඟිනි *iṇgini*].

ශ්වේතපත්‍ර, *Ṣwéta-patra*, *s.* (ශ්වේත white, පත්‍ර feather) goose; white coloured swan.

ශ්වේතපත්‍රා, *Ṣwéta-patrá*, *s.* plant, *trianthema decandra*, [Colloq. මහසාරණ *maha-sáraṇa*].

ශ්වේතපාටලා, *Ṣwéta-páṭalá*, *s.* trumpet flower, *bignonia suave-olens.*

ශ්වේත පාෂාණ, *Ṣwéta-páshána*, *s.* (ශ්වේත white, පාෂාණ stone) white arsenic.

ශ්වේතපුංඛ, *Ṣwéta-puṇkha*, *s.* plant, *nerium*, [Coll: පිලගස් *pila-gas*],

ශ්වේතපුෂ්ප, *Ṣwéta-pushpa*, *s.* (ශ්වේත white, පුෂ්ප flower) small tree, *vitex trifolia:* [Tamil, නොච්චි *nochchi* and නිර්නොච්චි *nír-nochchi*].

ශ්වේතපුෂ්පක, *Ṣwéta-pushpaka*.
ශ්වේතපුෂ්පා, *Ṣwéta-pushpá*,
ශ්වේතපුෂ්පී. *Ṣwéta-pushpí*,
} *s.* (ශ්වේත white, පුෂ්ප flower) the white variety of the *nerium odorum.*

ශ්වේත ප්‍රසූනක, *Ṣwéta-prasúnaka*, *s.* tree, *tapai cratæva.*

ශ්වේතභණ්ඩා, *Ṣwéta-bhaṇḍá*, *s.* flower, *clitoria ternatea*, [Colloq. නිල්කටරොළු *nil-kaṭaroḷu*].

ශ්වේතමධුරා, *Ṣwéta-madhurá*, *s.* variety of muruṇga, [Colloq. වැල් මුරුංගා *weḷ-muruṇgá*].

ශ්වේතමුෂ්ටි, *Ṣwéta-mushṭi*, *s.* tree, not ascertained, [Colloq. රේරුගස් *réru-gas*].

ශ්වේතමූලා, *Ṣwéta-múlá*, *s.* plant, *trianthema decandra*, [Colloq. මහසාරණ *maha-sáraṇa*].

ශ්වේතරක්ත, *Ṣwéta-rakta*, *s.* pale-red or pink, (the colour).

ශ්වේතරාස්නා, *Ṣwéta-rásná*, *s.* white *rasan*: see රාස්නා *rásná.*

ශ්වේතවචා, *Ṣwéta-wachá*, *s.* (ශ්වේත and වචා orris root) white orris root.

ශ්වේතවර්ණ, *Ṣwéta-warṇa*, *s.* (ශ්වේත and වර්ණ colour) colour white, [Colloq. සුදුපාට *sudu-páṭa*].

ශ්වේතවාහ, *Ṣwétawáha*, *s.* tree, *terminalia glabra*, [Colloq. කුඹුක් *kuṃbuk*].

ශ්වේතවිෂා, *Ṣwéta-vishá*, *s.* medicinal drug, *lagenandra lancifolia*, [Colloq. අතිවිඩයන් *ativiḍayan*].

ශ්වේතශර්ෂප, *Ṣwéta-ṣarshapa*, *s.* white mustard, [Colloq. හෙළ අබ *heḷa-aba*].

ශ්වේතසාර, *Ṣwétasára*, *s.* (ශ්වේත white, සාර pith or essence) tree, *acacia suma* or *a. catechu.*

ශ්වේතසීස, *Ṣwéta-sísa*, *s.* (ශ්වේත and සීස lead) white lead, [Colloq. සුදුඊයම් *sudu-íyam*].

ශ්වේතසුරසා, *Ṣwéta-surasá*, *s.* (ශ්වේත and සුරසා rasan) white variety of the *nyctanthes arbor tristis*, [Colloq. සේපාල *sépála* and සේපාලිකා *sépáliká*].

ශ්වේතහංස, *Ṣwéta-haṇsa*, *s.* white swan.

ශ්වේත හස්ති, *Ṣwéta-hasti*, *s.* (ශ්වේත and හස්ති elephant) Indra's elephant; white elephant, [Colloq. ඇලි ඇතා *eli-etá*].

ශ්වේතා, *Ṣwétá*, *s.* (ශ්විත *ṣvita* to be white, අ *a* aff.) cowri, [Colloq. කවඩි *kawaḍi*]; grass, *andropogon aciculatum;* flower, *clitoria ternatea*, [Colloq. නිල් කටරොළු *nil-kaṭaroḷu*]; crystal, [Colloq. පළිඟු *paḷiṇgu*]; bambu manna, [Colloq. උණ මකුළු *uṇa-makuḷu*]; hogweed; clayed or candied sugar.

ශ්වේතාර්ක, *Ṣwétárka*, *s.* (ශ්වේත *ṣwéta* and අර්ක *arka* swallow wort) gigantic swallow wort or mudar, *calotropis gigantea*, with white blossoms, [Colloq. හෙළවරා *heḷa-wará*].

ෂ

The thirty-first consonant of the Siṇhalese alphabet, the second of the sibilants, and expressed by *sh.*

ෂට්, *Shaṭ*, *a.* *six*, see ෂෂ් *shash.*

ෂට්ක, *Shaṭka*, *a.* six, six-fold.

ෂට්පද, *Shaṭpada*, *s.* (ෂට් six, පද foot) bee, [Colloq. මීමැස්සා *mímessá*]; louse, [Colloquial: උකුණා *ukuṇá*].

ෂට්පද ප්‍රිය, *Shṭpada-priya*, *s.* (ෂට්පද bee, ප්‍රිය fond of) pollen of the flower of the iron-wood tree, *mesua ferrea*, [Colloq. නාමල්රේණු *námal-réṇu*].

ෂට්පදේෂ්ට, *Shaṭpadéshṭa*, *s.* tree, *adina* or *nauclea cordifolia*, [Colloq. කොළොම් *koḷom*].

ෂඩ්ගුණ, *Shadguṇa*, *s.* (ෂෂ් *shash* six, ගුණ expedient) six regal expedients of defence, viz. pacification, war, marching, halting or maintaining a post, sowing dissension, recourse to protection: *a.* six-fold, six times.

ෂඩ්ග්‍රන්ථ, *Shaḍ-grantha*, *s.* variety of the *cæsalpinea bonduc*, [Colloq. කුඹුරුවැල් *kuṃburuwel*].

ෂඩ්ග්‍රන්ථා, *Shaḍ-granthá*, *s.* (ෂෂ් *shash* six, ග්‍රන්ථ *grantha* knot) orris root, *acorus calamus*, [Colloq. වදකහ *wadakaha*].

ෂඩ්ග්‍රන්ථිකා, *Shaḍ-granthiká*, *s.* zedoary, *curcuma aromatica*, [Colloq. හරංකහ *haraṇkaha*]: also, *kaempferia galanga*, [Colloquial: හිඟුරුපියලි *hiṇgurupiyali*].

ෂඩ්වර්ණ, *Shaḍ-warṇa*, *s.* (ෂෂ් *shash* six, වර්ණ colour) six colours which emanated from and surrounded the person of Buddha, in alternate circles, viz. blue, yellow, crimson, white, red, and prabháswara or a compound of the five.

ෂඩ්විධ, *Shaḍvidha*, *a.* (ෂෂ් *shash* and විධි *vidhi* sort) of six sorts, six-fold.

ෂඩඞ්ග, *Shaḍaṅga*, *s.* (ෂෂ් *shash* and අඞ්ග *aṅga* member) six parts of the body collectively, as the two arms, two legs, the head, and waist.

ෂඩඞ්ගජිත්, *Shaḍaṅgajit*, *s.* (ෂඩඞ්ග and ජිත් who conquers) name of Vishṇu.

ෂඩභිඥ, *Shaḍabhijña*, *s.* (ෂෂ් *shash* six, with අභි *abhi* and ඥ one who knows) name or title of Buddha; Rahat.

ෂඩභිඥා, *Saḍabhijñá*, *s.* (ෂෂ් *shash* and අභිඥා *abhijñá* profound knowledge) six branches of knowledge, peculiar to Buddha and the Rahats, and attained by devout abstraction, viz. divine perception, supernatural knowledge, superhuman power of hearing, knowledge or recollection of previous states of existence, faculty of knowing the hearts of others and an acquaintance with the various species of Ṛiddhi or power of flying through the air.

ෂඩානන, *Shaḍánana*, *s.* (ෂෂ් *shash* six, ආනන *ánana* face) name of Kataragama deviyó, who is sometimes represented with six faces, four to the cardinal points, and two to the nadir and zenith.

ෂඩාලම්බන, *Shaḍálambana*, *s.* (ෂෂ් *shash* six, five senses and thought, ආලම්බන *álambana* fixing) any object of sense or intellect.

ෂඩෘතු, *Shadṛitu*, *s.* (ෂෂ් *shash* six, ඍතු *ṛitu* season) six seasons.

ෂණ්ඩ, *Shaṇḍa*, *s.* multitude, quantity of lotuses.

ෂෂ්, *Shash*, *a.* six, [Colloq. හය *haya*].

ෂෂ්ටි, *Shashṭi*, *a.* sixty, [Colloq. හැට *heṭa*].

ෂෂ්ටික, *Shashṭika*, *s.* kind of rice of quick growth, [Colloq. හැටදා වී *heṭadá-ví*].

ෂෂ්ටි සංවත්සර, *Shashṭi-saṇwatsara*, *s.* (ෂෂ්ටි sixty, සංවත්සර year) Indian cycle of sixty years.

ෂෂ්ඨ, *Shashṭha*, *a.* sixth.

ෂෂ්ඨක, *Shashṭhaka*, *s.* frankincense, incense, [Colloq. තුවරලා *tuwaralá*].

ෂෝඩශ, *Shóḍaṣa*, *s.* (ෂෂ් *shash* six, දශ *daṣa* ten) sixteen, sixteenth.

ස

The thirty-second consonant of the Siṇhalese alphabet, the third sibilant, and corresponding to *s*.

සං, *Saṇ*, *ind.* in composition, with, together, being the optional form of writing සම් *sam* before a consonant; before consonants of the first five classess (except Ka-warga which is usually written with the anuswára or bindu) the bindu may be again changed to the nasal of the class to which the letter it precedes belongs; before the semi vowels, the sibilants, and හ *ha* it remains unchanged: see සම් *sam*.

සංක්ෂය, *Saṇkshaya*, *s.* (සං intense, ක්ෂය decay) destruction of the world; loss, destruction in general.

සංක්ෂේප, *Saṇkshépa*, *s.* (සං and ක්ෂිප *kshipa* to throw) abridgement, abbreviation; conciseness, compression.

සංක්ෂෝභ, *Saṇkshóbha*, *s.* (සං before, ක්ෂුභ *kshubha* to tremble) shaking, trembling; overthrowing; upsetting.

සංකට, *Saṇkaṭa*, *a.* narrow, contracted.

සංකර, *Saṇkara*, *s.* name of Ṣiva; the name of a celebrated teacher of the Védánta philosophy; mixing, blending, confounding: *a.* auspicious, propitious.

සංකරණවා, *Saṇkaraṇawá*, see සන්කරණවා *sankaraṇawá*.

සංකල්ප, *Saṇkalpa*, *s.* (සං and කල්ප thought) volition, will, resolve, mental determination.

සංකා, *Sanká*, *s.* doubt, uncertainty; fear, terror, apprehension.

සංකාර භූමිය, *Sankára-bhúmiya*, *s.* dunghill.

සංකාශ, *Sankása*, *a.* in composition; like, similar, near, proximate.

සංකිච්ච, *Sankichcha*, *s.* name of Buddha in one of his incarnations.

සංකීර්ණ, *Sankírṇa*, *a.* (සං and කෘ *krí* to scatter) miscellaneous, mixed, compounded; spread, scattered, diffused.

සංකීර්ත්තිය, *Sankírttiya*, *s.* (සං and කෘත *krita* to praise) praise, honor, glorification.

සංකු, *Sanku*, *s.* (සකි *saki* to doubt or apprehend) trunk of a lopped tree; pillar, post; enemy, adversary; fear, terror; compass.

සංකුර, *Sankura*, *a.* formidable, frightful, fearful.

සංකෝච, *Sankócha*, සංකෝචන, *Sankóchana*, } *s.* (සං and කුචි *kuchi* to contract) shutting, closing, contracting; binding, tying; kind of fish, skate.

සංක්‍රම, *Sankrama*, සංක්‍රමණ, *Sankramaṇa*, } *s.* (සං before, ක්‍රම to go) difficult progress, clambering up rocks, etc.; going, moving, travelling; the passage of a planetary body through the zodiac.

සංක්‍රාන්ති, *Sankránti*, *s.* passage of the sun or other planetary body from one sign of the zodiac into another; going, proceeding.

සංක්ලේශ, *Sanklésa*, *s.* (සං and ක්ලිශ *klisa* to suffer or inflict pain) source or origin of passion, klésa: see ක්ලේශ *klésa:* *a.* filthy, corrupt, pollute.

සංඛ, *Sankha*, *s.* conch shell, chank, *voluta gravis;* one of Kuvéra's treasures; large number, ten or one-hundred billions.

සංඛජ, *Sankhaja*, *s.* (සංඛ shell, ජ born) large pearl of the shape of a pigeon's egg.

සංඛනාභ, *Sankhanábha*, *s.* perfume: see සක්නැබ *saknęba.*

සංඛමුඛ, *Sankha-mukha*, *s.* (සංඛ conch, මුඛ face) alligator, [Colloq. කිඹුලා *kimbulá*].

සංඛමුණ්ඩකං, *Sankha-muṇḍakan*, *s.* (සංඛ conch, මුඩි *muḍi* to shave, කන් *kan* aff.) one of the thirty-two punishments inflicted by kings, rubbing the skull with a stone and gravel till it is completely bare of flesh as a conch shell.

සංඛලික, *Sankhalika*, *s.* fetter, chain for the legs and feet.

සංඛාර, *Sankhára*, Páli form of සංස්කාර *sanskárá*, which see.

සංඛ්‍යා, *Sankhyá*, *s.* (සං before, ඛ්‍යා to tell) number, a number, numeral; deliberation, reasoning, reflection.

සංඛ්‍යාත, *Sankhyáta*, *a.* numbered, counted, reckoned.

සංඛ්‍යාපථය, *Sankhyá-pathaya*, *s.* (සංඛ්‍යා number, පථ *patha* way) arithmetic, science of numbers, [Colloq. ගණන් ශාස්ත්‍රය *gaṇan-śástraya*].

සංඛ්‍යාව, *Sankhyáwa*, *s.* a number, numeral: pl. සංඛ්‍යා *sankhyá.*

සංගණවා, *Sanganawá*, *v.* to hide, to conceal: pret. සැංගුවා *sęnguwá.*

සංගම්, *Sangam*, *s.* war, [Colloq. යුද්ධය *yuddhaya.*]

සංගසූරිය, *Sangasúriya*, *s.* screw-hole.

සංගායනාව, *Sangáyanáwa*, *s.* (සං with ගායනා *gáyaná* singing, chanting) oral exhibition, holding forth, public recitation, but particularly three noted convocations held immediately after the death of Buddha, for the purpose of settling the Buddhist Canon; on the first occasion 500 priests were present, the second 700, and the third 1000.

සංගිප්පුව, *Sangíppuwa*, *s.* thanks, praise, [Colloq. ප්‍රශංසාව *praśansáwa*].

සංග්‍රහ, *Sangraha*, *s.* (සං with, together, ග්‍රහ to take) compilation, abridgement; brevity; taking, seizing; help, favour, protection; entertainment of strangers.

සංග්‍රහකරණවා, *Sangraha-karaṇawá*, *v.* to compile, to help, to entertain.

සංග්‍රහණි, *Sangrahaní*, *s.* (සං and ග්‍රහණි dysentery) dysentery, diarrhea.

සංග්‍රාම, *Sangráma*, *s.* (සංග්‍රාම to fight) war, battle, [Colloq. යුද්ධය *yuddhaya*].

සංග්‍රාහ, *Sangráha*, *s.* the grip of a shield; seizing, gripping; clenching the fist.

සංගෘහිත, *Sangrihíta*, *a.* compiled, collected, abridged, abbreviated.

සංඝ, *Sangha*, *s.* multitude, number, collection; Buddhist priesthood, a convocation of priests, five of whom constitute a sangha.

සංඝට්ටන, *Sanghaṭṭana*, *s.* (සං with ඝට්ට *ghaṭṭa* to strike) meeting, encountering; the shock or encounter of rams, bulls, etc.

සංඝටිත, *Sanghaṭita*, *a.* encountered, met; united, joined.

සංඝයා, *Sanghayá*, see සංඝ *sangha.*

සංඝරතන, *Sangha-ratna*, *s.* (සංඝ and රතන gem) one of the three gems of Buddhism, viz. the priesthood: see ත්‍රිවිධරතන *trividharatna*.

සංඝාත, *Sanghāta*, *s.* assemblage, multitude; killing, striking, hurting.

සංඝාදිසේස, *Sanghādisésa*, *s*, the second class of sins which are legislated for in the sacred code of the priesthood; there are thirteen crimes specified under this class in the Prátimóksha to which the priests are liable; when any of them is committed it must be confessed in the presence of a sanghayá, or a secret convocation of not less than five priests who after the confession have the power to adjudge the punishment.

සංඝානුස්මෘති, *Sanghánusmṛiti*, *s.* (සංඝ sangha, අනුස්මෘති *anusmṛiti* reflection) respect or veneration for the priesthood.

සංචර, *Sanchara*, *s.* (සං with චර to go) way, road, [Colloq. පාර *pára*]; going, walking, proceeding.

සංචරණය, *Sancharaṇaya*, *s.* going, walking, proceeding.

සංචල, *Sanchala*, *s.* (සං and චල to shake) moving, shaking, motion.

සංචලය, *Sanchalaya*, *s.* agitation, disturbance.

සංචාර, *Sanchára*, *s.* resort, haunt, place of resort; defile; difficult progress.

සංචාරක, *Sanchāraka*, *s.* (සං and චර *chara* to go, ක aff.) traveller, wanderer, pilgrim, [Colloq. වන්දනාකාරයා *wandanákárayá*].

සංචාරණයකරණවා, *Sanchāraṇaya-karaṇawá*, *v.* to walk about, to move about.

සංචිත, *Sanchita*, *a.* (සං and චි to collect) collected, gathered together.

සංඡන්න, *Sanchhanna*, *a.* (සං and ඡන්න covered) covered, enveloped.

සංජීව, *Sanjíwa*, *a.* (සං with ජීව life) living, existent, being.

සංඥාපනය, *Sanjñápanaya*, *s.* introduction, preface.

සංයත, *Sanyata*, *a.* (සං and යම *yama* to restrain) bound, fettered, confined, imprisoned; restrained, subdued, as the passions.

සංයතකාරි, *Sanyatakári*, *s.* (සංයත and කාර *kára* who does, ඉන් *in* aff.) ascetic, one endeavouring to subdue his passions by severe austerity.

සංයම, *Sanyama*, *s.* (සං completely, යම to restrain) restraint, forbearance.

සංයාචන, *Sanyáchana*, *s.* (සං intensitive, යාච *yácha* to beg) prayer, petition, earnest request, supplication, entreaty.

සංයාත්‍රා, *Sanyátrá*, *s.* (සං and යාත්‍රා going) visiting foreign countries, travelling by water, voyaging.

සංයාම, *Sanyáma*, *s.* (සං and යාම to restrain) forbearance, check, control, restraint.

සංයුක්ත, *Sanyukta*, *a.* (සං and යුජ *yuja* to join) joined with, connected, attached; endowed with, possessed of.

සංයුග, *Sanyuga*, *s.* (සං and යුජ *yuja* to join) war, battle; union, mixture.

සංයුත්නිකාය, *Sanyut-nikáya*, } *s.* (සංයුත *sanyuta*
සංයුත්සඟිය, *Sanyut-sangiya*, } and සඟිය compilation) third of the five Sangis or books of the Sútra Piṭaka: see සඟිය *sangiya*.

සංයුත, *Sanyuta*, *a.* connected, joined; mixed, blended; attached to.

සංයෝග, *Sanyóga*, *s.* union, association, conjunction.

සංයෝජන, *Sanyójana*, *s.* (සං with යුජ *yuja* to join) ordering, arranging, disposing, compounding.

සංරක්ෂණ, *Sanrakshaṇa*, *s.* (සං before, රක්ෂ *raksha* to guard) preserving, guarding, protecting, watching.

සංරම්භය, *Sanrambhaya*, *s.* (සං and රභ *rabha* to sound) wrath, rage; pride, arrogance.

සංලිප්ත, *Sanlipta*, *s.* (සං before, ලිප්ත smeared) junction, union, adhering: *a.* smeared, plastered; envenomed; united; stained;

සංවත්සර, *Sanwatsara*, *s.* (සං complete, වත්සර year) year, [Colloq. අවුරුද්ද *awurudda*].

සංවදන, *Sanwadana*, *s.* (සං with වදන speaking) communication, tidings, intelligence; charm, amulet; subduing, overcoming by magical drugs or mystical gems.

සංවර්ණ, *Sanwarṇa*, *s.* (සං before, වර්ණ to extol) praise, adulation, panegyric.

සංවර්තය, *Sanwartaya*, *s.* (සං and වෘත *wṛita* to be) destruction of the sakwaḷa or universe; beleric myrobalan, [Colloq. බුළු *buḷu*].

සංවර්ධන, *Sanwardhana*, *s.* (සං and වෘධ *wṛidha* to increase or prosper) augmenting, increasing; prosperity, thriving.

සංවර, *Sanwara*, *s.* rain, [Colloq. වැස්ස *wessa*]; water, [Colloq. වතුර *watura*]; self control; mound, [Colloq. ගොඩැල්ල *goḍella*]; bridge, [Colloq. පාලම *pálama*]; also, see the next.

සංවරසීල, *Sanwarasíla*, *s.* (සංවර self control, සීල duty or observance) the practice of religious ascetics or priests, closing the senses against all outward objects.

සංවාසය, *Sanwásaya*, *s.* (සං together, වාස an abode) dwelling together as man and wife; copulation; house dwelling.

සංවිඝ්න, *Sanvighna*, *s.* (සං and විඝ්න obstacle) danger, difficulty, impediment.

සංවිත්, *Sanvit*, *s.* (සං and විද් *vida* to know) intellect, understanding; mark, sign, signal; name, appellation; promise, agreement.

සංවිධාන, *Sanvidhána*, *s.* (සං and විධ *vidha* to command) rule, authority, command.

සංවිභාග, *Sanvibhága*, *s.* (සං and විභාග discussion) investigation, deliberation, examination.

සංවුත, *Sanwuta*, *a.* attended, accompanied, surrounded; overcome, subdued.

සංවුතින්ද්‍රියා, *Sanwutindriyá*, *s.* (සංවුත *sanwuta* overcome, ඉන්ද්‍රිය *indriya* an organ of sense) one whose passions are subdued, stoic, ascetic.

සංවේග, *Sanwéga*, *s.* (සං intensitive, විජ *vija* to agitate) hurry, flurry, haste proceeding from fear; emotion, agitation.

සංවේද, *Sanwéda*, *s.* (සං and විද් *vida* to know) perception, consciousness; intellect, understanding.

සංවෘත්ත, *Sanwritta*, *a.* (සං and වෘත *writa* to screen) hidden, concealed; possessed of, endowed.

සංවෘති, *Sanwriti*, see සංවර්තය *sanwartaya*.

සංශ්ලේෂ, *Sanslésha*, *s.* (සං before, ශ්ලිෂ *slisha* to unite) embrace, union, contact.

සංශය, *Sansaya*, *s.* uncertainty, doubt.

සංශුද්ධි, *Sansuddhi*, } සංශෝධන, *Sansódhana*, } *s.* (සං before, ශුධ *sudha* to be or make pure) cleaning, correcting, purifying; paying, discharging.

සංශ්‍රද්ධා, *Sansraddhá*, *s.* (සං and ශ්‍රද්ධා religious belief) firm belief and strict performance of religious duties.

සංශ්‍රය, *Sansraya*, *s.* protection, safety, refuge.

සංස්කාර, *Sanskára*, *a.* (සං implying perfection, කෘ *kri* to make, අණ් *an* affix with සුට් *sut* augment) apprehension, conception, completing, perfecting, accomplishing, finishing; embellishment, decoration, faculty; purificatory rite or ceremony.

සංස්කෘත, *Sanskrita*, *s.* (සං excellence or perfection, කෘත *krita* done) classical and sacred language of the Hindus: *a.* wrought, made; artificially produced; decorated, ornamented; cooked, dressed; best, excellent.

සංස්තර, *Sanstara*, *s.* (සං and ස්තෘ *stri* to spread) bed, couch, bed of leaves.

සංස්ථ, *Sanstha*, *s.* (සං and ස්ථා *sthá* to stay) dweller, an inhabitant: *a.* staying, stopping, fixed, stationary; staying with, associated, domesticated; lucky, fortunate.

සංස්ථා, *Sansthá*, *s.* state or condition of being; stop, stay, end, completion.

සංස්ථාන, *Sansthána*, *s.* (සං and ස්ථා *sthá* to be) form, figure, shape; fabrication, construction; mark, spot, sign.

සංස්ථිත, *Sansthita*, *a.* firm, remaining, stationary; established, fixed.

සංස්මරණ, *Sansmarana*, *s.* (සං intensitive, ස්මරණ remembering) remembering, calling to mind.

සංස්මෘති, *Sansmriti*, *s.* (සං and ස්මෘ *smri* to remember) remembering, remembrance, recollection.

සංසක්ත, *Sansakta*, *a.* near, adjoining, contiguous; possessing, endowed with; connected or acquainted with.

සංසක්ති, *Sansakti*, *s.* union, intimacy, devotion to.

සංසන්දනය, *Sansandanaya*, *s.* consultation, conversation, comparing.

සංසය, *Sansaya*, *s.* doubt, uncertainty.

සංසර්ග, *Sansarga*, *s.* the union of the sexes, copulation; union, proximity, approximation, contact; acquaintance, intimacy.

සංසර්ගාභාව, *Sansargábháwa*, *s.* (සංසර්ග *sansarga* union, of body and sentient faculty, අභාව *abháwa* non-existence) logical non-entity or annihilation of three kinds, prior, incidental, and final; or absence of birth or production, destruction of present being, and necessary end or cessation of existence.

සංසර, *Sansara*, } සංසරණ, *Sansarana*, } *s.* (සං together, සෘ *sri* to go) world, birth, production of living beings; high-way, principal road; going, proceeding.

සංසාර, *Sansára*, *s.* (සං together, සෘ *sri* to go) world, habitation of mortals, mundane existence; transmigration, renewed or continued existence, metempsychosis.

සංසාරගාමි, *Sansáragámi*, *s.* (සංසාර and ගාමි who goes) mortal, inhabitant of this world, one transmigrating.

සංසාරදුක්ඛ, *Sansára-dukkha*, *s.* (සංසාර and දුක්ඛ sorrow) misery of transmigration: see ක්ලේශ *klésa;* sorrow inseparable from existence.

සංසාරස්ථ, *Sansárastha*, *a.* (සංසාර and ස්ථ *stha* to stay) in a state of transmigration, not yet arrived at or attained to Nirwáṇa.

සංසාරසාගරය, *Sansára-ságaraya*, *s.* (සංසාර and සාගර ocean) metempsychosis, doomed to such a state of transmigration, that Nirwáṇa or final emancipation is next to impossible.

සංසිද්ධ, *Sansiddha*, *a.* (සං before, සිද්ධ accomplished) perfected, fully done or accomplished.

සංසිද්ධිය, *Sansiddhiya*, *s.* (සං and සිද්ධි *siddhi* completion) perfection, completion, accomplishment, [Colloq. සම්පූර්ණභාවය *sampúrṇabháwaya*].

සංසිඳුවනවා, *Sansinduwanawá*, *v.* the causal form of the next: pret. සංසිඳෙව්වා *sansindewwá*.

සංසිඳෙනවා, *Sansindenawá*, *v.* to be appeased, to be made calm or tranquil: pret. සංසිඳුනා *sansinduná*.

සංශුද්ධිය, *Sansuddhiya*, *s.* (සං completely, ශුද්ධි *suddhi* purification) purity, sanctity, holiness, entire purification of the affections and passions.

සංස්වේදජ, *Sansédaja*, සංස්වේදයෝනිය, *Sanséda-yóniya*, } *s.* (සං and ස්වේද vermes, ජ born, and යෝනි *yóni* place of birth or production) one of the four states of animal existence, including worms, flies, and insects in general.

සංසේප, *Sansépa*, corruption of සංක්ෂේප *sankshépa*, which see.

සංසේවන, *Sansévana*, *s.* (සං and සේව *séwa* to serve) waiting on, serving; connection, contact, intimacy.

සංසෝධනය, *Sansódhanaya*, *s.* (සං and සෝධන *sódhana* purifying) cleaning, cleansing, purifying, literally or metaphorically.

සංහත, *Sanhuta*, *a.* joined, attached or approximated to: struck, hurt, wounded, killed.

සංහාර, *Sanhára*, *s.* destruction, loss; abridgement; collection; restraining.

සංහිත, *Sanhita*, *a.* attached, joined; collected, assembled.

සංහිතා, *Sanhitá*, *s.* a compilation, digest, code, junction, sandhi, proximity.

සක්, *Sak*, *s.* conch shell perforated at the spiral end and used as a musical instrument; chank from සංඛ *sankha;* wheel, circle, from චක්‍ර *chakra*; eye, from චක්ෂුස් *chakshus;* multitude, collection; Ṣakra, from ශක්‍ර *sakra;* hiding, concealment; antimony: see also, සක්වාලිහිණියා *sakwálihiṇiyá*.

සක් අවි, *Sak-avi*, *s.* poet, bard, panegyrist; weapon of Ṣakra or Indra, thunderbolt, [Colloq. හෙන *hena*].

සක්ක, *Sakka*, *s.* jaw; Páli form of Ṣakra; man of the Sákya race; province inhabited by the descendants of the Ṣákya race: *a.* clever, skilful, able.

සක්කාර, *Sakkára*, *s.* charity, hospitality, entertainment of strangers.

සක්ඛලිත, *Sakkhalita*, *a.* stumbled; fettered, obstructed, hindered, impeded, opposed.

සක්ගෙඩිය, *Sakgediya*, *s.* (සක් and ගෙඩි *gedi* any globular substance) conch shell, chank.

සක්දෙව්, *Sak-dew*, *s.* (සක් and දෙව් a god) Ṣakra or Indra: see ශක්‍ර *ṣakra*.

සක්නිය, *Sakniya*, *s.* drug.

සක්නැබ, *Saknęba*, *s.* (සක් shell, නැබ navel) perfume, according to some a dried substance made from a shell-fish and said to resemble the conch or chank shell; according to others a vegetable perfume.

සක්පණ, *Sakpaṇa*, *s.* (සක් discus, පණ hand) name of Vishṇu, alluding to his holding the chakra or discus in his hand.

සක්පුපල, *Sakpu-pala*, *s.* clearing nut, *strychnos potatorum*, [Colloq. ඉඟිනිඇට *ingini-ęta*].

සක්පුර, *Sak-pura*, *s.* city of Ṣakra.

සක්මණ, *Sakmaṇa*, *s.* walking for exercise or amusement; place for walking, terrace, etc.

සක්මන්, *Sakman*, *s.* walking, going.

සක්මන්කරණවා, *Sakmankaraṇawá*, *v.* to walk about for pleasure, to perambulate.

සක්මන්කෙරීම, *Sakmankeríma*, *s.* walking.

සක්ලකුණ, *Sak-lakuṇa*, *s.* marks on the body indicative of the attainment of the Buddhaship, or of universal empire.

සක්වළ, *Sakwaḷa*, *s.* (සක් region, වළ circumference) the universe, comprehending, according to native geography, the various continents, islands, hells, and Brahma lókas, with Maha-méru in the centre, and a circular range of rocks surrounding the whole.

සක්වළගල, *Sakwaḷa-gala*, *s.* (සක්වළ and ගල rock) range of mountains supposed to encircle the universe, and to form its boundaries; see the last.

සක්වළගැබ, *Sakwaḷa-gęba*, *s.* (සක්වළ and ගැබ womb) interior of the universe, or the space included within the mountainous range encircling the universe.

සක්වා, *Sakwá*, } *s.* (සක්වා and
සක්වාලිහිණියා, *Sakwá-lihiniyá*, } ලිහිණියා the falco genus) ruddy goose, or as it is usually called the Brahminy kite, *heliastur indus*, [Colloq. රාජාලියා *rájáliyá*]: see සකුනග්ඝි *sakunagghi*.

සක්විති, *Sakviti*, *s.* universal emperor, Elu form of චක්‍රවර්ත්ති *chakrawartti:* see සක්වළ *sakwaḷa*.

සක්විතිරජ, *Sakvitiraja*, } *s.* (සක්විති and රජ or
සක්විතිරද, *Sakvitirada*, } රද king) universal emperor, a character attained by severe religious abstraction and austerities, and second only to the Buddhaship.

සක්විතිරාජ්‍යය, *Sakviti-rájyaya*, *s.* universal empire; see the last.

සක්සඳ, *Saksanda*, *s.* shrub, *aristolochia indica*, [Colloq. සප්සඳ *sapsanda*].

සක්සින්නම්, *Saksinnam*, *s.* conch shell perforated at the spiral end, and used as a horn.

සක්සොඳ, *Saksonda*, see සක්සඳ *saksanda*.

සක, *Saka*, *s.* doubt; chank or conch shell; wheel, circle; sovereign, any prince who gives name to an era: see ශකවර්ෂ *ṣakawarsha*; in Páli, his. his own, one's own.

සකට, *Sakaṭa*, *s.* cart, vehicle drawn by oxen; scraggy shrub or small tree, *streblus aspera*, [Colloq. ගැටනෙටුල් *geṭa-neṭul*]; demon slain by Krishṇa.

සකටධූර, *Sakaṭadhúra*, *s.* (සකට and ධූර yoke) yoke of a cart, ox or bullock; cart, conveyance; leader of a multitude of carts.

සකටරිපු, *Sakaṭa-ripu*, *s.* (සකට demon, රිපු enemy) name of Vishṇu, from his slaying the demon Sakaṭa.

සකටලෝචන, *Sakaṭalóchana*, *s.* plant, *aymrus agallocha*, [Colloq. ගුගුල් *gugul*].

සකදුනු, *Sakadunu*, *s.* (සක Indra, දුනු bow) rainbow, [Colloq. දේදුන්න *dédunna*].

සකදුරු, *Sakaduru*, *s.* date tree, *phœnix zeylanica*, [Colloq. ඉඳි *indi*].

සකප්, *Sakap*, *a.* sorrowful, beautiful, comely, fortunate, happy, auspicious.

සකපෝරුව, *Saka-póruwa*, *s.* potter's wheel.

සකර්ණ, *Sakarṇa*, *s.* (ස with කර්ණ ear) hearing, listening, attending, regarding.

සකර්මක, *Sakarmaka*, *a.* (in grammar) relating to the transitive verb.

සකර, *Sakara*, *s.* raw sugar, from ශර්කරා *ṣarkará*.

සකල, *Sakala*, *a.* all, whole, entire.

සකලඥෙය, *Sakalajñeya*, *a.* (සකල all, ඥෙය knowledge) omniscient; all wise.

සකලමුක්ත, *Sakalamukta*, *a.* (සකල entire, මුක්ත released) Nirwáṇa, final emancipation, annihilation.

සකලාශ්‍රවය, *Sakaláṣrawaya*, *s.* (සකල *sakala* all, ආශ්‍රව *áṣrawa* transgression) the four sources of sin, viz. passion, existence, religious belief, and ignorance.

සකලිකාව, *Sakalikáwa*, *s.* (ස with කලිකා *kaliká* unblown flower) unblown flower, [Colloq. මල් කැකුළ *mal-keḳuḷa*].

සකස්, *Sakas*, *a.* well, good, excellent, [Colloq. යහපත් *yahapat*]; fit, proper; pure, purified, consecrated; prepared, compounded, etc.; Elu form of සංස්කෘත *sanskrita*.

සකස්කඩය, *Sakaskaḍaya*, *s.* name of a book written in Páli containing a sketch of the life of Buddha.

සකස්කරණවා, *Sakaskaraṇawá*, *v.* to arrange, to place in order.

සකසා, *Sakasá*, *ad.* well, excellently; fitly, properly.

සකිය, *Sakiya*, *s.* friend, [Colloq. යහළුවා *yahaḷuwá*]; companion, from සඛි *sakhi*; button or circular piece of wood or glass, etc. terminating the string of a book, from චක්‍ර *chakra;* messenger, courier.

සකිලිටු, *Sakiliṭu*, *a.* (ස from සං *san* completely, කිලිටු filthy) polluted, contaminated, unclean, unholy.

සකී, *Sakí*, *s.* female friend, [Colloq. යහලු ස්ත්‍රී *yahalu-strí*]; niece by the sister's side.

සකු, *Saku*, *s.* name of Wesawaṇa, or Kuvéra, the Indian Plutus; Sanskrit language: pl. of සක්ක *sakka: a.* quick, speedy, swift.

සකුන්ත, *Sakunta*, *s.* blue jay, *cissa ornata, (*order *Passeres)*, [Colloq. කැහිබෙල්ලා *keḥi-bellá*]; Indian peregrine: see සකුනග්ඝි *sakunagghi*; kind of maritime or fishing falcon, called white-bellied sea eagle, *halietus leucoguste, (*order *Accipitres)*.

සකුන්ති, *Sakunti*, *s.* bird in general: see සකුන *sakuna*.

සකුන, *Sakuna*, *s.* bird in general, [Colloq. කුරුල්ලා *kurullá*].

සකුනග්ඝි, *Sakunagghi*, *s.* (සකුන bird, ඝස *ghasa* to eat) Indian peregrine, *falco peregrinator;* Pondicherry eagle, *falco ponticeriana*, [Colloq. උකුස්සා *ukussá*].

සකුනි, *Sakuni*, *s.* bird: see the last.

සකුනී, *Sakuní*, *s.* hen sparrow, *passer domesticus*, [Colloq. ගේ කිරිල්ලි *gé-kirilli*].

සකුරා, *Sakurá*, *s.* (සකුරු *sakuru* and අ *a* aff.) sugar-maker, man of the jaggery caste.

සකුරි, *Sakuri*, *s.* woman of the jaggery caste.

සකුරු, *Sakuru*, *s.* raw or coarse kind of sugar, clayed or candied sugar, jaggery.

සකුල්, *Sakul*, *s.* mark, spot, sign, signal, [Colloq. ලකුණ *lakuṇa*].

සකුල්‍ය, *Sakulya*, *s.* (ස for සං *saṉ* with or same, කුල්‍ය family) kinsman; one of the same family and of common origin, [Colloq. නෑයා *néyá*].

සකුල, *Sakula*, *a.* (ස and කුල tribe) having a family, belonging to a family, or race.

සකුලාක්‍ෂක, *Sakulákshaka*, *s.* fragrant grass, *cyperus rotundus*, [Colloq. කලාඳුරු *kaláṉduru*].

සකුළු, *Sakuḷu*, *a.* hard, [Colloq. දැඩි *dęḍi*]; sharp, pungent, acrid, [Colloq. දිවට සැරඇති *divaṭa-sęraęti*].

සකුස්, *Sakus*, *s.* haste, speed, rapidity, swiftness, [Colloq. ඉක්මණ *ikmaṇa*].

සකෙව්, *Sakew*, *s.* abridgement, abbreviation, from සංක්‍ෂේප *saṇkshépa*.

සකෘත්, *Sakṛit*, *s.* (සක *saka* to be able, to expel) fæces, excrement: *ind.* once; with, together with.

සකෘදාගාමි, *Sakṛidágámi*, *s.* (සකෘත් *sakṛit* once, ආගාමි *ágámi* came) second of the four states of existence previous to the attainment of Nirwáṇa or final emancipation.

සකෘදාගාමි ඵලය, *Sakṛidágámi-phalaya*, *s.* (සකෘදාගාමි and ඵල *phala* fruit, reward) enjoyments of the state of Sakṛidágmi: see the last.

සකෘදාගාමි මාර්ගය, *Sakṛidágámi-márgaya*, *s.* path leading to the second of the four states, which is called සකෘදාගාමි *sakṛidágámi*.

සඛා, *Sakhá*, } *s.* friend, associate, [Colloq. මිත්‍රයා
සඛි, *Sakhi*, } *mitrayá*].

සග, *Saga*, *s.* Swarga, paradise: see ස්වර්ග *swarga*; chapter, section, from the Sanskrit සර්ග *sarga*.

සගච්ඡ, *Sagachchha*, *s.* (ස for සහ *saha* with ගච්ඡ going) fellow-traveller, companion, [Colloquial: කැටුව ගමන්කරන්නා *kętuwa gamankarannà*].

සගණ, *Sagaṇa*, *a.* (ස sa, ගණ class) poetical foot ස *sa*; consisting of three syllables; the two first being short, and the last, long, Anapæst.

සගයා, *Sagayá*, *s.* celestial being, deity; young man, lad, [Colloq. කොල්ලා *kollá*].

සගර, *Sagara*, *s.* celebrated Hindu sovereign.

සගවැසි, *Sagawęsi*, *s.* (සග Swarga, වැසි who dwells) a god, deity.

සගුණ, *Saguna*, *a.* (ස for සය *saya* six, with ගුණ part) six-fold.

සඟර, *Saṉgara*, *s.* ointment, unction; abridgment.

සඟරම්, *Saṉgaram*, *s.* war, [Coll: යුද්ධය *yuddhaya*].

සඟරාව, *Saṉgaráwa*, *s.* compilation and abridgment, from සංග්‍රහ *saṉgraha*.

සඟරුවන, *Saṉgaruwana*, see සංඝරත්න *sangharatna*.

සඟල, *Saṉgala*, *s.* pair, couple, two, [Colloq. කුට්ටම *kuṭṭama*].

සඟලසිවුර, *Saṉgala-siwura*, *s.* (සඟල and සිවුර robe) double robe worn by the Upasampadá, or highest order of priest.

සඟවනවා, *Saṉgawanawá*, *v.* to cause to be hidden or concealed: pret. සැඟෙව්වා *sęṉgewwá*: causal form of සංගනවා *saṉganawá*.

සඟවැල, *Saṉga-węla*, *s.* (සඟ priests, වැල row or line) row of priests.

සඟිය, *Saṉgiya*, *s.* (සං *saṉ* with, together, ගම *gama* to go, ඉන් *in* aff.) compilation, collection, but particularly the five sangis or divisions of the teachings of Buddha, viz. dik, mędum, sanyut, aṅgóttara, and kudugot; these are accompanied with commentaries and glosses called aṭuwá or arthakathá, which are further explained in ṭíkás or supplementary commentaries, and the most difficult passages are collected and explained in separate works, hence called ganthi pada.

සඟුරුවන්, *Saṉguruwan*, see සංඝරත්න *saṉgharatna*.

සඟුල්, *Saṉgul*, *s.* pair, couple, [Colloq. කුට්ටම *kuṭṭama*].

සඞ්කර, *Saṅkara*, } *s.* dust, sweepings; crackling
සඞ්කාර, *Saṅkára*, } of a flame; mixing, confounding.

සඞ්කු, *Saṅku*, *s.* hole.

සඞ්ග, *Saṅga*, *s.* (සං *saṉ* with ගමු *gamu* to go) meeting, encountering; company; wish, desire, longing for; addiction or devotion to; confluence of rivers; joining.

සඞ්ගත, *Saṅgata*, *s.* union, meeting; observance of religious ordinances, the practices of a Buddhist priest.

සඞ්ගම, *Saṅgama*, *s.* (සං *saṉ* together, ගම to go) meeting, union, mixture, junction.

සඞ්ගර, *Saṅgara*, *s.* war, battle, [Colloq. යුද්ධය *yuddhaya*]: misfortune, calamity; promise, assent, agreement; bribe; friendship; power; heap, multitude.

සඞ්ගීති, *Sańgíti, s.* (සං *saṇ* together, ගා *gá* to sign) science of music and dancing; exhibition of song and music at public entertainments: see සංගායනාව *sangáyanáwa.*

සඞ්ගීතිකාරක, *Sańgítikáraka, s.* (සඞ්ගීති and කාර who does, ක aff.) musician, public exhibitor of song and music on festival occasions; priest of Buddha, public reader and expounder of the baṇa.

සච්ච, } *Sachcha*, Páli form of සත්‍ය *satya.*
සච්ච, }

සච්චයෝගී, } *Sachcha-yógí, s.* (සච්ච and යෝගී
සච්චයෝගී, } ascetic) sincere devotee.

සච්චවේදිත, } *Sachchawédita, s.* (සච්ච and වේදිත
සච්චවේදිත, } known) arrived at the knowledge of the four great truths, as a Rahat: see චතුස්සත්‍ය *chatussatya.*

සචල, *Sachala, a.* (සං *san* with චල to shake) shaking, moving, trembling.

සචිව, *Sachira, s.* friend, counsellor, minister.

සචේතනික, *Sachétanika, a.* (ස for සහ *saha* with චේතනා *chétaná* thought, ඉක *ika* aff.) sentient, endued with powers of thought or intellect; knowing, aware.

සජ්ජ, *Sajja, a.* (ෂසජ *shasja* to move, to go) armed, accoutred; prepared, got ready; adorned, ornamented, decorated.

සජ්ජන, *Sajjana, s.* (සත් *sat* good, ජන *jana* man) virtuous or excellent man, [Colloq. සත්පුරුෂයා *satpurushayá*]; putting on armour, guard, sentry; preparing.

සජ්ජරස, *Sajja-rasa,* see සර්ජරස *sarja-rasa.*

සජ්ජිත, *Sajjita, a.* armed, accoutred; dressed, decorated, ornamented.

සජ්ජුලසෝ, *Sajjulasó, s.* resin, [Colloq. දුම්මල *dummala*].

සජ්ජෝ, *Sajjó, s.* tree, *vateria acuminata,* [Colloq. හල් *hal*].

සජාති, *Sajáti, a.* (ස for සහ *saha* similar, with ජාති kind) of the same sort or species, of the same tribe.

සජාතීය, *Sajátiya, s.* of the same tribe or species.

සජීව, *Sajíwa, a.* (ස for සහ *saha* with ජීව life) alive, living.

සජෝත, *Sajóta, a.* (ස for සහ *saha* with, having, ජුති *juti* light) shining, glittering, brilliant.

සඤ්චය, *Sañchaya, s.* (සං *saṇ* before, චි *chi* to collect) heap, quantity; multitude.

සඤ්චර, *Sañchara, s.* difficult passage; road, route; course.

සඤ්චලන, *Sañchalana, s.* (සං *saṇ* and චල *chala* to shake) trembling, shaking.

සඤ්චාර, *Sañchára,* see සඤ්චර *sañchara.*

සඤ්ජ, *Sañja, s.* (සං *san* before, ජන *jana* to be born or created by whom) name of Brahma, as creator, also of Şiva; the name of an opponent of Buddha.

සඤ්ජාත, *Sañjáta, a.* born, produced.

සඤ්ඤක, *Saññaka, s.* name applied to half of Anuswára or bindu sign "ං" attached to a consonant.

සඥ, *Sajña, a.* knock-kneed.

සඥක, *Sajñaka, a.* (සඥා *sajñá* and ක aff.) apprehended, comprehended; marked, signed.

සඥප්ති, *Sajñapti,* see සඥාපන *sajñápana.*

සඥා, *Sajñá, s.* (සං *saṇ* and ඥා to know) name, appellation; gesture; sign, gesticulation; thought, mind, intellect: technical name of any grammatical affix.

සඥාකරණවා, *Sajñákaraṇawá, v.* to make signs, to beckon.

සඥාපන, *Sajñápana, s.* apprising, informing.

සඥාව, *Sajñáwa, s.* sign, mark, token; gesture, gesticulation, indication of sentiment, etc. by gesture, hint, intimation; any grammatical term; technical name of any affix, etc.

සඥි, *Sajñi, s.* one of the Brahma lókas.

සඥිත, *Sajñita, a.* (සඥා *sajñá* mark, ඉත *ita* affix) marked, spotted, signed; called.

සඥී, *Sajñí, a.* (සඥා *sajñá* and ඉන් *in* aff.) marked, signed; known.

සට්ටම්බි, *Saṭṭambi, s.* pedagogue, schoolmaster. (Tamil.)

සට්ටම, *Saṭṭama, s.* buttocks, rump, posterior: pl. සට්ටම් *saṭṭam.*

සට, *Saṭa, s.* an imitative sound; ascetic's clotted hair.

සටකපට, *Saṭakapaṭa, s.* (සට and කපට fraud) quarrel, tumult, uproar, wordy war.

සටද, *Saṭada, s.* perfume, odour, scent.

සටන්කරණවා, *Saṭankaraṇawá, v.* to make war; to fight, to contest.

සටන, *Saṭana, s.* (හඨ *hatha* to use violence) fight, conflict, contest, war, battle: pl. සටන් *saṭan.*

සටහන් කපනවා, *Saṭahan-kapanawá, v,* to write on letters as practised by natives when beginning to write on olas.

සටහන, *Saṭahana*. *s.* (ස before, ඨා *ṭhá* to be, to stay) mark, sign, sketch, outline; memorandum: pl. සටහන් *saṭuhan*.

සටි, *Saṭi*, } *s.* zedoary, *kæmpferia galanga*, [Coll: සටී, *Saṭí*, } හිඟුරුපියලි *hiṅgurupiyali*].

සටීක, *Saṭíka*, *a.* (ස with ටීකා *ṭíká* commentary) accompanied or explained by a commentary.

සඩංගුකරණවා, *Saḍaṅgukaraṇawá*, *v.* to quarrel.

සඩංගුව, *Saḍaṅguwa*, *s.* quarrel, broil, fray, tumult.

සඩංගුවෙනවා, *Saḍaṅgu-wenawá*, *v.* to fall out; to quarrel.

සඩුගඳ, *Saḍu-gaṇḍa*, *s.* stink, musty smell.

සඩුව, *Saḍuwa*, *s.* chaff, [Colloq. ලෙලි *leli*, පොතු *potu*].

සණ්ඩ, *Saṇḍa*, *s.* eunuch, [Colloq. නපුංසකයා *napuṇsakayá*]; bull at liberty; multitude of lotus flowers; wood, forest.

සණ්ඩාසය, *Saṇḍásaya*, *s.* pair of large pincers; smith's vice, [Colloq. දඬුඅඬුව *daṇḍuaṇḍuwa*].

සණ්ඩුකරණවා, *Saṇḍukaraṇawá*, *v.* to scold, to abuse; to fight, to quarrel.

සණ්ඩුකාරයා, *Saṇḍukárayá*, *s.* quarrelsome man.

සණ්ඩුකාරී, *Saṇḍukárí*, *s.* (සණ්ඩුව *saṇḍuwa* and කාර *kára* who does, ඊ *í* fem. aff.) scold, virago.

සණ්ඩුව, *Saṇḍuwa*, *s.* fray, tumult, wordy war.

සණගල, *Saṇagala*, *s.* grindstone, stone for the trituration of perfumes, etc.

සත්, *Sat*, *s.* a being, sentient creature; umbrella, from ඡත්‍ර *chhatra*, [Colloq. කුඩය *kuḍaya*]: *a.* true, good, virtuous, [Colloq. යහපත් *yahapat*]; excellent, best; right, proper; being, existing; in composition, good, right, fit, etc.

සත්කදම්බ, *Satkadamba*, *s.* (සත් good, කදම්බ kadamba tree) species of kadamba, *anthocephalus cordifolia:* see වෘත්තපුෂ්ප *writta-pushpa*.

සත්කාර, *Satkára*, *s.* (සත් and කාර doing) hospitality, entertainment of strangers; practice of prescribed duties to elders, superiors, etc; proper conduct, virtue.

සත්කාරකරණවා, *Satkára-karaṇawá*, *v.* to treat, to entertain.

සත්කුළපව්, *Satkuḷa-paw*, see සප්තකූටපර්වත *saptakúṭa-parwata*.

සත්කෘති, *Satkṛiti*, *s.* (සත් good, කෘති doing) doing good, acting properly, virtue, morality.

සත්ත, *Satta*, Páli form of සප්ත *sapta*.

සත්තක, *Sattaka*, *s.* certainty: *a.* true, certain, sure.

සත්තකකරණවා, *Sattaka-karaṇawá*, *v.* to assure, to affirm, to certify, to confirm by oath or ordeal.

සත්තකූටපබ්බත, *Sattakúṭa-pabbata*, see සප්තකූට පර්වත *saptakúṭa-parwata*.

සත්තභූමික, *Satta-bhúmika*, *a.* (සත්ත seven, භූමි ground, ඉක *ika* aff.) seven-storied, as a house.

සත්තම, *Sattama*, *a.* (සත් good, තමස් *tamas* aff.) best, excellent, eminent; respectable, venerable; seventh.

සත්තා, *Sattá*, *a.* (සත් being, තා aff.) being, existence; goodness, excellence, merit.

සත්තාහ, *Sattáha*, *s.* (සත්ත *satta* seven, අහ *áha* day) week, [Colloq. සුමානේ *sumáné*].

සත්තුටු, *Sattuṭu*, *s.* man professing to cure the bite of serpents by charms and incantations.

සත්තුරඟ, *Sat-turaṅga*, *s.* (සත් seven, තුරඟ horse) sun, alluding to his chariot being drawn by seven horses, [Colloq. ඉර *ira*].

සත්ථ, *Sattha*, *s.* company of traders, caravan, from සාර්ථ *sártha*.

සත්ථවාහක, *Sattha-wáhaka*. *s.* (සත්ථ and වාහක who carries) trader, travelling merchant, head of a caravan.

සත්ථා, *Satthá*, *s.* name of Buddha; Páli form of ශාස්තෘ *śástri*.

සත්දල, *Satdala*, *s.* tree, *alstonia* (or *echites*) *scholaris*, [Colloq. රුක්අත්තන *ruk-attana*].

සත්දහතළා, *Satdahataḷá*, *s.* corruptly for සදත්තළා *sadattaḷá*, which see.

සත්පත්, *Sat-pat*. *s.* (සත් seven, පත් leaf) tree, *alstonia scholaris*, having six and seven leaves on a stalk, [Colloq. රුක්අත්තන *ruk-attana*].

සත්පත්‍ර, *Sat-patra*, *s.* (සත් good, පත්‍ර leaf) new leaf of a water lily.

සත්පුරුෂ, *Satpurusha*, *a.* (සත් good, පුරුෂ man) good, virtuous, moral; excellent, best.

සත්පුරුෂකම, *Satpurushakama*, *s.* virtue.

සත්පුරුෂයා, *Satpurushayá*, *s.* virtuous man, good man.

සත්පෙති දෑසමන්, *Satpeti-dēsaman*, *s.* double jasmine.

සත්ඵල, *Sat-phala*, *s.* (සත් good, ඵල fruit) pomegranate, *punica granatum*, [Colloq. දෙළුම් *deḷum*].

සත්බුමු, *Satbumu*, *a.* (සත් seven, බුමු for බිම *bima* ground or floor) seven storied.

සත්‍ය, *Satya*, *s.* truth, direct truth, perceived without human speculation, doctrines of Buddha:

see චතුස්සත්‍ය *chatussatya;* first or golden age; oath: *a*, true, certain; sincere, honest, speaking the truth.

සත්‍යක, *Satyaka*, *s.* attestation or asseveration; ratification of a bargain.

සත්‍යක්‍රියාව, *Satya-kriyáwa*, *s.* (සත්‍ය truth, oath, ක්‍රියා *kriyá* act, doing) asseveration, invoking a deity, etc. to witness to the truth.

සත්‍යකෘති, *Satyakṛiti*, *s.* (සත්‍ය certain, කෘති doing) ratification of a bargain.

සත්‍යඥානය, *Satya-jñánaya*, *s.* (සත්‍ය truth, ඥාන *jñána* knowledge) knowledge of the four great truths of Buddhism: see චතුස්සත්‍ය *chatussatya*.

සත්‍යතාවය, *Satyatáwaya*, *s.* (සත්‍ය and තාව *táwa* aff. of the abstract) veracity, integrity, honour, uprightness.

සත්‍යධර්මය, *Satya-dharmaya*, *s.* (සත්‍ය and ධර්ම *dharma* practice) truth, true doctrine.

සත්‍යනාමා, *Satya-námá*, *s.* plant, *hydrocotyle asiatica*, [Colloq. හින් ගොටුකොල *hín-goṭukola*, or මකුළුවැන්න *makuḷuwenna*].

සත්‍ය පාරමිතාව, *Satya-páramitáwa*, *s.* (සත්‍ය truth, පාරමිතා *páramitá* gone, passed) veracity, the undeviating practice of truth, one of the ten páramitás: see පාරමිතා *páramitá*.

සත්‍යයුග, *Satya-yuga*, *s.* (සත්‍ය and යුග age) the first of the four Yugas or ages, the period of general purity and virtue.

සත්‍ය වචනය, *Satya-wachanaya*, *s.* true word, reliable saying.

සත්‍යවත්, *Satyawat*, *a.* (සත්‍ය and වත් poss. aff.) true, veracious, practising or possessing truth.

සත්‍යවාදිකම, *Satyawádikama*, *s.* veracity, speaking the truth.

සත්‍යවාදින්, *Satyawádin*, *s.* (සත්‍ය and වාදින් who speaks) person of integrity: *a.* speaking truth.

සත්‍යසංවස, *Satya-saṇwasa*, *s.* (සත්‍ය and සං with වස to dwell) adherence to the truth, observance or practice of truth, veracity.

සත්‍යසන්ධ, *Satyasandha*, *a.* (සත්‍ය truth, සං *saṇ* before, ධා *dhá* to have or hold) veracious, adhering to or observing the truth.

සත්‍යාපන, *Satyápana*, *s.* ratification of a bargain.

සත්රුවන, *Satruwana*, *s.* (සත් seven, රුවන jewel) the seven gems or treasures of a universal emperor, viz. his car, his elephant, his horse, the resplendent gem which gives whatsoever is desired, his queen, his grahapati, and his eldest son.

සතෘෂ්, *Satṛish*, *a.* (ස for සහ *saha* with තෘෂ් thirst, desire) thirsty, greedy, cupidinous.

සත්සමාගම, *Satsamágama*, *s.* association with the good.

සත්ව, *Satwa*, *s.* the quality of excellence or goodness; animal, a being; being, existence; certainty.

සත්වන, *Satwana*, *ind.* seventh, seventhly, [Colloq. සත් වෙනි *sat-weni*].

සත්වයා, *Satwayá*, *s.* sentient being, living creature: pl. සත්වයෝ *satwayó*.

සත්වලෝකය, *Satwa-lókaya*, *s.* (සත්ව being, ලෝක *lóka* world) mundane existence, this world in opposition to the world of the gods and brahma lókas.

සත්වා, *Satwá*, *s.* merchant, trader, [Colloq. වෙළෙන්දා *weḷendá*].

සත්සඳ, *Satsaṇda*, see සක්සඳ *saksaṇda*.

සත්සර, *Satsara*, *s.* way, road, path, [Colloq. පාර *pára*]; the seven lakes in the Himálaya mountain; name of Buddha.

සත්හු, *Sathu*, plural of සත් *sat*.

සත, *Sata*, *s.* seven; umbrella, from ඡත්‍ර *chhatra;* weapon, instrument, tool: see ශස්ත්‍ර *sastra*.

සතත්, *Satat*, *s.* name of Brahma, as the all pervading spirit.

සතත, *Satata*, *a.* eternal, continual.

සතතජ්වරය, *Satatajwaraya*, *s.* (සතත continual, ජ්වර *jwara* fever) synochus or continued fever.

සතධා, *Satadhá*, *s.* (සත hundred, blossoms, ධා to have) bent grass, *panicum dactylon:* *a.* in a hundred ways, a hundred fold.

සතධාර, *Satadhára*, *s.* (සත hundred, ධාරා *dhárá* edge) thunderbolt, [Colloq. හෙන *hena*]: *a.* flowing in many streams.

සතන්, *Satan*, *s.* acc. or gen. plural of සත් *sat*, living creature; also, mind, heart.

සතන්සෙත්, *Satan-set*, *s.* (සතන් beings, සෙත් who tranquilises) name of Buddha.

සතප්පවනවා, *Satappawanawá*, *v.* to cause to sleep: pret. සැතැප්පුවා *seṭeppuwá;* the causal form of සැතපෙනවා *seṭapenawá*.

සතපත්, *Satapat*, *s.* bird, [Colloq. කුරුල්ලා *kurullá*]; lotus, *nelumbium speciosum*, [Colloq. නෙළුම් *neḷum*].

සතපති, *Satapati*, *s.* (සත hundred, පති chief) centurion, commander of a hundred.

සතපා, *Satapá*, *s.* centipede, [Colloq. පත්තෑයා *pattẹyá*].

සතපාක, *Satapáka*, *a.* (සත hundred, පාක boiled) hundred times boiled, as oil, etc.

සතපුෂ්ප, *Satapushpa*, see ශතපුෂ්පා *ṣatapushpá*.

සතර, *Satara*, *s.* the number four; science, scripture, etc: see ශාස්ත්‍ර *ṣástra;* name of Buddha: and of Vishṇu.

සතර අගතිය, *Satara-agatiya*, *s.* (සතර four, අගති *agati* injustice) four causes of regal injustice or oppression, viz. lust, anger, fear, and ignorance.

සතර අනුදිග, *Satara-anudiga*, *s.* the four intermediate points of the compass.

සතර අපාය, *Satara-apáya*, *s.* (සතර and අපාය hell) four states of existence regarded as retributive punishments, viz. hell, birth as an irrational being, the condition of a préta or hobgoblin, and of an asura or titan.

සතර ආයර්‍යඵලය, *Satara-áryaphalaya*, see චතුරාර්‍ය ඵලය *chaturárya-palaya.*

සතර ආයර්‍යසත්‍යය, *Satara-áryasatyaya*, see චතුරාර්‍ය සත්‍යය *chaturárya-satyaya.*

සතර ඉරියව්ව, *Satara-iriyawwa*, *s.* (සතර and ඉරියව්ව being) the four states of being, viz. sitting, standing, walking, and sleeping.

සතර උපාය, *Satara-upáya*, *s.* (සතර and උපාය expedient) the four resorts of kings against an enemy, viz. sowing dissension, punishment, reconciliation, gifts.

සතර ඍද්ධිපාද, *Satara-ṛiddhipáda*, *s.* (සතරඍද්ධි and පාද foot, or foundation) devout abstract meditation: see ධ්‍යාන *dhyána*.

සතර ඍද්ධිය, *Satara-ṛiddhiya*, *s.* (සතර and ඍද්ධි *ṛiddhi* superhuman power) four sorts of ṛiddhi or the supernatural power possessed by the Rahats of flying through the air.

සතරකර, *Satarakara*, *s.* name of Vishṇu.

සතරගතිය, *Satara-gatiya*, see සතර අපාය *satara-apáya.*

සතරඟුල්, *Satarangul*, *s.* (සතර four, අඟුල් *angul* finger) tree, *cassia fistula*, [Colloq. ඇහැළ *ehela*]; four fingers; four inches.

සතර දම්, *Satara-dam*, *s.* doctrines of Buddha.

සතරදිග, *Satara-diga*, *s.* (සතර and දිග quarter) the four cardinal points.

සතර පාරාජිකාව, *Satara-párájikáwa*, *s.* (සතර and පාරාජිකා *párájiká* crime) the four great crimes which cause the expulsion of a priest, and the loss of all his privileges, viz. sexual intercourse, theft, murder or being accessory to it, and false assumption of the character of Rahat.

සතර පැත්ත, *Satara-petta*, see සතරදිග *sataradiga.*

සතර ප්‍රතිසන්ධිය, *Satara-pratisandhiya*, *s.* (සතර and ප්‍රතිසන්ධි *pratisandhi* production) the four modes in which living beings are engendered, viz. oviparous, viviparous, vermiparous, and ópapátika or supernatural birth, as the sudden appearance of the gods.

සතර ඵලය, *Satara-phalaya*, *s.* enjoyment of bliss in the four paths, viz. Sówán, Sakṛidágámi, Anágámi, and Arhat, which see in their proper places.

සතරමග, *Satara-maga*, *s.* the four paths or stages of sanctification which one must arrive at before he could attain Nirwáṇa.

සතර මහදිවයින, *Satara-mahadiwaina*, } *s.* (සතර
සතර මහද්වීපය, *Satara-mahadvípaya*, } and මහ දිවයින or ද්වීප *dvípa* continent) the four continents or grand divisions of the universe, situated on the outside of the seven ranges of rocks surrounding Mahaméru, at the cardinal points, and named as follows, Púrwavidéha, the eastern continent; Aparagóyána, the western; Jambudvipa, the southern; and Uturukuru, the northern.

සතර මහනිධාන, *Sataramaha-nidhána*, *s.* (සතර and මහනිධාන treasure) four great treasures possessed by a universal emperor.

සතර වරම් දෙවියෝ, *Satara-waram-deviyó*, *s.* (සතර and වරම් chief, දෙවියෝ gods) the four regents of the cardinal points, and guardian deities of their several quarters, each being chief of a class of demons, viz. Dhṛitaráshṭra chief of the Gándharwas, on the east; Virúḍha, chief of the Kumbháṇḍas, on the south; Virúpáksha, chief of the Nágas, on the west; and Kuwéra, chief of the Yakshas, on the north.

සතර සංග්‍රහ වස්තුව, *Satara-sangraha-wastuwa*, *s.* (සතර and සංග්‍රහ වස්තුව favour, protection) the four chief moral virtues, viz. almsgiving, affability, promoting the prosperity of others, and loving others as ourselves.

සතර සතිපට්ඨාන, *Satara-satipaṭṭhána*, *s.* (සතර and සතිපට්ඨාන fixing attention) four objects of contemplation for subduing the passions, viz. body, sensation, mind, and the dharma or doctrines of Buddha.

සතරැස්, *Satareṣ*, *a.* (සතර *satara* four, ඇස් *eṣ* side) square, four sided.

සතළිස, *Sataḷisa*, *ind.* number forty.

සතළොස, *Satalosa, ind.* (සත seven, දස *dasa* ten, ල *la* substituted for ද *da*) seventeen, [Colloq. දහහත *dahahata*].

සතා, *Satá, s.* existent creature, any living being; animal, reptile: pl. සත්තු *sattu.*

සතාසූ, *Satásu, ind.* (සත *sata* seven, අසූ *asu* eighty) eighty-seven, [Colloq. අසූහත *asúhata*].

සති, *Sati, s.* (සර *sara* to go, ති aff.) mind, intellect, understanding; end, destruction; gift, giving.

සතිකය, *Satikaya, s.* (සත *sata* seven, days, ඉක *ika* aff.) week, [Colloq. සුමානේ *sumáné*].

සතිපට්ඨාන, *Satipaṭṭhána, s.* (සති understanding, පට්ඨාන fixing) name of a sútra or oral declaration of Buddha, inculcating a system of abstract meditation for subduing the passions and attaining beatitude.

සතිය, *Satiya, s.* (සත *sata* seven, days, ඉ *i* aff.) week; understanding, reason: see සති *sati.*

සතිස්නරක, *Satis-naraka, s.* (ස six, තිස *tisa* thirty, නරක hell) the thirty-six hells or divisions of Tartarus.

සතිස, *Satisa, ind.* (ස six, තිස thirty) thirty-six, [Colloq. තිස්හය *tishaya*].

සතිසම්මෝහ, *Satisammóha, s.* (සති understanding, සම්මෝහ overpowering) loss of sense or reason, fainting, syncope.

සතු, *Satu, s.* fungus, mushroom: *a.* possessing, having.

සතුට, *Satuṭa, s.* joy, delight, gladness.

සතුටු, *Satuṭu, a.* content, happy, cheerful, merry.

සතුටුකරණවා, *Satuṭukaraṇawá, v.* to please, to content, to gladden.

සතුටුවෙනවා, *Satuṭuwenawá, v.* to be pleased, to be contented.

සතුන්, *Satun,* plural of සතා *satá.*

සතුරා, *Saturá, s.* enemy, adversary, opponent: pl. සතුරෝ *saturó.*

සතුරු, *Saturu, s.* enemy: *a.* inimical.

සතුරුකම, *Saturukama, s.* hostility, enmity.

සතොස්, *Satos, s.* joy, delight, glee; Elu form of සන්තොස *santosa.*

සතැවුලිය, *Satẹwuliya, s.* repentance, sorrow.

සද්ද, *Sadda, s.* sound, noise; voice.

සද්දකරණවා, *Saddakaraṇawá, v.* to make a noise.

සද්දාව, *Saddáwa, s.* belief and practice of moral duties; corruptly for සද්ධා *saddhá,* Páli form of ශ්‍රද්ධා *ṣraddhá,* belief, faith.

සධර්ම, *Saddharma,* } *s.* (සත් *sat* true, excellent,
සද්ධර්ම, *Saddharma,* } ධර්ම *dharma* doctrine) doctrines of Buddha, Buddhism.

සද්ධර්මාන්තර්ධාන, *Saddharmántardhána, s.* (සධර්ම *saddharma* and අන්තර්ධාන *antardhána* disappearance) event foretold by Buddha, that in consequence of the prevalence of evil in the Kaliyuga or age of sin, his doctrines would become obsolete, his precepts disregarded, and his system of religion extinct.

සද්ධා, *Saddhá,* } *s.* faith: see ශ්‍රද්ධා *ṣraddhá.*
සධා, *Saddhá,* }

සද්භූත, *Sadbhúta, a.* (සත් *sat* good, භූත been) true, certain; good, virtuous.

සදෘශ, *Sadṛiṣa, a.* (ස for සම *sama* same, දෘශ to see) like, similar, resembling; fit, proper, right.

සදෘශය, *Sadṛiṣaya, s.* resemblance, comparison.

සද, *Sada, s.* assembly; sound, noise, from ශබ්ද *ṣabda.*

සදත්තලා, *Sadattalá, s.* one of the seven lakes said to be on the Himálayan mountains; commonly called ඡද්දන්තවිල *chhaddanta-vila.*

සදන, *Sadana, s.* (සද *sada* to go) house; water: *part.* of සදනවා *sadanawá;* conquering, overcoming, subduing; restraining, taming.

සදනවා, *Sadanawá, v.* to make, to form, to construct: pret. සෑදුවා *sẹduwá.*

සදල්ල, *Sadalla, s.* elevated terrace surrounding a house, piazza, [Colloq. උඩුමහල්තලය *uḍumahaltalaya*].

සදලු, *Sadalu, s* heart, [Colloq. හිත *hita*]: see the last.

සදවනවා, *Sadawanawá, v.* to cause to make or form; causal form of සදනවා *sadanawá*: pret. සෑදෙව්වා *sẹdewwá.*

සදස්, *Sadas, s.* (සද *sada* to go) assembly, meeting; the eyes in peacock's tail.

සදස්පිල්, *Sadas-pil,* } *s.* (සදස් and පිල් or පිලි
සදස්පිලි, *Sadas-pili,* } feather) eye in a peacock's tail.

සදහම්, *Sadaham, s.* (ස for සත් *sat* good, දහම් doctrine) Buddhism, the doctrines of Buddha; Elu form of සද්ධර්ම *saddharma.*

සදා, *Sadá, ind.* (ස for සර්ව *sarwa* all, දා affix of time) always, at all times, [Colloq. සෑමදා *sẹmadá*].

සදාකල්, *Sadákal, s.* all times, eternity.

සදාකාල, *Sadákála, s.* (සදා always, කාල time) continual duration, for ever.

සදාගති, *Sadágati, s.* (සදා always, ගති going, duration) sun, [Colloq. ඉර *ira*]; air, wind, [Colloq. හුළඟ *huḷaṅga*].

සදාතන, *Sadátana, s.* name of Vishṇu: *a.* eternal, everlasting.

සදාපුෂ්පි, *Sadápushpi*, *s.* plant, *calotropis gigantea*, [Colloq. වරා *wará*].

සදාඵල, *Sadá-phala*, *s.* (සදා always, ඵල fruit) coconut tree, [Colloquial: පොල්ගහ *pol-gaha*]; glomerous fig tree, *ficus glomerata*, [Colloq. අට්ටික්කා *aṭṭikká*]; wood apple tree, *ægle marmelos*, [Colloq බෙලි *beli*]; plant, *phyllanthus niruri*, [Colloq. පිටවක්කා *piṭawakká*].

සදාභද්‍රා, *Sadá-bhadrá*, *s.* (සදා always, භද්‍ර *bhadra* good) shrub, *gmelina arborea*, [Colloq. දෙමට *demaṭa*].

සදිය, *Sadiya*, *s.* plot, trick, artifice, treachery.

සදිරඟ, *Sadiranga*, *s.* ? game at chess.

සදිව්‍යලෝකය, *Sadiwya-lókaya*, see සදෙව්ලොව *sadew-lowa*.

සදිස, *Sadisa*, *a.* like, resembling, similar, from සදෘශ *sadṛiṣa*.

සදී, *Sadí*, *s.* food, eating.

සදුල, *Sadula*, *s.* arrow-grass, *heteropopogon hirtus*, [Colloq. ඊතණ *ítaṇa*].

සදෙව්ලොව, *Sadew-lowa*, *s.* (ස six, දෙව් a god, ලොව world) the six divine worlds or the residences of six classes of gods, viz. Cháturmahárájika or the four regents of the cardinal points; Táwatiosa or Indra's heaven; Yáma; Nirmáṇa ratiya; and Paranirmita-wasawarti.

සදෙස, *Sadesa*, *a.* (ස with දෙස country) near, proximate; of the same country or place.

සදොලමල, *Sadola-mala*, *s.* resinous substance which exudes from the sal tree, *shorea robusta* or *vateria acuminata*, and from which an oil is prepared for blacking the native manuscript books.

සදොස්, *Sados*, *a.* guilty, faulty.

සදොසි, *Sadosi*, *a.* (ස with දොස *dosa* wrath, ඉ *i* aff.) wrathful, angry; vicious, depraved; vitiated, morbid.

සදෑස්, *Sadẹs*, *s.* eye in a peacock's tail.

සඳ, *Sanda*, *s.* moon; north; joint; evening; eye in the peacock's tail; woman, female; time; scent, odour; sorrow, distress; doubt, uncertainty; desire; dew; mind: *a.* noble, high, eminent; best, excellent.

සඳකට, *Sandakaṭa*, } *s.* (සඳ moon, කට or කඩ
සඳකඩ, *Sandakaḍa*, } ornament) name of Íṣwara.

සඳකඩපහණ, *Sandakaḍa-pahaṇa*, *s.* (සඳ and කඩ part, පහණ stone) flight of steps in the shape of a crescent.

සඳකත්, *Sanda-kat*, *s.* (සඳ and කත් ray) moon-beam; peacock; the woman-evening.

සඳකත, *Sandakata*, *s.* (සඳ and කත gem) sort of gem: see චන්ද්‍රකාන්ත *chandrakánta*.

සඳකිඳුරා, *Sanda-kindurá*, *s.* (සඳ and කිඳුරා kindurá) class of imaginary beings inhabiting hills and forests, with the head and neck of a woman and the body and legs of a goat; satyr.

සඳකැන්, *Sandakẹn*, *s.* peacock, [Colloq. මොණරා *monará*]; ray of the moon.

සඳගෝමි, *Sandagómi*, *s.* the venerable Sanda.

සඳතෙන, *Sanda-tena*. *s.* (සඳ moon, තෙන son) planet Mercury or its regent.

සඳපට, *Sandapaṭa*, *s.* piece of cloth; sheet, [Colloq. ඇතිරිල්ල *ẹtirilla*].

සඳපාන, *Sandapána*, *s.* (සඳ and පාන light) moon-light, (literally moon-lamp).

සඳබරණ, *Sanda-baraṇa*, *s.* (සඳ and අබරණ *abaraṇa* ornament) name of Ṣiva; peacock.

සඳමඩුල, *Sandamaḍula*, *s.* (සඳ and මඩුල orb) disc of the moon.

සඳමිදුලු, *Sandamidulu*, *s.* (සඳ joint, මිදුලු marrow) marrow of the joints.

සඳමුහුළු, *Sanda-muhuḷu*, *s.* (සඳ moon, මුහුළු crest) name of Ṣiva.

සඳරාජ, *Sandarája*, *s.* plant, St. John's wort, *hypericum campestre*.

සඳරැස්, *Sandarẹs*, *s.* (සඳ and රැස් ray) moon-beam.

සඳල්ල, *Sandalla*, see සදල්ල *sadalla*.

සඳලිඟු, *Sanda-lingu*, *s.* token, sign, mark, spot, [Colloq. ලකුණ *lakuna*].

සඳලු, *Sandalu*, see සදලු *sadalu*.

සඳවිමණ, *Sanda-vimana*, *s.* (සඳ and විමණ mansion) palace of the moon, serving also as a car.

සඳසාවා, *Sanda-sáwá*, *s.* (සඳ and සාවා hare) spots on the moon's disc, so called from their fancied resemblance to a hare.

සඳහන්කරණවා, *Sandahankaraṇawá*, *v.* to mention, to remind.

සඳහන, *Sandahana*, *s.* (සඳ moon, හන mark, or සඳ mind, හන for සන් *san* mark or impression on) horoscope; thought, reflection, recollection, memorandum; kind or affectionate thought, solicitude: pl. සඳහන් *sandahan*.

සඳහස, *Sandahasa*, *s.* sabre, scimitar.

සඳහා, *Sandahá*, } *ind.* particle signifying for,
සඳා, *Sandá*, } because, on account of, etc.

සඳු, *Sandu*, *s.* moon, [Colloq. හඳ *handa*].

සඳුදා, *Sandudá*, *s.* (සඳ and දා day) Monday.

සඳුන්, *Sandun*, *s.* sandal-wood, *santalum album;* also called රත්කිහිරිය *rat-kihiriya*, *(order Santalaceæ);* Elu form of චන්දන *chandana;* woman.

සඳුන්පලු, *Sandun-palu*, *s.* (සඳුන් and පලු sprout) leaf or shoot of the sandal-wood tree.

සධනික, *Sadhanika*, *a.* (ස for සහ *saha* with ධන *dhana* wealth, ඉක *ika* aff.) rich, wealthy, opulent.

සධර්ම, *Sadharma*, *a.* (ස for සමාන *samána* same, ධර්ම merit, practice) like, equal, resembling; of the same sect or caste, performing like duties.

සධවා, *Sadhawá*, *s.* (ස for සහ *saha* with ධව *dhawa* husband) wife, woman whose husband is living.

සධාතුක, *Sadhátuka*, *a.* (ස with ධාතු *dhátu* constituent part of the body, ක aff.) having a tooth or bone of Buddha, as a dágaba, etc. without which it is not considered duly consecrated.

සන්, *San*, *s.* sign, mark, token; hint, signal; Elu form of සංඥාව *sajñáwa;* hiding, concealment; sound, song, singing; cook.

සන්කටුව, *San-kaṭuwa*, *s.* spur.

සන්කරණවා, *Sankaraṇawá*, *v.* to make signs, to express anything by gesture, to beckon; to spur.

සන්කුණ්ඩ ඇල්වී, *Sankuṇḍa-ęlví*, *s.* kind of paddy, *oryza sativa.*

සන්ත, *Santa*, *a.* (සම *sama* to tranquilize, තන් *tan* aff.) calm, tranquil, pacified; true, virtuous, good; worshipped, praised, adored; existing; the hands joined and opened.

සන්තක, *Santaka*, *a.* belonging to, possessing, having, dependent upon.

සන්තකකරණවා, *Santakakaraṇawá*, *v.* to cause to belong.

සන්තකවෙනවා, *Santakawenawá*, *v.* to become one's own.

සන්තත, *Santata*, *a.* (සම් *sam* before, තන *tana* to spread) eternal, continual; spread, extended, continuous: *adv.* continually, perpetually, eternally.

සන්තතජ්වර, *Santatajwara*, *s.* (සන්තත and ජ්වර fever) continued fever.

සන්තතිය, *Santatiya*, *s.* (සම් *sam* before, තන *tana* to spread) race, lineage; offspring, progeny; descent, succession; continuous line, row, range; extent, expanse, spreading, stretching.

සන්තප්ත, *Santapta*, *a.* (සම් *sam* and තප *tapa* to heat) suffering pain or distress, distressed, afflicted, wretched; burnt, scorched, inflamed with passion, etc.

සන්තර්ජනය, *Santarjanaya*, *s.* (සම් *sam* and තර්ජ *tarja* to threaten) threatening, menacing, terrifying by threats.

සන්තර්ජනය කරණවා *Santarjanaya-karaṇawá*, *v.* to nourish, to sustain.

සන්තර්පණය, *Santarpaṇaya*, *s.* (සම් *sam* and තර්ප *tarpa* to satisfy) satisfaction, satiety, fulness; that which delights in smell or taste, what gives health and vigour to the body.

සන්තාන, *Santána*, *s.* (සම් *sam* and තන *tana* to spread) family, race, lineage; thought, reflection; offspring, progeny; spreading, expansion, diffusion.

සන්තාප, *Santápa*, *s.* (සම් *sam* and තප *tapa* to burn) heat, burning heat; affliction, grief, sorrow, repentance, distress; passion.

සන්තා ලතා, *Santá-latá*, *s.* (සන්තා and ලතා creeper) celestial creeper, double jasmine.

සන්ති, *Santi*, *s.* (ෂණ *shaṇa* to give, ති aff.) end, destruction; gift, giving.

සන්තුෂ්ට, *Santushṭa*, *a.* (සම් *sam* intensive prefix, තුෂ්ට pleased) pleased, delighted, rejoiced.

සන්තුෂිත, *Santushita*, *s.* (සම් *sam* and තුෂ *tusha* to be glad, ඉත *ita* aff.) one of the six divine world: see තුසිත භවන *tusita-bhawana.*

සන්තෝෂ, *Santósha*, *s.* (සම් *sam* and තුෂ *tusha* to be pleased) joy, pleasure, delight, satisfaction, happiness.

සන්තෝෂකරණවා, *Santóshakaraṇawá*, *v.* to gladden, to please.

සන්තෝෂවෙනවා, *Santóshawenawá*, *v.* to rejoice, to be glad.

සන්තෝස, *Santósa*, *a.* joyful: see සන්තෝෂ *santósha.*

සන්ත්‍රස, *Santrasa*, }
සන්ත්‍රාස, *Santrása*, } *s.* (සම් *sam* intensive, ත්‍රස or ත්‍රාස to fear) fear, dread, alarm, terror.

සන්ථව, *Santhawa*, *s.* acquaintance, intimacy, friendship; proximity.

සන්ථාගාරය, *Santhágáraya*, *s.* (සන්ථව *santhawa* and අගාර *ágára* house) council chamber, place of meeting, place of public resort, hall or room where friends associate.

සන්දංශ, *Sandanṣa*, *s.* (සම් *sam* with දංශ to bite) pair of tongs or nippers.

සන්දර්භය, *Sandarbhaya*, *s.* (සම් *sam* together, දර්භ *darbha* gathering) weaving garlands, collecting flowers into a wreath or fillet.

සන්දර්ශනය, *Sandarṣanaya*, *s.* (සම් *sam* intensely, දර්ශන *darṣana* seeing) looking intensely, examining, inspection.

සන්දිකරණවා, *Sandikaraṇawá*, *v.* to join, as two pieces of wood.

සන්දිය, *Sandiya*, *s.* joint; union, etc: see සන්ධි *sandhi;* time, occasion, opportunity.

සන්දිෂ්ට, *Sandishṭa*, *s.* (සම් *sam* with දිශ *diṣa* to shew) news, tidings, information: *a.* told, communicated, related; promised, agreed, assented.

සන්දීපක, *Sandípaka*, *a.* (සම් *sam* with දීපක shining) illuminating, irradiating; manifesting, illustrating.

සන්දෙනවා, *Sandenawá*, *v.* to give a signal, to make a sign.

සන්දේශය, *Sandéṣaya*, *s.* epistle, message, news, tidings, information.

සන්දේහ, *Sandéha*, *s.* fear, apprehension; doubt, uncertainty.

සන්දෝහ, *Sandóha*, *s.* multitude, assemblage.

සන්දෘෂ්ට, *Sandrishṭa*, *a.* (සම් *sam* and දෘෂ්ට seen) seen, beheld; foreseen, anticipated.

සන්ධි, *Sandhi*, *s.* (සම් *sam* together, ධා *dhá* to have) union, junction, connection, combination; joint, articulation of the body; peace, pacification; hole, chasm, hole made in or underneath a wall for hostile or felonious purposes, breach, mine; union of letters either at the end and beginning of different words or in the middle of compound terms, to avoid dissonance or hiatus; conception, production, quitting one body by death and at the same instant becoming united to a fœtus at that instant conceived.

සන්ධිචෝර, *Sandhi-chóra*, } *s.* (සන්ධි breach, චෝර or චෞර thief)
සන්ධිචෞර, *Sandhi-chaura*, } house-breaker.

සන්ධිත, *Sandhita*, *a.* tied, bound, strung, fastened together; allied, reconciled, united.

සන්ධිවෙලා, *Sandhiwelá*, *s.* (සන්ධි union, වෙලා time) particular period, which connects the part of the day or fortnight, as morning, noon, and evening, new moon, the first, or thirteenth day of the fortnight, and full moon.

සන්ධ්‍යා, *Sandhyá*, *s.* (සන්ධි *sandhi* joint, යත් *yat* aff.) twilight, either morning or evening; a period of time, forenoon, afternoon, or midday, but particularly the afternoon; boundary, limit; joining, union.

සන්ධ්‍යාකාල, *Sandhyá-kála*, *s.* twilight, evening.

සන්ධ්‍යා වේලාව, *Sandhyá-wéláwa*, *s.* (සන්ධ්‍යා and වේලා *wélá* time) twilight; afternoon, afterpart of the day, [Colloq. සවස *sawasa*].

සන්ධ්‍යා සමය, *Sandhyá-samaya*, *s.* (සන්ධ්‍යා and සමය time) evening, twilight.

සන්නකරණවා, *Sannakaraṇawá*, *v.* to paraphrase; to translate.

සන්නද්ධ, *Sannaddha*, *a.* (සම් *sam* before, නහ *naha* to bind, ක්ත *kta* aff.) armed, mailed, accoutred; arranged, arrayed.

සන්නය, *Sannaya*, *s.* (සම් *sam* together, නී *ní* to get or guide) a translation accompanying the original, paraphrase; multitude, number; quantity; rear, rear guard: pl. සන්න *sanna.*

සන්නස, *Sannasa*, *s.* grant, deed granting certain privileges: pl. සන්නස් *sannas.*

සන්නාලියා, *Sannáliyá*, *s.* tailor, [Colloq. ඇඳුම් මහන්නා *ẹndum-mahanná*].

සන්නාසියා, *Sannásiyá*, *s.* devotee, Hindu ascetic.

සන්නාහය, *Sannáhaya*, *s.* (සම් *sam* before, නහ *naha* to bind) armour, mail, either of iron or thick quilted cotton.

සන්නිකර්ෂ, *Sannikarsha*, *s.* (සම් *sam* together, නි before කෘෂ *kṛisha* to attract) proximity, nearness.

සන්නිකෘෂ්ට, *Sannikṛishṭa*, *a.* (සම් *sam* and නි before කෘෂ *kṛisha* to attract, ක්ත *kta* aff.) near, proximate.

සන්නිධ, *Sannidha*, *s.* (සම් *sam* together, නි before ධා *dhá* to have) proximity, vicinity.

සන්නිධාන, *Sannidhána*, *s.* proximity, nearness, appearance, perceptibility, presence.

සන්නිධි, *Sannidhi*, *s.* (සම් *sam* and නි before ධා *dhá* to have) proximity, approximation; perceptibility, presence, appearance; storing, hoarding.

සන්නිනායන්, *Sanninâyan*, *s.* plant, *vernonia anthelmintica (Compositæ);* also called නායන් *náyan.*

සන්නිපතිත, *Sannipatita*, *a.* (සම් *sam* and නි before පත *pata* to go, ඉත *ita* aff.) assembled, collected; mixed, blended.

සන්නිපාත, *Sannipáta*, *s.* (සම් *sam* and නි before පත *pata* to go) collection, assemblage, multitude; mixture, miscellaneous multitude; morbid state of the three humours.

සන්නිභ, *Sannibha*, *a.* like, resembling, similar.

සන්නිය, *Sanniya*, *s.* fit, cholera, convulsion arising from a morbid state of the three humours.

සන්නිශ්‍රිත, *Sannisrita*, *s.* joined with, cherished, served, honored; having, possessing.

සන්න්‍යාස, *Sannyása*, *s.* (සම් *sam* and නි *ni* before අස *asa* to throw, to cast off) abandonment of all worldly affections and possessions; Indian spikenard.

සන්න්‍යාසි, *Sannyási*, *s.* (සන්න්‍යාස *sannyása* abandonment of the world, ඊ *í* aff.) ascetic, devotee, religious mendicant entirely devoted to the practice of religious duties.

සන්නෙ, *Sanne*, *s.* translation, version, paraphrase.

සන්මාන, *Sanmána*, *s.* (සත් *sat* good, මාන respect) respect for the good.

සන්මාර්ග, *Sanmárga*, *s.* (සත් *sat* good, මාර්ග way) good or virtuous conduct.

සන්වැති, *Sanweti*, *s.* end of a Yuga or a period of the world.

සන්සළු, *Sansaḷu*, *s.* (සම *sama* skin, සළු cloth, dress) name of Ṣiva, who is habited in an elephant's skin.

සන්සාරය, *Sansáraya*, *s.* transmigration: see සංසාර *sansára*.

සන්සිඳුවනවා, *Sansinduwanawá*, *v.* to allay, to soothe, to appease: see සංසිඳුවනවා *sansinduwanawá*.

සන්සුන්, *Sansun*, *a.* (සම් *sam* completely, සුන් from සිඳෙනවා *sindenawá* to be tranquil) tranquil, calm, pacified; quiet, unruffled,

සන්සේප, *Sansépa*, *s.* brevity, abridgment, conciseness; properly සංක්ෂේප *sankshépa*, which see.

සන්සේපයෙන්, *Sansépayen*, *ad.* briefly.

සන්හතිය, *Sanhatiya*, *s.* more correctly සංහති *sanhati*, assemblage, union, combination.

සන්හිඳීම, *Sanhindíma*, *s.* allayment; verbal noun of සන්හිඳෙනවා *sanhindenawá*.

සන්හිඳෙනවා, *Sanhindenawá*, *v.* to cut, to rescind, to destroy; to be allayed, appeased, or soothed: pret. සන්හිඳුනා *sanhinduná*.

සන්හුන්, *Sanhun*, *a.* tranquil, calm: see සන්සුන් *sansun*.

සන, *Sana*, *s.* mark, sign: see සන් *san;* sea, ocean: hemp, *cannabis sativa;* flux; instant, moment, also, සැන *sena;* flapping of an elephant's ears.

සනත්, *Sanat*, *s.* name of Brahma: *ind.* always, perpetually.

සනරාමර, *Sanarámara*, *a.* (ස for සහ *saha* with නර *nara* man, අමර *amara* a god; with gods and men collectively.

සනසනවා, *Sanasanawá*, *v.* (ෂ්ණිහ *shṇiha* to love, නවා aff.) to comfort, to console: pret. සැනසුවා *senasuwá*.

සනහ, *Sanaha*, *s.* (ෂ්ණිහ *shṇiha* to be greasy or bland) oil, oily or unctuous substance; love, affection; bathing, ablution.

සනහස්, *Sanahas*, } *s.* love, affection; kind or
සනහස, *Sanahasa*, } affectionate speech: see the last.

සනා, *Saná*, *s.* love, affection, regard: *ind.* always, perpetually, eternally.

සනාතන, *Sanátana*, *s.* (සනා always, තන aff.) name of Vishṇu, Ṣiva, and Brahma: *a.* eternal, continual, perpetual; firm, fixed, permanent.

සනාතනී, *Sanátaní*, *s.* (සනාතන *sanátana* Vishṇu, ඊ *í* fem. aff.) Lakshmí the wife of Vishṇu.

සනාභි, *Sanábhi*, *a.* like, resembling.

සනිටුහන්, *Saniṭuhan*, *s.* thought, mind, reflection, [Colloq. කල්පනාව *kalpanáwa*]; mark, token.

සනිටුහන්කරණවා, *Saniṭuhan-karaṇawá*, *v.* to distinguish, to notice, to mark; to recollect, to think on, to fix the mind on any object or purpose; to indite, to compose.

සනීප, *Sanípa*, *s.* health, freedom from disease; ease, pleasure: *a.* healthy.

සප්, *Sap*, *s.* snake.

සප්ත, *Sapta*, *s.* number seven.

සප්තක, *Saptaka*, *a.* seven, [Colloq. හත *hata*].

සප්තකී, *Saptakí*, *s.* woman's girdle.

සප්තකූට පර්වත, *Saptakúṭa-parwata*, *s.* (සප්ත seven, කූට peak, පර්වත rock) seven circular ranges of rocks said to surround Maha Méru and to form the boundaries of so many circumambient waters or oceans, viz. Yugandharaya, Íṣadharaya, Karavíkaya, Sudarṣanaya, Némindaraya, Vinatakaya, and Aṣwakarṇaya.

සප්තජිහ්වා, *Sapta-jihwá*, *s.* (සප්ත seven, ජිහ්වා tongue) disease, the formation of several fleshy fibres under the tongue.

සප්තතන්තු, *Sapta-tantu*, *s.* (සප්ත and තන *tana* to spread, තු aff.) sacrifice, oblation.

සප්තදශ, *Sapta-daṣa*, *ind.* (සප්ත and දශ ten) seventeen, [Colloq. දහහත *dahahata*].

සප්තධාතුව, *Sapta-dhátuwa*, *s.* (සප්ත and ධාතු *dhátu* element) seven constituent parts of the body, viz. chyle, blood, flesh, adeps, marrow, bone, and semen.

සප්තපර්ණ, *Sapta-parṇa*, *s.* (සප්ත seven, පර්ණ leaf) tree, *alstonia, scholaris*, [Colloq. රුක් අත්තන

ruk-attana]; sort of sweetmeat, made of the expressed juice of the grape, pomegranate, and date, with sugar, spices, honey and ghee.

සපත ප්‍රකරණ, *Sapta-prakaraṇa*, *s.* (සපත and ප්‍රකරණ book) the seven chapters or books of the abhidharma-piṭaka: see පිටක *piṭaka*.

සපතම, *Saptama*, *a.* seventh, [Colloq. **හත්වෙනි** *hat-weni*].

සපතමහ ශෛලය, *Saptamaha-ṣailaya*, see **සපතකූට පර්වත** *saptakúṭa-parwata*.

සපතමි, *Saptami*, *s.* (සපතම *saptama* and ඊ *i* aff.) seventh or locative case in Páli grammar; the seventh day of the lunar fortnight.

සපත රතන, *Sapta-ratna*, *s.* the seven gems of a universal emperor: see **සත්රුවන** *satruwana*.

සපතලා, *Saptalá*, *s.* (සපත seven, leaves, etc. ලා to have) jasmine, [Colloq. **සේපාල** *sépála*]; trumpet flower, *stereospermum suaveolens*, [Colloq. **පලොල්** *paḷol*]; plant, *herpestis monniera*, [Coll: **ලුණුවිල** *luṇuvila*].

සපත විඥාන, *Sapta-vijñána*, *s.* (සපත and විඥාන intellect) seven Brahma Lókas.

සපතසාගර, *Sapta-ságara*, *s.* (සපත and සාගර ocean) the seven seas surrounding Maha Méru)

සපතාර්චි, *Saptárchi*, *s.* (සපත seven, අර්චි *archi* flame) Agni or fire; planet Saturn.

සපතාශ්ව, *Saptáṣwa*, *s.* (සපත and අශ්ව *aṣwa* horse) the sun, [Colloq. **ඉර** *ira*].

සපතාහ, *Saptáha*, *s.* (සපත *sapta* and අහන් *ahan* day) week, [Colloq. **සුමානය** *sumánaya*].

සප්තුඩු, *Saptuḍu*, } *a.* man professing to render
සප්දිව්, *Sapdiw*, } serpents harmless, or to counteract the effects of poison, by charms and incantations.

සප්පයා, *Sappayá*, *s.* animal: pl. **සප්පයෝ** *sappayó*.

සප්පාය, *Sappáya*, *s.* ease, pleasure, enjoyment.

සප්පායන්වෙනවා, *Sappáyan-wenawá*, *v.* to take food, (used respectfully).

සප්පුරිස, *Sappurisa*, Páli form of **සත්පුරුෂ** *sat-purusha*.

සප්රද, *Sap-rada*, *s.* (සප් snake, රද king) name of Ananta, king of the Nágas or serpent race.

සප්සඳ, *Sapsaṇda*, *s.* twining shrub with bitter roots, *aristolochia indica*, (*Aristolochiaceæ*).

සප්හල, *Sap-hala*, *s.* name of Káma, the Indian god of love.

සප, *Sapa*, *s.* (සප to revile, to curse) an oath; imprecation, curse, cursing; abuse, scurrility; chewing, mastication; Elu form of **සර්ප** *sarpa* snake, serpent.

සපක්ෂ, *Sapaksha*, *s.* (ස for සමාන *samána* same, පක්ෂ party) partizan, follower, adherent.

සපත්, *Sapat*, *s.* wealth: *a.* arrived at, come to, attained.

සපත්තා, *Sapattá*, *s.* enemy, [Colloquial: **සතුරා** *saturá*].

සපත්තු කුට්ටම, *Sapattu-kúṭṭama*, *s.* pair of shoes.

සපත්තු මල, *Sapattu-mala*, *s.* Chinese rose or shoe flower, *hibiscus rosa sinensis*.

සපත්තුව, *Sapattuwa*, *s.* shoe; pl. **සපත්තු** *sapattu*. (Portuguese.)

සපත්න, *Sapatna*, *s.* enemy, adversary.

සපත, *Sapata*, *s.* sea, ocean, [Colloq. **මුද** *múda*].

සපතේරුවා, *Sapatéruwá*, *s.* shoemaker.

සපථ, *Sapatha*, *s.* (සප to swear, අථ *atha* aff.) oath, asseveration; imprecation, cursing, wishing ill to.

සපද, *Sapada*, *s.* (ස six, පද foot) bee, [Colloq. **මීමැස්සා** *mímęssá*].

සපදංශ, *Sapadaṇṣa*, *s.* (සප and දංශ tooth) teeth of serpents in which the venomous fluid is deposited; horse-radish tree, *moringa pterygosperma*, [Colloq. **මුරුංගා** *muruṇgá*].

සපදන්, *Sapadan*, *s.* (ස for සහ *saha* and පදාන *padána* gift) Dative case.

සපදාන, *Sapadána*, *s.* gift or alms.

සපදානචාරිකාඞ්ග, *Sapadána-chárikáṅga*, *s.* (ස and පදාන gifts, alms, චාරික *chárika* who goes, අඞ්ග *aṅga* religious ordinance) ordinance of the Buddhist priesthood, enjoining it upon the priests to procure a subsistence as mendicants asking alms from house to house: see **තෙළෙස්ධුතාඞ්ග** *teḷesdhutáṅga*.

සපන්, *Sapan*, *a.* clever, skilled in.

සපන, *Sapana*, *s.* oath, ordeal; abuse, malediction: *a.* rich, opulent, powerful; able, skilful, clever.

සපනවා, *Sapanawá*, *v.* to bite, to seize by the teeth; to chew, to eat, to masticate: pret. **සැපුවා** *sępuwá*.

සපනා, *Sapaná*, *s.* rich or clever man: pl. **සපන්නු** *sapannu*.

සපයනවා, *Sapayanawá*, *v.* to procure, to obtain.

සපර්ෂත්, *Saparshat*, see **සපරිවාර** *sapariwára*.

සපරද, *Saparada*, *s.* (සප serpent, රද king) name of Ananta, king of the Nágas or serpent race.

සපරිවාර, *Sapariwára*, } *a.* (ස for සහ *saha* with
සපරිස, *Saparisa*, } පරිවාර retinue) surrounded with a retinue, attended, accompanied.

සපල, *Sapala*. *s.* prosperity, improvement: see **සඵල** *saphala*.

සපා, *Sapá*, s. serpent, snake, from සර්ප *sarpa;* bee, from ෂට්පද *shatpada;* also, *past. part.* of සපනවා *sapanawá.*

සපාකනවා, *Sapákanawá*, v. to bite.

සපියෝ, *Sapiyó*, s. union, association, conjunction; war, conflict, contest, battle.

සපිරි, *Sapiri*, a. whole, entire; complete, [Colloq. සම්පූර්ණ *sampúrṇa*].

සපිරිවර, *Sapiriwara*, see සපරිවාර *sapariwára.*

සපු, *Sapu*, s. champaca tree, which produces a very fragrant flower of a light yellow hue and useful timber, *michelia champaca (Magnoliaceæ);* snake, serpent, from සර්ප *sarpa;* pleasure, happiness, enjoyment.

සපු ආනවාළු කෙසෙල්, *Sapu-ánawálu-kesel*, s. kind of plantain, *musa sapientum.*

සපු මල, *Sapu-mala*, s. flower of the champaca: see සපු *sapu.*

සපු මිලිල, *Sapu-milila*, s. chaste tree, producing valuable timber, *vitex altissima (Verbenaceæ);* also called මිල්ල *milla*, මිලිල *milila* and මී අං මිලිල *mían-milila.*

සපුරිස, *Sapurisa*, s. (ස for සත් *sat* good, පුරිස man) harmonious and eloquent language: *a.* good, excellent, best, virtuous.

සපැමිණි, *Sapęmiṇi*, a. arrived at; attained, come to.

සඵර, *Saphara*, see ශඵර *ṣaphara.*

සඵල, *Saphala*, a. (ස for සහ *saha* with ඵල fruit) productive, fruitful, bearing fruit, yielding profit.

සඵලකම, *Saphalakama*, s. fruitfulness, prosperity.

සඵලකරණවා, *Saphalakáraṇawá*, v. to improve, to prosper.

සඵලවෙනවා, *Saphalawenawá*, v. to be improved, to be prosperous: pret. සඵලවුනා *saphalawuná.*

සබ්බ, *Sabba*, Páli form of සර්ව *sarwa.*

සබ්බඤ්ඤු, *Sabbaññu*, s. Buddha; Páli form of සර්වඥ *sarwajña.*

සබ්බදස්සී, *Sabbadassí*, Páli form of සර්වදර්ශී *sarvadarṣí.*

සබ, *Saba*, s. assembly, company, from සභා *sabhá.*

සබත් දවස, *Sabat-dawasa*, s. Sabbath. (Eng.)

සබඳ, *Sabanda*, s. (ස for සහ *saha* with බඳ connected) friend, companion, associate, [Colloq. මිත්‍රයා *mitrayá*]; also, name of the Genitive case: *a.* connected with.

සබන්, *Saban*, s. soap.

සබන්කුකුළා, *Saban-kukuḷá*, s. Ceylon spur fowl, *galloperdix bicalcarata (Phasianidæ*, order *Gallinæ);* also called හබන්කුකුළා *haban-kukuḷá.*

සබය, *Sabaya*, see සභාව *sabháwa.*

සබර, *Sabara*, s. young of any animal; hunter, bowyer, barbarian; sheat fish, *silurus pelorius*, [Colloq. පෙටියා *peṭiyá*]; timber tree, *barringtonia racemosa*, [Colloquial: දිය මිදෙල්ල *diyamidella*].

සබරල, *Sabarala*, s. plant, *alocasia macrorhizon:* see හබරල *habarala.*

සබරි, *Sabari*, s. medicinal plant, *hoya hirsuta*, [Colloq. මීනුග *mí-nuga*].

සබල, *Sabala*, s. variegated colour; water.

සබා, *Sabá*, s. assembly, convocation, from සභා *sabhá.*

සබාසල, *Sabá-sala*, s. (සබා and සල hall) place of assembly.

සබ්‍රම්සරුන්, *Sabramsarun*, Elu form of the next.

සබ්‍රහ්මචාරී, *Sabrahmachárí*, s. (ස for සහ *saha* with බ්‍රහ්මචාරී religious student) fellow student, one engaged in the same studies, and observing the same austerities.

සභ්‍ය, *Sabhya*, s. (සභා *sabhá* and ය *ya* aff.) person of honourable parentage, an assistant at an assembly: *a.* relating to an assembly.

සභා, *Sabhá*, see සභාව *sabháwa.*

සභාග, *Sabhága*, a. (ස for සමාන *samána* like, භාග part, sort) like, similar, of the same tribe or sort, especially animals which have no natural antipathy.

සභාව, *Sabháwa*, s. (ස for සහ *ṣaha* together, භා *bhá* to shine) assembly, meeting; house or place in which an assembly is met, court of justice, etc.

සභිරු, *Sabhíru*, a. (ස for සහ *saha* with භිරු fear) afraid, terrified.

සම්, *Sam*, plural of සම *sama*, skin: *ind.* particle and prefix implying union, with, together; beauty or perfection, intensity; as a prefix, it corresponds to con, co, com, etc.

සම්කරු, *Samkaru*, s. (සම *sama* skin, කරු who does) shoemaker; tanner.

සම්දිටු, *Samdiṭu*, s. (සම් correct, දිටු sight) correct religious views; Elu form of සම්‍යක්දෘෂ්ටිය *samyak-dṛishṭiya.*

සම්පජ්ජලිත, *Sampajjalita*, a. (සම් and ප before, ජලිත *jalita* shining) glittering, brilliant, resplendent.

සම්පජාන, *Sampajána*, *s.* (සම් and ප before, ඤා *ñá* to know) knowledge, acquaintance.

සම්පත්, *Sampat*, see සම්පත්තිය *sampattiya*.

සම්පත්කාරයා, *Sampatkárayá*, *s.* wealthy man.

සම්පත්තිය, *Sampattiya*, }
සම්පද්, *Sampad*, } *s.* (සම් implying, perfection, පද *pada* to go, ක්ත *kta* aff.) prosperity, success, increase of wealth, power, or happiness; wealth, property, possessions.

සම්පදන්, *Sampadan*, see සම්පත්තිය *sampattiya*.

සම්පදාන, *Sampadána*, Páli form of සම්ප්‍රදාන *sampradána*.

සම්පන්න, *Sampanna*, *a.* (සම් with පද *pada* to go, ක්ත *kta* aff.) accomplished, completed, effected, obtained; possessed of, endowed with.

සම්පයුක්ත, *Sampayukta*, see සම්ප්‍රයුක්ත *samprayukta*.

සම්පර්ක, *Samparka*, *s.* (සම් and පෘච *pricha* to be in contact) mixture, mingling, contact, union, junction.

සම්පරාය, *Samparáya*, *s*, (සම් and පර *para* before ඉන *ina* to go) futurity; adversity, calamity; war, battle.

සම්පරායක, *Samparáyaka*, }
සම්පරායික, *Samparáyika*, } *s.* war, battle, contest, [Colloq. යුද්ධය *yuddhaya*].

සම්පරිකීර්ණ, *Samparikírṇa*, *a.* (සම් and පරි before කීර්ණ mixed) mixed, blended, combined, mingled.

සම්පාත, *Sampáta*, *s.* (සම් and පත *pata* to fall) descending, falling, coming down, lighting as a bird.

සම්පාදක, *Sampádaka*, *a.* (සම් before, පද *pada* to go, ක aff.) productive, fruitful.

සම්පාදන, *Sampádana*, *s.* (සම් and පද *pada* to go causal form) gaining, acquiring, reaching, attaining; forming, creating.

සම්පාදනය කරගන්නවා, *Sampádanaya-karagannawá*, *v.* to gain, to acquire.

සම්පාදනය කරණවා, *Sampádanaya-karaṇawá*, *v.* to procure, to supply, to produce, to provide.

සම්පාදිත, *Sampádita*, *a.* attained, gained, acquired, gotten; made, formed.

සම්පුට, *Samputa*, *s.* (සම් together, පුට to contract) casket, covered box, [Colloquial: කරඬුව *karaṇḍuwa*].

සම්පූර්ණ, *Sampúrṇa*, *a.* (සම් intensitive, පූර්ණ full, finished) whole, entire; complete, finished.

සම්පූර්ණකරණවා, *Sampúrṇa-karaṇawá*, *v.* to accomplish, to fulfil.

සම්පූර්ණභාවය, *Sampúrṇabhdwaya*, *s.* perfection, completion, accomplishment.

සම්පූර්ණ මිම්ම, *Sampúrṇa-mimma*, *s.* complete measure of any kind.

සම්පූර්ණය, *Sampúrṇaya*, *s.* perfection, completion, fulness, pleasure, joy.

සම්පූර්ණවෙනවා, *Sampúrṇa-wenawá*, *v.* to be accomplished or fulfilled.

සම්ප්‍රදාන, *Sampradána*, *s.* (සම් and ප්‍ර before දා *dá* to give) gift, giving; dative case in grammar.

සම්ප්‍රදලිත, *Sampradálita*, *a.* (සම් and ප්‍ර before දල *dala* to pierce, break) cleft, rent.

සම්ප්‍රයුක්ත, *Samprayukta*, *a.* (සම් and ප්‍ර before යුජ *yuja* to join, ක්ත *kta* aff.) joined, connected, associated.

සම්ප්‍රයෝග, *Samprayóga*, *s.* (සම් and ප්‍ර before යුජ *yuja* to join) connection, relation, mutual proportion; order, natural and connected series or arrangement.

සම්ප්‍රසාරණ, *Samprasáraṇa*, *s.* (සම් and ප්‍ර before සෘ *sri* to go) mutual substitution of ඉ *i*, උ *u*, ඍ *ṛi*, ඏ *ḷú*, found their respective semivowels ය *ya*, ව *wa*, ර *ra*, and ල *la*.

සම්ප්‍රහාර, *Samprahára*, *s.* (සම් and ප්‍ර before හර *hara* to take) war, battle; striking, wounding, killing.

සම්ප්‍රාප්ත, *Samprápta*, *a.* (සම් and ප්‍රාප්ත obtained) attained, obtained, gotten; effected, accomplished; arrived, approached.

සම්ප්‍රාප්තවෙනවා, *Samprápta-wenawá*, *v.* to approach, to arrive, to come to.

සම්ඵ, *Sampha*, *ind.* a particle signifying vain, unmeaning.

සම්ඵප්‍රලාප, *Samphapralápa*, *s.* (සම්ඵ vain, ප්‍රලාප speech) vain or trifling talk, idle chat, nonsense.

සම්ඵුටක, *Samphuṭaka*, see සම්පුට *sampuṭa*.

සම්ඵුල්ල, *Samphulla*, *a.* (සම් completely, ඵුල්ල blown) blown, blossomed, opened as a flower.

සම්බකරණවා, *Sambakaraṇawá*, *v.* to find, to procure, to obtain, to accumulate as riches.

සම්බකෙරීම, *Sambakeríma*, *s.* accumulation, gain.

සම්බද්ධ, *Sambaddha*, *a.* (සම් with බන්ධ *bandha* to bind, ක්ත *kta* aff.) connected with, endowed with, possessing as a predicate or property; bound, tied, attached.

සම්බන්ධ, *Sambandha*, *s.* (සම් with බන්ධ to bind) connection, natural or essential connection, as of a property with a substance: *a.* adjunct, annexed or connected, inherent; fit, proper.

සම්බන්ධකරණවා, *Sambandha-karaṇawá*, *v.* to join, to connect.

සම්බර, *Sambara*, *s.* (සම්බ *samba* to accumulate) water, [Colloq. වතුර *watura*]; restraint, forbearance, self control; also, සංවර *saṇwara;* name of a demon or daitya.

සම්බරාරි, *Sambarári*, *s.* (සම්බර *sambara* daitya, අරි *ari* foe) name of Káma, the Indian deity of love.

සම්බල, *Sambala*, *s.* (සම්බ to go, to collect, අල *ala* aff.) provender for a journey, stock for travelling accommodation.

සම්බවෙනවා, *Sambawenawá*, *v.* to meet, to encounter; to find: pret. සම්බවුනා *sambawuná*.

සම්බාධ, *Sambádha*, *s.* (සම් before, බාධ to impede) fear, dread; opposition, impediment: *a.* narrow, contracted, impassable.

සම්බාධන, *Sambádhana*, *s.* (සම් and බාධ *bádha* to impede) gate, barrier; obstructing, opposing.

සම්බාහනය, *Sambáhanaya*, *s.* (සම් before, වහ *waha* to obtain, pleasure or ease) rubbing the body, kneading the limbs, shampooing.

සම්බු, *Sambu*, } *s.* bivalve shell; conch shell.
සම්බුක, *Sambuka*, }

සම්බුද්දිය, *Sambuddiya*, *s.* one's own accord, self-will.

සම්බුද්ධ, *Sambuddha*, *a.* (සම් implying perfection or intensity, බුද්ධ wise) all-wise, possessed of perfect knowledge or wisdom; epithet of Buddha.

සම්බෝධ, *Sambódha*, *s.* (සම් completely, බුධ *budha* to know, causal form) explaining, instructing, informing.

සම්බෝධිය, *Sambódhiya*, *s.* (සම්බුධ *sambuddha* and අණ් *aṇ* aff.) Buddhaship, character of Buddha.

සම්භක්ත, *Sambhakta*, *a.* (සම් intensitive, භජ *bhaja* to serve, ක්ත *kta* aff.) attached or devoted to, served, worshipped.

සම්භකරණවා, *Sambhakaraṇawá*, *v.* another form of සම්බකරණවා *sambakaraṇawá*, which see.

සම්භව, *Sambhawa*, } *s.* (සම් and භව being) cause, origin, motive;
සම්භවය, *Sambhawaya*, } birth, production.

සම්භාර, *Sambhára*, *s.* (සම් before, භෘ *bhṛi* to maintain) multitude, number, quantity, heap, assemblage; maintaining, supporting.

සම්භාවනා, *Sambháwaná*, *s.* worship, honor; possibility; sense of the Potential Mood.

සම්භාසන, *Sambhásana*, *s.* (සම් together, භාසන talking) conversation, discourse.

සම්භූ, *Sambhu*, *s.* (සම් auspicious particle, භූ *bhú* to be) name of Ṣiva, and Brahma; sage, venerable person; parent, progenitor.

සම්භූත, *Sambhúta*, *a.* (සම් and භූ to be, ක්ත *kta* aff.) born, produced.

සම්භූතනය, *Sambhútanaya*, *s.* (සම්භූ Ṣiva, තනය son) name of Kártikéya or Kataragama-deviyó; and of Gaṇéṣa.

සම්භෝග, *Sambhóga*, *s.* (සම් with භෝග enjoyment) enjoyment, pleasure, delight; coition, sensuality; use, employment.

සම්භ්‍රම, *Sambhrama*, *s.* (සම් before, භ්‍රම to revolve) haste, hurry, confusion.

සම්මට්ටිය, *Sammaṭṭiya*, *s.* whip, scourge, [Colloq. කසය *kasaya*].

සම්මතය, *Sammataya*, *s.* (සම් with මන *mana* to think, ත *ta* aff.) agreement, assent, similarity of opinion: *a.* elected or appointed by general consent, as the first kings of the Súrya race.

සම්මති, *Sammati*, *s.* order, command; see the last.

සම්මද, *Sammada*, *s.* (සම් with මද to delight) happiness, joy, pleasure.

සම්මර්ද, *Sammarda*, *s.* (සම් together, මෘද *mṛida* to trample) war, battle, [Colloq. යුද්ධය *yuddhaya*].

සම්මර්ෂණය, *Sammarshaṇaya*, *s.* (සම් intensitive, මෘෂ *mṛisha* to see) investigation, discrimination.

සම්මා, *Sammá*, *ind.* true, right; accurate, correct.

සම්මා ආජීව, *Sammá-ájíwa*, *s.* (සම්මා right, ආජීව livelihood) suitable profession, livelihood obtained in a proper manner, without destroying life, or contracting any other impurity.

සම්මා කර්මාන්ත, *Sammá-karmánta*, see සම්‍යක් කර්මාන්ත *samyak-karmánta*.

සම්මාදම් කරණවා, *Sammádam-karaṇawá*, *v.* to raise a subscription; to give in a subscription; to contribute.

සම්මාදම, *Sammádama*, *s.* subscription: pl. සම්මාදම් *sammádam*.

සම්මාදිට්ඨි, *Sammádiṭṭhi*, see සම්‍යක්දෘෂ්ටිය *samyak-dṛishṭiya*.

සම්මානිත, *Sammánita*, *a.* (සම් prep, මන *mana* to honour, ක්ත *kta* aff.) honoured, respected, venerated.

සම්මා වාචා, *Sammá-wáchá*, *s.* (සම්මා true, වාචා speech) speaking the truth, veracity.

සම්මා වායාම, *Sammá-wáyáma*, *s.* (සම්මා and වායාම labour) honest labour, industry, application, effort, [Colloq. උත්සාහය *utsáhaya*].

සම්මා සංකල්ප, *Sammá-saṇkalpa*, *s.* (සම්මා and සංකල්ප thought) purity of intention.

සම්මිශ්‍ර, *Sammiṣra*, *a.* (සම් together, මිශ්‍ර mixed) mixed, mingled, blended.

සම්මුඛ, *Sammukha*, *s.* (සම් with මුඛ face) encountering, facing, in front of.

සම්මුඛවෙනවා, *Sammukha-wenawá*, *v.* to meet, to encounter.

සම්මුතිය, *Sammutiya*, *s.* assembly for consultation; consent: pl. සම්මුති *sammuti*.

සම්මූඪ, *Sammúḍha*, *a.* (සම් entirely, මුහ *muha* to be foolish) ignorant, senseless.

සම්මූර්ච්ඡන, *Sammúrchchhana*, *s.* (සම් before, මූර්ච්ඡ *múrchchha* to faint) fainting, insensibility; permeation, pervading.

සම්මූළ්හ, *Sammúlha*, see සම්මූඪ *sammúdha*.

සම්මෝද, *Sammóda*, *s.* (සම් intensive, මුද *muda* to be happy) pleasure, delight.

සම්‍යක්, *Samyak*. *a.* good, holy, true, right; accurate, correct.

සම්‍යක්කර්මාන්ත, *Samyak-karmánta*, *s.* (සම්‍යක් and කර්මාන්ත action) correct conduct, upright or holy life.

සම්‍යක්දෘෂ්ටිය, *Samyak-drishṭiya*, *s.* (සම්‍යක් true, දෘෂ්ටි *drishṭi* sight) correct religious opinions, orthodoxy, restricted by the Buddhists to those of their own sect.

සම්‍යක් ප්‍රතිපත්තිය, *Samyak-pratipattiya*, *s.* (සම්‍යක් and ප්‍රතිපත්ති *pratipatti* conduct) due observance of religious duties, especially the particular observances of the priesthood.

සම්‍යක් ලබ්ධි, *Samyak-labdhi*, see සම්‍යක් දෘෂ්ටිය *samyak-drishṭiya*.

සම්‍රාජ, *Samrája*, *s.* (සම් *sam* all, රජ *rája* to rule) a Chakrawarti or universal emperor, a paramount sovereign.

සම්වන්, *Samwan*, *s.* colour black.

සම්සළු, *Samsaḷu*, *s.* (සම *sama* skin, සළු dress) name of Ṣiva.

සම, *Sama*, *s.* skin of any animal; tanned skin, leather, from චර්ම *charma*: *a.* like, similar; same, even, equal; full, complete.

සමකම, *Samakama*, *s.* (සම like, කම being) likeness, similarity.

සමකරණවා, *Samakaraṇawá*, *v.* to compare.

සමග්‍ර, *Samagra*, *a.* (සම and ග්‍රහ *graha* to take) all, whole, entire. full, complete.

සමග, *Samaga*, *ind.* particle signifying association, with, together with.

සමගන්ධික, *Samagandhika*, *s.* fragrant grass, *andropogon muricatus*, [Colloq. සැවැන්දරා *sewendara*].

සමගහනවා, *Samagahanawá*, *v.* to skin, to flay, to excoriate.

සමගි, *Samagi*, *a.* united, joined, associated; reconciled.

සමගිකම, *Samagikama*. *s.* peace.

සමගිකරණවා, *Samagikaraṇawá*, *v.* to reconcile.

සමගිතාව, *Samagitáwa*, *s.* agreement, union of minds, reconciliation.

සමගිවෙනවා, *Samagiwenawá*, *v.* to agree together, to be united.

සමගොත්, *Samagot*, *s.* (සම same, ගොත් tribe) relation, kinsman. [Colloq. නෑයා *néyá*].

සමඞ්ගා, *Samaṅgá*, *s.* (සම් *sam* together, අගි *agi* to go) Indian madder, *oldenlandia umbellata*; plant, *sida cordifolia*, [Colloq. සුළු බැලිල *sulu-belila*]; species of madder, *rubia manjitha*, [Colloq. වැල්මදට *welmadata*].

සමච්චල්, *Samachchal*, *a.* jocular.

සමච්චල් කරණවා, *Samachchal-karaṇawá*, *v.* to joke, to jest.

සමච්චලය, *Samachchalaya*, *s.* joke, jest, ridicule, banter: pl. සමච්චල් *samachchal*.

සමජ්‍ය, *Samajyá*, *s.* (සම් *sam* together, අජ *aja* to go) assembly, meeting; fame, celebrity.

සමජ, *Samaja*, *s.* forest, wood: see the last.

සමඥා, *Samjñá*, *s.* (සම all, ඥා to know) name, appellation; fame, reputation.

සමණ, *Samaṇa*, *s.* priest or Buddhist ascetic, also, written මහණ *mahaṇa* from ශ්‍රමණ *ṣramaṇa*; master, owner; mental tranquillity, calmness; from (සම *sama* to be tranquil); name given to the canopy carried in Buddhist processions.

සමණදම්, *Samaṇadam*, *s.* (සමණ and දම් practice) duties of a Buddhist priest or ascetic.

සමණදම් රකිනවා, *Samaṇadam-rakinawá*, *v.* to observe the duties of a Buddhist priest.

සමත්, *Samat*, *s.* bird in general; Indian cuckoo, *cuculus micropterus* (order *Picariae*); beggar, mendicant; rich person, wealthy man; brevity, conciseness.

සමත, *Samata*, *s.* Indian cuckoo: see the last word: *a.* clever, skilful, from සමර්ථ *samartha*; all, the whole, from සමස්ත *samasta*.

සමතල, Samatala, a. (සම even, තල surface) level, even, flat.

සමතලා, Samatalá, s. plane: see the last.

සමතලාකරණවා, *Samatalá-karaṇawá*, *v.* to plane.

සමතා, Samatá, s. clever man, skilful man.

සමතික්‍රම, *Samatikrama*, *s.* (සම් *sam* and අති *ati* before, ක්‍රම to go) going beyond, transgression.

සමතිස්පෙරුම්, *Samatis-perum*, *s.* (සම complete, තිස් thirty, පෙරුම් virtue) thirty perfections, or extraordinary virtues practised by Buddha.

සමතුන්, *Samatun*, *s.* clever person.

සමතැස්, *Samatẹs*, *s.* (සමත *samata* universal, ඇස් *ẹs* eye) name of Buddha, [Colloq. බුදුන් *budun*].

සමත්‍රිංශත්, *Sama-triṇsat*, *a.* (සම complete, ත්‍රිංශත් thirty) thirty, consisting of or having thirty.

සමත්‍රිංශත් පාරමිතා, *Sama-triṇsat-páramitá*, see පාරමිතා *páramitá*.

සමථ, *Samatha*, *s.* (සම to be tranquil. ථ aff.) calm, tranquillity.

සමදරා, *Samadará*, *s.* small tree, *samadera indica, (Simarubaceæ).*

සමධිගම, *Samadhigama*, *s.* (සම් *sam* and අධි *adhi* before ගමු *gamu* to go) arriving, obtaining, acquiring.

සමන්, *Saman*, *s.* generic name of jasmine, *jasminum sambac*, [Colloq. පිච්ච *pichcha*]; Buddha; union, association.

සමන් ඇල්වි, *Saman-ẹlvi*, *s.* kind of paddy, *oryza sativa.*

සමන්ත, *Samanta*, } *s.* (සම් *sam* with අන්ත
සමන්තක, *Samantaka*, } *anta* end) limit, term, boundary.

සමන්තකූටය, *Samantakúṭaya*, *s.* name of Adam's Peak.

සමන්ත චක්ෂු, *Samanta-chakshu*, *s.* (සමන්ත and චක්ෂු eye) name of Buddha: see සමතැස් *samatẹs*.

සමන්තතෝ, *Samantató*, *ind.* (සමන්ත and තෝ aff.) all round, on every side, wholly, altogether.

සමන්ත දුග්ධා, *Samanta-dugdhá*, *s.* (සමන්ත every way, දුග්ධ *dugdha* milk) milk hedge plant, *euphorbia tirucalli*, [Colloq. නවහන්දි *nawahandi*]; tree, *euphorbia antiquorum*, [Colloq. දළුක් *daluk*].

සමන්තභද්‍ර, *Samanta-bhadra*, *s.* (සමන්ත every way, භද්‍ර auspicious) generic name of Buddha.

සමන්තභුජ්, *Samanta-bhuj*, *s.* (සමන්ත and භුජ් what eats) fire, [Colloq. ගින්දර *gindara*].

සමන්නනවා, *Samannanawá*, *v.* to join together: pret. සැමැන්නුවා *sẹmẹnnuwá*.

සමන්නාගත, *Samannágata*, *a.* (සම් *sam* and අනු *anu* following, with ආ *á* and ගමු *gamu* to go, ත aff.) being possessed of, endowed with.

සමන්පිච්ච, *Saman-pichcha*, *s.* jasmine. *jasminum sambac*, [Colloq. පිච්ච *pichcha*].

සමන්බදුරු, *Saman-baduru*, *s.* name of Buddha; Elu form of සමන්තභද්‍ර *samanta-bhadra*.

සමන්වාගත, *Samanwágata*, see සමන්නාගත *samannágata*.

සමන්විත, *Samanvita*, *a.* (සම් *sam* intensitive, අන්විත *anvita* endowed with) possessed of, endowed with, possessing, affected with, full of.

සමනන්, *Samanan*, *s.* husband; master, lord, [Colloq. ස්වාමියා *swámiyá*].

සමනල, *Samanala*, *s.* mountain called Adam's peak.

සමනලයා, *Samanalayá*, *s.* butterfly: pl. සමනලයෝ *samanalayó*.

සමභාග, *Samabhága*, *a.* (සම same, භාග part) of the same size, measure, or weight.

සමම්, *Samam*, *ind.* with, together.

සමය, *Samaya*, *s.* multitude, assemblage; profit, gain; religious belief; obligation or observance, established moral or ceremonial custom; time; oath, affirmation; leisure, interval, opportunity; season, fit or proper time.

සමයන්, *Samayan*, *s.* proper season for the performance of the ceremonies of demon-worship, as morning twilight, midday, and evening twilight.

සමර්ථ, *Samarttha*, *a.* (සම් *sam* with අර්ථ *artha* to ask) strong, powerful; able, adequate to, capable; clever, skilful.

සමර්ථකම, *Samartthakama*, *s.* cleverness, ability.

සමර්ථයා, *Samartthayá*, *s.* clever man, skilful man, powerful man.

සමර, *Samara*, } *s.* name of Káma, the deity of
සමරු, *Samaru*, } love; recollection, from සමර *samara;* war, battle, contest, conflict.

සමරුන්, *Samarun*, *s.* thought, recollection; from සමර *samara;* also see සමාර *samára*.

සමල, *Samala*, *s.* (ස for සහ *saha* with මල dirt) fœces: *a.* dirty, muddy, filthy.

සමලංකෘත, *Samalaṇkrita*, *a.* (සම් *sam* and අලං *alaṇ* implying excellence, කෘත done) adorned, ornamented, decorated.

සමවත්, *Samawat*, Elu form of සමාපත්තිය *samápattiya*.

සමවතීර්ණ, *Samawatírṇa*, *a.* (සම් *sam* with අව *awa* below, තෘ *tri* to cross, ක්ත *kta* aff.) descended, gone down.

සමවදිනවා, *Sama-wadinawá*, *v.* to come, to arrive; to enter.

සමවන්, *Samawan*, *a.* blue.

සමවර්ති, *Samawartti*, *s.* (සම all, equal, වෘත *wṛita* to select, ඊ *í* aff.) name of Yama, ruler of Tartarus, and judge of the final destinies of men.

සමවාය, *Samawáya*, *s.* (සම් *sam* and අව *awa* before, අය *aya* to go) multitude, assemblage, collection, aggregate, quantity.

සමවෙනවා, *Samawenawá*, *v.* to become equal or similar.

සමස්, *Samas*, *s.* alarm, sudden fear; compound term, from සමාස *samása;* brevity, abridgment.

සමස්ත, *Samasta*, *a.* (සම් *sam* together, අස *asa* to throw, direct) all, whole, entire, complete; compound, compounded; abbreviated.

සමස්තලෝකය, *Samasta-lókaya*, *s.* whole world.

සමසම, *Samasama*, *a.* (සම repeated) same, even, equal.

සමහන්, *Samahan*, *s.* union, association, copulation.

සමහර, *Samahara*, *s.* part, portion, division; half moon.

සමහරවිට, *Samahara-viṭa*, *ad.* sometimes.

සමහරු, *Samaharu*, *s.* (සමහර *samahara* and උ *u* aff.) some persons.

සමා, *Samá*, *s.* forgiveness, pardon, from ක්ෂමා *kshamá;* time; the earth: *a.* even, equal, similar.

සමාකරණවා, *Samákaraṇawá*, *v.* to cause to forgive.

සමාගත, *Samágata*, *a.* (සම් *sam* and ආගත *ágata* come) arrived, approached, met, encountered; united, joined.

සමාගම්කාරයා, *Samágamkárayá*, *s.* member of any society, companion.

සමාගම් පවත්වනවා, *Samágam-pawatwanawá*, *v.* to associate.

සමාගම, *Samágama*, *s.* (සම් *sam* together, ආගම *ágama* coming) company, assembly, especially performing like duties; union, junction: pl. සමාගම් *samágam.*

සමාචාර, *Samáchára*, *s.* (සම් *sam* and ආචාර *áchára* salutation) respectful salutation, civility, politeness.

සමාඥා, *Samájñá*, *s.* (සම් *sam* and ආ *á* *prep.* ඥා to know) fame, reputation, [Colloq. කීර්තිය *kírttiya*].

සමාදන්කරණවා, *Samádan-karaṇawá*, *v.* (සමාදම *samádama* and කරණවා to do) to gather, to collect religious donations, etc.

සමාදන්වෙනවා, *Samádan-wenawá*, *v.* to participate.

සමාදම, *Samádama*, *s.* collecting, gathering, accumulation: pl. සමාදම් *samádam.*

සමාදර, *Samádara*, *s.* the earth, [Colloq. පොළව *poḷawa*].

සමාදාන, *Samádána*, *s.* peace, concord; receiving suitable donations: *a.* peaceful, tranquil.

සමාදානකරණවා, *Samádána-karaṇawá*, *v.* to promote peace, to reconcile.

සමාදානකාරයා, *Samádánakárayá*, *s.* a peaceable man.

සමාදානවෙනවා, *Samádána-wenawá*, *v.* to be reconciled.

සමාදිය, *Samádiya*, see සමාධි *samádhi.*

සමාධාන, *Samádhána*, *s.* (සම් *sam* intensive, ආ *á* before, ධා *dhá* to have or hold) religious meditation: see the next.

සමාධි, *Samádhi*, }
සමාධියෝග, *Samádhi-yóga*, } *s.* (සම් *sam* and ආ *á* *prep.* ධා *dhá* to have) deep and devout meditation, restraining the senses and confining the mind to contemplation on the true nature of existence, as the vanity and instability of all human good; religious vow or obligation; composing or reconciling differences.

සමාන, *Samána*, *s.* one of the five vital airs, that which is considered essential to digestion: *a.* like, similar, one, uniform, same.

සමානකරණවා, *Samánakaraṇawá*, *v.* to compare, to liken.

සමානකෙරීම, *Samánakeríma*, *s.* comparison.

සමානවෙනවා, *Samánawenawá*, *v.* to be or become equal.

සමාප්ත, *Samápta*, *a.* (සම් *sam* and ආප *ápa* to get, ක්ත *kta* aff.) finished, done, concluded, [Colloq. කම්මුතුවූ *kammutuwú*].

සමාප්ති, *Samápti*, *s.* end, completion, perfection.

සමාපත්තිය, *Samápattiya*, *s.* end, completion, perfection, conclusion, finish; deep and devout meditation.

සමාපන්න, *Samápanna*, *s.* (සම් *sam* with ආ *á* before, පද *pada* to go, ක්ත *kta* aff.) got, gained, obtained; finished, done, completed; effected, concluded, perfected, accomplished.

සමාර *Samára*, *s.* part, portion; end, conclusion.

සමාරාධිත, *Samárádhita*, *a.* (සම් *sam* and ආරාධිත *árádhita* requested) solicited, requested, beseeched; begun, commenced, undertaken.

සමාරෝහා, *Samároha*, *s.* date tree, *phœnix zeylanica*, [Colloq. ඉඳිගස *indi-gasa*].

සමාව, *Samáwa*, *s.* pardon, forgiveness.

සමාවෙනවා, *Samáwenawá*, *v.* to pardon, to forgive: pret. සමාවුනා *samáwuná*.

සමාස, *Samása*, *s.* (සම් *sam* together, අස *asa* to throw, to direct) contraction, abridgment, composition of words, formation of compound terms.

සමාසාදිත, *Samásádita*, *a.* (සම් *sam* with and ආ *á* before, සද *sada* to go, ඉත *ita* aff.) done, completed, effected, obtained, accomplished.

සමාහාර, *Samáhára*, *s.* (සම් *sam* with ආ *á* before, හර *hara* to take, convey) aggregation, collection, assemblage; contraction, abridgment.

සමාහිත, *Samáhita*, *a.* (සම් *sam* with ආ *á prep.* ධා *dhá* to have or hold) absorbed in meditation, absent, abstracted; finished, completed.

සමිත්, *Samit*, *s.* (සම් *sam* together, ඊ *í* to go) war, battle, [Colloq. යුද්ධය *yuddhaya* or සටන *saṭana*].

සමිත, *Samita*, *a.* (සම *sama* to tranquillize, ඉත *ita* aff.) pacified, appeased, calm, tranquil.

සමිති, *Samiti*, *s.* assembly, company; also see සමිත් *samit*.

සමිඳු, *Samidu*, *s.* master, owner, [Colloq. හිමියා *himiyá*].

සමිඳුරු, *Samiduru*, *s.* lord, master; Elu form of ස්වාමිදරුවෝ *swámidaruwó*.

සමිධ, *Samidha*, *s.* fuel; wood, grass, etc. employed as fuel.

සමිර, *Samira*, *s.* air, wind: see සමීර *samíra*,

සමීප, *Samípa*, *a.* (සම් *sam* together, ආප *ápa* water, ඊ *í sub.* for ආ *á*) near, contiguous, proximate, at hand.

සමීර, *Samíra*, *s.* (සම *sama* all sides, ඊර *íra* to go) air, wind, [Colloq. හුළඟ *hulaṅga*].

සමීරණ, *Samírana*, *s*, air, wind; speed, celerity, haste; journeyer, traveller; white variety of *calotropis gigantea*, [Colloquial: හෙළවරා *helawará*].

සමු, *Samu*, *s.* leave, permission.

සමුච්චය, *Samuchchaya*, *s.* (සම් *sam* together, උත් *ut* before, චි *chi* to collect) assemblage, collection; conjunction of words or sentences; the power of the article 'and' or 'also.'

සමුච්ඡින්න, *Samuchchhinna*, *a.* (සම් *sam* completely, උත් *ut* before, ඡිද *chhida* to cut, ක්ත *kta* aff.) destroyed, cut off, extirpated.

සමුච්ඡේද, *Samuchchhéda*, *s.* destroying, destruction.

සමුච්ඡ්‍රිත, *Samuchchhrita*, *a.* high, elevated, lofty.

සමුජ්වලිත, *Samujwalita*, *a.* (සම් *sam* intensitive, උත් *ut* and ජ්වලිත shining) splendid, brilliant, radiant, [Colloq. දීප්තිමත්වූ *díptimatwú*].

සමුට්ඨානය, *Samuṭṭhánaya*, *s.* (සම් *sam* and උද් *ud* before, ඨා *ṭhá* to stand) rising, getting up.

සමුත්ක්‍රම, *Samutkrama*, *s.* (සම් *sam* and උද් *ud* up, above, ක්‍රම to go) rise, ascent, going up, [Colloq. නැඟීම *neǵíma*].

සමුත්ථාන, *Samutthána*, *s.* (සම් *sam* intensitive, උද් *ud* up, ස්ථා *sthá* to be) rising, getting up; effort, industry; growth, increase; healing a wound or sore.

සමුත්ථිත, *Samutthita*, *a.* arisen, got up, increased; derived; cured.

සමුත්පන්න, *Samutpanna*, *a.* (සම් *sam* and උද් *ud* up, පද *pada* to go, ක්ත *kta* aff.) born, produced.

සමුත්පාද, *Samutpáda*, *s.* birth, production.

සමුද්ග, *Samudga*, } *s.* (සම් *sam* and උද් *ud* and
සමුද්ගක, *Samudgaka*, } ගම *gama* to go) casket, covered box.

සමුද්ගත, *Samudgata*, *a.* (සම් *sam* and උද් *ud* up, ගම *gama* to go, ක්ත *kta* aff.) risen, ascended.

සමුද්ගම, *Samudgama*, *s.* rising, ascent.

සමුද්ගය, *Samudgaya*, see සමුද්ග *samudga*.

සමුද්ධත, *Samuddhata*, *a.* proud, haughty, arrogant; ill-mannered, behaving ill or improperly; raised, drawn-up.

සමුද්ධරණ, *Samuddharaṇa*, *s.* (සම් *sam* and උද් *ud* before, ධර *dhara* to have) drawing up, raising, lifting, as water from a well; eradicating, pulling up by the roots.

සමුද්භව, *Samudbhawa*, *s.* (සම් *sam* and උද් *ud* up, භූ *bhú* to be) birth, production.

සමුද්‍ර, *Samudra*, *s.* sea, ocean, [Colloq. මූද *múda*].

සමුද්‍රකඵ, *Samudra-kapha*, *s.* (සමුද්‍ර the ocean, කඵ phlegm) cuttle fish.

සමුද්‍රග, *Samudraga*, *s.* (සමුද්‍ර sea, ග who goes) trader by sea; seaman: *a.* ocean-going, sea-faring.

සමුද්‍රඵේන, *Samudraphena*, *s.* (සමුද්‍ර and ඵේන froth or foam) cuttle fish bone; the froth or foam of the sea, [Colloq. මුහුදුපෙන *múdu-pena*].

සමුද්‍රය, *Samudraya*, see සමුද්‍ර *samudra*.

සමුද්‍රලවණ, *Samudra-lawaṇa*, *s.* (සමුද්‍ර sea, ලවණ salt) sea salt, [Colloq. මුහුදුලුණු *múdu-luṇu*].

සමුද්‍රාන්ත, *Samudránta*, *s.* (සමුද්‍ර *samudra* and අන්ත *anta* end, boundary) sea shore; nutmeg, *myristica fragrans*, [Colloq. සාදික්කා *sádikká*].

සමුද්‍රාන්තා, *Samudrántá*, *s.* cotton plant, *eriodendron anfractuosum*, [Colloq. කපුගස *kapu-gasa*];

twining plant, *tragia involucrata*, [Colloq. වැල් කහඹිලියා *wel-kahambiliyá*].

සමුද්‍රාරු, *Samudráru*, s. (සමුද්‍ර *samudra* sea, ඍ *ṛi* to go) shark, [Colloquial: මෝරා *mórá*]; large fabulous fish, perhaps intending the whale, hyperbolically described.

සමුද්‍රිය, *Samudriya*, a. marine, oceanic, maritime.

සමුදක්ත, *Samudakta*, a. (සම් *sam* intensitive, උද් *ud* up, අඤ්ච *añcha* to go, ක්ත *kta* aff.) drawn, raised, lifted or thrown up from a deep place.

සමුදය, *Samudaya*, s. (සම් *sam* and උද් *ud* up, ඉ *i* to go) birth, production; multitude, number, heap, quantity; ascent, rise; effort, exertion.

සමුදයසත්‍ය, *Samudaya-satya*, s. (සමුදය and සත්‍ය truth) according to Buddhism, one of the four truths connected with existence, viz. production.

සමුදාය, *Samudáya*, s. war, battle, [Colloq. යුද්ධය *yuddhaya*].

සමුදාව, *Samudáwa*, s. multitude, assemblage; host, army.

සමුදීම, *Samudíma*, s. (සමු and දීම giving) granting permission.

සමුදුර, *Samudura*, s. sea, ocean, [Colloq. මූද *múda*].

සමුදෙනවා, *Samu-denawá*, v. to grant permission.

සමුන්න, *Samunna*, a. (සම් *sam* and උන්දි *undi* to be wet or moist) wet, moist, moistened, [Colloq. තෙමුනු *temunu*].

සමුන්නත, *Samunnata*, a. (සම් *sam* and උද් *ud* before, නම *nama* to bow, ක්ත *kta* aff.) high, lofty, elevated, exalted, dignified; proud, arrogant.

සමුන්නද්ධ, *Samunnaddha*, a. conceited of learning; proud, arrogant; produced, born.

සමුප්පාද, *Samuppáda*, see සමුත්පාද *samutpáda*.

සමුපේත, *Samupéta*, a. (සම් *sam* with උප *upa* near, ඉ *i* to go ත aff.) possessed of, endowed with, inherent.

සමුසු, *Samusu*, a. (ස for සහ *saha* with මුසු mixed) compounded, blended, mingled.

සමූහ, *Samúha*, s. (සම් *sam* together, ඌහ *uha* to reason) assemblage, aggregate in general, heap, number, multitude, quantity.

සමෙත, *Sameta*, a. (සම් *sam* and ඉත *ita* gone) near; approximated, approached.

සමෘද්ධ, *Samṛiddha*, a. filled, completed; grown, increased, augmented; happy, prosperous, thriving.

සමෘද්ධිය, *Samṛiddhiya*, s. thriving, increase; prosperity, success; power, supremacy, sway.

සය, *Saya*, s. (ශී *si* to sleep) sleep, sleeping; bed, couch; hunger, drying up, waste: *ind.* number six, also, හය *haya*.

සයං, *Sayaṉ*, *ind.* own, self.

සයන, *Sayana*, } s. (ශී *si* to sleep) sleep, sleeping; reposing, reclining; bed, couch.
සයනය, *Sayanaya*,

සයනයකරණවා, *Sayanaya-karaṇawá*, v. to lie down, to sleep.

සයම්භූ, *Sayambhú*, s. (සයං *sayaṉ* self, භූ to be) name of Buddha: *a.* self-existing.

සයමුල්, *Saya-mul*, s. plant producing the chay root used as a red dye, Indian madder, *oldenlandia (or Hedyotis) umbellata (Rubiaceæ)*; also called සායන් මුල් *sáyan-mul*.

සයරෝගය, *Saya-rógaya*, s. consumption.

සයාස්ථ, *Sayástha*, s. (ශී *si* to sleep, ස්ථා *sthá* to stay or be) bed, couch, [Colloq. ඇඳ *ęnda*].

සයු, *Sayu*, s. (ස six, ඍතු season) the six seasons.

සයුර, *Sayura*, } s. sea, ocean, Elu form of සාගර *ságara*.
සයුරු, *Sayuru*,

සර්ග, *Sarga*, s. (සෘජ *sṛija* to quit, etc.) relinquishment, abandoning, letting loose; voiding, as excrement; chapter, book, section; creation.

සර්ගබන්ධ, *Sarga-bandha*, s. (සර්ග section, බන්ධ binding) principal or great poem, one comprising many cantos.

සර්ජ, *Sarja*, } s. hal tree, *vateria acuminata* [Colloq. හල් *hal*]; another tree, *pentaptera arjuna;* resinous exudation of the hal tree, [Colloq. දුම්මල *dummala*].
සර්ජක, *Sarjaka*,

සර්ජන, *Sarjana*, s. (සෘජ *sṛija* to abandon) abandoning, quitting; voiding as excrement; making, creating.

සර්ජරස, *Sarja-rasa*, s. (සර්ජ hal, රස juice) resin in general, or the resinous exudation of the hal tree, [Colloq. දුම්මල *dummala*].

සර්ජි, *Sarji*, } s. (සෘජ *sṛija* to abandon, ඉක *ika* aff.) natron, alkali, or the impure carbonate of soda, used as a soap for cleaning linen.
සර්ජික, *Sarjika*,

සර්ප, *Sarpa*, s. (සෘප *sṛipa* to go, to glide) snake, serpent; gentle or twining motion: *a.* serpentine, gliding, flowing, creeping.

සර්පකූට නයා, *Sarpakúṭa-nayá*, s. kind of venomous snake.

සර්පනාලි, *Sarpanáli*, s. plant, *amorphophallus campanulatus*, [Colloq. කිඩාරන් *kiḍáran*].

සර්පඵණජ, *Sarpa-phaṇaja*, *s.* (සර්ප and ඵණ hood, ජ born) snake-stone, gem or pearl said to resemble in form the berry of the *abrus precatorius*, [Colloq. ඔලිඳ *olinda*], and to be found in the head of the snake.

සර්පභුජ්, *Sarpabhuj*, *s.* (සර්ප and භුජ *bhuja* to eat) peacock; crane.

සර්පමණි, *Sarpa-maṇi*, see සර්පඵණජ *sarpa-phaṇaja*.

සර්පමාරී, *Sarpa-márí*, *s.* (සර්ප snake, මාරී what kills) garuḍa; ichneumon or mungoos, *hyrpestes griseus;* peacock, *pavo cristatus*, [Colloq. මොණරා *moṇará*]; plant, *solanum nigrum*, [Colloq. කළු කෑම්මෙරිය *kaḷu-kęmmériya*].

සර්පයා, *Sarpayá*, *s.* serpent.

සර්පරාජ, *Sarparája*, *s.* (සර්ප and රාජ king) cobra capella, [Colloq. නාගයා *nágayá*]; Vásuki sovereign of the serpent race.

සර්පහන්, *Sarpahan*, see සර්පමාරී *sarpa-márí*.

සර්පාක්‍ෂ, *Sarpáksha*, *s.* (සර්ප *sarpa* snake, අක්‍ෂි *akshi* eye) seed of the wild olive, *elæocarpus serratus*, [Colloq. වෙරළු *weraḷu*].

සර්පාරි, *Sarpári*, see සර්පමාරී *sarpamárí*.

සර්පි, *Sarpi*, *s.* (සර්ප *sarpa* to glide, ඉන් *in* aff.) butter; gliding: see සර්පින් *sarpin*.

සර්පිණී, *Sarpiṇí*, *s.* female serpent.

සර්පින්, *Sarpin*, *a.* (සෘප *sṛipa* to go, etc. ඉන් *in* aff.) going gently or tortuously, gliding, winding, creeping.

සර්පිස, *Sarpisa*, *s.* ghee, clarified butter, [Colloq. ගිතෙල් *gitel*].

සර්ප්පී, *Sarppí*, *s.* (සර්ප *sarpa* and ඊ *í* aff.) female of the snake: see සර්පින් *sarpin*.

සර්ප්පේෂ්ට, *Sarppéshṭa*, *s.* sandal-wood, [Colloq. හඳුන් *handun*].

සර්ම, *Sarma*, *s.* happiness, pleasure; sky, heaven.

සර්ව, *Sarwa*, *a.* all, whole, entire.

සර්වග්‍රන්ථිකා, *Sarwa-granthiká*, *s.* (සර්ව all, ග්‍රන්ථි knot, කා aff.) root of the long pepper plant, *piper longum*, [Colloq. තිප්පිලි මුල් *tippili-mul*].

සර්වජිත්, *Sarwa-jit*, *s.* (සර්ව and ජිත් who or what conquers) name of Buddha; the twenty-first year of the cycle: *a.* all-subduing, irresistible.

සර්වඥ, *Sarwajña*, *s.* (සර්ව all, ඥ who knows) name of Buddha; Śiva: *a.* omniscient, all-wise.

සර්වඥතා, *Sarwajñatá*, / **සර්වඥතාඥානය**, *Sarwajñatájñánaya*, } *s.* (සර්වඥ and තා abstract aff.) omniscience, as an attribute of Buddha.

සර්වඥශාසන, *Sarwajña-śásana*, *s.* (සර්වඥ and ශාසන reign) the whole system of Buddhism considered as a prevailing dispensation.

සර්වත්‍ර, *Sarwatra*, *ind.* (සර්ව all, ත්‍ර aff.) everywhere, in all places; always, at all times.

සර්වත්‍රග, *Sarwatraga*, / **සර්වත්‍රගාමිනී**, *Sarwatra-gáminí*, } *s.* (සර්වත්‍ර always, ගාමිනී going) air, wind, [Colloq. හුළඟ *hulanga*].

සර්වතස්, *Sarwatas*, *s.* (සර්ව all, තසි *tasi* aff.) every way, all round; wholly, entirely.

සර්වතාපන, *Sarwatápana*, *s.* (සර්ව and තාපන inflaming) lust, passion; Káma or the god of love.

සර්වතික්තා, *Sarwa-tiktá*, *s.* (සර්ව and තික්ත *tikta* bitter) creeper, snake gourd, *trichosanthes anguina*, [Colloq. පතෝල *patóla*].

සර්වතෝභද්‍ර, *Sarwató-bhadra*, *s.* (සර්වතස් *sarwatas* on every side, භද්‍ර auspicious) building of a square form with an entrance opposite each point of the compass; carriage of Vishṇu; form of military array; square mystical diagram; whimsical form of verse, so contrived that the same words and meanings occur whether the line be read backwards or forwards or in several other directions; margosa tree, *azadirachta indica*, [Colloq. කොහොඹ *kohomba*].

සර්වතෝභද්‍රා, *Sarwatóbhadrá*, *s.* timber tree, *gmelina arborea*, [Colloq. ඇත්දෙමට *ęt-demaṭa*].

සර්වථා, *Sarwathá*, *ind.* (සර්ව all, ථා aff.) always, by all means; assuredly, certainly.

සර්වදර්ශින්, *Sarwa-darṣin*, *s.* (සර්ව and දර්ශින් who sees) name of Buddha.

සර්වදරථ, *Sarwa-daratha*, *s.* (සර්ව and දරථ inflaming) passion, lust.

සර්වදා, *Sarwadá*, *ind.* (සර්ව all, දා aff. of time) always, at all times.

සර්වදුඃඛක්‍ෂය, *Sarwa-duḥkhakshaya*, *s.* (සර්ව and දුඃඛ pain, ක්‍ෂය destruction) final emancipation from existence, Nirwáṇa.

සර්වධාරී, *Sarwadhárí*, *s.* (සර්ව and ධර *dhara* to hold) the twenty-second year of the cycle.

සර්වභෞම, *Sarwa-bhuma*, *s.* (සර්ව and භෞම terrestrial) universal emperor, lord paramount of the whole world.

සර්වමය, *Sarwamaya*, *a.* (සර්ව and මය aff.) general, universal, comprehending.

සර්වරස, *Sarwa-rasa*, *s.* (සර්ව and රස taste) resin, exudation of the pine or hal tree.

සර්වලා, *Sarwalá*, *s.* (සර්ව all, ලූ *lú* to cut) iron crow.

සර්වලෝකනාථ, *Sarwa-lókanátha*, *s.* (සර්ව and ලෝක world, නාථ lord) name of Buddha.

සර්සංහාරක, *Sarwa-sanhâraka*, s. (සර් all, සම් *sam* and හාර *hára* what takes) compounded of all perfumes, precious oil.

සර්සිද්ධි, *Sarwa-siddhi*, s. (සර් and සිද්ධි completion) bael tree, *ægle marmelos*, [Colloq. බෙලි *beli*].

සර්වාඞ්ගය, *Sarwáńgaya*, s. (සර් *sarwa* all, අඞ්ග *ańga* limb) whole body.

සර්වානුභූති, *Sarwánubhúti*, s. bind-weed, *ipomœa turpethum*, [Colloq. ත්‍රස්තාවාලු *trastawálu*].

සර්වාර්තක, *Sarwártaka*, s. (සර් *sarwa* and අර්ථ *arttha* wealth, ක aff.) fabulous gem which bestows every thing desired by its possessor.

සර්වාර්ථසිද්ධ, *Sarwártha-siddha*, s. (සර් *sarwa* and අර්ථ *artha* meaning, wealth, etc. සිද්ධ who completes) name of Buddha.

සර්වාවසර, *Sarwáwasara*, s. (සර් *sarwa* and අවසර *awasara* cessation) midnight, [Colloq. මද්දුම රෑ *maddima-ré*].

සර්වේශ්වර, *Sarwéṣwara*, s. (සර් *sarwa* and ඊශ්වර *íṣwara* lord) name of Ṣiva.

සර්වෝපධි, *Sarwópadhi*, s. (සර් *sarwa* all, උප *upa* near, ධා *dhá* to have) all the incidents or circumstances of existence, as passion, ignorance, etc.

සර්ෂප, *Sarshapa*, s. variety of mustard, *sinapis dichotoma*.

සර්ෂප තෛල, *Sarshapa-taila*, s. (සර්ෂප and තෛල oil) mustard oil, [Colloq. අබතෙල් *aba-tel*].

සර, *Sara*, s. lake, pool, [Colloq. පොකුණ *pokuṇa* or විල *vila*]; arrow, [Colloq. ඊගහ *í-gaha*]; water, [Colloq. වතුර *watura*]; sort of reed or grass, *saccharum sara*; lotus or its edible root, *nelumbium speciosum*; pith, sap, from සාර *sára*; woman; going, proceeding.

සරක්, *Sarak*, s. cattle, oxen in general.

සරක්කු, *Sarakku*, s. drug, medicament; camp, intrenchment.

සරක, *Saraka*, s. spirituous liquor; drinking vessel.

සරකා, *Saraká*, see හරකා *haraká*.

සරග, *Saraga*, s. deer, [Colloq. මුවා *muwá*].

සරගටි, *Saragaṭi*, s. war, conflict, battle, [Colloq. යුද්ධය *yuddhaya* or සටන *saṭana*].

සරඞ්ග, *Saranga*, s. elephant, [Colloq. ඇතා *ętá*]; deer, [Colloq. මුවා *muwá*]; species of cuckoo, *cuculus passerinus*, [Colloq. කොහා *kohá*], or hornbill, *tockus gingalensis*, [Colloq. කෑදැත්තා *kęndattá*]; tree; parasol; flamingo, *phœnicopterus roseus*: see සාරඞ්ග *sáranga*.

සරජස්, *Sarajas*, s. (ස for සහ *saha* with රජස් menses) woman during menstruation.

සරට, *Saraṭa*, } s. lizard, [Colloq. හූනා *húná*];
සරටා, *Saraṭá*, } chameleon, [Colloq. කටුස්සා *kaṭussá*]; guana, [Colloq. තලගොයා *talagoyá*]; safflower, plant.

සරටි, *Saraṭi*, s. (සෘ *sṛi* to go, අටි *aṭi* aff.) elephant keeper, [Colloq. ඇත්ගොව්වා *ętgowwá*]; air, wind; cloud: see සරට *saraṭa*.

සරණ්ඩ, *Saraṇḍa*, s. bird in general; rogue, cheat; chameleon; libertine, lecher.

සරණ, *Saraṇa*, s. (සර *sara* to go) preservation, protection, defence; that which protects or preserves; foot; going, proceeding; village, town.

සරණං, *Saraṇaṅ*, s. name of Nirwáṇa.

සරණගත, *Saraṇagata*, a. gone for refuge.

සරණපාවාගන්නවා, *Saraṇa-páwágannawá*, v. to marry.

සරණපාවාදෙනවා, *Saraṇa-páwádenawá*, v. to give in marriage.

සරණයනවා, *Saraṇa-yanawá*, v. to contract marriage, to take refuge in, to trust.

සරණවි, *Saraṇavi*, s. (සරණ foot, අවි *avi* weapon) cock, [Colloq. කුකුළා *kukuḷá*].

සරණවෙනවා, *Saraṇawenawá*, v. to help, to assist, to marry.

සරණවැල, *Saraṇa-węla*, s. (සරණ and වැල ring) rings for the ankles.

සරණසීලය, *Saraṇa-sílaya*, s. (සරණ protection, සීල *síla* observance) believing in the three gems for protection, viz. Buddha, his doctrines, and priesthood.

සරණළු, *Saraṇaḷu*, s. latter part of the day, evening.

සරණා, *Saraṇá*, s. tree, *celastrus emarginatus*, [Colloq. කටුපිල *kaṭupila*]; also, *pæderia fetida*.

සරණි, *Saraṇi*, s. (සර to go, අණි *aṇi* aff.) road, path, way, [Colloq. මග *maga*].

සරත්, *Sarat*, s. riches, wealth, property; thread: see සරු *saru*.

සරත් කාලය, *Sarat-kálaya*, s. autumn, sultry season.

සරද, *Sarada*, s. autumn or the sultry season.

සරදම්කරණවා, *Saradam-karaṇawá*, v. to mock.

සරදම, *Saradama*, s. joke, jest: pl. සරදම් *saradam*.

සරදා, *Saradá*, s. year; sultry season.

සරදුන්, *Saradun*, s. bow, [Colloq. දුන්න *dunna*].

සරධි, *Saradhi*, s. (සර arrow, ධි what has) quiver, [Colloq. හීකොපුව *hí-kopuwa*].

සරබ, *Saraba*, see ශරභ *ṣarabha*.

සරබූ, *Sarabú*, *s.* sort of lizard.

සරභූ, *Sarabhú*, *s.* (සර the grass, භූ born) name of Kártikéya, or Kataragama-deviyó who was reared in a thicket of that grass.

සරම්ප ලෙඩ, *Sarampa-leḍa*, *s.* measles.

සරමින්, *Saramin*, *part.* going.

සරය, *Saraya*, *s.* coagulum of curd or milk: see සර *sara*.

සරයොන්, *Sarayon*, *s.* (සර the grass, යොන් place of production) Kártikéya: see සරභූ *sarabhú*.

සරරිපු, *Sara-ripu*, *s.* enemy, adversary, [Colloq. සතුරා *saturá*], opponent, [Colloq. විරුද්ධකාරයා *viruddhakárayá*]

සරල, *Sarala*, *s.* tree, species of pine, *pinus longifolia;* hare, [Colloq. හාවා *háwá*]: *a.* honest, upright, sincere.

සරලද්‍රුම, *Sarala-druma*, *s.* (සරල and ද්‍රුම tree) species of pine, *pinus longifolia*.

සරලා, *Saralá*, *s.* bind-weed, *ipomœa turpethum*, [Colloq. ත්‍රස්තාවැලු *trastawálu*].

සරස්, *Saras*, *s.* large pond or lake; water: see සරස *sarasa*.

සරස්වතී, *Saraswatí*, *s.* (ස for සහ *saha* with රස *rasa* taste, flavour, වත් *wat* aff.) wife of Brahmá, the goddess of speech and the arts, etc.; speech, the faculty or its exercise; river, the Sarsuti which rises in the mountains on the North East of the province of Delhi.

සරස්වා, *Saraṣwá*, *s.* (සරස් water, වාත් *wát* *poss.* aff.) ocean, [Colloq. මූද *múda*].

සරස, *Sarasa*, *s.* pool, pond, [Colloq. පොකුණ *pokuṇa* or විල *vila*]: *a.* horizontal, across, crosswise; savoury, tasty, sapid.

සරසනවා, *Sarasanawá*, *v.* to decorate, to ornament: pret. සැරසුවා *sẹrasuwá*.

සරසවි, *Sarasavi*, *s.* speech, either the faculty or its exercise: see සරස්වතී *saraswatí*.

සරසවියකල්, *Sarasaviyakal*, *s.* name of Brahmá, [Colloq. මහබ්‍රහ්මයා *maha-brahmayá*].

සරසා, *Sarasá*, *s.* bee, [Colloquial: මීමැස්සා *mímẹssá*].

සරසික, *Sarasika*, *s.* (සරස *sarasa* pond, ඉක *ika* aff.) Indian crane.

සරසිජ, *Sarasija*, *s.* (සරසි in a pond, ජ born) fish; lotus.

සරසි, *Sarasí*, *s.* pond, pool, [Colloq. පොකුණ *pokuṇa* or විල *vila*].

සරසිරුහ, *Sarasíruha*, *s.* (සරසි and රුහ what grows) lotus, *nelumbium speciosum*, [Colloq. නෙළුම් *neḷum*].

සරසුන්, *Sarasun*, *s.* (සර lotus, අසුන් *asun* seat) name of Brahma; bow; ornamenting, adorning, accoutering.

සරහනවා, *Sarahanawa*, *v.* to decorate, to ornament, to adorn, to accoutre: pret. සැරහුවා *sẹrahuwá*.

සරළු, *Saraḷu*, *s.* little, small quantity, as a handful, etc. [Colloq. ටිකක් *ṭikak*].

සරා, *Sará*, *s.* lotus, [Colloq. නෙළුම් *neḷum*]; pond, lake, [Colloq. විල *vila* or කලපුව *kalapuwa*]; year, [Colloq. අවුරුද්ද *awurudda*]; name of Káma the Indian Cupid; autumn, sultry season, from සරද *sarada*: *a.* full, complete, perfect.

සරාකල්, *Sarákal*, *s.* (සරා and කල් time) autumn.

සරාඝාත, *Sarágháta*, *s.* (සර *sara* arrow, ආඝාත *ágháta* striking) shooting with a bow.

සරාජික, *Sarájika*, *a.* (ස for සහ *saha* with රාජ *rája* to desire, to shine, ඉක *ika* aff.) having the passions unsubdued, sensual, etc.; shining, bright, resplendent.

සරාන, *Sarána*, *s.* quiver?

සරාභ්‍යාස, *Sarábhyása*, *s.* (සර *sara* arrow, අභ්‍යාස *abhyása* exercise) archery, practice with the bow and arrow.

සරාරෝප, *Sarárópa*, *s.* (සර *sara* and ආරෝප *árópa* receptacle) bow, [Colloq. දුන්න *dunna*].

සරාව, *Saráwa*, *s.* lid, cover; shallow cup or vessel.

සරාවතී, *Saráwati*, see සරස්වතී *saraswatí*.

සරාසඳ, *Sará-saṇda*, *s.* (සරා autumn, සඳ moon) autumnal moon.

සරාසන, *Sarásana*, *s.* (සර *sara* arrow, අස *asa* to throw) bow, [Colloq. දුන්න *dunna*].

සරාසය, *Sarásaya*, *s.* kind of coloured cloth worn chiefly by a Chetty woman.

සරි, *Sari*, *s.* resemblance, likeness, similarity; procuring, obtaining: *a.* right, accurate, correct, similar, proper, fit; just, equitable.

සරිත්, *Sarit*, *s.* (සෘ *sṛi* to go, ඉති *iti* aff.) river in general; woman, wife.

සරිත්පති, *Saritpati*, *s.* (සරිත් river, පති lord) ocean, [Colloq. මුහුද *muhuda*].

සරිමන්, *Sariman*, *s.* bearing, bringing forth; going, proceeding.

සරිය, *Sariya*, *s.* extent, capacity.

සරිල, *Sarila*, *s.* water; also, සලිල *salila*, [Colloq. වතුර *watura*].

සරිලනවා, *Sarilanawá*, *v.* to find, to get, to meet: pret. සරිලෑවා *sarilẹwá*.

සරිලෑම, *Sarilẹma*, *s.* procuring, getting, acquiring, encountering, meeting.

සරිසප, *Sarisapa*, *s.* mustard; snake, from සරිසෘප *sarisṛipa*.

සරිසෘප, *Sarisṛipa*, *s.* (සෘප *sṛipa* to go reiterative form) snake, [Colloq. සර්පයා *sarpayá*].

සරීර, *Saríra*, *s.* body.

සරීරජ, *Sariraja*, *s.* (සරීර body, ජ born) sickness, disease, son, offspring; Káma, the deity of love.

සරීරාවරණ, *Sarírâwaraṇa*, *s.* (සරීර *saríra* and ආවරණ *áwaraṇa* enclosing) skin, [Colloq. හම *hama*].

සරු, *Saru*, *s.* hilt of a sword: *a.* prosperous, flourishing; bold, fearless; thin, small, fine, minute.

සරුංගලේ, *Saruṇgalé*, *s.* paper kite.

සරුටි, *Saruṭi*, *s.* elephant keeper, [Colloq. ඇත් ගොව්වා *ẹtgowwá*].

සරුප්, *Sarup*, *a.* proper, fit, suitable, right, just.

සරුපය, *Sarupaya*, *s.* word: pl. සරුප *sarupa*.

සරුසාර, *Sarusára*, *s.* fertility, productiveness.

සරූප, *Sarúpa*, *s.* (ස for සමාන *samána* like, රූප form) natural state or condition, nature: *a.* like, resembling.

සරෙයන්, *Sareyan*, *s.* Sergeant.

සරොජ, *Saroja*, *s.* (සරස් *saras* pond, ජ produced) lotus, [Colloq. නෙළුම් *neḷum*]; fish.

සරොජී, *Sarojí*, *s.* (සරොජ *saroja* lotus, ඉනී *iní* aff.) name of Brahmá.

සරොම, *Saroma*, *s.* native dress made of cloth the ends of which are joined together: pl. සරොම් *sarom*.

සරෝරුහ, *Saróruha*, *s.* (සරස් *saras* pond, රුහ produced) lotus, *nelumbium speciosum*, [Colloq. නෙළුම් *neḷum*].

සල්, *Sal*, *s.* hal tree, *vateria acuminata;* earthen vessel, chatty; mountain, from සෛල *saila;* market, fair, bazaar; time; riches, wealth, property.

සල්ගස, *Sal-gasa*, *s.* hal tree, *vateria acuminata*.

සල්පිල, *Salpila*, *s.* shop, elevated bank or terrace in front of a house used as such, bazaar.

සල්ල, *Salla*. *s.* dart, javelin; peg, pin; porcupine's quill; hal tree, *vateria acuminata*.

සල්ලක්ඛණ, *Sallakkhaṇa*, see සලක්ෂණ *salakshaṇa*.

සල්ලකී, *Sallakí*, *s.* (සල *sala* to go) porcupine, *hystrix leucurus*, [Colloq. ඉත්තෑවා *ittẹwá*]; gum olibanum tree, *boswellia thurifera*.

සල්ලය, *Sallaya*, see සල්ල *salla*.

සල්ලවිධිය, *Salla-vidhiya*, *s.* (සල්ල dart, විධි *vidhi* rule) surgery, practice of surgery.

සල්ලාගාර, *Sallágára*, *s.* (සල්ල *salla* and අගාර *agára* house) porcupine, [Colloq. ඉත්තෑවා *ittẹwá*].

සල්ලාප, *Sallápa*, *s.* (ස for සහ *saha* with ලප *lapa* to speak) conversation, discourse.

සල්ලාල, *Sallála*, *a.* sensual, lecherous, lustful.

සල්ලාලකම, *Sallálakama*, *s.* lechery.

සල්ලාලයා, *Sallálayá*, *s.* lecher, libertine, catamite: pl. සල්ලාලයෝ *sallálayó*.

සල්ලිපෙතිමල්, *Sallipeti-mal*, *s.* plant, not ascertained.

සල්ලිය, *Salliya*, *s.* money in general; small coin, ¼ of a pice: pl. සල්ලි *salli*.

සල්ලෙඛ, *Sallekha*, *s.* (ස for සහ *saha* with ලිඛ *likha* to write) making thin, reducing: *a.* easy, facile.

සල්ලේඛනය, *Sallékhanaya*, *s.* (ස for සහ *saha* with ලිඛ *likha* to write) writing, scripture.

සල්ව, *Salwa*, *s.* silk cotton tree: *a.* greedy, ravenous, rapacious.

සල, *Sala*, *s.* house or hall; rock, a rocky mountain, place for devotees; hal tree, *vateria acuminata;* pebble; hare; delay, loitering; chatty, earthen vessel; shaking, moving; quill of a porcupine; arrow; dart, spear.

සලක්ෂණ, *Salakshaṇa*, *s.* (ස for සහ *saha* with ලක්ෂණ mark) regarding, considering; distinct, possessing marks or tokens.

සලකණවා, *Salakaṇawá*, *v.* (ස for සහ with ලක mark, ණවා *verb.* aff.) to regard, to consider, to notice, to respect, to observe: pret. සැලකුවා *sẹlakuwá*.

සලකුණ, *Salakuṇa*, } *s.* mark, sign, token, char-
සලකුණු, *Salakuṇu*, } acteristic.

සලකුණුකරණවා, *Salakuṇukaraṇawá*, *v.* to mark, to sign.

සලකුළු, *Salakuḷu*, *s.* theft, [Colloq. සොරකම *sorakama*].

සලඩඹු, *Saladambu*, *s.* hindrance, impediment, [Colloq. වැලහීම *wẹlahíma*].

සලදල, *Saladala*, *s.* (සල shaking, දල leaf) the sacred bó-tree, *ficus religiosa*, [Colloq. බෝගහ *bó-gaha*].

සලඳ *Salanda*, *s.* hindrance, obstacle, impediment.

සලන්පත, *Salanpata*, *s.* fan: pl. සලන්පත් *salanpat*.

සලනවා, *Salanawá*, *v.* to move, to stir, to shake as a sieve, to riddle, to throw on the ground: pret. සැළුවා *seluwá*.

සලපත්, *Salapat*, *s.* (සල moving, පත් leaf) bó-tree, *ficus religiosa*, [Colloq. බෝගහ *bó-gaha*]; priest's fan, [Colloq. වටාපත *watápata*].

සලපෝරුව, *Sala-póruwa*, *s.* moving board or plank.

සලඹ, *Salamba*, *s.* rings or bracelets of a dancer; see the next.

සලභ, *Salabha*, *s.* (සල to go, අභ *abha* aff.) grass-hopper, locust, [Colloq. පොලඟැටියා *polangetiyá*].

සලස්න, *Salasna*, *s.* (සල් *sal* and අස්න *asna* seat) throne of Indra on the summit of Méru; stone seat or bench.

සලස්වනවා, *Salaswanawá*, *v.* to cause, to make: pret. සැලැස්සුවා *selessuwá*.

සලසනවා, *Salasanawá*, *v.* to cause, to make, to do: pret. සැලසුවා *selasuwá*.

සලා, *Salá*, *s.* stones, pebbles; eddy, whirlpool.

සලාකා, *Saláká*, *s.* (සල *sala* to go, අක *áka* aff.) javelin, dart; arrow; porcupine; fibrous stick used as a brush or pencil; rib of an umbrella, etc.; rod, peg, pin, probe, etc. slip of bamboo.

සලාකාදානය, *Saláká-dánaya*, *s.* (සලාකා bit of wood, දාන *dána* alms) bestowing religious donations on the priests, of cloth, rice, etc. by lot, in which the names written on bits of wood are deposited in a vessel, and the person whose name is first drawn out receives the donation.

සලාටු, *Salátu*, *a.* unripe, immature, [Colloq. අමු *amu*, නොපැසුණු *nopesunu*], moist as fruit.

සලාද, *Saláda*, *s.* salad. (Dutch.)

සලාව, *Saláwa*, *s.* eddy, whirlpool.

සලිමලි, *Salimali*, *s.* silk cotton tree, *eriodendron anfractuosum*, [Colloq. ඉඹුල් *imbul*].

සලිල, *Salila*, *s.* (සල *sala* to go, ඉල *ila* aff.) water, [Colloq. වතුර *watura*]: *a.* cold, frigid.

සලිල කුන්තල, *Salila-kuntala*, *s.* (සලිල and කුන්තල hair) aquatic plant, *vallisneria octandra*.

සලිලජ, *Salilaja*, *s.* (සලිල and ජ born) lotus; fish.

සලිලධාර, *Salila-dhára*, *s.* (සලිල water, ධාර what has) sea, ocean, [Colloq. මූද *múda*].

සලෙලි, *Saleli*, *s.* young woman.

සලෙලු, *Salelu*, *s.* youth, young man.

සලෝභී, *Salóbhí*, *s.* (ස for සහ *saha* with ලෝභ *lóbha* covetousness) ඉන් *in* aff.) miser, niggard.

සව්, *Saw*, *s.* Elu form of සර්ව *sarwa*, all; scholar, from ශ්‍රාවක *sráwaka*.

සව්නේ, *Sawné*, *s.* every thing that can be known.

සව්නේදත්, *Sawnédat*, *a.* one acquainted with every thing that can be known, or is fit to be known.

සව්ම, *Sawma*, *s.* planet Mercury, [Colloq. බුදහු *budahu*].

සව්‍ය, *Sawya*, *a.* left, left hand; south; southern; reverse, contrary, backward.

සව්වා, *Sawwá*, *s.* scholar, disciple, from ශ්‍රාවක *sráwaka*, [Colloq. ගෝලයා *góلayá*].

සව්සත, *Sawsata*, *s.* every living being or every science.

සව්සිරි, *Sawsiri*, *s.* all prosperity.

සව, *Sawa*, *s.* dead body, corpse, [Colloq. මළකඳ *malakanda*].

සවග, *Sawaga*, *s.* (ස six, වග class) schism in Buddhism so called, which originated with six refractory priests in the days of Buddha.

සවත්, *Sawat*, } *s.* (ස six, වත් face) name of
සවත, *Sawata*, } Kártikéya or Kataragama deviyó, the Indian god of war: see ෂඩානන *shadánana*.

සවතිඳු, *Sawatindu*, *s.* (සවත *sawata* and ඉඳු *indu* lord) Kataragama-deviyó, leader of the celestial hosts.

සවන්, *Sawan*, see සවන *sawana*.

සවන්දීම, *Sawandíma*, *s.* giving ear, listening.

සවන, *Sawana*, } *s.* (සව all, න who knows)
සවනිය, *Sawaniya*, } name of Buddha, sacrifice, any ceremony in which offerings and oblations are presented; the ear; Elu form of සර්වඥ *sarwajña*.

සවනිය, *Sawaniya*, *a.* what is fit or possible to be heard, audible: see the last.

සවර්ණ, *Sawarna*, *a.* (ස for සමාන *samána* like, වර්ණ colour, tribe) like, resembling; of the same tribe, class, or kind, homogeneous.

සවර, *Sawara*, *s.* barbarian: see සබර *sabara*; water.

සවල, *Sawala*, see සබල *Sabala*.

සවස, *Sawasa*, *s.* after part of the day, afternoon, evening.

සවසාන, *Sawasána*, *s.* (සව corpse, සාන repose) cemetery, [Colloq. මිනිපිට්ටනිය *mini-pittaniya*].

සවි, *Savi*, *s.* strength, force, muscular power; prowess, intrepidity.

සවිකරණවා, *Savikaranawá*, *v.* to fasten, to make strong.

සවිචාර, *Savichára*, *s.* (ස for සහ *saha* with විචාර enquiring) investigation, enquiry; deliberation, reflection.

සවිඥානක, *Savijñánaka*, *a.* (ස for සහ *saha* with විඥාන sensation, ක aff.) sentient, possessing the powers of feeling; animate.

සවිතෘ, *Savitṛi*, *s.* sun.

සවිතර්ක, *Savitarka*, *a.* (ස for සහ with විතර්ක reasoning) rational, possessing or employing the reasoning faculty.

සවිතු, *Savitu*, *s.* sun.

සවිධ, *Savidha*, *a.* (ස for සමාන *samána* same, විධ manner, sort) near, proximate; of the same kind, homogeneous.

සවින්දව, *Savindawa*, *s.* rock salt: corrupt form of සෛන්ධව *saindhawa.*

සවින්දවයා, *Savindawayá*, *s.* mule, for සෛන්ධවයා *saindhawayá*: a Sindh horse (a breed much prized).

සවිය, *Saviya*, *s.* strength: see සවි *savi.*

සවිවැනි, *Sawiweni*, *s.* last day of a Kalpa.

සවිෂා, *Savishá*, see අතිවිඩයන් *atiriḍayan.*

සවුකෙන්ද, *Sawukenda*, *s.* plant, *kæmpferia rotunda*, also called යවකෙන්ද *yawakenda.*

සවුඩොදොල්, *Sawudodol*, *s.* kind of sweet meat.

සවුහාල්, *Sauhál*, *s.* sago, *sagus lævis.*

සවෙනි, *Saweni*, *ind.* sixth, sixthly.

සවැනි, *Ṣaweni*, *s.* name of Buddha=සර්වඥ *sarwajña*, all-wise.

සශ්‍රීක, *Sasríka*, *a.* (ස for සහ *saha* with ශ්‍රී plenty, ක aff.) prosperous, flourishing, thriving.

සශ්‍රීකකම, *Sasríkakama*, *s.* flourishing condition, prosperity, thriving.

සස්, *Sas*, Elu form of ශස්‍ය *ṣasya.*

සස්කර, *Saskara*, *s.* (සස් harvest, කර who does) husbandman, [Colloq. ගොවියා *goviyá*].

සසැති, *Sasti*, *s.* side-look, leer.

සස්න, *Sasna*, see සසුන් *sasun.*

සස්වදන්, *Sas-wadan*, *s.* (සස් truth, වදන් speech) Tápasa or religious ascetic.

සස්වාමික, *Saswámika*, *a.* (සහ *saha* with ස්වාමි lord, ක aff.) having an owner or husband, married.

සස, *Sasa*, *s.* hare, [Colloq. හාවා *háwá*], or rabbit; truth, verity, from සත්‍ය *satya;* carpenter, wheelwright; tree, *symplocos racemosa;* spots on the moon supposed to resemble a hare.

සසංක, *Sasanka*, *s.* (සස *sasa* hare, අංක *anka* mark) moon, [Colloq. හඳ *haṉda*].

සසක්, *Sasak*, *s.* sandal wood, *santalum album*, [Colloq. හඳුන් *haṉdun*]; moon, [Colloq. හඳ *haṉda*].

සසඟ, *Sasaṉga*, *s.* union, association, conjunction: *a.* associated.

සසදර, *Sasadara*, *s.* (සස hare, දර what has) moon, [Colloq. හඳ *haṉda*], the spots on her disc having a fancied resemblance to a hare.

සසන, *Sasana*, *s.* immolation, offering living victims.

සසර, *Sasara*, *s.* the world, habitation of mortals, mundane existence as opposed to Nirwáṇa or annihilation.

සසල්, *Sasal*, *s.* shaking, motion; the eye.

සසල, *Sasala*, *s.* thunder, [Colloq. අහස ගෙරවිම *ahasa-geravíma*]; rumbling of the clouds; shaking, moving.

සසලදල, *Sasaladala*, *s.* (සසල shaking, දල leaf) bó-tree, *ficus religiosa*, [Colloq. බෝගහ *bó-gaha*].

සසලේ, *Sasalé*, *s.* sandal wood, *santalum album*, [Colloq. හඳුන් *haṉdun*]; moon, [Colloq. හඳ *haṉda*].

සසවදන්, *Sasa-wadan*, *s.* (සස truth, වදන් speech) devotee, religious ascetic; veracity, probity.

සසාදන, *Sasádana*, *s.* (සස *sasa* and අදන *adana* what eats) hawk, falcon.

සසි, *Sasi*, *s.* (සස *sasa* and ඉනි *ini* aff.) moon.

සසිරිකය, *Sasirikaya*, *s.* world or residence of the gods, [Colloq. දෙව්ලොව *dewlowa*].

සසු, *Sasu*, *s.* corn, grain; from ශස්‍ය *ṣasya.*

සසුන්, *Sasun*, *s.* governing, ruling, commanding: see ශාසන *ṣásana.*

සහ, *Saha*, *s.* fire; friend: *a.* patient, enduring, suffering: *ind.* particle and prefix signifying union, association, with, together.

සහකාර, *Sahakára*, *s.* fragrant sort of mango, [Colloq. මී අඹ *mi-aṃba*]: *a.* working or living together, associating.

සහකාරක, *Sahakáraka*, *a.* (සහ with කර *kara* to do, ක aff.) assisting, working together.

සහකාරයා, *Sahakárayá*, *s.* companion, friend.

සහගත, *Sahagata*, *s.* (සහ with ගත gone) accompanying, going or associating with.

සහගුම්, *Sahagum*, *s.* (සහ with ගුම් thunder) roaring, thundering.

සහචර, *Sahachara*, *s.* (සහ with චර to go) companion, contemporary: *a.* accompanying, associating with.

සහජ, *Sahaja*, *s.* (සහ with ජ born) brother of whole blood, [Colloq. සහෝදරයා *sahódarayá*]: *a.* co-existent; cognate; hereditary.

සහජාත, *Sahajáta*, *s.* cognate, born together.

සහද, *Sahada*, *s.* one born in the same womb; brother.

සහදම්, *Sahadam*, *s.* wife faithful to her marriage vow.

සහදෙවා, *Sahadewá*, } *s.* (සහ with දෙව *dewa*
සහදෙවි, *Sahadeví*, } who sports) plant, species of *sida*, [Colloq. බැවිල *bęvila*]; twining shrub, *ichnocarpus frutescens*, [Colloq. කිරිවැල් *kiri-węl*]: see also ගොඩමානිල් *goḍa-mánil*.

සහන, *Sahana*, *s.* (සහ to bear) bearing, enduring: *a.* patient.

සහනයකරණවා, *Sahanaya-karaṇawá*, *v.* to comfort, to console, to encourage under affliction.

සහනයවෙනවා, *Sahanaya-wenawá*, *v.* to be comforted.

සහපිරිවර, *Saha-piriwara*, *a.* (සහ with පිරිවර attendants) attended, accompanied.

සහභාවි, *Sahabhávi*, *s.* (සහ with භාව *bháwa* quality, ඉ *i* aff.) friend, companion, adherent or partizan.

සහම්පති, *Sahampati*, *s.* epithet of Mahá Brahmá.

සහමුලින්, *Sahamulin*, *ad.* entirely, fundamentally.

සහය, *Sahaya*, *s.* help, favour, assistance, [Colloq. උපකාරය *upakáraya*].

සහයුරු, *Sahayuru*, *s.* mango, [Colloq. මී අඹ *mí-am̱ba*]; Elu form of සහකාර *sahakára*.

සහල්, *Sahal*, *s*, rice in general, from සාලි *sáli*, [Colloq. හාල් *hál*].

සහල්ල, *Sahalla*, *s.* cupboard, basket suspended from the ends of a pingo-load.

සහල, *Sahala*, *s.* friend, companion, adherent, [Colloq. මිත්‍රයා *mitrayá*].

සහලඟුරු, *Sahalan̲guru*, *s.* burning charcoal, embers.

සහස්, *Sahas*, *s.* strength, power; thousand, from සහස්‍ර *sahsra*: *ad.* quickly, rashly, [Colloq. ඉක්මණට *ikmaṇaṭa*].

සහස්දත්, *Sahasdat*, *s.* (සහස් and දත් tooth) sort of sheat fish.

සහස්නෙත්, *Sahasnet*, *s.* name of Indra: see සහස්‍රාක්‍ෂ *sahasráksha*.

සහස්පත්, *Sahaspat*, *s.* (සහස් and පත් leaf) lotus: Elu form of සහස්‍රපත්‍ර *sahasra-patra*.

සහස්‍ය, *Sahasya*, *s.* month Pausha, (December—January), [Colloq. දුරුත්ත *durutta*].

සහස්රෑස්, *Sahasręs*, *s.* (සහස් and රෑස් ray) sun, [Colloq. ඉර *ira*].

සහස්‍ර, *Sahasra*, *s.* thousand, [Colloq. දාහ *dáha*].

සහස්‍ර කිරණ, *Sahasra-kiraṇa*, *s.* (සහස්‍ර and කිරණ ray) sun, [Colloq. ඉර *ira*].

සහස්‍ර දංෂ්ට්‍ර, *Sahasra-danshṭra*, *s.* (සහස්‍ර and දංෂ්ට්‍ර tooth) sort of sheat fish, *silurus pelorius*.

සහස්‍ර නේත්‍ර, *Sahasra-nétra*, see සහස්‍රාක්‍ෂ *sahasráksha*.

සහස්‍ර පත්‍ර, *Sahasra-patra*, *s.* (සහස්‍ර and පත්‍ර leaf) lotus, *nelumbium speciosum*, [Colloq. නෙළුම් *neḷum*].

සහස්‍රපාක, *Sahasrapáka*, *s.* boiling down a thousand times, medical term applied to decoctions which undergo such a long process.

සහස්‍ර රශ්මි, *Sahasra-rasmi*, *s.* (සහස්‍ර thousand, රශ්මි ray) sun, [Colloq. ඉර *ira*].

සහස්‍ර වදන, *Sahasra-wadana*, *s.* (සහස්‍ර and වදන face) name of Vishṇu.

සහස්‍ර වීර්‍ය්‍ය, *Sahasra-víryá*, *s.* (සහස්‍ර and වීර්‍ය්‍ය splendour) bent grass, *panicum dactylon;* variety of *heteropogon hirtus*, [Colloq. එළ ඉතණ *ela-ítaṇa*].

සහස්‍රවේධි, *Sahasrawédhi*, *s.* (සහස්‍ර and වේධි what pierces) assafœtida, [Colloq. පෙරුංකායම් *peruṇ-káyam*].

සහස්‍රවේධී, *Sahasrawédhí*, *s.* sort of cane, *calamus fasciculatus*.

සහස්‍රස්ථාමධනු, *Sahasrasthâma-dhanu*, *s.* (සහස්‍ර thousand, ස්ථාම strength, ධනු bow) bow requiring a thousand men to bend it.

සහස්‍රාංශු, *Sahasráṇṣu*, see සහස්‍රරශ්මි *sahasra-raṣmi*.

සහස්‍රාක්‍ෂ, *Sahasráksha*, *s.* (සහස්‍ර thousand, අක්‍ෂ *aksha* eye) name of Indra, who in consequence of the curse of Gautama was covered over with marks resembling the female organ, which were subsequently changed to eyes by the relenting saint.

සහසතුරු, *Sahasaturu*, *s.* snake, serpent.

සහසා, *Sahasá*, *ind.* quickly, precipitately, inconsiderately.

සහසැස්, *Sahasęs*, *s.* (සහස් *sahas* thousand, ඇස් *ęs* eye) Indra, Elu form of සහස්‍රාක්‍ෂ *sahasráksha*, which see.

සහසැස්සතුරු, *Sahasęs-saturu*, *s.* (සහසැස් and සතුරු enemy) Titan.

සහළු, *Sahaḷu*, *s.* likeness, similarity, resemblance, [Colloq. සමානකම *samánakama*].

සහාය, *Saháya*, *s.* help, assistance; companion, associate, follower; ruddy goose, *tadorna casarca*, (*Anatidæ*, order *Auseres*).

සහායත්ව, *Sahâyatwa*, *s.* (සහාය and ත්ව aff. of the abstract) fellowship, companionship, friendship, [Colloq. මිත්‍රකම *mitrakama*].

සහාර, *Sahára*, see සහකාර *sahakára*.

සහිත, *Sahita*, *s.* (සහ *saha* with ඉත *ita* aff.) accompanied by, in company with, associated with, etc.; born, endured.

සහිඳලුණු, *Sahiṉda-luṇu*, *s.* rock-salt.

සහිනවා, *Sahinawá*, *v.* to chip: pret. සැස්සා *sessá*.

සහිෂ්ණු, *Sahishṇu*, *a.* (සහ *saha* to endure, ඉෂ්ණු *ishṇu* aff.) patient, enduring, resigned.

සහේතුක, *Sahétuka*, *a.* (ස for සහ *saha* with හේතු cause, ක aff.) fortunate, lucky, prosperous; meritorious, virtuous; having a cause or origin.

සහොක්තිය, *Sahoktiya*, *s.* (සහ *saha* with උක්ති *ukti* speech) figure of rhetoric; either the employment of a word in a double meaning, or connecting different circumstances in one sentence by the use of the term සහ *saha*, with, along with.

සහෝදර, *Sahódara*, } *s.* (සහ *saha* with උදර
සහෝදරයා, *Sahódarayá*, } *udara* belly) brother of whole blood, one by the same father and mother.

සහෝදරී, *Sahódari*, *s.* sister.

සහෘද, *Sahṛida*, *s.* (සහ *saha* with හෘද heart) friend, intimate: *a.* good-hearted, sincere.

සළුව, *Saḷuwa*, *s.* dress, vesture, habiliment; gestures of a dancer or public reciter of poetic compositions: pl. සළු *saḷu*.

සා, *Sá*, *s.* hunger, famine; branch of a tree, from සාඛා *sákhá*; hare, [Colloq. හාවා *háwá*]; evening; star Arcturus, or fifteenth lunar asterism, consisting of but one star.

සාංකාකරණවා, *Sáṅkákaraṇawá*, *v.* to suspect, to doubt.

සාංකාව, *Sáṅkáwa*, *s.* terror, apprehension, grief, sorrow; doubt, uncertainty: pl. සාංකා *sáṅká*.

සාංඝික, *Sáṅghika*, *a*, (සංඝ *saṅgha* Saṅgha, අණ් *aṇ* pleonasm, ඉක *ika* aff.) belonging or common to the Saṅgha or priesthood: see සංඝ *saṅgha*.

සාක්කිය, *Sákkiya*, *s.* evidence, testimony.

සාක්කුව, *Sákkuwa*, *s.* pocket: pl. සාක්කු *sákku*.

සාක්‍ෂ්‍ය, *Sákshya*, *s.* testimony, evidence.

සාක්‍ෂාත්, *Sákshát*, *ind.* (ස *sa* for සහ *saha* with අක්‍ෂි *akshi* eye, අත *ata* to go) before, in presence, in sight of; evidently, manifestly.

සාක්‍ෂිකාරයා, *Sákshikárayá*, *s.* (සාක්‍ෂි and කාර *kára* who does) a witness.

සාක්‍ෂිකියනවා, *Sákshi-kiyanawá*, *v.* to give evidence.

සාක්‍ෂිය, *Sákshiya*, *s.* (ස *sa* for සහ *saha* with අක්‍ෂි *akshi* eye, ඉනි *ini* aff.) attesting, testifying, evidence.

සාක්‍ෂි, *Sákshi*, *s.* witness (in law).

සාක, *Sáka*, *s.* potherb in general, any leaf, flower, fruit, stalk, or root, used as a vegetable; branch of a tree; teak tree, *tectona grandis*, [Colloq. තේක්ක *tékka*]; era of Saka, commencing 78 years after Christ, and the one in common use.

සාකච්ඡා, *Sákachchhá*, *s.* (සහ *saha* with කථ *katha* to talk) conversation, discourse.

සාකච්ඡාකරණවා, *Sákachchhá-karaṇawá*, *v.* to converse, to discourse.

සාකට, *Sákaṭa*, *s.* (සකට *sakaṭa* cart, අණ් *aṇ* aff.) draught ox: *a.* relating to cart, etc.

සාකටික, *Sákaṭika*, *s.* (සකට *sakaṭa* cart, අණ් *aṇ* and ඉක *ika* affs.) cart driver, travelling merchant: *a.* going in or on a cart.

සාකය, *Sákaya*, *s.* small tree, *cratæva Roxburghii* or *c. religiosa*, [Colloq. ලුණුවරණ *luṇuwaraṇa*].

සාකල්‍ය, *Sákalya*, } *s.* (සකල *sakala* all, whole,
සාකල්‍යක, *Sákalyaka*, } යඤ් *yañ* aff.) the whole, the entire.

සාකා, *Sáká*, *s.* vegetable in general.

සාඛ්‍ය, *Sákhya*, *s.* (සඛි *sakhi* friend, යඤ් *yañ* aff.) friendship, [Colloq. මිත්‍රකම *mitrakama*].

සාඛා, *Sákhá*, *s.* branch, branch of a tree, [Colloq. අත්ත *atta*]; any subdivision.

සාඛානගර, *Sákhá-nagara*, *s.* (සාඛා subdivision, නගර city) suburb.

සාඛාමිග, *Sákhá-miga*, *s.* (සාඛා branch, මිග animal) monkey, ape, [Colloq. වඳුරා *waṉdurá*, රිළවා *riḷawá*].

සාඛාව, *Sákháwa*, *s.* branch, the branch of a tree; subdivision: pl. සාඛා *sákhá*.

සාඛී, *Sákhí*, *s.* (සාඛ *sákha* and ඊ *í* aff.) tree in general, [Colloq. ගහ *gaha*].

සාගතය, *Ságataya*, *s.* famine: pl. සාගත *ságata*.

සාගර, *Ságara*, *s.* (සගර *sagara* king, අණ් *aṇ* aff.) ocean; deer.

සාගරක, *Ságaraka*, *s* (සාගර sea, ක aff.) sea-salt, [Colloq. මූදුලුණු *múdu-luṇu*]: *a.* marine, oceanic.

සාගරගාමිනී, *Ságara-gáminí*, *s.* (සාගර and ගාමිනී going to) river in general, [Colloq. ගඟ *ganga*].

සාගරනේමි, *Ságara-némi*, *s.* (සාගර and නේමි circumference) earth, [Colloq. පොළව *polawa*].

සාගරය, *Ságaraya*, see සාගර *ságara*.

සාගරාලය, *Ságarálaya*, *s.* (සාගර *ságara* sea, ආලය *álaya* abode) name of Varuṇa the deity of water.

සාගින්න, *Ságinna*, *s.* (සා hunger, ගින්න fire, literally, fire of hunger) hunger.

සාටක, *Sáṭaka*, } *s.* (සට *saṭa* to go, ක aff.) cloth,
සාටිකා, *Sáṭiká*, } petticoat.

සාටි, *Sáṭi*, *s.* (සට *saṭa* to go, ඊ *i* aff.) petticoat; garment, mantle.

සාණ, *Sáṇa*, see ශාන *ṣána*.

සාත්තුකරණවා, *Sáttukaraṇawá*, *v.* to nourish, to cherish, to nurse, to minister to.

සාත්තුකෙරීම, *Sáttukeríma*, *s.* nourishing, cherishing, attending, as the sick or aged.

සාත්තුනායක, *Sáttunáyaka*, *s.* (සාත්තු caravan, නායක leader) chief of a company of travelling merchants, head or guide of a caravan.

සාත්තුව, *Sáttuwa*, *s.* nourishing, cherishing, attending, as the sick or aged.

සාත, *Sáta*, *s.* joy, pleasure, happiness: *a.* given; destroyed.

සාතලා, *Sátalá*, *s.* plant, *herpestis monnirea*, [Coll: ලුණුවිල *luṇuvila*].

සාතවාහන, *Sáta-wáhana*, *s.* (සාත a Gandharwa, changed according to the legend to a lion, on which this prince was discovered riding when a child, and වාහන vehicle) name of the sovereign Sáliváhana: see ශාලිවාහන *ṣáliwáhana*.

සාතාවාරිය, *Sátáwáriya*, *s. asparagus:* see හාතාවාරිය *hátáwáriya*.

සාති, *Sáti*, *s.* (ශො *shó* to reduce or diminish, ක්ති *kti* aff.) destruction; end, cessation.

සාද්ධ්‍ය, *Sáddhya*, *s.* matter in debate, subject of a proposition: *a.* to be perfected or accomplished; to be inferred or concluded, (in logic.); to be cured or curable, (in medicine).

සාද, *Sáda*, *s.* mud; young grass; purity, cleanness; lassitude, exhaustion; perishing, decay.

සාදන, *Sádana*, *s.* (සද *sada* to go) house, dwelling; dispelling, destroying, wearying, exhausting.

සාදනවා, *Sádanawá*, *v.* to make, to construct, to form, to manufacture: pret. සෑදුවා *séduwá*.

සාදගන්නවා, *Sádagannawá*, *v.* to make for one's self.

සාදික්කා, *Sádikká*, *s.* nutmeg tree, *myristica fragrans*.

සාදිලිංගම්, *Sádilingam*, *s.* vermillion.

සාදෘශ්‍ය, *Sádṛiṣya*, *s.* (සදෘශ *sadṛiṣa* resemblance, යඤ් *yañ* aff.) resemblance, similarity, [Colloq. සමානකම *samánakama*].

සාධ්වස, *Sádhwasa*, *s.* fear, terror, [Colloq. භය *bhaya*].

සාධ්වී, *Sádhví*, *s.* virtuous wife.

සාධන, *Sádhana*, *s.* (සාධ *sádha* to complete) accomplishing, effecting; thing, substance; wealth; instrument, agent.

සාධර්ම, *Sádharma*, *s.* (සා for සහ *saha* with ධර්ම duty, etc.) common or universal duty, as humanity, justice, etc.

සාධාරණ, *Sádháraṇa*, *s.* (සා for සහ *saha* with ධාරණ having) justice, equity: *a.* common, belonging to all or many, generic; just, right, fit, proper, equitable; good, virtuous, excellent.

සාධිත, *Sádhita*, *a.* (සාධ *sádha* to accomplish, ඉත *ita* aff.) accomplished, finished; amerced, fined.

සාධු, *Sádhu*, *ind.* (සාධ *sádha* to accomplish, to perfect, උ *u* aff.) particle or interjection of assent and approval, well done, bravo! exclamation in hearing bana or Buddhist doctrine, corresponding to Amen! *a.* excellent, good, virtuous; pleasing, beautiful; right, fit, proper; pure, classical, (as applied to language).

සාධුකාර, *Sádhukára*, *s.* (සාධු and කාර doing) cheering, praising, acclamation of approval.

සාධුකාරදෙනවා, *Sádhukára-denawá*, *v.* to exclaim Sádhu, as in Buddhist ceremonies.

සාධුපුෂ්ප, *Sádhu-pushpa*, *s.* (සාධු and පුෂ්ප flower) flower, *hibiscus mutablis*.

සාධුඵල, *Sádhu-phala*, *s.* fruit of the jujube, *zizyphus jujuba*, [Colloq. මසන් *masan*]; Páli form of ස්වාදුඵල *swádu-phala*.

සාධුවෘක්ෂ, *Sádhu-wṛiksha*, *s.* (සාධු handsome, etc. වෘක්ෂ tree) cadamba tree, *anthocephalus (or nauclea) cadamba*.

සාන්කා, *Sánká*, see සාංකා *sánká*.

සාන්තදාන්ත, *Sántadánta*, *a.* (සාන්ත and දාන්ත tamed) having the passions completely subdued, calm, tranquil: see ශාන්තිය *ṣántiya*.

සාන්තුවරයා, *Sántuwarayá*, *s.* Saint, term used by Roman Catholics from the Portuguese.

සාන්ද්‍ර, *Sándra*, *a.* (සා for සහ *saha* with අදි *adi* to bind, ර *ra* aff.) gross, thick, coarse; close, compact.

සාන්දෘෂ්ටික, *Sándrishṭika, s.* (සම් *sam* with දෘෂ්ටි sight, ක aff.) first-sight, present perception, immediate consequence.

සානවා, *Sánawá, v.* to plough: see හානවා *hánawá.*

සානාය, *Sánáya, s.* tent. screen.

සාණි, *Sáni, s.* plant, from the fibres of which a coarse cloth is prepared, *corchorus olitorius:* see පට්ට *paṭṭa.*

සානු, *Sánu, s.* table land, level ground on the top or edge of a mountain; point, end, tip; a shoot, sprout; sun.

සාප්පුව, *Sáppuwa, s.* a retail shop.

සාපකරණවා, *Sápakaraṇawá, v.* to curse.

සාපනු, *Sápanu, s.* cock, [Colloq. කුකුළා *kukuḷá*].

සාපය, *Sápaya,* see ශාප *ṣápa.*

සාපරාධ, *Sáparádha, a.* (සා for සහ *saha* with අපරාධ *aparáḍha* crime) criminal, guilty.

සාපිපාස, *Sápipása, s.* (සා hunger, පිපාස thirst) hunger and thirst.

සාඵල්‍ය, *Sáphalya, s.* (සඵල *saphala* fruitful, අණ් *aṇ* pleonasm, යත් *yat* aff.) fruitfulness, productiveness, profitableness.

සාම්පරායික, *Sámparáyika, s.* (සම්පරාය *samparáya* and අණ් *aṇ* and ඉක *ika* affs.) war, battle, [Colloquial: යුද්ධය *yuddhaya* or සටන *saṭana*]; futurity.

සාම්බුව, *Sámbuwa, s.* whole piece of cloth containing many separate ones as a dozen of handkerchiefs in one piece.

සාම්‍ය, *Sámya, s.* (සම *sama* same, යත් *yat* aff.) equality, sameness, likeness, similarity.

සාමග්‍රී, *Sámyagrí, s.* entireness, wholeness, the whole; train, retinue; implements, instruments; stock, effects.

සාම්‍යාර්ථ, *Sámyartha, s.* (සාමි *sámi* master, අර්ථ *arttha* meaning) possession, the sense of the genitive case in grammar.

සාම්‍රාජ්‍ය, *Sámrájya, s.* (සම්‍රාජ් *samráj* emperor, with ෂ්‍යඤ් *shyañ* aff.) imperial rule, empire.

සාමඬුළු, *Sámaṇḍuḷu, s.* (සා branch, මඬුළු area) shade formed by the extended branches of a tree used as a place to recline in.

සාමණේර, *Sámaṇéra, s.* Buddhist priest in his noviciate, pupil of a priest.

සාමන්ත, *Sámanta, s.* (සමන්ත *samanta* end, term, අණ් *aṇ* aff. of relation) neighbourhood; chief of a district; neighbour; attendant of a chieftain; a leader, captain, champion: *a.* bordering, neighbouring; limitative, boundary, bounding.

සාමර්ථ්‍ය, *Sámarthya, s.* ability, skill, power; (in grammar) mutual relation of words.

සාමවායික, *Sámawáyika, s.* (සමවාය *samawáya* assembly, අණ් *aṇ* pleonasm, ඉක *ika* aff.) principal minister or counsellor.

සාමවේදය, *Sámawédaya, s.* the Sáma Véda of the Hindus.

සාමාන්‍ය, *Sámánya, s.* (සමාන *samána* common, අණ් *aṇ* aff. යත් *yat*) kind, sort; sixth or genitive case in grammar: *a.* common, general, universal.

සාමාන්‍යවශයෙන්, *Sámánya-waṣayen, ad.* generally.

සාමි, *Sámi, s.* lord, from ස්වාමි *swámi*: *ind. part.* half.

සාමික, *Sámika, a.* (සාමි master, ක aff.) owned, claimed, having a master or owner.

සාමිදරුවෝ, *Sámidaruwó, s.* lord, master: see ස්වාමිදරුවෝ *swámidaruwó.*

සාමුද්‍ර, *Sámudra, s.* (සමුද්‍ර *samudra* sea, අණ් *aṇ* aff of relation) spot or mark on the body; cuttle fish bone: *a.* marine, oceanic, sea born.

සාමුද්‍රික, *Sámudrika, s.* (සාමුද්‍ර *sámudra* spot or mole, ඉක *ika* aff.) interpreter of spots on the body; a work on the same subject: *a.* relating to spots on the body, supposed to indicate good or bad fortune.

සාමුද්‍රිකා ලක්ෂණය, *Sámudriká-lakshaṇaya, s.* signs on the human body which indicate good or bad fortune.

සාමුව, *Sámuwa, s.* (සා branch, මුව animal) monkey, [Colloq. වඳුරා *waṇḍurá,* රිළවා *riḷawá*]; Elu form of ශාඛාමෘග *ṣákhámriga.*

සාය, *Sáya, s.* petticoat; hunger, famine, scarcity or privation of food.

සායංකාල, *Sáyaṇkála, s.* (සායං evening, කාල time) even tide, evening, [Colloq. සවස *sawasa*].

සායක, *Sáyaka, s.* (ශෝ *sho* to destroy, ක aff.) sword; arrow.

සායම්, *Sáyam, ind.* evening.

සායම්කරණවා, *Sáyamkaraṇawá, v.* to tinge, to dye.

සායම්පොවනවා, *Sáyam-powanawá, v.* to dye.

සායම් මුල්, *Sáyam-mul, s.* chay root plant, *oldenlandia umbellata*: see සයමුල් *saya-mul.*

සායම, *Sáyama, s.* colour, dye, paint, tinge: pl. සායම් *sáyam.*

සායාහ්න වේලාව, *Sáyáhna-wéláwa,* see සායංකාල *sáyaṇkála.*

සාර්ථ, *Sártha,* } *s.* (ස for සහ *saha* with අර්ථ *artha*
සාර්ත්ථ, *Sárttha,* } wealth, meaning) company of

traders, caravan; multitude in general: *a.* wealthy, opulent; of like meaning or purport; significant, importing.

සාර්ථක, *Sárthaka*, *a.* (සාර්ථ and ක aff.) advantageous, profitable; edifying, instructive; productive, fruitful; significant, having meaning.

සාර්ථවාහ, *Sárthawáha*, *s.* (සාර්ථ company, caravan, වාහ who conveys) merchant, trader: see සාත්තුනායක *sáttunáyaka*.

සාර්පි, *Sárpi*, *s.* (සර්ප *sarpa* snake, අණ් *aṇ* aff.) ninth lunar asterism of which the serpents are the presiding deities.

සාර, *Sára*, *s*, (සර *sara* to go) pith or sap of trees; essence of any thing, essential or vital part; marrow; coagulum of curds, etc. cream, fresh butter; strength, vigor: *a.* best, excellent, fertile.

සාරකල්ප, *Sára-kalpa*, *s.* (සාර excellent, කල්ප Kalpa) the third of the four Kalpas in which three Buddhas were born; the present is the fourth: see භද්‍රකල්ප *bhadra-kalpa*.

සාරගන්ධ, *Sára-gandha*, *s.* (සාර essence, ගන්ධ smell) sandal-wood, *santalum album*, [Colloq. සඳුන් *sa͟ndun* and රත්කිහිරිය *ratkihiriya*].

සාරඝ, *Sáragha*, *s.* honey; bees wax.

සාරඞ්ග, *Sárañga*, *s.* the Chátaka, *cuculus melanoleucos*, [Colloq. කැඳැත්තා *kẹ͟ndẹttá*]; the kókila or Indian cuckoo, [Colloq. කොවුලා *kowulá*]; deer, [Colloq. මුවා *muwá*].

සාරජ, *Sáraja*, *s.* (සාර cream, ජ produced) fresh butter.

සාරණ, *Sáraṇa*, *s.* (සර *sara* to go, etc.) potherb, *marsilia quadrifolia*, [Colloq. දිය ඇඹුල් ඇඹිලිය *diya-ẹmbul-ẹmbiliya*]; hog plum, *spondias mangifera*, [Colloq. ඇඹරැල්ල *ẹmbarẹlla*]; dysentery, diarrhœa, [Colloq. අතිසාරය *atisáraya*].

සාරණවා, *Sáraṇawá*, *v.* to dig the ground, etc: pret. සෑරුවා *sẹruwá*.

සාරණී, *Sáraṇi*, *s.* (සර *sara* to go, ණී aff.) shrubby, twining plant, *pœderia fetida* or *convolvulus fœtidus*; small river; drain, canal.

සාරණික, *Sáraṇika*, *s.* (සරණි *saraṇi* road, අණ් *aṇ* and ඉක *ika* affs.) traveller.

සාරණිකඝ්න, *Sáraṇikaghna*, *s.* (සාරණික traveller, ඝ්න who kills) robber, highwayman.

සාරතරු, *Sárataru*, *s.* (සාර sap, තරු tree) plantain tree, which has no timber in the stem, *musa sapientum*, [Colloq. කෙසෙල්ගහ *kesel-gaha*].

සාරථි, *Sárathi*, *s.* (සෘ *sṛi* to go, causal form අථින් *athin* aff.) coachman, charioteer.

සාරදා, *Sáradá*, *s.* (සාර essence, of wisdom and eloquence, දා who gives) name of Saraswatí, the goddess of speech and eloquence, and wife of Brahmá; name of Durgá, the wife of Ṣiva.

සාරදී, *Sáradí*, *s.* medicinal plant, *cassia auriculata*, [Colloquial: රණවරා *raṇawará*]; another plant, [Colloq. කටුරෝහිණී *kaṭuróhiṇí*].

සාරධී, *Sáradhí*, *s.* plant, *gloriosa superba*, [Colloq. නියඟලා *niya͟ngalá*].

සාරම්භය, *Sárambhaya*, *s.* (සා for සං *saṇ* with රභි *rabhí* to sound) pride, arrogance; beginning, commencement.

සාරමණ්ඩ, *Sára-maṇḍa*, *s.* one of the four Kalpas.

සාරමේය, *Sáraméya*, *s.* (සරමා *saramá* bitch, අණ් *aṇ* aff.) dog, [Colloq. බල්ලා *ballá*].

සාරය, *Sáraya*, *s.* bees wax: see සාර *sára*.

සාරලෝහ, *Sáralóha*, *s.* steel, [Colloq. වානේ *wáṇé*].

සාරවත්, *Sárawat*, *a.* fruitful, productive.

සාරවීරතරු, *Sáravírataru*, *s.* tree, *dichrostachys cinerea*, [Colloq. අඳර *andara*].

සාරවෙනවා, *Sárawenawá*, *v.* to succeed, to become fertile.

සාරශ්‍රේෂ්ඨ, *Sáraṣréshṭha*, *s.* tree, *adenanthera pavonina*, [Colloq. මහරි *mahari* or මදටිය *madaṭiya*].

සාරස, *Sárasa*, *s.* (සරස් *saras* pond, etc. අණ් *aṇ* aff.) lotus, *nelumbium speciosum*, [Colloq. නෙළුම් *neḷum*]; woman's zone or girdle; Indian crane; moon: *a.* belonging to a lake or pond.

සාරා, *Sárá*, *s.* durba grass; plant, *dolichos* or *vigna catjang*, [Colloq. ලීමෑ *límẹ*]: *a.* best, excellent.

සාරි, *Sári*, *s.* man or piece at chess or backgammon, etc: see ශාරිකා *ṣáriká*.

සාරිඵලක, *Sári-phalaka*, *s.* chequered cloth or table for playing draughts; chess-board.

සාරිභව, *Sáribhawa*, *s.* conch shell.

සාරිවාහ, *Sáriwáha*, *s.* (සාරි and වාහ who conveys) merchant, [Colloq. වෙළෙන්දා *weḷendá*]: see සාර්ථවාහ *sárthawáha*.

සාරී, *Sárí*, see ශාරිකා *ṣáriká*.

සාරීරික, *Sárírika*, *a.* (සරීර *sarira* body, අණ් *aṇ* pleonasm, ඉක *ika* aff.) corporeal, belonging or relating to the body.

සාල්, *Sál*, *s.* rice in general, from සාලි *sáli*: see ශාල *ṣála*.

සාල, *Sála*, *s.* tree, *vateria acuminata*, [Colloq. හල් ගහ *hal-gahu*].

සලකලකණි, *Sála-kalyáṇi*, *s.* (සාල tree, *shorea robusta*, කලකණ *kalyána* excellent, ඉ *i* aff.) superior kind of the hal tree: see ශාල *ṣála*.

සාලඞුරු, *Sálaṅguru*, *s.* lighted or burning charcoal, embers.

සාලද්‍රැමය, *Sála-drumaya*, *s.* (සාල and ද්‍රැම *druma* tree) hal tree: see ශාල *ṣála*.

සාලනියඃිාස, *Sála-niryása*, *s.* resinous exudation of the hal tree: see ශාලනියඃිාස *ṣála-niryása*.

සාලපර්ණි, *Sála-parṇí*, *s.* medicinal plant: see ශාලපර්ණි *ṣála-parṇí*.

සාලපුෂ්ප, *Sála-pushpa*, *s.* (සාල and පුෂ්ප flower) shrub, *hibiscus mutabilis*.

සාලය, *Sálaya*, *s.* drawing room; hall.

සාලයා, *Sálayá*, *s.* kind of sea fish.

සාලරස, *Sálarasa*, see ශාලනියඃිාස *ṣálaniryása*.

සාල වෘක්ෂ, *Sála-wṛiksha*, see සාල ද්‍රැමය *sála-drumaya*.

සාලසාර, *Sála-sára*, *s.* assafœtida, [Colloq. පෙරුංකායම් *peruṇkáyam*].

සාලාකී, *Sálákí*, *s.* (සලාකා *salákú* probe, etc. ඊ *í* aff.) surgeon; barber, spearman, etc.

සාලාප, *Sálápa*, *s.* (සහ *saha* with අලාප *álápa* word) conversation.

සාලාව, *Sáláwa*, *s.* house; hall, largest or principal room in a house: pl. සාලා *sálá*.

සාලාවෘක, *Sálá-wṛika*, *s.* (සාලා and වෘක wolf) jackal, [Colloq. නරියා *nariyá*]; dog, [Colloq. බල්ලා *ballá*].

සාලිකා, *Sáliká*, *s.* (සාරිකා *sárika* and ලි *li* substituted for රි *ri*) small bird, *turdus*: see ශාරිකා *ṣáriká*; weaver; shrub, *desmodium gangeticum*.

සාලිස, *Sálisa*, *ind.* number forty, [Colloq. සතළිස *sataḷisa*].

සාලූක, *Sálúka*, *s.* root of the water-lily.

සාලූර, *Sálúra*, *s.* (සල *sala* to go, ඌර *ura* aff.) frog, [Colloq. ගෙමඩියා *gemaḍiyá*].

සාලෝද්‍යානය, *Sálódyánaya*, *s.* (සාල *sála* tree, *shorea robusta*, උද්‍යාන *udyána* garden) forest of sal trees, *vateria acuminata*.

සාව, *Sáwa*, *s.* (සව *sawa* dead body, අණ් *aṇ* aff.) tawny, the colour; young of any animal: *a.* tawny; relating to a dead body.

සාවක, *Sáwaka*, *s.* young of any animal: *a.* generative, productive, obstetric, parturient; Páli form of ශ්‍රාවක *ṣráwaka*, hearer, disciple.

සාවද්‍ය, *Sáwadya*, *a.* (සා for සහ *saha* with වද්‍ය crime) guilty, criminal.

සාවන, *Sáwana*, *s.* month of thirty solar days: *a.* natural, (in Astronomy) as සාවනදින *sáwana-dina*, a natural day, from sun rise to sun rise.

සාවර, *Sáwara*, *s.* fault, offence; sin, wickedness; tree, *symplocos racemosa*; wet or damp ground.

සාවශේෂ, *Sáwaṣésha*, *a.* (සා for සහ *saha* with අවශේෂ *awaṣésha* remainder) remaining, incomplete.

සාවා, *Sáwá*, *s.* hare, also called හාවා *háwá*.

සාවිත්‍ර, *Sávitra*, *s.* sun, [Colloq. ඉර *ira*]; name of Ṣiva.

සාහචය්‍ය, *Sáhachrya*, *s.* (සහචර *sahachara* companion, අණ් *aṇ* aff.) association, company, society.

සාහස, *Sáhasa*, *s.* (සහස *sahasa* strength, අණ් *aṇ* aff.) perpetration of any act of violence or rapine; oppression, cruelty; rape, ravishment.

සාහසික, *Sáhasika*, *s.* (සාහස *sáhasa* violence, ඉක *ika* aff.) robber, freebooter: *a.* violent, felonious, rapacious; brutal, cruel.

සාහිත්‍ය, *Sáhitya*, *s.* (සහිත *sahita* with, together, අණ් *aṇ* aff.) society, association, connection, combination, poetry, belles-lettres.

සාළුව, *Sáḷuwa*, *s.* shawl: pl. සාළු *sáḷu*. (Port.)

සි, *Si*, *s.* top of a tree.

සිංගාරම, *Ssṇgárama*, *s.* drum or tabour; any musical instrument: pl. සිංගාරම් *siṇgáram*.

සිංගිත්ත, *Siṇgitta*, *s.* little, bit, small portion, [Colloq. ටිකක් *ṭikak*].

සිංඝාතන, *Siṇghátana*, *s.* rust of iron, [Colloq. යබොර *yabora*].

සිංඝාන, *Siṇghána*, } *s.* (සිඝි *sighi* to smell, ආනක *ánaka* aff.) mucus
සිංඝානිකා, *Siṇghániká*, } of the nose, [Colloq. සොටු *soṭu*].

සිංඝිනි, *Siṇghiní*, *s.* (සිඝි *sighi* and ඉනි *ini* aff.) nose, [Colloq. නාහේ *náhé*].

සිංහ, *Siṇha*, *s.* lion; leo, the sign of the zodiac; in composition, pre-eminent.

සිංහකේශර, *Siṇha-késara*, *s.* (සිංහ lion, කේශර mane, etc.) plant, *mimusops elengi*, [Colloq. මූන මල් *múna-mal*]; lion's mane.

සිංහගජ්නාව, *Siṇha-garjanáwa*, *s.* (සිංහ and ගජ්නා *garjaná* thunder) roaring of a lion.

සිංහදෙන, *Siṇha-dena*, *s.* a lioness.

සිංහනාද, *Siṇhanáda*, *s.* (සිංහ and නාද cry) war cry, war hoop, shouting or roaring upon making an onset; roar of a lion.

සිංහනාදකරණවා, *Siṇhanáda-karaṇawá*, *v.* to roar as a lion.

සිංහපඤ්ජරය, *Sinha-pañjaraya, s.* (සිංහ and පඤ්ජර *pañjara* aviary) window, loop hole, [Colloq. ජනේලය *janélaya*].

සිංහපර්ණී, *Sinha-parni, s.* (සිංහ and පර්ණ *parna* leaf) small tree, *adhatoda vasica* or *justicia adhenatoda.* [Colloq. අගල්ආදර *agal-ádára*].

සිංහපුච්ඡි, *Sinha-puchchhi, s.* (සිංහ and පුච්ඡ *puchchha* tail) plant, *hedysarum lagopodiodes,* [Coll: පුස්වැන්න *puswenna*].

සිංහමුඛී, *Sinha-mukhí, s.* medicinal plant, *justicia adhenatoda.* [Colloq. අගල්ආදර *agal-ádára*].

සිංහයා, *Sinhayá,* see සිංහ *sinha.*

සිංහයානා, *Sinha-yáná,* } *s.* (සිංහ lion, යාන *yána*
සිංහරථා *Sinha-rathá,* } or රථ *ratha* vehicle) name of Durgá, being mounted on a lion.

සිංහල, *Sinhala, s.* (සිංහ and ලා *lá* to have or get) Ceylon, which was peopled by the descendants of විජය *Vijaya* son of සිංහබාහු *Sinhabáhu* who, according to fable, was begotten by a lion: *a.* belonging to Ceylon, native of Ceylon.

සිංහල අසමෝදගන්, *Sinhala-asamódagam, s.* saxifrage, *pimpinella anisum* or *p. heyneana:* see වල් අසමෝදගන් *wal-asamódagan.*

සිංහල කපු, *Sinhala-kapu, s.* (සිංහල Ceylon, කපු cotton) Ceylon cotton, *gossypium indicum.*

සිංහලේ, *Sinhalé, a.* belonging or relating to Kandy, used to distinguish a man of the Kandian or upper provinces from an inhabitant of the maritime districts.

සිංහවින්නා, *Sinhavinná, s.* fern, *drymoglossum heterophyllum,* [Colloq. මස්වැන්න *maswenna*].

සිංහ සෙය්‍යාව, *Sinha-seyyáwa, s.* (සිංහ lion, සෙය්‍යා *seyyá* reclining) sleeping attitude of a lion.

සිංහාන, *Sinhána, s.* rust of iron, mucus of the nose.

සිංහාස්‍ය, *Sinhásya, s.* (සිංහ *sinha* lion, ආස්‍ය *ásya* face) small tree, *adhatoda vasica,* [Colloq. අගල් ආදර *agal-ádára*], the flowers of which are compared to the face of the lion.

සිංහාසනය, *Sinhásanaya, s.* (සිංහ *sinha* and ආසන *ásana* seat) throne being supported by lions, etc: pl. සිංහාසන *sinhásana.*

සිංහාසනාරූඪ, *Sinhásanárúdha, a.* ascended the throne.

සිංහිකා, *Sinhiká, s.* (සිංහී lioness, ක *ka* aff. of comparison) mother of Ráhu the personified ascending node; medicinal plant, *justicia adhenatoda,* [Colloq. වං අපල *wan-epala* or අගල් ආදර *agal-ádára*].

සිංහී, *Sinhí, s.* egg plant, *solanum melongena,* [Colloq. එලබටු *elabatu*]; prickly night shade, *s. jacquini,* [Colloq. තිබ්බටු *tibbatu*]; mother of Ráhu; lioness.

සික්කා, *Sikká, s.* string by which a weight is suspended; strings of a කද *kada* pole for carrying a burden with a basket at each end.

සික්ඛා, *Sikkhá,* Páli form of ශික්ෂා *sikshá.*

සික්ත, *Sikta, a.* (සිච *sicha* to sprinkle, ක්ත *kta* aff.) sprinkled, wetted.

සික්ථ, *Siktha, s.* handful or mouthful of boiled rice; boiled rice; bees wax.

සික්ථකා, *Sikthaká, s.* bees wax. [Colloq. මී ඉටි *mí-iti*].

සික, *Sika, s.* crest; flame, from ශිඛා *sikhá.*

සිකත, *Sikata, s.* sand, see the next.

සිකතා, *Sikatá, s.* sand, [Colloq. වැලි *weli*]; sandy soil; gravel or stone, (the disease).

සිකනලා, *Sikanalá, s.* chameleon, *Calotes versicolor, c. ophiomachus,* or *camæleo ougaris,* [Coll: කටුස්සා *katussá*]; Brahminy lizard, [Colloq. හූනා *húná*], (order *Sauria.*)

සිකල්, *Sikal, s.* mud, mire, clay. [Colloq. මඩ *mada*].

සිකා, *Siká, s.* crest of peacocks.

සිකි, *Siki, s.* (සික *sika* crest, ඉ *i* aff.) peacock, [Colloq. මොණරා *monará*]; fire, [Colloq. ගින්දර *gindara*]; flag, banner, [Colloq. කොඩිය *kodiya*], Elu form of ශිඛී *sikhí.*

සිකියහන්, *Siki-yahan, s.* (සිකි peacock, යහන් vehicle) name of Kártikéya or Kataragama-deviyó, the Indian god of war.

සිකිදල, *Sikidala, s.* flame, [Colloq. ගිනිදළුව *ginidaluwa*].

සිකුරතවැසි, *Sikuratawesi, s.* Titan, Asur.

සිකුරා, *Sikurá, s.* planet Venus or its regent: see ශුක්‍ර *sukra.*

සිකුරාදා, *Sikurádá, s.* (සිකුරා and දා day) Friday.

සිකුරු, *Sikuru, s.* intoxicating liquor. [Colloq. අරක්කු *arakku*]; whiteness, [Colloq. සුදු *suda*]: see සිකුරා *sikurá.*

සිකුරුපියලි, *Sikurupiyali,* see සිඟුරුපියලි *singurupiyali.*

සිඛාව, *Sikháwa, s.* flame, [Colloq. ගිනිදැල්ල *ginidella*]: see ශිඛා *sikhá.*

සිගල්, *Sigal, s.* jackal: see ශෘගාල *srigála.*

සිගු, *Sigu, s.* horn, etc: see ශෘංග *sringa;* haste, speed: see ශීඝ්‍ර *sighra.*

සිඟන්නා, *Singanná*, s. beggar, mendicant: pl. සිඟන්නෝ *singannó*.

සිඟනවා, *Singanawá*, v. to beg, to solicit alms or charity; also called හිඟනවා *hinganawá*.

සිඟල්, *Singal*, s. jackal.

සිඟාන, *Singána*, s. agricultural instrument, sort of hoe.

සිඟාරම්කරණවා, *Singáramkaranawá*, v. to drum.

සිඟාරම්කාරයා, *Singáramkárayá*, s. drummer, [Colloq. බෙරගහන්නා *bera-gahanná*].

සිඟිමිග, *Singi-miga*, s. (සිඟි horn, මිග animal) crab, [Colloq. කකුළුවා *kakuluwá*].

සිඟු, *Singu*, s. peak, top, summit; horn; mark; sign; minutely, fine; Elu form of ශෘඞ්ග *sringa*.

සිඟුරුපියලි, *Singurupiyali*, s. small aromatic plant, *kaempferia galanga (Scitamineæ);* commonly called හිඟුරුපියලි *hingurupiyali*.

සිඟුවලඟ, *Singuwalanga*, s. (සිඟු delicate, වලඟ waist) woman.

සිඞ්ගාර, *Singára*, s. dancing accompanied with song and music.

සිඞ්ගි, *Singi*, s. gold; horn; fish, *silurus pungentissimus;* creeping plant, *dæmia extensa*, [Colloq. මැඩහඟු *medahangu*]; small tree or shrub with large flowers, *adhatoda vasica*, [Colloq, අගල් අඳුර *agaládára;* Páli form of ශෘඞ්ගි *sringi*.

සිටවනවා, *Sitawanawá*, v. to cause to stand, to plant: pret. සිටෙව්වා *sitewwá*.

සිටවීම, *Sitavíma*, s. planting, fixing, placing.

සිටානෝ, *Sitánó*, s. (සෙට්ඨි *setthi* noble) nobleman.

සිටිනවා, *Sitinawá*, v. (ස්ථා *sthá* to be or stay) to be, to remain, to stay.

සිටියා, *Sitiyá*, past tense of the above; stood.

සිටීම, *Sitíma*, verbal noun of සිටිනවා *sitinawá*.

සිටු, *Situ*, s. nobleman: see සිටානෝ *sitánó*.

සිටුතනතුර, *Situ-tanatura*, s. (සිටු and තානතුර an office) nobility, dignity of a nobleman.

සිටුවනවා, *Situwanawá*, v. (causal form of සිටිනවා *sitinawá* to be, to stay) to fix, to place, to establish; to set, to plant, as trees: pret. සිටෙව්වා *sitewwá*.

සිත්, *Sit*, see සිත *sita*.

සිත් ඇලෙනවා, *Sit-elenawá*, v. (සිත *sita* the mind, ඇලෙනවා to adhere) to wish, to desire, to covet.

සිත් ඔතැනි, *Sit-oteni*, a. (සිත *sita* mind, ඔතැනි feeble) disheartened, discouraged, abject.

සිත්කලු, *Sitkalu*, a. delightful, pleasing, agreeable, attractive.

සිත්ගන්නවා, *Sitgannawá*, v. (සිත *sita* mind, ගන්නවා to take) to please, to gratify.

සිත්තරා, *Sittará*, s. painter, colourer, limner: pl. සිත්තරු *sittaru*.

සිත්විකල, *Sit-vikala*, a. (සිත *sita* the mind, විකල confused) troubled, perplexed, perturbed.

සිත්විකලවීම, *Sit-vikalavíma*, s. perplexity, perturbation.

සිත, *Sita*, s. the mind, reasoning faculty, from චිත්තය *chittaya;* fourth lunar asterism, from චිත්‍ර *chitra;* white; planet Venus; silver; sandal wood; white arsenic.

සිතකූලක, *Sitakúlaka*, s. medicinal plant, *sida cordifolia*, [Colloq. සුළුබැලිල *sulu-belila*].

සිතච්ඡත්‍ර, *Sitachchhatra*, s. (සිත white, ඡත්‍ර umbrella) white umbrella, one of the emblems of royalty.

සිතච්ඡත්‍රි, *Sitachchhatri*, s. sort of fennel, *anethum sowa*.

සිතද්‍රු, *Sitadru*, s. plant, commonly called මොරටා *moratá*.

සිතද්‍රෝණ, *Sitadróna*, s. borago, *borago zeylanica*, [Colloq. යොන්තුඹ *yon-tumba*].

සිතධාතු, *Sitadhátu*, s. (සිත white, ධාතු mineral) chalk.

සිතනවා, *Sitanawá*, v. to think, to reflect, to consider: pret. සිතුවා *situwá*.

සිතපක්ෂ, *Sitapaksha*, s. (සිත white, පක්ෂ feather, half) goose; light fortnight of the moon.

සිතපුෂ්ප, *Sita-pushpa*, s. (සිත and පුෂ්ප flower) fragrant grass, *cyperus rotundus*, [Colloq. කලාඳුරු *kalánduru*]; another grass, *saccharum spontaneum*.

සිතපුෂ්පා, *Sitapushpá*, s. Arabian jasmine, *jasminum sambac*, [Colloq. පිච්ච *pichcha*].

සිතරශ්මි, *Sita-rasmi*, s. (සිත and රශ්මි ray) moon, [Colloq. හඳ *handa*].

සිතසර්ෂප, *Sita-sarshapa*, s. (සිත white, සර්ෂප mustard) white mustard, variety of *brassica juncea* or *cleome viscosa*, [Colloq. හෙළඅබ *hela-aba*].

සිතා, *Sitá*, s. clayed or candied sugar; Arabian jasmine: see සිතපුෂ්ප *sita-pushpa;* plant, species of *clitoria*, [Colloq. කටරොළු *katarolu*].

සිතාංක, *Sitánka*, s. (සිත *sita* and අංක *anka* mark or spot) fish, *lacertus scincus*.

සිතාණ්ඩිකා, *Sitándiká*, s. plant, *trianthera decandra*, [Colloq. මහ සාරණ *maha-sárana* and සුළු සාරණ *sulu-sárana*].

සිතාභ්‍ර, *Sitábhra*, *s.* (සිත *sita* and අභ්‍ර *abhra* cloud) camphor, [Colloq. කපුරු *kapuru*].

සිතාම්බර, *Sitámbara*, *s.* (සිත *sita* white, අම්බර *ambara* vesture) ascetic wearing white garments.

සිතාම්බුජ, *Sitámbuja*, *s.* (සිත *sita* white, අම්බුජ *ambuja* lotus) white lotus.

සිතාර්ජක, *Sitárjaka*, *s.* (සිත *sita* and අර්ජක *arjaka* basil) plant, according to one authority, *cleome pentaphylla;* or to another, white basil, *ocimum gratissimum.*

සිතාලතා, *Sitá-latá*, *s.* (සිතා white, ලතා creeper) durba grass, with white blossoms.

සිතාසිය, *Sitásiya*, *s.* Subpœna, summons: pl. සිතාසි *sitási.*

සිතාසිකරණවා, *Sitásikaraṇawá*, *v.* to subpœna.

සිති, *Siti*, *s.* colour white, [Colloq. සුදු පාට *sudu-páṭa*]; also black, [Colloq. කළු *kaḷu*].

සිතිකණ්ඨ, *Sitikanṭha*, *s.* (සිති black, කණ්ඨ throat) name of Ṣiva.

සිතියම්කරණවා, *Sitiyam-karaṇawá*, *v.* to paint, to draw.

සිතියම, *Sitiyama*, *s.* painting, delineation, map: pl. සිතියම් *sitiyam;* Elu form of චිත්‍රකර්ම *chitra-karma.*

සිතියර, *Sitiyara*, *s.* painter, colourer: pl. සිතියරු *sitiyaru.*

සිතිවිල්ල, *Sitivilla*, *s.* thought, reflection; anxious thought, solicitude: pl. සිතිවිලි *sitivili.*

සිතීම, *Sitíma*, *s.* thought, consideration: see සිතිවිල්ල *sitivilla.*

සිතු, *Situ*, *s.* mind; thought, wish.

සිතුම, *Situma*, see සිතිවිල්ල *sitivilla.*

සිතුමිණ, *Situmiṇa*, } සිතුමිණිරුවන, *Situmiṇiruwana*, } *s.* (සිතු thought, මිණ gem) fabulous gem which bestows on the possessor whatever is wished.

සිතුයම, *Situyama*, *s.* painting, colouring, delineating, [Colloq. පින්තාරුව *pintáruwa*].

සිතුවක්කාර, *Situwakkára*, *a.* (සිතු thought, කාර doing) self-willed, obstinate.

සිතුවක්කාරකම, *Situwakkárakama*, *s.* obstinacy, stubbornness.

සිතුවක්කාරයා, *Situwakkárayá*, *s.* obstinate or stubborn man.

සිතෙනවා, *Sitenawá*, *v.* thought occurs; it is thought: pret. සිතුනා *situná.*

සිතෝදර, *Sitódara*, *s.* (සිත *sita* white, උදර *udara* belly) name of Kuvéra who is whitened by a leprous taint.

සිද්දකරණවා, *Siddakaraṇawá*, *v.* to cause, to occasion, to effect.

සිද්දවීම, *Siddavíma*, *s.* event, occurrence.

සිද්දවෙනවා, *Siddawenawá*, *v.* to happen, to occur: pret. සිද්දවුනා *siddawuná.*

සිධ, } සිද්ධ, } *Siddha*, *s.* (සිධ *sidha* to effect, ක්ත *kta* aff.) divine personage of undefined attributes and character; sort of demigod; sage, seer; twenty-first of the astronomical Yógas; adept, magician: *a.* accomplished, effected, completed; happened; demonstrated, proved; decided, valid in law.

සිද්ධකරණවා, *Siddhakaraṇawá*, *v.* to effect, to accomplish, to bring about, to fulfil, to attain.

සිද්ධදේව, *Siddha-déwa*, *s.* name of Ṣiva.

සිද්ධධාතු, *Siddha-dhátu*, } සිද්ධරස, *Siddha-rasa*, } *s.* (සිධ adept, (in alchemy), ධාතු or රස mineral) quicksilver, [Colloq. රසදිය *rasadiya*].

සිද්ධාන්ත, *Siddhánta*, *s.* (සිධ *siddha* completed, අන්ත *anta* end, conclusion) demonstrated or established conclusion, as the concurrent doctrines of all the authorities on a subject similarly interpreted.

සිද්ධාන්ත සංග්‍රහය, *Siddhánta-sangrahaya*, *s.* (සිධාන්ත and සංග්‍රහ *sangraha* compilation) grammar of the Elu or ancient language of Ceylon.

සිද්ධාර්ථ, *Siddhárttha*, *s.* (සිධ *siddha* complete, අර්ථ *arttha* meaning, wealth) name of Gautama; white mustard; banyan tree; fifty-third year of the Indian cycle.

සිද්ධි, *Siddhi*, *s.* (සිධ *sidha* to accomplish, ක්ති *kti* aff.) fulfilment, accomplishment, the entire completion of any undertaking, or attainment of any object; final emancipation from existence, Nirwáṇa or annihilation; prosperity, success.

සිද්ධිගුරු, *Siddhinguru*, *s.* dried ginger.

සිද, *Sida*, *a.* Siddha or divine personage; Elu form of සිද්ධ *siddha.*

සිදත්, *Sidat*, Elu form of සිද්ධාන්ත *siddhánta.*

සිදත්සඟරාව, *Sidatsangaráwa*, see සිද්ධාන්තසංග්‍රහය *siddhánta-sangrahaya.*

සිදඹු, *Sidambu*, *s.* (සිද and අඹු *ambu* woman) wife of a Siddha.

සිදරං, *Sidaran*, *s.* common citron.

සිදු, *Sidu*, *s.* generic title of Buddha; hole; lake; birth; river; small tree, *vitex negundo* [Colloq. සුදුනික *sudu-nika*]; sea, ocean, [Colloq. මුද *múda*]; from සින්ධු *sindhu;* fulfilment, accomplishment: see සිද්ධ *siddha;* purity, holiness, from ශුද්ධ *suddha.*

සිදුපෙන, *Sidupena*, see මුදුපෙන *múdu-pena*.

සිදුර, *Sidura*, *s.* hole, perforation, cavity, elephant; Elu form of සින්ධුර *sindhura:* pl. සිදුරු *siduru*.

සිදුවර, *Siduwara*, *s.* see සිදු *sidu;* small tree, *vitex negundo*, [Colloq. සුදුනික *sudu-nika*]; Elu form of සින්ධුවාර *sindhuwára*.

සිදුවරණ, *Siduwaraṇa*, *s.* small tree, *vitex negundo*, [Colloq. නික *nika*].

සිදුහතු, *Siduhatu*, *s.* name of Buddha; mustard: see සිතසර්ෂප *sita-sarshapa* and සිද්ධාර්ථ *siddhártha*.

සිඳ, *Sinda*, *s.* cutting, excision, from ච්ඡේද *chchhéda*.

සිඳදමනවා, *Sindadamanawá*, *v.* to cut off, to extirpate.

සිඳිනවා, *Sindinawá*, *v.* to cut, to cut off; to pluck up, as hair; to express oil: pret. සින්දා *sindá*.

සිඳිම, *Sindíma*, *s.* plucking off, expression of oil: verbal noun of the last.

සිඳු, *Sindu*, *s.* horse, [Colloq. අශ්වයා *aşwayá*]; sea.

සිඳුවනවා, *Sinduwanawá*, *v.* to cause to express oil: pret. සිඳෙව්වා *sindewwá;* causal form of සිඳිනවා *sindinawá*.

සිඳෙනවා, *Sindenawá*, *v.* to be expressed as oil; to be dried as water in a well or river: pret. සිඳුනා *sinduná;* neuter form of සිඳිනවා *sindinawá*.

සිධම, *Sidhma*, *s.* blotch, scab.

සිධ්මල, *Sidhmala*, *s.* (සිධම scab, ල aff.) scab; sort of leprosy: *a.* scabby.

සිධ්‍ය, *Sidhya*, *s.* (සිධ *sidha* to accomplish, ය *ya* aff.) eighth lunar asterism, containing stars in Cancer.

සින්, *Sin*, *s.* sitting, reclining.

සින්දුක, *Sinduka*, see සින්ධුක *sindhuka*.

සින්දුකාරයා, *Sindukárayá*, *s.* songster.

සින්දුව, *Sinduwa*, *s.* song, ballad: pl. සින්දු *sindu*.

සින්දුවාර, *Sinduwára*, see සින්ධුවාර *sindhuwára*.

සින්දූර, *Sindúra*, *s.* red lead, minium.

සින්දූරී, *Sindúrí*, *s.* species of *crinum*, *c. asiaticum* or *c. zeylanicum:* see තොලබෝ *tolabó* and ගොඩ මානිල් *goda-mánil;* plant, *woodfordia floribunda*, [Colloq. මලිත *malita*].

සින්ධු, *Sindhu*, *s.* ocean, sea; river Indus; country along the Indus or Sindhu; elephant; small tree, *vitex negundo*: see the next; river in general.

සින්ධුක, *Sindhuka*, *s.* small tree, *vitex negundo*, [Colloq. සුදුනික *sudu-nika*]: see සිදුවර *siduwara*.

සින්ධු කඵ, *Sindhu-kapha*, *s.* (සින්ධු sea, කඵ phlegm) cuttle fish bone.

සින්ධුජ, *Sindhuja*, *s.* (සින්ධු and ජ born) rock-salt, [Colloq. සහිඳලුණු *sahinda-luṇu*]: *a.* river or sea born, aquatic.

සින්ධුජා, *Sindhujá*, *s.* (සින්ධු ocean, ජ *ja* born) name of Lakshmí, the Indian Venus.

සින්ධුනාථ, *Sindhu-nátha*, *s.* (සින්ධු river, නාථ lord) ocean, [Colloq. මහමුද *mahamúda*].

සින්ධුර, *Sindhura*, *s.* elephant, [Colloq. අලියා *aliyá*].

සින්ධු ලවණ, *Sindhu-lawaṇa*, *s.* rock-salt.

සින්ධුවාර, *Sindhuwára*, *s.* (සින්ධු and වෘ *wṛi* to choose) horse of good breed, brought probably from the Sindh or the borders of India and Persia; small tree, *vitex negundo*, [Colloq. සුදුනික *sudu-nika*].

සින්ධුවාරච්ඡද, *Sindhuwárachchhada*,
සින්ධුවාරිකා, *Sindhuwáriká*,
සින්ධුවාරිත, *Sindhuwárita*,
s. tree, *vitex negundo*, [Colloq. නිකගස් *nika-gas*].

සින්ධුශයන, *Sindhu-şayana*, *s.* (සින්ධු ocean, ශයන couch) name of Vishṇu.

සින්ධූද්භව, *Sindhúdbhawa*, *s.* (සින්ධු Sindhu, උද්භව *udbhawa* produced) rock-salt, [Colloq. සහිඳලුණු *sahinda-lunu*].

සින්ධූර, *Sindhúra*, *s.* red lead, minium: see සින්දූර *sindúra*].

සින්නක්කරය, *Sinnakkaraya*, *s.* transfer, deed.

සිනාව, *Sináwa*, *s.* laughter, merriment.

සිනාවෙනවා,
සිනාසෙනවා,
සිනාහෙනවා,
v. to laugh, to be merry: pret. සිනාසුනා *sinásuná*.

සිනිඳස, *Sinidasa*, *s.* love, affection, kindness.

සිනිදු, *Sinidu*, *a.* smooth, oily, unctuous, greasy; thin, fine; amiable, kind, affectionate; Elu form of ස්නිග්ධ *snigdha*.

සිනිබලා, *Sinibalá*, *s.* tamarind: see සියඹලා *siyambalá*.

සිනිබාලී, *Sinibálí*, *s.* (සිනි digit of the moon, බල *bala* to contain) day preceding that of new moon, or that on which the moon rises scarcely visible.

සිප්පිය, *Sippiya*, *s.* oyster-shell.

සිප්පියා, *Sippiyá*, *s*, pearl oyster, [Colloq. මුතු බෙල්ලා *mutu-bellá*].

සිප, *Sipa*, *s.* an art, etc.: see ශිල්ප *şilpa;* embracing, saluting.

සිපගන්නවා, *Sipagannawá*, *v.* to embrace, to fold in the arms.

සිපත, *Sipata*, *s.* (අසි *asi* sword, පත leaf, blade) blade of a sword, [Colloq. කඩුතලේ *kadu-talé*].

සිපද, *Sipada*, see සිපද *sípada*.

සිපි, *Sipi*, s. (සිප *sipa* art, ඉ *i* aff.) artist, artificer, artizan.

සිපියෝ, *Sipiyó*, s. union.

සිපිරිගේ, *Sipirigé*, s. prison.

සිපිරියා, *Sipiriyá*, s. Jailor.

සිපිවිෂ්ට, *Sipivishṭa*, s. corruptly for ශිපිවිෂ්ට *ṣipivishṭa*, bald man; leper.

සිපුම්, *Sipum*, s. embracing, saluting.

සිඵා, *Siphá*, s. fibrous root; spikenard, *valeriana jatamansi;* river; turmeric, *curcuma longa*, [Colloq. කහ *kaha*]; root of the water lily.

සිඵාකන්ද, *Siphákanda*, s. (සිඵා and කන්ද root) root of a water lily.

සිඵාරුහ, *Sipháruha*, s. (සිඵා fibrous root, රුහ what grows) banyan tree, [Colloq. මහනුග *maha nuga*].

සිඹලි, *Simbali*, s. silk cotton tree, from ශාල්මලි *ṣálmali*.

සිඹිනවා, *Simbinawá*, v. to kiss, to smell: pret. සිම්බා *simbá*.

සිඹීම, *Simbíma*, s. smelling, kissing; verbal noun of සිඹිනවා *simbinawá*.

සිම්, *Sim*, s. boundary, a limit, from සීමා *símá*.

සිඹ, *Simba*, s. large shrub, *cassia alata*, [Colloq. රටතෝර *raṭa-tóra*]; legume, pod.

සිඹා, *Simbá*, s. legume, pod; see the last.

සිඹි. *Simbi*, s. kind of kidney bean, *phaseolus trilobus*, [Colloq. මුංවැන්න *muṇwęnna*].

සිමි, *Simi*, } s. master, lord; Elu form of ස්වාමි
සිමියා, *Simiyá*, } *swámi*.

සිමෙන්ති, *Simenti*, s. cement. (Eng.)

සිය, *Siya*, s. relation, kindred, [Colloq. නෑයෝ *ṇęyó*]; roof; hundred: *adj.* own, individual, self: see also සියය *siyaya*.

සියක්දහස, *Siyakdahasa*, s. one hundred thousand.

සියකුලය, *Siyakulaya*, s. one's own caste or family.

සියකෙළ, *Siyakeḷa*, s. Indra's thunderbolt.

සියදන්, *Siyadan*, } s. legitimate son.
සියදම්, *Siyadam*, }

සියන්, *Siyan*, s. kinsmen; plural of සිය *siya*.

සියන් දුඹුළු, *Siyan-dumbuḷu*, s. soot.

සියපත්, *Siyapat*, s. (සිය hundred, පත් leaf) lotus, *nelumbium speciosum*, [Colloq. නෙළුම් *neḷum*], or *nymphæa lotus*, [Colloq. ඕලු *ólu*], from ශතපත්‍ර *ṣata-patra*.

සියපද, *Siya-pada*, s. (සිය and පද foot) centipede, [Colloq. පත්තෑයා *pattęyá*].

සියඹලා, *Siyambalá*, s. tamarind tree, *tamarindus indica (Leguminosæ)*.

සියය, *Siyaya*, s. hundred, the number.

සියරු, *Siyarú*, s. (සිය own, රු state) one's own form; natural or peculiar state or disposition.

සියරැලි, *Siyarẹli*, a. (සිය hundred, රැලි wave, flash) forked as lightning.

සියල්, *Siyal*, } s. all, the whole.
සියල්ල, *Siyalla*, }

සියලඟ, *Siyalanga*, s. (සියල් *siyal* all, අඟ *anga* limb) whole body.

සියලු, *Siyalu*, a. all, whole.

සියහ, *Siyaha*, *ind.* continually, perpetually; Elu form of සතත *satata*.

සියහුතන්, *Siyahutan*, s. name of Indra; fire, or Agni the deity of fire.

සියුන්, *Siyun*, } a. sharp, piercing, cutting; fine,
සියුම්, *Siyum*, } delicate, minute.

සියුරු, *Siyuru*, s. bartavelle or Greek partridge, *perdix rufa*, [Colloq. ඇටිකුකුළා *ẹtikukulá*]; Elu form of චකෝර *chakóra*.

සියුරු හැඬලීම, *Siyuru-hẹndalíma*, s. act of whistling.

සියො, *Siyo*, s. union, junction, association; relation, kindred.

සියොත්, *Siyot*, s. bird in general; Ceylon hornbill, *tockus gingalinsis*, [Colloq. කෑදැත්තා *kẹndattá*]; Elu form of චාතක *chátaka*.

සියොත් පියෙස්, *Siyot-piyes*, s. heavens, sky, atmosphere, [Colloq. අහස *ahasa*].

සියොතුන්, *Siyotun*, see සියොත් *siyot*.

සියොලඟ, *Siyolanga*, see සියලඟ *siyalanga*.

සිර, *Sira*, s. confinement, imprisonment, incarceration; also, the head.

සිරකන්, *Sirakan*, s. female ornament.

සිරකරණවා, *Sirakaraṇawá*, v. to imprison, to stop the progress of anything.

සිරකාරයා, *Sirakárayá*, s. prisoner: pl. සිරකාරයෝ *sirakárayó*.

සිරගෙය, *Sirageya*, s. prison, gaol: see හිරගෙය *hirageya*.

සිරස, *Sirasa*, s. head.

සිරා, *Sirá*, s. any vessel of the body, really or supposed of a tubular form, as a nerve, gut, tendon, [Colloq. නහර *nahara*].

සිරාජාල, *Sirájála*, s. (සිරා and ජාල multitude) arteries collectively.

සිරි, *Siri*, s. fortune, success, prosperity; beauty, splendour; fame, glory; wealth; virtue, moral merit; Lakshmí, the goddess of plenty: see ශ්‍රී *ṣrí*: plough; tree, *cathartocarpus fistula;* likeness, resemblance; species of reed, *saccharum cylindricum*; sword, [Colloq. කඩුව *kaduwa*]; dagger; arrow, [Colloq. ඊගහ *ígaha*]; murderer, killer; locust.

සිරිකඩ, *Sirikada*, *s.* sandal wood tree, [Colloq. සඳුන් *sandun*]; spray.

සිරිකත, *Sirikata*, *s.* (සිරි and කත woman) name of Lakshmí, from ශ්‍රීකාන්තාව *sṛikántáwa*.

සිරිකමල, *Sirikamala*, *s.* sandal wood, [Colloq. සඳුන් *sandun*].

සිරිගන, *Sirigana*, *s.* (සිරි virtue, ගන multitude) epithet or title of Buddha, [Colloquial. බුදුන් *budun*].

සිරිඟර, *Siringara*, *s.* wanton sport; copulation, love, passion or sentiment as an object of poetical description or dramatic representation; Elu form of ශෘංගාර *sṛiṅgára*.

සිරිඞි, *Siriṅgi*, *s.* sort of poison, used for tipping arrows, etc.; sort of sheat fish, *silurus pungentissimus*; gold.

සිරිත, *Sirita*, *s.* custom, traditionary practice or observance: pl. **සිරිත්** *sirit*.

සිරිතේක්කු, *Siritékku*, *s.* shrub, *siphonanthus indica*.

සිරිදා, *Siridá*, *s.* (සිරි wealth, දා who gives) name of Wesamuni or Kuvéra the Indian god of wealth.

සිරිදිය, *Siridiya*, *s.* name of Vishṇu.

සිරින්, *Sirin*, *ind.* as, like, resembling.

සිරින, *Sirina*, *s.* tortoise, [Colloq. ඉබ්බා *ibbá*, කෑස්බෑවා *kęsbęwá*]; oyster, [Colloq. බෙල්ලා *bellá*]; shell fish in general.

සිරිනෑ, *Sirinę*, *s.* tortoise: see the last.

සිරිපති, *Siripati*, *s.* name of Vishṇu.

සිරිපද, *Siripada*, *s.* the illustrious foot.

සිරිපන, *Siripana*, *s.* (සිරි plough, පන hand) name of Balabhadra.

සිරිපා, *Siripá*, *s.* the foot of Buddha, Adam's Peak (literally the illustrious foot): see ශ්‍රීපාද *sṛipáda*.

සිරිබර, *Siribara*, *s.* (සිරි and බර load) great wealth or fame: *a.* abounding with prosperity, wealthy.

සිරිබෝ, *Siribó*, *s.* variety called *piper* or *chavica siriboa* of the pepper plant, *piper betel (Piperaceæ);* also called රට බුලත්වැල් *raṭa-bulat-węl*; necklace resembling in form the flowers of the betel creeper.

සිරිමත්, *Sirimat*, *s.* (සිරි and මත් poss. aff.) name of Vishṇu, also of Kuvéra and of Buddha: *a.* wealthy, opulent; prosperous, fortunate, etc.

සිරිය, *Siriya*, *s.* a dagger or small sword.

සිරියරා, *Siriyará*, *s.* a carpenter, [Colloq. වඩුවා *waḍuwá*]: pl. **සිරියරු** *siriyaru*.

සිරියල්, *Siriyal*, *s.* yellow orpiment, Elu form of හරිතාල *haritála*.

සිරිරු, *Siriru*, *s.* body, Elu form of ශරීර *ṣaríra*.

සිරිල, *Sirila*, *s.* messenger, courier; bael tree, *ægle marmelos*, [Colloq. බෙලි *beli*].

සිරිලක, *Sirilaka*, *s.* name of Ceylon, Elu form of ශ්‍රීලංකා *sṛílaṅká*.

සිරිවටු, *Siriwaṭu*, *s.* plant, *sida cordifolia*: see **සිරිවැඩිබැලිල** *siriwęḍi-bęlila*.

සිරිවස්ලකුණු, *Siriwas-lakuṇu*, *s.* (සිරිවස *siriwasa* and ලකුණු mark) name of Vishṇu.

සිරිවස, *Siriwasa*, *s.* name of Vishṇu; a particular mark or curl of hair on the breast of Vishṇu; Elu form of ශ්‍රීවත්ස *ṣríwatsa*.

සිරිවැඩිබැලිල, *Siriwęḍi-bęlila*, }
සිරිවැඩිබැවිල, *Siriwęḍi-bęvila*, } *s.* plant, according to one authority, *sida cordifolia*, according to another *hibiscus rigidus*.

සිරිවැඩිය, *Siriwęḍiya*, see the last.

සිරිසඳ, *Sirisanda*, *s.* (සිරි prosperity, සඳ pre-eminence) name of Lakshmí, goddess of wealth, etc.

සිරිහිමි, *Sirihimi*, *s.* (සිරි Lakshmí, හිමි lord) name of Vishṇu.

සිරු, *Siru*, *s.* cricket, one which destroys the core of trees, [Colloq. නගුල *nagula*].

සිරුර, *Sirura*, }
සිරුරු, *Siruru*, } *s.* body, from ශරීර *ṣaríra*.

සිරුරුකිස, *Sirurukisa*, *s.* (සිරුරු body, කිස action) any natural evacuation; washing the body, ablution; personal decoration, etc.

සිල්, *Sil*, *s.* hole, perforation; moral observance or obligation, prescribed duty, etc.: see සීල *síla*.

සිල්කරණවා, *Silkaraṇawá*, *s.* make a hole through.

සිල්ගන්නවා, *Sil-gannawá*, *v.* to promise the obedience to the commands of Buddha.

සිල්පි, *Silpi*, *s.* artisan.

සිල්රකිනවා, *Sil-rakinawá*, *v.* to observe the precepts of Buddha.

සිල්වත්, *Silwat*, *a.* (සිල් and වත් poss. aff.) observant of moral and religious duties, pious.

සිල්වතා, *Silwatá*, *s.* pious man.

සිල, *Sila*, *s.* hole, perforation; also **හිල** *hila*.

සිලම්බුව, *Silambuwa*, *s.* rings or bangles worn on the ankles by dancers.

සිලව්කරණවා, *Silawkaraṇawá*, *v.* to balance an account: see හිලව්ව *hilawwa*.

සිලව්කෙරීම, *Silawkeríma*, *s.* balancing any account, liquidation.

සිලව්ව, *Silawwa*, *s.* substitution: see හිලව්ව *hilawwa*.

සිලවටුවා, *Sila-waṭuwá*, *s.* bird called the wood sand-piper, *totarns glareola (Scolopacidæ*, order *Grallæ)*.

සිලි, *Sili*, *s.* fruit.

සිලිමුව, *Silimuwa*, see ශිලීමුඛ *ṣilímukha*.

සිලිල්, *Silil*, *s.* water, [Colloq වතුර *watura*]; drug and perfume: see ඉරිවේරිය *iriwériya*.

සිලිල්දන්, *Silildan*, *s.* the lotus, [Colloq. නෙළුම් *neḷum*].

සිලිල්ද, *Sililda*, *s.* (සිලිල් water, ද what gives) cloud, rainy cloud, [Colloq. වලාකුළ *walákuḷa*].

සිලිල්නා, *Sililná*, *s.* (සිලිල් and නා lord) name of Varuṇa, the deity who presides over all waters.

සිලිල, *Silila*, *s.* water, [Colloq. වතුර *watura*]; cold, [Colloq. සීතල *sítala*].

සිලිලද, *Sililadá*, see සිලිල්ද *sililda*.

සිලිලාර, *Sililára*, *s.* sea, ocean, [Colloq. මූද *múda*]; stream of water, drain, etc.

සිලිලි, *Sílili*, see සිලිල *silila*.

සිලිලිද, *Sililidá*, see සිලිල්ද *sililda*.

සිලුටු, *Siluṭu*, *a.* smooth, polished; clinging, adhering to.

සිලුච්චය, *Siluchchaya*, *s.* rat snake, [Colloq. ගැරඬියා *gẹraṇḍiyá*]; mountain: see ශිලෝච්චය *ṣilóchchaya*.

සිව්, *Siw*, *adj.* four, consisting of four, [Colloq. හතර *hatara*].

සිව් අත්, *Siw-at*, *s.* (සිව් four, අත් hands) name of Vishṇu.

සිව්ගහණ, *Siw-gahaṇa*, *s.* (සිව් four, ගහණ nose) one having four noses, epithet of මහාබ්‍රහ්මයා *mahá-brahmayá*.

සිව්දිවු, *Siwdiwu*, see සතරමහ ද්විපය *sataramaha-dvípaya*.

සිව්දිවුහිමි, *Siwdiwuhimi*, *s.* (සිව් four, දිවු continent, හිමි lord) universal monarch, universal emperor.

සිව්දිසාව, *Siw-disáwa*, *s.* the four quarters.

සිව්දෙස්, *Siw-dès*, *s.* (සිව් and දෙස් quarter) four cardinal points; ray, sun-beam.

සිව්දෑගඳ, *Siwdẹ-gaṇda*, *s.* (සිව් four, දෑ sort, ගඳ perfume) class of four perfumes, viz. saffron, frankincense, gum benjamin or olibanum, and Yávana, a sort of incense said to be produced in the country of the Yavanas.

සිව්පදය, *Siwpadaya*, *s.* (සිව් and පද *pada* foot) verse, metre of stanzas consisting of four lines.

සිව්පසය, *Siwpasaya*, *s.* (සිව් and පස *pasa* necessary or utensil) the four requisites of a priest, viz. the yellow robe, alms, a residence, and sick diet.

සිව්පාවා, *Siwpáwá*, *s.* (සිව් and පා foot, වා aff.) quadruped: pl. සිව්පාවෝ *siwpáwó*.

සිව්පිළිසිඹියාව, *Siwpiḷisimbiyáwa*, *s.* (සිව් four, පිළි intensitive prefix, සිඹියා *simbiyá* discrimination) four attainments peculiar to the highest order of Rahats, viz. a knowledge of ethics, of dharma or religious doctrines, of the grammatical comments and expositions of the dharma, and a supernatural discrimination.

සිව්බලකෙළි, *Siwbalakeḷi*, *s.* game of chess.

සිව්බා, *Siwbá*, *s.* (සිව් and බා arm) name of Vishṇu.

සිව්මැදුර, *Siwmẹdura*, *s.* window, an air hole, [Colloq. ජනේලය *janélaya*].

සිව්මැලි, *Siwmẹli*, *a.* happy, at ease; soft, delicate; Elu form of සුකුමාල *sukumála*.

සිවර, *Siwra*, *s.* priest's yellow robe, from චීවර *chívara*.

සිව්රඟකෙළි, *Siwraṅga-keḷi*, *s.* (සිව් four, අඟ *aṅga* member, කෙළි game) game of chess.

සිව්රඟසෙනඟ, *Siwraṅga-senaga*, *s.* (සිව් and ර augment, අඟ *aṅga* limb, සෙනඟ host) complete army, composed of elephants, horses, chariots, and infantry.

සිව්රද, *Siwrada*, *s.* (සිව් and රද king) four regents of the four cardinal points.

සිව්රු, *Siwru*, *s.* bartavelle or Greek partridge, *perdix rufa*: see සියුරු *siyuru*.

සිව්රැස්, *Siwrẹs*, *s.* (සිව් four, ඇස් *ẹs* angle) plant, see හිරැස්ස *hirẹssa*: *a.* quadrangular, four cornered; square, four sided.

සිව්වණක්, *Siwwaṇak*, *a.* (සිව් and වණ *waṇa* sort) of four sorts or classes.

සිව්වත්, *Siwwat*, } *s.* (සිව් and වත් face) name of
සිව්වත, *Siwwata*, } Brahma: see සිව්හිස් *siw-his*.

සිව්වරම්, *Siw-waram*, *s.* (සිව් and වරම් best) regents of the four cardinal points.

සිව්වරම් දෙවියෝ, *Siwwaram-deviyó*, *s.* four guardian gods of the cardinal points.

සිව්වස්, *Siwwas*, *s.* name of Vishṇu.

සිව්හිස්, *Siw-his*, *s.* (සිව් four, හිස් head) name of Brahma, who is represented with four heads.

සිවංගුරු, *Siwaṅguru*, *s.* red chalk.

සිවලා, *Siwalá*, *s.* jackal: pl. සිවල්ලු *siwallu*.

සිවි, *Sivi*, *s.* ray, sun-beam; skin, skin of any animal: see සිවිය *siviya*; king so named.

සිවිකා, *Siviká*, *s.* (සිව *siva* pleasure, ඉක *ika* aff.) palanquin, litter.

සිවිගෙය, *Sivigeya*, *s.* (සිවි and ගෙය house) howdah, palanquin carried on the back of an elephant, litter.

සිවිය, *Siviya*, *s.* lamina, coat, tegument, tunicle; skin; rind, bark, or integuments of fruit, etc.; bladder; *piper chavya*, Elu form of චව්‍ය *chawyá*.

සිවියවැල්, *Siviya-wel*, *s.* species of pepper plant, *piper charya (Piperaceæ)*.

සිවිර, *Sivira*, *s.* camp; royal camp or residence.

සිවිරත, *Sivirata*, see සිවිගෙය *sivigeya*.

සිවුදු, *Siwudu*, *s.* hole, perforation.

සිස්, *Sis*, *s.* head, from ශීර්ෂ *sírsha*: *a.* empty, void, vain, unimportant.

සිස්කම, *Siskama*, *s.* emptiness, vanity, vacuum.

සිස්පලා, *Sispalá*, *s.* bird in general.

සිසාරණවා, *Sisáraṇawá*, *v.* to circumambulate, to perambulate; to move circulary: pret. සිසැරුවා *siséruwá*.

සිසාළ, *Sisáḷa*, *part.* moved round, [Colloq. කරකැවූ *karakewú*].

සිසි, *Sisi*, *s.* moon, [Colloq. හඳ *haṇda*].

සිසිපිය, *Sisipiya*, *s.* (සිසි moon, පිය beloved) blue lotus, *nymphæa stellata*, [Colloq. මානෙල් *mánel*]; also, *jasminum mulliflorum* or *pubescens*.

සිසිපුත්, *Sisiput*, *s.* (සිසි moon, පුත් son) the planet Mercury, [Colloq. බුදහු *budahu*].

සිසිල්, *Sisil*, *a.* cold.

සිසිල්කරණවා, *Sisilkaraṇawá*, *v.* to cool.

සිසිල, *Sisila*, *s.* cold, cold season: *a.* cold.

සිසුරු, *Sisuru*, *s.* clever or skilful man, [Colloq. සමර්ථයා *samarthayá*]; hole.

සිහල, *Sihla*, *s.* incense, gum benjamin or olibanum.

සිහ, *Siha*, *s.* lion, from සිංහ *sinha*; mother of Ráhu; (in composition) pre-eminent.

සිහතෙන, *Sihatena*, } *s.* (සිහ and තෙන son)
සිහතෙනේ, *Sihatené*, } name of Ráhu.

සිහසුන, *Sihasuna*, *s.* throne, from සිංහාසන *sinhásana*.

සිහි, *Sihi*, see සිහිය *Sihiya*.

සිහිත, *Sihita*, *s.* reproach, reflection; abuse, scurrility.

සිහින්, *Sihin*, *a.* small, thin, fine, delicate.

සිහින් අරත්ත, *Sihin-aratta*, *s.* (සිහින් small, අරත්ත mimosa octendra) species of *mimosa;* perfume, root of a plant.

සිහින් ඇල්වි, *Sihin-elví*, *s.* (සිහින් small) kind of paddy, *oryza sativa*.

සිහින්කරණවා, *Sihinkaraṇawá*, *v.* to make small.

සිහින් දඹල, *Sihin-dambala*, *s.* plant, variety of *phaseolus*.

සිහින් මිදි, *Sihin-midi*, *s.* tree, *premna spinosa* or *longifolia*.

සිහින් මැඩහඟු, *Sihin-medahangu*, *s.* plant, variety of *dæmia extensa*.

සිහින් වී, *Sihin-ví*, *s.* kind of paddy, *oryza satira*.

සිහිය, *Sihiya*, *s.* remembrance, memory, recollection; reason, understanding, from සමර *samara*.

සිහිල්, *Sihil*, *a.* cold, frigid.

සිහිල, *Sihila*, *s.* sandal wood tree, [Colloq. සඳුන් *sandun*]; coldness, frigidity.

සිහිලබනවා, *Sihilabanawá*, *v.* to revive, to recover from insensibility.

සිළු, *Siḷu*, *s.* head, top, peak; crown or tiara; crest of the peacock; flame, from සිඛා *sikhá;* planet Saturn, [Colloq. සෙනසුරා *senasurá*]; lighted wick.

සිළුමිණ, *Siḷumiṇa*, *s.* (සිළු head or a crest, මිණ gem) hair of the head, Buddha's hair: see the next; chief gem in a crest.

සිළුමිණිසෑය, *Siḷumiṇiséya*, *s.* (සිළුමිණි and සෑය monument) monumental receptacle in the world of Brahma, said to have been constructed by that deity for the purpose of depositing the hair of Buddha which was cut off at the period of his entering the priesthood.

සී, *Sí*, *s.* (සී to sleep) sleep, repose; lion; laughing, laughter; ploughing: *a.* best, excellent.

සීක, *Síka*, *a.* (සී to sleep, ක aff.) slothful, indolent, apathetic.

සීකම, *Síkam*, *s.* (සීය *síya* plough, කම action) ploughing, cultivation, agriculture.

සීකර, *Síkara*, *s.* (සීක to scatter or sprinkle, අර *ara* aff.) thin drizzling rain, rain driven by the wind.

සීග්‍ර, *Sígra*, *a.* corruptly for ශීඝ්‍ර *sighra*, expeditious, fine (applied to workmanship).

සීගතු, *Sígatu*, *s.* wrinkles caused by cold, chilblains.

සීට්ටුව, *Síṭṭuwa*, *s.* document or order written on a palmyra or talipot leaf: receipt, bill: pl. සීට්ටු *síṭṭu*.

සීතා, *Sítá*, *s.* furrow, track of a plough share; daughter of Janaka and wife of Rámachandra; name of Lakshmí.

සීතාපති, *Sítá-pati, s.* (සීතා and පති lord) name of Ráma.

සිතාම්බුජ, *Sítámbuja,* } *s.* white lotus, [Colloq.
සිතාම්භෝජ, *Sitámbhója,* } ඕලු *ólu*].

සිතාර්ජක, *Sitárjaka, s.* plant, species of the *ocimum,* [Colloq. අඳුතලා *andutalá*].

සිදන්, *Sídan, s.* flux tinged with blood, indicating the emptiness of the bowels.

සිදන්ත, *Sídanta,* } *s.* (සද *sada* to
සිදන්තසාගරය, *Sídanta-ságaraya,* } be congealed, අන්ත *anta* aff.) the seven seas surrounding Mahá Méru, so called from the intense cold and unruffled state of the water.

සිධු, *Sidhu, s.* spirit distilled from molasses.

සින්, *Sín,* see සිහින් *sihin.*

සින් ඉද්ද, *Sín-idda, s.* (සින් thin, ඉද්ද wrightea) plant, probably a species of *oleander.*

සින් එඬරු, *Sín-endaru, s.* species of castor oil plant, *ricinus communis.*

සින් එන්සාල්, *Sín-ensál, s.* (සින් and එන්සාල් cardamums) *elettaria cardamomum* (minor), small cardamums.

සින් ඩෙබර, *Sín-debara, s.* small species of jujube, variety of *zizyphus jujuba.*

සින් දුමුඩ, *Sín-dumuda, s.* sort of bind-weed, *convolvulus (or lettsomia) nervosus.*

සින් නාරන්, *Sín-náran, s.* small variety of the mandarin orange, *citrus nobilis.*

සින් මිදි, *Sín-midi, s.* species of the *premna spinosa.*

සින් මුං, *Sín-mun, s.* variety of the kidney bean, *phaseolus vulgaris.*

සින් මැඩහඟු, *Sín-medahangu, s.* plant, variety of *dæmia extensa.*

සින් රැත්ත, *Sín-retta, s.* plant, variety of *mimosa octandra.*

සිනා, *Sína, s.* fool, blockhead; large snake.

සිනක්කාරං, *Sinakkáran, s.* alum.

සිනච්චට්ටි, *Sínachchatti, s.* metal of which bullets, and pans are made, cast iron.

සිනය, *Sínaya, s.* dream, from ස්වප්න *swapna.*

සිනි, *Síni, s.* sugar.

සිනිය, *Síniya, s.* bell; thorny shrub, *acacia farnisiana (Leguminosæ).*

සිනුක්, *Sínuk, s.* milk hedge plant, *euphorbia tortilis (Euphorbiaceæ).*

සිනුව, *Sínuwa, s.* bell: pl. සිනු *sinu.*

සිපද, *Sípada, s.* stanza of four lines: see සිව්පද *siwpada;* also the elephantiasis, Páli form of ශ්ලීපද *slípada.*

සිපාලිකා, *Síphálíká,* see ශේපාලිකා *séphálíká.*

සීමන්ත, *Símanta, s.* (සීමා *símá* limit, අන්ත *anta* end) separation of the hair on each side, so as to leave a distinct line on the top of the head.

සීමන්තිනී, *Símantiní, s.* (සීමන්ත *símanta* separation of the hair, ඉනී *ini* aff.) woman in general, [Colloq. ස්ත්‍රී *strí*].

සීමාව, *Símáwa, s.* boundary, limit, landmark, etc. bank, shore; rectitude, observance of due bounds in morals: pl. සීමා *símá.*

සීමැදුර, *Simedura, s.* window, [Colloq. ජනේලය *janélaya*].

සිය, *Siya, s.* hundred: see සියා *hiya.*

සිරද, *Sírada, s.* (සි and රද king) lion, [Colloq. සිංහයා *sinhayá*].

සිරළුවා, *Síraluwá, s.* one who has forsaken the Buddhist priesthood, ex-priest.

සිරු, *Síru, s.* plough; cricket (insect).

සිරුමාරු, *Sírumáru, s.* good behaviour; steadiness; care.

සිරෙණවා, *Sírenawá,* neuter form of සූරණවා *súranawá.*

සිරැස්, *Sírẹs,* } see හිරැස්ස *híressa.*
සිරැස්ස, *Síressa,* }

සීල පාරමිතාව, *Síla-páramitáwa, v.* (සීල prescribed duty, පාරමිතාව páramitáwa) peculiar duty or practice of a Bódhisat, or any candidate for the Buddhaship, viz. enduring corporal punishment, suffering every worldly privation, as of riches, wife, children, etc. and lastly resigning life itself in the performance of religious duties: see පාරමිතාව *páramitáwa.*

සීලව්‍රතය, *Síla-wrataya, s.* (සීල and ව්‍රත *wrata* practice) observance of religious and moral obligations, piety.

සීලස්කන්ධ, *Sílaskandha, s.* (සීල and ස්කන්ධ multitude) religious observances collectively.

සීලාචාර, *Síláchára, s.* civilized manners: see සීල ව්‍රතය *sílawrataya.*

සීලාචාරකම, *Síláchárakama, s.* courtesy, politeness; good manners, civility.

සිවන, *Sívana, s.* (සිව to sew, ණය *nya* aff.) sewing, stitching.

සිවනා, *Sivaná, s.* service, employment.

සිවල, *Sívala,* } *s.* (සි to sleep, on the water, වල
සිවැල, *Sívela,* } aff.) aquatic plant, *rallisneria;* benzoin or storax.

සීස, *Sísa,* } *s.* (සි to bind, ක්ති *kti* aff.) lead,
සීසක, *Sísaku,* } [Colloq. ඊයම් *íyam*].

සිසන්න, *Sísanna,* see සිහන්න *síhanna.*

සිසපත්‍රක, *Sísa-patraka*, see සිස *sísa*.

සිසානවා, *Sisánawá, v.* (සිය *siya* plough, සානවා to plough) to plough, to till: pret. සිසෑවා *siséwá;* also called හිහානවා *hihánawá*.

සිහ, *Síha, s.* Páli form of සිංහ *sinha*, lion.

සිහන්න, *Síhanna, s.* sense, recollection.

සිහපපාත, *Síha-papáta, s.* (සිහ lion, පපාත precipice) one of the seven lakes in the Himálaya so named.

සිහල, *Síhala*, see සිංහල *Sinhala*.

සිහුණ්ඩ, *Síhunda*, } *s.* milk hedge plant, *euphorbia*
සිහුණ්ඩි, *Síhundi*. } *antiquorum*, [Colloq. දලුක් *daluk*].

සු, *Su, ind.* a particle and prefix analogous to good, well; also implying reverence, worship, honour; increase, prosperity; excess, exceeding.

සුං, *Sun*, see සුන් *sun*.

සුංගම, *Sungama, s.* toll, tribute, custom, etc: pl. සුංගම් *sungam*.

සුංගා, *Sungá, s.* sort of sheat fish, *silurus pungentissimus*.

සුංගාඩම, *Sungádama, s.* rudder, helm: pl. සුංගාඩම් *sungádam*, [Colloq. සුක්කානම *sukkánama*].

සුංගාඩම් ඔරුව, *Sungádam-oruwa, s.* (සුංගාඩම *sungádama* helm, ඔරුව boat) large boat, dhoney.

සුක්කානම, *Sukkánama, s.* rudder, helm: pl. සුක් කානම් *sukkánam*.

සුකට, *Sukata, s.* merit, power or virtue of good works, [Colloq. කුසල *kusala*].

සුකන්ද, *Sukanda, s.* (සු good, කන්ද root) onion, *allium cepa*, [Colloq. ලූනු *lúnu*]; yam, [Colloq. අල *ala*]; sort of grass, *scirpus kyssoor;* esculent root, *amorphophallus campanulatus*, [Colloq. කිඩාරන් *kidáran*].

සුකර්මන්, *Sukarman*, } *s.* (සු good, කර්ම act, action)
සුකර්මා, *Sukarmá*, } artist or architect of the gods; one of the astronomical Yógas: *a.* virtuous, good, acting virtuously, doing what is right and fit.

සුකර, *Sukara, a.* (සු pleasure, කර to make or confer) easy, practicable, attainable.

සුකවල්ලභ, *Suka-wallabha, s.* (සුක parrot, වල්ලභ beloved) pomegranate, *punica granatum*, [Coll: දෙළුම් *delum*].

සුකවාහ, *Sukawáha, s.* (සුක and වාහ who is borne) name of Kámadéwa, the Indian Cupid.

සුකාක්‍රීඩා, *Sukákrídá, s.* shrub, *adenanthera pavonina*, [Colloquial: මදටිය *madatiya*]: see මහරි *mahari*.

සුකාදන, *Sukádana, s.* (සුක *suka* parrot, අදන *adana* eating) pomegranate: see සුකවල්ලභ *sukuwallabha*.

සුකාශ, *Sukása, s.* species of *momordica*, [Colloq. වැල්තුඹ *wel-tumba*].

සුකුමාර, *Sukumára, s.* (සු very, exceedingly, කුමාර soft, young) variety of the sugar cane, *saccharum officinarum;* kind of grain, *panicum colonum;* tree, kind of wild *champaca: a.* soft, smooth, tender; youthful, young.

සුකුමාරක, *Sukumáraka, s.* tree: see කොල්ලන් කොල *kollan-kola*.

සුකුමාරා, *Sukumárá, s.* double jasmine; great flowered jasmine; plantain, [Colloq. කෙසෙල් *kesel*].

සුකෘත, *Sukrita, s.* (සු well, කෘත made or done) virtue, moral merit; fortune, auspiciousness: *a.* virtuous, pious; befriended, assisted, etc.

සුකෘතකර්ම, *Sukrita-karma, s.* (සුකෘත and කර්ම act) act of virtue, moral action.

සුකෘති, *Sukriti, s.* virtue, well doing; the practice of religious austerities: see සුකෘත *sukrita*.

සුඛ, *Sukha, s.* (සු good, ඛ organ of sense) happiness, pleasure, delight; heaven, paradise: *a.* happy, joyful, delighted.

සුඛදා, *Sukhadá, s.* (සුඛ pleasure, ද who or what gives) woman; courtezan of Indra's heaven: *a.* conferring or affording pleasure.

සුඛවර්චක, *Sukha-warchaka*, see සුවර්චස *suwarchasa*.

සුඛවාසන, *Sukha-wásana, s.* (සුඛ pleasure, වාසන perfume) perfume for the mouth.

සුඛාවහ, *Sukháwaha, a.* (සුඛ *sukha* and ආ *á* prer. වහ to convey) conferring pleasure, delighting, pleasing.

සුඛිත, *Sukhita, a.* (සුඛ *sukha* and ඉත aff.) joyful, delighted, happy, pleased.

සුඛිතයා, *Sukhitayá, s.* one who is at ease and happy.

සුඛී, *Sukhí, s.* (සුඛ *sukha* pleasure, ඉන් *in* aff.) religious ascetic.

සුඛුම, *Sukhuma*, Páli form of සූක්ෂ්ම *súkshma*.

සුඛුමාළ, *Sukhumála, a.* (සු very, ඛුමාළ for කුමාර *kumára* soft) at ease, enjoying, happy; tender, soft, delicate.

සුගත්, *Sugat*, } *s.* (සු well, excellent, ගත් or ගත
සුගත, *Sugata*, } gone) name of Buddha, alluding to his attainment of Nirvána or final emancipation.

සුගතාගම, *Sugatágama, s.* (සුගත *sugata* and ආගම *ágama* religion) Buddhist religion.

සුගති, *Sugati*, *s*. (සු good, ගති state) heaven or paradise, obtaining happiness or Swarga.

සුගතිඳු, *Sugatindu*, *s*. (සුගත *sugata* and ඉඳු *indu* chief) name of Buddha: see සුගත *sugata;* name of Indra.

සුගතිය, *Sugatiya*, *s*. happy state, heaven: see සුගති *sugati*.

සුගතේන්ද්‍ර, *Sugaténdra*, see සුගතිඳු *sugatindu*.

සුගඳ, *Suganda*, *s*. (සු good, ගඳ smell) odour, fragrance, etc.: see the next.

සුගන්ධ, *Sugandha*, *s*. (සු good, ගන්ධ smell) blue lotus, *nymphœa stellata*, [Colloq. මානෙල් *má-nel*]; small cummin seed; sandal wood tree, *santalum album*, [Coll: සඳුන් *sandun*]; sulphur, [Colloq. ගෙන්දගම් *gendagam*]; fragrance, odour; tree, කිණිහිරිය *kinihiriya*, commonly *Kaniyar*, *pterospermum acerifolium;* also, කිණදෙඹ *kína-domba*.

සුගන්ධක, *Sugandhaka*, *s*. (සුගන්ධ and කන් *kan* aff.) sulphur; orange, *citrus aurantium*, [Colloq. දොඩම් *dodam*]; sort of gourd, *momordica mixta*.

සුගන්ධකුසුම, *Sugandha-kusuma*, see සුගන්ධිකුසුම *sugandhi-kusuma*.

සුගන්ධමුද්ගා, *Sugandha-mudgá*, *s*. small grain or seed used by natives to put into their curries, [Colloq. උළුවා *uluwá*].

සුගන්ධමූල, *Sugandha-múla*, see සුගන්ධිමූල *sugandhi-múla*.

සුගන්ධමූලා, *Sugandha-múlá*, *s*. sarsaparilla, *hemi-desmus indicus*, [Colloq. ඉරමසු *iramasu*].

සුගන්ධය, *Sugandhaya*, see සුගන්ධ *sugandha*.

සුගන්ධා, *Sugandhá*, *s*. ichneumon plant, *mimosa octandra*, [Colloq. අරත්ත *aratta*]; zedoary, *curcuma zerumbet*, [Colloq. හරන්කහ *harankaha*]; holy basil, *ocimum sanctum*, [Colloq. මදුරුතලා *madurutalá*]; jasmine of various sorts, [Colloq. පිච්ච *pichcha*]; plant, *Lagenandra lancifolia*, [Colloq. අතිවිඩයම් *atividayam*].

සුගන්ධාගරු, *Sugandhá-garu*, *s*. agallochum having the fragrance of jasmine flowers.

සුගන්ධි, *Sugandhi*, *s*. (සුගන්ධ *sugandha* and ඉ *i* substituted for අ *a*) perfume, fragrance; fragrant sort of mango; white lotus, [Colloq. ඕලු *ólu*]; fragrant grass, *cyperus rotundus*, [Colloq. කලාඳුරු *kalánduru*]; another sort, *scirpus kyssoor;* coriander seed: *a*. fragrant, sweet-smelling.

සුගන්ධික, *Sugandhika*, *s*. (සුගන්ධ *sugandha* and ක aff.) large sort of rice; incense; sulphur; white lotus.

සුගන්ධිකුසුම, *Sugandhi-kusuma*, *s*. (සුගන්ධි fragrant, කුසුම flower) sort of *nerium*, with yellowish flowers.

සුගන්ධිකුසුමා, *Sugandhi-kusumá*, *s*. pot-herb, *trigo-nella corniculata*.

සුගන්ධිතා, *Sugandhitá*, *s*. (සුගන්ධි and තා aff.) fragrance, pleasing scent produced by the trituration of perfumes, etc.

සුගන්ධිමූල, *Sugandhi-múla*, *s*. (සුගන්ධි and මූල root) root of the *andropogon muricatum*, [Colloq. සෑවැන්දරා *sewendará*].

සුගන්ධී, *Sugandhí*, *s*. Ceylon cardamoms, *elettaria cardamomum*, [Colloq. එන්සාල් *ensál*].

සුගම, *Sugama*, *a*. (සු well, ගම going) accessible, good, as a road) easy, practicable; plain, intelligible.

සුගහන, *Sugahana*, *a*. (සු well or thoroughly, ගහ *gaha* to be thick) thick, close, impervious.

සුග්‍රීව, *Sugríwa*, *s*. (සු and ග්‍රීව neck) monkey king, friend and confederate of Rámachandra; one of the horses of Kṛishṇa's car; goose; serpent of Pátála: *a*. handsome-necked.

සුගෘහ, *Sugṛiha*, *s*. (සු handsome, ගෘහ house or nest) the tailor bird, *orthotomus sutorius:* see තාවිකා *táviká*.

සුගෘහීත, *Sugṛihíta*, *a*. (සු well, ගෘහ *gṛiha* to seize, ක්ත *kta* aff.) seized, caught; held fast or firmly seized: taken or applied properly or auspiciously.

සුඟ, *Sunga*, *s*. quantity, collection; considerable quantity; Indian fig tree, *ficus bengalensis*, [Colloq. මහනුග *maha-nuga*]; hog plum, *spondias mangifera*, [Colloq. ඇඹරැල්ල *embarella*]: *a*. small.

සුඟත්, *Sungat*, *a*. small.

සුඟු, *Sungu*, *s*. horn, from ශෘඞ්ග *sṛinga*; assafœtida, [Colloq. පෙරුංකායම් *perunkáyam*].

සුචක්ෂුස්, *Suchakshus*, *s*. learned or wise man; glomerous fig tree, *ficus glomerata*, [Colloq. අට්ටික්කා *aṭṭikká*].

සුචපල, *Suchapala*, *a*. (සු thoroughly, චපල tremulous, etc.) very rash or inconsiderate; shaking, tremulous; violently agitated, alarmed.

සුචරිත්‍රා, *Sucharitrá*, *s*. (සු good, චරිත්‍ර *charitra* custom) virtuous wife.

සුචරිත, *Sucharita*, } සුචරිත ක්‍රියාව, *Sucharita-kriyáwa*, } *s*. (සු good, චරිත and ක්‍රියාව conduct) morality, virtue, proper conduct.

සුචිකර්ණිකා, *Suchi-karṇiká*, *s*. (සුචි white, කර්ණිකා pericarp) white lotus, [Colloq. ඕලු *ólu*].

සුචිත්‍ර, *Suchitra*, *a.* (සු well, චිත්‍ර variegated) variegated.

සුචිත්‍රක, *Suchitraka*, *s.* (සු and චිත්‍රක variegated) king-fisher, [Colloq. පිළිහුඩුවා *pilihuduwá*].

සුචිරස්, *Suchiras*, *s.* (සු very, චිරස් long time) very long time.

සුචිරායුස්, *Suchiráyus*, *s.* (සුචිර *suchira* and ආයුස් *áyus* life) a god, divinity; longevity.

සුචූරල්, *Suchural*, *s.* cock, [Colloq. කුකුලා *kukulá*].

සුජන, *Sujana*, *s.* (සු good, ජන person) Indra's charioteer: *a.* virtuous, good, respectable.

සුජීවන, *Sujíwana*, see සුචිරායුස් *suchiráyus*.

සුණුකරණවා, *Suṇukaraṇawá*, *v.* to pulverize, to reduce to powder; to destroy: pret. සුණුකෙරුවා *suṇukeruwá*.

සුණුකෙරිම, *Suṇukerima*, *s.* pulverization.

සුණුගල, *Suṇu-gala*, *s.* (සුණු chunam, ගල stone) limestone.

සුණුවිසුණු, *Suṇuvisuṇu*, *s.* (සුණු destruction, විසුණු the same) ruin, extirpation.

සුණුවිසුණු කරණවා, *Suṇuvisuṇu-karaṇawá*, *v.* to reduce to perfect ruin.

සුත, *Suta*, *s.* (සු to bear or bring forth, ක්ත *kta* aff.) son, [Colloq. පුතා *putá*]; prince: see also සූත්‍ර *sútra*.

සුතජීව, *Sutajíwa*, *s.* (සුත son, ජීව life) tree from the fruit of which necklaces are made of supposed prolific efficacy, *nagelia putranjiva* or *putranjiva Ruxburghii;* plant, Indian shot, *canna indica*, [Colloq. බුත්සරණ *butsaraṇa*].

සුතනු, *Sutanu*, *s.* (සු good, excellent, තනු body or thin, delicate) woman, [Colloq. ස්ත්‍රී *strí*]: *a.* very thin.

සුතපස්, *Sutapas*, *s.* (සු very profoundly, තපස් religious austerity or තප *tapa* to heat, අසි *asi* aff.) hermit, ascetic; the sun.

සුතරම්, *Sutaram*, *ind.* (සු good, තරම් aff.) more excellently.

සුතශ්‍රේණි, *Sutaṣréṇi*, *s.* (සුත son or offspring, ශ්‍රේණි line) floating plant, *salvinia cucullata;* medicinal plant, *hoya hirsuta*, [Colloq. මීනුග *mí-nuga*].

සුතා, *Sutá*, *s.* (සු to bear, etc. ක්ත *kta* aff.) daughter, [Colloq. දුව *duwa*]; plant, *hedysarum alhagi*.

සුතික්තක, *Sutiktaka*, *s.* (සු very, තික්ත bitter, කන් *kan* aff.) kind of gentian used as febrifuge, *gentiana cherayta;* coral tree, *erythrina indica*, [Colloq. එරබදු *erabadu*].

සුතීක්ෂ්ණ, *Sutikshṇa*, *s.* (සු exceedingly, තීක්ෂ්ණ sharp) tree, *moringa pterygosperma*, [Colloq. මුරුංගා *murungá*]: *a.* very sharp, very pungent; acutely painful.

සුතු, *Sutu*, *s.* shell fish in general.

සුතුංග, *Sutuṅga*, *s.* (සු very, තුංග tall) coconut tree, *cocos nucifera*, [Colloq. පොල්ගහ *pol-gaha*].

සුතුරු, *Suturu*, *s.* thread, Elu form of සූත්‍ර *sútra*.

සුතොට, *Sutoṭa*, *s.* name of Vishṇu.

සුද්ද, *Sudda*, see ශුද්ධ *ṣuddha*.

සුද්ධකම, } *Suddhakama*, *s.* purity, holiness.
සුධකම,

සුද්ධකරණවා, *Suddhakaraṇawá*, *v.* to clean, to purify.

සුද්ධජංඝා, *Suddhajaṅghá*, *s.* axe, [Colloq, පොරව *porawa*].

සුද්ධවන්තයා, *Suddhawantayá*, *s.* Saint.

සුද්ධවල්ලිකා, *Suddha-wallikú*, *s.* (සුධ pure, වල්ලි pedicle, කන් *kan* aff.) plant, *tinospora cordifolia* or *menispermum glabrum*.

සුද්ධසිල, *Suddha-sila*, *s.* (සුධ pure, faultless, සිල observance) undeviating performance of religious duties.

සුද්ධාජීව, *Suddhájíwa*, *s.* (සුධ *suddha* pure, ආජීව *ájíwa* livelihood) subsistence procured by lawful means, without destroying life, etc.

සුද්ධාවාසය, *Suddháwásaya*, *s.* (සුධ *suddha* and ආවාස *áwása* residence) class of six Brahmalókas so called, which are the next previous stage to Nirwáṇa.

සුද්ධෝදන, *Suddhódana*, *s.* father of Gautama Buddha in his last incarnation.

සුද්ධෝදනසුත, *Suddhódana-sutu*, *s.* (සුධෝදන and සුත son) a patronymic of Gautama the founder of Buddhism.

සුද, *Suda*, *s.* the colour white; purity, cleanness; resemblance, likeness, similarity.

සුද අත් *Suda-at*, *s.* (සුද purity, අත් end, limit) harem, seraglio; Elu form of ශුද්ධාන්ත *ṣuddhánta*.

සුදඟ, *Sudaṅga*, *s.* name of Balabhadrayá; brother of Vishṇu.

සුදත්, *Sudat*, *s.* women's apartments in the palace of a prince; harem, seraglio.

සුදන්තය, *Sudantaya*, *s.* (සු excellent, දන්ත tooth) actor, dancer.

සුදන්ති, *Sudantí*, *s.* (සුදන්ත *sudanta* and ඊ *í* fem. aff.) female elephant of the North West quarter.

සුදන, *Sudana*, *s.* (සු good, excellent, දන person) good man.

සුදනා, *Sudaná*, *s.* good man (poetical term).

සුදබිඳිම, *Sudabindíma*, *s.* fluor albus; gleet.

සුදම්, *Sudam*, } *s.* council of the gods: see
සුදම්සබ, *Sudam-saba*, } සුධර්මන් *sudharman*.

සුදර්ශන, *Sudarṣana*, *s.* (සු good, දර්ශන sight or appearance) discus of Kṛishṇa; mount Méru; rose apple, *jambosa vulgaris*, [Colloq. ජම්බු *jambu*]; vulture; city of Indra; fourth of the seven circular ranges of rocks surrounding Maha Méru: *a.* handsome, good-looking.

සුදර්ශනා, *Sudarsaná*, *s.* drug; woman; handsome woman; plant, *menispermum glabrum*; order, command.

සුදසුන්, *Sudasun*, *s.* (සු good, දසුන් appearance) sky, atmosphere, [Colloq. අහස *ahasa*]; comparison; Ṣakra's diamond thunderbolt; the discus of Kṛishṇa: see සුදර්ශන *sudarṣana*.

සුදාන්ත, *Sudánta*, *s.* (සු well, දාන්ත tamed) follower of Buddha, Buddhist: *a.* well-tamed or restained.

සුදාය, *Sudáya*, *s.* (සු good, දාය gift) special gift, as a nuptial present, etc.

සුදි, *Sudi*, *s.* light half of the lunar month; virtuous man.

සුදු, *Sudu*, *a.* white; pure, holy, from ශුද්ධ *ṣuddha*.

සුදුඅත්තන, *Sudu-attana*, *s.* (සුදු white) thorn apple, *datura stramonium*.

සුදුඅන්නාසි, *Sudu-annási*, *s.* variety of the pineapple, *ananas sativa*.

සුදුඅරලිය, *Sudu-araliya*, *s.* temple tree.

සුදුඅවර, *Sudu-awara*, *s.* plant, sabre-podded bean, *dolichos gladiatus*.

සුදුඅවරි, *Sudu-awari*, *s.* Indigo plant, variety of *indigofera tinctoria*.

සුදුඇතඹිලු, *Sudu-ẹtólu*, *s.* variety of water lily, *nymphæa lotus*.

සුදුඇල්වී, *Sudu-ẹlví*, *s.* kind of paddy, *oryza sativa*.

සුදුඉද්ද, *Sudu-idda*, *s.* common flowering plant, peculiar to Ceylon, *Wrightea zeylanica (Apocynaceæ)*.

සුදුඉන්නර, *Sudu-innara*, *s.* hooded milfoil, *urticularia nivea*.

සුදුඉරිඟු, *Sudu-iringu*, *s.* Indian corn or maize, *zea mays*.

සුදුඋක්ගස්, *Sudu-ukgas*, *s.* sugar-cane, *saccharum officinarum*.

සුදුඔලිඳ, *Sudu-olinda*, *s.* (සුදු white) liquorice, or a plant the root of which is used as such, *abrus precatorius*.

සුදුකටරොළු, *Sudu-kaṭaroḷu*, *s.* plant, variety of *clitoria ternatea*.

සුදුකටුපතුක්, *Sudu-kaṭupatuk*, *s.* plant, variety of *opuntia Dillenii*.

සුදුකතුරුමුරුංගා, *Sudu-katuru-murungá*, *s.* plant, variety of *sesbania grandiflora*.

සුදුකඳල, *Sudu-kandala*, *s.* esculent root, variety of *colocasia antiquorum*.

සුදුකඳහතු, *Sudu-kandahatu*, *s.* variety of mushroom.

සුදුකන්නන්නෝරු, *Sudu-kannannóru*, *s.* kind of plantain, *musa sapientum*.

සුදුකරණවා, *Sudukaraṇawá*, *v.* to make white.

සුදුකාපිරි, *Sudu-kápiri*, *s.* endive, *cichorium endivia*.

සුදුකිඹුල්වැන්න, *Sudu-kimbulwẹnna*, *s.* persicaria or buckbean, *polygonum tomentosum (Polygonaceæ)*.

සුදුකිරිඇල්වී, *Sudu-kiriẹlví*, *s.* kind of paddy, *oryza sativa*.

සුදුකිරිඳි, *Sudu-kirindi*, *s.* plant, *eclipta prostrata*.

සුදුකුමාරවී, *Sudu-kumáraví*, *s.* kind of paddy, *oryza sativa*.

සුදුකොකා, *Sudu-koká*, *s.* little egret, *herodius garzetta*, *(ardeidæ*, order *Herodiones)*.

සුදුකොට්ටම්බා, *Sudu-koṭṭambá*, *s.* plant, variety of *terminalia catappa*.

සුදුකොත්විලවි, *Sudu-kotvilavi*, *s.* kind of paddy, *oryza sativa*.

සුදුකොතලා, *Sudu-kotalá*, *s.* sort of myrtle, *myrtus tomentosa*, or variety of *torenia asiatica*.

සුදුකොබලිල, *Sudu-kobalila*, *s.* shrub, *bauhinia acuminata*.

සුදුකොල්ලු, *Sudu-kollu*, *s.* plant, *glycine villosa* or variety of *dolichos biflora*.

සුදුකොලොන්දු, *Sudu-kolondu*, *s.* plant, *chrysanthemum indicum*.

සුදුකොස්ඇටවි, *Sudu-kosẹṭavi*, *s.* kind of paddy, *oryza sativa*.

සුදුකැකිරි, *Sudu-kẹkiri*, *s.* bitter gourd, colocynth, *citrullus colocynthis*, [Colloq. යක්කොමඩු *yakkomaḍu*].

සුදුගස්පුරුක්, *Sudu-gaspuruk*, *s.* plant, not ascertained.

සුදුගහල, *Sudu-gahala*, *s.* plant, variety of *colocasia antiquorum*.

සුදු ගෙඳකොල, *Sudu-gendakola*, *s.* (සුදු white) purslane, variety of *portulacea oleracea.*

සුදු ගොඩබිඳර, *Sudu-godabindara*, *s.* plant, *habenaria undulata.*

සුදු ගොනකොල, *Sudu-gonakola*, *s.* plant, *stemodia camphorata* or species of *adenosma.*

සුදු ගොරක, *Sudu-goraka*, *s.* mangosteen, *garcinia mangostana.*

සුදු ගැරඬියා, *Sudu-gerandiyá*, *s.* kind of snake.

සුදු ජම්බල, *Sudu-jambala*, *s.* variety of citron, shaddock, *citrus decumana.*

සුදු තම්පලා, *Sudu-tampalá*, *s.* plant, the leaves of which are eaten as a vegetable, *amaranthus gangeticus* or *a. oleraceus, (Amarantaceæ).*

සුදු තලා, *Sudu-talá*, *s.* white basil, *ocimum album.*

සුදු තුඹ, *Sudu-tumba*, *s.* plant, *leucas marrubioides (Labiatæ).*

සුදු තෙල්ඕලු, *Sudu-telólu*, *s.* species of the water lily, *nymphæa lotus.*

සුදුද්දය, *Sududdaya*, *s.* the invisible, epithet of නිර්වාණ *nirwána*, which see. (Páli.)

සුදු දඩින්නරු, *Sudu-dadinnaru*, *s.* annual plant, *buchnera asiatica.*

සුදු දඹල, *Sudu-dambala*, *s.* the kidney bean, *phaseolus vulgaris.*

සුදු දුරදඹල, *Sudu-dúradambala*, *s.* species of bean, *dolichos tetragonolobus.*

සුදු දිවිපහුරු, *Sudu-divipahuru*, *s.* plant, *ipomæa pes-tigridis:* see දිවිපහුරු *divipahuru.*

සුදුදුරු, *Sududuru*, *s.* white cummin seed.

සුදු නවරිකෙසෙල්, *Sudu-nawari-kesel*, *s.* plantain, variety of *musa sapientum.*

සුදු නික, *Sudu-nika*, *s.* flowering shrub, white variety of *vitex negundo (Verbenaceæ):* see නිල් නික *nil-nika.*

සුදු නිවිති, *Sudu-niviti*, *s.* pot-herb, *basella alba.*

සුදු නෙළුම්, *Sudu-nelum*, *s.* species of lotus, *nelumbium speciosum.*

සුදු පන්නටිවි, *Sudu-pannativí*, *s.* kind of paddy, *oryza sativa.*

සුදු පරෙයියාමල්, *Sudu-pareyiyá-mal*, *s.* parasitic plant, *dendrobium crumenatum (Orchideæ).*

සුදුපාට, *Sudu-páta*, *s.* colour white.

සුදු පාසානම්, *Sudu-pásánam*, *s.* white arsenic.

සුදු පිටවක්කා, *Sudu-pitawakká*, *s.* plant, variety of *phyllanthus.*

සුදු පිත්තල, *Sudu-pittala*, *s.* (සුදු white, පිත්තල brass) compound metal, sort of bell metal.

සුදු පුරුක්, *Sudu-puruk*, *s.* (සුදු white) flowering shrub, *justicia Betonica (Acanthaceæ).*

සුදු පෙතිදඹල, *Sudu-petidambala*, *s.* plant, producing beans, *dolichos*, variety of *d. lablab.*

සුදු පෙතිපියුම්, *Sudu-petipiyum*, *s.* kind of lotus.

සුදු පේර, *Sudu-péra*, *s.* variety of guava, *psidium guyava.*

සුදු බටතණ, *Sudu-batatana*, *s.* panic grass, *panicum grossarium.*

සුදු බතල, *Sudu-batala*, *s.* variety of sweet potato, *ipomæa batatas.*

සුදු බාලොලියා, *Sudu-báloliyá*, *s.* plant, variety of *desmodium triquetrum.*

සුදු බින්දද, *Sudu-bindada*, *s.* variety of spurge, *euphorbia thymifolia.*

සුදු බූදදකිරිය, *Sudu-búdadakíriya*, *s.* another variety of spurge, *euphorbia pilulifera.*

සුදු බෝවිටියා, *Sudu-bóvitiyá*, *s.* plant, variety of *osbeckia aspera.*

සුදු බැවිල, *Sudu-bevila*, *s.* variety of *sida humilis.*

සුදු මල්ගෝවා, *Sudu-malgówá*, *s.* cabbage, *brassica oleracea-capitata.*

සුදු මහනාරන්, *Sudu-mahanáran*, *s.* tree, species of *citrus.*

සුදු මාවී, *Sudu-máví*, *s.* kind of paddy, *oryza sativa.*

සුදු මීපත්ඇල්වී, *Sudu-mípat-elví*, *s.* kind of paddy, *oryza sativa.*

සුදු මුත්තෑස්වී, *Sudu-muttesví*, *s.* kind of paddy, *oryza sativa.*

සුදු මුල්, *Sudu-mul*, *s.* cabbage, *brasica oleracea*, [Colloq. ගෝවා *gówá*].

සුදු මුවයිරිඟු, *Sudu-muwairingu*, *s.* kind of maize.

සුදු මොට්ටුතණ, *Sudu-mottu-tana*, *s.* species of grass, *kyllingia monocephala.*

සුදුමැලි, *Sudumeli*, *a.* (සුදු white, මැලි wan) pale, of a yellowish white colour.

සුදු මෑ, *Sudu-mé*, *s.* species of bean, *dolichos sesquipedalis.*

සුදු යක්වනස්ස, *Sudu-yakwanassa*, *s.* plant, variety of *anisomeles ovata.*

සුදුර්ලභ, *Sudurlabha*, *a.* (සු very, දුර්ලභ difficult) very difficult to be attained, unattainable, impracticable.

සුදු රටපඹ, *Sudu-ratapamba*, *s.* species of fern, *lygodium.*

සුදු රටපොහොට්ටු, *Sudu-ratapohottu*, *s.* globe amaranth, *amarantus globosa.*

සුදු රටවදමල්, *Sudu-rata-wadamal*, *s.* variety of shoe flower, *hibiscus rosa sinensis.*

සුදු රතඹලා, *Sudu-ratambalá*, *s.* (සුදු white) plant, *ixora alba.*

සුදු රතු, *Sudu-ratu*, *s.* (සුදු white, රතු red) light red colour.

සුදුරු, *Suduru*, *s.* Sudra, cultivator.

සුදුල්ලභ, *Sudullabha*, Páli form of සුදුර්ලභ *sudurlabha.*

සුදු ලියන්, *Sudu-liyan*, *s.* tree, *phyllanthus cyanospermus (Euphorbiaceæ).*

සුදු ලූනු, *Sudu-lúnu*, *s.* (සුදු white, ලූනු onion) garlic, *allium sativum.*

සුදු වට, *Sudu-waṭa*, *s.* radish, *raphanus sativus*, [Colloq. රාබු *rábu*].

සුදු වතුජම්බු, *Sudu-watu-jambu*, *s.* tree, *jambosa alba.*

සුදු වදමල්, *Sudu-wadamal*, *s.* species of shoe flower, *hibiscus syriacus.*

සුදු වම්බටු, *Sudu-wambaṭu*, *s.* variety of brinjal, *solanum melongena.*

සුදු වරා, *Sudu-wará*, *s.* periwinkle, *vinca rosea.*

සුදු වල්, *Sudu-wal*, *s.* plant, *colocasia antiquorum:* see ගහල *gahala.*

සුදු වී, *Sudu-ví*, *s.* kind of paddy, *oryza sativa.*

සුදු වෙල්ලංගිරිය, *Sudu-wellangiriya*, *s.* plant, variety of *capparis horrida* or of *paramignya monophylla.*

සුදු වැලිවැන්න, *Sudu-wẹliwẹnna*, *s.* cock's comb, *celosia corymbosa*, or variety of *dimorphocalyx glabellus.*

සුදුශ්චර, *Suduṣchara*, *s.* (සු very, දුශ්චර difficult) very arduous or painful.

සුදු සඳුන්, *Sudu-sandun*, *s.* (සුදු white, සඳුන් sandal) white sandal wood, *santalum album.*

සුදු සිඳු, *Sudu-sindu*, *s.* (සුදු and සිඳු horse) white horse.

සුදුසු, *Sudusu*, *a.* fit, proper.

සුදු සෙන්දිරික්කා, *Sudu-sendirikká*, *s.* Marvel of Peru, variety of *mirabilis jalapa.*

සුදු සෙව්වන්දිමල්, *Sudu-sewwandi-mal*, *s.* species of rose, *rosa bankiæ.*

සුදු හන්දිරන්වී, *Sudu-handiranví*, *s.* kind of paddy, *oryza sativa.*

සුදු හබරල, *Sudu-habarala*, *s.* plant, with an esculent root, *alocasia macrorhiza.*

සුදු හමස්මෑ, *Sudu-hamasmẹ*, *s.* bean, *dolichos sesquipedalis.*

සුදු හාතලිවී, *Sudu-hátaliví*, *s.* kind of paddy, *oryza sativa.*

සුදු හාවා, *Sudu-háwá*, *s.* white hare.

සුදු හින්බෝවිටියා, *Sudu-hinbówiṭiyá*, *s.* (සුදු white) plant, variety of *osbeckia octandra.*

සුදු හැල්වී, *Sudu-hẹlví*, *s.* kind of paddy, *oryza sativa.*

සුදූර, *Sudúra*, *a.* (සු very, දූර far) very far, distant.

සුධර්ම, *Sudharma*, } *s.* (සු excellent, ධර්ම virtue,
සුධර්මන්, *Sudharman*, } අනි *ani* aff.) council or assembly of the gods.

සුධර්මා, *Sudharmá*, *s.* (සු and ධර්ම *dharma* practice) man attentive to the proper maintenance of his family.

සුධා, *Sudhá*, *s.* (සු pleasure, ධෙ *dhe* to drink or ධා to support, life, අණ් *aṇ* aff.) nectar, the beverage of immortality and sustenance of the gods; plaster, mortar; milk-hedge plant, *euphorbia tirucalli*, [Colloq. නවහඬි *nawahandi*]; tree, *euphorbia antiquorum*, [Colloq. දලුක් *daluk*]; plant, *aletris hyacinthoides;* juice; honey or nectar of flowers; emblic myrobalan, *phyllanthus emblica*, [Colloq. නෙල්ලි *nelli*].

සුධාංශු, *Sudhánṣu*, } *s.* (සුධා nectar, අංශු *anṣu*
සුධාකර, *Sudhákara*, } ray of light or ආකර *ákara* mine) moon, supposed to be the repository of the beverage of the gods.

සුධාධවල, *Sudhá-dhawala*, *a.* (සුධා mortar, ධවල white) white with plaster or mortar.

සුධාභෝජන, *Sudhábhójana*, *s.* fabled food of the gods, ambrosia.

සුධාවර්ෂ, *Sudháwarsha*, *s.* shower of ambrosia.

සුධාවර්ෂින්, *Sudhá-warshin*, *s.* (සුධා nectar, වර්ෂින් who rains) name or epithet of Buddha.

සුධිති, *Sudhiti*, *s.* (සු well, ධා *dhá* to hold, ක්ති *kti* aff.) axe, [Colloq. පොරොව *porowa*].

සුධී, *Sudhí*, } *s.* (සු and ධ්‍යෛ *dhyai* to think,
සුධීර, *Sudhíra*, } ක්ති *kti* aff.) learned man or teacher, scholar.

සුධෝද්භව, *Sudhódbhawa*, *s.* (සුධා *sudhá* nectar, උද්භව *udbhawa* produced) Dhanwantari the physician of Swarga.

සුධෝද්භවා, *Sudhódbhawá*, *s.* chebulic myrobalan, *terminalia chebula*, [Colloq. අරළු *araḷu*].

සුන්, *Sun*, *s.* dust, any pulverized substance, from චූර්ණ *chúrṇa*, variously written සුන්න *sunna*, සුණු *suṇu* and හුණු *huṇu;* multitude, quantity, heap; destruction, ruin; emptiness, vacuity: *a.* cut, powdered.

සුන්කරණවා, *Sunkaraṇawá*, see සුණු කරණවා *suṇukaraṇawá.*

සුඳුර, *Sundara*, *s.* name of Káma the god of love: *a.* handsome, beautiful, elegant; well, excellent.

සුඳුරී, *Sundarí*, *s.* (සුඳුර *sundara* handsome, ඊ *í* fem. aff.) handsome woman; small timber tree, *heritiera minor:* turmeric, *curcuma longa*, [Coll: කහ *kaha*].

සුන්න, *Sunna*, *s.* powder, dust, any pulverized substance; lime, chunam, etc. Elu form of චූර්ණ *chúrṇa*.

සුන්නා, *Sunná*, *s.* lime burner, one of that caste.

සුන්පිට, *Sunpiṭa*, *s.* mirror, looking-glass. [Colloq. කැඩපත *kędapata*].

සුන්බත්, *Sun-bat*, *s.* (සුන් empty, බත් boiled rice) famine, privation of food.

සුන්බුන්, *Sunbun*, *s.* small ware; lumber: *a.* cut and broken.

සුන්වන්, *Sunwan*, *s.* pulverization, state of being pulverized.

සුන්සාල්, *Sunsál*, *s.* (සුන් and සාල් rice) pulverized or ground rice.

සුනංගු, *Sunaṇgu*, *a.* late, slow.

සුනංගුකරණවා, *Sunaṇgukaraṇawá*, *v.* to delay; to keep long.

සුනංගුවෙනවා, *Sunaṇguwenawá*, *v.* to get late; to lose time.

සුනඛයා, *Sunakhayá*, *s.* dog, [Colloq. බල්ලා *ballá*]: pl. සුනඛයෝ *sunakhayó*.

සුනත, *Sunata*, *a.* (සුන් *sun* emptiness, අත *ata* hand) empty handed, poor, destitute.

සුනඳ, *Sunanda*, *s.* club of Balaráma.

සුනන්දා, *Sunandá*, *s.* (සු well, නදි *nadi* to please, අ *a* aff.) goddess Umá; woman; plant, *aristolochia indica*, [Colloquial: සප්සඳ *sapsaṇda*]: *a.* pleasing, delighting.

සුනන, *Sunana*, *s.* dimbul tree, *ficus glomerata;* also called අට්ටික්කා *aṭṭikká*.

සුනයන, *Sunayana*, *s.* (සු excellent, beautiful, නයන eye) a deer, [Colloq. මුවා *muwá*].

සුනයනා, *Sunayaná*, *s.* සුනයන *sunayana* with the fem. aff. added) woman, [Colloq. ස්ත්‍රී *strí*].

සුනාසීර, *Sunásíra*, *s.* (සු good, නාසීර the van of an army) name of Indra, chief of the inferior gods.

සුනික්ෂිප්ත, *Sunikshipta*, *a.* (සු and නි prefixed to, ක්ෂිප්ත thrown) cast, sent, thrown; dismissed, deserted, abandoned.

සුනිර්මල, *Sunirmala*, *a.* perfectly pure.

සුනිර්මිත, *Sunirmmita*, *a.* (සු well, නිර්මිත formed) well formed or executed.

සුනිර්වේෂ්ටණ, *Sunirwéṭhaṇa*, *s.* (සු and නි prefixed to වේෂ්ටණ twisting) confusing, involving, intertwining.

සුනිල්, *Sunil*, Elu form of සුනීල *suníla*.

සුනිවස්ත්‍ර, *Suni-wastra*, *a.* (සු and නි prefixed to වස්ත්‍ර dress) well clothed, ornamented, accoutred, decorated.

සුනිෂණ්ණ, *Sunishaṇṇa*, } *s.* (සු well, නි and
සුනිෂණ්ණක, *Sunishaṇṇaka*, } ෂද *shada* to go or නිෂණ්ණ sitting, reclining, on the ground, ක්ත *kta* aff.) pot-herb, species of *Polygonum*, [Colloq. කිඹුල්වැන්න *kimbulwęnna*].

සුනිෂණ්ණකපත්‍රක, *Sunishaṇṇaka-patraka*, *s.* medicinal plant, *marsilea quadrifolia*, [Colloq. ඇඹුලැඹිලිය *ęmbulęmbiliya*].

සුනිසන්නක, *Sunisannaka*, Páli form of the last.

සුනිසිත, *Sunisita*, *a.* (සු and නි prefixed to සිත sharp) sharp, keen.

සුනී, *Suní*, *s.* bitch, [Colloq. බැල්ලි *bęlli*].

සුනීත, *Sunita*, *a.* (සු and නී to gain, ක්ත *kta* aff.) tamed, docile; well-behaved, modest.

සුනීති, *Suníti*, *s.* (සු good, නීති manners) propriety of behaviour, good manners, decorum.

සුනීථ, *Sunítha*, *a.* (සු well, නී to obtain, ථක් *thak* aff.) virtuous, moral, good, of proper disposition or conduct.

සුනීල, *Suníla*, *s.* (සු much, නීල blue or black) pomegranate tree, *punica granatum*, [Colloq. දෙළුම් *delum*]; root of the *andropogon muricatus*, [Colloq. සෑවැන්දරා *sęwęndurá*]: *a.* very black or blue, dark.

සුනීලක, *Sunílaka*, *s.* (සුනීල and කන් *kan* added) emerald or sapphire; blue shrike.

සුනු, *Sunu*, *s.* dust: sharpness; hearing; offspring, progeny, a son, etc; destroying: powder, pulverized substance: chunam or caustic lime: see සුන්න *sunna*.

සුනුවන්, *Sunuwan*, Elu form of සුනයන *sunayana*, which see.

සුනෙට, *Suneṭa*, *s.* name of Vishṇu.

සුනෙර, *Sunera*, }
සුනෙරගිර, *Suneragira*, } *s.* name of Maha Méru.
සුනෙරු, *Suneru*, }

සුනොට, *Sunoṭa*, see සුනෙට *suneṭa*.

සුප්ත, *Supta*, *s.* (ෂ්වප *shwapa* to sleep, ක්ත *kta* aff.) sleep, deep or sound sleep: *a.* sleeping, asleep.

සුප්ති, *Supti*, *s.* (ස්වප *swapa* and ක්ති *kti* aff.) sleep, sleeping; numbness, insensibility, paralysis; drowsiness, sleepiness.

සුප්‍රතිෂ්ඨ, *Supratishṭha*, *s.* tree, *eugenia jambolana*, [Colloq. මාදම් *mádam*].

සුප්‍රතිෂ්ඨා, *Supratishṭhá*, *s.* (සු and ප්‍රති intensitives, ෂ්ඨා *sthá* to stay or be, අණ් *aṇ* aff.) form of metre, stanza of four lines containing five syllables each.

සුප්‍රතිෂ්ඨිත, *Supratishṭhita*, *a.* (සු and ප්‍රති intensitives, ෂ්ඨා *sthá* to stay, ක්ත *kta* aff.) fixed, established; firm, solid, immoveable; consecrated: celebrated.

සුප්‍රතීක, *Supratíka*, *s.* (සු handsome, ප්‍රතීක form) elephant of the north east quarter; name of Káma: *a.* well-made, handsome.

සුප්‍රපර්ණී, *Supra-parṇi*, *s.* kidney bean, *phaseolus trilobus*, [Colloq. මුංවැන්න *muṇwẹnna*].

සුප්‍රභ, *Suprabha*, *a.* (සු excellent or excessive, ප්‍රභ light, lustre) splendid, brilliant, glorious.

සුප්‍රයුක්ත, *Suprayukta*, *a.* (සු well, ප්‍රයුක්ත joined) joined, attached, closely connected, in contact.

සුප්‍රලාප, *Supralápa*, *s.* (සු and ප්‍රලාප speaking) eloquence, eloquent discourse.

සුපක්ව, *Supakwa*, *s.* (සු well, thoroughly, පක්ව ripe) mango or a variety of it, *mangifera indica*, [Colloq. අඹ *amba*]: *a.* ripe.

සුපත්‍ර, *Supatra*, *s.* (සු good, පත්‍ර leaf) leaf of the cinnamon tree, *cinnamomum zeylanicum* [Colloq. කුරුඳුකොළ *kurundu-kola*]; white lotus, *nelumbium speciosum*, [Colloquial: හෙළනෙළුම් *hela-nelum*].

සුපථ, *Supatha*, *s.* (සු good, පථ road) good road; good conduct.

සුපද්මා, *Supadmá*, *s.* orris root.

සුපර්ණ, *Suparna*, *s.* (සු handsome, පර්ණ leaf or feather) being of a superhuman character, as garuḍa and other birds of an equally fanciful description; tree, *cassia fistula*; a cock.

සුපර්ණක, *Suparṇaka*, *s.* (සුපර්ණ and කන් *kan* added) tree, *cassia fistula*, [Colloq. ඇහැළ *ẹhẹla*]; another tree, *alstonia scholaris*, [Colloq. රුක් අත්තන *ruk-attana*: see the last.

සුපර්වන්, *Suparwan*, *s.* (සු good or much, පර්වන් knot or joint) a god, deity; arrow; bambu, [Colloq. උණගහ *uṇagaha*]; lunar day on which religious ceremonies are particularly performed, as the new moon, etc.

සුපරිශුද්ධ, *Suparisuddha*, *a.* (සු well, පරිශුද්ධ clean) completely or thoroughly pure, holy, sacred.

සුපාක, *Supáka*, *s.* plant: see වැල්තුඹ *wẹl-tumba*.

සුපාන, *Supána*, *s.* (සු and පාන to drink) drinking well, easily, or deeply.

සුපින, *Supina*, *s.* dream, dreaming. [Colloq. හීනය *hínaya*]; sleep. (Páli.)

සුපිපි, *Supipi*, *a.* (සු well, පිපි blown) blown, expanded, as a flower.

සුපිරිසිදු, *Supirisidu*, *a.* perfectly holy.

සුපු, *Supu*, *s.* sleeping, sleep, repose.

සුපුන්, *Supun*, *a.* (සු and පුන් full) full, complete, whole, perfect.

සුපුල්, *Supul*, *a.* (සු well, පුල් opening) well expanded, as a flower.

සුපුෂ්ප, *Supushpa*, *s.* (සු excellent, පුෂ්ප flower) coral tree, *erythrina indica*, [Colloq. එරබදු *arabadu*]; sirisha tree, *mimosa sirisha*; cloves, [Colloq. කරාබු *karábu*].

සුපුෂ්පිත, *Supushpita*, *a.* blown, expanded.

සුපුෂ්පී, *Supushpí*, *s.* plantain, *musa sapientum*, [Colloq. කෙසෙල් *kesel*]; sort of fennel, *anethum sowa* and *pammorium*; flower, *clitoria ternatea*, [Colloq. නිල්කටරොළු *nil-kaṭaroḷu*].

සුපූර, *Supúra*, *s.* (සු well, පූර full, of seeds) sort of lime or citron.

සුපැතුම්, *Supẹtum*, *s.* good hope.

සුඵල, *Suphala*, *s.* (සු good, ඵල fruit) wood apple, *feronia elephantum*, [Colloq. දිවුල් *diwul*]; pomegranate, *punica granatum*, [Colloq. දෙළුම් *deḷum*]; jujube, *zizyphus jujuba*, [Colloq. මසන් *masan*]; sort of bean, *phaseolus mungo*, [Colloq. මුංඇට *muṇ-ẹta*].

සුබ, *Suba*, *s.* prosperity, success; good fortune, luck, auspiciousness: *a.* prosperous, lucky, fortunate: see සුභ *subha*.

සුබත්, *Subat*, *s.* (සු good, බත් boiled rice, food) abundance, plenty.

සුභ, *Subha*, *s.* (සුභ to shine, to be beautiful or handsome, ක *ka* aff.) good fortune, auspiciousness, happiness; one of the astronomical Yógas: *a.* happy, well, right; handsome, beautiful; splendid, shining.

සුභංකර, *Subhaṅkara*, *s.* (සුභ *subha* happiness, කර to make) propitious, auspicious, conferring happiness or fortune.

සුභකෘත, *Subha-kṛita*, *a.* (සුභ handsome, කෘත done) adorned, ornamented, decorated.

සුභග, *Subhaga*, *s.* (සු good, භග fortune, etc.) borax; asóka tree, *saraca indica*, [Colloq. දිය රතඹලා *diya-ratambalá*, හෝපළු *hópaḷu*]; champaca tree, *michelia champaca*, [Colloq. සපු *sapu*]: *a.* pleasing to the eye; grateful to the sight; beloved, liked; fortunate, auspicious.

සුභද්‍ර, *Subhadra*, *s.* (සු exceeding, භද්‍ර auspicious) name of Vishṇu: *a.* propitious, auspicious, fortunate.

සුභද්‍රක, *Subhadraka*, *s.* (සුභද්‍ර and කන් *kan* added) care of the gods; bael tree, *ægle marmelos*, [Colloq. බෙලි *beli*].

සුභද්‍රා, *Subhadrá*, *s.* creeper, *ichnocarpus frutescens*, [Colloq. කිරිවැල් *kiri-wel*].

සුභ නිමිත්ත, *Subha-nimitta*, *s.* (සුභ good, නිමිත්ත mark) good feature, mark of beauty: auspicious omen, etc.

සුභවාසන, *Subha-wásana*, *s.* (සුභ auspicious, වාසන perfuming) perfume for the mouth.

සුභසිද්ධවිම, *Subhasiddhavíma*, *s.* prosperity, welfare.

සුභා, *Subhá*, *s.* sort of turmeric, *curcuma zerumbet*, [Colloq. හරන්කහ *harankaha*].

සුභාඤ්ජන, *Subháñjana*, *s.* tree, *moringa pterygosperma*, [Colloq. මුරුංගා *murungá*]: see සෝභාඤ්ජන *sóbháñjana*.

සුභාන්විත, *Subhánvita*, *a.* (සුභ *subha* good fortune, අන්විත *anvita* endowed with) happy, prosperous, fortunate.

සුභානු, *Subhánu*, *s.* (සු excellent, භා to chine, නු aff.) sixteenth year of the Indian cycle.

සුභාරංචිය, *Subháranchiya*, *s.* good news, Gospel.

සුභාෂිත, *Subháshita*, *s.* (සු good, භාෂ *bhásha* to speak, ක්ත *kta* aff.) eloquence: *a.* spoken well or eloquently.

සුභික්ෂ, *Subhiksha*, *s.* (සු well, භික්ෂා *bhikshá* food) plenty, abundance of food, etc.

සුභික්ෂා, *Subhikshá*, *s.* (සුභික්ෂ *subhiksha* and අ *a* aff.) tree, *Woodfordia floribunda*, [Colloq. මයිල *mayila*].

සුභිරක, *Subhíraka*, *s.* Palas tree, *butea frondosa*, [Colloq. ගස්කැල *gas-kela*].

සුඹස, *Sumbasa*, *s.* elevations of earth raised by the white ant, white ant hill: pl. සුඹස් *sumbas*.

සුඹුළු, *Sumbuḷu*, *s.* tegument, tunicle, covering; bark or rind of trees; dress.

සුඹුළුමාරා, *Sumbuḷu-mártá*, *s.* tree, not ascertained.

සුමං, *Suman*, *s.* good road.

සුමංගල, *Sumangala*, *a.* (සු very, මංගල auspicious) very fortunate or auspicious.

සුමගුල්, *Sumagul*, Elu form of the last.

සුමත, *Sumata*, *a.* (සු well, මන *mana* to mind, ක්ත *kta* aff.) friendly, well or kindly disposed.

සුමති, *Sumati*, *s.* (සු good, මති understanding) friendship, kindness; intelligence, good capacity.

සුමධුර, *Sumadhura*, *a.* (සු very, මධුර sweet) pleasant, gentle, soothing; sweet, saccharine.

සුමනඃඵල, *Sumanaḥ-phala*, *s.* citron, *citrus medica*, [Colloq. ලප්නාරන් *lapnáran*]; elephant or wood apple, *feronia elephantum*, [Colloq. දිවුල් *diwul*].

සුමන්දුව, *Sumanduwa*, *s.* difficulty, distress, trouble, disturbance.

සුමන, *Sumana*, *s.* wheat; thorn apple, *datura stramonium;* shoe flower, *hibiscus rosa-sinensis*, [Colloq. වදමල් *wada-mal*]; nutmeg, *myristica fragrans*, [Colloq. සාදික්කා *sádikká*]: *a.* handsome, beautiful.

සුමනකූට, *Sumanakúṭa*, *s.* (සුමන and කූට peak) Adam's Peak.

සුමනපත්, *Sumana-pat*, *s.* mace, [Colloq. වසාවාසි *wasáwási*].

සුමනස්, *Sumanas*, *s.* (සු well, excellent, මනස් the mind) a god, an immortal; pandit, learned man or teacher; plant, *cæsalpinia bonduc*, [Colloq. කුඹුරුවැල් *kumburuwel*]; wheat; nimba tree, *azadirachta indica*, [Colloquial: කොහොඹ *kohomba*].

සුමනස, *Sumanasa*, *s.* flower in general: see the last.

සුමනා, *Sumaná*, *s.* great flowered jasmine, *jasminum grandiflorum*, [Colloq. දෑසමන් *désaman*].

සුමනෝරජස්, *Sumanó-rajas*, *s.* (සුමනස *sumanasa* and රජස් dust) pollen of a flower.

සුමර්දිත, *Sumardita*, *a.* (සු well, මෘද *mṛida* to grind) subdued, reduced, overcome, vanquished: grinded, pounded to dust.

සුමානපතා, *Sumánapatá*, *ad.* weekly.

සුමානය, *Sumánaya*, *s.* a week: pl. සුමාන *sumána*.

සුමු, *Sumu*, *s.* (සු excellent, මු countenance) multitude, heap, quantity, from සමූහ *samúha;* pleasure, enjoyment: *a.* beautiful, elegant, handsome.

සුමුඛ, *Sumukha*, *s.* (සු and මුඛ countenance) name of Gaṇésa; also of Garuḍa; pandit, learned man: *a.* pleasing, agreeable, lovely: handsome, hand some faced.

සුමුඛී, *Sumukhí*, *s.* (සුමුඛ *sumukha* and ඊ *í* fem. aff.) handsome woman; mirror.

සුමුග, *Sumuga*, *s.* casket; Elu form of සමුද්ග *samudga*.

සුමුත්පල, *Sumutpala*, *s.* blue lotus, *nymphæa stellata*, [Colloq. මානෙල් *mánel*].

සුමුදු, *Sumudu*, *s.* (සු very, මුදු soft) sea, ocean, [Colloq. මූද *múda*]: *a.* soft, tender, delicate.

සුමේධ, *Sumédha*, *a.* (සු good, මේධස් *médhas* apprehension) sensible, intelligent, of good capacity or understanding.

සුමේධා, *Sumédhá*, *s.* heart-pea: see the last.

සුමේරු, *Suméru*, *s.* (සු excellent, මේරු Méru) sacred mountain Méru.

සුයාමය, *Suyámaya*, *s.* a god so called, chief of one of the divine worlds.

සුර, *Sura*, *s.* (සුර to shine, to be radiant) a god, deity; sun; sage, learned man.

සුර අජර, *Sura-ajara*, *s.* (සුර god, අජර teacher) Bṛihaspati teacher of gods; Elu form of the සුරාචාර්ය *suráchárya*.

සුර ඉසුරු, *Sura-isuru*, *s.* (සුර and ඉසුරු lord) name of Indra; also of Ṣiva.

සුර ඍෂි, *Sura-ṛishi*, *s.* (සුර and ඍෂි Ṛishi) divine Ṛishi.

සුරක්ත, *Surakta*, *s.* (සු well, රක්ත red) deeply or well-coloured, or dyed, deep red, crimson; strongly affected or impassioned.

සුරක්ෂිත, *Surakshita*, *a.* (සු and රක්ෂ *raksha* to preserve, ක්ත *kta* aff.) fortified, defended; preserved, guarded; kept, observed, as a religious precept.

සුරක, *Suraka*, *s.* resemblance, similitude.

සුරකල, *Surakala*, *s.* (සුර god, කල waterpot) vessel filled with holy water, etc. and used on festival occasions.

සුරගඟ, *Suraganga*, *s.* (සුර god, ගඟ river) Ganges or river of heaven.

සුරගුරු, *Suraguru*, *s.* (සුර and ගුරු teacher) Bṛihaspati preceptor of the gods, [Colloq. බෘහස්පති *Bṛihaspati*].

සුරඟ, *Suranga*, *s.* (සු well, රඟ colour) orange, *citrus aurantium*, [Colloq. පැනිදොඩම් *penidoḍam*]; red sanders or red sandal wood, *pterocarpus santalinus*, [Colloquial: රත්සඳුන් *ratsandun*]; vermillion: see also the next.

සුරඟන, *Surangana*, *s.* (සුර god, අඟන *angana* woman) goddess; an apsará or courtezan of the gods.

සුරජ්‍යෙෂ්ඨ, *Surajyeshṭha*, *s.* (සුර and ජ්‍යෙෂ්ඨ elder) name of Brahma.

සුරත්, *Surat*, } see සුරක්ත *surakta*.
සුරත්ත, *Suratta*, }

සුරත, *Surata*, *s.* (සු well, රම *rama* to sport or play, ක්ත *kta* aff.) coition; right hand: *a.* compassionate, tender.

සුරතල්, *Suratal*, *s.* childishness, infant sport or talk, conversing or sporting with children: *a.* puerile, docile.

සුරතල්කරණවා, *Suratalkaraṇawá*, *v.* to play with a child, to sport, to fondle a child.

සුරතා, *Suratá*, *s.* (සුර god, තා aff. of the abstract) godhead, divinity.

සුරතුරු, *Suratura*, *s.* (සුර and තුරු tree) celestial tree, tree of plenty in Indra's heaven; the *pinus devadaru*.

සුරදුරු, *Suradáru*, *s.* (සුර and දුරු wood) sort of pine, *pinus devadaru*.

සුරදිරද, *Suradirada*, *s.* (සුර and දිරද elephant) Indra's elephant: see සුරද්විප *suradvipa;* Indra's city.

සුරදුම්, *Suradum*, *s.* celestial tree: see සුරතුරු *suratura*.

සුරදූතයා, *Suradútayá*, *s.* angel, messenger of th gods.

සුරදෙට, *Suradeṭa*, Elu form of සුරජ්‍යෙෂ්ඨ *surajyeshṭha*.

සුරදෙව්, *Suradew*, *s.* (සුර god, දෙව් deity) name of Brahma, the supreme being, the god of gods.

සුරද්විප, *Sura-dvipa*, *s.* (සුර and ද්විප elephant) elephant of the gods, either that of Indra or of either of the other rulers of the different quarters.

සුරධනුස්, *Sura-dhanus*, *s.* (සුර and ධනුස් bow) rainbow, or bow of Indra, [Colloq. දේදුන්න *dédunna*].

සුරධූප, *Sura-dhúpa*, *s.* (සුර and ධූප incense) resin; turpentine.

සුරනදී, *Sura-nadí*, see සුරගඟ *sura-ganga*.

සුරනී, *Suraní*, *s.* goddess.

සුරපති, *Surapati*, *s.* (සුර and පති master) Indra, ruler of Swarga, and chief of the inferior gods.

සුරපථ, *Sura-patha*, *s.* (සුර deity, පථ patha) sky, visible heavens, [Colloq. අහස *ahasa*].

සුරපර්ණකා, *Sura-parṇaká*, *s.* (සුර a god, පර්ණ leaf, කන් *kan* aff.) tree, *mallotus philippensis* or *rottleria tinctoria*, [Colloq. හම්පිරිල්ල *hampirilla*].

සුරපා, *Surapá*, s. (සුර deity, පා tree) divine tree: සුරතුර *suratura*.

සුරපිතෘ, *Sura-pitṛi*, s. (සුර a god, පිතෘ father) name of Brahma.

සුරපුන්නාග, *Sura-punnága*, s. tree, *calophyllum spectabile*, [Colloq. දොඹකින *domba-kíṇa*].

සුරපුර, *Surapura*, s. divine city; heaven.

සුරබොජුන්, *Surabojun*, } s. (සුර and බොජුන් or
සුරබොදුන්, *Surabodun*, } බොදුන් food) ambrosia, food of the immortals.

සුරභි, *Surabhi*, s. (සු well, රභි to begin) fragrance, perfume, sweet-smelling substance; *michelia champaca*, [Colloq. සපු *sapu*]; nutmeg, *myristica fragrans*, [Colloq. සාදික්කා *sádikká*]; spring; resin; gum olibanum tree; cow of plenty, granting every wish; holy basil; jasmine of several sorts; gold; sulphur: *a.* fragrant, sweet-smelling; pleasing, beloved; celebrated, famous.

සුරභිච්ඡද, *Surabhichchhada*, s. (සුරභි fragrant, ඡද rind) cinnamon, *cinnamomum zeylanicum*, [Colloq. කුරුඳු *kurundu*]: see also the next.

සුරභිත්වච්, *Surabhitwach*, s. (සුරභි and ත්වච් bark) large cardamoms, *elettaria cardamomum (major)*, [Colloq. එන්සාල් *ensál*].

සුරභිධේනු, *Surabhi-dhénu*, s. (සුරභි and ධේනු cow) fabulous cow: see සුරභි *surabhi*.

සුරභී, *Surabhí*, see සුරභි *surabhi*.

සුරභිපත්‍රා, *Surabhí-patrá*, } s. (සුරභි and පත්‍ර
සුරභිපත්‍රිකා, *Surabhí-patriká*, } *patra* leaf) tree, *eugenia jambolana*, [Colloq. මාදම් *mádam*].

සුරභිපුන්නාග, *Surabhípunnága*, s. tree, *calophyllum spectabile*, [Colloq. කිනදොඹ *kína-domba*].

සුරභිමුද්ගකා, *Surabhímudgaká*, s. small grain or seed used by natives to put into their curries, [Colloq. උළුවා *uḷuwá*].

සුරඹ, *Suramba*, s. (සුර a god, අඹ *amba* female) a celestial nymph, an apsara.

සුරඹිකාව, *Surambikáwa*, see සුරඹ *suramba*.

සුරමග, *Sura-maga*, s. (සුර deity, මග way) sky, heavens, firmament, [Colloq. අහස *ahasa*].

සුරමත, *Sura-mata*, s. (සුර a god, මත charm) incantations to the gods, etc.

සුරමන්ත්‍රී, *Sura-mantrí*, s. (සුර and මන්ත්‍රී who counsels) name of Bṛihaspati, regent of the planet Jupiter, and preceptor of the gods.

සුරරජ, *Sura-raja*, } s. (සුර a god, රජ or රද king)
සුරරද, *Sura-rada*; } name of Ṣakra; teacher of the gods.

සුරල, *Surala*, s. kind of drum beaten with the fingers: pl. සුරල් *sural*.

සුරලෝ, *Suraló*, } s. (සුර deity, ලෝක world)
සුරලෝක, *Suralóka*, } Swarga, the paradise of the gods.

සුරවර, *Surawara*, s. name of Indra.

සුරවි, *Suravi*, s. (සුර a god, අවි *avi* weapon) rainbow, [Colloq. දේදුනන *dédunna*].

සුරවීර, *Suravíra*, s. divine hero.

සුරශත්‍රු, *Sura-ṣatru*, s. (සුර deity, ශත්‍රු enemy) titan, Asura.

සුරස, *Surasa*, s. (සු good, රස taste, flavour) juice; gum, myrrh; cassia bark; holy basil, *ocimum sanctum*, [Colloq. මදුරුතලා *madurutalá*]: plant, *vitex trifolia*, [Tamil, නොච්චි *nochchi*]: *a.* sweet; sapid, juicy.

සුරසතුරු, *Sura-saturu*, see සුරශත්‍රු *suraṣatru*.

සුරසව්, *Surasaw*, s. (සු excellent, රස *rasa* flavour or juice) holy basil, *ocimum sanctum*, [Colloq. මදුරුතලා *madurutalá*]; sort of fennel, *anethum sowa*; moon plant, *asclepias acida*.

සුරසුන්දරිය, *Surasundariya*, } s. (සුර a god, සුන්දරී
සුරසුන්දරී, *Surasundarí*, } beauty) apsara or courtezan of heaven.

සුරසෑව්, *Suraṣew*, s. (සුර and සෑව් bow) rainbow, [Colloq. දේදුන්න *dédunna*].

සුරා, *Surá*, s. toddy, liquor extracted from the coconut tree, and from which arrack is distilled.

සුරාඞ්ගනා, *Suraṅganá*, s. nymph, fairy, sylph.

සුරාචාර්ය, *Surácharya*, s. (සුර *sura* a god, ආචාර්ය *ácharya* teacher) name of Bṛihaspati preceptor of the gods.

සුරාජක, *Surájaka*, s. plant, *eclipta prostrata*.

සුරාජා, *Surájá*, s. (සු particle of eminence, රාජ *rája* to shine, අ *a* aff.) a god, divinity.

සුරාධූර්ත, *Surádhúrta*, s. (සුරා liquor, ධූර්ත addicted to) drunken, sottish, intoxicated, living the life of a sot.

සුරාපගා, *Surápagá*, s. (සුර *sura* god, අපගා *apagá* river) celestial river, the Ganges.

සුරාභාග, *Surábhága*, s. (සුරා spirits, භාග part) yeast, barm, [Colloq. රා මණ්ඩි *rá-maṇḍi*].

සුරාරි, *Surári*, s. (සුර *sura* deity, අරි *ari* enemy) Asura, an infernal being opposed to the gods; sprite, goblin, etc.

සුරාලය, *Surálaya*, s. (සුර *sura* deity or සුරා spirits, ආලය *álaya* abode) sacred mountain Méru, the extremity of the world's axis and residence of the gods; Swarga or paradise; tavern.

සුරාව්හ, *Surávha, s.* (සුර *sura* a god, ආව්හ *áwha* appellation) kind of pine, *pinus devadaru;* the name alludes to its being called the tree of the gods.

සුරාව, *Suráwa, s.* toddy, liquor extracted from the coconut tree, from which arrack is distilled.

සුරාශ්‍රය, *Suráṣraya,* see සුරාලය *surálaya;* plant, [Colloq. යොහොඹු *yohombu*].

සුරිඳු, *Surindu, s.* (සුර *sura* a god, ඉඳු *indu* chief) name of Indra, the sovereign of the gods.

සුරු, *Suru, s.* warrior, hero: *a.* clever, skilful, capable: accustomed, brave, heroic, intrepid; also, beautiful, handsome.

සුරුක්කම, *Surukkama, s.* speed, expedition; brevity, retrenchment, smallness; carefulness: pl. සුරුක්කම් *surukkam.* (Tamil.)

සුරුකම, *Surukama, s.* skill, ability, cleverness: see සුරු *suru.*

සුරුඟ, *Suruṅga, s.* murunga tree, *moringa pterygosperma.*

සුරුඟා, *Suruṅgá, s.* (සු well, රඤ *rañja* to be intent on) hole made through the walls of a building for military or felonious purposes, mine, breach.

සුරුචිර, *Suruchira, a.* (සු very, රුචිර beautiful) handsome, elegant; best, pre-eminent.

සුරුට්ටුකාරයා, *Suruṭṭukárayá, s.* seller of cigars.

සුරුට්ටුව, *Suruṭṭuwa, s.* cigar: pl. සුරුට්ටු *suruṭṭu.*

සුරුතල්, *Surutal, s.* childishness, infant pastimes: *a.* childish, docile: see සුරතල් *suratal.*

සුරුව්ව, *Suruwwa, s.* economy, frugality, [Colloq. ප්‍රවේසම *prawésama*].

සුරුසුරු, *Surusuru, ind.* imitative sound, crackling of anything burning, or the hissing of boiling water.

සුරූප, *Surúpa, s.* (සු own or well, රූප image) form, image, likeness, resemblance: *a.* handsome, well-formed; wise, learned.

සුරේජ්‍ය, *Suréjya, s.* (සුර *sura* deity, ඉජ්‍ය *ijya* preceptor) name of Bṛihaspati, teacher of the gods.

සුරේන්ද්‍ර, *Suréndra, s.* (සුර *sura* a god, ඉන්ද්‍ර *indra* chief) name of Indra, chief of the gods inhabiting Swarga.

සුරේන්ද්‍රමන්ත්‍රී, *Suréndra-mantrí, s.* (සුරේන්ද්‍ර and මන්ත්‍රී counsellor) Bṛihaspati, preceptor of the gods.

සුරේශ්වර, *Suréṣwara. s.* (සුර *sura* and ඊශ්වර *íṣwara* lord) name or personification of Ṣiva.

සුරේෂ්ට, *Suréshṭa, s.* (සුර *sura* and ඉෂ්ට *ishṭa* wished) tree, *vateria acuminata,* [Colloq. හල් *hal*]; small tree with edible legumes, *æschynomene grandiflora.*

සුරෝත්තම, *Suróttama, s.* (සුර *sura* deity, උත්තම *uttama* best) sun, [Colloq. ඉර *ira*].

සුරැකි, *Surẹki, a.* well-guarded, defended; preserved, protected; Elu form of සුරක්ෂිත *surakshita.*

සුල්, *Sul, s.* stake, pillar: *a.* little, thin, small: see the next.

සුල, *Sula, s.* torch, flambeau, chool.

සුලඟ, *Sulanga, s.* air, wind, breeze; god of the wind: pl. සුලං *sulaṅ.*

සුලඟිල්ල, *Sulangilla, s.* (සුල් *sul* little, ඇඟිල්ල *ẹngilla* finger) little finger: pl. සුලඟිලි *sulangili.*

සුලබ, *Sulaba,* } *a.* (සු very, ලභ acquiring) easy,
සුලභ, *Sulabha,* } feasible, attainable.

සුලා, *Sulá, s.* friend, companion, [Colloq. මිත්‍රයා *mitrayá*].

සුලිය, *Suliya, s.* curve or groove of a screw, etc.; mischief, wickedness, imposture, deceit; spiral curve of a conch, the eddy in a river: pl. සුලි *suli.*

සුලු, *Sulu, a.* little, small, short; insignificant.

සුලු ඉරමසු, *Sulu-iramasu, s.* plant, variety of the *Indian sarsaparilla, hemidesmus indicus.*

සුලුකම, *Sulukama, s.* smallness.

සුලු කුඹුක්, *Sulu-kumbuk, s.* tree, variety of the *terminalia alata,* or of *t. glabra.*

සුලු කූර, *Sulu-kúra, s.* sort of amaranth, *amarantus polygamus,* [Colloq. වලු තම්පලා *walu-tampalá.*

සුලු කැල, *Sulu-kẹla, s.* small sort of *butea frondosa.*

සුලු දිය, *Sulu-diya, s.* urine.

සුලු නයි, *Sulu-nayi, s.* small creeping plant, *adhatoda repens.*

සුලුනෙයි, *Suluneyi, s.* plant, *rungia longifolia (Acanthaceæ).*

සුලුප්පුව, *Suluppuwa, s.* sloop: pl. සුලුප්පු *suluppu.*

සුලු බුරුද, *Sulu-buruda, s.* sort of hog-weed, *boerhavia diffusa,* [Colloq. පිටසුදු පලා *piṭasudu-palá*].

සුලු බැලිල, *Sulu-bẹlila, s.* plant, perhaps a variety of the *sida cordifolia.*

සුලුව, *Suluwa, s.* trifling matter.

සුලුවග, *Suluwaga, s.* class of books so called, the third of the winaya piṭaka: see පිටක *piṭaka.*

සුලෝචන, *Sulóchana, s.* (සු excellent, ලෝචන eye) deer: *a.* fine-eyed.

සුලෝචනා, *Sulóchaní*, *s.* handsome woman.

සුලෝහක, *Sulóhaka*, *s.* (සු and ලෝහ iron, ක aff.) brass, [Colloq. පිත්තල *pittala*].

සුලෝහිත, *Sulóhita*, *s.* (සු very, ලෝහිත red) one of the seven tongues of Agni the god of fire: *a.* very red, blood colour.

සුව, *Suwa*, *s.* (from සුඛ *sukha* joy) enjoyment, pleasure, happiness; health; Nirwáṇa or final emancipation; the young of any animal; parrot; *mimosa sirisha* from සුක *suka;* in composition implying own, self, from ස්ව *swa.*

සුවකරණවා, *Suwakaraṇawá*, *v.* to cure, to heal, to restore.

සුවකාය, *Suwakáya*, *s.* (සුව own, කාය body) personal identity.

සුවච්චල, *Suwachchala*, see සුවර්චලා *suwarchalá;* natron.

සුවච, *Suwacha*, *a.* (සු well, වච word, speech) obedient, attentive, docile; speaking much and eloquently.

සුවචකම, *Suwachakama*, *s.* obedience, attention.

සුවචන, *Suwachana*, *s.* (සු well, වච to speak, ණ්‍ය *nya* aff.) speaking much or well, eloquence.

සුවචස්, *Suwachas*, see සුවච *suwacha.*

සුවට, *Suwaṭa*, *a.* (සු good, වට round) round, globular.

සුවත්, *Suwat*, *s.* (සු good, වත් way) good road.

සුවතුරු, *Suwaturu*, *s.* (සුව and තුරු tree) plant, called mudar, *calotropis gigantea*, [Colloq. වරා *wará*]; sirisha tree, *mimosa sirisha;* also මදටිය *madaṭiya*, *adeananthera pavonia.*

සුවද, *Suwada*, *s.* colour white: *a.* conferring or producing pleasure.

සුවදු, *Suwadu*, } *s.* sea, ocean, [Colloq. මූද *múda*].
සුවදූ, *Suwadú*, }

සුවඳ, *Suwaṇḍa*, *s.* perfume, scent, odour, fragrance; plant, peculiar to Ceylon, *kayea stylosa (Gulliferæ).*

සුවඳ ඇල්වි, *Suwaṇḍa-ęlví*, *s.* kind of paddy, *oryza sativa.*

සුවඳ කෙසෙල්, *Suwaṇḍa-kesel*, *s.* variety of plantain, *musa sapientum.*

සුවඳ තලා, *Suwaṇḍa-talá*, *s.* (සුවඳ fragrant, තලා basil) plant, *ocimum basilicum.*

සුවඳලා, *Suwaṇḍalá*, *s.* (සුවඳ and ලා exudation, gum) incense, gum benjamin; perfume in general.

සුවඳ වී, *Suwaṇḍa-ví*, *s.* kind of paddy, *oryza sativa.*

සුවඳ සපු, *Suwaṇḍa-sapu*, *s.* (සුවඳ and සපු champaka) variety of champaka, *michelia graveolens*, or *m. champaka.*

සුවඳහොට, *Suwaṇḍahoṭa*, *s.* plant having a very fragrant root, *andropogon muricatus*, [Colloq. සෑවැන්දරා *sęwęndará*].

සුවඳැල්, *Suwaṇḍęl*, *s.* variety of plantain, *musa sapientum.*

සුවන්, *Suwan*, *s.* sound, noise, from ස්වාන *swána;* gold; dog; name of Garuḍa; ochre, etc. see සුවර්ණ *suwarṇa.*

සුවන්කරු, *Suwankaru*, *s.* goldsmith, [Colloq. බඩාලා *baḍálá*].

සුවන්න, *Suwanna*, *s.* gold, [Colloq. රත්රන් *ratran*]: see සුවර්ණ *suwarṇa.*

සුවන්බෘ, *Suwanbẹ*, *s.* dawn, daybreak, morn, [Colloq. පාන්දර *pándara*]; charioteer of the sun.

සුවන් යහන්, *Suwan-yahan*, *s.* (සුවන් garuḍa, යහන් vehicle) name of Vishṇu.

සුවන්වන්, *Suwanwan*, *s.* (සුවන් gold, වන් colour) bright yellow, gold colour.

සුවනා, *Suwana*, *s.* sun, [Colloq. ඉර *ira*]; fire, [Colloq. ගින්දර *gindara*]; moon, [Colloq. හඳ *haṇḍa*].

සුවපත්, *Suwapat*, *a.* (සුව health, පත් attained) healthy, convalescent; joyful, happy, delighted.

සුවපහස, *Suwa-pahasa*, *s.* (සුව and පහස contact, enjoyment, ස්පර්ශ *sparṣa*) health, enjoyment of health.

සුවබෘ, *Suwabẹ*, see සුවන්බෘ *suwanbẹ.*

සුවය, *Suwaya*, *s.* cure, restoration to health, health.

සුවර්චක, *Suwarchaka*, *s.* (සු well, වර්ච to shine, ක aff.) natron; alkali or impure carbonate of soda, [Colloq. සුවසලුණු *suwasa-luṇu*]; gold; vulture; eagle; weight equal to five kalaṇdas, or about 176 grains troy: *a.* beautiful skin, of a bright colour, brilliant.

සුවර්චලා, *Suwarchalá*, *s.* (සු and වර්ච to shine, අල *ala* aff.) linseed, *linum utilatissimum;* also කොබෝවක්කා *kobówakká*, cucurbitaceous plant with red fruit, *momordica monadelpha.*

සුවර්ණ, *Suwarṇa*, *s.* (සු excellent, වර්ණ tribe or colour) gold, [Colloq. රත්රන් *ratran*]; sort of sandal wood; kind of red chalk or ochre; wealth, property; tree, *cassia fistula*, [Colloq. ඇහැළ *ẹhẹla*]; also, යොහොඹු *yohombu*, species of jasmine, *jasminum auriculatum*: *a.* of good tribe, colour, etc.; brilliant.

සුවණ්ණක, *Suwarṇaka*, *s.* (සුවණ්ණ and ක aff.) tree, *cassia fistula*, [Colloq. ඇහැළ *ehela*].

සුවණ්ණකාර, *Suwarṇakára*, *s.* (සුවණ්ණ and කාර workman) goldsmith, [Colloq. බඩාලා *badálá*].

සුවණ්ණ ගෛරික, *Suwarṇa-gairika*, *s.* (සුවණ්ණ gold, ගෛරික red chalk) sort of ochre.

සුවණ්ණා, *Suwarṇá*, *s.* black aloe wood; turmeric, *curcuma longa*, [Colloq. කහ *kaha*]; bitter gourd, *citrullus colocynthus*, [Colloq. යක්කොමඩු *yak-komadu*]; plant, *sida cordifolia*, etc.: see the last.

සුවරු, *Suwaru*, *s.* goldsmith; worker on metal; cook, dresser of provisions.

සුවල්ලි, *Suwalli*, *s.* (සු excellent, වල්ලි stalk) shrub, *vernonia* or *serratula anthelmintica*, [Colloq. බෝදි ඇට *bódi-eta*].

සුවස, *Suwasa*, Elu form of සුවච්ක *suwarchaka*.

සුවස ලුණු, *Suwasa-luṇu*, *s*, (සුවස and ලුණු salt) natron; alkali, impure carbonate of soda.

සුවසේ, *Suwasé*, *ind.* (සුව health, etc. සේ aff.) happily, comfortably, joyfully; prosperously in health.

සුවසේ ඉන්නවා, *Suwasé-innawá*, *v.* to live in health.

සුවහ, *Suwaha*, *s.* (සු well, වහ to bear) patient, enduring; bearing or conveying well or pleasantly.

සුවහස්, *Suwahas*, *ind.* numeral, lak, hundred thousand.

සුවහා, *Suwahá*, *s.* flower, *nyctanthes arbor-tristis*, [Colloq. සේපාලිකා *sépáliká*]; shrub, *mimosa octandra;* gum olibanum tree; Indian lute.

සුවාස, *Suwása*, *s.* (සු well, වාස abode) pleasant or reputable dwelling; agreeable perfume.

සුවාසූදහසක්, *Suwásúdahasak*, *s.* (සුව *suwa* for සිව් *siw* eighty, දහසක් thousand) eighty-four thousand.

සුවිඥෙය, *Suvijñeya*, *s.* (සු very, විඥා *vijñá* knowledge, එය *eya* aff.) profound or extensive knowledge; keen penetration.

සුවිද්, *Suvid*, *s.* (සු well, විද් who knows) pandit, learned man.

සුවිනිත, *Suvinita*, *a.* (සු very, විනිත well behaved) well-trained, properly-behaved; obedient, attentive, docile, tractable.

සුවිපක්, *Suvipak*, *a.* (සු well, විපක් ripe) completely ripe, mature.

සුවිපුල, *Suvipula*, *a.* large, great, bulky, [Colloq. මහත් *mahat*].

සුවිභක්ත, *Suvibhakta*, *a.* (සු very, විභක්ත divided) well-divided, allotted, apportioned.

සුවිසාල, *Suvisála*, *s.* very large or extensive.

සුවීර, *Suvíra*, *s.* (සු excellent, වීර power, efficacy) courage, bravery, intrepidity, valour; collyrium prepared from an infusion of the *amomum anthorizon*.

සුව්‍රත, *Suwrata*, *s.* (සු well, ව්‍රත vow) a religious donation: *a.* virtuous, strict, rigidly observing any religious vow or obligation.

සුශ්‍රුත, *Suṣruta*, *s.* a medical work so called: *a.* well-heard.

සුශික්ෂිත, *Suṣikshita*, *a.* (සු well, ශික්ෂිත tamed) obedient, attentive, docile; trained, disciplined.

සුශුක්ල, *Suṣukla*, *a.* (සු very, ශුක්ල white) very white, [Colloq. ඉතාසුදු *itá-sudu*].

සුෂ්ඨු, *Sushṭhu*, *ind.* much, very much; well, excellent.

සුෂවී, *Sushaví*, *s.* sort of pungent seed, either black species of cummin seed or the *nigella indica*, [Colloq. කළුදුරු *kaḷuduru*]; creeping plant, *momordica charantia*, [Colloq. කරවිල *karavila*].

සුෂුප්ති, *Sushupti*, *s.* (සු well, ස්වප *shwapa* to sleep, ක්ති *kti* aff.) deep sleep, profound repose, entire insensibility.

සුෂේණිකා, *Sushéṇiká*, *s.* black teori plant, *ipomœa trupatum*, [Colloq. ත්‍රස්තවාලු *trastawálu*]; heart seed, *cardiospermum haliacacabum*, [Colloq. වැල් පෙනෙල *wel-penela*].

සුෂ්ක, *Suska*, see ශුෂ්ක *ṣushka*.

සුස්ථිර, *Susthira*, *a.* (සු well, ස්ථිර steady) very firm, steady, stable.

සුස්ම, *Susma*, *s.* breath, breathing, respiration; also සුසුම *susuma*.

සුසංස්කෘත, *Susaṇskṛita*, *a.* (සු well, සංස්කෘත made perfect) well-dressed, seasoned, prepared with condiments, sauces, etc.; entirely perfected, very highly finished.

සුසම්පත්, *Susampat*, *s.* (සු well, සම්පත් prosperity) good fortune, prosperity.

සුසම, *Susama*, *a.* (සු and සම equal) beautiful, handsome, pleasing; same, even, all.

සුසර්ජිත, *Susarjita*, *s.* (සු and සෘජ *srija* to adorn, ක්ත *kta* aff.) adorned, accoutred, decorated.

සුසාන, *Susána*, *s.* burying ground, sepulchre, cemetery, from ශ්මශාන *ṣmasána*, [Colloq. මිනිපිට්ටනිය *minipiṭṭaniya*].

සුසාර, *Susára*, s. (සු good, සාර essence) variety of *acacia catechu* or *a. suma;* sandal wood tree, *santalum album*, [Colloq. සඳුන් *sandun*].

සුසිර, *Susira*, s. lute: see ශුෂිර *sushira*.

සුසිරි, *Susiri*, s. (සු and සිරි prosperity) good fortune, auspiciousness; moral merit; the sound of any wind instrument.

සුසිත, *Susíta*, s. (සු excellent, සිත cold) yellow fragrant sandal wood.

සුසිතල, *Susítala*, a. (සු and සිතල cold) cool, refreshing; frigid, freezing.

සුසිල, *Susíla*, a. (සු well, සිල nature, etc.) well-disposed, of good temper or disposition; observant of religious duties, virtuous, pious.

සුසිලවන්ත, *Susílawanta*, a. good-natured, good-tempered: see the last.

සුසිලවන්තයා, *Susílawantayá*, s. good natured person.

සුසු, *Susu*, s. going, moving, proceeding; child, infant; pupil.

සුසුම්ලනවා, *Susumlanawá*, v. (සුසුම *susuma* breath, ලනවා to eject) to sigh, to sob or groan: pret. සුසුම්ලෑවා *susumlẹwá*.

සුසුම්ලෑම, *Susumlẹma*, s. sighing.

සුසුම, *Susuma*, s. breath, breathing; also සුස්ම *susma*.

සුසුරු, *Susuru*, s. hole, perforation; wind instrument; trunk of an elephant; also සුසිර *susira*.

සුහද, *Suhada*, s. good-heart; friend.

සුහිත, *Suhita*, a. (සු well, හිත placed, etc.) fit, right, suitable; kind, friendly.

සුහුදු, *Suhudu*, s. cook, particularly of a king or nobleman; a friend.

සුහුනා, *Suhuná*, s. lizard; also සූනා *súná*.

සුහුරු, *Suhuru*, s. uterine brother; pig, from සූකර *súkara*.

සුහුල්, *Suhul*, s. mother-in-law.

සුහෘද්, *Suhṛid*, s. (සු excellent, හෘද් heart) friend; ally.

සුහෘද්ජන, *Suhṛidjana*, s. (සුහෘද් and ජන man) friend; ally.

සුහෘද, *Suhṛida*, a. good-hearted, kind, friendly.

සූක්ත, *Súkta*, s. (සු *su* well, උක්ත *ukta* said) hymn in the Rig Veda.

සූක්ෂ්ම, *Súkshma*, s. (සූච *súcha* to inform or make known, ස්ම *sma* aff.) an atom; ingenuity, subtlety, discretion, fraud, cheating: *a.* little, small, minute, atomic; fine, delicate; ingenious, subtle.

සූක්ෂ්මපත්‍ර, *Súkshma-patra*, s. (සූක්ෂ්ම fine, පත්‍ර leaf) coriander seed, *coriandrum sativum;* wild kind of cummin, *nigella indica;* gum Arabic tree.

සූක්ෂ්මපත්‍රා, *Súkshma-patrá*, s. climbing plant, *tinospora cordifolia*, [Colloq. රසකිඳ *rasakiṇḍa*].

සූක්ෂ්මපත්‍රිකා, *Súkshma-patriká*, s. plant, *mollugo cerviana*, [Colloq. පත්පාඩගම් *patpáḍagam*].

සූක්ෂ්මපත්‍රී, *Súkshma-patrí*, s. creeping plant, *asparagus falcatus*, [Colloq. හාතාවාරිය *hátáwáriya*].

සූක්ෂ්මා, *Súkshmá*, s. species of jasmine, *jasminum auriculatum*, [Colloq. බෝලිද්ද *bólidda*]; small cardamums, *elettaria cardamomum (minor)*, [Colloq. රට එන්සාල් *raṭa-ensál*].

සූක්ෂ්මෛලා, *Súkshmailá*, s. small cardamums, *elettaria cardamomum*, [Colloquial: සිහින් එන්සාල් *sihin-ensál*].

සූකකීට, *Súkakíṭa*, s. (සූක awn, කීට insect) caterpillar, [Colloq. දළඹුවා *dalambuwá*].

සූකතුණ්ඩ, *Súka-tuṇḍa*, s. vermillion, [Colloq. සාදිලිංගම් *sádilingam*].

සූකරයා, *Súkarayá*, s. hog: pl. සූකරයෝ *súkarayó*.

සූකරී, *Súkarí*, s. sort of moss, *lycopodium imbricatum*.

සූකිරි, *Súkiri*, s. sugar candy.

සූචක, *Súchaka*, s. (සූච to make known, ක aff.) spy, informer; teacher, instructor; needle.

සූචි, *Súchi*, s. (සූච *súcha* to make known, or සිව *siva* to sew, ච *cha* aff.) needle, [Colloq. ඉදිකටුව *idikaṭuwa*]; indication of a passion or feeling by signs, gesture, gesticulation; piercing, perforating; index, catalogue.

සූචික, *Súchika*, s. (සූච *súcha* needle, ක aff.) tailor, [Colloq. මහන්නා *mahanná*].

සූචිකා, *Súchiká*, s. needle; elephant's trunk.

සූචිනී, *Súchiní*, s. needle, [Colloq. ඉදිකටුව *idikaṭuwa*].

සූටික්කා, *Súṭikká*, s. generic name (in combination) of the sun bird, *(Cynnyridæ*, order *Passeres):* see රන් සූටික්කා *ran-súṭikká*, මොදර සූටික්කා *modara-súṭikká*, and මල් සූටික්කා *mal-súṭikká*.

සූඩයා, *Súḍayá*, s. small sea fish, anchovy.

සූත්‍ර, *Sútra*, s. (සිව *siva* to sew, ත්‍ර aff. and ඉ *i* changed to උ *u* or සු *su* to hear, etc.) a thread in general; rule, precept in morals or science, short, obscure, and technical sentence, enjoining some observance in law or religion, or intimating some rule in grammar, logic, etc.; oral declaration of Buddha.

සූත්‍රපිටක, *Sútra-piṭaka*, s. (සූත්‍ර and පිටක basket) first of the three piṭakas or collections of the writings and doctrines of Buddha, containing the orations delivered by Buddha *viva voce*, and collected and arranged in their present form after his death; it consists of five books, called සඟි *sangi*, viz. දික් *dik*, මැදුම් *medum*, සංයුත් *sanyut*, අඞ්ගුත්තර *anguttara*, and කුදුගොත් *kudugot*.

සූත්‍රපුෂ්පිකා, *Sútra-pushpiká*, *s.* cotton tree, *gossypium indicum*, *g. herbaceum*, *g. barbadease*, [Colloq. කපුගස *kapu-gasa*].

සූත්‍රලා, *Sútralá*, *s.* (සූත්‍ර thread, ලා to have or get) spindle or distaff.

සූත්‍රාමන්, *Sútráman*, *s.* (සු *su* well, ත්‍රෛ *trai* to preserve, මනින් *manin* aff.) name of Indra.

සූත්‍රී, *Sútrí*, *s.* (සූත්‍ර *sútra* thread, ඉනි *ini* aff.) crow, [Colloq. කපුටා *kaputá*].

සූත, *Súta*, *s.* (සූ to bring forth, ක්ත *kta* aff.) quicksilver, [Colloq. රසදිය *rasadiya*]; charioteer; carpenter: *a.* born, engendered; sent, dispatched.

සූතක, *Sútaka*, *s.* quicksilver; birth, production; impurity from child-birth or miscarriage.

සූති, *Súti*, *s.* (සූ and ක්ති *kti* aff.) birth, production; delivery, parturition; offspring, progeny, sewing.

සූතිකා, *Sútiká*, *s.* woman recently delivered.

සූතිකාගෘහ, *Sútiká-griha*, } *s.* (සූතිකා and ගෘහ
සූතිගෘහ, *Súti-griha*, } house) part of a house appropriated to the women, or to a lying-in woman especially.

සූද, *Súda*, *s.* cook; sauce, seasoning; made dish, any thing seasoned.

සූදයා, *Súdayá*, *s.* (සූද sauce, යා aff.) cook; see the last.

සූදශාලාව, *Súda-śáláwa*, *s.* (සූද and ශාලා *śálá* house) kitchen, cook-house, [Colloq. කුස්සිය *kussiya*].

සූදා, *Súdá*, see සූදයා *súdayá*.

සූදානම්කරණවා, *Súdánamkaranawá*, *v.* to make ready.

සූදානම්වෙනවා, *Súdánamwenawá*, *v.* to get ready, to prepare one's self.

සූදානම, *Súdánama*, *s.* preparation, provision, readiness, making ready; care: pl. සූදානම් *súdánam*.

සූදුව, *Súduwa*, *s.* gaming, gambling: pl. සූදු *súdu*.

සූදුකාරයා, *Súdukárayá*, *s.* gambler: pl. සූදුකාරයෝ *súdukárayó*.

සූදුකෙළිනවා, *Sudukelinawá*, *v.* to gamble.

සූදුකෙළිය, *Súdukeliya*, *s.* gambling.

සූදුපල, *Súdupala*, *s.* place of gambling.

සූන්මද, *Súnmada*, *a.* (සු *su* very, උන්මද *unmada* mad) mad, crazy, insane.

සූන, *Súna*, *s.* (සූ to bear, ක්ත *kta* aff.) bringing forth, parturition; flower: *a.* empty, vacant; born, produced; swelled, increased.

සූනා, *Súná*, *s.* (සූ and නා aff.) daughter; uvula; shambles, slaughter house; hurting, injuring; lizard.

සූනින්, *Súnin*, *s.* (සූනා *súná* shambles, ඉනි *ini* aff.) butcher, hunter, one who practices the death of animals.

සූනියම්කපනවා, *Súniyam-kapanawá*, *v.* to destroy, bewitchment.

සූනියම්කරණවා, *Súniyamkaranawá*, *v.* to bewitch.

සූනියම, *Súniyama*, *s.* bewitching, by spells and incantations; magical ceremony, magic: pl. සූනියම් *súniyam*.

සූනු, *Súnu*, *s.* (සූ to bear, නු aff.) son; sun; younger brother; daughter.

සූප්පක, *Súppaka*, *s.* one of the lunar asterisms: see විශාඛ *viśákha*.

සූප, *Súpa*, *s.* (සූ and ප aff.) sauce, condiment in general; cook; vessel; arrow.

සූපකාර, *Súpakára*, } *s.* (සූප sauce, කාර who
සූපකාරක, *Súpakáraka*, } makes) cook, [Colloq. කෝකියා *kókiyá*].

සූපධූපන, *Súpa-dhúpana*, *s.* (සූප and ධූපන perfuming) assafœtida, [Colloq. පෙරුන්කායම් *perunkáyam*].

සූපශාස්ත්‍රය, *Súpa-śástraya*, *s.* (සූප and ශාස්ත්‍ර *śástra* science) cookery.

සූපාඞ්ග, *Súpánga*, *s.* (සූප *súpa* and අඞ්ග *anga* member) assafœtida, [Colloq. පෙරුන්කායම් *perunkáyam*].

සූම, *Súma*, *s.* sky, heaven, [Colloq. අහස *ahasa*].

සූමන්, *Súman*, *s.* bó-tree, *ficus religiosa*, [Colloq. බෝගහ *bó-gaha*].

සූයාම, *Súyáma*, see සුයාම *suyáma*.

සූර්‍ය්‍ය, *Súrya*, *s.* (සෘ *sri* to go, ක්‍ය *kya* aff.) sun; solar light; tulip tree, *thespesia populnea* (*Malvaceæ*): *a.* solar.

සූර්‍ය්‍යකාන්ත, *Súryakánta*, *s.* (සූර්‍ය්‍ය sun, කාන්ත gem) gem, sometimes applied to crystal, but usually to a stone of fabulous existence and properties; shrub, *hibiscus phœniceus*.

සූර්‍ය්‍යකාන්ති, *Súryakánti*, *s.* (සූර්‍ය්‍ය and කාන්ති lustre) sunflower, *helianthus annuus*; flower of the sesamum; sunshine.

සූර්‍ය්‍යකාරී, *Súryakárí*, *s.* creeper, borago, *borago zeylanica*: see ශූන්‍යකා *śúnyaká*.

සූර්‍යග්‍රහ, *Súryagraha*, *s.* (සූර්‍ය sun, ග්‍රහ planet, or to seize) sun; eclipse of the sun; the personified ascending and descending node, or Kétu and Ráhu.

සූර්‍යග්‍රහණ, *Súryagrahaṇa*, *s.* (සූර්‍ය and ග්‍රහණ seizing) eclipse of the sun, supposed to be caused by Ráhu's attempt to swallow that luminary: see රාහු *ráhu*.

සූර්‍යපුත්‍ර, *Súrya-putra*, *s.* (සූර්‍ය and පුත්‍ර son) name of Varuṇa; also of Saturn and of Yama.

සූර්‍යබන්ධු, *Súrya-bandhu*, *s.* (සූර්‍ය and බන්ධු relation) lotus, *nymphœa stellata*, [Colloq. පියුම් *piyum*]; name of Buddha, alluding to his being of the Súrya race.

සූර්‍යබිම්බය, *Súrya-bimbaya*, } *s.* (සූර්‍ය sun,
සූර්‍යමණ්ඩලය, *Súrya-maṇḍalaya*, } මණ්ඩල *maṇḍala* orb) disc of the sun.

සූර්‍යමණි, *Súrya-maṇi*, *s.* (සූර්‍ය and මණි jewel) shrub, *hibiscus phœniceus;* sunstone, crystal lens or a fabulous sort of gem.

සූර්‍යයා, *Súryayá*, *s.* sun.

සූර්‍යලතා, *Súrya-latá*, *s.* (සූර්‍ය and ලතා creeper) plant, *cleome viscosa*, [Colloq. වල් අබ *wal-aba*]: see සූර්‍යාවර්ත *súryáwarta*.

සූර්‍යා, *Súryá*, *s.* wife of the sun; drug, bitter gourd.

සූර්‍යාවර්ත, *Súryáwarta*, *s.* (සූර්‍ය *súrya* and ආවර්ත *áwarta* revolving) flower, *cleome viscosa;* sunflower, *helianthus indicus;* plant, *gynandropsis pentaphylla*, [Colloq. වේලා *wélá*]; headache supposed to be produced by the sun.

සූර්‍යාහ්ව, *Súryáhwa*, *s.* (සූර්‍ය *súrya* and ආහ්වා *áhwá* appellation) gigantic swallow wort or mudar, *calotropis gigantea*. [Colloq. වරා *wará*].

සූර්‍යෝද්ගමන, *Súryódgamana*, } *s.* (සූර්‍ය *súrya*
සූර්‍යෝදය, *Súryódaya*, } sun, උද්ගමන *udgamana* or උදය *udaya* arising) sunrise.

සූරණවා, *Súraṇawá*, *v.* to scratch, to scrub, to grate: pret. සීරුවා *síruwá*.

සූරණස්කන්ද, *Súraṇaskanda*, *s.* plant, *amorphophallus campanulatus*, [Colloq. කිඩාරන් *kiḍáran*].

සූරසූත, *Súrasúta*, *s.* (සූර sun, සූත charioteer) Arjuna, personification of the dawn, as the charioteer of the sun.

සූරි, *Súri*, *s.* pandit, learned man; dock or country sorrel, *rumex vesicarius*.

සූරිය, *Súriya*, *s.* Tulip tree, *thespesia populnea:* see සූර්‍ය *súrya*.

සූරියමාරා, *Súriyamárá*, *s.* forest tree, *albizzia odoratissima* (*Leguminosæ*).

සූරී, *Súrí*, *s.* (සූර *súra* to dispel, ignorance, etc. ඉනි *ini* aff.) pandit, scholar, learned man; name of Bṛihaspati preceptor of the gods: *a.* wise, learned.

සූල්‍යවිදාරණී, *Súlyaridáraṇi*, *s.* (සූල *súla* and විදාරණ *vidáraṇa* what tears) species of kidney bean, green gram, *phaseolus mungo*, [Colloq. මුංඇට *muṇeṭa*].

සූලනයි, *Súlanayi*, *s.* plant, *jussiœa repens*, [Colloq. බේරුදියනිල්ල *bérudiyanilla*].

සූලා, *Súlá*, *s.* instrument used for putting criminals to death, stake for impaling them.

සූලායුධය, *Súláyudhaya*, *s.* instrument for impaling criminals.

සූලින්, *Súlin*, *s.* (සූල *súla* pike, ඉනි *ini* aff.) name of Ṣiva, who carries a trident in his hand.

සූලුනයි, *Súlunayi*, see සූලනයි *súlanayi*.

සූස්තරය, *Sústaraya*, *s.* corrupt form of සූත්‍ර *sútra*, machine, invention, contrivance, advice: pl. සූස්තර *sústara*.

සෙ, *Se*, *s.* colour white, from ශ්වේත *ṣwéta*; sunshine: see සේ *sé*.

සෙංකොට්ටම්, *Seṅkoṭṭam*, *s.* marking nut: see තෙබු *tebu*.

සෙක්කුව, *Sekkuwa*, *s.* chekkoo: pl. සෙක්කු *sekku*. (Tamil.)

සෙකිත්, *Sekit*, *s.* deer, [Colloq. මුවා *muwá*].

සෙඛ, *Sekha*, Páli form of ශෛක්ෂ *ṣaiksha*.

සෙඞ්ගමාලේ, *Seṅgamálé*, *s.* a disease in which the body assumes a yellow colour, the jaundice: pl. සෙඞ්ගමාල *seṅgamála*.

සෙට්ටියා, *Seṭṭiyá*, *s.* Chetty: pl. සෙට්ටි *seṭṭi*.

සෙට්ඨං, *Seṭṭhaṇ*, Páli form of ශ්‍රේෂ්ඨ *ṣréshṭha*.

සෙට, *Seṭa*, *s.* to-morrow: *a.* noble, eminent, from ශ්‍රේෂ්ඨ *ṣréshṭha*.

සෙටු, *Seṭu*, *a.* eminent, noble, [Colloq. උතුම්වූ *utumwú*].

සෙණ්ඩුවාළුව, *Seṇḍuwáḷuwa*, *s.* yard, court yard.

සෙත්, *Set*, } *s.* tranquillity of mind, internal peace
සෙත, *Seta*, } or abstraction; peace, tranquillity, calmness; ease, happiness; name of Nirwáṇa; auspiciousness, fortune, good luck.

සෙතු, *Setu*, *s.* tree, *cratœva Roxburghii*, [Colloq. ලුණුවරණ *luṇuwaraṇa*].

සෙද, *Seda*, *ind.* quickly, soon.

සෙදල්, *Sedal*, *ind.* speed, haste, celerity.

සෙදෙල, *Sedela*, } *s.* crane; tiger, from ශාර්දූල
සෙදොල, *Sedola*, } *ṣárdúla*.

සෙදෑල්, *Sedel*, see සෙදල් *sedal*.

සෙදෑගෑමි, *Sedẹ́gẹ́mi*, see ශකෘදගාමි *ṣakṛidágámi.*

සෙන්, *Sen*, *s.* multitude, host, army, from සේනා *séná;* kite, the bird, *aquilinæ* order *accipitres*, [Colloq. රාජාලියා *rájáliyá* or උකුස්සා *ukussá*].

සෙන්කලේ, *Senkalé*, *s.* knuckle, shin, shank: pl. සෙන්කල *senkala.* (Dutch).

සෙන්දිරික්කා, *Sendirikká*, *s.* plant, Marvel of Peru, commonly called four o'clock flower, *mirabilis jalapa (Nyctaginæ).*

සෙන්පා, *Senpá*, *s.* (සෙන් army, පා who preserves) general.

සෙන, *Sena*, *s.* thunderbolt or the electrical fluid; reclining, repose; falling, dropping, descending.

සෙනඟ, *Senanga*, *s.* host, army, multitude, crowd, mob.

සෙනවා, *Senawá*, *v.* to fall, to laugh, to smile.

සෙනසුරා, *Senasurá*, *s.* planet Saturn.

සෙනසුරාදා, *Senasurádá*, *s.* (සෙනසුරා Saturn, දා day) Saturday.

සෙනසුරුදිෂ්ටිය, *Senasuru-dishṭiya*, *s.* evil influence of Saturn.

සෙනහඬ, *Senahanda*, *s.* (සෙන thunderbolt, හඬ sound) thunder.

සෙනාකොල, *Senákola*, *s.* senna leaves.

සෙනෙවි, *Senevi*, *s.* general, leader of an army.

සෙනෙවිරද, *Senevirada*, *s.* (සෙනෙවි and රද king) commander of the forces, generally the king's first minister.

සෙනෙහස, *Senehasa*, *s.* oil; affection.

සෙනෙහෙ, *Senehe*, *s.* oil, [Colloq. තෙල් *tel*].

සෙප්පඩිවිජ්ජාව, *Seppaḍi-vijjáwa*, *s.* deceit, trickery; juggling, sleight of hand.

සෙප්පම, *Seppama*, *s.* health, ease, enjoyment: pl. සෙප්පම් *seppam.*

සෙප්පුව, *Seppuwa*, *s.* casket, small box, especially the betel box: pl. සෙප්පු *seppu.*

සෙබළා, *Sebalá*, *s.* soldier, warrior, hero.

සෙම්, *Sem*, *s.* phlegm, etc. see සෙම *sema.*

සෙම්කුළු, *Semkuḷu*, see හෙම්කුළු *hemkuḷu.*

සෙම්ප්‍රතිශ්‍යාව, *Sempratiṣyáwa*, *s.* (සෙම් phlegm, ප්‍රතිශ්‍යාව cold) catarrh.

සෙම්බුනෙරෙංචි, *Sembunerenchi*, *s.* prostrate plant, common among grass, *tribulus terrestris (Zygophyllaceæ).*

සෙම්බුව, *Sembuwa*, *s.* copper pot: pl. සෙම්බු *sembu.*

සෙම්හ, *Semha*, Páli form of ශ්ලේෂ්ම *ṣleshma.*

සෙම, *Sema*, *s.* phlegmatic humour, saliva, from ශ්ලේෂ්මා *ṣleshmá;* peace, tranquillity, from සම *sama.*

සෙමර, *Semara*, *s.* Indian Yak, *bos-grunniens;* chámara or tail of the *bos-grunniens;* Elu form of චාමර *chámara.*

සෙමින්, *Semin*, *ind.* slowly, gently; calmly, peaceably.

සෙමෙ, *Seme*, *s.* time in general, from සමය *samaya.*

සෙමෙර, *Semera*, *s.* see සෙමර *semara*, above; also a fan made of the tail of the *bos-grunniens* to whisk off flies, etc.

සෙය්‍ය, *Seyya*, *a.* best, excellent, most excellent, Páli form of ශ්‍රෙයස් *ṣreyas.*

සෙය්‍යාව, *Seyyáwa*, *s.* reclining, repose, [Colloq. නිදාගැණීම *nidágẹṇima*].

සෙයින්, *Seyin*, *ind.* particle affixed to some words adverbially, as බොහෝ සෙයින් *bohó-seyin*, abundantly, sometimes incorrectly used to signify for, because, etc.

සෙයිලම, *Seyilama*, *s.* Ceylon. (Eng.)

සෙර, *Sera*, feminine form of සොරා *sorá*, thief.

සෙරි, *Seri*, see සේරි *séri.*

සෙරෙප්පුව, *Sereppuwa*, *s.* one of a pair of slippers, or sandals: pl. සෙරෙප්පු *sereppu.*

සෙරුස්, *Sereṣ*, *s.* (සෙ white, රුස් ray) moon, [Colloq. හඳ *handa*].

සෙල්, *Sel*, *s.* unfruitfulness; chaff; rock, stone, mountain, from ශෛල *ṣaila.*

සෙල්ගර, *Selgara*, } *s.* twine.
සෙල්ගාර, *Selgára*, }

සෙල්ල, *Sella*, *s.* spear, lance, pike, dart.

සෙල්ලම්කරණවා, *Sellamkaraṇawá*, *v.* to sport, etc.

සෙල්ලම්ගන්නවා, *Sellamgannawá*, *v.* to take pleasure.

සෙල්ලම, *Sellama*, *s.* sport, pleasure, pastime, amusement; wanton sport: pl. සෙල්ලම් *sellam.*

සෙල්වග, *Selwaga*, *s.* chapter on rocks, etc.

සෙල්වෙනවා, *Selwenawá*, *v.* to move, to shake, to be agitated: pret. සෙල්වුනා *selwuná.*

සෙල, *Sela*, *s.* hill, mountain, [Colloq. කන්ද *kanda*].

සෙලවෙනවා, *Selawenawá*, *v.* to shake, to tremble: pret. සෙලවුනා *selawuná.*

සෙව්‍ය, *Sewya*, see සේව්‍ය *séwya.*

සෙවක, *Sewaka*, see සේවක *séwaka.*

සෙවන්, *Sewan*, *s.* service: see සේවන *séwana.*

සෙවන, *Sewana*. *s.* shade, shelter, shady or secluded place, separation, wilderness; bucket, baling vessel.

සෙවනකරණවා, *Sewanakaraṇawá*, *v.* to shelter, to cause to shade.

සෙවනමැඩිය, *Sewanamẹḍiya*, *s.* large species of fig tree, *ficus asperrima (Urticaceæ).*

සෙවනිය, *Sewaniya*, *s.* coolness, shade: see සෙවෙනි *seweni*.

සෙවනැල්ල, *Sewanella*, *s.* shadow, shelter: pl. සෙවනැලි *sewanli*: see සෙවන *sewana*.

සෙවීම, *Sevíma*, *s.* search, enquiry; verbal noun of සොයනවා *soyanawá*.

සෙවුම, *Sewuma*, verbal noun of සොයනවා *soyanawá*: pl. සෙවුම් *sewum*.

සෙවුවන්දි, *Sewuwandi*, *s.* rose, *rosa semperflorens*, [Colloq. රෝසමල් *rósa-mal*].

සෙවෙනවා, *Sewenawá*, *v.* to be thick or impervious, to be extended as branches, to be sought after.

සෙවෙනි, *Seweni*, *s.* shade, shade or sequestered place, thicket; roof.

සෙවෙල්, *Sewel*, *s.* moss; aquatic plant, *vallisneria octandra;* Elu form of ශෛවාල *saiwála*.

සෙවෙල, *Sewela*, *s.* slime: pl. සෙවෙල් *sewel*.

සෙස්ස, *Sessa*, *s.* remainder, remnant.

සෙසු, *Sesu*, *adj.* remaining, left over, from ශේෂ *sésha*.

සෙහෙටි, *Seheṭi*, *s.* young woman, maid.

සෙළු, *Seḷu*, } *s.* nakedness, nudity; falco tribe:
සෙළුව, *Seḷuwa*, } see සේළු *séḷu*.

සෙළුවෙන්, *Seḷuwen*, *ad.* naked, in a state of nudity.

සේ, *Sé*, *s.* quickness; rays, image; colour white, from ශ්වේත *swéta;* bridge, causeway in a field, etc. from සේතු *sétu;* shade, from ඡායා *chháyá;* manner, likeness: *a.* clever, skilful, sharp, knowing, shrewd, from ඡේක *chhéka: ind.* an affix to words signifying as, like, similar; also, equivalent to the ablative case, and forming adverbs, as දුක්සේ *duksé* with sorrow or sorrowfully.

සේක්, *Sék*, *f. part.* of the honorific, සේක *séka*.

සේක, *Séka*, *s.* (සිච *sicha* to sprinkle) sprinkling, aspersion, as of a fluid: *ind.* an honorific affix.

සේකපාත්‍ර, *Sékapátra*, *s.* (සේක sprinkling, පාත්‍ර vessel) bucket, baling vessel.

සේකර, *Sékara*, *s.* (සේ white, කර ray) moon, [Colloq. හඳ *haṇda*].

සේඛර, *Sékhara*, *s.* (සිඛි *sikhi* to go, අරන් *aran* aff.) garland of flowers worn on the crown of the head; crest; root of the *moringa pterygosperma*, [Colloq. මුරුංගා *murungá*].

සේචක, *Séchaka*, *s.* (සිච *sicha* to sprinkle, ක aff.) cloud: *a.* sprinkling, aspergent.

සේචන, *Séchana*, *s.* (සිච *sicha* and ණ්‍ය *ṇya* aff.) bucket, baling vessel; sprinkling, aspersion; dripping, oozing.

සේඩු, *Séḍu*, *s.* water melon, *citrullus vulgaris*, [Colloq. කොමඩු *komaḍu*]; sort of cucumber, *cucumis madraspatanus*.

සේත, *Séta*, Páli form of ශ්වේත *swéta*.

සේතානි, *Sétáni*, *s.* tree bearing the clearing nut, *strychnos potatorum*, [Colloq. ඉඟිනි *ingini*].

සේතු, *Sétu*, *s.* (සි *si* to bind, තුන් *tun* aff.) mound, bank, causeway, elevated piece of ground separating fields and serving for the passage of travellers, etc., [Colloq. වේල්ල *wélla* or නියර *niyara*]; bridge, [Colloq. පාලම *pálama*]; pass, defile; small tree, *cratæva Roxburghii*, [Colloq. ලුණුවරණ *luṇuwaraṇa*].

සේතුබන්ධ, *Sétubandha*, *s.* (සේතු bridge, බන්ධ binding) ridge of rocks extending from the south extremity of the Coromandel coast towards the island of Ceylon, supposed to have been formed by Hanumán by command of Ráma, as a bridge for the passage of his forces, when going against Ráwaṇa; any dyke or dam, etc.

සේද, *Séda*, *s.* silk, satin; sweat, perspiration; heat, warmth; Páli form of ස්වේද *swéda*.

සේදජ, *Sédaja*, *s.* (සේද warmth, etc. ජ produced) insect, worm.

සේදීම, *Sedíma*, *s.* act of washing.

සේදෙනවා, *Sédenawá*, *v.* to be washed: pret. සේදුනා *sédunú*.

සේන්දුකරණවා, *Séndukaraṇawá*, *v.* to balance any account, to discount; to deduct; to put in place of.

සේන්දුකෙරීම, *Séndukerima*, *s.* balancing any account.

සේන්දුවෙනවා, *Sénduwenawá*, *v.* to arrive at.

සේන, *Séna*, *s.* reclining, reposing; also see ශේන *héna*.

සේනා, *Séná*, *s.* (සි *si* to bind, නක් *nak* aff.) army; host, multitude.

සේනාඞ්ග, *Sénáṅga*, *s.* (සේනා army, අඞ්ග *aṅga* limb or member) component part or member of an army as elephants, cavalry, infantry, or chariots.

සේනාණි, *Sénáṇi*, *s.* (සේනා army, ණී to lead) general, commander of an army; name of Kártikéya, the leader of the celestial hosts.

සේනාධිපතියා, *Sénádhipatiyá*, *s.* (සේනා and අධිපති *adhipati* chief) general, leader of an army: pl. සේනාධිපති *sénádhipati*.

සේනාපතියා, *Sénápatiyá*, *s.* (සේනා and පති *pati* master) general: see the last.

සේනාරක්ෂ, *Sénáraksha*, *s.* (සේනා and රක්ෂ what preserves) guard, piquet, sentinel, etc.

සේනාව, *Sénáwa*, *s.* army, host: see සේනා *séná*.

සේපාල, *Sépála*, } *s.* plant producing very
සේපාලිකා, *Sépáliká*, } fragrant flowers, *nyctanthes arbor-tristis (Oleaceæ):* see සේඵාලිකා *sépháliká*.

සේඵ, *Sépha*, } *s.* (සි *sí* to sleep, ඵ aff.) penis,
සේඵස්, *Séphas*, } [Colloq. පුරුෂ නිමිත්ත *purusa-nimitta*].

සේඵාලිකා, *Sépháliká*, *s.* (සේඵා sleeping, අලි *ali* bee, කන් *kan* aff.) plant, see සේපාල *sépála*.

සේම, *Séma*, *ind.* (සේ as, ම intensive aff.) as, even so, etc.

සේර, *Séra*, *s.* vegetable plant used especially with beef.

සේරම, *Sérama*, *ind.* all, the whole.

සේරා, *Sérá*, *s.* wild duck, Indian whistling teal, *dendrocygora javanica (*order *Anseres)*: pl. සේරු *séru*.

සේරි, *Séri*, *a.* uncontrolled, self-willed; Páli form of ස්වෛරි *swairi*, which see.

සේරිචාරිකාව, *Séricháríkáwa*, *s.* (සේරි and චාරිකා *cháriká* going, etc.) freedom, the power of going anywhere.

සේරිවාණිජ, *Sériwáṇija*, *s.* (සේරි and වාණිජ merchant) independent travelling merchant, one going where and how he likes.

සේරුව, *Séruwa*, *s.* measure, thirty-second part of a bushel: pl. සේරු *séru*.

සේලය, *Sélaya*, *s.* cloth, dress, a whole piece of cloth, also a long piece of cloth presented at a marriage ceremony to the bride's mother by the bridegroom: pl. සේල *séla:* see also, හේලෙ *héle*.

සේලු, *Sélu*, *s.* tree, *cordia myxa*, [Colloq. ලෝළු *lólu*].

සේව්‍ය, *Séwya*, *s.* (සේව *séwa* to serve, යත් *yat* aff.) root of the *andropogon muricatus*, [Colloq. සැවැන්දරා *sewendará*]; plant, *barringtonia acutangula*, [Colloq. එලමිදෙල්ල *ela-midella*]: *a.* to be served, or obeyed, to be worshipped or honoured.

සේවක, *Séwaka*, *s.* (සේව to serve, ක aff.) slave, servant, attendant: *a.* servile, dependant.

සේවකයා, *Séwakayá*, *s.* slave, servant, menial: pl. සේවකයෝ *séwakayó*.

සේවත්, *Séwat*, *s.* woman that would not forsake her husband.

සේවධි, *Séwadhi*, *s.* (සේව happiness or සේවා *séwá* service, ධා *dhá* to have, කි *ki* aff.) treasure as belonging to Kuvéra, a nidhi or substance of extraordinary rarity and value, possessed only by the god of wealth.

සේවනය, *Séwanaya*, *s.* (සේව to serve or සිව *siwa* to sew, ණය *ṇya* aff.) serving, service; sewing, darning, stitching; sack.

සේවනයකරණවා, *Séwanayakaraṇawá*, *v.* to familiarize with, to associate with; to serve; to attend.

සේවය, *Séwaya*, *s.* serving, servitude, dependance.

සේවයකෙරීම, *Séwayakeríma*, *s.* service, ministry.

සේවා, *Séwá*, *s.* (සේව *séwa* to serve, අ *a* aff.) service, servitude; worship, homage.

සේවාකම්කරණවා, *Séwákamkaraṇawá*, *v.* to war, to battle; to serve as a soldier.

සේවාකම, *Séwákama*, *s.* military service, battle, fighting: pl. සේවාකම් *séwákam*.

සේවාපන්නය, *Séwápannaya*, *s.* army, [Colloq. සේනාව *sénáwa*].

සේවායා, *Séwáyá*, *s.* (සේවා and යා aff.) soldier, lascoreen: pl. සේවායෝ *séwáyó*.

සේවාරාල, *Séwárála*, *s.* lascoreen, peon, more commonly හේවාරාල *héwárála*.

සේවාල, *Séwála*, *s.* (සි *sí* to sleep, වාලන් *wálan* aff.) aquatic plant, *blyxa* or *vallisneria octandra:* see ශෛවාල *ṣaiwála*.

සේවාසමුදාව, *Séwá-samudáwa*, *s.* (සේවා and සමුදාව company) army.

සේවිසි, *Sévisi*, *s.* corruptly for හේවිසි *hévisi*, tom-tom, drumming.

සේවිසිකරණවා, *Sévisikaraṇawá*, *v.* to beat a drum with sticks.

සේවිසිකාරයා, *Sévisikárayá*, see හේවිසිකාරයා *hévisikárayá*.

සේසත, *Sésata*, *s.* (සේ white, සත umbrella) white umbrella, one of the insignia of royalty; Elu form of ශ්වෙතච්ඡත්‍ර *ṣwétachchhatra:* pl. සේසත් *sésat*.

සේසය, *Sésaya*, *s.* remnant, what is left, remainder, an atom: see ශේෂ *ṣesha*.

සේසුහු, *Sésuhu*, *s.* name of Saturn.

සේහස, *Séhasa*, *s.* white-coloured swan.

සෛංහල, *Saiṇhala*, *s.* (සිංහල *siṇhala* Ceylon, අණ් *aṇ* aff.) cinnamon bark, [Colloq. කුරුඳුපොතු *kurundu-potu*]: *a.* belonging or relating to Ceylon, Siṇhalese.

සෛංහික, *Sainhika*, s. (සිංහිකා *sinhiká* mother of Ráhu, අණ් *an* patronymic aff.) Ráhu the personified ascending node: *a.* leonine, relating to a lion.

සෛංහිකේය, *Sainhikéya*, s. Ráhu, the personified ascending node.

සෛකත, *Saikata*, s. (සිකතා *sikatá* sandy soil, අණ් *an* aff.) sand bank, island with sandy shores.

සෛකතික, *Saikatika*, a. living in doubt and error.

සෛනික, *Sainika*, s. (සේනා *séná* army, අණ් *an* and ඉක *ika* affs.) guard, sentinel, piquet, body of forces in array.

සෛන්ධව, *Saindhawa*, s. (සින්ධු *sindhu* river, etc. අණ් *an* aff.) horse; rock salt: *a.* marine, aquatic, ocean or river born.

සෛන්ධවයා, *Saindhawayá*, s. mule, a Sindh horse (a breed much prized): pl. සෛන්ධවයෝ *saindhawayó*.

සෛන්ධව ලවණ, *Saindhawa-lawana*, s. (සෛන්ධව and ලවණ salt) rock salt.

සොට්ටි, *Sotti*, a. lifeless (applied only to the hand when lifeless).

සොට්ටියා, *Sottiyá*, s. cripple, deformed man, sometimes written සොත්තියා *sottiyá*: pl. සොට්ටි *sotti*.

සොට, *Sota*, s. snout, beak, mouth, etc.

සොටිය, *Sotiya*, s. spear, dart, missile, weapon resembling a spear.

සොටු, *Sotu*, s. mucus of the nose.

සොඬ, *Sonda*, s. poison; trunk of an elephant; snout, mouth; desire, longing, inclination.

සොඬල, *Sondala*, s. plant having a bulbous root, *modecca palmata.*

සොත්තියා, *Sottiyá*, see සොට්ටියා *sattiyá*.

සොඳ, *Sonda*, a. good, excellent, delightful, pleasing, agreeable.

සොඳුර, *Sondura*, s. a wife, a mistress; term of endearment, from සුන්දරී *sundarí*.

සොඳුරු, *Sonduru*. s. woman, wife: *a.* pleasing, agreeable, delightful.

සොබන, *Sobana*, a. pleasing, agreeable; beautiful, elegant; shining, brilliant; fit, proper, becoming.

සොබිනවා, *Sobinawá*, v. to be fit, proper: see the last.

සොම්, *Som*, s. mildness, gentleness, placidity, from සෞම්‍ය *saumya;* joy, pleasure, happiness, from සෞමනස්‍ය *saumanasya.*

සොම්කරු, *Somkaru*, s. barber, [Colloq. පනික්කියා *panikkiyá*].

සොම්නස්, *Somnas*, } s. joy, pleasure, delight,
සොම්නස, *Somnasa*, } from සෞමනස්‍ය *saumanasya*, [Colloq. සන්තෝෂය *santóshaya*].

සොම්ම, *Somma*, see සෞම්‍ය *saumya.*

සොම්මාර, *Sommára*, } s. one who works in
සොම්මාරු, *Sommáru*, } leather.

සොමි, *Somi*, s. moon, from සෝම *sóma;* Buddha, regent of Mercury, from සෞම්‍ය *saumya;* north: *a.* mild, gentle, placid.

සොමිදා, *Somidá*, s. (සොමි and දා element) semen virile.

සොමිදින, *Somidina*, s. Monday, [Colloq. සඳුදා *sandudá*]; also, Wednesday.

සොමියුරු, *Somiyuru*, s. likeness of the moon.

සොමිප, *Somípa*, s. corruption of සමීප *samípa.*

සොමු, *Somu*, s. smoothness.

සොමුකරණවා, *Somukaranawá*, v. to smooth by rubbing, to polish.

සොයනවා, *Soyanawá*, v. to seek, to search, to explore; to examine, to investigate; to cover, to roof: pret. සෙව්වා *sewwá.*

සොර, *Sora*, see සොරා *sorá.*

සොරකම්කරණවා, *Sorakamkaranawá*, v. to steal, to thieve, to pilfer, to rob.

සොරකම, *Sorakama*, s. theft, stealing, robbery: pl. සොරකම් *sorakam.*

සොරගහ, *Soragaha*, s. large timber tree, *dipterocarpus zeylanicus:* see හොර *hora.*

සොරඟ, *Soranga*, s. jail, prison.

සොරස, *Sorasa*, s. corruptly for ස්වරස *swarasa*, juice, juice of any fruit, flower, the vital part of any thing; sediment.

සොරහුව, *Sorahuwa*, s. spout, artificial drain, gutter, common sewer.

සොරා, *Sorá*, s. thief, pilferer, robber, from චෞර *chóra*: pl. සොරු *soru.*

සොරොව්ව, *Sorowwa*, s. drain, gutter, common sewer, etc.

සොල්, *Sol*, a. unprofitable, useless.

සොල්දරය, *Soldaraya*, } s. upstair: pl. සොල්දර
සොල්දරේ, *Soldaré*, } *soldara.*

සොල්දාදුවා, *Soldáduwá*, s. soldier, (English.): pl. සොල්දාදුවෝ *soldáduwó.*

සොල්ප, *Solpa*, corruption of ස්වල්ප *swalpa.*

සොල්මන් අඬ, *Solman-anda*, } s. any ominous
සොල්මන, *Solmana*, } sound, sound heard in the dead of the night, supposed to be the roaming of demons or hobgoblins; cry of the screech owl or devil-bird, *syrnium indrani;* signal, watchword or cry of lovers.

සොල්මනා, *Solmaná, s.* scarecrow, instrument made of bamboo with a spring to eject water, and placed in the rice fields for deterring birds, etc. from destroying the grain.

සොල්ලනවා, *Sollanawá, v.* to shake: pret. සෙල්ලුවා *selluwá:* see the next.

සොලවනවා *Solawanawá. v.* to shake, to move, to agitate: pret. සෙලෙව්වා *selewwá.*

සොලොච්චිය, *Solochchiya, s.* hook and eye, clasp: pl. සොලොච්චි *solochchi.*

සොලෝව, *Solówa, s.* poetical stanza: see ශ්ලෝක *ṣlóka.*

සොව, *Sowa, s.* singing, [Colloq. ගිකිම *gikíma*]; agreeableness, [Colloq. එකඟකම *ekangakama*]; shame, [Colloq. ලජ්ජාව *lajjáwa*]; fragrance, [Colloq. සුවඳ *suwaṇda*].

සොවාන්, *Sowán,* see සෝවාන් *sówán.*

සොසානික, *Sosánika, a.* (සුසාන *susána* cemetery, අණ් *aṇ* aff. of relation, ඉක *ika* aff.) belonging to a burying ground or cemetery, etc.

සොසානිකාඞ්ග, *Sosánikáńga, s.* (සොසානික *sosánika* and අඞ්ග *ańga* ordinance) ordinance of the Buddhist priesthood, enjoining it upon the priests to repair to some burying ground or cemetery in the middle of the night for the purpose of devout religious meditation: see තෙළෙස්ධුතාඞ්ග *teḷesdhutáńga.*

සොහොන්පල, *Sohonpala, s.* graveyard.

සොහොන්භූමිය, *Sohonbhúmiya, s.* burying ground, cemetery.

සොහොන, *Sohona, s.* tomb, sepulchre, cemetery, from ශ්මසාන *ṣmasána:* pl. සොහොන් *sohon.*

සොහොවුරා, *Sohowurá,* } *s.* uterine brother, Elu
සොහොවුරු, *Sohowuru,* } form of සහෝදර *sahódara;* name of Yama.

සොහොවුරුකල්, *Sohowurukal, s.* name of Yama, the deity who sits in judgment on the dead; and distributes rewards and punishments.

සොළස, *Soḷasa, ind.* sixteen, the number, [Colloq. දහසය *dahasaya*].

සොළොස්කලා, *Soḷoskalá, s.* (සොළොස *soḷosa* and කලා digit) sixteen digits of the moon.

සොළොස, *Soḷosa,* see සොළස *soḷasa.*

සෝ, *Só, s.* swelling, tumour, from සෝඵ *sópha;* sorrow, grief, distress, affliction, from සෝක *sóka;* ear, [Colloq. කණ *kaṇa*]; rapid. stream, current of a river, from ස්‍රෝතස් *srótas: ind.* own, self, peculiar, from ස්ව *swa.*

සෝක, *Sóka, s.* sorrow.

සෝකවෙනවා, *Sókawenawá, v.* to be grieved or sorrowful.

සෝගත්, *Sógat, s.* Buddhist, Elu form of සෞගත *saugata.*

සෝගන්ධික, *Sógandhika,* Páli form of සෞගන්ධික *saugandhika,* which see.

සෝචන, *Sóchana, s.* (සුච *sucha* to grieve, ණ්‍ය *ṇya* aff.) sorrow, grief, grieving.

සෝචි, *Sóchi, s.* (සුච *sucha* to be or make pure, ඉ *i* aff.) light, lustre, radiance, flame.

සෝඨ, *Sóṭha, s.* (සුඨ *suṭha* to be prevented or stopped) fool, blockhead; rogue, cheat.

සෝඩස, *Sóḍasa, ind.* number sixteen, [Colloq. දහසය *dahasaya*].

සෝඩිය, *Sóḍiya, s.* the alphabet.

සෝණිතෝපල, *Sóṇitó-pala, s.* (සෝණිත *sóṇita* blood, deep red, උපල *upala* stone) ruby.

සෝත්කණ්ඨ, *Sótkaṇṭha, a.* (ස *sa* with උත්කණ්ඨා *utkaṇṭhá* sorrow) regretting, bewailing, grieving.

සෝත්ප්‍රාස, *Sótprása, s.* (ස *sa* with උත්ප්‍රාස *utprása* excess or effort) irony, sneering, praise and covert censure: *a.* excessive, much, violent.

සෝත, *Sóta,* Páli form of ස්‍රෝතස් *srótas.*

සෝතාපත්ති, *Sótápatti,* see ස්‍රෝතාපත්ති *srótápatti.*

සෝථඝ්නී, *Sóthaghní, s.* hogweed, *boerhaavia diffusa,* [Colloq. පිටසුදුපලා *piṭasudu-palá*]; potherb, *marsilia quadrifolia,* [Colloq. සාරණ *sáraṇa*].

සෝදනවා, *Sódanawá, v.* to wash, to cleanse, to purify, from සෝධන *sódhana:* pret. සේදුවා *séduwá.*

සෝදර, *Sódara, s.* (ස with or common, උදර *udara* belly, womb) brother of whole blood, uterine brother.

සෝදිසිකරණවා, *Sódisikaraṇawá, v.* to examine, to investigate.

සෝදිසිකෙරීම, *Sódisikeríma, s.* examination, investigation.

සෝදිසිය, *Sódisiya, s.* investigation or enquiry: pl. සෝදිසි *sódisi.*

සෝන්මාද, *Sónmáda, s.* (ස *sa* with උන්මාද *unmáda* madness) mad, insane, [Colloq. පිස්සු *pissu*].

සෝන, *Sóna, s.* (සු *su* to hear, to be obedient) dog; cemetery.

සෝප්පිය, *Sóppiya, s.* as much spirituous liquor as is drank at once : pl. සෝප්පි *sóppi.*

සෝපකාර, *Sópakára, s.* (ස *sa* with උපකාර *upakára* instrument or assistance) equipped, stocked, furnished or provided; assisted, abetted, befriended.

සෝපප්ලව, *Sópaplawa*, *s.* (ස *sa* with උපප්ලව *upaplawa* portent, eclipse) sun or moon in eclipse.

සෝපය, *Sópaya*, *s.* swelling: pl. සෝප *sópa*.

සෝපාක, *Sópáka*, *s.* man of chandála caste: see ශ්වපාක *swapáka*.

සෝපාන, *Sópána*, *s.* (ස *sa* with උප *upa* above, up, අන *ana* to go) stairs, steps or a staircase.

සෝපාව, *Sópáwa*, *s.* sofa. (Eng.)

සෝපි, *Sópi*, *s.* foreigner, stranger, one who wanders about for the purpose of religious worship visiting holy places, etc. pilgrim.

සෝඵ, *Sópha*, *s.* (ශු *su* to go, ඵ aff.) swelling, intumescence.

සෝඵඝ්නි, *Sóphaghní*, *s.* (සෝඵ swelling, ඝ්නි what destroys) hogweed, *boerhaavia diffusa*, [Colloq. පිටසුදුපලා *piṭasudu-palá*]; plant, *trianthema decandra*, [Colloq. මහසාරණ *maha-sárana*].

සෝඵහෘත්, *Sóphahrit*, *s.* (සෝඵ swelling, හෘත් what removes) marking nut plant.

සෝභකෘත්, *Sóbhakṛit*, *s.* (සෝභා *sóbhá* and කෘත් what makes) thirtieth year of the Indian cycle; marking nut plant.

සෝභතා, *Sóbhatá*, *s.* (ශුභ *subha* to shine, තා aff.) beauty, elegance, etc.

සෝභනත්වය, *Sóbhanatwaya*, see the last.

සෝභමාන, *Sóbhamána*, *s.* (ශුභ *subha* to shine ශානච් *ṣánach* aff) beautiful, handsome; splendid, shining, brilliant.

සෝභාඤ්ජන, *Sóbháñjana*, *s.* horse radish tree, *moringa pterygosperma*, [Colloq. මුරුංගා *murungá*].

සෝභාවත්, *Sóbhámat*, *a.* (සෝභා and මත් aff.) radiant, illustrious, splendid.

සෝභාරංජිත, *Sóbhá-ranjita*, *a.* (සෝභා beauty, රංජිත possessing) radiant, splendid, brilliant.

සෝභාව, *Sóbháwa*, see ශෝභා *ṣóbhá*.

සෝභාවන්ත, *Sóbháwanta*, see සෝභමාන *sóbhamána*.

සෝම, *Sóma*, *s.* (ශු *su* to bear, as young, මන් *man* aff.) moon, [Colloquial. හඳ *handa*]; name of Kuvéra; moon-plant, *asclepias acida*, also its juice; water; nectar; deified progenitor; creeping plant, *sarcostemma Brunonianum* [Colloq. මුව කිරිය *muwakiriya*]; plant, *herpestis monniera*, [Colloq. ලුණුවිල *luṇuvila*].

සෝමන්, *Sóman*, *s.* moon, [Colloq. හඳ *handa*].

සෝමන, *Sómana*, *s.* coloured or variegated cloth: pl. සෝමන් *sóman*.

සෝමපා, *Sómapá*, *s.* (සෝම and පා who drinks) sacrificer who drinks the juice of the acid *asclepias*.

සෝමබන්ධු, *Sóma-bandhu*, *s.* (සෝම moon, බන්ධු friend) white esculent water lily which expands at night.

සෝමයාජින්, *Sómayájin*, see සෝමපා *sómapá*.

සෝමයෝනි, *Sóma-yóni*, *s.* (සෝම and යෝනි place of production) sort of sandal wood.

සෝමරාජින්, *Sómarájin*, *s.* (සෝම moon, රාජ *rája* to shine, ණිනි *ṇini* aff.) plant, *vernonia* or *serratula anthelmintica*, [Colloq. බෝදිඇට *bódi-eṭa*]; medicinal plant, *vernonia anthelmintica*, [Colloq. නායන් *náyan* and සන්නිනායන් *sannináyan*]: see සෝමවල්ලි *sómawallí* and සෝමවෘක්ෂ *sóma-wriksha*.

සෝමරාජි, *Sómarájí*, *s.* plant, *vernonia* or *serratula anthelmintica*. [Colloq. බෝදි ඇට *bódi-eṭa*].

සෝමලතා, *Sómalatá*, *s.* (සෝම and ලතා creeper) moon plant, or acid, *asclepias*.

සෝමවල්ක, *Sómawalka*, *s.* (සෝම and වල්ක bark) plant. *acacia suma* or *a. catechu*, seed tonic, *sappan* or *cæsalpinia bonducella*, [Colloq. සප් පන් *sappan* or පතඟි *patangi*]; also කුඹුරුවැල් *kumburuwel*.

සෝමවල්ලිකා, *Sómawalliká*, *s.* (සෝම moon, වල්ලී *wallí* creeper) twining plant, *menispermum glabrum;* medicinal plant, *vernonia anthelmintica*: see සෝමරාජින් *sómarájin ;* moon-plant.

සෝමවල්ලී, *Sómawallí*, *s.* plant, *alternanthera triandra*, [Colloq. මුකුණුවැන්න *mukuṇuwenna*]; climbing plant, *tinospora cordifolia*, [Colloq. රසකිඳ *rasakinda*]; creeping plant, *sarcostema Brunonianum*, [Colloq. මුවකිරිය *muwakiriya*].

සෝමවාර, *Sóma-wára*, *s.* (සෝම moon, වාර day) Monday. [Colloq. සඳුදා *sandudá*].

සෝමවෘක්ෂ, *Sóma-wriksha*, *s.* (සෝම and වෘක්ෂ tree) medicinal plant: see සෝමරාජින් *sómarájin*.

සෝමස්ත්‍රී, *Sómastrí*, *s.* resin, [Colloq. දුම්මල *dummala*].

සෝමසඤ්ඥ, *Sómasajña*, *s.* (සෝම moon, සඤ්ඥ *sajñá* appellation) camphor, [Colloq. කපුරු *kapuru*].

සෝමාඛ්‍ය, *Sómákhya*, *s.* (සෝම *sóma* and අඛ්‍ය *ákhyá* appellation) red lotus, *nymphæa rubra*.

සෝමාල, *Sómála*, *a.* (සෝම *sóma* and අල *ala* to resemble) soft, bland.

සෝරාෂ්ට්‍රික, *Sóráshṭrika*, *s.* (සුරාෂ්ට්‍ර *suráshṭra* Surat, අණ් *aṇ* and ඉක *ika* affs.) sort of poison, probably either a vegetable or mineral.

සෝල්ලුකරණවා, *Sóllukaranawá*, *v.* to cut, to carve.

සෝල්ලු ලිය, *Sóllu-liya*, *s.* (සෝල්ලු carved, ලිය stick) walking-stick, [Colloq. හැරමිටිය *herami-tiya*].

සෝලිකරණවා, *Sólikaranawá*, *v.* to injure, to stand as an obstacle.

සෝලිය, *Sóliya*, *s.* injury, harm, fault, error: pl. සෝලි *sóli*.

සෝවාන්, *Sówán*, *s.* first of the four stages or paths, leading to Nirwáṇa, attained by devout meditation and the other duties of an ascetic.

සෝවාන්ඵලය, *Sówán-phalaya*, *s.* happiness in the first stage of sanctification.

සෝවාන්මාර්ගය, *Sówán-márgaya*, see සෝවාන් *só-wán.*

සෝවැති, *Sóweti*, *s.* grooves or curves in the hood of the cobra capella.

සෝහම, *Sóhama*, *s.* the cuticle.

සෝළස, *Sóḷasa*, *ind.* number sixteen; also සෝඩස *sóḍasa*, [Colloq. දහසය *dahasaya*].

සෞකර්‍ය්‍ය, *Saukarya*, *s.* easy and extempore composition, or preparation of food or medicine; hoggishness.

සෞකර, *Saukara*, *a.* (සූකර *súkara* hog, අණ් *aṇ* affix of relation) hoggish, swinish, etc.

සෞකරික, *Saukarika*, *s.* (සූකර *súkara* and ඉක *ika* aff.) hunter, [Colloq. වැද්දා *weddá*].

සෞඛ්‍ය, *Saukhya*, *s.* (සුඛ *sukha* happiness, අණ් *aṇ* pleonasm) pleasure, happiness.

සෞගත, *Saugata*, } සෞගතික, *Saugatika*, } *s.* (සුගත *sugata* name of Buddha, අණ් *aṇ* affix of relation) Buddhist, follower of the doctrines of Sugata or Buddha.

සෞගන්ධ්‍ය, *Saugandhya*, *s.* odour, fragrance; sulphur.

සෞගන්ධ, *Saugandha*, *s.* (සුගන්ධ *sugandha* fragrance, අණ් *aṇ* aff.) fragrant grass; fragrance.

සෞගන්ධික, *Saugandhika*, *s.* (සෞගන්ධ *saugandha* and ඉක *ika* aff.) white water lily, *nymphæa lotus*, [Colloq. ඕලු *ólu*]; dealer in perfumes; fragrant grass; ruby.

සෞච, *Saucha*, *s.* (සුචි *suchi* purity, අණ් *aṇ* aff.) purification by ablution, cleaning, cleansing; state or property of freedom from defilement, purity.

සෞචි, *Sauchi*, } සෞචික, *Sauchika*, } *s.* (සූචි *súchi* needle, ඉන් *in* aff.) tailor, [Colloq. මහන්නා *mahanná*].

සෞචේය, *Sauchéya*, *s.* (සුචි *suchi* cleaning, අණ් *aṇ* aff.) washerman, [Colloq. රදවා *radawá*].

සෞත්‍ර, *Sautra*, *a.* (සූත්‍ර *sútra* thread, rule, අන් *an* aff.) preceptive, formula, according to rule or precept.

සෞත්‍රාන්තික, *Sautrántika*, *a.* (සෞත්‍ර *sautra* and අන්ත *anta* within, ඉක *ika* aff.) according to rule, regular: see the last.

සෞද්ධෝදනි, *Sauddhódani*, *s.* (සුද්ධෝදන *suddhó-dana* prince of the Ikshwáku family, අන් *an* aff. of descent) Buddha, founder of the Buddhist religion.

සෞදාමනී, *Saudámaní*, } සෞදාමිනී, *Saudáminí*, } *s.* (සුදාමන් *sudáman* cloud, අන් *an* aff.) lightning; particular kind of lightning, [Colloq. විදු ලිය *viduliya*].

සෞධ, *Saudha*, *s.* (සුධා *sudhá* plaster, අන් *an* aff.) mansion; palace; opal.

සෞන්දර්‍ය්‍ය, *Saundarya*, *s.* (සුන්දර *sundara* handsome, අන් *an* aff.) beauty, loveliness.

සෞනික, *Saunika*, *s.* (සූනා *súná* slaughter house, අණ් *aṇ* aff.) butcher, poulterer, vendor of the flesh of beasts or birds.

සෞභද්‍රේය, *Saubhadréya*, *s.* (සු *su* very, භද්‍ර *bhad-ra* auspicious, අන් *an* aff.) beleric myrobalan, *terminalia belerica*, [Colloq. බුළු *buḷu*].

සෞභාග්‍ය, *Saubhágya*, *s.* (සුභග *subhaga* auspicious, අන් *an* aff.) auspiciousness, good fortune, fourth of the astronomical Yógas; red lead.

සෞභාඤ්ජන, *Saubháñjana*, *s.* murunga tree: see ශෝභාඤ්ජන *ṣóbháñjana*.

සෞම්‍ය, *Saumya*, *s.* (සෝම *sóma* moon, etc. යත් *yat* aff.) Buddha, regent of the planet Mercury and son of Sóma or the moon; forty-third year of the Indian cycle; red chalk, red orpiment: *a.* handsome, pleasing; mild, gentle, placid.

සෞම්‍යකම, *Saumyakama*, *s.* mildness, placidity.

සෞම්‍යගුණය, *Saumya-guṇaya*, *s.* (සෞම්‍ය gentle, etc. ගුණ *guṇa* quality) gentleness, mildness, placidity; condescension, affability.

සෞම්‍යධාතු, *Saumya-dhátu*, *s.* (සෞම්‍ය lunar, ධාතු element) phlegm, phlegmatic humour.

සෞම්‍යා, *Saumyá*, *s.* plant, *allyssicarpus bupleuri-folius*, [Colloq. අස්වැන්න *aswenna*].

සෞමේධික, *Saumédhika*, *s.* (සු *su* excellent, මේධා *médhá* apprehension, ඉක *ika* aff.) sage, seer, one possessing supernatural knowledge or power.

සෞමේරුක, *Sauméruka*, *s.* (සුමේරු *suméru* mountain, අණ් *aṇ* affix of origin, කන් *kan* aff.) gold, [Colloq. රත්රන් *ratran*].

සෞර, *Saura*, *s.* (සූර *súra* sun, අණ් *aṇ* aff.) planet Saturn; month, solar month consisting of thirty risings and settings of the sun: *a.* solar.

සෞරභ්‍ය, *Saurabhya*, *s.* (සුරභි *surabhi* fragrant, pleasing, ඤ්‍යත් *ṇyat* aff.) pleasingness, agreeableness; fragrance, odour; fame, reputation, etc. name of Kuvéra.

සෞරභ, *Saurabha*, *s.* (සුරභි *surabhi* fragrant, අණ් *aṇ* aff.) fragrance, saffron, *curcuma longa*, [Colloq. කහ *kaha*].

සෞරවීර්‍ය, *Sauravírya*, *s.* (සූර *súra* valiant, වීර්‍ය same) heroism, valour, intrepidity.

සෞරාෂ්ට්‍ර, *Sauráshṭra*, *s.* (සුරාෂ්ට්‍ර *suráshṭra* country, අණ් *aṇ* aff.) bell metal; also the country of Surat.

සෞරාෂ්ට්‍රක, *Sauráshṭraka*, *s.* sort of white or bell metal, [Colloq. ලෝකඩ *lókaḍa*].

සෞරාෂ්ට්‍රික, *Sauráshṭrika*, *s.* (සෞරාෂ්ට්‍ර *sauráshṭra* and කන් *kan* aff.) sort of poison: see සෝරාෂ්ට්‍රික *sóráshṭrika*.

සෞරි, *Sauri*, *s.* name of Saturn, [Colloq. සෙනසුරා *senasurá*].

සෞරික, *Saurika*, *s.* (සුර *sura* deity, ඉක *ika* aff.) heaven, paradise, [Colloq. ස්වර්ගය *swargaya*].

සෞවර්චක, *Sauwarchaka*, } *s.* (සුවර්චල *suwar-*
සෞවර්චල, *Sauwarchala*, } *chala* district, අණ් *aṇ* aff.) sóchal salt; natron, alkali, [Colloq. සුවස ලුණු *suwasaluṇu*].

සෞවස්තික, *Sauwastika*, *s.* (ස්වස්ති *swasti* a term of salutation, ඨක් *ṭhak* aff.) a family Brahman or priest: *a.* salutatory, benedictory.

සෞවීර, *Sauvíra*, *s.* (සුවීර *suvíra* country so called, අණ් *aṇ* aff. of derivation) fruit of the jujube, *zizyphus jujuba*, [Colloq. මහඩෙබර *maha-ḍebara* and මසන් *masan*]; antimony, [Sinhalese, හොයඳුන් *hoyandun*]; sour gruel; district, in the west of India, connected with the country along the Indus.

සෞවීරක, *Sauvíraka*, *s.* vinegar, [Colloq. කාඩි *káḍi*].

සෞෂ්ඨව, *Saushṭawa*, *s.* (සුෂ්ඨු *sushṭu* excellent, etc. අඤ් *añ* aff.) excess, exceedingness, much; excellence.

සෞහාර්ද, *Sauhárda*, *s.* (සුහෘද් *suhrid* friend, අණ් *aṇ* aff.) friendship, [Colloquial: මිත්‍රකම *mitra-kama*].

සැ, *Sẹ*, see සෑ *sẹ́*.

සැංගිම, *Sẹngima*, *s.* hiding, concealment; verbal noun of සංගණවා *sanganawá*.

සැංගෙණවා, *Sẹngeṇawá*, *v.* to abscond: pret. සැංගුණා *sẹnguṇá*: see සැඟවෙනවා *sẹngawenawá*.

සැක්තිය, *Sẹktiya*, *s.* corrupt form of ශක්තිය *ṣaktiya*, strength, power.

සැක්‍රයා, *Sẹkrayá*, *s.* name of Indra, corrupt form of ශක්‍ර *ṣakra*, which see.

සැක, *Sẹka*, *s.* doubt, uncertainty; sorrow, distress, from ශංකා *ṣanká*: *a.* doubtful.

සැකවෙනවා, *Sẹkawenawá*, *v.* to be doubtful.

සැකි, *Sẹki*, *adj.* (සක්ක *sakka* strength) possible, able; more commonly written හැකි *hẹki*.

සැකිල්ල, *Sẹkilla*, *s.* articulation of the bones; skeleton; chain, fetter.

සැකී, *Sẹkí*, *part.* having entertained doubts.

සැකුළු, *Sẹkuḷu*, *a.* hard, solid, strong.

සැකෙවින්, *Sẹkevin*, *ad.* briefly.

සැඟවිල්ල, *Sẹngavilla*, *s.* act of hiding, concealment, a secret: pl. සැඟවිලි *sẹngavili*.

සැඟවීම, *Sẹngavíma*, *s.* the act of hiding.

සැඟවුම, *Sẹngawuma*, *s.* concealment, disappearance, invisibility: pl. සැඟවුම් *sẹngawum*.

සැඟවෙනවා, *Sẹngawenawá*, *v.* to abscond, to hide one's-self: pret. සැඟවුනා *sẹngawuná*.

සැට්ටය, *Sẹṭṭaya*, *s.* jacket or petticoat worn by women: pl. සැට්ට *sẹṭṭa*.

සැට, *Sẹṭa*, *ind.* number sixty, Elu form of ෂෂ්ටි *shashṭi*.

සැටදා ඇල්, *Sẹṭadá-ẹl*, *s.* (සැට sixty, දා day, ඇල් rice) species of grains.

සැටි, *Sẹṭi*, *s.* form, manner, nature.

සැටිමල්, *Sẹṭimal*, *s.* chatty.

සැටිරි, *Sẹṭiri*, *s.* archer, bowyer; wild man, savage, [Colloq. වැද්දා *wẹddá*].

සැඩ, *Sẹḍa*, *s.* thief; ascending: *a.* strong, hard; cruel, rough; Elu form of චණ්ඩ *chaṇḍa*.

සැඩපවන, *Sẹḍapawana*, *s.* (සැඩ and පවන wind) gale: pl. සැඩපවන් *sẹḍapawan*.

සැඩපහර, *Sẹḍapahara*, *s.* (සැඩ strong, පහර course) stream of a river, torrent, rapid.

සැඩපළු, *Sẹḍapaḷu*, *s.* tress or clump of hair, hair clotted, lock of hair.

සැඩරැස්, *Sẹḍares*, *s.* (සැඩ powerful, රැස් ray) sun, [Colloq. ඉර *ira*].

සැඩ වතුර, *Sẹḍa-watura*, see සැඩපහර *sẹḍapahara*.

සැඩිදෙමළු, *Sẹḍidemaḷu*, *s.* captives settled by king Duṭugemunu.

සැඬොල්, *Sẹḍol*, *s.* man of a servile tribe, or one following degraded profession; Elu form of චණ්ඩාල *chaṇḍála*.

සැණ, *Sęna*, *s.* moment, instant, the time which elapses while snapping the thumb and finger ten times, from ක්ෂණ *kshana.*

සැණකෙළිය, *Sęnakęliya*, *s.* (සැණ and කෙළිය festival) festival celebrated in the Siŋhalese month ඉල් *il* (October-November), when the moon is full near the Pleiades; any public rejoicing, festivity.

සැත්, *Sęt*, *s.* weapon, from ශස්ත්‍ර *sastra;* knowledge, science, etc.: see ශාස්ත්‍ර *sástra*: pl. of සැද *sęda.*

සැත්ත, *Sętta*, *s.* multitude, collection, heap; collection of flowers, nosegay, pond covered with flowers.

සැත්තෑව, *Settéwa*, *ind.* number seventy.

සැත්තෑවෙනි, *Settéweni*, *a.* seventieth.

සැත, *Sęta*, *s.* weapon, Elu form of ශස්ත්‍ර *sastra.*

සැතපීම, *Sętapíma*, *s.* reposing, reclining; verbal noun of සැතපෙනවා *sętapenawá.*

සැතපුම්, *Sętapum*, *s.* ease, repose.

සැතපෙනවා, *Sętapenawá*, *v.* to sleep, to repose, (used respectfully), to recline: pret. සැතපුනා *sętapuná.*

සැති, *Sęti*, *s.* the mind, from ස්වාන්ත *swánta;* also plural of සැත්ත *sętta;* cluster of flowers.

සැතිරි, *Sętiri*, *s.* female adversary or opponent.

සැතැප්ම, *Sętępma*, *s.* (සැතපෙනවා *sętapenawá* to repose) the distance at which a cooly rests, a mile.

සැතැවුලි, *Sętęwuli*, *s.* grief, sorrow, contrition, from සන්තාප *santápa*, [Colloq. ශෝකය *sókaya*].

සැද, *Sęda*, *s.* pair of panniers for carrying burdens; saddle, trappings of a horse.

සැදීම, *Sędíma*, *s.* making, forming, constructing; verbal noun of සාදනවා *sádanawá.*

සැදුම, *Sęduma*, *s.* ornament, decoration: pl. සැදුම් *sędum.*

සැදුල්, *Sędul*, } *s.* arrow-grass; tiger, from ශාර්දූල *śárdúla.*
සැදුල, *Sędula*, }

සැදෙනවා, *Sędenawá*, *v.* to ornament, to decorate, to adorn; to be made, to grow (as a plant, child, tumour): pret. සැදුනා *sęduná.*

සැදොල්, *Sędol*, *s.* small tiger, [Colloq. දිවියා *diviyá*]; cheetah.

සැදෑස්, *Sędęs*, } *s.* peacock's tail.
සැදෑස්පිල්, *Sędęspil*, }

සැදැහැ, *Sędęha*, *s.* faith, religious belief, Elu form of ශ්‍රද්ධා *śraddhá.*

සැදැහැමත්, *Sędęhęmat*, *a.* (සැදැහැ faith, මත් poss. aff.) pious, religious, faithful.

සැදෑගැමි, *Sędęgęmi*, see සකෘදාගාමි *sakridágámi.*

සැඳි, *Sęndi*, plural of සැඳ *sęnda.*

සැඳෑ, *Sęndę*, *s.* latter part of the day, afternoon, evening, from සන්ධ්‍යා *sandhyá.*

සැඳ, *Sęnda*, *s.* spoon, ladle: pl. සැඳි *sęndi*: see the next.

සැන්දෑව, *Sendéwa*, *s.* afternoon, evening, from සන්ධ්‍යා *sandhyá.*

සැනසිල්ල, *Sęnasilla*, *s.* comfort, consolation, from සනසනවා *sanasanawá.*

සැනසීම, *Sęnasíma*, *s.* comfort, consolation; verbal noun of සනසනවා *sanasanawá.*

සැනිදින, *Sęnidina*, *s.* Saturday, [Colloq. සෙනසුරාදා *senasurádá*].

සැණෙකින්, *Sęnekin*, *s.* in an instant.

සැප, *Sępa*, *s.* joy, happiness, pleasure, enjoyment; oath, from සප *sapa.*

සැපත්, *Sępat*, *s.* coming, approaching; wealth, possessions, property.

සැපත, *Sępata*, *s.* pleasure, enjoyment; wealth, substance, from සම්පත් *sampat.*

සැපතිම, *Sępatim*, *s.* agreement, engagement, condition, promise, [Colloq. පොරොන්දුව *poronduwa*].

සැපපහසු, *Sępapahasu*, *s.* (සැප and පහසු the same) health, enjoyment of health.

සැපමිණි, *Sępamiṇi*, *a.* arrived, accepted.

සැපවිහරණය, *Sępa-viharaṇaya*, *s.* (සැප pleasure, විහරණ *viharaṇa* existing) life of enjoyment, living or dwelling at ease.

සැපැමිණි, *Sępęmini*, *a.* approached, arrived, [Coll: පැමිණීම *pęmiṇima*]..

සැබ්ද, *Sębda*, *s.* sound, noise in general, corrupt form of ශබ්ද *śabda.*

සැබව, *Sębawa*, *ind.* verily, truly, certainly.

සැබෝගස, *Sębó-gasa*, *s.* plant, troublesome weed, *achyranthes aspera*, [Colloq. ගස්කරල්හැබ *gaskaralhęba*].

සැබෑව, *Sębéwa*, *s.* truth, verity: pl. සැබෑ *sębé.*

සැම්බිලිය *Sęmbiliya*, *s.* box: pl. සැම්බිලි *sęmbili:* see හැම්බිලිය *hęmbiliya.*

සැම, *Sęma*, *ind.* all, the whole.

සැමි, *Sęmi*, *s.* lord, master, owner, husband, variously written සාමි *sámi*, සාමු *sámu*, සිමි *simi*, etc.

සැමිටිය, *Sęmiṭiya*, *s.* (සැ with මිටි *miṭi* fist) stick, twig; whip, scourge: pl. සැමිටි *sęmiṭi.*

සැමියා, *Sęmiyá*, *s.* husband: see සැමි *sęmi.*

සැමුනි, *Sęmuni, s.* (සැ Şákya, මුනි muni) name of Buddha, Elu form of ශාක්‍යමුනි *şákyamuni.*

සැර, *Sęra, a.* swift, expeditious, quick; strong, powerful; going, moving.

සැරකරණවා, *Sęra-karaṇawá, v.* to scold, to threaten, to rebuke, to make stronger.

සැරකාරයා, *Sęrakárayá, s.* one that threatens: pl. සැරකාරයෝ *sęrakárayó.*

සැරකෙරිම, *Sęrakerima, s.* verbal noun of සැරකරණවා *sęrakaraṇawá.*

සැරටියා, *Sęraṭiyá, s.* elephant driver: pl. සැරටියෝ *sęraṭiyó.*

සැරමිටිය, *Sęramiṭiya, s.* walking stick: see සැරයටිය *sęrayaṭiya.*

සැරය, *Sęraya, s.* quickness, speed, velocity; energy, determination, promptitude; arrow; time, occasion: pl. සැර *sęra.*

සැරයටිය, *Sęrayaṭiya, s.* (සැර walking, යටිය stick) walking stick, staff, crook: pl. සැරයටි *sęrayaṭi.*

සැරයොන්, *Sęrayon, s.* Skanda or Kártikéya: see කඳකුමරු *kaṇḍakumaru.*

සැරව, *Sęrawa, s.* pus, matter, flowing from an ulcer, etc.

සැරවේදිය, *Sęrawédiya, s.* (සැර arrow, වේදිය science or shooting) archery, art or practice of shooting with the bow.

සැරසිම, *Sęrasíma, s.* ornament, decoration; verbal noun of සරසනවා *sarasanawá.*

සැරසුම, *Sęrasuma, s.* dressing, decoration.

සැරිසර, *Sęrisara, s.* motion, going, proceeding, [Colloq. ගමන *gamana*].

සැරිසරණවා, *Sęrisaraṇawá, v.* to walk about, to traverse; to walk for pleasure or amusement, to transmigrate: pret. සැරිසැරුවා *sęrisęruwá.*

සැරිර, *Sęrira, s.* the body, animal frame, for ශරීර *şarira.*

සැරුම්, *Sęrum,* see සැරිසර *sęrisara.*

සැල්, *Sęl, s.* delay, neglect, procrastination; cold, frigidity; rice; also see සැල *sęla.*

සැල්දිරි, *Sęldiri, s.* celery. (Dutch.)

සැල, *Sęla, s.* delay; large earthen vessel, jar, water pot; stone, rock; publicity, manifestation; shaking, moving, also written සල *sala.*

සැලකරණවා, *Sęlakaraṇawá, v.* to signify, to make known, to declare; to inform, to mention, to remind: pret. සැලකෙරුවා *sęlakeruwá.*

සැලකිම, *Sęlakíma, s.* regard, respectful attention.

සැලසිම, *Sęlasíma, s.* causing; verbal noun of සලසනවා *salasanawá.*

සැලිය, *Sęliya, s.* earthen cooking vessel; Elu form of ස්ථාලී *sthálí:* pl. සැලි *sęli.*

සැලුම, *Sęluma, s.* shaking, trembling, involuntary motion: pl. සැලුම් *sęlum.*

සැලෙනවා, *Sęlenawá, v.* to shake, to tremble, to be agitated, to drop or fall down: pret. සැලුනා *sęluná.*

සැලැස්සුම, *Sęlęssuma, s.* causing; verbal noun of සලස්සනවා *salassanawá.*

සැව්, *Sęw, s.* bow, Elu form of චාප *chápa.* [Colloq. දුන්න *dunna*].

සැව්රි, *Sęwri, s.* name of Vishṇu.

සැවත්, *Sęwat, s.* wealth, happiness.

සැවය, *Sęwaya, s.* dead body, corpse, [Colloq. මළකඳ *maḷakaṇda*]; the cast slough of a snake, from ඡවි *chhavi.*

සැවු, *Sęwu, s.* going, moving; also, a bow.

සැවුලා, *Sęwulá, s.* cock, [Colloq. කුකුළා *kukuḷá*].

සැවොම, *Sęwoma, s.* all.

සැවැඳන, *Sęwęndana,* / සැවැඳරා, *Sęwęndará,* / සැවැන්න, *Sęwęnna,* } *s.* very fragrant grass, *andropogon muricatus (Gramineæ).*

සැස්සා, *Sęssá,* past tense of සසිනවා *sasinawá,* to chip.

සැස, *Sęsa, s.* hare, from ශශ *şaşa,* [Colloq. හාවා *háwá*].

සැසළුම්, *Sęsaḷum, s.* thunder, [Colloq. හෙන *hena*].

සැසි, *Sęsi, s.* name of Gautama; moon.

සැසිය, *Sęsiya, s.* session. (Eng.)

සැහැන්, *Sęhęn, s.* evening; also written සැන්දෑ *sęndę,* etc.

සැහැමුනි, *Sęhęmuni, s.* (සැහැ for සැ *sę* Sákya, මුනි muni) name of Gautama.

සැහැයුරු, *Sęhęyuru, s.* mango, [Colloq. අඹ *amba*].

සැහැල්ලු, *Sęhęllu, a.* light, not heavy; easy, facile.

සැහැල්ලුකරණවා, *Sęhęllukaraṇawá, v.* to lighten, to relieve.

සැහැල්ලුකෙරිම, *Sęhęllukerima,* verbal noun of the above.

සැළලිහිණියා, *Sęḷalihiṇiyá. s.* bird, called the southern black maina, *gracula religiosa (*order *Passeres).*

සෑ, *Sę́, s.* Şákya race: see සෑය *sę́ya.*

සෑකුල, *Sę́kula, s.* the Şákya race.

සෑකුළු, *Sę́kuḷu, a.* hard, rough; mixed, compounded.

සෑදිම, *Sę́díma, s.* making, forming, construction; verbal noun of සාදනවා *sádanawá.*

සෑදෙව්වා, *Sę́dewwá, v.* caused to be made.

සැනතිය, *Séntiya*, *s.* peace, reconciliation, patience, gentleness; corrupt form of ශාන්තිය *śántiya*.

සැම, *Séma*, *ind.* all, every, the whole.

සැමගස්, *Séma-gas*, *s.* tree, *acacia suma*.

සැමදම, *Sémadáma*, *ad.* every day, ever.

සැමුනි, *Sémuni*, *s.* (සැ Śákya, මුනි muni) name of Gautama; Elu form of ශාක්‍යමුනි *śákyamuni*.

සැය, *Séya*, *s.* heap of wood, funeral pile, from චිතක *chitaka*.

සැහුම, *Séhuma*, verbal noun of the next.

සැහෙණවා, *Séheṇawá*, *v.* to be fit, to be sufficient, to be satisfied: pret. සැහුනා *séhuná*.

ස්‍යන්දන, *Syandana*, *s.* dropping, oozing, trickling; going, moving.

ස්‍රංසින්, *Sraṇsin*, *s.* (ස්‍රංස *sraṇsa* to fall down, ඉනි *ini* aff.) tree, Patana oak, *careya arborea*, [Colloq. කහට *kahaṭa*]: *a.* falling or hanging down, pendulous, depending.

ස්‍රවත්, *Srawat*, *a.* oozing, flowing, dropping.

ස්‍රවන්ති, *Srawanti*, *s.* river in general, [Colloq. ගඟ *gaṉga*].

ස්‍රවා, *Srawá*, *s.* plant, bowstring hemp, *sanseviera zeylanica*, [Colloq. නියඳ *niyaṉda*].

ස්‍රෂ්ට්‍ර, *Srashṭri*, *s.* (සෘජ *srija* to create. තෘච් *trich* aff.) name of Brahma; also of Śiva; creator, maker.

ස්‍රස්ත, *Srasta*, *a.* (ස්‍රංස *sraṇsa* to fall, ක්ත *kta* aff.) fallen down off or from, dropped.

ස්‍රාව, *Sráwa*, *s.* (ස්‍රැ *sru* to ooze) oozing, dropping, flowing.

සෘජ්, *Srij*, *s.* (සෘජ *srija* to create, to quit, ක්ති *kti* aff.) a creator; chaplet, or wreath of flowers, garland.

සෘණි, *Sriṇi*, *s.* enemy; elephant hook.

සෘති, *Sriti*, *s.* (සෘ to go, ක්ති *kti* aff.) road, path, way, [Colloq. පාර *pára*]; going, proceeding.

ස්‍රැව, *Sruwa*, *s.* (ස්‍රැ to flow, ක *ka* aff.) sacrificial vessel or ladle used for pouring ghee or oiled butter at a sacrifice.

ස්‍රැවා, *Sruwá*, *s.* plant, *sanseviera zeylanica:* see ස්‍රවා *srawá*.

ස්‍රෝත, *Sróta*, } *s.* (ශ්‍රු *śru* to hear, or ස්‍රැ *sru* to
ස්‍රෝතස්, *Srótas*, } flow, අසුන් *asun* aff.) ear, [Coll: කණ *kaṇa*]; current, natural or rapid stream, flow or course of water; river in general; organ of sense.

ස්‍රෝතාපත්තිය, *Srótápattiya*, *s.* (ස්‍රෝතස් *srótas* current, ආපත්ති *ápatti* arrival, obtaining) first of the four roads leading to Nirwáṇa.

ස්කන්ද, *Skanda*, *s.* (ස්කන්ද to go, අච් *ach* aff.) name of Kártikéya, Kataragama-deviyó the son of Śiva, and military deity of the Hindus.

ස්කන්ධ, *Skandha*, *s.* (ක *ka* head, ධා *dhá* to hold, ස *sa* initial augment, ක *ka* aff.) shoulder, head of the humerus; body; trunk of a tree; multitude, quantity; army; five objects of sense, viz. form, taste, smell, seeing, touch; book, section, chapter.

ස්කන්ධදේශ, *Skandha-déśa*, *s.* (ස්කන්ධ shoulder, දේශ part) withers of an elephant, or the part where the rider sits.

ස්කන්ධඵල, *Skandha-phala*, *s.* (ස්කන්ධ trunk, ඵල fruit) glomerous fig-tree, *ficus glomerata*, [Colloq. අට්ටික්කා *aṭṭikká*]; bael tree, *œgle marmelos*, [Colloq බෙලි *beli*]; coconut tree, *cocos nucifera*, [Colloq. පොල්ගහ *pol-gaha*].

ස්කන්ධාවාර, *Skandháwára*, *s.* (ස්කන්ධ *skandha* army, ආ *á* before, වෘ *wri* to screen, or guard, අණ් *aṇ* aff.) camp, fortified entrenchment.

ස්කන්ධි, *Skandhi*, *s.* (ස්කන්ධ *skandha* trunk, ඊ *í* aff.) tree in general, [Colloq. ගහ *gaha*].

ස්කෝප්පය, *Skóppaya*, *s.* name of a playing card; spades: pl. ස්කෝප්ප *skóppa*. (Dutch.)

ස්කෝලය, *Skólaya*, *s.* school: pl. ස්කෝල *skóla*. (English.)

ස්තන්‍ය, *Stanya*, *s.* (ස්තන *stana* breast, යත් *yat* aff.) milk, [Colloq. කිරි *kiri*].

ස්තන, *Stana*, *s.* (ස්තන to sound, අ *a* aff.) female breast or bosom.

ස්තනන, *Stanana*, *s.* (ස්තන *stana* to sound,) sound, noise in general; rumbling of clouds, thunder.

ස්තනපා, *Stanapá*, *s.* (ස්තන breast, පා who drinks) infant at the breast.

ස්තනිත, *Stanita*, *s.* (ස්තන *stana* sound, ක්ත *kta* aff.) rattling of thunder; rumbling of thunder clouds: noise of clapping the hands.

ස්තබ්ධ, *Stabdha*, *a.* (ස්තභි *stabhi* to stop, ක්ත *kta* aff.) stopped, blocked or shut up; firm, hard, stiff; dull, stupid, insensible.

ස්තම්බ, *Stamba*, *s.* shrub, plant that has no decided stem; post in general; post to which an elephant is tied; stupidity, insensibility.

ස්තම්භ, *Stambha*, *s.* (ස්තභි *stabhi* to stop, etc. අච් *ach* aff.) post, pillar; stupidity, insensibility; hindrance, obstruction; suppression of any faculty by magical means.

ස්තම්භන, *Stambhana*, *s.* stopping, hindering, obstruction: see the last.

ස්තව, *Stawa*, *s.* (ෂ්ටු *shṭu* to praise, අප් *ap* aff.) praise, eulogium, panegyric, [Colloq. ප්‍රශංසාව *praṣaṇsáwa*].

ස්තවක, *Stawaka*, *s.* (ස්තව and ක added or ස්ථා *sthá* to stay, අවක *awaka* aff.) cluster of blossoms, nosegay; multitude in general; praise, etc.

ස්තාලය, *Stálaya*, } *s* stall, stable: pl. ස්තාල *stála*.
ස්තාලේ, *Stálé*, } (Eng.)

ස්තිමිත, *Stimita*, *s.* (ෂ්ටිම *shṭima* to be wet, ක්ත *kta* aff.) wet, moist, [Colloq. තෙත *teta*].

ස්තුත, *Stuta*, *a.* (ෂ්ටු *shṭu* to praise, ක්ත *kta* aff.) praised, panegyrised, etc.

ස්තුති, *Stuti*, *s.* praise, panegyric, eulogium, thanks.

ස්තුතිකරණවා, *Stutikaraṇawá*, *v.* to thank.

ස්තුතිකෙරිම, *Stutikerima*, *s.* the act of giving thanks.

ස්තුතිපාඨක, *Stuti-páṭhaka*, *s.* (ස්තුති and පාඨක reader) bard, one who accompanies a chief or an army to recite the titles and praises of the one, and to inspire the other by chaunting martial exploits, etc.

ස්තූප, *Stúpa*, *s.* (ස්තූප to heap, to pile) heap, pile of earth, [Colloq. ගොඩ *goḍa*].

ස්තෙන, *Stena*, *s.* (ස්තෙන to steal, අ *a* aff.) thief, [Colloq. හොරා *horá*]; thieving, stealing.

ස්තෝක, *Stóka*, *s.* bird called chátaka, *cuculus melano leucos*: *a.* little, small, [Colloq. පුංචි *puṇchi*].

ස්තෝත්‍ර, *Stótra*, *s.* (ෂ්ටු *shṭu* to praise, ත්‍ර aff.) praise, eulogium.

ස්තෝම, *Stóma*, *s.* heap, number, multitude; praise, eulogium; the head.

ස්ත්‍රී, *Strí*, *s.* woman or female in general: pl. ස්ත්‍රීයෝ *striyó*.

ස්ත්‍රීක්කය, *Strikkaya*, *s.* iron used by washerman in smoothing clothes: pl. ස්ත්‍රීක්ක *strikka*.

ස්ත්‍රීගුහ්‍ය, *Striguhya*, *s.* (ස්ත්‍රී and ගුහ්‍ය privity) female organ of generation.

ස්ත්‍රීජිත, *Strijita*, *s.* hen-pecked husband.

ස්ත්‍රීධර්ම, *Strí-dharma*, *s.* (ස්ත්‍රී woman, ධර්ම peculiar property) diety of a woman, menstrual excretion.

ස්ත්‍රීරඤ්ජන, *Strí-rañjana*, *s.* (ස්ත්‍රී and රඤ්ජන delighting) betel, or the mixture of betel leaf, areca nut, caustic lime, etc. eaten by the Siṇhalese, and by women especially.

ස්ත්‍රීලිංග, *Strí-liṇga*, *s.* (ස්ත්‍රී and ලිංග mark) pudendum muliebre; feminine gender in grammar.

ස්ත්‍රෙක්කෙ, *Strekke*, *s.* tie (Dutch.)

ස්ථ, *Stha*, *a.* staying, abiding, what or who is or stays.

ස්ථග, *Sthaga*, *a.* fraudulent, dishonest, roguish, [Colloq. වංචාවූ *waṇcháwú*].

ස්ථණ්ඩිල, *Sthaṇḍila*, *s.* level square piece of ground, prepared for a sacrifice; boundary, limit, landmark.

ස්ථපති, *Sthapati*, *s.* (ස්ථ who is or stays, පති lord) sovereign, chief; architect, master-carpenter or builder; wheel-wright; charioteer.

ස්ථල, *Sthala*, *s.* (ස්ථල to be firm, අච් *ach* aff.) place, site, soil, dry or firm ground, mound, hillock.

ස්ථලශෘංගාට, *Sthalasriṇgáṭa*, *s.* thorny plant, *tribulus terrestris*, [Colloq. නෙරෙංචි *nereṇchi*].

ස්ථවිර, *Sthavira*, *s.* (ෂ්ඨා *shṭhá* to stay, a long time, කිරච් *kirach* aff.) name of Brahma; an old man; a title of respect applied to the senior or head priest of a vihára, terunnánsé: *a.* old, aged; fixed, firm, steady.

ස්ථවිරයන්, *Sthavirayan*, *s.* aged or venerable priest: see the last.

ස්ථවිරී, *Sthavirí*, *s.* (ස්ථවිර *sthavira* and ඊ *í* fem. aff.) aged female priest.

ස්ථාණු, *Sthánu*, *s.* (ෂ්ඨා *shṭhá* to stay, ණු aff.) stake, pin; spear, dart: *a.* fixed, firm, steady.

ස්ථානය, *Sthánaya*, *s.* (ෂ්ඨා *shṭhá* to stay, න *na* aff.) spot, place, site, situation; stay, staying, continuance; leisure, interval: pl. ස්ථාන *sthána*.

ස්ථානාන්තර, *Sthánántara*, *s.* (ස්ථාන *sthána* place, අන්තර *antara* interval) office, employment, dignity.

ස්ථානීය, *Sthániya*, *s.* (ස්ථාන *sthána* place, ඡ *chha* aff.) city, town: *a.* relating to or fit for a place.

ස්ථාපන, *Sthápana*, *s.* (ෂ්ඨා *shṭhá* to stay or stand causal form ල්‍යුට් *lyut* or යුච් *yuch* aff.) placing, founding, fixing, erecting; fixing or concentrating the thoughts upon the object of meditation, abstraction; ordering, arranging, directing; posture, attitude.

ස්ථාපනා, *Sthápaná*, *s.* ordering, arranging, managing.

ස්ථාපනී, *Sthápaní*, *s.* plant, *cissampelos pareira*, [Colloq. දියමිත්ත *diyamitta*].

ස්ථාපිත, *Sthápita*, *s.* placed, deposited.

ස්ථාම, *Stháma*, *s.* strength, power.

ස්ථායී, *Sthávi*, *a.* (ෂ්ඨා *shṭhá* to stay, ණිනි *ṇini* aff. යුක් *yuk* augment) steady, firm; unchangeable, invariable.

ස්ථාල, *Sthála*, s. (ෂ්ඨා *shṭhá* to stand, ආල *ála* aff.) caldron; any culinary utensil.

ස්ථාලී, *Sthálí*, s. earthen pot or boiler; trumpet flower, *stereospermum suaveolens*, [Colloq. පලොල් *paḷol*].

ස්ථාවර, *Stháwara*, s. (ෂ්ඨා *shṭhá* to stand, වරච් *warach* aff.) mountain, [Colloq. කන්ද *kanda*]: *a.* fixed, stationary, stable, immoveable; regular, established.

ස්ථාවිර, *Sthávira*, s. old age, anility, [Colloq. මහළුකම *mahaḷukama*].

ස්ථිත, *Sthita*, a. (ෂ්ඨා *shṭhá* to be or stay, ක්ත *kta* aff.) steady, firm, immoveable; agreed, engaged; risen, gotten up; stayed, stopped; determined, resolved, established.

ස්ථිති, *Sthiti*, s. staying, being fixed or stationary; limit, boundary; cessation, pause; determination, etc.

ස්ථිර, *Sthira*, s. (ෂ්ඨා *shṭhá* to stay or be, කිර *kira* aff.) deity; mountain; final emancipation: *a.* firm, fixed, steady, immoveable; permanent, durable, lasting; constant, faithful.

ස්ථිරකරණවා, *Sthirakaraṇawá*, v. to confirm, make firm.

ස්ථිරකෙරීම, *Sthirakeríma*, s. confirmation.

ස්ථිරගන්ධ, *Sthiragandha*, s. (ස්ථිර lasting, ගන්ධ smell) champaka tree, *michelia champaca*, [Colloq. සපු *sapu*].

ස්ථිරගන්ධා, *Sthiragandhá*, s. (ස්ථිර and ගන්ධ *gandha* smell) screw-pine, *pandanus fascicularis*, [Coll: මුදුකෙයියා *múdukeyiyá*]; trumpet flower: see ස්ථාලී *sthálí*.

ස්ථිරජිහ්ව, *Sthirajihwa*, s. (ස්ථිර immoveable, ජිහ්වා *jihwá* tongue) fish in general.

ස්ථිරද්‍රුම, *Sthiradruma*, s. tree, *bassia longifolia*, [Colloq. මීගස *mí-gasa*].

ස්ථිරපුෂ්ප, *Sthira-pushpa*, s. (ස්ථිර lasting, පුෂ්ප flower) champaka tree: see ස්ථිරගන්ධ *sthira-gandha*; tree, *mimusops elengi*, [Colloq. මූනමල් *múna-mal*].

ස්ථිරරඞ්ගා, *Sthira-rańgá*, s. (ස්ථිර and රඞ්ග *rańga* colour) indigo plant, [Colloquial: අවරි *awari*]; species of *curcuma*.

ස්ථිරා, *Sthirá*, s. earth, [Colloq. පොළව *poḷawa*]; plant, *alyssicarpus bupleurifolius*, [Colloq. අස්වැන්න *aswęnna*].

ස්ථිරායු, *Sthiráyu*, s. (ස්ථිර *sthira* long, ආයු *áyu* life) silk cotton tree, *bombax heptaphylla*; long life, longevity.

ස්ථූණා, *Sthúṇá*, s. (ෂ්ඨා *sthá* to stay, න *na* aff.) iron image; post or pillar of a house; anvil.

ස්ථූල, *Sthúla*, s. (ස්ථූල to increase, fatten, etc. අ *a* aff.) heap, quantity: *a.* fat, corpulent; stupid, dull, ignorant; large, great.

ස්ථූලකන්ද, *Sthúlakanda*, s. (ස්ථූල large, කන්ද root) two sorts of esculent roots, *colocasia antiquorum*, [Colloq. ගහල *gahala*]; yam, *alocasia indica*, [Colloq. රට අල *raṭa-ala*].

ස්ථූලපුෂ්ප, *Sthúla-pushpa*, s. (ස්ථූල and පුෂ්ප flower) tree, *æschynomene grandiflora*.

ස්ථූලබෘහති, *Sthúla-bṛihati*, s. egg plant, *solanum melongena*, [Colloq. වම්බටු *wambaṭu*].

ස්ථූලශෘඞ්ගාටක, *Sthúla-sṛińgáṭaka*, s. thorny plant, [Colloq. ගොකටු *gokaṭu*].

ස්ථෙය, *Sthéya*, s. (ෂ්ඨා *shṭhá* to stand, යත් *yat* aff.) judge, arbitrator; domestic priest: *a.* to be fixed or determined, etc.

ස්ථෙයස්, *Sthéyas*, a. (ස්ථිර *sthira* and ඉයසුන් *iyasun* aff.) firm, stable, fixed, eternal, permanent, [Colloq. ස්ථිර *sthira*].

ස්නපන, *Snapana*, s. (ෂ්ණා *shṇá* to bathe or purify by bathing, causal form ණ්‍ය *ṇya* aff.) ablution; washing; sprinkling, wetting.

ස්නසා, *Snasá*, s. (ස්නස *snasa* to eject, අච් *ach* aff.) tendon, muscle.

ස්නාන, *Snána*, s. (ෂ්ණා *shṇá* to bathe, ල්‍යුට් *lyut* aff.) bathing, ablution, purification by bathing.

ස්නානකරණවා, *Snánakaraṇawá*, v. to bathe.

ස්නායු, *Snáyu*, s. tendon, muscle, described as a tubular vessel attached to the bones at either end and carrying vital air.

ස්නාව, *Snáwa*, s. tendon, muscle.

ස්නිග්ධ, *Snigdha*, s. (ෂ්ණිහ *shṇiha* to be unctuous, ක්ත *kta* aff.) bees' wax; two sorts of pine, *pinus devadara* and *longifolia*: *a.* smooth, oily, unctuous, greasy; amiable, affectionate, kind; coarse, thick.

ස්නිග්ධතා, *Snigdhatá*, s. (ස්නිග්ධ affectionate, තා aff.) affection, kindness; unctuousness, oiliness.

ස්නිග්ධපත්‍ර, *Snigdha-patra*, s. (ස්නිග්ධ unctuous, පත්‍ර leaf) jujube tree, *zizyphus jujuba*, [Colloq. මසන් *masan*]; tree, *ficus glomerata*, [Colloq. දිඹුල් *dimbul* or අට්ටික්කා *aṭṭikka*].

ස්නු, *Snu*, s. table land, level summit or edge of a mountain.

ස්නුක්, *Snuk*, s. tree, *euphorbia antiquorum*, [Colloq. දළුක් *daluk*].

ස්නුත, *Snuta*, a. (ෂ්ණු *shṇu* to flow, ක්ත *kta* aff.) flowing, trickling, dropping, oozing.

ස්නුෂා, *Snushá*, *s.* (ෂ්ණු *shṇu* to distil, ස *sa* aff.) milk hedge plant, *euphorbia tirucalli*, [Colloq. නවහඬි *nawahandi*]; daughter-in-law.

ස්නුහ, *Snuha*, *s.* (ෂ්ණුහ *shṇuha* to vomit) milk hedge plant, the name alludes to its milk being used as an emetic: see the preceding word.

ස්නුහා, *Snuhá*, *s.* small thorny tree, *euphorbia neriifolia*, [Colloq. පතුක් *patuk*].

ස්නුහි, *Snuhi*, see ස්නුහ *snuha*.

ස්නේහ, *Snéha*, *s.* (ෂ්ණිහ *shṇiha* to be unctuous, etc.) love, affection, kindness; oil, unguent, grease, any greasy or unctuous substance.

ස්නේහබීජ, *Snéha-bíja*, *s.* (ස්නේහ oil, බීජ seed, grain) gingely, *sesamum indicum*, [Colloq. තෙල් තල *tel-tala*].

ස්නේහවන්ත, *Snéhawanta*, *a.* (ස්නේහ and වන්ත poss. aff.) beloved, dear.

ස්නේහවන්තයා, *Snéhawantayá*, *s.* beloved one.

ස්නේහවීජ, *Snéhavíja*, *s.* plant, *hoya*, [Colloq. රුකඟුන *rukanguna*].

ස්නේහිත, *Snéhita*, *a.* (ස්නේහ *snéha* affection, ඉත *ita* aff.) kind, affectionate; beloved.

ස්නේහී, *Snéhí*, *s.* (ස්නේහ *snéha* and ඊ *í* aff.) friend: *a.* affectionate, etc.

ස්පර්ශ, *Sparṣa*, *s.* touch, contact; air, wind.

ස්පර්ශලජ්ජා, *Sparṣa-lajjá*, *s.* (ස්පර්ශ touch, ලජ්ජා ashamed) sensitive plant, *mimosa pudica*, [Colloq. නිදිකුම්බ *nidikumba*].

ස්පර්ශා, *Sparṣá*, *s.* unchaste woman, a wanton.

ස්පෂ්ට, *Spashṭa*, *a.* evident, manifest, apparent; clear, easy, intelligible.

ස්පෘක්කා, *Spṛikká*, *s.* plant, pot-herb, *trigonella corniculata*, [Colloq. පික්මල් *pik-mal*].

ස්පෘෂ්ටි, *Spṛishṭi*, *s.* touch, feeling, contact.

ස්පෘසි, *Spṛisi*, *s.* plant, *solanum jacquini*, [Colloq. කටුවැල්බටු *kaṭuwelbaṭu*].

ස්ඵට, *Sphaṭa*, *s.* (ස්ඵුට *sphuṭa* to unfold, to swell, අ *a* aff.) snake's expanded neck or hood.

ස්ඵටික, *Sphaṭika*, *s.* (ස්ඵුට *sphuṭa* to expand, කත් *kat* aff.) crystal, [Colloq. පළිඟු *palingu*].

ස්ඵටිකමාණික්‍ය, *Sphaṭika-máṇikya*, see the last.

ස්ඵටිකාචල, *Sphaṭikáchala*, *s.* (ස්ඵටික *sphaṭika* crystal, අචල *achala* mountain) mount Kailása, the favourite haunt of Ṣiva.

ස්ඵරණ, *Spharaṇa*, *s.* (ස්ඵර to move, ලයුට් *lyut* aff.) throbbing, trembling, [Colloq. චංචල *chanchala*].

ස්ඵාටික, *Spháṭika*, see ස්ඵටික *sphaṭika*.

ස්ඵාති, *Spháti*, *s.* increase, growth; swelling, intumescence.

ස්ඵාර, *Sphára*, ස්ඵාරණ, *Sphárana*, } *s.* (ස්ඵුර *sphura* to move, ආ *á* substituted for the radical vowel) throbbing, quivering: *a.* great, large.

ස්ඵුට, *Sphuṭa*, *a.* (ස්ඵුට to blow, blossom, rend, tear, etc. ක *ka* aff.) blown, opened, expanded; apparent, manifest, evident; burst, broken, rent, torn.

ස්ඵුටන, *Sphuṭana*, *s.* rending, tearing, etc.

ස්ඵුටා, *Sphuṭá*, *s.* (ස්ඵුට *sphuṭa* to expand, ආ *á* aff.) expanded hood of a snake.

ස්ඵුටි, *Sphuṭi*, *s.* kibe, swelling of the feet; sort of melon, *cucumis momordica*.

ස්ඵුටිත, *Sphuṭita*, *a.* blown, expanded, etc.

ස්ඵුර්ජක, *Sphurjaka*, *s* (ස්ඵුර්ජ *sphurja* to sound, as thunder) sort of ebony, *diospyros glutinosa*.

ස්ඵුර, *Sphura*, *s.* (ස්ඵුර to tremble) throbbing, trembling.

ස්ඵුරණ, *Sphuraṇa*, *s.* (ස්ඵුර to shake, ලයුට් *lyut* aff.) quivering, trembling, throbbing, pulsation.

ස්ඵුරත්, *Sphurat*, *s.* (ස්ඵුර to swell, etc. ශතෘ *ṣatri* aff.) swelling, expanding; quivering: see the last.

ස්ඵුලණ, *Sphulaṇa*, see ස්ඵුරණ *sphuraṇa*.

ස්ඵුලිඞ්ග, *Sphuliṅga*, *s.* (ස්ඵුත් *sphut* imitative sound, ලිගි *ligi* to go) spark of fire, [Colloq. ගිනිපුපුර *ginipupura*].

ස්ඵූර්ජ, *Sphúrja*, *s.* (ස්ඵූර්ජ to sound as thunder, අච් *ach* aff.) thunder, Indra's thunderbolt.

ස්ඵෝට, *Sphóṭa*, *s.* (ස්ඵුට *sphuṭa* to break or open, අණ් *aṇ* aff.) boil, tumour, [Colloq. ගඩගෙඩිය *gaḍagediya*]; breaking, bursting.

ස්ඵෝටක, *Sphóṭaka*, *s.* boil, tumour; plant, *plumbago rosea*, [Colloq. රත්නිටුල් *ratniṭul*]: see the preceding word.

ස්ඵෝටනි, *Sphóṭani*, *s.* gimlet, auger, [Colloq. අවගාරය *awagáraya*, බුරුමය *burumaya*].

ස්මය, *Smaya*, *s.* pride, arrogance; surprize, astonishment.

ස්මර, *Smara*, *s.* (ස්මෘ *smṛi* to remember, අච් *ach* aff.) recollection; name of Káma the god of love.

ස්මරණ, *Smaraṇa*, *s.* recollecting, remembering, memory, recollection, [Colloq. සිහිය *sihiya*].

ස්මරධ්වජ, *Smara-dhwaja*, *s.* (ස්මර Káma, ධ්වජ banner, emblem) penis; vulva; the Makara, a fabulous marine monster and emblem of Káma.

ස්මෘත්‍යුපස්ථාන, *Smṛityupasthána*, *s.* (ස්මෘති *smṛiti* memory, උප *upa* near, ෂ්ඨා *shṭhá* to be) the proximate cause of recollection, association, recollection.

ස්මෘත, *Smṛita, a.* (ස්මෘ to remember, ක්ත *kta* aff.) recollected, remembered, called to mind.

ස්මෘති, *Smṛiti, s.* recollection, remembrance, memory; understanding, [Colloq. සිහිය *sihiya*].

ස්මෘතිශාස්ත්‍රය, *Smṛiti-sástraya, s.* a work on law, code, digest.

ස්මෘතිහේතු, *Smṛiti-hétu, s.* the proximate cause of recollection, association, recollection.

ස්ව, *Swa, s.* kinsman; self, identity, individuality; also, wealth, property: *a.* own.

ස්වකීය, *Swakíya, a.* (ස්ව own, කීය aff.) own, one's own.

ස්වගුප්තා, *Swaguptá, s.* (ස්ව self, ගුප්ත *gupta* preserved, defended) cowach, *carpopogon* (or *dolichos) pruriens,* [Colloq. වඳුරුමෑ *wandurumé*].

ස්වච්ඡ, *Swachchha, s.* talc, [Colloq. මිනිරන් *miniran*]: *a.* clear, pure.

ස්වච්ඡන්ද, *Swachchhanda, a.* (ස්ව own, ඡන්ද inclination) unrestrained, uncontrolled, self-willed.

ස්වච්ඡන්දික, *Swachchhandika, a.* (ස්වච්ඡන්ද *swachchhanda* and ඉක *ika* aff.) voluntary, independant, uncontrolled.

ස්වජ, *Swaja, s.* (ස්ව self, ජ born) son; sweat, perspiration; blood.

ස්වතන්ත්‍ර, *Swatantra, a.* (ස්ව own, තන්ත්‍ර will, inclination) unrestrained, uncontrolled, self-willed; independant, free.

ස්වදන, *Swadana, s.* (ස්වද to taste, ල්‍යුට් *lyut* aff.) eating, enjoying.

ස්වන, *Swana,* } *s.* (ස්වන to sound, අප් *ap* aff.)
ස්වනි, *Swani,* } sound in general, [Colloq. ශබ්දය *ṣabdaya*].

ස්වප්න, *Swapna, s.* (ෂ්වප *shwapa* to sleep, න aff.) sleep; dreaming, dream.

ස්වප්නකෘත්, *Swapna-krit, s.* (ස්වප්න sleep, කෘත් making) potherb of narcotic properties, *marsilea quadrifolia,* [Colloq. දිය ඇඹුල් ඇඹිලිය *diya-embul-embiliya*].

ස්වප්නාන්ත, *Swapnánta, a.* (ස්වප්න *swapna* dream, අන්ත *anta* within) dreaming, in a dream; sleeping, asleep.

ස්වභාව, *Swabháwa, s.* (ස්ව own, භාව property) nature, natural state, property or disposition.

ස්වභූ, *Swabhú, s.* (ස්ව self, භූ born) name of Brahma and of Vishṇu.

ස්වමීප, *Swamípa,* corruptly for සමීප *samípa.*

ස්වයංගුප්තා, *Swayanguptá, s.* (ස්වයම් *swayam* self, ගුප්ත *gupta* defended) *carpopogon pruriens:* see ස්වගුප්තා *swaguptá.*

ස්වයංජාත, *Swayanjáta, s.* (ස්වයම් *swayam* self, ජාත produced) fabulous sort of rice which springs up spontaneously for the use of Chakrawartis, and other eminent personages.

ස්වයථු, *Swayathu, s.* swelling, intumescence.

ස්වයම්, *Swayam, ind.* self, spontaneously, of one's own self or own accord.

ස්වයම්භූ, *Swayambhú, s.* (ස්වයම් and භූ to exist) name of Buddha; name of Brahma.

ස්වයම්භූඥාන, *Swayambhújñána, s.* (ස්වයම්භූ self, excellent, ඥාන knowledge) self-derived wisdom.

ස්වර්ග්‍ය, *Swargya, a.* (ස්වර්ග *swarga* heaven, යත් *yat* aff.) celestial, heavenly, paradisaical.

ස්වර්ග, *Swarga, s,* (සු *su* happiness, ඍජ *ṛija* to go or obtain) paradise of Indra on the top of Maha Méru, and the residence of deified mortals and the gods, heaven (in the Christian sense).

ස්වර්ගමෝක්ෂ, *Swargamóksha, s.* (ස්වර්ග and මෝක්ෂ release) final happiness, release or bliss in heaven.

ස්වර්ගීය, *Swarggiya,* see ස්වර්ග්‍ය *swargya.*

ස්වර්ණ, *Swarṇa, s.* (සු *su* excellent, ඍණ *ṛiṇa* to go, අ *a* aff.) gold, [Colloq. රත්රන් *ratran*]: sort of turmeric, *curcuma zerumbet,* [Colloq. හරන්කහ *harankaha*].

ස්වර්ණකාර, *Swarṇakára, s.* (ස්වර්ණ and කාර maker, worker) goldsmith, [Colloq. බඩාලා *badálá*].

ස්වර්ණගෛරික, *Swarṇa-gairika, s.* (ස්වර්ණ and ගෛරික red chalk) kind of ochre, golden ochre.

ස්වර්ණචූඩ, *Swarṇa-chúḍa, s.* (ස්වර්ණ gold, චූඩ crest) blue jay, *cissa ornata (*order *Passeres);* cock, *(*order *Gallinæ),* [Colloq. කුකුළා *kukuḷá*].

ස්වර්ණපුෂ්ප, *Swarṇa-pushpa, s.* (ස්වර්ණ and පුෂ්ප flower) tree, *cassia fistula,* [Colloq. ඇහැල *ehela*]; champaka tree, *michelia champaca,* [Colloq. සපු *sapu*].

ස්වර්ණපුෂ්පී, *Swarṇa-pushpi, s.* medicinal sort of moon-plant.

ස්වර්ණබීජ, *Swarṇa-bíja, s.* white water lily, *nelumbium speciosum,* [Colloq. හෙළ නෙළුම් *hela-nelum*].

ස්වර්ණවර්ණා, *warṇa-warṇá, s.* (ස්වර්ණ and වර්ණ *warṇa* colour) turmeric, *curcuma longa,* [Colloq. කහ *kaha*].

ස්වර්ණ ශිවිකා, *Swarṇa-ṣiviká, s.* (ස්වර්ණ gold, ශිවිකා litter) golden litter, one constructed of or ornamented with gold.

ස්වර්ණාරි, *Swarṇári, s.* (ස්වර්ණ *swarṇa* and අරි *ari* hostile) sulphur, [Colloq. කෙන්දගම් *kendagam*].

ස්වර්ණදී, *Swarnadí, s.* the celestial river, sometimes written ස්වර්ණදී *swarṇadí.*

ස්වර්භානු, *Swarbhánu, s.* (ස්වර් heaven, භානු shining) Ráhu the personified ascending node.

ස්වර්ලෝක, *Swarlóka, s.* (ස්වර් and ලෝක world) heaven.

ස්වර, *Swara, s.* (ස්වර to sound, අච් *ach* aff.) accent; vowel; sound in general; tune, voice; air breathed through the nostrils, snoring.

ස්වරත, *Swarata, s.* species of *hoya,* [Colloq. රුකඟුන *rukanguna*]: see ස්නේහරිජ *snéharija.*

ස්වරභඞ්ග, *Swarabhanga,* } *s.* (ස්වර sound, note,
ස්වරභේද, *Swarabhéda,* } භඞ්ග or භේද breaking) fluttering of the voice, as indicative of agitation or feeling.

ස්වරස්ථාන, *Swarasthána, s.* (ස්වර and ස්ථාන place) seat or organ of sound.

ස්වරස, *Swarasa, s.* (ස්ව own, රස taste) natural or peculiar flavour or taste; expressed or extracted juice.

ස්වරිත, *Swarita, s.* (ස්වර *swara* note, accent, ඉතච් *itach* aff.) accented; articulated; sounded as a note, pitched.

ස්වරුචි, *Swaruchi, a.* (ස්ව own, රුචි inclination) wilful, self-willed, uncontrolled, [Colloq. නොහික්මුණාවූ *nohikmuṇáwú*].

ස්වරූප, *Swarúpa, s.* (ස්ව own, රූප form) natural state or condition, nature; form, likeness.

ස්වල්ප, *Swalpa, a.* (සු *su* very, අල්ප *alpa* little or few) very small, very few.

ස්වල්පය, *Swalpaya, s.* a little.

ස්වස්ති, *Swasti, ind.* (සු *su* well, අස *asa* to be, ති aff.) particle of benediction; auspicious particle, etc.

ස්වස්තික, *Swastika, s.* (ස්වස්ති and කන් *kan* aff.) any lucky or auspicious object; meeting of four roads; temple of a particular form with a portico in front; mystical figure in the form of 卍

ස්වස්ථ, *Swastha, a.* (ස්ව self, ස්ථ staying) confident, resolute, firm, relying upon one's self; well at ease, in health.

ස්වසෘ, *Swasṛi, s.* sister, [Colloq. සහෝදරී *sahódari*].

ස්වාගත, *Swágata, s.* (සු *su* well, ආගත *ágata* come) welcome, salutation.

ස්වාති, *Swáti, s.* (සු *su* well, අත *ata* to go or be, ඉන් *in* aff.) star Arcturus, or fifteenth lunar asterism consisting of but one star.

ස්වාද, *Swáda, s.* (ස්වාද to taste, අච් *ach* aff.) taste, flavour; tasting, eating, drinking.

ස්වාදු, *Swádu, s.* (ස්වාද *swáda* to taste, be agreeable, උ *u* aff.) treacle, molasses; a grape: *a.* sweet; agreeable, desired.

ස්වාදුකණ්ටක, *Swádu-kaṇṭaka, s.* (ස්වාදු sweet, කණ්ටක thorn) plant, *flacourtia Ramontchi* or *f. sapida,* [Colloq. උගුරැස්ස *ugurèssa*]; prostrate plant, *tribulus terrestris,* [Colloq. සෙම්බුනෙරෙංචි *sembu-nerenchi*].

ස්වාදුකන්ද, *Swádu-kanda, s.* (ස්වාදු and කන්ද root) carrot, *daucus carota;* kind of yam, *ipomæa digitata,* [Colloq. කිරිබඩු *kiribadu*].

ස්වාදුතික්තක, *Swádu-tiktaka, s.* creeper bearing edible gourd, *trichosanthes cucumerina,* [Colloq. දුම්මැල්ල *dummèlla*].

ස්වාදුපුෂ්ප, *Swádu-pushpa, s.* (ස්වාදු agreeable, පුෂ්ප flower) flower or blossom of the bael tree, *ægle marmelos,* [Colloq. බෙලි *beli*]; tree, *bassia longifolia,* [Colloq. මීගස *migasa*].

ස්වාදුපුෂ්පී, *Swádu-pushpí,* see මයිල *mayila.*

ස්වාදුඵල, *Swádu-phala, s.* (ස්වාදු and ඵල fruit) fruit of the jujube, *zizyphus jujuba,* [Colloq. ඩෙබර *ḍebara* or මසන් *masan*]; tree, *phyllanthus emblica,* [Colloq. නෙල්ලි *nelli*]; palmyra tree, *borassus flabelliformis,* [Colloq. තල් *tal*].

ස්වාදුඵලා, *Swádu-phalá, s.* grape vine, *vitis vinifera,* [Colloq. මිදිවැල් *midiwel*].

ස්වාදුරෝමසා, *Swádu-rómasá, s.* cucumber, [Colloq. කැකිරි *kekiri*].

ස්වාධීන, *Swádhína, a.* (ස්ව *swa* self, අධීන *adhína* dependant) independant, uncontrolled.

ස්වාන්ත, *Swánta, s.* (ස්වන *swana* to sound, ක්ත *kta* aff.) mind, faculty of thought and feeling, [Colloq. හිත *hita*]; cave, cavern: *part.* sounded.

ස්වාන, *Swána, s.* sound, noise.

ස්වානජිහ්වාදල, *Swánajihwádala, s.* small thorny tree, *euphorbia neriifolia,* [Colloq. පතුක් *patuk*].

ස්වාප, *Swápa, s.* (ෂ්වප *shwapa* to sleep) sleep, sleeping; paralysis, palsy, loss of sensation; dreaming, a dream; temporary and partial palsy from pressure on a nerve, numbness, sleep of a limb.

ස්වාපද, *Swápada, s.* wild beast.

ස්වාමි, *Swámí,* } *s.* (ස්වාමි lord, දරුවා *daruwá* child,
ස්වාමිදරුවෝ, *Swámidaruwó,* } offspring) master, lord; husband, lover: owner, proprietor, [Colloq. ස්වාමියා *swámiyá*].

ස්වාර්ථ, *Swártha, s.* (ස්ව *swa* own, අර්ථ *arttha* wealth or signification) property, substance; same effect or meaning, a pleonasm.

ස්වාස්ථ්‍ය, *Swásthya*, *s.* (ස්වස්ථ *swastha* and අණ් *aṇ* aff.) fortitude, firmness; self dependance; health; content, complacency, satisfaction.

ස්වීය, *Sviya*, *a.* (ස්ව *swa* own, ඡ *chha* aff.) own, relating or belonging to self.

ස්වේච්ඡා, *Swéchchhá*, *s.* (ස්ව *swa* and ඉච්ඡා *ichchhá* wish) wilfulness, following one's own purpose or inclination.

ස්වේද, *Swéda*, *s.* (ෂ්විද *shrida* to perspire, etc.) warmth, heat; perspiration, sweat; warm vapour, steam.

ස්වේදජ, *Swédaja*, *a.* (ස්වේද sweat or warm vapour, ජ produced) engendered by heat and damp, as insects and worms.

ස්වේදන, *Swédana*, *s.* perspiration, sweat, [Colloq. ඩාඩිය *ḍáḍiya*].

ස්වෛර, *Swaira*, } *a.* (ස්ව *swa* self, ඊර *íra* to
ස්වෛරින්, *Swairin*, } go or be, අණ් *aṇ* aff.) self-willed, unrestrained; following one's own inclination.

හ

The thirty-third consonant of the Siṇhalese alphabet, expressed by the letter *h*.

හං, *Haṇ*, *s.* skin: see සම් *sam*.

හංගණවා, *Haṇgaṇawá*, *v.* to hide, to conceal: pret. හැංගුවා *hęṇguwá*.

හංපලඬා, *Haṇpalaṇḍá*, *s.* tree, peculiar to Ceylon, *terminalia parviflora (Combretaceæ)*.

හංස, *Haṇsa*, *s.* (හන *hana* to hurt, ස aff.) goose, gander, swan, of which three varieties are enumerated; one of the vital airs; sun; horse, (in composition): best, excellent.

හංසක, *Haṇsaka*, *s.* ornament for the feet, described as being made like a goose's foot; flamingo, *phœnicopterus roseus (Phœnicopteridæ*, order *Anseres)*.

හංසකූට, *Haṇsakúṭa*, *s.* hump on the shoulder of the Indian ox.

හංසපදී, *Haṇsapadí*, *s.* (හංස swan, පද *pada* foot, ඊ *í* aff.) scandent shrub, *vitis* (or *cissus*) *pedata*, [Colloq. මැඩිය වැල් *mędiya-węl*]; plant, *clitoria ternata*, [Colloq. නිල් කටරොළු *nil-kaṭaroḷu*]; kind of medicinal plant, [Colloq. වලාවැන්න *waláwęnna*].

හංසපාද, *Haṇsapáda*, *s.* vermillion, [Colloq. සාදිලිංගම් *sádiliṇgam*].

හංසපාදි, *Haṇsapádi*, see හංසපදී *haṇsapadí*.

හංසඵේන, *Haṇsaphéna*, *s.* opium, [Colloq. අබිං *abiṇ*].

හංසයා, *Haṇsayá*, see හංස *haṇsa*.

හංසරථ, *Haṇsa-ratha*, *s.* (හංස goose, රථ vehicle) name of Brahma.

හංසවතී, *Haṇsawatí*, *s.* (හංස goose, මතුප් *matup* aff.) creeper, *vitis pedata*: see හංසපදී *haṇsapadí*.

හංසවාහන, *Haṇsawáhana*, see හංසරථ *haṇsaratha*.

හක්, *Hak*, *s.* conch-shell; hook (in the expression hook and eyes). (Dutch.)

හක් ඇටය, *Hak-ęṭaya*, conch shell of which finger rings are also made.

හක්ක, *Hakka*. *s.* jaw: see හකුපාඩාව *hakupáḍáwa*.

හක්ගෙඩිය, *Hakgeḍiya*, *s.* conch shell: pl. හක්ගෙඩි *hakgeḍi*.

හක්මණ, *Hakmaṇa*, see සක්මණ *sakmaṇa*.

හක්මන්කරණවා, *Hakmankaraṇawá*, *v.* to walk up and down.

හක, *Haka*, *s.* the chank or conch shell: see සක *saka*.

හකඹල, *Hakaṃbala*, *s.* plant, not ascertained.

හකු, *Haku*, plural of හක්ක *hakka*.

හකුපාඩාව, *Hakupáḍáwa*, *s.* jaw: see හක්ක *hakka*.

හකුරල, *Hakurala*, *s.* plant, not ascertained.

හකුරා, *Hakurá*, *s.* man of the jaggery caste: pl. හකුරෝ *hakuró*.

හකුරී, *Hakurí*, *s.* woman of the jaggery caste: pl. හකුරියෝ *hakuriyó*.

හකුරු, *Hakuru*, *s.* jaggery, coarse kind of hard native sugar: see සකුරු *sakuru*.

හකුරු සියඹලා, *Hakuru-siyaṃbalá*, *s.* plant, related to the tamarind.

හකුලනවා, *Hakulanawá*. *v.* to fold, to double: pret. හැකුලුවා *hękuluwá*: see අකුලනවා *akulanawá*.

හගිස්වනවා, *Hagiswanawá*, *v.* to convince, to convict, to confront accusing parties: pret. හැගිස්සුවා *hęgiswuwá*.

හඟ, *Haṇga*, *s.* horn: see අඟ *aṇga*.

හඟල, *Haṇgala*, see අඟල *aṇgala*.

හඟවනවා, *Haṇgawanawá*, *v.* to cause to be known; to disclose, to reveal; to publish, to declare, causal form of හැඟෙනවා *hęṇgenawá*: pret. හැඟෙව්වා *hęṇgewwá*.

හඟුතණ, *Haṇgn-taṇa*, *s.* kind of grass.

හඟුනු, *Haṇgunu*, see අඟුන *aṇguna*.

හඟුළු, *Haṇguḷu*, *s.* double boat, two canoes tied together: see අඟුල *aṇgula*.

හට්ටිය, *Haṭṭiya*, *s.* earthen cooking vessel: pl. හට්ටි *haṭṭi*,

හටගන්නවා, *Haṭagannawá*, *v.* to be produced, to spring up, to grow, to originate.

හටන, *Haṭana*, see සටන *saṭana*.

හඨ, *Haṭha*, *s.* (හඨ to treat with violence, අ *a* aff.) violence, rapine; aquatic plant, *pistia stratiotes*. [Colloq. දියපරණලා *diyaparaṇalá*].

හඨපර්ණි, *Haṭha-parṇi*, *s.* (හඨ pistia, පර්ණ *parṇa* leaf) aquatic plant, *Blyxa Roxburghii* or *vallisneria octandra*, [Colloq. දිය හවරිය *diya-hawariya*].

හඩික, *Haḍika*, *s.* sweeper, servant of the meanest function.

හඬ, *Haṇḍa*, *s.* sound, noise; thunder; voice: see අඬ *aṇḍa*.

හඬගසනවා, *Haṇḍagasanawá*, *v.* to call out: pret. හඬගෑසුවා *haṇḍagęsuwá*.

හඬනවා, *Haṇḍanawá*, *v.* to sound, to make a noise; to cry, to weep: pret. හැඬුවා *hęṇḍuwá*.

හඬා, *Haṇḍá*, *part.* having wept.

හණ, *Haṇa*, *s.* san or saun hemp, *crotalaria juncea* (*Leguminosæ*).

හණගල, *Haṇa-gala*, *s.* rub-stone, whet stone.

හණනූල්, *Haṇa-núl*, *s.* hempen thread.

හණලනුව, *Haṇa-lanuwa*, *s.* hempen string or cord.

හණහූ, *Haṇahú*, *s.* (හණ and හූ string) hempen thread or string, cord.

හත්, *Hat*, *s.* cubit, [Colloq. රියන *riyana*]: see හත *hata*.

හත්කම, *Hatkama*, *s.* (හත *hata* hand, කම action) handicraft, manual work or employment.

හත්ත, *Hatta*, *s.* fungus, mushroom: pl. හතු *hatu*.

හත්තන, *Hattana*, *s.* thorn apple, *datura fastuosa*; also, අත්තන *attana*.

හත්තිය, *Hattiya*, *s.* hat made of bamboo leaves worn by Kandian workmen.

හත්ථි, *Hatthi*, Pali form of හස්ති *hasti*.

හත්නු, *Hatnú*, *s.* (හන *hana* to kill, ත්නු aff.) sickness, disease; weapon.

හත්වෙනි, *Hatweni*, *a.* seventh.

හත්සේ, *Hatsé*, *ind.* speedily, quickly.

හත, *Hata*, *s.* thirteenth lunar asterism, from හස්ත *hasta*: *ind.* number seven, also, written සත *sata*: *a.* struck, hurt; killed, lost, destroyed.

හතර, *Hatara*, *ind.* number four.

හතරකොණ, *Hatarakoṇa*, *s.* the four cardinal points and the four intermediate points of the compass.

හතරඟුල, *Hataraṅgula*, *s.* four inches.

හතරදිග, *Hataradiga*, see හතරකොණ *hatarakoṇa*.

හතරවරම් දෙවියෝ, *Hatarawaram-deviyó*, see සතරවරම් දෙවියෝ *satarawaram-deviyó*.

හතරෙන්පංගුව, *Hataren-paṅguwa*, *s.* quarter, fourth part.

හතරැස්, *Hatarœs*, *a.* square.

හතළිස්වෙනි, *Hataḷisweni*, *a.* fortieth.

හතළිහ, *Hataḷiha*, *s.* forty: see සතළිස *sataḷisa*.

හති ඇල්වී, *Hati-ęlvi*, *s.* kind of paddy, *oryza sativa*.

හතිදමනවා, *Hatidamanawá*, *v.* to pant.

හතිය, *Hatiya*, *s.* panting, loss of breath: pl. හති *hati*.

හතු, *Hatu*, plural of හත්ත *hatta*.

හතුරා, *Haturá*, *s.* enemy, or adversary: pl. හතුරෝ *haturó*: see සතුරා *saturá*.

හතුරී, *Haturí*, *s.* female enemy: pl. හතුරියෝ *haturiyó*.

හතුරුකම්කරණවා, *Haturukamkaraṇawá*, *v.* to do an unfriendly act; to act like an enemy.

හතුරුකම, *Haturukama*, *s.* enmity: pl. හතුරුකම් *haturukam*.

හද්දින්න, *Haddinna*, *s.* the Pleiades.

හද, *Hada*, *s.* heart, seat of thought, etc. from හෘද *hrida*; affection, love; mist or appearance of water in sandy deserts, mirage.

හදන්, *Hadan*, *s.* privity, male or female; mark, spot, sign, token, signal.

හදනවා, *Hadanawá*, *v.* to make, to form; to construct, to build; to prepare, from සාදනවා *sádanawá*: pret. හැදුවා *hęduwá*.

හදමස්, *Hadamas*, } *s.* (හද heart, මස් flesh or වත
හදවත, *Hadawata*, } substance) mind, breast, site of the heart.

හදවනවා, *Hadawanawá*, *v.* to cause to make: pret. හැදෙව්වා *hędewwá*.

හදුරණවා, *Hadúraṇawá*, *v.* to say, to repeat, to recite, to commit to memory by continual repetition: pret: හැදූරුවා *hędęruwá*.

හදිආයුධ, *Hadi-áyudha*, *s.* injurious weapons.

හදිකරණවා, *Hadikaraṇawá*, *v.* to injure.

හදිය, *Hadiya*, *s.* enmity, malice; treachery, treason, accident: pl. හදි *hadi*.

හදිස්සිය, *Hadissiya*, *s.* accident, suddenness: pl. හදිස්සි *hadissi*.

හදිස්සියෙන්, *Hadissiyen*, *ad.* speedily, quickly, suddenly, unexpectedly.

හඳ, *Haṇda*, *s.* the moon.

හඳපත්‍රිල, *Han̲dapatrila*, *s.* hedge-hyssop, *gratiola cordifolia.*

හඳපාන, *Han̲dapána*, *s.* moon-light.

හඳහන, *Han̲dahana*, *s.* horoscope: pl. හඳහන් *han̲dahan.*

හඳුදා, *Han̲dudá*, *s.* Monday: see සඳුදා *san̲dudá.*

හඳුන්, *Han̲dun*, *s.* sandal wood, *santalum album;* masculine gender, mark.

හඳුන්දිරියා, *Han̲dun-diriyá*, *s.* large tiger cat, *felis viverrina.*

හඳුන්මඩලා, *Han̲dunmaḍalá*, *s.* tree, not ascertained.

හඳුනනවා, *Han̲dunanawá*, *v.* to know, to be intimate or acquainted with.

හඳුම්පත, *Han̲dumpata*, *s.* breast.

හන්, *Han*, see හම් *ham* also සන් *san*: *a:* blunt.

හන්තු, *Hantu*, *s.* (හන *hana* to kill, තු aff.) death, [Colloq. මරණය *maraṇaya*].

හන්දිකරණවා, *Handikaraṇawá*, *v.* to joint.

හන්දිය, *Handiya*, *s.* joint: pl. හන්දි *handi.*

හන්දිරන්වී, *Hadiran-ví*, *s.* kind of paddy, *oryza sativa.*

හන්නාලියා, *Hannáliyá*, *s.* tailor, [Colloq. මහන්නා *mahanná*]: see සන්නාලියා *sannáliyá.*

හන්වඩුගහනවා, *Hanwaḍugahanawá*, *v.* to brand.

හන්වඩුව, *Hanwaḍuwa*, *s.* brand: pl. හන්වඩු *hanwaḍu.*

හන්ස, *Hansa*, *s.* goose, swan: see හංස *hansa.*

හන්හාවා, *Hanháwá*, *s.* brown flying squirrel, *pteromys petaurista.*

හනන, *Hanana*, *s.* (හන to hurt, injure, kill, ල්‍යුට් *lyuṭ* aff.) killing, destroying; injuring, hurting; striking.

හනනවා, *Hananawá*, *v.* to mix, to compound, to knead, also, අනනවා *ananawá:* pret. හැනුවා *hęnuwá.*

හනස්ස, *Hanassa*, *s.* covering of the flower of the coconut tree, the dried coconut flower: pl. හනසු *hanasu.*

හනහු, *Hanahu*, *s.* sort of grain, *eleusine coracana*, [Colloq. කුරක්කන් *kurakkan*].

හනික, *Hanika*, *ind.* (Páli සනිකං *sanikaṃ* the same) particle, implying speed, speedily, hastily.

හනු, *Hanu*, *s.* (හන *hana* to hurt, උ *u* aff.) jaw: see හක්ක *hakka;* medicinal plant, [Colloq. සක්නැබ *saknęba*].

හනුපුට්ටුව, *Hanu-puṭṭuwa*, *s.* locked jaw.

හනුමත්, *Hanuman*, *s.* (හනු jaw, මතුප් *matup* aff.) monkey chief, Hanuman, the ally and spy of Ráma against Rávaṇa: see රාවණ *Rávaṇa.*

හනුව, *Hanuwa*, see හනු *hanu.*

හනුස්තම්භ, *Hanustambha*, *s.* (හනු jaw, ස්තම්භ stiff) locked jaw.

හනූෂ, *Hanúsha*, *s.* (හන *hana* to kill, ඌෂ *úsha* aff.) goblin, demon.

හප්පනවා, *Happanawá*, *v.* to cause to strike against or touch: pret. හැප්පුවා *hęppuwá.*

හප, *Hapa*, *s.* anything chewed, rubbish, refuse.

හපන්, *Hapan*, *a.* superior, either in wealth, learning, or skill; rich, wealthy, powerful; clever, skilful, expert.

හපන්කම, *Hapankama*, *s.* cleverness, expertness: pl. හපන්කම් *hapankam.*

හපනවා, *Hapanawá*, *v.* to bite, to gnaw; to hit, to strike against: see සපනවා *sapanawá:* pret. හැපුවා *hępuwá*].

හපනා, *Hapaná*, *s.* clever man, adept: pl. හපන්නු *hapannu.*

හපාකනවා, *Hapákanawá*, *v.* to bite, to gnaw.

හපු, *Hapu*, see සපු *sapu.*

හපුෂා, *Hapushá*, *s.* small medicinal plant, *sphæranthus indicus*, [Coll. මුඩමහණ *muḍamahaṇa*]

හපුස්රා, *Hapusrá*, *s.* plant, [Colloq, වෙල්මඩ *wel maḍa*].

හබක, *Habaka*, *s.* trap with snare: pl. හබක් *habak.*

හබන්කුකුළා, *Habankukuḷá*, see සබන්කුකුළා *sabankukuḷá.*

හබය, *Habaya*, *s.* complaint, lawsuit, contest, dispute: pl. හබ *haba.*

හබර, *Habara*, see සබර *sabara.*

හබරළ, *Habaraḷa*, *s.* tuberous cultivated plant with ornamental leaves, *colocasia antiquorum (Araceæ):* see සබරළ *sabaraḷa.*

හබරළිය, *Habaraḷiya*, *s.* plant, not ascertained.

හබරළියා, *Habaraḷiyá*, *s.* a sea fish.

හබල, *Habala*, *s.* oar: pl. හබල් *habal.*

හබලපෙති, *Habalapeti*, *s.* soaked roasted and pounded rice, beaten rice.

හබුරු, *Haburu*, see සබරළ *sabaraḷa.*

හඹනවා, *Ham̲banawá*, *v.* to pursue, to follow, to chase, to drive away: pret. හැඹුවා *hęm̲buwá* also, අඹනවා *am̲banawá.*

හඹවනවා, *Ham̲bawanawá*, *v.* to cause to drive away: pret. හැඹෙව්වා *hęm̲bewwá;* causal form of හඹනවා *ham̲banawá.*

හඹා, *Ham̲bá*, *s.* haste, speed, rapidity; also participle of හඹනවා *ham̲banawá.*

හම්, *Ham*, plural of හම *hama.*

හම්පරඬැල්ල, *Hamparandella*, *s.* plant used in dyeing, *rottlera tinctoria*: see හම්පිරිල *hampirila.*

හම්පලඬ, *Hampalanda*, *s.* shrub, *combretum decandrum.*

හම්පින්න, *Hampinna*, *s.* plant, *desmodium pulchellum (Liguminosæ).*

හම්පිරිල, *Hampirila*, *s.* plant used in dyeing, *mallotus philippensis* or *rottlera tinctoria.*

හම්පිල්ල, *Hampilla*, *s.* flowering shrub, *flemingia strobilifera (Leguminosæ).*

හම්බකරණවා, *Hambakaranawá*, *v.* to find, to procure; to earn.

හම්බකෙරීම, *Hambakerima*, *s.* earning.

හම්බවෙනවා, *Hambawenawá*, *v.* to meet, to be found: pret. හම්බවුනා *hambawuná.*

හම්බාන්කාරයා, *Hambánkárayá*, *s.* (හම්බාන *hambána* boat, කාර *kára* who does) boatman, one who voyages in a dhóney, coast Moorman.

හම්බාන, *Hambána*, *s.* large boat, Malabar vessel, dhóney: pl. හම්බාන් *hambán.*

හම්බුපන්, *Hambupan*, *s.* plant, reed mace, *typha angustifolia (Typhaceæ).*

හම්භා, *Hambhá*, *s.* lowing of kine.

හම්සෙරෙප්පුව, *Ham-sereppuwa*, *s.* leathern slipper, sandals.

හම, *Hama*, *s.* skin, leather: pl. හම් *ham*: see සම *sama.*

හමගහනවා, *Hamagahanawá*, *v.* to flay, to skin.

හමදිනවා, *Hamadinawá*, *v.* to cleanse, to sweep: pret. හැමදුවා *hemaduwá.*

හමනනවා, *Hamananawá*, *v.* to equalize, to assimilate: pret. හැමනුවා *hemanuwá.*

හමනලයා, *Hamanalayá*, *s.* butterfly: see සමනලයා *samanalayá.*

හමනවා, *Hamanawá*, *v.* to blow as the wind: pret. හැමුවා *hemuwá.*

හමල, *Hamala*, *s.* collection, aggregation, assemblage.

හමස් කුරක්කන්, *Hamas-kurakkan*, *s.* sort of grain, *eleusine coracana.*

හමස්මෑ, *Hamasmé*, *s.* (හ six, මස *masa* month, මෑ bean) sort of bean, *dolichos sesquipedalis.*

හමා, *Hamá*, *s.* a person decrepit, infirm and feeble through age.

හමාර, *Hamára*, *s.* half, conclusion.

හමාරකරණවා, *Hamárakaranawá*, *v.* to conclude, to bring to a close.

හමාරවෙනවා, *Hamárawenawá*, *v.* to conclude, to be finished, to end.

හමාසය, *Hamásaya*, *s.* six months.

හමු, *Hamu*, *ind.* particle, signifying presence, before, in presence of: see අමු *amu.*

හමුළු, *Hamulu*, see හමල *hamala.*

හමුව, *Hamuwa*, *ad.* before, in presence or front of.

හය, *Haya*, *s.* (හය or හි *hi* to go, අච් *ach* aff.) horse, [Colloq. අශ්වයා *aswayá*]: name of Indra; number six; yak, *bos-grunniens*; (In prosody) foot of four short syllables.

හයගන්ධා, *Hayagandhá*, *s.* (හය horse, ගන්ධ *gandha* smell) plant, *physalis flexuosa.*

හයන, *Hayana*, *s.* (හය to go, ල්‍යුට් *lyut* aff.) covered carriage, [Colloq. කරත්තය *karattaya*]; also, a year.

හයනවා, *Hayanawá*, *v.* to open, to pull.

හයප්‍රිය, *Hayapriya*, *s.* (හය horse, ප්‍රිය fond of) barley, [Colloq. යව *yawa*].

හයමාරක, *Hayamáraka*, *s.* (හය and මාරක what kills) shrub, *nerium odorum*; temple tree, *plumeria acutifolia*, [Colloq. අලරිය *alariya*].

හයරුපු, *Haya-rupu*, *s.* (හය horse, රුපු enemy) buffalo, [Colloq. මීහරකා *miharaká*].

හයා, *Hayá*, *part.* of හයනවා *hayanawá.*

හයාග, *Hayága*, *s.* bow, [Colloq. දුන්න *dunna*].

හයාගණ ඉන්නවා, *Hayágana-innawá*, *v.* to be opened as, කට හයාගණ ඉන්නවා *kata-hayágana innawá*, to have the mouth opened, to gape.

හයානන්ද, *Hayánanda*, *s.* (හය *haya* horse, අනන්ද *ánanda* delighting) kidney bean, *phaseolus mungo*, [Colloq. මුංඇට *muneta*].

හයාරි, *Hayári*, see හයමාරක *hayamáraka.*

හයිකරණවා, *Hayikaranawá*, *v.* to make strong: see සවිකරණවා *savikaranawá.*

හයිය, *Hayiya*, *s.* (සවි *savi* strength) strength, force, muscular power.

හයියෙන්, *Hayiyen*, *ad.* strongly, forcibly, powerfully, aloud.

හර්ම්‍ය, *Harmya*, *s.* palace, mansion, residence of a man of wealth or rank.

හර්‍යක්ෂ, *Haryaksha*, *s.* (හරි *hari* green, අක්ෂි *akshi* eye. ය *ya* aff.) lion, [Colloq. සිංහයා *sinhayá*].

හර්ෂ, *Harsha*, *s.* (හෘෂ *hrisha* to be pleased, අ *a* aff.) joy, pleasure, delight, happiness, [Colloq. ප්‍රීතිය *prítiya*].

හර්ෂණ, *Harshana*, *s.* (හෘෂ *hrisha* to be pleased, ල්‍යුට් *lyut* aff.) cause of pleasure, anything which confers pleasure: *a.* causing delight, delightful, delighting, pleasurable, pleasant.

හර්ෂමාණ, *Harshamána*, s. (හර්ෂ and මාණ poss. aff.) resin tree: *a.* joyful, cheerful, happy.

හර, *Hara*, s. (හර to take, අ *a* aff.) name of Ṣiva; string of pearls; an ass, [Colloq. බූරුවා *búruwá*]; pith, core of a tree, [Colloq. අරටුව *araṭuwa*]; the presiding deity of the North East: see හාර *hára*: *a.* who or what takes or seizes, carries or conveys.

හරක්, *Harak*, plural of හරකා *haraká*.

හරක් අං, *Harak-aṇ*, s. horns of bullocks.

හරක්කටු, *Harakkaṭu*, s. bones of bullocks.

හරක්මස්, *Harakmas*, s. beef.

හරක, *Haraka*, s. (හර to take, steal, ක aff.) name of Ṣiva; rogue, cheat; taker, conveyer, seizer.

හරකම, *Harakama*, s. hardness, strength.

හරකල්, *Harakal*, s. (හර Ṣiva, කල් wife) name of Durgá.

හරකා, *Haraká*, s. ox, bull, bullock: pl. හරක් *harak*.

හරණ, *Haraṇa*, s. (හර to take, ල්‍යුට් *lyuṭ* aff.) taking, accepting, receiving; seizing, carrying off or away; gold; arm; hand: see අරණ *araṇa*.

හරන්කහ, *Harankaha*, s. (හරන් or අරන් *aran* forest, කහ turmeric) sort of turmeric, *curcuma zerumbet (Scitamineæ)*.

හරඹ, *Haraṃba*, s. fencing, practising with the sword; gymnastics.

හරඹකරණවා, *Haraṃbakaraṇawá*, v. to fence with the sword, to practise in fighting on foot.

හරවනවා, *Harawanawá*, v. to turn, to inflect: pret. හැරෙව්වා *herewwá*.

හරස්, *Haras*, a. cross, transverse.

හරස්කපනවා, *Haraskapanawá*, v. to stand across.

හරස්කරණවා, *Haraskaraṇawá*, v. to obstruct, to place across.

හරස්කෙරීම, *Haraskeríma*, s. obstruction, placing across.

හරසර, *Harasara*, s. (හර Ṣiva, සර wife) Durgá; affection, esteem, regard, assistance.

හරහට, *Harahaṭa*, ind. crosswise, horizontally, across, athwart.

හරහනවා, *Harahanawá*, v. to decorate, to adorn: pret. හැරහුවා *herahuwá*.

හරාද්‍රි, *Harádri*, s. (හර *hara* Ṣiva, අද්‍රි *adri* mountain) mount Kailása the favourite resort of Ṣiva.

හරාව, *Haráwa*, s. field newly asweddumised, and detached from the range of fields; sometimes written අරාව *aráwa;* fishing season.

හරළ, *Haráḷa*, s. alligator, [Colloq. කිඹුලා *kiṃbulá*].

හරි, *Hari*, s. (හර *hara* to take, ඉ *i* aff.) name of Kṛishṇa or Vishṇu; Yama; Indra; ray of light; kókila or Indian cuckoo, *cucullus micropterus;* lion, [Colloq. සිංහයා *siṇhayá*]; green colour; golden colour, or yellow: *a.* right, fit, proper, just; accurate; punctual, exact, precise.

හරිකම, *Harikama*, s. correctness: pl. හරිකම් *harikam.*

හරිකරණවා, *Harikaraṇawá*, v. to procure; to earn.

හරිගස්සනවා, *Harigassanawá*, v. to correct, to rectify; to adapt, to fit: pret. හරිගැස්සුවා *harigessuwá.*

හරිචන්දන, *Hari-chandana*, s. (හරි Vishṇu or yellow, චන්දන sandal) yellow and fragrant sort of sandal wood, variety of *santalum album*, one of the trees of paradise, [Colloq. රන්වන් සඳුන් *ranwan-saṇdun*]; saffron, *curcuma longa*, [Coll: කහ *kaha*]; farina of a lotus.

හරිණ, *Hariṇa*, s. (හර *hara* to take, ඉන *ina* aff.) deer, [Colloq. මුවා *muwá*]; yellowish white.

හරිණලෝචනී, *Hariṇalóchani*, s. (හරිණ deer, ලෝචන *lóchana* eye, ඊ *í* fem. aff.) woman, with handsome eyes, [Colloq. ස්ත්‍රී *strí*].

හරිණවා, *Hariṇawá*, v. to leave, to forsake, to cast off, to reject, to dismiss: pret. හැරියා *heriyá.*

හරිණී, *Hariṇi*, s. creeping plant, *gloriosa superba*, [Colloq. නියඟලා *niyagalá*].

හරිත, *Harita*, s. (හර *hara* to take, ඉත *ita* aff.) green colour, [Colloq. නිල්පාට *nil-páṭa*]; lion, [Colloq. සිංහයා *siṇhayá*].

හරිතක, *Haritaka*, s. (හරිත green, ක aff.) potherb.

හරිතා, *Haritá*, s. bent grass; turmeric, [Colloq. කහ *kaha*].

හරිතාල, *Haritála*, s. (හරිත *harita* green, අල *ala* to posses, අණ් *aṇ* aff.) yellow orpiment, [Colloq. හිරියල් *hiriyal*].

හරිතාලක, *Haritálaka*, s. (හරිතාල and කන් *kan* aff.) green pigeon, *carpophaga ænea*, [Colloq. බටගොයා *baṭagoyá*]; theatrical decoration, painting the person, etc.

හරිතාලි, *Haritálí*, s. bent grass, *panicum dactylon.*

හරිතුරඞ්ග, *Hariturańga*, s. name of Ṣakra or Indra.

හරිද්‍රා, *Haridrá*, s. (හරි green, ද්‍රු *dru* to flow or ooze) turmeric, either the plant or powdered root, *curcuma longa*, [Colloq. කහ *kaha*].

හරිද්‍රාණ්‍ය, *Haridránya*, *s.* bulbous plant, *curcuma zanthorrhiza*, or *coscinium fenestratum*, [Colloq. වෙනිවැල් *weniwel*].

හරිද්‍රාභ, *Haridrábha*, *s.* (හරිද්‍රා turmeric, ආභ *ábha* resembling) tree, *pentaptera arjuna;* zedoary, *curcuma zerumbet*: see හරන්කහ *harankaha*.

හරිද්‍රාරාග, *Haridrá-rága*, *a.* (හරිද්‍රා and රාග colour) fickle, capricious, unsteady, in affection or attachment.

හරිදශ්ව, *Haridaswa*, *s.* (හරිත් *harit* green, අශ්ව *aswa* horse) the sun, [Colloq. ඉර *ira*].

හරිවාර, *Haridwára*, *s.* a town so called, where the Ganges descends into the plains of Hindustan.

හරින්මණි, *Harinmani*, *s.* (හරිත් *harit* green, මණි gem) emerald, [Colloq. පච්ච ගල *pachcha-gala*].

හරිනේත්‍ර, *Harinétra*, *s.* (හරි Vishnu, නේත්‍ර eye) white lotus, *nymphæa lotus*, [Colloq. ඕලු *ólu*].

හරිප්‍රිය, *Haripriya*, *s.* (හරි and ප්‍රිය beloved) tree, *anthocephalus* (or *naculea*) *cadamba;* dark sort of sandal wood, variety of *santalum album*, [Colloq. රත්හිරිය *rathiriya*]; fragrant root of the *andropogon muricatus*, [Colloq. සැවැන්දරා මුල් *sewendará-mul*].

හරිප්‍රියා, *Haripriyá*, *s.* (හරිප්‍රිය *haripriya* and අ *a* fem. aff.) name of Lakshmí, sacred basil, *ocimum sanctum*, [Colloq. මදුරුතලා *madurutalá*]; the earth, [Colloq. පොළව *polawa*].

හරිබීජ, *Haribíja*, *s.* (හරි and බීජ semen) yellow orpiment. [Colloq. හිරියල් *hiriyal*].

හරිමඤ්ජරී, *Harimañjarí*, *s.* plant, *acalypha indica*, [Colloq. කුප්පමේනිය *kuppaméniya*].

හරිමන්ථ, *Harimantha*, *s.* (හරි fire, or horse, මන්ථ to agitate) tree, *premna longifolia;* chick pea.

හරිමන්ථක, *Harimanthaka*, *s.* chick pea.

හරිලනවා, *Harilanawá*, *v.* to meet, to encounter, to find.

හරිවාහන, *Hariwáhana*, *s.* (හරි Vishnu, වාහන vehicle) Garuda the bird of Vishnu.

හරිවිකාරයා, *Harivikárayá*, *s.* groom, [Colloq. කුදිරකාරයා *kudirakárayá*].

හරිසඳුන්, *Harisandun*, see හරිචන්දන *harichandana*.

හරිහය, *Harihaya*, *s.* (හරි green, හය horse) Indra; the sun, [Colloq. ඉර *ira*].

හරීතකී, *Harítakí*, *s.* (හරි *hari* green, ඉත *ita* gone, ක *ka* aff.) yellow or chebulic myrobalan, *terminalia chebula*, [Colloq. අරළු *aralu*], of which seven varieties are distinguished.

හරේණු, *Harénu*, *s.* pulse, pease.

හරේණුක, *Harénuka*, *s.* creeping plant, [Colloq. වල්ගාමිරිස් *walgá-miris*].

හල්, *Hal*, *s.* hal tree, peculiar to Ceylon, *vateria acuminata* or *v. indica (Dipterocarpaceæ);* mark over a consonant indicating the suppression of the vowel.

හල්බෙඹිය, *Halbémbiya*, *s.* small flowered bead tree: see හාල්බැඹිය *hálbembiya*.

හල්මිලිල, *Halmilila*, } *s.* valuable timber tree,
හල්මිල්ල, *Halmilla*, } called Trincomalee wood, *Berrya ammonilla (Tiliaceæ)*.

හලකුණ, *Halakuna*, *s.* a mark.

හලකුණුකරණවා, *Halakunukaranawá*, *v.* to make a mark.

හලදු, *Haladu*, *s.* turmeric, *curcuma longa*, [Colloq. කහ *kaha*].

හලධර ප්‍රිය, *Haladhara-priya*, see හලිප්‍රිය *halipriya*.

හලන්දා, *Halandá*, *s.* tree snake, *dendrophis picta*, *(Ophidia)*.

හලනවා, *Halanawá*, *v.* to throw down, to shake, to winnow, to sift: pl. හැලුවා *heluwá:* see සලනවා *salanawá*.

හලඹ, *Halamba*, *s.* devil dancer's rings filled with tinkling metal, the feetlet or armlet sacred to the gods.

හලල, *Halala*, *s.* the fire-fly, [Colloq. කලාමැදිරියා *kalámediriyá*].

හලලනවා, *Halalanawá*, *v.* to toss, to stir, to move, to agitate: pret. හැලලුවා *helaluwá*.

හලලූයා, *Halaluyá*, *s.* hallelujah. (Eng.)

හලවිය, *Halaviya*, *s.* (හල a plough, අවිය *aviya* weapon) name of Balabhadra.

හලහ, *Halaha*, *s.* measure of capacity, six láhas.

හලහල, *Halahala*, see හලාහල *haláhala*.

හලා, *Halá*, *s.* fire-fly, [Colloq. කලාමැදිරියා *kalá-mediriyá*]; whirlpool, female friend.

හලායුධ, *Haláyudha*, *s.* (හල *hala* and ආයුධ *áyudha* weapon) Balaráma.

හලාහල, *Haláhala*, *s.* sort of poison; kind of snake.

හලි, *Hali*, *s.* (හල *hala* to plow, ඉන් *in* aff.) furrow; agriculture.

හලිද්‍ර, *Halidra*, *s.* disease or affection of the urine: ප්‍රමේහ *praméha*.

හලිද්‍රා, *Halidrá*, see හරිද්‍රා *haridrá*.

හලිනී, *Haliní*, *s.* plant, *gloriosa superba*, [Colloq. නියඟලා *niyangalá*].

හලිප්‍රිය, *Halipriya*, *s.* (හලි Balaráma, ප්‍රිය beloved) tree, *anthocephalus* or *nauclea cadamba*, [Colloq. කොලොම්ගස් *kolom-gas*].

හලී, *Halí*, s. (හල *hala* plough, ඊ *í* aff.) Baladéva; ploughman, cultivator, [Colloq. ගොවියා *goviyá*].

හව්, *Haw*, see සව් *saw*.

හව්‍ය, *Hawya*, s. offering to the gods.

හව්‍යවාහ, *Hawyawáha*, s. (හව්‍ය and වාහ who bears) fire, [Colloq. ගින්දර *gindara*].

හව්‍යාශ, *Hawyáṣa*, s. (හව්‍ය *hawya* and අශ *aṣa* who eats) fire.

හව්රුද්ද, *Hawrudda*, see අවුරුද්ද *awurudda*.

හව්ලනවා, *Hawlanawá*, see අවුලනවා *awulanawá*.

හව, *Hawa*, s. (හු *hu* to sacrifice, අ *a* aff.) sacrifice, oblation; also call, calling.

හවඩිය, *Hawaḍiya*, s. metal waist chain: pl. හවඩි *hawaḍi*.

හවන, *Hawana*, s. (හු *hu* and ල්‍යුට් *lyuṭ* aff.) sacrifice, oblation.

හවනවා, *Hawanawá*, v. to curse, to utter imprecations against: see අවනවා *awanawá*.

හවරිමදු, *Hawari-madu*, s. (හවරිය *hawariya* tress, මදු convolvulus) sort of bindweed, *ipomœa tridentata (Convolvulaceœ)*: also called හින් මදු *hín-madu*.

හවරිය, *Hawariya*, s. tress of false hair worn by women, the tuft of a bullock's tail: pl. හවරි *hawari*.

හවස, *Hawasa*, s. evening: see සවස *sawasa*.

හවි, *Havi*, s. mountain, hill, [Colloq. කන්ද *kanda*]: see හවිස් *havis*.

හවිය, *Haviya*, see සවි *savi*.

හවිස්, *Havis*, s. (හු *hu* to offer, ඉසි *isi* aff.) clarified butter, ghee, [Colloq. ගිතෙල් *gitel*]; article to be offered as an oblation, usually ghee.

හවුරු, *Hawuru*, s. wall of earth, etc. cast up before a city as a defence.

හවුල්කාරයා, *Hawulkárayá*, s. partner.

හවුල්වෙනවා, *Hawulwenawá*, v. to become a partner: pret. හවුල්වුනා *hawulwuná*.

හවුල, *Hawula*, s. partnership, companionship, share, part: pl. හවුල් *hawul*.

හවුහරණය, *Hawuharaṇaya*, s. means of subsistence; help, succour, support.

හස්, *Has*, s. laughter, merriment; joy, delight; hansa or swan: see හංස *haṇsa*.

හස්කර, *Haskara*, s. (හස් for සස් *sas* corn, කර who does) husbandman, cultivator, [Colloq. ගොවියා *goviyá*].

හස්ත්‍ය, *Hastya*, a. (හස්ත *hasta* hand, යත් *yat* aff.) done with the hand, manual.

හස්ත්‍යාලංකාර, *Hastyalaṇkára*, s. (හස්ති *hasti* elephant, අලංකාර *alaṇkára* ornament) housings of an elephant.

හස්ත්‍යශ්වාදි, *Hastyaṣwádi*, s. elephants, horses, etc.

හස්ත්‍යාචාර්ය, *Hastyácharya*, s. (හස්ති *hasti* elephant, ආචාර්ය *áchárya* teacher or master) elephant keeper.

හස්ත්‍යාරෝහ, *Hastyároha*, s. (හස්ති *hasti* and ආරෝහ *áróha* who mounts) elephant rider or driver.

හස්ත, *Hasta*, s. hand, [Colloq. අත *ata*]; elephant's trunk; thirteenth lunar asterism designated by a hand, and containing five stars, one of which is Gamma or Delta corvi; cubit measured by the hand and arm, or from the elbow to the middle finger.

හස්තංගත, *Hastaṇgata*, corruptly for අස්තංගත *astaṇgata*.

හස්තංගතවෙනවා, *Hastaṇgatawenawá*, v. to set, applied only to the setting of the sun.

හස්තකර්මාන්තකාරයා, *Hastakarmántakárayá*, s. manufacturer.

හස්තකර්මාන්තය, *Hastakarmántaya*, s. manufacture, handicraft.

හස්තපයෝධර, *Hasta-payódhara*, s. thorn apple, *datura fastuosa*, [Colloq. අත්තන *attana*].

හස්තපුට, *Hastapuṭa*, s. (හස්ත and පුට concavity) joined hands, as in the attitude of worship.

හස්තප්‍රාප්ත, *Hastaprápta*, a. (හස්ත and ප්‍රාප්ත come, arrived) got, gained, obtained, (literally fallen into the hands).

හස්තබා, *Has-tabá*, s. (හස් seal, තබා having placed) having put the seal (on it, etc.)

හස්තමුද්‍රා, *Hasta-mudrá*, s. (හස්ත and මුද්‍රා sign) beckoning, indication of sentiment by the fingers.

හස්තමුද්‍රාභාෂා, *Hastamudrá-bháshá*, see the last.

හස්තවිකාර, *Hasta-vikára*, s. (හස්ත and විකාර gesture) signs, beckoning, etc.

හස්තාමලක, *Hastámalaka*, s. (හස්ත *hasta* and අමල *ámala* gem so called) fabulous gem, described as of a white colour, transparent and very brilliant, perhaps a species of crystal is intended.

හස්ති, *Hasti*, s. (හස්ත *hasta* trunk, ඉනි *ini* aff.) elephant, [Colloq. ඇතා *ẹtá*].

හස්තික, *Hastika*, s. (හස්ති elephant, ක aff.) multitude of elephants.

හස්තිකර්ණ, *Hastikarṇa*, s. (හස්ති and කර්ණ ear) plant with large flaggy leaves, *alocasia macrorrhiza*, [Colloq. හබරල *habarala*]; castor oil plant, *ricinus communis*, [Colloquial: එඬරු *endaru*]; ornamental tree, *butea frondosa*, [Colloq. ගස් කැල *gas-kela*].

හස්තිකා, *Hastiká*, *s.* (හස්ත *hasta* hand, ඉකා *iká* aff.) blow with the hand or fist, cuff, box.

හස්තිකුන්ත, *Hastikunta*, *s.* iron hook used in guiding an elephant, [Colloq. හෙණ්ඩුව *henduwa*].

හස්තිකුම්භ, *Hastikumbha*, *s.* (හස්ති and කුම්භ forehead) temples and forehead of an elephant, whence the juice exudes during rut.

හස්තිකෝල, *Hasti-kóla*, see හස්තිපිප්පලි *hasti-pippali*.

හස්තිදන්ත, *Hastidanta*, *s.* (හස්ති and දන්ත tooth) radish, *raphanus sativus;* ivory, [Colloq. ඇත්දත් *etdat*]; pin or bracket projecting from a wall to hang anything on.

හස්තින්, *Hastin*, see හස්ති *hasti*.

හස්තිනඛ, *Hasti-nakha*, *s.* (හස්ති and නඛ nail) sort of covered way, raised place of earth or masonry covering the access to the gate of a city or fort.

හස්තිනී, *Hastiní*, *s.* (හස්තින් *hastin* and ඊ *í* fem. aff.) female elephant, [Colloq. ඇතින්නී *etinní*].

හස්තිප, *Hastipa*, *s.* (හස්ති and පා *pá* to cherish, ක *ka* aff.) elephant rider or driver, [Colloq. ඇත් ගොව්වා *etgowwá*].

හස්තිපර්ණී, *Hasti-parní*, *s.* (හස්ති and පර්ණ *parna* leaf, ඊ *í* aff.) species of gourd, *momordica mixta.*

හස්තිපිප්පලි, *Hasti-pippali*, *s.* (හස්ති and පිප්පලි pepper) large sort of long pepper, variety of *piper longum*, [Colloq. ගජතිප්පිලි *gaja-tippili*].

හස්තිපුෂ්ප, *Hasti-pushpa*, *s.* stamina of the flowers of the iron-wood tree, *mesua ferrea*, [Colloq. නාමල්රේණු *námal-rénu*].

හස්තිමද, *Hasti-mada*, *s.* (හස්ති and මද juice) juice that exudes from the frontals of an elephant when in rut.

හස්තියා, *Hastiyá*, *s.* elephant: pl. හස්තියෝ *hastiyó*.

හස්තිරත්න, *Hasti-ratna*, *s.* (හස්ති and රත්න gem) royal elephant, one of the gems or treasures of kings.

හස්තිශුණ්ඩා, *Hasti-sundá*, *s.* (හස්ති and ශුණ්ඩා trunk) elephant's trunk; flower, *heliotropium indicum.*

හස්ති, *Hastí*, *s.* elephant, [Colloq. ඇතා *etá*].

හස්තේකරණ, *Hastékarana*, *s.* (හස්ත *hasta* hand, seventh case, කරණ making) marriage.

හස්න, *Hasna*, *s.* message, news, report, from සස්න *sasna*, [Colloq. ආරංචි *áranchi*].

හස, *Hasa*, *s.* laughter; swan, goose; husbandry, agriculture; sorrow, affliction, distress; going, proceeding.

හසන්ති, *Hasantí*, *s.* Arabian jasmine; portable, fire pan, small furnace.

හසන, *Hasana*, *s.* (හස to laugh, ල්‍යුට් *lyut* aff.) laughter, laughing.

හසනි, *Hasaní*, see හසන්ති *hasantí*.

හසර, *Hasara*, *s.* road, path, way, [Colloq. මග *maga*].

හසවාහන, *Hasawáhana*, *s.* name of Brahma.

හසිත, *Hasita*, *s.* smiling, laughter; also, the bow of Káma.

හසුන්, *Hasun*, *s.* message, an epistle, from ශාසන *sásana.*

හසුවෙනවා, *Hasuwenawá*, see අසුවෙනවා *asuwenawá.*

හහිනවා, *Hahinawá*, *v.* to cut with an adze or knife, to hoe, to chip, to smooth the sides of a bank or dam: pret. හැස්සා *hessá*.

හළ, *Hala*, participle (of හරිණවා *harinawá* to remove), removed away from, put at a distance, dismissed, expelled.

හළසේක, *Halaséka*, past tense (honorific) of හරිණවා *harinawá*, removed, sent away.

හළු, *Halu*, *s.* light, lustre, from ආලෝක *áloka;* similarity, resemblance: see අළු *alu*.

හළුගෙ, *Haluge*, *s.* people of the washer caste.

හළුව, *Haluwa*, *s.* cloth, shawl: see සළුව *saluwa.*

හළුහල්ලා, *Haluhallá*, *s.* tulip tree, *liriodendron liliifera.*

හා, *Há*, *ind.* a connective particle, and, with; also, a prohibitive particle which may be rendered by, hold, stay, do not do it, in which case the in is generally repeated.

හාකන්, *Hákan*, *s.* (හාවා *háwá* hare, කන් ear) hairy plant with spikes of purple and white flowers, *justicia echioides.*

හාකරණවා, *Hákaranawá*, *v.* to join, to unite.

හාඟිල්ල, *Hángilla*, *s.* (හය *haya* six, ඇඟිල්ල *engilla* finger) species of bindweed, *ipomœa digitata*, [Colloq. කිරිබඩු *kiribadu*]: *a.* six fingered.

හාටක, *Hátaka*, *s.* (හට *hata* to shine, ක aff.) gold, [Colloq. රත්රන් *ratran*]: *a.* golden, of gold.

හාත්පස, *Hátpasa*, *ind.* particle signifying circumjacency, around, about; completion, entirely, completely.

හාත්‍ර, *Hátra*, *s.* hire, wages, [Colloq. කුලි *kuli* or පඩි *paḍi*].

හාතණ, *Hátaṇa*, *s.* (හාවා *háwá* hare, තණ grass) species of panic grass, *panicum brizoides*.

හාතාවාරිය, *Hátáwáriya*, *s.* creeping plant, *asparagus falcatus* or *a. officinalis (Liliaceæ)*: see සතාවරි *satáwarí*.

හාදකම, *Hádakama*, *s.* friendship: pl. හාදකම් *hádakam*.

හාදයා, *Hádayá*, *s.* companion, associate, friend, from සහෘද *sahṛida*.

හාදවෙනවා, *Hádawenawá*, *v.* to associate with, to be friendly with, to become attached to or associated with.

හාදුව, *Háduwa*, *s.* kiss, [Colloquial: තොත්තුව *tottuwa*].

හාන්රෙද්ද, *Hánredda*, *s.* swaddling cloth.

හාන්සිපුටුව, *Hánsi-puṭuwa*, *s.* easy chair.

හාන්සිවෙනවා, *Hánsiwenawá*, *v.* to lean or recline: pret. හාන්සිවුනා *hánsiwuná*.

හාන, *Hána*, *s.* (හා to leave, ල්‍යුට් *lyuṭ* aff.) abandoning, relinquishing.

හානවා, *Hánawá*, *v.* to plough: pret. හෑවා *hẹwá*.

හානිය, *Hániya*, *s.* (හා to leave, etc. නි aff.) famine, destruction, loss, privation, abandonment, relinquishment; decreasing, wane: pl. හානි *háni*.

හාමත්වෙනවා, *Hámatwenawá*, *v.* to be weakened by hunger.

හාමත, *Hámata*, *s.* weakness from hunger: pl. හාමත් *hámat*.

හාමහේ, *Hámahé*, *s.* dearth, famine.

හාමිනේ, *Háminé*, *s.* lady: pl. හාමිනේලා *háminélá*.

හාමු, *Hámu*, *s.* lord, master; respectful term applied to children of Mudaliyars, from ස්වාමි *swámi*.

හාමුකරණවා, *Hámukaraṇawá*, *v.* to mix.

හාමුණ, *Hámuṇa*, *s.* six amuṇas.

හාමුදුරුවෝ, *Hámuduruwó*, *s.* lord, master, from ස්වාමිදරුවෝ *swámidaruwó*.

හාමුවෙනවා, *Hámuwenawá*, *v.* to be mixed up with.

හායකා, *Háyaká*, *s.* broom-like shrub with yellow flowers, *cortalaria laburnifolia*, [Colloq. යක්බෙරිය *yakbériya*].

හායන, *Háyana*, *s*, year; ray, flame.

හාර්චිය, *Hárchiya*, *s.* brooch, breast-pin: pl. හාර්චි *hárchi*.

හාර්ත, *Hárta*, *s.* Hárt, name of a playing card. (Dutch.)

හාර්ත අසියා, *Hárta-ásiyá*, *s.* ace of hárts. (Dutch).

හාර්ද, *Hárda*, *s.* (හෘද *hṛida* heart, අණ් *aṇ* aff.) affection, kindness: *a.* to be taken away, to be taken.

හාර්නල්, *Hárnal*, *s.* hair-pin. (Dutch.)

හාර්‍ය, *Hárya*, *s.* beleric myrobalan, *terminalia belerica*, [Colloq. බුළු *buḷu*].

හාර්‍යවෘක්ෂ, *Hárya-wṛiksha*, *s.* gold-coloured sandal wood, *santalum album*, [Colloq. රන්වන් සඳුන් *ranwan-saṇdun*].

හාර, *Hára*, *s.* number four, contracted from හතර *hatara*; (In Arithmetic) divisor, denominator of a fraction; string or garland of pearls, etc. porter, carrier; taking, conveying.

හාරක, *Háraka*, *s.* thief, [Colloq. හොරා *horá*] plunderer, ravisher; tree, *trophis aspera*; (In Arithmetic) divisor.

හාරණවා, *Háraṇawá*, *v.* to dig, excavate: pret. හෑරුවා *hẹruwá*.

හාරයෂ්ටි, *Hárayashṭi*, *s.* (හාර conveying, යෂ්ටි stick) pole for carrying burdens, the weight being suspended at both ends, it is carried across the shoulder; necklace.

හාරි, *Hári*, *a.* handsome, charming.

හාරිත, *Hárita*, *s.* (හරිත *harita* green, අණ් *aṇ* aff.) green or wood pigeon, *columba intermedia* (order *Columbæ*); green colour.

හාරිද්‍ර, *Háridra*, *s.* (හරිද්‍රා *haridrá* turmeric, අණ් *aṇ* aff.) kadamba tree, *anthocephalus (*or *nauclea cadamba*; yellow, colour of turmeric.

හාරී, *Hárí*, *a.* pleasant, agreeable, delightful.

හාරේ, *Háré*, *s.* pus, matter.

හාල්, *Hál*, *s.* unboiled rice, rice in general: see සාල්

හාල් ඇල්වි, *Hál-ẹlwí*, *s.* kind of hill paddy, *oryza sativa*.

හාල්ගැරඬියා, *Hál-gẹraṇḍiyá*, *s.* kind of rat snake, variety of *ptyas mucosus*.

හාල්දණ්ඩා, *Háldaṇḍá*, *s.* kind of tree snake, *dendrophis picta*, (order *Ophidia)*.

හාල්පන්, *Hálpan*, *s.* club rush, *fimbristylis globulosa (Cyperaceæ)*.

හාල්පානුදිය, *Hálpánudiya*, }
හාල්පානුදියර, *Hálpánudiyara*, } *s.* water in which raw rice has been washed.

හාල්බැඹිය, *Hálbẹmbiya*, *s.* small flowered bead tree, *cipadissa fruticosa* or *mallea Rothii (Meliaceæ)*.

හාල්මැස්සා, *Hálmẹssá*, *s.* (හාල් rice, මැස්සා fish) small sea fish, resembling white-bait.

හාල, *Hála*, *s.* rice; Balaráma, plough: pl. හාල් *hál.*

හාලා, *Hálá*, *s.* wine, spirituous or vinous liquor, [Colloq. මත්බීම *mat-bíma*].

හාලාහල, *Háláhala*, see හලාහල *haláhala.*

හාලි, *Háli*, see ශාලි *sáli.*

හාලියා, *Háliyá*, *s.* cinnamon peeler: pl. හාලි *háli.*

හාව, *Háwa*, } *s.* any feminine act of හාවභාව, *Háwabháwa*, } amorous pastime, or tending to excite amorous sensations, coquetry, blandishment, dalliance.

හාවා, *Háwá*, *s.* general name for the hare, usually the blacknecked Indian hare, *lepus nigricollis*: pl. හාවෝ *háwó.*

හාවිම *Háwima*, *s.* becoming united.

හාවෙනවා, *Háwenawá*, *v.* to become united, to be united by a metallic cement: pret. හාවුනා *háwuná.*

හාස්කම්කරණවා, *Háskamkaraṇawá*, *v.* to do wonders or miracles.

හාස්කම, *Háskama*, *s.* a miracle: pl. හාස්කම් *háskam.*

හාස්‍ය, *Hásya*, *s.* (හාස *hása* laughter, යත් *yat* aff.) laughter, laughing, mirth.

හාස, *Hása*, *s.* (හස *hasa* to laugh, අණ් *aṇ* aff.) laughing, laughter.

හිංසක, *Hiṇsaka*, *s.* (හිසි *hisi* to injure, ක aff.) beast of prey; enemy: *a.* mischievous, malignant; ferocious, savage.

හිංසන, *Hiṇsana*, *s.* injuring, hurting.

හිංසා, *Hiṇsá*, *s.* (හිසි *hisi* to kill, අ *a* aff.) injury, mischief, usually distinguished as of three kinds, mental (as malice), verbal (as abuse), personal (striking, wounding, beating, etc.).

හිංසාකර්ම, *Hiṇsá-karma*, *s.* (හිංසා and කර්ම act) incantation to destroy, practice of malice or employment of mystical texts for malevolent and injurious purposes.

හිංසාකරණවා, *Hiṇsákaraṇawá*, *v.* to injure, to hurt.

හිංසාත්මක, *Hiṇsátmaka*, *a.* injurious.

හිංසාරු, *Hiṇsáru*, *s.* (හිංසා and ඎ *ṛi* to effect) tiger, [Colloq. දිවියා *diviyá*, කොටියා *koṭiyá*].

හිංසාලු, *Hiṇsálu*, *a.* (හිංසා injury, ආලුච් *áluch* aff.) mischievous, hurtful.

හිංසි, *Hiṇsi*, *s.* tree, kind of bilimbi, *averrhoa carambola*, [Colloq. කාමරංගා *kámaraṇgá*].

හිංසිර, *Hiṇsira*, see හිංසාරු *hiṇsáru.*

හිංස්‍ර, *Hiṇsra*, *a.* (හිසි *hisi* to hurt, රක් *rak* aff.) mischievous, hurtful, injurious; murderous, fierce, savage.

හික්, *Hik*, *s.* timber tree, yielding medicinal gum, *odina Woodier (Anacardiaceæ).*

හික්කාව, *Hikkáwa*, *s.* hiccough: pl. හික්කා *hikká.*

හික්මවනවා, *Hikmawanawá*, *v.* to tame, to subdue, to train, discipline, to render docile: pret. හික්මෙව්වා *hikmewwá.*

හික්මියා, *Hikmiyá*, *s.* musk rat, *sorex cærulescens*: pl. හික්මියෝ *hikmiyó.*

හික්මුන්කම, *Hikmunkama*, *s.* state of being well trained or disciplined.

හික්මුනු, *Hikmunu*, *past part.* of the next.

හික්මෙනවා, *Hikmenawá*, *v.* to become tame or docile, etc: pret. හික්මුනා *hikmuná.*

හිකනලා, *Hikanalá*, *s.* ground lizard or skink, *euprepus rufescens* or *tiliqua carinata (Scincidæ*, order *Sauria).*

හිඟ, *Higa*, *s.* deficiency, defalcation, wanting to make up a sum; remainder, balance: *a.* scarce, deficient.

හිඟු, *Higu*, *a.* wanting, deficient, quick.

හිඟන්නා, *Hiṇganná*, *s.* beggar: pl. හිඟන්නෝ *hiṇgannó.*

හිඟනවා, *Hiṇganawá*, *v.* to beg: pret. හිඟුවා *hiṇguwá*: see සිඟනවා *siṇganawá.*

හිඟමන, *Hiṇgamana*, *s.* charity, mendicity, alms: pl. හිඟමන් *hiṇgaman.*

හිඟිනි, *Hiṇgini*, *s.* tree bearing the clearing nut, *strychnos potatorum*; also written ඉඟිනි *iṇgini.*

හිඟු, *Hiṇgu*, *s.* speed, haste.

හිඟුපත් ඇල්වි, *Hiṇgupat-ǽlví*, *s.* kind of paddy, *oryza sativa.*

හිඟුරල, *Hiṇgurala*, *s.* kind of yam.

හිඟුරු, *Hiṇguru*, *s.* ginger, properly written ඉඟුරු *iṇguru*, *zingiber officinalis*; climbing prickly plant with saponaceous legumes, *acacia concinna (Leguminosæ).*

හිඟුරුපට්ටා, *Hiṇguru-paṭṭá*, *s.* climbing medicinal plant: see the last.

හිඟුරුපියලි, *Hiṇgurupiyali*, *s.* small aromatic plant: see සිඟුරුපියලි *siṇgurupiyali.*

හිඟුල්, *Hiṇgul*, *s.* plant, *amoora Rohituka (Meliaceæ)*; vermillion, [Colloquial: සාදිලිංගම් *sádiliṇgam*].

හිඞ්ගු, *Hiṇgu*, *s.* assafætida, [Colloq. පෙරුංකායම් *peruṇkáyam*].

හිඞ්ගුනිර්‍යාස, *Hingu-niryása*, *s.* (හිඞ්ගු and නිර්‍යාස exudation) assafœtida (gum); nimb or margosa tree, *azadirachta indica*, [Colloq. කොහොඹ *kohomba*].

හිඞ්ගුපත්‍රිකා, *Hingu-patriká*, *s.* (හිඞ්ගු and පත්‍ර *patra* leaf, ඉක *ika* aff.) plant, *monochoria hastæfolia*, [Colloq. දිය හබරල *diya-habarala*].

හිංගුපත්‍රි, *Hingu-patri*, *s.* leaf and drug, perhaps the leaf of the assafœtida plant.

හිඞ්ගුල, *Hingula*, } *s.* vermillion, [Colloq. සාදිලිංගම් *sádilingam*].
හිඞ්ගුලි, *Hinguli*, }

හිඞ්ගුලිකා, *Hinguliká*, *s.* sort of prickly night shade, *solanum jacquini*, [Colloq. කටුවැල්බටු *katuwel-batu*].

හිඞ්ගුලී, *Hinguli*, *s.* species of egg plant or brinjal, *solanum xanthocarpum*, [Colloq. එලබටු *ela-batu*].

හිඞ්ගුලු, *Hingulu*, *s.* vermillion.

හිජ්ජ, *Hijja*, } *s.* plant, *barringtonia acutangula*, [Colloq. එලමිදෙල්ල *ela-midella*].
හිජ්ජල, *Hijjala*, }

හිට, *Hita*, *par.* beginning from.

හිටපන්, *Hitapan*, second person singular imperfect mood of හිටිනවා *hitinawá*.

හිටවනවා, *Hitawanawá*, *v.* to cause to stand, to plant: pret. හිටෙව්වා *hitewwá*.

හිටානෝ, *Hitánó*, *s.* very wealthy man.

හිටිතණ, *Hititana*, *s.* kind of grass.

හිටිනවා, *Hitinawá*, *v.* to stop, to stay, to be, to stand: pret. හිටියා *hitiyá:* see සිටිනවා *sitinawá*.

හිටුදුව, *Hitu-duwa*, *s.* daughter of a හිටානෝ *hitánó*.

හිටුදේවි, *Hitu-dévi*, *s.* wife of a හිටානෝ *hitánó*.

හිටුවනවා, *Hituwanawá*, *v.* to cause to stop or stand, to establish, to plant: pret. හිටෙව්වා *hitewwá:* see සිටුවනවා *situwanawá*.

හිණ්ඩන, *Hindana*, *s.* (හිඩි *hidi* to go, ල්‍යුට් *lyut* aff.) wandering, roaming.

හිණ්ඩිර, *Hindira*, } *s.* cuttle fish bone, considered to be the indurated foam of the sea, [Colloq. මුදු පෙන *'mudu-pena*]; egg plant, *solanum melongena*, [Colloq. වම්බටු *wambatu*].
හිණ්ඩීර, *Hindíra*, }

හිණ, *Hina*, *s.* stairs, ladder; lap, waist: see ඉණ *ina*.

හිණි, *Hini*, *s.* ladder, pair of stairs.

හිණිමඟ, *Hinimaga*, *s.* (හිණි and මඟ way) ladder: pl. හිණිමං *hiniman*.

හිත්, *Hit*, plural of හිත *hita*.

හිත් ඇලෙනවා, *Hit-elenawá*, *v.* to adhere with affection.

හිත්ඔතෑනි, *Hit-oténi*, see සිත්ඔතෑනි *sit-oténi*.

හිත්ගන්නවා, *Hit-gannawá*, see සිත්ගන්නවා *sit-gannawá*.

හිත්දැඩි, *Hitdedi*, *a.* stubborn, obstinate, hard-hearted.

හිත්දැඩිකම, *Hitdedikama*, *s.* stubbornness.

හිත, *Hita*, *s.* (ධා *dhá* to have or hold, ක්ත *kta* aff.) good, benefit; in Elu, the mind: see සිත *sita:* *a.* suitable, proper, fit, worthy, right; friendly, affectionate, kind: pl. හිත් *hit*.

හිතකාමී, *Hitakámí*, *s.* well-wisher: *a.* wishing well, concerned for another's welfare.

හිතනවා, *Hitanawá*, *v.* to think: pret. හිතුවා *hituwá*.

හිතුබුද්ධිය, *Hitubuddhiya*, *s.* self-will, caprice.

හිතුල්, *Hitul*, see කිතුල් *kitul*.

හිතුවක්කාරකම, *Hituwakkárakama*, *s.* doing as one likes; self-will.

හිතුවක්කාරයා, *Hituwakkárayá*, *s.* one who is self-willed; one who acts as he chooses.

හිතෙසි, *Hitési*, *s.* (හිත *hita* friendly, එසි *esi* who seeks, wishes) philanthropist, benevolent person: *a.* sincerely attached, sincerely faithful.

හිතෛෂී, *Hitaishí*, *a.* (හිත *hita* and ඓෂී *aishí* who seeks) wishing well to.

හිතෝපදේශ, *Hitópadésa*, } *s.* (හිත *hita* and උපදේස *upadésa* advice) friendly or proper advice; proverbs.
හිතෝපදේස, *Hitópadésa*, }

හිද, *Hida*, *s.* mind, heart as the faculty of reason: see හෘද *hrida;* natural pond, collection of water; a term used to direct elephants.

හිදස්, *Hidas*, *s.* hole, perforation, peep-hole.

හිඳිකටුව, *Hidikatuwa*, *s.* (හිඳි *hindi* from සිඳි *sindi* cutting, piercing, කටුව thorn) needle: see ඉඳි කටුව *idikatuwa*.

හිඳ, *Hinda*, participle (of හිඳිනවා *hindinawá* which see), having plucked, or expressed, having sat: *pass part.* of හිඳිනවා *hindinawá*.

හිඳගන්නවා, *Hindagannawá*, *v.* to sit down: pret. හිඳගත්තා *hindagattá*.

හිඳිනවා, *Hindinawá*, *v.* to sit; to evaporate by boiling; to pluck off (as feather); to express (as oil).

හිඳිලුණු, *Hindi-lunu*, *s.* salt prepared by evaporation.

හිඳුවනවා, *Hinduwanawá*, *v.* to place, to seat, to set, causal form of හිඳිනවා *hindinawá*.

හිඳෙනවා, *Hindenawá*, v. to dry up, to be expressed or dried: pret. හිඳුනා *hindunā*.

හිනතාල, *Hintála*, s. (හින *hina* defective, small, තාල palm) according to Sinhalese authorities the kitul tree, *caryota urens;* according to others, the marshy date, *phœnix paludosa*.

හින්දෝල, *Hindóla*, s. (හි particle, දුල to shake) swing, [Colloq. උංචිල්ලාව *unchilláwa*].

හින්නා, *Hinná*, s. very minute ant; also, wart: pl. හින්නෝ *hinnó*.

හින්නාවා, *Hinnáwá*, s. wicker worker, weaver of mats; washer for the Cháliya caste.

හිනවළු, *Hinawaḷu*, s. tree, not ascertained.

හිනහ, *Hinaha*, s. laughter, laughing.

හිනහවෙනවා, *Hinahawenawá*, } v. to laugh: pret. **හිනාවෙනවා**, *Hináwenawá*, } හිනාවුනා *hináwuná*.

හිබිලි, *Hibili*, s. mode of fishing; basket used for fishing in shallow water.

හිබුටුවැල්, *Hibuṭuwel*, } s. creeping plant, *salacia* **හිඹුටුවැල්**, *Himbuṭuwel*, } *reticulata (Celastraceæ)*.

හිම්, *Him*, s. boundary, limit, also written සිම් *sim* and ඉම් *im*.

හිම, *Hima*, s. frost, cold; dew, snow, thicket, jungle, snowy season; moon, camphor, [Colloq. කපුරු *kapuru*]; sandal wood tree, *santalum album*, [Colloquial: සඳුන් *sandun*]; Himálaya mountains; boundary: see සීමා *símá*.

හිමකල, *Himakala*, s. snowy season.

හිමගර්භ, *Hima-garbha*, s. (හිම snow, ගර්භ receptacle) condensed cloud.

හිමගල, *Hima-gala*, s. (හිම cold, ගල rock) Himálaya mountains.

හිමගිර, *Himagira*, s. (හිම and ගිර rock) Himálaya rock.

හිමජා, *Himajá*, s. (හිම Himálaya personified, ජ *ja* born) name of Párvatí; zedoary, *curcuma zedoaria;* aromatic plant, *kæmpferia galanga*, [Coll: හිඟුරුපියලි *hingurupiyali*].

හිමද්විෂ, *Hima-drisha*, s. (හිම and ද්විෂ enemy) sun, [Colloq. ඉර *ira*].

හිමපව්, *Himapaw*, s. (හිම cold, පව් mountain) Himálaya range.

හිමය, *Himaya*, see හිම *hima*.

හිමරශ්මි, *Hima-raṣmi*, } s. (හිම and රශ්මි or රැස් **හිමරැස්**, *Hima-reṣ*, } ray) moon, [Colloq. සඳ *handa*].

හිමව්, *Himaw*, s. Himálaya rock.

හිමව්කුළු, *Himaw-kuḷu*, s. (හිමව් Himálaya, කුළු peak) Himálaya range of mountains.

හිමවත්, *Himawat*, } s. (හිම cold, මතුප් *matup* **හිමවන්ත**, *Himawanta*, } possessive aff.) Himálaya **හිමවාන්**, *Himawán*, } mountain.

හිමවාලුකා, *Hima-wáluká*, s. (හිම and වාලුකා sand) camphor, [Colloq. කපුරු *kapuru*].

හිමශෛල, *Hima-ṣaila*, s. (හිම and ශෛල rock) Himálaya mountains.

හිමසෙල්, *Himasel*, Elu form of හිමශෛල *hima-ṣaila*.

හිමසෙව්, *Himasew*, s. (හිම and සෙව් crest) peacock, [Colloq. මොණරා *moṇará*].

හිමා, *Himá*, s. small cardamoms, [Colloq. සිහින් එන්සාල් *sihin-ensál*]; fragrant grass, *cyperus rotundus*, [Colloq. කලාඳුරු *kalánduru*].

හිමාංශු, *Himáṇṣu*, s. (හිම *hima* and අංශු *aṇṣu* ray) moon, [Colloq. සඳ *handa*]; camphor, [Colloq. කපුරු *kapuru*].

හිමාගම, *Himágama*, s. (හිම *hima* frost snow, අගම *ágama* arrival) cold season, winter.

හිමාද්‍රි, *Himádri*, see හිමාලය *himálaya*.

හිමාරි, *Himári*, s. (හිම *hima* cold, අරි *ari* enemy) fire, [Colloq. ගිනි *gini*]; sun, [Colloq. ඉර *ira*].

හිමාලපර්වත, *Himála-parwata*, } s. (හිම *hima* cold, **හිමාලය**, *Himálaya*, } frost, snow, අලය *álaya* abode) Himálaya range of mountains, which bounds India on the north and separates it from Tartary, (the Imaus and Emodus of the ancients,) giving rise to the Ganges, the Indus, Brahmaputra, etc.

හිමාලයා, *Himálayá*, s. medicinal plant, [Colloq. තලිස්පතුරු *talispaturu*].

හිමාවතී, *Himáwatí*, s. plant, according to some a sort of moon plant brought from the Himálaya; or *cambogia stalagmoides*.

හිමාහ්වා, *Himáhwa*, s. (හිම *hima* cold, ආහ්වා *áhwá* appellation) camphor, [Colloq. කපුරු *kapuru*].

හිමි, *Himi*, s. lord, master, owner: *a.* possessing, as proprietor, from ස්වාමි *swámi*.

හිමිකම, *Himikama*, s. ownership, possession, proprietorship.

හිමිකරණවා, *Himikaraṇawá*, v. to put in possession, to give a Billet.

හිමිකාරයා, *Himikárayá*, s. owner, proprietor: pl. හිමිකාරයෝ *himikárayó*.

හිමිකෙරුවා, *Himikeruwá*, past tense of හිමිකරණවා *himikaraṇawá*.

හිමියා, *Himiyá*, see හිමි *himi*.

හිමිවෙනවා, *Himiwenawá*, v. to inherit, become owner: pret. හිමිවුනා *himiwuná*.

හිමෙලු, *Himélu*, a. (හිම *hima* cold, එලු *elu* aff.) suffering from cold, chilly, frozen.

හිය, *Hiya*, s. an arrow.

හියවුර, *Hiyawura*, s. (හිය and වුර for උර *ura* receptacle) an archer's quiver.

හියාරණවා, *Hiyáraṇawá*, v. to fold, to wrap round, causal form of හියැරෙණවා *hiyẹreṇawá*: pret. හියැරුවා *hiyẹruwá*.

හියොර, *Hiyora*, see හියවුර *hiyawura*.

හියැරෙණවා, *Hiyẹreṇawá*, v. to diffuse, to pervade: pret. හියැරුණා *hiyẹruṇá*.

හිර, *Hira*, s. imprisonment, confinement, incarceration; prisoner: a. tight, confined, imprisoned, also written සිර *sira:* see ඉර *ira*.

හිරකරණවා, *Hirakaraṇawá*, v. to imprison, to tighten, to block up.

හිරකාරයා, *Hirakárayá*, s. prisoner: pl. හිරකාරයෝ *hirakárayó*.

හිරකෙරීම, *Hirakeríma*, s. act of confining in prison; blocking up.

හිරගලාවැටෙනවා, *Hira-galáwẹṭenawá*, v. to set, to descend, as the sun.

හිරගෙය, *Hirageya*, } s. (හිර and ගෙය house)
හිරගේ, *Hiragé*, } prison, jail.

හිරගේණවා, *Hiragéṇawá*, v. to bring a woman, as a wife; to wed.

හිරණ්‍ය, *Hiraṇya*, s. gold, [Colloq. රත්රන් *ratran*]; either of the precious metals, crude bullion, unwrought gold or silver; wealth, property.

හිරණ්‍යගර්භ, *Hiraṇya-garbha*, s. (හිරණ්‍ය and ගර්භ embroy) name of Brahma.

හිරණ්‍යද, *Hiraṇyada*, s. (හිරණ්‍ය and ද what gives) ocean, [Colloq. මහමූද *mahamúda*].

හිරණ්‍යදා, *Hiraṇyadá*, s. the earth, [Colloq. පොළව *poḷawa*].

හිරණ්‍යපුෂ්පි, *Hiraṇya-pushpi*, s. (හිරණ්‍ය and පුෂ්ප *pushpa* flower) plant variety of *basella alba*, [Colloq. නිවිති *niviti*]; kind of yam, [Colloq. ඌරල *úrala*].

හිරණ්‍යරේතා, *Hiraṇya-rétá*, s. (හිරණ්‍ය gold, රේතස් *rétas* semen) fire, [Colloq. ගින්දර *gindara*].

හිරබිම, *Hira-bima*, s. (හිර and බිම ground) strait or confined place; place of confinement.

හිරමඬල, *Hiramaṇḍala*, s. (හිර and මඬල disc) sun's disc.

හිරමණය, *Hiramaṇaya*, s. coconut scraper: pl. හිරමණ *hiramaṇá*.

හිරමණතලේ, *Hiramaṇá-talé*, s. blade of the coconut scraper.

හිරමණදැත්ත, *Hiramaṇá-dẹtta*, s. (හිරමණ *hiramaṇa* and දැත්ත tooth) plant, *zapania nodiflora*.

හිරමණේ, *Hiramaṇé*, see හිරමණය *hiramaṇaya*.

හිරවරණ, *Hirawaraṇa*, s. (හිර sun, අවරණ *awaraṇa* defending, screening) umbrella, [Colloq. කුඩේ *kuḍé*].

හිරවෙනවා, *Hirawenawá*, v. to be confined, to be straitened through want of room: pret. හිරවුනා *hirawuná*.

හිරි, *Hiri*, s. line, stroke; partial palsy, numbness or sleep of a limb; shame, confusion: a. benumbed.

හිරිඅංකුට්ටා, *Hiri-aṅkuṭṭá*, s. kind of fish.

හිරික්කේඩුව, *Hirikkéḍuwa*, s. weariness, fatigue, lassitude.

හිරිකඩ, *Hirikaḍa*, s. spray.

හිරිකඩගහනවා, *Hirikaḍa-gahanawá*, v. to fall in spray.

හිරිකිත, *Hirikita*, s. unpleasant feeling caused by dirt or filth in any place one has to walk over.

හිරිගතිය, *Hirigatiya*, s. numbness.

හිරිගල්, *Hiri-gal*, s. coral or lime stone.

හිරිතල, *Hiritala*, s. (හිරිත් *hirit* and අල *ala* root) species of yam, produced in the jungle, *dioscorea oppositifolia (Dioscoraceæ)*.

හිරිබෙන, *Hiribena*, see හ්‍රීවේර *hriwéra*.

හිරිමල, *Hirimala*, s. unripe or tender, applied to certain fruits and vegetables, as කජු හිරිමල *kaju-hirimala*, tender cashew nut, කෙසෙල් හිරිමල *kesel-hirimala*, tender or unripe plantain.

හිරියල්, *Hiriyal*, s. yellow orpiment; Elu form of හරිතාල *haritála*.

හිරිවේරිය, *Hiriwériya*, see හ්‍රීවේර *hriwéra*.

හිරිවැටෙනවා, *Hiriwẹṭenawá*, v. (හිරි numbness, etc. වැටෙනවා to fall) to fall asleep, to become numb, as a limb; to be on edge, as the teeth.

හිරිහැර, *Hirihẹra*, s. wrong, oppression, tyranny, annoyance: a. troublesome, tedious.

හිරිහැරකරණවා, *Hirihẹrakaraṇawá*, v. to oppress, trouble, to teaze.

හිරු, *Hiru*, s. sun, [Colloq. ඉර *ira*]; line, row; swallow-wort or mudar, *calotropis gigantea*, [Colloq. වරා *wará*].

හිරුතෙනේ, *Hirutené*, s. (හිරු and තනේ son) planet Saturn, [Colloq. සෙනසුරා *senasurá*].

හිරුපිත්, *Hiru-pit*, s. (හිරු and පිත් son) name of Yama, [Colloq. යමරජ *yama-raja*].

හිරුපුත්, *Hiru-put*, see හිරුතෙනේ *hirutené*.

හිල්, *Hil*, plural of හිල *hila*.

හිල්කරණවා, *Hilkaraṇawá*, *v.* to make a hole, to bore, to tap.

හිල්කෙරීම, *Hilkerima*, *s.* act of boring, tapping, piercing.

හිල, *Hila*, *s.* a hole through, perforation: see සිල *sila*.

හිලමෝචි, *Hilamóchi*, } *s.* plant, *Hingtsha*
හිලමෝචිකා, *Hilamóchiká*, } *repens*.

හිලව්කරණවා, *Hilawkaraṇawá*, *v.* to deduct one account from another in balancing, to liquidate, to adjust an account.

හිලව්කෙරීම, *Hilawkerima*, *s.* verbal noun of හිලව්කරණවා *hilawkaraṇawá*.

හිලව්ව, *Hilawwa*, *s.* deduction: *ind.* in lieu, in the place of, instead of.

හිලව්වෙනවා, *Hilawwenawá*, *v.* to be deducted: pret. හිලව්වුනා *hilawwuná*.

හිලවුව, *Hilawuwa*, *s.* substitute: pl. හිලවු *hilawu*.

හිලා, *Hilá*, *s.* oyster, [Colloq. බෙල්ලා *bellá*].

හිවනවා, *Hiwanawá*, *v.* to cover, to shade, to shelter; to twine, to entwist: pret. හිවුවා *hiwuwá*.

හිවලා, *Hiwalá*, *s.* jackal, *canis aureus*, [Colloq. නරියා *nariyá*].

හිවි, *Hivi*, *a.* high, tall, [Colloq. උස්වූ *uswú*].

හිවිගෑවසි, *Hivi-gęwasi*, *a.* entwined, entwisted, interwoven.

හිස්, *His*, *a.* empty, vacant, void, unoccupied: see සිස් *sis*.

හිස්කබල, *Hiskabala*, *s.* (හිස *hisa* and කබල skull) skull, cranium.

හිස්කම, *Hiskama*, *s.* emptiness, vacancy: pl. හිස්කම් *hiskam*.

හිස්කරණවා, *Hiskaraṇawá*, *v.* to empty, to make void.

හිස්කසු, *Hiskasu*, *s.* yoke of a cart.

හිස්කෙරීම, *Hiskerima*, verbal noun of හිස්කරණවා *hiskaraṇawá*.

හිස්පිඩු, *His-piḍu*, *s.* temples or frontals of an elephant.

හිස්බිජු, *Hisbiju*, see බට්ටා *baṭṭá*.

හිස, *Hisa*, *s.* head, from ශීර්ෂ *śirsha;* also, written ඉස *isa*.

හිසරුජාව, *Hisa-rujáwa*, *s.* (හිස and රුජා *rujá* ache) disease or pain of the head, head-ache.

හිහි, *Hihi*, *s.* height, altitude, [Colloq. උසස්කම *usaskama*].

හී, *Hí*, *s.* arrow: *ind.* being able: see හැකි *hęki*.

හීකොපුව, *Hí-kopuwa*, *s.* case or sheath for arrows.

හීගස, *Hígasa*, } *s.* arrow, also, ඊගස *ígasa*.
හීගහ, *Hígaha*, }

හීත, *Híta*, *s.* cold season (winter) coldness: see සීත *sita*.

හීතණ, *Hítaṇa*, *s.* (හිය *hiya* arrow, තණ grass) sort of grass, *heteropogon hirtus (Gramineæ)*; also called ඊතණ *itaṇa*.

හීතල, *Hítala*, *s.* (හිය *hiya* and තල blade) the blade of an arrow.

හීන්, *Hín*, *a.* thin, small, fine; also, written සීන් *sín*.

හීන් අක්මැල්ල, *Hín-akmęlla*, *s.* plant, *spilanthes pseudoacmella*.

හීන් අඳර, *Hín-andara*, *s.* tree, variety of *dichrostachys cinerea*.

හීන් අනෝදා, *Hín-anódá*, *s.* plant, variety of *abutilon asiaticum*.

හීන් අරමැස්ස, *Hín-aramęssa*, *s.* plant, *hoya pauciflora*.

හීන් අවරි, *Hín-awari*, *s.* plant, species of *indigofera*.

හීන් ඇත්අඩිය, *Hín-ętaḍiya*, *s.* plant, *elytraria lyrata*.

හීන් ඇපල, *Hín-ępala*, *s.* hairy plant, the bark yielding fibre, *urena sinuata (Malvaceæ)*.

හීන් ඇඹල, *Hín-ęmbala*, *s.* buck wheat, *menyanthes cristata*.

හීන් ඇඹිල්ල, *Hín-ęmbilla*, *s.* small tree, peculiar to Ceylon, *antidesma alexiteria (Euphorbiaceæ)*.

හීන් ඇඹුලැඹිලිය, *Hín-ęmbulęmbiliya*, *s.* wood sorrel, *oxalis corniculata (Geraniaceæ)*.

හීන් ඇඳුරු, *Hín-ęnduru*, *s.* dill, *anethum graveolens*.

හීන් ඉකිරි, *Hín-ikiri*, *s.* plant, variety of *accanthus ilicifolius*.

හීන් ඉත්තවැල, *Hín-ittawęla*, *s.* sort of ivy, plant peculiar to Ceylon, *heptapleurum* or *hedera emarginatum*.

හීන් ඉද්ද, *Hín-idda*, *s.* plant, species of *wrightia*.

හීන් ඉඳි, *Hín-indi*, *s.* (හීන් small, ඉඳි date) species of the date palm tree, almost stemless, *phœnix farinifera*.

හීන් ඉරමසු, *Hín-iramasu*, *s.* variety of Indian sarsaparilla, *hemidesmus indicus*.

හීන් ඊරිය, *Hín-íriya*, *s.* species of nutmeg, *myristica salisifolia*.

හීන් උඳුපියලි, *Hín-undupiyali*, *s.* creeping plant with ternate leaves and jointed legumes, *desmodium triflorum (Leguminosæ)*.

හින් එන්සාල්, *Hín-ensál*, *s.* small cardamoms, *elettaria cardamomum.*

හින් එරමිණියා, *Hín-eramiṇiyá*, *s.* thorny shrub with minute flowers, *zizyphus œnoplia (Rhamnaceæ).*

හින් එල බලල්තණ, *Hín-ela-baḷaltaṇa*, *s.* species of grass, *poa tenella.*

හින් එල වල්තණ, *Hín-ela-waltaṇa*, *s.* species of grass.

හින් එලවැල්ල, *Hín-elawella*, *s.* kind of reed, variety of *calamus viralis.*

හින් කටිල්ලා, *Hín-kaṭillá*, *s.* kind of fish.

හින් කටුපිල, *Hín-kaṭupila*, *s.* thorny shrub, *fluggea leucopyrus (Euphorbiaceæ).*

හින් කඩොල්, *Hín-kaḍol*, *s.* small tree growing near the sea. *ægiceris majus (Myrsineæ).*

හින් කපුරු, *Hín-kapuru*, *s.* (හින් small, කපුරු camphor) species of valerian, *valeriana villosa.*

හින් කබරස්ස, *Hín-kabarassa*, *s.* flowering plant, *smilax zeylanica (Liliaceæ).*

හින්කරණවා, *Hínkaraṇawá*, *v.* to make thin, fine, or small.

හින් කරඹ, *Hín-karamba*, *s.* shrub producing berries, *carissa spinarum (Apocynaceæ).*

හින් කලවැල්, *Hín-kalawel*, *s.* creeping plant, variety of *derris scandens.*

හින් කලාඳුරු, *Hín-kaláṉduru*, *s.* plant, variety of *cyperus rotundus.*

හින් කලුවාල, *Hín-kaluwála*, *s.* plant, variety of *alpinia galanga.*

හින් කවුඩුදල, *Hín-kawuḍudala*, *s.* plant, *oldenlendia biflora*

හින් කහඹිලියා, *Hín-kahaṃbiliyá*, *s.* plant, species of *fluerya* or *girardinia.*

හින් කිඹු, *Hín-kimbu*, *s.* plant, *cotula minima.*

හින් කිරිඳි, *Hín-kiriṉdi*, *s.* plant, species of *rourea* or *coix.*

හින් කිරිවැල, *Hín-kiriwela*, *s.* plant, variety of *ichnocarpus frutescens.*

හින් කුඩුමැට්ට, *Hín-kuḍumeṭṭa*, *s.* plant, *ischænum aristatum.*

හින් කුරුළුතණ, *Hín-kuruḷutaṇa*, *s.* mullet grass, *milium ramosum.*

හින් කූඩලු, *Hín-kúḍalu*, *s.* plant, species of *impatiens.*

හින් කෙයියා, *Hín-keyiyá*, *s.* species of screw pine, *pandanus pumila.*

හින්කෙරීම, *Hínkeríma*, verbal noun of හින්කරණවා *hínkaraṇawá.*

හින්කෙරුවා, *Hínkeruwá*, *pret.* of හින්කරණවා *hínkaraṇawá.*

හින් කොක්මොට, *Hín-kokmoṭa*, *s.* plant, pipe wort variety of *eriocaulon quinquangulare.*

හින් කොතලා, *Hín-kotalá*, *s.* plant, variety of *torenia asiatica.*

හින් කොන්ටේරු, *Hín-kontéru*, *s.* plant, *digitaria longifolia.*

හින්කොල ගැටපන්, *Hínkola-geṭapan*, *s.* club rush *scirpus pigmæus.*

හින් කොහොඹ, *Hín-kohoṃba*, *s.* small tree, variety of *azadirachta indica.*

හින් කැකිරි, *Hín-kekiri*, *s.* kind of cucumber *mukia scabrella (Cucurbitaceæ).*

හින් කැබෙල්ල, *Hín-kebella*, *s.* plant, *aporosa lanceolata (Euphorbiaceæ).*

හින් කැරැව්, *Hín-kerew*, *s.* plant with three-sided culms or stems, *scleria lævis (Cyperaceæ).*

හින් ගල්කූර, *Hín-galkúra*, *s.* plant, *melochia corchorifolia.*

හින් ගිරාපලා, *Hín-girápalá*, *s.* plant, variety of *commelina clavata.*

හින් ගෙඳකොල, *Hín-geṉdakola*, *s.* sort of purslane *portuluca quadrifida (Portuculaceæ).*

හින් ගෙරිඬුට, *Hín-gerieṭa*, *s.* plant, variety of *linociera purpurea.*

හින් ගොකටු, *Hín-gokaṭu*, see ගොකටු *gokaṭu.*

හින් ගොටුකොල, *Hín-goṭukola*, *s.* pennywort, *hydrocotyle asiatica (Umbelliferæ).*

හින් ගොයිවැල්, *Hín-goyiwel*, *s.* creeper, variety of *flagellaria indica.*

හින් ගොරඩිය, *Hín-goraḍiya*, *s.* twining plant, with legumes and yellow flowers, *cylista tomemtosa.*

හින් ගැටකොල, *Hín-geṭakola*, *s.* plant, variety of *hedyotis auricularia.*

හින් ගැටපන්, *Hín-geṭapan*, *s.* sort of club rush *scirpus atropurpureus.*

හින්ගැටියා, *Híngeṭiyá*, see බූගැටියා *búgeṭiyá.*

හින් තක්කඩ, *Hín-takkaḍa*, *s.* shrub with white one-petalled flowers, *scævola Lobelia (Goodenoviaceæ).*

හින් තඹල, *Hín-taṃbala*, *s.* shrub or small tree with white flowers and red berries, *ehretia buxifolia (Boragineæ).*

හින් තම්පලා, *Hín-tampalá*, *s.* (හින් small, තම්පලා amaranth) plant, variety of *nothosærua brachiala.*

හින් තලා, *Hín-talá*, *s.* species of basil, *ocimum canum (Labiatæ).*

හින්තාල, *Híntála*, see හින්තාල *hintála*.

හින් තිඹිරි, *Hín-timbiri*, *s.* species of *diospyros*.

හින් තෙලිකාපලා, *Hín-teliká-palá*, *s.* annual plant, *pharnaceum mollugo*.

හින් තොලබෝ, *Hín-tolabó*, *s.* plant, variety of *crinum asiaticum*.

හින් තෝවැල්ල, *Hín-tówęlla*, *s.* creeper or clasping plant, *vitis* or *cissus repanda*.

හින් තැඹිලිය, *Hín-tęmbiliya*, *s.* plant, variety of *eugenia bracteata*.

හින් දං, *Hín-dan*, *s.* tree, peculiar to Ceylon, *eugenia caryophyllæa (Myrtaceæ)*.

හින් දත්කැටියා, *Hín-datkętiyá*, *s.* plant, variety of *pittosporum zeylanicum*.

හින් දියජවාල, *Hín-diya-jáwála*, *s.* plant, *burmannia trifolia*.

හින් දියසියඹලා, *Hín-diya-siyambalá*, *s.* tree, variety of *æschynomene indica*.

හින් දිවිඅඩිය, *Hín-diviadiya*, *s.* plant: see දිවිපහුරු *divipahuru*.

හින් දුමුඩා, *Hín-dumudá*, *s.* sort of bindweed, *convolvulus nervosus*.

හින් දෙබර, *Hín-debara*, *s.* tree, not ascertained.

හින් දෙහි, *Hín-dehi*, *s.* (හින් small, දෙහි lime) species of lime, *citrus acida*.

හින් දොඩම්පනා, *Hín-dodampaná*, *s.* plant, variety of *glycosmis longifolia*.

හින්දෑරි, *Hindéri*, *a.* lean, thin, emaciated.

හින් නාපිරිත්ත, *Hín-nápiritta*, *s.* shrub, *hibiscus surratensis (Malvaceæ)*.

හින් නාරං, *Hín-náran*, *s.* (හින් small, නාරං citrus nobilis) variety of the mandarin orange, *citrus nobilis*.

හින් නියදඬු, *Hín-niyadandu*, *s.* plant, *amomum villosum*.

හින් නිල්වැල්ල, *Hín-nilwęlla*, *s.* plant, not ascertained.

හින් නෙළු, *Hín-nelu*, *s.* plant, species of *strobilanthes*.

හින් නෙළුම්, *Hín-nelum*, *s.* species of lotus, *nelumbium*.

හින් පට්ටාඇපල, *Hín-pattá-ępala*, *s.* plant, variety of *urena lobata*.

හින් පත්කුරුඳු, *Hín-patkurundu*, *s.* species of cinnamon, *cinnamomum*.

හින් පත්මයා, *Hín-patmayá*, *s.* plant, not ascertained.

හින් පනාඩෑත්ත, *Hín-panádętta*, *s.* plant, not ascertained.

හින් පඹ, *Hín-pamba*, *s.* (හින් small) fern, *lygodium flexuosum (Filices)*.

හින් පිනිබරුතණ, *Hín-pinibaru-tana*, *s.* kind of grass, variety of *anthistiria tremula*.

හින් පිහිඹිය, *Hín-pihimbiya*, *s.* tree, not ascertained.

හින් පුස්වැල *Hín-puswęla*, *s.* creeping plant, variety of *entada scandens*.

හින් පේර, *Hín-péra*, *s.* guava tree, variety of *psidium guyava*.

හින් පොතුකොල, *Hín-potukola*, *s.* kind of rush, variety of *scleria oryzoides*.

හින් පෝටෑ, *Hín-póté*, *s.* creeping plant, species of *pothos scandens*.

හින් බදුල්ල, *Hín-badulla*, *s.* tree, peculiar to Ceylon, *semicarpus parvifolia (Anacardiaceæ)*.

හින් බිංකොහොඹ, *Hín-binkohomba*, *s.* plant, *andrographis paniculata (Acanthaceæ)*.

හින් බින්තල්, *Hín-bintal*, *s.* plant, with yellow flowers, *curculigo orchioides (Amaryllideæ)*.

හින් බොරුපන්, *Hín-borupan*, *s.* club-rush, variety of *heleocharis plantaginea*.

හින් බෝවිටියා, *Hín-bóritiyá*, *s.* flowering plant, *osbeckia octandra (Melastomaceæ)*.

හින් මකුළු, *Hín-makulu*, *s.* plant, variety of *hydnocarpus venenata*.

හින් මදු, *Hín-madu*, *s.* annual plant, with sagittate three-toothed leaves, *ipomœa tridentata (Convolvulaceæ)*; also called හවරිමදු *hawarimadu*.

හින් මාරා, *Hín-márá*, *s.* tree, variety of *albizzia lebek*.

හින් මාරිය, *Hín-máriya*, *s.* tree, not ascertained.

හින් මාරුකු, *Hín-máruku*, *s.* sort of grass.

හින් මිදි, *Hín-midi*, *s.* (හින් small, මිදි premna) tree, variety of *premna serratifolia*.

හින් මිරිස්, *Hín-miris*, *s.* species of chillies, *capsicum*.

හින් මුඩමහණ, *Hín-mudamahana*, *s.* (හින් small, මුඩමහණ name of plant) plant, *epaltes divaricata (Compositæ)*.

හින් මූදුගැටකොල, *Hín-múdu-gętakola*, *s.* plant, variety of *hydrophylax maritima*.

හින් මූදුගැටපන්, *Hín-múdu-gętapan*, *s.* species of club rush, *scirpus*.

හින් මොට්ටු, *Hín-mottu*, *s.* winter cherry, *physalis minima*.

හින් මොනරකුඩිම්බිය, *Hín-monarakudimbiya*, *s.* plant, variety of *vernonia cinerea*.

හින් මොනරපෙතන්, *Hín-monarapetan*, *s.* plant, variety of *dianella ensifolia*.

හින් මෑ, *Hín-mé*, *s.* (හින් small) sort of bean, species of *dolichos* or *phaseolus*.

හින් යක්වනස්ස, *Hín-yakwanassa*, *s.* variety of *anisomeles ovata*.

හින් යොතුවැන්න, *Hín-yotuwenna*, *s.* the violet, *viola enneasperma*.

හින් රටඑලමල්, *Hín-rața-elamal*, *s.* plant, variety of *hedychium gracile*.

හින් රටපඹ, *Hín-rațapamba*, *s.* species of fern, *lygodium*.

හින් රටබටු, *Hín-rațabațu*, *s.* plant, species of *solanum*.

හින් රතු වල්ඉඟුරු, *Hín-ratu-walinguru*, *s.* variety of ginger, *zingiber cylindricum*.

හින් රවනරැවුල, *Hín-rawanarewula*, *s.* plant, species of *spinifex*.

හින් රිල්ල, *Hín-rilla*, *s.* plant, not ascertained.

හින් වල්ඉඟුරු, *Hín-walinguru*, *s.* variety of ginger, *zingiber cylindricum*.

හින් වල්කොල්ලු, *Hín-walkollu*, *s.* sort of gram or pea, variety of *atylosia rugosa*.

හින් වල්මාරුකු, *Hín-walmáruku*, *s.* sort of panic grass, *panicum flavidum*.

හින් විල්නානු, *Hín-vilnánu*, *s.* plant, not ascertained.

හින් විල, *Hín-vila*, *s.* plant, variety of *bonnaya veronicæfolia*.

හින් වෙල් ඇත්කලාඳුරු, *Hín-wel-etkalánduru*, *s.* variety of cyperus, *cyperus pygmæus*, or of *c. kyllingaoides*.

හින් වෙල්කාවුළු, *Hín-welkáwulu*, *s.* variety of balsam, *impatiens oppositifolia*.

හින් වේවැල, *Hín-wéwela*, *s.* (හින් small, වේවැල cane) the rattan or cane, variety of *calamus Roxburghii*.

හින් වැල්ගැටපන්, *Hín-welgetapan*, *s.* species of club rush, *scirpus squarrosus*.

හින් වැලිදං, *Hín-welidan*, *s.* plant, variety of *eugenia caryophyllæa*.

හින් වැලිහතු, *Hín-welihatu*, *s.* sort of mushroom.

හින් සාරණ, *Hín-sárana*, *s.* plant, *trianthema monogyna (Ficoideæ)*.

හින් සේරු, *Hín-séru*, *s.* plant, *webera internodis*.

හින් හබරලිය, *Hín-habaraliya*, *s.* plant, species of *colocasia*.

හින් හවරි, *Hín-hawari*, *v.* plant, perhaps species of *ipomæa*.

හින් හාල්පන්, *Hín-hálpan*, *s.* club rush, species of *fimbristylis*.

හින් හිඹුටුවැල්, *Hín-himbutuwel*, *s.* (හින් *hín* small) creeping plant, *salacia prinoides (Celastraceæ)*.

හින් හැඩයා, *Hín-hedayá*, *s.* plant, variety of *lycopodium hookeri*.

හින් හැඩවක, *Hín-hedawaka*, *s.* tree, species of *chætocarpus*.

හීන, *Hína*, *a.* (හා *há* to quit, ක්ත *kta* aff.) deficient, defective; blameable, bad, vile: left, abandoned, quitted: wasted, worn, decayed.

හීනකරණවා, *Hínakaranawá*, *v.* to make deficient.

හීනවෙනවා, *Hínawenawá*, *v.* to become deficient, to decline.

හීනජාතිය, *Hínajátiya*, *s.* (හීන vile, ජාති *játi* caste) outcast, vile or degraded class or tribe.

හීනටි, *Hínați*, *s.* (හින් *hín* small, ඇට *eta* grain) species of fine paddy, variety of *oryza sativa*.

හීනටි ඇල්වී, *Hínați-elví*, *s.* kind of hill paddy, *oryza sativa*.

හීනදකිනවා *Hína-dakinawá*, *v.* to dream.

හීනය, *Hínaya*, *s.* dream: pl. හීන *hína*: see සින *sina*.

හීනවාදී, *Hínawádí*, *a.* (හීන left, defective, වාද *wáda* speech, ඉනි *ini* aff.) dumb, speechless.

හීනසේවා, *Hína-séwá*, *s.* association with low persons.

හීනාඞ්ග, *Hínáńga*, *a.* crippled, maimed, defective.

හීනාශය, *Hínásaya*, *s.* (හීන *hína* vile, ආශය *ásaya* purpose) sordidness, baseness.

හීම, *Híma*, *s.* tree, yielding light wood used for catamarans, *gyrocarpus jacquini (Combretaceæ)*.

හීමාපවුර, *Hímápawura*, *s.* stone fence or boundary wall surrounding a field.

හීමාව, *Hímáwa*, *s.* limit, boundary: see සීමා *símá*.

හීය, *Híya*, *s.* arrow; plough, ploughing.

හීර, *Híra*, } *s.* (හෘ *hara* to take. ඊර *íra* aff.)
හීරක, *Híraka*, } diamond, [Colloq. දියමන්ති *diyamanti*]; the vajra or thunderbolt of Indra.

හීරලුවා, *Híraluwá*, *s.* apostate from the Buddhist priesthood; one who has put away his priestly robes.

හීරික, *Hírika*, see හීර *híra*.

හිරිමාංස, *Hírimánsa*, *s.* (හිරි blood, from රුධිර *rudhira*, රුහිර *ruhira*, හුරිර *hurira*, හුරි *huri* හිරි *hiri* and මාංස flesh) blood and flesh, flesh with blood.

හීරි, *Hírí*, *s.* sow, also written ඊරි *íri*.

හිරෙණවා, *Hírenawá*, *v.* to be scratched: pret. හිරුණ *híruná*.

හිරැස්ස, *Hirẹssa. s.* climbing plant, with four winged stems, edible when tender, and with red berries. *vitis* (or *cissus*) *quadrangularis (Ampelideæ);* also written සිව්රැස්ස *siwrẹssa.*

හිල්, *Hil*, see හිල *hila.*

හිල්බත්, *Hil-bat, s.* (හිල් cold, බත් boiled rice, food) rice prepared over-night and eaten cold, morning food.

හිල, *Hila, s.* cold, coldness, frigidity: pl. හිල් *hil.*

හිලෑ, *Hilẹ, a.* tame, docile.

හිලෑකරණවා, *Hilẹkaraṇawá, v.* to tame.

හිලෑකෙරීම, *Hilẹkeríma, s.* act of taming.

හිවිට, *Hiviṭa, s.* (හිය *hiya* plough, විට mark) furrow.

හිවුර, *Hiwura, s.* quiver.

හිවැල, *Hiwẹla, s.* (හිය *hiya* and වැල creeper) coulter of a plough.

හිස්සා, *Hissá*, corruptly for හිංසා *hinsá.*

හිස්සාකරණවා, *Hissákaraṇawá, v.* to trouble, to torment, to tease.

හිස්සාකෙරීම, *Hissákeríma, s.* tormenting, troubling, teasing.

හිහානවා *Hihánawá, v.* to plough.

හුංගා, *Hungá, s.* small sort of prickly fish found in rivers: pl. හුංගෝ *hungó.*

හුඟ, *Hunga, s.* much, many, abundance, considerable quantity, collection; also written සුඟ *sunga.*

හුඟක්, *Hungak, s.* a great deal, a considerable quantity.

හුඟු, *Hungu, ind.* particle or adverb signifying haste, speedily, rapidly.

හුණ්ඩුව, *Huṇḍuwa, s.* corn measure = ¼ quart: pl. හුණ්ඩු *huṇḍu.*

හුණගස, *Huṇa-gasa, s.* bamboo tree, *bambusa vulgaris;* also called උණ *uṇa.*

හුණමකුළු, *Huṇamakuḷu, s.* (හුණ bamboo, මකුළු manna) an earthy concretion of a milkwhite colour formed in the tube of the bamboo, called bamboo manna.

හුණු, *Huṇu, s.* lime, chunam: *a.* fallen; see also සුනු *sunu.*

හුණුකිරිල්ල, *Huṇukirilla, s.* plant, *phyllanthus zeylanicus (Euphorbiaceæ).*

හුණුකැටියවැල්, *Huṇukẹṭiya-wẹl, s.* twining plant with peltate leaves, *stephania.*

හුණුගානවා, *Huṇugánawá, v.* to daub with chunam, to white wash.

හුණු බදම, *Huṇu-badáma, s.* mortar, plaster.

හුණු හැන්ද, *Huṇu-hẹnda, s.* a trowel.

හුත, *Huta, s.* (හු to sacrifice, ක්ත *kta* aff.) sacrifice, [Colloq. යාගය *yágaya*]: *a.* offered with fire, burnt as an oblation.

හුතභුජ්, *Hutabhuj, s.* (හුත oblation, භුජ් who eats) Agṇi, the god of fire.

හුතස්, *Hutas*, see හුතාශ, *hutáṣa.*

හුතසන, *Hutasana*, see හුතාශන *hutáṣana.*

හුතාශ, *Hutáṣa, s.* (හුත *huta* and අශ *aṣa* who eats) fire or its deity.

හුතාශන, *Hutáṣana, s.* (හුත *huta* and අශන *aṣana* food) fire, [Colloq. ගිනි *gini*].

හුතැස්, *Hutẹs, s.* fire.

හුතැස්යොන්, *Hutẹsyon, s.* (හුතැස් fire. යොන් place of production) name of Kataragama-deviyó, god of war, in allusion to the fable of his birth from the fire into which Ṣiva had cast his semen.

හුතැස, *Hutẹsa*, Elu form of හුතාශ *hutáṣa.*

හුද, *Huda, s.* white colour: *ind.* particle implying speed, hastily, quickly.

හුදකලාව, *Hudakaláwa, a.* alone, [Colloq. තනියම *taniyama*].

හුදී, *Hudí*, } *s.* virtuous or excellent man,
හුදීසත්, *Hudísat*, } [Colloq. සත්පුරුෂයා *satpurushayá*].

හුදු, *Hudu*, see සුදු *sudu.*

හුන්, *Hun, a.* been, seated.

හුන්නා, *Hunná, s.* man of the lime burner's caste: pl. හුන්නෝ *hunnó.*

හුන, *Huna, s.* sacrifice.

හුනග, *Hunaga, s.* species of fig-tree, *ficus oppositifolia;* also called කොටදිඹුලා *koṭadimbulá.*

හුනත්, *Hunat, a.* expended, consumed, finished: see සුනත් *sunat.*

හුනත්කරණවා, *Hunatkaraṇawá, v.* to ruin, to destroy.

හුනනවා, *Hunanawá*, see උනනවා *unanawá.*

හුනු, *Hunu, s.* sharpness, falling, hearing.

හුඹස්මැටි, *Humbas-mẹṭi, s.* clay of the white ants' hill.

හුඹස, *Humbasa*, } *s.* white ants' hill: pl. හුඹස්
හුඹහ, *Humbaha*, } *humbas.*

හුය, *Huya, s.* thread.

හුයනවා, *Huyanawá, v.* to decorticate, to peel.

හුයින්, *Huyin, s.* (auxiliary case of හූ *hú* thread) with thread.

හුරතල්, *Huratal, a.* fondled; fond, childish.

හුරිරු, *Huriru, s.* blood, [Colloq. ලේ *lé*]: see උරිරු *uriru.*

හුරිරුපා, *Hurirupá,* } *s.* (හුරිරු blood, පා or පු who
හුරිරුපු, *Hurirupu,* } drinks) goblin, sprite or demon haunting cemeteries, etc.

හුරු, *Huru, a.* right-handed, dexterous, apt.

හුරු අත, *Huru-ata, s.* right-hand, hand which one has been accustomed to use.

හුරුකන්ඳු, *Hurukandu, s.* plant peculiar to Ceylon, *kurrimia zeylanica, (Celastraceæ);* also called පෙලං *pelaŋ* and ඇත්හෙරලිය *ętheraliya.*

හුරුකම, *Hurukama, s.* dexterity, handiness.

හුරුබුහුටි, *Hurubuhuṭi, a.* well-made, well-proportioned, bold, daring.

හුරුල්ල, *Hurulla, s.* two palmsful of betel, offered to a superior: pl. හුරුලු *hurulu.*

හුරුල්ලා, *Hurullá, s.* kind of sea fish, similar to the herring: pl. හුරුල්ලෝ *hurulló.*

හුල්, *Hul, s.* chief of a degraded tribe; omen, portent; air, wind, breeze: see උල් *ul.*

හුල, *Hula, s.* pike, dart, iron pin or spit, pl. හුල් *hul*: see සුල *sula.*

හුලං ඉද්ද, *Hulaŋ-idda, s.* plant, perhaps variety of *Wrightea zeylanica.*

හුලංකිරිය, *Hulaŋkiriya, s.* plant, species of arrow-root, peculiar to Ceylon, *phrynium zeylanicum* or *maranta spicata (Scitamineæ).*

හුලංගහනවා, *Hulaŋgahanawá, v.* to blow as the wind.

හුලංතලා, *Hulaŋtalá, s.* goat weed or white weed, *ageratum conyzoides (Compositæ).*

හුලං මාරා, *Hulaŋ-márá, s.* tree, *albizzia stipulata (Leguminosæ);* also called කබල්මාරා *kabalmárá.*

හුලංසැරේ, *Hulaŋseré, s.* force of the wind.

හුලංහික්, *Hulaŋhik, s.* tree producing fine timber, *chickrassia tabularis (Meliaceæ).*

හුලඟ, *Hulaŋga, s.* wind.

හුලඟිල්ල, *Hulaŋgilla, s.* the little finger.

හුලවාලියා, *Hulawáliyá, s.* headman of the Rodiyas.

හුලහ, *Hulaha, s.* point, extremity, edge: pl. හුලස් *hulas: a.* aside, out of the way.

හුලිජ්ජ, *Hulijja, s.* urine.

හුලිජ්ජ බොක්ක, *Hulijja-bokka, s.* the bladder.

හුවමාරු, *Huwamáru, s.* barter, exchange, traffic.

හුවමාරුකරණවා, *Huwamárukaraṇawá, v.* to exchange, to barter.

හුවමාරුව, *Huwamáruwa, s.* exchange, barter, reciprocity.

හුස්ම, *Husma, s.* breath, breathing.

හුස්ම අරිණවා, *Husma-ariṇawá, v.* to respire, to breathe.

හුස්මගන්නවා, *Husmagannawá, v.* to draw into the lungs, to inhale air, to take breath.

හුළ, *Huḷa, s.* torch, flambeau. (Tamil.)

හුළු, *Huḷu, s.* tile: see also සුළුව *suluwa.*

හුළුඅත්ත, *Huḷuatta, s.* dried branches of the coconut prepared to be used as a torch.

හුළු එළිය, *Huḷu-eliya, s.* torch-light.

හුළුකැන්, *Huḷukęn, s.* rice gruel, conji, starch, [Colloq. කැඳ *kęnda*].

හුළුගානවා, *Huḷugánawá, v.* to catch fish in fresh water by means of torch-light: pret. හුළුගෑවා *huḷugęwá.*

හුළුදැල්, *Huḷudęl, s.* sparks flying from torch-light.

හුළුනා, *Huḷuná, s.* thief, robber, [Colloq. හොරා *horá*].

හුළුමස්, *Huḷumas, s.* (හුළ *huḷa* torch, මස් fish) fish caught by torch light.

හූ, *Hú, s.* string, thread, from සූත්‍ර *sútra,* [Colloq. නූල් *núl*]: *ind.* a particle of shouting or halloing, eh, hallo.

හූකියනවා, *Húkiyanawá, v.* to halloo.

හූති, *Húti, s.* calling, shouting to.

හූනා, *Húná, s.* house lizard, *hemidactylus maculatus* or *peripia peronii (Geckotidæ* order *Sauria).*

හූනියම්කපනවා, *Húniyamkapanawá, v.* to avert the evil consequences of witchcraft or enchantment.

හූනියම්කරණවා, *Húniyamkaraṇawá, v.* to practise witchcraft, to bewitch, to enchant.

හූනියම, *Húniyama, s.* magic, enchantment: see සූනියම *súniyama.*

හූරණවා, *Húraṇawá, v.* to scrape off: pret. හිරුවා *hiruwá.*

හූරල, *Húrala,* see බින්තල් *bintal.*

හූරව, *Húrawa, s.* (හූ cry of fear or wrath, රව sound) jackal, [Colloq. නරියා *nariyá*].

හූලෑව, *Húlęwa, s.* a disease, hydrocele, swelled testicles.

හූව, *Húwa, s.* sound of calling, halloo: see හූ *hú.*

හූවට, *Húwaṭa, s.* (හූ thread, වට ball) ball of thread.

හූවැටිය, *Húwęṭiya, s.* roll or ball of thread.

හෙ, *He, ind.* a vocative particle.

හෙට්ටියා, *Heṭṭiyá, s.* a Chetty man.

හෙට්ටිරාල, *Heṭṭirála,* see the last.

හෙට්ඨා, *Heṭṭhá, ind.* underneath, beneath.

හෙට, *Heṭa, s.* to-morrow.

හෙණ්ඩුව, *Heṇḍuwa, s.* iron hook used in guiding an elephant.

හෙති, *Heti*, *v.* they are able; they fall.

හෙතු, *Hetu*, *s.* plant, species of the *marsilea*, [Colloq. ඇඹුලැඹිලිය *embulembiliya*].

හෙද, *Heda*, see සෙද *seda*.

හෙන්ත්‍රොක්කේ, *Hentrokké*, *s.* kind of jacket worn by native men.

හෙන්ද්‍රික්කා, *Hendrikká*, *s.* plant, Marvel of Peru, see සෙන්දිරික්කා *sendirikká*.

හෙන, *Hena*, *s.* pouring out; lightning; falling.

හෙනකඳයා, *Henakandayá*, *s.* green whip snake, *passerita mycterizans (Dryophidæ*, order *Ophidia)*; also called ඇහැටුල්ලා *chetullá*.

හෙනගහනවා, *Henagahanawá*, *v.* to be struck by lightning.

හෙනගුලිය, *Henaguliya*, *s.* thunderbolt.

හෙනවා, *Henawá*, *v.* to fall, to drop.

හෙප්, *Hep*, *s.* spear, large iron headed pike, peculiar to the Veddás who use it for spearing wild beasts; natural pond.

හෙප්පුව, *Heppuwa*, *s.* small metal box: see සෙප්පුව *seppuwa*.

හෙප්විල, *Hepvila*, *s.* natural pond, [Colloq. පොකුණ *pokuṇa*].

හෙපත්, *Hepat*, *s.* swan.

හෙබ, *Heba*, *s.* natural pond.

හෙබියේ, *Hebiyé*, *s.* one who is beautiful, shining, comely.

හෙබීම, *Hebíma*, verbal noun of හොබනවා *hobanawá*.

හෙම්, *Hem*, Elu form of හේම *héma*, gold; cold; snow; frost, from හිම *hima*.

හෙම්කුළ, *Hemkuḷa*, *s.* rock Mahámeru.

හෙම්කුළු, *Hemkuḷu*, *s.* (හෙම gold, කුළු peak) name of the Yugandhara rock which surrounds Mount Méru.

හෙම්බිරිස්සාව, *Hembirissáwa*, see සෙම්ප්‍රතිශ්‍යාව *sempratiṣyáwa*.

හෙම්මළු, *Hemmaḷu*, see හෝපල *hópala*.

හෙම්සළු, *Hemsaḷu*, *s.* (හෙම් gold, සළු cloth) name of Vishṇu.

හෙම, *Hema*, *ind.* suffix signifying identity, same, etc., as in එහෙම *ehema*=එසේම *eséma* in that same manner.

හෙමගහ, *Hema-gaha*, *s.* tree, *gyrocarpus jacquini* or *asiaticus:* see හිම *híma*.

හෙමලම්බ, *Hemalamba*, *s.* thirtieth year of the Indian cycle.

හෙමින්, *Hemin*, *ad.* softly, slowly: see සෙමින් *semin*.

හෙමිහිට, *Hemihiṭa*, *ad.* softly, slowly: see සෙමින් *semin*.

හෙමෝනම්, *Hemónam*, *v.* if we are able.

හෙය, *Heya*, *s.* bridge, [Colloq. පාලම් *pálama*]; causeway, mound in a paddy field, from සේතු *sétu;* cause, from හේතු *hétu*.

හෙයි, *Heyi*, *v.* he falls; he is able.

හෙයින්, *Heyin*, *s.* (auxiliary case of හේ *hé*,) by reason of, because of.

හෙර, *Hera*, *s.* female thief.

හෙරණ, *Heraṇa*, *s.* novice, Buddhist priest of the Sámaṇéra order.

හෙරළිගෙඩිය, *Heraḷigeḍiya*, } *s.* jack fruit, *arto-*
හෙරළිය, *Heraḷiya*, } *carpus integrifolia.*

හෙරෙණවා, *Hereṇawá*, *v.* to sink: see එරෙණවා *ereṇawá*.

හෙල්, *Hel*, *a.* white; plural of හෙල *hela:* see සෙල් *sel*.

හෙල්බිජු, *Hel-biju*, *s.* Ceylon cardamoms, *elettaria cardamomum (major)*, [Colloquial: එන්සාල් *ensál*].

හෙල්මැළි, *Helmeḷi*, *s.* white esculent water lily, *nymphæa lotus.*

හෙල්ලෙනවා, *Hellenawá*, *v.* to shake: pret. හෙල්ලුනා *helluná*.

හෙල්ලේ, *Hellé*, *s.* lance, spear: pl. හෙල්ල *hella*.

හෙල, *Hela*, *s.* whiteness; hillock, declivity; tree, *cordia myxa*, [Colloq. ලෝලු *lólu*]; carpet, rug.

හෙල අබ, *Hela-aba*, *s.* (හෙල white, අබ mustard) white mustard, variety of *brassica juncea* or *cleome viscosa.*

හෙල ඊතණ, *Hela-ítana*, *s.* (හෙල white, ඊතණ kind of grass) grass, variety of *heteropogon hirtus;* also called ඊතණ *ítaṇa*.

හෙල එඬරු, *Hela-eṇḍaru*, *s.* (හෙල and එඬරු castor oil) variety of the castor oil plant, *communis ricinus.*

හෙල කණේරු, *Hela-kaṇéru*, *s.* (හෙල and කණේරු plumeria) plant, *nerium odorum*, or *plumeria alba.*

හෙල කිරි, *Hela-kiri*, see එලකිරි *elakiri*.

හෙල කිරිබදු, *Hela-kiribadu*, *s.* variety of *ipomœa digitata.*

හෙල කිහිරි, *Hela-kihiri*, *s.* pale variety of *acacia suma* or *catechu.*

හෙල කුඩය, *Hela-kuḍaya*, *s.* (හෙල and කුඩ *kuḍa* umbrella) white umbrella: see ශ්වේතච්ඡත්‍ර *ṣwétachchhatra*.

හෙලඟිතෙල්, *Helangitel*, *s.* (හෙල term applied to black cattle as opposed to buffaloes, ගි ghee, තෙල් oil) butter.

හෙල තඹර, *Hela-tambara*, *s.* white lotus.

හෙල තොටිල, *Hela-toṭila*, *s.* plant, variety of *bignonia indica*.

හෙල දම්, *Hela-dam*, *s.* white sort of දං *dan* fruit.

හෙලදෙන්, *Heladen*, *s.* cow: see එලදෙන් *eladen*.

හෙල නික, *Hela-nika*, *s.* white variety of *vitex negundo*.

හෙල නෙලඹු, *Hela-nelambu*, } *s.* white water lily,
හෙල නෙලුම්, *Hela-nelum*, } variety of *nelumbium speciosum*.

හෙල පලොල්, *Hela-paḷol*, *s.* (හෙල white, පලොල් trumpet flower) variety of *stereospermum suaveolens*.

හෙල පියුම්, *Hela-piyum*, see හෙල නෙලුම් *hela-nelum*.

හෙල බටු, *Hela-baṭu*, *s.* (හෙල and බටු night shade) variety of egg plant, *solanum xanthocarpum*; also written එලබටු *ela-baṭu*.

හෙල බින්තඹුරු, *Hela-bintamburu*, *s.* (හෙල pale, බින්තඹුරු convolvulus) variety of *ipomœa baladamboe*.

හෙලඹුල, *Helambula*, *s.* (හෙල and ඇඹුල *embula* the same) white water lily, or variety of *nymphæa lotus*.

හෙල මහනෙල්, *Hela-mahanel*, *s.* (හෙල and මහනෙල් nymphæa) variety of *nymphæa stellata*.

හෙල ලූනු, *Hela-lúnu*, *s.* (හෙල white, ලූනු onion) garlic, *allium sativum*; also called සුදුලූනු *sudu-lúnu*.

හෙල ලොත්, *Hela-lot*, *s.* (හෙල and ලොත් symplocos recemosa) pale variety of the lódh tree, *symplocos racemosa*.

හෙල වද, *Hela-wada*, *s.* variety of shoe flower, *hibiscus rosa sinensis*.

හෙල වදකසා, *Hela-wadakasá*, *s.* white variety of orris root or sweet flag, *acorus calamus*.

හෙල වරා, *Hela-wará*, *s.* white variety of *calotropis gigantea*.

හෙල සඳුන්, *Hela-sandun*, *s.* white variety of sandal wood, *santalum album*; also called සුදු හඳුන් *sudu-handun*.

හෙල හිතණ, *Hela-hitaṇa*, see හෙල ඊතණ *hela-ítaṇa*.

හෙව, *Hewa*, *past part*, of හොවනවා *howanawá*.

හෙවත්, *Hewat*, *ind.* particle of alternative or option, either, or.

හෙවන, *Hewana*, *s.* shade, shelter: see සෙවන *sewana*.

හෙවනකරණවා, *Hewanakaraṇawá*, *v.* to shelter or screen from light and heat, to shade.

හෙවනිය, *Hewaniya*, *s.* shade, shelter, preservation: see සෙවනිය *sewaniya*.

හෙවනැල්ල, *Hewanella*, *s.* shadow: see සෙවනැල්ල *sewanella*.

හෙවෙනවා, *Hewenawá*, *v.* to be sheltered: see සෙවෙනවා *sewenawá*.

හෙළ, *Heḷa*, *s.* (සිහළ *síhaḷa*; සිළ *síla*, සෙළ *seḷa*, හෙළ *heḷa*) the ancient name of Ceylon, generally followed by දිව් *diw* island.

හෙළනවා, *Heḷanawá*, *v.* to throw, to cast, to drop, to cause to fall: pret. හෙළුවා *heḷuwá*.

හෙළාතළා දොඩනවා, *Heḷátalá-doḍanawá*, *v.* to speak contemptuously.

හෙළාදකිනවා, *Heḷádakinawá*, *v.* to speak disparagingly, to contemn, to slight: pret. හෙළාදැක්කා *heḷádekká*.

හෙළු, *Heḷu*, *s.* nudity.

හෙළුබස, *Heḷubasa*, Elu or ancient language of Ceylon.

හෙළුබැල්ල, *Heḷubella*, *s.* nakedness.

හේ, *Hé*, *s.* tameness, docility; cause: see හේතු *hétu*; see also හෙය *heya*.

හේක්කා, *Hékká*, *s.* hiccough, [Colloq. ඉක්කාව *ikkáwa*].

හේකණ්ඩෙ, *Hékaṇḍe*, *s.* disagreeable companion, nuisance, bore.

හේත්තුකරණවා, *Héttukaraṇawá*, *v.* to joint, to cause to lean or incline, to recline.

හේත්තුව, *Héttuwa*, *s.* junction, joint: pl. හේත්තු *héttu*.

හේත්තුවීම, *Héttuvíma*, *s.* leaning.

හේත්තුවෙනවා, *Héttuwenawá*, *v.* to lean or recline upon or against: pret. හේත්තුවුනා *héttuwuná*.

හේති, *Héti*, *s.* (හි *hi* to go or හන *hana* to kill, ක්ති *kti* aff.) weapon; ray of the sun; flame.

හේතු, *Hétu*, *s.* (හි *hi* to go, තු aff.) cause, origin, motive; moral merit, the cause of happiness or prosperity; reason or argument for an inference or deduction.

හේතුක, *Hétuka*, *s.* (හේතු cause, ක aff.) active cause, instrument or agent: *a.* causal, instrumental: meritorious, possessed of moral merit.

හේදඬු, *Hédaṇḍu*, *s.* (හේ bridge, දඬු wood) foot bridge over a brook or mountain stream, generally a single tree.

හේදම්මන්ඩෙට, *Hédammandeṭa*, } *s.* eye-service,
හේදමට, *Hédamaṭa*, } perfunctory discharge of duties; with indifference.

හේන්කොටනවා, *Hénkoṭanawá*, *v.* to make clearings in a chena land for the purpose of bringing it under dry grain cultivation.

හේන්කැකිරි, *Hén-kekiri*, *s.* (හේන *héna* and කැකිරි cucumber) annual plant or clasper, *bryonia cordifolia*.

හේන, *Héna*, *s.* ground prepared for cultivation by the cutting and burning of jungle; high jungle ground cultivated at intervals generally of from five to fourteen years, but in some cases at longer intervals: pl. හේන් *hén*.

හේනයා, *Hénayá*, *s.* washerman.

හේනාවා, *Hénáwá*, *s.* white-tailed Indian porcupine, *Hystriyx leucurus*.

හේම, *Héma*, *s.* gold, [Colloq. රත්රන් *ratran*].

හේමකාර, *Hémakára*, *s.* (හේම and කාර who works) goldsmith, [Colloq. බඩාලා *baḍálá*].

හේමතරු, *Hémataru*, *s.* thorn apple, *datura fastuosa*, [Colloq. අත්තන *attana*].

හේමදුග්ධ, *Hémadugdha*, } *s.* (හේම and දුග්ධ
හේමදුග්ධක, *Hémadugdhaka*, } milk) glomerous fig tree, *ficus glomerata*, [Colloq. අට්ටික්කා *aṭṭikká*].

හේමදුග්ධි, *Héma-dugdhi*, *s.* medicinal sort of moonplant, *ipomœa bona-nox*, [Colloquial: අලංගා *álangá*].

හේමද්‍රුම, *Héma-druma*, *s.* shrub, *cassia auriculata*, [Colloq. රණවරා *raṇawará*].

හේමධුස්තූර, *Héma-dhustúra*, *s.* wood-apple tree, *feronia elephantum*, [Colloq. දිවුල් *diwul*].

හේමන්, *Héman*, *s.* gold, [Colloq. රත්රන් *ratran*].

හේමන්කරණවා, *Hémankaraṇawá*, *v.* to calm one's fears; to soothe; to cause to lean; to unite.

හේමන්ත, *Hémanta*, *s.* (හන *hana* to hurt, etc.) cold season; winter, the two months, අග්‍රහායණ *agraháyaṇa* (November–December) and පෞෂ *paushya* (December–January).

හේමන්ත ඍතුව, *Hémanta-ṛituwa*, } *s.* snowy
හේමන්ත කාලය, *Hémanta-kálaya*, } season, cold season.

හේමපුෂ්ප, *Héma-pushpa*, } *s.* (හේම golden,
හේමපුෂ්පක, *Héma-pushpaka*, } පුෂ්ප flower) asóka tree, *saraca indica* or *jonesia asoca*, [Colloq. දිය රතඹලා *diya-ratambalá* or දිය රත්මල් *diyaratmal*]; champaka tree, *michelia champaca*, [Colloq. සපු *sapu*]; lódh tree, *symplocos racemosa*.

හේම පුෂ්පිකා, *Héma-pushpiká*, *s.* (හේමපුෂ්ප *hémapushpa* and ඉක *ika* aff.) yellow jasmine, *jasminum chrysanthemum*; species of *cucurligo*.

හේමයි, *Hémayi*, *ind.* particle expressive of doubt or conjecture; perhaps, probably.

හේමරස, *Héma-rasa*, *s.* (හේම gold, රස flavour) plant, *stalagmitis cambogoides*.

හේමල, *Hémala*, *s.* (හේම and ලා *lá* to have or take, ක *ka* aff.) goldsmith, [Colloquial: බඩාලා *baḍálá*]; chameleon, *calotes*, [Colloq. කටුස්සා *kaṭussá*]; lizard, *hemidactylus maculatus* or *peripia peronii*, [Colloq. හූනා *húná*].

හේමවත, *Hémawata*, *s.* inferior chief of the Yakshas or devils so called, and subordinate to Kuvéra.

හේම සඥක, *Héma-sajñaka*, *s.* (හේම gold, සඥ *sajñá* appellation, ක aff.) iron-wood tree, *mesua ferrea*, [Colloq. නා *ná*].

හේමා, *Hémá*, *s.* planet Mercury, [Colloq. බුදහු *budahu*]; an apsara or courtezan of Swarga; winter: see හේමන්ත *hémanta*.

හේමාඞ්ග, *Hémáṅga*, *s.* (හේම *héma* gold, අඞ්ග *aṅga* body) name of Garuḍa; also Brahma; lion; the mountain Suméru; champaka tree, *michelia champaca*, [Colloq. සපු *sapu*].

හේමාද්‍රි, *Hémádri*, *s.* (හේම *héma* snd අද්‍රි *adri* mountain) Mount Méru.

හේර, *Héra*, *s.* king, name of a playing card, (Dutch.); sort of crown or tiara, turmeric.

හේරකඳයා, *Hérakaṉdayá*, *s.* thin long-bellied bullock.

හේරම්බ, *Héramba*, *s.* name of Ganésa; buffalo; hero inflated with his own valour and prowess.

හේලන, *Hélana*, *s.* (හිල *hila* to disregard, ල්‍යුට් *lyuṭ* aff.) disregard, disrespect, contempt; wantoning, dalliance.

හේලය, *Hélaya*, see හේලේ *hélé*.

හේලා, *Hélá*, *s.* wanton dalliance, lascivious endearment; disrespect, contempt; moonlight.

හේලි, *Héli*, *s.* dalliance, wanton sport; the sun.

හේලේ, *Hélé*, *s.* cloth or dress twelve cubits long: pl. හෙල *héla*.

හේවා, *Héwá*, see සේවා *séwá*.

හේවාකම, *Héwákama*, *s.* war, warfare, service of a lascoreen, military service: pl. හේවාකම් *héwákam*.

හේවාකම්කරණවා, *Héwákamkaraṇawá*, *v.* to fight in battle.

හේවාපන්නේ, *Héwápanné*, *s.* soldiers.

හේවායා, *Héwáyá*, *s.* soldier, warrior.

හේවාරල, *Héwárála*, *s.* lascoreen.

හේවාවසම, *Héwáwasama*, *s.* military service.

හේවාසමුදාව, *Héwásamudáwa*, *s.* (හේවා and සමුදාව multitude) army, one on actual service.

හේෂා, *Héshá*, } *s.* (හෙෂ *hesha* to neigh,
හේෂාරව, *Hésháraワa*, } to bray) neighing as a horse, or braying as an ass.

හේෂින්, *Héshin*, *s.* (හේෂා *héshá* and ඉනි *ini* aff.) horse, [Colloq. අශ්වයා *aswayá*].

හේසා, *Hésá*, see හේෂා *héshá*.

හෛම, *Haima*, *s.* (හිම *hima* cold, or හෙම *hema* gold, අණ් *an* aff.) hoar frost: *a.* cold, frigid, freezing; golden.

හෛමන්ත, *Haimanta*, *s.* winter season: see හේමන්ත *hémanta*: *a.* wintry, cold, suitable to the winter.

හෛමවතී, *Haimawatí*, *s.* (හිමවත් *himawat* snowy mountains skirting India, අණ් *an* aff.) chebulic or yellow myrobalan, *terminalia chebula*, [Colloq. අරළු *aralu*]; medicinal kind of moon-plant, perhaps variety of *ipomœa bona-nox*, [Colloq. ඇලංගා *álangá*]; white kind of orris root, *acorus calamus*; name of Párvatí; the Ganges.

හෛයඞ්ගවීන, *Haiyanga-vína*, *s.* (හ්‍යස් *hyas* yesterday, ගෝදෝහ *gódóha* milk, හියඞ්ග *hiyanga* substituted for them, අණ් *an* aff.) clarified butter prepared a day before it is used; fresh butter.

හොක්ක, *Hokka*, *s.* part of the cheek alongside the jaws.

හොට, *Hota*, *s.* bill of a bird: see සොට *sota*.

හොටකළුකොකා, *Hotakalu-koká*, *s.* plumed egret, *herodins intermedia* (order *Herodiones*).

හොටළු, *Hotalu*, *s.* small house, cottage.

හොටිය, *Hotiya*, see සොටිය *sotiya*.

හොටු, *Hotu*, *s.* snot: see සොටු *sotu*.

හොටෑ, *Hoté*, *a.* smaller than the usual size, applied to coconuts, etc, as opposed to ලුව *luwa*, bulky, large, fully developed as fruits, nuts, etc.

හොණ්ඩරය, *Hondaraya*, *s.* hundredweight. (Eng.)

හොඬපර, *Hondapara*, *s.* (හොඬ trunk of an elephant, පර dillenia) tree, bearing large fragrant flowers, *dillenia indica* or *d. speciosa* (*Dilleneaceæ*); also called වම්පර *wampara*.

හොඬය, *Honduya*, *s.* elephant's trunk or proboscis: see සොඬ *sonda*.

හොඬල, *Hondala*, *s.* clasping plant, passion flower, *modecca palmata* (*Passifloraceæ*); also called පොතුහොඬ *potu-honda*.

හොඬවැල, *Hondawela*, see සොඬ *sonda*.

හොත්, *Hot*, *a.* reclined, reposed, from හෝනවා *hónawá*; affix answering to "if."

හොත්තාවූ, *Hottáwú*, *a.* who or which was lying down.

හොද්ද, *Hodda*, *s.* soup, gravy, condiment.

හොඳ, *Honda*, *s.* good, welfare, benefit: *a.* good virtuous.

හොඳකම, *Hondakama*, *s.* goodness: pl. හොඳකම් *hondakam*.

හොඳකරණවා, *Hondakaranawá*, *v.* to do good, to heal, to make good.

හොඳකෙරීම, *Hondakeríma*, *s.* act of doing good healing, making good.

හොඳනොහොඳ, *Honda-nohonda*, *s.* good and evil

හොඳ බෙරලිය, *Honda-beraliya*, *s.* tree, peculiar to Ceylon, *doona macrophylla* (*Dipterocarpaceæ*).

හොඳයි, *Hondayi*, *ind.* it is good, well.

හොඳවෙනවා, *Hondawenawá*, *v.* to become good to reform, to recover: pret. හොඳවුනා *hondawuna*

හොනරවාල වී, *Honarawála-wí*, *s.* kind of paddy *oryza sativa*.

හොනරවාලු කෙසෙල්, *Honarawálu-kesel*, *s.* kind of plantain, variety of *musa sapientum*.

හොපලු, *Hopalu*, see හෝපලු *hópalu*.

හොබන, *Hobana*, see සොබන *sobana*.

හොබනවා, *Hobanawá*, *v.* to press down: pret. හෙබුවා *hebuwá*: see සොබනවා *sobanawá*.

හොබින, *Hobina*, *a.* decent, proper, becoming, also written ඔබින *obina*.

හොබිනවා, *Hobinawá*, *v.* to be proper, suitable or becoming.

හොමුවගු, *Homuwagu*, see හෝමුවගු *hómuwagu*.

හොය, *Hoya*, *s.* small river, branch of a river rivulet.

හොයඳුන් *Hoyandun*, *s.* antimony.

හොයනවා, *Hoyanawá*, *v.* to seek, to find, to roof see සොයනවා *soyanawá*.

හොයල, *Hoyala*, *s.* sandy bank or plain, island of alluvial formation.

හොර, *Hora*, *s.* large timber tree, peculiar to Ceylon, producing resin and oil, *dipterocarpus zeylanicus* (*Dipterocarpaceæ*): *a.* thievish, trickish, lazy, unwilling to work.

හොරකම්කරණවා, *Horakamkaranawá*, *v.* to steal

හොරකම, *Horakama*, *s.* theft, trick: pl. හොරකම්

හොරකරණවා, *Horakaranawá*, *v.* to be restive unwilling to move, as an animal tied to a cart to act unfairly.

හොරගහ, *Hora-gaha*, see සොරගහ *sora-gaha*.

හොරණෑව, *Horaṇéwa*, *s.* trumpet: pl. හොරණෑ *horaṇé*.

හොර පුරුෂයා, *Hora-purushayá*, *s.* (හොර thief, පුරුෂ *purusha* husband) paramour.

හොරපොලා, *Horapolá*, *s.* kind of sea fish.

හොරලෙඩ, *Horaleḍa*, *s.* feigned sickness.

හොරවෙනවා, *Horawenawá*, *v.* to become obstinate in refusing to go right on, as a draft-horse, or draft-ox; to lose one's credit, or trust-worthiness: pret. හොරවුනා *horawuná*.

හොරා, *Horá*, *s.* thief, rogue: pl. හොරු *horu*.

හොරාකනවා, *Horákanawá*, *v.* to eat or graze, etc. unperceived.

හොරි, *Hori*, *s.* cutaneous eruption, itch.

හොරිකබල, *Horikabala*, *s.* (හොරි and කබල piece) scab, scales formed by itch.

හොරිගෙඩිය, *Horigeḍiya*, see හොරි *hori*.

හොරු, *Horu*, *s.* boat, canoe, also written ඔරු *oru*.

හොරොව්ව, *Horowwa*, see සොරොව්ව *sorowwa*.

හොල්ලනවා, *Hollanawá*, *v.* to shake violently: pret. හෙල්ලුවා *helluwá*.

හොවනවා, *Howanawá*, *v.* to put to sleep, causal of හෝනවා *hónawá*.

හොවාගෙණ, *Howágeṇa*, *part.* having caused to sleep or lie down.

හොවිනවා, *Hovinawá*, *v.* to sleep, to rest, to repose.

හොවිල්ල, *Hovilla*, *s.* palanquin, litter, etc. [Colloq. දෝලාව *dóláwa*]; swing; acute or shooting pain, as colic, etc.

හොවිලි, *Havili*, *s.* palanquin, [Colloq. දෝලාව *dóláwa*].

හොස්ස, *Hossa*, *s.* snout, mouth.

හොහපුටුවා, *Hohapuṭuwá*, *s.* small sort of mosquito.

හොහුම්, *Hohum*, *s.* thunder, [Colloquial: හෙන *hena*].

හෝ, *Hó*, *ind.* particle and affix of alternative or option, either, or; prefix implying depreciation, bad, inferior: see හොය *hoya*: *ind.* interjection of calling out or challenging.

හෝඩිය, *Hóḍiya*, *s.* alphabet.

හෝත්‍ර, *Hótra*, *s.* (හු *hu* to sacrifice, ත්‍ර aff.) burnt offering, oblation with fire; article intended or fit for such oblation, generally ghee, or clarified butter.

හෝතෘ, *Hótṛi*, *s.* priest who officiates at a sacrifice.

හෝතලා, *Hótalá*, *s.* plant, not ascertained.

හෝතුඹ, *Hótumba*, *s.* plant, perhaps species of *momordica*.

හෝතුරු, *Hóturu*, see හෝත්‍ර *hótra*.

හෝදනවා, *Hódanawá*, *v.* to wash: see සෝදනවා *sódanawá*.

හෝදිසිකරණවා, *Hódisikaraṇawá*, *v.* to enquire.

හෝදිසිය, *Hódisiya*, *s.* enquiry, examination.

හෝන්, *Hón*, see සොහොන් *sohon*.

හෝන්පල, *Hónpala*, *s.* burying ground: see සොහොන *sohona*.

හෝනවා, *Hónawá*, *v.* to sleep, to repose.

හෝපල, *Hópala*, හෝපලු, *Hópalu*, } *s.* (හෝ implying depreciation, පලු mimusops hexandra) tree, *saraca indica* or *jonesia asoca*, [Colloq. දියරතඹලා *diya-ratambalá* or දිය රත්මල් *diya-ratmal*]; tree, *dalbergia oujeinensis*, [Colloq. කොබු *kobu*]; the rattan or common cane, *calamus Roxburghii* or *c. rotang*, [Colloquial: වේවැල් *wéwel*]; tree, *mimosa sirisha*; tree, *hibiscus mutabilis*.

හෝම, *Hóma*, *s.* (හු *hu* to sacrifice, මන් *man* aff.) burnt offering, casting of clarified butter, etc., into the sacred fire.

හෝමාග්නිය, *Hómágniya*, *s.* sacrificial fire.

හෝමි, *Hómi*, *s.* (හු *hu* and මි aff.) clarified butter; fire; water.

හෝමිදි, *Hómidi*, *s.* (හෝ aquatic, මිදි premna serratifolia) species of *premna*.

හෝමිගහ, *Hómi-gaha*, *s.* tree, species of *bassia*.

හෝමුවගු, *Hómuwagu*, *s.* sort of cane or rattan, *calamus rotang*.

හෝමැදිරිය, *Hómediriya*, *s.* tree, peculiar to Ceylon, *diospyros Thwaitesii* or *d. condolleana*, *(Ebenaceæ)*.

හෝරත, *Hórata*, *s.* (හෝ bad, රත red) plant, *ixora cocchinea* [Colloq. රතඹලා *ratambalá*].

හෝරා, *Hórá*, *s.* (හෝඩ *hóḍa* to go, to proceed, ර *ra* substituted for ඩ *ḍa*) rising of a sign of the zodiac; part of the duration of a sign, twenty-fourth part of a day, an hour.

හෝල්ලුකරණවා, *Hóllukaraṇawá*, *v.* to chop and reduce to a point.

හෝවැල, *Hówela*, *s.* (හෝ implying depreciation, වැල ripe jak) rotten jak fruit; bank of a river.

හෝහම, *Hóhama*, *s.* outer skin.

හැංගුම, *Hẹnguma*, verbal noun of the next.

හැංගෙණවා, *Hẹngenawá*, *v.* to hide one's self, to abscond: pret. හැංගුනා *hẹnguná*: see සැඟවෙනවා *sẹngawenawá*.

හැක, *Hẹka*, *s.* doubt: see සැක *sẹka*.

හැකකරණවා, *Hẹkakaraṇawá*, *v.* to doubt.

හැකරිල්ල, *Hękarilla*, *s.* species of night-shade, *solanum verbascifolium (Solanaceæ).*

හැකරැල්ලා, *Hękarellá*, *s.* ringed creature with many short feet, millepede. *julus ater* or *julus carnifex.*

හැකවෙනවා, *Hękawenawá*, *v.* to be afraid. to be discouraged, to be suspicious: pret. හැකවුනා *hękawuná.*

හැකි, *Hęki*, see සැකි *sęki.*

හැකිර, *Hękira*, *s.* sand bank or sandy soil.

හැකිල්ල, *Hękilla*, *s.* fetter, chain.

හැකිලීම, *Hękilíma*, *s.* shrinking, withering: verbal noun of හකුලනවා *hakulanawá.*

හැකිලෙනවා, *Hękilenawá*, *v.* to close, to shrink and wither as a flower, from හකුලනවා *hakulanawá:* pret. හැකුලුනා *hękuluná.*

හැකුලුම, *Hękuluma*, *s.* alarm, sudden fear; doubt, uncertainty: pl. හැකුලුම් *hękulum.*

හැඟුම, *Hęnguma*, verbal noun of the next.

හැඟෙනවා, *Hęngenawá*, *v.* to know, to apprehend, to be sensible of; to feel, to perceive: pret. හැඟුනා *hęnguná.*

හැට්ටය, *Hęttaya*, see සැට්ටය *sęttaya.*

හැට්ටිය, *Hęttiya*, *s.* earthen cooking vessel: see සැට්ටිය *sęttiya.*

හැට, *Hęta*, *s.* sixty: see සැට *sęta.*

හැටදා කුරක්කන්, *Hętadá-kurakkan*, *s.* sort of grain, variety of *eleusine indica* or of *e. coracana.*

හැටදා වී, *Hętadá-ví*, *s.* kind of rice of quick growth, *oryza sativa.*

හැටිය, *Hętiya*, *s.* manner: see සැටිය *sętiya.*

හැඩ, *Hęda*, *s.* form, person, appearance; see සැඩ *sęda.*

හැඩකංසා, *Hęda-kansá*, *s.* kind of opium plant, variety of *papaver somniferum.*

හැඩගහනවා, *Hędagahanawá*, *v.* to turn from a direct line, to incline, to slant.

හැඩපල්ල, *Hędapalla*, *s.* clotted hair, lock of hair: pl. හැඩපලු *hędapalu.*

හැඩපාර, *Hędapára*, *s.* stream, strong current.

හැඩයා, *Hędayá*, *s.* club-moss, variety of *lycopodium Hookeri:* see කුඩාහැඩයා *kudáhędayá.*

හැඩවක, *Hędawaka*, } *s.* timber tree, *chætocarpus castanocarpus (Euphorbiaceæ).*
හැඩෝක, *Hędóka*, }

හැඬිම, *Hęndíma*, *s.* weeping; verbal noun of හඬනවා *handanawá.*

හැත්, *Hęt*, plural of හැද *hęda.*

හැත්ත, *Hętta*, *s.* herd, flock, litter, brood, crowd: see සැත්ත *sętta.*

හැත්තෑව, *Hettęwa*, *s.* seventy.

හැත්තෑවෙනි, *Hettęweni*, *a.* seventieth.

හැතපෙනවා, *Hętapenawá*, see සැතපෙනවා *sętapenawá.*

හැති, *Hęti*, *s.* panting: see හත්ත *hatta:* also pl. of හැත්ත *hętta;* cluster of flowers.

හැතිකැක්කුම, *Hętikękkuma*, *s.* shortness of breath, panting.

හැතිරි, *Hętirí*, see සැතිරි *sętirí.*

හැතැක්ම, *Hetękma*, } *s.* a mile.
හැතැප්ම, *Hetępma*, }

හැඳිගානවා, *Hęndigánawá*, *v.* to stir with a spoon: pret. හැඳිගෑවා *hęndigęwá.*

හැඳිල්ලා, *Hęndillá*, *s.* kind of sea fish.

හැන්ද, *Hęnda*, *s.* spoon: pl. හැඳි *hęndi.*

හැන්දෑව, *Hęndęwa*, *s.* evening.

හැන්නැද්දා, *Hennęddá*, *s.* head fisherman.

හැඹිලිය, *Hęmbiliya*, *s.* small box or purse made of rush: pl. හැඹිලි *hęmbili.*

හැම, *Hęma*, *s.* all, every, as හැමදෙනා *hęmadená* all persons.

හැමනිල්ල, *Hęmanilla*, *s.* plant, *dysophylla auricularia (Labiatæ).*

හැමියා, *Hęmiyá*, *s.* husband (not respectful): see සැමි *sęmi.*

හැර, *Hęra*, *s.* taking, seizing, from හර *hara* besides, except: *past part.* of හරිණවා *harinawá* to leave.

හැරගහනවා, *Hęragahanawá*, *v.* to tie withes round trees as hoops by which to ascend.

හැරපට, *Hęrapata*, *s.* a withe put round a tree in the form of a ring to facilitate climbing, as is done by toddy-drawers.

හැරමිටිය, *Hęramitiya*, *s.* walking stick: pl. හැරමිටි *hęramiti.*

හැරය, *Hęraya*, *s.* a binding used in climbing coconut trees.

හැරලනවා, *Hęralanawá*, see ඇරලනවා *ęralanawá*

හැරව, *Hęrawa*, *s.* pus, matter: see සැරව *sęrawa*

හැරවීම, *Hęravíma*, *s.* act of turning or causing to turn.

හැරීම, *Hęríma*, *s.* turning; verbal noun of හරිණවා *harinawá.*

හැරෙණවා, *Hęrenawá*, *v.* to turn, to change place, to change opinion or sentiments: pret. හැරුණා *hęruná.*

හැල්, *Hel*, *s.* cold, frigidity; winter, one of the six seasons of the year, (December–January); rice growing on hilly ground, from සාලි *sáli;* house.

හැල් කසාම්බිලිය, *Hel-kasámbiliya*, *s.* armed shrub, *hedysarum alhagi* or species of *fleuriya* or *giradiniya.*

හැල්පත, *Helpata*, *s.* rice field overflowed with water, swamp, bog: see හැල *hela.*

හැල්ම, *Helma*, *s.* trot.

හැල, *Hela*, *s.* swamp, marshy land, bog.

හැලලී, *Helalí*, *pret.* of හලලනවා *halalanawá*, to agitate, to stir, [Colloq. කැලඹී *kelambí*].

හැලි, *Heli*, *a.* white, of a white colour, also written ඇලි *eli*, [Colloq සුදු *sudu*].

හැලිදඹ, *Heli-damba*, *s.* (හැලි white, දඹ jambu) white jambu, *jambosa vulgaris.*

හැලිය, *Heliya*, *s.* earthern pot: see සැලිය *seliya.*

හැලීම, *Helíma*, *s.* casting down; verbal noun of හලනවා *halanawá.*

හැලෙනවා, *Helenawá*, *v.* to fall, to drop: pret. හැලුනා *heluná.*

හැව, *Hewa*, *s.* the cast skin of a serpent.

හැවංපන්, *Hewan-pan*, *s.* kind of shrub, *cyperus dehiscens (Cyperaceæ).*

හැවඅරිණවා, *Hewaarinawá*, *v.* to cast the skin as a serpent.

හැවිකාරය, *Hevikáraya*, *s.* anxiety, solicitude.

හැවිල්ල, *Hevilla*, *s.* curse, malediction: pl. හැවිලි *hevili.*

හැවිලෙනවා, *Hevilenawá*, see ඇවිලෙනවා *evilenawá.*

හැවීම, *Hevíma*, see the last; also written ඇවීම *evíma*, etc.

හැවොම, *Hewoma*, *s.* all, every one.

හැස්සා, *Hessá*, *pret.* of හහිනවා *hahinawá*, to chip, to make smooth with the adze.

හැසිරීම, *Hesiríma*, *s.* behaviour, conduct.

හැසිරෙණවා, *Hesirenawá*, *v.* to go, to move, literally or figuratively; to behave, to act, etc: pret. හැසුරුණා *hesuruná.*

හැසුනු, *Hesunu*, *a.* crowded, impassable, narrow; thick, congealed, consistent, as liquids.

හැළ, *Hela*, see හැල *hela.*

හැළ කිඹුලා, *Hela-kimbulá*, *s.* crocodile common in tanks near Jaffna, *Crocodilus palustris (order Sauria).*

හැළඹ, *Helamba*, *s.* large timber tree, *stephegyne (or nauclea) parviflora, (Rubiaceæ).*

හැළලිහිණියා, *Helalihiniyá*, *s.* hill maina, *gracula religiosa*, small bird usually called, maina in Bengal, *Turdus salica*, of which several varieties are distinguished by the Hindus: see සැළලිහිණියා *selalihiniyá.*

හෑම, *Héma*, verbal noun of හානවා *hánawá:* see සෑම *séma.*

හෑරීම, *Hérima*, *s.* digging.

හෑරෙණවා, *Hérenawá*, *v.* to be dug, to be excavated, to be deepened: pret. හෑරුණා *héruná;* Involitive or passive form of හාරණවා *háranawá.*

හ්‍රද, *Hrada*, *s.* deep lake, large or deep piece of water, ray of light.

හ්‍රදරෝගය, *Hradarógaya*, *s.* disease of the heart, liver complaint, consumption; corrupt form of හෘද්රෝග *hridróga* or හෘදයරෝග *hridayaróga.*

හ්‍රදිනි, *Hradini*, *s.* river in general; lightning.

හ්‍රෂිත, *Hrashita*, *a.* (හෘෂ *hrisha* to be pleased, ක්ත *kta* aff.) corruptly for හෘෂිත *hrishita.*

හ්‍රස්ව, *Hraswa*, *a.* short, dwarfish, low in stature, [Colloq. මිටි *miti*]; short, as a vowel.

හ්‍රස්වපුෂ්ප, *Hraswa-pushpa*, *s.* (හ්‍රස්ව short, පුෂ්ප flower) liquorice creeper, *abrus precatorius*, [Colloq. ඔලිඳවැල් *olindawel*].

හ්‍රස්වා, *Hraswá*, *s.* plant, *grewia lævigata*, [Colloq. ගස්කැලිය *gas-keliya*].

හ්‍රිවේර, *Hrivéra*, see හ්‍රීවේර *hrívéra.*

හ්‍රී, *Hrí*, } *s.* (හ්‍රී to be ashamed) shame, bash-
හ්‍රීකා, *Hríká*, } fulness, [Colloq. ලජ්ජාව *lajjáwa*].

හ්‍රීත, *Hríta*, *a.* ashamed, bashful, modest.

හ්‍රීවේර, *Hrívéra*, *s.* (හ්‍රී shame, වේර saffron) drug and perfume, synonymous with වාල *wála* and වාලක *wálaka*; also written හිරිවේරිය *hirivériya* and ඉරිවේරිය *irivériya.*

හෘණියා, *Hriniyá*, *s.* censure, reproach; shame, bashfulness.

හෘත්පිණ්ඩ, *Hritpindâ*, *s.* (හෘත් for හෘද් *hrid* heart, පිණ්ඩ lump of flesh) heart.

හෘත්ශූල, *Hritsúla*, *s.* heart-disease.

හෘත්සාක්ෂිය, *Hrit-sákshiya*, *s.* conscience.

හෘත, *Hrita*, *a.* taken, taken away, seized; accepted.

හෘති, *Hriti*, *s.* (හෘ to take, ක්ති *kti* aff.) taking, conveying.

හෘද්, *Hrid*, *s.* heart; mind, seat or faculty of thought and feeling.

හෘද්මය, *Hridmaya*, *s.* (හෘද් heart, මය produced) one of the eighty morbid airs, producing slight uneasiness in the region of the breast.

හෘද්මාංසය, *Hṛidmáṇsaya*, see හෘදයවස්තුව *hṛidaya-wastuwa*.

හෘද්මෝහ, *Hṛidmóha*, *s.* (හෘද් and මෝහ overpowering) one of eighty morbid airs, which is the cause of insensibility: see හෘද්මය *hṛidmaya*.

හෘද්‍ය, *Hṛidya*, *s.* (හෘද් *hṛid* heart, etc. යත් *yat* aff.) mantra or incantation for effecting any one's subjection or fascination; also cassia bark: *a.* dear, beloved, cherished, desired; grateful, pleasant, agreeable; affectionate; kind: produced in or from the heart.

හෘද්‍යගන්ධ, *Hṛidyagandha*, *s.* (හෘද්‍ය grateful, ගන්ධ smell) bael tree, *ægle marmelos*, [Colloq. බෙලි *beli*]; small cardamoms, *elettaria cardamomums*, (minor), [Colloq. හින්එන්සාල් *hín-ensál*]; sochal salt.

හෘද්‍යගන්ධා, *Hṛidya-gandhá*, *s.* great flowered jasmine.

හෘද්රෝග, *Hṛidróga*, *s.* heart disease, heart-burn.

හෘද්රෝග වෛරී, *Hṛidróga-wairí*, *s.* tree, *pentaptera arjuna*.

හෘදය, *Hṛidaya*, see හෘද් *hṛid*.

හෘදයංගම, *Hṛidayaṇgama*, *a.* (හෘදය *hṛidaya* and ගම to go) apposite and proper, as speech; affecting; touching.

හෘදයවස්තුව, *Hṛidaya-wastuwa*, *s.* (හෘදය and වස්තුව substance) flesh of the heart in contradistinction to the faculty.

හෘදයස්ථාන, *Hṛidayasthána*, *s.* (හෘදය heart, ස්ථාන place) breast, chest.

හෘදයාලු, *Hṛidayálu*, *a.* (හෘදය *hṛidaya* and ආලුච් *áluch* aff.) good-hearted.

හෘල්ලාස, *Hṛillása*, *s.* hiccough.

හෘෂ්ට, *Hṛishṭa*, *a.* pleased, glad, delighted; laughing, smiling, astonished, having the hair of the body erect with pleasure.

හෘෂ්ටි, *Hṛishṭi*, *s.* pleasure, delight, happiness.

හෘෂිත, *Hṛishita*, *a.* astonished, pleased, delighted. having the hair of the body erect with pleasure,

හෘෂීක, *Hṛishíka*, *s.* organ of sense.

හෘෂීකේශ, *Hṛishíkéṣa*, *s.* (හෘෂීක *hṛishíka* and ඊශ *íṣa* lord) name of Kṛishṇa or Vishṇu.

හ්ලාද, *Hláda*, *s.* (හ්ලාද to be glad, අ *a* aff.) pleasure, joy, [Colloq. ප්‍රීතිය *prítiya*].

හ්ලාදිනී, *Hládiní*, *s.* (හ්ලාද *hláda* pleasure, ඉනි *ini* aff.) gum olibanum tree.

APPENDIX.

NOTE. Words with an asterisk * have already been given in this book, but are here entered afresh, with new meanings.

අ

අං අදිනවා, *Aṇ-adinawá*, *v.* to pull horns.

අං ඇදීම, *Aṇ-ędíma*, *s.* horn-pulling, a native pastime supposed to have the effect of averting sickness.

අං කටිල්ලා, *Aṇ-katillá*, *s.* kind of sea fish.

අංකුට, *Aṇkuṭa*, *s.* corruptly for අඞ්ගුෂ්ඨ *aṅgushṭha*, the thumb, [Colloq. මාපටැඟිල්ල *mápaṭęṅgilla*].

අංකෝල, *Aṇkóla*, *s.* plant, *hoya:* see රුකඟුණ *rukaṇguṇa;* sometimes written අඞ්කෝල *aṅkóla.*

* අංශක, *Aṇsaka*, *s.* (of a dial) degree.

අංශුමත්ඵලා, *Aṇsumat-phalá*, *s.* plantain tree, [Colloq. කෙසෙල් *kesel*].

අංශුමතී, *Aṇsumatí*, *s.* plant, *alyssicarpus bupleurifolius*, [Colloq. අස්වැන්න *aswęnna*]; knot grass, *ærua lanata* or *illecebrum lanatum*, [Colloq. පොල්පලා *polpalá*].

අක්වරුව, *Akwaruwa*, *s.* chaff, as separated from good paddy, [Colloq. බොල් *bol*].

අක්ෂත, *Akshata*, *s.* fried grain, [Colloq. පොරි *pori*]: *a.* uninjured, whole, unbroken.

අක්ෂභ, *Akshabha*, *s.* natron; alkali, impure carbonate of soda, [Colloq. සුවසලුණු *suwasa-luṇu*].

* අක්ෂණ, *Akshaṇa*, *s.* (vide අකුණ *akuṇa*) the electric fluid, lightning.

අක්ෂර විපර්යාස, *Akshara-viparyása*, *s.* change of letters.

අක්ෂ සම්බන්ධ, *Aksha-sambandha*, *s.* axile (in bot).

අක්ෂික, *Akshika*, *s.* sea salt, [Colloq. මුහුදුලුණු *múdu-luṇu*]; tree, *dalbergia Oujeiniensis.*

අක්ෂිබ, *Akshiba*; } *s.* tree, *Morinda citrifolia*,
අක්ෂීබ, *Akshíba*, } [Colloq. අහු *ahu*]; horse radish tree, *moringa pterygosperma*, [Colloq. මුරුංගා *muruṇgá*].

අක්ෂෝට, *Akshóṭa*, *s.* tree bearing the clearing nut, *strychnos potatorum*, [Colloq. ඉඟිනි ඇට *iṅginięṭa*]; tree, described as a Pílu, growing on the hills.

අකටපි, *Akaṭapi*, *s.* steel, [Colloq. වාණේ *wáṇé*].

* අකර්මක, *Akarmaka*, *a.* grammatical term applied to verbs which do not pass over to an object; Intransitive or Neuter.

අකර්මශීලි, *Akarmaśíli*, *a.* idle; indolent.

* අකර, *Akara*, *s.* mine: see ආකරය *ákaraya.*

අකල්ක, *Akalka*, *a.* (අ neg කල්ක dirt) pure, clean, free from dirt.

අකවටු, *Akawaṭu*, see කැසපට *kęsapaṭa.*

අකාර, *Akára*, the letter අ *a.*

අකුත්සිත, *Akutsita*, *a.* unreproached, respectable.

අකුරුකරවනවා, *Akurukarawanawá*, *v.* to teach reading, to impart instruction.

අකුසු, *Akusu*, *s.* hook used to guide an elephant.

අග්ඝිකා, *Agghiká*, *s.* festoon of flowers.

අග්නි කදම්බිකා, *Agni-kadambiká*, see දේවදලී *déwadáli.*

අග්නිකා, *Agniká*, *s.* marking nut tree, *semicarpus Gardneri*, [Colloq. බඩුල්ල *badulla*].

අග්නිකේත, *Agnikéta*, *s.* red lotus, *nymphæa rubra*, [Colloq. රත්නෙළුම් *ratneḷum*].

අග්නිජිහ්වා, *Agni-jihwá*, *s.* flame of fire; medicinal plant, *gloriosa superba*, [Colloquial: නියඟලා *niyaṇgalá*].

අග්නි දීපනය, *Agni-dípanaya*, *s.* appetite, strengthening of the digestive faculty.

අග්නි පුෂ්ප, *Agni-pushpa*, *s.* creeping plant, *Sarcostemma Brunonianum*, [Colloq. මුවකිරිය *muwa-kiriya*].

අග්නිප්‍රස්තර, *Agniprastara*, *s.* silica; fire-stone, flint.

අග්නිමන්ථ, *Agnimantha*, *s*. tree, *premna spinosa* or *longifolia*, [Colloq. සිහින් මිදි *sihin-midi*].

අග්නිමුඛී, *Agnimukhí*, *s*. marking nut tree, *semicarpus Gardneri*, [Colloq. බදුල්ල *badulla*].

අග්නිරන්ධ්‍ර, *Agni-randhra*, *s*. tree, *dalbergia oujeiniensis*, [Colloq. කොබු *kobu*].

අග්නිස්තම්භ, *Agnistambha*, *s*. pillar of fire.

අග්‍රගන්ධ, *Agragandha*, *s*. medicinal plant, *spilanthes acmella*, [Colloq. අක්මැල්ල *akmella*].

අගඩා, *Agaḍá*, *s*. leech lime, [Colloq. කුඩලුදෙහි *kúdalu-dehi*].

අගඩි, *Agaḍi*, *s*. tree, *terminalia belerica*, [Colloq. බුළු *bulu*].

අගත්ති, *Agatti*, *s*. kind of pebbles; plant, *nerium*, [Colloq. පිලගස් *pila-gas*].

අගත, *Agata*, see අගාවත *agáwata*.

අගතැන්පත්, *Agatenpat*, *a*. (අග first, තැන් place, පත් come) come to the first place; supreme.

අගණේය, *Aganéya*, *v*. is worth.

අගරුකය, *Agarukaya*, *s*. odoriferous creeper: see කළුවැල් *kaluwel*.

අගවන්, *Agawan*, *a*. supreme.

අගසැව්, *Agasew*. *s*. chief disciple.

අගාවත, *Agáwata*, *s*. lower side of a paddy field or range of paddy fields.

අගොස්තු, *Agostu*, *s*. July-August, Sinhalese, නිකිණි මස *nikini-masa*.

අගෝචර, *Agóchara*, *s*. that which is not within the province of; wrong sphere; improper place or object.

අඟර, *Angara*, *s*. anointing the body with unguents of sandal, etc. after bathing.

අඟානිය, *Anganiya*, *s*. stall where meat is sold, sometimes written අඟාණිය *anganiya*.

අඟාරණවා, *Angáranawá*, *v*. to waddle: pret. ඇඟෑරුවා *engéruwá*.

අඟුටුමිටියා, *Angutumitiyá*, *s*. dwarf, [Colloq. මිට්ටා *mittá*].

අඟුරු කබල, *Anguru-kabala*, *s*. pan or potsherd containing live coals.

අඟුරෙලිවි, *Angureli-vi*, *s*. kind of paddy, *oryza sativa*.

අඞ්ගද, *Angada*, *s*. bracelet worn upon the upper arm.

අඞ්ගභංගිනී, *Angabhangini*, *s*. vine creeper, *vitis vinifera*, [Colloq. මිදිවැල් *midi-wel*].

අඞ්ගසූත්‍රය, *Anga-sútraya*, *s*. principal rule.

අඞ්ගානි, *Angáni*, *s*. meat-stall; flesh-market.

අඞ්ගාරවල්ලිනී, *Angárawallini*, *s*. creeping plant bind-weed, *convolvulus flavus*, [Colloq. තැල්වැල් *telwel*].

අඞ්ගාරිකාම්ල, *Angárikámla*, *s*. carbonic acid.

අඞ්ගුලිමාල, *Angulimála*, *s*. name of a demon.

අච්ඡාදන, *Achchhádana*, *s*. dressing of clothes garment, coverings. (Páli.)

අච්‍යුත, *Achyuta*, *s*. name of Vishṇu, [Colloq. විෂ්ණු *vishṇu*]; Nirwáṇa, annihilation of being or human passion, [Colloq. නිර්වාණය *nirwáṇaya*].

අචලකුජා, *Achalakujá*, *s*. plant, *vernonia* or *serratula anthelmintica*, [Colloq. බෝදිඇට *bódi-eta*].

අචාරිපළු, *Achāripaḷu*, *s*. plant, called cowitch *mucuna pruriens*, variety *biflora*, *(Liguminosæ)*.

අජ්ඣටා, *Ajjhaṭá*, *s*. plant, *phyllanthus nirури*: see පිටවක්කා *piṭawakká*.

අජ්ඣායන, *Ajjháyana*, *s*. reading, causing to be read.

අජගර, *Ajagara*, *s*. rock snake, *python molurus* [Colloq. පිඹුරා *pimburá*].

අජටා, *Ajaṭá*, *s*. name of a plant, *flacourtia cataphracta*, [Colloq. රට උගුරැස්ස *raṭa-ugurессa*].

අජටාකාසය, *Ajaṭákásaya*, *s*. lowest region of the atmosphere.

අජපල්, *Ajapal*, *s*. plant, *costus speciosus*, [Colloq. කොට්ටම් *kottam*, or තෙබු *tebu*].

අජශෘඞ්ගී, *Ajasṛingi*, *s*. creeping plant, *dæmia extensa*, [Colloq. මැඩහංගු *medahangu*].

අජහත්ස්වාර්ථා, *Ajahataswárthá*, *s*. (අ neg. ජහත් *jahat* leaving, ස්වාර්ථ *swártha* its own sense) figure of speech, metonymy, one name being put for another, as 'the spears enter' for the spearmen.

අජාජී, *Ajáji*, *s*. black and white cummin seed [Colloq. දෙදුරු *deduru*].

අඤ්ජනංඑලිය, *Añjanan-eliya*, *s*. the art of communicating with disembodied spirits by means of physical phenomena, spiritualism.

අඤ්ජලිකර්මය, *Añjalikarmaya*, *s*. respectful salutation performed by raising the joined hands to the forehead.

අටතැලි, *Aṭateli*, *s*. goldsmith, [Colloq. බඩාලා *badálá*].

අටන, *Aṭana*, *s*. walking, roaming about, [Colloq. ඇවිදීම *evidíma*].

අටනාකුල, *Aṭanákula*, *s*. (අට eight, නා elephant, කුල tribe) eight classes of elephants.

අටමස්සක්, *Aṭamassak*, *s*. eight massas, a massa being equal to about eightpence or thirty-three cents.

අටර, *Aṭara*, s. eighteen, [Colloq. දහඅට *daha-aṭa*].

අටරූෂ, *Aṭarúsha*, s. plant, *justicia adhatoda*, [Colloq. අඩාතෝඩා *áḍátóḍá*].

අටරේ, *Aṭaré*, s. tree, *allophylus cobbe*, [Colloq. කොබ්බෑගස *kobbé-gasa*].

අටලු වාසල්, *Aṭalu-wásal*, s. අටලු upper rooms or pavilions on the flat roof of an Indian house, and වාසල් gates.

අටසමවත්, *Aṭasamawat*, s. eight attainments or endowments, which are eight successive states induced by ecstatic meditation. (Sanskrit අෂ්ට සමාපත්ති *ashṭasamápatti*).

අටසාළිස, *Aṭasáḷisa*, s. number forty-eight, [Coll: හතළිස්අට *hataḷis-aṭa*].

අටළොස් අක්ෂෞහිණිය, *Aṭaḷos-akshauhiṇiya*, s. eighteen Akshauhiṇis, an Akshauhiṇi being a complete army consisting of 109,350 foot, 65,610 horse, 21,870 chariots, and 21,870 elephants.

අටළොස්හත් පවුර, *Aṭaḷoshat-pawura*, s. wall of eighteen cubits.

අඩප්පරය, *Aḍapparaya*, see ඇකන්සාව *ékansáwa*.

අඩුතුන්කෙළක්, *Aḍutun-keḷak*, s. 2½ kóṭis=25 millions.

අඩේ, *Aḍé*, / අඩෝ, *Aḍó*, } vocative particle, you, fellow.

අඬගා, *Aṇḍagá*, p. p. having called out.

අඬහැර, *Aṇḍahera*, s. two species of *crotalaria*, [Colloquial: අඬනහිරිය *aṇḍanahiriya*]; hedge hyssop, *herpestis monniera*, [Colloq. ලුණුවිල *luṇuvila*].

අණ්ණව, *Aṇṇawa*, Páli form of අර්ණව *arṇawa*, which see.

අණ්ණාවි, *Aṇṇavi*, s. reader or instructor in a Roman Catholic chapel. (Tamil aṇṇávi.)

අණබෙරය, *Aṇaberaya*, see අඬබෙරය *aṇḍaberaya*.

අණව, *Aṇawa*, s. ocean, [Colloq. මුහුද *muhuda*].

අත්ඇඳි පුටුව, *Ateṇḍi-puṭuwa*, s. arm chair.

අත්අරුණු, *Ateruṇu*, a. deserted, abandoned.

අත්කව්තුන, *Atkawtuka*, s. armlet, bracelet: see also, අතනූල් බැඳීම *atanúl-beṇḍíma*.

අත්තඩි පුටුව, *Attaḍi-puṭuwa*, s. arm chair.

අත්තනෝමත, *Attanómata*, s. one's own opinion.

අත්දුටු, *Atduṭu*, a. known by experience; known to be efficacious, as a medicine.

අත්පස ගේ, *Atpasa-gé*, s. privy, [Colloq. වැසිකිළිය *wesikiḷiya*].

අත්පිස්නාව, *Atpisnáwa*, s. towel.

අත්බැව්, *Atbew*,=ආත්මභාවය, *Átmabháwaya*, s. state of one's existence after death.

අත්මාරුව, *Atmáruwa*, s. change of hands.

අත්‍යන්තයෝග, *Atyanta-yóga*, s. grammatical term used to express duration of time or continuity of space.

අත්වැණුම, *Atweṇuma*, s. self-praise, self-exultation.

අත්හදාබලනවා, *Athadábalanawá*, v. to make an experiment; to give a trial.

අතකුරවී, *Atakúra-ví*, s. kind of paddy, *oryza sativa*.

අතත්ගුණ, *Atatguṇa*, s. term in Siṇhalese grammar used to designate a quality or attribute which is not inherent in the subject, as ඉකුත් සයුරු *ikut sayuru* (one) who has crossed the ocean.

අතනූල් බැඳීම, *Atanúl-beṇḍíma*, s. charm thread tied in the hand of a bride at the marriage ceremony.

අතපත්තුව, *Atapattuwa*, s. messenger staff of a Disáwa or Agent of a Province.

අතපොළා, *Atapoḷá*, v. having clapped the hands.

අතරවන්, *Atarawan*,=අථර්වවේදය, *Atharva-wéda-ya*, s. name of the fourth Véda.

අතිච්ඡත්‍රක, *Atichchhatraka*, s. plant, *leucas zeylanica*, [Colloq. ගැටතුඹ *geṭa-tuṃba*].

අතිජාත, *Atijáta*, a. high born; applied to a son who excels his father in virtuous qualities, etc.

අතිපතන, *Atipatana*, s. destruction, [Colloq. විනාශය *vináṣaya*].

අතිපරිහාස්‍ය, *Atiparihásya*, s. object of great ridicule.

අතිබලා, *Atibalá*, s. medicinal plant, *sida humilis*, [Colloq. මහබැවිල *maha-bevila*].

අතිමන්ද, *Atimanda*, s. plant, lead-wort, *plumbago rosea*, [Colloq. රත්නෙටුල් *ratneṭul*].

අතිමුක්ත, *Atimukta*, s. creeper, *borago zeylanica*, [Colloq. යොන්තුඹ *yon-tuṃba*]; sort of jasmine, *jasminum sambac*, [Colloquial. ගැට පිච්ච *geṭa-pichcha*].

අතිමුක්තක, *Atimuktaka*, s. tree, *dalbergia oujeiniensis*, [Colloq. කොබු *kobu*].

අතිරේක, *Atiréka*, a. much, excessive.

අතිරේකපත්‍රය, *Atiréka-patraya*, s. supplement or 'Extra-ordinary' issued *e. g.* in connection with a newspaper.

අතිශයෝක්ති, *Aatiṣayókti*, s. (අතිශය *atiṣaya* excess, උක්ති *ukti* speech) hyperbole; verbosity, prolixity.

අතිසය, *Atisaya*, *a.* much, excessive. (Páli.)

අතිසාරභේෂජ, *Atisára-bhéshaja*, *s.* small tree, *cratæva Roxburghii*, [Colloq. ලුණුවරණ *lunuwarana*].

අතිසෞරභ, *Atisaurabha*, *s.* mango tree, *mangifera indica* or *m. zeylanica*, [Colloq. අඹගස් *ambagas*].

අතුංගයා, *Atungayá*, *s.* (අ neg. තුංග tall, යා pers. aff.) one who is not tall, dwarf, [Colloq. මිට්ටා *mittá*].

අතුකෝරාල, *Atukórála*, *s.* assistant to a Kórála who is a Revenue Officer under a Raté-mahatmayá.

අතුර, *Atura*,=අන්තරාය, *Antaráya*, *s.* obstacle, danger, impediment.

අතුරුවේ, *Aturuwé*, *s.* middle of the way.

අතුරුසිදුරු, *Aturu-siduru*, *s.* (අතුරු interval, සිදුරු hole, interstice) intermediate space.

අතුල්තලය, *Atultalaya*, *s.* palm of the hand.

අතුල්සුඟ, *Atulsunga*, *s.* the little palms of the hand.

අද්ද, *Adda*, *s.* green ginger, [Colloq. අමු ඉඟුරු *amu-inguru*].

අද්‍ය, *Adya*, *ind.* to-day.

අද්‍රවා, *Adrawá*, *s.* plant, *alyssicarpus bupleurifolius*, [Colloq. අස්වැන්න *aswenna*].

අද්‍රිජ, *Adrija*, *s.* rock moss, [Colloq. ගල්සෙවෙල් *gal-sewel*].

අද, *Ada*, *a.* wet, moist: *p.* having come.

අදස්, *Adas*, *s.* mirror, [Colloq. කැඩපත *kedapata*].

අදස්න, *Adasna*, *s.* mustard, [Colloq. අබ *aba*].

අදිකරණි, *Adikarani*, *s.* anvil, [Colloq. කිනිරේ *kiniré*].

අදිටන්, *Aditan*, *s.* firm resolution; Elu form of අධිෂ්ඨාන *adhishthána*.

අදින්න, *Adinna*, *a*, not given, (Páli.)

අදිමොක්, *Adimok*,=අධිමෝක්ෂ, *Adhimóksha*, *s.* steadfastness, determination, certainty, confidence.

අදිරන්, *Adiran*, *s.* quicksilver, [Colloq, රසදිය *rasadiya*].

අදිරෂ්ඨ, *Adirashta*, *s.* fried grain, parched corn, [Colloq. විලඳ *vilanda*].

අදිසන්බව, *Adisanbawa*, *s.* foam of the sea, [Colloq. මුහුදුපෙන *múdu-pena*].

අදූෂිත, *Adúshita*, *a.* not contaminated, not polluted, not calumniated, not violated or blamed.

අදොස්, *Ados*,=අද්වේෂ *Adwésha*, *s.* freedom from hatred or enmity.

අඳනා, *Andaná*, *a.* painting, anointing, putting on as a garment.

අඳුන්කුළ, *Andunkula*,=අඤ්ජනකූට *Añjanakúta*, which see.

අඳෝ, *Andó*, *int.* Alas! Fy!

අඳෝනා, *Andóná*, *s.* weeping, lamentation, complaint.

අද්වය, *Adwaya*, *a.* without a second.

අද්විතීය, *Adwitíya*, *a.* (අ negative, ද්විතීය second) only, sole, without a second.

අධ්‍යක්ෂා, *Adhyakshá*, *s.* tree, *buchanania latifolia*, [Colloq. කිරිපළු *kiripalu*].

අධ්‍යාත්මික, *Adhyátmika*, *a.* spiritual, relating to the inner man or supreme spirit.

අධ්‍යාය, *Adhyáya*, *s.* section or division of a book, chapter, [Colloq. පරිච්ඡේදය *parichchhédaya*].

අධ්‍යාස, *Adhyása*, *s.* inhabiting, residing in; presiding over, sitting on or upon.

අධනී, *Adhani*, *s.* poor man, one destitute of wealth, [Colloq. දුප්පතා *duppatá*].

අධර්මචාරී, *Adharmachárí*, *s.* one who is immoral or irreligious, one who does not practise virtue.

අධරපල්ලව, *Adharapallawa*, *s.* (අධර lip, පල්ලව sprout, shoot, tender leaves) tender leaves-like lips.

අධිමුක්ති, *Adhimukti*, *s.* release, confidence, faith.

අධිතඵල, *Adhíta-phala*, *s.* tree, *phyllanthus emblica*, [Colloq. නෙල්ලි *nelli*].

අන් අලප්, *An-alap*,=අන්‍යාලාප, *Anyálápa*, which see.

අන්කරු, *Ankaru*, *s.* (in gram.) third person.

අන්කෙල්, *Ankel*, *s.* plant: see අඟුණ *anguna*.

අන්තර්වෘද්ධ, *Antarwriddha*, *a.* endogenous.

අන්තරට්ටාල, *Antarattála*, *s.* inside upper rooms or pavilions.

අන්තරාල, *Antarála*, *s.* included space, [Colloq. මැද *meda*].

අන්තරීක්ෂ, *Antariksha*, *s.* sky, heaven, [Colloq. අහස *ahasa*].

අන්තස්සර, *Antassara*, *s.* walking inside, within.

අන්තිම කෘත්‍ය, *Antima-kritya*, *s.* (අන්තිම last, කෘත්‍ය duties) what is done to a dead body; funeral duties.

අන්තෝසීමා, *Antó-símá*, *s.* within the boundary.

අන්දුබන්ධන, *Andubandhana*, *s.* fetters, [Colloq. විලංගු *vilangu*].

අන්ධයෂ්ටි, *Andhayashti*, *s.* blind man's staff or rod.

අන්නෑය, *Annéya*, *s.* injustice.

අන්‍යකාරක, *Anyakáraka*,=අන්කරු *ankaru*, which see.

අන්‍යතම, *Anyatama*, *a.* either, any, any one of many, distinct from many.

අන්‍යතීර්ථක, *Anyatirthaka*, *s.* other religionist.

අන්‍ය පර්ණි, *Anya-parṇi*, *s.* plant, *alyssicarpus bupleurifolius*, [Colloq. අස්වැන්න *aswęnna*].

අන්‍යාය, *Anyáya*, *s.* injustice.

අන්‍යාලාප, *Anyálápa*, *s.* [in Rhetor.] Metaphor; (as defined in Sidat Sangaráwa) "a sort of allegorical metaphor."

අන්‍යෝන්‍ය, *Anyónya*, *a.* (අන්‍ය *anya* repeated) mutual.

අන්වර්ථ, *Anwartha*, *a.* (අනු *anu*+අර්ථ *artha*) carrying out the sense of the root from which a word is derived.

අන්විත, *Anvita*, *s.* (අනු *anu* with ඉත *ita* gone) joined, connected with, possessed of, possessing.

අනංමනං, *Anaṇmanaṇ*, *s.* nonsensical talk.

අනත්, *Anat*, *s.* injustice, disadvantage: *a.* endless.

අනතිරිපා, *Anatiripá*,=ආනන්තර්‍ය පාපය, *Ánantarya-pápaya*, *s.* sin visited with immediate punishment in the next state of existence.

අනන්තක, *Anantaka*, *s.* timber tree, *calophyllum inophyllum*, [Colloq. දොඹ *domba*].

අනන්තරභව, *Anantara-bhawa*, *s.* (අන් *an*+අන්තර *antara* without interval, and භව existence) the next birth, state of existence immediately following.

අනන්තරෝක්ත, *Anantarókta*, *a.* (අනන්තර *anantara* and උක්ත *ukta*) mentioned immediately after.

අනන්තා, *Anantá*, *s.* twining plant with stinging hairs, *tragia involucrata*, [Colloq. වැල්කහඹිලියා *wel-kahambiliyá*]; sarsaparilla, *hemidesmus indicus*, [Colloq. ඉරමුසු *iramasu*]; grass, variety of *heteropogon hirtus*, [Colloq. හෙලඊතණ *hela-ítaṇa*].

අනන්තාපරිමාන, *Anantáparimána*, *a.* endless and immeasurable.

අනනුච්ඡවික, *Ananuchchhavika*, *a.* unfit, improper, [Colloq. නුසුදුසු *nusudusu*].

අනභිවෘද්ධිය, *Anabhiwṛiddhiya*, *s.* (අන් *an* and අභිවෘද්ධිය *abhiwṛiddhiya* prosperity) injury; harm; evil.

අනමතග්ග, *Anamatagga*, *a.* (අන් *an* not+අමත *amata* Nirvána, අග්ග *agga* end) which does not end in Nirváṇa. Turnour renders it, without beginning or end.

අනයිති, *Anayiti*, *a.* not belonging.

අනලස්වූයේ, *Analaswúyé*, *s.* one who is diligent; one who is not idle, [Colloq. අලසනොවූ *alasanowú*].

අනවස්ථිත, *Anawasthita*, *s.* (අ neg. අවස්ථිත *awasthita* steady) unsteady, unstable, inconstant, violating moral and legal restraint.

අනහංකාර, *Anahaṇkára*, *s.* freedom from pride or arrogance.

අනා, *Aná*,=අනාගත *Anágata*, *a.* future.

අනාගතඥානය, *Anágatajñánaya*, *a.* knowledge of the future.

අනාථනාථවූ, *Anáthanáthawú*, *a.* (අනාථ without a master or protector, නාථ *nátha* master, lord or protector) protector of those who have no protector, helper of the helpless, refuge of the distressed.

අනාද්‍යන්තවූ, *Anádyantawú*, *a.* having neither beginning nor end.

අනාර්‍යතික්ත, *Anárya-tikta*, *s.* plant, peculiar to Ceylon, *munronia pumila*, [Colloq. බින්කොහොඹ *bin-kohomba*].

අනිකී, *Anikí*, *s.* the other one, feminine form of අනිකා *aniká*.

අනිමිත්ත, *Animitta*, *a.* (අ negative, නිමිත්ත cause) without a cause.

අනිමිත්තඵල, *Animitta-phala*, *s.* causeless produce or fruit.

අනිවාර්‍ය, *Aniwárya*, *a.* not to be checked or opposed.

අනිස්ථිරකම, *Anisthirakama*, *s.* corruptly for අස්ථිරකම *asthirakama*, impermanence, inconstancy, instability.

අනිසේ, *Anisé*,=අනිත්‍ය, *Anitya*, *a.* inconstant, unstable.

අනුකරණ, *Anukaraṇa*, *s.* (අනු before කරණ making) imitation, making or doing anything in imitation of another; resemblance, similarity.

අනුක්‍රමණිකා, *Anukramaṇiká*, *s.* (අනු and ක්‍රමණ *kramaṇa* with ඉකා *iká* affix) table or chapter of contents, [Colloq. පටුන *paṭuna*].

අනුච්ඡවික, *Anuchchhavika*, *s.* suitable, fit, proper, [Colloq. සුදුසු *sudusu*].

අනුචිත, *Anuchita*, *a.* (අන් *an* neg. උචිත *uchita* proper) improper, wrong, [Colloq. නුසුදුසු *nusudusu*].

අනුඥාත, *Anujñáta*, *a.* permitted, sanctioned.

අනුදිත, *Anudita*, *a.* (අන් *an* neg. උදිත *udita* risen or said) unrisen, unsaid, unuttered.

අනුපද, *Anupada*, *s.* a word or passage repeated: *ind.* step by step.

අනුපදිසෙස්, *Anupadises*, see අනුපාදිසේස *anupádisésa.*

අනුපාකාර, *Anupákára*, *s.* (අනු inferior, secondary, පාකාර wall, rampart) second wall or rampart.

අනුපුටුව, *Anu-púṭṭuwa*, *s.* incorrectly for හනුපුට්ටුව *hanu-púṭṭuwa*, lock-jaw.

අනුභූත, *Anubhúta*, *s.* (අනු and භූත been) understood, apprehended, resulted, followed as a consequence, perceiving, understanding.

අනුමිතිය, *Anumitiya*, *s.* inference, deduction.

අනුයොන්, *Anuyon*, *s.* (අනු and යොන් origin, place of birth) secondary origin or place of birth.

අනුරුත්, *Anurut*, *s.* (අනු *anu*+අරුත් *arut* sense): see අන්වර්ථ *anwartha.*

අනුල්ලංඝන, *Anullańghana*, *s.* (අ+න්+උල්ලංඝන *ullańghana*) non-transgression.

අනුෂ්ටුප් ඡන්දස, *Anushṭup-chhandasa*, *s.* (අනුෂ්ටුප් metre so called and ඡන්දස poetical metre) measure of verse, the stanza consisting of four lines of eight syllables each. The fifth syllable of each line being short, the sixth long, and the seventh alternately long and short, whilst the first four syllables and the eighth are arbitrary.

අනුෂ්ඨාන, *Anushṭhána*, *s.* fixing, establishing, doing or engaging in anything, commencement, or course of proceeding.

අනුස්වාර, *Anuswára*, *s.* nasal letter (ං) or dot placed after a vowel, commonly called බින්දුව *binduwa.*

* අනුසර, *Anusara*, *s.* (අනු after, සර to go) conformity, following.

අනෝත්තප, *Anótapa*, *s.* absence of fear of sinning, recklessness.

අප්‍රණිහිත, *Apraṇihita*, *a.* (අ negative, ප්‍රණිහිත placed) not fixed or placed, not entrusted or acknowledged, not obtained, imprudent, unwary, not careful, not determined.

අප්‍රත්‍යක්ෂ ක්‍රියාව, *Apratyaksha-kriyáwa*, see අපසක් කිරිය *apasakkiriya*

අප්‍රතිමල්ල, *Apratimalla*, *a.* (අ neg. ප්‍රතිමල්ල rival) unrivalled, matchless.

අප්‍රමාණශුභ, *Apramáṇa-ṣubha*, *s.* (අප්‍රමාණ immeasurable, ශුභ good) good or welfare beyond measure.

අප්‍රාණික, *Apráṇika*, *a.* (අ neg. ප්‍රාණික living) not living, not possessed of life.

අප්‍රිය සම්ප්‍රයෝග, *Apriya-samprayóga*, *s.* (අ neg. ප්‍රිය beloved, සම්ප්‍රයෝග union) association with those who are not agreeable.

අපක්‍රමණය, *Apakramaṇaya*, *s.* straying, wandering; flight.

අපක්ව, *Apakwa*, *a.* (අ negative, පක්ව ripe) unripe, [Colloq. නොපැසුණු *nopẹsunu*].

අපත්‍ථ්‍ය විහරණ, *Apatthya-viharaṇa*, *s.* (අපථ්‍ය *apathya* improper, unsuitable, විහරණ mode of living) improper living.

අපත්‍ථ්‍යාහාර, *Apatthyáhára*, *s.* (අ neg. පථ්‍ය *pathya* suitable, ආහාර *áhára* food) improper food, food injurious in certain diseases.

අපත්‍ර, *Apatra*, *s.* small thorny tree, *euphorbia neriifolia*, [Colloq. පතුක් *patuk*].

අපත්විම, *Apatvíma*, *s.* decease, death, demise.

අපතේ, *Apaté*, *s.* waste.

අපනයන, *Apanayana*, *s.* act of removing, taking away, withdrawing; acquittance of a debt or obligation, [Colloq. පහකෙරීම *pahakeríma*].

අපනීත, *Apaníta*, *a.* (අප from, නී *ní* to take) taken away, removed, paid, discharged, [Colloq. පහකළ *pahakaḷa*].

අපරාධීන, *Aparádhína*, *a.* (අ neg. පර *para* other, අධීන *adhína* dependent) not dependent on others, independent.

අපරීක්ෂාකාර, *Aparíkshákára*, *s.* (අ neg. පරීක්ෂා examination, කාර doer) one who acts inconsiderately, rashly.

අපවත්විම, *Apawatvíma*, see අපත්විම *apatvíma.*

අපවරක, *Apawaraka*, *s.* inner apartment, lying-in-chamber; room, [Colloq. කාමරය *kámaraya*].

අපශබ්ද, *Apaṣabda*, *s.* (අප low, ශබ්ද sound) low word, incorrect speech, ungrammatical language.

අපසක්කිරිය, *Apasakkiriya*, *s.* act not perceptible by the senses.

අපායගාමී, *Apáyagámi*, *a.* (අපාය hell, ගාමි going) going to hell.

අපායභාග්, *Apáyabhág*, *s.* one suffering the torments of hell.

අපාර්ථ, *Apárttha*, *s.* (අප *apa* before අර්ථ *arttha*) incoherence in meaning, contradictory sense, inconsistence: *a.* unmeaning, useless.

අපාර, *Apára*, *s.* (අ neg. පාර shore) opposite bank of a river: *a.* unbounded, boundless, interminable.

අපිරිසේ, *Apirisé*=අපර්යන්ත, *Aparyanta*, *a.* unlimited.

අපිස්සන්තොස්බව, *Apis-satosbawa*, s. contentment.

අපූර්වරචිත, *Apúrwa-rachita*, a. recently made, [Colloq. අලුත් *alut*].

අබ්ධිකඵ, *Abdhikapha*, } s. (අබ්ධි sea, කඵ foam or
අබ්ධිජ, *Abdhija*, } ජ that which is produced) foam of the sea, [Colloq. මුදුපෙන *múdu-pena*].

අබ්බ. *Abba*, s. talc, plumbago, [Colloq. මිනිරන් *miniran*].

අබබ්බ, *Ababba*,=අභව්‍ය *abhawya*, which see.

අබවස්ති, *Abawashi*, s. in the open air.

අබවස, *Abawasa*, s. open place.

අබහය්, *Abahai*,=අභය, *Abhaya*, s. name of a king.

අබිම්මවා, *Abimmawá*, *part.* transgressing, not caring for, disregarding.

* අභය, *Abhaya*, s. ichneumon plant, *mimosa octandra*, [Colloq. අරත්ත *aratta*]; fragrant grass, *andropogon muricatus*, [Colloquial. සැවැන්දරා *sęwendará*].

අභයා, *Abhayá*, s. tree, *terminalia chebula*, [Colloq. අරළු *aralu*].

අභිඝාත, *Abhighâta*, s. (අභි before හන *hana* to strike) striking, wounding, pain, torture, removal, contact.

අභිඥාන, *Abijñána*, s. (අභි before, ඥා *jñá* to know) mark. spot, sign, token, ascertaining.

අභිධෙය, *Abhidhéya*, s. that which is named—in contradistinction to අභිධාන *abhidhána*, the name given.

අභිනනව, *Abhinnawa*, a. unbroken, [Colloq. නොබිඳි *nobindi*].

අභිප්‍රේත, *Abhipréta*, a. meant, intended, wished, [Colloq. කැමති *kęmati*].

අභිමුඛස්ථවූ, *Abhimukhasthawú*, a. standing in the presence of.

අභිරුකා, *Abhiruká*, } s. creeping plant, *asparagus*
අභිරුපති, *Abhirupati*, } *falcatus*, [Colloq. හාතාවාරිය *hátáwáriya*].

අභූතපූර්ව, *Abhútapúrwa*, a. not been before.

අභේදෝපචාර, *Abhédópachára*, s. (අ neg. භේද *bhéda* breach, distinction, උපචාර *upachára* approach, neighbourhood, usage) ellipsis, a form of speech that leaves something to be inferred, figure of rhetoric, called metonymy.

අඹල, *Ambala*, part of අඹරණවා *ambaranawá*, to whirl, to wave in the air.

අඹුසැමියෝ, *Ambusęmiyó*, s. (අඹු wife, සැමි husband) husband and wife.

අම්බරෝද්ගතවන, *Ambaródgatawana*, s. up lifted forest.

අම්බෂ්ඨා, *Ambashthá*, s. creeping plant, *cissampelos Pareira*, [Colloq. දියමිත්ත *diyamitta*]; plant, *marsilea quadrifolia*, [Colloq. ඇඹුලැඹිලිය *ęmbulęmbiliya*].

* අම්බුද, *Ambuda*, s. medicinal plant, *plectranthus zeylanicus*, [Colloq. ඉරිවේරිය *iriwériya*]; cloud.

අම්බුප්‍රසාදනී, *Aambu-prasádaní*, s. tree bearing the clearing nut, *strychnos potatorum*, [Colloq. ඉඟිනි *ingini*].

අම්බුවාහිනී, *Ambuwáhiní*, s. tree bearing the trumpet flower, *stereospermum suaveolens*, [Colloq. පළොල් *palol*].

අම්ලකර වායුව, *Amlakara-wáyuwa*, s. oxygen.

අම්ල කාඤ්ජිකා, *Amla-káñjiká*, s. vinegar, [Colloq. විනාකිරි *vinákiri*]; toddy or boiled rice water in a state of spontaneous fermentation, used in the preparation of medicine, [Colloq. කාඩි *kádi*].

අම්ලකේසර, *Amla-késara*, s. citron, *citrus medica*, [Colloq. ලප්නාරං *lapnáran*].

අම්ලපත්‍ර, *Amla-patra*, s. plant, *marsilea quadrifolia*, [Colloq. ඇඹුලැඹිලිය *ęmbulęmbiliya*].

අම්ලපත්‍රිකා *Amla-patriká*, s. tamarind tree, *tamarindus indica*, [Colloq. සියඹලා *siyambalá*].

අම්ලපුෂ්පක, *Amla-pushpaka*, s. tree, mountain ebony, *bauhinia purpurea*, [Colloq. කොබලිල *kobalila*].

අම්ලපූර, *Amla-púra*, see අම්ලපත්‍රිකා *amlapatriká*.

අම්ලලෝණිකා, *Amla-lóniká*, see අම්ලපත්‍ර *amlapatra*.

අම්ලා, *Amlá*, s. banana or plantain, *musa sapientum*, [Colloquial: කෙසෙල් *kesel*]; lime, *citrus limetta*, [Colloq. දෙහි *dehi*].

අමන්ත්‍රී, *Amantri*, s. (අ neg. මන්ත්‍රී councillor) one who has no counsellor.

අමන්නේය, *Amannéya*, v. blows, shall, or, will blow.

අමයි, *Amayi*, v. blows, spreads, diffuses.

අමරපුර, *Amarapura*, s. (අමර god, පුර city) city of the gods, heaven, [Colloq. දිව්‍යලෝකය *divyalókaya*].

අමරපුර සමාගම, *Amarapura-samágama*, s. (අමරපුර capital of Burma, සමාගම society) the Amarapura sect of Buddhists in Ceylon who are in communion with the priests of Burma. This sect was introduced into Ceylon, about 1800 A. D. by Ambagahapitiye, a priest of the Cháliya caste.

අමර පුෂ්පිකා, *Amara-pushpiká*, *s.* kind of dill or fennel, *anethum sowa*, [Colloq. ශතපුෂ්ප *ṣata-pushpa*].

අමරභව, *Amarabhawa*, *s.* plant, *amyrus agallocha*, [Colloq. ගුගුල් *gugul*].

අමරාවතී, *Amaráwati*, *s.* city of Indra, [Colloq. ශක්‍රපුරය *ṣakrapuraya*].

අමලා, *Amalá*, *s.* plant, *phyllanthus niruri*. [Colloq. පිටවක්කා *piṭawakká*].

අමා ඔසු, *Amáosu*,=අමෘත ඖෂධය, *Amṛita-aushadhaya*, *s.* medicine conferring immortality, nectareous medicine.

අමාකර, *Amákara*, *s.* (අමා nectar, ආකර *ákara* mine) the moon as the source of nectar, [Colloq. හඳ *haṉda*].

අමානන, *Amánana*, *s.* (අ neg. මානන esteem, regard) disregard, disrespect, [Colloq. නින්දාකෙරීම *nindákeríma*].

අමුක්කුව, *Amukkuwa*, *s.* trigger.

අමුලා, *Amulá*, *s.* plant, *Wrightia zeylanica*, [Coll: ඉද්ද *idda*].

අමූල්‍ය, *Amúlya*, *a.* (අ neg. මූල්‍ය price) invaluable, not to be purchased.

අමෘතපලා, *Amṛitapalá*, *s.* tree, *phyllanthus emblica*, [Colloq. නෙල්ලි *nelli*].

අමෘතපානය, *Amṛitapánaya*, *s.* (අමෘත nectar, පාන *pána* drinking) beverage of immortality.

අමෘතා, *Amṛitá*, *s.* tree, *terminalia chebula*, [Colloq. අරළු *araḷu*]; climbing plant, *tinospora cordifolia*, [Colloq. රසකිඳ *rasakiṉda*].

අමෘතාභිෂේක, *Amṛitábhishéka*, *s.* sprinkling with nectar.

අමෘතෝද්භවා, *Amṛitódbhawá*, *s.* heart pea, *cardiospermum halicacabum*, used in Ceylon for culinary and medicinal purposes, [Colloq. දූදු *dúdu*].

අමෙත, *Ameta*,
අමෙතිය, *Ametiya*, } =අමාත්‍ය, *amátya*, *s.* minister, counsellor.

අමෝඝා, *Amóghá*, *s.* tree, *stereospermum suaveolens*, [Colloq. පලොල් *paḷol*]; climbing anthelmintic shrub, *erycibe paniculata*, [Colloq. වළඟසාල් *waḷaṉgasál*].

අයකැමි, *Ayakęmi*, *s.* one who keeps an account of income or receipts, accountant.

අයගම, *Ayagama*, *s.* (අය tax or income, ගම village) royal village, [Colloq. නින්දගම *nindagama*].

අයජති, *Ayajati*, *v.* they invite, [Colloq. ආරාධනාකරති *árádhanákarati*].

අයත්, *Ayat*, *a.* belonging to, dependent upon, [Colloq. අයිති *ayiti*].

අයදුම් පත්‍රය, *Ayadum-patraya*, *s.* petition, application.

අයා, *Ayá*, *s.* Ceylon cardamoms, *elettaria cardamomum*, [Colloq. එන්සාල් *ensál*].

අයිනාදන්, *Ayinádan*, *s.* අයින් *ayin*+ආ *á*+දන් *dan*=අදින්නාදාන, *Adinnádána*, taking what is not given, *i. e.* stealing, theft.

අයිමි, *Ayimi*, *v.* I came.

අයිරාවණ, *Ayiráwaṇa*, *s.* Indra's elephant.

අයෝඝන, *Ayóghana*, *s.* (අයෝ for අයස් *ayas* iron, ඝන what strikes) hammer, a forge hammer, [Colloq. කුළුගෙඩිය *kuḷugeḍiya*].

අයෝනිසෝමනස්කාර, *Ayónisómanaskára*, *s.* (අ neg. යෝනිසෝ wisely, really, මනස්කාර attention) want of careful consideration or close attention.

අයෝසාර, *Ayósára*, *s.* (අයෝ for අයස් *ayas* iron, සාර essence, strength) iron, [Colloq. යකඩ *yakaḍa*].

අර්කලතා, *Arkalatá*, *s*, plant, *xyris indica*, [Colloq. රම්මනිස්ස *rammanissa*].

අර්චන, *Archana*, *s.* offering, [Colloq. පූජාව *pújáwa*].

අර්ච්චිස්, *Archchis*, *s.* flame of fire.

අර්ජක, *Arjaka*, *s.* medicinal plant, *spilanthes acmella*, [Colloq. අක්මැල්ල *akmęlla*].

අර්ජනී, *Arjaní*, *s.* Ceylon cardamoms, *elettaria cardamomum*, [Colloq. එන්සාල් *ensál*].

* අර්ජුන, *Arjuna*, *s.* tree, *terminalia glabra*, [Colloq. කුඹුක් *kuṉbuk*].

අර්ථකථා, *Arthakathá*, *s.* (අර්ථ meaning, කථා discourse) commentary, exposition of meaning, generally applied to commentaries on the text of the Tri-piṭaka or the three depositories of the doctrines of Buddha.

අර්ථ ක්‍රියා, *Artha-kriyá*, *s.* verbal appellative.

අර්ථ චර්‍ය්‍යා, *Artha-charyá*, *s.* (අර්ථ good, benefit, චර්‍ය්‍යා conduct) beneficial conduct, beneficence.

අර්ථනිරුක්තිය, *Arthaniruktiya*, *s.* explanation of words.

අර්ථප්‍රසාධනී, *Artha-prasádhaní*, *s.* bulbous stemless plant, *crinum zeylanicum*, [Colloq. ගොඩමානිල් *goḍa-mánil*].

අර්ථබෝධකයා, *Arthabódhakayá*, *s.* one who expounds the meaning; expositor.

අර්ථ ව්‍යාඛ්‍යාන, *Artha-wyákhyána*, *s.* paraphrase.

අර්ථාන්විත, *Arthánvita*, *a.* (අර්ථ *artha* meaning or wealth, අන්විත *anvita* possessed of) significant, rich.

අර්ථානර්ථ, *Arthánartha*, s. (අර්ථ *artha* good, අනර්ථ *anartha* evil) good and evil, advantage and disadvantage, [Colloq. වැඩ අවැඩ *wẹḍa-awẹḍa*].

අර්ථානුසාරය, *Arthánusáraya*, s. conformity to the meaning.

අර්ථී, *Arthí*, s. one who asks or seeks, servant, follower.

අර්ධගෝත්‍රය, *Ardha-gótraya*, s. (අර්ධ half, ගෝත්‍ර *gótra* caste or tribe) half-caste, half-tribe.

අර්ධගෝලය, *Ardha-gólaya*, s. (අර්ධ and ගෝලය globe) hemisphere.

අර්ධචන්ද්‍රා, *Ardha-chandrá*, s. heart-seed, *cardiospermum haliacacabam*, [Colloq. වැල් පෙනෙල *wẹl-penela*].

අර්ධජානුක, *Ardha-jánuka*, a. (අර්ධ half, ජානු knee, ක aff.) with the knee half bent.

අර්ශෝඝ්න, *Arṣóghna*, s. plant, *amorphophallus campanulatus*, [Colloq. කිඩාරම් *kiḍáram*]; marking nut tree, *semicarpus gardneri*, [Colloq. බඩුල්ල *badulla*].

අර්ශෝඝ්නී, *Arṣóghní*, s. climbing plant: see හිරුස්ස *hirẹssa*.

අර්හ, *Arha*, a. fit, proper, suitable, worthy of, [Colloq. සුදුසු *sudusu*].

අරතර, *Aratara*,=දැඩිතර, *Ḍẹḍitara*, s. excessively.

අරමණ්ඩ, *Aramanda*, s. plant, *gynandropsis pentaphylla*, [Colloq. වේලා *wélá*].

අරරුට්, *Araruṭ*, s. arrowroot. (Eng.)

අරලිය, *Araliya*, s. temple tree: see අලරිය *alariya*.

අරාව, *Aráwa*, s. portion of land newly asweddumised and lying detached from the range of fields.

අරිගණ, *Arigaṇa*, s. (අරි=ආර්ය *Árya* venerable, ගණ multitude) the saints, those who have entered the four paths of sanctification, [Colloq. ආර්ය සමූහයා *árya-samúhayá*].

අරිපුඟුල්, *Aripuṉgul*,=ආර්යපුද්ගල *Áryapudgala*, which see.

අරියු, *Ariyu*,=ආරාධිත, *Árádhita*, s. propitiated, invited, entreated, satisfied, pleased.

අරුණිකා, *Aruṇiká*, s. small grain or seed used by natives to put into their curries, [Colloq. උළුවා හාල් *uḷuwáhál*].

* අරුණු, *Aruṇu*,=ආරූඪ, *Árúḍha*: see ආරූඪශබ්ද, *árúḍha-ṣabda*.

අරුත්, *Arut*, s. meaning.

අරුත්පල, *Arut-pala*, [in Sinhalese Rhetoric.] energy produced by perspicuity.

අරුත්විලොම්, *Arutvilom*, a. contrary to the sense conveyed by the root from which a word is apparently derived.

අරුෂ්කර, *Arushkara*, s. marking nut tree, *semicarpus gardneri*, [Colloq. බඩුල්ල *badulla*].

අල්පමාරිෂ, *Alpamárisha*, s. sort of amaranth, *amarantus polygamus*, [Colloq. සුලුකූර *sulukúra* or වලුතම්පලා *walutampalá*].

අල්පායුෂ්කයෝ, *Alpáyushkayó*, s. (අල්ප *alpa* short, ආයුෂ්කයෝ *áyushkayó* those who have a term of life) those who live a short life, short-lived.

අල්පාර්හ, *Alpárha*, a. of little worth.

අල්ලා, *Allá*, v. having caught, past participle of අල්ලනවා *allanawá*, to catch.

අලංකාරෝක්තිය, *Alaṉkáróktiya*. s. rhetorical expression; ornaments of speech.

අලගර්ද, *Alagarda*, s. water-snake, [Colloq. දියනයා *diya-nayá*].

අලඹයටි, *Alaṃbayaṭi*, s. (අලඹ support, යටි stick) walking-stick, [Colloq. හැරමිටිය *hẹramiṭiya*].

අලම්බුෂා, *Alambushá*, s. name of a certain Apsara or heavenly nymph.

අලර්ක, *Alarka*, s. white variety of *calotropis gigantea*, [Colloq. හෙලවරා *hela-wará*]; mad dog or one rendered furious.

අලීක, *Alíka*, s. untruth, falsehood, a lie, [Colloq. බොරුව *boruwa*].

අලුත්හඳ, *Aluthaṉda*, s. new moon.

අව්‍යණ්ඩා, *Awyaṇḍá*, s. cowach, *carpopogon pruriens*, [Colloq. වඳුරුමෑ *waṉdurumẹ*].

අව්‍යථා, *Awyathá*, s. tree, *terminalia chebula*, [Coll: අරළු *araḷu*].

අව්‍යයශබ්ද, *Awyaya-ṣabda*, indeclinable word, particle.

අව්‍යාකෘත, *Awyákṛita*, s. (අ neg. ව්‍යාකෘත separated) elementary substance from which all things were created: a. undecomposed, simple.

අව්‍යුත්පන්න, *Awyutpanna*, a. ignorant, unlearned.

අවක්ෂේපණ, *Awakshépaṇa*, s. throwing down.

අවකේශි, *Awakéṣi*, a. barren.

අවගාරය, *Awagáraya*, s. auger.

අවදැරැ, *Awaḍẹrẹ*, v. having torn or divided.

අවධාන, *Awadhána*, s. attention, care, [Colloq. එකඟ *ekaṉga*].

අවධූනන, *Awadhúnana*, s. shaking, trembling, trampling on, causing to shake, [Colloq. සෙලවීම *selavíma*].

අවපීඩන, *Awapíḍana*, s. sternutatory, a drug which produces sneezing.

අවපෑළවිය, *Awa-pẹḷaviya*, *s.* first day of the dark half of a lunar month.

අවරෝහ, *Awaróha*, *s.* mounting, descending, pendant branch.

අවල්ගුජ, *Awalguja*, *s.* plant, *vernonia* or *serratula anthelmintica*, [Colloq. බෝදිඇට *bódi-ẹṭa*].

අවලකුණු, *Awalakuṇu*, *s.* unlucky omens, bad signs.

අවශ්‍යබන්ධු, *Awaṣya-bandhu*, *s.* close relative.

අවස්ථාන, *Awasthána*, *s.* situation, station, place or period of staying, [Colloq. සිටීම *siṭíma*].

අවස, *Awasa*,=ආවාස, *Áwása*, *s.* residence.

අවාක්පුෂ්පි, *Awákpushpí*, *s.* creeper, borago, *borago zeylanica*, [Colloq. යොන්තුඹ *yontumba*].

අවාපුරය, *Awápuraya*, *s.* hell, [Colloquial: නිරය *niraya*].

අවිච්චා, *Avichchá*, *s.* bird called Indian pitta, *pitta coronata*, (order *Passeres*); also called අවිච්චියා *avichchiyá*.

අවිනිශ්චිත, *Aviniṣchita*, *a.* not ascertained, not determined, not decided.

අවිප්‍රවාසය, *Aviprawásaya*, *s.* (අ negative, විප්‍රවාස *viprawása* residence in a foreign country) residence in one's own country.

අවිලංඝනීය, *Avilanghaníya*, *a.* not to be transgressed or exceeded; prescribed, fixed.

අවිසරඹ, *Avisaramba*, } *s.* fight with weapons;
අවිසරම, *Avisarama*, } battle.

අවිහිංසක, *Avihiṇsaka*, *a.* not doing harm; innocent; harmless.

අවිහිංසා, *Avihiṇsá*, *s.* harmlessness, innocence.

අවිහිත, *Avihita*, *a.* undone, uneffected, unprescribed, [Colloq. නොකළ *nokaḷa*].

අවීර්‍ය, *Avírya*, *a.* dispirited, disheartened.

අවුදින්, *Awudin*, = ඇවිත්, *Ẹvit*, *part.* having come.

අවුරු, *Awurú*, *s.* embankment.

අවුල්පත්, *Awulpat*, *s.* cakes and other sweet things eaten after a meal.

අවෛර, *Awaira*, *s.* absence of hatred.

අශ්මජ, *Aṣmaja*, *s.* red chalk; iron.

අශ්මජිත්, *Aṣmajit*, }
අශ්මභිද්, *Aṣmabhid*, } *s.* knot-grass, *ærua lanata* or *illecebrum lanatum*,
අශ්මභේද, *Aṣmabhéda*, } [Colloq. පොල්පලා *polpalá*].

අශ්මරස, *Aṣmarasa*, } *s.* iron, [Colloq. යකඩ *yakaḍa*]; sort of collyrium pre-
අශ්මසාර, *Aṣmasára*, } pared with the calx of brass or with the *amomum anthorrhiza*, [Colloq. රසාඤ්ජන *rasáñjana*].

අශ්‍ර, *Aṣra*, *s.* tear, blood.

අශ්වගන්ධා, *Aṣwagandhá*, } *s.* plant, *Withania som-*
අශ්වගන්ධි, *Aṣwagandhi*, } *nifera*, [Colloq. අමුක්කරා *amukkará*].

අශ්වත්ථපත්‍රකා, *Aṣwattha-patraká*, *s.* tree, *stereospermum suaveolens*, [Colloq. පලොල් *paḷol*].

අශ්වදන්තක, *Aṣwadantaka*, *s.* tree, *adhatoda vasica*, [Colloq. අගල්අඩුර *agaládúra*].

අශ්වනාහේ, *Aswanáhé*, *s.* muzzle of a horse.

අශිෂ්ට, *Aṣishṭa*, *a.* ill-regulated, ill-behaved; rude, barbarous, profligate.

අෂ්ටක්ෂණ, *Ashṭakshaṇa*, *s.* eight favorable opportunities of acquiring merit.

අෂ්ටකෝණ, *Ashṭakóṇa*, *s.* octagon.

අෂ්ටපර්ෂත්, *Ashṭa-parshat*, *s.* (අෂ්ට eight, පර්ෂත් assembly) eight classes of persons who were Buddha's attendants:—Kshatriya, Brahmins, householders, Buddhist monks, gods of the Cháturmahárájika world, gods of the Táwatiṇsa heaven, gods of the Vasawattimára world, and angels of the Brahma world.

අෂ්ටම, *Ashṭama*, *a.* eighth, [Colloq. අටවෙනි *aṭaweni*].

අෂ්ටමාධිපති, *Ashṭamádhipati*, *s.* the ruler of the eighth place in a horoscope.

අෂ්ටාදශ පුරාණ, *Ashṭádaṣa-puráṇa*, *s.* the eighteen Puráṇas, sacred and poetical works comprising the whole body of Hindu theology.

අෂ්ටාදශවිද්‍යා, *Ashṭádaṣa-vidyá*, *s.* eighteen branches of learning.

අෂ්ටාර්‍යපුද්ගල, *Ashṭárya-pudgala*, *s.* the eight holy personages who have attained the four Paths and four Fruitions.

අෂ්ටෝත්තර, *Ashṭóttara*, *a.* (අෂ්ට *ashṭa*+උත්තර *uttara*) plus eight, exceeded by eight.

අස්ඔබ්බවීම, *As-obbavíma*, *s.* stamping with a seal; prohibition.

අස්ගොව්වා, *Asgowwá*, *s.* horse-keeper.

අස්ත්‍යර්ථධාතු, *Astyartha-dhátu*, *s.* (අස්ති *asti*+අර්ථ *artha*+ධාතු) verbal root conveying the sense of අස්ති *asti*, "to be."

අස්ථි, *Asthi*, *s.* bone, [Colloq. ඇට *ẹṭa*].

අස්මත් ශබ්දාර්ථ, *Asmat-ṣabdártha*, *s.* (අස්මත් I, we+ශබ්ද *ṣabda* word, and අර්ථ *artha* sense) conveying the sense of the word 'අස්මත්' 'I or we.'

අස්ලිස, *Aslisa*, *s.* ninth lunar mansion containing five stars.

අස්වන්, *Aswan*, *s.* under crop.

අස්වනාත, *Aswanáta*, *s.* uncultivated portion of a field bordering a jungle.

අසවයා, *Aswayá*, corruptly for අශ්වයා *aṣwayá*.

අස්වස්, *Aswas*, *s.* consolation, inhaling air.

අස්වසා, *Aswasá*, *p.* having consoled, [Colloq. සනසා *sanasá*].

අස්වාමික, *Aswámika*, *a.* having no master or husband.

අස්වැද්දුම, *Aswędduma*, *s.* land recently converted into a field.

අස්වැසීම, *Aswęsíma*, *s.* act of consoling.

අස්සල, *Assala*, *s.* stable.

අසංඛත, *Asaṇkhata*, *a.* unorganised, immaterial.

අසංඛ්‍යාත, *Asaṇkhyáta*, *a.* uncounted.

අසංසර්ග, *Asaṇsarga*, *s.* non-association.

අසඞ්ගත, *Asańgata*, *a.* improper, unfit, unsuitable.

අසජ්ජන, *Asajjaṇa*, *s.* bad man. (Páli.)

අසඤ්ඤත, *Asaññáta*, *a.* unrestrained, intemperate. (Páli.)

අසඥතලය, *Asajñátalaya*, *s.* state of total unconsciousness, one of the Brahma worlds.

අසත්‍යභාෂක, *Asatyabháshaka*, *a.* speaking lies.

අසබහව්, *Asabahaw*,=අසම්භාවනීය *asambháwaníya*, which see.

අසභ්‍ය, *Asabhya*, *a.* unsuitable for an assembly, vulgar, low.

අසම්භාවනීය, *Asambháwaníya*, *a.* inconceivable, incomprehensible.

අසම්භාවනීය ක්‍රියා, *Asambháwaníya-kriyá*, [in Grammar] conditional or subjunctive mood.

අසම්භීත, *Asambhíta*, *a.* undaunted, [Colloq. භය නැති *bhayanęti*].

අසම්භෝග, *Asambhóga*, *s.* non-enjoyment.

අසමසමවූ, *Asamasamawú*, *a.* unrivalled, having no equal, matchless.

අසරණසරණවූ, *Asaraṇa-saraṇawú*, *s.* help of the helpless; refuge to those who have no refuge or protection.

අසස් පසස්, *Asas-pasas*,=ආශ්වාස ප්‍රශ්වාස *Áṣwása-praṣwása*, *s.* inhaled breath and exhaled breath.

අසාරූප්‍ය, *Asárupya*, *s.* unsuitablity, inconsistency.

අසාවදාරා, *Asáwadárá*, *p.* (honorific) having heard or questioned.

අසිපත්‍රක, *Asipatraka*, *s.* sugar cane. *saccharum officinarum*, [Colloq. උක්ගස් *ukgas*].

අසුරවිජයලත්, *Asuravijayalat*, *a.* who obtained victory over the Asuras or titans.

අසුරාචාර්ය, *Asurácharya*, *s.* teacher of the Asuras or titans, epithet of Sukra, regent of Venus.

අසූකෙළක්, *Asúkeḷak*, *s.* eighty kótis=800,000,000 millions.

අසෝ, *Asó*,=අසවල්, *Asawal*, *s.* such a one, such and such.

අහංකාරෝක්තිය, *Ahankáróktiya*, *s.* egotism; speaking highly of one's-self.

අහකාවෙලා, *Ahakáwelá*, *s.* after having done, or finished. (Vulgar.)

* **අහරකුක්කා**, *Aharakukká*, *s.* snake, *tropodonotus stolatus (Colubridæ*, order *Ophidiæ)*.

අහවාටිය, *Ahawáṭiya*, *s.* margin, border, edge.

අහස්දිය, *Ahas-diya*, *s.* rain-water.

අහසගෙරවීම, *Ahasageravíma*, *s.* thunder.

අහිරාවය, *Ahiráwaya*, *s.* sound made by a snake, [Colloq. සර්ප හඬ *sarpa-haṇḍa*].

අහිරික, *Ahirika*, *a.* shameless, impudent, [Colloq. ලජ්ජානැති *lajjáneti*].

අහිරිකබව, *Ahirikabawa*, *s.* state of being lost to shame.

අහේතුක ප්‍රතිසන්ධි, *Ahétuka-pratisandhi*, *s.* miserable conception, entering a miserable state of existence in a future world.

අහේපිළිසඳ, *Ahépiḷisaṇda*, see the last.

අහේම, *Ahéma*, *s.* distress.

අළහ, *Aḷaha*, *v.* they gave.

අළුකරවලා, *Aḷukarawalá*, *s.* snake: see කරවලා *karawalá*.

* **අළුකොබෙයියා**, *Aḷukobeyiyá*, *s.* spotted dove, *turtur suratensis*, (order *Columbæ*); also called කොබෙයියා *kobeyiyá*.

අළුගිරවා, *Aḷugirawá*, *s.* Layard's parrakeet, *palæornis calthropæ* (order *Psittaci*).

අළුමීකරවලා, *Aḷumí-karawalá*, *s.* snake: see කරවලා *karawalá*.

ආ

ආක්‍රමණ, *Ákramaṇa*, *s.* going over or beyond; subduing, attacking.

ආක්‍රාන්ත, *Ákránta*, *a.* overcome, distressed, surpassed.

ආකඩ්ඪන, *Ákaḍḍhana*, *s.* drawing, attraction.

ආකර්ණිත, *Ákarṇita*, *a.* heard, [Colloq ඇසූ *ęsú*].

ආකර්ෂණ, *Ákarshaṇa*, *s.* drawing, attraction.

ආකාඞ්ක්ෂා, *Ákáṅkshá*, *s.* wish, purpose, intention, enquiry, looking at, to, towards.

ආකාශධාතු, *Ákáṣadhátu*, *s.* element of air, space.

ආකාශවිද්‍යා, *Ákáṣavidyá*, *s.* meteorology.

ආකිඤ්චඤ්ඤායතන, *Ákiñchaññáyatana*, *s.* name of the third of the Arúpa Brahma lóka, peopled by beings who believe that nothing exists.

ආකු, *Áku*, *s.* Elu form of ආඛු *ákhu*, mouse or rat [Colloq. මියා *míyá*].

ආකුඤ්චන, *Ákuñchana*, *s.* contraction, [Colloq. ඇකිලීම *ẹkilíma*].

ආකුඤ්චිත, *Ákuñchita*, *s.* bent, curved, contracted, [Colloq. ඇකුළු *ẹkuḷú*].

ආකුලිත, *Ákulita*, *a.* bewildered, flurried, agitated, distressed.

ආකුලි, *Ákulí*, *s.* shrub, *cassia auriculata*, [Colloq. රණවරා *raṇawará*].

ආකුලිකෘත, *Ákulí-kṛita*, *a.* made ආකුල *ákula*, *i. e.* confounded, incoherent.

ආකෝටන, *Ákóṭana*, *s.* beating down.

ආකෝටිත, *Ákóṭita*, *a.* beaten down.

ආඛුපාෂාණ, *Ákhupáshána*, *s.* white arsenic, [Colloq. මීපාසානම් *mí-pásánam*].

ආගත, *Ágata*, *p.* come, arrived, [Colloq. ආවාවූ *áwáwú*].

ආගන්තුක සත්කාරය, *Ágantuka-satkáraya*, *s.* hospitality.

ආගාරික, *Ágárika*, *a.* belonging to a house.

ආච්ඡේද, *Áchchhéda*, *s.* cutting off, excision; plunder, robbery.

ආචන්ද්‍රාර්කස්ථායී, *Áchandrárkastháyí*, *s.* lasting as long as the moon and sun endure.

ආචමන, *Áchamana*, *s.* rinsing the mouth, gargling the throat, etc.

ආචාරධර්මයෙහි, *Áchára-dharmayehi*, *s.* in duties of courtesy, acts of civility, customary duties.

ආචීර්ණ, *Áchiṇṇa*, *a.* accustomed, practised, performed, sanctioned.

ආජ්‍ය, *Ájya*, *s.* clarified butter, [Colloq. ගිතෙල් *gitel*].

ආඥාව, *Ájñáwa*, *s.* command, order.

ආඬි, *Áṉḍi*, *s.* kind of sea fish.

ආත්ම, *Átma*, *s.* soap-berry plant, *sapindus emarginatus*, [Colloq. පෙනෙලගස් *penela-gas*].

ආත්මගුප්තා, *Átma-guptá*, *s.* cowach, *carpopogon pruriens*, [Colloq. වඳුරුමෑ *waṉdurumẹ*].

ආත්මජීවනීය, *Átma-jíwaníya*, *s.* milk, [Colloq. කිරි *kiri*].

ආත්මබාන්ධව, *Átmabándhawa*, *s.* one's own kinsman, first cousin.

ආත්මවර්ණනාව, *Átma-warṇanáwa*, *s.* self-praise; self-glorification; self-exultation.

ආත්මසංනිර්යාතන, *Átmasaṉniryátana*, *s.* (ආත්ම+සං+නිර්යාතන delivering, etc.) giving up one's self, revenging one's self.

ආත්‍යයික, *Átyaika*, *a.* (අත්‍යය *atyaya* destruction) ill-omened, unpropitious, destructive, painful.

ආතඞ්ක, *Átaṅka*, *s.* disease, pain, [Colloq. ලෙඩ *leḍa*.]

ආතෝද්‍ය, *Átódya*, *s.* musical instrument.

ආද්‍යධාතුව, *Ádyadhátuwa*, *s.* protoplast.

ආදරණීය, *Ádaraṇíya*, *a.* venerable, respectable, lovely.

ආදාහන කරණවා, *Ádáhana-karaṇawá*, *v.* to cremate.

ආදිකොට, *Ádikoṭa*, *part.* taking as the first, commencing with, et-cetera, [Colloq. පළමුකොට *paḷamukoṭa*].

ආදිත්‍යවල්ලී, *Ádityawallí*, *s.* plant, *ventilago maderaspatana*, [Colloq. කොබෝවක්කා *kobówakká*].

ආදර්ශය, *Ádṛiṣaya*, *s.* example.

ආධ්‍යා, *Ádhyá*, *s.* recollection, remembering, especially with regret.

ආධාන, *Ádhána*, *s.* taking, receiving, pledge, deposit; surety.

ආධාරාධෙයභාව, *Ádhárádhéyabháwa*, *s.* influence or action of the support or recipient upon the thing received or supported.

ආධික්‍ය, *Ádhikya*, *s.* excess.

ආධිපත්‍ය, *Ádhipatya*, *s.* supremacy, power, sovereignty.

ආධුනික, *Ádhunika*, *s.* young student, beginner.

ආධෙය, *Ádhéya*, *a.* to be placed, received, deposited.

ආන්දොල, *Ándóla*, } *s.* swinging, swing, oscillation.
ආන්දොලන, *Ándólana*, }

ආන්දොලිත, *Ándólita*, *a.* swung, shaken.

ආනඤ්ච, *Ánañcha*, *s.* infinity, immensity, boundlessness, (Páli.)

ආනන්තර්යකර්ම, *Ánantarya-karma*, *s.* five sinful deeds which will be visited with immediate punishment, *i. e.* in the next birth, viz. matricide, parricide, the murder of a Rahat, shedding the blood of a Buddha, and schism.

ආප්පේ, *Áppé*, *s.* cake made of a rice-flour, hopper: pl. ආප්ප *áppa*.

ආපීන, *Ápína*, *s.* udder, well: *a.* stout, fat.

ආබද්ධ, *Ábaddha*, *p. a.* fastened, joined, united.

ආභස්සර, *Ábhassara*, *s.* world of the radiant gods, a Brahma world so called.

ආභාෂ, *Ábhásha*, *s.* introduction.

ආභිධර්මික, *Ábhidharmmika*, *s.* connected with or versed in Abhidhamma or the Buddhist Metaphysics.

ආභීර, *Ábhíra*, *s.* cow-herd, [Colloquial: එඬේර *eṇḍérá*].

ආභිෂණ, *Ábhishaṇá*, *s.* plant, *cæsalpinea bonduc*, [Colloq. කුඹුරුවැල් *kumburuwel*].

ආම්බම, *Ámbama*, *s.* training.

ආමණ්ඩකී, *Ámaṇḍakí*, *s.* tree, *phyllanthus emblica*, [Colloq. නෙල්ලි *nelli*].

ආමය, *Ámaya*, *s.* sickness, disease.

ආමර්ෂ, *Ámarṣa*, *s.* advice, counsel.

ආමර්ෂ, *Ámarsha*, *s.* anger, wrath, [Colloq. ක්‍රෝධය *kródhaya*].

ආමාතිසාරය, *Ámátisáraya*, *s.* dysentery, the excretion being mixed with hard and fetid matter.

ආමුඛ, *Ámukha*, *s.* prelude, prologue, commencement of a drama.

ආයති, *Áyati*, *s.* length, future time.

ආයතිභව, *Áyatibhawa*, *s.* future state of existence.

ආයස, *Áyasa*, *s.* iron, weapon: *a.* made of iron.

ආයාචනා, *Áyáchaná*, *s.* petition, prayer, [Colloq. ඉල්ලීම *illíma*].

ආයාත, *Áyáta*, *a.* come, [Colloq. ආවාවූ *áwáwú*].

ආයුක්ත, *Áyukta*, *s.* agent, deputy, minister.

ආයුර්වාචක, *Áyurwáchaka*, *a.* expressing, "age."

ආයුරාරෝග්‍ය, *Áyurárógya*, *s.* long life and health.

ආයුසංස්කාර, *Áyusaṇskára*, *s.* term of life.

ආයෝජන, *Áyójana*, *s.* effort, endeavour, [Colloq. උත්සාහය *utsáhaya*].

ආයෝධන, *Áyódhana*, *s.* war, battle, conflict, [Colloq. යුද්ධය *yuddhaya*].

ආර්ද්‍ර, *Árdra*, *a.* wet, moist, [Colloq. තෙත්වූ *tetwú*].

ආර්ද්‍ර නාගර, *Árdra-nágara*, *s.* green ginger, [Colloq. අමුඉඟුරු *amu-inguru*].

ආර්‍ය්‍ය පුද්ගල, *Árya-pudgala*, *s.* holy personage, saint.

ආර්‍ය්‍යාෂ්ටාංගිකමාර්ග, *Áryáshṭáṅgika-márga*, *s.* the eight-fold holy path, viz. right views, right thoughts, right speech, right actions, right living, right exertion, right recollection, right meditation; (Childers.)

ආර්‍ය්‍යාපවාද, *Áryápawáda*, *s.* speaking evil of the saints.

ආර, *Ára*, *s.* stream, [Tamil, áru].

ආරක්ෂක, *Árakshaka*, *s.* watchman, patrole.

ආරක්ෂිත, *Árakshita*, *a.* protected.

ආරකූට, *Árakúṭa*, *s.* brass, [Colloquial: පිත්තල *pittala*].

ආරග්වධ, *Áragwadha*, *s.* medicinal tree, *cassia fistula*, [Colloq. ඇහැළ *ehela*].

ආරණ්‍යක, *Áraṇyaka*, *a.* wild, sylvan, inhabiting forests.

ආරණ්‍යජ, *Áraṇyaja*, *s.* forest-born, wild.

ආරාධිත, *Árádhita*, *a.* worshipped, propitiated, accomplished, effected.

ආරාමික, *Árámika*, *s.* temple servant, gardener.

ආරූඪශබ්ද, *Árúḍha-ṣabda*, *a.* word conveying a sense different from that of its apparent root.

ආරේවත, *Áréwata*, *s.* medicinal tree, *cassia fistula*, [Colloq. ඇහැළ *ehela*].

ආරෝග්‍යශාලාව, *Árógya-ṣáláwa*, *s.* hospital.

ආරෝචනය, *Áróchanaya*, *s.* making known, announcement, declaring. (Páli).

ආරෝහක, *Áróhaka*, *s.* rider; one who mounts.

ආලග්න, *Álagna*, *a.* adhering, [Colloquial: ඇලුන *eluna*].

ආලපන, *Álapana*, see අලප් *alap*; vocative case.

ආලවාල, *Álawála*, *s.* basin for water round the root of a tree.

ආලාපාලු, *Álápálu*, *s.* damage caused by cattle trespass.

*ආලි, *Áli*, *s.* main channel, spill, dam, bund of a tank.

ආලිංගිත, *Áliṅgita*, *a.* embraced.

ආලින්දය, *Álindaya*, *s.* terrace before a house, raised place or terrace for sleeping upon.

ආලිප්ත, *Álipta*, *a.* smeared, plastered, [Colloq. ගෑවාවූ *géwáwú*].

ආලිස්සම්, *Álissam*, *s.* disregard, carelessness, [Colloq. නොසැලකීම *noselakíma*].

ආලු, *Álu*, *s.* yam, edible root.

ආලෝකන, *Álókana*, *s.* seeing, [Colloq. බැලීම *belíma*].

ආලෝල, *Álóla*, *s.* trembling, agitation, [Colloq. කැලඹීම *kelambíma*].

ආවතේව කරන්නා, *Áwatéwa-karanná*, *s.* (ආවතේව+කරන්නා) attendant, keeper.

ආවර්තිත, *Áwarttita*, *a.* turned round, revolved.

ආවිෂ්ට, *Ávishṭa*, *a.* entered, possessed (as by a demon, etc.) engrossed (by any sentiment or feeling).

ආවේඨන, *Áwéṭhana*, *s.* entwining, surrounding, enclosing.

ආවෘත, *Áwṛita*, *a.* enclosed, surrounded, covered, abounding with.

* ආශ්‍රය, *Áṣraya*, *s.* (in common usage) companionship, association, intercourse.

ආශ්‍රයකරණවා, *Áṣraya-karaṇawá*, *v.* to associate with; to hold intercourse with.

ආශ්‍රිත, *Áṣrita*, *a.* inhabiting, resorting to, following, using, receiving, taking one's station at or on, as at a window, etc.; a dependant.

ආශ්ලේෂ, *Áṣlésha*, *s.* embracing, site of any act; intimate connection.

ආශ්වාසකරණවා, *Áṣwásakaraṇawá*, *v.* to inhale, to draw the air in.

ආශංකා, *Áṣaṅká*, *s.* fear, apprehension, doubt, uncertainty.

ආශිංසනයකරණවා, *v.* to bless, etc.

ආස්තෘත, *Ástṛita*, *a.* covered, strewn, [Colloq. ඇතුරූ *ęturú* or අතුළ *atuḷa*].

ආස්ඵෝටන, *Ásphóṭana*, *s.* blowing, expanding; contracting, closing; slapping.

ආස්ඵෝතා, *Ásphótá*, *s.* plant, [Colloq. කටරොළු *kaṭaroḷu*], which see.

ආස, *Ása*,=අහස *ahasa*, *s.* sky.

ආසක්ති, *Ásakti*, *s.* attachment, desire; intimate union, meeting, junction.

ආසිවිස, *Ásívisa*, *s.* snake. (Páli.)

ආසුර, *Ásura*, *s.* black salt.

ආසුරි, *Ásurí*, *s.* mustard, *brassica juncea*, [Colloq. අබ *aba*].

ආසේධ, *Ásédha*, *s.* legal restraint of four kinds, viz. කාලාසේධ *kálásédha*, limit of time, ස්ථානාසේධ *sthánásédha*, confinement to a place, ප්‍රවාසාසේධ *prawásásédha*, prohibition against removal or departure, කර්මාසේධ *karmásédha*, restriction from employment.

ආහ්ලාද, *Áhláda*, *s.* joy, delight, gladness, [Colloq. සතුට *satuṭa*].

ආහ්වාන, *Áhwána*, *s.* calling, call, summons, name, invocation.

ආහරණ, *Áharaṇa*, *s.* taking, seizing; extracting, causing.

ආහරබොක්ක, *Áhara-bokka*, *s.* receptacle of food, stomach.

ආහාර්‍යමාන, *Áháryamána*, *a.* taken; brought.

ආහිත, *Áhita*, *a.* placed, deposited, made, done; containing.

ඉ

ඉ, *I*, prefix implying intensity, *e. g.* ඉබොහෝ *ibohó*, very much; ඉවහල් *iwahal*, very helpful.

ඉක්ම, *Ikma*, *part.* having gone beyond, trespassed, transgressed, passed.

ඉක්ෂුගන්ධ, *Ikshugandha*, *s.* plant: see වැලුක් *wẹluk*.

ඉක්ෂුගන්ධා, *Ikshugandhá*, *s.* plant, *barleria prionitis*, [Colloq. ඉකිරි *ikiri* or කටුකරඬු *kaṭukaraṇḍu*]; plant, *tribulus terrestris*, [Colloq. සෙම්බුනෙරෙංචි *sembunereṇchi*].

ඉක්ෂුපත්‍ර, *Ikshupatra*, *s.* species of grain, jowar, *panicum spicatum*.

ඉක්ෂුබිදාරිකා, *Ikshu-bidáriká*, *s.* plant, *ipomœa digitata*, [Colloq. කිරිබඬු *kiribadu*].

ඉක්ෂුර, *Ikshura*, *s.* plant, *barleria prionitis*, [Colloq, ඉකිරි *ikiri* or කටුකරඬු *kaṭukaraṇḍu*].

ඉකුත්දෑ, *Ikutdẹ*, *s.* past birth, [Colloq. පසුගිය ජාතිය *pasugiya-játiya*].

ඉකුත්වත්, *Ikutwat*, *s.* past narrative, history of the past.

ඉච්ඡාවිඝාත, *Ichchhávighátha*, *s.* defeat of one's wishes.

ඉටා, *Iṭá*, *part.* of ඉටනවා *iṭanawá*, to resolve, [Colloq. අධිෂ්ඨානකොට *adhishṭhánakoṭa*].

ඉටුමිතුරු, *Iṭumituru*, *s.* cherished friend, beloved friend.

ඉඩෝරකාලය, *Iḍóra-kálaya*, *s.* hot or dry season.

ඉණකඩක්, *Iṇakaḍak*, *s.* waist-cloth.

ඉත්ථම්භූත, *Itthambhúta*, *a.* (ඉත්ථම් thus, so, භූත been) grammatical term to express the state of one's feeling or disposition towards another.

ඉතසිතින්, *Itasitin*, *s.* with friendly feeling.

ඉතිකින්, *Itikin*, *s.* from hence, [Colloq. මෙයින් *meyin*].

ඉතිහස, *Itihasa*, see ඉතිහාස *itihása*.

ඉදි, *Idi*, Elu form of ඍජු *ṛiju* and of ඍද්ධි *ṛiddhi*, *q. v.*

ඉදිකළ, *Idikaḷa*, *a.* made.

ඉදු, *Idu*,=ඉදි, *Idi*, which see.

ඉදුහු, *Iduhu*, *s.* superhuman power, [Colloq. ඍද්ධිය *ṛiddhiya*].

ඉඳලොලු, *Indalolu*, *s.* kind of mushroom.

ඉඳි ඇල්වී, *Indi-ęlví*, *s.* kind of paddy, *oryza sativa*.

ඉඳින්, *Indin*, imperative Mood of ඉඳිනවා *indinawá*, addressed to equals or inferiors.

ඉඳිපත් ඇල්වී, *Indipat-ęlví*, *s.* kind of paddy, *oryza sativa*.

ඉඳුරුකොකා, *Indurukoká*, *s.* grey heron: see කලපුව කරවැල්කොකා *kalapuwa-karawęlkoká*.

ඉඳුරුදික්පති, *Indurudikpati*, *s.* regent of the east, ruler of Swarga or paradise, [Colloq. ශක්‍රයා *ṣakrayá*].

ඉඳුරුපුර, *Indurupura*, *s*, city of Indra, Amarávatí, capital of Indra.

ඉන්, *In*,=එයින් *Eyin*, from it, from them.
ඉඳදී, *Indadí*,=ඉන්දෙද්දී *Indeddí*, whilst being.
ඉන්දීවරී, *Indíwari*, *s.* creeping plant, *asparagus falcatus* or *a. officinalis*, [Colloq. හාතාවාරිය *hátáwáriya*].
ඉන්‍ද්‍රගෝප, *Indragópa*, *s.* insect, (coccinella of various kinds).
ඉන්‍ද්‍රජාලික, *Indrajálika*, *s.* juggler, conjuror.
ඉන්‍ද්‍රදික්, *Indradik*, *s.* the direction over which Indra rules.
ඉන්‍ද්‍රද්‍රු, *Indradru*, *s.* tree, *terminalia glabra*, [Coll: කුඹුක් *kumbuk*].
ඉන්‍ද්‍රයව, *Indra-yawa*, *s.* medicinal nut or seed, from the tree, *nerium antidysentericum*, [Colloq. කෙළිඳඇට *kelinda-eta*].
ඉන්‍ද්‍රලුප්ත, *Indralupta*, *s.* kind of small worm which eats away the roots of the hair, [Colloq. උඳුගොවුවා *undugowuwá*]; morbid baldness, falling of the hair of the head.
ඉන්‍ද්‍රවජ්‍රා, *Indra-wajrá*, *s.* verse of four Pádas, each of which contains two antibacchics, one amphibrach and two long syllables.
ඉන්‍ද්‍රවල්ලී, *Indrawallí*, *s.* medicinal plant, *plumbago zeylanica*, [Colloq. එලනෙටුල් *elanetul*].
ඉන්‍ද්‍රවාරුණිකා, *Indrawáruniká*, *s.* kind of cucumber, large variety of the *cucumis pubescens*, [Colloq. මහගොන්කැකිරි *maha-gonkekiri*].
ඉන්‍ද්‍රවාරුණී, *Indrawáruni*, *s.* sort of cucumber, [Colloq. තියඹරා *tiyambará*].
ඉන්‍ද්‍රාණී, *Indrání*, *s.* shrub, species of *vitex*, [Colloq. නික *nika*].
ඉන්‍ද්‍රියබෝධනී, *Indriyabódhaní*, *s.* medicinal plant, *hydrocotyle asiatica*, [Colloq. මකුළුවැන්න *makuluwenna*].
ඉන්‍ද්‍රෝපල, *Indrópala*, see ඉන්‍ද්‍රනීල *indraníla*.
ඉන්නියර, *Inniyara*, *s.* limitary dam or ridge of a field.
ඉන්මතු, *Inmatu*, *adv.* after that.
ඉනත්කරණවා, *Inatkaranawá*, *v.* to vaccinate.
ඉනි, *Iní*, *v.* released, untied, set loose.
ඉපන්, *Ipan*,=උපන් *upan*, *a.* born.
ඉපිලෙනවා, *Ipilenawá*, *v.* to float.
ඉපැදෙ, *Ipede*, *v.* being born.
ඉබියතුර, *Ibiyatura*, see ගෙඩියතුර *gedi-yatura*.
ඉබෝ, *Ibó*, *s.* (ඉ=අති *ati* or ඉතා *itá* very, බෝ=බොහෝ *bohó* many) very many.
ඉභකණා, *Ibhakaná*, *s.* climbing plant: see ඇත්වගපුල් *etwagapul*.

ඉඹුල් ලාටු, *Imbul-látu*, *s.* gum of the silk cotton tree.
ඉර්වාරු, *Irwáru*, *s.* generic name for cucumber, [Colloq. කැකිරි *kekiri*].
ඉර්වාරුකිණී, *Irwárukiní*, *s.* kind of cucumber, large variety of the *cucumis pubescens*, [Colloq. මහගොන්කැකිරි *maha-gonkekiri*].
ඉරමඬල, *Iramandala*, *s.* disc of the sun.
ඉරුරැස්, *Iru-res*, *s.* rays of the sun.
ඉරුවේ, *Iruwé*, see ඍග්වේද *rigwéda*.
ඉරෙණවා, *Irenawá*, *v.* to be split or torn: pret. ඉරුණ *iruná*.
ඉවකරණවා, *Ivakaranawá*, *v.* to search by scent.
ඉවත්ව, *Iratwa*, *v.* standing aside.
ඉවහල්, *Ivahal*, *s.* very useful.
ඉෂ්ටදේවතාවා, *Ishtadéwatáwá*, *s.* tutelary deity, one particularly worshipped.
ඉස්පිල්ල, *Ispilla*, *s.* the symbol ි or ී for ඉ *i* or ඊ *í* respectively, placed over a consonant.
* ඉස්බ, *Isba*, *s.* verbal root meaning 'to take rest.'
ඉස්සරවෙනවා, *Issarawenawá*, *v.* to get the start of, to go ahead.
ඉස්සාමච්ඡරිය, *Issámachchhariya*, *s.* envy and avaric, [Colloq. ඊර්ෂ්‍යාව *írshyáwa*, මසුරුකම *masurukama*].
ඉසහෙණමුගුරු, *Isahena-muguru*, *s.* clubs falling on the head.
ඉසුරණ, *Isurana*, *a.* scattered, sprinkled, dispersed.
ඉසුරු, *Isuru*, see ඊශ්වර *iswara*.
ඉසුරුමදයෙන්, *Isurumadayen*, *s.* in the pride of wealth.

ඊ

ඊ, *Í*,=එහි *ehi*, as "ඊ උවටා ලෙසින් *Í uwata lesin*"=එහි (ඒ විහාරයෙහි උපස්ථායකයන් පරිද්දෙන් *É viháráyehi upastháyakayan paridden*) like the ministers in it (in that temple).
ඊදෝලි, *Ídóli*,=ඊල්දෝලි *Íldóli*, *s.* palanquin and litter.
ඊනියා, *Íniyá*,=මේ අන්දමේ *Mé-andamé*, of this nature, such as this.
ඊප්සිත, *Ípsita*, *a.* desired, wished.

උ

උංචිල්ලාව, *Unchilláwa*, *s.* swing.
උකාගත්, *Ukágat*, *a.* taken up, raised, lifted up.

*උකුස්සා, *Ukussá*, *s.* pale harrier, *circus macrurus;* crested goshawk, *astur trivirgatus;* Indian goshawk, *a. badius,* also called කුරුළුගොයා *kurulugoyá;* jungle sparrow hawk, *accipiter virgatus;* black shouldered kite, *elanus caeruleus;* common peregrine, *falco peregrinus;* Indian peregrine, *p. peregrinator;* common kestrel *cerchneis tinnunculur*, also called කුරුළුගොයා *kurulugoyá (*order *Accipitres).*

උග්‍රගන්ධඵල, *Ugragandha-phala*, *s.* variety of the mandarin orange, *citrus noblis*, [Colloq හින් නාරන් *hín-náran*].

උග්ඝටිතඤ්ඤු, *Ugghațitaññu*, *a.* understanding what is revealed.

උගතමනා, *Ugatamaná*, *a.* fit to be learned.

උච්චාර්‍යමාන, *Uchcháryamána*, *a.* being uttered or pronounced.

උචිත, *Uchıta*, *a.* fit, proper, [Colloq. සුදුසු *sudusu*].

උජ්ජුමානක, *Ujjumánaka*, see කදුරු *kaduru.*

උජ්ජ්වලිත, *Ujjwalita*, *s.* lighted, shining, flaming, etc.

උජාරිකා, *Ujáriká*, *s.* boils in armpit.

උජාරු, *Ujáru*, *s.* vain shew, ostentation, display.

උඩත්ත, *Udatta*, medicinal plant, not ascertained.

උඩත්පිරිසෙයින්, *Udatpiriseyin*, *ad.* at the most.

උඩබල, *Udabala*, *s.* plant, *hedyotis nitida*, [Colloq. පිටසුදුපලා *pitasudu-palá*].

උඩුකුරු, *Udukuru*, *a.* looking upwards, with the face turned up.

උඩුගඟ, *Uduganga*, *s.* upper part of the river; towards the source of the river.

උඩුදෙලි, *Ududeli* *s.* mustache.

උඩුමහල්තලය, *Udumahaltalaya*, *s.* upper story of a palace.

උඩුහෝ, *Uduhó*, *s.* upper part of a river.

උණ්හීස, *Unhísa*, *s.* crown, turban; curly hair with which a Buddha is born.

උණුලොම්, *Unulom*, see ඌර්ණරෝම *úrnaróma.*

උත්ක්ෂේපණීයකර්ම, *Utkshépaníyakarma*, *s.* excommunication of a Buddhist priest for a grave offence.

උත්කට, *Utkata*, *s.* cinnamon bark, *cinnamomum zeylanicum*, [Colloq. කුරුඳුපොතු *kurundupotu*].

උත්තංස, *Uttansa*, *s.* earring; crest.

උත්තමා, *Uttamá*, *s.* medicine compounded of the three noted myrobalans or medicinal nuts, අරළු *aralu*, බුළු *bulu*, නෙල්ලි *nelli:* see තිපල් *tipal.*

උත්තරඞ්ග, *Uttaranga*, *s.* wooden arch surmounting a door frame: *a.* flooded, inundated.

උත්තරපක්ෂය, *Uttarapakshaya*, *s.* second part of an argument, reply, refutation; minor proposition in a syllogism; latter half of a lunar month.

උත්තරවෘත්තිය, *Uttarawrittiya*, *s.* (in Logic) the consequent clause in a conditional sentence; apodosis.

උත්තරාංශය, *Uttaránsaya*, *s.* symbol "ෙ *e*" "ේ *é*", attached to a consonant as in කෙ *ke*, කේ *ké.*

උත්තරාග්‍රය, *Uttarágraya*, *s.* north pole.

උත්තරිතර, *Uttaritara*, *s.* superior, better, more eminent, higher.

උත්තානපත්‍ර, *Uttánapatra*, *s.* castor oil plant, *ricinus communis*, [Colloq. එඬරු *endaru*].

උත්ථිත, *Utthita*, *s.* risen, born, produced, happened, occurring.

උත්පලවන, *Utpalawana*, *s.* jumping, springing upon.

උත්පලශාරිවා, *Utpala-sáriwá*, *s.* sarsaparilla, *hemidesmus indicus*, [Colloq. ඉරමුසු *iramasu*].

උත්ඵුල්ල, *Utphulla*, *a.* expanded, blown, as a flower; risen as bread, leavened, [Colloq. පිපුන *pipuna*].

උතුරුකන් හුලඟ, *Uturukan-hulanga*, *s.* wind from the northern point of the Compass.

උතුරුදිගිඳු, *Uturu-digindu*, *s.* name of Kuvéra regent of the north and chief of the Yakshas, [Colloq. වෙසමුණු *wesamunu*].

උතුරුපුටුපය, *Uturuputupaya*, *s.* the second of the lunar asterisms called Bhádrapadá.

උතුවදන, *Utuwadana*, *s.* tree, *phyllanthus emblica*, [Colloq. නෙල්ලි *nelli*].

උතුළ, *Utula*, *a.* overflowed.

උද්ග්‍රහණ, *Udgrahana*, *s.* learning, [Colloq. ඉගෙනගැණිම *igenageníma*].

උද්ගීර්ණ, *Udgírna*, *v.* vomited, thrown out, [Colloq. වැමෙරූ *wemérú*].

උද්දාල, *Uddála*, *s.* low tree with edible roots, *cordia myxa*, [Colloq. ලෝලු *lólu*].

උද්ධරණ, *Uddharana*, *s.* raising or lifting any thing, eradicating, vomiting.

උද්ධූත, *Uddhúna*, *a.* raised, pulled up, lifted up, thrown up.

උද්භාවන, *Udbháwana*, *s.* neglect, inattention, disregard.

උද්‍යම, *Udyama*, *s.* strenuous and continued effort, strenuous exertion, [Colloq. උත්සාහය *utsáhaya*].

උද්වර්තන, *Udwartana*, *s.* going up, rising, grinding, pounding, rubbing or kneading the body.

උද්වහනය, } උවහනය, } *Udwahanaya*, *s.* bearing, [Colloq. ඉසිලීම *isilíma*].

උද්වේග, *Udwéga*, *s.* regret, anxiety, distress: betel nut.

* උදක්, *Udak*, *a.* only, merely.

උදග්‍ර, *Udagra*, *a.* high, tall; pointing upwards, excessive, [Colloq. අධික *adhika*]; fierce, intense, large, vast.

උදන්, *Udan*, see උදාන *udána*.

උදයඅත්, *Udaya-at*, *s.* east, [Colloq. නැගෙණහිර *negeṇahira*].

උදය පර්වතය, *Udaya-parwataya*, *s.* the eastern mountain behind which the sun is supposed to rise.

උදරබන්ධනය, *Udarabandhanaya*, *s.* belt for the waist, [Colloq. ඔට්ටුකච්චිය *oṭṭukachchiya*].

උදරාග්නිය, *Udarágniya*, *s.* hunger, [Colloq. බඩගින්න *baḍaginna*].

උදශ්චිත්, *Udaşchit*, *s.* butter milk with an equal proportion of water.

උදාගල්, *Udágal*, } *s.* fabulous rock in the east.
උදාගිරි, *Udágiri*, }

උදීච්‍ය, *Udíchya*, *s.* medicinal plant, *plectranthus zeylanicus*, [Colloq. ඉරිවේරිය *iriwériya*].

උදුම්බරපර්ණි, *Udumbara-parṇi*, *s.* medicinal plant, *croton polyandrum:* [Colloq. දැත්ත ගස් *detta-gas*].

උන්නත, *Unnata*, *a.* high, elevated.

උන්මත්ත, *Unmatta*, *s.* thorn apple, *datura fastuosa*, [Colloq. අත්තන *attana*].

උනඹර, *Unambara*. *s.* heretical or unorthodox ascetic.

උනුන්, *Unun*, pron.=උන් *un*+උන් *un* one another, each other, mutually.

උපකථා, *Upakathá*, *s.* anecdote.

උපකුංචිකා, *Upakunchiká*, *s.* black cummin seed, *nigella indica*, [Colloq. කළුදුරු *kaḷuduru*].

උපකුල්‍යා, *Upakulyá*, *s.* long pepper, *piper longum*, [Colloq. තිප්පිලි *tippili*].

උපගන්ධිකා, *Upagandhiká*, *s.* kind of basil, *ocimum gratissimum*, [Colloq. වේලා *wélá*].

උපචය, *Upachaya*, *s.* heap, accumulation, elevation, prosperity.

උපචිත්‍රා, *Upachitrá*, *s.* medicinal plant, *croton polyandrum*, [Colloq. දැත්ත *detta*]; plant, *hoya hirsuta*, [Colloq. මිනුග *mínuga*].

උපද්‍රව රහිත, *Upadrawa-rahita*, *a.* free from danger, safe.

* උපදන්, *Upadan*, *s.* taking, restraining, cause, motive; material cause; proximate cause.

උපදේශ රත්නය, *Upadéşa-ratnaya*, *s.* jewel of advice, precious piece of advice.

උපදේශ වාක්‍යය, *Upadéşa-wákyaya*, *s.* instruction in morality; moral maxims.

උපනුපන්, *Upanupan*, *a.* born and born, viz. in various births.

උපපීඩක, *Upapíḍaka*, *a.* inflicting pain.

උපමාවිෂය, *Upamávishaya*, *s.* range of similitude or comparison.

උපමේය, *Upaméya*, *s.* (in gram.) that to which a similitude is exhibited as opposed to උපමා *upamá* or උවම් *uwam* that from which the comparison is drawn; object compared.

උපරජ, *Upa-raja*, *s.* viceroy: see යුවරජ *yuwa-raja* and උපරාජ *upa-rája*.

උපරි, *Upari*, *prep.* above, higer up, upwards, over, above the head, [Colloq. උඩ *uḍa*].

උපරිගමන, *Uparigamana*, *s.* going upwards, passing over.

උපරිභාග, *Uparibhága*, *s.* upper part.

උපලාලන, *Upalálana*, *s.* soothing, conciliating, lulling, [Colloq. නැළවීම *neḷavíma*].

උපවේශන, *Upawéşana*, *s.* sitting, resting; voiding by stool.

උපස්ථිත, *Upasthita*, *a.* approached, staying near to, arrived.

උපසපන්, *Upasapan*,=උපසම්පන්න, *Upa-sampanna*, *a.* having priest's orders, ordained.

උපාඛ්‍යාන, *Upákhyána*, *s.* anecdote; tale, narrative.

උපාගත, *Upágata*, *a.* approached, arrived; occurred.

උපාඞ්ගසූත්‍ර, *Upánga-sútra*, *s.* secondary or subsidiary rules.

උපාය චින්තන, *Upáya-chintana*, *s.* devising means to an end.

උපායඥ, *Upáyajña*, *a.* one skilled in contriving means or expedients.

උපුටාගෙණ, *Upuṭágeṇa*, *v.* having extracted or compiled from.

උපෝදිකා, *Upódiká*, *s.* Malabar nightshade, plant with leaves resembling spinage, *basella alba*, [Colloq. නිවිතිවැල් *niviti-wel*].

උපෝසථ, *Upósatha*, *s.* quarters of the moon observed sacred by the Buddhist, [Colloq. පෝය *póya*].

උබබස්, *Ubabas*, see උභයභාෂා *ubhayabháshá*.

උභතෝකෝටික, *Ubhatókóṭika*, *s.* dilemma, an argument conclusive both ways.

උභයභාෂා, *Ubhaya-bháshá*, *s.* dialogue, (in Rhet.)

උභයලෝක, *Ubhaya-lóka*, *s.* two worlds, this and the next life.

උම්බලකඩ, *Umbalakada*, *s.* Maldive fish.

උම්මත්ත, *Ummatta*, Páli form of උන්මත්ත *unmatta*.

උමංදාව, *Umandáwa*, *s.* book so called, the birth story of Buddha giving an account of his උමඟ *umaga* an underground passage.

උමංදොර, *Umandora*, *s.* the entrance to the උමඟ *umaga*.

උමතුවන්සේ, *Umatuwansé*, *s.* as insane persons.

උයිත්, *Uyit*, *pron.* and he.

උරඟ, *Uranga*, *s.* snake, serpent, one who creeps.

උරස්තලය, *Urastalaya*, *s.* the chest, breast.

උරුබුක, *Urubuka*, *s.* castor oil plant, *ricinus communis*, [Colloq. එඬරු *endaru*].

උරෝජාත, *Urójáta*, see උරදා *uradá*.

උරුලුවන්බානවා, *Uruluwanbánawá*, } *v.* to whistle.
උරුලෑපිඹිනවා, *Urulé-pimbinawá*, }

උල්ලඞ්ඝනය කරණවා, *Ullanghanaya-karanawá*, *v.* to overstep, transgress, leap over.

උල්ලඞ්ඝිත, *Ullanghita*, *a.* passed over or beyond, transgressed, jumped across.

උල්ලාඝ, *Ullágha*, *a.* recovered from sickness, clever, happy, pure.

උල්ලෝල, *Ullóla*, see උලෙල *ulela*.

උල්වර, *Ulwara*, *s.* plant, *barleria prionitis*, [Coll: කටුකරඬු *katukarandu*].

උල්වැරණිය, *Ul-weraniya*, *s.* medicinal plant.

උලක්කු, *Ulakku*, *s.* one fourth part of a ප්‍රස්ථ *prastha* or නැළිය *neliya*, [Colloq. පත *pata*].

* උලමා, *Ulamá*, *s.* brown wood owl, *syrnium indrani*, (order *Accipitres*).

උවටු, *Uwatu*, *s.* servant; attendant: see උපස්ථායක යා *upastháyakayá*.

උවදන්, *Uwadan*,=උපදාන, *Upadána*, present to a king or a great man, [Colloq. පඬුර *pandura*].

උවම්, *Uwam*, see උපමා *upamá*.

උවමේ, *Uwamé*, see උපමේය *upaméya*.

උවමැනව, *Uwamenawa*, *v.* be pleased to be or become.

උවැසි, *Uwesi*, see උපාසක *upásaka*.

උශීර, *Usíra*, *s.* fragrant grass, *andropogon muricatus*, [Colloq. සැවැන්දරා *sewendará*].

උෂ්ට්‍ර, *Ushtra*, *s.* camel, [Colloq. ඔටුවා *otuwá*].

උෂණා, *Ushaná*, *s.* long pepper, *piper longum*, [Colloq. තිප්පිලි *tippili*].

උසස්කම, *Usaskama*, *s.* height, altitude.

උසිරණා, *Usiraná*, *s.* magnet, loadstone, [Colloq. කාන්දම *kándama*].

උසුන්මුල්, *Usunmul*, *a.* eradicated, pulled by the roots.

උහු, *Uhu*, *pron.* his, him.

උළුපැන්ගේ, *Ulupengé*, *s.* bathing establishment of Sinhalese kings.

ඌ

* ඌ, *Ú*, *pron.* they, she.

ඌනපූරණය, *Únapúranaya*, *s.* supplying of deficiency; supplement.

ඌනමාත්‍ර, *Únamátra*, *a.* less syllabic quantity.

ඌනවිංශතිය, *Úna-vinsatiya*, *s.* twenty minus one, nineteen.

ඌනාතිරේක, *Únátiréka*, *s.* deficiency and excess.

ඌර්ධ්වගත, *Úrdhwagata*, *a.* gone upwards.

ඌර්ධ්වලෝම, *Úrdhwalóma*, *s.* kind of reed, *imperata arundinacea*, [Colloq. ඉලුක් *iluk*].

ඌර්මිවේගය, *Úrmiwégaya*, *s.* force of the waves.

ඌරල්වෙනවා, *Úralwenawá*, *v.* to stick in fast, to be penetrated.

ඌරුපු, *Úrupu*, } *s.* castor oil plant, *ricinus com-*
ඌරුබු, *Úrubu*, } *munis*, [Colloq. එඬරු *endaru*].

ඌරුයුගලය, *Úruyugalaya*, *s.* two thighs.

ඌරුස්තම්භ, *Úrustambha*, *s.* paralysis of the lower extremities; rheumatism of the thigh.

ඌල්, *Úl*, *s.* spring of water; fountain, [Colloq. උල්පත *ulpata*].

ඌසිකාන්දම්, *Úsikándam*, *s.* [Tamil.] magnet, loadstone.

ඍ

ඍක්ෂ, *Riksha*, *s.* plant, *oroxylum indicum*, [Colloq. තොටිල *totila*]; star; bear.

ඍක්ෂගන්ධා, *Riksha-gandhá*, *s.* sort of plant, *withania somnifera*, [Colloq. අමුක්කරා *amukkará*].

ඍග්වේද, *Rigwéda*, *s.* earliest of the four Vedas consisting of hymns; addressed to the great powers of nature, to Indra, to Fire, to the Sun, to the Moon, etc.: see වේද *wéda*.

ඍජුකෝණය, *Rijukónaya*, *s.* right angle.

ඍජුරේඛාව, *Rijurékháwa*, *s.* right line.

ඍතු භේදය, *Ritubhédaya*, *s.* difference in the seasons.

ඍතු වර්ධනී, *Ritu-vardhani*, *s.* tree, *phyllanthus emblica*, [Colloq. නෙල්ලි *nelli*].

ඍද්ධිවන්ත, *Riddhiwanta*, } *a.* endowed with
ඍද්ධිසම්පන්න, *Riddisampanna*, } superhuman power.

ඍෂ්‍යගතා, *Ṛishyagatá*, *s.* creeping plant, *asparagus falcatus*, [Colloq. හාතාවාරිය *hátáwáriya*].

ඍෂ්‍යගන්ධා, *Ṛishya-gandhá*, } *s.* medicinal plant,
ඍෂ්‍යපේශී, *Ṛishya-pési*, } variety of *sida humilis*, [Colloq. බිංබෑලිල *binbęlila*, and බෑවිල *bęvila*].

ඍෂ්‍යප්‍රොක්තා, *Ṛishya-proktá*, *s.* cowach, *carpopogon pruriens*, [Colloq. වඳුරුමෑ *wandurumę*]; creeping plant, *asparagus falcatus*, [Colloq. හාතාවාරිය *hátáwáriya*]; sida.

ඍෂී, *Ṛishí*, *s.* screw-pine, *pandanus fascicularis* or *p. odoratissimus* [Colloq. වෑටකෙයියා *węṭakeyiyá*].

එ

එක්පෙතිපියුම්, *Ekpeti-piyum*, *s.* variety of *nymphæa stellata*, [Colloq. හෙල මානෙල් *hela-mánel*].

එක්බිත්තෙහි, *Ekbittehi*,=ඉක්බිත්තෙහි *Ikbittehi*, afterwards.

එක්වීම, *Ekvíma*, *s.* union, coming in contact with; association with.

එක්වෑටිය, *Ekwęṭiya*, *s.* necklace of large pearls.

එක්සමයෙක්හි, *Eksamayekhi*, *s.* once upon a time.

එකක්, *Ekak*,=එකියක්, *Ekiyak*, as බාල එකක් *bála-ekak*, a young woman.

එකඩමස, *Ekaḍamasa*, *s.* one half of a month.

එකපෑහෑර, *Ekapęhęra*, *s.* one time, at once, all at once.

එකවිරු, *Ekaviru*, *s.* the sole hero, unrivalled hero.

එකසර, *Ekasara*, *a.* walking alone.

එකහමාර, *Ekahamára*, *s.* one and half.

එකාවන්, *Ekáwan*, *a.* continually.

එකාෂ්ඨිලී, *Ekáshṭhílí*, *s.* creeping plant, *cissampelos Pareira*, [Colloq. දියමිත්ත *diyamitta*].

එකූන විසති, *Ekúna-vísati*, one minus twenty, nineteen. (Páli.)

එකෝන විංශති, *Ekóna-vinsati*, one minus twenty, nineteen. (Sanskrit.)

එඬේරකම්කරණවා, *Endérakam-karaṇawá*, *v.* to tend cattle.

එධ, *Edha*, } *s*, fuel, firewood, [Colloquial: දර
එධස්, *Edhas*, } *dara*].

එන්නත්කරණවා, *Ennatkaraṇawá*, see ඉනාත්කරණවා *inatkaraṇawá*.

එනු, *Enu*, *s.* act of coming.

එපවත්, *Epawat*, *s.* that fact.

එයින්, *Eyin*,=එහෙයින් *Eheyin*, *conj.* therefore.

එරණ්ඩක, *Eraṇḍaka*, *s.* castor oil plant, *ricinus communis*, [Colloq. එඬරු *enḍaru*].

එල්බිජු, *Elbiju*, *s.* Ceylon cardamoms, *elettaria cardamomum*, [Colloq. එන්සාල් *ensál*].

එලනෙළුම්, *Ela-nelum*, *s.* white water lily, variety of *nelumbium spiciosum*.

එලපුළු, *Elapuḷu*, *s.* mandarin orange, variety of *citrus aurantium*, [Colloq. ජවනාරං *jawanáran*].

එලව්, *Elaw*, *s.* funeral: see ඉලව්ව *ilawwa*.

එලවනවා, *Elawanawá*, *v.* to produce, to bring.

එලවයි, *Elawayi*, *v.* produces, brings, [Colloq. ගෙණදෙයි *geṇadeyi*].

එලාපර්ණී, *Eláparṇí*, *s.* plant, *mimosa octandra*.

* එලි, *Eli*, *s.* similar letters at the end of each line in a verse in poetry; rhyme.

එලිපත්ත, *Elipatta*, *s.* threshold.

එලිහඳයා, *Elihandayá*, *s.* kind of sea fish.

එසේ මෙසේ, *Esé-mesé*, *a.* insignificant, worthless, of no consequence.

එළුපොර, *Eḷupora*, *s.* fight between two rams.

ඒ

ඒකධර්මානුසාරිවූ, *Éka-dharmánusáriwú*, *s.* following the same kind of duties.

ඒකපදික මාර්ගය, *Éka-padika-márgaya*, *s.* (ඒක+පදික+මාර්ග) footpath.

ඒකශ්‍රුති, *Ékaṣruti*, *s.* hearing but once.

ඒකාතපත්‍ර, *Ékáta-patra*, see එක්සත් *eksat*.

ඒකාදශ, *Ékádaṣa*, *s.* eleven, [Colloq. එකොළහ *ekoḷaha*].

ඒජන්ත, *Éjanta*, *s.* Agent.

ඒඩගජ, *Éḍagaja*, *s.* medicinal plant, used for the cure of ringworms, *cassia tora*.

ඒරණ්ඩඵලා, *Éranḍa-phalá*, *s.* medicinal plant, *Croton polyandrum*, [Colloq. දෑත්ත ගස් *dętta-gas*].

ඒරාෂ්ටක, *Éráshṭaka*, *s.* unpropitious aspect of a planet.

*ඒරියකඳ, *Ériyakanda*, *s.* pole of a double bullock bandy to which the yoke is fastened.

ඒරුවෙනවා, *Éruwenawá*, *v.* to be offended, to scold.

ඒල්, *Él*, *s.* small cardamoms; ripe fruit of *bassia latifolia*.

ඒලාපත්‍ර, *Élá-patra*, *s.* one of the chiefs of the Nágas or serpent race.

ඒවංගියේ, *Éwangiyé*, *s.* at that time, then, thereupon.

ඒසා, *Ésá*,=ඒ සමාන, *É-samána*, like that, such.

ඒසිකාස්තම්භ, *Ésikástambha*, *s.* pillar in front of a city gate; also a threshold.

* ඓරාවත, *Airáwata*, *s.* small variety of the mandarin orange, *citrus nobilis*, [Colloq. හින්නාරං *hín-náraṉ*].

ඔ

ඔකාවස්, *Okáwas*,=ඉක්ෂ්වාකුවංශ *Ikshwáku-waṉṣa*, the race of Ikshwáku the first prince of the Solar dynasty who reigned at Ayódhyá.

ඔදවැඩීම, *Odawęḍíma*, *s.* increase of sap, juice, mirth, joy.

ඔප්පුකරණවා, *Oppukaraṇawá*, *v.* to prove.

ඔප්පොහුකරණවා, *Oppohu-karaṇawá*, *v.* to postpone.

ඔපදමනවා, *Opadamanawá*, *v.* to polish, to make bright.

ඔපවැටෙනවා, *Opawęṭenawá*, *v.* to look bright.

ඔබ්බ, *Obba*, *s.* further side.

ඔම්පාව, *Ompáwa*, *s.* jest.

ඔයිත්, *Oyit*, *pron.* she, [Colloq. ඒ ස්ත්‍රී *é strí*].

ඔරහිඳ, *Orahiṉda*, *s.* reclining on the breast.

ඔරු, *Oru*, *s.* thigh; Elu form of ඌරු *úru*, [Colloq. කළව *kaḷawa*].

ඔල, *Ola*, *a.* violent, fierce, savage.

* ඔලෙයියා, *Oleyiyá*, *s.* Asiatic golden plover, *charadius fulvus*, also called රේනවටුවා *réna-waṭuwá*; large sand plover *ægialitis geoffroyi* (order *Grallæ)*.

ඔව්හු, *Owhu*, *pron.* they.

ඔවදන්, *Owadan*, *s.* advice, [Colloq. අවවාද *awa-wáda*].

ඔවාගෙණ, *Owágeṇa*, *v.* having put on (as an ornament*)*.

ඔෂ්ඨී, *Oshṭhí*, *s.* creeping plant, *bryonia grandis*, [Colloq. කෙම්වැල *kemwęla*].

ඔස්සවටුවා, *Ossawaṭuwá*, *s.* grey partridge *ortygorais pondiceriana* (order *Gallinæ)*.

* ඔහු, *Ohu*, *pron.* his, him.

ඕ

ඕ, *Ó*, *pron.* she.

ඕඩ්‍ර, *Ódra*, *s.* northern part of Orissa; Chinese rose.

ඕදාත, *Ódáta*, *a.* white.

ඕනා, *Óná*, *part.* cramming, falling.

ඕලවටුවා, *Ólawaṭuwá*, *s.* bird called long-toed stint, *tringa subminuta* (order *Grallæ*)*.*

ඕළාරික, *Óḷárika*, *a.* large, gross, coarse, material. (Páli.)

ඕළු අල, *Óḷu-ala*, *s.* root of ඕළු, esculent water lily.

ඖදුම්බරගිරි, *Audumbaragiri*, *s.* name of a Buddhist temple, better known by its Siṉhalese equivalent දිඹුලාගල විහාරය *dimbuḷágala-viháraya.*

ඇ

* ඇක්ම, *Ękma*, *p. p.* of ඇක්මෙනවා *ękmenawá*, to walk or tread upon.

ඇඟය, *Ęṉgaya*,
ඇඟේ, *Ęṉgé*, } *s.* three oxen yoked together.

* ඇටිකුකුළා, *Ęṭikukuḷá*, *s.* common coucal *centropus rufipennis;* Ceylonese coucal, *c. chlororhyncus*, (order *Piçariæ)*.

ඇටිස්සා, *Ęṭissá*, *s.* kind of fish.

ඇණවීම, *Ęṇavíma*, *s.* giving orders, [Colloq, අණකෙරිම *aṇakeríma*].

ඇණිය, *Ęṇiya*, *s.* array of troops, fore-part of a ship, prow: *a.* small, trifling.

ඇත්තල, *Ęttala*, *s.* elephant stall.

ඇත්දත් වැටකොළු, *Ętdat-węṭakoḷu*, see ඇත්දන් වැටකොළු *ętdan-węṭakoḷu.*

ඇතජරා, *Ętajará*, *s.* (ඇත් *ęt*+අජරා *ajará*) elephant keeper.

ඇතිදැඩිකරණවා, *Ętidęḍikaraṇawá*, *v.* to bring up as a child, to train, to educate.

ඇතුරුවන්, *Ęturuwan*, *s.* those who ride on elephants.

ඇතුළුගම, *Ętuḷugama*, *s.* the interior of the village, within the village.

ඇතොවුර, *Ętowura*, see අන්තඃපුරය *antaḥpuraya*.

ඇදැල්ලා, *Ędęllá*, *s.* kind of sea fish.

ඇඳිගම්වී, *Ęṉdigam-ví*, *s.* kind of paddy, *oryza sativa.*

ඇඳුම්මහන්නා, *Ęṉdum-mahanná*, *s.* tailor.

ඇඹනියෝ, *Ęmbaniyó*, *s.* wife, [Colloq. භාර්‍යාව *bháryáwa*].

ඇඹල ඇල්වී, *Ęmbala-ęlví*, *s.* kind of paddy, *oryza sativa.*

ඇඹුල් කෙසෙල්, *Ęmbul-kesel*, *s.* plantain tree, *musa sapientum.*

ඇඹුල් මෝරු, *Ęmbul-móru*, *s.* vinegar.

ඇඹෙනියෝ, *Ęmbeniyó*, *s.* wife.

ඇම්මුන මැනව, *Ęmmuna-męnawa*, *v.* be pleased to have patience, to wait or forbear.

ඇරගෙණ, *Ęrageṇa*, *v.* having taken,=අරගෙණ, *arageṇa*; having opened for one's self.

ඇල්කොකා, *Ęlkoká*, *s.* black-necked stork, *xenorhyncus asiaticus* (order *Herodiones)*.

ඇල්ගෙවි, *Ęlgevi*, *s.* a female who looks after Chénas of hill-paddy cultivation.

ඇලපිල්ල, *Ęlapilla*, *s.* vowel symbol "ා" placed by the right hand side of a consonant as in කා *ká*, ගා *gá*, conveying the sound of ඇ *á*.

* ඇලි, *Ęli*, plural of ඇල්ල *ęlla*.

ඇලිකිඹුලා, *Ęli-kimbulá*, *s.* crocodile found in the larger rivers, *crocodilus porosus* (order *Sauria*).

ඇලිමිනිස්සු, *Ęli-minissu*, *s.* white men, albinos.

ඇලියවී, *Ęliya-ví*, *s.* kind of paddy, *oryza sativa*.

ඇලිවී, *Ęli-ví*, see the last.

ඇවරිය, *Ęwariya*, *s.* comb of plantain.

ඇවිණිදොර, *Ęvini-dora*, *s.* door of a shop or boutique.

ඇවිලි අවන්නාවූ, *Ęvili-awannáwú*, *a.* heaping curses.

ඇවුරුම්, *Ęwurum*, *s.* obstruction, covering.

ඇස් ඇඳිරිය, *Ęs-ęndiriya*, *s.* dimness of sight.

ඇසනොපහළවිරි, *Ęsanopahaḷaviri*, *a.* (ඇස eye, නොපහළ not struck or met, විරි before) which had not met the eye before=which had been seen before.

ඇසවාගෙණ, *Ęsawágeṇa*, *v.* continuing to flow.

ඇසිවෑසන්, *Ęsiwęsan*,=ආශිර්විෂයන් *Áṣírvishayan*, *s.* snakes, venomous serpents.

ඇසුවිරු, *Ęsúvirú*, *a.* heard of in time past.

ඇගි, *Ęgí*, *s.* this and other ways.

ඇත් මෑත්, *Ęt-męt*,=ඒ අත මේ අත *é-ata mé-ata*, this side and that side; distance, this way or that way.

ඇඳනවා, *Ęndanawá*, *v.* to couple trees for drawing toddy; to yoke or fasten together by means of ropes or withes, as oxen: pret. ඇඳුවා *ęnduwá*.

ඇඳුත්ත, *Ęndutta*, *s.* yoke (of oxen).

ඇපා, *Ępá*,=ආදිපාද *Ádipáda*, *v.* heir apparent to the throne, the first official next to the sovereign.

ක

කංසතාලම්, *Kaṇsatálam*, *s.* cymbal, [Colloq. කයිතාලම *kayitálama*].

ක අත්, *Ka-at*,=කාගේ අත *Kágé-ata*, *s.* whose hand.

කක්කල්කෑස්ස, *Kakkal-kęssa*, *s.* hooping cough.

කක්කෝල, *Kakkóla*, *s.* annual hairy plant, *hibiscus angulosus*, [Colloq. කපුකිනිස්ස *kapukinissa*].

කක කකයේ සිනාසි, *Kaka-kakayé-sinási*, = කක් කක්ගාලා හිනාවෙලා *Kak-kakgálá-hináwelá*, *s.* laughing with the sound, කක් කක් *kak-kak*.

කකුභ, *Kakubha*, *s.* tree, *terminalia glabra*, [Coll: කුඹුක් *kumbuk*].

කකුළුසුඟු, *Kakuḷusuṇgu*, see කර්කටකශෘංගි *karkaṭaka-ṣringi*.

කගටය, *Kagaṭaya*, *s.* creeping plant, *ipomœa pestigridis*, [Colloq. දිවිපහුරු *divipahuru*].

කගල්වේරිය, *Kagalwériya*, *s.* plant, wild liquorice, *abrus precatorius*. [Colloq. ඔලිඳවැල් *olinda-węl*].

කඞ්කණ, *Kańkaṇa*, *s.* bracelet, armlet, rings used for ornamenting the arms and ankles, [Colloq. වළල්ල *walalla*].

කඞ්කෙලි, *Kańkelli*, } *s.* tree, *jonesia asoca*.
කඞ්කෙලිනි, *Kańkeliní*, }

කඞ්ගුනි, *Kańguní*, *s.* sort of turmeric, *curcuma zerumbet*, [Colloq. හරන්කහ *harankaha*]; also, sort of panic seed.

කච්චිපෝටවී, *Kachchipóṭa-ví*, *s.* kind of paddy, *oryza sativa*.

කච්ඡ, *Kachchha*, *s.* marshy ground, morass, ground bordering water; hem of a garment tucked into a waistband.

කච්ඡුඝ්නි, *Kachchhughni*, *s.* medicinal plant, *sphæranthus indicus*, [Colloquial: මුඩමහණ *muḍamahaṇa*].

කච්ඡුරා, *Kachchhurá*, *s.* twining plant, *tragia montana*, [Colloq. වැල්කහඹිලියා *węl-kahambiliyá*].

කඤ්ච, *Kañcha*, *s.* iron-wood tree, *mesua ferrea*, [Colloq. නාගහ *nágaha*].

කඤ්ජ, *Kañja*, *s.* frankincense, incense, [Colloq. තුවරලා *tuwarálá*].

කඤ්ජනා, *Kañjaná*, *s.* saffron, turmeric, *curcuma longa*, [Colloq. කහ *kaha*].

කඤ්ජර, *Kañjara*, *s.* areca-nut tree, *areca catechu*, [Colloq. පුවක්ගස *puwak-gasa*].

කඤ්ජිකා, *Kañjiká*, *s.* plant, *siphonanthus indica*.

කට්ටුමරම්, *Kattumaram*, *s.* raft used in fishing.

කට්ඵල, *Kaṭphala*, *s.* plant, *murraya Koenigii*, [Colloq. කරපිංච *karapiñcha*]; timber tree with yellow flowers, *gmelina arborea*, [Colloq. ඇත්දෙමට *ętdemaṭa*]; tree, *adenanthera pavonina*, [Colloq. මදටිය *madaṭiya*].

කට්වඞ්ග, *Kaṭwańga*, *s.* plant, *oroxylum indicum*, [Colloq. තොටිල *toṭila*].

කට්වී, *Kaṭví*, see කටුරෝහිණී *kaṭuróhiṇí*.

කටක, *Kaṭaka*, *s.* bangles as in කනක කටක *kanaka-kaṭaka*, gold bangles, ("Ummagga-játaka).

කටකරවි, *Kaṭaka-ravi*, *s.* the sun in the Sign Cancer. (corruptly for කර්කටකරවි *karkaṭaka-ravi*.)

කටඞ්කටේරි, *Kṭańkaṭéri*, *s.* creeper, *coscinium fenestratum*, [Colloq. වෙනිවැල් *weniwęl*].

කටටියෙමි, *Kaṭaṭiyemi*, = කරණු කැමැත්තෙමි *karaṇu-kęmęttemi*, I wish to do.

කටභී, *Kaṭabhi*, *s.* heart pea, *cardiospermum halicacabum*, used in Ceylon for culinary and medicinal purposes, [Colloq. දුදු *dúdu*, or පෙනලවැල් *penela-węl*].

කටම්භරා, *Kaṭambhará*, *s.* medicinal plant, [Colloq. කටුකරෝසන *kaṭukarósana*]; also sort of bindweed, *ipomœa tridentata*, [Colloquial: අපසු මදු *ápasu-madu*].

කටහෙළන, *Kaṭaheḷana*, *s.* putting in the mouth.

කටිකය, *Kaṭikaya*, see කර්කටකශෘඞ්ගි *karkaṭaka-sṛiṅgi*.

කටිසජ්ජනා, *Kaṭisajjaná*, see මෙවුල්දම් *mewuldam*.

කටුඅල, *Caṭu-ala*, *s.* edible root of a prickly creeper, commonly called කටුවල *kaṭuwala*.

කටුකරෝසන, *Kaṭukarósana*, see කටුකරෝහිණී *kaṭukaróhiṇí*.

කටුකෝල්, *Kaṭukól*. *s.* breaches, [Colloq. කැඩුම් බිඳුම් *kędum-bindum*].

කටුකෝශාතකී, *Kaṭukósátakí*, *s.* creeping plant, *genus luffa*, [Colloq. තිත්ත වැටකොළු *titta-węṭakoḷu*].

කටුගන්ධික, *Kaṭugandhika*, *s.* tree, *alstonia* (or *echites*) *scholaris*, [Colloq. රුක් අත්තන *ruk-attana*].

කටුග්‍රන්ථි, *Kaṭugranthi*, *s.* root of the long pepper, *piper longum*, [Colloq. තිප්පිලිමුල් *tippili-mul*].

කටුතික්තා, *Kaṭutiktá*, *s.* bitter gourd, *citrullus colocynthus*, [Colloq. තිත්තලබු *titta-labu*]; creeper, *trichosanthes cucumerina*, [Colloq. දුම්මැල්ල *dummęlla*].

කටුතුම්බී, *Kaṭutumbí*, *s.* bitter gourd.

කටුපර්ණී, *Kaṭuparṇi*, *s.* cinnamon bark, *cinnamomum zeylanicum*, [Colloq. කුරුඳුපොතු *kurundu-potu*].

කටුපුංඛික, *Kaṭupuṅkhika*, *s.* tree, *celastrus emarginatus*, [Colloq. කටුපිල *kaṭupila*].

කටුපුල්ලෙ, *Kaṭupulle*, *s.* police staff of a Disáwa.

කටුඵල, *Kaṭuphala*, *s.* kind of perfume, [Colloq. තකුල් *takul*, or කපුකිනිස්ස *kapukinissa*].

කඨිඤ්ජර, *Kaṭhiñjara*, see අඳුතලා *andutalá*.

කඨිල්ලක, *Kaṭhillaka*, *s.* creeping plant, the fruit of which is used in making curry, *momordica charantia*, [Colloq. කරවිල *karivila*].

කඨිල්ලා, *Kaṭhillá*, *s.* hog-weed, [Colloq. සාරණ *sárana*].

කඩඉරුව, *Kaḍairuwa*, *s.* outermost plank sawn out.

කඩකෑම, *Kaḍakęma*, *s.* articles of food prepared in a boutique, hoppers, etc.

කඩම්බි, *Kaḍambí*, *s.* Malabar nightshade, *basella alba*, [Colloq. නිවිතිවැල් *niviti-węl*].

කඩමලය, *Kaḍamalaya*, *s.* trap to seize animals.

කඩයප්පන්, *Kaḍayappan*, *s.* hoppers sold in boutiques.

කඩරෙද්ද, *Kaḍaredda*, *s.* dirty or tattered cloth; piece of cloth.

කඩසරක්කු, *Kaḍasarakku*, *s.* curry stuff, such as coriander, parsley, carroway seed, etc.

කඩිය, *Kaḍiya*, *s.* piece of cloth used between the legs for the purpose of tucking up the lower garments, [Colloq. අමුඩය *amuḍaya*].

කණ්ටකාරි, *Kaṇṭakári*, *s.* species of egg plant, *solanum trilobatum*, [Colloq. වැල්තිබ්බටු *węl-tibbaṭu*].

කණ්ටකාරිකා, *Kaṇṭakáriká*, *s.* plant, kind of night shade, used medicinally, *solanum jacquini*, [Colloq. කටුවැල්බටු *kaṭuwęlbaṭu*].

කණ්ටකාලි, *Kaṇṭakáli*, *s.* cotton tree, *eriodendron anfractuosum*, [Colloq. ඉඹුල් ගහ *imbul-gaha*].

කණ්ටකිඵල, *Kaṇṭakí-phala*, *s.* jack tree, *artocarpus integrifolia*, [Colloq. කොස් *kos*].

කණ්ඨීරව, *Kaṇṭhírawa*, *s.* lion, [Colloq. සිංහයා *sinhayá*].

කණන, *Kaṇana*, *part.* digging.

කණමැදිරියා, *Kaṇamędiriyá*, *s.* firefly.

කණහුනහොත්, *Kaṇahunahot*, *v.* if it falls in the ear.

කණාඞ්ඝ්‍රි, *Kaṇáṅghri*, *s.* root of the long pepper, *piper longum*, [Colloq. තිප්පිලිමුල් *tippili-mul*].

කණිකා, *Kaṇiká*, *s.* tree, *premna spinosa* or *longifolia*, [Colloq. සිහින්මිදි *sihin-midi*].

කණිනවා, *Kaṇinawá*, see කනිනවා *kaninawá*.

කණිසම, *Kaṇisama*, *s.* size, extent, about.

කණේරු, *Kaṇéru*, *s.* kind of tree, *plumeria acuminata*, [Colloq. අරලිය *araliya*].

කත්කෙහෙල්, *Katkehel*, *s.* kind of plantain.

කත්තුමල්ලිය, *Kattumalliya*, *s.* mortise.

කතක, *Kataka*, *s.* tree bearing the clearing nut, *strychnos potatorum*, [Colloq. ඉඟිනිඇට *ingini-ęṭa*].

කථා ශරීරය, *Kathá-ṣaríraya*, *s.* subject of the narrative.

කථාශේෂ භාවෝපගත, *Katháṣésha-bháwópagatá* *a.* dead, deceased.

කථාශේෂය, *Katháṣéshaya*, *s.* (කථා speech, ශේෂ what remains, remnant) death.

කථිත, *Kathita, a.* said, told, related.

කථෝපකථන, *Kathópa-kathana, s.* dialogue.

කදම්බපුෂ්පී, *Kadamba-pushpí, s.* medicinal plant, *sphæranthus indicus*, [Colloq. මුඩමහණ *muḍa-mahaṇa*].

කදමල්, *Kadamal, s.* a very fragrant flower: see රුක්ගස *ruk-gasa.*

කදලිපුෂ්ප, *Kadali-pushpa, s.* flower of the plantain, [Colloq. කෙසෙල්මුව *keselmuwa*].

කදමැටි, *Kadámeṭi, s.* crystal, quartz, glass.

කදුළුගෙඩි, *Kaduḷu-geḍi, s.* tree, *butea frondosa*, [Colloq. කැල *kéla*].

කඳයුරුකුල, *Kaṉdayurukula, s.* of the Kandayuru family.

කඳරලා, *Kaṉdaralá, s.* kind of large sea fish.

කන්ජික, *Kanjika, s.* tree, formerly called *galedupa indica* or *dalbergia arborea*, now *pongamia glabra*, [Colloq. මගුල්කරඳ *magul-karaṉda*].

කඳකුමර, *Kandakumara, s.* plant, wild liquorice, *abrus precatorius*, [Colloq. ඔලිඳවැල් *olindawel*]; kind of basil, *ocimum gratissimum*, [Colloq. වෙලා *wélá*].

කඳාරිෂ්ටා, *Kandárishṭá, s.* plant, *grewia lævigata*, [Colloq. ගස්කැලිය *gas-kéliya*].

කන්නන්නෝරු, *Kannannóru, s.* kind of plantain.

කන්‍යකා, *Kanyaká,* } *s.* socotrine aloe, [Colloq.
කන්‍යා, *Kanyá,* } කෝමාරිකා *kómáriká*].

කන්වයින, *Kanwayina, s.* pillow.

කන්වේරිය, *Kanwériya, s.* night shade, species of *solanum.*

කන්හවන්ට, *Kanhawanṭa, s.* tree bearing the trumpet flower, *stereospermum suaveolens*, [Coll: පළොල් *paḷol*].

කනකපුෂ්ප, *Kanaka-pushpa, s.* tree, *cochlospermum gossypium*, [Colloq. කිණිහිරිය *kiṇihiriya*].

කනකපුෂ්පක, *Kanaka-pushpaka, s.* tree, *michelia champaca*: see සපු *sapu.*

කනකා, *Kanaká, s.* cassia plant: see තෝර *tóra.*

කනකාහ්ව, *Kanakáhwa, s.* iron-wood tree, *mesua ferrea*, [Colloq. නාගස් *ná-gas*].

කනකිති, *Kanakiti, s.* species of night shade, *solanum Xanthocarpum*, [Colloq. එලබටු *elabaṭu*].

කනතුල, *Kanatula, s.* sort of turmeric, *curcuma zerumbet*, [Colloq. හරන්කහ අල *harankaha-ala*].

කනතුරු, *Kanaturu, s.* last fruits of a season.

කනන්ග, *Kananga*, see භිසනාග *bhisanága.*

කනබිජු, *Kanabiju, s.* long pepper, *piper longum*, [Colloq. තිප්පිලි *tippili*]; shrub, the leaves of which are used as tea and bark as a buff dye, *cassia auriculata*, [Colloq. රණවරා ඇට *raṇa-wará-eṭa*].

කනමුල්, *Kanamul, s.* root of the long pepper, *piper longum*, [Colloq. තිප්පිලිමුල් *tippili-mul*].

කනස්සල්ල, *Kanassalla, s.* distress, sorrow, sadness, trouble.

කප්පාසි, *Kappási, s.* silk cotton, [Colloq. කපු *kapu*]. (Páli.)

කප්පිත්තා, *Kappittá, s.* Captain. (Eng.)

කප්පිලිකරණවා, *Kappilikaraṇawá, v.* to make කප්පිලි *kappili*, which see.

කප්පිලිය, *Kappiliya, s.* prepared end of a pillar on which a beam rests.

කපත්‍ර, *Kapatra, s.* plant, *euphorbia neriifolia*, [Colloq. පතුක් *patuk*].

කපර්දක, *Kapardaka, s.* small shell used as a coin, [Colloq. කවඩි *kawaḍi*].

කපි, *Kapi, s.* incense; emblic myrobalan; kind of bonduc.

කපිකච්ඡු, *Kapikachchhu, s.* cowach, *carpopogon pruriens*, [Colloq. වඳුරුමෑ *waṉdurumé*].

කපිත්ථ, *Kapittha,* } *s.* wood apple, *feronia ele-*
කපිප්‍රිය, *Kapipriya,* } *phantum*, [Colloquial: දිවුල් *diwul*].

කපිලා, *Kapilá, s.* water melon, *citrullus vulgaris*, [Colloq. කොමඩු *komaḍu*]; name of cucumber, [Colloq. කැකිරිවැල් *kekiri-wel*]; small tree, with white fragrant flowers, *murraya exotica*, ඇට්ටේරිය *eṭṭériya*].

කපිවල්ලි, *Kapiwalli, s.* elephant or wood apple; climbing plant with an aromatic seed something of the nature of pepper, *pothos officinalis*, [Coll: ඇත්වගපුල් *etwagapul*].

කපෝතවංකා, *Kapótawaṅká, s.* plant, *ventilago maderaspatana*, [Colloq. කොබෝවක්කා *kobó-wakká*].

කඵා, *Kaphá, s.* sort of bind-weed with twining stem, large pointed leaves, and pale rose-coloured flowers, *ipomœa sepiaria*, [Colloq. රසතැල් *rasa-tel*].

කබඬා, *Kabaṉdá, s.* cow-dung.

* කබර, *Kabara, s.* medicinal plant, [Colloq. පැපිළිය *pepiḷiya* or පත්පාඩගම් *patpáḍagam*].

කබරතෙල්, *Kabara-tel, s.* oil prepared from කබරගොයා *kabaragoyá*, which see.

* කබරා, *Kabará, s.* kind of sea fish.

කබාකුරුත්තුව, *Kabákuruttuwa, s.* female jacket.

කඹුට, *Kaṃbuṭa*, participle of කඹුරණවා, *kaṃbu-raṇawá*, to serve, to do menial work.

කඹුරු ඇල්වී, *Kamburu-ẹlví*, s. kind of paddy, *oryza sativa*.
කඹුළ, *Kambuḷa*, a. who did menial work.
කම්කටුළු, *Kamkaṭuḷu*, s. trouble, distress, pain, agony.
කම්පල, *Kampala*, s. result of any action.
කම්බෝජි, *Kambóji*, s. fern, *drymoglossum heterophyllum*, [Colloq: මස්වැන්න *maswẹnna*].
* කම, *Kama*,=ක්‍ෂමා *kshamá*, s. patience.
කමදරසමස්, *Kamadarasamas*, Elu form of කර්මධාර සමාස, *karmadhára-samása*, which see.
* කමල, *Kamala*, s. lotus, *nelumbium speciosum*, [Colloq. නෙළුම් *neḷum*]: see the next.
කමල පත්‍ර, *Kamala-patra*, s. plant, kind of mint, [Colloq. කොල්ලන්කොල *kollankola*].
කමලාලිය, *Kamaláliya*, see කමල්කල් *kamalkal*.
කමසේ, *Kamasé*, ind. according to pleasure; as one likes.
කමුක, *Kamuka*, s. areca-nut, *areca catechu*, [Coll: පුවක් *puwak*]. (Páli.)
කයිවාරු, *Kayiwáru*, s. congratulation, boasting.
කර්කටකප්‍රියා, *Karkaṭaka-priyá*, s. Malabar nightshade, *basella alba*, [Colloq. නිවිතිවැල් *nivitiwẹl*].
කර්කටිකා, *Karkaṭiká*, s. tree, *zizyphus jujuba*, [Colloq. ඩෙබර *ḍebara* or මසන් *masan*].
කර්කටි, *Karkaṭí*, s. name of cucumber, [Colloq. කැකිරි *kẹkiri*].
කර්කරී, *Karkarí*, see දේවදළි *déwadáli*.
කර්කශච්ඡද, *Karkaṣachchhada*, s. small tree, *Streblus aspera* or *trophis aspera*, [Colloq. ගැටනි ටුල් *gẹṭanitul*].
කර්කෝටක, *Karkóṭaka*,
කර්කෝටකී, *Karkóṭakí*,
කර්කෝටී, *Karkóṭí*, s. species of *momordiká*, [Colloq. වැල්තුඹ *wẹl-tumba*].
කර්චූරක, *Karchúraka*, s. small aromatic plant, *kaempferia galanga*, [Colloq. හිඟුරුපියලි *hingurupiyali*].
කර්ණපාශ, *Karṇapáṣa*, s. earring, [Colloq. කන්වැල *kanwẹla*].
කර්ණපූර, *Karṇapúra*, s. blue lotus, *nymphæa stellata*, [Colloq. නිල් මානෙල් *nil-mánel*]: see හෝපලු *hópalu*.
කර්ණරසායන, *Karṇarasáyana*, a. sweet to the ear, euphonious.
කර්ණාවතංශ, *Karṇáwatanṣa*, s. ear-ornaments, [Colloq. තෝඩු *tóḍu*].
කර්ණිකාර, *Karṇikára*, s. tree, *cochlospermum gossypium*, [Colloq. කිණිහිරිය *kiṇihiriya*].
කර්තන, *Kartana*, s. cutting, [Colloquial: කැපීම *kẹpíma*].
කර්තව්‍ය, *Kartavya*, a. what ought to be done, duty, [Colloq. කටයුත්ත *katayutta*].
කර්පර, *Karpara*, s. blue vitriol, [Colloq. තුත්තම් *tuttam*].
කර්මධාරය, *Karmadháraya*, s. grammatical term, one of the Samásas or compound words.
කර්මාර, *Karmára*, s. bamboo tree, *bambusa vulgaris*, [Colloq. උණගස් *uṇagas*].
කර්මේන්ද්‍රිය, *Karméndriya*, s. (කර්ම *karma* + ඉන්ද්‍රිය *indriya*) organ of action.
කර්ෂක, *Karshaka*, s. pigeon pea, *cajanus indica*, [Colloq. රටතෝර *raṭa-tóra*].
කර්ෂඵල, *Karsha-phala*, s. tree, *terminalia belerica*, [Colloq. බුළු *buḷu*].
කරක, *Karaka*, s. pomegranate tree, *punica granatum*, [Colloq. දෙළුම් *deḷum*].
කරකඳ, *Karakanda*, s. date tree, *phœnix zeylanica*, [Colloq. ඉඳි *indi*].
කරජ, *Karaja*, s. tree, formerly called *galedupa indica* or *dalbergia arborea*, now *pongamia glabra*, [Colloq. මගුල් කරඳ *magul karanda*]; plant from the fibres of which bow strings are made, *sanseviera zeylanica*, [Colloq. වක්නිය *wakniya*, or නියඳ *niyanda*]; perfume, according to some a dried substance made from a shell-fish and said to resemble the conch or chank shell; according to others a vegetable perfume, [Colloq. සක්නැබ *saknẹba*].
කරඤ්ජක, *Karañjaka*, see මගුල්කරඳ *magul-karanda*.
කරඤ්ජාන්‍ය, *Karañjánya*, s. medicinal plant, [Coll: සිරිල *sirila*].
කරත්තපාර, *Karatta-pára*, s. cart-road.
කරතංගය, *Karatangaya*, s. seed of the opium plant, [Colloq. කන්සා ඇට *kansá-ẹta*].
කරතිරුව, *Karatíruwa*, s. carpenters' term for a quarter.
කරප, *Karapa*, see කරක්ගෙඩිය *karakgeḍiya*.
කරපයමස්වා, *Karapaya-maswá*, s. having handcuffed and put fetters on.
කරබි, *Karabí*, s. black cummin seed, *nigella indica*, [Colloq. කළුදුරු *kaḷuduru*].
කරභි, *Karabhi*, s. species of *momordica*, [Colloq. වැල්තුඹ *wẹl-tumba*].
කරමදින, *Karamadina*, s. fruit of the *myristica horsfieldia*, [Colloq. රුක්ගෙඩි *ruk-geḍi*, or පුවඟු පල *puwangu-pala*].

කරමල් කටුස්සා, *Karamal-kaṭussá*, *s.* lizard, kind of chameleon, *(Agames* order *Sauria)*.

කරමස්සා, *Karamassá*, *s.* kind of sea fish.

කරමිල්, *Karamil*, see හිරුස්ස *hiręssa*.

කරමුරලා, *Karamuralá*, *s.* kind of sea fish.

කරරුහ, *Kararuha*, see සක්නැබ *saknęba*.

කරල්හැබ, *Karalhęba*, see කරල්සැබෝ *karalsębó*.

කරවිරහා, *Karavíraha*, *s.* red arsenic, [Colloq. රත්හිරියල් *rat-hiriyal*].

කරවුවර, *Karawuwara*, *s.* royal revenue.

කරසක්, *Karasak*, *s.* kind of conch shell.

කරහාට, *Karaháṭa*, කරහාටක, *Karaháṭaka*, } *s.* thorny shurb, *randia dumetorum*, [Colloq. කුකුරුමුවන් *kukurumuwan*]; also, fibrous root of a lotus.

කරාල, *Karála*, *s.* medicinal plant, *spilanthes acmella*, [Colloq. අක්මැල්ල *akmęlla*].

කරාවිය, *Karáviya*, *s.* belly of the lute.

කරිණ්ඩක, *Kariṇḍaka*, *s.* plant, *oroxylum indicum*, [Colloq. තොටිල *toṭila*].

කරිපිප්පලි, *Karipippalí*, see ඇත්වගපුල් *ętwagapul*].

කරී, *Karí*, *s.* tree with acrid juice, *excœcaria agallocha*, [Colloq. තෙලකිරිය *telakíriya*].

කරීර, *Karíra*, *s.* temple tree, *plumeria acutifolia*, [Colloq. අලරිය *alariya*].

කරීෂ, *Karísha*, *s.* dried cow-dung, [Colloq. ගොම වැරටි *goma-węraṭi*].

කරුණානිධානවූ, *Karuṇá-nidhánawú*, *s.* abode of kindness, receptacle of benevolence.

කල්කණ්ඩු, *Kalkaṇḍu*, *s.* sugar candy. (Tamil.)

කල්පක, *Kalpaka*, *s.* barber, one who makes, [Colloq. පනික්කියා *panikkiyá*]; also, see කපුවා *kapuwá*.

කල්පවෘක්ෂ, *Kalpa-wṛiksha*, *s.* wish-conferring tree.

කල්පිත, *Kalpita*, *a.* made, put in order, prepared, arranged.

කල්‍යක, *Kalyaka*, *s.* small aromatic plant, *kaempferia galanga*, [Colloquial: සිඟුරුපියලි *singuru-piyali*].

කල්‍යා, *Kalyá*, *s.* coriander, *coriandrum sativum*, [Colloq. කොත්තමල්ලි *kottamalli*]; sort of turmeric, *curcuma zerumbet*, [Colloq. හරන්කහ *harankaha*].

කල්‍යාණ, *Kalyáṇa*, *s.* gold, [Colloq. රත්රන් *rat-ran*].

කල්‍යාණිශාඛවෘක්ෂක, *Kalyáṇi-śákhawṛikshaka*, *s.* hal tree, *vateria acuminata*, [Colloq. හල්ගස *hal-gasa*].

කලකිරීම, *Kalakiríma*, *s.* discouragement, a disheartening.

කලඳුරු, *Kalaṉduru*, *s.* same as කලාඳුරු *kaláṉduru*; also a species of worms.

* කලබ, *Kalaba*, [from Sanskrit, කලාප *kalápa*]; an assemblage, bundle:—මල්කලබ *malkalaba* nosegay: see කලප් *kalap*.

කලඹක්, *Kalaṃbak*, *s.* bundle, cluster.

කලමියා, *Kalamiyá*, *s.* kind of sea fish.

කලහකාරයින්, *Kalahakárayin*, *s.* those who quarrel, rioters.

කලාපිනි, *Kalápini*, *s.* plant, species of night shade, *solanum nigrum*, [Colloq. කළුකැම්මෙරිය *kaḷu-kęmmériya*].

කලිඞ්ගක, *Kaliṅgaka*, *s.* medicinal nut or seed, from the tree, *nerium antidysentericum*, [Colloq. කෙළිඳඇට *keḷiṉda-ęṭa*].

කලිද්‍රුම, *Kalidruma*, *s.* tree, *terminalia belerica*, [Colloq. බුළුගස් *buḷu-gas*].

කලිමන්, *Kaliman*, *s.* desire, wish; avarice.

කලිමාරක, *Kalimáraka*, *s.* medicinal plant, [Colloq. සිරිල *sirila*].

කලී, *Kalí*, *ind.* expletive particle=වනාහී *wanáhí*.

කවඩයා, *Kawaḍayá*, *s.* kind of sea fish.

කවරි, *Kawari*, *s.* kind of basil, *ocimum gratissimum*, [Colloq. වෙලාගස් *wélá-gas*].

කවිම්මන්‍ය, *Kavimmanya*, *s.* one who fancies himself a poet or learned man.

කවිසිකේශ, *Kavisikéśa*, *s.* curly hair.

කවිසියා, *Kavisiyá*, *s.* Kaffir.

කවීන්ද්‍ර, *Kavíndra*, *s.* (කවි *kavi*+ඉන්ද්‍ර *indra*) an eminent poet.

කවුඩු ඇල්වී, *Kawuḍu-ęlví*, *s.* kind of paddy, *oryza sativa*.

කශ්චිත්, *Kaşchit*, *pron.* some-body, some-one, a certain one.

* කෂ්ට, *Kashṭa*, *a.* suffering pain, impervious, impenetrable.

* කසින, *Kasina*, (භාවනා *bháwaná*, etc.)

කසුන්පය, *Kasunpaya*,=කාඤ්චන පාත්‍ර *káñchana-pátra*, *s.* golden bowl or vessel.

කහලාර, *Kahlára*, *s.* white esculent water lily, [Colloq. හෙල්මැලි *helmęli*].

කහ ඇල්වී, *Kaha-ęlví*, *s.* kind of paddy.

* කහ කුරුල්ලා, *Kaha-kurullá*, *s.* common bush bulbul, *iora tiphia*.

කහට ඇල්වී, *Kahaṭa-ęlví*, *s.* kind of paddy.

කහට වී, *Kahaṭa-ví*, *s.* kind of paddy.

කහට හඳිරන්වී, *Kahata-handiranví*, *s.* kind of paddy.

කහනයා, *Kaha-nayá*, s. yellow cobra: see නයා *nayá*.

කහපත් ඇල්වී, *Kahapat-ęlví*, s. kind of paddy.

කහ මාවී, *Kaha-márí*, s. kind of paddy.

කහමිලිල, *Kaha-milila*, s. timber tree: see මිලිල *milila*.

කහමුන්, *Kahamun*, s. seed of the *cassia auriculata*, [Colloq. රණවරා ඇට *raṇawará-ęta*].

කහර, *Kahara*, s. thorny shrub, *randia dumetorum*, [Colloq. කුකුරුමුවන් *kukurumuwan*].

කහහූනා, *Kaha-húná*, s. yellow lizard (*Geckotidæ* order *Sauria*).

කළුඊයම්, *Kaḷu-íyam*, s. (කළු black, ඊයම් lead) black lead.

කළු ඇල්වී, *Kaḷu-ęlví*, s. kind of paddy, *oryza satira*.

කළු කත්කෙහෙල්, *Kaḷu-katkehel*, s. kind of plantain.

කළු කන්නන්නෝරු, *Kaḷu-kannannóru*, s. kind of plantain.

කළු කරඇල්වී, *Kaḷu-karaęlví*,
කළු කුණ්ඩවී, *Kaḷu-kuṇḍaví*,
කළු කුමාරවී, *Kaḷu-kumáraví*, } s. kind of paddy *oryza sativa*.

කළු කෙසෙල්, *Kaḷu-kesel*, s. kind of plantain.

කළු කොත්විලවී, *Kaḷu-kotvilaví*, s. kind of paddy.

කළුකැම්මෙරිය, *Kaḷukęmmériya*, see කළුකන්මේරිය *kaḷu-kanmériya*.

කළු ත්‍රස්තාවාලු, *Kaḷu-trastawálu*, s. plant, black species of teori, *ipomæa turpethum*.

කළුදොදොල්, *Kaḷu-dodol*, s. kind of sweetmeat of black colour.

කළු නවරි කෙසෙල්, *Kaḷu-nawari-kesel*, s. kind of plantain.

කළු පරව්, *Kaḷu-paraw*, s. kind of sea fish.

කළුමස්, *Kaḷumas*, s. fresh water fish, so called, *ophiocephalus striatus*, [Colloq. ලූලා *lúlá*].

කළුමාවී, *Kaḷu-máví*, s. kind of paddy, *oryza sativa*.

කළුරුවා, *Kaḷuruwá*, s. pupil of the eye.

කළු හඬිරන්වී, *Kaḷu-handiranví*, s. kind of paddy.

කළු හිනටිවී, *Kaḷu-hínaṭiví*, s. kind of paddy.

කාංගණ, *Káṅgana*, s. black cloth.

* කාංස්‍ය, *Káṅsya*, s. white copper or brass; bell metal, bronze, [Colloq. ලෝකඩ *lókaḍa*].

කාකකුට්මල, *Kákakuṭmala*, s. variety of water lily.

කාකචිඤ්චි, *Kákachiñchi*, s. plant, *abrus precatorius*, [Colloq, ඔලිඳ *olinda*].

කාකත, *Kákata*, s. Saraswatí, wife of Brahma.

කාකතාලීය, *Kákatálíya*, s. accident, unforeseen event; unexpected circumstance.

කාකතික්තා, *Kákatiktá*, s. creeping plant, bind-weed, *convolvulus flavus*, [Colloq. තැල්වැල් *tęlwęl*].

කාකනන්දිකා, *Kákanandiká*, s. plant, *abrus precatorius*, [Colloq. ඔලිඳ *olinda*].

කාකමාචි, *Kákamáchi*, s. plant, species of night shade, *solanum nigrum*, [Colloq. කළුකැම්මෙරිය *kaḷukęmmériya*].

කාකමුද්ගා, *Kákamudgá*, s. kind of kidney bean, *phaseolus trilobus*. [Colloquial: මුංවැන්න *muṇwęnna*].

කාකවල්ලී, *Kákawallí*, s. creeping plant, bind-weed, *convolvulus flavus*, [Colloq. තැල්වැල් *tęlwęl*].

කාකාදනී, *Kákádani*, see කාකනන්දිකා *kákanandiká*.

කාකෝත්පල, *Kákótpala*, s. kind of lotus.

කාඤ්චනභූෂණ, *Káñchana-bhúshaṇa*, s. red chalk, [Colloq. සිවංගුරු *siwaṅguru*].

කාඤ්චික, *Káñchika*, s. talipot tree, *corypha umbraculifera*, [Colloq. තලගහ *tala-gaha*].

කාඤ්ජිකා, *Káñjiká*, see අම්ලකාඤ්ජිකා *amlakáñjiká*.

කාණ්ඩතික්තක, *Káṇḍa-tiktaka*, s. plant peculiar to Ceylon, *munronia pumila*, [Colloq. බින්කොහොඹ *bin-kohomba*].

කාන්තධාතු, *Kánta-dhátu*, s. red chalk, [Colloq. සිවංගුරු *siwaṅguru*].

* කාන්තා, *Kántá*, s. woman; sugar cane, [Colloq. උක්ගස *ukgasa*].

කානනාධිප, *Kánanádhipa*, s. mango tree, *mangifera indica* or *m. zeylanica*, [Colloq. අඹ *amba*].

කාප්පුව, *Káppuwa*, s. bracelet: pl. කාප්පු *káppu*.

කාමදා, *Kámadá*, s. plant, *ipomæa digitata*, [Colloq. කිරිබඩු *kiribadu*]; fabulous cow, cow of plenty.

කාමපඞ්ක, *Kámapaṅka*, s. (කාම lust, පඞ්ක mire, mud) mud of lust.

කාමභෝගී, *Kámabhógí*, s. one enjoying sensual pleasures, a lustful man.

කාමරාග, *Kámarága*, s. sensual desire.

කාමවිෂය, *Kámavishaya*, s. object of sensual gratification.

කාමා, *Kámá*, s. species of croton, *croton lacciferum*, [Colloq. කැප්පිටියා *kęppiṭiyá*].

කාමාචාර, *Kámáchára*, s. acting according to one's wish or pleasure.

කාමුකා, *Kámuká*, s. medicinal plant, *spilanthes acmella*, [Colloq. අක්මැල්ල *akmęlla*].

කාමුරණ්ඩ, *Kámuraṇda*, s. shrub with yellow flowers, *crotalaria laburnifolia*, [Colloq. යක්බේරිය *yakbériya*].

කාමුරු, *Kámuru*, s. cloves, [Colloq. කරාබු *karábu*].

කායද්වාරය, *Káyadwáraya*, s. door of the body. body as an organ of action.

කායබල, *Káyabala*, s. strength of body.

කායස්ථා, *Káyasthá*, s. tree, *terminalia chebula*, [Colloq. අරළු *araḷu*].

කාකිවල්ලී, *Kárkawallí*, s. plant, wild liquorice, *abrus precatorius*, [Colloq. ඔලිඳ *olinda*].

කාරණ්ඩව, *Káraṇḍawa*, s. sort of duck.

කාරම්බෙත්, *Káram-bét*, s. caustic.

කාරම්භා, *Kárambhá*, s. lofty tree, which produces fragrant flowers, *myristica horsfieldia*, [Colloq. පුවඟු *puwangu* or රුක්ගස *ruk-gasa*].

කාරවි, *Káraví*, s. kind of dill or fennel, *anethum sowa*, [Colloq, ශතපුෂ්ප *ṣatapushpa*].

කාරසවද, *Kárasawada*, s. medicinal tree, *cassia fistula*, [Colloq. ඇහැළ *ęhęla*].

කාරාගාර, *Kárágára*, s. prison, [Colloq. හිරගේ *hiragé*].

කාලකපිත්ත, *Kálakapitta*, s. medicinal plant, *spilanthes acmella*, [Colloq. අක්මැල්ල *akmęlla*].

කාලකභාව, *Kálakabháwa*, s. state of being black or dark coloured.

කාලකූටක, *Kálakuṭaka*, see වච්චනාවි *wachchanávi*.

කාලජීරක, *Kála-jíraka*, s. black cummin seed, *nigella indica*, [Colloq. කළුදුරු *kaḷuduru*].

* කාලම, *Kálama*, s. trumpet.

කාලමාල, *Kálamála*, s. medicinal plant, *spilanthus acmella*, [Colloq. අක්මැල්ල *akmęlla*].

කාලමෙෂී, *Kálameshí*, s. plant, *vernonia* or *serratula anthelmintica*, [Colloq. බෝදිඇට *bódi-ęṭa*].

කාලමෙෂිකා, *Kálameshiká*, s. heart-seed, *cardiospermum haliacacabum*, [Colloq. වැල් පෙනෙල *węl-penela*].

* කාලය, *Kálaya*, s. species of bean, *vigna* (or *dolichos*) *catiang*, [Colloq. ලිමෑ *límę*]: see කලා *kála*.

කාලවිශේෂ, *Kála-viṣésha*, s. special time.

කාලස්කන්ධ, *Kálaskandha*, s. tree, *diospyros embryopteris*, [Colloq. තිඹිරි *timbiri*]; see කොල්ලං ගහ *kollan-gaha*.

කාලසේය, *Kálaséya*, s. whey, [Colloq. මෝරු *móru*].

කාලා, *Kálá*, s. indigo plant: see අවරිය *awariya*.

කාලාභ්‍ර, *Kálábhra*, s. black cloud.

කාලාවාටය, *Káláwáṭaya*, s. black hole or pit.

කාලිඞ්ග, *Kálinga*, s. medicinal nut or seed, from the tree, *nerium antidysentricum*, [Colloq. කෙළිඳ *keḷinda*].

කාලින්දී, *Kálindí*, s. the Jumna river, [Colloq. යමුනාගඞ්ග *yamuná-ganga*].

කාලී, *Kálí*, s. species of water lily, *nymphæa lotus*, [Colloq. ඕලු *ólu*]; heart-seed, *cardiospermum haliacacabum*, [Colloquial: වැල්පෙනෙල *węl-penela*].

කාලේයක, *Káléyaka*, s. creeper, *coscinium fenestratum*, [Colloq. වෙනිවැල් *weniwęl*].

කාලෝපල, *Kálópala*, s. magnet, loadstone, [Coll: කාන්දම් *kándam*].

කාව්‍ය ලක්ෂ්‍ය, *Káwya-lakshya*, s. examples from poetry.

කාවිය, *Káviya*, s. buoy in net.

කාවේරි, *Kávéri*, s. river in the Deccan, the Kávéri.

කාශ්මර්‍ය, *Káṣmarya*, } s. timber tree with yellow
කාශ්මරී, *Káṣmarí*, } flowers, *gmelina arborea*, [Colloq. ඇත්දෙමට *ętdemaṭa*],

කාෂ්ඨ මධුක, *Káshṭha-madhuka*, s. liquorice plant, *glycirrhiza glabrum*, [Colloq. වැල්මී *węlmí*].

කාෂ්ඨවාහන, *Káshṭhawáhana*, s. wood-vehicle.

කාෂ්ඨිලා, *Káshṭhílá*, s. plantain, [Colloq. කෙසෙල් *kesel*].

*කාහල, *Káhala*,=හොරණෑව *horanęwa*, s. trumpet; or horn, either a cow horn, or an instrument of that shape.

කිංජල්ක, *Kinjalka*, s. plant, *costus speciosus*, [Colloq. කොට්ටම් *koṭṭam* or තෙබු *tebu*]; filament of a lotus; flower of the *mesua ferrea*.

කිකී, *Kikí*, s. blue jay: see කිරලා *kiralá*.

කිට්ට, *Kiṭṭa*, s. excrement, rust of iron dust.

කිටිප, *Kiṭipa*, s. blue vitriol. sulphate of copper. see තුත්තම් *tuttam*.

කිඩාරන් අල, *Kiḍáran-ala*, s. medicinal root, *amorphophallus campanulatus*.

කිණිගෞරා, *Kiṇigawrá*, s. brinjal plant, prickly night-shade, *solanum*, [Colloq. බටු *baṭu*].

කිණිහි, *Kiṇihí*, s. spiny shrub, kind of night-shade, *solanum indicum*, [Colloq. තිබ්බටු *tibbaṭu*]: plant, *achyranthes aspera*, [Colloq. කරල්හැබ *karalhęba*].

කිතක, *Kitaka*, (Páli.) for කෘදන්ත *kṛidanta*.

කින්නර, *Kinnara*, s. demigod attached to the service of Kuvéra, celestial musician, [කිම් *kim* what (contemptuously) නර *nara* man].

කිනම්, *Kinam*, a.=Páli, කින්නාම *kinnáma*, having what name, *e. g.* තෝ කිනම්ද *tó kinamda?* what is your name? plural, කිනම්මු *kinammu*, *e. g.* තගේ අඹුවන්ගේ මැනියෝ පියානෝ කිනම්මුදෑ? *tagé ambuwangé męniyó piyánó kinammudę?* what are your wife's mother and father called?

කිනිත්තා, *Kinittá*, *s*. kind of sea fish.

කිඹිසිනි, *Kimbisini*, *a*. closed, turned upside down.

* කිඹුල්හූනා, *Kimbul-húná*, *s*. kind of lizard, *hemidactylus triedrus Geckotidæ* order *Sauria*.

* කිම්පුරුෂ, *Kim-purusha*, see කින්නර *kinnara*.

කිමිජ, *Kimija*, *a*. produced by a worm, silken.

කියග, *Kiyaga*, imperative Mood of කිය with "ග" affix, *e. g.* "කියග මඟිය *kiyaga magiya*" Tell me, O traveller, etc. (පැරකුම්බා සිරිත *perakumbá sirita*); "කියග තපස්විය *kiyaga tapasviya*" Tell me, O hermit, (අමාවතුර *amáwatura*).

කියැකි, *Kiyęki*,=කියහැකි *kiyahęki*, able to say.

කිරඟන, *Kirangana*, *s*. (කිරි *kiri* elephant, අඟන *angana* female) she elephant.

කිරාත, *Kiráta*, }

කිරාතතික්තා, *Kiráta-tiktá*, } *s*. plant, peculiar to Ceylon, *munronia pumila*, [Colloq. බිංකොහොඹ *binkohomba*].

කිරාතුන්, *Kirátun*, *s*. plant, *gentiana cherayta*. (Námávali, 133.)

කිරිදොදොල්, *Kiri-dodol*, *s*. kind of sweetmeat.

කිරි රුක, *Kiri-ruka*, *s*. tree, *buchanania latifolia*, [Colloq. කිරිපළු *kiripalu*].

කිලා, *Kilá*, *s*. thorny shrub, *carissa carandas*, [Colloq. මහකරඹ *maha-karamba*].

කිලිකිප්ප, *Kilikippa*, }

කිලිකිලි, *Kilikili*, } *s*. shrub with yellow flowers, *crotalaria laburnifolia*, [Colloq. යක්බේරිය *yakbériya*].

කිලිම, *Kilima*, *s*. sort of pine, *pinus devadaru*, [Colloq. දේවදාර *déwadára*].

කිලුටුකම, *Kilutukama*, *s*. pollution, filthiness.

කිව, *Kiwa*,=කිවාය *kíwáya*, she said; also=කිවහොත් *kiwahot* or කිවොත් *kíwot*, if one should say.

කිවද, *Kiwada*, *v*. although he said.

කිස්දොවුන්මල්, *Kisdowunmal*, same as කිස්දොවුන් *hisdowun*.

කිසලං, *Kisalan*, *s*. medicinal plant, *eclipta erecta*, [Colloq. කිකිරිඳිය *kíkirindiya*]; sprout.

කිසුණු පිරියම්, *Kisunu-piriyam*, *s*.=(Páli) කසිණ පරිකම්ම, *kasina-parikamma*, process by means of which mystic meditation may be induced.

කිසෙයයත්, *Kiseyayat*,=කෙසේද කිවොත් *keséda kíwot*, to say how it was, if I am asked how it was I should say.

කිහි, *Kihi*,=කිසි *kisi*, *e. g.* පව්කම් කෙරීමට කිහිකමක් දක්වයි කී *pawkam kerímata kihikamak dakwayi kí*" (අමාවතුර *amáwatura*.). Show me some instrument for the commission of sinful deeds.

කීටක, *Kítaka*, *s*. worm, insect.

කීටමාරිකා, *Kítamáriká*, *s*. kind of medicinal plant, [Colloq. වලාවැන්න *waláwęnna*].

කීටවිජයා, *Kítavijayá*, *s*. tree, *terminalia glabra*, [Colloq. කුඹුක් *kumbuk*.

කීනදොඹ, *Kínadomba*, see දේවවල්ලභ *déwa-wallabha*.

කීලබද්ධව, *Kílabaddhawa*, *a*. tied to a post or pillar.

කීවා, *Kíwá*,=කියාපු දේ *kiyápu-dé*, *s*. that which was said, *e. g.* මම තොප කීවා කරමි *mama topa kíwá karami*, I (will) do that which was said by you.

කීසපර්ණී, *Kísaparni*, *s*. plant, *achyranthes aspera*, [Colloq. කරල්සැබෝ *karalsębó*].

කුංකුමප්පු, *Kunkumappu*, *s*. saffron.

කුංජරී, *Kunjari*, *s*. large creeper with large leaves and white flowers, turning to yellow, *bauhinia racemosa*, [Colloq. මයිල *mayila*].

කුංජල, *Kunjala*, *s*. water lily.

කුක්කුටාණ්ඩ, *Kukkutánda*, *s*. eggs.

කුක්කුරාගාරය, *Kukkurágáraya*, *s*. house where dogs are confined.

කුක්ෂිශූල, *Kukshisúla*, *s*. pain in the belly [Colloq. බඩරුජාව *badarujáwa*].

කුකුණ්ඨ, *Kukuntha*, *e*. sort of kidney bean: see ලීමෑ *límę*.

කුකුසා, *Kukusá*, *s*. repentance.

කුටජ, *Kutaja*, *s*. tree, *nerium antidysentericum*, [Colloq කෙළිඳගස් *kelinda-gas*].

කුටජඵල, *Kutaja-phala*, *s*. medicinal nut or seed, from the tree, [Colloq. කෙළිඳඇට *kelinda-eta*].

කුටන්නට, *Kutannata*, *s*. plant, *oroxylum indicum*, [Colloq. තොටිල *totila*]; bulbous plant or grass used medicinally, *cyperus rotundus*, [Colloq. කලාඳුරු *kalánduru*].

කුටිච, *Kuticha*, *s*. Ceylon cardamoms, *elettaria cardamomum*, [Colloq. එන්සාල් *ensál*].

කුටිර, *Kutira*, *s*. hut, cottage.

කුටිලකණ්ටක, *Kutilakantaka*, *s*. tree, *acacia catechu*, also called, *a. suma* and *a. sundra*, [Colloq. කිහිරි *kihiri*].

කුටිලාලය, *Kutilálaya*, *s*. sort of turmeric, *curcuma zerumbet*, [Colloq. හරන්කහ *harankaha*].

කුටුම්බසන්ථාපනය, *Kutumba-santhápanaya*, *s*. supporting a family.

කුඨ, *Kutha*, *s*. tree, [Colloq. ගහ *gaha*].

කුඨාර, *Kuthára*, }

කුඨාරි, *Kuthári*, } *s*. axe, hatchet, [Colloq. පොරව *porawa*, කෙටේරිය *ketériya*].

කුට්මල, *Kuṭmala*, s. new bud, [Colloq. කැකුල *kẹkula*].

කුඨේරක, *Kuṭheraka*, s. plant, species of the *ocimum*, [Colloq. අඳුතලා *andutalá*].

කුඩාකළුවා, *Kuḍákaḷuwá*, s. a black and jointed creeper, grown in moist soil.

කුඩා සුදනා, *Kuḍá-sudaná*, s. a plant bearing small white flower grown on summits of cold mountains.

කුඩුම්බිය, *Kuḍumbiya*, s. tuft of hair on the top of the head.

කුඩෙනි, *Kuḍeni*, s. O little one, [Colloq. පොඩ්ඩො *poḍḍo*].

කුණ්ඩලඵල, *Kuṇḍala-phala*, s. tree, *morinda citrifolia* and *m. tinctoria*, [Colloq. අහු *ahu*].

කුණ්ඩලී, *Kuṇḍalí*, s. climbing plant, *tinospora cordifolia*, [Colloq. රසකිඳ *rasakinda*].

කුණ්ඩිකා, *Kuṇḍiká*, see කෙණ්ඩිය *keṇḍiya*.

කුතුම්බක, *Kutumbaka*, s. plant, *leucas zeylanica*, [Colloq. ගැටතුඹ *gẹṭatumba*].

කුද්දාල, *Kuddála*, s. tree, mountain ebony, *bauhinia purpurea*, [Colloq. කොබලිල *kobalila*].

කුද්දෝ, *Kuddó*, s. kind of sea fish.

කුදිරකාරයා, *Kudirakárayá*, s. groom.

කුදුමැදුර, *Kudumẹdura*, s. (කුදු small, මැදුර=මන්දිරය *mandiraya* house) cottage.

කුඳුරු, *Kunduru*, s. earth, *terra firma*.

කුන්තය, *Kuntaya*, s. dart, lance, [Colloq. හෙල්ලය *hellaya*].

කුන්තානිය, *Kuntániya*, s. pick-axe.

කුන්දර, *Kundara*, s. shrub, *Lamonia alata*, [Colloq. තුම්පත්කුරුඳු *tumpat-kurundu*]; sort of grass.

කුනටි, *Kunaṭí*, s. coriander, red arsenic.

කුනටු, *Kunaṭu*, s. creeping plant bearing a pungent leaf, called betel pepper, *piper betle*, [Colloq. බුලත් *bulat*].

කුනාශක, *Kunáṣaka*, s. twining plant with stinging hairs, *tragia involucrata*, [Colloq. වැල්කහඹිලියා *wẹl-kahambiliyá*].

කුප්පවා, *Kuppawá*=කෝපකරවා *kópakarawá*, *part.* having provoked or made angry.

කුප්පායම, *Kuppáyama*, s. village or habitation of a Roḍiya.

කුපුරිස්, *Kupuris*, s. mean, contemptible man; coward, wretch.

කුබ්ජපර්ණිකා, *Kubja-parṇiká*, s. creeping plant, *dæmia extensa*, [Colloq. මැඩහඟු *mẹḍahangu*].

කුබේරබිජු, *Kubéra-biju*, s. medicinal nut, *cæsalpinia bonduc*, [Colloq. කුඹුරුඇට *kumburu-ẹṭa*].

කුඹහ, *Kumbaha*, s. wooden pipe placed under ground through which water is conveyed from one division of a field into another.

කුඹු, *Kumbu*, same as කුම්භ *kumbha*, *q. v.*

කුඹුස්ස, *Kumbussa*, see කුඹහ *kumbaha*.

කුම්බික පල, *Kumbika-pala*, s. fruit of the Patana oak, *careya arborea*, [Colloq. කහටගෙඩි *kahaṭa geḍi*].

කුම්භක, *Kumbhaka*, s. plumbago, [Colloq. මිණිරන් *miṇiran*].

කුම්භී, *Kumbhí*, s. timber tree, *gmelina arborea*, [Colloq. ඇත්දෙමට *ẹtdemaṭa*].

කුම්භිකා, *Kumbhíká*, s. aquatic plant, *pistia stratiotes*, [Colloq. දියපරණලා *diyaparaṇalá*]; tree bearing the trumpet flower, *stereospermum suaveolens*, [Colloq. පළොල් *paḷol*].

කුම්භෝලු, *Kumbhólu*, s. plant, *amyrus agallocha*; balm: see ගුගුල් *gugul*.

කුමතේරුකරණවා, *Kumatérukaraṇawá*, v. to inspect land with a view to appraise it or assess damages.

* කුමර, *Kumara*, s. plant, *gynandropsis pentaphylla*, [Colloq. වේලා *wélá*].

* කුමාරක, *Kumáraka*, s. plant, peculiar to Ceylon, *munronia pumila*, [Colloq. බින් කොහොඹ *bin-kohomba*]; small tree, *cratæva Roxburghii* or *c. religiosa*, [Colloq. ලුණුවරණ *luṇuwaraṇa*].

* කුමාරිකා, *Kumáriká*, } s. kind of medicinal plant,
කුමාරි, *Kumári*, } aloe, *aloe vulgaris*, [Coll: කෝමාරිකා *kómáriká*].

කුමාරෝදය, *Kumáródaya*, s. birth of a child, or the god of war.

* කුමු, *Kumu*, s. tortoise, [Colloq. ඉබ්බා *ibbá*].

කුමුටු, *Kumuṭu*, v. plunged in.

කුමුඩු, *Kumuḍu*, s. plant, *cephalandra indica* or *coccinea*, [Colloq. කෝවක්කා *kówakká*].

කුමුදිකා, *Kumudiká*, s. aromatic plant, *murraya Koenigii*, [Colloq. කරපිංච *karapiñcha*].

කුමුදිනවා, *Kumudinawá*, v. to plunge, to dive.

කුමැති, *Kumẹti*, s. bad minister.

කුරඹ, *Kuramba*, s. tree, sweet lovilovi, *flacourtia Ramontchi*, [Colloq. උගුරැස්ස *ugurẹssa*].

කුර රජ, *Kura-raja*, s. dust raised by the hoofs of an animal.

කුරවක, *Kurawaka*, s. plant, species of *barleria prionitis*, [Colloquial. රතු කටුකරඬු *ratu-kaṭu-karandu*].

කුරු ඇල්වී, *Kuru-ẹlví*, s. kind of paddy, *oryza sativa*.

කුරුබිලිය, *Kurubiliya*, s. small hole; narrow passage.

කුරුම්බැට්ට, *Kurumbeṭṭa*, s. very young coconut.

කුරු මාවී, *Kuru-mávi*, s. kind of paddy.

කුරුවි, *Kuruvi*, s. kókila or Indian cuckoo, [Coll: කොවුලා *kowulá*].

කුරුවිලි, *Kuruvili*, s. kind of sea fish.

කුරුවී, *Kuru-ví*, s. kind of paddy.

කුරුස, *Kurusa*, s. broken rice.

කුරුහ් *Kuruh*, s. tree, [Colloq. ගස *gasa*].

කුරු හෙරලි, *Kuru-herali*, s. kind of small jack.

කුරුළුතුඩුවී, *Kuruḷutuḍu-ví*, s. kind of paddy.

කුලක, *Kulaka*, s. medicinal plant, *Croton polyandrum*, [Colloq. දෙත්ත *deṭṭa*].

කුලකිඳුර, *Kulakidára*, s. grey pelican, *pelicanus phillipinensis* (order *Steganopodes*).

කුලච්චි, *Kulachchi*, s. alum, [Colloq. සීනක්කාරං *sínakkáraṇ*].

කුලජා, *Kulajá*, s. plant, not ascertained.

කුලටා, *Kulaṭá*, s. sort of plant, *withania somnifera* [Colloq. අමුක්කරා *amukkará*].

කුලටී, *Kulaṭí*, s. red-arsenic.

කුලත්ථ, *Kulattha*, s. kind of pulse, grain, [Colloq. කොල්ලු *kollu*].

කුලදූෂණය, *Kuladúshaṇaya*, s. bringing disgrace on a family.

කුලදේවතා, *Kuladéwatá*, s. tutelary deity, particular god of one's family.

කුලල්බට, *Kulalbaṭa*, s. kind of reed, *arundu tibialis*.

කුලාක්ෂක, *Kulákshaka*, s. species of garlic or onion, *allium ascalohicum*, [Colloq. රතුළූනු *ratulúnu*].

කුලාල, *Kulála*, s. potter, [Colloq. බඩහැලයා *baḍaheḷayá*]; wild cock.

කුලාල භාණ්ඩ, *Kulála-bhánḍa*, s. pottery, [Colloq. වළන් *walan*].

කුලිශ, *Kuliṣa*, } s. diamond, [Colloq. දියමන්ති
කුලිස, *Kulisa*, } *diyamanti*]; Indra's thunderbolt.

කුළුඳුල, *Kulunḍula*,=අඩපත *aḍa-pata*, s. half a pint.

කුලැටි, *Kuléṭi*, a. wild, disobedient, unmanageable.

කුවල, *Kuwala*, s. tree, *zizyphus jujuba*, [Colloq. මසන් *masan*]; water lily, [Colloq. මහනෙල් *mahanel*].

කුවලකර්ණ, *Kuwalakarṇa*, s. variety of the *nymphœa stellata*, species of water lily, [Colloq. නිල්මානෙල් *nil-mánel*].

කුශ, *Kuṣa*, s. kind of reed, *imperata arundinacea*, [Colloq. ඉළුක් *iḷuk*].

කුශලප්‍රශ්න, *Kuṣala-praṣna*, s. enquiry after one's health or welfare.

* කුෂ්ඨඝ්නී, *Kushṭhaghni*, s. species of night shade, *solanum nigrum*, [Colloq. කළුකැම්මෙරිය *kaḷu-kemmériya*].

කුස්තුම්බුරු, *Kustumburu*, s. coriander, *coriandrum sativum*. [Colloq. කොත්තමල්ලි *kottamalli*].

කුසකන්, *Kusakan*, s. dried saffron, *curcuma longa*, [Colloq. වියලි කහ *viyali-kaha*].

කුසපත්‍රා, *Kusa-patrá*, s. species of the sensitive plant, *mimosa pudica*, [Colloq. නිදිකුම්බ *nidi-kumba*].

* කුසීද, *Kusída*, a. idle, slothful.

කුසුම්භ, *Kusumbha*, s. plant, the Marvel of Peru, called also the four o'clock flower, *mirablis jalapa*, [Colloq. වනුප් *wanup* or හෙන්ද්‍රික්කා *hendrikká*].

කුසුම්රස, *Kusum-rasa*, s. pollen of flowers.

කුළගිරි, *Kuḷagiri*, s. range of rocks round Mahá-méru.

කුළාරගේ, *Kuḷára-gé*,=කූටාගාර ගෘහ *kúṭágára-gṛiha*, s. upper room, apartment on the top of a house.

කුළුගෙය, *Kuḷugeya*, s. apartment on the top of a house.

කුළුරස, *Kuḷu-rasa*, s. sharp, pungent taste.

කුළුහරකා, *Kuḷu-haraká*, s. wild ox.

කූජන, *Kújana*, s. cooing, uttering an inarticulate sound.

කූටකභේදි, *Kúṭaka-bhédi*, see කටුරෝහිණී *kaṭu-róhiṇi*.

කූටසාක්ෂි, *Kúṭasákshi*, s. false witness, [Colloq. බොරුසාක්ෂි *boru-sákshi*].

කූටාගාර කුක්ෂිය, *Kúṭágára-kukshiya*, s. inside a room on the top of a house.

කූඩම, *Kúḍam*, s. shed, rest-house, inn, [Colloq. තානායම *tánáyama*].

කූනම් මඩුව, *Kúnam-maḍuwa*, s. establishment of palanquin bearers of the kings of Kandy.

කූපමණ්ඩූක, *Kúpa-maṇḍúka*, s. frog in a well, one ignorant of the world; one who never leaves his home.

කූරුව, *Kúruwa*, s. the elephant department.

කෙ, *Ke*, pron. who, what, [Colloq. කවරෙක් *kawarek*].

කෙම්පා, *Kempá*, s. plant, *acalypha indica*, [Colloq. කුප්පමේනිය *kuppaméniya*].

කෙම්බිජු, *Kembiju*, s. plant, *cephalandra indica* or *coccinea*, [Colloq. කෝවක්කා *kówakká*].

කෙම්ලිය, *Kemliya*, *s.* same as කෙම්වැල *kemwela*, which see.

කෙමෙක, *Kemeka*,=කර්මයක්ය *karmayakya*, *s.* is a deed or action.

කෙරළන්, *Keraḷan*, *s.* inhabitants of කෙරල *kerala* the modern Malabar coast.

කෙලතොල්ලා, *Kelatollá*, *s.* idiot; driveller.

කෙලෙස්ගිරි, *Kelesgiri*,=කෛලාස පර්වතය *kailása-parwataya*, *s.* mountain Kailása, fabulous residence of Kuvéra, and the favourite haunt of Ṣiva.

කෙලෙස් බැරිසේ, *Keles-bẹrisé*, *s.* (කෙලෙස් sinful desire, බැරි heavy, සේ manner) the manner or fact of being overwhelmed with sinful desires.

කෙස්පත, *Kespata*, *s.* quantity of hair of the head.

කෙස්ස, *Kessa*, *s.* key.

කෙසරසතු, *Kesarasatu*, *s.* castor oil, [Colloq. එඬරු තෙල් *enḍaru-tel*].

කෙසා, *Kesá*, *particle.* what manner.

කෙසි සිදුර, *Kesi-sidura*, *s.* key-hole.

කෙහෙල්ගෙඩිය, *Kehelgeḍiya*, *s.* plantain fruit.

කෙළපැමිණි, *Keḷapẹmiṇi*, *a.* attained to perfection, arrived at the end.

කෙළමෝල, *Keḷamóla*, *s.* rice-pounder without the iron ring at the end.

කෙළිල්ලෙන්, *Keḷillen*, *s.* sitting on the hams; in a squatting posture.

කේකාරවය, *Kékárawaya*, *s.* cry of a peacock.

කේඬැරි, *Kénḍẹri*, *a.* slender or unhealthy as a plant.

කේතුමාලාලඞ්කාර, *Kétumálálaṅkára*, *s.* (කේතු flag, මාලා a row, අලංකාර *alaṅkára* an ornament) the rays proceeding from Buddha's head resembling a banner.

කේර, *Kéra*, *s.* coconut, *cocos nucifera*, [Colloq. පොල් *pol*]; plumbago, [Colloq. මිණිරන් *miṇiran*].

කේරමජ්ජ, *Kéramajja*, *s.* stalk of a coconut branch, [Colloq. පොල්පිති *polpiti*].

කේලම්කියන්නා, *Kélam-kiyanná*, *s.* backbiter, slanderer.

කේශකය, *Késakaya*, *s.* medicinal plant, yielding leaves of narcotic and intoxicating qualities, used by smokers, *cannabis sativa*, [Colloq. කන්සා *kansá*]. (Tamil kañchá.)

කේශකලාපය, *Késakalápaya*, *s.* quantity of hair.

කේශරඤ්ජන, *Késarañjana*, *s.* medicinal plant, *eclipta erecta*, [Colloq. කිකිරිඳිය *kikirinḍiya*].

කේශවාවාස, *Késawáwása*, *s.* sacred fig-tree, *ficus religiosa*, [Colloq. බෝගස *bógasa*].

කේශික, *Késika*, *s.* having fine or luxuriant hair, relating to the hair.

කෛණ්ඩර්ය, *Kaiṇḍarya*, *s.* aromatic plant, *murraya Koenigii*, [Colloq. කරපිංච *karapiṇcha*].

කෛපෝට්ටු, *Kaipóṭṭu*, *s.* that which is put on the hand as an ornament or for defence.

කෛවාරු, *Kaiwáru*, *s.* flattery, self-praise, boasting, bragging, (sometimes written කයිවාරු *kayiwáru*).

කොක්නාවා, *Koknáwá*, *s.* wolf.

* කොක, *Koka*, *s.* tree, *cochlospermum gossypium*, කිණිහිරිය *kiṇihiriya*].

කොකවිසල්, *Kókavisal*, *s.* tree, *alstonia scholaris*, [Colloq. රුක් අත්තන *ruk-attana*].

කොටර, *Koṭara*, *s.* small tree, *streblus asper* or *trophis aspera*, [Colloq. ගැටනෙටුල් *gẹtaneṭul*].

කොටාරය, *Koṭáraya*, *s.* granary, treasury, store.

කොටිකන් වවුලා, *Koṭikan-wawulá*, *s.* margin-eared bat.

කොටින්, *Koṭin*,=කොට *koṭa*, *v.* having done.

කොටි, *Koṭí*, *s.* sort of jasmine, *jasminum sambac*, [Colloq. ගැටපිච්ච *gẹṭa-pichcha*].

කොටුදොරා, *Koṭudorá*, *s.* kind of sea fish.

කොතඹුරු, *Kotamburu*, *s.* coriander, *coriandrum sativum*, [Colloq. කොත්තමල්ලි *kottamalli*].

කොද, *Koda*,=කවරේද *kawaréda*, *v.* who.

කොදිව්, *Kodiw*, see කොදෙව් *kodew*.

කොබු, *Kobu*, *s.* tree, *dalbergia ougeiniensis*.

කොමඩු ඇල්වී, *Komaḍu-ẹlví*, *s.* kind of paddy.

කොමුල්, *Komul*, *s.* shrub: see දෙමට *demaṭa*.

කොයට, *Koyaṭa*, = කොතැනට *kotẹnaṭa*, *v.* to what place.

කොරහන, *Korahana*, *s.* place where there are stones in river beds.

කොල්ලෑගස්, *Kollẹ́-gas*, *s.* small thorny tree, *euphorbia neriifolia*, [Colloq. පතුක් *patuk*].

කොල, *Kola*, vocative particle, expression of contempt or disrespect=බොල *bola*, අඩේ *aḍé*.

කොලරා රෝගය, *Kolara-rógaya*, *s.* cholera.

කොලවැද්දා, *Kolawẹddá*, *s.* golden Paradoxure.

කොලොප්පම, *Koloppama*, *s.* row, stir: pl. කොලොප්පම් *koloppam*.

කොලොස්, *Kolos*, *s.* the gum of the *canarium zeylanicum*, [Colloq. කැකුණමල *kẹkuṇa-maḷa*].

කොලෝග, *Kológa*, *s.* tree, *terminalia chebula*, [Colloq. අරළු *araḷu*].

කොවුලා, *Kowulá*, see කොවුල්ලා *kowullá*.

කොස්ඇටබුරුමය, *Koseta-burumaya*, *s.* gimlet.

කොස්තාපල්, *Kostápal*, *s.* Constable. (Eng.)

කොස්වාලිහිණියා, *Koswálihiniyá*, *s.* kind of heron.

කොහොන්, *Kohon*, *s.* cheat, rogue, juggler; deception, juggling.

කොහොළකම්, *Koholakam*,=කෝලම් *kólam*, *s.* antics, mimicry.

කොළොම්පුරය, *Kolompuraya*, *s.* city of Colombo.

කෝකිලාක්‍ෂ, *Kókiláksha*, *s.* plant, *barleria prionitis*, [Colloq. ඉකිරි *ikiri* or කටුකරඬු *katukarandu*].

කෝගිනි, *Kógini*, *s.* fire of anger.

කෝටර, *Kótara*, *s.* hollow of a tree, [Colloq. ගස් බෙනය *gas-benaya*].

කෝඩුකාරයා, *Kódukárayá*, *s.* one who visits a place for the first time.

කෝඩුව, *Kóduwa*, *s.* first visit to a place.

කෝණංගියා, *Kónangiyá*, *s.* buffoon.

කෝදුව, *Kóduwa*, *s.* yard-wand, carpenter's rule, measure of length=1 cubit.

කෝරඞ්ගි, *Kórańgi*, *s.* small cardamoms, *elettaria cardamomum*, [Colloq. සින් එන්සාල් *sín-ensál*].

කෝරණ්ඩ, *Koranda*, *s.* plant, *barleria prionitis*, [Colloq. කටුකරඬු *katukarandu*].

කෝලය, *Kólaya*, *s.* small grain or seed used by natives to put into their curries, sort of grass, *trigonella fœnugracum*, [Colloq. උළුවා *uluwá*].

කෝවාරි, *Kówári*, *s.* sarsaparilla, *hemidesmus indicus*, [Colloq. ඉරමසු *iramasu*].

කෝෂඵලා, *Kóshaphalá*, *s.* night shade, *solanum nigrum*, [Colloq. කෑම්මේරිය *kemmériya*]; heart-seed creeper, *cardiospermum halicacabum*, [Coll: පෙනෙලවැල් *penelawel*]; cultivated plant, *luffa acutangula*, [Colloq. වැටකොළු *wetakolu*].

කෞටා, *Kautá*, *s.* medicinal nut or seed, from the tree, *nerium antidysentericum*, [Colloq. කෙළිඳ ඇට *kelinda-eta*].

කෞරිය, *Kauriya*, *s.* creeping plant, the fruit of which is used in making curry, *momordica charantia*, [Colloq. කරිවිල *karivila*].

කෑටුවගමන්කරන්නා, *Ketuwa-gamankaranná*, *s.* one who goes along with another.

කෑඩුන, *Keduna*, *a.* broken.

කෑණිමඩල, *Kenimadala*, *s.* frame of a roof, circular peak of a house.

කෑඳිත්ත, *Kenditta*, *s.* small quantity of rice gruel.

කෑන්, *Ken*, *s.* ray of light; multitude.

කෑමියන්, *Kemiyan*, *s.* workmen, [Colloq. කර්මාන්ත කාරයන් *karmántakárayan*].

කෑලිබව, *Kelibawa*, *s.* blackness, [Colloq. කළුව *kaluwa*].

කෑලෑකෝරාල, *Kelekórála*, *s.* officer in charge of forests.

කෑහැට, *Keheta*, } *s.* thin, lean, [Colloq. කෙට්ටු
කෑහැටු, *Kehetu*, } *kettu*].

කෑම අල්මාරිය, *Kémá-almáriya*, *s.* meat safe.

කෑම බිම, *Kéma-bima*, *s.* food and drink.

කෑම ශාලාව, *Kéma-sáláwa*, *s.* dining hall.

ක්‍රාන්තිපාත, *Krántipáta*, *s.* nodes of the ecliptic, equinoctial points.

ක්‍රාන්තිමණ්ඩල, *Kránti-mandala*, *s.* the ecliptic.

ක්‍රාන්තිවලය, *Krántiwalaya*, *s.* space within the tropics.

ක්‍රියාධිකාර, *Kriyádhikára*, *s.* chapter on verbs.

ක්‍රියානිෂ්පත්ති, *Kriyá-nishpatti*, *s.* accomplishment of an act.

ක්‍රියානුරූප පරිද්දෙන්, *Kriyánurúpa-paridden*, *s.* according to actions.

කෘත්‍රිම, *Krittrima*, *s.* incense; adopted son; common *bit noben*, [Colloq. පාංශුලුණු *pánsu-lunu*]: *a.* made, artificial.

* කෘතක, *Kritaka*, *s.* nitre, saltpetre, [Colloq. බලල් ලුණු *balal-lunu*]; kind of medicinal salt, brought from the continent of India, [Colloq. රෝමලුණු *róma-lunu*].

කෘතච්ඡද්‍රා, *Kritachchhadrá*, *s.* cultivated plant, *buffa acutangula*, [Colloq. වැටකොළු *wetakolu*].

කෘතමාල, *Kritamála*, *s.* medicinal tree, *cassia fistula*, [Colloq. ඇහැළ *ehela*].

කෘතයුග, *Kritayuga*, *s.* the first of the four ages of the world, sometimes called සත්‍යයුග *satya yuga*, the age of Truth.

කෘතවේධනා, *Kritawédhaná*, see කෘතච්ඡද්‍රා *kritachchhadrá*.

කෘදන්ත, *Kridanta*, *s.* grammatical term applied to words ending in කෘත් *krit* affixes, *i. e.* *Participle.*

* කෘෂ්ණකාන්ත, *Krishna-kánta*, *s.* loadstone, [Coll: කාන්දම් *kándam*].

කෘෂ්ණතුලසි, *Krishna-tulasí*, *s.* tree, *nyctanthes arbor tristis*, [Colloq. කළුතලා *kalu-talá*].

කෘෂ්ණනිම්බක, *Krishna-nimbaka*, *s.* aromatic plant, *murraya koenigii*, [Colloq. කරපිංච *karapincha*].

කෘෂ්ණපාකඵල, *Krishna-pákaphala*, *s.* tree: see කරඹ *karamba*.

කෘෂ්ණඵලා, *Krishna-phalá*, *s.* plant, *vernonia* or *serratula anthelmintica*, [Colloq, බෝදිඇට *bódi-eta*].

කෘෂණමඤ්ජරිකා, *Kṛishṇa-mañjariká*, s. medicinal plant, *spilanthes acmella*, [Colloq. අක්මැල්ල *akmęlla*].

කෘෂණමඤ්ජරී, *Kṛsihṇa-mañjarí*, see කෘෂණතුලසි *kṛishṇa-tulasí*.

කෘෂණමණ්ඩලය, *Kṛishṇa-maṇḍalaya*, s. pupil of the eye.

කෘෂණරක්තිකා, *Kṛishṇa-raktiká*, } s. plant, wild
කෘෂණලා, *Kṛishṇalá*, } liquorice, *abrus precatorius*, [Colloq. ඔලිඳ *olinda*].

කෘෂණලෝහ, *Kṛishṇa-lóha*, s. iron, [Colloq. යකඩ *yakaḍa*].

කෘෂණවල්ලී, *Kṛishṇawallí*, s. sarsaparilla, *hemidesmus indicus*, [Colloq. ඉරමසු *iramasu*].

* කෘෂණවෘන්තා, *Kṛishṇa-wṛintá*, s. tree, *stereospermum suaveolens*, [Colloq. පලොල් *palol*]; plant, *cæsalpinia bonduc*, [Colloq. කුඹුරුවැල් *kumburuwel*].

කෘෂණසීසක, *Kṛishṇa-sísaka*, s. black lead, [Colloq. කළුඊයම් *kaḷu-íyam*].

කෘෂණාඞ්ගනා, *Kṛishṇáṅganá*, s. black woman.

කෘෂණාර්ජක, *Kṛishṇárjaka*, s. medicinal plant, *spilanthes acmella*, [Colloq. අක්මැල්ල *akmęlla*].

කෘෂිකර්ම, *Kṛishikarma*, s. agriculture, ploughing.

ක්ලීතක, *Klítaka*, s. liquorice plant, *glycirrhiza glabrum*, [Colloq. වැල්මී *wełmí*].

ක්ලීතකිකා, *Klítakiká*, s. indigo plant, [Colloq. අවරිය *awariya*].

ක්ලම, *Klama*, s. fatigue, weariness, [Colloq. වෙහෙස *wehesa*].

ක්ෂණභඞ්ගුර, *Kshaṇa-bhaṅgura*, a. liable to break in an instant.

ක්ෂිණාශ්‍රව, *Kshináṡrawa*, s. one who has overcome sinful passions.

ක්ෂිතිජ, *Kshitija*, s. Mars: a. earth-born.

ක්ෂිතිමණ්ඩල, *Kshiti-maṇḍala*, e. earth, globe.

* ක්ෂීරවෘක්ෂ, *Kshíra-wṛiksha*, s. holy fig tree, *ficus religiosa*, [Colloq. බෝගස් *bó-gas*].

ක්ෂීරාර්ණව, *Kshírárṇawa*, s. (ක්ෂීර *kshíra* milk, අර්ණව *arṇawa* ocean) the milky ocean.

ක්ෂීරිකා, *Kshíriká*, s. tree, *buchanania latifolia*, [Colloq. කිරිපළු *kiripaḷu*].

ක්ෂීරිභක්තා, *Kshíribhaktá*, s. plant, *ventilago maderaspatana*, [Colloq. කොබෝවක්කා *kobówakká*].

ක්ෂුද්‍රබුද්ධිය, *Kshudra-buddhiya*, s. little understanding: a. silly, ignorant.

ක්ෂුද්‍රසහ, *Kshudrasaha*, s. medicinal plant: see මුංවැන්න *muṉwęnna*.

ක්ෂුප, *Kshupa*, s. small tree, bush, shrub.

ක්ෂුරක, *Kshuraka*, s. tree, *adenanthera pavonina*, [Colloq. මදටියගස් *madaṭiya-gas*].

ක්ෂේන්ද්‍ර, *Kshéndra*, s. wheat, [Colloq. තිරිඟු *tiringu*].

ක්ෂේමක, *Kshémaka*, s. small aromatic plant, *kaempferia galanga*, [Colloq. සිඟුරුපියලි *singurupiyali*]; sort of turmeric, *curcuma zerumbet*, [Colloq. හරන්කහ *harankaha*].

ක්ෂේමභූමිය, *Kshéma-bhúmiya*, } s. place of safety.
ක්ෂේමස්ථාන, *Kshémasthána*, }

ඛණ්ඩහාර, *Khaṇḍahára*, s. whey, [Colloq. මෝරු *móru*].

ඛනිජ, *Khanija*, s. that which is produced from a mine.

ඛරලෝහක, *Kharalóhaka*, s. brass, [Colloq. පිත්තල *pittala*].

ඛල්ව, *Khalwa*, s. horse gram, Madras gram, *dolichos biflorus*, [Colloq. කොල්ලු *kollu*].

ඛලී, *Khalí*, s. kind of porridge, [Colloq. තලප *talapa*].

ඛානෝදක, *Khánódaka*, s. coconut, *cocos nucifera*, [Colloq. පොල් *pol*].

ඛින්න, *Khinna*, s. fatigued, wearied.

ගංඅස, *Gaṉ-asa*, s. bank of a river, side of a river.

ගංකනයා, *Gaṉ-kanayá*, s. kind of river fish.

ගංගාධාරය, *Gaṉgádháraya*, s. river bed.

ගංජන, *Ganjana*, s. garlic, *allium sativum*, [Colloq. සුදුලූණු *sudulúnu*].

ගංබිත්තිය, *Gaṉ-bittiya*, s. bank of a river, [Colloq. ගංඉවුර *gaṉ-iwura*].

ගගඩු, *Gagadu*, see බින්දුම්මල *bin-dummala*.

ගගරසින්බා, *Gagarasinbá*, s. shrub or small tree, *ehretia buxifolia*, [Colloquial: හින්තඹල *hintambala*].

ගඟලෝ, *Gaṉgaló*, s. climbing plant, *tinospora cordifolia*, [Colloq. රසකිඳ *rasakinda*].

ගඟුල්හැලි, *Gaṉgulhęli*, s. rapids, waterfalls, [Coll: ඇල්ල *ęlla*].

ගඞ්ගෝදක, *Gaṅgódaka*, s. (ගඞ්ගා *gaṅgá*+උදක *udaka*) river-water.

ගජචක්‍ර, *Gaja-chakra*, s. (ගජ and චක්‍ර circle) a large number of elephants assembled.

ගජපුට, *Gagapuṭa*, s. small hollow for a fire over which to prepare medical decoctions, extracts, etc.

ගජෝ, *Gajó*, s. plant, *atylosia candollei*, [Colloq. ඇත්තෝර *ęttóra*].

ගඩුවා, *Gaḍuwá*, s. roguish cat, [Colloq. හොර බළලා *hora-baḷalá*].

ගණ්ඩාන්ත, *Gaṇḍánta*, s. (ගණ්ඩ *gaṇḍa*+අන්ත *anta*) end of the cheek.

ගණ්ඩාලි, *Gaṇḍálí*, *s.* fragrant grass, *cyperus rotundus*, [Colloq. කලාඳුරු *kalánduru*].

ගණදෙටු, *Gaṇadeṭu*, see ගණනායක *gaṇanáyaka*.

ගණන්පියනවා, *Gaṇanpiyanawá*, *v.* to settle accounts.

ගණන්ශාස්ත්‍රය, *Gaṇanṣástraya*, *s.* science of com puting numbers; arithmetic.

ගණනායක, *Gaṇanáyaka*, *s.* chief of an assemblage of priests.

ගණපූරක, *Gaṇapúraka*, *s.* completing a chapter of priests.

ගණාචාර්‍ය, *Gaṇácharya*, *s.* teacher of a troop of disciples.

ගණිකාරිකා, *Gaṇikáriká*, *s.* tree, *premna spinosa*, or *longifolia*, [Colloq. සිහින්මිදි *sihin-midi*].

ගණිච්චිය, *Gaṇichchiya*, *s.* notice, attention.

ගණුදෙනු, *Gaṇudenu*, *s.* dealings, receiving and giving.

ගණුදෙනුකරණවා, *Gaṇudenu-karaṇawá*, *v.* to deal, to have intercourse.

ගත්කරු, *Gatkaru*, *s.* book-maker, author.

ගත්තරයා, *Gattarayá*, *s.* descendant of captives, or condemned thieves, etc.: pl. ගත්තරු *gattaru*.

ගතකරණවා, *Gatakaraṇawá*, *v.* to pass time, spend.

ගතලකුණු, *Gatalakuṇu*, *s.* marks on the body, features.

ගතිනිමිත්ත, *Gatinimitta*, *s.* signs which a dying man sees and which indicate the place where he will be born.

ගතැටිවුව, *Gteṭiwuwa*, *v.* became desirous of taking, wished to take.

ගද්‍ය, *Gadya*, *s.* prose.

ගද්‍යමයරචනා, *Gadyamaya-rachaná*, *s.* prose composition.

ගද්‍රභ, *Gadrabha*, *s.* incorrectly for ගර්දභ *gardabha*, ass.

ගදෙව්, *Gadew*, *s.* celestial musician, singer in general.

ගන්ආරච්චි, *Gan-árachchi*, *s.* an Árachchi of a village.

ගන්ගාතය, *Gangátaya*, *s.* leg of an animal killed in the chase given to the proprietor of the land.

* ගන්ධපත්‍ර, *Gandha-patra*, *s.* tree, *premna spinosa* or *longifolia*, [Colloq. සිහින්මිදි *sihin-midi*].

ගන්ධපත්‍රිකා, *Gandha-patriká*, see අඳුතලා *andutalá*.

ගන්ධඵලී, *Gandhaphalí*, *s.* lofty tree which produces fragrant flowers, *myristica horsfieldia*, [Colloq. පුවඟු *puwangu*, or රුක්අත්තන *ruk-attana*].

ගන්ධමූලිකා, *Gandha-múliká*, *s.* hedge hyssop, blue flowers, juice mixed with petroleum used to cure rheumatism, *herpestis* (or *gratiola*) *monniera*, [Colloq. ලුණුවිල *luṇuvila*].

ගන්ධහස්ති, *Gandha-hasti*, *s.* elephant of the best kind.

* ගන්ධාරී, *Gandhárí*, *s.* medicinal plant, yielding leaves of narcotic and intoxicating qualities much used by smokers, *cannabis sativa*, [Colloq. කන්සා *kansá*].

ගන්නිලේ, *Gannilé*, *s.* service field in a village held by the Gammahe or the village headman for the time being. Share under a ගම්වසම *gamwasama*, the district of a village headman ගම්මහේ *gammahé* or ගමරාල *gamarála*, who enjoys the pangu or share. He must inform all the tenants of the orders of the නින්ද *ninda* proprietor, land-lord or king, as the case may be. He must accommodate all the persons who come from the land-lord to the village and carry his messages to the tenants and others. He must also supply provisions in some cases.

ගන්වසම, *Ganwasama*, *s.* tenement held by headmen of villages from the Crown subject to certain services.

ගන්හන්, *Ganhan*, *s.* kind of resin, [Colloq. දුම්මල *dummala*].

ගනඝොස, *Ganagosa*, *s.* rumbling of clouds, thun der.

ගනරන්, *Ganaran*, *s.* solid gold.

ගනසා, *Ganasá*, *s.* camphor, [Colloquial: කපුරු *kapuru*]; thick branches.

ගනහඬ, *Gana-hanḍa*, *s.* noise or rumbling of clouds.

ගනු, *Ganu*, *s.* singing.

ගප්සා, *Gapsá*, *s.* abortion, miscarriage.

ගබ්ගේ, *Gabgé*, *s.* lying-inchamber.

ගබඩාගම, *Gabaḍá-gama*, *s.* (ගබඩා store, ගම village) a Royal village.

ගබඩා නිලමේ, *Gabaḍá-nilamé*, *s.* officer in charge of the Royal stores.

ගම්පහරණ, *Gampaharaṇa*, } *s.* robbing villages.
ගම්පැහැරීම, *Gampeherima*, }

ගම්බඩහීනටිවි, *Gambaḍa-hínaṭiví*, *s.* kind of paddy.

ගම්මහේ, *Gammahé*, *s.* a village headman, headman of Véddás.

ගම් මුලාදෑනියා, *Gam-muládeniyá*, *s.* village headman.

ගම්වර, *Gamwara*, *s*, gift of villages.

ගම්වසම්, *Gamwasam*, *a.* belonging to a village.

ගම්සබේ, *Gamsabé*, *s.* a village council.

ගමන්කරණවා, *Gamankaraṇawá*, *v.* to travel, to go, to move.

ගමන්යන්නා, *Gamanyanná*, *s.* traveller, wayfarer.

ගමනාගමන, *Gamanágamana*, *s.* going and coming.

ගයින්, *Gayin*, *s.* with a stanza.

ගර්භපාතිනි, *Garbhapátini*, *s.* creeping plant, with handsome flowers, *gloriosa superba*, [Colloq. නියඟලා *niyangalá*].

ගර්භාශය, *Garbháṣaya*, *s.* womb, receptacle of the fœtus.

ගරාදිවැට, *Garádi-weṭa*, *s.* (ගරාදි and වැට fence) rails.

ගරායකා, *Garáyaká*, *s.* house-demon.

ගරාවැටෙනවා, *Garáweṭenawá*, *v.* to fall down as by a flood, etc.

ගරුකාපත්ති, *Garukápatti*, *s.* (ගරුක *garuka* and ආපත්ති *ápatti* crime) a heavy crime for which a Buddhist priest is liable to be expelled from the priesthood.

ගරුඩාසන, *Garuḍásana*, *s.* one whose vehicle is Garuḍa king of the feathered tribes, epithet of Vishṇu.

ගල් අඟුරු, *Gal-anguru*, *s.* coal.

ගල්අද්දො, *Gal-addo*, *s.* workers in precious stones, lapidaries.

ගල් ආනවාළු කෙසෙල්, *Gal-ánawáḷu-kesel*, *s.* kind of plantain.

ගල්කාසයා, *Galkásayá*, *s.* villainous character, rogue, scamp.

ගල් කොරලියා, *Gal-koraliyá*, } *s.* kind of sea fish.
ගල් කොස්සා, *Gal-kossá*, }

ගල්ගානාහන්ගිඩියා, *Galgáná-hangiḍiyá*, *s.* chief of stone cutters under the Kandyan kings.

ගල්තුම්බයා, *Gal-tumbayá*, *s.* kind of sea fish.

ගල්පළන පෙණුම, *Galpaḷana-peṇuma*, *s.* wedge used in splitting stones.

ගල්පොත්ත, *Galpotta*, *s.* range or surface of rocks.

ගල්පාසි, *Galpási*, *s.* rock-moss.

ගල්බඩ ඇල්වි, *Galbaḍa-ẹlví*, *s.* kind of paddy.

ගල්මල, *Gal-mala*, *s.* coral flower.

ගල්ල, *Galla*, *s.* common terminations of names of places, as අත්තනගල්ල *attanagalla*, කෑගල්ල *kẹgalla*, etc.

ගල්ලත්ගම, *Gallat-gama*, *s.* a species of villages much in the nature of a ninda gama village and sometimes bearing that name.

ගල්ලියා, *Galliyá*, *s.* kind of sea fish.

ගල්වළ, *Galwaḷa*, *s.* quarry, pit from which stones are cut or dig out.

ගල්වැස්ස, *Gal-wẹssa*, *s.* hail.

ගලං, *Galaṇ*, *s.* ginger, [Colloq. ඉඟුරු *inguru*].

ගලන, *Galana*, *a.* flowing, dropping, oozing.

ගවක්ෂීර, *Gawakshíra*, *s.* cow-milk.

ගවරපිරි, *Gawarapiri*, *a.* full of gayals, *bos gavæus:* ගවාලූක *gawáluka*.

ගවේධුකා, *Gawédhuká*, *s.* plant, *grewia lævigata*, [Colloq. ගස්කැලිය *gaskẹliya*]; red chalk, [Coll: සිවංගුරු *siwanguru*].

ගස්කොලන්, *Gaskolan*, *s.* trees and leaves, trees in general.

ගස්බිලය, *Gas-bilaya*, *s.* hole in a tree.

ගස්බෙනය, *Gasbenaya*, *s.* cleft or hole in a tree.

ගස්මන්දා, *Gasmandá*, *s.* a term for a Roḍiya.

ගහනවූ, *Gahanawú*, *a.* thick, impervious, abounding in.

ගහමුල, *Gahamula*, *s.* foot or root of a tree.

ගහෝනි, *Gahóni*, *s.* ornamental covers made of cloth to throw over a pingo-load of presents.

ගළුගුළුවා, *Gaḷuguluwá*, see ගුලුගුරුවා *guluguruwá*.

ගාඞ්ගෙරුකි, *Gáṅgeruki*, *s.* plant, *grewia lævigata*, [Colloq. ගස්කැලිය *gaskẹliya*].

ගාමණී, *Gámaṇi*, *s.* excellent; chief; superintendent of a village.

ගාමන්ත, *Gámanta*, *s.* borders of a village.

ගාමි, *Gámi*, *s.* termination meaning going, as in අපායගාමි *apáyagámi*, going to hell.

ගායත්‍රි, *Gáyatri*, see කිහිරි *kihiri*.

ගාර්දියේ, *Gárdiyé*, *s.* of the Guard.

ගාලව, *Gálawa*, *s.* tree, lódhra, *symplocos racemosa:* see ලොත්සුඹුළු *lotsumbuḷu*.

ගිගුම්දෙනවා, *Gigumdenawá*, *v.* to roar, to thunder.

ගින්දර, *Gindara*, } *s.* fire.
ගින්න, *Ginna*, }

ගින්නටියා, *Ginnaṭiyá*, *s.* kind of sea fish.

ගිනිකන, *Ginikana*, *s.* bright, dazzling light, brilliant luster that dazzles the eyes.

ගිනිගන්නවා, *Ginigannawá*, *v.* catches fire; fire is emitted spontaneously.

ගිනිගල, *Ginigala*, *s.* a stone which produces fire on striking against steel, flint.

ගිනිගහනවා, *Ginigahanawá*, *v.* to produce fire by collision to do mischief.

ගිනිදලුව, *Ginidaluwa*, *s.* flame of fire.

ගිනිවතුර, *Giniwatura*, *s.* aqua fortis.

ගිම්සමය, *Gim-samaya*, *s.* (ගිම් heat, සමය season) the hot season, the summer.

ගිම්හාණඍතුව, *Gimháṇa-ṛituwa*, } *s.* hot season,
ගිම්හාණකාලය, *Gimháṇa-kálaya*, } dry weather.

ගියා, *Giyá*, *v.* went.

ගිරාමිණි, *Girámiṇi*, *s.* green-coloured gem.

ගිරිමෘත්, *Girimṛit*, *s.* red chalk, [Colloq. සිවංගුරු *siwanguru*].

ගිරිදුළුළු, *Giriduḷuḷu*, } *s.* impassable places on
ගිරිදුර්ග, *Giridurga*, } rocks.

ගිලීම, *Gilíma*, *s.* act of swallowing, act of sinking in water.

ගිහිකිස, *Gihikisa*, *s.* duties of a householder or layman.

ගිහිවෑසි, *Gihiwęsi*, *s.* layman.

ගීතිකාකාරණවා, *Gítikákaraṇawá*, *v.* to sing.

ගුඩදරු, *Guḍadáru*, } *s.* sugar cane, [Colloq. උක්
ගුඩමූල, *Guḍamúla*, } ගස් *uggas*].

ගුඩයෝෂපලා, *Guḍayóshapalá*, *s.* pumpkin gourd; ash-pumpkin, [Colloq. පුහුල් *puhul*].

ගුඩුගුඩාව, *Guḍuguḍáwa*, *s.* the whole round shell of a coconut used to smoke from.

ගුණ්‍යය, *Guṇyaya*, *s.* multiplicand.

ගුණකය, *Guṇakaya*, *s.* multiplier.

ගුණකාමී, *Guṇakámí*, *a.* loving virtue.

ගුණලවය, *Guṇalawaya*, *s.* small merit, little virtue or moral worth.

ගුණාඞ්ගය, *Guṇáńgaya*, *s.* attribute, quality, trait of character.

ගුණාඞ්ගසඞ්ගත, *Guṇáńgasańgata*, *a.* endowed with virtuous qualities.

ගුණාරෝපණයකොට, *Guṇárópaṇayakoṭa*, *part.* having attributed certain virtues; having given credit for the possession of certain virtuous qualities.

ගුණිත, *Guṇita*, *a.* multiplied (arithmetically), collected.

ගුණිතය, *Guṇítaya*, *s.* product.

* ගුදම, *Gudama*, *s.* godown, store (of arrack, etc.); out house.

ගුප්තා, *Guptá*, *s.* cowach: see වඳුරුමෑ *waṇdurumę́*.

ගුර්දූර, *Gurdúra*, *s.* lard. (Port.)

ගුර්වක්ෂර, *Gurwakshara*, *s.* (ගුරු *guru* heavy and අක්ෂර *akshara* letters) the long vowels.

ගුර, *Gura*, *s.* long vowel, long syllable.

ගුරුන්නැහේ, *Gurunnęhé*, *s.* a term of respect in addressing a tom tom beater.

ගුරුභාවය, *Gurubháwaya*, *s.* weight, gravity, importance.

ගුරුවො, *Guruwo*, *s.* a mixed race (or caste) of Siṇhalese and Moors who profess the Mohammedan religion.

ගුරුළුගෝමී, *Guruḷugómí*, *s.* learned man so called.

ගුරූපදේශ, *Gurúpadésa*, *s.* (ගුරු *guru* teacher, උපදේශ *upadésa* advice) advice of teachers, precepts.

ගුල්මඝ්න, *Gulmaghna*, *s.* temple tree, *plumeria acuminata*, [Colloq. අලරිය *alariya*].

ගුලුඇණ, *Gulu-ęṇé*, *s.* nail used to fasten a turner's board.

ගුවන්තලය, *Guwantalaya*, *s.* sky, firmament, aerial region.

ගූඪචර, *Gúḍhachara*, *s.* secret spy, emissary.

ගූඪවිලාප, *Gúḍha-vilápa*, *s.* concealed or secret sorrow, or lamentation.

ගූඪාකාර, *Gúḍhákára*, *s.* hidden or concealed manner.

ගූඪාර්ථ, *Gúḍhártha*, *s.* concealed meaning, recondite, abstruse, mysterious.

ගෙන්ගෙට, *Gengeṭa*, *s.* from house to house.

ගෙපියසි, *Gepiyasi*, *s.* house-roof.

ගෙබ, *Geba*, the Elu form of ගර්භ *garbha*, womb.

ගෙබරාල, *Gebarála*, *s.* store-keeper, whose duty it is to measure the paddy, rice, oil, etc., received into and issued out of a temple ගබඩාව *gabaḍáwa*, or store.

ගෙමඩ, *Gemaḍa*, *s.* tender top, shoot of the palm or plantain kind; see also දෙමට *demaṭa*.

ගෙයක්පණහා, *Geyak-paṇahá*, *adv.* from house to house, [Colloq. ගෙයක්පාසා *geyak-pásá*].

ගෙයඟන, *Geyaṇgana*, *s.* house-yard, compound.

ගෙරවීම, *Geravíma*, *s.* thunder, rumbling of clouds.

ගෙරිසරක්, *Gerisarak*, *s.* cattle meaning oxen and buffaloes.

ගෙවතුපණම, *Gewatu-paṇama*, *s.* ground-rent.

ගෙවලයා, *Gewalayá*, *s.* ghost harassing the inmates of a house.

ගෙවිල, *Gevila*, } *s.* tank or pond near a house.
ගෙසර, *Gesara*, }

ගෙසිකි, *Gesiki*, *s.* house-peacock.

ගොංගා, *Gongá*, *s.* kind of fish.

ගොකන් සමුදුර, *Gokan-samudura*, *s.* the sea to the east of Batticoloa.

ගොකුරදිය, *Gokuradiya*, *s.* (ගොකුර and දිය water) the water in a hole made by a cow's hoof.

ගොජී, *Gojí*, *s.* small tree, *streblus aspera*, [Colloq. ගෑටනෙටුල් *gętaneṭul*].

ගොටළු, *Goṭaḷu*, *s.* small horse: see ඝෝටක *ghóṭaka*.

ගොඩකරණවා, *Goḍakaraṇawá*, *v.* to fill up a valley or hole, to heap up.

ගොඩමඩ, *Goḍamaḍa*, *s.* high and low lands.

ගොටුගෑහෙනවා, *Goṭugẹhenawá*, *v.* to become shrivelled or contracted as a leaf, opposed to spreading.

ගොඩ මාවී, *Goḍa-máví*, *s.* kind of paddy.

ගොඩලිබිම, *Goḍali-bima*, *s.* hilly ground.

ගොණෑස්, *Goṇẹs*, *s.* rafter.

ගොන්තැඹිලි, *Gontẹmbili*, *s.* king coconut of a whitish colour.

ගොබ්කොල, *Gobkola*, see ගොක්කොල *gokkola*.

ගොබ්බයො, *Gobbayo*, *s.* frogs, (peculiar to Southern Province).

ගොම්මංවේලාව, *Gommanwelúwa*, *s.* (ගොන් *gon* oxen, cattle, මං road, වේලාව time) dusk of the evening, time when cattle come to the road, returning from pasture land.

ගොම්මුල, *Gommula*, *s.* plant, *leucas zeylanica*, [Colloq. ගැටතුඹ *gẹta-tumba*].

* ගොමු, *Gomu*, *s.* thicket, clump of trees.

ගොයම්කරවනවා, *Goyamkarawanawá*, *v.* to raise paddy, to cause fields to be cultivated with paddy.

ගොයිගානවා, *Goyigánawá*, *v.* to smooth the bed of a field.

ගොයිගැටේ, *Goyigẹṭé*, *s.* knot made by the goyiyá in the first wisp of straw that comes up during the threshing. This knot is hid in the paddy that is being threshed and is never removed from the heap until the final measurement and division of the crop.

ගොලෑ, *Golẹ́*, *a.* very tender, generally applied to arecanut.

ගොවිඳුකල්, *Govindukal*, } *s.* wife of Vishṇu.
ගොවිඳුසඳ, *Govindusanda*, }

ගොවුද, *Gowuda*, see ගොවද *gowada*.

ගොළ, *Goḷa*, *s.* a blow given by the fist.

ගෝග්‍රන්ථි, *Gó-granthi*, *s.* dried cow dung, [Colloq. ගොමවැරටි *gomawẹraṭi*].

ගෝචර, *Góchara*, *s.* provender, prey, [Colloq. ගොදුර *godura*]; object of sense; house or mansion of a planet, or its presence in any sign which is that of a person's nativity.

ගෝචරපල, *Góchara-pala*, *s.* pasturage, [Colloq. ගොදුරුබිම *goduru-bima*].

ගෝඩා, *Góḍá*, *s.* sediment of arrack, refuse of fermented toddy.

ගෝඩුම්බා, *Góḍumbá*, *s.* kind of cucumber, large variety of the *cucumis pubescens*, [Colloq. මහගොන්කෑකිරි *mahagonkẹkiri*]; also, water-melon, [Colloq. කොමඩු *komaḍu*].

ගෝත්‍රනාම, *Gótra-náma*, *s.* name of the tribe or family.

ගෝත්‍රභූචිත්ත, *Gótrabhúchitta*, *s.* mind in a fit state to receive sanctification.

ගෝන්දි, *Góndi*, *a.* when, (vulgar).

ගෝපාලිකා, *Gópáliká*, *s.* cowherdess.

ගෝපිකා, *Gópiká*, *s.* protectress; female cowherd.

ගෝපිත, *Gópita*, *s.* protected, concealed, hidden.

ගෝපුරද්වාර, *Gópuradwára*, *s.* town-gate.

ගෝල්ලා, *Góllá*, *s.* kind of sea fish.

ගෝලාඞ්ගුල, *Góláṅgula*, *s.* the black monkey: see කළුවඳුරා *kaḷu-wandurá*.

ගෝලිච්චාකරණවා, *Gólichchá-karaṇawá*, *v.* to make noise.

ගෝවඳනි, *Gówandani*, *s.* lofty tree which produces fragrant flowers, *myristica horsfieldia*, [Colloq පුවඟු *puwangu*, or රුක්අත්තන *ruk-attana*].

ගෝශකෘත්, *Góṣakṛit*, *s.* cow dung, [Colloq. ගොම *goma*].

ගෝස්තනිකා, *Góstaniká*, *s.* vine creeper, [Colloq. මිදිවැල් *midi-wẹl*].

ගෝස්මය, *Gósmaya*, *s.* hurried breath as of a cock.

ගෝසතර, *Gósatara*, *s.* art of healing cattle diseases.

ගෝසීස සඳුන්, *Gósísa-sandun*, *s.* sandal of gold colour.

ගෝහඟ, *Góhanga*, *s.* the oxen's horn.

ගෝළ, *Góḷa*, *s.* short in stature, dwarfish.

ගෞරාඞ්ගනා, *Gauráṅganá*, *s.* white woman.

ගෞරිය, *Gauriya*, *s.* sarsaparilla, *hemidesmus indicus*, [Colloq. ඉරමසු *iramasu*].

ගැටගැහෙනවා, *Gẹṭagẹhenawá*, *v.* to become contracted or tied down.

ගැටතෝඩු, *Gẹṭatóḍu*, *s.* kind of betel, [Colloq. බුලත් *bulat*].

ගැටනෙටුල්, *Gẹṭaneṭul*, see ගැටනිටුල් *gẹṭaniṭul*.

ගැටපහටු, *Gẹṭapahaṭu*, *s.* a musical instrument.

ගැටවහකම, *Gẹṭawahakama*, *s.* (Provincial) care, attention, = ප්‍රවේසම *prawésama*.

ගැටවා, *Gẹṭawá*, *s.* stripling.

ගැටහූපලඳනාව, *Gẹṭahú-palandanáwa*, *s.* ornament made of knotted thread.

ගැටිස්සා, *Gẹṭissá*, *s.* lad, stripling; kind of sea fish: pl. ගැටිස්සො *gẹṭisso*.

ගැටිම, *Gẹṭima*, *s.* abusing, rubbing, striking together.

ගැතිකම, *Gẹtikama*, *s.* work of a servant, servitude.

ගැතිබව, *Gẹtibawa*, *s.* condition of a servant.

ගැප්, *Gẹp*, *s.* fœtus, embryo.

ගැප්ගේ, *Gẹp-gé*, *s.* lying-in-chamber.

ගැයුම, *Gẹyum*, *s.* singing.

ගැරවිල්කුණ, *Gẹravil-kuna*, *s.* carcase of an earth-worm.

ගැලතුම, *Gẹlatuma*, *s.* tying together oxen and buffaloes for threshing paddy.

ගැලින, *Gẹlina*, *s.* was stuck (as in mud).

ගැහැටි, *Gẹhẹti*, *s.* a rural man, a rustic.

ගැහැවි, *Gẹhẹvi*, *s.* master of a family; householder.

ගැළපීම, *Gẹlapíma*, *s.* uniting, conciliating.

* ග්‍රන්ථ, *Grantha*, *s.* Alphabet used in south India in writing Sanskrit.

ග්‍රන්ථකර්තෘ, *Grantha-kartṛi*, *s.* the auther of a book.

ග්‍රන්ථචෞර්‍ය්‍යය, *Grantha-chauryaya*, *s.* plagiarism, infringement of the law of copyright.

ග්‍රන්ථාරම්භය, *Granthárambhaya*, *s.* commencement of a literary work.

ග්‍රහණධාරණ, *Grahaṇa-dháraṇa*, *s.* (ග්‍රහණ and ධාරණ mental retention) receiving and keeping of instruction.

ග්‍රහණයකොට, *Grahaṇayakoṭa*, *part.* having seized.

ග්‍රහ යාග, *Graha-yága*, *s.* (ග්‍රහ planet, යාග ceremony) a ceremony to appease the planets.

ග්‍රහ ශාන්ති, *Graha-sánti*, see above.

ග්‍රාම්‍ය ජන, *Grámya-jana*, *s.* the inhabitant of a village, an uneducated man, a fool.

ග්‍රාම්‍යාර්ථදෝෂ, *Grámyártha-dósha*, *s.* fault in composition consisting in vulgarisms, or rusticity of language.

ග්‍රාමණිකා, *Gráma-ṇiká*, *s.* a plebeian woman, a village woman.

ගෘධ්‍රකූට, *Gṛidhra-kúṭa*, *s.* (ගෘධ්‍ර vulture, කූට rock) a rock where vultures build their nests. Vulture Peak, name of a mountain in India.

ගෘහකාරක, *Gṛihakáraka*, *s.* house builder, architect.

ගෘහදීර්ඝිකා, *Gṛiha-dírghiká*, *s.* an oblong pond near a house.

ගෘහමයූර, *Gṛiha-mayúra*, *s.* house-peacock.

ගෘහස්ථභාවය, *Gṛihasthabháwaya*, *s.* life of a householder or layman, [Colloq. ගිහිබව *gihibawa*].

ගෘහසිඛි, *Gṛiha-sikhi*, *s.* house-peacock.

ගෘහාඞ්ගනා, *Gṛiháṅganá*, *s.* house woman.

ගෘහාභිනිෂ්ක්‍රමණ, *Gṛihábhinishkramaṇa*, *s.* going out of the house.

ගෘහෝපකරණය, *Gṛihópakaraṇaya*, *s.* household furniture.

ඝ

ඝටිත, *Ghaṭita*, *a.* in contact with, joined, devised, made of.

ඝටිකායන්ත්‍රය, *Ghaṭiká-yantraya*, *s.* water clock, Indian clock, plate of metal on which hours are struck.

ඝණ්ටාරාවය, *Ghaṇṭáráwaya*, *s.* (ඝණ්ටා bell, රාවය sound) the sound of the bell.

* ඝන, *Ghana*, *s.* sort of cucumber, [Colloq. තියඹරා *tiyam̃bará*]; chillies.

ඝනකර්කශපත්‍රක, *Ghanakarkaṣa-patraka*, *s.* plant, growing in marshy place, [Colloq. දියබෙරලිය *diyaberaliya*].

ඝනාවස්ථා, *Ghanáwasthá*, *s.* rainy season.

ඝනීභූත, *Ghaníbhúta*, *a.* become thick.

ඝර්මසූර්‍ය්‍යා, *Gharma-súryá*, *s.* (ඝර්ම hot, සූර්‍ය්‍යා sun) the summer sun.

* ඝොණ්ටා, *Ghonṭá*, *s.* medicinal plant, species of *sida humilis*, [Colloq. මහබැවිල *maha-bẹvila*].

ඝ්‍රාණප්‍රසාද, *Ghráṇa-prasáda*, *s.* pleasing sensation to the nose.

ච

චංචල, *Chaṇchala*, see චඤ්චල *chañchala*.

චක්‍රදච, *Chakradácha*, *s.* plant, *atylosia candollei*, [Colloq. ඇත්තෝර *ẹttóra*].

චක්‍රධර, *Chakradhara*, *s.* one who holds a wheel or discus; epithet of Vishṇu.

චක්‍රා, *Chakrá*, *s.* creeping plant, *ipomœa pes-tigridis*, [Colloq. දිවිපහුරු *divipahuru*].

චක්‍රාකාරක, *Chakrákáraka*, *s.* stemless plant with long leaves, from the fibres of which cord and bow strings are made, called bow-string hemp, *sanseviera zeylanica*, [Colloq නියඳ *niyan̆da*].

චඤ්චලාංගුලි, *Chañchaláṅguli*, *s.* coconut palm, *cocos nucifera*, [Colloq. පොල්ගහ *polgaha*].

චඤ්චු, *Chañchu*, *s.* the bill of a bird.

චණ්ඩාත, *Chaṇḍáta*, *s.* temple tree, *plumeria acutifolia*, [Colloq. අලරිය *alariya*].

චත්‍රා, *Chatrá*, *s.* ginger, [Colloq. ඉඟුරු *in̆guru*].

චත්වාරිංශත්, *Chatwáriṇsat*, *s.* forty, [Colloq. හතළිහ *hataḷiha*].

චතුඃෂෂ්ටි, *Chatuḥshashṭi*, *s.* sixty four, [Colloq. හැටහතර *hẹtahatara*].

චතුප්පාදක, *Chatuppádaka*, *a.* four footed. (Páli.)

චතුර්ජාත, *Chaturjáta*, *s.* four kinds of perfumes, viz. kind of mint, [Colloq, කොල්ලන්කොළ *kollankola*]; bark of cinnamon, *cinnamomum zeylanicum*, [Colloquial: කුරුඳුපොතු *kurun̆dupotu*]; small cardamoms, *elettaria cardamomum*, [Colloq. එන්සාල් *ensál*]; pollen or farma of the iron-wood tree.

චතුර්දිශා, *Chaturdiṣá*, *s.* four directions of the compass, east, west, north and south.

චතුර්යුග, *Chatur-yuga*, *s.* four ages of the world, viz. Kṛita, golden, Trétá, Dwápara, and Kali-yuga, age of vice.

චතුර්විංශති, *Chatur-vinṣati*, *s.* twenty four, [Coll: විසිහතර *visihatara*].

චතුර්විධ, *Chaturvidha*, *a.* four fold.

චතුරාර්‍ය්‍යසත්‍යය, *Chaturárya-satyaya*, *s.* the four sublime truths as inculcated by Buddha—suffering, cause of suffering, cessation of suffering, and the path leading to the cessation of suffering.

චතුරාර්‍ය්‍ය ඵලය, *Chaturárya-phalaya*, *s.* the four sublime fruitions, viz. fruitions in the four paths, Sówán, Sakradágámi, Anágámi and Arhat states of existence.

චතුෂ්ක, *Chatushka*, *s.* four, [Colloq. හතර *hatara*].

* චන්ද්‍ර, *Chandra*, *s.* small aromatic plant, *kaempferia galanga*, [Colloq. හිඟුරුපියලි *hinguru-piyali*].

චන්ද්‍රකාන්තා, *Chandrakántá*, *s.* species of night shade, [Colloq. බටු *batu*].

චන්ද්‍රකාන්තිය, *Chandrakántiya*, *s.* kind of medicinal oil.

චන්ද්‍රකාර, *Chandrakára*, *s.* white sandal wood, *santalum album*, [Colloq. සුදුහඳුන් *suduhandun*].

චන්ද්‍රකාලි, *Chandrakáli*, *s.* creeping plant, species of *pothos scandens*, [Colloq. සුළු පෝටා *sulupótá*].

චන්ද්‍රකිරණ, *Chandra-kiraṇa*, *s.* moon beam.

චන්ද්‍රපාන, *Chandrapána*, *s.* thorn apple, *datura stramonium*, [Colloq. සුදුඅත්තන *sudu-attana*].

චන්ද්‍රමාසය, *Chandra-másaya*, *s.* lunar month.

චන්ද්‍රයා, *Chandrayá*, *s.* moon.

චන්ද්‍රවාසින්, *Chandrawásin*, *s.* inhabitants of the moon.

චන්ද්‍රිකාශාලා, *Chandriká-ṣálá*, *s.* upper room, room in the upper apartments of a house.

* චපල, *Chapala*, *s.* quicksilver, [Colloq. රසදිය *rasadiya*]; plant, species of *flemingia*, [Colloq. උඳු *undu*].

* චපලා, *Chapalá*, *s.* screw-pine, *pandanus fascicularis* or *p. odoratissimus*, [Colloq. වැටකේ *weṭaké*].

චමත්කාර, *Chamatkára*, *s.* astonishment, show, row, riot; elaborate style or high poetical composition.

චමූපති, *Chamúpati*, *s.* commander of an army.

චර්මාසන, *Charmásana*, *s.* seat on leather, skin or hide.

චර්වණ, *Charwaṇa*, *s.* chewing, masticating.

චරුපර්ණි, *Charu-parṇi*, *s.* sort of bindweed, *ipomæa tridentata*, [Colloq. අපසුමඩු *ápasu-madu*].

චලදල, *Chaladala*, *s.* holy fig tree, [Colloq. බෝගහ *bó-gaha*].

චවිකා, *Chaviká*, *s.* climbing plant with an aromatic seed something of the nature of pepper, *piper chavya*, [Colloq. සිවිය *siviya*]; small flowering plant, *evolvulus alsinoides*, [Colloq. විෂ්ණුක්‍රාන්ති *vishṇukránti*].

චවිකාඞ්ඝ්‍රික, *Chavikánghrika*, *s.* long pepper root, *piper longum*, [Colloquial. තිප්පිලි මුල් *tippili-mul*].

චාඞ්ගේරි, *Chángéri*, *s.* plant, species of the *marsilea*, [Colloq. ඇඹුලැඹිලිය *embulembiliya*].

චාතුර්දිශික, *Cháturdiṣika*, *a.* belonging to the four directions of the compass.

චාතුර්ද්වීපික, *Cháturdvípika*, *a.* belonging to the four continents.

චිකිත්සා ශාලාව, *Chikitsá-ṣáláwa*, *s.* hospital.

චිත්තවිභ්‍රමය, *Chitta-vibhramaya*, *s.* error of judgment, mental aberration or derangement of intellect.

චිත්තාරාධනා, *Chittárádhaná*, *s.* satisfying or winning the heart.

චිත්තාස්වාදය, *Chittáswádaya*, *s.* intellectual gratification, mental enjoyment.

චිත්‍රවධ, *Chitra-wadha*, *s.* various kinds of torture.

චින්තනයෙහි, *Chintanayehi*, *s.* in the thinking.

චිරපාකි, *Chirapáki*, *s.* wood apple, *feronia elephantum*, [Colloq. දිවුල් *diwul*].

චිරස්ථිති, *Chirasthiti*, *s.* long continuance, perpetuation.

චිරිවිල්ව, *Chirivilwa*, *s.* tree, formerly called *galedupa indica* or *dalbergia arborea*, now *pongamia glabra*, [Colloq. මගුල්කරඳ *magulkaranda*].

චීනච්චට්ටි, *Chínachchaṭṭi*, see සිනච්චට්ටි *sínachchaṭṭi*.

චීනපිෂ්ට, *Chínapishṭa*, *s.* minium, or red lead, [Colloq. සින්දූරං *sindúran*].

චීවරවංස, *Chívara-wansa*, *s.* (චීවර and වංස a bamboo) a bamboo to put in a Buddhist priest's robe.

චුති, *Chuti*, *s.* departure.

චුතිචිත්ත, *Chutichitta*, *s.* conciousness of death or of leaving one world to be born in another.

චේතනා ශක්තිය, *Chétaná-ṣaktiya*, *s.* intellectual power or faculty.

චෛත්‍යවෘක්‍ෂ, *Chaitya-wriksha*, *s.* holy fig tree, *ficus religiosa*, [Colloq. බෝගස *bó-gasa*]; any sacred tree held in religious veneration.

චෛවගුලං, *Chaiwagulaṇ*, *s.* camphor, [Colloq. කපුරු *kapuru*].

චෝදක, *Chódaka*, *s.* one who rebukes or exhorts.

චෝරඝාත, *Chóragháta*, *s.* the killing of a thief.

ඡ

ඡණක්‍රීඩා, *Chhaṇa-kríḍá*, *s.* festival sports.

ඡත්‍රපර්ණී, *Chhatra-parṇi*, *s.* tree, *ficus arnottiana*, [Colloq. පුලිල *pulila* or කවුඩුබෝ *kawuḍubó*].

ඡත්‍රාඞ්ගි, *Chhatráṅgi*, *s.* creeping plant, *vitis quadrangularis*, [Colloq. සිරැස්ස *siréssa*].

ඡර්දිඝ්න, *Chhardighna*, *s.* fried grain, parched corn, [Colloq. විලඳ *vilanda*].

ඡවිගත, *Chhavigata*, *a.* lying on the skin.

ඡාගභක්‍ෂිණී, *Chhága-bhakshiṇi*, *s.* bow string hemp, *sanseviera zeylanica*, [Colloq. නියඳ *niyanda*].

ඡින්නගන්ධනිකා, *Chhinna-gandhaniká*, *s.* medicinal plant, *sphæranthus indicus*, or *s. hirtus*, [Colloq. මුඩමහණ *muḍamahaṇa*].

ජ

ජගත්කර්තෘවූ, *Jagat-kartriwú*, *a.* who is the creator of the world.

ජගද්විවරණය, *Jagad-viwaraṇaya*, *s.* description of the world.

ජගදන්ත, *Jagadanta*, *s.* (ජගත් *jagat* world, අන්ත *anta* end) the end of the world.

ජගදන්තර, *Jagadantara*, *s.* (ජගත් *jagat* and අන්තර *antara* between) within or inside the world.

ජගදානන්දලෝචනවූ, *Jagadánanda-lóchanawú*, *a.* like an eye gladdening the world.

ජගදායුවිවරණය, *Jagadáyu-viwaraṇaya*, *s.* explanatory account of the age of the world.

ජඝන්‍යචන්දන, *Jaghanya-chandana*, *s.* red sandal wood, variety of *santalum album*, [Colloq. රන්වන් සඳුන් *ranwan-sandun*].

ජඝනස්ථල, *Jaghanasthala*, *s.* region of the hip and loins.

* ජඝනේඵලා, *Jaghanéphalá*, *s.* plant, species of night shade, *solanum nigrum*, [Colloq. කළුකෑම්මෙරිය *kaḷukemmériya*].

ජඞ්ගලමාංස, *Jaṅgala-mánsa*, *s.* flesh of wild animals, as opposed to sea fish.

ජඞ්ගලවර්ග, *Jaṅgala-warga*, *s.* chapter relating to wild beasts or plants.

ජන්තුහෘත්, *Jantuhrit*, *s.* climbing anthelmintic shrub, *erycibe paniculata*, [Colloq. වලංගසාල් *walangasál*].

ජන්මප්‍රවේණි, *Janma-prawéṇi*, *s.* natural inheritance.

ජන්මාන්තරගතවිය, *Janmántaragatariya*, *v.* went to another state of existence, departed this life.

*ජනනී, *Janani*, *s.* nutmeg tree, *myristica fragrans*, [Colloq. සාදික්කා *sádikká*].

ජනානන්දකරවූ, *Jánánandakarawú*, *a.* causing joy to people.

ජනේහිත, *Janéhita*, *s.* silver, [Colloq. රිදී *ridí*].

ජපාපුෂ්ප, *Japá-pushpa*, *s.* China rose.

ජබාදු, *Jabádu*, *s.* frankincense, [Colloq. කට්ටකුමංචල් *kaṭṭakumaṇchal*].

ජම්භ, *Jambha*, *s.* orange, *citrus aurantium*, [Colloq. දොඩම් *doḍam*].

ජමාලයා, *Jamálayá*, *s.* a skilful or clever person, [Colloq. සමර්ථයා *samarthayá*]. (Provincial).

ජමීරය, *Jamíraya*, *s.* medicinal plant, *sida humilis*, [Colloq. බෑවිල *bevila*].

ජයග්‍රහණය, *Jayagrahaṇaya*, *s.* conquest, victory, [Colloq. ජයගැණීම *jayageníma*].

ජයඝෝෂාව, *Jaya-ghóshawa*, *s.* triumph of victory.

ජයපානය, *Jayapánaya*, *s.* draught of victory.

ජයප්‍රකාශිත, *Jaya-prakáśita*, *a.* (ජය victory, ප්‍රකාශිත published) manifesting victory, triumphant.

ජයබෙරය, *Jaya-beraya*, } *s.* victory drum, procla-
ජයභේරි, *Jaya-bhéri*, } mation of victory.

ජයා, *Jayá*, *s.* medicinal plant, yielding leaves of narcotic and intoxicating qualities much used by smokers, *cannabis satira*, [Colloq. කන්සා *kansá*]. (Tamil, Kañchá).

ජයාර්ජනී, *Jayárjaní*, *s.* Ceylon cardamoms *elettaria cardamomum*, [Colloq. එන්සාල් *ensál*].

ජරාපත්, *Jarápat*, *s.* decayed, old, dilapidated.

ජල්පන, *Jalpana*, *a.* saying, repeating, chattering, prating.

ජලදායක, *Jaladáyaka*, *s.* (ජල water, දායක one who gives) a cloud.

ජලදුර්ග, *Jaladurga*, *s.* place inaccessible by reason of water.

ජලධාරාව, *Jaladhárawa*, *s.* stream of water, shower.

ජලභරිත, *Jalabharita*, *a.* (ජල and භරිත laden) heavy with water, containing much water.

ජලයන්ත්‍රිකා ගෘහ, *Jalayantriká-griha*, *s.* a summer house.

ජලරේඛාව, *Jala-rékháwa*, *s.* line inscribed on water.

ජලස්කන්ධය, *Jalaskandhaya*, *s.* body or volume of water.

ජලාඤ්ජලි, *Jaláñjali*, *s.* (ජල *jala* water, අඤ්ජලි *añjali* the cavity formed by putting the hands together hollowing them) a handful of water.

ජලාධාරය, *Jaládháraya*, *s.* basin of a river, etc. reservoir.

ජලාභිවෘද්ධි, *Jalábhiwṛiddhi*, *a.* (ජල *jala* and අභිවෘද්ධි *abhiwṛiddhi* increasing) increasing of water, water rising high.

ජලෞඝ, *Jalógha*, *s.* current or stream of water, flood.

ජලෝදර, *Jalódara*, *s.* (ජල *jala*+උදර *udara*) dropsy.

ජවනචිත්ත, *Jawana-chitta*, *s.* mind which runs after any object.

ජවිස, *Javisa*, *s.* medicinal drug, *lagenandra lancifolia*, [Colloq. අතිවිඩයන් *atividayan*].

ජාඩි, *Jádi*, *s.* salt fish.

ජාඩිය, *Jádiya*, *s.* jar, fish preserved in a jar.

ජාතක උරුමේ *Játaka-urumé*, *s.* (ජාතක birth, උරුමේ right, inheritance) the right of inheritance by the father's side.

ජාතකර්ම, *Játa-karma*, *s.* delivery, &c. of a new born infant; ceremony performed, when the navel string is divided, touching the infant's tongue thrice with ghee, appropriate prayers, etc.

ජාතකුල, *Játakula*, *s.* family or tribe in which one is born.

ජාතභූමි, *Játa-bhúmi*, *s.* native country or place.

ජාතිභේදය, *Játi-bhédaya*, *s.* caste distinction.

ජාතිලිඞ්ග, *Játilinga*, *s.* vermillion, [Colloq. සාදිලිංගම් *sádilingam*].

ජාතිසෝද, *Játisóda*, *s.* tree, *croton tiglium*, [Colloq. ජයපාල *jayapála*].

ජාතිකපත්‍ර, *Játika-patra*, *s.* mace: see ජාතිපත්‍ර *játipatra*.

ජානකී, *Jánakí*, *s.* name of Sítá, daughter of Janaka.

ජානකීහරණ, *Jánakí-harana*, *s.* "the taking away of Sítá" a Sanskrit poem so called attributed to king Kumáradása of Ceylon.

ජාරබා, *Járabá*, *s.* ornamental and medicinal tree, *cassia fistula*, [Colloq. ඇහැළ *ehela*].

ජින්ජිබීර, *Jinjibíra*, *s.* ginger-beer. (English.)

ජිහවමඞ්ගල, *Jihwa-mangala*, *s.* frankincense, incense, [Colloq. තුවරලා *tuwaralá* or කට්ටකුමංචල් *kattakumanchal*].

ජීවග්‍රාහ, *Jívagráha*, *s.* taking alive.

ජීවදන්ති, *Jívadantí*, *s.* climbing plant, *vitis* or *cissus quadrangularis*, [Colloq. හිරැස්ස *hiressa*].

ජීවන්තක, *Jívantaka*, *s.* species of amaranth, *amaranthus cruentus*, [Colloq. රත්තම්පලා *rattampalá*].

ජීවම්කරණවා, *Jívamkaranawá*, *v.* to enchant.

ජීවම, *Jívama*, *s.* enchantment.

ජීවලෝක, *Jívalóka*, *s.* world of living beings.

ජීවාන්තකවායු, *Jívántaka-wáyu*, *s.* nitrogen.

ජීවිතක්ෂය, *Jívitakshaya*, *s.* loss of life.

ජූරි, *Júri*, *s.* jury. (English).

ජූලමස්සා, *Júlamassá*, *s.* kind of sea fish.

ජූලි, *Júli*, see ජූරි *júri*.

ජේත්තුව, *Jéttuwa*, *s.* pompous shew or finery in dress, pride.

ජේතවනාරාමය, *Jétawanárámaya*, *s.* famous Vihára so called.

ජෝතිපාසාණ, *Jótipásána*, *s.* burning glass, (made of crystal).

ජ්වරඝ්න, *Jwaraghna*, *s.* medicinal plant, *mollugo cerviana*, [Colloq. පත්පාඩගම් *patpádagam*].

ජ්වරහරා, *Jwarahará*, *s.* bulbous stemless plant, *crinum zeylanicum* or *c. ornatum*, [Colloq. ගොඩමානිල් *goda-mánil*].

ඣ

ඣිණ්ටිකා, *Jhintiká*, *s.* creeping plant, peculiar to Ceylon, *argyreia populifolia*, [Colloq. ගිරිතිල්ල *giritilla*].

ඣින්තුඩිය, *Jhintudiya*, *s.* sandal wood, *santalum album*, [Colloq. සඳුන් *sandun*].

ඤ

ඤාතිව්‍යසනය, *Ñátiwyásanaya*, *s.* loss of kinsmen.

ඤාතිසම්බන්ධය, *Ñátisambandhaya*, *s.* connection as relatives.

ඤානාභිමානය, *Ñánábhimánaya*, *s.* pride of learning, pedantry, concert.

ඤෙයමණ්ඩලය, *Ñeyya-mandalaya*, *s.* circle of knowledge.

ට

ටිකානොවූ, *Ṭikanowú*, *a.* which is not little.

ටිකිරි, *Ṭikiri*, *a.* little.

ඩ

ඩාහුක, *Ḍáhuka*, *s.* gallinule.

ඩිම්බපෝෂණ, *Ḍimbapóshana*, *s.* (ඩිම්බ chrysalis, young animal+පෝෂණ *póshana*) rearing young animals.

ඩෝලායන්ත්‍රය, *Ḍóláyantraya*, *s.* same as වණ්ඩුව *waṇḍuwa*, which see.

ත

තක්සේරුව, *Takséruwa*, *s.* appraisement, valuation. (Portuguese.)

තක්සේරුකරණවා, *Takséru-karaṇawá*, *v.* to value, to appraise.

තකතිරුවා, *Takatiruwá*, *v.* worthless character, villain.

තකහනියාම, *Takahaniyáma*, *adv.* on purpose, [Colloq. ඒ ගෑණම *é geṇama*]. (Provincial.)

තට්ටම්පෝරුව, *Taṭṭampóruwa*, *s.* the flat part of the buttocks

තට්ටුමාරුව, *Taṭṭumáruwa*, *s.* a field, héna or other land cultivated by joint owners in turns—thus if a field belongs to three families in taṭṭumáru possession, each family will cultivate the whole every third year—if it were held in common each family will take one third of the produce every year.

තටංපෝරුව, *Taṭaṇpóruwa*, *s.* a sort of bell or frame work of wood or other matter hung on fruit trees to drive away squirrels, etc.; more commonly ටකපෝරුව *ṭakapóruwa*.

තටු ඇල්වි, *Taṭu-elvi*, *s.* kind of paddy.

තටුපත, *Taṭupata*, *s.* wing of a bird.

තඩාග, *Taḍága*, *s.* moss, [Colloq. සෙවෙල් *sewel*]; pond: see තටාක *taṭáka*.

තඩිගහනවා, *Taḍigahanawá*, see තඩිබානවා *taḍibánawá*.

තණ්ඩුලඛණ්ඩ, *Taṇḍula-khaṇḍa*, *s.* pieces of rice, film, [Colloq. කුඩු *kuḍu*].

තණ්ඩුලවාරි, *Taṇḍulawári*, *v.* water in which rice has been washed, [Coll. දොවුන්දිය *dowundiya*].

තණසුල, *Taṇasula*, *s.* (තණ grass, සුල or හුල *hula* torch) a torch made of dried grass or other leaves.

තත්කාල, *Tatkála*, *s.* that time.

තත්ගුණ, *Tatguṇa*, *s.* a grammatical term to express an inherent quality, as, දසබල *dasabala*, one having ten powers.

තත්තකාරයා, *Tattakáraya*, *s.* carpenter, [Colloq. වඩුවා *waḍuwá*].

තත්පරකම්, *Tatparakam*, *s.* trying, endeavour, close attention.

තත්පරායණ, *Tatparáyaṇa*, *a.* attached to it, devoted.

තත්පරිදි, *Tat-paridi*, *s.* that manner or fact.

තත්භව, *Tatbhawa*, see තබව *tabawa*.

තත්ලෙසින්, *Tatlesin*, *s.* in that manner or way.

තදනන්තර, *Tadanantara*, *s.* the time after that, that interval.

තදනන්තරව, *Tadanantarawa*, *adv.* immediately, after that.

තන්, *Tan*, *s.* place.

තන්තිරිකඩ, *Tantirikaḍa*, *s.* temporary boutiques opened in the night near a mosque during the Mohammedan fast days.

තන්වඟි, *Tanwańgi*, *s.* a woman of slender make.

තනිකම, *Tanikama*, *s.* state of being alone, loneliness, supposed influence of devil when a woman is alone.

තනියම, *Taniyama*, *a.* alone, single.

තපෝගුණ, *Tapóguṇa*, *s.* asceticism, practice of a hermit.

තඹර අරණ, *Tam̲bara-araṇa*, *s.* assemblage of lotuses.

තඹරකර, *Tam̲barakara*, *s.* the sun, [Colloq. ඉර *ira*].

* තඹාක්ක, *Tam̲bákka*, *s.* a composite metal copper mixed with gold.

* තමා, *Tamá*,=ඒකාන්තයෙන් *Ékántayen*, *adv.* indeed, certainly.

* තමි, *Tamí*, *s.* saffron, turmeric, *curcuma longa*, [Colloq. කහ *kaha*].

තමෝගුණ, *Tamóguṇa*, *s.* the quality of darkness or ignorance.

තර්කණය, *Tarkaṇaya*, *s.* an argument, inference.

තර්කවිද්‍යා, *Tarka-vidyá*, *s.* science of logic.

තර්කශාස්ත්‍රාර්ණවය, *Tarka-śástrárṇawaya*, *s.* ocean of logical science.

තර්කසිද්ධාන්ත, *Tarka-siddhánta*, *s.* demonstrated conclusion, established truth.

තර්කානුසාරය, *Tarkánusáraya*, *s.* process of reasoning; conformity to logic.

තරකොට, *Tarakoṭa*, *adv.* firmly, strongly.

තරගේ, *Tara-gé*, *s.* prison, gaol, [Colloq. හිරගේ *hiragé*].

තරගය *Taran̲gaya*, *s.* debate, verbal contest.

තරගවෙනවා, *Taran̲gawenawá*, *a.* to compete, to strive.

තරගේ, *Taran̲gé*, *s.* verbal dispute, controversy, reasoning.

තරඞ්ග, *Tarańga*, see තරග *taran̲ga*.

තරඞ්ගමාලාව, *Tarańgamáláwa*, *s.* a round and continued wave.

තරණය, *Taraṇaya*, *s.* act of crossing over.

තරයේ, *Tarayé*, *adv.* firmly, fast, [Colloq. හයියෙන් *hayiyen*].

තරලමිණ, *Taralamiṇa*, *s.* central gem in a necklace, luminous gem.

තරසරව, *Tarasarawa*, *a.* firm and strong,=ස්ථිරසාරව *sthirasárawa*.

තරකඳවුර, *Tárákandayura*, *s.* strong camp.

තරදොර, *Tarádora*, *s.* strong door or gate.

තරුණාද්‍රි, *Taruṇádri*, *s.* tree, *adina cordifolia* or *nauclea*, [Colloq. කොළොම්ගස *kolom-gasa*].

තරුපිච්ඡා, *Tarupichchhá*, } *s.* gum, [Colloq. ලාටු
තරුමජ්ජක, *Tarumajjaka*, } *látu*].

තරේ, *Taré*, see තරයේ *tarayé*.

තල්වම්බටු, *Tal-wambaṭu*, *s.* kind of brinjal or egg plant.

තලකැලැල්, *Tala-kelal*, *s.* a mole on the body.

තලගහ, *Tala-gaha*, *s.* talipot tree.

තලත්තානි, *Talattáni*, } *a.* elderly, respectable by
තලත්තැනි, *Talatteni*, } age.
තලතුනා, *Talaṭuná*, }

තලනබටු, *Talanabaṭu*, see එලබටු *elabaṭu*.

තලප්පාව, *Talappáwa*, *s.* turban.

තලපුන්නක්කු, *Tala-punnakku*, *s.* poonac prepared from the refuse of sesamum.

තලාතුමිණිරං, *Talátu-miṇiraṇ*, *s.* plumbago used to serve as an ornament for talipot leaves.

තශබ්ද, *Tṣabda*, } *s.* word expressive of ත second
තසද, *Tasada*, } person in both numbers.

තසදකරු, *Tasadakaru*, *s.* in Grammar the second person.

තහන්චිකලා, *Tahanchikalá*, *s.* placed under restriction. (S. P.)

*තාච්චිය, *Táchchiya*, } *s.* brass pan. (Port.)
තාච්චුව, *Táchchuwa*, }

තාපිජ, *Tápija*, *s.* mineral substance of a dark colour, used medicinally; it is apparently the common pyritic iron ore, [Colloq. මැසිඳ *meṣidé*].

*තාම්‍රපර්ණි, *Támra-parṇi*, *s.* an ancient name of Ceylon, P. තම්බපණ්ණි *tambapaṇṇi*, hence the Taprobane of the ancient Greeks and Romans.

තාලවටු, *Tálawaṭu*, *s.* fan, [Colloq. පවන්පත *pawanpata*].

තාවුරු, *Táwuru*, *a.* firm, [Colloq. තදවූ *tadawú*].

තික්තකරෝහිණි, *Tiktakaróhiṇi*, see තික්තා *tiktá*.

තික්තය, *Tiktaya*, *s.* plant, peculiar to Ceylon, *munronia pumila* [Colloq. බින්කොහොඹ *bin-kohomba*].

තිකටු, *Tikaṭu*, see ගොකටු *gokaṭu*.

තිනුම්, *Tinum*, *s.* shaking, trembling, [Colloq. සෙලවීම *selavíma*].

තිප්පොල, *Tippola*, *s.* lair.

තිබුකස්, *Tibukas*, } *s.* tree, *diospyros embryopteris:*
තිබුරු, *Tiburu*, } see තිඹිරි *timbiri*.

තිර්‍යග්යෝනි, *Tiryagyóni*, *s.* state of existence as irrational animals.

තිලගන්ධ, *Tilagandha*, *s.* plant, *oleander*, [Colloq. බොලිද්ද *bolidda*].

තිලෝකය, *Tilókaya*, see තුන්ලෝ *tunló*.

තිවග, *Tiwaga*, *s.* three kinds of fragrant substances, viz. clove, *caryophyllus aromaticus*, [Colloq. කරාබු *karábu*]; mace, [Colloq. වසාවාසි *wasáwási*]; nutmeg, *myristica fragrans*, [Colloq. සාදික්කා *sádikká*]; the three myrobalans; the three spices, viz. black and long pepper, and dry ginger.

තිසරු, *Tisaru*, *s.* sort of frogs moving on the surface of water; also, swan, goose, gander.

තිසුල, *Tisula*, *s.* trident, three pointed pike or spear.

තිහිරි, *Tihiri*, *s.* bark of a tree worn by ascetics.

තීක්ෂ්ණමය, *Tíkshṇamaya*, } *s.* steel, tempered
තීක්ෂ්ණලෝහ, *Tíkshṇalóha*, } iron, [Colloq. වාණේ *wáné*].

තුඩතුඩ, *Tuḍatuḍa*, *s.* mouth to mouth, in every mouth.

තුඩුපත, *Tuḍu-pata*, *s.* (තුඩු mouth, පත leaf, writing) order or grant given by word of mouth and recorded on an óla.

* තුණ්ඩිල, *Tuṇḍila*, *s.* vegetable used in making curry; purslane, *portulaca oleracea*, [Colloq. ගෙද *genda*].

තුණ්ඩිලයා, *Tuṇḍilayá*, *s.* one who speaks harshly or severely.

තුණ්ඩිලජාතකය, *Tuṇḍila-játakaya*, *s.* so called Birth story of Buddha.

තුන්කුළු, *Tunkuḷu*, see තිකුළු *tikuḷu*.

තුන්තරාබෝධිය, *Tuntará-bódhiya*, *s.* the three kinds of Bódhi; viz. Arhatship, Pratyéka Buddhaship, and Supreme Buddhaship.

තුන්නකය, *Tunnakaya*, } *s.* the three fraternities
තුන්නිකාය, *Tunnikáya*, } of Buddhist priests in Ceylon, viz. those of the Abhayagiri, Jétawana, and Mahavihára monasteries.

තුන්බුමු, *Tunbumu*, *a.* three storied.

තුන්බෝ පිහිටුවා, *Tunbó-pihiṭuwá*, *s.* having planted a bó tree, built a monastery, and a house with the images of Buddha in it.

තුන්මංසල, *Tunmansala*, *s.* place where three roads meet, a hall at the junction of three roads, a term used colloquially to denote destitute condition.

තුන්යම්රෑ, *Tunyam-ré*, } *s.* three watches of the
තුන්යම, *Tunyama*, } night, whole night.

තුන්යලක්, *Tunyalak*, *s.* three times.

තුන්රැස්, *Tunręs*, *s.* creeping plant with large white flowers and medicinal root, bind-weed, *ipomœa turpethum*, [Colloq. ත්‍රස්තවාලු *trastawálu*].

තුන්වන්මිටු, *Tunwanmitu*, *s.* tuberous plant, the fruit used for curries, *momordica dioika*, [Colloq. තුඹකරවිල *tumba-kararila*].

තුන්විතක්, *Tunvitak*, *s.* three kinds of thought, viz. lustful thought, malevolent thought, and cruel thought.

තුන්සිවුර, *Tunsiwura*, *s.* the three robes of a Buddhist priest, viz. අඳනය *andunaya*, under garment, තනිපට සිවුර *tanipata-siwura*, robe made of one single piece; outer garment, ordinary dress used at the Pansala; දෙපට සිවුර *depata-siwura*, robe made of two pieces doubled, generally used when going out of the Pansala.

තුන්හවුල් ඉඩම්, *Tunhawul-idam*, *s.* term applied to designate Crown lands planted by private individuals, the planter being entitled to one-third share.

තුඹුපට, *Tumbupata*, *s.* copper coloured cloth.

තුරුරැව්, *Tururęw*, } *s.* sound of music.
තුරුහඬ, *Turuhanda*, }

තුල්‍යතාවය, *Tulyatáwaya*, *s.* equilibrium, equality.

තුලාන, *Tulána*, *s.* a division of country, district, —the term is peculiar to the District of Nuwara-kaláviya.

තුලාබර, *Tulábara*, see තුලාභාරය *tulábháraya*.

තූතු, *Tútu*, *s.* fragments of a broken vessel.

තූතුකරමින්, *Tútukaramin*, } *part.* smashing,
තූතුකෙරෙමින්, *Tútukeremin*, } reducing to pieces, tearing up,=ඉරාදමමින් *irádamamin*.

තූතුකොට, *Tútukota*, *part.* having rejected with contempt.

තූරල්කරණවා, *Túralkaranawá*, *v.* cease, as rain; clear up, as weather.

තෙජාත, *Tejáta*, } *s.* three kinds of drugs,
තෙජාතක, *Tejátaka*, } viz. cinnamon, *cinnamomum zeylanicum*, [Colloq. කුරුඳු *kurundu*]; Ceylon cardamoms, *elettaria cardamomum*, [Colloq. එන්සාල් *ensál*]; kind of mint, [Colloq. කොල්ලංකොල *kollankola*].

තෙප්පම්කාරයා, *Teppamkárayá*, *s.* one who pushes a raft, or one who uses a raft to catch fish.

තෙපණස්වෙනි, *Tepanasweni*, *a.* fifty third.

තෙමඬුලු, *Temadulu*, *s.* (තෙ three+මඬුලු *mandulu* circles) term applied to denote the navel and the two knees of Buddhist priests' clothing of proper height and length.

තෙමුණු, *Temunu*, *p. p.* wetted.

තෙරුවන්, *Teruwan*, *s.* the three Gems, viz. Buddha, his Law, and his Scriptures.

තෙල්කුළාව, *Telkuláwa*, *s.* phial of oil.

තෙල්දිනි, *Teldini*, *s.* ant, [Colloq. කුඹියා *kúmbiyá*].

තෙල්ධාතුව, *Teldhátuwa*, *s.* the serous secretion that spreads amongst the muscular fibres of the body.

තෙල්වළ, *Telwala*, *s.* depression on the top of the head of infants where oil is rubbed.

තෙලිත්තක්, *Telittak*, *s.* small quantity of oil.

තෙවග, *Tewaga*, *s.* three kinds of fragrant substances: see තිවග *tiwaga*.

තෙවිද, *Tevida*, the Elu form of ත්‍රිවිධ *trividha*.

තෙළෙස්වක, *Teleswaka*, *s.* thirteenth day of a lunar fortnight.

තේකොල, *Tékola*, *s.* Tea.

තේජවන්ත, *Téjawanta*, *a.* glorious.

තේරූවා, *Téruwá*, *v.* selected, explained, expounded.

තෛලං, *Tailan*, *s.* purified opium.

තෛලමඤ්ජු, *Tailamañju*, *s.* sesamum oil, gingely oil, [Colloq. තලතෙල් *talatel*].

තොණ්ඩයා, *Tondayá*, *s.* small sea fish.

තොප්පි සළුව, *Toppi-saluwa*, *s.* hat cloth (a Kandyan word).

තොපනූ, *Topanú*, *a.* in which you were not, as "තොපනූ අවස" time in which you did not exist or live. (කාව්‍යශේඛර *káwyasékhara*.)

තොරලියා, *Toraliyá*, *s.* kind of sea fish.

තෝඤ්චිවෙනවා, *Tóñchiwenawá*, *v.* to delay, to hesitate.

තෝන්, *Tón*, see තෝං *tón*.

තෝම, *Tóma*, *s.* cinnamon bark, *cinnamomum zeylanicum*, [Colloq. කුරුඳුපොතු *kurundupotu*].

තෝමාල, *Tómála*, *s.* red arsenic, [Colloq. මනෝසිල *manósila*].

තෝල්කයා, *Tólkayá*, *s.* interpreter.

තෝල්ක මහත්මයා, *Tólka-mahatmayá*, *s.* respectful form of the above.

තෝල, *Tóla*, } *s.* weight of gold or silver.
තෝලක, *Tólaka*, }

තැටමිල්ල, *Tẹṭamilla*, s. straining at stools.

තැත්, *Tẹt*, s. effort, endeavour.

තැත්කරණවා, *Tẹtkaraṇawá*, v. to try, to endeavour.

තැන්පත්, *Tẹnpat*, a. who holds the post or office of, e. g. ගුරුතැන්පත් *gurutẹnpat*.

*තැන්පත්කරණවා, *Tẹnpatkaraṇawá*, v. to deposit, to keep, to burn.

තැබෑරුම, *Tẹbẹ́ruma*, s. tavern, place where liquors are vended.

තැලිවළ, *Tẹliwaḷa*, s. that part of the chest where the heart beats or throbs.

තැලිවැල්, *Tẹliwẹl*, s. kind of medicinal plant.

තෑගිපත්‍රය, *Tẹ́gipatraya*, s. deed of gift.

ත්‍යක්තලජ්ජාඇති, *Tyakta-lajjáeti*, a. lost to shame, impudent.

ත්‍රපු, *Trapu*, s. white lead, [Colloq. සුදුඊයම් *sudu-íyam*].

ත්‍රිකාලවර්තී, *Trikálawartti*, s. existing in the present, past, and future times.

ත්‍රිකෝණාකාර, *Trikóṇákára*, s. the form of a triangle.

ත්‍රිතය, *Tritaya*, a. third.

ත්‍රිදෝෂ, *Tridósha*, s. three humors of the human body, viz. wind, air, and bile.

ත්‍රිධා, *Tridhá*, adv. in three ways.

ත්‍රිපාදී, *Tripádí*, s. kind of medicinal plant, [Colloq. වලාවැන්න *waláwẹnna*].

ත්‍රිමාසාවසානය, *Trimásáwasánaya*, s. expiration of three months.

ත්‍රිලෝක, *Trilóka*, s. three worlds, viz. human, divine, and Asura worlds.

ත්‍රිවේද, *Trivéda*, s. three Vedas, viz. Rig, Yajur, and Sáma.

ත්‍රිශීර්ෂක, *Tri-şírshaka*, s. plant, *amorphophallus campanulatus*, [Colloq. කිඩාරන් *kiḍáran*].

ත්‍රිසිංහලය, *Trisiṇhalaya*, s. three-fold division of Ceylon, consisting of Ruhuṇu, Máyá, and Pihiṭi-Southern, Central, and Northern Divisions respectively.

තෘණජාති, *Tṛiṇajáti*, s. grass in general, herbage, trees and plants, vegetable world.

තෘණධ්වජ, *Tṛiṇadhwaja*, s. sugar cane, [Colloq. උක්ගහ *ukgaha*].

තෘෂ්ණාව, *Tṛishṇáwa*, s. desire, wish, anxious longing, lust.

තෘෂාවහා, *Tṛisháwahá*, s. kind of medicinal plant, [Colloq. වලාවැන්න *waláwẹnna*].

ත්‍රෛරාශිය, *Trai-ráşiya*, s. simple proportion.

ත්‍ර්‍යක්ෂම, *Tryakshma*, s. coconut tree, *cocos nucifera*, [Colloq. පොල්ගහ *polgaha*].

ත්වච්ඡාර, *Twachchhára*, s. bamboo tree, *bambusa vulgaris*, [Colloq. උණගස් *uṇagas*].

ත්වචඵල, *Twacha-phala*, s. shrub, the leaves of which are used as tea and the bark as a buff dye, *cassia auriculata*. [Colloq. රණවරා *raṇawará*].

ත්වචිසාර, *Twachisára*, see ත්වච්ඡාර *twachchhára*.

ථීන, *Thína*, s. idleness, sloth, dulness. (Páli.)

ද

දක්ෂිණාග්‍ර, *Dakshiṇágra*, s. (දක්ෂිණ *dakshiṇa* south, අග්‍ර *agra* end) that which points to the south, that which has the head or top to the south; south pole of the world.

දක්ෂිණායන, *Dakshiṇáyana*, s. (දක්ෂිණ *dakshiṇa* and අයන *ayana* going) the sun's progress south of the equator, the winter solstice.

දකුණුලක, *Dakuṇa-laka*, s. the South Ceylon, Ruhuṇa division.

දඟදමනවා, *Daṇgadamanawá*, v. to twist ropes or strings.

දඟවැටෙනවා, *Daṇga-wẹṭenawá*, v. to be twisted.

දජය, *Dajaya*, see ධ්වජය *dhwajaya*.

දඩකෙළිය, *Daḍakeḷiya*, s. hunting excursion.

දඩරන්, *Daḍaran*, s. tree, *adina cordifolia* or *nauclea*, [Colloq. කොළොම්ගහ *kolom-gaha*].

දඬුමොණරයන්ත්‍රය, *Daṇḍumoṇara-yantraya*, s. sor of balloon or flying apparatus.

දඬුරියන, *Daṇḍuriyana*, s. cubic measure rule.

දණ්ඩනායක, *Daṇḍanáyaka*, s. general, commander in-chief, magistrate, head police officer.

*දණ්ඩනීතිය, *Daṇḍanítiya*, s. Penal Code; polity, system of civil and military administration.

දණ්ඩපාතය, *Daṇḍapátaya*, s. fine.

දණ්ඩාඥා, *Daṇḍájñá*, s. an order for punishment.

දත්මැලියම්, *Datmẹliyam*, s. tartar of the teeth.

දත්රජ, *Datraja*, s. king-tooth, principal tooth, fore-tooth.

දත්වෑයා, *Datwẹ́yá*, s. worm supposed to eat away the teeth.

දදකැල, *Dadakẹla*, s. assemblage of Brahmins, multitude of stars.

දධිත්ථ, *Dadhittha*, s. wood apple, *feronia elephantum*, [Colloq. ගිවුල් *giwul* or දිවුල් *diwul*].

දන්තශඨා, *Dantaşaṭhá*, s. plant, species of the *marsilea*. [Colloq. ඇඹුල්ඇඹිලිය *ẹmbulẹmbiliya*].

දනතා, *Dantá*, *s.* small tree or shrub with large flowers, *adhatoda vasica*, [Colloq. අගල්අදර *agaládára* or වංඅපල *waṇepala*].

*දනුව, *Danuwa*,=ධ්වනි *dhwani*, *s* sound, noise.

දපන, *Dapana*, *a.* charming, muttering prayers.

දබ්බ, *Dabba*, *s.* material, substance (Páli)=Skt. ද්‍රව්‍ය *drawya*.

දබ්බි, *Dabbí*, *s.* (Páli) spoon,=Skt. දර්වි *darvi*.

දඹුබත්, *Dambubat*, see දන්දික *dandika*.

දම්දෙව්සුදු, *Damdewsudu*, *s.* shrub, *siphonanthus indica*, [Colloq. සිරිතේක්කු *siritékku*].

දම්සෙනෙවි, *Damsenevi*, *s.* the chief of divines.

දමිටු, *Damitu*, see දෑමිටු *demitu*.

දයාමය, *Dayámaya*, *a.* merciful, kind-hearted.

දර්ශනපථය, *Darṣanapathaya*, *s.* range or extent of vision.

දලියා, *Daliyá*, *s.* a cockroach: pl. දලි *dali*.

දලුපොත, *Dalupota*, *s.* land lately brought into cultivation as a paddy field or more recently than the original field.

දලුමුරේ, *Dalumuré*, *s.* turn to supply betel for a temple proprietor.

දශඥනබල, *Daṣajñána-bala*, *s.* ten-fold knowing power; ten kinds of knowledge.

දශදනවස්තු, *Daṣadána-wastu*, *s.* ten kinds of articles given away to priests as gifts, viz. food, drink, dwelling, raiment, vehicle, garlands, unguent, perfume, beds, oil for lamps.

දශනාගකුල, *Daṣa-nágakula*, *s.* ten kinds of elephants, viz. කාලවක *kálavaka*, ගාංගෙය්‍ය *gańgeyya*, පණ්ඩර *paṇḍara*, තම්බ *tamba*, පිඞ්ගල *pińgala*, ගන්ධ *gandha*, මඞ්ගල *mańgala*, හේම *héma*, උපෝසථ *upósatha*, ඡද්දන්ත *chhaddanta*.

දශමභාගය, *Daṣama-bhágaya*, *s.* decimal fraction, tenth part.

දශසහශ්‍රී, *Daṣasahasrí*, } *s.* ten thousand.
දසදහස, *Dasadahasa*, }

දසදිග, *Dasadiga*, *s.* ten directions, viz. east, west, north, south, north-east, south-east, north-west, south-west, nadir, and the zenith.

දසන්වරණ, *Dasanwaraṇa*, *s.* that which covers the teeth, lips.

දසනඛසමෝධාන, *Dasanakha-samódhána*, *s.* bringing the ten finger-nails together (in clasping the rounds).

දසබිම්බර, *Dasabimbara*, *s.* term applied to a vast army sufficient to occupy ten earths as large as our own.

දහනමුඛී, *Dahanamukhí*, *s.* the marking-nut tree, *semicarpus gardneri*, formerly called *s. anacardium*, [Colloq. බඩුල්ල *badulla*].

දහනෝපල, *Dahanópala*, *s.* crystal, common rock crystal, [Colloq. පළිඟු *paḷingu*].

දහම්සොඬ, *Dahamsonḍa*, *s.* fond of or attached to Dharma or Law of Buddha.

දහස්ගුණයක්, *Dahas-guṇayak*, *s.* one thousand times.

දහස, *Dahasa*, *s.* thousand: pl. දහස් *dahas*.

දළනෙත, *Daḷaneta*, *s.* Sakra having an eye on his fore-head.

*දා, *Dá*, *a*, begotten by.

දාගල, *Dágala*, *s.* the small stone used in the hand for grinding condiments, etc. upon a slab, [Coll: දූගල *dú-gala*].

දාඨාධාතු, *Dáṭhádhátu*, *s.* the relic of the canine tooth of Buddha.

දාඨාධාතුඝර, *Dáṭhádhátughara*, *s.* (දාඨාධාතු and ඝර house) the building containing the relic of the canine tooth of Buddha.

දාදුකැටය, *Dádukeṭaya*, *s.* a dice used in gaming.

දානමාන, *Dánamána*, *s.* gift and respect.

දානවසතර, *Dánawa-satara*, *s.* art or science of the Asuras or Titans.

දාමරික, *Dámarika*, *s.* rebel, competitor for the throne.

* දායාද, *Dáyáda*, *s.* heir, kinsman; dowry.

දාරකයා, *Dárakayá*, *s.* a son.

දාරාභරණ, *Dárábharaṇa*, *s.* maintenance of a wife.

දාරිද්‍ර, *Dáridra*, *s.* poverty.

දාලන, *Dálana*, *a.* splitting.

දාවාග්නිය, *Dáwágniya*, *s.* fire in a forest, conflagration of a forest.

දාසිපටිය, *Dási-paṭiya*, *s.* a neck tie.

දාසිය, *Dásiya*, *s.* a maid servant; neck tie.

දික්කසාද, *Dikkasáda*, *s.* divorce.

දික්පුරුදු, *Dikpurudu*, *s.* acquaintance with the different quarters or directions.

දික්සුද්ධිය, *Diksuddhiya*, *s.* sanctity of the different points of the compass.

දිග්ගේ, *Dig-gé*, *s.* porch of a Déwála, a long hall to which alone worshippers have access.

දිගවෙලිකරණවා, *Digawelikaraṇawá*, *v.* to tether.

දිගැසිය, *Digasiya*, *s.* the long-eyed one, epithet of a handsome woman.

දිගායුස, *Digáyusa*, *s.* long life.

දිගින්නා, *Diginná*, *s.* kind of sea fish.

දිගුණය, *Digunaya*, s. the two-fold quantity, (Elu form of විගුණ *driguna*).
දිගෙල්කරණවා, *Digelkaranawá*, v. to tether.
* දිට, *Dita*, v. saw,=දුටුවේය *dutuwéya*.
දිටිල, *Ditila*. v. it is said that he saw.
දිටුඅත්, *Dituat*, s. meaning which was seen.
දිතිසුත, *Ditisuta*, s. sun, [Colloq. සූර්‍යයා *súryayá*].
දින ඉසුරු, *Dina-isuru*, s. lord of the day, epithet of the sun.
දිනචරිතය, *Dina-charitaya*, s. daily conduct or behaviour.
දිනාන්ත, *Dinánta*, s. close of day, evening, sunset.
*දිනිසුරු, *Dinisuru*, see දිනඉසුරු *dina-isuru*.
දිමුත්, *Dimut*, see දිමුතු *dimutu*.
දියකඩේ, *Diyakadé*, s. current of the sea or of a river.
දියකුස, *Diyakusa*, s. the whole orb or circle of the world, within the world.
දියග, *Diyaga*,=දිපිය *dipiya*, v. give away (imperative mood).
දියඝොස, *Diyagosa*, s. shout of victory.
දියදඹ, *Diyadamba*, s. tree, *æschynomini sasban*.
දියපිටනංවා, *Diyapita-nanwá*, *part.* having sent him over the waters, having exiled or transported.
දියබිඳු, *Diyabindu*, s. drops of water.
දියබෙදුම, *Diyabeduma*, s. water shed, division of a water-course into channels or branches.
දියඹෙ, *Diyambe*, s. part of a sheet of water where the water is deep.
දියවක, *Diyawaka*, s. second day of a lunar fortnight.
දියාළුව, *Diyáluwa*, see දිය අළුව *diya-aluwa*.
දියෑස, *Diyesa*, s. eye of the world.
දිරිතර, *Diritara*, s. very courageous person.
දිරිය, *Diriya*, s. courage.
දිලෙන, *Dilena*, a. shining, brilliant.
දිව්‍යචන්දන පුෂ්ප, *Divyachandana-pushpa*, s. tree, clove, *caryophyllus aromaticus*, [Colloq. කරාබු *karábu*].
*දිව්‍යාප්සරාව, *Divyápsaráwa*, s. divine nymph.
දිවගඳ, *Divaganda*, see දිවසුවඳ *diva-suwanda*.
දිවමන්, *Divaman*, a. living, [Colloq. ජීවමාන *jíva-mána*].
දිවමල්, *Divamal*, s. divine flowers.
දිවසුවඳ, *Diva-suwanda*, s. the heavenly smell or scent.
දිවාකරායමාන, *Divákaráyamána*, a. resembling the sun.
දිවාවිහරණ, *Diváviharana*, s. walking about in the day time.
* දිවෙල, *Divela*,=ආජීව *ájíwa*, රක්‍ෂාව *rakshάwa*, s. livelihood.
දිස්ත්‍රික්කේ, *Distrikké*, s. district. (Eng.)
දිස්ත්‍රික් උසාවිය, *Distrik-usáviya*, s. district court.
දිසාන්තර, *Disántara*, s. (දිසා and අන්තර *antara* between) between the cardinal points.
දිසාවේ නඩුව, *Disáwé-naduwa*, s. provincial court higher than ගම්සබාව *gamsabáwa*. (Kandyan.)
දීප්තා, *Díptá*, s. tree, *adina cordifolia* or *nauclea*, [Colloq. කොළොම්ගහ *kolom-gaha*].
දීපස්තම්භය, *Dípastambhaya*, s. light-house.
දීර්ඝාක්‍ෂ, *Dírghάksha*, s. long eye, (දීර්ඝ *dírgha*+අක්‍ෂ *aksha*).
දීර්ඝායු, *Dírghάyu*, s. tree, *ficus religiosa*, [Colloq. බෝගහ *bógaha*].
දීර්ඝායුස, *Dírgháyusa*, s. long life.
දුඃඛදායක, *Duhkhadáyaka*, a. causing sorrow, pain, or misery.
දුඃස්පර්ශ, *Duhsparsa*, s. twining plant with stinging hairs: see වැල්කහඹිලියා *wel-kahambiliyá*].
දුඃස්පර්ශනී, *Duhsparsaní*, s. date tree, *phœnix zeylanica*, [Colloq. ඉඳිගහ *indi-gaha*].
දුඃස්පර්ශා, *Duhsparsá*, see බටු *batu*.
දුක්මන්, *Dukman*, s. a sorrowful heart.
දුකසේ, *Dukasé*, adv. with difficulty.
දුණු, *Dunu*,=ජීර්ණ *jirna*, a. old, infirm, decayed.
දුදුල, *Dudula*, s. bottle gourd, *lagenaria vulgaris*, [Colloq. දියලබු *diyalabu*].
දුබික්, *Dubik*, s. Elu form of දුර්භික්‍ෂ *durbhiksha*.
දුම්අල්ලනවා, *Dum-allanawá*, v. to apply smoke.
දුර්ණය, *Durnaya*, s. misconduct, impropriety, impolicy.
දුර්ණීතිය, *Durnnítiya*, s. misconduct, impolicy.
*දුර්දර්ශ, *Durdarsa*, a. dazzling, painful to the sight.
දුර්දර්ශන, *Durdarsana*, s. bad sight, evil sight: *adj.* difficult to be seen: unsightly, ugly.
දුර්දාන්ත, *Durdánta*, a. untameable, intractable, difficult to be restrained or disciplined.
දුර්බුද්ධි, *Durbuddhi*, a. silly, ignorant.
දුර්බෝධ, *Durbódha*, s. misapprehension, misunderstanding.
*දුර්භාෂිත, *Durbháshita*, s. wrong or evil saying, abuse.
දුර්මත, *Durmata*, s. wrong belief or opinion.
දුර්වාර, *Durwára*, a. irresistible, not to be checked or prevented.

දුර්විරචිත, *Durvirachita*, *a.* ill-made, ill-written, ill-contrived.

දුරතික්‍රම, *Duratikrama*, *a.* difficult to be suppressed or overcome; insuperable, unconquerable; difficult of accomplishment.

දුරවබෝධ, *Durawabódha*, *a.* incomprehensible, difficult to be understood.

දුරාචාර, *Duráchára*, *a.* wicked, depraved, deviating from established practices.

*දුරාවාරෙ, *Durávare*, *adv.* not plentifully, here and there (seldom found as fruit on trees).

දුරාසද, *Durásada*, *a.* difficult of attainment or access; unequalled, unrivalled; intolerable.

දුරුක්ත, *Durukta*, *a.* ill-said.

දුරුක්ති, *Durukti*, *s.* bad saying.

දුරුත්තර, *Duruttara*, *a.* unanswerable; difficult to be crossed.

දුරුපචාර, *Durupachára*, *a.* difficult of cure; unmanageable.

දුල්‍ය, *Dulya*, *s.* pomegranate tree, *punica granatum*, [Colloq. දෙළුම් *de!um*].

දුෂ්ටචේතනා, *Dushṭa-chétaná*, *s.* wicked thought.

දුසිරිකම්, *Dusirikam*, *s.* sinful acts, bad ways.

දුහුල්සුඹුල, *Duhul-sumbula*, *s.* a roll of silk cloth to serve as a support for a burden, circle, hoop.

දූතක්‍රියා, *Dúta-kriyá*, *s.* the delivery of a message, the bearing of a message.

දූදරුවෝ, *Dúdaruwó*, *s.* sons and daughters.

දූරිභූත, *Dúribhúta*, *a.* removed.

දූරේනිදානය, *Dúrénidánaya*, *s.* first of the three epochs into which the life of Gótama Bódhisatta and Buddha is divided;–the epoch which extends from his resolve to become Buddha to his birth in the Tusita heaven.

දූවිලි, *Dúvili*, see දූලි *dúli*.

දෙඅතුර, *Deatura*, *s.* interval between two events.

දෙකපෝල, *Dekapóla*, *s.* the two cheeks.

දෙගල්, *Degal*, *s.* two rocks.

දෙටු, *Deṭu*, *a.* chief, eldest.

දෙටුපිත්, *Deṭpit*, *s.* eldest son.

*දෙණ, *Deṇa*, *s.* bier, hearse.

දෙණිකඩ, *Deṇikaḍa*, } *s.* a narrow valley running
*දෙණිය, *Deṇiya*, } up between the spurs of a range of hills and cultivated with paddy; high ground as distinguished from low or marshy ground.

දෙතිස්කථා, *Detis-kathá*, *s.* the thirty-two subjects of conversation.

දෙතිස්කුණපය, *Detiskuṇapaya*, *s.* the thirty-two defilements, or constituents of the body, as phlegm, sweat, mucus, etc.

දෙදෙව්ලොව, *Dedewlowa*, *s.* the two divine worlds, viz. චාතුර්මහාරාජික *cháturmahárájika* and තවුතිසා *tawutisá* 1st and 2nd, respectively of the six heavens.

දෙනට, *Denaṭa*, *s.* the twenty-fourth lunar mansion.

දෙනානකය, *Denánakaya*, *s.* name of a Buddhist fraternity, commonly called ජේතවන නිකාය *jétawana-nikáya*.

දෙනිඹ, *Denimba*, *s.* two kinds of margosa, *azadirachta indica*, [Colloq. කොහොඹ *kohomba*]; plant, peculiar to Ceylon, *munronia pumila*, [Colloq බින්කොහොඹ *bin-kohomba*].

දෙපදය, *Depadaya*, *s.* the two lines of a stanza or verse in poetry; two verses.

දෙබටු, *Debaṭu*, *s.* two kinds of solanum: see බටු *baṭu* and කටුවැල්බටු *kaṭuwelbaṭu*.

දෙබිහින්නන්, *Debihinnan*, *s.* brothers and sisters.

දෙබේ, *Debé*, *s.* two divisions.

දෙමදු, *Demadu*, *s.* liquorice, *glycirrhiza glabrum*, [Colloq. වැල්මී *welmí*]; blossoms of *bassia longifolia*, [Colloq. මීමල් *mí-mal*].

දෙමයිල්, *Demayil*, *s.* uncle and aunt; uncle and son-in-law, as දෙමයිල් නාරජහු *demayil-nárajahu*, in Saddharmálaṇkára.

දෙමළගත්තරු, *Demaḷa-gattaru*, *s.* (දෙමළ Tamil, ගත්තරු captives) a caste so called, supposed to be descendants of Tamil Captives taken by Sinhalese kings. These people are found chiefly in the villages of Indigastuḍuwa, Bonḍupiṭiya in the Pasdun Kóralé in the Western Province, Wallambagala, Galkanda, in the Bentoṭa Walalláviṭi Kóralé and Galahén-kanda and some other villages in the Gangaboḍa Pattu of Galle: S. P.

දෙමිරිස්, *Demiris*, *s.* two kinds of chillies, called මිරිස් *miris* and වල්ගාමිරිස් *walgá-miris*.

දෙයදර, *Deyadara*, *s.* (දෙ two, අදර *adara* lips) the two lips.

දෙයිද්ද, *Deyidda*, *s.* two kinds of jasmin, called සිනිද්ද *sinidda* and බොලිද්ද *bolidda*.

දෙරියන්හමාර, *Deriyanhamára*, *s.* two cubits and half a cubit.

දෙරියන, *Deriyana*, *s.* two cubits, one yard.

දෙරසන්මාලේ, *Derisan-málé*, *s.* immense wealth (S. P.) [Colloq. ලොකු වස්තුව *loku-wastuwa*].

දෙව්කොඩි, *Dewkodi*, *s.* divine flags.

දෙව්ඳුහැනුවර, *Dewdehe-nuwara*, s. city so called, more commonly known Déwadaha.

දෙව, *Dewa*, *part.* having milked.

දෙවරැද්දිරි වී, *Dewareddiri-ví*, s. kind of paddy, *oryza satira*.

දෙවිඳුසැව්, *Devindusew*, s. (දෙවිඳු and සැව් a bow) the Indra's bow, rain bow, [Colloq. දේදුන්න *dé-dunna*].

දෙවියත, *Deviyata*, s. two spans.

දෙව්විමන්, *Devi-viman*, s. divine mansion.

* දෙස්, *Des*, s. witness, evidence. [Colloq. සාක්ෂි *sákshi*].

දෙහිරු, *Dehiru*, s. large black bee; hornet.

දෙහිය, *Dehiya*, s. second ploughing.

* දේව, *Déwa*, s. bulbous stemless plant, *crinum zeylanicum* or *c. ornatum*, [Colloq. ගොඩමානිල් *goda-mánil*]; sort of pine, *pinus deradaru*, [Colloq. දේවදුර *déwadára*].

දේවකෙඳිරි, *Déwa-kendiri*, s. horse radish tree, *moringa pterygosperma*, [Colloquial: මුරුංගා *murungá*].

දේවමන්දිරය, *Déwamandiraya*, s. divine mansion, church (as a building).

දේවාධිපත්‍යය, *Déwádhipatyaya*, s. divine supremacy.

දේවාලගම, *Déwála-gama*, s. (දේවාල a Hindu temple, ගම village) a village or land belonging to the temple of some heathen deity.

දේශ අල, *Désa-ala*, see රට අල *rata-ala*.

දේහදිය, *Déha-diya*, s. urine, [Colloq. නර මූත්‍ර *nara-mútra*].

දෛවපර, *Daiwapara*, a. fated, willed, predestined, trusting to fate.

දො, *Do*, s. light, two (as in දොහොත *dohota* for දෙ *de*+අත *ata*).

දොදොල්, *Dodol*, s. kind of sweetmeat prepared by the natives.

දෝලායමාන, *Dóláyamána*, a. swinging, doubting, vacillating.

දෝසත, *Dósata* / දෝසතර, *Dósatara*, } s. astronomy, astrology.

දෝසි, *Dósi*, s. preserves. (Port.)

දෝහදදුඃඛ, *Dóhada-duhkha*, s. longing of pregnant women, [Colloq. දොළදුක *doladuka*].

දෝහදලක්ෂණ, *Dóhada-lakshana*, s. signs of pregnancy, longing of a pregnant woman as a sign of impregnation.

දැමි, *Demi*, s. just, righteous.

දැමිකම්, *Demikam*, s. righteous act.

දැමීම, *Demíma*, s. placing, putting, subduing, overcoming.

දැවටු, *Dewatu*, see දැහැටු *dehetu*.

දැවටෙනවා, *Dewatenawá*, v. to twist, to hang or loiter about as in the expression දැවටිදැවටී ඉන්නවා *dewati-dewatí innawá*.

*දැවපන්නේ, *Dewapanné*, s. also, belonging to the forest department as දැවපන්නේ ආරච්චි *dewa-panné árachchi*, දැවපන්නේ මුදියන්සේ *dewa-panné mudiyansé*.

දැවෙනවා, *Dewenawá*, v. n. to burn: pl. දැවුනා *dewuná*.

දැහැටු, *Dehetu*, s. the dried roots of කරඳ *karanda* and කුඹුක් *kumbuk*, used for cleaning the teeth. At the present day this practice prevails in the Matara district, chiefly among the priesthood.

දැහැත්අත, *Dehet-ata*, s. roll of betel leaves given to a Buddhist priest, quid of betel.

දැහැත්කනවා, *Dehet-kanawá*, v. to have a chew of betel used only when speaking of the Buddhist priests.

දැහැත්විඩ, *Dehet-vida*, s. a quid of betel offered to a Buddhist priest.

*දැහැන, *Dehena*, s. meditation; that profound and abstract meditation which brings its object fully before the mind: ධ්‍යානය *dhyánaya*.

දෑපල, *Dépala*, s. nutmeg, [Colloq. සාදික්කා *sá-dikká*].

දෑවාණ අතල, *Dewána-atala*, s. crystal pavement or floor.

*ද්‍රෝණ, *Dróna*, s. plant, *leucas zeylanica*, [Colloq. ගැටතුඹ *getatumba*].

ද්‍රෝණිමුඛ, *Drónimukha*, see ද්‍රෝණමුඛය *dróna-mukhaya*.

ද්වාදශාංශක, *Dwádasánsaka*, s. twelfth portion or degree in astrology.

ද්වාරත්‍රය, *Dwáratraya*, s. the three doors, viz. body, word, and mind.

ද්විභාග, *Dvibhága*, s. half.

ධ

*ධන, *Dhana*, s. the sign plus or affirmative quantity (in Algebra).

ධනගර්භය, *Dhana-garbhaya*, s. a store house.

ධනුර්වේධය, *Dhanurwédhaya*, s. perforation or piercing with a bow.

ධනෝපාර්ජන, *Dhanópárjana*, s. acquisition of wealth.

ධර්මභාණ්ඩාගාරය, *Dharmabháṇḍágáraya*, *s.* a library of sacred books; treasury of Dharma or Buddhist Law.

ධර්මභාණ්ඩාගාරික, *Dharma-bháṇḍágárika*, *s.* Treasurer or Depositary of the Buddhist Law.

ධර්මශික්ෂක, *Dharma-ṣikshaka*, *s.* divinity student, one who learns religious truth.

ධර්මානුකූල, *Dharmánukúla*, *s.* (ධර්ම *dharma* moral precepts, අනුකූල *anukúla* in accordance with) religious; conformable to Dharma.

ධර්මානුගත, *Dharmánugata*, *a.* conformable to virtue or Buddhist Law.

ධර්මාභියෝගය, *Dharmábhiyógaya*, *s.* practice of virtue, observance of Law.

ධර්මාන්විත, *Dharmánvita*, *a.* religious, connected with the Buddhist Law.

ධරණීපාල, *Dharaṇipála*, *s.* protector of the earth, king.

ධාතුජාති, *Dhátu-játi*, *s.* kinds of minerals, mineral kingdom.

ධාතුමන්දිර, *Dhatu-mandira*, *s.* a house where the relics are kept.

ධාතුවිද්‍යා, *Dhátu-vidyá*, *s.* mineralogy.

ධාරානගණලද, *Dháránaganalada*, *s.* sharpened or whetted.

ධූර්තස්ත්‍රී, *Dhúrta-strí*, *s.* knavish or roguish woman.

ධ්‍රැව වෘත්තය, *Dhruwa-writtaya*, *a.* polar circle.

ධෞත, *Dhauta*, *a.* washed, bright, white.

න

නක්ෂත්‍රපාඨක, *Nakshatra-páṭhaka*, *s.* astrologer, one well versed in astronomy.

නක්ෂත්‍රවිද්‍යා, *Nakshatra-vidyá*, *s.* science of stars, astrology.

නඛපඤ්ජර, *Nakhapañjara*, *s.* enclosure within the nails, claws or talons clasped.

නඛසමෝධාන, *Nakha-samódhána*, *s.* clasping of the hands, literally, bringing the nails together.

නගරගුත්තිකයෝ, *Nagaraguttikayó*, *s.* city-guards or protectors.

නගාමැරූ අල, *Nagámerú-ala*, *s.* (literally, the yam that killed the younger sister) *Habenaria* or Butterfly Orchid, (Tamil 'Tankayákolli').

* නට, *Naṭa*, *a.* perished, destroyed, died.

නටනලිය, *Naṭanaliya*, see කහඹිලියා *kahambiliyá*.

නටුවමෝ, *Naṭuwamó*, *v.* we have perished.

නඩය, *Naḍaya*, *s.* ambulance hall.

*නඩලම, *Naḍalama*, *s.* something to cause annoyance.

නතමාල, *Natamála*, *s.* plant, *galedupa arborea*, [Colloq. කරඳ *karaṇḍa*].

නතිඳු, *Natiṇḍu*, *s.* god Nátha.

නද්‍යාශ්‍රිත, *Nadyáṣrita*, *s.* antimony, [Colloq. හොයඳුන් *hoyaṇdun*].

නප්තෘ, *Naptri*, *s.* grandson.

නභාන්තර, *Nabhántara*, *s.* (නභස් *nabhas* and අන්තර *antara* between) the region below the clouds.

නම්බිරාල, *Nambirála*, } *s.* headman corresponding
නම්බුරාල, *Namburála*, } to an overseer, a term used in Moorish villages.

* නම, *Nama*, *s.* a term applied to a Buddhist priest, expressive of respect.

නමාගත්හ, *Namágatha*, *v.* they bent for themselves; started to go.

නමැති, *Nameti*, *a.* having the name, named.

නයතුරහ, *Nayaturaha*, *s.* debt or debts.

නයනාඤ්ජනිකා, *Nayanáñjaniká*, *s.* antimony, [Colloq. හොයඳුන් *hoyaṇdun*].

නයියන්ඩි නැටීම, *Nayiyaṇḍi-neṭíma*, *s.* dance of the Yakdessá or devil priest during a perahera in a déwála.

නර්තකී, *Nartakí*, *s.* actress, female dancer or singing girl.

නර්තන, *Nartana*, *s.* dancing, gesticulation; acting.

නර්මදා, *Narmadá*, *s.* river Narmadá, which rising in the Vindhyá mountains, runs westward to the gulf of Cambay.

නරපවර, *Nara-pawara*, *s.* chief amongst men.

නරපා, *Narapá*, *s.* protector of men, king.

නරබීජ, *Narabíja*, *s.* seed of the *cassia auriculata*, [Colloq. රණවරා ඇට *raṇawará-eṭa*].

නරශ්‍රෙෂ්ඨ, *Naraṣréshṭha*, *s.* chief amongst men.

නරුපට, *Narupaṭa*, *s.* cloth round a woman's waist, or the ends of cloth passed round the loins so as to hold the whole together.

නරේන්ද්‍ර, *Naréndra*, *s.* chief of men, king.

නලකූබර, *Nalakúbara*, *s.* son of Kuvéra.

නලද, *Nalada*, *s.* plant having a very fragrant root, *andropogon muricatus*, [Colloq. සැවැන්දරා *sewendará*]; Indian spikenard, [Colloq. ජටාමාංස *jaṭámánsa*].

නලඹල, *Nalambala*, *a.* shaken by the wind.

නව ඇඟිලිය, *Nawa-engiliya*, *s.* castor oil plant, *ricinus communis*, [Colloq. එඬරු *eṇdaru*].

නවකම, *Nawakam*, *s.* new work.

නවගුණ මන්ත්‍ර, *Nawaguna-mantra*, *s.* repeating the nine attributes of Buddha, viz. worthy of receiving honor and worship; perfectly enlightened; endowed with knowledge and conduct; deity of felicitous advent; unrivalled trainer of the refractory human steer; teacher of gods and men; the one who has comprehended the truth; the Sanctified being.

නවනාට්‍යරස, *Nawanátya-rasa*, *s.* nine dramatic tastes or sentiments, love, mirth, tenderness, anger, heroism, terror, disgust, surprise, tranquillity or paternal affection.

නවයොවුන්, *Nawayowun*, *s.* early part of youth, prime of life.

නවරුවන්, *Nawaruwan*, see නවවිධරත්නය *nawa-vidha-ratnaya.*

නවලෝකෝත්තර ධර්ම, *Nawalókóttara-dharma*, *s.* the four stages of sanctification, the four states, their fruition, and the Nirwána.

නවවිධරත්නය, *Nawavidha-ratnaya*, *s.* the nine gems, viz. ruby, pearl, agate, diamond, lapis lazuli, coral, sapphire, topaz, and emerald.

නවසත්තාවාස, *Nawasattáwása*, *s.* the nine worlds of the sentient beings.

නවෝද්ධෘත, *Nawóddhrita*, *s.* ghee, clarified butter, [Colloq. වෙඬරු *wendaru*].

නෂ්ටබුද්ධි, *Nashtabuddhi*, *s.* one who has lost his powers of understanding; simpleton.

නස්‍ය, *Nasya*, *s.* (corruptly නස්න *nasna*) medicine taken by the nose, a sternutatory.

නහමක්, *Nahamak*, *s.* prohibitive particle, a prefix meaning no, not, as නහමක්කරව *nahamakka-rawa*, don't do.

* නාගගන්ධ, *Nága-gandha*, *s.* red lead, minium, [Colloq. සින්දූරන් *sindúran*].

නාගවතී, *Nágawatí*, *s.* name of a city: see also, රසතැල්ල *rasatella.*

නාගිනී, *Náginí*, *s.* female elephant, [Colloq. ඇතින්න *etinna*].

නාච්චිරේ, *Náchchiré*, *s.* a term of respect used in addressing a woman of the goldsmith caste.

නාටිකාඞ්ගනාව, *Nátikánganáwa*, *s.* actress, female dancer.

නාථදේව, *Náthadéwa*, } *s.* god Nátha.
නාථේන්ද්‍ර, *Náthéndra*, }

නාදිවු, *Nádiwu*, *s.* plant, *asclepias psendosarsa.*

නානාභරණ, *Nánábharana*, *s.* various ornaments.

නානායක්කාරයා, *Nánáyakkárayá*, *s.* disguised emissary or informer.

නානාලම්බනයෙහි, *Nánálambanayehi*, *s.* in or on various objects of sense.

නාභිසිත, *Nábhisita*, see රසාඤ්ජන *rasáñjana.*

නාම්බතල්කඳ, *Námba-talkanda*, *s.* trunk of a young palmyra tree.

නාමධාරී, *Námadhárí*, *s.* one who bears a name.

නාමමාත්‍රය, *Námamátraya*, *s.* mere name.

නාමරූප, *Námarúpa*, *s.* body and mind, material and immaterial part of which man is formed.

නාමෙනෙවි, *Námenevi*, *s.* female nága or snake.

නාළිඅල්ලනවා, *Náli-allanawá*, *v.* to feel the pulse.

නාළිවැටෙනවා, *Náli-wetenawá*, *v.* to beat as the pulse.

නිඃශේෂ, *Nihsésha*, *a.* complete, entire, without a remainder.

නිකමට, *Nikamata*, *adv.* freely; without any object in view.

නිකල්, *Nikal*, *s.* an ancient coin.

නිකායත්‍රය, *Nikáyatraya*, see තුන්නිකාය *tunnikáya.*

නිත්‍යජීවී, *Nityajívi*, *a.* ever-living.

* නිද්‍රා, *Nidrá*, *s.* tree, *croton tigliyum*, [Colloq. ජයපාල *jayapála*].

නිද්‍රාග්‍රන්ථි, *Nidrá-granthi*, *s.* state of being sleepy, drowsiness.

නිද්‍රාඵල, *Nidrá-phala*, *s.* kind of *solanum*, [Colloq. බටු *batu*].

නිදානත්‍රය, *Nidánatraya*, *s.* the three epochs into which the life of Gótama, Bodhisatta and Buddha is divided. The first extends from his first resolve to become Buddha to his birth in the Tusita heaven; the second from the latter period to his attainment of Buddhahood, and the third from his attainment of Buddhahood to his death.

නිදිග්ධි, *Nidigdhi*, *s.* kind of night-shade, *solanum indicum*, [Colloq. තිබ්බටු *tibbatu*].

නිදැල්ලේ, *Nidellé*, *ad.* in a single state, not put in a pair, as cattle; alone.

නින්න, *Ninna*, *a.* deep, low-lying. (Páli.)

නින්නාද, *Ninnáda*, *s.* sound, noise, [Colloq. හඬ *handa*]; incorrectly for නිනාද *ninúda.*

නිපතිත, *Nipatita*, *a.* fallen, [Colloquial. වැටුන *wetuna*].

නිබද්ධ, *Nibaddha*, *a.* adhered to, connected with.

නිබුල්ලු, *Nibullu*, *s.* twins.

නිම්බපතරා, *Nimbapatará*, *s.* leaves of the margosa tree.

නිම්නභූමි, *Nimna-bhúmi*, *s.* valley, (vide මිටියාවත *mitiyáwata*).

* නිමල, *Nimala*, *s.* red arsenic, [Colloq. රත්හිරියල් *rat-hiriyal*].

නිමලජල, *Nimala-jala*, *s.* (නිමල free from filth, ජල water) pure water.

නිමාගොස්, *Nimá-gos, part.* having been finished, [Colloq. කම්මුතුවි *kammutuwi*].

නිමිතිගල්, *Nimitigal, s.* boundary stones.

නිමේෂාන්තර, *Niméshántara, s.* the time between the two twinklings of the eye.

නියමුවා, *Niyamuwá, s.* pilot, steersman, [Colloq. නැව්පදින්නා *new-padinná*].

නියලී, *Niyalí, a.* attached.

නියසක, *Niyasaka,* see සක්නැබ *saknęba.*

නියංමිට, *Niyanmita, s.* handle of the plough.

නිර්ගුම්බ, *Nirgumba, a.* not entangled.

නිර්ජට, *Nirjata, a.* not confused, not interwoven.

නිර්ධාරණ, *Nirdhárana, s.* certainty, ascertainment, singling out.

නිර්භින්න, *Nirbhinna, a.* undistinguished, equal, like; pierced, divided.

නිර්මාණ, *Nirmána, s.* creation, manufacture, [Coll: මැව්ම *męvma*].

නිර්මිත, *Nirmita, a.* created, made, artificial.

* නිර්මූල, *Nirmúla, s.* creeping plant, *cercostemma brunonianum,* [Colloq. මුවකිරිය *muwakiriya*].

නිර්මූලන, *Nirmúlana, s.* destroying totally, rooting up.

නිර්යාතන, *Niryátana, s.* delivery of a deposit, replacing any thing lost.

* නිර්යාස, *Niryása, s.* gum of the cotton tree, [Colloq. ඉඹුල්මැලියම් *imbul-męliyam*]; any natural exudation of a plant, as gum, milk, etc.

නිර්යාසගත, *Niryásagata, a.* ripe, mature, [Colloq. පැසුනු *pęsunu*].

නිර්ලෝභ, *Nirlóbha, a.* not covetous.

නිර්වාප, *Nirwápa, s.* putting out, as a fire or light, [Colloq. නිවීම *nivíma*].

නිරක්ෂරේඛාව, *Niraksha-rékháwa, s.* equator.

නිරග්ගික, *Niraggika, a.* having no fire.

නිරලම්බ, *Niralamba, s.* having nothing to hang on, having no help.

නිරහංකාර, *Nirahankára, a.* humble, free from pride.

නිරායුධ, *Niráyudha, a.* unarmed, without weapons.

නිරාශ්වාස, *Niráswása, s.* having no breath.

* නිරි, *Niri,* (in නිරිසතා *niri-satá,*) *s.* miserable being.

නිරික්ෂි, *Nirikshí, s.* large timber tree with edible seeds, yielding oil, *sterculia fœtida,* [Colloq. තෙලඹු *telambu*].

නිරිතකොණ, *Niritakona, s.* south-west point of the compass.

නිරුක්ති ප්‍රතිසම්භිදාව, *Nirukti-pratisambhidáwa, s.* knowledge of the origin of words; intuitive knowledge possessed by Buddhas.

නිරුචිත, *Nirochita, a.* improper.

නිරුත්සාහ, *Nirutsáha, s.* want of effort, ease, facility.

නිල්ගස්, *Nilgas, s.* indigo plant, [Colloq. අවරි *awari*].

නිලමක්කාරයා, *Nilamakkárayá, s.* officer, native headman.

* නිවට, *Niwata, s.* a class of ascetics who go about naked.

නිවර්තන, *Niwartana, s.* returning, stopping, ceasing, giving back.

නිවර්තනය, *Niwartanaya, s.* tropic (as of Cancer).

නිවහන, *Niwahana, s.* the last drawn line of a map; dwelling place, resting place.

නිවුන්නු, *Niwunnu, s.* twins.

නිවෙඨන, *Niwethana, v.* to unravel, to untwine.

නිවැසි, *Niwęsi, a.* dwelling, inhabiting.

නිශ්චිත, *Nischita, a.* certain, ascertained, determined, sentenced, pronounced.

නිශ්‍රීක, *Nisríka, a.* miserable, ugly, wretched.

නිශාකර, *Nisákara, s.* the moon, one who makes the night.

නිශාභාගය, *Nisábhágaya, s.* night time.

නිෂ්ක්ලෙශි, *Nishklési, s.* one not subject to sinful passion.

නිෂ්කණ්ටක, *Nishkantaka, a.* without thorns; free from trouble.

නිෂ්පාර්ශ්ව, *Nishpárswa, s.* impartial not favouring one party against another.

නිෂ්ප්‍රයෝජන, *Nishprayójana, a.* vain, fruitless, without profit; groundless.

නිෂීදන, *Nishídana, s.* sitting; that which is spread to sit upon.

නිස්කුටි, *Niskuti, s.* Ceylon cardamoms, *elettaria cardamomum,* [Colloq. එන්සාල් *ensál*].

නිස්ත්‍රිංශත් පත්‍රිකා, *Nistrinsat-patriká, s.* tree, *euphorbia antiquorum,* [Colloq. දළුක් *daluk*].

නිස්සන්තාප, *Nissantápa, a.* not warmed, having no mental pain.

නිස්සයමුක්ත, *Nissayamukta, a.* no longer subject to the care and protection of a superior priest; term applied to one who has completed his term of apprenticeship under an elderly monk, and passed the prescribed examination.

නිස්සරණාධ්‍යාස, *Nissaranádhyása, s.* intention of attaining Nirvána.

* නිස්සාර, *Nissára*, s. castor oil plant, *ricinus communis*, [Colloq. එඬරු *enḍaru*].

නිස්‍රාව, *Nisráwa*, s. scum of boiled rice.

නිස්සේණි, *Nisséṇi*, s. ladder; stairs.

නිස්සෝභා, *Nissóbhá*, a. dejected, having no brightness.

නිසවත්ත, *Nisawatta*, = ප්‍රකෝෂ්ඨ *prakóshṭha*, s. court yard attached to a house, open space surrounded by buildings.

නිසේවිත, *Nisévita*, a. served, obeyed, frequented; practised.

නිහඬ, *Nihaṉḍa*, s. obstacle, preventing offence, [Colloq. බාධාව *bádháwa*].

නිහතමානී, *Nihatamání*, s. one whose pride is brought low.

නීචානන්තා, *Níchánantá*, s. silk cotton tree, [Coll: කපුගස් *kapu-gas*].

නීතිශික්ෂක, *Nítiṣikshaka*, s. law student.

නින්සාර, *Nínsára*, s. tree, *cochlospermum gossypium*, [Colloq. කිණිහිරිය *kiṇihiriya*].

නීරෝහිණී, *Níróhiṇi*, s. creeping plant, variety of *pothos scandens*, [Colloq. මහපෝටා *maha-póṭá*].

*නීලපත්‍ර, *Níla-patra*, s. wheat, [Colloquial. තිරිඟු *tiriṉgu*].

නීලපුරි, *Nílapuri*, s. creeping plant, *desmodium triflorum*, [Colloq. උඳුපියලි *uṉdupiyali*].

නීලමඤ්ජරී, *Nílamañjarí*, s. tree, *nyctanthes arbortristis*, [Colloq. කළුතලා *kaḷu-talá*].

නීලය, *Nílaya*, s. kind of black salt used in the preparation of medicine, [Colloq. කළුලුණු *kaḷuluṇu*]: see also, රුකඟුන *rukaṉguna*.

නීලරත්න, *Nílaratna*, s. emerald, [Colloq. පච්චගල් *puchcha-gal*].

නීලා, *Nílá*, s. plant, *persea semicarpifolia*, variety peculiar to Ceylon, *p. angustifolia*, [Colloq. වෑවරණි *wẹwaraṇi*].

නීලිකාලි, *Nílikáli*, s. blue, [Colloq. නිල් *nil*].

නීලෝත්පල, *Nílótpala*, s. blue lotus, *nymphæa stellata*, [Colloq. නිල්මානෙල් *nil-mánel*].

නීවරණ, *Níwaraṇa*, s covering, [Colloq. වෑසිම *wẹsima*].

නීවිපට්ට, *Nívipaṭṭa*, s. cloth round a woman's waist or the ends of the cloth passed round the loins so as to hold the whole together, [Colloq. නෙරිය *neriya*].

නුකුසීදව, *Nukuṣídawa*, s. not being idle.

නුදුටුවිරූම්හ, *Nuduṭurirúmha*, v. we have not seen before.

නුරාගය, *Nurágaya*, s. amorous look, lustful desire, contracted form of අනුරාගය *anurágaya*.

නුවන්පිළිකය, *Nuwan-piḷikaya*, s. fistula at the corner of the eye at the upper end of the nose.

නෙක්කන්ති, *Nekkanti*, s. tree: see දේවදාර *déwadára*].

නෙත්තිමාලෙ, *Nettimále*, s. ornamental head dress of an elephant in a procession.

නෙත්දල, *Netdala*, s. tears, [Colloq. කඳුළු *kaṉduḷu*].

නෙතඳුන්, *Netaṉdun*, s. (නෙත eye, අඳුන් *aṉdun* collyrium, antimony) a substance applied to the eye to make the eye healthy.

නෙරණ, *Neraṇa*, a. projecting, protruding.

නෙරුක්කම්, *Nerukkam*, s. oppression, tyranny, harshness.

නෙළුම්බුදෙලි, *Neḷumbudeḷi*, s. the root of lotus.

නේත්‍රපුද්‍යෙතන, *Nétra-pudyetana*, s. plant, not identified.

නේත්‍රප්‍රතිෂ්ඨාපන, *Nétra-pratishṭhápana*, s. setting eyes to an image.

නේත්‍රාඤ්ජන, *Nétráñjana*, s. antimony: see අඳුන් *aṉdun*.

නේමිසාර, *Némisára*, s. tree, species of *santalum*, [Colloq. කළුකිහිරි *kaḷu-kihiri*].

නේවසඤ්ඤා නාසඤ්ඤායතනය, *Néwasaññá-násaññáyatanaya*, a. abode where there is neither consciousness nor unconsciousness, the fourth Formless Brahma heaven.

නේසජ්ජිකධුතාංග, *Nésajjika-dhutaṉga*, s. a religious observance which restrains a man from sleeping or lying down; one who observes this can only sit, stand, and walk.

නෛරන්තර්‍යාභ්‍යාස, *Nairaktaryábhyása*, s. practising continually without any interruption.

නෛරුක්තික, *Nairuktika*, s. one who knows the formation of words, a grammarian.

නොඇද, *Noẹda*, a. not crooked.

නොකන්නෙමි, *Nokannemi*, v. I shall not eat.

නොකමන්නු, *Nokamannu*, s. those from whom rice, etc. were prohibited by the state to be eaten, (vide ගත්තර *gattara*).

නොකරමි, *Nokarami*, v. I do not do.

නොකරන්නෙමි, *Nokarannemi*, v. I shall or will not do.

නොකල්හි, *Nokalhi*, s. at an improper or unusual time, unseasonably, [Colloq. අකාලයෙහි *akálayehi*].

නොකියමි, *Nokiyami*, v. I do not say.

නොකෑමි, *Nokėmi*, *v.* I have not eaten, I did not eat.

නොතෝරමි, *Notórami*, *v.* I do not select or explain.

නොදැනී, *Nodėní*, *part.* not being known.

නොදැනුවත්ව, *Nodėnuwatwa*, *adv.* without the knowledge of.

නොනැවත, *Nonėwata*, *part.* not stopping.

නොපතල, *Nopatala*, *s.* not widely known, not public, not spread.

නොපියා, *Nopiyá*, *part.* not having left.

නොපිරිය, *Nopiriya*, *a.* unpleasant.

නොපිළිවන්, *Nopiliwan*, *a.* impossible, unable.

නොපැටියේ, *Nopėtiyé*, *s.* that which is not begun.

නොබට, *Nobata*, *a.* not descended.

නොමිතුරු, *Nomituru*, *a.* unfriendly.

නොමිලයේ, *Nomilayé*, *adv.* freely, free of cost.

නොයමි, *Noyami*, *v.* I do not go.

නොඉඳුල්, *Noyindul*, *a.* not partaking of the fragments of others' meals.

නොලත්විරූ, *Nolatvirú*, *a.* not received before.

නොහැකි, *Noheki*, *a.* unable, impossible.

නැට්ටුම්කාරි, *Nettumkári*, *s.* dancing girl.

නැට්ටුවා, *Nettuwá*, *s.* dancer.

නැටුම්කාරි, *Netumkári*, *s.* dancing girl.

නැඳවට, *Nedawata*, *s.* peculiar to diagram: see නන්ද්‍යාවර්ත *nandyáwarta.*

නැනග, *Nenaga*, *s.* god of wisdom, Ganésa; one endowed with supreme wisdom.

නැමුණු, *Nemunu*, *a.* bent, crooked, stooped.

නැල්ලවටුවා, *Nella-watuwá*, *s.* kind of snipe.

ප

පග්ඝරණ, *Paggharana*, *s.* shedding.

පච්චගල, *Pachcha-gala*, *s.* emerald.

පච්ච සිනක්කාරන්, *Pachcha-sínakkáran*, *s.* blue vitriol.

පචන, *Pachana*, *s.* cooking.

පඤ්චගති, *Pañcha-gatı*, *s.* (පඤ්ච five, ගති state) five states of existence into which a being may be reborn on death, viz. hell, brute creation, the state of the manes or departed spirits, men, and gods.

පඤ්චචෙතොඛිල, *Pañchachetokhila*, *s.* the doubt in five places, viz. Buddha, Dhamma, Sangha, Şikshá, Sabbrahmachári.

පඤ්ච දුශ්චරිත, *Pañcha-duşcharita*, *s.* five evil practices.

පඤ්චධන, *Pañcha-dhana*, *s.* five sorts of wealth.

පඤ්චනිවරණ, *Pañcha-níwarana*, *s.* the five coverings, viz. කාමච්ඡන්ද නිවරණ *kámachchhanda-níwarana*, or cleaving unto the gratification of five senses, ව්‍යාපාද නිවරණ *wyápáda-níwarana*, the hatred that one bears towards another to kill him, ථිනමිද්ධ නිවරණ *thínamiddha-níwarana*, subduing endeavour and strength, උද්ධච්චකුක්කුච්චනිවරණ *uddhachchakukkuchcha-níwarana*, having unsettled mind as ashes on which a stone is cast and repenting of what is done and undone, විචිකිච්ඡානිවරණ *wichikichchhá-níwarana*, the doubt of eight places, viz. Buddha, Dharma, Sangha, etc.

පඤ්චම ධ්‍යාන, *Pañchama-dhyána*, *s.* the fifth of five dhyana.

පඤ්චමහා ගති, *Pañchamahá-gati*, *s.* being born in the following five places, viz, 1. in hell, 2. in the womb of animals, 3. as a préta, 4. being born as a man, 5. as a god or Brahma.

පඤ්චමහානදී, *Pañchamahá-nadí*, *s.* the five great rivers, viz. Gangá, Yamuná (Jumna), Achiravati, Sarabhú, Mahí.

පඤ්චමහාපුරුෂයෝග, *Pañchamahá-purushayóga*, *s.* the five positions in which some planets are situated over a man.

පඤ්චමහාභූතයෝ, *Pañchamahá-bhútayó*, *s.* fire, air, earth, water, and ether.

පඤ්චමාර, *Pañcha-mára*, *s.* Buddhist term applied to five Máras or hindrances, viz. 1. ඛන්ධමාර *khandhamára*, the five elements of existence generally called පඤ්චස්කන්ධය *pañchaskandhaya.* 2. ක්ලේසමාර *kilésa-mára*, depraved nature. 3. මච්චුමාර *machchumára*, death. 4. අභිසංඛාර මාර *abhisankháramára*, accumulation of කර්ම *karma*, merit and demerit. 5. දෙවපුත්තමාර *dewaputtamára*, the Tempter.

පඤ්චරාජ කකුදභාණ්ඩ, *Pañcharája-kakudabhánda*, *s.* five insignia of royalty, viz. sword, umbrella, diadem, slippers, and fan.

පඤ්චවාණ, *Pañcha-vána*, *s.* one armed with five arrows, an epithet of Kámadéva, the Indian Cupid.

පඤ්චවිමුක්ති, *Pañcha-vimukti*, *s.* the five විමුත්ති *vimutti*, the five-fold relinquishment, viz. the first in the cessation of human passion on entrance into the මාර්ග (márga) paths, the second on attaining the fruition of the paths; the third is the relinquishment which consists in extrepation, the fourth in cessation, and the fifth in escape from existence.

පඤ්චවිලෝකන, *Pañcha-vilókana*, see මාතුවිලෝකන *mátu-vilókana*.

පඤ්චාඞ්ගිකතූර්යනාද, *Pañcháńgika-túryanáda*, *s.* five kinds of musical instruments, ආතත *atata*, such as timbrels which have one face, විතත *vitata*, those that have two faces one on each side, විතතාතත *vitátata*, musical instruments which have one face on each side and one in the middle, ඝන *ghana*, such instruments as plates which are called කයිතාලම්තැටි *kayitálam-teti*, etc. සුසිර *susira*, various kinds of flutes, etc.

පට්ටකාර, *Pattakára*, *s.* tailor, [Colloq. මහන්නා *mahanná*].

පට්ටින්, *Pattin*, *s.* red lódh, [Colloq. රත්ලොත් *rat-lot*].

පට්ටිල, *Pattila*, *s.* pale variety of the lódh tree, *symplocos racemosa*, [Colloq. හෙලලොත් *hela-lot*]; plant, *cæsalpinia bonducella*.

පට්ටෝඩම, *Pattódam*, *s.* kind of ornament.

පටියත්ත, *Patiyatta*, *a.* prepared, made, ready. Sanskrit ප්‍රතියත්ත *pratiatta*.

පටුතර, *Patutara*, *s.* very skilful or clever.

පඨන, *Pathana*, *s.* reading, reciting.

පඩත්තලකම, *Padattalakama*, *s.* influence, importance, post of captain or commander.

*පණවනවා, *Panawanawá*, *v.* to enact a law; to erect (a seat); to set suits to opposite winds.

පණහා, *Panahá*, *adv.* from one to another, one after the other,=පාසා *pásá*.

පණිවා,, *Paniwá*, *s.* plant: see අඳුතලා *andutalá*]; destruction of animal life.

පණුගාය, *Panugáya*, *s.* worm complaint.

පණුහොරි, *Panu-hori*, *s.* itch.

පත්කරණ, *Patkarana*, *s.* a written deed or instrument.

පත්කුඩය, *Patkudaya*, *s.* a shelter or umbrella for sun and rain made of leaves.

පත්තනිකුජ්ජන, *Pattanikujjana*, *s.* upsetting of a bowl.

පත්තාර, *Pattára*, *s.* plank attached to a boat.

පත්තිදාන, *Pattidána*, *s.* transference to any one, living or dead, of merit acquired by one's self.

පත්තියම් අල්ලනවා, *Pattiyam-allanawá*, *v.* to observe a prescribed diet.

පත්තුරු, *Patturu*, *s.* tree, *terminalia belerica*, [Colloq. බුළු *bulu*].

පත්දල, *Patdala*, *s.* tree, *gracinia* or *xanthocymus pictorius*, [Colloq. කොළොම්ගහ *kolom-gaha*].

පතඞ්ගිකා, *Patańgiká*, *s.* sort of bee.

පතිද්‍රුම, *Patidruma*, *s.* tree yielding tough wood, *pterospermum suberifolium*, [Colloq. වෙලංගහ *welan-gaha*].

පතුල්සුංදෙක, *Patulsun-deka*, *s.* the two little soles of the feet.

පථ්‍යාහාර, *Pathyáhára*, *s.* suitable diet for a sick person.

පද්මරවින්දා, *Padmaravindá*, } *s.* lotus having one
පද්මසාරණි, *Padmasárani*, } petal, [Colloq. එක්පෙතිපියුම් *ekpetipiyum*].

පදන්ගේ, *Padan-gé*, *s.* the house in which hermits practise or observe Dhyána, [Colloq. යෝගකරණ ගෙය *yógakarana-geya*].

පදාර්ථවිද්‍යා, *Padártha-vidyá*, *s.* natural philosophy.

පදික, *Padika*, *s.* infantry.

* පන්, *Pan*, *s.* wages, hire, price (Skt. පණ *pana*).

පන්කාඩු, *Pankádu*, *s.* vanity, big talk, vain shew.

පන්තිස්බලිය, *Pantis-baliya*, *s.* thirty five kinds of බලි *bali* or offerings to propitiate malignant planets.

පනසඵල, *Panasa-phala*, *s.* jack fruit.

පනාපතුරු, *Panápaturu*, *s.* first stage of the production of jack fruit.

පනාපිට, *Panápita*, as in ඇස්පනාපිට *es-panápita*,= ඇස් ඉස්සරහපිට *es-issarahapita*, *adv.* before one's eyes, or in one's presence.

පනාපුප්පි, *Panápuppi*, *s.* bud of jack fruits, [Colloq. පනාමල *panámala*]; young jack fruit, *artocarpus integrifolia*, [Colloq. පොලහ *polaha*].

පබ්බාජන, *Pabbájana*, *s.* made of bulrush.

පබ්භාර, *Pabbhára*, *s.* bending.

පබන්ධ, *Pabandha*, *s.* unbroken series; continuity.

පමාකරණවා, *Pamákaranawá*, *v.* to delay, to detain.

පමුණු, *Pamunu*, *s.* belonging, පමුණුකොට *pamunukota*, අයිතිකොට *ayitikota*, assigned to.

පමුදිත, *Pamudita*, *s.* being highly pleased at the happiness of others.

පයිරුපාසන, *Payirupásana*, *s.* being associated, keeping company with.

පර්කටි, *Parkati*, *s.* tree: see පුලිල *pulila*.

පර්ණවා, *Parnawá*, *s.* plant, species of the *ocimum*: see අඳුතලා *andutalá*.

පර්ණි, *Parni*, *s.* kind of dill or fennel, *anethum sowo*, [Colloq. ශතපුෂ්ප *satapushpa*].

පර්පටිය, *Parpatiya*, *s.* cowry, [Colloq. කවඩි *kavadi*].

පර්වතදුර්ග, *Parwata-durga*, *s.* rocks difficult of access.

පරකීර්තිය, *Parakírtiya*, s. tree, *morinda citrifolia* and *tinctoria*, [Colloq. අහු *ahu*].

පරගණ, *Paragaṇa*, a. making a noise, [Colloq. ඝෝෂාකරණ *ghóshákaraṇa*].

පරඟනවා, *Paranganawá*, v. to filter, to strain, [Colloq. පෙරණවා *peraṇawá*].

පරචිත්තවිජානනඥාන, *Parachitta-vijánana-jñána*, s. the knowledge of understanding the heart or the thoughts of others.

පරද්දනවා, *Paraddanawá*, v. to defeat, to vanquish.

පරප්‍රබෝධ, *Paraprabódha*, s. instruction of others, making others to comprehend.

පරභෘත, *Parabhṛita*, s. Indian cuckoo: a. nourished by others.

පරම්පරානුයාත, *Paramparánuyáta*, a. descended from generation to generation or lineally descended.

පරමුවා, *Paramuwá*, s. kind of sea fish.

පරයමින්, *Parayamin*, part. over coming, surpassing, excelling.

පරවම්හණ, *Parawamhana*, s. despising others, disgracing others.

පරවිටිය, *Paraviṭiya*, s. line, lineage, successive series, [Colloq. පරම්පරාව *paramparáwa*].

පරාභිභවනයකරණවා, *Parábhibhawanaya-karaṇawá*, v. to subdue others.

පරාවා, *Paráwá*, s. kind of sea fish: pl. පරව් *paraw*.

පරිඝෝෂය, *Parighóshaya*, s. sound; improper or blamable discourse; muttering or rumbling of clouds.

පරිචය, *Parichaya*, s. intimacy, familiarity, acquaintance.

පරිඥෙය, *Parijñéya*, s. that ought to be known.

* **පරිත්ත**, *Paritta*, s. a Brahma world, little, few.

පරිදහන, *Paridahana*, s. name of a Játaka.

පරිදේව, *Paridéwa*, s. crying, lamenting.

පරිපුච්ඡා, *Paripuchchhá*, s. enquiry, questioning, asking, [Colloq. ඇසීම *ęsíma*].

පරිභ්‍රමණය, *Pari-bhramaṇaya*, s. revolution.

පරිමිත ආණ්ඩුව, *Parimita-ánduwa*, s. monarchical government; limited monarchy.

පරිරක්ෂණය, *Pari-rakshaṇaya*, s. preservation, protection, [Colloquial: ආරක්ෂාකෙරීම *árakshákeríma*].

පරිවර්ජිත, *Pariwarjita*, a. abandoned, left, quitted, devoid of, [Colloq. දුරුකළ *durukaḷa*].

පරිශීලනයකරණවා, *Pariṣílanaya-karaṇawá*, v. to practise, to exercise, (as the memory, etc.).

පරිෂත්, *Parishat*, s. assembly, meeting, audience, congregation, [Colloq. පිරිස *pirisa*].

පරිසේක, *Pariséka*, s. sprinkling water, ablution.

පරිසේවන, *Parisévana*, s. washing with water.

පල්බොරු, *Palboru*, s. sheer lie, gross falsehood.

පලංකෂ, *Palaṇkasha*, s. plant, *amyrus agallocha*: see ගුගුල් *gugul*.

පලන්, *Palan*, part. worn, put on,=පැලැන්ඳවූ *pęlęndáwú*.

පලලේ, *Palalé*, s of the same age with another.

පලහිලව්ව, *Palahilawwa*, s. intercourse, dealing.

පලාලපුඤ්ජ, *Palálapuñja*, s. a heap of straw.

පලාසය, *Palásaya*, s. coral tree, *erythrina indica*, [Colloq. එරබදු *erabadu*].

පලිස්කාරයා, *Paliskárayá*, s. shield bearer.

පලු, *Palu*, s. tender leaves, fruits.

පලුග්ග, *Palugga*, a. fallen down, crumbled. (Páli.)

පවත්නා, *Pawatná*, a. existing, continuing.

පවිත්‍රක, *Pavitraka*, s. sacred fig tree, *ficus religiosa*, [Colloq. බෝගහ *bó-gaha*].

පවිත්‍රකරණවා, *Pavitrakaraṇawá*, v. to purify, to make clean.

පවුරුණ, *Pawuruṇa*, s. treatise, book; Elu form of ප්‍රකරණ *prakaraṇa*.

පශ්චාත්භක්ත, *Paṣchátbhakta*, s. afternoon meal.

පශ්චිමජනතා, *Paṣchima-janatá*, s. multitude of people that will be born hereafter.

පස් ඇඹුල්, *Pas-ęmbul*, s. (පස් five, ඇඹුල් sour) five kinds of sour substances or acids, viz. lime, *citrus limetta*, [Colloq. දෙහි *dehi*]; orange, *citrus aurantium*, [Colloquial: දොඩම් *dodam*]; mandarin orange, *citrus nobilis*, [Colloq නාරං *náraṇ*]; leech-lime, [Colloq. කුඩලු *kúḍalu*]; acid fruit, *garcinia cambogia*, [Colloq. ගොරක *goraka*].

පස් පැඟිරි, *Pas-pęngiri*, s. five kinds of zest, viz. නාරං *náraṇ*; දොඩම් *doḍam*; දෙහි *dehi*; කුඩලු යකිනාරං *yakináraṇ*.

පස් පැණි, *Pas-pęni*, s. five kinds of honey, viz. honey made by the common bee, [Colloq. මීපැණි *mípęni*]; by the wasp, [Colloq. බඹරපැණි *bamara-pęni*]; by the kaneyiyá fly, [Colloq. කනමී පැණි *kanamí-pęni*]; by the humble bee, [Colloq. දඬුවැල් පැණි *danduwęl-pęni*]; the juice of the sugar cane, [Colloq. උක්පැණි *ukpęni*]

පස්බත, *Pas-bata*, s. afternoon, food taken in the afternoon.

පස්මල්, *Pas-mal, s.* five kinds of flowers, or flower like substances, viz. white mustard, variety of *brassica juncea* or *cleome viscosa*, [Colloq. හෙල අබ *hela-aba*]; pulverized or ground rice, [Colloq. සුන්සාල් *sunsál*]; arabian jasmine, *jasminum sambac*, [Colloq. දෑසමන් *dḙsaman*]; species of the panic grass, *hetero-pogon hirtus*, [Colloq. ඉතණ *itaṇa*]; fried or parched grain, [Colloq. විලඳ *vilanda*].

පස්මෙහෙකරු, *Pas-mehekaru, s.* the five handicraft castes or trades, viz. carpenter, weaver, washer-man, barber, and shoe or sandal maker, [Colloq. වඩුවා *waḍuwá*, රෙදිවියන්නා *redi-viyanná*, රදවා *radawá*, පනික්කියා *panikkiyá*, සම්කරුවා *sam-karuwá*].

පස්විකා, *Pasviká, s.* having considered, Sans. ප්‍රත්‍යවේක්ෂා *pratyawékshá*.

පස්සහදෙමි, *Passahadḙmi, s.* priest in full orders, Sámanéra, a priest not in full orders, she who prepares to be a priestess, a priestess in full orders.

* පස, *Pasa. s.* a noose.

පසඟිලි, *Pasangili, s.* castor oil plant; five fingers.

පසත, *Pasata, s.* the palm of the hand hollowed as if to hold liquids.

පසදුරු, *Pasaduru, s.* (පස five, දුරු cummin) the aggregate of five spices, viz. white cummin seed, [Colloq. සුදුදුරු *sududuru*]; black cummin seed, *nigella indica*, [Colloquial: කළුදුරු *kaḷuduru*]; caraway seed, *carum carui*, [Colloq. මහදුරු *mahaduru*]; parsley, *petroselinum sativum*, [Coll: අසමෝදගම් *asamódagam*]; kind of dill or fennel, *anethum sowa*, [Colloq. ශතපුෂ්ප *ṣatapushpa*].

පසල්දනව්, *Pasal-danaw, s.* adjoining country.

පසළොස්චරණ ධර්ම, *Pasaḷoscharaṇa-dharma, s.* fifteen good practices, viz. a moral life, guarding the senses, moderation in eating, watchfulness, faith, shame, fear of sin, learning, energy, recollection, wisdom, and the four Jhánas or stages of mystic meditation. (Childers.)

පසාදන, *Pasádana, s.* tree lódhra, *symplocos racemosa:* see ලෝද්‍ර *lódhra*.

පසුබත්, *Pasu-bat, s.* after noon meal.

පහන්කිච්චා, *Pahankichchá, s.* magpie, (up cuntry word): see පොල්ලිච්චා *pollichchá*.

පහන්වැස්ස, *Pahanwḙssa, s.* hail, (Vide ගල්වැස්ස *galwḙssa*).

පහන්සිළ, *Pahansiḷa, s.* flame of a candle.

පහිඹුව, *Pahimbuwa, s.* mark X branded on cattle.

පළ, *Paḷa, a.* known, public, notorious, [Colloq. ප්‍රකාශවූ *prakáṣawú*].

* පා, *Pá*,=පාඨය, *páṭhaya, s.* reading; also an honorific affix=පාද *páda*, as in රතෑසිපා *ratḙ-sipá*.

පාංශුලුණු, *Pánṣu-luṇu, s.* salt extracted from soil, rock or fossil salt.

පාටිහාරිය පක්ෂ, *Páṭihániya-paksha, s.* the season during which Buddhist priests stay in one place:—this staying is called "Washiṭinawá."

පාඨන, *Páṭhana, s.* lecturing, teaching, causing to read.

පාණ්ඩරවර්ණ, *Páṇḍara-warṇa, s.* pale or yellowish white colour.

පාණ්ඩුඵල, *Páṇḍu-phala, s.* creeper, *trichosanthes cucumerina*, [Colloq. දුම්මැල්ල *dummḙlla*].

පාණිප්‍රහාර, *Páṇi-prahára, s.* clapping, striking the hands together.

පාත්‍රි, *Pátrí, s.* small or portable furnace.

පාදදර, *Pá-dadara, s.* cobra, snake, serpent, [Coll: නාගයා *nágayá*].

පාදධෝවන, *Páda-dhówana, s.* washing the feet.

පාදුකාව, *Pádukáwa, s.* circular hole cut in a water closet.

පාදෞවුන්, *Pádowun, s.* washing the feet.

පාන්එළිය, *Pán-eḷiya, s.* lamp light.

පානීයාහරණ, *Páníyáharaṇa, a.* extracting water, taking water, removing water.

පානුදි, *Pánudi, s.* tree, *terminalia belerica*, [Coll: බුළු *buḷu*].

පාපනිවර්තනය, *Pápa-niwartanaya, s.* putting a stop to sin.

පාපමරා, *Pápamará, s.* creeping plant, *cissampelos Pareira*, [Colloq. දියමිත්ත *diyamitta*].

පාපරෝග, *Pápa-róga, s.* leprosy, consumption, etc.

පාපිල්ල, *Pápilla, s.* symbol for උ *u* and ඌ *ú* attached to the tail or lower part of a consonant as in කු *ku*, කූ *kú*, ඛු *khu*, ඛූ *khú*.

පාපිය, *Pápiya, s.* one who commits sin, one who has sin, a sinner.

පායාසය, *Páyásaya, s.* rice cooked with milk, [Colloq. කිරිබත් *kiribat*].

පාර්ථිව, *Párthiva, s.* culinary salt: [Colloq. උද්භිද ලුණු *udbhida-luṇu*].

*පාර්වතී, *Párwatí, s.* olibanum tree, *boswellia thurifera:* another tree, *celtis orientalis*; kind of plantain or banana, *musa sapientum*, [Colloq. ඇටකෙහෙල් *ḙṭakehel*].

*පාර, *Pára*, *s.* quicksilver, [Colloq. රසදිය *rasadiya*].

පාරලෞකික, *Páralawkika*, *a.* relating to the next world.

පාරාවතපදී, *Páráwatapadí*, *s.* heartpea, *cardiospermum halicacabum*, [Colloq. දූදු *dúdu* or වැල්පෙනෙල *wel-penela*].

පාරිභෝගික, *Páribhógika*, *a.* used, employed.

පාරුපණ, *Párupana*, *s.* putting on as a robe, [Coll: පෙරවීම *peravíma*].

පාවචන, *Páwachana*, *s.* term applied to denote the text of the canoncial works of Buddhism. (Páli.)

පාෂාණ්ඩ, *Páshánda*, *s.* one who does not live according to the doctrines of Védas.

පාෂාණීභූතව, *Páshánibhútawa*, *part.* having become a stone, petrified, [Colloq. ගල්වෙලා *galwelá*].

පාස්කාව, *Páskáwa*,=පාස්කුව *páskuwa*, *s.* festival of the Easter, Paschal season.

පාහේ, *Páhé*, *adv.* somewhat, as if, seemingly.

* පිඞ්ග, *Pinga*, *s.* vine creeper, *vitis vinifera*, [Colloq. මිදිවැල් *midiwel*].

* පිඞ්ගල, *Pingala*, *s.* medicinal plant, *plectranthus zeylanicus*, [Colloq. ඉරිවේරිය *iriwériya*].

පිච්ඡලත්වච්, *Pichchhalatwach*, *s.* plant, perhaps a variety of the *sida cordifolia*, [Colloq. සුලුබැලිල *sulu-belila*].

පිච්ඡිලච්ඡද, *Pichchhilachchhada*, *s.* tree, *zizyphus jujuba*, [Colloq. මසන් *masan*].

පිච්ඡිල පත්‍රිකා, *Pichchhila-patriká*, *s.* kind of medicinal plant, aloe, *aloe vulgaris*, [Colloq. කෝමාරිකා *kómáriká*].

පිඤ්ජයා, *Piñjayá*, see ජයා *jayá*, and කන්සා *kansá*,

පිටගැස්ම, *Pitagesma*, *s.* tetanus.

පිටල්ල, *Pitalla*, *s.* basket, cupboard.

පිටවෙනවා, *Pitawenawá*, *v.* to go out.

පිටිතොලහයා(බැඳ), *Pititolahayá(benda)*, *s.* having tied his hands behind his back.

පිටිදකුම්හ, *Pitidakumha*, *v.* we shall see his back, *i. e.* put him to flight, [Colloq. ජයගණිමි *jayaganimi*].

පිටිනුවර, *Pitinuwara*, *s.* outer city, suburb.

පිටොතුවෙනවා, *Pitotuwenawá*, *v.* to go out.

පිඩිපිට, *Pidipita*, see සට්ටම *sattama*.

පිඩුපල, *Pidupala*, *s.* mango fruit, [Colloq. අඹ *amba*].

පිඩුව, *Piduwa*, *s.* alms; lump or ball of rice.

පිණ්ඩචාරික, *Pindachárika*, *a.* going about begging alms.

පිණ්ඩපර්ණී, *Pindaparni*, *s.* turmeric, *curcuma longa*, [Colloq. කහ *kaha*].

පිණ්ඩිතක, *Pinditaka*, *s.* thorny shrub, *randia dumetorum*, [Colloq. කුකුරුමුවං *kukurumuwan*].

පිණ්ඩිපුෂ්ප, *Pindipushpa:* see හෝපලු *hópalu*.

පිණ, *Piná*, *part.* being satisfied, being filled with.

පිත්තඝාති, *Pittagháti*, *s.* plant, *mollugo ceroina*, [Colloq. පත්පාඩගම් *patpádagam*].

පිතෘඝාතකර්ම, *Pitrighátakarma*, *s.* killing a father, the sin resulting from parricide.

* පින්, *Pin*, *s.* pollen of the lotus flower, [Colloq. නෙළුම්රේණු *nelum-rénu*].

පින්කිරියවත්, *Pinkiriyawat*, *s.* Register of meritorious works.

පින්තාරුව, *Pintáruwa*, *s.* painting.

පින්නපාතකරණවා *Pinnapáta-karanawá*, see පිණ්ඩපාතකරණවා *pindapáta-karanawá*.

පින්සෙණ්ඩුලි, *Pinsendu-lí*, *s.* soft-wood.

පියදු, *Piyadu*, *s.* sent, employed.

පියදුපත, *Piyadu-pata*, *s.* (පියදු sent, and පත leaf) letter which was sent.

පියමහ, *Piyamaha*, *s.* Brahma the great father of all; also, paternal grand father.

පියයුරු රස, *Piyayuru-rasa*, *s.* woman's milk.

පියල්ල, *Piyalla*, *s.* drinking vessel.

පියවරසනෙන්, *Piyawara-sanen*, *s.* (පියවර footstep, and සන *sana* sound or mark) by the sound or mark of the footsteps.

පියවසාව, *Piyawasáwa*, *s.* that part of a dágaba which serves as an altar for offering flowers upon.

පියවිලි, *Piyavili*, *s.* carpet, cloth spread on the ground to walk upon, [Colloq. පාවාඩ *páwáda*].

පිරිබඩගන්වනවා, *Piribadaganwanawá*, *v.* to smear with cow-dung, etc.

පිරිවානාකල්හි, *Piriwáná-kalhi*, *s.* at the time of reciting.

පිලිහොඳවෙනවා, *Pilihondawenawá*, *v.* to arrive at puberty.

පිෂ්ටපාන්තකරී, *Pishtapántakarí*, *s.* fruit of the tree, *zizyphus jujuba*, [Colloq. මසන්ගෙඩි *masan gedi*].

පිසූ, *Pisú*, *a.* boiled.

පිහනරාළ, *Pihanarála*, *s.* cook.

පිහිතාපාය, *Pihitápáya*, *s.* having the hell shut.

පිළාගෙඩිය, *Pilágediya*, *s.* cancer, carbuncle.

පිළිදෙගුන්, *Piliḍegun*, *s.* protection, preservation.

පිළිවදන්දෙනවා, *Piḷiwadan-denawá*, *v.* to give an answer, to reply.

පිළිවිසීම, *Piḷivisíma*, *s.* questioning, making an inquiry.

පිළිසඳ, *Piḷisan̲da*, *s.* the link which connects the existing life and the future life.

පිළිහසුන්, *Piḷihasun*, *s.* reply, answer.

පීඨාපීඨ, *Píṭápiṭa*, *s.* a stool, a chair, a seat of the religious students made of Kusa grass.

* පීතපුෂ්පක, *Pítapushpaka*, *s.* plant: see රතතෝර *raṭa-tóra*.

පීවරබාහු, *Píwara-báhu*, *s.* stout arm.

පීළනය, *Píḷanaya*, *s.* calamity.

පුඩුකොට, *Puḍukoṭa*, *part.* having collected.

පුණ්‍යපරායණ, *Puṇya-paráyaṇa*, *a.* attached or devoted to religious duties or meritorious works.

පුත්‍රපෞත්‍ර, *Putra-pautra*, *s.* sons and grandsons.

පුදඔලක්කන්, *Pudaólakkan*, *s.* offerings and presents.

පුනරුප්පාදය, *Punaruppádaya*, *s.* being born again, rebirth.

පුරං, *Puran̲*, *s.* fallow ground.

පුරංමැඩවුම, *Puran̲-meḍawuma*, *s.* first turning up of mud in a field.

පුරංහීය, *Puran̲-híya*, *s.* first ploughing.

පුරජ්ජේරු, *Purajjéru*, *s.* vain shew, conceit, big talk.

පුරවඩනවා, *Pura-wadanawá*, *v.* commencing the work of a field by clearing jungle, preparatory to tilling.

පුරවලියම, *Purawaliyama*, *s.* midicinal application to the eyes.

පුරාකෘත, *Purákṛita*, *a.* done formerly, done long ago.

පුරාජේරු, *Purájéru*, see පුරජ්ජේරු *purajjéru*.

පුරුෂනිමිත්ත, *Purusha-nimitta*, *s.* male organs of generation.

පුලස්තිපුර, *Pulasti-pura*, *s.* Polonnaruwa, a town in Ceylon.

පුලිනතලය, *Pulinatalaya*, *s.* sandbank.

පුවත්පත්, *Puwatpat*, *s.* (පුවත් news, intelligence, පත් leaf, paper) newspaper.

පුෂ්පෝද්භව, *Pushpódbhawa*, *s.* (පුෂ්ප *pushpa* flower, උද්භව *udbhawa* origin, product) fruit.

පුෂ්‍යලතා, *Pushya-latá*, *s.* pumpkin gourd, ash-pumpkin, [Colloq. පුහුල් *puhul*].

පූකරුවා, *Púkaruwá*, *s.* one who makes cake or bread.

පූච්චම්කියනවා, *Púchcham-kiyanawá*, *v.* to brag, to boast.

පූච්චම, *Púchchama*, *s.* bragging, boasting.

පූණ්ඩුකරණවා, *Púṇḍukaraṇawá*, *v.* to bring into contact, to join, to bring together.

පූර්වභෝග, *Púrwabhóga*, *s.* prior possession or enjoyment.

පූර්වවර්තනය, *Púrwa-wartanaya*, *s.* previous existence.

පූර්වේනිවාසානුස්මෘති, *Púrweniwásánusmṛiti*, *s.* recollection of former births.

පූර්වෝපාය, *Púrwópáya*, *s.* previous or precautionary measures.

පෙත්මග, *Petmaga*, *s.* ladder.

පෙත, *Peta*, *s.* range, series, line.

පෙතිපිළිම, *Peti-piḷima*, *s.* painted likeness of a person as opposed to a statue or carved image.

පෙන්දෙල්ලා, *Pen̲dellá*, *s.* kind of sea fish.

පෙරබත, *Perabata*, *s.* forenoon meal.

පෙරලා, *Perala*, *adv.* back again, turning back.

පෙරළිකරණවා, *Peraḷikaraṇawá*, *v.* to make war, to fight, to quarrel.

පෙරළිවෙනවා, *Peraḷiwenawá*, *v.* war is being carried on.

පෙරෝදියර, *Peródiyara*, *s.* pus, purulent matter exuding from a sore; sap of a tree.

* පෙල්ල, *Pella*, *s.* time, [Colloq. වාරය *wáraya*].

පෙළවහකරණවා, *Peḷawaha-karaṇawá*, *v.* marry.

පෙළාන්තර, *Peḷántara*, *s.* between the rows.

පේම, *Péma*, *s.* love, affection.

පෛශුන්‍ය, *Paiṣunya*, *s.* slander, [Colloq. කේලාම් *kélám*].

පොකුණුපල්, *Pokuṇupal*, *s.* keeper or protector of ponds.

පොකුරුවැසි, *Pokuruwęsi*, *s.* rain of flowers, especially of lotus flowers.

පොටගල, *Poṭagala*, see වැලුක් *weluk*.

පොඩිත්ත, *Poḍitta*, *s.* very little.

පොපියුම්, *Popiyum*, *s.* shaking shivering.

පොරොඩු, *Porodu*, *s.* cloth or covering laid over the saddle or furniture of an elephant, horse, etc.

පොරෝකාරයා, *Porókárayá*, *s.* feller of wood, applied to one who supplied firewood to the king's kitchen in the Kandyan times.

පොල්කිච්චා, *Polkichchá*, *s.* magpie, robin: see පොල්ලිච්චා *pollichchá*.

පොලෑල්, *Poleַl*, *s.* kind of paddy.

පොහොකරුණු, *Pohokaruṇu*, *s.* observance of the Buddhist sabbath.

පොහොසත්මි, *Pohosatmi*, *v.* I am rich, I am able.

පෞෂ්ටික, *Paushṭika*, *a.* protective, nutritive, nutritious.

පැකි, *Pęki*, *s.* fruit, [Colloq. ගෙඩි *gędi*].

පැකුළුනන්ට, *Pękulunanṭa*, *s.* to those who have fallen or stumbled, [Colloq. වැටුනවුන්ට *wętuna-wunṭa*].

පැදරු, *Pędaru*, *s.* sail, (*cf.* රුවල් පැදරු ඇති *ruwal pędaru ęti*).

පැදුම් මුහුද, *Pędum-muhuda*, *s.* eastern sea.

පැලගහ, *Pęla-gaha*, *s.* young tree, as පැලපොල් ගස් *pęlapol-gas*.

පැලහ, *Pęlaha*, *v.* they fled, took to their heels.

පැවතුම්, *Pęwatum*, *s.* existence.

පැසිබත, *Pęsi-bata*, *s.* rice prepared from small particles of pounded grains of paddy.

* පැහැ, *Pęhę*, *s.* an interjection.

පැහැරපියා, *Pęhęrapiyá*, *part.* having quitted, deserted, neglected, left, struck.

පැලවෙනවා, *Pęlawenawá*, *v.* to germinate, to shoot as a plant: to spring up as seedlings: pret. පැලවුනා *pęlawuná*.

පැලහෙන්නී, *Pęlahenní*, *s.* (feminine form of පැලහෙන්නා *pęlahenná*) one who is being burnt.

ප්‍රකර්ෂවාද, *Prakarsha-wáda*, *s.* strong controversy.

ප්‍රණිපාතන, *Praṇipátana*, *s.* worshipping.

ප්‍රත්‍යක්ෂ බෙහෙත්, *Pratyaksha-behet*, *s.* medicines which have been tried and found efficacious.

ප්‍රත්‍යය සන්නිශ්‍රිතශීල, *Pratyaya-sannisríta-síla*, *s.* observance of sil by using food, medicine, robes, and seats, given by upásaka or religious men for the preservation of life and not for decoration or gratification of sensual desires.

ප්‍රත්‍යුපස්ථාන, *Pratyupasthána*, *s.* rendering assistance in return.

ප්‍රත්‍යෙකබුද්ධ, *Pratyéka-buddha*, *a.* an inferior class of Buddha.

ප්‍රත්‍යෙකභාග, *Pratyéka-bhága*, *s.* a single portion, a separate portion.

ප්‍රතාප ගුණ, *Pratápa-guṇa*, *s.* the good result produced by punishment.

ප්‍රතික්‍රමණ ශාලා, *Pratikramaṇa-śálá*, *s.* ambulance hall.

ප්‍රතිඝානුනය, *Pratighánúnaya*, *s.* subduing hatred and pleasure, obtaining satisfaction of hatred.

ප්‍රතිච්ඡාදක, *Pratichchhádaka*, *a.* covering.

ප්‍රතිනියත, *Prati-niyata*, *s.* fixed.

ප්‍රතිපදාව, *Pratipadáwa*, *s.* the first day of the lunar fortnight, the first day of the moon's increase or decrease.

ප්‍රතිපීඩිත, *Prati-píḍita*, *a.* come to calamity, suffering distress.

ප්‍රතිමාගෘහ, *Pratimá-griha*, *s.* a house in which images are put in.

ප්‍රතිරූප දේශය, *Pratirúpa-déṣaya*, *s.* opposite of ප්‍රත්‍යන්ත දේශය *pratyanta-déṣaya*.

ප්‍රතිලෝභ, *Pratilóbha*, *s.* desire, [Colloq. ආශාව *áṣáwa*].

ප්‍රතිවිරුද්ධ, *Prati-viruddha*, *a.* contrary, hostile, inimical, [Colloq. සතුරු *saturu*].

ප්‍රතිසංස්කරණ, *Pratisaṇskaraṇa*, *s.* repairing of what is rotten or decayed.

ප්‍රතිසන්ධිචිත්ත, *Pratisandhi-chitta*, *s.* the thought which joins the present existence with that of the next birth.

ප්‍රතිසම්භිදා, *Pratisambhidá*, *s.* (see පටිසම්භිදා *pati-sambhidá*, in Childers Dictionary, knowledge of අර්ථධර්ම නිරුක්ති ප්‍රතිභාන *artha-dharma-nirukti-pratibhána*), discrimination.

ප්‍රතිසාරණ, *Pratisáraṇa*, *s.* an action of Vinaya.

ප්‍රථමබෝධිය, *Prathama-bódhiya*, *s.* state of Arhat or saint in the fourth and final stage of sanctification.

ප්‍රදාලන, *Pradálana*, *s.* splitting, cleaving, [Colloq. පැළීම *pęlíma*].

ප්‍රදීපායමාණ, *Pradípáyamáṇa*, *a.* being like a lamp.

ප්‍රබන්ධවාසය, *Prabandha-wásaya*, *s.* living or dwelling continually.

ප්‍රභාගය, *Prabhágaya*, *s.* compound fraction.

ප්‍රමත්තවූ, *Pramattawú*, *a.* intoxicated, careless, blundering.

ප්‍රයත්න, *Prayatna*, *s.* continued or persevering effort, exertion, active effort, [Colloq. උත්සාහය *utsáhaya*].

ප්‍රයාස, *Prayása*, *s.* trouble, labour, fatigue, [Colloq. වෙහෙස *wehesa*].

ප්‍රසවවේදනා, *Prasawa-wédaná*, *s.* pain caused on account of giving birth to a child.

ප්‍රසවබන්ධන, *Prasawa-bandhana*, *s.* stalk of a flower.

ප්‍රසාධිතව, *Prasádhitawa*, *part.* being ornamented or decorated, accomplished, completed.

ප්‍රසූතිමන්දිර, *Prasúti-mandira*, *s.* lying in home.

ප්‍රහාරෝපමවූ, *Prahárópamawú*, *a.* like a blow or stroke.

ප්‍රාණවායු, *Práṇa-wáyu*, *s.* vital air.

ප්‍රාප්තිදානය, *Prápti-dánaya*, see පත්තිදාන *patti-dána*.

ප්‍රිය ඵලවන්නේය, *Priya-elawannéya*, *v.* causes joy, delights.

ප්‍රිය විප්‍රයෝග, *Priya-viprayóga*, *s.* separation from one who is dear or beloved.

පෘථිවිගර්භ ශාස්ත්‍රය, *Prithivigarbha-śástraya*, *s.* geology.

පෘථිවිතලය, *Prithivitalaya*, *s.* the earth.

පෘථිවි විද්‍යා, *Prituví-vidyá*, *s.* geology.

පෘෂ්ඨ, *Prishtha*, *s.* back, [Colloq. පිට *pita*].

ප්‍රෞඪ, *Prawdha*, *a.* full grown, bold, arrogant, impudent; full, (as the moon); forward, (as the hand to seize any thing); raised, lifted.

ඵ

* ඵල, *Phala*, *s.* quotient, (in Arithmetic).

ඵලපල්ලව, *Phala-pallawa*, *s.* fruits and tender leaves or shoots.

බ

* බක, *Baka*, *s.* great, [Colloq. මහ *maha*].

බගිරිනකය, *Bagirinakaya*, *s.* one of the three Buddhist fraternities in Ceylon, more commonly known as අභයගිරිනිකාය *Abhayagiri-nikáya*.

බටුබටුවන්, *Batubatuwan*, *s.* as many as went down; whoever descended.

බටුයේ, *Batuyé*, *s.* one who descended, [Colloq. බැස්සේ *bessé*].

බඩපිපිම, *Bada-pipíma*, *s.* flatulence.

බඩවාග්නිය, *Badawágniya*, *s.* submarine fire.

බණ්ඩිය, *Bandiya*, *s.* belly.

බණ්ඩියා, *Bandiyá*, *s.* one with a big belly.

බණවස්න, *Bana-wasna*, *s.* cover laid over a sacred Buddhist work.

බණවා, *Banawá*, *part.* having addressed.

බත්කොමුනොකොට, *Batkomunokota*, *part.* not over boiling rice.

බත්ගමයා, *Batgamayá*, *s.* man of the Paduwá caste, [Colloq. පදුවා *paduwá*].

බත්බෑළයා, *Batbelayá*, *s.* one who does cooly work for the sake of his meals.

බත්වඩන නිලමේ, *Batwadana-nilamé*, *s.* food steward.

බත්වලඳ, *Batwalanda*, *s.* rice eating dish, earthen plate or dish.

බදරිකා, *Badariká*, *s.* berry or pod of the cotton.

බඹුරා, *Bamburá*, *s.* (from Skt. බර්බර *barbara*,) low man, barbarian, out-cast.

බම්බලෝසි, *Bambalósi*, *s.* shaddock.

බම්බු, *Bambu*, *s.* Brahma.

බම, *Bama*, *s.* whirling, giddiness, dizziness.

බමරබස්සා, *Bamarabassá*, see බිම්බස්සා *bimbassá*.

බමරලියා, *Bamaraliyá*, see රෑබස්සා *ré-bassá*.

බයගන්වනවා, *Bayaganwanawá*, *v.* to frighten, to intimidate.

බයවෙනවා, *Bayawenawá*, *v.* to fear, to be afraid: pret. බයවුනා *bayawuná*.

බයාදුකම, *Bayádukama*, *s.* timidity, fearfulness.

බරපණ, *Barapana*, *s.* what is paid for copying a book, (corruptly බරපෑන් *barapen*).

බරෝතිය, *Barótiya*, *s.* term applied to a flanel covering for the chest to keep it warm. (Port.)

බලඇණි, *Bala-eni*, *s.* division of military forces, [Colloq. යුද්ධසේනාව *yuddha-sénáwa*].

බලතා, *Balatá*, *s.* person of authority, superintendent, protector, guard.

බලවාහන, *Balawáhana*, *s.* forces and vehicles.

බලසෞගන්ධික, *Bala-saugandhika*. see ගෙන්දගම් *gendagam*.

බලාපුව, *Balápuwa*, *s.* tract of fields. (S. P.)

බලියාම, *Baliyáma*, *s.* titan, [Colloq. අසුරයා *asurayá*].

බලිසයනය, *Balisayanaya*, *s.* sleep looking or turning the head upwards.

බවලත් උදවිය, *Bawalat-udaviya*, *s.* woman kind, women, female members of society.

බවසුව, *Bawasuwa*, *s.* happiness in existence.

බහුදර්ශීවූ, *Bahudarśíwú*, *a.* seeing many things.

බහුප්පාද, *Bahuppáda*, *a.* many footed.

බහුපත්‍ර, *Bahu-patra*, see දියබෙරලිය *diyaberaliya*.

බහුපුට, *Bahuputa*, *s.* talc, plumbago, [Colloq. මිනිරන් *miniran*].

බහුඵලා, *Bahuphalá*, *s.* plant, species of night shade, *solanum nigrum*, [Colloq. කළුකැම්මේරිය *kalukemmériya*].

බහුබීජක, *Bahubíjaka*, *s.* annual hairy plant, *hibiscus angulosus* or *h. abelmoschus*, [Colloq. තකුල් *takul* or කපුකිණිස්ස *kapukinissa*]; kind of plantain or banana, [Colloq. ඇටකෙහෙල් *eta-kehel*].

බහුවර, *Bahuwara*, see බහුවාතක *bahuwátaka*.

බාගිය, *Bágiya*, *s.* corruptly for භාග්‍යය *bhágyaya*, which see.

* බානවා, *Bánawá*,=බයවෙනවා, *bayawenawá*, *v.* to fear, to be afraid of.

බානසුල්ලහ, *Bánasullaha*, *v.* they are timid.

බාපනය, *Bápanaya*, see වාපනය *wápanaya*.

බාලපරාය, *Bálaparáya*, *s.* young age, youth.

* බාලි, *Báli*, *s.* plant, *abrus precatorius*, [Colloq. ඔලිඳ *olinda*].

* බාලි, *Bálí*, *s.* small cardamoms, *elettaria cardamomum*, [Colloq. සිහින් එන්සාල් *sihin-ensál*].

බාෂ්ප, *Báshpa*, *s.* tears, [Colloq. කඳුළු *kandulu*].

* බාසුරු, *Básuru*, *a.* hero by means of his arms, lion.

බාහ්‍ය, *Báhya*, see බාහිර *báhira*.

බාහ්‍යාභ්‍යන්තර, *Báhyábhyantara*, *s.* out side and in side: *a.* external and internal, [Colloq. ඇතුළ පිට *etula pita*].

බාහිරශාස්ත්‍ර, *Báhira-śástra*, *s.* secular sciences, sciences not connected with religion.

බාහුභූෂණ, *Báhubhúshana*, *s.* a bracelet for the arm.

බාහුල්‍යවෘත්ති, *Báhulya-writti*, *s.* existence in abundance.

බික්සඟ, *Biksanga*, *s.* community of Buddhist priests.

බිඩලු, *Bidalu*, *s.* clods, splinters.

බිණුවා, *Binuwá*, *v.* said, spoke, [Colloq. කීවා *kíwá*].

බින්කාර, *Binkára*, *s.* goglet, [Colloq. කෙණ්ඩිය *kendiya*].

බින්නකරණවා, *Binnakaranawá*, *v.* to break, [Coll: කඩනවා *kadanawá*].

බින්නබහිනවා, *Binnabahinawá*, *v.* applied to the act of a husband living permanently in the house of his wife.

බින්නෑගිම, *Binnegíma*, *s.* first ploughing.

බිම්නා, *Bimná*, *s.* long earth worm, [Colloq. ගැඩවිලා *gedavilá*].

බිම්පිසකරවා, *Bimpisakarawá*, *part.* having levelled the ground.

බිම්බෑවිල, *Bim-bevila*, *s.* plant, variety of *sida humilis*.

බිම්මද, *Bimmada*, *s.* mango, *mangifera indica*, or *m. zeylanica*, [Colloq. අඹ *amba*].

බිම්රක්ෂා, *Bimrakshá*, *s.* kind of resin, [Colloq. දුම්මල *dummala*].

බිමහෙව, *Bimahewa*, *part.* having fallen on the ground.

බියකරු, *Biyakaru*, *a.* causing fear, terrific.

බියසුලුවෙති, *Biyasuluweti*, *v.* become timid.

බිලඟ, *Bilanga*, *s.* jack tree, *artocarpus integrifolia*, [Colloq. කොස් *kos*].

බිලිතටු, *Bili-tatu*, *s.* altar or platform on which offerings are presented to demons or planets.

බිලිවෑද්දා, *Biliweddá*, *s.* one who catches fish by an angling rod.

බිස්කඩ, *Biskada*, *s.* foot scraper.

* බිස්ස, *Bissa*, *s.* granary.

බිසක්, *Bisak*, *s.* physician, doctor, [Colloq. වෙදා *wedá*].

බිජක, *Bíjaka*, *s.* citron, *citrus medica*, [Colloq. ලප්නාරං *lapnárań*].

බිජගර්භ, *Bíja-garbha*, *s.* inside a seed: *adj.* that which has seed inside.

බිරුපත්, *Bírupat*, *s.* creeping plant, *asparagus falcatus*, [Colloq. හාතාවාරිය *hátáwáriya*].

බුද්ධපබ්බජිත, *Buddha-pabbajita*, *a.* become a Buddhist monk in his old age, or an old monk.

බුද්ධාලම්බනප්‍රීති, *Buddhálambana-príti*, *s.* pleasure obtained by remembering Buddha.

බුද්ධෝත්පාදකාලය, *Buddhótpáda-kálaya*, *s.* (බුද්ධ *buddha* + උත්පාද *utpáda* + කාලය *kálaya*) time in which a (Supreme) Buddha is born in this world.

බුන්දත්, *Bundat*, *s.* god Ganésa, [Colloq. ගණදෙවියෝ *ganadeviyó*].

බුන්වෙරලෑති, *Bunweraleti*, *a.* having an indented shore.

බුමුතුරුණු, *Bumuturunu*, *s.* cloth spread on the floor on state or festive occasions.

බුසා, *Busá*, *s.* banana or plantain tree, [Colloq. කෙහෙල්ගහ *kehelgaha*].

බූටියා, *Bútiyá*, *s.* play things: pl. බූටි *búti*.

බූපදි, *Búpadi*, *s.* plant, oleander, [Colloq. බොලිද්ද *bolidda*].

බූමාටු, *Búmátu*, *a.* terrestrial (deities).

බූසිනියාවෙනවා, *Búsiniyáwenawá*, *v.* to be extirpated, another form of බූසනයාවෙනවා *búsanayá wenawá*.

බෙදීම, *Bedíma*, *s.* division.

බෙදෙනවා, *Bedenawá*, *v.* to be divided.

බෙරගහන්නා, *Beragahanná*, *s.* tom-tom beater.

බෙරපියවිකරවා, *Berapiyavikarawá*, } *part.* having proclaimed by beat of tom-tom.
බෙරලවා, *Bera-lawá*,
බෙරහසුරුවා, *Berahasuruwá*,

* බෙරු, *Beru*, *s.* indigo plant, [Colloq. නිල්ගස් *nil gas*, අවරි *awari*].

බෙලිදඬු, *Belidandu*, see පෙලිදඬු *pelidandu*.

බෙහෙව, *Behewa*, *v.* are abundant or many, [Colloq. බොහෝය *bohóya*].

බෙහෙවින්, *Behevin*, *adv.* abundantly, [Colloq. බොහෝසෙයින් *bohóseyin*].

බොල්පාන, *Bolpána*, *s.* water in which rice has been cleaned.

බෝංචි, *Bónchi*, *s.* beans.

බෝදන, *Bódana*, *s.* purslane, *portulaca oleracea*, [Colloq. ගෙඳ *genda*].

බෝදිරි, *Bódiri*, *s.* kind of coconut.

බෝදිලියා, *Bódiliyá*, see බෝදිරිමවු *bódirimawu*.

බෝපල, *Bópala*, *s.* tree, called මී *mí*, from the nuts of which a kind of medicinal oil is prepared.

බෝම, *Bóma*, *s.* shortened form of බොහොම *bohoma*.

බෝමැඩ, *Bómęda*, *s.* terrace around the bó tree.

බෝලකඩල, *Bóla-kadala*, *s.* round kind of gram, which some people are fond of eating.

බෝලගහනවා, *Bólagahanawá*, *v.* playing at marble or cricket.

බෝහන්වෙනවා, *Bóhanwenawá*, *v.* to perish, to go to pot [Colloquial and vulgar].

බෞද්ධධ්වජය, *Bauddhadhwajaya*, *s.* Buddhist banner or flag.

බැංකුව, *Bęnkuwa*, *s.* bank, place where money is deposited.

බැගෑහඬ, *Bęgé-handa*, *s.* piteous cry.

බැටළුපොව්, *Bętalupow*, *s.* lamb, young sheep.

බැමිණිටිසාය, *Bęminitisáya*, *s.* famine caused by the wish of a certain Brahmin woman.

බැරුක්කේ, *Bęrękké*, *s.* barracks.

* බෑනා, *Bęná*, *s.* brother.

බ්‍රහ්මදණ්ඩ, *Brahmadanda*, *s.* plant, *ligusticum ajwaen*, [Colloq. අසමෝදගම් *asamódagam*].

බ්‍රහ්මධර්ම, *Brahma-dharma*, *s.* living without being defiled by woman, doctrines of Brahma.

බ්‍රහ්මමූලි, *Brahma-múli*, *s.* medicinal plant, *herpestis monniera*, [Colloq. ලුනුවිල *lunuvila*].

බෘන්දාරක, *Brindáraka*, *s.* a god.

භ

භර්තෘස්වාමියා, *Bhartri-swámiyá*, *s.* nourisher, cherisher, husband.

භරිත, *Bharita*, *a.* filled, nourished.

භවක්ෂය, *Bhawakshaya*, *s.* cessation of existence, annihilation.

භාගප්‍රභාගය, *Bhága-prabhágaya*, *s.* complex fraction.

භාගානුබන්ධය, *Bhágánubandhaya*, *s.* mixed number.

භාජ්‍යය, *Bhájyaya*, *a.* dividend.

භාජකය, *Bhájakaya*, *a.* divisor.

භාවාර්ථය, *Bháwárthaya*, *s.* purport, *general* sense as oppsed to පදගතාර්ථය *padagatárthaya*, *literal* meaning.

භාෂාන්තර, *Bháshántara*, *s.* different language.

භාස්කරායමාන, *Bháskaráyamána*, *a.* shining like the sun.

භාස්වර, *Bháswara*, *a.* shining, radiant, [Colloq. බබලන *babalana*].

භීමදර්ශනවූ, *Bhímadarsanawú*, *a*, of frightful appearance, horrific.

භීෂණෝත්පාදක, *Bhíshanótpádaka*, *a.* causing fear, terror-inspiring, [Colloq. භය උපදවන *bhaya-upadawana*].

භුවනත්‍රය, *Bhuwanatraya*, *s.* the three worlds, viz. world of men, gods, and asuras or titans.

භූතවේය, *Bhútawéya*, *s.* a medicinal plant: see තලා *talá*.

භූමිලතා, *Bhúmilatá*, *s.* bindweed, bearing a red flower, *ipomœa beladamboe* or *i. rugosa*, [Colloq. බින්තඹුරු *bintamburu*].

භූයෝවෘත්ති, *Bhúyówritti*, *s.* frequency, abundance.

භෝගාවලි, *Bhógáwali*, *s.* coils of a snake; expanded hood of a snake; also praise or eulogium.

භ්‍රාජමාන, *Bhrájamána*, *a.* shining, brilliant, [Coll: බබලන *babalana*].

භ්‍රාජිත, *Bhrájita*, *a.* luminous, resplendent, [Colloq. බැබලූ *bębalú*].

භ්‍රාතෘ, *Bhrátri*, *s.* brother.

ම

මංගලවෘත්තාන්තය, *Mangalawrittántaya*, *s.* glad tidings; Gospel.

මක්කා, *Makká*,=මක් *mak*, what.

මකරධ්වජ, *Makaradhwaja*, *s.* one whose banner is the fabulous monster called Makara; name of Anangayá, the Indian Cupid.

මකස, *Makasa*, *s.* musquito, gnat, [Colloq. මදුරුවා *maduruwá*].

මකළ, *Makala*, *s.* monkey or ape, [Colloq. රිළවා *rilawá*].

මගධභාෂා, *Magadha-bháshá*, *s.* language used in the country of Magadha,—another term for the Páli language.

මගධ නැළිය, *Magadha-nęliya*, *s.* the Nęli measure of capacity used by the inhabitants of Magadha, South Behar, equal to sixteen Nęlis in modern use.

මගීවෙස, *Magíwesa*, *s.* disguise of a way-fairer or traveller.

මඟුල්බත, *Magul-bata*, s. feast at a wedding or any similar occasion.

මගෙ බඩකයිද, *Mage-bada-kayida*, a. Kandyan phrase, meaning "what does it matter to me," "it is no concern of mine."

මඞ්ගල්‍යසන්නිශ්‍රිත, *Mańgalya-sannisrita*, adj. (මඞ්ගල්‍ය auspicious, සන්නිශ්‍රිත mixed) mixed with auspicious deeds, belonging to a marriage.

මච්ඡමාංස, *Machchha-mánsa*, s. fish and meat.

මටකම්, *Maṭakam*, s. act of polishing; polished work.

මණ්ඩඩියා, *Manḍadiyá*, s. the man in charge of a fishing net called manḍa.

මණ්ඩනායමාන, *Manḍanáyamána*, a. becoming an ornament, or like an ornament.

මණ්ඩලකුෂ්ඨය, *Manḍala-kushṭhaya*, s. erysipelas, ringworm.

මණ්ඩලික, *Manḍalika*, s. district, circular figure or diagram; sort of leprosy with large round spots.

මණ්ඩිත, *Manḍita*, a. ornamented, decorated, [Coll: අලංකාරකළ *alankára-kaḷa*].

මණ්ඩුකරාවය, *Manḍukaráwaya*, s. noise made by a frog, [Colloq. ගෙමඩිහඬ *gemaḍi-hanḍa*].

මණිකයිවඩම්, *Manikayiwaḍam*, s. jewel ornaments worn on the wrist.

මත්තං, *Mattan*, s. thorn apple, *datura fastuosa*, [Colloq. අත්තන *attana*].

මත්තිය, *Mattiya*, s. small kind of plant, heart pea, *cardiospermum halicacabum*, [Colloq. දූදු *dúdu* or පෙනෙලවැල් *penelawel*].

මත්ස්‍යමාංස, *Matsya-mánsa*, s. fish and meat.

* මති, *Mati*, s. tree, *ægle marmelos*, [Colloq. බෙලිගස *beligasa*].

මතුනු, *Matunu*, s. my body.

මදවික්ක, *Mada-vikka*, s. toddy seller.

මදුරස, *Madu-rasa*, s. mora tree, the fruit of which gives a delicious taste.

මදුරසා, *Madurasá*, s. kind of creeper.

මධ්‍යාහ්න රේඛාව, *Madhyáhna-rékháwa*, s. meridian line.

මධුධාතු, *Madhu-dhátu*, see මැසිඳු *mesidé*.

මධුපටලය, *Madhu-paṭalaya*, s. beehive, honey comb, [Colloq. මීවදය *míwadaya*].

මධුමාර්ජික, *Madhumárjika*, s. date tree, *phœnix zeylanica*, [Colloq. ඉඳිගහ *indigaha*].

මධූෂිත, *Madhúshita*, s. bee's wex, [Colloq. මීඉටි *míiṭi*].

මන්ජිට්ටා, *Manjiṭṭá*, s. kind of tree.

* මන්ද, *Manda*, s. meshes in the net; rope for noosing elephants.

මන්දනල, *Mandanala*, same as මන්දමාරුත *manda-máruta*.

* මන්දාකිනි, *Mandákini*, s. a river supposed to be in heaven generally called අහස්ගඟ *ahas-ganga*.

මන්දිය, *Mandiya*, s. flow of water between ebb and tide.

මනකලි, *Manakalí*, a. captivating the heart, delighting the mind, pleasing, handsome.

මනාචාර, *Manáchára*, s. good conduct.

මනුෂ්‍යෝත්පාදනය, *Manushyótpádanaya*, s. creation of man, bringing man into existence.

මනෝදුශ්චරිත, *Manóduscharita*, s. sins of thought.

මනෝනේත්‍රය, *Manónétraya*, s. mental eye.

මනෝරඤ්ජන, *Manórañjana*, s. gratifying the mind.

මනෝරථසිද්ධි, *Manóratha-siddhi*, s. accomplishment of the desire in one's mind.

මනෝහරා, *Manóhará*, s. species of waterlily, [Colloq. නිල්ඕලු *nil-ólu*].

මබස්පත, *Mabaspata*, s. my letter, or what I said.

මයුක, *Mayuka*, s. kind of tree, used as medicine.

මයුරුක, *Mayuruka*, s. wood apple tree.

මයුරුකර, *Mayurukara*, s. neck of the peacock.

මයූරතුතු, *Mayúratutu*, s. blue vitriol, [Colloq. පල්මාණික්කන් *palmáṇikkan*].

මයූරපක්ෂ, *Mayúra-paksha*, s. peacock's tail or the feathers of his tail, [Colloq. මොණරපිල් *moṇara-pil*].

මරණෝපමවූ, *Maraṇópamawú*, a. resembling death.

මරමරා, *Maramará*, part. continuing to strike, giving repeated blows.

* මරා, *Mará*, part. having struck or killed.

මරිෂ්ට, *Marishṭa*, s. whey, [Colloq. මෝරු *móru*].

මරීචිමඤ්ජරී, *Maríchi-mañjarí*, s. cluster or pencil of rays.

මරුත්තුකොට, *Maruttukoṭa*, v. to disobey, to transgress, to break. (Telingu.)

මරුත්තු නොකොට, *Maruttu-nokoṭa*, part. not breaking, [Colloq. කඩනොකර *kaḍanokara*].

මරුමුවපත්, *Marumuwa-pat*, a. come to the mouth of death.

මල් අවිච්චියා, *Mal-avichchiyá*, see ශාරිකා *sáriká*.

මල්කලය, *Mal-kalaya*, s. flower pot, pot filled with flowers.

මල්කවඩියා, *Mal-kawaḍiyá*, see ශාරිකා *sáriká*.

මල්ගුලාව, *Mal-guláwa*, s. bunch of flowers, nosegay.

මල්ගොටුව, *Mal-goṭuwa*, *s.* leaves folded to form a cavity holding flowers.

මල්පල්ලව, *Malpallawa*, *s.* flowers and tender buds.

මල්පු, *Malpu*, *s.* clay pot.

මල්වට, *Malwaṭa*, *s.* bunch of flowers.

මල්සුමුග, *Malsumuga*, *s.* box containing flowers, nosegay, bouquet of flowers.

මලඉත්ත, *Malaitta*, see මලිත *malita*, and මයිල *mayila*.

මලගය, *Malagaya*, *s.* tree, Patana oak, *careya arborea*, [Colloq. කහටගහ *kahaṭa-gaha*].

* මලඟ, *Malan̲ga*. *s.* woman.

මලපු, *Malapu*, *s.* wood apple.

මලයජවෘක්ෂ, *Malayaja-wriksha*, *s.* sandal-wood, *santalum album*, [Colloq. සඳුන් *san̲dun*].

මලායන, *Maláyana*,=මැලවෙන *mẹlawena*, මැලවී යන *mẹlavi-yana*, *a.* withering, fading.

මලින්දා, *Malindá*, *s.* tree, commonly called මයිල *mayila*, bearing beautiful flowers.

මලු, *Malu*, *s.* relations.

මලුකම්, *Malukam*, *s.* admission into the Upasampadá order of Buddhist monks.

* මලුපු, *Malupu*, *s.* jasmine creeper or shrub: see මලිගිය *maligiya*; bunch of flowers.

මලෝලඹු, *Malólam̲bu*, *s.* hanging flowers.

මස් ඇස්, *Mas-ẹs*, *s.* kind of plant used as vegetable; medicinal plant.

මස්සබාදුව, *Massabáduwa*, *s.* rape.

මසවුළු, *Masawuḷu*, *s.* meat and sweetmeats taken after a meal.

* මහ ඉඟිනි, *Maha-in̲gini*, *s.* tree, *strychnos nux-vomica*, [Colloq. ගොඩකදුරු *goḍa-kaduru*].

මහ කපිත, *Maha-kapita*, *s.* slime apple.

මහගබඩානිලමේ, *Maha-gabaḍánilamé*, *s.* Principal guardian of the Royal stores.

මහණවින්, *Mahaṇavin*, *s.* by the great ocean,= මහාර්ණවයෙන් *mahárṇawayen*.

මහදිසාව, *Maha-diṣáwa*, *s.* governor of a province.

මහදුරු, *Mahaduru*, *s.* large cummin seed.

මහපස්මුල්, *Maha-pasmul*, see පංචමූල *pañcha-múla*.

මහබද්දේ, *Mahabaddé*, *s.* caste so called, generally known as people of the Cháliya or Halágama caste.

මහබිනික්මණ, *Mahabinikmaṇa*, *s.* (මහ great, අබිනික්මණ *abinikmana* going out) a Buddhistic term used to express the abandonment of household life by Buddha with a view to lead a monastic life for the purpose of attaining Buddha-hood.

මහමී, *Maha-mí*, *s.* honey made by the wasp, [Colloq. බඹරපැණි *bam̲bara-pẹṇi*].

මහ මොහොට්ටාල, *Maha-mohoṭṭála*, *s.* chief secretary.

මහරා, *Mahará*, *s.* kind of tree; same as මහරිරුක *mahari-ruka*; fermented toddy.

මහලුපැවිදි, *Mahalupẹvidi*, *s.* ordination as a Buddhist monk of the superior order.

මහලේ තනතුර, *Mahalé-tanatura*, *s.* officer of chief Secretary.

මහවුල, *Mahawula*, *s.* pillow.

මහාකාය, *Mahákáya*, *s.* the great body.

මහාද්භූත, *Mahádbhuta*, *a.* very wonderful or uncommon.

මහාපත්‍ර, *Mahá-patra*, *s.* red variety of the castor oil plant, *recinus communis*, [Colloq. රත්එඬරු *rat-en̲daru*].

මහාර්හ, *Mahárha*, *a.* costly, valuable; very worthy.

* මහාසාර, *Mahására*, *s.* tree, species of *santalum*, [Colloq. කළුකිහිරි *kaḷu-kihiri*].

මහාසාවද්‍ය, *Mahásáwadya*, *a.* very wrong, faulty.

මහිමය, *Mahimaya*, *s.* glory, power, dignity honour, greatness, grandeur.

මහීපාල, *Mahípála*, *s.* protector of the earth; king.

මහෝත්සව, *Mahótsawa*, *s.* great festival or occasion of public rejoicings.

මළකුර, *Maḷakura*, *s.* (මළ+අකුර *akura*) term applied to mute consonants, *i. e.* consonants without the inherent vowel sound attached to them, *e. g.* ක් *k*, ඛ් *kh*, ග් *g*, etc. [Colloq. අල් අකුර *al-akura*].

මළපත, *Maḷapata*, *s.* (මළ dead+පත leaf, writing) letter announcing the death of any person; obituary.

මාකදර, *Mákadara*, *s.* garlic, *allium sativum*, [Colloq. සුදුළූණු *sudu-lúṇu*].

මාකඳර, *Mákan̲dara*, *s.* mango tree, [Colloq. අඹගහ *am̲ba-gaha*].

මාඝ, *Mágha*, *s.* one of the months of the Hindu year corresponding to January–February; name of a poet the author of "Siṣupála Badha" or as it is named after him the Mághakávya, one of the great profane poems of Hindu literature.

මාතඞ්ගයා, *Mátaṅgayá*, *s.* a man of mean birth.

මාතන, *Mátana*, *s.* small hairy species of night shade, *solanum ferox*, [Colloq. මලබටු *mala-baṭu*].

මාතලි, *Mátali*, *s.* plant, *justicia adhatoda*, [Colloq. අඩාතෝඩා *áḍátóḍá*].

මාතුපෝෂක, *Mátupóshaka*, *s.* one who supports own mother.

මාතෙලිජ්ජා, *Mátelijjá*, *s.* kind of sea fish.

මාධවීලතා, *Mádhaví-latá*, *s.* creeping plant, liquorice, [Colloq. වැල්මි *welmi*].

මාන්වෙනවා, *Mánwenawá*, *v.* to split in two, as the head (vulgar).

මානුෂාධිපත්‍යය, *Mánushádhipatyaya*, *s.* supremacy over men.

මානුස, *Mánusa*, Páli form for man.

මානෙල් අල, *Mánel-ala*, *s.* root of the white esculent water lily, *nymphœa stellata.*

මාපස, *Mápasa*, *s.* my side.

මාපා, *Mápá*, *s.* a rank, prime minister or viceroy; also, a form of swearing by one's self.

මාමද, *Mámada*, *s.* plant, *acorus calamus*, [Colloq. වදකහ *wadakaha*].

මායූරුක, *Máyuruka*, *s.* wood apple, *feronia elephantum*, [Colloq. දිවුල් *diwul*].

මාරුත්, *Márut*, *s.* plant, *euphorbia entiquorum*, [Colloq. දළුක් *daluk*]; kind of beautiful flower, *rosa semperflorens*, [Colloq. සෙවුවන්දි *sewuwandi*, or රෝස *rósa*].

මාරේස, *Máresa*, *s.* beams of the moon.

මාලක්කාරයා, *Málakkárayá*, *s.* flower seller.

මාලගොව්වා, *Málagowwá*, *s.* flower keeper, gardener.

මාලි, *Máli*, see මාරුත් *márut.*

මාලිමා යන්ත්‍රය, *Málimá-yantraya*, *s.* mariner's compass.

මාස්කන්න, *Máskanna*, *s.* crop for the මහ *maha* season of paddy harvest.

මිටියන්කරණවා, *Miṭiyankaraṇawá*, *v.* to clinch a nail.

මිණිකොඬොල, *Miṇikoṇḍola*, *s.* ear-rings set with gems.

මිණිමෙවුල්, *Miṇimewul*, *s.* girdle set with gems.

මිණිහිරි වැව, *Miṇihiri-wewa*, *s.* tank Minihiri, commonly called මින්නේරිය *minnériya.*

මිථ්‍යාභාෂණය, *Mithyábháshaṇaya*, *s.* speaking what is not true, lying, [Colloq. බොරුකීම *borukíma*].

මිථ්‍යාමති, *Mithyá-mati*, *s.* erroneous view or opinions.

මිථ්‍යාලබ්ධි, *Mithyá-labdhi*, *s.* false faith, heresy.

මිථ්‍යාලෝක, *Mithyálóka*, *s.* false light.

මිථ්‍යාහේතු, *Mithyá-hétu*, *s.* false cause.

මිනින්නඹු, *Mininnambu*, } *s.* midwife, [Colloquial:
මිනීනඹු, *Minínambu*, } වින්නඹු *vinnambu*].

මියඬුරුසුස්ම, *Miyaṇḍurususma*, *s.* deep sigh.

මිලිනය, *Milinaya*, *s.* swan.

මිලීන, *Milína*, *s.* dark colour.

මිශ්‍රභාගය, *Miṣrabhágaya*, *s.* mixed number.

මිශ්‍රරාශිය, *Miṣrarásiya*, *s.* compound proportion.

මිශ්‍ර ව්‍යවහාරය, *Miṣra-vyawahéraya*, *s.* practice.

මිසිනි, *Misiní*, *s.* small cardamoms, *elettaria cardamomum*, [Colloq. සින්එන්සාල් *sín-ensál*].

මිහිරිය, *Mihiriya*, *s.* honey.

මීකටුවැල්බටු, *Mí-kaṭuwelbaṭu*, *s.* species of egg plant, *solanum trilobatum*, [Colloq. වැල්තිබ්බටු *wel-tibbaṭu*].

මීනපලා, *Mínapalá*, *s.* soap-berry plant, *sapindus emarginatus*, [Colloq. පෙනෙලගස් *penela-gas*].

මීනයකෙළිය, *Mínaya-keḷiya*, *s*, the play of Ananga, god of love.

මීනියා, *Míniyá*, *a.* of this kind, manner or size,= මේ හැටි *mé-heṭi*, මෙවැනි *meweni*, මේ අකාර *mé-ákára.*

මීපටලය, *Mí-paṭalaya*, *s.* honey-comb; bee hive.

මීපය, *Mípaya*, same as මීපා *mípá.*

මීබොන, *Míbona*, *s.* drinking honey.

මීවැදැල්ල, *Mí-wedella*, *s.* bee hive; honey-comb.

මුංමා, *Muṇmá*, *s.* deceit.

මුංමාකොට, *Muṇmákoṭa*, *s.* having deceived.

මුංයුස, *Muṇyusa*, *s.* pease porridge, pease soup; water in which *phaseolus mungo* has been boiled.

මුංවන්, *Muṇwan*, *a.* having the colour of මුං *muṇ*, *phaseolus mungo*, or green gram.

මුග්ගරය, *Muggaraya*, *s.* club: see මුගුර *mugura.*

මුට්ටය, *Muṭṭaya*, *s.* a bag of rice containing about two bushels.

මුඩුසෙවෙනි, *Muḍuseweni*, *s.* house without a roof on it.

මුත්තිකා, *Muttiká*, *s.* pearl oyster, [Colloq. මුතු බෙල්ලා *mutu-bellá*].

මුතනය, *Mutanaya*, *s.* bulbous plant or grass used medicinally, *cyperus rotundus*, [Colloq. කලාඳුරු *kaláṇduru*].

මුද්දය, *Muddáya*, *s.* tree, *nephelium longanum*, [Colloq. මොර *mora*].

මුදුන්දි, *Mudundí*, *part.* placing on the head.

මුදුන්මල්කඩක්, *Mudunmalkaḍak*, *s.* chaplet of flowers worn on the top of the head.

මුදුන්මිණ, *Mudunmiṇa*, *s.* gem on the top of a crown.

මුදුනෙන් පිළිගන්නවා, *Mudunen-piḷigannawá*, *v.* to receive on the top of the head, *i. e.* respectfully.

මුදුනෙන් පිළිගෙණ, *Mudunen-piligena*, past participal of above.

මුබ, *Muba*, *s.* this way, here; (pron. sec. pers. sing.) you.

මුල්ග්‍රන්ථය, *Mul-granthaya*, *s.* original composition. text.

මුවදොර, *Muwadora*, *s.* mouth of a river, place where a river disembogues, [Colloquial: මෝය *móya*].

මුවනොසෑහෙණසේ, *Muwa-noséhenasé*, *s.* unspeakably, words being insufficient to express.

මුවෙන්, *Muwen*, *s.* with the mouth.

මුස්තක, *Mustaka*, *s.* fragrant grass, *cyperus rotundus*, [Colloq. කලාඳුරු *kalánduru*].

මුසල්, *Musal*, see මුෂල *mushala*.

මුහුල, *Muhula*, *s.* hair: see also, මූනමල් *múnamal*.

මූදුපරගානාසේ, *Múduparagánásé*, *adv.* like the roaring of the sea.

මූදුබත්වූහ, *Múdubatwúha*, *v.* they became a prey to the sea, *i. e.* they were drowned in the sea.

මූදුලුණු, *Múdu-lunu*, *s.* sea salt.

මූදෙවියා, *Múdeviyá*, *s.* miserable-looking man, one whose sight is disagreeable, (used in the Galle district).

මූර්තිමත්, *Múrtimat*, *a.* material; substantial, having shape or form; incarnate.

මූර්ති රහිතවූ, *Múrti-rahitawú*, *a.* void of form or shape; immaterial.

මූලඝාතන, *Múlaghátana*, *s.* eradicating, utter distruction.

මූලභාෂා, *Múlabháshá*, *s.* the original language, [Colloq. පාලිභාසාව *páli-bhásáwa*].

මූලාඞ්කය, *Múlánkaya*, *s.* factor (in Arithmetic, and Algebra).

මූලෝච්ඡින්න, *Múlóchchhinna*, *a.* utterly destroyed, altogether cut off.

මෙතුට, *Metuta*, *s.* peacock.

මෙහෙණිසස්න, *Meheni-sasna*, *s.* nunnery, college of priestesses or nuns.

මෙහෙයම්, *Meheyam*, *v.* to command, to direct, to drive, to dispatch.

මේ ඇන්නෑවක්, *Mé-ennéwak*, *a.* phrase meaning "what a bore or nuisance is this"! "this is very annoying."

මේකරු, *Mékaru*, *s.* servant, cook.

මේනිමවනවා, *Mé-nimawanawá*, *v.* to take meals, to eat (used respectfully).

මේල්, *Mél*, *s.* clerk, writer.

මෛත්‍රීනිවාස, *Maitri-nivása*, *s.* abode of mercy or benevolence.

මොට්ටකරණවා, *Mottakaranawá*, *v.* to make blunt.

මොබ, *Moba*, *adv.* here, this way, [Colloq. මෙහි *mehi*].

මොරපුටු, *Moraputu*, *s.* easy chair formed in the shape of peacock's tail.

මොහඳුර, *Mohandura*, *s.* darkness of ignorance.

*මොහොට්ටාල, *Mohottála*, *s.* Clerk.

මොහොට්ටි නිලේ, *Mohotti-nilé*, *s.* post of Clerk.

මොහොර, *Mohora*, *s.* (මහ *maha*+උර *ura*) great rampart=මහාප්‍රාකාරය *mahá-prákáraya*.

මෝචි, *Móchi*, *s.* medicine prepared from the refuse of the seeds of the *bassia longifolia*, after the oil has been expressed, [Colloq. මිවුරුවට *mímuruwata*].

මෝහෝද්භූත, *Móhódbhúta*, *a.* caused by ignorance.

මෞර්‍ය්‍යවංශ, *Maurya-wansa*, *s.* Mayurya race.

මැදුවන්, *Meduwan*, *s.* straw.

මැදකන්න, *Meda-kanna*, *s.* middle crop or harvest, between the යල *yala* and මහ *maha* seasons.

ය

යකෙස් බිජු, *Yakes-biju*, *s.* seed of the *cæsalpinia bonduc*, [Colloq. කුඹුරුඇට *kumburueta*].

යකුන්නැටීම, *Yakun-netima*, *s.* devil ceremony at which certain persons dance to propitiate a malignant demon.

යටත්පිරිසෙයින්, *Yatatpiriseyin*, *adv.* at the bottom end as far down as.

යථාර්ථ, *Yathártha*, *adv.* according to the sense: *adj.* right, proper.

යදමින්මසා, *Yadamin-masá*, *part.* having fastened with iron chains.

යන්ත්‍රාගාරය, *Yantrágáraya*, *s.* machinery house, as a Printing Office, sewing machine, etc.

යනුවෙන්, *Yanuwen*,=යනුකිහෙයින් *yanu-kíheyin*. *s.* as it is so said.

යමහල, *Yama-hala*, *s.* (යම Yama, regent of the death, and හල house) house or abode of Yama, Indian Pluto.

යවට, *Yawata*, *s.* (ය iron, වට ball) ball of iron, [Colloq. යකඩ ගුලිය *yakada-guliya*].

යවදානි, *Yawadáni*, see යවධාන්‍යක *yawadhányaka*.

යාකරණවා, *Yákaranawá*, *v.* to annex, to attach or adjoin.

යාගු, *Yágu*, *s.* rice gruel, decoction, congee, [Colloq. කැඳ *kenda*].

යුගකන්, *Yugakan*, *s.* two ears.

යුගදල, *Yugadala*, *s.* mountain ebony, *bauhinia purpurea*, [Colloq. කොබලිල *kobalila*].

යුද්ධභූමිය, *Yuddha-bhúmiya*, *s.* field of battle.

යුද්ධෝන්මත්තව, *Yuddhónmattawa*, *part.* being maddened or infuriated for war.

යෙත්, *Yet*, *v.* they say.

යෙදෙනසේ, *Yedenasé*, *adv.* as fit, according to circumstances.

යෙමි, *Yemi*, *v.* I say; I go.

යෙලයාලක්, *Yelayálak*, *s.* one and a half යාල *yála* or thirty Amunams of grain.

යොත්ත, *Yotta*, *s.* wooden trough for baling water with a long handle.

යොන්හිඳි, *Yonhiṇdi*, see යොන් ඉඳි *yon-iṇdi*.

යොහොඹු, *Yohombu*, *s.* species of jasmine, *jasminum sambac*, [Colloq. පිච්චමල් *pichchamal*].

ර

රජතමය, *Rajatamaya*, *a.* made of silver, silvery.

රජදත්, *Rajadat*, *s.* upper and fore-tooth, applied to the two middle ones.

රට්ටු, *Raṭṭu*, *s.* foreigners, outsiders, strangers.

රණපණ්ඩිතයා, *Raṇa-paṇḍitayá*, *s.* skilful warrior.

රණබිජු, *Raṇa-biju*, *s.* seed of the *cassia auriculata*, [Colloq. රණවරා ඇට *raṇawará-eṭa*].

රණබිම, *Raṇa-bima*, *s.* field of battle, [Colloq. යුද්ධ භූමිය *yuddha-bhúmiya*].

රණභේරි, *Raṇa-bhéri*, *s.* war-drum.

රත්නමාලි චෛත්‍යය, *Ratnamáli-chaityaya*, *s.* name of a Buddhist dágaba, commonly called රුවන් වැලි සෑය *ruwanweli-séya*.

රත්පොඩි, *Ratpoḍi*, *s.* vermillion, [Colloq. සාදිලිංගම් *sádiliṅgam*].

රතනාගාර, *Ratanágára*, *s.* house where gems are deposited.

රතැඹුල, *Ratembula*, *s.* species of water lily, *nymphœa lotus*.

රතැස්දර, *Ratesdara*, *s.* one who has red eyes, devil in general.

රන්ධ්‍රගවේෂී, *Randhragawéshí*, *s.* one who hunts for the faults of others.

රන්සැත්, *Ranseṭ*, *s.* golden caparison.

රම්බා, *Rambá*, *s.* plantain, one of the apsaras or courtezans of Swarga.

රව්හිණ, *Rawhina*, *s.* god, planet Mercury, [Colloq. බුදහු *budahu*].

රවිකිඤ්ඤෙ, *Ravikiññe*, *s.* violin, (Portuguese or Dutch).

රසඳුන්, *Rasaṇdun*, *s.* sort of collyrium, prepared either with the calx of brass, or with the *amonium anthorrhiza*.

රසාස්වාද, *Rasáswáda*, *s.* enjoyment of taste, [Colloq. රසවිඳීම *rasaviṇdíma*].

රාක්ෂසී, *Rákshasí*, *s.* female demon, female imp.

රාගනිශ්‍රිත, *Rága-nisríta*, *a.* calculated to excite sensual desire.

රාජපූජ්‍යය, *Rája-pújyaya*, *a.* worthy of being honored by kings.

රාජාගාර, *Rájágára*, *s.* royal mansion.

රාජාරාම, *Rájaráma*, *s.* royal garden or park.

රාමඩුලු, *Rámaḍulu*, *s.* place where toddy is sold, tavern.

රාමසුත, *Rámasuta*, *s.* assafœtida, [Colloq. පෙරුංකායම් *peruṅkáyam*].

රාමුව, *Rámuwa*, *s.* frame of wooden work.

රාමුවා, *Rámuwá*, *s.* kind of large sea fish.

රාවය, *Ráwaya*, *s.* sound, noise.

රාවරය, *Ráwaraya*, *s.* moisture.

රාශි ගණන, *Rási-gaṇana*, *s.* proportion.

රික්වෙස්ට්නඩුසාලාව, *Rikweṣṭ-naḍusáláwa*, *s.* Court of Requests.

* රිදී, *Ridí*, *s.* washer-woman.

රිදීකල, *Ridíkala*, *s.* washer-woman, (Kávyasékhara).

රිවි ඉරමසු, *Rivi-iramasu*, *s.* twining shrub with bitter roots, *aristolochia indica*, [Colloq. සප්සඳ *sapsaṇda*].

රීරු, *Ríru*, *s.* that which has glided.

රුප්පා, *Ruppá*, *s* shade, grove.

රුපු අනඟ, *Rupu-ananga*, *s.* enemy of Cupid epithet of Íṣwara, who is more commonly called Ṣiva.

රුපු අසුර, *Rupu-asura*, *s.* enemy of the titans epithet of Vishṇu.

රෙදිපෙරෙදි, *Rediperedi*, *s.* clothes.

රේඛා ගණිතශාස්ත්‍රය, *Rékhá-gaṇitaṣástraya*, *s.* Geometry.

රේගුව, *Beguwa*, *s.* custom-house.

රෝමරාජිකා, *Rómarájiká*, } *s.* line of hair extending to the navel.
රෝමරාජි, *Rómarájí*, }

රෝහිතමත්ස්‍ය, *Róhita-matsya*, *s.* fish of the carp tribe: see ලේලු *lélu*.

රුස්, *Reṣ*, *s.* rays.

රුස්පිරිස්නැති, *Reṣpiris-neṭi*, *a.* reckless, (vulgar).

රේකණ, *Rékuṇá*, *s.* one who is blind at night.

රූපානේ *Répáné*, *s.* night time.

ල

ලක්‍ෂපුස්නා, *Laksha-pusná*. *a.* worth a lac,=ලක්‍ෂයක් වටින *lakshayak-waṭina*.

ලකවැල, *Lakawęla*, *s.* rosary.

ලගණහු, *Laganahu*, *s.* those who take lodgings.

ලගුළ, *Laguḷa*, *s.* a fighting club.

ලඝුකොට, *Laghukoṭa*, *part.* considering it to be a trifling matter; treating lightly.

ලඝුතර, *Laghutara*, *a.* very small, light, or trifling.

ලට්ට, *Laṭṭa*, *s.* kind of tree, commonly known as මී *mí*, (*Bassia longifolia*).

ලදරු පිරිමි, *Ladaru-pirimi*, *s.* male children, young men.

ලදින්, *Ladin*,=ලැබ *lęba*, *part.* having received.

ලන්තන, *Lantana*, *s.* a plant, commonly called ගඳපාන *gandapána*, which see.

ලප්, *Lap*, *s.* mark, stain.

ලබුසා, *Labusá*, *s.* pumpkin.

ලවග, *Lawaga*, *s.* forest on fire, conflagration of a forest; wood on fire.

ලවණත, *Lawaṇata*, *s.* lips, (sometimes written ලවනත *lawanata*).

ලවණස්තම්බය, *Lawaṇastambaya*, *s.* pillar of salt, [Colloq. ලුණුකණුව *luṇukaṇuwa*].

ලස්නොවි, *Lasnoví*, *part.* not being idle, slow, or lazy.

ළුරට, *Laḷu-raṭa*, *s.* a country in India, more commonly called ලාඩදේශය *láḍa-désaya*.

ලාක්‍ෂණික, *Lákshaṇika*, *a.* technical.

ලාකිරි. *Lákiri*, see ලාකඩ *lákaḍa*.

ලානය, *Lánaya*, *s.* (ලා to take) act of taking, [Colloq. ගැණීම *gęníma*].

ලාබාල, *Lábála*, *a.* tender and young, infantile.

ලාවන්, *Láwan*, *s.* leeches, [Colloq. කුඩැල්ලෝ *kúḍęlló*].

ලාහෙලා, *Láhelá*, *adv.* quickly, forcibly.

ලිපිදෝෂ, *Lipidósha*, *s.* clerical errors.

ලිම්පිත, *Limpita*, *a.* anointed, smeared with.

ලියකොමල, *Liyakomala*, *a.* soft like a creeper.

ලෙන් ඇනි, *Len-ęni*, *part.* having run through the heart, as a weapon used by an enemy.

ලේකැන්, *Lékęn*, *s.* large quantity of blood.

ලේඛන චර්ම, *Lékhana-charma*, *s.* skin on which to write, [Colloq. ලියනහම් *liyana-ham*].

ලේඛනාගාරය, *Lékhanágáraya*, *s.* office where one writes.

ලොටතන, *Loṭatana*, *s.* tender paps.

ලොත්ගස, *Lot-gasa*, see ලොත්සුඹුල *lotsumbula*.

ලොව්තුරා, *Lowturá*, *a.* eminent in the world, epithet of Buddha, as opposed to පසේබුදුන් *Pasé Budun*, a secondary or inferior Buddha.

ලෝකයා, *Lókayá*, *s.* the world, meaning the inhabitants of the world, people in general.

ලෝකුඹුනිරේ, *Lókumbu-niré*, *s.* a hell so called.

ලෝකේශ්වර, *Lókéṣwara*, *s.* (ලෝක *lóka*+ඊශ්වර *íṣwara*) chief of the world.

ලෝකෝද්භවය, *Lókódbhawaya*, *s.* origin of the world.

ලෝපල්ලා, *Lópallá*, *s.* king, sovereign, [Colloq. රජ *raja*].

ලැමද, *Lęmada*, *s.* bosom, breast.

ලැවි, *Lęvi*, *s.* archer, bowman.

ව

වංකොස්, *Waṅkos*, *s.* very young jack fruit, commonly called පොලොස් *polos*.

වක්තව්‍ය, *Waktawya*, *adj.* fit to be said, [Colloq. කියයුත්ත *kiyayutta*].

වක්තෘ, *Waktṛi*, *s.* speaker.

වකගසනවා, *Wakagasanawá*, *v.* to bend, to make crooked; to gather up the limbs, [Colloq. වකුටු කරණවා *wakuṭukaraṇawá*].

වගාකරණවා, *Wagákaraṇawá*, *v.* to improve as a plantation, to cure a disease.

වගාව, *Wagáwa*, *s.* plantation, planted portion of land.

වගුතුවෙනවා, *Wagutuwenawá*, *v.* to thrive, to be successful, to improve.

වජ්‍රබුද්ධි, *Wajra-buddhi*, *s.* one who has an intellect as sharp as diamond; one of sharp intellect.

වජිරත, *Wajirata*, *s.* god Ṣakra.

* වට, *Waṭa*, *s.* ball as in යවට *yawaṭa*, [Colloq. ගුලිය *guliya*].

වටදාගෙය, *Waṭadágeya*, *s.* circular relic-house.

වටා, *Waṭá*, *adv.* around, having surrounded, [Colloq. වටකර *waṭakara*]: *part.* having ground or pounded.

වතක්, *Watak*, *v.* a custom or ceremony, [Colloq. සිරිතක් *siritak*].

වතුරණ, *Waturaṇa*, *s.* cloth spread as a carpet.

වන්ටය, *Wanṭaya*, *s.* stalk of a flower or fruit, [Colloq. නැට්ට *neṭṭa*].

වන්නාට, *Wannáṭa*, *adv.* be it so; let be.

වනපොත්, *Wanapot*, *s.* committing to memory.

වයෝකල්‍යාණ, *Wayókalyáṇa*, *s.* one of the five perfections of a woman, perpetual or unfading youth, appearing as if she had borne only one child, although mother of ten children.

වර්ගබන්ධන, *Wargabandhana*, *s.* coming together as a flock of birds, etc.

වරහමිහිර, *Warahamihira*, *s.* a philosopher so called.

වල්ලිබ, *Walliba*, *s.* a kind of pumpkin.

වලත, *Walata*, *s.* skirts of a forest or jungle, [Colloq. වනාන්තරය *wanántaraya*].

වලද, *Walada*, *s.* a spot.

වලයබරණ, *Walayabaraṇa*, *s.* bracelet, armlet, [Colloq. වළල්ල *walalla*].

වලාඉදු, *Waláidu*, *s.* thunder.

වලාපරාටියා, *Waláparáṭiyá*, *s.* kind of sea fish.

වලාපිය, *Walápiya*, *v.* evaded.

වසන්තභද්‍ර, *Wasantabhadra*, *s.* Indian cuckoo or kókila.

* වසම, *Wasama*, *s.* division of a district over which a headman is placed.

වසවෙනවා, *Wasawenawá*, *v.* to turn out to be a poison.

වසාරාජිකා, *Wasárájiká*, see වසාරොද *wasároda*.

වසුච්ඡිද්‍රා, *Wasuchchhidrá*, *s.* common bamboo, *bambusa vulgaris*, [Colloq. උණගස් *uṇagas*].

වසුන්පියන, *Wasun-piyana* *s.* lid placed over pots containing a pingo-load of rice.

වහන්දෑ, *Wahandẹ́*,=වහන්සේලා, *wahansélá*, *s.* an honorific mode of addressing Buddhist priests.

වහල්හබය, *Wahal-habaya*, *s.* king's court.

වහිර්වෘද්ධ, *Wahirwṛiddha*, *s.* growing from without, exogenous.

වාක්‍යප්‍රසංගය, *Wákya-prasangaya*, *s.* connected language or discourse, connected reasoning or argument.

වාක්‍යයෝජනා, *Wákya-yójaná*, *s.* construction of a sentence.

වාග්ඩම්බරය, *Wágḍambaraya*, *s.* graceful or eloquent language.

වාග්දණ්ඩනය, *Wágdaṇḍanaya*, *s.* reproof, reprimand; restraint or control of speech.

වාග්දේවතාවා, *Wágdéwatáwá*, *s.* the god of language, Vṛihaspati.

වාග්දේවී, *Wágdévi*, *s.* name of Saraṣwati, goddess of speech.

වාග්මාත්‍ර, *Wág-mátra*, *s.* mere speech, words alone.

වාග්ව්‍යවහාරය, *Wágwyawaháraya*, *s.* use of words.

වාග්ව්‍යාපාර, *Wágwyápára*, *s.* manner, style or habit of speaking, customary phraseology.

වාගීශ්වර, *Wágíṣwara*, *s.* orator, learned man.

වාජි, *Wáji*, *s.* a sort of plant, *(physalis floxuosa)*; *Withania somnifera*, [Colloq. අමුක්කරා *amukkará*].

වාඩිහාල්, *Wáḍi-hál*, *s.* rice pounded, (a term used in harvest time), [Colloq. හබලපෙති *habala-peti*].

වාතකී, *Wátakí*, *s.* species of night shade, *solanum Xanthocarpum*, [Colloq. එලබටු *elabaṭu*].

වාතිනි, *Wátini*, *s.* sun flower, [Colloq. සූර්යකාන්ති *súryakánti*].

වානප්‍රස්ථ, *Wána-prastha*, *s.* wild sapota tree, *bassia longifolia*, [Colloq. මීගහ *mí-gaha*].

වාරිමුල්, *Wárimul*, see හාටාවාරිය *hátáwáriya*.

වාලහන්, *Wálahan*, *s.* one-seventh of the produce of a paddy field given to those who are employed in reaping and threshing the corn.

වාසිබැණ, *Wásibẹṇa*, *part.* having boasted, defied, or challenged.

වාසිලනවා, *Wásilanawá*, *v.* to threaten, to boast, to bray.

වාසිලබනවා, *Wásilabanawá*, *v.* to get an advantage or superiority.

විකෙව්, *Vikew*, *s.* confusion perplexity, fear proceeding from ignorance or error, [Colloq. සැකය *sẹkaya.*]

විඛ්‍යාත, *Vikhyáta*, *a.* known, notorious, famous avowed, confessed, [Colloq. ප්‍රසිද්ධ *prasiddha*].

විචාරවිද්‍යාව, *Vichára-vidyáwa*, *s.* science of reasoning or logic, [Colloq. තර්කශාස්ත්‍රය *tarka-sástraya*]

විජම්පෙල, *Vijam-pela*,= අභිධර්මපාඨ *abhidharma páṭha*, *s.* text of the Abhidharma Piṭaka.

විඩව්, *Viḍaw*, *s.* fissure.

විතාන, *Vitána*, විතානරාල, *Vitánarála*, විතාරණ, *Vitáraṇa*, } *s.* one of the four village headmen under the Dutch, forming village council, the other three were ගමරාල *gamarála* පතිරන්නැහෙ *patirannẹhe*, මන්නාහෙ *mannahe*

විද්වජ්ජන, *Vidwajjana*, *s.* learned persons.

විද්‍යාධ්වජ, *Vidyádhwaja*, *s.* one who has knowledge for his flag, standard bearer of knowledge; one eminent for his learning.

විද්‍යුල්ලතා, *Vidyullatá*, *s.* creeping plant with handsome flowers, *gloriosa superba*, [Colloq. නියගලා *niyangalá*].

විදානදුරයා, *Vidána-durayá*, *s.* headman of the Paduwá caste.

විදානහේනයා, *Vidána-hénayá*, *s.* headman of the Washer caste in the Kandyan country.

විත්න, *Vinna*, *s.* grove (Skt. වන්‍ය *wanya*), as in කොස්විත්න *kosvinna*, නාවිත්න *návinna*, names of villages, so called probably from the large number of jack, or ironwood trees, etc. found in them.

විප්‍රලම්භ, *Vipralambha*, *s.* disappointing or deceiving by a false affirmative or by not keeping a promise; separation, especially of lovers; disunion, quarrel.

විභවානුරූපයෙන්, *Vibhawánurúpayen*, *adv.* according to one's wealth or ability.

විභීෂණ, *Vibhísana*, *s.* brother of Rávaṇa.

වියොලේ, *Viyolé*, *s.* violin, fiddle. (Dutch.)

විලිකුන්කදලි, *Vilikun-kadali*, *s.* ripe plantain.

විලොල, *Vilola*, *a.* shaking, tremulous, unsteady.

විශ්‍රාමශාලාව, *Viṣráma-ṣáláwa*, *s.* rest-house, inn, caravansera.

විශ්ලේෂ, *Viṣlésha*, *s.* separation of lovers, disunion; disjunction.

විශ්වාස උච්චාරණය, *Viṣwása-uchcháraṇaya*, *s.* the Creed.

විශ්වේශ, *Viṣweṣa*, } *s.* lord of the world,
විශ්වේශ්වර, *Viṣwéṣwara*, } [Colloq. ලෝක නායක *lóka-náyaka*].

විශාලා, *Viṣálá*, *s.* city Oujein; kind of cucumber, large variety of the *cucumis pubescens*, [Colloq. මහගොන්කැකිරි *maha-gonkẹkiri*].

විශීර්ණ, *Viṣírṇa*, *a.* dried up, withered, wasted, impaired, decayed.

විශුද්ධ ලවණ, *Viṣuddha-lawaṇa*, *s.* very pure salt.

විශේෂාර්ථය, *Viṣésharthaya*, *s.* special meaning, peculiar sense.

විෂමභාගය, *Visamubhágaya*, *s.* improper fraction.

විස්ක්‍රිඤ්ඤ, *Viskriñña*, *s.* small biscuits.

විසදෘශ, *Visadṛiṣa*, *a.* unlike, dissimilar.

විසිත්ත, *Visitta*, *s.* visit. (Eng.)

විසිත්තකාමරේ, *Visitta-kámaré*, *s.* drawing room.

විසිත්තෙයනවා, *Visitte-yanawá*, *v.* to go on a visit.

විළඞ්ග, *Viḷaṅga*, *s.* climbing anthelmintic shrub, *erycibe paniculata*, [Colloq. වලඟසාල් *walaṅga-sál*].

විබදු අරච්චි, *Vibadu-árachchi*, *s.* an Árachchi attached to the paddy-tax department.

විබදු ලේකම, *Vibadu-lékama*, *s.* a writer of the paddy waṭṭóru.

වෙදමවු, *Weda-mawu*, see වංඇපල *waṇ-ẹpala*.

වෙදහල්, *Wedahal*, *s.* medical hall, hospital.

වෙන්කත, *Wenkata*, *s.* Ṣrí, wife of Vishṇu, [Colloq. ශ්‍රීකාන්තාව *ṣrikántáwa*].

වෙනදා, *Wenadá*, *adv.* on other days, usually.

වෙල්දුරයා, *Welduraya*, *s.* Irrigation headman of the low caste.

වෙල්මුඩ, *Welmuḍa*, see මුඩමහණ *muḍamahaṇa*.

වෙල්විදානේ, *Wel-vidáné*, *s.* Irrigation headman.

වේදසාක්ෂිකයා, *Wédasákshikayá*, *s.* Martyr.

වේරම්භවාතය, *Wérambha-wátaya*, *s.* wind blowing one yoduna above, or blowing from the four quarters.

වේලවීම, *Wélavíma*, *s.* causing to dry up.

වෛතුල්‍යවාදි, *Waitulyawádi*, *s.* Buddhist schismatics, who held heterodox opinions.

වැණිගිය, *Wẹṇigiya*, *a.* shaken.

වැයික්කිය, *Wẹyikkiya*, *s.* division or district over which an officer has jurisdiction.

වැලිගල, *Wẹli-gala*, *s.* sand-stone.

වැවුම්කැරය, *Wẹwumkẹraya*, *s.* planting voucher.

ව්‍යවස්ථාදායක, *Wyawasthádáyaka*, *a.* enacting laws.

ව්‍යවස්ථානුරූප, *Wyawasthánurúpa*, *a.* conformable to law, legal.

ව්‍යාකුලීකෘත, *Wyákulíkṛita*, *a.* confused, confounded, bewildered.

ව්‍යාඝ්‍රතල, *Wyághratala*, } *s.* plant from the
ව්‍යාඝ්‍රනඛ, *Wyághranakha*, } fibres of which bow strings are made, *sanseviera zeylanica*, [Colloq. නියඳ *niyaṇḍa*].

ව්‍යාපාර, *Wyápára*, *s.* trade, business, occupation.

ව්‍යාපාරයා, *Wyáparayá*, *s.* trader, merchant.

වෘක්ෂලතාවිද්‍යා, *Wrikshalatá-vidyá*, *s.* Botany.

ශ

ශකට, *Ṣakaṭa*, *s.* car or carriage, [Colloq. කරත්තය *karattaya*].

ශබ්දශාස්ත්‍රඥ, *Ṣabda-ṣástrañja*, *s.* one acquainted with verbal science or grammar.

ශබ්දානුසාරයෙන්, *Ṣabdánusárayen*, *s.* in conformity with or in accordance with the sound.

ශබ්දාලංකාරය, *Ṣabdálaṅkáraya*, *s.* elegance of words or language, rhetoric, ornaments of speech.

ශරභපර්‍යඞ්ක, *Ṣarabha-paryaṅka*, *s.* a chair or bed like a ශරභ *ṣarabha*, grass-hopper.

ශරච්චන්ද්‍ර, *Ṣarachchandra*, *s.* moon in autumn.

ශරීරය, *Ṣaríraya*, *s.* the body.

ශශලාඤ්ඡන, *Ṣaṣa-láñchhana*, *s.* monk, or likeness of a hare.

ශාරීරික, *Ṣárírika*, *a.* bodily, corporeal.

ශාලිගෝපිකා, *Ṣáligópiká*, *s.* protectress of a field of rice, female watcher of a héna cultivated with ẹl-ví.

ශිරෝවිරේචන, *Ṣiró-viréchana*, *s* cleansing and cooling the head by medicinal applications.

ශිලාලේඛනය, *Ṣilálékhanaya*, *s.* inscription on a stone.

ශිෂ්ටාචාර, *Ṣishṭáchára*, *s.* good or refined manners, civility, politeness.

ශිෂ්‍යානුශිෂ්‍ය පරම්පරාව, *Ṣishyánuṣishya-paramparáwa*, *s.* succession from pupil to pupil of a Buddhist priest, pupillary succession.

ශුද්ධගිනිස්ථානය, *Ṣuddhaginisthánaya*, *s.* purgatory. (R. C.)

ශුෂ්කා, *Ṣushká*, *s.* foam of the sea [Colloq. මුදු පෙන *múdu-pena*].

ශූන්‍යාක්ෂර, *Ṣúnyákshara*, *s.* empty letters, letters which are mere cyphers or useless.

ශ්‍රවණයකරණවා, *Ṣrawaṇaya-karaṇawá*, *v.* to hear.

ශ්‍රවා, *Ṣrawá*, *s.* plant, *marsdenia tenacissima*, [Colloq. මුරුවාදුල් *muruwádúl*].

ස

සංක්ෂිප්ත, *Sankshipta*, *a.* contracted, abridged, concise, compressed, abbreviated.

සංකේත, *Sankéta*, *s.* gesture, sign, gesticulation; agreement; engagement.

සක්කායදිට්ඨි, *Sakkáyadiṭṭhi*, *s.* believing that man has a soul, delusion of self.

සක්‍රමේන්තුව, *Sakraméntuwa*, *s.* Sacrament. (Eng.)

සකසුරුවම්, *Sakasuruwam*, *s.* economy.

සකිල, *Sakila*, *s.* thriving.

සඞ්කලන, *Sankalana*, *s.* heaping as corn, etc.; addition (in arithmetic).

සඤ්චිත, *Sañchita*, *a.* collected, assembled, gathered, accumulated, [Colloq. රැස්කළ *reskaḷa*].

සඤ්ඤත, *Saññata*, *a.* checked, restrained, controlled, bound, (Páli form of Sanskrit සංයත *saṇyata*).

සජ්ඣායනා, *Sajjháyaná*, *s.* reading, recital, (Páli).

සටවක, *Saṭawaka*, which is sometimes written සැට වක *seṭawaka*, *s.* sixth day of a lunar fortnight.

සත්කර්මය, *Satkarmaya*, *s.* Sacrament.

සත්ප්‍රසාදය, *Satprasádaya*, *s.* Sacrament of the Lord's Supper. (R. C.)

සත්‍යාතික්‍රාමිකවූ, *Satyátikrámikawú*, *a.* transgressing the truth; overstepping the bounds of credibility.

සත්වවිද්‍යා, *Satwavidyá*, *s.* zoology.

සතරපූර්වනිමිති, *Satarapúrwa-nimiti*, *s.* the four signs seen by prince Siddhárttha which induced him to renounce house-hold life and embrace a life of asceticism with a view to attaining Buddhahood, viz. sight of an old decrepit man, a man suffering from disease, a dead man, and an ascetic.

සතරමහභූතයෝ, *Sataramaha-bhútayó*, *s.* the four great elements, viz. fire, air, earth, and water.

සද්ගුණ, *Sadguna*, *s.* good quality, virtue.

සදාචාර, *Sadáchára*, *s.* good conduct.

සදාස්ථායිවූ, *Sadásthayiwú*, *a.* everlasting.

සඳවත්, *Saṇdawat*, *s.* moon faced, fair faced.

සන්තාන පත්‍රය, *Santána-patraya*, *s.* articles of convention entired into between the Kandyan chiefs and the British Government on the acquisition of the Kandyan territories.

සන්තානවෙනවා, *Santánawenawá*, *v.* to make peace with.

සන්නිපාත උණ, *Sannipáta-uṇa*, *s.* Typhoid fever.

සනිප පුටුව, *Sanipa-puṭuwa*, *s.* easy chair.

සප්තබෞද්ධාඞ්ගධර්මය, *Saptabauddhánga-dharmaya*, *s.* (සප්ත seven, බෞද්ධ *bauddha* Buddhist, අංග *anga* qualification or attainment, ධර්ම *dharma* duty or religious practice) viz. 1. සමාධි *samádhi*, 2. සති *sati*, 3. ප්‍රීති *príti*, 4. පචද්ධි *pañchaddhi*, 5. විරිය *viriya*, 6. ධම්මවිචය *dhamma-vichaya*, 7. උපෙක්ඛා *upekkhá*.

සප්තවිධරත්නය, *Saptavidha-ratnaya*, *s.* the seven gems or treasures of a Chakrawarti king, viz. chariot wheel, wife, jewel, elephant, horse, son, prime minister.

සප්තාඞ්ග, *Saptánga*, *s.* the seven attributes or requisites of a kingdom, viz. the king, the minister, an ally, treasure, territory, fortress, and an army.

සපිනි, *Sapíni*, *s.* sort of bindweed, *ipomœa tridentata*, [Colloq. අපසුමඩු *ápasu-madu*].

සබුක්කුව, *Sambukkuwa*, *s.* whip.

සම්පජාන මුසාවාදය, *Sampajána-musáwádaya*, *s.* a deliberate lie.

සම්බාහාල්, *Sambá-hál*, *s.* a white superior kind of rice, *oryza sativa*.

සම්මාන, *Sammána*, *s.* respect, homage; measure.

සම්මාර්ජන, *Sammárjana*, *s.* sweeping, brushing, clearing.

සම්වරු, *Samwaru*, see සොම්මාර *sommára*.

සමකාලික, *Samakálika*, *s.* contemporary.

සමන්වාගෙණ, *Samanwágeṇa*, *part.* having brought under subjection.

සමරමැටි, *Samarameṭi*, *s.* kind of clay, used as a yellow paint.

සමරේඛාව, *Sama-rékháwa*, *s.* parallel line.

සමස්ත ශාස්ත්‍රශාලාව, *Samasta-ṣástra-ṣáláwa*, *s.* University.
සමාන්තර, *Samántara*, *s.* having the same intermediate space, as parallel lines.
සමානකම, *Samánakama*, *s.* equality.
සමානජාතිත්වය, *Samána-játitwaya*, *s.* homogeneousness, similarity in kind.
සමුක්කාව, *Samukkáwa*, *s.* telescope.
සමුද්‍රකට, *Samudra-kaṭa*, *s.* creeping plant, *ipomœa pestigridis*, [Colloq. දිවිපහුරු *divipahuru*].
සමුද්‍රමජ්ජනය, *Samudra-majjanaya*, *s.* drowning or dipping in the sea.
සර්වදර්ශී, *Sarwadarṣi*, *a.* all seeing, omniscient.
සර්වබලධාරී, *Sarwabaladhári*, *a.* Almighty.
සර්වවල්ලම, *Sarwawallama*, *a.* Almighty.
සර්වවිද්‍යා සාගර, *Sarwavidyá-ságara*, *s.* ocean of all knowledge, one possessed of the whole circle of knowledge.
සර්වව්‍යාපී, *Sarwa-wyápí*, *a.* all pervading.
සර්වශක්ති, *Sarwa-ṣakti*, *s.* Almighty, an attribute given to God in Hindu theology.
සර්වෝපද්‍රව, *Sarwópadrawa*, *a.* all misfortunes, all afflictions.
සර්වෝපරිස්ථ, *Sarwóparistha*, *a.* (සර්ව *sarwa* all, උපරි *upari* over, ස්ථ *stha* standing) standing over all; supreme being.
සරදි, *Saradi*, *s.* tree, *alstonia* (or *echitis*) *scholaris*, [Colloq. රුක් අත්තන *ruk-attana*].
සරයන්, *Sarayan*, *s.* sergeant.
සරාගී, *Sarági*, *s.* one subject to lust, sensual, lascivious.
සරුවත්, *Saruwat*, *s.* sherbet.
සරෝවර, *Sarówara*, *s.* noble lake.
සලස්ම, *Salasma*, *s.* small tree, *cartæva Roxburghii*, or *c. religiosa*, [Colloq. ලුණුවරණ *luṇuwaraṇa*].
සලාගම, *Salágama*, *s.* another term for people of the Cháliya caste.
සලාම්, *Salám*, *s.* a salutation.
සලාරිස්, *Saláris*, *s.* commission allowed at a Fiscal's sale.
සවාරි, *Sawári*, *s.* drive as in a carriage.
සවෝදි, *Sawódi*, *s.* toast.
සවෝදිපුරණවා, *Sawódi-puraṇawá*, *v.* to propose a toast.
සවෝදිබොනවා, *Sawódi-bonawá*, *v.* to drink to one's health.
සස්ගාලා, *Sasgálá*, *s.* abruptly.
සළා වැටුම, *Saláwẹṭuma*, *s.* a whirlpool, [Colloq. වක්කලම *wakkalama*].

සාංවත්සරික, *Sáṅwatsarika*, *s.* yearly, anniversary.
සාංඛ්‍ය, *Sáṅkhya*, *s.* system of the philosophy founded by Kapila.
සාතන්, *Sátan*, *s.* Satan. (Eng.)
සාධා, *Sádhá*, *part.* having destroyed, as in "සතුරන් සාධා *satura sádhá*."
සාන්තවූ, *Sántawú*, *s.* Holy.
සාමාග්‍රී, *Sámágri*, *s.* union, fellowship, entirety, [Colloq. එකතුකම *ekatukama*].
සාරිබ, *Sáriba*, *s.* sarsaparilla, *hemidesmus indicus*, [Colloq. ඉරමසු *iramasu*].
සාවධාන, *Sáwadhána*, *a.* attentive.
සාවාලයා, *Sáwálayá*, *s.* kind of sea fish.
* සිංගි, *Siṅgi*, *s.* kind of poison.
සිංගිත්තා, *Siṅgittá*, *s.* the little one.
සිංහචර්මාච්ඡාදිත, *Siṅha-charmáchchhádita*, *a.* covered with the skin of a lion.
* සිකුරු, *Sikuru*, *a.* sure and certain, (Colloquial).
සිඤ්ඤෝ, *Siñño*, *s.* master. (Port.)
සිටුදේවි, *Siṭudéví*, *s.* wife of a nobleman, or of a wealthy man.
සිථිලය, *Sithilaya*, *s.* soft, as opposed to ධනිත *dhanita*, aspirated.
සිදාදි, *Sidádi*, *s.* city, town. (Port.)
සිදුබිජු, *Sidubiju*, *s.* mustard seed, *brassica juncea*, [Colloq. අබ *aba*].
සිඹගන්නවා, *Simbagannawá*, *v.* to kiss each other.
සියාවස, *Siyáwasa*, *s.* one of the lunar mansions.
සිරසනග්න, *Sirasa-nagna*, *a.* bare-headed.
සිරිපල, *Siripala*, *s.* tree, *ægle marmelos*, [Colloq. බෙලි *beli*].
සිල්වාරම, *Silwárama*, *s.* a little (of time or quantity.)
සිව්සයුරු, *Siwsayuru*, *s.* the four oceans.
සිසැරිම්, *Sisẹrim*, *s.* turning round, surrounding.
සිහින්එන්සාල්, *Sihin-ensál*, see සින්එන්සාල් *sin ensál*.
සිහින්බොග, *Sihin-bóga*, *s.* dry or fine grain.
සිනමුල්, *Sínamul*, *s.* china root, a medicinal root.
සිහපඤ්ජර, *Sihapañjara*, *s.* kind of window.
සුඛෝපදේශය, *Sukhópadéṣaya*, *s.* (සුඛ *sukha* health, උපදේශ *upadéṣa* advice) counsels about health, a book so called.
සුජාත, *Sujáta*, *a.* well born.
සුණුවම්, *Suṇuwam*, *s.* chunam work.
සුදවස්වැසි, *Sudawaswẹsi*, *s.* the dwellers of the Brahma world, called සුද්ධාවාස *suddháwása*.
සුදුකඳ, *Sudu-kanda*, *s.* plant, *ipomœa digitata*, [Colloq. කිරිබදු *kiribadu*].

සුදුවතුර, *Sudu-watura*, *s.* toddy, a term used during the time of harvest operations.

සුදුවා, *Suduwá*, *s.* chunam, a term used during the time of harvest operations.

සුන්තුරු, *Sunturu*, *s.* an axe.

සුප්‍රිම්උසාවිය, *Suprím-usáviya*, *s.* Supreme Court.

සුඹුළුව, *Sumbuluwa*, *s.* coil or roll of cloth used as a padding by the carrier of any load or weight, [Colloq. දරණුව *daranuwa*].

සුරතාවෝ, *Suratáwo*, } *s.* Angels. (R. C.)
සුරදූත, *Suradúta*, }

සුරුබුහුටි, *Surubuhuti*, *a.* of small make, slender; also, well-proportioned.

සුරුබුහුටිකම, *Surubuhutikama*, *s.* state of being well-made or well-proportioned.

සුරුවම්, *Suruwam*, *s.* images of Saints. (R. C.): *a.* economical, thrifty.

සුලුප්පුව, *Suluppuwa*, *s.* sloop.

සුලුපස්මුල, *Sulu-pasmula*, *s.* five minor roots, viz. species of night shade, *solanum Xanthocarpum*, [Colloq. එලබටු *ela-batu*]; *solanum jacquini*, [Colloq. කටුවැල්බටු *katuwelbatu*]; plant, *alyssicarpus bupleurifolius*, [Colloq. අස්වැන්න *aswenna*]; knot-grass, *œrua lanata* or *illecebrum lanatum*, [Colloq. පොල්පලා *polpalá*]; plant, *trebulus languinosus*, [Colloq. ගොකටු *gokatu*].

සුවිශේසකයෝ, *Suvisésakayó*, *s.* Evangelists.

සුවිශේසය, *Suvisésaya*, *s.* Gospel. (R. C.)

සුහුඹුල්, *Suhumbul*, *a.* growing luxuriantly.

සුහුරුබඩු, *Suhurubadu*, *s.* brother-in-law, [Colloq. මස්සිනා *massiná*].

සූර්‍ය්‍යතාපය, *Súrya-tápaya*, *s.* heat of the sun.

සූර්‍ය්‍යමාසය, *Súrya-másaya*, *s.* solar month.

සූරයා, *Súrayá*, *s.* a shrewd man, a cunning man.

සූසැට, *Súseta*, *s.* sixty four.

සෙක්‍රතාරිස්, *Sekratáris*, *s.* Secretary. (Eng.)

සෙනසුන්, *Senasun*, *s.* dwelling, residence, etc.

සෙබඩු, *Sebadu*, *s.* pea-hen, [Colloq. මොණරකිකිළි *monara-kikili*].

සෙල්මුවා, *Selmuwá*, *s.* made of stone, [Colloq. ගලින්කළ *galin-kala*].

සෙව්නා, *Sewná*, *a.* served or attended by.

සේකව, *Sékawa*, *adv.* cleverly, quickly.

සේවතුන්, *Séwatun*, *s.* maid-servants.

සේවාභට, *Séwábhata*, *s.* warrior, soldier.

සොකඩයා, *Sokadayá*, *s.* weak or feeble person.

සොකඩෙ, *Sokade*, *s.* clappers of bambu tied around the necks of cattle.

සෝපානපඞ්ක්ති, *Sópána-pańkti*, *s.* flight of steps, series of ladders, [Colloq. පඩිපෙළ *padipela*].

සෝමවංශ, *Sóma-wansa*, *s.* lunar dynasty.

සෝර්ති, *Sórti*, *s.* sorts.

සෑදලේ, *Sédalé*, *s.* saddle.

ස්ඛලිත, *Skhalita*, *a.* impeded, stumbled, obstructed.

ස්ත්‍යාන, *Styána*, *s.* dulness of the mind or body.

ස්ථවිරපාදයෝ, *Sthavirapádayó*, *s.* elderly Buddhist priest, worthy of being revered; venerable priest of Buddha. (the plural honorific form.)

ස්නාවක, *Snáwaka*, *s.* Baptist. (R. C.)

ස්පර්ධාකරණ, *Spardhákarana*, *a.* rivalling, vying, surpassing.

ස්ප්‍රිතුව, *Sprítuwa*, *s.* Spirit.

ස්ප්‍රිතුසාන්තු, *Spritu-sántu*, *s.* Holy Spirit. (R. C.)

ස්මරණාර්ථකචිහ්න, *Smaranárthaka-chihna*, *s.* mark for the sake of remembrance, memento.

ස්වප්නමාලේ, *Swapnamálé*, *s.* a book treating on dreams.

ස්වභාවික, *Swabhávika*, *s.* natural.

ස්වභාවෝක්ති, *Swabháwókti*, *s.* description of inherent attributes, specification of generic or specific qualities.

ස්වභාෂා, *Swabháshá*, *s.* one's own language, native language.

ස්වභාෂා ග්‍රන්ථය, *Swabháshá-granthaya*, *s.* work written in the native language.

ස්වයංනියුක්ත, *Swayanniyukta*, *s.* self appointed, self authorized.

ස්වයංභාෂණ, *Swayanbháshana*, *s.* soliloquy.

ස්වයම්භාවය, *Swayambháwaya*, *s.* self existence.

ස්වර්ගපතිත, *Swarga-patita*, *s.* (ස්වර්ග and පතිත fallen) fallen from heaven.

ස්වර්ගාපවර්ග, *Swargápawarga*, *s.* heaven and exemption from further transmigration.

ස්වරාන්ත ශබ්ද, *Swaránta-sabda*, *s.* (ස්වර *swara* vowel, අන්ත *anta* ending, ශබ්ද word) in grammar, noun that has its base ending in a vowel, as, සුර *sura*, god, මිතුරු *mituru* friend.

ස්වෙච්ඡාවෙන්, *Swechchháwen*, *adv.* of one's own free-will.

හ

හඟිනවා, *Hanginawá*, *v.* to think, to suppose.

හතරමංහන්දිය, *Hataraman-handiya*, *s.* place where four roads meet.

හතිකැක්කුම, *Hati-kekkuma*, *s.* shortness of breath, panting.

හඳහන්බැලීම, *Haṇdahan-bęlíma*, *s.* inspection of horoscopes.

* හන්, *Han*, *part.* of හඳිනවා *haṇdinawá*,=හඳනාලද *haṇdanálada*, or අඳිනාලද *aṇdinálada*, worn, put on as a garment.

හන්ද, *Handá*, particle, same as සන්ද *sandá*, on account of.

හන්දුරු, *Handuru*, *s.* caste so called, Vellála: see ගොයිගම *goyigama*.

හබකරණවා, *Habakaraṇawá*, *v.* to quarrel.

හබවෙනවා, *Habawenawá*, *v.* dispute arises.

හම්බාවා, *Hambáwá*, *s.* flying squirrel.

හයරිපු, *Hayaripu*, see හයරුපු *haya-rupu*.

හරක්ගාල, *Harak-gála*, *s.* cow-pen, fold for cattle.

හරය, *Haraya*, *s.* (in arithmetic) divisor, denominator of a fraction.

හරස්වුනා, *Haraswuná*, *v.* came across.

හරිය, *Hariya*, *s.* extent.

හරිහම්බකරණවා, *Harihambakaraṇawá*, *v.* to earn.

හල්පතාක්කය, *Halpatákkaya*, *s.* outer verandah.

හල්පිට්ටු, *Hal-piṭṭu*, *s.* kind of cake prepared from the fruit of the hal tree, *vateria acuminata.*

හල්දුම්මල, *Hal-dummala*, *s.* resin of the hal tree.

හලත්සද, *Halatsada*, *s.* Elu form of හලන්ත ශබ්ද *halanta-ṣabda*, which see below.

හලන්ත ශබ්ද, *Halanta-ṣabda*, *s.* (හල් *hal*+අන්ත *anta* and ශබ්ද) in grammar, a noun that has its base ending in a consonant: as, පුත් *put*, son; ගොන් *gon*, ox.

* හව්, *Haw*, *s.* Elu form of භාවය *bháwaya*, which see.

හව්කිරිය, *Hawkiriya*,=භාවක්‍රියාව *bháwa-kriyáwa*, word expressive of a state or the abstract idea, verbal noun.

හවස්වරුව, *Hawaswaruwa*, *s.* afternoon.

හවස්වෙනවා, *Hawaswenawá*, *v.* evening comes on.

හස්කර, *Haskara*, *part.* having stamped, [Colloq. මුද්දරකරලා *muddarakaralá*].

හස්තතල, *Hastatala*, *s.* the palm.

හසකුරු, *Hasakuru*, *s.* grammatical term applied to the thirty-four consonants of the Siṇhalese Alphabet commencing from ක *ka* and ending with හ *ha*.

හසළ, *Hasaḷa*, *p. part.* learnt, instructed, familiar with.

හසුරුවනවා, *Hasuruwanawá*, *v.* regulate; cause to act or move.

හසුරුසන, *Hasurusana*, *s.* snapping the fingers.

හානිකරණවා, *Hánikaraṇawá*, *v.* to destroy.

හාල්පන් පිදුම, *Hálpan-píduma*, *s.* sprouting of the rice-rush (or club rush) applied to a paddy disease, a blight which affects the young paddy plants, due to the prolonged rains. From want of sun the young plant fails to mature the ear and a shoot of grass appears in its stead.

හාස්‍යජනක, *Hásyajanaka*, } *s.* ridiculous, cal-
හාස්‍යොත්පාදක, *Hásyotpádaka*, } culated to raise laughter, [Colloq. හිනා උපදවන *hiná-upadawana*].

* හික්, *Hik*,=ශික්ෂා *ṣikshá*, *s.* one of the Védáṇgas or sciences attached to the Védas: the proper pronunciation of the vocal sounds which occur in them, as explained by Páṇini, learning, acquisition of knowledge.

හික්මෙණසුලු, *Hikmeṇa-sulu*, *a.* docile, teachable, trainable.

* හිඟන්නා, *Hiṇganná*, *s.* one who has not had an attack of illness,=වසූරිය නැල්ලූ අය *wasúriya nęllú-aya.*

හිඟුල, *Hiṇgula*, *s.* vermillion.

හින්ද, *Hindá*, past tense of හිඳිනවා *hiṇdinawá*: also, *ind.* particle [Colloq.], on account of.

හිමිදිරිය, *Himidiriya*, *s.* twilight.

හිමේ, *Himé*, *s.* jungle.

හිරුගොත්, *Hirugot*, *s.* (හිරු sun, ගොත් race) solar race or dynasty, descendant of the sun.

හිල්වෙනවා, *Hilwenawá*, *v.* a hole breaks out or opens.

හිසකෙස්, *Hisakes*, } *s.* hair on the head.
හිසකේ, *Hisaké*, }

හිදන්, *Hídan*, see සිදන් *sídan*.

හින්සෙරේ, *Hínsęré*, *adv.* slowly.

හිනැස්සා, *Hínęssá*, *s.* tall, thin person.

හිපගිලිය, *Hípagiliya*, *s.* quiver, [Colloq. ඊකොපුව *ikopuwa*].

හිවුර, *Híwura*, see හියවුර *hiyawura*.

හිලේකම්මිටිය, *Hí-lékam-miṭiya*, *s.* Register of ploughed lands. According to some authorities it is a corrupt form of හින් ලේකම්මිටිය *hínlékam-miṭtya*, Minor or Supplementary Register.

හුණකපුරු, *Huṇa-kapuru*, *s.* same as උණමකුළු *uṇa-makuḷu*, which see.

හුණුගල්, *Huṇu-gal*, *s.* coral stones.

හුදක්, *Hudak*, *adv.* solely, only, as in හුදක් ඒ සල්රුක් දෙක මතුනොවෙයි, *hudak é salruk-deka matunoweyi*,=තනිකර ඒ සල්ගස් දෙක පමණක්

නොවෙයි *tanikara é salgas deka pamaṇak nowe-yi*, not only those two trees to the exclusion of others.

හුනස්න, *Hunasna*, *s.* (හුන් *hun* been, අස්න *asna* seat) seat on which one is seated.

හුරතල්කරණවා, *Huratalkaraṇawá*, *v.* to fondle; to pet.

හෙතෙම, *Hetema*, *pron*, he.

හෙබුනේ, *Hebuné*, } pret. of හොබනවා *hobana-*
හෙබුවා, *Hebuwá*, } *wá*, which see.

හෙලිල්ලඹු, *Helillambu*, *s.* (හෙලිලි *helili* white, and අඹු *ambu* woman) white or fair woman.

හෙවිල්ලනවා, *Hevillanawá*, *v.* to thatch or cover a roof with tiles, etc.

* හේ, *Hé*, *pron.* that: same as ඒ *é*.

හේත්වවයව, *Hétwawayawa*, } *s.* term in Logic to
හේතුඅවයව, *Hétu-awayawa*, } express the minor premise in a syllogism.

හේතුකොටගෙන, *Hétukoṭageṇa*, *part.* (හේතු cause කොටගෙණ having taken as) by reason of, owing to, on account of.

හේදණ්ඩ, *Hédaṇḍa*, *s.* different form of හේදඬු *hédaṇḍu*, which see.

*හේම, *Héma*, particle colloquially used, equivalent to 'also,' '&c,' as in "උඹ පොත් හේම ගෙණාවාද? *umba pot héma genáwáda?*" "did you bring the books and other things.?"

* හේමා, *Hémá*, see හේමයි *hémayi*.

හේවිසි, *Hévisi*, *s.* tom-tom beating.

හේවිසිගහනවා, *Hévisi-gahanawá*, *v.* to beat tom-tom as in a procession or occasion of a religious festival.

හොටබරියා, *Hoṭabariyá*, *s.* pig.

හොඳ අප්පා, *Honda-appá*, *s.* (literally good father) paternal younger uncle.

හොඳ අම්මා, *Honda-ammá*, *s.* feminine of above.

හෝතඹුවා, *Hótambuwá*, *s.* reddish mungoose.

හෝයියා, *Hóyiyá*, *interj.* hurrah (expressive of triumph).

හැද, *Heda*, see සැද *seda*.

හැදිම, *Hedíma*, *s.* growing, training; formation.

හැදෙනවා, *Hedenawá*, *v.* to grow, to thrive.

හැදෑරීම, *Hedéríma*, verbal noun from හදාරණවා *hadáraṇawá*, which see.

හැඳිඅළුව, *Hendi-aḷuwa*, *s.* place where coconut shell ladles are put.

හැප්පෙනවා, *Heppenawá*, *v.* to strike against any object. (corruptly for හැපෙනවා *hepenawá*.)

හැපින්නී, *Hepinní*, *s.* female snake.

හැඹිලිකටුව, *Hembili-kaṭuwa*, *s.* needle used in stitching a betel-bag.

හැමදාම, *Hemadáma*, *adv.* every day.

හැමදීම, *Hemadíma*, } *s.* sweeping, as with
හැමදුම, *Hemaduma*, } broom. [Colloq. අතුගෑම *atugéma*].

හැල්ල, *Hella*, *s.* cold, coldness. [Colloq. සීතගුණය *síta-guṇaya*, සීතල *sítala*]; also, eddy or rapids.

හැලප, *Helapa*, *s.* kind of food prepared from millet.

හැසිරවීම, *Hesiravíma*, *s.* regulating.

හෑල්ල, *Hélla*, *s.* [Colloq.] "rigmarole,": pl. හෑලි *héli*.

හෘදසාක්ෂිය, *Hridasáksihiya*, *s.* conscience: corrupt form of හෘදයසාක්ෂිය, *hridaya-sákshiya*, or හෘත්සාක්ෂිය *hrit-sákshiya*, which see.